Copyright © 2023 National Fire Protection Association®. All Rig

NFPA® 1

Fire Code

2024 Edition

This edition of NFPA 1, *Fire Code*, was prepared by the Technical Committees on Building Systems and Special Occupancies; Fundamentals of the Fire Code; and Special Equipment, Processes and Hazardous Materials. It was released by the Correlating Committee on Fire Code. It was issued by the Standards Council on August 25, 2023, with an effective date of September 14, 2023, and supersedes all previous editions.

This document has been amended by one or more Tentative Interim Amendments (TIAs) and/or Errata. See "Codes & Standards" at www.nfpa.org for more information.

This edition of NFPA 1 was approved as an American National Standard on September 14, 2023.

Origin and Development of NFPA 1

This *Code* was originally developed as a result of the requests of many members of the National Fire Protection Association for a document covering all aspects of fire protection and prevention that used the other developed NFPA codes and standards. NFPA staff initiated this work in 1971 upon a directive from the NFPA Board of Directors. The original code was written around a format that served as a guide for the development of a local fire prevention code. Prerogatives of local officials were excluded from the main text of the document but were included within appendices as guidance for exercising desired prerogatives.

In the late 1980s, the Fire Marshals Association of North America (now the International Fire Marshals Association [IFMA]) undertook the task of developing a code that was more self-contained, adding administrative sections and extracting heavily from other NFPA codes and standards. The draft was submitted to the Fire Prevention Code Committee. The committee examined changes in the built environment as it is affected by fire and incorporated significant portions of the *Life Safety Code*®. A special task group on hazardous materials examined technological changes in the handling, storage, and use of flammable and combustible materials. Chapters extracting hazardous material requirements placed a greater emphasis on protection of life and property from chemical products made and used in the environment. A major rewrite resulted in the 1992 edition of the *Fire Prevention Code*.

The 1997 edition updated the text extracted from other NFPA codes and standards and added compliance with additional NFPA codes and standards as part of the requirements of NFPA 1.

The 2000 edition of NFPA 1 was a complete revision that updated the text extracted from other NFPA codes and standards. Additional direct references from NFPA codes and standards that are essential to a code official's use of the document were added. The committee also added a new section on performance-based design as a tool for code officials and design professionals. NFPA 1 was restructured to be more functional with respect to administration, code enforcement, and regulatory adoption processes.

The 2003 edition of NFPA 1, *Uniform Fire Code*™, was a complete revision. It incorporated provisions from the Western Fire Chiefs, *Uniform Fire Code*™, under a partnership between NFPA and Western Fire Chiefs, while it updated and expanded the provisions extracted from other key NFPA codes and standards. To emphasize the partnership, the document was renamed NFPA 1, *Uniform Fire Code*™. The *Uniform Fire Code* is a trademark of the Western Fire Chiefs Association. NFPA 1, *Uniform Fire Code*™, was restructured into parts to be more compatible with the regulatory adoption procedures, including administration and code enforcement, occupancies, processes, equipment, and hazardous materials provisions. The Committee included a newly expanded chapter on performance-based design as an enhanced tool for code officials and design professionals. Additional extracts and references from NFPA codes and standards that are essential to a code official's use of the document were added, bringing the number of referenced NFPA codes and

NFPA and National Fire Protection Association are registered trademarks of the National Fire Protection Association, Quincy, Massachusetts 02169.

standards to over 125. Additional chapters on hazardous materials were included that incorporate the provisions covered in the *Uniform Fire Code*™.

The 2006 edition of NFPA 1, *Uniform Fire Code*, was a complete revision of the code that incorporated the provisions from NFPA 230, *Standard for the Fire Protection of Storage*. The Technical Committee on Uniform Fire Code had been given responsibility for NFPA 230 by the NFPA Standards Council, so they incorporated the requirements into NFPA 1 rather than maintain a separate standard.

The 2006 edition of NFPA 1 also included new chapters on classification of occupancy, motion picture studios, outdoor tire storage, and general storage, along with other extracted provisions updated and expanded the from other key NFPA codes and standards that were essential to a code official's use of the document. The number of NFPA codes and standards referenced in this edition was 117.

With the 2009 edition of NFPA 1, the title of the document was changed from *Uniform Fire Code* to *Fire Code*. The revision updated all the extracted provisions from the 117 codes and standards that were included as mandatory reference publications in the 2006 edition. The revisions also included an expansion of Section 12.5 on interior finish to contain extracted provisions from NFPA *101*; an expansion of Section 12.6 on furnishings, contents, decorations, and treated fabrics to contain extracted provisions from NFPA *101*; a new Section 18.4, which moved fire flow requirements for buildings from Annex H; a new Section 32.5 for regulating locations for motion picture and television production studios, soundstages, and approved production facilities with extracted provisions from NFPA 140; and new Sections 40.3 through 40.7 on combustible dust explosion protection and fire prevention with extracted provisions from NFPA 654. Additional information on hazardous materials classifications was added to Annex B. This revision also added three annexes to the 2009 edition, including Annex O, In-Building Public Safety Radio Enhancement Systems; Annex P, Fire Department Service Delivery Concurrency Evaluation; and Annex Q, Fire Fighter Safety Building Marking System. The number of NFPA codes and standards referenced in this edition was 119.

Six annexes published in the 2006 edition were deleted from the 2009 edition, including Annex E, Model Citation Program; Annex F, Model Fees and Charges Program; Annex H, Fire Flow Requirements for Buildings; Annex J, Protection of Outdoor Storage; Annex M, Recommendations for Fighting Rubber Tire Fires in Sprinklered Buildings; and Annex N, AHJ Minimum Qualifications and Job Descriptions for Code Enforcement Personnel.

The 2012 edition of NFPA 1 included revisions to requirements for the fire code board of appeals (Section 1.10); certificates of fitness (Section 1.13); application limits of referenced standards (Section 2.1); emergency plan provisions (Section 10.9); prohibited storage of grills on balconies (10.11.6.2); new requirements for standardized elevator keys (11.3.6); new requirements for determination of fire department communication capabilities in buildings and two-way radio communication enhancement systems and deleted former Annex O (Section 11.10); medical gas and vacuum systems (Section 11.11); photovoltaic systems (Section 11.12); quality assurance of fire barrier penetrations and joints (12.3.2); and automatic sprinkler system requirement for new buildings three or more stories in height above grade (13.3.2.4). The 2012 edition also relocated former Annex P to the new Chapter 15, Fire Department Service Delivery Concurrency Evaluation; expanded Chapter 17, Wildland Urban Interface; added a new Chapter 36, Telecommunication Facilities and Information Technology Equipment; added a new Chapter 37, Fixed Guideway Transit and Passenger Rail Systems; added requirements for carbon monoxide detection in residential occupancies; relocated former Annex G to the new Chapter 54, Ozone Gas-Generating Equipment; extensively revised Chapter 60, Hazardous Materials, to extract from NFPA 400, *Hazardous Materials Code*; updated Chapter 66, Flammable and Combustible Liquids, per the current edition of NFPA 30, *Flammable and Combustible Liquids Code*; revised Chapter 67, Flammable Solids, to reference NFPA 400; revised Chapter 68, Highly Toxic and Toxic Solids and Liquids, to reference NFPA 400; completely revised Chapter 70, Oxidizer Solids and Liquids; revised Chapter 71, Pyrophoric Solids and Liquids, to reference NFPA 400; revised Chapter 72, Unstable (Reactive) Solids and Liquids, to reference NFPA 400; added a new Chapter 74, Ammonium Nitrate; added a new Chapter 75, Organic Peroxide Solids and Liquids; deleted Annex K, Explanation of Rack Storage Test Data and Procedures; deleted Annex L, Protection of Baled Cotton: History of Guidelines; and updated all extracts through the Annual 2011 revision cycle.

Key revisions for the 2015 edition of NFPA 1 included the prohibition of the use of sky lanterns (10.10.9.3); expanded application of photovoltaic system requirements to existing installations (Section 11.12); AHJ authorization to permit the removal of nonrequired, existing occupant-use hose (13.2.2.6); mandatory automatic sprinkler requirement for all new hotels without exception (13.3.2.15); enhanced attic protection for residential board and care occupancies with residential sprinkler systems (13.3.2.21.2.7); expanded occupancy-based fire alarm system provisions to correlate with NFPA *101* (Section 13.7); new occupant load factor for concentrated business use (14.8.1.2); completely revised fire hydrant location and distribution requirements and deleted former Annex E (Section 18.5); revisions to NFPA 654 extracts for dust explosion prevention (Chapter 40); new hot work permit limits from NFPA 51B (41.3.4.4); expanded existing commercial cooking equipment extinguishing system requirements from NFPA 96 (50.4.4.3.2); expanded ammonia refrigeration system maintenance and testing requirements (Section 53.3); updated hazardous materials maximum allowable quantities from NFPA 400 (60.4.2); new provisions for alcohol-based hand rub dispensers from NFPA *101* (60.5.2); revisions to aerosol product classifications from NFPA 30B (61.1.3); new requirements for cleaning and purging gas piping systems from NFPA 55 (63.3.1.19); new provisions for cooking oil storage tank systems in commercial kitchens from NFPA 30 (66.19.7); and updates of all extracts through the Annual 2014 revision cycle.

The 2018 edition of NFPA 1 included revisions to requirements for the application of referenced publications (1.4.1.1 and 2.1.1); references for the professional qualifications for fire inspectors, plan examiners, and fire marshals (1.7.2); new minimum fire prevention inspection frequencies for existing occupancies (10.2.7); updates to premises identification (10.11.1); new and updated marking and access criteria for photovoltaic systems (Section 11.12); new provisions for rubberized asphalt melters (Section 16.7); listing requirements for electric gates used on fire department access roads (18.2.4.2.6); new provisions on the outside storage of biomass feedstock (31.3.10); new requirements for the outdoor storage of wood and wood composite pallets or listed pallets equivalent to wood (34.10.3); a new chapter on marijuana growing, processing, or extraction facilities (Chapter 38); a revision of Chapter 40 to replace extracts from NFPA 654 with extracted provisions from NFPA 652 (Chapter 40); complete reorganization of aircraft fuel servicing provisions in accordance with NFPA 407 (Section 42.10); a new section on mobile and temporary cooking operations (Section 50.7); extensive revisions of Chapter 52 on energy storage systems (Chapter 52); a new Chapter 55 on cleaning and purging of flammable gas piping systems with reference to NFPA 56 (Chapter 55); new provisions for insulated liquid carbon dioxide systems extracted from NFPA 55 (Section 63.9); a new annex on fire-fighter breathing-air replenishment systems (Annex E); and updates of all extracts through the Annual 2017 revision cycle.

Key revisions for the 2021 edition included updates to in-building emergency responder communication enhancement system requirements for better alignment with NFPA 1221 (Section 11.10); new signage requirements for nonsprinklered high-rise buildings (13.3.2.25.2.4); new provisions for carbon dioxide enrichment equipment, indoor horticultural grow structures, and listing requirements for extraction equipment as they relate to cannabis facilities (Chapter 38); a new chapter on wastewater treatment and collection facilities (Chapter 39); a new chapter on additive manufacturing (3D printing, Chapter 46); energy storage system requirements extracted from NFPA 855 (Chapter 52); and updates of all extracts through the Annual 2020 revision cycle.

The 2024 edition of NFPA 1 includes revisions to the requirements for permits (1.13.8); new requirements for inspections during declared disasters (1.7.7.6); new requirements for pre-incident planning (Section 1.10); revisions to requirements for document retention for AHJs (1.12.1.1); new requirements for the outdoor use of electrically powered cooking appliances in residential occupancies (10.10.6); new requirements for charging of micromobility devices (Section 10.21); revisions to requirements for listing of relocatable power taps (11.1.4); revisions to requirements for in-building emergency responder communication enhancement systems, including new references to NFPA 1225 (Section 11.10); new requirements for timeframes for correcting impairments in water-based fire protection systems (13.1.9); new requirements for inspection and testing of private fire service mains (13.5.4); removal of all extracts from NFPA 241 and replacement with reference to NFPA 241 (Chapter 16); new requirements for handling and storage of batteries for automobile wrecking yards (22.9.6); revised classifications for mechanical refrigeration (Chapter 53); and updates to all extracts through the Annual 2023 revision cycle.

NFPA 1 reflects the technical knowledge of the committees responsible for the codes and standards referenced in, and from which text is extracted and incorporated into, the technical provisions of NFPA 1. This *Code* is intended to provide state, county, and local jurisdictions with an effective fire code.

Correlating Committee on Fire Code

Kenneth E. Bush, *Chair*
Maryland State Fire Marshals Office, MD [E]

Carl F. Baldassarra, Wiss, Janney, Elstner Associates, Inc., IL [SE]
Scott M. Bryant, Fire & Risk Alliance LLC, MD [U]
   Rep. Edison Electric Institute
Chris L. Butts, Sompo International, NC [I]
Shane M. Clary, Bay Alarm Company, CA [M]
   Rep. Automatic Fire Alarm Association, Inc.
Robert J. Davidson, Davidson Code Concepts, LLC, SC [SE]
John August Denhardt, American Fire Sprinkler Association (AFSA), TX [IM]
Ernest J. Gallo, Telcordia Technologies (Ericsson), NJ [U]
   Rep. Alliance for Telecommunications Industry Solutions
Marvin Dwayne Garriss, Synergy Consortium Group, LLC, GA [M]
   Rep. Fire Equipment Manufacturers' Association
Edward M. Hawthorne, DFW Dynamics, TX [U]
   Rep. American Petroleum Institute
Rick Heffernan, SDi, NJ [M]
   Rep. National Electrical Manufacturers Association
David W. Hollinger, Drexel University, PA [U]

Jeffrey M. Hugo, National Fire Sprinkler Association, Inc., MI [M]
James Kendzel, American Supply Association, IL [M]
William E. Koffel, Koffel Associates, Inc., MD [SE]
Kelly T. Nicolello, UL LLC, TX [RT]
Michael O'Brian, Code Savvy Consultants, MI [SE]
Raymond C. O'Brocki, American Wood Council, DE [M]
   Rep. American Wood Council
Wade Palazini, JENSEN HUGHES, RI [SE]
Leonard J. Ramo, Telgian Corporation, GA [SE]
Steven F. Sawyer, Retired, CT [E]
   Rep. International Fire Marshals Association
Catherine L. Stashak, Office of the Illinois State Fire Marshal, IL [E]
Kenneth Earl Tyree, Jr., West Virginia State Fire Marshals Office, WV [E]
Peter J. Willse, Portland Fire Marshal's Office, CT [E]

Alternates

Roland A. Asp, National Fire Sprinkler Association, Inc., MD [M]
   (Alt. to Jeffrey M. Hugo)
Kevin Ryan Hall, American Fire Sprinkler Association (AFSA), MD [IM]
   (Alt. to John August Denhardt)
Roy C. Kimball, Brooks Equipment Company, LLC, NC [M]
   (Alt. to Marvin Dwayne Garriss)
Richard G. Kluge, Ericsson, NJ [U]
   (Alt. to Ernest J. Gallo)

Brian L. Olsen, Phillips 66, OK [U]
   (Alt. to Edward M. Hawthorne)
Rodger Reiswig, Johnson Controls, VA [M]
   (Alt. to Shane M. Clary)
David P. Tyree, American Wood Council, CO [M]
   (Alt. to Raymond C. O'Brocki)

Nonvoting

Bruce E. Johnson, UL LLC, NY [RT]
   Rep. TC on Building Systems and Special Occupancies
James S. Peterkin, TLC Engineering, FL [U]
   Rep. TC on Fundamentals

Michael D. Snyder, Dekra Insight, MI [RT]
   Rep. TC on Special Equipment, Processes and Hazardous Materials

Jen Sisco, NFPA Staff Liaison

This list represents the membership at the time the Committee was balloted on the final text of this edition. Since that time, changes in the membership may have occurred. A key to classifications is found at the back of the document.

NOTE: Membership on a committee shall not in and of itself constitute an endorsement of the Association or any document developed by the committee on which the member serves.

Committee Scope: This committee shall have primary responsibility for documents on a Fire Prevention Code that includes appropriate administrative provisions, to be used with the National Fire Codes for the installation, operation, and maintenance of buildings, structures, and premises for the purpose of providing safety to life and property from fire and explosion. This includes development of requirements for, and maintenance of, systems and equipment for fire control and extinguishment. Safety to life of occupants of buildings and structures is under the primary jurisdiction of the Committee on Safety to Life.

Technical Committee on Building Systems and Special Occupancies

Bruce E. Johnson, *Chair*
UL LLC, NY [RT]

Musfiqul Azad, Prokausholee Bangladesh, Bangladesh [SE]
Laura Bennett-Hourigan, Walt Disney World Parks & Resorts, FL [U]
Justin B. Biller, Emerson Graham + Associates, VA [SE]
Ralph E. Bless, Jr., Telgian Corporation, GA [SE]
Kenneth E. Bush, Maryland State Fire Marshals Office, MD [E]
Chris L. Butts, Sompo International, NC [I]
Michael Connolly, Jacobs Engineering, MD [SE]
Timothy R. Costello, Wiss, Janney, Elstner Associates, Inc., NJ [SE]
Andrew Fukuda, Honolulu Fire Department, HI [L]
Marvin Dwayne Garriss, Synergy Consortium Group, LLC, GA [M]
 Rep. Fire Equipment Manufacturers' Association
Kevin Ryan Hall, American Fire Sprinkler Association (AFSA), MD [IM]
Sarina L. Hart, Koffel Associates, Inc., MD [SE]
Edward M. Hawthorne, DFW Dynamics, TX [U]
 Rep. American Petroleum Institute
Terin Hopkins, National Fire Sprinkler Association (NFSA), MD [M]
Jaewook Kwon, Loring Consulting Engineers, Inc., NY [SE]
Maria B. Marks, Siemens Industry, Inc., MD [M]
 Rep. Automatic Fire Alarm Association, Inc.
Balakrishnan V. Nair, TUV-SUD, Singapore [SE]
Sam Newman, Flame King, CA [M]

Raymond C. O'Brocki, American Wood Council, DE [M]
 Rep. American Wood Council
James S. Peterkin, TLC Engineering, PA [U]
 Rep. NFPA Health Care Section
Richard Jay Roberts, Honeywell Fire Safety, IL [M]
Bruce L. Rottner, H2M Architects & Engineers, NJ [SE]
Mohammed A. Saeefan, Saudi Aramco, Saudi Arabia [U]
Michael L. Savage, Sr., Marion County Building Safety, FL [E]
Steven F. Sawyer, Retired, CT [E]
 Rep. New England Association of Fire Marshals
Kenneth R. Schneider, UA-ITF, MO [L]
Michael Sheehan, SLS Consulting, Inc., FL [SE]
 Rep. Property Markets Group (PMG)
Alex Spataru, The Adept Group, Inc., CA [SE]
Catherine L. Stashak, Office of the Illinois State Fire Marshal, IL [E]
Michael J. Thomas, California State University, Los Angeles, CA [RT]
Kenneth Earl Tyree, Jr., West Virginia State Fire Marshals Office, WV [E]
Carl F. Weaver, Greater Orlando Aviation Authority, FL [U]
Peter J. Willse, Portland Fire Marshal's Office, CT [E]
Jeremy Zeedyk, National Energy Management Institute Committee (NEMIC), CT [IM]

Alternates

Daniel Buuck, National Association of Home Builders (NAHB), DC [U]
 (Voting Alt.)
Shane M. Clary, Bay Alarm Company, CA [M]
 (Alt. to Maria B. Marks)
Ty Darby, International Association of Fire Fighters (IAFF), OR [L]
 (Alt. to Andrew Fukuda)
John August Denhardt, American Fire Sprinkler Association (AFSA), TX [IM]
 (Alt. to Kevin Ryan Hall)
Matthew Michael DonMoyer, NBC Universal Parks and Resorts, FL [U]
 (Alt. to Laura Bennett-Hourigan)

Chris Hill, Edwards/Carrier/UTC/Kidde Safety, FL [M]
 (Alt. to Richard Jay Roberts)
Roy C. Kimball, Brooks Equipment Company, LLC., NC [M]
 (Alt. to Marvin Dwayne Garriss)
Kelly T. Nicolello, UL LLC, TX [RT]
 (Alt. to Bruce E. Johnson)
Brian L. Olsen, Phillips 66, OK [U]
 (Alt. to Edward M. Hawthorne)
Vincent Powers, National Fire Sprinkler Association (NFSA), MD [M]
 (Alt. to Terin Hopkins)

Tracy L. Vecchiarelli, NFPA Staff Liaison

This list represents the membership at the time the Committee was balloted on the final text of this edition. Since that time, changes in the membership may have occurred. A key to classifications is found at the back of the document.

NOTE: Membership on a committee shall not in and of itself constitute an endorsement of the Association or any document developed by the committee on which the member serves.

Committee Scope: This committee shall have primary responsibility for documents on building fire protection and life safety systems, construction operations, occupancy fire safety and definitions for the purpose of providing safety to life and property from fire and explosion.

Technical Committee on Fundamentals of the Fire Code

James S. Peterkin, *Chair*
TLC Engineering, PA [U]
Rep. NFPA Health Care Section

Mohammed Abdulah Alkhaldi, Saudi Aramco Refinery, Saudi Arabia [U]

Anthony C. Apfelbeck, Altamonte Springs Building/Fire Safety Division, FL [E]

Tracey D. Bellamy, Telgian Corporation, GA [SE]

H. Butch Browning, Jr., Louisiana Office of State Fire Marshal, LA [E]
Rep. International Association of Fire Chiefs

Kenneth E. Bush, Maryland State Fire Marshals Office, MD [E]

Chris L. Butts, Sompo International, NC [I]

Daniel Buuck, National Association of Home Builders (NAHB), DC [U]
Rep. National Association of Home Builders (NAHB)

Ramjee Pradeep Chand, Ezone Rest Assured, India [M]

Shane M. Clary, Bay Alarm Company, CA [M]
Rep. Automatic Fire Alarm Association, Inc.

Michael Scott Custer, Fort Detrick Fire Department, MD [E]

Andrew Fukuda, Honolulu Fire Department, HI [L]

Marvin Dwayne Garriss, Synergy Consortium Group, LLC, GA [M]
Rep. Fire Equipment Manufacturers' Association

Kevin Ryan Hall, American Fire Sprinkler Association (AFSA), MD [IM]

Sarina L. Hart, Koffel Associates, Inc., MD [SE]

Terin Hopkins, National Fire Sprinkler Association (NFSA), MD [M]

Michael A. Jackson, Philadelphia Fire Department, PA [E]

James Kendzel, American Supply Association, IL [M]
Rep. American Supply Association

Scott T. Laramee, AON Property Risk, CA [I]

Brian Mosberian, Phoenix Fire Department, AZ [E]

Kelly T. Nicolello, UL LLC, TX [RT]

Michael O'Brian, Code Savvy Consultants, MI [SE]

Raymond C. O'Brocki, American Wood Council, DE [M]
Rep. American Wood Council

Brian L. Olsen, Phillips 66, OK [U]
Rep. American Petroleum Institute

Wade Palazini, JENSEN HUGHES, RI [SE]

Gary S. Santoro, Self Employed, FL [SE]

Steven F. Sawyer, Retired, CT [E]
Rep. New England Association of Fire Marshals

Randy H. Schubert, Ericsson, NJ [U]
Rep. Alliance for Telecommunications Industry Solutions

Robert E. Solomon, SLS Consulting, Inc., MA [SE]

Catherine L. Stashak, Office of the Illinois State Fire Marshal, IL [E]

Kenneth Earl Tyree, Jr., West Virginia State Fire Marshals Office, WV [E]

Christopher Weniger, Hillsborough Township Fire Commission, NJ [E]

Alternates

Ty Darby, International Association of Fire Fighters (IAFF), OR [L]
(Alt. to Andrew Fukuda)

John August Denhardt, American Fire Sprinkler Association (AFSA), TX [IM]
(Alt. to Kevin Ryan Hall)

Ernest J. Gallo, Telcordia Technologies (Ericsson), NJ [U]
(Alt. to Randy H. Schubert)

Edward M. Hawthorne, DFW Dynamics, TX [U]
(Alt. to Brian L. Olsen)

Jeffrey M. Hugo, National Fire Sprinkler Association, Inc., MI [M]
(Alt. to Terin Hopkins)

Bruce E. Johnson, UL LLC, NY [RT]
(Alt. to Kelly T. Nicolello)

Roy C. Kimball, Brooks Equipment Company, LLC., NC [M]
(Alt. to Marvin Dwayne Garriss)

Rodger Reiswig, Johnson Controls, VA [M]
(Alt. to Shane M. Clary)

Annie Renee Therrien, SLS Consulting, Inc., NC [SE]
(Alt. to Robert E. Solomon)

Janet A. Washburn, Bonita Springs Fire Control District, FL [E]
(Alt. to H. Butch Browning, Jr.)

Jen Sisco, NFPA Staff Liaison

This list represents the membership at the time the Committee was balloted on the final text of this edition. Since that time, changes in the membership may have occurred. A key to classifications is found at the back of the document.

NOTE: Membership on a committee shall not in and of itself constitute an endorsement of the Association or any document developed by the committee on which the member serves.

Committee Scope: This committee shall have primary responsibility for documents on the basic goals, objectives, performance requirements, classification of occupancy, general safety requirements, building services, fire department access, and definitions for the purpose of providing safety to life and property from fire and explosion.

Technical Committee on Special Equipment, Processes and Hazardous Materials

Michael D. Snyder, *Chair*
Dekra Insight, MI [RT]

Chris L. Butts, Sompo International, NC [I]
John Caliri, SLS Consulting, Inc., GA [SE]
Kathryn M. Cifa, Bechtel National, Inc., VA [SE]
Benjamin Craig, Insight Risk/D.B.A. REM Risk Consultants, TX [SE]
Robert J. Davidson, Davidson Code Concepts, LLC, SC [SE]
Jeffery Charles Dunkel, National Fire Sprinkler Association (NFSA), KS [M]
Andrew Fukuda, Honolulu Fire Department, HI [L]
Michael Anthony Galfano, UA-ITF, IL [L]
Marvin Dwayne Garriss, Synergy Consortium Group, LLC, GA [M]
  Rep. Fire Equipment Manufacturers' Association
Joseph Henry Griner, Griner Engineering, FL [SE]
Kevin Ryan Hall, American Fire Sprinkler Association (AFSA), MD [IM]
James Herrmann, Williams County Emergency Management, ND [U]

David W. Hollinger, Drexel University, PA [U]
Kevin J. Kelly, Victaulic, PA [M]
Richard G. Kluge, Ericsson, NJ [U]
  Rep. Alliance for Telecommunications Industry Solutions
William E. Koffel, Koffel Associates, Inc., MD [SE]
Kelly T. Nicolello, UL LLC, TX [RT]
Brian L. Olsen, Phillips 66, OK [U]
  Rep. American Petroleum Institute
Nicholas Ozog, Wiss, Janney, Elstner Associates, Inc., IL [SE]
Geoffrey A. Raifsnider, Global Finishing Solutions, WI [M]
Leonard J. Ramo, Telgian Corporation, GA [SE]
Ryan Sandler, ADT Commercial LLC./Red Hawk Fire Security, CA [M]
  Rep. Automatic Fire Alarm Association, Inc.
Catherine L. Stashak, Office of the Illinois State Fire Marshal, IL [E]
Peter J. Willse, Portland Fire Marshal's Office, CT [E]

Alternates

Ty Darby, International Association of Fire Fighters (IAFF), OR [L]
  (Alt. to Andrew Fukuda)
Edward M. Hawthorne, DFW Dynamics, TX [U]
  (Alt. to Brian L. Olsen)
Bruce E. Johnson, UL LLC, NY [RT]
  (Alt. to Kelly T. Nicolello)
Roy C. Kimball, Brooks Equipment Company, LLC., NC [M]
  (Alt. to Marvin Dwayne Garriss)
Joshua P. McDonald, American Fire Sprinkler Association (AFSA), TX [IM]
  (Alt. to Kevin Ryan Hall)

Chad Putney, Portsmouth Fire Department (NH), NH [M]
  (Alt. to Ryan Sandler)
Ronald W. Ritchey, National Fire Sprinkler Association (NFSA), IN [M]
  (Alt. to Jeffery Charles Dunkel)
Randy H. Schubert, Ericsson, NJ [U]
  (Alt. to Richard G. Kluge)

Alex Ing, NFPA Staff Liaison

This list represents the membership at the time the Committee was balloted on the final text of this edition. Since that time, changes in the membership may have occurred. A key to classifications is found at the back of the document.

NOTE: Membership on a committee shall not in and of itself constitute an endorsement of the Association or any document developed by the committee on which the member serves.

Committee Scope: This committee shall have primary responsibility for documents on special equipment and processes in buildings, the storage, use and handling of hazardous materials indoors and outdoors, and definitions for the purpose of providing safety to life and property from fire and explosion.

Contents

Chapter 1	Administration	1–13
1.1	Scope.	1–13
1.2	Purpose.	1–13
1.3	Application.	1–13
1.4	Equivalencies, Alternatives, and Modifications.	1–14
1.5	Units.	1–14
1.6	Enforcement.	1–15
1.7	Authority.	1–15
1.8	Duties and Powers of the Incident Commander.	1–16
1.9	Liability.	1–17
1.10	Pre-incident Planning.	1–17
1.11	Fire Code Board of Appeals.	1–17
1.12	Records and Reports.	1–18
1.13	Permits and Approvals.	1–18
1.14	Certificates of Fitness.	1–24
1.15	Plan Review.	1–25
1.16	Technical Assistance.	1–26
1.17	Notice of Violations and Penalties.	1–26
1.18	Fees.	1–26

Chapter 2	Referenced Publications	1–27
2.1	General.	1–27
2.2	NFPA Publications.	1–27
2.3	Other Publications.	1–29
2.4	References for Extracts in Mandatory Sections.	1–34

Chapter 3	Definitions	1–35
3.1	General.	1–35
3.2	NFPA Official Definitions.	1–35
3.3	General Definitions.	1–35
3.4	Special Performance-Based Definitions.	1–56

Chapter 4	General Requirements	1–57
4.1	Goals and Objectives.	1–57
4.2	Assumptions.	1–58
4.3	Compliance Options.	1–58
4.4	Fundamental Requirements.	1–58
4.5	General Requirements.	1–59

Chapter 5	Performance-Based Option	1–61
5.1	General.	1–61
5.2	Performance Criteria.	1–62
5.3	Retained Prescriptive Requirements.	1–62
5.4	Design Scenarios.	1–63
5.5	Evaluation of Proposed Designs.	1–64
5.6	Safety Factors.	1–64
5.7	Documentation Requirements.	1–64

Chapter 6	Classification of Occupancy	1–65
6.1	Classification of Occupancy.	1–65

Chapter 7	Reserved	1–70

Chapter 8	Reserved	1–70

Chapter 9	Reserved	1–70

Chapter 10	General Safety Requirements	1–70
10.1	Fundamental Requirements.	1–70
10.2	Owner/Operator/Tenant Responsibilities.	1–70
10.3	Occupancy.	1–70
10.4	Emergency Action Plans.	1–71
10.5	Building Evacuation.	1–71
10.6	Fire Drills.	1–71
10.7	Reporting of Fires and Other Emergencies.	1–71
10.8	Tampering with Fire Safety Equipment.	1–71
10.9	Smoking.	1–72
10.10	Open Flames, Candles, Open Fires, and Incinerators.	1–72
10.11	Fire Protection Markings.	1–73
10.12	Seasonal and Vacant Buildings and Premises.	1–74
10.13	Combustible Vegetation.	1–74
10.14	Special Outdoor Events, Carnivals, and Fairs.	1–74
10.15	Portable and Vehicle-Mounted Generators.	1–77
10.16	Outside Storage.	1–78
10.17	Parade Floats.	1–78
10.18	Powered Industrial Trucks.	1–78
10.19	Storage of Combustible Materials.	1–78
10.20	Indoor Play Structures.	1–79
10.21	Powered Micromobility Devices.	1–79
10.22	Alcohol-Based Hand-Rub (ABHR) Dispensers.	1–80

Chapter 11	Building Services	1–81
11.1	Electrical Fire Safety.	1–81
11.2	Heating, Ventilation, and Air-Conditioning.	1–82
11.3	Elevators, Escalators, and Conveyors.	1–82
11.4	Utilities.	1–83
11.5	Heating Appliances.	1–83
11.6	Waste Chutes, Incinerators, and Laundry Chutes.	1–84
11.7	Stationary Generators and Standby Power Systems.	1–84
11.8	Smoke Control.	1–85
11.9	Emergency Command Center.	1–85
11.10	In-Building Emergency Responder Communication Enhancement Systems.	1–85
11.11	Medical Gas and Vacuum Systems.	1–85
11.12	Photovoltaic Systems.	1–85

Chapter 12	Features of Fire Protection	1–88
12.1	General.	1–88
12.2	Construction.	1–88
12.3	Fire-Resistive Materials and Construction.	1–88
12.4	Fire Doors and Other Opening Protectives.	1–89
12.5	Interior Finish.	1–92
12.6	Contents and Furnishings.	1–95
12.7	Fire Barriers.	1–97
12.8	Smoke Partitions.	1–102
12.9	Smoke Barriers.	1–103

Chapter 13	Fire Protection Systems	1–105
13.1	General.	1–105
13.2	Standpipe Systems.	1–106
13.3	Sprinkler Systems.	1–107
13.4	Fire Pumps.	1–120
13.5	Water Supply.	1–121
13.6	Portable Fire Extinguishers.	1–121
13.7	Detection, Alarm, and Communications Systems.	1–130
13.8	Other Fire Protection Systems.	1–161
13.9	Non-Listed Fire Protection or Suppression Devices and Equipment.	1–161

Chapter 14	Means of Egress	1–162
14.1	Application.	1–162
14.2	Exit Access Corridors.	1–162
14.3	Exits.	1–162
14.4	Means of Egress Reliability.	1–163
14.5	Door Openings.	1–163
14.6	Enclosure and Protection of Stairs.	1–172
14.7	Exit Passageways.	1–172
14.8	Capacity of Means of Egress.	1–172
14.9	Number of Means of Egress.	1–175
14.10	Arrangement of Means of Egress.	1–176

14.11	Discharge from Exits.	1-178
14.12	Illumination of Means of Egress.	1-179
14.13	Emergency Lighting.	1-179
14.14	Marking of Means of Egress.	1-180
14.15	Secondary Means of Escape.	1-182

Chapter 15 Fire Department Service Delivery Concurrency Evaluation ... 1-182
- 15.1 Application. ... 1-182
- 15.2 Level of Service Objectives. ... 1-182
- 15.3 Evaluator Qualifications. ... 1-183
- 15.4 Fire Department Service Delivery Concurrency Evaluation Documentation. ... 1-183
- 15.5 Independent Review. ... 1-183
- 15.6 Approval. ... 1-183

Chapter 16 Safeguarding Construction, Alteration, and Demolition Operations ... 1-183
- 16.1 General Requirements. ... 1-183
- 16.2 Alteration of Buildings. ... 1-183
- 16.3 Fire Safety During Demolition. ... 1-183
- 16.4 Torch-Applied Roofing Systems. ... 1-183
- 16.5 Tar Kettles and Rubberized Asphalt Melters. ... 1-183
- 16.6 Asbestos Removal. ... 1-186
- 16.7 Lead Removal. ... 1-186

Chapter 17 Wildland Urban Interface ... 1-186
- 17.1 General. ... 1-186
- 17.2 Plans. ... 1-188
- 17.3 Wildland Fire-Prone Areas. ... 1-188

Chapter 18 Fire Department Access and Water Supply ... 1-190
- 18.1 General. ... 1-190
- 18.2 Fire Department Access. ... 1-190
- 18.3 Water Supplies. ... 1-192
- 18.4 Fire Flow Requirements for Buildings. ... 1-192
- 18.5 Fire Hydrants. ... 1-193

Chapter 19 Combustible Waste and Refuse ... 1-196
- 19.1 General. ... 1-196
- 19.2 Combustible Waste and Refuse. ... 1-196

Chapter 20 Occupancy Fire Safety ... 1-197
- 20.1 Assembly Occupancies. ... 1-197
- 20.2 Educational Occupancies. ... 1-203
- 20.3 Day-Care Occupancies. ... 1-204
- 20.4 Health Care Occupancies. ... 1-206
- 20.5 Residential Board and Care Occupancies. ... 1-209
- 20.6 Ambulatory Health Care Centers. ... 1-211
- 20.7 Detention and Correctional Occupancies. ... 1-212
- 20.8 Hotels and Dormitories. ... 1-214
- 20.9 Apartment Buildings. ... 1-215
- 20.10 Lodging or Rooming Houses. ... 1-215
- 20.11 One- and Two-Family Dwellings and Manufactured Housing. ... 1-216
- 20.12 Mercantile Occupancies. ... 1-216
- 20.13 Business Occupancies. ... 1-216
- 20.14 Industrial Occupancies. ... 1-217
- 20.15 Storage Occupancies. ... 1-217
- 20.16 Special Structures and High-Rise Buildings. ... 1-218
- 20.17 Historic Buildings and Cultural Resources. ... 1-218

Chapter 21 Airports and Heliports ... 1-218
- 21.1 Hangars. ... 1-218
- 21.2 Terminals. ... 1-219
- 21.3 Rooftop Heliport Construction and Protection. ... 1-220

Chapter 22 Automobile Wrecking Yards ... 1-223
- 22.1 General. ... 1-223
- 22.2 Permits. ... 1-223
- 22.3 Fire Apparatus Access Roads. ... 1-223
- 22.4 Welding and Cutting. ... 1-223
- 22.5 Housekeeping. ... 1-223
- 22.6 Fire Extinguishers. ... 1-223
- 22.7 Tire Storage. ... 1-223
- 22.8 Burning Operations. ... 1-223
- 22.9 Motor Vehicle Fluids and Hazardous Materials. ... 1-223

Chapter 23 Cleanrooms ... 1-223
- 23.1 General. ... 1-223
- 23.2 Applicability. ... 1-223
- 23.3 Permits. ... 1-223

Chapter 24 Drycleaning ... 1-223
- 24.1 General. ... 1-223
- 24.2 Permits. ... 1-223

Chapter 25 Grandstands and Bleachers, Folding and Telescopic Seating, Tents, and Membrane Structures ... 1-223
- 25.1 General. ... 1-223
- 25.2 Tents. ... 1-225
- 25.3 Grandstands. ... 1-226
- 25.4 Folding and Telescopic Seating. ... 1-227
- 25.5 Permanent Membrane Structures. ... 1-228
- 25.6 Temporary Membrane Structures. ... 1-229

Chapter 26 Laboratories Using Chemicals ... 1-230
- 26.1 General. ... 1-230
- 26.2 Permits. ... 1-230

Chapter 27 Manufactured Home and Recreational Vehicle Sites ... 1-231
- 27.1 General. ... 1-231
- 27.2 Manufactured Home Sites. ... 1-231
- 27.3 Recreational Vehicle Parks and Campgrounds. ... 1-231

Chapter 28 Marinas, Boatyards, Marine Terminals, Piers, and Wharves ... 1-231
- 28.1 Marinas, Boatyards, and Other Recreational Marine Facilities. ... 1-231
- 28.2 Marine Terminals, Piers, and Wharves. ... 1-234
- 28.3 Construction, Conversion, Repair, and Lay-Up of Vessels. ... 1-235

Chapter 29 Parking Garages ... 1-235
- 29.1 General. ... 1-235

Chapter 30 Motor Fuel Dispensing Facilities and Repair Garages ... 1-235
- 30.1 Motor Fuel Dispensing Facilities. ... 1-235
- 30.2 Repair Garages for Vehicles Powered by Flammable and Combustible Liquids. ... 1-236
- 30.3 Repair Garages for Vehicles Powered by Alternate Fuels. ... 1-237
- 30.4 Operational Requirements. ... 1-243

Chapter 31 Forest Products and Biomass Feedstocks ... 1-243
- 31.1 General. ... 1-243
- 31.2 Permits. ... 1-243
- 31.3 Protection of Storage of Forest Products. ... 1-243

Chapter 32 Motion Picture and Television Production Studio Soundstages and Approved Production Facilities ... 1-247
- 32.1 General. ... 1-247
- 32.2 Permits. ... 1-247
- 32.3 Fire Watch. ... 1-247
- 32.4 Decorative Materials. ... 1-248

2024 Edition

32.5	Smoking.	1–248
32.6	Pyrotechnic Special Effects and Open Flames.	1–248
32.7	Fire Department Access.	1–248
32.8	Housekeeping.	1–248
32.9	Soundstages and Approved Production Facilities.	1–248
32.10	Production Locations.	1–249

Chapter 33 Outside Storage of Tires ... 1–250
33.1	General.	1–250
33.2	Individual Piles.	1–250
33.3	Emergency Response Plan.	1–251
33.4	Fire Control Measures.	1–251
33.5	Site Access.	1–251
33.6	Signs and Security.	1–251
33.7	Outdoor Storage of Altered Tire Material.	1–251

Chapter 34 General Storage ... 1–251
34.1	General.	1–251
34.2	Classification of Commodities.	1–252
34.3	Commodity Classes.	1–252
34.4	Building Construction.	1–255
34.5	Storage Arrangement.	1–255
34.6	General Fire Protection.	1–255
34.7	Building Equipment, Maintenance, and Operations.	1–256
34.8	Protection of Rack Storage.	1–257
34.9	Protection of Rubber Tires.	1–257
34.10	Protection of Roll Paper.	1–258
34.11	Storage of Idle Pallets.	1–258

Chapter 35 Animal Housing Facilities ... 1–259
35.1	General.	1–259
35.2	Permits.	1–259

Chapter 36 Telecommunication Facilities and Information Technology Equipment ... 1–259
36.1	General.	1–259

Chapter 37 Fixed Guideway Transit and Passenger Rail Systems ... 1–259
37.1	General.	1–259

Chapter 38 Cannabis Growing, Processing, or Extraction Facilities ... 1–260
38.1	Application.	1–260
38.2	Permits.	1–260
38.3	Fire Protection Systems.	1–260
38.4	Means of Egress.	1–260
38.5	Growing or Production of Cannabis.	1–260
38.6	Processing or Extraction.	1–261
38.7	Transfilling.	1–264

Chapter 39 Wastewater Treatment and Collection Facilities ... 1–264
39.1	General.	1–264

Chapter 40 Dust Explosion and Fire Prevention ... 1–264
40.1	Application.	1–264
40.2	Permits.	1–264
40.3	Retroactivity.	1–264
40.4	General.	1–264
40.5	Dust Hazards Analysis (DHA).	1–264
40.6	Operating Procedures and Practices.	1–265
40.7	Housekeeping.	1–265
40.8	Hot Work.	1–267
40.9	Personal Protective Equipment.	1–267
40.10	Inspection, Testing, and Maintenance.	1–267
40.11	Training and Hazard Awareness.	1–267
40.12	Contractors.	1–268
40.13	Emergency Planning and Response.	1–268
40.14	Incident Investigation.	1–268
40.15	Management of Change.	1–268
40.16	Documentation Retention.	1–268
40.17	Management Systems Review.	1–268
40.18	Employee Participation.	1–268

Chapter 41 Welding, Cutting, and Other Hot Work ... 1–269
41.1	General.	1–269
41.2	Responsibility for Hot Work.	1–269
41.3	Fire Prevention Precautions.	1–270
41.4	Sole Proprietors and Individual Operators.	1–272
41.5	Public Exhibitions and Demonstrations.	1–272
41.6	Arc Welding Equipment.	1–272

Chapter 42 Refueling ... 1–272
42.1	General.	1–272
42.2	Automotive Fuel Servicing.	1–272
42.3	Storage of Liquids.	1–273
42.4	Piping for Liquids.	1–276
42.5	Fuel Dispensing Systems.	1–278
42.6	Building Construction Requirements.	1–280
42.7	Operational Requirements.	1–280
42.8	Additional Requirements for CNG, LNG, Hydrogen, and LP-Gas.	1–285
42.9	Marine Fueling.	1–285
42.10	Aircraft Fuel Servicing.	1–289
42.11	Alternate Fuels.	1–305
42.12	On-Demand Mobile Fueling.	1–305

Chapter 43 Spraying, Dipping, and Coating Using Flammable or Combustible Materials ... 1–308
43.1	Application.	1–308
43.2	Automated Electrostatic Spray Equipment.	1–322
43.3	Handheld Electrostatic Spray Equipment.	1–322
43.4	Drying, Curing, and Fusion Processes.	1–322
43.5	Miscellaneous Spray Operations.	1–322
43.6	Powder Coating.	1–324
43.7	Organic Peroxides and Plural Component Coatings.	1–324
43.8	Containers. [33:17.7.2]	1–324
43.9	Styrene Cross-Linked Composites Manufacturing (Glass Fiber–Reinforced Plastics).	1–324
43.10	Dipping, Coating, and Printing Processes.	1–325
43.11	Training.	1–326

Chapter 44 Solvent Extraction ... 1–326
44.1	General.	1–326
44.2	Application.	1–326
44.3	Permits.	1–326
44.4	Special Requirements.	1–326

Chapter 45 Combustible Fibers ... 1–326
45.1	General.	1–326
45.2	Electrical Wiring.	1–326
45.3	No Smoking.	1–326
45.4	Vehicles and Material Handling Equipment.	1–326
45.5	Loose Storage of Combustible Fibers.	1–326
45.6	Baled Storage.	1–327
45.7	Storage of Hay, Straw, and Other Similar Agricultural Products.	1–327
45.8	Hazardous Materials.	1–327

Chapter 46 Additive Manufacturing (3D Printing) ... 1–328
46.1	Application.	1–328
46.2	Nonindustrial Additive Manufacturing.	1–328
46.3	Industrial Additive Manufacturing.	1–328

Chapter 47 Reserved ... 1–328

Chapter 48	Reserved	1–328
Chapter 49	Reserved	1–328
Chapter 50	**Commercial Cooking**	1–329
50.1	Application.	1–329
50.2	General Requirements for Cooking Operations in Buildings and Mobile and Temporary Cooking Operations.	1–329
50.3	Protection of Coverings and Enclosure Materials.	1–329
50.4	Fire-Extinguishing Equipment for Cooking Operations in Buildings.	1–330
50.5	Fire-Extinguishing Equipment for Mobile and Temporary Cooking Operations.	1–332
50.6	Procedures for the Use, Inspection, Testing, and Maintenance of Equipment.	1–333
50.7	Minimum Safety Requirements for Cooking Equipment.	1–335
50.8	Mobile and Temporary Cooking Operations.	1–336
Chapter 51	**Industrial Ovens and Furnaces**	1–339
51.1	General.	1–339
51.2	Location.	1–339
51.3	Safety Controls.	1–339
Chapter 52	**Energy Storage Systems**	1–339
52.1	General.	1–339
52.2	Remediation Measures.	1–341
52.3	System Interconnection.	1–341
52.4	Operation and Maintenance.	1–341
52.5	Electrochemical Energy Storage Systems.	1–341
52.6	Capacitor Energy Storage Systems.	1–341
52.7	Fuel Cell Energy Storage Systems.	1–341
52.8	Storage of Used or Off-Specification Batteries.	1–341
Chapter 53	**Mechanical Refrigeration**	1–341
53.1	General.	1–341
53.2	Safety Features.	1–342
53.3	Operations, Maintenance, Testing, and Decommissioning.	1–344
Chapter 54	**Ozone Gas–Generating Equipment**	1–344
54.1	Scope.	1–344
54.2	Location.	1–344
54.3	Piping, Valves, and Fittings.	1–345
54.4	Automatic Shutdown.	1–345
54.5	Manual Shutdown.	1–345
Chapter 55	**Cleaning and Purging of Flammable Gas Piping Systems**	1–345
55.1	Application.	1–345
55.2	Permits.	1–345
Chapter 56	Reserved	1–345
Chapter 57	Reserved	1–345
Chapter 58	Reserved	1–345
Chapter 59	Reserved	1–345
Chapter 60	**Hazardous Materials**	1–345
60.1	General Requirements.	1–345
60.2	Special Definitions.	1–346
60.3	Classification of Materials, Wastes, and Hazard of Contents.	1–347
60.4	Permissible Storage and Use Locations.	1–347
60.5	Fundamental Requirements.	1–353
60.6	Emergency Action Planning, Fire Risk Control, and Chemical Hazard Requirements for Industrial Processes.	1–360
60.7	Performance Alternative.	1–360
Chapter 61	**Aerosol Products**	1–361
61.1	General Provisions.	1–361
61.2	Basic Requirements.	1–362
61.3	Storage in Warehouses and Storage Areas.	1–364
61.4	Mercantile Occupancies.	1–365
61.5	Operations and Maintenance.	1–366
Chapter 62	Reserved	1–367
Chapter 63	**Compressed Gases and Cryogenic Fluids**	1–367
63.1	General Provisions.	1–367
63.2	Building-Related Controls.	1–369
63.3	Compressed Gases.	1–374
63.4	Cryogenic Fluids.	1–389
63.5	Bulk Oxygen Systems.	1–396
63.6	Gas Hydrogen Systems.	1–396
63.7	Bulk Liquefied Hydrogen Systems.	1–396
63.8	Gas Generation Systems.	1–396
63.9	Insulated Liquid Carbon Dioxide Systems.	1–396
63.10	Storage, Handling, and Use of Ethylene Oxide for Sterilization and Fumigation.	1–399
63.11	Carbon Dioxide Beverage Systems.	1–399
63.12	Liquid Oxygen in Home Care.	1–400
Chapter 64	**Corrosive Solids and Liquids**	1–401
64.1	General.	1–401
Chapter 65	**Explosives, Fireworks, and Model Rocketry**	1–401
65.1	General.	1–401
65.2	Display Fireworks.	1–401
65.3	Pyrotechnics Before a Proximate Audience.	1–401
65.4	Flame Effects Before an Audience.	1–401
65.5	Fireworks Manufacturing.	1–401
65.6	Model Rocketry.	1–401
65.7	Rocketry Manufacturing.	1–401
65.8	High Power Rocketry.	1–401
65.9	Explosives.	1–401
Chapter 66	**Flammable and Combustible Liquids**	1–402
66.1	General.	1–402
66.2	Reserved.	1–402
66.3	Definitions.	1–402
66.4	Classification of Liquids.	1–403
66.5	Reserved.	1–404
66.6	Fire and Explosion Prevention and Risk Control.	1–404
66.7	Electrical Systems.	1–408
66.8	Application of Area Classification.	1–408
66.9	Storage of Ignitible (Flammable or Combustible) Liquids in Containers — General Requirements.	1–408
66.10	Reserved.	1–417
66.11	Reserved.	1–417
66.12	Reserved.	1–417
66.13	Reserved.	1–417
66.14	Hazardous Materials Storage Lockers.	1–417
66.15	Outdoor Storage.	1–418
66.16	Automatic Fire Protection for Inside Liquid Storage Areas.	1–420
66.17	Processing Facilities.	1–452
66.18	Dispensing, Handling, Transfer, and Use of Ignitible (Flammable or Combustible) Liquids.	1–459
66.19	Specific Operations.	1–461
66.20	Reserved.	1–465

2024 Edition

66.21	Storage of Ignitible (Flammable or Combustible) Liquids in Tanks — Requirements for All Storage Tanks.	1–465
66.22	Storage of Ignitible (Flammable or Combustible) Liquids in Tanks — Aboveground Storage Tanks.	1–471
66.23	Storage of Ignitible (Flammable or Combustible) Liquids in Tanks — Underground Tanks.	1–480
66.24	Storage Tank Buildings.	1–480
66.25	Storage Tank Vaults.	1–484
66.26	Reserved.	1–485
66.27	Piping Systems.	1–485
66.28	Bulk Loading and Unloading Facilities for Tank Cars and Tank Vehicles.	1–489
66.29	Wharves.	1–491
Chapter 67	**Flammable Solids**	1–494
67.1	General.	1–494
Chapter 68	**Highly Toxic and Toxic Solids and Liquids**	1–494
68.1	General.	1–494
Chapter 69	**Liquefied Petroleum Gases and Liquefied Natural Gases**	1–494
69.1	General Provisions.	1–494
69.2	LP-Gas Equipment and Appliances.	1–494
69.3	Installation of LP-Gas Systems.	1–496
69.4	LP-Gas Liquid Transfer.	1–509
69.5	Storage of Cylinders Awaiting Use, Resale, or Exchange.	1–512
69.6	Vehicular Transportation of LP-Gas.	1–514
69.7	LP-Gases at Utility Plants.	1–516
69.8	Liquefied Natural Gas (LNG) Facilities.	1–516
Chapter 70	**Oxidizer Solids and Liquids**	1–516
70.1	General.	1–516
Chapter 71	**Pyrophoric Solids and Liquids**	1–516
71.1	General.	1–516
Chapter 72	**Unstable (Reactive) Solids and Liquids**	1–516
72.1	General.	1–516
Chapter 73	**Water-Reactive Solids and Liquids**	1–516
73.1	General.	1–516
Chapter 74	**Ammonium Nitrate**	1–517
74.1	General.	1–517
Chapter 75	**Organic Peroxide Solids and Liquids**	1–517
75.1	General.	1–517
Annex A	**Explanatory Material**	1–518
Annex B	**Sample Ordinance Adopting the NFPA 1, *Fire Code***	1–719
Annex C	**Fire Fighter Safety Building Marking System**	1–720
Annex D	**Firefighter Breathing-Air Replenishment Systems**	1–721
Annex E	**Fire Sprinkler Disclosure Statement for One- and Two-Family Dwellings**	1–721
Annex F	**Informational References**	1–722
Index		1–730

NFPA 1

Fire Code

2024 Edition

IMPORTANT NOTE: This NFPA document is made available for use subject to important notices and legal disclaimers. These notices and disclaimers appear in all publications containing this document and may be found under the heading "Important Notices and Disclaimers Concerning NFPA Standards." They can also be viewed at www.nfpa.org/disclaimers or obtained on request from NFPA.

UPDATES, ALERTS, AND FUTURE EDITIONS: *New editions of NFPA codes, standards, recommended practices, and guides (i.e., NFPA Standards) are released on scheduled revision cycles. This edition may be superseded by a later one, or it may be amended outside of its scheduled revision cycle through the issuance of Tentative Interim Amendments (TIAs). An official NFPA Standard at any point in time consists of the current edition of the document, together with all TIAs and Errata in effect. To verify that this document is the current edition or to determine if it has been amended by TIAs or Errata, please consult the National Fire Codes® Subscription Service or the "List of NFPA Codes & Standards" at www.nfpa.org/docinfo. In addition to TIAs and Errata, the document information pages also include the option to sign up for alerts for individual documents and to be involved in the development of the next edition.*

NOTICE: An asterisk (*) following the number or letter designating a paragraph indicates that explanatory material on the paragraph can be found in Annex A.

A reference in brackets [ ] following a section or paragraph indicates material that has been extracted from another NFPA document. Extracted text may be edited for consistency and style and may include the revision of internal paragraph references and other references as appropriate. Requests for interpretations or revisions of extracted text shall be sent to the technical committee responsible for the source document.

Information on referenced and extracted publications can be found in Chapter 2 and Annex F.

Chapter 1 Administration

1.1 Scope.

1.1.1* The scope includes, but is not limited to, the following:

(1) Inspection of permanent and temporary buildings, processes, equipment, systems, and other fire and related life safety situations
(2) Investigation of fires, explosions, hazardous materials incidents, and other related emergency incidents
(3) Review of construction plans, drawings, and specifications for life safety systems, fire protection systems, access, water supplies, processes, hazardous materials, and other fire and life safety issues
(4) Fire and life safety education of fire brigades, employees, responsible parties, and the general public
(5) Existing occupancies and conditions, the design and construction of new buildings, remodeling of existing buildings, and additions to existing buildings
(6) Design, installation, alteration, modification, construction, maintenance, repairs, servicing, and testing of fire protection systems and equipment
(7) Installation, use, storage, and handling of medical gas systems
(8) Access requirements for fire department operations
(9) Hazards from outside fires in vegetation, trash, building debris, and other materials
(10) Regulation and control of special events including, but not limited to, assemblage of people, exhibits, trade shows, amusement parks, haunted houses, outdoor events, and other similar special temporary and permanent occupancies
(11) Interior finish, decorations, furnishings, and other combustibles that contribute to fire spread, fire load, and smoke production
(12) Storage, use, processing, handling, and on-site transportation of flammable and combustible gases, liquids, and solids
(13) Storage, use, processing, handling, and on-site transportation of hazardous materials
(14) Control of emergency operations and scenes
(15) Conditions affecting fire fighter safety
(16) Arrangement, design, construction, and alteration of new and existing means of egress

1.1.2 Title. The title of this *Code* shall be NFPA 1, *Fire Code*, of the National Fire Protection Association (NFPA).

1.2* Purpose. The purpose of this *Code* is to prescribe minimum requirements necessary to establish a reasonable level of fire and life safety and property protection from the hazards created by fire, explosion, and dangerous conditions.

1.3 Application.

1.3.1 This *Code* shall apply to both new and existing conditions.

1.3.2* Referenced Standards.

1.3.2.1 Details regarding processes, methods, specifications, equipment testing and maintenance, design standards, performance, installation, or other pertinent criteria contained in those codes and standards listed in Chapter 2 of this *Code* shall be considered a part of this *Code*.

1.3.2.2* Where no applicable codes, standards, or requirements are set forth in this *Code* or contained within other laws, codes, regulations, ordinances, or bylaws adopted by the authority having jurisdiction (AHJ), compliance with applicable codes and standards of NFPA or other nationally recognized standards, as are approved, or approved performance-based options in accordance with Chapter 5, shall be deemed as prima facie evidence of compliance with the intent of this *Code*.

1.3.2.3 Nothing herein shall diminish the authority of the AHJ to determine compliance with codes or standards for those activities or installations within the AHJ's responsibility.

1.3.2.4 Retroactivity of Referenced Standards to Existing Conditions. Unless otherwise specified by 1.3.2.4.1 through 1.3.2.4.3, the current provisions of the referenced standards shall not apply to facilities, equipment, structures, or installations that existed or were approved for construction or installation prior to the effective date of this *Code*.

1.3.2.4.1 Where specified by a reference standard for existing occupancies, conditions, or systems, the provisions of the referenced standards shall be retroactive.

1.3.2.4.2 Facilities, equipment, structures, and installations, installed in accordance with a reference standard, shall be maintained in accordance with the edition of the standard in effect at the time of installation.

1.3.2.4.3 In those cases where the AHJ determines that the existing situation constitutes an imminent danger, the AHJ shall be permitted to apply retroactively any portions of the current referenced standards deemed appropriate.

1.3.3 Conflicts.

1.3.3.1 When a requirement differs between this *Code* and a referenced document, the requirement of this *Code* shall apply.

1.3.3.2 When a conflict between a general requirement and a specific requirement occurs, the specific requirement shall apply.

1.3.4 Multiple Occupancies. Where two or more classes of occupancy occur in the same building or structure and are so intermingled that separate safeguards are impractical, means of egress facilities, construction, protection, and other safeguards shall comply with the most restrictive fire safety requirements of the occupancies involved.

1.3.5 Vehicles and Vessels. Vehicles, vessels, or other similar conveyances, when in fixed locations and occupied as buildings, as described by Section 11.6 of NFPA *101* shall be treated as buildings and comply with this *Code*.

1.3.6 Buildings.

1.3.6.1 Buildings permitted for construction after the adoption of this *Code* shall comply with the provisions stated herein for new buildings.

1.3.6.2* Buildings in existence or permitted for construction prior to the adoption of this *Code* shall comply with the provisions stated herein or referenced for existing buildings *(see 10.3.2)*.

1.3.6.3 Repairs, renovations, alterations, reconstruction, change of occupancy, and additions to buildings shall conform to this *Code*, NFPA *101*, and the building code.

1.3.6.4 Newly introduced equipment, materials, and operations regulated by this *Code* shall comply with the requirements for new construction or processes.

1.3.7 Severability. If any provision of this *Code* or the application thereof to any person or circumstance is held invalid, the remainder of the *Code* and the application of such provision to other persons or circumstances shall not be affected thereby.

1.4 Equivalencies, Alternatives, and Modifications.

1.4.1 Equivalencies. Nothing in this *Code* is intended to prevent the use of systems, methods, or devices of equivalent or superior quality, strength, fire resistance, effectiveness, durability, and safety to those prescribed by this *Code*, provided technical documentation is submitted to the AHJ to demonstrate equivalency and the system, method, or device is approved for the intended purpose.

1.4.1.1* Compliance with Subsequent Editions of Referenced Publications. The AHJ shall be authorized to accept subsequent editions of publications referenced in this *Code* as evidence of compliance with the specified edition. When the AHJ accepts compliance with a subsequent edition of a referenced publication, compliance with subsequent edition shall be considered evidence of compliance with this *Code's* specified edition.

1.4.1.1.1* Compliance with subsequent editions of reference publications shall be achieved by complying with the entire subsequent edition of the referenced publication.

1.4.1.1.2* Compliance with individual specific sections contained in subsequent editions of referenced publications, and not the entire reference publication, shall only be approved by the AHJ through technical documentation submitted in compliance with 1.4.1 or 1.4.2.

1.4.2 Alternatives. The specific requirements of this *Code* shall be permitted to be altered by the AHJ to allow alternative methods that will secure equivalent fire safety, but in no case shall the alternative afford less fire safety than, in the judgment of the AHJ, that which would be provided by compliance with the provisions contained in this *Code*.

1.4.3* Modifications. The AHJ is authorized to modify any of the provisions of this *Code* upon application in writing by the owner, a lessee, or a duly authorized representative where there are practical difficulties in the way of carrying out the provisions of the *Code*, provided that, in the judgment of the AHJ, the intent of the *Code* shall be complied with, public safety secured, and substantial justice done.

1.4.4 Buildings with equivalency, alternatives, or modifications approved by the AHJ shall be considered as conforming with this *Code*.

1.4.5 Each application for an equivalent, alternative, or modified fire protection feature shall be filed with the AHJ and shall be accompanied by such evidence, letters, statements, results of tests, or other supporting information as required to justify the request. The AHJ shall keep a record of actions on such applications, and a signed copy of the AHJ's decision shall be provided for the applicant.

1.4.6 Approval. The AHJ shall approve such equivalent, alternative, or modified construction systems, materials, or methods of design when it is substantiated that the standards of this *Code* are at least equaled. If, in the opinion of the AHJ, the standards of this *Code* are not equaled by the alternative requested, approval for permanent work shall be refused. Consideration shall be given to test or prototype installations.

1.4.7 Tests.

1.4.7.1 Whenever evidence of compliance with the requirements of this *Code* is insufficient or evidence that any material or method of construction does not conform to the requirements of this *Code*, or to substantiate claims for alternative construction systems, materials, or methods of construction, the AHJ shall be permitted to require tests for proof of compliance to be made by an approved agency at the expense of the owner or his/her agent.

1.4.7.2 Test methods shall be as specified by this *Code* for the material in question. If appropriate test methods are not specified in this *Code*, the AHJ is authorized to accept an applicable test procedure from another recognized source.

1.4.7.3 Copies of the results of all such tests shall be retained in accordance with Section 1.12.

1.5 Units.

1.5.1 International System of Units. Metric units of measurement in this *Code* are in accordance with the modernized metric system known as the International System of Units (SI).

1.5.2 Primary and Equivalent Values. If a value for a measurement as given in this *Code* is followed by an equivalent value in other units, the first stated value shall be regarded as the requirement. A given equivalent value could be approximate.

1.6 Enforcement. This *Code* shall be administered and enforced by the AHJ designated by the governing authority. *(See Annex B for sample wording for enabling legislation.)*

1.7 Authority.

1.7.1 Administration. The provisions of this *Code* shall apply without restriction, unless specifically exempted.

1.7.2* Minimum Qualifications to Enforce This *Code*. The AHJ shall establish minimum qualifications for all persons assigned the responsibility of enforcing this *Code*.

1.7.2.1 Fire inspectors and plans examiners shall meet the minimum professional qualifications established in NFPA 1030.

1.7.2.2 The AHJ shall be authorized to approve alternative qualifications for personnel conducting fire inspections and plan examination under 1.7.2.1 if the AHJ determines the individual possesses the knowledge, skills, and abilities to perform the job performance requirements of the position.

1.7.2.3 Fire marshals shall meet the minimum professional qualifications established in NFPA 1030.

1.7.2.4 The AHJ shall be authorized to approve alternative qualifications for personnel performing the position of fire marshal under 1.7.2.3 if the AHJ determines the individual possesses the knowledge, skills, and abilities to perform the job performance requirements of the position.

1.7.3 Interpretations, Rules, and Regulations.

1.7.3.1 The AHJ is authorized to render interpretations of this *Code* and to make and enforce rules and supplemental regulations in order to carry out the application and intent of its provisions.

1.7.3.2 Such interpretations, rules, and regulations shall be in conformance with the intent and purpose of this *Code* and shall be available to the public during normal business hours.

1.7.4 Enforcement Assistance. Police and other enforcement agencies shall have authority to render necessary assistance in the enforcement of this *Code* when requested to do so by the AHJ.

1.7.5 Delegation of Authority. The AHJ shall be permitted to delegate to other qualified individuals such powers as necessary for the administration and enforcement of this *Code*.

1.7.6 Reliance on Other Enforcement Officials.

1.7.6.1* The AHJ shall be authorized to rely on plan reviews, inspections, opinions, and approvals rendered by other enforcement officials in determining compliance with this *Code*.

1.7.6.2 When the AHJ relies on inspections, plan reviews, opinions, and approvals rendered by other enforcement officials in determining compliance with this *Code*, the other enforcement officials shall be deemed to be acting as agents under their own authority and not as agents of the AHJ enforcing this *Code*.

1.7.7 Inspection.

1.7.7.1* The AHJ shall be authorized to inspect, at all reasonable times, any building or premises for dangerous or hazardous conditions or materials as set forth in this *Code*.

1.7.7.2 To the full extent permitted by law, any AHJ engaged in fire prevention and inspection work shall be authorized at all reasonable times to enter and examine any building, structure, marine vessel, vehicle, or premises for the purpose of making fire safety inspections.

1.7.7.3 Before entering, the AHJ shall obtain the consent of the occupant thereof or obtain a court warrant authorizing entry for the purpose of inspection except in those instances where an emergency exists.

1.7.7.4 As used in 1.7.7.3, emergency shall mean circumstances that the AHJ knows, or has reason to believe, exist and that can constitute imminent danger.

1.7.7.5 Persons authorized to enter and inspect buildings, structures, marine vessels, vehicles, and premises as herein set forth shall be identified by credentials issued by the governing authority.

N 1.7.7.6* Building, fire and life safety, fire protection systems and equipment, and other AHJ code-related inspections shall be permitted to be modified or delayed as permitted by the AHJ due to national, regional, or locally declared disasters.

1.7.8 Authority to Order Corrections and Abate.

1.7.8.1 The AHJ shall have authority to order any person(s) to remove or remedy such dangerous or hazardous condition or material. Any person(s) failing to comply with such order shall be in violation of this *Code*.

1.7.8.2 Where conditions exist and are deemed hazardous to life or property by the AHJ, the AHJ shall have the authority to summarily abate such hazardous conditions that are in violation of this *Code*.

1.7.8.3* Where such hazardous conditions exist, abatement actions by the AHJ shall include the authority to order the immediate disconnection or reconnection of utilities to a structure or property.

1.7.9 Interference with Enforcement. Persons shall not interfere or cause conditions that would interfere with an AHJ carrying out any duties or functions prescribed by this *Code*.

1.7.10 Impersonation. Persons shall not use a badge, uniform, or other credentials to impersonate the AHJ.

1.7.11 Investigation.

1.7.11.1 Authority. The AHJ shall have the authority to investigate the cause, origin, and circumstances of any fire, explosion, release of hazardous materials, or other hazardous condition.

1.7.11.2 Evidence. The AHJ shall have the authority to take custody of all physical evidence relating to the origin and cause of a fire, explosion, release of hazardous materials, or other hazardous condition.

1.7.11.3 Limiting Access. The AHJ shall have the authority to limit access to emergencies or other similar situations.

1.7.12 Plans and Specifications.

1.7.12.1 The AHJ shall have the authority to require plans and specifications to ensure compliance with applicable codes and standards.

1.7.12.2 Plans shall be submitted to the AHJ prior to construction unless otherwise permitted by 1.7.12.4.

1.7.12.3 The construction documents for each phase shall be complete in themselves, so that review and inspection can properly be made. Preliminary plans of the total building shall be submitted with the construction documents, and with sufficient detail, so that proper evaluation can be made. Areas and items not included in the phase to be permitted shall be shown as not included. [5000:1.7.6.3.3.3]

1.7.12.4 The AHJ is authorized to exempt detached one- and two-family dwellings and accessory structures from the submittal of plans and permit requirements in 1.7.12.8.

1.7.12.5 Plans shall be submitted to the AHJ prior to the change of occupancy of any existing building.

1.7.12.6 Plans shall be submitted to the AHJ prior to the alteration of the means of egress or fire protection systems of any existing building.

1.7.12.7 Plans shall be submitted to the AHJ for other conditions as deemed necessary by the AHJ to determine compliance with the applicable codes and standards.

1.7.12.8 The AHJ shall be authorized to require permits for conditions listed in 1.7.12.2, 1.7.12.5, and 1.7.12.6, unless otherwise permitted by 1.7.12.4.

1.7.12.9 No construction work shall proceed until the AHJ has reviewed the plans for compliance with the applicable codes and standards and the applicable permits have been issued.

1.7.13 Inspection of Construction and Installation.

1.7.13.1 The AHJ shall be notified by the person performing the work when the installation is ready for a required inspection.

1.7.13.2 Whenever any installation subject to inspection prior to use is covered or concealed without having first been inspected, the AHJ shall have the authority to require that such work be exposed for inspection.

1.7.13.3 When any construction or installation work is being performed in violation of the plans and specifications as approved by the AHJ, a written notice shall be issued to the responsible party to stop work on that portion of the work that is in violation.

1.7.13.4 The notice shall state the nature of the violation, and no work shall be continued on that portion until the violation has been corrected.

1.7.14 Certificate of Occupancy. When the building code requires a certificate of occupancy, the certificate of occupancy shall not be issued until approved by the AHJ for fire code enforcement.

1.7.15 Stop Work Order. The AHJ shall have the authority to order an operation, construction, or use stopped when any of the following conditions exists:

(1) Work is being done contrary to provision of this *Code*.
(2) Work is occurring without a permit required by Section 1.13.
(3) An imminent danger has been created.

1.7.16 Imminent Dangers and Evacuation.

1.7.16.1 When, in the opinion of the AHJ, an imminent danger exists, the AHJ shall be authorized to order the occupants to vacate, or temporarily close for use or occupancy, a building, the right-of-way, sidewalks, streets, or adjacent buildings or nearby areas.

1.7.16.2 Where, in the opinion of the AHJ, an imminent danger exists, the AHJ shall be authorized to order the immediate disconnection or reconnection of utilities to a structure or property.

1.7.16.3 The AHJ shall be authorized to employ the necessary resources to perform the required work in order to mitigate the imminent danger.

1.7.16.4 Costs incurred by the AHJ in the performance of emergency work shall be the responsibility of the property owner or other responsible party creating such imminent danger.

1.7.17 Standby and Fire Watch Personnel.

1.7.17.1 The AHJ shall have the authority to require standby fire personnel, emergency medical services personnel, or an approved fire watch when potentially hazardous conditions or a reduction in a life safety feature exist due to the type of performance, display, exhibit, occupancy, contest, or activity; an impairment to a fire protection feature; or the number of persons present.

1.7.17.2 The owner, agent, or lessee shall employ one or more qualified persons, as required and approved, to be on duty.

1.7.17.2.1 The cost of standby fire personnel or emergency medical services personnel shall be at no cost to the AHJ.

1.7.17.3* Such standby fire personnel, emergency medical services personnel, or fire watch personnel shall be subject to the AHJ's orders at all times and shall be identifiable and remain on duty during the times such places are open to the public, when such activity is being conducted, or as required by the AHJ.

1.7.18 Public Fire Education.

1.7.18.1 The AHJ shall have the authority to develop and implement a public fire safety education program as deemed necessary for the general welfare with respect to the potential fire hazards within the jurisdiction.

1.7.18.2 The AHJ shall have the authority to ensure duly authorized public fire safety education programs or public fire safety messages are disseminated to the general public.

1.8 Duties and Powers of the Incident Commander.

1.8.1 Authority. The incident commander conducting operations in connection with the extinguishment and control of any fire, explosion, hazardous materials incident, natural disaster, rescue, and/or other emergency shall have authority to direct all operations of fire extinguishment, mitigation of a hazardous materials incident, natural disaster, rescue, and/or control and to take necessary precautions to save life, protect property, and prevent further injury or damage.

1.8.2 Controlling Scene. During any emergency described in 1.8.1, including the investigation of the cause of such emergency, the incident commander or authorized representative shall be permitted to control or prohibit the approach to the scene of such emergency by any vehicle, vessel, or person.

1.8.3 Obstruction of Operations. Persons shall not obstruct the operations of the fire department or disobey any command of the incident commander or authorized representative or any part thereof, or any order of a police officer assisting the fire department.

1.8.4 Scene Barrier. The incident commander or authorized representative in charge of an emergency scene shall have the authority to establish barriers to control access in the vicinity of such emergency and to place, or cause to be placed, ropes, guards, barricades, or other obstructions across any street or alley to delineate such emergency scene barrier.

1.8.5 Persons, except as authorized by the incident commander in charge of the emergency, shall not be permitted to cross barriers established in accordance with 1.8.4.

1.9 Liability.

1.9.1 The AHJ, and other individuals charged by the AHJ, or the incident commander of emergency operations, charged with the enforcement of this *Code* or any other official duties, acting in good faith and without malice in the discharge of their duties, shall not thereby be rendered personally liable for any damage that could accrue to persons or property as a result of any act or by reason of any act or omission in the discharge of their duties.

1.9.2 The fire department and AHJ, acting in good faith and without malice in the discharge of the organizations' public duty, shall not thereby be rendered liable for any damage that could accrue to persons or property as a result of any act or by reason of any act or omission in the discharge of such duties.

1.9.3 Any suit brought against the AHJ, the incident commander, or such individuals because of such act or omission performed in the enforcement of any provision of such codes or other pertinent laws or ordinances implemented through the enforcement of this *Code* or enforced by the code enforcement agency shall be defended by this jurisdiction until final termination of such proceedings, and any judgment resulting therefrom shall be assumed by this jurisdiction.

1.9.4 This *Code* shall not be construed to relieve from or lessen the responsibility of any person owning, operating, or controlling any building or structure for any damages to persons or property caused by defects, nor shall the code enforcement agency or its parent jurisdiction be held as assuming any such liability by reason of the inspections authorized by this *Code* or any permits or certificates issued under this *Code*.

N **1.10 Pre-incident Planning.** The fire department and the AHJ shall be authorized to conduct pre-incident planning activities in accordance with NFPA 1660.

1.11 Fire Code Board of Appeals.

1.11.1 Establishment of Fire Code Board of Appeals. A Board of Appeals shall be established to rule on matters relating to the fire code and its enforcement.

1.11.1.1 Membership.

1.11.1.1.1 The members of the Board of Appeals shall be appointed by the governing body of the jurisdiction.

1.11.1.1.2 The Board of Appeals shall consist of five or seven principal members and one ex officio member representative of the AHJ. Each principal member shall be permitted to have an alternate with similar experience to serve in his or her stead when necessary.

1.11.1.1.2.1 The jurisdiction governing body shall have the authority to appoint alternates who shall serve when a principal member is unable to fulfill their obligations. Alternates shall have the full authority and responsibility of principal members when serving in place of a principal member.

1.11.1.1.3 Members and alternate members shall be appointed based on their education, experience, and knowledge.

1.11.1.1.4 Members and alternates shall be appointed to a 3-year term.

1.11.1.1.5 Members and alternates shall be composed of individuals experienced in the following fields or professions:

(1) Engineering or architectural design
(2) General contracting
(3) Fire protection contracting
(4) Fire department operations or fire code enforcement
(5) Building code enforcement
(6) Legal
(7) General public

1.11.1.1.5.1 Members and alternates shall not be employees, agents, or officers of the jurisdiction.

1.11.1.1.5.2 Members and alternates shall be residents of the jurisdiction.

1.11.1.1.5.3 No more than one member shall represent the same field or profession listed in 1.11.1.1.5.

1.11.1.1.6 The representative of the AHJ shall be an ex officio member and shall be entitled to participate in all discussions. The ex officio member shall not be entitled to a vote.

1.11.1.1.7 No member of the Board of Appeals shall sit in judgment on any case in which the member holds a direct or indirect property or financial interest in the case.

1.11.1.1.8 The board shall select one of its members to serve as chair and one member to serve as vice chair.

1.11.2 Rules and Procedures of the Board of Appeals. The Board of Appeals shall have the authority to establish rules and regulations for conducting its business that are consistent with the provisions of this *Code*.

1.11.3 Authority of the Board of Appeals.

1.11.3.1 The Board of Appeals shall provide for the reasonable interpretation of the provisions of this *Code* and issue rulings on appeals of the decisions of the AHJ.

1.11.3.2 The ruling of the Board of Appeals shall be consistent with the letter of the *Code* or when involving issues of clarity, ensuring that the intent of the *Code* is met with due consideration for public safety and fire fighter safety.

1.11.3.3 The Board of Appeals shall have the authority to grant alternatives or modifications through procedures outlined in Section 1.4 of the *Code*.

1.11.3.4 The Board of Appeals shall not have the authority to waive the requirements of the *Code*.

1.11.3.5 The Board of Appeals decisions shall not be precedent setting.

1.11.4 Means of Appeals.

1.11.4.1 Any person with standing shall be permitted to appeal a decision of the AHJ to the Board of Appeals when it is claimed that any one or more of the following conditions exist:

(1) The true intent of the *Code* has been incorrectly interpreted.
(2) The provisions of the *Code* do not fully apply.
(3) A decision is unreasonable or arbitrary as it applies to alternatives or new materials.

1.11.4.2 An appeal shall be submitted to the AHJ in writing within 30 calendar days of notification of violation. The appeal shall outline all of the following:

(1) The *Code* provision(s) from which relief is sought
(2) A statement indicating which provisions of 1.11.4.1 apply
(3) Justification as to the applicability of the provision(s) cited in 1.11.4.1
(4) A requested remedy
(5) Justification for the requested remedy stating specifically how the *Code* is complied with, public safety is secured, and fire fighter safety is secured

1.11.4.3* Documentation supporting an appeal shall be submitted to the AHJ at least 7 calendar days prior to the Board of Appeals hearing.

1.11.5 Meetings and Records.

1.11.5.1 Meetings of the Board of Appeals shall be held at the call of the chair, at such other times as the board determines, and within 30 calendar days of the filing of a notice of appeal.

1.11.5.2 All hearings before the Board of Appeals shall be open to the public.

1.11.5.3 The Board of Appeals shall keep minutes of its proceedings showing the vote of each member on every question or, if the member is absent or fails to vote, these actions shall be recorded.

1.11.5.4 The Board of Appeals shall keep records of its examinations and other official actions.

1.11.5.5 Minutes and records of the Board of Appeals shall be public record.

1.11.5.6 A quorum shall consist of not less than a simple majority of appointed members or alternates.

1.11.5.7 In varying the application of any provision of this *Code*, or in modifying an order of the AHJ, a two-thirds vote of the quorum shall be required.

1.11.6 Decisions.

1.11.6.1 Every decision of the Board of Appeals shall be entered in the minutes of the board meeting.

1.11.6.2 A decision of the Board of Appeals to modify an order of the AHJ shall be in writing and shall specify the manner in which such modification is made, the conditions upon which it is made, the reasons therefore, and justification linked to specific code sections.

1.11.6.3 Every decision shall be promptly filed in the office of the AHJ and shall be open for public inspection.

1.11.6.4 A certified copy shall be sent by mail or delivered in person to the appellant, and a copy shall be publicly posted in the office of the AHJ for 2 weeks after filing.

1.11.6.5 The decision of the Board of Appeals shall be final, subject to such remedy as any aggrieved party might have through legal, equity, or other avenues of appeal or petition.

1.11.6.6 If a decision of the Board of Appeals reverses or modifies a refusal, order, or disallowance of the AHJ, or varies the application of any provision of this *Code*, the AHJ shall take action immediately in accordance with such decision.

1.12 Records and Reports.

1.12.1 A record of examinations, approvals, equivalencies, and alternates shall be maintained by the AHJ and shall be available for public inspection during business hours in accordance with applicable laws.

Δ **1.12.1.1** Documents requested from a property owner shall be maintained by the AHJ.

1.12.2 The AHJ shall keep a record of all fire prevention inspections, including the date of such inspections and a summary of any violations found to exist, the date of the services of notices, and a record of the final disposition of all violations.

1.12.3 The AHJ shall keep a record of all permits and plans reviewed, including the dates of such reviews and a summary of any comments, denials, or approvals.

1.12.4 Emergency Response Records.

1.12.4.1 The fire department shall keep a record of fire and other emergency responses occurring within its jurisdiction and of facts concerning the same, including statistics as to the extent and damage caused by such fires or emergencies.

Δ **1.12.4.2** The fire department shall report its incident record data, collected in accordance with 1.12.4, to the recognized agency responsible for collecting such data.

1.12.5 All records required to be kept shall be maintained until their usefulness has been served or as required by law.

1.13 Permits and Approvals.

1.13.1 The AHJ shall be authorized to establish and issue permits, certificates, and approvals pertaining to conditions, operations, or materials hazardous to life or property pursuant to Section 1.13.

1.13.2 Applications for permits shall be made to the AHJ on forms provided by the jurisdiction and shall include the applicant's answers in full to inquiries set forth on such forms.

1.13.2.1 Applications for permits shall be accompanied by such data as required by the AHJ and fees as required by the jurisdiction.

1.13.2.2 The AHJ shall review all applications submitted and issue permits as required.

1.13.2.3 If an application for a permit is rejected by the AHJ, the applicant shall be advised of the reasons for such rejection.

1.13.2.4 Permits for activities requiring evidence of financial responsibility by the jurisdiction shall not be issued unless proof of required financial responsibility is furnished.

1.13.3 Conditions of Approval.

1.13.3.1 Any conditions of the initial approval by the AHJ of a use, occupancy, permit, or construction shall remain with the use, occupancy, permit, or construction unless modified by the AHJ.

1.13.3.2 The AHJ shall be permitted to require conditions of approval be memorialized via recording in the public records, as part of the plat, permit, or other method as approved by the AHJ.

1.13.4 Approvals by Other AHJs.

1.13.4.1 The AHJ shall have the authority to require evidence to show that other regulatory agencies having jurisdiction over the design, construction, alteration, repair, equipment, maintenance, process, and relocation of structures have issued appropriate approvals.

1.13.4.2 The AHJ shall not be held responsible for enforcement of the regulations of such other regulatory agencies unless specifically mandated to enforce those agencies' regulations.

1.13.5 Misrepresentation.

1.13.5.1 Any attempt to misrepresent or otherwise deliberately or knowingly design; install; service; maintain; operate; sell; represent for sale; falsify records, reports, or applications; or other related activity in violation of the requirements prescribed by this *Code* shall be a violation of this *Code*.

1.13.5.2 Such violations shall be cause for immediate suspension or revocation of any related approvals, certificates, or permits issued by this jurisdiction.

1.13.5.3 Such violations shall be subject to any other criminal or civil penalties as available by the laws of this jurisdiction.

1.13.6 Permits.

1.13.6.1 A permit shall be predicated upon compliance with the requirements of this *Code* and shall constitute written authority issued by the AHJ to maintain, store, use, or handle materials; to conduct processes that could produce conditions hazardous to life or property; or to install equipment used in connection with such activities.

1.13.6.2 Any permit issued under this *Code* shall not take the place of any other approval, certificate, license, or permit required by other regulations or laws of this jurisdiction.

1.13.6.3 Where additional permits, approvals, certificates, or licenses are required by other agencies, approval shall be obtained from those other agencies.

1.13.6.4 The AHJ shall have the authority to require an inspection prior to the issuance of a permit.

1.13.6.5 A permit issued under this *Code* shall continue until revoked or for the period of time designated on the permit.

1.13.6.6 The permit shall be issued to one person or business only and for the location or purpose described in the permit.

1.13.6.7 Any change that affects any of the conditions of the permit shall require a new or amended permit.

1.13.6.8 The AHJ shall have the authority to grant an extension of the permit time period upon presentation by the permittee of a satisfactory reason for failure to start or complete the work or activity authorized by the permit.

1.13.6.9 A copy of the permit shall be posted or otherwise readily accessible at each place of operation and shall be subject to inspection as specified by the AHJ.

1.13.6.10 Any activity authorized by any permit issued under this *Code* shall be conducted by the permittee or the permittee's agents or employees in compliance with all requirements of this *Code* applicable thereto and in accordance with the approved plans and specifications.

1.13.6.11 No permit issued under this *Code* shall be interpreted to justify a violation of any provision of this *Code* or any other applicable law or regulation.

1.13.6.12 Any addition or alteration of approved plans or specifications shall be approved in advance by the AHJ, as evidenced by the issuance of a new or amended permit.

1.13.6.13* Permits shall be issued by the AHJ and shall indicate the following:

(1) Operation, activities, or construction for which the permit is issued
(2) Address or location where the operation, activity, or construction is to be conducted
(3) Name, address, and phone number of the permittee
(4) Permit number
(5) Period of validity of the permit
(6) Inspection requirements
(7) Name of the agency authorizing the permit (AHJ)
(8) Date of issuance
(9) Permit conditions as determined by the AHJ

1.13.6.14 Any application for, or acceptance of, any permit requested or issued pursuant to this *Code* shall constitute agreement and consent by the person making the application or accepting the permit to allow the AHJ to enter the premises at any reasonable time to conduct such inspections as required by this *Code*.

1.13.7 Revocation or Suspension of Permits.

1.13.7.1 The AHJ shall be permitted to revoke or suspend a permit or approval issued if any violation of this *Code* is found upon inspection or in case any false statements or misrepresentations have been submitted in the application or plans on which the permit or approval was based.

1.13.7.2 Revocation or suspension shall be constituted when the permittee is duly notified by the AHJ.

1.13.7.3 Any person who engages in any business, operation, or occupation, or uses any premises, after the permit issued therefore has been suspended or revoked pursuant to the provisions of this *Code*, and before such suspended permit has been reinstated or a new permit issued, shall be in violation of this *Code*.

1.13.8 Permits shall be required in accordance with Table 1.13.8(a) through Table 1.13.8(d).

Δ **Table 1.13.8(a) Permit Requirements**

Operations and Materials	Permit Required	Cross Reference Section Number
Additive manufacturing	To conduct industrial additive manufacturing operations	46.1.2
Aerosol products	To store or handle an aggregate quantity of Level 2 or Level 3 aerosol products in excess of 500 lb (226.8 kg)	61.1.2
Aircraft fuel servicing	To provide aircraft fuel servicing	42.1.2
Aircraft hangars	For servicing or repairing aircraft	21.1.1
Aircraft refueling vehicles	To operate aircraft refueling vehicles	42.1.2
Airport terminal buildings	For construction and alteration	21.2.2.1
Ammonium nitrate	For storage	74.1.3
Amusement parks	For construction, alteration, or operation of amusement park fire protection safety features	10.14.1
Animal housing facilities	For operation	35.2
Asbestos removal	For the removal of asbestos	16.6.2
Automatic fire suppression systems	For installation, modification, or removal from service of any automatic fire suppression system*	13.1.1.1; 50.4.2; 1.7.12.6
Automobile wrecking yards	To operate automobile wrecking yards	22.2
Automotive fuel servicing	To provide automotive fuel servicing	42.1.2
Biomass feed stock storage	To store more than 250,000 ft^3 (7080 m^3)	31.2
Candles, open flames, and portable cooking	To use in connection with assembly areas, dining areas of restaurants, or drinking establishments	17.3.2; 20.1.1.1
Cannabis growing, processing, or extraction facilities	For the construction, alteration, or operation of a cannabis growing, processing, or extraction facility	38.2
Carnivals and fairs	To conduct a carnival or fair	10.14.1
Cellulose nitrate film	To store, handle, use, or display	20.15.7.2
Cellulose nitrate plastic	To store or handle more than 25 lb (11.3 kg)	43.1.1.7
Change of occupancy	For the change of occupancy classification of an existing building	1.7.12.5
Cleaning and purging of flammable gas piping systems	Cleaning and purging	55.2
Cleanrooms	For construction, alteration, or operation	23.3
Combustible fibers	For storage or handling of combustible fibers greater than 100 ft^3 (2.8 m^3)	45.1.4
Combustible material storage	To store more than 2500 ft^3 (70.8 m^3) gross volume	10.19.2; 19.1.1; 31.2
Commercial cooking	Placement, operation, or construction	50.1.2
Commercial rubbish-handling operation	To operate	19.1.1
Compressed gases	1. To store, use, or handle compressed gases in excess of the amounts listed in Table 1.13.8(b) 2. When the compressed gases in use or storage exceed the amounts listed in Table 1.13.8(b), a permit is required to install, repair damage to, abandon, remove, place temporarily out of service, close, or substantially modify a compressed gas system 3. For additional permit requirements for compressed gases facility closures, see 63.1.2 4. Insulated liquid carbon dioxide (CO$_2$) systems in accordance with 63.9.2	63.1.2; 63.9.2
Construction	For the construction of a building or structure	1.7.12.2
Covered mall buildings	Annual requirement for facilities that utilize mall area for exhibits or displays with four conditions	20.1.5.5.1

(continues)

Δ **Table 1.13.8(a)** Continued

Operations and Materials	Permit Required	Cross Reference Section Number
Crop maze	To operate a crop maze	10.14.12.1
Cryogens	To produce, store, or handle cryogens in excess of amounts listed in Table 1.13.8(c) *Exception: Where federal or state regulations apply or for fuel systems of a vehicle.*	63.1.2
Cutting and welding operation	For operations within a jurisdiction	31.3.2.1.12; 41.1.5; 41.3.5
Display fireworks (1.3G)	For possession, transportation, storage, manufacture, sale, handling, and discharge of display fireworks within the jurisdiction	65.2.3; 65.5.2
Drycleaning plants	To engage in business of drycleaning or to change to a more hazardous cleaning solvent	24.2
Dust-producing operations	To operate a grain elevator, flour mill, starch mill, feed mill, or plant pulverizing aluminum, coal, cocoa, magnesium, spices, sugar, or other similar combustible material	40.2
Energy storage systems	To install and operate energy storage systems having an aggregate capacity exceeding the threshold quantities in Table 1.3 of NFPA 855	52.1.3
Exhibit and trade shows	For operation of all exhibits and trade shows held within a jurisdiction	20.1.5.5.1
Explosives	1. Manufacture, sell, dispose, purchase, storage, use, possess, or transport of explosives within the jurisdiction 2. For additional permit requirements for blasting operations, see 65.9.2	65.9.2
Fire alarm and detection systems and related equipment	For installation, modification, or removal from service of any fire alarm and detection systems and related equipment*	13.1.1.1; 1.7.12.6
Fire apparatus access roads	For the construction of a fire apparatus access road	18.1.2
Fire hydrants and water-control valves	To use a fire hydrant or operate a water-control valve intended for fire suppression purposes	13.1.1.1
Fire pumps and related equipment	For installation of, modification to, or removal from service of any fire pumps, jockey pumps, controllers, and generators*	13.1.1.1; 1.7.12.6
Flame effects	Use of flame effects before an audience	65.4.2
Flammable and combustible liquids	1. To use or operate, repair, or modify a pipeline for the on-site transportation of flammable or combustible liquids 2. To store, handle, or use Class I liquids in excess of 5 gal (18.9 L) in a building or in excess of 10 gal (37.9 L) outside of a building *Exception to item (2): A permit is not required for the following:* *(a) The storage or use of Class I liquids in the fuel tank of a motor vehicle, aircraft, motorboat, mobile power plant, or mobile heating plant unless such storage in the opinion of the chief would cause an unsafe condition* *(b) The storage or use of paints, oils, varnishes, or similar flammable mixtures when such liquids are stored for maintenance, painting, or similar purposes for a period of not more than 30 days* 3. To store, handle, or use Class II or Class III-A liquids in excess of 25 gal (94.6 L) in a building or in excess of 60 gal (227.1 L) outside a building *Exception to item (3): Fuel oil used in connection with oil-burning equipment* 4. To remove Class I or Class II liquids from an underground storage tank used for fueling motor vehicles by any means other than the approved, stationary on-site pumps normally used for dispensing purposes 5. To install, construct, alter, or operate tank vehicles, equipment, tanks, plants, terminals, wells, fuel-dispensing stations, refineries, distilleries, and similar facilities where flammable and combustible liquids are produced, processed, transported, stored, dispensed, or used 6. To install, alter, clean, repair, line with a protective coating, remove, abandon, place temporarily out of service, or otherwise dispose of a flammable or combustible liquid tank	66.1.6

(continues)

Δ Table 1.13.8(a) Continued

Operations and Materials	Permit Required	Cross Reference Section Number
	7. To change the type of contents stored in a flammable or combustible liquid tank to a material other than those for which the tank was designed and constructed	
Fruit ripening	To operate a fruit-ripening process	63.1.2
General storage	To store materials indoors or outdoors, representing a broad range of combustibles, including plastics, rubber tires, and roll paper	34.1.2
Grandstands, bleachers, and folding and telescopic seating	For construction, location, erection, or placement of grandstands, bleachers, and folding and telescopic seating	25.1.2
Hazardous materials	1. To store, transport on site, dispense, use, or handle hazardous materials in excess of the amounts listed in Table 1.13.8(d) 2. To install, repair, abandon, remove, place temporarily out of service, close, or substantially modify a storage facility or other area regulated by Chapter 60 when the hazardous materials in use or storage exceed the amounts listed in Table 1.13.8(d)	60.1.3
High-piled combustible storage	To use any building or portion thereof as a high-piled storage area exceeding 500 ft^2 (46.45 m^2)	20.15.8.2
High-powered rocketry	For the manufacture, sale, and use of high-powered rocketry	65.8.2; 65.7.2
Hot work operations	To conduct hot work	17.3.2; 41.1.5; 41.3.5
In-building emergency responder communications enhancement systems	To install and operate an in-building emergency responder communication enhancement system	11.10.1
Industrial ovens and furnaces	For operation of industrial ovens and furnaces covered by Chapter 51	51.1.2
Laboratories using chemicals	For construction, alteration, or operation	26.2
Lead removal	For lead removal operations	16.7.2
Liquefied petroleum gases	1. To store, use, handle, or dispense LP-Gas of 125 gal (0.5 m^3) (water capacity) aggregate capacity or greater 2. To install or modify LP-Gas systems	42.1.2 69.1.2
Liquid- or gas-fueled vehicles	To display, compete, or demonstrate liquid- or gas-fueled vehicles or equipment in assembly buildings	20.1.5.5.1
Lumberyards and woodworking plants	For storage of lumber exceeding 100,000 board ft	31.2
Manufactured home and recreational vehicle sites	Installation, construction, and location	27.1.4
Marinas, boatyards, marine terminals, piers, and wharves	To operate, locate, or construct	28.1.1.5
Marine craft fuel servicing	To provide marine craft fuel servicing	41.1.5
Means of egress	For the modification of a means of egress system in an existing building	1.7.12.6
Membrane structures, tents, and canopies — permanent	For construction, location, erection, or placement	25.1.2
Membrane structures, tents, and canopies — temporary	To erect or operate an air-supported temporary membrane structure or tent having an area in excess of 200 ft^2 (18.6 m^2) or a canopy in excess of 400 ft^2 (37.2 m^2) *Exception: Temporary membrane structures, tents, or canopy structures used exclusively for camping.*	25.1.2
Mobile cooking operations	Placement, operation, or construction	50.1.2
Motion picture and television production studio soundstages and approved production facilities	1. To design, construct, operate, and maintain soundstages and approved production facilities used in motion picture and television industry productions 2. Electrical power connections 3. For additional permit requirements for operations, see 32.2.2	32.2; 32.10.1.1

(continues)

Δ Table 1.13.8(a)   Continued

Operations and Materials	Permit Required	Cross Reference Section Number
Oil- and gas-fueled heating appliances	To install oil- and gas-fired heating appliances	11.5.1.8
On-demand mobile fueling	To conduct on-demand mobile fueling operations	42.1.2; 42.12
Open fires	1. For kindling or maintaining an open fire 2. For additional permit requirements for open fires, see 10.10.4†	10.10.4; 10.10.1
Open flame devices	The use of tar pots, decorative torches, and other devices, machines, or processes liable to start or cause an unwanted fire.	10.10.9.1
Organic coatings	For operation and maintenance of a facility that manufactures organic coatings	43.1.1.7
Organic peroxide formulations	To store, transport on site, use, or handle materials in excess of amounts listed in Table 1.13.8(c) and Table 1.13.8(d)	75.1.3
Outside storage of tires	To store more than 500 tires outside	33.1.2
Oxidizers	To store, transport on site, use, or handle materials in excess of amounts listed in Table 1.13.8(c) and (d)	70.1.4
Ozone gas–generating equipment	Location and operation	54.1.3
Parade floats	To use a parade float for public performance, presentation, spectacle, entertainment, or parade	10.17.1
Photovoltaic systems	Installation and placement	11.12.1.2
Places of assembly	To operate a place of assembly	10.14.1; 20.1.1.1
Pyrotechnic articles	For the manufacture, storage, sale, or use of pyrotechnic articles within the jurisdiction	65.2.3; 65.3.3; 65.5.2
Pyrotechnics before a proximate audience	For the display and use of pyrotechnic materials before a proximate audience	65.3.3
Pyroxylin plastics	For storage, handling, assembly, or manufacture of pyroxylin plastics	43.1.1.7
Private fire hydrants	For installation, modification, or removal from service of any private fire hydrants	13.1.1.1
Refrigeration equipment	To install or operate a mechanical refrigeration unit or system regulated by this *Code*	53.1.2
Repair garages	For operation of repair garages	30.1.1.3; 30.2.1.1
Rocketry manufacturing	For the manufacture of model rocket motors	65.7.2
Rooftop heliports	For construction, modification, or operation of a rooftop heliport	21.3.2.1
Rubberized asphalt melters	For operation	16.5.3.2
Solvent extraction	For storage, use, and handling	44.3
Spraying or dipping of flammable finish	For installation or modification of any spray room, spray booth, or preparation workstation, or to conduct a spraying or dipping operation utilizing flammable or combustible liquids or powder coating	43.1.1.7
Standpipe systems	For installation, modification, or removal from service of any standpipe system*	13.1.1.1; 1.7.12.6
Special amusement buildings	Operation	20.1.4.1.3
Special outdoor events	For the location and operation of special outdoor events	10.14.1
Tar kettles	To place a tar kettle, a permit must be obtained prior to the placement of a tar kettle	16.5.1.2; 17.3.2
Temporary cooking	Placement, operation, or construction	50.1.2
Tire storage	To use an open area or portion thereof to store tires in excess of 500 tires	33.1.2; 34.1.2
Torch-applied roofing operation	For the use of a torch for application of roofing materials	16.4.1

(continues)

△ Table 1.13.8(a) *Continued*

Operations and Materials	Permit Required	Cross Reference Section Number
Wastewater treatment and collection facilities	For the operation or construction	39.1.2
Water supply system for fire flow	For the construction of a water supply system for fire flow	18.1.2
Wildland-fire-prone areas	For use of hazardous areas within fire-prone areas	17.3.2
Wood products	To store wood chips, hogged material, wood by-products, lumber, or plywood in excess of 200 ft³ (5.7 m³)	31.2

*Maintenance performed in accordance with this *Code* is not considered a modification and does not require a permit.
†Cooking and recreational fires are exempt and do not require a permit.

Table 1.13.8(b) Permit Amounts for Compressed Gases

Type of Gas	Amount* ft³	Amount* m³
Corrosive	200	0.57
Flammable	200	0.57
Highly toxic	Any amount	
Inert and simple asphyxiant	6000	169.9
Oxidizing (including oxygen)	504	14.3
Pyrophoric	Any amount	
Toxic	Any amount	
Unstable (reactive)	Any amount	

Note: See Chapters 41, 42, 60, 63, and 69 for additional requirements and exceptions.
*Cubic feet measured at normal temperature and pressure.

Table 1.13.8(c) Permit Amounts for Cryogens

Type of Cryogen	Inside Building (gal)	Outside Building (gal)
Corrosive	Over 1	Over 1
Flammable	Over 1	60
Toxic/highly toxic	Over 1	Over 1
Nonflammable	60	500
Oxidizer (includes oxygen)	10	50

Note: See Chapter 63.

△ **1.14 Certificates of Fitness.**

1.14.1 Authorization. The AHJ shall have the authority to require certificates of fitness and collect fees for individuals or companies performing any of the following activities:

(1) Inspection, servicing, or recharging of portable fire extinguishers
(2) Installation, servicing, modification, or recharging of fixed fire extinguishing systems
(3) Installation, servicing, or modification of fire alarm or fire communication systems
(4) Installation, modification, or servicing of gas- or oil-burning heating systems
(5) Chimney sweep operations
(6) Installation, inspection, servicing, or modification of range-hood systems
(7) Installation or servicing of private fire service mains and their appurtenances
(8) Crowd management services required by the *Code*
(9) Utilization of pyrotechnics before a proximate audience
(10) Installation, modification, or maintenance of liquefied petroleum gas or liquefied natural gas tanks or systems
(11) Installation or modification of medical gas systems where a permit is required by Table 1.13.8(a)
(12) Installation, modification, or maintenance of standpipe systems
(13) Installation, modification, or maintenance of automatic sprinkler systems
(14) Installation, modification, or maintenance of fire pumps
(15) Installation, modification, or maintenance of tanks, wells, or drafting points used for fire protection water supplies

1.14.2 Mandatory. The AHJ shall require certificates of fitness and collect fees for individuals or companies performing any of the following activities:

(1) Use of explosive materials
(2) Fireworks displays involving display fireworks, 1.3G

1.14.3 The AHJ shall be responsible for the issuance of certificates of fitness required by the AHJ.

1.14.4 All applications for a certificate of fitness shall be filed with the AHJ on forms provided by the AHJ.

1.14.5 Certification of Applicant.

1.14.5.1 Every individual or company applying for a certificate of fitness shall furnish to the AHJ evidence of a familiarity with applicable codes, regulations, standards, listings, guidelines, and construction and safety practices for the activity for which the certificate of fitness is issued.

1.14.5.2* The AHJ shall also utilize certification programs provided by national organizations acceptable to the AHJ, where available, to determine evidence of compliance with 1.14.5.1.

1.14.5.3 The AHJ shall investigate every application for a certificate of fitness.

1.14.5.4* The investigation shall include an examination of the applicant's experience and training in the field of the certificate of fitness for which application has been made.

Δ **Table 1.13.8(d) Permit Amounts for Hazardous Materials**

Type of Material	US Unit	Metric Unit
Cellulose nitrate	25 lb	11.3 kg
Combustible fiber	100 ft^3	2.8 m^3
Combustible liquids	See Table 1.13.8(a)	
Corrosive gases	See Table 1.13.8(b)	
Corrosive liquids	55 gal	208 L
Corrosive solids	500 lb	227 kg
Cryogens	See Table 1.13.8(c)	
Display fireworks (1.3G)	Any amount	
Explosives	Any amount	
Flammable gases	See Table 1.13.8(b)	
Flammable liquids	See Table 1.13.8(a)	
Flammable solids	100 lb	45.4 kg
Highly toxic gases	See Table 1.13.8(b)	
Highly toxic liquids	Any amount	
Highly toxic solids	Any amount	
LP-Gas	See Table 1.13.8(b)	
Nitrate film (cellulose)	Any amount	
Organic peroxides:	See Table 1.13.8(a)	
Class I	Any amount	
Class II	Any amount	
Class III	10 lb	4.5 kg
Class IV	20 lb	9 kg
Class V	Not required	
Unclassified detonable	Any amount	
Oxidizing gases	See Table 1.13.8(b)	
Oxidizing liquids:	See Table 1.13.8(a)	
Class 4	Any amount	
Class 3	1 gal	3.8 L
Class 2	10 gal	38 L
Class 1	55 gal	208 L
Oxidizing solids:	See Table 1.13.8(a)	
Class 4	Any amount	
Class 3	10 lb	4.5 kg
Class 2	100 lb	45 kg
Class 1	500 lb	227 kg
Pyrophoric gases	See Table 1.13.8(b)	
Pyrophoric liquids	Any amount	
Pyrophoric solids	Any amount	
Toxic gases	See Table 1.13.8(b)	
Toxic liquids	10 gal	38 L
Toxic solids	100 lb	45 kg
Unstable (reactive) gases	See Table 1.13.8(b)	
Unstable (reactive) liquids:		
Class 4	Any amount	
Class 3	Any amount	
Class 2	5 gal	19 L
Class 1	10 gal	38 L
Unstable (reactive) solids:		
Class 4	Any amount	
Class 3	Any amount	
Class 2	50 lb	22.7 kg
Class 1	100 lb	45 kg
Water reactive liquids:		
Class 3	Any amount	
Class 2	5 gal	19 L
Class 1	10 gal	38 L
Water reactive solids:		
Class 3	Any amount	
Class 2	50 lb	22.7 kg
Class 1	100 lb	45 kg

Note: See Chapter 60 for additional requirements and exceptions.

1.14.5.5 When the AHJ determines that an applicant is not fit to receive the certificate of fitness because of the applicant's inability to comply with the provisions of this *Code*, the AHJ shall refuse to issue the certificate of fitness.

1.14.5.6 If the refusal is based on the applicant's inability to pass an examination given to determine competency, the applicant shall not be permitted to apply again for the certificate of fitness within a 10-day period following the examination.

1.14.6 Certificates of fitness shall not be transferable.

1.14.7 Certificates of fitness shall be issued for the period of time as indicated on the certificate of fitness as determined by the AHJ, but such period of time shall not exceed 3 years.

1.14.8 Applications for renewal of a certificate of fitness shall be filed in the same manner as an application for an original certificate.

1.14.9 Each individual or company holding a certificate of fitness shall notify the AHJ in writing of any address change within 10 days after such change.

1.14.10 A certificate of fitness shall be in the form of an identification card. The card shall contain the following information:

(1) Purpose for which the certificate of fitness is issued
(2) Date of expiration
(3) Information necessary to easily identify the individual to whom the certificate of fitness is issued
(4) Signature of the individual to whom the certificate of fitness is issued
(5) Name and signature of the AHJ or a designated representative
(6) Statement printed thereon in bold type the following: THIS CERTIFICATE IS NOT AN ENDORSEMENT OF THIS INDIVIDUAL OR COMPANY BY THE AUTHORITY HAVING JURISDICTION.

1.14.11 Any individual or company to whom a certificate of fitness has been granted shall, upon request, produce and show proper identification and the certificate of fitness to anyone for whom that individual seeks to render services or to the AHJ.

1.14.12 Revocation or Suspension of Certificates of Fitness.

1.14.12.1 The AHJ shall be permitted to revoke or suspend a certificate of fitness issued if any violation of this *Code* is found upon inspection or where any false statements or misrepresentations are submitted in the application on which the approval was based.

1.14.12.2 Revocation or suspension shall be constituted when notification is served, posted, or mailed to the address of record for the certificate holder.

1.14.12.3 Failure on the part of an individual to give such notification of a change of address required by 1.14.9 shall constitute grounds for revocation of the certificate of fitness.

1.14.12.4 Revocations or suspensions of a certificate of fitness by the AHJ are appealable to the Board of Appeals as established in Section 1.11.

1.15 Plan Review.

1.15.1 Where required by the AHJ for new construction, modification, or rehabilitation, construction documents and shop drawings shall be submitted, reviewed, and approved prior to the start of such work as provided in Section 1.15.

1.15.2 The applicant shall be responsible to ensure that the following conditions are met:

(1) The construction documents include all of the fire protection requirements.
(2) The shop drawings are correct and in compliance with the applicable codes and standards.
(3) The contractor maintains an approved set of construction documents on site.

1.15.3 It shall be the responsibility of the AHJ to promulgate rules that cover the following:

(1) Criteria to meet the requirements of Section 1.15
(2) Review of documents and construction documents within established time frames for the purpose of acceptance or providing reasons for nonacceptance

1.15.4 Review and approval by the AHJ shall not relieve the applicant of the responsibility of compliance with this *Code*.

1.15.5 When required by the AHJ, revised construction documents or shop drawings shall be prepared and submitted for review and approval to illustrate corrections or modifications necessitated by field conditions or other revisions to approved construction documents.

1.15.6* When required by the AHJ, plans and design documents shall be prepared by a registered design professional.

1.16 Technical Assistance.

1.16.1 The AHJ shall be permitted to require a review by an approved independent third party with expertise in the matter to be reviewed at the submitter's expense.

1.16.2 The independent reviewer shall provide an evaluation and recommend necessary changes of the proposed design, operation, process, or new technology to the AHJ.

1.16.3 The AHJ shall be authorized to require design submittals to bear the stamp of a registered design professional.

1.16.4 The AHJ shall make the final determination as to whether the provisions of this *Code* have been met.

1.17 Notice of Violations and Penalties.

1.17.1 Where Required. Whenever the AHJ determines violations of this *Code*, a written notice shall be issued to confirm such findings.

1.17.2 Serving Notice of Violation.

1.17.2.1 Any order or notice of violation issued pursuant to this *Code* shall be served upon the owner, operator, occupant, registered agent, or other person responsible for the condition or violation by one of the following means:

(1) Personal service
(2) Mail to last known address of the owner, operator, or registered agent

1.17.2.2 For unattended or abandoned locations, a copy of such order or notice of violation shall be posted on the premises in a conspicuous place at or near the entrance to such premises, and the order or notice shall be disseminated in accordance with one of the following:

(1) Mailed to the last known address of the owner, occupant, or registered agent
(2) Published in a newspaper of general circulation wherein the property in violation is located

1.17.2.3 Refusal of an owner, occupant, operator, or other person responsible for the violation to accept the violation notice shall not be cause to invalidate the violation or the notice of violation. When acceptance of a notice of violation is refused, valid notice shall have deemed to have been served under this section provided the methods of service in 1.17.2.1 or 1.17.2.2 have been followed.

1.17.3 Destruction or Removal of Notice. The mutilation, destruction, or removal of a posted order or violation notice without authorization by the AHJ shall be a separate violation of this *Code* and punishable by the penalties established by the AHJ.

1.17.4 Penalties.

1.17.4.1 Any person who fails to comply with the provisions of this *Code*, fails to carry out an order made pursuant to this *Code*, or violates any condition attached to a permit, approval, or certificate shall be subject to the penalties established by the AHJ.

1.17.4.2 Violations of the provisions of this *Code* shall be punishable by a fine or imprisonment as determined by a penalty schedule adopted by the AHJ or specified by state law/rules.

1.17.4.3 Where the AHJ has not adopted a separate penalty schedule, or if state laws or rules do not specify a penalty, violations of this *Code* shall be subject to a $100.00 penalty per day for each violation.

1.17.4.4 Failure to comply with the time limits of an order or notice of violation issued by the AHJ shall result in each day that the violation continues being regarded as a separate offense and shall be subject to a separate penalty.

1.17.4.5 A separate notice of violation shall not be required to be served each day for a violation to be deemed a separate offense.

1.17.5 Abatement. Where a violation creates an imminent danger, the AHJ is authorized to abate such hazard in accordance with 1.7.16.

Δ **1.18* Fees.** The AHJ shall be authorized to establish a schedule of fees.

Chapter 2 Referenced Publications

2.1 General. The documents referenced in this chapter or portions of such documents are referenced within this *Code* and shall be considered part of the requirements of this document.

(1)* Documents referenced in this chapter or portion of such documents shall only be applicable to the extent called for within other chapters of this *Code*.
(2) Where the requirements of a referenced code or standard differ from the requirements of this *Code*, the requirements of this *Code* shall govern.

2.1.1* Compliance with Subsequent Editions of the Referenced Publications. Compliance with subsequent editions of the referenced publications shall be considered evidence of compliance with the editions specified in this *Code*.

2.1.1.1* Compliance with subsequent editions of reference publications shall be achieved by complying with the entire subsequent edition of the referenced publication.

2.1.1.2* Compliance with individual specific sections contained in subsequent edition referenced publications, and not the entire reference publication, shall only be approved by the AHJ through technical documentation submitted in compliance with 1.4.1 or 1.4.2.

N 2.1.2* Referenced Publications Within Extracted Sections. A publication referenced within an extracted section shall be the edition referenced within the extract document.

Δ 2.2 NFPA Publications. National Fire Protection Association, 1 Batterymarch Park, Quincy, MA 02169-7471.

NFPA 2, *Hydrogen Technologies Code*, 2023 edition.
NFPA 4, *Standard for Integrated Fire Protection and Life Safety System Testing*, 2024 edition.
NFPA 10, *Standard for Portable Fire Extinguishers*, 2022 edition.
NFPA 11, *Standard for Low-, Medium-, and High-Expansion Foam*, 2021 edition.
NFPA 12, *Standard on Carbon Dioxide Extinguishing Systems*, 2022 edition.
NFPA 12A, *Standard on Halon 1301 Fire Extinguishing Systems*, 2022 edition.
NFPA 13, *Standard for the Installation of Sprinkler Systems*, 2022 edition.
NFPA 13D, *Standard for the Installation of Sprinkler Systems in One- and Two-Family Dwellings and Manufactured Homes*, 2022 edition.
NFPA 13R, *Standard for the Installation of Sprinkler Systems in Low-Rise Residential Occupancies*, 2022 edition.
NFPA 14, *Standard for the Installation of Standpipe and Hose Systems*, 2024 edition.
NFPA 15, *Standard for Water Spray Fixed Systems for Fire Protection*, 2022 edition.
NFPA 17, *Standard for Dry Chemical Extinguishing Systems*, 2024 edition.
NFPA 20, *Standard for the Installation of Stationary Pumps for Fire Protection*, 2022 edition.
NFPA 22, *Standard for Water Tanks for Private Fire Protection*, 2023 edition.
NFPA 24, *Standard for the Installation of Private Fire Service Mains and Their Appurtenances*, 2022 edition.
NFPA 25, *Standard for the Inspection, Testing, and Maintenance of Water-Based Fire Protection Systems*, 2023 edition.

NFPA 30, *Flammable and Combustible Liquids Code*, 2024 edition.
NFPA 30A, *Code for Motor Fuel Dispensing Facilities and Repair Garages*, 2024 edition.
NFPA 30B, *Code for the Manufacture and Storage of Aerosol Products*, 2023 edition.
NFPA 31, *Standard for the Installation of Oil-Burning Equipment*, 2020 edition.
NFPA 32, *Standard for Drycleaning Facilities*, 2021 edition.
NFPA 33, *Standard for Spray Application Using Flammable or Combustible Materials*, 2021 edition.
NFPA 34, *Standard for Dipping, Coating, and Printing Processes Using Flammable or Combustible Liquids*, 2021 edition.
NFPA 35, *Standard for the Manufacture of Organic Coatings*, 2021 edition.
NFPA 36, *Standard for Solvent Extraction Plants*, 2021 edition.
NFPA 37, *Standard for the Installation and Use of Stationary Combustion Engines and Gas Turbines*, 2024 edition.
NFPA 40, *Standard for the Storage and Handling of Cellulose Nitrate Film*, 2022 edition.
NFPA 45, *Standard on Fire Protection for Laboratories Using Chemicals*, 2024 edition.
NFPA 51, *Standard for the Design and Installation of Oxygen–Fuel Gas Systems for Welding, Cutting, and Allied Processes*, 2023 edition.
NFPA 51B, *Standard for Fire Prevention During Welding, Cutting, and Other Hot Work*, 2024 edition.
NFPA 52, *Vehicular Natural Gas Fuel Systems Code*, 2023 edition.
NFPA 54, *National Fuel Gas Code*, 2024 edition.
NFPA 55, *Compressed Gases and Cryogenic Fluids Code*, 2023 edition.
NFPA 56, *Standard for Fire and Explosion Prevention During Cleaning and Purging of Flammable Gas Piping Systems*, 2023 edition.
NFPA 58, *Liquefied Petroleum Gas Code*, 2024 edition.
NFPA 59, *Utility LP-Gas Plant Code*, 2024 edition.
NFPA 59A, *Standard for the Production, Storage, and Handling of Liquefied Natural Gas (LNG)*, 2023 edition.
NFPA 61, *Standard for the Prevention of Fires and Dust Explosions in Agricultural and Food Processing Facilities*, 2020 edition.
NFPA 68, *Standard on Explosion Protection by Deflagration Venting*, 2023 edition.
NFPA 69, *Standard on Explosion Prevention Systems*, 2019 edition.
NFPA 70®, *National Electrical Code*®, 2023 edition.
NFPA 72®, *National Fire Alarm and Signaling Code*®, 2022 edition.
NFPA 75, *Standard for the Fire Protection of Information Technology Equipment*, 2020 edition.
NFPA 76, *Standard for the Fire Protection of Telecommunications Facilities*, 2020 edition.
NFPA 80, *Standard for Fire Doors and Other Opening Protectives*, 2022 edition.
NFPA 82, *Standard on Incinerators and Waste and Linen Handling Systems and Equipment*, 2019 edition.
NFPA 85, *Boiler and Combustion Systems Hazards Code*, 2023 edition.
NFPA 86, *Standard for Ovens and Furnaces*, 2023 edition.
NFPA 88A, *Standard for Parking Structures*, 2023 edition.

NFPA 90A, *Standard for the Installation of Air-Conditioning and Ventilating Systems*, 2024 edition.

NFPA 90B, *Standard for the Installation of Warm Air Heating and Air-Conditioning Systems*, 2024 edition.

NFPA 91, *Standard for Exhaust Systems for Air Conveying of Vapors, Gases, Mists, and Particulate Solids*, 2020 edition.

NFPA 92, *Standard for Smoke Control Systems*, 2021 edition.

NFPA 96, *Standard for Ventilation Control and Fire Protection of Commercial Cooking Operations*, 2024 edition.

NFPA 99, *Health Care Facilities Code*, 2024 edition.

NFPA 99B, *Standard for Hypobaric Facilities*, 2024 edition.

NFPA *101®*, *Life Safety Code®*, 2024 edition.

NFPA 102, *Standard for Grandstands, Folding and Telescopic Seating, Tents, and Membrane Structures*, 2021 edition.

NFPA 105, *Standard for Smoke Door Assemblies and Other Opening Protectives*, 2022 edition.

NFPA 110, *Standard for Emergency and Standby Power Systems*, 2022 edition.

NFPA 111, *Standard on Stored Electrical Energy Emergency and Standby Power Systems*, 2022 edition.

NFPA 115, *Standard for Laser Fire Protection*, 2020 edition.

NFPA 120, *Standard for Fire Prevention and Control in Coal Mines*, 2023 edition.

NFPA 122, *Standard for Fire Prevention and Control in Metal/Nonmetal Mining and Metal Mineral Processing Facilities*, 2023 edition.

NFPA 130, *Standard for Fixed Guideway Transit and Passenger Rail Systems*, 2023 edition.

NFPA 140, *Standard on Motion Picture and Television Production Studio Soundstages, Approved Production Facilities, and Production Locations*, 2024 edition.

NFPA 150, *Fire and Life Safety in Animal Housing Facilities Code*, 2022 edition.

NFPA 160, *Standard for the Use of Flame Effects Before an Audience*, 2021 edition.

NFPA 170, *Standard for Fire Safety and Emergency Symbols*, 2021 edition.

NFPA 204, *Standard for Smoke and Heat Venting*, 2021 edition.

NFPA 211, *Standard for Chimneys, Fireplaces, Vents, and Solid Fuel–Burning Appliances*, 2024 edition.

NFPA 220, *Standard on Types of Building Construction*, 2024 edition.

NFPA 221, *Standard for High Challenge Fire Walls, Fire Walls, and Fire Barrier Walls*, 2024 edition.

NFPA 232, *Standard for the Protection of Records*, 2022 edition.

NFPA 241, *Standard for Safeguarding Construction, Alteration, and Demolition Operations*, 2022 edition.

NFPA 252, *Standard Methods of Fire Tests of Door Assemblies*, 2022 edition.

NFPA 253, *Standard Method of Test for Critical Radiant Flux of Floor Covering Systems Using a Radiant Heat Energy Source*, 2023 edition.

NFPA 257, *Standard on Fire Test for Window and Glass Block Assemblies*, 2022 edition.

NFPA 259, *Standard Test Method for Potential Heat of Building Materials*, 2023 edition.

NFPA 260, *Standard Methods of Tests and Classification System for Cigarette Ignition Resistance of Components of Upholstered Furniture*, 2024 edition.

NFPA 261, *Standard Method of Test for Determining Resistance of Mock-Up Upholstered Furniture Material Assemblies to Ignition by Smoldering Cigarettes*, 2023 edition.

NFPA 265, *Standard Methods of Fire Tests for Evaluating Room Fire Growth Contribution of Textile or Expanded Vinyl Wall Coverings on Full Height Panels and Walls*, 2023 edition.

NFPA 286, *Standard Methods of Fire Tests for Evaluating Contribution of Wall and Ceiling Interior Finish to Room Fire Growth*, 2024 edition.

NFPA 288, *Standard Methods of Fire Tests of Horizontal Fire Door Assemblies Installed in Horizontal Fire Resistance–Rated Assemblies*, 2022 edition.

NFPA 289, *Standard Method of Fire Test for Individual Fuel Packages*, 2023 edition.

NFPA 301, *Code for Safety to Life from Fire on Merchant Vessels*, 2023 edition.

NFPA 302, *Fire Protection Standard for Pleasure and Commercial Motor Craft*, 2020 edition.

NFPA 303, *Fire Protection Standard for Marinas and Boatyards*, 2021 edition.

NFPA 307, *Standard for the Construction and Fire Protection of Marine Terminals, Piers, and Wharves*, 2021 edition.

NFPA 312, *Standard for Fire Protection of Vessels During Construction, Conversion, Repair, and Lay-Up*, 2021 edition.

NFPA 318, *Standard for the Protection of Semiconductor Fabrication Facilities*, 2022 edition.

NFPA 326, *Standard for the Safeguarding of Tanks and Containers for Entry, Cleaning, or Repair*, 2020 edition.

NFPA 385, *Standard for Tank Vehicles for Flammable and Combustible Liquids*, 2022 edition.

NFPA 400, *Hazardous Materials Code*, 2022 edition.

NFPA 407, *Standard for Aircraft Fuel Servicing*, 2022 edition.

NFPA 408, *Standard for Aircraft Hand Portable Fire Extinguishers*, 2022 edition.

NFPA 409, *Standard on Aircraft Hangars*, 2022 edition.

NFPA 410, *Standard on Aircraft Maintenance*, 2020 edition.

NFPA 415, *Standard on Airport Terminal Buildings, Fueling Ramp Drainage, and Loading Walkways*, 2022 edition.

NFPA 418, *Standard for Heliports*, 2021 edition.

NFPA 423, *Standard for Construction and Protection of Aircraft Engine Test Facilities*, 2022 edition.

NFPA 460, *Standard for Aircraft Rescue and Firefighting Services at Airports, Recurring Proficiency of Airport Fire Fighters, and Evaluating Aircraft Rescue and Firefighting Foam Equipment*, 2024 edition.

NFPA 484, *Standard for Combustible Metals*, 2022 edition.

NFPA 495, *Explosive Materials Code*, 2023 edition.

NFPA 498, *Standard for Safe Havens and Interchange Lots for Vehicles Transporting Explosives*, 2023 edition.

NFPA 501, *Standard on Manufactured Housing*, 2022 edition.

NFPA 501A, *Standard for Fire Safety Criteria for Manufactured Home Installations, Sites, and Communities*, 2021 edition.

NFPA 502, *Standard for Road Tunnels, Bridges, and Other Limited Access Highways*, 2023 edition.

NFPA 505, *Fire Safety Standard for Powered Industrial Trucks Including Type Designations, Areas of Use, Conversions, Maintenance, and Operations*, 2024 edition.

NFPA 601, *Standard for Security Services in Fire Loss Prevention*, 2020 edition.

NFPA 652, *Standard on the Fundamentals of Combustible Dust*, 2019 edition.

NFPA 654, *Standard for the Prevention of Fire and Dust Explosions from the Manufacturing, Processing, and Handling of Combustible Particulate Solids*, 2020 edition.

NFPA 655, *Standard for Prevention of Sulfur Fires and Explosions,* 2017 edition.

NFPA 664, *Standard for the Prevention of Fires and Explosions in Wood Processing and Woodworking Facilities,* 2020 edition.

NFPA 701, *Standard Methods of Fire Tests for Flame Propagation of Textiles and Films,* 2023 edition.

NFPA 703, *Standard for Fire-Retardant-Treated Wood and Fire-Retardant Coatings for Building Materials,* 2024 edition.

NFPA 704, *Standard System for the Identification of the Hazards of Materials for Emergency Response,* 2022 edition.

NFPA 731, *Standard for the Installation of Premises Security Systems,* 2023 edition.

NFPA 750, *Standard on Water Mist Fire Protection Systems,* 2019 edition.

NFPA 770, *Standard on Hybrid (Water and Inert Gas) Fire-Extinguishing Systems,* 2021 edition.

NFPA 780, *Standard for the Installation of Lightning Protection Systems,* 2023 edition.

NFPA 801, *Standard for Fire Protection for Facilities Handling Radioactive Materials,* 2020 edition.

NFPA 804, *Standard for Fire Protection for Advanced Light Water Reactor Electric Generating Plants,* 2020 edition.

NFPA 805, *Performance-Based Standard for Fire Protection for Light Water Reactor Electric Generating Plants,* 2020 edition.

NFPA 820, *Standard for Fire Protection in Wastewater Treatment and Collection Facilities,* 2024 edition.

NFPA 855, *Standard for the Installation of Stationary Energy Storage Systems,* 2023 edition.

NFPA 909, *Code for the Protection of Cultural Resource Properties — Museums, Libraries, and Places of Worship,* 2021 edition.

NFPA 914, *Code for the Protection of Historic Structures,* 2023 edition.

NFPA 1030, *Standard for Professional Qualifications for Fire Prevention Program Positions,* 2024 edition.

NFPA 1122, *Code for Model Rocketry,* 2018 edition.

NFPA 1123, *Code for Fireworks Display,* 2022 edition.

NFPA 1124, *Code for the Manufacture, Transportation, and Storage of Fireworks and Pyrotechnic Articles,* 2022 edition.

NFPA 1125, *Code for the Manufacture of Model Rocket and High-Power Rocket Motors,* 2022 edition.

NFPA 1126, *Standard for the Use of Pyrotechnics Before a Proximate Audience,* 2021 edition.

NFPA 1127, *Code for High Power Rocketry,* 2018 edition.

NFPA 1140, *Standard for Wildland Fire Protection,* 2022 edition.

NFPA 1142, *Standard on Water Supplies for Suburban and Rural Fire Fighting,* 2022 edition.

NFPA 1192, *Standard on Recreational Vehicles,* 2021 edition.

NFPA 1194, *Standard for Recreational Vehicle Parks and Campgrounds,* 2021 edition.

NFPA 1225, *Standard for Emergency Services Communications,* 2022 edition.

NFPA 1660, *Standard on Community Risk Assessment, Pre-Incident Planning, Mass Evacuation, Sheltering, and Re-entry Programs,* 2024 edition.

NFPA 1730, *Standard on Organization and Deployment of Fire Prevention Inspection and Code Enforcement, Plan Review, Investigation, and Public Education Operations,* 2019 edition.

NFPA 1900, *Standard for Aircraft Rescue and Firefighting Vehicles, Automotive Fire Apparatus, Wildland Fire Apparatus, and Automotive Ambulances,* 2024 edition.

NFPA 1910, *Standard for Marine Firefighting Vessels and the Inspection, Maintenance, Testing, Refurbishing, and Retirement of In-Service Emergency Vehicles,* 2024 edition.

NFPA 1963, *Standard for Fire Hose Connections,* 2019 edition.

NFPA 2001, *Standard on Clean Agent Fire Extinguishing Systems,* 2022 edition.

NFPA 2010, *Standard for Fixed Aerosol Fire Extinguishing Systems,* 2020 edition.

NFPA 2113, *Standard on Selection, Care, Use, and Maintenance of Flame-Resistant Garments for Protection of Industrial Personnel Against Short-Duration Thermal Exposures from Fire,* 2020 edition.

NFPA 5000®, *Building Construction and Safety Code®,* 2024 edition.

2.3 Other Publications.

2.3.1 ANSI Publications. American National Standards Institute, Inc., 25 West 43rd Street, 4th Floor, New York, NY 10036.

ANSI B11.19, *Performance Requirements for Risk Reduction Measures: Safeguarding and other Means of Reducing Risk,* 2019.

ANSI/BHMA A156.3, *Exit Devices,* 2020.

ANSI/AWWA G200, *Distribution Systems Operation and Management,* 2021.

2.3.2 APA Publications. 7910 Woodmont Avenue, Suite 1220, Bethesda, MD 20814.

APA 87-1, *Standard for the Construction and Approval for Transportation of Fireworks, Novelties, and Theatrical Pyrotechnics,* 2001.

Δ **2.3.3 API Publications.** American Petroleum Institute, 1220 L Street, NW, Washington, DC 20005-4070.

API-ASME Code for Unfired Pressure Vessels for Petroleum Liquids and Gases, Pre-July 1, 1961.

API Specification 12B, *Bolted Tanks for Storage of Production Liquids,* 15th edition, 2014.

API Specification 12D, *Field-welded Tanks for Storage of Production Liquids,* 12th edition, 2017.

API Specification 12F, *Shop-welded Tanks for Storage of Production Liquids,* 13th edition, 2019.

API 607, *Fire Test for Quarter-Turn Valves and Valves Equipped with Nonmetallic Seats,* 7th edition, 2016.

API 620, *Design and Construction of Large, Welded, Low-Pressure Storage Tanks,* 12th edition, Addendum 2 (2018), 2013.

API 650, *Welded Tanks for Oil Storage,* 12th edition, Addendum 3 (2018), 2013.

API 653, *Tank Inspection, Repair, Alteration, and Reconstruction,* 5th edition, Addendum 1 (2014), Addendum 2 (2018), Addendum 3 (2021), 2014.

2.3.4 ASCE Publications. American Society of Civil Engineers, 1801 Alexander Bell Drive, Reston, VA 20191-4400.

ASCE/SEI 7, *Minimum Design Loads and Associated Criteria for Buildings and Other Structures,* 2016.

2.3.5 ASHRAE Publications. ASHRAE, 1791 Tullie Circle, NE, Atlanta, GA 30329-2305.

ANSI/ASHRAE 15, *Safety Standard for Refrigeration Systems,* 2019.

ANSI/ASHRAE 34, *Designation and Safety Classification of Refrigerants*, 2019.

Δ **2.3.6 ASME Publications.** American Society of Mechanical Engineers, Two Park Avenue, New York, NY 10016-5990.

ASME A13.1, *Scheme for the Identification of Piping Systems*, 2020.

ASME A17.1, *Safety Code for Elevators and Escalators*, 2019.

ASME A17.3, *Safety Code for Existing Elevators and Escalators*, 2020.

ANSI/ASME B31.1, *Power Piping*, 2020.

ANSI/ASME B31.3, *Process Piping*, 2020.

ANSI/ASME B31.4, *Pipeline Transportation Systems for Liquids and Slurries*, 2019.

ASME *Boiler and Pressure Vessel Code*, 2021.

ASME *Boiler and Pressure Vessel Code*, Section VIII, "Rules for the Construction of Unfired Pressure Vessels," 2021.

Δ **2.3.7 ASTM Publications.** ASTM International, 100 Barr Harbor Drive, P.O. Box C700, West Conshohocken, PA 19428-2959.

ASTM A395, *Standard Specification for Ferritic Ductile Iron Pressure-Retaining Castings for Use at Elevated Temperatures*, 1999, reapproved 2018.

ASTM D56, *Standard Test Method for Flash Point by Tag Closed Cup Tester*, 2021a.

ASTM D92, *Standard Test Method for Flash and Fire Points by Cleveland Open Cup Tester*, 2018.

ASTM D86, *Standard Test Method for Distillation of Petroleum Products at Atmospheric Pressure*, 2020b.

ASTM D93, *Standard Test Methods for Flash Point by Pensky-Martens Closed Cup Tester*, 2020.

ASTM D323, *Standard Method of Test for Vapor Pressure of Petroleum Products (Reid Method)*, 2020a.

ASTM D396, *Standard Specification for Fuel Oils*, 2021.

ASTM D635, *Standard Test Method for Rate of Burning and/or Extent and Time of Burning of Plastics in a Horizontal Position*, 2018.

ASTM D1929, *Standard Test Method for Determining Ignition Temperature of Plastics*, 2020.

ASTM D2843, *Standard Test Method for Density of Smoke from the Burning or Decomposition of Plastics*, 2019.

ASTM D2859, *Standard Test Method for Ignition Characteristics of Finished Textile Floor Covering Materials*, 2016, reapproved 2021.

ASTM D2898, *Standard Practice for Accelerated Weathering of Fire-Retardant-Treated Wood for Fire Testing*, 2010, reapproved 2017.

ASTM D3278, *Standard Test Methods for Flash Point of Liquids by Small Scale Closed-Cup Apparatus*, 2021.

ASTM D3699, *Standard Specification for Kerosene*, 2019.

ASTM D3828, *Standard Test Methods for Flash Point by Small Scale Closed Cup Tester*, 2016a, reapproved 2021.

ASTM D5391, *Standard Test Method for Electrical Conductivity and Resistivity of a Flowing High Purity Water Sample*, 2014.

ASTM D5456, *Standard Specification for Evaluation of Structural Composite Lumber Products*, 2021e1.

ASTM D6448, *Standard Specification for Industrial Burner Fuels from Used Lubricating Oils*, 2016.

ASTM D6751, *Standard Specification for Biodiesel Fuel Blend Stock (B100) for Middle Distillate Fuel*, 2020a.

ASTM D6823, *Standard Specification for Commercial Burner Fuels with Used Lubricating Oils*, 2008, reapproved 2021.

ASTM D7666, *Standard Specification for Triglyceride Burner Fuel*, 2019.

ASTM E84, *Standard Test Method for Surface Burning Characteristics of Building Materials*, 2021a.

ASTM E108, *Standard Test Methods for Fire Tests of Roof Coverings*, 2020a.

ASTM E119, *Standard Test Methods for Fire Tests of Building Construction and Materials*, 2020.

ASTM E136, *Standard Test Method for Assessing Combustibility of Materials Using a Vertical Tube Furnace at 750 Degrees C*, 2019a.

ASTM E648, *Standard Test Method for Critical Radiant Flux of Floor-Covering Systems Using a Radiant Heat Energy Source*, 2019ae1.

ASTM E681, *Standard Test Method for Concentration Limits of Flammability of Chemicals (Vapors and Gases)*, 2009, reapproved 2015.

ASTM E814, *Standard Test Method for Fire Tests of Penetration Firestop Systems*, 2013a, reapproved 2017.

ASTM E1354, *Standard Test Method for Heat and Visible Smoke Release Rates for Materials and Products Using an Oxygen Consumption Calorimeter*, 2017.

ASTM E1537, *Standard Test Method for Fire Testing of Upholstered Furniture*, 2016.

ASTM E1590, *Standard Test Method for Fire Testing of Mattresses*, 2022.

ASTM E1591, *Standard Guide for Obtaining Data for Fire Growth Models*, 2020.

ASTM E1966, *Standard Test Method for Fire-Resistive Joint Systems*, 2015, reapproved 2019.

ASTM E2019, *Standard Test Method for Minimum Ignition Energy of a Dust Cloud in Air*, 2003, reapproved 2019.

ASTM E2174, *Standard Practice for On-Site Inspection of Installed Firestops*, 2020a.

ASTM E2307, *Standard Test Method for Determining Fire Resistance of Perimeter Fire Barriers Using Intermediate-Scale, Multi-story Test Apparatus*, 2020.

ASTM E2336, *Standard Test Methods for Fire Resistive Grease Duct Enclosure Systems*, 2020.

ASTM E2393, *Standard Practice for On-Site Inspection of Installed Fire Resistive Joint Systems and Perimeter Fire Barriers*, 2020a.

ASTM E2404, *Standard Practice for Specimen Preparation and Mounting of Textile, Paper or Polymeric (Including Vinyl) and Wood Wall or Ceiling Coverings, Facings and Veneers, to Assess Surface Burning Characteristics*, 2017.

ASTM E2573, *Standard Practice for Specimen Preparation and Mounting of Site-Fabricated Stretch Systems to Assess Surface Burning Characteristics*, 2019.

ASTM E2599, *Standard Practice for Specimen Preparation and Mounting of Reflective Insulation, Radiant Barrier and Vinyl Stretch Ceiling Materials for Building Applications to Assess Surface Burning Characteristics*, 2018.

ASTM E2652, *Standard Test Method for Assessing Combustibility of Materials Using a Tube Furnace with a Cone-Shaped Airflow Stabilizer, at 750 Degrees C*, 2018.

ASTM E2768, *Standard Test Method for Extended Duration Surface Burning Characteristics of Building Materials (30 min Tunnel Test)*, 2011, reapproved 2018.

ASTM E2965, *Standard Test for Determination of Low Levels of Heat Release Rate for Materials and Products Using an Oxygen Combustion Calorimeter*, 2017.

ASTM E3082, *Standard Test Methods for Determining the Effectiveness of Fire Retardant Treatments for Natural Christmas Trees*, 2020.

ASTM F852/F852M, *Standard for Portable Gasoline, Kerosene, and Diesel Containers for Consumer Use*, 2022.

ASTM F2200, *Standard Specification for Automated Vehicular Gate Construction*, 2020.

Δ **2.3.8 CGA Publications.** Compressed Gas Association, 14501 George Carter Way, Suite 103, Chantilly, VA 20151.

CGA C-7, *Guide to Classification and Labeling of Compressed Gases*, 2020.

ANSI/CGA G-13, *Storage and Handling of Silane and Silane Mixtures*, 2016.

CGA P-1, *Standard for Safe Handling of Compressed Gases in Containers*, 2022.

ANSI/CGA P-18, *Standard for Bulk Inert Gas Systems*, 2020.

CGA P-20, *Standard for the Classification of Toxic Gas Mixtures*, 2017.

CGA P-23, *Standard for Categorizing Gas Mixtures Containing Flammable and Nonflammable Components*, 2015.

CGA S-1.1, *Pressure Relief Device Standards — Part 1 — Cylinders for Compressed Gases*, 2022.

CGA S-1.2, *Pressure Relief Device Standards — Part 2 — Portable Containers for Compressed Gases*, 2019.

CGA S-1.3, *Pressure Relief Device Standards — Part 3 — Stationary Storage Containers for Compressed Gases*, 2020.

2.3.9 CTA Publications. Canadian Transportation Agency, Queen's Printer, Ottawa, Ontario, Canada. (Available from the Canadian Communications Group Publication Centre, Ordering Department, Ottawa, Canada K1A 0S9.)

Transportation of Dangerous Goods Regulations.

2.3.10 EI Publications. Energy Institute, 61 New Cavendish Street, London W1G 7AR, United Kingdom.

EI 1529, *Aviation Fueling Hose and Hose Assemblies*, 2014 (reaffirmed 2019).

Δ **2.3.11 FM Publications.** FM Approvals LLC, 1151 Boston-Providence Turnpike, P.O. Box 9102, Norwood, MA 02062.

ANSI/FM 4880, *American National Standard for Evaluating the Fire Performance of Insulated Building Panel Assemblies and Interior Finish Materials*, 2017.

FM 6051/6052, *Approval Standard for Safety Containers and Filling, Supply, and Disposal Containers — for Ignitible (Flammable) Liquids*, November 2017.

FM 6083, *Approval Standard for Plastic Plugs for Steel Drums*, October 2006.

FM 6921, *Approval Standard for Oily Containers for Combustible Waste*, 2004.

2.3.12 ICC Publications. International Code Council, 500 New Jersey Avenue, NW, 6th Floor, Washington, DC 20001-2070.

ICC A117.1, *Accessible and Usable Buildings and Facilities*, 2017.

2.3.13 IEC Publications. International Electrotechnical Commission, 3, rue de Varembé, P.O. Box 131, CH-1211 Geneva 20, Switzerland.

IEC 61340-4-4, *Electrostatics—Part 4-4: Standard Test Methods for Specific Applications — Electrostatic Classification of Flexible Intermediate Bulk Containers (FIBC)*, 2018.

Δ **2.3.14 IIAR Publications.** International Institute of Ammonia Refrigeration, 1001 N. Fairfax Street, Suite 503, Alexandria, VA 22314.

ANSI/IIAR 2, *Standard for Design of Safe Closed-Circuit Ammonia Refrigeration Systems*, 2021.

ANSI/IIAR 6, *Standard for the Inspection, Testing, and Maintenance of Closed-Circuit Ammonia Refrigeration Systems*, 2019.

ANSI/IIAR 7, *Standard for Developing Operating Procedures for Closed-Circuit Ammonia Mechanical Refrigeration Systems*, 2019.

ANSI/IIAR 8, *Standard for Decommissioning of Closed-Circuit Ammonia Mechanical Refrigeration Systems*, 2020.

2.3.15 ISO Publications. International Organization for Standardization, ISO Central Secretariat, BIBC II, Chemin de Blandonnet 8, CP 401, 1214 Vernier, Geneva, Switzerland.

ISO 10156, *Gas Cylinders — Gases and Gas Mixtures — Determination of Fire Potential and Oxidizing Ability for the Selection of Cylinder Valve Outlets*, 2017.

ISO 10298, *Gas Cylinders — Gases and Gas Mixtures — Determination of Toxicity for the Selection of Cylinder Valve Outlets*, amendment 1 (2021), 2018.

N 2.3.16 ITSDF Publications. Industrial Truck Standards Development Foundation, Suite 460, 1750 K Street NW, Washington, DC 20006.

ANSI/ITSDF B56.1, *Safety Standard for Low Lift and High Lift Trucks*, 2020.

2.3.17 NBBPVI Publications. National Board of Boiler and Pressure Vessel Inspectors, 1055 Crupper Avenue, Columbus, OH 43229.

NBBI NB23, *National Board Inspection Code*, 2021.

2.3.18 NRFC Publications. National Railroad Freight Committee, 222 South Riverside Plaza, Chicago, IL 60606-5945.

Uniform Freight Classification (UFC), 2005.

2.3.19 RVIA Publications. Recreation Vehicle Industry Association, 1896 Preston White Drive, P.O. Box 2999, Reston, VA 20195-0999.

RVIA/ANSI A119.5, *Park Model Recreational Vehicle Standard*, 2020.

Δ 2.3.20 UL Publications. Underwriters Laboratories Inc., 333 Pfingsten Road, Northbrook, IL 60062-2096.

UL 8, *Water Based Agent Fire Extinguishers*, 2016, revised 2020.

UL 9, *Fire Tests of Window Assemblies*, 2009, revised 2020.

UL 10B, *Fire Tests of Door Assemblies*, 2008, revised 2020.

UL 10C, *Positive Pressure Fire Tests of Door Assemblies*, 2016, revised 2021.

UL 25, *Meters for Flammable and Combustible Liquids and LP-Gas*, 2021.

UL 30, *Metal Safety Cans*, 1995, revised 2019.

UL 38, *Manual Signaling Boxes for Fire Alarm Systems*, 2008, revised 2018.

UL 58, *Steel Underground Tanks for Flammable and Combustible Liquids*, 2018.

UL 79, *Power-Operated Pumps for Petroleum Dispensing Products*, 2016, revised 2021.

UL 79A, *Power-Operated Pumps for Gasoline and Gasoline/Ethanol Blends with Nominal Ethanol Concentrations up to 85 Percent (E0–E85)*, 2015 (2016), revised 2020.

UL 80, *Steel Tanks for Oil Burner Fuels and Other Combustible Liquids*, 2007, revised 2019.

UL 87A, *Power-Operated Dispensing Devices for Gasoline and Gasoline/Ethanol Blends with Nominal Ethanol Concentrations up to 85 Percent (E0–E85)*, 2015, revised 2020.

UL 142, *Steel Aboveground Tanks for Flammable and Combustible Liquids*, 2019, revised 2021.

UL 142A, *Special Purpose Aboveground Tanks for Specific Flammable or Combustible Liquids*, 2018, revised 2021.

UL 147A, *Nonrefillable (Disposable) Type Fuel Gas Cylinder Assemblies*, 2018, revised 2019.

UL 147B, *Nonrefillable (Disposable) Type Metal Container Assemblies for Butane*, 2016, revised 2019.

UL 154, *Carbon Dioxide Fire Extinguishers*, 2005, revised 2021.

UL 162, *Foam Equipment and Liquid Concentrates*, 2018, revised 2022.

UL 197, *Commercial Electric Cooking Appliances*, 2010, revised 2020.

UL 263, *Fire Tests of Building Construction and Materials*, 2011, revised 2021.

UL 294, *Access Control System Units*, 2018.

UL 296A, *Waste Oil-Burning Air-Heating Appliances*, 2018.

UL 299, *Dry Chemical Fire Extinguishers*, 2012, revised 2021.

UL 300, *Fire Testing of Fire Extinguishing Systems for Protection of Commercial Cooking Equipment*, 2019.

UL 305, *Panic Hardware*, 2012, revised 2017.

UL 325, *Door, Drapery, Gate, Louver, and Window Operators and Systems*, 2017, revised 2020.

UL 330A, *Hose and Hose Assemblies for Use with Dispensing Devices Dispensing Gasoline and Gasoline/Ethanol Blends with Nominal Ethanol Concentrations up to 85 Percent (E0–E85)*, 2019, revised 2020.

UL 340, *Tests for Comparative Flammability of Liquids*, 2017.

UL 499, *Electric Heating Appliances*, 2014, revised 2021.

UL 555, *Fire Dampers*, 2006, revised 2020.

UL 555S, *Smoke Dampers*, 2014, revised 2020.

UL 567, *Emergency Breakaway Fittings, Swivel Connectors and Pipe Connection Fittings for Petroleum Products and LP-Gas*, 2021.

UL 567A, *Emergency Breakaway Fittings, Swivel Connectors and Pipe-Connection Fittings for Gasoline and Gasoline/Ethanol Blends with Nominal Ethanol Concentrations up to 85 Percent (E0–E85)*, 2015 revised 2019.

UL 626, *Water Fire Extinguishers*, 2005, revised 2021.

UL 647, *Unvented Kerosene-Fired Room Heaters and Portable Heaters*, 1993, revised 2010.

UL 710B, *Recirculating Systems*, 2011, revised 2021.

UL 711, *Rating and Fire Testing of Fire Extinguishers*, 2018.

UL 723, *Test for Surface Burning Characteristics of Building Materials*, 2018.

UL 790, *Test Methods for Fire Tests of Roof Coverings*, 2022.

UL 842, *Valves for Flammable Fluids*, 2007, 2022.

UL 842A, *Valves for Gasoline and Gasoline/Ethanol Blends with Nominal Ethanol Concentrations up to 85 Percent (E0–E85)*, 2015, revised 2019.

UL 900, *Air Filter Units*, 2015.

UL 913, *Intrinsically Safe Apparatus and Associated Apparatus for Use in Class I, II, and III Division 1, Hazardous (Classified) Locations*, 2013, revised 2019.

UL 924, *Emergency Lighting and Power Equipment*, 2016, revised 2020.

UL 962A, *Furniture Power Distribution Units*, 2018, revised 2021.

UL 971, *Nonmetallic Underground Piping for Flammable Liquids*, 2021.

UL 1026, *Household Electric Cooking and Food Serving Appliances*, 2021, revised 2021.

UL 1037, *Antitheft Alarms and Devices*, 2016, revised 2017.

UL 1040, *Fire Test of Insulated Wall Construction*, 1996, revised 2022.

UL 1278, *Movable and Wall- or Ceiling-Hung Electric Room Heaters*, 2014, revised 2022.

UL 1313, *Nonmetallic Safety Cans for Petroleum Products*, 2015.

UL 1315, *Metal Waste Paper Containers*, 2017.

UL 1316, *Fibre Reinforced Underground Storage Tanks for Flammable and Combustible Liquids*, 2018, revised 2019.

UL 1363, *Relocatable Power Taps*, 2018.

UL 1363A, *Outline of Investigation for Special Purpose Relocatable Power Taps*, 2010.

UL 1369, *Above Ground Piping for Flammable and Combustible Liquids*, 2018, revised 2020.

CAN/UL 1389, *Plant Oil Extraction Equipment for Installation and Use in Ordinary (Unclassified) Locations and Hazardous (Classified) Locations*, 2019, revised 2021.

UL 1479, *Fire Tests of Penetration Firestops*, 2015, revised 2021.

UL 1484, *Residential Gas Detectors*, 2016, revised 2022.

UL 1564, *Industrial Battery Chargers*, 2015, revised 2020.

UL 1573, *Stage and Studio Luminaires and Connector Strips*, 2003, revised 2019.

UL 1640, *Portable Power-Distribution Equipment*, 2016, revised 2021.

UL 1715, *Fire Test of Interior Finish Material*, 1997, revised 2022.

UL 1803, *Factory Follow-up on Third Party Certified Portable Fire Extinguishers*, 2012, revised 2021.

UL 1973, *Batteries for Use in Stationary and Motive Auxiliary Power Applications*, 2022.

UL 1975, *Fire Tests for Foamed Plastics Used for Decorative Purposes*, 2006.

UL 1994, *Luminous Egress Path Marking Systems*, 2015, revised 2020.

UL 2011, *Outline of Investigation for Machinery*, 2019, revised 2021.

UL 2034, *Single and Multiple Station Carbon Monoxide Alarms*, 2017, revised 2018.

UL 2075, *Gas and Vapor Detectors and Sensors*, 2013, revised 2021.

UL 2079, *Tests for Fire Resistance of Building Joint Systems*, 2015, revised 2020.

UL 2080, *Fire Resistant Tanks for Flammable and Combustible Liquids*, 2000.

UL 2085, *Protected Aboveground Tanks for Flammable and Combustible Liquids*, 1997, revised 2010.

UL 2129, *Halocarbon Clean Agent Fire Extinguishers*, 2017, revised 2021.

UL 2208, *Solvent Distillation Units*, 2010, revised 2020.

UL 2245, *Below-Grade Vaults for Flammable Liquid Storage Tanks*, 2006.

UL 2258, *Aboveground Nonmetallic Tanks for Fuel Oil and Other Combustible Liquids*, 2018, revised 2019.

CAN/UL 2272, *Electrical Systems for Personal E-Mobility Devices*, 2016, revised 2019.

UL 2358, *Outline of Investigation for Fire Tests of Pre-Lit Artificial Seasonal Use Trees and Other Seasonal Decorative Items*, 2013.

UL 2368, *Fire Exposure Testing of Rigid Nonmetallic and Composite Nonmetallic Intermediate Bulk Containers for Flammable and Combustible Liquids*, 2012, revised 2018.

UL 2524, *In-building 2-Way Emergency Radio Communication Enhancement Systems*, 2019.

UL 2586, *Hose Nozzle Valves for Flammable and Combustible Liquids*, 2021.

UL 2586A, *Hose Nozzle Valves for Gasoline and Gasoline/Ethanol Blends with Nominal Ethanol Concentrations up to 85 Percent (E0–E85)*, 2015, revised 2019.

CAN/UL 2849, *Electrical Systems for eBikes*, 2020.

UL 2930, *Outline of Investigation for Cord-and-Plug-Connected Health Care Facility Outlet Assemblies*, 2020.

UL 3400, *Outline of Investigation for Additive Manufacturing Facility Safety Management*, 2017.

UL 9540, *Energy Storage Systems and Equipment*, 2020, revised 2021.

UL 60601-1, *Medical Electrical Equipment, Part 1: General Requirements for Safety*, 2003, revised 2006.

UL 60950-1, *Information Technology Equipment — Safety — Part 1: General Requirements*, 2007, revised 2019.

UL 62368-1, *Audio/Video, Information and Communication Technology Equipment — Part 1: Safety Requirements*, 2019, revised 2021.

2.3.21 ULC Publications. ULC Standards, 171 Nepean Street, Suite 400, Ottawa, ON K2P 0B4, Canada.

CAN/ULC 8800, *Horticultural Lighting Equipment and Systems*, 2019, revised 2022.

CAN/ULC-S503, *Carbon-Dioxide Fire Extinguishers*, 2005.

CAN/ULC-S504, *Dry Chemical Fire Extinguishers*, 2012, revised 2021.

CAN/ULC-S507, *Water Fire Extinguishers*, 2005, revised 2021.

CAN/ULC-S508, *Rating and Testing of Fire Extinguishers*, 2018.

CAN/ULC-S512, *Halogenated Agent Hand and Wheeled Fire Extinguishers*, 2005.

CAN/ULC-S554, *Water Based Agent Fire Extinguishers*, 2016.

CAN/ULC-S566, *Halocarbon Clean Agent Fire Extinguishers,* 2017, revised 2021.

2.3.22 UN Publications. United Nations Headquarters, New York, NY 10017.

Recommendations on the Transport of Dangerous Goods, 19th revised edition, 2015.

Manual of Tests and Criteria, Part II, 7th edition, 2019.

2.3.23 US Government Publications. US Government Publishing Office, 732 North Capitol Street, NW, Washington, DC 20401-0001.

FAA AC 150/5390-2C, *Heliport Design Advisory Circular,* April 24, 2012.

Interstate Commerce Commission (ICC), *Rules for Construction of Unfired Pressure Vessels,* US Department of Transportation, Washington, DC.

Resource Conservation and Recovery Act (RCRA), US Department of Transportation, Washington, DC, 1976.

Title 16, Code of Federal Regulations, Part 1500.41, "Method of Testing Primary Irritant Substances."

Title 16, Code of Federal Regulations, Part 1632, "Standard for the Flammability of Mattresses and Mattress Pads," (FF 4-72).

Title 21, Code of Federal Regulations, Part 210, "Processing, Packing, or Holding Drugs; General."

Title 21, Code of Federal Regulations, Part 211, "Current Good Manufacturing Practice for Finished Pharmaceuticals."

Title 27, Code of Federal Regulations, Part 555.

Title 29, Code of Federal Regulations, Part 1910.242(b), "Compressed Air Used for Cleaning."

Title 29, Code of Federal Regulations, Part 1910.1000, "Air Contaminants."

Title 29, Code of Federal Regulations, Part1910.1200, "Hazard Communication."

Title 46, Code of Federal Regulations, Parts 30, 32, 35, and 39, "Shipping."

Title 49, Code of Federal Regulations, Parts 100 through 199.

Title 49, Code of Federal Regulations, Part 173, "Shippers — General Requirements for Shipments and Packages."

Title 49, Code of Federal Regulations, Part 173, Annex H, "Method of Testing for Sustained Combustibility."

Title 49, Code of Federal Regulations, Part 180.205, "General Requirements for Requalification of Specification Cylinders."

Title 49, Code of Federal Regulations, Part 571.108, "Lamps, Reflective Devices, and Associated Equipment."

2.3.24 Other Publications.

Merriam-Webster's Collegiate Dictionary, 11th edition, Merriam-Webster, Inc., Springfield, MA, 2003.

Δ **2.4 References for Extracts in Mandatory Sections.**

NFPA 10, *Standard for Portable Fire Extinguishers,* 2022 edition.

NFPA 13, *Standard for the Installation of Sprinkler Systems,* 2022 edition.

NFPA 14, *Standard for the Installation of Standpipe and Hose Systems,* 2024 edition.

NFPA 20, *Standard for the Installation of Stationary Pumps for Fire Protection,* 2022 edition.

NFPA 25, *Standard for the Inspection, Testing, and Maintenance of Water-Based Fire Protection Systems,* 2023 edition.

NFPA 30, *Flammable and Combustible Liquids Code,* 2024 edition.

NFPA 30A, *Code for Motor Fuel Dispensing Facilities and Repair Garages,* 2024 edition.

NFPA 30B, *Code for the Manufacture and Storage of Aerosol Products,* 2023 edition.

NFPA 31, *Standard for the Installation of Oil-Burning Equipment,* 2020 edition.

NFPA 33, *Standard for Spray Application Using Flammable or Combustible Materials,* 2021 edition.

NFPA 34, *Standard for Dipping, Coating, and Printing Processes Using Flammable or Combustible Liquids,* 2021 edition.

NFPA 36, *Standard for Solvent Extraction Plants,* 2021 edition.

NFPA 45, *Standard on Fire Protection for Laboratories Using Chemicals,* 2024 edition.

NFPA 51B, *Standard for Fire Prevention During Welding, Cutting, and Other Hot Work,* 2024 edition.

NFPA 52, *Vehicular Natural Gas Fuel Systems Code,* 2023 edition.

NFPA 55, *Compressed Gases and Cryogenic Fluids Code,* 2023 edition.

NFPA 58, *Liquefied Petroleum Gas Code,* 2024 edition.

NFPA 59A, *Standard for the Production, Storage, and Handling of Liquefied Natural Gas (LNG),* 2023 edition.

NFPA 61, *Standard for the Prevention of Fires and Dust Explosions in Agricultural and Food Processing Facilities,* 2020 edition.

NFPA 68, *Standard on Explosion Protection by Deflagration Venting,* 2023 edition.

NFPA 69, *Standard on Explosion Prevention Systems,* 2019 edition.

NFPA 70®, National Electrical Code®, 2023 edition.

NFPA 72®, National Fire Alarm and Signaling Code®, 2022 edition.

NFPA 80, *Standard for Fire Doors and Other Opening Protectives,* 2022 edition.

NFPA 88A, *Standard for Parking Structures,* 2023 edition.

NFPA 90A, *Standard for the Installation of Air-Conditioning and Ventilating Systems,* 2024 edition.

NFPA 96, *Standard for Ventilation Control and Fire Protection of Commercial Cooking Operations,* 2024 edition.

NFPA 101®, Life Safety Code®, 2024 edition.

NFPA 140, *Standard on Motion Picture and Television Production Studio Soundstages, Approved Production Facilities, and Production Locations,* 2024 edition.

NFPA 211, *Standard for Chimneys, Fireplaces, Vents, and Solid Fuel–Burning Appliances,* 2019 edition.

NFPA 303, *Fire Protection Standard for Marinas and Boatyards,* 2021 edition.

NFPA 307, *Standard for the Construction and Fire Protection of Marine Terminals, Piers, and Wharves,* 2021 edition.

NFPA 312, *Standard for Fire Protection of Vessels During Construction, Conversion, Repair, and Lay-Up,* 2021 edition.

NFPA 400, *Hazardous Materials Code,* 2022 edition.

NFPA 407, *Standard for Aircraft Fuel Servicing,* 2022 edition.

NFPA 415, *Standard on Airport Terminal Buildings, Fueling Ramp Drainage, and Loading Walkways,* 2022 edition.

NFPA 418, *Standard for Heliports,* 2021 edition.

NFPA 440, *Guide for Aircraft Rescue and Firefighting Operations and Airport/Community Emergency Planning,* 2024 edition.

NFPA 470, *Hazardous Materials/Weapons of Mass Destruction (WMD) Standard for Responders,* 2022 edition.

NFPA 652, *Standard on the Fundamentals of Combustible Dust,* 2019 edition.

NFPA 654, *Standard for the Prevention of Fire and Dust Explosions from the Manufacturing, Processing, and Handling of Combustible Particulate Solids,* 2020 edition.

NFPA 805, *Performance-Based Standard for Fire Protection for Light Water Reactor Electric Generating Plants,* 2020 edition.

NFPA 855, *Standard for the Installation of Stationary Energy Storage Systems,* 2023 edition.

NFPA 914, *Code for the Protection of Historic Structures,* 2023 edition.

NFPA 1030, *Standard for Professional Qualifications for Fire Prevention Program Positions,* 2024 edition.

NFPA 1124, *Code for the Manufacture, Transportation, and Storage of Fireworks and Pyrotechnic Articles,* 2022 edition.

NFPA 1140, *Standard for Wildland Fire Protection,* 2022 edition.

NFPA 1142, *Standard on Water Supplies for Suburban and Rural Fire Fighting,* 2022 edition.

NFPA 1730, *Standard on Organization and Deployment of Fire Prevention Inspection and Code Enforcement, Plan Review, Investigation, and Public Education Operations,* 2019 edition.

NFPA 5000®, *Building Construction and Safety Code®,* 2024 edition.

Chapter 3 Definitions

3.1 General. The definitions contained in this chapter shall apply to the terms used in this *Code.* Where terms are not defined in this chapter or within another chapter, they shall be defined using their ordinarily accepted meanings within the context in which they are used. *Merriam-Webster's Collegiate Dictionary,* 11th edition, shall be the source for the ordinarily accepted meaning.

3.2 NFPA Official Definitions.

3.2.1* Approved. Acceptable to the AHJ.

3.2.2* Authority Having Jurisdiction (AHJ). An organization, office, or individual responsible for enforcing the requirements of a code or standard, or for approving equipment, materials, an installation, or a procedure.

3.2.3* Code. A standard that is an extensive compilation of provisions covering broad subject matter or that is suitable for adoption into law independently of other codes and standards.

3.2.4 Guide. A document that is advisory or informative in nature and that contains only nonmandatory provisions. A guide may contain mandatory statements such as when a guide can be used, but the document as a whole is not suitable for adoption into law.

3.2.5 Labeled. Equipment or materials to which has been attached a label, symbol, or other identifying mark of an organization that is acceptable to the authority having jurisdiction and concerned with product evaluation, that maintains periodic inspection of production of labeled equipment or materials, and by whose labeling the manufacturer indicates compliance with appropriate standards or performance in a specified manner.

3.2.6* Listed. Equipment, materials, or services included in a list published by an organization that is acceptable to the AHJ and concerned with evaluation of products or services, that maintains periodic inspection of production of listed equipment or materials or periodic evaluation of services, and whose listing states that either the equipment, material, or service meets appropriate designated standards or has been tested and found suitable for a specified purpose.

3.2.7 Recommended Practice. A document that is similar in content and structure to a code or standard but that contains only nonmandatory provisions using the word "should" to indicate recommendations in the body of the text.

3.2.8 Shall. Indicates a mandatory requirement.

3.2.9 Should. Indicates a recommendation or that which is advised but not required.

3.2.10 Standard. An NFPA Standard, the main text of which contains only mandatory provisions using the word "shall" to indicate requirements and that is in a form generally suitable for mandatory reference by another standard or code or for adoption into law. Nonmandatory provisions are not to be considered a part of the requirements of a standard and shall be located in an appendix, annex, footnote, informational note, or other means as permitted in the NFPA Manuals of Style. When used in a generic sense, such as in the phrase "standards development process" or "standards development activities," the term "standards" includes all NFPA Standards, including Codes, Standards, Recommended Practices, and Guides.

3.3 General Definitions.

3.3.1* Absolute Pressure. Pressure based on a zero reference point, the perfect vacuum. [55, 2023] (FCC-HAZ)

3.3.2 Access Box. An approved secure box, accessible by the AHJ's master key or control, containing entrance keys or other devices to gain access to a structure or area. (FCC-FUN)

3.3.3 Addition. An increase in the building area, aggregate floor area, building height, or number of stories of a structure. [5000, 2024] (FCC-FUN)

3.3.4 Additive Manufacturing. A process of joining materials to make objects from 3D model data, usually layer upon layer, sometimes referred to as 3D printing. (FCC-HAZ)

3.3.4.1 Industrial Additive Manufacturing. 3D printing operations that utilize combustible powders or metals, an inert gas supply, or a combustible dust collection system or that create a hazardous electrical classification area outside of the equipment. (FCC-HAZ)

3.3.4.2 Nonindustrial Additive Manufacturing. 3D printing operations that do not create a hazardous electrical classification area outside of the equipment and do not utilize an inert gas supply or combustible dust collection system. (FCC-HAZ)

N **3.3.5* Aerosol Container.** A metal can or plastic container, up to a maximum size of 1000 ml (33.8 fl oz), or a glass bottle, up to a maximum size of 118 ml (4 fl oz), that is designed and intended to dispense an aerosol. [30B, 2023] (FCC-HAZ)

3.3.6* Aerosol Products. A nonrefillable combination of an aerosol container, aerosol propellant, and aerosol valve, with or without a base product, that is dispensed through the aerosol valve. [30B, 2023] (FCC-HAZ)

N **3.3.7 Aerosol Propellant.** A liquefied or compressed gas that is used in whole or in part, such as a cosolvent, to expel a liquid or any other material from the same self-pressurized container or from a compartmented container. [30B, 2023] (FCC-HAZ)

N **3.3.8* Aerosol Valve.** A self-closing device attached to an aerosol container to allow dispensing of the contents of an aerosol product. [30B, 2023] (FCC-HAZ)

Δ **3.3.9 Airport (Aerodrome).** An area on land or water that is used or intended to be used for the landing and takeoff of aircraft and includes buildings and facilities. [440, 2024] (FCC-OCP)

3.3.10 Airport Ramp. Any outdoor area, including aprons and hardstands, where aircraft can be positioned, stored, serviced, or maintained, irrespective of the nature of the surface of the area. [415, 2022] (FCC-OCP)

3.3.11* Aisle Width. The horizontal dimension between the face of the loads in racks under consideration. [13, 2022] (FCC-OCP)

3.3.12 Alarm. An indication of the existence of a condition that requires immediate response. [72, 2019] (FCC-OCP)

3.3.13 Alarm Signal. See 3.3.256.1.

3.3.14 Alcohol-Based Hand Rub. An alcohol-containing preparation designed for application to the hands for reducing the number of visible microorganisms on the hands and containing ethanol or isopropanol in an amount not exceeding 95 percent by volume. (FCC-HAZ)

3.3.15 Alleyway. An accessible clear space between storage piles or groups of piles suitable for housekeeping operations, visual inspection of piling areas, and initial fire-fighting operations. (FCC-OCP)

3.3.16 ANSI/ASME. The designation for American National Standards Institute publication sponsored and published by the American Society of Mechanical Engineers. (FCC-FUN)

3.3.17 Area.

3.3.17.1 *Back Stock Area.* The area of a mercantile occupancy that is physically separated from the sales area and not intended to be accessible to the public. [30B, 2023] (FCC-HAZ)

3.3.17.2 *Control Area.* A building or portion of a building or outdoor area within which hazardous materials are allowed to be stored, dispensed, used, or handled in quantities not exceeding the maximum allowable quantities (MAQ). [400, 2022] (FCC-HAZ)

3.3.17.3 *Fire Area.* An area of a building separated from the remainder of the building by construction having a fire resistance of at least 1 hour and having all communicating openings properly protected by an assembly having a fire resistance rating of at least 1 hour. [30, 2024] (FCC-OCP)

3.3.17.4 *Fire Flow Area.* The floor area, in square feet, used to determine the required fire flow. (FCC-FUN)

3.3.17.5 *Indoor Area.* An area that is within a building or structure having overhead cover, other than a structure qualifying as "weather protection." [55, 2023] (FCC-HAZ)

3.3.17.6 *Organic Peroxide Storage Area.* An area used for the storage of organic peroxide formulations. [400, 2022] (FCC-HAZ)

3.3.17.7 *Outdoor Area.* An area that is not an indoor area. [55, 2023] (FCC-HAZ)

3.3.17.8 *Permissible Areas.*

3.3.17.8.1 *Designated Area.* A specific location designed and approved for hot work operations that is maintained fire-safe, such as a maintenance shop or a detached outside location, that is of noncombustible or fire-resistive construction, essentially free of combustible and flammable contents, and suitably segregated from adjacent areas. [51B, 2024] (FCC-HAZ)

3.3.17.8.2 *Permit-Required Area.* Any location other than a designated area that is approved for hot work and is made fire-safe by removing or protecting combustibles from ignition sources. [51B, 2024] (FCC-HAZ)

3.3.17.9 *Sales Display Area.* The area of a mercantile occupancy that is open to the public for the purpose of viewing and purchasing goods, wares, and merchandise. Individuals are free to circulate among the items, which are typically displayed on shelves, on racks, or on the floor. [30B, 2023] (FCC-HAZ)

3.3.17.10 *Smoking Area.* A designated area where smoking is permitted within a premises in which smoking is otherwise generally prohibited. (FCC-OCP)

3.3.17.11* *Spray Area.* Any fully enclosed, partly enclosed, or unenclosed area in which flammable or combustible vapors, mists, residues, dusts, or deposits are present due to the operation of spray processes, including (1) any area in the direct path of a spray application process; (2) the interior of a spray booth, spray room, or limited finishing workstation, as herein defined; (3) the interior of any exhaust plenum, eliminator section, or scrubber section; (4) the interior of any exhaust duct or exhaust stack leading from a spray application process; (5) the interior of any air recirculation path up to and including recirculation particulate filters; (6) any solvent concentrator (pollution abatement) unit or solvent recovery (distillation) unit; and (7) the inside of a membrane enclosure. The following are not part of the spray area: (1) fresh air make-up units; (2) air supply ducts and air supply plenums; (3) recirculation air supply ducts downstream of recirculation particulate filters; and (4) exhaust ducts from solvent concentrator (pollution abatement) units. [33, 2021] (FCC-HAZ)

3.3.18 ASME. American Society of Mechanical Engineers. [58, 2024] (FCC-HAZ)

3.3.19 ASME Container (or Tank). See 3.3.73.1.

3.3.20 ASTM. American Society for Testing and Materials, now known as "ASTM International." [55, 2023] (FCC-HAZ)

3.3.21 Automatic Emergency Shutoff Valve. A designated fail-safe automatic closing valve designed to shut off the flow of gases or liquids that is initiated by a control system where the control system is activated by either manual or automatic means. [55, 2023] (FCC-HAZ)

N **3.3.22 Automatic Sprinkler.** A fire suppression or control device that operates automatically when its heat-activated element is heated to its thermal rating or above, allowing water to discharge over a specified area. [13, 2022] (FCC-OCP)

3.3.23* Baled Cotton. A natural seed fiber wrapped and secured in industry-accepted materials, usually consisting of burlap, woven polypropylene, or sheet polyethylene, and secured with steel, synthetic, or wire bands, or wire; also includes linters (lint removed from the cottonseed) and motes (residual materials from the ginning process). (FCC-HAZ)

>**3.3.23.1** *Block.* A basic yard storage unit for baled cotton comprising multiple-row storage with clear spaces on all sides. (FCC-HAZ)

>**3.3.23.2*** *Densely Packed Baled Cotton.* Cotton, made into banded bales, with a packing density of at least 22 lb/ft^3 (360 kg/m^3), and dimensions complying with the following: a length of 55 in. (ca. 1400 mm ± 20 mm), a width of 21 in. (ca. 530 mm ± 20 mm), and a height of 27.6 in. to 35.4 in. (700 mm to 900 mm). (FCC-HAZ)

>**3.3.23.3** *Fire-Packed Baled Cotton.* A cotton bale within which a fire has been packed as a result of a process in which ginning is the most frequent cause. (FCC-HAZ)

>**3.3.23.4** *Naked Cotton Bale.* An unwrapped cotton bale secured with wire or steel straps. (FCC-HAZ)

3.3.24 Barrel. A unit of volume used in the petroleum industry that is equal to 42 gal (159 L). [30, 2024] (FCC-HAZ)

3.3.25 Basement. Any story of a building wholly or partly below grade plane that is not considered the first story above grade plane. *(See also 3.3.289.1 in NFPA 5000®, First Story Above Grade Plane.)* [5000, 2024] (FCC-FUN)

3.3.26 Battery System. A system that consists of these interconnected subsystems: (1) stationary storage batteries, (2) battery chargers, and (3) a collection of rectifiers, inverters, converters, and associated electrical equipment as required for a particular application. (FCC-HAZ)

3.3.27 Battery Types, Stationary.

>**3.3.27.1** *Lithium-Ion Battery.* A storage battery that consists of lithium ions imbedded in a carbon graphite or nickel metal-oxide substrate. The electrolyte is a carbonate mixture or a gelled polymer. The lithium ions are the charge carriers of the battery. (FCC-HAZ)

>**3.3.27.2** *Lithium Metal Polymer Battery.* A storage battery that is comprised of nonaqueous liquid or polymerized electrolytes, which provide ionic conductivity between lithiated positive active material electrically separated from metallic lithium or lithiated negative active material. (FCC-HAZ)

>**3.3.27.3** *Nickel Cadmium (NiCad) Battery.* An alkaline storage battery in which the positive active material is nickel oxide, the negative contains the cadmium, and the electrolyte is potassium hydroxide. (FCC-HAZ)

>**3.3.27.4*** *Valve-Regulated (VRLA).* A lead-acid battery consisting of sealed cells furnished with a valve that opens to vent the battery whenever the internal pressure of the battery exceeds the ambient pressure by a set amount. (FCC-HAZ)

3.3.28 Block. See 3.3.23.1.

3.3.29 Board of Appeals. A group of persons appointed by the governing body of the jurisdiction adopting this *Code* for the purpose of hearing and adjudicating differences of opinion between the AHJ and the citizenry in the interpretation, application, and enforcement of this *Code*. (FCC-FUN)

3.3.30* Boiling Point (BP). The temperature at which the vapor pressure of a liquid equals the surrounding atmospheric pressure. [30, 2024] (FCC-HAZ)

3.3.31* Boil-Over. An event in the burning of certain oils in an open-top tank when, after a long period of quiescent burning, there is a sudden increase in fire intensity associated with expulsion of burning oil from the tank. [30, 2024] (FCC-HAZ)

3.3.32* Building. Any structure used or intended for supporting or sheltering any use or occupancy. [101, 2024] (FCC-FUN)

>**3.3.32.1*** *Airport Terminal Building.* A structure used primarily for air passenger enplaning or deplaning, including ticket sales, flight information, baggage handling, and other necessary functions in connection with air transport operations. This term includes any extensions and satellite buildings used for passenger handling or aircraft flight service functions. Aircraft loading walkways and "mobile lounges" are excluded. [415, 2022] (FCC-OCP)

>**3.3.32.2** *Apartment Building.* See 3.3.203.2.

>**3.3.32.3** *Attached Building.* A building having only one common wall with another building having other types of occupancies. (FCC-HAZ)

>**3.3.32.4** *Bulk Merchandising Retail Building.* See 3.3.203.4.

>**3.3.32.5*** *Existing Building.* A building erected or officially authorized prior to the effective date of the adoption of this edition of the *Code* by the agency or jurisdiction. [101, 2024] (FCC-FUN)

>**3.3.32.6*** *High-Rise Building.* A building where the floor of an occupiable story is greater than 75 ft (23 m) above the lowest level of fire department vehicle access. [5000, 2024] (FCC-FUN)

>**3.3.32.7*** *Important Building.* A building that is considered not expendable in an exposure fire. [30, 2024] (FCC-HAZ)

>**3.3.32.8** *Mini-Storage Building.* See 3.3.203.31.1.

>**3.3.32.9** *Satellite.* A structure that can be adjacent to but separated from the airport terminal building, accessible above ground or through subway passages, and used to provide flight service operations, such as passenger check-in, waiting rooms, food service, enplaning or deplaning, etc. [415, 2022] (FCC-OCP)

>**3.3.32.10*** *Special Amusement Building.* A building or portion thereof that is temporary, permanent, or mobile and contains a ride or device that conveys patrons where the

patrons can be contained or restrained, or provides a walkway along, around, or over a course in any direction as a form of amusement or entertainment, and arranged so that the egress path is not readily apparent due to visual or audio distractions, contains an intentionally confounded egress path, or is not readily available due to the mode of conveyance through the building or structure. [*101*, 2024] (FCC-OCP)

3.3.32.11 *Storage Tank Building.* A three-dimensional space that is enclosed by a roof and walls that cover more than one-half of the possible area of the sides of the space, is of sufficient size to allow entry by personnel, will likely limit the dissipation of heat or dispersion of vapors, and restricts access for fire fighting. [30, 2024] (FCC-HAZ)

3.3.33 Bulk Hydrogen Compressed Gas System. See 3.3.283.1.

3.3.34 Bulk Inert Gas System. See 3.3.283.2.

3.3.35 Bulk Liquefied Hydrogen Gas System. See 3.3.283.3.

3.3.36 Bulk Oxygen System. See 3.3.283.4.

3.3.37 Bulk Plant or Terminal. That portion of a property where liquids are received by tank vessel, pipelines, tank car, or tank vehicle and are stored or blended in bulk for the purpose of distributing such liquids by tank vessel, pipeline, tank car, tank vehicle, portable tank, or container. (FCC-HAZ)

3.3.38 Burn-It. A fire-fighting strategy that allows for the free burn of a tire fire. (FCC-OCP)

3.3.39 Bury-It. A fire-fighting strategy in which a tire pile is buried with soil, sand, gravel, cement dust, or other cover material. (FCC-OCP)

3.3.40 Cannabis Extraction Equipment. Equipment or appliances used for the extraction of botanical material, such as essential oils, from cannabis. (FCC-OCP)

3.3.41 Cannabis Extraction Facility. A building used for the solvent-based extraction process of cannabis. (FCC-OCP)

3.3.42 Carbon Dioxide Enrichment Process. A process where carbon dioxide gas is intentionally introduced into an indoor environment for the purpose of accelerating plant growth. (FCC-OCP)

3.3.43* Cathodic Protection. A technique to resist the corrosion of a metal surface by making the surface the cathode of an electrochemical cell. [55, 2023] (FCC-HAZ)

3.3.44 Cathodic Protection Tester. A person who demonstrates an understanding of the principles and measurements of all common types of cathodic protection systems applicable to metal piping and container systems and who has education and experience in soil resistivity, stray current, structure-to-soil potential, and component electrical isolation measurements of metal piping and container systems. [55, 2023] (FCC-HAZ)

3.3.45 Certificate of Fitness. A written document issued by the AHJ to any person for the purpose of granting permission to such person to conduct or engage in any operation or act for which certification is required. (FCC-FUN)

3.3.46 CFR. The Code of Federal Regulations of the United States Government. (FCC-FUN)

3.3.47 CGA. Compressed Gas Association. (FCC-FUN)

3.3.48 Chemical Fume Hood. A ventilated enclosure designed to contain and exhaust fumes, gases, vapors, mists, and particulate matter generated within the hood interior. [45, 2024] (FCC-OCP)

3.3.49 Chemical Name. The scientific designation of a chemical in accordance with the nomenclature system developed by the International Union of Pure and Applied Chemistry or the Chemical Abstracts Service rules of nomenclature, or a name that clearly identifies a chemical for the purpose of conducting an evaluation. (FCC-HAZ)

3.3.50 Chemical Plant. A large integrated plant or that portion of such a plant, other than a refinery or distillery, where liquids are produced by chemical reactions or used in chemical reactions. [30, 2024] (FCC-HAZ)

3.3.51* Chip. A wood chip of various species used in the manufacture of pulp. (FCC-OCP)

3.3.52* Cleaning Media. Materials used to clean piping systems. [55, 2023] (FCC-HAZ)

3.3.53 Cleanroom. A room in which the concentration of airborne particles is controlled to specified limits, including areas below the raised floor and above the ceiling grid if these areas are part of the air path and within the rated construction. [5000, 2024] (FCC-OCP)

3.3.54 Clear Space. An area free of combustible materials but that can contain noncombustible materials that cannot transmit an exposure fire. (FCC-OCP)

3.3.55 Closed System Use. See 3.3.298.1.

3.3.56 Closed-Top Diking. A dike with a cover intended to minimize the entrance of precipitation into the diked area. [30, 2024] (FCC-HAZ)

3.3.57 Code.

Δ **3.3.57.1** *Building Code.* The building code enforced by the jurisdiction or agency enforcing this *Code*. [*101*, 2021] (FCC-FUN)

3.3.57.2 *Electrical Code.* The electrical code adopted by the jurisdiction. (FCC-FUN)

3.3.57.3 *Mechanical Code.* The mechanical or mechanical construction code adopted by the jurisdiction. [55, 2023] (FCC-HAZ)

3.3.57.4 *Plumbing Code.* The plumbing code adopted by the jurisdiction. (FCC-FUN)

3.3.58 Cold Deck. A single ranked pile of logs with individual logs of regular or irregular length usually 20 ft to 50 ft (6.1 m to 15.2 m) long, but greater than 8 ft (2.4 m) long. (FCC-OCP)

3.3.59 Column (Paper). A single vertical stack of rolls of paper. (FCC-OCP)

3.3.60 Combustible (Material). A material that, in the form in which it is used and under the conditions anticipated, will ignite and burn; a material that does not meet the definition of noncombustible or limited-combustible. [*101*, 2024] (FCC-FUN)

3.3.61* Combustible Dust. A finely divided combustible particulate solid that presents a flash fire hazard or explosion hazard when suspended in air or the process-specific oxidizing medium over a range of concentrations. [652, 2019] (FCC-HAZ)

3.3.62* Combustible Fiber. Any material in a fibrous or shredded form that readily ignites when heat sources are present. (FCC-HAZ)

3.3.63 Combustible Liquid. See 3.3.180.1.

3.3.64 Combustible Particulate Solid. See 3.3.264.1.

3.3.65 Combustible Refuse. All combustible or loose rubbish, litter, or waste materials generated by an occupancy that are refused, rejected, or considered worthless and are disposed of by incineration on the premises where generated or periodically transported from the premises. (FCC-OCP)

3.3.66* Combustible Waste. Combustible or loose waste material that is generated by an establishment or process and, if salvageable, is retained for scrap or reprocessing on the premises where generated or transported to a plant for processing. (FCC-OCP)

3.3.67 Combustion. A chemical process of oxidation that occurs at a rate fast enough to produce heat and usually light in the form of either a glow or flame. (FCC-FUN)

3.3.68 Commodity. The combination of products, packing material, and container that determines commodity classification. [13, 2022] (FCC-OCP)

3.3.69* Common Path of Travel. The portion of exit access that must be traversed before two separate and distinct paths of travel to two exits are available. [101, 2024] (FCC-OCP)

3.3.70 Compartment.

3.3.70.1* *Fire Compartment.* A space within a building that is enclosed by fire barriers on all sides, including the top and bottom. [101, 2024] (FCC-OCP)

3.3.70.2* *Smoke Compartment.* A space within a building enclosed by smoke barriers on all sides, including the top and bottom. [101, 2024] (FCC-OCP)

3.3.71 Condition, Existing. See 3.3.109.

3.3.72 Construction Documents. Documents that consist of scaled design drawings and specifications for the purpose of construction of new facilities or modification to existing facilities. *(See also 3.3.255, Shop Drawings.)* (FCC-FUN)

3.3.73 Container. A vessel, including cylinders, tanks, portable tanks, and cargo tanks, used for transporting or storing materials. (FCC-HAZ)

3.3.73.1 *ASME Container.* A container constructed in accordance with the ASME Code. [58, 2024] (FCC-HAZ)

3.3.73.2 *Compressed Gas Container.* A pressure vessel designed to hold compressed gas at an absolute pressure greater than 1 atmosphere at 68°F (20°C) that includes cylinders, containers, and tanks. [55, 2023] (FCC-HAZ)

3.3.73.3* *Container (Flammable or Combustible Liquid).* A vessel of 119 gal (450 L) or less capacity used for transporting or storing liquids, excluding intermediate bulk containers. [30, 2024] (FCC-HAZ)

3.3.73.3.1 *Closed Container.* A container as herein defined, so sealed by means of a lid or other device that neither liquid nor vapor will escape from it at ordinary temperatures. [30, 2024] (FCC-HAZ)

3.3.73.4 *Cryogenic Fluids Container.* A cryogenic vessel used for transportation, handling, or storage. (FCC-HAZ)

3.3.73.5 *Intermediate Bulk Container.* Any closed vessel having a liquid capacity not exceeding 3000 L (793 gal) and intended for storing and transporting liquids, as defined in Title 49, Code of Federal Regulations, Parts 100 through 199 or in Part 6 of the United Nations *Recommendations on the Transport of Dangerous Goods.* [30, 2024] (FCC-HAZ)

3.3.73.6 *[LP-Gas] Container.* Any vessel, including cylinders, tanks, portable tanks, and cargo tanks, used for the transporting or storing of LP-Gases. [58, 2024] (FCC-HAZ)

3.3.74 Control Area. See 3.3.17.2.

3.3.75* Conventional Pallet. A material-handling aid designed to support a unit load with openings to provide access for material-handling devices. *(See Figure A.3.3.75.)* [13, 2022] (FCC-OCP)

3.3.76 Cooking Fire. The noncommercial, residential burning of materials not exceeding 3 ft (0.9 m) in diameter and 2 ft (0.6 m) in height, other than rubbish in which the fuel burned is contained in an outdoor fireplace, a barbecue grill, or a barbecue pit for the purpose of preparing food. (FCC-FUN)

3.3.77 Cordwood. Logs 8 ft (2.4 m) or less in length customarily intended for pulpwood or fuel uses. (FCC-OCP)

3.3.78 Corrosive Material. See 3.3.189.3.

3.3.79 Crude Petroleum. Hydrocarbon mixtures that have a flash point below 150°F (65.6°C) and that have not been processed in a refinery. [30, 2024] (FCC-HAZ)

3.3.80 Cryogenic Fluid. A fluid with a boiling point lower than −130°F (−90°C) at an absolute pressure of 14.7 psi (101.3 kPa). [55, 2023] (FCC-HAZ)

3.3.80.1 *Flammable Cryogenic Fluid.* A cryogenic fluid that forms flammable mixtures in air when in its vapor state. [55, 2023] (FCC-HAZ)

3.3.80.2 *Inert Cryogenic Fluid.* A cryogenic fluid that vaporizes to produce an inert gas when in its vapor state. [55, 2023] (FCC-HAZ)

3.3.80.3 *Oxidizing Cryogenic Fluid.* An oxidizing gas in the cryogenic state. [55, 2023] (FCC-HAZ)

3.3.81* Cultural Resource Properties. Buildings, structures, or sites, or portions thereof, that are culturally significant, or that house culturally significant collections for museums, libraries, and places of worship. [914, 2023] (FCC-OCP)

3.3.82 Cylinder. A pressure vessel designed for absolute pressures higher than 40 psi (276 kPa) and having a circular cross-section. It does not include a portable tank, multiunit tank car tank, cargo tank, or tank car. [55, 2023] (FCC-HAZ)

3.3.83 Cylinder Containment Vessel. A gastight recovery vessel designed so that a leaking compressed gas container can be placed within its confines, thereby encapsulating the leaking container. [55, 2023] (FCC-HAZ)

3.3.84* Cylinder Pack. An arrangement of cylinders into a cluster where the cylinders are confined into a grouping or arrangement with a strapping or frame system and connections are made to a common manifold. The frame system is allowed to be on skids or wheels to permit movement. [**55,** 2023] (FCC-HAZ)

Δ **3.3.85 Damage-Limiting Construction.** For the purposes of this *Code,* any set of construction elements, used individually or in combination, which will act to limit damage from an explosion, including open structures, pressure relieving construction, or pressure resistant construction. [**30,** 2024] (FCC-HAZ)

3.3.86* Deficiency. For the purposes of inspection, testing, and maintenance of water-based fire protection systems, a condition that will or has the potential to adversely impact the performance of a system or portion thereof but does not rise to the level of an impairment. [**25,** 2023] (FCC-OCP)

3.3.86.1 *Critical Deficiency.* A deficiency that, if not corrected, can have a material effect on the ability of the fire protection system or unit to function as intended in a fire event. [**25,** 2023] (FCC-OCP)

Δ **3.3.86.2** *Noncritical Deficiency.* A deficiency that does not have a material effect on the ability of the fire protection system or unit to function in a fire event, but correction is needed to meet the requirements of this *Code* and NFPA 25 or for the proper inspection, testing, and maintenance of the system or unit. [**25,** 2023] (FCC-OCP)

3.3.87 Deflagration. Propagation of a combustion zone at a velocity that is less than the speed of sound in the unreacted medium. [**68,** 2023] (FCC-HAZ)

3.3.88 Delivered Audio Quality (DAQ). A measure of speech intelligibility over a transmission medium. (FCC-FUN)

3.3.89 Desolventizing. The act of removing a solvent from a material. (FCC-HAZ)

3.3.90 Detector. A device suitable for connection to a circuit that has a sensor that responds to a physical stimulus such as gas, heat or smoke. [**72,** 2019] (FCC-OCP)

3.3.90.1 *Air Sampling–Type Detector.* A detector that consists of a piping or tubing distribution network that runs from the detector to the area(s) to be protected. An aspiration fan in the detector housing draws air from the protected area back to the detector through air-sampling ports, piping, or tubing. At the detector, the air is analyzed for fire products. [**72,** 2019] (FCC-OCP)

3.3.90.2 *Automatic Fire Detector.* A device designed to detect the presence of a fire signature and to initiate action. For the purpose of this *Code,* automatic fire detectors are classified as follows: Automatic Fire Extinguishing or Suppression System Operation Detector, Fire–Gas Detector, Heat Detector, Other Fire Detectors, Radiant Energy–Sensing Fire Detector, and Smoke Detector. [**72,** 2019] (FCC-OCP)

3.3.90.3 *Automatic Fire Extinguishing or Suppression System Operation Detector.* A device that automatically detects the operation of a fire extinguishing or suppression system by means appropriate to the system employed. [**72,** 2019] (FCC-OCP)

3.3.90.4* *Combination Detector.* A device that either responds to more than one of the fire phenomena or employs more than one operating principle to sense one of these phenomena. Typical examples are a combination of a heat detector with a smoke detector or a combination rate-of-rise and fixed-temperature heat detector. This device has listings for each sensing method employed. [**72,** 2019] (FCC-OCP)

3.3.90.5 *Electrical Conductivity Heat Detector.* A line-type or spot-type sensing element in which resistance varies as a function of temperature. [**72,** 2019] (FCC-OCP)

3.3.90.6 *Fire–Gas Detector.* A device that detects gases produced by a fire. [**72,** 2019] (FCC-OCP)

3.3.90.7* *Fixed-Temperature Detector.* A device that responds when its operating element becomes heated to a predetermined level. [**72,** 2019] (FCC-OCP)

3.3.90.8* *Flame Detector.* A radiant energy–sensing fire detector that detects the radiant energy emitted by a flame. *(Refer to A.17.8.2 of NFPA 72.)* [**72,** 2019] (FCC-OCP)

3.3.90.9 *Gas Detector.* A device that detects the presence of a specified gas concentration. Gas detectors can be either spot-type or line-type detectors. [**72,** 2019] (FCC-OCP)

3.3.90.10 *Heat Detector.* A fire detector that detects either abnormally high temperature or rate of temperature rise, or both. [**72,** 2019] (FCC-OCP)

3.3.90.11 *Line-Type Detector.* A device in which detection is continuous along a path. Typical examples are rate-of-rise pneumatic tubing detectors, projected beam smoke detectors, and heat-sensitive cable. [**72,** 2019] (FCC-OCP)

3.3.90.12* *Multi-Criteria Detector.* A device that contains multiple sensors that separately respond to physical stimulus such as heat, smoke, or fire gases, or employs more than one sensor to sense the same stimulus. This sensor is capable of generating only one alarm signal from the sensors employed in the design either independently or in combination. The sensor output signal is mathematically evaluated to determine when an alarm signal is warranted. The evaluation can be performed either at the detector or at the control unit. This detector has a single listing that establishes the primary function of the detector. [**72,** 2019] (FCC-OCP)

3.3.90.13* *Multi-Sensor Detector.* A device that contains multiple sensors that separately respond to physical stimulus such as heat, smoke, or fire gases, or employs more than one sensor to sense the same stimulus. A device capable of generating multiple alarm signals from any one of the sensors employed in the design, independently or in combination. The sensor output signals are mathematically evaluated to determine when an alarm signal is warranted. The evaluation can be performed either at the detector or at the control unit. This device has listings for each sensing method employed. [**72,** 2019] (FCC-OCP)

3.3.90.14 *Other Fire Detectors.* Devices that detect a phenomenon other than heat, smoke, flame, or gases produced by a fire. [**72,** 2019] (FCC-OCP)

3.3.90.15 *Pneumatic Rate-of-Rise Tubing Heat Detector.* A line-type detector comprising small-diameter tubing, usually copper, that is installed on the ceiling or high on the walls throughout the protected area. The tubing is terminated in a detector unit containing diaphragms and associated contacts set to actuate at a predetermined pressure. The

DEFINITIONS

system is sealed except for calibrated vents that compensate for normal changes in temperature. [72, 2019] (FCC-OCP)

3.3.90.16 *Projected Beam–Type Detector.* A type of photoelectric light obscuration smoke detector wherein the beam spans the protected area. [72, 2019] (FCC-OCP)

3.3.90.17 *Radiant Energy–Sensing Fire Detector.* A device that detects radiant energy, such as ultraviolet, visible, or infrared, that is emitted as a product of combustion reaction and obeys the laws of optics. [72, 2019] (FCC-OCP)

3.3.90.18* *Rate Compensation Detector.* A device that responds when the temperature of the air surrounding the device reaches a predetermined level, regardless of the rate of temperature rise. [72, 2019] (FCC-OCP)

3.3.90.19* *Rate-of-Rise Detector.* A device that responds when the temperature rises at a rate exceeding a predetermined value. [72, 2019] (FCC-OCP)

3.3.90.20 *Smoke Detector.* A device that detects visible or invisible particles of combustion. [72, 2019] (FCC-OCP)

3.3.90.21 *Spark/Ember Detector.* A radiant energy–sensing fire detector that is designed to detect sparks or embers, or both. These devices are normally intended to operate in dark environments and in the infrared part of the spectrum. [72, 2019] (FCC-OCP)

3.3.90.22 *Spot-Type Detector.* A device in which the detecting element is concentrated at a particular location. Typical examples are bimetallic detectors, fusible alloy detectors, certain pneumatic rate-of-rise detectors, certain smoke detectors, and thermoelectric detectors. [72, 2019] (FCC-OCP)

3.3.91 Detonation. Propagation of a combustion zone at a velocity greater than the speed of sound in the unreacted medium. [68, 2023] (FCC-HAZ)

3.3.92 Dispensing. The pouring or transferring of a material from a container tank, or similar vessel whereby vapors, dusts, fumes, mists, or gases could be liberated to the atmosphere. [5000, 2024] (FCC-HAZ)

3.3.93 Distillery. A plant or that portion of a plant where liquids produced by fermentation are concentrated and where the concentrated products are also mixed, stored, or packaged. [30, 2024] (FCC-HAZ)

3.3.94 Distributor. A business engaged in the sale or resale, or both, of compressed gases or cryogenic fluids, or both. [55, 2023] (FCC-HAZ)

3.3.95 Donor Antenna. Antennas used with in-building emergency responder communications enhancement systems that provide the connection between the wide-area communications system of interest and the in-building system. (FCC-FUN)

3.3.96 Dormitory. See 3.3.203.9.

3.3.97 DOT. US Department of Transportation. (FCC-FUN)

3.3.98 Driveway. A clear space suitable for fire-fighting operations by motorized fire apparatus. (FCC-FUN)

3.3.99* Dwelling Unit. One or more rooms arranged for complete, independent housekeeping purposes, with space for eating, living, and sleeping; facilities for cooking; and provisions for sanitation. [5000, 2024] (FCC-OCP)

3.3.99.1 *One- and Two-Family Dwelling Unit.* See 3.3.203.25.1.

3.3.100 Emergency. A fire, explosion, or hazardous condition that poses an immediate threat to the safety of life or damage to property. (FCC-FUN)

3.3.101 Emergency Relief Vent. An opening, construction method, or device that will automatically relieve excessive internal pressure due to an exposure fire. [30, 2024] (FCC-HAZ)

3.3.102 Emergency Shutoff Valve. A designated valve designed to shut off the flow of gases or liquids. [55, 2023] (FCC-HAZ)

Δ **3.3.103* Energy Storage Systems (ESS).** One or more devices, assembled together, capable of storing energy to supply electrical energy at a future time. [855, 2023] (FCC-HAZ)

Δ **3.3.104 Ethylene Oxide Drum.** For the purposes of this *Code*, containers built to UN specification 1A1. [55, 2023] (FCC-HAZ)

3.3.105 Excess Flow Control. A fail-safe system or approved means designed to shut off flow due to a rupture in pressurized piping systems. [55, 2023] (FCC-HAZ)

3.3.106 Excess Flow Valve. A valve inserted into a compressed gas cylinder, portable tank, or stationary tank that is designed to positively shut off the flow of gas in the event that its predetermined flow is exceeded. (FCC-HAZ)

3.3.107* Exhausted Enclosure. An appliance or piece of equipment that consists of a top, a back, and two sides that provides a means of local exhaust for capturing gases, fumes, vapors, and mists. [55, 2023] (FCC-HAZ)

3.3.108* Existing. That which is already in existence on the date this edition of the *Code* goes into effect. [101, 2024] (FCC-FUN)

3.3.109 Existing Condition. Any situation, circumstance, or physical makeup of any structure, premise, or process that was ongoing or in effect prior to the adoption of this *Code*. (FCC-FUN)

3.3.110* Exit. That portion of a means of egress that is separated from all other spaces of the building or structure by construction, location, or equipment as required to provide a protected way of travel to the exit discharge. [101, 2024] (FCC-OCP)

3.3.110.1* *Horizontal Exit.* A way of passage from one building to an area of refuge in another building on approximately the same level, or a way of passage through or around a fire barrier to an area of refuge on approximately the same level in the same building that affords safety from fire and smoke originating from the area of incidence and areas communicating therewith. [101, 2024] (FCC-OCP)

3.3.111 Exit Access. That portion of a means of egress that leads to an exit. [101, 2024] (FCC-OCP)

3.3.112 Exit Discharge. That portion of a means of egress between the termination of an exit and a public way. [101, 2024] (FCC-OCP)

3.3.113 Explosion. The bursting or rupture of an enclosure or a container due to the development of internal pressure from a deflagration. [69, 2019] (FCC-HAZ)

3.3.114* Explosion Control. A means of either preventing an explosion through the use of explosion suppression, fuel reduction, or oxidant reduction systems or a means to prevent the structural collapse of a building in the event of an explosion through the use of deflagration venting, barricades, or related construction methods. [55, 2023] (FCC-HAZ)

3.3.115* Explosive Material. A chemical compound, mixture, or device, the primary or common purpose of which is to function by explosion. [5000, 2024] (FCC-HAZ)

3.3.116 Extraction Room (Cannabis). The room or space in which the solvent–based extraction process of cannabis occurs. (FCC-OCP)

3.3.117 Facility. As applied to access and water supply, a structure or use in a fixed location including exterior storage, use, and handling areas that relates to the occupancies and operations covered by this *Code*. (FCC-FUN)

3.3.117.1 *Animal Housing Facility.* Area of a building or structure, including interior and adjacent exterior spaces, where animals are fed, rested, worked, exercised, treated, exhibited, or used for production. (FCC-OCP)

3.3.117.2 *Hazardous Material Storage Facility.* See 3.3.157.

3.3.117.3 *Limited Care Facility.* See 3.3.203.16.

3.3.117.4 *Motor Fuel Dispensing Facility.* See 3.3.203.22.

3.3.117.4.1 *Fleet Vehicle Motor Fuel Dispensing Facility.* See 3.3.203.22.1.

3.3.117.4.2 *Marine Motor Fuel Dispensing Facility.* See 3.3.203.22.2.

3.3.117.4.3 *Motor Fuel Dispensing Facility Located Inside a Building.* See 3.3.203.22.3.

3.3.118 Fail-Safe. A design arrangement incorporating one or more features that automatically counteracts the effect of an anticipated source of failure or which includes a design arrangement that eliminates or mitigates a hazardous condition by compensating automatically for a failure or malfunction. (FCC-HAZ)

3.3.119* Festival Seating. A form of audience/spectator accommodation in which no seating, other than a floor or finished ground level, is provided for the audience/spectators gathered to observe a performance. [101, 2024] (FCC-OCP)

3.3.120 Fines (Wood). Small pieces or splinters of wood by-products that can pass through a 0.25 in. (6.4 mm) screen. (FCC-HAZ)

3.3.121 Finish.

3.3.121.1 *Interior Ceiling Finish.* The interior finish of ceilings. [101, 2024] (FCC-OCP)

3.3.121.2* *Interior Finish.* The exposed surfaces of walls, ceilings, and floors within buildings. [101, 2024] (FCC-OCP)

3.3.121.3* *Interior Floor Finish.* The interior finish of floors, ramps, stair treads and risers, and other walking surfaces. [101, 2024] (FCC-OCP)

3.3.121.4* *Interior Wall Finish.* The interior finish of columns, fixed or movable walls, and fixed or movable partitions. [101, 2024] (FCC-OCP)

3.3.122 Fires, Classification of.

3.3.122.1 *Class A Fires.* Class A fires are fires in ordinary combustible materials, such as wood, cloth, paper, rubber, and many plastics. [10, 2018] (FCC-OCP)

3.3.122.2 *Class B Fires.* Class B fires are fires in flammable liquids, combustible liquids, petroleum greases, tars, oils, oil-based paints, solvents, lacquers, alcohols, and flammable gases. [10, 2018] (FCC-OCP)

3.3.122.3 *Class C Fires.* Class C fires are fires that involve energized electrical equipment. [10, 2018] (FCC-OCP)

3.3.122.4 *Class D Fires.* Class D fires are fires in combustible metals, such as magnesium, titanium, zirconium, sodium, lithium, and potassium. [10, 2018] (FCC-OCP)

3.3.122.5 *Class K Fires.* Class K fires are fires in cooking appliances that involve combustible cooking media (vegetable or animal oils and fats). [10, 2018] (FCC-OCP)

3.3.123 Fire, Recreational. See 3.3.239.

3.3.124 Fire Alarm System. See 3.3.283.10.

3.3.125 Fire Apparatus Access Road. The road or other means developed to allow access and operational setup for fire-fighting and rescue apparatus. (FCC-FUN)

3.3.126 Fire Compartment. See 3.3.70.1.

3.3.127 Fire Door Assembly. Any combination of a fire door, a frame, hardware, and other accessories that together provide a specific degree of fire protection to the opening. [80, 2019] (FCC-OCP)

3.3.128 Fire Flow. The flow rate of a water supply, measured at 20 psi (137.9 kPa) residual pressure, that is available for fire fighting. (FCC-FUN)

3.3.129 Fire Hazard. Any situation, process, material, or condition that, on the basis of applicable data, can cause a fire or explosion or that can provide a ready fuel supply to augment the spread or intensity of a fire or explosion, all of which pose a threat to life or property. [914, 2019] (FCC-FUN)

Δ **3.3.130* Fire Hydrant.** A valved connection on a water supply system having one or more outlets and that is used to supply hose and fire department pumpers with water. [1140, 2022] (FCC-FUN)

3.3.131* Fire Lane. A fire apparatus access road, which is marked with approved signs or other approved notices. (FCC-FUN)

3.3.132 Fire Monitoring. Provisions implemented to provide early warning of smoldering fire conditions in the hot work area following completion of the established fire watch time period. [51B, 2024] (FCC-HAZ)

3.3.133 Fire Point. The lowest temperature at which a liquid will ignite and achieve sustained burning when exposed to a test flame in accordance with ASTM D92, *Standard Test Method for Flash and Fire Points by Cleveland Open Cup Tester*. [30, 2024] (FCC-HAZ)

3.3.134 Fire Retardant. A liquid, solid, or gas that tends to inhibit combustion when applied on, mixed in, or combined with combustible materials. (FCC-OCP)

3.3.135 Fire Watch. The assignment of a person or persons to an area for the express purpose of notifying the fire department, the building occupants, or both of an emergency; preventing a fire from occurring; extinguishing small fires; protecting the public from fire and life safety dangers. (FCC-FUN)

3.3.136* Fireworks. Any composition or device for the purpose of producing a visible or an audible effect for entertainment purposes by combustion, deflagration, or detonation, that meets the definition of *Consumer Fireworks* or *Display Fireworks* as set forth in NFPA 1124. [1124, 2022] (FCC-HAZ)

3.3.136.1* *Display Fireworks.* Large fireworks devices that are explosive materials intended for use in fireworks displays and designed to produce visible or audible effects by combustion, deflagration, or detonation, as set forth in 27 CFR 555, 49 CFR 172, and APA 87-1, *Standard for the Construction and Approval for Transportation of Fireworks, Novelties, and Theatrical Pyrotechnics.* [1124, 2022] (FCC-HAZ)

3.3.137* Flame Spread. The propagation of flame over a surface. [101, 2024] (FCC-OCP)

3.3.138 Flame Spread Index. A comparative measure, expressed as a dimensionless number, derived from visual measurements of the spread of flame versus time for a material tested in accordance with ASTM E84, *Standard Test Method for Surface Burning Characteristics of Building Materials*, or UL 723, *Test for Surface Building Characteristics of Burning Materials.* [101, 2024] (FCC-OCP)

3.3.139 Flammable Vapors. Flammable vapors are the concentration of flammable constituents in air that exceed 25 percent of their lower flammability limit (LFL). (FCC-HAZ)

3.3.140 Flash Point (FP). The minimum temperature of a liquid at which sufficient vapor is given off to form an ignitible mixture with the air, near the surface of the liquid or within the vessel used, as determined by the appropriate test procedure and apparatus specified in Section 4.4 of NFPA 30. [30, 2024] (FCC-HAZ)

3.3.141 Floor Area.

3.3.141.1* *Gross Floor Area.* The floor area within the inside perimeter of the outside walls, or the outside walls and fire walls of a building, or outside and/or inside walls that bound an occupancy or incidental use area with no deduction for hallways, stairs, closets, thickness of interior walls, columns, elevator and building services shafts, or other features, but excluding floor openings associated with atriums and communicating spaces. [5000, 2024] (FCC-OCP)

3.3.141.2 *Net Floor Area.* The floor area within the inside perimeter of the outside walls, or the outside walls and fire walls of a building, or outside and/or inside walls that bound an occupancy or incidental use area with deductions for hallways, stairs, closets, shafts, thickness of interior walls, columns, and other features. [5000, 2024] (FCC-OCP)

3.3.142 Forecasting. The ability to predict fire progression in a scrap tire storage location prior to the completion of the inventory fire break using heavy equipment. (FCC-OCP)

3.3.143* Fugitive Emissions. Releases of flammable vapor that continuously or intermittently occur from process equipment during normal operations. [30, 2024] (FCC-HAZ)

3.3.144 Gallon, US Standard. 1 US gal = 0.833 Imperial gal = 231 in.^{3} = 3.785 L. [58, 2024] (FCC-HAZ)

3.3.145 Garage. A building or portion of a building in which one or more self-propelled vehicles carrying volatile Class I liquid for fuel or power are kept for use, sale, storage, rental, repair, exhibition, or demonstrating purposes, and all that portion of a building that is on or below the floor or floors in which such vehicles are kept and that is not separated therefrom by suitable cutoffs. [5000, 2024] (FCC-OCP)

3.3.146 Gas.

3.3.146.1* *Compressed Gas.* A material, or mixture of materials, that (1) is a gas at 68°F (20°C) or less at an absolute pressure of 14.7 psi (101.3 kPa) and (2) has a boiling point of 68°F (20°C) or less at an absolute pressure of 14.7 psi (101.3 kPa) and that is liquefied, nonliquefied, or in solution, except those gases that have no other health or physical hazard properties are not considered to be compressed gases until the pressure in the packaging exceeds an absolute pressure of 40.6 psi (280 kPa) at 68°F (20°C). [55, 2023] (FCC-HAZ)

3.3.146.1.1 *Compressed Gas Mixtures.* A mixture of two or more compressed gases contained in a packaging, the hazard properties of which are represented by the properties of the mixture as a whole. (FCC-HAZ)

3.3.146.1.2 *Compressed Gases in Solution.* Nonliquefied gases that are dissolved in a solvent. (FCC-HAZ)

3.3.146.1.3 *Liquefied Compressed Gases.* Gases that are contained in a packaging under the charged pressure and are partially liquid at a temperature of 68°F (20°C). (FCC-HAZ)

3.3.146.1.4 *Nonliquefied Compressed Gases.* Gases, other than those in solution, that are contained in a packaging under the charged pressure and are entirely gaseous at a temperature of 68°F (20°C). (FCC-HAZ)

3.3.146.2 *Corrosive Gas.* A gas that causes visible destruction of or irreversible alterations in living tissue by chemical action at the site of contact. [55, 2023] (FCC-HAZ)

Δ **3.3.146.3* *Flammable Gas.*** A material that is a gas at 68°F (20°C) or less at an absolute pressure of 14.7 psi (101.3 kPa). [55, 2023] (FCC-HAZ)

3.3.146.4 *Flammable Liquefied Gas.* A liquefied compressed gas that, when under a charged pressure, is partially liquid at a temperature of 68°F (20°C) and is flammable. [55, 2023] (FCC-HAZ)

3.3.146.5 *Highly Toxic Gas.* A chemical that has a median lethal concentration (LC_{50}) in air of 200 ppm by volume or less of gas or vapor, or 2 mg/L or less of mist, fume, or dust, when administered by continuous inhalation for 1 hour (or less if death occurs within 1 hour) to albino rats weighing between 0.44 lb and 0.66 lb (200 g and 300 g) each. [55, 2023] (FCC-HAZ)

3.3.146.6* *Inert Gas.* A nonreactive, nonflammable, noncorrosive gas such as argon, helium, krypton, neon, nitrogen, and xenon. [55, 2023] (FCC-HAZ)

3.3.146.7 *Liquefied Gas.* A gas, other than in solution, that in a packaging under the charged pressure exists both as a liquid and a gas at a temperature of 68°F (20°C). [30, 2024] (FCC-HAZ)

3.3.146.8 *Liquefied Natural Gas (LNG).* A fluid in the cryogenic liquid state that is composed predominantly of methane and that can contain minor quantities of ethane, propane, nitrogen, and other components normally found in natural gas. [59A, 2023] (FCC-HAZ)

3.3.146.9* *Liquefied Petroleum Gas (LP-Gas).* Any material having a vapor pressure not exceeding that allowed for commercial propane that is composed predominantly of the following hydrocarbons, either by themselves (except propylene) or as mixtures: propane, propylene, butane (normal butane or isobutane), and butylenes. [58, 2024] (FCC-HAZ)

3.3.146.10 *Nonflammable Gas.* A gas that does not meet the definition of a flammable gas. [55, 2023] (FCC-HAZ)

3.3.146.11* *Other Gas.* A gas that is not a corrosive gas, flammable gas, highly toxic gas, oxidizing gas, pyrophoric gas, toxic gas, or unstable reactive gas with a hazard rating of Class 2, Class 3, or Class 4 gas. [55, 2023] (FCC-HAZ)

3.3.146.12 *Oxidizing Gas.* A gas that can support and accelerate combustion of other materials more than air does. [55, 2023] (FCC-HAZ)

3.3.146.13 *Pyrophoric Gas.* A gas with an autoignition temperature in air at or below 130°F (54.4°C). [55, 2023] (FCC-HAZ)

3.3.146.14 *Scavenged Gas.* A residual process gas that is collected for treatment or release at a location remote from the site of use. (FCC-HAZ)

3.3.146.15 *Simple Asphyxiant Gas.* A gas that does not provide sufficient oxygen to support life and that has none of the other physical or health hazards. (FCC-HAZ)

3.3.146.16 *Toxic Gas.* A gas with a median lethal concentration (LC_{50}) in air of more than 200 ppm but not more than 2000 ppm by volume of gas or vapor, or more than 2 mg/L but not more than 20 mg/L of mist, fume, or dust, when administered by continuous inhalation for 1 hour (or less if death occurs within 1 hour) to albino rats weighing between 0.44 lb and 0.66 lb (200 g and 300 g) each. [55, 2023] (FCC-HAZ)

3.3.146.17* *Unstable Reactive Gas.* A gas that, in the pure state or as commercially produced, will vigorously polymerize, decompose, or condense; become self-reactive; or otherwise undergo a violent chemical change under conditions of shock, pressure, or temperature. [55, 2023] (FCC-HAZ)

3.3.147* **Gas Cabinet.** A fully enclosed, noncombustible enclosure used to provide an isolated environment for compressed gas cylinders in storage or use. [55, 2023] (FCC-HAZ)

3.3.148 Gas Manufacturer/Producer. A business that produces compressed gases or cryogenic fluids, or both, or fills portable or stationary gas cylinders, containers, or tanks. [55, 2023] (FCC-HAZ)

3.3.149 Gas Room. A separately ventilated, fully enclosed room in which only compressed gases, cryogenic fluids, associated equipment, and supplies are stored or used. [55, 2023] (FCC-HAZ)

3.3.150* **Gaseous Hydrogen (GH_2) System.** An assembly of equipment that consists of, but is not limited to, storage containers, pressure regulators, pressure relief devices, compressors, manifolds, and piping and that terminates at the source valve. [55, 2023] (FCC-HAZ)

3.3.151* **Grade Plane.** A reference plane upon which vertical measurements of a building are based representing the average of the finished ground level adjoining the building at all exterior walls. [5000, 2024] (FCC-OCP)

3.3.152 Ground Kettle. A container that could be mounted on wheels and is used for heating tar, asphalt, or similar substances. (FCC-OCP)

3.3.153 Handling. The deliberate movement of material by any means to a point of storage or use. (FCC-FUN)

3.3.154* **Hazard of Contents.**

3.3.154.1 *High Hazard.* High hazard contents shall include materials defined as hazardous materials in Chapter 3, whether stored, used, or handled. *(See also 6.3.2.4.1.2 and 6.3.2.4.1.3 of NFPA 5000®.)* [5000:6.3.2.4.1.1] [5000:6.3.2.4.1.2] (FCC-HAZ)

3.3.154.1.1 *High Hazard Level 1 Contents.* High hazard Level 1 contents shall include materials that present a detonation hazard including, but not limited to, the following: (1) Explosives; (2) Unclassified detonable organic peroxides; (3) Class 4 oxidizers; (4) Detonable pyrophoric materials; (5) Class 3 detonable and Class 4 unstable (reactive) materials. [5000:6.3.2.4.2, 6.3.2.4.1.3] (FCC-HAZ)

3.3.154.1.2 *High Hazard Level 2 Contents.* High hazard Level 2 contents shall include materials that present a deflagration hazard or a hazard from accelerated burning including, but not limited to, the following: (1) Class I, Class II, or Class III-A ignitible (flammable or combustible) liquids that are used or stored in normally open containers or systems, or in closed containers or systems at gauge pressures of more than 15 psi (103 kPa); (2) Combustible dusts stored, used, or generated in a manner creating a severe fire or explosion hazard; (3) Flammable gases and flammable cryogenic liquids; (4) Class I organic peroxides; (5) Class 3 solid or liquid oxidizers that are used or stored in normally open containers or systems, or in closed containers or systems at gauge pressures of more than 15 psi (103 kPa); (6) Nondetonable pyrophoric materials; (7) Class 3 nondetonable unstable (reactive) materials; (8) Class 3 water-reactive materials. [5000:6.3.2.4.3] (FCC-HAZ)

3.3.154.1.3 *High Hazard Level 3 Contents.* High hazard Level 3 contents shall include materials that readily support combustion or present a physical hazard including, but not limited to, the following: (1) Level 2 and Level 3 aerosols; (2) Class I, Class II, or Class III-A ignitible (flammable or combustible) liquids that are used or stored in normally closed containers or systems at gauge pressures of less than 15 psi (103 kPa); (3) Flammable solids, other than dusts classified as high hazard Level 2, stored, used, or generated in a manner creating a high fire hazard; (4) Class II and Class III organic peroxides; (5) Class 2 solid or liquid oxidizers; (6) Class 3 solid or liquid oxidizers that are used or stored in normally closed containers or systems at gauge pressures of less than 15 psi (103 kPa); (7) Oxidizing gases and oxidizing cryogenic liquids; (8) Class 2 unstable (reactive) materials; (9) Class 2 water-reactive materials. [5000:6.3.2.4.4] (FCC-HAZ)

3.3.154.1.4 *High Hazard Level 4 Contents.* High hazard Level 4 contents shall include materials that are acute health hazards including, but not limited to, the following: (1) Corrosives; (2) Highly toxic materials; (3) Toxic materials. [5000:6.3.2.4.5] (FCC-HAZ)

3.3.154.1.5 *High Hazard Level 5 Contents.* High hazard Level 5 contents shall include hazardous production materials (HPM) used in the fabrication of semiconductors or semiconductor research and development. [5000:6.3.2.4.6] (FCC-HAZ)

3.3.154.2* *Low Hazard Contents.* Low hazard contents shall be classified as those of such low combustibility that no self-propagating fire therein can occur. [5000:6.3.2.2] (FCC-FUN)

3.3.154.3* *Ordinary Hazard Contents.* Ordinary hazard contents shall be classified as those that are likely to burn with moderate rapidity or to give off a considerable volume of smoke. [5000:6.3.2.3] (FCC-FUN)

3.3.155* Hazard Rating. The numerical rating of the health, flammability, self-reactivity, and other hazards of the material, including its reaction with water. [55, 2023] (FCC-HAZ)

3.3.156 Hazardous Material. See 3.3.189.4.

3.3.157 Hazardous Material Storage Facility. A building, a portion of a building, or exterior area used for the storage of hazardous materials in excess of exempt amounts. (FCC-HAZ)

3.3.158 Hazardous Materials Storage Locker. A movable prefabricated structure, manufactured primarily at a site other than the final location of the structure and transported completely assembled or in a ready-to-assemble package to the final location, and intended to meet local, state, and federal requirements for outside storage of hazardous materials. [30, 2024] (FCC-HAZ)

3.3.159* Hazardous Reaction or Hazardous Chemical Reaction. Reactions that result in dangers beyond the fire problems relating to flash point and boiling point of either the reactants or of the products. [30, 2024] (FCC-HAZ)

3.3.160 Heat Transfer Fluid (HTF). A liquid that is used as a medium to transfer heat energy from a heater or vaporizer to a remote heat consumer (e.g., injection molding machine, oven, or dryer, or jacketed chemical reactor). [30, 2024] (FCC-HAZ)

3.3.161* Heliport. An identifiable area located on land, on water, or on a structure, that also includes any existing buildings or facilities thereon, used or intended to be used for landing and takeoff of helicopters. [418, 2016] (FCC-OCP)

3.3.162 Hogged Material. Mill waste consisting mainly of hogged bark but possibly including a mixture of bark, chips, dust, or other by-products from trees; also includes material designated as hogged fuel. (FCC-OCP)

3.3.163 Home.

   3.3.163.1 *Day-Care Home.* See 3.3.203.6.

   3.3.163.2 *Nursing Home.* See 3.3.203.24.

3.3.164 Horizontal Exit. See 3.3.110.1.

3.3.165* Immediately Dangerous to Life and Health (IDLH). A concentration of airborne contaminants, normally expressed in parts per million (ppm) or milligrams per cubic meter, that represents the maximum level from which one could escape within 30 minutes without any escape-impairing symptoms or irreversible health effects. [55, 2023] (FCC-HAZ)

3.3.166* Imminent Danger. A condition, use, or practice in an occupancy or structure that poses a hazard that could reasonably be expected to cause death, serious physical harm, or serious property loss. (FCC-FUN)

N **3.3.167 Impairment.** A condition where a fire protection system or unit or portion thereof is out of order, and the condition can result in the fire protection system or unit not functioning in a fire event. [25, 2020] (FCC-OCP)

3.3.168 In-Building Emergency Responder Communications Enhancement System. A combination of components, RF-emitting devices, antennas, cables, power supplies, control circuitry, and programming installed at a specific location to improve wireless communication at that location. (FCC-OCP)

Δ **3.3.169* Incident Commander (IC).** The individual responsible for all incident activities, including the development of strategies and tactics and the ordering and the release of resources. [470, 2022] (FCC-FUN)

3.3.170 Incidental Liquid Use or Storage. Use or storage as a subordinate activity to that which establishes the occupancy or area classification. [30, 2024] (FCC-HAZ)

3.3.171 Indicating Valve. See 3.3.300.1.

3.3.172 Indoor Horticultural Grow Structure. An enclosed structure installed within buildings that creates a controlled environment for enhanced horticultural growing conditions using an artificial light source. (FCC-OCP)

N **3.3.173 Initiating Device.** A system component that originates transmission of a signal indicating a change-of-state condition. [72, 2022] (FCC-OCP)

3.3.174 Initiating Device Circuit. A circuit to which automatic or manual initiating devices are connected where the signal received does not identify the individual device operated. [72, 2016] (FCC-OCP)

3.3.175 Inside Liquid Storage Area. See 3.3.17.6.

3.3.176* ISO Module. An assembly of tanks or tubular cylinders permanently mounted in a frame conforming to International Organization for Standardization (ISO) requirements. [55, 2023] (FCC-HAZ)

3.3.177 Jurisdiction. A governmental unit or political division or a subdivision. (FCC-FUN)

3.3.178 Limit.

   3.3.178.1* *Ceiling Limit.* The maximum concentration of an airborne contaminant to which one can be exposed. [5000, 2024] (FCC-HAZ)

   3.3.178.2* *Permissible Exposure Limit (PEL).* The maximum permitted 8-hour, time-weighted average concentration of an airborne contaminant. [55, 2023] (FCC-HAZ)

   3.3.178.3* *Short-Term Exposure Limit (STEL).* The concentration to which it is believed that workers can be exposed continuously for a short period of time without suffering from irritation, chronic or irreversible tissue damage, or narcosis of a degree sufficient to increase the likelihood of accidental injury, impairment of self-rescue, or the material reduction of work efficiency, without exceeding the daily permissible exposure limit (PEL). [55, 2023] (FCC-HAZ)

3.3.179 Limited-Combustible (Material). See 4.5.10. [5000, 2024]

3.3.180 Liquid. A material that has a melting point that is equal to or less than 68°F (20°C) at a boiling point that is greater than 68°F (20°C) and 14.7 psia (101.3 kPa). When not otherwise identified, the term *liquid* shall mean all ignitible (flammable and combustible) liquids. [5000, 2024] (FCC-HAZ)

3.3.180.1 *Combustible Liquid.* An ignitible liquid that is classified as a Class II or Class III liquid. *(See 66.4.1.2 and 66.4.1.3.)* [30, 2024] (FCC-HAZ)

3.3.180.2 *Flammable Liquid.* An ignitible liquid that is classified as a Class I liquid. *(See 66.4.1.1.)* [30, 2024] (FCC-HAZ)

3.3.180.3 *Highly Volatile Liquid.* A liquid with a boiling point of less than 68°F (20°C). (FCC-HAZ)

3.3.180.4* *Ignitible Liquid.* Any liquid or liquid mixture that has a measurable closed-cup flash point. [30, 2024] (FCC-HAZ)

3.3.180.5 *Liquid Class.* A uniform system of classifying ignitible liquids. *(See 66.4 and Chapter 4 of NFPA 30.)* (FCC-HAZ)

3.3.180.6 *Stable Liquid.* Any liquid not defined as unstable. [30, 2024] (FCC-HAZ)

3.3.181 Log. Felled tree from which all the branches have been removed. (FCC-OCP)

3.3.182 Loose House. A separate detached building in which unbaled combustible fibers are stored. (FCC-HAZ)

3.3.183 Lumber. Wood from felled trees having a section produced by lengthwise sawing or chipping of logs or other solid wood of large dimensions and possible crosscutting and/or further machining to obtain a certain size and includes boards, dimension lumber, timber, and similar wood products. (FCC-OCP)

3.3.184 Manual Emergency Shutoff Valve. A designated valve designed to shut off the flow of gases or liquids that is manually operated. [55, 2023] (FCC-HAZ)

3.3.185 Manual Fire Alarm Box. A manually operated device used to initiate a fire alarm signal. [72, 2016] (FCC-OCP)

3.3.186 Manual Pull Station. See 3.3.185, Manual Fire Alarm Box.

3.3.187 Marine Terminal. A facility comprised of one or more berths, piers, wharves, loading and unloading areas, warehouses, and storage yards and used for transfer of people and/or cargo between waterborne and land transportation modes. [307, 2021] (FCC-OCP)

3.3.188 Marine Vessel. A water craft or other artificial contrivance used as a means of transportation in or on the water. (FCC-OCP)

3.3.189 Material.

3.3.189.1 *Combustible (Material).* See 3.3.60.

3.3.189.2 *Compatible Material.* A material that, when in contact with an oxidizer, will not react with the oxidizer or promote or initiate its decomposition. (FCC-HAZ)

3.3.189.3* *Corrosive Material.* A chemical that causes visible destruction of, or irreversible alterations in, living tissue by chemical action at the site of contact. [400, 2022] (FCC-HAZ)

3.3.189.4* *Hazardous Material.* A chemical or substance that is classified as a physical hazard material or a health hazard material, whether the chemical or substance is in usable or waste condition. *(See also 3.3.189.6, Health Hazard Material, and 3.3.189.12, Physical Hazard Material.)* [400, 2022] (FCC-HAZ)

3.3.189.5 *Hazardous Production Material (HPM).* A solid, liquid, or gas associated with semiconductor manufacturing that has a degree-of-hazard rating of 3 or 4 in health, flammability, instability, or water reactivity in accordance with NFPA 704 and that is used directly in research, laboratory, or production processes that have as their end product materials that are not hazardous. [5000, 2024] (FCC-HAZ)

3.3.189.6 *Health Hazard Material.* A chemical or substance classified as a toxic, highly toxic, or corrosive material in accordance with definitions set forth in this *Code*. [400, 2022] (FCC-HAZ)

3.3.189.7* *Highly Toxic Material.* A material that produces a lethal dose or lethal concentration that falls within any of the following categories: (1) a chemical that has a median lethal dose (LD_{50}) of 50 mg/kg or less of body weight when administered orally to albino rats weighing between 200 g and 300 g each; (2) a chemical that has a median lethal dose (LD_{50}) of 200 mg/kg or less of body weight when administered by continuous contact for 24 hours, or less if death occurs within 24 hours, with the bare skin of albino rabbits weighing between 2 kg and 3 kg each or albino rats weighing 200 g to 300 g each; (3) a chemical that has a median lethal concentration (LC_{50}) in air of 200 parts per million by volume or less of gas or vapor, or 2 mg/L or less of mist, fume, or dust, when administered by continuous inhalation for 1 hour, or less if death occurs within 1 hour, to albino rats weighing between 200 g and 300 g each. [400, 2022] (FCC-HAZ)

3.3.189.8 *Hogged Material.* See 3.3.162.

3.3.189.9* *Incompatible Material.* Materials that, when in contact with each other, have the potential to react in a manner that generates heat, fumes, gases, or by-products that are hazardous to life or property. [400, 2022] (FCC-HAZ)

3.3.189.10 *Limited-Combustible (Material).* See 4.5.10. [5000, 2024]

3.3.189.11 *Noncombustible Material.* See 4.5.9. [5000, 2024]

3.3.189.12 *Physical Hazard Material.* A chemical or substance classified as an explosive, flammable cryogen, flammable gas, flammable solid, ignitible (flammable or combustible) liquid, organic peroxide, oxidizer, oxidizing cryogen, pyrophoric, unstable (reactive), or water-reactive material. [400, 2022] (FCC-HAZ)

3.3.189.13 *Pyrophoric Material.* A chemical with an autoignition temperature in air at or below 130°F (54.4°C). [400, 2022] (FCC-HAZ)

3.3.189.14* *Toxic Material.* A material that produces a lethal dose or a lethal concentration within any of the following categories: (1) a chemical or substance that has a median lethal dose (LD_{50}) of more than 50 mg/kg but not more than 500 mg/kg of body weight when administered orally to albino rats weighing between 200 g and 300 g each; (2) a chemical or substance that has a median lethal dose (LD_{50}) of more than 200 mg/kg but not more than 1000 mg/kg of body weight when administered by continuous contact for 24 hours, or less if death occurs within 24 hours, with the bare skin of albino rabbits weighing between 2 kg and 3 kg each; (3) a chemical or substance that has a median lethal concentration (LC_{50}) in air of more than 200 parts per million but not more than 2000 parts per million by volume of gas or vapor, or more than 2 mg/L but not more than 20 mg/L, of mist, fume, or dust when administered by continuous inhalation for 1 hour, or less if death occurs within 1 hour, to albino rats weighing between 200 g and 300 g each. [400, 2022] (FCC-HAZ)

3.3.189.15* *Unstable (Reactive) Material.* A material that, in the pure state or as commercially produced, will vigorously polymerize, decompose or condense, become self-reactive, or otherwise undergo a violent chemical change under conditions of shock, pressure, or temperature. [400, 2022] (FCC-HAZ)

3.3.189.16* *Water-Reactive Material.* A material that explodes, violently reacts, produces flammable, toxic, or other hazardous gases; or evolves enough heat to cause self-ignition or ignition of nearby combustibles upon exposure to water or moisture. [400, 2022] (FCC-HAZ)

3.3.190* *Maximum Allowable Quantity (MAQ).* The quantity of hazardous material permitted in a control area. (FCC-HAZ)

3.3.191* *Means of Egress.* A continuous and unobstructed way of travel from any point in a building or structure to a public way consisting of three separate and distinct parts: (1) the exit access, (2) the exit, and (3) the exit discharge. [*101*, 2024] (FCC-OCP)

3.3.192 *Means of Escape.* A way out of a building or structure that does not conform to the strict definition of means of egress but does provide an alternate way out. [*101*, 2024] (FCC-OCP)

3.3.193 *Mezzanine.* An intermediate level between the floor and the ceiling of any room or space. [*101*, 2024] (FCC-FUN)

N **3.3.194*** *Micromobility Device, Powered.* Motorized bicycles, motorized scooters, or other personal transportation devices powered by lithium-ion or lithium metal batteries. (FCC-FUN)

3.3.195 *Miscella.* A mixture, in any proportion, of the extracted oil or fat and the extracting solvent. (FCC-HAZ)

3.3.196* *Mobile Supply Unit.* Any supply source that is equipped with wheels so it is able to be moved around. [55, 2023] (FCC-HAZ)

3.3.197* *Mobile or Temporary Cooking.* Any cooking apparatus or equipment operated on a one-time basis, interim basis, or for less than 90 days in the same location, other than at a fixed location, building, or structure that has been inspected and permitted under another section of this *Code*, regulation, or statute. (FCC-HAZ)

3.3.198 *Motor Vehicle Fluid.* A fluid that is a flammable, combustible, or hazardous material, such as crankcase fluids, fuel, brake fluids, transmission fluids, radiator fluids, and gear oil. (FCC-OCP)

3.3.199 *Nesting.* A method of securing cylinders upright in a tight mass using a contiguous three-point contact system whereby all cylinders in a group have a minimum of three contact points with other cylinders or a solid support structure (e.g., a wall or railing). [55, 2023] (FCC-HAZ)

3.3.200* *Normal Temperature and Pressure (NTP).* A temperature of 70°F (21°C) at an absolute pressure of 14.7 psi (101.3 kPa). [55, 2023] (FCC-HAZ)

N **3.3.201*** *Nuisance Alarm.* An unwanted activation of a signaling system or an alarm initiating device in response to a stimulus or condition that is not the result of a potentially hazardous condition. [72, 2022] (FCC-OCP)

3.3.202 *Observation.* For the purposes of cannabis extraction equipment field verification, a practice or condition not technically noncompliant with other regulations or requirements, but could lead to noncompliance if left unaddressed. (FCC-OCP)

Δ **3.3.203** *Occupancy.* See NFPA *101*. (FCC-FUN)

3.3.203.1* *Ambulatory Health Care Occupancy.* An occupancy used to provide services or treatment simultaneously to four or more patients that provides, on an outpatient basis, one or more of the following: (1) treatment for patients that renders the patients incapable of taking action for self-preservation under emergency conditions without the assistance of others; (2) anesthesia that renders the patients incapable of taking action for self-preservation under emergency conditions without the assistance of others; (3) treatment for patients who, due to the nature of their injury or illness, are incapable of taking action for self-preservation under emergency conditions without the assistance of others. [*101*, 2024] (FCC-FUN)

3.3.203.2* *Apartment Building.* A building or portion thereof containing three or more dwelling units with independent cooking and bathroom facilities. [*101*, 2024] (FCC-FUN)

3.3.203.3* *Assembly Occupancy.* An occupancy (1) used for a gathering of 50 or more persons for deliberation, worship, entertainment, eating, drinking, amusement, awaiting transportation, or similar uses; or (2) used as a special amusement building, regardless of occupant load. [*101*, 2024] (FCC-FUN)

3.3.203.4 *Bulk Merchandising Retail Building.* A building in which the sales area includes the storage of combustible materials on pallets, in solid piles, or in racks in excess of 12 ft (3660 mm) in storage height. [*101*, 2024] (FCC-FUN)

3.3.203.5* *Business Occupancy.* An occupancy used for the transaction of business other than mercantile. [*101*, 2024] (FCC-FUN)

3.3.203.6* *Day-Care Home.* A building or portion of a building in which more than 3 but not more than 12 clients receive care, maintenance, and supervision, by other than their relative(s) or legal guardian(s), for less than 24 hours per day. [*101*, 2024] (FCC-FUN)

3.3.203.7* *Day-Care Occupancy.* An occupancy in which four or more clients receive care, maintenance, and supervision, by other than their relatives or legal guardians, for less than 24 hours per day. [*101*, 2024] (FCC-FUN)

3.3.203.8* *Detention and Correctional Occupancy.* An occupancy, other than one whose primary intended use is health care, ambulatory health care, or residential board and care, used to lawfully incarcerate or lawfully detain one or more persons under varied degrees of restraint or security where such occupants are mostly incapable of self-preservation because of security measures not under the occupants' control. [*101*, 2024] (FCC-FUN)

3.3.203.8.1 *Detention and Correctional Use Condition.* For application of the life safety requirements in Section 20.7, the resident user category is divided into the five use conditions. (FCC-FUN)

3.3.203.8.1.1 *Use Condition I — Free Egress.* A condition under which free movement is allowed from sleeping areas and other spaces where access or occupancy is permitted to the exterior via means of egress that meet the requirements of NFPA *101*. [*101*:22.1.2.1.1] (FCC-FUN)

3.3.203.8.1.2 *Use Condition II — Zoned Egress.* A condition under which free movement is allowed from sleeping areas and any other occupied smoke compartment to one or more other smoke compartments. [*101*:22.1.2.1.2] (FCC-FUN)

3.3.203.8.1.3 *Use Condition III — Zoned Impeded Egress.* A condition under which free movement is allowed within individual smoke compartments, such as within a residential unit comprised of individual sleeping rooms and a group activity space, with egress impeded by remote-controlled release of means of egress from such a smoke compartment to another smoke compartment. [*101*:22.1.2.1.3] (FCC-FUN)

3.3.203.8.1.4 *Use Condition IV — Impeded Egress.* A condition under which free movement is restricted from an occupied space, and remote-controlled release is provided to allow movement from all sleeping rooms, activity spaces, and other occupied areas within the smoke compartment to another smoke compartment. [*101*:22.1.2.1.4] (FCC-FUN)

3.3.203.8.1.5 *Use Condition V — Contained.* A condition under which free movement is restricted from an occupied space, and staff-controlled manual release at each door is provided to allow movement from all sleeping rooms, activity spaces, and other occupied areas within the smoke compartment to another smoke compartment. [*101*:22.1.2.1.5] (FCC-FUN)

3.3.203.9* *Dormitory.* A building or a space in a building in which group sleeping accommodations are provided for more than 16 persons who are not members of the same family in one room, or a series of closely associated rooms under joint occupancy and single management, with or without meals, but without individual cooking facilities. [*101*, 2024] (FCC-FUN)

3.3.203.10* *Educational Occupancy.* An occupancy used for educational purposes through the twelfth grade by six or more persons for 4 or more hours per day or more than 12 hours per week. [*101*, 2024] (FCC-FUN)

3.3.203.11* *Health Care Occupancy.* An occupancy used to provide medical or other treatment or care simultaneously to four or more patients on an inpatient basis, where such patients are mostly incapable of self-preservation due to age, physical or mental disability, or because of security measures not under the occupants' control. [*101*, 2024] (FCC-FUN)

3.3.203.12* *High-Risk Occupancy.* An occupancy that has a history of high frequency of fires, high potential for loss of life or economic loss, or that has a low or moderate history of fires or loss of life but the occupants have a high dependency on the built-in fire protection features or staff to assist in evacuation during a fire or other emergency. [*1730*, 2019] (FCC-FUN)

3.3.203.13 *Hospital.* A building or portion thereof used on a 24-hour basis for the medical, psychiatric, obstetrical, or surgical care of four or more inpatients. [*101*, 2024] (FCC-FUN)

3.3.203.14* *Hotel.* A building or groups of buildings under the same management in which there are sleeping accommodations for more than 16 persons and primarily used by transients for lodging with or without meals. [*101*, 2024] (FCC-FUN)

3.3.203.15* *Industrial Occupancy.* An occupancy in which products are manufactured or in which processing, assembling, mixing, packaging, finishing, decorating, or repair operations are conducted. [*101*, 2024] (FCC-FUN)

3.3.203.16* *Limited Care Facility.* A building or portion of a building used on a 24-hour basis for the housing of four or more persons who are incapable of self-preservation because of age; physical limitations due to accident or illness; or limitations such as intellectual disability/developmental disability, mental illness, or chemical dependency. [*101*, 2024] (FCC-FUN)

3.3.203.17 *Lodging or Rooming House.* A building or portion thereof that does not qualify as a one- or two-family dwelling, that provides sleeping accommodations for a total of 16 or fewer people on a transient or permanent basis, without personal care services, with or without meals, but without separate cooking facilities for individual occupants. [*101*, 2024] (FCC-FUN)

3.3.203.18* *Low-Risk Occupancy.* An occupancy that has a history of low frequency of fires and minimal potential for loss of life or economic loss. [*1730*, 2019] (FCC-FUN)

3.3.203.19* *Mercantile Occupancy.* An occupancy used for the display and sale of merchandise. [*101*, 2024] (FCC-FUN)

3.3.203.19.1 *Class A Mercantile Occupancy.* All mercantile occupancies having an aggregate gross area of more than 30,000 ft² (2800 m²) or occupying more than three stories for sales purposes. [*101*, 2024] (FCC-FUN)

3.3.203.19.2 *Class B Mercantile Occupancy.* All mercantile occupancies of more than 3000 ft² (280 m²), but not more than 30,000 ft² (2800 m²), aggregate gross area and occupying not more than three stories for sales purposes. Class B also includes all mercantile occupancies of not more than

3000 ft² (280 m²) gross area and occupying two or three stories for sales purposes. [*101*, 2024] (FCC-FUN)

3.3.203.19.3 *Class C Mercantile Occupancy.* All mercantile occupancies of not more than 3000 ft² (280 m²) gross area and used for sales purposes occupying one story only, excluding mezzanines. [*101*, 2024] (FCC-FUN)

3.3.203.20 *Mixed Occupancy.* A multiple occupancy where the occupancies are intermingled. [*101*, 2024] (FCC-FUN)

3.3.203.21* *Moderate-Risk Occupancy.* An occupancy that has a history of moderate frequency of fires or a moderate potential for loss of life or economic loss. [*1730*, 2019] (FCC-FUN)

3.3.203.22 *Motor Fuel Dispensing Facility.* That portion of a property where motor fuels are stored and dispensed from fixed equipment into the fuel tanks of motor vehicles or marine craft or into approved containers, including all equipment used in connection therewith. [*30A*, 2024] (FCC-OCP)

3.3.203.22.1 *Fleet Vehicle Motor Fuel Dispensing Facility.* A motor fuel dispensing facility at a commercial, industrial, governmental, or manufacturing property where motor fuels are dispensed into the fuel tanks of motor vehicles that are used in connection with the business or operation of that property by persons within the employ of such business or operation. [*30A*, 2024] (FCC-OCP)

3.3.203.22.2 *Marine Motor Fuel Dispensing Facility.* A motor fuel dispensing facility at or adjacent to shore, a pier, a wharf, or a floating dock where motor fuels are dispensed into the fuel tanks of marine craft. [*30A*, 2024] (FCC-OCP)

3.3.203.22.3* *Motor Fuel Dispensing Facility Located Inside a Building.* That portion of a motor fuel dispensing facility located within the perimeter of a building or building structure that also contains other occupancies. [*30A*, 2024] (FCC-OCP)

3.3.203.23 *Multiple Occupancy.* A building or structure in which two or more classes of occupancy exist. [*101*, 2024] (FCC-FUN)

3.3.203.24 *Nursing Home.* A building or portion of a building used on a 24-hour basis for the housing and nursing care of four or more persons who, because of mental or physical incapacity, might be unable to provide for their own needs and safety without the assistance of another person. [*101*, 2024] (FCC-FUN)

3.3.203.25 *One- and Two-Family Dwelling.* One- and two-family dwellings include buildings containing not more than two dwelling units in which each dwelling unit is occupied by members of a single family with not more than three outsiders, if any, accommodated in rented rooms. (FCC-FUN)

3.3.203.25.1 *One- and Two-Family Dwelling Unit.* A building that contains not more than two dwelling units, each dwelling unit occupied by members of a single family with not more than three outsiders, if any, accommodated in rented rooms. [*101*, 2024] (FCC-FUN)

3.3.203.26* *Parking Structure.* A building, structure, or portion thereof used for the parking, storage, or both, of motor vehicles. [*88A*, 2023] (FCC-OCP)

3.3.203.26.1 *Basement and Underground Parking Structures.* Parking structures that are located below grade. A basement parking structure has other occupancies above it and an underground parking structure has no occupancy other than parking above it. Basement and underground parking structures are considered as specific cases of enclosed parking structures. (FCC-OCP)

3.3.203.26.2 *Enclosed Parking Structure.* Any parking structure that is not an open parking structure. [*88A*, 2023] (FCC-OCP)

3.3.203.26.3 *Open Parking Structure.* A parking structure that meets the requirements of Section 5.6 of NFPA 88A. [*88A*, 2023] (FCC-OCP)

3.3.203.27 *Repair Garages.*

3.3.203.27.1 *Major Repair Garage.* A building or portions of a building where major repairs, such as engine overhauls, painting, body and fender work, and repairs that require draining of the motor vehicle fuel tank are performed on motor vehicles, including associated floor space used for offices, parking, or showrooms. (FCC-OCP)

3.3.203.27.2 *Minor Repair Garage.* A building or portions of a building used for lubrication, inspection, and minor automotive maintenance work, such as engine tune-ups, replacement of parts, fluid changes (e.g., oil, antifreeze, transmission fluid, brake fluid, air conditioning refrigerants, etc.), brake system repairs, tire rotation, and similar routine maintenance work, including associated floor space used for offices, parking, or showrooms. (FCC-OCP)

3.3.203.28* *Residential Board and Care Occupancy.* An occupancy used for lodging and boarding of four or more residents, not related by blood or marriage to the owners or operators, for the purpose of providing personal care services. [*101*, 2024] (FCC-FUN)

3.3.203.29* *Residential Occupancy.* An occupancy that provides sleeping accommodations for purposes other than health care or detention and correctional. [*101*, 2024] (FCC-FUN)

3.3.203.30 *Separated Occupancy.* A multiple occupancy where the occupancies are separated by fire resistance–rated assemblies. [*101*, 2024] (FCC-FUN)

3.3.203.31* *Storage Occupancy.* An occupancy used primarily for the storage or sheltering of goods, merchandise, products, or vehicles. [*101*, 2024] (FCC-FUN)

3.3.203.31.1* *Mini-Storage Building.* A storage occupancy partitioned into individual storage units that are rented or leased for the purposes of storing personal or business items where a majority of the individual storage units are not greater than 750 ft² (70 m²). [*5000*, 2024] (FCC-FUN)

3.3.204 **Occupant Load.** The total number of persons that might occupy a building or portion thereof at any one time. [*101*, 2024] (FCC-OCP)

3.3.205 **Open System Use.** See 3.3.298.2.

3.3.206 **Operating Pressure.** The pressure at which a system operates. (FCC-HAZ)

3.3.207* **Operating Unit (Vessel) or Process Unit (Vessel).** The equipment in which a unit operation or unit process is conducted. *(See also 3.3.294, Unit Operation or Unit Process.)* [**30, 2024**] (FCC-HAZ)

3.3.208 Operations. A general term that includes, but is not limited to, the use, transfer, storage, and processing of liquids. [**30**, 2024] (FCC-HAZ)

3.3.209 Organic Peroxide. Any organic compound having a double oxygen or peroxy (-O-O-) group in its chemical structure. [**400**, 2022] (FCC-HAZ)

3.3.209.1 *Organic Peroxide Formulation.* A pure or technically pure organic peroxide or a mixture of organic peroxides with an active oxygen (aO) concentration greater than 1 percent alone or in combination with one or more materials. The transport type for organic peroxide formulations is determined by the UN *Manual of Tests and Criteria, Part II.* Terms such as *accelerator, catalyst, initiator,* and *curing agent* are sometimes used to describe organic peroxide formulations and are misleading because they can also refer to materials that are not or do not contain organic peroxides, some of which might present increased hazard when mixed with organic peroxides. [**400**, 2022] (FCC-HAZ)

3.3.209.1.1 *Class I Organic Peroxide.* Describes organic peroxide formulations that are more severe than a Class II but do not detonate and that are characterized as "explosive in package" or by a very fast burning rate. Includes those characterized for transport as Type B, those characterized for transport as Type C and Type D with a large-scale burning rate equal to or greater than 300 kg/min, and those characterized for transport as Type C and Type D with a small-scale burning rate equal to or greater than 9.0 kg/min × m² unless the large-scale burning rate is less than 300 kg/min. [**400**, 2022] (FCC-HAZ)

3.3.209.1.2 *Class II Organic Peroxide.*

3.3.209.1.2.1 *Class IIA Organic Peroxide.* Describes organic peroxide formulations that burn very rapidly and that present a severe reactivity hazard, and those characterized for transport as Type C and Type D with a large-scale burning rate equal to or greater than 140 kg/min but less than 300 kg/min and those characterized for transport as Type E with a large-scale burning rate equal to or greater than 140 kg/min. Includes those characterized as Type C and Type D if the small-scale burning rate is equal to or greater than 2.2 kg/min × m², but less than 9.0 kg/min × m², and Type E if the small-scale burning rate is equal to or greater than 2.2 kg/min × m². [**400**, 2022] (FCC-HAZ)

Δ **3.3.209.1.2.2** *Class IIB Organic Peroxide.* Describes organic peroxide formulations that burn very rapidly and that present a severe reactivity hazard, and those characterized for transport as Type C with a large-scale burning rate of less than 140 kg/min. Includes those characterized for transport as Type D and Type E with a large-scale burning rate equal to or greater than 60 kg/min but less than 140 kg/min, those characterized as Type C if the small-scale burning rate is less than 2.2 kg/min × m², and those characterized as Type D and Type E if the small-scale burning rate is equal to or greater than 0.9 kg/min × m² but less than 2.2 kg/min × m². [**400**, 2022] (FCC-HAZ)

Δ **3.3.209.1.3** *Class III Organic Peroxide.* Describes organic peroxide formulations that burn rapidly and present a moderate reactivity hazard. Includes those characterized for transport as Type D with a large-scale burning rate less than 60 kg/min, those characterized for transport as Type E with a large-scale burning rate equal to or greater than 10 kg/min but less than 60 kg/min, those characterized for transport as Type F with a large-scale burning rate equal to or greater than 10 kg/min, and those characterized as Type D and Type E if the small-scale burning rate is less than 0.9 kg/min × m² and Type F irrespective of the small-scale burning rate. [**400**, 2022] (FCC-HAZ)

3.3.209.1.4 *Class IV Organic Peroxide.* Describes organic peroxide formulations that burn in the same manner as ordinary combustibles and present a minimal reactivity hazard. Includes those characterized for transport as Type E or Type F with a large-scale burning rate less than 10 kg/min. [**400**, 2022] (FCC-HAZ)

3.3.209.1.5 *Class V Organic Peroxide.* Describes organic peroxide formulations that burn with less intensity than ordinary combustibles or those that do not sustain combustion and present no reactivity hazard, and those characterized for transport as Type G without additional subsidiary risks. [**400**, 2022] (FCC-HAZ)

3.3.209.2 *Organic Peroxide Storage Area.* See 3.3.17.6.

3.3.210 OSHA. The Occupational Safety and Health Administration of the US Department of Labor. [**55**, 2023] (FCC-HAZ)

3.3.211 Overcrowded. A situation where the occupant load exceeds the exit capacity or the posted occupant load. (FCC-FUN)

3.3.212* Oxidizer. Any solid or liquid material that readily yields oxygen or other oxidizing gas or that readily reacts to promote or initiate combustion of combustible materials and that can, under some circumstances, undergo a vigorous self-sustained decomposition due to contamination or heat exposure. [**400**, 2022] (FCC-HAZ)

3.3.212.1 *Class 1.* An oxidizer that does not moderately increase the burning rate of combustible materials with which it comes into contact or a solid oxidizer classified as Class 1 when tested in accordance with the test protocol set forth in Section G.1 of NFPA 400. [**400**, 2022] (FCC-HAZ)

3.3.212.2 *Class 2.* An oxidizer that causes a moderate increase in the burning rate of combustible materials with which it comes into contact or a solid oxidizer classified as Class 2 when tested in accordance with the test protocol set forth in Section G.1 of NFPA 400. [**400**, 2022] (FCC-HAZ)

3.3.212.3 *Class 3.* An oxidizer that causes a severe increase in the burning rate of combustible materials with which it comes into contact or a solid oxidizer classified as Class 3 when tested in accordance with the test protocol set forth in Section G.1 of NFPA 400. [**400**, 2022] (FCC-HAZ)

3.3.212.4 *Class 4.* An oxidizer that can undergo an explosive reaction due to contamination or exposure to thermal or physical shock and that causes a severe increase in the burning rate of combustible materials with which it comes into contact. [**400**, 2022] (FCC-HAZ)

3.3.213 Ozone Generator. Equipment that causes the production of ozone. (FCC-HAZ)

3.3.214 Paper. Felted sheets made from natural fibrous materials, usually vegetable but sometimes mineral or animal, and formed on a fine wire screen by means of water suspension. (FCC-OCP)

3.3.215 Patch Kettle. Any pot or container with a capacity of less than 6 gal (22.7 L) used for preheating tar, asphalt, pitch, or similar substances for the repair of roofs, streets, floors, pipes, or similar objects. (FCC-OCP)

3.3.216 Permissible Exposure Limit (PEL). See 3.3.178.2.

3.3.217 Permit. A document issued by the AHJ for the purpose of authorizing performance of a specified activity. (FCC-FUN)

3.3.218 Peroxide-Forming Chemical. A chemical that, when exposed to air, forms explosive peroxides that are shock sensitive, pressure sensitive, or heat sensitive. (FCC-HAZ)

3.3.219* Personal Care. The care of residents who do not require chronic, convalescent medical or continuous skilled nursing care. [*101*, 2024] (FCC-FUN)

3.3.220 Pesticide. Any substance or mixture of substances intended for preventing, destroying, repelling, or mitigating any pest or for use as a plant regulator, defoliant, or desiccant. (FCC-OCP)

3.3.221 Physical Hazard. A chemical for which there is scientifically valid evidence that the chemical is an organic peroxide or oxidizer. (FCC-HAZ)

3.3.222* Pier. A structure, usually of greater length than width and projecting from the shore into a body of water with direct access from land, that can be either open deck or provided with a superstructure. [307, 2021] (FCC-OCP)

3.3.223 Portable Generator. A portable piece of equipment with an internal combustion engine-driven device that provides electrical power. (FCC-FUN)

N **3.3.224 Pre-Incident Plan.** A document developed by gathering general and detailed data that is used by responding personnel in effectively managing emergencies for the protection of occupants, responding personnel, property, and the environment. (FCC-FUN)

3.3.225 Pressure-Regulating Device. A device designed for the purpose of reducing, regulating, controlling, or restricting water pressure. [14, 2024] (FCC-OCP)

3.3.225.1 *Pressure-Reducing Valve.* A valve designed for the purpose of reducing the downstream water pressure under both flowing (residual) and nonflowing (static) conditions. [14, 2024] (FCC-OCP)

3.3.225.2 *Pressure-Restricting Device.* A valve designed for the purpose of reducing the downstream water pressure under flowing (residual) conditions only. [14, 2024] (FCC-OCP)

3.3.226* Pressure Vessel. A container, process vessel, or other component designed in accordance with the ASME *Boiler and Pressure Vessel Code*, DOT, or other approved standards. [400, 2022] (FCC-HAZ)

3.3.227 Primary Containment. The first level of containment, consisting of the inside portion of that container that comes into immediate contact on its inner surface with the material being contained. (FCC-HAZ)

3.3.228* Process or Processing. An integrated sequence of operations. [30, 2024] (FCC-HAZ)

3.3.229 Process Unit (Vessel). See 3.3.207, Operating Unit (Vessel) or Process Unit (Vessel). (FCC-HAZ)

3.3.230 Proprietary Information. Information regarding compounds or ingredients used in a process or production that do not qualify as trade secrets but that provide an industry or business with a competitive advantage. (FCC-HAZ)

3.3.231 Protection for Exposures. Fire protection for structures on property adjacent to liquid storage that is provided by (1) a public fire department or (2) a private fire brigade maintained on the property adjacent to the liquid storage, either of which is capable of providing cooling water streams to protect the property adjacent to the liquid storage. [30, 2024] (FCC-HAZ)

3.3.232 Public Way. A street, alley, or other similar parcel of land essentially open to the outside air deeded, dedicated, or otherwise permanently appropriated to the public for public use and having a clear width and height of not less than 10 ft (3050 mm). [*101*, 2024] (FCC-FUN)

3.3.233 Purging. A method used to free the internal volume of a piping system of unwanted contents that results in the existing contents being removed or replaced. [55, 2023] (FCC-HAZ)

3.3.234 Pyrophoric. A chemical that spontaneously ignites in air at or below a temperature of 130°F (54.5°C). (FCC-HAZ)

3.3.235 Quality Assurance. The procedures conducted by the registered design professionals (RDPs) responsible for design and the registered design professionals responsible for inspection that provide evidence and documentation to the RDPs, the owner, and the AHJ that the work is being constructed in accordance with the approved construction documents. [5000, 2024] (FCC-OCP)

3.3.236 Quality Assurance Program. A predefined set of observations, special inspections, tests, and other procedures that provide an independent record to the owner, AHJ, and RDP responsible for design that the construction is in general conformance with the approved construction documents. [5000, 2024] (FCC-OCP)

3.3.237* Rack. Any combination of vertical, horizontal, and diagonal members that supports stored materials. (FCC-OCP)

3.3.237.1 *Double-Row Racks.* Racks less than or equal to 12 ft (3.7 m) in depth or single-row racks placed back to back having an aggregate depth up to 12 ft (3.7 m), with aisles having an aisle width of at least 3.5 ft (1.1 m) between loads on racks. [13, 2022] (FCC-OCP)

3.3.237.2* *Movable Racks.* Racks on fixed rails or guides. (FCC-OCP)

3.3.237.3 *Multiple-Row Racks.* Racks greater than 12 ft (3.7 m) in depth or single- or double-row racks separated by aisles less than 3.5 ft (1.1 m) wide having an overall width greater than 12 ft (3.7 m). [13, 2022] (FCC-OCP)

3.3.237.4* *Portable Racks.* Racks that are not fixed in place and can be arranged in any number of configurations. [13, 2022] (FCC-OCP)

3.3.237.5 *Single-Row Racks.* Racks that have no longitudinal flue space and that have a depth up to 6 ft (1.8 m) with aisles having a width of at least 3.5 ft (1.1 m) between loads on racks. [13, 2022] (FCC-OCP)

3.3.238* **Ramp.** A walking surface that has a slope steeper than 1 in 20. [*101*, 2024] (FCC-OCP)

3.3.239 Recreational Fire. The noncommercial burning of materials other than rubbish for pleasure, religious, ceremonial, cooking, or similar purposes in which the fuel burned is not contained in an incinerator, a barbecue grill, or a barbecue pit, and the total fuel area is not exceeding 3 ft (0.9 m) in diameter and 2 ft (0.6 m) in height. (FCC-FUN)

Δ **3.3.240 Refinery.** A plant in which ignitible (flammable or combustible) liquids are produced on a commercial scale from crude petroleum, natural gasoline, or other hydrocarbon sources. [30, 2024] (FCC-HAZ)

N **3.3.241 Refrigerant Concentration Limit (RCL).** The refrigerant concentration limit, in air, determined in accordance with ANSI/ASHRAE 34, *Designation and Safety Classification of Refrigerants,* and intended to reduce the risks of acute toxicity, asphyxiation, and flammability hazards in normally occupied, enclosed spaces. (FCC-HAZ)

3.3.242 Registered Design Professional (RDP). An individual who is registered or licensed to practice his/her respective design profession as defined by the statutory requirements of the professional registration laws of the state or jurisdiction in which the project is to be constructed. [5000, 2024] (FCC-FUN)

3.3.243 Relocatable Power Tap. A device for indoor use consisting of an attachment plug on one end of a flexible cord and two or more receptacles on the opposite end, and has overcurrent protection. (FCC-FUN)

3.3.244 RF Emitting Device. A device that emits a radio frequency signal as part of a two-way radio communications enhancement system. (FCC-FUN)

3.3.244.1 *Active RF Emitting Device.* Any type of circuit component that requires an ac or dc power source with the ability to electrically control electron flow and/or amplification of RF signal, including but not limited to signal boosters, repeaters, bi-directional amplifiers, and fiber distributed antenna systems. (FCC-FUN)

3.3.244.2 *Passive RF Emitting Device.* A device that does not require an external ac or dc source of power for its operation and does not provide amplification of the RF signal, including but not limited to coax, couplers, splitters, and passive antennas. (FCC-FUN)

3.3.245 RF Radio Frequency (RF). A measurement representing the oscillation rate of electromagnetic radiation spectrum, or electromagnetic radio waves, from public safety frequency bands as specified by the fire code official. (FCC-FUN)

3.3.246 Row. A minimum yard storage unit comprised of adjoining cotton bales. (FCC-OCP)

3.3.247 Rubberized Asphalt Melter (Melter). Portable equipment used for the heating of rubberized asphalt material that is a mix of asphalt, rubber polymer, and filler material. (FCC-OCP)

3.3.248 Rural. Those areas that are not unsettled wilderness or uninhabitable territory but are sparsely populated with densities below 500 persons per square mile. [1142, 2017] (FCC-FUN)

Δ **3.3.249* Safety Can.** A listed container of not more than 5.3 gal (20 L) capacity having a flame mitigation device, such as a flame arrester in each fill and pour opening or expanded metal mesh in the container, and having a spring-closing lid and spout cover designed to safely relieve internal pressure when exposed to fire. [30, 2024] (FCC-HAZ)

3.3.250* Safety Data Sheet (SDS). The document that describes composition of a material, hazardous properties and hazard mitigation, and disposal information. [400, 2022] (FCC-HAZ)

3.3.251 Sales Display Area. See 3.3.17.9.

3.3.252 Salvage Vehicle. A vehicle that is dismantled for parts or awaiting destruction. (FCC-OCP)

3.3.253 Self-Closing. Equipped with an approved device that ensures closing after opening. [*101*, 2024] (FCC-OCP)

3.3.254 Separation of Hazards. Physically separated by a specified distance, construction, or appliance. [55, 2023] (FCC-HAZ)

Δ **3.3.255 Shop Drawings.** Scaled working drawings, equipment cutsheets, and design calculations. *(See 3.3.62, Plan, of NFPA 1030.)* [1030, 2024] (FCC-OCP)

3.3.256* Signal. An indication of a condition communicated by electrical, visible, audible, wireless, or other means. [72, 2016] (FCC-OCP)

3.3.256.1* *Alarm Signal.* A signal that results from the manual or automatic detection of an alarm condition. [72, 2016] (FCC-OCP)

3.3.256.2* *Fire Alarm Signal.* A signal that results from the manual or automatic detection of a fire alarm condition. [**72**, 2016] (FCC-OCP)

3.3.256.3* *Supervisory Signal.* A signal that results from the detection of a supervisory condition. [72, 2016] (FCC-OCP)

3.3.256.4* *Trouble Signal.* A signal that results from the detection of a trouble condition. [72, 2016] (FCC-OCP)

3.3.257 Simple Asphyxiant Gas. See 3.3.146.15.

3.3.258 Smoke Alarm. A single or multiple-station alarm responsive to smoke. [72, 2016] (FCC-OCP)

3.3.259* Smoke Barrier. A continuous membrane, or a membrane with discontinuities created by protected openings, where such membrane is designed and constructed to restrict the movement of smoke. [5000, 2024] (FCC-OCP)

3.3.260 Smoke Compartment. See 3.3.70.2.

3.3.261* Smoke Partition. A continuous membrane that is designed to form a barrier to limit the transfer of smoke. [*101*, 2024] (FCC-OCP)

3.3.262 Smoking. The use or carrying of a lighted pipe, cigar, cigarette, tobacco, or any other type of smoking substance. (FCC-FUN)

3.3.263 Smoking Area. See 3.3.17.10.

3.3.264 Solid.

3.3.264.1* *Combustible Particulate Solid.* An oxidizable, solid-phase material comprising distinct particles or pieces. [69, 2019] (FCC-HAZ)

3.3.264.2* *Flammable Solid.* A solid substance, other than a substance defined as a blasting agent or explosive, that is liable to cause fire resulting from friction or retained heat from manufacture, that has an ignition temperature below 212°F (100°C), or that burns so vigorously or persistently when ignited that it creates a serious hazard. [400, 2022] (FCC-HAZ)

3.3.265 Solid Material. A material that has a melting point, decomposes, or sublimes at a temperature greater than 68°F (20°C). [5000, 2024] (FCC-HAZ)

3.3.266* Solid Shelving. Shelving that is fixed in place, slatted, wire mesh, or other type of shelves located within racks. The area of a solid shelf is defined by perimeter aisle or flue space on all four sides or by the placement of loads that block openings that would otherwise serve as the required flue spaces. Solid shelves having an area equal to or less than 20 ft^2 (1.9 m^2) are defined as open racks. Shelves of wire mesh, slats, or other materials more than 50 percent open and where the flue spaces are maintained are defined as open racks. [13, 2022] (FCC-OCP)

3.3.267 Special Use. See 3.3.298.3.

3.3.268 Spray Area. See 3.3.17.11.

3.3.269* Spray Booth. A power-ventilated enclosure for a spray application operation or process that confines and limits the escape of the material being sprayed, including vapors, mists, dusts, and residues that are produced by the spraying operation and conducts or directs these materials to an exhaust system. [33, 2021] (FCC-HAZ)

3.3.270* Spray Room. A power-ventilated fully enclosed room with a specified fire resistance rating used for spraying of flammable or combustible materials. [33, 2021] (FCC-HAZ)

N **3.3.271 Sprinkler System.**

N **3.3.271.1 *Sprinkler System (NFPA 13/13R).*** A system, commonly activated by heat from a fire and discharges water over the fire area, that consists of an integrated network of piping designed in accordance with fire protection engineering standards that includes a water supply source, a control valve, a waterflow alarm, and a drain. The portion of the sprinkler system above ground is a network of specifically sized or hydraulically designed piping installed in a building, structure, or area, generally overhead, and to which sprinklers are attached in a systematic pattern. [13, 2022] (FCC-OCP)

N **3.3.271.2 *Sprinkler System (NFPA 13D)*** A system that consists of an integrated network of piping designed in accordance with fire protection engineering standards that includes a water supply source, a water control valve, and a drain. The portion of the sprinkler system above ground is a network of specifically sized or hydraulically designed piping installed in a building, structure, or area, generally overhead, and to which sprinklers are attached in a systematic pattern. The system is commonly activated by heat from a fire and discharges water over the fire area. [13D, 2022] (FCC-OCP)

3.3.272 Standard Cubic Foot (scf) of Gas. An amount of gas that occupies one cubic foot at an absolute pressure of 14.7 psi (101 kPa) and a temperature of 70°F (21°C). [55, 2023] (FCC-HAZ)

3.3.273 Standard Temperature and Pressure (STP). A temperature of 70°F (21°C) and a pressure of 1 atmosphere (14.7 psi or 760 mm Hg). (FCC-HAZ)

3.3.274 Standpipe System. See 3.3.283.13.

3.3.275 Storage.

3.3.275.1 *Banded Tire Storage.* Storage in which a number of tires are strapped together. (FCC-OCP)

3.3.275.2 *Cartoned Storage.* Storage consisting of corrugated cardboard or paperboard containers that fully enclose the commodity. (FCC-OCP)

3.3.275.3 *Detached Storage.* Storage in a separate building or in an outside area located away from all structures. (FCC-OCP)

3.3.275.4 *High-Piled Storage.* Solid-piled, palletized, rack storage, bin box, and shelf storage of Class I through Class IV commodities more than 12 ft (3.7 m) in height and solid-piled, palletized, rack storage, bin box, and shelf storage of Group A plastic commodities more than 5 ft (1.5 m) in height. [13, 2022] (FCC-OCP)

3.3.275.5 *Isolated Storage.* Storage in a different storage room or in a separate and detached building located at a safe distance. (FCC-HAZ)

3.3.275.6 *Laced Tire Storage.* Tires stored where the sides of the tires overlap, creating a woven or laced appearance. [See Figure A.34.9.1(g).] [13, 2022] (FCC-OCP)

3.3.275.7* *Miscellaneous Tire Storage.* The storage of rubber tires that is incidental to the main use of the building; storage areas do not exceed 2000 ft^2 (186 m^2), and on-tread storage piles, regardless of storage method, do not exceed 25 ft (7.6 m) in the direction of the wheel holes. Acceptable storage arrangements include (a) on-floor, on-side storage up to 12 ft (3.7 m) high; (b) on-floor, on-tread storage up to 5 ft (1.5 m) high; (c) double-row or multirow fixed or portable rack storage on-side or on-tread up to 5 ft (1.5 m) high; (d) single-row fixed or portable rack storage on-side or on-tread up to 12 ft (3.7 m) high; and (e) laced tires in racks up to 5 ft (1.5 m) in height. [13, 2022] (FCC-OCP)

3.3.275.8 *On-Side Tire Storage.* Tires stored horizontally or flat. [13, 2022] (FCC-OCP)

3.3.275.9 *On-Tread Tire Storage.* Tires stored vertically or on their treads. [13, 2022] (FCC-OCP)

3.3.275.10 *Palletized Tire Storage.* Storage on portable racks of various types utilizing a conventional pallet as a base. [13, 2022] (FCC-OCP)

3.3.275.11 *Segregated Storage.* Storage located in the same room or inside area that is physically separated by distance from incompatible materials. (FCC-OCP)

3.3.275.12 *Yard Storage.* Storage of commodities in outdoor areas. (FCC-OCP)

3.3.276 Story. The portion of a building located between the upper surface of a floor and the upper surface of the floor or roof next above. [*5000*, 2024] (FCC-FUN)

3.3.276.1 *Occupiable Story.* A story occupied by people on a regular basis. [*101*, 2024] (FCC-FUN)

3.3.277 Street. A public thoroughfare that has been dedicated for vehicular use by the public and can be used for access by fire department vehicles. [*101*, 2024] (FCC-FUN)

3.3.278* Street Floor. A story or floor level accessible from the street or from outside the building at the finished ground level, with the floor level at the main entrance located not more than three risers above or below the finished ground level, and arranged and utilized to qualify as the main floor. [*101*, 2024] (FCC-FUN)

3.3.279 Structural Element. The columns and girders, beams, trusses, joists, braced frames, moment-resistant frames, and vertical and lateral resisting elements, and other framing members that are designed to carry any portion of the dead or live load and lateral forces, that are essential to the stability of the building or structure. [*5000*, 2024] (FCC-FUN)

3.3.280* Structure. That which is built or constructed. [*101*, 2024] (FCC-FUN)

3.3.280.1* *Open Structure.* A structure that supports equipment and operations not enclosed within building walls. [*101*, 2024] (FCC-FUN)

3.3.281* Suburb or Suburban. Those moderately inhabited areas with population densities of at least 500 persons per square mile but less than 1000 persons per square mile. [*1142*, 2017] (FCC-FUN)

3.3.282 Summarily Abate. To immediately judge a condition to be a fire hazard to life or property and to order immediate correction of such condition. (FCC-FUN)

3.3.283 System. Several items of equipment assembled, grouped, or otherwise interconnected for the accomplishment of a purpose or function. (FCC-FUN)

3.3.283.1* *Bulk Hydrogen Compressed Gas System.* A gaseous hydrogen (GH$_2$) system with a storage capacity of more than 5000 scf (141.6 Nm^3) of compressed hydrogen gas. [*55*, 2023] (FCC-HAZ)

Δ **3.3.283.2*** *Bulk Inert Gas System.* An assembly of equipment that consists of, but is not limited to, storage containers, pressure regulators, pressure relief devices, vaporizers, manifolds, and piping, with a storage capacity of more than 20,000 scf (566 Nm^3) of inert gas, and that terminates at the source valve. [*55*, 2023] (FCC-HAZ)

3.3.283.3* *Bulk Liquefied Hydrogen System.* A liquefied hydrogen (LH$_2$) system with a storage capacity of more than 39.7 gal (150 L) of liquefied hydrogen. [*55*, 2023] (FCC-HAZ)

3.3.283.4* *Bulk Oxygen System.* An assembly of equipment, such as oxygen storage containers, pressure regulators, pressure relief devices, vaporizers, manifolds, and interconnecting piping, that has a storage capacity of more than 20,000 scf (566 Nm^3) of oxygen and that terminates at the source valve. [*55*, 2023] (FCC-HAZ)

3.3.283.5 *Central Station Service Alarm System.* A system or group of systems in which the operations of circuits and devices are transmitted automatically to, recorded in, maintained by, and supervised from a listed central station that has competent and experienced servers and operators who, upon receipt of a signal, take such action as required by *NFPA 72*. Such service is to be controlled and operated by a person, firm, or corporation whose business is the furnishing, maintaining, or monitoring of supervised alarm systems. [*72*, 2016] (FCC-OCP)

Δ **3.3.283.6** *Compressed Gas System.* An assembly of equipment designed to contain, distribute, or transport compressed gases. [*55*, 2023] (FCC-HAZ)

3.3.283.7 *Continuous Gas Detection System.* A gas detection system in which the instrument is maintained in continuous operation and the interval between sampling of any point does not exceed 30 minutes. [*55*, 2023] (FCC-HAZ)

3.3.283.8 *Cylinder Containment System.* A gastight recovery system comprising equipment or devices that can be placed over a leak in a compressed gas container, thereby stopping or controlling the escape of gas from the leaking container. [*55*, 2023] (FCC-HAZ)

3.3.283.9 *Dedicated Smoke-Control System.* A system that is intended for the purpose of smoke control only, which are separate systems of air moving and distribution equipment that do not function under normal building operating conditions. (FCC-FUN)

3.3.283.10 *Fire Alarm System.* A system or portion of a combination system that consists of components and circuits arranged to monitor and annunciate the status of fire alarm or supervisory signal-initiating devices and to initiate the appropriate response to those signals. [*72*, 2016] (FCC-OCP)

Δ **3.3.283.11** *Fire Protection System.* Any fire alarm device or system or fire-extinguishing device or system, or combination thereof, that is designed and installed for detecting, controlling, or extinguishing a fire or otherwise alerting occupants, or the fire department, or both, that a fire has occurred. [*1140*, 2022] (FCC-OCP)

3.3.283.12 *Nondedicated Smoke-Control System.* A smoke-control system that shares components with some other system(s), such as the building HVAC system, which changes its mode of operation to achieve the smoke-control objective. (FCC-FUN)

3.3.283.13* *Standpipe System.* An arrangement of piping, valves, hose connections, and associated equipment installed in a building or structure, with the hose connections located in such a manner that water can be discharged in streams or spray patterns through attached hose and nozzles, for the purpose of extinguishing a fire, thereby protecting a building or structure and its contents in addition to protecting the occupants. [*14*, 2024] (FCC-OCP)

3.3.283.14 *Treatment System.* An assembly of equipment capable of processing a hazardous gas and reducing the gas concentration to a predetermined level at the point of discharge from the system to the atmosphere. [*55*, 2023] (FCC-HAZ)

3.3.283.15* *Vapor Processing System.* A system designed to capture and process vapors displaced during transfer or filling operations by use of mechanical or chemical means. [30, 2024] (FCC-HAZ)

3.3.283.16* *Vapor Recovery System.* A system designed to capture and retain, without processing, vapors displaced during transfer or filling operations. [30, 2024] (FCC-HAZ)

3.3.284 Tank.

3.3.284.1 *Aboveground Storage Tank.* A horizontal or vertical tank that is listed and intended for fixed installation, without backfill, above or below grade and is used within the scope of its approval or listing. [30A, 2024] (FCC-HAZ)

3.3.284.2 *Aboveground Tank.* A storage tank that is installed above grade, at grade, or below grade without backfill. [30, 2024] (FCC-HAZ)

3.3.284.2.1 *Protected Aboveground Tank.* An atmospheric aboveground storage tank with integral secondary containment and thermal insulation that has been evaluated for resistance to physical damage and for limiting the heat transferred to the primary tank when exposed to a hydrocarbon pool fire and is listed in accordance with UL 2085, *Protected Aboveground Tanks for Flammable and Combustible Liquids,* or an equivalent test procedure. [30:22.2.3] (FCC-HAZ)

3.3.284.3 *ASME Tank.* See 3.3.73.1, ASME Container.

3.3.284.4* *Portable Tank.* Any vessel having a liquid capacity over 60 gal (230 L) intended for storing liquids and not intended for fixed installation. [30, 2024] (FCC-HAZ)

3.3.284.5 *Secondary Containment Tank.* A tank that has an inner and outer wall with an interstitial space (annulus) between the walls and that has a means for monitoring the interstitial space for a leak. [30, 2024] (FCC-HAZ)

3.3.284.6* *Stationary Tank.* A packaging designed primarily for stationary installations not intended for loading, unloading, or attachment to a transport vehicle as part of its normal operation in the process of use. [55, 2023] (FCC-HAZ)

3.3.284.7 *Storage Tank.* Any vessel having a liquid capacity that exceeds 60 gal (230 L), is intended for fixed installation, and is not used for processing. [30, 2024] (FCC-HAZ)

3.3.285 TC. Transport Canada. [55, 2023] (FCC-HAZ)

3.3.286 Temporary Wiring. Approved wiring for power and lighting during a period of construction, remodeling, maintenance, repair, or demolition, and decorative lighting, carnival power and lighting, and similar purposes. (FCC-FUN)

3.3.287 3D Printer. A machine used in the additive manufacturing process for fabricating objects through the deposition of a material using a printhead, nozzle, or another printer technology. (FCC-HAZ)

3.3.288 Tire.

3.3.288.1 *Rubber Tires.* Pneumatic tires for passenger automobiles, aircraft, light and heavy trucks, trailers, farm equipment, construction equipment (off-the-road), and buses. [13, 2022] (FCC-OCP)

3.3.288.2 *Scrap Tire.* A tire that can no longer be used for its original purpose due to wear or damage. (FCC-OCP)

3.3.289 Toxic Material. See 3.3.189.14.

3.3.290* Traffic Calming Device. A roadway design element utilized to reduce vehicle speeds, decrease motor vehicle volumes, and increase safety for pedestrians and nonmotorized vehicles. (FCC-FUN)

3.3.291* Transfilling. The process of transferring a gas, either in compressed or liquid form from one cylinder or container to another cylinder or container. (FCC-HAZ)

3.3.292* Tube Trailer. A truck or semitrailer on which a number of very long compressed gas tubular cylinders have been mounted and manifolded into a common piping system. [55, 2023] (FCC-HAZ)

3.3.293 Unauthorized Discharge. A release or emission of materials in a manner that does not conform to the provisions of this *Code* or applicable public health and safety regulations. (FCC-HAZ)

3.3.294 Unit Operation or Unit Process. A segment of a physical or chemical process that might or might not be integrated with other segments to constitute the manufacturing sequence. [30, 2024] (FCC-HAZ)

3.3.295 Unit Process. See 3.3.294, Unit Operation or Unit Process.

3.3.296 Unit (Vessel), Operating or Process. See 3.3.207.

3.3.297 Unstable (Reactive) Material. See 3.3.189.15.

3.3.298* Use [Hazardous Materials]. To place a material, including solids, liquids, and gases, into action. [400, 2022] (FCC-HAZ)

3.3.298.1* *Closed System Use.* Use of a solid or liquid hazardous material in a closed vessel or system that remains closed during normal operations where vapors emitted by the product are not liberated outside of the vessel or system and the product is not exposed to the atmosphere during normal operations and all uses of compressed gases. [400, 2022] (FCC-HAZ)

3.3.298.2* *Open System Use.* Use of a solid or liquid hazardous material in a vessel or system that is continuously open to the atmosphere during normal operations and where vapors are liberated or the product is exposed to the atmosphere during normal operations. [400, 2022] (FCC-HAZ)

3.3.298.3 *Special Use.* A use that includes, but is not limited to, events or occurrences during which life safety–threatening situations or fire hazards exist or are likely to exist as determined by the AHJ. (FCC-FUN)

3.3.299 Valet Trash Collection. A service that collects occupant-generated trash or recyclable materials from dwelling units, where the trash is left outside of dwelling units for scheduled pickup. (FCC-OCP)

3.3.300 Valve.

3.3.300.1 *Indicating Valve.* A valve that has components that show if the valve is open or closed. Examples are outside screw and yoke (OS&Y) gate valves and underground gate valves with indicator posts. (FCC-OCP)

3.3.300.2 *Reduced Flow Valve.* A valve equipped with a restricted flow orifice that is designed to reduce the maximum flow from the valve under full flow conditions. (FCC-HAZ)

3.3.300.3 *Valve Outlet Cap or Plug.* A removable device that forms a gastight seal on the outlet to the control valve that is provided on a source containing a compressed gas or cryogenic fluid. [55, 2023] (FCC-HAZ)

3.3.300.4 *Valve Protection Cap.* A rigid, removable cover provided for container valve protection during handling, transportation, and storage. [55, 2023] (FCC-HAZ)

3.3.300.5 *Valve Protection Device.* A device attached to the neck ring or body of a cylinder for the purpose of protecting the cylinder valve from being struck or from being damaged by the impact resulting from a fall or an object striking the cylinder. (FCC-HAZ)

3.3.301 Vapor Pressure. The pressure, measured in pounds per square inch, absolute (psia), exerted by a liquid, as determined by ASTM D323, *Standard Test Method for Vapor Pressure of Petroleum Products (Reid Method)*. [30, 2024] (FCC-HAZ)

3.3.302 Vapor Processing System. See 3.3.283.15.

3.3.303 Vapor Recovery System. See 3.3.283.16.

3.3.304 Vehicle-Mounted Generator. A mobile piece of equipment with an internal-combustion-engine-driven device that provides electrical power and is mounted on a motorized vehicle or trailer for transport. (FCC-FUN)

3.3.305 Warehouse.

3.3.305.1 *General-Purpose Warehouse.* A separate, detached building or portion of a building used only for warehousing-type operations and classified as a "storage — low hazard" or "storage — ordinary hazard" occupancy by the building code and by NFPA *101*. [30, 2024] (FCC-HAZ)

3.3.305.2* *Liquid Warehouse.* A separate, detached building, an attached building, or a portion of a building used for warehousing-type operations for liquids in quantities that exceed the maximum allowable quantity (MAQ). [30, 2024] (FCC-HAZ)

3.3.306 Water Capacity. The amount of water at 60°F (16°C) required to fill a container. [58, 2024] (FCC-HAZ)

3.3.307* **Wharf.** A structure at the shoreline that has a platform built along and parallel to a body of water with either an open deck or a superstructure. [307, 2021] (FCC-OCP)

Δ **3.3.308*** **Wildland/Urban Interface.** A geographical area where structures and other human development meet or intermingle with wildland or vegetative fuels, resulting in the potential for ignition of the structures within the area from flames or firebrands of a wildland fire. [1140, 2022] (FCC-OCP)

3.3.309 Wood Panel. Board or sheet made from veneers, particles, or fibers of wood and includes plywood, oriented strand board, and similar wood products. (FCC-OCP)

3.3.310 Written Notice. A notification in writing delivered in person to the individual or parties intended, or delivered at, or sent by certified or registered mail to, the last residential or business address of legal record. (FCC-FUN)

3.4 Special Performance-Based Definitions.

3.4.1 Alternative Calculation Procedure. A calculation procedure that differs from the procedure originally employed by the design team but that provides predictions for the same variables of interest. [*101*, 2024] (FCC-FUN)

3.4.2 Analysis.

Δ **3.4.2.1** *Sensitivity Analysis.* An analysis performed to determine the degree to which a predicted output will vary given a specified change in an input parameter, usually in relation to models. [*101*, 2024] (FCC-FUN)

3.4.2.2 *Uncertainty Analysis.* An analysis intended to (1) identify key sources of uncertainties in the predictions of a model, (2) assess the potential impacts of these uncertainties on the predictions, and (3) assess the likelihood of these potential impacts. Per this definition, sensitivity analysis performs some but not all of the functions of uncertainty analysis. [805, 2020] (FCC-FUN)

3.4.3 Data Conversion. The process of developing the input data set for the assessment method of choice. [*101*, 2024] (FCC-FUN)

3.4.4 Design Fire Scenario. See 3.4.9.1.

Δ **3.4.5*** **Design Specification.** A building characteristic and other conditions that are under the control of the design team. [*101*, 2024] (FCC-FUN)

3.4.6 Design Team. A group of stakeholders including, but not limited to, representatives of the architect, client, and any pertinent engineers and other designers. [*101*, 2024] (FCC-FUN)

3.4.7* **Exposure Fire.** A fire that starts at a location that is remote from the area being protected and grows to expose that which is being protected. [*101*, 2024] (FCC-FUN)

3.4.8* **Fire Model.** Mathematical prediction of fire growth, environmental conditions, and potential effects on structures, systems, or components based on the conservation equations or empirical data. [805, 2020] (FCC-FUN)

3.4.9* **Fire Scenario.** A set of conditions that defines the development of fire, the spread of combustion products throughout a building or portion of a building, the reactions of people to fire, and the effects of combustion products. [*101*, 2024] (FCC-FUN)

3.4.9.1 *Design Fire Scenario.* A fire scenario selected for evaluation of a proposed design. [*101*, 2024] (FCC-FUN)

Δ **3.4.10*** **Fuel Load.** The total quantity of combustible contents of a building, space, or fire area. [*101*, 2024] (FCC-FUN)

3.4.11 Incapacitation. A condition under which humans do not function adequately and become unable to escape untenable conditions. [*101*, 2024] (FCC-FUN)

3.4.12 Input Data Specification. Information required by the verification method. [*101*, 2024] (FCC-FUN)

3.4.13 Occupant Characteristics. The abilities or behaviors of people before and during a fire. [*101*, 2024] (FCC-FUN)

3.4.14* **Performance Criteria.** Threshold values on measurement scales that are based on quantified performance objectives. [*101*, 2024] (FCC-FUN)

3.4.15* Proposed Design. A design developed by a design team and submitted to the AHJ for approval. [*101*, 2024] (FCC-FUN)

3.4.16 Safe Location. A location remote or separated from the effects of a fire so that such effects no longer pose a threat. [*101*, 2024] (FCC-FUN)

3.4.17 Safety Factor. A factor applied to a predicted value to ensure that a sufficient safety margin is maintained. [*101*, 2024] (FCC-FUN)

3.4.18 Safety Margin. The difference between a predicted value and the actual value where a fault condition is expected. [*101*, 2024] (FCC-FUN)

3.4.19 Sensitivity Analysis. See 3.4.2.1.

3.4.20 Stakeholder. An individual, or representative of same, having an interest in the successful completion of a project. [*101*, 2024] (FCC-FUN)

3.4.21 Uncertainty Analysis. See 3.4.2.2.

3.4.22 Verification Method. A procedure or process used to demonstrate or confirm that the proposed design meets the specified criteria. [*101*, 2024] (FCC-FUN)

Chapter 4   General Requirements

4.1* Goals and Objectives.

4.1.1* Goals. The goals of this *Code* shall be to provide a reasonable level of safety, property protection, and public welfare from the hazards created by fire, explosion, and other hazardous conditions.

4.1.2* Objectives. To achieve the goals stated in 4.1.1, the goals and objectives of 4.1.3 through 4.1.5 shall be used to determine the intent of this *Code*.

4.1.3* Safety. This *Code* shall provide for life safety by reducing the probability of injury or death from fire, explosions, or events involving hazardous materials.

4.1.3.1 Safety from Fire.

4.1.3.1.1* Safety-from-Fire Goals. The fire safety goals of this *Code* shall be as follows:

(1) To provide an environment for the occupants in a building or facility and for the public near a building or facility that is reasonably safe from fire and similar emergencies
(2) To protect fire fighters and emergency responders

4.1.3.1.2 Safety-from-Fire Objectives.

4.1.3.1.2.1 Buildings and facilities shall be designed, constructed, and maintained to protect occupants who are not intimate with the initial fire development for the amount of time needed to evacuate, relocate, or defend in place.

4.1.3.1.2.2* Buildings shall be designed and constructed to provide reasonable safety for fire fighters and emergency responders during search and rescue operations.

4.1.3.1.2.3 Buildings shall be designed, located, and constructed to reasonably protect adjacent persons from injury or death as a result of a fire.

4.1.3.1.2.4 Buildings shall be designed, located, and constructed to provide reasonable access to the building for emergency responders.

4.1.3.1.2.5* Operations shall be conducted at facilities in a safe manner that minimizes, reduces, controls, or mitigates the risk of fire injury or death for the operators, while protecting the occupants not intimate with initial fire development for the amount of time needed to evacuate, relocate, or defend in place.

4.1.3.2 Safety During Building Use.

4.1.3.2.1* Safety-During-Building-Use Goal. The safety-during-building-use goal of this *Code* shall be to provide an environment for the occupants of the building that is reasonably safe during the normal use of the building.

4.1.3.2.2 Safety-During-Building-Use Objectives.

4.1.3.2.2.1 Buildings shall be designed and constructed to reduce the probability of death or injury of persons from falling during normal use of the building.

4.1.3.2.2.2 Buildings shall be designed and constructed to provide for reasonably safe crowd movement during emergency and nonemergency conditions.

4.1.3.2.2.3 Buildings shall be designed and constructed to provide reasonable life safety for occupants and workers during construction and demolition.

4.1.3.2.2.4 Buildings shall be designed and constructed to provide reasonable notification to occupants of fire and other emergency situations.

4.1.3.2.2.5 Buildings shall be designed and constructed to provide reasonable signage and lighting to identify hazards, exits, means of egress, and other building safety features.

4.1.3.3 Safety from Hazardous Materials.

4.1.3.3.1 Safety-from-Hazardous-Materials Goal. The safety-from-hazardous-materials goal of this *Code* shall be to provide an environment for the occupants in a building or facility and to those adjacent to a building or facility that is reasonably safe from exposures to adverse affects from hazardous materials present therein.

4.1.3.3.2 Safety-from-Hazardous-Materials Objectives.

4.1.3.3.2.1 The storage, use, or handling of hazardous materials in a building or facility shall be accomplished in a manner that provides a reasonable level of safety for occupants and for those adjacent to a building or facility from health hazards, illness, injury, or death during normal storage, use, or handling operations and conditions.

4.1.3.3.2.2* The storage, use, or handling of hazardous materials in a building or facility shall be accomplished in a manner that provides a reasonable level of safety for occupants and for those adjacent to a building or facility from illness, injury, or death due to the following conditions:

(1) An unplanned release of the hazardous material
(2) A fire impinging upon the hazardous material or the involvement of the material in a fire
(3) The application of an external force on the hazardous material that is likely to result in an unsafe condition

4.1.4 Property Protection.

4.1.4.1 Property Protection Goal. The property protection goal of this *Code* shall be to limit damage created by a fire, explosion, or event associated with hazardous materials to a reasonable level to the building or facility and adjacent property.

4.1.4.2 Property Protection Objectives.

4.1.4.2.1* Prevention of Ignition. The facility shall be designed, constructed, and maintained, and operations associated with the facility shall be conducted, to prevent unintentional explosions and fires that result in failure of or damage to adjacent compartments, emergency life safety systems, adjacent properties, adjacent outside storage, and the facility's structural elements.

4.1.4.2.2* Fire Spread and Explosions. In the event that a fire or explosion occurs, the building or facility shall be sited, designed, constructed, or maintained, and operations associated with the facility shall be conducted and protected, to reasonably reduce the impact of unwanted fires and explosions on the adjacent compartments, emergency life safety systems, adjacent properties, adjacent outside storage, and the facility's structural elements.

4.1.4.2.3 Structural Integrity. The facility shall be designed, constructed, protected, and maintained, and operations associated with the facility shall be conducted, to provide a reasonable level of protection for the facility, its contents, and adjacent properties from building collapse due to a loss of structural integrity resulting from a fire.

4.1.4.2.4 Hazardous Materials. The facility shall be designed, constructed, and maintained, and operations associated with the facility shall be conducted, to provide reasonable property protection from damage resulting from fires, explosions, and other unsafe conditions associated with the storage, use, and handling of hazardous materials therein.

4.1.5 Public Welfare.

4.1.5.1* Public Welfare Goal. The public welfare goal of this *Code* shall be to maintain a high probability that buildings and facilities that provide a public welfare role for a community continue to perform the function for their intended purpose following a fire, explosion, or hazardous materials event.

4.1.5.2* Public Welfare Objective. Buildings and facilities that provide a public welfare role for a community shall be designed, constructed, maintained, and operated to provide reasonable assurance of continued function following a fire, explosion, or hazardous materials event.

4.1.6* Security Features. Where buildings are designed and constructed to include security features to protect occupants or contents, such features shall not compromise compliance with requirements of this *Code*.

4.2 Assumptions.

4.2.1* Single Fire Source.

4.2.1.1 The fire protection methods of this *Code* shall assume that multiple simultaneous fire incidents will not occur.

4.2.1.2 The single fire source assumption shall not preclude the evaluation of multiple design fire scenarios as required by Section 5.4.

4.2.2* Single Hazardous Material Release.

4.2.2.1 The protection methods of this *Code* shall assume that multiple simultaneous unauthorized releases of hazardous materials from different locations will not occur.

4.2.2.2 The single hazardous material release assumption shall not preclude the evaluation of multiple design scenarios as required by Section 5.4.

4.2.3* Incidents Impinging on Hazardous Materials. The protection methods of this *Code* shall assume that a fire, explosion, hazardous materials release, or external force that creates a dangerous condition has the potential to impinge on hazardous materials being stored, handled, or used in the building or facility under normal conditions. *(See Section 5.4 for performance-based design scenarios.)*

4.3 Compliance Options.
Compliance with the goals and objectives of Section 4.1 shall be provided in accordance with either of the following:

(1) The prescriptive-based provisions per 4.3.1
(2) The performance-based provisions per 4.3.2

4.3.1 Prescriptive-Based Option.

4.3.1.1 A prescriptive-based option shall be in accordance with Chapter 1 through Chapter 4, Chapter 6, and Chapter 10 through Chapter 75 of this *Code*.

4.3.1.2 Where specific requirements contained in Chapter 20 for occupancies differ from general requirements contained in Chapter 1 through Chapter 4 and Chapter 10 through Chapter 75, the requirements of Chapter 20 shall govern.

4.3.2 Performance-Based Option.

4.3.2.1 A performance-based option shall be in accordance with Chapter 1 through Chapter 5 of this *Code*.

4.3.2.2 Prescriptive requirements shall be permitted to be used as part of the performance approach, if they, in conjunction with the performance features, meet the overall goals and objectives of this *Code*.

4.4 Fundamental Requirements.

4.4.1 Multiple Safeguards.

4.4.1.1 The design of every building or structure intended for human occupancy shall be such that reliance for property protection and safety to life does not depend solely on any single safeguard.

4.4.1.2 Additional safeguard(s) shall be provided for property protection and life safety in the event that any single safeguard is ineffective due to inappropriate human actions, building failure, or system failure.

4.4.2 Appropriateness of Safeguards. Every building or structure shall be provided with means of egress and other safeguards of the kinds, numbers, locations, and capacities appropriate to the individual building or structure, with due regard to the following:

(1) Characteristics of the occupancy
(2) Capabilities of the occupants
(3) Number of persons exposed
(4) Fire protection available
(5) Capabilities of response personnel

(6) Height and type of construction of the building or structure
(7) Other factors necessary to provide occupants with a reasonable degree of safety
(8) Other factors necessary to protect the building and contents from damage

4.4.3 Means of Egress.

4.4.3.1 Unobstructed Egress.

4.4.3.1.1 In every occupied building or structure, means of egress from all parts of the building shall be maintained free and unobstructed.

4.4.3.1.2 No lock or fastening shall be permitted that prevents free escape from the inside of any building other than in health care occupancies and detention and correctional occupancies where staff are continually on duty and effective provisions are made to remove occupants in case of fire or other emergency.

4.4.3.1.3 Means of egress shall be accessible to the extent necessary to ensure reasonable safety for occupants having impaired mobility.

4.4.3.2 Awareness of Egress System.

4.4.3.2.1 Every exit shall be clearly visible, or the route to reach every exit shall be conspicuously indicated.

4.4.3.2.2 Each means of egress, in its entirety, shall be arranged or marked so that the way to a place of safety is indicated in a clear manner.

4.4.3.2.3 Lighting. Illumination of means of egress shall be provided. [*See 5.3.4(10).*]

4.4.4* Occupant Notification. In every building or structure of such size, arrangement, or occupancy that a fire itself could not provide adequate occupant warning, fire alarm systems shall be provided where necessary to warn occupants of the existence of fire.

4.4.5 Vertical Openings. Every vertical opening between the floors of a building shall be suitably enclosed or protected, as necessary, to provide the following:

(1) Reasonable safety to occupants while using the means of egress by preventing spread of fire, smoke, or fumes through vertical openings from floor to floor to allow occupants to complete their use of the means of egress
(2) Limitation of damage to the buildings and its contents

4.4.6 System Design/Installation. Any fire protection system, building service equipment, feature of protection, or safeguard provided to achieve the goals of this *Code* shall be designed, installed, and approved in accordance with applicable codes and standards referenced in Chapter 2.

4.5 General Requirements.

4.5.1 Authority Having Jurisdiction (AHJ).

4.5.1.1 The AHJ shall determine whether the provisions of this *Code* are met.

4.5.1.2 Where it is evident that a reasonable degree of safety is provided, any requirement shall be permitted to be modified if its application would be hazardous under normal occupancy conditions in the judgment of the AHJ.

4.5.2 Historic Structures and Cultural Resource Buildings. The provisions of this *Code* shall be permitted to be modified by the AHJ for buildings or structures identified and classified as historic structures in accordance with Section 20.17.

4.5.3 Provisions in Excess of *Code* Requirements. Nothing in this *Code* shall be construed to prohibit a better type of building construction, an additional means of egress, or an otherwise more safe condition than that specified by the minimum requirements of this *Code*.

4.5.4 Conditions for Occupancy. No new construction or existing building shall be occupied in whole or in part in violation of the provisions of this *Code* unless the following conditions exist:

(1) A plan of correction has been approved.
(2) The occupancy classification remains the same.
(3) No serious life safety hazard exists as judged by the AHJ.

4.5.5 Warrant of Fitness.

4.5.5.1 Where compliance with this *Code* is effected by means of a performance-based design, the owner shall annually certify compliance with the conditions and limitations of the design by submitting a warrant of fitness acceptable to the AHJ.

4.5.5.2 The warrant of fitness shall attest that the building features, systems, and use have been inspected and confirmed to remain consistent with design specifications outlined in the documentation required by 5.1.8 and 5.7.3 and that they continue to satisfy the goals and objectives specified in Section 4.1. *(See 5.1.11.)*

4.5.6 Construction, Repair, and Improvement Operations.

4.5.6.1 Buildings or portions of buildings shall be permitted to be occupied during construction, repair, alterations, or additions only where required means of egress and required fire protection features are in place and continuously maintained for the portion occupied or where alternative life safety measures and building protection measures acceptable to the AHJ are in place.

4.5.6.2 Escape Facilities.

4.5.6.2.1 In buildings under construction, adequate escape facilities shall be maintained at all times for the use of construction workers.

4.5.6.2.2 Escape facilities shall consist of doors, walkways, stairs, ramps, fire escapes, ladders, or other approved means or devices arranged in accordance with the general principles of the *Code* insofar as they can reasonably be applied to buildings under construction.

4.5.6.3 Flammable, hazardous, or explosive substances or equipment for repairs or alterations shall be permitted in a building while the building is occupied if the condition of use and safeguards provided do not create any additional danger or impediment to egress beyond the normally permissible conditions in the building and is such that materials are safeguarded when the building is unoccupied.

4.5.7* Changes of Occupancy.

4.5.7.1 In any building or structure, whether or not a physical alteration is needed, a change from one occupancy classification to another shall be permitted only where such a structure, building, or portion thereof conforms with the requirements of this *Code* that apply to new construction for the proposed new use, except as follows:

(1) Where, in the opinion of the AHJ, the proposed occupancy or change in use is not more hazardous than the existing use, based on life safety and fire risk, the AHJ shall be permitted to approve such change of occupancy provided compliance with the requirements of this *Code* for buildings of like occupancy or use are specifically incorporated to safeguard the life, health, and welfare of persons.

(2) Change of tenants or ownership shall not be construed to be a change of occupancy classification where the nature of use and assigned occupancy classification remain the same.

4.5.7.2 Where specifically permitted elsewhere in the *Code*, existing construction features shall be permitted to be continued in use in conversions.

4.5.8 Maintenance, Inspection, and Testing.

4.5.8.1 Whenever or wherever any device, equipment, system, condition, arrangement, level of protection, fire-resistive construction, or any other feature is required for compliance with the provisions of this *Code*, such device, equipment, system, condition, arrangement, level of protection, fire-resistive construction, or other feature shall thereafter be continuously maintained. Maintenance shall be provided in accordance with applicable NFPA requirements or requirements developed as part of a performance-based design, or as directed by the AHJ. [*101*:4.6.12.1]

4.5.8.2 No existing life safety feature shall be removed or reduced where such feature is a requirement for new construction. [*101*:4.6.12.2]

4.5.8.3* Existing life safety features obvious to the public, if not required by the *Code*, shall be either maintained or removed. [*101*:4.6.12.3]

4.5.8.4* Existing life safety features that exceed the requirements for new buildings shall be permitted to be decreased to those required for new buildings. [*101*:4.6.7.4]

4.5.8.5* Existing life safety features that do not meet the requirements for new buildings, but that exceed the requirements for existing buildings, shall not be further diminished. [*101*:4.6.7.5]

4.5.8.6 Any device, equipment, system, condition, arrangement, level of protection, fire-resistive construction, or any other feature requiring periodic testing, inspection, or operation to ensure its maintenance shall be tested, inspected, or operated as specified elsewhere in this *Code* or as directed by the AHJ. [*101*:4.6.12.5]

4.5.8.7 Maintenance, inspection, and testing shall be performed under the supervision of a responsible person who shall ensure that testing, inspection, and maintenance are made at specified intervals in accordance with applicable NFPA standards or as directed by the AHJ. [*101*:4.6.12.6]

4.5.9 Noncombustible Material.

4.5.9.1 A material that complies with any one of the following shall be considered a noncombustible material:

(1)* The material, in the form in which it is used, and under the conditions anticipated, will not ignite, burn, support combustion, or release flammable vapors when subjected to fire or heat.

(2) The material is reported as passing ASTM E136, *Standard Test Method for Assessing Combustibility of Materials Using a Vertical Tube Furnace at 750°C*.

(3) The material is reported as complying with the pass/fail criteria of ASTM E136 when tested in accordance with the test method and procedure in ASTM E2652, *Standard Test Method for Assessing Combustibility of Materials Using a Tube Furnace with a Cone-shaped Airflow Stabilizer, at 750°C*. [**5000**:7.1.4.1.1]

4.5.9.2 Where the term *limited-combustible* is used in this *Code*, it shall also include the term *noncombustible*. [**5000**:7.1.4.1.2]

Δ 4.5.10* Limited-Combustible Material. A material shall be considered a limited-combustible material where one of the following is met:

(1) The conditions of 4.5.10.1 and 4.5.10.2, and the conditions of either 4.5.10.3 or 4.5.10.4, shall be met.
(2) The conditions of 4.5.10.5 shall be met.
[**5000**:7.1.4.2]

4.5.10.1 The material does not comply with the requirements for a noncombustible material in accordance with 4.5.9. [**5000**:7.1.4.2.1]

4.5.10.2 The material, in the form in which it is used, exhibits a potential heat value not exceeding 3500 Btu/lb (8141 kJ/kg) when tested in accordance with NFPA 259. [**5000**:7.1.4.2.2]

4.5.10.3 The material shall have a structural base of noncombustible material with a surfacing not exceeding a thickness of $\frac{1}{8}$ in. (3.2 mm) where the surfacing exhibits a flame spread index not greater than 50 when tested in accordance with ASTM E84, *Standard Test Method for Surface Burning Characteristics of Building Materials*, or UL 723, *Test for Surface Burning Characteristics of Building Materials*. [**5000**:7.1.4.2.3]

4.5.10.4 The material shall be composed of materials that in the form and thickness used neither exhibit a flame spread index greater than 25 nor exhibit evidence of continued progressive combustion when tested in accordance with ASTM E84 or UL 723 and are of such composition that all surfaces that would be exposed by cutting through the material on any plane would neither exhibit a flame spread index greater than 25 nor exhibit evidence of continued progressive combustion when tested in accordance with ASTM E84 or UL 723. [**5000**:7.1.4.2.4]

4.5.10.5 Materials shall be considered limited-combustible materials where tested in accordance with ASTM E2965, *Standard Test Method for Determination of Low Levels of Heat Release Rate for Materials and Products Using an Oxygen Consumption Calorimeter*, at an incident heat flux of 75 kW/m² for a 20-minute exposure, and both the following conditions are met:

(1) The peak heat release rate shall not exceed 150 kW/m² for longer than 10 seconds.
(2) The total heat released shall not exceed 8 MJ/m².
[**5000**:7.1.4.2.5]

4.5.10.6 Where the term *limited-combustible* is used in this *Code*, it shall also include the term *noncombustible*. [**5000**:7.1.4.2.6]

Chapter 5 Performance-Based Option

5.1* General.

5.1.1 Application. The requirements of this chapter shall apply to facilities designed to the performance-based option permitted by Section 4.3.

5.1.2 Goals and Objectives. The performance-based design shall meet the goals and objectives of this *Code* in accordance with Section 4.1 and Section 4.2.

5.1.3* Approved Qualifications. The performance-based design shall be prepared by a person with qualifications acceptable to the AHJ.

5.1.4* Plan Submittal Documentation. When a performance-based design is submitted to the AHJ for review and approval, the owner shall document, in an approved format, each performance objective and applicable scenario, including any calculation methods or models used in establishing the proposed design's fire and life safety performance.

5.1.5* Independent Review. The AHJ shall be permitted to require an approved, independent third party to review the proposed design and provide an evaluation of the design to the AHJ at the expense of the owner.

5.1.6 Sources of Data. Data sources shall be identified and documented for each input data requirement that is required to be met using a source other than a required design scenario, an assumption, or a facility design specification.

5.1.6.1 The degree of conservatism reflected in such data shall be specified, and a justification for the source shall be provided.

5.1.6.2 Copies of all references relied upon by the performance-based design to support assumptions, design features, or any other part of the design shall be made available to the AHJ if requested.

5.1.7 Final Determination. The AHJ shall make the final determination as to whether the performance objectives have been met.

5.1.8* Operations and Maintenance Manual. An approved Operations and Maintenance (O&M) Manual shall be provided by the owner to the AHJ and the fire department and shall be maintained at the facility in an approved location.

5.1.9* Information Transfer to the Fire Service. Where a performance-based design is approved and used, the designer shall ensure that information regarding the operating procedures of the performance-based designed fire protection system is transferred to the owner and to the local fire service for inclusion in the pre-fire plan.

5.1.10* Design Feature Maintenance.

5.1.10.1 The design features required for the facility to meet the performance goals and objectives shall be maintained by the owner and be readily accessible to the AHJ for the life of the facility.

5.1.10.2 The facility shall be maintained in accordance with all documented assumptions and design specifications.

5.1.10.2.1 Any proposed changes or variations from the approved design shall be approved by the AHJ prior to the actual change.

5.1.10.2.2 Any approved changes to the original design shall be maintained in the same manner as the original design.

5.1.11* Annual Certification. Where a performance-based design is approved and used, the property owner shall annually certify that the design features and systems have been maintained in accordance with the approved original performance-based design and assumptions and any subsequent approved changes or modifications to the original performance-based design.

5.1.12 Hazardous Materials.

5.1.12.1 Performance-based designs for facilities containing high hazard contents shall identify the properties of hazardous materials to be stored, used, or handled and shall provide adequate and reliable safeguards to accomplish the following objectives, considering both normal operations and possible abnormal conditions:

(1) Minimize the potential occurrence of unwanted releases, fire, or other emergency incidents resulting from the storage, use, or handling of hazardous materials
(2) Minimize the potential failure of buildings, equipment, or processes involving hazardous materials by ensuring that such buildings, equipment, or processes are reliably designed and are suitable for the hazards present
(3) Minimize the potential exposure of people or property to unsafe conditions or events involving an unintended reaction or release of hazardous materials
(4) Minimize the potential for an unintentional reaction that results in a fire, explosion, or other dangerous condition
(5) Provide a means to contain, treat, neutralize, or otherwise handle plausible releases of hazardous materials to minimize the potential for adverse impacts to persons or property outside of the immediate area of a release
(6) Provide appropriate safeguards to minimize the risk of and limit damage and injury that could result from an explosion involving hazardous materials that present explosion hazards
(7) Detect hazardous levels of gases or vapors that are dangerous to health and alert appropriate persons or mitigate the hazard when the physiological warning properties for such gases or vapors are inadequate to warn of danger prior to personal injury
(8) Maintain power to provide for continued operation of safeguards and important systems that are relied upon to prevent or control an emergency condition involving hazardous materials
(9) Maintain ventilation where ventilation is relied upon to minimize the risk of emergency conditions involving hazardous materials
(10) Minimize the potential for exposing combustible hazardous materials to unintended sources of ignition and for exposing any hazardous material to fire or physical damage that can lead to endangerment of people or property

5.1.12.2 A process hazard analysis and off-site consequence analysis shall be conducted when required by the AHJ to ensure that people and property are satisfactorily protected from potentially dangerous conditions involving hazardous materials. The results of such analyses shall be considered when determining active and passive mitigation measures used in accomplishing the objectives of 4.1.3.3.2 and 4.1.4.2.

5.1.12.3 Written procedures for pre-start-up safety reviews, normal and emergency operations, management of change, emergency response, and accident investigation shall be developed prior to beginning operations at a facility designed in accordance with Section 5.1. Such procedures shall be developed with the participation of employees.

5.1.13 Special Definitions. A list of special terms used in this chapter shall be as follows:

(1) Design Fire Scenario. *(See 3.4.9.1.)*
(2) Design Specification. *(See 3.4.5.)*
(3) Design Team. *(See 3.4.6.)*
(4) Exposure Fire. *(See 3.4.7.)*
(5) Fire Model. *(See 3.4.8.)*
(6) Fire Scenario. *(See 3.4.9.)*
(7) Fuel Load. *(See 3.4.10.)*
(8) Input Data Specification. *(See 3.4.12.)*
(9) Occupant Characteristics. *(See 3.4.13.)*
(10) Performance Criteria. *(See 3.4.14.)*
(11) Proposed Design. *(See 3.4.15.)*
(12) Safety Factor. *(See 3.4.17.)*
(13) Safety Margin. *(See 3.4.18.)*
(14) Sensitivity Analysis. *(See 3.4.2.1.)*
(15) Stakeholder. *(See 3.4.20.)*
(16) Uncertainty Analysis. *(See 3.4.2.2.)*
(17) Verification Method. *(See 3.4.22.)*

5.2 Performance Criteria.

5.2.1 General. A design shall meet the objectives specified in Section 4.1 if, for each required design scenario, assumption, and design specification, the performance criteria of 5.2.2 are met.

5.2.2* Specific Performance Criteria.

5.2.2.1* Fire Conditions. No occupant who is not intimate with ignition shall be exposed to instantaneous or cumulative untenable conditions.

5.2.2.2* Explosion Conditions. The facility design shall provide an acceptable level of safety for occupants and for individuals immediately adjacent to the property from the effects of unintentional detonation or deflagration.

5.2.2.3* Hazardous Materials Exposure. The facility design shall provide an acceptable level of safety for occupants and for individuals immediately adjacent to the property from the effects of an unauthorized release of hazardous materials or the unintentional reaction of hazardous materials.

5.2.2.4* Property Protection. The facility design shall limit the effects of all required design scenarios from causing an unacceptable level of property damage.

5.2.2.5* Public Welfare. For facilities that serve a public welfare role as defined in 4.1.5, the facility design shall limit the effects of all required design scenarios from causing an unacceptable interruption of the facility's mission.

5.2.2.6 Occupant Protection from Untenable Conditions. Means shall be provided to evacuate, relocate, or defend in place occupants not intimate with ignition for sufficient time so that they are not exposed to instantaneous or cumulative untenable conditions from smoke, heat, or flames.

5.2.2.7 Emergency Responder Protection. Buildings shall be designed and constructed to reasonably prevent structural failure under fire conditions for sufficient time to enable fire fighters and emergency responders to conduct search and rescue operations.

5.2.2.8* Occupant Protection from Structural Failure. Buildings shall be designed and constructed to reasonably prevent structural failure under fire conditions for sufficient time to protect the occupants.

5.3 Retained Prescriptive Requirements.

5.3.1 Systems and Features. All fire protection systems and features of the building shall comply with applicable NFPA standards for those systems and features.

5.3.2 Electrical Systems. Electrical systems shall comply with applicable NFPA standards for those systems.

5.3.3 General. The design shall comply with the following requirements in addition to the performance criteria of Section 5.2 and the methods of Section 5.4 through Section 5.7:

(1) Fundamental requirements in Section 10.1
(2) Fire drills in Section 10.6
(3) Smoking in Section 10.9
(4) Open flame, candles, open fires, and incinerators in Section 10.10
(5) Fire protection markings in Section 10.11
(6) Seasonal and vacant buildings and premises in Section 10.12
(7) Combustible vegetation in Section 10.13
(8) Safeguards during building construction, alteration, and demolition operations in Chapter 16

5.3.4 Means of Egress. The design shall comply with the following NFPA *101* requirements in addition to the performance criteria of Section 5.2 and the methods of Section 5.4 through Section 5.7:

(1) Changes in level in means of egress: 7.1.7 of NFPA *101*
(2) Guards: 7.1.8 of NFPA *101*
(3) Door openings: 7.2.1 of NFPA *101*
(4) Stairs: 7.2.2 of NFPA *101*

Exception: The provisions of 7.2.2.5.1, 7.2.2.5.2, 7.2.2.6.2, 7.2.2.6.3, and 7.2.2.6.4 of NFPA 101 shall be exempted.

(5) Ramps: 7.2.5 of NFPA *101*

Exception: The provisions of 7.2.5.3.1, 7.2.5.5, and 7.2.5.6.1 of NFPA 101 shall be exempted.

(6) Fire escape ladders: 7.2.9 of NFPA *101*
(7) Alternating tread devices: 7.2.11 of NFPA *101*
(8) Capacity of means of egress: Section 7.3 of NFPA *101*

Exception: The provisions of 7.3.3 and 7.3.4 of NFPA 101 shall be exempted.

(9) Impediments to egress: 7.5.2 of NFPA *101*
(10) Illumination of means of egress: Section 7.8 of NFPA *101*
(11) Emergency lighting: Section 7.9 of NFPA *101*
(12) Marking of means of egress: Section 7.10 of NFPA *101*

5.3.5 Equivalency. Equivalent designs for the features covered in the retained prescriptive requirements mandated by 5.3.1 through 5.3.4 shall be addressed in accordance with the equivalency provisions of Section 1.4.

5.4* Design Scenarios.

5.4.1 General.

5.4.1.1 The proposed design shall be considered to meet the goals and objectives if it achieves the performance criteria for each required design scenario. The AHJ shall approve the parameters involved with required design scenarios.

5.4.1.2* Design scenarios shall be evaluated for each required scenario using a method acceptable to the AHJ and appropriate for the conditions. Each scenario shall be as challenging and realistic as any that could realistically occur in the building.

5.4.1.3* Scenarios selected as design scenarios shall include, but not be limited to, those specified in 5.4.2 through 5.4.5.

5.4.1.3.1 Design fire scenarios demonstrated by the design team to the satisfaction of the AHJ as inappropriate for the building use and conditions shall not be required to be evaluated fully.

5.4.1.3.2 Fire Design Scenario 8 (see 5.4.2.8) shall not be required to be applied to fire protection systems or features for which both the level of reliability and the design performance in the absence of the system or feature are acceptable to the AHJ.

5.4.1.4 Each design scenario used in the performance-based design proposal shall be translated into input data specifications, as appropriate for the calculation method or model.

5.4.1.5 Any design scenario specifications that the design analyses do not explicitly address or incorporate and that are, therefore, omitted from input data specifications shall be identified, and a sensitivity analysis of the consequences of that omission shall be performed.

5.4.1.6 Any design scenario specifications modified in input data specifications, because of limitations in test methods or other data generation procedures, shall be identified, and a sensitivity analysis of the consequences of the modification shall be performed.

5.4.2 Required Design Scenarios — Fire.

5.4.2.1* **Fire Design Scenario 1.** Fire Design Scenario 1 involves an occupancy-specific design scenario representative of a typical fire for the occupancy.

5.4.2.1.1 This design scenario shall explicitly account for the following:

(1) Occupant activities
(2) Number and location of occupants
(3) Room size
(4) Furnishings and contents
(5) Fuel properties and ignition sources
(6) Ventilation conditions

5.4.2.1.2 The first item ignited and its location shall be explicitly defined.

5.4.2.2* **Fire Design Scenario 2.** Fire Design Scenario 2 involves an ultrafast-developing fire in the primary means of egress with interior doors open at the start of the fire. This design scenario shall address the concern regarding a reduction in the number of available means of egress.

5.4.2.3* **Fire Design Scenario 3.** Fire Design Scenario 3 involves a fire that starts in a normally unoccupied room that can potentially endanger a large number of occupants in a large room or other area. This design scenario shall address the concern regarding a fire starting in a normally unoccupied room and migrating into the space that can, potentially, hold the greatest number of occupants in the building.

5.4.2.4* **Fire Design Scenario 4.** Fire Design Scenario 4 involves a fire that originates in a concealed wall or ceiling space adjacent to a large occupied room. This design scenario shall address the concern regarding a fire originating in a concealed space that does not have either a detection system or suppression system and then spreading into the room within the building that can, potentially, hold the greatest number of occupants.

5.4.2.5* **Fire Design Scenario 5.** Fire Design Scenario 5 involves a slow-developing fire, shielded from fire protection systems, in close proximity to a high occupancy area. This design scenario shall address the concern regarding a relatively small ignition source causing a significant fire.

5.4.2.6* **Fire Design Scenario 6.** Fire Design Scenario 6 involves the most severe fire resulting from the largest possible fuel load characteristic of the normal operation of the building. This design scenario shall address the concern regarding a rapidly developing fire with occupants present.

5.4.2.7* **Fire Design Scenario 7.** Fire Design Scenario 7 involves an outside exposure fire. This design scenario shall address the concern regarding a fire starting at a location remote from the area of concern and either spreading into the area, blocking escape from the area, or developing untenable conditions within the area.

5.4.2.8* **Fire Design Scenario 8.** Fire Design Scenario 8 involves a fire originating in ordinary combustibles in a room or area with each passive or active fire protection system or feature independently rendered ineffective. This set of design scenarios shall address concerns regarding each fire protection system or fire protection feature, considered individually, being unreliable or becoming unavailable. This scenario shall not be required to be applied to fire protection systems or features for which both the level of reliability and the design performance in the absence of the system are acceptable to the AHJ.

5.4.3 Required Design Scenarios — Explosion.

5.4.3.1* **Explosion Design Scenario 1.**

5.4.3.1.1 Explosion Design Scenario 1 is the detonation or deflagration of explosive materials being manufactured, stored, handled, or used in a facility.

5.4.3.1.2 Explosion Design Scenario 1 shall address the concern regarding safety of individuals not intimate with the explosion and property protection of adjacent properties and buildings.

5.4.4* Required Design Scenarios — Hazardous Materials.

5.4.4.1 Hazardous Materials Design Scenario 1. Hazardous Materials Design Scenario 1 involves an unauthorized release of hazardous materials from a single control area. This design scenario shall address the concern regarding the spread of hazardous conditions from the point of release.

5.4.4.2 Hazardous Materials Design Scenario 2. Hazardous Materials Design Scenario 2 involves an exposure fire on a location where hazardous materials are stored, used, handled, or dispensed. This design scenario shall address the concern regarding how a fire in a facility affects the safe storage, handling, or use of hazardous materials.

5.4.4.3 Hazardous Materials Design Scenario 3. Hazardous Materials Design Scenario 3 involves the application of an external factor to the hazardous material that is likely to result in a fire, explosion, toxic release, or other unsafe condition. This design scenario shall address the concern regarding the initiation of a hazardous materials event by the application of heat, shock, impact, or water onto a hazardous material being stored, used, handled, or dispensed in the facility.

5.4.4.4 Hazardous Materials Design Scenario 4.

5.4.4.4.1 Hazardous Materials Design Scenario 4 involves an unauthorized discharge with each protection system independently rendered ineffective. This set of design hazardous materials scenarios shall address concern regarding each protection system or protection feature, considered individually, being unreliable or becoming unavailable.

5.4.4.4.2* Hazardous Materials Design Scenario 4 shall not be required to be applied to protection systems or features for which both the level of reliability and the design performance in the absence of the system are acceptable to the AHJ.

5.4.5 Required Design Scenarios — Safety During Building Use.

5.4.5.1* Building Use Design Scenario 1. Building Use Design Scenario 1 involves an event in which the maximum occupant load is in the assembly building and an emergency event occurs blocking the principal exit/entrance to the building. This design scenario shall address the concern of occupants having to take alternative exit routes under crowded conditions.

5.4.5.2 Building Use Design Scenario 2. Building Use Design Scenario 2 involves a fire in an area of a building undergoing construction or demolition while the remainder of the building is occupied. The normal fire suppression system in the area undergoing construction or demolition has been taken out of service. This design scenario shall address the concern regarding the inoperability of certain building fire safety features during construction and demolition in a partially occupied building.

5.5 Evaluation of Proposed Designs.

5.5.1 General.

5.5.1.1 A proposed design's performance shall be assessed relative to each performance objective in Section 4.1 and each applicable scenario in Section 5.4, with the assessment conducted through the use of appropriate calculation methods.

5.5.1.2 The choice of assessment methods shall require the approval of the AHJ.

5.5.2 Use. The design professional shall use the assessment methods to demonstrate that the proposed design achieves the goals and objectives, as measured by the performance criteria in light of the safety margins and uncertainty analysis, for each scenario, given the assumptions.

5.5.3 Input Data.

5.5.3.1* Data.

5.5.3.1.1 Input data for computer fire models shall be obtained in accordance with ASTM E1591, *Standard Guide for Obtaining Data for Fire Growth Models*.

5.5.3.1.2 Data for use in analytical models that are not computer-based fire models shall be obtained using appropriate measurement, recording, and storage techniques to ensure the applicability of the data to the analytical method being used.

5.5.3.2 Data Requirements. A complete listing of input data requirements for all models, engineering methods, and other calculation or verification methods required or proposed as part of the performance-based design shall be provided.

5.5.3.3 Uncertainty and Conservatism of Data. Uncertainty in input data shall be analyzed and, as determined appropriate by the AHJ, addressed through the use of conservative values.

5.5.4 Output Data. The assessment methods used shall accurately and appropriately produce the required output data from input data based on the design specifications, assumptions, and scenarios.

5.5.5* Validity. Evidence shall be provided confirming that the assessment methods are valid and appropriate for the proposed facility, use, and conditions.

5.6* Safety Factors. Approved safety factors shall be included in the design methods and calculations to reflect uncertainty in the assumptions, data, and other factors associated with the performance-based design.

5.7 Documentation Requirements.

5.7.1* General.

5.7.1.1 All aspects of the design, including those described in 5.7.2 through 5.7.14, shall be documented.

5.7.1.2 The format and content of the documentation shall be acceptable to the AHJ.

5.7.2* Technical References and Resources.

5.7.2.1 The AHJ shall be provided with sufficient documentation to support the validity, accuracy, relevance, and precision of the proposed methods.

5.7.2.2 The engineering standards, calculation methods, and other forms of scientific information provided shall be appropriate for the particular application and methodologies used.

5.7.3 Facility Design Specifications. All details of the proposed facility design that affect the ability of the facility to meet the stated goals and objectives shall be documented.

5.7.4 Performance Criteria. Performance criteria, with sources, shall be documented.

5.7.5 Occupant Characteristics. Assumptions about occupant characteristics shall be documented.

5.7.6 Design Scenarios. Descriptions of design hazard scenarios shall be documented.

5.7.7 Input Data. Input data to models and assessment methods, including sensitivity analysis, shall be documented.

5.7.8 Output Data. Output data from models and assessment methods, including sensitivity analysis, shall be documented.

5.7.9 Safety Factors. Safety factors utilized shall be documented.

5.7.10 Prescriptive Requirements. Retained prescriptive requirements shall be documented.

5.7.11* Modeling Features.

5.7.11.1 Assumptions made by the model user, and descriptions of models and methods used, including known limitations, shall be documented.

5.7.11.2 Documentation shall be provided that the assessment methods have been used validly and appropriately to address the design specifications, assumptions, and scenarios.

5.7.12 Evidence of Modeler Capability. The design team's relevant experience with the models, test methods, databases, and other assessment methods used in the performance-based design proposal shall be documented.

5.7.13 Performance Evaluation. The performance evaluation summary shall be documented.

5.7.14 Use of Performance-Based Design Option. Design proposals shall include documentation that provides anyone involved in ownership or management of the facility with all of the following notification:

(1) The facility was approved as a performance-based design with certain specified design criteria and assumptions.
(2) Any remodeling, modification, renovation, change in use, or change in the established assumptions requires a re-evaluation and reapproval.

Chapter 6   Classification of Occupancy

6.1 Classification of Occupancy.

6.1.1 General.

6.1.1.1 Occupancy Classification. The occupancy of a building or structure, or portion of a building or structure, shall be classified in accordance with 6.1.2 through 6.1.13. Occupancy classification shall be subject to the ruling of the AHJ where there is a question of proper classification in any individual case. [*101*:6.1.1.1]

6.1.1.2 Special Structures. Occupancies in special structures shall conform to the requirements of Section 20.16. [*101*:6.1.1.2]

6.1.2 Assembly. For requirements, see Section 20.1. [*101*:6.1.2]

6.1.2.1* Definition — Assembly Occupancy. An occupancy (1) used for a gathering of 50 or more persons for deliberation, worship, entertainment, eating, drinking, amusement, awaiting transportation, or similar uses; or (2) used as a special amusement building, regardless of occupant load. [*101*:6.1.2.1]

6.1.2.2 Other. (Reserved)

6.1.3 Educational. For requirements, see Section 20.2. [*101*:6.1.3]

6.1.3.1* Definition — Educational Occupancy. An occupancy used for educational purposes through the twelfth grade by six or more persons for 4 or more hours per day or more than 12 hours per week. [*101*:6.1.3.1]

6.1.3.2 Other Occupancies. Other occupancies associated with educational institutions shall be in accordance with the appropriate parts of this *Code* and NFPA *101*. [*101*:6.1.3.2]

6.1.3.3 Incidental Instruction. In cases where instruction is incidental to some other occupancy, the section of this *Code* and NFPA *101* governing such other occupancy shall apply. [*101*:6.1.3.3]

6.1.4 Day Care. For requirements, see Section 20.3. [*101*:6.1.4].

6.1.4.1* Definition — Day-Care Occupancy. An occupancy in which four or more clients receive care, maintenance, and supervision, by other than their relatives or legal guardians, for less than 24 hours per day. [*101*:6.1.4.1]

6.1.4.2 Other. (Reserved)

6.1.5 Health Care. For requirements, see Section 20.4. [*101*:6.1.5]

6.1.5.1* Definition — Health Care Occupancy. An occupancy used to provide medical or other treatment or care simultaneously to four or more patients on an inpatient basis, where such patients are mostly incapable of self-preservation due to age, physical or mental disability, or because of security measures not under the occupants' control. [*101*:6.1.5.1]

6.1.5.2 Other. (Reserved)

6.1.6 Ambulatory Health Care. For requirements, see Section 20.6. [*101*:6.1.6]

6.1.6.1* Definition — Ambulatory Health Care Occupancy. An occupancy used to provide services or treatment simultaneously to four or more patients that provides, on an outpatient basis, one or more of the following:

(1) Treatment for patients that renders the patients incapable of taking action for self-preservation under emergency conditions without the assistance of others
(2) Anesthesia that renders the patients incapable of taking action for self-preservation under emergency conditions without the assistance of others
(3) Emergency or urgent care for patients who, due to the nature of their injury or illness, are incapable of taking action for self-preservation under emergency conditions without the assistance of others

[*101*:6.1.6.1]

6.1.6.2 Other. (Reserved)

6.1.7 Detention and Correctional. For requirements, see Section 20.7. [*101*:6.1.7]

6.1.7.1* Definition — Detention and Correctional Occupancy. An occupancy, other than one whose primary intended use is health care, ambulatory health care, or residential board and care, used to lawfully incarcerate or lawfully detain one or more persons under varied degrees of restraint or security where such occupants are mostly incapable of self-preservation because of security measures not under the occupants' control. [*101*:6.1.7.1]

6.1.7.2* Nonresidential Uses. Within detention and correctional facilities, uses other than residential housing shall be in accordance with the appropriate chapter of this *Code* and

NFPA *101*. (See 22.1.3.3 and 23.1.3.3 of NFPA *101*.) [*101*:6.1.7.2]

6.1.8 Residential. For requirements, see Sections 20.5 and 20.8 through 20.11. [*101*:6.1.8]

6.1.8.1 Definition — Residential Occupancy. An occupancy that provides sleeping accommodations for purposes other than health care or detention and correctional. [*101*:6.1.8.1]

6.1.8.1.1* Definition — One- and Two-Family Dwelling Unit. A building that contains not more than two dwelling units, each dwelling unit occupied by members of a single family with not more than three outsiders, if any, accommodated in rented rooms. [*101*:6.1.8.1.1]

6.1.8.1.2 Definition — Lodging or Rooming House. A building or portion thereof that does not qualify as a one- or two-family dwelling, that provides sleeping accommodations for a total of 16 or fewer people on a transient or permanent basis, without personal care services, with or without meals, but without separate cooking facilities for individual occupants. [*101*:6.1.8.1.2]

6.1.8.1.3* Definition — Hotel. A building or groups of buildings under the same management in which there are sleeping accommodations for more than 16 persons and primarily used by transients for lodging with or without meals. [*101*:6.1.8.1.3]

6.1.8.1.4* Definition — Dormitory. A building or a space in a building in which group sleeping accommodations are provided for more than 16 persons who are not members of the same family in one room, or a series of closely associated rooms, under joint occupancy and single management, with or without meals, but without individual cooking facilities. [*101*:6.1.8.1.4]

6.1.8.1.5 Definition — Apartment Building. A building or portion thereof containing three or more dwelling units with independent cooking and bathroom facilities. [*101*:6.1.8.1.5]

6.1.8.2 Other. (Reserved)

6.1.9 Residential Board and Care. For requirements, see Section 20.5. [*101*:6.1.9]

6.1.9.1* Definition — Residential Board and Care Occupancy. An occupancy used for lodging and boarding of four or more residents, not related by blood or marriage to the owners or operators, for the purpose of providing personal care services. [*101*:6.1.9.1]

6.1.9.2 Other. (Reserved)

6.1.10 Mercantile. For requirements, see Section 20.12. [*101*:6.1.10]

6.1.10.1* Definition — Mercantile Occupancy. An occupancy used for the display and sale of merchandise. [*101*:6.1.10.1]

6.1.10.2 Other. (Reserved)

6.1.11 Business. For requirements, see Section 20.13. [*101*:6.1.11]

6.1.11.1* Definition — Business Occupancy. An occupancy used for the transaction of business other than mercantile. [*101*:6.1.11.1]

6.1.11.2 Other. (Reserved)

6.1.12 Industrial. For requirements, see Section 20.14. [*101*:6.1.12]

6.1.12.1* Definition — Industrial Occupancy. An occupancy in which products are manufactured or in which processing, assembling, mixing, packaging, finishing, decorating, or repair operations are conducted. [*101*:6.1.12.1]

6.1.12.2 Other. (Reserved)

6.1.13 Storage. For requirements, see Section 20.15. [*101*:6.1.13]

6.1.13.1* Definition — Storage Occupancy. An occupancy used primarily for the storage or sheltering of goods, merchandise, products, or vehicles. [*101*:6.1.13.1]

6.1.13.2 Other. (Reserved)

6.1.14 Multiple Occupancies.

6.1.14.1 General.

6.1.14.1.1* Multiple occupancies shall comply with the requirements of 6.1.14.1 and one of the following:

(1) Mixed occupancies — 6.1.14.3
(2) Separated occupancies — 6.1.14.4
[*101*:6.1.14.1.1]

6.1.14.1.2 Where exit access from an occupancy traverses another occupancy, the multiple occupancy shall be treated as a mixed occupancy. [*101*:6.1.14.1.2]

6.1.14.1.3* Where incidental to another occupancy, areas used as follows shall be permitted to be considered part of the predominant occupancy and shall be subject to the provisions of this *Code* and NFPA *101* that apply to the predominant occupancy:

(1) Mercantile, business, industrial, or storage use
(2)* Nonresidential use with an occupant load fewer than that established by Section 6.1 for the occupancy threshold
[*101*:6.1.14.1.3]

6.1.14.2 Definitions.

6.1.14.2.1 Multiple Occupancy. A building or structure in which two or more classes of occupancy exist. [*101*:6.1.14.2.1]

6.1.14.2.2 Mixed Occupancy. A multiple occupancy where the occupancies are intermingled. [*101*:6.1.14.2.2]

6.1.14.2.3 Separated Occupancy. A multiple occupancy where the occupancies are separated by fire barriers. [*101*:6.1.14.2.3]

6.1.14.3 Mixed Occupancies.

6.1.14.3.1 Each portion of the building shall be classified as to its use in accordance with Section 6.1. [*101*:6.1.14.3.1]

6.1.14.3.2* The building shall comply with the most restrictive requirements of the occupancies involved, unless separate safeguards are approved. [*101*:6.1.14.3.2]

6.1.14.4 Separated Occupancies. (See also 6.1.14.4.2.) [*101*:6.1.14.4]

6.1.14.4.1 Where separated occupancies are provided, each part of the building comprising a distinct occupancy, as described in this chapter, shall be completely separated from other occupancies by fire-barriers as specified in 6.1.14.4.2, 6.1.14.4.3, and Table 6.1.14.4.1(a) and Table 6.1.14.4.1(b), unless separation is provided by approved existing separations or as otherwise permitted by 6.1.14.4.6. [*101*:6.1.14.4.1]

6.1.14.4.2 Occupancy separation fire barriers shall be classified as 3-hour fire-resistance-rated, 2-hour fire-resistance-rated, or 1-hour fire-resistance-rated and shall meet the requirements of Chapter 8 of NFPA *101*. [*101*:6.1.14.4.2]

6.1.14.4.3 The fire barrier minimum fire resistance rating specified in Table 6.1.14.4.1(a) and Table 6.1.14.4.1(b) shall be permitted to be reduced by 1 hour, but in no case shall it be reduced to less than 1 hour, where the building is protected throughout by an approved automatic sprinkler system in accordance with NFPA 13 and supervised in accordance with 13.3.1.8, unless prohibited by the dagger footnote entries in the tables. [*101*:6.1.14.4.3]

6.1.14.4.4 Occupancy separation fire barriers shall be vertical, horizontal, or both or, when necessary, of such other form as required to provide complete separation between occupancy divisions in the building. [*101*:6.1.14.4.4]

6.1.14.4.5* Each separated portion of the building shall comply with the requirements for the occupancy therein. [*101*:6.1.14.4.5]

6.1.14.4.6 Where permitted in Chapters 11 through 43 of NFPA *101*, atrium walls shall be permitted to serve as part of the separation required by 6.1.14.4.1 for creating separated occupancies on a story-by-story basis, provided all of the following are met:

(1) The atrium is separated from adjacent areas by walls that are smoke partitions in accordance with Section 8.4 of NFPA *101*.
(2) Doors in the smoke partitions required by 6.1.14.4.6(1) are equipped with positive latching hardware.
(3) The atrium meets the provisions of 8.6.7 of NFPA *101* that are applicable to new atriums.

[*101*:6.1.14.4.6]

Table 6.1.14.4.1(a) Required Separation of Occupancies (hours),* Part 1

Occupancy	Assembly ≤300	Assembly >300 to ≤1000	Assembly >1000	Educational	Day-Care >12 Clients	Day-Care Homes	Health Care	Ambulatory Health Care	Detention & Correctional	One- & Two-Family Dwellings	Lodging or Rooming Houses	Hotels & Dormitories
Assembly ≤300	—	0	0	2	2	1	2†	2	2†	2	2	2
Assembly >300 to ≤1000	0	—	0	2	2	2	2†	2	2†	2	2	2
Assembly >1000	0	0	—	2	2	2	2†	2	2†	2	2	2
Educational	2	2	2	—	2	2	2†	2	2†	2	2	2
Day-Care >12 Clients	2	2	2	2	—	1	2†	2	2†	2	2	2
Day-Care Homes	1	2	2	2	1	—	2†	2	2†	2	2	2
Health Care	2†	2†	2†	2†	2†	2†	—	2†	2†	2†	2†	2†
Ambulatory Health Care	2	2	2	2	2	2	2†	—	2†	2	2	2
Detention & Correctional	2†	2†	2†	2†	2†	2†	2†	2†	—	2†	2†	2†
One- & Two-Family Dwellings	2	2	2	2	2	2	2†	2	2†	—	1	1
Lodging or Rooming Houses	2	2	2	2	2	2	2†	2	2†	1	—	1
Hotels & Dormitories	2	2	2	2	2	2	2†	2	2†	1	1	—
Apartment Buildings	2	2	2	2	2	2	2†	2	2†	1	1	1
Board & Care, Small	2	2	2	2	2	2	2†	2	2†	1	2	2
Board & Care, Large	2	2	2	2	2	2	2†	2	2†	2	2	2
Mercantile	2	2	2	2	2	2	2†	2	2†	2	2	2
Mercantile, Mall	2	2	2	2	2	2	2†	2	2†	2	2	2
Mercantile, Bulk Retail	3	3	3	3	3	3	2†	2†	2†	3	3	3
Business	1	2	2	2	2	2†	1	2†	2	2	2	2
Industrial, General Purpose	2	2	3	3	3	3	2†	2	2†	2	2	2
Industrial, Special-Purpose	2	2	2	3	3	3	2†	2	2†	2	2	2
Industrial, High Hazard	3	3	3	3	3	3	2†	2†	NP	3	3	3
Storage, Low & Ordinary Hazard	2	2	3	3	3	2	2†	2	2†	2	2	2
Storage, High Hazard	3	3	3	3	3	3	2†	2†	NP	3	3	3

NP: Not permitted.

*Minimum Fire Resistance Rating. The fire resistance rating is permitted to be reduced by 1 hour, but in no case to less than 1 hour, where the building is protected throughout by an approved automatic sprinkler system in accordance with NFPA 13 and supervised in accordance with 13.3.1.8.
†The 1-hour reduction due to the presence of sprinklers in accordance with the asterisk footnote is not permitted.
[*101*:Table 6.1.14.4.1(a)]

Table 6.1.14.4.1(b) Required Separation of Occupancies (hours)*, Part 2

Occupancy	Apartment Buildings	Board & Care, Small	Board & Care, Large	Mercantile	Mercantile, Mall	Mercantile, Bulk Retail	Business	Industrial, General Purpose	Industrial, Special-Purpose	Industrial, High Hazard	Storage, Low & Ordinary Hazard	Storage, High Hazard
Assembly ≤300	2	2	2	2	2	3	1	2	2	3	2	3
Assembly >300 to ≤1000	2	2	2	2	2	3	2	2	2	3	2	3
Assembly >1000	2	2	2	2	2	3	2	3	2	3	3	3
Educational	2	2	2	2	2	3	2	3	3	3	3	3
Day-Care >12 Clients	2	2	2	2	2	3	2	3	3	3	3	3
Day-Care Homes	2	2	2	2	2	3	2	3	3	3	2	3
Health Care	2†	2†	2†	2†	2†	2†	2†	2†	2†	2†	2†	2†
Ambulatory Health Care	2	2	2	2	2	2†	1	2	2	2†	2	2†
Detention & Correctional	2†	2†	2†	2†	2†	2†	2†	2†	2†	NP	2†	NP
One- & Two-Family Dwellings	1	1	2	2	2	3	2	2	2	3	2	3
Lodging or Rooming Houses	1	2	2	2	2	3	2	2	2	3	2	3
Hotels & Dormitories	1	2	2	2	2	3	2	2	2	3	2	3
Apartment Buildings	—	2	2	2	2	3	2	2	2	3	2	3
Board & Care, Small	2	—	1	2	2	3	2	3	3	3	3	3
Board & Care, Large	2	1	—	2	2	3	2	3	3	3	3	3
Mercantile	2	2	2	—	0	3	2	2	2	3	2	3
Mercantile, Mall	2	2	2	0	—	3	2	3	3	3	2	3
Mercantile, Bulk Retail	3	3	3	3	3	—	2	2	2	3	2	2
Business	2	2	2	2	2	2	—	2	2	2	2	2
Industrial, General Purpose	2	3	3	2	3	2	2	—	1	1	1	1
Industrial, Special-Purpose	2	3	3	2	3	2	2	1	—	1	1	1
Industrial, High Hazard	3	3	3	3	3	3	2	1	1	—	1	1
Storage, Low & Ordinary Hazard	2	3	3	2	2	2	2	1	1	1	—	1
Storage, High Hazard	3	3	3	3	3	2	2	1	1	1	1	—

NP: Not permitted.
*Minimum Fire Resistance Rating. The fire resistance rating is permitted to be reduced by 1 hour, but in no case to less than 1 hour, where the building is protected throughout by an approved automatic sprinkler system in accordance with NFPA 13 and supervised in accordance with 13.3.1.8.
†The 1-hour reduction due to the presence of sprinklers in accordance with the asterisk footnote is not permitted.
[*101:*Table 6.1.14.4.1(b)]

Chapter 7 Reserved

Chapter 8 Reserved

Chapter 9 Reserved

Chapter 10 General Safety Requirements

10.1 Fundamental Requirements.

10.1.1 Every new and existing building or structure shall be constructed, arranged, equipped, maintained, and operated in accordance with this *Code* so as to provide a reasonable level of life safety, property protection, and public welfare from the actual and potential hazards created by fire, explosion, and other hazardous conditions.

10.1.2* *Life Safety Code.* Every new and existing building shall comply with this *Code* and NFPA *101*.

10.1.3 Building Code. Where a building code has been adopted, all new construction shall comply with this *Code* and the building code.

10.1.4 Structural Hazards.

10.1.4.1 Where structural elements have visible damage, the AHJ shall be permitted to require a technical analysis prepared in accordance with Section 1.16 to determine if repairs are necessary to restore structural integrity.

10.1.4.2 Where the technical analysis recommends repairs to the structure, such repairs shall be made.

10.1.5 Any person who deliberately, or through negligence, sets fire to or causes the burning of any combustible material in such a manner as to endanger the safety of any person or property shall be deemed to be in violation of this *Code*.

10.1.6 The AHJ shall have the authority to prohibit any or all open flames or other sources of ignition where circumstances make such conditions hazardous.

10.1.7 Listed and Labeled. Listed and labeled equipment, devices, and materials shall be installed and used in accordance with the listing limitations and the manufacturers' instructions.

10.2 Owner/Operator/Tenant Responsibilities.

10.2.1 The owner, operator, tenant, or authorized representative shall be responsible for compliance with this *Code*.

10.2.2 The owner, operator, tenant, or authorized representative of a building shall notify the AHJ prior to a change of occupancy as specified in 4.5.7 and 10.3.4.

10.2.3 The AHJ shall be permitted to require the owner, operator, tenant, or authorized representative to provide tests or test reports, without expense to the AHJ, as proof of compliance with the intent of this *Code*.

10.2.4 The owner, operator, tenant, or authorized representative of a building that is deemed unsafe by the AHJ shall abate, through corrective action approved by the AHJ, the condition causing the building to be unsafe either by repair, rehabilitation, demolition, or other corrective action approved by the AHJ.

10.2.5 The owner, operator, tenant, or authorized representative, or any person in control of a building or premises shall keep records of all maintenance, inspections, and testing of fire protection systems, fire alarm systems, smoke control systems, emergency evacuation and relocation drills, emergency action plans, emergency power, elevators, and other equipment as required by the AHJ.

10.2.6 All records required to be kept shall be maintained until their useful life has been served, as required by law, or as required by the AHJ.

10.2.7 Minimum Fire Prevention Inspection Frequencies for Existing Occupancies.

Δ **10.2.7.1** Fire prevention inspections shall occur on existing premises in accordance with the minimum inspection frequency schedule specified in Table 10.2.7.1.

10.2.7.2 Where required or permitted by the AHJ, the required fire prevention inspection shall be conducted by an approved party that is qualified in accordance with NFPA *1030*.

10.2.7.3 The AHJ shall be permitted to approve alternative qualifications for the approved party specified in 10.2.7.2.

10.2.7.4 The provisions of 10.2.7 shall not apply to detached one- and two-family dwellings or townhomes.

10.3 Occupancy.

10.3.1 No new construction or existing building shall be occupied in whole or in part in violation of the provisions of this *Code* or the certificate of occupancy issued under the building code.

10.3.2 Existing buildings that are occupied at the time of adoption of this *Code* shall be permitted to remain in use provided that the following conditions are met:

(1) The use and occupancy classification has been approved and is unchanged from the time of the approval.
(2) No condition deemed hazardous to life or property exists that would constitute an imminent danger.

10.3.3* Buildings or portions of buildings, except for routine maintenance or repair, shall not be occupied during construction, repair, or alteration without the approval of the AHJ if required means of egress are impaired or required fire protection systems are out of service.

10.3.4 Change of Use or Occupancy Classification.

10.3.4.1 In any building or structure, whether or not a physical alteration is needed, a change from one use or occupancy classification to another shall comply with 4.6.7 of NFPA *101*. [*101*:4.6.11]

Table 10.2.7.1 Minimum Inspection Frequency

Occupancy Risk Classification	Frequency
High	Annually
Moderate	Biennially
Low	Triennially
Critical infrastructure	Per AHJ

[*1730*:Table 6.7]

10.3.4.2 Occupancy classifications and subclassifications, as defined, shall be in accordance with Chapter 6.

10.4 Emergency Action Plans.

10.4.1 Where Required. Emergency action plans shall be provided for high-rise, health care, ambulatory health care, residential board and care, assembly, day-care centers, special amusement buildings, hotels and dormitories, detention and correctional occupancies, educational, underground and windowless structures, facilities storing or handling materials covered by Chapter 60, or where required by the AHJ.

10.4.2 Plan Requirements.

10.4.2.1* Emergency action plans shall include the following:

(1) Procedures for reporting of emergencies
(2) Occupant and staff response to emergencies
(3)* Evacuation, relocation, and shelter-in-place procedures appropriate to the building, its occupancy, emergencies, and hazards
(4) Appropriateness of the use of elevators
(5) Design and conduct of fire drills
(6) Type and coverage of building fire protection systems
(7) Specific details, locations, and operational features of security features that could impact or be integrated with life safety systems
(8) Design and conduct of life safety, security, lockdown, and other drills not associated with fire
(9) Operational features that are to be integrated with a voice evacuation system, a mass notification system, or both, to meet design and operational requirements of other installation standards
(10) Other items required by the AHJ

[*101*:4.8.2.1]

10.4.2.2 Emergency action plans shall be submitted to the AHJ for review when required by the AHJ.

10.4.2.3* Emergency action plans shall be reviewed and updated as required by the AHJ. [*101*:4.8.2.3]

10.5 Building Evacuation.

10.5.1 Persons shall not fail to leave a building when notified to do so or when directed by the AHJ as a result of a known or perceived emergency.

10.5.2* Persons shall not fail to leave any overcrowded premises when ordered to do so by the AHJ.

10.5.3* Persons shall not fail to leave a building when a fire alarm system is activated or when required by a fire drill, unless otherwise provided for in an approved building fire evacuation plan or during routine system testing or maintenance.

10.5.4 For non-fire incidents, persons shall not fail to comply with actions required by an emergency action plan when a mass notification or other emergency notification signal is activated.

10.6* Fire Drills.

10.6.1 Where Required. Emergency egress and relocation drills conforming to the provisions of this *Code* shall be conducted as specified by the provisions of Chapter 20 of this *Code*, Chapters 11 through 42 of NFPA *101*, or by appropriate action of the AHJ. Drills shall be designed in cooperation with the local authorities. [*101*:4.7.1]

10.6.2* Drill Frequency. Emergency egress and relocation drills, where required by Chapter 20 of this *Code*, Chapters 11 through 43 of NFPA *101*, or the AHJ, shall be held with sufficient frequency to familiarize occupants with the drill procedure and to establish conduct of the drill as a matter of routine. Drills shall include suitable procedures to ensure that all persons subject to the drill participate. [*101*:4.7.2]

10.6.3 Orderly Evacuation. When conducting drills, emphasis shall be placed on orderly evacuation rather than on speed. [*101*:4.7.3]

10.6.4* Simulated Conditions. Drills shall be held at expected and unexpected times and under varying conditions to simulate the unusual conditions that can occur in an actual emergency. [*101*:4.7.4]

10.6.5 Relocation Area. Drill participants shall relocate to a predetermined location and remain at such location until a recall or dismissal signal is given. [*101*:4.7.5]

10.6.6* A written record of each drill shall be completed by the person responsible for conducting the drill and maintained in an approved manner. [*101*:4.7.6]

10.7 Reporting of Fires and Other Emergencies.

10.7.1 Fire Reporting.

10.7.1.1 The person discovering any unwanted fire, regardless of magnitude, shall immediately notify the fire department.

10.7.1.2 Facilities that have established on-premises firefighting organizations and have coordinated and arranged procedures approved by the AHJ shall not need to notify the fire department.

10.7.1.3* The owner, manager, occupant, or any person in control of such building or premises, upon discovery of an unwanted fire or evidence of a previous unwanted fire that had apparently been extinguished, shall immediately notify the fire department.

10.7.1.4 Persons shall not make, issue, post, or maintain any regulation or order, written or verbal, that would require any person to take any unnecessary delaying action prior to reporting a fire to the fire department.

10.7.2 Persons shall not deliberately or maliciously turn in an alarm of fire when in fact that person knows that no fire exists.

10.7.3 Notification of unauthorized discharge of hazardous materials shall be in accordance with Chapter 60.

10.7.4 Any person who willfully makes any false, fraudulent, misleading, or unfounded report or statement or willfully misrepresents any fact with the intention of misleading any fire department personnel or who interferes with the operation of the fire department shall be in violation of this *Code*.

10.8 Tampering with Fire Safety Equipment.

10.8.1 Persons shall not render any portable or fixed fire-extinguishing system or device or any fire-warning system or device inoperative or inaccessible.

10.8.1.1 As necessary during emergencies, maintenance, drills, prescribed testing, alterations, or renovations, portable or fixed fire-extinguishing systems or devices or any fire-warning system or device shall be permitted to be made inoperative or inaccessible.

10.8.2 Persons shall not render a fire protection system or device inoperative during an emergency unless by direction of the incident commander.

10.8.3 Persons, except a person authorized by the AHJ, shall not remove, unlock, destroy, or tamper with in any manner any locked gate, door, or barricade; chain; enclosure; sign; tag; or seal that has been required by the AHJ pursuant to this *Code*.

10.9 Smoking.

10.9.1 Where smoking is considered a fire hazard, the AHJ shall be authorized to order the owner in writing to post "No Smoking" signs in conspicuous, designated locations where smoking is prohibited.

10.9.2 In areas where smoking is permitted, noncombustible ashtrays shall be provided.

10.9.3 Removal or destruction of any required "No Smoking" sign shall be prohibited.

10.9.4 Smoking or depositing any lighted or smoldering substance in a place where required "No Smoking" signs are posted shall be prohibited.

10.10 Open Flames, Candles, Open Fires, and Incinerators.

10.10.1 Permits. Permits, where required, shall comply with Section 1.13.

10.10.1.1 Permits shall not be required for cooking and recreational fires.

10.10.1.2 Where burning is conducted on public property or the property of someone other than the permit applicant, the permit applicant shall demonstrate that permission has been obtained by the appropriate government agency, the owner, or the owner's authorized agent.

10.10.1.3 When limits for atmospheric conditions or hours restrict burning, such limits shall be designated in the permit restrictions.

10.10.1.4 Instructions or stipulations of permit shall be followed.

10.10.2* The AHJ shall have the authority to prohibit any or all open flames, use of fireworks, candles, and open, recreational, and cooking fires or other sources of ignition, or establish special regulations on the use of any form of fire or smoking material where circumstances make such conditions hazardous.

10.10.3 Outdoor Fires.

10.10.3.1* Outdoor fires shall not be built, ignited, or maintained in or upon hazardous fire areas, except by permit from the AHJ.

10.10.3.2 Permanent barbecues, portable barbecues, outdoor fireplaces, or grills shall not be used for the disposal of rubbish, trash, or combustible waste material.

10.10.4 Open Fires.

10.10.4.1 Permitted open fires shall be located not less than 50 ft (15 m) from any structure.

10.10.4.2 Burning hours shall be prescribed by the AHJ.

10.10.4.3 Recreational fires shall not be located within 25 ft (7.6 m) of a structure or combustible material unless contained in an approved manner.

10.10.4.4 Conditions that could cause a fire to spread to within 25 ft (7.6 m) of a structure shall be eliminated prior to ignition.

10.10.5 Fire Attendant.

10.10.5.1 Open, recreational, and cooking fires shall be constantly attended by a competent person until such fire is extinguished.

10.10.5.2 This person shall have a garden hose connected to the water supply or other fire-extinguishing equipment readily available for use.

10.10.6 Cooking Equipment.

10.10.6.1 Unless permitted by 10.10.6.2, for other than one- and two-family dwellings, outdoor cooking appliances, grills, or other similar devices intended for cooking, heating, or any other purpose shall not be used, kindled, or stored in any of the following locations:

(1) On any balcony
(2) Under any overhanging portion of a structure
(3) Within 10 ft (3 m) of any structure

N **10.10.6.2** In residential occupancies protected throughout by an approved sprinkler system, which includes the areas in 10.10.6.1(1) and 10.10.6.1(2) or of Type I or Type II construction, electrically powered cooking appliances listed and labeled in accordance with UL 1026, *Standard for Household Electric Cooking and Food Serving Appliances,* and operated in accordance with the manufacturer's instructions shall be permitted to be used or stored in any of the locations in 10.10.6.1.

N **10.10.6.2.1** Electric cooking equipment intended for exterior use in accordance with 10.10.6.2 shall not be used in any enclosed space.

N **10.10.6.2.2** A minimum clearance of 24 in. (610 mm) shall be maintained from the building and combustibles, unless otherwise permitted by the manufacturer's instructions.

10.10.6.3* Listed equipment permanently installed in accordance with its listing, applicable codes, and manufacturer's instructions shall be permitted.

10.10.7 Installation of Patio Heaters. The installation of patio heaters shall comply with 69.3.13.

10.10.8 Incinerators and Fireplaces.

10.10.8.1 Incinerators, outdoor fireplaces, permanent barbecues, and grills shall not be built, installed, or maintained without prior approval of the AHJ.

10.10.8.2 Incinerators, outdoor fireplaces, permanent barbecues, and grills shall be maintained in good repair and in a safe condition at all times.

10.10.8.3 Openings in incinerators, outdoor fireplaces, permanent barbecues, and grills shall be provided with an approved spark arrester, screen, or door.

10.10.9 Open-Flame Devices.

10.10.9.1* Welding torches, tar pots, decorative torches, and other devices, machines, or processes liable to start or cause an unwanted fire shall not be operated or used in or upon any areas, except by permit from the AHJ.

10.10.9.2 Flame-employing devices, such as lanterns or kerosene road flares, and fuses shall not be operated or used as a signal or marker in or upon any areas unless at the scene of emergencies or railroad operations. *(See Chapter 16 and Chapter 65 for additional guidance.)*

10.10.9.3 The use of unmanned, free-floating sky lanterns and similar devices utilizing an open flame shall be prohibited.

10.10.10* Discontinuance. The AHJ shall be authorized to require any fire to be immediately discontinued if the fire or smoke generated by such fire is determined to constitute a hazardous condition.

10.11 Fire Protection Markings.

10.11.1* Premises Identification.

10.11.1.1* New and existing buildings shall have approved address numbers placed in a position to be plainly legible and visible from the street or road fronting the property.

10.11.1.2 Address numbers shall be a minimum of 4 in. (100 mm) high with a minimum stroke width of ½ in. (13 mm).

10.11.1.3 Address numbers shall contrast with their background.

10.11.1.4 Address numbers shall be arabic numerals or alphabet letters.

10.11.1.5* Telecommunications equipment utilized to communicate address data to E911 communication centers shall be programmed and maintained to accurately convey such address information to the E911 communication center.

10.11.1.6 The assignment of addresses to buildings shall be in accordance with a method approved by the AHJ.

10.11.1.7 Addresses shall not be changed unless approved by that AHJ.

10.11.1.8 Address numbers for suites within a multiple tenant building or complex shall be individually identified in a manner approved by the AHJ.

10.11.2 Shaftways to Be Marked for Fire Fighter Safety.

10.11.2.1 Every outside opening accessible to the fire department that opens directly on any hoistway or shaftway communicating between two or more floors in a building shall be plainly marked with a sign in accordance with 10.11.2.2 and 10.11.2.3.

10.11.2.2 Shaftway signs shall be in red letters at least 6 in. (152 mm) high on a white background stating "SHAFTWAY."

10.11.2.3 Such warning signs shall be placed so as to be readily discernible from the outside of the building.

10.11.3* Stairway Identification.

10.11.3.1 New enclosed stairs serving three or more stories and existing enclosed stairs, other than those addressed in 10.11.3.1.16, serving five or more stories shall comply with 10.11.3.1.1 through 10.11.3.1.15. [*101*:7.2.2.5.4.1]

10.11.3.1.1 The stairs shall be provided with special signage within the enclosure at each floor landing. [*101*:7.2.2.5.4.1(A)]

10.11.3.1.2 The signage shall indicate the floor level. [*101*:7.2.2.5.4.1(B)]

10.11.3.1.3 The signage shall indicate the terminus of the top and bottom of the stair enclosure. [*101*:7.2.2.5.4.1(C)]

10.11.3.1.4 The signage shall indicate the identification of the stair enclosure. [*101*:7.2.2.5.4.1(D)]

10.11.3.1.5 The signage shall indicate the floor level of, and the direction to, exit discharge. [*101*:7.2.2.5.4.1(E)]

10.11.3.1.6 The signage shall be located inside the stair enclosure. [*101*:7.2.2.5.4.1(F)]

10.11.3.1.7 The bottom of the signage shall be located a minimum of 48 in. (1220 mm) above the floor landing, and the top of the signage shall be located a maximum of 84 in. (2135 mm) above the floor landing. [*101*:7.2.2.5.4.1(G)]

10.11.3.1.8 The signage shall be in a position that is visible from within the stair enclosure when the door is in the open or closed position. [*101*:7.2.2.5.4.1(H)]

10.11.3.1.9 The signage shall comply with 14.14.8.1 and 14.14.8.2. [*101*:7.2.2.5.4.1(I)]

10.11.3.1.10 The floor level designation shall also be tactile in accordance with ICC A117.1, *Accessible and Usable Buildings and Facilities*. [*101*:7.2.2.5.4.1(J)]

10.11.3.1.11 The signage shall be painted or stenciled on the wall or on a separate sign securely attached to the wall. [*101*:7.2.2.5.4.1(K)]

10.11.3.1.12 The stairway identification shall be located at the top of the sign in minimum 1 in. (25 mm) high lettering and shall be in accordance with 14.14.8.2. [*101*:7.2.2.5.4.1(L)]

10.11.3.1.13* Signage that reads NO ROOF ACCESS shall designate stairways that do not provide roof access. Lettering shall be a minimum of 1 in. (25 mm) high and shall be in accordance with 14.14.8.2. [*101*:7.2.2.5.4.1(M)]

10.11.3.1.14 The floor level number shall be located below the stairway identifier in minimum 5 in. (125 mm) high numbers and shall be in accordance with 14.14.8.2. Mezzanine levels shall have the letter "M" or other appropriate identification letter preceding the floor number, while basement levels shall have the letter "B" or other appropriate identification letter preceding the floor level number. [*101*:7.2.2.5.4.1(N)]

10.11.3.1.15 Identification of the lower and upper terminus of the stairway shall be on the sign in minimum 1 in. (25 mm) high letters or numbers and shall be in accordance with 14.14.8.2. [*101*:7.2.2.5.4.1(O)]

10.11.3.1.16 Previously approved existing signage shall not be required to comply with 10.11.3.1.12 through 10.11.3.1.15. [*101*:7.2.2.5.4.1(P)]

10.11.3.2 Wherever an enclosed stair requires travel in an upward direction to reach the level of exit discharge, special signs with directional indicators showing the direction to the level of exit discharge shall be provided at each floor level landing from which upward direction of travel is required, unless otherwise provided in 10.11.3.2.1 and 10.11.3.2.2, and both of the following also shall apply:

(1) Such signage shall comply with 14.14.8.1 and 14.14.8.2.

(2) Such signage shall be visible when the door leaf is in the open or closed position.
[*101*:7.2.2.5.4.2]

10.11.3.2.1 The requirement of 10.11.3.2 shall not apply where signs required by 10.11.3.1.1 are provided. [*101*:7.2.2.5.4.2(A)]

10.11.3.2.2 The requirement of 10.11.3.2 shall not apply to stairs extending not more than one story below the level of exit discharge where the exit discharge is clearly obvious. [*101*:7.2.2.5.4.2(B)]

10.11.3.3 These signs shall be maintained in an approved manner.

10.11.3.4 Existing approved signs shall be permitted.

10.12 Seasonal and Vacant Buildings and Premises.

10.12.1 Every person owning or having charge or control of any vacant building, premises, or portion thereof shall remove all combustible storage, waste, refuse, and vegetation and shall lock, barricade, or otherwise secure the building or premises to prohibit entry by unauthorized persons.

10.12.1.1 The requirement of 10.12.1 shall not apply to buildings used on a seasonal basis, or the temporary vacancy of a building for tenant change or remodeling purposes.

10.12.2 All fire protection systems shall be maintained in service in seasonal and vacant buildings, unless otherwise approved by the AHJ.

10.12.2.1* With the approval of the AHJ, fire protection and fire alarm systems in seasonal and vacant buildings shall be permitted to be removed from service.

10.12.2.2 When required by the AHJ, other systems or components pertaining to fire protection shall be maintained.

10.12.3 The AHJ shall have the authority to require an inspection and test of any fire protection system or fire alarm system that has been out of service for 30 days or more before restored back into service.

10.13 Combustible Vegetation.

10.13.1 Interior Vegetation. Interior vegetation shall comply with 12.6.9.

10.13.2 Exterior Vegetation.

10.13.2.1 Cut or uncut weeds, grass, vines, and other vegetation shall be removed when determined by the AHJ to be a fire hazard.

10.13.2.2 When the AHJ determines that total removal of growth is impractical due to size or environmental factors, approved fuel breaks shall be established.

10.13.2.3 Designated areas shall be cleared of combustible vegetation to establish the fuel breaks.

10.14 Special Outdoor Events, Carnivals, and Fairs.

10.14.1 Permits. Permits, where required, shall comply with Section 1.13.

10.14.2 The AHJ shall be permitted to regulate all outdoor events such as carnivals and fairs as it pertains to access for emergency vehicles; access to fire protection equipment; placement of stands, concession booths, and exhibits; and the control of hazardous conditions dangerous to life and property.

10.14.3 Life Safety Evaluation. The AHJ shall be permitted to order a life safety evaluation in accordance with this subsection.

10.14.3.1* General. Where a life safety evaluation is required by other provisions of the *Code*, it shall comply with all of the following:

(1) The life safety evaluation shall be performed by persons acceptable to the AHJ.
(2) The life safety evaluation shall include a written assessment of safety measures for conditions listed in 10.14.3.2 and of the building systems and facility management in accordance with 10.14.3.3.
(3) The life safety evaluation shall be approved annually and shall be updated for special or unusual conditions in accordance with the provisions of 13.4.2 of NFPA *101* for existing assembly occupancies.

[*101*:12.4.2.1]

10.14.3.2 Conditions to Be Assessed. Life safety evaluations shall include an assessment of all of the following conditions and related appropriate safety measures:

(1) Nature of the events and the participants and attendees
(2) Access and egress movement, including crowd density problems
(3) Medical emergencies
(4) Fire hazards
(5) Permanent and temporary structural systems
(6) Severe weather conditions
(7) Earthquakes
(8) Civil or other disturbances
(9) Hazardous materials incidents within and near the facility
(10) Relationships among facility management, event participants, emergency response agencies, and others having a role in the events accommodated in the facility

[*101*:12.4.2.2]

10.14.3.3* Building Systems and Facility Management Assessments. Life safety evaluations shall include assessments of both building systems and facility management upon which reliance is placed for the safety of facility occupants, and such assessments shall consider scenarios appropriate to the facility. [*101*:12.4.2.3]

10.14.3.3.1 Building Systems. Prior to issuance of the building permit, the design team shall provide the AHJ with building systems documentation in accordance with 10.14.3.4. [*101*:12.4.2.3.1]

10.14.3.3.2 Facility Management. Prior to issuance of the certificate of occupancy, the facility management shall provide the AHJ with facility management documentation in accordance with 10.14.3.5. [*101*:12.4.2.3.2]

10.14.3.3.3 Life Safety Evaluation.

10.14.3.3.3.1 Prior to issuance of the building permit, the persons performing the life safety evaluation shall confirm that the building systems provide safety measures. [*101*:12.4.2.3.3.1]

10.14.3.3.3.2 Prior to issuance of the certificate of occupancy, the owner shall confirm that the facility management and operational plans provide appropriate safety measures. [*101*:12.4.2.3.3.2]

10.14.3.3.3.3 The life safety evaluation shall be performed by persons acceptable to the AHJ. [*101*:12.4.2.3.3.3]

10.14.3.4 Life Safety Building Systems Document. The AHJ shall be provided with a life safety building systems document providing the information required in 10.14.3.4.2 through 10.14.3.4.4. [*101*:12.4.2.4]

10.14.3.4.1 Document Distribution. The persons performing the life safety evaluation, the AHJ, the A/E design team, and the building owner shall receive a copy of the life safety building systems document prior to issuance of the building permit. [*101*:12.4.2.4.1]

Δ **10.14.3.4.2 Life Safety Narrative.** A life safety narrative shall be provided describing the following, as applicable:

(1) Building occupancy, construction type, and intended uses and events
(2) Building area and population capacity of the proposed facility
(3) Principal fire and life safety features/strategies for the building, including, as applicable, the following:
 (a) Egress
 (b) Access control
 (c) Fire barriers, smoke barriers, and smoke partitions
 (d) Fire suppression systems
 (e) Smoke control/protection
 (f) Fire detection and alarm
 (g) PA system
 (h) Emergency elevator operation
 (i) Emergency power and lighting
 (j) Provisions for patrons with disabilities
 (k) Fire department access
 (l) Fire/emergency command center
(4) Exterior construction design parameters used/applied

[*101*:12.4.2.4.2]

10.14.3.4.3 Life Safety Floor Plans. Life safety floor plans of each level shall be provided, as applicable, with the following:

(1) Occupant load, exit location, egress capacity, main entrance/exit, horizontal exits, travel distance, and exit discharge
(2) Fire barriers, smoke barriers, and smoke partitions
(3) Areas of smoke-protected assembly occupancy
(4) Separate smoke-protected areas or zones
(5) Areas of other occupancy type and separations
(6) Unprotected vertical openings
(7) Event plans for each anticipated type of event depicting the following:
 (a) Seating configuration
 (b) Exhibit booth layout
 (c) Stage location
 (d) Occupant load, egress capacity required, exits provided, and travel distance
 (e) Any floor or stage use restrictions
 (f) Plan and/or section drawing indicating where sprinkler protection is omitted
 (g) Areas of refuge — interior and exterior

[*101*:12.4.2.4.3]

Δ **10.14.3.4.4 Engineering Analysis and Calculations.** Where active or passive smoke control is used, an engineering analysis shall be provided and shall include the following, as applicable:

(1) Smoke protection analysis to substitute the use of smoke-protected assembly seating as follows:
 (a) Performance-based design methods approved by the AHJ
 (b) Smoke control requirements per NFPA 92
 (c) Smoke control assumptions, such as fire scenario description, fire size quantification, and smoke development/smoke movement analysis
 (d) Proposed testing protocol for smoke control system and pass/fail criteria
 (e) Timed egress analysis assumed flow rates and travel speeds
(2) Sprinkler protection calculations, including an engineering analysis substantiating locations in accordance with 13.3.2.5.3 where sprinkler protection would be ineffective due to height and combustible loading
(3) Load diagram of rigging/load capacity of gridiron, fly loft, or long-span roof structure used for hanging overhead objects

[*101*:12.4.2.4.4]

10.14.3.5 Life Safety Management Document. The AHJ shall be provided with a life safety management document providing the information required in 10.14.3.5.2 through 10.14.3.5.7. [*101*:12.4.2.5]

10.14.3.5.1 Document Distribution. The persons performing the life safety evaluation, the AHJ, the A/E design team and the building owner shall receive a copy of the life safety management document prior to issuance of the certificate of occupancy. [*101*:12.4.2.5.1]

10.14.3.5.2 Facility Management and Operational Plans. Facility management and operational plans shall address the following, as applicable:

(1) Best practices adopted or recognized
(2) Emergency plans
(3) Evacuation plans
(4) Shelter-in-place plans, including capacities and protection considerations
(5) Crowd management training plan
(6) Safety plans, which include the following:
 (a) Training plans
 (b) Safety equipment plans
(7) Fire alarm, smoke control system protocol, and testing plans
(8) First aid or medical treatment plans, which include the following:
 (a) Defined levels of service
 (b) Standing orders adopted
 (c) Supply and equipment plan
(9) Housekeeping plans — biological, medical, hazardous materials cleaning
(10) Emergency communication plans, which include the following:
 (a) Chain of authority and incident command system employed
 (b) Contact information for the following:
  i. Venue personnel
  ii. Emergency management and response organizations (such as fire, police, medical, utility, transportation, and key stakeholders)
 (c) Communication systems

(d) Standard announcement for incidents or emergency situations
(11) Risk and threat assessment for venue and surrounding area for the following:
 (a) Severe weather
 (b) Hazardous materials
 (c) Terrorism
 (d) Hostile intruder
(12) Operating procedures and protocols for risks, such as the following:
 (a) Severe weather preparedness and monitoring plans
 (b) Hazardous materials incidence response plans
 (c) Terrorism response plans
 (d) Hostile intruder response plans
(13) First responder response/arrival routes plans
(14) Alcohol management plans
(15) Food safety plans
(16) Rigging and temporary performance structure, which includes the following:
 (a) Design and safety review plans
 (b) Emergency action plans
(17) Chemical and hazardous materials information and data
(18) Barrier and wall protection plans for motor sports or similar events
[*101*:12.4.2.5.2]

Δ **10.14.3.5.3 Records.** Records of the facility management plans, including procedures and location, shall be maintained for the following:

(1) Crowd management training
(2) Safety training
(3) Fire alarm, smoke control system maintenance, and test records
(4) First aid or medical treatment and regulation compliance
[*101*:12.4.2.5.3]

10.14.3.5.4 Building Systems Reference Guide. A building systems reference guide shall be provided in accordance with 10.14.3.5.4.1 through 10.14.3.5.4.3. [*101*:12.4.2.5.4]

10.14.3.5.4.1 A basic life safety building systems reference guide shall be developed and maintained. [*101*:12.4.2.5.4.1]

10.14.3.5.4.2 The life safety building systems reference guide shall contain the important and key information for the venue management's use when planning events/activities for the safety of patrons, performers/participants, employees, and vendors. [*101*:12.4.2.5.4.2]

Δ **10.14.3.5.4.3** The life safety building systems document in accordance with 10.14.3.4 shall be permitted to be used, and additionally the life safety building systems reference guide shall include the following, as applicable:

(1) Occupant capacity of every space/room
(2) Egress flow diagrams, including assumed flow rates, and capacities of all aisles and hallways, including public and nonpublic areas
(3) Capacities of all exterior doors and/or choke points in immediate perimeter areas
(4) Limitations or assumptions for ingress control that could be in place during an emergency egress/evacuation, including control gates, queuing barriers, and turnstiles
(5) Capacities of immediate perimeter exterior walkways, including assumed flow rates for exterior areas
(6) Assumed egress paths for normal conditions — transportation modes
(7) Management-level sequencing charts for alarm and emergency communication systems, the manual, or override options/instructions that include the following:
 (a) List of codes or alarm signals
 (b) Location of manual overrides
 (c) Description of sequence of operations during an alarm, such as exhaust fans operate or doors open
(8) Principal fire and life safety features/strategies, such as sprinklers, smoke control, fire alarm notifications, PA system, emergency power, and fire department access
(9) Assumptions when developing occupancy plans for venue floor, open areas, and nonevent spaces, such as the following:
 (a) Event floor plans/setup diagrams for each typical event/activity
 (b) Fire sprinkler and smoke protection capabilities
(10) Severe weather shelter areas, locations, structure considerations (limitations), capacities (occupancy and density factor)
(11) Command center, which includes the following:
 (a) Location (formal or informal)
 (b) Structural integrity considerations
 (c) Redundant locations and/or capabilities
 (d) Jurisdictional rights — assumed and/or applied
(12) Locations and capacities of wheelchair spaces and seats with movable aisle armrests
(13) Locations and capacities of areas of refuge and other safe areas
(14) Rigging or structural load capacities of grids, truss structure, fly lofts, ceilings, floors, ramps, and staging
(15) List of locations of emergency equipment such as fire extinguishers, fire hose cabinets, fire hydrants, and AEDs
(16) Sequencing of electrical service, such as the following:
 (a) Emergency generators and charts of all areas illuminated during power outages
 (b) Multiple electrical feed capabilities
(17) List of mechanical, movable equipment in the facility
(18) Potential hazards in the surrounding neighborhood, including train tracks and propane stations
(19) Assumptions or accommodations considered and used in design
[*101*:12.4.2.5.4.3]

10.14.3.5.5 The facility management plans shall be maintained and adjusted as necessary for changes to the venue structure, operating purposes and style, and event occupancy. [*101*:12.4.2.5.5]

10.14.3.5.6 Facility management and operational plans shall be submitted to the AHJ annually. [*101*:12.4.2.5.6]

10.14.3.5.7 For events and activities at the venue that are outside the normal operating conditions or vary from the normal facility management plans, the following shall apply:

(1) Facility management shall perform an event/activity-specific facility management plan for the AHJ to review.
(2) Approval of the AHJ for the specific facility management plan shall occur prior to such event.
[*101*:12.4.2.5.7]

10.14.4 Standby Fire Personnel. Where required by the AHJ, standby fire personnel shall be provided and comply with 1.7.17.

10.14.5 Portable Fire Extinguishers. A minimum of one portable fire extinguisher shall be provided for each concession stand where required by the AHJ in accordance with Section 13.6.

10.14.6 Smoke Alarms. A minimum of one single station smoke alarm shall be located in all stock or equipment trailers when they are used for sleeping purposes.

10.14.7 Carbon Monoxide Alarm. A minimum of one single station carbon monoxide alarm shall be located in all stock or equipment trailers when they are used for sleeping purposes and contain fuel-fired appliances.

10.14.8 Electrical Equipment. Electrical equipment and installations shall comply with Section 11.1.

10.14.9 Cooking. Concession stands utilized for cooking shall comply with both of the following:

(1) Have a minimum of 10 ft (3 m) of clearance on sides where an exposure exists
(2) Not be located within 10 ft (3 m) of amusement rides or devices

10.14.10 Communications. Where required by the AHJ, a method of notifying the fire department in the event of an emergency shall be provided.

10.14.10.1 Methods of notifying the fire department shall consist of a telephone, an alarm system connected to the fire department or other approved agency, or other approved means.

10.14.10.2 Methods of notifying the fire department shall be readily available to the public.

10.14.11 Internal Combustion Power Sources.

10.14.11.1 Fueling. Fuel tanks shall be of adequate capacity to permit uninterrupted operation during normal operating hours.

10.14.11.2 Refueling. Refueling shall be conducted only when not in use.

10.14.11.3 Protection. Internal combustion power sources shall be isolated from contact with the public by either physical guards, fencing, or an enclosure.

10.14.11.4 Fire Extinguishers. A minimum of one portable fire extinguisher with a rating of not less than 2-A:10-B:C shall be provided.

10.14.12 Crop Maze.

10.14.12.1 Permits. Permits, where required, shall comply with Section 1.13.

10.14.12.2 General.

10.14.12.2.1 The owner or operator of a crop maze amusement attraction shall advise all employees of the fire and life safety regulations established in this subsection prior to the employees assuming their respective duties.

10.14.12.2.2 The owner or operator of a crop maze or their employees shall provide safety instructions to the visitors and patrons of a crop maze prior to their entrance to the maze.

10.14.12.2.3 Employee Monitor.

10.14.12.2.3.1 A minimum of two employees shall be on duty to monitor a crop maze during hours of operation.

10.14.12.2.3.2 A minimum of one of the employees shall be located on an elevated platform a minimum of 10 ft (3 m) above the maze.

10.14.12.2.4 The owner or operator of a crop maze shall contact the local fire department and provide the fire department with the opportunity to prepare a pre-plan of the crop maze amusement attraction prior to the start of seasonal operations.

10.14.12.2.5 Motorized vehicles shall not be parked within 75 ft (23 m) of a crop maze.

10.14.12.2.6 A fuel break of a minimum of 20 ft (6 m) wide shall be cleared between a crop maze and any vehicles or vegetation outside the maze.

10.14.12.2.7 Public Address System.

10.14.12.2.7.1 A public address system shall be readily available to employees at a crop maze to assist them in making announcements to the visitors or patrons of a crop maze in the event of an emergency.

10.14.12.2.7.2 A bull horn or loud speaker shall suffice as a public address system.

10.14.12.2.8 The entrance and exit from a crop maze shall not be blocked or obstructed at any time the maze is open for business and occupied by the public.

10.14.12.2.9 No more than 200 persons per acre, including adults and children, shall occupy the crop maze at any one time.

10.14.12.3 Prohibited.

10.14.12.3.1* No open flame-producing devices or equipment shall be permitted within the confines of the crop maze.

10.14.12.3.2 No smoking shall be permitted within the confines of the crop maze.

10.14.12.4 Fireworks.

10.14.12.4.1 Fireworks shall not be discharged within a minimum of 300 ft (91 m) of any crop maze at any time.

10.14.12.4.2 The use of display fireworks shall comply with Chapter 65 in addition to the requirements of 10.14.12.4.

10.15 Portable and Vehicle-Mounted Generators.

10.15.1 Scope.

10.15.1.1 Portable and vehicle-mounted generators shall comply with Section 10.15.

Δ **10.15.1.2** Section 10.15 shall not apply to portable and vehicle-mounted generators used solely for mobile and temporary cooking operations. *(See Section 50.8.)*

10.15.1.3 Section 10.15 shall not apply to stationary generators. *(See Section 11.7.)*

10.15.2 Portable generators manufactured after January 1, 2021, other than vehicle-mounted generators, shall be listed and labeled in accordance with the carbon monoxide mitigation requirements in UL 2201, *Carbon Monoxide Emission Rate of Portable Generators*.

10.15.3 Portable and vehicle-mounted generators shall be operated and maintained in accordance with the manufacturer's instructions.

10.15.4 Portable and vehicle-mounted generators shall not be refueled while operating.

10.15.5 Operation of Portable and Vehicle-Mounted Generators.

10.15.5.1* Portable and vehicle-mounted generators shall only be operated or refueled outdoors a minimum of 20 ft (6.1 m) from any building openings, including windows, doors, and air intakes.

10.15.5.2* Portable and vehicle-mounted generators shall not be operated within buildings or enclosed areas, except as permitted in 10.15.5.

10.15.6 Portable and vehicle-mounted generators shall be permitted to be operated and refueled in a building or room that has been constructed for such use in accordance with the building code.

10.15.7 Portable and vehicle-mounted generators shall be positioned so the exhaust is directed away from openings in buildings, tents, and membrane structures.

10.15.8* Portable and vehicle-mounted generators shall be grounded in accordance with *NFPA 70*.

10.15.9 Extension cords and temporary wiring used to connect portable and vehicle-mounted generators shall comply with Chapter 11 and shall be provided with GFCI protection.

10.15.10 Connections to a premise wiring system shall comply with all of the following:

(1)* Connection to a premise served by commercial power shall be made through a listed transfer switch installed, used, and maintained in accordance with *NFPA 70*.
(2) Connections to buildings not served by utility power shall comply with *NFPA 70*.

10.16* Outside Storage.

10.16.1 Outside storage of combustible materials shall not be located within 10 ft (3 m) of a property line.

10.16.2 The separation distance shall be allowed to be reduced to 3 ft (0.9 m) for storage not exceeding 6 ft (1.8 m) in height.

10.16.3 The separation distance shall be allowed to be reduced where the AHJ determines that no hazard to the adjoining property exists.

10.16.4 Combustible material shall not be stored beneath a building or structure unless specifically constructed or protected for this purpose.

10.16.5 Combustible storage in the open shall not exceed 20 ft (6.1 m) in height.

10.17 Parade Floats.

10.17.1 Permits. Permits, where required, shall comply with Section 1.13.

10.17.2 Fire Protection. Motorized parade floats and towing apparatus shall be provided with a minimum 2-A:10-B:C-rated portable fire extinguisher readily accessible to the operator.

10.18 Powered Industrial Trucks. Powered industrial trucks shall be operated and maintained in accordance with NFPA 505.

10.19* Storage of Combustible Materials.

10.19.1 General. Storage of combustible materials shall be orderly.

10.19.2 Permits. Permits, where required, shall comply with Section 1.13.

10.19.3 Ceiling Clearance.

10.19.3.1 Storage shall be maintained 2 ft (0.61 m) or more from the ceiling in nonsprinklered areas of buildings.

Δ **10.19.3.2** Unless greater distances are required by 10.19.3.3, 10.19.3.4, or 10.19.3.5, or lesser distances permitted by 10.19.3.6, clearance between the deflector and the top of storage shall be 18 in. (457 mm) or greater. [25:5.2.1.2.1]

N **10.19.3.3** Clearance between the deflector and the top of storage shall be 36 in. (914 mm) or greater for special sprinklers. [25:5.2.1.2.2]

N **10.19.3.4** Where standards other than NFPA 13 specify greater clearance to storage minimums, they shall be followed. [25:5.2.1.2.3]

N **10.19.3.5** Clearance from the top of storage to sprinkler deflectors shall be 36 in. (914 mm) or greater where rubber tires are stored. [25:5.2.1.2.4]

N **10.19.3.6** In-rack sprinklers shall not be required to meet the obstruction criteria and clearance from storage requirements. [25:5.2.1.2.5]

N **10.19.3.7** Clearance between the deflector and the top of storage shall be permitted to be less than 18 in. (457 mm) where shown to be permitted by the installation standard. [25:5.2.1.2.6]

10.19.4 Means of Egress. Combustible material shall not be stored in exits.

10.19.5 Equipment Rooms.

10.19.5.1 Combustible material shall not be stored in boiler rooms, mechanical rooms, or electrical equipment rooms.

10.19.5.2 Materials and supplies for the operation and maintenance of the equipment in the room shall be permitted.

10.19.6 Attic, Under-Floor, and Concealed Spaces. Attic, under-floor, and concealed spaces used for storage of combustible materials shall comply with the protection from hazards requirements for storage rooms in NFPA *101*.

10.19.7 Fueled Equipment. Fueled equipment, including but not limited to motorcycles, mopeds, lawn-care equipment, and portable cooking equipment, shall not be stored, operated, or repaired within a building except under one of the following conditions:

(1) The building or room has been constructed for such use in accordance with the building code.
(2) The use is allowed by other provisions of this *Code*.

10.20 Indoor Play Structures.

10.20.1 Play structures installed indoors and exceeding 10 ft (3.1 m) in height or 160 ft^2 (14.9 m^2) in area shall comply with the specifications in 10.20.1.1 through 10.20.1.5.

10.20.1.1 Indoor play structures shall be constructed of noncombustible materials or of combustible materials that comply with the following:

(1) Wood shall be fire-retardant-treated wood.
(2) Light-transmitting plastics shall comply with the requirements in 10.20.1.2.
(3) Foam plastics (including the pipe foam used in soft-contained play equipment structures) shall have a maximum heat-release rate not greater than 100 kW when tested in accordance with UL 1975, *Fire Tests for Foamed Plastics Used for Decorative Purposes*, or NFPA 289 using the 20 kW ignition source.
(4) Aluminum composite material (ACM) shall meet the requirements of Class A interior finish in accordance with Chapter 10 of NFPA *101* when tested as an assembly in the maximum thickness intended for use.
(5) Textiles and films shall comply with the flame propagation performance criteria contained in Test Method 1 or Test Method 2, as appropriate, of NFPA 701.
(6) Plastic materials used to construct rigid components of soft-contained play equipment structures (such as tubes, windows, panels, junction boxes, pipes, slides, and decks) shall exhibit a peak rate of heat release not exceeding 400 kW/m^2 when tested in accordance with ASTM E1354, *Standard Test Method for Heat and Visible Smoke Release Rates for Materials and Products Using an Oxygen Consumption Calorimeter*, at an incident heat flux of 0.24 in. (6 mm) 50 kW/m^2 in the horizontal orientation at a thickness of 0.24 in. (6 mm).
(7) The balls used in ball pools, in soft-contained play equipment structures, shall comply with all of the following:
   (a) The balls shall have a maximum heat release rate not greater than 100 kW when tested in accordance with UL 1975 or NFPA 289 using the 20 kW ignition source.
   (b) The minimum specimen test size for balls shall be 36 in. × 36 in. (0.91 m × 0.91 m) by an average of 21 in. (0.56 m) deep.
   (c) The balls shall be held in a box constructed of galvanized steel poultry netting wire mesh.
(8) Foam plastics shall be covered by fabric, coating, or film meeting the flame propagation performance criteria contained in Test Method 1 or Test Method 2, as appropriate, of NFPA 701.
(9) The floor covering within the play structure shall exhibit a Class I interior floor finish classification, as described in Chapter 10 of NFPA *101*, when tested in accordance with NFPA 253 or with ASTM E648, *Standard Test Method for Critical Radiant Flux of Floor-Covering Systems Using a Radiant Heat Energy Source*.

10.20.1.2* Light-transmitting plastics used for indoor play structures shall meet all of the following criteria:

(1) They shall have a self-ignition temperature of 650°F (343°C) or greater when tested in accordance with ASTM D1929, *Standard Test Method for Determining Ignition Temperature of Plastics*.
(2) They shall have a smoke developed index not greater than 450 when tested in the manner intended for use in accordance with ASTM E84, *Standard Test Method for Surface Burning Characteristics of Building Materials*, or UL 723, *Test for Surface Burning Characteristics of Building Materials*, or not greater than 75 when tested in the thickness intended for use in accordance with ASTM D2843, *Standard Test Method for Density of Smoke from the Burning or Decomposition of Plastics*.
(3) They shall meet the criteria of one of the following classifications:
   (a) CC1 — Plastic materials that have a burn length of 1 in. (25 mm) or less and flame extinguishment when tested at a nominal thickness of 0.060 in. (1.5 mm), or in the thickness intended for use, in accordance with ASTM D635, *Standard Test Method for Rate of Burning and/or Extent and Time of Burning of Plastics in a Horizontal Position*
   (b) CC2 — Plastic materials that have a burning rate of 2½ in./min (64 mm/min) or less when tested at a nominal thickness of 0.060 in. (1.5 mm), or at a thickness intended for use, in accordance with ASTM D635

10.20.1.3 Where interior finish materials are added to an individual indoor play structure exceeding 300 ft^2 (28 m^2) in area, the interior finish material shall comply with the applicable occupancy chapter in NFPA 101.

10.20.1.4 Indoor play structures shall have a minimum horizontal separation from other structures of 20 ft (6.1 m).

10.20.1.5* Indoor play structures complying with the requirements of 10.20.1.1 and 10.20.1.2 shall not exceed 600 ft^2 (56 m^2) in area, unless a fire hazards analysis is approved by the AHJ.

N **10.21 Powered Micromobility Devices.**

N **10.21.1 General.** Where more than five powered micromobility devices will be charged inside or within 10 ft (3 m) of a building or structure, the charging operation shall be in accordance with Section 10.21.

N **10.21.2 Charging Equipment.** Powered micromobility devices shall be charged in accordance with their listing and the manufacturer's instructions using either the original-equipment-manufacturer-supplied listed charging equipment or listed charging equipment specified in the manufacturer's instructions.

N **10.21.3 Listing.** Powered micromobility devices and portable battery packs shall be listed and labeled in accordance with UL 2272, *Electrical Systems for Personal E-Mobility Devices*, or UL 2849, *Electrical Systems for eBikes*, as applicable.

N **10.21.4 Battery Charging.** Battery charging for powered micromobility devices shall be in accordance with all of the following:

(1) The charging equipment for each device shall be plugged directly into a listed receptacle.
(2) Extension cords and relocatable power taps shall not be utilized.
(3) Storage of combustible materials, combustible waste, or hazardous materials shall not be permitted within 10 ft (3 m) of the charging equipment.
(4) The charging operation shall not be located in any exit access corridor or exit enclosure

N **10.22* Alcohol-Based Hand-Rub (ABHR) Dispensers.** Where permitted by Chapters 11 through 43 of NFPA *101*, ABHR dispensers shall be permitted provided they meet all of the criteria in 10.22.1 through 10.22.5. [*101*:8.7.3.3]

N **10.22.1 Personal Use Containers.** The requirements of Section 10.22 shall not apply to individual personal use ABHR containers with a volume not exceeding 16.9 oz (500 mL). [*101*:8.7.3.3.1]

N **10.22.2 ABHR Dispenser Capacity.** The capacity of ABHR dispensers shall comply with all of the following:

(1) The maximum individual dispenser fluid capacity shall be as follows:
   (a) 0.53 gal (2.0 L) for dispensers in corridors and areas open to corridors
   (b) 1.06 gal (4.0 L) for dispensers in corridors and areas open to corridors in buildings protected throughout by an approved, supervised automatic sprinkler system in accordance with Section 13.3
   (c) 1.06 gal (4.0 L) for dispensers in rooms or suites of rooms separated from corridors
(2) Where aerosol containers are used, the maximum capacity of the aerosol dispenser shall be 18 oz (0.51 kg) and shall be limited to Level 1 aerosols as defined in NFPA 30B.
(3) In buildings without an automatic sprinkler system, not more than an aggregate 10 gal (37.8 L) of ABHR solution or 1135 oz (32.2 kg) of Level 1 aerosols, or a combination of liquids and Level 1 aerosols not to exceed, in total, the equivalent of 10 gal (37.8 L) or 1135 oz (32.2 kg), shall be in use outside of a storage cabinet in a single smoke compartment or fire compartment or story, whichever is less in area. One dispenser complying with 10.22.2(1) per room and located in that room shall not be included in the aggregated quantity.
(4) In buildings protected throughout by an approved, supervised automatic sprinkler system in accordance with Section 13.3, not more than an aggregate 20 gal (75.6 L) of ABHR solution shall be in use outside of a storage cabinet in a single smoke compartment or fire compartment or story, whichever is less in area. One dispenser complying with 10.22.2(1) per room and located in that room shall not be included in the aggregated quantity. [*101*:8.7.3.3.2]

N **10.22.3 ABHR Dispenser Location.** The locations of ABHR dispensers shall comply with all of the following:

(1) Dispensers shall not be installed in the following locations:
   (a) Above an ignition source for a horizontal distance of 1 in. (25 mm) to each side of the ignition source
   (b) To the side of an ignition source within a 1 in. (25 mm) horizontal distance from the ignition source
   (c) Beneath an ignition source within a 1 in. (25 mm) vertical distance from the ignition source
(2) Dispensers installed directly over carpeted floors shall be permitted only in sprinklered areas of the building.
(3) ABHR dispensers shall be separated from each other by horizontal spacing of not less than 48 in. (1220 mm). [*101*:8.7.3.3.3]

N **10.22.4 ABHR Dispenser Operation and Testing.** The operation of the dispenser shall comply with the following:

(1) Dispensers shall not release their contents except when activated, either manually or automatically by touch-free activation.
(2) Any activation of a dispenser shall only occur when an object is placed within 4 in. (100 mm) of the sensing device.
(3) An object placed within an activation zone and left in place shall not cause more than one activation.
(4) Dispensers shall not dispense more solution than the amount required for hand hygiene consistent with label instructions.
(5) Dispensers shall be designed, constructed, and operated in a manner that ensures accidental or malicious activation of dispensing devices is minimized.
(6) Dispensers shall be tested in accordance with the manufacturer's care and use instructions each time new refills are installed. [*101*:8.7.3.3.4]

N **10.22.5 Spill Containment and Maintenance.** Maintenance and spill containment of the dispenser shall comply with the following:

(1) Spill containment for dispensers shall be provided.
(2) Any ABHR spilled during a refill process shall be removed following the refill operation.
(3) Catch basins or spill collection means shall be kept free of accumulated ABHR material and refuse. [*101*:8.7.3.3.5]

Chapter 11 Building Services

11.1 Electrical Fire Safety.

11.1.1 General. Section 11.1 shall apply to permanent and temporary electrical appliances, equipment, fixtures, and wiring.

11.1.2 Permanent Wiring, Fixtures, and Equipment.

11.1.2.1 All new electrical wiring, fixtures, appliances and equipment shall be installed in accordance with *NFPA 70*.

11.1.2.2 Unless determined to present an imminent danger, existing electrical wiring, fixtures, appliances, and equipment shall be permitted to be maintained in accordance with the edition of *NFPA 70* in effect at the time of the installation.

11.1.2.2.1* Where the AHJ determines that there is sufficient evidence that existing electrical wiring, fixtures, appliances, or equipment is potentially unsafe, the AHJ is authorized to require an evaluation of the existing electrical wiring, fixtures, appliances, electrical loads, or equipment, or portion thereof, by a qualified person.

11.1.2.2.2 The qualified person shall provide a report to the AHJ with an assessment of the condition of the electrical wiring, fixtures, appliances, electrical loads, or equipment along with recommendations for any needed repairs to correct the unsafe condition(s).

11.1.2.3 Permanent wiring abandoned in place shall be tagged or otherwise identified at its termination and junction points as "Abandoned in Place" or removed from all accessible areas and insulated from contact with other live electrical wiring or devices.

11.1.3 Multiplug Adapters.

11.1.3.1 Multiplug adapters, such as multiplug extension cords, cube adapters, strip plugs, and other devices, shall be listed and used in accordance with their listing.

11.1.3.2 Multiplug adapters shall not be used as a substitute for permanent wiring or receptacles.

11.1.4 Relocatable Power Taps.

11.1.4.1 Relocatable power taps shall be listed to UL 1363, *Relocatable Power Taps*, or UL 1363A, *Outline of Investigation for Special Purpose Relocatable Power Taps*, where applicable, except as permitted by 11.1.4.2 or 11.1.4.3.

N **11.1.4.2** Relocatable power taps incorporated into furniture shall be listed and labeled in accordance with UL 962A, *Furniture Power Distribution Units*.

N **11.1.4.3** Relocatable power taps used in health care occupancies shall be listed and labeled in accordance with UL 1363A, *Outline of Investigation for Special Purpose Relocatable Power Taps*, or UL 2930, *Outline of Investigation for Cord and Plug Connected Health Care Facility Outlet Assemblies*, and UL 60601-1, *Medical Electrical Equipment, Part 1: General Requirements for Safety*.

11.1.4.4 The relocatable power taps shall be directly connected to a permanently installed receptacle, except as permitted by 11.1.4.5.

11.1.4.5 Relocatable power tap cords shall not extend through walls, ceilings, or floors; under doors or floor coverings; or be subject to environmental or physical damage.

11.1.5* Extension Cords.

11.1.5.1 Extension cords shall be plugged directly into an approved receptacle, power tap, or multiplug adapter and shall, except for approved multiplug extension cords, serve only one portable appliance.

11.1.5.2 The ampacity of the extension cords shall not be less than the rated capacity of the portable appliance supplied by the cord.

11.1.5.3 The extension cords shall be maintained in good condition without splices, deterioration, or damage.

11.1.5.4 Extension cords shall be grounded when servicing grounded portable appliances.

11.1.5.5 Extension cords and flexible cords shall not be affixed to structures; extend through walls, ceilings, or floors, or under doors or floor coverings; or be subject to environmental or physical damage.

11.1.5.6* Extension cords shall be permitted to be used on portable appliances to the nearest receptacle where receptacle spacing is in accordance with *NFPA 70*.

11.1.6 Temporary Installations.

11.1.6.1 Scope. The provisions of 11.1.6 apply to temporary electric power and lighting installations. [*70*:590.1]

11.1.6.2 All Wiring Installations.

11.1.6.2.1 Other Articles. Except as specifically modified in Article 590 of *NFPA 70*, all other requirements of *NFPA 70* for permanent wiring shall apply to temporary wiring installations. [*70*:590.2(A)]

11.1.6.2.2 Approval. Temporary wiring methods shall be acceptable only if approved based on the conditions of use and any special requirements of the temporary installation. [*70*:590.2(B)]

11.1.6.3 Time Constraints.

11.1.6.3.1 During the Period of Construction. Temporary electric power and lighting installations shall be permitted during the period of construction, remodeling, maintenance, repair, or demolition of buildings, structures, equipment, or similar activities. [*70*:590.3(A)]

11.1.6.3.2 90 Days. Temporary electric power and lighting installations shall be permitted for a period not to exceed 90 days for holiday decorative lighting and similar purposes. [*70*:590.3(B)]

11.1.6.3.3 Emergencies and Tests. Temporary electric power and lighting installations shall be permitted during emergencies and for tests, experiments, and developmental work. [*70*:590.3(C)]

11.1.6.3.4 Removal. Temporary wiring shall be removed immediately upon completion of construction or purpose for which the wiring was installed. [*70*:590.3(D)]

11.1.7 Building Disconnect.

11.1.7.1* Means shall be provided for the fire department to disconnect the electrical service to a building, structure, or facility when the electrical installation is covered under the scope of *NFPA 70*.

11.1.7.2 The disconnecting means shall be maintained accessible to the fire department.

11.1.7.3 Identification of Disconnecting Means.

11.1.7.3.1 Each disconnecting means shall be legibly marked to indicate its purpose unless located and arranged so the purpose is evident. In other than one- or two-family dwellings, the marking shall include the identification and location of the circuit source that supplies the disconnecting means unless located and arranged so the identification and location of the circuit source is evident. The marking shall be of sufficient durability to withstand the environment involved. [*70*:110.22(A)]

11.1.8 Covers. All panelboard and switchboards, pull boxes, junction boxes, switches, receptacles, and conduit bodies shall be provided with covers compatible with the box or conduit body construction and suitable for the conditions of use.

11.2 Heating, Ventilation, and Air-Conditioning.

11.2.1 Air-Conditioning, Heating, Ventilating Ductwork, and Related Equipment. Air-conditioning, heating, ventilating ductwork, and related equipment shall be in accordance with NFPA 90A or NFPA 90B, as applicable, unless such installations are approved existing installations, which shall be permitted to be continued in service. [*101*:9.2.1]

11.2.2 Ventilating or Heat-Producing Equipment. Ventilating or heat-producing equipment shall be in accordance with NFPA 31, NFPA 54, *NFPA 70*, NFPA 91, or NFPA 211, as applicable, unless such installations are approved existing installations, which shall be permitted to be continued in service. [*101*:9.2.2]

11.3 Elevators, Escalators, and Conveyors.

11.3.1 Firefighters' Emergency Operations.

11.3.1.1 All new elevators shall conform to the firefighters' emergency operations requirements of ASME A17.1/CSA B44, *Safety Code for Elevators and Escalators*. [*101*:9.4.3.1]

11.3.1.2 All existing elevators having a travel distance of 25 ft (7620 mm) or more above or below the level that best serves the needs of emergency personnel for firefighting or rescue purposes shall conform to the firefighters' emergency operations requirements of ASME A17.3, *Safety Code for Existing Elevators and Escalators*. [*101*:9.4.3.2]

11.3.2 Number of Cars. The number of elevator cars permitted in a hoistway shall be in accordance with 8.6.9.4 of NFPA *101*. [*101*:9.4.4]

11.3.3* Elevator Machine Rooms. Elevator machine rooms that contain solid-state equipment for elevators, other than existing elevators, having a travel distance exceeding 50 ft (15 m) above the level of exit discharge, or exceeding 30 ft (9.1 m) below the level of exit discharge, shall be provided with a natural or mechanical means to maintain temperature during firefighters' emergency operations for elevator operation *(see 11.3.1)*. The operating temperature shall be established by the elevator equipment manufacturer's specifications. When standby power is connected to the elevator, the means to control the temperature in the machine room shall be connected to standby power, if applicable. [*101*:9.4.5]

11.3.4 Elevator Testing.

11.3.4.1 Elevators shall be subject to periodic inspections and tests as specified in ASME A17.1/CSA B44, *Safety Code for Elevators and Escalators*. [*101*:9.4.6.1]

11.3.4.2 All elevators equipped with firefighters' emergency operations in accordance with 11.3.1 shall be subject to a monthly operation with a written record of the findings made and kept on the premises as required by ASME A17.1/CSA B44, *Safety Code for Elevators and Escalators*. [*101*:9.4.6.2]

11.3.4.3 The elevator inspections and tests required by 11.3.4.1 shall be performed at frequencies complying with one of the following:

(1) Inspection and test frequencies specified in Appendix N of ASME A17.1/CSA B44, *Safety Code for Elevators and Escalators*
(2) Inspection and test frequencies specified by the AHJ [*101*:9.4.6.3]

11.3.5 Openings to Exit Enclosures. Conveyors, elevators, dumbwaiters, and pneumatic conveyors serving various stories of a building shall not open to an exit enclosure. [*101*:9.4.7]

11.3.6 Standardized Fire Service Elevator Keys.

11.3.6.1 Buildings with elevators equipped with Phase I emergency recall, Phase II emergency in-car operation, or a fire service access elevator shall be equipped to operate with a standardized fire service key complying with ASME A17.1/CSA B44, *Safety Code for Elevators and Escalators*, except as otherwise permitted by 11.3.6.

11.3.6.2 Existing buildings with elevators equipped with Phase I emergency recall or Phase II emergency in-car operation shall be permitted to comply with 11.3.6.3.

11.3.6.3 Existing Buildings. Existing buildings shall be in compliance with the provisions of 11.3.6.3.1 one year after adoption by the AHJ.

11.3.6.3.1 Where a standardized key cylinder cannot be installed in an existing elevator key switch assembly, the building's nonstandardized fire service elevator keys shall be provided in an access box in accordance with 11.3.6.3.1.1 through 11.3.6.3.1.6.

11.3.6.3.1.1 The access box shall be compatible with an existing rapid-entry access box system in use in the jurisdiction and approved by the AHJ.

11.3.6.3.1.2 The front cover shall be permanently labeled with the words "Fire Department Use Only — Elevator Keys."

11.3.6.3.1.3 The access box shall be mounted at each elevator bank at the lobby nearest to the lowest level of fire department access.

11.3.6.3.1.4 The access box shall be mounted at a location approved by the AHJ.

11.3.6.3.1.5 Contents of the access box shall be limited to the fire service elevator key. Additional elevator access tools, keys, and information pertinent to emergency planning or elevator access shall be permitted when authorized by the AHJ.

11.3.6.3.1.6 In buildings with two or more elevator banks, a single access box shall be permitted to be used where such elevator banks are separated by not more than 30 ft

(9140 mm). Additional access boxes shall be provided for each individual elevator or elevator bank separated by more than 30 ft (9140 mm).

11.3.6.3.1.7 A single access box shall be permitted to be located adjacent to a fire command center, or the nonstandard fire service elevator key shall be secured in an access box used for other purposes and located in accordance with 18.2.2.1 when approved by the AHJ.

11.3.7 Elevators for Occupant-Controlled Evacuation Prior to Phase I Emergency Recall Operations and Fire Service Access Elevators. An approved method to prevent automatic sprinkler water from infiltrating into the hoistway enclosure from the operation of the automatic sprinkler system outside the enclosed occupant evacuation elevator lobby shall be provided where the hoistway serves elevators in accordance with any of the following:

(1) Occupant-controlled evacuation elevators in accordance with Section 7.14 of NFPA *101*
(2) Occupant-controlled evacuation elevators in accordance with the building code
(3) Fire service access elevators in accordance with the building code

11.4 Utilities. Equipment using fuel gas and related gas piping shall be in accordance with NFPA 54 or NFPA 58. *(See Chapter 69 for LP-Gas fuel supply and storage installations.)*

11.4.1 Existing installations shall be permitted to be continued in service, subject to approval by the AHJ.

11.4.2 Aboveground gas meters, regulators, and piping exposed to vehicular damage shall be protected in accordance with 60.5.1.9.

11.5 Heating Appliances.

11.5.1 General.

11.5.1.1 The installation of stationary liquid fuel–burning appliances, including but not limited to industrial-, commercial-, and residential-type steam, hot water, or warm air heating appliances; domestic-type range burners; space heaters; and portable liquid fuel–burning equipment shall comply with Section 11.5 and NFPA 31.

11.5.1.2 Section 11.5 shall also apply to all accessories and control systems, whether electric, thermostatic, or mechanical, and all electrical wiring connected to liquid fuel–burning appliances. [31:1.1.2]

11.5.1.3 Section 11.5 shall also apply to the installation of liquid fuel storage and supply systems connected to liquid fuel–burning appliances. [31:1.1.3]

11.5.1.4 Section 11.5 shall also apply to those multifueled appliances in which a liquid fuel is one of the standard or optional fuels. [31:1.1.4]

11.5.1.5* Section 11.5 shall not apply to internal combustion engines, oil lamps, or portable devices not specifically covered in NFPA 31. *(See Chapter 11 of NFPA 31 for portable devices that are covered in NFPA 31.)* [31:1.1.5]

11.5.1.6 The installation of gas-fired heating appliances shall comply with Section 11.5 and NFPA 54. *(See Chapter 69 for LP-Gas fuel supply and storage installations.)*

11.5.1.7 All heating appliances shall be approved or listed.

11.5.1.8 Permits. Permits, where required, shall comply with Section 1.13.

11.5.1.9 Electrical wiring and utilization equipment used in connection with oil-burning appliances or equipment shall be installed in accordance with Section 11.1. [31:4.4.1]

11.5.1.10 Acceptable Liquid Fuels.

11.5.1.10.1* The type and grade of liquid fuel used in a liquid fuel–burning appliance shall be that type and grade for which the appliance is listed and approved or is stipulated by the manufacturer. Liquid fuels shall meet one of the following specifications and shall not contain gasoline or any other flammable liquid:

(1) ASTM D396, *Standard Specification for Fuel Oils*
(2) ASTM D3699, *Standard Specification for Kerosine*
(3) ASTM D6448, *Industrial Burner Fuels from Used Lube Oils*
(4) ASTM D6751, *Standard Specification for Biodiesel Fuel Blend Stock (B100) for Middle Distillate Fuels*
(5) ASTM D6823, *Standard Specification for Commercial Boiler Fuels with Used Lubricating Oils*
(6) ASTM D7666, *Standard Specification for Triglyceride Burner Fuel*

[31:4.5.1]

11.5.1.10.2 Appliances that burn crankcase oil or used oil shall not be used in a residential occupancy. Such appliances shall only be used if all of the following conditions are met:

(1) The installation is in a commercial or industrial occupancy.
(2) The oil-burning appliance is designed to burn crankcase oil or used oil and is listed for such use.
(3) The appliance is installed in accordance with the manufacturer's instructions and with the terms of its listing.
(4) The installation meets the applicable requirements of Section 4.6 of NFPA 31 and Chapter 12 of NFPA 31.

[31:4.5.2]

11.5.1.10.3* Where heavy oils are used, the following shall be required:

(1) The oil-burning appliance shall be designed to burn such fuels.
(2) Means shall be provided to maintain the oil at its proper atomizing temperature.
(3) Automatically operated burners that require preheating of oil shall be arranged so that no oil can be delivered for combustion until the oil is at the proper atomizing temperature.
(4)* Use of an oil-fired appliance that is listed in accordance with UL 296A, *Waste Oil-Burning Air-Heating Appliances*, shall be deemed as meeting the intent of 11.5.1.10.3(1) through 11.5.1.10.3(3).

[31:4.5.3]

11.5.1.10.4 A properly sized and rated oil filter or strainer shall be installed in the oil supply line to an oil burner. [31:4.5.4]

11.5.1.11 Clothes Dryers.

11.5.1.11.1 Clothes dryers shall be cleaned to maintain the lint trap and keep the mechanical and heating components free from excessive accumulations of lint.

11.5.1.11.2 The requirements of 11.5.1.11.1 shall not apply to clothes dryers in individual dwelling units of residential occupancies.

11.5.2 Kerosene Burners and Oil Stoves.

11.5.2.1 Kerosene burners and oil stoves shall be equipped with a primary safety control furnished as an integral part of the appliance by the manufacturer to stop the flow of oil in the event of flame failure. Barometric oil feed shall not be considered a primary safety control.

11.5.2.2 A conversion range oil burner shall be equipped with a thermal (heat-actuated) valve in the oil supply line, located in the burner compartment of the stove.

11.5.2.3 Kerosene heaters shall be listed and labeled in accordance with UL 647, *Unvented Kerosene-Fired Room Heaters and Portable Heaters,* and their use shall meet all of the following:

(1) Adequate ventilation shall be provided.
(2) Kerosene heaters shall not be placed on carpeting.
(3) Kerosene heaters shall be located not less than 3 ft (0.9 m) from combustible furnishings and drapes.
(4) Only approved Type 1-K water clear kerosene shall be used.
(5) Kerosene heaters shall be allowed to cool before refueling.

11.5.3 Portable Electric Heater.

11.5.3.1 The AHJ shall be permitted to prohibit use of portable electric heaters in occupancies or situations where such use or operation would present an undue danger to life or property.

11.5.3.2 Portable electric heaters shall be designed and located so that they cannot be easily overturned.

11.5.3.3 All portable electric heaters shall be listed.

11.5.4 Vents. All chimneys, smokestacks, or similar devices for conveying smoke or hot gases to the outer air and the stoves, furnaces, incinerators, boilers, or any other heat-producing devices or appliances shall be installed and maintained in accordance with NFPA 54 and NFPA 211.

11.6 Waste Chutes, Incinerators, and Laundry Chutes.

11.6.1 Enclosure.

11.6.1.1 Waste chutes and laundry chutes shall be separately enclosed by walls or partitions in accordance with the provisions of Section 12.7. [*101*:9.5.1.1]

11.6.1.2 Chute intake openings shall be protected in accordance with Section 12.7. [*101*:9.5.1.2]

11.6.1.3 The doors of chutes specified in 11.6.1.2 shall open only to a room that is designed and used exclusively for accessing the chute opening. [*101*:9.5.1.3]

11.6.1.4 Chute service opening rooms shall be separated from other spaces in accordance with Section 8.7 of NFPA *101*. [*101*:9.5.1.4]

11.6.1.5 The requirements of 11.6.1.1 through 11.6.1.4 shall not apply where otherwise permitted by the following:

(1) Existing installations having properly enclosed service chutes and properly installed and maintained chute intake doors shall be permitted to have chute intake doors open to a corridor or normally occupied space.
(2) Waste chutes and laundry chutes shall be permitted to open into rooms not exceeding 400 ft^2 (37 m^2) that are used for storage, provided that the room is protected by automatic sprinklers.

[*101*:9.5.1.5]

11.6.2 Installation and Maintenance. Waste chutes, laundry chutes, and incinerators shall be installed and maintained in accordance with NFPA 82 unless such installations are approved existing installations, which shall be permitted to be continued in service. [*101*:9.5.2]

11.7 Stationary Generators and Standby Power Systems.

11.7.1 Scope.

11.7.1.1 Stationary generators and standby power systems shall comply with Section 11.7.

11.7.1.2 Section 11.7 shall not apply to portable generators. *(See Section 10.15.)*

11.7.2* Stationary Combustion Engines and Gas Turbines Installation. Stationary generator sets shall be installed in accordance with NFPA 37 and *NFPA 70*.

11.7.3 Emergency and Legally Required Standby Power Systems.

11.7.3.1 General. New stationary generators for emergency use or for legally required standby power required by this *Code*, the building code, or other codes and standards shall be installed in accordance with NFPA 110.

11.7.3.2 Acceptance. Newly installed stationary generators for emergency use or for legally required standby power for fire protection systems and features shall demonstrate the capacity of the energy converter, with its controls and accessories, to survive without damage from common and abnormal disturbances in actual load circuits by any of the following means:

(1) By tests on separate prototype models
(2) By acceptance tests on the system components as performed by the component suppliers
(3) By listing for emergency service as a completely factory-assembled and factory-tested apparatus

11.7.4 Stored Electrical Energy Emergency and Legally Required Standby Power System Installation. Stored electrical energy systems required by this *Code*, the building code, or other NFPA codes and standards shall be installed in accordance with NFPA 111 and *NFPA 70*.

11.7.5 Maintenance and Testing.

11.7.5.1 Stationary generators used for emergency or legally required standby power shall be tested and maintained in accordance with NFPA 110 and NFPA 37.

11.7.5.2 Stationary generators required by this *Code*, the building code, or other NFPA codes and standards shall be maintained in accordance with NFPA 110.

11.7.5.3 Stored electrical energy systems required by this *Code*, the building code, or other NFPA codes and standards shall be maintained in accordance with NFPA 111.

11.8* Smoke Control.

11.8.1 Newly installed smoke-control systems shall be inspected by the AHJ and tested in accordance with the criteria established in the approved design documents, NFPA 204 and NFPA 92.

11.8.2 Smoke-control systems shall have an approved maintenance and testing program to ensure operational integrity in accordance with this section. Components of such systems shall be operated, maintained, and tested in accordance with their operation and maintenance manuals.

11.8.2.1 Testing. Operational testing of the smoke-control system shall be in accordance with NFPA 92, and shall include all equipment related to the system including, but not limited to, initiating devices, fans, dampers, controls, doors, and windows.

11.8.2.1.1 An approved written schedule for such operational tests shall be established.

11.8.2.2 Test records shall be maintained on the premises and must indicate the date of such testing, the qualified service personnel, and any corrective measures needed or taken.

11.8.3 All smoke-control systems and devices shall be maintained in a reliable operating condition and shall be replaced or repaired where defective.

11.8.4 The AHJ shall be notified when any smoke-control system is out of service for more than 4 hours in a 24-hour period and again upon restoration of service of such systems.

11.8.5 The AHJ shall be permitted to require the building to be evacuated or an approved fire watch to be provided for all portions left unprotected by the fire protection system shutdown until the fire protection system has been returned to service.

11.9 Emergency Command Center. Where required, emergency command centers shall comply with Section 11.9.

11.9.1 The location, design, content, and fire department access of the emergency command center shall be approved by the fire department.

11.9.2 The emergency command center shall be separated from the remainder of the building by a fire barrier having a fire resistance rating of not less than 1 hour.

11.9.3 New emergency command center rooms shall be a minimum of 200 ft² (19 m²) with a minimum dimension of 10 ft (3050 mm).

11.9.3.1 Existing emergency command center rooms shall be maintained with the minimum square footage and dimensions previously approved by the AHJ.

11.9.4 The following shall be provided in the emergency command center:

(1) The fire department communication unit
(2) A telephone for fire department use with controlled access to the public telephone system
(3) Schematic building plans indicating the typical floor plan and detailing the building core means of egress, fire protection systems, fire-fighting equipment, and fire department access
(4) Work table
(5) If applicable, hazardous material management plans for the building

11.9.5 Where otherwise required, the following devices or functions shall be provided within the emergency command center:

(1) The emergency voice/alarm communication system unit
(2) Fire detection and alarm system annunciator unit
(3) Annunciator visually indicating the location of the elevators and whether they are operational
(4) Status indicators and controls for air-handling systems
(5) Controls for unlocking stairway doors simultaneously
(6) Sprinkler valve and waterflow detector display panels
(7) Emergency and standby power status indicators
(8) Fire pump status indicators
(9) Generator supervision devices and manual start and transfer features
(10) Public address system, where specifically required by other sections of this *Code*
(11) Controls required for smoke control

11.9.6 Emergency Command Center Acceptance Testing. Devices, equipment, components, and sequences shall be individually tested in accordance with appropriate standards and manufacturers' documented instructions.

11.10* In-Building Emergency Responder Communication Enhancement Systems.

11.10.1 Permits.

11.10.1.1 Where required by the AHJ, an installation permit shall comply with Section 1.13.

11.10.1.2 Where required by the AHJ, a renewable permit in accordance with 18.7.7 of NFPA 1225 shall be issued at the conclusion of successful acceptance testing.

Δ **11.10.2*** In all new and existing buildings, an approved emergency communication enhancement system shall be installed where the minimum radio signal strength into the building cannot be maintained in accordance with NFPA 1225.

Δ **11.10.3** In-building emergency responder communication enhancement systems shall comply with the design, installation, testing, inspection, and maintenance requirements in NFPA 1225.

11.10.4 Listed and Labeled. In-building emergency responder communication enhancement systems installed within buildings shall be listed and labeled in accordance with UL 2524, *In-building 2-Way Emergency Radio Communication Enhancement Systems*.

11.11 Medical Gas and Vacuum Systems. Medical gas and vacuum systems shall comply with NFPA 99.

11.12 Photovoltaic Systems.

11.12.1 General.

11.12.1.1 Photovoltaic systems shall be designed and installed in accordance with Section 11.12.

N **11.12.1.2** Permits, where required, shall comply with Section 1.13.

11.12.1.3 Electrical portions of photovoltaic systems shall be designed and installed in accordance with *NFPA 70*.

11.12.2 Building-Mounted Photovoltaic (PV) and Building Integrated Photovoltaic (BIPV) Installations.

11.12.2.1* Marking. Photovoltaic systems shall be permanently marked as specified in 11.12.2.1.1 through 11.12.2.1.6.3.

11.12.2.1.1* Rapid Shutdown Marking. Buildings with a rooftop-mounted PV system and buildings with a BIPV system installed as the roof covering shall be provided with permanent labels as described in 11.12.2.1.1.1 through 11.12.2.1.1.9.

11.12.2.1.1.1 Rapid Shutdown Type. The type of PV system rapid shutdown shall be labeled as described in 11.12.2.1.1.1.1 or 11.12.2.1.1.1.2.

11.12.2.1.1.1.1 Buildings with Rapid Shutdown. PV systems that shut down the PV system and reduce shock hazard in the array and conductors leaving the array shall be labeled as follows:

SOLAR PV SYSTEM IS EQUIPPED WITH RAPID SHUTDOWN.

TURN RAPID SHUTDOWN SWITCH TO THE "OFF" POSITION TO SHUT DOWN PV SYSTEM AND REDUCE SHOCK HAZARD IN ARRAY.

11.12.2.1.1.1.2 PV systems that only shut down conductors outside the array shall be labeled as follows:

SOLAR PV SYSTEM IS EQUIPPED WITH RAPID SHUTDOWN.

TURN RAPID SHUTDOWN SWITCH TO THE "OFF" POSITION TO SHUT DOWN CONDUCTORS OUTSIDE THE ARRAY. CONDUCTORS WITHIN ARRAY REMAIN ENERGIZED IN SUNLIGHT.

11.12.2.1.1.2 The label required by 11.12.2.1.1.1 shall be both of the following:

(1) Reflective
(2) Lettered as follows:
  (a) All letters capitalized
  (b) All letters having a minimum height of ⅜ in. (9.5 mm)
  (c) All letters in white on a red background

11.12.2.1.1.3 The label required by 11.12.2.1.1.1 shall include a simple diagram of a building with a roof.

11.12.2.1.1.4 Diagram sections in red shall signify sections of the PV system that are not shut down when the rapid shutdown switch is operated.

11.12.2.1.1.5 Sections of the diagram in green shall signify sections of the PV system that are shut down when the rapid shutdown switch is operated.

11.12.2.1.1.6 Buildings with PV systems shall have both of the following:

(1) A permanent label located at each service equipment location to which the PV systems are connected or at a readily visible location approved by the fire department
(2) The location of rapid shutdown initiation devices indicated on the permanent label

11.12.2.1.1.7 Buildings with More Than One Rapid Shutdown Type. For buildings that have PV systems with both rapid shutdown types, or a rapid shutdown type and a PV system with no rapid shutdown, a detailed plan view diagram of the roof shall be provided showing each PV system and a dotted line around areas that remain energized after the rapid shutdown switch is operated.

11.12.2.1.1.8 Rapid Shutdown Switch. The rapid shutdown switch shall have a permanent label located at a readily visible location on or no more than 3 ft (1 m) from the switch that includes the following words:

RAPID SHUTDOWN SWITCH FOR SOLAR PV SYSTEM

11.12.2.1.1.9 The label required by 11.12.2.1.1.8 shall be both of the following:

(1) Reflective
(2) Lettered as follows:
  (a) All letters capitalized
  (b) All letters having a minimum height of ⅜ in. (9.5 mm)
  (c) All letters in white on red background

11.12.2.1.2 Marking.

11.12.2.1.2.1 Each PV system disconnecting means shall plainly indicate whether in the open (off) or closed (on) position.

11.12.2.1.2.2 Each PV system disconnecting means shall be permanently marked "PV SYSTEM DISCONNECT" or equivalent.

11.12.2.1.2.3 Additional markings shall be permitted based upon the specific system configuration.

11.12.2.1.2.4 For PV system disconnecting means where the line and load terminals may be energized in the open position, the device shall be marked with the following words or equivalent wording approved by the fire department:

WARNING: ELECTRIC SHOCK HAZARD TERMINALS ON THE LINE AND LOAD SIDES MAY BE ENERGIZED IN THE OPEN POSITION

11.12.2.1.2.5 The warning sign(s) or label(s) shall comply with 110.21(B) of *NFPA 70*.

11.12.2.1.3 Marking and Labeling Required. Unless located and arranged so the purpose is evident, the following wiring methods and enclosures that contain PV power source conductors shall be marked with the words WARNING: PHOTOVOLTAIC POWER SOURCE or SOLAR PV DC CIRCUIT by means of permanently affixed labels or other approved permanent marking approved by the fire department:

(1) Exposed raceways, cable trays, and other wiring methods
(2) Covers or enclosures of pull boxes and junction boxes
(3) Conduit bodies in which any of the available conduit openings are unused

11.12.2.1.3.1 Marking and Labeling Required.

(A) The labels or markings shall be visible after installation.

(B) All letters shall be as follows:

(1) Capitalized
(2) Minimum height of ⅜ in. (9.5 mm)
(3) White on a red background

(C) Labels shall appear on every section of the wiring system that is separated by enclosures, walls, partitions, ceilings, or floors.

(D) Spacing between labels or markings, or between a label and a marking, shall not be more than 10 ft (3 m).

(E) Labels required by 11.12.2.1.3 shall be suitable for the environment where they are installed.

(F) Labels required by 11.12.2.1.3 shall be maintained and replaced if removed or damaged, or if the label becomes illegible.

11.12.2.1.4 Identification of Power Sources.

11.12.2.1.4.1 A permanent plaque or directory shall be installed at each service equipment location, or at a readily visible location approved by the fire department.

11.12.2.1.4.2 Where installations consist of multiple co-located power production sources, the permanent plaque or directory shall be permitted to identify the sources as a group(s).

11.12.2.1.4.3 Plaques or directories permitted by 11.12.2.1.4.2 shall not be required to identify each power source individually.

11.12.2.1.4.4 The plaque or directory shall denote the location of each power source disconnecting means for the building or structure and be grouped with other plaques or directories for other on-site sources.

11.12.2.1.4.5 The plaque or directory shall be marked with the wording "CAUTION: MULTIPLE SOURCES OF POWER."

11.12.2.1.4.6 Any posted diagrams shall be correctly oriented with respect to the diagram's location. The marking shall comply with 110.21(B) of *NFPA 70*.

11.12.2.1.5 Installer Information. A label shall be installed adjacent to the main disconnect indicating the name and emergency telephone number of the company currently servicing the PV system.

11.12.2.1.6 Markings for Building Integrated PV (BIPV) Systems.

11.12.2.1.6.1 BIPV systems installed as the roof covering shall have markings to identify any areas with electrical hazards hidden from view.

11.12.2.1.6.2 Marking shall be both of the following:
(1) Reflective
(2) Visible from grade beneath the eaves or other approved location

11.12.2.1.6.3 The AHJ shall be permitted to reduce or exempt marking requirements for BIPV systems installed as the roof covering when they are installed in accordance with 690.12(B)(2) of *NFPA 70*.

11.12.3 Rooftop Access and Ventilation.

11.12.3.1 General.

11.12.3.1.1 Access pathways, setbacks, and spacing requirements shall be required to provide emergency access to the roof, provide pathways to specific areas of the roof, provide for smoke ventilation opportunity areas, and to provide emergency egress from the roof.

11.12.3.1.2 The AHJ shall be permitted to reduce or modify roof access based upon fire department ventilation procedures or alternative methods that ensure adequate fire department access, pathways, and smoke ventilation.

11.12.3.1.3 The AHJ shall be permitted to reduce or modify roof access for BIPV systems installed as the roof covering when they are listed in accordance with 690.12(B)(2) of *NFPA 70*.

11.12.3.2 One- and Two-Family Dwellings and Townhouses.

11.12.3.2.1 Photovoltaic systems installed on one- and two-family dwellings and townhouses shall provide roof access in accordance with 11.12.3.2.

11.12.3.2.2 Designation of ridges shall not apply to roofs with 2 in 12 or less pitch.

11.12.3.2.3* Access Pathways.

11.12.3.2.3.1 Not less than two 36 in. (914 mm) wide access pathways on separate roof planes, from gutter to ridge, shall be provided on all buildings.

11.12.3.2.3.2 One access pathway shall be provided on the street or driveway side of the roof.

11.12.3.2.3.3 For each roof plane with a PV array, a 36 in. (914 mm) wide access pathway from gutter to ridge shall be provided on the same roof plane as the PV array, on an adjacent roof plane, or straddling the same and adjacent roof planes.

11.12.3.2.3.4 Access pathways shall be located in areas with minimal obstructions such as vent pipes, conduit, or mechanical equipment.

11.12.3.2.4 Setbacks at Ridge.

11.12.3.2.4.1 For PV arrays occupying up to 33 percent of the plan view roof area, a minimum 18 in. (457 mm) setback shall be provided on either side of a horizontal ridge.

11.12.3.2.4.2 For PV arrays occupying more than 33 percent of the plan view roof area, a minimum of 36 in. (914 mm) setback shall be provided on either side of a horizontal ridge.

11.12.3.2.5 Alternative Setbacks at Ridge.

11.12.3.2.5.1 For one- and two-family dwellings with an automatic sprinkler system installed within the dwelling in accordance with 13.3.2.18, for PV arrays occupying up to 66 percent of the plan view roof area, a minimum 18 in. (457 mm) setback shall be provided on either side of a horizontal ridge.

11.12.3.2.5.2 For PV arrays occupying more than 66 percent of the plan view roof area on sprinklered one- and two-family dwellings, a minimum 36 in. (914 mm) setback shall be provided on either side of a horizontal ridge.

11.12.3.3 Buildings Other Than One- and Two-Family Dwellings and Townhouses.

11.12.3.3.1 Roof Access.

11.12.3.3.1.1 Photovoltaic systems installed on any building other than one- and two-family dwellings and townhouses shall provide roof access in accordance with 11.12.3.3.

11.12.3.3.1.2 Where the AHJ determines that the roof configuration is similar to a one- and two-family dwelling or townhouse, the AHJ shall allow the roof access requirements of 11.12.3.2.

11.12.3.3.1.3 Detached, nonhabitable structures, including, but not limited to, parking shade structures, carports, solar trellises, and similar structures, shall not be required to provide roof access.

11.12.3.3.2 Perimeter Pathways.

11.12.3.3.2.1 A minimum 48 in. (1219 mm) wide perimeter pathway shall be provided around the edges of the roof for buildings with a length or width of 250 ft (76.2 m) or less along either axis.

11.12.3.3.2.2 A minimum 6 ft (1829 mm) wide perimeter pathway shall be provided around the edges of the roof for buildings having length or width greater than 250 ft (76.2 m) along either axis.

11.12.3.3.3 Other Pathways. Pathways shall be over areas capable of supporting firefighters accessing the roof and shall be provided between array sections as follows:

(1) Pathways shall be provided in a straight line 48 in. (1219 mm) or greater in width to all ventilation hatches and roof standpipes.
(2) Pathways shall be provided 48 in. (1219 mm) or greater in width around roof access hatches with at least one 48 in. (1219 mm) or greater in width pathway to the parapet or roof edge.
(3) Pathways shall be provided at intervals no greater than 150 ft (46 m) throughout the length and width of the roof.

11.12.3.3.4 Smoke Ventilation.

11.12.3.3.4.1 A minimum 48 in. (1219 mm) wide pathway shall be provided bordering all sides of non-gravity-operated smoke and heat vents and bordering at least one side of gravity-operated smoke and heat vents.

11.12.3.3.4.2 Ventilation options between array sections shall be at least one of the following:

(1)* A pathway 96 in. (2438 mm) or greater in width
(2)* A pathway 48 in. (1219 mm) or greater in width and bordering on existing roof skylights at intervals no greater than 150 ft (46 m) throughout the length and width of the roof
(3)* A pathway 48 in. (1219 mm) or greater in width and bordering 48 in. (1219 mm) by 96 in. (2438 mm) with venting cutouts options every 20 ft (6096 mm)

11.12.3.3.5 Minimizing Obstructions in Pathways. Pathways shall be located in areas with minimal obstructions such as vent pipes, conduit, or mechanical equipment to reduce trip hazards and maximize ventilation opportunities.

11.12.3.4 Emergency Escape and Rescue Openings.

11.12.3.4.1 Where rooftop-mounted PV systems or BIPV systems installed as the roof covering are installed on a roof plane directly below an emergency escape and rescue opening, a minimum 36 in. (914 mm) wide access pathway shall be provided to at least one emergency escape and rescue opening for each sleeping room.

11.12.3.4.2 The AHJ shall be permitted to reduce or exempt access pathways at emergency escape and rescue openings for BIPV systems installed as the roof covering when they are listed in accordance with 690.12(B)(2) of *NFPA 70*.

11.12.4 Ground-Mounted Photovoltaic System Installations. Ground-mounted photovoltaic systems shall be installed in accordance with 11.12.4.1 and 11.12.4.2.

11.12.4.1* Clearances. A clear area of 10 ft (3048 mm) around ground-mounted photovoltaic installations shall be provided.

11.12.4.2* Vegetation Management Plan. A vegetation management plan or noncombustible base acceptable to the AHJ shall be approved and maintained under and around the installation where required by the AHJ.

Chapter 12 Features of Fire Protection

12.1 General. This chapter shall apply to new, existing, permanent, or temporary buildings.

12.2* Construction.

12.2.1* Where required by this *Code*, a type of building construction shall comply with NFPA 220.

12.2.2 Fire safety construction features for new and existing occupancies shall comply with this *Code* and the referenced edition of *NFPA 101*.

12.3 Fire-Resistive Materials and Construction.

12.3.1 The design and construction of fire walls and fire barrier walls that are required to separate buildings or subdivide a building to prevent the spread of fire shall comply with Section 12.3 and NFPA 221.

12.3.2 Quality Assurance for Penetrations and Joints. A quality assurance program for the installation of devices and systems installed to protect penetrations and joints shall be prepared and monitored by the RDP responsible for design. Inspections of firestop systems and fire-resistive joint systems shall be in accordance with 12.3.2.1 and 12.3.2.2. [5000:40.9]

12.3.2.1 Inspection of firestop systems of the types tested in accordance with ASTM E814, *Standard Test Method for Fire Tests of Penetration Firestop Systems*, or UL 1479, *Fire Tests of Penetration Firestops*, shall be conducted in accordance with ASTM E2174, *Standard Practice for On-Site Inspection of Installed Firestop Systems*. [5000:40.9.1]

12.3.2.2 Inspection of fire-resistive joint systems of the types tested in accordance with ASTM E1966, *Standard Test Method for Fire-Resistive Joint Systems*, or UL 2079, *Tests for Fire Resistance of Building Joint Systems*, shall be conducted in accordance with ASTM E2393, *Standard Practice for On-Site Inspection of Installed Fire Resistive Joint Systems and Perimeter Fire Barriers*. [5000:40.9.2]

12.3.3* Maintenance of Fire-Resistive Construction, Draft-Stop Partitions, and Roof Coverings.

12.3.3.1 Required fire-resistive construction, including fire barriers, fire walls, exterior walls due to location on property, fire-resistive requirements based on type of construction, draft-stop partitions, and roof coverings, shall be maintained and shall be properly repaired, restored, or replaced where damaged, altered, breached, penetrated, removed, or improperly installed.

12.3.3.2 Where required, fire-rated gypsum wallboard walls or ceilings that are damaged to the extent that through openings exist, the damaged gypsum wallboard shall be replaced or returned to the required level of fire resistance using a listed repair system or using materials and methods equivalent to the original construction.

12.3.3.3 Where readily accessible, required fire-resistance-rated assemblies in high-rise buildings shall be visually inspected for integrity at least once every 3 years.

12.3.3.3.1 The person responsible for conducting the visual inspection shall demonstrate appropriate technical knowledge and experience in fire-resistance-rated design and construction acceptable to the AHJ.

12.3.3.3.2 A written report prepared by the person responsible for conducting the visual inspection shall be submitted to the AHJ documenting the results of the visual inspection.

12.4 Fire Doors and Other Opening Protectives.

Δ **12.4.1*** The installation and maintenance of assemblies and devices used to protect openings in walls, floors, and ceilings against the spread of fire and smoke within, into, or out of buildings shall comply with Section 12.4 and NFPA 80.

12.4.1.1* With the exception of fabric fire safety curtain assemblies, Section 12.4 addresses assemblies that have been subjected to standardized fire tests. *(See Chapter 20 of NFPA 80.)* [80:1.1.1]

12.4.1.2* Incinerator doors, record room doors, and vault doors are not covered in Section 12.4. [80:1.1.2]

12.4.1.3* Requirements for horizontally sliding, vertically sliding, and swinging doors as used in this *Code* do not apply to hoistway doors for elevators and dumbwaiters. [80:1.1.3]

12.4.1.4* Section 12.4 does not cover fire resistance glazing materials and horizontally sliding accordion or folding assemblies fabricated for use as walls and tested as wall assemblies in accordance with ASTM E119, *Standard Test Methods for Fire Tests of Building Construction and Materials,* or UL 263, *Fire Tests of Building Construction and Materials.* [80:1.1.4]

12.4.2 Care and Maintenance of Fire Doors and Other Opening Protectives.

12.4.2.1* Subsection 12.4.2 shall cover the inspection, testing, and maintenance of fire doors, fire shutters, fire windows, and opening protectives other than fire dampers, fabric fire safety curtains, and fire protective curtain assemblies. [80:5.1.1.1]

12.4.2.2 The requirements of Section 12.4 shall apply to new and existing installations. [80:5.1.1.2]

12.4.2.3 Operability.

12.4.2.3.1* Doors, shutters, and windows shall be operable at all times. [80:5.1.2.1]

12.4.2.3.2 Doors, shutters, and windows shall be kept closed and latched or arranged for automatic closing. [80:5.1.2.2]

12.4.2.3.3 Prevention of Door Blockage.

12.4.2.3.3.1 Door openings and their surrounding areas shall be kept clear of anything that could obstruct or interfere with the free operation of the door. [80:5.1.2.3.1]

12.4.2.3.3.2 Where necessary, a barrier shall be built to prevent the piling of material against sliding doors. [80:5.1.2.3.2]

12.4.2.3.3.3 Blocking or wedging of doors in the open position shall be prohibited. [80:5.1.2.3.3]

12.4.2.4 Replacement. Where it is necessary to replace fire doors, shutters, windows or their frames, glazing materials, hardware, and closing mechanisms, replacements shall meet the requirements for fire protection and shall be installed and tested as required by this section for new installations. [80:5.1.3]

12.4.2.5 Field Labeling.

Δ **12.4.2.5.1** Field labeling shall be performed only by individuals or companies that have been certified or listed, or by individuals or companies that are representatives of a labeling service that that maintains periodic inspections of production of labeled equipment or materials and by whose labeling the manufacturer indicates compliance with appropriate standards or performance in a specified manner. [80:5.1.4.1]

12.4.2.5.2 Individuals performing the service shall provide proof of qualifications to the AHJ prior to performing work, as described in 12.4.2.5.1. [80:5.1.4.2]

12.4.2.5.3 At a minimum, field labels shall contain the following information:

(1) The words "field inspected" or "field labeled"
(2) The words "fire door" or "fire door frame"
(3) The marking of a third-party certification agency
(4) The fire protection rating
(5) A unique serial number (if provided by the listing agency)
(6) The fire test standard designation to which the assembly was tested

[80:5.1.4.3]

12.4.2.5.4 Field modifications shall not be permitted to be made to a non-fire-rated door assembly to achieve a fire rating unless the field modification is completed under label service. [80:5.1.4.4]

12.4.2.5.5 Doors in which a field modification in accordance with 12.4.2.5.4 has been completed shall be labeled. [80:5.1.4.5]

12.4.2.5.6 When an opening with a non-fire-rated door requires a fire door, the door assembly shall be replaced. [80:5.1.4.6]

12.4.2.6* Field Modifications.

12.4.2.6.1 In cases where a field modification to a fire door or a fire door assembly is desired, and is not permitted by 4.1.3.2 through 4.1.3.2.5 of NFPA 80, the laboratory with which the product or component being modified is listed shall be contacted through the manufacturer and a written or graphic description of the modifications shall be presented to that laboratory. [80:5.1.5.1.1]

12.4.2.6.2 Field modifications shall be permitted without a field visit from the laboratory upon written authorization from that laboratory. [80:5.1.5.1.2]

12.4.2.6.3 When the manufacturer is no longer available, the laboratory shall be permitted to provide an engineering evaluation supporting the field modification. [80:5.1.5.1.3]

12.4.2.7 Removal of Door or Window. Where a fire door or fire window opening no longer functions as an opening, or the door or window is removed and not replaced, the opening shall be filled to maintain the required rating of the wall assembly. [80:5.1.6]

12.4.2.8* Inspection and Testing.

12.4.2.8.1* Installation Inspection. Upon completion of the installation, door, shutters, and window assemblies shall be inspected and tested in accordance with 12.4.2.8.4. [80:5.2.1]

12.4.2.8.2* Inspection Records. A record of all inspections and testing shall be signed by the inspector and kept for inspection by the AHJ. [80:5.2.2]

12.4.2.8.2.1 Records of acceptance tests shall be retained for the life of the assembly. [80:5.2.2.1]

12.4.2.8.2.2* Unless a longer period is required by 12.4.2.10, records shall be retained for a period of at least 3 years. [80:5.2.2.2]

Δ **12.4.2.8.2.3*** The records shall be on a medium that will survive the retention period. Paper or electronic media shall be permitted. [80:5.2.2.3]

12.4.2.8.2.4 A record of all inspections and testing shall be provided that includes, but is not limited to, the following information:

(1) Date of inspection
(2) Name of facility
(3) Address of facility
(4) Name of person(s) performing inspections and testing
(5) Company name and address of inspecting company
(6) Signature of inspector of record
(7) Individual record of each inspected and tested fire door assembly
(8)* Opening identifier and location of each inspected and tested fire door assembly
(9)* Type and description of each inspected and tested fire door assembly
(10)* Verification of visual inspection and functional operation
(11) Listing of deficiencies in accordance with 12.4.2.8.3, 12.4.2.9, and 12.4.2.10

[80:5.2.2.4]

12.4.2.8.3 Acceptance Testing.

12.4.2.8.3.1* Acceptance testing of fire door and window assemblies shall be performed by a qualified person with knowledge and understanding of the operating components of the type of assembly being subject to testing. [80:5.2.3.1]

12.4.2.8.3.2* Before testing, a visual inspection shall be performed to identify any damaged or missing parts that can create a hazard during testing or affect operation or resetting. [80:5.2.3.2]

12.4.2.8.3.3 Acceptance testing shall include the closing of the door by all means of activation. [80:5.2.3.3]

12.4.2.8.3.4 A record of these inspections and testing shall be made in accordance with 12.4.2.8.2. [80:5.2.3.4]

12.4.2.8.3.5 Swinging Doors with Builders Hardware or Fire Door Hardware.

12.4.2.8.3.5.1 Fire door assemblies shall be visually inspected from both sides to assess the overall condition of door assembly. [80:5.2.3.5.1]

12.4.2.8.3.5.2* Inspection Mark. Upon completion of inspection, an inspection mark shall be permitted to be applied to the assembly. [80:5.2.3.5.3]

N **12.4.2.8.3.6 Swinging Doors with Fire Door Hardware.** [80:5.2.3.6]

N **12.4.2.8.3.6.1** Fire door assemblies shall be visually inspected from both sides to assess the overall condition of the door assembly. [80:5.2.3.6.1]

12.4.2.8.3.7 Horizontally Sliding, Vertically Sliding, and Rolling Doors.

12.4.2.8.3.7.1 Fire door assemblies shall be visually inspected from both sides to assess the overall condition of door assembly. [80:5.2.3.7.1]

12.4.2.8.3.8 Closing Devices.

12.4.2.8.3.8.1 All fire doors, fire shutters, and fire window assemblies shall be inspected and tested to check for proper operation and full closure. [80:5.2.3.8.1]

12.4.2.8.3.8.2 Resetting of the automatic-closing device shall be done in accordance with the manufacturer's instructions. [80:5.2.3.8.2]

12.4.2.8.3.8.3 Rolling Steel Fire Doors.

12.4.2.8.3.8.3.1 Rolling steel fire doors shall be drop-tested twice. [80:5.2.3.8.3.1]

12.4.2.8.3.8.3.2 The first test shall be to check for proper operation and full closure. [80:5.2.3.8.3.2]

12.4.2.8.3.8.3.3 A second test shall be done to verify that the automatic-closing device has been reset correctly. [80:5.2.3.8.3.3]

12.4.2.8.3.9* Fusible links, release devices, and any other moveable parts shall not be painted or coated with other materials that could interfere with the operation of the assembly. [80:5.2.3.9]

12.4.2.8.4* Periodic Inspection and Testing.

12.4.2.8.4.1* Periodic inspections and testing shall be performed not less than annually. [80:5.2.4.1]

N **12.4.2.8.4.2*** For doors complying with Chapters 11 and 13 in NFPA 80, periodic inspections and testing shall be performed by a trained rolling steel fire door systems technician. [80:5.2.4.2]

12.4.2.8.4.3 As a minimum, the provisions of 12.4.2.8.3 shall be included in the periodic inspection and testing procedure. [80:5.2.4.3]

12.4.2.8.4.4 Inspection shall include an operational test for automatic-closing doors and windows to verify that the assembly will close under fire conditions. [80:5.2.4.4]

12.4.2.8.4.5 The assembly shall be reset after a successful test. [80:5.2.4.4.1]

12.4.2.8.4.6 Resetting of the release mechanism shall be done in accordance with the manufacturer's instructions. [**80:**5.2.4.4.2]

12.4.2.8.4.7* Hardware shall be examined, and inoperative hardware, parts, or other defective items shall be replaced without delay. [**80:**5.2.4.5]

12.4.2.8.4.8 Tin-clad and kalamein doors shall be inspected for dry rot of the wood core. [**80:**5.2.4.6]

12.4.2.8.4.9 Chains, cables or ropes employed shall be inspected for excessive wear, stretching, degradation, and binding. [**80:**5.2.4.7]

N **12.4.2.8.4.10** Undamaged and unmarked wired glass in existing labeled fire door assemblies shall be permitted to remain in accordance with codes applicable at the time of installation. [**80:**5.2.4.8]

12.4.2.9 Retrofit Operators.

12.4.2.9.1 The operator, governor, and automatic-closing device on rolling steel fire doors shall be permitted to be retrofitted with a labeled retrofit operator under the conditions specified in 12.4.2.9.2 through 12.4.2.9.5. [**80:**5.3.1]

12.4.2.9.2 The retrofit operator shall be labeled as such. [**80:**5.3.2]

12.4.2.9.3 The retrofit operator shall be installed in accordance with its installation instructions and listing. [**80:**5.3.3]

12.4.2.9.4 The installation shall be acceptable to the AHJ. [**80:**5.3.4]

12.4.2.9.5 The retrofit operator shall be permitted to be provided by a manufacturer other than the original manufacturer of the rolling steel fire door on which it is retrofitted, provided its listing allows it to be retrofitted on that manufacturer's doors. [**80:**5.3.5]

12.4.2.10* Performance-Based Option.

12.4.2.10.1 As an alternate means of compliance with 12.4.2.8.4, subject to the AHJ, fire door assemblies shall be permitted to be inspected, tested, and maintained under a written performance-based program. [**80:**5.4.1]

12.4.2.10.2 Goals established under a performance-based program shall provide assurance that the fire door assembly will perform its intended function when exposed to fire conditions. [**80:**5.4.2]

12.4.2.10.3 Technical justification for inspection, testing, and maintenance intervals shall be documented in writing. [**80:**5.4.3]

12.4.2.10.4 The performance-based option shall include historical data acceptable to the AHJ. [**80:**5.4.4]

12.4.2.11 Maintenance.

12.4.2.11.1* Repairs shall be made, and defects that could interfere with operation shall be corrected without delay. [**80:**5.5.1]

12.4.2.11.2 Damaged glazing material shall be replaced with labeled glazing. [**80:**5.5.2]

12.4.2.11.3 Replacement glazing materials shall be installed in accordance with their individual listing. [**80:**5.5.3]

12.4.2.11.4* Any breaks in the face covering of doors shall be repaired without delay. [**80:**5.5.4]

Δ **12.4.2.11.5** Where a fire door, assembly, or any part thereof is damaged to the extent that it could impair the door's proper emergency function, the following actions shall be performed:

(1) The fire door, assembly, or any part thereof shall be repaired with listed or labeled parts or parts obtained from the original manufacturer.
(2) The fire door assembly shall be tested to ensure emergency operation and closing upon completion of the repairs.

[**80:**5.5.5]

12.4.2.11.6 If repairs cannot be made with parts that are listed or labeled or that are obtained from the original manufacturer or retrofitted in accordance with 12.4.2.9, the fire door assembly or any part thereof shall be replaced. [**80:**5.5.6]

12.4.2.11.7 When fastener holes are left in a door or frame due to changes or removal of hardware or plant-ons, the holes shall be repaired by the following methods:

(1) Install steel fasteners that completely fill the holes.
(2) Fill the screw or bolt holes with the same material as the door or frame.
(3) Fill holes with material listed for this use and installed in accordance with the manufacturer's procedures.

[**80:**5.5.7]

12.4.2.11.8 Holes, other than those as described by 12.4.2.11.7, shall be treated as a field modification in accordance with 12.4.2.6. [**80:**5.5.8]

N **12.4.2.11.9** Field painting of rolling steel fire doors and service counter fire doors shall be considered maintenance work. [**80:**5.5.9]

12.4.2.11.10* Upon completion of maintenance or repair work, fire door assemblies shall be inspected and tested in accordance with 12.4.2.8.3. [**80:**5.5.10]

12.4.2.11.10.1 A record of inspections and testing, as required by 12.4.2.11.10, shall be made in accordance with 12.4.2.8.2. [**80:**5.5.10.1]

12.4.2.11.10.2 A record of maintenance performed on existing fire door assemblies shall include the following information:

(1) Date of maintenance
(2) Name of facility
(3) Address of facility
(4) Name of person(s) performing maintenance
(5) Company name and address of maintenance personnel
(6) Signature of maintenance personnel performing the work
(7) Individual listings of each inspected and tested fire door assembly
(8)* Opening identifier and location of each repaired fire door assembly
(9)* Type and description of each repaired fire door assembly
(10)* Description or listing of the work performed on each fire door assembly

[**80:**5.5.10.2]

12.5* Interior Finish.

12.5.1 Interior finish in buildings and structures shall meet the requirements of NFPA *101* and this *Code*.

12.5.2* General.

12.5.2.1 Classification of interior finish materials shall be in accordance with tests made under conditions simulating actual installations, provided that the AHJ is permitted to establish the classification of any material for which classification by a standard test is not available. [*101*:10.2.1.1]

12.5.2.2 Fixed or movable walls and partitions, paneling, wall pads, and crash pads applied structurally or for decoration, acoustical correction, surface insulation, or other purposes shall be considered interior finish and shall not be considered decorations or furnishings. [*101*:10.2.1.2]

12.5.2.3 Lockers shall be considered interior finish. [*101*:10.2.1.3]

12.5.2.4 Washroom water closet partitions shall be considered interior finish. [*101*:10.2.1.4]

12.5.2.5 Fire-retardant coatings shall be in accordance with 12.5.7. [*101*:10.2.1.5]

12.5.3* Use of Interior Finishes.

12.5.3.1 Requirements for interior wall and ceiling finish shall apply as follows:

(1) Where specified elsewhere in this *Code* for specific occupancies *(see Chapter 7 and Chapters 11 through 43 of NFPA 101)*
(2) As specified in 12.5.4 through 12.5.7

[*101*:10.2.2.1]

12.5.3.2* Interior floor finish shall comply with 12.5.8 under any of the following conditions:

(1) Where floor finish requirements are specified elsewhere in this *Code*
(2) Where the fire performance of the floor finish cannot be demonstrated to be equivalent to floor finishes with a critical radiant flux of at least 0.1 W/cm^2

[*101*:10.2.2.2]

12.5.4* Interior Wall or Ceiling Finish Testing and Classification. Where interior wall or ceiling finish is required elsewhere in this *Code* to be classified for fire performance and smoke development, it shall be classified in accordance with 12.5.4.1 or 12.5.4.2, except as indicated in 12.5.5. [*101*:10.2.3]

12.5.4.1 Interior Wall and Ceiling Finish Materials Tested in Accordance with NFPA 286.

12.5.4.1.1 Interior wall and ceiling finish materials shall be classified in accordance with NFPA 286 and comply with 12.5.4.2. [*101*:10.2.3.1.1]

Δ **12.5.4.1.2*** Materials tested in accordance with 12.5.4.1.1 and complying with 12.5.4.2 shall also be considered to comply with the requirements of a Class A in accordance with 12.5.4.3. [*101*:10.2.3.1.2]

12.5.4.2 Acceptance Criteria for NFPA 286. The interior finish shall comply with the following:

(1) During the 40 kW exposure, flames shall not spread to the ceiling.
(2) The flame shall not spread to the outer extremity of the sample on any wall or ceiling.
(3) Flashover, as described in NFPA 286, shall not occur.
(4) The peak heat release rate throughout the test shall not exceed 800 kW.
(5) For new installations, the total smoke released throughout the test shall not exceed 1000 m^2.

[*101*:10.2.3.2]

12.5.4.3* Interior Wall and Ceiling Finish Materials Tested in Accordance with ASTM E84 or UL 723. Interior wall and ceiling finish materials shall be classified in accordance with ASTM E84, *Standard Test Method for Surface Burning Characteristics of Building Materials,* or UL 723, *Test for Surface Burning Characteristics of Building Materials,* except as indicated in 12.5.4.4 and 12.5.4.5, and shall be grouped in the following classes in accordance with their flame spread and smoke developed indexes:

(1) Class A: Flame spread index 0–25; smoke developed index 0–450.
(2) Class B: Flame spread index 26–75; smoke developed index 0–450.
(3) Class C: Flame spread index 76–200; smoke developed index 0–450.

[*101*:10.2.3.3]

12.5.4.3.1 Existing interior finish shall be exempt from the smoke developed index criteria of 12.5.4.3. [*101*:10.2.3.3.1]

12.5.4.3.2 The classification of interior finish specified in 12.5.4.3 shall be that of the basic material used by itself or in combination with other materials. [*101*:10.2.3.3.2]

12.5.4.3.3 Wherever the use of Class C interior wall and ceiling finish is required, Class A or Class B shall be permitted, and where Class B interior wall and ceiling finish is required, Class A shall be permitted. [*101*:10.2.3.3.3]

12.5.4.4 Materials complying with the requirements of 12.5.4.1 shall not be required to be tested in accordance with 12.5.4.3. [*101*:10.2.3.4]

12.5.4.5 Materials described in 12.5.5 shall be tested as described in the corresponding sections. [*101*:10.2.3.5]

12.5.5* Interior Wall and Ceiling Finish Materials with Special Requirements. The materials indicated in 12.5.5.1 through 12.5.5.16 shall be tested as indicated in the corresponding sections. [*101*:10.2.4]

12.5.5.1 Thickness Exemption. The provisions of 12.5.4 shall not apply to materials having a total thickness of less than $\frac{1}{28}$ in. (0.9 mm) that are applied directly to the surface of walls and ceilings where all of the following conditions are met:

(1) The wall or ceiling surface is a noncombustible or limited combustible material.
(2) The material applied meets the requirements of Class A interior wall or ceiling finish when tested in accordance with 12.5.4.3, using fiber cement board as the substrate material.
(3) The material applied is not one of the following:
    (a) A textile wall or ceiling covering
    (b) An expanded vinyl wall or ceiling covering

[*101*:10.2.4.1]

12.5.5.1.1 If a material having a total thickness of less than $\frac{1}{28}$ in. (0.9 mm) is applied to a surface that is not noncombustible or not limited-combustible, the provisions of 12.5.4 shall apply. [*101*:10.2.4.1.1]

12.5.5.1.2 Approved existing installations of materials applied directly to the surface of walls and ceilings in a total thickness of less than $\frac{1}{28}$ in. (0.9 mm) shall be permitted to remain in use, and the provisions of 12.5.4 shall not apply. [*101*:10.2.4.1.2]

12.5.5.2* Exposed Portions of Structural Members. In other than new interior exit stairways, new interior exit ramps, and new exit passageways, exposed portions of structural members complying with the requirements for Type IV (2HH) construction in accordance with NFPA 220 or with the building code shall be exempt from testing and classification in accordance with 12.5.4. [*101*:10.2.4.2]

12.5.5.3 Cellular or Foamed Plastic.

12.5.5.3.1 Cellular or foamed plastic materials shall not be used as interior wall and ceiling finish unless specifically permitted by 12.5.5.3.2 or 12.5.5.3.3.1. [*101*:10.2.4.3.1]

12.5.5.3.2 The requirements of 12.5.5.3 shall apply both to exposed foamed plastics and to foamed plastics used in conjunction with a textile or vinyl facing or cover. [*101*:10.2.4.3.2]

12.5.5.3.3* Cellular or foamed plastic materials shall be permitted where subjected to large-scale fire tests that substantiate their combustibility and smoke release characteristics for the use intended under actual fire conditions. [*101*:10.2.4.3.3]

12.5.5.3.3.1 One of the following fire tests shall be used for assessing the combustibility of cellular or foamed plastic materials as interior finish:

(1) NFPA 286 with the acceptance criteria of 12.5.4.2
(2) UL 1715, *Fire Test of Interior Finish Material* [including smoke measurements, with total smoke release not to exceed 10,764 ft^2 (1000 m^2)]
(3) UL 1040, *Fire Test of Insulated Wall Construction*
(4) ANSI/FM Approvals 4880, *American National Standard for Evaluating the Fire Performance of Insulated Building Panel Assemblies and Interior Finish Materials*

[*101*:10.2.4.3.3.1]

12.5.5.3.3.2* The tests shall be performed on a finished foamed plastic assembly related to the actual end-use configuration, including any cover or facing, and at the maximum thickness intended for use. [*101*:10.2.4.3.3.2]

12.5.5.3.3.3 Cellular or foamed plastic materials tested in accordance with UL 1040, *Fire Test of Insulated Wall Construction*, or ANSI/FM Approvals 4880, *American National Standard for Evaluating the Fire Performance of Insulated Building Panel Assemblies and Interior Finish Materials*, shall also be tested for smoke release using NFPA 286 with the acceptance criteria of 12.5.4.2. [*101*:10.2.4.3.3.3]

12.5.5.3.4 Cellular or foamed plastic shall be permitted for trim not in excess of 10 percent of the specific wall or ceiling area to which it is applied, provided that it is not less than 20 lb/ft^3 (320 kg/m^3) in density, is limited to ½ in. (13 mm) in thickness and 4 in. (100 mm) in width, and complies with the requirements for Class A or Class B interior wall and ceiling finish as described in 12.5.4.3; however, the smoke developed index shall not be limited. [*101*:10.2.4.3.4]

12.5.5.4* Textile Wall Coverings. Where used as interior wall finish materials, textile materials shall be tested in the manner intended for use, using the product mounting system, including adhesive, and shall comply with the requirements of 12.5.4.1, 12.5.5.4.1, or 12.5.5.4.3. [*101*:10.2.4.4]

12.5.5.4.1* Products tested in accordance with NFPA 265 shall comply with the criteria of 12.5.5.4.2. [*101*:10.2.4.4.1]

12.5.5.4.2* The interior finish shall comply with all of the following when tested using method B of the test protocol of NFPA 265:

(1) During the 40 kW exposure, flames shall not spread to the ceiling.
(2) The flame shall not spread to the outer extremities of the samples on the 8 ft × 12 ft (2440 mm × 3660 mm) walls.
(3) Flashover, as described in NFPA 265, shall not occur.
(4) For new installations, the total smoke released throughout the test shall not exceed 1000 m^2.

[*101*:10.2.4.4.2]

12.5.5.4.3 Textile materials meeting the requirements of Class A when tested in accordance with ASTM E84, *Standard Test Method for Surface Burning Characteristics of Building Materials*, or UL 723, *Test for Surface Burning Characteristics of Building Materials*, using the specimen preparation and mounting method of ASTM E2404, *Standard Practice for Specimen Preparation and Mounting of Textile, Paper or Polymeric (Including Vinyl) and Wood Wall or Ceiling Coverings, Facings and Veneers, to Assess Surface Burning Characteristics*, shall be permitted as follows:

(1) On the walls of rooms or areas protected by an approved automatic sprinkler system.
(2) On partitions that do not exceed three-quarters of the floor-to-ceiling height or do not exceed 8 ft (2440 mm) in height, whichever is less.
(3) On the lower 48 in. (1220 mm) above the finished floor on ceiling-height walls and ceiling-height partitions.
(4) Previously approved existing installations of textile material meeting the requirements of Class A when tested in accordance with ASTM E84, *Standard Test Method for Surface Burning Characteristics of Building Materials* or UL 723, *Test for Surface Burning Characteristics of Building Materials*, shall be permitted to be continued to be used.

[*101*:10.2.4.4.3]

12.5.5.5* Expanded Vinyl Wall Coverings. Where used as interior wall finish materials, expanded vinyl wall coverings shall be tested in the manner intended for use, using the product mounting system, including adhesive, and shall comply with the requirements of either 12.5.4.1, 12.5.5.4.1, or 12.5.5.4.3. [*101*:10.2.4.5]

12.5.5.6 Textile Ceiling Coverings. Where used as interior ceiling finish materials, textile materials shall be tested in the manner intended for use, using the product mounting system, including adhesive, and shall meet one of the following:

(1) Comply with the requirements of 12.5.4.1
(2) Meet the requirements of Class A when tested in accordance with ASTM E84, *Standard Test Method for Surface Burning Characteristics of Building Materials* or UL 723, *Test for Surface Burning Characteristics of Building Materials* using the specimen preparation and mounting method of ASTM E2404, *Standard Practice for Specimen Preparation and Mounting of Textile, Paper or Polymeric (Including Vinyl) and Wood Wall or Ceiling Coverings, Facings and Veneers, to Assess*

Surface Burning Characteristics, and used on the ceilings of rooms or areas protected by an approved automatic sprinkler system [*101*:10.2.4.6]

12.5.5.7 Expanded Vinyl Ceiling Coverings. Where used as interior ceiling finish materials, expanded vinyl materials shall be tested in the manner intended for use, using the product mounting system, including adhesive, and shall meet one of the following:

(1) Comply with the requirements of 12.5.4.1
(2) Meet the requirements of Class A when tested in accordance with ASTM E84, *Standard Test Method for Surface Burning Characteristics of Building Materials* or UL 723, *Test for Surface Burning Characteristics of Building Materials*, using the specimen preparation and mounting method of ASTM E2404, *Standard Practice for Specimen Preparation and Mounting of Textile, Paper or Polymeric (Including Vinyl) and Wood Wall or Ceiling Coverings, Facings and Veneers, to Assess Surface Burning Characteristics*, and used on the ceilings of rooms or areas protected by an approved automatic sprinkler system

[*101*:10.2.4.7]

12.5.5.8 Lockers.

12.5.5.8.1 Combustible Lockers. Where lockers constructed of combustible materials other than wood are used, the lockers shall be considered interior finish and shall comply with 12.5.4, except as permitted by 12.5.5.8.2. [*101*:10.2.4.8.1]

12.5.5.8.2 Wood Lockers. Lockers constructed entirely of wood and of noncombustible materials shall be permitted to be used in any location where interior finish materials are required to meet a Class C classification in accordance with 12.5.4. [*101*:10.2.4.8.2]

12.5.5.9 Solid Thermoplastics.

12.5.5.9.1 Solid thermoplastics including, but not limited to, polypropylene, high-density polyethylene (HDPE), solid polycarbonate, solid polystyrene, and solid acrylic materials that melt and drip when exposed to flame shall not be permitted as interior wall or ceiling finish unless the material complies with the requirements of 12.5.4.1. [*101*:10.2.4.9.1]

12.5.5.9.2 The tests shall be performed on a finished assembly and on the maximum thickness intended for use. [*101*:10.2.4.9.2]

12.5.5.10 Site-Fabricated Stretch Systems.

12.5.5.10.1 For new installations, site-fabricated stretch systems containing all three components described in the definition in Chapter 3 shall be tested in the manner intended for use and shall comply with the requirements of 12.5.4.1 or with the requirements of Class A in accordance with 12.5.4.3. [*101*:10.2.4.10.1]

12.5.5.10.2 If the materials are tested in accordance with ASTM E84, *Standard Test Method for Surface Burning Characteristics of Building Materials*, or UL 723, *Test for Surface Burning Characteristics of Building Materials*, specimen preparation and mounting shall be in accordance with ASTM E2573, *Standard Practice for Specimen Preparation and Mounting of Site-Fabricated Stretch Systems to Assess Surface Burning Characteristics*. [*101*:10.2.4.10.2]

12.5.5.11 Reflective Insulation Materials.

12.5.5.11.1 Reflective insulation materials shall be tested in the manner intended for use and shall comply with the requirements of 12.5.4 or 12.5.4.3. [*101*:10.2.4.11.1]

Δ **12.5.5.11.2** If the materials are tested in accordance with ASTM E84, *Standard Test Method for Surface Burning Characteristics of Building Materials*, or UL 723, *Test for Surface Burning Characteristics of Building Materials*, specimen preparation and mounting shall be in accordance with ASTM E2599, *Standard Practice for Specimen Preparation and Mounting of Reflective Insulation, Radiant Barrier and Vinyl Stretch Ceiling Materials for Building Applications to Assess Surface Burning Characteristics*. [*101*:10.2.4.11.2]

12.5.5.12 Metal Ceiling and Wall Panels.

Δ **12.5.5.12.1** Listed factory finished metal ceiling and wall panels meeting the requirements of Class A in accordance with 12.5.4, shall be permitted to be finished with one additional application of paint. [*101*:10.2.4.12.1]

12.5.5.12.2 Such painted panels shall be permitted for use in areas where Class A interior finishes are required. The total paint thickness shall not exceed $\frac{1}{28}$ in. (0.9 mm). [*101*:10.2.4.12.2]

12.5.5.13 Laminated Products Factory Produced with a Wood Substrate.

12.5.5.13.1 Laminated products factory produced with a wood substrate shall be tested in the manner intended for use and shall comply with the requirements of 12.5.4.1 or 12.5.4.3. [*101*:10.2.4.13.1]

12.5.5.13.2 If the materials are tested in accordance with ASTM E84, *Standard Test Method for Surface Burning Characteristics of Building Materials*, or UL 723, *Test for Surface Burning Characteristics of Building Materials*, specimen preparation and mounting shall be in accordance with ASTM E2579, *Standard Practice for Specimen Preparation and Mounting of Wood Products to Assess Surface Burning Characteristics*, using the product-mounting system, including adhesive, of actual use. [*101*:10.2.4.13.2]

12.5.5.14 Facings or Wood Veneers Intended to be Applied on Site over a Wood Substrate.

12.5.5.14.1 Facings or veneers intended to be applied on site over a wood substrate shall be tested in the manner intended for use and shall comply with the requirements of 12.5.4.1 or 12.5.4.3. [*101*:10.2.4.14.1]

12.5.5.14.2 If the materials are tested in accordance with NFPA 286 they shall use the product-mounting system, including adhesive, described in 5.8.9 of NFPA 286. [*101*:10.2.4.14.2]

12.5.5.14.3 If the materials are tested in accordance with ASTM E84, *Standard Test Method for Surface Burning Characteristics of Building Materials*, or UL 723, *Test for Surface Burning Characteristics of Building Materials*, specimen preparation and mounting shall be in accordance with ASTM E2404, *Standard Practice for Specimen Preparation and Mounting of Textile, Paper or Polymeric (Including Vinyl) and Wood Wall or Ceiling Coverings, Facings and Veneers, to Assess Surface Burning Characteristics*. [*101*:10.2.4.14.3]

12.5.5.15* Light-Transmitting Plastics.

12.5.5.15.1 Light-transmitting plastics used as interior wall and ceiling finish shall be permitted based on large-scale fire tests per 12.5.5.3.3.1, which substantiate the combustibility characteristics of the plastics for the use intended under actual fire conditions. [*101*:10.2.4.15.1]

12.5.5.15.2 The tests shall be performed on a light-transmitting plastic assembly related to the actual end-use configuration and on the maximum thickness intended for use. [*101*:10.2.4.15.2]

12.5.5.16 Decorations and Furnishings. Decorations and furnishings that do not meet the definition of interior finish, as defined in 3.3.121.2, shall be regulated by the provisions of Section 12.6. [*101*:10.2.4.16]

12.5.6 Trim and Incidental Finish.

12.5.6.1 General. Interior wall and ceiling trim and incidental finish, other than wall base in accordance with 12.5.6.2 and bulletin boards, posters, and paper in accordance with 12.5.6.3, not in excess of 10 percent of the specific wall and ceiling areas of any room or space to which it is applied shall be permitted to be Class C materials in occupancies where interior wall and ceiling finish of Class A or Class B is required. [*101*:10.2.5.1]

12.5.6.2 Wall Base. Interior floor trim material used at the junction of the wall and the floor to provide a functional or decorative border, and not exceeding 6 in. (150 mm) in height, shall meet the requirements for interior wall finish for its location or the requirements for Class II interior floor finish as described in 12.5.8.4 using the test described in 12.5.8.3. [*101*:10.2.5.2]

12.5.6.2.1 If a Class I floor finish is required, the interior floor trim shall be Class I. [*101*:10.2.5.2.1]

12.5.6.3 Bulletin Boards, Posters, and Paper.

12.5.6.3.1 Bulletin boards, posters, and paper attached directly to the wall shall not exceed 20 percent of the aggregate wall area to which they are applied. [*101*:10.2.5.3.1]

12.5.6.3.2 The provision of 12.5.6.3.1 shall not apply to artwork and teaching materials in sprinklered educational or day-care occupancies in accordance with 20.2.4.4.3(3), 20.2.4.4.3(4), 20.3.4.2.3.5.3(3), and 20.3.4.2.3.5.3(4). [*101*:10.2.5.3.2]

12.5.7* Fire-Retardant Coatings.

12.5.7.1* The required flame spread index or smoke developed index of existing surfaces of walls, partitions, columns, and ceilings shall be permitted to be secured by applying approved fire-retardant coatings to surfaces having higher flame spread index values than permitted. [*101*:10.2.6.1]

Δ **12.5.7.1.1** Such treatments shall be tested or shall be listed and labeled for application to the material to which they are applied and shall comply with the requirements of NFPA 703. [*101*:10.2.6.1.1]

12.5.7.2* Surfaces of walls, partitions, columns, and ceilings shall be permitted to be finished with factory-applied fire-retardant-coated products that have been listed and labeled to demonstrate compliance with the requirements of ASTM E2768, *Standard Test Method for Extended Duration Surface Burning Characteristics of Building Materials (30 min Tunnel Test)*, on the coated surface. [*101*:10.2.6.2]

12.5.7.3 Fire-retardant coatings or factory-applied fire-retardant-coated products shall possess the desired degree of permanency and shall be maintained so as to retain the effectiveness of the treatment under the service conditions encountered in actual use. [*101*:10.2.6.3]

12.5.8* Interior Floor Finish Testing and Classification.

12.5.8.1* Carpet and carpet-like interior floor finishes shall comply with ASTM D2859, *Standard Test Method for Ignition Characteristics of Finished Textile Floor Covering Materials*. [*101*:10.2.7.1]

12.5.8.2 Floor coverings, other than carpet for which 12.5.3.2 establishes requirements for fire performance, shall have a minimum critical radiant flux of 0.1 W/cm^2. [*101*:10.2.7.2]

12.5.8.3* Interior floor finishes shall be classified in accordance with 12.5.8.4, based on test results from NFPA 253 or ASTM E648, *Standard Test Method for Critical Radiant Flux of Floor-Covering Systems Using a Radiant Heat Energy Source*. [*101*:10.2.7.3]

12.5.8.4 Interior floor finishes shall be grouped in the classes specified in 12.5.8.4.1 and 12.5.8.4.2 in accordance with the critical radiant flux requirements. [*101*:10.2.7.4]

12.5.8.4.1 Class I Interior Floor Finish. Class I interior floor finish shall have a critical radiant flux of not less than 0.45 W/cm^2, as determined by the test described in 12.5.8.3. [*101*:10.2.7.4.1]

12.5.8.4.2 Class II Interior Floor Finish. Class II interior floor finish shall have a critical radiant flux of not less than 0.22 W/cm^2, but less than 0.45 W/cm^2, as determined by the test described in 12.5.8.3. [*101*:10.2.7.4.2]

12.5.8.5 Wherever the use of Class II interior floor finish is required, Class I interior floor finish shall be permitted. [*101*:10.2.7.5]

12.5.9 Automatic Sprinklers.

Δ **12.5.9.1** Other than as required in 12.5.5, where an approved automatic sprinkler system is installed in accordance with Section 13.3, Class C interior wall and ceiling finish materials shall be permitted in any location where Class B is required, and Class B interior wall and ceiling finish materials shall be permitted in any location where Class A is required. [*101*:10.2.8.1]

Δ **12.5.9.2** Where an approved automatic sprinkler system is installed in accordance with Section 13.3, throughout the fire compartment or smoke compartment containing the interior floor finish, Class II interior floor finish shall be permitted in any location where Class I interior floor finish is required, and where Class II is required, the provisions of 12.5.8.2 shall apply. [*101*:10.2.8.2]

12.6 Contents and Furnishings.

12.6.1* Draperies, Curtains, and Other Hanging or Suspended Furnishings and Decorations. Where required by the applicable provisions of this *Code*, draperies, curtains, and other hanging or suspended furnishings and decorations shall meet the flame propagation performance criteria contained in Test Method 1 or Test Method 2, as appropriate, of NFPA 701. [*101*:10.3.1]

12.6.2 Upholstered Furniture.

12.6.2.1* Smoldering Ignition of Upholstered Furniture. Newly introduced upholstered furniture, except as otherwise permitted by Chapters 11 through 43 of *NFPA 101*, shall be resistant to a cigarette ignition (i.e., smoldering) in accordance with one of the following:

(1) The components of the upholstered furniture shall meet the requirements for Class I when tested in accordance with NFPA 260.
(2) Mocked-up composites of the upholstered furniture shall have a char length not exceeding 1½ in. (38 mm) when tested in accordance with NFPA 261.

[*101*:10.3.2.1]

12.6.2.2* Rate of Heat Release Testing of Upholstered Furniture.

12.6.2.2.1 Where required by the applicable provisions of this *Code*, upholstered furniture and other seating furniture, unless the furniture is located in a building protected throughout by an approved automatic sprinkler system, shall have limited rates of heat release when tested in accordance with ASTM E1537, *Standard Test Method for Fire Testing of Upholstered Furniture*, as follows:

(1) The peak rate of heat release for the single furniture item shall not exceed 80 kW.
(2) The total heat released by the single furniture item during the first 10 minutes of the test shall not exceed 25 MJ.

[*101*:10.3.2.2.1]

12.6.2.2.2 When tests are conducted in accordance with 12.6.2.2, the formation of flaming droplets during the test shall be reported. [*101*:10.3.2.2.2]

12.6.3 Mattresses.

12.6.3.1* Smoldering Ignition of Mattresses. Newly introduced mattresses, except as otherwise permitted by Chapters 11 through 43 of *NFPA 101*, shall have a char length not exceeding 2 in. (51 mm) when tested in accordance with 16 CFR 1632, "Standard for the Flammability of Mattresses and Mattress Pads" (FF 4-72, Amended). [*101*:10.3.3.1]

12.6.3.2* Rate of Heat Release and Mass Loss Testing of Mattresses. Where required by the applicable provisions of this *Code*, mattresses shall comply with 12.6.3.2.1 or 12.6.3.2.2, unless the mattress is located in a building protected throughout by an approved automatic sprinkler system. [*101*:10.3.3.2]

12.6.3.2.1 The mattress shall have limited rates of heat release when tested in accordance with ASTM E1590, *Standard Test Method for Fire Testing of Mattresses*, as follows:

(1) The peak rate of heat release for the single mattress shall not exceed 100 kW.
(2) The total heat released by the mattress during the first 10 minutes of the test shall not exceed 25 MJ.

[*101*:10.3.3.2.1]

12.6.3.2.2 The mattress shall have a mass loss not exceeding 15 percent when tested in accordance with the fire test in Annex A3 of ASTM F1085, *Standard Specification for Mattress and Box Springs for Use in Berths in Marine Vessels*. [*101*:10.3.3.2.2]

12.6.3.2.3 When tests are conducted in accordance with 12.6.3.2, the formation of flaming droplets during the test shall be reported. [*101*:10.3.3.2.3]

12.6.4* Explosive or Highly Flammable Furnishings or Decorations. Furnishings or decorations of an explosive or highly flammable character shall not be used. [*101*:10.3.4]

12.6.5 Fire-Retardant Coatings. Fire-retardant coatings shall be maintained to retain the effectiveness of the treatment under service conditions encountered in actual use. [*101*:10.3.5]

12.6.6* Foamed Plastics. Where required by the applicable provisions of this *Code*, furnishings and contents made with foamed plastic materials that are unprotected from ignition shall have a heat release rate not exceeding 100 kW when tested in accordance with UL 1975, *Fire Tests for Foamed Plastics Used for Decorative Purposes*, or when tested in accordance with NFPA 289 using the 20 kW ignition source. [*101*:10.3.6]

12.6.7 Lockers. Lockers shall be considered interior finish and shall comply with the requirements of 12.5.5.8. [*101*:10.3.7]

12.6.8 Containers for Waste or Linen.

12.6.8.1 Where required by Chapters 11 through 43 of NFPA *101*, newly introduced containers for waste or linen, with a capacity of 20 gal (75.7 L) or more, shall meet both of the following:

(1) Such containers shall be provided with lids.
(2) Such containers and their lids shall be constructed of noncombustible materials or of materials that meet a peak rate of heat release not exceeding 300 kW/m^2 when tested at an incident heat flux of 50 kW/m^2 in the horizontal orientation and at a thickness as used in the container but not less than ¼ in. (6.3 mm), in accordance with ASTM E1354, *Standard Test Method for Heat and Visible Smoke Release Rates for Materials and Products Using an Oxygen Consumption Calorimeter*.

[*101*:10.3.8.1]

12.6.8.2 Where required by Chapters 11 through 43 of NFPA *101*, newly introduced metal wastebaskets and other metal waste, or linen containers with a capacity of 20 gal (75.7 L) or more shall be listed in accordance with UL 1315, *Safety Containers for Waste Paper*, and shall be provided with a noncombustible lid. [*101*:10.3.8.2]

12.6.9 Combustible Vegetation.

12.6.9.1 Combustible vegetation, including natural cut Christmas trees, shall be in accordance with 12.6.9.

12.6.9.1.1 Christmas tree placement within buildings shall comply with Table 12.6.9.1.1.

12.6.9.2 In any occupancy, limited quantities of combustible vegetation shall be permitted where the AHJ determines that adequate safeguards are provided based on the quantity and nature of the combustible vegetation.

12.6.9.3 Vegetation and Christmas trees shall not obstruct corridors, exit ways, or other means of egress.

12.6.9.4 Combustible vegetation and natural cut Christmas trees shall not be located near heating vents or other fixed or

Table 12.6.9.1.1 Provisions for Christmas Trees by Occupancy

Occupancy	No Trees Permitted	Cut Tree Permitted With Automatic Sprinkler Systems	Cut Tree Permitted Without Automatic Sprinkler Systems	Balled Tree Permitted
Ambulatory health care				X
Apartment buildings		Within unit	Within unit	X
Assembly	X			
Board and care	X			
Business		X		X
Day-care		X		X
Detention and correctional	X			
Dormitories	X			
Educational	X			
Health care				X
Hotels	X			
Industrial		X	X	X
Lodging and rooming				X
Mercantile		X		X
One and two family		X	X	X
Storage		X	X	X

portable heating devices that could cause it to dry out prematurely or to be ignited.

12.6.9.5 Flammability of Combustible Artificial Decorative Vegetation.

Δ **12.6.9.5.1** Combustible artificial decorative vegetation shall meet one of the following:

(1) The flame propagation performance criteria of Test Method 1 or Test Method 2, as appropriate, of NFPA 701
(2) A maximum heat release rate of 100 kW when tested to NFPA 289, using the 20 kW ignition source

[*101*:10.3.9.1]

12.6.9.5.2 Each individual artificial decorative vegetation item shall be labeled to demonstrate compliance with 12.6.9.5.1 in an approved manner.

12.6.9.6 Provisions for Natural Cut Trees.

12.6.9.6.1 Where a natural cut tree is permitted, the bottom end of the trunk shall be cut off with a straight fresh cut at least ½ in. (13 mm) above the end prior to placing the tree in a stand to allow the tree to absorb water.

12.6.9.6.2 The tree shall be placed in a suitable stand with water.

12.6.9.6.3 The water level shall be maintained above the fresh cut and checked at least once daily.

12.6.9.6.4* The tree shall be removed from the building immediately upon evidence of dryness.

12.6.9.6.5 Fire-Retardant Treatments for Natural Cut Christmas Trees. Where fire-retardant treatments are applied to natural cut Christmas trees, the fire-retardant treatment shall comply with both Test Method 1 and Test Method 2 of ASTM E3082, *Standard Test Methods for Determining the Effectiveness of Fire Retardant Treatments for Natural Christmas Trees*. [*101*:10.3.9.2]

12.6.9.7 Electrical Equipment.

Δ **12.6.9.7.1** Electrical wiring and listed luminaires used on combustible artificial decorative vegetation shall be listed for that application. [*101*:10.3.9.3.1]

12.6.9.7.2 Electrical wiring and luminaires used on natural vegetation shall be listed for that application.

12.6.9.7.3 Electrical lights shall be prohibited on metal artificial trees.

12.6.9.8 Open Flames.

12.6.9.8.1 Candles and open flames shall not be used on or near combustible artificial decorative vegetation. [*101*:10.3.9.4]

12.6.9.8.2 Candles and open flames shall not be used on or near natural vegetation.

12.7 Fire Barriers.

12.7.1 General. Fire barriers used to provide enclosure, subdivision, or protection under NFPA *101* and this *Code* shall be classified in accordance with one of the following fire resistance ratings:

(1) 3-hour fire resistance rating
(2) 2-hour fire resistance rating
(3) 1-hour fire resistance rating
(4) ½-hour fire resistance rating

[*101*:8.3.1.1]

12.7.2* Fire barriers shall comply with one of the following:

(1) The fire barriers are continuous from outside wall to outside wall or from one fire barrier to another, or a combination thereof, including continuity through all concealed spaces, such as those found above a ceiling, including interstitial spaces.
(2) The fire barriers are continuous from outside wall to outside wall or from one fire barrier to another, and from the floor to the bottom of the interstitial space, provided that the construction assembly forming the bottom of the interstitial space has a fire resistance rating not less than that of the fire barrier.

[*101*:8.3.1.2]

12.7.3 Walls used as fire barriers shall comply with the requirements of NFPA 221 applicable to fire barrier walls. [*101*:8.3.1.3]

12.7.4 Smoke Barrier Used as a Fire Barrier. A smoke barrier shall be permitted to be used as a fire barrier, provided that it meets the requirements of Section 8.3 of NFPA *101*. [*101*:8.3.1.4]

12.7.5 Walls.

12.7.5.1 The fire-resistive materials, assemblies, and systems used shall be limited to those permitted in this *Code* and this subsection. [*101*:8.3.2.1]

12.7.5.1.1* Fire resistance glazing tested in accordance with ASTM E119, *Standard Test Methods for Fire Tests of Building Construction and Materials*, or UL 263, *Fire Tests of Building Construction and Materials*, shall be permitted. [*101*:8.3.2.1.1]

12.7.5.2 The construction materials and details for fire-resistive assemblies and systems for walls described shall comply with all other provisions of this *Code*, except as modified herein. [*101*:8.3.2.2]

12.7.5.3 Interior walls and partitions of nonsymmetrical construction shall be evaluated from both directions and assigned a fire resistance rating based on the shorter duration obtained in accordance with ASTM E119, *Standard Test Methods for Fire Tests of Building Construction and Materials*, or UL 263, *Fire Tests of Building Construction and Materials*. When the wall is tested with the least fire-resistive side exposed to the furnace, the wall shall not be required to be subjected to tests from the opposite side. [*101*:8.3.2.3]

12.7.6 Opening Protectives.

12.7.6.1 General. Every opening in a fire barrier shall be protected to limit the spread of fire from one side of the fire barrier to the other. [*101*:8.3.3.1]

12.7.6.2 Minimum Fire Protection Rating.

12.7.6.2.1 Fire protection ratings for products required to comply with 12.7.6 shall be as determined and reported by a nationally recognized testing agency in accordance with NFPA 252; NFPA 257; UL 10B, *Fire Tests of Door Assemblies*; UL 10C, *Positive Pressure Fire Tests of Door Assemblies*; or UL 9, *Fire Tests of Window Assemblies*. [*101*:8.3.3.2.1]

12.7.6.2.2* The minimum fire rating for opening protectives in fire barriers, fire-rated smoke barriers, and fire-rated smoke partitions shall be in accordance with Table 12.7.6.2.2, except as otherwise permitted in 12.7.6.2.3 or 12.7.6.2.4. [*101*:8.3.3.2.2]

12.7.6.2.3 Existing fire door assemblies having a minimum ¾-hour fire protection rating shall be permitted to continue to be used in vertical openings and in exit enclosures in lieu of the minimum 1-hour fire protection rating required by Table 12.7.6.2.2. [*101*:8.3.3.2.3]

12.7.6.2.4 Where a 20-minute fire-protection-rated door is required in existing buildings, an existing 1¾ in. (44 mm) solid-bonded wood-core door, an existing steel-clad (tin-clad) wood door, or an existing solid-core steel door shall be permitted, unless otherwise specified by Chapters 11 through 43 of NFPA *101*. [*101*:8.3.3.2.4]

12.7.6.2.5 Existing doors permitted by 12.7.6.2.4 shall have a positive latch and a closer. [*101*:8.3.3.2.5]

Δ **12.7.6.2.6** Openings required to have a fire protection rating by Table 12.7.6.2.2 shall be protected by approved, listed and labeled fire door assemblies and fire window assemblies and their accompanying hardware, including all frames, closing devices, anchorage, and sills in accordance with the requirements of NFPA 80 except as otherwise specified in NFPA *101*. [*101*:8.3.3.2.6]

12.7.6.3* Fire Doors.

12.7.6.3.1* Required fire door assemblies shall be installed, inspected, tested, and maintained in accordance with NFPA 80. [*101*:8.3.3.3.1]

12.7.6.3.2 All fire door assemblies shall be labeled. [*101*:8.3.3.3.2]

12.7.6.3.3 Labels on fire door assemblies shall be maintained in a legible condition. [*101*:8.3.3.3.3]

12.7.6.3.4 In existing installations, steel door frames without a label shall be permitted where approved by the AHJ. [*101*:8.3.3.3.4]

12.7.6.3.5 Unless otherwise specified, fire doors shall be self-closing or automatic-closing. [*101*:8.3.3.3.5]

12.7.6.4 Floor Fire Door Assemblies.

12.7.6.4.1 Floor fire door assemblies used to protect openings in fire-resistance-rated floors shall be tested in accordance with NFPA 288 and shall achieve a fire resistance rating not less than the assembly being penetrated. [*101*:8.3.3.4.1]

12.7.6.4.2 Floor fire doors assemblies shall be listed and labeled. [*101*:8.3.3.4.2]

12.7.6.5 Fire Windows.

12.7.6.5.1 Fire window assemblies shall be installed, inspected, tested, and maintained in accordance with NFPA 80. [*101*:8.3.3.5.1]

12.7.6.5.2 All fire window assemblies shall be labeled. [*101*:8.3.3.5.2]

12.7.6.5.3* Fire window assemblies shall be permitted in fire barriers having a required fire resistance rating of 1 hour or less and shall be of an approved type with the appropriate fire protection rating for the location in which they are installed. [*101*:8.3.3.5.3]

12.7.6.6 Glazing.

Δ **12.7.6.6.1** Glazing materials that have been listed and labeled to indicate the type of opening to be protected for fire protection purposes shall be permitted to be used in approved opening protectives in accordance with Table 12.7.6.2.2 and NFPA 80. [*101*:8.3.3.6.1]

12.7.6.6.2 Fire-rated glazing assemblies shall be permitted as follows:

(1) Those marked as complying with hose stream requirements (H) shall be permitted in applications that do not require compliance with hose stream requirements.
(2) Those marked as complying with temperature rise requirements (T) shall be permitted in applications that do not require compliance with temperature rise requirements.
(3) Those marked with ratings that exceed the ratings required by NFPA *101* shall be permitted.

[*101*:8.3.3.6.2]

12.7.6.6.3 New fire-protection glazing shall be marked in accordance with Table 12.7.6.6.3 and Table 12.7.6.2.2, and such marking shall be permanently affixed. [*101*:8.3.3.6.3]

Δ **Table 12.7.6.2.2 Minimum Fire Ratings for Opening Protectives in Fire-Resistance-Rated Assemblies and Fire-Rated Glazing Markings**

Component	Walls and Partitions (hr)	Fire Door Assemblies (hr)	Door Vision Panel Maximum Size (in.²)	Fire-Rated Glazing Marking Door Vision Panel	Minimum Side Light/Transom Assembly Rating (hr) — Fire Protection	Minimum Side Light/Transom Assembly Rating (hr) — Fire Resistance	Fire-Rated Glazing Marking Side Light/Transom Panel — Fire Protection	Fire-Rated Glazing Marking Side Light/Transom Panel — Fire Resistance	Minimum Fire Window Rating[a,b] (hr) — Fire Protection	Minimum Fire Window Rating[a,b] (hr) — Fire Resistance	Fire Window Marking — Fire Protection	Fire Window Marking — Fire Resistance
Elevator hoistways	2	1½	155 in.²[c]	D-H-90 or D-H-W-90	NP	2	NP	D-H-W-120	NP	2	NP	W-120
	1	1	155 in.²[c]	D-H-60 or D-H-W-60	NP	1	NP	D-H-W-60	NP	1	NP	W-60
	½	⅓	85 in.²[d]	D-20 or D-W-20	⅓	⅓	D-H-20	D-W-20	⅓	⅓	OH-20	W-30
Elevator lobby (per 7.2.13.4 of NFPA *101*)	1	1	100 in.²[a]	≤100 in.², D-H-T-60 or D-H-W-60[a]; >100 in.², D-H-W-60	NP	1	NP	D-H-W-60	NP	1	NP	W-60
Vertical shafts, (including stairways, exits, and refuse chutes)	2	1½	Maximum size tested	D-H-90 or D-H-W-90	NP	2	NP	D-H-W-120	NP	2	NP	W-120
	1	1	Maximum size tested	D-H-60 or D-H-W-60	NP	1	NP	D-H-W-60	NP	1	NP	W-60
Replacement panels in existing vertical shafts	½	⅓	Maximum size tested	D-20 or D-W-20	⅓	⅓	D-H-20	D-W-20	⅓	⅓	OH-20	W-30
Horizontal exits	2	1½	Maximum size tested	D-H-90 or D-H-W-90	NP	2	NP	D-H-W-120	NP	2	NP	W-120
Horizontal exits served by bridges between buildings	2	¾	Maximum size tested[e]	D-H-45 or D-H-W-45	¾[e]	¾[e]	D-H-45	D-H-W-45	¾	¾	OH-45	W-120
Exit access corridors[f]	1	⅓	Maximum size tested	D-20 or D-W-20	¾	¾	D-H-45	D-H-W-45	¾	¾	OH-45	W-60
	½	⅓	Maximum size tested	D-20 or D-W-20	⅓	⅓	D-H-20	D-H-W-20	⅓	⅓	OH-20	W-30
Other fire barriers	3	3	100 in.²[a]	≤100 in.², D-H-180 or D-H-W-180; >100 in.², D-H-W-180	NP	3	NP	D-H-W-180	NP	3	NP	W-180
	2	1½	Maximum size tested	D-H-90 or D-H-W-90	NP	2	NP	D-H-W-120	NP	2	NP	W-120
	1	¾	Maximum size tested[e]	D-H-45 or D-H-W-45	¾[e]	¾[e]	D-H-45	D-H-W-45	¾	¾	OH-45	W-60
	½	⅓	Maximum size tested	D-20 or D-W-20	⅓	⅓	D-H-20	D-W-20	⅓	⅓	OH-20	W-30
Smoke barriers[f]	1	⅓	Maximum size tested	D-20 or D-W-20	¾	¾	D-H-45	D-H-W-45	¾	¾	OH-45	W-60
	½	⅓	Maximum size tested	D-20 or D-W-20	⅓	⅓	D-H-20	D-H-W-20	⅓	⅓	OH-20	W-30
Smoke partitions[f,g]	1	⅓	Maximum size tested	D-20 or D-W-20	¾	¾	D-H-45	D-H-W-45	¾	¾	OH-45	W-60
	½	⅓	Maximum size tested	D-20 or D-W-20	⅓	⅓	D-H-20	D-H-W-20	⅓	⅓	OH-20	W-30

For SI units, 1 in.² = 0.00064516 m².
NP: Not permitted.
[a]Fire resistance glazing tested to ASTM E119, *Standard Test Methods for Fire Tests of Building Construction and Materials* shall be permitted in the maximum size tested. *(See 12.7.6.6.8).*
[b]Fire-rated glazing in exterior windows shall be marked in accordance with Table 12.7.6.6.3.
[c]See ASME A17.1/CSA B44, *Safety Code for Elevators and Escalators*, for additional information.
[d]See ASME A17.3, *Safety Code for Existing Elevators and Escalators*, for additional information.
[e]Maximum area of individual exposed lights shall be 1296 in.² (0.84 m²) with no dimension exceeding 54 in. (1.37 m) unless otherwise tested. [**80**:Table 4.4.5, Note b, and **80**:4.4.5.1]
[f]Fire doors are not required to have a hose stream test per UL 10B, *Fire Tests of Door Assemblies*, or UL 10C, *Positive Pressure Fire Tests of Door Assemblies*.
[g]For residential board and care, see 32.2.3.1 and 33.2.3.1 of NFPA *101*.
[*101*:Table 8.3.3.2.2]

Table 12.7.6.6.3 Marking Fire-Rated Glazing Assemblies

Fire Test Standard	Marking	Definition of Marking
ASTM E119 or UL 263	W	Meets wall assembly criteria
NFPA 257 or UL 9	OH	Meets fire window assembly criteria, including the hose stream test
NFPA 252, UL 10B, or UL 10C	D	Meets fire door assembly criteria
	H	Meets fire door assembly hose stream test
	T	Meets 450°F (232°C) temperature rise criteria for 30 minutes
	XXX	The time, in minutes, of fire resistance or fire protection rating of the glazing assembly

12.7.6.6.4 New fire resistance glazing shall be marked in accordance with Table 12.7.6.6.3 and Table 12.7.6.2.2, and such marking shall be permanently affixed. [*101*:8.3.3.6.4]

12.7.6.6.5 Fire protection glazing shall be permitted in fire barriers having a required fire resistance rating of 1 hour or less and shall be of an approved type with the appropriate fire protection rating for the location in which the barriers are installed. [*101*:8.3.3.6.5]

12.7.6.6.6* Glazing in fire window assemblies, other than in existing fire window installations of wired glass and other fire-rated glazing material, shall be of a design that has been tested to meet the conditions of acceptance of NFPA 257 or UL 9, *Fire Tests of Window Assemblies*. [*101*:8.3.3.6.6]

12.7.6.6.7 Fire protection glazing in fire door assemblies, other than in existing fire-rated door assemblies, shall be of a design that has been tested to meet the conditions of acceptance of NFPA 252, UL 10B, *Fire Tests of Door Assemblies*, or UL 10C, *Positive Pressure Fire Tests of Door Assemblies*. [*101*:8.3.3.6.7]

12.7.6.6.8 Fire resistance glazing tested in accordance with ASTM E119, *Standard Test Methods for Fire Tests of Building Construction and Materials*, or UL 263, *Fire Tests of Building Construction and Materials*, shall be permitted in fire doors and fire window assemblies in accordance with their listings. [*101*:8.3.3.6.8]

12.7.6.6.9 Nonsymmetrical fire protection glazing systems shall be tested with each face exposed to the furnace, and the assigned fire protection rating shall be the shortest duration obtained from the two tests conducted in compliance with NFPA 257 or UL 9, *Fire Tests of Window Assemblies*. [*101*:8.3.3.6.9]

Δ **12.7.6.6.10** The total combined area of fire protection glazing in fire window assemblies and fire door assemblies used in fire barriers shall not exceed 25 percent of the area of the fire barrier that is common with any room, unless the installation is an existing fire window of wired glass or other fire protection glazing in approved frames. [*101*:8.3.3.10]

12.7.6.6.11 Existing installations of wired glass of ¼ in. (6.3 mm) thickness previously approved for fire protection purposes shall be permitted to remain in use. [*101*:8.3.3.6.11]

12.7.6.7 Sidelights and Transoms. Glazing used in sidelights and transoms adjacent to 20-minute doors in 1-hour corridor fire barriers shall be tested in accordance with 12.7.6.2, including hose stream, and shall attain a minimum 45-minute fire protection rating. [*101*:8.3.3.7]

12.7.7 Opening Protectives.

12.7.7.1 Every opening in a fire barrier shall be protected to limit the spread of fire and restrict the movement of smoke from one side of the fire barrier to the other. [*101*:8.3.3.1]

12.7.8 Penetrations.

12.7.8.1 General.

12.7.8.1.1 The provisions of 12.7.8 shall govern the materials and methods of construction used to protect through-penetrations and membrane penetrations in fire walls, fire barrier walls, and fire-resistance-rated horizontal assemblies. [*101*:8.3.4.1.1]

12.7.8.1.2 The provisions of 12.7.8 shall not apply to approved existing materials and methods of construction used to protect existing through-penetrations and existing membrane penetrations in fire walls, fire barrier walls, or fire-resistance-rated horizontal assemblies, unless otherwise required by Chapters 11 through 43 of NFPA *101*. [*101*:8.3.4.1.2]

Δ **12.7.8.1.3** Penetrations shall be protected by a tested system installed and maintained in accordance with the manufacturer's instructions. [*101*:8.3.4.1.3]

12.7.8.2 Firestop Systems and Devices Required.

12.7.8.2.1 Penetrations for cables, cable trays, conduits, pipes, tubes, combustion vents and exhaust vents, wires, and similar items to accommodate electrical, mechanical, plumbing, and communications systems that pass through a wall, floor, or floor/ceiling assembly constructed as a fire barrier shall be protected by a firestop system or device. [*101*:8.3.4.2.1]

12.7.8.2.2 Testing. The firestop system or device shall be tested in accordance with ASTM E814, *Standard Test Method for Fire Tests of Penetration Firestop Systems*, or UL 1479, *Fire Tests of Penetration Firestops*, at a minimum positive pressure differential of 0.01 in. water column (2.5 Pa) between the exposed and the unexposed surface of the test assembly. [*101*:8.3.4.2.2]

12.7.8.2.3 F Ratings. Firestop systems and devices shall have an F rating of not less than 1 hour, and not less than the required fire resistance rating of the fire barrier penetrated. [*101*:8.3.4.2.3]

12.7.8.2.4 T Ratings.

12.7.8.2.4.1 Penetrations in fire-resistance-rated horizontal assemblies shall have a T rating of not less than 1 hour, and not less than the fire resistance rating of the horizontal assembly. [*101*:8.3.4.2.4.1]

12.7.8.2.4.2 A T rating shall not be required for either of the following:

(1) Floor penetrations contained within the cavity of a wall assembly

(2) Penetrations through floors or floor assemblies where the penetration is not in direct contact with combustible material [*101*:8.3.4.2.4.2]

12.7.8.2.5 Alternative Firestop Requirements.

12.7.8.2.5.1 The requirements of 12.7.8.2 shall not apply where otherwise permitted by any one of the following:

(1) Where penetrations are tested and installed as part of an assembly tested and rated in accordance with ASTM E119, *Standard Test Methods for Fire Tests of Building Construction and Materials*, or UL 263, *Fire Tests of Building Construction and Materials*
(2) Where penetrations through floors are enclosed in a shaft enclosure designed as a fire barrier
(3) Where concrete, grout, or mortar has been used to fill the annular spaces around cast-iron, copper, or steel piping, conduit, or tubing that penetrates one or more concrete or masonry fire-resistance-rated assemblies, and all of the following applies:
   (a) The nominal diameter of each penetrating item does not exceed 6 in. (150 mm),
   (b) The opening size does not exceed 1 ft^2 (0.09 m^2).
   (c) The thickness of the concrete, grout, or mortar is the full thickness of the assembly.
(4) Where penetration is limited to one floor, the firestopping material is capable of preventing the passage of flame and hot gases sufficient to ignite cotton waste when subjected to the time-temperature fire conditions of ASTM E119, *Standard Test Methods for Fire Tests of Building Construction and Materials*, or UL 263, *Fire Tests of Building Materials*, under a minimum positive pressure differential of 0.01 in. water column (2.5 Pa) at the location of the penetration for the time period equivalent to the required fire resistance rating of the assembly penetrated, and the firestopping materials are used with the following penetrating items:
   (a) Steel, ferrous, or copper cables
   (b) Cable or wire with steel jackets
   (c) Cast-iron, steel, or copper pipes
   (d) Steel conduit or tubing

[*101*:8.3.4.2.5.1]

12.7.8.2.5.2 The maximum nominal diameter of the penetrating item, as indicated in 12.7.8.2.5.1(4)(a) through 12.7.8.2.5.1(4)(d), shall not be greater than 4 in. (100 mm) and shall not exceed an aggregate 100 in.^{2} (64,520 mm^2) opening in any 100 ft^2 (9.3 m^2) of floor or wall area. [*101*:8.3.4.2.5.2]

12.7.8.3 Sleeves. Where the penetrating item uses a sleeve to penetrate the wall or floor, the sleeve shall be securely set in the wall or floor, and the space between the item and the sleeve shall be filled with a material that complies with 12.7.8.2. [*101*:8.3.4.3]

12.7.8.4 Insulation and Coverings. Insulation and coverings for penetrating items shall not pass through the wall or floor unless the insulation or covering has been tested as part of the firestop system or device. [*101*:8.3.4.4]

12.7.8.5 Vibration Isolation Equipment or Systems. Where vibration isolation of equipment or systems is employed, the vibration restraint(s) shall be located outside of the partition, wall, or floor assembly for which the equipment or systems pass through. [*101*:8.3.4.5]

12.7.8.6 Transitions.

12.7.8.6.1 Where piping penetrates a fire-resistance-rated wall or floor assembly, combustible piping shall not connect to noncombustible piping unless it can be demonstrated that the transition will not reduce the fire resistance rating, except in the case of previously approved installations. [*101*:8.3.4.6.1]

12.7.8.6.2 Unshielded couplings shall not be used to connect noncombustible piping to combustible piping unless it can be demonstrated that the transition complies with the fire-resistive requirements of 12.7.8.2. [*101*:8.3.4.6.2]

12.7.8.7 Membrane Penetrations.

12.7.8.7.1 Membrane penetrations for cables, cable trays, conduits, pipes, tubes, combustion vents, exhaust vents, wires, and similar items to accommodate electrical, mechanical, plumbing, and communications systems that pass through a membrane of a wall, floor, or floor/ceiling assembly constructed as a fire barrier shall be protected by a firestop system or device and shall comply with 12.7.8.2 through 12.7.8.6.2. [*101*:8.3.4.7.1]

Δ **12.7.8.7.2** The firestop system or device shall be tested in accordance with ASTM E814, *Standard Test Method for Fire Tests of Penetration Firestop Systems*, or UL 1479, *Fire Tests of Penetration Firestops*, at a minimum positive pressure differential of 0.01 in. water column (2.5 Pa) between the exposed and the unexposed surface of the test assembly, unless one of the following conditions applies:

(1) Membrane penetrations of ceilings that are not an integral part of a fire-resistance-rated floor/ceiling or roof/ceiling assembly
(2) Membrane penetrations of steel, ferrous, or copper conduits, piping, or tubing, and steel electrical outlet boxes and wires, or combustion vents or exhaust vents where the annular space is protected with an approved material and the aggregate area of the openings does not exceed 100 in.^{2} (64,520 mm^2) in any 100 ft^2 (9.3 m^2) of ceiling area
(3) Electrical outlet boxes and fittings provided that such devices are listed for use in fire-resistance-rated assemblies and are installed in accordance with their listing
(4) The annular space created by the membrane penetration of a fire sprinkler shall be permitted, provided that the space is covered by a metal escutcheon plate

[*101*:8.3.4.7.2]

12.7.8.7.3 Where walls or partitions are required to have a minimum 1-hour fire resistance rating, recessed fixtures shall be installed in the wall or partition in such a manner that the required fire resistance is not reduced, unless one of the following criteria is met:

(1) Any steel electrical box not exceeding 16 in.^{2} (10,300 mm^2) in area shall be permitted where the aggregate area of the openings provided for the boxes does not exceed 100 in.^{2} (64,520 mm^2) in any 100 ft^2 (9.3 m^2) of wall area, and, where outlet boxes are installed on opposite sides of the wall, the boxes shall be separated by one of the following means:
   (a) Horizontal distance of not less than 24 in. (610 mm)
   (b) Horizontal distance of not less than the depth of the wall cavity, where the wall cavity is filled with cellulose loose-fill, rock wool, or slag wool insulation

(c)* Solid fireblocking
(d) Other listed materials and methods

(2) Membrane penetrations for any listed electrical outlet box made of any material shall be permitted, provided that such boxes have been tested for use in fire-resistance-rated assemblies and are installed in accordance with the instructions included in the listing.

(3) The annular space created by the membrane penetration of a fire sprinkler shall be permitted, provided that the space is covered by a metal escutcheon plate.

(4) Membrane penetrations by electrical boxes of any size or type, which have been listed as part of a wall opening protective material system for use in fire-resistance-rated assemblies and are installed in accordance with the instructions included in the listing, shall be permitted.

[*101*:8.3.4.7.3]

12.7.8.8 Ducts and Air-Transfer Openings. Openings for air-handling ductwork or air movement shall be protected in accordance with 11.2.1. [*101*:8.3.4.8]

12.7.9 Joints.

12.7.9.1 General.

12.7.9.1.1 The provisions of 12.7.9 shall govern the materials and methods of construction used to protect joints in fire barriers, in between fire barriers, and at the perimeter of fire barriers where fire barriers meet other fire barriers, the floor or roof deck above, or the outside walls. [*101*:8.3.5.1.1]

12.7.9.1.2 The provisions of 12.7.9 shall not apply to approved existing materials and methods of construction used to protect existing joints in fire barriers, unless otherwise required by Chapters 11 through 43 of NFPA *101*. [*101*:8.5.1.2]

12.7.9.2 Joint System Requirements.

12.7.9.2.1 Joints made within or at the perimeter of fire barriers, between fire-resistance-rated assemblies, or where fire barriers meet other fire barriers, the floor or roof deck above, or the outside walls shall be protected with a joint system that is designed and tested to prevent the spread of fire for a time period equal to that of the assembly in which the joint is located. [*101*:8.3.5.2.1]

12.7.9.2.2 Joints made within or at the perimeter of fire barriers used as smoke barriers shall be capable of restricting the transfer of smoke in accordance with 8.5.7.4 of NFPA *101*. [*101*:8.3.5.2.2]

12.7.9.2.3 Joints shall be installed in accordance with a tested system, and installed and maintained in accordance with the manufacturer's instructions. [*101*:8.3.5.2.3]

12.7.9.2.4 Testing of the joint system in a fire barrier shall be representative of the actual installation suitable for the required engineering demand without compromising the fire resistance rating of the assembly or the structural integrity of the assembly. [*101*:8.3.5.2.4]

12.7.9.2.5 Such materials, systems, or devices shall be tested as part of the assembly in accordance with the requirements of ASTM E1966, *Standard Test Method for Fire-Resistive Joint Systems*, or UL 2079, *Tests for Fire Resistance of Building Joint Systems*. [*101*:8.3.5.2.5]

12.7.9.2.6 All joint systems shall be tested at their maximum joint width in accordance with the requirements of ASTM E1966, *Standard Test Method for Fire-Resistive Joint Systems*, or UL 2079, *Tests for Fire Resistance of Building Joint Systems*, under a minimum positive pressure differential of 0.01 in. water column (2.5 N/m^2) for a time period equal to that of the assembly. [*101*:8.3.5.2.6]

12.7.9.2.7 All test specimens shall comply with the minimum height or length required by the standard. [*101*:8.3.5.2.7]

12.7.9.2.8 Wall assemblies shall be subjected to a hose stream test in accordance with ASTM E119, *Standard Test Methods for Fire Tests of Building Construction and Materials*, or UL 263, *Fire Tests of Building Construction and Materials*. [*101*:8.3.5.2.8]

12.7.9.3 Joints made between a fire barrier and a non-fire-resistance-rated floor or roof sheathing, slab, or deck above shall be protected by an approved continuity head of wall joint system installed and tested in accordance with ASTM E2837, *Standard Test Method for Determining the Fire Resistance of Continuity Head-of-Wall Joint Systems Installed Between Rated Wall Assemblies and Nonrated Horizontal Assemblies*, and the system shall have an F rating and T rating of not less than the required fire resistance rating of the fire barrier. [*101*:8.3.5.3]

12.7.9.4* Exterior Curtain Walls and Perimeter Joints.

12.7.9.4.1 Voids created between the fire-resistance-rated floor assembly and the exterior curtain wall shall be protected with a perimeter joint system that is designed and tested in accordance with ASTM E2307, *Standard Test Method for Determining Fire Resistance of Perimeter Fire Barriers Using Intermediate-Scale, Multistory Apparatus*. [*101*:8.3.5.4.1]

12.7.9.4.2 The perimeter joint system shall have an F rating equal to the fire resistance rating of the floor assembly. [*101*:8.3.5.4.2]

12.8 Smoke Partitions.

12.8.1* General. Where required elsewhere in this *Code*, smoke partitions shall be provided to limit the transfer of smoke. [*101*:8.4.1]

12.8.2 Continuity. Smoke partitions shall comply with the following:

(1) They shall extend from the floor to the underside of the floor or roof deck above, through any concealed spaces, such as those above suspended ceilings, and through interstitial structural and mechanical spaces.

(2)* They shall be permitted to extend from the floor to the underside of a monolithic or suspended ceiling system where all of the following conditions are met:

(a) The ceiling system forms a continuous membrane.
(b) A smoke-tight joint is provided between the top of the smoke partition and the bottom of the suspended ceiling.
(c) The space above the ceiling is not used as a plenum.

(3) Smoke partitions enclosing hazardous areas shall be permitted to terminate at the underside of a monolithic or suspended ceiling system where all of the following conditions are met:

(a) The ceiling system forms a continuous membrane.
(b) A smoke-tight joint is provided between the top of the smoke partition and the bottom of the suspended ceiling.

(c) Where the space above the ceiling is used as a plenum, return grilles from the hazardous area into the plenums are not permitted. [*101*:8.4.2]

12.8.3 Opening Protectives.

12.8.3.1 Doors in smoke partitions shall comply with 12.8.3.2 through 12.8.3.6. [*101*:8.4.3.1]

12.8.3.2 Doors shall comply with the provisions of 7.2.1 of NFPA *101*. [*101*:8.4.3.2]

12.8.3.3 Doors shall not include louvers. [*101*:8.4.3.3]

12.8.3.4* Door clearances shall be in accordance with NFPA 80. [*101*:8.4.3.4]

12.8.3.5 Doors shall be self-closing or automatic-closing in accordance with 14.5.4. [*101*:8.4.3.5]

12.8.3.6 Shutters that protect openings shall be automatic-closing upon operation of approved smoke detectors installed in accordance with the provisions of *NFPA 72*. [*101*:8.4.3.6]

12.8.4 Penetrations. The provisions of 12.8.4 shall govern the materials and methods of construction used to protect through-penetrations and membrane penetrations of smoke partitions. [*101*:8.4.4]

12.8.4.1 Penetrations for cables, cable trays, conduits, pipes, tubes, vents, wires, and similar items to accommodate electrical, mechanical, plumbing, and communications systems that pass through a smoke partition shall be protected by a system or material that is capable of limiting the transfer of smoke. [*101*:8.4.4.1]

12.8.4.2 Vibration Isolation Equipment or Systems. Where vibration isolation of equipment or systems is employed, the vibration restraint(s) shall be located outside of the partition, wall, or floor assembly through which the equipment or systems pass. [*101*:8.4.4.2]

12.8.5 Joints.

12.8.5.1 The provisions of 12.8.5 shall govern the materials and methods of construction used to protect joints in between and at the perimeter of smoke partitions or, where smoke partitions meet other smoke partitions, the floor or roof deck above, or the outside walls. The provisions of 12.8.5 shall not apply to approved existing materials and methods of construction used to protect existing joints in smoke partitions, unless otherwise required by Chapters 11 through 43 of NFPA *101*. [*101*:8.4.5.1]

12.8.5.2 Joints made within or at the perimeter of smoke partitions shall be protected with a joint system that is capable of limiting the transfer of smoke. [*101*:8.4.5.2]

12.8.6 Air-Transfer Openings.

12.8.6.1 General. The provisions of 12.8.6 shall govern the materials and methods of construction used to protect air-transfer openings in smoke partitions. [*101*:8.4.6.1]

12.8.6.2* Smoke Dampers. Air-transfer openings in smoke partitions shall be provided with approved smoke dampers designed and tested in accordance with the requirements of UL 555S, *Smoke Dampers*, to limit the transfer of smoke. [*101*:8.4.6.2]

12.8.6.3 Smoke Damper Ratings. Smoke damper leakage ratings shall be not less than Class II. Elevated temperature ratings shall be not less than 250°F (140°C). [*101*:8.4.6.3]

12.8.6.4 Smoke Detectors. Smoke dampers in air-transfer openings shall close upon detection of smoke by approved smoke detectors installed in accordance with *NFPA 72*. [*101*:8.4.6.4]

12.9 Smoke Barriers.

12.9.1* General. Where required by Chapters 11 through 43 of NFPA *101*, smoke barriers shall be provided to subdivide building spaces for restricting the movement of smoke. [*101*:8.5.1]

12.9.2* Continuity.

12.9.2.1 Smoke barriers required by NFPA *101* shall be continuous from an outside wall to an outside wall, from a floor to a floor, or from a smoke barrier to a smoke barrier, or by use of a combination thereof. [*101*:8.5.2.1]

12.9.2.2 Smoke barriers required by NFPA *101* shall be continuous through all concealed spaces, such as those found above a ceiling, including interstitial spaces. [*101*:8.5.2.2]

12.9.2.3 A smoke barrier required for an occupied space below an interstitial space shall not be required to extend through the interstitial space, provided that the construction assembly forming the bottom of the interstitial space provides resistance to the passage of smoke equal to that provided by the smoke barrier. [*101*:8.5.2.3]

12.9.3 Fire Barrier Used as Smoke Barrier. A fire barrier shall be permitted to be used as a smoke barrier, provided that it meets the requirements of Section 12.9. [*101*:8.5.3]

12.9.4 Opening Protectives.

12.9.4.1* Doors in smoke barriers shall close the opening, leaving only the minimum clearance necessary for proper operation, and shall be without louvers or grilles. For other than previously approved existing doors, the clearance under the bottom of the doors shall be a maximum of ¾ in. (19 mm). [*101*:8.5.4.1]

12.9.4.2 Where required by Chapters 11 through 43 of NFPA *101*, doors in smoke barriers that are required to be smoke-leakage-rated shall comply with the requirements of 8.2.2.4 of NFPA *101*. [*101*:8.5.4.2]

12.9.4.3 Latching hardware shall be required on doors in smoke barriers, unless specifically exempted by Chapters 11 through 43 of NFPA *101*. [*101*:8.5.4.3]

12.9.4.4* Doors in smoke barriers shall be self-closing or automatic-closing in accordance with 14.5.4 and shall comply with the provisions of 7.2.1 of NFPA *101*. [*101*:8.5.4.4]

12.9.4.5 Fire window assemblies shall comply with 12.7.6. [*101*:8.5.4.5]

12.9.5 Ducts and Air-Transfer Openings.

12.9.5.1 General. The provisions of 12.9.5 shall govern the materials and methods of construction used to protect ducts and air-transfer openings in smoke barriers. [*101*:8.5.5.1]

12.9.5.2 Smoke Dampers.

12.9.5.2.1 Where a smoke barrier is penetrated by a duct or air-transfer opening, a smoke damper designed and tested in accordance with the requirements of UL 555S, *Smoke Dampers*, shall be installed. [*101*:8.5.5.2.1]

12.9.5.2.2 Where a smoke barrier is also constructed as a fire barrier, a combination fire/smoke damper designed and tested in accordance with the requirements of UL 555, *Fire Dampers*, and UL 555S, *Smoke Dampers*, shall be installed. [*101*:8.5.5.2.2]

12.9.5.3 Smoke Damper Exemptions. Smoke dampers shall not be required under any of the following conditions:

(1) Where specifically exempted by provisions in Chapters 11 through 43 of NFPA *101*
(2) Where ducts or air-transfer openings are part of an engineered smoke control system and the smoke damper will interfere with the operation of a smoke control system
(3) Where the air in ducts continues to move and the air-handling system installed is arranged to prevent recirculation of exhaust or return air under fire emergency conditions
(4) Where the air inlet or outlet openings in ducts are limited to a single smoke compartment
(5) Where ducts penetrate floors that serve as smoke barriers
(6) Where ducts penetrate smoke barriers forming a communicating space separation in accordance with 8.6.6(4)(a) of NFPA *101*

[*101*:8.5.5.3]

12.9.5.4 Installation, Testing, and Maintenance.

12.9.5.4.1 Air-conditioning, heating, ventilating ductwork, and related equipment, including smoke dampers and combination fire and smoke dampers, shall be installed in accordance with NFPA 90A, NFPA 90B, NFPA 105, or NFPA 80, as applicable. [*101*:8.5.5.4.1]

12.9.5.4.2 Smoke dampers and combination fire and smoke dampers required by this *Code* shall be inspected, tested, and maintained in accordance with NFPA 105. [*101*:8.5.5.4.2]

12.9.5.4.3 The equipment specified in 12.9.5.4.1 shall be installed in accordance with the requirements of 12.9.5, the manufacturer's installation instructions, and the equipment listing. [*101*:8.5.5.4.3]

12.9.5.5 Access and Identification.

12.9.5.5.1 Access to the dampers shall be provided for inspection, testing, and maintenance. [*101*:8.5.5.5.1]

12.9.5.5.2 Smoke and combination fire and smoke dampers in new construction shall be provided with an approved means of access, as follows:

(1) The means of access shall be large enough to allow inspection and maintenance of the damper and its operating parts.
(2) The access shall not affect the integrity of fire-resistance-rated assemblies or smoke barrier continuity.
(3) The access openings shall not reduce the fire resistance rating of the assembly.
(4) Access doors in ducts shall be tight-fitting and suitable for the required duct construction.
(5) Access and maintenance shall comply with the requirements of the mechanical code.

[*101*:8.5.5.5.2]

12.9.5.5.3 Identification. Access points to fire and smoke dampers in new construction shall be permanently identified by one of the following:

(1) A label having letters not less than ½ in. (13 mm) in height and reading as one of the following:
  (a) FIRE/SMOKE DAMPER
  (b) SMOKE DAMPER
  (c) FIRE DAMPER
(2) Symbols as approved by the AHJ

[*101*:8.5.5.5.3]

12.9.5.6 Smoke Damper Ratings. Smoke damper leakage ratings shall be not less than Class II. Elevated temperature ratings shall be not less than 250°F (140°C). [*101*:8.5.5.6]

12.9.5.7 Smoke Detectors.

Δ **12.9.5.7.1** Required smoke dampers in ducts penetrating smoke barriers shall close upon detection of smoke by approved smoke detectors in accordance with *NFPA 72* unless one of the following conditions exists:

(1) The ducts penetrate smoke barriers above the smoke barrier doors, and the door release detector actuates the damper.
(2) Approved smoke detector installations are located within the ducts in existing installations.

[*101*:8.5.5.7.1]

12.9.5.7.2 Where a duct is provided on one side of the smoke barrier, the smoke detectors on the duct side shall be in accordance with 12.9.5.7.1. [*101*:8.5.5.7.2]

12.9.5.7.3 Required smoke dampers in air-transfer openings shall close upon detection of smoke by approved smoke detectors in accordance with *NFPA 72*. [*101*:8.5.5.7.3]

12.9.6 Penetrations.

12.9.6.1 The provisions of 12.9.6 shall govern the materials and methods of construction used to protect through-penetrations and membrane penetrations of smoke barriers. [*101*:8.5.6.1]

12.9.6.2 Penetrations for cables, cable trays, conduits, pipes, tubes, vents, wires, and similar items to accommodate electrical, mechanical, plumbing, and communications systems that pass through a wall, floor, or floor/ceiling assembly constructed as a smoke barrier, or through the ceiling membrane of the roof/ceiling of a smoke barrier assembly, shall be protected by a system or material capable of restricting the transfer of smoke. [*101*:8.5.6.2]

12.9.6.3 Where a smoke barrier is also constructed as a fire barrier, the penetrations shall be protected in accordance with the requirements of 12.7.8 to limit the spread of fire for a time period equal to the fire resistance rating of the assembly and the requirements of 12.9.6 to restrict the transfer of smoke, unless the requirements of 12.9.6.4 are met. [*101*:8.5.6.3]

12.9.6.4 Where sprinklers penetrate a single membrane of a fire-resistance-rated assembly in buildings equipped throughout with an approved automatic fire sprinkler system, noncombustible escutcheon plates shall be permitted, provided that the space around each sprinkler penetration does not exceed ½ in. (13 mm), measured between the edge of the membrane and the sprinkler. [*101*:8.5.6.4]

12.9.6.5 In new construction, through-penetrations shall be protected by an approved through-penetration firestop system installed and tested in accordance with the requirements of UL 1479, *Fire Tests of Penetration Firestops*, for air leakage and shall comply with one of the following:

(1) A maximum 5 ft^3/min per ft^2 (0.025 m^3/s per m^2) of penetration opening for each through-penetration firestop system
(2) A maximum total cumulative leakage of 50 ft^3/min (0.024 m^3/s) for any 100 ft^2 (9.3 m^2) of wall area or floor area

[*101*:8.5.6.5]

Δ **12.9.6.6 Vibration Isolation Equipment or Systems.** Where vibration isolation of equipment or systems is employed, the vibration restraint(s) shall be located outside of the partition, wall or floor assembly through which the equipment or systems pass. [*101*:8.5.6.7]

12.9.7 Joints.

12.9.7.1 The provisions of 12.9.7 shall govern the materials and methods of construction used to protect joints in between and at the perimeter of smoke barriers or, where smoke barriers meet other smoke barriers, the floor or roof deck above, or the outside walls. The provisions of 12.9.7 shall not apply to approved existing materials and methods of construction used to protect existing joints in smoke barriers, unless otherwise required by Chapters 11 through 43 of NFPA *101*. [*101*:8.5.7.1]

12.9.7.2 Joints made within, between, or at the perimeter of smoke barriers shall be protected with a joint system that is tested in accordance with the requirements of UL 2079, *Tests for Fire Resistance of Building Joint Systems*, for air leakage, and the L rating of the joint system shall not exceed 5 ft^3/min per ft (0.00775 m^3/s per m) of the joint. [*101*:8.5.7.2]

12.9.7.3 Smoke barriers that are also constructed as fire barriers shall be protected with a joint system that is designed and tested to resist the spread of fire for a time period equal to the required fire resistance rating of the assembly and restrict the transfer of smoke in accordance with 12.9.7.2. [*101*:8.5.7.3]

12.9.7.4 Testing of the joint system in a smoke barrier that also serves as fire barrier shall be representative of the actual installation. [*101*:8.5.7.4]

Chapter 13 Fire Protection Systems

13.1 General.

13.1.1 The AHJ shall have the authority to require that construction documents for all fire protection systems be submitted for review and approval and a permit be issued prior to the installation, rehabilitation, or modification. *(For additional information concerning construction documents, see Section 1.15.)* Further, the AHJ shall have the authority to require that full acceptance tests of the systems be performed in the AHJ's presence prior to final system certification.

13.1.1.1 Permits. Permits, where required, shall comply with Section 1.13.

13.1.2 The property owner shall be responsible for the inspection, testing, and maintenance of the equipment and systems.

13.1.3 Integrated Fire Protection and Life Safety System Test.

13.1.3.1 Basic Testing. Where required by Chapters 11 through 43 of NFPA *101*, installations involving two or more integrated fire protection or life safety systems shall be tested to verify the proper operation and function of such systems in accordance with 13.1.3.1.1 and 13.1.3.1.2. [*101*:9.11.4.1]

13.1.3.1.1 When a fire protection or life safety system is tested, the response of integrated fire protection and life safety systems shall be verified. [*101*:9.11.4.1.1]

13.1.3.1.2 After repair or replacement of equipment, required retesting of integrated systems shall be limited to verifying the response of fire protection or life safety functions initiated by repaired or replaced equipment. [*101*:9.11.4.1.2]

13.1.3.2* NFPA 4 Testing. Where required by 9.3.5 or Chapters 11 through 43 of *NFPA 101*, the following integrated fire protection and life safety systems shall be tested in accordance with 13.1.3.1 and 13.1.3.2.1 through 13.1.3.2.2:

(1) Integrated fire protection and life safety systems in high-rise buildings
(2) Integrated fire protection and life safety systems that include a smoke control system

[*101*:9.11.4.2]

13.1.3.2.1 For new buildings, integrated testing in accordance with NFPA 4 shall be conducted prior to the issuance of a certificate of occupancy. [*101*:9.11.4.2.1]

13.1.3.2.2 For existing buildings, integrated testing in accordance with NFPA 4 shall be conducted at intervals not exceeding 10 years unless otherwise specified by an integrated system test plan prepared in accordance with NFPA 4. [*101*:9.11.4.2.2]

13.1.4 Obstructions shall not be placed or kept near fire hydrants, fire department inlet connections, or fire protection system control valves in a manner that would prevent such equipment or fire hydrants from being immediately visible and accessible.

13.1.5 A minimum 36 in. (915 mm) of clear space shall be maintained to permit access to and operation of fire protection equipment, fire department inlet connections, or fire protection system control valves. The fire department shall not be deterred or hindered from gaining immediate access to fire protection equipment.

13.1.5.1 An approved clear and unobstructed path shall be provided and maintained for access to the fire department inlet connections.

Δ **13.1.6 Records.**

N **13.1.6.1** Records shall be made for all inspections, tests, and maintenance of the system and its components. [**25**:4.3.1]

N **13.1.6.1.1** Records shall be maintained by the property owner. [**25**:4.3.1.1]

N **13.1.6.1.2** Records shall be permitted to be stored and accessed electronically. [**25**:4.3.1.2]

N **13.1.6.2** Records shall include the following:

(1) The procedure/activity performed (e.g., inspection, test, or maintenance)
(2) The organization that performed the activity
(3) The required frequency of the activity

(4) The results and date of the activity
(5) The name and contact information of the qualified contractor or owner, including lead person for activity

[25:4.3.2]

N **13.1.6.3** Records shall be made available to the authority having jurisdiction upon request. [25:4.3.3]

N **13.1.6.4** As-built system installation drawings, hydraulic calculations, original acceptance test records, and device manufacturer's data sheets shall be retained for the life of the system. [25:4.3.4]

N **13.1.6.5** Subsequent records shall be retained for a period of 1 year after the next inspection, test, or maintenance of that type required by the standard. [25:4.3.5]

13.1.7 Existing systems shall be in accordance with 1.3.6.2 and 10.3.2.

13.1.8 All fire protection systems and devices shall be maintained in a reliable operating condition and shall be replaced or repaired where defective or recalled.

13.1.9* Whenever impairments, critical deficiencies, or noncritical deficiencies are identified in water-based fire protection systems maintained in accordance with NFPA 25, both of the following shall apply:

(1) Impairments or deficiencies shall be corrected or repaired in a timeframe approved by the AHJ.
(2) Until impairments or deficiencies are corrected or repaired, an approved impairment or deficiency program shall be implemented in accordance with 13.3.3.6.5 or 13.3.3.6.6.

13.1.10 The AHJ shall be notified when any fire protection system is out of service and on restoration of service.

13.1.11 In the event of a failure of a fire protection system or an excessive number of accidental activations, the AHJ shall be permitted to require an approved fire watch until the system is repaired.

13.1.12* For occupancies of an especially hazardous nature or where special hazards exist in addition to the normal hazard of the occupancy, or where access for fire apparatus is unduly difficult, or where the size or configuration of the building or contents limits normal fire suppression efforts, the AHJ shall have the authority to require additional safeguards consisting of additional fire protection systems, fire safety equipment, more than one type of fire protection system or safety equipment, or special systems suitable for the protection of the hazard involved.

13.1.13 The AHJ shall have the authority to require locking fire department connection (FDC) plugs or caps on all water-based fire protection systems.

13.2 Standpipe Systems.

13.2.1 General.

13.2.1.1 The design and installation of standpipe systems shall be in accordance with Section 13.2 and NFPA 14.

13.2.1.2 Where standpipe and hose systems are installed in combination with automatic sprinkler systems, installation shall be in accordance with the appropriate provisions established by NFPA 13 and NFPA 14. [*101*:9.10.2]

13.2.2 Where Required.

13.2.2.1 Where required by this *Code* or the referenced codes and standards listed in Chapter 2, standpipe systems shall be installed in accordance with 13.2.1.

13.2.2.2 New buildings shall be equipped with a Class I standpipe system installed in accordance with the provisions of Section 13.2 where any of the following conditions exist:

(1) Four or more stories in height above grade plane where the building is protected by an approved automatic sprinkler system
(2) Three or more stories in height above grade plane where the building is not protected by an approved automatic sprinkler system
(3)* More than 50 ft (15 m) above grade plane and containing intermediate stories or balconies
(4) More than one story below grade plane
(5) More than 20 ft (6.1 m) below grade plane

13.2.2.3 High-rise buildings shall be protected throughout by a Class I standpipe system in accordance with Section 13.2. [*101*:11.8.3.2]

13.2.2.4 New and Existing Detention and Correctional Facilities. Standpipe and hose systems shall be provided in accordance with Section 9.10 of NFPA *101* as follows, unless otherwise permitted by 13.2.2.4.1:

(1) Class I standpipe systems shall be provided for any building three or more stories in height.
(2) Class III standpipe and hose systems shall be provided for all nonsprinklered buildings three or more stories in height.

[*101*:22.3.5.5; *101*:23.3.5.5]

13.2.2.4.1 The requirements of 13.2.2.4 shall not apply where otherwise permitted by the following:

(1) Formed hose, 1 in. (25 mm) in diameter, on hose reels shall be permitted to provide Class II service.
(2) Separate Class I and Class II systems shall be permitted in lieu of a Class III system.

[*101*:22.3.5.6; *101*:23.3.5.6]

13.2.2.5* The AHJ shall be authorized to permit the removal of existing occupant-use hose lines where all of the following are met:

(1) This *Code* does not require their installation.
(2) The current building code does not require their installation.
(3) The AHJ determines that the occupant-use hose line will not be utilized by trained personnel or the fire department.

13.2.3 Inspection, Testing, and Maintenance.

13.2.3.1 A standpipe system installed in accordance with this *Code* shall be properly inspected, tested, and maintained to provide at least the same level of performance and protection as designed.

13.2.3.2 The owner shall be responsible for inspecting, testing, and maintaining the standpipe system and keeping it in good working condition.

13.2.3.3 A standpipe system installed in accordance with this *Code* shall be inspected, tested, and maintained in accordance with NFPA 25.

13.2.3.4 Existing Systems.

13.2.3.4.1 Where an existing standpipe system, including yard piping and fire department connection, is modified, the new piping shall be independently tested in accordance with 12.4.1 of NFPA 14. [*14*:14.2.1]

13.2.3.4.2 Modifications that cannot be isolated, such as new valves or the point of connection for new piping, shall not require testing in excess of system static pressure. [*14*:14.2.2]

N **13.2.3.4.3*** The AHJ shall be authorized to require the replacement of existing pressure-regulating devices installed on a 2½ in. (66 mm) hose valve on Class I or Class III standpipe hose valves with standard hose valves where all the following are met:

(1) The static pressure at any 2½ in. (65 mm) hose connection shall not exceed 175 psi (12.1 bar).
(2) The standpipe system shall meet the requirements of Section 13.2.

13.3 Sprinkler Systems.

13.3.1 General.

13.3.1.1* Sprinkler systems shall be installed and maintained in full operating condition in the occupancies specified in this *Code* or in the codes or standards referenced in Chapter 2.

13.3.1.2 Installations shall be in accordance with NFPA 13, NFPA 13R, or NFPA 13D as appropriate.

13.3.1.3 Existing systems shall be in accordance with 1.3.6.2 and 10.3.2.

13.3.1.4 Sprinkler piping serving not more than six sprinklers for any hazardous area shall be permitted to be connected directly to a domestic water supply system having a capacity sufficient to provide 0.15 gpm/ft^2 (6.1 mm/min) throughout the entire enclosed area. [*101*:9.7.1.2]

13.3.1.5 Sprinkler piping serving hazardous areas as described in 13.3.1.4 shall be provided with an indicating shutoff valve, supervised in accordance with 13.3.1.8 or NFPA 13, and installed in an accessible, visible location between the sprinklers and the connection to the domestic water supply. [*101*:9.7.1.3]

13.3.1.6* In areas protected by automatic sprinklers, automatic heat-detection devices required by other sections of this *Code* shall not be required. [*101*:9.7.1.4]

13.3.1.7 Automatic sprinkler systems installed to make use of an alternative permitted by this *Code* shall be considered required systems and shall meet the provisions of this *Code* that apply to required systems. [*101*:9.7.1.5]

13.3.1.8 Supervision.

13.3.1.8.1 Supervisory Signals.

13.3.1.8.1.1* Where supervised automatic sprinkler systems are required by another section of this *Code*, supervisory initiating devices shall be installed and monitored for integrity in accordance with *NFPA 72*, and a distinctive supervisory signal shall be provided to indicate a condition that would impair the satisfactory operation of the sprinkler system. [*101*:9.7.2.1.1]

13.3.1.8.1.2 Supervisory signals shall sound and shall be displayed either at a location within the protected building that is constantly attended by qualified personnel or at an approved, remotely located receiving facility. [*101*:9.7.2.1.2]

13.3.1.8.2 Alarm Signal Transmission.

13.3.1.8.2.1 Where supervision of automatic sprinkler systems is required by another section of this *Code*, waterflow alarms shall be transmitted to an approved, proprietary alarm-receiving facility, a remote station, a central station, or the fire department. [*101*:9.7.2.2.1]

13.3.1.8.2.2 The connection described in 13.3.1.8.2.1 shall be in accordance with 13.7.1.1. [*101*:9.7.2.2.2]

13.3.2 Where Required.

13.3.2.1 Where required by this *Code* or the referenced codes and standards listed in Chapter 2, automatic sprinkler systems shall be installed in accordance with 13.3.1.

13.3.2.2 Basements exceeding 2500 ft^2 (232 m^2) in new buildings shall be protected throughout by an approved automatic sprinkler system.

13.3.2.3 New buildings housing emergency fire, rescue, or ambulance services shall be protected throughout by approved supervised automatic sprinkler systems.

13.3.2.4 New buildings three or more stories in height above grade shall be protected throughout by an approved automatic sprinkler system in accordance with Section 13.3 unless otherwise permitted by 13.3.2.5.

13.3.2.5 New Assembly Occupancies.

13.3.2.5.1 The following assembly occupancies shall be protected throughout by an approved, electrically supervised automatic sprinkler system in accordance with 13.3.1.2:

(1) Dance halls
(2) Discotheques
(3) Nightclubs
(4) Bars
(5) Restaurants
(6) Assembly occupancies with festival seating

[*101*:12.3.5.1]

13.3.2.5.2 Any building containing one or more assembly occupancies where the aggregate occupant load of the assembly occupancies exceeds 300 shall be protected by an approved, supervised automatic sprinkler system in accordance with NFPA 13 as follows *(see also 12.1.6, 12.2.6, 12.3.2, and 12.3.6 of NFPA 101)*:

(1) Throughout the story containing the assembly occupancy
(2) Throughout all stories below the story containing the assembly occupancy
(3) In the case of an assembly occupancy located below the level of exit discharge, throughout all stories intervening between that story and the level of exit discharge, including the level of exit discharge

[*101*:12.3.5.2]

13.3.2.5.3 The requirements of 13.3.2.5.2 shall not apply to the following:

(1)* Assembly occupancies consisting of a single multipurpose room of less than 12,000 ft^2 (1115 m^2) that are not used for exhibition or display and are not part of a mixed occupancy

(2) Gymnasiums, skating rinks, and swimming pools used exclusively for participant sports with no audience facilities for more than 300 persons
(3)* Locations in stadia and arenas as follows:
   (a) Over the floor areas used for contest, performance, or entertainment, provided that the roof construction is more than 50 ft (15 m) above the floor level, and use is restricted to low fire hazard uses
   (b) Over the seating areas, provided that use is restricted to low fire hazard uses
   (c) Over open-air concourses where an approved engineering analysis substantiates the ineffectiveness of the sprinkler protection due to building height and combustible loading
(4) Locations in unenclosed stadia and arenas as follows:
   (a) Press boxes of less than 1000 ft² (93 m²)
   (b) Storage facilities of less than 1000 ft² (93 m²) if enclosed with not less than 1-hour-fire-resistance-rated construction
   (c) Enclosed areas underneath grandstands that comply with 25.3.4
[*101*:12.3.5.3]

13.3.2.5.4 Where another provision of Chapter 12 of NFPA *101* requires an approved, electrically supervised automatic sprinkler system, it shall be installed in accordance with NFPA 13. [*101*:12.3.5.4]

13.3.2.5.5 Fire Protection. Every stage shall be protected by an approved, supervised automatic sprinkler system in compliance with Section 13.3. [*101*:12.4.7.10]

13.3.2.5.5.1 Protection shall be provided throughout the stage and in storerooms, workshops, permanent dressing rooms, and other accessory spaces contiguous to stages. [*101*:12.4.7.10.1]

13.3.2.5.5.2 Sprinklers shall not be required for stages 1000 ft² (93 m²) or less in area and 50 ft (15 m) or less in height where the following criteria are met:
(1) Curtains, scenery, or other combustible hangings are not retractable vertically.
(2) Combustible hangings are limited to borders, legs, a single main curtain, and a single backdrop.
[*101*:12.4.7.10.2]

13.3.2.5.5.3 Sprinklers shall not be required under stage areas less than 48 in. (1220 mm) in clear height that are used exclusively for chair or table storage and lined on the inside with ⅝ in. (16 mm) type X gypsum panels or an approved equivalent. [*101*:12.4.7.10.3]

13.3.2.6 Existing Assembly Occupancies.

13.3.2.6.1 Where the occupant load exceeds 100, the following assembly occupancies shall be protected throughout by an approved, electrically supervised automatic sprinkler system in accordance with Section 13.3:
(1) Dance halls
(2) Discotheques
(3) Nightclubs
(4) Assembly occupancies with festival seating
[*101*:13.3.5.1]

13.3.2.6.2 Any assembly occupancy used or capable of being used for exhibition or display purposes shall be protected throughout by an approved automatic sprinkler system in accordance with Section 13.3 where the exhibition or display area exceeds 15,000 ft² (1400 m²). [*101*:13.3.5.2]

13.3.2.6.3 The sprinklers specified by 13.3.2.6.2 shall not be required where otherwise permitted in the following locations:
(1) Locations in stadia and arenas as follows:
   (a) Over the floor areas used for contest, performance, or entertainment
   (b) Over the seating areas
   (c) Over open-air concourses where an approved engineering analysis substantiates the ineffectiveness of the sprinkler protection due to building height and combustible loading
(2) Locations in unenclosed stadia and arenas as follows:
   (a) Press boxes of less than 1000 ft² (93 m²)
   (b) Storage facilities of less than 1000 ft² (93 m²) if enclosed with not less than 1-hour fire-resistance-rated construction
   (c) Enclosed areas underneath grandstands that comply with 25.3.4
[*101*:13.3.5.3]

13.3.2.6.4 Where another provision of this chapter and Chapter 13 of NFPA *101* requires an automatic sprinkler system, the sprinkler system shall be installed in accordance with NFPA 13. [*101*:13.3.5.4]

13.3.2.6.5 Fire Protection. Every stage shall be protected by an approved automatic sprinkler system in compliance with Section 13.3. [*101*:13.4.7.10]

Δ **13.3.2.6.5.1** Protection shall be provided throughout the stage and in storerooms, workshops, permanent dressing rooms, and other accessory spaces contiguous to stages. [*101*:13.4.7.10.1]

13.3.2.6.5.2 Sprinklers shall not be required for stages 1000 ft² (93 m²) or less in area where the following criteria are met:
(1) Curtains, scenery, or other combustible hangings are not retractable vertically.
(2) Combustible hangings are limited to borders, legs, a single main curtain, and a single backdrop.
[*101*:13.4.7.10.2]

13.3.2.6.5.3 Sprinklers shall not be required under stage areas less than 48 in. (1220 mm) in clear height that are used exclusively for chair or table storage and lined on the inside with ⅝ in. (16 mm) type X gypsum panels or an approved equivalent. [*101*:12.4.7.10.3]

13.3.2.7 New Educational Occupancies.

13.3.2.7.1 Educational occupancy buildings shall be protected throughout by an approved, supervised automatic sprinkler system in accordance with Section 13.3 except as otherwise permitted by 13.3.2.7.2. [*101*:14.3.5.1]

13.3.2.7.2 The requirement of 13.3.2.7.1 shall not apply to any of the following:
(1) Non-relocatable buildings having an area not exceeding 1000 ft² (93 m²)
(2) Non-relocatable buildings containing a single classroom
(3) Relocatable buildings complying with all of the following:
   (a) Building area does not exceed 1000 ft² (93 m²)
   (b) Building contains a single classroom

(c) Building is located not less than 30 ft (9.1 m) from another building

[*101*:14.3.5.2]

13.3.2.7.3 Every portion of educational buildings below the level of exit discharge shall be protected throughout by an approved, supervised automatic sprinkler system in accordance with Section 13.3. [*101*:14.3.5.3]

13.3.2.7.4 Buildings with unprotected openings in accordance with 8.6.6 of NFPA *101* shall be protected throughout by an approved, supervised automatic sprinkler system in accordance with Section 13.3. [*101*:14.3.5.4]

13.3.2.7.5 Where another provision of Chapter 14 of NFPA *101* requires an automatic sprinkler system, the sprinkler system shall be installed in accordance with NFPA 13. [*101*:14.3.5.5]

13.3.2.8 Existing Educational Occupancies.

13.3.2.8.1 Where student occupancy exists below the level of exit discharge, every portion of such floor shall be protected throughout by an approved automatic sprinkler system in accordance with Section 13.3. [*101*:15.3.5.1]

13.3.2.8.2 Where student occupancy does not exist on floors below the level of exit discharge, such floors shall be separated from the rest of the building by 1-hour fire resistance–rated construction or shall be protected throughout by an approved automatic sprinkler system in accordance with Section 13.3. [*101*:15.3.5.2]

13.3.2.8.3 Automatic sprinkler protection shall not be required where student occupancy exists below the level of exit discharge, provided that both of the following criteria are met:

(1) The approval of the AHJ shall be required.
(2) Windows for rescue and ventilation shall be provided in accordance with 15.2.11.1 of NFPA *101*.

[*101*:15.3.5.3]

13.3.2.8.4 Buildings with unprotected openings in accordance with 8.6.6 of NFPA *101* shall be protected throughout by an approved, supervised automatic sprinkler system in accordance with Section 13.3. [*101*:15.3.5.4]

13.3.2.8.5 Where another provision of Chapter 15 of NFPA *101* requires an automatic sprinkler system, the sprinkler system shall be installed in accordance with Section 13.3. [*101*:15.3.5.5]

13.3.2.9 New Health Care Occupancies.

13.3.2.9.1* Buildings containing health care occupancies shall be protected throughout by an approved, supervised automatic sprinkler system in accordance with Section 13.3, unless otherwise permitted by 13.3.2.9.3. [*101*:18.3.5.1]

13.3.2.9.2 The sprinkler system required by 13.3.2.9.1 shall be installed in accordance with NFPA 13. [*101*:18.3.5.4]

Δ **13.3.2.9.3** In Type I and Type II construction, alternative protection measures shall be permitted to be substituted for sprinkler protection without causing a building to be classified as nonsprinklered in specified areas where the AHJ has prohibited sprinklers. [*101*:18.3.5.5]

13.3.2.9.4* Listed quick-response or listed residential sprinklers shall be used throughout smoke compartments containing patient sleeping rooms. [*101*:18.3.5.6]

13.3.2.9.5* Sprinklers shall not be required in clothes closets of patient sleeping rooms in hospitals where the area of the closet does not exceed 6 ft^2 (0.55 m^2), provided that the distance from the sprinkler in the patient sleeping room to the back wall of the closet does not exceed the maximum distance permitted by NFPA 13. [*101*:18.3.5.10]

13.3.2.9.6* Sprinklers in areas where cubicle curtains are installed shall be in accordance with NFPA 13. [*101*:18.3.5.11]

13.3.2.10 Existing Health Care Occupancies.

13.3.2.10.1 Buildings containing nursing homes shall be protected throughout by an approved, supervised automatic sprinkler system in accordance with Section 13.3 and Section 9.7 of NFPA *101*, unless otherwise permitted by 13.3.2.10.8. [*101*:19.3.5.1]

13.3.2.10.2 All high-rise buildings containing health care occupancies shall be protected throughout by an approved, supervised automatic sprinkler system installed in accordance with Section 13.3 within 12 years of the adoption of this *Code*, or by the date established by the AHJ prior to the adoption of this edition of this *Code*, whichever is earlier. [*101*:19.4.3]

13.3.2.10.3 Where a jurisdiction adopts this edition of the *Code* and previously adopted the 2018 edition, the sprinklering required by 13.3.2.10.2 shall be installed within 9 years of the adoption of this *Code*. [*101*:19.4.3.2]

13.3.2.10.4 Where a jurisdiction adopts this edition of the *Code* and previously adopted the 2015 edition, the sprinklering required by 13.3.2.10.2 shall be installed within 6 years of the adoption of this *Code*. [*101*:19.4.3.3]

13.3.2.10.5 Where a jurisdiction adopts this edition of the *Code* and previously adopted the 2012 edition, the sprinklering required by 13.3.2.10.2 shall be installed within 3 years of the adoption of this *Code*. [*101*:19.4.3.4]

13.3.2.10.6 Where required by 19.1.6 of NFPA *101*, buildings containing hospitals or limited care facilities shall be protected throughout by an approved, supervised automatic sprinkler system in accordance with Section 13.3 and Section 9.7 of NFPA *101*, unless otherwise permitted by 13.3.2.10.8. [*101*:19.3.5.3]

13.3.2.10.7* The sprinkler system required by 13.3.2.10.1 or 13.3.2.10.6 shall be installed in accordance with NFPA 13. [*101*:19.3.5.4]

13.3.2.10.8 In Type I and Type II construction, alternative protection measures shall be permitted to be substituted for sprinkler protection in specified areas where the AHJ has prohibited sprinklers, without causing a building to be classified as nonsprinklered. [*101*:19.3.5.5]

13.3.2.10.9* Where this *Code* permits exceptions for fully sprinklered buildings or smoke compartments, the sprinkler system shall meet all of the following criteria:

(1) It shall be in accordance with Section 13.3.
(2) It shall be installed in accordance with NFPA 13, unless it is an approved existing system.
(3) It shall be electrically connected to the fire alarm system.
(4) It shall be fully supervised.

(5) In Type I and Type II construction, where the AHJ has prohibited sprinklers, approved alternative protection measures shall be permitted to be substituted for sprinkler protection in specified areas without causing a building to be classified as nonsprinklered.
[*101*:19.3.5.7]

13.3.2.10.10* Where this *Code* permits exceptions for fully sprinklered buildings, suites, or smoke compartments and specifically references this paragraph, the sprinkler system shall meet all of the following criteria:

(1) It shall be installed throughout the building, suite, or smoke compartment in accordance with Section 13.3.
(2) It shall be installed in accordance with NFPA 13, unless it is an approved existing system.
(3) It shall be electrically connected to the fire alarm system.
(4) It shall be fully supervised.
(5) It shall be equipped with listed quick-response or listed residential sprinklers throughout all smoke compartments containing patient sleeping rooms.
(6)* Standard-response sprinklers shall be permitted to be continued to be used in approved existing sprinkler systems where quick-response and residential sprinklers were not listed for use in such locations at the time of installation.
(7) Standard-response sprinklers shall be permitted for use in hazardous areas protected in accordance with 19.3.2.1 of NFPA *101*.
[*101*:19.3.5.8]

13.3.2.10.11 Isolated hazardous areas shall be permitted to be protected in accordance with 13.3.1.4. For new installations in existing health care occupancies, where more than two sprinklers are installed in a single area, waterflow detection shall be provided to sound the building fire alarm or to notify, by a signal, any constantly attended location, such as PBX, security, or emergency room, at which the necessary corrective action shall be taken. [*101*:19.3.5.9]

13.3.2.10.12* Sprinklers shall not be required in clothes closets of patient sleeping rooms in hospitals where the area of the closet does not exceed 6 ft^2 (0.55 m^2), provided that the distance from the sprinkler in the patient sleeping room to the back wall of the closet does not exceed the maximum distance permitted by NFPA 13. [*101*:19.3.5.10]

13.3.2.10.13* Newly introduced cubicle curtains in sprinklered areas shall be installed in accordance with NFPA 13. [*101*:19.3.5.11]

13.3.2.11 New Detention and Correctional Facilities.

13.3.2.11.1 All buildings classified as Use Condition II, Use Condition III, Use Condition IV, or Use Condition V shall be protected throughout by an approved, supervised automatic sprinkler system in accordance with 13.3.2.11.2. [*101*:22.3.5.2]

Δ **13.3.2.11.2** The automatic sprinkler system required by 13.3.2.11.1 shall meet all of the following criteria:

(1) It shall be in accordance with Section 13.3.
(2) It shall be installed in accordance with NFPA 13.
(3) It shall be electrically connected to the fire alarm system.
(4) It shall electrically supervised in accordance with 9.7.2 of NFPA *101*.
[*101*:22.3.5.3]

13.3.2.12 Existing Detention and Correctional Facilities.

13.3.2.12.1* Where required by Table 23.1.6.1 of NFPA *101*, facilities shall be protected throughout by an approved, supervised automatic sprinkler system in accordance with 13.3.2.12.2. [*101*:23.3.5.2]

13.3.2.12.2 Where this *Code* permits exceptions for fully sprinklered detention and correctional occupancies or sprinklered smoke compartments, the sprinkler system shall meet all of the following criteria:

(1) It shall be in accordance with Section 13.3.
(2) It shall be installed in accordance with NFPA 13.
(3) It shall be electrically connected to the fire alarm system.
(4) It shall be fully supervised.
[*101*:23.3.5.3]

13.3.2.13 New Hotels and Dormitories.

13.3.2.13.1 All buildings shall be protected throughout by an approved, electrically supervised automatic sprinkler system in accordance with 13.3.2.13.2. [*101*:28.3.5.1]

13.3.2.13.2 Where an automatic sprinkler system is installed, either for total or partial building coverage, the system shall be in accordance with Section 13.3, as modified by 13.3.2.13.3. In hotel or dormitory occupancies up to and including four stories in height that are located in buildings not exceeding 60 ft (18.3 m) in height above grade plane, systems in accordance with NFPA 13R shall be permitted. [*101*:28.3.5.3]

13.3.2.13.2.1 Where located in a building of Type III, Type IV, or Type V construction designed in accordance with 4.6.3(5) of NFPA *101* and where the roof assembly is located more than 55 ft (17 m) above the lowest level of required fire department vehicle access, attics shall comply with 13.3.2.13.2.1.1, 13.3.2.13.2.1.2, and one of the following:

(1) Attics shall be provided with sprinkler protection.
(2) Attics shall be constructed with noncombustible materials.
(3) Attics shall be constructed with fire-retardant-treated wood.
(4) Attics shall be filled with noncombustible insulation.
[*101*:28.3.5.3.1]

13.3.2.13.2.1.1 The height of the roof assembly shall be determined by measuring the distance from the lowest level of required fire department vehicle access adjacent to the building to the eave of the highest pitched roof, the intersection of the highest roof to the exterior wall, or the top of the highest parapet, whichever yields the greatest distance. [*101*:28.3.5.3.1.1]

13.3.2.13.2.1.2 Required fire department vehicle access roads used in 13.3.2.13.2.1.1 shall include only those roads that are necessary for required fire department vehicle access in accordance with Section 18.2. [*101*:28.3.5.3.1.2]

13.3.2.13.3 The provisions for draft curtains and closely spaced sprinklers in NFPA 13 shall not be required for openings complying with 8.6.9.1 of NFPA *101* where the opening is within the guest room or guest suite. [*101*:28.3.5.4]

13.3.2.14 Existing Hotels and Dormitories.

13.3.2.14.1 All high-rise buildings, other than those where each guest room or guest suite has exterior exit access in accordance with 7.5.3 of NFPA *101*, shall be protected throughout by an approved, supervised automatic sprinkler system in accordance with 13.3.2.14.2. [*101*:29.3.5.1]

13.3.2.14.2* Where an automatic sprinkler system is installed, either for total or partial building coverage, the system shall be in accordance with Section 13.3, as modified by 13.3.2.14.3 and 13.3.2.14.4. In buildings four or fewer stories in height and not exceeding 60 ft (18.3 m) in height above grade plane, systems in accordance with NFPA 13R shall be permitted. [*101*:29.3.5.3]

13.3.2.14.3 The provisions for draft curtains and closely spaced sprinklers in NFPA 13 shall not be required for openings complying with 8.6.9.1 of NFPA *101* where the opening is within the guest room or guest suite. [*101*:29.3.5.4]

13.3.2.14.4 In guest rooms and in guest room suites, sprinkler installations shall not be required in closets not exceeding 24 ft^2 (2.2 m^2) and in bathrooms not exceeding 55 ft^2 (5.1 m^2). [*101*:29.3.5.5]

13.3.2.15 New Apartment Buildings.

13.3.2.15.1 All buildings shall be protected throughout by an approved, supervised automatic sprinkler system installed in accordance with 13.3.2.15.1 through 13.3.2.15.6. [*101*:30.3.5.1]

13.3.2.15.1.1 Where an automatic sprinkler system is installed, the system shall be installed in accordance with Section 13.3 and electrically supervised in accordance with 9.7.2 in NFPA *101*, as modified by 13.3.2.15.5. [*101*:30.3.5.1.1]

13.3.2.15.1.2 In apartment buildings up to and including four stories in height, that are located in buildings not exceeding 60 ft (18.3 m) in height above grade plane, systems in accordance with NFPA 13R shall be permitted. [*101*:30.3.5.1.2]

13.3.2.15.2 Attics. Where located in a building of Type III, Type IV, or Type V construction designed in accordance with 4.6.3(5) of NFPA *101* and where the roof assembly is located more than 55 ft (17 m) above the lowest level of required fire department vehicle access, attics shall comply with 13.3.2.15.2.1, 13.3.2.15.2.2, and one of the following:

(1) Attics shall be provided with sprinkler protection.
(2) Attics shall be constructed with noncombustible materials.
(3) Attics shall be constructed with fire-retardant-treated wood.
(4) Attics shall be filled with noncombustible insulation.

[*101*:30.3.5.2]

13.3.2.15.2.1 The height of the roof assembly shall be determined by measuring the distance from the lowest level of required fire department vehicle access adjacent to the building to the eave of the highest pitched roof, the intersection of the highest roof to the exterior wall, or the top of the highest parapet, whichever yields the greatest distance. [*101*:30.3.5.2.1]

13.3.2.15.2.2 Required fire department vehicle access roads used in 13.3.2.15.2.1 shall include only those roads that are necessary for required fire department vehicle access in accordance with Section 18.2. [*101*:30.3.5.2.2]

Δ **13.3.2.15.3*** In buildings sprinklered in accordance with NFPA 13, closets shall meet the following requirements:

(1) Closets of less than 12 ft^2 (1.1 m^2) in individual dwelling units shall not be required to be sprinklered.

(2) Closets that contain equipment such as washers, dryers, furnaces, or water heaters shall be sprinklered, regardless of size. [*101*:30.3.5.3]

13.3.2.15.4 Convenience Openings. The draft curtain and closely spaced sprinkler requirements of NFPA 13 shall not be required for convenience openings complying with 8.6.9.1 of NFPA *101* where the convenience opening is within the dwelling unit. [*101*:30.3.5.4]

13.3.2.16 Existing Apartment Buildings.

13.3.2.16.1* Where an automatic sprinkler system is installed, either for total or partial building coverage, the system shall be installed in accordance with Section 13.3, as modified by 13.3.2.16.2 and 13.3.2.16.3. In buildings four or fewer stories in height and not exceeding 60 ft (18.3 m) in height above grade plane, systems in accordance with NFPA 13R shall be permitted. [*101*:31.3.5.2]

13.3.2.16.2 In individual dwelling units, sprinkler installation shall not be required in closets not exceeding 24 ft^2 (2.2 m^2) and in bathrooms not exceeding 55 ft^2 (5.1 m^2). Closets that contain equipment such as washers, dryers, furnaces, or water heaters shall be sprinklered, regardless of size. [*101*:31.3.5.3]

13.3.2.16.3* In buildings sprinklered in accordance with NFPA 13 bathrooms not greater than 55 ft^2 (5.1 m^2) in individual dwelling units shall not be required to be sprinklered. [*101*:31.3.5.4]

13.3.2.16.4 The draft curtain and closely spaced sprinkler requirements of NFPA 13 shall not be required for convenience openings complying with 8.6.9.1 of NFPA *101* where the convenience opening is within the dwelling unit. [*101*:31.3.5.5]

13.3.2.16.5 Buildings using Option 3 in accordance with NFPA *101* shall be provided with automatic sprinkler protection installed in accordance with 13.3.2.16.5.1 through 13.3.2.16.5.4. [*101*:31.3.5.6]

13.3.2.16.5.1 Automatic sprinklers shall be installed in the corridor, along the corridor ceiling, utilizing the maximum spacing requirements of the standards referenced by 13.3.1.2. [*101*:31.3.5.6.1]

13.3.2.16.5.2 An automatic sprinkler shall be installed within every dwelling unit that has a door opening to the corridor, with such sprinkler positioned over the center of the door, unless the door to the dwelling unit has not less than a 20-minute fire protection rating and is self-closing. [*101*:31.3.5.6.2]

13.3.2.16.5.3 The workmanship and materials of the sprinkler installation specified in 13.3.2.16.5 shall meet the requirements of 13.3.1.2. [*101*:31.3.5.6.3]

13.3.2.16.5.4 Where Option 3 is being used to permit the use of 1¾ in. (44 mm) thick, solid-bonded wood-core doors in accordance with 31.2.2.1.3 of NFPA *101*, sprinklers shall be provided within the exit enclosures in accordance with NFPA 13. [*101*:31.3.5.6.4]

13.3.2.16.6 Buildings using Option 4 in accordance with NFPA *101* shall be protected throughout by an approved automatic sprinkler system in accordance with 13.3.2.16.1 and meeting the requirements of Section 13.3 for supervision for buildings seven or more stories in height. [*101*:31.3.5.7]

13.3.2.16.7* Where sprinklers are being used as an option to any requirement in this *Code*, the sprinklers shall be installed throughout the space in accordance with the requirements of that option. [*101*:31.3.5.8]

13.3.2.17 Lodging or Rooming Houses.

13.3.2.17.1 All new lodging or rooming houses shall be protected throughout by an approved automatic sprinkler system in accordance with 13.3.2.17.2. [*101*:26.3.6.1]

13.3.2.17.2 Where an automatic sprinkler system is required or is used as an alternative method of protection, either for total or partial building coverage, the system shall be installed in accordance with Section 13.3 and electrically supervised in accordance with 9.7.2. [*101*:26.3.6.2]

13.3.2.17.2.1 Automatic sprinkler system waterflow shall actuate the fire alarm system in accordance with Section 13.7. [*101*:26.3.6.2.1]

13.3.2.17.2.2 In buildings four or fewer stories in height and not exceeding 60 ft (18.3 m) in height above grade plane, systems in accordance with NFPA 13R shall be permitted. [*101*:26.3.6.2.2]

13.3.2.17.2.3* Systems in accordance with NFPA 13D shall be permitted where all of the following requirements are met:

(1) The lodging or rooming house shall not be part of a mixed occupancy.
(2) Entrance foyers shall be sprinklered.
(3) Lodging or rooming houses with sleeping accommodations for more than eight occupants shall be treated as two-family dwellings with regard to the water supply.

[*101*:26.3.6.2.3]

13.3.2.17.2.4 In buildings sprinklered in accordance with NFPA 13, closets less than 12 ft² (1.1 m²) in area in individual dwelling units shall not be required to be sprinklered. [*101*:26.3.6.2.4]

13.3.2.17.2.5 In buildings sprinklered in accordance with NFPA 13, closets that contain equipment such as washers, dryers, furnaces, or water heaters shall be sprinklered, regardless of size. [*101*:26.3.6.2.5]

13.3.2.17.2.6 In existing lodging or rooming houses, sprinkler installations shall not be required in closets not exceeding 24 ft² (2.2 m²) and in bathrooms not exceeding 55 ft² (5.1 m²). [*101*:26.3.6.2.6]

13.3.2.18 One- and Two-Family Dwellings.

13.3.2.18.1 All new one- and two-family dwellings shall be protected throughout by an approved automatic sprinkler system in accordance with 13.3.2.18.2. [*101*:24.3.5.1]

13.3.2.18.2 Where an automatic sprinkler system is installed, either for total or partial building coverage, the system shall be in accordance with Section 13.3. [*101*:24.3.5.2]

13.3.2.19 New Residential Board and Care Occupancies.

13.3.2.19.1 Large Facilities.

13.3.2.19.1.1 General. All buildings shall be protected throughout by an approved automatic sprinkler system installed in accordance with NFPA 13 and provided with quick-response or residential sprinklers throughout. [*101*:32.3.3.5.1]

13.3.2.19.1.2 Supervision. Automatic sprinkler systems shall be provided with electrical supervision in accordance with 13.3.1.8. [*101*:32.3.3.5.5]

13.3.2.19.2 Small Facilities.

13.3.2.19.2.1* All facilities, other than those meeting the requirement of 13.3.2.19.2.2, shall be protected throughout by an approved automatic sprinkler system, installed in accordance with 13.3.2.19.2.3, using quick-response or residential sprinklers. [*101*:32.2.3.5.1]

13.3.2.19.2.2* In conversions, sprinklers shall not be required in small board and care homes serving eight or fewer residents when all occupants have the ability as a group to move reliably to a point of safety within 3 minutes. [*101*:32.2.3.5.2]

13.3.2.19.2.3 Where an automatic sprinkler system is installed, for either total or partial building coverage, all of the following requirements shall be met:

(1) The system shall be in accordance with NFPA 13 and shall initiate the fire alarm system in accordance with 13.7.2.19.
(2) The adequacy of the water supply shall be documented to the AHJ.

[*101*:32.2.3.5.3]

13.3.2.19.2.3.1 In buildings four or fewer stories in height and not exceeding 60 ft (18.3 m) in height above grade plane, systems in accordance with NFPA 13R shall be permitted. All habitable areas and closets shall be sprinklered. [*101*:32.2.3.5.3.1]

Δ **13.3.2.19.2.3.2*** An automatic sprinkler system with a 30-minute water supply, and complying with all of the following requirements and with NFPA 13D shall be permitted:

(1) All habitable areas and closets shall be sprinklered.
(2) Where a roof, deck, or balcony greater than 4 ft (1.2 m) wide is provided above, sprinklers shall be installed to protect attached exterior balconies, attached exterior decks, and ground floor patios serving buildings of Type V construction.
(3) Facilities with more than eight residents shall be treated as two-family dwellings with regard to water supply.

[*101*:32.2.3.5.3.2]

13.3.2.19.2.4 Automatic sprinkler systems installed in accordance with NFPA 13 and NFPA 13R shall be provided with electrical supervision in accordance with 13.3.1.8. [*101*:32.2.3.5.4]

13.3.2.19.2.5 Automatic sprinkler systems installed in accordance with NFPA 13D shall be provided with valve supervision by one of the following methods:

(1) Single listed control valve that shuts off both domestic and sprinkler systems and separate shutoff for the domestic system only
(2) Electrical supervision in accordance with 13.3.1.8
(3) Valve closure that causes the sounding of an audible signal in the facility

[*101*:32.2.3.5.5]

13.3.2.19.2.6 Sprinkler piping serving not more than six sprinklers for any isolated hazardous area shall be permitted to be installed in accordance with 13.3.1.4 and shall meet all of the following requirements:

(1) In new installations, where more than two sprinklers are installed in a single area, waterflow detection shall be

provided to initiate the fire alarm system required by 13.7.2.19.

(2) The duration of water supplies shall be as required by 13.3.2.19.2.3.2.

[*101*:32.2.3.5.6]

13.3.2.19.2.7 Attics shall be protected in accordance with 13.3.2.19.2.7.1 or 13.3.2.19.2.7.2. [*101*:32.2.3.5.7]

13.3.2.19.2.7.1 Where an automatic sprinkler system is required by 13.3.2.19.2, attics used for living purposes, storage, or fuel-fired equipment shall be protected with automatic sprinklers that are part of the required, approved automatic sprinkler system in accordance with 13.3.1.2. [*101*:32.2.3.5.7.1]

13.3.2.19.2.7.2 Where an automatic sprinkler system is required by 13.3.2.19.2, attics not used for living purposes, storage, or fuel-fired equipment shall meet one of the following criteria:

(1) Attics shall be protected throughout by a heat detection system arranged to activate the building fire alarm system in accordance with Section 13.7.
(2) Attics shall be protected with automatic sprinklers that are part of the required, approved automatic sprinkler system in accordance with 13.3.1.2.
(3) Attics shall be of noncombustible or limited-combustible construction.
(4) Attics shall be constructed of fire-retardant-treated wood in accordance with NFPA 703.

[*101*:32.2.3.5.7.2]

N **13.3.2.19.2.7.3** The provisions of 13.3.2.19.2.7.1 and 13.3.2.19.2.7.2 shall be permitted to be applied separately to portions of the attic separated by partitions that have a minimum ½-hour fire resistance rating and that extend to the underside of the floor or roof deck above. [*101*:32.2.3.5.7.3]

13.3.2.20 Existing Residential Board and Care Facilities.

13.3.2.20.1 Large Facilities.

13.3.2.20.1.1* General. Where an automatic sprinkler system is installed, for either total or partial building coverage, the system shall be installed in accordance with Section 13.3, as modified by 13.3.2.20.1.1.1 through 13.3.2.20.1.1.3. [*101*:33.3.3.5.1]

13.3.2.20.1.1.1 In buildings four or fewer stories above grade plane, systems in accordance with NFPA 13R shall be permitted. [*101*:33.3.3.5.1.1]

13.3.2.20.1.1.2 In facilities having prompt or slow evacuation capability, automatic sprinklers shall not be required in closets not exceeding 24 ft² (2.2 m²) and in bathrooms not exceeding 55 ft² (5.1 m²), provided that such spaces are finished with noncombustible or limited-combustible materials. [*101*:33.3.3.5.1.2]

13.3.2.20.1.1.3 Initiation of the fire alarm system shall not be required for existing installations in accordance with 13.3.2.20.1.6. [*101*:33.3.3.5.1.3]

13.3.2.20.1.2 Impractical Evacuation Capability. All facilities having impractical evacuation capability shall be protected throughout by an approved, supervised automatic sprinkler system in accordance with NFPA 13. [*101*:33.3.3.5.2]

13.3.2.20.1.3 High-Rise Buildings. All high-rise buildings shall be protected throughout by an approved, supervised automatic sprinkler system in accordance with 13.3.2.20.1. Such systems shall initiate the fire alarm system in accordance with 13.7.1.4. [*101*:33.3.3.5.3]

13.3.2.20.1.4 Attics shall be protected in accordance with 13.3.2.20.1.4.1 or 13.3.2.20.1.4.2. [*101*:33.3.3.5.4]

13.3.2.20.1.4.1 Where an automatic sprinkler system is installed, attics used for living purposes, storage, or fuel-fired equipment shall be protected with automatic sprinklers that are part of the required, approved automatic sprinkler system in accordance with 13.3.1.2. [*101*:33.3.3.5.4.1]

13.3.2.20.1.4.2 Where an automatic sprinkler system is installed, attics not used for living purposes, storage, or fuel-fired equipment shall meet one of the following criteria:

(1) Attics shall be protected throughout by a heat detection system arranged to activate the building fire alarm system in accordance with Section 13.7.
(2) Attics shall be protected with automatic sprinklers that are part of the required, approved automatic sprinkler system in accordance with 13.3.1.2.
(3) Attics shall be of noncombustible or limited-combustible construction.
(4) Attics shall be constructed of fire-retardant-treated wood in accordance with NFPA 703.

[*101*:33.3.3.5.4.2]

13.3.2.20.1.5 Supervision. Automatic sprinkler systems shall be supervised in accordance with Section 13.3; waterflow alarms shall not be required to be transmitted off-site. [*101*:33.3.3.5.5]

13.3.2.20.1.6 Domestic Water Supply Option. Sprinkler piping serving not more than six sprinklers for any isolated hazardous area in accordance with 13.3.1.4 shall be permitted; in new installations where more than two sprinklers are installed in a single area, waterflow detection shall be provided to initiate the fire alarm system required by 13.7.2.22. [*101*:33.3.3.5.6]

13.3.2.20.2 Small Facilities.

13.3.2.20.2.1 Where an automatic sprinkler system is installed, for either total or partial building coverage, all of the following requirements shall be met:

(1) The system shall be in accordance with Section 13.3 and shall initiate the fire alarm system in accordance with 13.7.2.21, as modified by 13.3.2.20.2.1.1 through 13.3.2.20.2.1.6.
(2) The adequacy of the water supply shall be documented to the AHJ.

[*101*:33.2.3.5.3]

13.3.2.20.2.1.1* In prompt evacuation capability facilities, all of the following shall apply:

(1) An automatic sprinkler system in accordance with NFPA 13D shall be permitted.
(2) Automatic sprinklers shall not be required in closets not exceeding 24 ft² (2.2 m²) and in bathrooms not exceeding 55 ft² (5.1 m²), provided that such spaces are finished with lath and plaster or materials providing a 15-minute thermal barrier.

[*101*:33.2.3.5.3.1]

13.3.2.20.2.1.2 In slow and impractical evacuation capability facilities, all of the following shall apply:

(1) An automatic sprinkler system in accordance with NFPA 13D, with a 30-minute water supply, shall be permitted.
(2) All habitable areas and closets shall be sprinklered.
(3) Automatic sprinklers shall not be required in bathrooms not exceeding 55 ft^2 (5.1 m^2), provided that such spaces are finished with lath and plaster or materials providing a 15-minute thermal barrier.

[*101*:33.2.3.5.3.2]

Δ **13.3.2.20.2.1.3** In prompt and slow evacuation capability facilities, where an automatic sprinkler system is in accordance with NFPA 13 sprinklers shall not be required in closets not exceeding 24 ft^2 (2.2 m^2) and in bathrooms not exceeding 55 ft^2 (5.1 m^2), provided that such spaces are finished with lath and plaster or materials providing a 15-minute thermal barrier. [*101*:33.2.3.5.3.3]

13.3.2.20.2.1.4 In prompt and slow evacuation capability facilities in buildings four or fewer stories above grade plane, systems in accordance with NFPA 13R shall be permitted. [*101*:33.2.3.5.3.4]

13.3.2.20.2.1.5 In impractical evacuation capability facilities in buildings four or fewer stories above grade plane, systems in accordance with NFPA 13R shall be permitted. All habitable areas and closets shall be sprinklered. Automatic sprinklers shall not be required in bathrooms not exceeding 55 ft^2 (5.1 m^2), provided that such spaces are finished with lath and plaster or materials providing a 15-minute thermal barrier. [*101*:33.2.3.5.3.5]

13.3.2.20.2.1.6 Initiation of the fire alarm system shall not be required for existing installations in accordance with 13.3.2.20.3. [*101*:33.2.3.5.3.6]

13.3.2.20.2.2 All impractical evacuation capability facilities shall be protected throughout by an approved, supervised automatic sprinkler system in accordance with 13.3.2.20.2.1. [*101*:33.2.3.5.3.7]

13.3.2.20.3 Sprinkler piping serving not more than six sprinklers for any isolated hazardous area shall be permitted to be installed in accordance with 13.3.1.4 and shall meet all of the following requirements:

(1) In new installations, where more than two sprinklers are installed in a single area, waterflow detection shall be provided to initiate the fire alarm system required by 13.7.2.21.
(2) The duration of water supplies shall be as required for the sprinkler systems addressed in 13.3.2.20.2.1.

[*101*:33.2.3.5.6]

13.3.2.20.4 Attics shall be protected in accordance with 13.3.2.20.4.1 or 13.3.2.20.4.2. [*101*:33.2.3.5.7]

13.3.2.20.4.1 Where an automatic sprinkler system is installed, attics used for living purposes, storage, or fuel-fired equipment shall be protected with automatic sprinklers that are part of the required, approved automatic sprinkler system in accordance with 13.3.1.2. [*101*:33.2.3.5.7.1]

13.3.2.20.4.2 Where an automatic sprinkler system is installed, attics not used for living purposes, storage, or fuel-fired equipment shall meet one of the following criteria:

(1) Attics shall be protected throughout by a heat detection system arranged to activate the building fire alarm system in accordance with Section 13.7.
(2) Attics shall be protected with automatic sprinklers that are part of the required, approved automatic sprinkler system in accordance with 13.3.1.2.
(3) Attics shall be of noncombustible or limited-combustible construction.
(4) Attics shall be constructed of fire-retardant-treated wood in accordance with NFPA 703.
(5) Attics shall be protected by heat alarms arranged to provide occupant notification in accordance with 13.7.2.21.3.

[*101*:33.2.3.5.7.2]

N **13.3.2.20.4.3** The provisions of 13.3.2.20.4.1 and 13.3.2.20.4.2 shall be permitted to be applied separately to portions of the attic separated by partitions that have a minimum ½-hour fire resistance rating and that extend to the underside of the floor or roof deck above. [*101*:32.2.3.5.7.3]

13.3.2.21 New Mercantile Occupancies.

13.3.2.21.1 Mercantile occupancies shall be protected by an approved automatic sprinkler system in accordance with NFPA 13 in any of the following specified locations:

(1) Throughout all mercantile occupancies three or more stories in height
(2) Throughout all mercantile occupancies exceeding 12,000 ft^2 (1115 m^2) in gross area
(3) Throughout stories below the level of exit discharge where such stories have an area exceeding 2500 ft^2 (232 m^2) and are used for the sale, storage, or handling of combustible goods and merchandise
(4) Throughout multiple occupancies protected as mixed occupancies in accordance with 6.1.14 where the conditions of 13.3.2.21.1(1), 13.3.2.21.1(2), or 13.3.2.21.1(3) apply to the mercantile occupancy

[*101*:36.3.5.1]

Δ **13.3.2.21.2 Extinguishing Requirements.** Bulk merchandising retail buildings shall be protected throughout by an approved, supervised automatic sprinkler system in accordance with Section 13.3 and the applicable provisions of the following:

(1) This *Code*
(2) NFPA 30
(3) NFPA 30B

[*101*:36.4.5.5]

13.3.2.21.3 Mall Buildings.

13.3.2.21.3.1 Automatic Extinguishing Systems.

13.3.2.21.3.1.1 The mall structure and all anchor buildings shall be protected throughout by an approved, supervised automatic sprinkler system in accordance with NFPA 13 and 13.3.2.21.3.1.2. [*101*:36.4.4.14.1]

13.3.2.21.3.1.2 The system shall be installed in such a manner that any portion of the system serving tenant spaces can be taken out of service without affecting the operation of the portion of the system serving the mall concourse. [*101*:36.4.4.14.2]

13.3.2.21.3.2 Hose Connections.

13.3.2.21.3.2.1 There shall be a hose outlet connected to a system sized to deliver 250 gal/min (946 L/min) at the most hydraulically remote outlet. [5000:27.4.4.8.2.1]

13.3.2.21.3.2.2 The outlet shall be supplied from the mall concourse zone sprinkler system and shall be hydraulically calculated. [5000:27.4.4.8.2.2]

13.3.2.21.3.2.3 Hose outlets shall be provided at each of the following locations:

(1) Within the mall concourse at the entrance to each exit passage or corridor
(2) At each floor level landing within enclosed stairways opening directly onto the mall concourse
(3) At exterior public entrances to the mall concourse

[5000:27.4.4.8.2.3]

13.3.2.22 Existing Mercantile Occupancies.

13.3.2.22.1 Mercantile occupancies, other than one-story buildings that meet the requirements of a street floor, as defined in 3.3.278, shall be protected by an approved automatic sprinkler system in accordance with NFPA 13 in any of the following specified locations:

(1) Throughout all mercantile occupancies with a story over 15,000 ft² (1400 m²) in area
(2) Throughout all mercantile occupancies exceeding 30,000 ft² (2800 m²) in gross area
(3) Throughout stories below the level of exit discharge where such stories have an area exceeding 2500 ft² (232 m²) and are used for the sale, storage, or handling of combustible goods and merchandise
(4) Throughout multiple occupancies protected as mixed occupancies in accordance with 6.1.14 where the conditions of 13.3.2.22.1(1), 13.3.2.22.1(2), or 13.3.2.22.1(3) apply to the mercantile occupancy

[*101*:37.3.5.1]

Δ **13.3.2.22.2** Bulk merchandising retail buildings shall be protected throughout by an approved, supervised automatic sprinkler system in accordance with Section 13.3 and the applicable provisions of the following:

(1) This *Code*
(2) NFPA 30
(3) NFPA 30B

[*101*:37.4.5.5]

13.3.2.23 Underground and Limited Access Structures. Underground and limited-access structures, and all areas and floor levels traversed in traveling to the exit discharge, shall be protected by an approved, supervised automatic sprinkler system in accordance with Section 13.3, unless such structures meet one of the following criteria:

(1) They have an occupant load of 50 or fewer persons in new underground or limited-access portions of the structure.
(2) They have an occupant load of 100 or fewer persons in existing underground or limited-access portions of the structure.
(3) The structure is a one-story underground or limited-access structure that is permitted to have a single exit per Chapters 12 through 43 of NFPA *101*, with a common path of travel not greater than 50 ft (15 m).

[*101*:11.7.3.4]

13.3.2.24 High-Rise Buildings.

13.3.2.24.1 New high-rise buildings shall be protected throughout by an approved automatic sprinkler system in accordance with Section 13.3.

13.3.2.24.2* Existing high-rise buildings shall be protected throughout by an approved automatic sprinkler system in accordance with this chapter and 13.3.2.24.2.1 through 13.3.2.24.2.3.

13.3.2.24.2.1 Each building owner shall, within 180 days of receiving notice, file an intent to comply with this regulation with the AHJ for approval.

13.3.2.24.2.2 The AHJ shall review and respond to the intent-to-comply submittal within 60 days of receipt.

13.3.2.24.2.3* The entire building shall be required to be protected by an approved automatic sprinkler system within 12 years of adoption of this *Code*.

13.3.2.24.2.4 Public Disclosure Signage. In high-rise buildings that are not protected throughout by an approved automatic sprinkler system, signage shall be posted complying with 13.3.2.24.2.4(A) through 13.3.2.24.2.4(D).

(A) Signage shall be posted at all main building entrances as approved by the AHJ.

(B) The lettering on the sign shall be at least 1 in. (25 mm) high.

(C) The lettering shall be placed on a contrasting background.

(D) The wording shall state as follows:

WARNING:

This high-rise building is not protected throughout with an automatic fire sprinkler system.

13.3.2.25* New Storage Occupancies.

13.3.2.25.1 High-Piled Storage. An automatic sprinkler system shall be installed throughout all occupancies containing areas greater than 2500 ft² (232 m²) for the high-piled storage of combustibles.

13.3.2.25.2* General Storage. An automatic sprinkler system shall be installed throughout all occupancies containing areas greater than 12,000 ft² (1115 m²) for the storage of combustibles.

13.3.2.25.3 An automatic sprinkler system shall be installed throughout all occupancies containing storage commodities classified as Group A Plastics in excess of 5 ft (1.5 m) in height over an area exceeding 2500 ft² (232 m²) in area.

13.3.2.25.4 Bulk Storage of Tires. Buildings and structures where the volume for the storage of tires exceeds 20,000 ft³ (566 m³) shall be equipped throughout with an approved automatic fire sprinkler system. [5000:30.3.4.2]

13.3.2.25.5 Mini-Storage Building. An automatic sprinkler system shall be installed throughout all mini-storage buildings greater than 2500 ft² (232 m²) and where any of the individual storage units are separated by less than a 1-hour fire-resistance-rated barrier. [5000:30.3.4.3]

13.3.2.26 Woodworking Operations. An approved automatic fire sprinkler system shall be installed in buildings containing woodworking operations exceeding 2500 ft² (232 m²) that use equipment, machinery, or appliances; that generate finely divided combustible waste; or that use finely divided combustible materials. [**5000**:29.3.5.1.2]

Δ **13.3.2.27 New and Existing Day Care.**

N **13.3.2.27.1 New Day Care.**

N **13.3.2.27.1.1** All new day care occupancies shall be protected throughout by an approved, supervised automatic sprinkler system in accordance with Section 9.7 of NFPA *101*. [*101*:16.3.5.1]

N **13.3.2.27.1.2** Required sprinkler systems shall be installed in accordance with 9.7.1.1(1) of NFPA *101* and supervised in accordance with 9.7.2 of NFPA *101*. [*101*:16.3.5.2]

N **13.3.2.27.1.3** Buildings with unprotected openings in accordance with 8.6.6 of NFPA *101* shall be protected throughout by an approved, supervised automatic sprinkler system in accordance with Section 9.7 of NFPA *101*. [*101*:16.3.5.3]

N **13.3.2.27.1.4** Where required by 16.1.6 of NFPA *101*, buildings containing a day care occupancy shall be protected throughout by an approved, supervised automatic sprinkler system in accordance with Section 9.7 of NFPA *101*. [*101*:16.3.5.4]

N **13.3.2.27.2 Existing Day Care.**

N **13.3.2.27.2.1** Any required sprinkler system shall be in accordance with Section 9.7 of NFPA *101*. [*101*:17.3.5.1]

N **13.3.2.27.2.2** Required sprinkler systems, other than approved existing systems, shall be installed in accordance with 9.7.1.1(1) of NFPA *101*. [*101*:17.3.5.2]

N **13.3.2.27.2.3** Buildings with unprotected openings in accordance with 8.6.6 of NFPA *101* shall be protected throughout by an approved, supervised automatic sprinkler system in accordance with Section 9.7 of NFPA *101*. [*101*:17.3.5.3]

N **13.3.2.27.2.4** Where required by 17.1.6 of NFPA *101*, buildings containing a day care occupancy shall be protected throughout by an approved, supervised automatic sprinkler system in accordance with Section 9.7 of NFPA *101*. [*101*:17.3.5.4]

13.3.2.28 New Industrial Occupancies. Industrial occupancies, other than low-hazard industrial occupancies, shall be protected by an approved automatic sprinkler system in accordance with NFPA 13 in any of the following locations:

(1) Throughout all industrial occupancies three or more stories in height
(2) Throughout all industrial occupancies exceeding 12,000 ft² (1115 m²) in fire area
(3) Where the total area of all floors, including mezzanines, exceeds 24,000 ft² (2230 m²)

[**5000**:29.3.5.1.1.1]

13.3.3 Inspection, Testing, and Maintenance.

13.3.3.1 A sprinkler system installed in accordance with this *Code* shall be properly maintained to provide at least the same level of performance and protection as designed. The owner shall be responsible for maintaining the system and keeping it in good working condition.

13.3.3.2 A sprinkler system installed in accordance with this *Code* shall be inspected, tested, and maintained in accordance with NFPA 25.

13.3.3.3 Ceiling Tiles and Ceiling Assemblies. Where automatic sprinklers are installed, ceilings necessary for the proper actuation of the fire protection device in accordance with NFPA 13 shall be maintained.

13.3.3.4 General Requirements.

13.3.3.4.1 Responsibility of the Property Owner or Designated Representative.

13.3.3.4.1.1* Responsibility for Inspection, Testing, Maintenance, and Impairment. The property owner or designated representative shall be responsible for the proper inspection, testing, maintenance, and impairment management of water-based fire protection systems in accordance with NFPA 25. [**25**:4.1.1]

13.3.3.4.1.1.1 Inspection, testing, maintenance, and impairment procedures shall be implemented in accordance with those established in NFPA 25 and in accordance with the manufacturer's instructions. [**25**:4.1.1.1]

N **13.3.3.4.1.1.2** The property owner or designated representative shall have manufacturers' literature available to provide specific instructions for inspecting, testing, and maintaining valves and associated equipment. [**25**:4.1.1.2]

13.3.3.4.1.1.3 Inspection, testing, and maintenance shall be performed by qualified personnel. [**25**:4.1.1.3]

13.3.3.4.1.1.3.1* The owner shall coordinate with the entity conducting the inspection, testing, and maintenance activities to minimize any water damage caused by the discharge of water. [**25**:4.1.1.4]

13.3.3.4.1.1.4* Where the property owner or designated representative is not the occupant, the property owner or designated representative shall be permitted to delegate the authority for inspecting, testing, maintenance, and the managing of impairments of the fire protection system to a designated representative. [**25**:4.1.1.5]

13.3.3.4.1.1.5 Where a designated representative has received the authority for inspecting, testing, maintenance, and the managing of impairments, the designated representative shall comply with the requirements identified for the property owner or designated representative throughout this *Code*. [**25**:4.1.1.6]

Δ **13.3.3.4.1.2* Freeze Protection.** The property owner or designated representative shall ensure that water-filled piping is maintained at a minimum temperature of 40°F (4°C) unless an antifreeze solution complying with NFPA 25 is utilized. [**25**:4.1.2]

13.3.3.4.1.2.1* All areas of the building containing water-filled piping that does not have another means of freeze protection shall be maintained at a minimum temperature of 40°F (4°C). [**25**:4.1.2.1]

13.3.3.4.1.2.2* The requirements of 13.3.3.4.1.2 shall not apply where water-filled piping is located in unconditioned building spaces or areas outside the building envelope and are not subject to freezing. [**25**:4.1.2.2]

13.3.3.4.1.2.3 Aboveground water-filled pipes that pass through open areas, cold rooms, passageways, or other areas exposed to temperatures below 40°F (4°C), protected against freezing by insulating coverings, frostproof casings, listed heat tracing systems, or other reliable means shall be maintained at temperatures between 40°F (4°C) and 120°F (48.9°C). [**25:**4.1.2.3]

13.3.3.4.1.2.4 Where other approved means of freeze protection for water-filled piping as described in 13.3.3.4.1.2.3 are utilized they shall be inspected, tested, and maintained in accordance with NFPA 25. [**25:**4.1.2.4]

13.3.3.4.1.2.5 Valve enclosures for preaction valves, deluge valves, and dry pipe valves subject to freezing shall be inspected daily during cold weather to verify a minimum temperature of 40°F (4°C). [**25:**4.1.2.5]

13.3.3.4.1.2.5.1 Valve enclosures equipped with low-temperature alarms shall be allowed to be inspected weekly. [**25:**4.1.2.5.1]

13.3.3.4.1.2.5.2 Low-temperature alarms, if installed in valve enclosures, shall be inspected annually toward the beginning of the heating season prior to the onset of freezing conditions to verify that they are free of physical damage. [**25:**4.1.2.5.2]

13.3.3.4.1.3* **Accessibility.** The property owner or designated representative shall provide ready accessibility to components of water-based fire protection systems that require inspection, testing, and maintenance. [**25:**4.1.3]

13.3.3.4.1.4 Notification of System Shutdown or Testing. The property owner or designated representative shall notify the AHJ, the fire department, if required, and the alarm-receiving facility before testing or shutting down a system or its supply. [**25:**4.1.4]

13.3.3.4.1.4.1 The notification of system shutdown or test shall include the purpose for the shutdown or test, the system or component involved, the estimated time of shutdown or test, and the expected duration of the shutdown or test. [**25:**4.1.4.1]

13.3.3.4.1.4.2 The AHJ, the fire department, and the alarm-receiving facility shall be notified when the system, supply, or component is returned to service or when the test is complete. [**25:**4.1.4.2]

N **13.3.3.4.1.4.3*** Where a nitrogen supply is used as part of the dry pipe or preaction system design in accordance with NFPA 13, it shall be maintained, repaired, or replaced with a nitrogen supply capable of maintaining design concentrations. [**25:**4.1.4.3]

13.3.3.4.1.5* **Corrections and Repairs.**

13.3.3.4.1.5.1* The property owner or designated representative shall correct or repair deficiencies or impairments. [**25:**4.1.5.1]

13.3.3.4.1.5.1.1* Upon discovery of any component and equipment under recall or replacement programs by the owner's maintenance personnel, designated representative, or contractor, the owner shall be notified in writing. [**25:**4.1.5.1.1]

13.3.3.4.1.5.1.2* The property owner or designated representative shall correct, remedy, repair, or replace components and equipment under recall or replacement program. [**25:**4.1.5.1.2]

13.3.3.4.1.5.2 Corrections and repairs shall be performed by qualified personnel. [**25:**4.1.5.2]

13.3.3.4.1.6* **Changes in Occupancy, Use, Process, or Materials.** The property owner or designated representative shall not make changes in the occupancy, the use or process, or the materials used or stored in the building without evaluation of the fire protection system(s) for its capability to protect the new occupancy, use, or materials. [**25:**4.1.6]

13.3.3.4.1.6.1 The evaluation required by 13.3.3.4.1.6 shall not be considered part of the normal inspection, testing, and maintenance required by this *Code*. [**25:**4.1.6.1]

13.3.3.4.1.6.2* The evaluation shall consider factors that include, but are not limited to, the following:

(1) Occupancy changes such as converting office or production space into warehousing
(2) Process or material changes such as metal stamping to molded plastics
(3) Building revisions such as relocated walls, added mezzanines, and ceilings added below sprinklers
(4) Removal of heating systems in spaces with piping subject to freezing
(5) Changes to the storage method, arrangement, height, or commodities
(6) Changes in water supplies

[**25:**4.1.6.2]

13.3.3.4.1.7* **Addressing Changes in Hazard.**

13.3.3.4.1.7.1 Where changes in the occupancy, hazard, water supply, storage commodity, storage arrangement, building modification, or other condition that affects the installation criteria of the system are identified, the property owner or designated representative shall promptly take steps to evaluate the adequacy of the installed system in order to protect the building or hazard in question. [**25:**4.1.7.1]

13.3.3.4.1.7.2 Where the evaluation reveals that the installed system is inadequate to protect the building or hazard in question, the property owner or designated representative shall make the required corrections. [**25:**4.1.7.2]

13.3.3.4.1.7.3 Corrections shall be approved. [**25:**4.1.7.3]

13.3.3.4.1.8 Control Valve Location. The location of control valves shall be identified at the system riser or other approved locations. [**25:**4.1.8]

13.3.3.4.1.9* **Information Sign.**

13.3.3.4.1.9.1 A permanently marked metal or rigid plastic information sign shall be placed at each system riser. [**25:**4.1.9.1]

13.3.3.4.1.9.2 Each sign shall be secured with a corrosion-resistant wire, chain, or other approved means and shall indicate at least the following information:

(1) Location of the area served by the system
(2) Location of auxiliary drains and low-point drains for dry pipe and preaction systems
(3) Presence and location of antifreeze or other auxiliary systems
(4) Presence and location(s) of heat tape
(5) Location of control valves as required by 13.3.1.1

[**25:**4.1.9.2]

13.3.3.4.1.10* Hydraulic Design Information Sign. The hydraulic design information sign shall be inspected annually to verify that it is provided, attached securely to the sprinkler riser, and is legible. [25:5.2.5]

13.3.3.4.1.10.1 A hydraulic design information sign that is missing or illegible shall be replaced. [25:5.2.5.1]

13.3.3.4.1.10.2 A pipe schedule system shall have a hydraulic design information sign that reads "Pipe Schedule System." [25:5.2.5.2]

Δ **13.3.3.4.1.11 Antifreeze Information Sign.** An antifreeze information sign shall be placed on the antifreeze system control valve indicating, the manufacture type and brand of the antifreeze solution, the concentration by volume of the antifreeze solution used, and the volume of the antifreeze solution used in the system. [25:4.1.10]

13.3.3.4.1.12 Impairments.

13.3.3.4.1.12.1 Where an impairment to a water-based fire protection system occurs or is identified during inspection, testing, or maintenance activities, the procedures outlined in Chapter 15 of NFPA 25 shall be followed, including the attachment of a tag to the impaired system. [25:4.1.11.1]

13.3.3.4.1.12.2 Where a water-based fire protection system is returned to service following an impairment, the system shall be verified to be working properly by means of an appropriate inspection or test as described in the table "Summary of Component Replacement [Action] Requirements" in the applicable chapters of NFPA 25. [25:4.1.11.2]

13.3.3.4.2 Manufacturer's Corrective Action. Manufacturers shall be permitted to make modifications to their own listed product in the field with listed devices that restore the original performance as intended by the listing, where acceptable to the AHJ. [25:4.2]

13.3.3.4.3 Records.

13.3.3.4.3.1* Records shall be made for all inspections, tests, and maintenance of the system and its components. [25:4.3.1]

13.3.3.4.3.1.1* Records shall be maintained by the property owner. [25:4.3.1.1]

13.3.3.4.3.1.2* Records shall be permitted to be stored and accessed electronically. [25:4.3.1.2]

13.3.3.4.3.2 Records shall indicate the following:

(1) The procedure/activity performed (e.g., inspection, test, or maintenance)
(2) The organization that performed the activity
(3) The required frequency of the activity
(4) The results and date of the activity
(5) The name and contact information of the qualified contractor or owner, the qualified personnel performing the activity

[25:4.3.2]

13.3.3.4.3.3* Records shall be made available to the AHJ upon request. [25:4.3.3]

13.3.3.4.3.4 As-built system installation drawings, hydraulic calculations, original acceptance test records, and device manufacturer's data sheets shall be retained for the life of the system. [25:4.3.4]

13.3.3.4.3.5 Inspection, testing, and maintenance records shall be retained for a minimum period of 1 year after the next inspection, test, or maintenance of that type required by the *Code*. [25:4.3.5]

13.3.3.5 Sprinkler Systems.

13.3.3.5.1 Maintenance — Sprinklers.

13.3.3.5.1.1 Replacement Sprinklers. Sprinklers with any of the following qualifications shall be replaced:

(1) Sprinklers manufactured prior to 1920.
(2) Sprinklers showing signs described in 5.2.1.1.1 of NFPA 25.
(3) Sprinklers with unsatisfactory performance when tested in accordance with 5.3.1 of NFPA 25.
(4)* Sprinklers affected by a fire as determined by the authority having jurisdiction.

[25:5.4.1.1]

N **13.3.3.5.1.2*** Where a threaded sprinkler has been removed from a fitting or welded outlet for any reason, the sprinkler shall not be reinstalled. [25:5.4.1.2]

13.3.3.5.1.3* Replacement sprinklers shall have the proper characteristics for the application intended, which include the following:

(1) Style
(2) Orifice size and K-factor
(3) Temperature rating
(4) Coating, if any
(5) Deflector type (e.g., upright, pendent, sidewall)
(6) Design requirements

[25:5.4.1.3]

13.3.3.5.1.3.1* Spray sprinklers shall be permitted to replace old-style sprinklers. [25:5.4.1.3.1]

13.3.3.5.1.3.2* Where replacing residential sprinklers manufactured prior to 2003 that are no longer available from the manufacturer and are installed using a design density less than 0.05 gpm/ft^2 (204 mm/min), a residential sprinkler with an equivalent K-factor (± 5 percent) shall be permitted to be used provided the currently listed coverage area for the replacement sprinkler is not exceeded. [25:5.4.1.3.2]

13.3.3.5.1.3.3 Replacement sprinklers for piers and wharves shall comply with NFPA 307. [25:5.4.1.3.3]

13.3.3.5.1.4 Only new, listed sprinklers shall be used to replace existing sprinklers. [25:5.4.1.4]

13.3.3.5.1.5* Special and quick-response sprinklers as defined by NFPA 13 shall be replaced with sprinklers of the same orifice, size, temperature range and thermal response characteristics, and K-factor. [25:5.4.1.5]

13.3.3.5.1.6* Stock of Spare Sprinklers. A supply of at least six spare sprinklers shall be maintained on the premises so that any sprinklers that have operated or been damaged in any way can be promptly replaced. [25:5.4.1.6]

13.3.3.5.1.6.1 The sprinklers shall correspond to the types and temperature ratings of the sprinklers in the property. [25:5.4.1.6.1]

13.3.3.5.1.6.2 The stock of spare sprinklers shall be kept in a cabinet located where the temperature to which they are subjected will at no time exceed the maximum ceiling temperatures specified in Table 13.3.3.5.1.6.2 for each of the sprinklers within the cabinet. [25:5.4.1.6.2]

13.3.3.5.1.6.3 Where dry sprinklers of different lengths are installed, spare dry sprinklers shall not be required, provided that a means of returning the system to service is furnished. [25:5.4.1.6.3]

13.3.3.5.1.6.4 The number of spare sprinklers in the cabinet shall be based on the number of sprinklers in the protected facility as follows:

(1) For protected facilities having under 300 sprinklers — no fewer than 6 sprinklers
(2) For protected facilities having 300 to 1000 sprinklers — no fewer than 12 sprinklers
(3) For protected facilities having over 1000 sprinklers — no fewer than 24 sprinklers

[25:5.4.1.6.4]

13.3.3.5.1.6.5* One sprinkler wrench as specified by the sprinkler manufacturer shall be provided in the cabinet for each type of sprinkler installed to be used for the removal and installation of sprinklers in the system. [25:5.4.1.6.5]

13.3.3.5.1.6.6 A list of the sprinklers installed in the property shall be posted in the sprinkler cabinet. [25:5.4.1.6.6]

13.3.3.5.1.6.6.1* The list shall include the following:

(1) Sprinkler identification number (SIN) if equipped; or the manufacturer, model, orifice, deflector type, thermal sensitivity, and pressure rating
(2) General description
(3) Quantity of each type to be contained in the cabinet
(4) Issue or revision date of the list

[25:5.4.1.6.6.1]

13.3.3.5.1.7* Sprinklers shall not be altered in any respect or have any type of ornamentation, paint, or coatings applied after shipment from the place of manufacture. [25:5.4.1.7]

13.3.3.5.1.8 Sprinklers and automatic spray nozzles used for protecting commercial-type cooking equipment and ventilating systems shall be replaced annually. [25:5.4.1.8]

13.3.3.5.1.8.1 Where automatic bulb-type sprinklers or spray nozzles are used and annual examination shows no buildup of grease or other material on the sprinklers or spray nozzles, such sprinklers and spray nozzles shall not be required to be replaced. [25:5.4.1.8.1]

13.3.3.5.1.9 Electrically operated sprinklers shall be maintained in accordance with the manufacturer's requirements. [25:5.4.1.9]

13.3.3.5.1.10 Protective Coverings.

13.3.3.5.1.10.1* Sprinklers protecting spray areas and mixing rooms in resin application areas installed with protective coverings shall continue to be protected against overspray residue so that they will operate in the event of fire. [25:5.4.1.10.1]

13.3.3.5.1.10.2 Sprinklers installed as described in 13.3.3.5.1.10.1 shall be protected using cellophane bags having a thickness of 0.003 in. (0.076 mm) or less or thin paper bags. [25:5.4.1.10.2]

13.3.3.5.1.10.3 Coverings shall be replaced periodically so that heavy deposits of residue do not accumulate. [25:5.4.1.10.3]

13.3.3.5.2* Maintenance — Dry Pipe Systems. Dry pipe systems shall be kept dry at all times. [25:5.4.2]

13.3.3.5.2.1 During nonfreezing weather, a dry pipe system shall be permitted to be left wet if the only other option is to remove the system from service while waiting for parts or during repair activities. [25:5.4.2.1]

13.3.3.5.2.2 Refrigerated spaces or other areas within the building interior where temperatures are maintained at or below 40°F (4°C) shall not be permitted to be left wet. [25:5.4.2.2]

13.3.3.5.2.3 Air driers shall be maintained in accordance with the manufacturer's instructions. [25:5.4.2.3]

13.3.3.5.2.4 Compressors used in conjunction with dry pipe sprinkler systems shall be maintained in accordance with Chapter 13 of NFPA 25 and the manufacturer's instructions. [25:5.4.2.4]

13.3.3.6 Impairments.

13.3.3.6.1 General.

13.3.3.6.1.1 Minimum Requirements.

Δ **13.3.3.6.1.1.1** Sub-subsection 13.3.3.6 shall provide the minimum requirements for a fire protection system impairment program. [25:15.1.1.1]

Δ **Table 13.3.3.5.1.6.2 Temperature Ratings, Classifications, and Color Codings**

Maximum Ceiling Temperature °F	°C	Temperature Rating °F	°C	Temperature Classification	Color Code	Glass Bulb Colors
100	38	135–170	57–77	Ordinary	Uncolored or black	Orange or red
150	66	175–225	79–107	Intermediate	White	Yellow or green
225	107	250–300	121–149	High	Blue	Blue
300	149	325–375	163–191	Extra high	Red	Purple
375	191	400–475	204–246	Very extra high	Green	Black
475	246	500–575	260–302	Ultra high	Orange	Black
625	329	650	343	Ultra high	Orange	Black

[25:Table 5.4.1.6.2]

13.3.3.6.1.1.2 Measures shall be taken during the impairment to ensure that increased risks are minimized and the duration of the impairment is limited. [25:15.1.1.2]

13.3.3.6.2 Impairment Coordinator.

13.3.3.6.2.1 The property owner or designated representative shall assign an impairment coordinator to comply with the requirements of 13.3.3.6. [25:15.2.1]

13.3.3.6.2.2 In the absence of a specific designee, the property owner or designated representative shall be considered the impairment coordinator. [25:15.2.2]

13.3.3.6.2.3 Where the lease, written use agreement, or management contract specifically grants the authority for inspection, testing, and maintenance of the fire protection system(s) to the tenant, management firm, or managing individual, the tenant, management firm, or managing individual shall assign a person as impairment coordinator. [25:15.2.3]

13.3.3.6.3 Tag Impairment System.

13.3.3.6.3.1* A tag shall be used to indicate that a system, or part thereof, has been removed from service. [25:15.3.1]

13.3.3.6.3.2* The tag shall be posted at each fire department connection and the system control valve, and other locations required by the AHJ, indicating which system, or part thereof, has been removed from service. [25:15.3.2]

13.3.3.6.4 Impaired Equipment.

13.3.3.6.4.1 The impaired equipment shall be considered to be the water-based fire protection system, or part thereof, that is removed from service. [25:15.4.1]

13.3.3.6.4.2 The impaired equipment shall include, but shall not be limited to, the following:

(1) Sprinkler systems
(2) Standpipe systems
(3) Fire hose systems
(4) Underground fire service mains
(5) Fire pumps
(6) Water storage tanks
(7) Water spray fixed systems
(8) Foam-water sprinkler systems
(9) Water mist systems
(10) Fire service control valves
(11) Water supply

[25:15.4.2]

13.3.3.6.5* Preplanned Impairment Programs.

13.3.3.6.5.1 All preplanned impairments shall be authorized by the impairment coordinator. [25:15.5.1]

13.3.3.6.5.2 Before authorization is given, the impairment coordinator shall be responsible for verifying that the following procedures have been implemented:

(1) The extent and expected duration of the impairment have been determined.
(2) The areas or buildings involved have been inspected and the increased risks determined.
(3) Recommendations to mitigate any increased risks have been submitted to management or the property owner or designated representative.
(4) Where a fire protection system is out of service for more than 10 hours in a 24-hour period, the impairment coordinator shall arrange for one of the following:

  (a) Evacuation of the building or portion of the building affected by the system out of service
  (b)* An approved fire watch
  (c)* Establishment of a temporary water supply
  (d)* Establishment and implementation of an approved program to eliminate potential ignition sources and limit the amount of fuel available to the fire

(5) The fire department has been notified.
(6) The insurance carrier, the alarm company, property owner or designated representative, and other authorities having jurisdiction have been notified.
(7) The supervisors in the areas to be affected have been notified.
(8) A tag impairment system has been implemented. *(See 13.3.3.6.3.)*
(9) All necessary tools and materials have been assembled on the impairment site.

[25:15.5.2]

13.3.3.6.6* Emergency Impairments.

13.3.3.6.6.1 Emergency impairments shall include, but are not limited to, interruption of water supply, frozen or ruptured piping, and equipment failure, and includes impairments found during inspection, testing, or maintenance activities. [25:15.6.1]

13.3.3.6.6.2* The coordinator shall implement the steps outlined in 13.3.3.6.5. [25:15.6.2]

13.3.3.6.7* Restoring Systems to Service. When all impaired equipment is restored to normal working order, the impairment coordinator shall verify that the following procedures have been implemented:

(1) Any necessary inspections and tests have been conducted to verify that affected systems are operational. The appropriate chapter of NFPA 25 shall be consulted for guidance on the type of inspection and test required.
(2) Supervisors have been advised that protection is restored.
(3) The fire department has been advised that protection is restored.
(4) The property owner or designated representative, insurance carrier, alarm company, and other AHJs have been advised that protection is restored.
(5) The impairment tag has been removed.

[25:15.7]

13.4 Fire Pumps.

13.4.1 General.

13.4.1.1 Where provided, fire pumps shall be installed in accordance with NFPA 20 and Section 13.4.

13.4.1.2 Permits. Permits, where required, shall comply with Section 1.13.

13.4.1.3 Pump Operation.

13.4.1.3.1 Service Personnel Qualifications and Experience.

13.4.1.3.1.1 Service personnel shall be qualified and experienced in the inspection, testing, and maintenance of fire protection systems. [20:4.3.4.1]

13.4.1.3.1.2 Qualified personnel shall include, but not be limited to, one or more of the following:

(1) Personnel who are factory trained and certified for fire pump system servicing of the specific type and brand of system being designed
(2) Personnel who are certified by a nationally recognized fire protection certification organization acceptable to the AHJ
(3) Personnel who are registered, licensed, or certified by a state or local authority
(4) Personnel who are employed and qualified by an organization listed by a nationally recognized testing laboratory for the servicing of fire protection systems

[20:4.3.4.2]

13.4.1.3.1.3 Additional evidence of qualification or certification shall be permitted to be required by the AHJ. [20:4.3.4.3]

13.4.2* Valve Supervision.

13.4.2.1 Supervised Open. Where provided, the suction valve, discharge valve, bypass valves, and isolation valves on the backflow prevention device or assembly shall be supervised open by one of the following methods:

(1) Central station, proprietary, or remote station signaling service
(2) Local signaling service that will cause the sounding of an audible signal at a constantly attended point
(3) Locking valves open
(4) Sealing of valves and approved weekly recorded inspection where valves are located within fenced enclosures under the control of the owner

[20:4.18.1]

13.4.2.2 Supervised Closed. Control valves located in the pipeline to the hose valve header shall be supervised closed by one of the methods allowed in 13.4.2.1. [20:4.18.2]

13.4.3 Diesel Engine Driver System Operation.

13.4.3.1 Emergency Starting and Stopping.

13.4.3.1.1 The sequence for emergency manual operation, arranged in a step-by-step manner, shall be posted on the fire pump engine. [20:11.6.6.1]

13.4.3.1.2 It shall be the engine manufacturer's responsibility to list any specific instructions pertaining to the operation of this equipment during the emergency operation. [20:11.6.6.2]

13.4.3.2* Certified Pump Curve.

13.4.3.2.1 A copy of the manufacturer's certified pump test curve shall be available for comparison with the results of the field acceptance test. [20:14.2.4.1]

13.4.3.2.1.1 For water mist positive displacement pumping units, a copy of the manufacturer's certified shop test data for both variable speed and non-variable speed operation shall be available for comparison of the results of the field acceptance test. [20:14.2.4.1.1]

13.4.3.2.1.2 For multistage multiport pumps, a copy of the manufacturer's certified shop test data for each discharge outlet shall be available for comparison with the results of the field acceptance test. [20:14.2.4.1.2]

13.4.3.2.1.3 For self-regulating variable speed fire pump units, a copy of the manufacturer's test curves for self-regulating variable speed constant boost mode, self-regulating variable speed constant discharge mode, and bypass constant speed mode shall be available. [20:14.2.4.1.3]

Δ **13.4.4 Periodic Inspection, Testing, and Maintenance.** Fire pumps shall be inspected, tested, and maintained in accordance with NFPA 25. [20:14.4]

13.4.5 Component Replacement. Component replacement in a fire pump shall be in accordance with NFPA 20.

13.5 Water Supply.

13.5.1 Private fire service mains shall be installed in accordance with NFPA 13 and NFPA 24.

13.5.1.1 NFPA 24 shall not apply to underground mains serving sprinkler systems designed and installed in accordance with NFPA 13R that are less than 4 in. (100 mm) in nominal diameter. [24:1.1.4]

13.5.1.2 NFPA 24 shall not apply to underground mains serving sprinkler systems designed and installed in accordance with NFPA 13D. [24:1.1.5]

13.5.2 Where no adequate and reliable water supply exists for fire-fighting purposes, the requirements of NFPA 1142 shall apply.

13.5.3* The installation of devices to protect the public water supply from contamination shall comply with the provisions of NFPA 13, NFPA 13D, NFPA 13R, NFPA 24, and the plumbing code.

13.5.3.1 Backflow prevention devices shall be inspected, tested, and maintained in accordance with the requirements of NFPA 25.

13.5.4 Inspection, Testing, and Maintenance.

Δ **13.5.4.1** A private fire service main installed in accordance with this *Code* shall be properly inspected, tested, and maintained to provide at least the same level of performance and protection as designed.

N **13.5.4.2** The owner of the private fire service main shall be responsible for maintaining the system and keeping it in good working condition.

13.5.4.3 A private fire service main installed in accordance with this *Code* shall be inspected, tested, and maintained in accordance with NFPA 25.

13.6 Portable Fire Extinguishers.

13.6.1 General Requirements.

13.6.1.1 Scope. The selection, installation, inspection, maintenance, recharging, and testing of portable fire extinguishers shall be in accordance with NFPA 10 and Section 13.6.

13.6.1.1.1 The requirements given herein are minimum. [10:1.1.1]

13.6.1.1.2 The requirements shall not apply to permanently installed systems for fire extinguishment, even where portions of such systems are portable (such as hose and nozzles attached to a fixed supply of extinguishing agent). [10:1.1.2]

13.6.1.2* Where Required. Fire extinguishers shall be provided where required by this *Code* as specified in Table 13.6.1.2 and the referenced codes and standards listed in Chapter 2.

Table 13.6.1.2 Portable Fire Extinguishers Required

Occupancy Use	Where Required
Ambulatory health care occupancies	Yes
Apartment occupancies[a]	Yes
Assembly occupancies[b]	Yes
Business occupancies	Yes
Day-care occupancies	Yes
Detention and correctional occupancies[c,d]	Yes
Educational occupancies	Yes
Health care occupancies	Yes
Hotel and dormitory occupancies	Yes
Industrial occupancies	Yes
Lodging and rooming house occupancies	Yes
Mercantile occupancies	Yes
Occupancies in special structures	Yes
One- and two-family dwelling occupancies	No
Residential board and care occupancies	Yes
Storage occupancies[e]	Yes

[a]Portable fire extinguishers shall be permitted to be located at exterior locations or interior locations so that all portions of the buildings are within 75 ft (22.8 m) of travel distance to an extinguishing unit.
[b]Portable fire extinguishers are not required in seating or outdoor performance areas.
[c]Access to portable fire extinguishers shall be permitted to be locked.
[d]Portable fire extinguishers shall be permitted to be located at staff locations only.
[e]In storage areas where forklift, powered industrial truck, or cart operators are the primary occupants, fixed extinguishers, as specified in NFPA 10, need not be provided when:

(1) Use of vehicle-mounted extinguishers is approved by the AHJ.
(2) Each vehicle is equipped with a 10 lb, 40-A:80-B:C extinguisher affixed to the vehicle using a mounting bracket approved by the extinguisher manufacturer or the AHJ for vehicular use.
(3) Not less than two spare extinguishers of equal or greater rating are available onsite to replace a discharged extinguisher.
(4) Vehicle operators are trained in the proper operation and use of the extinguisher.
(5) Inspections of vehicle-mounted extinguishers are performed daily.

13.6.1.3 Listing and Labeling.

13.6.1.3.1* Portable fire extinguishers used to comply with Section 13.6 shall be listed and labeled and shall meet or exceed all the requirements of UL 711, CAN/ULC-S508, *Standard for the Rating and Fire Testing of Fire Extinguishers*, and one of the following applicable performance standards:

(1) Carbon dioxide types: UL 154, CAN/ULC-S503, *Standard for Carbon-Dioxide Fire Extinguishers*
(2) Dry chemical types: UL 299, CAN/ULC-S504, *Standard for Dry Chemical Fire Extinguishers*
(3) Water types: UL 626, CAN/ULC-S507, *Standard for Water Fire Extinguishers*
(4) Halon types: CAN/ULC-S512, *Standard for Halogenated Agent Hand and Wheeled Fire Extinguishers*
(5) Film-forming foam types: UL 8, CAN/ULC-S554, *Water Based Agent Fire Extinguishers*
(6) Halocarbon types: UL 2129, CAN/ULC-S566, *Standard for Halocarbon Clean Agent Fire Extinguishers*

[**10**:4.1.1]

Δ **13.6.1.3.2*** Each fire extinguisher shall be marked with the following:

(1) Identification of the listing and labeling organization
(2) Product category indicating the type of extinguisher
(3) Extinguisher classification as indicated in Section 5.3 of NFPA 10
(4) Performance and fire test standards that the extinguisher meets or exceeds

[**10**:4.1.2]

13.6.1.3.2.1 Halon extinguishers listed and labeled to UL 1093, *Standard for Halogenated Agent Fire Extinguishers*, shall be permitted to be used to comply with the requirements of Section 13.6 when installed, inspected, and maintained in accordance with Section 13.6. [**10**:4.1.2.2]

13.6.1.3.3 Electrical Conductivity. Extinguishers listed for the Class C rating shall not contain an agent that is a conductor of electricity. [**10**:4.1.4]

Δ **13.6.1.3.3.1** In addition to successfully meeting the requirements of UL 711, CAN/ULC-S508, water-based agents that are listed for the Class C rating shall be tested in accordance with ASTM D5391, *Standard Test for Electrical Conductivity and Resistivity of a Flowing High Purity Water Sample*. [**10**:4.1.4.1]

13.6.1.3.3.2 Fire extinguishers containing water-based agents that have a conductivity higher than 1.00 µS/cm at 77°F (25°C) shall be considered a conductor of electricity and therefore shall not be rated Class C. [**10**:4.1.4.2]

13.6.1.3.3.3 Paragraphs 13.6.1.3.3.1 and 13.6.1.3.3.2 shall apply only to water-based extinguishers manufactured after August 15, 2002. [**10**:4.1.4.3]

Δ **13.6.1.4* Identification of Contents.** A fire extinguisher shall have a label, tag, or stencil attached to it providing the following information:

(1) The content's product name as it appears on the manufacturer's Material Safety Data Sheet (MSDS)
(2) Listing of the hazardous material identification in accordance with *Hazardous Materials Identification System (HMIS) Implementation Manual* [in Canada, *Globally Harmonized System of Classification and Labeling of Chemicals (GHS)*]
(3) List of any hazardous materials that are in excess of 1.0 percent of the contents
(4) List of each chemical in excess of 5.0 percent of the contents
(5) Information as to what is hazardous about the agent in accordance with the MSDS
(6) Manufacturer's or service agency's name, mailing address, and phone number

[**10**:4.2]

13.6.1.5 Obsolete Fire Extinguishers. The following types of fire extinguishers are considered obsolete and shall be removed from service:

(1) Soda acid
(2) Chemical foam (excluding film-forming agents)
(3) Carbon tetrachloride, methyl bromide, and chlorobromomethane (CBM)
(4) Cartridge-operated water
(5) Cartridge-operated loaded stream
(6) Copper or brass shell (excluding pump tanks) joined by soft solder or rivets
(7) Carbon dioxide extinguishers with metal horns

(8) Solid charge–type AFFF extinguishers (paper cartridge)
(9) Pressurized water fire extinguishers manufactured prior to 1971
(10) Any extinguisher that needs to be inverted to operate
(11) Any extinguisher manufactured prior to 1955
(12) Any extinguishers with 4B, 6B, 8B, 12B, and 16B fire ratings
(13) Stored-pressure water extinguishers with fiberglass shells (pre-1976)

[10:4.4]

13.6.1.5.1 Dry chemical stored-pressure extinguishers with an indicated manufacturing date of 1984 or prior shall be removed from service. [10:4.4.1]

13.6.1.5.1.1 Paragraph 13.6.1.5.1 shall not apply to wheeled-type dry chemical stored-pressure fire extinguishers. [10:4.4.1.1]

13.6.1.5.2* Any fire extinguisher that can no longer be serviced in accordance with the manufacturer's maintenance manual is considered obsolete and shall be removed from service. [10:4.4.2]

13.6.2 Selection of Portable Fire Extinguishers.

13.6.2.1 General Requirements. The selection of fire extinguishers for a given situation shall be determined by the applicable requirements of Sections 5.2 through 5.5 of NFPA 10 and the following factors:

(1) Type of fire most likely to occur
(2) Size of fire most likely to occur
(3) Hazards in the area where the fire is most likely to occur
(4) Energized electrical equipment in the vicinity of the fire
(5) Ambient temperature conditions
(6) Other factors *(see Section H.2 of NFPA 10)*

[10:5.1]

13.6.2.1.1 Portable fire extinguishers shall be installed as a first line of defense to cope with fires of limited size, except as required by 5.5.4.5 of NFPA 10. [10:5.1.1]

13.6.2.1.2 The selection of extinguishers shall be independent of whether the building is equipped with automatic sprinklers, standpipe and hose, or other fixed protection equipment. [10:5.1.2]

13.6.2.2 Classification of Fires. See 3.3.115.

13.6.2.3 Extinguisher Classification System.

13.6.2.3.1 The classification of fire extinguishers shall consist of a letter that indicates the class of fire on which a fire extinguisher has been found to be effective. [10:5.3.1]

13.6.2.3.1.1 Fire extinguishers classified for use on Class A or Class B hazards shall be required to have a rating number preceding the classification letter that indicates the relative extinguishing effectiveness. [10:5.3.1.1]

13.6.2.3.1.2 Fire extinguishers classified for use on Class C, Class D, or Class K hazards shall not be required to have a number preceding the classification letter. [10:5.3.1.2]

13.6.2.3.2 Fire extinguishers shall be selected for the class(es) of hazards to be protected in accordance with 13.6.2.3.2.1 through 13.6.2.3.2.5. *(For specific hazards, see Section 5.5.4 of NFPA 10.)* [10:5.3.2]

13.6.2.3.2.1* Fire extinguishers for the protection of Class A hazards shall be selected from types that are specifically listed and labeled for use on Class A fires. *(For halon agent–type extinguishers, see 13.6.2.3.2.6.)* [10:5.3.2.1]

13.6.2.3.2.2* Fire extinguishers for the protection of Class B hazards shall be selected from types that are specifically listed and labeled for use on Class B fires. *(For halon agent–type extinguishers, see 13.6.2.3.2.6.)* [10:5.3.2.2]

13.6.2.3.2.3* Fire extinguishers for the protection of Class C hazards shall be selected from types that are specifically listed and labeled for use on Class C hazards. *(For halon agent–type fire extinguishers, see 13.6.2.3.2.6.)* [10:5.3.2.3]

13.6.2.3.2.4* Fire extinguishers and extinguishing agents for the protection of Class D hazards shall be of the types specifically listed and labeled for use on the specific combustible metal hazard. [10:5.3.2.4]

13.6.2.3.2.5 Fire extinguishers for the protection of Class K hazards shall be selected from types that are specifically listed and labeled for use on Class K fires. [10:5.3.2.5]

13.6.2.3.2.6* Use of halon agent fire extinguishers shall be limited to applications where a clean agent is necessary to extinguish fire efficiently without damaging the equipment or area being protected, or where the use of alternative agents has the potential to cause a hazard to personnel in the area. [10:5.3.2.6]

13.6.2.3.2.6.1* Placement of portable fire extinguishers containing halogenated agents shall conform to minimum confined space volume requirement warnings contained on the fire extinguisher nameplates. [10:5.3.2.6.1]

13.6.2.3.2.7* Wheeled fire extinguishers shall be considered for hazard protection in areas in which a fire risk assessment has shown the following:

(1) High hazard areas are present
(2) Limited available personnel are present, thereby requiring an extinguisher that has the following features:
   (a) High agent flow rate
   (b) Increased agent stream range
   (c) Increased agent capacity

[10:5.3.2.7]

13.6.2.4 Classification of Hazards.

13.6.2.4.1 Classifying Occupancy Hazard. Rooms or areas shall be classified as being light hazard, ordinary hazard, or extra hazard. [10:5.4.1]

13.6.2.4.1.1* Light Hazard. Light hazard occupancies shall be classified as locations where the quantity and combustibility of Class A combustibles and Class B flammables are low and fires with relatively low rates of heat release are expected. These occupancies consist of fire hazards having normally expected quantities of Class A combustible furnishings, and/or the total quantity of Class B flammables typically expected to be present is less than 1 gal (3.8 L) in any room or area. [10:5.4.1.1]

13.6.2.4.1.2* Ordinary Hazard. Ordinary hazard occupancies shall be classified as locations where the quantity and combustibility of Class A combustible materials and Class B flammables are moderate and fires with moderate rates of heat release are expected. These occupancies consist of fire hazards that only occasionally contain Class A combustible materials beyond normal anticipated furnishings, and/or the total quantity of Class B flammables typically expected to be present is from 1 gal to 5 gal (3.8 L to 18.9 L) in any room or area. [10:5.4.1.2]

13.6.2.4.1.3* Extra Hazard. Extra hazard occupancies shall be classified as locations where the quantity and combustibility of Class A combustible material are high or where high amounts of Class B flammables are present and rapidly developing fires with high rates of heat release are expected. These occupancies consist of fire hazards involved with the storage, packaging, handling, or manufacture of Class A combustibles, and/or the total quantity of Class B flammables expected to be present is more than 5 gal (18.9 L) in any room or area. [10:5.4.1.3]

13.6.2.4.1.4 Limited areas of greater or lesser hazard shall be protected as required. [10:5.4.1.4]

N **13.6.2.4.2* Selection of Fire Extinguishers.**

N **13.6.2.4.2.1 General.** Where fire extinguishers have more than one letter classification (such as 3-A:40-B:C), they shall be permitted to satisfy the requirements of each letter class. [10:5.5.1]

N **13.6.2.4.2.2 Selection for Building Protection.** Fire extinguishers for building protection shall be selected for Class A fires, regardless of the presence of any fixed fire suppression systems. [10:5.5.2]

13.6.2.4.2.3 Selection for Occupancy Hazards. Fire extinguishers shall be selected for the occupancy hazards contained therein regardless of the presence of any fixed fire suppression systems. [10:5.5.3]

Δ **13.6.2.4.2.3.1** Fire extinguishers for occupancy hazard protection shall be provided by fire extinguishers for Class A, B, C, D, or K fire hazards present or anticipated to be present. [10:5.5.3.1]

13.6.2.4.2.3.2 Fire extinguishers selected for building protection shall be permitted to also be considered for occupancy hazard protection. [10:5.5.3.2]

13.6.2.5 Selection for Specific Hazards.

13.6.2.5.1 Class B Fires.

13.6.2.5.1.1* Extinguishers for Pressurized Liquid and Pressurized Gas Fires. Large-capacity dry chemical extinguishers of 10 lb (4.54 kg) or greater and with a discharge rate of 1 lb/sec (0.45 kg/sec) or more shall be selected to protect these hazards. [10:5.5.4.1]

13.6.2.5.1.1.1* Thee-Dimensional Fires. Large-capacity dry chemical extinguishers of 10 lb (4.54 kg) or greater and a discharge rate of 1 lb/sec (0.45 kg/sec) or more shall be selected to protect these hazards. [10:5.5.4.2]

13.6.2.5.2 Obstacle Fires. Selection of a fire extinguisher for this type of hazard shall be based on one of the following:

(1) Extinguisher containing a vapor-suppressing foam agent
(2)* Multiple extinguishers containing non-vapor-suppressing Class B agents intended for simultaneous application
(3) Larger capacity extinguishers of 10 lb (4.54 kg) or greater and with a minimum discharge rate of 1 lb/sec (0.45 kg/sec)

[10:5.5.4.4]

Δ **13.6.2.5.3* Water-Soluble Liquid Fires (Polar Solvents).** Aqueous film-forming foam (AFFF) and film-forming fluoroprotein foam (FFFP) foam types of fire extinguishers shall not be selected for the protection of water-soluble flammable or combustible liquids, unless specifically referenced on the fire extinguisher's nameplate. [10:5.5.5.4]

13.6.2.5.4* Class K Cooking Media Fires. Fire extinguishers provided for the protection of cooking appliances that use combustible cooking media (e.g., vegetable or animal oils and fats) shall be listed and labeled for Class K fires. [10:5.5.4.5]

13.6.2.5.4.1 Class K fire extinguishers manufactured after January 1, 2002, shall not be equipped with extended-wand-type discharge devices. [10:5.5.4.5.1]

13.6.2.5.4.2 Fire extinguishers installed specifically for the protection of cooking appliances that use combustible cooking media (e.g., animal or vegetable oils and fats) without a Class K rating shall be removed from service. [10:5.5.4.5.2]

Δ **13.6.2.5.4.3*** Where a hazard is protected by an automatic fire protection system, a placard shall be placed near the extinguisher that states that the fire protection system shall be actuated prior to using the fire extinguisher. [10:5.5.4.5.3]

Δ **13.6.2.5.5* Electronic Equipment Fires.**

N **13.6.2.5.5.1** Fire extinguishers for the protection of delicate electronic equipment shall be selected from types specifically listed and labeled for Class C hazards. *(See 13.6.2.3.2.3.)* [10:5.5.4.6]

13.6.2.5.5.2* Dry chemical fire extinguishers shall not be installed for the protection of delicate electronic equipment. [10:5.5.4.6.2]

13.6.2.5.6 Areas Containing Oxidizers.

13.6.2.5.6.1 Only water or foam extinguishers shall be installed in areas where pool chemicals containing chlorine or bromine are stored. [10:5.5.4.7.1]

13.6.2.5.6.2 Multipurpose dry chemical fire extinguishers shall not be installed in areas where pool chemicals containing chlorine or bromine are stored. [10:5.5.4.7.2]

Δ **13.6.2.5.6.3** Fire extinguishers intended for use where oxidizers are stored or used shall be selected and installed based on the specific recommendations contained within the material's safety data sheet (SDS) for the oxidizer, surrounding conditions, and NFPA 400. [10:5.5.4.7.3]

Δ **13.6.2.5.7 Class D Combustible Metal Fires.**

N **13.6.2.5.7.1** Fire extinguishers or containers of Class D extinguishing agents provided for the protection of Class D fires shall be listed and labeled for Class D fires. [10:5.5.4.8.1]

13.6.2.5.7.2* Class D fire extinguishers and agents shall be compatible with the specific metal for which protection is provided. [10:5.5.4.8.2]

13.6.2.6 Selection for Specific Locations.

Δ **13.6.2.6.1*** Where portable fire extinguishers are required to be installed, the following documents shall be reviewed for the occupancies outlined in their respective scopes:

(1) This *Code*
(2) NFPA 2
(3) NFPA 22

(4) NFPA 30
(5) NFPA 30A
(6) NFPA 33
(7) NFPA 40
(8) NFPA 45
(9) NFPA 51
(10) NFPA 51B
(11) NFPA 52
(12) NFPA 58
(13) NFPA 59
(14) NFPA 59A
(15) NFPA 72
(16) NFPA 75
(17) NFPA 76
(18) NFPA 96
(19) NFPA 99
(20) NFPA 99B
(21) NFPA *101*
(22) NFPA 102
(23) NFPA 115
(24) NFPA 120
(25) NFPA 122
(26) NFPA 130
(27) NFPA 140
(28) NFPA 150
(29) NFPA 160
(30) NFPA 232
(31) NFPA 241
(32) NFPA 301
(33) NFPA 302
(34) NFPA 303
(35) NFPA 307
(36) NFPA 326
(37) NFPA 385,
(38) NFPA 400
(39) NFPA 403
(40) NFPA 407
(41) NFPA 408
(42) NFPA 409
(43) NFPA 410
(44) NFPA 418
(45) NFPA 423
(46) NFPA 484
(47) NFPA 495
(48) NFPA 498
(49) NFPA 501A
(50) NFPA 502
(51) NFPA 505
(52) NFPA 655
(53) NFPA 731
(54) NFPA 801
(55) NFPA 804
(56) NFPA 805
(57) NFPA 820
(58) NFPA 909
(59) NFPA 914
(60) NFPA 1123
(61) NFPA 1125
(62) NFPA 1126
(63) NFPA 1141
(64) NFPA 1192
(65) NFPA 1194
(66) NFPA 1221
(67) NFPA 1901
(68) NFPA 1906
(69) NFPA 1925
(70) *NFPA 5000*
[**10**:5.5.5.1]

13.6.2.6.2 In no case shall the requirements of the documents in 13.6.2.6.1 be less than those specified in Section 13.6 and Chapter 2. [**10**:5.5.5.2]

13.6.3 Installation of Portable Fire Extinguishers.

13.6.3.1 General.

13.6.3.1.1* Number of Extinguishers. The minimum number of fire extinguishers needed to protect a property shall be determined as outlined in 13.6.3. [**10**:6.1.1]

13.6.3.1.1.1 The installation of extinguishers shall be independent of whether the building is equipped with automatic sprinklers, standpipe and hose, or other fixed protection equipment. [**10**:6.1.1.1]

Δ **13.6.3.1.1.2** Additional extinguishers shall be permitted to be installed to provide more protection. [**10**:6.1.1.2]

13.6.3.1.1.3 Fire extinguishers having ratings less than those specified in Table 13.6.3.2.1.1 and Table 13.6.3.3.1.1 shall be permitted to be installed, provided they are not used in fulfilling the minimum protective requirements of this subsection, except as modified in 13.6.3.2.1.3, 13.6.3.2.1.4, and 13.6.3.3.1.1.1. [**10**:6.1.1.3]

N **13.6.3.1.1.4** Where multiple fire extinguishers with different ratings or operating characteristics are co-located to protect multiple hazard classes or specific hazards, each extinguisher shall be provided with clear and legible signage or placards to indicate their specific hazard use or protection rating. [**10**:6.1.1.4]

N **13.6.3.1.1.4.1** Individual signage or placards shall be provided for each extinguisher in the grouping and shall be placed immediately above or adjacent to each installed extinguisher. [**10**:6.1.1.4.1]

N **13.6.3.1.1.4.2** Where extinguishers are installed in cabinets, the required signage or placard shall be permitted to be placed on the face of the cabinet door provided it does not interfere with cabinet visibility, conspicuity, or fire resistance rating. [**10**:6.1.1.4.2]

13.6.3.1.2 Extinguisher Readiness. Portable fire extinguishers shall be maintained in a fully charged and operable condition and shall be kept in their designated places at all times when they are not being used. [**10**:6.1.2]

13.6.3.1.3 Placement.

13.6.3.1.3.1 Fire extinguishers shall be conspicuously located where they are readily accessible and immediately available in the event of fire. [**10**:6.1.3.1]

13.6.3.1.3.2 Fire extinguishers shall be located along normal paths of travel, including exits from areas. [**10**:6.1.3.2]

13.6.3.1.3.3 Visibility.

13.6.3.1.3.3.1 Fire extinguishers shall be installed in locations where they are visible except as permitted by 13.6.3.1.3.3.2 or 13.6.3.1.3.3.3. [**10**:6.1.3.3.1]

13.6.3.1.3.3.2* In rooms and in locations where visual obstructions cannot be completely avoided, signs or other means shall be provided to indicate the extinguisher location. [10:6.1.3.3.2]

N **13.6.3.1.3.3.3** Fire extinguishers shall be permitted to be installed in fire extinguisher cabinets provided the extinguisher is visible or signs or other means are provided to indicate the extinguisher location. [10:6.1.3.3.3]

13.6.3.1.3.3.4 Where signs or other means are used to indicate fire extinguisher location they shall be located in close proximity to the extinguisher. [10:6.1.3.3.4]

13.6.3.1.3.3.5 Where signs or other means are used to indicate fire extinguisher location they shall be visible from the normal path of travel. [10:6.1.3.3.5]

13.6.3.1.3.4* Portable fire extinguishers other than wheeled extinguishers shall be installed using any of the following means:

(1)* Securely on a hanger intended for the extinguisher
(2) In a bracket incorporating releasing straps or bands supplied by the extinguisher manufacturer
(3) In a listed bracket incorporating releasing straps or bands approved for such purpose
(4) In approved cabinets or wall recesses

[10:6.1.3.4]

N **13.6.3.1.3.4.1** Hangers and brackets shall not be fabricated in the field. [10:6.1.3.4.1]

13.6.3.1.3.5 Wheeled fire extinguishers shall be located in designated locations. [10:6.1.3.5]

13.6.3.1.3.6 Fire extinguishers installed in or on vehicles shall be installed in approved strap-type brackets specifically designed for this application. [10:6.1.3.6]

N **13.6.3.1.3.7** Fire extinguishers installed under conditions where they are subject to dislodgement shall be installed in approved strap-type brackets specifically designed to prevent dislodgement. [10:6.1.3.7]

13.6.3.1.3.8 Fire extinguishers installed under conditions or in locations where they are subject to physical damage (e.g., from impact, vibration, the environment) shall be protected against such damage. [10:6.1.3.8]

13.6.3.1.3.9 Installation Height.

13.6.3.1.3.9.1 Fire extinguishers having a gross weight not exceeding 40 lb (18.14 kg) shall be installed so that the top of the fire extinguisher is not more than 5 ft (1.53 m) above the floor. [10:6.1.3.9.1]

13.6.3.1.3.9.2 Fire extinguishers having a gross weight greater than 40 lb (18.14 kg) (except wheeled types) shall be installed so that the top of the fire extinguisher is not more than 3½ ft (1.07 m) above the floor. [10:6.3.1.9.2]

13.6.3.1.3.9.3 In no case shall the clearance between the bottom of the hand portable fire extinguisher and the floor be less than 4 in. (102 mm). [10:6.3.1.9.3]

13.6.3.1.3.10 Label Visibility.

13.6.3.1.3.10.1 Fire extinguishers shall be installed so that the fire extinguisher's operating instructions face outward. [10:6.1.3.10.1]

13.6.3.1.3.10.2 Hazardous materials identification systems (HMIS) labels, 6-year maintenance labels, hydrostatic test labels, or other labels shall not be located or placed on the front of the extinguisher. [10:6.1.3.10.2]

13.6.3.1.3.10.3* The restrictions of 13.6.3.1.3.10.2 shall not apply to the original manufacturer's labels, labels that specifically relate to the extinguisher's operation or fire classification, or inventory control labels specific to that extinguisher. [10:6.3.1.3.10.3]

13.6.3.1.3.11 Cabinets.

Δ **13.6.3.1.3.11.1 Locked Cabinets.**

N **13.6.3.1.3.11.1.1** Cabinets housing fire extinguishers shall not be locked, except where fire extinguishers are subject to malicious use and cabinets include a means of emergency access. [10:6.1.3.11.1.1]

13.6.3.1.3.11.1.2 Cabinets housing fire extinguishers with breakfront panels shall be provided with breaker bars or hammers, designed for accessing the extinguisher during a fire emergency. [10:6.1.3.11.1.2]

Δ **13.6.3.1.3.11.2 Location.**

N **13.6.3.1.3.11.2.1** The location of fire extinguishers in cabinets that are not visible from the normal path of travel shall be provided with signs or other means to indicate the extinguisher location. [10:6.1.3.11.2.1]

N **13.6.3.1.3.11.2.2** Signs or other means as stated in 13.6.3.1.3.11.2.1 shall be visible from the normal path of travel. [10:6.1.3.11.2.2]

N **13.6.3.1.3.11.3** Fire extinguishers mounted in cabinets or wall recesses shall be placed so that the fire extinguisher's operating instructions face outward. [10:6.1.3.11.3]

13.6.3.1.3.11.4* Where fire extinguishers are installed in closed cabinets that are exposed to elevated temperatures, the cabinets shall be provided with screened openings and drains. [10:6.1.3.11.4]

13.6.3.1.3.11.5 Cabinets or wall recesses for fire extinguishers shall be installed such that the extinguisher mounting heights specified in 13.6.3.1.3.9.1 and 13.6.3.1.3.9.2 are met. [10:6.1.3.11.5]

13.6.3.1.3.11.6* For fire resistance–rated walls, only surface-mounted cabinets or listed fire-rated cabinets shall be installed. [10:6.1.3.11.6]

13.6.3.1.3.12* Fire extinguishers shall not be exposed to temperatures outside of the listed temperature range shown on the fire extinguisher label. [10:6.1.3.12]

13.6.3.1.4 Antifreeze.

13.6.3.1.4.1 Fire extinguishers containing only plain water shall be protected to temperatures as low as −40°F (−40°C) by the addition of an antifreeze that is stipulated on the fire extinguisher nameplate. [10:6.1.4.1]

13.6.3.1.4.2 Calcium chloride solutions shall not be used in stainless steel fire extinguishers. [10:6.1.4.2]

13.6.3.1.5 Electronic Monitoring and Alarm System. Where an electronic monitoring and alarm system is installed, 13.6.3.1.5.1 and 13.6.3.1.5.2 shall apply. [10:6.1.5]

13.6.3.1.5.1 The connection to the electronic monitoring device shall be continuously supervised for integrity. [**10**:6.1.5.1]

13.6.3.1.5.2 The power source for the electronic monitoring device shall be supervised for continuity of power. [**10**:6.1.5.2]

13.6.3.2 Installations for Class A Hazards.

13.6.3.2.1 Fire Extinguisher Size and Placement for Class A Hazards.

13.6.3.2.1.1 Minimal sizes of fire extinguishers for the listed grades of hazards shall be provided on the basis of Table 13.6.3.2.1.1, except as modified by 13.6.3.2.1.3 and 13.6.3.2.1.4. [**10**:6.2.1.1]

13.6.3.2.1.2 The minimum number of extinguishers for Class A hazards shall be sufficient to meet the requirements of 13.6.3.2.1.2.1 through 13.6.3.2.1.2.3. [**10**:6.2.1.2]

13.6.3.2.1.2.1 The minimum number of fire extinguishers for Class A hazards for each floor of a building shall be determined by dividing the total floor area by the maximum area to be protected per extinguisher as determined by Table 13.6.3.2.1.1. *(See Annex E of NFPA 10.)* [**10**:6.2.1.2.1]

13.6.3.2.1.2.2 Fire extinguishers shall be located so that the maximum travel distances shall not exceed 75 ft (22.9 m), except as modified by 13.6.3.2.1.3. [**10**:6.2.1.2.2]

13.6.3.2.1.2.3 Where the quantity of extinguishers required to satisfy 13.6.3.2.1.2.2 exceeds the number calculated in 13.6.3.2.1.2.1, additional extinguishers shall be installed. [**10**:6.2.1.2.3]

13.6.3.2.1.3 Fire extinguishers of lesser rating shall be permitted to be installed but shall not be considered as fulfilling any part of the requirements of Table 13.6.3.2.1.1, except as permitted in 13.6.3.2.1.3.1 and 13.6.3.2.1.3.2. [**10**:6.2.1.3]

13.6.3.2.1.3.1 Up to two water-type extinguishers, each with 1-A rating, shall be permitted to be used to fulfill the requirements of one 2-A rated extinguisher. [**10**:6.2.1.3.1]

13.6.3.2.1.3.2 Two 2½ gal (9.46 L) water-type extinguishers shall be permitted to be used to fulfill the requirements of one 4-A rated extinguisher. [**10**:6.2.1.3.2]

Δ **Table 13.6.3.2.1.1 Fire Extinguisher Size and Placement for Class A Hazards**

Criteria	Light-Hazard Occupancy	Ordinary-Hazard Occupancy	Extra-Hazard Occupancy
Minimum-rated single extinguisher	2-A	2-A	4-A
Maximum floor area per unit of A	3000 ft^2 (279 m^2)	1500 ft^2 (139 m^2)	1000 ft^2 (92.9 m^2)
Maximum floor area per extinguisher	11,250 ft^2 (1045 m^2)	11,250 ft^2 (1045 m^2)	11,250 ft^2 (1045 m^2)
Maximum travel distance to extinguisher	75 ft (22.9 m)	75 ft (22.9 m)	75 ft (22.9 m)

For SI units, 1 ft = 0.305 m; 1 ft^2 = 0.0929 m^2.
Note: For maximum floor area explanations, see E.3.3 of NFPA 10.
[**10**:Table 6.2.1.1]

13.6.3.2.1.4 Up to one-half of the complement of fire extinguishers specified in Table 13.6.3.2.1.1 shall be permitted to be replaced by uniformly spaced 1½ in. (38 mm) hose stations for use by the occupants of the building. [**10**:6.2.1.4]

13.6.3.2.1.4.1 Where hose stations are so provided, they shall conform to NFPA 14. [**10**:6.2.1.4.1]

13.6.3.2.1.4.2 The location of hose stations and the placement of fire extinguishers shall be such that the hose stations do not replace more than every other fire extinguisher. [**10**:6.2.1.4.2]

13.6.3.2.1.5 Where the area of the floor of a building is less than that specified in Table 13.6.3.2.1.1, at least one fire extinguisher of the minimum size required shall be provided. [**10**:6.2.1.5]

13.6.3.2.1.6 The protection requirements shall be permitted to be fulfilled with fire extinguishers of higher rating, provided the travel distance to such larger fire extinguishers does not exceed 75 ft (22.9 m) and the maximum floor area per unit of A is not exceeded. [**10**:6.2.1.6]

13.6.3.3 Installations for Class B Hazards.

13.6.3.3.1 Spill Fires.

13.6.3.3.1.1 Minimum ratings of fire extinguishers for the listed grades of hazard shall be provided in accordance with Table 13.6.3.3.1.1. [**10**:6.3.1.1]

13.6.3.3.1.1.1 Two or more fire extinguishers of lower rating shall not be used to fulfill the protection requirements of Table 13.6.3.3.1.1, except as permitted by 13.6.3.3.1.1.2 and 13.6.3.3.1.1.3. [**10**:6.3.1.1.1]

13.6.3.3.1.1.2 Up to three AFFF or FFFP fire extinguishers of at least 2½ gal (9.46 L) capacity shall be permitted to be used to fulfill extra hazard requirements. [**10**:6.3.1.1.2]

13.6.3.3.1.1.3 Two AFFF or FFFP fire extinguishers of at least 1.6 gal (6 L) capacity shall be permitted to be used to fulfill ordinary hazard requirements. [**10**:6.3.1.1.3]

Table 13.6.3.3.1.1 Fire Extinguisher Size and Placement for Class B Hazards

Type of Hazard	Basic Minimum Extinguisher Rating	Maximum Travel Distance to Extinguishers ft	m
Light	5-B	30	9.14
	10-B	50	15.25
Ordinary	10-B	30	9.14
	20-B	50	15.25
Extra	40-B	30	9.14
	80-B	50	15.25

Note:
The specified ratings do not imply that fires of the magnitudes indicated by these ratings will occur, but, rather, they are provided to give the operators more time and agent to handle difficult spill fires that have the potential to occur.
[**10**:Table 6.3.1.1]

13.6.3.3.1.2 Fire extinguishers of lesser rating, designed for small specific hazards within the general hazard area, shall be permitted to be installed but shall not be considered as fulfilling any part of the requirements of Table 13.6.3.3.1.1, unless permitted by 13.6.3.3.1.1.1 or 13.6.3.3.1.1.2. [**10:**6.3.1.2]

13.6.3.3.1.3 Fire extinguishers shall be located so that the maximum travel distances do not exceed those specified in Table 13.6.3.3.1.1. [**10:**6.3.1.3]

13.6.3.3.1.4 The protection requirements shall be permitted to be fulfilled with fire extinguishers of higher ratings, provided the travel distance to such larger fire extinguishers does not exceed 50 ft (15.25 m). [**10:**6.3.1.4]

13.6.3.3.2 Flammable Liquids of Appreciable Depth.

13.6.3.3.2.1 Portable fire extinguishers shall not be installed as the sole protection for flammable liquid hazards of appreciable depth where the surface area exceeds 10 ft^2 (0.93 m^2). [**10:**6.3.2.1]

13.6.3.3.2.2 For flammable liquid hazards of appreciable depth, a Class B fire extinguisher shall be provided on the basis of at least 2 numerical units of Class B extinguishing potential per 1 ft^2 (0.09 m^2) of flammable liquid surface of the largest hazard area. [**10:**6.3.2.2]

13.6.3.3.2.3 AFFF- or FFFP-type fire extinguishers shall be permitted to be provided on the basis of 1-B of protection per 1 ft^2 (0.09 m^2) of hazard. *(For fires involving water-soluble flammable liquids, see 5.5.4.4 of NFPA 10.)* [**10:**6.3.2.3]

13.6.3.3.2.4 Two or more fire extinguishers of lower ratings, other than AFFF- or FFFP-type fire extinguishers, shall not be used in lieu of the fire extinguisher required for the largest hazard area. [**10:**6.3.2.4]

13.6.3.3.2.5 Up to three AFFF- or FFFP-type fire extinguishers shall be permitted to fulfill the requirements, provided the sum of the Class B ratings meets or exceeds the value required for the largest hazard area. [**10:**6.3.2.5]

13.6.3.3.2.6 Travel distances for portable fire extinguishers shall not exceed 50 ft (15.25 m). *(See Annex E of NFPA 10.)* [**10:**6.3.2.6]

13.6.3.3.2.6.1 Scattered or widely separated hazards shall be individually protected. [**10:**6.3.2.6.1]

13.6.3.3.2.6.2 A fire extinguisher in the proximity of a hazard shall be located to be accessible in the presence of a fire without undue danger to the operator. [**10:**6.3.2.6.2]

13.6.3.3.3 Obstacle, Gravity/Three-Dimensional, and Pressure Fire Hazards.

13.6.3.3.3.1 Where hand portable fire extinguishers are installed or positioned for obstacle, gravity/three-dimensional, or pressure fire hazards, the actual travel distance to hazard shall not exceed 30 ft (9 m) unless otherwise specified *(See 5.5.5.1 of NFPA 10.)* [**10:**6.3.3.1]

13.6.3.3.3.2 Where wheeled fire extinguishers of 125 lb (56.7 kg) agent capacity or larger are installed or positioned for obstacle, gravity/three-dimensional, or pressure fire hazards, the actual travel distance to hazard shall not exceed 100 ft (30.5 m) unless otherwise specified. *(See 5.5.3.1 of NFPA 10.)* [**10:**6.3.3.2]

13.6.3.4* Installations for Class C Hazards.

13.6.3.4.1 Fire extinguishers with Class C ratings shall be required where energized electrical equipment can be encountered. [**10:**6.4.1]

13.6.3.4.2 The requirement in 13.6.3.4.1 shall include situations where fire either directly involves or surrounds electrical equipment. [**10:**6.4.2]

13.6.3.4.3 Because fire is a Class A or Class B hazard, the fire extinguishers shall be sized and located on the basis of the anticipated Class A or Class B hazard. [**10:**6.4.3]

13.6.3.5 Installations for Class D Hazards.

13.6.3.5.1 Fire extinguishers or extinguishing agents with Class D ratings shall be provided for fires involving combustible metals. [**10:**6.5.1]

13.6.3.5.2 Fire extinguishers or extinguishing agents (media) shall be located not more than 75 ft (22.9 m) of travel distance from the Class D hazard. *(See Section E.6 of NFPA 10.)* [**10:**6.5.2]

13.6.3.5.3* Portable fire extinguishers or extinguishing agents (media) for Class D hazards shall be provided in those work areas where combustible metal powders, flakes, shavings, chips, or similarly sized products are generated. [**10:**6.5.3]

13.6.3.5.4* Size determination shall be on the basis of the specific combustible metal, its physical particle size, area to be covered, and recommendations by the fire extinguisher manufacturer based on data from control tests. [**10:**6.5.4]

13.6.3.6 Installations for Class K Hazards.

13.6.3.6.1 Class K fire extinguishers shall be provided for hazards where there is a potential for fires involving combustible cooking media (vegetable or animal oils and fats). [**10:**6.6.1]

13.6.3.6.2 Maximum travel distance shall not exceed 30 ft (9.1 m) from the hazard to the extinguishers. [**10:**6.6.2]

13.6.3.7 Solid-Fuel Cooking Appliances. All solid fuel cooking appliances (whether or not under a hood) with fire boxes of 5 ft^3 (0.14 m^3) volume or less shall have at least a listed 2-A rated water-type fire extinguisher or a 1.6 gal (6 L) wet chemical fire extinguisher that is listed for Class K fires. [**10:**6.3.7]

13.6.4 Inspection, Maintenance, and Recharging.

13.6.4.1* General.

13.6.4.1.1 Responsibility. The owner or designated agent or occupant of a property in which fire extinguishers are located shall be responsible for inspection, maintenance, and recharging. *(See 13.6.4.1.2.)* [**10:**7.1.1]

13.6.4.1.2 Personnel.

13.6.4.1.2.1* Persons performing maintenance and recharging of extinguishers shall be certified. [**10:**7.1.2.1]

13.6.4.1.2.1.1 Persons training to become certified shall be permitted to perform maintenance and recharging of extinguishers under the direct supervision and in the immediate presence of a certified person. [**10:**7.1.2.1.1]

13.6.4.1.2.1.2 Certification requires that a person pass a test administered by an organization acceptable to the AHJ. [**10:**7.1.2.1.2]

13.6.4.1.2.1.3 The test shall, at a minimum, be based upon knowledge of the chapters and annexes of NFPA 10. [**10:**7.1.2.1.3]

13.6.4.1.2.1.4 The testing process shall permit persons to use NFPA 10 during the test. [**10:**7.1.2.1.4]

13.6.4.1.2.1.5 Persons passing the test required in 13.6.4.1.2.1.2 shall be issued a document or a certificate. [**10:**7.1.2.1.5]

13.6.4.1.2.1.6 The document or certificate shall be made available when requested by the AHJ. [**10:**7.1.2.1.6]

13.6.4.1.2.2 Persons performing maintenance and recharging of extinguishers shall be trained and shall have available the appropriate manufacturer's servicing manual(s), the correct tools, recharge materials, lubricants, and manufacturer's replacement parts or parts specifically listed for use in the fire extinguisher. [**10:**7.1.2.2]

13.6.4.1.2.3* Persons performing inspections shall not be required to be certified. [**10:**7.1.2.3]

Δ **13.6.4.1.3 Replacement Fire Extinguishers.** Fire extinguishers removed from service shall be immediately replaced with extinguishers that are suitable for the type of hazard(s) being protected and shall be of at least equal rating. [**10:**7.1.3]

N **13.6.4.1.3.1** When the removal and replacement of fire extinguishers from installed locations is necessary or desired, the owner or owner's agent shall be notified. [**10:**7.1.3.1]

13.6.4.1.4 Tags or Labels.

13.6.4.1.4.1 Tags or labels intended for recording inspections, maintenance, or recharging shall be affixed so as not to obstruct the fire extinguisher use, fire extinguisher classification, or manufacturer's labels. [**10:**7.1.4.1]

13.6.4.1.4.2 Labels indicating fire extinguisher use or classification or both shall be permitted to be placed on the front of the fire extinguisher. [**10:**7.1.4.2]

13.6.4.2 Inspection.

13.6.4.2.1 Inspection Frequency.

13.6.4.2.1.1* Fire extinguishers shall be manually inspected when initially placed in service. [**10:**7.2.1.1]

13.6.4.2.1.2* Fire extinguishers and Class D extinguishing agents shall be inspected either manually or by means of an electronic monitoring device/system at intervals not exceeding 31 days. [**10:**7.2.1.2]

13.6.4.2.1.2.1 Fire extinguishers and Class D extinguishing agents shall be inspected at least once per calendar month. [**10:**7.2.1.2.1]

13.6.4.2.1.3* Fire extinguishers and Class D extinguishing agents shall be manually inspected daily or weekly when conditions exist that indicate the need for more frequent inspections. [**10:**7.2.1.3]

13.6.4.2.1.4 Extinguishers that are electronically monitored for location only, such as those monitored by means of a switch to indicate when the extinguisher is removed from its bracket or cabinet, shall be manually inspected in accordance with 13.6.4.2.2. [**10:**7.2.1.4]

13.6.4.2.2 Inspection Procedures. Periodic inspection or electronic monitoring of fire extinguishers shall include a check of at least the following items:

(1) Location in designated place
(2) Visibility of the extinguisher or means of indicating the extinguisher location
(3) Access to the extinguisher
(4) Pressure gauge reading or indicator in the operable range or position
(5) Fullness determined by weighing or hefting
(6) Condition of tires, wheels, carriage, hose, and nozzle for wheeled extinguishers
(7) Indicator for nonrechargeable extinguishers using push-to-test pressure indicators

[**10:**7.2.2]

13.6.4.2.2.1 The owner or the owner's agent shall determine the method of extinguisher inspection such as manual inspection, electronic monitoring, or any combination of the two. [**10:**7.2.2.1]

13.6.4.2.2.2 Any method(s) of inspection other than manual inspection shall require the approval of the authority having jurisdiction. [**10:**7.2.2.2]

13.6.4.2.2.3* In addition to 13.6.4.2.2, fire extinguishers shall be visually inspected in accordance with 13.6.4.2.2.4 if they are located where any of the following conditions exists:

(1) High frequency of fires in the past
(2) Severe hazards
(3) Locations that make fire extinguishers susceptible to mechanical injury or physical damage
(4) Exposure to abnormal temperatures or corrosive atmospheres

[**10:**7.2.2.3]

13.6.4.2.2.4 Where required by 13.6.4.2.2.3, the following inspection procedures shall be in addition to those addressed in 13.6.4.2.2:

(1) Verify that operating instructions on nameplates are legible and face outward
(2) Check for broken or missing safety seals and tamper indicators
(3) Examine for obvious physical damage, corrosion, leakage, or clogged nozzle

[**10:**7.2.2.4]

13.6.4.2.2.5 Inspection Procedure for Containers of Class D Extinguishing Agent. Periodic inspection of containers of Class D extinguishing agent used to protect Class D hazards shall include verification of at least the following:

(1) Located in designated place
(2) Visibility of the container or means of indicating the container location
(3) Access to the container
(4) Lid is sealed
(5) Fullness by hefting or weighing
(6) No obvious physical damage to container

[**10:**7.2.2.5]

13.6.4.2.3 Corrective Action. When an inspection of any fire extinguisher reveals a deficiency in any of the conditions in

13.6.4.2.2 or 13.6.4.2.2.4, immediate corrective action shall be taken. [**10**:7.2.3]

13.6.4.2.3.1 Rechargeable Fire Extinguishers. When an inspection of any rechargeable fire extinguisher reveals a deficiency in any of the conditions in 13.6.4.2.2(3), 13.6.4.2.2(4), 13.6.4.2.2(5), or 13.6.4.2.2(1) through 13.6.4.2.2(3), the extinguisher shall be subjected to applicable maintenance procedures. [**10**:7.2.3.1]

13.6.4.2.3.2 Nonrechargeable Dry Chemical Fire Extinguisher. When an inspection of any nonrechargeable dry chemical fire extinguisher reveals a deficiency in any of the conditions listed in 13.6.4.2.2(3), 13.6.4.2.2(4),13.6.4.2.2(6), or 13.6.4.2.2.4(1) through 13.6.4.2.2.4(3), the extinguisher shall be removed from further use, discharged, and destroyed at the direction of the owner or returned to the manufacturer. [**10**:7.2.3.2]

13.6.4.2.3.3 Nonrechargeable Halon Agent Fire Extinguisher. When an inspection of any nonrechargeable fire extinguisher containing a halon agent reveals a deficiency in any of the conditions listed in 13.6.4.2.2(3), 13.6.4.2.2(4), 13.6.4.2.2(6), or 13.6.4.2.2.4(1) through 13.6.4.2.2.4(3), the extinguisher shall be removed from service, shall not be discharged, and shall be returned to the manufacturer, a fire equipment dealer, or a distributor to permit recovery of the halon. [**10**:7.2.3.3]

13.6.4.2.4 Inspection Record Keeping.

13.6.4.2.4.1 Manual Inspection Records.

13.6.4.2.4.1.1 Where manual inspections are conducted, records for manual inspections shall be kept on a tag or label attached to the fire extinguisher, on an inspection checklist maintained on file, or by an electronic method. [**10**:7.2.4.1.1]

13.6.4.2.4.1.2 Where manual inspections are conducted, the month and year the manual inspection was performed and the initials of the person performing the inspection shall be recorded. [**10**:7.2.4.1.2]

N **13.6.4.2.4.1.3** Where an external visual examination is performed in accordance with 7.3.2.1.1 of NFPA 10, a record in accordance with 13.6.4.3.2 shall be required in lieu of the record required by 13.6.4.2.4.1.2. [**10**:7.2.4.1.3]

13.6.4.2.4.1.4 Personnel making manual inspections shall keep records of all fire extinguishers inspected, including those found to require corrective action. [**10**:7.2.4.1.4]

13.6.4.2.4.1.5 Records for manual inspection shall be kept to demonstrate that at least the last 12 monthly inspections have been performed. [**10**:7.2.4.1.5]

13.6.4.2.4.2* Electronic Inspection Records.

13.6.4.2.4.2.1 Where electronically monitored systems are employed for inspections, records shall be kept for fire extinguishers found to require corrective action. [**10**:7.2.4.2.1]

13.6.4.2.4.2.2 Records for electronic monitoring shall be kept to demonstrate that at least the last 12 monthly inspections have been performed. [**10**:7.2.4.2.2]

13.6.4.2.4.2.3 For electronically monitored fire extinguishers, where the extinguisher causes a signal at a control unit when a deficiency in any of the conditions listed in 13.6.4.2.2 occurs, record keeping shall be provided in the form of an electronic event log at the control panel. [**10**:7.2.4.2.3]

13.6.4.3 Extinguisher Maintenance.

13.6.4.3.1 Maintenance Procedures. Where required by another section of this *Code* or NFPA 10, maintenance procedures shall include the procedures detailed in the manufacturer's service manual and a thorough examination of the basic elements of the fire extinguisher, including the following:

(1) Mechanical parts of all fire extinguishers
(2) Extinguishing agent
(3) Expelling means
(4) Physical condition

[**10**:7.3.1]

13.6.4.3.2* Annual Maintenance Record Keeping.

13.7 Detection, Alarm, and Communications Systems.

13.7.1 General.

13.7.1.1 Where building fire alarm systems or automatic fire detectors are required by other sections of this *Code*, they shall be provided and installed in accordance with *NFPA 70*, *NFPA 72*, and Section 13.7.

13.7.1.2* Building Alarm and Signaling Systems. Protected premises systems that serve the alarm and signaling needs of a building or buildings shall include one or more of the following systems or functions:

(1) Manual fire alarm signal initiation
(2) Automatic fire alarm and supervisory signal initiation
(3) Monitoring of abnormal conditions in fire suppression systems
(4) Actuation of fire suppression systems
(5) Actuation of emergency control functions
(6) Actuation of fire alarm notification appliances
(7) In-building fire emergency voice/alarm communications
(8) Automatic carbon monoxide alarm and supervisory signal initiation
(9) Actuation of carbon monoxide notification appliances
(10) Guard's tour supervisory service
(11) Process monitoring supervisory systems
(12) Actuation of off-premises signals
(13) Combination systems

[**72**:23.3.3.1]

13.7.1.3 All apparatus requiring rewinding or resetting to maintain normal operation shall be rewound or reset as promptly as possible after each test and alarm. [**72**:14.5.4]

13.7.1.4 The provisions of Section 13.7 shall apply only where specifically required by another section of this *Code*. [***101***:9.6.1.1]

13.7.1.4.1 Fire detection, alarm, and communications systems installed to make use of an alternative permitted by this *Code* shall be considered required systems and shall meet the provisions of this *Code* applicable to required systems. [***101***:9.6.1.2]

13.7.1.4.2* To ensure operational integrity, the fire alarm system shall have an approved maintenance and testing program complying with the applicable requirements of *NFPA 70* and *NFPA 72*. [***101***:9.6.1.5]

13.7.1.4.3 Fire alarm system impairment procedures shall comply with *NFPA 72*. [***101***:9.6.1.6]

13.7.1.5* Impaired and Nuisance Alarm Prone Systems.

13.7.1.5.1 Impaired fire alarm systems shall include, but shall not be limited to, required systems that are not fully operational, are no longer monitored as required by the AHJ, or are under renovation or repair.

13.7.1.5.2 The system owner or designated representative shall immediately notify the AHJ in an approved manner when a fire alarm system is impaired.

13.7.1.5.3 The AHJ shall be authorized to require standby fire personnel or an approved fire watch in accordance with 1.7.16 at premises in which required fire alarm systems are impaired or classified as chronic nuisance alarm prone systems.

13.7.1.5.4 Fire alarm systems that have produced five or more nuisance alarms in a 365-day period shall be classified as chronic nuisance alarm prone systems.

N 13.7.1.5.5* Fire alarm systems classified as chronic-nuisance-alarm-prone systems shall comply with the following:

(1) The system shall be inspected by qualified inspection, testing, and service personnel, in accordance with *NFPA 72*, for the cause of the nuisance alarms.
(2) Corrective action shall be taken to address the cause of the nuisance alarms.
(3) A report indicating the cause and corrective action taken to mitigate future nuisance alarms from the fire alarm system shall be provided to the AHJ by the owner.

N 13.7.1.5.6* It is prohibited for an owner to operate a fire alarm system that is classified as a chronic-nuisance-alarm-prone system unless corrective actions taken in accordance with 13.7.1.5.5 have occurred to mitigate the cause of the nuisance alarms.

13.7.1.5.7* The AHJ shall be authorized to require central station service be provided for chronic nuisance alarm prone systems.

13.7.1.5.8* Fire alarm supervising stations and fire alarm service companies shall immediately notify the AHJ when any of the following conditions exists:

(1) A fire alarm system is impaired.
(2) Required system monitoring is no longer being provided.
(3) Required testing, service, and maintenance is no longer being provided.
(4) A fire alarm system cannot be serviced or repaired to make it fully operational.
(5) A fire alarm system cannot be serviced or repaired to eliminate chronic nuisance alarms.

13.7.1.5.9 The system owner shall replace required fire alarm systems that cannot be serviced or repaired to eliminate system impairments or chronic nuisance alarms.

13.7.1.6* Nonrequired Coverage.

13.7.1.6.1 Detection installed for reasons of achieving specific fire safety objectives, but not required by any laws, codes, or standards, shall meet all of the requirements of this *Code*, with the exception of prescriptive spacing criteria of Chapter 17 of *NFPA 72*. [**72:**17.5.3.3.1]

13.7.1.6.2 Where nonrequired detectors are installed for achieving specific fire safety objectives, additional detectors not necessary to achieve the objectives shall not be required. [**72:**17.5.3.3.2]

13.7.1.7 Signal Initiation.

13.7.1.7.1 Where required by other sections of this *Code*, actuation of the fire alarm system shall occur by any or all of the following means of initiation but shall not be limited to such means:

(1) Manual fire alarm initiation
(2) Automatic detection
(3) Extinguishing system operation

[***101:***9.6.2.1]

13.7.1.7.2 Manual fire alarm boxes shall be used only for fire-protective signaling purposes. Combination fire alarm and guard's tour stations shall be permitted. [***101:***9.6.2.2]

13.7.1.7.3 A manual fire alarm box shall be provided as follows, unless modified by another section of this *Code*:

(1) For new alarm system installations, the manual fire alarm box shall be located within 60 in. (1525 mm) of exit doorways.
(2) For existing alarm system installations, the manual fire alarm box either shall be provided in the natural exit access path near each required exit or within 60 in. (1525 mm) of exit doorways.

[***101:***9.6.2.3]

13.7.1.7.4 Manual fire alarm boxes shall be mounted on both sides of grouped openings over 40 ft (12.2 m) in width, and within 60 in. (1525 mm) of each side of the opening. [***101:***9.6.2.4]

13.7.1.7.5* Additional manual fire alarm boxes shall be located so that, on any given floor in any part of the building, no horizontal distance on that floor exceeding 200 ft (61 m) shall need to be traversed to reach a manual fire alarm box. [***101:***9.6.2.5]

13.7.1.7.6* For fire alarm systems using automatic fire detection or waterflow detection devices to initiate the fire alarm system in accordance with Chapters 11 through 43 of *NFPA 101*, not less than one manual fire alarm box, located as required by the AHJ, shall be provided to initiate a fire alarm signal. [***101:***9.6.2.6]

13.7.1.7.7* Manual fire alarm boxes shall be accessible, unobstructed, and visible. [***101:***9.6.2.7]

13.7.1.7.8 Where a sprinkler system provides automatic detection and alarm system initiation, it shall be provided with an approved alarm initiation device that operates when the flow of water is equal to or greater than that from a single automatic sprinkler. [***101:***9.6.2.8]

13.7.1.7.9 Where a total (complete) coverage smoke detection system is required by another section of this *Code*, automatic detection of smoke in accordance with *NFPA 72* shall be provided in all occupiable areas in environments that are suitable for proper smoke detector operation. [***101:***9.6.2.9]

13.7.1.8 Smoke Alarms.

13.7.1.8.1 Where required by another section of this *Code*, single-station and multiple-station smoke alarms shall be in accordance with *NFPA 72* unless otherwise provided in 13.7.1.8.4, 13.7.1.8.5.4, 13.7.1.8.5.7, or 13.7.1.8.6. [***101:***9.6.2.10.1]

13.7.1.8.2 Where automatic smoke detection is required by Chapters 11 through 43 of NFPA *101*, smoke alarms shall not be used as a substitute. [*101*:9.6.2.10.2]

13.7.1.8.3 Smoke Alarms in Sleeping Rooms.

13.7.1.8.3.1 In new construction, where required by Chapters 11 through 43 of NFPA *101*, the alarm notification signal in sleeping rooms resulting from activation of smoke alarms shall be a 520 Hz low-frequency signal complying with *NFPA 72*. [*101*:9.6.2.10.3]

Δ **13.7.1.8.4*** The interconnection of smoke alarms shall apply only to new construction. [*101*:9.6.2.10.7.1]

13.7.1.8.5 Specific Location Requirements. The installation of smoke alarms and smoke detectors shall comply with 13.7.1.8.5.1 through 13.7.1.8.5.13. [**72**:29.11.3.4]

13.7.1.8.5.1 Smoke alarms and smoke detectors shall not be located where ambient conditions, including humidity and temperature, are outside the limits specified by the manufacturer's published instructions. [**72**:29.11.3.4(1)]

13.7.1.8.5.2 Smoke alarms and smoke detectors shall not be located within unfinished attics or garages or in other spaces where temperatures can fall below 40°F (4.4°C) or exceed 100°F (38°C). [**72**:29.11.3.4(2)]

13.7.1.8.5.3* Where the mounting surface could become considerably warmer or cooler than the room, such as a poorly insulated ceiling below an unfinished attic or an exterior wall, smoke alarms and smoke detectors shall be mounted on an inside wall. [**72**:29.11.3.4(3)]

Δ **13.7.1.8.5.4*** Smoke alarms and smoke detectors shall not be installed between 10 ft (3.0 m) and 20 ft (6.1 m) along a horizontal flow path from a stationary or fixed cooking appliance, unless the devices comply with the following:

(1) Prior to January 1, 2023, smoke alarms and smoke detectors shall be equipped with an alarm silencing means, use photoelectric detection, or be listed for resistance to common nuisance sources from cooking in accordance with the 8th edition of UL 217, *Smoke Alarms*, the 7th edition of UL 268, *Smoke Detectors for Fire Alarm Systems*, or subsequent editions.
(2) Effective January 1, 2023, smoke alarms and smoke detectors shall be listed for resistance to common nuisance sources from cooking in accordance with the 8th edition of UL 217, the 7th edition of UL 268, or subsequent editions.

[**72**:29.11.3.4(4)]

13.7.1.8.5.5 Smoke alarms and smoke detectors shall not be installed within an area of exclusion determined by a 10 ft (3.0 m) radial distance along a horizontal flow path from a stationary or fixed cooking appliance. When the 10 ft (3.0 m) area of exclusion would prohibit the placement of a smoke alarm or smoke detector required by other sections of this *Code*, and when the kitchen or cooking area and adjacent spaces have no clear interior partitions or headers, smoke alarms or smoke detectors shall be permitted for installation at a radial distance between 6 ft (1.8 m) and 10 ft (3.0 m) from any stationary or fixed cooking appliance unless the devices comply with the following:

(1) Prior to January 1, 2023, the devices shall use photoelectric detection or be listed for resistance to common nuisance sources from cooking in accordance with the 8th edition of UL 217, the 7th edition of UL 268, or subsequent editions.
(2) Effective January 1, 2023 the devices shall be listed for resistance to common nuisance sources from cooking nuisance alarms in accordance with the 8th edition of UL 217, the 7th edition of UL 268, or subsequent editions.

[**72**:29.11.3.4(5)]

13.7.1.8.5.6* Smoke alarms and smoke detectors shall not be installed within a 36 in. (910 mm) horizontal path from a door to a bathroom containing a shower or tub unless listed for installation in close proximity to such locations. [**72**:29.11.3.4(6)]

13.7.1.8.5.7* Smoke alarms and smoke detectors shall not be installed within a 36 in. (910 mm) horizontal path from the supply registers of a forced air heating or cooling system and shall be installed outside of the direct airflow from those registers. [**72**:29.11.3.4(7)]

13.7.1.8.5.8 Smoke alarms and smoke detectors shall not be installed within a 36 in. (910 mm) horizontal path from the tip of the blade of a ceiling-suspended (paddle) fan unless the room configuration restricts meeting this requirement. [**72**:29.11.3.4(9)]

13.7.1.8.5.9 Where stairs lead to other occupiable levels, a smoke alarm or smoke detector shall be located so that smoke rising in the stairway cannot be prevented from reaching the smoke alarm or smoke detector by an intervening door or obstruction. [**72**:29.11.3.4(9)]

13.7.1.8.5.10 For stairways leading up from a basement, smoke alarms or smoke detectors shall be located on the basement ceiling near the entry to the stairs. [**72**:29.11.3.4(10)]

13.7.1.8.5.11* For tray-shaped ceilings (coffered ceilings), smoke alarms and smoke detectors shall be installed on the highest portion of the ceiling or on the sloped portion of the ceiling within 12 in. (300 mm) vertically down from the highest point. [**72**:29.11.3.4(11)]

13.7.1.8.5.12 Smoke alarms and detectors installed in rooms with joists or beams shall comply with the requirements of 17.7.4.2.4 of *NFPA 72*. [**72**:29.11.3.4(12)]

13.7.1.8.5.13 Heat alarms and detectors installed in rooms with joists or beams shall comply with the requirements of 17.6.3 of *NFPA 72*. [**72**:A.29.11.3.4(13)]

13.7.1.8.6 System smoke detectors in accordance with *NFPA 72* and arranged to function in the same manner as single-station or multiple-station smoke alarms shall be permitted in lieu of smoke alarms. [*101*:9.6.2.10.8]

13.7.1.8.7 Smoke alarms, other than battery-operated smoke alarms as permitted by other sections of this *Code*, shall be powered in accordance with the requirements of *NFPA 72*. [*101*:9.6.2.10.6]

13.7.1.8.8* In new construction, where two or more smoke alarms are required within a dwelling unit, suite of rooms, or similar area, they shall be arranged so that operation of any smoke alarm shall cause the alarm in all smoke alarms within the dwelling unit, suite of rooms, or similar area to sound, unless otherwise permitted by one of the following:

(1) The requirement of 13.7.1.8.8 shall not apply where permitted by another section of this *Code*.
(2) The requirement of 13.7.1.8.8 shall not apply to configurations that provide equivalent distribution of the alarm signal.

[*101*:9.6.2.10.7.2]

13.7.1.8.9 The alarms described in 13.7.1.8.8 shall sound only within an individual dwelling unit, suite of rooms, or similar area and shall not actuate the building fire alarm system, unless otherwise permitted by the AHJ. [*101*:9.6.2.10.9]

13.7.1.8.10 Smoke alarms shall be permitted to be connected to the building fire alarm system for the purpose of annunciation in accordance with *NFPA 72*. [*101*:9.6.2.10.10]

13.7.1.9 Occupant Notification.

13.7.1.9.1 Occupant notification shall be provided to alert occupants of a fire or other emergency where required by other sections of this *Code*. [*101*:9.6.3.1]

13.7.1.9.2 Occupant notification shall be in accordance with 13.7.1.9.4 through 13.7.1.9.11.2, unless otherwise provided in 13.7.1.9.2.1 through 13.7.1.9.2.4. [*101*:9.6.3.2]

13.7.1.9.2.1* Elevator lobby, hoistway, and associated machine room smoke detectors used solely for elevator recall, and heat detectors used solely for elevator power shutdown, shall not be required to activate the building evacuation alarm if the power supply and installation wiring to such detectors are monitored by the building fire alarm system, and if the activation of such detectors initiates a supervisory signal at a constantly attended location. [*101*:9.6.3.2.1]

13.7.1.9.2.2* Smoke detectors used solely for closing dampers or heating, ventilating, and air-conditioning system shutdown shall not be required to activate the building evacuation alarm, provided that the power supply and installation wiring to the detectors are monitored by the building fire alarm system, and the activation of the detectors initiates a supervisory signal at a constantly attended location. [*101*:9.6.3.2.2]

13.7.1.9.2.3* Smoke detectors located at doors for the exclusive operation of automatic door release shall not be required to activate the building evacuation alarm, provided that the power supply and installation wiring to the detectors are monitored by the building fire alarm system, and the activation of the detectors initiates a supervisory signal at a constantly attended location. [*101*:9.6.3.2.3]

13.7.1.9.2.4 Detectors in accordance with 22.3.4.3.1(2) and 23.3.4.3.1(2) of *NFPA 101* shall not be required to activate the building evacuation alarm. [*101*:9.6.3.2.4]

13.7.1.9.3 Where required by Chapters 11 through 43 of *NFPA 101*, the audible alarm notification signal provided in sleeping rooms resulting from the activation of the fire alarm system or sleeping room smoke detector shall be a 520 Hz low-frequency signal complying with *NFPA 72*. [*101*:9.6.3.3]

13.7.1.9.4 Where permitted by Chapters 11 through 43 of *NFPA 101*, a presignal system shall be permitted where the initial fire alarm signal is automatically transmitted without delay to a municipal fire department, to a fire brigade (if provided), and to an on-site staff person trained to respond to a fire emergency. [*101*:9.6.3.4]

13.7.1.9.5 Where permitted by Chapters 11 through 43 of *NFPA 101*, a positive alarm sequence shall be permitted, provided that it is in accordance with *NFPA 72*. [*101*:9.6.3.5]

13.7.1.9.6 Unless otherwise provided in 13.7.1.9.6.1 through 13.7.1.9.6.8, notification signals for occupants to evacuate shall be by audible and visible signals in accordance with *NFPA 72* and ICC A117.1, *Accessible and Usable Buildings and Facilities*, or other means of notification acceptable to the AHJ. [*101*:9.6.3.6]

13.7.1.9.6.1 Areas not subject to occupancy by persons who are deaf or hard of hearing shall not be required to comply with the provisions for visible signals. [*101*:9.6.3.6.1]

13.7.1.9.6.2 Visible-only signals shall be provided where specifically permitted in health care occupancies in accordance with Chapters 18 and 19 of *NFPA 101*. [*101*:9.6.3.6.2]

13.7.1.9.6.3 Existing alarm systems shall not be required to comply with the provision for visible signals. [*101*:9.6.3.6.3]

13.7.1.9.6.4 Visible signals shall not be required in lodging or rooming houses in accordance with Chapter 26 of *NFPA 101*. [*101*:9.6.3.6.4]

13.7.1.9.6.5 Visible signals shall not be required in exit stair enclosures. [*101*:9.6.3.6.5]

13.7.1.9.6.6 Visible signals shall not be required in elevator cars. [*101*:9.6.3.6.6]

13.7.1.9.6.7* Public mode visual notification appliances in accordance with *NFPA 72* shall not be required in designated areas as permitted by Chapters 11 through 43 of *NFPA 101*, provided that they are replaced with approved alternative visible means. [*101*:9.6.3.6.7]

13.7.1.9.6.8* Where visible signals are not required, as permitted by 13.7.1.9.6.7, documentation of such omission shall be maintained in accordance with 9.13.3 of *NFPA 101*. [*101*:9.6.3.6.8]

13.7.1.9.7 The general evacuation alarm signal shall operate in accordance with one of the methods prescribed by 13.7.1.9.7.1 through 13.7.1.9.7.3. [*101*:9.6.3.7]

13.7.1.9.7.1 The general evacuation alarm signal shall operate throughout the entire building other than the locations described in 13.7.1.9.7.4 and 13.7.1.9.7.5. [*101*:9.6.3.7.1]

13.7.1.9.7.2* Where total evacuation of occupants is impractical due to building configuration, only the occupants in the affected zones shall be initially notified, and provisions shall be made to selectively notify occupants in other zones to afford orderly evacuation of the entire building, provided that such arrangement is approved by the AHJ. [*101*:9.6.3.7.2]

13.7.1.9.7.3 Where occupants are incapable of evacuating themselves because of age, physical or mental disabilities, or physical restraint, all of the following shall apply:

(1) The private operating mode, as described in *NFPA 72* shall be permitted to be used.

(2) Only the attendants and other personnel required to evacuate occupants from a zone, area, floor, or building shall be required to be notified.
(3) Notification of personnel as specified in 13.7.1.9.7.3(2) shall include means to readily identify the zone, area, floor, or building in need of evacuation.
[*101*:9.6.3.7.3]

13.7.1.9.7.4 The general evacuation signal shall not be required in exit stair enclosures. [*101*:9.6.3.7.4]

13.7.1.9.7.5 The general evacuation signal shall not be required in elevator cars. [*101*:9.6.3.7.5]

13.7.1.9.8 Audible alarm notification appliances shall be of such character and so distributed as to be effectively heard above the average ambient sound level that exists under normal conditions of occupancy. [*101*:9.6.3.8]

13.7.1.9.9 Audible alarm notification appliances shall produce signals that are distinctive from audible signals used for other purposes in a given building. [*101*:9.6.3.9]

13.7.1.9.10 Automatically transmitted or live voice evacuation or relocation instructions shall be permitted to be used to notify occupants and shall comply with either 13.7.1.9.10.1 or 13.7.1.9.10.2. [*101*:9.6.3.10]

13.7.1.9.10.1 Automatically transmitted or live voice evacuation or relocation instructions shall be in accordance with *NFPA 72*. [*101*:9.6.3.10.1]

13.7.1.9.10.2 Where permitted by Chapters 11 through 43 of NFPA *101*, automatically transmitted or live voice announcements shall be permitted to be made via a voice communication or public address system that complies with all of the following:
(1) Occupant notification, either live or recorded, shall be initiated at a constantly attended receiving station by personnel trained to respond to an emergency.
(2) An approved secondary power supply shall be provided for other than existing, previously approved systems.
(3) The system shall be audible above the expected ambient noise level.
(4) Emergency announcements shall take precedence over any other use.
[*101*:9.6.3.10.2]

13.7.1.9.11 Unless otherwise permitted by another section of this *Code*, audible and visible fire alarm notification appliances shall comply with either 13.7.1.9.11.1 or 13.7.1.9.11.2. [*101*:9.6.3.11]

13.7.1.9.11.1 Audible and visible fire alarm notification appliances shall be used only for fire alarm system or other emergency purposes. [*101*:9.6.3.11.1]

13.7.1.9.11.2 Emergency voice/alarm communication systems shall be permitted to be used for other purposes in accordance with *NFPA 72*. [*101*:9.6.3.11.2]

13.7.1.10 Emergency Forces Notification.

13.7.1.10.1 Where required by another section of this *Code*, emergency forces notification shall be provided to alert the municipal fire department and fire brigade (if provided) of fire or other emergency. [*101*:9.6.4.1]

13.7.1.10.2 Where emergency forces notification is required by another section of this *Code*, the fire alarm system shall be arranged to transmit the alarm automatically via any of the following means acceptable to the AHJ and shall be in accordance with *NFPA 72*:
(1) Auxiliary fire alarm system
(2) Central station fire alarm system
(3) Proprietary supervising station fire alarm system
(4) Remote supervising station fire alarm system
[*101*:9.6.4.2]

13.7.1.10.3 For existing installations where none of the means of notification specified in 13.7.1.10.2(1) through 13.7.1.10.2(4) are available, an approved plan for notification of the municipal fire department shall be permitted. [*101*:9.6.4.3]

13.7.1.10.4 For other than existing installations, where fire alarm systems are required to provide emergency forces notification, supervisory signals and trouble signals shall sound and be visibly displayed either at an approved, remotely located receiving facility or at a location within the protected building that is constantly attended by qualified personnel. [*101*:9.6.4.4]

13.7.1.10.5* The use of a system that transmits signals directly to an emergency forces call center shall comply with *NFPA 72*.

13.7.1.11 Emergency Control Functions.

13.7.1.11.1 Emergency control functions shall be installed in accordance with the requirements of *NFPA 72*. [*101*:9.6.6.1]

13.7.1.11.2 Where required by another section of this *Code*, the following functions shall be actuated:
(1) Release of hold-open devices for doors or other opening protectives
(2) Stairwell or elevator shaft pressurization
(3) Smoke management or smoke control systems
(4) Unlocking of doors
(5) Elevator recall and shutdown
(6) HVAC shutdown
[*101*:9.6.6.2]

13.7.1.12 Location of Controls. Operator controls, alarm indicators, and manual communications capability shall be installed at a convenient location acceptable to the AHJ. [*101*:9.6.7]

13.7.1.13 Annunciation.

13.7.1.13.1 Where alarm annunciation is required by another section of this *Code*, it shall comply with 13.7.1.13.2 through 13.7.1.13.13. [*101*:9.6.8.1]

13.7.1.13.2 Alarm Annunciation. Where required by other governing laws, codes, or standards, the location of an operated initiating device shall be annunciated by visible means. [*72*:10.18.1]

13.7.1.13.2.1 Visible annunciation of the location of an operated initiating device shall be by an indicator lamp, alphanumeric display, printout, or other approved means. [*72*:10.18.1.1]

13.7.1.13.2.2 The visible annunciation of the location of operated initiating devices shall not be canceled by the means used to deactivate alarm notification appliances. [*72*:10.18.1.2]

Δ **13.7.1.13.3 Supervisory and Trouble Annunciation.** Where required by other governing laws, codes, or standards, supervisory or trouble conditions shall be annunciated by visible means. [72:10.18.2]

13.7.1.13.3.1 Visible annunciation shall be by an indicator lamp, an alphanumeric display, a printout, or other means. [72:10.18.2.1]

Δ **13.7.1.13.3.2** The visible annunciation of supervisory or trouble conditions shall not be canceled by the means used to deactivate supervisory or trouble notification appliances. [72:10.18.2.2]

13.7.1.13.4* Annunciator Access and Location.

13.7.1.13.4.1 All required annunciation means shall be readily accessible to responding personnel. [72:10.18.3.1]

13.7.1.13.4.2 All required annunciation means shall be located as required by the AHJ to facilitate an efficient response to the situation. [72:10.18.3.2]

13.7.1.13.5 Alarm Annunciation Display. Visible annunciators shall be capable of displaying all zones in alarm. [72:10.18.4]

13.7.1.13.5.1 If all zones in alarm are not displayed simultaneously, the zone of origin shall be displayed. [72:10.18.4.1]

13.7.1.13.5.2 If all zones in alarm are not displayed simultaneously, there shall be an indication that other zones are in alarm. [72:10.18.4.2]

13.7.1.13.6* Annunciation Zoning.

13.7.1.13.6.1 For the purpose of alarm annunciation, each floor of the building shall be considered as a separate zone. [72:10.18.5.1]

13.7.1.13.6.2 For the purposes of alarm annunciation, if a floor of the building is subdivided into multiple zones by fire or smoke barriers and the fire plan for the protected premises allows relocation of occupants from the zone of origin to another zone on the same floor, each zone on the floor shall be annunciated separately. [72:10.18.5.2]

13.7.1.13.6.3 Where the system serves more than one building, each building shall be annunciated separately. [72:10.18.5.3]

13.7.1.13.7 Alarm annunciation at the control center shall be by means of audible and visible indicators. [101:9.6.8.2]

13.7.1.13.8 For the purposes of alarm annunciation, each floor of the building, other than floors of existing buildings, shall be considered as not less than one zone, unless otherwise permitted by 13.7.1.13.9.4, 13.7.1.13.9.5, 13.7.1.13.9.6, or as another section of this *Code*. [101:9.6.8.3]

13.7.1.13.9 Where a floor area exceeds 22,500 ft² (2090 m²), additional fire alarm zoning shall be provided, and the length of any single fire alarm zone shall not exceed 300 ft (91 m) in any direction, except as provided in 13.7.1.13.9.1 through 13.7.1.13.9.6, or otherwise modified by another section of this *Code*. [101:9.6.8.4]

13.7.1.13.9.1 Where permitted by another section of this *Code*, fire alarm zones shall be permitted to exceed 22,500 ft² (2090 m²), and the length of a zone shall be permitted to exceed 300 ft (91 m) in any direction. [101:9.6.8.4.1]

13.7.1.13.9.2 Where the building is protected by an automatic sprinkler system in accordance with NFPA 13, the area of the fire alarm zone shall be permitted to coincide with the allowable area of the sprinkler system. [101:9.6.8.4.2]

13.7.1.13.9.3 Where the building is protected by a water mist system in accordance with 9.8.1 and Table 9.8.1 of NFPA *101*, the area of the fire alarm zone shall be permitted to coincide with the allowable area of the water mist system. [101:9.6.8.4.3]

13.7.1.13.9.4 Unless otherwise prohibited by another section of this *Code*, where a building not exceeding four stories in height is protected by an automatic water mist system in accordance with 9.8.1 of NFPA *101*, the water mist system shall be permitted to be annunciated on the fire alarm system as a single zone. [101:9.6.8.4.4]

13.7.1.13.9.5 Unless otherwise prohibited by another section of this *Code*, where a building not exceeding four stories in height is protected by an automatic sprinkler system in accordance with NFPA 13, the sprinkler system shall be permitted to be annunciated on the fire alarm system as a single zone. [101:9.6.8.4.5]

13.7.1.13.9.6 Where the building is protected by an automatic sprinkler system in accordance with NFPA 13D or NFPA 13R, the sprinkler system shall be permitted to be annunciated on the fire alarm system as a single zone. [101:9.6.8.4.6]

Δ **13.7.1.13.10** A system trouble signal shall be annunciated by means of audible and visible indicators in accordance with *NFPA 72*. [101:9.6.8.5]

13.7.1.13.11 A system supervisory signal shall be annunciated by means of audible and visible indicators in accordance with *NFPA 72*. [101:9.6.8.6]

13.7.1.13.12 Where the system serves more than one building, each building shall be annunciated separately. [101:9.6.8.7]

13.7.1.13.13 Where permitted by another section of this *Code*, the alarm zone shall be permitted to coincide with the permitted area for smoke compartments. [101:9.6.8.8]

13.7.1.14 Carbon Monoxide (CO) Detection and Warning Equipment. Where required by another section of this *Code*, carbon monoxide (CO) detection and warning equipment shall be provided in accordance with *NFPA 72*. [101:9.12]

13.7.1.15* Risk Analysis for Mass Notification Systems.

13.7.1.15.1* Where required by another section of this *Code*, a risk analysis for mass notification systems shall be provided in accordance with the requirements of Chapter 24 of *NFPA 72*. [101:9.14.1]

13.7.1.15.2 Where a mass notification system is required by the risk analysis in 13.7.1.15.1, the system shall be in accordance with the requirements of Chapter 24 of *NFPA 72*. [101:9.14.2]

13.7.2 Where Required and Occupancy Requirements.

13.7.2.1 New Assembly Occupancies.

13.7.2.1.1 General.

13.7.2.1.1.1 New assembly occupancies with occupant loads of more than 300 and all theaters with more than one audience-viewing room shall be provided with an approved fire alarm system in accordance with Section 13.7 and 13.7.2.1, unless otherwise permitted by 13.7.2.1.1.2. [*101*:12.3.4.1.1]

13.7.2.1.1.2 New assembly occupancies that are a part of a multiple occupancy protected as a mixed occupancy *(see 6.1.14 of NFPA 101)* shall be permitted to be served by a common fire alarm system, provided that the individual requirements of each occupancy are met. [*101*:12.3.4.1.2]

13.7.2.1.2 Initiation.

13.7.2.1.2.1 Initiation of the required fire alarm system shall be by both of the following means:

(1) Manual means in accordance with 13.7.1.7.1(1), unless otherwise permitted by one of the following:
   (a) The requirement of 13.7.2.1.2.1(1) shall not apply where initiation is by means of an approved automatic fire detection system in accordance with 13.7.1.7.1(2) that provides fire detection throughout the building.
   (b) The requirement of 13.7.2.1.2.1(1) shall not apply where initiation is by means of an approved automatic sprinkler system in accordance with 13.7.1.7.1(3) that provides fire detection and protection throughout the building.
(2) Where automatic sprinklers are provided, initiation of the fire alarm system by sprinkler system waterflow, even where manual fire alarm boxes are provided in accordance with 13.7.2.1.2.1(1)

[*101*:12.3.4.2.1]

13.7.2.1.2.2 The initiating device shall be capable of transmitting an alarm to a receiving station, located within the building, that is constantly attended when the assembly occupancy is occupied. [*101*:12.3.4.2.2]

13.7.2.1.2.3* In new assembly occupancies with occupant loads of more than 300, automatic detection shall be provided in all hazardous areas that are not normally occupied, unless such areas are protected throughout by an approved, supervised automatic sprinkler system in accordance with Section 13.3. [*101*:12.3.4.2.3]

13.7.2.1.3 Notification. The required fire alarm system shall activate an audible and visible alarm in a constantly attended receiving station within the building when occupied for purposes of initiating emergency action. [*101*:12.3.4.3]

13.7.2.1.3.1 Positive alarm sequence in accordance with 13.7.1.9.5 shall be permitted. [*101*:12.3.4.3.1]

13.7.2.1.3.2 Reserved.

13.7.2.1.3.3 Occupant notification shall be by means of voice announcements in accordance with 13.7.1.9.10, initiated by the person in the constantly attended receiving station. [*101*:12.3.4.3.3]

13.7.2.1.3.4 Occupant notification shall be by means of visible signals in accordance with 13.7.1.9.6, initiated by the person in the constantly attended receiving station, unless otherwise permitted by 13.7.2.1.3.5. [*101*:12.3.4.3.4]

13.7.2.1.3.5* Visible signals shall not be required in the assembly seating area, or the floor area used for the contest, performance, or entertainment, where the occupant load exceeds 1000 and an approved, alternative visible means of occupant notification is provided. *(See 13.7.1.9.6.7.)* [*101*:12.3.4.3.5]

13.7.2.1.3.6 The announcement shall be permitted to be made via a voice communication or public address system in accordance with 13.7.1.9.10.2. [*101*:12.3.4.3.6]

13.7.2.1.3.7 Where the AHJ determines that a constantly attended receiving station is impractical, both of the following shall be provided:

(1) Automatically transmitted evacuation or relocation instructions shall be provided in accordance with *NFPA 72*.
(2) The system shall be monitored by a supervising station in accordance with *NFPA 72*.

[*101*:12.3.4.3.7]

13.7.2.1.4 Carbon Monoxide Detection.

13.7.2.1.4.1 New assembly occupancies shall be provided with carbon monoxide detection and warning equipment in accordance with 13.7.1.14 in the locations specified as follows:

(1) On the ceilings of rooms containing permanently installed fuel-burning appliances or fuel-burning fireplaces
(2) Centrally located within occupiable spaces served by the first supply air register from permanently installed fuel-burning HVAC systems
(3)* Centrally located within occupiable spaces adjacent to an attached garage

[*101*:12.3.4.4.1]

13.7.2.1.4.2 Carbon monoxide detectors as specified in 13.7.2.1.4.1 shall not be required in the following locations:

(1) Garages
(2) Occupiable spaces with attached garages that are open parking structures as defined in 3.3.203.26.3.
(3) Occupiable spaces with attached garages that are mechanically ventilated in accordance with the mechanical code

[*101*:12.3.4.4.2]

13.7.2.1.5 Risk Analysis for Mass Notification Systems. A risk analysis in accordance with 13.7.1.15 shall be performed for new assembly occupancies with an occupant load of 500 or more to determine whether a mass notification system is required. [*101*:12.3.4.5]

13.7.2.2 Existing Assembly Occupancies.

13.7.2.2.1 General.

13.7.2.2.1.1 Existing assembly occupancies with occupant loads of more than 300 and all theaters with more than one audience-viewing room shall be provided with an approved fire alarm system in accordance with Section 13.7 and 13.7.2.2, unless otherwise permitted by 13.7.2.2.1.2, 13.7.2.2.1.3, or 13.7.2.2.1.4. [*101*:13.3.4.1.1]

13.7.2.2.1.2 Existing assembly occupancies that are a part of a multiple occupancy protected as a mixed occupancy *(see 6.1.14 of NFPA 101)* shall be permitted to be served by a common fire alarm system, provided that the individual requirements of each occupancy are met. [*101*:13.3.4.1.2]

13.7.2.2.1.3 Voice communication or public address systems complying with 13.7.2.2.3.6 shall not be required to comply with Section 13.7. [*101*:13.3.4.1.3]

13.7.2.2.1.4 The requirement of 13.7.2.2.1.1 shall not apply to existing assembly occupancies where, in the judgment of the AHJ, adequate alternative provisions exist or are provided for the discovery of a fire and for alerting the occupants promptly. [*101*:13.3.4.1.4]

13.7.2.2.2 Initiation.

13.7.2.2.2.1 Initiation of the required fire alarm system shall be by both of the following means, and the system shall be provided with an emergency power source:

(1) Manual means in accordance with 13.7.1.7.1(1), unless otherwise permitted by one of the following:
 (a) The requirement of 13.7.2.2.2.1(1) shall not apply where initiation is by means of an approved automatic fire detection system in accordance with 13.7.1.7.1(2) that provides fire detection throughout the building.
 (b) The requirement of 13.7.2.2.2.1(1) shall not apply where initiation is by means of an approved automatic sprinkler system in accordance with 13.7.1.7.1(3) that provides fire detection and protection throughout the building.
(2) Where automatic sprinklers are provided, initiation of the fire alarm system by sprinkler system waterflow, even where manual fire alarm boxes are provided in accordance with 13.7.2.2.2.1(1)

[*101*:13.3.4.2.1]

13.7.2.2.2.2 The initiating device shall be capable of transmitting an alarm to a receiving station, located within the building, that is constantly attended when the assembly occupancy is occupied. [*101*:13.3.4.2.2]

13.7.2.2.2.3* In existing assembly occupancies with occupant loads of more than 300, automatic detection shall be provided in all hazardous areas that are not normally occupied, unless such areas are protected throughout by an approved automatic sprinkler system in accordance with Section 13.3. [*101*:13.3.4.2.3]

13.7.2.2.3 Notification. The required fire alarm system shall activate an audible alarm in a constantly attended receiving station within the building when occupied for purposes of initiating emergency action. [*101*:13.3.4.3]

13.7.2.2.3.1 Positive alarm sequence in accordance with 13.7.1.9.5 shall be permitted. [*101*:13.3.4.3.1]

13.7.2.2.3.2 A presignal system in accordance with 13.7.1.9.4 shall be permitted. [*101*:13.3.4.3.2]

13.7.2.2.3.3 Occupant notification shall be by means of voice announcements in accordance with 13.7.1.9.10 initiated by the person in the constantly attended receiving station. [*101*:13.3.4.3.3]

13.7.2.2.3.4 Reserved.

13.7.2.2.3.5 Reserved.

13.7.2.2.3.6 The announcement shall be permitted to be made via a voice communication or public address system in accordance with 13.7.1.9.10.2. [*101*:13.3.4.3.6]

13.7.2.2.3.7 Where the AHJ determines that a constantly attended receiving station is impractical, automatically transmitted evacuation or relocation instructions shall be provided in accordance with *NFPA 72*. [*101*:13.3.4.3.7]

13.7.2.3 New Educational Occupancies.

13.7.2.3.1 General.

13.7.2.3.1.1 New educational occupancies shall be provided with a fire alarm system in accordance with Section 9.6 of NFPA *101*. [*101*:14.3.4.1.1]

13.7.2.3.1.2 The requirement of 13.7.2.3.1.1 shall not apply to buildings meeting all of the following criteria:

(1) Buildings having an area not exceeding 1000 ft^2 (93 m^2)
(2) Buildings containing a single classroom
(3) Buildings located not less than 30 ft (9.1 m) from another building

[*101*:14.3.4.1.2]

13.7.2.3.2 Initiation.

13.7.2.3.2.1 General. Initiation of the required fire alarm system, other than as permitted by 13.7.2.3.2.3, shall be by manual means in accordance with 13.7.1.7.1(1). [*101*:14.3.4.2.1]

13.7.2.3.2.2 Automatic Initiation. In buildings provided with automatic sprinkler protection, the operation of the sprinkler system shall automatically activate the fire alarm system in addition to the initiation means required in 13.7.2.3.2.1. [*101*:14.3.4.2.2]

13.7.2.3.2.3 Alternative Protection System. Manual fire alarm boxes shall be permitted to be eliminated in accordance with 13.7.2.3.2.3.1 or 13.7.2.3.2.3.2. [*101*:14.3.4.2.3]

13.7.2.3.2.3.1* Manual fire alarm boxes shall be permitted to be eliminated where all of the following conditions apply:

(1) Interior corridors are protected by smoke detectors in accordance with Section 13.7.
(2) Auditoriums, cafeterias, and gymnasiums are protected by heat-detection devices or other approved detection devices.
(3) Shops and laboratories involving dusts or vapors are protected by heat-detection devices or other approved detection devices.
(4) Provision is made at a central point to manually activate the evacuation signal or to evacuate only affected areas.

[*101*:14.3.4.2.3.1]

13.7.2.3.2.3.2* Manual fire alarm boxes shall be permitted to be eliminated where both of the following conditions apply:

(1) The building is protected throughout by an approved, supervised automatic sprinkler system in accordance with Section 13.3.
(2) Provision is made at a central point to manually activate the evacuation signal or to evacuate only affected areas.

[*101*:14.3.4.2.3.2]

13.7.2.3.3 Notification.

13.7.2.3.3.1 Occupant Notification.

13.7.2.3.3.1.1 Occupant notification shall be accomplished automatically in accordance with 13.7.1.9. [*101*:14.3.4.3.1.1]

13.7.2.3.3.1.2 The occupant notification required by 13.7.2.3.3.1.1 shall utilize an emergency voice/alarm communication system in accordance with 13.7.1.9 where the building has an occupant load of more than 100. [*101*:14.3.4.3.1.2]

13.7.2.3.3.1.3 Positive alarm sequence shall be permitted in accordance with 13.7.1.9.5. [*101*:14.3.4.3.1.3]

13.7.2.3.3.1.4 In accordance with 13.7.1.9.11.2, the emergency voice/alarm communication system shall be permitted to be used for other emergency signaling or for class changes. [*101*:14.3.4.3.1.4]

13.7.2.3.3.1.5 To prevent students from being returned to a building that is burning, the recall signal shall be separate and distinct from any other signals, and such signal shall be permitted to be given by use of distinctively colored flags or banners. [*101*:14.3.4.3.1.5]

13.7.2.3.3.1.6 If the recall signal required by 13.7.2.3.3.1.5 is electric, the push buttons or other controls shall be kept under lock, the key for which shall be in the possession of the principal or another designated person in order to prevent a recall at a time when there is an actual fire. [*101*:14.3.4.3.1.6]

13.7.2.3.3.1.7 Regardless of the method of recall signal, the means of giving the recall signal shall be kept under lock. [*101*:14.3.4.3.1.7]

13.7.2.3.3.2 Emergency Forces Notification. Emergency forces notification shall be accomplished in accordance with 13.7.1.10. [*101*:14.3.4.3.2]

13.7.2.3.4 Carbon Monoxide Alarms and Carbon Monoxide Detection Systems.

13.7.2.3.4.1 Carbon monoxide detectors in accordance with 13.7.1.14 shall be provided in new educational occupancies in the locations specified as follows:

(1) Carbon monoxide detectors shall be installed on the ceilings of rooms containing permanently installed fuel-burning appliances.
(2) Carbon monoxide detectors shall be installed centrally located within occupiable spaces served by the first supply air register from a permanently installed, fuel-burning HVAC system.
(3) Carbon monoxide detectors shall be installed centrally located within occupiable spaces adjacent to a communicating attached garage.
(4) Carbon monoxide detectors shall be installed centrally located within occupiable spaces adjacent to an attached garage with a separation wall constructed of gypsum panels.

[*101*:14.3.4.4.1]

13.7.2.3.4.2 Carbon monoxide detectors as specified in 13.7.2.3.4.1 shall not be required in the following locations:

(1) Garages
(2) Occupiable spaces with communicating attached garages that are open parking structures as defined in 3.3.203.26.3
(3) Occupiable spaces with communicating attached garages that are mechanically ventilated in accordance with the applicable mechanical code
(4) Occupiable spaces that are separated from attached garages by walls constructed of gypsum panels where the garage is an open parking structure as defined in 3.3.203.26.3
(5) Occupiable spaces that are separated from attached garages by walls constructed of gypsum panels where the garage is mechanically ventilated in accordance with the mechanical code

[*101*:14.3.4.4.3]

13.7.2.3.5 Risk Analysis for Mass Notification Systems. A risk analysis in accordance with 13.7.1.15 shall be performed to determine if a mass notification system is required. [*101*:14.3.4.5]

13.7.2.4 Existing Educational Occupancies.

13.7.2.4.1 General.

13.7.2.4.1.1 Existing educational occupancies shall be provided with a fire alarm system in accordance with Section 9.6 of NFPA *101*. [*101*:15.3.4.1.1]

13.7.2.4.1.2 The requirement of 13.7.2.4.1.1 shall not apply to buildings meeting all of the following criteria:

(1) Buildings having an area not exceeding 1000 ft^2 (93 m^2)
(2) Buildings containing a single classroom
(3) Buildings located not less than 30 ft (9.1 m) from another building

[*101*:15.3.4.1.2]

13.7.2.4.2 Initiation.

13.7.2.4.2.1 General. Initiation of the required fire alarm system shall be by manual means in accordance with 13.7.1.7(1), unless otherwise permitted by one of the following:

(1) Manual fire alarm boxes shall not be required where permitted by 13.7.2.4.2.3.
(2) In buildings where all normally occupied spaces are provided with a two-way communication system between such spaces and a constantly attended receiving station from where a general evacuation alarm can be sounded, the manual fire alarm boxes shall not be required, except in locations specifically designated by the AHJ.

[*101*:15.3.4.2.1]

13.7.2.4.2.2 Automatic Initiation. In buildings provided with automatic sprinkler protection, the operation of the sprinkler system shall automatically activate the fire alarm system in addition to the initiation means required in 13.7.2.4.2.1. [*101*:15.3.4.2.2]

13.7.2.4.2.3 Alternative Protection System. Manual fire alarm boxes shall be permitted to be eliminated in accordance with 13.7.2.4.2.3.1 or 13.7.2.4.2.3.2. [*101*:15.3.4.2.3]

13.7.2.4.2.3.1* Manual fire alarm boxes shall be permitted to be eliminated where all of the following conditions apply:

(1) Interior corridors are protected by smoke detectors using an alarm verification system as described in *NFPA 72*.
(2) Auditoriums, cafeterias, and gymnasiums are protected by heat-detection devices or other approved detection devices.
(3) Shops and laboratories involving dusts or vapors are protected by heat-detection devices or other approved detection devices.
(4) Provision is made at a central point to manually activate the evacuation signal or to evacuate only affected areas.

[*101*:15.3.4.2.3.1]

13.7.2.4.2.3.2* Manual fire alarm boxes shall be permitted to be eliminated where both of the following conditions apply:

(1) The building is protected throughout by an approved, supervised automatic sprinkler system in accordance with Section 13.3.
(2) Provision is made at a central point to manually activate the evacuation signal or to evacuate only affected areas. [*101*:15.3.4.2.3.2]

13.7.2.4.3 Notification.

13.7.2.4.3.1 Occupant Notification.

13.7.2.4.3.1.1* Occupant notification shall be accomplished automatically in accordance with 13.7.1.9. [*101*:14.3.4.3.1.1]

13.7.2.4.3.1.2 Reserved.

13.7.2.4.3.1.3 Positive alarm sequence shall be permitted in accordance with 13.7.1.9.5. [*101*:15.3.4.3.1.3]

13.7.2.4.3.1.4 Where acceptable to the AHJ, the fire alarm system shall be permitted to be used for other emergency signaling or for class changes, provided that the fire alarm is distinctive in signal and overrides all other use. [*101*:15.3.4.3.1.4]

13.7.2.4.3.1.5 To prevent students from being returned to a building that is burning, the recall signal shall be separate and distinct from any other signals, and such signal shall be permitted to be given by use of distinctively colored flags or banners. [*101*:15.3.4.3.1.5]

13.7.2.4.3.1.6 If the recall signal required by 13.7.2.4.3.1.5 is electric, the push buttons or other controls shall be kept under lock, the key for which shall be in the possession of the principal or another designated person in order to prevent a recall at a time when there is an actual fire. [*101*:15.3.4.3.1.6]

13.7.2.4.3.1.7 Regardless of the method of recall signal, the means of giving the recall signal shall be kept under lock. [*101*:15.3.4.3.1.7]

13.7.2.4.3.2 Emergency Forces Notification.

13.7.2.4.3.2.1 Wherever any of the school authorities determine that an actual fire exists, they shall immediately call the local fire department using the public fire alarm system or other available facilities. [*101*:15.3.4.3.2.1]

13.7.2.4.3.2.2 Emergency forces notification shall be accomplished in accordance with 13.7.1.10 where the existing fire alarm system is replaced. [*101*:15.3.4.3.2.2]

13.7.2.5 New Day-Care Occupancies.

13.7.2.5.1 General. New day-care occupancies, other than day-care occupancies housed in one room having at least one door opening directly to the outside at grade plane or to an exterior exit access balcony in accordance with 14.10.3, shall be provided with a fire alarm system in accordance with Section 13.7 and 13.7.2.5. [*101*:16.3.4.1]

13.7.2.5.2 Initiation. Initiation of the required fire alarm system shall be by manual means and by operation of any required smoke detectors and required sprinkler systems. *(See 13.7.2.5.5.)* [*101*:16.3.4.2]

13.7.2.5.3 Occupant Notification.

13.7.2.5.3.1 Occupant notification shall be in accordance with 13.7.1.9. [*101*:16.3.4.3.1]

13.7.2.5.3.2 Positive alarm sequence shall be permitted in accordance with 13.7.1.9.5. [*101*:16.3.4.3.2]

13.7.2.5.3.3 Private operating mode in accordance with 13.7.1.9.7.3 shall be permitted. [*101*:16.3.4.3.3]

13.7.2.5.4 Emergency Forces Notification. Emergency forces notification shall be accomplished in accordance with 13.7.1.10. [*101*:16.3.4.4]

13.7.2.5.5 Detection. A smoke detection system in accordance with 13.7.1 shall be installed in new day-care occupancies, other than those housed in one room having at least one door opening directly to the outside at grade plane or to an exterior exit access balcony in accordance with 14.10.3, and such system shall comply with both of the following:

(1) Detectors shall be installed on each story in front of the doors to the stairways and in the corridors of all floors occupied by the day-care occupancy.
(2) Detectors shall be installed in lounges, recreation areas, and sleeping rooms in the day-care occupancy.
[*101*:16.3.4.5]

13.7.2.5.6 New Day-Care Homes.

13.7.2.5.6.1 Smoke alarms shall be installed within day-care homes in accordance with 13.7.1.8. [*101*:16.6.3.4.1]

13.7.2.5.6.2 Where a day-care home is located within a building of another occupancy, such as in an apartment building or office building, any corridors serving the day-care home shall be provided with a smoke detection system in accordance with 13.7.1.4 except as otherwise provided in 13.7.2.5.6.3. [*101*:16.6.3.4.2]

13.7.2.5.6.3 The corridor smoke detection system addressed in 13.7.2.5.6.2 shall not be required where all of the following conditions are met:

(1) The day-care home is in a building of another occupancy that is not required to have a fire alarm system by some other provision of this *Code*.
(2) Smoke alarms are installed in accordance with 13.7.1.8 in the corridor serving the day-care home.
(3) Smoke alarms are installed within the day-care home as required by 13.7.2.5.6.1.
(4) Additional smoke alarms are installed within the day-care home within 15 ft (4.6 m) of all sleeping rooms.
(5) The smoke alarms required by 13.7.2.5.6.3(2), 13.7.2.5.6.3(3), and 13.7.2.5.6.3(4) are interconnected, as required by *NFPA 72*, so that each sounds an alarm when any of these smoke alarms detects smoke.
[*101*:16.6.3.4.3]

13.7.2.5.6.4 Single-station or multiple-station smoke alarms or smoke detectors shall be provided in all rooms used for sleeping in accordance with 13.7.1.8. [*101*:16.6.3.4.4]

13.7.2.5.6.5 Single-station or multiple-station carbon monoxide alarms or detectors shall be provided in accordance with 13.7.1.14 in day-care homes where client sleeping occurs and one or both of the following conditions exist:

(1) Fuel-fired equipment is present.

(2) An enclosed parking structure is attached to the day-care home.
[*101*:16.6.3.4.6]

13.7.2.6 Existing Day-Care Occupancies.

13.7.2.6.1 General. Existing day-care occupancies, other than day-care occupancies housed in one room, shall be provided with a fire alarm system in accordance with Section 13.7 and 13.7.2.6. [*101*:17.3.4.1]

13.7.2.6.2 Initiation. Initiation of the required fire alarm system shall be by manual means and by operation of any required smoke detectors and required sprinkler systems. *(See 13.7.2.6.5.)* [*101*:17.3.4.2]

13.7.2.6.3 Occupant Notification.

13.7.2.6.3.1 Occupant notification shall be in accordance with 13.7.1.9. [*101*:17.3.4.3.1]

13.7.2.6.3.2 Positive alarm sequence shall be permitted in accordance with 13.7.1.9.5. [*101*:17.3.4.3.2]

13.7.2.6.3.3 Private operating mode in accordance with 13.7.1.9.7.3 shall be permitted. [*101*:17.3.4.3.3]

13.7.2.6.4 Emergency Forces Notification.

13.7.2.6.4.1 Emergency forces notification, other than for day-care occupancies with not more than 100 clients, shall be accomplished in accordance with 13.7.1.10. [*101*:17.3.4.4.1]

13.7.2.6.4.2 Emergency forces notification shall be accomplished in accordance with 13.7.1.10 where the existing fire alarm system is replaced. [*101*:17.3.4.4.2]

13.7.2.6.5 Detection. A smoke detection system in accordance with 13.7.1 shall be installed in existing day-care occupancies, other than those housed in one room or those housing clients capable of self-preservation where no sleeping facilities are provided, and such system shall comply with both of the following:

(1) Detectors shall be installed on each story in front of the doors to the stairways and in the corridors of all floors occupied by the day-care occupancy.
(2) Detectors shall be installed in lounges, recreation areas, and sleeping rooms in the day-care occupancy.
[*101*:17.3.4.5]

13.7.2.6.6 Existing Day-Care Homes.

13.7.2.6.6.1 Smoke alarms shall be installed within day-care homes in accordance with 13.7.1.8. [*101*:17.6.3.4.1]

13.7.2.6.6.2 Where a day-care home is located within a building of another occupancy, such as in an apartment building or office building, any corridors serving the day-care home shall be provided with a smoke detection system in accordance with 13.7.1.7 except as otherwise provided in 13.7.2.6.6.3. [*101*:17.6.3.4.2]

13.7.2.6.6.3 The corridor smoke detection system addressed in 13.7.2.6.6.2 shall not be required where all of the following conditions are met:

(1) The day-care home is in a building of another occupancy that is not required to have a fire alarm system by another provision of this *Code*.
(2) Smoke alarms are installed in accordance with 13.7.1.8 in the corridor serving the day-care home.
(3) Smoke alarms are installed within the day-care home as required by 13.7.2.6.6.1.
(4) Additional smoke alarms are installed within the day-care home within 15 ft (4.6 m) of all sleeping rooms.
(5) The smoke alarms required by 13.7.2.6.6.3(2), 13.7.2.6.6.3(3), and 13.7.2.6.6.3(4) are interconnected, as required by *NFPA 72*, so that each sounds an alarm when any of these smoke alarms detects smoke.
(6) The exemption of 13.7.2.6.6.5 for existing battery-powered smoke alarms does not apply.
[*101*:17.6.3.4.3]

13.7.2.6.6.4 Single-station or multiple-station smoke alarms or smoke detectors shall be provided in all rooms used for sleeping in accordance with 13.7.1.8, other than as permitted by 13.7.2.6.6.5. [*101*:17.6.3.4.4]

13.7.2.6.6.5 Approved existing battery-powered smoke alarms, rather than house electrical service–powered smoke alarms required by 13.7.2.6.6.4, shall be permitted where the facility has testing, maintenance, and battery replacement programs that ensure reliability of power to the smoke alarms. [*101*:17.6.3.4.5]

13.7.2.7 New Health Care Occupancies.

13.7.2.7.1 General. New health care occupancies shall be provided with a fire alarm system in accordance with Section 13.7 and 13.7.2.7. [*101*:18.3.4.1]

13.7.2.7.2* Initiation.

13.7.2.7.2.1 Initiation of the required fire alarm systems shall be by manual means in accordance with 13.7.1.7 and by means of any required sprinkler system waterflow alarms, detection devices, or detection systems, unless otherwise permitted by 13.7.2.7.2.2 and 13.7.2.7.2.3. [*101*:18.3.4.2.1]

13.7.2.7.2.2 Manual fire alarm boxes in patient sleeping areas shall not be required at exits if located at all nurses' control stations or other continuously attended staff location, provided that both of the following criteria are met:

(1) Such manual fire alarm boxes are visible and continuously accessible.
(2) Travel distances required by 13.7.1.7.5 are not exceeded.
[*101*:18.3.4.2.2]

13.7.2.7.2.3 The system smoke detector installed in accordance with 18.3.2.5.3(13) of NFPA *101* shall not be required to initiate the fire alarm system. [*101*:18.3.4.2.3]

13.7.2.7.3 Notification. Positive alarm sequence in accordance with 13.7.1.9.5 shall be permitted. [*101*:18.3.4.3]

13.7.2.7.3.1 Occupant Notification. Occupant notification shall be accomplished automatically in accordance with 13.7.1.9, unless otherwise modified by the following:

(1) Paragraph 13.7.1.9.2.3 shall not be permitted to be used.
(2)* Where the private operating mode in accordance with *NFPA 72* is used, alarm notification appliances shall not be required in patient care spaces where alarm notification adversely affects patient care.
(3) The provision of 18.3.2.5.3(13)(c) of NFPA *101* shall be permitted to be used.
[*101*:18.3.4.3.1]

13.7.2.7.3.2 Emergency Forces Notification.

13.7.2.7.3.2.1 Emergency forces notification shall be accomplished in accordance with 13.7.1.10, except that the provision of 18.3.2.5.3(13)(d) of NFPA *101* shall be permitted to be used. [*101*:18.3.4.3.2.1]

13.7.2.7.3.2.2 Reserved.

13.7.2.7.3.3 Annunciation and Annunciation Zoning.

13.7.2.7.3.3.1 Annunciation and annunciation zoning shall be provided in accordance with 13.7.1.13, unless otherwise permitted by 13.7.2.7.3.3.2 or 13.7.2.7.3.3.3. [*101*:18.3.4.3.3.1]

13.7.2.7.3.3.2 The alarm zone shall be permitted to coincide with the permitted area for smoke compartments. [*101*:18.3.4.3.3.2]

13.7.2.7.3.3.3 The provision of 13.7.1.13.9.2, which permits sprinkler system waterflow to be annunciated as a single building zone, shall be prohibited. [*101*:18.3.4.3.3.3]

13.7.2.7.4 Emergency Control Functions. Operation of any activating device in the required fire alarm system shall be arranged to accomplish automatically any control functions to be performed by that device. (*See 13.7.1.11.*) [*101*:18.3.4.4]

13.7.2.7.5 Detection.

13.7.2.7.5.1 General. Detection systems, where required, shall be in accordance with Section 13.7. [*101*:18.3.4.5.1]

13.7.2.7.5.2 Detection in Spaces Open to Corridors. See 18.3.6.1 of NFPA *101*. [*101*:18.3.4.5.2]

13.7.2.7.5.3* Nursing Homes. An approved automatic smoke detection system shall be installed in corridors throughout smoke compartments containing patient sleeping rooms and in spaces open to corridors as permitted in nursing homes by 18.3.6.1 of NFPA *101*, unless otherwise permitted by one of the following:

(1) Corridor systems shall not be required where each patient sleeping room is protected by an approved smoke detection system.
(2) Corridor systems shall not be required where patient room doors are equipped with automatic door-closing devices with integral smoke detectors on the room side installed in accordance with their listing, provided that the integral detectors provide occupant notification.

[*101*:18.3.4.5.3]

N **13.7.2.7.5.4 Carbon Monoxide Detection.**

N **13.7.2.7.5.4.1** Carbon monoxide detection, where required by 13.7.2.7.5.4.2 shall be in accordance with 13.7.1.14. [*101*:18.3.4.6.1]

N **13.7.2.7.5.4.2** Carbon monoxide detection shall be provided in the following locations:

(1) Carbon monoxide detectors shall be installed on the ceilings of rooms containing permanently installed fuel-burning appliances, including fireplaces.
(2) Carbon monoxide detectors shall be installed within 36 in. (910 mm) of the first supply air register from a permanently installed, fuel-burning HVAC system.

[*101*:18.3.4.6.2]

13.7.2.8 Existing Health Care Occupancies.

13.7.2.8.1 General. Existing health care occupancies shall be provided with a fire alarm system in accordance with Section 13.7 and 13.7.2.8. [*101*:19.3.4.1]

13.7.2.8.2* Initiation.

13.7.2.8.2.1 Initiation of the required fire alarm systems shall be by manual means in accordance with 13.7.1.7 and by means of any required sprinkler system waterflow alarms, detection devices, or detection systems, unless otherwise permitted by 13.7.2.8.2.2 through 13.7.2.8.2.5. [*101*:19.3.4.2.1]

13.7.2.8.2.2 Manual fire alarm boxes in patient sleeping areas shall not be required at exits if located at all nurses' control stations or other continuously attended staff location, provided that both of the following criteria are met:

(1) Such manual fire alarm boxes are visible and continuously accessible.
(2) Travel distances required by 13.7.1.7.5 are not exceeded.

[*101*:19.3.4.2.2]

13.7.2.8.2.3 The system smoke detector installed in accordance with 19.3.2.5.3(13) of NFPA *101* shall not be required to initiate the fire alarm system. [*101*:19.3.4.2.3]

13.7.2.8.2.4 Fixed extinguishing systems protecting commercial cooking equipment in kitchens that are protected by a complete automatic sprinkler system shall not be required to initiate the fire alarm system. [*101*:19.3.4.2.4]

13.7.2.8.2.5 Detectors required by 19.7.5.3 and 19.7.5.5 of NFPA *101* shall not be required to initiate the fire alarm system. [*101*:19.3.4.2.5]

13.7.2.8.3 Notification. Positive alarm sequence in accordance with 13.7.1.9.5 shall be permitted in health care occupancies protected throughout by an approved, supervised automatic sprinkler system in accordance with NFPA 13. [*101*:19.3.4.3]

13.7.2.8.3.1 Occupant Notification. Occupant notification shall be accomplished automatically in accordance with 13.7.1.9, unless otherwise modified by the following:

(1)* In lieu of audible alarm signals, visible alarm-indicating appliances shall be permitted to be used in critical care areas.
(2) Where visual devices have been installed in patient sleeping areas in place of an audible alarm, they shall be permitted where approved by the AHJ.
(3) The provision of 19.3.2.5.3(13)(c) of NFPA *101* shall be permitted to be used.
(4)* Where the private operating mode in accordance with *NFPA 72* is used, alarm notification appliances shall not be required in patient care spaces where alarm notification adversely affects patient care.

[*101*:19.3.4.3.1]

13.7.2.8.3.2 Emergency Forces Notification.

13.7.2.8.3.2.1 Emergency forces notification shall be accomplished in accordance with 13.7.1.10, except that the provision of 19.3.2.5.3(13)(d) of NFPA *101* shall be permitted to be used. [*101*:19.3.4.3.2.1]

13.7.2.8.3.2.2 Smoke detection devices or smoke detection systems equipped with reconfirmation features shall not be required to automatically notify the fire department, unless the alarm condition is reconfirmed after a period not exceeding 120 seconds. [*101*:19.3.4.3.2.2]

13.7.2.8.3.3 Reserved.

13.7.2.8.4 Emergency Control Functions. Operation of any activating device in the required fire alarm system shall be arranged to accomplish automatically any control functions to be performed by that device. *(See 13.7.1.11.)* [*101*:19.3.4.4]

13.7.2.8.5 Detection.

13.7.2.8.5.1 Corridors. An approved automatic smoke detection system in accordance with Section 13.7 shall be installed in all corridors of limited care facilities, unless otherwise permitted by one of the following:

(1) Where each patient sleeping room is protected by an approved smoke detection system, and a smoke detector is provided at smoke barriers and horizontal exits in accordance with Section 13.7, the corridor smoke detection system shall not be required on the patient sleeping room floors.
(2) Smoke compartments protected throughout by an approved, supervised automatic sprinkler system in accordance with 13.3.2.10.9 shall be permitted.

[*101*:19.3.4.5.1]

13.7.2.8.5.2 Detection in Spaces Open to Corridors. See 19.3.6.1 of NFPA *101*. [*101*:19.3.4.5.2]

13.7.2.9 New Ambulatory Health Care Occupancies.

13.7.2.9.1 General. New ambulatory health care facilities shall be provided with fire alarm systems in accordance with Section 13.7 and 13.7.2.9, except as modified by 13.7.2.9.2 through 13.7.2.9.5. [*101*:20.3.4.1]

13.7.2.9.2 Initiation. Initiation of the required fire alarm systems shall be by manual means in accordance with 13.7.1.7 and by means of any detection devices or detection systems required. [*101*:20.3.4.2]

13.7.2.9.3 Notification. Positive alarm sequence in accordance with 13.7.1.9.5 shall be permitted. [*101*:20.3.4.3]

13.7.2.9.3.1 Occupant Notification.

13.7.2.9.3.1.1 Occupant notification shall be accomplished automatically, without delay, in accordance with 13.7.1.9 upon operation of any fire alarm activating device. [*101*:20.3.4.3.1.1]

13.7.2.9.3.1.2* Where the private operating mode in accordance with *NFPA 72* is used, alarm notification appliances shall not be required in patient care spaces where alarm notification adversely affects patient care. [*101*:20.3.4.3.1.2]

13.7.2.9.3.2 Emergency Forces Notification.

13.7.2.9.3.2.1 Emergency forces notification shall be accomplished in accordance with 13.7.1.10. [*101*:20.3.4.3.2.1]

13.7.2.9.3.2.2 Reserved.

N **13.7.2.9.4 Carbon Monoxide Detection.**

N **13.7.2.9.4.1** Carbon monoxide detection, where required by 13.7.2.9.4.2, shall be in accordance with 13.7.1.14. [*101*:20.3.4.5.1]

N **13.7.2.9.4.2** Carbon monoxide detection shall be provided in the following locations:

(1) Carbon monoxide detectors shall be installed on the ceilings of rooms containing permanently installed fuel-burning appliances, including fireplaces.
(2) Carbon monoxide detectors shall be installed within 36 in. (910 mm) of the first supply air register from a permanently installed, fuel-burning HVAC system.

[*101*:20.3.4.5.2]

13.7.2.9.5 Emergency Control Functions. Operation of any activating device in the required fire alarm system shall be arranged to accomplish automatically, without delay, any control functions required to be performed by that device. *(See 13.7.1.11.)* [*101*:20.3.4.4]

13.7.2.10 Existing Ambulatory Health Care Occupancies.

13.7.2.10.1 General. Existing ambulatory health care facilities shall be provided with fire alarm systems in accordance with Section 13.7 and 13.7.2.10, except as modified by 13.7.2.10.2 through 13.7.2.10.4. [*101*:21.3.4.1]

13.7.2.10.2 Initiation. Initiation of the required fire alarm systems shall be by manual means in accordance with 13.7.1.7 and by means of any detection devices or detection systems required. [*101*:21.3.4.2]

13.7.2.10.3 Notification. Positive alarm sequence in accordance with 13.7.1.9.5 shall be permitted. [*101*:21.3.4.3]

13.7.2.10.3.1 Occupant Notification.

13.7.2.10.3.1.1 Occupant notification shall be accomplished automatically, without delay, in accordance with 13.7.1.9 upon operation of any fire alarm activating device. [*101*:21.3.4.3.1.1]

13.7.2.10.3.1.2* Where the private operating mode in accordance with *NFPA 72* is used, alarm notification appliances shall not be required in patient care spaces where alarm notification adversely affects patient care. [*101*:21.3.4.3.1.2]

13.7.2.10.3.2 Emergency Forces Notification.

13.7.2.10.3.2.1 Emergency forces notification shall be accomplished in accordance with 13.7.1.10. [*101*:21.3.4.3.2.1]

13.7.2.10.3.2.2 Smoke detection devices or smoke detection systems equipped with reconfirmation features shall not be required to automatically notify the fire department, unless the alarm condition is reconfirmed after a period not exceeding 120 seconds. [*101*:21.3.4.3.2.2]

13.7.2.10.4 Emergency Control Functions. Operation of any activating device in the required fire alarm system shall be arranged to accomplish automatically, without delay, any control functions required to be performed by that device. *(See 13.7.1.11.)* [*101*:21.3.4.4]

13.7.2.11 New Detention and Correctional Occupancies.

13.7.2.11.1 General. New detention and correctional occupancies shall be provided with a fire alarm system in accordance with Section 13.7 and 13.7.2.11, except as modified by 13.7.2.11.2 through 13.7.2.11.4.3. [*101*:22.3.4.1]

13.7.2.11.2 Initiation. Initiation of the required fire alarm system shall be by manual means in accordance with 13.7.1.7, by means of any required detection devices or detection systems, and by means of waterflow alarm in the sprinkler system required by 13.3.2.11.1, unless otherwise permitted by the following:

(1) Manual fire alarm boxes shall be permitted to be locked, provided that staff is present within the area when it is occupied and staff has keys readily available to unlock the boxes.
(2) Manual fire alarm boxes shall be permitted to be located in a staff location, provided that both of the following criteria are met:
    (a) The staff location is attended when the building is occupied.
    (b) The staff attendant has direct supervision of the sleeping area.

[*101*:22.3.4.2]

13.7.2.11.3 Notification.

13.7.2.11.3.1 Occupant Notification. Occupant notification shall be accomplished automatically in accordance with 13.7.1.9, and the following also shall apply:

(1) A positive alarm sequence shall be permitted in accordance with 13.7.1.9.5.
(2)* Any smoke detectors required by this chapter shall be permitted to be arranged to alarm at a constantly attended location only and shall not be required to accomplish general occupant notification.

[*101*:22.3.4.3.1]

13.7.2.11.3.2 Emergency Forces Notification.

13.7.2.11.3.2.1 Fire department notification shall be accomplished in accordance with 13.7.1.10, unless otherwise permitted by one of the following:

(1) A positive alarm sequence shall be permitted in accordance with 13.7.1.9.5.
(2) Any smoke detectors required by this chapter shall not be required to transmit an alarm to the fire department.
(3) This requirement shall not apply where staff is provided at a constantly attended location that meets one of the following criteria:
    (a) It has the capability to promptly notify the fire department.
    (b) It has direct communication with a control room having direct access to the fire department.

[*101*:22.3.4.3.2.1]

13.7.2.11.3.2.2 Where the provision of 13.7.2.11.3.2.1(3) is utilized, the fire plan, as required by 20.7.2.1.3, shall include procedures for logging of alarms and immediate notification of the fire department. [*101*:22.3.4.3.2.2]

13.7.2.11.4* Detection. An approved automatic smoke detection system shall be in accordance with Section 13.7, as modified by 13.7.2.11.4.1 through 13.7.2.11.4.3, throughout all resident sleeping areas and adjacent day rooms, activity rooms, or contiguous common spaces. [*101*:22.3.4.4]

13.7.2.11.4.1 Smoke detectors shall not be required in sleeping rooms with four or fewer occupants. [*101*:22.3.4.4.1]

13.7.2.11.4.2 Other arrangements and positioning of smoke detectors shall be permitted to prevent damage or tampering, or for other purposes. [*101*:22.3.4.4.2]

13.7.2.11.4.2.1 Other arrangements, as specified in 13.7.2.11.4.2, shall be capable of detecting any fire, and the placement of detectors shall be such that the speed of detection is equivalent to that provided by the spacing and arrangements required by the installation standards referenced in Section 13.7. [*101*:22.3.4.4.2.1]

13.7.2.11.4.2.2 Detectors shall be permitted to be located in exhaust ducts from cells, behind grilles, or in other locations. [*101*:22.3.4.4.2.2]

13.7.2.11.4.2.3 The equivalent performance of the design permitted by 13.7.2.11.4.2.2 shall be acceptable to the AHJ in accordance with the equivalency concepts specified in Section 1.4. [*101*:22.3.4.4.2.3]

13.7.2.11.4.3* Smoke detectors shall not be required in Use Condition II open dormitories where staff is present within the dormitory whenever the dormitory is occupied. [*101*:22.3.4.4.3]

13.7.2.12 Existing Detention and Correctional Occupancies.

13.7.2.12.1 General. Existing detention and correctional occupancies shall be provided with a fire alarm system in accordance with Section 13.7 and 13.7.2.12, except as modified by 13.7.2.12.2 through 13.7.2.12.4.4. [*101*:23.3.4.1]

13.7.2.12.2 Initiation. Initiation of the required fire alarm system shall be by manual means in accordance with 13.7.1.7 and by means of any required detection devices or detection systems, unless otherwise permitted by the following:

(1) Manual fire alarm boxes shall be permitted to be locked, provided that staff is present within the area when it is occupied and staff has keys readily available to unlock the boxes.
(2) Manual fire alarm boxes shall be permitted to be located in a staff location, provided that both of the following criteria are met:
    (a) The staff location is attended when the building is occupied.
    (b) The staff attendant has direct supervision of the sleeping area.

[*101*:23.3.4.2]

13.7.2.12.3 Notification.

13.7.2.12.3.1 Occupant Notification. Occupant notification shall be accomplished automatically in accordance with 13.7.1.9, and the following also shall apply:

(1) A positive alarm sequence shall be permitted in accordance with 13.7.1.9.5.
(2)* Any smoke detectors required by this chapter shall be permitted to be arranged to alarm at a constantly attended location only and shall not be required to accomplish general occupant notification.

[*101*:23.3.4.3.1]

13.7.2.12.3.2 Emergency Forces Notification.

13.7.2.12.3.2.1 Fire department notification shall be accomplished in accordance with 13.7.1.10, unless otherwise permitted by one of the following:

(1) A positive alarm sequence shall be permitted in accordance with 13.7.1.9.5.

(2) Any smoke detectors required by this chapter shall not be required to transmit an alarm to the fire department.
(3) This requirement shall not apply where staff is provided at a constantly attended location that meets one of the following criteria:
   (a) It has the capability to promptly notify the fire department.
   (b) It has direct communication with a control room having direct access to the fire department.

[*101*:23.3.4.3.2.1]

13.7.2.12.3.2.2 Where the provision of 13.7.2.12.3.2.1(3) is utilized, the fire plan, as required by 20.7.2.1.3, shall include procedures for logging of alarms and immediate notification of the fire department. [*101*:23.3.4.3.2.2]

13.7.2.12.4 Detection. An approved automatic smoke detection system shall be in accordance with Section 13.7, as modified by 13.7.2.12.4.1 through 13.7.2.12.4.4, throughout all resident housing areas. [*101*:23.3.4.4]

13.7.2.12.4.1 Smoke detectors shall not be required in sleeping rooms with four or fewer occupants in Use Condition II or Use Condition III. [*101*:23.3.4.4.1]

13.7.2.12.4.2 Other arrangements and positioning of smoke detectors shall be permitted to prevent damage or tampering, or for other purposes. [*101*:23.3.4.4.2]

13.7.2.12.4.2.1 Other arrangements, as specified in 13.7.2.12.4.2, shall be capable of detecting any fire, and the placement of detectors shall be such that the speed of detection is equivalent to that provided by the spacing and arrangements required by the installation standards referenced in Section 13.7. [*101*:23.3.4.4.2.1]

13.7.2.12.4.2.2 Detectors shall be permitted to be located in exhaust ducts from cells, behind grilles, or in other locations. [*101*:23.3.4.4.2.2]

13.7.2.12.4.2.3 The equivalent performance of the design permitted by 13.7.2.12.4.2.2 shall be acceptable to the AHJ in accordance with the equivalency concepts specified in Section 1.4. [*101*:23.3.4.4.2.3]

13.7.2.12.4.3* Smoke detectors shall not be required in Use Condition II open dormitories where staff is present within the dormitory whenever the dormitory is occupied and the building is protected throughout by an approved, supervised automatic sprinkler system in accordance with 13.3.2.12.2. [*101*:23.3.4.4.3]

13.7.2.12.4.4 In smoke compartments protected throughout by an approved automatic sprinkler system in accordance with 13.3.2.12.2, smoke detectors shall not be required, except in corridors, common spaces, and sleeping rooms with more than four occupants. [*101*:23.3.4.4.4]

13.7.2.13 New and Existing One- and Two-Family Dwellings.

13.7.2.13.1 Smoke alarms or a smoke detection system shall be provided in accordance with either 13.7.2.13.1.1 or 13.7.2.13.1.2, as modified by 13.7.2.13.1.3. [*101*:24.3.4.1]

13.7.2.13.1.1* Smoke alarms shall be installed in accordance with 13.7.1.8 in all of the following locations:

(1) All sleeping rooms
(2)* Outside of each separate sleeping area, in the immediate vicinity of the sleeping rooms
(3) On each level of the dwelling unit, including basements

[*101*:24.3.4.1.1]

13.7.2.13.1.2 Dwelling units shall be protected by an approved smoke detection system in accordance with Section 13.7 and equipped with an approved means of occupant notification. [*101*:24.3.4.1.2]

13.7.2.13.1.3 In existing one- and two-family dwellings, approved smoke alarms powered by batteries shall be permitted. [*101*:24.3.4.1.3]

13.7.2.13.2 Carbon Monoxide and Carbon Monoxide Detection Systems.

13.7.2.13.2.1 Carbon monoxide alarms or carbon monoxide detectors in accordance with 13.7.1.14 and 13.7.2.13.2 shall be provided in new one- and two-family dwellings where either of the following conditions exists:

(1) Dwelling units with communicating attached garages, unless otherwise exempted by 13.7.2.13.2.3
(2) Dwelling units containing fuel-burning appliances or fuel-burning fireplaces

[*101*:24.3.4.2.1]

13.7.2.13.2.2* Where required by 13.7.2.13.2.1, carbon monoxide alarms or carbon monoxide detectors shall be installed in the following locations:

(1) Outside of each separate dwelling unit sleeping area in the immediate vicinity of the sleeping rooms
(2) On every occupiable level of a dwelling unit, including basements, and excluding attics and crawl spaces

[*101*:24.3.4.2.2]

13.7.2.13.2.3 Carbon monoxide alarms and carbon monoxide detectors as specified in 13.7.2.13.2.1(1) shall not be required in the following locations:

(1) In garages
(2) Within dwelling units with communicating attached garages that are open parking structures as defined by the building code
(3) Within dwelling units with communicating attached garages that are mechanically ventilated in accordance with the mechanical code

[*101*:24.3.4.2.3]

13.7.2.14 New and Existing Lodging or Rooming Houses.

13.7.2.14.1 General.

13.7.2.14.1.1 Lodging and rooming houses, other than those meeting 13.7.2.14.1.2, shall be provided with a fire alarm system in accordance with Section 13.7. [*101*:26.3.4.1.1]

13.7.2.14.1.2 A fire alarm system in accordance with Section 13.7 shall not be required in existing lodging and rooming houses that have an existing smoke detection system meeting or exceeding the requirements of 13.7.2.14.5.1 where that detection system includes not less than one manual fire alarm box per floor arranged to initiate the smoke detection alarm. [*101*:26.3.4.1.2]

13.7.2.14.2 Initiation. Initiation of the required fire alarm system shall be by manual means in accordance with 13.7.1.7, or by alarm initiation in accordance with 13.7.1.7.1(3) in buildings protected throughout by an approved automatic sprinkler system in accordance with 13.3.2.17. [*101*:26.3.4.2]

13.7.2.14.3 Notification. Occupant notification shall be provided automatically in accordance with 13.7.1.9, as modified by 13.7.2.14.3.1 and 13.7.2.14.3.2. [*101*:26.3.4.3]

Δ **13.7.2.14.3.1*** Visible signals shall not be required where the proprietor resides in the building and there are five or fewer rooms for rent. [*101*:26.3.4.3.1]

13.7.2.14.3.2 Positive alarm sequence in accordance with 13.7.1.9.5 shall be permitted. [*101*:26.3.4.3.2]

13.7.2.14.4 Detection. (Reserved)

13.7.2.14.5 Smoke Alarms.

13.7.2.14.5.1 Approved smoke alarms, other than existing smoke alarms meeting the requirements of 13.7.2.14.5.3, shall be installed in accordance with 13.7.1.8 in every sleeping room. [*101*:26.3.4.5.1]

13.7.2.14.5.2 In other than existing buildings, the smoke alarms required by 13.7.2.14.5.1 shall be interconnected in accordance with 13.7.1.8.4. [*101*:26.3.4.5.2]

13.7.2.14.5.3 Existing battery-powered smoke alarms, rather than house electric-powered smoke alarms, shall be permitted where the facility has demonstrated to the AHJ that the testing, maintenance, and battery replacement programs will ensure reliability of power to the smoke alarms. [*101*:26.3.4.5.3]

13.7.2.14.6 Carbon Monoxide Alarms and Carbon Monoxide Detection Systems.

13.7.2.14.6.1 Carbon monoxide alarms or carbon monoxide detectors in accordance with 13.7.1.14 and 13.7.2.14.6 shall be provided in new and existing lodging or rooming houses where either of the following conditions exists:

(1) Lodging or rooming houses with communicating attached garages, unless otherwise exempted by 13.7.2.14.6.3
(2) Lodging or rooming houses containing fuel-burning appliances or fuel-burning fireplaces

[*101*:26.3.4.6.1]

13.7.2.14.6.2* Where required by 13.7.2.14.6.1, carbon monoxide alarms or carbon monoxide detectors shall be installed in the following locations:

(1) Outside of each separate sleeping area in the immediate vicinity of the sleeping rooms
(2) On every occupiable level, including basements, and excluding attics and crawl spaces

[*101*:26.3.4.6.2]

13.7.2.14.6.3 Carbon monoxide alarms and carbon monoxide detectors as specified in 13.7.2.14.6.1(1) shall not be required in the following locations:

(1) In garages
(2) Within lodging or rooming houses with communicating attached garages that are open parking structures as defined by the building code
(3) Within lodging or rooming houses with communicating attached garages that are mechanically ventilated in accordance with the mechanical code

[*101*:26.3.4.6.3]

13.7.2.15 New Hotels and Dormitories.

13.7.2.15.1 General. A fire alarm system in accordance with Section 13.7, except as modified by 13.7.2.15.2 through 13.7.2.15.6, shall be provided. [*101*:28.3.4.1]

13.7.2.15.2 Initiation. The required fire alarm system shall be initiated by each of the following:

(1) Manual means in accordance with 13.7.1.7
(2) Manual fire alarm box located at the hotel desk or other convenient central control point under continuous supervision by responsible employees
(3) Required automatic sprinkler system
(4) Required automatic detection system other than sleeping room smoke detectors

[*101*:28.3.4.2]

Δ **13.7.2.15.3 Notification.**

13.7.2.15.3.1* Occupant notification shall be provided automatically in accordance with 13.7.1.9. [*101*:28.3.4.3.1]

13.7.2.15.3.2 In hotels and dormitories that are required by 13.7.2.15 to have a fire alarm system, the audible alarm notification signal provided in sleeping rooms of guest rooms or guest suites that is activated by the fire alarm system shall be a 520 Hz low-frequency signal in accordance with 13.7.1.8.3. [*101*:28.3.4.3.2]

13.7.2.15.3.3 Positive alarm sequence in accordance with 13.7.1.9.5 shall be permitted. [*101*:28.3.4.3.3]

13.7.2.15.3.4* Guest rooms and guest suites required to be equipped with accessible communication features shall be provided with a visible notification appliance. [*101*:28.3.4.3.4]

13.7.2.15.3.5 In occupiable areas, other than guest rooms and guest suites, visible notification appliances shall be provided. [*101*:28.3.4.3.5]

13.7.2.15.3.6 Annunciation and annunciation zoning in accordance with 13.7.1.13 shall be provided in buildings three or more stories in height or having more than 50 guest rooms or guest suites. Annunciation shall be provided at a location readily accessible from the primary point of entry for emergency response personnel. [*101*:28.3.4.3.6]

13.7.2.15.3.7 Emergency forces notification shall be provided in accordance with 13.7.1.10. [*101*:28.3.4.3.7]

13.7.2.15.4 Detection. A corridor smoke detection system in accordance with Section 13.7 shall be provided in buildings other than those protected throughout by an approved, supervised automatic sprinkler system in accordance with 13.7.2.15. [*101*:28.3.4.5]

13.7.2.15.5* Smoke Alarms. Smoke alarms shall be installed in accordance with 13.7.1.8 in every guest room and every living area and sleeping room within a guest suite. [*101*:28.3.4.6]

13.7.2.15.6 Carbon Monoxide Alarms and Carbon Monoxide Detection Systems.

13.7.2.15.6.1 Carbon monoxide alarms or carbon monoxide detectors in accordance with 13.7.1.14 and 13.7.2.15.6 shall be provided in new hotels and dormitories where either of the following conditions exists:

(1) Guest rooms or guest suites with communicating attached garages, unless otherwise exempted by 13.7.2.15.6.3
(2) Guest rooms or guest suites containing a permanently installed fuel-burning appliance or fuel-burning fireplace

[*101*:28.3.4.7.1]

13.7.2.15.6.2 Where required by 13.7.2.15.6.1, carbon monoxide alarms or carbon monoxide detectors shall be installed on every occupiable level of a guest room and guest suite and in the immediate vicinity of the sleeping rooms.[*101*:28.3.4.7.2]

13.7.2.15.6.3 Carbon monoxide alarms and carbon monoxide detectors as specified in 13.7.2.15.6.1(1) shall not be required in the following locations:

(1) In garages
(2) Within guest rooms or guest suites with communicating attached garages that are open parking structures as defined by the building code
(3) Within guest rooms or guest suites with communicating attached garages that are mechanically ventilated in accordance with the mechanical code

[*101*:28.3.4.7.3]

13.7.2.15.6.4 Where fuel-burning appliances or fuel-burning fireplaces are installed outside guest rooms or guest suites, carbon monoxide detectors shall be installed in accordance with the manufacturer's published instructions in the locations specified as follows:

(1) On the ceilings of rooms containing permanently installed fuel-burning appliances or fuel-burning fireplaces
(2) Centrally located within occupiable spaces served by the first supply air register from a permanently installed, fuel-burning HVAC system
(3) Centrally located within occupiable spaces adjacent to a communicating attached garage

[*101*:28.3.4.7.4]

13.7.2.15.6.5 Where carbon monoxide detectors are installed in accordance with 13.7.2.15.6.4(1), the alarm signal shall be automatically transmitted to an approved on-site location or to an off-premises location in accordance with *NFPA 72*. [*101*:28.3.4.7.5]

13.7.2.15.7 Risk Analysis for Mass Notification.

Δ **13.7.2.15.7.1** A risk analysis in accordance with 13.7.1.15 shall be performed for grade K through 12, college, or university dormitories with an occupant load greater than 100 to determine whether a mass notification is required. [*101*:28.3.4.4.1]

13.7.2.15.7.2 Applicable portions of an existing risk analysis shall be permitted to be used when a new building is added to the campus. [*101*:28.3.4.4.2]

13.7.2.16 Existing Hotels and Dormitories.

13.7.2.16.1 General. A fire alarm system in accordance with Section 13.7, except as modified by 13.7.2.16.2 through 13.7.2.16.3.5, shall be provided in buildings, other than those where each guest room has exterior exit access in accordance with 14.10.3 and the building is three or fewer stories in height. [*101*:29.3.4.1]

13.7.2.16.2 Initiation. The required fire alarm system shall be initiated by each of the following:

(1) Manual means in accordance with 13.7.1.7, unless there are other effective means to activate the fire alarm system, such as complete automatic sprinkler or automatic detection systems, with manual fire alarm box in accordance with 13.7.2.16.2(2) required
(2) Manual fire alarm box located at the hotel desk or other convenient central control point under continuous supervision by responsible employees
(3) Required automatic sprinkler system
(4) Required automatic detection system other than sleeping room smoke detectors

[*101*:29.3.4.2]

Δ **13.7.2.16.3 Notification.**

13.7.2.16.3.1 Occupant notification shall be provided automatically in accordance with 13.7.1.9. [*101*:29.3.4.3.1]

13.7.2.16.3.2 Positive alarm sequence in accordance with 13.7.1.9.5, and a presignal system in accordance with 13.7.1.9.4, shall be permitted. [*101*:29.3.4.3.2]

13.7.2.16.3.3 Reserved.

13.7.2.16.3.4 Reserved.

13.7.2.16.3.5 Reserved.

13.7.2.16.3.6* Where the existing fire alarm system does not provide for automatic emergency forces notification in accordance with 13.7.1.10, provisions shall be made for the immediate notification of the public fire department by telephone or other means in case of fire, and, where there is no public fire department, notification shall be made to the private fire brigade. [*101*:29.3.4.3.6]

13.7.2.16.3.7 Where a new fire alarm system is installed or the existing fire alarm system is replaced, emergency forces notification shall be provided in accordance with 13.7.1.10. [*101*:29.3.4.3.7]

13.7.2.16.4 Detection. (Reserved)

13.7.2.16.5* Smoke Alarms. An approved single-station smoke alarm shall be installed in accordance with 13.7.1.8 in every guest room and every living area and sleeping room within a guest suite. [*101*:29.3.4.5]

13.7.2.16.5.1 The smoke alarms shall not be required to be interconnected. [*101*:29.3.4.5.1]

13.7.2.16.5.2 Single-station smoke alarms without a secondary (standby) power source shall be permitted. [*101*:29.3.4.5.2]

13.7.2.16.6 Carbon Monoxide Alarms and Carbon Monoxide Detection Systems.

13.7.2.16.6.1 Carbon monoxide alarms or carbon monoxide detectors in accordance with 13.7.1.14 and 13.7.2.16.6 shall be provided in existing hotels and dormitories where either of the following conditions exists:

(1) Guest rooms or guest suites with communicating attached garages, unless otherwise exempted by 13.7.2.16.6.3

(2) Guest rooms or guest suites containing a permanently installed fuel-burning appliance or fuel-burning fireplace [*101*:29.3.4.6.1]

13.7.2.16.6.2 Where required by 13.7.2.16.6.1, carbon monoxide alarms or carbon monoxide detectors shall be installed on every occupiable level of a guest room and guest suite and in the immediate vicinity of the sleeping rooms. [*101*:29.3.4.6.2]

13.7.2.16.6.3 Carbon monoxide alarms and carbon monoxide detectors as specified in 13.7.2.16.6.1(1) shall not be required in the following locations:

(1) In garages
(2) Within guest rooms or guest suites with communicating attached garages that are open parking structures as defined by the building code
(3) Within guest rooms or guest suites with communicating attached garages that are mechanically ventilated in accordance with the mechanical code

[*101*:29.3.4.6.3]

13.7.2.16.6.4 Where fuel-burning appliances or fuel-burning fireplaces are installed outside guest rooms or guest suites, carbon monoxide detectors shall be installed in accordance with the manufacturer's published instructions in the locations specified as follows:

(1) On the ceilings of rooms containing permanently installed fuel-burning appliances or fuel-burning fireplaces
(2) Centrally located within occupiable spaces served by the first supply air register from a permanently installed, fuel-burning HVAC system
(3) Centrally located within occupiable spaces adjacent to a communicating attached garage

[*101*:29.3.4.6.4]

13.7.2.16.6.5 Where carbon monoxide detectors are installed in accordance with 13.7.2.16.6.4, the alarm signal shall be automatically transmitted to an approved on-site location or to an off-premises location in accordance with *NFPA 72*. [*101*:29.3.4.6.5]

13.7.2.17 New Apartment Buildings.

13.7.2.17.1 General.

13.7.2.17.1.1 New apartment buildings four or more stories in height or with more than 11 dwelling units, other than those meeting the requirements of 13.7.2.17.1.2, shall be provided with a fire alarm system in accordance with Section 13.7, except as modified by 13.7.2.17.2 through 13.7.2.17.6. [*101*:30.3.4.1.1]

13.7.2.17.1.2 A fire alarm system shall not be required in buildings where each dwelling unit is separated from other contiguous dwelling units by fire barriers *(see Section 12.7)* having a minimum 1-hour fire resistance rating, and where each dwelling unit has either its own independent exit or its own independent stairway or ramp discharging at the finished ground level. [*101*:30.3.4.1.2]

13.7.2.17.2 Initiation.

13.7.2.17.2.1 Initiation of the required fire alarm system shall be by manual means in accordance with 13.7.1.7, unless the building complies with 13.7.2.17.2.2. [*101*:30.3.4.2.1]

13.7.2.17.2.2 Initiation of the required fire alarm system by manual means shall not be required in buildings four or fewer stories in height, containing not more than 16 dwelling units, and protected throughout by an approved, supervised automatic sprinkler system installed in accordance with 13.3.2.15. [*101*:30.3.4.2.2]

13.7.2.17.2.3 In buildings protected throughout by an approved, supervised automatic sprinkler system in accordance with 13.3.2.15, required fire alarm systems shall be initiated upon operation of the automatic sprinkler system. [*101*:30.3.4.2.3]

13.7.2.17.3 Notification.

13.7.2.17.3.1 Occupant notification shall be provided automatically in accordance with Section 13.7, and both of the following shall also apply:

(1) Visible signals shall be installed in units required to be equipped with accessible communication features.
(2) Positive alarm sequence in accordance with 13.7.1.9.5 shall be permitted.

[*101*:30.3.4.3.1]

13.7.2.17.3.2* In apartment buildings that are required by 13.7.2.17.1 to have a fire alarm system, the audible alarm notification signal provided in sleeping rooms of dwelling units that is activated by the fire alarm system shall be a 520 Hz low-frequency signal in accordance with 13.7.1.9.9. [*101*:30.3.4.3.2]

13.7.2.17.3.3 Annunciation, and annunciation zoning, in accordance with 13.7.1.13 shall be provided, unless the building complies with either 13.7.2.17.3.4 or 13.7.2.17.3.5. Annunciation shall be provided at a location readily accessible from the primary point of entry for emergency response personnel. [*101*:30.3.4.3.3]

13.7.2.17.3.4 Annunciation, and annunciation zoning, shall not be required in buildings two or fewer stories in height and having not more than 50 dwelling units. [*101*:30.3.4.3.4]

13.7.2.17.3.5 Annunciation, and annunciation zoning, shall not be required in buildings four or fewer stories in height containing not more than 16 dwelling units and protected throughout by an approved, supervised automatic sprinkler system installed in accordance with 13.3.2.15. [*101*:30.3.4.3.5]

13.7.2.17.3.6 Emergency forces notification shall be accomplished in accordance with 13.7.1.10. [*101*:30.3.4.3.6]

13.7.2.17.4 Detection. (Reserved)

13.7.2.17.5* Smoke Alarms. Smoke alarms shall be installed in accordance with 13.7.1.8 in every sleeping area, outside every sleeping area in the immediate vicinity of the bedrooms, and on all levels of the dwelling unit, including basements. [*101*:30.3.4.5]

13.7.2.17.5.1* In apartment buildings that are required by 13.7.2.17 to have a fire alarm system, the audible alarm notification signal provided in sleeping rooms that is activated by smoke alarms shall be a 520 Hz low-frequency signal in accordance with 13.7.1.8.3. [*101*:30.3.4.5.1]

13.7.2.17.6 Carbon Monoxide Alarms and Carbon Monoxide Detection Systems.

13.7.2.17.6.1 Carbon monoxide alarms or carbon monoxide detectors in accordance with 13.7.1.14 and 13.7.2.17.6 shall be provided in new apartment buildings where either of the following conditions exists:

(1) Dwelling units with communicating attached garages, unless otherwise exempted by 13.7.2.17.6.3
(2) Dwelling units containing a permanently installed fuel-burning appliance or fuel-burning fireplace

[*101*:30.3.4.6.1]

13.7.2.17.6.2 Where required by 13.7.2.17.6.1, carbon monoxide alarms or carbon monoxide detectors shall be installed in the following locations:

(1) Outside of each separate dwelling unit sleeping area in the immediate vicinity of the sleeping rooms
(2) On every occupiable level of a dwelling unit

[*101*:30.3.4.6.2]

13.7.2.17.6.3 Carbon monoxide alarms and carbon monoxide detectors as specified in 13.7.2.17.6.1(1) shall not be required in the following locations:

(1) In garages
(2) Within dwelling units with communicating attached garages that are open parking structures as defined by the building code
(3) Within dwelling units with communicating attached garages that are mechanically ventilated in accordance with the mechanical code

[*101*:30.3.4.6.3]

Δ **13.7.2.17.6.4*** Where fuel-burning appliances or fuel-burning fireplaces are installed outside dwelling units, carbon monoxide detectors shall be installed in accordance with the manufacturer's published instructions in the locations specified as follows:

(1) On the ceilings of rooms containing permanently installed fuel-burning appliances or fuel-burning fireplaces
(2) Centrally located position within occupiable spaces served by the first supply air register from a permanently installed, fuel-burning HVAC system
(3) Centrally located position within occupiable spaces adjacent to a communicating attached garage

[*101*:30.3.4.6.4]

Δ **13.7.2.17.6.5** Where carbon monoxide detectors are installed in accordance with 13.7.2.17.6.4(1), the alarm signal shall be automatically transmitted to an approved on-site location or to an off-premises location in accordance with *NFPA 72*. [*101*:30.3.4.6.5]

13.7.2.18 Existing Apartment Buildings.

13.7.2.18.1 General.

13.7.2.18.1.1 Existing apartment buildings four or more stories in height or with more than 11 dwelling units, other than those meeting the requirements of 13.7.2.18.1.2, shall be provided with a fire alarm system in accordance with Section 13.7, except as modified by 13.7.2.18.1.2 through 13.7.2.18.5. [*101*:31.3.4.1.1]

13.7.2.18.1.2 A fire alarm system shall not be required where each dwelling unit is separated from other contiguous dwelling units by fire barriers (*see Section 12.7*) having a minimum ½-hour fire resistance rating, and where each dwelling unit has either its own independent exit or its own independent stairway or ramp discharging at the finished ground level. [*101*:31.3.4.1.2]

13.7.2.18.2 Initiation.

13.7.2.18.2.1 Initiation of the required fire alarm system shall be by manual means in accordance with 13.7.1.7, unless the building complies with 13.7.2.18.2.2. [*101*:31.3.4.2.1]

13.7.2.18.2.2 Initiation of the required fire alarm system by manual means shall not be required in buildings four or fewer stories in height, containing not more than 16 dwelling units, and protected throughout by an approved, supervised automatic sprinkler system installed in accordance with 13.7.2.18. [*101*:31.3.4.2.2]

13.7.2.18.2.3 In buildings using Option 2 as defined by NFPA *101*, the required fire alarm system shall be initiated by the automatic fire detection system in addition to the manual initiation means of 13.7.2.18.2.1. [*101*:31.3.4.2.3]

13.7.2.18.2.4 In buildings using Option 3 as defined by NFPA *101*, the required fire alarm system shall be initiated upon operation of the automatic sprinkler system in addition to the manual initiation means of 13.7.2.18.2.1. [*101*:31.3.4.2.4]

13.7.2.18.2.5 In buildings using Option 4 as defined by NFPA *101*, the required fire alarm system shall be initiated upon operation of the automatic sprinkler system in addition to the manual initiation means of 13.7.2.18.2.1. [*101*:31.3.4.2.5]

13.7.2.18.3 Notification.

13.7.2.18.3.1 Occupant notification shall be provided automatically in accordance with Section 13.7, and all of the following shall also apply:

(1) Visible signals shall be installed in units required to be equipped with accessible communication features.
(2) Positive alarm sequence in accordance with 13.7.1.9.5 shall be permitted.
(3) Existing approved presignal systems shall be permitted in accordance with 13.7.1.9.4.

[*101*:31.3.4.3.1]

13.7.2.18.3.2 An annunciator panel, whose location shall be approved by the AHJ, connected with the required fire alarm system shall be provided, unless the building meets the requirements of 13.7.2.18.3.3 or 13.7.2.18.3.4. [*101*:31.3.4.3.2]

13.7.2.18.3.3 Annunciation shall not be required in buildings two or fewer stories in height and having not more than 50 rooms. [*101*:31.3.4.3.3]

13.7.2.18.3.4 Annunciation shall not be required in buildings four or fewer stories in height containing not more than 16 dwelling units and protected throughout by an approved, supervised automatic sprinkler system installed in accordance with 13.3.2.16. [*101*:31.3.4.3.4]

13.7.2.18.3.5 Emergency forces notification shall be accomplished in accordance with 13.7.1.10. [*101*:31.3.4.3.5]

13.7.2.18.4 Detection.

13.7.2.18.4.1* In buildings using Option 2 as defined by NFPA *101*, a complete automatic fire detection system in accordance with 9.6.1.3 of NFPA *101* and 13.7.2.18.4.2 shall be required. [*101*:31.3.4.4.1]

13.7.2.18.4.2 Automatic fire detection devices shall be installed as follows:

(1) Smoke detectors shall be installed in all common areas and work spaces outside the living unit, such as exit stairs, egress corridors, lobbies, storage rooms, equipment rooms, and other tenantless spaces in environments that are suitable for proper smoke detector operation.
(2) Heat detectors shall be located within each room of the living unit.

[*101*:31.3.4.4.2]

13.7.2.18.5 Smoke Alarms.

13.7.2.18.5.1* In buildings other than those equipped throughout with an existing, complete automatic smoke detection system, smoke alarms shall be installed in accordance with 13.7.1.8, as modified by 13.7.2.18.5.2, outside every sleeping area in the immediate vicinity of the bedrooms and on all levels of the dwelling unit, including basements. [*101*:31.3.4.5.1]

13.7.2.18.5.2 Smoke alarms required by 13.7.2.18.5.1 shall not be required to be provided with a secondary (standby) power source. [*101*:31.3.4.5.2]

13.7.2.18.5.3 In buildings other than those equipped throughout with an existing, complete automatic smoke detection system or a complete, supervised automatic sprinkler system in accordance with 13.3.2.16, smoke alarms shall be installed in every sleeping area in accordance with 13.7.1.8, as modified by 13.7.2.18.5.4. [*101*:31.3.4.5.3]

13.7.2.18.5.4 Smoke alarms required by 13.7.2.18.5.3 shall be permitted to be battery powered. [*101*:31.3.4.5.4]

13.7.2.19 New, Small (Not More Than 16 Residents) Residential Board and Care Occupancies.

13.7.2.19.1 General. A fire alarm system shall be provided in accordance with Section 13.7. [*101*:32.2.3.4.1]

13.7.2.19.2 Initiation. Initiation of the required fire alarm system shall be by manual means in accordance with 13.7.1.7.1(1). [*101*:32.2.3.4.2]

13.7.2.19.3 Occupant Notification. Occupant notification shall be provided automatically, without delay, in accordance with 13.7.1.9. [*101*:32.2.3.4.3]

13.7.2.19.4 Carbon Monoxide Alarms and Carbon Monoxide Detection Systems.

13.7.2.19.4.1 Carbon monoxide alarms or carbon monoxide detectors in accordance with 13.7.1.14 and 13.7.2.19.4 shall be provided in new, small board and care facilities where either of the following conditions exists:

(1) Where small board and care facilities have communicating attached garages, unless otherwise exempted by 13.7.2.19.4.3
(2) Where small board and care facilities contain fuel-burning appliances or fuel-burning fireplaces

[*101*:32.2.3.4.4.1]

13.7.2.19.4.2 Where required by 13.7.2.19.4.1, carbon monoxide alarms or carbon monoxide detectors shall be installed in the following locations:

(1) Outside each separate sleeping area in the immediate vicinity of the sleeping rooms
(2) Within sleeping rooms containing fuel-burning appliances or fuel-burning fireplaces
(3) On every occupiable level, including basements and excluding attics and crawl spaces
(4) Centrally located within occupiable spaces adjacent to a communicating attached garage, unless otherwise exempted by 13.7.2.19.4.3

[*101*:32.2.3.4.4.2]

13.7.2.19.4.3 Carbon monoxide alarms and carbon monoxide detectors as specified in 13.7.2.19.4.1(1) shall not be required in the following locations:

(1) In garages
(2) Within small board and care facilities with communicating attached garages that are open parking structures as defined by the building code
(3) Within small board and care facilities with communicating attached garages that are mechanically ventilated in accordance with the mechanical code

[*101*:32.2.3.4.4.3]

13.7.2.19.5 Smoke Alarms.

13.7.2.19.5.1 Approved smoke alarms shall be provided in accordance with 13.7.1.8. [*101*:32.2.3.4.5.1]

13.7.2.19.5.2 Smoke alarms shall be installed on all levels, including basements but excluding crawl spaces and unfinished attics. [*101*:32.2.3.4.5.2]

13.7.2.19.5.3 Additional smoke alarms shall be installed in all living areas, as defined in 3.3.24.5 of NFPA *101*. [*101*:32.2.3.4.5.3]

13.7.2.19.5.4 Each sleeping room shall be provided with an approved smoke alarm in accordance with 13.7.1.8. [*101*:32.2.3.4.5.4]

13.7.2.20 New, Large (More than 16 Residents) Residential Board and Care Occupancies.

13.7.2.20.1 General. A fire alarm system shall be provided in accordance with Section 13.7. [*101*:32.3.3.4.1]

13.7.2.20.2 Initiation. The required fire alarm system shall be initiated by each of the following:

(1) Manual means in accordance with 13.7.1.7
(2) Manual fire alarm box located at a convenient central control point under continuous supervision of responsible employees
(3) Required automatic sprinkler system
(4) Required detection system

[*101*:32.3.3.4.2]

13.7.2.20.3 Annunciator Panel. An annunciator panel, connected to the fire alarm system, shall be provided at a location readily accessible from the primary point of entry for emergency response personnel. [*101*:32.3.3.4.3]

13.7.2.20.4 Occupant Notification. Occupant notification shall be provided automatically, without delay, in accordance with 13.7.1.9. [*101*:32.3.3.4.4]

13.7.2.20.5 High-Rise Buildings. High-rise buildings shall be provided with an approved emergency voice communication/alarm system in accordance with 13.7.2.29.3. [*101*:32.3.3.4.5]

13.7.2.20.6* Emergency Forces Notification. Emergency forces notification shall meet the following requirements:

(1) Emergency forces notification shall be accomplished in accordance with 13.7.1.10.
(2) Smoke detection devices or smoke detection systems shall be permitted to initiate a positive alarm sequence in accordance with 13.7.1.9.5 for not more than 120 seconds.

[*101*:32.3.3.4.6]

13.7.2.20.7 Smoke Alarms.

13.7.2.20.7.1 Approved smoke alarms shall be installed in accordance with 13.7.1.8 inside every sleeping room, outside every sleeping area in the immediate vicinity of the bedrooms, and on all levels within a resident unit. [*101*:32.3.3.4.7.1]

13.7.2.20.7.2 Smoke alarms shall not be required to be installed in locations where smoke detection is otherwise required per 13.7.2.20.8. [*101*:32.3.3.4.7.2]

13.7.2.20.8 Smoke Detection Systems.

13.7.2.20.8.1 Corridors and spaces open to the corridors, other than those meeting the requirement of 13.7.2.20.8.3, shall be provided with smoke detectors that comply with *NFPA 72* and are arranged to initiate an alarm that is audible in all sleeping areas. [*101*:32.3.3.4.8.1]

13.7.2.20.8.2 Reserved.

13.7.2.20.8.3 Smoke detection systems shall not be required in unenclosed corridors, passageways, balconies, colonnades, or other arrangements with one or more sides along the long dimension fully or extensively open to the exterior at all times. [*101*:32.3.3.4.8.3]

13.7.2.20.9 Carbon Monoxide Alarms and Carbon Monoxide Detection Systems.

13.7.2.20.9.1 Carbon monoxide detectors in accordance with 13.7.1.14 and 13.7.2.20.9 shall be provided in new large board and care facilities where any of the following conditions exists:

(1) Where facilities have communicating attached garages, unless otherwise exempted by 13.7.2.20.9.3
(2) Where fuel-burning appliances or fuel-burning fireplaces are in the facility

[*101*:32.3.3.4.9.1]

13.7.2.20.9.2 Where required by 13.7.2.20.9.1, carbon monoxide detectors shall be installed in all of the following locations:

(1) Within rooms containing fuel-burning appliances or fuel-burning fireplaces, unless otherwise exempted by 13.7.2.20.9.4
(2) Centrally located within occupiable spaces served by the first supply air register from a fuel-burning HVAC system
(3) On every occupiable level
(4) Within adjacent communicating occupiable spaces to an attached garage, unless otherwise exempted by 13.7.2.20.9.3

[*101*:32.3.3.4.9.2]

13.7.2.20.9.3 Carbon monoxide detectors as specified in 13.7.2.20.9.1(1) shall not be required in the following locations:

(1) In garages
(2) Within facilities with communicating attached garages that are open parking structures as defined by the building code
(3) Within facilities with communicating attached garages that are mechanically ventilated in accordance with the mechanical code

[*101*:32.3.3.4.9.3]

13.7.2.20.9.4 Within resident units containing fuel-burning appliances or fuel-burning fireplaces, carbon monoxide alarms shall be permitted to be used.[*101*:32.3.3.4.9.4]

13.7.2.21 Existing, Small (Not More Than 16 Residents) Residential Board and Care Occupancies.

13.7.2.21.1 Fire Alarm Systems. A fire alarm system shall be provided in accordance with Section 13.7, unless the provisions of 13.7.2.21.1.1 or 13.7.2.21.1.2 are met. [*101*:33.2.3.4.1]

Δ **13.7.2.21.1.1** A fire alarm system shall not be required where interconnected smoke alarms complying with 13.7.2.21.4 and not less than one manual fire alarm box per floor arranged to continuously sound the smoke detector alarms are provided. [*101*:33.2.3.4.1.1]

13.7.2.21.1.2 Other manually activated continuously sounding alarms acceptable to the AHJ shall be permitted in lieu of a fire alarm system. [*101*:33.2.3.4.1.2]

13.7.2.21.2 Initiation. Initiation of the required fire alarm system shall be by manual means in accordance with 13.7.1.7.1(1). [*101*:33.2.3.4.2]

13.7.2.21.3 Occupant Notification. Occupant notification shall be in accordance with 13.7.1.9. [*101*:33.2.3.4.3]

13.7.2.21.4* Smoke Alarms.

13.7.2.21.4.1 Approved smoke alarms shall be provided in accordance with 13.7.1.8, unless otherwise indicated in 13.7.2.21.4.6 and 13.7.2.21.4.7. [*101*:33.2.3.4.4.1]

13.7.2.21.4.2 Smoke alarms shall be installed on all levels, including basements but excluding crawl spaces and unfinished attics. [*101*:33.2.3.4.4.2]

13.7.2.21.4.3 Additional smoke alarms shall be installed for living rooms, dens, day rooms, and similar spaces. [*101*:33.2.3.4.4.3]

13.7.2.21.4.4 Reserved.

13.7.2.21.4.5 Smoke alarms shall be powered from the building electrical system and, when activated, shall initiate an alarm that is audible in all sleeping areas. [*101*:33.2.3.4.4.5]

13.7.2.21.4.6 Smoke alarms in accordance with 13.7.2.21.4.1, 13.7.2.21.4.2, and 13.7.2.21.4.3 shall not be required where buildings are protected throughout by an approved automatic sprinkler system, in accordance with 13.3.2.20.2, that uses quick-response or residential sprinklers, and are protected with approved smoke alarms installed in each sleeping room, in accordance with 13.7.1.8, that are powered by the building electrical system. [*101*:33.2.3.4.4.6]

13.7.2.21.4.7 Smoke alarms in accordance with 13.7.2.21.4.1, 13.7.2.21.4.2, and 13.7.2.21.4.3 shall not be required where buildings are protected throughout by an approved automatic sprinkler system, in accordance with 13.3.2.20.2, that uses quick-response or residential sprinklers, with existing battery-powered smoke alarms in each sleeping room, and where, in the opinion of the AHJ, the facility has demonstrated that testing, maintenance, and a battery replacement program ensure the reliability of power to the smoke alarms. [*101*:33.2.3.4.4.7]

13.7.2.22 Existing, Large (More Than 16 Residents) Residential Board and Care Occupancies.

13.7.2.22.1 General. A fire alarm system in accordance with Section 13.7 shall be provided, unless all of the following conditions are met:

(1) The facility has an evacuation capability of prompt or slow.
(2) Each sleeping room has exterior exit access in accordance with 14.10.3.
(3) The building does not exceed three stories in height.

[*101*:33.3.3.4.1]

13.7.2.22.2 Initiation. The required fire alarm system shall be initiated by each of the following means:

(1) Manual means in accordance with 13.7.1.7, unless there are other effective means (such as a complete automatic sprinkler or detection system) for notification of fire as required
(2) Manual fire alarm box located at a convenient central control point under continuous supervision of responsible employees
(3) Automatic sprinkler system, other than that not required by another section of this *Code*
(4) Required detection system, other than sleeping room smoke alarms

[*101*:33.3.3.4.2]

13.7.2.22.3 Reserved.

13.7.2.22.4 Occupant Notification. Occupant notification shall be provided automatically, without delay, by internal audible alarm in accordance with 13.7.1.9. [*101*:33.3.3.4.4]

13.7.2.22.5 Reserved.

13.7.2.22.6 Emergency Forces Notification.

13.7.2.22.6.1* Where the existing fire alarm system does not provide for automatic emergency forces notification in accordance with 13.7.1.10, provisions shall be made for the immediate notification of the public fire department by either telephone or other means, or, where there is no public fire department, notification shall be made to the private fire brigade. [*101*:33.3.3.4.6.1]

13.7.2.22.6.2 Where a new fire alarm system is installed, or the existing fire alarm system is replaced, emergency forces notification shall be provided in accordance with 13.7.1.10. [*101*:33.3.3.4.6.2]

13.7.2.22.7 Smoke Alarms. Smoke alarms shall be provided in accordance with 13.7.2.22.7.1, 13.7.2.22.7.2, or 13.7.2.22.7.3. [*101*:33.3.3.4.7]

13.7.2.22.7.1 Each sleeping room shall be provided with an approved smoke alarm in accordance with 13.7.1.8 that is powered from the building electrical system. [*101*:33.3.3.4.7.1]

13.7.2.22.7.2 Existing battery-powered smoke alarms, rather than building electrical-service-powered smoke alarms, shall be accepted where, in the opinion of the AHJ, the facility has demonstrated that testing, maintenance, and battery replacement programs ensure the reliability of power to the smoke alarms. [*101*:33.3.3.4.7.2]

13.7.2.22.7.3 Sleeping room smoke alarms shall not be required in facilities having an existing corridor smoke detection system that complies with Section 13.7 and is connected to the building fire alarm system. [*101*:33.3.3.4.7.3]

13.7.2.22.8 Smoke Detection Systems.

13.7.2.22.8.1 All living areas, as defined in 3.3.24.5 of NFPA *101*, and all corridors shall be provided with smoke detectors that comply with *NFPA 72* and are arranged to initiate an alarm that is audible in all sleeping areas, as modified by 13.7.2.22.8.2 and 13.7.2.22.8.3. [*101*:33.3.3.4.8.1]

13.7.2.22.8.2 Smoke detection systems shall not be required in living areas of buildings having a prompt or slow evacuation capability protected throughout by an approved automatic sprinkler system installed in accordance with 13.7.2.22.1. [*101*:33.3.3.4.8.2]

13.7.2.22.8.3 Smoke detection systems shall not be required in unenclosed corridors, passageways, balconies, colonnades, or other arrangements with one or more sides along the long dimension fully or extensively open to the exterior at all times. [*101*:33.3.3.4.8.3]

13.7.2.23 New Mercantile Occupancies.

13.7.2.23.1 General. New Class A mercantile occupancies shall be provided with a fire alarm system in accordance with Section 13.7. [*101*:36.3.4.1]

Δ **13.7.2.23.2 Initiation.** Initiation of the required fire alarm system shall be by any one of the following means:

(1) Manual means in accordance with 13.7.1.7.1(1)
(2) Approved automatic fire detection system in accordance with 13.7.1.7.1(2) that provides protection throughout the building and the provision of 13.7.1.7.6 shall apply.
(3) Approved automatic sprinkler system in accordance with 13.7.1.7.1(3) that provides protection throughout the building and the provision of 13.7.1.7.6 shall apply.

[*101*:36.3.4.2]

13.7.2.23.3 Notification.

13.7.2.23.3.1 Occupant Notification. During all times that the mercantile occupancy is occupied, the required fire alarm system, once initiated, shall perform one of the following functions:

(1) It shall activate an alarm in accordance with 13.7.1.9 throughout the mercantile occupancy.
(2) Positive alarm sequence in accordance with 13.7.1.9.5 shall be permitted.

[*101*:36.3.4.3.1]

13.7.2.23.3.2 Emergency Forces Notification. Emergency forces notification shall be provided and shall include notifying both of the following:

(1) Fire department in accordance with 13.7.1.10
(2) Approved, local emergency organization, if provided

[*101*:36.3.4.3.2]

13.7.2.24 Existing Mercantile Occupancies.

13.7.2.24.1 General. Existing Class A mercantile occupancies shall be provided with a fire alarm system in accordance with Section 13.7. [*101*:37.3.4.1]

Δ **13.7.2.24.2 Initiation.** Initiation of the required fire alarm system shall be by one of the following means:

(1) Manual means in accordance with 13.7.1.7.1(1)
(2) Approved automatic fire detection system in accordance with 13.7.1.7.1(2) that provides protection throughout the building and the provision of 13.7.1.7.6 shall apply.
(3) Approved automatic sprinkler system in accordance with 13.7.1.7.1(3) that provides protection throughout the building and the provision of 13.7.1.7.6 shall apply.

[*101*:37.3.4.2]

13.7.2.24.3 Notification.

13.7.2.24.3.1 Occupant Notification. During all times that the mercantile occupancy is occupied, the required fire alarm system, once initiated, shall perform one of the following functions:

(1) It shall activate an alarm in accordance with 13.7.1.9 throughout the mercantile occupancy, and both of the following also shall apply:
   (a) Positive alarm sequence in accordance with 13.7.1.9.5 shall be permitted.
   (b) A presignal system in accordance with 13.7.1.9.4 shall be permitted.
(2) Occupant notification shall be made via a voice communication or public address system in accordance with 13.7.1.9.10.2.

[*101*:37.3.4.3.1]

13.7.2.24.3.2 Emergency Forces Notification. Emergency forces notification shall be provided and shall include notifying both of the following:

(1) Fire department in accordance with 13.7.1.10
(2) Approved, local emergency organization, if provided

[*101*:37.3.4.3.2]

13.7.2.25 New Business Occupancies.

13.7.2.25.1 General. A fire alarm system in accordance with Section 13.7 shall be provided in all new business occupancies where any one of the following conditions exists:

(1) The building is three or more stories in height.
(2) The occupancy is subject to 50 or more occupants above or below the level of exit discharge.
(3) The occupancy is subject to 300 or more total occupants.

[*101*:38.3.4.1]

13.7.2.25.2 Initiation. Initiation of the required fire alarm system shall be by any one of the following means:

(1) Manual means in accordance with 13.7.1.7.1(1)
(2) Approved automatic fire detection system in accordance with 13.7.1.7.1(2) that provides protection throughout the building and the provision of 13.7.1.7.6 shall apply.
(3) Approved automatic sprinkler system in accordance with 13.7.1.7.1(3) that provides protection throughout the building and the provision of 13.7.1.7.6 shall apply.

[*101*:38.3.4.2]

13.7.2.25.3 Occupant Notification. During all times that the building is occupied *(see 7.2.1.1.3 of NFPA 101)*, the required fire alarm system, once initiated, shall perform one of the following functions:

(1) It shall activate a general alarm in accordance with 13.7.1.9.

(2) A positive alarm sequence in accordance with 13.7.1.9.5 shall be permitted.

[*101*:38.3.4.3]

13.7.2.25.4 Emergency Forces Notification. Emergency forces notification shall be provided and shall include notifying both of the following:

(1) Fire department in accordance with 13.7.1.10
(2) Approved local emergency organization, if provided

[*101*:38.3.4.4]

13.7.2.25.5* Risk Analysis for Mass Notification. A risk analysis in accordance with 13.7.1.15 shall be performed for new business occupancies containing a classroom where the building is owned, rented, leased, or operated by a college or university to determine whether a mass notification system is required. [*101*:38.3.4.5]

13.7.2.25.5.1 A risk analysis to determine the need for a mass notification system in accordance with Section 13.7.1.15 shall be conducted for buildings containing a classroom where the building is owned, rented, leased, or operated by a college or university to determine whether a mass notification system is required. [*101*:38.3.4.5]

13.7.2.26 Existing Business Occupancies.

13.7.2.26.1 General. A fire alarm system in accordance with Section 13.7 shall be provided in all existing business occupancies where any one of the following conditions exists:

(1) The building is three or more stories in height.
(2) The occupancy is subject to 100 or more occupants above or below the level of exit discharge.
(3) The occupancy is subject to 1000 or more total occupants.

[*101*:39.3.4.1]

13.7.2.26.2 Initiation. Initiation of the required fire alarm system shall be by one of the following means:

(1) Manual means in accordance with 13.7.1.7.1(1)
(2) Approved automatic fire detection system in accordance with 13.7.1.7.1(2) that provides protection throughout the building and the provision of 13.7.1.7.6 shall apply.
(3) Approved automatic sprinkler system in accordance with 13.7.1.7.1(3) that provides protection throughout the building and the provision of 13.7.1.7.6 shall apply.

[*101*:39.3.4.2]

13.7.2.26.3 Occupant Notification. During all times that the building is occupied *(see 7.2.1.1.3 of NFPA 101)*, the required fire alarm system, once initiated, shall perform one of the following functions:

(1) It shall activate a general alarm in accordance with 13.7.1.9, and both of the following also shall apply:
   (a) Positive alarm sequence in accordance with 13.7.1.9.5 shall be permitted.
   (b) A presignal system in accordance with 13.7.1.9.4 shall be permitted.
(2) Occupant notification shall be permitted to be made via a voice communication or public address system in accordance with 13.7.1.9.10.2.

[*101*:39.3.4.3]

13.7.2.26.4 Emergency Forces Notification. Emergency forces notification shall be accomplished in accordance with 13.7.1.10 when the existing fire alarm system is replaced. [*101*:39.3.4.4]

13.7.2.27 New and Existing Industrial Occupancies.

Δ **13.7.2.27.1 General.** A fire alarm system shall be required in accordance with Section 13.7 for industrial occupancies, unless the total occupant load of the building is under 100 persons and unless, of these, fewer than 25 persons are above or below the level of exit discharge. [*101*:40.3.4.1]

13.7.2.27.2 Initiation. Initiation of the required fire alarm system shall be by any of the following means:

(1) Manual means in accordance with 13.7.1.7.1(1)
(2) Approved automatic fire detection system in accordance with 13.7.1.7.1(2) throughout the building, plus a minimum of one manual fire alarm box in accordance with 13.7.1.7.6
(3) Approved, supervised automatic sprinkler system in accordance with 13.7.1.7.1(3) throughout the building, plus a minimum of one manual fire alarm box in accordance with 13.7.1.7.6

[*101*:40.3.4.2]

13.7.2.27.3 Notification.

13.7.2.27.3.1 The required fire alarm system shall meet one of the following criteria:

(1) It shall provide occupant notification in accordance with 13.7.1.9.
(2) It shall sound an audible and visible signal in a constantly attended location for the purposes of initiating emergency action.

[*101*:40.3.4.3.1]

13.7.2.27.3.2 Positive alarm sequence in accordance with 13.7.1.9.5 shall be permitted. [*101*:40.3.4.3.2]

13.7.2.27.3.3 Existing presignal systems in accordance with 13.7.1.9.4 shall be permitted. [*101*:40.3.4.3.3]

13.7.2.27.3.4 In high-hazard industrial occupancies, as described in 40.1.2.1.3 of NFPA *101*, the required fire alarm system shall automatically initiate an occupant evacuation alarm signal in accordance with 13.7.1.9. [*101*:40.3.4.3.4]

13.7.2.28 New and Existing Storage Occupancies.

Δ **13.7.2.28.1 General.** A fire alarm system shall be required in accordance with Section 13.7 for storage occupancies, except as modified by 13.7.2.28.1.1, 13.7.2.28.1.2, and 13.7.2.28.1.3. [*101*:42.3.4.1]

13.7.2.28.1.1 Storage occupancies limited to low-hazard contents shall not be required to have a fire alarm system. [*101*:42.3.4.1.1]

13.7.2.28.1.2 Storage occupancies with ordinary- or high-hazard contents not exceeding an aggregate floor area of 100,000 ft^2 (9300 m^2) shall not be required to have a fire alarm system. [*101*:42.3.4.1.2]

13.7.2.28.1.3 Storage occupancies protected throughout by an approved automatic sprinkler system in accordance with Section 13.3 shall not be required to have a fire alarm system. [*101*:42.3.4.1.3]

13.7.2.28.2 Initiation. Initiation of the required fire alarm system shall be by any of the following means:

(1) Manual means in accordance with 13.7.1.7.1(1)
(2) Approved automatic fire detection system in accordance with 13.7.1.7.1(2) throughout the building, plus a minimum of one manual fire alarm box in accordance with 13.7.1.7.6
(3) Approved, supervised automatic sprinkler system in accordance with 13.7.1.7.1(3) throughout the building, plus a minimum of one manual fire alarm box in accordance with 13.7.1.7.6

[*101*:42.3.4.2]

13.7.2.28.3 Notification.

13.7.2.28.3.1 The required fire alarm system shall meet one of the following criteria:

(1) It shall provide occupant notification in accordance with 13.7.1.9.
(2) It shall sound an audible and visible signal in a constantly attended location for the purposes of initiating emergency action.

[*101*:42.3.4.3.1]

13.7.2.28.3.2 Positive alarm sequence in accordance with 13.7.1.9.5 shall be permitted. [*101*:42.3.4.3.2]

13.7.2.28.3.3 Existing presignal systems in accordance with 13.7.1.9.4 shall be permitted. [*101*:42.3.4.3.3]

13.7.2.28.3.4 In high-hazard storage occupancies, the required fire alarm system shall automatically initiate an occupant evacuation alarm signal in accordance with 13.7.1.9. [*101*:42.3.4.3.4]

13.7.2.29 Special Structures and High-Rise Buildings.

13.7.2.29.1 Open Structures. Open structures shall be exempt from the requirement for detection, alarm, and communications systems. [*101*:11.2.3.4]

13.7.2.29.2 Towers. Towers, as defined in 3.3.303 of NFPA *101*, designed for occupancy by not more than three persons shall be exempt from requirements for detection, alarm, and communications systems. [*101*:11.3.3.4]

13.7.2.29.3 New High-Rise Buildings.

13.7.2.29.3.1* A fire alarm system using an approved emergency voice/alarm communication system shall be installed in accordance with Section 13.7 and NFPA *101*. [*101*:11.8.4.1]

13.7.2.29.3.2 Two-way telephone service shall be in accordance with 13.7.2.29.3.2.1 and 13.7.2.29.3.2.2. [*101*:11.8.4.2]

13.7.2.29.3.2.1 Two-way telephone communication service shall be provided for fire department use. [*101*:11.8.4.2.1]

13.7.2.29.3.2.1.1 The two-way telephone communication system shall be in accordance with NFPA *72*. [*101*:11.8.4.2.1.1]

13.7.2.29.3.2.1.2 The two-way telephone communication system shall operate between the emergency command center and every elevator car, every elevator lobby, and each floor level of exit stairs. [*101*:11.8.4.2.1.2]

13.7.2.29.3.2.2 The requirement of 13.7.2.29.3.2.1 shall not apply where the fire department radio system is approved as an equivalent system. [*101*:11.8.4.2.2]

13.7.2.29.3.2.3 Risk Analysis for Mass Notification Systems. For high-rise buildings with a total occupant load of 5000 or more persons, or where the floor of an occupiable story is greater than 420 ft (128 m) above the lowest level of fire department vehicle access, a risk analysis in accordance with

13.7.1.15 shall be performed to determine whether a mass notification system is required. [*101*:11.8.4.3]

13.7.2.30 Carbon Monoxide Detectors.

Δ **13.7.2.30.1*** Where carbon monoxide protection of a building is required, carbon monoxide detectors shall be installed in accordance with all of the following, unless a performance-based design in accordance with Section 17.3 of *NFPA 72* is used:

(1)* On the ceiling in the same room as permanently installed fuel-burning appliances
(2)* Centrally located on every habitable level and in every HVAC zone of the building
(3)* Outside of each separate dwelling unit, guest room, and guest suite sleeping area within 21 ft (6.4 m) of any door to a sleeping room, with the distance measured along a path of travel
(4)* Other locations where required by applicable laws, codes, or standards

[**72**:17.12.1]

13.7.2.30.2 Carbon monoxide detectors shall meet the following requirements:

(1) Carbon monoxide detectors shall be listed in accordance with applicable standards, such as UL 2075, *Gas and Vapor Detectors and Sensors*.
(2) Carbon monoxide detectors shall be set to respond to the sensitivity limits specified in UL 2034, *Single and Multiple Station Carbon Monoxide Alarms*.

[**72**:17.12.2]

13.7.2.30.3 All carbon monoxide detectors shall be located and mounted so that accidental operation will not be caused by jarring or vibration. [**72**:17.12.4]

13.7.2.30.4 The location of carbon monoxide detectors shall be based on an evaluation of potential ambient sources and flows of carbon monoxide, moisture, temperature, dust, or fumes and of electrical or mechanical influences to minimize nuisance alarms. [**72**:17.12.5]

13.7.2.30.5 The selection and placement of carbon monoxide detectors shall take into account both the performance characteristics of the detector and the areas into which the detectors are to be installed to prevent nuisance and unintentional alarms or improper operation after installation. [**72**:17.12.6]

13.7.2.30.6 Unless tested and listed for recessed mounting, carbon monoxide detectors shall not be recessed into the mounting surface. [**72**:17.12.7]

N **13.7.2.30.7*** Carbon monoxide detectors that are installed in air duct systems shall not be used as a substitute for open area protection. [**72**:17.12.3]

13.7.2.30.8 Protection During Construction.

13.7.2.30.8.1 Where detectors are installed for signal initiation during construction, they shall be replaced prior to the final commissioning of the system. [**72**:17.12.8.1]

13.7.2.30.8.2 Where detection is not required during construction, detectors shall not be installed until after all other construction trades have completed cleanup. [**72**:17.12.8.2]

13.7.2.30.9 Carbon Monoxide Detectors for Control of Carbon Monoxide Spread.

13.7.2.30.9.1 System designers shall consider the spread of carbon monoxide through an occupancy through the HVAC system. [**72**:17.12.9.1]

13.7.2.30.9.2 Interaction with smoke control systems, if such is provided, shall be coordinated. [**72**:17.12.9.2]

13.7.3 Fire Alarm Systems.

13.7.3.1 General.

13.7.3.1.1 Equipment.

13.7.3.1.1.1 Equipment constructed and installed in conformity with this *Code* shall be listed for the purpose for which it is used. [**72**:10.3.1]

13.7.3.1.1.2 System components shall be installed, tested, inspected, and maintained in accordance with the manufacturer's published instructions and this *Code*. [**72**:10.3.2]

13.7.3.1.1.3* All devices and appliances that receive their power from the initiating device circuit (IDC) or signaling line circuit (SLC) of a control unit shall be listed for use with the control unit. [**72**:10.3.3]

13.7.3.1.1.4 All apparatus requiring rewinding or resetting to maintain normal operation shall be restored to normal after each abnormal condition. [**72**:10.3.4]

13.7.3.2 Documentation and Notification.

13.7.3.2.1 Approval and Acceptance. The AHJ shall be notified prior to installation or alteration of equipment or wiring. [**72**:10.20.2]

13.7.3.2.2 Minimum Required Documentation.

Δ **13.7.3.2.2.1** Where documentation is required by the authority having jurisdiction, the following list shall represent the minimum documentation required for new systems and additions or alterations to existing systems:

(1)* Written narrative providing intent and system description
(2) Riser diagram
(3) Floor plan layout showing locations of all devices, control equipment, and supervising station and shared communications equipment with each sheet showing the following:
  (a) Point of compass (north arrow)
  (b) A graphic representation of the scale used
  (c) Room use identification
  (d) Building features that will affect the placement of initiating devices and notification appliances
(4) Sequence of operation in either an input/output matrix or narrative form
(5) Equipment technical data sheets
(6) Manufacturers' published instructions, including operation and maintenance instructions
(7) Battery capacity and safety margin calculations (where batteries are provided)
(8) Voltage drop calculations for notification appliance circuits
(9) Mounting height elevation for wall-mounted devices and appliances

(10) Where occupant notification is required, minimum sound pressure levels that must be produced by the audible notification appliances in applicable covered areas
(11) Locations of alarm notification appliances, including candela ratings for visual alarm notification appliances
(12)* Pathway diagrams between the control unit and shared communications equipment within the protected premises
(13) Completed record of completion in accordance with 13.7.3.2.3.6 and 13.7.3.2.6.2
(14) For software-based systems, a copy of site-specific software, including specific instructions on how to obtain the means of system and software access (password)
(15) Record (as-built) drawings
(16) Records, record retention, and record maintenance in accordance with Section 7.7 of *NFPA 72*
(17) Completed record of inspection and testing in accordance with 13.7.3.2.4.6 and 13.7.3.2.6.2

[**72:**7.2.1]

13.7.3.2.2.2 System design documents shall identify the name and contact information of the system designer. [**72:**7.2.2]

13.7.3.2.2.3 All fire alarm drawings shall use symbols described in NFPA 170 or other symbols acceptable to the authority having jurisdiction. [**72:**7.2.3]

13.7.3.2.3 Completion Documentation.

13.7.3.2.3.1 The requirements of 13.7.3.2.3 shall apply only where required by other governing laws, codes, or standards; by other parts of *NFPA 72*; or by project specifications or drawings. [**72:**7.5.1]

13.7.3.2.3.2 Before requesting final approval of the installation, if required by the AHJ, the installing contractor shall furnish a written statement stating that the system has been installed in accordance with approved plans and tested in accordance with the manufacturer's published instructions and the appropriate NFPA requirements. [**72:**7.5.2]

Δ **13.7.3.2.3.3** All systems, including new systems and additions or alterations to existing systems, shall include the following documentation:

(1) An owner's manual and manufacturer's published instructions covering all system equipment
(2) Record (as-built) drawings in accordance with 13.7.3.2.3.5
(3) A completed record of completion form in accordance with 13.7.3.2.3.6
(4) For software-based systems, record copy of the site-specific software in accordance with 13.7.3.2.3.7

[**72:**7.5.3.1]

13.7.3.2.3.4 For new emergency communications systems, an owner's manual shall be provided and shall contain the following documentation:

(1) Detailed narrative description of the system inputs, evacuation signaling, ancillary functions, annunciation, intended sequence of operations, expansion capability, application considerations, and limitations
(2) Written sequence of operation for the system including an operational input/output matrix
(3) Operator instructions for basic system operations, including alarm acknowledgment, system reset, interpretation of system output (LEDs, CRT display, and printout), operation of manual evacuation signaling and ancillary function controls, and change of printer paper
(4) Detailed description of routine maintenance and testing as required and recommended and as would be provided under a maintenance contract, including testing and maintenance instructions for each type of device installed, which includes the following:
  (a) Listing of the individual system components that require periodic testing and maintenance
  (b) Step-by-step instructions detailing the requisite testing and maintenance procedures, and the intervals at which those procedures shall be performed, for each type of device installed
  (c) Schedule that correlates the testing and maintenance procedures that are required by this section
(5) Service directory, including a list of names and telephone numbers of those who provide service for the system
(6) Product data sheets for all system equipment

[**72:**7.5.4]

13.7.3.2.3.5 Record Drawings (As-Builts).

13.7.3.2.3.5.1 Record drawings shall consist of current updated shop drawings reflecting the actual installation of all system equipment, components, and wiring. [**72:**7.5.5.1]

13.7.3.2.3.5.2 A sequence of operations in input/output matrix or narrative form shall be provided with the record drawings to reflect actual programming at the time of completion. [**72:**7.5.5.2]

13.7.3.2.3.5.3 Where necessary, revised calculations in accordance with 7.4.10 of *NFPA 72* shall be provided depicting any changes due to installation conditions. [**72:**7.5.5.3]

13.7.3.2.3.5.4 Record drawings shall be turned over to the owner with a copy placed inside the documentation cabinet in accordance with Section 7.7 of *NFPA 72*. [**72:**7.5.5.4]

13.7.3.2.3.5.5 Record drawings shall include approval documentation resulting from variances, performance-based designs, risk analyses, and other system evaluations or variations. [**72:**7.5.5.5]

13.7.3.2.3.6 Record of Completion.

13.7.3.2.3.6.1 The record of completion shall be documented in accordance with 13.7.3.2.3.6 using either the record of completion forms, Figure 7.8.2(a) through Figure 7.8.2(f) of *NFPA 72*, or an alternative document that contains only the elements of Figure 7.8.2(a) through Figure 7.8.2(f) of *NFPA 72* applicable to the installed system. [**72:**7.5.6.1]

13.7.3.2.3.6.2 The record of completion documentation shall be completed by the installing contractor and submitted to the authority having jurisdiction and the owner at the conclusion of the job. The record of completion documentation shall be permitted to be part of the written statement required in 13.7.3.2.3.2 and part of the documents that support the requirements of 13.7.3.2.3.8. When more than one contractor has been responsible for the installation, each contractor shall complete the portions of the documentation for which that contractor has responsibility. [**72:**7.5.6.2]

13.7.3.2.3.6.3 The preparation of the record of completion documentation shall be the responsibility of the qualified and experienced person in accordance with 10.5.2 of *NFPA 72*. [**72:**7.5.6.3]

13.7.3.2.3.6.4 The record of completion documentation shall be updated in accordance with 13.7.3.2.3.6.6 to reflect all system additions or modifications. [**72:**7.5.6.4]

13.7.3.2.3.6.5 The updated copy of the record of completion documents shall be maintained in a documentation cabinet in accordance with 7.7.2 of *NFPA 72*. [**72:**7.5.6.5]

13.7.3.2.3.6.6 Revisions.

13.7.3.2.3.6.6.1 All modifications made after the initial installation shall be recorded on a revised version of the original completion documents, which shall serve as a supplement to the original, unaltered completion documents. [**72:**7.5.6.6.1]

13.7.3.2.3.6.6.2 The revised record of completion document shall include a revision date. [**72:**7.5.6.6.2]

13.7.3.2.3.6.6.3* Where the original or the latest overall system record of completion cannot be obtained, a new system record of completion shall be provided that documents the system configuration as discovered during the current project's scope of work. [**72:**7.5.6.6.3]

13.7.3.2.3.6.7 Electronic Record of Completion.

13.7.3.2.3.6.7.1 Where approved by the AHJ, the record of completion shall be permitted to be filed electronically instead of on paper. [**72:**7.5.6.7.1]

13.7.3.2.3.6.7.2 If filed electronically, the record of completion document shall be accessible with standard software and shall be backed up. [**72:**7.5.6.7.2]

13.7.3.2.3.7 Site-Specific Software.

13.7.3.2.3.7.1 For software-based systems, a copy of the site-specific software shall be provided to the system owner or owner's designated representative. [**72:**7.5.7.1]

13.7.3.2.3.7.1.1 The site-specific software documentation shall include both the user passcode and either the system programming password or specific instructions on how to obtain the programming password from the system manufacturer. [**72:**7.5.7.1.2]

13.7.3.2.3.7.1.2 The passwords provided shall enable currently certified qualified programming personnel to access, edit, modify, and add to the existing system's site-specific software. [**72:**7.5.7.1.3]

Δ **13.7.3.2.3.7.2** A copy of the site-specific software shall be stored on-site in nonvolatile memory. [**72:**7.5.7.2]

13.7.3.2.3.8* Verification of Compliant Installation.

13.7.3.2.3.8.1 Where required by the AHJ, compliance of the completed installation with the requirements of *NFPA 72* shall be certified by a qualified and impartial third-party organization acceptable to the AHJ. [**72:**7.5.8.1]

13.7.3.2.3.8.2 Verification of compliant installation shall be performed according to testing requirements and procedures specified in 14.4.1 and 14.4.2 of *NFPA 72*. [**72:**7.5.8.2]

13.7.3.2.3.8.3 Verification shall ensure that:

(1) All components and functions are installed and operate per the approved plans and sequence of operation.
(2) All required system documentation is complete and is archived on site.
(3) For new supervising station systems, the verification shall also ascertain proper arrangement, transmission, and receipt of all signals required to be transmitted off-premises and shall meet the requirements of 14.4.1 and 14.4.2 of *NFPA 72*.
(4) For existing supervising station systems that are extended, modified, or reconfigured, the verification shall be required for the new work only, and reacceptance testing in accordance with Chapter 14 of *NFPA 72* shall be acceptable.
(5) Written confirmation has been provided that any required corrective actions have been completed

[**72:**7.5.8.3]

13.7.3.2.3.9 Documentation of central station service shall be in accordance with 26.3.4 of *NFPA 72*. [**72:**7.5.9]

13.7.3.2.3.10 Documentation of remote station service shall be in accordance with 26.5.2 of *NFPA 72*. [**72:**7.5.10]

13.7.3.2.4 Inspection, Testing, and Maintenance Documentation.

13.7.3.2.4.1 Test plan documentation shall be provided in accordance with 14.2.10 of *NFPA 72*. [**72:**7.6.1]

13.7.3.2.4.2 Acceptance testing documentation shall be provided in accordance with 14.6.1 of *NFPA 72*. [**72:**7.6.2]

13.7.3.2.4.3 Reacceptance test documentation shall be provided in accordance with 14.6.1 of *NFPA 72*. [**72:**7.6.3]

13.7.3.2.4.4 Periodic inspection and testing documentation shall be provided in accordance with 14.6.2 through 14.6.4 of *NFPA 72*. [**72:**7.6.4]

13.7.3.2.4.5 Impairment documentation shall be provided in accordance with Section 10.20 of *NFPA 72*. [**72:**7.6.5]

13.7.3.2.4.6 Record of Inspection and Testing. The record of all inspections, testing, and maintenance as required by 14.6.2.4 of *NFPA 72* shall be documented using either the record of inspection and testing forms, Figure 7.8.2(g) through Figure 7.8.2(l) of *NFPA 72*, or an alternative record that includes all the applicable information shown in Figure 7.8.2(g) through Figure 7.8.2(l) of *NFPA 72*. [**72:**7.6.6]

13.7.3.2.5 Records, Record Retention, and Record Maintenance.

13.7.3.2.5.1 Records.

13.7.3.2.5.1.1 A complete record of the tests and operations of each system shall be kept until the next test and for 1 year thereafter unless more stringent requirements are required elsewhere in *NFPA 72*. [**72:**7.7.1.1]

13.7.3.2.5.1.2* The records shall be available for examination and, if required, reported to the authority having jurisdiction. Archiving of records by any means shall be permitted if hard copies of the records can be provided promptly when requested. [**72:**7.7.1.2]

13.7.3.2.5.1.3 If off-premises monitoring is provided, records of all signals, tests, and operations recorded at the supervising station, including the public emergency alarm reporting system, shall be maintained by the off-premise monitoring service provider for not less than 1 year unless more stringent requirements are required elsewhere in *NFPA 72*. [**72:**7.7.1.3]

13.7.3.2.5.1.4 Required documents regarding system design and function shall be maintained for the life of the system. [**72:**7.7.1.4]

13.7.3.2.5.1.5 The emergency communications system and fire alarm system as-built plans and other related documentation shall be permitted to be maintained together, including the appearance of both systems on the same drawings. [**72:**7.7.1.5]

13.7.3.2.5.1.6 Revisions and alterations to systems shall be recorded and records maintained with the original system design documents. [**72:**7.7.1.6]

13.7.3.2.5.2 Document Accessibility.

13.7.3.2.5.2.1 With every new system, a documentation cabinet shall be installed at the system control unit or at another approved location at the protected premises. [**72:**7.7.2.1]

13.7.3.2.5.2.2 The documentation cabinet shall be sized so that it can contain all necessary documentation. [**72:**7.7.2.2]

13.7.3.2.5.2.3* All record documentation shall be stored in the documentation cabinet. No record documentation shall be stored in the control unit. [**72:**7.7.2.3]

13.7.3.2.5.2.4 Where the documentation cabinet is not in the same location as the system control unit, its location shall be identified at the system control unit. [**72:**7.7.2.4]

13.7.3.2.5.2.5 The documentation cabinet shall be prominently labeled SYSTEM RECORD DOCUMENTS. [**72:**7.7.2.5]

13.7.3.2.5.2.6* The building owner or the building owner's representative shall, on an annual basis, review any electronic documentation media formats and associated interfacing hardware for compatibility and update, if necessary. [**72:**7.7.2.6]

13.7.3.2.5.2.7 The contents of the cabinet shall be accessible by authorized personnel only. [**72:**7.7.2.7]

13.7.3.2.5.2.8 Emergency communications system and fire alarm system record documentation shall be permitted to be maintained together in the same documentation cabinet. [**72:**7.7.2.8]

13.7.3.2.5.3 Document Security.

13.7.3.2.5.3.1 Security for system's documentation shall be determined by the stakeholders. [**72:**7.7.3.1]

13.7.3.2.5.3.2* Where such documents cannot be protected from public access, it shall be permitted to remove sensitive information from record documents provided the owner retains complete documentation that will be made accessible to the authority having jurisdiction at an owner designated location. [**72:**7.7.3.2]

13.7.3.2.6 Forms.

13.7.3.2.6.1 General.

13.7.3.2.6.1.1 The requirements of 13.7.3.2.6 shall apply only where required by other governing laws, codes, or standards; by other parts of this *Code*, or by project specifications or drawings. [**72:**7.8.1.1]

13.7.3.2.6.1.2 Where specific forms are required by other governing laws, codes, or standards; by other parts of *NFPA 72*; or by project specifications or drawings, form layouts and content that differ from those in 13.7.3.2.6 shall be permitted provided that the minimum required content is included. [**72:**7.8.1.2]

13.7.3.2.6.2 Forms for Documentation. Forms for documentation shall comply with Section 7.8.2 of NFPA 72.

13.7.3.3 Manually Actuated Alarm-Initiating Devices.

13.7.3.3.1 Manually actuated alarm-initiating devices shall be listed in accordance with applicable standards such as UL 38, *Manual Signaling Boxes for Fire Alarm Systems*. [**72:**17.15.1]

13.7.3.3.2 Manually actuated alarm-initiating devices for initiating signals other than for fire alarm shall be permitted if the devices are differentiated from manual fire alarm boxes by a color other than red and labeling. [**72:**17.15.2]

13.7.3.3.3 Combination manual fire alarm boxes and guard's signaling stations shall be permitted. [**72:**17.15.3]

13.7.3.3.4 Manually actuated alarm-initiating devices shall be securely mounted. [**72:**17.15.4]

13.7.3.3.5 Manually actuated alarm-initiating devices shall be mounted on a background of contrasting color. [**72:**17.15.5]

13.7.3.3.6 The operable part of a manually actuated alarm-initiating device shall be not less than 42 in. (1.07 m) and not more than 48 in. (1.22 m) from the finished floor. [**72:**17.15.6]

13.7.3.3.7 Manually actuated alarm-initiating devices shall be permitted to be single action or double action. [**72:**17.15.7]

13.7.3.3.8* Listed protective covers shall be permitted to be installed over single- or double-action manually actuated alarm-initiating devices. [**72:**17.15.8]

13.7.3.3.9 Manual fire alarm boxes shall comply with 13.7.3.3.9.1 through 13.7.3.3.9.6. [**72:**17.15.9]

13.7.3.3.9.1 Manual fire alarm boxes shall be used only for fire alarm initiating purposes. [**72:**17.15.9.1]

13.7.3.3.9.2 Manual fire alarm boxes shall be installed so that they are conspicuous, unobstructed, and accessible. [**72:**17.15.9.2]

13.7.3.3.9.3* Unless installed in an environment that precludes the use of red paint or red plastic, manual fire alarm boxes shall be red in color. [**72:**17.15.9.3]

13.7.3.3.9.4 Manual fire alarm boxes shall be located within 5 ft (1.5 m) of each exit doorway on each floor. [**72:**17.15.9.4]

13.7.3.3.9.5* Additional manual fire alarm boxes shall be provided so that the travel distance to the nearest manual fire alarm box will not exceed 200 ft (61 m), measured horizontally on the same floor. [**72:**17.15.9.5]

13.7.3.3.9.6 Manual fire alarm boxes shall be mounted on both sides of grouped openings over 40 ft (12.2 m) in width, and within 5 ft (1.5 m) of each side of the grouped opening. [**72:**17.15.9.6]

13.7.3.3.10 When fire alarm systems are not monitored, an approved permanent sign shall be installed adjacent to each manual fire alarm box. The sign shall read as follows:

> Local alarm only:
>
> (1) Activate alarm
>
> (2) Exit building
>
> (3) Call fire department

13.7.3.4* Indication of Central Station Service. The prime contractor shall conspicuously indicate that the alarm system providing service at a protected premises complies with all the requirements of this *Code* through the use of a systematic follow-up program under the control of the organization that has listed the prime contractor. [**72**:26.3.4]

13.7.3.4.1 Documentation indicating *Code* compliance of the alarm system shall be issued by the organization that has listed the prime contractor. [**72**:26.3.4.1]

13.7.3.4.2 The documentation shall include, at a minimum, the following information:

(1) Name of the prime contractor involved with the ongoing *Code* compliance of the central station service
(2)* Full description of the alarm system as installed
(3) Issue and expiration dates of the documentation
(4) Name, address, and contact information of the organization issuing the document
(5) Identification of the AHJ(s) for the central station service installation

[**72**:26.3.4.2]

13.7.3.4.3 The documentation shall be physically posted within 3 ft (1 m) of the control unit, and copies of the documentation shall be made available to the AHJ(s) upon request. [**72**:26.3.4.3]

13.7.3.4.4 A central repository of issued documentation, accessible to the AHJ, shall be maintained by the organization that has listed the prime contractor. [**72**:26.3.4.4]

13.7.3.4.5* Alarm system service that does not comply with all the requirements of Section 26.3 of *NFPA 72* shall not be designated as central station service. [**72**:26.3.4.5]

13.7.3.4.6* For the purpose of Section 26.3 of *NFPA 72*, the subscriber shall notify the prime contractor, in writing, of the identity of the authority(ies) having jurisdiction. [**72**:26.3.4.6]

13.7.3.4.7 The AHJ(s) identified in 13.7.3.4.2(5) shall be notified within 30 calendar days of the expiration or cancellation by the organization that has listed the prime contractor. [**72**:26.3.4.7]

13.7.3.4.8 The subscriber shall surrender expired or canceled documentation to the prime contractor within 30 days of the termination date. [**72**:26.3.4.8]

13.7.3.5 Automatic Fire Detection and Alarm Service.

13.7.3.5.1 Automatic fire detectors shall be located, maintained, and tested in accordance with *NFPA 72*.

13.7.4 Automatic Fire Detectors.

13.7.4.1 General Requirements.

13.7.4.1.1 The requirements of 13.7.4.1.1 through 13.7.4.1.4 shall apply to all initiating devices. [**72**:17.4.1]

13.7.4.1.2 Mechanical Protection.

13.7.4.1.2.1 Initiating devices subject to mechanical damage shall be protected. [**72**:17.4.2.1]

13.7.4.1.2.2 If guards or covers are employed, they shall be listed for use with the initiating device. [**72**:17.4.2.2]

13.7.4.1.2.3* The protection shall not prevent the initiating device from achieving the objectives of the system by adversely affecting the use, operation, or performance of the initiating device. [**72**:17.4.2.3]

13.7.4.1.3 Initiating devices shall be installed in a manner that provides accessibility for periodic inspection, testing, and maintenance. [**72**:17.4.3]

13.7.4.1.4 Initiating devices shall be supported independently of their attachment to the circuit conductors. [**72**:17.4.4]

13.7.4.1.5 Duct Detector Installation.

13.7.4.1.5.1 Smoke detectors shall be installed, tested, and maintained in accordance with *NFPA 72*. [**90A**:11.4.4.1]

13.7.4.1.5.2 In addition to the requirements of 11.4.3 of NFPA 90A where an approved fire alarm system is installed in a building, the smoke detectors required by the provisions of Section 11.4 of NFPA 90A shall be connected to the fire alarm system in accordance with the requirements of *NFPA 72*. [**90A**:11.4.4.2]

13.7.4.1.5.2.1 Smoke detectors used solely for closing dampers or for heating, ventilating, and air-conditioning system shutdown shall not be required to activate the building evacuation alarm. [**90A**:11.4.4.2.1]

13.7.4.1.5.3 Where smoke detectors required by Section 11.4 of NFPA 90A are installed in a building not equipped with an approved fire alarm system as specified by 13.7.4.1.5.2, the following shall occur:

(1) Smoke detector activation required by Section 11.4 of NFPA 90A shall cause a visual signal and an audible signal in a normally occupied area.
(2) Smoke detector trouble conditions shall be indicated visually or audibly in a normally occupied area and shall be identified as air duct detector trouble.

[**90A**:11.4.4.3]

13.7.4.1.5.4 Smoke detectors powered separately from the fire alarm system for the sole function of stopping fans shall not require standby power. [**90A**:11.4.4.4]

13.7.4.2 Requirements for Smoke and Heat Detectors.

13.7.4.2.1 Recessed Mounting. Unless tested and listed for recessed mounting, detectors shall not be recessed into the mounting surface. [**72**:17.5.1]

13.7.4.2.2* Partitions. Where partitions extend to within 15 percent of the ceiling height, the spaces separated by the partitions shall be considered as separate rooms. [**72:**17.5.2]

13.7.4.3 Location.

13.7.4.3.1* Unless otherwise modified by 17.6.3.2.2, 17.6.3.3.2, or 17.6.3.7 of *NFPA 72*, spot-type heat-sensing fire detectors shall be located on the ceiling not less than 4 in. (100 mm) from the sidewall or on the sidewalls between 4 in. and 12 in. (100 mm and 300 mm) from the ceiling. [**72:**17.6.3.1.3.1]

13.7.4.3.2 Unless otherwise modified by 17.6.3.2.2, 17.6.3.3.2, or 17.6.3.7 of *NFPA 72*, line-type heat detectors shall be located on the ceiling or on the sidewalls not more than 20 in. (510 mm) from the ceiling. [**72:**17.6.3.1.3.2]

13.7.4.3.3* Spot-Type Smoke Detectors.

13.7.4.3.3.1* Spot-type smoke detectors shall be located on the ceiling or, if on a sidewall, between the ceiling and 12 in. (300 mm) down from the ceiling to the top of the detector. [**72:**17.7.4.2.1]

13.7.4.3.3.2* To minimize dust contamination, smoke detectors, where installed under raised floors, shall be mounted only in an orientation for which they have been listed. [**72:**17.7.4.2.2]

13.7.4.3.3.3 On smooth ceilings, spacing for spot-type smoke detectors shall be in accordance with 13.7.4.3.3.3.1 through 13.7.4.3.3.3.4. [**72:**17.7.4.2.3]

13.7.4.3.3.3.1* In the absence of specific performance-based design criteria, one of the following requirements shall apply:

(1) The distance between smoke detectors shall not exceed a nominal spacing of 30 ft (9.1 m) and there shall be detectors within a distance of one-half the nominal spacing, measured at right angles from all walls or partitions extending upward to within the top 15 percent of the ceiling height.
(2)* All points on the ceiling shall have a detector within a distance equal to or less than 0.7 times the nominal 30 ft (9.1 m) spacing (0.7 S).
[**72:**17.7.4.2.3.1]

13.7.4.3.3.3.2 In all cases, the manufacturer's published instructions shall be followed. [**72:**17.7.4.2.3.2]

13.7.4.3.3.3.3 Other spacing shall be permitted to be used depending on ceiling height, different conditions, or response requirements. [**72:**17.7.4.2.3.3]

13.7.4.3.3.3.4 For the detection of flaming fires, the guidelines in Annex B of *NFPA 72* shall be permitted to be used. [**72:**17.7.4.2.3.4]

13.7.4.3.3.4* For solid joist and beam construction, spacing for spot-type smoke detectors shall be in accordance with 13.7.4.3.3.4.1 through 13.7.4.3.3.4.5. [**72:**17.7.4.2.4]

13.7.4.3.3.4.1 Solid joists shall be considered equivalent to beams for smoke detector spacing guidelines. [**72:**17.7.4.2.4.1]

13.7.4.3.3.4.2 For level ceilings, the following shall apply:

(1) For ceilings with beam depths of less than 10 percent of the ceiling height (0.1 H), the following shall apply:

　(a) Smooth ceiling spacing shall be permitted.

　(b) Spot-type smoke detectors shall be permitted to be located on ceilings or on the bottom of beams.

(2) For ceilings with beam depths equal to or greater than 10 percent of the ceiling height (0.1 H), the following shall apply:

　(a) Where beam spacing is equal to or greater than 40 percent of the ceiling height (0.4 H), spot-type detectors shall be located on the ceiling in each beam pocket.

　(b) Where beam spacing is less than 40 percent of the ceiling height (0.4 H), the following shall be permitted for spot detectors:

　　i. Smooth ceiling spacing in the direction parallel to the beams and at one-half smooth ceiling spacing in the direction perpendicular to the beams

　　ii. Location of detectors either on the ceiling or on the bottom of the beams

(3)* For beam pockets formed by intersecting beams, including waffle or pan-type ceilings, the following shall apply:

　(a) For beam depths less than 10 percent of the ceiling height (0.1 H), spacing shall be in accordance with 13.7.4.3.3.4.2(1).

　(b) For beam depths greater than or equal to 10 percent of the ceiling height (0.1 H), spacing shall be in accordance with 13.7.4.3.3.4.2(2)(b).

(4)* For corridors 15 ft (4.6 m) in width or less having ceiling beams or solid joists perpendicular to the corridor length, the following shall apply:

　(a) Smooth ceiling spacing shall be permitted.

　(b) Location of spot-type smoke detectors shall be permitted on ceilings, sidewalls, or the bottom of beams or solid joists.

(5) For rooms of 900 ft² (84 m²) or less, the following shall apply:

　(a) Use of smooth ceiling spacing shall be permitted.

　(b) Location of spot-type smoke detectors shall be permitted on ceilings or on the bottom of beams

[**72:**17.7.4.2.4.2]

13.7.4.3.3.4.3* For sloping ceilings with beams running parallel up slope, the following shall apply:

(1) Spot-type detector(s) shall be located on the ceiling within beam pocket(s).
(2) The ceiling height shall be taken as the average height over slope.
(3) Spacing shall be measured along a horizontal projection of the ceiling.
(4) Smooth ceiling spacing shall be permitted within beam pocket(s) parallel to the beams.
(5) For beam depths less than or equal to 10 percent of the ceiling height (0.1 H), spot-type detectors shall be located with smooth ceiling spacing perpendicular to the beams.
(6) For beam depths greater than 10 percent of the ceiling height (0.1 H), the following shall apply for spacing perpendicular to the beams:

　(a) For beam spacing greater than or equal to 40 percent of the ceiling height (0.4 H), spot-type detectors shall be located in each beam pocket.

　(b) For beam spacing less than 40 percent of the ceiling height (0.4 H), spot-type detectors shall not be required in every beam pocket but shall be spaced not greater than 50 percent of smooth ceiling spacing. [**72:**17.7.4.2.4.3]

13.7.4.3.3.4.4* For sloping ceilings with beams running perpendicular across slope, the following shall apply:

(1) Spot-type detector(s) shall be located at the bottom of the beams.
(2) The ceiling height shall be taken as the average height over slope.
(3) Spacing shall be measured along a horizontal projection of the ceiling.
(4) Smooth ceiling spacing shall be permitted within beam pocket(s).
(5) For beam depths less than or equal to 10 percent of the ceiling height (0.1 H), spot-type detectors shall be located with smooth ceiling spacing.
(6) For beam depths greater than 10 percent of the ceiling height (0.1 H), spot-type detectors shall not be required to be located closer than (0.4 H) and shall not exceed 50 percent of smooth ceiling spacing.

[**72:**17.7.4.2.4.4]

13.7.4.3.3.4.5* For sloped ceilings with beam pockets formed by intersecting beams, the following shall apply:

(1) Spot-type detector(s) shall be located at the bottom of the beams.
(2) The ceiling height shall be taken as the average height over slope.
(3) Spacing shall be measured along a horizontal projection of the ceiling.
(4) For beam depths less than or equal to 10 percent of the ceiling height (0.1 H), spot-type detectors shall be spaced with not more than three beams between detectors and shall not exceed smooth ceiling spacing.
(5) For beam depths greater than 10 percent of the ceiling height (0.1 H), spot-type detectors shall be spaced with not more than two beams between detectors, but shall not be required to be spaced closer than (0.4 H), and shall not exceed 50 percent of smooth ceiling spacing.

[**72:**17.7.4.2.4.5]

13.7.4.3.3.4.6 For sloped ceilings with solid joists, the detectors shall be located on the bottom of the joist. [**72:**17.7.4.2.4.6]

13.7.4.3.4 Air Sampling–Type Smoke Detector.

13.7.4.3.4.1 General.

13.7.4.3.4.1.1 In the absence of specific performance-based design criteria, each sampling port of an air sampling–type smoke detector shall be treated as a spot-type detector for the purpose of location and spacing in accordance with 17.7.4 of *NFPA 72*. [**72:**17.7.4.6.1.1]

13.7.4.3.4.1.2 Air sampling–type smoke detectors shall produce trouble signals if the airflow is outside the manufacturer's specified range. [**72:**17.7.4.6.1.2]

13.7.4.3.4.1.3 If provided, atmospheric contaminant filtration shall be listed for use with the detector and installed and maintained in accordance with the air sampling–type smoke detector manufacturer's published instructions. [**72:**17.7.4.6.1.3]

13.7.4.3.4.2 Pipe Network.

13.7.4.3.4.2.1 Maximum air sample transport time from the farthest sampling port to the detector shall not exceed 120 seconds. [**72:**17.7.4.6.2.1]

13.7.4.3.4.2.2 Sampling pipe networks shall be designed on the basis of, and shall be supported by, computer-based fluid dynamics design calculations to ensure required performance. [**72:**17.7.4.6.2.2]

13.7.4.3.4.2.3 The sampling pipe network design calculations shall include pressure, volumetric flow, and alarm sensitivity at each sampling port. [**72:**17.7.4.6.2.3]

13.7.4.3.4.2.4 Software applications for the design of pipe networks shall be listed for use with the manufacturer's equipment. [**72:**17.7.4.6.2.4]

13.7.4.3.4.2.5 Sampling system piping shall be conspicuously identified as "SMOKE DETECTOR SAMPLING TUBE — DO NOT DISTURB," as follows:

(1) At changes in direction or branches of piping
(2) At each side of penetrations of walls, floors, or other barriers
(3) At intervals on piping that provide visibility within the space, but no greater than 20 ft (6.1 m)

[**72:**17.7.4.6.2.5]

13.7.4.3.4.2.6* Sampling ports shall be identified as such. [**72:**17.7.4.6.2.6]

13.7.4.3.4.2.7* If provided, test ports at the end (most remote location) of a pipe run installed in the pipe network solely for the purpose of validating consistency in performance (also referred to as benchmark test points) shall be included in the design calculations and allowed, but not required, to comply with the requirements of 13.7.4.3.4.2. [**72:**17.7.4.6.2.7]

13.7.4.3.4.2.8 If the piping and fittings are painted, the painting shall be performed in accordance with the air sampling–type smoke detector manufacturer's published instructions. [**72:**17.7.4.6.2.8]

13.7.4.3.4.2.9* Pipe network materials, sizing, and installation shall be in accordance with the manufacturer's published requirements and suitable for use in the environment in which they are installed. [**72:**17.7.4.6.2.9]

13.7.4.3.4.2.10 Where used, capillary tubing shall be sized and affixed in accordance with the manufacturer's published instructions and computer-based design calculations. [**72:**17.7.4.6.2.10]

13.7.4.3.5* Projected Beam–Type Smoke Detectors.

13.7.4.3.5.1 Projected beam–type smoke detectors shall be located in accordance with the manufacturer's published instructions. [**72:**17.7.4.7.1]

13.7.4.3.5.2 The effects of stratification shall be evaluated when locating the detectors. [**72:**17.7.4.7.2]

13.7.4.3.5.3 The beam length shall not exceed the maximum permitted by the equipment listing. [**72:**17.7.4.7.3]

13.7.4.3.5.4 If reflectors are used with projected beams, the reflectors shall be installed in accordance with the manufacturer's published instructions. [**72:**17.7.4.7.4]

13.7.4.3.5.5 A projected beam–type smoke detector shall be considered equivalent to a row of spot-type smoke detectors for level and sloping ceiling applications. [72:17.7.4.7.5]

13.7.4.3.5.6 Projected beam–type detectors and reflectors shall be mounted on stable surfaces to prevent false or erratic operation due to movement. [72:17.7.4.7.6]

13.7.4.3.5.7 The beam shall be designed so that small angular movements of the light source or receiver do not prevent operation due to smoke and do not cause nuisance or unintentional alarms. [72:17.7.4.7.7]

13.7.4.3.5.8* Unless otherwise permitted by 13.7.4.1.2.2, the design and installation of projected beam-type detectors shall address the potential for the obstruction of the light path. [72:17.7.4.7.8]

13.7.4.3.6* Protection During Construction.

13.7.4.3.6.1 Where detectors are installed for signal initiation during construction, they shall be cleaned and verified to be operating in accordance with the listed sensitivity, or they shall be replaced prior to the final acceptance test of the system. [72:17.7.2.1]

13.7.4.3.6.2 Where detectors are installed but not operational during construction, they shall be protected from construction debris, dust, dirt, and damage in accordance with the manufacturer's recommendations and verified to be operating in accordance with the listed sensitivity, or they shall be replaced prior to the final acceptance test of the system. [72:17.7.2.2]

13.7.4.3.6.3 Where detection is not required during construction, detectors shall not be installed until after all other construction trades have completed cleanup. [72:17.7.2.3]

Δ 13.7.4.3.7 Ceiling Tiles and Ceiling Assemblies. Where automatic detectors are installed in accordance with *NFPA 72*, ceilings necessary for the proper actuation of the fire protection device shall be maintained.

13.7.4.3.8 High Air Movement Areas.

13.7.4.3.8.1 Location. Smoke detectors shall not be located directly in the airstream of supply registers. [72:17.7.7.3.2]

13.7.4.3.8.2* Spacing.

13.7.4.3.8.2.1 Smoke detector spacing shall be reduced where the airflow in a defined space exceeds 8 minutes per air change (total space volume) (equal to 7.5 air changes per hour). [72:17.7.7.3.3.1]

13.7.4.3.8.2.2 Where spacing must be adjusted for airflow, spot-type smoke detector spacing shall be adjusted in accordance with Table 13.7.4.3.8.2.2 or Figure 13.7.4.3.8.2.2 before making any other spacing adjustments required by this *Code*. [72:17.7.7.3.3.2]

13.7.4.3.8.2.3 Air-sampling or projected beam smoke detectors shall be installed in accordance with the manufacturer's published instructions. [72:17.7.7.3.3.3]

13.7.4.4 Inspection, Testing, and Maintenance. The inspection, testing, and maintenance for fire alarm and fire detection systems shall be in accordance with *NFPA 72*.

Δ Table 13.7.4.3.8.2.2 Smoke Detector Spacing Based on Air Movement (Not to Be Used for Under-Floor or Above-Ceiling Spaces)

Minutes per Air Change	Air Changes per Hour	Spacing per Detector ft^2	Spacing per Detector m^2
1	60	125	12
2	30	250	23
3	20	375	35
4	15	500	46
5	12	625	58
6	10	750	70
7	8.6	875	81
8	7.5	900	84
9	6.7	900	84
10	6	900	84

[72:Table 17.7.7.3.3.2]

Δ **FIGURE 13.7.4.3.8.2.2** High Air Movement Areas (Not to Be Used for Under-Floor or Above-Ceiling Spaces). [72:Figure 17.7.7.3.3.2]

13.8 Other Fire Protection Systems.

13.8.1 Where other fire protection systems are required to be installed by the provisions of this *Code*, or are installed with the approval of the AHJ as an alternative or equivalency, the design and installation of the system shall comply with the appropriate standards listed in Table 13.8.1.

13.8.2 Other fire protection systems permitted by 13.8.1 shall be tested and maintained in accordance with 4.5.8.

13.9 Non-Listed Fire Protection or Suppression Devices and Equipment.

13.9.1 It shall be unlawful to market, sell, advertise, or distribute any device or equipment as suitable for fire protection or fire suppression purposes unless the device or equipment is listed for such purpose by a nationally recognized testing laboratory or as otherwise permitted by 13.9.2.

Δ **Table 13.8.1 Other Required Fire Protection Systems**

Type of System	NFPA Standard
Low-, medium-, and high-expansion foam systems	NFPA 11
Carbon dioxide systems	NFPA 12
Halon 1301 systems	NFPA 12A
Sprinklers in one- and two-family dwellings and manufactured homes	NFPA 13D
Sprinklers in residential occupancies up to and including four stories in height	NFPA 13R
Water spray systems	NFPA 15
Dry-chemical extinguishing systems	NFPA 17
Wet-chemical extinguishing systems	NFPA 17A
Water mist systems	NFPA 750
Hybrid (water and inert gas) fire-extinguishing systems	NFPA 770
Clean agent fire-extinguishing systems	NFPA 2001
Aerosol extinguishing systems	NFPA 2010

13.9.2 The requirements of 13.9.1 shall not apply where NFPA standards, other adopted standards, or the adopted code allow the use of non-listed fire protection or suppression equipment.

Chapter 14   Means of Egress

14.1 Application. Means of egress in new and existing buildings shall comply with this *Code* and NFPA *101*.

14.2 Exit Access Corridors. Corridors used as exit access and serving an area having an occupant load exceeding 30 shall be separated from other parts of the building by walls having not less than a 1-hour fire resistance rating in accordance with Section 12.7, unless otherwise permitted by one of the following:

(1) This requirement shall not apply to existing buildings, provided that the occupancy classification does not change.
(2) This requirement shall not apply where otherwise provided in Chapters 11 through 43 of NFPA *101*.

[*101*:7.1.3.1]

14.3 Exits.

14.3.1 Where this *Code* requires an exit to be separated from other parts of the building, the separating construction shall meet the requirements of Section 8.2 of NFPA *101* and the following:

(1)* The separation shall have a minimum 1-hour fire resistance rating where the exit connects three or fewer stories.
(2) The separation specified in 14.3.1(1), other than an existing separation, shall be supported by construction having not less than a 1-hour fire resistance rating.
(3)* The separation shall have a minimum 2-hour fire resistance rating where the exit connects four or more stories, unless one of the following conditions exists:

   (a) In existing non-high-rise buildings, existing exit stair enclosures shall have a minimum 1-hour fire resistance rating.
   (b) In existing buildings protected throughout by an approved, supervised automatic sprinkler system in accordance with Section 13.3, existing exit stair enclosures shall have a minimum 1-hour fire resistance rating.
   (c) The minimum 1-hour enclosures in accordance with 28.2.2.1.2, 29.2.2.1.2, 30.2.2.1.2, and 31.2.2.1.2 of NFPA *101* shall be permitted as an alternative to the requirement of 14.3.1(3).

(4) The minimum 2-hour fire-resistance-rated separation required by 14.3.1(3) shall be constructed of an assembly of noncombustible or limited-combustible materials and shall be supported by construction having a minimum 2-hour fire resistance rating, unless otherwise permitted by 14.3.1(6).
(5)* Structural elements, or portions thereof, that support exit components and either penetrate into a fire-resistance-rated assembly or are installed within a fire-resistance-rated wall assembly shall be protected, as a minimum, to the fire resistance rating required by 14.3.1(1) or 14.3.1(3).
(6) Fire-retardant-treated wood enclosed in noncombustible or limited-combustible materials shall be permitted in accordance with NFPA 220.
(7) Openings in the separation shall be protected by fire door assemblies equipped with door closers complying with 14.5.4.
(8)* Openings in exit enclosures shall be limited to door assemblies from normally occupied spaces and corridors and door assemblies for egress from the enclosure, unless one of the following conditions exists:

   (a) Vestibules that separate normally unoccupied spaces from an exit enclosure shall be permitted, provided the vestibule is separated from adjacent spaces by corridor walls and related opening protectives as required for the occupancy involved but not less than a smoke partition in accordance with Section 8.4 of NFPA *101*.
   (b) In buildings of Type I or Type II construction, as defined in NFPA 220 *(see 8.2.1.2 of NFPA 101)*, fire-protection-rated door assemblies to normally unoccupied building service equipment support areas as addressed in Section 7.14 of NFPA *101* shall be permitted, provided the space is separated from the exit enclosure by fire barriers as required by 14.3.1(3).
   (c) Openings in exit passageways in mall buildings as provided in Chapters 36 and 37 of NFPA *101* shall be permitted.
   (d) In buildings of Type I or Type II construction, as defined in NFPA 220 *(see 8.2.1.2 of NFPA 101)*, existing fire-protection-rated door assemblies to interstitial spaces shall be permitted, provided that such spaces meet all of the following criteria:

   i. The space is used solely for distribution of pipes, ducts, and conduits.
   ii. The space contains no storage.
   iii. The space is separated from the exit enclosure in accordance with Section 12.7.

   (e) Existing openings to mechanical equipment spaces protected by approved existing fire-protection-rated door assemblies shall be permitted, provided that the following criteria are met:

   i. The space is used solely for non-fuel-fired mechanical equipment.

ii. The space contains no storage of combustible materials.
iii. The building is protected throughout by an approved, supervised automatic sprinkler system in accordance with Section 13.3 or the mechanical equipment space is provided with sprinkler protection in accordance with Section 13.3 and provided with complete smoke detection in accordance with Section 13.7.

(9) Penetrations into, and openings through, an exit enclosure assembly shall be limited to the following:

  (a) Door assemblies permitted by 14.3.1(8)
  (b)* Electrical conduit serving the exit enclosure
  (c) Pathways for devices for security and communication systems serving the exit enclosure, where pathways are installed in metal conduit
  (d)* Required exit door openings
  (e) Ductwork and equipment necessary for independent stair pressurization
  (f) Water or steam piping necessary for the heating or cooling of the exit enclosure
  (g) Sprinkler piping
  (h) Standpipes
  (i) Existing penetrations
  (j) Penetrations for fire alarm circuits, where the circuits are installed in metal conduit

(10) Penetrations or communicating openings shall be prohibited between adjacent exit enclosures.
(11) All penetrations in fire barriers separating the exit from other parts of the building shall be protected in accordance with 12.7.8.
(12) Membrane penetrations shall be permitted on the exit access side of the exit enclosure and shall be protected in accordance with 12.7.5.6.

[*101*:7.1.3.2.1]

14.3.2 An exit enclosure shall provide a continuous protected path of travel to an exit discharge. [*101*:7.1.3.2.2]

14.3.3* An exit enclosure shall not be used for any purpose that has the potential to interfere with its use as an exit and, if so designated, as an area of refuge. *(See also 14.6.3.)* [*101*:7.1.3.2.3]

14.4 Means of Egress Reliability.

14.4.1* Maintenance. Means of egress shall be continuously maintained free of all obstructions or impediments to full instant use in the case of fire or other emergency. [*101*:7.1.10.1]

14.4.2 Furnishings and Decorations in Means of Egress.

14.4.2.1 No furnishings, decorations, or other objects shall obstruct exits or their access thereto, egress therefrom, or visibility thereof. [*101*:7.1.10.2.1]

14.4.2.2 No obstruction by railings, barriers, or gates shall divide the means of egress into sections appurtenant to individual rooms, apartments, or other occupied spaces. Where the AHJ finds the required path of travel to be obstructed by furniture or other movable objects, the authority shall be permitted to require that such objects be secured out of the way or shall be permitted to require that railings or other permanent barriers be installed to protect the path of travel against encroachment. [*101*:7.1.10.2.2]

14.4.2.3 Mirrors shall not be placed on exit door leaves. Mirrors shall not be placed in or adjacent to any exit in such a manner as to confuse the direction of egress. [*101*:7.1.10.2.3]

14.4.2.4 Every door opening and every principal entrance that is required to serve as an exit shall be designed and constructed so that the path of egress travel is obvious and direct. Windows that, because of their physical configuration or design and the materials used in their construction, have the potential to be mistaken for door openings shall be made inaccessible to the occupants by barriers or railings. [*101*:7.2.1.1.2]

14.4.3 Impediments to Egress. Any device or alarm installed to restrict the improper use of a means of egress, and any device or system installed to monitor or record use of a means of egress, shall be designed and installed so that it cannot, even in case of failure, impede or prevent emergency use of such means of egress, unless otherwise provided in 14.5.3 and Chapters 18, 19, 22, and 23 of NFPA *101*. [*101*:7.1.9]

14.5 Door Openings.

14.5.1 Swing and Force to Open.

14.5.1.1* Swinging-Type Door Assembly Requirement. Any door assembly in a means of egress shall be of the side-hinged or pivoted-swinging type, and shall be installed to be capable of swinging from any position to the full required width of the opening in which it is installed, unless otherwise specified as follows:

(1) Door assemblies in dwelling units, as provided in Chapter 24 of NFPA *101*, shall be permitted.
(2) Door assemblies in residential board and care occupancies, as provided in Chapters 32 and 33 of NFPA *101*, shall be permitted.
(3) Horizontal-sliding or vertical-rolling security grilles or door assemblies that are part of the required means of egress, where permitted in Chapters 11 through 43 of NFPA *101*, shall be permitted, provided that all of the following criteria are met:

  (a) Such grilles or door assemblies shall remain secured in the fully open position during the period of occupancy by the general public.
  (b) On or adjacent to the grille or door opening, there shall be a readily visible, durable sign in letters not less than 1 in. (25 mm) high on a contrasting background that reads as follows: THIS DOOR TO REMAIN OPEN WHEN THE SPACE IS OCCUPIED.
  (c) Door leaves or grilles shall not be brought to the closed position when the space is occupied.
  (d) Door leaves or grilles shall be operable from within the space without the use of any special knowledge or effort.
  (e) Where two or more means of egress are required, not more than half of the means of egress shall be equipped with horizontal-sliding or vertical-rolling grilles or door assemblies.

(4) Horizontal-sliding door assemblies shall be permitted under any of the following conditions:

  (a) Horizontal-sliding door assemblies in detention and correctional occupancies, as provided in Chapters 22 and 23 of NFPA *101*, shall be permitted.

(b) Special-purpose horizontally sliding accordion or folding door assemblies complying with 7.2.1.13 of NFPA *101* shall be permitted.
(c) Unless prohibited by Chapters 11 through 43 of NFPA *101*, horizontal-sliding door assemblies serving a room or area with an occupant load of fewer than 10 shall be permitted, provided that all of the following criteria are met:

  i. The area served by the door assembly has no high-hazard contents.
  ii. The door assembly is readily operable from either side without special knowledge or effort.
  iii. The force required to operate the door assembly in the direction of door leaf travel is not more than 30 lbf (133 N) to set the door leaf in motion and is not more than 15 lbf (67 N) to close the door assembly or open it to the minimum required width.
  iv. The door assembly complies with any required fire protection rating, and, where rated, is self-closing or automatic-closing by means of smoke detection in accordance with 14.5.4 and is installed in accordance with NFPA 80.
  v. Corridor door assemblies required to be self-latching shall have a latch or other mechanism that ensures that the door leaf will not rebound into a partially open position if forcefully closed.

(d) Where private garages, business areas, industrial areas, and storage areas with an occupant load not exceeding 10 contain only low- or ordinary-hazard contents, door openings to such areas and private garages shall be permitted to be horizontal-sliding door assemblies.

(5) Vertical-rolling door assemblies shall be permitted in door openings to private garages, business areas, industrial areas, and storage areas where such areas have an occupant load not exceeding 10 and contain only low or ordinary hazard contents.
(6) Revolving door assemblies complying with 7.2.1.10 of NFPA *101* shall be permitted.
(7) Existing fusible link–operated horizontal-sliding or vertical-rolling fire door assemblies shall be permitted to be used as provided in Chapters 39, 40, and 42 of NFPA *101*.
[*101*:7.2.1.4.1]

14.5.1.2* Door Leaf Swing Direction. Door leaves required to be of the side-hinged or pivoted-swinging type shall swing in the direction of egress travel under any of the following conditions:

(1) Where serving a room or area with an occupant load of 50 or more, except under any of the following conditions:
  (a) Door leaves in horizontal exits shall not be required to swing in the direction of egress travel where permitted by 7.2.4.3.8.1 or 7.2.4.3.8.2 of NFPA *101*.
  (b) Door leaves in smoke barriers shall not be required to swing in the direction of egress travel in existing health care occupancies, as provided in Chapter 19 of NFPA *101*.
(2) Where the door assembly is used in an exit enclosure, unless the door opening serves an individual living unit that opens directly into an exit enclosure
(3) Where the door opening serves a high hazard contents area
[*101*:7.2.1.4.2]

14.5.1.3* Door Leaf Encroachment.

14.5.1.3.1 During its swing, any door leaf in a means of egress shall leave not less than one-half of the required width of an aisle, a corridor, a passageway, or a landing unobstructed, unless both of the following conditions are met:

(1) The door opening provides access to a stair in an existing building.
(2) The door opening meets the requirement of 14.5.1.3.2.
[*101*:7.2.1.4.3.1]

14.5.1.3.2 When fully open, any door leaf in a means of egress shall not project more than 7 in. (180 mm) into the required width of an aisle, a corridor, a passageway, or a landing, unless the door leaf is equipped with an approved self-closing device and is not required by the provisions of 14.5.1.2 to swing in the direction of egress travel. [*101*:7.2.1.4.3.2]

14.5.1.3.3 Surface-mounted latch release hardware on the door leaf shall be exempt from being included in the maximum 7 in. (180 mm) projection requirement of 14.5.1.3.2, provided that both of the following criteria are met:

(1) The hardware is mounted to the side of the door leaf that faces the aisle, corridor, passageway, or landing when the door leaf is in the open position.
(2) The hardware is mounted not less than 34 in. (865 mm), and not more than 48 in. (1220 mm), above the floor.
[*101*:7.2.1.4.3.3]

14.5.1.4 Screen Door Assemblies and Storm Door Assemblies. Screen door assemblies and storm door assemblies used in a means of egress shall be subject to the requirements for direction of swing that are applicable to other door assemblies used in a means of egress. [*101*:7.2.1.4.4]

14.5.1.5 Door Unlatching and Leaf Operating Forces.

14.5.1.5.1 The forces required to fully unlock and unlatch any door leaf manually in a means of egress shall not exceed 15 lbf (67 N) where the door hardware operates by push, pull, or slide, or 28 in.-lbf (3.16 N-m) where the door hardware operates by rotation. [*101*:7.2.1.4.5.1]

14.5.1.5.2 The forces required to fully open any door leaf manually in a means of egress shall not exceed 30 lbf (133 N) to set the leaf in motion, and 15 lbf (67 N) to open the leaf to the minimum required width, unless otherwise specified as follows:

(1) The door opening forces for interior side-hinged or pivoted-swinging door leaves without closers shall not exceed 5 lbf (22 N).
(2) The door opening forces for existing door leaves in existing buildings shall not exceed 50 lbf (222 N) applied to the latch stile.
(3) The door opening forces for horizontal-sliding door leaves in detention and correctional occupancies shall be as provided in Chapters 22 and 23 of NFPA *101*.
(4) The opening forces for power-operated door leaves shall be as provided in 7.2.1.9 of NFPA *101*.
[*101*:7.2.1.4.5.2]

14.5.1.5.3 The forces specified in 14.5.1.5 shall be applied to the latch stile. [*101*:7.2.1.4.5.3]

14.5.2 Locks and Latches.

14.5.2.1 Door leaves shall be arranged to be opened readily from the egress side whenever the building is occupied. [*101*:7.2.1.5.1]

14.5.2.2 Locks and latches shall not require the use of a key, a tool, or special knowledge or effort for operation from the egress side. [*101*:7.2.1.5.2]

14.5.2.3* Latch-Release Devices. All locks, latches, and all other fastening device on a door leaf shall be provided with a releasing device on the egress side of the door that has an obvious method of operation and that is readily operated under all lighting conditions. [*101*:7.2.1.5.3]

14.5.2.3.1 The releasing mechanism for locks and latches shall be located as follows:

(1) Not less than 34 in. (865 mm) above the finished floor for other than existing installations
(2) Not more than 48 in. (1220 mm) above the finished floor

[*101*:7.2.1.5.3.1]

14.5.2.3.2* The operation of the releasing mechanism shall release all latching and all locking devices of the door leaf with not more than one motion in a single linear or rotational direction, unless otherwise specified in 14.5.2.3.4, 14.5.2.3.5, 14.5.2.3.7 or 14.5.2.3.8. [*101*:7.2.1.5.3.2]

14.5.2.3.3 The releasing mechanism for new installations shall be capable of being operated with one hand and shall not require tight grasping, tight pinching, or twisting of the wrist to operate. [*101*:7.2.1.5.3.3]

14.5.2.3.4* Egress door assemblies from individual living units and guest rooms of residential occupancies shall be permitted to be provided with devices, including automatic latching devices, that require not more than one additional releasing motion, provided that releasing does not require simultaneous operations, and provided that such devices are operable from the inside without the use of a key or tool and are mounted at a height not exceeding 48 in. (1220 mm) above the finished floor. [*101*:7.2.1.5.3.4]

14.5.2.3.5 Existing security devices permitted by 14.5.2.3.4 shall be permitted to have two additional releasing motions. [*101*:7.2.1.5.3.5]

14.5.2.3.6 Existing security devices permitted by 14.5.2.3.4, other than automatic latching devices, shall be located not more than 60 in. (1525 mm) above the finished floor. [*101*:7.2.1.5.3.6]

14.5.2.3.7 Two releasing motions shall be permitted for existing hardware on a door leaf serving an area having an occupant load not exceeding three, provided that releasing does not require simultaneous operations. [*101*:7.2.1.5.3.7]

14.5.2.3.8 Two releasing motions shall be permitted in existing educational occupancies in accordance with 15.2.2.2.4 of NFPA *101* and in existing day care occupancies in accordance with 17.2.2.2.6 of NFPA *101*. [*101*:7.2.1.5.3.8]

14.5.2.4 The requirements of 14.5.2.1 and 14.5.2.2 shall not apply where otherwise provided in Chapters 18 through 23 of NFPA *101*. [*101*:7.2.1.5.4]

14.5.2.5* The requirement of 14.5.2.1 shall not apply to door leaves of listed fire door assemblies after exposure to elevated temperature in accordance with the listing, based on laboratory fire test procedures. [*101*:7.2.1.5.5]

14.5.2.6 Key-Operated Locks.

14.5.2.6.1 Where permitted in Chapters 11 through 43 of NFPA *101*, key operation shall be permitted, provided that the key cannot be removed when the door leaf is locked from the side from which egress is to be made. [*101*:7.2.1.5.6.1]

14.5.2.6.2* Exterior door assemblies and interior door assemblies to an individual tenant space or to a single tenant space shall be permitted to have key-operated locks from the egress side, provided that all of the following criteria are met:

(1) This alternative is permitted in Chapters 11 through 43 of NFPA *101* for the specific occupancy.
(2) Doors remain unlocked when the building or space is occupied.
(3) Doors marked with a readily visible, durable sign in letters not less than 1 in. (25 mm) high on a contrasting background that reads as follows and is located on or adjacent to the door leaf: THIS DOOR TO REMAIN UNLOCKED WHEN THIS SPACE IS OCCUPIED, or THIS DOOR TO REMAIN UNLOCKED WHEN THE BUILDING IS OCCUPIED, as applicable.
(4) The locking device is of a type that is readily distinguishable as locked.
(5) A key is immediately available to any occupant inside the building when it is locked.

[*101*:7.2.1.5.6.2]

14.5.2.6.3 The alternative provisions of 14.5.2.6.2 shall be permitted to be revoked by the AHJ for cause. [*101*:7.2.1.5.6.3]

14.5.2.7* Stair Enclosure Re-entry. Every door assembly in a stair enclosure serving more than four stories, unless permitted by 14.5.2.7.2, shall meet one of the following conditions:

(1) Re-entry from the stair enclosure to the interior of the building shall be provided.
(2) An automatic release shall be provided that meets all of the following:
 (a) The automatic release shall unlock all stair enclosure door assemblies to allow re-entry.
 (b) The automatic release shall be actuated with the initiation of the building fire alarm system.
 (c) Door electromechanical or electromagnetic locking hardware for new installations shall be listed in accordance with UL 294, *Access Control System Units*, or UL 1034, *Burglary-Resistant Electric Locking Mechanisms*.
(3) Selected re-entry shall be provided in accordance with 14.5.2.7.1.

[*101*:7.2.1.5.7]

14.5.2.7.1 Door assemblies on stair enclosures shall be permitted to be equipped with hardware that prevents re-entry into the interior of the building, provided that all of the following criteria are met:

(1) There shall be not less than two levels where it is possible to leave the stair enclosure to access another exit.
(2) There shall be not more than four stories intervening between stories where it is possible to leave the stair enclosure to access another exit.

(3) Re-entry shall be possible on the top story or next-to-top story served by the stair enclosure, and such story shall allow access to another exit.
(4) Door assemblies allowing re-entry shall be identified as such on the stair side of the door leaf.
(5) Door assemblies not allowing re-entry shall be provided with a sign on the stair side indicating the location of the nearest door opening, in each direction of travel, that allows re-entry or exit.

[*101*:7.2.1.5.7.1]

Δ **14.5.2.7.2** The requirements of 14.5.2.7, except as provided in 14.5.2.7.3, shall not apply to the following:

(1) Existing installations in buildings that are not high-rise buildings as permitted in Chapters 11 through 43 of NFPA *101*
(2) Existing installations in high-rise buildings as permitted in Chapters 11 through 43 of NFPA *101* where the occupancy is within a building protected throughout by an approved, supervised automatic sprinkler system in accordance with Section 13.3
(3) Existing approved stairwell re-entry installations as permitted by Chapters 11 through 43 of NFPA *101*
(4) Stair enclosures serving a building permitted to have a single exit in accordance with Chapters 11 through 43 of NFPA *101*
(5) Stair enclosures in health care occupancies where otherwise provided in Chapter 18 of NFPA *101*
(6) Stair enclosures in detention and correctional occupancies where otherwise provided in Chapter 22 of NFPA *101*

[*101*:7.2.1.5.7.2]

14.5.2.7.3 When the provisions of 14.5.2.7.2 are used, signage on the stair door leaves shall be required as follows:

(1) Door assemblies allowing re-entry shall be identified as such on the stair side of the door leaf.
(2) Door assemblies not allowing re-entry shall be provided with a sign on the stair side indicating the location of the nearest door opening, in each direction of travel, that allows re-entry or exit.

[*101*:7.2.1.5.7.3]

Δ **14.5.2.8** If a door allows access to the roof of the building, the door to the roof either shall be kept locked preventing access to the roof or shall allow re-entry from the roof. [*101*:7.2.1.5.8]

14.5.2.9 Where pairs of door leaves are required in a means of egress, one of the following criteria shall be met:

(1) Each leaf of the pair shall be provided with a releasing device that does not depend on the release of one leaf before the other.
(2) Approved automatic flush bolts shall be used and arranged such that both of the following criteria are met:
    (a) The door leaf equipped with the automatic flush bolts shall have no doorknob or surface-mounted hardware on the egress side of the door.
    (b) Unlatching of any leaf shall not require more than one operation.

[*101*:7.2.1.5.9]

Δ **14.5.2.10*** On doors required to release all latching and all locking devices of the door leaf with not more than one releasing motion in accordance with 14.5.2.3.2, devices shall not be installed in connection with any door assembly where such devices prevent or are intended to prevent the free use of the leaf for purposes of egress, unless otherwise provided in 14.5.3. [*101*:7.2.1.5.10]

14.5.3* Special Locking Arrangements.

14.5.3.1* Delayed-Egress Electrical Locking Systems.

14.5.3.1.1 Approved, delayed-egress electrical locking systems shall be permitted to be installed on door assemblies serving low- and ordinary-hazard contents in buildings protected throughout by an approved, supervised automatic fire detection system in accordance with Section 13.7 or an approved, supervised automatic sprinkler system in accordance with Section 13.3, and where permitted in Chapters 11 through 43 of NFPA *101*, provided that the following criteria are met:

(1) The delay of the delayed-egress electrical locking system shall deactivate allowing unobstructed egress upon actuation of one of the following:
    (a) Approved, supervised automatic sprinkler system in accordance with Section 13.3
    (b) Not more than one heat detector of an approved, supervised automatic fire detection system in accordance with Section 13.7
    (c) Not more than two smoke detectors of an approved, supervised automatic fire detection system in accordance with Section 13.7
(2) The delay of the delayed-egress electrical locking system shall deactivate allowing unobstructed egress upon loss of power controlling the lock or locking mechanism.
(3)* An irreversible process shall release the electrical lock in the direction of egress within 15 seconds, or 30 seconds where approved by the AHJ, upon application of a force to the release device required in 14.5.2.3 under all of the following conditions:
    (a) The force shall not be required to exceed 15 lbf (67 N).
    (b) The force shall not be required to be continuously applied for more than 3 seconds.
    (c) The initiation of the release process shall activate an audible signal in the vicinity of the door opening.
    (d) Once the electrical lock has been released by the application of force to the releasing device, rearming the delay electronics shall be by manual means only.
(4)* A readily visible, durable sign that conforms to the visual characters requirements of ICC A117.1, *Accessible and Usable Buildings and Facilities*, shall be located on the door leaf adjacent to the release device in the direction of egress, and shall read as follows:
    (a) PUSH UNTIL ALARM SOUNDS, DOOR CAN BE OPENED IN 15 SECONDS, for doors that swing in the direction of egress travel
    (b) PULL UNTIL ALARM SOUNDS, DOOR CAN BE OPENED IN 15 SECONDS, for doors that swing against the direction of egress travel
(5) The egress side of doors equipped with delayed-egress electrical locking systems shall be provided with emergency lighting in accordance with Section 7.9 of NFPA *101*.
(6)* Door electromechanical or electromagnetic locking hardware for new installations shall be listed in accordance with UL 294, *Access Control System Units*, or UL 1034, *Burglary-Resistant Electric Locking Mechanisms*.

[*101*:7.2.1.6.1.1]

Δ 14.5.3.1.2 The provisions of 14.5.3.2 for sensor-release of electrical locking systems and 14.5.3.3 for door hardware release of electrically locked egress door assemblies shall not apply to door assemblies with delayed-egress electrical locking systems. [*101*:7.2.1.6.1.2]

14.5.3.2* Sensor-Release of Electrical Locking Systems.

14.5.3.2.1 Where permitted in Chapters 11 through 43 of NFPA *101*, door assemblies in the means of egress shall be permitted to be equipped with sensor-release electrical locking system hardware provided that all of the following criteria are met:

(1) A sensor shall be provided on the egress side, arranged to electrically unlock the door leaf in the direction of egress upon detection of an approaching occupant.
(2) Door leaves shall automatically electrically unlock in the direction of egress upon loss of power to the sensor or to the part of the locking system that electrically locks the door leaves.
(3) Door locks shall be arranged to electrically unlock in the direction of egress from a manual release device complying with all of the following criteria:
   (a) The manual release device shall be located on the egress side, 40 in. to 48 in. (1015 mm to 1220 mm) vertically above the floor, and within 60 in. (1525 mm) of the secured door openings, except as otherwise permitted by 14.5.3.2.1(3)(b).
   (b) The requirement of 14.5.3.2.1(3)(a) to locate the manual release device within 60 in. (1525 mm) of the secured door opening shall not apply to previously approved existing installations.
   (c) The manual release device shall be readily accessible and clearly identified by a sign that reads as follows: PUSH TO EXIT.
   (d) When operated, the manual release device shall result in direct interruption of power to the electrical lock — independent of the locking system electronics — and the lock shall remain unlocked for not less than 30 seconds.
(4) Activation of the building fire-protective signaling system, if provided, shall automatically electrically unlock the door leaves in the direction of egress, and the door leaves shall remain electrically unlocked until the fire-protective signaling system has been manually reset.
(5) The activation of manual fire alarm boxes that activate the building fire-protective signaling system specified in 14.5.3.2.1(4) shall not be required to unlock the door leaves.
(6) Activation of the building automatic sprinkler or fire detection system, if provided, shall automatically electrically unlock the door leaves in the direction of egress, and the door leaves shall remain electrically unlocked until the fire-protective signaling system has been manually reset.
(7) The egress side of sensor-release electrically locked egress doors, other than existing sensor-release electrically locked egress doors, shall be provided with emergency lighting in accordance with Section 14.13.
(8)* Door electromechanical or electromagnetic locking hardware for new installations shall be listed in accordance with UL 294, *Access Control System Units*, or UL 1034, *Burglary-Resistant Electric Locking Mechanisms*.

[*101*:7.2.1.6.2.1]

14.5.3.2.2 The provisions of 14.5.3.1 for delayed-egress electrical locking systems and 14.5.3.3 for door hardware release of electrically locked egress door assemblies shall not apply to door assemblies with sensor-release of electrical locking systems. [*101*:7.2.1.6.2.2]

14.5.3.3 Door Hardware Release of Electrically Locked Egress Door Assemblies.

Δ **14.5.3.3.1** Door assemblies in the means of egress shall be permitted to be equipped with approved electrical locking systems released by the operation of door hardware provided that all of the following conditions are met:

(1) The hardware for egress-side occupant release of the electrical lock is affixed to the door leaf.
(2) The hardware has an obvious method of operation that is readily operated in the direction of egress under all lighting conditions.
(3) The hardware is capable of being operated with one hand in the direction of egress.
(4) Operation of the hardware directly and immediately interrupts the power supply to the electric lock to unlock the door assembly in the direction of egress.
(5)* Loss of power to the listed releasing hardware automatically unlocks the door assembly in the direction of egress.
(6) Door electromechanical or electromagnetic locking hardware for new installations is listed in accordance with UL 294, *Access Control System Units*, or UL 1034, *Burglary-Resistant Electric Locking Mechanisms*.

[*101*:7.2.1.6.3.1]

14.5.3.4* Elevator Lobby Exit Access Door Assemblies Locking.

14.5.3.4.1 Where permitted in Chapters 11 through 43 of NFPA *101*, door assemblies separating the elevator lobby from the exit access required by 14.9.1.6.1 shall be permitted to be electrically locked, provided that all the following criteria are met:

(1) Door electromechanical or electromagnetic locking hardware is listed in accordance with UL 294, *Access Control System Units*, or UL 1034, *Burglary-Resistant Electric Locking Mechanisms*.
(2) The building is protected throughout by a fire alarm system in accordance with Section 13.7.
(3) The building is protected throughout by an approved, supervised automatic sprinkler system in accordance with Section 13.3.
(4) Waterflow in the sprinkler system required by 14.5.3.4.1 is arranged to initiate the building fire alarm system.
(5) The elevator lobby is protected by an approved, supervised smoke detection system in accordance with Section 13.7.
(6) Detection of smoke by the detection system required by 14.5.3.4.1 is arranged to initiate the building fire alarm system and notify building occupants.
(7) Initiation of the building fire alarm system by other than manual fire alarm boxes unlocks the electrical locks on the elevator lobby door assembly.
(8) Loss of power to the elevator lobby electrical lock system unlocks the electrical locks on the elevator lobby door assemblies.
(9) Once unlocked, the elevator lobby door assemblies remain electrically unlocked until the building fire alarm system has been manually reset.

(10) Where the elevator lobby door assemblies remain mechanically latched after being electrically unlocked, latch-releasing hardware in accordance with 14.5.2.3 is affixed to the door leaves.
(11) A two-way communication system is provided for communication between the elevator lobby and a central control point that is constantly staffed.
(12) The central control point staff required by 14.5.3.4.1 is capable, trained, and authorized to provide emergency assistance.

[*101*:7.2.1.6.4.1]

14.5.3.4.2 Elevator lobby exit access doors equipped with electrical locking systems shall not be required to comply with 14.5.3.1, 14.5.3.2, or 14.5.3.3. [*101*:7.2.1.6.4.2]

14.5.3.5* Panic Hardware and Fire Exit Hardware.

Δ **14.5.3.5.1** Where a side-hinged door assembly, a pivoted-swinging door assembly, or a balanced door assembly is required to be equipped with panic or fire exit hardware, such hardware shall meet all of the following criteria:

(1) It shall consist of a cross bar or a push pad, with the length of the actuating portion of the cross bar or push pad extending not less than one-half of the width of the door leaf measured from the latch stile unless otherwise required by 14.5.3.5.2.
(2) It shall be mounted as follows:
  (a) New installations shall be not less than 34 in. (865 mm) and not more than 48 in. (1220 mm) above the floor.
  (b) Existing installations shall be not less than 30 in. (760 mm) and not more than 48 in. (1220 mm) above the floor.
(3) It shall be constructed so that a horizontal force not to exceed 15 lbf (66 N) actuates the cross bar or push pad and latches.

[*101*:7.2.1.7.1]

14.5.3.5.2 Where panic or fire exit hardware is installed on a balanced door assembly or pivoted-swinging door assembly, the panic or fire exit hardware shall be of the push-pad type, and the pad shall extend approximately one-half the width of the door leaf, measured from the latch stile. [*101*:7.2.1.7.2]

14.5.3.5.3* Only approved fire exit hardware shall be used on fire-protection-rated door assemblies. New panic hardware and new fire exit hardware shall comply with UL 305, *Panic Hardware*, and ANSI/BHMA A156.3, *Exit Devices*. [*101*:7.2.1.7.3]

14.5.3.5.4 Required panic hardware and fire exit hardware, in other than detention and correctional occupancies as otherwise provided in Chapters 22 and 23 of NFPA *101*, shall not be equipped with any locking device, set screw, or other arrangement that prevents the release of the latch when pressure is applied to the releasing device. [*101*:7.2.1.7.4]

14.5.3.5.5 Devices that hold the latch in the retracted position shall be prohibited on fire exit hardware, unless such devices are listed and approved for such a purpose. [*101*:7.2.1.7.5]

14.5.4 Self-Closing Devices.

14.5.4.1* A door leaf normally required to be kept closed shall not be secured in the open position at any time and shall be self-closing or automatic-closing in accordance with 14.5.4.2, unless otherwise permitted by 14.5.4.3. [*101*:7.2.1.8.1]

14.5.4.2 In any building of low- or ordinary-hazard contents, as defined in 3.3.154.2 and 3.3.154.3, or where approved by the AHJ, door leaves shall be permitted to be automatic-closing, provided that all of the following criteria are met:

(1) Upon release of the hold-open mechanism, the leaf becomes self-closing.
(2) The release device is designed so that the leaf instantly releases manually and, upon release, becomes self-closing, or the leaf can be readily closed.
(3) The automatic releasing mechanism or medium is activated by the operation of approved smoke detectors installed in accordance with the requirements for smoke detectors for door leaf release service in *NFPA 72*.
(4) Upon loss of power to the hold-open device, the hold-open mechanism is released and the door leaf becomes self-closing.
(5) The release by means of smoke detection of one door leaf in a stair enclosure results in closing all door leaves serving that stair.

[*101*:7.2.1.8.2]

14.5.4.3 The elevator car doors, and the associated hoistway enclosure doors, at the floor level designated for recall in accordance with the requirements of 11.3.1 shall be permitted to remain open during Phase I Emergency Recall Operation. [*101*:7.2.1.8.3]

14.5.4.4 Delayed Action Closers. Doors required to be self-closing and not required to be automatic closing shall be permitted to be equipped with delayed action closers. [*101*:7.2.1.8.4]

14.5.5* Powered Door Leaf Operation.

14.5.5.1* General. Where means of egress door leaves are operated by power by any automatic mechanism or are provided with power-assisted manual operation, the design shall be such that, in the event of power failure, the leaves open manually to allow egress travel or close when necessary to safeguard the means of egress. [*101*:7.2.1.9.1]

14.5.5.1.1 New power-operated swinging doors, power-operated sliding doors, and power-operated folding doors shall comply with ANSI/BHMA A156.10, *Power Operated Pedestrian Doors*. [*101*:7.2.1.9.1.1]

14.5.5.1.2 New power-assisted swinging doors and low-energy power-operated swinging doors shall comply with ANSI/BHMA A156.19, *Power Assist and Low Energy Power Operated Doors*. [*101*:7.2.1.9.1.2]

14.5.5.1.3 New low-energy power-operated sliding doors and low-energy power-operated folding doors shall comply with ANSI/BHMA A156.38, *Low Energy Power Operated Sliding and Folding Doors*. [*101*:7.2.1.9.1.3]

14.5.5.1.4 The forces required to manually open the door leaves specified in 14.5.5.1 shall not exceed those required in 14.5.1.5, except that the force required to set the leaf in motion shall not exceed 50 lbf (222 N). [*101*:7.2.1.9.1.4]

14.5.5.1.5 The door assembly shall be designed and installed so that, when a force is applied to the door leaf on the egress side, the door leaf shall be capable of swinging from any position to provide full use of the required width of the opening in which it is installed. (See 14.5.1.) [*101*:7.2.1.9.1.5]

14.5.5.1.6 A readily visible, durable sign in letters not less than 1 in. (25 mm) high on a contrasting background that reads as follows shall be located on the egress side of each door opening:

IN EMERGENCY, PUSH TO OPEN

[*101*:7.2.1.9.1.6]

14.5.5.1.7 Sliding, power-operated door assemblies in an exit access serving an occupant load of fewer than 50 that manually open in the direction of door leaf travel, with forces not exceeding those required in 14.5.1.5, shall not be required to have the swing-out feature required by 14.5.5.1.5. The required sign shall be in letters not less than 1 in. (25 mm) high on a contrasting background and shall read as follows:

IN EMERGENCY, SLIDE TO OPEN

[*101*:7.2.1.9.1.7]

14.5.5.1.8* In the emergency breakout mode, a door leaf located within a two-leaf opening shall be exempt from the minimum 32 in. (810 mm) single-leaf requirement of 7.2.1.2.3.2(1) of NFPA *101*, provided that the clear width of the single leaf is not less than 30 in. (760 mm). [*101*:7.2.1.9.1.8]

14.5.5.1.9 For a biparting sliding door assembly in the emergency breakout mode, a door leaf located within a multiple-leaf opening shall be exempt from the minimum 32 in. (810 mm) single-leaf requirement of 7.2.1.2.3.2(1) of NFPA *101* if a clear opening of not less than 32 in. (810 mm) is provided by all leafs broken out. [*101*:7.2.1.9.1.9]

14.5.5.1.10 Door assemblies complying with 14.5.9 shall be permitted to be used. [*101*:7.2.1.9.1.10]

14.5.5.1.11 The requirements of 14.5.5.1.1 through 14.5.5.1.10 shall not apply in detention and correctional occupancies where otherwise provided in Chapters 22 and 23 of NFPA *101*. [*101*:7.2.1.9.1.11]

14.5.5.2 Self-Closing or Self-Latching Door Leaf Operation. Where door leaves are required to be self-closing or self-latching and are operated by power by any automatic device, or are provided with power-assisted manual operation, they shall be permitted in the means of egress where they meet the following criteria:

(1) Door leaves can be opened manually in accordance with 14.5.5.1 to allow egress travel in the event of power failure.
(2) New door leaves remain in the closed position, unless actuated or opened manually.
(3) When actuated, new door leaves remain open for not more than 30 seconds.
(4) Door leaves held open for any period of time close — and the power-assist mechanism ceases to function — upon operation of approved smoke detectors installed in such a way as to detect smoke on either side of the door opening in accordance with the provisions of *NFPA 72*.
(5) Door leaves required to be self-latching are either self-latching or become self-latching upon operation of approved smoke detectors per 14.5.5.2(4).
(6) New power-assisted swinging door assemblies comply with ANSI/BHMA A156.19, *Power Assist and Low Energy Power Operated Doors*.

[*101*:7.2.1.9.2]

14.5.6 Revolving Door Assemblies.

14.5.6.1 Revolving door assemblies, whether used or not used in the means of egress, shall comply with all of the following:

(1) New revolving doors shall comply with ANSI/BHMA A156.27, *Power and Manual Operated Revolving Pedestrian Doors*, and shall be installed in accordance with the manufacturer's installation instructions.
(2) Revolving door wings shall be capable of book-fold or breakout for egress in accordance with ANSI/BHMA A156.27, unless they are existing revolving doors approved by the AHJ.
(3) When revolving door wings are collapsed into the book-fold position, the parallel egress paths formed shall provide an aggregate width of 36 in. (915 mm), unless they are approved existing revolving door assemblies.
(4) Revolving door assemblies shall not be used within 10 ft (3050 mm) of the foot or the top of stairs or escalators.
(5) A dispersal area acceptable to the AHJ shall be located between stairs or escalators and the revolving door assembly.
(6) The revolutions per minute (rpm) of door wings shall not exceed the following:
   (a) The values in Table 14.5.6.1 for existing revolving doors.
   (b) The values in ANSI/BHMA A156.27 for new revolving doors.
(7) Each revolving door assembly shall have a conforming side-hinged swinging door assembly in the same wall as the revolving door within 10 ft (3050 mm) of the revolving door, unless one of the following conditions applies:
   (a) Revolving door assemblies shall be permitted without adjacent swinging door assemblies, as required by 14.5.6.1(6), in street floor elevator lobbies, provided that no stairways or door openings from other parts of the building discharge through the lobby and the lobby has no occupancy other than as a means of travel between the elevators and street.
   (b) The requirement of 14.5.6.1(6) shall not apply to existing revolving door assemblies where the number of revolving door assemblies does not exceed the number of swinging door assemblies within 20 ft (6100 mm) of the revolving door assembly.

[*101*:7.2.1.10.1]

Table 14.5.6.1 Existing Revolving Door Assembly Maximum Speed

Inside Diameter		Power-Driven Speed Control (rpm)	Manual Speed Control (rpm)
ft/in.	mm		
6 ft 6 in.	1980	11	12
7 ft	2135	10	11
7 ft 6 in.	2285	9	11
8 ft	2440	9	10
8 ft 6 in.	2590	8	9
9 ft	2745	8	9
9 ft 6 in.	2895	7	8
10 ft	3050	7	8

[*101*:Table 7.2.1.10.1]

14.5.6.2 Where permitted in Chapters 11 through 43 of NFPA *101*, revolving door assemblies shall be permitted as a component in a means of egress, provided that all of the following criteria are met:

(1) Revolving door openings shall not be given credit for more than 50 percent of the required egress capacity.
(2) Each revolving door opening shall not be credited with more than a 50-person capacity or, if of not less than a 9 ft (2745 mm) diameter, a revolving door assembly shall be permitted egress capacity based on the clear opening width provided when collapsed into a book-fold position.
(3) Revolving door wings shall be capable of being collapsed into a book-fold position when a force not exceeding 130 lbf (580 N) is applied to the wings within 3 in. (75 mm) of the outer edge.

[*101*:7.2.1.10.2]

14.5.6.3 Revolving door assemblies not used as a component of a means of egress shall have a collapsing force not exceeding 180 lbf (800 N) applied at a point 3 in. (75 mm) from the outer edge of the outer wing stile and 40 in. (1015 mm) above the floor. [*101*:7.2.1.10.3]

14.5.6.4 The requirement of 14.5.6.3 shall not apply to revolving door assemblies, provided that the collapsing force is reduced to a force not to exceed 130 lbf (580 N) under all of the following conditions:

(1) Power failure, or removal of power to the device holding the wings in position
(2) Actuation of the automatic sprinkler system, where such a system is provided
(3) Actuation of a smoke detection system that is installed to provide coverage in all areas within the building that are within 75 ft (23 m) of the revolving door assemblies
(4) Actuation of a clearly identified manual control switch in an approved location that reduces the holding force to a force not to exceed 130 lbf (580 N)

[*101*:7.2.1.10.4]

14.5.7 Turnstiles and Similar Devices.

14.5.7.1 Turnstiles or similar devices that restrict travel to one direction or are used to collect fares or admission charges shall not be placed so as to obstruct any required means of egress, unless otherwise specified in 14.5.7.1.1, 14.5.7.1.2, and 14.5.7.1.3. [*101*:7.2.1.11.1]

14.5.7.1.1 Approved turnstiles not exceeding 39 in. (990 mm) in height that turn freely in the direction of egress travel shall be permitted where revolving door assemblies are permitted in Chapters 11 through 43 of NFPA *101*. [*101*:7.2.1.11.1.1]

14.5.7.1.2 Where turnstiles are approved by the AHJ and permitted in Chapters 11 through 43 of NFPA *101*, each turnstile shall be credited for a capacity of 50 persons, provided that such turnstiles meet all of the following criteria:

(1) They freewheel in the egress direction when primary power is lost, and freewheel in the direction of egress travel upon manual release by an employee assigned in the area.
(2) They are not given credit for more than 50 percent of the required egress width.
(3) They are not in excess of 39 in. (990 mm) in height and have a clear width of not less than 16½ in. (420 mm).

[*101*:7.2.1.11.1.2]

14.5.7.1.3* Security access turnstiles that impede travel in the direction of egress utilizing a physical barrier shall be permitted to be considered as a component of the means of egress, where permitted in Chapters 11 through 43 of NFPA *101*, provided that all the following criteria are met:

(1) The building is protected throughout by an approved, supervised automatic sprinkler system in accordance with Section 13.3.
(2) Each security access turnstile lane configuration has a minimum clear passage width of 22 in. (560 mm).
(3) Any security access turnstile lane configuration providing a clear passage width of less than 32 in. (810 mm) shall be given an egress capacity of 50 persons.
(4) Any security access turnstile lane configuration providing a clear passage width of 32 in. (810 mm) or more shall be given an egress capacity as calculated in accordance with Section 14.8.
(5) Each secured physical barrier shall automatically retract or swing to an unobstructed open position in the direction of egress, under each of the following conditions:

   (a) Upon loss of power to the turnstile or any part of the access control system that secures the physical barrier
   (b) Upon actuation of a readily accessible and clearly identified manual release device that results in direct interruption of power to each secured physical barrier, remains in the open position for not less than 30 seconds, and is positioned at one of the following locations:
      i. The manual release device is located on the egress side of each security access turnstile lane.
      ii. The manual release device is located at an approved location where it can be actuated by an employee assigned to the area.
   (c) Upon actuation of the building fire-protective signaling system, if provided, and for which the following apply:
      i. The physical barrier remains in the open position until the fire-protective signaling system is manually reset.
      ii. The actuation of manual fire alarm boxes that actuate the building fire-protective signaling system is not required to meet the requirements specified in 14.5.7.1.3(5)(c)(i).
   (d) Upon actuation of the building automatic sprinkler or fire detection system, and for which the physical barrier remains in the open position until the fire-protective signaling system is manually reset

[*101*:7.2.1.11.1.3]

14.5.7.2 Turnstiles exceeding 39 in. (990 mm) in height shall meet the requirements for revolving door assemblies in 14.5.6 or the requirements of 14.5.7.1.3 for security access turnstiles. [*101*:7.2.1.11.2]

14.5.7.3 Turnstiles located in, or furnishing access to, required exits shall provide not less than 16½ in. (420 mm) clear width at and below a height of 39 in. (990 mm) and at least 22 in. (560 mm) clear width at heights above 39 in. (990 mm). [*101*:7.2.1.11.3]

14.5.8 Door Openings in Folding Partitions. Where permanently mounted folding or movable partitions divide a room into smaller spaces, a swinging door leaf or open doorway shall be provided as an exit access from each such space, unless otherwise specified in 14.5.8.1 or 14.5.8.2. [*101*:7.2.1.12]

Δ **14.5.8.1** A door leaf or opening in the folding partition shall not be required, provided that all of the following criteria are met:

(1) The subdivided space is used by not more than 20 persons at any time.
(2) The use of the space is under adult supervision.
(3) The partitions are arranged so that they do not extend across any aisle or corridor used as an exit access to the required exits from the story.
(4) The partitions conform to the interior finish and other requirements of this *Code*.
(5) The partitions are of an approved type, have a simple method of release, and are capable of being opened quickly and easily by experienced persons in case of emergency.

[*101*:7.2.1.12.1]

Δ **14.5.8.2** The door leaf or opening in the folding partition shall not be required where each space on both sides of the folding partition is provided with compliant means of egress without requiring travel through the folding partition. [*101*:7.2.1.12.2]

14.5.9 Special-Purpose Horizontally Sliding Accordion or Folding Door Assemblies. Special-purpose horizontally sliding accordion or folding door assemblies shall be permitted in means of egress, provided that all of the following criteria are met:

(1) The door is readily operable from the egress side without special knowledge or effort.
(2) The force that, when applied to the operating device in the direction of egress, is required to operate the door is not more than 15 lbf (67 N).
(3) The force required to operate the door in the direction of travel is not more than 30 lbf (133 N) to set the door in motion and is not more than 15 lbf (67 N) to close the door or open it to the minimum required width.
(4) The door is operable using a force of not more than 50 lbf (222 N) when a force of 250 lbf (1100 N) is applied perpendicularly to the door adjacent to the operating device, unless the door opening is an existing special-purpose horizontally sliding accordion or folding exit access door assembly serving an area with an occupant load of fewer than 50.
(5) The door assembly complies with the fire protection rating, if required, and, where rated, is self-closing or automatic-closing by means of smoke detection in accordance with 14.5.4 and is installed in accordance with NFPA 80.

[*101*:7.2.1.13]

14.5.10 Inspection of Door Openings.

14.5.10.1* Where required by Chapters 11 through 43 of NFPA *101*, the following door assemblies shall be inspected and tested not less than annually in accordance with 14.5.10.2 through 14.5.10.7:

(1) Door leaves equipped with panic hardware or fire exit hardware in accordance with 14.5.3.5
(2) Door assemblies in exit enclosures
(3) Door hardware release of electrically locked egress door assemblies
(4) Door assemblies with special locking arrangements subject to 14.5.3.4

[*101*:7.2.1.14.1]

14.5.10.2* The inspection and testing interval for fire-rated and nonrated door assemblies shall be permitted to exceed 12 months under a written performance-based program. [*101*:7.2.1.14.2]

14.5.10.2.1 Goals established under a performance-based program shall provide assurance that the door assembly will perform its intended function. [*101*:7.2.1.14.2.1]

14.5.10.2.2 Technical justification for inspection, testing, and maintenance intervals shall be documented. [*101*:7.2.1.14.2.2]

14.5.10.2.3 The performance-based option shall include historical data. [*101*:7.2.1.14.2.3]

14.5.10.3 A written record of the inspections and testing shall be signed and kept for inspection by the AHJ. [*101*:7.2.1.14.3]

14.5.10.4 Functional testing of door assemblies shall be performed by individuals who can demonstrate knowledge and understanding of the operating components of the type of door being subjected to testing. [*101*:7.2.1.14.4]

14.5.10.5 Door assemblies shall be visually inspected from both sides of the opening to assess the overall condition of the assembly. [*101*:7.2.1.14.5]

14.5.10.6 As a minimum, the following items shall be verified:

(1) Floor space on both sides of the openings is clear of obstructions, and door leaves open fully and close freely.
(2) Forces required to set door leaves in motion and move to the fully open position do not exceed the requirements in 14.5.1.5.
(3) Latching and locking devices comply with 14.5.2.
(4) Releasing hardware devices are installed in accordance with 14.5.2.3.1.
(5) Door leaves of paired openings are installed in accordance with 14.5.2.9.
(6) Door closers are adjusted properly to control the closing speed of door leaves in accordance with accessibility requirements.
(7) Projection of door leaves into the path of egress does not exceed the encroachment permitted by 14.5.1.3.
(8) Powered door openings operate in accordance with 14.5.5.
(9) Signage required by 14.5.1.1(3), 14.5.2.6, 14.5.3, and 14.5.5 is intact and legible.
(10) Door openings with special locking arrangements function in accordance with 14.5.3.
(11) Security devices that impede egress are not installed on openings, as required by 14.5.2.10.
(12) Where required by 7.2.2.5.5.7 of NFPA *101*, door hardware marking is present and intact.
(13) Emergency lighting on sensor-release of electrical locking systems and doors equipped with delayed-egress electrical locking systems is present in accordance with Section 14.13.

[*101*:7.2.1.14.6]

14.5.10.7* Door openings not in proper operating condition shall be repaired or replaced without delay. [*101*:7.2.1.14.7]

14.6 Enclosure and Protection of Stairs.

14.6.1 Enclosures.

14.6.1.1 All inside stairs serving as an exit or exit component shall be enclosed in accordance with Section 14.3. [*101*:7.2.2.5.1.1]

14.6.1.2 Inside stairs, other than those serving as an exit or exit component, shall be protected in accordance with Section 8.6 of NFPA *101*. [*101*:7.2.2.5.1.2]

14.6.1.3 In existing buildings, where a two-story exit enclosure connects the story of exit discharge with an adjacent story, the exit shall be permitted to be enclosed only on the story of exit discharge, provided that not less than 50 percent of the number and capacity of exits on the story of exit discharge are independent of such enclosures. [*101*:7.2.2.5.1.3]

14.6.2* Exposures.

14.6.2.1 Where nonrated walls or unprotected openings enclose the exterior of a stairway, other than an existing stairway, and the walls or openings are exposed by other parts of the building at an angle of less than 180 degrees, the building enclosure walls within 10 ft (3050 mm) horizontally of the nonrated wall or unprotected opening shall be constructed as required for stairway enclosures, including opening protectives. [*101*:7.2.2.5.2.1]

14.6.2.2 Construction shall extend vertically from the finished ground level to a point 10 ft (3050 mm) above the topmost landing of the stairs or to the roofline, whichever is lower. [*101*:7.2.2.5.2.2]

14.6.2.3 The fire resistance rating of the separation extending 10 ft (3050 mm) from the stairs shall not be required to exceed 1 hour where openings have a minimum ¾-hour fire protection rating. [*101*:7.2.2.5.2.3]

△ **14.6.3* Usable Space.** Enclosed, usable spaces within exit enclosures shall be prohibited, including under stairs, unless otherwise permitted by 14.6.3.2. [*101*:7.2.2.5.3]

14.6.3.1 Open space within the exit enclosure shall not be used for any purpose that has the potential to interfere with egress. [*101*:7.2.2.5.3.1]

14.6.3.2 Enclosed, usable space shall be permitted under stairs, provided that both of the following criteria are met:

(1) The space shall be separated from the stair enclosure by the same fire resistance as the exit enclosure.
(2) Entrance to the enclosed, usable space shall not be from within the stair enclosure. *(See also 14.3.3.)*

[*101*:7.2.2.5.3.2]

14.7* Exit Passageways.

14.7.1* General. Exit passageways used as exit components shall conform to the general requirements of Section 7.1 of NFPA *101* and to the special requirements of Section 14.7. [*101*:7.2.6.1]

14.7.2 Enclosure. An exit passageway shall be separated from other parts of the building as specified in Section 14.3, and the following alternatives shall be permitted:

(1) Fire windows in accordance with 12.7.6 shall be permitted to be installed in the separation in a building protected throughout by an approved, supervised automatic sprinkler system in accordance with Section 13.3.
(2) Existing fixed wired glass panels in steel sash shall be permitted to be continued in use in the separation in buildings protected throughout by an approved, supervised automatic sprinkler system in accordance with Section 13.3.

[*101*:7.2.6.2]

14.7.3 Stair Discharge. An exit passageway that serves as a discharge from a stair enclosure shall have not less than the same fire resistance rating and opening protective fire protection rating as those required for the stair enclosure. [*101*:7.2.6.3]

14.7.4 Width.

14.7.4.1 The width of an exit passageway shall be sized to accommodate the aggregate required capacity of all exits that discharge through it, unless one of the following conditions applies:

(1)* Where an exit passageway serves occupants of the level of exit discharge as well as other stories, the capacity shall not be required to be aggregated.
(2) As provided in Chapters 36 and 37 of NFPA *101*, an exit passageway in a mall structure shall be permitted to accommodate occupant loads independently from the mall concourse and the tenant spaces. *(See 36.2.2.7.2 and 37.2.2.7.2 of NFPA 101.)*

[*101*:7.2.6.4.1]

14.7.4.2 In new construction, the minimum width of any exit passageway into which an exit stair discharges, or that serves as a horizontal transfer within an exit stair system, shall meet the following criteria:

(1) The minimum width of the exit passageway shall be not less than two-thirds of the width of the exit stair.
(2) Where stairs are credited with egress capacity in accordance with 14.8.3.2, the exit passageway width shall be sized to accommodate the same capacity as the stair, with such capacity determined by use of the capacity factors in Table 14.8.3.1.

[*101*:7.2.6.4.2]

14.8 Capacity of Means of Egress.

14.8.1 Occupant Load.

14.8.1.1 Sufficient Capacity.

14.8.1.1.1 The total capacity of the means of egress for any story, balcony, tier, or other occupied space shall be sufficient for the occupant load thereof unless one of the following conditions exists:

(1) The AHJ shall be permitted to establish the occupant load as the number of persons for which existing means of egress is adequate, provided that measures are established to prevent occupancy by a greater number of persons.
(2) The egress capacity shall have been previously approved as being adequate.

[*101*:7.3.1.1.1]

14.8.1.1.2 For other than existing means of egress, where more than one means of egress is required, the means of egress shall be of such width and capacity that the loss of any one means of egress leaves available not less than 50 percent of the required capacity. [*101*:7.3.1.1.2]

14.8.1.2* Occupant Load Factor. The occupant load in any building or portion thereof shall be not less than the number of persons determined by dividing the floor area assigned to that use by the occupant load factor for that use as specified in Table 14.8.1.2, Figure 14.8.1.2(a), and Figure 14.8.1.2(b). Where both gross and net area figures are given for the same occupancy, calculations shall be made by applying the gross area figure to the gross area of the portion of the building devoted to the use for which the gross area figure is specified and by applying the net area figure to the net area of the portion of the building devoted to the use for which the net area figure is specified. [*101*:7.3.1.2]

14.8.1.3 Occupant Load Increases.

14.8.1.3.1 The occupant load in any building or portion thereof shall be permitted to be increased from the occupant load established for the given use in accordance with 14.8.1.2 where all other requirements of this *Code* are also met, based on such increased occupant load. [*101*:7.3.1.3.1]

14.8.1.3.2 The AHJ shall be permitted to require an approved aisle, seating, or fixed equipment diagram to substantiate any increase in occupant load and shall be permitted to require that such a diagram be posted in an approved location. [*101*:7.3.1.3.2]

14.8.1.4 Exits Serving More than One Story. Where an exit serves more than one story, only the occupant load of each story considered individually shall be used in computing the required capacity of the exit at that story, provided that the required egress capacity of the exit is not decreased in the direction of egress travel. [*101*:7.3.1.4]

14.8.1.5 Capacity from a Point of Convergence. Where means of egress from a story above and a story below converge at an intermediate story, the capacity of the means of egress from the point of convergence shall be not less than the sum of the required capacity of the two means of egress. [*101*:7.3.1.5]

14.8.1.6 Egress Capacity from Balconies and Mezzanines. Where any required egress capacity from a balcony or mezzanine passes through the room below, that required capacity shall be added to the required egress capacity of the room in which it is located. [*101*:7.3.1.6]

14.8.2 Measurement of Means of Egress.

14.8.2.1 The width of means of egress shall be measured in the clear at the narrowest point of the egress component under consideration, unless otherwise provided in 14.8.2.2 or 14.8.2.3. [*101*:7.3.2.1]

14.8.2.2 Projections within the means of egress of not more than 4½ in. (114 mm) on each side shall be permitted at a height of 38 in. (965 mm) and below. In the case of stair and landing handrails forming part of a guard, in accordance with 7.2.2.4.5.3 of NFPA *101*, such projections shall be permitted at a height of 42 in. (1065 mm) and below. [*101*:7.3.2.2]

14.8.2.3 In health care and ambulatory health care occupancies, projections shall be permitted in corridors in accordance with Chapters 18 through 21 of NFPA *101*. [*101*:7.3.2.3]

Δ **Table 14.8.1.2 Occupant Load Factor**

Use	(ft²/person)[a]	(m²/person)[a]
Assembly Use	-	-
Concentrated use, without fixed seating	7 net	0.65 net
Less concentrated use, without fixed seating	15 net	1.4 net
Bench-type seating	1 person/ 18 linear in.	1 person/ 455 linear mm
Fixed seating	Use number of fixed seats	Use number of fixed seats
Waiting spaces	See 12.1.7.2 and 13.1.7.2 of NFPA 101	See 12.1.7.2 and 13.1.7.2 of NFPA 101
Kitchens	100	9.3
Library stack areas	100	9.3
Library reading rooms	50 net	4.6 net
Swimming pools	50 (water surface)	4.6 (water surface)
Swimming pool decks	30	2.8
Exercise rooms with equipment	50	4.6
Exercise rooms without equipment	15	1.4
Stages	15 net	1.4 net
Lighting and access catwalks, galleries, gridirons	100 net	9.3 net
Casinos and similar gaming areas	11	1
Skating rinks	50	4.6
Business Use (other than below)	150	14
Concentrated Business Use[b]	50	4.6
Airport control tower observation levels	40	3.7
Collaboration rooms/ spaces ≤450 ft² (41.8 m²) in area[b]	30	2.8
Collaboration rooms/ spaces >450 ft² (41.8 m²) in area[b]	15	1.4
Day-Care Use	35 net	3.3 net
Detention and Correctional Use	120	11.1
Educational Use	-	-
Classrooms	20 net	1.9 net
Shops, laboratories, vocational rooms	50 net	4.6 net
Health Care Use	-	-
Inpatient treatment departments	240	22.3
Sleeping departments	120	11.1
Ambulatory health care	150	14
Industrial Use	-	-
General and high hazard industrial	100	9.3
Special-purpose industrial	MP	MP
Mercantile Use	-	-
Sales area on street floor[c,d]	30	2.8
Sales area on two or more street floors[d]	40	3.7
Sales area on floor below street floor[d]	30	2.8

(continues)

Δ Table 14.8.1.2 Continued

Use	(ft²/person)[a]	(m²/person)[a]
Sales area on floors above street floor[d]	60	5.6
Floors or portions of floors used only for offices	See business use.	See business use.
Floors or portions of floors used only for storage, receiving, and shipping, and not open to general public	300	27.9
Mall structures[e]	Per factors applicable to use of space[f]	
Residential Use	-	-
Hotels and dormitories	200	18.6
Apartment buildings	200	18.6
Board and care, large	200	18.6
Storage Use	-	-
In storage occupancies	MP	MP
In mercantile occupancies	300	27.9
In other than storage and mercantile occupancies	500	46.5

MP: The occupant load is the maximum probable number of occupants present at any time.

[a]All factors are expressed in gross area unless marked "net."

[b]See A.14.8.1.2.

[c]For determining occupant load in mercantile occupancies where, due to differences in the finished ground level of streets on different sides, two or more floors directly accessible from streets (not including alleys or similar back streets) exist, each such floor is permitted to be considered a street floor. The occupant load factor is one person for each 40 ft² (3.7 m²) of gross floor area of sales space.

[d]For determining occupant load in mercantile occupancies with no street floor, as defined in 3.3.279, but with access directly from the street by stairs or escalators, the floor at the point of entrance to the mercantile occupancy is considered the street floor.

[e]For any food court or other assembly use areas located in the mall concourse that are not included as a portion of the gross leasable area of the mall structure, the occupant load is calculated based on the occupant load factor for that use as specified in Table 14.8.1.2. The remaining mall concourse area is not required to be assigned an occupant load.

[f]The portions of the mall concourse not used as gross leasable area are not required to be assessed an occupant load based on Table 14.8.1.2. However, means of egress from a mall concourse are required to be provided for an occupant load determined by dividing the gross leasable area of the mall building (not including anchor buildings) by the appropriate lowest whole number occupant load factor from Figure 14.8.1.2(a) or Figure 14.8.1.2(b).

Each individual tenant space is required to have means of egress to the outside or to the mall concourse based on occupant loads calculated by using the appropriate occupant load factor from Table 14.8.1.2.

Each individual anchor store is required to have means of egress independent of the mall concourse.

[*101*:Table 7.3.1.2]

Δ FIGURE 14.8.1.2(a) Mall Structure Occupant Load Factors (US Customary Units). [*101*:Figure 7.3.1.2(a)]

FIGURE 14.8.1.2(b) Mall Structure Occupant Load Factors (SI Units). [*101*:Figure 7.3.1.2(b)]

14.8.3* Egress Capacity.

14.8.3.1 Egress capacity for approved components of means of egress shall be based on the capacity factors shown in Table 14.8.3.1, unless otherwise provided in 14.8.3.2. [*101*:7.3.3.1]

14.8.3.2* For stairways wider than 44 in. (1120 mm) and subject to the 0.3 in. (7.6 mm) width per person capacity factor, the capacity shall be permitted to be increased using the following equation:

$$C = 146.7 + \left(\frac{Wn - 44}{0.218} \right) \quad [14.8.3.2]$$

where:
 C = capacity, in persons, rounded to the nearest integer
 Wn = nominal width of the stair as permitted by 14.8.3.2 (in.)
 [*101*:7.3.3.2]

Table 14.8.3.1 Capacity Factors

Area	Stairways (width/person) in.	Stairways (width/person) mm	Level Components and Ramps (width/person) in.	Level Components and Ramps (width/person) mm
Board and care	0.4	10	0.2	5
Health care, sprinklered	0.3	7.6	0.2	5
Health care, nonsprinklered	0.6	15	0.5	13
High-hazard contents	0.7	18	0.4	10
All others	0.3	7.6	0.2	5

[*101*:Table 7.3.3.1]

14.8.3.3 The required capacity of a corridor shall be the occupant load that utilizes the corridor for exit access divided by the required number of exits to which the corridor connects, but the corridor capacity shall be not less than the required capacity of the exit to which the corridor leads. [*101*:7.3.3.3]

14.8.3.4 Minimum Width.

Δ **14.8.3.4.1** The width of any means of egress, unless otherwise provided in 14.8.3.4.1.1 through 14.8.3.4.1.3, shall be as follows:

(1) Not less than that required for a given egress component in this chapter or Chapter 7 or Chapters 11 through 43 of NFPA *101*
(2) Not less than 36 in. (915 mm) where another part of this chapter and Chapters 11 through 43 of NFPA *101* do not specify a minimum width

[*101*:7.3.4.1]

14.8.3.4.1.1* The width of exit access serving not more than six people, and having a length not exceeding 50 ft (15 m) shall meet both of the following criteria:

(1) The width shall be not less than 18 in. (455 mm), at and below a height of 38 in. (965 mm), and not less than 28 in. (710 mm) above a height of 38 in. (965 mm).
(2) A width of not less than 36 in. (915 mm) for new exit access, and not less than 28 in. (710 mm) for existing exit access, shall be capable of being provided without moving permanent walls.

[*101*:7.3.4.1.1]

14.8.3.4.1.2 In existing buildings, the width of exit access shall be permitted to be not less than 28 in. (710 mm). [*101*:7.3.4.1.2]

14.8.3.4.1.3 The requirement of 14.8.3.4.1 shall not apply to the following:

(1) Doors as otherwise provided for in 7.2.1.2 of NFPA *101*
(2) Aisles and aisle accessways in assembly occupancies as otherwise provided in Chapters 12 and 13 of NFPA *101*
(3) Industrial equipment access as otherwise provided in 40.2.5.3 of NFPA *101*

[*101*:7.3.4.1.3]

14.8.3.4.2 Where a single exit access leads to an exit, its capacity in terms of width shall be not less than the required capacity of the exit to which it leads. [*101*:7.3.4.2]

14.8.3.4.3 Where more than one exit access leads to an exit, each shall have a width adequate for the number of persons it accommodates. [*101*:7.3.4.3]

14.9 Number of Means of Egress.

14.9.1 General.

14.9.1.1 The number of means of egress from any balcony, mezzanine, story, or portion thereof shall be not less than two, except under one of the following conditions:

(1) A single means of egress shall be permitted where permitted in Chapters 11 through 43 of NFPA *101*.
(2) A single means of egress shall be permitted for a mezzanine or balcony where the common path of travel limitations of Chapters 11 through 43 of NFPA *101* are met.

[*101*:7.4.1.1]

14.9.1.2 The number of means of egress from any story or portion thereof, other than for existing buildings as permitted in Chapters 11 through 43 of NFPA *101*, shall be as follows:

(1) Occupant load more than 500 but not more than 1000 — not less than 3
(2) Occupant load more than 1000 — not less than 4

[*101*:7.4.1.2]

14.9.1.3 Accessible means of egress in accordance with 14.10.4 that do not utilize elevators shall be permitted to serve as any or all of the required minimum number of means of egress. [*101*:7.4.1.3]

14.9.1.4 The occupant load of each story considered individually shall be required to be used in computing the number of means of egress at each story, provided that the required number of means of egress is not decreased in the direction of egress travel. [*101*:7.4.1.4]

14.9.1.5 Doors other than the hoistway door; the elevator car door; and doors that are readily openable from the car side without a key, a tool, special knowledge, or special effort shall be prohibited at the point of access to an elevator car. [*101*:7.4.1.5]

14.9.1.6 Elevator Landing and Lobby Exit Access.

14.9.1.6.1 Each elevator landing and lobby shall have access to at least one exit. [*101*:7.4.1.6.1]

14.9.1.6.2 The elevator landing and lobby exit access required by 14.9.1.6.1 shall not require the use of a key, a tool, special knowledge, or special effort, unless permitted by 14.9.1.6.3. [*101*:7.4.1.6.2]

14.9.1.6.3 Doors separating the elevator lobby from the exit access required by 14.9.1.6.1 shall be permitted to be electronically locked in accordance with 14.5.3.4. [*101*:7.4.1.6.3]

14.9.2 Spaces About Electrical Equipment.

14.9.2.1 600 Volts, Nominal, or Less.

14.9.2.1.1 Number of Means of Egress. The minimum number of means of egress for working space about electrical equipment, other than existing electrical equipment, shall be in accordance with 110.26(C) of NFPA *70*. [*101*:7.4.2.1.1]

14.9.2.1.2 Door Unlatching and Direction of Door Swing. The method of door unlatching and direction of door swing for working space about electrical equipment, other than existing electrical equipment, shall be in accordance with 110.26(C)(3) of *NFPA 70*. [*101*:7.4.2.1.2]

14.9.2.2 Over 600 Volts, Nominal.

14.9.2.2.1 Number of Means of Egress. The minimum number of means of egress for working space about electrical equipment, other than existing electrical equipment, shall be in accordance with 110.33(A) of *NFPA 70*. [*101*:7.4.2.2.1]

14.9.2.2.2 Door Unlatching and Direction of Door Swing. The method of door unlatching and direction of door swing for working space about electrical equipment, other than existing electrical equipment, shall be in accordance with 110.33(A)(3) of *NFPA 70*. [*101*:7.4.2.2.2]

14.10 Arrangement of Means of Egress.

14.10.1 General.

14.10.1.1 Exits shall be located, and exit access shall be arranged, so that exits are readily accessible at all times. [*101*:7.5.1.1]

14.10.1.1.1* Where exits are not immediately accessible from an open floor area, continuous passageways, aisles, or corridors leading directly to every exit shall be maintained and shall be arranged to provide access for each occupant to not less than two exits by separate ways of travel, unless otherwise provided in 14.10.1.1.3 and 14.10.1.1.4. [*101*:7.5.1.1.1]

14.10.1.1.2 Exit access corridors shall provide access to not less than two approved exits, unless otherwise provided in 14.10.1.1.3 and 14.10.1.1.4. [*101*:7.5.1.1.2]

14.10.1.1.3 The requirements of 14.10.1.1.1 and 14.10.1.1.2 shall not apply where a single exit is permitted in Chapters 11 through 43 of NFPA *101*. [*101*:7.5.1.1.3]

14.10.1.1.4 Where common paths of travel are permitted for an occupancy in Chapters 11 through 43 of NFPA *101*, such common paths of travel shall be permitted but shall not exceed the limit specified. [*101*:7.5.1.1.4]

14.10.1.2 Corridors shall provide exit access without passing through any intervening rooms other than corridors, lobbies, and other spaces permitted to be open to the corridor, unless otherwise provided in 14.10.1.2.2 and 14.10.1.2.3. [*101*:7.5.1.2]

14.10.1.2.1* Exit access shall be arranged so that there are no dead ends in corridors, unless permitted by, and limited to the lengths specified in, Chapters 11 through 43 of NFPA *101*. [*101*:7.5.1.2.1]

14.10.1.2.2 Approved existing corridors that require passage through a room to access an exit shall be permitted to continue to be used, provided that all of the following criteria are met:

(1) The path of travel is marked in accordance with Section 14.14.
(2) Doors to such rooms comply with 7.2.1 of NFPA *101*.
(3) Such arrangement is not prohibited by the applicable occupancy chapter in NFPA *101*.

[*101*:7.5.1.2.2]

14.10.1.2.3 Corridors that are not required to be fire resistance rated shall be permitted to discharge into open floor plan areas. [*101*:7.5.1.2.3]

14.10.1.3 Remoteness shall be provided in accordance with 14.10.1.3.1 through 14.10.1.3.7. [*101*:7.5.1.3]

14.10.1.3.1 Where more than one exit, exit access, or exit discharge is required from a building or portion thereof, such exits, exit accesses, or exit discharges shall be remotely located from each other and be arranged to minimize the possibility that more than one has the potential to be blocked by any one fire or other emergency condition. [*101*:7.5.1.3.1]

14.10.1.3.2* Where two exits, exit accesses, or exit discharges are required, they shall be located at a distance from one another not less than one-half the length of the maximum overall diagonal dimension of the building or area to be served, measured in a straight line between the nearest edge of the exits, exit accesses, or exit discharges, unless otherwise provided in 14.10.1.3.3 through 14.10.1.3.5. [*101*:7.5.1.3.2]

14.10.1.3.3 In buildings protected throughout by an approved, supervised automatic sprinkler system in accordance with Section 13.3, the minimum separation distance between two exits, exit accesses, or exit discharges, measured in accordance with 14.10.1.3.2, shall be not less than one-third the length of the maximum overall diagonal dimension of the building or area to be served. [*101*:7.5.1.3.3]

14.10.1.3.4* In other than high-rise buildings, where exit enclosures are provided as the required exits specified in 14.10.1.3.2 or 14.10.1.3.3 and are interconnected by not less than a 1-hour fire-resistance-rated corridor, exit separation shall be measured along the shortest line of travel within the corridor [*101*:7.5.1.3.4]

14.10.1.3.5 In existing buildings, where more than one exit, exit access, or exit discharge is required, such exits, exit accesses, or exit discharges shall be exempt from the diagonal measurement separation distance criteria of 14.10.1.3.2 and 14.10.1.3.3, provided that such exits, exit accesses, or exit discharges are remotely located in accordance with 14.10.1.3.1. [*101*:7.5.1.3.5]

14.10.1.3.6 In other than existing buildings, where more than two exits, exit accesses, or exit discharges are required, at least two of the required exits, exit accesses, or exit discharges shall be arranged to comply with the minimum separation distance requirement. [*101*:7.5.1.3.6]

14.10.1.3.7 The balance of the exits, exit accesses, or exit discharges specified in 14.10.1.3.6 shall be located so that, if one becomes blocked, the others are available. [*101*:7.5.1.3.7]

14.10.1.4 Interlocking or scissor stairs shall comply with 14.10.1.4.1 and 14.10.1.4.2. [*101*:7.5.1.4]

14.10.1.4.1 New interlocking or scissor stairs shall be permitted to be considered only as a single exit. [*101*:7.5.1.4.1]

14.10.1.4.2* Existing interlocking or scissor stairs shall be permitted to be considered separate exits, provided that they meet all of the following criteria:

(1) They are enclosed in accordance with Section 14.3.
(2) They are separated from each other by 2-hour fire-resistance-rated noncombustible construction.
(3) No protected or unprotected penetrations or communicating openings exist between the stair enclosures.

[*101*:7.5.1.4.2]

14.10.1.5 Exit access from rooms or spaces shall be permitted to be through adjoining or intervening rooms or areas, provided that such rooms or areas are accessory to the area served. Foyers, lobbies, and reception rooms constructed as required for corridors shall not be construed as intervening rooms. Exit access shall be arranged so that it is not necessary to pass through any area identified under Protection from Hazards in Chapters 11 through 43 of NFPA *101*. [*101*:7.5.1.5]

14.10.2 Impediments to Egress. See also 7.1.9 of NFPA *101*, and 14.5.2. [*101*:7.5.2]

14.10.2.1* Access to an exit shall not be through kitchens, storerooms other than as provided in Chapters 36 and 37 of NFPA *101*, restrooms, closets, bedrooms or similar spaces, or other rooms or spaces subject to locking, unless passage through such rooms or spaces is permitted for the occupancy by Chapters 18, 19, 22, or 23 of NFPA *101*. [*101*:7.5.2.1]

14.10.2.2* Exit access and exit doors shall be designed and arranged to be clearly recognizable. [*101*:7.5.2.2]

14.10.2.2.1 Hangings or draperies shall not be placed over exit doors or located so that they conceal or obscure any exit, unless otherwise provided in 14.10.2.2.2. [*101*:7.5.2.2.1]

14.10.2.2.2 Curtains shall be permitted across means of egress openings in tent walls, provided that all of the following criteria are met:

(1) They are distinctly marked in contrast to the tent wall so as to be recognizable as means of egress.
(2) They are installed across an opening that is at least 6 ft (1830 mm) in width.
(3) They are hung from slide rings or equivalent hardware so as to be readily moved to the side to create an unobstructed opening in the tent wall that is of the minimum width required for door openings.

[*101*:7.5.2.2.2]

14.10.3 Exterior Ways of Exit Access.

14.10.3.1 Exit access shall be permitted to be by means of any exterior balcony, porch, gallery, or roof that conforms to the requirements of this chapter and Chapter 7 of NFPA *101*. [*101*:7.5.3.1]

14.10.3.2 The long side of the balcony, porch, gallery, or similar space shall be at least 50 percent open and shall be arranged to restrict the accumulation of smoke. [*101*:7.5.3.2]

14.10.3.3 Exterior exit access balconies shall be separated from the interior of the building by walls and opening protectives as required for corridors, unless the exterior exit access balcony is served by at least two remote stairs that can be accessed without any occupant traveling past an unprotected opening to reach one of the stairs, or unless dead ends on the exterior exit access do not exceed 20 ft (6100 mm). [*101*:7.5.3.3]

14.10.3.4 Exterior exit access shall be arranged so that there are no dead ends in excess of those permitted for dead-end corridors in Chapters 11 through 43 of NFPA *101*. [*101*:7.5.3.4]

14.10.4 Accessible Means of Egress.

14.10.4.1* Areas accessible to people with severe mobility impairment, other than in existing buildings, shall have not less than two accessible means of egress, unless otherwise provided in 14.10.4.1.2 through 14.10.4.1.4. [*101*:7.5.4.1]

14.10.4.1.1 Access within the allowable travel distance shall be provided to not less than one accessible area of refuge or one accessible exit providing an accessible route to an exit discharge. [*101*:7.5.4.1.1]

14.10.4.1.2 A single accessible means of egress shall be permitted from buildings or areas of buildings permitted to have a single exit. [*101*:7.5.4.1.2]

14.10.4.1.3 Accessible means of egress shall not be required in health care occupancies protected throughout by an approved, supervised automatic sprinkler system in accordance with Section 13.3. [*101*:7.5.4.1.3]

14.10.4.1.4 Exit access travel along the accessible means of egress shall be permitted to be common for the distances permitted as common paths of travel. [*101*:7.5.4.1.4]

14.10.4.2 Where two accessible means of egress are required, the exits serving such means of egress shall be located at a distance from one another not less than one-half the length of the maximum overall diagonal dimension of the building or area to be served. This distance shall be measured in a straight line between the nearest edge of the exit doors or exit access doors, unless otherwise provided in 14.10.4.2.1 through 14.10.4.2.3. [*101*:7.5.4.2]

14.10.4.2.1 Where exit enclosures are provided as the required exits specified in 14.10.4.2 and are interconnected by not less than a 1-hour fire-resistance-rated corridor, exit separation shall be permitted to be measured along the line of travel within the corridor. [*101*:7.5.4.2.1]

14.10.4.2.2 The requirement of 14.10.4.2 shall not apply to buildings protected throughout by an approved, supervised automatic sprinkler system in accordance with Section 13.3. [*101*:7.5.4.2.2]

14.10.4.2.3 The requirement of 14.10.4.2 shall not apply where the physical arrangement of means of egress prevents the possibility that access to both accessible means of egress will be blocked by any one fire or other emergency condition as approved by the AHJ. [*101*:7.5.4.2.3]

14.10.4.3 Each required accessible means of egress shall be continuous from each accessible occupied area to a public way or area of refuge in accordance with 7.2.12.2.2 of NFPA *101*. [*101*:7.5.4.3]

14.10.4.4 Where an exit stair is used in an accessible means of egress, it shall comply with 7.2.12 of NFPA *101* and either shall incorporate an area of refuge within an enlarged story-level landing or shall be accessed from an area of refuge. [*101*:7.5.4.4]

14.10.4.5 To be considered part of an accessible means of egress, an elevator shall be in accordance with 7.2.12.2.4 of NFPA *101*. [*101*:7.5.4.5]

14.10.4.6 To be considered part of an accessible means of egress, a smoke barrier in accordance with Section 12.9 with not less than a 1-hour fire resistance rating, or a horizontal exit in accordance with 7.2.4 of NFPA *101*, shall discharge to an area of refuge in accordance with 7.2.12 of NFPA *101*. [*101*:7.5.4.6]

14.10.4.7 Accessible stories that are four or more stories above or below a story of exit discharge shall have not less than one elevator complying with 14.10.4.5, except as modified in 14.10.4.8. [*101*:7.5.4.7]

14.10.4.8 Where elevators are required by 14.10.4.7, the smokeproof enclosure required by 7.2.12.2.4 of NFPA *101* shall not be required in buildings protected throughout by an approved, supervised automatic sprinkler system in accordance with NFPA 13. [*101*:7.5.4.8]

14.10.4.9 An area of refuge used as part of a required accessible means of egress shall be in accordance with 7.2.12 of NFPA *101*. [*101*:7.5.4.9]

14.11 Discharge from Exits.

14.11.1* Exit Termination. Exits shall terminate directly, at a public way or at an exterior exit discharge, unless otherwise provided in 14.11.1.3 through 14.11.1.5. [*101*:7.7.1]

14.11.1.1 Yards, courts, open spaces, or other portions of the exit discharge shall be of the required width and size to provide all occupants with a safe access to a public way. [*101*:7.7.1.1]

14.11.1.2 New exit discharge paths to a public way shall have a width of not less than 36 in. (915 mm) and existing exit discharge paths to a public way shall have a width of not less than 28 in. (710 mm). [*101*:7.7.1.2]

14.11.1.3 The requirement of 14.11.1 shall not apply to interior exit discharge as otherwise provided in 14.11.2. [*101*:7.7.1.3]

14.11.1.4 The requirement of 14.11.1 shall not apply to rooftop exit discharge as otherwise provided in 14.11.6. [*101*:7.7.1.4]

14.11.1.5 Means of egress shall be permitted to terminate in an exterior area for detention and correctional occupancies as otherwise provided in Chapters 22 and 23 of NFPA *101*. [*101*:7.7.1.5]

Δ **14.11.2 Exit Discharge Through Interior Building Areas.** Exits shall be permitted to discharge through interior building areas, provided that all of the following are met:

(1) Not more than 50 percent of the required number of exit stairs serving normally occupied areas of each floor, and not more than 50 percent of the exit enclosure capacity required for normally occupied areas of each floor, shall discharge through areas on any level of discharge, except as otherwise permitted by one of the following:

(a) One hundred percent of the exits shall be permitted to discharge through areas on any level of discharge in detention and correctional occupancies as otherwise provided in Chapters 22 and 23 of NFPA *101*.

(b) In existing buildings, the 50 percent limit on egress capacity shall not apply if the 50 percent limit on the required number of exits is met.

(c) Not more than 75 percent of the required number and capacity of exit stairs serving normally occupied areas of each floor shall be permitted to discharge through vestibules or foyers on any level of discharge where the level of discharge is protected throughout by an approved automatic sprinkler system in accordance with Section 13.3, and such vestibules or foyers meet the requirements of 14.11.2(3)(b).

(2) Each level of discharge shall discharge directly outside at the finished ground level or discharge directly outside and provide access to the finished ground level by outside stairs or outside ramps.

(3) The interior exit discharge shall be protected by one of the following methods:

(a) The level of discharge shall be protected throughout by an approved automatic sprinkler system in accordance with Section 13.3, or the portion of the level of discharge used for interior exit discharge shall be protected by an approved automatic sprinkler system in accordance with Section 13.3 and shall be separated from the nonsprinklered portion of the floor by fire barriers with a fire resistance rating meeting the requirements for the enclosure of exits. *(See 14.3.1.)*

(b) The interior exit discharge area shall be in a vestibule or foyer that meets all of the following criteria:

i. The depth from the exterior of the building shall be not more than 10 ft (3050 mm), and the length shall be not more than 30 ft (9.1 m).

ii. The foyer shall be separated from the remainder of the level of discharge by fire barriers with a minimum 1-hour fire resistance rating, and existing installations of wired glass in steel frames shall be permitted to be continued in use.

iii. The foyer shall serve only as means of egress and shall include an exit directly to the outside.

(4) The interior exit discharge shall lead to a free and unobstructed way to the exterior of the building, and such way shall be readily apparent or shall be identifiable by exit signage from the point of discharge from the exit.

(5) The entire area on the level of discharge shall be separated from areas below by construction having a fire resistance rating not less than that required for the exit enclosure, unless otherwise provided in 14.11.2(6).

(6) Levels below the level of discharge in an atrium shall be permitted to be open to the level of discharge where such level of discharge is protected in accordance with 8.6.7 of NFPA *101*.

[*101*:7.7.2]

14.11.3 Arrangement and Marking of Exit Discharge.

14.11.3.1 Where more than one exit discharge is required, exit discharges shall be arranged to meet the remoteness criteria of 14.10.1.3. [*101*:7.7.3.1]

14.11.3.2 The exit discharge shall be arranged and marked to make clear the direction of egress travel from the exit discharge to a public way. [*101*:7.7.3.2]

14.11.3.3* Stairs and ramps that continue more than one-half story below the level of discharge shall be provided with an approved means to prevent or dissuade occupants from traveling past the level of discharge during emergency building evacuation. [*101*:7.7.3.3]

14.11.4 Components of Exit Discharge. Doors, stairs, ramps, corridors, exit passageways, bridges, balconies, escalators, moving walks, and other components of an exit discharge shall comply with the detailed requirements of this chapter for such components. [*101*:7.7.4]

14.11.5 Signs. See 10.11.3. [*101*:7.7.5]

14.11.6 Discharge to Roofs. Where approved by the AHJ, exits shall be permitted to discharge to roofs or other sections of the building or an adjoining building where all of the following criteria are met:

(1) The roof/ceiling assembly construction has a fire resistance rating not less than that required for the exit enclosure.
(2) A continuous and safe means of egress from the roof is available.

[*101*:7.7.6]

14.12 Illumination of Means of Egress.

14.12.1 General.

14.12.1.1* Illumination of means of egress shall be provided in accordance with Section 14.12 for every building and structure where required in Chapters 11 through 43 of NFPA *101*. For the purposes of this requirement, exit access shall include only designated stairs, aisles, corridors, ramps, escalators, and passageways leading to an exit. For the purposes of this requirement, exit discharge shall include only designated stairs, aisles, corridors, ramps, escalators, walkways, and passageways leading to a public way. [*101*:7.8.1.1]

14.12.1.2 Illumination of means of egress shall be continuous during the time that the conditions of occupancy require that the means of egress be available for use, unless otherwise provided in 14.12.1.2.2. [*101*:7.8.1.2]

14.12.1.2.1 Artificial lighting shall be employed at such locations and for such periods of time as are necessary to maintain the illumination to the minimum criteria values herein specified. [*101*:7.8.1.2.1]

14.12.1.2.2* Unless prohibited by Chapters 11 through 43 of NFPA *101*, automatic lighting control devices shall be permitted to temporarily turn off the illumination within the means of egress, provided that each lighting control device complies with all of the following:

(1) In new installations, the lighting control device is listed.
(2) The lighting control device is equipped to automatically energize any controlled lights required for compliance with Section 14.13 upon loss of normal power and is evaluated for this purpose.
(3) Illumination timers are provided and are set for a minimum 15-minute duration.
(4) The lighting control device is activated by any occupant movement in the area served by the lighting units.
(5) In new installations, the lighting control device is activated by activation of the building fire alarm system, if provided.
(6) The lighting control device does not turn off any lights relied upon for activation of photoluminescent exit signs or path markers.
(7) The lighting control device does not turn off any battery-equipped emergency luminaires, unit equipment, or exit signs.

[*101*:7.8.1.2.2]

14.12.1.2.3* Energy-saving sensors, switches, timers, or controllers shall be approved and shall not compromise the continuity of illumination of the means of egress required by 14.12.1.2. [*101*:7.8.1.2.3]

14.12.1.3 The floors and other walking surfaces within an exit and within the portions of the exit access and exit discharge designated in 14.12.1.1 shall be illuminated as follows:

(1) During conditions of stair use, the minimum illumination for new stairs shall be at least 10 foot-candles (108 lux), measured at the walking surfaces.
(2) The minimum illumination for floors and other walking surfaces, other than new stairs during conditions of stair use, shall be to values of at least 1 foot-candle (10.8 lux), measured at the floor.
(3) In assembly occupancies, the illumination of the walking surfaces of exit access shall be at least 0.2 foot-candle (2.2 lux) during periods of performances or projections involving directed light.
(4)* The minimum illumination requirements shall not apply where operations or processes require low lighting levels.

[*101*:7.8.1.3]

14.12.1.4* Required illumination shall be arranged so that the failure of any single lighting unit does not result in an illumination level of less than 0.2 foot-candle (2.2 lux) in any designated area. [*101*:7.8.1.4]

14.12.1.5 The equipment or units installed to meet the requirements of Section 14.14 also shall be permitted to serve the function of illumination of means of egress, provided that all requirements of Section 14.12 for such illumination are met. [*101*:7.8.1.5]

14.12.2 Sources of Illumination.

14.12.2.1 Illumination of means of egress shall be from a source considered reliable by the AHJ. [*101*:7.8.2.1]

14.12.2.2 Battery-operated electric lights and other types of portable lamps or lanterns shall not be used for primary illumination of means of egress. Battery-operated electric lights shall be permitted to be used as an emergency source to the extent permitted under Section 14.13. [*101*:7.8.2.2]

14.13 Emergency Lighting.

14.13.1 General.

14.13.1.1* Emergency lighting facilities for means of egress shall be provided in accordance with Section 14.13 for the following:

(1) Buildings or structures where required in Chapters 11 through 43 of NFPA *101*
(2) Underground and limited-access structures as addressed in Section 11.7 of NFPA *101*
(3) High-rise buildings as required by NFPA *101*
(4) Doors equipped with delayed-egress locks
(5) Stair shafts and vestibules of smokeproof enclosures, for which the following also apply:

  (a) The stair shaft and vestibule shall be permitted to include a standby generator that is installed for the smokeproof enclosure mechanical ventilation equipment.
  (b) The standby generator shall be permitted to be used for the stair shaft and vestibule emergency lighting power supply.

(6) New sensor-release of electrical locking systems in accordance with 14.5.3.2

[*101*:7.9.1.1]

14.13.1.2 For the purposes of 14.13.1.1, exit access shall include only designated stairs, aisles, corridors, ramps, escalators, and passageways leading to an exit. For the purposes of 14.13.1.1, exit discharge shall include only designated stairs, ramps, aisles, walkways, and escalators leading to a public way. [*101*:7.9.1.2]

14.13.1.3 Where maintenance of illumination depends on changing from one energy source to another, a delay of not more than 10 seconds shall be permitted. [*101*:7.9.1.3]

14.13.2 Periodic Testing of Emergency Lighting Equipment.

14.13.2.1 Required emergency lighting systems shall be tested in accordance with one of the four options offered by 14.13.2.1.1, 14.13.2.1.2, or 14.13.2.1.3, or 14.13.2.1.4. [*101*:7.9.3.1]

14.13.2.1.1 Testing of required emergency lighting systems shall be permitted to be conducted as follows:

(1) Functional testing shall be conducted monthly with a minimum of 3 weeks and a maximum of 5 weeks between tests, for not less than 30 seconds, except as otherwise permitted by 14.13.2.1.1(2).
(2) The test interval shall be permitted to be extended beyond 30 days with the approval of the AHJ.
(3) Functional testing shall be conducted annually for a minimum of 1½ hours if the emergency lighting system is battery powered.
(4) The emergency lighting equipment shall be fully operational for the duration of the tests required by 14.13.2.1.1(1) and 14.13.2.1.1(3).
(5) Written records of visual inspections and tests shall be kept by the owner for inspection by the AHJ.

[*101*:7.9.3.1.1]

14.13.2.1.2 Testing of required emergency lighting systems shall be permitted to be conducted as follows:

(1) Self-testing/self-diagnostic battery-operated emergency lighting equipment shall be provided.
(2) Not less than once every 30 days, self-testing/self-diagnostic battery-operated emergency lighting equipment shall automatically perform a test with a duration of a minimum of 30 seconds and a diagnostic routine.
(3) Self-testing/self-diagnostic battery-operated emergency lighting equipment shall indicate failures by a status indicator.
(4) A visual inspection shall be performed at intervals not exceeding 30 days.
(5) Functional testing shall be conducted annually for a minimum of 1½ hours.
(6) Self-testing/self-diagnostic battery-operated emergency lighting equipment shall be fully operational for the duration of the 1½ hour test.
(7) Written records of visual inspections and tests shall be kept by the owner for inspection by the AHJ.

[*101*:7.9.3.1.2]

14.13.2.1.3 Testing of required emergency lighting systems shall be permitted to be conducted as follows:

(1) Computer-based, self-testing/self-diagnostic battery-operated emergency lighting equipment shall be provided.
(2) Not less than once every 30 days, emergency lighting equipment shall automatically perform a test with a duration of a minimum of 30 seconds and a diagnostic routine.
(3) The emergency lighting equipment shall automatically perform annually a test for a minimum of 1½ hours.
(4) The emergency lighting equipment shall be fully operational for the duration of the tests required by 14.13.2.1.3(2) and 14.13.2.1.3(3).
(5) The computer-based system shall be capable of providing a report of the history of tests and failures at all times.

[*101*:7.9.3.1.3]

14.13.2.1.4 Testing of required emergency lighting systems shall be permitted to be conducted in accordance with 7.9.2.4 of NFPA *101*. [*101*:7.9.3.1.4]

14.14 Marking of Means of Egress.

14.14.1 General.

14.14.1.1 Where Required. Means of egress shall be marked in accordance with Section 14.14 where required in Chapters 11 through 43 of NFPA *101*. [*101*:7.10.1.1]

14.14.1.2 Exits.

14.14.1.2.1* Exits, other than main exterior exit doors that obviously and clearly are identifiable as exits, shall be marked by an approved sign that is readily visible from any direction of exit access. [*101*:7.10.1.2.1]

14.14.1.2.2* Horizontal components of the egress path within an exit enclosure shall be marked by approved exit or directional exit signs where the continuation of the egress path is not obvious. [*101*:7.10.1.2.2]

14.14.1.3 Exit Stair Door Tactile Signage. Tactile signage shall be provided to meet all of the following criteria, unless otherwise provided in 14.14.1.4:

(1) Tactile signage shall be located at each exit door requiring an exit sign.
(2) Tactile signage shall read as follows: EXIT
(3) Tactile signage shall comply with ICC A117.1, *Accessible and Usable Buildings and Facilities*.

[*101*:7.10.1.3]

14.14.1.4 Existing Exemption. The requirements of 14.14.1.3 shall not apply to existing buildings, provided that the occupancy classification does not change. [*101*:7.10.1.4]

14.14.1.5 Exit Access.

14.14.1.5.1 Access to exits shall be marked by approved, readily visible signs in all cases where the exit or way to reach the exit is not readily apparent to the occupants. [*101*:7.10.1.5.1]

14.14.1.5.2* New sign placement shall be such that no point in an exit access corridor is in excess of the rated viewing distance or 100 ft (30 m), whichever is less, from the nearest sign. [*101*:7.10.1.5.2]

14.14.1.6* Floor Proximity Exit Signs. Where floor proximity exit signs are required in Chapters 11 through 43 of NFPA *101*, such signs shall comply with 14.14.3, 14.14.4, 14.14.5, and 14.14.6 for externally illuminated signs and 14.14.7 for internally illuminated signs. Such signs shall be located near the floor level in addition to those signs required for doors or corridors. The bottom of the sign shall be not less than 6 in. (150 mm), but not more than 18 in. (455 mm), above the floor. For exit doors, the sign shall be mounted on the door or adjacent to the door, with the nearest edge of the sign within 4 in. (100 mm) of the door frame. [*101*:7.10.1.6]

14.14.1.7* Floor Proximity Egress Path Marking. Where floor proximity egress path marking is required in Chapters 11 through 43 of NFPA *101*, an approved floor proximity egress path marking system that is internally illuminated shall be installed within 18 in. (455 mm) of the floor. Floor proximity egress path marking systems shall be listed in accordance with UL 1994, *Luminous Egress Path Marking Systems*. The system shall provide a visible delineation of the path of travel along the designated exit access and shall be essentially continuous, except as interrupted by doorways, hallways, corridors, or other such architectural features. The system shall operate continuously or at any time the building fire alarm system is activated. The activation, duration, and continuity of operation of the system shall be in accordance with 7.9.2 of NFPA *101*. The system shall be maintained in accordance with the product manufacturing listing. [*101*:7.10.1.7]

14.14.1.8* Visibility. Every sign required in Section 14.14 shall be located and of such size, distinctive color, and design that it is readily visible and shall provide contrast with decorations, interior finish, or other signs. No decorations, furnishings, or equipment that impairs visibility of a sign shall be permitted. No brightly illuminated sign (for other than exit purposes), display, or object in or near the line of vision of the required exit sign that could detract attention from the exit sign shall be permitted. [*101*:7.10.1.8]

14.14.1.9 Mounting Location. The bottom of new egress markings shall be located at a vertical distance of not more than 6 ft 8 in. (2030 mm) above the top edge of the egress opening intended for designation by that marking. Egress markings shall be located at a horizontal distance of not more than the required width of the egress opening, as measured from the edge of the egress opening intended for designation by that marking to the nearest edge of the marking. [*101*:7.10.1.9]

14.14.2 Directional Signs.

14.14.2.1 A sign complying with 14.14.3, with a directional indicator showing the direction of travel, shall be placed in every location where the direction of travel to reach the nearest exit is not apparent. [*101*:7.10.2.1]

14.14.2.2 Directional exit signs shall be provided within horizontal components of the egress path within exit enclosures as required by 14.14.1.2.2. [*101*:7.10.2.2]

14.14.3* Sign Legend.

14.14.3.1 Signs required by 14.14.1 and 14.14.2 shall read as follows in plainly legible letters, or other appropriate wording shall be used:

EXIT

[*101*:7.10.3.1]

14.14.3.2* Where approved by the AHJ, pictograms in compliance with NFPA 170 shall be permitted. [*101*:7.10.3.2]

14.14.4* Power Source. Where emergency lighting facilities are required by the applicable provisions of Chapters 11 through 43 of NFPA *101* for individual occupancies, the signs, other than approved self-luminous signs and listed photoluminescent signs in accordance with 14.14.7.2, shall be illuminated by the emergency lighting facilities. The level of illumination of the signs shall be in accordance with 14.14.6.3 or 14.14.7 for the required emergency lighting duration as specified in 7.9.2.1 of NFPA *101*. However, the level of illumination shall be permitted to decline to 60 percent at the end of the emergency lighting duration. [*101*:7.10.4]

14.14.5 Illumination of Signs.

14.14.5.1* General. Every sign required by 14.14.1.2, 14.14.1.5, or 14.14.8.1, other than where operations or processes require low lighting levels, shall be suitably illuminated by a reliable light source. Externally and internally illuminated signs shall be legible in both the normal and emergency lighting mode. [*101*:7.10.5.1]

14.14.5.2* Continuous Illumination.

14.14.5.2.1 Every sign required to be illuminated by 14.14.6.3, 14.14.7, and 14.14.8.1 shall be continuously illuminated as required under the provisions of Section 14.12, unless otherwise provided in 14.14.5.2.2. [*101*:7.10.5.2.1]

14.14.5.2.2* Illumination for signs shall be permitted to flash on and off upon activation of the fire alarm system. [*101*:7.10.5.2.2]

14.14.6 Externally Illuminated Signs.

14.14.6.1* Size of Signs.

14.14.6.1.1 Externally illuminated signs required by 14.14.1 and 14.14.2, other than approved existing signs, unless otherwise provided in 14.14.6.1.2, shall read EXIT or shall use other appropriate wording in plainly legible letters sized as follows:

(1) For new signs, the letters shall be not less than 6 in. (150 mm) high, with the principal strokes of letters not less than ¾ in. (19 mm) wide.
(2) For existing signs, the required wording shall be permitted to be in plainly legible letters not less than 4 in. (100 mm) high.
(3) The word EXIT shall be in letters of a width not less than 2 in. (51 mm), except the letter I, and the minimum spacing between letters shall be not less than ⅜ in. (9.5 mm).
(4) Sign legend elements larger than the minimum established in 14.14.6.1.1(1) through 14.14.6.1.1(3) shall use letter widths, strokes, and spacing in proportion to their height.

[*101*:7.10.6.1.1]

14.14.6.1.2 The requirements of 14.14.6.1.1 shall not apply to marking required by 14.14.1.3 and 14.14.1.7. [*101*:7.10.6.1.2]

14.14.6.2* Size and Location of Directional Indicator.

14.14.6.2.1 Directional indicators, unless otherwise provided in 14.14.6.2.2, shall comply with all of the following:

(1) The directional indicator shall be located outside of the EXIT legend, not less than ⅜ in. (9.5 mm) from any letter.
(2) The directional indicator shall be of a chevron type, as shown in Figure 14.14.6.2.1.
(3) The directional indicator shall be identifiable as a directional indicator at a distance of 40 ft (12 m).
(4) A directional indicator larger than the minimum established for compliance with 14.14.6.2.1(3) shall be proportionately increased in height, width, and stroke.

(5) The directional indicator shall be located at the end of the sign for the direction indicated. [*101*:7.10.6.2.1]

14.14.6.2.2 The requirements of 14.14.6.2.1 shall not apply to approved existing signs. [*101*:7.10.6.2.2]

14.14.6.3* Level of Illumination. Externally illuminated signs shall be illuminated by not less than 5 foot-candles (54 lux) at the illuminated surface and shall have a contrast ratio of not less than 0.5. [*101*:7.10.6.3]

14.14.7 Internally Illuminated Signs.

14.14.7.1 Listing. Internally illuminated signs shall be listed in accordance with UL 924, *Emergency Lighting and Power Equipment*, unless they meet one of the following criteria:

(1) They are approved existing signs.
(2) They are existing signs having the required wording in legible letters not less than 4 in. (100 mm) high.
(3) They are signs that are in accordance with 14.14.1.3 and 14.14.1.6.

[*101*:7.10.7.1]

14.14.7.2* Photoluminescent Signs. The face of a photoluminescent sign shall be continually illuminated while the building is occupied. The illumination levels on the face of the photoluminescent sign shall be in accordance with its listing. The charging illumination shall be a reliable light source, as determined by the AHJ. The charging light source shall be of a type specified in the product markings. [*101*:7.10.7.2]

14.14.8 Special Signs.

14.14.8.1 Sign Illumination.

14.14.8.1.1* Where required by other provisions of this *Code*, special signs shall be illuminated in accordance with 14.14.5, 14.14.6.3, and 14.14.7. [*101*:7.10.8.1.1]

14.14.8.1.2 Where emergency lighting facilities are required by the applicable provisions of Chapters 11 through 43 of NFPA *101*, the required illumination of special signs shall additionally be provided under emergency lighting conditions. [*101*:7.10.8.1.2]

14.14.8.2 Characters. Special signs, where required by other provisions of this *Code*, shall comply with the visual character requirements of ICC A117.1, *Accessible and Usable Buildings and Facilities*. [*101*:7.10.8.2]

14.14.8.3* No Exit.

14.14.8.3.1 Any door, passage, or stairway that is neither an exit nor a way of exit access and that is located or arranged so that it is likely to be mistaken for an exit shall be identified by a sign that reads as follows:

NO
EXIT

[*101*:7.10.8.3.1]

14.14.8.3.2 For other than previously approved existing NO EXIT signs, the sign shall comply with all of the following:

(1) The word NO shall be in letters not less than 2 in. (51 mm) high, with a stroke width of not less than 3⁄8 in. (9.5 mm).
(2) The word EXIT shall be in letters not less than 1 in. (25 mm) high.
(3) Larger signs shall retain the same letter-height-to-stroke-width ratio for the word NO and a 2:1 letter-height ratio between the words NO and EXIT.
(4) The word EXIT shall be located below the word NO.

[*101*:7.10.8.3.2]

14.15 Secondary Means of Escape.

14.15.1 Secondary means of escape shall comply with NFPA *101*.

14.15.2 Where approved on secondary means of escape, security bars, grates, grilles, or similar devices shall be equipped with approved release mechanisms that are releasable from the inside without the use of a tool, a key, special knowledge, or force greater than that which it takes for normal operation of the door or window.

Chapter 15 Fire Department Service Delivery Concurrency Evaluation

15.1 Application.

15.1.1 The AHJ shall be permitted to require a proposed development in the jurisdiction undergo a fire department service delivery concurrency evaluation.

15.1.1.1 Proposed developments that would increase the fire department's service population by less than 1 percent or increase the fire department's total protected building square footage by less than 1 percent shall not be subject to a fire department service delivery concurrency evaluation.

15.1.1.2 Paragraph 15.1.1.1 shall not apply to proposed developments that would exceed a 240-second travel time from an existing fire station and also exhibit one of the following characteristics:

(1) Total development square footage greater than 100,000 ft² (9290 m²)
(2) Increasing the fire department's service population by 500 or more

15.1.1.3* Paragraph 15.1.1.1 shall not apply to proposed developments that exhibit operational challenges to the fire department for which the fire department currently does not have the service levels in place to meet the hazard.

15.2 Level of Service Objectives.

15.2.1 The fire department shall provide the developer with the current level of service standards for fire protection, emergency medical, prevention, and other operational services provided by the fire department.

FIGURE 14.14.6.2.1 Chevron-Type Indicator. [*101*:Figure 7.10.6.2.1]

15.2.2 The level of service for the proposed development shall not be less than the fire department's current level of service for fire protection, emergency medical, prevention, and other operational services.

15.2.2.1 The AHJ shall be permitted to approve a reduced level of service for the proposed development if a service mitigation plan has been adopted by the jurisdiction.

15.3 Evaluator Qualifications. The fire department service delivery concurrency evaluation shall be prepared by a person with qualifications acceptable to the AHJ.

15.4 Fire Department Service Delivery Concurrency Evaluation Documentation.

15.4.1 The fire department service delivery concurrency evaluation shall include, but not be limited to, the following:

(1) The current level of service for fire protection, emergency medical, and prevention services
(2) The post-development level of service for fire protection, emergency medical, and prevention services
(3) Mitigation recommendations if the level of service in the post-development condition falls below the current level of service
(4) Short- and long-term funding sources for implementation of the mitigation recommendations

15.4.2 The fire department service delivery concurrency evaluation shall be provided in a format approved by the AHJ.

15.4.3 The fire department service delivery concurrency evaluation shall utilize data sources and standards approved by the AHJ.

15.5 Independent Review. The AHJ shall be permitted to require an approved, independent third-party evaluation of the fire department service delivery concurrency evaluation at the expense of the developer.

15.6 Approval.

15.6.1 The AHJ shall make the final determination as to whether the level of service objectives have been met for the proposed development and, if applicable, the mitigation strategies are funded and appropriate.

15.6.2 If a fire department service delivery concurrency evaluation is required by the AHJ, development shall not proceed until the report has been accepted by the AHJ.

Chapter 16 Safeguarding Construction, Alteration, and Demolition Operations

16.1 General Requirements.

16.1.1 Structures undergoing construction, alteration, or demolition operations, including those in underground locations, shall comply with NFPA 241 and this chapter.

16.1.2 A fire protection plan shall be established where required by the AHJ.

16.1.3* In buildings under construction, adequate escape facilities shall be maintained at all times for the use of construction workers. Escape facilities shall consist of doors, walkways, stairs, ramps, fire escapes, ladders, or other approved means or devices arranged in accordance with the general principles of Chapter 14 and NFPA *101* insofar as they can reasonably be applied to buildings under construction. [*101*:4.6.10.3]

16.1.4 Fire apparatus access roads provided in accordance with 18.2.3 shall be both of the following:

(1) Provided at the start of a project and shall be
(2) Maintained throughout construction

16.1.5 Permanent fire apparatus access road markings shall not be required until the building is complete or occupied for use.

16.2 Alteration of Buildings.

16.2.1 Where the building is protected by fire protection systems, such systems shall be maintained operational at all times during alteration.

16.2.2 Where alteration requires modification of a portion of the fire protection system, both of the following shall apply:

(1) The remainder of the system shall be kept in service.
(2) The fire department shall be notified.

16.2.3 When it is necessary to shut down the system, the AHJ shall have the authority to require alternate measures of protection until the system is returned to service.

16.2.4 The fire department shall be notified when the system is shut down and when the system is returned to service.

16.2.5 All required exit components shall be maintained in accordance with this *Code* as deemed necessary by the AHJ.

16.2.6 Fire-resistive assemblies and construction shall be maintained.

16.3 Fire Safety During Demolition.

16.3.1 If a building intended to be demolished contains a sprinkler system, such system shall not be rendered inoperative without approval of the AHJ.

16.3.2 Demolition operations involving the use of cutting and welding shall be done in accordance with Chapter 41.

Δ **16.3.3** Combustible waste material shall not be burned at the demolition site unless approved by the AHJ.

N **16.3.4** Combustible materials shall be removed from the site as often as necessary to minimize the hazards therefrom. *(See 16.2.3 and Section 10.10.)*

16.3.5 Where in the opinion of the AHJ the demolition site is of a hazardous nature, qualified personnel shall serve as an on-site fire watch.

16.4 Torch-Applied Roofing Systems.

16.4.1 Permits. Permits, where required, shall comply with Section 1.13.

16.4.2 Torch-applied roofing systems shall be installed in accordance with Chapter 9 of NFPA 241.

16.5 Tar Kettles and Rubberized Asphalt Melters.

16.5.1 General.

16.5.1.1 The provisions of Section 16.5 shall apply to any type of equipment including, but not limited to, chassis-mounted equipment used for preheating or heating tar, asphalt, rubberized asphalt, pitch, or similar substances for roofs, floors, pipes, or similar objects.

16.5.1.2 Permits. Permits, where required, shall comply with Section 1.13.

16.5.2 Tar Kettles.

16.5.2.1 Operating kettles shall not be located inside of or on the roof of any building.

Δ **16.5.2.2 Tar Kettle Location.**

N **16.5.2.2.1** The kettle shall be operated in a controlled area.

N **16.5.2.2.2** The controlled area shall be identified by the use of traffic cones, barriers, and other suitable means as approved by the AHJ.

16.5.2.3 Kettle Supervision.

16.5.2.3.1 An operating kettle shall be attended by a minimum of one employee who is knowledgeable of the operations and hazards.

16.5.2.3.2 The employee shall comply with both of the following:

(1) Be within 25 ft (7.6 m) of the kettle
(2) Have the kettle within sight

16.5.2.4 Fire Extinguishers.

16.5.2.4.1 Two approved 4-A:40-B:C fire extinguishers shall be provided and maintained within 25 ft (7.6 m) of the operating kettle.

16.5.2.4.2* A minimum of one approved 4-A:40-B:C fire extinguisher shall be provided and maintained on the roof in close proximity to the roofing operations while the roofing material is being applied.

16.5.2.4.3 Fire extinguishers shall be mounted in an accessible and visible or identified location.

16.5.2.5 Exits.

16.5.2.5.1 Roofing kettles shall not block exits, means of egress, gates, roadways, or entrances.

16.5.2.5.2 Kettles shall not be closer than 10 ft (3 m) from exits or means of egress.

16.5.2.6 Fuel System.

16.5.2.6.1 Fuel containers shall be constructed and approved for the use for which they were designed.

16.5.2.6.2 Liquefied petroleum gas (LP-Gas) containers, hose, regulators, and burners shall conform to the requirements in Chapter 69.

16.5.2.6.3 LP-Gas cylinders shall be secured to prevent accidental tipover.

16.5.2.7 Regulators shall be required on any cylinders.

16.5.2.8 Where, in the opinion of the AHJ, physical damage to the container is a danger, protection shall be provided to prevent such physical damage.

16.5.2.9 LP-Gas containers for roofing kettles shall not be used in any building.

16.5.2.10 Maintenance.

16.5.2.10.1 Roofing kettles and all integral working parts shall be both of the following:

(1) In good working condition
(2) Maintained free of excessive residue

16.5.2.10.2 All piping used for pumping heated material to the roof shall be installed in a manner to prevent loss of heated material.

16.5.2.10.3 Flexible steel piping shall not be used on the vertical extension of piping systems.

16.5.2.10.4 Flexible steel piping shall be limited to those connections that are immediately adjacent to the pump kettle or discharge outlet.

Δ **16.5.2.10.5** No single length of flexible piping shall exceed 6 ft (1.8 m) in length.

N **16.5.2.10.6** All piping shall be able to withstand a pressure of at least four times the working pressure of the pump.

16.5.2.11 Roofing Kettle Doors.

16.5.2.11.1 All roofing kettles shall have doors permanently attached.

16.5.2.11.2 Roofing kettle doors shall be both of the following:

(1) Installed in a workmanlike manner
(2) Provided with handles that allow them to be opened without the operator having to stand in front of same

16.5.2.11.3 All kettles shall have an approved, working visible temperature gauge that indicates the temperature of the material being heated.

16.5.2.12 All kettle doors shall be tightly closed and latched when in transit.

16.5.2.13 Construction.

16.5.2.13.1 The materials and methods of construction of roofing kettles shall be acceptable to the AHJ.

16.5.2.13.2 Minimum Requirements.

16.5.2.13.2.1 Paragraph 16.5.2.13.2 shall apply to all roofing kettles or tar pots in excess of 1 gal (3.8 L) capacity.

16.5.2.13.2.2 No roofing kettle shall have a capacity in excess of 5 barrels (bbl).

Δ **16.5.2.13.2.3** Roofing kettles of 2 bbl capacity or less shall be constructed of steel sheet having a thickness of not less than 0.105 in. (No. 12 Manufacturers' Standard Gauge).

N **16.5.2.13.2.4** Kettles of more than 2 bbl capacity shall be constructed of steel sheet having a thickness of not less than 0.135 in. (No. 10 Manufacturers' Standard Gauge).

N **16.5.2.13.2.5** All supports, corners, and the top and bottom of the fire box shall be bound with angle iron or other reinforcements approved by the AHJ.

N **16.5.2.13.2.6** All doors shall be hinged, closely fitted, and adequately latched.

N **16.5.2.13.2.7** Fire boxes shall be either of sufficient height from the ground or provided with a system of shields or insulation to prevent heat damage to the street surface.

Δ **16.5.2.13.2.8** Lids that can be gravity operated shall be provided on all roofing kettles.

N **16.5.2.13.2.9** The tops and covers of all kettles shall be constructed of steel sheet having a thickness of not less than 0.075 in. (1.90 mm) (No. 14 Manufacturers' Standard Gauge) that is close fitting and attached to the kettle with hinges that allow gravity to close the lid.

16.5.2.13.2.10 The chassis shall be substantially constructed and capable of carrying the load imposed upon it whether it is standing still or being transported.

16.5.2.13.2.11 Fuel containers, burners, and related appurtenances of roofing kettles in which LP-Gas is used for heating shall comply with all the requirements of Chapter 69.

16.5.2.13.2.12 Fuel containers that operate under air pressure shall comply with both of the following:

(1) Not exceed 20 gal (76 L) in capacity
(2) Be subject to the approval of the AHJ

Δ **16.5.2.13.2.13** All fuel containers shall be

(1) Maintained in accordance with applicable NFPA codes and standards
(2) Be at least 10 ft (3 m) from the burner flame or at least 2 ft (0.6 m) therefrom when properly insulated from heat or flame

16.5.3 Rubberized Asphalt Melters for Roof Deck Systems.

16.5.3.1 General.

16.5.3.1.1 Fully enclosed chassis-mounted and portable rubberized asphalt melters shall comply with 16.5.3.

16.5.3.1.2 Fully enclosed chassis-mounted and portable rubberized asphalt melters for heating a mix of asphalt and inert material for application on roof decks shall use an indirect method of heating that complies with all of the following:

(1) The heating system shall use a fully enclosed oil or air system that transfers heat from a burner to the oil or air around the outside of a material vat which then heats the rubberized material.
(2) The material vat shall not be subject to direct burner or flame impingement.
(3) The temperature rise in the material vat shall be gradual and controlled.

16.5.3.2 Permits.

16.5.3.2.1 Permits, where required, shall comply with Section 1.13.

Δ **16.5.3.2.2*** Permits for the operation of a rubberized asphalt melter on a roof deck shall not be deemed a permit for torches or burners.

16.5.3.3 Rubberized Asphalt Melter Location. The melter shall be located and operated in a controlled area identified by the use of traffic cones, barriers, and other suitable means as designated by the AHJ.

16.5.3.3.1 Melters shall not be located or operated on combustible roof decks.

16.5.3.3.2 The design load of the roof deck shall be both of the following:

(1) Capable of supporting the weight of the melter when loaded to capacity with rubberized asphalt material
(2) As determined on building drawings or by a design professional acceptable to the AHJ

16.5.3.3.3 Melters shall be chocked in place on the roof deck at locations identified by the design professional and acceptable to the AHJ.

16.5.3.3.4 Rubberized asphalt cakes for use in melters shall be located on the roof at a location agreed upon by the design professional and the AHJ.

16.5.3.3.5 Rubberized asphalt melters shall not be located inside of any building.

16.5.3.4 Exits.

16.5.3.4.1 Melters shall not block exits or a means of egress or escape to an exit.

16.5.3.4.2 Melters shall not be closer than 10 ft from exits.

16.5.3.5 Fire Extinguishers.

16.5.3.5.1 Two approved 4-A:40-B:C fire extinguishers shall be provided and maintained within 25 ft of the melter.

16.5.3.5.2 A minimum of one approved 4-A:40-B:C fire extinguisher shall be provided in close proximity to the roofing material application.

16.5.3.5.3 Each worker shall be instructed on the proper use of fire extinguishers and in the event of a fire to turn off all melter engines and burners and notify the fire department.

16.5.3.6 Melter Operation.

Δ **16.5.3.6.1** Melters shall be operated according to manufacturer instructions.

N **16.5.3.6.2** Melters shall operate using integral control systems that include shut off controls for the diesel fired burner and temperature controls for the oil system and the material vat.

16.5.3.6.3 The diesel burner shall fire into an oil or air jacketed tank for uniform transfer.

16.5.3.6.4 Melters shall have melter lids permanently attached and closed at all times during operation.

16.5.3.7 Melter Supervision.

16.5.3.7.1 An operating melter shall be constantly attended by an employee who is knowledgeable and solely dedicated to the operation of the equipment and associated hazards.

16.5.3.7.2 The employee shall comply with both of the following:

(1) Be within 25 ft of the melter
(2) Have the melter within sight

16.5.3.7.3 The employee shall remain in the area of the melter for a minimum of one-hour after the device is shut down.

16.5.3.7.4 The roofing contractor shall have the capability to immediately notify the fire department of an emergency on the site.

16.5.3.8 Fuel System.

△ **16.5.3.8.1** Fuel containers shall be constructed and approved for the use for which they were designed.

N **16.5.3.8.2** Melter fuel tanks shall be attached to the frame of the melter.

16.5.3.8.3 Melters shall be diesel fuel or electrically powered.

16.5.3.8.4 Portable fuel tanks shall not be utilized to power melters.

16.5.3.8.5 Diesel tanks and engines integral to melters shall be maintained in accordance with manufacturer instructions.

16.5.3.8.6 Refueling of diesel tanks shall be performed when the melter is off.

16.5.3.8.6.1 A refueling and spill prevention plan acceptable to the AHJ shall be utilized.

16.5.3.8.6.2 Refueling shall be conducted using approved safety cans.

16.5.3.8.6.3 No open flames shall be present within 20 ft of the refueling operation.

△ **16.5.3.9 Maintenance.** Melters and all integral working parts shall be both in good working condition and maintained free of excessive residue.

16.5.3.10 Minimum Requirements.

△ **16.5.3.10.1** Melters shall be operated as a complete unit as designed and built by the manufacturer.

N **16.5.3.10.2** Field changes that override controls or safety features shall not be permitted.

△ **16.5.3.10.3** Material vats on melters shall have a capacity of 230 gal or less.

N **16.5.3.10.4** Material vats shall be a permanent integral part of the melter unit.

16.5.3.10.5 The melter chassis shall be substantially constructed and capable of carrying the load imposed upon it whether it is standing still or being transported.

16.6 Asbestos Removal.

16.6.1 Notification. The AHJ and the fire department shall be notified 24 hours prior to the commencement and closure of asbestos removal operations.

16.6.2 Permits. Permits, where required, shall comply with Section 1.13.

16.6.3 Signs. Approved signs shall be posted at the entrance, exit and exit access door, decontamination areas, and waste disposal areas for asbestos removal operations.

16.6.3.1 The signs shall state that asbestos is being removed from the area, that asbestos is a suspected carcinogen, and that proper respiratory protection is required.

16.6.3.2 Signs shall have a reflective surface.

N **16.6.3.3** Sign lettering shall be a minimum of 2 in. (51 mm) high.

N **16.7 Lead Removal.**

N **16.7.1 Notification.** The AHJ and the fire department shall be notified 24 hours prior to the commencement and closure of lead removal operations.

N **16.7.2 Permits.** Permits, where required, shall comply with Section 1.13.

N **16.7.3 Signs.** Approved signs shall be posted at the entrance, exit and exit access door, decontamination areas, and waste disposal areas for lead removal operations.

N **16.7.3.1** The signs shall state that lead is being removed from the area.

N **16.7.3.2** Signs shall have a reflective surface.

N **16.7.3.3** Sign lettering shall be a minimum of 2 in. (51 mm) high.

Chapter 17   Wildland Urban Interface

17.1 General. The planning, construction, maintenance, education, and management elements for the protection of life and property from wildfire shall meet the requirements of this chapter and NFPA 1140.

17.1.1 In cases in which the local jurisdiction declares that an area within the jurisdiction is a wildland urban interface as determined by an assessment tool based upon accepted fire services practices, or where new structures will be located in a wildland/urban interface or intermix area, the AHJ shall perform, or cause to be performed, a wildland fire hazard assessment of each structure ignition zone in the development to determine relative risk, the extent of wildland fire hazard, and applicable mitigation measures.

△ **17.1.2*** The structure assessment shall, at a minimum, include the following:

(1) Identification and documentation of the wildland fire hazards in the ignition zone(s) for each structure within wildland fire hazard areas, according to the elements and conditions in 17.1.4
(2) Determination of mitigation measures for vegetation, other combustibles, and the structure, including the periodic maintenance associated with such measures
(3) Establishment of priorities relative to mitigating the risks from wildland fire
(4) Evaluation of the site for conflagration hazards associated with the property to provide information for fire operations strategies should the site or surrounding properties become involved with fire
[1140:424.2.2]

△ **17.1.3** The wildland fire hazard assessment shall be the basis for recommended mitigation measures relative to the vegetation, other combustibles, and structures on the site. [1140:24.2.3]

△ **17.1.4* Structure Assessment Elements and Conditions.** As a minimum, the structure assessment shall cover elements and conditions indicated in 17.1.5 through 17.1.9. [1140:24.3]

△ **17.1.5 Overview of the Surrounding Environment.** The structure assessment shall document the conditions of 17.1.5.1 through 17.1.5.5 in the assessment of the surrounding environment, as they will place the structure in the most risk from ignition by a wildland fire. [1140:24.3.1]

Δ **17.1.5.1*** The structure assessment shall document the location of the structure in relation to predominant topographical features, such as flat open areas, ridges, saddles, steep slopes, natural chimneys like steep narrow draws, or small canyons, that will increase the ignition potential of the structure. [1140:24.3.1.1]

Δ **17.1.5.2*** The structure assessment shall document local weather conditions, including wind, relative humidity, temperature, and fine fuel moisture content. [1140:24.3.1.2]

Δ **17.1.5.3*** The structure assessment shall document nearby structures using the same criteria as the primary structure. [1140:24.3.1.3]

Δ **17.1.5.4*** The structure assessment shall document any neighboring properties that could impact the ignition zone of the property being assessed. [1140:24.3.1.4]

Δ **17.1.5.5*** The structure assessment shall document the structure's location on the slope relative to the structure's potential exposure to heat from a wildland fire. [1140:24.3.1.5]

Δ **17.1.6 From Chimney to Eaves.** The structure assessment shall document the conditions of 17.1.6.1 through 17.1.6.6 to observe construction and vegetation as they place the structure in the most risk from ignition by a wildland fire. [1140:24.3.2]

Δ **17.1.6.1*** The structure assessment shall document the type and construction of roofing materials. [1140:24.3.2.1]

Δ **17.1.6.2*** The structure assessment shall document the condition of roofing materials and assemblies. [1140:24.3.2.2]

Δ **17.1.6.3*** The structure assessment shall document all skylights in roof assemblies. [1140:24.3.2.3]

Δ **17.1.6.4*** The structure assessment shall document the potential of roof gutters and areas where exterior walls meet roof or deck surfaces to collect litter on surfaces or in crevices. [1140:24.3.2.4]

Δ **17.1.6.5*** The structure assessment shall document the construction materials of gutters, downspouts, and connectors. [1140:24.3.2.5]

Δ **17.1.6.6*** The structure assessment shall document the materials and construction used in eaves of roof overhangs. [1140:24.3.2.6]

Δ **17.1.7 From Top of Exterior Wall to Foundation.** The structure assessment shall document the conditions of 17.1.7.1 through 17.1.7.6 to observe construction and vegetation as they place the structure in the most risk from ignition by a wildland fire. [1140:24.3.3]

Δ **17.1.7.1*** The structure assessment shall document the materials and construction used in exterior walls and exterior siding. [1140:24.3.3.1]

Δ **17.1.7.2** The structure assessment shall document the materials used for gutter downspouts and connectors on exterior walls. [1140:24.3.3.2]

Δ **17.1.7.3*** The structure assessment shall document the materials used in windows and other openings in vertical surfaces. [1140:24.3.3.3]

Δ **17.1.7.4*** The structure assessment shall document the location, size, and screening of ventilation openings. [1140:24.3.3.4]

Δ **17.1.7.5*** The structure assessment shall document all attached accessory structures as part of the primary structure. [1140:24.3.3.5]

Δ **17.1.7.6*** The structure assessment shall document areas next to or under a structure where combustible materials that present a source of flame exposure to the structure might collect. [1140:24.3.3.6]

Δ **17.1.8* From Foundation to the Immediate Landscaped Area.** The structure assessment shall document the conditions of 17.1.8.1 through 17.1.8.5 to observe construction and vegetation, as they place the structure in the most risk from ignition by a wildland fire. [1140:24.3.4]

Δ **17.1.8.1*** The structure assessment shall document all vegetative fuels and other combustible materials adjacent to and within 30 ft (9 m) of the structure for their potential to contribute to the intensity and spread of wildland fire. [1140:24.3.4.1]

Δ **17.1.8.2*** The structure assessment shall document the presence and location of all heat and flame sources within 30 ft (9 m) of the primary structure. [1140:24.3.4.2]

Δ **17.1.8.3*** The structure assessment shall document all projections attached to the primary structure. [1140:24.3.4.3]

Δ **17.1.8.4*** The structure assessment shall document detached structures within 30 ft (9 m) of the primary structure that might be ignited by flames, radiant heat, or firebrands from wildland fires. [1140:24.3.4.4]

Δ **17.1.8.5*** The structure assessment shall document vehicle parking areas within 30 ft (9 m) of any surface of the structure. [1140:24.3.4.5]

Δ **17.1.9 From the Immediate Landscaped Area to the Extent of the Structure Ignition Zone.** The structure assessment shall document the conditions of 17.1.9.1 through 17.1.9.8 to observe construction and vegetation, as they place the structure in the most risk from ignition by a wildland fire. [1140:24.3.5]

Δ **17.1.9.1*** The structure assessment shall document vegetation within the area between the outer edge of the immediate landscaped area and the extent of the structure ignition zone as potential fuel that can convey the fire to the structure. [1140:24.3.5.1]

Δ **17.1.9.2*** The structure assessment shall document the species and location of trees and the separation of tree crowns within the area between the outer edge of the immediate landscaped area and the extent of the structure ignition zone. [1140:24.3.5.2]

Δ **17.1.9.3*** The structure assessment shall document the presence and location of all heat and flame sources within the area between the outer edge of the immediate landscaped area and the extent of the structure ignition zone. [1140:24.3.5.3]

Δ **17.1.9.4*** The structure assessment shall document detached structures within the area between the outer edge of the immediate landscaped area and the extent of the structure ignition zone that might be ignited by flames, radiant heat, or firebrands from wildland fires. [1140:24.3.5.4]

△ **17.1.9.5*** The structure assessment shall document vehicle parking areas within the area between the outer edges of the immediate landscaped area and the extent of the structure ignition zone. [1140:24.3.5.5]

△ **17.1.9.6*** The structure assessment shall document all projections attached to the primary structure that extend beyond the immediate landscaped area. [1140:24.3.5.6]

△ **17.1.9.7** The structure assessment shall document all other factors that can affect the risk of ignition or the spread of wildland fire on improved property within the structure ignition zone, including the risk of structure fires spreading to vegetation. [1140:24.3.5.7]

△ **17.1.9.8** Any structure that fails to comply with the requirements of Chapter 25 of NFPA 1140 shall be deemed to increase the risk of the spread of wildland fire to improved property and the risk of fires on improved property spreading to wildland fuels. [1140:24.3.5.8]

17.1.10 Development of Wildland Fire Hazard Mitigation Plan.

△ **17.1.10.1** From the information gathered in each structure assessment, the AHJ shall require or cause to be developed a wildland fire hazard mitigation plan and schedule to address the wildland fire hazards identified in the specific structure ignition zone assessment. [1140:24.4.1]

△ **17.1.10.2** The AHJ shall work with applicable agencies and organizations to resolve any conflicts between recommended wildland fire hazard mitigation measures and mitigation measures or objectives of other hazards. [1140:24.4.2]

△ **17.1.10.3*** This plan shall include, but not be limited to, the following:

(1) Specific mitigation recommendations based on the hazard assessment to reduce the ignition potential around and including the structure
(2) Construction modification or retrofit necessary to reduce the identified hazards as a minimum or to comply with the provisions of Chapter 25 of NFPA 1140
(3) Fuel modification recommendations as specified in Chapter 26 of NFPA 1140
(4) A hazard mitigation implementation and maintenance schedule approved by the AHJ

[1140:24.4.3]

△ **17.1.10.4*** The history of wildland fire in the area under assessment shall be considered in determining required hazard mitigation plan. [1140:24.4.4]

△ **17.1.10.5*** The AHJ shall approve the mitigating measures relative to access, water supply, and construction based upon the structure assessment established in 17.1.2. [1140:24.4.5]

△ **17.1.10.6** From the information gathered in each structure assessment, the AHJ shall require or cause to be developed a wildland fire hazard severity map of each residential development area addressed. [1140:24.4.6]

△ **17.1.10.7** The map shall include, but not be limited to, the following data elements:

(1) Lot designations
(2) Structure locations on each lot
(3) Locations of wildland fire evacuation centers or safety zones
(4) Hazard severity for each lot

(5) Overlapping ignition zones
(6) Location of fire hydrants, cisterns, or other water sources for fire fighting

[1140:24.4.7]

17.1.11 Mitigation Implementation and Enforcement.

△ **17.1.11.1** The AHJ shall require the property owner to develop and comply with the approved wildland fire hazard mitigation plan and schedule according to 17.1.10.1. [1140:24.5.1]

△ **17.1.11.2** No permit associated with construction shall be issued if the provisions of this *Code* are not addressed. [1140:24.5.2]

△ **17.1.11.3** No permit associated with occupancy shall be issued until the provisions of this *Code* are satisfied. [1140:24.5.3]

17.2 Plans. The plans for construction and development within the wildland urban interface shall be submitted to the AHJ for review and approval.

17.3 Wildland Fire–Prone Areas.

17.3.1* Safeguards. Safeguards to prevent the occurrence of fires and to provide adequate fire protection and mitigation measures in hazardous fire areas shall be provided and maintained in accordance with Section 17.3.

17.3.2* Permits and Approvals. Permits for use of hazardous areas shall not be issued when public safety would be at risk, as determined by the AHJ. *(See Section 1.13 for additional requirements for permits.)*

17.3.3 Restricted Entry.

17.3.3.1 The AHJ shall determine and publicly announce when hazardous fire areas shall be closed to entry, and when such areas shall again be opened to entry.

17.3.3.2 Unauthorized persons shall not be permitted to enter or remain in closed hazardous fire areas.

17.3.3.3 Signs. Approved signs prohibiting entry by unauthorized persons shall be placed on every closed area and access point.

17.3.4 Use of Flammable Materials and Procedures.

17.3.4.1 Smoking. Lighting, igniting, or otherwise setting fire to any smoking material shall be prohibited unless within structures or smoking areas approved by the AHJ. *(See Section 10.9 for additional requirements on smoking.)*

17.3.4.2 Tracer Bullets, Tracer Charges, Rockets, and Model Aircraft.

17.3.4.2.1 Tracer bullets and tracer charges shall not be possessed, fired, or caused to be fired into or across hazardous fire areas.

17.3.4.2.2 Rockets, model planes, gliders, and balloons powered with an engine, propellant, or other feature liable to start or cause fire shall not be fired or projected into or across hazardous fire areas.

17.3.4.3 Explosives and Blasting. Explosives shall not be possessed, kept, stored, sold, offered for sale, given away, used, discharged, transported, or disposed of within hazardous fire areas except as permitted by the AHJ. *(See Chapter 65 for additional guidance.)*

17.3.4.4 Fireworks. Fireworks shall not be used or possessed in hazardous fire areas unless permitted by the AHJ. *(See Chapter 65 for additional guidance.)*

17.3.4.5 Apiaries. Lighted and smoldering material used in connection with smoking bees shall not be allowed in or upon hazardous fire areas except as permitted by the AHJ.

17.3.5 Clearance of Brush and Vegetative Growth.

17.3.5.1 Electrical Transmission Lines.

17.3.5.1.1 Clearance of brush and vegetative growth from electrical transmission and distribution line(s) shall be provided and maintained in accordance with 17.3.5.1.

17.3.5.1.2 A combustible-free space around poles and towers shall consist of a clearing of not less than 10 ft (3.05 m) in each direction from the outer circumference of the pole or tower during such periods of time as designated by the AHJ.

17.3.5.1.3 Trimming Clearance.

17.3.5.1.3.1 At the time of trimming, clearances not less than those established by Table 17.3.5.1.3.1 shall be provided.

17.3.5.1.3.2 The radial clearances in Table 17.3.5.1.3.1 are minimum clearances that shall be established at time of trimming between the vegetation and the energized conductors and associated live parts.

17.3.5.1.4 Clearances not less than those established by Table 17.3.5.1.4 shall be maintained during such periods of time as designated by the AHJ.

17.3.5.1.4.1 The site-specific clearance achieved, at the time of pruning, shall vary based on species' growth rates, the utility company specific trim cycle, the potential line sway due to wind, line sway due to electrical loading and ambient temperature, and the tree's location in proximity to the high voltage lines.

Table 17.3.5.1.3.1 Minimum Clearances Between Vegetation and Electrical Lines at Time of Trimming

Line Voltage	Minimal Radial Clearance from Conductor ft	m
2400–72,000	4	1.2
72,001–110,000	6	1.8
110,001–300,000	10	3.0
300,001 or more	15	4.6

Table 17.3.5.1.4 Minimum Clearances Between Vegetation and Electrical Lines to Be Maintained

Line Voltage	Minimum Clearance in.	mm
750–35,000	6	152
35,001–60,000	12	305
60,001–115,000	19	483
115,001–230,000	30.5	775
230,001–500,000	115	2920

17.3.5.1.4.2 The AHJ shall establish minimum clearances different than those specified by Table 17.3.5.1.4 when evidence substantiating such other clearances is submitted to the AHJ and approved.

17.3.5.1.5* Electrical Power Line Emergencies. During emergencies, the utility company shall perform the required work to the extent necessary to clear the hazard.

17.3.5.2 Structures.

17.3.5.2.1 Persons owning, leasing, controlling, operating, or maintaining buildings or structures in, upon, or adjoining hazardous fire areas, and persons owning, leasing, or controlling land adjacent to such buildings or structures, shall maintain an effective defensible space in accordance with 17.3.5.2.1.1 through 17.3.5.2.1.11.5.

Δ **17.3.5.2.1.1*** Surface fuels, including native vegetation and plants used for landscaping within the defined landscaping zones, shall be treated or removed. [1140:26.2.1]

Δ **17.3.5.2.1.2** Live vegetation within the fuel modification area shall have dead material removed and shall be thinned and pruned in conformance with the wildland fire mitigation plan, as approved by the AHJ. [1140:26.2.2]

Δ **17.3.5.2.1.3** Dead and downed fuels within 30 ft (9 m) of all buildings shall be removed or treated to maintain the fuel modification area in conformance with the wildland fire mitigation plan, as approved by the AHJ. [1140:26.2.3]

Δ **17.3.5.2.1.4** Vegetation under trees within the fuel modification area shall be maintained at a height that will preclude ground fire from spreading in the tree crown. [1140:26.2.4]

Δ **17.3.5.2.1.5*** Tree crowns within the structure ignition zone shall be spaced to prevent structure ignition from radiant heat. [1140:26.2.5]

Δ **17.3.5.2.1.6** The fuel modification plan shall include a maintenance element identifying and defining the responsibility for continued and periodic maintenance. [1140:26.2.6]

17.3.5.2.1.7 Chimneys and Flues.

Δ **17.3.5.2.1.7.1** Every fireplace and wood stove chimney and flue shall be provided with an approved spark arrester constructed of a minimum 12-gauge welded wire or woven wire mesh, with openings not exceeding ½ in. (12.7 mm). [1140:25.8.1]

Δ **17.3.5.2.1.7.2** Vegetation shall not be allowed within 10 ft (3 m) of a chimney outlet. [1140:25.8.2]

Δ **17.3.5.2.1.8* Accessory Structure(s).** Accessory structures shall be constructed to meet the requirements of Chapter 25 of NFPA 1140 or shall be separated from the main structure by a minimum of 30 ft (9 m). [1140:25.9]

17.3.5.2.1.9 Mobile and Manufactured Homes.

Δ **17.3.5.2.1.9.1** Permanently located mobile and manufactured homes with an open space beneath shall have a skirt of noncombustible materials, exterior fire-retardant-treated wood, or other ignition-resistant material. [1140:25.10.1]

Δ **17.3.5.2.1.9.2** Any enclosed space beneath the mobile or manufactured home shall be vented according to 25.3.3 of NFPA 1140. [1140:25.10.2]

Δ **17.3.5.2.1.10 Vehicle Parking Areas.** Vehicle parking areas within the immediate landscaped zone shall be maintained free of dry grasses and fine fuels that could be ignited by hot exhaust systems or firebrands. [1140:25.11]

17.3.5.2.1.11 Exterior Exposure Hazards.

Δ **17.3.5.2.1.11.1*** Heat and flame sources that are unprotected or unsupervised shall not be permitted within 30 ft (9 m) of the primary structure. [1140:25.12.1]

Δ **17.3.5.2.1.11.2** Incinerators, outdoor fireplaces, permanent barbecues, and grills shall not be built, installed, or maintained in hazardous fire areas without prior approval of the AHJ. [1140:25.12.2]

Δ **17.3.5.2.1.11.3** Openings in incinerators, outdoor fireplaces, permanent barbecues, and grills shall be provided with an approved spark arrester, screen, or door. [1140:25.12.3]

Δ **17.3.5.2.1.11.4** Propane tanks and other combustible liquids storage shall conform to NFPA 58 and the wildland fire hazard mitigation plan required in 17.1.10. [1140:25.12.4]

Δ **17.3.5.2.1.11.5** Other combustible materials within 30 ft (9 m) of any structure shall be removed or stored in conformance with the wildland fire hazard mitigation plan as approved by the AHJ. [1140:25.12.5]

17.3.5.2.2 Where required by the AHJ because of extra hazardous conditions, additional areas shall be maintained to include additional defensible space from buildings or structures, trees adjacent to or overhanging a building shall be maintained free of deadwood, and the roof of a structure shall be free of leaves, needles, or other dead vegetative growth.

17.3.5.3 Roadways. Areas within 10 ft (3 m) on each side of portions of highways and private streets shall be cleared of combustible vegetation and other combustible growth. Single specimens of trees, shrubbery, or cultivated ground cover such as green grass, ivy, succulents, or similar plants used as ground covers shall be permitted to be exempt provided that they do not form a means of readily transmitting fire.

17.3.6 Unusual Circumstances. The AHJ shall determine that difficult terrain, danger of erosion, or other unusual circumstances could require additional safeguards.

17.3.7 Fire Roads, Firebreaks, and Emergency Access.

17.3.7.1 The provisions of 17.3.7 and Section 18.2 shall be used to determine the design, clearances, and provisions for emergency access (ingress and egress).

17.3.7.2 Unauthorized vehicles shall not be driven upon fire roads or firebreaks. Vehicles shall not be parked in a manner that obstructs the entrance to a fire road or firebreak.

17.3.7.3 Radio and television aerials, guy wires, and other obstructions shall not be installed or maintained on fire roads or firebreaks unless the vertical clearance is sufficient to allow the movement of fire and emergency apparatus.

17.3.7.4 Motorcycles, motor scooters, and motor vehicles shall not be operated within hazardous fire areas, except upon clearly established public or private roads.

17.3.8 Tampering with Fire Safety Equipment. See Section 10.8 for requirements on tampering with fire safety equipment.

17.3.9 Maintenance. See 4.5.8 for requirements on maintenance.

Chapter 18 Fire Department Access and Water Supply

18.1 General. Fire department access and water supplies shall comply with this chapter.

18.1.1 Application.

18.1.1.1 This chapter shall apply to public and privately owned fire apparatus access roads.

18.1.1.2 This chapter shall apply to public and privately owned fire hydrant systems and water supplies.

18.1.2 Permits. Permits, where required, shall comply with Section 1.13.

18.1.3 Plans.

18.1.3.1 Fire Apparatus Access. Plans for fire apparatus access roads shall be submitted to the AHJ for review and approval prior to construction.

18.1.3.2 Fire Hydrant Systems. Plans and specifications for fire hydrant systems shall be submitted to the AHJ for review and approval prior to construction.

18.2 Fire Department Access.

18.2.1 Fire department access and fire apparatus access roads shall be provided and maintained in accordance with Section 18.2.

18.2.2* Access to Structures or Areas.

18.2.2.1 Access Box(es). The AHJ shall have the authority to require an access box(es) to be installed in an accessible location where access to or within a structure or area is difficult because of security. The access box(es) shall be of an approved type listed in accordance with UL 1037.

18.2.2.2 Access to Gated Subdivisions or Developments. The AHJ shall have the authority to require fire department access be provided to gated subdivisions or developments through the use of an approved device or system.

18.2.2.3 Access Maintenance. The owner or occupant of a structure or area, with required fire department access as specified in 18.2.2.1 or 18.2.2.2, shall notify the AHJ when the access is modified in a manner that could prevent fire department access.

18.2.3 Fire Apparatus Access Roads.

18.2.3.1 Required Access.

18.2.3.1.1 Approved fire apparatus access roads shall be provided for every facility, building, or portion of a building hereafter constructed or relocated.

18.2.3.1.2 Fire apparatus access roads shall consist of roadways, fire lanes, parking lot lanes, or a combination thereof.

18.2.3.1.3* The provisions of 18.2.3.1 through 18.2.3.2.2.1 shall be permitted to be modified by the AHJ where any of the following conditions exists:

(1) One- and two-family dwellings protected by an approved automatic sprinkler system in accordance with Section 13.1

(2) Existing one- and two-family dwellings
(3) Private garages having an area not exceeding 400 ft² (37 m²)
(4) Carports having an area not exceeding 400 ft² (37 m²)
(5) Agricultural buildings having an area not exceeding 400 ft² (37 m²)
(6) Sheds and other detached buildings, not classified as a residential occupancy, having an area not exceeding 400 ft² (37 m²)

18.2.3.1.4 When fire apparatus access roads cannot be installed due to location on property, topography, waterways, nonnegotiable grades, or other similar conditions, the AHJ shall be authorized to require additional fire protection features.

18.2.3.2 Access to Building.

18.2.3.2.1 A fire apparatus access road shall extend to within 50 ft (15 m) of at least one exterior door that can be opened from the outside and that provides access to the interior of the building.

18.2.3.2.1.1 Where a one- or two-family dwelling, or townhouse, is protected with an approved automatic sprinkler system that is installed in accordance with Section 13.3, the distance in 18.2.3.2.1 shall be permitted to be increased to 150 ft (46 m).

18.2.3.2.2 Fire apparatus access roads shall be provided such that any portion of the facility or any portion of an exterior wall of the first story of the building is located not more than 150 ft (46 m) from fire apparatus access roads as measured by an approved route around the exterior of the building or facility.

Δ **18.2.3.2.2.1** Where buildings are protected throughout with an approved automatic sprinkler system that is installed in accordance with NFPA 13, NFPA 13R, or NFPA 13D, the distance in 18.2.3.2.2 shall be permitted to be increased to 450 ft (137 m).

18.2.3.3* Multiple Access Roads. More than one fire apparatus access road shall be provided when it is determined by the AHJ that access by a single road could be impaired by vehicle congestion, condition of terrain, climate conditions, or other factors that could limit access.

18.2.3.4 Traffic Signal Pre-emption. Where fire department apparatus are equipped with traffic signal pre-emption devices, newly installed traffic signals shall be equipped with traffic signal pre-emption.

18.2.3.5 Specifications.

18.2.3.5.1 Dimensions.

18.2.3.5.1.1* Fire apparatus access roads shall have an unobstructed width of not less than 20 ft (6.1 m).

18.2.3.5.1.1.1* Where approved by the AHJ, the width of fire apparatus access roads shall be permitted to be less than the minimum specified in 18.2.3.5.1.1.

18.2.3.5.1.1.2 The width of fire apparatus access roads shall be increased when the minimum width specified in 18.2.3.5.1.1 is not adequate to accommodate fire apparatus.

18.2.3.5.1.2 Fire apparatus access roads shall have an unobstructed vertical clearance of not less than 13 ft 6 in. (4.1 m).

18.2.3.5.1.2.1 Vertical clearance shall be permitted to be reduced where approved by the AHJ, provided such reduction does not impair access by fire apparatus, and approved signs are installed and maintained indicating the established vertical clearance when approved.

18.2.3.5.1.2.2 Vertical clearances shall be increased when vertical clearances are not adequate to accommodate fire apparatus.

18.2.3.5.2* Surface. Fire apparatus access roads shall be designed and maintained to support the imposed loads of fire apparatus and shall be provided with an all-weather driving surface.

18.2.3.5.3 Turning Radius.

18.2.3.5.3.1 The turning radius of a fire apparatus access road shall be as approved by the AHJ.

18.2.3.5.3.2 Turns in fire apparatus access roads shall maintain the minimum road width.

18.2.3.5.3.3 Fire apparatus access roads connecting to roadways shall be provided with curb cuts extending at least 2 ft (0.61 m) beyond each edge of the fire apparatus access road.

18.2.3.5.4 Dead Ends. Dead-end fire apparatus access roads in excess of 150 ft (46 m) in length shall be provided with approved provisions for the fire apparatus to turn around.

18.2.3.5.5 Bridges.

18.2.3.5.5.1 When a bridge is required to be used as part of a fire apparatus access road, it shall be constructed and maintained in accordance with nationally recognized standards.

18.2.3.5.5.2 The bridge shall be designed for a live load sufficient to carry the imposed loads of fire apparatus.

18.2.3.5.5.3 Vehicle load limits shall be posted at both entrances to bridges where required by the AHJ.

18.2.3.5.6 Grade.

18.2.3.5.6.1 The gradient for a fire apparatus access road shall not exceed the design limitations of the fire apparatus of the fire department and shall be subject to approval by the AHJ.

18.2.3.5.6.2* The angle of approach and departure for any means of fire apparatus access road shall not exceed 1 ft drop in 20 ft (0.3 m drop in 6 m) or the design limitations of the fire apparatus of the fire department, and shall be subject to approval by the AHJ.

18.2.3.5.7 Traffic Calming Devices. The design and use of traffic calming devices shall be approved by the AHJ.

18.2.3.6 Marking of Fire Apparatus Access Road.

18.2.3.6.1 Where required by the AHJ, approved signs, approved roadway surface markings, or other approved notices shall be provided and maintained to identify fire apparatus access roads or to prohibit the obstruction thereof or both.

18.2.3.6.2 A marked fire apparatus access road shall also be known as a fire lane.

18.2.4* Obstruction and Control of Fire Apparatus Access Road.

18.2.4.1 General.

18.2.4.1.1 The required width of a fire apparatus access road shall not be obstructed in any manner, including by the parking of vehicles.

18.2.4.1.2 Minimum required widths and clearances established under 18.2.3.5 shall be maintained at all times.

18.2.4.1.3* Facilities and structures shall be maintained in a manner that does not impair or impede accessibility for fire department operations.

18.2.4.1.4 Entrances to fire apparatus access roads that have been closed with gates and barriers in accordance with 18.2.4.2.1 shall not be obstructed by parked vehicles.

18.2.4.2 Closure of Accessways.

18.2.4.2.1 The AHJ shall be authorized to require the installation and maintenance of gates or other approved barricades across roads, trails, or other accessways not including public streets, alleys, or highways.

18.2.4.2.2 Where required, gates and barricades shall be secured in an approved manner.

18.2.4.2.3 Roads, trails, and other accessways that have been closed and obstructed in the manner prescribed by 18.2.4.2.1 shall not be trespassed upon or used unless authorized by the owner and the AHJ.

18.2.4.2.4 Public officers acting within their scope of duty shall be permitted to access restricted property identified in 18.2.4.2.1.

18.2.4.2.5 Locks, gates, doors, barricades, chains, enclosures, signs, tags, or seals that have been installed by the fire department or by its order or under its control shall not be removed, unlocked, destroyed, tampered with, or otherwise vandalized in any manner.

18.2.4.2.6 Gates shall comply with 18.2.4.2.6.1 and 18.2.4.2.6.2.

18.2.4.2.6.1 Electric gate operators and systems, where provided, shall be installed, maintained, listed, and labeled in accordance with UL 325, *Door, Drapery, Gate, Louver, and Window Operators and Systems*.

18.2.4.2.6.2 Gates intended for automatic operation shall be designed, constructed, installed, and maintained to comply with ASTM F2200, *Standard Specification for Automated Vehicular Gate Construction*.

18.2.4.2.7 When authorized by the AHJ, public officers acting within their scope of duty shall be permitted to obtain access through secured means identified in 18.2.4.2.1.

18.3 Water Supplies.

18.3.1* An approved water supply capable of supplying the required fire flow for fire protection shall be provided to all premises upon which facilities, buildings, or portions of buildings are hereafter constructed or moved into the jurisdiction. The approved water supply shall be in accordance with Section 18.4.

18.3.1.1* Where no adequate or reliable water distribution system exists, approved reservoirs, pressure tanks, elevated tanks, fire department tanker shuttles, or other approved systems capable of providing the required fire flow shall be permitted.

18.4 Fire Flow Requirements for Buildings.

18.4.1* Scope.

18.4.1.1* The procedure determining fire flow requirements for buildings hereafter constructed or moved into the jurisdiction shall be in accordance with Section 18.4.

18.4.1.2 Section 18.4 shall not apply to structures other than buildings.

18.4.2 Modifications.

18.4.2.1 Decreases in Fire Flow Requirements.

18.4.2.1.1* Fire flow requirements shall be permitted to be decreased by the AHJ for isolated buildings or a group of buildings in rural areas or suburban areas where the development of full fire flow requirements is impractical as determined by the AHJ.

18.4.2.1.2 The AHJ shall be authorized to establish conditions on fire flow reductions approved in accordance with 18.4.2.1.1 including, but not limited to, fire sprinkler protection, type of construction of the building, occupancy, development density, building size, and setbacks.

18.4.2.2 Increases in Fire Flow Requirements. The minimum required fire flow shall be permitted to be increased by the AHJ where conditions indicate an unusual susceptibility to group fires or conflagrations. An upward modification shall not be more than twice that required for the building under consideration.

18.4.3 Fire Flow Area.

18.4.3.1 General. The fire flow area shall be the total floor area of all floor levels of a building except as modified in 18.4.3.2.

18.4.3.2 Type I (443), Type I (332), and Type II (222) Construction. The fire flow area of a building constructed of Type I (443), Type I (332), and Type II (222) construction shall be the area of the three largest successive floors.

18.4.4 Fire Flow Requirements for Buildings.

18.4.4.1 One- and Two-Family Dwellings Not Exceeding 5000 ft^2 (464.5 m^2).

18.4.4.1.1 The minimum fire flow and flow duration requirements for one- and two-family dwellings having a fire flow area that does not exceed 5000 ft^2 (464.5 m^2) shall be 1000 gpm (3785 L/min) for 1 hour.

18.4.4.1.2* A reduction in required fire flow of 75 percent shall be permitted where the one- and two-family dwelling is provided with an approved automatic sprinkler system.

18.4.4.1.3* Where one- and two-family dwellings are proposed to be constructed in areas where water distribution systems providing fire flow were designed and installed prior to the effective date of this *Code*, the AHJ shall be authorized to accept the previously designed system fire flow where the one- and two-family dwellings are provided with approved automatic sprinkler systems.

18.4.4.1.4 A reduction in fire flow shall be permitted for building separation distance in accordance with 18.4.4.1.4 and Table 18.4.4.1.4.

18.4.4.1.4.1 Where multiple buildings are located on a single lot, the building separation distance shall be the distance between the buildings.

18.4.4.1.4.2 Where a building abuts a lot line, the building separation distance shall be the distance between the building and the lot line.

18.4.4.1.4.3 Where a building is contiguous to a public right of way or no-build easement, the separation distance shall be the distance between the building to the opposite side of the right of way or no-build easement.

18.4.4.1.4.4 Where multiple buildings are located on a single lot and abut a lot line, the building separation distance for determining fire flow reduction shall be the smallest of the two distances.

18.4.4.1.5* The reductions in 18.4.4.1.2, 18.4.4.1.3, and 18.4.4.1.4 shall not reduce the required fire flow to less than 500 gpm (1900 L/min).

18.4.4.2 One- and Two-Family Dwellings Exceeding 5000 ft^2 (464.5 m^2).

18.4.4.2.1 Fire flow and flow duration for dwellings having a fire flow area in excess of 5000 ft^2 (464.5 m^2) shall not be less than that specified in Table 18.4.4.2.1.

18.4.4.2.2 Required fire flow shall be reduced by 75 percent and the duration reduced to 1 hour where the one- and two-family dwelling is provided with an approved automatic sprinkler system.

18.4.4.2.3 A reduction in the required fire flow shall be permitted where a one- and two-family dwelling is separated from all lot lines in accordance with Table 18.4.4.1.4.

18.4.4.2.4 Required fire flow for one- and two-family dwellings protected by an approved automatic sprinkler system shall not exceed 2000 gpm (7571 L/min) for 1 hour.

18.4.4.2.5* The reductions in 18.4.4.2.2, and 18.4.4.2.3 shall not reduce the required fire flow to less than 500 gpm (1900 L/min) for 1 hour.

Table 18.4.4.1.4 Permitted Fire Flow Reduction for Building Separation

Separation Distance Between Buildings on a Single Lot		Separation Distance to Lot Line or Easement[a]		Permitted Fire Flow Reduction
ft	m	ft	m	
>30 and ≤50	>9.1 and ≤15.2	>15 and ≤25	>4.6 and ≤7.6	25%
>50	>15.2	>25	>7.6	40%

[a] See 18.4.5.1.4.3.

18.4.4.3 Buildings Other Than One- and Two-Family Dwellings.

18.4.4.3.1* The minimum fire flow and flow duration for buildings other than one- and two-family dwellings shall be as specified in Table 18.4.4.2.1.

18.4.4.3.2 Required fire flow shall be reduced by 75 percent when the building is protected throughout by an approved automatic sprinkler system. The resulting fire flow shall not be less than 1000 gpm (3785 L/min).

18.4.4.3.3 Required fire flow shall be reduced by 75 percent when the building is protected throughout by an approved automatic sprinkler system, which utilizes quick response sprinklers throughout. The resulting fire flow shall not be less than 600 gpm (2270 L/min).

18.4.4.3.4* Required fire flow for buildings protected by an approved automatic sprinkler system shall not exceed 2000 gpm (7571 L/min) for 2 hours.

18.4.4.3.5 Required fire flow for open parking structures that are not protected throughout by an approved automatic sprinkler system shall be reduced by 75 percent where all of the following conditions are met:

(1) The structure complies with the building code.
(2) The structure is of Type I or Type II construction.
(3) The structure is provided with a Class I standpipe system in accordance with NFPA 14. Class I standpipe systems of the manual dry type shall be permitted.
(4) The resulting fire flow is not less than 1000 gpm (3785 L/min).

18.4.4.4* Required Fire Flow and Automatic Sprinkler System Demand. For a building with an approved fire sprinkler system, the fire flow demand and the fire sprinkler system demand shall not be required to be added together. The water supply shall be capable of delivering the larger of the individual demands.

18.5 Fire Hydrants.

18.5.1 Fire Hydrant Locations and Distribution. Fire hydrants shall be provided in accordance with Section 18.5 for all new buildings, or buildings relocated into the jurisdiction unless otherwise permitted by 18.5.1.1 or 18.5.1.2.

18.5.1.1 Fire hydrants shall not be required where the water distribution system is not capable of providing a fire flow of greater than 500 gpm (1893 L/min) at a residual pressure of 20 psi (139.9 kPa).

18.5.1.2* Fire hydrants shall not be required where modification or extension of the water distribution system is deemed to be impractical by the AHJ.

18.5.1.3 The provisions of 18.5.1.1 and 18.5.1.2 shall not eliminate the fire flow requirements of Section 18.4.

18.5.1.4* The distances specified in Section 18.5 shall be measured along fire apparatus access roads in accordance with 18.2.3.

Table 18.4.4.2.1 Minimum Required Fire Flow and Flow Duration for Buildings

\multicolumn{5}{c}{Fire Flow Area ft² (× 0.0929 for m²)}	Fire Flow gpm† (× 3.785 for L/min)	Flow Duration (hours)
I(443), I(332), II(222)*	II(111), III(211)*	IV(2HH), V(111)*	II(000), III(200)*	V(000)*		
0–22,700	0–12,700	0–8200	0–5900	0–3600	1500	2
22,701–30,200	12,701–17,000	8201–10,900	5901–7900	3601–4800	1750	
30,201–38,700	17,001–21,800	10,901–12,900	7901–9800	4801–6200	2000	
38,701–48,300	21,801–24,200	12,901–17,400	9801–12,600	6201–7700	2250	
48,301–59,000	24,201–33,200	17,401–21,300	12,601–15,400	7701–9400	2500	
59,001–70,900	33,201–39,700	21,301–25,500	15,401–18,400	9401–11,300	2750	
70,901–83,700	39,701–47,100	25,501–30,100	18,401–21,800	11,301–13,400	3000	3
83,701–97,700	47,101–54,900	30,101–35,200	21,801–25,900	13,401–15,600	3250	
97,701–112,700	54,901–63,400	35,201–40,600	25,901–29,300	15,601–18,000	3500	
112,701–128,700	63,401–72,400	40,601–46,400	29,301–33,500	18,001–20,600	3750	
128,701–145,900	72,401–82,100	46,401–52,500	33,501–37,900	20,601–23,300	4000	4
145,901–164,200	82,101–92,400	52,501–59,100	37,901–42,700	23,301–26,300	4250	
164,201–183,400	92,401–103,100	59,101–66,000	42,701–47,700	26,301–29,300	4500	
183,401–203,700	103,101–114,600	66,001–73,300	47,701–53,000	29,301–32,600	4750	
203,701–225,200	114,601–126,700	73,301–81,100	53,001–58,600	32,601–36,000	5000	
225,201–247,700	126,701–139,400	81,101–89,200	58,601–65,400	36,001–39,600	5250	
247,701–271,200	139,401–152,600	89,201–97,700	65,401–70,600	39,601–43,400	5500	
271,201–295,900	152,601–166,500	97,701–106,500	70,601–77,000	43,401–47,400	5750	
Greater than 295,900	Greater than 166,500	106,501–115,800	77,001–83,700	47,401–51,500	6000	
		115,801–125,500	83,701–90,600	51,501–55,700	6250	
		125,501–135,500	90,601–97,900	55,701–60,200	6500	
		135,501–145,800	97,901–106,800	60,201–64,800	6750	
		145,801–156,700	106,801–113,200	64,801–69,600	7000	
		156,701–167,900	113,201–121,300	69,601–74,600	7250	
		167,901–179,400	121,301–129,600	74,601–79,800	7500	
		179,401–191,400	129,601–138,300	79,801–85,100	7750	
		Greater than 191,400	Greater than 138,300	Greater than 85,100	8000	

*Types of construction are based on NFPA 220.
†Measured at 20 psi (139.9 kPa).

18.5.1.5 Where fire apparatus access roads are provided with median dividers incapable of being crossed by fire apparatus, or where fire apparatus access roads have traffic counts of more than 30,000 vehicles per day, hydrants shall be placed on both sides of the fire apparatus access road on an alternating basis, and the distances specified by Section 18.5 shall be measured independently of the hydrants on the opposite side of the fire apparatus access road.

18.5.1.6 Fire hydrants shall be located not more than 12 ft (3.7 m) from the fire apparatus access road.

18.5.2 Detached One- and Two-Family Dwellings. Fire hydrants shall be provided for detached one- and two-family dwellings in accordance with both of the following:

(1) The maximum distance to a fire hydrant from the closest point on the building shall not exceed 600 ft (183 m).
(2) The maximum distance between fire hydrants shall not exceed 800 ft (244 m).

18.5.3 Buildings Other than Detached One- and Two-Family Dwellings. Fire hydrants shall be provided for buildings other than detached one- and two-family dwellings in accordance with both of the following:

(1) The maximum distance to a fire hydrant from the closest point on the building shall not exceed 400 ft (122 m).
(2) The maximum distance between fire hydrants shall not exceed 500 ft (152 m).

18.5.4 Minimum Number of Fire Hydrants for Fire Flow.

18.5.4.1 The minimum number of fire hydrants needed to deliver the required fire flow for new buildings in accordance with Section 18.4 shall be determined in accordance with Section 18.5.4.

18.5.4.2 The aggregate fire flow capacity of all fire hydrants within 1000 ft (305 m) of the building, measured in accordance with 18.5.1.4 and 18.5.1.5, shall be not less than the required fire flow determined in accordance with Section 18.4.

18.5.4.3* The maximum fire flow capacity for which a fire hydrant shall be credited shall be as specified by Table 18.5.4.3. Capacities exceeding the values specified in Table 18.5.4.3 shall be permitted when local fire department operations have the ability to accommodate such values as determined by the fire department.

18.5.4.4 Fire hydrants required by 18.5.2 and 18.5.3 shall be included in the minimum number of fire hydrants for fire flow required by 18.5.4.

18.5.5 Inspection, Testing, and Maintenance.

18.5.5.1 Private water supply systems shall be inspected, tested, and maintained in accordance with NFPA 25.

Table 18.5.4.3 Maximum Fire Hydrant Fire Flow Capacity

Distance to Building[a]		Maximum Capacity[b]	
(ft)	(m)	(gpm)	(L/min)
≤ 250	≤ 76	1500	5678
> 250 and ≤ 500	> 76 and ≤ 152	1000	3785
> 500 and ≤ 1000	> 152 and ≤ 305	750	2839

[a] Measured in accordance with 18.5.1.4 and 18.5.1.5.
[b] Minimum 20 psi (139.9 kPa) residual pressure.

18.5.5.2 Public water supply systems providing fire flow shall be inspected, tested, and maintained in accordance with ANSI/AWWA G200, *Standard for Distribution Systems Operation and Management.*

18.5.6 Accessibility. Fire hydrants and connections to other approved water supplies shall be accessible to the fire department.

18.5.7 Clear Space Around Hydrants.

18.5.7.1 A 36 in. (914 mm) clear space shall be maintained around the circumference of fire hydrants except as otherwise required or approved.

18.5.7.2 A clear space of not less than 60 in. (1524 mm) shall be provided in front of each hydrant connection having a diameter greater than 2½ in. (64 mm).

18.5.8 Protection. Where required by the AHJ, fire hydrants subject to vehicular damage shall be protected unless located within a public right of way.

18.5.9 Hydrants Out of Service. Where water supplies or fire hydrants are out of service for maintenance or repairs, a visible indicator acceptable to the AHJ shall be used to indicate that the hydrant is out of service.

18.5.10 Marking of Hydrants.

18.5.10.1 Fire hydrants shall be marked with an approved reflector affixed to the roadway surface where required by the AHJ.

18.5.10.2 Fire hydrants shall be marked with an approved flag or other device affixed to or proximate to the fire hydrant where required by the AHJ.

18.5.10.3* Where required by the AHJ, fire hydrants shall be color coded or otherwise marked with an approved system indicating the available flow capacity.

Chapter 19 Combustible Waste and Refuse

19.1 General.

19.1.1 Permits. Permits, where required, shall comply with Section 1.13.

△ **19.1.2** Persons owning or having control of any property shall not allow any combustible waste material to accumulate in any area or in any manner that creates a fire hazard to life or property.

△ **19.1.3** Combustible waste or refuse shall be properly stored or disposed of to prevent unsafe conditions.

△ **19.1.4** Fire extinguishing capabilities approved by the AHJ including, but not limited to, fire extinguishers, water supply and hose, and earth-moving equipment shall be provided at waste disposal sites.

△ **19.1.5** Burning debris shall not be dumped at a waste disposal site except at a remote location on the site where fire extinguishment can be accomplished before compacting, covering, or other disposal activity is carried out. *(See Section 10.10 for additional guidance.)*

19.1.6 Vehicles or Conveyances Used to Transport Combustible Waste or Refuse.

△ **19.1.6.1** Vehicles or conveyances used to transport combustible waste or refuse over public thoroughfares shall have all cargo space covered and maintained tight enough to ensure against ignition from external fire sources and the scattering of burning and combustible debris that can come in contact with ignition sources.

△ **19.1.6.2** Transporting burning waste or refuse shall be prohibited.

△ **19.1.6.3** Trucks or automobiles, other than mechanical handling equipment and approved industrial trucks as listed in NFPA 505 shall not enter any fiber storage room or building but shall be permitted to be used at loading platforms.

19.2 Combustible Waste and Refuse.

19.2.1 Rubbish Containers.

19.2.1.1 General. Rubbish containers kept outside of rooms or vaults shall not exceed 40.5 ft^3 (1.15 m^3) capacity.

△ **19.2.1.1.1** Containers exceeding a capacity of 5⅓ ft^3 [40 gal (0.15 m^3)] shall be provided with lids.

△ **19.2.1.1.2** Such containers and lids as described in 19.2.1.1.1 shall be constructed of noncombustible materials or nonmetallic materials complying with 19.2.1.2.

19.2.1.2 Nonmetallic Containers.

△ **19.2.1.2.1*** Nonmetallic rubbish containers exceeding a capacity of 5⅓ ft^3 [40 gal (0.15 m^3)] shall be manufactured of materials having a peak rate of heat release not exceeding 300 kW/m^2 at a flux of 50 kW/m^2 when tested in the horizontal orientation, at a thickness as used in the container but not less than of 0.25 in. (6 mm), in accordance with ASTM E1354, *Test Method for Heat and Visible Smoke Release Rates for Materials and Products Using an Oxygen Consumption Calorimeter.*

△ **19.2.1.2.2** Such containers shall be permanently labeled indicating capacity and peak rate of heat release.

19.2.1.3 Removal. Combustible rubbish stored in containers outside of noncombustible vaults or rooms shall be removed from buildings at least once each working day.

19.2.1.4 Rubbish Within Dumpsters. Dumpsters and combustible waste containers with an individual capacity of 1.5 yd^3 [40.5 ft^3 (1.15 m^3)] or more shall not be stored in buildings or placed within 10 ft (3050 mm) of combustible walls, openings, or combustible roof eave lines of buildings unless otherwise permitted by 19.2.1.4.1 or 19.2.1.4.2.

△ **19.2.1.4.1** The requirement of 19.2.1.4 shall not apply to building areas protected by an approved automatic sprinkler system and enclosed by fire barriers having a fire resistance rating not less than of 1 hour.

△ **19.2.1.4.2** The requirement of 19.2.1.4 shall not apply to structures meeting all of the following requirements:

(1) Structures shall be Type I or Type II construction.
(2) Structures shall be located not less than 10 ft (3050 mm) from other structures.
(3) Structures shall be used only for storage of dumpsters and combustible waste containers.

19.2.1.5 Commercial Rubbish-Handling Operations. Occupancies exclusively performing commercial rubbish handling or recycling shall maintain rubbish or product to be processed or recycled in one of the following ways:

(1) In approved vaults
(2) In covered metal or metal-lined receptacles or bins
(3) Completely baled and stacked in an orderly manner in an approved location

△ **19.2.1.6** Approved metal receptacles with self-closing covers shall be provided for the storage or disposal of oil-soaked waste or cloths.

Chapter 20 Occupancy Fire Safety

20.1 Assembly Occupancies.

20.1.1 Application. New and existing assembly occupancies shall comply with Section 20.1 and NFPA *101*.

20.1.1.1 Permits. Permits, where required, shall comply with Section 1.13.

20.1.1.2 Indoor play structures shall also comply with Section 10.20.

20.1.2 Flame-Retardant Requirements.

20.1.2.1 Combustible scenery of cloth, film, vegetation (dry), and similar materials shall comply with one of the following:

(1) They shall meet the flame propagation performance criteria contained in Test Method 1 or Test Method 2, as appropriate, of NFPA 701.
(2) They shall exhibit a heat release rate not exceeding 100 kW when tested in accordance with NFPA 289 using the 20 kW ignition source.

[*101*:12.4.7.11.1; *101*:13.4.7.11.1]

20.1.2.2 Foamed plastics *(see definition of cellular or foamed plastic in 3.3.43 of NFPA 101)* shall be permitted to be used if they exhibit a heat release rate not exceeding 100 kW when tested in accordance with NFPA 289 using the 20 kW ignition source or by specific approval of the AHJ. [*101*:12.4.7.11.2; *101*:13.4.7.11.2]

20.1.2.3 Scenery and stage properties not separated from the audience by proscenium opening protection shall be of noncombustible materials, limited-combustible materials, or fire-retardant-treated wood. [*101*:12.4.7.11.3; *101*:13.4.7.11.3]

20.1.2.4 In assembly occupancies, any single fuel package shall have a heat release rate not to exceed 100 kW where tested in accordance with one of the following:

(1) UL 1975, *Fire Tests for Foamed Plastics Used for Decorative Purposes*
(2) NFPA 289 using the 20 kW ignition source

[*101*:12.4.7.11.4; *101*:13.4.7.11.4]

20.1.3 Interior Finish.

20.1.3.1 General. Interior finish shall be in accordance with Section 12.5. [*101*:12.3.3.1]

20.1.3.2 Corridors, Lobbies, and Enclosed Stairways. Interior wall and ceiling finish materials complying with Section 12.5 shall be Class A or Class B in all corridors and lobbies and shall be Class A in enclosed stairways. [*101*:12.3.3.2; *101*:13.3.3.2]

20.1.3.3 Assembly Areas. Interior wall and ceiling finish materials complying with Section 12.5 shall be Class A or Class B in general assembly areas having occupant loads of more than 300 and shall be Class A, Class B, or Class C in assembly areas having occupant loads of 300 or fewer. [*101*:12.3.3.3; *101*:13.3.3.3]

20.1.3.4 Screens. Screens on which pictures are projected shall comply with requirements of Class A or Class B interior finish in accordance with Section 12.5. [*101*:12.3.3.4; *101*:13.3.3.4]

20.1.3.5 Interior Floor Finish.

20.1.3.5.1 New interior floor finish shall comply with Section 12.5. [*101*:12.3.3.5.1]

20.1.3.5.2 New interior floor finish in exit enclosures and exit access corridors and in spaces not separated from them by walls complying with 12.3.6 of NFPA *101* shall be not less than Class II. [*101*:12.3.3.5.2]

20.1.3.5.3 New interior floor finish shall comply with 12.5.9.1 or 12.5.9.2, as applicable. [*101*:12.3.3.5.3]

20.1.3.5.4 Existing Interior Floor Finish. (No requirements.) [*101*:13.3.3.5]

20.1.4* Special Amusement Buildings.

20.1.4.1 General.

20.1.4.1.1* Special amusement buildings, regardless of occupant load, shall meet the requirements for assembly occupancies in addition to the requirements of 20.1.4, unless the special amusement building is a multilevel play structure that is not more than 10 ft (3050 mm) in height and has aggregate horizontal projections not exceeding 160 ft^2 (15 m^2). [*101*:12.4.9.1.1; *101*:13.4.9.1.1]

20.1.4.1.2* Special amusement buildings shall be subclassified as follows:

(1) Class A: Permanently installed special amusement buildings that include an amusement ride or device in which patrons are contained or restrained and are unable to evacuate without the assistance of the ride operator
(2) Class B: Permanently installed special amusement buildings that do not include an amusement ride or device, or that include an amusement ride or device from which patrons are able to self-evacuate
(3) Class C: Temporary or mobile special amusement buildings

[*101*:12.4.9.1.2; *101*:13.4.9.1.2]

N 20.1.4.1.3 Permits, where required, shall comply with Section 1.12.

20.1.4.2 Means of Egress.

20.1.4.2.1 Exit Marking.

20.1.4.2.1.1 Exit marking shall be in accordance with Section 14.14. [*101*:12.4.9.2.1.1; *101*:13.4.9.2.2.1]

20.1.4.2.1.2 Floor proximity exit signs shall be provided in accordance with 14.14.1.6. [*101*:12.4.9.2.1.2; *101*:13.4.9.2.1.2]

20.1.4.2.1.3* In special amusement buildings where mazes, mirrors, or other designs are used to confound the egress path, approved directional exit marking that becomes apparent in an emergency shall be provided. [*101*:12.4.9.2.1.3; *101*:13.4.9.2.1.3]

20.1.4.2.2 Illumination.

20.1.4.2.2.1* Unless otherwise permitted by 20.1.4.2.2.2, actuation of the automatic sprinkler system, or any other suppression system, or actuation of a smoke detection system having an approved verification or cross-zoning operation capability shall provide for both of the following:

(1) Increase in illumination in the means of egress to that required by Section 14.12

(2) Termination of any conflicting or confusing sounds and visuals
[*101*:12.4.9.2.2.1; *101*:13.4.9.2.2.1]

20.1.4.2.2.2* Class A special amusement buildings shall not be required to comply with 20.1.4.2.2.1 where all of the following conditions apply:

(1) The emergency action plan required by 20.1.4.6.2 provides specific evacuation instructions to all attraction operators for cycling out the attraction when it is determined that meeting the requirements of 20.1.4.2.2.1 presents a hazard to ride patrons.
(2) A means of manually complying with 20.1.4.2.2.1 is provided to the primary attraction operator.
(3) Attraction operators are trained on the alternative procedures for evacuations.
(4) The AHJ approves the modifications.

[*101*:12.4.9.2.2.2; *101*:13.4.9.2.2.2]

20.1.4.3 Interior Finish. Interior wall and ceiling finish materials complying with Section 12.5 shall be Class A throughout. [*101*:12.4.9.3; *101*:13.4.9.3]

20.1.4.4 Detection, Alarm, and Communications Systems.

20.1.4.4.1 General.

20.1.4.4.1.1 Class A and Class B special amusement buildings shall be provided with an approved fire alarm system and smoke detection system in accordance with 13.7.1 and 20.1.4.4. [*101*:12.4.9.4.1.1; *101*:13.4.9.4.1.1]

20.1.4.4.1.2 Class C special amusement buildings shall be provided with an approved automatic smoke detection system in accordance with Section 13.7. [*101*:12.4.9.4.1.2; *101*:13.4.9.4.1.2]

20.1.4.4.2* Initiation.

20.1.4.4.2.1 In Class A and Class B special amusement buildings, the required fire alarm system shall be initiated by each of the following:

(1) Manual fire alarm box located at a constantly attended location under continuous supervision by competent persons when the special amusement building is open to patrons
(2) Required automatic sprinkler system
(3) Required automatic detection systems

[*101*:12.4.9.4.2.1, *101*:13.4.9.4.2.1]

20.1.4.4.2.2 In Class C special amusement buildings, actuation of any smoke detection system device shall activate an audible and visible alarm in a constantly attended receiving station within the building when occupied for purposes of initiating emergency action. [*101*:12.4.9.4.2.2, *101*:13.4.9.4.2.2]

20.1.4.4.3 Smoke Detection. Where the nature of the special amusement building is such that it operates in reduced lighting levels, the building shall be protected throughout by an approved automatic smoke detection system in accordance with Section 13.7. [*101*:12.4.9.4.3; *101*:13.4.9.4.3]

20.1.4.4.4* Notification.

20.1.4.4.4.1 Occupant notification for Class A and Class B special amusement buildings shall be in accordance with 13.7.2.1.3. [*101*:12.4.9.4.4.1, *101*:13.4.9.4.4.1]

20.1.4.4.4.2 Occupant notification for Class C special amusement buildings shall be in accordance with 13.7.2.1.3; however, positive alarm sequence shall not be permitted. [*101*:12.4.9.4.4.2, *101*:13.4.9.4.4.2]

20.1.4.4.4.3* An automatic means for sounding the general evacuation alarm shall be provided when the constantly attended location is not staffed. [*101*:12.4.9.4.4.3, *101*:13.4.9.4.4.3]

20.1.4.5 Extinguishment Requirements.

20.1.4.5.1* Automatic Sprinklers. Every special amusement building, other than buildings or structures not exceeding 10 ft (3050 mm) in height and not exceeding 160 ft^2 (15 m^2) in aggregate horizontal projection, shall be protected throughout by an approved, supervised automatic sprinkler system installed and maintained in accordance with Section 13.3. [*101*:12.4.9.5.1; *101*:13.4.9.5.1]

20.1.4.5.2 Where the special amusement building required to be sprinklered by 20.1.4.5.1 is movable or portable, the sprinkler water supply shall be permitted to be provided by an approved temporary means. [*101*:12.4.9.5.2; *101*:13.4.9.5.2]

20.1.4.6 Operating Features.

20.1.4.6.1* Furnishings, Decorations, and Scenery. Furnishings shall be in accordance with 20.1.5.4. [*101*:12.4.9.6.1, *101*:13.4.9.6.1]

20.1.4.6.2* Emergency Action Plan. In Class A special amusement buildings, the emergency action plan shall be reviewed and approved by the AHJ. [*101*:12.4.9.6.2, *101*:13.4.9.6.2]

20.1.5 Operating Features.

20.1.5.1 Means of Egress Inspection.

20.1.5.1.1 The building owner or agent shall inspect the means of egress to ensure it is maintained free of obstructions, and correct any deficiencies found, prior to each opening of the building to the public. [*101*:12.7.1.1; *101*:13.7.1.1]

20.1.5.1.2 The building owner or agent shall prepare and maintain records of the date and time of each inspection on approved forms, listing any deficiencies found and actions taken to correct them. [*101*:12.7.1.2; *101*:13.7.1.2]

20.1.5.1.3 Inspection of Door Openings. Door openings shall be inspected in accordance with 14.5.10. [*101*:12.7.1.3]

20.1.5.2 Special Provisions for Food Service Operations.

20.1.5.2.1 All devices in connection with the preparation of food shall be installed and operated to avoid hazard to the safety of occupants. [*101*:12.7.2.1; *101*:13.7.2.1]

20.1.5.2.2 All devices in connection with the preparation of food shall be of an approved type and shall be installed in an approved manner. [*101*:12.7.2.2; *101*:13.7.2.2]

20.1.5.2.3 Food preparation facilities shall be protected in accordance with Chapter 50 and shall not be required to have openings protected between food preparation areas and dining areas. [*101*:12.7.2.3; *101*:13.7.2.3]

20.1.5.2.4 Portable cooking equipment that is not flue-connected shall be permitted only as follows:

(1) Equipment fueled by small heat sources that can be readily extinguished by water, such as candles or alcohol-burning equipment, including solid alcohol, shall be

permitted to be used, provided that precautions satisfactory to the AHJ are taken to prevent ignition of any combustible materials.
(2) Candles shall be permitted to be used on tables used for food service where securely supported on substantial noncombustible bases located to avoid danger of ignition of combustible materials and only where approved by the AHJ.
(3) Candle flames shall be protected.
(4) "Flaming sword" or other equipment involving open flames and flamed dishes, such as cherries jubilee or crêpes suzette, shall be permitted to be used, provided that precautions subject to the approval of the AHJ are taken.
(5) Listed and approved LP-Gas commercial food service appliances shall be permitted to be used where in accordance with Chapter 69.

[*101*:12.7.2.4; *101*:13.7.2.4]

20.1.5.2.4.1 Permits. Permits, where required, shall comply with Section 1.13.

20.1.5.3 Open Flame Devices and Pyrotechnics. No open flame devices or pyrotechnic devices shall be used in any assembly occupancy, unless otherwise permitted by one of the following:

(1) Pyrotechnic special effect devices shall be permitted to be used on stages before proximate audiences for ceremonial or religious purposes, as part of a demonstration in exhibits, or as part of a performance, provided that both of the following criteria are met:
  (a) Precautions satisfactory to the AHJ are taken to prevent ignition of any combustible material.
  (b) Use of the pyrotechnic device complies with Section 65.3.
(2) Flame effects before an audience shall be permitted in accordance with Section 65.4.
(3) Open flame devices shall be permitted to be used in the following situations, provided that precautions satisfactory to the AHJ are taken to prevent ignition of any combustible material or injury to occupants:
  (a)* For ceremonial or religious purposes
  (b) On stages and platforms where part of a performance
  (c) Where candles on tables are securely supported on substantial noncombustible bases and candle flame is protected
(4) The requirement of 20.1.5.3 shall not apply to heat-producing equipment complying with 11.2.2.
(5) The requirement of 20.1.5.3 shall not apply to food service operations in accordance with 20.1.5.2.
(6) Gas lights shall be permitted to be used, provided that precautions are taken, subject to the approval of the AHJ, to prevent ignition of any combustible materials.

[*101*:12.7.3; *101*:13.7.3]

20.1.5.3.1 Permits. Permits, where required, shall comply with Section 1.13.

20.1.5.4 Furnishings, Decorations, and Scenery.

20.1.5.4.1* Fabrics and films used for decorative purposes, all draperies and curtains, and similar furnishings shall be in accordance with the provisions of 12.6.1. [*101*:12.7.4.1; *101*:13.7.4.1]

20.1.5.4.2 The AHJ shall impose controls on the quantity and arrangement of combustible contents in assembly occupancies to provide an adequate level of safety to life from fire. [*101*:12.7.4.2; *101*:13.7.4.2]

20.1.5.4.3* Exposed foamed plastic materials and unprotected materials containing foamed plastic used for decorative purposes or stage scenery shall have a heat release rate not exceeding 100 kW where tested in accordance with one of the following:

(1) UL 1975, *Fire Tests for Foamed Plastics Used for Decorative Purposes*
(2) NFPA 289 using the 20 kW ignition source

[*101*:12.7.4.3; *101*:13.7.4.3]

20.1.5.4.4 The requirement of 20.1.5.4.3 shall not apply to individual foamed plastic items and items containing foamed plastic where the foamed plastic does not exceed 1 lb (0.45 kg) in weight. [*101*:12.7.4.4; *101*:13.7.4.4]

20.1.5.5 Special Provisions for Exposition Facilities.

20.1.5.5.1 Permits. Permits, where required, shall comply with Section 1.13.

20.1.5.5.2 General. No display or exhibit shall be installed or operated to interfere in any way with access to any required exit or with the visibility of any required exit or required exit sign; nor shall any display block access to fire-fighting equipment. [*101*:12.7.5.1; *101*:13.7.5.1]

20.1.5.5.3 Materials Not on Display. A storage room having an enclosure consisting of a smoke barrier having a minimum 1-hour fire resistance rating and protected by an automatic extinguishing system shall be provided for combustible materials not on display, including combustible packing crates used to ship exhibitors' supplies and products. [*101*:12.7.5.2; *101*:13.7.5.2]

20.1.5.5.4 Exhibits.

20.1.5.5.4.1 Exhibits shall comply with 20.1.5.5.4.2 through 20.1.5.5.4.11. [*101*:12.7.5.3.1; *101*:13.7.5.3.1]

20.1.5.5.4.2 The travel distance within the exhibit booth or exhibit enclosure to an exit access aisle shall not exceed 50 ft (15 m). [*101*:12.7.5.3.2; *101*:13.7.5.3.2]

20.1.5.5.4.3 The upper deck of multilevel exhibits exceeding 300 ft^2 (28 m^2) shall have not less than two remote means of egress. [*101*:12.7.5.3.3; *101*:13.7.5.3.3]

20.1.5.5.4.4 Exhibit booth construction materials shall be limited to the following:

(1) Noncombustible or limited-combustible materials
(2) Wood exceeding ¼ in. (6.3 mm) nominal thickness
(3) Wood that is pressure-treated, fire-retardant wood meeting the requirements of NFPA 703
(4) Flame-retardant materials complying with one of the following:
  (a) They shall meet the flame propagation performance criteria contained in Test Method 1 or Test Method 2, as appropriate, of NFPA 701.
  (b) They shall exhibit a heat release rate not exceeding 100 kW when tested in accordance with NFPA 289 using the 20 kW ignition source.
(5) Textile wall coverings, such as carpeting and similar products used as wall or ceiling finishes, complying with the provisions of 12.5.3 and 12.5.5

(6) Plastics limited to those that comply with 20.1.3 and Section 12.5
(7) Foamed plastics and materials containing foamed plastics having a heat release rate for any single fuel package that does not exceed 100 kW where tested in accordance with one of the following:
   (a) UL 1975, *Fire Tests for Foamed Plastics Used for Decorative Purposes*
   (b) NFPA 289 using the 20 kW ignition source
(8) Cardboard, honeycombed paper, and other combustible materials having a heat release rate for any single fuel package that does not exceed 150 kW where tested in accordance with one of the following:
   (a) UL 1975, *Fire Tests for Foamed Plastics Used for Decorative Purposes*
   (b) NFPA 289, using the 20 kW ignition source

[*101*:12.7.5.3.4; *101*:13.7.5.3.4]

20.1.5.5.4.5 Curtains, drapes, and decorations shall comply with 12.6.1. [*101*:12.7.5.3.5; *101*:13.7.5.3.5]

20.1.5.5.4.6 Acoustical and decorative material including, but not limited to, cotton, hay, paper, straw, moss, split bamboo, and wood chips shall be flame-retardant-treated to the satisfaction of the AHJ. [*101*:12.7.5.3.6; *101*:13.7.5.3.6]

20.1.5.5.4.6.1 Materials that cannot be treated for flame retardancy shall not be used. [*101*:12.7.5.3.6.1; *101*:13.7.5.3.6.1]

20.1.5.5.4.6.2 Foamed plastics, and materials containing foamed plastics and used as decorative objects such as, but not limited to, mannequins, murals, and signs, shall have a heat release rate for any single fuel package that does not exceed 150 kW where tested in accordance with one of the following:
(1) UL 1975, *Fire Tests for Foamed Plastics Used for Decorative Purposes*
(2) NFPA 289 using the 20 kW ignition source

[*101*:12.7.5.3.6.2; *101*:13.7.5.3.6.2]

20.1.5.5.4.6.3 Where the aggregate area of acoustical and decorative materials is less than 10 percent of the individual floor or wall area, such materials shall be permitted to be used subject to the approval of the AHJ. [*101*:12.7.5.3.6.3; *101*:13.7.5.3.6.3]

20.1.5.5.4.7 The following shall be protected by automatic extinguishing systems:
(1) Single-level exhibit booths exceeding 300 ft^2 (28 m^2) and covered with a ceiling
(2) Each level of multilevel exhibit booths, including the uppermost level where the uppermost level is covered with a ceiling

[*101*:12.7.5.3.7; *101*:13.7.5.3.7]

20.1.5.5.4.7.1 The requirements of 20.1.5.5.4.7 shall not apply where otherwise permitted by the following:
(1) Ceilings that are constructed of open grate design or listed dropout ceilings in accordance with NFPA 13 shall not be considered ceilings within the context of 20.1.5.5.4.7.
(2) Vehicles, boats, and similar exhibited products having over 100 ft^2 (9.3 m^2) of roofed area shall be provided with smoke detectors acceptable to the AHJ.
(3)* The requirement of 20.1.5.5.4.7(2) shall not apply where fire protection of multilevel exhibit booths is consistent with the criteria developed through a life safety evaluation of the exhibition hall in accordance with 12.4.2 and 13.4.2 of NFPA *101*, subject to approval of the AHJ. [*101*:12.7.5.3.7.1; *101*:13.7.5.3.7.1]

20.1.5.5.4.7.2 A single exhibit or group of exhibits with ceilings that do not require sprinklers shall be separated by a distance of not less than 10 ft (3050 mm) where the aggregate ceiling exceeds 300 ft^2 (28 m^2). [*101*:12.7.5.3.7.2; *101*:13.7.5.3.7.2]

20.1.5.5.4.7.3 The water supply and piping for the sprinkler system shall be permitted to be of an approved temporary means that is provided by a domestic water supply, a standpipe system, or a sprinkler system. [*101*:12.7.5.3.7.3; *101*:13.7.5.3.7.3]

20.1.5.5.4.8 Open flame devices within exhibit booths shall comply with 20.1.5.3. [*101*:12.7.5.3.8; *101*:13.7.5.3.8]

20.1.5.5.4.9 Cooking and food-warming devices in exhibit booths shall comply with 20.1.5.2 and all of the following:
(1) Gas-fired devices shall comply with the following:
   (a) Natural gas-fired devices shall comply with Section 11.4.
   (b) The requirement of 20.1.5.5.4.9(1)(a) shall not apply to compressed natural gas where permitted by the AHJ.
   (c) The use of LP-Gas cylinders shall be prohibited.
   (d) Nonrefillable LP-Gas cylinders shall be approved for use where permitted by the AHJ.
(2) The devices shall be isolated from the public by not less than 48 in. (1220 mm) or by a barrier between the devices and the public.
(3) Multi-well cooking equipment using combustible oils or solids shall comply with Chapter 50.
(4) Single-well cooking equipment using combustible oils or solids shall meet all of the following criteria:
   (a) The equipment shall have lids available for immediate use.
   (b) The equipment shall be limited to 2 ft^2 (0.2 m^2) of cooking surface.
   (c) The equipment shall be placed on noncombustible surface materials.
   (d) The equipment shall be separated from each other by a horizontal distance of not less than 24 in. (610 mm).
   (e) The requirement of 20.1.5.5.4.9(4)(d) shall not apply to multiple single-well cooking equipment where the aggregate cooking surface area does not exceed 2 ft^2 (0.2 m^2).
   (f) The equipment shall be kept at a horizontal distance of not less than 24 in. (610 mm) from any combustible material.
(5) A portable fire extinguisher in accordance with Section 13.6 shall be provided within the booth for each device, or an approved automatic extinguishing system shall be provided.

[*101*:12.7.5.3.9; *101*:13.7.5.3.9]

20.1.5.5.4.10 Combustible materials within exhibit booths shall be limited to a one-day supply. Storage of combustible materials behind the booth shall be prohibited. *(See 20.1.5.4.2 and 20.1.5.3.)* [*101*:12.7.5.3.10; *101*:13.7.5.3.10]

20.1.5.5.4.11 Plans for the exposition, in an acceptable form, shall be submitted to the AHJ for approval prior to setting up any exhibit. [*101*:12.7.5.3.11; *101*:13.7.5.3.11]

20.1.5.5.4.11.1 The plan shall show all details of the proposed exposition. [*101*:12.7.5.3.11.1; *101*:13.7.5.3.11.1]

20.1.5.5.4.11.2 No exposition shall occupy any exposition facility without approved plans. [*101*:12.7.5.3.11.2; *101*:13.7.5.3.11.2]

20.1.5.5.4.12 Vehicles. Vehicles on display within an exposition facility shall comply with 20.1.5.5.4.12.1 through 20.1.5.5.4.12.5. [*101*:12.7.5.4; *101*:13.7.5.4]

20.1.5.5.4.12.1 All fuel tank openings shall be locked and sealed in an approved manner to prevent the escape of vapors; fuel tanks shall not contain in excess of one-half their capacity or contain in excess of 10 gal (38 L) of fuel, whichever is less. [*101*:12.7.5.4.1; *101*:13.7.5.4.1]

20.1.5.5.4.12.2 At least one battery cable shall be removed from the batteries used to start the vehicle engine, and the disconnected battery cable shall then be taped. [*101*:12.7.5.4.2; *101*:13.7.5.4.2]

20.1.5.5.4.12.3 Batteries used to power auxiliary equipment shall be permitted to be kept in service. [*101*:12.7.5.4.3; *101*:13.7.5.4.3]

20.1.5.5.4.12.4 Fueling or defueling of vehicles shall be prohibited. [*101*:12.7.5.4.4; *101*:13.7.5.4.4]

20.1.5.5.4.12.5 Vehicles shall not be moved during exhibit hours. [*101*:12.7.5.4.5; *101*:13.7.5.4.5]

20.1.5.5.4.13 Prohibited Materials.

20.1.5.5.4.13.1 The following items shall be prohibited within exhibit halls:

(1) Compressed flammable gases
(2) Ignitible (flammable or combustible) liquids
(3) Hazardous chemicals or materials
(4) Class II or greater lasers, blasting agents, and explosives

[*101*:12.7.5.5.1; *101*:13.7.5.5.1]

20.1.5.5.4.13.2 The AHJ shall be permitted to allow the limited use of any items specified in 20.1.5.5.4.13.1 under special circumstances. [*101*:12.7.5.5.2; *101*:13.7.5.5.2]

20.1.5.6 Crowd Managers.

20.1.5.6.1 Assembly occupancies shall be provided with a minimum of one trained crowd manager or crowd manager supervisor. Where the occupant load exceeds 250, additional trained crowd managers or crowd manager supervisors shall be provided at a ratio of one crowd manager or crowd manager supervisor for every 250 occupants, unless otherwise permitted by one of the following:

(1) This requirement shall not apply to assembly occupancies used exclusively for religious worship with an occupant load not exceeding 500.
(2) The ratio of trained crowd managers to occupants shall be permitted to be reduced where, in the opinion of the AHJ, the existence of an approved, supervised automatic sprinkler system and the nature of the event warrant.

[*101*:12.7.6.1; *101*:13.7.6.1]

20.1.5.6.2* The crowd manager and crowd manager supervisor shall receive approved training in crowd management techniques. [*101*:12.7.6.2; *101*:13.7.6.2]

20.1.5.6.3 Duties and responsibilities for the crowd manager and crowd manager supervisor shall be documented within a written emergency plan as required by 12.7.13 and 13.7.3 of NFPA *101*. [*101*:12.7.6.3; *101*:13.7.6.3]

20.1.5.6.4* The training for the duties and responsibilities of crowd managers shall include the following:

(1) Understanding crowd manager roles and responsibilities
(2) Understanding safety and security hazards that can endanger public assembly
(3) Understanding crowd management techniques
(4) Introduction to fire safety and fire safety equipment
(5) Understanding methods of evacuation and movement
(6) Understanding procedures for reporting emergencies
(7) Understanding crowd management emergency response procedures
(8) Understanding the paths of travel and exits, facility evacuation and emergency response procedures and, where provided, facility shelter-in-place procedures
(9) Familiarization with the venue and guest services training
(10) Other specific event-warranted training

[*101*:12.7.6.4; *101*:13.7.6.4]

Δ **20.1.5.6.5** The training for the duties and responsibilities of crowd manager supervisors shall include the following:

(1) The duties described in 20.1.5.6.4
(2) Understanding crowd manager supervisor roles and responsibilities
(3) Understanding incident management procedures
(4) Understanding the facility evacuation plan
(5) Understanding the facility command structure

[*101*:12.7.6.5; *101*:13.7.6.5]

20.1.5.7* Fire Detail. Fire details, if deemed necessary in any assembly occupancy, shall be determined by the AHJ.

20.1.5.8* Drills.

20.1.5.8.1 The employees or attendants of assembly occupancies shall be trained and drilled in the duties they are to perform in case of fire, panic, or other emergency to effect orderly exiting. [*101*:12.7.7.1; *101*:13.7.7.1]

20.1.5.8.2 Employees or attendants of assembly occupancies shall be instructed in the proper use of portable fire extinguishers and other manual fire suppression equipment where provided. [*101*:12.7.7.2; *101*:13.7.7.2]

20.1.5.8.3* In the following assembly occupancies, an audible announcement shall be made, or a projected image shall be shown, prior to the start of each program that notifies occupants of the location of the exits to be used in case of a fire or other emergency:

(1) Theaters
(2) Motion picture theaters
(3) Auditoriums
(4) Other similar assembly occupancies with occupant loads exceeding 300 where there are noncontinuous programs

[*101*:12.7.7.3; *101*:13.7.7.3]

20.1.5.8.4 The requirement of 20.1.5.8.3 shall not apply to assembly occupancies in schools where used for nonpublic events. [*101*:12.7.7.4; *101*:13.7.7.4]

20.1.5.9 Smoking.

20.1.5.9.1 Smoking in assembly occupancies shall be regulated by the AHJ. [*101*:12.7.8.1; *101*:13.7.8.1]

20.1.5.9.2 In rooms or areas where smoking is prohibited, plainly visible signs shall be posted that read as follows:

NO SMOKING

[*101*:12.7.8.2; *101*:13.7.8.2]

20.1.5.9.3 No person shall smoke in prohibited areas that are so posted, unless permitted by the AHJ under both of the following conditions:

(1) Smoking shall be permitted on a stage only where it is a necessary and rehearsed part of a performance.
(2) Smoking shall be permitted only where the smoker is a regular performing member of the cast.

[*101*:12.7.8.3; *101*:13.7.8.3]

20.1.5.9.4 Where smoking is permitted, suitable ashtrays or receptacles shall be provided in convenient locations. [*101*:12.7.8.4; *101*:13.7.8.4]

20.1.5.10 Seating.

20.1.5.10.1 Secured Seating.

20.1.5.10.1.1 Seats in assembly occupancies accommodating more than 200 persons shall be securely fastened to the floor, except where fastened together in groups of not less than three and as permitted by 20.1.5.10.1.2 and 20.1.5.10.2. [*101*:12.7.9.1.1; *101*:13.7.9.1.1]

20.1.5.10.1.2 Balcony and box seating areas that are separated from other areas by rails, guards, partial-height walls, or other physical barriers and have a maximum of 14 seats shall be exempt from the requirement of 20.1.5.10.1.1. [*101*:12.7.9.1.2; *101*:13.7.9.1.2]

20.1.5.10.2 Unsecured Seating.

20.1.5.10.2.1 Seats not secured to the floor shall be permitted in restaurants, night clubs, and other occupancies where fastening seats to the floor might be impracticable. [*101*:12.7.9.2.1; *101*:13.7.9.2.1]

20.1.5.10.2.2 Unsecured seats shall be permitted, provided that, in the area used for seating, excluding such areas as dance floors and stages, there is not more than one seat for each 15 ft^2 (1.4 m^2) of net floor area, and adequate aisles to reach exits are maintained at all times. [*101*:12.7.9.2.2; *101*:13.7.9.2.2]

20.1.5.10.2.3 Seating diagrams shall be submitted for approval by the AHJ to permit an increase in occupant load per 14.8.1.3. [*101*:12.7.9.2.3; *101*:13.7.9.2.3]

20.1.5.10.3 Festival Seating. Festival seating, as defined in 3.3.119, shall be prohibited within a building, unless otherwise permitted by one of the following:

(1) Festival seating shall be permitted in assembly occupancies where the festival seating occupant load is 250 or less.
(2) Festival seating shall be permitted in assembly occupancies where the festival seating occupant load exceeds 250, provided that an approved life safety evaluation has been performed. *(See 10.16.3.)*
(3) Festival seating shall be permitted in assembly occupancies without dance halls, discotheques, and nightclubs, where the festival seating occupant load is 1000 or less.

[*101*:12.2.5.6.1; *101*:13.2.5.6.1]

20.1.5.10.4 Occupant Load Posting.

20.1.5.10.4.1 Every room constituting an assembly occupancy and not having fixed seats shall have the occupant load of the room posted in a conspicuous place near the main exit from the room. [*101*:12.7.9.3.1; *101*:13.7.9.3.1]

20.1.5.10.4.2 Approved signs shall be maintained in a legible manner by the owner or authorized agent. [*101*:12.7.9.3.2; *101*:13.7.9.3.2]

20.1.5.10.4.3 Signs shall be durable and shall indicate the number of occupants permitted for each room use. [*101*:12.7.9.3.3; *101*:13.7.9.3.3]

20.1.5.11 Clothing. Clothing and personal effects shall not be stored in corridors, and spaces not separated from corridors, unless otherwise permitted by one of the following:

(1) In new assembly occupancies, this requirement shall not apply to corridors, and spaces not separated from corridors, that are protected by an approved, supervised automatic sprinkler system in accordance with Section 13.3. [*101*:12.7.12(1)]
(2) In existing assembly occupancies, this requirement shall not apply to corridors, and spaces not separated from corridors, that are protected by an approved automatic sprinkler system in accordance with Section 13.3. [*101*:13.7.12(1)]
(3) This requirement shall not apply to corridors, and spaces not separated from corridors, that are protected by a smoke detection system in accordance with Section 13.3. [*101*:12.7.12(2); *101*:13.7.12(2)]
(4) This requirement shall not apply to storage in metal lockers, provided that the required egress width is maintained. [*101*:12.7.12(3); *101*:13.7.12(3)]

[*101*:12.7.12; *101*:13.7.12]

20.1.5.12 Projection Rooms.

20.1.5.12.1 Film or video projectors or spotlights utilizing light sources that produce particulate matter or toxic gases, or light sources that produce hazardous radiation, without protective shielding shall be located within a projection room complying with 12.3.2.1.2 and 13.3.2.1.2 of NFPA *101*. [*101*:12.4.8.3; *101*:13.4.8.3]

20.1.5.12.2 Every projection room shall be of permanent construction consistent with the building construction type in which the projection room is located and shall comply with the following:

(1) Openings shall not be required to be protected.
(2) The room shall have a floor area of not less than 80 ft^2 (7.4 m^2) for a single machine and not less than 40 ft^2 (3.7 m^2) for each additional machine.
(3) Each motion picture projector, floodlight, spotlight, or similar piece of equipment shall have a clear working space of not less than 30 in. (760 mm) on each side and at its rear, but only one such space shall be required between adjacent projectors.

[*101*:12.4.8.4; *101*:13.4.8.4]

20.1.5.13 Integrated Fire Protection and Life Safety Systems. Integrated fire protection and life safety systems shall be tested in accordance with 13.1.3.1. [*101*:12.7.14; *101*:13.7.14.1]

20.2 Educational Occupancies.

20.2.1 Application. New and existing educational occupancies shall comply with Section 20.2 and NFPA *101*.

20.2.2 Flexible Plan and Open Plan Buildings.

20.2.2.1 Flexible plan and open plan buildings shall comply with the requirements of 20.2.2 as modified by 20.2.2.2 through 20.2.2.5. [*101*:14.4.4.1; *101*:15.4.4.1]

20.2.2.2 Each room occupied by more than 300 persons shall have two or more means of egress entering into separate atmospheres. [*101*:14.4.4.2; *101*:15.4.4.2]

20.2.2.3 Where three or more means of egress are required, the number of means of egress permitted to enter into the same atmosphere shall not exceed two. [*101*:14.4.4.3; *101*:15.4.4.3]

20.2.2.4 Flexible plan buildings shall be permitted to have walls and partitions rearranged periodically only if revised plans or diagrams have been approved by the AHJ. [*101*:14.4.4.4; *101*:15.4.4.4]

20.2.2.5 Flexible plan buildings shall be evaluated while all folding walls are extended and in use as well as when they are in the retracted position. [*101*:14.4.4.5; *101*:15.4.4.5]

Δ **20.2.3 Interior Finish.**

20.2.3.1 General. Interior finish shall be in accordance with Section 12.5. [*101*:14.3.3.1; *101*:15.3.3.1]

20.2.3.2 Interior Wall and Ceiling Finish. Interior wall and ceiling finish materials complying with Section 12.5 shall be permitted as follows:

(1) Exits — Class A [*101*:14.3.3.2(1); *101*:15.3.3.2(1)]
(2) In new educational occupancies, other than exits — Class A or Class B [*101*:14.3.3.2(2)]
(3) In existing educational occupancies, corridors and lobbies — Class A or Class B [*101*:15.3.3.2(2)]
(4) Low-height partitions not exceeding 60 in. (1525 mm) and used in locations other than exits — Class A, Class B, or Class C [*101*:14.3.3.2(3); *101*:15.3.3.2(3)]

[*101*:14.3.3.2; *101*:15.3.3.2]

20.2.3.3 Interior Floor Finish.

20.2.3.3.1 New interior floor finish shall comply with Section 12.5. [*101*:14.3.3.3.1]

20.2.3.3.2 New interior floor finish in exit enclosures and exit access corridors and spaces not separated from them by walls complying with 14.3.6 of NFPA *101* shall be not less than Class II. [*101*:14.3.3.3.2]

20.2.3.3.3 New interior floor finish shall comply with 12.5.8.1 or 12.5.8.2, as applicable. [*101*:14.3.3.3.3]

20.2.3.3.4 Existing Interior Floor Finish. (Reserved) [*101*:15.3.3.3]

20.2.4 Operating Features.

Δ **20.2.4.1 Emergency Action Plan.**

N **20.2.4.1.1** Emergency action plans shall be provided in accordance with Section 10.4. [*101*:14.7.1.1; *101*:15.7.1.1]

N **20.2.4.1.2** The operation of security features, fire protection systems, and life safety systems shall be documented in the building's emergency action plan. [*101*:14.7.1.2; *101*:15.7.1.2]

20.2.4.2 Emergency Egress Drills.

20.2.4.2.1* Emergency egress drills shall be conducted in accordance with Section 10.6 and the applicable provisions of 20.2.4.2.3 as otherwise provided in 20.2.4.2.2. [*101*:14.7.2.1; *101*:15.7.2.1]

20.2.4.2.2 Approved training programs designed for education and training and for the practice of emergency egress to familiarize occupants with the drill procedure, and to establish conduct of the emergency egress as a matter of routine, shall be permitted to receive credit on a one-for-one basis for not more than four of the emergency egress drills required by 20.2.4.2.3, provided that a minimum of four emergency egress drills are completed prior to the conduct of the first such training and practice program. [*101*:14.7.2.2; *101*:15.7.2.2]

20.2.4.2.3 Emergency egress drills shall be conducted as follows:

(1) Not less than one emergency egress drill shall be conducted every month the facility is in session, unless both of the following criteria are met:
  (a) In climates where the weather is severe, the monthly emergency egress drills shall be permitted to be deferred.
  (b) The required number of emergency egress drills shall be conducted, and not less than four shall be conducted before the drills are deferred.
(2) All occupants of the building shall participate in the drill.
(3) One additional emergency egress drill, other than for educational occupancies that are open on a year-round basis, shall be required within the first 30 days of operation.

[*101*:14.7.2.3; *101*:15.7.2.3]

20.2.4.2.4* Where permitted by the AHJ, up to two of the emergency egress drills required by 20.2.4.2.3 shall be permitted to consist of alternative emergency drills for one or both of the following:

(1) Targeted violence events
(2) Natural hazard events
[*101*:14.7.2.4; *101*:15.7.2.4]

20.2.4.2.5 All emergency drill alarms shall be sounded on the fire alarm system. [*101*:14.7.2.5; *101*:15.7.2.5]

20.2.4.3 Inspection.

20.2.4.3.1* It shall be the duty of principals, teachers, or staff to inspect all exit facilities daily to ensure that all stairways, doors, and other exits are in proper condition. [*101*:14.7.3.1; *101*:15.7.3.1]

20.2.4.3.2 Open plan buildings shall require extra surveillance to ensure that exit paths are maintained clear of obstruction and are obvious. [*101*:14.7.3.2; *101*:15.7.3.2]

20.2.4.3.3 Inspection of Door Openings. Door openings shall be inspected in accordance with 14.5.10. [*101*:14.7.3.3; *101*:15.7.3.3]

20.2.4.4 Furnishings and Decorations.

20.2.4.4.1 Draperies, curtains, and other similar furnishings and decorations in educational occupancies shall be in accordance with the provisions of 12.6.1. [*101*:14.7.4.1; *101*:15.7.4.1]

20.2.4.4.2 Clothing and personal effects shall not be stored in corridors, unless otherwise permitted by one of the following:

(1) This requirement shall not apply to corridors protected by an automatic sprinkler system in accordance with Section 13.3.
(2) This requirement shall not apply to corridor areas protected by a smoke detection system in accordance with 13.7.1.4.
(3) This requirement shall not apply to storage in metal lockers, provided that the required egress width is maintained.

[*101*:14.7.4.2; *101*:15.7.4.2]

20.2.4.4.3 Artwork and teaching materials shall be permitted to be attached directly to the walls in accordance with the following:

(1) In new educational occupancies, the artwork and teaching materials shall not exceed 20 percent of the wall area in a building that is not protected throughout by an approved, supervised automatic sprinkler system in accordance with Section 13.3. [*101*:14.7.4.3(1)]
(2) In existing educational occupancies, the artwork and teaching materials shall not exceed 20 percent of the wall area in a building that is not protected throughout by an approved automatic sprinkler system in accordance with Section 13.3. [*101*:15.7.4.3(1)]
(3) In new educational occupancies, the artwork and teaching materials shall not exceed 50 percent of the wall area in a building that is protected throughout by an approved, supervised automatic sprinkler system in accordance with Section 13.3. [*101*:14.7.4.3(2)]
(4) In existing educational occupancies, the artwork and teaching materials shall not exceed 50 percent of the wall area in a building that is protected throughout by an approved automatic sprinkler system in accordance with Section 13.3. [*101*:15.7.4.3(2)]

[*101*:14.7.4.3; *101*:15.7.4.3]

20.2.4.5 Unvented Fuel-Fired Heating Equipment. Unvented fuel-fired heating equipment, other than gas space heaters in compliance with NFPA 54 shall be prohibited. [*101*:14.5.2.2; *101*:15.5.2.2]

20.2.4.6 Integrated Fire Protection and Life Safety Systems. Integrated fire protection and life safety systems shall be tested in accordance with 13.1.3.1. [*101*:14.7.6; *101*:15.7.6.1]

20.3 Day-Care Occupancies.

20.3.1 Application. New and existing day-care occupancies shall comply with Section 20.3 and NFPA *101*.

20.3.1.1 In new day-care occupancies, where a facility houses more than one age group or self-preservation capability, the strictest requirements applicable to any group present shall apply throughout the day-care occupancy or building, as appropriate to a given area, unless the area housing such a group is maintained as a separate fire area. [*101*:16.1.1.6]

20.3.1.2 In existing day-care occupancies, where a facility houses clients of more than one self-preservation capability, the strictest requirements applicable to any group present shall apply throughout the day-care occupancy or building, as appropriate to a given area, unless the area housing such a group is maintained as a separate fire area. [*101*:17.1.1.6]

20.3.1.3* Rooms or spaces used for temporary child care, during short-term activities of the child's relative or guardian within the same building, shall not be required to meet the provisions of this chapter. [*101*:16.1.1.7; *101*:17.1.1.7]

20.3.1.4 General. Occupancies that include preschools, kindergartens, and other schools whose purpose is primarily educational for children 30 months of age or older, even though the children who attend such schools are of preschool age, shall comply with the provisions of Chapter 14 or Chapter 15 of NFPA *101*, as applicable. [*101*:16.1.2.1;*101*:17.1.2.1]

20.3.1.5 Adult Day-Care Occupancies.

20.3.1.5.1 Adult day-care occupancies shall include any building or portion thereof used for less than 24 hours per day to house more than three adults requiring care, maintenance, and supervision by other than their relative(s). [*101*:16.1.2.2.1; *101*:17.1.2.2.1]

20.3.1.5.2 Clients in adult day-care occupancies shall be ambulatory or semiambulatory and shall not be bedridden. [*101*:16.1.2.2.2; *101*:17.1.2.2.2]

20.3.1.5.3 Clients in adult day-care occupancies shall not exhibit behavior that is harmful to themselves or to others. [*101*:16.1.2.2.3; *101*:17.1.2.2.3]

20.3.2 General Requirements.

20.3.2.1 Unvented fuel-fired heating equipment, other than gas space heaters in compliance with NFPA 54 shall be prohibited. [*101*:16.5.2.2; *101*:17.5.2.2]

20.3.2.2* Door Latches. Every door latch to closets, storage areas, kitchens, and other similar spaces or areas shall be such that clients can open the door from inside the space or area. [*101*:16.2.2.2.4; *101*:17.2.2.2.4]

20.3.2.3 Bathroom Doors. Every bathroom door lock shall be designed to allow opening of the locked door from the outside by an opening device that shall be readily accessible to the staff. [*101*:16.2.2.2.5; *101*:17.2.2.2.5]

20.3.2.4 Flexible Plan and Open Plan Buildings.

20.3.2.4.1 In new day-care occupancies, flexible plan and open plan buildings shall comply with the requirements of 20.3.2.4 as modified by 20.3.2.4.3 through 20.3.2.4.6. [*101*:16.4.4.1]

20.3.2.4.2 In existing day-care occupancies, flexible plan and open plan buildings shall comply with the requirements of 20.3.2.4 as modified by 20.3.2.4.3 and 20.3.2.4.4. [*101*:17.4.4.1]

20.3.2.4.3 Flexible plan buildings shall be permitted to have walls and partitions rearranged periodically only if revised plans or diagrams have been approved by the AHJ. [*101*:16.4.3.2; *101*:17.4.4.2]

20.3.2.4.4 Flexible plan buildings shall be evaluated while all folding walls are extended and in use as well as when they are in the retracted position. [*101*:16.4.4.3; *101*:17.4.4.3]

20.3.2.4.5 In new day-care occupancies, each room occupied by more than 300 persons shall have two or more means of egress entering into separate atmospheres. [*101*:16.4.4.4]

20.3.2.4.6 In new day-care occupancies, where three or more means of egress are required from a single room, the number of means of egress permitted to enter into a common atmosphere shall not exceed two. [*101*:16.4.4.5]

20.3.3 Interior Finish.

20.3.3.1 General. Interior finish shall be in accordance with Section 12.5. [*101*:16.3.3.1; *101*:17.3.3.1]

20.3.3.2 New Interior Wall and Ceiling Finish. New interior wall and ceiling finish materials complying with Section 12.5 shall be Class A in stairways, corridors, and lobbies; in all other occupied areas, new interior wall and ceiling finish shall be Class A or Class B. [*101*:16.3.3.2]

20.3.3.3 Existing Interior Wall and Ceiling Finish. Existing interior wall and ceiling finish materials complying with Section 12.5 shall be Class A or Class B throughout. [*101*:17.3.3.2]

20.3.3.4 Interior Floor Finish.

20.3.3.4.1 New interior floor finish shall comply with Section 12.5. [*101*:16.3.3.3.1]

20.3.3.4.2 New interior floor finish in exit enclosures and exit access corridors and spaces not separated from them by walls complying with 14.3.6 of NFPA *101* shall be not less than Class II. [*101*:16.3.3.3.2]

20.3.3.4.3 New interior floor finish shall comply with 12.5.8.1 or 12.5.8.2, as applicable. [*101*:16.3.3.3.3]

20.3.3.4.4 Existing Interior Floor Finish. (Reserved) [*101*:17.3.3.3]

20.3.4 Day-Care Homes.

20.3.4.1 Classification.

20.3.4.1.1 In new day-care homes, the requirements of 20.3.4 shall apply to day-care homes in which more than 3, but not more than 12, clients receive care, maintenance, and supervision by other than their relative(s) or legal guardian(s) for less than 24 hours per day, generally within a dwelling unit. *(See also 16.6.1.4 of NFPA 101.)* [*101*:16.6.1.1.2]

20.3.4.1.2* In existing day-care homes, the requirements of Section 17.6 of NFPA *101* shall apply to existing day-care homes in which more than 3, but not more than 12, clients receive care, maintenance, and supervision by other than their relative(s) or legal guardian(s) for less than 24 hours per day, generally within a dwelling unit. An existing day-care home shall be permitted the option of meeting the requirements of Section 16.6 of NFPA *101* in lieu of Section 17.6 of NFPA *101*. Any existing day-care home that meets the requirements of Chapter 16 of NFPA *101* shall be judged as meeting the requirements of this chapter. *(See also 17.6.1.4 of NFPA 101.)* [*101*:17.6.1.1.2]

20.3.4.1.3 In new day-care homes, where a facility houses more than one age group or one self-preservation capability, the strictest requirements applicable to any group present shall apply throughout the day-care home or building, as appropriate to a given area, unless the area housing such a group is maintained as a separate fire area. [*101*:16.6.1.1.3]

20.3.4.1.4 In existing day-care homes, where a facility houses clients of more than one self-preservation capability, the strictest requirements applicable to any group present shall apply throughout the day-care home or building, as appropriate to a given area, unless the area housing such a group is maintained as a separate fire area. [*101*:17.6.1.1.3]

20.3.4.1.5 Facilities that supervise clients on a temporary basis with a parent or guardian in close proximity shall not be required to meet the provisions of 20.3.4. [*101*:16.6.1.1.4; *101*:17.6.1.1.4]

20.3.4.1.6 Places of religious worship shall not be required to meet the provisions of 20.3.4 where operating a day-care home while services are being held in the building. [*101*:16.6.1.1.5; *101*:17.6.1.1.5]

20.3.4.2 Operating Features.

Δ **20.3.4.2.1 Emergency Action Plans.**

N **20.3.4.2.1.1*** Emergency action plans shall be provided in accordance with Section 10.4. [*101*:16.7.1.1; *101*:17.7.1.1]

N **20.3.4.2.1.2** The operation of security features, fire protection systems, and life safety systems shall be documented in the building's emergency action plan. [*101*:16.7.1.2; *101*:17.7.1.2]

20.3.4.2.2 Emergency Egress and Relocation Drills.

20.3.4.2.2.1* Emergency egress and relocation drills shall be conducted in accordance with Section 10.6 and the applicable provisions of 20.3.4.2.2.2. [*101*:16.7.2.1; *101*:17.7.2.1]

20.3.4.2.2.2 Emergency egress and relocation drills shall be conducted as follows:

(1) Not less than one emergency egress and relocation drill shall be conducted every month the facility is in session, unless both of the following criteria are met:
   (a) In climates where the weather is severe, the monthly emergency egress and relocation drills shall be permitted to be deferred.
   (b) The required number of emergency egress and relocation drills shall be conducted, and not less than four shall be conducted before the drills are deferred.
(2) The monthly frequency specified by 20.3.4.2.2.2(1) shall be permitted to be bimonthly in adult day-care centers.
(3) All occupants of the building shall participate in the drill.
(4) One additional emergency egress and relocation drill, other than for day-care occupancies that are open on a year-round basis, shall be required within the first 30 days of operation.

[*101*:16.7.2.2; *101*:17.7.2.2]

20.3.4.2.3 Inspections.

20.3.4.2.3.1 Fire prevention inspections shall be conducted monthly by a trained senior member of the staff, after which a copy of the latest inspection report shall be posted in a conspicuous place in the day-care facility. [*101*:16.7.3.1; *101*:17.7.3.1]

20.3.4.2.3.2* It shall be the duty of site administrators and staff members to inspect all exit facilities daily to ensure that all stairways, doors, and other exits are in proper condition. [*101*:16.7.3.2; *101*:17.7.3.2]

20.3.4.2.3.3 Open plan buildings shall require extra surveillance to ensure that exit paths are maintained clear of obstruction and are obvious. [*101*:16.7.3.3; *101*:17.7.3.3]

20.3.4.2.3.4 Inspection of Door Openings. Door openings shall be inspected in accordance with 14.5.10. [*101*:16.7.3.4; *101*:17.7.3.4]

20.3.4.2.3.5 Furnishings and Decorations.

20.3.4.2.3.5.1 Draperies, curtains, and other similar furnishings and decorations in day-care occupancies, other than in day-care homes, shall be in accordance with the provisions of 12.6.1. [*101*:16.7.4.1; *101*:17.7.4.1]

20.3.4.2.3.5.2 Clothing and personal effects shall not be stored in corridors, unless otherwise permitted by one of the following:

(1) This requirement shall not apply to corridors protected by an automatic sprinkler system in accordance with Section 13.3.
(2) This requirement shall not apply to corridor areas protected by a smoke detection system in accordance with Section 13.7.
(3) This requirement shall not apply to storage in metal lockers, provided that the required egress width is maintained.

[*101*:16.7.4.2; *101*:17.7.4.2]

20.3.4.2.3.5.3 Artwork and teaching materials shall be permitted to be attached directly to the walls in accordance with the following:

(1) In new day-care homes, the artwork and teaching materials shall not exceed 20 percent of the wall area in a building that is not protected throughout by an approved, supervised automatic sprinkler system in accordance with Section 13.3. [*101*:16.7.4.3(1)]
(2) In existing day-care homes, the artwork and teaching materials shall not exceed 20 percent of the wall area in a building that is not protected throughout by an approved automatic sprinkler system in accordance with Section 13.3. [*101*:17.7.4.3(1)]
(3) In new day-care homes, the artwork and teaching materials shall not exceed 50 percent of the wall area in a building that is protected throughout by an approved, supervised automatic sprinkler system in accordance with Section 13.3. [*101*:16.7.4.3(2)]
(4) In existing day-care homes, the artwork and teaching materials shall not exceed 50 percent of the wall area in a building that is protected throughout by an approved automatic sprinkler system in accordance with Section 13.3. [*101*:17.7.4.3(2)]

[*101*:16.7.4.3; *101*:17.7.4.3]

20.3.4.2.3.5.4 The provision of 12.6.3 for cigarette ignition resistance of newly introduced upholstered furniture and mattresses shall not apply to day-care homes. [*101*:16.7.4.4; *101*:17.7.4.4]

20.3.4.2.3.6* Day-Care Staff. Adequate adult staff shall be on duty in the facility and alert at all times where clients are present. [*101*:16.7.5; *101*:17.7.5]

20.3.4.2.3.7 Integrated Fire Protection and Life Safety Systems. Integrated fire protection and life safety systems shall be tested in accordance with 13.1.3.1. [*101*:16.7.6; *101*:17.7.6.1]

20.4 Health Care Occupancies.

20.4.1 Application. New and existing health care occupancies shall comply with Section 20.4, NFPA *101*, and NFPA 99.

20.4.2* Operating Features.

20.4.2.1 Evacuation and Relocation Plan and Fire Drills.

20.4.2.1.1 The administration of every health care occupancy shall have, in effect and available to all supervisory personnel, written copies of a plan for the protection of all persons in the event of fire, for their evacuation to areas of refuge, and for their evacuation from the building when necessary. [*101*:18.7.1.1; *101*:19.7.1.1]

20.4.2.1.2 All employees shall be periodically instructed and kept informed with respect to their duties under the plan required by 20.4.2.1.1. [*101*:18.7.1.2; *101*:19.7.1.2]

20.4.2.1.3 A copy of the plan required by 20.4.2.1.1 shall be readily available at all times in the telephone operator's location or at the security center. [*101*:18.7.1.3; *101*:19.7.1.3]

20.4.2.1.4 The provisions of Section 10.6 and 20.4.2.1.2 through 20.4.2.2.3 shall apply.

20.4.2.1.5* Fire drills in health care occupancies shall include the simulation of emergency fire conditions and, except as indicated in 20.4.2.1.8, include activation of the fire alarm system notification appliances. [*101*:18.7.1.4; *101*:19.7.1.4]

20.4.2.1.6 Infirm or bedridden patients shall not be required to be moved during drills to safe areas or to the exterior of the building. [*101*:18.7.1.5; *101*:19.7.1.5]

20.4.2.1.7 Drills shall be conducted quarterly on each shift to familiarize facility personnel (nurses, interns, maintenance engineers, and administrative staff) with the signals and emergency action required under varied conditions. [*101*:18.7.1.6; *101*:19.7.1.6]

20.4.2.1.8 When drills are conducted between 9:00 p.m. and 6:00 a.m. (2100 hours and 0600 hours), a coded announcement shall be permitted to be used instead of activating the fire alarm system notification appliances. [*101*:18.7.1.7; *101*:19.7.1.7]

20.4.2.1.9 Employees of health care occupancies shall be instructed in life safety procedures and devices. [*101*:18.7.1.8; *101*:19.7.1.8]

20.4.2.2 Procedure in Case of Fire.

20.4.2.2.1* Protection of Patients.

20.4.2.2.1.1 For health care occupancies, the proper protection of patients shall require the prompt and effective response of health care personnel. [*101*:18.7.2.1.1; *101*:19.7.2.1.1]

20.4.2.2.1.2 The basic response required of staff shall include the following:

(1) Removal of all occupants directly involved with the fire emergency
(2) Transmission of an appropriate fire alarm signal to warn other building occupants and summon staff

(3) Confinement of the effects of the fire by closing doors to isolate the fire area
(4) Relocation of patients as detailed in the health care occupancy's fire safety plan

[*101*:18.7.2.1.2; *101*:19.7.2.1.2]

20.4.2.2.2 Fire Safety Plan. A written health care occupancy fire safety plan shall provide for all of the following:

(1) Use of alarms
(2) Transmission of alarms to fire department
(3) Emergency phone call to fire department
(4) Response to alarms
(5) Isolation of fire
(6) Evacuation of immediate area
(7) Evacuation of smoke compartment
(8) Preparation of floors and building for evacuation
(9) Extinguishment of fire
(10) Location and operation of doors disguised with murals as permitted by 18.2.2.2.7 and 19.2.2.2.7 of NFPA *101*.

[*101*:18.7.2.2; *101*:19.7.2.2]

20.4.2.2.3 Staff Response.

20.4.2.2.3.1 All health care occupancy personnel shall be instructed in the use of and response to fire alarms. [*101*:18.7.2.3.1; *101*:9.7.2.3.1]

20.4.2.2.3.2 All health care occupancy personnel shall be instructed in the use of the code phrase to ensure transmission of an alarm under the following conditions:

(1) When the individual who discovers a fire must immediately go to the aid of an endangered person
(2) During a malfunction of the building fire alarm system

[*101*:18.7.2.3.2; *101*:19.7.2.3.2]

20.4.2.2.3.3 Personnel hearing the code announced shall first activate the building fire alarm using the nearest manual fire alarm box and then shall execute immediately their duties as outlined in the fire safety plan. [*101*:18.7.2.3.3; *101*:19.7.2.3.3]

20.4.2.3 Maintenance of Means of Egress.

20.4.2.3.1 Proper maintenance shall be provided to ensure the dependability of the method of evacuation selected. [*101*:18.7.3.1; *101*:19.7.3.1]

20.4.2.3.2 Health care occupancies that find it necessary to lock means of egress doors shall, at all times, maintain an adequate staff qualified to release locks and direct occupants from the immediate danger area to a place of safety in case of fire or other emergency. [*101*:18.7.3.2; *101*:19.7.3.2]

20.4.2.3.3* Where required by the AHJ, a floor plan shall be provided to indicate the location of all required means of egress corridors in smoke compartments having spaces not separated from the corridor by partitions. [*101*:18.7.3.3; *101*:19.7.3.3]

20.4.2.4* Smoking. Smoking regulations shall be adopted and shall include not less than the following provisions:

(1) Smoking shall be prohibited in any room, ward, or individual enclosed space where flammable liquids, flammable gases, or oxygen is used or stored and in any other hazardous location, and such areas shall be posted with signs that read NO SMOKING or shall be posted with the international symbol for no smoking.
(2) In health care occupancies where smoking is prohibited and signs are prominently placed at all major entrances, secondary signs with language that prohibits smoking shall not be required.
(3) Smoking by patients classified as not responsible shall be prohibited.
(4) The requirement of 20.4.2.4(3) shall not apply where the patient is under direct supervision.
(5) Ashtrays of noncombustible material and safe design shall be provided in all areas where smoking is permitted inside the building.
(6) Metal containers with self-closing cover devices into which ashtrays can be emptied shall be readily available to all areas where smoking is permitted inside the building.

[*101*:18.7.4; *101*:19.7.4]

20.4.2.5 Furnishings, Mattresses, and Decorations.

20.4.2.5.1* Draperies, curtains, and other loosely hanging fabrics and films serving as furnishings or decorations in health care occupancies shall be in accordance with the provisions of 12.6.1 *(see 18.3.5.11 or 19.3.5.11 of NFPA 101)*, and the following also shall apply:

(1) Such curtains shall include cubicle curtains.
(2) Such curtains shall not include curtains at showers and baths.
(3) Such draperies and curtains shall not include draperies and curtains at windows in patient sleeping rooms in sprinklered smoke compartments.
(4) Such draperies and curtains shall not include draperies and curtains in other rooms or areas where the draperies and curtains comply with all of the following:

 (a) Individual drapery or curtain panel area does not exceed 48 ft^2 (4.5 m^2).
 (b) Total area of drapery and curtain panels per room or area does not exceed 20 percent of the aggregate area of the wall on which they are located.
 (c) For existing healthcare occupancies, smoke compartment in which draperies or curtains are located is sprinklered in accordance with 13.3.2.10.

[*101*:18.7.5.1; *101*:19.7.5.1]

20.4.2.5.2 Newly introduced upholstered furniture within health care occupancies shall comply with one of the following provisions, unless otherwise provided in 20.4.2.5.3:

(1) The furniture shall meet the criteria specified in 12.6.2.2.1 and 12.6.3.2.1.
(2) The furniture shall be in a building protected throughout by an approved, supervised automatic sprinkler system in accordance with NFPA 13.

[*101*:18.7.5.2; *101*:19.7.5.2]

20.4.2.5.3 The requirements of 20.4.2.5.2, 12.6.2.2.1, and 12.6.3.2.1 shall not apply to upholstered furniture belonging to the patient in sleeping rooms of existing nursing homes where the following criteria are met:

(1) A smoke detector shall be installed where the patient sleeping room is not protected by automatic sprinklers.
(2) Battery-powered single-station smoke detectors shall be permitted.

[*101*:19.7.5.3]

20.4.2.5.4 Newly introduced mattresses within health care occupancies shall comply with one of the following provisions, unless otherwise provided in 20.4.2.5.5:

(1) The mattresses shall meet the criteria specified in 12.6.3 and 12.6.3.2.
(2) The mattresses shall be in a building protected throughout by an approved, supervised automatic sprinkler system in accordance with NFPA 13.

[*101*:18.7.5.4; *101*:19.7.5.4]

20.4.2.5.5 The requirements of 20.4.2.5.4, 12.6.3, and 12.6.3.2 shall not apply to mattresses belonging to the patient in sleeping rooms of existing nursing homes where the following criteria are met:

(1) A smoke detector shall be installed where the patient sleeping room is not protected by automatic sprinklers.
(2) Battery-powered single-station smoke detectors shall be permitted.

[*101*:19.7.5.5]

20.4.2.5.6 Combustible decorations shall be prohibited in any health care occupancy, unless one of the following criteria is met:

(1) They are flame-retardant or are treated with approved fire-retardant coating that is listed and labeled for application to the material to which it is applied.
(2)* The decorations meet the flame propagation performance criteria contained in Test Method 1 or Test Method 2, as appropriate, of NFPA 701.
(3) The decorations exhibit a heat release rate not exceeding 100 kW when tested in accordance with NFPA 289 using the 20 kW ignition source.
(4)* The decorations, such as photographs, paintings, and other art, are attached directly to the walls, ceiling, and non-fire-rated doors in accordance with the following:
  (a) Decorations on non-fire-rated doors do not interfere with the operation or any required latching of the door and do not exceed the area limitations of 20.4.2.5.6(4)(b), 20.4.2.5.6(4)(c), or 20.4.2.5.6(4)(d).
  (b) Decorations do not exceed 20 percent of the wall, ceiling, and door areas inside any room or space of a smoke compartment that is not protected throughout by an approved automatic sprinkler system in accordance with Section 13.3.
  (c) Decorations do not exceed 30 percent of the wall, ceiling, and door areas inside any room or space of a smoke compartment that is protected throughout by an approved supervised automatic sprinkler system in accordance with Section 13.3.
  (d) Decorations do not exceed 50 percent of the wall, ceiling, and door areas inside patient sleeping rooms having a capacity not exceeding four persons, in a smoke compartment that is protected throughout by an approved, supervised automatic sprinkler system in accordance with Section 13.3.
(5)* In existing health care occupancies, they are decorations, such as photographs or paintings, in such limited quantities that a hazard of fire development or spread is not present.

[*101*:18.7.5.6; *101*:19.7.5.6]

20.4.2.5.7 Soiled Linen and Trash Receptacles.

20.4.2.5.7.1* Soiled linen or trash collection receptacles with capacities greater than 64 gal (242 L) shall be located in a hazardous area when not attended. [*101*:18.7.5.7.1; *101*:19.7.5.7.1]

20.4.2.5.7.2* Containers greater than 64 gal (242 L) used solely for recycling clean waste or for patient records awaiting destruction shall be permitted to be excluded from the requirements of 20.4.2.5.7.1 where all the following conditions are met:

(1) Each container is limited to a maximum capacity of 96 gal (363 L).
(2) Containers for combustibles shall be labeled and listed as meeting the requirements of FM Approvals 6920/6921, *Oily Waste Cans and Containers for Combustible Waste*; however, such testing, listing, and labeling shall not be limited to FM Approvals.

[*101*:18.7.5.7.2; *101*:19.7.5.7.2]

20.4.2.5.7.3 The provisions of 12.6.8, applicable to containers for waste or linen, shall not apply. [*101*:18.7.5.7.3; *101*:19.7.5.7.3]

20.4.2.5.8 The provisions of 19.2.1.1 through 19.2.1.2 applicable to soiled linen and trash receptacles shall not apply.

20.4.2.6* Portable Space-Heating Devices. Portable space-heating devices shall be prohibited in all health care occupancies, unless both of the following criteria are met:

(1) Such devices are permitted to be used only in nonsleeping staff and employee areas.
(2) Such devices are listed and labeled for use as a freestanding, movable heater in accordance with UL 1278, *Movable and Wall- or Ceiling-Hung Electric Room Heaters*.

[*101*:18.7.8; *101*:19.7.8]

20.4.2.7 Integrated Fire Protection and Life Safety Systems. Integrated fire protection and life safety systems shall be tested in accordance with 13.1.3.1. [*101*:18.7.10; *101*:19.7.10.1]

20.4.3 Interior Finish.

20.4.3.1 General. Interior finish shall be in accordance with Section 12.5. [*101*:18.3.3.1; *101*:19.3.3.1]

20.4.3.2 New Interior Wall and Ceiling Finish. New interior wall and ceiling finish materials complying with Section 12.5 shall be permitted throughout if Class A, except as indicated in 20.4.3.2.1 or 20.4.3.2.2. [*101*:18.3.3.2]

20.4.3.2.1 New walls and ceilings shall be permitted to have Class A or Class B interior finish in individual rooms having a capacity not exceeding four persons. [*101*:18.3.3.2.1]

20.4.3.2.2 New corridor wall finish not exceeding 48 in. (1220 mm) in height that is restricted to the lower half of the wall shall be permitted to be Class A or Class B. [*101*:18.3.3.2.2]

20.4.3.2.3 Existing Interior Wall and Ceiling Finish. Existing interior wall and ceiling finish materials complying with Section 12.5 shall be permitted to be Class A or Class B. [*101*:19.3.3.2]

20.4.3.3 Interior Floor Finish.

20.4.3.3.1 New interior floor finish shall comply with Section 12.5. [*101*:18.3.3.3.1]

20.4.3.3.2 New interior floor finish in exit enclosures and exit access corridors and spaces not separated from them by walls complying with 18.3.6 of NFPA *101* shall be Class I or Class II. [*101*:18.3.3.3.2]

20.4.3.3.3 New interior floor finish shall comply with 12.5.8.1 or 12.5.8.2, as applicable. [*101*:18.3.3.3.3]

20.4.3.4 Interior Finish (Nonsprinklered Smoke Compartment Rehabilitation).

20.4.3.4.1 General. Interior finish within the modification area shall be in accordance with Section 12.5. [*101*:18.4.5.6.1]

20.4.3.4.2 Interior Wall and Ceiling Finish. Newly installed interior wall and ceiling finish materials complying with Section 12.5 shall be permitted throughout nonsprinklered smoke compartments if the materials are Class A, except as otherwise permitted in 20.4.3.4.2.1 or 20.4.3.4.2.2. [*101*:18.4.5.6.2]

20.4.3.4.2.1 Walls and ceilings shall be permitted to have Class A or Class B interior finish in individual rooms having a capacity not exceeding four persons. [*101*:18.4.5.6.2.1]

20.4.3.4.2.2 Corridor wall finish not exceeding 48 in. (1220 mm) in height and restricted to the lower half of the wall shall be permitted to be Class A or Class B. [*101*:18.4.5.6.2.2]

20.4.3.5 Interior Floor Finish.

20.4.3.5.1 Newly installed interior floor finish shall comply with Section 12.5. [*101*:18.4.5.6.3.1]

20.4.3.5.2 The requirements for newly installed interior floor finish in exit enclosures and corridors not separated from them by walls complying with 19.3.5.7 of NFPA *101* shall be as follows:

(1) Unrestricted in smoke compartments protected throughout by an approved, supervised automatic sprinkler system in accordance with 19.3.5.7 of NFPA *101*
(2) Not less than Class I in smoke compartments not protected throughout by an approved, supervised automatic sprinkler system in accordance with 19.3.5.7 of NFPA *101*

[*101*:18.4.5.6.3.2]

20.4.3.5.3 Existing Interior Floor Finish. No restrictions shall apply to existing interior floor finish. [*101*:19.3.3.3]

20.5 Residential Board and Care Occupancies.

20.5.1 Application. New and existing residential board and care occupancies shall comply with Section 20.5 and NFPA *101*.

20.5.2 Operating Features.

20.5.2.1 Emergency Action Plan.

20.5.2.1.1* The administration of every residential board and care facility shall have, in effect and available to all supervisory personnel, written copies of a plan for protecting all persons in the event of fire, for keeping persons in place, for evacuating persons to areas of refuge, and for evacuating persons from the building when necessary. [*101*:32.7.1.1; *101*:33.7.1.1]

20.5.2.1.2 The emergency action plan shall include special staff response, including the fire protection procedures needed to ensure the safety of any resident, and shall be amended or revised whenever any resident with unusual needs is admitted to the home. [*101*:32.7.1.2; *101*:33.7.1.2]

20.5.2.1.3 All employees shall be periodically instructed and kept informed with respect to their duties and responsibilities under the plan, and such instruction shall be reviewed by the staff not less than every 2 months. [*101*:32.7.1.3; *101*:33.7.1.3]

20.5.2.1.4 A copy of the plan shall be readily available at all times within the facility. [*101*:32.7.1.4; *101*:33.7.1.4]

20.5.2.2 Resident Training.

20.5.2.2.1 All residents participating in the emergency action plans shall be trained in the proper actions to be taken in the event of fire. [*101*:32.7.2.1; *101*:33.7.2.1]

20.5.2.2.2 The training required by 20.5.2.2.1 shall include actions to be taken if the primary escape route is blocked. [*101*:32.7.2.2; *101*:33.7.2.2]

20.5.2.2.3 If a resident is given rehabilitation or habilitation training, training in fire prevention and the actions to be taken in the event of a fire shall be a part of the training program. [*101*:32.7.2.3; *101*:33.7.2.3]

20.5.2.2.4 Residents shall be trained to assist each other in case of fire to the extent that their physical and mental abilities permit them to do so without additional personal risk. [*101*:32.7.2.4; *101*:33.7.2.4]

20.5.2.3 Emergency Egress and Relocation Drills. Emergency egress and relocation drills shall be conducted in accordance with 20.5.2.3.1 through 20.5.2.3.6. [*101*:32.7.3; *101*:33.7.3]

20.5.2.3.1 Emergency egress and relocation drills shall be conducted not less than six times per year on a bimonthly basis, with not less than two drills conducted during the night when residents are sleeping, as modified by 20.5.2.3.5 and 20.5.2.3.6. [*101*:32.7.3.1; *101*:33.7.3.1]

20.5.2.3.2 The emergency drills shall be permitted to be announced to the residents in advance. [*101*:32.7.3.2; *101*:33.7.3.2]

20.5.2.3.3* The drills shall involve the actual evacuation of all residents to an assembly point, as specified in the emergency action plan, and shall provide residents with experience in egressing through all exits and means of escape required by the *Code*. [*101*:32.7.3.3; *101*:33.7.3.3]

20.5.2.3.4 Exits and means of escape not used in any drill shall not be credited in meeting the requirements of this *Code* for board and care facilities. [*101*:32.7.3.4; *101*:33.7.3.4]

20.5.2.3.5 Actual exiting from windows shall not be required to comply with 20.5.2.3; opening the window and signaling for help shall be an acceptable alternative. [*101*:32.7.3.5; *101*:33.7.3.5]

20.5.2.3.6 Residents who cannot meaningfully assist in their own evacuation or who have special health problems shall not be required to actively participate in the drill. [*101*:32.7.3.6; *101*:33.7.3.6]

20.5.2.4 Smoking.

20.5.2.4.1* Smoking regulations shall be adopted by the administration of board and care occupancies. [*101*:32.7.4.1; *101*:33.7.4.1]

20.5.2.4.2 Where smoking is permitted, noncombustible safety-type ashtrays or receptacles shall be provided in convenient locations. [*101*:32.7.4.2; *101*:33.7.4.2]

20.5.2.5* Furnishings, Bedding, and Decorations.

20.5.2.5.1 New draperies, curtains, and other similar loosely hanging furnishings and decorations shall comply with 20.5.2.5.1.1 and 20.5.2.5.1.2. [*101*:32.7.5.1; *101*:33.7.5.1]

20.5.2.5.1.1 New draperies, curtains, and other similar loosely hanging furnishings and decorations in board and care facilities shall be in accordance with the provisions of 12.6.1, unless otherwise permitted by 20.5.2.5.1.2. [*101*:32.7.5.1.1; *101*:33.7.5.1.1]

Δ **20.5.2.5.1.2** In other than common areas, new draperies, curtains, and other similar loosely hanging furnishings and decorations shall not be required to comply with 20.5.2.5.1.1 where the building is protected throughout by an approved automatic sprinkler system installed in accordance with 13.3.2.19.2 for small facilities or 32.3.3.5 or 33.3.3.5 of NFPA *101* for large facilities. [*101*:32.7.5.1.2; *101*:33.7.5.1.2]

20.5.2.5.2* New upholstered furniture within board and care facilities shall comply with 20.5.2.5.2.1 or 20.5.2.5.2.2. [*101*:32.7.5.2; *101*:33.7.5.2]

20.5.2.5.2.1 New upholstered furniture shall be tested in accordance with the provisions of 12.6.2.2.1(1) and 12.6.3.2.1. [*101*:32.7.5.2.1; *101*:33.7.5.2.1]

20.5.2.5.2.2 Upholstered furniture belonging to residents in sleeping rooms shall not be required to be tested, provided that a smoke alarm is installed in such rooms; battery-powered single-station smoke alarms shall be permitted in such rooms. [*101*:32.7.5.2.2; *101*:33.7.5.2.2]

20.5.2.5.2.3* Newly introduced mattresses within board and care facilities shall comply with 20.5.2.5.2.3.1 or 20.5.2.5.2.3.2. [*101*:32.7.5.3; *101*:33.7.5.3]

20.5.2.5.2.3.1 Newly introduced mattresses shall be tested in accordance with the provisions of 12.6.3.2 and 12.6.3.2.2. [*101*:32.7.5.3.1; *101*:33.7.5.3.1]

20.5.2.5.2.3.2 Mattresses belonging to residents in sleeping rooms shall not be required to be tested, provided that a smoke alarm is installed in such rooms; battery-powered single-station smoke alarms shall be permitted in such rooms. [*101*:32.7.5.3.2; *101*:33.7.5.3.2]

20.5.2.5.3 No stove or combustion heater shall be located to block escape in case of fire caused by the malfunction of the stove or heater. [*101*:32.2.5.2.2; *101*:33.2.5.2.2]

20.5.2.5.4 Unvented fuel-fired heaters shall not be used in any residential board and care facility. [*101*:32.2.5.2.3; *101*:33.2.5.2.3]

20.5.3 Interior Finish.

20.5.3.1 Small Facilities.

20.5.3.1.1 General. Interior finish shall be in accordance with Section 12.5. [*101*:32.2.3.3.1; *101*:33.2.3.3.1]

20.5.3.1.2 New Interior Wall and Ceiling Finish. New interior wall and ceiling finish materials complying with Section 12.5 shall be Class A, Class B, or Class C. [*101*:32.2.3.3.2]

20.5.3.1.3 Existing Interior Wall and Ceiling Finish. Existing interior wall and ceiling finish materials complying with Section 12.5 shall be as follows:

(1) Class A or Class B in facilities other than those having prompt evacuation capability
(2) Class A, Class B, or Class C in facilities having prompt evacuation capability

[*101*:33.2.3.3.2]

20.5.3.1.4 Interior Floor Finish.

20.5.3.1.4.1 New interior floor finish shall comply with Section 12.5. [*101*:32.2.3.3.3.1]

20.5.3.1.4.2 New interior floor finish shall comply with 12.5.8.1 or 12.5.8.2, as applicable. [*101*:32.2.3.3.3.2]

20.5.3.1.4.3 Existing Interior Floor Finish. (No requirements.) [*101*:33.2.3.3.3]

20.5.3.2 Large Facilities.

20.5.3.2.1 General. Interior finish shall be in accordance with Section 12.5. [*101*:32.3.3.3.1; *101*:33.3.3.3.1]

20.5.3.2.2 New Interior Wall and Ceiling Finish. New interior wall and ceiling finish materials complying with Section 12.5 shall be in accordance with the following:

(1) Exit enclosures — Class A
(2) Lobbies and corridors — Class B
(3) Rooms and enclosed spaces — Class B

[*101*:32.3.3.3.2]

20.5.3.2.3 Existing Interior Wall and Ceiling Finish. Existing interior wall and ceiling finish materials complying with Section 12.5 shall be Class A or Class B. [*101*:33.3.3.3.2]

20.5.3.2.4 Interior Floor Finish.

20.5.3.2.4.1 New interior floor finish shall comply with Section 12.5. [*101*:32.3.3.3.3.1]

20.5.3.2.4.2 New interior floor finish in exit enclosures and exit access corridors and spaces not separated from them by walls complying with 32.3.3.6 of NFPA *101* shall be not less than Class II. [*101*:32.3.3.3.3.2]

20.5.3.2.4.3 New interior floor finish shall comply with 12.5.8.1 or 12.5.8.2, as applicable. [*101*:32.3.3.3.3.3]

20.5.3.2.4.4 Existing Interior Floor Finish. Existing interior floor finish, other than approved existing floor coverings, shall be Class I or Class II in corridors or exits. [*101*:33.3.3.3.3]

20.5.3.3 Apartment Buildings Housing Board and Care Occupancies.

20.5.3.3.1 New Interior Finish.

20.5.3.3.1.1 The requirements of 20.9.3 shall apply only to the parts of means of egress serving the apartment(s) used as a residential board and care occupancy, as modified by 20.5.3.3.1.2. [*101*:32.4.3.1.1]

20.5.3.3.1.2 If a new board and care occupancy is created in an existing apartment building, the requirements of 31.3.3 of NFPA *101* shall apply to the parts of the means of egress serving the apartment(s) used as a residential board and care occupancy. [*101*:32.4.3.1.2]

20.5.3.3.2 Existing Interior Finish. The requirements of 20.9.3 shall apply only to the parts of means of egress serving the apartment(s) used as a residential board and care occupancy. [*101*:33.4.3.1]

20.6 Ambulatory Health Care Centers.

20.6.1 Application. New and existing ambulatory health care centers shall comply with Section 20.6 and NFPA *101*.

20.6.2* Operating Features.

20.6.2.1 Evacuation and Relocation Plan and Fire Drills.

20.6.2.1.1 The administration of every ambulatory health care facility shall have, in effect and available to all supervisory personnel, written copies of a plan for the protection of all persons in the event of fire, for their evacuation to areas of refuge, and for their evacuation from the building when necessary. [*101*:20.7.1.1; *101*:21.7.1.1]

20.6.2.1.2 All employees shall be periodically instructed and kept informed with respect to their duties under the plan required by 20.6.2.1.1. [*101*:20.7.1.2; *101*:21.7.1.2]

20.6.2.1.3 A copy of the plan required by 20.6.2.1.1 shall be readily available at all times when the facility is open. [*101*:20.7.1.3; *101*:21.7.1.3]

20.6.2.1.4 The provisions of Section 10.7 and 20.6.2.1.5 through 20.6.2.2.3 shall apply.

20.6.2.1.5* Fire drills in ambulatory health care facilities shall include the simulation of emergency fire conditions. [*101*:20.7.1.4; *101*:21.7.1.4]

20.6.2.1.6 Patients shall not be required to be moved during drills to safe areas or to the exterior of the building. [*101*:20.7.1.5; *101*:21.7.1.5]

20.6.2.1.7 Drills shall be conducted quarterly on each shift to familiarize facility personnel (including but not limited to nurses, interns, maintenance engineers, and administrative staff) with the emergency action required under varied conditions. [*101*:20.7.1.6; *101*:21.7.1.6]

20.6.2.1.8 Employees of ambulatory health care facilities shall be instructed in life safety procedures and devices. [*101*:20.7.1.7; *101*:21.7.1.7]

20.6.2.2 Procedure in Case of Fire.

20.6.2.2.1* Protection of Patients.

20.6.2.2.1.1 For ambulatory health care facilities, the proper protection of patients shall require the prompt and effective response of ambulatory health care personnel. [*101*:20.7.2.1.1; *101*:21.7.2.1.1]

20.6.2.2.1.2 The basic response required of staff shall include the following:

(1) Removal of all occupants directly involved with the fire emergency
(2) Transmission of an appropriate fire alarm signal to warn other building occupants and summon staff
(3) Confinement of the effects of the fire by closing doors to isolate the fire area
(4) Relocation of patients as detailed in the facility's fire safety plan

[*101*:20.7.2.1.2; *101*:21.7.2.1.2]

20.6.2.2.2 Fire Safety Plan. A written fire safety plan shall provide for all of the following:

(1) Use of alarms
(2) Transmission of alarms to fire department
(3) Response to alarms
(4) Isolation of fire
(5) Evacuation of immediate area
(6) Evacuation of smoke compartment
(7) Preparation of floors and building for evacuation
(8) Extinguishment of fire

[*101*:20.7.2.2; *101*:21.7.2.2]

20.6.2.2.3 Staff Response.

20.6.2.2.3.1 All personnel shall be instructed in the use of and response to fire alarms. [*101*:20.7.2.3.1; *101*:21.7.2.3.1]

20.6.2.2.3.2 All personnel shall be instructed in the use of the code phrase to ensure transmission of an alarm under either of the following conditions:

(1) When the individual who discovers a fire must immediately go to the aid of an endangered person
(2) During a malfunction of the building fire alarm system

[*101*:20.7.2.3.2; *101*:21.7.2.3.2]

20.6.2.2.3.3 Personnel hearing the code announced shall first activate the building fire alarm using the nearest fire alarm box and then shall execute immediately their duties as outlined in the fire safety plan. [*101*:20.7.2.3.3; *101*:21.7.2.3.3]

20.6.2.3 Maintenance of Exits.

20.6.2.3.1 Proper maintenance shall be provided to ensure the dependability of the method of evacuation selected. [*101*:20.7.3.1; *101*:21.7.3.1]

20.6.2.3.2 Ambulatory health care occupancies that find it necessary to lock exits shall, at all times, maintain an adequate staff qualified to release locks and direct occupants from the immediate danger area to a place of safety in case of fire or other emergency. [*101*:20.7.3.2; *101*:21.7.3.2]

20.6.2.4* Smoking. Smoking regulations shall be adopted and shall include not less than the following provisions:

(1) Smoking shall be prohibited in any room, ward, or compartment where flammable liquids, flammable gases, or oxygen is used or stored and in any other hazardous location, and such areas shall be posted with signs that read NO SMOKING or shall be posted with the international symbol for no smoking.
(2) In ambulatory health care facilities where smoking is prohibited and signs are placed at all major entrances, secondary signs with language that prohibits smoking shall not be required.
(3) Smoking by patients classified as not responsible shall be prohibited.
(4) The requirement of 20.6.2.4(3) shall not apply where the patient is under direct supervision.
(5) Ashtrays of noncombustible material and safe design shall be provided in all areas where smoking is permitted.
(6) Metal containers with self-closing cover devices into which ashtrays can be emptied shall be readily available to all areas where smoking is permitted.

[*101*:20.7.4; *101*:21.7.4]

20.6.2.5 Furnishings, Mattresses, and Decorations.

20.6.2.5.1* Draperies, curtains, and other loosely hanging fabrics and films serving as furnishings or decorations in ambulatory health care occupancies shall be in accordance with the provisions of 12.6.1, and the following also shall apply:

(1) Such curtains shall include cubicle curtains.
(2) Such curtains shall not include curtains at showers.

[*101*:20.7.5.1; *101*:21.7.5.1]

20.6.2.5.2 Newly introduced upholstered furniture shall comply with 12.6.2.1 and one of the following provisions:

(1) The furniture shall meet the criteria specified in 12.6.2.2.
(2) The furniture shall be in a building protected throughout by an approved, supervised automatic sprinkler system in accordance with NFPA 13.

[*101*:20.7.5.2; *101*:21.7.5.2]

20.6.2.5.3 Newly introduced mattresses shall comply with 12.6.3 and one of the following provisions:

(1) The mattresses shall meet the criteria specified in 12.6.3.2.
(2) The mattresses shall be in a building protected throughout by an approved, supervised automatic sprinkler system in accordance with Section 13.3.

[*101*:20.7.5.3; *101*:21.7.5.3]

20.6.2.5.4 Combustible decorations shall be prohibited, unless one of the following criteria is met:

(1) They are flame-retardant.
(2) The decorations meet the flame propagation performance criteria contained in Test Method 1 or Test Method 2, as appropriate, of NFPA 701.
(3) The decorations exhibit a heat release rate not exceeding 100 kW when tested in accordance with NFPA 289 using the 20 kW ignition source.
(4)* The decorations, such as photographs, paintings, and other art, are attached directly to the walls, ceiling, and non-fire-rated doors in accordance with the following:

   (a) Decorations on non-fire-rated doors do not interfere with the operation or any required latching of the door and do not exceed the area limitations of 20.6.2.5.4(4)(b) or 20.6.2.5.4(4)(c).
   (b) Decorations do not exceed 20 percent of the wall, ceiling, and door areas inside any room or space of a smoke compartment that is not protected throughout by an approved, automatic sprinkler system in accordance with Section 13.3.
   (c) Decorations do not exceed 30 percent of the wall, ceiling, and door areas inside any room or space of a smoke compartment that is protected throughout by an approved, supervised automatic sprinkler system in accordance with Section 13.3.

[*101*:20.7.5.4; *101*:21.7.5.4]

20.6.2.5.5 Soiled Linen and Trash Receptacles.

20.6.2.5.5.1 Soiled linen or trash collection receptacles with capacities greater than 64 gal (242 L) shall be located in a hazardous area when not attended. [*101*:20.7.5.5.1; *101*:21.7.5.5.1]

20.6.2.5.5.2* Containers greater than 64 gal (242 L) used solely for recycling clean waste or for patient records awaiting destruction shall be permitted to be excluded from the requirements of 20.6.2.5.5.1 where all the following conditions are met:

(1) Each container shall be limited to a maximum capacity of 96 gal (363 L).
(2) Containers for combustibles shall be labeled and listed as meeting the requirements of FM Approvals 6920/6921, *Oily Waste Cans and Containers for Combustible Waste*; however, such testing, listing, and labeling shall not be limited to FM Approvals.

[*101*:20.7.5.5.2; *101*:21.7.5.5.2]

20.6.2.5.5.3 The provisions of 12.6.8, applicable to containers for waste or linen, shall not apply. [*101*:20.7.5.5.3; *101*:21.7.5.5.3]

20.6.2.5.5.4 The provisions of 19.2.1.1 through 19.2.1.2 applicable to soiled linen and trash receptacles shall not apply.

20.6.2.6 Portable Space-Heating Devices. Portable space-heating devices shall be prohibited in all ambulatory health care occupancies, unless both of the following criteria are met:

(1) Such devices are used only in nonsleeping staff and employee areas.
(2) Such devices are listed and labeled for use as a freestanding, movable heater in accordance with UL 1278, *Movable and Wall- or Ceiling-Hung Electric Room Heaters*.

[*101*:20.7.8; *101*:21.7.8]

20.6.2.7 Integrated Fire Protection and Life Safety Systems. Integrated fire protection and life safety systems shall be tested in accordance with 13.1.3.1. [*101*:20.7.10; *101*:21.7.10.1]

20.6.3 Interior Finish.

20.6.3.1 General. Interior finish shall be in accordance with Section 12.5. [*101*:20.3.3.1; *101*:21.3.3.1]

20.6.3.2 Interior Wall and Ceiling Finish.

20.6.3.2.1 Interior wall and ceiling finish material complying with Section 12.5 shall be Class A or Class B in exits and in exit access corridors. [*101*:20.3.3.2.1; *101*:21.3.3.2.1]

20.6.3.2.2 Interior wall and ceiling finishes shall be Class A, Class B, or Class C in areas other than those specified in 20.6.3.2.1. [*101*:20.3.3.2.2; *101*:21.3.3.2.2]

20.6.3.3 New Interior Floor Finish.

20.6.3.3.1 New interior floor finish shall comply with Section 12.5. [*101*:20.3.3.3.1]

20.6.3.3.2 New interior floor finish in exit enclosures shall be Class I or Class II. [*101*:20.3.3.3.2]

20.6.3.3.3 New interior floor finish shall comply with 12.5.8.1 or 12.5.8.2, as applicable. [*101*:20.3.3.3.3]

20.6.3.4 Existing Interior Floor Finish. (Reserved) [*101*:21.3.3.3]

20.7 Detention and Correctional Occupancies.

20.7.1 Application. New and existing detention and correctional occupancies shall comply with Section 20.7 and NFPA *101*.

20.7.2 Operating Features.

20.7.2.1 Attendants, Evacuation Plan, and Fire Drills.

20.7.2.1.1 Detention and correctional facilities, or those portions of facilities having such occupancy, shall be provided with 24-hour staffing, and the following requirements also shall apply:

(1) Staff shall be within three floors or a 300 ft (91 m) horizontal distance of the access door of each resident housing area.
(2) For Use Condition III, Use Condition IV, and Use Condition V, the arrangement shall be such that the staff involved starts the release of locks necessary for emergency evacuation or rescue and initiates other necessary emergency actions within 2 minutes of alarm.
(3) The following shall apply to areas in which all locks are unlocked remotely in compliance with 22.2.11.1.8 or 23.2.11.1.8 of NFPA *101*.
   (a) Staff shall not be required to be within three floors or 300 ft (91 m) of the access door.
   (b) The 10-lock, manual key exemption of 22.2.11.1.8.2 or 23.2.11.1.8.2 of NFPA *101* shall not be permitted to be used in conjunction with the alternative requirement of 20.7.2.1.1(3)(a).

[*101*:22.7.1.1; *101*:23.7.1.1]

20.7.2.1.2* Provisions shall be made so that residents in Use Condition III, Use Condition IV, and Use Condition V shall be able to notify staff of an emergency. [*101*:22.7.1.2; *101*:23.7.1.2]

20.7.2.1.3* The administration of every detention or correctional facility shall have, in effect and available to all supervisory personnel, written copies of a plan for the protection of all persons in the event of fire, for their evacuation to areas of refuge, and for evacuation from the building when necessary. [*101*:22.7.1.3; *101*:23.7.1.3]

20.7.2.1.3.1 All employees shall be instructed and drilled with respect to their duties under the plan. [*101*:22.7.1.3.1; *101*:23.7.1.3.1]

20.7.2.1.3.2 The plan shall be coordinated with, and reviewed by, the fire department legally committed to serve the facility. [*101*:22.7.1.3.2; *101*:23.7.1.3.2]

20.7.2.1.4 Employees of detention and correctional occupancies shall be instructed in the proper use of portable fire extinguishers and other manual fire suppression equipment. [*101*:22.7.1.4; *101*:23.7.1.4]

20.7.2.1.4.1 The training specified in 20.7.2.1.4 shall be provided to new staff promptly upon commencement of duty. [*101*:22.7.1.4.1; *101*:23.7.1.4.1]

20.7.2.1.4.2 Refresher training shall be provided to existing staff at not less than annual intervals. [*101*:22.7.1.4.2; *101*:23.7.1.4.2]

20.7.2.2* Combustible Personal Property. Books, clothing, and other combustible personal property allowed in sleeping rooms shall be stored in closable metal lockers or an approved fire-resistant container. [*101*:22.7.2; *101*:23.7.2]

20.7.2.3 Heat-Producing Appliances. The number of heat-producing appliances, such as toasters and hot plates, and the overall use of electrical power within a sleeping room shall be controlled by facility administration. [*101*:22.7.3; *101*:23.7.3]

20.7.2.4* Furnishings, Mattresses, and Decorations.

20.7.2.4.1 Draperies and curtains, including privacy curtains, in detention and correctional occupancies shall be in accordance with the provisions of 12.6.1. [*101*:22.7.4.1; *101*:23.7.4.1]

20.7.2.4.2 Newly introduced upholstered furniture within new detention and correctional occupancies shall be tested in accordance with the provisions of 12.6.2.1(2). [*101*:22.7.4.2]

20.7.2.4.3 Newly introduced upholstered furniture within existing detention and correctional occupancies shall meet the criteria specified in 12.6.2.1(2) and 12.6.2.2.1. [*101*:23.7.4.2]

20.7.2.4.4 Newly introduced mattresses within new detention and correctional occupancies shall be tested in accordance with the provisions of 10.3.3. [*101*:22.7.4.3]

20.7.2.4.5 Newly introduced mattresses within existing detention and correctional occupancies shall meet the criteria specified in 12.6.3.2 and 13.6.3.2.2 of NFPA *101*. [*101*:23.7.4.3]

20.7.2.4.6 Combustible decorations shall be prohibited in any detention or correctional occupancy unless they are flame retardant and approved. [*101*:22.7.4.4; *101*:23.7.4.4]

20.7.2.4.7 Wastebaskets and other waste containers shall be of noncombustible or other approved materials. Waste containers with a capacity exceeding 20 gal (76 L) shall be provided with a noncombustible lid or lid of other approved material. [*101*:22.7.4.5; *101*:23.7.4.5]

20.7.2.5 Keys. All keys necessary for unlocking doors installed in a means of egress shall be individually identified by both touch and sight. [*101*:22.7.5; *101*:23.7.5]

20.7.2.6 Portable Space-Heating Devices. Portable space-heating devices shall be prohibited in all detention and correctional occupancies. [*101*:22.7.6; *101*:23.7.6]

20.7.2.7 Door Inspection. Doors and door hardware in means of egress shall be inspected annually by an appropriately trained person. The inspection shall be documented. [*101*:22.7.7; *101*:23.7.7]

20.7.2.8 Integrated Fire Protection and Life Safety Systems. Integrated fire protection and life safety systems shall be tested in accordance with 13.1.3.1. [*101*:22.7.8; *101*:23.7.8.1]

20.7.3 Interior Finish.

20.7.3.1 General. Interior finish shall be in accordance with Section 12.5. [*101*:22.3.3.1; *101*:23.3.3.1]

20.7.3.2 New Interior Wall and Ceiling Finish. New interior wall and ceiling finish materials complying with Section 12.5 shall be Class A or Class B in corridors, in exits, and in any space not separated from corridors and exits by partitions capable of retarding the passage of smoke; and Class A, Class B, or Class C in all other areas. The provisions of 12.5.9.1 shall not apply. [*101*:22.3.3.2]

20.7.3.3 Existing Interior Wall and Ceiling Finish. Existing interior wall and ceiling finish materials complying with Section 12.5 shall be Class A or Class B in corridors, in exits, and in any space not separated from corridors and exits by partitions capable of retarding the passage of smoke; and Class A, Class B, or Class C in all other areas. [*101*:23.3.3.2]

20.7.3.4 New Interior Floor Finish.

20.7.3.4.1 New interior floor finish shall comply with Section 12.5. [*101*:22.3.3.3.1]

20.7.3.4.2 New interior floor finish in exit enclosures and exit access corridors shall be not less than Class II. The provisions of 12.5.9.2 shall not apply to new detention and correctional occupancies. [*101*:22.3.3.3.2]

20.7.3.4.3 New interior floor finish shall comply with 12.5.8.1 or 12.5.8.2, as applicable. [*101*:22.3.3.3.3]

20.7.3.5 Existing Interior Floor Finish.

20.7.3.5.1 Existing interior floor finish complying with Section 12.5 shall be Class I or Class II in corridors and exits. [*101*:23.3.3.3.1]

20.7.3.5.2 Existing floor finish material of Class A or Class B in nonsprinklered smoke compartments and Class A, Class B, or Class C in sprinklered smoke compartments shall be permitted to be continued to be used, provided that it has been evaluated based on tests performed in accordance with 12.5.4. [*101*:23.3.3.3.2]

20.7.3.6 Interior Finish (Nonsprinklered Existing Building Renovations).

20.7.3.6.1 Interior Wall and Ceiling Finish. Interior wall and ceiling finish materials complying with Section 12.5 shall be Class A in corridors, in exits, and in any space not separated from corridors and exits by partitions capable of retarding the passage of smoke; and Class A, Class B, or Class C in all other areas. [*101*:22.4.5.8.1]

20.7.3.6.2 Interior Floor Finish.

20.7.3.6.2.1 Interior floor finish shall comply with Section 12.5. [*101*:22.4.5.8.2.1]

20.7.3.6.2.2 Interior floor finish in exit enclosures and exit access corridors shall be not less than Class I. [*101*:22.4.5.8.2.2]

20.7.3.6.2.3 Interior floor finish shall comply with 12.5.8.1 or 12.5.8.2, as applicable. [*101*:22.4.5.8.2.3]

20.8 Hotels and Dormitories.

20.8.1 Application. New and existing hotels and dormitories shall comply with Section 20.8 and NFPA *101*.

20.8.2 Operating Features.

20.8.2.1 Hotel Emergency Organization.

20.8.2.1.1* Employees of hotels shall be instructed and drilled in the duties they are to perform in the event of fire, panic, or other emergency. [*101*:28.7.1.1; *101*:29.7.1.1]

20.8.2.1.2* Drills of the emergency organization shall be held at quarterly intervals and shall cover such points as the operation and maintenance of the available first aid fire appliances, the testing of devices to alert guests, and a study of instructions for emergency duties. [*101*:28.7.1.2; *101*:29.7.1.2]

20.8.2.2 Emergency Duties. Upon discovery of a fire, employees shall carry out all of the following duties:

(1) Activation of the facility fire protection signaling system, if provided
(2) Notification of the public fire department
(3) Other action as previously instructed [*101*:28.7.2; *101*:29.7.2]

20.8.2.3 Drills in Dormitories. Emergency egress and relocation drills in accordance with Section 10.6 shall be held with sufficient frequency to familiarize occupants with all types of hazards and to establish conduct of the drill as a matter of routine. Drills shall be conducted during peak occupancy periods and shall include suitable procedures to ensure that all persons subject to the drill participate. [*101*:28.7.3; *101*:29.7.3]

20.8.2.4 Emergency Instructions for Residents or Guests.

20.8.2.4.1* A floor diagram reflecting the actual floor arrangement, exit locations, and room identification shall be posted in a location and manner acceptable to the AHJ on, or immediately adjacent to, every guest room door in hotels and in every resident room in dormitories. [*101*:28.7.4.1; *101*:29.7.4.1]

20.8.2.4.2* Fire safety information shall be provided to allow guests to make the decision to evacuate to the outside, to evacuate to an area of refuge, to remain in place, or to employ any combination of the three options. [*101*:28.7.4.2; *101*:29.7.4.2]

20.8.2.4.3 Emergency Action Plans. Emergency action plans in accordance with Section 10.4 shall be provided. [*101*:28.7.5]

20.8.2.5 Contents and Furnishings.

20.8.2.5.1 New draperies, curtains, and other similar loosely hanging furnishings and decorations shall meet the flame propagation performance criteria contained in Test Method 1 or Test Method 2, as appropriate, of NFPA 701. [*101*:28.7.6.1; *101*:29.7.6.1]

20.8.2.5.2 Upholstered Furniture and Mattresses.

20.8.2.5.2.1 Newly introduced upholstered furniture shall meet the criteria specified in 12.6.2.1 and 12.6.2.2. [*101*:28.7.6.2.1; *101*:29.7.6.2.1]

20.8.2.5.2.2 Newly introduced mattresses shall meet the criteria specified in 12.6.3 and 12.6.3.2. [*101*:28.7.6.2.2; *101*:29.7.6.2.2]

20.8.2.5.3 Furnishings or decorations of an explosive or highly flammable character shall not be used. [*101*:28.7.6.3; *101*:29.7.6.3]

20.8.2.5.4 Fire-retardant coatings shall be maintained to retain the effectiveness of the treatment under service conditions encountered in actual use. [*101*:28.7.6.4; *101*:29.7.6.4]

20.8.2.6 Fuel-Fired Heaters. Unvented fuel-fired heaters, other than gas space heaters in compliance with NFPA 54, shall not be used. [*101*:28.5.2.2; *101*:29.5.2.2]

20.8.2.7 Integrated Fire and Life Safety Protection Systems. Integrated fire protection and life safety systems shall be tested in accordance with 13.1.3.1. [*101*:28.7.8, *101*:29.7.8.1]

20.8.3 Interior Finish.

20.8.3.1 General. Interior finish shall be in accordance with Section 12.5. [*101*:28.3.3.1; *101*:29.3.3.1]

20.8.3.2 New Interior Wall and Ceiling Finish. New interior wall and ceiling finish materials complying with Section 12.5 shall be permitted as follows:

(1) Exit enclosures — Class A

(2) Lobbies and corridors — Class A or Class B
(3) Other spaces — Class A, Class B, or Class C
[*101*:28.3.3.2]

20.8.3.3 Existing Interior Wall and Ceiling Finish. Existing interior wall and ceiling finish materials complying with Section 12.5 shall be permitted as follows:

(1) Exit enclosures — Class A or Class B
(2) Lobbies and corridors — Class A or Class B
(3) Other spaces — Class A, Class B, or Class C
[*101*:29.3.3.2]

20.8.3.4 New Interior Floor Finish.

20.8.3.4.1 New interior floor finish shall comply with Section 12.5. [*101*:28.3.3.3.1]

20.8.3.4.2 New interior floor finish in exit enclosures and exit access corridors and spaces not separated from them by walls complying with 28.3.6.1 of NFPA *101* shall be not less than Class II. [*101*:28.3.3.3.2]

20.8.3.4.3 New interior floor finish shall comply with 12.5.8.1 or 12.5.8.2, as applicable. [*101*:28.3.3.3.3]

20.8.3.5 Interior Floor Finish (Existing Nonsprinklered Buildings). In nonsprinklered buildings, newly installed interior floor finish in exits and exit access corridors shall be not less than Class II in accordance with 12.5.8. [*101*:29.3.3.3]

20.9 Apartment Buildings.

20.9.1 Application. New and existing apartment buildings shall comply with Section 20.9 and NFPA *101*.

20.9.2 Operating Features.

20.9.2.1 Emergency Instructions for Residents of Apartment Buildings. Emergency instructions shall be provided annually to each dwelling unit to indicate the location of alarms, egress paths, and actions to be taken, both in response to a fire in the dwelling unit and in response to the sounding of the alarm system. [*101*:30.7.1; *101*:31.7.1]

20.9.2.2 Fuel-Fired Heaters. Unvented fuel-fired heaters, other than gas space heaters in compliance with NFPA 54, shall not be used. [*101*:30.5.2.2; *101*:31.5.2.2]

20.9.2.3 Inspection of Door Openings. Door openings shall be inspected in accordance with 14.5.10. [*101*:30.7.3; *101*:31.7.3]

20.9.2.4 Integrated Fire Protection and Life Safety Systems. Integrated fire protection and life safety systems shall be tested in accordance with 13.1.3.1. [*101*:30.7.4, *101*:31.7.4.1]

20.9.3 Interior Finish.

20.9.3.1 General. Interior finish shall be in accordance with Section 12.5. [*101*:30.3.3.1; *101*:31.3.3.1]

20.9.3.2 New Interior Wall and Ceiling Finish. New interior wall and ceiling finish materials complying with Section 12.5 shall be permitted as follows:

(1) Exit enclosures — Class A
(2) Lobbies and corridors — Class A or Class B
(3) Other spaces — Class A, Class B, or Class C
[*101*:30.3.3.2]

20.9.3.3 Existing Interior Wall and Ceiling Finish. Existing interior wall and ceiling finish materials complying with Section 12.5 shall be permitted as follows:

(1) Exit enclosures — Class A or Class B
(2) Lobbies and corridors — Class A or Class B
(3) Other spaces — Class A, Class B, or Class C
[*101*:31.3.3.2]

20.9.3.4 New Interior Floor Finish.

20.9.3.4.1 New interior floor finish shall comply with Section 12.5. [*101*:30.3.3.3.1]

20.9.3.4.2 New interior floor finish in exit enclosures and exit access corridors and spaces not separated from them by walls complying with 30.3.6 of NFPA *101* shall be not less than Class II. [*101*:30.3.3.3.2]

20.9.3.4.3 New interior floor finish shall comply with 12.5.8.1 or 12.5.8.2, as applicable. [*101*:30.3.3.3.3]

20.9.3.5 Existing Interior Floor Finish. In buildings utilizing Option 1 or Option 2, as defined in 31.1.1.1 of NFPA *101*, newly installed interior floor finish in exits and exit access corridors shall be not less than Class II in accordance with 12.5.8. [*101*:31.3.3.3]

20.9.4 Contents and Furnishings.

20.9.4.1 Contents and furnishings shall not be required to comply with Section 12.6. [*101*:30.7.2.1; *101*:31.7.2.1]

20.9.4.2 Furnishings or decorations of an explosive or highly flammable character shall not be used outside of dwelling units. [*101*:30.7.2.2; *101*:31.7.2.2]

20.9.4.3 Fire-retardant coatings shall be maintained to retain the effectiveness of the treatment under service conditions encountered in actual use. [*101*:30.7.2.3; *101*:31.7.2.3]

20.10 Lodging or Rooming Houses.

20.10.1 Application. New and existing lodging or rooming houses shall comply with Section 20.10 and NFPA *101*.

20.10.2 Fuel-Fired Heaters. Unvented fuel-fired heaters, other than gas space heaters in compliance with NFPA 54, shall not be used. [*101*:26.5.2.2]

20.10.3 Interior Finish.

20.10.3.1 General. Interior finish shall be in accordance with Section 12.5. [*101*:26.3.3.1]

20.10.3.2 Interior Wall and Ceiling Finish. Interior wall and ceiling finish materials complying with Section 12.5 shall be Class A, Class B, or Class C. [*101*:26.3.3.2]

20.10.3.3 Interior Floor Finish.

20.10.3.3.1 Newly installed interior floor finish shall comply with Section 12.5. [*101*:26.3.3.3.1]

20.10.3.3.2 Newly installed interior floor finish shall comply with 12.5.8.1 or 12.5.8.2, as applicable. [*101*:26.3.3.3.2]

20.10.4 Contents and furnishings shall not be required to comply with Section 12.6. [*101*:26.7.1.1]

20.10.4.1 Furnishings or decorations of an explosive or highly flammable character shall not be used. [*101*:26.7.1.2]

20.10.4.2 Fire-retardant coatings shall be maintained to retain the effectiveness of the treatment under service conditions encountered in actual use. [*101*:26.7.1.3]

20.11 One- and Two-Family Dwellings and Manufactured Housing.

20.11.1 Application. New and existing one- and two-family dwellings shall comply with Section 20.11 and NFPA *101*.

Δ **20.11.2 Fuel-Fired Heaters.** Unvented fuel-fired heaters shall not be used unless they are listed and approved. [*101*:24.5.1.2]

20.11.3 Interior Finish.

20.11.3.1 General. Interior finish shall be in accordance with Section 12.5. [*101*:24.3.3.1]

20.11.3.2 Interior Wall and Ceiling Finish. Interior wall and ceiling finish materials complying with Section 12.5 shall be Class A, Class B, or Class C. [*101*:24.3.3.2]

20.11.3.3 Interior Floor Finish. (Reserved) [*101*:24.3.3.3]

20.11.4 Fire Protection of Floors. In new construction, floor assemblies shall be provided with a continuous membrane of gypsum wallboard having a nominal thickness of not less than ½ in. (13 mm), or equivalent, to protect the floor framing members from a fire exposure from below.

20.11.4.1 Protection in accordance with 20.11.4 shall not be required where the building is protected by an approved automatic sprinkler system installed in accordance with 13.3.1.2.

20.11.4.2 Protection in accordance with 20.11.4 shall not be required for floor assemblies located directly over a crawl space not intended for storage or fuel-fired equipment.

20.11.4.3 Portions of floor assemblies shall be permitted to be unprotected where the aggregate area of the unprotected portions does not exceed 80 ft^2 (7.4 m^2) per story and where fire blocking is installed along the perimeter of the unprotected portion to separate the unprotected portion from the remainder of the floor assembly.

20.11.4.4* Protection in accordance with 20.11.4 shall not be required in floor assemblies using wood joists with nominal dimensions not less than 2 in. (51 mm) in thickness by 10 in. (254 mm) in width, or other approved floor assemblies providing equivalent performance.

20.11.4.5 Protection in accordance with 20.11.4 shall not be required in floor assemblies using wood joist structural composite lumber that are compliant with ASTM D5456 and that have dimensions not less than 1½ in. (38 mm) in thickness by 9¼ in. (235 mm) in width.

20.11.4.6 Penetrations by mechanical, plumbing, fire protection, and electrical systems through the membrane protection required by 20.11.4 shall not be required to be protected.

20.11.5 Manufactured Housing. New manufactured housing shall comply with Section 20.11 and NFPA 501.

20.12 Mercantile Occupancies.

20.12.1 Application. New and existing mercantile occupancies shall comply with Section 20.12 and NFPA *101*.

20.12.2 Operating Features.

20.12.2.1 Emergency Plans. Emergency action plans complying with Section 10.4 shall be provided in high-rise buildings. [*101*:36.7.1; *101*:37.7.1]

20.12.2.2 Drills. In every Class A or Class B mercantile occupancy, employees shall be periodically trained in accordance with Section 10.6. [*101*:36.7.2; *101*:37.7.2]

20.12.2.3 Extinguisher Training. Employees of mercantile occupancies shall be periodically instructed in the use of portable fire extinguishers. [*101*:36.7.3; *101*:37.7.3]

20.12.2.4 Food Service Operations. Food service operations shall comply with Chapter 50. [*101*:36.7.4; *101*:37.7.4]

20.12.2.5 Inspection of Door Openings. Door openings shall be inspected in accordance with 14.5.10. [*101*:36.7.7; *101*:37.7.7]

20.12.2.6 Integrated Fire Protection and Life Safety Systems. Integrated fire protection and life safety systems shall be tested in accordance with 13.1.3.1. [*101*:36.7.8; *101*:37.7.8.1]

20.12.3 Interior Finish.

20.12.3.1 General. Interior finish shall be in accordance with Section 12.5. [*101*:36.3.3.1; *101*:37.3.3.1]

20.12.3.2 Interior Wall and Ceiling Finish. Interior wall and ceiling finish materials complying with Section 12.5 shall be Class A, Class B, or Class C. [*101*:36.3.3.2; *101*:37.3.3.2]

20.12.3.3 Interior Floor Finish.

20.12.3.3.1 New interior floor finish shall comply with Section 12.5. [*101*:36.3.3.3.1]

20.12.3.3.2 New interior floor finish in exit enclosures shall be Class I or Class II. [*101*:36.3.3.3.2]

20.12.3.3.3 New interior floor finish shall comply with 12.5.8.1 or 12.5.8.2, as applicable. [*101*:36.3.3.3.3]

Δ **20.12.3.3.4 Existing Interior Floor Finish.** (No requirements.) [*101*:37.3.3.3]

20.13 Business Occupancies.

20.13.1 Application. New and existing business occupancies shall comply with Section 20.13 and NFPA *101*.

20.13.2 Operating Features.

20.13.2.1 Emergency Action Plans. Emergency action plans complying with Section 10.4 shall be provided in high-rise buildings. [*101*:38.7.1; *101*:39.7.1]

20.13.2.2 Drills. In all business occupancy buildings occupied by more than 500 persons, or by more than 100 persons above or below the street level, employees and supervisory personnel shall be periodically instructed in accordance with Section 10.6 and shall hold drills periodically where practicable. [*101*:38.7.2; *101*:39.7.2]

20.13.2.3 Portable Fire Extinguisher Training. Designated employees of business occupancies shall be trained periodically to know the locations and proper use of portable fire extinguishers. [*101*:38.7.3; *101*:39.7.3]

20.13.2.4 Food Service Operations. Food service operations shall comply with Chapter 50. [*101*:38.7.4; *101*:39.7.4]

20.13.2.5 Inspection of Door Openings. Door openings shall be inspected in accordance with 14.5.10. [*101*:38.7.7; *101*:39.7.7]

20.13.3 Interior Finish.

20.13.3.1 General. Interior finish shall be in accordance with Section 12.5. [*101*:38.3.3.1; *101*:39.3.3.1]

20.13.3.2 Interior Wall and Ceiling Finish.

20.13.3.2.1 Interior wall and ceiling finish materials complying with Section 12.5 shall be Class A or Class B in exits and in exit access corridors. [*101*:38.3.3.2.1; *101*:39.3.3.2.1]

20.13.3.2.2 Interior wall and ceiling finishes shall be Class A, Class B, or Class C in areas other than those specified in 20.13.3.2.1. [*101*:38.3.3.2.2; *101*:39.3.3.2.2]

20.13.3.3 Interior Floor Finish.

20.13.3.3.1 New interior floor finish shall comply with Section 12.5. [*101*:38.3.3.3.1]

20.13.3.3.2 New interior floor finish in exit enclosures shall be Class I or Class II. [*101*:38.3.3.3.2]

20.13.3.3.3 New interior floor finish shall comply with 12.5.8.1 or 12.5.8.2, as applicable. [*101*:38.3.3.3.3]

Δ **20.13.3.3.4 Existing Interior Floor Finish.** (No requirements.) [*101*:39.3.3.3]

20.14 Industrial Occupancies.

20.14.1 Application. New and existing industrial occupancies shall comply with Section 20.14 and NFPA *101*.

20.14.2 Permits. Permits, where required, shall comply with Section 1.13.

20.14.3 Operating Features.

20.14.3.1 Inspection of Door Openings. Door openings shall be inspected in accordance with 14.5.10. [*101*:40.7.3]

20.14.3.2 Integrated Fire Protection and Life Safety Systems. Integrated fire protection and life safety systems shall be tested in accordance with 13.1.3.1. [*101*:40.7.4.1]

20.14.4 Interior Finish.

20.14.4.1 General. Interior finish shall be in accordance with Section 12.5. [*101*:40.3.3.1]

20.14.4.2 Interior Wall and Ceiling Finish. Interior wall and ceiling finish materials complying with Section 12.5 shall be Class A, Class B, or Class C in operating areas and shall be as required by 7.1.4 of NFPA *101* in exit enclosures. [*101*:40.3.3.2]

20.14.4.3 Interior Floor Finish.

20.14.4.3.1 Interior floor finish in exit enclosures and in exit access corridors shall be Class I or Class II in accordance with 12.5.8.4. [*101*:40.3.3.3.1]

20.14.4.3.2 Interior floor finish in areas other than those specified in 20.14.4.3.1 shall not be required to comply with 12.5.8. [*101*:40.3.3.3.2]

20.15 Storage Occupancies.

20.15.1 Application. New and existing storage occupancies shall comply with NFPA *101*, Chapter 34, appropriate codes or standards referenced in Chapter 2, and Section 20.15.

20.15.2 Permits. Permits, where required, shall comply with Section 1.13.

20.15.3 Operating Features.

20.15.3.1 Inspection of Door Openings. Door openings shall be inspected in accordance with 14.5.10. [*101*:42.9.3]

20.15.3.2 Integrated Fire Protection and Life Safety Systems. Integrated fire protection and life safety systems shall be tested in accordance with 13.1.3.1. [*101*:42.9.4.1]

20.15.4 Interior Finish.

20.15.4.1 General. Interior finish shall be in accordance with Section 12.5. [*101*:42.3.3.1]

20.15.4.2 Interior Wall and Ceiling Finish. Interior wall and ceiling finish materials shall be Class A, Class B, or Class C in accordance with Section 12.5 in storage areas and shall be as required by 7.1.4 of NFPA *101* in exit enclosures. [*101*:42.3.3.2]

20.15.4.3 Interior Floor Finish.

20.15.4.3.1 Interior floor finish in exit enclosures and in exit access corridors shall be Class I or Class II. [*101*:42.3.3.3.1]

20.15.4.3.2 Interior floor finish in areas other than those specified in 20.15.4.3.1 shall not be required to comply with 12.5.8. [*101*:42.3.3.3.2]

20.15.5 Bulk Storage Elevators. Bulk storage elevators shall comply with 20.15.5 and NFPA 61.

20.15.5.1* Application. The requirements of 20.15.5 shall apply to all of the following:

(1) All facilities that receive, handle, process, dry, blend, use, mill, package, store, or ship dry agricultural bulk materials, their by-products, or dusts that include grains, oilseeds, agricultural seeds, legumes, sugar, flour, spices, feeds, dry dairy/food powders, and other related materials

(2) All facilities designed for manufacturing and handling starch, including drying, grinding, conveying, processing, packaging, and storing dry or modified starch, and dry products and dusts generated from these processes

(3) Those seed preparation and meal-handling systems of oilseed processing plants not covered by NFPA 36

[*61*:1.3.1]

20.15.5.2 Subsection 20.15.5 shall not apply to oilseed extraction processes that are covered by NFPA 36. [*61*:1.3.2]

20.15.5.3 Applicability.

20.15.5.3.1 Unless otherwise noted, the provisions of 20.15.5 on bulk storage elevators shall not be applied to facilities, equipment, structures, or installations that were existing or approved for construction or installation prior to the effective date of this *Code*, except in those cases where it is determined by the AHJ that the existing situation involves a distinct hazard to life or adjacent property.

20.15.5.3.2 The requirements of Chapter 11 of NFPA 61 shall apply to all facilities.

20.15.6 Record Storage.

20.15.6.1 Records protection equipment, facilities, and records-handling techniques that provide protection from the hazards of fire shall comply with 20.15.6 and NFPA 232.

20.15.6.2* Because of the volume of records, 20.15.6.1 shall not cover large archives or records storage buildings.

20.15.7 Cellulose Nitrate Motion Picture Film Storage.

20.15.7.1 Application. The storage and handling of cellulose nitrate film records shall comply with 20.15.7 and NFPA 40.

20.15.7.2 Permits. Permits, where required, shall comply with Section 1.13.

20.15.8 High-Piled Storage.

20.15.8.1 Application. Buildings containing high-piled storage shall comply with Chapter 13, Chapter 34, and 20.15.8.

20.15.8.2 Permits. Permits, where required, shall comply with Section 1.13.

20.16 Special Structures and High-Rise Buildings.

20.16.1 Application.

20.16.1.1 New and existing special structures and high-rise buildings shall comply with NFPA *101*.

20.16.1.2 Motion picture and television production studio soundstages and approved production facilities shall comply with Chapter 32.

20.17 Historic Buildings and Cultural Resources.

20.17.1 Historic buildings shall comply with this *Code* or with the provisions of NFPA 914.

20.17.2 Buildings that store or display cultural resources, including museum or library collections, or spaces within other buildings used for such culturally significant purposes, shall comply with this *Code* or with the provisions of NFPA 909.

20.17.3 The provisions of this *Code* relating to the construction, repair, alteration, enlargement, restoration, and moving of buildings or structures shall not be mandatory for the following:

(1) Existing buildings or structures identified and classified by the state or local government authority as historic buildings where such buildings comply with NFPA 914
(2)* Buildings or spaces within buildings that store or display cultural resources and comply with the provisions of NFPA 909

Chapter 21 Airports and Heliports

21.1 Hangars. The construction and protection of aircraft hangars from fire shall comply with this section; NFPA 409, NFPA 410, and Sections 40.6 and 42.6 of NFPA *101*.

21.1.1 Permits. Permits, where required, shall comply with Section 1.13.

21.1.2 Fire Department Access. Fire apparatus access roads shall be provided and maintained in accordance with Section 18.2 for all aircraft hangars.

21.1.3 Smoking.

21.1.3.1 Smoking shall be prohibited in aircraft hangars.

21.1.3.2 Smoking shall be in accordance with Section 10.9.

21.1.4* Means of Egress Provisions for Aircraft Servicing Hangars.

21.1.4.1 The requirements of Sections 40.1 through 40.5 of NFPA *101* shall be met, except as modified by 21.1.4.2 through 21.1.4.4. [*101*:40.6.1]

21.1.4.2 The requirements for exits from aircraft servicing areas shall comply with 21.1.4.2.1 through 21.1.4.2.4. [*101*:40.6.2]

21.1.4.2.1 There shall be not less than two means of egress from each aircraft servicing area. [*101*:40.6.2.1]

21.1.4.2.2 Exits from aircraft servicing areas shall be provided at intervals not exceeding 150 ft (46 m) on all exterior walls. [*101*:40.6.2.2]

21.1.4.2.3 Where horizontal exits are provided, doors shall be provided in the horizontal exit fire barrier at intervals not exceeding 100 ft (30 m). [*101*:40.6.2.3]

21.1.4.2.4 Where egress doors are provided in doors that accommodate aircraft, such doors shall be permitted for compliance with 21.1.4.2.1 through 21.1.4.2.3. [*101*:40.6.2.4]

21.1.4.3 Means of egress from mezzanine floors in aircraft servicing areas shall be arranged so that the travel distance to the nearest exit from any point on the mezzanine does not exceed 75 ft (23 m), and such means of egress shall lead directly to a properly enclosed stair discharging directly to the exterior, to a suitable cutoff area, or to outside stairs. [*101*:40.6.3]

21.1.4.4 Dead ends shall not exceed 50 ft (15 m) for other than high-hazard contents areas and shall not be permitted for high-hazard contents areas. [*101*:40.6.4]

21.1.5* Means of Egress Provisions for Aircraft Storage Hangars.

21.1.5.1 The requirements of Sections 42.1 through 42.5 of NFPA *101* shall be met, except as modified by 21.1.5.1.1 through 21.1.5.1.3. [*101*:42.6.1]

21.1.5.1.1 There shall be not less than two means of egress from each aircraft storage area. [*101*:42.6.1.1]

21.1.5.1.2 Exits from aircraft storage areas shall be provided at intervals not exceeding 150 ft (46 m) on all exterior walls. [*101*:42.6.1.2]

21.1.5.1.3 Where horizontal exits are provided, doors shall be provided in the horizontal exit fire barrier at intervals not exceeding 100 ft (30 m). [*101*:42.6.1.3]

21.1.5.1.4 Where egress doors are provided in doors that accommodate aircraft, such doors shall be permitted for compliance with 21.1.5.1.1, 21.1.5.1.2, and 21.1.5.1.3. [*101*:42.6.1.4]

21.1.5.2 Means of egress from mezzanine floors in aircraft storage areas shall be arranged so that the travel distance to the nearest exit from any point on the mezzanine does not exceed 75 ft (23 m), and such means of egress shall lead directly to a properly enclosed stair discharging directly to the exterior, to a suitable cutoff area, or to outside stairs. [*101*:42.6.2]

21.1.5.3 Dead ends shall not exceed 50 ft (15 m) for other than high-hazard contents areas and shall not be permitted for high-hazard contents areas. [*101*:42.6.3]

21.2 Terminals.

21.2.1 Application.
Airport terminal buildings shall comply with the requirements of Section 21.2 and NFPA 415.

21.2.2 General.

21.2.2.1 Permits. Permits, where required, shall comply with Section 1.13.

21.2.2.2 Fire Department Access. Fire apparatus access roads for all airport terminal buildings shall be provided and maintained in accordance with Section 18.2.

21.2.3 Smoking.

21.2.3.1 Smoking shall be prohibited in fuel ramp areas and loading walkways.

21.2.3.2 Smoking shall be in accordance with Section 10.9.

21.2.4 General.

21.2.4.1 Airport terminal buildings shall be of Type I, Type II, or Type IV construction, as defined in NFPA 220.

21.2.4.2* Interior finish materials shall be limited to Class A or Class B regardless of the occupant load. [**415**:4.1.2]

21.2.4.3 Aircraft fueling facilities and ramps shall be designed in accordance with NFPA 407 and Chapter 5 of NFPA 415. [**415**:4.1.3]

21.2.4.4 Belowgrade areas and blind spaces in airport terminal buildings shall be protected against flammable fuel and vapor penetration or shall be mechanically ventilated to provide at least four complete air changes per hour. The mechanical ventilation system shall be installed in accordance with NFPA 91. [**415**:4.1.4]

21.2.4.5 Glazing Material–Covered Openings Facing the Ramp.

21.2.4.5.1 Openings covered with glazing material that have the lowest part of the glazing material not less than 7 ft (2.1 m) above each finished floor level shall not be required to comply with 21.2.4.5.3. [**415**:4.1.5.1]

21.2.4.5.2 Openings covered with glazing material listed for use in a fire barrier and installed in accordance with the listing shall not be required to comply with 21.2.4.5.3. [**415**:4.1.5.2]

21.2.4.5.3 Where potential fuel spill points are located less than 100 ft (30.5 m) horizontally from glazing material–covered openings in airport terminal building walls facing the airport ramp, they shall be provided with an automatically activated water spray system in accordance with 21.2.4.5.3.1 or an automatically activated, listed fire shutter system in accordance with 21.2.4.5.3.2. (*See Annex C of NFPA 415.*) [**415**:4.1.5.3]

21.2.4.5.3.1 Where an automatically activated water spray system(s) is provided, it shall be installed in accordance with NFPA 15. [**415**:4.1.5.3.1]

21.2.4.5.3.1.1 The system shall be designed to provide a density of at least 0.25 gpm/ft^2 [10.2 (L/min)/m^2] over the entire exterior surface area of the glazing assembly. [**415**:4.1.5.3.1.1]

21.2.4.5.3.1.2 Where multiple water spray systems are used, the water supply shall be capable of supplying all systems that could be expected to operate as a result of one fire incident. [**415**:4.1.5.3.1.2]

21.2.4.5.3.1.3 The detection system design analysis for the water spray system shall include consideration of false alarms and detector response time. [**415**:4.1.5.3.1.3]

21.2.4.5.3.2 Where an automatically activated, listed fire shutter is provided, it shall be installed in accordance with its listing. [**415**:4.1.5.3.2]

21.2.5 Heating, Ventilating, and Air Conditioning.

21.2.5.1 Heating, ventilating, and air-conditioning systems shall be installed in accordance with Section 11.2 and Section 11.5, as applicable.

21.2.5.2* Air supply intake and exhaust openings for air-conditioning or ventilating equipment serving the terminal building, if located on the ramp side, shall be not less than 10 ft (3 m) above the grade level of the ramp and shall be at least 50 ft (15 m) from any point of flammable vapor release. [**415**:4.2.2]

21.2.5.3* Openings to rooms that contain coal-, gas-, or oil-fired equipment or any other open-flame device and that face the ramp side of the terminal shall be above ramp grade and 50 ft (15 m) from any point of flammable vapor release. [**415**:4.2.3]

21.2.5.4 Stacks or chimneys from a boiler, heater, or incinerator shall terminate at least 20 ft (6.1 m) above ramp grade and above the roof of the building. Stacks or chimneys from boilers or heaters that use solid fuel or from any incinerator shall be fitted with double screening to control fly ash and sparks. Such stacks or chimneys shall be located so the outlet is at least 100 ft (30.5 m) horizontally from any aircraft position or point of flammable vapor release. [**415**:4.2.4]

21.2.5.5 Incinerators shall conform to the requirements of Chapter 4 of NFPA 82. [**415**:4.2.5]

21.2.5.6 Exhaust hood ventilation systems for restaurant and flight kitchens shall conform to the applicable portions of Chapter 50. [**415**:4.2.6]

21.2.6 Exits.

21.2.6.1 Airport terminal building means of egress shall conform to the requirements of NFPA *101*. [**415**:4.3.1]

21.2.6.2* In addition to the exit signage requirements specified in NFPA *101*, doors serving as exits that discharge onto an airport ramp and are provided solely for the purpose of meeting emergency egress requirements from public areas shall be placarded "Emergency Exit Only" in letters at least 2 in. (50 mm) high. [**415**:4.3.2]

21.2.7* Fire Protection — Sprinkler Systems.

21.2.7.1 An airport terminal building with more than 12,000 ft^2 (1115 m^2) total floor area for the assembly portion of the occupancy shall be provided with an automatic sprinkler system installed in accordance with Section 13.3. [**415:**4.5.1.1]

21.2.7.2 Terminal buildings with less than 12,000 ft^2 (1115 m^2) total floor area for the assembly portion of the occupancy shall not be required to be provided with an automatic sprinkler system. [**415:**4.5.1.2]

21.2.7.3 Passenger-handling areas shall be classified as Ordinary Hazard Group 1 Occupancy, as defined in NFPA 13, for the purpose of sprinkler system design. [**415:**4.5.1.3]

21.2.7.4 Baggage, package, and mail-handling areas shall be classified as Ordinary Hazard Group 2 Occupancy, as defined in NFPA 13, for the purpose of sprinkler system design. [**415:**4.5.1.4]

21.2.7.5* Other areas of the airport terminal building shall be classified in accordance with Chapter 5 of NFPA 13, based on the occupancy of the area. [**415:**4.5.1.5]

21.2.7.6 Covered Plane-Loading Positions. Airport terminal buildings having canopy areas or roofed-over recesses at aircraft loading positions that, in effect, place the aircraft totally or substantially under such canopies or roofs shall have the canopies or roofs protected by automatic sprinkler systems in accordance with NFPA 409. [**415:**4.5.1.6]

21.2.8 Fire Alarm and Communications Systems. A fire alarm and communications system shall be installed as required by 13.7.2.1. [**415:**4.5.2]

21.2.8.1 Means to alert the public fire department or the airport fire station shall be available through manual fire alarm pull stations. Manual fire alarm services shall be installed in accordance with *NFPA 72*. [**415:**4.5.2.1]

21.2.8.2* Annunciation for all building fire alarm signals shall be provided near the front entrance of the building. [**415:**4.5.2.2]

21.2.8.3 If the public fire department has two-way voice communication with a constantly attended location, 21.2.8.2 shall not apply. [**415:**4.5.2.3]

21.2.9 Fire Hydrants. Fire hydrants shall be provided on both the ramp and the street sides of airport terminal buildings. Such hydrants shall be located so that no portion of the terminal building is more than 500 ft (152.4 m) from a hydrant. [**415:**4.5.3]

21.2.10 Standpipe and Hose Systems. Standpipe and hose systems shall be provided for all airport terminal buildings in excess of two stories [35 ft (10.7 m)] in height or 100 ft (30.5 m) in shortest horizontal dimension. Standpipe and hose systems shall be installed in accordance with Section 13.2. [**415:**4.5.4]

21.2.10.1 Class I standpipe systems shall be provided in buildings protected throughout by an approved automatic sprinkler system. Each 2½ in. (63.5 mm) hose connection shall be equipped with a 2½ in. × 1½ in. (63.5 mm × 38 mm) reducer and cap. [**415:**4.5.4.1]

21.2.10.2 Class III standpipe systems shall be provided in nonsprinklered buildings. Paragraphs 5.3.3.1 and 5.3.3.2 of NFPA 14 for Class III systems shall be applicable to this requirement. [**415:**4.5.4.2]

21.2.11 Portable Fire Extinguishers. Portable fire extinguishers shall be provided throughout the airport terminal building in accordance with Section 13.6. [**415:**4.5.6]

21.3 Rooftop Heliport Construction and Protection.

21.3.1 Application. Rooftop heliport construction and protection shall comply with Section 21.3 and NFPA 418.

21.3.1.1 Section 21.3 shall not apply to ground level helicopter hangars. All hangars not covered by this section shall comply with NFPA 409.

21.3.1.2 Temporary landing sites and emergency evacuation facilities shall not be required to comply with Section 21.3.

21.3.2 General.

21.3.2.1 Permits. Permits, where required, shall comply with Section 1.13.

21.3.2.2 Fire Department Access. Fire apparatus access roads for all buildings with a rooftop heliport shall be provided and maintained in accordance with Section 18.2.

21.3.2.3 Smoking.

21.3.2.3.1 Smoking shall be prohibited at rooftop heliports.

21.3.2.3.2 Smoking shall be in accordance with Section 10.9.

21.3.3 General Requirements — Land-Based Facilities.

21.3.3.1* Plans.

21.3.3.1.1 The design drawings for the construction and protection of the heliport shall be approved by the AHJ. [**418:**4.2.1]

21.3.3.1.2 The design of the heliport, including all the aeronautical components, shall be in accordance with FAA AC 150/5390-2C, *Heliport Design Advisory Circular*. [**418:**4.2.2]

21.3.3.1.3 The final approach and takeoff (FATO) area, the approach/departure path, and the touchdown and liftoff (TLOF) area shall be designated on the design drawings. [**418:**4.2.3]

21.3.3.2 Tank and Equipment Locations.

21.3.3.2.1 Storage, handling, and use of flammable and combustible liquids shall be in accordance with Chapter 66. [**418:**4.3.1]

21.3.3.2.2 Oxygen and other medical gases shall be stored and used in accordance with NFPA 99. [**418:**4.3.2]

21.3.3.2.3 Aboveground flammable liquid storage tanks, compressed gas storage tanks, fuel storage tanks, and liquefied gas storage tanks shall be laterally located at least 50 ft (15.2 m) from the edge of the FATO area as defined in FAA AC 150/5390-2C, *Heliport Design Advisory Circular*. [**418:**4.3.3]

21.3.3.3 Firefighting Access.

21.3.3.3.1 The heliport shall have at least two access points for firefighting/rescue personnel. The access points shall be located at least 90 degrees from each other as measured from the center of the landing pad (TLOF). [**418:**4.4.1]

21.3.3.3.2 Fences shall not prevent access by firefighting/rescue personnel. [**418**:4.4.2]

21.3.3.4 Fuel Spill Control. The landing pad shall be designed so that fuel spills are directed away from access/egress points and passenger holding areas. [**418**:4.5]

21.3.3.5 No Smoking.

21.3.3.5.1 No smoking shall be permitted within 50 ft (15.2 m) of the landing pad edge. [**418**:4.6.1]

21.3.3.5.2 NO SMOKING signs shall be erected at access/egress points to the heliport. [**418**:4.6.2]

21.3.3.6 Fueling System. Fueling systems shall be designed in accordance with Section 42.10. [**418**:4.7]

21.3.3.6.1 Fueling equipment shall not hinder or obstruct access to exits or firefighting equipment. [**418**:4.7.1]

21.3.3.6.2 Fueling equipment shall be located a minimum of 25 ft (7.6 m) from hangars and fixed fire protection equipment. [**418**:4.7.2]

21.3.3.6.3 Fuel servicing equipment shall be designed to not penetrate the FATO and safety area obstruction clearance requirements in FAA AC 150/5390-2C, *Heliport Design Advisory Circular*. [**418**:4.7.3]

21.3.3.7* Means of Egress. At least two means of egress that lead to a public way shall be provided from the landing pad. [**418**:4.8]

21.3.3.7.1* The egress points shall be located at least 90 degrees from each other as measured from the center of the landing pad (TLOF). [**418**:4.8.1]

21.3.3.7.2 The egress points shall be located remotely from each other, not less than 30 ft (9.1 m) apart. [**418**:4.8.2]

21.3.3.7.3 No two egress points shall be located on the same side of the landing pad. [**418**:4.8.3]

21.3.4 Rooftop Landing Facilities.

21.3.4.1* Structural Support. Main structural support members that could be exposed to a fuel spill shall be made fire resistant using listed materials and methods to provide a fire-resistance rating of not less than 2 hours. [**418**:5.2]

21.3.4.2 Landing Pad Pitch. The rooftop landing pad shall be pitched to provide drainage at a slope of 0.5 percent to 2 percent. [**418**:5.3]

21.3.4.2.1 The pitch of the pad shall be designed to protect, at a minimum, the primary egress path, passenger holding area, rooftop hangar, and fire protection activation systems. [**418**:5.3.1]

21.3.4.2.2 Drainage flow shall not penetrate alternate egress points, stairways, ramps, hatches, and other openings not designed for drainage. [**418**:5.3.2]

21.3.4.3 Landing Pad Construction Materials.

21.3.4.3.1 The rooftop landing pad surface shall be constructed of approved noncombustible, nonporous materials. [**418**:5.4.1]

Δ **21.3.4.3.2** The contiguous building roof covering within 50 ft (15.2 m) of the landing pad edge shall have a Class A fire rating for exterior fire exposure, and shall be listed according to FM 4470, *Approval Standard for Single-Ply, Polymer-Modified Bitumen Sheet, Built-Up Roof (BUR) and Liquid Applied Roof Assemblies for Use in Class 1 and Noncombustible Roof Deck Construction*; UL 790, *Test Methods for Fire Tests of Roof Covering*, or ASTM E108, *Standard Test Methods for Fire Tests of Roof Coverings*. [**418**:5.4.2]

21.3.4.4* Means of Egress. Two means of egress from the rooftop landing pad to the building's egress system shall be provided. [**418**:5.5]

21.3.4.4.1* The egress points shall be located at least 90 degrees from each other as measured from the center of the landing pad (TLOF). [**418**:5.5.1]

21.3.4.4.2 The egress points shall be remotely located from each other, not less than 30 ft (9.1 m) apart. [**418**:5.5.2]

21.3.4.4.3 No two egress points shall be located on the same side of the rooftop landing pad. [**418**:5.5.3]

21.3.4.4.4* Means of egress from the landing pad shall not obstruct flight operations. [**418**:5.5.4]

21.3.4.5 Fire-Fighting Access. (Reserved)

21.3.4.6 Fire Protection.

21.3.4.6.1 General. A foam fire-extinguishing system with either a fixed discharge outlet(s) in accordance with 21.3.4.6.2 or a hose line(s) in accordance with 21.3.4.6.3 shall be designed and installed to protect the rooftop landing pad, unless otherwise permitted by the following:

(1) A foam fire-extinguishing system shall not be required for heliports located on open parking structures or buildings that are not normally occupied.
(2) For H-1 heliports, two portable foam extinguishers, each having a rating of 20-A:160-B, shall be permitted to be used to satisfy the requirement of 21.3.4.6.

[**418**:5.7.1]

21.3.4.6.1.1 Where trained personnel are not available, fixed fire protection outlet(s) shall be provided. [**418**:5.7.1.2]

N **21.3.4.6.1.1.1** Where trained personnel are not available, fixed fire protection outlet(s) shall be provided. [**418**:5.7.1.2]

21.3.4.6.1.2* The foam discharge rate for the fire-extinguishing system shall be 0.10 gpm/ft^2 (4.1 L/min·m^2) for aqueous film forming foam (AFFF). [**418**:5.7.1.3]

21.3.4.6.1.3 Where freezing is possible, freeze protection shall be provided. [**418**:5.7.1.4]

21.3.4.6.1.4 The foam components shall be installed in an area of the heliport and shall not penetrate, when not in use, the approach departure surface, transitional surfaces, TLOF, FATO, and safety areas as defined in FAA AC 150/5390-2C, *Heliport Design Advisory Circular*. [**418**:5.7.1.5]

21.3.4.6.2 Fixed Foam Fire-Extinguishing Systems.

Δ **21.3.4.6.2.1** Fixed foam fire-extinguishing systems shall be designed and installed in accordance with NFPA 11 or an equivalent standard, as appropriate, except as modified by Chapter 5 of NFPA 418. [**418**:5.7.2.1]

21.3.4.6.2.2* The design area of application of foam discharge for fixed discharge outlet systems shall be the entire rooftop landing pad. [**418**:5.7.2.2]

21.3.4.6.2.3 The duration of foam discharge for the fixed discharge outlet system shall be 10 minutes. [**418:**5.7.2.3]

21.3.4.6.2.4 A fixed nozzle discharge outlet system shall be one of the following: fixed stationary nozzles around the perimeter, two or more oscillating monitors/nozzles, or in-deck (deck-integrated firefighting system) nozzles within the perimeter of the deck. [**418:** 5.7.2.4]

21.3.4.6.2.5 Where fixed foam systems utilizing fixed deck nozzles or oscillating foam turrets, or both, are installed, system components shall be listed or approved. [**418:**5.7.2.5]

21.3.4.6.2.6 Activation of Systems.

21.3.4.6.2.6.1* The fixed discharge outlet system shall be activated manually. [**418:**5.7.2.6.1]

21.3.4.6.2.6.2* Manual actuation stations shall be located at each egress point from the rooftop landing pad and at an approved location inside the building from which the rooftop landing pad can be viewed. [**418:**5.7.2.6.2]

21.3.4.6.2.6.3 Manual foam activation stations shall be clearly labeled or identified as to the purpose and hazard protected. [**418:**5.7.2.6.3]

21.3.4.6.2.7 Where buildings are provided with a fire alarm system, the activation of the foam system shall be monitored by the building fire alarm system in accordance with *NFPA 72*. [**418:**5.7.2.6.4]

21.3.4.6.2.8 An approved manual control for foam system shutdown shall be accessible at all times, including the time of fire and system operation. [**418:**5.7.2.6.5]

21.3.4.6.3 Manual Fire-Fighting Equipment.

21.3.4.6.3.1* The area of application of foam discharge for hose line systems shall be the practical critical fire area for the category of the helicopter landing facility in accordance with Table 21.3.4.6.3.1. [**418:**5.7.3.1]

21.3.4.6.3.2 Supplementary Protection. The duration of foam discharge for the hose line systems shall be 10 minutes. [**418:**5.7.3.2]

21.3.4.6.4 Standpipes and hose stations, if used, shall be installed in accordance with Section 13.2. [**418:**5.7.4]

Δ **Table 21.3.4.6.3.1 Practical Critical Fire Areas for Hose Line Systems Only**

Heliport Category	Helicopter Overall Length*/D-Value	Practical Critical Fire Area ft²	Practical Critical Fire Area m²
H-1	Less than 50 ft (15.2 m)	375	34.8
H-2	50 ft (15.2 m) up to but not including 80 ft (24.4 m)	840	78.0
H-3	80 ft (24.4 m) up to but not including 120 ft (36.6 m)	1440	133.8

*Helicopter length, including the tail boom and the rotors.
[**418:** Table 5.7.3.1]

21.3.4.6.5 Water Supply.

21.3.4.6.5.1 The water supply for the foam system shall be from a source approved by the AHJ. [**418:**5.7.5.1]

21.3.4.6.5.2 Fire pumps, if used, shall be installed in accordance with Section 13.4. [**418:**5.7.5.2]

21.3.4.6.6 Foam Concentrate Supply.

21.3.4.6.6.1 The supply of foam concentrate shall be sufficient to supply the largest system. [**418:**5.7.6.1]

21.3.4.6.7 The foam concentrate for the fixed system or manual fire-fighting equipment shall be listed in accordance with UL 162, *Foam Equipment and Liquid Concentrates*, or FM 5130, *Approval Standard for Foam Extinguishing Systems*, and shall be on the qualified products list for MIL-F-24385, or equivalent. [**418:**5.7.6.2]

21.3.4.6.8 Fire Alarm. A means of communication shall be provided from the roof area to notify the fire department of emergencies. [**418:**5.7.7.1]

21.3.4.6.8.1 Where buildings are provided with a fire alarm system, a manual pull station shall be provided for each designated means of egress from the roof. *(See 21.3.4.4.1.)* [**418:**5.7.7.2]

21.3.4.6.9 Acceptance Testing.

Δ **21.3.4.6.9.1 Fixed Foam Fire-Extinguishing Systems.** The fixed foam discharge outlet system shall be tested to determine coverage of the rooftop landing pad using water, foam, or an alternative test fluid acceptable to the AHJ. [**418:**5.7.8.1]

21.3.4.6.9.1.1 The system shall cover 95 percent of the rooftop landing pad during the test. [**418:**5.7.8.1.1]

21.3.4.6.9.1.2 The access points for firefighting and for egress located on the landing pad shall be covered. [**418:**5.7.8.1.2]

21.3.4.6.9.2 Manual Firefighting Equipment. The hose handlines shall be flow tested to demonstrate that the design objectives are met. [**418:**5.7.8.2]

21.3.4.6.10 Inspection, Testing, and Maintenance.

Δ **21.3.4.6.10.1** Fire protection systems installed in accordance with NFPA 11 or NFPA 14 shall be inspected, tested, and maintained in accordance with NFPA 25. [**418:**5.7.9.1]

21.3.4.6.10.2 Foam systems installed in accordance with NFPA 11 shall be maintained in accordance with NFPA 11. [**418:**5.7.9.2]

21.3.5 Portable Fire Extinguishers.

21.3.5.1 Minimum Requirement. At least one portable fire extinguisher as specified in Table 21.3.5.1 shall be provided for each takeoff and landing area, parking area, and fuel storage area. [**418:**9.2]

21.3.5.2 Extinguishers Subject to Damage, Theft, or Tampering. Where the portable extinguisher cannot be maintained and safeguarded against damage, theft, or tampering, the portable fire extinguisher shall be omitted with the approval of the AHJ. [**418:**9.3]

Δ **Table 21.3.5.1 Minimum Ratings of Portable Fire Extinguishers for Heliport Categories**

Heliport Category	Helicopter Overall Length*/D-Value	Minimum Rating (UL)
H-1	Less than 50 ft (15.2 m)	4-A:80-B
H-2	50 ft (15.2 m) up to but not including 80 ft (24.4 m)	10-A:120-B
H-3	80 ft (24.4 m) up to but not including 120 ft (36.6 m)	30-A:240-B

*Helicopter length, including the tail boom and the rotors.
[**418:** Table 9.2]

Chapter 22   Automobile Wrecking Yards

22.1 General. Automobile wrecking yards shall be in accordance with this chapter.

22.2 Permits. Permits, where required, shall comply with Section 1.13.

22.3 Fire Apparatus Access Roads. Fire apparatus access roads shall be in accordance with Section 18.2.

22.4 Welding and Cutting. Welding and cutting operations shall be in accordance with Chapter 41.

22.5 Housekeeping. The yard shall be kept free of vegetation, debris, and any other material that is not necessary to the proper operation of the facility.

22.6 Fire Extinguishers. Fire extinguishers shall be placed and sized in accordance with Section 13.6.

22.7 Tire Storage. The storage of tires shall be in accordance with Chapters 33 and 34.

22.8 Burning Operations. Burning operations shall be in accordance with Section 10.10.

22.9 Motor Vehicle Fluids and Hazardous Materials.

22.9.1 General. The storage, use, and handling of motor vehicle fluids and hazardous materials shall be in accordance with Chapters 60 and 66.

22.9.2 Motor Vehicle Fluids.

22.9.2.1 Motor vehicle fluids shall be drained from salvage vehicles when such fluids are leaking.

22.9.2.2 Storage and handling of motor vehicle fluids shall be done in an approved manner.

22.9.2.3 Flammable and combustible liquids shall be stored and handled in accordance with Chapter 66.

22.9.3 Mitigation for Vehicle Fluid Leaks.

22.9.3.1 Supplies or equipment capable of mitigating leaks from fuel tanks, crankcases, brake systems, and transmissions shall be kept available on site.

22.9.3.2 Single-use plugging, diking, and absorbent materials shall be disposed of as hazardous waste and removed from the site in a manner approved by federal, state, and local requirements.

22.9.4 Air Bag Systems. Removed air bag systems shall be handled and stored in accordance with Chapter 60.

22.9.5 Lead-Acid Batteries.

22.9.5.1 Lead-acid batteries shall be removed from salvage vehicles when such batteries are leaking.

22.9.5.2 Lead-acid batteries that have been removed from vehicles shall be stored in an approved manner.

N **22.9.6 Other Battery Technologies.** Other battery technologies shall be handled and stored in accordance with NFPA 855.

Chapter 23   Cleanrooms

23.1 General. All semiconductor facilities containing a cleanroom or a clean zone, or both, shall comply with this chapter and NFPA 318.

23.2 Applicability. Unless otherwise noted in NFPA 318, the provisions of NFPA 318 shall not be applied to facilities, equipment, structures, or installations that were existing or approved for construction or installation prior to the effective date of this *Code*, except in those cases where it is determined by the AHJ that the existing situation involves a distinct hazard to life or adjacent property.

23.3 Permits. Permits, where required, shall comply with Section 1.13.

Chapter 24   Drycleaning

24.1 General.

24.1.1 Drycleaning plants shall comply with this chapter and NFPA 32.

24.1.2 Drycleaning plants or systems using solvents that have a flash point below 100°F (37.8°C) shall be prohibited.

24.2 Permits. Permits, where required, shall comply with Section 1.13.

Chapter 25   Grandstands and Bleachers, Folding and Telescopic Seating, Tents, and Membrane Structures

25.1 General.

25.1.1 The construction, location, protection, and maintenance of grandstands and bleachers, folding and telescopic seating, tents, and membrane structures shall meet the requirements of this chapter. Seating facilities located in the open air or within enclosed or semi-enclosed structures, such as tents, membrane structures, and stadium complexes, shall comply with this chapter, NFPA *101*, and NFPA 102.

25.1.2 Permits. Permits, where required, shall comply with Section 1.13.

25.1.3 Means of Egress.

25.1.3.1 Means of egress shall comply with the requirements of Chapter 14.

25.1.3.2 No guy wire or guy rope shall cross any means of egress at a height of less than 7 ft (2.1 m).

25.1.3.3 Tent stakes adjacent to any means of egress from any tent open to the public shall be railed off, capped, or covered so as not to present a hazard to the public.

25.1.3.4 New facilities shall comply with the means of egress provisions of NFPA *101* for the applicable occupancies.

25.1.3.5 Existing facilities shall comply with the means of egress provisions of NFPA *101* for the applicable occupancies.

25.1.4 Flammable Liquids and Gases.

Δ **25.1.4.1** Where required by the provisions of Chapters 11 through 43 of NFPA *101*, occupancies with storage and handling of hazardous materials shall comply with the following codes unless otherwise modified by other provisions of NFPA *101*: NFPA 30, NFPA 54, NFPA 55, NFPA 58, NFPA 400, and NFPA 495.[*101*:8.7.3.1]

25.1.4.2* No storage, use, or handling of hazardous materials shall be permitted in any location where such storage, use, or handling would jeopardize egress from the structure, unless otherwise permitted by a document listed in 25.1.4.1. [*101*:8.7.3.2]

25.1.4.3 Refueling of equipment with liquids having flash points below 100°F (38°C) shall not be permitted within the structure.

25.1.5 Fire Hazards.

25.1.5.1 The finished ground level enclosed by the structure, and the surrounding finished ground level not less than 10 ft (3050 mm) outside of the structure, shall be cleared of all flammable or combustible material and vegetation. [5000:32.3.5.1.1]

25.1.5.2 Where prohibited by the AHJ, smoking shall not be permitted in any temporary membrane structure. [*101*:11.10.2.2]

25.1.5.3 Hay, straw, shavings, or similar combustible materials that have not been treated to make them flame retardant to a degree acceptable to the AHJ shall not be permitted within any structure used as an assembly occupancy.

Exception: Animal bedding and fodders in quantities approved by the AHJ.

25.1.5.4 Open Flame Devices and Pyrotechnics. Use of open flame devices and pyrotechnics shall comply with 20.1.5.3.

25.1.6 Extinguishment Requirements.

25.1.6.1 Enclosed stadiums, arenas, and similar structures shall be protected throughout by an approved, electrically supervised automatic sprinkler system in accordance with Section 13.3, unless otherwise permitted by the following:

(1) Where the ceiling or roof, whichever is lower, of the playing/activity area is more than 55 ft (16.7 m) above the floor, sprinklers shall not be required above the playing/activity area where permitted by the AHJ.
(2) Sprinklers shall not be required above seating areas that view the playing/activity area.

[5000:32.3.5.2]

25.1.6.2 An enclosed area shall be protected by an approved sprinkler system in accordance with Section 13.3, unless such an area is one of the following:

(1) Enclosed stadiums, arenas, and similar structures
(2) Press boxes of less than 1000 ft² (93 m²)
(3) Storage facilities of less than 1000 ft² (93 m²), if enclosed with minimum 1-hour fire-resistance-rated construction
(4) Enclosed areas underneath grandstands or bleachers that comply with 16.4.10.5 of NFPA *5000*

[5000:32.3.5.3]

25.1.6.3 Portable Fire Extinguishers. Portable fire extinguishers shall be installed in assembly occupancies in accordance with Section 13.6, unless otherwise permitted by one of the following:

(1) The requirement of 25.1.6.3 shall not apply to seating areas.
(2) The requirement of 25.1.6.3 shall not apply to floor areas used for contests, performances, or entertainment.
(3) The requirement of 25.1.6.3 shall not apply to outside assembly occupancy areas.
(4) Portable extinguishers shall be permitted to be located in secure locations accessible to staff.

[5000:16.3.5.3]

25.1.6.4 Fire-extinguishing equipment shall be maintained in accordance with Section 13.6.

25.1.6.5 Employees shall be trained to operate fire-extinguishing equipment and shall be required to exhibit their skill when requested by the AHJ.

25.1.7 Detection, Alarm, and Communications Systems. Detection, alarm, and communications systems shall comply with Section 13.7 where required by 13.7.2.1 or 13.7.2.2.

25.1.8* Fire Detail. See 1.7.17 for fire detail requirements.

25.1.9 Electrical Installations.

Δ **25.1.9.1 Electrical Systems.** Electrical wiring and equipment shall be in accordance with Section 11.1 unless such installations are approved existing installations, which shall be permitted to be continued in service. [*101*:9.1.2]

25.1.9.2 The electrical system shall be installed, maintained, and operated in a safe and professional manner. When in use, portable electrical systems shall be inspected daily by a qualified person representing the owner, and any defects found shall be corrected before the public is admitted.

25.1.9.3 The electrical system and equipment shall be isolated from the public by proper elevation or guarding, and all electrical fuses and switches shall be enclosed in approved enclosures. Cables on the ground in areas traversed by the public shall be placed in trenches or protected by approved covers.

25.1.10 Heating Devices.

25.1.10.1 Fired Heaters.

25.1.10.1.1 Heating devices shall comply with Sections 11.2 and 11.5.

25.1.10.1.2 Only labeled heating devices shall be used. [*101*:11.9.5.1.1]

25.1.10.1.3 Fuel-fired heaters and their installation shall be approved by the AHJ. [*101*:11.9.5.1.2]

25.1.10.1.4 Air-Conditioning, Heating, Ventilating Ductwork, and Related Equipment. Air-conditioning, heating, ventilating ductwork, and related equipment shall be in accordance with NFPA 90A or NFPA 90B, as applicable, unless such installations are approved existing installations, which shall be permitted to be continued in service. [*101*:9.2.1]

25.1.10.1.5 Ventilating or Heat-Producing Equipment. Ventilating or heat-producing equipment shall be in accordance with NFPA 31, NFPA 54, *NFPA 70*, NFPA 91, or NFPA 211, as applicable, unless such installations are approved existing installations, which shall be permitted to be continued in service. [*101*:9.2.2]

25.1.10.1.6 Containers for liquefied petroleum gases shall be installed not less than 5 ft (1.5 m) from any tent or temporary membrane structure and shall be in accordance with the provisions of Chapter 69.

25.1.10.1.7 Tanks shall be secured in the upright position and protected from vehicular traffic. [*101*:11.10.7.1.4]

25.1.10.2 Electric Heaters.

25.1.10.2.1 Electric heaters shall comply with 25.1.10.2 and Section 11.5.

25.1.10.2.2 Only labeled heaters shall be permitted. [*101*:11.9.5.2.1]

25.1.10.2.3 Electric heaters, their placement, and their installation shall be approved by the AHJ. [*101*:11.9.5.2.2]

25.1.10.2.4 Heaters shall be connected to electricity by electric cable that is suitable for outside use and is of sufficient size to handle the electrical load. [*101*:11.9.5.2.3]

25.1.11 Cooking. Cooking operations shall comply with Chapter 50.

25.1.12 Generators.

25.1.12.1 Generators and other internal combustion power sources shall comply with Section 10.15 and 25.1.12.

25.1.12.2* Generators and other internal combustion power sources shall be separated from temporary membrane structures and tents by a minimum of 20 ft (6.1 m) and shall be protected from contact by fencing, enclosure, or other approved means.

25.1.12.3 Fueling. Fuel tanks shall be of adequate capacity to permit uninterrupted operation during normal operating hours. Refueling shall be conducted only when not in use.

25.1.12.4 Fire Extinguishers. A minimum of one portable fire extinguisher with a rating of not less than 2-A:10-B:C shall be provided.

25.2 Tents.

25.2.1 General.

25.2.1.1 Tents shall be permitted only on a temporary basis. [*101*:11.11.1.2]

25.2.1.2 Tents shall be erected to cover not more than 75 percent of the premises, unless otherwise approved by the AHJ. [*101*:11.11.1.3]

25.2.2 Flame Propagation Performance.

25.2.2.1 All tent fabric shall meet the flame propagation performance criteria contained in Test Method 2 of NFPA 701. [*101*:11.11.2.1]

25.2.2.2 One of the following shall serve as evidence that the tent fabric materials have the required flame propagation performance:

(1) The AHJ shall require a certificate or other evidence of acceptance by an organization acceptable to the AHJ.
(2) The AHJ shall require a report of tests made by other inspection authorities or organizations acceptable to the AHJ.

[*101*:11.11.2.3]

25.2.2.3 Where required by the AHJ, confirmatory field tests shall be conducted using test specimens from the original material, which shall have been affixed at the time of manufacture to the exterior of the tent. [*101*:11.11.2.4]

25.2.3 Location and Spacing.

25.2.3.1 There shall be a minimum of 10 ft (3050 mm) between stake lines. [*101*:11.11.3.1]

25.2.3.2 Adjacent tents shall be spaced to provide an area to be used as a means of emergency egress. Where 10 ft (3050 mm) between stake lines does not meet the requirements for means of egress, the distance necessary for means of egress shall govern. [*101*:11.11.3.2]

25.2.3.3 Tents not occupied by the public and not used for the storage of combustible material shall be permitted to be erected less than 10 ft (3050 mm) from other structures where the AHJ deems such close spacing to be safe from hazard to the public. [*101*:11.11.3.3]

25.2.3.4 Tents, each not exceeding 1200 ft^2 (112 m^2) in finished ground level area and located in fairgrounds or similar open spaces, shall not be required to be separated from each other, provided that safety precautions meet the approval of the AHJ. [*101*:11.11.3.4]

25.2.3.5 The placement of tents relative to other structures shall be at the discretion of the AHJ, with consideration given to occupancy, use, opening, exposure, and other similar factors. [*101*:11.11.3.5]

25.2.4 Fire Hazards.

25.2.4.1 The finished ground level enclosed by any tent, and the finished ground level for a reasonable distance, but for not less than 10 ft (3050 mm) outside of such a tent, shall be cleared of all flammable or combustible material or vegetation that is not used for necessary support equipment. The clearing work shall be accomplished to the satisfaction of the AHJ prior to the erection of such a tent. The premises shall be kept free from such flammable or combustible materials during the period for which the premises are used by the public. [*101*:11.11.4.1]

25.2.4.2 Smoking.

25.2.4.2.1 Smoking shall not be permitted in any tent, unless approved by the AHJ. [*101*:11.11.4.2.1]

25.2.4.2.2 In rooms or areas where smoking is prohibited, plainly visible signs shall be posted that read as follows:

NO SMOKING
[*101*:11.11.4.2.2]

25.2.5 Fire-Extinguishing Equipment. Portable fire-extinguishing equipment of approved types shall be furnished and maintained in tents in such quantity and in such locations as directed by the AHJ. [*101*:11.11.5]

25.3 Grandstands.

25.3.1 Seating.

25.3.1.1 Where grandstand seating without backs is used indoors, rows of seats shall be spaced not less than 22 in. (560 mm) back-to-back. [*101*:12.4.10.2.1]

25.3.1.2 The depth of footboards and seat boards in grandstands shall be not less than 9 in. (230 mm); where the same level is not used for both seat foundations and footrests, footrests independent of seats shall be provided. [*101*:12.4.10.2.2]

25.3.1.3 Seats and footrests of grandstands shall be supported securely and fastened in such a manner that they cannot be displaced inadvertently. [*101*:12.4.10.2.3]

25.3.1.4 Individual seats or chairs shall be permitted only if secured in rows in an approved manner, unless seats do not exceed 16 in number and are located on level floors and within railed-in enclosures, such as boxes. [*101*:12.4.10.2.4]

25.3.1.5 The maximum number of seats permitted between the farthest seat in an aisle in grandstands and bleachers shall not exceed that shown in Table 25.3.1.5. [*101*:12.4.10.2.5]

25.3.2 Special Requirements — Wood Grandstands.

25.3.2.1 An outdoor wood grandstand shall be erected within not less than two-thirds of its height and, in no case, within not less than 10 ft (3050 mm) of a building, unless otherwise permitted by one of the following:

(1) The distance requirement shall not apply to buildings having minimum 1-hour-fire-resistance-rated construction with openings protected against the fire exposure hazard created by the grandstand.
(2) The distance requirement shall not apply where a wall having minimum 1-hour-fire-resistance-rated construction separates the grandstand from the building.

[*101*:12.4.10.3.1]

25.3.2.2 An outdoor wood grandstand unit shall not exceed 10,000 ft² (929 m²) in finished ground level area or 200 ft (61 m) in length, and all of the following requirements also shall apply:

(1) Grandstand units of the maximum size shall be placed not less than 20 ft (6100 mm) apart or shall be separated by walls having a minimum 1-hour fire-resistance rating.
(2) The number of grandstand units erected in any one group shall not exceed three.
(3) Each group of grandstand units shall be separated from any other group by a wall having minimum 2-hour-fire-resistance-rated construction extending 24 in. (610 mm) above the seat platforms or by an open space of not less than 50 ft (15 m).

[*101*:12.4.10.3.2]

△ **Table 25.3.1.5 Maximum Number of Seats Between Farthest Seat and an Aisle**

Application	Outdoors	Indoors
Grandstands	11	6
Bleachers (*See 12.2.5.8.1.2 of NFPA 101*)	20	9

[*101*:Table 12.4.10.2.5]

25.3.2.3 The finished ground level area or length required by 25.3.2.2 shall be permitted to be doubled where one of the following criteria is met:

(1) Where the grandstand is constructed entirely of labeled fire-retardant-treated wood that has passed the standard rain test, ASTM D2898, *Standard Practice for Accelerated Weathering of Fire-Retardant-Treated Wood for Fire Testing*
(2) Where the grandstand is constructed of members conforming to dimensions for heavy timber construction [Type IV (2HH)]

[*101*:12.4.10.3.3]

25.3.2.4 The highest level of seat platforms above the finished ground level or the surface at the front of any wood grandstand shall not exceed 20 ft (6100 mm). [*101*:12.4.10.3.4]

25.3.2.5 The highest level of seat platforms above the finished ground level, or the surface at the front of a portable grandstand within a tent or membrane structure, shall not exceed 12 ft (3660 mm). [*101*:12.4.10.3.5]

25.3.2.6 The height requirements specified in 25.3.2.4 and 25.3.2.5 shall be permitted to be doubled where constructed entirely of labeled fire-retardant-treated wood that has passed the standard rain test, ASTM D2898, *Standard Practice for Accelerated Weathering of Fire-Retardant-Treated Wood for Fire Testing*, or where constructed of members conforming to dimensions for heavy timber construction [Type IV (2HH)]. [*101*:12.4.10.3.6]

25.3.3 Special Requirements — Portable Grandstands.

25.3.3.1 Portable grandstands shall conform to the requirements of Section 25.3 for grandstands and the requirements of 25.3.3.2 through 25.3.3.7. [*101*:12.4.10.4.1]

25.3.3.2 Portable grandstands shall be self-contained and shall have within them all necessary parts to withstand and restrain all forces that might be developed during human occupancy. [*101*:12.4.10.4.2]

25.3.3.3 Portable grandstands shall be designed and manufactured so that, if any structural members essential to the strength and stability of the structure have been omitted during erection, the presence of unused connection fittings shall make the omissions self-evident. [*101*:12.4.10.4.3]

25.3.3.4 Portable grandstand construction shall be skillfully accomplished to produce the strength required by the design. [*101*:12.4.10.4.4]

25.3.3.5 Portable grandstands shall be provided with base plates, sills, floor runners, or sleepers of such area that the permitted bearing capacity of the supporting material is not exceeded. [*101*:12.4.10.4.5]

25.3.3.6 Where a portable grandstands rest directly on a base of such character that it is incapable of supporting the load without appreciable settlement, mud sills of suitable material, having sufficient area to prevent undue or dangerous settlement, shall be installed under base plates, runners, or sleepers. [*101*:12.4.10.4.6]

25.3.3.7 All bearing surfaces of portable grandstands shall be in contact with each other. [*101*:12.4.10.4.7]

25.3.4 Spaces Underneath Grandstands.
Spaces underneath a grandstand shall be kept free of flammable or combustible materials, unless protected by an approved, supervised auto-

matic sprinkler system in accordance with Section 13.3 or unless otherwise permitted by one of the following:

(1) This requirement shall not apply to accessory uses of 300 ft² (28 m²) or less, such as ticket booths, toilet facilities, or concession booths where constructed of noncombustible or fire-resistive construction in otherwise nonsprinklered facilities.
(2) This requirement shall not apply to rooms that are enclosed in not less than 1-hour-fire-resistance-rated construction and are less than 1000 ft² (93 m²) in otherwise nonsprinklered facilities.

[*101*:12.4.10.5]

25.3.5 Guards and Railings.

25.3.5.1 Railings or guards not less than 42 in. (1065 mm) above the aisle surface or footrest or not less than 36 in. (915 mm) vertically above the center of the seat or seat board surface, whichever is adjacent, shall be provided along those portions of the backs and ends of all grandstands where the seats are more than 48 in. (1220 mm) above the floor or the finished ground level. [*101*:12.4.10.6.1]

25.3.5.2 The requirement of 25.3.5.1 shall not apply where an adjacent wall or fence affords equivalent safeguard. [*101*:12.4.10.6.2]

25.3.5.3 Where the front footrest of any grandstand is more than 24 in. (610 mm) above the floor, railings or guards not less than 33 in. (825 mm) above such footrests shall be provided. [*101*:12.4.10.6.3]

25.3.5.4 The railings required by 25.3.5.3 shall be permitted to be not less than 26 in. (660 mm) high in grandstands or where the front row of seats includes backrests. [*101*:12.4.10.6.4]

25.3.5.5 Cross aisles located within the seating area shall be provided with rails not less than 26 in. (660 mm) high along the front edge of the cross aisle. [*101*:12.4.10.6.5]

25.3.5.6 The railings specified by 25.3.5.5 shall not be required where the backs of the seats in front of the cross aisle project 24 in. (610 mm) or more above the surface of the cross aisle. [*101*:12.4.10.6.6]

25.3.5.7 Vertical openings between guardrails and footboards or seat boards shall be provided with intermediate construction so that a 4 in. (100 mm) diameter sphere cannot pass through the opening. [*101*:12.4.10.6.7]

25.3.5.8 An opening between the seat board and footboard located more than 30 in. (760 mm) above the finished ground level shall be provided with intermediate construction so that a 4 in. (100 mm) diameter sphere cannot pass through the opening. [*101*:12.4.10.6.8]

25.3.6 Maintenance of Outdoor Grandstands.

25.3.6.1 The owner shall provide for not less than annual inspection and required maintenance of each outdoor grandstand to ensure safe conditions. [*101*:12.7.10.1]

25.3.6.2 At least biennially, the inspection shall be performed by a professional engineer, registered architect, or individual certified by the manufacturer. [*101*:12.7.10.2]

25.3.6.3 Where required by the AHJ, the owner shall provide a copy of the inspection report and certification that the inspection required by 25.3.6.2 has been performed. [*101*:12.7.10.3]

25.4 Folding and Telescopic Seating.

25.4.1 Seating.

25.4.1.1 The horizontal distance of seats, measured back-to-back, shall be not less than 22 in. (560 mm) for seats without backs, and all of the following requirements shall also apply:

(1) There shall be a space of not less than 12 in. (305 mm) between the back of each seat and the front of each seat immediately behind it.
(2) If seats are of the chair type, the 12 in. (305 mm) dimension shall be measured to the front edge of the rear seat in its normal unoccupied position.
(3) All measurements shall be taken between plumb lines.

[*101*:12.4.11.2.1]

25.4.1.2 The depth of footboards (footrests) and seat boards in folding and telescopic seating shall be not less than 9 in. (230 mm). [*101*:12.4.11.2.2]

25.4.1.3 Where the same level is not used for both seat foundations and footrests, footrests independent of seats shall be provided. [*101*:12.4.10.2.3]

25.4.1.4 Individual chair-type seats shall be permitted in folding and telescopic seating only if firmly secured in groups of not less than three. [*101*:12.4.11.2.4]

25.4.1.5 The maximum number of seats permitted between the farthest seat in an aisle in folding and telescopic seating shall not exceed that shown in Table 25.3.1.5. [*101*:12.4.11.2.5]

25.4.2 Guards and Railings.

25.4.2.1 Railings or guards not less than 42 in. (1065 mm) above the aisle surface or footrest, or not less than 36 in. (915 mm) vertically above the center of the seat or seat board surface, whichever is adjacent, shall be provided along those portions of the backs and ends of all folding and telescopic seating where the seats are more than 48 in. (1220 mm) above the floor or the finished ground level. [*101*:12.4.11.3.1]

25.4.2.2 The requirement of 25.4.2.1 shall not apply where an adjacent wall or fence affords equivalent safeguard. [*101*:12.4.11.3.2]

25.4.2.3 Where the front footrest of folding or telescopic seating is more than 24 in. (610 mm) above the floor, railings or guards not less than 33 in. (825 mm) above such footrests shall be provided. [*101*:12.4.11.3.3]

25.4.2.4 The railings required by 25.4.2.3 shall be permitted to be not less than 26 in. (660 mm) high where the front row of seats includes backrests. [*101*:12.4.11.3.4]

25.4.2.5 Cross aisles located within the seating area shall be provided with rails not less than 26 in. (660 mm) high along the front edge of the cross aisle. [*101*:12.4.11.3.5]

25.4.2.6 The railings specified by 25.4.2.5 shall not be required where the backs of the seats in front of the cross aisle project 24 in. (610 mm) or more above the surface of the cross aisle. [*101*:12.4.11.3.6]

25.4.2.7 Vertical openings between guardrails and footboards or seat boards shall be provided with intermediate construction so that a 4 in. (100 mm) diameter sphere cannot pass through the opening. [*101*:12.4.11.3.7]

25.4.2.8 An opening between the seat board and footboard located more than 30 in. (760 mm) above the finished ground level shall be provided with intermediate construction so that a 4 in. (100 mm) diameter sphere cannot pass through the opening. [*101*:12.4.11.3.8]

25.4.3 Maintenance and Operation of Folding and Telescopic Seating.

25.4.3.1 Instructions in both maintenance and operation shall be transmitted to the owner by the manufacturer of the seating or his or her representative. [*101*:12.7.11.1]

25.4.3.2 Maintenance and operation of folding and telescopic seating shall be the responsibility of the owner or his or her duly authorized representative and shall include all of the following:

(1) During operation of the folding and telescopic seats, the opening and closing shall be supervised by responsible personnel who shall ensure that the operation is in accordance with the manufacturer's instructions.
(2) Only attachments specifically approved by the manufacturer for the specific installation shall be attached to the seating.
(3) An annual inspection and required maintenance of each grandstand shall be performed to ensure safe conditions.
(4) At least biennially, the inspection shall be performed by a professional engineer, registered architect, or individual certified by the manufacturer.

[*101*:12.7.11.2]

25.5 Permanent Membrane Structures.

25.5.1 Application.

25.5.1.1 Use of Membrane Roofs. Membrane roofs shall be used in accordance with the following:

(1) Membrane materials shall not be used where fire resistance ratings are required for walls or roofs.
(2) Where every part of the roof, including the roof membrane, is not less than 20 ft (6100 mm) above any floor, balcony, or gallery, a noncombustible or limited-combustible membrane shall be permitted to be used as the roof in any construction type.
(3) With approval of the AHJ, membrane materials shall be permitted to be used where every part of the roof membrane is sufficiently above every significant fire potential, such that the imposed temperature cannot exceed the capability of the membrane, including seams, to maintain its structural integrity.

[*101*:11.9.1.2]

25.5.1.2 Testing. Testing of membrane materials for compliance with the requirements of Section 25.5 for use of the categories of noncombustible and limited-combustible materials shall be performed on weathered-membrane material as defined in 3.3.184.8 of NFPA *101*. [*101*:11.9.1.3]

25.5.1.3 Flame Spread Index. The flame spread index of all membrane materials exposed within the structure shall be Class A in accordance with Section 12.5. [*101*:11.9.1.4]

25.5.1.4 Roof Covering Classification. Roof membranes shall have a roof covering classification, as required by the applicable building codes, when tested in accordance with ASTM E108, *Standard Test Methods for Fire Tests of Roof Coverings*, or UL 790, *Standard Test Methods for Fire Tests of Roof Coverings*. [*101*:11.9.1.5]

25.5.1.5 Flame Propagation Performance.

25.5.1.5.1 All membrane structure fabric shall meet the flame propagation performance criteria contained in Test Method 2 of NFPA 701. [*101*:11.9.1.6.1]

25.5.1.5.2 One of the following shall serve as evidence that the fabric materials have the required flame propagation performance:

(1) The AHJ shall require a certificate or other evidence of acceptance by an organization acceptable to the AHJ.
(2) The AHJ shall require a report of tests made by other inspection authorities or organizations acceptable to the AHJ.

[*101*:11.9.1.6.2]

25.5.1.5.3 Where required by the AHJ, confirmatory field tests shall be conducted using test specimens from the original material, which shall have been affixed at the time of manufacture to the exterior of the structure. [*101*:11.9.1.6.3]

25.5.2 Tensioned-Membrane Structures.

25.5.2.1 The design, materials, and construction of the building shall be based on plans and specifications prepared by a licensed architect or engineer knowledgeable in tensioned-membrane construction. [*101*:11.9.2.1]

25.5.2.2 Material loads and strength shall be based on physical properties of the materials verified and certified by an approved testing laboratory. [*101*:11.9.2.2]

25.5.2.3 The membrane roof for structures in climates subject to freezing temperatures and ice buildup shall be composed of two layers separated by an air space through which heated air can be moved to guard against ice accumulation. As an alternative to the two layers, other approved methods that protect against ice accumulation shall be permitted. [*101*:11.9.2.3]

25.5.2.4 Roof drains shall be equipped with electrical elements to protect against ice buildup that can prevent the drains from functioning. Such heating elements shall be served by on-site standby electrical power in addition to the normal public service. As an alternative to such electrical elements, other approved methods that protect against ice accumulation shall be permitted. [*101*:11.9.2.4]

25.5.3 Air-Supported and Air-Inflated Structures.

25.5.3.1 General. In addition to the general provisions of 25.5.1, the requirements of 25.5.3 shall apply to air-supported and air-inflated structures. [*101*:11.9.3.1]

25.5.3.2 Pressurization (Inflation) System. The pressurization system shall consist of one or more operating blower units. The system shall include automatic control of auxiliary blower units to maintain the required operating pressure. Such equipment shall meet the following requirements:

(1) Blowers shall be powered by continuous-rated motors at the maximum power required.
(2) Blowers shall have personnel protection, such as inlet screens and belt guards.
(3) Blower systems shall be weather protected.
(4) Blower systems shall be equipped with backdraft check dampers.

(5) Not less than two blower units shall be provided, each of which has capacity to maintain full inflation pressure with normal leakage.
(6) Blowers shall be designed to be incapable of overpressurization.
(7) The auxiliary blower unit(s) shall operate automatically if there is any loss of internal pressure or if an operating blower unit becomes inoperative.
(8) The design inflation pressure and the capacity of each blower system shall be certified by a professional engineer.

[*101*:11.9.3.2]

25.5.3.3 Standby Power System.

25.5.3.3.1* A fully automatic standby power system shall be provided. The system shall be either an auxiliary engine generator set capable of running the blower system or a supplementary blower unit that is sized for 1 times the normal operating capacity and is powered by an internal combustion engine. [*101*:11.9.3.3.1]

25.5.3.3.2 The standby power system shall be fully automatic to ensure continuous inflation in the event of any failure of the primary power. The system shall be capable of operating continuously for a minimum of 4 hours. [*101*:11.9.3.3.2]

25.5.3.3.3 The sizing and capacity of the standby power system shall be certified by a professional engineer. [*101*:11.9.3.3.3]

25.5.4 Maintenance and Operation.

25.5.4.1 Instructions in both operation and maintenance shall be transmitted to the owner by the manufacturer of the tensioned-membrane, air-supported, or air-inflated structure. [*101*:11.9.4.1]

25.5.4.2 Annual inspection and required maintenance of each structure shall be performed to ensure safety conditions. At least biennially, the inspection shall be performed by a professional engineer, registered architect, or individual certified by the manufacturer. [*101*:11.9.4.2]

25.6 Temporary Membrane Structures.

25.6.1 Application.

25.6.1.1 Required Approval. Membrane structures designed to meet all the requirements of Section 25.6 shall be permitted to be used as temporary buildings subject to the approval of the AHJ. [*101*:11.10.1.2]

25.6.1.2 Alternative Requirements. Temporary tensioned-membrane structures shall be permitted to comply with Section 25.2 instead of Section 25.6. [*101*:11.10.1.3]

25.6.1.3 Roof Covering Classification. Roof membranes shall have a roof covering classification, as required by the applicable building codes, when tested in accordance with ASTM E108, *Standard Test Methods for Fire Tests of Roof Coverings*, or UL 790, *Standard Test Methods for Fire Tests of Roof Coverings*. [*101*:11.10.1.4]

25.6.1.4 Flame Propagation Performance.

25.6.1.4.1 All membrane structure fabric shall meet the flame propagation performance criteria contained in Test Method 2 of NFPA 701. [*101*:11.10.1.5.1]

25.6.1.4.2 One of the following shall serve as evidence that the fabric materials have the required flame propagation performance:
(1) The AHJ shall require a certificate or other evidence of acceptance by an organization acceptable to the AHJ.
(2) The AHJ shall require a report of tests made by other inspection authorities or organizations acceptable to the AHJ.

[*101*:11.10.1.5.2]

25.6.1.4.3 Where required by the AHJ, confirmatory field tests shall be conducted using test specimens from the original material, which shall have been affixed at the time of manufacture to the exterior of the structure. [*101*:11.10.1.5.3]

25.6.2 Fire Hazards.

25.6.2.1 The finished ground level enclosed by any temporary membrane structure, and the finished ground level for a reasonable distance but for not less than 10 ft (3050 mm) outside of such a structure, shall be cleared of all flammable or combustible material or vegetation that is not used for necessary support equipment. The clearing work shall be accomplished to the satisfaction of the AHJ prior to the erection of such a structure. The premises shall be kept free from such flammable or combustible materials during the period for which the premises are used by the public. [*101*:11.10.2.1]

25.6.2.2 Where prohibited by the AHJ, smoking shall not be permitted in any temporary membrane structure. [*101*:11.10.2.2]

25.6.3 Fire-Extinguishing Equipment. Portable fire-extinguishing equipment of approved types shall be furnished and maintained in temporary membrane structures in such quantity and in such locations as directed by the AHJ. [*101*:11.10.3]

25.6.4 Tensioned-Membrane Structures.

25.6.4.1 The design, materials, and construction of the building shall be based on plans and specifications prepared by a licensed architect or engineer knowledgeable in tensioned-membrane construction. [*101*:11.10.4.1]

25.6.4.2 Material loads and strength shall be based on physical properties of the materials verified and certified by an approved testing laboratory. [*101*:11.10.4.2]

25.6.4.3 The membrane roof for structures in climates subject to freezing temperatures and ice buildup shall be composed of two layers separated by an air space through which heated air can be moved to guard against ice accumulation. As an alternative to the two layers, other approved methods that protect against ice accumulation shall be permitted. [*101*:11.10.4.3]

25.6.4.4 Roof drains shall be equipped with electrical elements to protect against ice buildup that can prevent the drains from functioning. Such heating elements shall be served by on-site standby electrical power in addition to the normal public service. As an alternative to such electrical elements, other approved methods that protect against ice accumulation shall be permitted. [*101*:11.10.4.4]

25.6.5 Air-Supported and Air-Inflated Structures.

25.6.5.1 General. In addition to the general provisions of 25.6.1, the requirements of 25.6.5 shall apply to air-supported and air-inflated structures. [*101*:11.10.5.1]

25.6.5.2 Pressurization (Inflation) System. The pressurization system shall consist of one or more operating blower units. The system shall include automatic control of auxiliary blower units to maintain the required operating pressure. Such equipment shall meet the following requirements:

(1) Blowers shall be powered by continuous-rated motors at the maximum power required.
(2) Blowers shall have personnel protection, such as inlet screens and belt guards.
(3) Blower systems shall be weather protected.
(4) Blower systems shall be equipped with backdraft check dampers.
(5) Not less than two blower units shall be provided, each of which has capacity to maintain full inflation pressure with normal leakage.
(6) Blowers shall be designed to be incapable of overpressurization.
(7) The auxiliary blower unit(s) shall operate automatically if there is any loss of internal pressure or if an operating blower unit becomes inoperative.
(8) The design inflation pressure and the capacity of each blower system shall be certified by a professional engineer.

[*101*:11.10.5.2]

25.6.5.3 Standby Power System.

25.6.5.3.1 A fully automatic standby power system shall be provided. The system shall be either an auxiliary engine generator set capable of running the blower system or a supplementary blower unit that is sized for 1 times the normal operating capacity and is powered by an internal combustion engine. [*101*:11.10.5.3.1]

25.6.5.3.2 The standby power system shall be fully automatic to ensure continuous inflation in the event of any failure of the primary power. The system shall be capable of operating continuously for a minimum of 4 hours. [*101*:11.10.5.3.2]

25.6.5.3.3 The sizing and capacity of the standby power system shall be certified by a professional engineer. [*101*:11.10.5.3.3]

25.6.6 Maintenance and Operation.

25.6.6.1 Instructions in both operation and maintenance shall be transmitted to the owner by the manufacturer of the tensioned-membrane, air-supported, or air-inflated structure. [*101*:11.10.6.1]

25.6.6.2 Annual inspection and required maintenance of each structure shall be performed to ensure safety conditions. At least biennially, the inspection shall be performed by a professional engineer, registered architect, or individual certified by the manufacturer. [*101*:11.10.6.2]

Chapter 26 Laboratories Using Chemicals

26.1 General.

Δ **26.1.1** The handling or storage of chemicals in laboratory buildings, laboratory units, and laboratory work areas whether located above or below grade shall comply with this chapter. Construction and protection of new laboratories shall also comply with NFPA 45.

Δ **26.1.2** Chapter 26 shall apply to laboratory buildings, laboratory units, and laboratory work areas whether located above or below grade in which chemicals, as defined in NFPA 704 with one or more of the following hazard ratings, are handled or stored: health — 2, 3, or 4; flammability — 2, 3, or 4; or instability — 2, 3, or 4. *(See also Section B.2 of NFPA 45.)* [45:1.1.1]

Δ **26.1.3** Chapter 26 shall apply to all educational laboratory units and instructional laboratory units in which any quantity of chemicals, as defined in NFPA 704 with one or more of the following hazard ratings, is handled or stored: health — 2, 3, or 4: flammability — 2, 3, or 4; or instability — 2, 3, or 4. *(See also Section B.2 of NFPA 45).* [45:1.1.2]

Δ **26.1.4** With the exception of 26.1.3, Chapter 26 shall not apply to the following:

(1)* Laboratories for which the following conditions apply:
   (a) Laboratory units that contain less than or equal to 1 gal (4 L) of flammable or combustible liquid
   (b) Laboratory units that contain less than 75 scf (2.2 standard m^3) of flammable gas, not including piped-in low-pressure utility gas installed in accordance with NFPA 54
(2)* Pilot plants
(3) Laboratories that handle only chemicals with a hazard rating of 0 or 1 for all of the following: health, flammability, and instability, as defined by NFPA 704
(4) Laboratories that are primarily manufacturing plants
(5) Incidental testing facilities
(6) Physical, electronic, instrument, laser, or similar laboratories that use chemicals only for incidental purposes, such as cleaning
(7)* Hazards associated with radioactive materials, as covered by NFPA 801
(8) Laboratories that work only with explosive material, as covered by NFPA 495
(9) A laboratory work area containing an explosion hazard great enough to cause property damage outside that laboratory work area or injury outside that laboratory work area requiring medical treatment beyond first aid

[45:1.1.3]

Δ **26.1.5** Chapter 26 contains requirements, but not all-inclusive requirements, for handling and storage of chemicals where laboratory-scale operations are conducted and shall not cover the following:

(1) The special fire protection required when handling explosive materials *(See NFPA 495.)*
(2) The special fire protection required when handling radioactive materials

[45:1.1.6]

26.1.6 Plans and Procedures.

Δ **26.1.6.1*** Fire prevention, maintenance, and emergency action plans and procedures shall be established.

26.2 Permits. Permits, where required, shall comply with Section 1.13.

Chapter 27 Manufactured Home and Recreational Vehicle Sites

27.1 General.

Δ **27.1.1** Manufactured home and recreational vehicle sites shall meet the requirements of this chapter.

Δ **27.1.2** This chapter shall not apply to recreational vehicles as defined in NFPA 1192 or to park trailers as defined in RVIA/ANSI A.119.5, *Park Model Recreational Vehicle Standard.*

Δ **27.1.3** This chapter shall not cover the design of recreational vehicles or other forms of camping units or the operational and maintenance practices of recreational vehicle parks and campgrounds.

N **27.1.4** Permits, where required, shall comply with Section 1.13.

27.2 Manufactured Home Sites. The fire safety requirements for the installation of manufactured homes and manufactured home sites, including accessory buildings, structures, and communities, shall comply with NFPA 501A.

27.3 Recreational Vehicle Parks and Campgrounds. The construction of recreational vehicle parks and campgrounds that offer temporary living sites for use by recreational vehicles and camping units shall comply with NFPA 1194.

Chapter 28 Marinas, Boatyards, Marine Terminals, Piers, and Wharves

28.1 Marinas, Boatyards, and Other Recreational Marine Facilities.

28.1.1 Scope. The construction and operation of marinas, boatyards, yacht clubs, boat condominiums, docking facilities associated with residential condominiums, multiple-docking facilities at multiple-family residences, and all associated piers, docks, and floats shall comply with NFPA 303 and Section 28.1. [**303**:1.1]

28.1.1.1 Section 28.1 also applies to support facilities and structures used for construction, repair, storage, hauling and launching, or fueling of vessels if fire on a pier would pose an immediate threat to these facilities, or if a fire at a referenced facility would pose an immediate threat to a docking facility. [**303**:1.1.1]

28.1.1.2 Section 28.1 applies to marinas and facilities servicing small recreational and commercial craft, yachts, and other craft of not more than 300 gross tons. [**303**:1.1.2]

28.1.1.3 Section 28.1 is not intended to apply to a private, noncommercial docking facility constructed or occupied for the use of the owners or residents of the associated single-family dwelling. [**303**:1.1.3]

28.1.1.4 No requirement in this chapter is to be construed as reducing applicable building, fire, and electrical codes. [**303**:1.1.4]

N **28.1.1.5** Permits, where required, shall comply with Section 1.13.

28.1.2 Fire Protection.

28.1.2.1 Portable Fire Extinguishers.

28.1.2.1.1 Placement.

28.1.2.1.1.1 Selection and installation of portable fire extinguishers shall be in accordance with NFPA 10 unless otherwise permitted by 28.1.2.1.1.1.1, 28.1.2.1.1.1.2, or 28.1.2.1.1.1.3. [**303**:6.1.1.1]

28.1.2.1.1.1.1 Placement of portable fire extinguishers on piers and along bulkheads where vessels are moored or are permitted to be moored shall meet the following criteria:

(1) Extinguishers listed for Class A, Class B, and Class C fires shall be installed at the pier/land intersection on a pier that exceeds 25 ft (7.62 m) in length.
(2) Additional fire extinguishers shall be placed such that the maximum travel distance to an extinguisher does not exceed 75 ft (22.86 m).
(3) Extinguishers shall be protected from environmental exposures to prevent damage and lack of operability.

[**303**:6.1.1.1.1]

28.1.2.1.1.1.2 All extinguishers installed on piers shall meet the rating requirements set forth in NFPA 10 for ordinary hazard. [**303**:6.1.1.1.2]

28.1.2.1.1.1.3 Fuel-Dispensing Areas.

(A) Portable fire extinguishers that meet the minimum requirements of NFPA 10 for extra hazard shall be installed on two sides of a fuel-dispensing area. [**303**:6.1.1.1.3.1]

(B) On piers or bulkheads where long fueling hoses are installed for fueling vessels, additional extinguishers installed on piers or bulkheads shall meet the requirements of NFPA 10 for extra hazard and 28.1.2.1.1.1.1 of this *Code*. [**303**:6.1.1.1.3.2]

28.1.2.1.2 Visibility and Identification. All portable fire extinguishers shall be clearly visible and marked. [**303**:6.1.2]

28.1.2.2* Fixed Fire-Extinguishing Systems.

28.1.2.2.1 Buildings on Piers and Covered Piers.

28.1.2.2.1.1 Buildings in excess of 500 ft² (46 m²) that are constructed on piers and covered piers in excess of 5000 ft² (460 m²) shall be protected by an approved automatic fire-extinguishing system unless otherwise permitted by 28.1.2.2.1.2 or 28.1.2.2.1.3. [**303**:6.2.1.1]

28.1.2.2.1.2 Buildings of Type I or Type II construction, as specified in NFPA 220 and without combustible contents, shall not be required to be protected by an automatic fire-extinguishing system. [**303**:6.2.1.2]

28.1.2.2.1.3* Existing facilities shall not be required to be protected by an automatic fire-extinguishing system where acceptable to the AHJ. [**303**:6.2.1.3]

28.1.2.2.2* Buildings Exceeding 5000 ft² (465 m²).

28.1.2.2.2.1 Marina and boatyard buildings in excess of 5000 ft² (465 m²) in total area shall be protected by an approved automatic fire-extinguishing system unless otherwise permitted by 28.1.2.2.2.2. [**303**:6.2.2.1]

28.1.2.2.2.2* Existing facilities shall not be required to be protected by an automatic fire-extinguishing system where acceptable to the AHJ. [**303**:6.2.2.2]

28.1.2.2.3 Combustible Piers and Substructures.

28.1.2.2.3.1 Combustible piers and substructures in excess of 25 ft (7.62 m) in width or in excess of 5000 ft^2 (465 m^2) in area, or within 30 ft (9.14 m) of other structures or superstructures required to be so protected, shall be protected in accordance with Section 4.3 of NFPA 307 unless otherwise permitted by 28.1.2.2.3.2, 28.1.2.2.3.3, or 28.1.2.2.3.4. [**303**:6.2.3.1]

28.1.2.2.3.2 Fixed piers shall not be required to be protected as specified in 28.1.2.2.3.1 where the vertical distance from the surface of mean high water level to the underside of the pier surface does not exceed 36 in. (914 mm). [**303**:6.2.3.2]

28.1.2.2.3.3 Floating piers shall not be required to be protected as specified in 28.1.2.2.3.1 where the vertical distance from the surface of the water to the underside of the pier surface does not exceed 36 in. (914 mm). [**303**:6.2.3.3]

28.1.2.2.3.4* Existing facilities shall not be required to be protected by an automatic fire-extinguishing system where acceptable to the AHJ. [**303**:6.2.3.4]

28.1.2.2.4 Indoor Rack Storage.

28.1.2.2.4.1* Where boats are stored on multilevel racks in buildings, an approved automatic fire-extinguishing system shall be installed throughout the building unless otherwise permitted by 28.1.2.2.4.2 or 28.1.2.2.4.3. [**303**:6.2.4.1]

28.1.2.2.4.2 An automatic fire-extinguishing system shall not be required for buildings less than 5000 ft^2 (465 m^2) having multilevel racks where provided with one of the following:

(1) An automatic fire detection and alarm system supervised by a central station complying with *NFPA 72*
(2) An automatic fire detection and alarm system supervised by a local protective signaling system complying with *NFPA 72* if the provisions of 28.1.2.2.4.2(1) are not technically feasible
(3) A full-time watch service if the provisions of 28.1.2.2.4.2(1) are not technically feasible

[**303**:6.2.4.2]

28.1.2.2.4.3* Existing facilities shall not be required to be protected by an automatic fire-extinguishing system where acceptable to the AHJ. [**303**:6.2.4.3]

28.1.2.2.5* An approved water supply shall be provided within 100 ft (30 m) of the pier/land intersection or fire department connection serving fire protection systems. [**303**:6.2.5]

28.1.2.2.6 Access between water supplies and pier/land intersections or fire department connections shall be by roadway acceptable to the AHJ. [**303**:6.2.6]

28.1.2.3* Fire Standpipe Systems.

28.1.2.3.1 Class I standpipe systems shall be provided for piers, bulkheads, and buildings where the hose lay distance from the fire apparatus exceeds 150 ft (45 m). [**303**:6.3.1]

28.1.2.3.2 Class I standpipes shall be provided in all buildings used for the rack storage of boats. [**303**:6.3.2]

28.1.2.3.3 Standpipe systems, where installed, shall be in accordance with NFPA 14, except for the provisions identified in 28.1.2.3.4. [**303**:6.3.3]

28.1.2.3.4 Hose racks, hoses, and standpipe cabinets shall not be required on piers and bulkheads. [**303**:6.3.4]

28.1.2.4 In-Out Dry Storage and Rack Storage.

28.1.2.4.1 Fire protection shall be provided as described in either 28.1.2.4.1.1 or 28.1.2.4.1.2. [**303**:6.4.1]

28.1.2.4.1.1 A Class II standpipe system shall be designed and installed in accordance with NFPA 14. [**303**:6.4.1.1]

28.1.2.4.1.2* Portable fire extinguishers shall be provided in accordance with NFPA 10. [**303**:6.4.1.2]

28.1.2.4.2 The fire protection provided in 28.1.2.4.1 shall be capable of reaching all boats, including those on the highest rack. [**303**:6.4.2]

28.1.2.5 Hydrants and Water Supplies. Hydrants and water supplies for fire protection in marinas and boatyards shall be provided in accordance with this *Code*, NFPA 13, NFPA 14, and NFPA 24. [**303**:6.5]

28.1.2.6* Exposure Protection. The hazards of fire exposure and appropriate protection methods shall be evaluated. [**303**:6.7]

28.1.2.7 Transmittal of Fire Emergency.

28.1.2.7.1 All marinas and boatyards shall have a means to notify the fire department rapidly in the event of an emergency. [**303**:6.8.1]

28.1.2.7.2 If a telephone is used to meet 28.1.2.8.1, the telephone installation shall meet the following criteria::

(1) The telephone shall be available for use at all times.
(2) Use of the telephone for emergency notification shall not require the use of a card, coin, or currency.
(3)* The street address of the facility and the emergency telephone number(s) shall be displayed prominently on a sign at the telephone.

[**303**:6.8.2]

28.1.2.8 Automatic Fire Detectors.

28.1.2.8.1 Automatic fire detection devices and installation shall be in accordance with *NFPA 72*. [**303**:6.9.1]

28.1.2.8.2 Automatic fire detectors shall be installed in the following interior or covered locations unless those locations are protected by a fixed automatic sprinkler system installed in accordance with NFPA 13:

(1) Rooms containing combustible storage or goods
(2) Rooms containing flammable liquid storage or use
(3) Rooms containing battery storage or maintenance
(4) Rooms containing paint and solvent storage or use
(5) Areas used for enclosed or covered storage of vessels
(6) Areas used for enclosed or covered maintenance of vessels
(7) Areas used for public assembly, dining, or lodging
(8) Kitchens and food preparation areas
(9) Dust bins and collectors
(10) Inside trash storage areas
(11) Rooms used for storing janitor supplies or linens
(12) Laundry rooms

(13) Furnace rooms
[**303**:6.9.2]

28.1.3 Berthing and Storage.

28.1.3.1 Wet Storage and Berthing.

28.1.3.1.1 Each berth shall be arranged such that a boat occupying the berth can be removed in an emergency without the necessity of moving other boats. [**303**:7.1.1]

28.1.3.1.2 Access to all piers, floats, and wharves shall be provided for municipal fire-fighting equipment. [**303**:7.1.2]

28.1.3.1.3* Electrical lighting shall be provided to ensure adequate illumination of all exterior areas, piers, and floats. [**303**:7.1.3]

28.1.3.1.4 Electrical lighting shall not interfere with navigation or aids to navigation. [**303**:7.1.4]

28.1.3.1.5 Only listed 120/240 V ac electrical equipment shall be operated unattended. [**303**:7.1.5]

28.1.3.2 Dry Storage.

28.1.3.2.1 General.

28.1.3.2.1.1 Heaters.

28.1.3.2.1.1.1 The use of portable heaters in boat storage areas shall be prohibited except where necessary to accomplish repairs. [**303**:7.2.1.1.1]

28.1.3.2.1.1.2 Portable heaters used in accordance with 28.1.3.2.1.1.1 shall be used only when personnel are in attendance. [**303**:7.2.1.1.2]

28.1.3.2.1.1.3 Open flame heaters shall not be used in boat storage areas. [**303**:7.2.1.1.3]

28.1.3.2.1.2 Ladders long enough to reach the deck of any stored boat shall be provided and readily accessible. [**303**:7.2.1.2]

28.1.3.2.1.3 The use of blow torches or flammable paint remover shall be prohibited unless permitted by 8.7.1 of NFPA 303. [**303**:7.2.1.3]

28.1.3.2.1.4 The use of gasoline or other flammable solvents for cleaning purposes shall be prohibited. [**303**:7.2.1.4]

28.1.3.2.1.5 Where a boat is to be dry-stored for the season or stored indoors for an extended period of time, such as while awaiting repairs, the following precautions shall be taken:

(1) The vessel shall be inspected for any hazardous materials or conditions that could exist, and corrective action shall be taken.
(2) Liquefied petroleum gas (LPG) and compressed natural gas (CNG) cylinders, reserve supplies of stove alcohol or kerosene, and charcoal shall be removed from the premises or stored in a separate, designated safe area.
(3) All portable fuel tanks shall be removed from the premises or emptied and, if emptied, the cap shall be removed and the tank left open to the atmosphere.
(4)* Permanently installed fuel tanks shall be stored at least 95 percent full.

[**303**:7.2.1.5]

28.1.3.2.1.6 No unattended electrical equipment shall be in use aboard boats. [**303**:7.2.1.6]

28.1.3.2.1.7 All storage areas shall be routinely raked, swept, or otherwise policed to prevent the accumulation of rubbish. [**303**:7.2.1.7]

28.1.3.2.1.8 Fire Department Access.

28.1.3.2.1.8.1 Access to boats stored outside shall be such that the hose-lay distance from the fire apparatus to any portion of the boat shall not exceed 150 ft (45 m). [**303**:7.2.1.8.1]

28.1.3.2.1.8.2 Access to buildings in which boats are stored shall be such that the hose-lay distance from the fire apparatus to all exterior portions of the building shall not exceed 150 ft (45 m). [**303**:7.2.1.8.2]

28.1.3.2.1.8.3 Wet standpipe systems shall be permitted to be used to meet the requirement in 28.1.3.2.1.8.1 or 28.1.3.2.1.8.2. [**303**:7.2.1.8.3]

28.1.3.2.2 Indoors.

28.1.3.2.2.1 When work is being carried out onboard a vessel in an unsprinklered storage building, management shall require an inspection of the vessel at the end of the day to ensure that no hazards resulting from the day's work are present. [**303**:7.2.2.1]

28.1.3.2.2.2 If a guard is employed, vessels addressed in 28.1.3.2.2.1 shall be included in the regular rounds. [**303**:7.2.2.2]

28.1.3.2.2.3 Class I flammable liquids shall not be stored in an indoor boat storage area. [**303**:7.2.2.3]

28.1.3.2.2.4 Work performed on boats stored indoors shall be performed by qualified personnel. [**303**:7.2.2.4]

28.1.3.2.2.5 Facility management shall maintain control over all personnel access to storage facilities and boats stored indoors. [**303**:7.2.2.5]

28.1.3.2.3 In-Out Dry Storage and Rack Storage.

28.1.3.2.3.1 Where boats are stored either inside or outside in single- or multiple-level racks, those boats shall have unimpeded vehicular access at one end and equipment shall be available to remove any stored boat. [**303**:7.2.3.1]

28.1.3.2.3.2 Where boats are stored in multilevel racks, either inside or outside, for seasonal storage or for in-out operation, the following precautions shall be taken:

(1) Drain plugs shall be removed (in sprinklered buildings).
(2) Batteries shall be disconnected or the master battery switch turned off.
(3) Fuel tank valves shall be closed.
(4) For seasonal storage, the requirements of 28.1.3.2.1 shall apply.

[**303**:7.2.3.2]

28.1.3.2.3.3 Repairs to boats that are on racks or that are inside an in-out dry storage building shall be prohibited. [**303**:7.2.3.3]

28.1.3.2.3.4 Portable power lines, such as drop cords, shall be prohibited from use on boats in an in-out dry storage building. [**303**:7.2.3.4]

28.1.3.2.3.5 The charging of batteries shall be prohibited in an in-out dry storage building. [**303**:7.2.3.5]

28.1.3.2.4* Battery Storage. Where due to size and weight the removal of batteries for storage or charging is impractical, batteries shall be permitted to remain onboard provided the following conditions are met:

(1) The battery compartment is arranged to provide adequate ventilation.
(2) A listed battery charger is used to provide a suitable charge.
(3) The power connection to the charger consists of a three-wire cord of not less than No. 14 AWG conductors connected to a source of 110 V to 125 V single-phase current, with a control switch and approved circuit protection device designed to trip at not more than 125 percent of the rated amperage of the charger.
(4) There is no connection on the load side of the charger to any other device except the battery, and the boat battery switch is turned off.
(5) The battery is properly connected to the charger, and the grounding conductor effectively grounds the charger enclosure.
(6) Unattended battery chargers are checked at intervals not exceeding 8 hours while in operation.

[**303:**7.2.4]

28.1.4 Operational Hazards.

28.1.4.1* Conditions on Individual Boats.

28.1.4.1.1 The management shall have an inspection made of each boat received for major repair or storage as soon as practicable after arrival of the boat and before commencement of any work aboard. [**303:**8.1.1]

28.1.4.1.2 The inspection required in 28.1.4.1.1 shall include the following determinations:

(1) Presence of combustible or flammable vapors in any compartment
(2) General maintenance and cleanliness, and location of any combustible or flammable materials that require removal or protection for the safe accomplishment of the particular work involved
(3) Quantity, type, and apparent condition of fire-extinguishing equipment onboard
(4) Listed and appropriate shore power inlet(s) and ship-to-shore cable(s), when present

[**303:**8.1.2]

28.1.4.1.3 The management shall, as a condition to accepting a boat received for major repair or storage, require the owner to correct any inadequacies found in 28.1.4.1.2 or to authorize management to do so. [**303:**8.1.3]

28.1.4.2 General Precautions.

28.1.4.2.1 Smoking in the working area shall be prohibited. [**303:**8.2.1]

28.1.4.2.2 Loose combustibles in the area of any hazardous work shall be removed. [**303:**8.2.2]

28.1.4.2.3 Unprotected battery terminals shall be covered to prevent inadvertent shorting from dropped tools or otherwise, and the ungrounded battery lead shall be disconnected. [**303:**8.2.3]

28.1.4.2.4 Personnel employed in the removal or installation of storage batteries shall be qualified. [**303:**8.2.4]

28.1.4.2.5 Where electric service is provided to boats in storage, the receptacle providing the power shall be protected with a ground-fault circuit-interrupter. [**303:**8.2.5]

28.1.4.2.6 The marina or boatyard operator shall post in a prominent location, or provide to boat operators using a marina or boatyard for mooring, repair, servicing, or storage, a list of safe operating procedures containing at least the following information:

(1) A prohibition against the use of any form of hibachis, charcoal, wood, or gas-type portable cooking equipment, except in specifically authorized areas that are not on the docks, on boats in the berthing area, or near flammables
(2) Procedures for disposal of trash
(3) Designation of nonsmoking areas
(4) Location of fire extinguishers and hoses
(5) Procedures for turning in a fire alarm
(6)* Fueling procedures
(7)* Emergency contact information and marina address for notifying emergency services to respond to an incident

[**303:**8.2.6]

28.1.4.2.7 The information on fueling procedures referred to in 28.1.4.2.6(6) shall include at least the following information:

(1) Procedures before fueling
  (a) Stop all engines and auxiliaries
  (b) Shut off all electricity, open flames, and heat sources
  (c) Check bilges for fuel vapors
  (d) Extinguish all smoking materials
  (e) Close access fittings and openings that could allow fuel vapors to enter the boat's enclosed spaces
  (f) Remove all personnel from the boat except the person handling the fueling hose
(2) Procedures during fueling
  (a) Maintain nozzle contact with fill pipe
  (b) Attend fuel-filling nozzle at all times
  (c) Wipe up spills immediately
  (d) Avoid overfilling
(3) Procedures after fueling and before starting engine
  (a) Inspect bilges for leakage or fuel odors
  (b) Ventilate until odors are removed

[**303:**8.2.7]

28.2 Marine Terminals, Piers, and Wharves.

28.2.1 Section 28.2 shall apply to marine terminals as defined herein. Special use piers and wharf structures that are not marine terminals, such as public assembly, residential, business, or recreational occupancies that differ in design and construction from cargo handling piers, require special consideration. The general principles of NFPA 307 for the construction and fire protection of piers and wharves shall be applicable to such structures and shall comply with NFPA 307 and Section 28.2.

28.2.1.1 Marine terminals, piers, and wharves shall comply with 28.1.4.2.7.

28.2.2* Section 28.2 shall not apply to marinas and boatyards. *(See Section 28.1.)* [**307:**1.3.2]

28.2.3 Section 28.2 shall not apply to the handling of the following:

(1)* Flammable or combustible liquids in bulk (*See Chapter 66.*)

(2)* Liquefied gases in bulk *(See Chapter 69.)* [**307**:1.3.3]

28.2.4 Nothing in Section 28.2 shall supersede any of the regulations of governmental or other regulatory authority. [**307**:1.1.2]

28.3 Construction, Conversion, Repair, and Lay-Up of Vessels.

28.3.1* The construction, conversion, repair, or lay-up of vessels shall comply with NFPA 312 and Section 28.3.

28.3.2 Nothing in Section 28.3 shall be construed as prohibiting the immediate dry-docking of a vessel whose safety is imperiled, as by being in a sinking condition or by being seriously damaged. [**312**:1.2.2]

28.3.3 In such cases, all necessary precautionary measures shall be taken as soon as practicable. [**312**:1.2.3]

28.3.4 Section 28.3 shall not apply to situations where it is in conflict with or superseded by requirements of any government regulatory agency. [**312**:1.1.2]

Chapter 29 Parking Garages

29.1 General.

29.1.1 The protection of new and existing parking garages, as well as the control of hazards in open parking structures, enclosed parking structures, and basement and underground parking structures shall comply with this chapter and Section 42.8 of NFPA *101*.

29.1.2 Construction and protection of new parking garages shall also comply with NFPA 88A.

29.1.3 The storage of self-propelled vehicles powered by GH_2 or LH_2 shall be in accordance with NFPA 2.

29.1.4 Chapter 29 shall not apply to parking garages in one- and two-family dwellings.

Chapter 30 Motor Fuel Dispensing Facilities and Repair Garages

30.1 Motor Fuel Dispensing Facilities.

30.1.1 Application.

30.1.1.1 Motor fuel dispensing facilities, marine/motor fuel dispensing facilities, motor fuel dispensing facilities located inside buildings, and fleet vehicle motor fuel dispensing facilities shall comply with Sections 30.1 and 30.4 and NFPA 30A. Hydrogen fueling facilities shall comply with NFPA 2.

30.1.1.2 This chapter shall not apply to refueling operations. *(For refueling operations, see Chapter 42.)*

30.1.1.3 Permits. Permits, where required, shall comply with Section 1.13.

30.1.2 Occupancy Classification. The occupancy classification of a motor fuel dispensing facility that is located inside a building or structure shall be a special purpose industrial occupancy as defined in NFPA *101* or as determined in accordance with the adopted building code. [**30A**:7.3.1]

30.1.3 Means of Egress. In a motor fuel dispensing facility that is located inside a building or structure, the required number, location, and construction of means of egress shall meet all applicable requirements for special purpose industrial occupancies, as set forth in NFPA *101* or as determined in accordance with the adopted building code. [**30A**:7.3.3]

30.1.4 Drainage. Where Class I or Class II liquids are dispensed, provisions shall be made to prevent spilled liquids from flowing into the interior of buildings. Such provisions shall be made by grading driveways, raising door sills, or other equally effective means. [**30A**:7.3.4]

30.1.5 Fixed Fire Protection.

30.1.5.1* For an unattended, self-serve, motor fuel dispensing facility, additional fire protection shall be provided where required by the AHJ. [**30A**:7.3.5.1]

30.1.5.2 Where required, an automatic fire suppression system shall be installed in accordance with the appropriate NFPA standard, manufacturers' instructions, and the listing requirements of the systems. [**30A**:7.3.5.2]

30.1.6 Fuel Dispensing Areas Inside Buildings.

30.1.6.1 The fuel dispensing area shall be separated from all other portions of the building by walls, partitions, floors, and floor–ceiling assemblies having a fire resistance rating of not less than 2 hours. [**30A**:7.3.6.1]

Δ **30.1.6.2** Interior finish shall be of noncombustible materials or of approved limited-combustible materials, as defined in this *Code*. [**30A**:7.3.6.2]

30.1.6.3 Door and window openings in fire-rated interior walls shall be provided with listed fire doors having a fire protection rating of not less than 1½ hours. Doors shall be self-closing. They shall be permitted to remain open during normal operations if they are designed to close automatically in a fire emergency by means of listed closure devices. Fire doors shall be installed in accordance with NFPA 80. They shall be kept unobstructed at all times. [**30A**:7.3.6.3]

30.1.6.4 Openings for ducts in fire-rated interior partitions and walls shall be protected by listed fire dampers. Openings for ducts in fire-rated floor or floor–ceiling assemblies shall be protected with enclosed shafts. Enclosure of shafts shall be with wall or partition assemblies having a fire resistance rating of not less than 2 hours. Openings for ducts into enclosed shafts shall be protected with listed fire dampers. [**30A**:7.3.6.4]

30.1.6.5 The fuel dispensing area shall be located at street level, with no dispenser located more than 50 ft (15 m) from the vehicle exit to, or entrance from, the outside of the building. [**30A**:7.3.6.5]

30.1.6.6 Number of Vehicles Simultaneously Served.

30.1.6.6.1 The fuel dispensing area shall be limited to that required to serve not more than four vehicles at one time. [**30A**:7.3.6.6.1]

30.1.6.6.2 Where only Class II and Class III liquids are dispensed at fleet vehicle motor fuel dispensing facilities, the number of vehicles serviced at any one time shall be permitted to be increased to 12. [**30A**:7.3.6.6.2]

30.1.6.7* Mechanical Exhaust System.

30.1.6.7.1 A mechanical exhaust system that serves only the fuel dispensing area shall be provided when two or more sides of the dispensing area are not open to the building exterior. [**30A:**7.3.6.7.1]

30.1.6.7.2 This system shall meet all of the following requirements:

(1) The system shall be interlocked with the dispensing system so that airflow is established before any dispensing device can operate. Failure of airflow shall automatically shut down the dispensing system.
(2) The exhaust system shall be designed to provide air movement across all portions of the floor of the fuel dispensing area and to prevent the flowing of ignitible vapors beyond the dispensing area.
(3) Exhaust inlet ducts shall not be less than 3 in. (76 mm) or more than 12 in. (305 mm) above the floor. Exhaust ducts shall not be located in floors or penetrate the floor of the dispensing area. Exhaust ducts shall discharge to a safe location outside the building.
(4) The exhaust system shall provide ventilation at a rate of not less than 1 ft^3/min/ft^2 (0.3 m^3/min/m^2) of floor area, based on the fuel dispensing area.
(5) The exhaust system shall meet all applicable requirements of NFPA 91.

[**30A:**7.3.6.7.2]

30.1.6.8 The floor of the dispensing area shall be liquidtight. Where Class I liquids are dispensed, provisions shall be made to prevent spilled liquids from flowing out of the fuel dispensing area and into other areas of the building by means of curbs, scuppers, special drainage systems, or other means acceptable to the AHJ. [**30A:**7.3.6.8]

30.1.6.9* Oil drainage systems shall be equipped with approved oil/water traps or separators if they connect to public sewers or discharge into public waterways. [**30A:**7.3.6.9]

30.2 Repair Garages for Vehicles Powered by Flammable and Combustible Liquids.

30.2.1 Application. The construction and protection of, as well as the control of hazards in, garages used for major repair and maintenance of motorized vehicles and any sales and servicing facilities associated therewith shall comply with Sections 30.2 and 30.4 and NFPA 30A.

30.2.1.1 Permits. Permits, where required, shall comply with Section 1.13.

Δ **30.2.2 Occupancy Classification.** The occupancy classification of a repair garage shall be a special purpose industrial occupancy as defined in NFPA *101* or as determined in accordance with the adopted building code. [**30A:**7.4.1]

Δ **30.2.3 Means of Egress.** In a repair garage, the required number, location, and construction of means of egress shall meet all applicable requirements for special purpose industrial occupancies, as set forth in NFPA *101* or as determined in accordance with the adopted building code. [**30A:**7.4.2]

30.2.4 Drainage. In areas of repair garages used for repair or servicing of vehicles, floor assemblies shall be constructed of noncombustible materials or, if combustible materials are used in the assembly, they shall be surfaced with approved, nonabsorbent, noncombustible material, except as indicated in 30.2.4.1. [**30A:**7.4.3]

30.2.4.1 Slip-resistant, nonabsorbent, interior floor finishes having a critical radiant flux not less than 9.87 Btu/in.^{2}-hr (0.45 W/cm^2), as determined by NFPA 253, shall be permitted. [**30A:**7.4.3.1]

30.2.4.2 Floors shall be liquidtight to prevent the leakage or seepage of liquids and shall be sloped to facilitate the movement of water, fuel, or other liquids to floor drains. [**30A:**7.4.3.2]

30.2.4.3 In areas of repair garages where vehicles are serviced, any floor drains shall be properly trapped and shall discharge through an oil/water separator to the sewer or to an outside vented sump. [**30A:**7.4.3.3]

30.2.5 Fixed Fire Protection. Automatic sprinkler protection installed in accordance with the requirements of Section 13.3 shall be provided throughout all buildings containing major repair garages, as herein defined, when any one of the following conditions exist:

(1) The building housing the major repair garage is two or more stories, including basements, and the aggregate area of the major repair garage exceeds 10,000 ft^2 (930 m^2).
(2) The major repair garage is one story and exceeds 12,000 ft^2 (1115 m^2).
(3) The major repair garage is servicing vehicles parked in the basement of the building.

[**30A:**7.4.5]

30.2.6 Gas Detection System. Repair garages used for repair of vehicle engine fuel systems fueled by nonodorized gases shall be provided with an approved flammable gas detection system. Gas detection systems in repair garages for hydrogen vehicles shall be in accordance with NFPA 2. [**30A:**7.4.6]

30.2.6.1 System Design.

30.2.6.1.1 The flammable gas detection system shall be calibrated to the types of fuels or gases used by the vehicles to be repaired. [**30A:**7.4.6.1.1]

30.2.6.1.2 The gas detection system shall be designed to activate when the level of flammable gas exceeds 25 percent of the lower flammable limit (LFL). [**30A:**7.4.6.1.2]

30.2.6.2 Operation. Activation of the gas detection system shall result in all of the following:

(1) Initiation of distinct audible and visual alarm signals in the repair garage
(2) Deactivation of all heating systems located in the repair garage
(3) Activation of the mechanical ventilation system, when the system is interlocked with gas detection

[**30A:**7.4.6.2]

30.2.6.3 Failure of the Gas Detection System. Failure of the gas detection system shall result in the deactivation of the heating system and activation of the mechanical ventilation system and, where the ventilation system is interlocked with gas detection, shall cause a trouble signal to sound in an approved location. [**30A:**7.4.6.3]

30.2.6.4 System Integrity. The circuits of the detection system required by 30.2.6 shall be monitored for integrity in accordance with *NFPA 72*. [**30A:**7.4.6.4]

30.2.7* Heating, Ventilating, and Air-Conditioning.

30.2.7.1* Forced air heating, air-conditioning, and ventilating systems serving a fuel dispensing area inside a building or a repair garage shall not be interconnected with any such systems serving other occupancies in the building. Such systems shall be installed in accordance with NFPA 90A. [**30A:7.5.1**]

30.2.7.2 Return air openings in areas of repair garages used for the repair or servicing of vehicles or in a fuel dispensing area shall be not less than 18 in. (455 mm) above floor level measured to the bottom of the openings. [**30A:7.5.2**]

30.2.7.3 Combined ventilation and heating systems shall not recirculate air from areas that are below grade level. [**30A:7.5.3**]

30.2.7.4* Exhaust duct openings shall be located so that they effectively remove vapor accumulations at floor level from all parts of the floor area. Where lighter-than-air gaseous fuel vehicles are repaired, exhaust duct openings shall be located so that they effectively remove vapor accumulations at the ceiling level. [**30A:7.5.4**]

30.2.8 Heat-Producing Appliances.

30.2.8.1 Heat-producing appliances shall be installed in accordance with the requirements of 30.2.8. They shall be permitted to be installed in the conventional manner except as provided in 30.2.8. [**30A:7.6.1**]

30.2.8.2 Listing and Restricted Locations.

30.2.8.2.1 Heat-producing appliances shall be listed for use in classified areas. [**30A:7.6.2.1**]

30.2.8.2.2 Solid fuel stoves, improvised furnaces, salamanders, and space heaters shall not be permitted in areas of repair garages used for repairing or servicing of vehicles or in a fuel dispensing area. [**30A:7.6.2.2**]

30.2.8.2.3 Heat-producing equipment in any lubrication room or service room where there is no dispensing or transferring of Class I or Class II liquids or LP-Gas, when installed in accordance with Chapter 7 of NFPA 30A, shall be listed. [**30A:7.6.2.3**]

30.2.8.3 Heat-producing appliances shall be permitted to be installed in a special room that is separated from areas that are classified as Division 1 or Division 2, in accordance with Chapter 8 of NFPA 30A, by walls that are constructed to prevent the transmission of vapors, that have a fire resistance rating of at least 1 hour, and that have no openings in the walls that lead to a classified area within 8 ft (2.4 m) of the floor. Specific small openings through the wall, such as for piping and electrical conduit, shall be permitted, provided the gaps and voids are filled with a fire-resistant material to resist transmission of vapors. All air for combustion purposes shall be taken from outside the building. This room shall not be used for storage of combustible materials, except for fuel storage as permitted by the standards referenced in 30.2.8.9. [**30A:7.6.3**]

30.2.8.4 Heat-producing appliances using gas or oil fuel shall be permitted to be installed in a lubrication or service room where there is no dispensing or transferring of Class I liquids, including the open draining of automotive gasoline tanks, provided the bottom of the combustion chamber is at least 18 in. (455 mm) above the floor and the appliances are protected from physical damage. [**30A:7.6.4**]

30.2.8.5 Heat-producing appliances using gas or oil fuel listed for use in garages shall be permitted to be installed in lubrication rooms, service rooms, or fuel dispensing areas where Class I liquids are dispensed or transferred, provided the equipment is installed at least 8 ft (2.4 m) above the floor. [**30A:7.6.5**]

30.2.8.6* Where major repairs are conducted on lighter-than-air-fueled vehicles, open flame heaters or heating equipment with exposed surfaces having a temperature in excess of 750°F (399°C) shall not be permitted in areas subject to ignitible concentrations of gas. [**30A:7.6.6**]

30.2.8.7 Electrical heat-producing appliances shall meet the requirements of Chapter 8 of NFPA 30A. [**30A:7.6.7**]

30.2.8.8 Fuels used shall be of the type and quality specified by the manufacturer of the heating appliance. Crankcase drainings shall not be used in oil-fired appliances, unless the appliances are specifically approved for such use. [**30A:7.6.8**]

30.2.8.9 Heat-producing appliances shall be installed to meet the requirements of NFPA 31, NFPA 54, NFPA 82, NFPA 90A, and NFPA 211, as applicable, except as hereinafter specifically provided. [**30A:7.6.9**]

30.3 Repair Garages for Vehicles Powered by Alternate Fuels.

30.3.1 Hydrogen.

30.3.1.1 Repair garages servicing self-propelled vehicles powered by GH_2 or LH_2 shall comply with NFPA 2.

30.3.1.2 Means of Egress. In a repair garage, the required number, location, and construction of means of egress shall meet all applicable requirements for special purpose industrial occupancies, as set forth in NFPA *101* or as determined in accordance with the adopted building code. [**30A:7.4.2**]

30.3.2 LP-Gas-Fueled Vehicles.

30.3.2.1 General Construction Requirements. In repair garages, where CNG-fueled vehicles, LNG-fueled vehicles, or LP-Gas-fueled vehicles are repaired, all applicable requirements of NFPA 52 or NFPA 58, whichever is applicable, shall be met.

30.3.2.2 Means of Egress. In a repair garage, the required number, location, and construction of means of egress shall meet all applicable requirements for special purpose industrial occupancies, as set forth in NFPA *101*, or as determined in accordance with the adopted building code. [**30A:7.4.2**]

30.3.2.3 Drainage. In areas of repair garages used for repair or servicing of vehicles, floor assemblies shall be constructed of noncombustible materials or, if combustible materials are used in the assembly, they shall be surfaced with approved, nonabsorbent, noncombustible material, except as indicated in 30.3.2.3.1. [**30A:7.4.3**]

30.3.2.3.1 Slip-resistant, nonabsorbent, interior floor finishes having a critical radiant flux not less than 9.87 Btu/in.^{2}-hr (0.45 W/cm^2), as determined by NFPA 253, shall be permitted. [**30A:7.4.3.1**]

30.3.2.3.2 Floors shall be liquidtight to prevent the leakage or seepage of liquids and shall be sloped to facilitate the movement of water, fuel, or other liquids to floor drains. [**30A:7.4.3.2**]

30.3.2.3.3 In areas of repair garages where vehicles are serviced, any floor drains shall be properly trapped and shall discharge through an oil/water separator to the sewer or to an outside vented sump. [**30A:7.4.3.3**]

30.3.2.4 Pits, Belowgrade Work Areas, and Subfloor Work Areas for LP-Gas Powered Vehicles.

30.3.2.4.1 Pits, belowgrade work areas, and subfloor work areas used for lubrication, inspection, and minor automotive maintenance work shall comply with the provisions of this chapter, in addition to other applicable requirements of NFPA 30A. [**30A:**7.4.4.1]

30.3.2.4.2 Walls, floors, and structural supports shall be constructed of masonry, concrete, steel, or other approved noncombustible materials. [**30A:**7.4.4.2]

30.3.2.4.3 In pits, belowgrade work areas, and subfloor work areas, the required number, location, and construction of means of egress shall meet the requirements for special purpose industrial occupancies in Chapter 40 of NFPA *101* or as determined in accordance with the adopted building code. [**30A:**7.4.4.3]

30.3.2.4.4 Pits, belowgrade work areas, and subfloor work areas shall be provided with exhaust ventilation at a rate of not less than 1 ft^3/min/ft^2 (0.3 m^3/min/m^2) of floor area at all times that the building is occupied or when vehicles are parked in or over these areas. Exhaust air shall be taken from a point within 12 in. (0.3 m) of the floor. [**30A:**7.4.4.4]

30.3.2.5 Fixed Fire Protection. Automatic sprinkler protection installed in accordance with the requirements of Section 13.3 shall be provided throughout all buildings containing repair garages, as herein defined, where any one of the following conditions exist:

(1) The building housing the repair garage is two or more stories, including basements, and the aggregate area of the repair garage exceeds 10,000 ft^2 (930 m^2).
(2) The repair garage is one story and exceeds 12,000 ft^2 (1115 m^2).
(3) The repair garage is servicing vehicles parked in the basement of the building.

30.3.2.6 Gas Detection System. Repair garages used for repair of vehicle engine fuel systems fueled by nonodorized gases shall be provided with an approved flammable gas detection system. Gas detection systems in repair garages for hydrogen vehicles shall be in accordance with NFPA 2. [**30A:**7.4.6]

30.3.2.6.1 System Design.

30.3.2.6.1.1 The flammable gas detection system shall be calibrated to the types of fuels or gases used by the vehicles to be repaired. [**30A:**7.4.6.1.1]

30.3.2.6.1.2 The gas detection system shall be designed to activate when the level of flammable gas exceeds 25 percent of the lower flammable limit (LFL). [**30A:**7.4.6.1.2]

30.3.2.6.2 Operation. Activation of the gas detection system shall result in all of the following:

(1) Initiation of distinct audible and visual alarm signals in the repair garage
(2) Deactivation of all heating systems located in the repair garage
(3) Activation of the mechanical ventilation system, when the system is interlocked with gas detection

[**30A:**7.4.6.2]

30.3.2.6.3 Failure of the Gas Detection System. Failure of the gas detection system shall result in the deactivation of the heating system and activation of the mechanical ventilation system and, where the ventilation system is interlocked with gas detection, shall cause a trouble signal to sound in an approved location. [**30A:**7.4.6.3]

30.3.2.6.4 System Integrity. The circuits of the detection system required by 30.3.2.6 shall be monitored for integrity in accordance with *NFPA 72*. [**30A:**7.4.6.4]

30.3.2.7 Heating, Ventilating, and Air-Conditioning.

30.3.2.7.1 Forced air heating, air-conditioning, and ventilating systems serving a fuel dispensing area inside a building or a repair garage shall not be interconnected with any such systems serving other occupancies in the building. Such systems shall be installed in accordance with NFPA 90A. [**30A:**7.5.1]

30.3.2.7.2 Return air openings in areas of repair garages for vehicles powered by LP-Gas used for the repair or servicing of vehicles or in a fuel dispensing area shall be not less than 18 in. (455 mm) above floor level measured to the bottom of the openings.

30.3.2.7.3 Combined ventilation and heating systems shall not recirculate air from areas that are below grade level for repair garages for vehicles powered by LP-Gas.

30.3.2.7.4 For repair garages for vehicles powered by LP-Gas, exhaust duct openings shall be located so that they effectively remove vapor accumulations at floor level from all parts of the floor area. Where lighter-than-air gaseous fuel vehicles are repaired, exhaust duct openings shall be located so that they effectively remove vapor accumulations at the ceiling level.

30.3.2.8 Heat-Producing Appliances.

30.3.2.8.1 Heat-producing appliances shall be installed in accordance with the requirements of 30.3.2.8. They shall be permitted to be installed in the conventional manner except as provided in 30.3.2.8. [**30A:**7.6.1]

30.3.2.8.2 Listing and Restricted Locations.

30.3.2.8.2.1 Heat-producing appliances shall be listed for use in classified areas. [**30A:**7.6.2.1]

30.3.2.8.2.2 Solid fuel stoves, improvised furnaces, salamanders, and space heaters shall not be permitted in areas of repair garages used for repairing or servicing of vehicles or in a fuel dispensing area. [**30A:**7.6.2.2]

30.3.2.8.2.3 Heat-producing equipment in any lubrication room or service room where there is no dispensing or transferring of Class I or Class II liquids or LP-Gas, when installed in accordance with Chapter 7 of NFPA 30A, shall be listed. [**30A:**7.6.2.3]

30.3.2.8.3 Heat-producing appliances shall be permitted to be installed in a special room that is separated from areas that are classified as Division 1 or Division 2, in accordance with Chapter 8 of NFPA 30A, by walls that are constructed to prevent the transmission of vapors, that have a fire resistance rating of at least 1 hour, and that have no openings in the walls that lead to a classified area within 8 ft (2.4 m) of the floor. Specific small openings through the wall, such as for piping and electrical conduit, shall be permitted, provided the gaps and voids are filled with a fire-resistant material to resist transmission of vapors. All air for combustion purposes shall be taken from outside the building. This room shall not be used for storage of combustible materials, except for fuel storage as permitted by the standards referenced in 30.2.8.9. [**30A:**7.6.3]

30.3.2.8.4 Heat-producing appliances using gas or oil fuel shall be permitted to be installed in a lubrication or service room where there is no dispensing or transferring of Class I liquids, including the open draining of automotive gasoline tanks, provided the bottom of the combustion chamber is at least 18 in. (455 mm) above the floor and the appliances are protected from physical damage. [**30A:**7.6.4]

30.3.2.8.5 Heat-producing appliances using gas or oil fuel listed for use in garages shall be permitted to be installed in lubrication rooms, service rooms, or fuel dispensing areas where Class I liquids are dispensed or transferred, provided the equipment is installed at least 8 ft (2.4 m) above the floor. [**30A:**7.6.5]

30.3.2.8.6 Where major repairs are conducted on lighter-than-air-fueled vehicles, open flame heaters or heating equipment with exposed surfaces having a temperature in excess of 750°F (399°C) shall not be permitted in areas subject to ignitible concentrations of gas. [**30A:**7.6.6]

30.3.2.8.7 Electrical heat-producing appliances shall meet the requirements of Chapter 8 of NFPA 30A. [**30A:**7.6.7]

30.3.2.8.8 Fuels used shall be of the type and quality specified by the manufacturer of the heating appliance. Crankcase drainings shall not be used in oil-fired appliances, unless the appliances are specifically approved for such use. [**30A:**7.6.8]

30.3.2.8.9 Heat-producing appliances shall be installed to meet the requirements of NFPA 31, NFPA 54, NFPA 82, NFPA 90A, and NFPA 211, as applicable, except as hereinafter specifically provided. [**30A:**7.6.9]

30.3.3 CNG Fueled Vehicles and LNG Fueled Vehicles.

30.3.3.1 Applicability.

30.3.3.1.1 Paragraph 30.3.3 shall apply to the construction of new buildings, existing buildings, and portions of buildings serving as repair garages and repair areas for CNG and LNG vehicles. [**30A:**7.8.1.1]

30.3.3.1.2 Major and minor repair areas, as defined in 30.3.3.4 for CNG and LNG vehicle repair, shall meet the requirements of 30.3.3. [**30A:**7.8.1.2]

30.3.3.2 Occupancy Classification. The occupancy classification of a repair garage shall be a special purpose industrial occupancy as defined in NFPA *101* or as determined in accordance with the adopted building code. [**30A:**7.8.2]

30.3.3.3 Means of Egress. In a repair garage, the required number, location, and construction of means of egress shall meet all applicable requirements for special purpose industrial occupancies as set forth in NFPA *101* or as determined in accordance with the adopted building code. [**30A:**7.8.3]

30.3.3.4 Definition and Classification of Repair Areas Serving CNG and LNG Vehicle Repair.

30.3.3.4.1 Applicability. This section shall classify repair areas for CNG and LNG vehicles based on vehicle fuel system pressure status and permissible repair activities. [**30A:**7.8.4.1]

30.3.3.4.2 CNG Repair Area Classification. CNG vehicle repair areas shall be classified according to Table 30.3.3.4.2. [**30A:**7.8.4.2]

30.3.3.4.3 LNG Repair Area Classification. LNG vehicle repair areas shall be classified according to Table 30.3.3.4.3. [**30A:**7.8.4.3]

30.3.3.4.3.1 All vehicles upon first entering the facility shall have a tank pressure less than 65 percent of the tank maximum allowable working pressure (MAWP) as per the ASME *Boiler Pressure Vessel Code.* [**30A:**7.8.4.3.1]

30.3.3.4.3.2 High-pressure fuel systems shall be depressurized in accordance with the original equipment manufacturers' recommended maintenance procedures. [**30A:**7.8.4.3.2]

30.3.3.5 Drainage. In areas of repair garages used for repair or servicing of vehicles, floor assemblies shall be constructed of noncombustible materials or combustible materials. [**30A:**7.8.5]

30.3.3.5.1 If combustible materials are used in the floor assembly, they shall meet the provisions of 30.3.3.5.2. [**30A:**7.8.5.1]

Table 30.3.3.4.2 Repair Area Classification Assignment for CNG Vehicles

Vehicle Status – Fuel System Pressure (psig) (Not to Exceed 3600 psig)	Type of Repair	Minimum Repair Area Classification
≤500	Minor ongoing repair work or unattended vehicle storage while undergoing minor repair	Minor repair area
≤500	Major ongoing repair work or unattended vehicle storage while undergoing major repair	Major repair area
>500	Ongoing major or minor repair work or unattended vehicle storage while undergoing major or minor repair	Major repair area

[**30A:**Table 7.8.4.2]

△ **Table 30.3.3.4.3 Repair Area Classification Assignment for LNG Vehicles**

Vehicle Status			
Vehicle Fuel System Pressure Status (psig)	Vehicle Fuel System Liquid Content Status (Onboard Fuel)	Type of Vehicle Repair	Minimum Repair Area Classification
<65% of tank MAWP*	Any liquid volume	Minor ongoing repair work or unattended vehicle storage while undergoing minor repair	Minor (ongoing repair work) or major repair area (unattended vehicle storage)
		Major ongoing repair work or unattended vehicle storage while undergoing major repair	Major repair

*See 30.3.3.4.3.1 and 30.3.3.4.3.2.
[**30A:**Table 7.8.4.3]

30.3.3.5.2 Combustible materials used in the floor assembly shall be surfaced with approved, nonabsorbent, noncombustible material, except as indicated in 30.3.3.5.3. [**30A:**7.8.5.2]

30.3.3.5.3 Major repair garages and major repair areas serving LNG-fueled vehicles shall comply with the following:

(1) Floor drains shall be designed with consideration for spilled LNG entering the drain.
(2) Drains shall be designed to prevent excessive pressure buildup.
(3) Drains shall not allow the migration of gas or liquid to adjacent areas of the facility.

[**30A:**7.8.5.3]

30.3.3.5.4 Where installed, slip-resistant, nonabsorbent interior floor finishes shall have a critical radiant flux of not less than 9.87 Btu/in.^{2}-hr (0.45 W/cm^2), as determined by NFPA 253. [**30A:**7.8.5.4]

30.3.3.5.5 Floors shall be liquidtight to prevent the leakage or seepage of liquids and be sloped to facilitate the movement of water, fuel, or other liquids to floor drains. [**30A:**7.8.5.5]

30.3.3.5.6 In areas of repair garages where vehicles are serviced, floor drains shall be properly trapped and discharge through an oil/water separator either to the sewer or to an outside vented sump. [**30A:**7.8.5.6]

30.3.3.6 Construction Requirements of CNG and LNG Repair Areas. In repair garages or areas where CNG or LNG vehicles are repaired, all the applicable requirements of NFPA 52 shall be met. [**30A:**7.8.6]

30.3.3.7 Roofs and Ceilings — Major and Minor Repair Areas.

30.3.3.7.1 Roof and ceiling structures — and their accessories or attachments — shall be constructed to not impede the free movement of gas toward ventilation fans and gas sensor locations. [**30A:**7.8.7.1]

30.3.3.7.2* Where gas movement in roof and ceiling structures is impeded, provisions to mitigate gas holdup shall be made. [**30A:**7.8.7.2]

30.3.3.8 Walls and Partitions — Major and Minor Repair Areas.

30.3.3.8.1* Walls and partitions separating major repair areas from other repair spaces, including mechanical equipment rooms, shall be constructed to minimize the migration of natural gas to the other repair spaces. [**30A:**7.8.8.1]

30.3.3.8.2 Walls and partitions separating major repair areas from occupied spaces other than repair areas shall be gastight. [**30A:**7.8.8.2]

30.3.3.8.3 Walls and partitions shall have a fire resistance rating of not less than 1 hour as defined in NFPA *101* or as determined in accordance with the adopted building code. [**30A:**7.8.8.3]

30.3.3.8.4 Penetrations of gastight walls for ducts, pipes, conduits, and structural members shall be sealed to prevent migration of natural gas. [**30A:**7.8.8.4]

30.3.3.8.5 Hinged doors separating major repair areas from all other interior areas shall be in accordance with the following:

(1) Be self-closing and equipped with seals
(2) Not be equipped with baffles, louvres, or other penetrations

[**30A:**7.8.8.5]

30.3.3.8.6 Rollup doors separating major repair areas from all other interior areas shall remain closed when not in use. [**30A:**7.8.8.6]

30.3.3.8.7 Windows located in walls or partitions separating major repair areas from other spaces shall be self-closing or non-opening. [**30A:**7.8.8.7]

30.3.3.9 Pits, Belowgrade Work Areas, and Subfloor Work Areas.

△ **30.3.3.9.1** Pits, belowgrade work areas, and subfloor work areas in LNG vehicle repair areas shall meet the requirements of 30.3.2.4. [**30A:**7.8.9.1]

△ **30.3.3.9.2** Pits used in major repair garages for LNG vehicles shall have a continuous ventilation system as per Table 8.3.3 of NFPA 30A or a ventilation system that is initiated automatically upon the detection of a gas concentration of 25 percent of the lower flammable limit (LFL). [**30A:**7.8.9.2]

30.3.3.9.3 Pit ventilation systems shall have provisions for manual activation inside and outside of the pit. [**30A:**7.8.9.3]

30.3.3.9.4 Manual activation shall not defeat the automatic activation stipulated in 30.3.3.9.2. [**30A:**7.8.9.4]

30.3.3.10 Fixed Fire Protection. CNG and LNG vehicle repair areas shall meet the requirements of 30.2.5. [**30A:**7.8.10]

30.3.3.11 Gas Detection System. Repair areas and overnight vehicle storage areas in garages servicing CNG and LNG vehicles shall be provided with an approved flammable gas detection system. [**30A:**7.8.11]

30.3.3.11.1 System Design. The flammable gas detection system shall be calibrated to the types of fuels or gases used by the vehicles to be repaired. [**30A:**7.8.11.1]

30.3.3.11.1.1 The gas detection system shall be designed to activate when the level of flammable gas exceeds 25 percent of the LFL. [**30A:**7.8.11.1.1]

30.3.3.11.1.2 Gas detection shall also be provided in lubrication or chassis repair pits in buildings serving LNG vehicles. [**30A:**7.8.11.1.2]

Δ **30.3.3.11.2* Operation.** Activation of the gas detection system shall result in all of the following automatic actions:

(1) Initiation of distinct audible and visual alarm signals in the repair garage
(2) Deactivation of all heating systems located in the repair garage
(3) De-energization of all spark-producing electrical systems and components and motors within 18 in. (455 mm) of the ceiling
(4) Activation of the purge ventilation system as specified in 30.3.3.12.4

[**30A:**7.8.11.2]

30.3.3.11.3 Failure of the Gas Detection System.

30.3.3.11.3.1 Failure of the gas detection system shall result in the deactivation of the heating system and the activation of the mechanical ventilation system. [**30A:**7.8.11.3.1]

30.3.3.11.3.2 Where the ventilation system is interlocked with gas detection, failure of the gas detection system shall cause a trouble signal to sound in an approved location. [**30A:**7.8.11.3.2]

30.3.3.11.4 System Integrity. The circuits of the detection system required by 30.3.3.9 shall be monitored for integrity. [**30A:**7.8.11.4]

30.3.3.12 Heating, Ventilating, and Air Conditioning.

30.3.3.12.1 Heating, ventilating, and air conditioning of repair garages and repair areas for servicing CNG and LNG vehicles shall meet the requirements of 30.2.7.1, 30.2.7.2, and 30.2.7.3. [**30A:**7.8.12.1]

30.3.3.12.2 Exhaust duct openings shall be located so that they effectively remove vapor accumulation at floor level from all parts of the floor area. [**30A:**7.8.12.2]

Δ **30.3.3.12.3** Exhaust duct openings shall be located so that they effectively remove vapor accumulations at the ceiling level within 18 in. (455 mm) of the ceiling. [**30A:**7.8.12.3]

30.3.3.12.4 Where required, purge ventilation shall comply with 30.3.3.12.4.1, 30.3.3.12.4.2, and 30.3.3.12.4.3. [**30A:**7.8.12.4]

30.3.3.12.4.1 Capacity. The purge ventilation capacity required for major repair areas shall be determined in accordance with the maintenance room volume as per Table 30.3.3.12.4.1. [**30A:**7.8.12.4.1]

30.3.3.12.4.2* Minor Repair Areas. For minor repair areas, a minimum purge ventilation rate of two air changes per hour (ACH) shall be provided. [**30A:**7.8.12.4.2]

30.3.3.12.4.3 Minimum Ventilation.

30.3.3.12.4.3.1 Ventilation shall meet the requirements of applicable mechanical standards, building codes, or local regulations. [**30A:**7.8.12.4.3.1]

30.3.3.12.4.3.2 In no case shall ventilation be less than 0.5 ACH. [**30A:**7.8.12.4.3.2]

Δ **30.3.3.12.4.3.3** Natural or mechanical ventilation shall extract air from within 20 in. (0.5 m) of the ceiling. [**30A:**7.8.12.4.3.3]

30.3.3.13 Heat-Producing Appliances and Other Sources of Ignition.

30.3.3.13.1 Heat-producing appliances shall be listed and installed in accordance with the manufacturer's instructions, governing codes, and the requirements of this section. [**30A:**7.8.13.1]

30.3.3.13.2 Solid fuel stoves, improvised furnaces, salamanders, and portable space heaters shall not be permitted. [**30A:**7.8.13.2]

30.3.3.13.3 The following shall be considered potential sources of ignition and prohibited from locations as specified elsewhere in this *Code* for CNG and LNG vehicle repair areas:

(1) Open flame heaters
(2) Heating systems and other equipment either not employing sealed combustion or with exposed surface temperatures exceeding 750°F (399°C)
(3) Unit heaters
(4) Water heaters not employing sealed combustion
(5) Fired pressure washers
(6) Arcing and sparking tools or equipment
(7) Gas-fired cutting torches

[**30A:**7.8.13.3]

Table 30.3.3.12.4.1 Minimum Purge Ventilation Requirements for Major Repair Areas

Minimum Air Changes per Hour (ACH)	Major Repair Area Volume, V (m³)
10.0	V < 400
8.5	400 ≤ V < 800
7.0	800 ≤ V < 1600
6.0	1600 ≤ V < 3200
5.0	3200 ≤ V < 6400
4.5	6400 ≤ V < 12800
4.0	V ≥ 12800

Source: Canadian Standards Association B401, *Vehicle Maintenance Facilities Code*, Table 4, 2018.
[**30A:**Table 7.8.12.4.1]

30.3.3.13.4 Fired Heating Equipment.

△ **30.3.3.13.4.1** Fired heating equipment installed in minor repair areas for CNG and LNG vehicles shall meet the following requirements:

(1) Fired heating equipment shall be located with flame and combustion air inlet elevation a minimum of 24 in. (0.61 m) above the floor level and a minimum of 42 in. (1.1 m) below the ceiling.
(2) Fired heating equipment and its combustion air intake shall not be located directly above where a vehicle is normally parked for servicing.
(3) Fired heating equipment shall be located a minimum horizontal distance of 1 m from all parts of the vehicle.

[30A:7.8.13.4.1]

△ **30.3.3.13.4.2** Where permitted by the manufacturer's installation instructions, 30.3.3.13.4.1 shall not apply to radiant heaters with surface temperatures not exceeding 750°F (399°C). [30A:7.8.13.4.2]

30.3.3.14 CNG and LNG Defueling Equipment.

30.3.3.14.1 General.

30.3.3.14.1.1 Installation of equipment for defueling CNG and LNG vehicles for repair and other purposes shall be in accordance with the following requirements:

(1) Defueling equipment and installations shall be designed in accordance with applicable codes and standards.
(2) Defueling equipment and installations shall be approved by the AHJ.
(3) Defueling and captive vent systems and equipment shall be designed to recover, store, flare, or vent gas in a safe manner.
(4) Where gas is vented, the vent outlet shall comply with the following:
 (a) Be a minimum of 15 ft (4.5 m) away from building ventilation and heating and air-conditioning exhaust and intake locations
 (b) Be at a minimum elevation of 10 ft (3 m) above surrounding buildings or equipment within 50 ft (15 m) of the vent location
 (c) Be directed in a vertically upward direction
 (d) Have an electrical area classification in accordance with Table 8.3.3 of NFPA 30A

[30A:7.8.14.1.1]

30.3.3.14.2 Defueling equipment and captive vent piping systems shall be designed in accordance with CSA B51, *Boiler, Pressure Vessel, and Pressure Piping Code*, or ASME B31.3, *Process Piping*, where applicable. [30A:7.8.14.2]

30.3.3.14.3 The location of defueling equipment shall consider the safe movement and parking of the defueling vehicle, as well as other vehicular traffic. [30A:7.8.14.3]

30.3.3.14.4 Defueling equipment shall be protected from vehicle impact. [30A:7.8.14.4]

30.3.3.14.5 The flexible hoses of the defueling equipment shall be designed to minimize the potential for hose contact with the ground, accidental hose damage, and tripping hazards. [30A:7.8.14.5]

30.3.3.14.6 Bonding and Grounding.

30.3.3.14.6.1 All defueling equipment, hoses, and piping systems shall be bonded to a common ground. [30A:7.8.14.6.1]

30.3.3.14.6.2 Convenient bonding of vehicle fuel containers to decanting equipment shall be provided. [30A:7.8.14.6.2]

30.3.3.14.6.3 The defueling hose shall be electrically conductive. [30A:7.8.14.6.3]

30.3.3.14.7 Captive Vent Systems.

30.3.3.14.7.1 Major and minor repair areas that have LNG vehicles parked for extended periods of time shall have provisions for a captive vent system to safely vent boil-off gas from the vehicle fuel container to a safe outdoor location. [30A:7.8.14.7.1]

30.3.3.14.7.2 The captive vent system shall be designed with engineering supervision. [30A:7.8.14.7.2]

30.3.3.14.7.3 The LNG captive vent system shall meet the following requirements:

(1) The captive vent system shall be designed for cryogenic temperatures and have a design pressure rating in accordance with the highest potential vent flow pressure.
(2) The captive vent piping system shall be without any in-line valves.
(3) A single captive vent shall not serve more than one vehicle fuel container.
(4) The captive vent systems using cryogenic flexible hoses shall be designed to minimize the potential for hose contact with the floor, accidental hose damage, and tripping hazards.
(5) The captive vent system hoses and piping systems shall be electrically conductive and grounded.
(6) Convenient bonding of the vehicle fuel container to the captive vent system shall be provided.

[30A:7.8.14.7.3]

30.3.4 Battery-Powered Electric Vehicles.

30.3.4.1 Occupancy Classification. The occupancy classification of a repair garage shall be a special purpose industrial occupancy as defined in NFPA *101*, or as determined in accordance with the adopted building code.

30.3.4.2 Means of Egress. In a repair garage, the required number, location, and construction of means of egress shall meet all applicable requirements for special purpose industrial occupancies, as set forth in NFPA *101*, or as determined in accordance with the adopted building code.

30.3.4.3 Construction. Walls, floors, and structural supports shall be constructed of masonry, concrete, steel, or other approved noncombustible materials.

30.3.4.4 Fixed Fire Protection.

30.3.4.4.1 Automatic sprinkler protection installed in accordance with the requirements of Section 13.3 shall be provided throughout the fire area containing the repair garage.

30.3.4.4.2 An automatic smoke detection system shall be installed throughout the fire area containing the repair garage in accordance with *NFPA 70*, *NFPA 72*, and Section 13.7 of this *Code*.

30.3.4.4.3 Emergency forces notification shall be in accordance with 13.7.1.10.

30.3.4.5 Charging equipment shall be installed in accordance with *NFPA 70*.

30.3.4.6 Used Electric Batteries. (Reserved)

30.4 Operational Requirements. Operations conducted in motor fuel dispensing facilities and repair garages shall comply with Section 42.7.

Chapter 31 Forest Products and Biomass Feedstocks

31.1* General. The storage, manufacturing, and processing of timber, lumber, plywood, veneers, biomass feedstock, and by-products shall be in accordance with this chapter and NFPA 664.

31.2 Permits. Permits, where required, shall comply with Section 1.13.

31.3 Protection of Storage of Forest Products.

31.3.1 Application.

31.3.1.1 The requirements of this chapter shall apply to the outside storage of the following:

(1) Lumber and wood panel products at retail and wholesale lumber storage yards
(2) Lumber and wood panel products at other than retail and wholesale storage yards
(3) Ties, poles, piles, posts, and other similar forest products at pressure-treating plant yards
(4) Outside storage of wood chips, hogged material, and wood by-products
(5) Logs
(6) Outside storage of biomass feedstocks

31.3.1.2 The requirements of this chapter shall not apply to forest products stored on piers and wharves as addressed in NFPA 307.

31.3.2 General Fire Protection. The requirements in this subsection shall apply to all facilities regulated by 31.3.3 through 31.3.8 except as modified by those subsections.

31.3.2.1 Operational Fire Prevention.

31.3.2.1.1* Combustible waste materials such as bark, sawdust, chips, and other debris shall not be permitted to accumulate in a quantity or location that constitutes an undue fire hazard.

31.3.2.1.2 Smoking shall be prohibited except in specified safe locations approved by the AHJ.

31.3.2.1.2.1 Signs that read "No Smoking" shall be posted in those areas where smoking is prohibited.

31.3.2.1.2.2 Signs indicating areas designated as safe for smoking shall be posted in those locations where smoking is permitted.

31.3.2.1.2.3 Smoking areas shall be provided with approved, noncombustible ash receptacles.

31.3.2.1.2.4 Smoking shall be specifically prohibited in and around railroad cars.

31.3.2.1.3 Access into yard areas by unauthorized persons shall be prohibited.

31.3.2.1.4 Storage areas shall be enclosed with a fence equipped with effective gates located as necessary to allow the entry of fire department apparatus.

31.3.2.1.5 Miscellaneous occupancy hazards such as vehicle storage and repair shops, cutting and welding operations, flammable liquid storage, liquefied petroleum gas storage, and similar operations shall be safeguarded in accordance with recognized good practice and this *Code*.

31.3.2.1.6 Vehicles and other power devices shall be of an approved type and shall be safely maintained and operated.

31.3.2.1.6.1* Vehicle fueling operations shall be conducted in specified safe locations, isolated from storage areas and principal operating buildings.

31.3.2.1.6.2 Diesel- or gasoline-fueled vehicles that operate on hogged material or chip piles, in log storage areas, or in lumber storage areas shall be equipped with fixed fire-extinguishing systems of a type approved for off-road vehicles.

31.3.2.1.7 All electrical equipment and installations shall conform to the provisions of Section 11.1.

31.3.2.1.8 Salamanders, braziers, open fires, and similar dangerous heating arrangements shall be prohibited.

31.3.2.1.9 Heating devices shall be limited to approved-type equipment installed in an approved manner.

31.3.2.1.10 Suitable safeguards shall be provided to minimize the hazard of sparks caused by equipment such as refuse burners, boiler stacks, vehicle exhausts, and locomotives.

31.3.2.1.10.1* Burning of shavings, sawdust, and refuse materials shall be conducted only in an approved, enclosed refuse burner equipped with an approved spark arrester and located at a safe distance from the nearest point of any yard. (See Section 10.10.)

31.3.2.1.10.2 The design and location of large burners presents special problems, and the AHJ shall be consulted.

31.3.2.1.11 Stacks from solid fuel-burning furnaces and boilers shall be equipped with spark-arresting equipment to prevent hot sparks from reaching the ground, and consideration shall be given to spark hazard in determining the height of such stacks.

31.3.2.1.12 Cutting, welding, or other use of open flames or spark-producing equipment shall not be permitted in the storage area unless by an approved permit system.

31.3.2.2 Exposure Protection. Exposure to the yard shall be protected in accordance with the requirements of 31.3.2.2.1 through 31.3.2.2.2.2.

31.3.2.2.1* Yard areas shall be separated from plant operations and other structures so that fire exposure into the yard is minimized.

31.3.2.2.1.1 Minimum separation shall be by means of a clear space permanently available for fire-fighting operations.

31.3.2.2.1.2 The width of the clear space shall be based on the severity of exposure, which varies with the area, height, occupancy, construction, and protection of the exposing structure and the type of stacking and height of adjacent stacks.

31.3.2.2.2* Forest, brush, and grass fire exposure shall be minimized by providing adequate clear space that is carefully kept free of combustible vegetation.

31.3.2.2.2.1 Clear space of a width at least equivalent to the fire apparatus access road shall be provided for grass exposures, and clear space of a width not less than 100 ft (30 m) shall be provided for light brush exposures.

31.3.2.2.2.2 In forested areas, a wider clear space than in 31.3.2.2.2.1 shall be provided.

31.3.2.3* Fire Detection and Extinguishment. A reliable means for prompt transmission of fire alarms to public fire departments and plant emergency organizations shall be provided.

31.3.3 Outside Storage of Lumber and Wood Panel Products at Retail and Wholesale Storage Yards.

31.3.3.1 Application.

31.3.3.1.1 The requirements of 31.3.3 shall apply to the following areas:

(1) Retail lumberyards handling forest products and other building materials
(2) Wholesale lumber storage yards, including distribution, holding, and transshipment areas

31.3.3.1.2* The requirements of 31.3.4 shall apply to other than large outside wholesale and retail distribution yards.

31.3.3.2 General.

31.3.3.2.1* The fire hazard potential inherent in lumber storage operations with large quantities of combustible materials shall be controlled by a positive fire prevention program under the direct supervision of upper level management that shall include the following:

(1) Selection, design, and arrangement of storage yard areas and materials-handling equipment based upon proven fire prevention and protection principles
(2) Means for early fire detection, transmission of alarm, and fire extinguishment
(3) Fire apparatus access roads to separate large stacks and provide access for effective fire-fighting operations
(4) Separation of yard storage from yard buildings and other exposing properties
(5) Effective fire prevention maintenance program, including regular yard inspections by trained personnel

31.3.3.2.2* Water supplies shall be provided in accordance with this *Code*.

31.3.3.3 Open Yard Storage.

31.3.3.3.1* Lumber stacks shall be on stable ground, and paved or surfaced with materials such as cinders, fine gravel, or stone.

31.3.3.3.2 The method of stacking shall be stable and in an orderly and regular manner.

31.3.3.3.3* The height of stacks shall not exceed 20 ft (6 m) with consideration for stability.

31.3.3.3.4 Where stacks are supported clear of the ground, 6 in. (150 mm) of clearance shall be provided for cleaning operations under the stacks.

31.3.3.3.5 Fire apparatus access roads shall be spaced so that a grid system of not more than 50 ft × 150 ft (15 m × 46 m) is produced.

31.3.3.3.6 Fire apparatus access roads shall comply with Section 18.2.

31.3.3.3.7 Stacking limits shall be designated to indicate yard area and alleyway limits in accordance with 31.3.3.3.7.1 or 31.3.3.3.7.2.

31.3.3.3.7.1 The stacking limits shall be designated with boundary posts having signs that indicate stacking limits unless otherwise permitted by 31.3.3.3.7.2.

31.3.3.3.7.2 Where yards have paved areas, painted boundary limits shall be permitted to be used to designate stacking limits.

31.3.3.4 Exposure Protection.

31.3.3.4.1 Exposure to the Yard.

31.3.3.4.1.1 Open yard stacking shall be located with not less than 15 ft (4.6 m) clear space to buildings.

31.3.3.4.1.2 Boundary posts with signs designating stacking limits shall be provided to designate the clear space to unsprinklered buildings in which hazardous manufacturing or other operations take place.

31.3.3.4.2* Exposure from the Yard.

31.3.3.4.2.1 Open yard stacking shall be located with not less than 15 ft (4.6 m) clear space to adjacent property lines.

31.3.3.4.2.2 Alternative forms of exposure protection shall be permitted where approved by the AHJ.

31.3.4 Outside Storage of Lumber and Wood Panel Products at Other Than Retail and Wholesale Storage Yards.

31.3.4.1* Application. The requirements of 31.3.4 shall apply to large yard storage areas containing lumber, wood panels, and other similar wood products not intended for retail or wholesale distribution at the site.

31.3.4.2* General. The fire hazard potential inherent in forest product storage operations with large quantities of combustible materials shall be controlled by a positive fire prevention program under the direct supervision of upper level management that shall include the following:

(1) Selection, design, and arrangement of storage yard areas and materials-handling equipment based on sound fire prevention and protection principles
(2) Means for early fire detection, transmission of alarm, and fire extinguishment
(3) Fire apparatus access roads to separate large stacks and provide access for effective fire-fighting operations
(4) Separation of yard storage from mill or other plant operations and other exposing properties
(5) Effective fire prevention maintenance program, including regular yard inspections by trained personnel

31.3.4.3* Open Yard Storage.

31.3.4.3.1* Water supplies shall be provided in accordance with this *Code*.

31.3.4.3.2 Access to the plant and yard from public highways shall be provided by all-weather roadways capable of supporting fire department apparatus.

31.3.4.3.3 The storage site shall be reasonably level, on solid ground, and paved or surfaced with materials such as cinders, fine gravel, or stone.

31.3.4.3.4 Stack height shall be limited to 20 ft (6 m).

31.3.5 Outside Storage of Ties, Poles, Piles, Posts, and Other Similar Forest Products at Pressure-Treating Plant Yards.

31.3.5.1 Application.

31.3.5.1.1* The requirements of 31.3.5 shall apply to yard storage areas containing treated and untreated ties, poles, piles, posts, and other similar forest products in yards connected with pressure-treating plants.

31.3.5.1.2 The requirements of 31.3.5 shall not apply to pressure-treating buildings, processes, or storage of treating materials.

31.3.5.2* General. The fire hazard potential inherent in tie storage operations with large quantities of combustible materials shall be controlled by a positive fire prevention program under the direct supervision of upper level management that shall include the following:

(1) Selection, design, and arrangement of storage yard areas and materials-handling equipment based upon sound fire prevention and protection principles
(2) Means for early fire detection, transmission of alarm, and fire extinguishment
(3) Fire apparatus access roads to separate large stacks and provide access for effective fire-fighting operations
(4) Separation of yard storage from mill buildings and other exposing properties
(5) Effective fire prevention maintenance program, including regular yard inspections by trained personnel

31.3.5.3* Tie Yard Protection.

31.3.5.3.1* Unobstructed alleyways of sufficient width for hand or cart fire hose laying operations shall be provided between piles.

31.3.5.3.1.1 Alleyways shall not be less than 2 ft (0.6 m) in width.

31.3.5.3.1.2 Where a minimum alleyway width of 4 ft (1.2 m) is provided, the length of the rows shall be not more than 100 ft (30 m).

31.3.5.3.1.3 Where an alleyway width less than 4 ft (1.2 m) is provided, the length of the rows shall be not more than 75 ft (23 m).

31.3.5.3.2* Water supplies shall be provided in accordance with this *Code*.

31.3.5.3.3 Access to the plant and yard from public highways shall be provided by all-weather roadways capable of supporting fire department apparatus.

31.3.5.3.4 The storage site shall be reasonably level, on solid ground, and paved or surfaced with materials such as cinders, fine gravel, or stone.

31.3.5.3.5* Stack heights shall be limited to 20 ft (6 m).

31.3.6 Outside Storage of Wood Chips and Hogged Material.

31.3.6.1* Application. The requirements of 31.3.6 shall apply to yard storage areas containing wood chips and hogged material.

31.3.6.2 General.

31.3.6.2.1* The fire hazard potential inherent in storage piles shall be controlled by a positive fire prevention program under the direct supervision of upper level management that shall include the following:

(1) Selection, design, and arrangement of storage yard areas and materials-handling equipment based upon sound fire prevention and protection principles
(2) Establishment of control over the various factors that lead to spontaneous heating, including provisions for monitoring the internal condition of the pile
(3) Means for early fire detection and extinguishment
(4) Fire apparatus access roads around the piles and access roads to the top of the piles for effective fire-fighting operations
(5) Facilities for calling the public fire department and facilities needed by the fire department for fire extinguishment
(6) Effective fire prevention maintenance program, including regular yard inspections by trained personnel

31.3.6.2.2* The following items shall be addressed when establishing operating procedures:

(1) The storage site shall be reasonably level, solid ground, or shall be paved with blacktop, concrete, or other hard-surface material.
(2) Sites shall be cleaned before transferring wood products to the site.
(3) Operating plans for the buildup and reclaiming of the pile shall be based on a turnover time of not more than 1 year under ideal conditions.
(4)* Piles containing other than screened chips made from cleaned and barked logs shall be minimized.
(5)* The pile size shall be limited.
(6) Pile heights shall be kept low, particularly piles that inherently carry a larger percentage of fines and are subject to greater compaction.
(7) Thermocouples shall be installed during pile buildup, or other means for measuring temperatures within the pile shall be provided with regular (normally weekly) reports to management.
(8)* The pile shall be wetted regularly to help keep fines from drying out and help maintain the moisture content of the surface layer of the pile.

31.3.6.3* Pile Protection.

31.3.6.3.1* Piles shall be constructed with an access roadway to the top of the pile in order to reach any part of the pile.

31.3.6.3.2* Piles shall not exceed 60 ft (18 m) in height, 300 ft (90 m) in width, and 500 ft (150 m) in length.

31.3.6.3.2.1 Where pile height and width are such that all portions of the pile cannot be reached by direct hose streams from the ground, arrangements shall be made to provide fire-fighting service in these areas, and small fire stream supplies shall be available on the top of the pile for handling small surface fires and for wetting the pile in dry weather.

31.3.6.3.2.2 When more than one pile exists, they shall be subdivided by fire apparatus access roads having not less than 30 ft (9 m) of clear space at the base of the piles.

31.3.6.3.2.3 Low barrier walls around piles shall be provided to clearly define pile perimeters, prevent creeping, and facilitate cleanup of fire apparatus access roads.

31.3.6.3.3 Where suitable, a small, motorized vehicle amply equipped with portable extinguishing equipment or a water tank and pump shall be provided.

31.3.6.3.3.1 Lightweight ladders that can be placed against the side of the pile shall be placed at convenient locations throughout the yard for use by the plant emergency organization.

31.3.6.3.3.2 Training of the plant emergency organization also shall include procedures and precautions to be observed by yard crews employing power equipment in fighting internal fires.

31.3.6.3.4* Portable fire extinguishers for Class A fires shall be provided in accordance with Section 13.6 on all vehicles operating on the pile in addition to the normal Class B units for the vehicle.

31.3.6.3.5* Water supplies shall be provided in accordance with this *Code*.

31.3.6.3.6 All motor and switchgear enclosures shall be provided with approved, portable fire extinguishers suitable for the hazard involved in accordance with Section 13.6.

31.3.6.3.7* Power-operated, shovel-type or scoop-type vehicles, dozers, or similar equipment shall be available for use in moving stored material for fire fighting.

31.3.6.3.8 Temporary conveyors and motors on the surface or adjacent to the piles shall not be permitted.

31.3.6.3.9 Physical protection shall be provided to prevent heat sources such as steam lines, air lines, electrical motors, and mechanical drive equipment from becoming buried or heavily coated with combustible material.

31.3.6.3.10 Tramp metal collectors or detectors shall be required on all conveyor and blower systems.

31.3.6.4 Exposure Protection.

31.3.6.4.1* Incinerators or open refuse burning shall not be permitted in any area where sparks could reach the storage piles.

31.3.6.4.2* A clear space of not less than 15 ft (4.6 m) shall be maintained between piles and exposing structures, yard equipment, or stock, depending on the degree of exposure hazard.

31.3.6.4.3* Pile-to-pile clearance of not less than 30 ft (9 m) at the base of the pile shall be provided.

31.3.6.5 Emergency Action Plan. The facility shall have an emergency action plan for monitoring, controlling, and extinguishing spot fires.

31.3.7* Storage and Processing of Wood Chips, Hogged Material, Fines, Compost, and Raw Products at Yard Waste Recycling Facilities.

31.3.7.1 The storage and processing of wood chips, hogged material, fines, compost, and raw products produced from yard waste recycling facilities shall comply with 31.3.6 and 31.3.7.

31.3.7.2 When not protected by a fixed fire-extinguishing system in accordance with Chapter 13, piles shall not exceed 25 ft (7.6 m) in height, 150 ft (45 m) in width, and 250 ft (76.2 m) in length.

31.3.7.3 Static Pile Protection.

31.3.7.3.1 Static piles shall be monitored by an approved means to measure temperatures within the piles.

31.3.7.3.2 Internal pile temperatures shall be recorded weekly.

31.3.7.3.3 Records shall be kept on file at the facility and made available for inspection.

31.3.7.3.4 The facility shall have an operational plan indicating procedures and schedules for the inspection, monitoring, and restricting of excessive internal temperatures in static piles.

31.3.7.4 Fire Protection.

31.3.7.4.1 Conveyor tunnels and combustible enclosures that pass under a pile shall be protected with automatic sprinklers complying with Section 13.3.

31.3.7.4.2 Combustible or enclosed conveyor systems shall be protected with automatic sprinklers complying with Section 13.3.

31.3.8 Outside Storage of Logs.

31.3.8.1 Application.

31.3.8.1.1* The requirements of 31.3.8 shall apply to log yard storage areas containing saw, plywood veneer, or pulpwood logs stored in ranked piles commonly referred to as cold decks.

31.3.8.1.2 The requirements of 31.3.8 shall not apply to cordwood.

31.3.8.2* General. The fire hazard potential inherent in log storage operations with large quantities of combustible materials shall be controlled by a positive fire prevention program under the direct supervision of upper level management that shall include the following:

(1) Selection, design, and arrangement of storage yard areas and materials-handling equipment based on sound fire prevention and protection principles
(2) Means for early fire detection, transmission of alarm, and fire extinguishment
(3) Fire apparatus access roads to separate large piles and provide access for effective fire-fighting operations
(4) Separation of yard storage from mill operations and other exposing properties
(5) Effective fire prevention maintenance program, including regular yard inspections by trained personnel

31.3.8.3* Log Yard Protection.

31.3.8.3.1 The storage site shall be reasonably level, on solid ground, and paved or surfaced with materials such as cinders, fine gravel, or stone.

31.3.8.3.2 Access to the plant and yard from public highways shall be provided by all-weather roadways capable of supporting fire department apparatus.

31.3.8.3.3* All sides of each cold deck shall be accessible by means of fire apparatus access roads.

31.3.8.3.3.1 A fire apparatus access road width of 1½ times the pile height but not less than 20 ft (6 m) shall be provided, with fire apparatus access roads between alternate rows of two pile groups providing a clear space of at least 100 ft (30 m).

31.3.8.3.3.2* Each cold deck shall not exceed 500 ft (150 m) in length, 300 ft (90 m) in width, and 20 ft (6 m) in height.

31.3.8.3.3.3* Fire apparatus access roads for access across each end, with a clear space of not less than 100 ft (30 m) to adjacent pile rows or other exposed property, shall be provided.

31.3.8.3.3.4* The size of cold decks shall be permitted to be increased where additional fire flow and fixed fire protection equipment is provided and the approval of the AHJ is obtained.

31.3.8.3.4 Water supplies shall be provided in accordance with this *Code*.

31.3.8.3.5 Dynamite shall never be used as a means to reclaim frozen log piles.

31.3.8.3.6* During dry weather, piles shall be wet down.

31.3.9 Wood Processing and Woodworking Facilities. Dust control shall be in accordance with NFPA 664 for combustible dust-producing operations that occupy areas of more than 5000 ft² (464 m²), or to areas where dust-producing equipment requires an aggregate dust collection flow rate of more than 1500 ft³/min (2549 m³/hr).

31.3.10 Outside Storage of Biomass Feedstock.

31.3.10.1 The fire hazard potential inherent in biomass feedstock storage operations with large quantities of combustible materials shall be controlled by a positive fire prevention program under the direct supervision of upper level management that shall include the following:

(1) Selection, design, and arrangement of storage yard areas and materials-handling equipment based upon proven fire prevention and protection principles
(2) Means for early fire detection, transmission of alarm, and fire extinguishment
(3) Establishment of control over the various factors that lead to spontaneous heating, including provisions for monitoring the internal condition of the pile
(4) Fire apparatus access roads to separate large stacks and provide access for effective fire-fighting operations
(5) Separation of yard storage from yard buildings and other exposing properties
(6) Effective fire prevention maintenance program, including regular yard inspections by trained personnel

31.3.10.2 Bale stacks shall not exceed 25 ft (7.6 m) in height, 150 ft (45 m) in width, and 250 ft (76.2 m) in length.

31.3.10.3 The storage site shall be reasonably level, on solid ground.

31.3.10.4 Access to the plant and yard from public highways shall be provided by all-weather roadways capable of supporting fire department apparatus.

31.3.10.5 All sides of each storage site shall be accessible by means of fire apparatus access roads.

31.3.10.6 Where more than one pile exists, they shall be subdivided by fire apparatus access roads having not less than 30 ft (9 m) of clear space at the base of the piles.

31.3.10.7 Power-operated, shovel-type or scoop-type vehicles, dozers, bale movers, or similar equipment shall be available for use in moving stored material for fire fighting.

31.3.10.8 Training of the plant emergency organization also shall include procedures and precautions to be observed by yard crews employing power equipment in fighting internal fires.

31.3.10.9 Portable fire extinguishers for Class A fires shall be provided in accordance with Section 13.6 on all vehicles operating in the storage yard in addition to the normal Class B units for the vehicle.

31.3.10.10 Lightning protection shall be provided for the outside storage yard in accordance with NFPA 780.

31.3.10.11 Outside storage yards shall be secured against unauthorized access in an approved manner.

31.3.10.12 Water supplies shall be provided in accordance with this *Code*.

Chapter 32 Motion Picture and Television Production Studio Soundstages and Approved Production Facilities

32.1 General. The design, construction, operation, and maintenance of soundstages and approved production facilities used in motion picture and television industry productions shall comply with NFPA 140 and Chapter 32.

32.2 Permits.

32.2.1 Permits, where required, shall comply with Section 1.13.

32.2.2 Where required by the AHJ, a permit shall be obtained for any of the following activities:

(1) Use of pyrotechnic special effects
(2) Use of open flames
(3) Welding
(4) Use of ignitible (flammable or combustible) liquids or gases
(5) Use of aircraft
(6) Presence of motor vehicles within a building
(7) Productions with live audiences
(8) Change of use or change of occupancy classification [140:4.2]
(9) Use of the site as a production location [140:5.2(1)]

32.3 Fire Watch.

32.3.1 Where required by the AHJ, a fire watch shall be provided for soundstages and approved production facilities where pyrotechnic special effects are used. [140:4.4.1]

32.3.2 A fire watch shall be required for production locations where pyrotechnic special effects are used, unless otherwise waived by the AHJ. [140:5.4.1]

Δ **32.3.3 Other Hazards.** Where required by the AHJ, a fire watch shall be provided for hazardous operations other than pyrotechnic special effects. [140:4.4.2] [140:5.4.2]

32.4 Decorative Materials.

Δ **32.4.1** Foamed plastic materials used for decorative purposes, scenery, sets, or props shall have a heat release rate not exceeding 100 kW where tested in accordance with UL 1975, *Fire Tests for Foamed Plastics Used for Decorative Purposes,* or where tested in accordance with NFPA 289 using the 20 kW ignition source. [**140:**4.5.1] [**140:**5.5]

32.4.2 Combustible drapes, drops, and any other similar combustible hangings or vertically placed materials shall comply with one of the following options:

(1) The materials meet the requirements of NFPA 701.
(2) The materials exhibit a heat release rate not exceeding 100 kW when tested in accordance with NFPA 289 using the 20 kW ignition source.
(3) The materials are present in such limited quantity that a hazard of fire development or spread is minimal.
(4) The materials are considered by the AHJ to exhibit acceptable fire performance.
(5) Approved interim measures are provided for the period during which the combustible materials are present. [**140:**4.5.2]

32.4.3 Cut greens shall be treated with an approved or listed fire retardant, and the process shall be repeated as often as necessary to maintain its effectiveness. [**140:**4.5.3]

32.5 Smoking.

32.5.1 Smoking shall be prohibited on soundstages and in approved production facilities unless otherwise provided in 32.5.2 or 32.5.3. [**140:**4.6.1] [**140:**5.6.1]

32.5.2 Smoking shall be permitted when it is a necessary part of a performance, and only when the smoker is a member of the cast. [**140:**4.6.2] [**140:**5.6.2]

32.5.3 Except where prohibited by the AHJ, smoking shall be permitted where all of the following conditions are met:

(1) The smoking area is outdoors.
(2) Hazardous materials are not present.
(3) Approved ash trays or receivers are provided. [**140:**4.6.3] [**140:**5.6.3]

32.6 Pyrotechnic Special Effects and Open Flames.

32.6.1 The use of pyrotechnic special effects and open flames shall be subject to the approval of the AHJ. [**140:**4.3.1] [**140:**5.3.1]

32.6.2 When an audience is present, NFPA 1126 shall be used to regulate any pyrotechnic use. [**140:**4.3.2] [**140:**5.3.2]

32.6.3 When an audience is present, NFPA 160 shall be used to regulate any flame effects use. [**140:**4.3.3] [**140:**5.3.3]

32.7* **Fire Department Access.** Fire department access shall be maintained as required by the AHJ. [**140:**4.9] [**140:**5.9]

32.8 Housekeeping. Soundstages and approved production facilities shall maintain housekeeping in accordance with Chapters 10 and 19 where applicable.

32.9 Soundstages and Approved Production Facilities.

32.9.1 General. Section 32.9 shall apply to new and existing motion picture and television soundstages and approved production facilities. [**140:**4.1]

32.9.2 Electrical Requirements.

32.9.2.1 Electrical equipment shall be in accordance with Section 11.1. [**140:**4.8.1]

32.9.2.2* Soundstages and approved production facilities shall be provided with a minimum of 35 W/ft^2 (377 W/m^2) dedicated for production lighting and power. [**140:**4.8.2]

32.9.2.3 The electrical distribution equipment used shall comply with UL 1640, *Portable Power-Distribution Equipment,* and the provisions of Article 530 of *NFPA 70.* [**140:**4.8.3]

32.9.2.4 The wiring method to electrical distribution equipment shall comply with the provisions of Article 530 of *NFPA 70.* [**140:**4.8.4]

32.9.2.5 The location of portable, mobile, or stationary power-generating equipment shall be subject to the approval of the AHJ. [**140:**4.8.5]

32.9.2.6 Exterior penetrations shall be located near the predesignated location for portable and mobile power-generating equipment. [**140:**4.8.6]

32.9.2.7 Auxiliary power cables supplied from mobile generators or adjacent buildings shall not be routed through fire-rated windows and doors. [**140:**4.8.7]

Δ **32.9.2.8** Portable feeder cables shall be permitted to temporarily penetrate fire-rated walls, floors, or ceilings provided that all of the following apply:

(1) The opening is of noncombustible material.
(2) When in use, the penetration is sealed with a temporary seal of a listed firestop material.
(3) When not in use, the opening shall be capped with a material of equivalent fire rating.

[**140:**4.8.8]

32.9.2.9 Where the penetration utilizes a conduit, metal-threaded caps shall be attached to the pipe by means of chain or cable and shall effectively cap the conduit when not in use. [**140:**4.8.9]

32.9.2.10 The lighting equipment used shall comply with UL 1573, *Stage and Studio Luminaires and Connector Strips,* and the provisions of Article 530 of *NFPA 70.* [**140:**4.8.10]

32.9.3 Means of Egress.

32.9.3.1 Means of egress shall be in accordance with NFPA *101* unless otherwise modified by 32.9.3.2 through 32.9.3.6. [**140:**4.10.1]

32.9.3.2 The maximum travel distance to an exit within the soundstage shall be 150 ft (45 m). [**140:**4.10.2]

32.9.3.3 Soundstages and approved production facilities shall have an aisle along the perimeter of the soundstage or facility as approved by the AHJ unless otherwise provided in 32.9.3.3.2. [**140:**4.10.3]

32.9.3.3.1 A clear unobstructed aisle height of 7 ft (2.1 m) shall be maintained. [**140:**4.10.3.1]

32.9.3.3.2 A soundstage or approved production facility with a gross area not exceeding 1500 ft^2 (139 m^2) shall be exempt from the perimeter aisle requirement of 32.9.3.3 provided there is a minimum of two means of egress. [**140:**4.10.3.2]

32.9.3.4 Emergency lighting shall be provided for the means of egress in accordance with NFPA *101*. [**140**:4.10.4]

32.9.3.5 Any door in a required means of egress from an area having an occupant load of 100 or more persons shall be permitted to be provided with a latch or lock only if it is panic hardware or fire exit hardware. [**140**:4.10.5]

32.9.3.6 Means of egress shall be kept clear of obstructions and tripping hazards. [**140**:4.10.6]

32.9.3.7 Emergency Instruction to Audience. When an audience is present, an announcement shall be made notifying the audience of the following:

(1) The location of exits to be used in case of fire or other emergency
(2) The means that will be used to notify the audience of fire or other emergency

[**140**:4.10.7]

32.9.4 Fire Protection.

32.9.4.1 Extinguishment Requirements.

32.9.4.1.1 Existing soundstages and existing approved production facilities equipped with automatic sprinkler systems shall maintain those systems in accordance with 13.3.3. [**140**:4.11.1.1]

32.9.4.1.2 A new soundstage or new approved production facility shall be equipped with an approved, supervised automatic sprinkler system. [**140**:4.11.1.2]

32.9.4.1.3 The automatic sprinkler system required by 32.9.4.1.2 shall be installed in accordance with Section 13.3 unless otherwise provided in 32.9.4.1.3.1 or 32.9.4.1.3.2. [**140**:4.11.1.3]

32.9.4.1.3.1* The requirements of NFPA 13 prohibiting obstructions to sprinkler discharge shall not be applicable if approved mitigation is employed. [**140**:4.11.1.3.1]

32.9.4.1.3.2* The requirements of NFPA 13 prohibiting obstructions to sprinkler discharge shall not be applicable if the building sprinkler system meets the design criteria for Extra Hazard, Group 2. [**140**:4.11.1.3.2]

32.9.4.1.4 The automatic sprinkler system required by 32.9.4.1.2 shall be maintained in accordance with 13.3.3. [**140**:4.11.1.4]

32.9.4.1.5 Portable fire extinguishers shall be installed and maintained in accordance with Section 13.6. [**140**:4.11.1.5]

32.9.4.2 Fire Alarm System. Fire alarm system notification appliances within soundstages and approved production facilities shall be permitted to be deactivated with the approval of the AHJ during videotaping, filming, or broadcasting of programs, provided the following conditions exist:

(1) In the event of alarm system activation, notification appliances shall activate at a location that is constantly attended during the videotaping, filming, or broadcasting of programs.
(2) The attendants of the location identified in 32.9.4.2(1) shall be provided with a means of communicating with the fire command center for the building, where one is provided, and with the occupants of the soundstage to initiate emergency action.
(3) Deactivation of notification appliances shall cause activation of a visual signal at an approved location, which shall remain illuminated while notification appliances on the soundstage are deactivated.
(4) The visual signal shall be identified by a sign that shall read, "When Illuminated, Soundstage Fire Alarm System Notification Appliances Are Deactivated."

[**140**:4.11.2]

32.9.5 Air Conditioning, Heating, and Ventilating. Air-conditioning, heating, and ventilating ductwork and related equipment shall be in good working order and in compliance with the requirements of the AHJ. [**140**:4.12]

32.10 Production Locations.

32.10.1 Electrical Requirements.

32.10.1.1 Electrical power connections made to the site electrical service shall be made by an approved electrician under permit from the AHJ. [**140**:5.8.1]

32.10.1.2 Portable cables shall be positioned to allow for emergency egress as approved by the AHJ. [**140**:5.8.2]

32.10.1.3* Auxiliary power cables supplied from mobile generators or adjacent buildings shall be permitted to be routed through fire-rated windows and doors with the approval of the AHJ. [**140**:5.8.3]

32.10.1.4 Where power from both mobile generators and site electrical services are used to energize equipment in the same proximate location at production locations, grounds for the two systems shall be bonded in accordance with *NFPA 70*. [**140**:5.8.4]

32.10.2* Means of Egress. The production location shall be provided with means of egress appropriate for the intended use as approved by the AHJ. [**140**:5.10]

32.10.3 Fire Protection.

32.10.3.1* Building areas used as production locations shall be designed, constructed, and maintained to protect the occupants not intimate with the initial fire development for the time needed to evacuate, relocate, or defend in place. [**140**:5.11.1]

32.10.3.2 Where an automatic sprinkler system is provided for compliance with 32.10.3.1, the automatic sprinkler system shall be installed in accordance with Section 13.3 unless otherwise provided in 32.10.3.4 or 32.10.3.5. [**140**:5.11.2]

32.10.3.3 In any production location building protected by an existing automatic sprinkler system, where solid- or hard-ceiling sets or platforms are introduced and create an obstruction to sprinkler discharge, the provisions of 32.10.3.4 or 32.10.3.5 shall be met. [**140**:5.11.3]

32.10.3.4* The requirements of NFPA 13 prohibiting obstructions to sprinkler discharge shall not be applicable if approved mitigation is employed. [**140**:5.11.4]

32.10.3.5* The requirements of NFPA 13 prohibiting obstructions to sprinkler discharge shall not be applicable if the building sprinkler system meets the design criteria for Extra Hazard, Group 2. [**140**:5.11.5]

32.10.3.6 Automatic sprinkler systems, where provided, shall be maintained in accordance with 13.3.3. [**140**:5.11.6]

32.10.3.7 Portable fire extinguishers shall be provided as required by the AHJ. [**140:**5.11.7]

32.10.3.8 Fire Hydrants and Fire Appliances. Hydrants, standpipes, and fire department connections (FDCs) shall not be obstructed, blocked, or rendered inoperable unless approved by the AHJ. [**140:**5.11.8]

32.10.4 Operating Features.

32.10.4.1 Waste or Refuse. Waste or refuse shall not be allowed to accumulate in any area or in any manner that creates a fire hazard. [**140:**6.1]

32.10.4.2 Ignitible (Flammable or Combustible) Liquids.

32.10.4.2.1 The use, mixing, dispensing, and storage of ignitible (flammable or combustible) liquids shall be in accordance with this *Code* and Chapter 66 and Chapter 69, as applicable, unless otherwise permitted by 32.10.4.2.2.[**140:**6.2.1]

32.10.4.2.2 Approved ignitible (flammable or combustible) liquids and liquefied petroleum gases used for special effects shall be permitted. [**140:**6.2.2]

32.10.4.3 Welding. Welding shall be in accordance with NFPA 51 and Chapter 41. [**140:**6.3]

32.10.4.4* Audience Life Safety. When an audience is present during productions, provisions for life safety and means of egress shall be subject to the approval of the AHJ. [**140:**6.4]

32.10.4.5 Emergency Services Notification. The production company shall provide a procedure acceptable to the AHJ for notifying the public emergency services of emergency incidents. [**140:**6.5]

Chapter 33 Outside Storage of Tires

33.1* General.

33.1.1 Facilities storing more than 500 tires outside shall be in accordance with Chapter 33.

33.1.2 Permits. Permits, where required, shall comply with Section 1.13.

33.1.3 Fire apparatus access roads to separate tire piles and for effective fire-fighting operations shall be in accordance with Table 33.1.3.

33.1.4 Separation of yard storage from buildings, vehicles, flammable materials, and other exposures shall be in accordance with Table 33.1.3.

33.1.5 Trees, plants, and vegetation within the separation areas shall be managed in accordance with Section 10.13.

33.1.6 Ignition Sources.

33.1.6.1 Smoking shall be prohibited within the tire storage area.

33.1.6.2 Sources of ignition such as cutting and welding, heating devices, and open fires shall be prohibited within the tire storage area.

33.1.6.3 Safeguards shall be provided to minimize the hazard of sparks from equipment such as refuse burners, boiler stacks, and vehicle exhaust when such hazards are located near the tire storage area.

33.1.7 Piles of tires or altered tire material shall not be located beneath power lines or structures.

33.1.8 Piles of tires or altered tire material shall be at least 50 ft (15 m) from the perimeter fence.

33.1.9 Provisions for surface water drainage and measures to provide protection of pyrolytic oil runoff shall be directed around and away from the outdoor tire storage site to an approved location.

33.1.10 Tires shall be removed from rims immediately upon arrival at the storage site.

33.1.11 Tires shall not be stored on wetlands, flood plains, ravines, canyons, or steeply graded surfaces.

33.2 Individual Piles.

33.2.1 New Outside Tire Storage Sites and Piles.

33.2.1.1 New individual outside tire storage piles containing more than 500 tires shall be limited in volume to 125,000 ft^3 (3540 m^3).

33.2.1.2 The dimensions of new tire storage piles shall not exceed 10 ft (3 m) in height, 50 ft (15 m) in width, and 250 ft (75 m) in length.

33.2.1.3 Individual piles shall be separated in accordance with Table 33.1.3.

33.2.2 Existing Individual Piles.

33.2.2.1 Existing outside tire storage piles shall be in accordance with the provisions of 33.2.1 within 5 years of the adoption of this *Code*.

Table 33.1.3 Representative Minimum Exposure Separation Distances in Feet (Meters) for Tire Storage

Exposed Face Dimension		Pile Height												
ft	m	8 ft	2.4 m	10 ft	3 m	12 ft	3.7 m	14 ft	4.3 m	16 ft	4.9 m	18 ft	5.5 m	20 ft	6.1 m
25	7.6	56	17	62	19	67	20	73	22	77	23	82	25	85	26
50	15.2	75	23	84	26	93	28	100	30	107	33	113	34	118	36
100	30	100	30	116	35	128	39	137	42	146	44	155	47	164	50
150	45	100	30	116	35	128	39	137	42	146	44	155	47	164	50
200	61	100	30	116	35	128	39	137	42	146	44	155	47	164	50
250	75	100	30	116	35	128	39	137	42	146	44	155	47	164	50

33.2.2.2 Existing individual outside tire storage piles containing more than 500 tires shall be limited in volume to 250,000 ft^3 (7080 m^3).

33.2.2.3 Existing pile dimensions shall not exceed 20 ft (6 m) in height, 50 ft (15 m) in width, and 250 ft (75 m) in length.

33.2.2.4 Individual piles shall be separated in accordance with Table 33.1.3.

33.3 Emergency Response Plan.

33.3.1 The operator of the outside tire storage facility shall develop an emergency response plan and submit it for approval by the AHJ.

33.3.2 The AHJ shall retain a copy of the approved emergency response plan.

33.3.3 The operator of the outside tire storage facility shall keep a copy of the approved emergency response plan at the facility.

33.3.4 The AHJ shall be immediately notified of and approve any proposed changes to the emergency response plan.

33.4 Fire Control Measures. Measures to aid in the control of fire shall be in accordance with Section 33.4.

33.4.1 Manual Fire-Fighting Equipment.

33.4.1.1 At a minimum, the following items shall be maintained on site and in working order:

(1) One 2-A:10-B:C fire extinguisher
(2) One 2.5 gal (10 L) water extinguisher
(3) One 10 ft (3 m) long pike pole
(4) One rigid rake
(5) One round point shovel
(6) One square point shovel

33.4.1.2 One dry chemical fire extinguisher with a minimum rating of 4-A:40-B:C shall be carried on each piece of fuel-powered equipment used to handle scrap tires.

33.4.1.3 On-site personnel shall be trained in the use and function of this equipment to mitigate tire pile ignition.

33.4.2 An approved water supply capable of supplying the required fire flow to protect exposures and perform fire suppression and overhaul operations shall be provided.

33.4.3* The AHJ shall be permitted to require additional tools and equipment for fire control and the protection of life and property.

33.5 Site Access.

33.5.1 Access to the site and each tire storage yard and pile shall be in accordance with Section 18.2 and this section.

33.5.2 Accesses shall be maintained clear of combustible waste or vegetation and shall remain accessible to the fire department at all times.

33.6 Signs and Security. Access by unauthorized persons and security of the site shall be in accordance with Section 33.6.

33.6.1 Signs bearing the name of the operator, the operating hours, emergency telephone numbers, and site rules shall be posted at site entrances.

33.6.2 The facility shall have noncombustible fencing at least 10 ft (3 m) high with intruder controls on top, in accordance with local laws, around the entire perimeter of the property.

33.6.3 Access.

33.6.3.1 Access to the facility shall be in accordance with Section 18.2.

33.6.3.2 An attendant shall be on site at all times when the site is open.

33.7 Outdoor Storage of Altered Tire Material. Outdoor storage of altered tire material in the form of chunks, chips, or crumbs shall be protected in accordance with 33.7.1 through 33.7.5.

33.7.1 A 10 ft (3 m) fence shall be maintained around the altered tire material storage area.

33.7.2 Altered tire material piles shall be kept 50 ft (15 m) from perimeter fencing.

33.7.3 Potential ignition sources such as welding, smoking, or other open flame uses shall not be allowed within 20 ft (6 m) of the altered tire pile.

33.7.4 Individual altered tire material piles shall not be located on site in excess of 90 days.

33.7.5* Individual altered tire material piles shall be kept sheltered from precipitation.

Chapter 34 General Storage

34.1 General.

34.1.1 Application. This chapter shall apply to the indoor and outdoor storage of materials representing the broad range of combustibles, including plastics, rubber tires, and roll paper.

34.1.1.1 Storage configurations shall include palletized storage, solid-piled storage, and storage in bin boxes, on shelves, or on racks.

34.1.1.2 Chapter 34 shall not apply to the following:

(1) Storage of commodities that, with their packaging and storage aids, would be classified as noncombustible
(2) Unpackaged bulk materials such as grain, coal, or similar commodities but excluding wood chips and sawdust, which are addressed in Chapter 31
(3) Inside or outside storage of commodities covered by this *Code*, except where specifically mentioned herein (e.g., pyroxylin plastics)
(4) Storage of high-hazard materials covered by this *Code*, except where specifically mentioned herein
(5) Storage on plastic shelves on racks
(6)* Miscellaneous tire storage
(7) Combustible fiber storage, which is covered in Chapter 45

34.1.2 Permits. Permits, where required, shall comply with Section 1.13.

34.1.3* Approved Storage Floor Plan. An approved storage floor plan that documents the permissible use of the storage area, based on the occupancy classification and the design basis of the automatic sprinkler system, shall be provided and mounted in an approved location.

34.2 Classification of Commodities.

34.2.1* Commodity classification and the corresponding protection requirements shall be determined based on the makeup of individual storage units. [13:20.3.1]

34.2.1.1 The type and amount of materials used as part of the product and its primary packaging as well as the storage pallet shall be considered in the classification of the commodity. [13:20.3.1.1]

34.2.1.2 When specific test data of commodity classification by a nationally recognized testing agency are available, the data shall be permitted to be used in determining classification of commodities. [13:20.3.1.2]

N **34.2.1.3** For the same storage arrangement, the following commodity classification ranking shall apply from lowest (Class I) to highest (exposed expanded plastic) severity as follows:

(1) Class I
(2) Class II
(3) Class III
(4) Class IV
(5) Cartoned nonexpanded plastic
(6) Cartoned expanded plastic
(7) Exposed nonexpanded plastic
(8) Exposed expanded plastic

[13: 20.3.1.3]

N **34.2.1.4** Protection criteria for commodities listed in 34.2.1.3 shall be permitted to protect lower commodities in the same list. [13:20.3.1.4]

34.2.2 Pallet Types.

34.2.2.1 General. When loads are palletized, the use of wood or metal pallets, or listed pallets equivalent to wood, shall be assumed in the classification of commodities. [13:20.3.2.1]

34.2.2.2 Plastic Pallet. A pallet having any portion of its construction consisting of a plastic material that has not been listed as equivalent to wood shall increase the class of commodity determined for a storage load in accordance with 20.3.2.2.1 or 20.3.2.2.2 of NFPA 13. [13:20.3.2.2]

Δ 34.3* Commodity Classes.

34.3.1* Class I. A Class I commodity shall be defined as a noncombustible product that meets one of the following criteria:

(1) Placed directly on wood pallets
(2) Placed in single-layer corrugated cartons, with or without single-thickness cardboard dividers, with or without pallets
(3) Shrink-wrapped or paper-wrapped as a unit load with or without pallets [13:20.4.1]

34.3.2* Class II. A Class II commodity shall be defined as a noncombustible product that is in slatted wooden crates, solid wood boxes, multiple-layered corrugated cartons, or equivalent combustible packaging material, with or without pallets. [13:20.4.2]

34.3.3* Class III.

34.3.3.1 A Class III commodity shall be defined as a product fashioned from wood, paper, natural fibers, or Group C plastics with or without cartons, boxes, or crates and with or without pallets. [13:20.4.3.1] [13:20.4.3]

34.3.3.2 A Class III commodity shall be permitted to contain a limited amount (5 percent or less by weight of nonexpanded plastic or 5 percent or less by volume of expanded plastic) of Group A or Group B plastics. [13:20.4.3.2]

34.3.3.3 Class III commodities containing a mix of both Group A expanded and nonexpanded plastics shall comply with Figure 34.3.3.3(a) where they are within cartons, boxes, or crates or with Figure 34.3.3.3(b) where they are exposed. [13:20.4.3.3]

III - Class III Commodity. Refer to 20.3.2 if a plastic pallet is used.
IV - Class IV Commodity. Refer to 20.3.2 if a plastic pallet is used.

Δ **FIGURE 34.3.3.3(a)** Commodities, Cartoned or Within a Wooden Container, Containing a Mixture of Expanded and Nonexpanded Group A Plastics. [13:Figure 20.4.3.3(a)]

FIGURE 34.3.3.3(b) Exposed Commodities Containing a Mixture of Expanded and Nonexpanded Group A Plastics. [13:Figure 20.4.3.3(b)]

III - Class III Commodity. Refer to 20.3.2 if a plastic pallet is used.
IV - Class IV Commodity. Refer to 20.3.2 if a plastic pallet is used.

34.3.4* Class IV. [13:20.4.4]

34.3.4.1 A Class IV commodity shall be defined as a product, with or without pallets, that meets one of the following criteria:

(1) Constructed partially or totally of Group B plastics
(2) Consists of free-flowing Group A plastic materials
(3) Cartoned, or within a wooden container, that contains greater than 5 percent and up to 15 percent by weight of Group A nonexpanded plastic
(4) Cartoned, or within a wooden container, that contains greater than 5 percent and up to 25 percent by volume of expanded Group A plastics
(5) Cartoned, or within a wooden container, that contains a mix of Group A expanded and nonexpanded plastics and complies with Figure 34.3.3.3(a)
(6) Exposed, that contains greater than 5 percent and up to 15 percent by weight of Group A nonexpanded plastic
(7) Exposed, that contains a mix of Group A expanded and nonexpanded plastics and complies with Figure 34.3.3.3(b)

[13:20.4.4.1]

34.3.4.2 The remaining materials shall be permitted to be noncombustible, wood, paper, natural fibers, or Group B or Group C plastics. [13:20.4.4.2]

34.3.5* **Classification of Plastics, Elastomers, and Rubber.** Plastics, elastomers, and rubber shall be classified as Group A, Group B, or Group C. [13:20.4.5]

34.3.5.1 Group A. The following materials shall be classified as Group A:

(1) ABS (acrylonitrile-butadiene-styrene copolymer)
(2) Acetal (polyformaldehyde)
(3) Acrylic (polymethyl methacrylate)
(4) Butyl rubber
(5) Cellulosics (cellulose acetate, cellulose acetate butyrate, ethyl cellulose)
(6) EPDM (ethylene-propylene rubber)
(7) FRP (fiberglass-reinforced polyester)
(8) Natural rubber
(9) Nitrile-rubber (acrylonitrile-butadiene-rubber)
(10) Nylon (nylon 6, nylon 6/6)
(11) PET (thermoplastic polyester)
(12) Polybutadiene
(13) Polycarbonate
(14) Polyester elastomer
(15) Polyethylene
(16) Polypropylene
(17) Polystyrene
(18) Polyurethane
(19) PVC (polyvinyl chloride — highly plasticized, with plasticizer content greater than 20 percent) (rarely found)
(20) PVF (polyvinyl fluoride)
(21) SAN (styrene acrylonitrile)
(22) SBR (styrene-butadiene rubber)

[13:20.4.5.1]

34.3.5.2* Group A plastics shall be further subdivided as either expanded or nonexpanded. [13:20.4.5.2]

34.3.5.3 A Group A expanded plastic commodity shall be defined as a product, with or without pallets, that meets one of the following criteria:

(1) Cartoned, or within a wooden container, that contains greater than 40 percent by volume of Group A expanded plastic
(2) Exposed, that contains greater than 25 percent by volume of Group A expanded plastic

[13:20.4.5.3]

34.3.5.4 A Group A nonexpanded plastic commodity shall be defined as a product, with or without pallets, that meets one of the following criteria:

(1) Cartoned, or within a wooden container, that contains greater than 15 percent by weight of Group A nonexpanded plastic

(2) Cartoned, or within a wooden container, that contains greater than 25 percent and up to 40 percent by volume of Group A expanded plastic
(3) Cartoned, or within a wooden container, that contains a mix of Group A nonexpanded and expanded plastics, in compliance with Figure 34.3.3.3(a)
(4) Exposed, that contains greater than 15 percent by weight of Group A nonexpanded plastic
(5) Exposed, that contains greater than 5 percent and up to 25 percent by volume of Group A expanded plastic
(6) Exposed, that contains a mix of Group A nonexpanded and expanded plastics, in compliance with Figure 34.3.3.3(b)

[13:20.4.5.4]

34.3.5.5 The remaining materials shall be permitted to be noncombustible, wood, paper, natural or synthetic fibers, or Group A, Group B, or Group C plastics. [13:20.4.5.5]

34.3.6 Group B. The following materials shall be classified as Group B:

(1) Chloroprene rubber
(2) Fluoroplastics (ECTFE — ethylene-chlorotrifluoro-ethylene copolymer; ETFE — ethylene tetrafluoroethylene copolymer; FEP — fluorinated ethylene-propylene copolymer)
(3) Silicone rubber

[13:20.4.6]

34.3.7 Group C. The following materials shall be classified as Group C:

(1) Fluoroplastics (PCTFE — polychlorotrifluoroethylene; PTFE — polytetrafluoroethylene)
(2) Melamine (melamine formaldehyde)
(3) Phenolic
(4) PVC (polyvinyl chloride — flexible — PVCs with plasticizer content up to 20 percent)
(5) PVDC (polyvinylidene chloride)
(6) PVDF (polyvinylidene fluoride)
(7) Urea (urea formaldehyde)

[13:20.4.7]

34.3.8* Plastic commodities shall be protected in accordance with Figure 34.3.8. *(See Section C.21 of NFPA 13.)* [13:20.4.8]

34.3.8.1 Group B plastics and free-flowing Group A plastics shall be protected the same as Class IV commodities. [13:20.4.8.1]

34.3.8.2 Group C plastics shall be protected the same as Class III commodities. [13:20.4.8.2]

34.3.9 Rubber Tires. Pneumatic tires for passenger automobiles, aircraft, light and heavy trucks, trailers, farm equipment, construction equipment (off-the-road), and buses shall be protected as rubber tire storage in accordance with Chapters 20 through 25 of NFPA 13. [13:20.4.9]

34.3.10* Classification of Rolled Paper Storage. For the purposes of this *Code*, the classifications of paper described in 34.3.10.1 through 34.3.10.4 shall apply and shall be used to determine the sprinkler system design criteria in accordance with Chapters 20 through 25 of NFPA 13. [13:20.4.10]

34.3.10.1 Heavyweight Class. Heavyweight class shall be defined so as to include paperboard and paper stock having a basis weight [weight per 1000 ft^2 (93 m^2)] of 20 lb (100 g/m^2). [13:20.4.10.1]

34.3.10.2 Mediumweight Class. Mediumweight class shall be defined so as to include all the broad range of papers having a basis weight [weight per 1000 ft^2 (93 m^2)] of 10 lb to 20 lb (50 g/m^2 to 100 g/m^2). [13:20.4.10.2]

34.3.10.3 Lightweight Class. Lightweight class shall be defined so as to include all papers having a basis weight [weight per 1000 ft^2 (93 m^2)] of 10 lb (50 g/m^2). [13:20.4.10.3]

34.3.10.4 Tissue. [13:20.4.10.4]

34.3.10.4.1 Tissue shall be defined so as to include the broad range of papers of characteristic gauzy texture, which, in some cases, are fairly transparent. [13:20.4.10.4.1]

34.3.10.4.2 For the purposes of this *Code*, tissue shall be defined as the soft, absorbent type, regardless of basis weight — specifically, crepe wadding and the sanitary class including facial tissue, paper napkins, bathroom tissue, and toweling. [13:20.4.10.4.2]

34.3.11* Plastic Motor Vehicle Components. Group A plastic automotive components and associated packaging material consisting of exposed, expanded Group A plastic dunnage, instrument panels, and plastic bumper fascia shall be permitted to be protected as defined in Chapter 23 of NFPA 13. [13:20.5.4]

Δ **34.3.12 Display/Storage of Up to Group A Plastics.** Group A plastics combined with Class I through Class IV commodities in a display/storage arrangement shall be permitted to be protected as display/storage of up to Group A plastics in accordance with Section 26.3 of NFPA 13. [13:20.4.11]

Δ **34.3.12.1 Baled Cotton.** Baled cotton shall be protected in accordance with Section 26.5 of NFPA 13. *(See Table A.3.3.23.)* [13:20.4.11.1]

34.3.13 Carton Records Storage. A Class III commodity consisting predominantly of paper records in cardboard cartons shall be permitted to be protected as cartoned record storage in accordance with Section 26.6 of NFPA 13. [13:20.4.12]

FIGURE 34.3.8 Decision Tree. [13:Figure 20.4.8]

34.3.14 Mixed Commodities. [13:20.4.13]

34.3.14.1 Protection requirements shall not be based on the overall commodity mix in a fire area. [13:20.4.13.1]

34.3.14.2 Unless the requirements of 34.3.14.3 or 34.3.14.4 are met, mixed commodity storage shall be protected by the requirements for the highest classified commodity and storage arrangement. [13:20.4.13.2]

34.3.14.3 The protection requirements for the lower commodity class shall be permitted to be utilized where all of the following are met:

(1) Up to 10 pallet loads of a higher hazard commodity, as described in 34.3.1 and 34.3.7, shall be permitted to be present in an area not exceeding 40,000 ft^2 (3720 m^2).
(2) The higher hazard commodity shall be randomly dispersed with no adjacent loads in any direction (including diagonally).
(3) Where the ceiling protection is based on Class I or Class II commodities, the allowable number of pallet loads for Class IV or Group A plastics shall be reduced to five. [13:20.4.13.3]

34.3.14.4 Mixed Commodity Segregation. The protection requirements for the lower commodity class shall be permitted to be utilized in the area of lower commodity class, where the higher hazard material is confined to a designated area and the area is protected to the higher hazard in accordance with the requirements of this *Code*. [13:20.4.13.4]

34.4 Building Construction.

34.4.1* Construction Type. Buildings used for storage of materials that are stored and protected in accordance with this chapter shall be permitted to be of any of the types described in NFPA 220.

34.4.2 Fire-Fighting Access. Access shall be provided to all portions of the premises for fire-fighting purposes.

34.4.3* Emergency Smoke and Heat Venting.

34.4.3.1 Protection outlined in this chapter shall apply to buildings with or without smoke and heat vents.

34.4.3.2 Protection outlined in this chapter shall apply to buildings with or without draft curtains.

34.4.3.3 Where local codes require smoke and heat vents in buildings protected by early suppression fast response (ESFR) sprinklers, the vents shall be manually operated or have an operating mechanism with a standard response fusible element rated not less than 360°F (182°C).

34.5 Storage Arrangement.

34.5.1* Piling Procedures and Precautions.

34.5.1.1 Any commodities that are hazardous in combination with each other shall be stored so they cannot come into contact with each other.

34.5.1.2 Safe floor loads shall not be exceeded.

34.5.1.3 Where storing water-absorbent commodities, normal floor loads shall be reduced to take into account the added weight of water that can be absorbed during fire-fighting operations.

34.5.2 Commodity Clearance.

34.5.2.1 The clearance between top of storage and sprinkler deflectors shall conform to NFPA 13.

34.5.2.2* If the commodity is stored above the lower chord of roof trusses, not less than 1 ft (0.3 m) of clear space shall be maintained to allow wetting of the truss, unless the truss is protected with 1-hour fireproofing.

34.5.2.3 Storage clearance from ducts shall be maintained in accordance with NFPA 91.

34.5.2.4 The clearance between stored materials and unit heaters, radiant space heaters, duct furnaces, and flues shall not be less than 3 ft (0.9 m) in all directions or shall be in accordance with the clearances shown on the approval agency label.

34.5.2.5* Clearance shall be maintained to lights or light fixtures to prevent ignition.

34.5.2.6 Clearance shall be maintained around the path of fire door travel to ensure the door's proper operation and inspection.

34.5.2.7 Operation and inspection clearance shall be maintained around fire-extinguishing and fire protection equipment.

34.5.3 Aisles.

34.5.3.1 For the storage of commodities that expand with the absorption of water, such as roll paper, wall aisles not less than 24 in. (0.6 m) wide shall be provided.

34.5.3.2 Aisles shall be maintained to retard the transfer of fire from one pile to another and to allow convenient access for fire fighting, salvage, and removal of storage.

34.5.4 Flammable and Combustible Liquids. Storage of flammable or combustible liquids shall be in accordance with Chapter 60.

34.6 General Fire Protection.

34.6.1* Sprinkler Systems. Sprinkler systems installed in buildings used for storage shall be in accordance with Section 13.3.

34.6.2 High-Expansion Foam.

34.6.2.1 High-expansion foam systems installed in addition to automatic sprinklers shall be installed in accordance with NFPA 11 except where modified by other requirements in this chapter.

34.6.2.2 High-expansion foam used to protect idle pallets shall have a fill time of not more than 4 minutes.

34.6.2.3 High-expansion foam systems shall be automatic in operation.

34.6.2.4 Detectors for high-expansion foam systems shall be listed and shall be installed at the ceiling at not more than one-half the listed spacing in accordance with *NFPA 72*.

34.6.2.5 Detection systems, concentrate pumps, generators, and other system components essential to the operation of the system shall have an approved standby power source.

34.6.3 Manual Protection.

34.6.3.1 Portable Fire Extinguishers.

34.6.3.1.1 Portable fire extinguishers shall be provided in accordance with Section 13.6, unless 34.6.3.1.2 applies.

34.6.3.1.2 Where 1½ in. (38 mm) hose lines are available to reach all portions of areas with Class A fire loads, up to one-half of the portable fire extinguishers required by Section 13.6 shall be permitted to be omitted.

34.6.3.2 Hydrants. At locations without public hydrants, or where hydrants are not within 250 ft (75 m), private hydrants shall be installed in accordance with Section 13.5.

34.6.4 Fire Organization.

34.6.4.1 Arrangements shall be made to allow rapid entry into the premises by the municipal fire department, police department, or other authorized personnel in case of fire or other emergency.

34.6.4.2* Due to the unique nature of storage fires and the hazards associated with fighting such fires, facility emergency personnel shall be trained to have knowledge of the following:

(1) Pile and building collapse potential during fire-fighting and mop-up operations due to sprinkler water absorption, use of hose streams, and the undermining of piles by fire that is likely to cause material or piles to fall (especially roll tissue paper), resulting in injury
(2) Operation of sprinkler systems and water supply equipment
(3) Location of the controlling sprinkler valves so that the correct sprinkler system can be turned on or off as necessary
(4) Correct operation of emergency smoke and heat vent systems where they have been provided
(5) Use of material-handling equipment while sprinklers are operating to effect final extinguishment
(6) Procedure for summoning outside aid immediately in an emergency
(7) Maintenance of the security features of the premises
(8) Operation of foam systems, evacuation procedures, and safety precautions during all foam operations

34.6.4.3 A fire watch shall be maintained when the sprinkler system is not in service.

34.6.5 Alarm Service.

34.6.5.1 Automatic sprinkler systems and foam systems, where provided, shall have approved central station, auxiliary, remote station, or proprietary waterflow alarm service unless otherwise permitted by 34.6.5.1.1 or 34.6.5.1.2.

34.6.5.1.1 Local waterflow alarm service shall be permitted when recorded guard service also is provided.

34.6.5.1.2 Local waterflow alarm service shall be permitted where the storage facilities are occupied on a 24-hour basis.

34.6.5.2 Alarm service shall comply with *NFPA 72*.

34.6.6 Security Service. Security service, where provided, shall comply with NFPA 601.

34.7 Building Equipment, Maintenance, and Operations.

34.7.1 Industrial Trucks.

34.7.1.1 Power-operated industrial trucks and their use shall comply with NFPA 505.

34.7.1.2 Industrial trucks using liquefied petroleum gas (LP-Gas) or liquid fuel shall be refueled outside of the storage building at a location designated for the purpose.

34.7.2 Building Service Equipment. Electrical equipment shall be installed in accordance with the provisions of Section 11.1.

34.7.3 Cutting and Welding Operations.

34.7.3.1 Where welding or cutting operations are necessary, the requirements of Chapter 41 shall apply.

34.7.3.2* Welding, soldering, brazing, and cutting shall be permitted to be performed on building components or contents that cannot be removed, provided that no storage is located below and within 25 ft (7.6 m) of the working area and flameproof tarpaulins enclose the area.

34.7.3.3 During any of the operations identified in 34.7.3.2, all of the following shall apply:

(1) The sprinkler system shall be in service.
(2) Extinguishers suitable for Class A fires with a minimum rating of 2-A shall be located in the working area.
(3) Where inside hose lines are available, charged and attended inside hose lines shall be located in the working area.
(4) A fire watch shall be maintained during the operations specified in 34.7.3.2 and for not less than 30 minutes following completion of open-flame operation.

34.7.4 Waste Disposal.

34.7.4.1 Approved containers for rubbish and other trash materials shall be provided.

34.7.4.2 Rubbish, trash, and other waste material shall be disposed of at regular intervals.

34.7.5 Smoking.

34.7.5.1 Smoking shall be prohibited except in locations designated as smoking areas.

34.7.5.2 Signs that read "No Smoking" shall be posted in prohibited areas.

34.7.6* Maintenance and Inspection.

34.7.6.1 Fire walls, fire doors, and floors shall be maintained in functional condition at all times.

34.7.6.2* All water-based fire protection systems and the water supplies shall be inspected, tested, and maintained in accordance with NFPA 25.

34.7.6.3 Storage Plan Maintenance.

34.7.6.3.1 Storage shall comply with the approved storage floor plan.

34.7.6.3.2* Compliance with the approved storage floor plan required by 34.1.3 shall be evaluated and verified not less than once per year.

34.7.6.3.3 Modifications or changes to the approved storage floor plan shall be approved by the AHJ prior to any modifications or changes.

34.7.7 Refrigeration Systems. Refrigeration systems, if used, shall be in accordance with ASHRAE 15, *Safety Code for Mechanical Refrigeration.*

34.7.8 Lighting. Where metal halide lighting is installed, it shall be selected, installed, and maintained such that catastrophic failure of the bulb shall not ignite materials below.

34.8 Protection of Rack Storage.

34.8.1 Application. Section 34.8 shall apply to the indoor storage of normal combustibles (Class I through Class IV) and plastics that are stored on racks.

34.8.2 Building Construction.

34.8.2.1 Fire protection of roof steel shall not be required when sprinkler systems are installed in accordance with Section 13.3.

34.8.2.2 Fire protection of steel building columns and vertical rack members that support the building shall not be required when ceiling sprinklers and in-rack sprinklers are installed in accordance with Section 13.3.

34.8.2.3 For sprinklered buildings with rack storage of over 15 ft (4.6 m) in height and only ceiling sprinklers installed, steel building columns within the rack structure and vertical rack members that support the building shall have a fire resistance rating not less than 1 hour, unless the installation meets the requirements of 16.1.4 of NFPA 13.

34.8.3 Storage Arrangement.

34.8.3.1* Rack Structure. Rack configurations shall be approved.

34.8.3.2* Rack Loading. Racks shall not be loaded beyond their design capacity.

34.8.3.3* Aisle Widths.

34.8.3.3.1 Aisle widths and depth of racks shall be determined by material-handling methods.

34.8.3.3.2 The width of aisles shall be considered in the design of the protection system.

34.8.3.3.3* Aisle widths shall be maintained by either fixed rack structures or control in placement of portable racks.

34.8.3.3.4 Any decrease in aisle width shall require a review of the adequacy of the protection system.

34.8.3.4 General Fire Protection.

34.8.3.4.1 High-Expansion Foam.

34.8.3.4.1.1* Where high-expansion foam systems are installed, they shall be automatic in operation and shall be in accordance with NFPA 11, except when modified by 34.8.3.4.

34.8.3.4.1.2 When high-expansion foam systems are used in combination with ceiling sprinklers, in-rack sprinklers shall not be required.

34.8.3.4.1.3 Detectors shall be listed and shall be installed in one of the following configurations:

(1) At one-half listed linear spacing [e.g., 15 ft × 15 ft (4.6 m × 4.6 m) rather than 30 ft × 30 ft (9.1 m × 9.1 m)] when the following conditions exist:
   (a) Detectors are installed at the ceiling only.
   (b) The clearance from the top of storage does not exceed 10 ft (3 m).
   (c) The height of storage does not exceed 25 ft (7.6 m).
(2) At the ceiling at listed spacing and on racks at alternate levels
(3) Where listed for rack storage installation and installed in accordance with ceiling detector listing to provide response within 1 minute after ignition using an ignition source equivalent to that used in a rack storage testing program

34.8.3.4.2 High-Expansion Foam Submergence.

34.8.3.4.2.1 The following requirements shall apply to storage of Class I, Class II, Class III, and Class IV commodities, as classified in Section 34.2, up to and including 25 ft (7.6 m) in height:

(1)* When high-expansion foam systems are used without sprinklers, the submergence time shall be not more than 5 minutes for Class I, Class II, or Class III commodities.
(2) When high-expansion foam systems are used without sprinklers, the submergence time shall be not more than 4 minutes for Class IV commodities.
(3) When high-expansion foam systems are used in combination with ceiling sprinklers, the submergence time shall be not more than 7 minutes for Class I, Class II, or Class III commodities.
(4) When high-expansion foam systems are used in combination with ceiling sprinklers, the submergence time shall be not more than 5 minutes for Class IV commodities.

34.8.3.4.2.2 The following requirements shall apply to storage of Class I, Class II, Class III, and Class IV commodities stored over 25 ft (7.6 m) high up to and including 35 ft (10.7 m) in height:

(1) Ceiling sprinklers shall be used in combination with the high-expansion foam system.
(2) The submergence time for the high-expansion foam shall be not more than 5 minutes for Class I, Class II, or Class III commodities.
(3) The submergence time for the high-expansion foam shall be not more than 4 minutes for Class IV commodities.

34.9 Protection of Rubber Tires.

34.9.1* Application.

34.9.1.1 Section 34.9 shall apply to new facilities with indoor storage of usable tires and to existing facilities being converted to the indoor storage of usable tires.

34.9.1.2 Existing buildings storing rubber tires shall be exempted from complying with Section 34.9.

34.9.1.3 This section shall not apply to scrap tire storage.

34.9.2 Building Arrangement.

34.9.2.1 Steel Columns. Steel columns shall be protected as follows unless protected in accordance with 16.1.4 of NFPA 13:

(1) For storage exceeding 15 ft to 20 ft (4.6 m to 6 m) in height, columns shall have 1-hour fireproofing.

(2) For storage exceeding 20 ft (6 m) in height, columns shall have 2-hour fireproofing for the entire length of the column, including connections with other structural members.

34.9.2.2 Fire Walls.

34.9.2.2.1 Four-hour fire walls shall be provided between the tire warehouse and tire manufacturing areas.

34.9.2.2.2 Fire walls shall be designed in accordance with NFPA 221.

34.9.2.3* Travel Distance to Exits. Travel distance to exits shall be in accordance with NFPA *101*.

34.9.3 Storage Arrangement.

34.9.3.1 Piling Procedures.

34.9.3.1.1* Piles that are not adjacent to or located along a wall shall be not more than 50 ft (15 m) in width.

34.9.3.1.2 Tires stored adjacent to or along one wall shall not extend more than 25 ft (7.6 m) from the wall.

34.9.3.1.3 Where tires are stored on-tread, the dimension of the pile in the direction of the wheel hole shall be not more than 50 ft (15 m).

34.9.3.1.4 The width of the main aisles between piles shall be not less than 8 ft (2.4 m).

34.9.3.2 Clearances.

34.9.3.2.1 Storage clearance from roof structures shall be not less than 18 in. (470 mm) in all directions.

34.9.3.2.2 A clearance of not less than 24 in. (610 mm) shall be maintained around the path of fire door travel unless a barricade is provided.

34.9.3.2.3 Where protection in accordance with this chapter is provided, stored tires shall be segregated from other combustible storage by aisles not less than 8 ft (2.4 m) wide.

34.10 Protection of Roll Paper.

34.10.1 Application. Section 34.10 shall apply to new facilities with indoor storage of roll paper, and to existing facilities being converted to the indoor storage of roll paper, except for the following types of roll paper:

(1) Waxed paper
(2) Synthetic paper
(3) Palletized roll paper storage other than that stored on a single floor pallet or raised floor platform

34.10.2* Building Construction. The protection outlined in Section 34.10 shall apply to buildings with or without fireproofing or other modes of steel protection, unless modified by the requirements of 34.5.2.2.

34.10.3 Storage Arrangement. The floor load design shall take into account the added weight of water that could be absorbed by the commodity during fire-fighting operations.

34.11 Storage of Idle Pallets.

34.11.1* General. Idle pallets shall be stored outside or in a separate building designated for pallet storage, unless permitted by 34.11.2.

34.11.2 Indoor Storage. Idle pallets shall be permitted to be stored in a building used for other storage or other purpose if the building is sprinklered in accordance with Section 13.3.

34.11.3* Outdoor Storage.

34.11.3.1 The storage of wood and wood composite pallets or listed pallets equivalent to wood at pallet manufacturing and pallet recycling facility sites shall comply with 34.11.4.

34.11.3.2 Idle pallets stored outside shall be stored in accordance with Table 34.11.3.2(a) and Table 34.11.3.2(b).

Table 34.11.3.2(a) Required Clearance Between Outside Idle Pallet Storage and Other Yard Storage

Pile Size	Minimum Distance ft	Minimum Distance m
Under 50 pallets	20	6
50–200 pallets	30	9
Over 200 pallets	50	15

Table 34.11.3.2(b) Required Clearance Between Outside Idle Pallet Storage and Building

Wall Construction	Under 50 Pallets ft	Under 50 Pallets m	50 to 200 Pallets ft	50 to 200 Pallets m	Over 200 Pallets ft	Over 200 Pallets m
Masonry with no openings	0	0	0	0	15	4.6
Masonry with wired glass in openings, outside sprinklers, and 1-hour doors	0	0	10	3	20	6
Masonry with wired or plain glass, outside sprinklers, and ¾-hour doors	10	3	20	6	30	9
Wood or metal with outside sprinklers	10	3	20	6	30	9
Wood, metal, or other	20	6	30	9	50	15

34.11.3.3 Idle pallet stacks shall not exceed 15 ft (4.6 m) in height nor shall cover an area of greater than 400 ft² (37 m²). Pallet stacks shall be arranged to form stable piles. A distance of not less than 8 ft (2.4 m) shall separate stacks. Piles shall be no closer than 8 ft (2.4 m) to any property line.

34.11.4 Outside Storage at Pallet Manufacturing and Pallet Recycling Facilities.

34.11.4.1* The outside storage of wood and wood composite pallets or listed pallets equivalent to wood on the same site as a pallet manufacturing or pallet recycling facility shall comply with 34.11.4.

34.11.4.2 Each site shall maintain a current site plan. The site plan shall be submitted to the authority having jurisdiction for review and approval and shall include all of the following:

(1) Lot lines
(2) Utilities
(3) Size, location, and type of construction of the buildings on the property
(4) Presence of fire protection systems
(5) Water supply sources for fire-fighting purposes
(6) Locations of hazardous material storage areas
(7) Location of pallet storage
(8) Equipment protected with a dust collection system
(9) Fire department access routes
(10) Designated smoking areas
(11) Locations of fire alarm control panels

34.11.4.3 The owner or designated representative shall submit a fire prevention plan for review and approval by the authority having jurisdiction that includes all of the following:

(1) Frequency of walk-through inspections to verify compliance with the approved fire prevention plan
(2) Hot work permit process in accordance with Chapter 41
(3) Preventive maintenance program for equipment associated with the pallet activities
(4) Inspection, testing, and maintenance of fire protection systems in accordance with Chapter 13
(5) Frequency of walk-through inspections to verify pallet stack height, area, and setbacks are in compliance with 34.11.4

34.11.4.4 The owner or designated representative shall prepare and train employees in an approved emergency action plan in accordance with Section 10.4.

34.11.4.5 The owner or designated representative shall prepare a security management plan based on a security risk assessment and shall make the plan and assessment available to the AHJ upon request.

34.11.4.6 Unless permitted by 34.11.4.11, stacks of pallets shall not be stored within 0.75 times the stack height or 8 ft (2.4 m), whichever is greater, of any property line.

34.11.4.7 Unless permitted by 34.11.4.11, stacks of pallets shall not be stored within 0.75 times the stack height of any important building on site.

34.11.4.8 Pallet stacks shall not exceed 20 ft (6 m) in height.

34.11.4.9* The size of pallet arrays shall comply with one of the following:

(1) Where the access to the pallet array is less than 20 ft (6 m) in width but at least 8 ft (2.4 m) in width, the nearest edge of any individual pallet stack shall be no more than 30 ft (9 m) from the access.
(2) Where the access to the pallet array is by a fire department access route complying with Section 18.2, the nearest edge of any individual pallet stack shall be no more than 50 ft (15 m) from the access.
(3) The individual pallet stack depth from access within pallet arrays at existing facilities that exceed 34.11.4.9(1) or 34.11.4.9(2) shall be as approved by the AHJ.

34.11.4.10* Fire flow requirements for the site shall be determined by the AHJ.

34.11.4.11 Portable fire extinguishers shall be selected, installed, and maintained in accordance with Section 13.6.

Δ **34.11.4.12*** The AHJ shall be permitted to allow pallet stacks closer to a property line or structure on-site where additional fire protection is provided.

Chapter 35 Animal Housing Facilities

35.1 General. Animal housing facilities shall comply with NFPA 150 and this chapter.

35.2 Permits. Permits, where required, shall comply with Section 1.13.

Chapter 36 Telecommunication Facilities and Information Technology Equipment

36.1 General.

Δ **36.1.1** Telecommunication facilities shall comply with NFPA 76.

Δ **36.1.2** Information technology equipment and information technology equipment areas shall comply with NFPA 75.

Chapter 37 Fixed Guideway Transit and Passenger Rail Systems

37.1 General. Fixed guideway transit and passenger rail system facilities shall comply with NFPA 130.

Chapter 38 Cannabis Growing, Processing, or Extraction Facilities

38.1* Application.

38.1.1* Chapter 38 shall apply to the growing and processing of cannabis within new and existing buildings.

38.1.2 The use, storage, transfilling, and handling of hazardous materials shall comply with this chapter, and other applicable provisions of this *Code*.

38.1.3 Chapter 38 shall not apply to the retail sale of cannabis where growing and processing does not occur.

38.1.4 Where a material, its use, or associated process poses multiple hazards, all hazards shall be addressed in accordance with applicable requirements of this *Code*.

38.1.5* The occupancy of buildings or portions of buildings where the growing or processing of cannabis occurs shall be in accordance with Chapter 6 and the applicable building code.

38.2 Permits. Permits, where required, shall comply with Section 1.13.

38.3 Fire Protection Systems. Fire protection systems shall be provided in accordance with Chapter 13.

38.4* Means of Egress. Means of egress shall be in accordance with Chapter 14.

38.5 Growing or Production of Cannabis.

38.5.1 Ventilation for Light Fixtures. Light fixture ductwork shall be installed in accordance with the manufacturer and NFPA 90A.

38.5.2 Odor Control. The use of ozone generators used for odor control shall comply with Chapter 54.

38.5.3 Carbon Dioxide Enrichment Equipment. The design, installation, and maintenance of equipment utilized for a carbon dioxide enrichment process with more than 100 lb (45.4 kg) of carbon dioxide or utilizing any quantity of carbon dioxide having a remote fill connection shall comply with 38.5.3.1 through 38.5.3.5.

38.5.3.1 Equipment. Pressure relief, vent piping, fill indicators, fill connections, vent terminations, piping systems, and the storage, use, and handling of the carbon dioxide shall be in accordance with NFPA 55.

38.5.3.2 Gas Detection System. A gas detection system complying with NFPA 55 shall be provided in rooms or indoor areas in which the carbon dioxide enrichment process is located, in rooms or indoor areas in which container systems are located, and in other areas where carbon dioxide could accumulate.

38.5.3.2.1 System Design. The system shall be designed as follows:

(1) Activates a low-level alarm upon detection of a carbon dioxide concentration of 5000 ppm (9000 mg/m^3).
(2) Activates a high-level alarm upon detection of a carbon dioxide concentration of 30,000 ppm (54,000 mg/m^3).

38.5.3.2.2 System Activation.

38.5.3.2.2.1 Activation of the low-level gas detection system alarm shall automatically initiate the following:

(1) Stop the flow of carbon dioxide to the piping system.
(2) Activate the mechanical exhaust ventilation system.
(3) Activate an audible and visible supervisory alarm signal at an approved location within the building.

38.5.3.2.2.2 Activation of the high-level gas detection system alarm shall automatically initiate the following:

(1) Stop the flow of carbon dioxide to the piping system.
(2) Activate the mechanical exhaust ventilation system.
(3) Activate an audible and visible evacuation alarm both inside and outside of the carbon dioxide enrichment area and the area in which the carbon dioxide containers are located.

38.5.3.3 Pressurization and Ventilation. Rooms or indoor areas in which carbon dioxide enrichment is provided shall be maintained at a negative pressure in relation to the surrounding areas in the building. A mechanical ventilation system shall be provided in accordance 3.3.57.3, mechanical code, and complies with all of the following:

(1) Mechanical ventilation in the room or area shall be at a rate of not less than 1 cfm/ft^2 [0.00508 m^3/(s • m^2)].
(2) When activated by the gas detection system, the mechanical ventilation system shall remain on until manually reset.
(3) The exhaust system intakes shall be taken from points within 12 in. (305 mm) of the floor.
(4) The ventilation system shall discharge to the outdoors in an approved location.

Δ **38.5.3.4 Signage.**

N **38.5.3.4.1** Hazard identification signs shall be posted at the entrance to the room and indoor areas where the carbon dioxide enrichment process is located, and at the entrance to the room or indoor area where the carbon dioxide containers are located.

N **38.5.3.4.2** Hazard identification signs shall be not less than 8 in. (200 mm) in width and 6 in. (150 mm) in height and indicate the following:

CAUTION: CARBON DIOXIDE (CO$_2$) GAS VENTILATE THE AREA BEFORE ENTERING. A HIGH CO$_2$ GAS CONCENTRATION IN THIS AREA CAN CAUSE ASPHYXIATION.

38.5.3.5 Container Refilling. Carbon dioxide containers located indoors shall not be refilled unless filled from a remote connection located outdoors.

38.5.4 Interior Finish, Contents, and Furnishings.

38.5.4.1 Interior finish, including the use of any plastic, mylar, or other thin film sheeting to enclose rooms or cover any walls or ceilings shall be in accordance with Sections 12.5 and 12.6.

38.5.4.2 Hanging of plastic from ceiling or from suspended overhead structures to create wall dividers shall not be permitted.

38.5.5 Fumigation.

38.5.5.1* General. Any cannabis growing facility that is fumigated shall comply with 38.5.5.

38.5.5.2* Sources of Ignition. Sources of ignition shall be shut off during the fumigation activity and remain shut off until the required ventilation is completed.

38.5.5.3 Notification.

38.5.5.3.1 The AHJ and fire department shall be notified in writing not less than 48 hours before the building, structure, or space is to be closed in connection with the utilization of any toxic or flammable fumigant.

38.5.5.3.2 Notification, as required by 38.5.5.3.1, shall include the following:

(1) The location of the enclosed space to be fumigated or fogged
(2) The occupancy
(3) The fumigants or insecticides to be utilized
(4) The person or persons responsible for the operation
(5) The date and time at which the operation will begin

38.5.5.3.3 Written notice of any fumigation or insecticidal fogging operation shall be given to all affected occupants of the building, structure, or space in which such operations are to be conducted with sufficient advance notice to allow the occupants to evacuate the building, structure, or space.

38.5.5.3.4 Written notice, as required by 38.5.5.3.3, shall inform the occupants as to the purposes, anticipated duration, and hazards associated with the fumigation or insecticidal fogging operation.

38.5.5.4 Signage.

38.5.5.4.1 Approved warning signs indicating the danger, type of chemical involved, and necessary precautions shall be posted on all doors and entrances to the premises, including interior rooms and areas.

38.5.5.4.2 Signage shall be located at the exterior main entry and at the entries to those areas being fumigated indicating the duration of the fumigation.

38.5.5.5 Watch Personnel.

38.5.5.5.1 During the period fumigation is in progress a watchperson shall remain on duty at the entrance or entrances to the enclosed fumigated space until after the fumigation is completed and the building, structure, or space is properly ventilated and safe for occupancy.

38.5.5.5.2 Sufficient watchpersons shall be provided to prevent any person from entering the enclosed space under fumigation unobserved.

38.5.5.6 Occupancy During Fumigation. Occupants of the building, structure, or space to be fumigated, except the personnel conducting the fumigation, shall be evacuated from such building, structure, or space prior to commencing fumigation operations.

38.5.5.7 Sealing of Building Structure, or Space. Paper, and other similar materials, used to wrap or cover a building, structure, or space in excess of that required for the sealing of cracks, casements, and similar openings shall meet the flame propagation performance criteria of Test Method 1 or Test Method 2 of NFPA 701.

38.5.5.8 Maintenance of Openings. All openings to the building, structure, or space to be fumigated or fogged shall be kept securely closed during such operation.

38.5.5.9 Venting and Cleanup. At the end of the exposure period the following procedures shall be followed:

(1) Fumigators shall safely and properly ventilate the premises and contents.
(2) Fumigant containers, residues, debris, and other materials used for such fumigation shall be properly disposed.
(3) Obstructions shall be cleared from gas-fired appliance vents.

38.5.6 Pesticide Application.

38.5.6.1 A warning sign shall be provided to indicate that pesticides have been applied.

38.5.6.2 A record of pesticide application shall be provided and shall include the following:

(1) The pesticide product or chemical used
(2) The date and time the pesticide was applied
(3) When the room or area is safe to reoccupy

38.6* Processing or Extraction.

38.6.1 General.

38.6.1.1 Extraction Room.

38.6.1.1.1 Extraction rooms in a cannabis extraction facility shall be constructed in accordance with the building code and this *Code*.

38.6.1.1.2* For other than CO_2 and nonhazardous extraction process, the cannabis extraction equipment and process shall be located in a room of noncombustible construction dedicated to the extraction process and the room shall not be used for any other purpose.

38.6.1.1.3 Cannabis extraction shall not be located in any building containing assembly, educational, day care, health care, ambulatory health care, residential board and care, residential, or detention and correctional facilities.

Δ **38.6.1.1.4*** **Means of Egress.** For extraction rooms using hazardous materials, each room shall be provided with means of egress complying with the following:

(1) Egress capacity for high-hazard contents areas shall be based on 0.7 in./person (18 mm/person) for stairs or 0.4 in./person (10 mm/person) for level components and ramps in accordance with 7.3.3.1 of NFPA *101*. [*101*:7.11.3]
(2) Not less than two means of egress shall be provided from each building or hazardous area thereof, unless all of the following criteria are met:
   (a) Rooms or spaces do not exceed 200 ft² (18.6 m²).
   (b) Rooms or spaces have an occupant load not exceeding three persons.
   (c) Rooms or spaces have a travel distance to the room door not exceeding 25 ft (7620 mm).
   [*101*:7.11.4]
(3) Means of egress, for rooms or spaces other than those that meet the criteria of 7.11.4(1) through 7.11.4(3) of NFPA *101* shall be arranged so that there are no dead ends in corridors. [*101*:7.11.5]
(4) Doors serving high-hazard content areas shall swing in the direction of egress travel. [*101*:7.11.6]
(5) Doors serving high-hazard contents areas with occupant loads in excess of five shall be permitted to be provided with a latch or lock only if the latch or lock is panic hardware or fire exit hardware complying with 7.2.1.7 of NFPA *101*. [*101*:7.11.7]

38.6.1.2 Staffing.

38.6.1.2.1* For other than approved, unattended processes, the extraction process shall be continuously staffed.

38.6.1.2.2* Staff monitoring the extraction process shall be trained in the following:

(1) The extraction process
(2)* The transfer of solvents, where applicable
(3) All emergency procedures

38.6.1.2.3 All staff training records shall be maintained on-site and made available to the AHJ upon request.

38.6.1.3 Indoor Horticultural Grow Structures.

38.6.1.3.1 Indoor horticultural grow structures installed and operated inside all occupancies covered by this *Code* that exceed 5 ft (1524 mm) in height and 32 ft² (3.0 m²) in floor area shall comply with the building code and this *Code*.

38.6.1.3.2 Materials. Horticultural grow structures shall be constructed of noncombustible materials or of combustible materials that comply with the following:

(1) Textiles and films complying with Test Method 2 of NFPA 701
(2) Plastic materials having a maximum heat-release rate not greater than 100 kW when tested in accordance with UL 1975, *Fire Tests for Foamed Plastics Used for Decorative Purposes*, or when tested in accordance with NFPA 289, using the 20 kW ignition source
(3) Exterior fire-retardant-treated wood complying with NFPA 703
(4) Light-transmitting plastics complying with 12.5.5.15 of this *Code*
(5) Aluminum composite material (ACM) meeting the requirements of Class A interior finish in accordance with Chapter 10 of NFPA *101* when tested as an assembly in the maximum thickness intended for use

Δ **38.6.1.3.3 Electrical Wiring and Equipment.** Electrical wiring and equipment shall be listed and labeled for the intended use and installed in accordance with *NFPA 70*.

N **38.6.1.3.4 Horticultural Lighting.** Where horticultural lighting is used, it shall be listed and labeled in accordance with CAN/ULC 8800, *Horticultural Lighting Equipment and Systems*, and installed in accordance with *NFPA 70*.

38.6.1.3.5 Heating Appliances. Where heating appliances are installed, these devices shall be installed in accordance with the manufacturer's instructions and comply with the requirements in Section 11.5 of this *Code*.

Δ **38.6.1.3.6 Fire Protection Systems.**

N **38.6.1.3.6.1** All required fire protection systems shall be in accordance with Chapter 13 of this *Code*.

N **38.6.1.3.6.2** Obstructions to sprinkler discharge and clearances between automatic sprinklers and the top of horticultural grow structures shall comply with 13.3.1.2.

38.6.1.3.7 Clearance from Ignition Sources. Clearance between indoor horticultural grow structures and ignition sources such as luminaires, heaters, and grow lamps shall be maintained in an approved manner.

38.6.1.3.8 Area Limits. Indoor horticultural grow structures shall not exceed an aggregate 200 ft² (18.6 m²) of floor area per fire area, unless a special investigation, approved by the AHJ, has demonstrated adequate fire safety.

38.6.1.4 Operator Training.

38.6.1.4.1 In addition to the provisions of 38.6.1.2, the operator of the cannabis extraction equipment shall also receive training in safe operation of the equipment.

38.6.1.4.2* Documentation of training required by 38.6.1.4.1 shall be maintained on-site and made available to the AHJ upon request.

38.6.1.5 Signage.

38.6.1.5.1 All applicable safety data sheets (SDS) shall be posted in the extraction room.

38.6.1.5.2 The NFPA 704 hazard rating diamond sign and no smoking signs shall be posted on the exterior of the extraction room door.

38.6.1.5.3 Applicable hazard warning signage shall be posted throughout the facility as applicable for emergency equipment.

38.6.1.6 Systems, Equipment, and Processes.

38.6.1.6.1 General.

38.6.1.6.1.1 Systems, equipment, and processes shall be in accordance with 38.6.1.6.1 through 38.6.1.6.6.3.

38.6.1.6.1.2 Systems, equipment, and processes shall include, but are not limited to, vessels, chambers, containers, cylinders, tanks, piping, tubing, valves, fittings, and pumps.

38.6.1.6.1.3 In addition to the requirements in 38.6.1.6, systems, equipment, and processes shall also comply with 60.5.1.6, other applicable provisions of this *Code*, the building code, and NFPA 90A.

Δ **38.6.1.6.1.4** Systems or equipment used for the extraction of cannabis oils and products from plant material shall be performed using equipment that has been listed in accordance with CAN/UL 1389, *Plant Oil Extraction Equipment for Installation and Use in Ordinary (Unclassified) Locations and Hazardous (Classified) Locations*.

38.6.1.6.2 Equipment.

38.6.1.6.2.1 Where an explosion condition exists, heating equipment such as vacuum ovens, heating mantels, heat guns, or other equipment shall not be used to heat flammable or combustible liquids or oils containing liquefied petroleum gasses.

38.6.1.6.2.2 Refrigerators, freezers, and other cooling equipment used to store or cool flammable liquids shall be listed for the storage of flammable/combustible liquids or be listed for Class I, Division 1 locations, as described in Article 501 of *NFPA 70*.

38.6.1.6.2.3* LPG tanks shall comply with 69.2.1.

38.6.1.6.3 Approval for Systems and Equipment with No Listing.

38.6.1.6.3.1 Where the system used for extraction of cannabis oils and products from plant material is not listed, the system shall have a designer of record.

38.6.1.6.3.2 The designer of record shall be a registered design professional.

38.6.1.6.4* Documentation for Equipment with No Listing. For systems and equipment not listed for the specific use, a technical report in accordance with Section 1.16 documenting the design or peer review of the equipment shall be prepared and submitted to the AHJ for review and approval.

38.6.1.6.5 Change of Extraction Medium.

38.6.1.6.5.1 Where the medium of extraction or solvent is changed from the material indicated in the technical report or as required by the manufacturer, the technical report shall be revised at the cost of the facility owner and submitted for review and approval by the AHJ prior to the use of the equipment with the new medium or solvent.

38.6.1.6.5.2 If the original designer of record is not available, then the new designer of record shall comply with 38.6.1.6.3.1.

38.6.1.6.6 Equipment Field Verification.

38.6.1.6.6.1 Prior to operation of the extraction equipment, the designer of record for the equipment shall inspect the site of the extraction process once equipment has been installed for compliance with the technical report and the building analysis.

38.6.1.6.6.2 The designer of record performing the field verification shall provide a report of findings and observations of the site inspection to the AHJ for review and approval prior to the approval of the extraction process.

38.6.1.6.6.3 The field inspection report authored by designer of record shall include the serial number of the equipment used in the process and shall confirm the equipment installed is the same model and type of equipment identified in the technical report.

38.6.2 Liquefied Petroleum Gas (LPG) Extraction.

38.6.2.1 General. Cannabis extraction facilities using liquefied petroleum gas solvents shall comply with 38.6.1 and 38.6.2.

38.6.2.2 Exhaust.

38.6.2.2.1 An approved exhaust system shall be provided for LPG extractions.

38.6.2.2.2 The exhaust systems shall be installed and maintained accordance with NFPA 91 or the mechanical code.

38.6.2.2.3 All LPG extraction operations, including processes for off-gassing spent plant material and oil retrieval, shall be conducted within a chemical fume hood or enclosure in compliance with NFPA 91 or the mechanical code.

38.6.2.3 Electrical.

38.6.2.3.1 All conductive equipment and conductive objects within the exhaust room shall be bonded and grounded with a resistance of less than 1.0×10^6 ohms in accordance with *NFPA 70*.

38.6.2.3.2 The area within a hood or enclosure used for LPG extractions shall be classified as a Class I, Division 1 hazardous location in accordance with *NFPA 70*.

38.6.2.3.3 Areas adjacent to Class I, Division 1 locations shall be classified in accordance with *NFPA 70*.

38.6.2.3.4 All electrical components within the extraction room shall be interlocked with the hazardous exhaust system such that room lighting and other extraction room electrical equipment will only operate when the exhaust system is in operation.

38.6.2.3.5 An emergency power system in accordance with Section 11.7 shall be provided for the following items:

(1) Extraction room lighting
(2) Extraction room ventilation system
(3) Solvent gas detection system

38.6.2.4 Extraction Room Gas Detection System.

38.6.2.4.1 An approved continuous gas detection system shall be provided.

38.6.2.4.2* The gas detection system shall alert the extraction operator in an approved manner at a gas detection threshold no greater than 25 percent of the gas LEL/LFL.

38.6.2.4.3 Gas detection systems shall be provided with constant noninterlocked power.

38.6.2.5 Protection. An automatic suppression system shall be provided within hoods or enclosures, including ductwork, in accordance with the following:

(1) An automatic water sprinkler system that meets all applicable requirements of NFPA 13
(2) A carbon dioxide extinguishing system that meets all applicable requirements of NFPA 12
(3) A dry chemical extinguishing system that meets all applicable requirements of NFPA 17
(4) A gaseous agent extinguishing system that meets all applicable requirements of NFPA 2001

38.6.2.6 Storage. LPG containers not in use shall not be stored within extraction rooms.

38.6.2.7 Facility Piping Systems. LPG liquid piping systems shall be in compliance with NFPA 58.

38.6.3 Flammable and Combustible Liquid Extraction.

38.6.3.1 General. Cannabis extraction facilities using flammable and combustible liquid solvents shall comply with 38.6.1 and 38.6.3.

38.6.3.2 Exhaust.

38.6.3.2.1* Extraction and post oil processing operations, including dispensing of flammable liquids between containers, shall be performed in one of the following locations:

(1) A chemical fume hood in accordance with Chapter 7 of NFPA 45
(2) An approved exhaust system installed in accordance with NFPA 91 or the mechanical code

38.6.3.2.2 Unheated processes at atmospheric pressure using less than 16 oz (473 ml) of flammable liquids shall not be required to comply with 38.6.3.2.1.

38.6.3.2.3 Classified electrical systems shall be in accordance with *NFPA 70*.

38.6.3.2.4 All electrical components within the chemical fume hood or exhausted enclosure shall be interlocked such that the exhaust system shall be in operation for lighting and components to be used.

38.6.3.3 Storage and Handling. The storage, use, and handling of flammable liquids shall be in compliance with this chapter and Chapter 66.

38.6.3.4 Heating of flammable or combustible liquids over an open flame shall be prohibited.

38.6.4 Carbon Dioxide Extraction.

38.6.4.1 General. Cannabis extraction facilities using carbon dioxide solvents shall comply with 38.6.1 and 38.6.4.

38.6.4.2 Storage and Handling. All CO_2 compressed gas cylinders shall be secured to a fixed object to prevent falling.

38.6.4.3 CO_2 Gas Detection.

38.6.4.3.1 An approved, listed CO_2 detector shall be installed in the CO_2 extraction room.

38.6.4.3.2 Auto calibrating and self-zeroing devices or detectors shall be prohibited.

38.6.4.3.3 The detector shall be set to alarm at 5000 ppm of CO_2.

38.6.4.4* CO_2 Discharges. The extraction equipment pressure relief devices and blow-off valves shall be piped to the exterior of the building.

38.7* Transfilling. Filling LPG extraction equipment supply containers shall be in compliance with 69.3.5, 69.4.2, and NFPA 58.

Chapter 39 Wastewater Treatment and Collection Facilities

Δ 39.1 General.

N **39.1.1** Wastewater treatment and collection facilities shall comply with NFPA 820.

N **39.1.2** Permits, where required, shall comply with Section 1.13.

Chapter 40 Dust Explosion and Fire Prevention

40.1 Application. Equipment, processes, and operations that involve the manufacture, processing, blending, repackaging, or handling of combustible particulate solids or combustible dusts regardless of concentration or particle size shall be installed and maintained in accordance with this chapter.

40.1.1 All facilities and operations that manufacture, process, blend, convey, repackage, generate, or handle combustible dusts or combustible particulate solids shall be in compliance with NFPA 652 and, as applicable, NFPA 61, NFPA 69, NFPA 85, NFPA 120, NFPA 484, NFPA 654, NFPA 655, and NFPA 664.

Δ 40.2 Permits.

N **40.2.1** Permits shall be required in accordance with this chapter and Table 1.13.8(a) through Table 1.13.8(d).

N **40.2.2** Permits, where required, shall comply with Section 1.13.

40.3 Retroactivity. This chapter shall be applied retroactively to new and existing facilities and processes. [**652**:8.1]

40.3.1 Existing facilities shall perform a dust hazards analysis (DHA) in accordance with Section 40.5.

40.4* General. The procedures and training in this chapter shall be delivered in a language that the participants can understand. [**652**:8.2]

40.5 Dust Hazards Analysis (DHA).

40.5.1* General Requirements.

40.5.1.1 Retroactivity. The requirements of this section shall be applied retroactively in accordance with 40.5.1.1.1 and 40.5.1.1.2. [**652**:7.1.1]

40.5.1.1.1* A DHA shall be completed for all new processes and facility compartments. [**652**:7.1.1.1]

40.5.1.1.2* For existing processes and facility compartments, a DHA shall be completed by September 7, 2020. [**652**:7.1.1.2]

40.5.1.1.3 The owner/operator shall demonstrate reasonable progress each year in completing DHAs prior to the deadline set in 40.5.1.1.2. [**652**:7.1.1.3]

40.5.1.2 The owner/operator of a facility where materials determined to be combustible or explosible in accordance with Chapter 5 of NFPA 652 are present in an enclosure shall be responsible to ensure a DHA is completed in accordance with the requirements of this section. [**652**:7.1.2]

40.5.1.3 The absence of previous incidents shall not be used as the basis for not performing a DHA. [**652**:7.1.3]

40.5.1.4 The DHA shall be reviewed and updated at least every 5 years. [**652**:7.1.4]

40.5.2 Criteria.

40.5.2.1* Overview. The DHA shall evaluate the fire, deflagration, and explosion hazards and provide recommendations to manage the hazards in accordance with Section 4.2 of NFPA 652. [**652**:7.2.1]

40.5.2.2* Qualifications. The DHA shall be performed or led by a qualified person. [**652**:7.2.2]

40.5.2.3 Documentation. The results of the DHA review shall be documented, including any necessary action items requiring change to the process materials, physical process, process operations, or facilities associated with the process. [**652**:7.2.3]

40.5.3 Methodology.

40.5.3.1 General. The DHA shall include the following:

(1) Identification and evaluation of the process or facility areas where fire, flash fire, and explosion hazards exist
(2) Where such a hazard exists, identification and evaluation of specific fire and deflagration scenarios shall include the following:
  (a) Identification of safe operating ranges
  (b)* Identification of the safeguards that are in place to manage fire, deflagration, and explosion events
  (c) Recommendation of additional safeguards where warranted, including a plan for implementation

[**652**:7.3.1]

40.5.3.2 Material Evaluation.

40.5.3.2.1 The DHA shall be based on data obtained in accordance with Chapter 5 of NFPA 652 for material that is representative of the dust present. [**652:**7.3.2.1]

40.5.3.3 Process Systems.

40.5.3.3.1* Each part of the process system where combustible dust is present or where combustible particulate solids could cause combustible dust to be present shall be evaluated, and the evaluation shall address the following:

(1) Potential intended and unintended combustible dust transport between parts of the process system
(2) Potential fugitive combustible dust emissions into a building or building compartments
(3) Potential deflagration propagation between parts of the process system

[**652:**7.3.3.1]

40.5.3.3.2 Each part of the process that contains a combustible particulate solid and that can potentially include both of the following conditions shall be considered a fire hazard and shall be documented as such:

(1) Oxidizing atmosphere
(2) Credible ignition source

[**652:**7.3.3.2]

40.5.3.3.3* Each part of the process that contains a sufficient quantity of combustible dust to propagate a deflagration and that can potentially include all the following conditions shall be considered a dust deflagration hazard and shall be documented as such:

(1) Oxidizing atmosphere
(2) Credible ignition source
(3) Credible suspension mechanism

[**652:**7.3.3.3]

40.5.3.4 Building or Building Compartments.

40.5.3.4.1 Each building or building compartment where combustible dust is present shall be evaluated. [**652:**7.3.4.1]

40.5.3.4.1.1 Where multiple buildings or building compartments present essentially the same hazard, a single evaluation shall be permitted to be conducted as representative of all similar buildings or building compartments. [**652:**7.3.4.1.1]

40.5.3.4.1.2 The evaluation shall address potential combustible dust migration between buildings or building compartments. [**652:**7.3.4.1.2]

40.5.3.4.1.3 The evaluation shall address potential deflagration propagation between buildings or building compartments. [**652:**7.3.4.1.3]

40.5.3.4.2* Each building or building compartment that contains a combustible particulate solid and that can potentially include both of the following conditions shall be considered a fire hazard and shall be documented as such:

(1) Oxidizing atmosphere
(2) Credible ignition source

[**652:**7.3.4.2]

40.5.3.4.2.1* The evaluation of dust deflagration hazard in a building or building compartment shall include a comparison of actual or intended dust accumulation to the threshold housekeeping dust accumulation that would present a potential for flash-fire exposure to personnel or compartment failure due to explosive overpressure. [**652:**7.3.4.2.1]

40.5.3.4.2.2 Threshold housekeeping dust accumulation levels and nonroutine dust accumulation levels (e.g., from a process upset) shall be in accordance with relevant industry- or commodity-specific NFPA standards. [**652:**7.3.4.2.2]

40.5.3.4.3 Each building or building compartment that contains a sufficient quantity of combustible dust to propagate a deflagration and that can potentially include all of the following conditions shall be considered a dust deflagration hazard and shall be documented as such:

(1) Oxidizing atmosphere
(2) Credible ignition source
(3) Credible suspension mechanism

[**652:**7.3.4.3]

40.6 Operating Procedures and Practices.

40.6.1* The owner/operator shall establish written procedures for operating its facility and equipment to prevent or mitigate fires, deflagrations, and explosions from combustible particulate solids. [**652:**8.3.1]

40.6.2* The owner/operator shall establish safe work practices to address hazards associated with maintenance and servicing operations. [**652:**8.3.2]

40.6.2.1 The safe work practices shall apply to employees and contractors. [**652:**8.3.2.1]

40.6.3 A periodic walk-through review of operating areas shall be conducted, on a schedule established by the owner/operator per the requirement in 40.10.3, to verify that operating procedures and safe work practices are being followed. [**652:**8.3.3]

40.7 Housekeeping.

40.7.1 General.

40.7.2* Methodology.

40.7.2.1 Procedure.

40.7.2.1.1* Housekeeping procedures shall be documented. [**652:**8.4.2.1.1]

40.7.2.1.2* The methods used for cleaning surfaces shall be selected on the basis of reducing the potential for creating a combustible dust cloud. [**652:**8.4.2.1.2]

40.7.2.1.3 Cleaning methods to be used shall be based on the characteristics of the material and quantity of material present. [**652:**8.4.2.1.3]

40.7.2.2 Vacuum Cleaning Method.

40.7.2.2.1* Portable Vacuum Cleaners.

40.7.2.2.1.1 Portable vacuum cleaners with a dirty side volume greater than 8 ft^3 shall comply with 9.7.3 and 9.7.4 of NFPA 652. [**652:**8.4.2.2.1.1]

40.7.2.2.1.2* When metal particles, dusts, or powders are being cleaned NFPA 484 shall be the reference source for proper use and limitations of both dry and wet portable vacuum cleaners. [**652:** 8.4.2.2.1.2]

40.7.2.2.1.3* The operation of portable vacuum cleaning devices shall be subject to a dust hazard analysis to ensure that the risk to personnel and facility operations from deflagrations is minimized. [652:8.4.2.2.1.3]

40.7.2.2.1.4 Hoses and vacuum tools shall be appropriate for use and be static dissipative or conductive. [652:8.4.2.2.1.4]

40.7.2.2.1.5 Portable vacuum cleaners shall not be used on processes generating hot embers or sparks. [652:8.4.2.2.1.5]

40.7.2.2.1.6* For portable vacuum cleaners used with combustible dusts having a minimum ignition energy less than 30 mJ, the path to ground shall be verified prior to use after each movement or new connection, or both. [652:8.4.2.2.1.6]

40.7.2.2.1.7* Portable vacuum cleaners that meet the following minimum requirements shall be permitted to be used to collect combustible particulate solids in unclassified (nonhazardous) areas:

(1) Materials of construction shall comply with 9.4.7.1 of NFPA 652.
(2) Hoses shall be conductive or static dissipative.
(3) All conductive components, including wands and attachments, shall be bonded and grounded.
(4) The fan or blower shall be on the clean side of the primary filtration media or wet separation chamber.
(5) Electrical motors shall not be located on the dirty side of the primary filtration media or wet separation chamber unless listed for Class II, Division 1 locations.
(6)* Where liquids or wet materials are picked up by the vacuum cleaner, paper filter elements shall not be used.
(7) Vacuum cleaners used for metal dusts shall meet the requirements of NFPA 484.

[652:8.4.2.2.1.7]

40.7.2.2.2* In Class II electrically classified (hazardous) locations, electrically powered vacuum cleaners shall be listed for the purpose and location or shall be a fixed-pipe suction system with a remotely located exhauster and an AMS installed in conformance with Section 9.3 of NFPA 652, and they shall be suitable for the dust being collected. [652:8.4.2.2.2]

40.7.2.2.3 Where flammable vapors or gases are present in Class II areas, vacuum cleaners shall be listed for both Class I and Class II hazardous locations. [652:8.4.2.2.3]

40.7.2.3* Sweeping, Shoveling, Scoop, and Brush Cleaning Method. The use of scoops, brooms, and brushes for sweeping and shoveling shall be a permitted cleaning method. [652:8.4.2.3]

40.7.2.4* Water Washdown Cleaning Method.

40.7.2.4.1 The use of water washdown shall be a permitted cleaning method. [652:8.4.2.4.1]

40.7.2.4.2 Where the combustible dust being removed is metal or metal-containing dust or powder within the scope of NFPA 484, the requirements of NFPA 484 shall be followed. [652:8.4.2.4.2]

40.7.2.4.3* Where the combustible dust being removed is a water-reactive material, additional precautions shall be taken to control the associated hazards. [652:8.4.2.4.3]

40.7.2.5 Water Foam Washdown Systems. (Reserved)

40.7.2.6 Compressed Air Blowdown Method.

40.7.2.6.1* Blowdowns using compressed air shall be permitted to be used as a cleaning method in accordance with the provisions of 40.7.2.6.2. [652:8.4.2.6.1]

40.7.2.6.2* Where blowdown using compressed air is used, the following precautions shall be followed:

(1) Prior to using compressed air, vacuum cleaning, sweeping, or water washdown methods are used to clean surfaces that can be safely accessed.
(2) Dust accumulations in the area after vacuum cleaning, sweeping, or water washdown do not exceed the threshold housekeeping dust accumulation.
(3) Compressed air hoses are equipped with pressure relief nozzles limiting the discharge pressure to 30 psi (207 kPa) in accordance with OSHA requirements in 29 CFR 1910.242(b), "Hand and Portable Powered Tools and Equipment, General."
(4) All electrical equipment, including lighting, potentially exposed to airborne dust in the area during cleaning is suitable for use in a Class II, Division 2, hazardous (classified) location in accordance with *NFPA 70*.
(5) All ignition sources and hot surfaces capable of igniting a dust cloud or dust layer are shut down or removed from the area.
(6) After blowdown is complete, residual dust on lower surfaces is cleaned prior to re-introduction of potential ignition sources.
(7) Where metal or metal-containing dust or powder under the scope of NFPA 484 is present, the requirements of NFPA 484 apply.

[652:8.4.2.6.2]

40.7.2.7 Steam Blow Down Method. (Reserved)

40.7.3 Training. Employee and contractor training shall include housekeeping procedures, required personal protective equipment (PPE) during housekeeping, and proper use of equipment. [652:8.4.3]

40.7.4 Equipment. (Reserved)

40.7.5 Vacuum Trucks.

40.7.5.1 Vacuum trucks shall be grounded and bonded. [652:8.4.5.1]

40.7.5.2 Vacuum truck hoses and couplings shall be static dissipative or conductive and grounded. [652:8.4.5.2]

40.7.6 Frequency and Goal.

40.7.6.1* Housekeeping frequency and accumulation goals shall be established to ensure that the accumulated fugitive dust levels on surfaces do not exceed the threshold housekeeping dust accumulation limits. [652:8.4.6.1]

40.7.6.2 The threshold housekeeping dust accumulation limits shall be in accordance with the industry- or commodity-specific NFPA standard. *(See 1.3.1 of NFPA 652.)* [652:8.4.6.2]

40.7.6.3* Provisions for unscheduled housekeeping shall include specific requirements establishing time to clean local dust spills or transient releases. [652:8.4.6.3]

40.7.7 Auditing and Documentation.

40.7.7.1* Housekeeping effectiveness shall be assessed based on the results of routine scheduled cleaning and inspection, not including transient releases. [**652**:8.4.7.1]

40.7.7.2 The owner/operator shall retain documentation that routine scheduled cleaning occurs in accordance with the frequency and accumulation goals established in 40.7.6.1. [**652**:8.4.7.2]

40.8 Hot Work.

40.8.1* In addition to the requirements of NFPA 51B, all hot work activities shall comply with the requirements in 40.8.2 through 40.8.5. [**652**:8.5]

40.8.2* The area affected by hot work shall be thoroughly cleaned of combustible dust prior to commencing any hot work. [**652**:8.5.2]

40.8.3 Equipment that contains combustible dust and is located within the hot work area shall be shut down, shielded, or both. [**652**:8.5.3]

40.8.4 When the hot work poses an ignition risk to the combustible dust within equipment, the equipment shall be shut down and cleaned prior to commencing such hot work. [**652**:8.5.4]

40.8.5 Floor and wall openings within the hot work area shall be covered or sealed. [**652**:8.5.5]

40.8.6 Use of portable electrical equipment that does not comply with the electrical classification of the area where it is to be used shall be authorized and controlled in accordance with the hot work procedure as outlined in Section 40.8. [**652**:8.5.6]

40.9 Personal Protective Equipment.

40.9.1 Workplace Hazard Assessment.

40.9.1.1* An assessment of workplace hazards shall be conducted as described in NFPA 2113. [**652**:8.6.1.1]

40.9.1.2 When the assessment in 40.9.1.1 has determined that flame-resistant garments are needed, personnel shall be provided with and wear flame-resistant garments. [**652**:8.6.1.2]

40.9.1.3* When flame-resistant clothing is required for protecting personnel from flash fires, it shall comply with the requirements of NFPA 2112. [**652**:8.6.1.3]

40.9.1.4* Consideration shall be given to the following:

(1) Thermal protective characteristics of the fabric over a range of thermal exposures
(2) Physical characteristics of the fabric
(3) Garment construction and components
(4) Avoidance of static charge buildup
(5) Design of garment
(6) Conditions under which garment will be worn
(7) Garment fit
(8) Garment durability/wear life
(9) Recommended laundering procedures
(10) Conditions/features affecting wearer comfort

[**652**:8.6.1.4]

40.9.1.5 Flame-resistant garments shall be selected, procured, inspected, worn, and maintained in accordance with NFPA 2113. [**652**:8.6.1.5]

40.9.1.6* The employer shall implement a policy regarding care, cleaning, and maintenance for flame-resistant garments. [**652**:8.6.1.6]

40.9.2 Limitations of PPE Application. (Flame-Resistant Garments)

40.9.2.1* When required by 40.9.1.2, flame-resistant or non-melting undergarments shall be used. [**652**:8.6.2.1]

40.9.2.2* When determined by 40.9.1.1 that flame-resistant garments are needed, only flame-resistant outerwear shall be worn over flame-resistant daily wear. [**652**:8.6.2.2]

40.9.3 Limitations of PPE to Combustible Dust Flash Fires. (Reserved)

40.9.4 Face, Hands, and Footwear Protection. (Reserved)

40.10 Inspection, Testing, and Maintenance.

40.10.1* Equipment affecting the prevention, control, and mitigation of combustible dust fires, deflagrations, and explosions shall be inspected and tested in accordance with the applicable NFPA standard and the manufacturers' recommendations. [**652**:8.7.1]

40.10.2 The inspection, testing, and maintenance program shall include the following:

(1) Fire and explosion protection and prevention equipment in accordance with the applicable NFPA standards
(2) Dust control equipment
(3) Housekeeping
(4) Potential ignition sources
(5)* Electrical, process, and mechanical equipment, including process interlocks
(6) Process changes
(7) Lubrication of bearings

[**652**:8.7.2]

40.10.3 The owner/operator shall establish procedures and schedules for maintaining safe operating conditions for its facility and equipment in regard to the prevention, control, and mitigation of combustible dust fires and explosions. [**652**:8.7.3]

40.10.4* Where equipment deficiencies that affect the prevention, control, and mitigation of dust fires, deflagrations, and explosions are identified or become known, the owner/operator shall establish and implement a corrective action plan with an explicit deadline. [**652**:8.7.4]

40.10.5* Inspections and testing activities that affect the prevention, control, and mitigation of dust fires, deflagrations, and explosions shall be documented. [**652**:8.7.5]

40.10.6 A periodic walk-through review of operating areas shall be conducted, on a schedule established by the owner/operator per the requirement in 40.10.3, to verify that the equipment is in safe operating condition. [**652**:8.7.6]

40.11 Training and Hazard Awareness.

40.11.1* Employees, contractors, temporary workers, and visitors shall be included in a training program according to the potential exposure to combustible dust hazards and the potential risks to which they might be exposed or could cause. [**652**:8.8.1]

40.11.2* General safety training and hazard awareness training for combustible dusts and solids shall be provided to all affected employees. [**652**:8.8.2]

40.11.2.1* Job-specific training shall ensure that employees are knowledgeable about fire and explosion hazards of combustible dusts and particulate solids in their work environment. [**652**:8.8.2.1]

40.11.2.2 Employees shall be trained before taking responsibility for a task. [**652**:8.8.2.2]

40.11.2.3* Where explosion protection systems are installed, training of affected personnel shall include the operations and potential hazards presented by such systems. [**652**:8.8.2.3]

40.11.3 Refresher training shall be provided as required by the AHJ and as required by other relevant industry- or commodity-specific NFPA standards. [**652**:8.8.3]

40.11.4 The training shall be documented. [**652**:8.8.4]

40.12 Contractors.

40.12.1 Owner/operators shall ensure the requirements of Section 40.12 are met. [**652**:8.9.1]

40.12.2* Only qualified contractors shall be employed for work involving the installation, repair, or modification of buildings (interior and exterior), machinery, and fire and explosion protection equipment that could adversely affect the prevention, control, or mitigation of fires and explosions. [**652**:8.9.2]

40.12.3* Contractor Training.

40.12.3.1 Contractors operating owner/operator equipment shall be trained and qualified to operate the equipment and perform the work. [**652**:8.9.3.1]

40.12.3.2 Contractor training shall be documented. [**652**:8.9.3.2]

40.12.3.3* Contractors working on or near a given process shall be made aware of the potential hazards from and exposures to fires and explosions. [**652**:8.9.3.3]

40.12.3.4 Contractors shall be trained and required to comply with the facility's safe work practices and policies in accordance with 40.6.2. [**652**:8.9.3.4]

40.12.3.5 Contractors shall be trained on the facility's emergency response and evacuation plan, including, but not limited to, emergency reporting procedures, safe egress points, and evacuation area. [**652**:8.9.3.5]

40.13 Emergency Planning and Response.

40.13.1* A written emergency response plan shall be developed for preparing for and responding to work-related emergencies including, but not limited to, fire and explosion. [**652**:8.10.1]

40.13.2 The emergency response plan shall be reviewed and validated at least annually. [**652**:8.10.2]

40.14* Incident Investigation.

40.14.1* The owner/operator shall have a system to ensure that incidents that result in a fire, deflagration, or explosion are reported and investigated in a timely manner. [**652**:8.11.1]

40.14.2 The investigation shall be documented and include findings and recommendations. [**652**:8.11.2]

40.14.3 A system shall be established to address and resolve the findings and recommendations. [**652**:8.11.3]

40.14.4* The investigation findings and recommendations shall be reviewed with affected personnel. [**652**:8.11.4]

40.15 Management of Change.

40.15.1* Written procedures shall be established and implemented to manage proposed changes to process materials, staffing, job tasks, technology, equipment, procedures, and facilities. [**652**:8.12.1]

40.15.2 The procedures shall ensure that the following are addressed prior to any change:

(1)* The basis for the proposed change
(2)* Safety and health implications
(3) Whether the change is permanent or temporary, including the authorized duration of temporary changes
(4) Modifications to operating and maintenance procedures
(5) Employee training requirements
(6) Authorization requirements for the proposed change
(7) Results of characterization tests used to assess the hazard, if conducted

[**652**:8.12.2]

40.15.3* Implementation of the management of change procedure shall not be required for replacements-in-kind. [**652**:8.12.3]

40.15.4 Design and procedures documentation shall be updated to incorporate the change. [**652**:8.12.4]

40.16* Documentation Retention.

40.16.1 The owner/operator shall establish a program and implement a process to manage the retention of documentation, including, but not limited to, the following:

(1) Training records
(2) Equipment inspection, testing, and maintenance records
(3)* Incident investigation reports
(4) Dust hazards analyses
(5)* Process and technology information
(6)* Management of change documents
(7) Emergency response plan documents
(8)* Contractor records

[**652**:8.13.1]

40.17 Management Systems Review.

40.17.1 The owner/operator shall evaluate the effectiveness of the management systems presented in this standard by conducting a periodic review of each management system. [**652**:8.14.1]

40.17.2 The owner/operator shall be responsible for maintaining and evaluating the ongoing effectiveness of the management systems presented in this standard. [**652**:8.14.2]

40.18* Employee Participation. Owner/operators shall establish and implement a system to consult with and actively involve affected personnel and their representatives in the implementation of this standard. [**652**:8.15]

Chapter 41 Welding, Cutting, and Other Hot Work

41.1 General.

41.1.1 Hot work shall comply with NFPA 51B and this chapter.

41.1.2 Chapter 41 shall apply to the following hot work processes:

(1) Welding and allied processes
(2) Heat treating
(3) Grinding
(4) Thawing pipe
(5) Powder-driven fasteners
(6) Hot riveting
(7)* Torch-applied roofing in conjunction with the requirements of Section 16.4
(8) Similar applications producing or using a spark, flame, or heat

[51B:1.3.1]

41.1.3 Chapter 41 shall not apply to the following:

(1) Candles
(2) Pyrotechnics or special effects
(3) Cooking operations
(4) Electric soldering irons
(5) Design and installation of gas cutting equipment and welding equipment covered in NFPA 51
(6) Additional requirements for hot work operations in confined spaces
(7) Lockout/tagout procedures during hot work

[51B:1.3.2]

41.1.4 Acetylene cylinder charging plants shall comply with NFPA 55.

41.1.5 Permits.

N **41.1.5.1** Permits shall be required in accordance with this chapter and Table 1.13.8(a) through Table 1.13.8(d).

41.1.5.2 Permits, where required, shall comply with Section 1.13.

41.1.5.3 Where an approved facility hot work permit program exists that meets the requirements of Chapter 41, the permit shall be permitted to be issued for an entire facility.

41.2 Responsibility for Hot Work.

41.2.1* Management. Management shall be responsible for the safe operations of hot work activity. [51B:4.1]

41.2.1.1 Management shall establish permissible areas for hot work. [51B:4.1.1]

41.2.1.2 Management shall designate a permit authorizing individual (PAI). [51B:4.1.2]

41.2.1.3 All equipment shall be examined to ensure it is in a safe operating condition. [51B:4.1.3]

41.2.1.4 When found to be incapable of reliable safe operation, the equipment shall be repaired by qualified personnel prior to its next use or be withdrawn from service and tagged out of service. [51B:4.1.4]

41.2.1.5 Management shall ensure that only approved apparatus, such as torches, manifolds, regulators or pressure-reducing valves, and acetylene generators, are used. [51B:4.1.5]

41.2.1.6 Management shall ensure that all individuals involved in the hot work operations, including contractors, are familiar with the provisions of Chapter 41. [51B:4.1.6]

41.2.1.6.1 Individuals involved in hot work operations shall be trained in the safe operation of their equipment and in the safe use of the process. [51B:4.1.6.1]

41.2.1.6.2 Individuals involved in hot work operations shall have an awareness of the inherent risks involved and understand the emergency procedures in the event of a fire. [51B:4.1.6.2]

41.2.1.7 Management shall advise all contractors about site-specific flammable materials, hazardous processes or conditions, or other potential fire hazards. [51B:4.1.7]

41.2.2 Permit Authorizing Individual (PAI). In conjunction with management, the PAI shall be responsible for the safe operation of hot work activities. [51B:4.2]

41.2.2.1* The PAI shall consider the safety of the hot work operator and fire watch with respect to personal protective equipment (PPE) for other special hazards beyond hot work. (*See 41.3.1.*) [51B:4.2.1]

41.2.2.2 The PAI shall determine site-specific flammable materials, hazardous processes, or other potential fire hazards that are present or likely to be present in the work location. [51B:4.2.2]

41.2.2.3 The PAI shall ensure the protection of combustibles from ignition by the following means:

(1)* Considering alternative methods to hot work
(2) Moving the work to a location that is free from combustibles
(3) If the work cannot be moved, moving the combustibles to a safe distance or having the combustibles properly shielded against ignition
(4) Scheduling hot work so that operations that could expose combustibles to ignition are not begun during hot work operations

[51B:4.2.3]

41.2.2.4 If the criteria of 41.2.2.3(2) through 41.2.2.3(4) cannot be met, hot work shall not be performed. [51B:4.2.4]

41.2.2.5 The PAI shall determine that appropriate fire protection and extinguishing equipment are located at the hot work site. [51B:4.2.5]

41.2.2.6 Where a fire watch is required (*see 41.3.6*), the PAI shall be responsible for ensuring that a fire watch is at the site. [51B:4.2.6]

41.2.2.7* Where a fire watch is not required, the PAI shall make a final check ½ hour after the completion of hot work operations to detect and extinguish smoldering fires. [51B:4.2.7]

41.2.3 Hot Work Operator. The hot work operator shall handle equipment safely and use it as follows so as not to endanger lives and property:

(1) The operator shall have the PAI's approval before starting hot work operations.
(2) All equipment shall be examined to ensure it is in a safe operating condition; if found to be incapable of reliable safe operation, the equipment shall be repaired by quali-

fied personnel prior to its next use or be withdrawn from service.

(3) The operator shall cease hot work operations if unsafe conditions develop and shall notify management, the area supervisor, or the PAI for reassessment of the situation. [51B:4.3]

41.2.4 Fire Watch.

41.2.4.1* The fire watch shall be trained to recognize the inherent hazards of the work site and hot work operations. [51B:4.4.1]

41.2.4.2 The fire watch shall ensure safe conditions are maintained during hot work operations. [51B:4.4.2]

41.2.4.3 The fire watch shall have the authority to stop the hot work operations if unsafe conditions develop. [51B:4.4.3]

41.2.4.4* The fire watch shall have fire-extinguishing equipment readily available and shall be trained in its use. [51B:4.4.4]

41.2.4.5 The fire watch shall be familiar with the facilities and procedures for sounding an alarm in the event of a fire. [51B:4.4.5]

41.2.4.6 The fire watch shall watch for fires in all exposed areas and try to extinguish them only when the fires are obviously within the capacity of the equipment available. If the fire watch determines that the fire is not within the capacity of the equipment, the fire watch shall sound the alarm immediately. [51B:4.4.6]

41.2.4.7* The fire watch shall be permitted to perform additional tasks, but those tasks shall not distract him or her from his or her fire watch responsibilities, except as outlined in Section 41.4. [51B:4.4.7]

41.2.5* Contractors. Before starting any hot work, contractors and their clients shall discuss the planned project completely, including the type of hot work to be conducted and the hazards in the area. [51B:4.5]

41.2.6 Mutual Responsibility. Management, contractors, the PAI, the fire watch, and the operators shall recognize their mutual responsibility for safety in hot work operations by complying with this *Code* and their specified responsibilities. [51B:4.6]

41.3 Fire Prevention Precautions.

41.3.1* Personal Protective Clothing. Clothing shall be selected to minimize the potential for ignition, burning, trapping hot sparks, and electric shock. [51B:5.1]

41.3.2 Fire Extinguishers. Fire extinguishers required by this *Code* shall be in accordance with Chapter 13 and NFPA 10. [51B:5.2]

41.3.3 Permissible Areas.

41.3.3.1 General. Hot work shall be permitted only in areas that are or have been made fire safe. [51B:5.3.1]

41.3.3.2 Designated or Permit-Required Areas. Hot work shall be performed in either designated areas or permit-required areas. [51B:5.3.2]

41.3.3.2.1 Designated Areas.

41.3.3.2.1.1 In order for a location to be a designated area, the area shall meet the requirements in 41.3.5.1. [51B:5.3.2.1.1]

41.3.3.2.1.2 Prior to the start of any hot work in a designated area, at a minimum, the hot work operator shall verify all of the following:

(1) The location is fire resistant.
(2) The requirements of 41.3.5.1.3 are met.
(3) Fire extinguishers are in working condition and readily available.
(4) Ventilation is working properly.
(5) Equipment is in working order.
[51B:5.3.2.1.2]

41.3.3.2.1.3 Permanent areas designated for hot work shall be reviewed at least annually by the PAI. [51B:5.3.2.1.3]

41.3.3.2.1.4 Signs shall be posted designating hot work areas as deemed necessary by the PAI. [51B:5.3.2.1.4]

41.3.3.2.2* Permit-Required Areas. Before hot work operations begin in a permit-required area, a documented hot work permit issued by the PAI shall be required in accordance with 41.3.5. [51B:5.3.2.2]

41.3.4* Nonpermissible Areas. Hot work shall not be permitted in the following:

(1) In areas not authorized by management
(2)* In buildings where fire protection systems are impaired, unless additional precautions are taken as determined by the PAI or AHJ
(3)* In the presence of explosive atmospheres
(4) In the presence of uncleaned or improperly prepared equipment, drums, tanks, or other containers that have previously contained materials that could develop explosive atmospheres
(5) In areas with potential fire or flash fire hazards associated with the presence of one or more combustible particulate solids (dusts)
[51B:5.4]

41.3.5* Hot Work Permit.

41.3.5.1 Before a hot work permit is issued, the following conditions in 41.3.5.1.1 through 41.3.5.1.15 shall be verified by the PAI. [51B:5.5.1]

41.3.5.1.1 The hot work equipment to be used shall be in satisfactory operating condition and in good repair. [51B:5.5.1.1]

41.3.5.1.2 Where combustible materials, such as paper clippings, wood shavings, or textile fibers, are on the floor, the floor shall be swept clean for a radius of 35 ft (11 m). [51B:5.5.1.2]

41.3.5.1.2.1* Combustible floors shall be kept wet, covered with damp sand, or protected by a listed welding blanket, welding pad, or equivalent. [51B:5.5.1.2.1]

41.3.5.1.2.2 Where floors have been wet down, personnel operating arc welding equipment or cutting equipment shall be protected from possible electric shock. [51B:5.5.1.2.2]

41.3.5.1.3* Combustibles shall be relocated at least 35 ft (11 m) in all directions from the hot work area. [51B:5.5.1.3]

41.3.5.1.3.1* If relocation is impractical, combustibles shall be shielded by a barrier constructed of noncombustible materials or otherwise protected by a listed welding curtain, welding blanket, welding pad, or equivalent. [51B:5.5.1.3.1]

41.3.5.1.3.2 To prevent the entrance of sparks, the edges of covers at the floor shall be tight, including at the point where covers overlap. [51B:5.5.1.3.2]

41.3.5.1.4 Openings or cracks in walls, floors, or ducts within 35 ft (11 m) of the hot work site shall be covered or sealed with listed fire-rated or noncombustible material to prevent the passage of sparks to adjacent areas. [51B:5.5.1.4]

41.3.5.1.5 Ducts and conveyor systems that might carry sparks to distant combustibles shall be shielded, shut down, or both. [51B:5.5.1.5]

41.3.5.1.6* If hot work is done near walls, partitions, ceilings, or roofs of combustible construction, they shall be protected by a listed welding curtain, welding blanket, welding pad, or equivalent. [51B:5.5.1.6]

41.3.5.1.7* If hot work is done on one side of a noncombustible wall, partition, ceiling, or roof, the criteria of one of the following shall apply:

(1) The PAI shall verify that no combustibles are at risk of ignition on the other side.
(2) Precautions shall be taken to prevent ignition of combustibles on the other side by relocating the combustibles.
(3) If it is impractical to relocate combustibles, a fire watch shall be provided on the side opposite from where the work is being performed.

[51B:5.5.1.7]

41.3.5.1.8 Hot work shall not be attempted on a partition, wall, ceiling, or roof that has a combustible covering or insulation, or on walls or partitions of combustible sandwich-type panel construction. [51B:5.5.1.8]

41.3.5.1.9 Hot work that is performed on pipes or other metal that is in contact with combustible walls, partitions, ceilings, roofs, or other combustibles shall not be undertaken if the work is close enough to cause ignition by conduction. [51B:5.5.1.9]

41.3.5.1.10 Fully charged and operable fire extinguishers that are appropriate for the type of possible fire shall be available immediately at the work area. [51B:5.5.1.10]

41.3.5.1.11 If existing hose lines are located within the hot work area defined by the permit, they shall be connected and ready for service but shall not be required to be unrolled or charged. [51B:5.5.1.11]

41.3.5.1.12* During hot work, special precautions shall be taken to avoid accidental activation of automatic fire protection systems. [51B:5.5.1.12]

41.3.5.1.13 The operator and nearby personnel shall be suitably protected against dangers such as heat, sparks, and slag. [51B:5.5.1.13]

41.3.5.1.14* In instances where the scope of work and the tools used to conduct hot work result in possible travel of slag, sparks, spatter, or similar mobile sources of ignition farther than 35 ft (11 m), the PAI shall be permitted to extend the distances and areas addressed in 41.3.5.1.2 through 41.3.5.1.4. [51B:5.5.1.14]

41.3.5.1.15* In instances where the scope of work and tools used to conduct hot work are known to be incapable of generating slag, sparks, spatter, or similar mobile sources of ignition capable of leaving the immediate area of the applied hot work, the PAI shall be permitted to reduce the distances and areas addressed in 41.3.5.1.2 through 41.3.5.1.4. [51B:5.5.1.15]

N **41.3.5.1.16** Where hot work operations are to be performed on tanks, containers, or piping that have contained ignitible liquids or other combustible materials, such operations shall be permitted only if the tanks, containers, or piping have been cleaned or purged in accordance with NFPA 326. [51B:A.5.5.1.16]

41.3.5.2 The PAI shall describe any separation, distance extension, or reduction on the hot work permit. [51B:5.5.2]

41.3.5.3 The PAI shall determine the time period for which the hot work permit is valid. [51B:5.5.3]

41.3.5.4 The hot work permit shall not be valid for a time period exceeding 24 hours. [51B:5.5.4]

41.3.5.5* The PAI shall re-inspect the hot work area at least once per shift during the hot work permit time period to ensure a fire-safe area. [51B:5.5.5]

41.3.6 Fire Watch and Fire Monitoring.

41.3.6.1* A fire watch shall be required by the PAI when hot work is performed in a location where other than a minor fire might develop or where any of the following conditions exist:

(1)* Combustible materials in building construction or contents closer than 35 ft (11 m) to the hot work operation
(2) Combustible materials more than 35 ft (11 m) away from the hot work operation but easily ignited by sparks
(3) Wall or floor openings within a 35 ft (11 m) radius that expose combustible materials in adjacent areas, including concealed spaces in walls or floors
(4) Combustible materials adjacent to the opposite side of partitions, walls, ceilings, or roofs and likely to be ignited

[51B:5.6.1]

41.3.6.1.1 A fire watch shall be maintained for at least 1 hour after completion of hot work operations in order to detect and extinguish smoldering fires. [51B:5.6.1.1]

41.3.6.1.2 The duration of the fire watch shall be permitted to be reduced to no less than 30 minutes if the PAI determines the absence of fire hazards warrants the reduction. [51B:5.6.1.2]

41.3.6.2* More than one fire watch shall be required if combustible materials that could be ignited by the hot work operation cannot be directly observed by the initial fire watch. [51B:5.6.2]

41.3.6.3* Following the completion of the established fire watch time period, fire monitoring shall be provided within the hot work area for up to an additional 3 hours as determined by the PAI. [51B:5.6.3]

41.3.7* Hot Tapping. Hot tapping or other cutting and welding on a flammable gas or liquid transmission or distribution utility pipeline shall be performed by a crew qualified to make hot taps. [51B:5.7]

41.3.8 Cylinders. Cylinder use and storage shall be in accordance with Chapter 63 and NFPA 55. [51B:5.8]

41.4 Sole Proprietors and Individual Operators.

41.4.1* Assignment of PAI and Fire Watch. In a site where hot work operations are not under the control of another authority, the individual hot work operator shall be permitted to serve as PAI and as fire watch, provided that the operator is trained and follows the provisions of Chapter 41. [51B:6.1]

41.4.2 Documented Hot Work Permit. A checklist shall be permitted to serve as the documented hot work permit. [51B:6.2]

41.5 Public Exhibitions and Demonstrations.

41.5.1 Application. The provisions of Section 41.5 shall apply to oxy–fuel gas welding and cutting operations at public exhibitions, demonstrations, displays, and trade shows, referred to hereinafter as the "site," in order to promote the safe use of compressed gases in public gatherings. [51B:7.1]

41.5.2 Supervision. Installation and operation of welding, cutting, and related equipment shall be done by, or under the supervision of, a competent operator, to ensure the personal protection of viewers and demonstrators as well as the protection from fire of materials in and around the site and the building itself. [51B:7.2]

41.5.3 Site.

41.5.3.1 Location. Sites involving the use and storage of compressed gases shall be located so as not to interfere with egress during an emergency. [51B:7.3.1]

41.5.3.2 Design. The site shall be constructed, equipped, and operated in such a manner that the demonstration minimizes the possibility of injury to viewers. [51B:7.3.2]

41.5.4 Fire Protection.

41.5.4.1 Fire Extinguishers. Each site shall be provided with a portable fire extinguisher of appropriate size and type in accordance with NFPA 10. [51B:7.4.1]

41.5.4.2 Shielding. The public, combustible materials, and compressed gas cylinders at the site shall be protected from flames, sparks, and molten metal. [51B:7.4.2]

41.5.4.3 Fire Department Notification. The fire department shall be notified in advance of the use of a site for public exhibitions, demonstrations, and trade shows. [51B:7.4.3]

41.5.5 Cylinders.

41.5.5.1 Gas Capacity Limitation.

41.5.5.1.1 Cylinders containing compressed gases for use at the site shall not be charged in excess of one-half their maximum permissible content. [51B:7.5.1.1]

41.5.5.1.2 Cylinders of nonliquefied gases and acetylene shall be charged to not more than one-half their maximum permissible charged gauge pressure [psi (kPa)]. [51B:7.5.1.2]

41.5.5.1.3 Cylinders of liquefied gases shall be charged to not more than one-half the maximum permissible capacity [lb (kg)]. [51B:7.5.1.3]

41.5.5.2 Storage.

41.5.5.2.1 Cylinders located at the site shall be connected for use. [51B:7.5.2.1]

41.5.5.2.2 A sufficient number of additional cylinders shall be permitted to be stored at the site to furnish approximately one day's consumption of each gas used. [51B:7.5.2.2]

41.5.5.2.3* Other cylinders shall be stored in an approved storage area, but not near a building exit. [51B:7.5.2.3]

41.5.5.3 Transporting Cylinders. Cylinders in excess of 40 lb (18 kg) total weight being transported to or from the site shall be carried on a hand truck or motorized truck. [51B:7.5.3]

41.5.5.4 Process Hose. Process hose shall be located and protected so that they will not be physically damaged. [51B:7.5.4]

41.5.5.5 Cylinder Valves. Cylinder valves shall be closed when equipment is unattended. [51B:7.5.5]

41.5.5.6 Valve Caps. If cylinders are designed to be equipped with valve protection caps, such caps shall be in place, except when the cylinders are in service or are connected and ready for service. [51B:7.5.6]

41.5.5.7 Cylinder Protection. Cylinders shall be secured so that they cannot be knocked over. [51B:7.5.7]

41.6 Arc Welding Equipment.

41.6.1 Installation. Electrical equipment shall be of an approved type and shall be installed and used in accordance with Section 11.1 and manufacturers' requirements.

41.6.2 Damaged cables shall be removed from service until repaired or replaced.

Chapter 42 Refueling

42.1 General.

42.1.1 Scope. Chapter 42 shall apply to refueling of automotive vehicles, marine vessels, and aircraft.

Δ **42.1.2 Permits.**

N **42.1.2.1** Permits shall be required in accordance with this chapter and Table 1.13.8(a) through Table 1.13.8(d).

N **42.1.2.2** Permits, where required, shall comply with Section 1.13.

42.2 Automotive Fuel Servicing.

42.2.1 Applicability.

42.2.1.1 Fueling processes at automotive service stations, service stations located inside buildings, and fleet vehicle service stations shall comply with NFPA 30A and Sections 42.2 through 42.8.

42.2.1.2 If approved by the AHJ, mobile fleet fueling at commercial, industrial, and governmental sites shall be conducted in accordance with 42.7.7.

Δ **42.2.1.3*** Sections 42.2 through 42.8 shall not apply to those motor fuel dispensing facilities where only liquefied petroleum gas (LP-Gas), liquefied natural gas (LNG), compressed natural gas (CNG), or hydrogen is dispensed as motor fuel, or where both gaseous fuel storage and dispensing equipment are at least 50 ft (15 m) from any other motor fuel storage or dispensing equipment of different chemical composition. [30A:1.1.3]

42.2.2 General Requirements.

42.2.2.1 Plans and Specifications. Plans and specifications shall be submitted for review and approval prior to the installation or construction of a motor vehicle fuel dispensing station.

42.2.2.1.1 A site plan shall be submitted that illustrates the location of flammable and combustible liquids, LP-Gas or CNG storage vessels, and their spatial relation to each other, property lines, and building openings.

42.2.2.1.2 Aboveground and underground storage vessels shall be shown on plans.

42.2.2.1.3 For each type of fuel dispensing facility, plans and specifications shall also include, but not be limited to, the following:

(1) Type and design of underground and aboveground liquid storage tanks
(2) Quantity and types of liquids to be stored
(3) Location and design of the fuel dispensers and dispenser nozzles
(4) Distances from dispensers to tanks, property lines, and buildings
(5) Vehicle access
(6) Fire appliances
(7) Vehicle impact protection
(8) Method of storage and dispensing
(9) Overfill prevention
(10) Spill containment
(11) Vents
(12) Vapor recovery
(13) Other equipment and accessories
(14) Seismic design in accordance with the building code
(15) Secondary containment
(16) Design and specifications for related piping, valves, and fittings
(17) Location and classification of electrical equipment, including emergency fuel shutdown devices
(18) Specifications for fuel storage and venting components
(19) Other information as required by the AHJ

42.3 Storage of Liquids.

42.3.1 Scope. Section 42.3 shall apply to the storage of liquid fuels and to the storage of related materials, such as lubricating oils and greases, cleaning solvents, and windshield washer solvents. [30A:4.1]

Δ **42.3.2 General Requirements.**

Δ **42.3.2.1** Liquids shall be stored in the following:

(1) Approved closed containers that do not exceed 60 gal (227 L) capacity and are located outside buildings
(2) Tanks or approved closed containers located inside motor fuel dispensing facilities or repair garages
(3) Aboveground tanks, underground tanks, and containers in accordance with the requirements of 42.3.3
(4) Tanks supplying marine service stations in accordance with 42.9.2

[30A:4.2.1]

42.3.2.2 A motor fuel dispensing facility located at a bulk plant shall be separated from areas in which bulk plant operations are conducted by a fence or other approved barrier. Dispensing devices at the motor fuel dispensing facility shall not be supplied by aboveground tanks located in the bulk plant. Storage tanks at motor fuel dispensing facilities shall not be connected by piping to aboveground tanks located in the bulk plant. [30A:4.2.2]

Δ **42.3.2.3** Class I liquids shall not be stored or handled in a building that has a basement or pit into which ignitible vapors can travel, unless the basement or pit is provided with ventilation that will prevent the accumulation of vapors. The ventilation system shall be capable of providing at least 1 cfm of exhaust per ft^2 of floor area (0.3 m^3/min per m^2), but not less than 150 ft^3/min (4 m^3/min). [30A:4.2.3]

42.3.2.4 Where tanks are at an elevation that produces a gravity head on the dispensing device, the tank outlet shall be equipped with a device, such as a normally closed solenoid valve, positioned adjacent to and downstream from the valve specified in 22.13.1 of NFPA 30 that is installed and adjusted so that liquid cannot flow by gravity from the tank if the piping or hose fails when the dispenser is not in use. [30A:4.2.4]

42.3.3 Storage of Liquids.

42.3.3.1* Aboveground Storage Tanks.

42.3.3.1.1 Tanks designed and built for underground use shall not be installed for aboveground use. [30A:4.3.2.2]

42.3.3.1.2 Tanks storing liquid motor fuels at an individual site shall be limited to a maximum individual capacity of 12,000 gal (45,400 L) and aggregate capacity of 48,000 gal (181,700 L) unless such tanks are installed in vaults complying with 42.3.3.2, in which case the maximum individual capacity shall be permitted to be 15,000 gal (57,000 L). [30A:4.3.2.3]

42.3.3.1.3 Tanks shall be located in accordance with Table 42.3.3.1.3. [30A:4.3.2.4]

42.3.3.1.4 The maximum individual tank capacity of 12,000 gal (45,400 L), where indicated in Table 42.3.3.1.3, shall be permitted to be increased to 20,000 gal (75,700 L) for Class II and Class III liquids at a fleet vehicle motor fuel dispensing facility and an aggregate capacity of 80,000 gal (304,000 L). [30A:4.3.2.5]

42.3.3.1.5 At fleet vehicle motor fuel dispensing facilities, no minimum separation shall be required between the dispensing device and a tank in a vault, a protected aboveground tank, or a fire-resistant tank. [30A:4.3.2.6]

42.3.3.1.6 The provisions of this subsection shall not prohibit the dispensing of liquid motor fuels in the open from a fuel dispensing system supplied by an existing aboveground tank, not to exceed 6000 gal (22,710 L), located at commercial, industrial, government, or manufacturing establishments, and intended for fueling vehicles used in connection with their business. Such dispensing shall be permitted provided the following conditions are met:

(1) An inspection of the premises and operations has been made and approval has been granted by the AHJ.
(2) The tank is safeguarded against collision, spillage, and overfill to the satisfaction of the AHJ.
(3) The tank system is listed or approved for such aboveground use.
(4) The tank complies with requirements for emergency relief venting, the tank and dispensing system meet the

Table 42.3.3.1.3 Minimum Separation Requirements for Aboveground Tanks

Tank Type	Individual Tank Capacity (gal)[a]	Minimum Distance (ft) From the Nearest Important Building on the Same Property	From Nearest Fuel Dispensing Device[b]	From Lot Line That Is or Can Be Built Upon[c]	From the Nearest Side of Any Public Way	Between Tanks
Tanks in vaults[d]	0–15,000	0	0	0	0	Separate compartments required for each tank
Protected aboveground tanks	Less than or equal to 6,000	5	0	15	5	3
	6,001–12,000	15	0	25	15	3
Fire-resistant tanks	0–12,000	25	25	50	25	3
Other tanks meeting the requirements of NFPA 30	0–12,000	50	50	100	50	3

For SI units, 1 ft = 0.30 m; 1 gal = 3.8 L.
[a]See 42.3.3.1.2 and 42.3.3.1.4.
[b]See 42.3.3.1.5.
[c]Including the opposite side of a public way.
[d]The separation distances given for vaults are measured from the outer perimeter of the vault.
[30A: Table 4.3.2.4]

electrical classification requirements of NFPA 30A, and the tank complies with the provisions of 42.3.2.4.
(5) The tank storage complies with Chapter 22 of NFPA 30. [30A:4.3.2.7]

42.3.3.1.7 Spill Control.

42.3.3.1.7.1 Aboveground tanks not installed in vaults shall be provided with spill control that meets the requirements of 21.7.1 and Section 22.11 of NFPA 30. [30A:4.3.2.8.1]

42.3.3.1.7.2 Tank fill connections shall be provided with a noncombustible spill containment device. [30A:4.3.2.8.2]

42.3.3.2 Vaults for Aboveground Tanks.

42.3.3.2.1 Scope. Paragraph 42.3.3.2 shall apply to installation of aboveground tanks in vaults and design and installation of such vaults. [30A:4.3.3.1]

42.3.3.2.2 General. Aboveground tanks shall be permitted to be installed in vaults that meet the requirements of 42.3.3.2. Except as modified by the provisions of 42.3.3.2, vaults shall meet all other applicable provisions of NFPA 30A. Vaults shall be constructed and listed in accordance with UL 2245, *Below-Grade Vaults for Flammable Liquid Storage Tanks*. Vaults shall be permitted to be either above or below grade. [30A:4.3.3.2]

42.3.3.2.3 Construction and Installation of Storage Tank Vaults.

42.3.3.2.3.1 Construction Requirements.

42.3.3.2.3.1.1 The top of an abovegrade vault that contains a tank storing Class I liquid or Class II or Class III liquid stored at a temperature at or above its flash point shall be constructed of noncombustible material and shall be designed to be weaker than the walls of the vault to ensure that the thrust of any explosion occurring inside the vault is directed upward before destructive internal pressure develops within the vault. [30A:4.3.3.3.1.1]

42.3.3.2.3.1.2 The top of an at-grade or belowgrade vault that contains a tank storing Class I liquid or Class II or Class III liquid stored at a temperature at or above its flash point shall be designed to relieve or contain the force of any explosion occurring inside the vault. [30A:4.3.3.3.1.2]

Δ **42.3.3.2.3.1.3** Adjacent vaults shall be permitted to share a common wall. [30A:4.3.3.3.1.3]

Δ **42.3.3.2.3.2 Installation Requirements.** Storage tank vaults shall be installed in accordance with the requirements of 42.3.3.2.3.2.1 and 42.3.3.2.3.2.2. [30A:4.3.3.3.2]

Δ **42.3.3.2.3.2.1** Each vault and its tank shall be anchored to resist uplifting by groundwater or flooding, including when the tank is empty. [30A:4.3.3.3.2.1]

Δ **42.3.3.2.3.2.2** Vaults that are not resistant to damage from the impact of a motor vehicle shall be protected by collision barriers. [30A:4.3.3.3.2.2]

42.3.3.2.4 Storage Tank Selection and Arrangement.

Δ **42.3.3.2.4.1** Tanks shall be listed for aboveground use. [30A:4.3.3.4.1]

Δ **42.3.3.2.4.2** Each tank shall be in its own vault and shall be completely enclosed by the vault. [30A:4.3.3.4.2]

Δ **42.3.3.2.4.3** Sufficient clearance between the tank and the vault shall be provided to allow for visual inspection and maintenance of the tank and its appurtenances. [30A:4.3.3.4.3]

Δ **42.3.3.2.4.4** Backfill shall not be permitted around the tank. [30A:4.3.3.4.4]

42.3.3.2.5 Tank Appurtenances.

42.3.3.2.5.1 Vent pipes that are provided for normal tank venting shall terminate outside the vault and at least 12 ft (3.6 m) above ground level and shall meet the requirements of 66.27.8.1. [**30A:**4.3.3.5.1]

42.3.3.2.5.2 Emergency vents shall be vaportight and shall be permitted to discharge inside the vault. Long-bolt manhole covers shall not be permitted for this purpose. [**30A:**4.3.3.5.2]

42.3.3.2.5.3 An approved means of overfill protection shall be provided for tanks. The use of ball float valves shall be prohibited. [**30A:**4.3.3.5.3]

42.3.3.2.5.4 Fill connections for vaults installed inside buildings shall comply with 66.22.13.4. [**30A:**4.3.3.5.4]

42.3.3.2.6 Ventilation Systems for Storage Tank Vaults.

Δ **42.3.3.2.6.1** Vaults that contain tanks storing Class I liquids [FP < 100°F (37.8°C)] shall be ventilated at a rate of not less than 1 cfm/ft^2 of floor area (0.3 m^3/min/m^2), but not less than 150 cfm (4 m^3/min). [**30A:**4.3.3.6.1]

Δ **42.3.3.2.6.2** Such ventilation shall operate continuously or shall be designed to operate upon activation of a vapor and liquid detection system. [**30A:**4.3.3.6.2]

Δ **42.3.3.2.6.3** Failure of the exhaust airflow shall automatically shut down the dispensing system. [**30A:**4.3.3.6.3]

Δ **42.3.3.2.6.4** The exhaust system shall be designed to provide air movement across all parts of the vault floor. [**30A:**4.3.3.6.4]

Δ **42.3.3.2.6.5** Supply and exhaust ducts shall extend to within 3 in. (75 mm), but not more than 12 in. (300 mm) of the floor. [**30A:**4.3.3.6.5]

Δ **42.3.3.2.6.6** The exhaust system shall be installed in accordance with the provisions of NFPA 91. [**30A:**4.3.3.6.6]

42.3.3.2.7 Detection and Alarm Systems for Storage Tank Vaults.

Δ **42.3.3.2.7.1** Each vault shall be provided with an approved vapor and liquid detection system that is equipped with on-site audible and visual warning devices with battery backup. [**30A:**4.3.3.7.1]

Δ **42.3.3.2.7.2** The vapor detection system shall sound an alarm when the system detects vapors that reach or exceed 25 percent of the lower flammable limit of the liquid stored. [**30A:**4.3.3.7.2]

Δ **42.3.3.2.7.3** Vapor detectors shall be located no higher than 12 in. (300 mm) above the lowest point in the vault. [**30A:**4.3.3.7.3]

Δ **42.3.3.2.7.4** The liquid detection systems shall sound an alarm upon detection of any liquid, including water. [**30A:**4.3.3.7.4]

Δ **42.3.3.2.7.5** Liquid detectors shall be located in accordance with the manufacturer's instructions. [**30A:**4.3.3.7.5]

Δ **42.3.3.2.7.6** Activation of either the vapor detection system or the liquid detection system shall cause a signal to be sounded at an approved, constantly attended location within the facility serving the tanks or at an approved location. [**30A:**4.3.3.7.6]

Δ **42.3.3.2.8 Location of Storage Tank Vaults.** In lieu of the separation distance requirements given in 66.22.4, separation distances between the vault and any of the following shall be permitted to be reduced to 0 ft (0 m), as measured from the outer perimeter of the vault wall:

(1) Any property line that is or can be built upon
(2) The near and far sides of a public way
(3) The nearest important building on the same property

[**30A:**4.3.3.8]

Δ **42.3.3.2.9 Inspection and Maintenance of Storage Tank Vaults and Equipment.** Vaults and their required equipment shall be maintained in accordance with the requirements of Chapter 25 of NFPA 30. [**30A:**4.3.3.9]

42.3.3.3 Additional Requirements for Fire-Resistant Aboveground Storage Tanks.

Δ **42.3.3.3.1** Fire-resistant tanks shall be tested and listed in accordance with UL 2080, *Fire Resistant Tanks for Flammable and Combustible Liquids*. Fire-resistant tanks shall also meet both of the following requirements:

(1) The construction that provides the required fire-resistive protection shall reduce the heat transferred to the primary tank in order to limit the temperature of the primary tank to an average maximum rise of 800°F (430°C) and a single point maximum rise of 1000°F (540°C) and to prevent release of liquid, failure of the primary tank, failure of the supporting structure, and impairment of venting for a period of not less than 2 hours when tested using the fire exposure specified in UL 2080.
(2) Reduction in sizing of the emergency vents in accordance with 22.7.3.5 of NFPA 30 shall not be permitted.

[**30A:**4.3.4]

42.3.3.4 Additional Requirements for Protected Aboveground Storage Tanks.

Δ **42.3.3.4.1** Protected aboveground tanks shall be tested and listed in accordance with UL 2085, *Protected Aboveground Tanks for Flammable and Combustible Liquids*. [**30A:**4.3.5]

Δ **42.3.3.4.2** Protected aboveground tanks shall also meet both of the following requirements:

(1) The construction that provides the required fire-resistive protection shall reduce the heat transferred to the primary tank in order to limit the temperature of the primary tank to an average maximum rise of 260°F (144°C) and a single point maximum rise of 400°F (204°C) and to prevent release of ignitible (flammable or combustible) liquid, failure of the primary tank, failure of the supporting structure, and impairment of venting for a period of not less than 2 hours when tested using the fire exposure specified in UL 2085, *Protected Aboveground Tanks for Flammable and Combustible Liquids*.
(2) Reduction in sizing of the emergency vents in accordance with 22.7.3.5 of NFPA 30 shall not be permitted.

[**30A:**4.3.5.1]

42.3.3.5 Additional Requirements for All Aboveground Tanks.

42.3.3.5.1 All openings shall be located above the maximum liquid level. [**30A:**4.3.6.1]

42.3.3.5.2 Means shall be provided for determining the liquid level in each tank, and this means shall be accessible to the delivery operator. [**30A:**4.3.6.2]

Δ **42.3.3.5.3**

N **42.3.3.5.3.1** Means shall be provided to sound an audible alarm when the liquid level in the tank reaches no more than 90 percent of capacity. [30A:4.3.6.3.1]

N **42.3.3.5.3.2** Means shall be provided to automatically stop the flow of liquid into the tank when the liquid level in the tank reaches no more than 95 percent capacity. [30A:4.3.6.3.2]

N **42.3.3.5.3.3** Tanks storing Class IIIB liquids with deliveries less than 95 L (25 gal) at one time shall not be required to comply with 42.3.3.5.3.1 and 42.3.3.5.3.2. [30A:4.3.6.3.3]

N **42.3.3.5.3.4** These provisions shall not restrict or interfere with the operation of either the normal vent or the emergency vent. [30A:4.3.6.3.4]

42.3.3.5.4 Means shall be provided to prevent the release of liquid by siphon flow. [30A:4.3.6.4]

42.3.3.5.5 Shutoff and check valves shall be equipped with a pressure-relieving device that will relieve the pressure generated by thermal expansion back to the tank. [30A:4.3.6.5]

42.3.3.5.6 Fuel shall not be dispensed from the tank by either gravity flow or pressurization of the tank. [30A:4.3.6.6]

42.3.3.5.7 Storage tank appurtenances shall be installed and calibrated in accordance with the manufacturer's instructions, published industry practices, or equivalent methods approved by the AHJ. [30A:4.3.6.7]

42.3.3.6 Physical Protection for All Outside Aboveground Tanks.

42.3.3.6.1 Security.

42.3.3.6.1.1 Tanks that are not enclosed in vaults shall be enclosed by a perimeter property security fence or a separate chain link fence, at least 6 ft (1.8 m) high. [30A:4.3.7.1.1]

42.3.3.6.1.2 The perimeter property security fence or separate chain link fence shall be separated from the tanks by at least 10 ft (3 m). [30A:4.3.7.1.2]

42.3.3.6.1.3 Gates in perimeter property security fences shall be secured against unauthorized entry. [30A:4.3.7.1.3]

42.3.3.6.2* Guard posts or other approved means shall be provided to protect tanks that are subject to vehicular damage. When guard posts are installed, the following design shall be acceptable:

(1) They shall be constructed of steel not less than 4 in. (100 mm) in diameter and shall be filled with concrete.
(2) They shall be spaced not more than 4 ft (1.2 m) on center.
(3) They shall be set not less than 3 ft (0.9 m) deep in a concrete footing of not less than 15 in. (380 mm) diameter.

[30A:4.3.7.2]

42.3.3.7 Corrosion Protection. Any portion of a tank or its piping that is in contact with the soil shall have properly engineered, installed, and maintained corrosion protection that meets the requirements of 66.21.4.5. [30A:4.3.8]

42.3.3.8 Storage of Liquids Inside Buildings. Storage of flammable and combustible liquids in motor fuel dispensing facility buildings and in repair garage buildings shall meet the requirements of 42.3.3.8. [30A:4.3.9]

42.3.3.8.1 Class I, II, and IIIA Liquids in Tanks Not Exceeding 120 Gal (454 L) Capacity and in Containers.

42.3.3.8.1.1 The aggregate quantity of Class I liquids stored in a tank that does not exceed 120 gal (454 L) capacity and in containers shall not exceed 120 gal (454 L). Liquids in storage shall be maintained in tanks or in approved containers that are closed or are fitted with an approved dispensing device that meets the requirements of 42.7.2.4.1. [30A:4.3.9.1.1]

42.3.3.8.1.2 Except as permitted under 42.3.3.8.1.3, the aggregate quantity of Class II and Class IIIA liquids stored in a tank that does not exceed 120 gal (454 L) capacity and in containers shall not exceed 240 gal (908 L). The quantity for each class shall not exceed 120 gal (454 L). Liquids in storage shall be maintained in tanks or in approved containers that are closed or are fitted with an approved dispensing device that meets the requirements of 42.7.2.4.1. [30A:4.3.9.1.2]

42.3.3.8.1.3 Where there are no Class I liquids stored, the aggregate quantities of Class II liquids shall not exceed 240 gal (908 L). [30A:4.3.9.1.3]

42.3.3.8.2 Class I, II, and IIIA Liquids in Tanks Exceeding 120 Gal (454 L) Capacity. Where installation of a tank that exceeds 120 gal (454 L) capacity in accordance with 42.3.3.1 is not practical because of building or property limitations, the tank shall be permitted to be installed in a building if it is enclosed as described in 42.3.3.2 and if the installation is specifically approved by the AHJ. [30A:4.3.9.2]

42.3.3.8.3 Class IIIB Liquids. The quantity of Class IIIB liquids in storage shall not be limited. Class IIIB liquids shall be permitted to be stored in and dispensed from tanks and containers that meet the requirements of Chapter 9 and Chapters 21 through 23 of NFPA 30, as applicable. Tanks storing Class IIIB liquids inside buildings shall be permitted to be located at, below, or above grade. Adequate drainage shall be provided. Tanks and containers that contain only crankcase drainings shall be considered as containing Class IIIB liquids. [30A:4.3.9.3]

42.3.3.9 Temporary Storage of Liquid Fuels. Aboveground tanks used for dispensing of motor fuels shall not be required to be permanently installed when located on premises not normally accessible to the public, provided that all of the following requirements are met:

(1) Approval of the AHJ shall be required prior to bringing the tank to a site in the jurisdiction. In reviewing a proposed installation, the condition of the tank, the site where the tank will be located, installation and testing procedures, and operational procedures shall be evaluated prior to approval.
(2) The approval shall include a definite time limit after which the tank shall be removed from the site and relocated to an approved location.
(3) The tank shall comply with 42.3.3 and all other applicable provisions of NFPA 30A and NFPA 30.
(4) A tank containing liquid shall not be moved unless it has been specifically investigated and approved for movement while full or partially full.

[30A:4.3.10]

42.4 Piping for Liquids.

42.4.1 Scope. Section 42.4 shall apply to piping systems consisting of pipe, tubing, flanges, bolting, gaskets, valves, fittings, flexible connectors, the pressure-containing parts of other components such as expansion joints and strainers, and devices that serve such purposes as mixing, separating, snubbing, distributing, metering, controlling flow, or secondary containment of liquids and associated vapors. [**30A:**5.1]

42.4.2 General Requirements for All Piping Systems.

42.4.2.1 The design, fabrication, assembly, test, and inspection of the piping system shall meet the requirements of Chapter 27 of NFPA 30. [**30A:**5.2.1]

42.4.2.2 Piping shall be located so that it is protected from physical damage. Piping that passes through a dike wall shall be designed to prevent excessive stresses that could result from settlement or fire exposure. [**30A:**5.2.2]

42.4.2.3 Any portion of a piping system that is in contact with the soil shall be protected from corrosion in accordance with good engineering practice. [**30A:**5.2.3]

42.4.2.4 All piping inside buildings but outside the motor fuel dispensing area shall be enclosed within a horizontal chase or a vertical shaft used only for this piping. Vertical shafts and horizontal chases shall be constructed of materials having a fire resistance rating of not less than 2 hours. [**30A:**5.2.4]

42.4.2.5 Each fill pipe shall be identified by color code or other marking to identify the product for which it is used. The color code or marking shall be maintained in legible condition throughout the life of the installation. [**30A:**5.2.5]

42.4.2.6 Shutoff and check valves shall be equipped with a pressure-relieving device that will relieve any pressure generated by thermal expansion of the contained liquid back to the storage tank. [**30A:**5.2.6]

Δ **42.4.2.7** Piping components made of low melting point materials shall be permitted to be used without backfill with the following sumps:

(1) Belowgrade underground tank sumps that are fitted with a cover
(2) Belowgrade piping connection sumps that are fitted with a cover
(3) Containment sumps, under the following conditions:
  (a) The sump is monitored to detect any leaks
  (b) Any leaks can be controlled
  (c) The components are either resistant to or shielded from damage by fire exposure
(4) Containment sumps, provided the piping components can successfully pass the test procedures described in API 607, *Fire Test for Quarter-Turn Valves and Valves Equipped with Nonmetallic Seats*

[**30A:**5.2.7]

N **42.4.3 Installation of Piping Systems.** Piping shall be installed in accordance with the manufacturers' instructions. [**30A:**5.3]

N **42.4.3.1 Bends.** The bending radius for piping and tubing that is bent shall not be less than recommended by the manufacturer. [**30A:**5.3.1]

N **42.4.3.2 Flexible Connections.**

N **42.4.3.2.1** Flexible piping connections shall be provided at the following points in the piping system:

(1) Where liquid, vapor return, and vent piping connect to underground tanks

(2) At the base of any vent riser
(3) Where required to relieve stress at points where the piping changes direction

[**30A:**5.3.2.1]

N **42.4.3.2.2** Acceptable means for providing flexibility in piping systems shall include the following:

(1) Listed flexible connectors that are approved for the purpose
(2) Piping that is inherently flexible and is approved for the purpose
(3) Other means acceptable to the piping manufacturer

[**30A:**5.3.2.2]

N **42.4.4 Testing.**

N **42.4.4.1 General.** All piping and secondary containment piping shall be tested before being covered, enclosed, or placed in service in accordance with the requirements of Section 27.7 of NFPA 30. [**30A:**5.4.1]

N **42.4.4.2* Secondary Containment Piping.** In addition to the test required in 42.4.4.1, secondary containment–type piping shall have the interstitial space (annulus) tested hydrostatically or with air pressure at minimum gauge pressure of 34.5 kPa (5 psi) or shall be tested in accordance with the listing or the manufacturer's instructions. The pressure source shall be closed from the system being tested to ensure that the test is being conducted on a closed system. [**30A:**5.4.2]

N **42.4.4.3 Maintenance Testing.** Existing piping shall be tested in accordance with 42.4.4.1 when the authority having jurisdiction has reasonable cause to believe that a leak exists. Piping that could contain flammable or combustible liquids shall not be tested pneumatically. Such tests shall be at the expense of the owner or operator. [**30A:**5.4.3]

N **42.4.4.4 Leak Detection.** On remote pressure pumping systems, each pump shall have installed, on the discharge side, a listed leak detection device that will provide an audible indication, a visible indication, or will restrict or shut off the flow of product if the piping and dispensing devices are not liquid-tight. [**30A:**5.4.4]

N **42.4.5 Detector Maintenance.** Each leak-detecting device shall be checked and tested at least annually according to the manufacturer's specifications to ensure proper installation and operation. [**30A:**5.5]

N **42.4.6 Vent Piping.**

N **42.4.6.1** Vent piping shall meet the requirements of Section 27.8 of NFPA 30. [**30A:**5.6.1]

N **42.4.6.2** Vent pipes for all tanks storing Class I liquids shall discharge only in an upward direction in order to disperse vapors and shall terminate at least 3.6 m (12 ft) above grade. [**30A:**5.6.2]

N **42.4.6.3** Tank vents that are installed within or attached to a canopy shall extend a minimum of 1.5 m (5 ft) above the highest projection of the canopy. [**30A:**5.6.3]

N **42.4.7 Vapor Recovery Piping.** A vapor return pipe inside the dispenser housing shall have a shear section or flexible connector so that the liquid emergency shutoff valve will function as described in 42.5.3.9. [**30A:**5.7]

42.5 Fuel Dispensing Systems.

42.5.1 Scope. Section 42.5 shall apply to the system and components that dispense fuel into the tanks of motor vehicles and marine craft. [**30A:**6.1]

42.5.2 General Requirements.

42.5.2.1 Dispensing devices installed outside at motor fuel dispensing stations shall be located as follows:

(1) 10 ft (3 m) or more from property lines
(2) 10 ft (3 m) or more from buildings, other than canopies, having combustible exterior wall surfaces or buildings having noncombustible exterior wall surfaces that are not a part of a 1 hr fire-resistive assembly
(3) Such that all parts of the vehicle being served will be on the premises of the service station
(4) Such that the nozzle, when the hose is fully extended, will not reach within 5 ft (1.5 m) of building openings

[**30A:**6.2.1]

42.5.2.2 Liquids shall not be dispensed by applying pressure to drums, barrels, and similar containers. Listed pumps taking suction through the top of the container or listed self-closing faucets shall be used. [**30A:**6.2.2]

Δ **42.5.2.3** Fuel dispensing systems, including dispensers, hoses, nozzles, breakaway fittings, swivels, flexible connectors, dispenser emergency shutoff valves, vapor recovery systems, and pumps that are used for alcohol-blended motor fuels shall be listed for the specific purpose and in accordance with the following:

(1) UL 79A, *Power-Operated Pumps for Gasoline and Gasoline/Ethanol Blends with Nominal Ethanol Concentrations up to 85 Percent (E0–E85)*
(2) UL 87A, *Power-Operated Dispensing Devices for Gasoline and Gasoline/Ethanol Blends with Nominal Ethanol Concentrations Up to 85 Percent (E0–E85)*
(3) UL 330A, *Outline of Investigation for Hose and Hose Assemblies for Use with Dispensing Devices Dispensing Gasoline and Gasoline/Ethanol Blends with Nominal Ethanol Concentrations up to 85 Percent (E0–E85)*
(4) UL 567A, *Emergency Breakaway Fittings, Swivel Connectors and Pipe-Connection Fittings for Gasoline and Gasoline/Ethanol Blends with Nominal Ethanol Concentrations up to 85 Percent (E0–E85)*
(5) UL 842A, *Valves for Gasoline and Gasoline/Ethanol Blends with Nominal Ethanol Concentrations up to 85 Percent (E0–E85)*
(6) UL 2586A, *Hose Nozzle Valves for Gasoline and Gasoline/Ethanol Blends with Nominal Ethanol Concentrations up to 85 Percent (E0–E85)*

[**30A:**6.2.3]

42.5.3 Requirements for Dispensing Devices.

42.5.3.1 Class I and Class II liquids shall be transferred from tanks by means of fixed pumps designed and equipped to allow control of the flow and prevent leakage or accidental discharge. [**30A:**6.3.1]

42.5.3.2 Dispensing devices for Class I and Class II liquids shall be listed. [**30A:**6.3.2]

42.5.3.2.1 Existing listed or labeled dispensing devices shall be permitted to be modified provided that the modifications made are "Listed by Report" by an approved testing laboratory or as otherwise approved by the AHJ. Modification proposals shall contain a description of the component parts used in the modification and the recommended methods of installation on specific dispensing devices. Modification proposals shall be made available to the AHJ upon request. [**30A:**6.3.2.1]

42.5.3.3 A control shall be provided that will permit the pump to operate only when a dispensing nozzle is removed from its bracket or normal position with respect to the dispensing device and the switch on this dispensing device is manually actuated. This control shall also stop the pump when all nozzles have been returned to their brackets or to their normal nondispensing position. [**30A:**6.3.3]

42.5.3.4 Dispensing devices shall be mounted on a concrete island or shall otherwise be protected against collision damage by means acceptable to the AHJ. Dispensing devices shall be securely bolted in place. If located indoors, dispensing devices shall also be located in a position where they cannot be struck by a vehicle that is out of control descending a ramp or other slope. Dispensing devices shall be installed in accordance with the manufacturer's instructions. [**30A:**6.3.4]

42.5.3.5 Dispensing devices used to fill portable containers with home heating fuels shall be located at least 20 ft (6 m) from any dispensing devices for motor fuels. [**30A:**6.3.5]

42.5.3.6 Inspections. Dispensing equipment shall be periodically inspected by a person who is knowledgeable in the operation of the equipment to verify that it is in proper working order and is not leaking. [**30A:**6.3.6]

42.5.3.6.1* Exterior Inspection. A visual inspection of the fuel dispenser and its associated hanging hardware (hose nozzle valve, hose, breakaway valve, and hose swivel) shall be conducted at least weekly and shall be documented. Documentation shall be available for review by the AHJ upon request. [**30A:**6.3.6.1]

42.5.3.6.2* Internal Dispenser Cabinet Inspection. An inspection of the fuel dispensing equipment that is located inside the dispenser cabinet shall be conducted. The interior of the fuel dispenser cabinet shall be inspected for signs of leaks, damage, corrosion, or weathering, with particular attention to the sump area and joints and castings of fluid handling components. The inspection shall be conducted at least monthly and shall be documented. Documentation shall be available for review by the AHJ upon request. [**30A:**6.3.6.2]

42.5.3.6.3 Maintenance. When maintenance to dispensing devices is necessary and such maintenance is capable of causing accidental release or ignition of liquid, the following precautions shall be taken before such maintenance is begun:

(1) Only persons knowledgeable in performing the required maintenance shall perform the work.
(2) All electrical power to the dispensing devices, to the pump serving the dispensing devices, and to all associated control circuits shall be shut off at the main electrical disconnect panel.
(3) The emergency shutoff valve at the dispenser, if installed, shall be closed.
(4) All vehicular traffic and unauthorized persons shall be prevented from coming within 20 ft (6 m) of the dispensing device.

[**30A:**6.3.6.3]

42.5.3.7 Motor vehicle traffic patterns at motor fuel dispensing facilities shall be designed to inhibit movement of vehicles that are not being fueled from passing through the dispensing area. [**30A**:6.3.7]

42.5.3.8 At unattended self-serve motor fuel dispensing facilities, coin- and currency-type devices shall be permitted only with the approval of the AHJ. [**30A**:6.3.8]

Δ **42.5.3.9** Where liquid is supplied to the dispensing device under pressure, a listed, rigidly anchored, double-poppet type emergency shutoff valve incorporating a fusible link or other thermally actuated device designed to close automatically in the event of severe impact or fire exposure, shall be installed in the supply line at the base of each individual island-type dispenser or at the inlet of each overhead dispensing device. [**30A**:6.3.9]

42.5.3.9.1 The emergency shutoff valve shall be installed in accordance with the manufacturer's instructions. [**30A**:6.3.9.1]

42.5.3.9.2 The emergency shutoff valve shall not incorporate a slip-joint feature. [**30A**:6.3.9.2]

42.5.3.9.3 The automatic-closing feature of this valve shall be tested at the time of installation and at least once a year thereafter by manually tripping the hold-open linkage. Records of such tests shall be kept at the premises or shall be made available for inspection by the AHJ within 24 hours of a verbal or written request. [**30A**:6.3.9.3]

42.5.3.10 Where a suction-type dispensing system includes a booster pump or where a suction-type dispensing system is supplied by a tank in a manner that produces a gravity head on the dispensing device, a vacuum-actuated shutoff valve with a shear section or equivalent-type valve, listed and labeled in accordance with CAN/UL/ULC 842, *Valves for Flammable and Combustible Liquids*, shall be installed directly under the dispensing device. [**30A**:6.3.10]

42.5.4 Requirements for Remote/Submersible Pumps. Subsection 42.5.4 shall apply to systems for dispensing Class I and Class II liquids where the liquids are transferred from storage to individual or multiple dispensing devices by pumps located other than at the dispensing devices. [**30A**:6.4]

42.5.4.1 Pumps shall be listed and shall be designed or equipped so that no part of the system will be subjected to pressures above its allowable working pressure. [**30A**:6.4.1]

42.5.4.2 Leak Detection.

42.5.4.2.1 Where all discharge piping is not visible, each pump shall have installed on the discharge side a listed leak detection device that will provide an audible indication or a visible indication or that will restrict or shut off the flow of product if the piping or a dispenser is leaking. [**30A**:6.4.2.1]

42.5.4.2.2 Each leak-detecting device shall be checked and tested at least annually according to the manufacturer's specifications to ensure proper installation and operation. [**30A**:6.4.2.2]

42.5.4.3 Pumps installed above grade outside of buildings shall be located not less than 10 ft (3 m) from lines of adjoining property that can be built upon and not less than 5 ft (1.5 m) from any building opening. Where an outside pump location is impractical, pumps shall be permitted to be installed inside buildings as provided for dispensers in 42.5.3.4 or in sumps as provided in 42.5.4.4. Pumps shall be anchored and protected against physical damage. [**30A**:6.4.3]

42.5.4.4 Sumps for subsurface pumps or piping manifolds of submersible pumps shall withstand the external forces to which they can be subjected without damage to the pump, tank, or piping. The sump shall be no larger than necessary for inspection and maintenance and shall be provided with a fitted cover. [**30A**:6.4.4]

42.5.5 Requirements for Dispensing Hose.

42.5.5.1 Listed hose assemblies shall be used to dispense fuel. Hose length at automotive motor fuel dispensing facilities shall not exceed 18 ft (5.5 m). Where hose length at marine motor fuel dispensing facilities exceeds 18 ft (5.5 m), the hose shall be secured so as to protect it from damage. [**30A**:6.5.1]

42.5.5.2 A listed emergency breakaway device designed to retain liquid on both sides of the breakaway point shall be installed on each hose dispensing Class I and II liquids. Such devices shall be installed and maintained in accordance with the manufacturer's instructions. [**30A**:6.5.2]

42.5.5.3 Where hose are attached to a hose-retrieving mechanism, the listed emergency breakaway device shall be installed between the point of attachment of the hose-retrieving mechanism to the hose and the hose nozzle valve. [**30A**:6.5.3]

42.5.6 Requirements for Fuel Delivery Nozzles.

42.5.6.1 An automatic closing-type hose nozzle valve, with a latch-open device and listed and labeled in accordance with CAN/UL/ULC 842, *Valves for Flammable and Combustible Liquids*; or CAN/UL/ULC 2586, *Hose Nozzle Valves for Flammable and Combustible Liquids*, shall be provided on island-type dispensing devices used to dispense Class I or Class II liquids. [**30A**:6.6.1]

42.5.6.1.1 Any modification of the dispensing nozzle shall be listed or approved by the manufacturer of the nozzle. [**30A**:6.6.1.1]

42.5.6.2* At any installation where an automatic closing-type dispensing nozzle is used, the nozzle valve shall include a feature that causes or requires the closing of the hose nozzle valve before product flow can be resumed or before the hose nozzle valve can be replaced in its normal position in the dispenser. [**30A**:6.6.2]

42.5.6.3 Automatic Closing Valve.

42.5.6.3.1 Overhead-type dispensing devices shall be provided with a listed, automatic closing-type hose nozzle valve without a latch-open device. [**30A**:6.6.3.1]

42.5.6.3.2 A listed, automatic closing-type hose nozzle valve with a latch-open device shall be permitted to be used if the hose nozzle valve will close automatically in the event the valve is released from a fill opening or upon impact. [**30A**:6.6.3.2]

42.5.6.4 Dispensing nozzles used at marine motor fuel dispensing facilities shall be of the listed automatic closing-type hose nozzle valve without a latch-open device. [**30A**:6.6.4]

42.5.7 Emergency Electrical Disconnects.

42.5.7.1 Fuel dispensing systems shall be provided with one or more clearly identified emergency shutoff devices or electrical disconnects. [**30A**:6.7.1]

Δ **42.5.7.2** At least one emergency shutoff device or electrical disconnect shall be installed in approved locations not less than 20 ft (6 m) or more than 100 ft (30 m) from the fuel dispensing devices that they serve. [30A:6.7.2]

N **42.5.7.3** Additional shutoff devices or electrical disconnects shall be permitted to be located less than 6 m (20 ft) or greater than 30 m (100 ft) from an individual dispenser. [30A:6.7.3]

Δ **42.5.7.4** Emergency shutoff devices or electrical disconnects shall disconnect power to all dispensing devices not supplied by circuits that are identified to be intrinsically safe; to all remote pumps serving the dispensing devices; to all associated power, control, and signal circuits; to all other electrical equipment in the hazardous (classified) locations; and to electrical receptacles over or adjacent to the hazardous (classified) locations. [30A:6.7.4]

42.5.7.5 Emergency shutoff devices or electrical disconnects shall mechanically or electrically isolate other fluid transfer systems serving the fuel dispensing area. [30A:6.7.5]

42.5.7.6 Intrinsically safe electrical equipment shall not be required to be disconnected by the emergency shutoff device or the electrical disconnect. [30A:6.7.6]

42.5.7.7 When more than one emergency shutoff device or electrical disconnect is provided, all devices shall be interconnected. [30A:6.7.7]

42.5.7.8 Resetting from an emergency shutoff condition shall require manual intervention. [30A:6.7.8]

42.5.7.9 The manner of resetting shall be approved. [30A:6.7.9]

42.5.7.10 At attended motor fuel dispensing facilities, the devices or disconnects shall be readily accessible to the attendant and labeled with an approved sign stating "EMERGENCY FUEL SHUTOFF" or equivalent language. [30A:6.7.10]

42.5.7.11 Unattended Motor Fuel Dispensing Facilities.

42.5.7.11.1 At unattended motor fuel dispensing facilities, the devices or disconnects shall be readily accessible to patrons. [30A:6.7.11.1]

42.5.7.11.2 At least one additional device or disconnect shall be readily accessible to each group of dispensing devices on an individual island. [30A:6.7.11.2]

42.5.7.11.3 The device(s) or disconnect(s) shall be labeled with an approved sign stating "EMERGENCY FUEL SHUTOFF" or equivalent language. [30A:6.7.11.3]

42.5.8 Vapor Recovery Systems.

42.5.8.1 Dispensing devices that incorporate vapor recovery shall be listed. [30A:6.8.1]

42.5.8.2 Hose nozzle valves used on vapor recovery systems shall be listed for the purpose. [30A:6.8.2]

42.5.8.3 Means shall be provided in the vapor return path from each dispensing outlet to prevent the discharge of vapors when the hose nozzle valve is in its normal nondispensing position. [30A:6.8.3]

42.6 Building Construction Requirements. The construction of buildings and portions of buildings that are motor fuel dispensing facilities or repair garages shall comply with Chapter 30.

42.7 Operational Requirements.

42.7.1 Scope. Section 42.7 applies to those requirements that relate to the operation of motor fuel dispensing facilities, fuel dispensing systems, repair garages, and repair areas. [30A:9.1]

42.7.2 Basic Requirements.

42.7.2.1* Inventory Control. Accurate daily inventory records shall be maintained and reconciled for all liquid fuel storage tanks for indication of possible leakage from tanks or piping. The records shall be kept on the premises or shall be made available to the AHJ for inspection within 24 hours of a written or verbal request. The records shall include, as a minimum and by product, daily reconciliation between sales, use, receipts, and inventory on hand. If there is more than one storage system serving an individual pump or dispensing device for any product, the reconciliation shall be maintained separately for each system. [30A:9.2.1]

42.7.2.2 Tank Filling and Bulk Delivery.

42.7.2.2.1 Delivery operations shall meet all applicable requirements of NFPA 385 and the requirements of 42.7.2.2.2 through 42.7.2.2.6. [30A:9.2.2.1]

42.7.2.2.2 No separation shall be required between the delivery vehicle and the fill connection of an underground storage tank. [30A:9.2.2.2]

42.7.2.2.3 The delivery vehicle shall be separated from any aboveground tank in accordance with Table 42.7.2.2.3. [30A:9.2.2.3]

42.7.2.2.3.1 Separation distances shall be imposed by the use of curbing, guard posts, or other approved methods. [30A:9.2.2.3.1]

42.7.2.2.3.2* Means shall be provided to prevent an accidental release originating from the delivery vehicle from flowing under the aboveground tank. [30A:9.2.2.3.2]

Table 42.7.2.2.3 Minimum Separation Distances Between Delivery Vehicles and Aboveground Tanks

Aboveground Tank Type	Separation Distance Between Delivery Vehicle and Aboveground Tank (ft)
Protected aboveground tanks	0
Tanks in abovegrade vaults (measured from vault wall)	0
Tanks filled by gravity	0
Fire-resistant tanks	15
Other tanks meeting the requirements of NFPA 30 storing Class II or Class III liquids	15
Other tanks meeting the requirements of NFPA 30 storing Class I liquids	25

[30A:Table 9.2.2.3]

42.7.2.2.4 Delivery Vehicle Location.

42.7.2.2.4.1 The delivery vehicle shall be located so that all parts of the vehicle are on the premises when delivery is made. [**30A:**9.2.2.4.1]

42.7.2.2.4.2 Where fuel dispensing facilities are located inside buildings, the fuel delivery vehicle shall be permitted to be located off premises at approved locations. [**30A:**9.2.2.4.2]

42.7.2.2.4.3 Existing fuel dispensing facilities shall not be required to meet 42.7.2.2.4.1. [**30A:**9.2.2.4.3]

42.7.2.2.5 Tank filling shall not begin until the delivery operator has determined that the tank has sufficient available capacity (i.e., ullage). [**30A:**9.2.2.5]

42.7.2.2.6 Tanks shall be filled through a liquidtight connection. [**30A:**9.2.2.6]

42.7.2.2.6.1 Where an aboveground tank is filled by means of fixed piping, either a check valve and shutoff valve with a quick-connect coupling or a check valve with a dry-break coupling shall be installed in the piping at a point where connection and disconnection is made between the tank and the delivery vehicle. This device shall be protected from tampering and physical damage. [**30A:**9.2.2.6.1]

42.7.2.2.6.2 Underground tanks and tanks in belowgrade vaults shall be filled through a liquidtight connection within a spill container. [**30A:**9.2.2.6.2]

42.7.2.3 Dispensing into Containers.

42.7.2.3.1* Class I or Class II liquids shall not be dispensed into portable containers unless the container is constructed of metal or is approved by the AHJ, has a tight closure, and is fitted with a spout or so designed that the contents can be poured without spilling. The hose nozzle valve shall be manually held open during the dispensing operation. [**30A:**9.2.3.1]

42.7.2.3.2 No sale or purchase of any Class I, Class II, or Class III liquids shall be made in containers unless such containers are clearly marked with the name of the product contained therein. [**30A:**9.2.3.2]

42.7.2.3.3 Portable containers of 12 gal (45 L) capacity or less shall not be filled while they are in or on a motor vehicle or marine craft. [**30A:**9.2.3.3]

42.7.2.4 Dispensing from a Tank That Does Not Exceed 120 Gal (454 L) and from Containers Inside Buildings. Dispensing of flammable and combustible liquids from a tank not exceeding 120 gal (454 L) capacity and from containers in a motor fuel dispensing facility or in a repair garage building shall meet the requirements of 42.7.2.4.1 and 42.7.2.4.2. *(See 42.3.3.8 for storage quantity limitations.)* [**30A:**9.2.4]

42.7.2.4.1 Not more than one container of Class I liquid shall be permitted to be provided with a dispensing pump inside a building at any one time. The number of tanks or containers of Class II or Class IIIA liquids fitted for dispensing at any one time shall not be limited, except as provided for in 42.3.3.8.2. The number of tanks or containers of Class IIIB liquids fitted for dispensing at any one time shall not be limited. [**30A:**9.2.4.1]

42.7.2.4.2 Class I, Class II, and Class IIIA liquids shall not be dispensed by applying pressure to tanks or containers. Listed pumps that take suction through the top of the tank or container or listed self-closing faucets shall be used. [**30A:**9.2.4.2]

42.7.2.5* Display of Materials. The storage or placement for display or sale of products shall be prohibited within 20 ft (6 m) of any fuel dispenser. [**30A:**9.2.5.6]

42.7.2.6 Basic Fire Control.

Δ **42.7.2.6.1 Sources of Ignition.** Lit smoking materials or igniters, including electronic cigarettes, shall not be used within 20 ft (6 m) of areas used for fueling, servicing fuel systems of internal combustion engines, or receiving or dispensing of Class I and Class II liquids. [**30A:**9.2.5.1]

N **42.7.2.6.2* Continuing Operation.** The engines of all equipment or vehicles being fueled shall be shut off except where continuing operation is essential for protecting life, property, or the environment. [**30A:**9.2.5.2]

42.7.2.6.3* Fire Extinguishers.

42.7.2.6.3.1 Portable fire extinguishers shall be selected, installed, inspected, and maintained in accordance with Section 13.6 and 42.7.2.6.3.2 through 42.7.2.6.3.5. [**30A:**9.2.5.3.1]

42.7.2.6.3.2 All portable fire extinguishers installed to achieve compliance with this *Code* shall be a minimum of 10 lb (4.54 kg) ABC dry chemical having an agent discharge rate of 1 lb/sec (0.45 kg/sec) or greater. [**30A:**9.2.5.3.2]

42.7.2.6.3.3 The maximum travel distance from a minimum 20 lb (9.1 kg) ABC dry chemical extinguisher having an agent discharge rate of 1 lb/sec (0.45 kg/sec) or greater shall be permitted to be 100 ft (30.5 m). [**30A:**9.2.5.3.3]

42.7.2.6.3.4 New Fire Extinguishers. Installed fire extinguishers, including replacements or exchanges, shall meet the requirements of 42.7.2.6.3. [**30A:**9.2.5.3.4]

42.7.2.6.3.5 Repair Garages.

42.7.2.6.3.5.1 At least one portable fire extinguisher shall be provided in any repair garage. [**30A:**9.2.5.3.5.1]

42.7.2.6.3.5.2 The maximum travel distance from any point in the vehicle service area to a portable fire extinguisher shall not exceed 50 ft (15 m). [**30A:**9.2.5.3.5.2]

42.7.2.6.3.6 Indoor Liquid Motor Fuel Dispensing Areas.

42.7.2.6.3.6.1 At least one portable fire extinguisher shall be provided at a position no less than 15 ft (4.6 m) but no more than 50 ft (15 m) from the fuel dispenser and within the identified path of egress from the fuel dispensing area. [**30A:**9.2.5.3.6.1]

42.7.2.6.3.6.2 An additional compliant extinguisher shall be provided within the egress path in cases where the travel distance and the egress requirements cannot be simultaneously met. [**30A:**9.2.5.3.6.2]

42.7.2.6.3.7 Outdoor Liquid Motor Fuel Dispensing Areas. At least one portable fire extinguisher shall be provided at all fuel dispensing islands, or group of islands, so as not to exceed a maximum travel distance of 75 ft (23 m) to any single portable fire extinguisher. [**30A:**9.2.5.3.7]

42.7.2.6.3.8 Gaseous Fuel Dispensing Areas. At least one portable fire extinguisher shall be provided for each gaseous fuel dispenser or group of dispensers so as not to exceed a maximum travel distance of 50 ft (15 m) but not less than 15 ft (4.6 m) to any single portable fire extinguisher. [**30A:**9.2.5.3.8]

42.7.2.6.4 Fire Suppression Systems. Where required, automatic fire suppression systems shall be installed in accordance with the appropriate NFPA standard, manufacturers' instructions, and the listing requirements of the systems. [**30A:**9.2.5.4]

42.7.2.6.5* Signs. Warning signs shall be conspicuously posted in the dispensing area and shall incorporate the following or equivalent wording:

WARNING It is unlawful and dangerous to dispense gasoline into unapproved containers.
No smoking.
Stop motor.
No filling of portable containers in or on a motor vehicle.
Place container on ground before filling.
Discharge your static electricity before fueling by touching a metal surface away from the nozzle.
Do not re-enter your vehicle while gasoline is pumping.
If a fire starts, **do not** remove nozzle — back away immediately.
Do not allow individuals under licensed age to use the pump.
[**30A:**9.2.5.5]

42.7.2.7 Waste Handling.

42.7.2.7.1 Crankcase drainings and waste liquids shall not be dumped into sewers, into streams, or on the ground. [**30A:**9.2.6.1]

Δ **42.7.2.7.2** Crankcase drainings and waste liquids shall be stored in approved tanks or containers outside any building or in tanks installed in accordance with Chapters 4 and 5 of NFPA 30A until they can be removed from the premises. [**30A:**9.2.6.2]

42.7.2.7.3 The contents of oil separators and traps of floor drainage systems shall be collected at sufficiently frequent intervals to prevent oil from being carried into sewers. [**30A:**9.2.6.3]

42.7.2.8 Housekeeping. The dispensing area and the area within any dike shall be kept free of vegetation, debris, and any other material that is not necessary to the proper operation of the motor fuel dispensing facility. [**30A:**9.2.7]

42.7.2.9 Fire Doors. Fire doors shall be kept unobstructed at all times. Appropriate signs and markings shall be used. [**30A:**9.2.8]

42.7.2.10 Maintenance of Aboveground Storage Tank Appurtenances. Storage tank appurtenances shall be maintained and operated in accordance with manufacturer's instructions, published industry practices, or equivalent methods approved by the AHJ. [**30A:**9.2.9]

42.7.3 Operating Requirements for Full-Service Motor Fuel Dispensing Facilities. Each motor fuel dispensing facility shall have an attendant or supervisor on duty whenever the facility is open for business. The attendant or supervisor shall dispense liquids into fuel tanks or into containers, except as covered in 42.7.4 and 42.7.5. [**30A:**9.3]

42.7.4 Operating Requirements for Attended Self-Service Motor Fuel Dispensing Facilities.

42.7.4.1 "Self-service motor fuel dispensing facility" shall mean that portion of a property where liquids used as motor fuels are stored and dispensed from fixed, approved dispensing equipment into the fuel tanks of motor vehicles by persons other than the facility attendant and shall also include, where provided, facilities for the sale of other retail products. [**30A:**9.4.1]

42.7.4.2 There shall be at least one attendant on duty while the self-service facility is open for business. The attendant's primary function shall be to supervise, observe, and control the dispensing of motor fuels. [**30A:**9.4.2]

42.7.4.3 The responsibility of the attendant shall be as follows:

(1) Prevent the dispensing of Class I liquids into portable containers not in compliance with 42.7.2.3.1
(2) Prevent the use of hose nozzle valve latch-open devices that do not comply with 42.5.6.1
(3) Control sources of ignition
(4) Immediately activate emergency controls and notify the fire department of any fire or other emergency
(5) Handle accidental spills and fire extinguishers if needed

[**30A:**9.4.3]

42.7.4.3.1 The attendant or supervisor on duty shall be mentally and physically capable of performing the functions and assuming the responsibility prescribed in 42.7.4. [**30A:**9.4.3.1]

42.7.4.4 Operating instructions shall be conspicuously posted in the dispensing area. [**30A:**9.4.4]

42.7.5 Operating Requirements for Unattended Self-Service Motor Fuel Dispensing Facilities.

42.7.5.1 Unattended self-service facilities shall be permitted, where approved by the AHJ. [**30A:**9.5.1]

42.7.5.2 Operating instructions shall be conspicuously posted in the dispensing area. The instructions shall include location of emergency controls and a requirement that the user stay outside of his/her vehicle and in view of the fueling nozzle during dispensing. [**30A:**9.5.2]

42.7.5.3 In addition to the warning signs specified in 42.7.2.6.5, emergency instructions shall be conspicuously posted in the dispenser area. The instructions shall incorporate the following or equivalent wording:

Emergency Instructions

In case of fire or spill:

(1) Use emergency stop button.

(2) Report accident by calling (*specify local fire number*). Report location.

[**30A:**9.5.3]

42.7.5.4 A listed, automatic closing–type hose nozzle valve with latch-open device shall be provided. The hose nozzle valve shall meet the requirements of 42.5.6.2. [**30A:**9.5.4]

42.7.5.5 A telephone or other approved, clearly identified means to notify the fire department shall be provided on the site in a location approved by the AHJ. [**30A:**9.5.5]

42.7.5.6* Additional fire protection shall be provided where required by the AHJ. [**30A:**9.5.6]

N 42.7.6 Operating Requirements for Fleet Vehicle Motor Fuel Dispensing Facilities.

N 42.7.6.1 The dispensing of motor fuels shall be conducted only by employees or other authorized affiliates of the business or operation. [**30A:**9.6.1]

N 42.7.6.2 If dispensing is conducted after normal working hours of the facility or when normal facility telecommunications are not available for use, then a telephone or other approved, clearly identified means to notify the fire department shall be provided on the site in a location approved by the authority having jurisdiction. [**30A:**9.6.2]

N 42.7.6.3 A listed, automatic closing–type hose nozzle valve that meets the requirements of 42.5.6.2 and has a latch-open device shall be provided. [**30A:**9.6.3]

N 42.7.6.4 Operating instructions shall be conspicuously posted in the dispensing area. [**30A:**9.6.4]

N 42.7.6.4.1 The instructions in 42.7.6.4 shall include the location of emergency controls and a requirement that the user stay outside of their vehicle and in view of the fueling nozzle during dispensing. [**30A:**9.6.4.1]

N 42.7.6.5 In addition to the warning signs specified in 42.7.2.6.4, emergency instructions shall be conspicuously posted in the dispenser area. [**30A:**9.6.5]

N 42.7.6.5.1 The instructions in 42.7.6.5 shall incorporate the following or equivalent wording:

Emergency Instructions

In case of fire or spill:

(1) Use emergency stop button.
(2) Report accident by calling (specify local fire number). Report location.

[**30A:**9.6.5.1]

42.7.7 Refueling from Tank Vehicles. The dispensing of Class I and Class II liquids in the open from a tank vehicle to a motor vehicle located at commercial, industrial, governmental, or manufacturing establishments and intended for fueling vehicles used in connection with their businesses shall be permitted only if all of the requirements of 42.7.7.1 through 42.7.7.9 have been met. [**30A:**9.7]

42.7.7.1 An inspection of the premises and operations shall be made and operations shall not be conducted unless approved by the AHJ. [**30A:**9.7.1]

42.7.7.2 The tank vehicle shall comply with the requirements of NFPA 385. [**30A:**9.7.2]

42.7.7.3 The dispensing hose shall not exceed 50 ft (15 m) in length. [**30A:**9.7.3]

42.7.7.4 The dispensing nozzle shall be a listed, automatic closing–type without a latch-open device. [**30A:**9.7.4]

42.7.7.5 Nighttime deliveries shall only be made in areas deemed adequately lighted by the AHJ. [**30A:**9.7.5]

42.7.7.6 The tank vehicle flasher lights shall be in operation while dispensing operations are in progress. [**30A:**9.7.6]

42.7.7.7 Expansion space shall be left in each fuel tank to prevent overflow in the event of temperature increase. [**30A:**9.7.7]

42.7.7.8 A means for bonding the tank vehicle to the motor vehicle shall be provided. Such bonding means shall be employed during fueling operations. [**30A:**9.7.8]

42.7.7.9 A spill kit designed for motor vehicle fuels shall be carried on the tank vehicle and employed in case of a fuel spill. [**30A:**9.7.9]

N 42.7.7.10 Portable Fire Extinguishers.

N 42.7.7.10.1 Fuel delivery tank vehicles shall be provided with at least one portable fire extinguisher selected, installed, inspected, and maintained as required by NFPA 10. [**30A:**9.7.10.1]

N 42.7.7.10.2 The fire extinguisher shall be a minimum 9.1 kg (20 lb) ABC dry chemical agent type and shall also be rated with an agent discharge rate of 0.45 kg/sec (1 lb/sec) or greater. [**30A:**9.7.10.2]

N 42.7.7.10.3 The fire extinguisher shall be readily accessible from the ground level whenever fuel dispensing or tank filling is under way. [**30A:**9.7.10.3]

N 42.7.7.10.4 Installed fire extinguishers, including replacements or exchanges, shall meet the requirements of 42.7.7.10. [**30A:**9.7.10.4]

N 42.7.8 Repair Areas.

N 42.7.8.1 General. Repairing of motor vehicles shall be restricted to areas specifically provided for such purposes. [**30A:**9.8.1]

N 42.7.8.1.1* Major repair of hydrogen vehicles shall comply with NFPA 2. [**30A:**9.8.1.1]

N 42.7.8.1.2 Major repair and minor repair of CNG and LNG vehicles shall comply with Sections 7.8 and 8.3 of NFPA 30A. [**30A:**9.8.1.2]

N 42.7.8.2 Welding and Open Flame Operations.

N 42.7.8.2.1 Operations involving open flame or electric arcs, including fusion gas and electric welding, shall be restricted to areas specifically provided for such purposes. Cutting and welding and related fire prevention precautions shall be in accordance with the requirements of NFPA 51B. [**30A:**9.8.2.1]

N 42.7.8.2.2 Electric arc welding generators or transformers shall conform to *NFPA 70*. Gas fusion welding apparatus and storage of compressed gas cylinders shall be in accordance with the provisions of NFPA 51. [**30A:**9.8.2.2]

N 42.7.8.2.3* The grounded side of an electric welding circuit shall be attached to the part being welded. [**30A:**9.8.2.3]

N 42.7.8.2.4 Compressed gases shall be stored in accordance with Chapter 4 of NFPA 51 and Chapters 4 and 7 of NFPA 55. [**30A:**9.8.2.4]

N 42.7.8.2.5 Gas fusion welding equipment shall be periodically inspected for worn or injured hoses and defective or damaged valves, gauges, and reducing devices. [**30A:**9.8.2.5]

N 42.7.8.2.6 Exterior storage of cylinders shall comply with NFPA 51 and Chapters 4 and 7 of NFPA 55. [**30A:**9.8.2.6]

N **42.7.8.3 Spray Painting and Undercoating.**

N **42.7.8.3.1** Spray painting shall meet the requirements of NFPA 33. [**30A:**9.8.3.1]

N **42.7.8.3.2** Where only a small portion of a vehicle is spray painted and no accumulations of paint residue are allowed to form, such occasional painting shall be permitted in the open in the structure if located not less than 6 m (20 ft) horizontally from all open flame devices or spark-producing electrical equipment or appliances. [**30A:**9.8.3.2]

N **42.7.8.3.3** Undercoating spray operations conducted in any area having adequate natural or mechanical ventilation shall be exempt from the requirements pertaining to spray finishing operations where the undercoating materials are nonflammable or where the solvents used have a flash point in excess of 37.8°C (100°F) (closed cup). There shall be no open flame devices or spark-producing electrical equipment or appliances within 6 m (20 ft) horizontally while such operations are conducted. Undercoating materials shall be dry before starting the engine of the undercoated vehicle. [**30A:**9.8.3.3]

N **42.7.8.3.4** Undercoating spray operations that do not meet the requirements of 42.7.8.3.3 shall meet all requirements of NFPA 33. [**30A:**9.8.3.4]

N **42.7.8.4 Drying Apparatus.** Drying and baking apparatus in connection with the spray application of flammable finishes shall conform to NFPA 33 and NFPA 86. [**30A:**9.8.4]

N **42.7.8.5 Repair of Fuel Tanks Containing Flammable or Combustible Liquids.**

N **42.7.8.5.1** Prior to repair work on fuel tanks of vehicles involving flame- or heat-producing devices, the tanks shall be drained and purged, or inerted, and tested in accordance with applicable procedures outlined in NFPA 326. [**30A:**9.8.5.1]

N **42.7.8.5.2** In lieu of draining the fuel tank outside the building, an approved portable pump and storage tank shall be permitted to be used. [**30A:**9.8.5.2]

N **42.7.8.5.3** Fuel drained from vehicle tanks that is not to be disposed of shall be stored in approved safety cans or returned to standard underground storage tanks. [**30A:**9.8.5.3]

N **42.7.8.5.4** Fuel to be disposed of shall be stored in tanks or drums suitable for such purpose that shall be located outside of the building until removed from the premises. Such containers shall be identified as having flammable contents. [**30A:**9.8.5.4]

N **42.7.8.6 Parts Cleaning.**

N **42.7.8.6.1** Cleaning of parts shall be performed with a nonflammable solvent or combustible liquid that has a flash point above 37.8°C (100°F) (closed cup) and used where there is adequate ventilation in the cleaning area and no sources of ignition are present. [**30A:**9.8.6.1]

N **42.7.8.6.2** Devices used to heat nonflammable solvents shall conform to the requirements of one or both of the following:

(1) NFPA 31
(2) NFPA 54
[**30A:**9.8.6.2]

N **42.7.8.6.3** The heating devices described in 42.7.8.6.2 shall be installed in accordance with the requirements of Section 7.6 of NFPA 30A. [**30A:**9.8.6.3]

N **42.7.8.6.4** A device for heating solvents that give off flammable or toxic vapors when heated shall be provided with a limit control to prevent the solvent from exceeding a temperature 10°C (50°F) below the point at which flammable or toxic vapors are released. [**30A:**9.8.6.4]

N **42.7.8.6.5** Direct-fired parts cleaners shall not be installed or used below grade. [**30A:**9.8.6.5]

N **42.7.8.7 Chassis Cleaning.**

N **42.7.8.7.1** Chassis cleaning shall not be performed with liquids having flash points below 60°C (140°F) (closed cup). If steam is used, it shall be supplied from a boiler located, installed, and safeguarded in accordance with the applicable requirements for heating equipment in Section 7.6 of NFPA 30A and in NFPA 31, NFPA 54, and NFPA 85. [**30A:**9.8.7.1]

N **42.7.8.7.2** Steam cleaning devices shall be of an approved type. [**30A:**9.8.7.2]

N **42.7.8.8 Storage and Handling of Flammable and Combustible Liquids, Liquefied Petroleum Gases, and Compressed Natural Gases.** Except as otherwise provided by this *Code*, the storage and handling of flammable and combustible liquids shall be in accordance with NFPA 30. The storage and handling of liquefied petroleum gas shall be in accordance with NFPA 58. The storage and handling of flammable compressed gas fuels shall be in accordance with NFPA 55, NFPA 52, and NFPA 2. [**30A:**9.8.8]

N **42.7.8.9 Housekeeping.**

N **42.7.8.9.1** An authorized employee, an officer of the firm, or the owner shall make daily inspections of the repair garage and shall be responsible for the prompt removal or repair of any hazardous condition, including proper maintenance of equipment and safety devices and the immediate removal of accumulations of combustible materials. [**30A:**9.8.9.1]

N **42.7.8.9.2** Clear aisle space shall be maintained to permit ready access to and the use of firefighting equipment. [**30A:**9.8.9.2]

N **42.7.8.9.3** Floors shall be kept clean and free of oil and grease. Only approved water solutions or detergents, floor-sweeping compounds, and grease absorbents shall be used for cleaning floors. [**30A:**9.8.9.3]

N **42.7.8.9.4** Metal lockers shall be provided for employees' clothes. [**30A:**9.8.9.4]

N **42.7.8.9.5** Approved metal receptacles with self-closing covers shall be provided for the storage or disposal of oil-soaked waste or cloths. [**30A:**9.8.9.5]

N **42.7.8.9.6** Combustible rubbish shall be placed in covered metal receptacles until removed to a safe place for disposal. Contents of such containers shall be removed daily. [**30A:**9.8.9.6]

N **42.7.8.9.7** Smoking shall be prohibited except in designated areas subject to the approval of the authority having jurisdiction. [**30A:**9.8.9.7]

42.7.9 LNG Vehicle Fueling System Monitoring and Management.

42.7.9.1* Repairs to LNG vehicles lasting 8 hours or more shall require pressure monitoring and management of the LNG tank. [**30A:**9.9.1]

42.8 Additional Requirements for CNG, LNG, Hydrogen, and LP-Gas.

42.8.1 Scope. Section 42.8 shall apply where CNG, LNG, compressed or liquefied hydrogen, LP-Gas, or combinations of these, are dispensed as motor vehicle fuels along with Class I or Class II liquids that are also dispensed as motor vehicle fuels. [**30A:**12.1]

42.8.2 General Requirements.

42.8.2.1 The installation and use of CNG and LNG systems shall meet the requirements of NFPA 52, except as modified by Section 42.8. The installation and use of hydrogen systems shall meet the requirements of NFPA 2, except as modified by Section 42.8. The installation and use of LP-Gas systems shall meet the requirements of NFPA 58, except as modified by Section 42.8. [**30A:**12.2.1]

42.8.2.2 A means shall be provided that connects to the dispenser supply piping and that prevents flow in the event that the dispenser is displaced from its mounting. [**30A:**12.2.2]

42.8.2.3* Dispensing devices for CNG, LNG, hydrogen, and LP-Gas shall be listed or approved. [**30A:**12.2.3]

42.8.2.4* Listed or approved hose assemblies shall be used to dispense fuel. Hose length at automotive motor fuel dispensing facilities shall not exceed 18 ft (5.5 m). [**30A:**12.2.4]

42.8.3 Fuel Storage.

42.8.3.1 Aboveground tanks storing CNG or LNG shall be separated from any adjacent property line that is or can be built upon, any public way, and the nearest important building on the same property by not less than the distances given in Section 8.4 of NFPA 52. [**30A:**12.3.1]

42.8.3.2 Aboveground tanks storing hydrogen shall be separated from any adjacent property line that is or can be built upon, any public way, and the nearest important building on the same property by not less than the distances given in NFPA 2. [**30A:**12.3.2]

42.8.3.3 Aboveground tanks storing LP-Gas shall be separated from any adjacent property line that is or can be built upon, any public way, and the nearest important building on the same property by not less than the distances given in Section 6.4 of NFPA 58. [**30A:**12.3.3]

42.8.3.4* Aboveground tanks storing CNG, LNG, or LP-Gas shall be separated from each other by at least 20 ft (6 m) and from dispensing devices that dispense liquid or gaseous motor vehicle fuels by at least 20 ft (6 m). [**30A:**12.3.4]

42.8.3.4.1 Dispensers and aboveground tanks storing CNG, LNG, or LP-Gas shall not require separation if handling fuels of the same chemical composition. [**30A:**12.3.4.1]

42.8.3.4.2 Where dispensers and aboveground tanks storing CNG, LNG, or LP-Gas are at least 50 ft (15 m) from any other aboveground motor fuel storage or dispensing equipment, the requirements of NFPA 52 or NFPA 58 shall apply. [**30A:**12.3.4.2]

42.8.3.5 Aboveground storage tanks for the storage of CNG, LNG, or LP-Gas shall be provided with physical protection in accordance with 42.3.3.6. [**30A:**12.3.5]

42.8.3.6 Horizontal separation shall not be required between aboveground tanks storing CNG, LNG, or LP-Gas and underground tanks containing Class I or Class II liquids, provided the structural limitations of the underground tanks are not exceeded. [**30A:**12.3.6]

42.8.4 Dispenser Installations Beneath Canopies. Where CNG or LNG dispensers are installed beneath a canopy or enclosure, either the canopy or enclosure shall be designed to prevent accumulation or entrapment of ignitible vapors or all electrical equipment installed beneath the canopy or enclosure shall be suitable for Class I, Division 2 hazardous (classified) locations. [**30A:**12.4]

42.8.5 Specific Requirements for LP-Gas Dispensing Devices.

Δ **42.8.5.1** Dispensing devices for LP-Gas shall meet all applicable requirements of NFPA 58. [**30A:**12.5.1]

42.8.5.2 Dispensing devices for LP-Gas shall be located as follows:

(1) At least 10 ft (3 m) from any dispensing device for Class I liquids
(2) At least 5 ft (1.5 m) from any dispensing device for Class I liquids where the following conditions exist:
  (a) The LP-Gas deliver nozzle and filler valve release no more than 0.1 oz (4 cm^3) of liquid upon disconnection.
  (b) The fixed maximum liquid level gauge remains closed during the entire refueling process.

[**30A:**12.5.2]

42.8.6 Electrical Equipment.

42.8.6.1 All electrical wiring and electrical utilization equipment shall be of a type specified by, and shall be installed in accordance with, Section 11.1. [**30A:**12.6.1]

42.8.6.2* Table 42.8.6.2 shall be used to delineate and classify areas for the purpose of installation of electrical wiring and electrical utilization equipment. [**30A:**12.6.2]

42.9 Marine Fueling.

42.9.1 Scope.

42.9.1.1 Section 42.9 shall apply to that portion of a property where liquids used as fuels are stored, handled, and dispensed from equipment located on shore or from equipment located on piers, wharves, or floating docks into the fuel tanks of marine craft, including incidental activity, except as covered elsewhere in NFPA 30A or in other NFPA standards. [**30A:**11.1.1]

42.9.1.2 Section 42.9 shall not apply to the following:

(1) Bulk plant or terminal loading and unloading facilities
(2) Transfer of liquids utilizing a flange-to-flange closed transfer piping system
(3) Marine motor fuel dispensing facilities where liquids used as fuels are stored and dispensed into the fuel tanks of marine craft of 300 gross tons (272 metric tons) or more

[**30A:**11.1.2]

42.9.1.3 For the purpose of Section 42.9, the word *pier* shall also mean dock, floating dock, and wharf. [**30A:**11.1.3]

Table 42.8.6.2 Electrical Equipment Classified Areas for Dispensing Devices

Dispensing Device	Extent of Classified Area Class I, Division 1	Extent of Classified Area Class I, Division 2
Compressed natural gas (CNG)	Entire space within the dispenser enclosure	5 ft (1.5 m) in all directions from dispenser enclosure
Liquefied natural gas (LNG)	Entire space within the dispenser enclosure	10 ft (3 m) in all directions from the dispenser enclosure
Liquefied petroleum gas (LP-Gas)	Entire space within the dispenser enclosure; 18 in. (46 cm) from the exterior surface of the dispenser enclosure to an elevation of 4 ft (1.22 m) above the base of the dispenser; the entire pit or open space beneath the dispenser and within 20 ft (6 m) horizontally from any edge of the dispenser when the pit or trench is not mechanically ventilated	Up to 18 in. (46 cm) above ground and within 20 ft (6 m) horizontally from any edge of the dispenser enclosure, including pits or trenches within this area when provided with adequate mechanical ventilation

[30A: Table 12.6.2]

42.9.2 Storage.

42.9.2.1 Liquids shall be stored in tanks or containers complying with 42.3.3. [30A:11.2.1]

42.9.2.2* Tanks that supply marine motor fuel dispensing facilities shall be located on shore or on a pier of the solid-fill type. [30A:11.2.2]

42.9.2.3 Pumps that are not integral to the dispensing device shall also be located on shore or on a pier of the solid-fill type. [30A:11.2.3]

42.9.2.4 Where tanks are located on a pier not of the solid-fill type, tanks shall be permitted with AHJ approval, providing the tank does not exceed 1100 gal (4164 L) aggregate capacity and meets Chapters 4 and 5 of NFPA 30A and NFPA 30. [30A:11.2.4]

42.9.2.5 Tanks at Elevation.

42.9.2.5.1 Where a tank is at an elevation that produces a gravity head on the dispensing device, the tank outlet shall be equipped with a device, such as a normally closed solenoid valve, that will prevent gravity flow from the tank to the dispenser. [30A:11.2.5.1]

42.9.2.5.2 This device shall be located adjacent to and downstream of the outlet valve specified by 66.22.13.1. [30A:11.2.5.2]

42.9.2.5.3 The device shall be installed and adjusted so that liquid cannot flow by gravity from the tank to the dispenser if the piping or hose fails when the dispenser is not in use. [30A:11.2.5.3]

42.9.3 Piping Systems.

42.9.3.1 Piping shall be installed in accordance with all applicable requirements of Chapter 5 of NFPA 30A. [30A:11.3.1]

42.9.3.2 Piping systems shall be supported and protected against physical damage and stresses arising from impact, settlement, vibration, expansion, contraction, and tidal action. [30A:11.3.2]

42.9.3.3 Means shall be provided to ensure flexibility of the piping system in the event of motion of the pier. Flexible piping shall be of a type designed to withstand the forces and pressures exerted upon the piping. [30A:11.3.3]

42.9.3.4 Where dispensing is from a floating structure or pier, approved oil-resistant flexible hose shall be permitted to be used between shore piping and the piping on a floating structure or pier and between separate sections of the floating structure to accommodate changes in water level or shoreline, provided that the hose is either resistant to or shielded from damage by fire. [30A:11.3.4]

42.9.3.5 A valve to shut off the liquid supply from shore shall be provided in each pipeline at or near the approach to the pier and at the shore end of each marine pipeline adjacent to the point where each flexible hose is attached. [30A:11.3.5]

42.9.3.6 Low melting point rigid piping shall be permitted to be used between underground shore piping and a floating structure or pier and on the floating structure or pier itself, provided that the piping is protected from physical damage and stresses arising from impact, settlement, vibration, expansion, contraction, or tidal action and provided that the hose is either resistant to or shielded from damage by fire exposure. [30A:11.3.6]

42.9.4 Fuel Dispensing System.

42.9.4.1 All hose shall be listed. Where hose length exceeds 18 ft (5.5 m), the hose shall be secured so as to protect it from damage. [30A:11.4.1]

42.9.4.1.1 Where hoses are attached to a hose-retrieving mechanism in a marine motor fuel dispensing facility, a listed emergency breakaway device shall not be required between the point of attachment of the hose-retrieving mechanism to the hose and the hose nozzle valve. [30A:11.4.1.1]

42.9.4.2 Dispensing nozzles shall be of the automatic-closing type without a latch-open device. [30A:11.4.2]

42.9.4.3 Dispensing devices shall be permitted to be located on open piers, on shore, or on piers of the solid-fill type and shall be located apart from other structures so as to provide room for safe ingress to and egress from marine craft. [30A:11.4.3]

42.9.4.4 Dispensing devices shall be located so that exposure to all other operational marina or pleasure boat berthing area facilities is minimized. Where tide and weather conditions permit, liquid fuel handling shall be outside the main berthing areas. Where located inside marina or pleasure craft berthing areas, fueling facilities shall be located so that, in case of fire aboard a marine craft alongside, the danger to other craft near the facility is minimized. [**30A:**11.4.4]

42.9.4.5 No vessel or marine craft shall be made fast to any other vessel or marine craft occupying a berth at a fuel dispensing location during fueling operations. [**30A:**11.4.5]

42.9.4.6 A marine motor fuel dispensing facility located at a bulk plant shall be separated by a fence or other approved barrier from areas in which bulk plant operations are conducted. Dispensing devices shall not be supplied by aboveground tanks located in the bulk plant. Marine motor fuel dispensing facility storage tanks shall not be connected by piping to aboveground tanks located in the bulk plant. [**30A:**11.4.6]

42.9.4.7 Each marine motor fuel dispensing facility shall have an attendant or supervisor on duty whenever the facility is open for business. The attendant's primary function shall be to supervise, observe, and control the dispensing of liquids. [**30A:**11.4.7]

42.9.5 Sources of Ignition.

42.9.5.1 All electrical components for dispensing liquids shall be installed in accordance with Chapter 8 of NFPA 30A. [**30A:**11.5.1]

42.9.5.2 All electrical equipment shall be installed and used in accordance with the requirements of Section 11.1 as it applies to wet, damp, and hazardous locations. [**30A:**11.5.2]

42.9.5.3 Clearly identified emergency electrical disconnects that are readily accessible in case of fire or physical damage at any dispensing unit shall be provided on each marine wharf. The disconnects shall be interlocked to shut off power to all pump motors from any individual location and shall be manually reset only from a master switch. Each such disconnect shall be identified by an approved sign stating EMERGENCY PUMP SHUTOFF in 2 in. (50 mm) red capital letters. [**30A:**11.5.3]

42.9.5.4* All electrical wiring for power and lighting shall be protected from a release from the liquid piping system. [**30A:**11.5.4]

42.9.5.5 Smoking materials, including matches and lighters, shall not be used within 20 ft (6 m) of areas used for fueling, servicing fuel systems for internal combustion engines, or receiving or dispensing of Class I liquids. Conspicuous NO SMOKING signs shall be posted within sight of the customer being served. [**30A:**11.5.5]

42.9.5.6* Continuing Operation. The engines of all equipment and vessels being fueled shall be shut off, except where continuing operation is essential for protecting life, property, or the environment. [**30A:**11.5.6]

42.9.6 Electrical Installations.

42.9.6.1 Where excessive stray currents are encountered, piping handling Class I and Class II liquids shall be electrically isolated from the shore piping. [**30A:**8.5.1]

42.9.6.2* Pipelines on piers shall be bonded and grounded. Bonding and grounding connections on all pipelines shall be located on the pier side of hose riser insulating flanges, if used, and shall be accessible for inspection. [**30A:**8.5.2]

42.9.6.3 The fuel delivery nozzle shall be put into contact with the vessel fill pipe before the flow of fuel commences, and this bonding contact shall be continuously maintained until fuel flow has stopped, to avoid the possibility of electrostatic discharge. [**30A:**8.5.3]

42.9.6.4* Bonding and Grounding.

42.9.6.4.1* Pipelines on piers shall be bonded and grounded. Bonding and grounding connections on all pipelines shall be located on the pier side of hose riser insulating flanges, if used, and shall be accessible for inspection. [**30A:**11.6.1]

42.9.6.4.2 The fuel delivery nozzle shall be put into contact with the vessel fill pipe before the flow of fuel commences and this bonding contact shall be continuously maintained until fuel flow has stopped to avoid possibility of electrostatic discharge. [**30A:**11.6.2]

42.9.7 Portable Fire Extinguishers.

Δ **42.9.7.1** Portable fire extinguishers shall be selected, installed, inspected, and maintained in accordance with NFPA 10 and 42.9.7.1.1 through 42.9.7.1.3. [**30A:**11.7.1]

N **42.9.7.1.1** All portable fire extinguishers installed to achieve compliance with this *Code* shall be a minimum 20 lb (9.1 kg) ABC dry chemical type having an agent discharge rate of 1 lb/sec (0.45 kg/sec) or greater. [**30A:**11.7.1.1]

N **42.9.7.1.2** The maximum travel distance to any single fire extinguisher shall not exceed 100 ft (30 m) as measured along the designated walkways and aisles of the dock, pier, wharf, or bulkhead. [**30A:**11.7.1.2]

N **42.9.7.1.3** The maximum travel distance measurement shall not include traversing stairs, steps, ladders, or a gantry but can include walking ramps. [**30A:**11.7.1.3]

N **42.9.7.1.4** Fire extinguishers shall be required to comply with 42.9.7.1.1 through 42.9.7.1.3 when installed, replaced, or exchanged. [**30A:**11.7.1.4]

42.9.7.2 Piers that extend more than 500 ft (152 m) in travel distance from shore shall be provided with a Class III standpipe that is installed in accordance with Section 13.2. [**30A:**11.7.2]

Δ **42.9.7.3** Materials shall not be placed on a pier in such a manner that they obstruct access to firefighting equipment or important piping system control valves. [**30A:**11.7.3]

N **42.9.7.3.1** Where the pier is accessible to vehicular traffic, an unobstructed roadway to the shore end of the wharf shall be maintained for access by firefighting apparatus. [**30A:**11.7.3.1]

42.9.8 Containers and Movable Tanks.

42.9.8.1 The temporary use of movable tanks in conjunction with the dispensing of liquids into the fuel tanks of marine craft on premises not normally accessible to the public shall be permitted. Such installations shall only be made with the approval of the AHJ. [**30A:**11.8.1]

42.9.8.2* Class I or Class II liquids shall not be dispensed into a portable container unless the container is constructed of metal or is approved by the AHJ, has a tight closure, and is fitted with a spout or is so designed that the contents can be dispensed without spilling. [**30A:**11.8.2]

42.9.8.3 Portable containers of 12 gal (45 L) capacity or less shall not be filled while they are in or on a marine craft. [**30A:**11.8.3]

42.9.9 Cargo Tank Fueling Facilities. The provisions of 42.9.2 shall not prohibit the dispensing of Class II liquids in the open from a tank vehicle to a marine craft located at commercial, industrial, governmental, or manufacturing establishments when the liquid is intended for fueling marine craft used in connection with those establishments' businesses if the requirements of 42.9.9.1 through 42.9.9.7 are met. [**30A:**11.9]

42.9.9.1 An inspection of the premises and operations shall be made and approval granted by the AHJ. [**30A:**11.9.1]

42.9.9.2 The tank vehicle shall comply with the requirements of NFPA 385. [**30A:**11.9.2]

42.9.9.3 The dispensing hose shall not exceed 50 ft (15 m) in length. [**30A:**11.9.3]

42.9.9.4 The dispensing nozzle shall be a listed, automatic-closing type without a latch-open device. [**30A:**11.9.4]

42.9.9.5 Nighttime deliveries shall only be made in areas deemed adequately lighted by the AHJ. [**30A:**11.9.5]

42.9.9.6 The tank vehicle flasher lights shall be in operation while dispensing. [**30A:**11.9.6]

42.9.9.7 Fuel expansion space shall be left in each fuel tank to prevent overflow in the event of temperature increase. [**30A:**11.9.7]

42.9.10 Operating Requirements.

42.9.10.1 The following shall be the responsibilities of the attendant:

(1) Prevent the dispensing of Class I liquids into portable containers that do not comply with 42.9.8.2
(2) Be familiar with the dispensing system and emergency shutoff controls
(3) Ensure that the vessel is properly moored and that all connections are made
(4) Be within 15 ft (4.6 m) of the dispensing controls during the fueling operation and maintain a direct, clear, unobstructed view of both the vessel fuel filler neck and the emergency fuel shutoff control

[**30A:**11.10.1]

42.9.10.2 Fueling shall not be undertaken at night except under well-lighted conditions. [**30A:**11.10.2]

42.9.10.3 During fueling operations, smoking shall be forbidden on board the vessel or marine craft and in the dispensing area. [**30A:**11.10.3]

42.9.10.4 Before opening the tanks of the vessel to be fueled, the following precautions shall be taken:

(1) All engines, motors, fans, and bilge blowers shall be shut down.
(2) All open flames and smoking material shall be extinguished and all exposed heating elements shall be turned off.
(3) Galley stoves shall be extinguished.
(4) All ports, windows, doors, and hatches shall be closed.

[**30A:**11.10.4]

42.9.10.5 After the flow of fuel has stopped, the following shall occur:

(1) The fill cap shall be tightly secured.
(2) Any spillage shall be wiped up immediately.
(3) If Class I liquid has been delivered, the entire vessel or marine craft shall remain open.
(4) Bilge blowers shall be turned on and allowed to run for at least 5 minutes before starting any engines or lighting galley fires. If bilge blowers are not available, 10 minutes of ventilation shall be required.

[**30A:**11.10.5]

42.9.10.6 No Class I liquids shall be delivered to any vessel having its tanks located below deck unless each tank is equipped with a separate fill pipe, the receiving end of which shall be securely connected to a deck plate and fitted with a screw cap. Such pipe shall extend into the tank. Vessels receiving Class II or Class IIIA liquids shall have the receiving end of the fill pipe securely connected to a deck plate and fitted with a screw cap. Such pipe shall be permitted to connect to a manifold system that extends into each separate tank. Each tank shall be provided with a suitable vent pipe that shall extend from the tank to the outside of the coaming or enclosed rails so that the vapors will dissipate away from the vessel. [**30A:**11.10.6]

42.9.10.7 Owners or operators shall not offer their vessel or marine craft for fueling unless the following conditions exist:

(1) The tanks being filled are properly vented to dissipate vapors to the outside atmosphere, and the fuel systems are liquidtight and vaportight with respect to all interiors.
(2) All fuel systems are designed, installed, and maintained in compliance with the specifications of the manufacturer of the vessel or marine craft.
(3) Communication has been established between the fueling attendant and the person in control of the vessel or craft receiving the fuel so as to determine the vessel's fuel capacity, the amount of fuel on board, and the amount of fuel to be taken on board.
(4) The electrical bonding and grounding systems of the vessel or craft have been maintained in accordance with the manufacturer's specifications.

[**30A:**11.10.7]

Δ **42.9.10.8** A sign with the following legends printed in 2 in. (50 mm) red letters on a white background shall be conspicuously posted at the dispensing area:

Before Fueling:

(1) Stop all engines and auxiliaries.

(2) Shut off all electricity, open flames, and heat sources.

(3) Check all bilges for fuel vapors.

(4) Extinguish all smoking materials.

(5) Close access fittings and openings that could allow fuel vapors to enter enclosed spaces of the vessel.

During Fueling:

(1) Maintain nozzle contact with fill pipe.

(2) Wipe up spills immediately.

(3) Avoid overfilling.

(4) Fuel filling nozzle must be attended at all times.

After Fueling:

(1) Inspect bilges for leakage and fuel odors.

(2) Ventilate until odors are removed.

[30A:11.10.8]

42.10 Aircraft Fuel Servicing.

42.10.1 Application. Section 42.10 applies to the fuel servicing of all types of aircraft using liquid petroleum fuel in accordance with NFPA 407.

42.10.1.1 Section 42.10 does not apply to any of the following:

(1) In-flight fueling
(2) Fuel servicing of flying boats or amphibious aircraft on water
(3) Draining or filling of aircraft fuel tanks incidental to aircraft fuel system maintenance operations or manufacturing
(4) Spacecraft

[407:1.1.1]

42.10.2 General Requirements.

42.10.2.1 Design and Construction.

42.10.2.1.1 General Requirements.

42.10.2.1.1.1 The requirements of 42.10.2 shall apply to all aviation fueling facilities, aircraft fueling vehicles, rooftop heliport fueling facilities, and self-service aviation fueling facilities. [407:4.1.1.1]

42.10.2.1.1.2 Aviation fueling facilities shall also comply with the requirements of 42.10.3. [407:4.1.1.2]

42.10.2.1.1.3 Aircraft fueling vehicles and carts shall also comply with the requirements of 42.10.4. [407:4.1.1.3]

42.10.2.1.1.4 Rooftop heliport fueling facilities shall also comply with the requirements of 42.10.3 and 42.10.5. [407:4.1.1.4]

42.10.2.1.1.5 Self-service aviation fueling facilities shall also comply with the requirements of 42.10.3 and 42.10.6. [407:4.1.1.5]

42.10.2.1.2 Fuel Dispensing Systems.

42.10.2.1.2.1 Any valve that controls the flow of fuel into or from an aircraft fuel servicing vehicle or cart, or into or from an aircraft shall have a deadman control(s). [407:4.1.3.1]

42.10.2.1.2.2 The deadman flow control in the nozzle shall be permitted for overwing fueling. [407:4.1.3.2]

42.10.2.1.2.3 Notches or latches in the handle of an overwing nozzle that could allow the valve to be locked open shall be prohibited. [407:4.1.3.3]

42.10.2.1.2.4 Nozzles for pressure fuel servicing shall be designed to be attached securely to the aircraft adapter before the nozzle can be opened. [407:4.1.3.4]

42.10.2.1.2.5 Disengaging the nozzle from the aircraft adapter shall not be possible until the nozzle is fully closed. [407:4.1.3.5]

42.10.2.1.2.6 Fuel servicing pump mechanisms shall be designed and arranged so that failure or seizure does not cause rupture of the pump housing, of a tank, or of any component containing fuel. [407:4.1.3.6]

42.10.2.1.2.7 Fuel pressure shall be controlled within the stress limits of the hose and plumbing by means of either an in-line pressure controller or, a system pressure relief valve, or other suitable means. [407:4.1.3.7]

42.10.2.1.2.8 The working pressure of any system component shall equal or exceed any pressure to which it could be subjected. [407:4.1.3.8]

42.10.2.1.3* Fueling Hose.

42.10.2.1.3.1 Performance Requirements. Hose and couplings shall comply with the requirements of EI 1529. [407:4.1.4.1]

42.10.2.1.3.2 Fueling Hose Apparatus. Nozzle receptacles and hose storage shall be arranged to avoid kinks and maintain the hose bend radius within the requirements of EI 1529 and EI 1540. [407:4.1.4.2]

42.10.2.1.3.3 Additional Requirements.

42.10.2.1.3.3.1 Each coupled length of hose shall be tested at the same minimum proof pressure rating for that grade of hose as defined in EI 1529. [407:4.1.4.3.1]

42.10.2.1.3.3.2 A test certificate shall be provided for each coupled length of hose and shall state the following:

(1) Manufacturer's name of hose
(2) Manufacturer's name of couplings
(3) Hose type
(4) Hose grade
(5) Size and length of hose
(6) Serial number or reference number of hose
(7) Quarter and year of manufacture of hose
(8) Model number of couplings
(9) Sizes of coupling ferrules
(10) Hydrostatic test pressures
(11) Coupled length serial number
(12) Identification of individual responsible for coupling the hose
(13) Name and address of company responsible for coupling the hose
(14) Date of certification

[407:4.1.4.3.2]

42.10.2.1.3.3.3 The coupling tests as specified in EI 1529 shall be performed for each hose grade, type, and manufacturer. [407:4.1.4.3.3]

42.10.2.1.3.3.4 Each coupling of a coupled length of hose shall be permanently marked with a serial number corresponding to its hydrostatic test certificate. [407:4.1.4.3.4]

42.10.2.1.3.3.5 The hose at the end of each coupling ferrule shall be permanently marked prior to hydrostatic testing to serve as a reference to determine whether a coupling has slipped during testing or while in service. [**407**:4.1.4.3.5]

42.10.2.1.3.3.6* Lengths of hose shall not be spliced together. [**407**:4.1.4.3.6]

42.10.2.1.3.3.7 Hydrostatic Testing. Hydrostatic testing shall be in accordance with ASTM D380. [**407**:4.1.4.3.7]

42.10.2.1.3.3.7.1 Following a hydrostatic test, all the water shall be drained and the hose shall be dried internally. [**407**:4.1.4.3.7.1]

42.10.2.1.3.3.7.2 Following a hydrostatic test, the open ends of the hose, including the threads of the couplings, shall be suitably covered to protect the threads and to prevent contamination. [**407**:4.1.4.3.7.2]

42.10.2.1.3.3.7.3 A hose that is recoupled for any reason shall be hydrostatically tested and recertified to the same criteria as a newly coupled hose. [**407**:4.1.4.3.7.3]

42.10.2.1.3.3.8 Hose shall be connected to rigid piping or coupled to a hose reel in a manner that prevents kinks or undue bending action or mechanical stress on the hose or hose couplings. [**407**:4.1.4.3.8]

42.10.2.1.4 Electrostatic Hazards and Bonding.

42.10.2.1.4.1 A provision for bonding shall be incorporated in the design of fuel servicing vehicles or carts and airport fueling systems to prevent differences in electrostatic potential. [**407**:4.1.5.1]

42.10.2.1.4.2 The maximum resistance between the bonding cable clip and the fueling system framework shall not exceed 25 ohms. [**407**:4.1.5.2]

42.10.2.1.4.3 Bonding cables shall be constructed of conductive, durable, and flexible material. [**407**:4.1.5.3]

42.10.2.1.4.4 Bonding connections shall be electrically and mechanically firm. [**407**:4.1.5.4]

42.10.2.1.4.5 Jacks, plugs, clamps, and connecting points shall be clean, unpainted metal to provide a positive electrical connection. [**407**:4.1.5.5]

42.10.2.1.4.6 EI 1529 Type C hose (semiconductive) shall be used to prevent electrostatic discharges but shall not be used to accomplish required bonding. [**407**:4.1.5.6]

42.10.2.1.4.7 EI 1529 Type A hose that does not have a semiconductive cover shall not be used. [**407**:4.1.5.7]

42.10.2.1.4.8 EI 1529 Type F hose (hard wall) and EI 1529 Type CT hose (cold temperature) shall be permitted because they have semiconductive covers. [**407**:4.1.5.8]

42.10.2.1.4.9* The design of airport fueling systems shall incorporate the provision of a 30-second relaxation period following the filter separator, monitors, or other filtration devices discharging into tanks. [**407**:4.1.5.9]

42.10.2.1.4.9.1 The relaxation period required by 42.10.2.1.4.9 shall not apply to the actual refueling of an aircraft. [**407**:4.1.5.9.1]

42.10.2.1.4.9.2 The relaxation period required by 42.10.2.1.4.9 shall not apply to fuels with static dissipater additives. [**407**:4.1.5.9.2]

42.10.2.1.5 Filters and Ancillary Equipment.

42.10.2.1.5.1 Filter vessels used in aviation fuel service shall have a functional automatic air vent (AAV) or automatic air eliminator (AAE). [**407**:4.1.8.1]

42.10.2.1.5.2 The AAV or AAE shall discharge to a closed system. [**407**:4.1.8.2]

42.10.2.1.6 Fire Extinguishers.

42.10.2.1.6.1* During fueling operations, fire extinguishers shall be available on aircraft servicing ramps or aprons, in accordance with NFPA 410. [**407**:4.1.10.1]

42.10.2.1.6.2 All fire extinguishers shall conform to the requirements of NFPA 10. [**407**:4.1.10.2]

42.10.2.1.6.3* ABC multipurpose dry chemical fire extinguishers (ammonium phosphate) shall not be placed on aircraft fueling vehicles, airport fuel servicing ramps or aprons, or at airport fuel facilities that are located within 150 m (500 ft) of aircraft operating areas. [**407**:4.1.10.3]

42.10.2.1.7 Marking and Labeling.

42.10.2.1.7.1 Each emergency fuel shutoff station location shall be placarded EMERGENCY FUEL SHUTOFF in letters at least 50 mm (2 in.) high. [**407**:4.1.11.1]

42.10.2.1.7.2 The method of operation shall be indicated by an arrow or by the word PUSH or PULL, as appropriate. [**407**:4.1.11.2]

42.10.2.1.7.3 Any action necessary to gain access to the shutoff device (e.g., BREAK GLASS) shall be shown clearly. [**407**:4.1.11.3]

42.10.2.1.7.4 Lettering shall be of a color contrasting sharply with the placard background for visibility. [**407**:4.1.11.4]

42.10.2.1.7.5 Placards shall be weather resistant. [**407**:4.1.11.5]

42.10.2.1.8 Aircraft Fueling Ramps.

42.10.2.1.8.1 Aircraft Radar Equipment.

42.10.2.1.8.1.1 Surveillance radar equipment in aircraft shall not be operated within 90 m (300 ft) of any fueling, servicing, or other operation in which flammable liquids, vapors, or mist could be present. [**407**:4.1.12.1.1]

42.10.2.1.8.1.2 Weather-mapping radar equipment in aircraft shall not be operated while the aircraft in which it is mounted is undergoing fuel servicing. [**407**:4.1.12.1.2]

42.10.2.1.8.2* Ground Radar Equipment.

42.10.2.1.8.2.1 Antennas of airport flight traffic surveillance radar equipment shall be located so that the beam will not be directed toward any fuel storage or loading racks within 90 m (300 ft). [**407**:4.1.12.2.1]

42.10.2.1.8.2.2 Aircraft fuel servicing shall not be conducted within the 90 m (300 ft) distance established by 42.10.2.1.8.2.1. [**407**:4.1.12.2.2]

42.10.2.1.8.2.3 Antennas of airport ground traffic surveillance radar equipment shall be located so that the beam will not be directed toward any fuel storage or loading racks within 30 m (100 ft). [**407**:4.1.12.2.3]

42.10.2.1.8.2.4 Aircraft fuel servicing or any other operations involving flammable liquids or vapors shall not be conducted within 30 m (100 ft) of antennas of airport ground traffic surveillance radar equipment. [407:4.1.12.2.4]

42.10.2.1.8.3 Emergency Fire Equipment Accessibility. Accessibility to aircraft by emergency fire equipment shall be considered in establishing aircraft fuel servicing positions. [407:4.1.12.3]

42.10.2.1.8.4 Ramp and Apron Drainage. Aircraft servicing ramps or aprons shall be sloped and drained in accordance with NFPA 415. [407:4.1.12.4]

42.10.2.1.8.4.1 The ramp or apron shall slope away from the rim or edge of fueling hydrants or fueling pits to prevent flooding. [407:4.1.12.4.1]

42.10.2.1.8.4.2 Fueling hydrant boxes or fueling pits that are connected to a ramp drainage system shall be fitted with vapor-sealing traps. [407:4.1.12.4.2]

42.10.2.2 Operations.

42.10.2.2.1 Training.

42.10.2.2.1.1* Only personnel trained in the safe operation of the equipment and the fuels they use, the operation of emergency controls, and the procedures to be followed in an emergency shall be permitted to handle fuel. [407:4.2.2.1]

42.10.2.2.1.2* Fuel servicing personnel shall be trained in the use of the available fire-extinguishing equipment they could be expected to use. [407:4.2.2.2]

42.10.2.2.2* Prevention and Control of Spills.

42.10.2.2.2.1 Following fueling of an aircraft or fuel servicing vehicle, all hoses shall be removed, including those from hydrant systems if applicable. [407:4.2.3.1]

42.10.2.2.2.2 All hoses shall also be properly stowed. [407:4.2.3.2]

42.10.2.2.2.3 Fuel nozzles shall not be dragged along the ground. [407:4.2.3.3]

42.10.2.2.2.4 Approved pumps, either hand operated or power operated, shall be used where aircraft are fueled from drums. [407:4.2.3.4]

42.10.2.2.2.4.1 Pouring or gravity flow shall not be permitted from a container with a capacity of more than 19 L (5 gal). [407:4.2.3.4.1]

42.10.2.2.2.5 Fuel Spill Procedures.

42.10.2.2.2.5.1 Where a spill is observed, the fuel servicing shall be stopped immediately by release of the deadman controls. [407:4.2.3.5.1]

42.10.2.2.2.5.2 In the event that a spill continues, the equipment emergency fuel shutoff shall be actuated. [407:4.2.3.5.2]

42.10.2.2.2.5.3 In the event that a spill continues from a hydrant system, the system emergency fuel shutoff shall be actuated. [407:4.2.3.5.3]

42.10.2.2.2.5.4 The supervisor shall be notified immediately. [407:4.2.3.5.4]

42.10.2.2.2.5.5 Cleaning operations shall be performed by personnel trained in accordance with 42.10.2.2.1.1. [407:4.2.3.5.5]

42.10.2.2.2.5.6 Operation shall not be resumed until the spill has been cleared and conditions are determined to be safe. [407:4.2.3.5.6]

42.10.2.2.2.5.7 The airport fire crew, if established, or the local fire department serving the airport shall be notified if a spill covers over 3 m (10 ft) in any direction or is over 5 m^2 (50 ft^2) in area, continues to flow, or is otherwise a hazard to persons or property. [407:4.2.3.5.7]

42.10.2.2.2.5.8 The spill shall be investigated to determine the cause, to determine whether emergency procedures were properly carried out, and to determine the necessary corrective measures. [407:4.2.3.5.8]

42.10.2.2.2.5.9 Corrective measures identified by the spill investigation shall be implemented as required by the authority having jurisdiction. [407:4.2.3.5.9]

42.10.2.2.2.6 Transferring fuel by pumping from one tank vehicle to another tank vehicle shall not be permitted except under emergency maintenance conditions. [407:4.2.3.6]

42.10.2.2.2.7 Not more than one tank vehicle shall be permitted to be connected to the same aircraft fueling manifold, unless means are provided to prevent fuel from flowing back into a tank vehicle due to a difference in pumping pressure. [407:4.2.3.7]

42.10.2.2.3 Emergency Fuel Shutoff.

42.10.2.2.3.1 Emergency fuel shutoff control stations shall be accessible at all times. [407:4.2.4.1]

42.10.2.2.3.2 A procedure shall be established to notify the fire department serving the airport in the event of a control station activation. [407:4.2.4.2]

42.10.2.2.3.3 If the fuel flow stops for an unknown reason, the emergency fuel shutoff system shall be checked first. [407:4.2.4.3]

42.10.2.2.3.4 The cause of the shutoff shall be identified and corrected before fuel flow is resumed. [407:4.2.4.4]

42.10.2.2.3.5 Emergency fuel shutoff systems shall be operationally checked at intervals not exceeding 6 months. [407:4.2.4.5]

42.10.2.2.3.6 Each individual device shall be checked at least once during every 12-month period. [407:4.2.4.6]

42.10.2.2.3.7 Suitable records shall be kept of tests required by this section. [407:4.2.4.7]

42.10.2.2.4* Bonding.

42.10.2.2.4.1 Prior to making any fueling connection to an aircraft or fuel servicing vehicle, the fueling equipment shall be bonded to the aircraft or fuel servicing vehicle by use of a cable, thus providing a conductive path to equalize the potential between the fueling equipment and the aircraft. [407:4.2.5.1]

42.10.2.2.4.1.1 The electrical bond shall be maintained until fueling connections have been removed, thus allowing separated charges that could be generated during the fueling operation to reunite. [**407**:4.2.5.1.1]

42.10.2.2.4.1.2 Grounding for the sole purpose of aircraft fueling shall not be permitted. [**407**:4.2.5.1.2]

42.10.2.2.4.2 Bonding for Overwing Fueling. In addition to the requirements in 42.10.2.2.4.1, where fueling overwing, the nozzle shall be bonded to a metallic component of the aircraft that is metallically connected to the tank filler port. [**407**:4.2.5.2]

42.10.2.2.4.2.1 The bond connection shall be made before the filler cap is removed. [**407**:4.2.5.2.1]

42.10.2.2.4.2.2 If a nozzle bond cable and plug receptacle or means for attaching a clip is available, the operator shall attach the nozzle bond cable before removing the cap in order to equalize the potential between the nozzle and the filler port. [**407**:4.2.5.2.2]

42.10.2.2.4.2.3 If no plug receptacle or means for attaching a clip is available, the operator shall touch the filler cap with the nozzle spout before removing the cap in order to equalize the potential between the nozzle and the filler port. [**407**:4.2.5.2.3]

42.10.2.2.4.2.4 The nozzle spout shall be kept in contact with the filler neck until the fueling is completed. [**407**:4.2.5.2.4]

42.10.2.2.4.3 Where a funnel is used in aircraft fueling, it shall be kept in contact with the filler neck as well as the fueling nozzle spout or the supply container to avoid the possibility of a spark at the fill opening. [**407**:4.2.5.3]

42.10.2.2.4.3.1* Only metal funnels shall be used. [**407**:4.2.5.3.1]

42.10.2.2.4.4 Where a hydrant servicer or cart is used for fueling, the hydrant coupler shall be connected to the hydrant system prior to bonding the fuel equipment to the aircraft. [**407**:4.2.5.4]

42.10.2.2.4.5 Bonding and fueling connections shall be disconnected in the reverse order of connection. [**407**:4.2.5.5]

42.10.2.2.4.6 Conductive hose shall be used to prevent electrostatic discharge but shall not be used to accomplish required bonding. [**407**:4.2.5.6]

42.10.2.2.5 Control of Fuel Flow.

42.10.2.2.5.1 Fuel flow shall be controlled by use of a dead-man control device. [**407**:4.2.6.1]

42.10.2.2.5.2 The use of any means that defeats the dead-man control shall be prohibited. [**407**:4.2.6.2]

42.10.2.2.6 Fire Protection.

42.10.2.2.6.1* During fueling operations, fire extinguishers shall be available on aircraft servicing ramps or aprons, in accordance with NFPA 410. [**407**:4.2.7.1]

42.10.2.2.6.2* Extinguishers shall be kept clear of elements such as ice and snow. [**407**:4.2.7.2]

42.10.2.2.6.3 Extinguishers located in enclosed compartments shall be readily accessible, and their location shall be marked clearly in letters at least 50 mm (2 in.) high. [**407**:4.2.7.3]

42.10.2.2.6.4 Fuel servicing personnel shall be trained in the use of the available fire-extinguishing equipment they could be expected to use. *(See A.42.10.2.2.1.2.)* [**407**:4.2.7.4]

42.10.2.2.7 Maintenance.

42.10.2.2.7.1 Fuel servicing equipment shall be maintained in safe operating condition. [**407**:4.2.8.1]

42.10.2.2.7.2 Malfunctioning equipment shall be removed from service. [**407**:4.2.8.2]

42.10.2.2.7.3 Where a valve or electrical device is used for isolation during maintenance or modification of a fuel system, it shall be tagged and locked out. [**407**:4.2.8.3]

42.10.2.2.7.4 The tag/lock shall not be removed until the operation is completed. [**407**:4.2.8.4]

42.10.2.2.7.5 All inspection and maintenance activities shall be recorded. [**407**:4.2.8.5]

42.10.2.2.7.6 Inspection and maintenance records shall be retained for a minimum of 12 months. [**407**:4.2.8.6]

42.10.2.2.8* Aircraft Fueling Hose. Any hose found to be defective, in accordance with 42.10.2.2.8.1 through 42.10.2.2.8.4, shall be removed from service. [**407**:4.2.9]

42.10.2.2.8.1 Suitable records shall be kept of required inspections and hydrostatic tests. [**407**:4.2.9.1]

42.10.2.2.8.2 Aircraft fueling hose shall be removed from service after 10 years from the date of manufacture. [**407**:4.2.9.2]

42.10.2.2.8.3 Aircraft fueling hose not placed into service within 2 years of the date of manufacture shall not be used. [**407**:4.2.9.3]

42.10.2.2.8.4 Daily Inspection. Aircraft fueling hose shall be inspected before use each day. [**407**:4.2.9.4]

42.10.2.2.8.4.1 The hose shall be extended as it normally would be for fueling. [**407**:4.2.9.4.1]

42.10.2.2.8.4.2 The hose shall be checked for evidence of any of the following defects:

(1) Blistering
(2) Carcass saturation or separation
(3) Exposure of the reinforcement material
(4) Slippage, misalignment, or leaks at couplings

[**407**:4.2.9.4.2]

42.10.2.2.8.5 Monthly Inspection. At least once each month the hose shall be completely extended and inspected as required in 42.10.2.2.8.4 and 42.10.2.2.8.5. [**407**:4.2.9.5]

42.10.2.2.8.5.1* The hose couplings and the hose shall be examined for structural weakness or soft spots. [**407**:4.2.9.5.1]

42.10.2.2.8.5.2 With the hose completely extended, it shall be pressurized to the working pressure of the fueling equipment to which it is attached and checked for defects, such as abnormal twisting or blistering. [**407**:4.2.9.5.2]

42.10.2.2.8.6 Quarterly Inspection.

42.10.2.2.8.6.1 The nozzle screens shall be examined for evidence of hose deterioration. [**407**:4.2.9.6.1]

42.10.2.2.8.7 Kinks or short loops in fueling hose shall be avoided. [**407**:4.2.9.7]

42.10.2.2.9* Lightning. A written procedure shall be established to set the criteria for when and where fueling operations are to be suspended at each airport as approved by the fueling agent and the airport authority. [**407**:4.2.10]

42.10.2.2.10 Aircraft Fuel Servicing.

42.10.2.2.10.1 Location of Aircraft During Fuel Servicing.

42.10.2.2.10.1.1 Aircraft fuel servicing shall be performed outdoors. [**407**:4.2.11.1.1]

42.10.2.2.10.1.2 Aircraft fuel servicing incidental to aircraft fuel system maintenance operations shall comply with the requirements of NFPA 410. [**407**:4.2.11.1.2]

42.10.2.2.10.1.3* Aircraft being fueled shall be positioned so that aircraft fuel system vents or fuel tank openings are not closer than 7.6 m (25 ft) to any terminal building, hangar, service building, or enclosed passenger concourse other than a loading walkway. [**407**:4.2.11.1.3]

42.10.2.2.10.1.4 Aircraft being fueled shall be positioned so that the vent or tank openings are not closer than 15 m (50 ft) of any combustion and ventilation air intake to any boiler, heater, or incinerator room. [**407**:4.2.11.1.4]

42.10.2.2.10.1.5 Accessibility to aircraft by emergency fire equipment shall be maintained for aircraft fuel servicing positions. [**407**:4.2.11.1.5]

42.10.2.2.10.2 Aircraft Occupancy During Fuel Servicing.

42.10.2.2.10.2.1 If passengers remain on board an aircraft during fuel servicing, at least one qualified person trained in emergency evacuation procedures shall be in the aircraft at or near a door at which there is a passenger loading walkway, integral stairs that lead downward, or a passenger loading stair or stand. [**407**:4.2.11.2.1]

42.10.2.2.10.2.1.1 A clear area for emergency evacuation of the aircraft shall be maintained at not less than one additional exit. [**407**:4.2.11.2.1.1]

42.10.2.2.10.2.1.2 Where fueling operations take place with passengers on board away from the terminal building, and stairways are not provided, such as during inclement weather (diversions), all slides shall be armed and the aircraft rescue and fire-fighting (ARFF) services shall be notified to respond in standby position in the vicinity of the fueling activity with at least one vehicle. [**407**:4.2.11.2.1.2]

42.10.2.2.10.2.1.3 Aircraft operators shall establish specific procedures covering emergency evacuation under such conditions for each type of aircraft they operate. [**407**:4.2.11.2.1.3]

42.10.2.2.10.2.1.4 All "NO SMOKING" signs shall be displayed in the cabin(s), and the no smoking rule shall be enforced. [**407**:4.2.11.2.1.4]

42.10.2.2.10.2.2 For each aircraft type, aircraft operators shall determine the areas through which it could be hazardous for boarding or deplaning passengers to pass while the aircraft is being fueled. [**407**:4.2.11.2.2]

42.10.2.2.10.2.2.1 Controls shall be established so that passengers avoid such areas. [**407**:4.2.11.2.2.1]

42.10.2.2.11 Fire Hazards on Aircraft Fuel Servicing Ramps.

42.10.2.2.11.1* Electrical Equipment Operated on Aircraft Fuel Servicing Ramps or Aprons.

42.10.2.2.11.1.1 Battery chargers on any fueling equipment shall not be connected or disconnected while fuel servicing is performed on an aircraft. [**407**:4.2.12.1.1]

42.10.2.2.11.1.2* Aircraft ground-power generators or other electrical ground-power supplies shall not be connected or disconnected while fuel servicing is performed on the aircraft. [**407**:4.2.12.1.2]

42.10.2.2.11.1.3 Electric tools or similar tools likely to produce sparks or arcs shall not be used while fuel servicing is performed on an aircraft. [**407**:4.2.12.1.3]

42.10.2.2.11.1.4 Other than aircraft fuel servicing vehicles, battery-powered vehicles, including battery-powered aircraft, that do not comply with the provisions of this standard shall not be operated within 3 m (10 ft) of fueling equipment or spills. [**407**:4.2.12.1.4]

42.10.2.2.11.1.5* Communication equipment located outside of the cab of fuel servicing vehicles and used during aircraft fuel servicing operations within 3 m (10 ft) of the fill or vent points of aircraft fuel systems shall be listed as intrinsically safe for Class I, Division 1, Group D hazardous (classified) locations in accordance with UL 913. [**407**:4.2.12.1.5]

42.10.2.2.11.2 Open Flames on Aircraft Fuel Servicing Ramps.

42.10.2.2.11.2.1 Entrances to fueling areas shall be posted with "NO SMOKING" signs. [**407**:4.2.12.2.1]

42.10.2.2.11.2.2 Open flames on aircraft fuel servicing ramps or aprons within 15 m (50 ft) of any aircraft fuel servicing operation or fueling equipment shall be prohibited. [**407**:4.2.12.2.2]

42.10.2.2.11.2.3 The category of open flames and lighted open flame devices shall include, but shall not be limited to, the following:

(1) Lighted cigarettes, cigars, or pipes
(2) Electronic cigarettes (e.g., personal vaporizers or electronic nicotine delivery systems)
(3) Exposed flame heaters, liquid, solid, or gaseous devices, including portable and wheeled gasoline or kerosene heaters
(4) Heat-producing welding or cutting devices and blowtorches
(5) Flare pots or other open-flame lights

[**407**:4.2.12.2.3]

42.10.2.2.11.2.4 The authority having jurisdiction can establish other locations where open flames and open-flame devices shall not be permitted. [**407**:4.2.12.2.4]

42.10.2.2.11.2.5 Personnel shall not carry lighters, matches, or electronic cigarettes on their person while engaged in fuel servicing operations. [**407**:4.2.12.2.5]

42.10.2.2.11.2.6 Lighters, matches, or electronic cigarettes shall not be permitted on or in fueling equipment. [**407**:4.2.12.2.6]

42.10.2.2.11.2.7 Equipment performing aircraft servicing functions shall not be positioned within a 3 m (10 ft) radius of aircraft fuel system vent openings. [**407**:4.2.12.2.7]

42.10.2.2.11.3 Operation of Aircraft Engines and Heaters.

42.10.2.2.11.3.1 Fuel servicing shall not be performed on a fixed wing aircraft while an onboard engine is operating, except as permitted by 42.10.2.2.11.3.2 or 42.10.2.2.13. [**407**:4.2.12.3.1]

42.10.2.2.11.3.2 Aircraft auxiliary power units (APUs) that direct exhaust away from the fueling operation shall be permitted to operate during fuel servicing. [**407**:4.2.12.3.2]

42.10.2.2.11.3.3 Combustion heaters on aircraft (e.g., wing and tail surface heaters, integral cabin heaters) shall not be operated during fueling operations. [**407**:4.2.12.3.3]

42.10.2.2.12 Defueling of Aircraft.

42.10.2.2.12.1 All requirements of this standard shall apply to defueling operations. [**407**:4.2.13.1]

42.10.2.2.12.2 Each operator shall establish procedures to prevent the overfilling of the tank vehicle, which is a special hazard when defueling. [**407**:4.2.13.2]

42.10.2.2.13 Rapid Refueling.

42.10.2.2.13.1 Rapid refueling of aircraft shall be limited to the following aircraft types:

(1) Helicopters
(2) Agricultural aircraft actively engaged in aerial application duties
(3) Medical aircraft actively engaged in the transport of medical patients
(4) Fire-fighting and search-and-rescue aircraft actively engaged in emergency operations

[**407**:4.2.14.1]

42.10.2.2.13.2 Only turbine engine aircraft fueled with JET A or JET A-1 fuels shall be permitted to be fueled while an onboard engine is operating. [**407**:4.2.14.2]

42.10.2.2.13.3 Aircraft permitted to be fueled while an onboard engine is operating shall have all sources of ignition of potential fuel spills located above the fuel inlet port(s) and above the vents or tank openings, including but not limited to the following:

(1) Engines
(2) Exhausts
(3) Auxiliary power units (APUs)
(4) Combustion-type cabin heater

[**407**:4.2.14.3]

42.10.2.2.13.4 Aircraft fueling while onboard engines are operating shall be permitted only under the following conditions:

(1) A pilot licensed by the appropriate governmental body shall be at the aircraft controls during the entire fueling operation.
(2) All passengers shall be deboarded to a safe location prior to rapid refueling operations, except as permitted in 42.10.2.2.13.3(3).
(3) Patients on board medical transport aircraft shall be permitted to remain on board the aircraft with medical personnel during rapid refueling operations if, in the opinion of the medical provider, removal from the aircraft would be detrimental to the patient's condition.
(4) Passengers shall not board or deboard during rapid refueling operations.
(5) Only designated personnel, properly trained in rapid refueling operations, shall operate the equipment. Written procedures shall include the safe handling of the fuel and equipment.
(6) All doors, windows, and access points allowing entry to the interior of the aircraft that are adjacent to, or in the immediate vicinity of, the fuel inlet ports shall be closed and shall remain closed during refueling operations.
(7) Fuel shall be permitted to be dispensed by one of the following methods:
   (a) Into an open port from approved deadman-type nozzles with a flow rate not to exceed 227 L/min (60 gpm)
   (b) Through close-coupled pressure fueling ports
(8) Where fuel is dispensed from fixed piping systems, the hose cabinet shall not extend into the rotor space.
(9) Clearance between aircraft fuel servicing vehicles and rotating components shall be maintained by one of the following methods:
   (a) A curb or other approved barrier shall be provided to restrict the fuel servicing vehicle from coming within 3 m (10 ft) of any aircraft rotating components.
   (b) Fuel servicing vehicles shall be kept 6 m (20 ft) away from any aircraft rotating components, and a trained person shall direct fuel servicing vehicle approach and departure.

[**407**:4.2.14.4]

42.10.3 Aviation Fueling Facilities.

42.10.3.1 Design and Construction.

42.10.3.1.1 General Requirements.

42.10.3.1.1.1 Each installation shall be designed and installed in conformity with the requirements of this standard and with any additional fire safety measures deemed necessary by the authority having jurisdiction. [**407**:5.1.1.1]

42.10.3.1.1.2 The system and each of its components shall be designed for the working pressure of the system. [**407**:5.1.1.2]

42.10.3.1.1.3 The emergency fuel shutoff system shall be designed and installed as an integral part of the airport fuel system. [**407**:5.1.1.3]

42.10.3.1.1.4 Operating controls for emergency fuel shutoff of the system shall be located to be readily accessible in the event of an accident or spill. [**407**:5.1.1.4]

42.10.3.1.1.5 In establishing each aircraft fuel dispensing location, consideration shall be given to the accessibility of the location in an emergency by fire-fighting personnel and equipment. [**407**:5.1.1.5]

42.10.3.1.1.6 System Design and Approval.

42.10.3.1.1.6.1 Design Approval. Work shall not be started on the construction or alteration of an airport fuel system until the design, plans, and specifications have been approved by the authority having jurisdiction. [**407**:5.1.1.6.1]

42.10.3.1.1.6.2 System Approval. The authority having jurisdiction shall inspect and approve the completed system before it is put into service. [**407**:5.1.1.6.2]

42.10.3.1.1.6.3 Hydrostatic Test.

42.10.3.1.1.6.3.1 After completion of the installation (including fill and paving), new airport fuel piping systems shall be subjected to a temperature-compensated hydrostatic test pressure equal to 150 percent of the system working pressure for at least 4 hours and shall be proven tight before the system is placed into service. [**407**:5.1.1.6.3.1]

42.10.3.1.1.6.3.2 For additions or modifications to existing airport fuel piping systems, hydrostatic testing of new piping prior to final tie-in to existing piping shall be permitted, with final closure (tie-in) welds examined in-process in accordance with ASME B31.3. [**407**:5.1.1.6.3.2]

42.10.3.1.2 Fuel Storage Tanks.

42.10.3.1.2.1* Fuel storage tanks shall conform to the applicable requirements of NFPA 30. [**407**:5.1.2.1]

42.10.3.1.2.2 The authority having jurisdiction shall determine the clearances required from runways, taxiways, and other aircraft movement and servicing areas to any aboveground fuel storage structure or fuel transfer equipment, with due recognition given to national and international standards establishing clearances from obstructions. [**407**:5.1.2.2]

42.10.3.1.3 Pumps and Piping Systems.

42.10.3.1.3.1 Underground piping or impact-protected aboveground piping shall be used in the vicinity of aircraft operating areas. [**407**:5.1.3.1]

42.10.3.1.3.2 Piping shall be laid on firm supports using clean, noncorrosive backfill. [**407**:5.1.3.2]

42.10.3.1.3.3 Transfer piping located within buildings not specifically designed for the purpose of fuel transfer shall be located within a steel casing of a pressure rating equal to that of the carrier pipe. [**407**:5.1.3.3]

42.10.3.1.3.3.1 The casing shall extend beyond the building. [**407**:5.1.3.3.1]

42.10.3.1.3.3.2 The casing shall terminate at a low point(s) with an automatic leak detection system. [**407**:5.1.3.3.2]

42.10.3.1.3.3.3 The casing shall be capable of being drained to a safe location. [**407**:5.1.3.3.3]

42.10.3.1.3.4 Piping, valves, and fittings shall be of steel or stainless steel, suitable for aviation fuel service and designed for the working pressure and mechanically and thermally produced structural stresses to which they could be subjected and shall comply with ASME B31.3. [**407**:5.1.3.4]

42.10.3.1.3.5 Cast-iron, copper, copper alloy, and galvanized steel piping, valves, and fittings shall not be permitted. [**407**:5.1.3.5]

42.10.3.1.3.6 Ductile iron valves shall be permitted. [**407**:5.1.3.6]

42.10.3.1.3.7 Aluminum piping, valves, and fittings shall be used only where specifically approved by the authority having jurisdiction. [**407**:5.1.3.7]

42.10.3.1.3.8 In the selection of pipe, valves, and fittings, the following shall be considered:

(1) Working pressure
(2) Bending and mechanical strength requirements (including settlement)
(3) Internal and external corrosion
(4) Impact stresses
(5) Method of system fabrication and assembly
(6) Location of piping and accessibility for repair or replacement
(7) Exposure to mechanical, atmospheric, or fire damage
(8) Expected period of service and effect of future operations

[**407**:5.1.3.8]

42.10.3.1.3.9 Gaskets in flanged connections shall resist fire temperatures for a duration comparable to the temperature resistance of the flange and bolts. [**407**:5.1.3.9]

42.10.3.1.3.10 Flanges and their associated bolts shall be steel or stainless steel. [**407**:5.1.3.10]

42.10.3.1.3.10.1 Flanges shall be rated to the ANSI pressure class suitable to the fuel system working pressures but in no cases shall be less than Class 150. [**407**:5.1.3.10.1]

Δ 42.10.3.1.3.10.2 Joints shall be designed and installed so that the mechanical strength of the joint will not be impaired if exposed to a fire. [**407**:5.1.3.10.2]

42.10.3.1.3.11 Allowances shall be made for thermal expansion and contraction by the use of pipe bends, welded elbows, or other flexible design. [**407**:5.1.3.11]

42.10.3.1.3.12 Pressure relief valves shall be provided in lines that can be isolated. [**407**:5.1.3.12]

Δ 42.10.3.1.3.13 Welded joints shall be made by qualified welders in accordance with the standards of the American Welding Society and ASME B31.3. [**407**:5.1.3.13]

42.10.3.1.3.14* Isolation valves or devices shall be provided to facilitate dismantling portions of the fueling system. [**407**:5.1.3.14]

42.10.3.1.3.15 Isolation valves shall be capable of being locked closed. [**407**:5.1.3.15]

42.10.3.1.3.16 Buried flanges and valves shall not be permitted. [**407**:5.1.3.16]

42.10.3.1.3.17* All fueling systems with underground piping shall have cathodic protection to mitigate corrosion. [**407**:5.1.3.17]

42.10.3.1.3.18 A heat-actuated shutoff valve shall be provided in the piping immediately upstream of loading hoses or swing arm connections. [**407**:5.1.3.18]

N **42.10.3.1.4 Electrostatic Hazards and Bonding.** The use of a grounding strap from the hydrant head to a grounding path shall not be permitted. [**407**:5.1.5]

42.10.3.1.5 Electrical Systems.

42.10.3.1.5.1 **Electrical Equipment.** All electrical equipment and wiring shall comply with the requirements of *NFPA 70*, Article 515, utilizing the Class I liquids requirements for all applications. [**407**:5.1.6.1]

42.10.3.1.6 Control of Fuel Flow.

42.10.3.1.6.1* Deadman Controls.

42.10.3.1.6.1.1 The valve that controls the flow of fuel to an aircraft or fueling vehicle shall have a deadman control. [**407**:5.1.7.1.1]

42.10.3.1.6.1.2 The fuel flow control means shall be one of the following:

(1) The hydrant pit valve
(2) At the feed-side of the fueling hose
(3) A separate valve on the fuel piping system
(4) On the hose nozzle for overwing servicing
(5) An electronic control to stop the pump

[**407**:5.1.7.1.2]

42.10.3.1.6.1.3 Deadman controls shall be designed to preclude defeating their intended purpose. [**407**:5.1.7.1.3]

42.10.3.1.6.2 Pressure Fuel Servicing System Controls.

42.10.3.1.6.2.1 The system shall be designed to minimize surge pressure. [**407**:5.1.7.2.1]

42.10.3.1.6.2.2* The overshoot shall not exceed 5 percent of actual flow rate in L/min (gal/min) at the time the deadman is released. [**407**:5.1.7.2.2]

42.10.3.1.6.2.3 The control valve shall be located and designed so that it will not be rendered inoperative by a surface accident, power failure, or spill. [**407**:5.1.7.2.3]

42.10.3.1.6.2.4 The control valve shall be fail-safe by closing completely in the event of control power loss. [**407**:5.1.7.2.4]

42.10.3.1.6.3* Hydrant Valves. Hydrant valves shall be designed so that the flow of fuel shall shut off when the hydrant coupler is closed. [**407**:5.1.7.3]

42.10.3.1.6.3.1 Hydrant valves shall be of the self-closing, dry-break type. [**407**:5.1.7.3.1]

42.10.3.1.6.4 Flow Control Valves. The flow control valve shall be an integral part of the hydrant valve or coupler. [**407**:5.1.7.4]

42.10.3.1.6.4.1 The fuel control valve shall be arranged so that it is not rendered inoperative by a surface accident, spill, or malfunction and shall shut off the flow of fuel if the operating energy fails. [**407**:5.1.7.4.1]

42.10.3.1.6.4.2 The fuel control system shall be designed to minimize overshoot. [**407**:5.1.7.4.2]

42.10.3.1.6.4.3 The system shall be designed to shut off fuel flow quickly and effectively, even if there is a reduction of pressure downstream of the flow control valve such as could result from a major line or hose break. [**407**:5.1.7.4.3]

42.10.3.1.6.4.4 A screen shall be provided ahead of the valve to trap foreign material that could interfere with complete closure of the valve. [**407**:5.1.7.4.4]

42.10.3.1.6.4.5 The hydrant valve that allows the flow of fuel to the aircraft shall have a deadman control. [**407**:5.1.7.4.5]

42.10.3.1.6.4.6 The use of any means that allows fuel to flow without the operator activating the deadman shall not be permitted. [**407**:5.1.7.4.6]

42.10.3.1.6.4.7 The deadman control shall be arranged so that the fueling operator can observe the operation while activating the control. [**407**:5.1.7.4.7]

42.10.3.1.6.4.8 Wireless deadman controls shall be permitted. [**407**:5.1.7.4.8]

42.10.3.1.6.5* Fuel Pressure. The pressure of the fuel delivered to the aircraft shall be automatically controlled so that it is not higher than that specified by the manufacturer of the aircraft being serviced. [**407**:5.1.7.5]

42.10.3.1.7 Filters and Ancillary Equipment.

42.10.3.1.7.1 All sections of the filtering system shall have electrical continuity with adjoining piping and equipment. [**407**:5.1.8.1]

42.10.3.1.7.2 In freezing climates, filter separator sumps and associated piping that could contain water shall be protected to prevent freezing and bursting. [**407**:5.1.8.2]

42.10.3.1.7.3 Heaters shall be constructed of noncorrosive materials. [**407**:5.1.8.3]

42.10.3.1.7.4 Piping, valves, meters, filters, air eliminators, connections, outlets, fittings, and other components shall be designed to meet the working pressure requirements of the system. [**407**:5.1.8.4]

42.10.3.1.8 Emergency Fuel Shutoff Systems.

42.10.3.1.8.1 Each tank vehicle loading station shall be provided with an emergency fuel shutoff system, in addition to the deadman control required by 42.10.3.1.6.4. [**407**:5.1.9.1]

42.10.3.1.8.2* The emergency fuel shutoff system shall shut down the flow of fuel in the entire system or in sections of the system. [**407**:5.1.9.2]

42.10.3.1.8.3 The emergency fuel shutoff system shall be of a fail-safe design. [**407**:5.1.9.3]

42.10.3.1.8.4* The method of fuel transfer (gravity, pumping, or use of hydraulic or inert gas pressure) shall be considered in the design of the emergency fuel shutoff system and the location of the emergency fuel shutoff valve. [**407**:5.1.9.4]

42.10.3.1.8.5 The emergency fuel shutoff system shall include shutoff stations located outside of probable spill areas and near the route that normally is used to leave the spill area or to reach the fire extinguishers provided for the protection of the area. [**407**:5.1.9.5]

42.10.3.1.8.6* At least one emergency shutoff control station shall be accessible to each fueling vehicle loading position or aircraft fueling position. [**407**:5.1.9.6]

42.10.3.1.8.7 The emergency fuel shutoff system shall be designed so that operation of a station shuts off fuel flow to all hydrants that have a common exposure. [**407**:5.1.9.7]

42.10.3.1.8.8 Emergency fuel shutoff systems shall be designed so that they shut off the flow of fuel if the operating power fails. [**407**:5.1.9.8]

42.10.3.1.8.9 Emergency fuel shutoffs shall not be located beneath piping, pumps, vents, or other components containing fuel or fuel vapors. [**407**:5.1.9.9]

42.10.3.1.9* Fire Protection. At least one fire extinguisher, with a minimum rating of 40-B:C and a minimum capacity of

9.0 kg (20 lb) of dry chemical agent shall be provided at each fueling vehicle loading position or rack. [407:5.1.10]

N **42.10.3.1.9.1*** A single fire extinguisher shall be permitted to serve up to two fueling vehicle loading positions or racks that are on a common island. [407:5.1.10.1]

N **42.10.3.1.9.2** Travel distance to extinguishers shall not exceed 15 m (50 ft). [407:5.1.10.2]

42.10.3.1.10 Marking and Labeling.

42.10.3.1.10.1 Emergency fuel shutoff signs shall be located at least 2.1 m (7 ft) above grade, measured to the bottom of the placard. [407:5.1.11.1]

42.10.3.1.10.2 Emergency fuel shutoff signs shall be positioned so that they can be seen readily from a distance of at least 15.2 m (50 ft). [407:5.1.11.2]

42.10.3.1.10.3 Systems provided with impressed current cathodic protection shall have appropriate signs, located at points of entry, warning against separation of units without prior deenergization or without proper jumpers across the sections to be disconnected. [407:5.1.11.3]

42.10.3.1.10.4 Fuel storage tanks shall be labelled in accordance with the requirements of NFPA 704. [407:5.1.11.4]

42.10.3.1.10.5 Fuel transfer piping shall be marked in accordance with EI 1542 as to the product type conveyed through the pipe and the proper direction of flow of the product. [407:5.1.11.5]

42.10.3.1.11 Aircraft Fuel Servicing Vehicle Loading and Unloading Racks.

42.10.3.1.11.1 The loading rack shall be equipped with an automatic shutdown system that stops the tank loading operation when the fuel servicing vehicle tank is full. [407:5.1.12.1]

42.10.3.1.11.2 All fuel servicing tank vehicle primary shutdown systems shall be compatible with the system utilized at the loading rack. [407:5.1.12.2]

42.10.3.1.11.3 The automatic secondary shutoff control shall not be used for normal filling control. [407:5.1.12.3]

42.10.3.1.11.4 New and existing loading systems shall comply with 42.10.3.1.11.1 through 42.10.3.1.11.3 by June 2, 2023. [407:5.1.12.4]

42.10.3.1.12 Fuel Servicing Hydrants, Pits, and Cabinets.

42.10.3.1.12.1 Fueling hydrants and fueling pits that are recessed below a ramp or apron surface and are subject to vehicle or aircraft traffic shall be fitted with a cover designed to sustain the load of vehicles or aircraft that taxi over all or part of them. [407:5.1.13.1]

Δ **42.10.3.1.12.2** Fueling hydrants and pits shall be located at least 15.2 m (50 ft) from any terminal building, hangar, service building, or enclosed passenger concourse (other than loading bridges). [407:5.1.13.2]

N **42.10.3.1.12.3** Fueling cabinets shall be located at least 3 m (10 ft) from any building. [407:5.1.13.3]

N **42.10.3.1.12.4** Fueling cabinets shall be located at least 6.1 m (20 ft) from any building opening. [407:5.1.13.4]

42.10.3.2 Operations.

42.10.3.2.1* Security. Access to fuel storage and fuel vehicle loading areas shall be secured. [407:5.2.1]

42.10.3.2.2 Control of Fuel Flow. If a wireless deadman control is used, the operator shall be located at the fueling point during the fueling operation. [407:5.2.6]

42.10.3.2.3 Fire Protection. During fueling operations, fire extinguishers shall be available on aircraft servicing ramps or aprons, in accordance with NFPA 410. [407:5.2.7]

42.10.4 Airport Fueling Vehicles.

42.10.4.1 Design and Construction.

42.10.4.1.1 General Requirements.

42.10.4.1.1.1 Aircraft fuel servicing tank vehicles that are operated on public roadways shall comply with the requirements of NFPA 385. [407:6.1.1.1]

42.10.4.1.1.2 In addition to any specific requirements in this chapter, only materials safe for use in the service intended and compatible with fuel applications shall be used in the construction of aircraft fuel servicing vehicles and hydrant fuel service carts. [407:6.1.1.2]

42.10.4.1.1.3 Magnesium shall not be used in the construction of any portion of an aircraft fuel servicing vehicle or cart. [407:6.1.1.3]

42.10.4.1.1.4 Trailer connections shall be designed to secure the trailer firmly and to prevent the towed vehicle from swerving from side to side at the speeds anticipated so that the trailer essentially remains in the path of the towing vehicle. [407:6.1.1.4]

42.10.4.1.2 Tanks.

42.10.4.1.2.1 Every cargo tank shall be supported by and attached to, or shall be a part of, the tank vehicle upon which it is carried in accordance with NFPA 385. [407:6.1.2.1]

42.10.4.1.2.2 Cargo tanks shall be constructed in accordance with 49 CFR 178.345, DOT 406, or other equivalent standard for international application. [407:6.1.2.2]

42.10.4.1.2.3 Aluminum alloys for high-strength welded construction shall be joined by an inert gas arc welding process using filler metals R-GR40A, E-GR40A (5154 alloy), R-GM50A, and EGM50A (5356 alloy) in accordance with AWS A5.10. [407:6.1.2.3]

42.10.4.1.2.4 Tank outlets shall be of substantial construction. [407:6.1.2.4]

42.10.4.1.2.5 Tank outlets shall be attached securely to the tank. [407:6.1.2.5]

42.10.4.1.2.6 Baffles. Every cargo tank or compartment over 2.3 m (7.5 ft) long shall be provided with baffles, the total number of which shall be such that the distance between any two adjacent baffles, or between any tank head or bulkhead and the baffle closest to it, shall in no case exceed 1.5 m (5 ft). [407:6.1.2.6]

42.10.4.1.2.6.1 The cross-sectional area of each baffle shall be not less than 80 percent of the cross-sectional area of the tank. [407:6.1.2.6.1]

42.10.4.1.2.6.2 The thickness of a baffle shall be not less than that required for the heads and bulkheads of the cargo tank in which it is installed. [**407**:6.1.2.6.2]

42.10.4.1.2.7 Venting shall be in accordance with 49 CFR, DOT 406. [**407**:6.1.2.7]

42.10.4.1.2.8 Cargo draw-off valves or faucets projecting beyond the frame of a tank vehicle shall be protected against damage. [**407**:6.1.2.8]

42.10.4.1.2.9 Fill Openings and Top Flashings.

42.10.4.1.2.9.1 Dome covers shall be provided with a forward mounted hinge and self-latching catches and shall be fitted with watertight fuel-resistant seals or gaskets designed to prevent spillage or leakage from overturn and to prevent water entry. [**407**:6.1.2.9.1]

42.10.4.1.2.9.2 Dome covers shall automatically close and latch with the forward motion of the vehicle. [**407**:6.1.2.9.2]

42.10.4.1.2.9.3 Drains from top flashing shall divert spilled fuel from possible sources of ignition, including the engine, the engine exhaust system, the electrical equipment, or an auxiliary equipment enclosure. [**407**:6.1.2.9.3]

42.10.4.1.2.9.4 The tank fill openings shall be protected against overturn damage by a rigid member(s) fixed to the tank and extending a minimum of 25 mm (1 in.) above any dome cover, handle, vent opening, or projection of the unit. [**407**:6.1.2.9.4]

42.10.4.1.2.9.5 Overturn protection shall be braced adequately to prevent collapse. [**407**:6.1.2.9.5]

42.10.4.1.2.9.6 Overturn protection shall be designed to channel rainwater, snow, or fuel to the exterior of the cargo tank and away from vehicle exhaust components. [**407**:6.1.2.9.6]

42.10.4.1.2.10 Tanks for Flammable Liquids Other than Fuel. Vehicle or cart fuel tanks and containers for other flammable liquids shall be made of metal and shall be designed, constructed, and located in a manner that precludes hazardous arrangements. [**407**:6.1.2.10]

42.10.4.1.2.10.1 Tanks shall be substantially protected by their location. [**407**:6.1.2.10.1]

42.10.4.1.2.10.2 Fill pipes shall not project beyond the vehicle profile. [**407**:6.1.2.10.2]

42.10.4.1.2.10.3 Tanks and containers shall vent away from sources of ignition during filling. [**407**:6.1.2.10.3]

42.10.4.1.2.10.4 Any arrangement not protected by location shall be listed for such use. [**407**:6.1.2.10.4]

42.10.4.1.2.10.5 The fuel tank arrangement shall allow for drainage without the tank's removal from its mountings. [**407**:6.1.2.10.5]

42.10.4.1.2.11 Tests. Cargo tanks, at the time of manufacture, shall be tested by a minimum air or hydrostatic pressure of 24.4 kg/m^2 (5 psi) applied to the whole tank (or each compartment thereof if the tanks are compartmented) for a period of at least 5 minutes. [**407**:6.1.2.11]

42.10.4.1.2.11.1 If the test is by air pressure, the entire exterior surface of all joints shall be coated with a solution of soap and water, heavy oil, or other substance that causes foaming or bubbling that indicates the presence of leaks. [**407**:6.1.2.11.1]

42.10.4.1.2.11.2 If the test is by hydrostatic pressure, it shall be gauged at the top of the tank, and the tank shall be inspected at the joints for the issuance of liquid to indicate leaks. [**407**:6.1.2.11.2]

42.10.4.1.2.11.3 Any leakage discovered by either of the methods described in 42.10.4.1.2.11.1 and 42.10.4.1.2.11.2, or by any other method, shall be considered evidence of failure to meet these requirements. [**407**:6.1.2.11.3]

42.10.4.1.3 Pumps and Piping System.

42.10.4.1.3.1 All portions of the flammable liquid feed system shall be constructed and located to minimize the fire hazard. [**407**:6.1.3.1]

42.10.4.1.3.2 Piping and plumbing shall be made of materials not adversely affected by the fluid or by other materials likely to be encountered. [**407**:6.1.3.2]

42.10.4.1.3.3 Piping and plumbing shall be of adequate strength for the purpose. [**407**:6.1.3.3]

42.10.4.1.3.4 Piping and plumbing shall be secured to avoid chafing or undue vibration. [**407**:6.1.3.4]

42.10.4.1.3.5 Piping and plumbing shall be supported adequately. [**407**:6.1.3.5]

42.10.4.1.3.6 Product piping shall be metal and rated for the system working pressure or at least 1030 kPa (150 psi), whichever is greater. [**407**:6.1.3.6]

42.10.4.1.3.7 Except as provided in 42.10.4.1.3.8, all joints shall be welded. [**407**:6.1.3.7]

42.10.4.1.3.8 Flanged connections or approved couplings shall be provided to avoid the need for cutting and welding where components are serviced or replaced. [**407**:6.1.3.8]

42.10.4.1.3.9 Gaskets in flanged connections shall be of a material and design that resist fire exposure for a time comparable to the flange and bolts. [**407**:6.1.3.9]

42.10.4.1.3.10 Gravity feed systems shall not be used. [**407**:6.1.3.10]

42.10.4.1.3.11 At the time of manufacture, the section of the fuel dispensing system that is under pressure during service shall be subjected to a hydrostatic test pressure equal to 150 percent of the working pressure of the system for at least 30 minutes and shall be proven tight before it is placed in service. [**407**:6.1.3.11]

42.10.4.1.3.11.1 Hose connections shall be permitted to be plugged during this test. [**407**:6.1.3.11.1]

42.10.4.1.3.12 Loading System.

42.10.4.1.3.12.1 Top Loading.

42.10.4.1.3.12.1.1 Drop tubes shall be used. [**407**:6.1.3.12.1.1]

42.10.4.1.3.12.1.2 Splash filling shall be prohibited. [**407**:6.1.3.12.1.2]

42.10.4.1.3.12.1.3 Drop tubes used in top loading or overhead loading of tank vehicles shall be designed to minimize turbulence. [**407**:6.1.3.12.1.3]

42.10.4.1.3.12.1.4 Drop tubes shall be metallic. [**407**:6.1.3.12.1.4]

42.10.4.1.3.12.1.5 Drop tubes shall extend to the bottom of the tank or to the inside of the sump to maintain submerged loading and to avoid splashing of the fuel. [**407**:6.1.3.12.1.5]

42.10.4.1.3.12.2 Bottom Loading.

42.10.4.1.3.12.2.1 The bottom-loading connection of a tank truck shall be a dry-break coupler that cannot be opened until it is engaged to the vehicle tank adapter. [**407**:6.1.3.12.2.1]

42.10.4.1.3.12.2.2 It shall not be possible to disconnect the hose coupler from the tank vehicle until the coupler valve is fully closed. [**407**:6.1.3.12.2.2]

42.10.4.1.3.12.2.3* The bottom loading fitting of the tank vehicle shall be a spring-loaded check valve that remains in a closed position until opened by connecting the coupler. [**407**:6.1.3.12.2.3]

42.10.4.1.3.12.2.4 A float-actuated shutoff or other automatic sensing device shall be provided to close the bottom-loading valve when the tank is filled. [**407**:6.1.3.12.2.4]

42.10.4.1.3.12.2.5 Any liquid bled from a sensing device during loading shall be piped to the bottom of the cargo tank. [**407**:6.1.3.12.2.5]

42.10.4.1.3.12.2.6 The fill pipe and valving on bottom-loaded tank vehicles shall be arranged to prevent fuel spray and turbulence in the cargo tank. [**407**:6.1.3.12.2.6]

42.10.4.1.3.12.2.7 The cargo tank vehicle shall be equipped with an automatic primary shutdown system that stops the tank loading operation when the tank is full, unless an automatic shutdown is provided on the loading rack in accordance with 42.10.3.1.11. [**407**:6.1.3.12.2.7]

42.10.4.1.3.12.2.8 The cargo tank vehicle shall be equipped with an automatic secondary shutdown system that stops the tank loading operation when the tank is full. [**407**:6.1.3.12.2.8]

42.10.4.1.3.12.2.9 The automatic secondary shutoff control shall not be used for normal filling control. [**407**:6.1.3.12.2.9]

42.10.4.1.3.13 Each outlet valve shall be provided with a fusible device that causes the valve to close automatically in case of fire. [**407**:6.1.3.13]

42.10.4.1.3.14 A shear section shall be provided between shutoff valve seats and discharge outlets that breaks under strain, unless the discharge piping is arranged to afford the same protection and leave the shutoff valve seat intact. [**407**:6.1.3.14]

42.10.4.1.3.15 Openings in cargo tank compartments that are connected to pipe or tubing shall be fitted with a spring-loaded check valve, a self-closing valve, or a similar device to prevent the accidental discharge of fuel in case of equipment malfunction or line breakage. [**407**:6.1.3.15]

42.10.4.1.3.15.1 Unless the valves required in 42.10.4.1.3.15 are located inside the tank, they shall be equipped with a shear section as described in 42.10.4.1.3.14. [**407**:6.1.3.15.1]

42.10.4.1.3.16 The operating mechanism for each tank outlet valve shall be adjacent to the fuel delivery system operating controls. [**407**:6.1.3.16]

42.10.4.1.3.16.1 The operating mechanism for each tank outlet valve shall be arranged so that the outlet valve(s) can be closed simultaneously and instantly in the event of a fire or other emergency. [**407**:6.1.3.16.1]

42.10.4.1.3.16.2 A means shall be provided to assure proper operation. [**407**:6.1.3.16.2]

42.10.4.1.4 Bonding.

42.10.4.1.4.1 All metallic components and vehicle or cart chassis shall be electrically bonded to prevent a difference in their electrostatic potential. [**407**:6.1.5.1]

42.10.4.1.4.2 Such bonding shall be inherent to the installation or by physical application of a suitable bonding mechanism. [**407**:6.1.5.2]

42.10.4.1.4.3 A provision shall be provided on the vehicle to bond the tank to a fill pipe or loading rack as specified in 42.10.4.2.5.10.1. [**407**:6.1.5.3]

42.10.4.1.4.4 Cables shall be provided on the vehicle or cart to allow the bonding operations specified in 42.10.2.2.4. [**407**:6.1.5.4]

42.10.4.1.5 Electrical System.

42.10.4.1.5.1 Battery Compartments. Batteries that are not in engine compartments shall be securely mounted in compartments to prevent accidental arcing. [**407**:6.1.6.1]

42.10.4.1.5.1.1 The compartment shall be separate from fueling equipment. [**407**:6.1.6.1.1]

42.10.4.1.5.1.2 Suitable shielding shall be provided to drain possible fuel spillage or leakage away from the compartment. [**407**:6.1.6.1.2]

42.10.4.1.5.1.3 The compartment shall be provided with a vent at the top of the compartment. [**407**:6.1.6.1.3]

42.10.4.1.5.2 Wiring. Wiring shall be of adequate size to provide the required current-carrying capacity and mechanical strength. [**407**:6.1.6.2]

42.10.4.1.5.2.1 Wiring shall be installed to provide protection from physical damage and from contact with spilled fuel either by its location or by enclosing it in metal conduit or other oil-resistant protective covering. [**407**:6.1.6.2.1]

42.10.4.1.5.2.2 All circuits shall have overcurrent protection. [**407**:6.1.6.2.2]

42.10.4.1.5.2.3 Junction boxes shall be weatherproofed. [**407**:6.1.6.2.3]

42.10.4.1.5.2.4 The vehicle shall be equipped with a battery disconnect switch. [**407**:6.1.6.2.4]

42.10.4.1.5.3 Spark plugs and other exposed terminal connections shall be insulated to prevent sparking in the event of contact with conductive materials. [**407**:6.1.6.3]

42.10.4.1.5.4* Motors, alternators, generators, and their associated control equipment located outside of the engine compartment or vehicle cab shall be of a type listed for use in accordance with *NFPA 70*, Class I, Division 1, Group D locations. [**407**:6.1.6.4]

42.10.4.1.5.5 Electrical equipment and wiring located within a closed compartment shall be of a type listed for use in accordance with *NFPA 70*, Class I, Division 1, Group D locations. [**407:**6.1.6.5]

42.10.4.1.5.6 Lamps, switching devices, and electronic controls, other than those covered in 42.10.4.1.5.4 and 42.10.4.1.5.5, shall be of the enclosed, gasketed, weatherproof type. [**407:**6.1.6.6]

42.10.4.1.5.7 Other electrical components not covered in 42.10.4.1.5.4 through 42.10.4.1.5.6 shall be of a type listed for use in accordance with *NFPA 70*, Class I, Division 2, Group D locations. [**407:**6.1.6.7]

42.10.4.1.5.8 Electronic equipment shall not be installed in compartments with other equipment that can produce flammable vapors, unless permitted by *NFPA 70*. [**407:**6.1.6.8]

42.10.4.1.5.9 Tractor Trailer Wiring. Electrical service wiring between a tractor and trailer shall be designed for heavy-duty service. [**407:**6.1.6.9]

42.10.4.1.5.9.1 The connector shall be of the positive-engaging type. [**407:**6.1.6.9.1]

42.10.4.1.5.9.2 The trailer receptacle shall be mounted securely. [**407:**6.1.6.9.2]

42.10.4.1.6 Control of Fuel Flow.

42.10.4.1.6.1* The valve that controls the flow of fuel to an aircraft shall have a deadman control. [**407:**6.1.7.1]

42.10.4.1.6.2 The fuel flow control valve shall be one of the following:

(1) The hydrant pit valve
(2) At the tank outlet on a tank vehicle
(3) A separate valve on the tank vehicle
(4) On the hose nozzle for overwing servicing

[**407:**6.1.7.2]

42.10.4.1.6.3 Deadman controls shall be designed to preclude defeating their intended purpose. [**407:**6.1.7.3]

42.10.4.1.6.4 Pressure Fuel Servicing System Controls.

42.10.4.1.6.4.1 The system shall be designed to minimize surge pressure. [**407:**6.1.7.4.1]

42.10.4.1.6.4.2* The overshoot shall not exceed 5 percent of actual flow rate in L/min (gal/min) at the time the deadman is released. [**407:**6.1.7.4.2]

42.10.4.1.6.4.3 The control valve shall be located and designed so that it will not be rendered inoperative by a surface accident, power failure, or spill. [**407:**6.1.7.4.3]

42.10.4.1.6.4.4 The control valve shall be fail-safe by closing completely in the event of control power loss. [**407:**6.1.7.4.4]

42.10.4.1.6.5 On tank full trailer or tank semitrailer vehicles, the use of a pump in the tractor unit with flexible connections to the trailer shall be prohibited unless one of the following conditions exists:

(1) Flexible connections are arranged above the liquid level of the tank in order to prevent gravity or siphon discharge in case of a break in the connection or piping.
(2) The cargo tank discharge valves required by 42.10.4.1.6.1 are arranged to be normally closed and to open only when the brakes are set and the pump is engaged.

[**407:**6.1.7.5]

42.10.4.1.6.6 Air Elimination. Aircraft fuel servicing tank vehicles having a positive displacement product pump shall be equipped with a product tank low-level shutdown system that prevents air from being ingested into the fueling system. [**407:**6.1.7.6]

42.10.4.1.7 Filters and Ancillary Equipment.

42.10.4.1.7.1 Cabinets.

42.10.4.1.7.1.1 All cabinets, other than those housing electronic equipment, shall be vented to prevent the accumulation of fuel vapors. *(See 42.10.4.1.5.)* [**407:**6.1.8.1.1]

42.10.4.1.7.1.2 All cabinets, other than those housing electronic equipment, shall be constructed of noncombustible materials. *(See 42.10.4.1.5.)* [**407:**6.1.8.1.2]

42.10.4.1.7.2 Product Recovery Tanks. The refueling system product recovery tank shall be equipped with a control that shuts down the vehicle's fuel dispensing system when the refueling system product recovery tank is three-quarters full. [**407:**6.1.8.2]

42.10.4.1.8 Emergency Fuel Shutoff Systems.

42.10.4.1.8.1 The vehicle shall have at least two emergency shutoff controls, one mounted on each side of the vehicle. [**407:**6.1.9.1]

42.10.4.1.8.2 The emergency fuel shutoff controls shall be quick-acting to close the outlet valve in case of emergency. [**407:**6.1.9.2]

42.10.4.1.8.3 The emergency fuel shutoff controls shall be remote from the fill openings and discharge outlets and shall be operable from a ground level standing position. [**407:**6.1.9.3]

42.10.4.1.8.4 All vehicles or carts equipped with a top deck or elevating platform shall have an additional emergency shutoff control operable from the deck or platform. [**407:**6.1.9.4]

42.10.4.1.9* Fire Protection.

42.10.4.1.9.1 Each aircraft fuel servicing tank vehicle shall have two listed fire extinguishers, each having a rating of at least 40-B:C and a minimum capacity of 9.0 kg (20 lb) of dry chemical agent, with one extinguisher mounted on each side of the vehicle. [**407:**6.1.10.1]

42.10.4.1.9.2 One listed fire extinguisher having a rating of at least 40-B:C and a minimum capacity of 9.0 kg (20 lb) of dry chemical agent shall be installed on each hydrant fuel servicing vehicle or cart. [**407:**6.1.10.2]

42.10.4.1.9.3 Extinguishers shall be readily accessible from the ground. [**407:**6.1.10.3]

42.10.4.1.9.4 The area of the paneling or tank adjacent to or immediately behind the extinguisher(s) on fueling vehicles or carts shall be painted a color contrasting with that of the extinguisher. [**407:**6.1.10.4]

42.10.4.1.9.5 Extinguishers shall be kept clear of elements such as ice and snow. [**407:**6.1.10.5]

42.10.4.1.9.6 Extinguishers located in enclosed compartments shall be readily accessible. [**407:**6.1.10.6]

42.10.4.1.9.7 The locations of extinguishers in enclosed compartments shall be marked clearly in letters of a contrasting color at least 50 mm (2 in.) high. [**407**:6.1.10.7]

42.10.4.1.9.8 Smoking Equipment.

42.10.4.1.9.8.1* Smoking equipment, such as cigarette lighter elements and ashtrays, shall not be provided. [**407**:6.1.10.8.1]

42.10.4.1.9.8.2 If a vehicle includes smoking equipment, it shall be removed or rendered inoperable. [**407**:6.1.10.8.2]

42.10.4.1.9.8.3 Subsection 42.10.4.1.9.8.2 shall be retroactive to existing vehicles. [**407**:6.1.10.8.3]

42.10.4.1.10 Marking and Labeling.

42.10.4.1.10.1 Aircraft fueling vehicles shall be marked with the name of the operator or the responsible organization. [**407**:6.1.11.1]

42.10.4.1.10.2 The marking shall be approved, legible signs on both sides of the exterior of the vehicle. [**407**:6.1.11.2]

42.10.4.1.10.3 Signage. Each aircraft fuel servicing vehicle or cart shall have a signage viewable from all sides of the vehicle. [**407**:6.1.11.3]

42.10.4.1.10.3.1 Signs shall have letters at least 75 mm (3 in.) high. [**407**:6.1.11.3.1]

42.10.4.1.10.3.2 Signs shall be of a color contrasting sharply with the sign background for visibility. [**407**:6.1.11.3.2]

Δ **42.10.4.1.10.3.3** The words FLAMMABLE, NO SMOKING, and the name of the product carried, such as JET A, JET B, GASOLINE, or AVGAS, shall appear on each sign. [**407**:6.1.11.3.3]

N **42.10.4.1.10.3.4** Placards shall be weather resistant. [**407**:6.1.11.3.4]

N **42.10.4.1.10.3.5** A NO SMOKING sign shall be posted prominently in the cab of every aircraft fuel servicing vehicle. [**407**:6.1.11.3.5]

N **42.10.4.1.10.3.6** Hazardous material placards meeting the requirements of 49 CFR 172.504 or equivalent shall be displayed on all four sides of fuel servicing vehicles. [**407**:6.1.11.3.6]

42.10.4.1.10.4 Emergency Fuel Shutoff Signs.

42.10.4.1.10.4.1 Each emergency fuel shutoff station location shall be placarded EMERGENCY FUEL SHUTOFF in letters at least 50 mm (2 in.) high. [**407**:6.1.11.4]

42.10.4.1.10.4.2 The method of operation shall be indicated by an arrow or by the word PUSH or PULL, as appropriate. [**407**:6.1.11.4.2]

42.10.4.1.10.4.3 Any action necessary to gain access to the shutoff device (e.g., BREAK GLASS) shall be shown clearly. [**407**:6.1.11.4.3]

42.10.4.1.10.4.4 Lettering shall be of a color contrasting sharply with the placard background for visibility. [**407**:6.1.11.4.4]

42.10.4.1.11 Drive Train.

42.10.4.1.11.1 Propulsion or power engine equipment shall be in a compartment housing that shall minimize the hazard of fire in the event of leakage or spillage of fuel during the servicing of an aircraft. [**407**:6.1.12.1]

42.10.4.1.11.2 The engine air intake shall retain the manufacturer's configuration to prevent the emission of flame in case of backfiring. [**407**:6.1.12.2]

42.10.4.1.11.3 Where provided, the sediment bowl in the fuel supply line shall be of steel or material of equivalent fire resistance. [**407**:6.1.12.3]

42.10.4.1.11.4 Full trailers and semitrailers, except tow carts with a gross vehicle weight rating (GVWR) under 1360 kg (3000 lb), shall be equipped with service brakes on all wheels. [**407**:6.1.12.4]

42.10.4.1.11.5 All full trailers and semitrailers, including tow carts with a GVWR under 1360 kg (3000 lb), shall be equipped with parking brakes. [**407**:6.1.12.5]

42.10.4.1.11.6 Self-propelled aircraft fuel servicing vehicles shall have an integral system or device that prevents the vehicle from being moved unless all of the following conditions are met:

(1) All fueling nozzles and hydrant couplers are properly stowed.
(2) All mechanical lifts are lowered to their stowed position.
(3) Bottom-loading couplers have been disconnected from the vehicle.

[**407**:6.1.12.6]

42.10.4.1.11.7 The vehicle shall have a means to override the system or device required by 42.10.4.1.11.6 so that the vehicle can be moved during an emergency. [**407**:6.1.12.7]

42.10.4.1.11.7.1 The override control shall be clearly marked and accessible. [**407**:6.1.12.7.1]

42.10.4.1.11.7.2 A light to indicate activation of the override shall be located in the cabin and visible outside. [**407**:6.1.12.7.2]

42.10.4.1.11.7.3 The override control shall be secured in the normal position with a breakaway seal. [**407**:6.1.12.7.3]

42.10.4.1.11.7.4 The override control shall deactivate the fueling system. [**407**:6.1.12.7.4]

42.10.4.1.12 Exhaust System.

42.10.4.1.12.1* The engine exhaust system shall be designed, located, and installed to minimize the hazard of fire in the event of any of the following:

(1) Leakage of fuel from the vehicle or cart (where applicable) fuel tank or fuel system
(2) Leakage from the fuel dispensing system of the vehicle or cart
(3) Spillage or overflow of fuel from the vehicle or cart (if applicable) fuel tank or the cargo tank
(4) Spillage of fuel during the servicing of an aircraft

[**407**:6.1.13.1]

42.10.4.1.12.2 Exhaust system components shall be secured and located clear of components carrying flammable liquids and separated from any combustible materials used in the construction of the vehicle. [**407**:6.1.13.2]

42.10.4.1.12.3 Suitable shielding shall be provided to drain possible fuel spillage or leakage away from exhaust system components safely. [**407**:6.1.13.3]

42.10.4.1.12.3.1 Diesel particulate filter (DPF) regeneration system piping shall be shielded from the engine discharge manifold to the outlet at the tailpipe. [**407**:6.1.13.3.1]

42.10.4.1.12.3.2 DPF regeneration–equipped vehicles shall have a listed diffuser installed at the outlet of the exhaust tailpipe. [**407**:6.1.13.3.2]

42.10.4.1.12.4 Exhaust gases shall not be discharged where they could ignite fuel vapors that could be released during normal operations or by accidental spillage or by leakage of fuel. [**407**:6.1.13.4]

42.10.4.1.12.4.1 DPF regeneration–equipped vehicles shall have a lockout mode that will prevent automatic regeneration when these vehicles are operated within 30 m (100 ft) of aircraft parking areas. [**407**:6.1.13.4.1]

42.10.4.1.12.5 A muffler (or silencer) cutout shall not be provided. [**407**:6.1.13.5]

42.10.4.1.12.6 Carbureted gasoline-powered engines on fuel servicing vehicles shall be provided with flame- and spark-arresting exhaust systems. [**407**:6.1.13.6]

42.10.4.1.12.7* Non-turbo-charged diesel engines on fuel servicing vehicles shall be equipped with flame- and spark-arresting exhaust systems. [**407**:6.1.13.7]

42.10.4.2 Operations.

42.10.4.2.1 Security.

42.10.4.2.1.1 Parking of Aircraft Fuel Servicing Tank Vehicles. Parking areas for unattended aircraft fuel servicing tank vehicles shall be arranged to provide the following:

(1) Dispersal of the vehicles in the event of an emergency
(2) A minimum of 3 m (10 ft) of clear space between parked vehicles for accessibility for fire control purposes
(3) Prevention of any leakage from draining to an adjacent building or storm drain that is not suitably designed to handle fuel
(4) A minimum of 15 m (50 ft) from any parked aircraft and buildings other than maintenance facilities and garages for fuel servicing tank vehicles

[**407**:6.2.1.1]

42.10.4.2.1.2 Parking of Aircraft Fuel Servicing Hydrant Vehicles and Carts. Parking areas for unattended aircraft fuel servicing hydrant vehicles or carts shall be arranged to provide the following:

(1) Dispersal of the vehicles in the event of an emergency
(2) Prevention of any leakage from draining to an adjacent building or storm drain that is not suitably designed to handle fuel

[**407**:6.2.1.2]

42.10.4.2.1.3* The authority having jurisdiction shall determine the suitability of tunnels, enclosed roadways, or other limited access areas for use by fuel servicing vehicles. [**407**:6.2.1.3]

42.10.4.2.2 Control of Fuel Flow.

42.10.4.2.2.1 The fueling operator shall monitor the fueling operation. [**407**:6.2.6.1]

42.10.4.2.2.2 During overwing fueling, the operator shall monitor the fill port. [**407**:6.2.6.2]

42.10.4.2.3 Maintenance.

42.10.4.2.3.1 Aircraft fuel servicing vehicles or carts shall not be operated unless they are in proper repair and free of accumulations of grease, oil, or other combustibles. [**407**:6.2.8.1]

42.10.4.2.3.2 Leaking vehicles or carts shall be removed from service, defueled, and parked in a safe area until repaired. [**407**:6.2.8.2]

42.10.4.2.3.3 Maintenance and servicing of aircraft fuel servicing vehicles and carts shall be performed outdoors or in a building approved for the purpose. [**407**:6.2.8.3]

42.10.4.2.3.4 At least monthly the operator shall perform a check to ensure complete closure of the bottom-loading valve on the tank vehicle. [**407**:6.2.8.4]

42.10.4.2.4 Exhaust System.

42.10.4.2.4.1 All vehicles that have engines equipped with an exhaust after-treatment device, such as a DPF, that requires the filter to be cleaned at high temperature (regenerated) while installed on the vehicle shall meet the requirements of 42.10.4.2.4.2 through 42.10.4.2.4.10. [**407**:6.2.10.1]

42.10.4.2.4.2 DPF regeneration shall be performed only in area(s) designated by the authority having jurisdiction. [**407**:6.2.10.2]

42.10.4.2.4.3 DPF regeneration shall not be performed within 30 m (100 ft) of any aircraft refueling operations. [**407**:6.2.10.3]

42.10.4.2.4.4* Vehicle Regeneration Area.

42.10.4.2.4.4.1 The immediate area surrounding the DPF exhaust outlet shall be concrete or other high temperature–resistant material and shall be clear of any grass, soil, or flammable materials. [**407**:6.2.10.4.1]

42.10.4.2.4.4.2 The area shall be in a remote location that is a minimum of 30 m (100 ft) from the nearest aircraft parking location, airport terminal, or flammable storage or a minimum of 15 m (50 ft) from any other building. [**407**:6.2.10.4.2]

42.10.4.2.4.4.3 The area shall be clearly marked with a minimum 61 cm by 30 cm (2 ft by 1 ft) sign reading "VEHICLE DPF REGENERATION AREA," which shall have letters at least 75 mm (3 in.) high and shall be of a color contrasting sharply with the sign background for visibility. [**407**:6.2.10.4.3]

42.10.4.2.4.5 The regeneration cycle shall be performed only by trained personnel, who shall remain with the vehicle until the regeneration cycle is complete. [**407**:6.2.10.5]

42.10.4.2.4.6 The vehicle shall be visually inspected for any signs of fluid leaks under or around the vehicle before regeneration is initiated. [**407**:6.2.10.6]

42.10.4.2.4.7 DPF regeneration shall not be initiated if there are any signs of any fluid leaks on or beneath the vehicle. [**407**:6.2.10.7]

42.10.4.2.4.8 Once a regeneration cycle is started, it shall be completed without interruption. [**407**:6.2.10.8]

42.10.4.2.4.9 After the regeneration process is successfully completed, the vehicle shall be permitted to return to normal service. [**407**:6.2.10.9]

42.10.4.2.4.10 Problems occurring during the regeneration cycle shall be corrected prior to the vehicle returning to normal service. [**407**:6.2.10.10]

42.10.4.2.4.11 Aircraft refueling operations shall not be initiated if the regenerative system indicates regeneration is required. [**407**:6.2.10.11]

42.10.4.2.5 Loading and Unloading.

42.10.4.2.5.1 Aircraft fuel servicing tank vehicles shall be loaded only at an approved loading rack. [**407**:6.2.11.1]

42.10.4.2.5.2 Aircraft fuel servicing tank vehicles shall not be loaded from a hydrant pit, unless permitted by the authority having jurisdiction under emergency circumstances. [**407**:6.2.11.2]

42.10.4.2.5.3 Filling of the vehicle cargo tank shall be under the observation and control of a qualified and authorized operator at all times. [**407**:6.2.11.3]

42.10.4.2.5.4 The required deadman and automatic overfill controls shall be in normal operating condition during the filling operation. [**407**:6.2.11.4]

42.10.4.2.5.5 The controls shall not be blocked open or otherwise bypassed. [**407**:6.2.11.5]

42.10.4.2.5.6 The engine of the tank vehicle shall be shut off before starting to fill the tank. [**407**:6.2.11.6]

42.10.4.2.5.7 To prevent leakage or overflow from expansion of the contents due to a rise in atmospheric temperature or direct exposure to the sun, no cargo tank or compartment shall be loaded to the point where it is liquid full. [**407**:6.2.11.7]

42.10.4.2.5.7.1 No cargo tank or compartment shall be loaded above the rated net capacity, as specified by the manufacturer's data plate. [**407**:6.2.11.7.1]

42.10.4.2.5.7.2 Space for thermal expansion, in no case less than 3 percent of the tank volume, shall be provided to prevent leakage. [**407**:6.2.11.7.2]

Δ **42.10.4.2.5.8** The driver, operator, or attendant of any tank vehicle shall not remain in the vehicle but shall not leave the vehicle unattended during the loading or unloading process. [**407**:6.2.11.8]

42.10.4.2.5.8.1 Delivery hose, when attached to a tank vehicle, shall be considered to be a part of the tank vehicle. [**407**:6.2.11.8.1]

42.10.4.2.5.9 No fuel shall be transferred to or from any tank vehicle until the parking brake and wheel chocks have been set to prevent motion of the vehicle. [**407**:6.2.11.9]

42.10.4.2.5.10 Top Loading.

42.10.4.2.5.10.1 Where loading tank trucks through open domes, a bond shall be established between the loading piping and the cargo tank to equalize potentials. [**407**:6.2.11.10.1]

42.10.4.2.5.10.2 The bond connection shall be made before the dome is opened and shall be removed only after the dome is closed. [**407**:6.2.11.10.2]

42.10.4.2.5.10.3 Drop tubes attached to loading assemblies extending into the vehicle tank shall extend to the bottom of the tank and shall be maintained in that position until the tank is loaded to provide submerged loading and avoid splashing or free falling of fuel through the tank atmosphere. [**407**:6.2.11.10.3]

42.10.4.2.5.10.4 Splash filling shall be prohibited. [**407**:6.2.11.10.4]

42.10.4.2.5.10.5 The flow rate into the tanks shall not exceed 25 percent of the maximum flow until the outlet is fully covered. [**407**:6.2.11.10.5]

42.10.4.2.5.10.6 Fixed drop tubes permanently mounted in the vehicle tank shall extend to the bottom of the tank or to the inside of the sump to maintain submerged loading and to avoid splashing of the fuel. [**407**:6.2.11.10.6]

42.10.4.2.5.10.7 The level in the tank shall be visually monitored at all times during top loading. [**407**:6.2.11.10.7]

42.10.4.2.5.11 Bottom Loading.

42.10.4.2.5.11.1 A bonding connection shall be made between the cargo tank and the loading rack before any fuel connections are made and shall remain in place throughout the loading operation. [**407**:6.2.11.11.1]

42.10.4.2.5.11.2 The operator shall initiate fuel flow by means of a dead-man control device. [**407**:6.2.11.11.2]

42.10.4.2.5.11.3 The operator shall ensure that the automatic high-level shutoff system is functioning properly for each compartment shortly after flow has been initiated. [**407**:6.2.11.11.3]

42.10.4.2.6 Positioning of Aircraft Fuel Servicing Vehicles and Carts During Fueling.

42.10.4.2.6.1 Aircraft fuel servicing vehicles and carts shall be positioned so that a clear path of egress from the aircraft for fuel servicing vehicles shall be maintained. [**407**:6.2.12.1]

42.10.4.2.6.2 The propulsion or pumping engine of aircraft fuel servicing vehicles or carts shall not be positioned under the wing of the aircraft during overwing fueling or where aircraft fuel system vents are located on the upper wing surface. [**407**:6.2.12.2]

42.10.4.2.6.3 Aircraft fuel servicing vehicles or carts shall not be positioned within a 3 m (10 ft) radius of aircraft fuel system vent openings. [**407**:6.2.12.3]

42.10.4.2.6.4 Parking brakes and chocks shall be set on all fuel servicing vehicles or carts before operators begin the fueling operation. [**407**:6.2.12.4]

42.10.4.2.6.5 During overwing aircraft fuel servicing where aircraft fuel system vents are located on the upper wing surface, equipment shall not be positioned under the trailing edge of the wing. [**407**:6.2.12.5]

N **42.10.4.2.6.6** Aircraft fuel servicing tank vehicles shall be positioned so that the vehicle is not closer than 7.6 m (25 ft) to any terminal building, hangar, service building, or enclosed passenger concourse other than a loading walkway. [**407**:6.2.12.6]

42.10.5 Rooftop Heliports.

42.10.5.1 Design and Construction.

42.10.5.1.1 General Requirements.

42.10.5.1.1.1 System Design and Approval.

42.10.5.1.1.1.1 Fueling on rooftop heliports shall be permitted only where approved by the authority having jurisdiction. [**407:**7.1.1.1.1]

42.10.5.1.1.1.2 In addition to the special requirements in this chapter, the heliport shall comply with the requirements of NFPA 418. [**407:**7.1.1.1.2]

42.10.5.1.1.1.3 Facilities for dispensing fuel with a flash point below 37.8°C (100°F) shall not be permitted at any rooftop heliport. [**407:**7.1.1.1.3]

42.10.5.1.1.1.4 In addition to the special requirements of this chapter, the fuel storage, piping, and dispensing system shall comply with the requirements of NFPA 30 and with applicable portions of this standard. [**407:**7.1.1.1.4]

42.10.5.1.1.1.5 The entire system shall be designed so that no part of the system is subjected to pressure above its working pressure. [**407:**7.1.1.1.5]

42.10.5.1.2 Fuel Storage Tanks.

42.10.5.1.2.1 Fuel storage tanks and components shall comply with the requirements of NFPA 30. [**407:**7.1.2.1]

42.10.5.1.2.2 The fuel storage system shall be located at or below ground level. [**407:**7.1.2.2]

42.10.5.1.3 Pumps and Piping Systems.

42.10.5.1.3.1 Pumps and piping systems shall comply with the requirements of NFPA 30. [**407:**7.1.3.1]

42.10.5.1.3.2 Pumps shall be located at or below ground level. [**407:**7.1.3.2]

42.10.5.1.3.3 Relay pumping shall not be permitted. [**407:**7.1.3.3]

42.10.5.1.3.4 Pumps installed outside of buildings shall be located not less than 1.5 m (5 ft) from any building opening. [**407:**7.1.3.4]

42.10.5.1.3.5 Pumps shall be anchored and protected against physical damage from collision. [**407:**7.1.3.5]

42.10.5.1.3.6 Pumps installed within a building shall be in a separate room with no opening into other portions of the building. [**407:**7.1.3.6]

42.10.5.1.3.7 The pump room shall be adequately ventilated. [**407:**7.1.3.7]

42.10.5.1.3.8 Electrical wiring and equipment in pump rooms shall conform to the requirements of *NFPA 70*, Article 515. [**407:**7.1.3.8]

42.10.5.1.3.9 Piping above grade shall be steel and, unless otherwise approved by the authority having jurisdiction, shall be suitably cased or shall be installed in a duct or chase. [**407:**7.1.3.9]

42.10.5.1.3.9.1 Such piping duct or chase shall be constructed so that a piping failure does not result in the entry of fuel liquid or vapor entering the building. [**407:**7.1.3.9.1]

42.10.5.1.3.9.2 All pipe casings, ducts, and chases shall be drained. [**407:**7.1.3.9.2]

42.10.5.1.3.10 Piping shall be anchored and shall be protected against physical damage for a height of at least 2.4 m (8 ft) above the ground. [**407:**7.1.3.10]

42.10.5.1.3.11 An isolation valve shall be installed on the suction and discharge piping of each pump. [**407:**7.1.3.11]

42.10.5.1.3.12 A check valve shall be installed at the base of each fuel piping riser to automatically prevent the reverse flow of the fuel into the pump room in the event of pump seal failure, pipe failure, or other malfunction. [**407:**7.1.3.12]

42.10.5.1.3.13 Piping within buildings shall comply with 42.10.3.1.3.3. [**407:**7.1.3.13]

42.10.5.1.4 Emergency Fuel Shutoff Systems.

42.10.5.1.4.1 At least two emergency fuel shutoff stations located on opposite sides of the heliport at exitways or at similar locations shall be provided. [**407:**7.1.9.1]

42.10.5.1.4.2 An additional emergency fuel shutoff station shall be located at ground level and shall be located at least 3 m (10 ft) from the pump but no further than 6 m (20 ft). [**407:**7.1.9.2]

42.10.5.1.5 Fire Protection.
Fire protection shall conform to the requirements of NFPA 418. [**407:**7.1.10]

42.10.5.2 Operations.

42.10.5.2.1 Personnel.
All heliport personnel shall be trained in the use of the available fire extinguishers and fixed extinguishing systems. [**407:**7.2.2]

42.10.5.2.2 Emergency Fuel Shutoff.
All heliport personnel shall be trained in the operation of emergency fuel shutoff controls. [**407:**7.2.4]

42.10.6 Self-Service Aircraft Fueling.

42.10.6.1 Design and Construction.

42.10.6.1.1 General Requirements.

42.10.6.1.1.1 System Design and Approval.
Self-service fueling shall be permitted, subject to the approval of the authority having jurisdiction. [**407:**8.1.1.1]

42.10.6.1.1.2 Dispensing devices shall be located on an island to protect against collision damage or shall be protected with pipe bollards or other approved protection. [**407:**8.1.1.2]

42.10.6.1.2 Fuel Storage Tanks.
In addition to the special requirements of this chapter, the fuel storage system shall comply with the requirements of NFPA 30. [**407:**8.1.2]

42.10.6.1.3 Pumps and Piping Systems.

42.10.6.1.3.1 In addition to the special requirements of this chapter, the piping and dispensing system shall comply with the requirements of NFPA 30. [**407:**8.1.3.1]

42.10.6.1.3.2 Listed or approved dispensing devices shall be used. [**407:**8.1.3.2]

42.10.6.1.4 Emergency Fuel Shutoff Systems.

42.10.6.1.4.1 The controls shall be designed to allow only authorized personnel to reset the system after an emergency fuel shutoff. [**407**:8.1.9.1]

42.10.6.1.4.2 The emergency fuel shutoff controls shall be installed in a location acceptable to the authority having jurisdiction and shall be more than 6 m (20 ft) but less than 30 m (100 ft) from the dispensers. [**407**:8.1.9.2]

42.10.6.1.4.3 A clearly identified means to notify the fire department shall be provided and shall be located in the immediate vicinity of each emergency fuel shutoff control. [**407**:8.1.9.3.]

42.10.6.1.4.4 Dispensing devices shall have a listed or approved emergency shutoff valve, incorporating a fusible link or other thermally actuated device designed to close automatically in case of fire. [**407**:8.1.9.4]

42.10.6.1.4.5 The emergency shutoff valve also shall incorporate a shear section that automatically shuts off the flow of fuel due to severe impact. [**407**:8.1.9.5]

42.10.6.1.4.6 The emergency shutoff valve shall be rigidly mounted at the base of the dispenser in accordance with the manufacturer's instructions. [**407**:8.1.9.6]

42.10.6.1.5* Fire Protection.

42.10.6.1.5.1 Each facility shall have a minimum of one fire extinguisher with a rating of at least 40-B:C and a minimum capacity of 9.0 kg (20 lb) of dry chemical agent located at the dispenser. [**407**:8.1.10.1]

42.10.6.1.5.2 At least one fire extinguisher with a rating of at least 40-B:C and a minimum capacity of 9.0 kg (20 lb) of dry chemical agent shall be provided at each emergency fuel shutoff control. [**407**:8.1.10.2]

42.10.6.1.6 Marking and Labeling.

42.10.6.1.6.1 Emergency instructions shall be conspicuously posted in the dispensing area and at the emergency fuel shutoff control. [**407**:8.1.11.1]

42.10.6.1.6.2 Emergency instructions shall incorporate the following or equivalent wording:

EMERGENCY INSTRUCTIONS IN CASE OF FIRE OR SPILL

(1) Use emergency fuel shutoff.

(2) Report accident by calling (specify local fire emergency reporting number) on phone.

(3) Report address of site (list address of site here).

[**407**:8.1.11.2]

42.10.6.1.6.3 Operating Instructions. Operating instructions shall be posted. [**407**:8.1.11.3]

42.10.6.1.6.4 The operating instructions shall include the following:

(1) Proper operation and use of all equipment
(2) Correct bonding procedures
(3) Procedures to be employed to dispense fuel safely
(4) Location and use of the emergency fuel shutoff controls
(5) Procedures to be used in the event of an emergency

[**407**:8.1.11.4]

42.10.6.2 Operations.

42.10.6.2.1 Security. Access to dispensing equipment shall be controlled by means of mechanical or electronic devices designed to resist tampering and to prevent access or use by unauthorized persons. [**407**:8.2.1]

42.10.6.2.2 Occupancy. The aircraft shall not be occupied during self-service fueling. [**407**:8.2.9]

42.11 Alternate Fuels.

42.11.1 Compressed Natural Gas (CNG) Vehicular Fuel Systems. The design and installation of CNG engine fuel systems on vehicles of all types shall comply with NFPA 52, *Vehicular Gaseous Fuel Systems Code*, and Section 42.11.

42.11.1.1* Scope.

42.11.1.1.1 Section 42.11 shall apply to the design, installation, operation, and maintenance of compressed natural gas (CNG) and liquefied natural gas (LNG) engine fuel systems on vehicles of all types and for fueling vehicle (dispensing) systems and facilities, and associated storage, including the following:

(1) Original equipment manufacturers (OEMs)
(2) Final-stage vehicle integrator/manufacturer (FSVIM)
(3) Vehicle fueling (dispensing) systems

[**52**:1.1.1]

42.11.1.1.2 Section 42.11 shall apply to the design, installation, operation, and maintenance of LNG engine fuel systems on vehicles of all types, to their associated fueling (dispensing) facilities, and to LNG-to-CNG facilities with LNG storage in ASME containers of 100,000 gal (379 m^3) or less. [**52**:1.1.2]

42.11.1.1.3* This section and NFPA 52 shall not apply to those aspects of vehicles and fuel supply containers that are covered by federal motor vehicle safety standards (FMVSSs). [**52**:1.1.3]

42.11.1.1.4 Section 42.11 shall include marine, highway, rail, off-road, and industrial vehicles. [**52**:1.1.4]

42.11.2 Liquefied Petroleum Gas (LP-Gas).

Δ **42.11.2.1** Fuel dispensing facilities for vehicles using LP-Gas shall comply with NFPA 58.

42.11.3* Liquefied Natural Gas (LNG). Fuel dispensing facilities for marine, highway, rail, off-road, and industrial vehicles using LNG and LNG storage in ASME containers of 70,000 gal (265 m^3) or less shall comply with NFPA 52.

42.12 On-Demand Mobile Fueling.

Δ **42.12.1* Scope.** Section 42.12 applies to the practice of mobile fueling of motor vehicles while the motor vehicle being fueled is parked. [**30A**:14.1]

Δ **42.12.1.1** Section 42.12 shall not apply to the following:

(1) Fueling from tank vehicles at commercial, industrial, governmental, or manufacturing establishments in accordance with 42.7.7.
(2) Fueling from portable containers in cases of emergency or for personal use.

[**30A**:14.1.1]

42.12.1.2 Dispensing Class I and Class II Liquids for On-Demand Mobile Fueling.

42.12.1.2.1 The dispensing of Class I and Class II liquids from a mobile fueling vehicle or metal safety cans into the fuel tank of a motor vehicle shall be permitted only if all of the requirements of 42.12.2 through 42.12.4 have been met. [**30A:**14.1.2.1]

42.12.1.2.2 The dispensing of all other motor fuels from mobile refueling vehicles into the fuel tank of a motor vehicle shall be permitted only if the following requirements are met:

(1) Completion of a risk assessment and operating plan addressing the identified hazards
(2) Approval of the AHJ
[**30A:**14.1.2.2]

42.12.2 Approvals and Mobile Fueling Locations.

42.12.2.1 Mobile fueling operations shall not be conducted unless approved by the AHJ and the owner of the property on which the fueling will occur. [**30A:**14.2.1]

42.12.2.2 Mobile fueling operations shall occur only at approved locations. [**30A:**14.2.2]

42.12.2.3* Safety and Emergency Response Plan.

42.12.2.3.1 The AHJ shall be permitted to require a safety and emergency response plan for locations where mobile fueling is approved. [**30A:**14.2.3.1]

42.12.2.3.2 When required, the safety and emergency response plan shall be available on each mobile fueling vehicle. [**30A:**14.2.3.2]

42.12.2.4 Training.

42.12.2.4.1* Mobile fueling vehicle operators shall possess evidence of training on proper fueling procedures and the safety and emergency response plan. [**30A:**14.2.4.1]

42.12.2.4.2 The vehicle operator training shall be approved by the AHJ. [**30A:**14.2.4.2]

42.12.2.5 Mobile fueling shall not take place within 25 ft (7.6 m) of buildings, property lines, or combustible storage. [**30A:**14.2.5]

42.12.2.6 An approved storm drain cover or equivalent method that will prevent any fuel from reaching the drain shall be used when mobile fueling occurs within 25 ft (7.6 m) of a storm drain. [**30A:**14.2.6]

Δ **42.12.2.7 Buildings and Parking Structures.** Mobile fueling operations shall be prohibited in buildings and in parking structures. [**30A:**14.2.7]

N **42.12.2.7.1*** Mobile fueling operations shall be permitted in open parking structures when approved. [**30A:**14.2.7.1]

N **42.12.2.7.2*** When approved, mobile fueling operations conducted in above-ground open parking structures shall comply with 42.12.2.7.2.1 through 42.12.2.7.2.16 in addition to the other requirements of Section 42.12. [**30A:**14.2.7.2]

N **42.12.2.7.2.1*** Open parking structures shall meet the definition in the jurisdiction's adopted building code. [**30A:**14.2.7.2.1]

N **42.12.2.7.2.2** Mobile fueling shall not occur in parking garages where other occupancies exist above or below. [**30A:**14.2.7.2.2]

N **42.12.2.7.2.3** Mobile fueling operations shall not occur within 25 ft (7.6 m) of attached occupancies. [**30A:**14.2.7.2.3]

N **42.12.2.7.2.4** Means shall be provided to prevent liquid spills from leaving the dispensing area. [**30A:**14.2.7.2.4]

N **42.12.2.7.2.5** The attendant shall remain at the dispensing nozzle during fuel flow. [**30A:**14.2.7.2.5]

N **42.12.2.7.2.6** The mobile refueling vehicle shall not be parked in the parking structure when not performing a dispensing event. [**30A:**14.2.7.2.6]

N **42.12.2.7.2.7** Mobile fueling vehicles shall comply with 42.12.3. [**30A:**14.2.7.2.7]

N **42.12.2.7.2.8** Operations shall comply with 42.12.4. [**30A:**14.2.7.2.8]

N **42.12.2.7.2.9*** Mobile fueling vehicles shall be positioned in a manner to preclude vehicles from driving over the dispensing hose. [**30A:**14.2.7.2.9]

N **42.12.2.7.2.10** Fuel dispensing shall occur at street level. [**30A:**14.2.7.2.10]

N **42.12.2.7.2.11** The mobile refueling vehicle and the vehicle being fueled shall both be on the same level within the structure. [**30A:**14.2.7.2.11]

N **42.12.2.7.2.12*** Fuel dispensing shall occur no more than 50 ft (15 m) from openings in exterior walls where the openings are accessible to firefighting apparatus. [**30A:**14.2.7.2.12]

N **(A)** Openings in 42.12.2.7.2.12 that are exterior walls shall be adjacent to roads, ways, or public streets. [**30A:**14.2.7.2.12.1]

N **42.12.2.7.2.13** The simultaneous fueling of more than one vehicle from a single mobile fueling vehicle shall be prohibited. [**30A:**14.2.7.2.13]

N **42.12.2.7.2.14** Operators shall place a drip pan or absorbent pad under each fuel fill opening prior to and during dispensing operations. [**30A:**14.2.7.2.14]

N **(A)** Drip pans and absorbent pads shall be safely removed from the site and handled and disposed of in accordance with local and state requirements. [**30A:**14.2.7.2.14.1]

N **42.12.2.7.2.15** Mobile fueling vehicles shall be equipped with a listed shutoff valve assembly and a fuel limit switch set to a maximum of 15 gal (57 L). [**30A:**14.2.7.2.15]

N **42.12.2.7.2.16** The AHJ shall be authorized to specify time-of-day and day-of-week limitations on mobile fueling operations. [**30A:**14.2.7.2.16]

42.12.2.8 Mobile fueling operations shall be prohibited on public streets and public ways unless approved by the AHJ. [**30A:**14.2.8]

42.12.2.9* Where approved by the AHJ, mobile fueling operations conducted on public streets and public ways shall comply with Section 42.12 and the following:

(1) The dispensing hose shall not cross an active traffic lane or vehicle pathway.

(2)* The mobile fueling vehicle and the dispensing hose shall not encumber a marked pedestrian crossing or bicycle lane or obstruct a pedestrian walkway.
(3) The mobile fueling vehicle's hazard warning signal and flashers shall be activated during dispensing operations.
(4) The AHJ shall be authorized to specify time-of-day and day-of-week limitations on mobile fueling operations.
[**30A:**14.2.9]

42.12.3 Mobile Fueling Vehicles and Equipment.

Δ **42.12.3.1*** Mobile fueling vehicles shall comply with all applicable local, state, and federal requirements and shall be one of the following:

(1) A tank vehicle complying with NFPA 385 with chassis-mounted tanks that do not exceed an aggregate capacity of 1600 gal (7274 L)
(2) A vehicle with chassis-mounted tanks, each of which does not exceed 110 gal (415 L), that does not exceed an aggregate capacity of 1200 gal (4542 L)
(3) A vehicle that carries a maximum of 60 gal (227 L) of motor fuel in listed metal safety cans not to exceed 5.3 gal (20 L) in capacity

[**30A:**14.3.1]

42.12.3.2 Dispensing hose assemblies shall be listed and the hose shall not exceed 50 ft (15 m) in length. [**30A:**14.3.2]

42.12.3.3 A listed breakaway device shall be provided at the nozzle. [**30A:**14.3.3]

42.12.3.4 Dispensing nozzles shall be a listed, automatic closing–type with a latch-open device. [**30A:**14.3.4]

42.12.3.5 A listed fuel shutoff switch and a listed shutoff valve assembly shall be provided on the delivery vehicle. [**30A:**14.3.5]

42.12.3.6 The pump shall be listed to UL 79, *Power-Operated Pumps for Petroleum Dispensing Products*. [**30A:**14.3.6]

42.12.3.7 The meter shall be listed to UL 25, *Meters for Flammable and Combustible Liquids and LP-Gas*. [**30A:**14.3.7]

42.12.3.8 Mobile fueling vehicles shall be provided with at least one portable fire extinguisher selected, installed, inspected, and maintained as required by NFPA 10. [**30A:**14.3.8]

42.12.3.8.1 The extinguisher shall be a minimum 10 lb (4.54 kg) ABC dry chemical agent–type and shall also be rated with an agent discharge rate of 1 lb/sec (0.45 kg/sec) or greater. [**30A:**14.3.8.1]

42.12.3.9 Mobile fueling vehicles shall be provided with a minimum 5 gal (18.9 L) spill kit designed to promptly and safely mitigate and dispose of leakage or spills. [**30A:**14.3.9]

42.12.3.10 NO SMOKING signs shall be prominently displayed on the mobile fueling vehicle. [**30A:**14.3.10]

42.12.3.11 The mobile fueling vehicles shall be fitted with 360-degree retro reflective tape or markings in compliance with 49 CFR 571.108, "*Lamps, Reflective Devices, and Associated Equipment*." [**30A:**14.3.11]

42.12.4 Operations.

Δ **42.12.4.1** Nighttime deliveries shall be made only in areas deemed adequately lighted by the AHJ. The source of lighting shall be permitted to originate from the mobile fueling vehicle. [**30A:**14.4.1]

42.12.4.2 The mobile fueling vehicle's hazard warning signal and flashers shall be activated during dispensing operations. [**30A:**14.4.2]

42.12.4.3 Safety cones or barriers shall be employed to protect the vehicle fueling area. [**30A:**14.4.3]

42.12.4.4 Expansion space shall be left in each motor vehicle fuel tank to prevent overflow in the event of temperature increase. [**30A:**14.4.4]

42.12.4.5* A means for bonding the mobile fueling vehicle to the motor vehicle shall be provided. Such bonding means shall be employed during fueling operations. [**30A:**14.4.5]

42.12.4.6 Sources of ignition shall be controlled in accordance with 42.7.2.6.1. [**30A:**14.4.6]

42.12.4.7 Mobile fueling vehicles shall be constantly attended during fueling operations. [**30A:**14.4.7]

42.12.4.8 Mobile fueling vehicles shall not obstruct emergency vehicle access roads. [**30A:**14.4.8]

42.12.4.9 Mobile fueling vehicles shall be positioned in a manner to preclude traffic from driving over the dispensing hose. [**30A:**14.4.9]

42.12.4.10 Inspection Program.

42.12.4.10.1 The mobile fueling operator shall have in place an approved vehicle inspection program. [**30A:**14.4.10.1]

42.12.4.10.2 Vehicles shall be inspected prior to each shift with records available to the AHJ upon request. [**30A:**14.4.10.2]

42.12.4.11 Operations Using Metal Safety Cans.

42.12.4.11.1 All metal safety cans shall be listed. [**30A:**14.4.11.1]

42.12.4.11.2 Metal safety cans shall be secured to the mobile fueling vehicle except when in use. [**30A:**14.4.11.2]

42.12.4.11.3 The AHJ shall be permitted to require additional measures in the handling of approved metal safety cans for refueling. [**30A:**14.4.11.3]

Chapter 43 Spraying, Dipping, and Coating Using Flammable or Combustible Materials

43.1 Application.

43.1.1* Operations involving the spray application of flammable and combustible materials shall comply with NFPA 33 and Section 43.1.

43.1.1.1* Section 43.1 shall apply to the spray application of flammable or combustible materials, as herein defined, either continuously or intermittently by any of the following methods:

(1) Compressed air atomization
(2) Airless or hydraulic atomization
(3) Electrostatic application methods
(4) Other means of atomized application

[**33**:1.1.1]

43.1.1.2 Section 43.1 shall also apply to the application of flammable or combustible materials, as herein defined, either continuously or intermittently by any of the following methods:

(1) Fluidized bed application methods
(2) Electrostatic fluidized bed application methods
(3) Other means of fluidized application

[**33**:1.1.2]

43.1.1.3 Section 43.1 shall also apply to the spray application of water-borne, water-based, and water-reducible materials that contain ignitible (flammable or combustible) liquids or that produce combustible deposits or residues. [**33**:1.1.3]

43.1.1.4 Section 43.1 shall apply to spray application processes or operations that are conducted indoors or outdoors within temporary membrane enclosures. [**33**:1.1.5]

N **43.1.1.5** Use of inflatable enclosures for flammable or combustible spray applications shall be prohibited.

43.1.1.6 Section 43.1 shall not apply to the following:

(1)* Spray operations that use less than 1 L (33.8 fl oz) of ignitible (flammable or combustible) liquid in any 8-hour period [**33**:1.1.4]
(2)* Spray application processes or operations that are conducted outdoors [**33**:1.1.6]
(3)* Use of portable spraying equipment that is not used repeatedly in the same location [**33**:1.1.7]
(4) Use of aerosol products in containers up to and including 1 L (33.8 oz) capacity that are not used repeatedly in the same location *[See A.43.1.1.6(3)]* [**33**:1.1.8]
(5) Spray application of noncombustible materials [**33**:1.1.9]
(6) Hazards of toxicity or to industrial health and hygiene [**33**:1.1.10]

Δ **43.1.1.7 Permits.**

N **43.1.1.7.1** Permits shall be required in accordance with this chapter and Table 1.13.8(a) through Table 1.13.8(d).

N **43.1.1.7.2** Permits, where required, shall comply with Section 1.13.

43.1.2 General Requirements.

43.1.2.1* **Location of Spray Application Operations.** Spray application operations and processes shall be located in industrial occupancies as defined by *NFPA 5000* and shall be confined to spray booths, spray rooms, spray areas, or in temporary membrane enclosures as defined in this *Code*. [**33**:4.1]

Δ **43.1.2.2*** **Locations in Other Occupancies.** Spray application operations and processes shall not be conducted in any building that is classified as an assembly, an educational, a day care, a health care, an ambulatory health care, a detention/correctional, a residential, a mercantile, a business, or a storage occupancy, unless the following requirements are met:

(1) The spraying is located in a room that is separated both vertically and horizontally from all surrounding areas by construction having a fire resistance rating of not less than 2 hours or in a spray room *(see 43.1.3.2)*.
(2) The room is protected by an approved automatic sprinkler system designed and installed in accordance with Section 13.3.

[**33**:4.1.1]

43.1.2.3* **Separation.** Spray application operations shall be separated from other operations, materials, or occupancies by location, fire barrier walls, and horizontal assemblies in accordance with *NFPA 5000*, or other means acceptable to the AHJ. [**33**:4.2]

43.1.3 Construction and Design of Spray Areas, Spray Rooms, and Spray Booths.

43.1.3.1* **Spray Areas.**

43.1.3.1.1 Walls, doors, and ceilings that intersect or enclose a spray area shall be both of the following:

(1) Constructed of noncombustible or limited-combustible materials or assemblies
(2) Securely and rigidly mounted or fastened

[**33**:5.1.1]

43.1.3.1.1.1 The interior surfaces of the spray area shall be smooth, designed and installed to prevent pockets that can trap residues, and designed to facilitate ventilation and cleaning. [**33**:5.1.1.1]

43.1.3.1.1.2 Air intake filters that are a part of a wall or ceiling assembly shall be listed in accordance with UL 900, *Air Filter Units*. [**33**:5.1.1.2]

43.1.3.1.2 The floor of the spray area shall be constructed of noncombustible material, limited-combustible material, or combustible material that is completely covered by noncombustible material. [**33**:5.1.2]

43.1.3.1.3 Aluminum shall not be used for structural support members, walls, or ceilings that enclose a spray area or for ventilation ductwork to or from an enclosed spray area unless otherwise permitted by 43.1.3.1.3.1. [**33**:5.1.3]

43.1.3.1.3.1 Aluminum shall be permitted to be used for interior components, such as platforms, spray apparatus components, and other ancillary devices. [**33**:5.1.3.1]

43.1.3.1.4 Enclosed spray areas shall be provided with means of egress that meet the applicable requirements of Chapter 40 of NFPA *101*. [**33**:5.1.4]

43.1.3.2 Spray Rooms. In addition to the requirements of 43.1.3.1, spray rooms shall be constructed of and separated vertically and horizontally from all surrounding areas by construction assemblies that have a fire resistance rating of not less than 2 hours. [**33**:5.2]

43.1.3.3 Spray Booths.

43.1.3.3.1 Spray booths shall meet the requirements of 43.1.3.1 and 43.1.3.3. [**33**:5.3.1]

43.1.3.3.2 If walls or ceiling assemblies are constructed of sheet metal, single-skin assemblies shall be no thinner than 0.0478 in. (1.2 mm), and each sheet of double-skin assemblies shall be no thinner than 0.0359 in. (0.9 mm). [**33**:5.3.2]

43.1.3.3.3 Structural sections of spray booths shall be permitted to be sealed with a caulk or sealant to minimize air leakage. [**33**:5.3.3]

Δ **43.1.3.3.4** Spray booths that are used exclusively for powder coating shall meet the requirements of Chapter 15 of NFPA 33. [**33**:5.3.4.1]

N **43.1.3.3.5** Spray booths that are used exclusively for powder coating shall be permitted to be constructed of fire-retardant combustible materials where approved by the authority having jurisdiction. [**33**:5.3.4.2]

43.1.3.3.5.1 Listed spray booth assemblies that are constructed of other materials shall be permitted. [**33**:5.3.4.3]

Δ **43.1.3.3.6** Spray application operations and processes that involve the use of finishing materials containing nitrocellulose shall be confined to water-wash spray booths as defined in NFPA 33 unless otherwise specified in 43.1.3.3.5.1. [**33**:5.3.5]

43.1.3.3.6.1 Spray application of finishing materials containing nitrocellulose shall be permitted in a dry-type spray booth provided that residue is removed from all baffle plates at least daily and all filters are changed at least daily. [**33**:5.3.5.1]

43.1.3.4 Conveyor Openings.
Conveyor openings that are necessary for transporting or moving work into and out of the spray area shall be as small as practical. [**33**:5.4]

Δ **43.1.3.5 Separation from Other Occupancies.**

N **43.1.3.5.1** Spray booths shall be separated from other operations by a minimum distance of 3 ft (915 mm) or by a partition, wall, or floor/ceiling assembly having a minimum fire resistance rating of 1 hour.

N **43.1.3.5.2** Multiple connected spray booths shall not be considered as "other operations" except as provided for in Section 13.3 of NFPA 33. [**33**:5.5.2]

N **43.1.3.5.3** Multiple spray booths connected by openings for moving the workpiece or that share a common wall shall not be considered as "other operations." [**33**:5.5.3]

N **43.1.3.5.4** For spray booths adjacent to rooms or equipment used for drying, curing or fusing, the separation requirements of Section 13.7 of NFPA 33 shall apply. [**33**:5.5.4]

43.1.3.5.5 Spray booths shall be installed so that all parts of the booth are readily accessible for cleaning. [**33**:5.5.5]

43.1.3.5.6 A clear space of not less than 3 ft (915 mm) shall be both of the following:

(1) Maintained on all sides and above the spray booth
(2) Kept free of any storage or combustible construction

[**33**:5.5.6]

43.1.3.5.6.1 The requirement in 43.1.3.5.6 shall not prohibit locating a spray booth closer than 3 ft (915 mm) to or directly against an interior partition, wall, or floor/ceiling assembly that has a fire resistance rating of not less than 1 hour, provided the spray booth can be maintained and cleaned. [**33**:5.5.6.1]

43.1.3.5.6.2 The requirement in 43.1.3.5.6 shall not prohibit locating a spray booth closer than 3 ft (915 mm) to an exterior wall or a roof assembly, provided the wall or roof is constructed of noncombustible material and provided the spray booth can be maintained and cleaned. [**33**:5.5.6.2]

43.1.3.6 Illumination and Observation Panels.

43.1.3.6.1 Panels for luminaires or observation shall be of heat-treated glass, laminated glass, wired glass, or hammered-wired glass and shall be sealed to confine vapors, mists, residues, dusts, and deposits to the spray area. [**33**:5.6.1]

Δ **43.1.3.6.1.1** Listed spray booth assemblies that have observation panels constructed of other materials shall be permitted. [**33**:5.6.1.1]

Δ **43.1.3.6.2** Panels shall be separated from the luminaire to prevent the surface temperature of the panel from exceeding 221°F (105°C). [**33**:5.6.2]

43.1.3.6.3 The panel frame and method of attachment shall be designed to not fail under fire exposure before the observation panel fails. [**33**:5.6.3]

43.1.3.6.4 Observation panels for spray booths that are used exclusively for powder coating processes shall be permitted to be constructed of fire-resistant combustible materials. [**33**:5.6.4]

43.1.3.7 Ventilation.
Spray areas that are equipped with ventilation distribution, baffle plates, or dry overspray collection filters shall meet the requirements of 43.1.3.7.1 through 43.1.3.7.5. [**33**:5.7]

43.1.3.7.1 Distribution plates or baffles shall be constructed of noncombustible materials and shall be readily removable or accessible for cleaning on both sides. [**33**:5.7.1]

43.1.3.7.2 Filters shall not be used when applying materials known to be highly susceptible to spontaneous heating or spontaneous ignition. [**33**:5.7.2]

43.1.3.7.3 Supports and holders for filters shall be constructed of noncombustible materials. [**33**:5.7.3]

43.1.3.7.4 Overspray collection filters shall be readily removable or accessible for cleaning or replacement. [**33**:5.7.4]

Δ **43.1.3.7.5** Filters shall not be alternately used for different types of coating materials if the combination of the materials might result in spontaneous heating or ignition. *(See also 43.1.8.8.)* [**33**:5.7.5]

43.1.4 Electrical and Other Sources of Ignition.

43.1.4.1* General.

43.1.4.1.1 Electrical wiring and utilization equipment shall meet all applicable requirements of Articles 500, 501, 502, 505, and 516 of *NFPA 70* and all applicable requirements of this chapter. [**33**:6.2.1]

43.1.4.1.1.1 Powered vehicles shall meet the requirements of 43.1.4.9. [**33**:6.2.1.1]

43.1.4.1.1.2 Resin application operations shall meet the requirements of Chapter 17 of NFPA 33. [**33**:6.2.1.2]

Δ **43.1.4.1.2*** For the purposes of this *Code,* the Zone system of electrical area classification shall be applied as follows:

(1) The inside of open or closed containers or vessels shall be considered a Zone 0 location.
(2) A Class I, Division 1 location shall be permitted to be alternatively classified as a Zone 1 location.
(3) A Class I, Division 2 location shall be permitted to be alternatively classified as a Zone 2 location.
(4) A Class II, Division 1 location shall be permitted to be alternatively classified as a Zone 21 location.
(5) A Class II, Division 2 location shall be permitted to be alternatively classified as a Zone 22 location.

[**33**:6.2.2]

43.1.4.1.3 For the purposes of electrical area classification, the Division system and the Zone system shall not be intermixed for any given source of release. [**33**:6.2.3]

Δ **43.1.4.1.4** In instances of areas within the same facility classified separately, Zone 2 locations shall be permitted to abut, but not overlap, Class I, Division 2 locations. Zone 0 or Zone 1 locations shall not abut Class I, Division 1 or Division 2 locations. [**33**:6.2.4]

43.1.4.1.5* Open flames, spark-producing equipment or processes, and equipment whose exposed surfaces exceed the autoignition temperature of the material being sprayed shall not be located in a spray area or in any surrounding area that is classified as Division 2, Zone 2, or Zone 22. [**33**:6.2.5]

43.1.4.1.5.1 This requirement shall not apply to drying, curing, or fusing apparatus covered by Section 43.4. [**33**:6.2.5.1]

43.1.4.1.6* Any utilization equipment or apparatus that is capable of producing sparks or particles of hot metal and that is located above or adjacent to either the spray area or the surrounding Division 2, Zone 2, or Zone 22 areas shall be of the totally enclosed type or shall be constructed to prevent the escape of sparks or particles of hot metal. [**33**:6.2.6]

43.1.4.2 Electrical Area Classification.

43.1.4.2.1* Class I Locations. A Class I location shall be any location where a flammable gas or vapor is present or might be present in the air in quantities sufficient to produce an explosive or ignitable mixture. [**33**:6.3.1]

Δ **43.1.4.2.1.1* Class I, Division 1 Locations.** As defined in 500.5(B)(1) of *NFPA 70*, a Class I, Division 1 location shall be any location where one of the following conditions exists:

(1) An ignitible concentration of flammable gas or vapor can exist under normal operating conditions.
(2) An ignitible concentration of flammable gas or vapor can exist frequently because of repair or maintenance operations or because of leakage.
(3) Breakdown or faulty operation of equipment or processes might release an ignitible concentration of flammable gas or vapor and might also cause simultaneous failure of electrical equipment in such a way as to directly cause the electrical equipment to become a source of ignition.

[**33**:6.3.1.1]

Δ **43.1.4.2.1.2* Class I, Division 2 Locations.** As defined in 500.5(B)(2) of *NFPA 70*, a Class I, Division 2 location shall be any location where one of the following conditions exists:

(1) A flammable gas or a Class I liquid [FP < 100°F (37.8°C)] is handled, processed, or used, but any flammable gas, vapor, or liquid is confined within a closed container or a closed system from which it can escape only in the case of an accidental rupture or breakdown of the container or system or in case of abnormal operation of the equipment.
(2) An ignitible concentration of flammable gas or vapor is normally prevented by positive mechanical ventilation but might exist because of failure or abnormal operation of the ventilating equipment.
(3) An ignitible concentration of flammable gas or vapor might occasionally be transmitted from an adjacent Class I, Division 1 location, unless such transmission is prevented by positive pressure ventilation from a source of clean air and effective safeguards against ventilation failure are provided.

[**33**:6.3.1.2]

Δ **43.1.4.2.1.3* Zone 0 Locations.** As defined in 505.5(B)(1) of *NFPA 70*, a Zone 0 location shall be any location where an ignitible concentration of flammable gas or vapor is present either continuously or for long periods of time. [**33**:6.3.1.3]

Δ **43.1.4.2.1.4* Zone 1 Locations.** As defined in 505.5(B)(2) of *NFPA 70*, a Zone 1 location shall be any location where one of the following conditions exists:

(1) An ignitible concentration of flammable gas or vapor is likely to exist under normal operating conditions.
(2) An ignitible concentration of flammable gas or vapor might exist frequently because of repair or maintenance operations or because of leakage.
(3) Breakdown or faulty operation of equipment or processes might release an ignitible concentration of flammable gas or vapor and might also cause simultaneous failure of electrical equipment in such a way as to directly cause the electrical equipment to become a source of ignition.
(4) An ignitible concentration of flammable gas or vapor might occasionally be transmitted from an adjacent Zone 0 location, unless such transmission is prevented by positive pressure ventilation from a source of clean air and effective safeguards against ventilation failure are provided.

[**33**:6.3.1.4]

Δ **43.1.4.2.1.5 Zone 2 Locations.** As defined in 505.5(B)(3) of *NFPA 70*, a Zone 2 location shall be any location where one of the following conditions exists:

(1) An ignitible concentration of a flammable gas or vapor is not likely to exist under normal operating conditions, and if an ignitible concentration does exist, it will only exist for a short period of time.
(2) A flammable gas or a Class I liquid [FP < 100°F (37.8°C)] is handled, processed, or used, but any flammable gas, vapor, or liquid is confined within a closed container or a closed system from which it can escape only in the case of an accidental rupture or breakdown of the container or system or in the case of abnormal operation of the equipment.
(3) An ignitible concentration of flammable gas or vapor is normally prevented by positive mechanical ventilation but might exist because of failure or abnormal operation of the ventilating equipment.
(4) An ignitible concentration of flammable gas or vapor might occasionally be transmitted from an adjacent Zone

1 location, unless such transmission is prevented by positive pressure ventilation from a source of clean air and effective safeguards against ventilation failure are provided. *(See also A.43.1.4.2.1.2.)* [**33**:6.3.1.5]

43.1.4.2.2 Class II Locations. A Class II location shall be any location that might be hazardous because of the presence of a combustible dust. [**33**:6.3.2]

Δ **43.1.4.2.2.1* Class II, Division 1 Locations.** As defined in 500.5(C)(1) of *NFPA 70*, a Class II, Division 1 location shall be any location where one of the following conditions exists:

(1) Combustible dust is in the air in quantities sufficient to produce explosive or ignitible mixtures under normal operating conditions.
(2) Mechanical failure or abnormal operation of machinery or equipment might cause an explosive or ignitible mixture of combustible dust in air and might also provide a source of ignition through simultaneous failure of electrical equipment, operation of protection devices, or from other causes.
(3) Group E combustible dusts might be present in quantities sufficient to be hazardous.

[**33**:6.3.2.1]

Δ **43.1.4.2.2.2* Class II, Division 2 Locations.** As defined in 500.5(C)(2) of *NFPA 70*, a Class II, Division 2 location shall be a location in which one of the following conditions exists:

(1) Combustible dust due to abnormal operations might be present in the air in quantities sufficient to produce explosive or ignitible mixtures.
(2) Combustible dust accumulations are present but are normally insufficient to interfere with the normal operation of electrical equipment or other apparatus, but could as a result of infrequent malfunctioning of handling or processing equipment become suspended in the air.
(3) Combustible dust accumulations on, in, or in the vicinity of the electrical equipment could be sufficient to interfere with the safe dissipation of heat from electrical equipment, or could be ignitible by abnormal operation or failure of electrical equipment.

[**33**:6.3.2.2]

Δ **43.1.4.2.2.3* Zone 20.** As defined in 506.5(B)(1) of *NFPA 70*, a Zone 20 location shall be any location where one of the following conditions exists:

(1) An ignitible concentration of combustible dust is present continuously.
(2) An ignitible concentration of combustible dust is present for long periods of time.

[**33**:6.3.2.3]

Δ **43.1.4.2.2.4* Zone 21.** As defined in 506.5(B)(2) of *NFPA 70*, a Zone 21 location shall be any location where one of the following conditions exists:

(1) An ignitible concentration of combustible dust is likely to exist occasionally under normal operating conditions.
(2) An ignitible concentration of combustible dust might exist frequently because of repair or maintenance operations or because of leakage.
(3) Equipment is operated or processes are carried on of such a nature that equipment breakdown or faulty operations could result in the release of an ignitible concentration of combustible dust and also cause simultaneous failure of electrical equipment in a mode to cause the electrical equipment to become a source of ignition.
(4) An ignitible concentration of combustible dust could be communicated from an adjacent Zone 20 location, unless communication is prevented by adequate positive pressure ventilation from a source of clean air and effective safeguards against ventilation failure are provided.

[**33**:6.3.2.4]

Δ **43.1.4.2.2.5* Zone 22.** As defined in 506.5(B)(3) of *NFPA 70*, a Zone 22 location shall be any location where one of the following conditions exists:

(1) An ignitible concentration of combustible dust is not likely to occur in normal operation, and if it does occur, will only persist for a short period.
(2) A combustible dust is handled, processed, or used, but the dust is normally confined within closed containers or closed systems from which it can escape only as a result of the abnormal operation of the equipment with which the dust is handled, processed, or used.
(3) An ignitible concentration of combustible dust could be communicated from an adjacent Zone 21 location, unless communication is prevented by adequate positive pressure ventilation from a source of clean air and effective safeguards against ventilation failure are provided.

[**33**:6.3.2.5]

43.1.4.3 Electrical Devices in Spray Areas.

Δ **43.1.4.3.1** The spray area as defined in 3.3.17.11 shall be Class I, Division 1; Zone 1; Class II, Division 1; or Zone 21, whichever is applicable. [**33**:6.4.1]

Δ **43.1.4.3.2** Electrical wiring and utilization equipment that is located in the spray area and is not subject to deposits of combustible residues shall be suitable for Class I, Division 1; Zone 1; Class II, Division 1; or Zone 21 locations, whichever is applicable. [**33**:6.4.2]

Δ **43.1.4.3.3*** Electrical wiring and utilization equipment that is located in the spray area and is subject to deposits of combustible residues shall be listed for such exposure and shall be suitable for Class I, Division 1; Zone 1; Class II, Division 1; or Zone 21 locations, whichever is applicable. [**33**:6.4.3]

43.1.4.4 Electrical Devices in Areas Adjacent to or Connected to Spray Areas. Electrical wiring and utilization equipment located in areas adjacent to or connected to the spray area, including but not limited to vestibules and tunnels, shall be classified in accordance with 43.1.4.4.1 through 43.1.4.4.5. [**33**:6.5]

Δ **43.1.4.4.1** Electrical wiring and utilization equipment located outside, but within 20 ft (6100 mm) horizontally and 10 ft (3050 mm) vertically, of an unenclosed spray area and not separated from the spray area by partitions extending to the boundaries of the area designated as Division 2, Zone 2; or Zone 22 in Figure 43.1.4.4.1 shall be suitable for Class I, Division 2; Zone 2; Class II, Division 2; or Zone 22 locations, whichever is applicable. [**33**:6.5.1]

Δ **43.1.4.4.2** If spray application operations are conducted within a closed-top, open-face or open-front booth or room, as shown in Figure 43.1.4.4.2(a) or Figure 43.1.4.4.2(b), any electrical wiring or utilization equipment located outside the booth or room but within 3 ft (915 mm) of any opening shall be suitable for Class I, Division 2; Zone 2; Class II, Division 2; or Zone 22 locations, whichever is applicable. [**33**:6.5.2]

Δ **43.1.4.4.3** If spray application operations are conducted within an open-top booth, any electrical wiring or utilization equipment located within the space 3 ft (915 mm) vertically from the top of the booth shall be suitable for Class I, Division 2; Zone 2; Class II, Division 2; or Zone 22 locations, whichever is applicable. In addition, any electrical wiring or utilization equipment located within 3 ft (915 mm) in all directions of openings other than the open top also shall be suitable for Class I, Division 2; Zone 2; Class II, Division 2; or Zone 22 locations, whichever is applicable. [**33**:6.5.3]

Δ **43.1.4.4.4** If spray application operations are confined to an enclosed spray booth or room, electrical area classification shall be as follows:

(1) The area within 3 ft (915 mm) of any opening shall be classified as Class I, Division 2; Zone 2; Class II, Division 2; or Zone 22 locations, whichever is applicable, as shown in Figure 43.1.4.4.4.

(2)* Where automated spray application equipment is used, the area outside the access doors shall be unclassified provided the door interlock prevents the spray application operations when the door is open.

(3) Where exhaust air is recirculated and all requirements of 43.1.5.5 are met, both of the following shall apply:

   (a) The interior of any recirculation path downstream of the recirculation particulate filter up to and including the air supply plenum shall be classified as Class I, Division 2; Zone 2; Class II, Division 2; or Zone 22 locations, whichever is applicable.

   (b) The interior of fresh air supply ducts shall be unclassified.

(4) Where exhaust air is not recirculated, the interior of fresh air supply ducts and fresh air supply plenums shall be unclassified. [**33**:6.5.4]

Δ **FIGURE 43.1.4.4.1** Electrical Area Classification for Unenclosed Spray Areas. [**33**:Figure 6.5.1]

Δ **FIGURE 43.1.4.4.2(a)** Class I, Division 2; Zone 2; Class II, Division 2; or Zone 22 Locations Adjacent to an Open-Face or Open-Front Spray Booth or Spray Room. [**33**:Figure 6.5.2(a)]

FIGURE 43.1.4.4.2(b) Class II, Division 1; or Zone 21 Locations Inside Powder Coating Booth and On the Manual Spray Platforms. Class II, Division 2; or Zone 22 Locations Adjacent to Automatic Gun Openings and Outer Edge of the Manual Spray Platform for Powder Coating Booth. [**33**:Figure 6.5.2(b)]

FIGURE 43.1.4.4.4 Class I, Division 2; Zone 2; Class II, Division 2; or Zone 22 Locations Adjacent to an Enclosed Spray Booth or Spray Room. [33:Figure 6.5.4]

43.1.4.4.5* Open containers, supply containers, waste containers, spray gun cleaners, and solvent distillation units that contain Class I liquids shall be located in areas ventilated in accordance with applicable requirements of 43.1.5. [33:6.5.5]

43.1.4.4.5.1 Electrical area classification shall be as follows:

(1) The area within 3 ft (915 mm) in all directions from any such container or equipment and extending to the floor or grade level shall be classified as Class I, Division 1 or Zone 1, whichever is applicable.
(2) The area extending 2 ft (610 mm) beyond the Division 1 or Zone 1 location shall be classified as Class I, Division 2 or Zone 2, whichever is applicable.
(3) The area extending 5 ft (1525 mm) horizontally beyond the area described in 43.1.4.4.5.1(2) up to a height of 18 in. (460 mm) above the floor or grade level shall be classified as Class I, Division 2 or Zone 2, whichever is applicable.
(4) The area inside any tank or container shall be classified as Class I, Division 1 or Zone 0, whichever is applicable.

[33:6.5.5.1]

43.1.4.4.5.2 Electrical wiring and utilization equipment installed in these areas shall be suitable for the location, as shown in Figure 43.1.4.4.5.2. [33:6.5.5.2]

43.1.4.5 Illumination.

43.1.4.5.1 Luminaires, like that shown in Figure 43.1.4.5.1, that are outside any classified area and are separated from the spray area by glass panels that meet the requirements of 43.1.3.6 shall not be required to be listed for use in hazardous (classified) locations. [33:6.6.1.1]

N **43.1.4.5.2** Such luminaires as stated in 43.1.4.5.1 shall be capable of being serviced from outside the spray area. [33:6.6.1.2]

43.1.4.5.3 Luminaires, like that shown in Figure 43.1.4.5.1, that are separated from the spray area by glass panels that meet the requirements of 43.1.3.6; and that are located within a Class I, Division 2; a Zone 2; a Class II, Division 2; or a Zone 22 location shall be listed for such locations. [33:6.6.2.1]

N **43.1.4.5.4** Such luminaires as stated in 43.1.4.5.3 shall be serviced from outside the spray area. [33:6.6.2.2]

43.1.4.5.5 Luminaires, like that shown in Figure 43.1.4.5.5, that are an integral part of the walls or ceiling of a spray area shall be permitted to be separated from the spray area by glass panels that are an integral part of the luminaire. [33:6.6.3.1]

FIGURE 43.1.4.4.5.2 Electrical Area Classification for Class I Liquid Operations Around Open Containers, Supply Containers, Waste Containers, Spray Gun Cleaners, and Solvent Distillation Units. [33:Figure 6.5.5.2]

FIGURE 43.1.4.5.1 Example of a Luminaire Mounted Outside the Spray Area and Serviced from Outside the Spray Area. [33:Figure 6.6.1.1]

FIGURE 43.1.4.5.5 Examples of Luminaires That Are Integral Parts of the Spray Area and That Are Serviced from Inside the Spray Area. [33:Figure 6.6.3.1]

N **43.1.4.5.6** Such luminaires as stated in 43.1.4.5.5 shall be listed for the following:

(1) Use in Class I, Division 2; Zone 2; Class II, Division 2; or Zone 22 locations, whichever is applicable
(2) Accumulations of deposits of combustible residues
[**33:**6.6.3.2]

N **43.1.4.5.7** Such luminaires as stated in 43.1.4.5.5 shall be permitted to be serviced from inside the spray area. [**33:**6.6.3.3]

43.1.4.5.8 Luminaires that are located inside the spray area shall meet the requirements of 43.1.4.3 and 43.1.4.6. [**33:**6.6.4]

43.1.4.6* Static Electricity. All electrically conductive objects in the spray area, except those objects required by the process to be at high voltage, shall be electrically connected to ground with a resistance of not more than 1 megohm (10^6 ohms). This requirement shall apply to containers of coating material, wash cans, guards, hose connectors, brackets, and any other electrically conductive objects or devices in the area. This requirement shall also apply to any personnel who enter the spray area. [**33:**6.7]

Δ **43.1.4.7* Flexible Power Cords.** For automated equipment and robotic equipment, flexible power cords shall be permitted to be used in hazardous (classified) locations and to be connected to the fixed part of an electrical circuit provided they meet all of the following conditions:

(1) They are listed for extra-hard usage.
(2) They are equipped with a grounding conductor that meets the requirements of Section 400.2 of *NFPA 70*.
(3) They are connected to terminals or conductors in an approved manner.
(4) They are supported by a positive mechanical clamp in such a manner that enables a cord to be readily replaced and prevents strain at the cord connections within the terminal enclosure.
(5)* They are provided with explosionproof seals for liquid applications or dusttight seals for powder applications where cords enter junction boxes, fittings, or enclosures.
(6) They are listed for deposits of combustible residue.
[**33:**6.8]

43.1.4.8 Portable Electric Luminaires. Portable electric luminaires used in spray areas shall meet the requirements of 43.1.4.3.3. [**33:**6.9]

43.1.4.9 Movement of Powered Vehicles. Powered vehicles shall be listed for the electrical area classification in which they are used, and unlisted powered vehicles shall not be moved into or out of a spray area or operated in a spray area unless the spray application operation or process is stopped and the ventilation system is maintained in operation. [**33:**6.10]

43.1.5 Ventilation.

43.1.5.1 General. Ventilating and exhaust systems shall be designed and installed in accordance with the applicable requirements of NFPA 91 except as amended by the requirements of 43.1.5. [**33:**7.1]

43.1.5.2 Performance Requirements. Each spray area shall be provided with mechanical ventilation that is capable of confining and removing vapors and mists to a safe location and is capable of confining and controlling combustible residues, dusts, and deposits. The concentration of the vapors and mists in the exhaust stream of the ventilation system shall not exceed 25 percent of the lower flammable limit. *(See Annex B of NFPA 33 for additional guidance on determining the lower flammable limit.)* [**33:**7.2]

43.1.5.2.1* Spray areas equipped with overspray collection filters shall have an effective means to ensure that the performance requirements of 43.1.5.2 are met. [**33:**7.2.1]

43.1.5.2.2 Powder Coating Systems. Powder coating systems also shall meet the requirements of Section 15.8 of NFPA 33. [**33:**7.2.2]

43.1.5.2.3 Mechanical ventilation shall be kept in operation at all times while spray operations are being conducted and for a sufficient time thereafter to allow the vapors from drying coated objects or material and residues to be exhausted. Where spray operations are conducted automatically without an attendant constantly on duty, the operating controls of the spray apparatus shall be arranged so that the spray apparatus cannot function unless the exhaust fans are operating. [**33:**7.2.3]

43.1.5.2.4 In confined spaces, where ventilation is not capable of meeting the requirements of 43.1.5.2, an inerting procedure shall be permitted to be used. Such procedures shall meet the applicable requirements of NFPA 69 and shall be acceptable to the AHJ. [**33:**7.2.4]

43.1.5.3* Make-Up Air. Clean make-up air shall be provided to compensate for the air exhausted from spray operations. The intake for this make-up air shall be located so that the air exhausted from spray operations is not recirculated. [**33:**7.3]

43.1.5.4 Routing of Exhaust Ducts. Air exhausted from liquid spray operations shall be conducted by ducts directly to the outside of the building. Exhaust ducts shall follow the shortest route to the point of discharge and shall meet the following conditions:

(1) Exhaust ducts shall not penetrate a fire wall or fire barrier wall.
(2) Exhaust discharge shall be directed away from any air intakes.
(3) Exhaust discharge point shall be at least 6 ft (1830 mm) from any exterior wall or roof.
(4) Exhaust discharge point shall be at least 10 ft (3048 mm) from openings into the building.
(5) Exhaust discharge point shall be at least 10 ft (3048 mm) above adjoining grade.
(6) Exhaust duct shall not discharge in the direction of any combustible construction that is within 25 ft (7625 mm) of the exhaust duct discharge point.
(7) Exhaust duct shall not discharge in the direction of any unprotected opening in any noncombustible or limited-combustible construction that is within 25 ft (7625 mm) of the exhaust duct discharge point.
(8) Exhaust duct shall not discharge in the direction of any exit discharge or public way that is within 25 ft (7625 mm) of the exhaust duct discharge point.

[**33:**7.4]

43.1.5.5* Recirculation of Exhaust. Air exhausted from spray areas shall not be recirculated unless all of the following requirements are met:

(1) Recirculation particulate filters as defined in this *Code* shall be used to remove particulates from the recirculated air.
(2) The concentration of vapors in the exhaust airstream shall not exceed 25 percent of the lower flammable limit.
(3) Listed equipment shall be used to monitor the concentration of vapors in all exhaust airstreams.
(4) The equipment specified in 43.1.5.5(3) shall initiate a local alarm and shall automatically shut down the spray operation if the concentration of any vapor in the exhaust airstream exceeds 25 percent of the lower flammable limit.
(5) All equipment installed to process and remove contaminants from the air exhausted from spray operations shall be approved by the AHJ.
(6)* For occupied spray areas where a portion of the exhaust air is recirculated within the spray area, toxicity and worker exposures shall be addressed.

[**33:**7.5]

N **43.1.5.6*** Where air recirculated from a spray application process is heated, the following requirements shall be met:

(1) The air heater shall be located downstream of the recirculation particulate filter and vapor concentration monitor.
(2) The air heating system shall not include an open flame.

(3) The surface temperature of the air heater shall not exceed 221°F (105°C).

[**33:**7.6]

43.1.5.7* Manifolding of Exhaust Ducts. Individual spray booths shall be separately ducted to the building exterior except as indicated in 43.1.5.7.1 or 43.1.5.7.2. [**33:**7.7]

Δ **43.1.5.7.1** Multiple spray booths whose combined frontal area does not exceed 18 ft² (1.7 m²) shall be permitted to be manifolded if the sprayed materials used will not react and cause ignition of the residue in the ducts. [**33:**7.7.1]

Δ **43.1.5.7.2** Where treatment of exhaust is necessary for air pollution control or for energy conservation, ducts shall be permitted to be manifolded if all of the following conditions are met:

(1) The sprayed materials used will not react and cause ignition of the residue in the ducts.
(2) No finishing materials containing nitrocellulose are used.
(3) An air-cleaning system is provided to reduce the amount of overspray carried into the duct manifold.
(4) Automatic sprinkler protection is provided at the junction of each booth exhaust with the manifold, in addition to the protection required by 43.1.7.
(5) The installation is approved by the AHJ.

[**33:**7.7.2]

43.1.5.8* Materials of Construction. Exhaust plenums and exhaust ducts and fasteners shall be constructed of steel, except as allowed in 43.1.5.8.1, 43.1.5.8.2, and 43.1.5.8.3. [**33:**7.8]

43.1.5.8.1 For spray booths used exclusively for powder coating, ducts shall be permitted to be constructed of fire-retardant combustible materials. [**33:**7.8.1]

43.1.5.8.2 Concrete shall be permitted to be used. The interior surfaces of the concrete exhaust plenum or exhaust duct shall be smooth and sealed to facilitate cleaning. [**33:**7.8.2]

43.1.5.8.3 Other materials of construction shall be permitted to be used in cases where the conveyed materials are not compatible with steel. [**33:**7.8.3]

43.1.5.9* Support of Exhaust Ducts. Exhaust ducts shall be supported to prevent collapse under fire conditions. [**33:**7.9]

43.1.5.9.1 Duct supports shall be designed to carry the weight of the duct system itself, plus the anticipated weight of any residues. If sprinkler protection is provided inside the duct system, then the duct supports also shall be designed to carry the anticipated weight of any accumulation of sprinkler discharge. [**33:**7.9.1]

43.1.5.9.2 Hangers and supports shall be fastened to the building or to the structure to minimize vibration and stress on the duct system. [**33:**7.9.2]

43.1.5.9.3 Hangers and supports shall be designed to allow for expansion and contraction. [**33:**7.9.3]

43.1.5.9.4 Exhaust ducts shall not use building walls, floors, ceilings, or roofs as component parts. [**33:**7.9.4]

43.1.5.9.5 The provisions of 43.1.5.9.4 shall not disallow the use of concrete exhaust plenums or exhaust ducts where some or all of the plenum or duct is part of the concrete floor. [**33:**7.9.5]

43.1.5.10 Exhaust Duct Access Openings. Exhaust ducts shall be provided with doors, panels, or other means to facilitate inspection, maintenance, cleaning, and access to fire protection devices. [**33**:7.10]

43.1.5.11 Exhaust Fans and Drives.

43.1.5.11.1 The rotating element of the exhaust fan shall be nonferrous, or the fan shall be constructed so that a shift of the impeller or shaft will not permit two ferrous parts of the fan to rub or strike. Necessary allowances shall be made for ordinary expansion and loading and to prevent contact between moving parts and the duct or fan housing. Fan blades shall be mounted on a shaft that shall maintain alignment even when the blades of the fan are heavily loaded. All bearings shall be of the self-lubricating type or shall be provided with accessible lubricating ports. [**33**:7.11.1]

43.1.5.11.2 Electric motors that drive exhaust fans shall not be placed inside any spray area unless they meet the provisions of 43.1.4.3.3. [**33**:7.11.2]

43.1.5.11.3 Belts shall not enter any spray area unless the belt and pulley within the spray area are completely enclosed. [**33**:7.11.3]

43.1.5.12* Drying Areas. Freshly sprayed workpieces shall be dried only in spaces that are ventilated to prevent the concentration of vapors from exceeding 25 percent of the lower flammable limit. *(See also Section 43.4.)* [**33**:7.12]

43.1.6 Storage, Handling, and Distribution of Flammable and Combustible Liquids.

43.1.6.1* General. Storage, handling, and mixing of ignitible (flammable and combustible) liquids shall meet all the applicable requirements of NFPA 30 and 43.1.6. [**33**:8.1]

Δ **43.1.6.2 General Occupancy Limits.** The maximum allowable quantities (MAQs) of ignitible (flammable or combustible) liquids allowed in each control area shall be in accordance with 66.9.5.1.

43.1.6.3 Mixing.

43.1.6.3.1 Dispensing or transfer of liquids from containers and filling of containers, including portable mixing tanks and "pressure pots," shall be done only in a spray area with the ventilation in operation or in a mixing room. [**33**:8.3.1]

43.1.6.3.2 Where the quantities of liquids required or the floor area necessary to provide a suitable mixing room exceeds the limits specified in 43.1.6.2.3 through 43.1.6.2.6, the mixing room shall meet all applicable requirements of this *Code* and NFPA 30. [**33**:8.3.2]

Δ **43.1.6.3.3** Mixing rooms shall meet all of the following requirements:

(1) Mixing rooms shall meet the construction requirements of 43.1.3.1.
(2) The area of a mixing room shall not exceed 150 ft^2 (14 m^2).
(3) If more than one mixing room is installed, the total quantity of liquids shall not exceed the limits stated in 43.1.6.3.5 or 43.1.6.3.6.
(4) Mixing rooms shall be designed to contain a spill of the contents in the room.
(5) Mixing rooms where dispensing, handling, or transferring of ignitible (flammable or combustible) liquids at temperatures at or above their flash point occurs shall be provided with mechanical ventilation capable of providing air movement not less than 1 ft^3/min/ft^2 (0.3 m^3/min/m^2) of floor area or 150 ft^3/min (4 m^3/min), whichever is greater.
(6) Ventilation systems provided in accordance with 43.1.6.3.3(5) shall be in operation during operating hours or whenever vapors are present.
(7) Mixing rooms shall be classified for purposes of electrical area classification in accordance with Chapter 7 of NFPA 30.
(8) Mixing rooms shall be provided with an approved automatic fire protection system that meets all applicable requirements of 43.1.7.
(9) Mixing rooms shall be provided with portable fire extinguishers located in accordance with NFPA 10.

[**33**:8.3.3]

43.1.6.3.4 The amount of liquid permitted in a single spray area shall not exceed 60 gal (227 L). [**33**:8.3.4]

Δ **43.1.6.3.5** Where a separate mixing room is provided and the mixing room is located adjacent to or within 6 ft (1830 mm) of an adjacent spray area or areas, as shown in Figure 43.1.6.3.5(a) and Figure 43.1.6.3.5(b), the combined quantities of liquids located in the spray areas and the mixing room shall not exceed 120 gal (454 L). [**33**:8.3.5]

43.1.6.3.6 Where a separate mixing room is provided and the mixing room is located more than 6 ft (1830 mm) from an adjacent spray area or areas, the quantity of liquid permitted in the mixing room shall not exceed 2 gal/ft^2 (80 L/m^2), up to a maximum of 300 gal (1135 L), as shown in Figure 43.1.6.3.6. The amount of liquid in the spray area shall not exceed 60 gal (227 L). [**33**:8.3.6]

43.1.6.4 Distribution Systems — Piping.

Δ **43.1.6.4.1*** Piping systems that convey ignitible (flammable or combustible) liquids between storage tanks, mixing rooms (paint kitchens), and spray areas shall be composed of steel or some other material having comparable properties of resistance to heat and physical damage. [**33**:8.4.1]

Maximum volumes of liquid allowed:
Spray area, 60 gal (227 L)
Spray area and mix room, 120 gal (454 L)

FIGURE 43.1.6.3.5(a) Mixing Room Within 6 ft (1830 mm) of Spray Area, Including Maximum Volume of Liquid Allowed. [**33**:Figure 8.3.5(a)]

N **43.1.6.4.1.1*** Piping systems shall be properly bonded and grounded. [**33**:8.4.1.1]

N **43.1.6.4.1.2** Piping systems shall be in accordance with Chapter 27 of NFPA 30. [**33**:8.4.1.2]

Δ **43.1.6.4.2*** Piping systems within the spray area shall be of steel or some other material having comparable resistance to heat and physical damage where possible. [**33**:8.4.2]

43.1.6.4.3* Tubing or hose shall be inspected and maintained in accordance with 43.1.8. [**33**:8.4.3]

Δ **43.1.6.4.4*** Where a pump is used to supply the liquid used in the spray application process, as well as in the cleaning process, piping, tubing, hose, and other accessories shall be designed to withstand the maximum working pressure of the pump or other means shall be provided to limit the discharge pressure of the pump. [**33**:8.4.4]

FIGURE 43.1.6.3.5(b) Mixing Room Within 6 ft (1830 mm) of Spray Area and with Direct Entry to Spray Area, Including Maximum Volume of Liquid Allowed. [**33**:Figure 8.3.5(b)]

FIGURE 43.1.6.3.6 Mixing Room More Than 6 ft (1830 mm) from Spray Area, Including Maximum Volume of Liquid Allowed. [**33**:Figure 8.3.6]

N **43.1.6.4.4.1** Where a pressure relief device is used, it shall be piped to a safe location. [**33**:8.4.4.1]

43.1.6.5 Distribution Systems — General.

43.1.6.5.1 Liquids shall be transported by means of closed containers, approved safety cans, or approved portable tanks or shall be transferred by means of a piping system. Open containers shall not be used for moving or storing liquids. [**33**:8.5.1]

43.1.6.5.2* Wherever liquids are transferred from one container to another, both containers shall be effectively bonded and grounded to dissipate static electricity. [**33**:8.5.2]

43.1.6.5.3 Containers that supply spray nozzles shall be of the closed type or shall be provided with metal covers that are kept closed. Containers that do not rest on the floor shall have supports or shall be suspended by wire cables. Containers that supply spray nozzles by gravity flow shall not exceed 10 gal (38 L) capacity. [**33**:8.5.3]

43.1.6.5.4 Original shipping containers shall not be subjected to air pressure for supplying spray nozzles. [**33**:8.5.4]

43.1.6.5.5 Containers that are pressurized to supply spray nozzles, air storage tanks, and coolers shall comply with all applicable requirements of the ASME *Boiler and Pressure Vessel Code*, Section VIII, for construction, tests, and maintenance. [**33**:8.5.5]

43.1.6.5.5.1 Containers that meet the following requirements need not meet the requirements of the ASME *Boiler and Pressure Vessel Code*, Section VIII, for construction, tests, and maintenance:

(1) Pressure containers less than 6 in. (150 mm) in diameter
(2) Pressure containers that operate at less than a gauge pressure of 15 psi (1.03 kPa)
(3) Siphon-type spray cups

[**33**:8.5.5.1]

43.1.6.5.6 If a heater is used to heat the liquid being sprayed, it shall be low-pressure steam, low-pressure hot water, or electric. [**33**:8.5.6]

Δ **43.1.6.5.6.1** If electric heaters are used to heat the liquid being sprayed, the electric heater shall be approved and listed for the specific location in which it is used. *(See 43.1.4.)* [**33**:8.5.6.1]

43.1.6.5.6.2 Heaters shall not be located in spray booths or other locations subject to the accumulation of deposits of combustible residue. [**33**:8.5.6.2]

43.1.6.5.7 Agitators, if used, shall be driven by compressed air, water, low-pressure steam, or electricity. [**33**:8.5.7]

Δ **43.1.6.5.7.1** If the agitators are powered by an electric motor, the motor shall meet the requirements of 43.1.4. [**33**:8.5.7.1]

43.1.6.5.8 Methods for cleaning paint circulation systems shall meet the requirements of Chapter 18 of NFPA 30. [**33**:8.5.8]

43.1.6.5.9 Compressed air shall be permitted to be used for cleaning paint delivery hose for individual applicators in a spray booth, provided both of the following requirements are met:

(1) The booth ventilation is operating.

(2) The maximum air pressure does not exceed the maximum working pressure of any component of the piping or hose system.

[33:8.5.9]

43.1.7 Protection.

43.1.7.1* General.

Δ 43.1.7.1.1 Spray areas, as defined in this *Code*, used for liquid spray operations and mixing rooms shall be protected with an approved automatic fire protection system. [33:9.1.1.1]

N 43.1.7.1.2 The automatic fire protection system requirement in 43.1.7.1.1 shall apply to both manual and automated spray application processes. [33:9.1.1.2]

N 43.1.7.1.3 **Mix Rooms.** [33:9.1.2]

N 43.1.7.1.3.1 Mix rooms shall be protected with an approved automatic fire protection system. [33:9.1.2.1]

N 43.1.7.1.3.2 Mix room intake or exhaust duct shall not require protection. [33:9.1.2.2]

43.1.7.1.4 Spray areas used for powder application operations shall be in accordance with Section 15.5 of NFPA 33. [33:9.1.3]

Δ 43.1.7.1.5 The fire protection system shall be monitored in accordance with *NFPA 72* when a fire alarm system exists. [33:9.1.4]

N 43.1.7.1.5.1 Where a building fire alarm system is not present, actuation of fire protection systems required by this standard shall initiate an audible alarm or visual indicator. [33:9.1.4.1]

43.1.7.1.6 **Portable Fire Extinguishers.** Portable fire extinguishers shall be provided and located in accordance with Section 13.6. [33:9.1.5]

43.1.7.2 **Ventilation Systems.** Air make-up systems and spray area exhaust systems shall remain functioning during any fire condition. [33:9.2]

43.1.7.2.1* Where air exhausted from spray areas is recirculated, an interlock shall shut down the recirculation of air during any fire condition unless it can be demonstrated that shutdown creates a greater hazard. [33:9.2.1]

N 43.1.7.2.2 Where air exhausted from spray areas or nonspray areas is used to supply air to other areas, both of the following shall apply:

(1) An interlock shall shut down the supply air.
(2) Ductwork and dampers shall redirect the air to the outdoors in accordance with 43.1.5.4.

[33:9.2.2]

43.1.7.2.3 Air make-up systems, spray area recirculation systems, and spray area exhaust systems shall be permitted to be shut down and dampers shall be permitted to close where the automatic fire protection system type requires that ventilation be discontinued. [33:9.2.3]

43.1.7.3* **Coating Material Delivery Systems.**

43.1.7.3.1 Where a pump is used to supply the liquid used in the spray application process, an automatic means shall be provided to shut off the supply of liquid in the event of fire. [33:9.3.1]

43.1.7.3.2 When pressurized tanks larger than 5 gal (19 L) are used to supply the liquid used in the spray application process, an automatic means shall be provided to shut off liquid flow at the tank outlet in the event of fire. [33:9.3.2]

43.1.7.4 **Conveyors.** For operations where the workpiece is automatically conveyed through the spray area, activation of the automatic fire protection system shall automatically stop any conveyors into and out of the spray area. [33:9.4]

43.1.7.5 **Protection Systems.** The automatic fire protection system shall be permitted to be, and shall be installed in accordance with, any of the following:

(1) An automatic water sprinkler system that meets all applicable requirements of NFPA 13
(2) An automatic foam water sprinkler system that meets all applicable requirements of NFPA 11
(3) A carbon dioxide extinguishing system that meets all applicable requirements of NFPA 12
(4) A dry chemical extinguishing system that meets all applicable requirements of NFPA 17
(5) A gaseous agent extinguishing system that meets all applicable requirements of NFPA 2001
(6) A water mist fire protection system that meets the applicable requirements of NFPA 750

[33:9.5]

43.1.7.6 **Automated Spray Application Operations.**

43.1.7.6.1 **Interlock.** For automated spray application operations, activation of the automatic fire protection system shall automatically accomplish all of the following:

(1) Activate a local alarm in the vicinity of the spraying operation
(2) Transmit an alarm signal to the facility's fire alarm system, if such a system is provided
(3) Shut down all spray application operations

[33:9.6.1.1]

43.1.7.6.1.1 The requirements of 43.1.7.6.1 shall not apply to operations where the supply of ignitible (flammable or combustible) liquids is located within the spray area and does not exceed 5 gal (18.9 L). [33:9.6.1.2]

43.1.7.6.1.2 For automated spray application operations, the additional requirements of 43.1.7.9 for automated liquid electrostatic spray application equipment shall also apply. [33:9.6.1.3]

Δ 43.1.7.6.2 **Emergency Shutdown.** For automated spray application operations, one or more manual emergency system shutdown stations shall be installed to serve each spray area in accordance with the following requirements:

(1) When activated, the stations shall accomplish at least the functions listed in 43.1.7.3, 43.1.7.4, and 43.1.7.6.1.
(2) At least one such station shall be within ready access of operating personnel.
(3) If access to the station required in 43.1.7.6.2(2) is likely to involve exposure to danger, an additional station shall be located adjacent to an exit from the area.

[33:9.6.1.4]

43.1.7.7* Automatic Sprinkler Systems.

43.1.7.7.1* The automatic sprinkler system shall be a wet pipe system, a dry pipe system, a preaction system, or an open-head deluge system, whichever is most appropriate for the portion of the spray operation being protected. [33:9.5.1.1]

43.1.7.7.2 The automatic sprinkler system shall be designed as follows:

(1) For spray application of styrene cross-link thermoset resin application areas, sprinklers shall be designed for Ordinary Hazard (Group 2) as defined in NFPA 13.
(2) For powder coating operations, sprinklers shall be designed for Ordinary Hazard (Group 2) as defined in NFPA 13.
(3) For all other spray areas, sprinklers shall be designed for Extra Hazard (Group 2) as defined in NFPA 13.

[33:9.5.1.2]

43.1.7.7.2.1 The sprinkler design area shall not be required to exceed the area of the booth or room in which spraying or resin application is conducted. [33:9.5.1.2.1]

43.1.7.7.3* The water supply shall be sufficient to supply all sprinklers likely to open in any one fire incident without depleting the available water for use in hose streams. [33:9.5.1.3]

43.1.7.7.3.1 Hose streams in accordance with NFPA 13 for the occupancy shall be included in the water suppression systems demands. [33:9.5.1.3.1]

43.1.7.7.4 Where sprinklers are installed to protect spray areas and mixing rooms only, water shall be permitted to be supplied from domestic water systems, provided the domestic supply can meet the demand for the design criteria of 43.1.7.7.2. [33:9.5.1.4]

43.1.7.7.5 The sprinkler system shall be controlled by a separate, listed indicating valve(s), operable from floor level. [33:9.5.1.5]

43.1.7.7.6* Dust Protection. Sprinkler systems protecting stacks or ducts with widths or diameters equal to or greater than 10 in. (0.25 m) but less than 12 ft (3.7 m) shall meet all of the following requirements:

(1) One sprinkler shall be located at the top of each vertical riser and at the midpoint of each offset. Additional sprinklers shall be spaced on 24 ft (7.3 m) centers if the rise is greater than 24 ft (7.3 m).
(2) Horizontal exhaust ducts shall have sprinklers located on 12 ft (3.7 m) centers beginning no more than 6 ft (1.7 m) from the duct entrance.
(3) If exhaust ducts are manifolded, a sprinkler shall be located in the manifold at the junction of each exhaust duct with the manifold.
(4) Sprinklers shall provide a minimum flow of 30 gpm (114 L/min) per sprinkler at a minimum of 15 psi (1 bar) pressure.
(5) Sprinklers shall be ordinary temperature rated, unless required to be higher due to operating temperatures measured in the ducts, in which case the operating temperature shall be at least 50°F (28°C) above the inside temperature of the duct.
(6)* The system demand shall include the discharge from the hydraulically most remote adjacent sprinklers in a common 100 linear ft (30.5 m) area of duct (horizontal and/or vertical).
(7)* The supply line to the duct sprinklers, if taken from the ceiling sprinkler system, shall be equipped with an accessible listed control valve.

[33:9.5.1.6]

43.1.7.7.6.1 Stacks and exhaust ducts shall be provided with a means for the inspection and maintenance of sprinklers. [33:9.5.1.6.1]

43.1.7.7.6.2 Sprinkler systems protecting stacks and ducts that are subject to freezing shall be of a nonfreezing type or be a manually controlled open-head system. [33:9.5.1.6.2]

43.1.7.7.7 Sprinklers shall be protected against overspray residue, either by location or covering, so that they will operate quickly in event of fire. [33:9.5.1.7]

43.1.7.7.7.1* Sprinklers shall be permitted to be covered by only clear, cellulose-based bags having a thickness of 0.003 in. (0.08 mm) or less or by thin paper bags. These coverings shall be replaced frequently so that heavy deposits of residue do not accumulate. [33:9.5.1.7.1]

43.1.7.7.7.2 Sprinklers that have been painted or coated by overspray or residues shall be replaced with new sprinklers. [33:9.5.1.7.2]

43.1.7.8* Automatic Carbon Dioxide, Dry Chemical, and Clean Agent Systems. The fire protection system shall be capable of discharging its contents into the entire protected area simultaneously, including the exhaust plenum and exhaust ductwork. [33:9.5.2]

43.1.7.9* Protection for Automated Liquid Electrostatic Spray Application Equipment.

43.1.7.9.1 Automated liquid electrostatic spray application equipment, both listed and unlisted, shall be further protected by listed optical flame detection, installed and supervised in accordance with NFPA 72. The optical flame detection shall, in event of ignition, react to the presence of flame within one-half (0.5) second and shall accomplish all of the following:

(1) Meet all the requirements of 43.1.7.6.1
(2) Disconnect power to the high-voltage elements in the spray area and de-energize the system

[33:9.6.2.1]

43.1.7.9.2 Automated liquid electrostatic spray application equipment that is unlisted shall be protected further by the following:

(1) In addition to meeting the requirements in 43.1.7.9.1, the optical flame detection system shall also activate one of the following over each zone in which fire has been detected:
　(a) An open head deluge system designed to discharge a minimum density of 0.6 gpm/ft^2 (24.4 mm/min)
　(b) A carbon dioxide extinguishing system
　(c) A dry chemical extinguishing system
　(d) A gaseous agent extinguishing system
　(e) A water mist fire protection system
(2) Manual activation stations shall be installed. At least one such station shall be within ready access of operating personnel. If access to this station is likely to involve exposure to danger, an additional station shall be located adjacent to an exit from the area. These devices shall activate

the fire protection system as specified in 43.1.7.9.2(1) and accomplish the requirements of 43.1.7.6.1 and 43.1.7.9.1(2).

(3) A wet pipe sprinkler system shall also be provided throughout the spray booth. This system shall meet all the applicable requirements of NFPA 13 for Extra Hazard (Group 2) occupancies.

(4) Automatic electrostatic equipment enclosures inside the booth systems shall be protected with an approved automatic fire protection system. Activation of this system shall automatically accomplish the requirements of 43.1.7.6.1 and 43.1.7.9.1(2).

[33:9.6.2.2]

Δ **43.1.7.10 Protection for Dry Particulate Scrubber.**

N **43.1.7.10.1** The use of dry particulate scrubbers shall be permitted provided that both of the following conditions are met:

(1) The virgin powder used for paint particulate scrubbing is noncombustible.
(2) The concentration of paint solids collected and mixed in the powder scrubbing material is maintained such that the mixture remains noncombustible.

[33:9.6.3.1]

N **43.1.7.10.2** The dry particulate scrubber chambers shall be protected by an approved automatic fire protection system. [33:9.6.3.2]

N **43.1.7.10.2.1** The automatic fire protection system shall be installed in accordance with any of the protection systems described in 43.1.7.5. [33:9.6.3.2.1]

N **43.1.7.10.3** Access for inspection and cleaning of sprinklers shall be provided. [33:9.6.3.3]

N **43.1.7.10.4*** Areas subject to buildup of overspray residues where protection is permanently obstructed shall be protected by approved fire protection systems. [33:9.6.3.4]

N **43.1.7.10.4.1** Areas subject to buildup of overspray residues shall be cleaned to minimize the fuel loading. [33:9.6.3.4.1]

N **43.1.7.10.5** The scrubber shall be designed to direct the flow from the fire extinguishing system to an approved location or shall be designed to contain a minimum of 20 minutes of flow. [33:9.6.3.5]

N **43.1.7.10.6** In addition to the requirements of 43.1.7.6.1, activation of the automatic fire protection system shall automatically accomplish all of the following:

(1) Shut down the operation of the dry particulate scrubbing system.
(2)* Automatically stop the air recirculation.

[33:9.6.3.6]

Δ **43.1.7.11 Protection for Electrostatic Precipitator Scrubber.**

N **43.1.7.11.1** The use of high-voltage electrostatic precipitator type scrubbers shall be permitted provided they meet the applicable requirements on Chapter 11 of NFPA 33. [33:9.7.1]

N **43.1.7.11.2** High voltage electrostatic precipitators shall be protected by an approved automatic fire protection system. [33:9.7.2]

N **43.1.7.11.2.1*** Activation of the fire protection system shall be by an approved automatic detection system. [33:9.7.2.1]

N **43.1.7.11.3*** Areas subject to buildup of overspray residues where protection is permanently obstructed shall be protected by approved fire protection systems. [33:9.7.3]

N **43.1.7.11.3.1** Areas subject to buildup of overspray residues shall be cleaned to minimize the fuel loading. [33:9.7.3.1]

N **43.1.7.11.4** The scrubber shall be designed to direct the flow from the fire-extinguishing system to an approved location or shall be designed to contain 20 minutes of flow. [33:9.7.4]

N **43.1.7.11.5** In addition to the requirements of 43.1.7.6.1, activation of the automatic fire protection system shall automatically accomplish all of the following:

(1) Meet the requirement of 11.3.8(3) of NFPA 33
(2) Meet the requirement of 11.3.8(4) of NFPA 33
(3)* Automatically stop the air recirculation

[33:9.7.5]

N **43.1.7.11.6** The high-voltage power supplies shall be capable of monitoring current draw and shutting down or reducing voltage to prevent the generation of an electrostatic discharge. [33:9.7.6]

Δ **43.1.7.12 Protection for High-Capacity Dry Paint Arrestor.**

N **43.1.7.12.1** The filtration media shall be protected by an approved automatic fire protection system in accordance with 43.1.7.5. [33:9.8.1]

N **43.1.7.12.2** If the filter itself is made from combustible material, the filter shall be housed in a noncombustible enclosure. [33:9.8.2]

N **43.1.7.12.2.1** The enclosure housing the filters shall be closed during spraying operations. [33:9.8.2.1]

N **43.1.7.12.2.2** The enclosure shall be protected by an approved automatic fire protection system in accordance with 43.1.7.5. [33:9.8.2.2]

N **43.1.7.12.2.3** The filters and enclosure shall be designed so as to prevent overspray residues from accumulating on the inside of the enclosure. [33:9.8.2.3]

N **43.1.7.12.3*** Areas subject to buildup of overspray residues where protection is permanently obstructed shall be protected by approved fire protection systems. [33:9.8.3]

N **43.1.7.12.4*** In addition to the requirements of 43.1.7.6.1, activation of the automatic fire protection system shall automatically stop air recirculation. [33:9.8.4]

43.1.8 Operations and Maintenance.

43.1.8.1* General. Maintenance procedures shall be established to ensure that all spray application apparatus and processes are operated and maintained in accordance with the manufacturers' specifications and the requirements of this *Code*. Maintenance shall be the responsibility of the users of the apparatus and processes. [33:10.1]

43.1.8.1.1* Spray application operations shall not be conducted outside predetermined spray areas. [33:10.1.1]

43.1.8.1.2 Inspection of extinguishing systems shall be conducted to ensure that the performance of the extinguishing system components will not be affected by overspray and residues. [33:10.1.2]

SPRAYING, DIPPING, AND COATING USING FLAMMABLE OR COMBUSTIBLE MATERIALS

N **43.1.8.1.3 Inspection, Testing, and Maintenance. [33:10.2]**

N **43.1.8.1.3.1** Safety devices such as detection, monitoring, actuation, interlock, and annunciation shall be maintained in accordance with the manufacturer's instructions. [33:10.2.1]

N **43.1.8.1.3.2** It shall be the responsibility of the equipment manufacturer to provide instructions for inspection, testing, and maintenance. [33:10.2.2]

N **43.1.8.1.3.3** It shall be the responsibility of the user to establish, schedule, and enforce the frequency and extent of the inspection, testing, and maintenance program, as well as the corrective action to be taken. [33:10.2.2]

N **43.1.8.1.3.4** All safety devices shall be tested for function at least annually. [33:10.2.4]

N **43.1.8.1.3.5** Safety device testing shall be documented. [33:10.2.5]

N **43.1.8.1.3.6** Calibration of equipment used to monitor the concentration of vapors shall be performed as follows:

(1) In accordance with the manufacturer's instructions
(2) At least annually

[33:10.2.6]

N **43.1.8.1.3.7** As part of record retention, records of inspection, testing, and maintenance activities shall be retained for a period of 3 years. [33:10.2.7]

43.1.8.2* Combustible Deposits.

43.1.8.2.1 All spray areas shall be kept free of excessive accumulation of deposits of combustible residues. [33:10.3.1]

43.1.8.2.2 Combustible coverings (thin paper, plastic) and strippable coatings shall be permitted to be used to facilitate cleaning operations in spray areas. [33:10.3.2]

43.1.8.2.2.1 Where plastic covering is used, it shall be of a static dissipative nature or shall have a maximum breakdown voltage of 4 kV to prevent accumulation of a hazardous static electric charge. [33:10.3.2.1]

43.1.8.2.3 If residue accumulates to excess in booths, duct or duct discharge points, or other spray areas, all spraying operations shall be discontinued until conditions have been corrected. [33:10.3.3]

Δ **43.1.8.3 High-Pressure Hose Lines.** High-pressure hose lines that convey ignitible (flammable or combustible) coating material in airless spray application operations shall be inspected daily and shall be repaired or replaced as necessary. Hose lines and equipment shall be located so that, in the event of a leak or rupture, coating material will not be discharged into any space containing a source of ignition. [33:10.4]

43.1.8.4 Maintenance Procedures.

Δ **43.1.8.4.1** Overspray collectors shall be inspected daily and clogged filters shall be discarded and replaced. Maintenance procedures shall be established to ensure that overspray collector filters are replaced before restriction to airflow is reduced below the minimum established by 43.1.5.2. [33:10.5.1]

43.1.8.4.2 At the close of the day's operation, all discarded overspray collector filters, residue scrapings, and debris contaminated with residue shall be removed immediately to a designated storage location, placed in a noncombustible container with a tight-fitting lid, or placed in a water-filled metal container. [33:10.5.2]

43.1.8.5* Waste Containers.

43.1.8.5.1 Approved waste containers shall be provided wherever rags or waste are impregnated with sprayed material, and all such rags or waste shall be deposited therein immediately after use. The contents of waste containers shall be placed in a designated storage location. [33:10.6.1]

43.1.8.5.2 Waste containers Class I [FP < 100°F (37.8°C)] liquids shall be located in ventilated areas that meet the requirements of 43.1.5. Such areas shall also meet the electrical area classification requirements of 43.1.4.4.5. [33:10.6.2]

43.1.8.5.3* Waste containers for Class I [FP < 100°F (37.8°C)] liquids shall be constructed of conductive materials and shall be bonded and grounded. [33:10.6.3]

43.1.8.5.4 Waste containers for Class I [FP < 100°F (37.8°C)] liquids shall be handled and stored in accordance with 43.1.6. [33:10.6.4]

43.1.8.6 Clothing. Employees' clothing contaminated with sprayed material shall not be left on the premises overnight unless kept in metal lockers. [33:10.7]

43.1.8.7 Cleaning Operations.

43.1.8.7.1 Scope. Paragraph 43.1.8.7 shall apply to the use of ignitible (flammable or combustible) liquids for the flushing and cleaning of equipment. [33:10.8.1]

43.1.8.7.2 Liquids. Class I and Class II [FP < 140°F (60°C)] liquids used in cleaning operations shall be in their original shipping containers or in listed safety containers. [33:10.8.2]

Δ **43.1.8.7.3 Location.** Cleaning operations using ignitible flammable or combustible liquids shall be conducted inside a spray area with operating ventilating equipment or in ventilated areas that meet the requirements of 43.1.5. Such areas shall also meet the electrical area classification requirements of 43.1.4.4.5. [33:10.8.3]

43.1.8.7.4* Equipment. Equipment using ignitible (flammable or combustible) liquids shall meet the requirements of 43.1.4.4.5 and shall be bonded and grounded. [33:10.8.4]

43.1.8.7.5 Manual Cleaning. Individual manual cleaning operations shall be limited to not more than 1 gal (4 L) of ignitible (flammable or combustible) liquid for each cleaning operator. [33:10.8.5]

43.1.8.7.6 Liquid Storage. Ignitible (flammable or combustible) liquids shall be handled and stored in accordance with 43.1.6. Containers used for handling, storing, or recovering Class I [FP < 100°F (37.8°C)] liquids shall be constructed of conductive materials and shall be bonded and grounded. [33:10.8.6]

43.1.8.8 Solvent Distillation Units (Solvent Recyclers).

43.1.8.8.1 Scope.

Δ **43.1.8.8.1.1** This section shall apply to solvent distillation units having distillation chambers or still pots that do not exceed 227 L (60 gal) nominal capacity and are used to recycle Class I, Class II, or Class IIIA liquids [FP < 93°C (200°F)]. [33:10.9.1.1]

Δ **43.1.8.8.1.2** This section shall not apply to research, testing, or experimental processes; to distillation processes carried out in petroleum refineries, chemical plants, or distilleries; or to distillation equipment used in dry cleaning operations. [**33**:10.9.1.2]

Δ **43.1.8.8.2 Equipment.** Solvent distillation units shall be approved or shall be listed in accordance with UL 2208, *Solvent Distillation Units*. [**33**:10.9.2]

Δ **43.1.8.8.3 Solvents.** Solvent distillation units shall only be used to distill liquids for which they have been investigated and that are listed on the unit's marking or contained within the manufacturer's literature. [**33**:10.9.3]

Δ **43.1.8.8.3.1** Unstable or reactive liquids or materials shall not be processed unless they have been specifically listed on the system's markings or contained within the manufacturer's literature. [**33**:10.9.3.1]

43.1.8.8.4 Location.

Δ **43.1.8.8.4.1** Solvent distillation units shall be located and operated in locations in accordance with their approval or listing. [**33**:10.9.4.1]

Δ **43.1.8.8.4.2** Solvent distillation units shall not be used in basements. [**33**:10.9.4.2]

Δ **43.1.8.8.4.3** Solvent distillation units shall be located away from potential sources of ignition, as indicated on the unit's marking. [**33**:10.9.4.3]

Δ **43.1.8.8.5 Liquid Storage.** Distilled liquids and liquids awaiting distillation shall be stored in accordance with NFPA 30. [**33**:10.9.5]

43.1.8.9* Spontaneous Ignition Hazards. The same spray booth shall not be alternately used for different types of coating materials if the combination of the materials is conducive to spontaneous ignition, unless all deposits of the first-used coating material are removed from the booth and exhaust ducts prior to spraying with the second coating material. [**33**:10.10]

43.1.8.10* Chlorinated Solvents. Coating materials containing chlorinated solvents shall not be used with spray application apparatus or fluid-handling equipment if the chlorinated solvent will come into contact with aluminum within a piping system, pump, enclosed container, or any enclosure that is capable of being pressurized by the potential reaction. This shall apply even if the container or system has been constructed with pressure relief devices. [**33**:10.11]

43.1.8.11 Smoking. Signs stating NO SMOKING OR OPEN FLAMES in large letters on contrasting color background shall be conspicuously posted at all spray areas and paint storage rooms. [**33**:10.12]

43.1.8.12* Hot Work. Welding, cutting, and other spark-producing operations shall not be permitted in or adjacent to spray areas until a written permit authorizing such work has been issued. The permit shall be issued by a person in authority following his or her inspection of the area to ensure that precautions have been taken and will be followed until the job is completed. [**33**:10.13]

43.2 Automated Electrostatic Spray Equipment. For information on the installation and use of automated electrostatic spray application apparatus, see Chapter 11 of NFPA 33.

43.3 Handheld Electrostatic Spray Equipment. For information on the installation and use of handheld electrostatic spray application apparatus, see Chapter 12 of NFPA 33.

43.4 Drying, Curing, and Fusion Processes. For information on drying, curing, and fusion apparatus used in connection with spray application of flammable and combustible materials, see Chapter 13 of NFPA 33.

43.5 Miscellaneous Spray Operations.

43.5.1 Vehicle Undercoating and Body Lining.

43.5.1.1 Spray undercoating or spray body lining of vehicles that is conducted in an area that has adequate natural or mechanical ventilation shall be exempt from the provisions of this *Code*, if all the requirements of 43.5.1.1.1 through 43.5.1.1.4 are met. [**33**:14.1.1]

43.5.1.1.1 There shall be no open flames or spark-producing equipment within 20 ft (6100 mm) of the spray operation while the spray operation is being conducted. [**33**:14.1.1.1]

43.5.1.1.2 There shall be no drying, curing, or fusion apparatus in use within 20 ft (6100 mm) of the spray operation while the spray operation is being conducted. [**33**:14.1.1.2]

43.5.1.1.3 Any solvent used for cleaning procedures shall have a flash point not less than 100°F (37.8°C). [**33**:14.1.1.3]

43.5.1.1.4 The coating or lining materials used shall meet one of the following criteria:

(1) Be no more hazardous than UL Class 30-40, when tested in accordance with UL 340, *Tests for Comparative Flammability of Liquids*
(2) Not contain any solvent or component that has a flash point below 100°F (37.8°C)
(3) Consist only of Class IIIB [FP ≥ 200°F (93°C)] liquids and not include any organic peroxide catalyst

[**33**:14.1.1.4]

43.5.1.2 Noncomplying Undercoating Operations. Spray undercoating operations that do not meet the requirements of 43.5.1 shall meet all applicable requirements of this *Code* pertaining to spray finishing operations. [**33**:14.1.2]

43.5.2 Preparation Workstations. If spray finishing operations are performed at or in a preparation workstation, the preparation workstation shall be considered an unenclosed spray area and shall meet all requirements of an unenclosed spray area. [**33**:14.2]

43.5.2.1 A preparation workstation that is designed and operated in accordance with 43.5.3 shall be considered a limited finishing workstation and not an unenclosed spray area. [**33**:14.2.1]

43.5.3 Limited Finishing Workstations.

43.5.3.1 A limited finishing workstation shall be designed and operated in accordance with the requirements of 43.5.3.2 through 43.5.3.10. [**33**:14.3.1]

43.5.3.2 A limited finishing workstation shall be designed and constructed to have all of the following:

(1) A dedicated make-up air supply and air supply plenum
(2) Curtains or partitions that are noncombustible or limited-combustible, as defined in 3.3.179 and 3.3.189.11 or that can successfully pass Test Method 2 in NFPA 701

(3) A dedicated mechanical exhaust and filtration system
(4)* An approved automatic extinguishing system that meets the requirements of 43.1.7
[**33:**14.3.2]

43.5.3.3 The amount of material sprayed in a limited finishing workstation shall not exceed 1 gal (3.8 L) in any 8-hour period. [**33:**14.3.3]

43.5.3.4 The limited finishing workstation shall meet all applicable requirements of 43.1.2 through 43.1.8 and Section 43.11. [**33:**14.3.4]

43.5.3.5 Curtains or partitions shall be fully closed during any spray application operations. [**33:**14.3.5]

Δ **43.5.3.6** The area inside the curtains or partitions shall be considered a Class I, Division 1; Zone 1; Class II, Division 1; or Zone 21 hazardous (classified) location, as defined by Article 500 of *NFPA 70*. [**33:**14.3.6]

Δ **43.5.3.6.1** A Class I, Division 2; Zone 2; Class II, Division 2; or Zone 22 hazardous (classified) location, as applicable, shall extend 3 ft (915 mm) both horizontally and vertically beyond the volume enclosed by the outside surface of the curtains or partitions as shown in Figure 43.5.3.6.1. [**33:**14.3.6.1]

43.5.3.6.2 For the purposes of this subsection, *interlocked* shall mean that the spray application equipment cannot be operated unless the exhaust ventilation system is operating and functioning properly and spray application is automatically stopped if the exhaust ventilation system fails. [**33:**14.3.6.2]

43.5.3.7 Any limited finishing workstation used for spray application operations shall not be used for any operation that is capable of producing sparks or particles of hot metal or for operations that involve open flames or electrical utilization equipment capable of producing sparks or particles of hot metal. [**33:**14.3.7]

43.5.3.8 Drying, curing, or fusion apparatus shall be permitted to be used in a limited finishing workstation if they meet

Δ **FIGURE 43.5.3.6.1** Class I, Division 2; Zone 2; Class II, Division 2; or Zone 22 Locations Adjacent to a Limited Finishing Workstation. [**33:**Figure 14.3.6.1]

the requirements of Section 43.4 and the requirements of 43.5.3.8.1 through 43.5.3.8.3. [**33**:14.3.8]

43.5.3.8.1 Where industrial air heaters are used to elevate the air temperature for drying, curing, or fusing operations, a high-limit switch shall be provided to automatically shut off the drying apparatus if the air temperature in the limited finishing workstation exceeds the maximum discharge-air temperature allowed by the standard that the heater is listed to or 221°F (105°C), whichever is less. [**33**:14.3.8.1]

43.5.3.8.2* A means shall be provided to show that the limited finishing workstation is in the drying or curing mode of operation and that it is to be unoccupied. [**33**:14.3.8.2]

43.5.3.8.3 Any containers of ignitible (flammable or combustible) liquids shall be removed from the limited finishing workstation before the drying apparatus is energized. [**33**:14.3.8.3]

43.5.3.9 Portable spot-drying, curing, or fusion apparatus shall be permitted to be used in a limited finishing workstation, provided that it is not located within the hazardous (classified) location defined in 43.5.3.5 when spray application operations are being conducted. [**33**:14.3.9]

43.5.3.10 Recirculation of exhaust air shall be permitted only if all provisions of 43.1.5.5 are met. [**33**:14.3.10]

43.6 Powder Coating.

43.6.1 For information on the installation and use of powder coating application apparatus, see Chapter 15 of NFPA 33.

43.6.2 Sprinklers shall be protected against overspray residue by either location or covering in order to operate quickly in event of fire. [**33**:15.5.8.6]

Δ **43.6.2.1** Sprinklers shall be permitted to be covered by either clear, cellulose-based bags that are equal to or less than 0.003 in. (0.08 mm) thick or by thin paper bags. [**33**:15.5.8.6.1]

43.6.2.2 The coverings permitted in 43.6.2.1 shall be replaced frequently so that heavy deposits of residue do not accumulate. [**33**:15.5.8.6.2]

43.6.3 Sprinklers that have been painted or coated by overspray or residues shall be replaced with new sprinklers. [**33**:15.5.8.7]

43.7 Organic Peroxides and Plural Component Coatings.

Δ **43.7.1* Scope.** Section 43.7 shall apply to the spray application operations that involve the use of organic peroxide formulations and other plural component coatings, not including styrene cross-linked composites manufacturing. [**33**:16.1]

43.7.2 General. Spray application operations that involve the use of organic peroxide formulations and other plural component coatings shall be conducted in spray areas that are protected by approved automatic sprinkler systems that meet the requirements of 43.1.7. [**33**:16.2]

43.7.3 Prevention of Contamination. Measures shall be taken to prevent the contamination of organic peroxide formulations with any foreign substance. Only spray guns and related handling equipment that are specifically manufactured for use with organic peroxide formulations shall be used. Separate fluid-handling equipment shall be used for the resin and for the catalyst, and they shall not be interchanged. [**33**:16.3]

43.7.3.1 The wetted portions of equipment and apparatus that handle organic peroxide formulations shall be constructed of stainless steel (300 series), polyethylene, Teflon®, or other materials that are specifically recommended for the application. [**33**:16.3.1]

43.7.3.2* Measures shall be taken to prevent contamination of organic peroxide formulations with dusts or overspray residues resulting from the sanding or spray application of finishing materials. [**33**:16.3.2]

43.7.3.3 Spills of organic peroxide formulations shall be promptly removed so there are no residues. Spilled material shall be permitted to be absorbed by use of a noncombustible absorbent, which is then disposed of promptly in accordance with the manufacturer's recommendations. [**33**:16.3.3]

Δ **43.7.4 Storage of Organic Peroxides.** Organic peroxide formulations shall be stored in accordance with the requirements of NFPA 400 and with the manufacturers' recommendations. [**33**:16.4]

43.7.5 Handling of Organic Peroxides. Measures shall be taken to prevent handling of organic peroxide formulations to avoid shock and friction, which can cause decomposition and violent reaction. [**33**:16.5]

43.7.6* Mixing of Organic Peroxides with Promoters. Organic peroxide formulations shall not be mixed directly with any cobalt compounds or other promoters or accelerators, due to the possibility of violent decomposition or explosion. To minimize the possibility of such accidental mixing, these materials shall not be stored adjacent to each other. [**33**:16.6]

43.7.7 Smoking. Smoking shall be prohibited, NO SMOKING signs shall be prominently displayed, and only nonsparking tools shall be used in any area where organic peroxide formulations are stored, mixed, or applied. [**33**:16.7]

43.7.8 Trained Personnel. Only designated personnel trained to use and handle organic peroxide formulations shall be permitted to use these materials. [**33**:16.8]

43.7.9 Material Safety Data Sheets. Where organic peroxide formulations are used, the material safety data sheet (MSDS) or its equivalent shall be consulted. [**33**:16.9]

N **43.8 Containers.** [**33**:17.7.2]

N **43.8.1** Excess catalyzed resin, while still in the liquid state, shall be drained into a steel container of no more than 55 gal (208 L) capacity. [**33**:17.7.2.1]

N **43.8.2** The container shall conform to all of the following:

(1) Be located in an area with sprinklers if inside the building
(2) Be allowed to be no more than 75 percent full
(3) Kept covered (but not sealed) except when adding or mixing material

[**33**:17.7.2.2]

43.9 Styrene Cross-Linked Composites Manufacturing (Glass Fiber–Reinforced Plastics).

43.9.1* Scope. Section 43.9 shall apply to manufacturing processes involving spray application of styrene cross-linked thermoset resins (commonly known as glass fiber–reinforced plastics) for hand lay-up or spray fabrication methods, that is, resin application areas, and where the processes do not produce vapors that exceed 25 percent of the lower flammable limit. [**33**:17.1]

43.9.2 Resin Application Equipment. The equipment and apparatus for spray application of the resin shall be installed and used in accordance with the requirements of Sections 43.7 and 43.9. [**33**:17.2]

43.9.3* Fire Protection. Resin application areas shall be protected in accordance with 43.1.7. [**33**:17.3]

43.9.4 Resin Storage. The quantity of ignitible (flammable and combustible) liquids located in the vicinity of resin application areas outside an inside storage room or storage cabinet in any one process area shall not exceed the greater of any of the following:

(1) A supply for one day
(2) The sum of 25 gal (95 L) of Class IA [FP < 73°F (22.8°C) and BP < 100°F (37.8°C)] liquids in containers and 120 gal (454 L) of Class IB, IC, II, or III [any flash point and BP > 100°F (37.8°C)] liquids in containers
(3) One approved portable tank not exceeding 660 gal (2500 L) of Class IB, IC, II, or III [any flash point and BP > 100°F (37.8°C)] liquids

[**33**:17.4]

43.9.5 Electrical and Other Hazards.

43.9.5.1 Electrical wiring and utilization equipment located in resin application areas that is not subject to deposits of combustible residues shall be installed in accordance with the requirements of *NFPA 70* for Ordinary Hazard locations. [**33**:17.5.1]

Δ **43.9.5.2** Electrical wiring and utilization equipment located in resin application areas that is subject to deposits of combustible residues shall be listed for such exposure and shall be suitable for Class I, Division 2 or Zone 2 locations, if applicable as defined in 43.1.4.2.1.2. [**33**:17.5.2]

43.9.5.3* All metal parts of resin application areas, exhaust ducts, ventilation fans, spray application equipment, workpieces or containers that receive the spray stream, and piping that conveys ignitible (flammable or combustible) liquids shall be electrically grounded. [**33**:17.5.3]

43.9.5.4 Space heating appliances or other hot surfaces in resin application areas shall not be located where deposits or residues accumulate. [**33**:17.5.4]

43.9.6 Ventilation.

43.9.6.1 Mechanical ventilation shall be designed and installed throughout the resin application area in accordance with the requirements of 43.1.5. [**33**:17.6.1]

43.9.6.1.1 Buildings that are not enclosed for at least three-quarters of their perimeter shall not be required to meet this requirement. [**33**:17.6.1.1]

43.9.6.2 Local ventilation shall be provided where personnel are under or inside of the workpiece being fabricated. [**33**:17.6.2]

43.9.7 Use and Handling.

43.9.7.1 The storage and use of organic peroxide formulations shall meet the requirements of Section 43.7. [**33**:17.7.1]

43.9.7.2 Excess catalyzed resin, while still in the liquid state, shall be drained into a steel container of no more than 55 gal (208 L) capacity. [**33**:17.7.2.1]

N **43.9.7.3** The container shall conform to all of the following:
(1) Be located in an area with sprinklers if inside the building
(2) Be allowed to be no more than 75 percent full
(3) Kept covered (but not sealed) except when adding or mixing material

[**33**:17.7.2.2]

43.9.7.4 In areas where chopper guns are used, paper, polyethylene film, or similar material shall be provided to cover the exposed surfaces of the walls and floor to allow the buildup of overchop to be removed. [**33**:17.7.3]

43.9.7.4.1 Accumulated overchop shall be disposed of when it has reached an average thickness of 2 in. (50 mm). [**33**:17.7.3.1]

43.9.7.4.2 Used paper, polyethylene film, or similar material shall be placed in a noncombustible container and disposed of when removed from the facility. [**33**:17.7.3.2]

43.10 Dipping, Coating, and Printing Processes.

Δ **43.10.1*** Section 43.10 shall apply to dipping, roll coating, flow coating, curtain coating, printing, cleaning, and similar processes, hereinafter referred to as "coating processes" or "processes," in which articles or materials are passed through tanks, vats, or containers, or passed over rollers, drums, or other process equipment that contain flammable or combustible liquid. [**34**:1.1.1]

43.10.1.1 Section 43.10 shall also apply to cleaning processes that utilize a solvent vapor, such as vapor degreasing processes. [**34**:1.1.2]

43.10.1.2 Section 43.10 shall also apply to processes that use water-borne, water-based, and water-reducible materials that contain ignitible (flammable or combustible) liquids or that produce combustible deposits or residues. [**34**:1.1.3]

43.10.1.3 Section 43.10 shall not apply to processes that use only noncombustible liquids for processing and cleaning. Section 43.10 shall also not apply to processes that use only Class IIIB [FP > 200°F (93°C)] liquids for processing or cleaning, provided the liquids or mixtures thereof maintain their Class IIIB [FP > 200°F (93°C)] liquid classification at their point of use. [**34**:1.1.4]

43.10.1.4 Section 43.10 shall not apply to processes that use a liquid that does not have a fire point when tested in accordance with ASTM D92, *Standard Test Method for Flash and Fire Points by Cleveland Open Cup Tester*, up to the boiling point of the liquid or up to a temperature at which the sample being tested shows an obvious physical change. [**34**:1.1.5]

43.10.1.5 Section 43.10 shall not apply to fluidized bed powder application. *(See Chapter 15 of NFPA 33.)* [**34**:1.1.6]

43.10.1.6* Section 43.10 shall not apply to quench tanks that are addressed in Chapter 51 of this *Code*.

43.10.2* Where unusual industrial processes are involved, the AHJ shall be permitted to require additional safeguards or modifications to the requirements of NFPA 34, provided equivalent safety is achieved.

43.11 Training.

43.11.1* General. All personnel involved in the spray application processes covered by this *Code* shall be instructed in the following:

(1) Potential safety and health hazards
(2) Operational, maintenance, and emergency procedures required
(3) Importance of constant operator awareness

[**33**:19.1]

43.11.1.1 Personnel required to handle or use flammable or combustible materials shall be instructed in the safe handling, storage, and use of the materials, as well as emergency procedures. [**33**:19.1.1]

43.11.1.2* All personnel required to enter or to work within confined or enclosed spaces shall be instructed as to the nature of the hazard involved, the necessary precautions to be taken, and the use of protective and emergency equipment required. [**33**:19.1.2]

43.11.1.3 All personnel shall be instructed in the proper use, maintenance, and storage of all emergency, safety, or personal protective equipment that they might be required to use in their normal work performance. [**33**:19.1.3]

43.11.1.4 Documentation shall be employed to record the type and date of training provided to each individual involved in these processes. [**33**:19.1.4]

Chapter 44 Solvent Extraction

44.1 General. Solvent extraction plants shall comply with NFPA 36 and Chapter 44.

44.2 Application.

Δ **44.2.1** Chapter 44 shall apply to the following:

(1)* The commercial scale extraction processing of animal and vegetable oils and fats by the use of Class I flammable hydrocarbon liquids, hereinafter referred to as "solvents" [**36**:1.1.1]
(2) Any equipment and buildings that are located within 100 ft (30 m) of the extraction process [**36**:1.1.2]
(3) The unloading, storage, and handling of solvents, regardless of distance from the extraction process [**36**:1.1.3]
(4) The means by which material to be extracted is conveyed from the preparation process to the extraction process [**36**:1.1.4]
(5) The means by which extracted desolventized solids and oils are conveyed from the extraction process [**36**:1.1.5]
(6) Preparation and meal finishing processes that are connected by conveyor to the extraction process, regardless of intervening distance [**36**:1.1.6]

44.2.2 Chapter 44 shall not apply to the following:

(1) The storage of raw materials or finished products [**36**:1.1.7]
(2) Extraction processes that use liquids that are miscible with water [**36**:1.1.8]
(3) Extraction processes that use flammable gases, liquefied petroleum gases, or nonflammable gases [**36**:1.1.9]

Δ **44.3 Permits.**

N **44.3.1** Permits shall be required in accordance with this chapter and Table 1.13.8(a) through Table 1.13.8(d).

N **44.3.2** Permits, where required, shall comply with Section 1.13.

Δ **44.4 Special Requirements.** This section shall prohibit the use of processes that employ oxygen-active compounds that are heat or shock sensitive, such as certain organic peroxides, within the area defined in 44.2.1(2). [**36**:1.1.10]

Chapter 45 Combustible Fibers

45.1 General.

45.1.1 The storage, use, and handling of combustible fibers shall comply with the requirements of Chapter 45.

45.1.2* Chapter 45 shall not apply to buildings completely protected by an approved automatic fire-extinguishing system; however, this exclusion does not preclude the need for good housekeeping.

45.1.3 Chapter 45 shall not apply to biomass feedstock regulated by Chapter 31.

Δ **45.1.4 Permits.**

N **45.1.4.1** Permits shall be required in accordance with this chapter and Table 1.13.8(a) through Table 1.13.8(d).

N **45.1.4.2** Permits, where required, shall comply with Section 1.13.

45.2 Electrical Wiring.

45.2.1 Electrical wiring and equipment in any combustible fiber storage room or building shall be installed in accordance with the requirements of *NFPA 70* for Class III hazardous locations.

45.2.2 The AHJ shall be responsible for designating the areas requiring hazardous location electrical classifications and shall classify the area in accordance with the classification system set forth in *NFPA 70*.

45.3 No Smoking.

45.3.1 No smoking or open flame shall be permitted in any area where combustible fibers are handled or stored, nor within 50 ft (15 m) of any uncovered pile of such fibers.

45.3.2 NO SMOKING signs shall be posted.

45.4 Vehicles and Material Handling Equipment. Trucks or automobiles, other than mechanical handling equipment and approved industrial trucks complying with NFPA 505, shall not enter any fiber storage room or building but shall be permitted to be used at loading platforms.

45.5 Loose Storage of Combustible Fibers.

45.5.1 Loose combustible fibers (not in bales or packages), whether housed or in the open, shall not be stored within 100 ft (30 m) of any building, except as hereinafter specified.

45.5.2 Quantities of loose combustible fibers up to 100 ft^3 (2.8 m^3) shall not be kept in any building unless stored in a metal or metal-lined bin that is equipped with a self-closing cover.

45.5.3 Rooms or Compartments for Quantities of Loose Combustible Fibers Ranging Between 100 ft³ (2.8 m³) and 500 ft³ (14.2 m³).

45.5.3.1 Quantities exceeding 100 ft³ (2.8 m³) of loose combustible fibers, but not exceeding 500 ft³ (14.2 m³), shall be permitted to be stored in rooms or compartments in which the floors, walls, and ceilings have a fire-resistance rating of not less than ¾ hour.

45.5.3.2 Each opening into such rooms or compartments from other parts of the building shall be equipped with an approved self-closing fire door.

45.5.4 Storage Vaults for Quantities of Loose Combustible Fibers Ranging Between 500 ft³ (14.2 m³) and 1000 ft³ (28.3 m³).

45.5.4.1 Quantities exceeding 500 ft³ (14.2 m³) of loose combustible fibers, but not exceeding 1000 ft³ (28.3 m³), shall be permitted to be stored in storage vaults enclosed with floors, walls, and ceilings that are 2-hour fire-resistance-rated fire barriers.

45.5.4.2 Such storage vaults shall be located outside of buildings or, if located inside, shall be protected with approved safety vents to the outside.

45.5.4.3 If such storage vaults are located inside a building, each opening into the storage vault from other parts of the building shall be protected on each side of the wall by an approved opening protective assembly having a fire resistance rating of 1½ hours.

45.5.4.4 If such storage vaults are located outside of buildings but have openings that expose other buildings (not sufficiently detached to be considered cutoff), each such opening shall be protected on each side of the wall by an approved opening protective assembly having a fire resistance rating of 1½ hours.

45.5.4.5 Roofs of outside vaults shall be of noncombustible material, but shall be permitted to be constructed so as to readily give way in case of an internal explosion.

45.5.5 Storage Vaults for Quantities of Loose Combustible Fibers Exceeding 1000 ft³ (28.3 m³).

45.5.5.1 Quantities exceeding 1000 ft³ (28.3 m³) of loose combustible fibers shall be permitted to be stored in storage vaults as indicated in 45.5.4.

45.5.5.2 The storage vault shall also be protected by an approved automatic sprinkler system designed and installed in accordance with Section 13.3.

45.5.6 Loose House.

45.5.6.1 Not more than 2500 ft³ (71 m³) of loose fibers shall be permitted to be stored in a detached loose house, with openings properly protected against the entrance of sparks.

45.5.6.2 The loose house shall be used for no other purpose.

45.6 Baled Storage.

45.6.1 Blocks or Piles.

45.6.1.1 No single block or pile shall contain more than 25,000 ft³ (708 m³) of combustible fibers, exclusive of aisles or clearances.

45.6.1.2 Blocks or piles of baled fiber shall be separated from adjacent storage by aisles not less than 5 ft (1.5 m) wide or by flash fire barriers consisting of continuous sheets of noncombustible material extending from the floor to a height of at least 1 ft (0.3 m) beyond the top of the piles and projecting not less than 1 ft (0.3 m) beyond the sides of the piles.

45.6.1.3 Baled cotton storage and combustibles shall be kept at least 4 ft (1.2 m) from fire door openings.

45.6.2 Sisal and Other Fibers.

45.6.2.1 Sisal and other fibers in bales bound with combustible tie ropes or jute and other fibers that are liable to swell when wet shall be stored in a manner that allows for expansion in any direction without endangering building walls, ceilings, or columns.

45.6.2.2 Not less than 3 ft (0.9 m) of clearance shall be left between walls and sides of piles, except that in storage compartments not more than 30 ft (9 m) in width, 1 ft (0.3 m) clearance at side walls shall be sufficient, provided that a center aisle not less than 5 ft (1.5 m) wide is maintained.

45.7 Storage of Hay, Straw, and Other Similar Agricultural Products.

45.7.1 Hay, straw, and other similar agricultural products shall not be stored adjacent to buildings or combustible material unless a cleared horizontal distance equal to the height of pile is maintained between such storage and combustible material and buildings.

45.7.2 Storage shall be limited to stacks of 100 tons (90,720 kg) each.

45.7.3 Either an approved 1-hour fire wall installed in accordance with NFPA 221 or a clear space of 20 ft (6.1 m) shall be maintained between such stacks.

45.7.4 Unlimited quantities of hay, straw, and other agricultural products shall be permitted to be stored in or near farm buildings located outside of closely built areas.

45.8 Hazardous Materials. Combustible fibers shall not be stored in rooms or buildings with hazardous gases, flammable liquids, dangerous chemicals, or other similar materials.

Chapter 46 Additive Manufacturing (3D Printing)

46.1 Application.

Δ **46.1.1** Additive manufacturing equipment and operations shall comply with this section and other applicable provisions of this *Code*.

Δ **46.1.1.1** Nonindustrial additive manufacturing shall comply with Section 46.2.

Δ **46.1.1.2** Industrial additive manufacturing shall comply with Section 46.3.

Δ **46.1.2 Permits.**

N **46.1.2.1** Permits shall be required in accordance with this chapter and Table 1.13.8(a) through Table 1.13.8(d).

N **46.1.2.2** Permits, where required, shall comply with Section 1.13.

46.1.3 Installation, Operation, and Maintenance. 3D printers and associated additive manufacturing equipment shall be installed, operated, and maintained in accordance with this *Code*, the listing, and the manufacturer's instructions.

46.2 Nonindustrial Additive Manufacturing. Nonindustrial additive manufacturing equipment and operations shall comply with 46.2.1 through 46.2.6. Additive manufacturing operations and equipment that do not comply with 46.2.1 through 46.2.5 shall comply with Section 46.3.

Δ **46.2.1** Equipment used in nonindustrial additive manufacturing shall be listed and labeled in accordance with UL 60950-1, *Information Technology Equipment — Safety — Part 1: General Requirements*; UL 62368-1, *Audio/Video, Information and Communication Technology Equipment — Part 1: Safety Requirements*; or UL 2011, *Outline of Investigation for Machinery*.

Δ **46.2.2** Nonindustrial additive manufacturing shall be self-contained and utilize maximum 8 gal (30 L) prepackaged production materials.

Δ **46.2.3** The operation of the nonindustrial additive manufacturing shall not create a hazardous electrical classified environment outside the unit as defined in *NFPA 70*, Article 500.

Δ **46.2.4** Nonindustrial additive manufacturing shall only use plastic filament production materials, which are listed with the 3D printer and identified in the manufacturer's instructions.

Δ **46.2.5** Nonindustrial additive manufacturing shall not utilize inert gas for creating an inert environment or a combustible dust collection system.

Δ **46.2.6** Nonindustrial additive manufacturing shall be permitted in all occupancy groups.

46.3 Industrial Additive Manufacturing. Industrial additive manufacturing equipment and operations shall comply with 46.3.1 through 46.3.9.

Δ **46.3.1** 3D printers used in industrial additive manufacturing shall be listed and labeled in accordance with UL 2011, *Outline of Investigation for Machinery*, or approved for the application based on a field evaluation conducted by an approved agency.

Δ **46.3.2** Industrial additive manufacturing operations that use, store, or produce combustible powders or dusts shall comply with Chapter 40 and this section.

Δ **46.3.3** 3D printing powders used in industrial additive manufacturing operations shall be tested for combustibility in accordance with NFPA 484 or NFPA 652, as applicable. A copy of test reports shall be provided to the AHJ upon request.

Δ **46.3.4** Industrial additive manufacturing operations that store, use, or produce combustible, nonmetallic powders shall comply with NFPA 654.

Δ **46.3.5** Industrial additive manufacturing operations that store or use combustible metals shall comply with NFPA 484.

Δ **46.3.6** Ancillary equipment provided for recycling, sieving, vacuuming, or handling combustible powders shall be designed and approved for such use.

Δ **46.3.7** Additive manufacturing processes that utilize inert gases shall comply with Chapter 60. A gas detection system shall be provided in rooms or indoor areas in which the inert gas is present. Gas sensors shall be provided in the areas where the gas is expected to accumulate and in other locations required by the AHJ.

Δ **46.3.7.1** The gas detection system shall be designed to activate an audible and visible supervisory alarm at a normally attended location upon detection of inert gas at the 8-hour time-weighted average concentration.

Δ **46.3.7.2** The gas detection system shall be designed to activate an audible and visible alarm within the room or immediate area where the system is located and automatically shut off flow of the inert gas to the 3D printing equipment upon detection of inert gas at the threshold limit value–short-term exposure limit concentration.

Δ **46.3.8*** Where required by the AHJ, a report evaluating the acceptability of technologies, processes, products, facilities, materials, and uses associated with the operation shall be provided in accordance with Section 1.4 and approved. The evaluation shall be conducted by an approved agency.

Δ **46.3.9** Industrial additive manufacturing shall only be conducted in the occupancy groups associated with the manufacturing operations and as permitted by NFPA 400 maximum allowable quantity tables.

Chapter 47 Reserved

Chapter 48 Reserved

Chapter 49 Reserved

Chapter 50 Commercial Cooking

50.1 Application.

50.1.1* The design, installation, operation, inspection, and maintenance of all public and private commercial cooking equipment and mobile and temporary cooking operations shall comply with this chapter and NFPA 96.

N **50.1.2** Permits shall be required in accordance with this chapter and Table 1.13.8(a) through Table 1.13.8(d).

N **50.1.3** Permits, where required, shall comply with Section 1.13.

50.1.4 This chapter shall apply to residential cooking equipment used for commercial cooking operations. [96:1.1.2]

50.1.5* Cooking equipment used in fixed, mobile, or temporary concessions, such as trucks, buses, trailers, pavilions, tents, or any form of roofed enclosure, shall comply with NFPA 96. [96:1.1.3]

50.1.6 This chapter shall not apply to cooking equipment located in a single dwelling unit. [96:1.1.4]

50.1.7* This chapter shall not apply to facilities where all of the following are met:

(1) Only residential equipment is used.
(2) Fire extinguishers are located in all kitchen areas in accordance with Section 13.6.
(3) The facility is not an assembly occupancy.
(4) The AHJ has approved the installation.

[96:1.1.5]

50.2 General Requirements for Cooking Operations in Buildings and Mobile and Temporary Cooking Operations.

50.2.1 General.

50.2.1.1 Cooking equipment used in processes producing smoke or grease-laden vapors shall be equipped with an exhaust system that complies with all the equipment and performance requirements of this chapter. [96:4.1.1]

50.2.1.1.1* Cooking equipment that has been listed in accordance with UL 197 or an equivalent standard for reduced emissions shall not be required to be provided with an exhaust system. [96:4.1.1.1]

50.2.1.1.2 The listing evaluation of cooking equipment covered by 50.2.1.1.1 shall demonstrate that the grease discharge at the exhaust duct of a test hood placed over the appliance shall not exceed 0.00018 oz/ft^3 (5 mg/m^3) when operated with a total airflow of 500 cfm (0.236 m^3/sec). [96:4.1.1.2]

50.2.1.2 All such equipment and its performance shall be maintained in accordance with the requirements of this chapter during all periods of operation of the cooking equipment. [96:4.1.2]

50.2.1.3 The following equipment shall be kept in working condition:

(1) Cooking equipment
(2) Hoods
(3) Ducts
(4) Fans
(5) Fire-extinguishing equipment
(6) Special effluent or energy control equipment

[96:4.1.3]

50.2.1.3.1 Maintenance and repairs shall be performed on all components at intervals necessary to maintain good working condition. [96:4.1.3.1]

50.2.1.4 All airflows shall be maintained. [96:4.1.4]

Δ **50.2.1.5 Responsibility.**

N **50.2.1.5.1*** The responsibility for inspection, testing, maintenance, and cleanliness of the ventilation control and fire protection, and cooking appliances of the commercial cooking operations, shall be that of the equipment owner. [96:4.1.5.1]

N **50.2.1.5.2*** Where the equipment owner is not the commercial cooking operator, the equipment owner shall be permitted to delegate the authority and responsibility for inspection, testing, maintenance, and cleanliness of the ventilation control, fire protection, and cooking appliances to the commercial cooking operator, management firm, or managing individual through specific provisions in the lease, written use agreement, or management contract. [96:50.2.1.5.2]

50.2.1.6 Multitenant applications shall require the concerted cooperation of design, installation, operation, and maintenance responsibilities by tenants and by the building owner. [96:4.1.7]

50.2.1.7 All interior surfaces of the exhaust system shall be accessible for cleaning and inspection purposes. [96:4.1.8]

50.2.2 Clearance.

50.2.2.1* Where enclosures are not required, hoods, grease removal devices, exhaust fans, and ducts shall have a clearance of at least 18 in. (457 mm) to combustible material, 3 in. (76 mm) to limited-combustible material, and 0 in. (0 mm) to noncombustible material. [96:4.2.1]

50.2.2.2 Where a hood, duct, or grease removal device is listed for clearances less than those required in 50.2.2.1, the listing requirements shall be permitted. [96:4.2.2]

50.2.3 Drawings.

50.2.3.1 Where inspections are required, notice shall be given to the AHJ on completion of the installation, or as otherwise directed. [96:4.6.3]

50.2.3.2 For cooking operations in buildings, a drawing(s) of the exhaust system installation along with copies of operating instructions for subassemblies and components used in the exhaust system, including electrical schematics, shall be kept on the premises and made available on request to the AHJ and maintenance persons. [96:4.6.4]

50.2.4 AHJ Notification.
If required by the AHJ, notification in writing shall be given of any alteration, replacement, or relocation of any exhaust or extinguishing system or part thereof or cooking equipment. [96:4.7]

50.3 Protection of Coverings and Enclosure Materials.

50.3.1 Measures shall be taken to prevent physical damage to any covering or enclosure material. [96:7.7.3.1]

50.3.2 Any damage to the covering or enclosure shall be repaired, and the covering or enclosure shall be restored to meet its intended listing and fire resistance rating and to be acceptable to the AHJ. [**96:**7.7.3.2]

50.3.3 In the event of a fire within a kitchen exhaust system, the duct, the enclosure, and the covering directly applied to the duct shall be inspected by qualified personnel to determine whether the duct, the enclosure, and the covering directly applied to the duct are structurally sound, capable of maintaining their fire protection functions, suitable for continued operation, and acceptable to the AHJ. [**96:**7.7.3.3]

50.3.4 Listed grease ducts shall be installed in accordance with the terms of the listing and the manufacturer's instructions. [**96:**7.7.3.4]

50.4 Fire-Extinguishing Equipment for Cooking Operations in Buildings.

50.4.1 Prior to installation of any fire-extinguishing system, construction documents shall be reviewed and approved by the AHJ.

50.4.2 Permits. Permits, where required, shall comply with Section 1.13.

50.4.3 General Requirements.

50.4.3.1 Fire-extinguishing equipment for the protection of grease removal devices, hood exhaust plenums, and exhaust duct systems shall be provided. [**96:**10.1.1]

50.4.3.2* Cooking equipment that produces grease-laden vapors and that might be a source of ignition of grease in the hood, grease removal device, or duct shall be protected by fire-extinguishing equipment. [**96:**10.1.2]

50.4.3.3 Fume incinerators, thermal recovery units, air pollution control devices, or other devices installed in the exhaust duct, shall be protected by an automatic fire-extinguishing system. [**96:**10.1.3]

50.4.4 Types of Equipment.

50.4.4.1 Fire-extinguishing equipment shall include both automatic fire-extinguishing systems as primary protection and portable fire extinguishers as secondary backup. [**96:**10.2.1]

50.4.4.2* A placard shall be conspicuously placed near each Class K extinguisher that states that the fire protection system shall be activated prior to using the fire extinguisher. [**96:**10.2.2]

50.4.4.2.1 The language and wording for the placard shall be approved by the AHJ. [**96:**10.2.2.1]

50.4.4.3* Automatic fire-extinguishing systems shall comply with ANSI/CAN/UL/ULC 300 or other equivalent standards and shall be installed in accordance with the requirements of the listing. [**96:**10.2.3]

50.4.4.3.1* In existing dry or wet chemical systems not in compliance with ANSI/CAN/UL/ULC 300, the fire-extinguishing system shall be made to comply with 50.4.4.3 when any of the following occurs:

(1) The cooking medium is changed from animal oils and fats to vegetable oils.
(2) The positioning of the cooking equipment is changed.
(3) Cooking equipment is replaced.
(4) The equipment is no longer supported by the manufacturer.
[**96:**10.2.3.1]

50.4.4.3.2 The provision became a requirement for all systems effective January 1, 2014. [**96:**10.2.3.2]

50.4.4.4 Grease removal devices, hood exhaust plenums, exhaust ducts, and cooking equipment that are not addressed in ANSI/CAN/UL/ULC 300 or other equivalent test standards shall be protected with an automatic fire-extinguishing system(s) in accordance with the applicable NFPA standard(s), all local building and fire codes, and the fire-extinguishing system's manufacturer's recommendations and shall be approved by the AHJ. [**96:**10.2.4]

50.4.4.5 Automatic fire-extinguishing equipment provided as part of listed recirculating systems shall comply with UL 710B. [**96:**10.2.5]

50.4.4.6 Automatic fire-extinguishing systems shall be installed in accordance with the terms of their listing, the manufacturer's instructions, and the following standards where applicable:

(1) NFPA 12
(2) NFPA 13
(3) NFPA 17
(4) NFPA 17A
(5) NFPA 750
(6) NFPA 770
[**96:**10.2.6]

50.4.4.7 Modifications to Existing Hood Systems.

50.4.4.7.1 Any abandoned pipe or conduit from a previous installation shall be removed from within the hood, plenum, and exhaust duct. [**96:**10.2.7.1]

50.4.4.7.2 Penetrations and holes resulting from the removal of conduit or piping shall be sealed with listed or equivalent liquidtight sealing devices. [**96:**10.2.7.2]

50.4.4.7.3 The addition of obstructions to spray patterns from the cooking appliance nozzle(s) such as baffle plates, shelves, or any modification shall not be permitted. [**96:**10.2.7.3]

50.4.4.7.4 Changes or modifications to the hazard area including cooking appliances after installation of the fire-extinguishing systems shall result in re-evaluation of the system design by a properly trained, qualified, and certified person(s). [**96:**10.2.7.4]

50.4.4.8 Hoods with Water Wash.

50.4.4.8.1 Areas requiring protection in accordance with 50.4.3.1 shall be permitted to be protected by a water-wash system that is listed as a fire-extinguishing system in compliance with ANSI/CAN/UL/ULC 300 or other equivalent standards and installed in accordance with the requirements of its listing. [**96:**10.2.8.1]

50.4.4.8.2 Each such area not provided with a listed water-wash fire-extinguishing system shall be provided with a fire-extinguishing system listed for the purpose. [**96:**10.2.8.2]

50.4.4.8.3 The water supply for water-wash fire-extinguishing systems shall be permitted to be supplied from the domestic water supply when the minimum water pressure and flow are provided in accordance with the terms of the listing. [**96:**10.2.8.3]

50.4.4.8.4 The water supply for water-wash fire-extinguishing systems shall be controlled by a listed indicating valve. [**96:**10.2.8.4]

50.4.4.8.5 Where a separate fire-extinguishing system is used for protection of cooking equipment only, a water-wash fire-extinguishing system listed for protection of the grease removal device(s), hood exhaust plenum(s), exhaust duct(s), or combination thereof shall be provided with instructions and appropriate means for electrical interface for simultaneous actuation. [**96:**10.2.8.5]

50.4.4.8.6 A water-wash system approved to be used for protection of the grease removal device(s), hood exhaust plenum(s), exhaust duct(s), or combination thereof shall include instructions and appropriate electrical interface for simultaneous actuation of the water-wash system from an automatic fire-extinguishing system, where the automatic fire-extinguishing system is used for cooking equipment protection only. [**96:**10.2.8.6]

50.4.4.8.7 Where the automatic fire-extinguishing system in accordance with NFPA 17A provides protection for the hood and duct in a hood containing a water-wash system, the water-wash system shall be made inoperable or delayed for a minimum of 60 seconds upon operation of the automatic fire-extinguishing system. [**96:**10.2.8.7]

50.4.4.8.8 Grease removal devices, hood exhaust plenums, and exhaust ducts on hoods with water wash shall be permitted to be protected by a sprinkler system with an individual control valve if the design of the hood prevents the water from reaching the cooking appliances. [**96:**10.2.8.8]

50.4.4.9 Water-Based Fire-Extinguishing System.

50.4.4.9.1 The water required for listed automatic fire-extinguishing systems shall be permitted to be supplied from the domestic water supply where the minimum water pressure and flow are provided in accordance with the terms of the listing. The water supply shall be controlled by a supervised water supply control valve. [**96:**10.2.9.1]

50.4.4.9.2 Where the water supply is from a dedicated fire protection water supply in a building with one or more fire sprinkler systems, separate indicating control valves and drains shall be provided and arranged so that the hood system and sprinkler systems can be controlled individually. [**96:**10.2.9.2]

50.4.4.10 Water Valve Supervision. Valves controlling the water supply to listed water-wash fire-extinguishing systems, automatic fire-extinguishing systems, or both shall be listed indicating type of valve and shall be supervised open by one of the following methods:

(1) Central station, proprietary, or remote station alarm service
(2) Local alarm service that will cause the sounding of an audible signal at a constantly attended point
(3) Locking valves open
(4)* Sealing of valves and approved weekly recorded inspection

[**96:**10.2.10]

50.4.5 Simultaneous Operation.

50.4.5.1 Fixed pipe extinguishing systems in a single hazard area *(see 3.3.44 of NFPA 96 for the definition of single hazard area)* shall be arranged for simultaneous automatic operation upon actuation of any one of the systems. [**96:**10.3.1]

50.4.5.1.1 Hoods installed end to end, back to back, or both, or sharing a common ductwork, not exceeding 75 ft (22.9 m) in distance from the farthest hood, and having a grease-producing appliance(s) located under one or more of the hoods, shall be considered a single hazard area requiring simultaneous automatic fire protection in all hoods and ducts. [**96:**10.3.1.1]

50.4.5.1.1.1 In hoods that are installed end to end, back to back, or both, and that share a common ductwork, the ductwork beyond 75 ft (22.9 m) from the farthest hood shall be protected by an independent fire-extinguishing system with its own detection system or by a fire-extinguishing system that activates simultaneously with the fire-extinguishing system(s) protecting the hoods. [**96:**10.3.1.1.1]

50.4.5.1.2 Hoods installed end to end, back to back, or both that do not share a common exhaust duct and are separated by a wall(s) or other means to ensure that grease-laden vapors exhausted under one hood cannot propagate to the other hoods, the hoods' fire-extinguishing system(s) shall be independent and shall not be required to simultaneously discharge. [**96:**10.3.1.2]

50.4.5.1.3 Fume incinerators, thermal recovery units, air pollution control devices, or other devices installed in the exhaust duct shall not be required to comply with 50.4.5.1.1. [**96:**10.3.1.3]

50.4.5.2 Simultaneous operation shall not be required where the one fixed pipe extinguishing system is an automatic sprinkler system. [**96:**10.3.2]

50.4.5.2.1 Where an automatic sprinkler system is used in conjunction with a water-based fire-extinguishing system served by the same water supply, hydraulic calculations shall consider both systems operating simultaneously. [**96:**10.3.2.1]

50.4.5.3 Simultaneous operation shall be required where a dry or wet chemical system is used to protect common exhaust ductwork by one of the methods specified in NFPA 17 or NFPA 17A. [**96:**10.3.3]

50.4.6 Fuel and Electric Power Shutoff.

50.4.6.1 Upon actuation of any fire-extinguishing system for a cooking operation, all sources of fuel and electric power that produce heat to all equipment protected by the system shall automatically shut off. [**17A:**4.4.4.1]

50.4.6.2 Steam supplied from an external source shall not be required to automatically shut off. [**96:**10.4.2]

50.4.6.3 Gas appliances not requiring protection but located under the same ventilation equipment where protected appliances are located shall also be automatically shut off upon actuation of the extinguishing system. [**17A:**4.4.4.2]

50.4.6.4 Shutoff devices shall require manual resetting prior to fuel or power being restored. [**96:**10.4.4]

50.4.6.5 Solid fuel cooking operations shall not be required to be shut down. [**96:**10.4.5]

50.4.7 Manual Actuation.

50.4.7.1 All systems shall have both automatic and manual methods of actuation. [**96:**10.5.1]

50.4.7.1.1* At least one manual actuator shall be located in a means of egress or at a location acceptable to the AHJ. [**96:**10.5.1.1]

50.4.7.1.2 The actuator shall clearly identify the hazard protected and be provided with instructions for its use. [**96:**10.5.1.2]

50.4.7.1.3* Manual actuators installed in locations where accidental operation could occur shall be provided with a guard where required by the AHJ. [**96:**10.5.1.3]

50.4.7.2 An automatic sprinkler system shall not require a method of manual actuation. [**96:**10.5.2]

50.4.8 System Annunciation.

50.4.8.1 Upon actuation of an automatic fire-extinguishing system, an audible alarm or visual indicator shall be provided to show that the system has actuated. [**96:**10.6.1]

50.4.8.2 Where a fire alarm signaling system is serving the occupancy where the extinguishing system is located, the actuation of the automatic fire-extinguishing system shall actuate the fire alarm signaling system in accordance with the requirements of *NFPA 72*. [**96:**10.6.2]

50.4.9 Special Design and Application.

50.4.9.1 Hoods containing automatic fire-extinguishing systems are protected areas; therefore, these hoods shall not be considered obstructions to overhead sprinkler systems and shall not require additional sprinkler coverage underneath. [**96:**10.7.1]

Δ **50.4.9.2** A single listed detection device shall be permitted for more than one appliance when installed in accordance with the system's listing.

50.4.10 Review and Certification.

50.4.10.1 Where required, complete drawings of the system installation, including the hood(s), exhaust duct(s), and appliances, along with the interface of the fire-extinguishing system detectors, piping, nozzles, fuel and electric power shutoff devices, agent storage container(s), and manual actuation device(s), shall be submitted to the AHJ. [**96:**10.8.1]

50.4.10.2* Installation Requirements.

50.4.10.2.1 Installation of systems shall be performed only by persons properly trained and qualified to install the specific system being provided. [**96:**10.8.2.1]

50.4.10.2.2 The installer shall provide certification to the AHJ that the installation is in agreement with the terms of the listing and the manufacturer's instructions and/or approved design. [**96:**10.8.2.2]

50.4.11 Portable Fire Extinguishers.

50.4.11.1* Portable fire extinguishers shall be selected and installed in kitchen cooking areas in accordance with Section 13.6 and shall be specifically listed for such use. [**96:**10.9.1]

50.4.11.2 Class K fire extinguishers shall be provided for cooking appliance hazards that involve combustible cooking media (vegetable oils and animal oils and fats). [**96:**10.9.2]

50.4.11.3 Portable fire extinguishers shall be provided for other hazards in kitchen areas and shall be selected and installed in accordance with Section 13.6. [**96:**10.9.3]

50.4.11.4 Carbon dioxide–type extinguishers shall not be permitted. [**96:**10.9.4]

50.4.11.5 Portable fire extinguishers shall be maintained in accordance with Section 13.6. [**96:**10.9.5]

50.5 Fire-Extinguishing Equipment for Mobile and Temporary Cooking Operations.

50.5.1 General Requirements.

50.5.1.1 Fire-extinguishing equipment for the protection of grease removal devices, hood exhaust plenums, and exhaust duct systems shall be provided. [**96:**11.1.1]

50.5.1.2* Cooking equipment that produces grease-laden vapors shall be protected by a fire-extinguishing system for the protection of grease removal devices, hood exhaust plenums, and exhaust duct systems. [**96:**11.1.2]

50.5.2 Types of Equipment.

50.5.2.1* A placard shall be conspicuously placed near each Class K extinguisher that states that the fire protection system shall be activated prior to using the fire extinguisher. [**96:**11.2.1]

50.5.2.1.1 The language and wording for the placard shall be approved by the AHJ. [**96:**11.2.1.1]

50.5.2.2* Automatic fire-extinguishing systems shall comply with ANSI/CAN/UL/ULC 300 or other equivalent standards and shall be installed in accordance with the terms of their listing and NFPA 17A. [**96:**11.2.2]

50.5.2.3 Modifications to Existing Hood Systems.

50.5.2.3.1 Any abandoned pipe or conduit from a previous installation shall be removed from within the hood, plenum, and exhaust duct. [**96:**11.2.3.1]

50.5.2.3.2 Penetrations and holes resulting from the removal of conduit or piping shall be sealed with listed or equivalent liquidtight sealing devices. [**96:**11.2.3.2]

50.5.2.3.3 The addition of obstructions to spray patterns from the cooking appliance nozzle(s) such as baffle plates, shelves, or any modification shall not be permitted. [**96:**11.2.3.3]

50.5.2.3.4 Changes or modifications to the hazard after installation of the fire-extinguishing systems shall result in re-evaluation of the system design by a properly trained, qualified, and certified person(s). [**96:**11.2.3.4]

50.5.3 Fuel and Electric Power Shutoff.

50.5.3.1 Upon actuation of any fire-extinguishing system for a cooking operation, all sources of fuel and electric power that produce heat to all equipment protected by the system shall automatically shut off. [**17A:**4.4.4.1]

50.5.3.2 Gas appliances not requiring protection but located under the same ventilation equipment where protected appliances are located shall also be automatically shut off upon actuation of the extinguishing system. [**17A:**4.4.4.2]

50.5.3.3 Shutoff devices shall require manual resetting prior to fuel or power being restored. [**96:**11.3.3]

50.5.3.3.1 Where an electrical gas valve is used for shutting off gas to appliances, a manually reset relay shall be used to restore electrical power to the gas valve. [**96**:11.3.3.1]

50.5.4 Manual Actuation.

50.5.4.1 All systems shall have both automatic and manual methods of actuation. [**96**:11.4.1]

50.5.4.1.1* At least one manual actuation device shall be located in a means of egress or at a location acceptable to the AHJ. [**96**:11.4.1.1]

50.5.4.1.2 The manual actuation device shall clearly identify the hazard protected and be provided with instructions for its use. [**96**:11.4.1.2]

50.5.4.1.3* Manual actuation devices installed in locations where accidental operation could occur shall be provided with a guard where required by the AHJ. [**96**:11.4.1.3]

50.5.4.2 An automatic sprinkler system shall not require a method of manual actuation. [**96**:11.4.2]

50.5.5 System Annunciation.

50.5.5.1 Upon actuation of an automatic fire-extinguishing system, an audible alarm or visual indicator shall be provided to show that the system has actuated. [**96**:11.5.1]

50.5.5.2 At least one listed audible and visual notification appliance shall be installed on the exterior surface of the vehicle readily audible and visible to the public. [**96**:11.5.2]

50.5.6 Review and Certification.

50.5.6.1 Where required, complete drawings of the system installation, including the hood(s), exhaust duct(s), and appliances, along with the interface of the fire-extinguishing system detectors, piping, nozzles, fuel and electric power shutoff devices, agent storage container(s), and manual actuation device(s), shall be submitted to the AHJ and located within the mobile cooking operation. [**96**:11.6.1]

50.5.6.2* Installation Requirements.

50.5.6.2.1 Installation of systems shall be performed only by persons properly trained and qualified to install the specific system being provided. [**96**:11.6.2.1]

50.5.6.2.2 The installer shall provide certification to the AHJ that the installation is in agreement with the terms of the listing and the manufacturer's instructions and/or approved design. [**96**:11.6.2.2]

50.5.7 Portable Fire Extinguishers.

50.5.7.1* Portable fire extinguishers shall be selected and installed in kitchen cooking areas in accordance with Section 13.6 and shall be specifically listed for such use. [**96**:11.7.1]

50.5.7.2 Class K fire extinguishers shall be provided for cooking appliance hazards that involve combustible cooking media (vegetable oils and animal oils and fats). [**96**:11.7.2]

Δ **50.5.7.3** Portable fire extinguishers shall be provided for solid fuel cooking operations in accordance with 15.7.5 of NFPA 96. [**96**:11.7.3]

50.5.7.4 Portable fire extinguishers shall be provided for other hazards in kitchen areas and shall be selected and installed in accordance with Section 13.6. [**96**:11.7.4]

50.5.7.5 Where internal combustion engine power sources are provided, at least one portable fire extinguisher 20-B:C shall be provided. [**96**:11.7.5]

50.5.7.6 Carbon dioxide–type extinguishers shall not be permitted. [**96**:11.7.6]

50.5.7.7 Portable fire extinguishers shall be maintained in accordance with Section 13.6. [**96**:11.7.7]

50.6 Procedures for the Use, Inspection, Testing, and Maintenance of Equipment.

50.6.1 Operating Procedures.

50.6.1.1 Exhaust systems shall be operated whenever cooking equipment is turned on. [**96**:12.1.1]

50.6.1.2 Filter-equipped exhaust systems shall not be operated with filters removed. [**96**:12.1.2]

50.6.1.3 Openings provided for replacing air exhausted through ventilating equipment shall not be restricted by covers, dampers, or any other means that would reduce the operating efficiency of the exhaust system. [**96**:12.1.3]

50.6.1.4* Instructions shall be provided to new employees on hiring and to all employees annually on the use of portable fire extinguishers and the manual actuation of the fire-extinguishing system. [**96**:12.1.4]

50.6.1.4.1 Responsibility for compliance with 50.6.1.4 shall be that of management of the commercial cooking operation. [**96**:12.1.4.1]

50.6.1.4.2 Records of compliance with 50.6.1.4 shall be maintained and shall be available to the AHJ. [**96**:12.1.4.2]

50.6.1.4.3 Instructions for manually operating the fire-extinguishing system shall be posted conspicuously in the kitchen and shall be reviewed with employees by the management. [**96**:12.1.4.3]

50.6.1.5 Listed exhaust hoods shall be operated in accordance with the terms of their listings and the manufacturer's instructions. [**96**:12.1.5]

50.6.1.6 Cooking equipment shall not be operated while its fire-extinguishing system or exhaust system is nonoperational or impaired. [**96**:12.1.6]

50.6.1.6.1 Where the fire-extinguishing system or exhaust system is nonoperational or impaired, the system shall be tagged as noncompliant, the system owner or the owner's representative shall be notified in writing of the impairment, and, where required, the AHJ shall be notified. [**96**:12.1.6.1]

50.6.1.7 Secondary filtration and pollution control equipment shall be operated in accordance with the terms of its listing and the manufacturer's recommendations. [**96**:12.1.7]

50.6.1.7.1 The requirement of 50.6.1.7 shall not apply to mobile and temporary cooking operations. [**96**:12.1.7.1]

50.6.1.8 Inspection and maintenance of "other equipment" as allowed in 9.3.1 of NFPA 96 shall be conducted by properly trained and qualified persons at a frequency determined by the manufacturer's instructions or the equipment listing. [**96**:12.1.8]

50.6.2 Inspection, Testing, and Maintenance of Fire-Extinguishing Systems.

50.6.2.1* Maintenance of the fire-extinguishing systems and listed exhaust hoods containing a constant or fire-activated water system that is listed to extinguish a fire in the grease removal devices, hood exhaust plenums, and exhaust ducts shall be made by properly trained, qualified, and certified person(s) acceptable to the AHJ at least every 6 months. [**96**:12.2.1]

50.6.2.2* All actuation and control components, including remote manual pull stations, mechanical and electrical devices, detectors, and actuators, shall be tested for proper operation during the inspection in accordance with the manufacturer's procedures. [**96**:12.2.2]

50.6.2.3 The specific inspection and maintenance requirements of the extinguishing system standards as well as the applicable installation and maintenance manuals for the listed system and service bulletins shall be followed. [**96**:12.2.3]

50.6.2.4* Fusible links of the metal alloy type and automatic sprinklers of the metal alloy type shall be replaced at least semiannually. [**96**:12.2.4]

50.6.2.5 The year of manufacture and the date of installation of the fusible links shall be marked on the system inspection tag. [**96**:12.2.6]

50.6.2.5.1 The tag shall be signed or initialed by the installer. [**96**:12.2.6.1]

50.6.2.5.2 The fusible links shall be destroyed when removed. [**96**:12.2.6.2]

50.6.2.6 Detection devices that are bulb-type automatic sprinklers and fusible links other than the metal alloy type shall be examined and cleaned or replaced annually. [**96**:12.2.7]

50.6.2.7 Fixed temperature-sensing elements other than the fusible metal alloy type shall be permitted to remain continuously in service, provided they are inspected and cleaned or replaced if necessary in accordance with the manufacturer's instructions, every 12 months or more frequently to ensure proper operation of the system. [**96**:12.2.8]

50.6.2.8 Where required, certificates of inspection and maintenance shall be forwarded to the AHJ. [**96**:12.2.9]

50.6.2.8.1 Records, including certificates of inspection and maintenance, shall be permitted to be forwarded to or shared with the AHJ either by hard copy or electronically. [**96**:12.2.9.1]

50.6.3 Inspection of Fire Dampers.

50.6.3.1 The requirements in 50.6.3 shall not apply to mobile and temporary cooking operations. [**96**:12.3.1]

50.6.3.2 Actuation components for fire dampers shall be inspected for proper operation in accordance with the manufacturer's listed procedures. [**96**:12.3.2]

50.6.3.3 Replacement of Fusible Links.

50.6.3.3.1 Fusible links on fire damper assemblies shall be replaced at least semiannually or more frequently as necessary. [**96**:12.3.3.1]

50.6.3.3.2 Replacement shall be made by a certified person acceptable to the AHJ. [**96**:12.3.3.2]

50.6.3.4* Documentation Tag.

50.6.3.4.1 The year of manufacture and the date of installation of the fusible links shall be documented. [**96**:12.3.4.1]

50.6.3.4.2 The tag shall be signed or initialed by the installer. [**96**:12.3.4.2]

50.6.4* Inspection for Grease Buildup. The entire exhaust system shall be inspected for grease buildup by a properly trained, qualified, and certified person(s) acceptable to the AHJ and in accordance with Table 50.6.4. [**96**:12.4]

50.6.5 Inspection, Testing, and Maintenance of Listed Hoods Containing Mechanical, Water Spray, or Ultraviolet Devices. Listed hoods containing mechanical or fire-actuated dampers, internal washing components, or other mechanically operated devices shall be inspected and tested by properly trained, qualified, and certified persons every 6 months or at frequencies recommended by the manufacturer in accordance with their listings. [**96**:12.5]

50.6.6 Cleaning of Exhaust Systems.

50.6.6.1* If, upon inspection, the exhaust system is found to be contaminated with deposits from grease-laden vapors, the contaminated portions of the exhaust system shall be cleaned by a properly trained qualified, and certified person(s) acceptable to the AHJ. [**96**:12.6.1]

50.6.6.1.1 A measurement system of deposition shall be established to trigger a need to clean when the exhaust system is inspected at the frequencies in Table 50.6.4. [**96**:12.6.1.1]

50.6.6.1.1.1 Hoods, grease removal devices, fans, ducts, and other appurtenances shall be cleaned to remove combustible contaminants to a maximum of 0.002 in. (50 µm). [**96**:12.6.1.1.1]

50.6.6.1.1.2 A grease depth gauge comb as shown in Figure 50.6.6.1.1.2 shall be placed upon the surface to measure grease depth. [**96**:12.6.1.1.2]

50.6.6.1.1.3 Where a measured depth of 0.078 in. (2000 µm) is observed, the surfaces shall be cleaned in accordance with 50.6.6.1. [**96**:12.6.1.1.3]

Table 50.6.4 Schedule of Inspection for Grease Buildup

Type or Volume of Cooking	Inspection Frequency
Systems serving solid fuel cooking operations	Monthly
*Systems serving high-volume cooking operations	Quarterly
Systems serving moderate-volume cooking operations	Semiannually
†Systems serving low-volume cooking operations	Annually

*High-volume cooking operations include 24-hour cooking, charbroiling, and wok cooking.
†Low-volume cooking operations include churches, day camps, seasonal businesses, and senior centers.
[**96**:Table 12.4]

FIGURE 50.6.6.1.1.2   Depth Gauge Comb. [96:Figure 12.6.6.1.1.2]

50.6.6.1.1.4 Where a measured depth of 0.125 in. (3175 μm) is observed in a fan housing, the surfaces shall be cleaned in accordance with 50.6.6.1. [96:12.6.1.1.4]

50.6.6.2 Hoods, grease removal devices, fans, ducts, and other appurtenances shall be cleaned to remove combustible contaminants prior to surfaces becoming heavily contaminated with grease or oily sludge. [96:12.6.2]

50.6.6.3 At the start of the cleaning process, electrical switches that could be activated accidentally shall be locked out. [96:12.6.3]

50.6.6.4 Components of the fire suppression system shall not be rendered inoperable during the cleaning process. [96:12.6.4]

50.6.6.5 Fire-extinguishing systems shall be permitted to be rendered inoperable during the cleaning process where serviced by properly trained and qualified persons. [96:12.6.5]

50.6.6.6 Flammable solvents or other flammable cleaning aids shall not be used. [96:12.6.6]

50.6.6.7 Cleaning chemicals shall not be applied on fusible links or other detection devices of the automatic extinguishing system. [96:12.6.7]

50.6.6.8 After the exhaust system is cleaned, it shall not be coated with powder or other substance. [96:12.6.8]

50.6.6.9 When cleaning procedures are completed, all access panels (doors) and cover plates shall be restored to their normal operational condition. [96:12.6.9]

50.6.6.10 When an access panel is removed, a service company label or tag preprinted with the name of the company and giving the date of inspection or cleaning shall be affixed near the affected access panels. [96:12.6.10]

50.6.6.11 Dampers and diffusers shall be positioned for proper airflow. [96:12.6.11]

50.6.6.12 When cleaning procedures are completed, all electrical switches and system components shall be returned to an operable state. [96:12.6.12]

50.6.6.13 After an exhaust system is inspected or cleaned, an adhesive label shall be securely attached to the hood. [96:12.6.13]

N **50.6.6.13.1** The label required by 50.6.6.13 shall provide a record of the following information:

(1)* Date service was performed indicated by a perforation
(2) Name of person performing the work
(3) Name, address, and phone number of service provider
[96:12.6.13.1]

N **50.6.6.13.2** The label required by 50.6.6.13 shall remain affixed until the next inspection or cleaning event. [96:12.6.13.2]

50.6.6.14 After an inspection for grease buildup is complete, a written report shall be provided to the system owner or owner's agent (see 50.2.1.5) within 2 weeks. [96:12.6.14]

N **50.6.6.14.1** The report required by 50.6.6.14 shall provide a record of the following information:

(1) Areas in need of cleaning where grease is found to exceed the limits specified in 50.6.6.1
(2) Areas that are inaccessible and were not inspected
(3) Areas that are accessible but were not inspected
(4) Location(s) of duct access panel(s)
(5) Location(s) of visible leakage(s) from ductwork
(6) Location(s) of leaking access panel(s)

50.6.6.15 After cleaning is complete, a written report shall be provided to the system owner or owner's agent (see 50.2.1.5) within 2 weeks. [96:12.6.15]

N **50.6.6.15.1** The report required by 50.6.6.15 shall provide a record of the following information:

(1) Date cleaning was performed
(2) Name of person who performed the cleaning
(3) Name, address, and phone number of service provider
[96:12.6.15.1]

N **50.6.6.15.2** The report required by 50.6.6.15 shall detail the following information:

(1) Areas that are inaccessible and were not cleaned
(2) Areas that are accessible but were not cleaned
(3) Location(s) of duct access panel(s)
(4) Location(s) of visible leakage(s) from ductwork
(5) Location(s) of leaking access panel(s)
[96:12.6.15.2]

50.6.6.16 Where required, the reports required by 50.6.6.15.1 and 50.6.6.15.2 shall be submitted to the AHJ. [96:12.6.16]

50.6.7 Cooking Equipment Maintenance.

50.6.7.1 Inspection and servicing of the cooking equipment shall be made at least annually by properly trained and qualified persons. [96:12.7.1]

50.6.7.2* Cooking equipment that collects grease below the surface, behind the equipment, or in cooking equipment flue gas exhaust, such as griddles, deep-fat fryers, or charbroilers, shall be inspected and, if found with grease accumulation, cleaned by a properly trained, qualified, and certified person(s) acceptable to the AHJ. [96:12.7.2]

50.7 Minimum Safety Requirements for Cooking Equipment.

50.7.1 Cooking Equipment.

50.7.1.1* Cooking equipment shall be approved based on one of the following criteria:

(1) Listings by a testing laboratory
(2) Test data acceptable to the AHJ
[96:13.1.1]

50.7.1.2 Installation.

50.7.1.2.1* All listed appliances shall be installed in accordance with the terms of their listings and the manufacturer's instructions. [96:13.1.2.1]

50.7.1.2.1.1 Solid fuel used for flavoring within a gas-operated appliance shall be in a solid fuel holder (smoker box) that is listed with the equipment. [**96:**13.1.2.1.1]

50.7.1.2.2* Cooking appliances requiring protection shall not be moved, modified, or rearranged without prior re-evaluation of the fire-extinguishing system by the system installer or servicing agent, unless otherwise allowed by the design of the fire-extinguishing system. [**96:**13.1.2.2]

50.7.1.2.2.1 A solid fuel holder shall not be added to an existing appliance until the fire-extinguishing system has been evaluated by the fire-extinguishing system service provider. [**96:**13.1.2.2.1]

50.7.1.2.3 The fire-extinguishing system shall not require re-evaluation where the cooking appliances are moved for the purposes of maintenance and cleaning, provided the appliances are returned to approved design location prior to cooking operations, and any disconnected fire-extinguishing system nozzles attached to the appliances are reconnected in accordance with the manufacturer's listed design manual. [**96:**13.1.2.3]

50.7.1.2.3.1* An approved method shall be provided that will ensure that the appliance is returned to an approved design location. [**96:**13.1.2.3.1]

50.7.1.2.4 All deep-fat fryers shall be installed with at least a 16 in. (406 mm) space between the fryer and surface flames from adjacent cooking equipment. [**96:**13.1.2.4]

50.7.1.2.5 Where a steel or tempered glass baffle plate is installed at a minimum 8 in. (203 mm) in height between the fryer and surface flames of the adjacent appliance, the requirement for a 16 in. (406 mm) space shall not apply. [**96:**13.1.2.5]

50.7.1.2.5.1 If the fryer and the surface flames are at different horizontal planes, the minimum height of 8 in. (203 mm) shall be measured from the higher of the two. [**96:**13.1.2.5.1]

50.7.2 Commercial Kitchen Cooking Oil Storage Tank Systems. Commercial kitchen cooking oil storage tank systems shall comply with 66.19.7.

50.8 Mobile and Temporary Cooking Operations.

50.8.1 General.

50.8.1.1 Mobile and temporary cooking operations shall comply with the requirements of this section, NFPA 96 and the applicable section for the type of cooking performed.

50.8.1.2 Where required by the AHJ, permits shall be required for the location, design, construction, and operation of mobile and temporary cooking operations.

50.8.1.3 Cooking equipment that is powered on during transit shall be listed as installed for such use. [**96:**17.1.2]

50.8.1.4 Fire Department Access. Mobile or temporary cooking operations shall not block fire apparatus access roads, fire lanes, fire hydrants, or other fire protection devices and equipment.

50.8.1.5 Communications.

50.8.1.5.1 Where required by the AHJ, an approved method of communication to emergency personnel shall be accessible to all employees.

50.8.1.5.2 The address of the current operational location shall be posted and accessible to all employees.

50.8.1.6 Storage of Flammable and Combustible Liquids. Flammable and combustible liquids shall not be stored inside mobile cooking vehicles or in temporary cooking areas unless stored in accordance with NFPA 30.

50.8.2 Location of Mobile and Temporary Cooking Operations.

50.8.2.1* Relative to Buildings. Mobile or temporary cooking operations shall be separated from the entrances and other exits of buildings or structures, combustible materials, vehicles, and other cooking operations by a clear space distance of 10 ft (3 m) or as prescribed by the AHJ. [**96:**17.2.1]

50.8.2.2 Relative to Other Mobile or Temporary Cooking. Mobile or temporary cooking operations shall be separated from other mobile or temporary cooking operations by a clear distance of 10 ft (3 m). [**96:**17.2.2]

50.8.2.3 When the mobile unit is parked, the vehicle shall be stabilized so that it will not move, either by jacking the vehicle or placing wheel chocks around the wheels. [**96:**17.2.3]

50.8.3 Tents.

50.8.3.1 Temporary cooking operations conducted in tents shall comply with NFPA 102 and Chapter 25. [**96:**17.3.1]

50.8.3.2 Seating for the public shall not be located within any mobile or temporary cooking vehicle.

N **50.8.4 Appliance Installation on Vehicles.**

N **50.8.4.1** Cooking equipment shall be approved based on one of the following criteria:

(1) Listings by a testing laboratory
(2) Test data acceptable to the authority having jurisdiction
[**96:**17.4.1]

N **50.8.4.1.1** Cooking equipment shall be installed in accordance with the manufacturer's instructions. [**96:**17.4.1.1]

N **50.8.4.2** Space and water heating appliances shall be listed and installed in accordance with the manufacturer's instructions. [**96:**17.4.2]

N **50.8.4.3** Any appliance originally manufactured for operation with a gaseous fuel other than LP-Gas shall not be used with LP-Gas unless it is converted for use in accordance with the manufacturer's instructions. [**96:**17.4.3]

N **50.8.4.4** Catalytic heating appliances shall be equipped with an approved automatic device to shut off the flow of gas in the event of combustion failure. [**96:**17.4.4]

N **50.8.4.5** Gas-fired appliances shall be provided with combustion air, flue outlets, and cooking exhaust systems in accordance with the manufacturer's instructions. [**96:**17.4.5]

N **50.8.5 LP-Gas Cooking Appliances.**

N **50.8.5.1** Gas-fired cooking appliances shall be equipped with shutoffs in accordance with 5.23.8(A) of NFPA 58. [**96:**17.5.1]

N **50.8.5.2** Cooking appliances installed on vehicles shall be readily accessible under all conditions. [**96:**17.5.2]

N **50.8.5.3** To minimize possible damage and impaired operation due to items shifting in transit, cooking appliances shall be constructed and secured in place or otherwise protected. [**96**:17.5.3]

N **50.8.5.4** Appliances shall be located such that a fire at any appliance will not block egress of persons from the vehicle. [**96**:17.5.4]

N **50.8.5.5** A permanent caution plate shall be installed in a location visible to operational personnel. [**96**:17.5.5]

N **50.8.5.6** The caution plate shall be in accordance with Figure 50.8.5.6 and comply with the following specifications:

(1) The triangle shall be black with a yellow Pantone 109 C exclamation mark.
(2) The word "CAUTION" shall be in black font on a yellow Pantone 109 C background.
(3) The fire symbol shall be black within a red Pantone 186 C diamond shape.
(4) All other text shall be in black Arial font.

[**96**:17.5.6]

N **50.8.5.7** Gas-fired cooking appliances shall be equipped with automatic devices designed to shut off the flow of gas to the main burner and the pilot in the event the pilot flame is extinguished. [**96**:17.5.7]

50.8.6 Internal Combustion Engine Power Sources.

50.8.6.1 Electric generator and internal combustion power sources used for mobile or temporary cooking shall comply with 50.8.6.

50.8.6.2 Electrical appliances, fixtures, equipment, or wiring other than low-voltage and automotive vehicle circuits or extensions thereof, installed within or on vehicles, shall comply with *NFPA 70*.

50.8.6.3 An internal combustion engine shall be permitted to be used to operate an electric power generator. [**96**:17.6.1]

50.8.6.4 Generator units that are not vehicle-mounted while in use shall meet the requirements of 50.8.6.4.1 through 50.8.6.4.3. [**96**:17.6.2]

50.8.6.4.1 Internal combustion engine power sources shall be located at least 12 ft (4 m) from mobile or temporary cooking operations. [**96**:17.6.2.1]

50.8.6.4.2 Internal combustion engine power sources shall be isolated from physical contact by the installation of physical guards, fencing, or an enclosure. [**96**:17.6.2.2]

50.8.6.4.3 Internal combustion engine power sources shall be positioned so that the exhaust complies with the following:

(1) Located at least 12 ft (4 m) from openings, air intakes, and means of egress
(2) In a position pointed away from any building
(3) In a position pointed away from any mobile or temporary cooking operations

[**96**:17.6.2.3]

50.8.7 Vehicle-Mounted Generators.

50.8.7.1 Vehicle-mounted generators shall meet the requirements of 50.8.7.2 through 50.8.7.5.

50.8.7.2 Internal combustion engine-driven generator units (subject to the provisions of NFPA 1192) shall be listed and installed in accordance with the manufacturer's instructions and shall be vapor resistant to the interior of the vehicle. [**1192**:6.4.5.1]

50.8.7.3 Where a generator compartment is used to isolate the installed generator from the vehicle's interior, or a compartment is provided for the future installation of a generator and is intended to isolate the future generator from the vehicle interior, the generator compartment shall be lined with galvanized steel not less than 26 MSG thick. [**1192**:6.4.5.2]

50.8.7.3.1 Seams and joints shall be lapped, mechanically secured, and made vapor resistant to the interior of the vehicle. [**1192**:6.4.5.2.1]

50.8.7.3.2 Alternative materials and methods of construction shall be permitted in accordance with Section 1.4. [**1192**:6.4.5.2.2]

50.8.7.4 Liquid fuel lines and exhaust systems shall not penetrate into the area. [**1192**:6.4.5.2.3]

50.8.7.5 Holes into the living area shall be sealed. [**1192**:6.4.5.2.4]

50.8.8 LP-Gas Systems.

Δ **50.8.8.1** LP-Gas systems for mobile cooking operations shall comply with NFPA 58 and NFPA 96.

50.8.8.1.1 LP-Gas cylinders shall be secured so that the relief valve is in communication with the vapor space of the cylinder. [**96**:17.8.1.1]

50.8.8.1.2 Where a shutoff valve is provided, it shall be readily accessible and identified with a sign permanently affixed to the vehicle in reflective decal material with letters a minimum of 2 in. (50 mm) high.

50.8.8.2 LP-Gas System Leak Detection.

50.8.8.2.1 All mobile and temporary cooking operations equipped with a propane appliance and an electrical system

N **FIGURE 50.8.5.6** Appliance Caution Plate. [96:Figure 17.5.6]

shall be equipped with a propane detector listed and marked on the device as being suitable for use in the vehicles under the requirements of UL 1484, and installed according to the terms of its listing. [96:17.8.2.1]

50.8.8.2.2 The LP-Gas leak detection system shall be tested monthly. [96:17.8.2.2]

50.8.8.2.3* LP-Gas systems shall be visually inspected daily for damage and proper operation prior to each use. [96:17.8.2.3]

50.8.8.2.4 Where problems are detected, the system shall not be used until immediate corrective action is taken. [96:17.8.2.4]

50.8.8.3 LP-Gas Systems on Vehicles (Other than Engine Fuel Systems).

50.8.8.3.1 LP-Gas Container Installation Requirements.

50.8.8.3.1.1 LP-Gas containers installed on vehicles shall not exceed 200 gal (0.8 m^3) aggregate water capacity. [96:17.8.4.1.3]

50.8.8.3.2 Disconnected LP-Gas containers and LP-Gas cylinders for purposes other than engine fuel systems shall not be transported or stored inside the vehicle. [96:17.8.4.2]

△ **50.8.8.3.3** All other LP-Gas containers and LP-Gas cylinders shall comply with 17.8.4.7 of NFPA 96 and Chapter 69. [96:17.8.4.3]

50.8.8.3.4 Where equipment such as a cargo heater or cooler is designed to be in operation while the vehicle is in transit, means such as an excess-flow valve to stop the flow of gas in the event of a line break shall be installed. [96:17.7.3.6]

50.8.8.3.5 Cylinders shall be retested every 5 to 12 years in accordance with the manufacturer's recommendations and 49 CFR 180.205:

(1) No letter after the requalification date means the cylinder must be retested within 12 years.
(2) "S" means the cylinder must be retested within 7 years.
(3) "E" means the cylinder must be retested within 5 years.
[96:17.7.3.7]

50.8.9 Electrical Wiring.

50.8.9.1 Vehicle-mounted generators shall comply with the provisions of *NFPA 70*, Article 551, Part III. [96:17.9.1]

50.8.9.2 The manufacturer of an engine generator unit intended for installation in a recreational vehicle shall provide instructions for the safe and effective installation, operation, and servicing of the generator. [96:17.9.2]

50.8.9.3 Refueling of internal combustion engine power sources shall be permitted only when the electric generators and internal combustion power sources are not in use. [96:17.9.3]

50.8.9.3.1 Refueling of internal combustion engines shall not be allowed during mobile or temporary cooking operations. [96:17.9.3.1]

50.8.9.3.2 Refueling of internal combustion engine power sources from a container shall be permitted when the engine is shut down and the surface temperature of the engine and fuel tank is below the autoignition temperature of the fuel. [96:17.9.3.2]

50.8.10 Carbon Monoxide Detectors.

50.8.10.1 If the heat source is nonelectric and open flames are used, at least one listed carbon monoxide detector shall be installed. [96:17.10.1]

50.8.11 Training.

△ **50.8.11.1** Prior to performing cooking operations, one worker shall be provided with initial training in emergency response procedures including the following:

(1) Using portable fire extinguishers and extinguishing systems
(2) Shutting off fuel sources
(3) Notifying the local fire department
(4) Refueling internal combustion engine power sources and LP-Gas container change-out
(5) Performing leak detection of LP-Gas
(6) Understanding fuel properties
[96:17.11.1]

△ **50.8.11.2** During the time of cooking operation at least one person in the vehicle shall be trained to provide the functions listed in 50.8.9.1. [96:17.11.2]

50.8.11.3 The provision of training shall be the responsibility of the owner, and the training program and materials shall be acceptable to the AHJ. [96:17.11.3]

50.8.11.4 Refresher training shall be provided annually. [96:17.11.4]

50.8.11.5 Initial and refresher training shall be documented, and the documentation shall be held in the mobile unit and made available to the AHJ upon request. [96:17.11.5]

50.8.11.6* The address of the current operational location shall be posted and accessible to all employees. [96:17.11.6]

50.8.12 Parking, Servicing, and Repair.

50.8.12.1 Wheel chocks shall be provided to prevent mobile and temporary cooking units from moving. [96:17.12.7]

50.8.13 General Precautions.

50.8.13.1 All fat fryers shall have a lid over the oil vat that can be secured to prevent the spillage of cooking oil during transit. This lid shall be secured at all times when the vehicle is in motion.

Chapter 51 Industrial Ovens and Furnaces

51.1 General.

51.1.1 Application. Industrial ovens and furnaces shall comply with this chapter and the applicable provisions of NFPA 86.

51.1.2 Permits.

N 51.1.2.1 Permits shall be required in accordance with this chapter and Table 1.13.8(a) through Table 1.13.8(d).

Δ 51.1.2.2 Permits, where required, shall comply with Section 1.13.

Δ 51.1.2.3 Applications for a permit shall be accompanied by plans for safe operation showing all essential details and calculations.

51.2 Location. Special consideration shall be given to the location of equipment using flammable liquids or when using gas fuels with a vapor density greater than air.

51.3 Safety Controls. Safety controls, as specified in NFPA 86, shall be sufficient in number and substantially constructed and arranged to maintain the required conditions of safety and prevent the development of fire and explosion hazards.

Chapter 52 Energy Storage Systems

52.1 General.

52.1.1* Energy storage systems (ESS) having an aggregate capacity exceeding the threshold quantities established in Table 1.3 of NFPA 855 shall comply with Chapter 52.

Δ **52.1.2 One- and Two-Family Dwelling and Townhouse Units.** ESS associated with one-and two-family dwellings and townhouse units shall be in accordance with Chapter 15 of NFPA 855. *(See 3.3.203.25.1, One- and Two-Family Dwelling Unit.)*

52.1.3 Permits.

N 52.1.3.1 Permits shall be required in accordance with this chapter and Table 1.13.8(a) through Table 1.13.8(d).

52.1.3.2 Permits, where required, shall comply with Section 1.13.

52.1.3.3 Prior to installation, plans shall be submitted and approved by the AHJ.

52.1.3.4 Construction documentation shall include the documents required in 4.1.2.1 of NFPA 855.

52.1.4 Documentation Location. A copy of the operations and maintenance manual shall be placed in an approved location to be accessible to AHJs and emergency responders. [855:4.2.3.2]

52.1.5 Emergency Operations Plan. An emergency operations plan shall be readily available for use by facility operations and maintenance personnel. [855:4.3.2.1]

52.1.5.1 The emergency operations plan shall be readily available to emergency responders as required in 52.1.5.

52.1.5.2 Emergency contact numbers for the owner representative/operations and maintenance staff shall be accessible to emergency responders as required in 52.1.5.

52.1.6 System Commissioning and Decommissioning. System commissioning of ESS shall be both of the following:

(1) Performed in accordance with Chapter 6 of NFPA 855
(2) Approved prior to putting the system into service

52.1.6.1 Commissioning Plan. A commissioning plan meeting the provisions of Chapter 6 in NFPA 855 shall be provided to the building owner or their authorized agent and the AHJ. [855:4.2.4]

52.1.6.2 A decommissioning plan shall be both of the following:

(1) Prepared in accordance with Chapter 8 of NFPA 855
(2) Approved prior to putting the system in service

52.1.6.3 The AHJ shall be notified prior to decommissioning an ESS. [855:8.2.1]

52.1.6.4 Recommissioning of existing ESS that have undergone alterations, additions, repositioning, or renovations to the system or any of its components shall be in accordance with Chapter 6 of NFPA 855.

52.1.7 Operation, Maintenance, and Testing. Operation, maintenance, and testing of ESS shall be in accordance with Chapter 7 of NFPA 855.

52.1.8* Installations and Locations. The installation of ESS and related systems shall be in accordance with NFPA 855.

52.1.9 Mobile ESS Equipment and Operations.

52.1.9.1 The charging, storage, and deployment of mobile ESS shall be in accordance with Section 4.5 of NFPA 855.

52.1.9.2 Operational permits might be required, see Table 1.13.8(a).

52.1.10 System Interconnections. All electrical connections and wiring to and from an ESS or the components of an ESS, and connections to fuel gas, liquid fuel, or water shall be in accordance with Chapter 5 of NFPA 855.

52.1.11 Combustible Storage.

52.1.11.1 Combustible materials not related to the ESS shall not be stored in dedicated rooms, cabinets, or enclosures containing ESS equipment. [855:4.5.1]

52.1.11.2 Combustible materials related to the ESS shall not be stored within 3 ft (0.9 m) from ESS equipment. [855:4.5.2]

52.1.11.3 Combustible materials in occupied work centers shall comply with Section 10.19 or other applicable fire codes. [855:4.5.4]

52.1.12 Equipment.

52.1.12.1 Repairs. Repairs of ESS shall only be performed by qualified persons and documented in the maintenance, testing, and events log required in 4.2.3 of NFPA 855. [855:4.6.2.1]

52.1.12.2 Retrofits.

52.1.12.2.1 Retrofits of ESS shall be approved and comply with the following unless modified in other sections:

(1) Battery systems and modules and capacitor systems and modules shall be listed in accordance with UL 1973 and installed in accordance with the manufacturer's instructions.

(2) ESS management and other monitoring systems shall be connected and installed in accordance with the manufacturer's instructions.
(3) The overall installation shall continue to comply with UL 9540 listing requirements, where applicable.
(4) Retrofits shall be documented in the maintenance, testing, and events log required in 4.2.3 of NFPA 855.
[855:4.6.3.1]

Δ **52.1.12.2.2** Changing out or retrofitting existing lead-acid or nickel-cadmium batteries shall be considered repairs when there is no increase in system size or capacity greater than 10 percent from the original design. [855:4.6.3.2]

Δ **52.1.12.2.3*** Lead-acid and nickel-cadmium battery systems that are used for dc power for control of substations and control or safe shutdown of generating stations under the exclusive control of the electric utility and located outdoors or in building spaces used exclusively for such installations. [855:4.7.7.3(2)]

52.1.12.2.4 Lead-acid and nickel-cadmium battery systems in uninterruptable power supplies listed and labeled in accordance with UL 1778 and used in standby power applications shall not be required to comply with 9.2.3.1 through 9.2.3.3 of NFPA 855. [855:9.2.3.4.3]

52.1.12.3 Replacements. Replacement of ESS shall be considered new ESS installations and comply with the provisions applicable to new ESS. [855:4.6.4.1]

52.1.13 Increase in Power Rating or Maximum Stored Energy.

Δ **52.1.13.1** A complete new ESS that is added to an existing installation of one or more systems shall be treated as a new system and meet the applicable requirements of this Code. [855:4.6.6.1]

52.1.13.2 An increase in maximum stored energy or power rating to an existing ESS shall be considered a retrofit and comply with 52.1.12.2. [855:4.6.6.2]

N **52.1.14* Electrical Installation.** The electrical installation shall be in accordance with NFPA 70 or IEEE C2 based on the location of the ESS in relation to and its interaction with the electrical grid. [855:4.7.1]

Δ **52.1.15 Environment.** The temperature, humidity, and other environmental conditions in which an ESS is located shall be maintained in accordance with the listing and the manufacturer's specifications. [855:4.6.7]

52.1.16 Security of Installations.

52.1.16.1 ESS shall be secured against unauthorized entry and safeguarded in an approved manner. [855:4.7.6.1]

52.1.16.2 Security barriers, fences, landscaping, and other enclosures shall not inhibit the required air flow to or exhaust from the ESS and its components. [855:4.7.6.2]

52.1.17 Fire Command Centers. In buildings containing ESS and equipped with a fire command center, the command center shall include signage or readily available documentation that describes the location and type of ESS, operating voltages, and location of electrical disconnects as required by NFPA 70. [855:4.7.10]

Δ **52.1.18 Reused Equipment.** Materials, equipment, and devices shall not be reused or reinstalled unless such elements have been reconditioned, tested, and placed in good and proper working condition and approved. [855:4.6.5]

52.1.19 Signage.

52.1.19.1 Approved signage shall be provided in the following locations:
(1) On the front doors to rooms or areas containing ESS or in approved locations near entrances to ESS rooms
(2) On the front doors to outdoor occupiable ESS containers
(3) In approved locations on outdoor ESS that are not enclosed in occupiable containers or otherwise enclosed
[855:4.7.4.1]

52.1.19.2* The signage required in 52.1.19.1 shall be in compliance with ANSI Z535 and include the following information as shown in Figure 52.1.19.2:
(1) "Energy Storage Systems" with symbol of lightning bolt in a triangle
(2) Type of technology associated with the ESS
(3) Special hazards associated as identified in Chapters 9 through 15 of NFPA 855
(4) Type of suppression system installed in the area of the ESS
(5) Emergency contact information
[855:4.7.4.2]

52.1.20 Impact Protection.

52.1.20.1 ESS shall be located or protected to prevent physical damage from impact where such risks are identified. [855:4.7.5.1]

52.1.20.2 Vehicle impact protection consisting of guard posts or other approved means shall be provided where ESS are subject to impact by motor vehicles. [855:4.7.5.2]

52.1.21 Means of Egress.

52.1.21.1 All areas containing ESS shall provide egress from the area in which they are located in accordance with the local building code. [855:4.7.8.1]

52.1.21.2 Required egress doors shall be provided with emergency lighting as required by the local building code. [855:4.7.8.2]

52.1.22 Spill Control. Rooms, buildings, or areas containing ESS with free-flowing liquid electrolyte in individual vessels having a capacity of more than 55 gal (208 L) or multiple vessels having an aggregate capacity exceeding 1000 gal (3785 L) shall be provided with spill control to prevent the flow of liquids to adjoining areas. [855:9.6.5.2.1]

```
┌─────────────────────────────────┐
│         ENERGY STORAGE          │
│   ⚡         SYSTEMS        ⚡   │
│                                 │
│ TYPE OF TECHNOLOGY              │
│ SPECIAL HAZARDS                 │
│ EMERGENCY CONTACT INFORMATION   │
│ SUPPRESSION SYSTEM              │
└─────────────────────────────────┘
```

Δ **FIGURE 52.1.19.2** Example of ESS Signage. [855:Figure 4.7.4.2]

N **52.1.23* Exhaust Ventilation During Normal Operation.** Where required by Table 9.6.5 of NFPA 855 or elsewhere in this standard, exhaust ventilation during normal operation shall be provided for rooms, enclosures, walk-in units, and cabinets as follows:

(1) ESS rooms and walk-in units shall use mechanical exhaust ventilation in accordance with 9.6.5.1.5 of NFPA 855.
(2) Outdoor ESS cabinets shall use either mechanical or natural exhaust ventilation in accordance with 9.6.5.1.4 or 9.6.5.1.5 of NFPA 855.

[855:9.6.5.1]

52.1.24 Fire Suppression and Control. Where fire suppression and control is provided it shall be in accordance with 4.4.4.3 of NFPA 855.

52.1.25 Ventilation. Where ventilation is provided it shall be in accordance with Section 4.9 of NFPA 855.

52.1.26 Smoke and Fire Detection. Where smoke and fire detection is provided it shall be in accordance with Section 4.10 of NFPA 855.

52.1.27 Water Supply. Where water supplies are provided they shall be in accordance with Section 4.13 of NFPA 855.

52.2 Remediation Measures. Remediation measures shall be provided in accordance with Section 4.16 of NFPA 855.

Δ **52.2.1 Hazard Support Personnel.** Where required by the AHJ for public safety, the owner or their authorized agent shall provide hazard support personnel at the owner's expense. [855:9.6.6.2]

52.2.2* Required hazard support personnel shall monitor the ESS continuously in a method approved by the AHJ from the time the fire department releases the emergency scene until the hazard is mitigated and the AHJ gives authorization to the owner or their authorized agent that onsite hazard support personnel are no longer required. [855:9.6.6.2.4]

52.2.3* On-duty hazard support personnel shall have the following responsibilities:

(1) Ensure the security and safety of the ESS site in accordance with the emergency operation plan and decommissioning plan
(2) Keep diligent watch for fires or signs of off-gassing, obstructions to means of egress, and other hazards for the time required in accordance with 9.6.6.2.4 of NFPA 855
(3) Ensure a means of communication is available to immediately contact the fire department if their assistance is needed to mitigate any hazards
(4) Take prompt measures for remediation of hazards
(5) Take prompt measures to assist in the evacuation of the public from the structures in accordance with the emergency operations plan
(6) Allow only authorized personnel to enter the ESS site
(7) Ensure authorized personnel are wearing proper PPE
(8) Where required by the AHJ, maintain a written or electronic log of all personnel entering/leaving the portion of the site containing the ESS
(9) Record all postincident tasks performed

[855:9.6.6.2.5]

52.3 System Interconnection. Where system interconnections are provided they shall be in accordance with Section 5.1 of NFPA 855.

52.4 Operation and Maintenance. Operations and maintenance shall be in accordance with Chapter 7 of NFPA 855.

52.5 Electrochemical Energy Storage Systems. Where electrochemical energy storage systems are provided they shall be in accordance with Chapter 9 of NFPA 855.

52.6 Capacitor Energy Storage Systems. Where capacitor energy storage systems are provided they shall be in accordance with Chapter 10 of NFPA 855.

52.7 Fuel Cell Energy Storage Systems. Where fuel cell energy storage systems are provided they shall be in accordance with Chapter 11 of NFPA 855.

52.8 Storage of Used or Off-Specification Batteries. Where storage of used or off-specification batteries is provided it shall be in accordance with Chapter 14 of NFPA 855.

Chapter 53 Mechanical Refrigeration

53.1* General.

53.1.1 Applicability.

53.1.1.1* Refrigeration unit and system installations having a refrigerant circuit containing more than 220 lb (100 kg) of Group A1 or 30 lb (13.6 kg) of any other group refrigerant shall be in accordance with Chapter 53 and the mechanical code.

53.1.1.2 Temporary and portable installations shall be exempt from the requirements of this chapter when approved.

53.1.1.3 Ammonia Refrigeration. Ammonia refrigeration systems shall be exempt from the requirements of this chapter, other than 53.1.2 and 53.1.3.

53.1.2 Permits and Plans.

N **53.1.2.1** Permits shall be required in accordance with this chapter and Table 1.13.8(a) through Table 1.13.8(d).

53.1.2.2 Permits, where required, shall comply with Section 1.13.

53.1.2.3 Plans and specifications for devices and systems required by this chapter shall be submitted to the AHJ for review and approval prior to installation.

53.1.3 Reference Codes and Standards.

53.1.3.1 Refrigeration systems using a refrigerant other than ammonia shall be in accordance with ANSI/ASHRAE 15, *Safety Standard for Refrigeration Systems*, and the mechanical code.

53.1.3.2 Refrigeration systems using ammonia as the refrigerant shall comply with ANSI/IIAR 2, *Standard for Equipment, Design, and Installation of Closed-Circuit Ammonia Mechanical Refrigerating Systems*; ANSI/IIAR 6, *Standard for Inspection, Testing, and Maintenance of Closed-Circuit Ammonia Refrigeration Systems*; ANSI/IIAR 7, *Developing Operating Procedures for Closed-Circuit Ammonia Mechanical Refrigerating Systems*; and ANSI/IIAR 8, *Decommissioning of Closed-Circuit Ammonia Mechanical Refrigerating Systems*.

53.2 Safety Features.

53.2.1 Emergency Pressure Control System. Refrigeration systems containing more than 6.6 lb (3 kg) of Group A2, A3, B2, or B3 refrigerant, as designated by ANSI/ASHRAE 34, *Designation and Safety Classification of Refrigerants*, shall be provided with an emergency pressure control system in accordance with 53.2.1.1 and 53.2.1.2.

53.2.1.1 High- and Intermediate-Pressure Zones. Each high- and intermediate-pressure zone in a refrigeration system shall be provided with a single automatic valve providing a crossover connection to a lower pressure zone. Automatic crossover valves shall comply with 53.2.1.1.1 through 53.2.1.1.4.

53.2.1.1.1 Overpressure Limit Set Point for Crossover Valves. Automatic crossover valves shall be provided to automatically relieve excess system pressure to a lower pressure zone if the pressure in a high- or intermediate-pressure zone rises to within 90 percent of the set point for emergency pressure relief devices.

53.2.1.1.2 Manual Operation. Where required by the AHJ, automatic crossover valves shall be capable of manual operation.

53.2.1.1.3 System Design Pressure. Refrigeration system zones that are connected to a higher pressure zone by an automatic crossover valve shall be designed to safely contain the maximum pressure that can be achieved by interconnection of the two zones.

53.2.1.1.4 Automatic Emergency Stop. Operation of an automatic crossover valve shall cause all compressors on the affected system to immediately stop in accordance with the following:

(1) Dedicated pressure-sensing devices located immediately adjacent to crossover valves shall be permitted as a means for determining operation of a valve.
(2) To ensure that the automatic crossover valve system provides a redundant means of stopping compressors in an overpressure condition, high-pressure cutout sensors associated with compressors shall not be used as a basis for determining operation of a crossover valve.

53.2.1.2 Low-Pressure Zone.

53.2.1.2.1 Overpressure Limit Set Point for Emergency Stop. The lowest pressure zone in a refrigeration system shall be provided with a dedicated means of determining a rise in system pressure to within 90 percent of the set point for emergency pressure relief devices.

53.2.1.2.2 Automatic Emergency Stop. Activation of the overpressure sensing device shall cause all compressors on the affected system to immediately stop.

53.2.2 Treatment, Flaring, and Diffusion Systems for Refrigerant Discharge.

53.2.2.1 Required Systems. Unless the AHJ determines, upon review of an engineering analysis prepared at the expense of the owner, that a significant fire, health, or environmental hazard would not result from an atmospheric release, refrigeration systems that are designed to discharge refrigerant vapor to the atmosphere shall be provided with an approved treatment, flaring, or diffusion system where required by 53.2.2.1.1 and 53.2.2.1.2.

53.2.2.1.1 Toxic and Highly Toxic Refrigerants. Systems containing toxic or highly toxic refrigerants shall discharge vapor to the atmosphere only through an approved treatment system in accordance with Chapter 63 or flaring system in accordance with 53.2.2.2.

53.2.2.1.2 Flammable Refrigerants. Systems containing flammable refrigerants shall discharge vapor to the atmosphere in accordance with the following:

(1) For refrigerants having a density equal to or greater than the density of air, discharge shall be through an approved treatment system in accordance with or flaring system in accordance with 53.2.2.2.
(2) For refrigerants having a density less than the density of air, discharge to the atmosphere shall be permitted, provided that the point of discharge is located outside of the structure at not less than 15 ft (4.6 m) above the adjoining grade level and not less than 20 ft (6.1 m) from any window, ventilation opening, or exit.

53.2.2.2 Design of Flaring Systems.

53.2.2.2.1 Flaring systems for incineration of Group A2, A3, B2, or B3 refrigerants, as designated by ANSI/ASHRAE 34, *Designation and Safety Classification of Refrigerants*, shall be designed to incinerate the entire discharge.

53.2.2.2.2 The products of refrigerant incineration shall not pose health or environmental hazards.

53.2.2.2.3 Incineration shall be automatic upon initiation of discharge, shall be designed to prevent blowback, and shall not expose structures or materials to threat of fire.

53.2.2.2.4 Standby fuel, such as LP-Gas, and standby power shall have the capacity to operate for one and one half the required time for complete incineration of refrigerant in the system.

53.2.3 Refrigeration Machinery Rooms. Where required by the mechanical code, refrigeration systems shall be provided with a refrigeration machinery room, which shall comply with 53.2.3.1 through 53.2.3.4.

53.2.3.1 Refrigerant Vapor Detection, Monitoring, Alarm, and Electrical Systems. Refrigeration machinery rooms shall have an approved refrigerant vapor detection, monitoring, and alarm system in accordance with 53.2.3.1.1 through 53.2.3.1.7 and the mechanical code.

53.2.3.1.1 Alarm Threshold. The refrigerant vapor detector shall activate approved visual and audible alarm signaling devices at a value not greater than the corresponding refrigerant concentration limit (RCL).

53.2.3.1.2 Location of Signaling Devices. Audible and visual alarm signaling devices shall be located inside the refrigeration machinery room and outside the room at each entrance into the room.

53.2.3.1.3 Audibility. Audible alarm signaling devices shall provide a sound level of at least 15 dB above the operating ambient noise sound pressure level of the space in which they are installed and shall provide approved, distinctive audible and visual alarms.

53.2.3.1.4* Emergency Shutoff Interface. Where the quantity of a Group A2, B2, A3, or B3 refrigerant in an independent circuit would exceed 25 percent of the LFL if released to the surrounding room, either of the following shall apply:

(1) Electrical equipment shall comply with the requirements of *NFPA 70* for Class I, Division 2.
(2) The refrigerant vapor detection system required by 53.2.3.1 shall automatically de-energize all electrical power within the space at vapor concentrations at or above 25 percent of the LFL.

53.2.3.1.5 Power and Supervision. Refrigerant vapor detection and alarm systems shall be powered and supervised as required for fire alarm systems in accordance with *NFPA 72*.

53.2.3.1.6 Monitoring and Annunciation. Refrigerant vapor detection and alarm systems shall transmit a signal to an approved location.

53.2.3.1.7 Installation and Maintenance. Detection and alarm systems shall be installed and maintained in accordance with the equipment manufacturers' specifications. *(Also see 53.3.2.1.)*

53.2.3.2* Prohibited Sources of Ignition. Open flames or devices having an exposed surface temperature exceeding 800°F (427°C) shall be prohibited in refrigeration machinery rooms except as follows:

(1) Momentary temperature excursions such as electrical contacts in Group A1 and B1 systems shall be permitted.
(2) Open flames or devices having an exposed surface temperature exceeding the following shall be permitted:
   (a) 800°F (427°C) shall be permitted in refrigeration machinery rooms used exclusively for direct-fired absorption equipment.
   (b) 1290°F (700°C) shall be permitted in the room for Group A2L and B2L refrigerants only.
(3) Existing nonconforming installations shall be permitted where approved by the AHJ, where the combustion system is interlocked with the refrigerant detection system to shut off at the permissible exposure limit (PEL).
(4) Direct-vented combustion equipment shall be permitted in accordance with the mechanical code.

53.2.3.3 Ventilation Systems.

53.2.3.3.1 Fans providing emergency purge ventilation for refrigerant escape from a refrigeration room shall have a clearly identified switch of the break-glass type providing on-only control immediately adjacent to, and outside of, each refrigerant machinery room means of egress.

53.2.3.3.2 An emergency purge control shall be provided with a manual reset only.

53.2.3.3.3 Purge fans shall also respond automatically to the refrigerant concentration detection system set to activate the ventilation system at the threshold levels set forth in 53.2.3.1.1.

53.2.3.3.4 Mechanical ventilation systems serving refrigeration rooms shall have switches to control the power to each fan.

53.2.3.3.5 The switches shall be key-operated or within a locked glass-covered or tamper-resistant enclosure at an approved location adjacent to and outside of the principal entrance to the refrigeration machinery room.

53.2.3.3.6 Keys necessary for operation of ventilation systems shall be located in a single approved location.

53.2.3.3.7 Switches controlling fans providing continuous ventilation shall be of the two-position, on/off type.

53.2.3.3.8 Switches controlling fans providing intermittent or emergency ventilation shall be of the three-position, automatic on/off type.

53.2.3.3.9 Switches shall be labeled identifying both the function and the specific fan being controlled.

53.2.3.3.10 Two colored and labeled indicator lamps responding to the differential pressure created by airflow shall be provided for each switch.

53.2.3.3.11 One lamp shall indicate flow, and the other shall indicate no flow.

53.2.3.3.12 Exhaust from mechanical ventilation systems in refrigeration rooms shall be discharged 20 ft (6.1 m) or more from a property line or openings into buildings.

53.2.3.3.13 Discharges capable of exceeding 25 percent of the LFL or 50 percent of the immediately dangerous to life and health (IDLH) value shall be equipped with approved treatment systems to reduce the discharge concentrations to these values or lower, except as provided in 53.2.3.3.13.1. *(Also see 53.2.2.1.)*

53.2.3.3.13.1 A treatment system shall not be required when an approved engineering analysis of plume dispersion demonstrates that the limiting value will not be exceeded at the property line.

53.2.3.4 Electrical.

53.2.3.4.1 The refrigeration machinery room shall not be required to be classified as a hazardous location for electrical equipment except as provided in the mechanical code or *NFPA 70*.

53.2.3.4.2 Refrigeration machinery rooms used exclusively for direct-fired absorption equipment shall be permitted not to be classified as a hazardous location for electrical equipment in accordance with *NFPA 70*.

53.2.3.4.3 Electrical equipment and electrical installations in refrigeration machinery rooms shall comply with Section 11.1.

53.2.3.4.4 Where treatment, detection, or alarm systems are required, such systems shall be connected to a secondary source of power to automatically supply electrical power in the event of loss of power from the primary source.

53.2.3.4.5 A clearly identified switch of the break-glass type or with an approved tamper-resistant cover shall provide off-only control of refrigerant compressors, refrigerant pumps, and normally closed, automatic refrigerant valves located in the machinery room. In addition, this equipment shall be automatically shut off whenever the refrigerant vapor concentration in the machinery room exceeds the vapor detector's upper detection limit or 25 percent of the LFL, whichever is lower.

53.2.3.4.5.1 In machinery rooms where only nonflammable refrigerants are used, only compressors shall be required to be stopped by vapor detection or the cut-off switch. *(Also see 53.2.3.1.4.)*

53.2.4 Signs and Labels.

53.2.4.1 General. Refrigeration units or systems shall be provided with approved hazard identification signs in accordance with NFPA 704, emergency operational signs, charts, and labels in accordance with the mechanical code, and the following:

(1) Name and address of the manufacturer or installer
(2) Type and total number of pounds of refrigerant contained in the system
(3) Field test pressure applied

53.2.4.2 Systems with More Than 110 lb (50 kg) of Refrigerant. Systems containing more than 110 lb (50 kg) of refrigerant shall be provided with signs having letters not less than ½ in. (12.7 mm) high, designating the following:

(1) Main shutoff valves to each vessel
(2) Mainstream or electrical controls
(3) Remote control switch
(4) Pressure-limiting device

53.3 Operations, Maintenance, Testing, and Decommissioning.

53.3.1 Operations and Maintenance.

53.3.1.1 General. Refrigeration systems shall be operated and maintained in a safe and operable condition, free from accumulations of oil, dirt, waste, excessive corrosion, other debris, or leaks, and in accordance with ASHRAE 15, *Safety Standard for Refrigeration Systems*, and the mechanical code.

53.3.1.2 Access to System. Refrigeration systems shall be maintained accessible to the fire department as required by the AHJ.

53.3.1.3 Storage in Machinery Rooms.

53.3.1.3.1 Flammable and combustible materials shall not be stored in refrigeration machinery rooms except for incidental materials necessary for the safe and proper operation and maintenance of the system.

53.3.1.3.2 Storage of materials in a refrigeration machinery room, including reserve supplies of refrigerants or refrigerant oils, shall be in accordance with other applicable chapters of this *Code*.

53.3.1.4 Changing of Refrigerant Type. Refrigerant types shall not be changed without prior notification and approval of the AHJ.

53.3.1.5 Records of Refrigerant Quantities. The person in charge of the premises on which a refrigeration unit or system subject to these regulations is installed or maintained shall keep a written record of refrigerant quantities brought onto and removed from the premises, which shall be made available to the AHJ upon request.

53.3.1.6 Permissible Refrigerant Discharges. Refrigerant shall be only permitted to be released to atmosphere in the following circumstances:

(1) Refrigeration systems operating at pressures below atmospheric and incorporating automatic purge cycles
(2) Incidental operation of automatic pressure relief valves resulting in minor release of the refrigerant charge
(3) Incidental minor releases associated with service operations after system pumpdown has been accomplished
(4) In an emergency

53.3.1.7 Notification of Fugitive Releases. Where required by the fire department, the fire department shall be notified upon discharges of refrigerant that are not in accordance with 53.3.1.6(1), 53.3.1.6(2), or 53.3.1.6(3).

53.3.2 Testing of Equipment.

53.3.2.1 Acceptance Testing. The following emergency devices or systems shall be tested to demonstrate their safety and effectiveness upon completion of the installation or alteration:

(1) Treatment and flaring systems
(2) Fans and associated equipment intended to operate emergency purge ventilation systems
(3) Refrigerant vapor detection and alarm systems

53.3.2.2 Periodic Testing. The following emergency devices or systems shall be tested in accordance with the manufacturers' specifications at intervals not exceeding one year:

(1) Treatment and flaring systems
(2) Fans and associated equipment intended to operate emergency purge ventilation systems
(3) Refrigerant vapor detection and alarm systems

53.3.2.3 Records of Required Testing. A written record of required testing shall be maintained on the premises.

53.3.2.4 Testing Personnel Qualifications. Tests of emergency devices or systems required by Chapter 53 shall be conducted by persons trained in such testing.

Chapter 54 Ozone Gas–Generating Equipment

54.1 Scope.

54.1.1 Equipment having a maximum ozone-generating capacity of not less than ½ lb (0.23 kg) over a 24-hour period shall comply with Chapter 54 unless otherwise permitted by 54.1.2.

54.1.2 Chapter 54 shall not apply to ozone-generating equipment used in one- and two-family dwellings or lodging or rooming house occupancies.

N **54.1.3** Permits shall be required in accordance with this chapter and Table 1.13.8(a) through Table 1.13.8(d).

N **54.1.4** Permits, where required, shall comply with Section 1.13.

54.2 Location.

54.2.1 General.

54.2.1.1 Ozone generators shall be located in approved cabinets or ozone generator rooms in accordance with Section 54.2 unless otherwise permitted by 54.2.1.2.

54.2.1.2 Ozone generators within approved pressure vessels located outside of buildings shall not be required to be located in a cabinet or ozone generator room.

54.2.2 Cabinets.

54.2.2.1 Ozone cabinets shall be constructed of approved materials compatible with ozone in accordance with nationally recognized standards.

54.2.2.2* Cabinets shall display an approved sign stating: OZONE GAS GENERATOR — HIGHLY TOXIC — OXIDIZER.

54.2.2.3 Cabinets shall be braced for seismic activity in accordance with the building code.

54.2.2.4 Cabinets shall be mechanically ventilated in accordance with all of the following:

(1) Not less than six air changes per hour shall be provided.
(2) Exhausted air shall be directed to a treatment system designed to reduce the discharge concentration of the gas to one-half of the immediately dangerous to life and health (IDLH) value at the point of discharge to the atmosphere.
(3) The average velocity of ventilation at makeup air openings with cabinet doors closed shall not be less than 200 ft/min (1.02 m/s).

54.2.3 Ozone Generator Rooms. Ozone generator rooms shall comply with all of the following:

(1) Not less than six air changes per hour shall be provided.
(2) Exhausted air shall be directed to a treatment system designed to reduce the discharge concentration of the gas to one-half of the IDLH value at the point of discharge to the atmosphere, or the ozone generator room shall be equipped with a continuous gas detection system that will shut off the ozone generator and sound a local alarm when concentrations above the permissible exposure limit occur.
(3) Ozone generator rooms shall not normally be occupied, and such rooms shall be kept free of combustible and hazardous material storage.
(4) Room access doors shall display an approved sign stating: OZONE GAS GENERATOR — HIGHLY TOXIC — OXIDIZER.

54.3 Piping, Valves, and Fittings.

54.3.1 General. Piping, valves, fittings, and related components used to convey ozone shall be in accordance with Section 54.3.

54.3.2 Secondary Containment.

54.3.2.1 Secondary containment, such as double-walled piping or exhausted enclosures, shall be provided for piping, valves, fittings, and related components, unless otherwise permitted by 54.3.2.3.

54.3.2.2 Secondary containment shall be capable of directing a sudden release to an approved treatment system.

54.3.2.3 Secondary containment shall not be required for welded stainless steel piping and tubing.

54.3.3 Materials. Materials shall be compatible with ozone and shall be rated for the design operating pressures.

54.3.4 Identification. Piping shall be identified: OZONE GAS — HIGHLY TOXIC — OXIDIZER.

54.4 Automatic Shutdown. Ozone generators shall be designed to automatically shut down when any one of the following occurs:

(1) The dissolved ozone concentration in the water being treated is above saturation when measured at the point where the water is exposed to the atmosphere.
(2) The process using generated ozone is shut down.
(3) The ventilation system for the cabinet or ozone generator room fails.
(4) The gas detection system fails.

54.5 Manual Shutdown. Manual shutdown controls shall be provided at the ozone generator and, if in a room, within 10 ft (3 m) of the main exit or exit access door.

Chapter 55 Cleaning and Purging of Flammable Gas Piping Systems

55.1 Application. Cleaning and purging activities for new and existing flammable gas piping found in electric generating plants and in industrial, institutional, and commercial applications shall comply with NFPA 56.

N **55.2 Permits.**

N **55.2.1** Permits shall be required in accordance with this chapter and Table 1.13.8(a) through Table 1.13.8(d).

N **55.2.2** Permits, where required, shall comply with Section 1.13.

Chapter 56 Reserved

Chapter 57 Reserved

Chapter 58 Reserved

Chapter 59 Reserved

Chapter 60 Hazardous Materials

60.1 General Requirements.

60.1.1 Applicability. Occupancies containing high-hazard contents shall comply with this chapter in addition to other applicable requirements of this *Code*. [5000:34.1.1.1]

Δ **60.1.2 Subjects Not Regulated.** Buildings, and portions thereof, containing high-hazard contents limited to any of the following shall not be required to comply with this chapter:

(1) Ignitible (flammable and combustible) liquids associated with application of flammable finishes and complying with Chapter 43.
(2) Ignitible (flammable and combustible) liquids associated with wholesale and retail sales and storage in mercantile occupancies and complying with Chapter 66
(3) Class IIIA and Class IIIB combustible liquid solvents in closed systems employing listed cleaning equipment complying with Chapter 24
(4) Refrigerants and refrigerant oil contained within closed-cycle refrigeration systems complying with Chapter 53 and the *Uniform Mechanical Code*, as referenced in Chapter 50 of *NFPA 5000*
(5) Ignitible (flammable and combustible) liquid beverages in liquor stores and distributors without bulk storage
(6) High-hazard contents stored or used in farm buildings or similar occupancies for on-premise agricultural use
(7) Corrosive materials in stationary batteries utilized for facility emergency power, uninterrupted power supply, or similar purposes, provided that the batteries are provided with safety venting caps and ventilation is provided in accordance with Chapter 52

(8) Corrosive materials displayed in original packaging in mercantile occupancies and intended for personal or household use or as building materials
(9) Aerosol products in storage or mercantile occupancies and complying with Chapter 61
(10) Ignitible (flammable and combustible) liquids storage tank buildings meeting the requirements of Chapter 24 of NFPA 30
(11) Ignitible (flammable and combustible) liquids storage tank vaults meeting the requirements of Chapter 25 of NFPA 30
(12) Ignitible (flammable and combustible) liquids process buildings meeting the requirements of Chapter 17 of NFPA 30
(13) Installation of fuel gas distribution systems and associated equipment in accordance with Section 11.4 and Chapter 69

[5000:34.1.1.2]

N **60.1.3 Permits.**

N **60.1.3.1** Permits shall be required in accordance with this chapter and Table 1.13.8(a) through Table 1.13.8(d).

N **60.1.3.2** Permits, where required, shall comply with Section 1.13.

60.1.4 Applicability of Sections.

60.1.4.1 Quantities Not Exceeding the Maximum Allowable Quantities per Control Area. Storage, use, and handling of hazardous materials in quantities not exceeding maximum allowable quantities permitted in control areas set forth in Section 60.1.4.1 shall be in accordance with Section 60.1 through Section 60.5.

60.1.4.2 Quantities Exceeding the Maximum Allowable Quantities per Control Area. Storage, use, and handling of hazardous materials in quantities in excess of the maximum allowable quantities permitted in control areas set forth in 60.1.4.2 shall comply with Section 60.2 through Section 60.6.

60.1.4.3 Limited Applicability of this Chapter for Specific Material Classes. Chapter 60 shall apply in its entirety to all hazardous materials except where Chapters 61 through 73 of this *Code* specify that only certain sections of this chapter shall apply to a specific material classification category.

60.1.5 Facility Closure.

60.1.5.1 Where required by the AHJ, no facility storing hazardous materials listed in 1.1.1 of NFPA 400 shall close or abandon an entire storage facility without notifying the AHJ at least 30 days prior to the scheduled closing. [**400:**1.9.1]

60.1.5.2 The AHJ shall be permitted to reduce the 30-day period specified in 60.1.5.1 when there are special circumstances requiring such reduction. [**400:**1.9.2]

60.1.5.3 Facilities out of service shall comply with NFPA 400.

60.1.5.4 Closure plans shall comply with NFPA 400.

60.1.5.5 Facilities shall have an emergency plan that complies with NFPA 400.

60.1.6 Hazardous Materials Management Plan (HMMP).

60.1.6.1* When required by the AHJ, new or existing facilities that store, use, or handle hazardous materials covered by this *Code* in amounts above the MAQ specified in 60.4.2.1.2 through 60.4.2.1.5 and 60.4.4.1.2 shall submit a hazardous materials management plan (HMMP) to the AHJ. [**400:**1.11.1]

60.1.6.2 The HMMP shall be reviewed and updated as follows:
(1) Annually
(2) When the facility is modified
(3) When hazardous materials representing a new hazard category not previously addressed are stored, used, or handled in the facility

[**400:**1.11.2]

Δ **60.1.6.3** The HMMP shall comply with the requirements of Chapter 6 of NFPA 400. [**400:**1.11.3]

60.1.7* Hazardous Materials Inventory Statement (HMIS). When required by the AHJ, a hazardous materials inventory statement (HMIS) shall be completed and submitted to the AHJ. [**400:**1.12.1]

60.2 Special Definitions.

60.2.1 Chemical Name. See 3.3.49.

60.2.2 Closed System Use. See 3.3.298.1.

60.2.3 Control Area. See 3.3.17.2.

60.2.4 Dispensing. See 3.3.92.

60.2.5 Flammable Solid. See 3.3.264.2.

60.2.6 Hazardous Material. See 3.3.189.4.

60.2.7 Health Hazard Material. See 3.3.189.6.

60.2.8 Highly Toxic Material. See 3.3.189.7.

60.2.9 Incompatible Material. See 3.3.189.9.

60.2.10 Liquid. See 3.3.180.

60.2.11 Open System Use. See 3.3.298.2.

60.2.12 Organic Peroxide. See 3.3.209.

60.2.12.1 Organic Peroxide Formulation. See 3.3.209.1.

60.2.12.1.1 Class I. See 3.3.209.1.1.

60.2.12.1.2 Class II. See 3.3.209.1.2.

60.2.12.1.3 Class III. See 3.3.209.1.3.

60.2.12.1.4 Class IV. See 3.3.209.1.4.

60.2.12.1.5 Class V. See 3.3.209.1.5.

60.2.13 Oxidizer. See 3.3.212.

60.2.13.1 Class 1. See 3.3.212.1.

60.2.13.2 Class 2. See 3.3.212.2.

60.2.13.3 Class 3. See 3.3.212.3.

60.2.13.4 Class 4. See 3.3.212.4.

60.2.14 Physical Hazard Material. See 3.3.189.12.

60.2.15 Pyrophoric Material. See 3.3.189.13.

60.2.16 Solid Material. See 3.3.265.

60.2.17 Toxic Material. See 3.3.189.14.

60.2.18 Unstable (Reactive) Material. See 3.3.189.15.

60.2.19 Use. See 3.3.298.

60.2.20 Water-Reactive Material. See 3.3.189.16.

60.3 Classification of Materials, Wastes, and Hazard of Contents.

60.3.1 Classification of High-Hazard Contents.

60.3.1.1 General.

60.3.1.1.1 High-hazard contents shall include materials defined as hazardous material in Chapter 3, whether stored, used, or handled. [400:4.2.1.1]

60.3.1.1.2 High-hazard contents shall include those materials defined as hazardous material solids, liquids, or gases limited to the hazard categories specified in 1.1.1 of NFPA 400 and classified in accordance with 60.3.1.1.2.1 through 60.3.1.1.2.4 whether stored, used, or handled. [400:4.2.1.2]

60.3.1.1.2.1 High-Hazard Level 1 Contents. High-hazard Level 1 contents shall include materials that present a detonation hazard, including, but not limited to, the following hazard categories:

(1) Class 4 oxidizers
(2) Detonable pyrophoric solids or liquids
(3) Class 3 detonable and Class 4 unstable (reactive) solids, liquids, or gases
(4) Detonable organic peroxides
[400:4.2.1.2.1]

60.3.1.1.2.2 High-Hazard Level 2 Contents. High-hazard Level 2 contents shall include materials that present a deflagration hazard or a hazard from accelerated burning, including, but not limited to, the following hazard categories:

(1) Combustible dusts that are stored, used, or generated in a manner that creates a severe fire or explosion hazard
(2) Class I organic peroxides
(3) Class 3 solid or liquid oxidizers that are used or stored in normally open containers or systems or in closed containers or systems at gauge pressures of more than 15 psi (103.4 kPa)
(4) Flammable gases
(5) Flammable cryogenic fluids
(6) Nondetonable pyrophoric solids, liquids, or gases
(7) Class 3 nondetonable unstable (reactive) solids, liquids, or gases
(8) Class 3 water-reactive solids and liquids
[400:4.2.1.2.2]

60.3.1.1.2.3 High-Hazard Level 3 Contents. High-hazard Level 3 contents shall include materials that readily support combustion or present a physical hazard, including, but not limited to, the following hazard categories:

(1) Flammable solids, other than dusts classified as high-hazard Level 2, that are stored, used, or generated in a manner that creates a high fire hazard
(2) Class IIA, Class IIB, and Class III organic peroxides
(3) Class 2 solid or liquid oxidizers
(4) Class 3 solid or liquid oxidizers that are used or stored in normally closed containers or systems at gauge pressures of less than 15 psi (103.4 kPa)
(5) Class 2 unstable (reactive) materials
(6) Class 2 water-reactive solids, liquids, or gases

(7) Oxidizing gases
(8) Oxidizing cryogenic fluids
[400:4.2.1.2.3]

60.3.1.1.2.4 High-Hazard Level 4 Contents. High-hazard Level 4 contents shall include materials that are acute health hazards, including, but not limited to, the following hazard categories:

(1) Corrosive solids, liquids, or gases
(2) Highly toxic solids, liquids, or gases
(3) Toxic solids, liquids, or gases
[400:4.2.1.2.4]

60.3.2 Mixtures. Mixtures shall be classified in accordance with the hazards of the mixture as a whole by an approved, qualified organization, individual, or testing laboratory. [400:4.3]

60.3.3* Multiple Hazards. Hazardous materials that have multiple hazards shall conform to the code requirements for each applicable hazard category. [400:4.4]

60.3.4* Classification of Waste. Waste comprised of or containing hazardous materials shall be classified in accordance with 60.3.1 through 60.3.3 as applicable. [400:4.5]

60.4 Permissible Storage and Use Locations.

60.4.1 General.

60.4.1.1 Control Areas or Special Protection Required. Hazardous materials shall be stored and used in any of the following:

(1) In control areas complying with 60.4.2
(2) In occupancies complying with requirements for Protection Level 1, Protection Level 2, Protection Level 3, or Protection Level 4 in accordance with 60.4.3
(3) In outdoor areas complying with 60.4.4
[400:5.1.1]

60.4.1.2 Weather Protection Structures. Weather protection, when provided, shall comply with 6.2.7.2 of NFPA 400. [400:5.4.3]

Δ **60.4.1.3 High-Hazard Contents.** Occupancies in which high-hazard contents are stored, used, or handled shall also comply with Chapter 6 of NFPA 400. [400:5.1.3]

60.4.2 Control Areas.

60.4.2.1 Hazardous materials shall be permitted to be stored and used in control areas in accordance with 60.4.2.1 and 60.4.2.2. [400:5.2.1]

60.4.2.1.1 General.

60.4.2.1.1.1 All occupancies shall be permitted to have one or more control areas in accordance with 60.4.2. [400:5.2.1.1.1]

Δ **60.4.2.1.1.2** The aggregate quantity of hazardous materials in storage and use shall not exceed the quantity for storage set forth in Table 60.4.2.1.1.3. [400:5.2.1.1.2]

60.4.2.1.1.2.1 The quantity of hazardous materials in an individual control area in laboratories classified as business occupancies shall not exceed the MAQ set forth in Table 60.4.2.1.1.3. [400:5.2.1.1.2.1]

60.4.2.1.1.3 The MAQ of hazardous materials per control area shall be as specified in Table 60.4.2.1.1.3 except as modified by

60.4.2.1.2 through 60.4.2.1.5. Ammonium nitrate shall also comply with Chapter 11 of NFPA 400. [**400:**5.2.1.1.3]

60.4.2.1.2 Quantity Limits for Occupancies Other than Mercantile, Storage, or Industrial Occupancies.

60.4.2.1.2.1 The MAQ of hazardous materials per control area in occupancies other than mercantile, storage, or industrial occupancies shall be as specified in Table 60.4.2.1.2.1. [**400:**5.2.1.2.1]

60.4.2.1.2.2 The MAQ set forth in Table 60.4.2.1.2.1 shall be the maximum aggregate quantity allowed in storage and use. [**400:**5.2.1.2.2]

60.4.2.1.3 Industrial Occupancies. The MAQ of hazardous materials per control area in industrial occupancies shall be as specified in Table 60.4.2.1.1.3, with increased quantities permitted where storage areas comply with 60.4.2.1.5. [**400:**5.2.1.3]

60.4.2.1.4 Storage Occupancies. The MAQ of hazardous materials per control area in storage occupancies shall be as specified in Table 60.4.2.1.1.3, with increased quantities permitted where storage areas comply with 60.4.2.1.5. [**400:**5.2.1.4]

60.4.2.1.5 Special Quantity Limits for Mercantile, Industrial, and Storage Occupancies.

60.4.2.1.5.1 General. Where storage in mercantile, industrial, and storage occupancies is in compliance with all of the special controls set forth in 60.4.2.1.5.2, the MAQ of selected hazardous materials shall be permitted to be increased in accordance with 60.4.2.1.5.3. [**400:**5.2.1.5.1]

60.4.2.1.5.2 Special Controls Required for Increased Quantities. Where quantities of hazardous materials are increased in accordance with 60.4.2.1.5.3, such materials shall be stored in accordance with the following limitations:

(1) Storage and display of solids shall not exceed 200 lb/ft^2 (976.4 kg/m^2) of floor area actually occupied by solid merchandise.
(2) Storage and display of liquids shall not exceed 20 gal/ft^2 (76 L/m^2) of floor area actually occupied by liquid merchandise.
(3) Storage and display height shall not exceed 6 ft (1.8 m) above the finished floor.
(4) Individual containers less than 5 gal (19 L) or less than 25 lb (11 kg) shall be stored or displayed on pallets, racks, or shelves.
(5) Racks and shelves used for storage or display shall be in accordance with 60.5.1.13.
(6) Containers shall be listed or approved for the intended use.
(7) Individual containers shall not exceed 100 lb (45.4 kg) capacity for solids or a 10 gal (38 L) capacity for liquids.
(8) Incompatible materials shall be separated in accordance with 60.5.1.12.
(9) Except for surfacing, floors shall be of noncombustible construction.
(10) Aisles 4 ft (1.2 m) in width shall be maintained on three sides of the storage or display area.
(11) Hazard identification signs shall be provided in accordance with 60.5.1.8.

[**400:**5.2.1.5.2]

60.4.2.1.5.3 Special Maximum Allowable Quantity Increases for Storage in Mercantile, Storage, and Industrial Occupancies. The aggregate quantity of nonflammable solid and nonflammable or noncombustible liquid hazardous materials permitted within a single control area of a mercantile, storage, or industrial occupancy shall be permitted to exceed the MAQ specified in Table 60.4.2.1.1.3, without complying with Protection Level 2, Protection Level 3, or Protection Level 4, provided that the quantities comply with Table 60.4.2.1.5.3(a) and Table 60.4.2.1.5.3(b) and that materials are displayed and stored in accordance with the special limitations in 60.4.2.1.5.2. [**400:**5.2.1.5.3]

60.4.2.2 Construction Requirements for Control Areas.

60.4.2.2.1 Number of Control Areas. The maximum number of control areas within a building shall be in accordance with Table 60.4.2.2.1. [**400:**5.2.2.1]

60.4.2.2.2 Where only one control area is present in a building, no special construction provisions shall be required. [**400:**5.2.2.2]

60.4.2.2.3 Where more than one control area is present in a building, control areas shall be separated from each other by fire barriers in accordance with Table 60.4.2.2.1. [**400:**5.2.2.3]

60.4.3 Protection Levels.

60.4.3.1 Where the quantity of hazardous materials in storage or use exceeds the MAQ for indoor control areas as set forth in 60.4.2, the occupancy shall comply with the requirements for Protection Level 1, Protection Level 2, Protection Level 3, or Protection Level 4, as required for the material in storage or use as defined in 6.2.2 through 6.2.5 of NFPA 400. [**400:**5.3.1]

60.4.3.2 Protection Level 5 shall apply to semiconductor fabrication facilities where required by the building code. [**400:**5.3.2]

60.4.3.3 Protection Level 1.

60.4.3.3.1 Buildings containing quantities of hazardous materials exceeding the MAQ of high-hazard level 1 contents permitted in control areas shall comply with applicable regulations for Protection Level 1, as set forth in the applicable sections of Chapter 6 and Chapters 11 through 21 of NFPA 400, and the building code. [**400:**5.3.3.1]

60.4.3.3.2 High-hazard level 1 contents shall include materials that present a detonation hazard as defined in 60.3.1.1.2.1. [**400:**5.3.3.2]

60.4.3.4 Protection Level 2.

60.4.3.4.1 Buildings, and portions thereof, containing quantities of hazardous materials exceeding the MAQ of high-hazard level 2 contents permitted in control areas shall comply with applicable regulations for Protection Level 2, as set forth in the applicable sections of Chapter 6 and Chapters 11 through 21 of NFPA 400, and the building code. [**400:**5.3.4.1]

60.4.3.4.2 High-hazard level 2 contents shall include materials that present a deflagration hazard or a hazard from accelerated burning as defined in 60.3.1.1.2.2. [**400:**5.3.4.2]

60.4.3.5 Protection Level 3.

60.4.3.5.1 Buildings, and portions thereof, containing quantities of hazardous materials exceeding the MAQ of high-hazard level 3 contents permitted in control areas shall comply with applicable regulations for Protection Level 3, as set forth in the applicable sections of Chapter 6 and Chapters 11 through 21 of NFPA 400, and the building code. [**400:**5.3.5.1]

Δ Table 60.4.2.1.1.3 Maximum Allowable Quantities (MAQ) of Hazardous Materials per Control Area

Material	Class	High Hazard Protection Level	Storage Solid Pounds	Storage Liquid Gallons (lb)	Storage Gas (at NTP) ft³ (lb)	Use — Closed Systems Solid Pounds	Use — Closed Systems Liquid Gallons (lb)	Use — Closed Systems Gas (at NTP) ft³ (lb)	Use — Open Systems Solid Pounds	Use — Open Systems Liquid Gallons (lb)
Physical Hazard Materials										
Combustible metals	See Note 1.	See Note 1.	See Note 1.	See Note 1.	See Note 1.	See Note 1.	See Note 1.	See Note 1.	See Note 1.	See Note 1.
Cryogenic fluid [55:Table 6.3.1.1]	Flammable	2	N/A	45^{e,f}	N/A	N/A	45^{e,f}	N/A	N/A	45^{e,f}
	Oxidizing	3	N/A	45^{a,b}	N/A	N/A	45^{a,b}	N/A	N/A	45^{a,b}
	Inert	N/A	N/A	NL	N/A	N/A	NL	N/A	N/A	NL
Explosives	See Note 1.	See Note 1.	See Note 1.	See Note 1.	See Note 1.	See Note 1.	See Note 1.	See Note 1.	See Note 1.	See Note 1.
Flammable gas^g [55:Table 6.3.1.1]	Gaseous	2	N/A	N/A	1000^{a,b}	N/A	N/A	1000^{a,b}	N/A	N/A
	Liquefied	2	N/A	N/A	(150)^{a,b}	N/A	N/A	(150)^{a,b}	N/A	N/A
	Liquefied petroleum (LP)	2	N/A	N/A	(300)^{h,j,j}	N/A	N/A	(300)^i	N/A	N/A
Ignitible (flammable or combustible liquid)^c	IA	3	N/A	30^{a,b}	N/A	N/A	See Note 1.	N/A	N/A	See Note 1.
	IB and IC	3	N/A	120^{a,b}	N/A	N/A	See Note 1.	N/A	N/A	See Note 1.
	Combination (IA, IB, IC)	3	N/A	120^{a,b,k}	N/A	N/A	See Note 1.	N/A	N/A	See Note 1.
	II	3	N/A	120^{a,b}	N/A	N/A	See Note 1.	N/A	N/A	See Note 1.
	IIIA	3	N/A	330^{a,b}	N/A	N/A	See Note 1.	N/A	N/A	See Note 1.
	IIIB	N/A	N/A	13,200^{a,d}	N/A	N/A	See Note 1.	N/A	N/A	See Note 1.
Flammable solid	N/A	3	125^{a,b}	N/A	N/A	125^{a,b}	N/A	N/A	25^{a,b}	N/A
Inert gas	Gaseous	N/A	N/A	N/A	NL	N/A	N/A	NL	N/A	N/A
	Liquefied	N/A	N/A	N/A	NL	N/A	N/A	NL	N/A	N/A
Organic peroxide	I	2	16^{a,b}	(16)^{a,b}	N/A	8^{a,b}	(8)^{a,b}	N/A	8^{a,b}	(8)^{a,b}
	IIA	3	100^{a,b}	(100)^{a,b}	N/A	50^b	(50)^b	N/A	50^b	(50)^b
	IIB	3	400	(400)^{a,b}	N/A	400^{a,b}	(400)^{a,b}	N/A	200^b	(200)^b
	III	3	840^{a,b}	(840)^{a,b}	N/A	840^{a,b}	(840)^{a,b}	N/A	840^b	(840)^b
	IV	N/A	NL	NL	N/A	NL	NL	N/A	NL	NL
	V	N/A	NL	NL	N/A	NL	NL	N/A	NL	NL
Oxidizer	4	1	1^{a,l}	(1)^{a,l}	N/A	¼^l	(¼)^l	N/A	¼^l	(¼)^l
	3^m	2 or 3	10^{a,b}	(10)^{a,b}	N/A	2^b	(2)^b	N/A	2^b	(2)^b
	2	3	250^{a,b}	(250)^{a,b}	N/A	250^b	(250)^b	N/A	50^b	(50)^b
	1	N/A	4000^{a,n}	(4000)^{a,n}	N/A	4000^n	(4000)^n	N/A	1000^n	(1000)^n
Oxidizing gas [55:Table 6.3.1.1]	Gaseous	3	N/A	N/A	1500^{a,b}	N/A	N/A	1500^{a,b}	N/A	N/A
	Liquefied	3	N/A	N/A	(150)^{a,b}	N/A	N/A	(150)^{a,b}	N/A	N/A
Pyrophoric	N/A	2	4^{a,l}	(4)^{a,l}	N/A	1^l	(1)^l	N/A	NP	NP
Pyrophoric gas [55:Table 6.3.1.1]	Gaseous	2	N/A	N/A	50^{a,l}	N/A	N/A	50^{a,l}	N/A	N/A
	Liquefied	2	N/A	N/A	(4)^{a,l}	N/A	N/A	(4)^{a,l}	N/A	N/A
Unstable (reactive)	4	1	1^{a,l}	(1)^{a,l}	N/A	¼^l	(¼)^l	N/A	¼^l	(¼)^l
	3	1 or 2	5^{a,b}	(5)^{a,b}	N/A	1^b	(1)^b	N/A	1^b	(1)^b
	2	2	50^{a,b}	(50)^{a,b}	N/A	50^b	(50)^b	N/A	10^b	(10)^b
	1	N/A	NL	NL	N/A	NL	NL	N/A	NL	NL
Unstable (reactive) gas [55:Table 6.3.1.1]	Gaseous	1	N/A	N/A	10^{a,l}	N/A	N/A	10^{a,l}	N/A	N/A
	4 or 3 detonable 3 non-detonable	2	N/A	N/A	50^{a,b}	N/A	N/A	50^{a,b}	N/A	N/A
	2	3	N/A	N/A	750^{a,b}	N/A	N/A	750^{a,b}	N/A	N/A
	1	N/A	N/A	N/A	NL	N/A	N/A	NL	N/A	N/A
Unstable (reactive) gas Liquefied [55:Table 6.3.1.1]		1	N/A	N/A	(1)^{a,l}	N/A	N/A	(1)^{a,l}	N/A	N/A
	4 or 3 detonable 3 non-detonable	2	N/A	N/A	(2)^{a,b}	N/A	N/A	(2)^{a,b}	N/A	N/A
	2	3	N/A	N/A	(150)^{a,b}	N/A	N/A	(150)^{a,b}	N/A	N/A
	1	N/A	N/A	N/A	NL	N/A	N/A	NL	N/A	N/A

(continues)

Shaded text = Revisions.   Δ = Text deletions and figure/table revisions.   • = Section deletions.   *N* = New material.

2024 Edition

Δ Table 60.4.2.1.1.3 Continued

Material	Class	High Hazard Protection Level	Storage Solid Pounds	Storage Liquid Gallons (lb)	Storage Gas (at NTP) ft³ (lb)	Use — Closed Systems Solid Pounds	Use — Closed Systems Liquid Gallons (lb)	Use — Closed Systems Gas (at NTP) ft³ (lb)	Use — Open Systems Solid Pounds	Use — Open Systems Liquid Gallons (lb)
Water-reactive	3	2	5^{a,b}	(5)^{a,b}	N/A	5^b	(5)^b	N/A	1^b	(1)^b
	2	3	50^{a,b}	(50)^{a,b}	N/A	50^b	(50)^b	N/A	10^b	(10)^b
	1	N/A	NL	NL	N/A	NL	NL	N/A	NL	NL
Health Hazard Materials										
Corrosive	N/A	4	5000^{a,b}	500^{a,b}	N/A	5000^b	500^b	N/A	1000^b	100^b
Corrosive gas [55:Table 6.3.1.1]	Gaseous	4	N/A	N/A	810^{a,b}	N/A	N/A	810^{a,b}	N/A	N/A
	Liquefied	4	N/A	N/A	(150)^{a,b}	N/A	N/A	(150)^{a,b}	N/A	N/A
Highly toxic	N/A	4	10^{a,b}	(10)^{a,b}	N/A	10^b	(10)^b	N/A	3^b	(3)^b
Highly toxic gas [55:Table 6.3.1.1]	Gaseous	4	N/A	N/A	20^{b,o}	N/A	N/A	20^{b,o}	N/A	N/A
	Liquefied	4	N/A	N/A	(4)^{b,o}	N/A	N/A	(4)^{b,o}	N/A	N/A
Toxic	N/A	4	500^{a,b}	(500)^{a,b}	N/A	500^b	(500)^b	N/A	125^b	(125)^b
Toxic gas	Gaseous	4	N/A	N/A	810^{a,b}	N/A	N/A	810^{a,b}	N/A	N/A
	Liquefied	4	N/A	N/A	(150)^{a,b}	N/A	N/A	(150)^{a,b}	N/A	N/A

For SI units, 1 lb = 0.454 kg; 1 gal = 3.785 L; 1 ft³ = 0.0283 m³. Where quantities are indicated in pounds and when the weight per gallon of the liquid is not provided to the AHJ, a conversion factor of 10 lb/gal (1.2 kg/L) shall be used.

NTP: Measured at normal temperature and pressure [70°F (21°C) and 14.7 psi (101.3 kPa)].

N/A: Not applicable. NL: Not limited. NP: Not permitted.

Notes:
(1) See Chapter 2 for the reference code or standard governing these materials and establishing the MAQs. In accordance with 1.1.1.2 of NFPA 400, materials having multiple hazards that fall within the scope of NFPA 400 shall comply with NFPA 400.
(2) Table values in parentheses correspond to the unit name in parentheses at the top of the column.
(3) The use of explosive materials required by federal, state, or municipal agencies while engaged in normal or emergency performance of duties is not required to be limited. The storage of explosive materials is required to be in accordance with the requirements of NFPA 495.
(4) The storage and use of explosive materials in medicines and medicinal agents in the forms prescribed by the official United States Pharmacopeia or the National Formulary are not required to be limited.
(5) The storage and use of propellant-actuated devices or propellant-actuated industrial tools manufactured, imported, or distributed for their intended purposes are required to be limited to 50 lb (23 kg) net explosive weight.

^{a}Quantities are permitted to be increased 100 percent where stored or used in approved cabinets, gas cabinets, exhausted enclosures, gas rooms explosives magazines, or safety cans, as appropriate for the material stored, in accordance with this *Code*. Where footnote b also applies, the increase for both footnote a and footnote b is permitted to be applied accumulatively.

^{b}Maximum quantities are permitted to be increased 100 percent in buildings equipped throughout with an automatic sprinkler system in accordance with NFPA 13. Where footnote a also applies, the increase for both footnote a and footnote b is permitted to be applied accumulatively.

^{c}Beverages, medicines, foodstuffs, cosmetics, and other products that contain not more than 20 percent by volume of water-miscible ignitible (flammable or combustible) liquids, with the remainder of the product consisting of components that do not burn, are not limited. (*See 9.1.4 of NFPA 30.*)

^{d}The permitted quantities are not limited in a building equipped throughout with an automatic sprinkler system installed in accordance with NFPA 13 and designed in accordance with the protection criteria contained in Chapter 16 of NFPA 30.

^{e}None allowed in unsprinklered buildings unless stored or used in gas rooms, approved gas cabinets, or exhausted enclosures, as specified in this *Code*.

^{f}With pressure-relief devices for stationary or portable containers vented directly outdoors or to an exhaust hood. [55:Table 6.3.1.1]

^{g}Flammable gases in the fuel tanks of mobile equipment or vehicles are permitted to exceed the MAQ where the equipment is stored and operated in accordance with this *Code*.

^{h}Additional storage locations are required to be separated by a minimum of 300 ft (92 m).

^{i}In mercantile occupancies, storage of LP-Gas is limited to a maximum of 200 lb (91 kg) in nominal 1 lb (0.45 kg) LP-Gas containers.

^{j}See NFPA 58 for liquefied petroleum gas (LP-Gas) requirements. LP-Gas is not within the scope of NFPA 400.

^{k}Containing not more than the MAQ of Class IA, Class IB, or Class IC flammable liquids, individually, per control area.

^{l}Permitted only in buildings equipped throughout with an automatic sprinkler system in accordance with NFPA 13.

^{m}A maximum quantity of 220 lb (99 kg) of solid or 22 gal (83 L) of liquid Class 3 oxidizer is permitted where such materials are necessary for maintenance purposes, operation, or sanitation of equipment. Storage containers and the manner of storage are required to be approved.

^{n}The permitted quantities are not limited in a building equipped throughout with an automatic sprinkler system in accordance with NFPA 13.

^{o}Allowed only where stored or used in gas rooms, approved gas cabinets, or exhausted enclosures, as specified in this *Code*.

[**400**:Table 5.2.1.1.3]

Δ **Table 60.4.2.1.2.1 Maximum Allowable Quantities (MAQ) of Hazardous Materials per Control Area in Occupancies Other Than Mercantile, Storage, or Industrial Occupancies**

Material	Class	Solid Pounds	Liquid Gallons (lb)	Gas (at NTP) ft^3 (lb)
Ignitible (flammable and combustible) liquid[a,b,c]	I and II	N/A	10	N/A
	IIIA	N/A	60	N/A
	IIIB	N/A	120[d]	N/A
Cryogenic fluid	Flammable	N/A	10	N/A
	Oxidizing	N/A	10	N/A
Explosives[e,f,g,h]	See Note 1.	See Note 1.	See Note 1.	See Note 1.
Flammable gas[b]	Gaseous	N/A	N/A	NP[i]
	Liquefied	N/A	N/A	NP[i,j]
	Liquefied petroleum (LP)	N/A	N/A	(20)[k]
Flammable solid	N/A	5	N/A	N/A
Oxidizers	4	NP	NP	NA
	3	10[l]	1[l]	NA
	2	250	25	NA
	1	4,000[m]	400[m]	NA
Oxidizing gas	Gaseous	N/A	N/A	NP[i]
	Liquefied	N/A	N/A	NP[i]
Organic peroxides	I	NP	NP	N/A
	IIA	NP	NP	N/A
	IIB	NP	NP	N/A
	III	25	(25)	N/A
	IV	NL	NL	N/A
	V	NL	NL	N/A
Pyrophoric materials	N/A	1[n]	(1)[n]	NP
Unstable (reactive)	4	¼	(¼)	NP
	3	1	(1)	NP
	2	10	(10)	NP[i]
	1	NL	NL	NP
Water-reactive	3	1	(1)	N/A
	2	10	(10)	N/A
	1	NL	NL	N/A
Corrosives	N/A	1,000	100	NP

(continues)

Δ Table 60.4.2.1.2.1 *Continued*

Material	Class	Solid Pounds	Liquid Gallons (lb)	Gas (at NTP) ft³ (lb)
Highly toxic	N/A	3	(3)	NP^o
Toxic	N/A	125	(125)	NP^o

For SI units, 1 lb = 0.454 kg; 1 gal = 3.785 L; 1 ft³ = 0.0283 m³. Where quantities are indicated in pounds and when the weight per gallon of the liquid is not provided to the AHJ, a conversion factor of 10 lb/gal (1.2 kg/L) shall be used.
NTP: Measured at normal temperature and pressure [70°F (21°C) and 14.7 psi (101 kPa)]. N/A: Not applicable. NP: Not permitted. NL: Not limited.
Notes:
(1) The hazardous material categories and MAQs that are shaded in this table are not regulated by NFPA 400 but are provided here for informational purposes. See Chapter 2 of NFPA 400 for the reference code or standard governing these materials and establishing the MAQs. In accordance with 1.1.1.2 of NFPA 400, materials having multiple hazards that fall within the scope of NFPA 400 shall comply with NFPA 400.
(2) Table values in parentheses correspond to the unit name in parentheses at the top of the column. The aggregate quantity in use and storage is not permitted to exceed the quantity listed for storage.
[a] Storage in excess of 10 gal (38 L) of Class I and Class II liquids combined or 60 gal (227 L) of Class IIIA liquids is permitted where stored in safety cabinets with an aggregate quantity not to exceed 180 gal (681 L).
[b] Fuel in the tank of operating mobile equipment is permitted to exceed the specified quantity where the equipment is operated in accordance with this *Code*.
[c] Medicines, foodstuffs, cosmetics, and other consumer products that contain not more than 50 percent by volume of water-miscible ignitible (flammable or combustible) liquids, with the remainder of the product consisting of components that do not burn, are not limited where packaged in individual containers that do not exceed a 1.3 gal (5 L) capacity. (*See 9.1.4 of NFPA 30.*)
[d] Storage shall be permitted to be increased 100 percent in educational, day care, and health care occupancies if the building is protected throughout with an automatic sprinkler system installed in accordance with NFPA 13.
[e] The use of explosive materials required by federal, state, or municipal agencies while engaged in normal or emergency performance of duties is not required to be limited. The storage of explosive materials is required to be in accordance with the requirements of NFPA 495.
[f] The storage and use of explosive materials in medicines and medicinal agents in the forms prescribed by the official United States Pharmacopeia or the National Formulary are not required to be limited.
[g] The storage and use of propellant-actuated devices or propellant-actuated industrial tools manufactured, imported, or distributed for their intended purposes are required to be limited to 50 lb (23 kg) net explosive weight.
[h] The storage and use of small arms ammunition, and components thereof, are permitted where in accordance with NFPA 495.
[i] Containers, cylinders, or tanks not exceeding 250 ft³ (7.1 m³) content measured at NTP and used for maintenance purposes, patient care, or operation of equipment shall be permitted.
[j] In residential occupancies consisting of lodging and rooming houses, hotels, dormitories, apartments, and residential board and care facilities, storage containers are not permitted to exceed 0.325 ft³ (0.0092 m³).
[k] In educational occupancies, allowed in laboratories only; additional 20 lb (9 kg) units are permitted where minimum 20 ft (6.1 m) separation is provided.
[l] A maximum quantity of 220 lb (99 kg) of solid or 22 gal (83 L) of liquid Class 3 oxidizer is permitted where such materials are necessary for maintenance purposes, operation, or sanitation of equipment. Storage containers and the manner of storage are required to be approved.
[m] Quantities are not limited in educational, day care, and health care occupancies protected throughout by automatic sprinkler systems in accordance with NFPA 13.
[n] Not permitted in health care occupancies.
[o] Gas containers or cylinders not exceeding 20 ft³ (0.57 m³) content measured at NTP are permitted to be stored or used within gas cabinets or exhausted enclosures of educational occupancies.
[**400**:Table 5.2.1.2.1]

Δ **Table 60.4.2.1.5.3(a) Maximum Allowable Quantity (MAQ) per Indoor and Outdoor Control Area for Selected Hazard Categories in Mercantile, Storage, and Industrial Occupancies**

	Maximum Allowable Quantity[a,b]			
	Solids		Liquids	
Hazard Category	lb	kg	gal	L
Physical Hazard Materials:				
Nonflammable and Noncombustible Solids and Liquids				
Oxidizers				
Class 3	1,500	680	150	568
Class 2	2,250	1,021	225	852
Class 1	18,000[c]	8,165[c]	1,800[c]	6,814[c]

Note: Maximum quantities for hazard categories not shown are required to be in accordance with Table 60.4.2.1.1.3.
[a]Maximum quantities are permitted to be increased 100 percent in buildings that are sprinklered in accordance with NFPA 13. Where footnote b also applies, the increase for both footnotes is permitted to be applied.
[b]Maximum quantities are permitted to be increased 100 percent where stored in approved storage cabinets in accordance with this *Code*. Where footnote a also applies, the increase for both footnotes is permitted to be applied.
[c]Quantities are not limited in buildings protected by an automatic sprinkler system complying with NFPA 13.
[**400**:Table 5.2.1.5.3(a)]

60.4.3.5.2 High-hazard level 3 contents shall include materials that readily support combustion or present a physical hazard as defined in 60.3.1.1.2.3. [**400**:5.3.5.2]

60.4.3.6 Protection Level 4.

60.4.3.6.1 Buildings, and portions thereof, containing quantities of hazardous materials exceeding the MAQ of high-hazard level 4 contents permitted in control areas shall comply with applicable regulations for Protection Level 4, as set forth in the applicable sections of Chapter 6 and Chapters 11 through 21 of NFPA 400, and the building code. [**400**:5.3.6.1]

60.4.3.6.2 High-hazard level 4 contents shall include materials that are acute health hazards as defined in 60.3.1.1.2.4. [**400**:5.3.6.2]

60.4.3.7 Detached Building Required for High-Hazard Level 2 and High-Hazard Level 3 Materials. Buildings required to comply with Protection Level 2 or Protection Level 3 and containing quantities of high-hazard contents exceeding the quantity limits set forth in Table 60.4.3.7 shall be in accordance with 6.2.3.4 or 6.2.4.4 of NFPA 400, as applicable. [**400**:5.3.7]

60.4.4* Outdoor Areas.

60.4.4.1 Outdoor Control Areas.

60.4.4.1.1 General.

60.4.4.1.1.1 Hazardous materials shall be permitted to be stored or used in outdoor control areas in accordance with 60.4.4.1.2 and 60.4.4.1.3. [**400**:5.4.1.1.1]

60.4.4.1.1.2 Where storage or use is in an outdoor control area, compliance with the outdoor storage and use requirements in Chapters 11 through 21 of NFPA 400 shall not be required. [**400**:5.4.1.1.2]

60.4.4.1.2 Maximum Allowable Quantity per Outdoor Control Area. Maximum allowable quantities of hazardous materials in an outdoor control area shall be as specified in Table 60.4.2.1.5.3(a) and Table 60.4.2.1.5.3(b) or Table 60.4.4.1.2. [**400**:5.4.1.2]

60.4.4.1.3 Number of Outdoor Control Areas.

60.4.4.1.3.1 A single outdoor control area shall be permitted on any property. [**400**:5.4.1.3.1]

60.4.4.1.3.2 Where a property exceeds 10,000 ft² (929 m²), a group of two outdoor control areas shall be permitted where approved and where each control area is separated by a minimum distance of 50 ft (15 m). [**400**:5.4.1.3.2]

60.4.4.1.3.3 Where a property exceeds 35,000 ft² (3252 m²), additional groups of outdoor control areas shall be permitted where approved, provided that each group is separated by a minimum distance of 300 ft (91 m). [**400**:5.4.1.3.3]

60.4.4.2 Outdoor Storage and Use Areas. Where the quantity of hazardous materials in outdoor storage or use exceeds the MAQ for outdoor control areas as set forth in Table 60.4.4.1.2, the outdoor area shall comply with the applicable outdoor requirements of Chapter 6 and Chapters 11 through 21 of NFPA 400. [**400**:5.4.2]

60.5 Fundamental Requirements.

60.5.1 General Requirements.

60.5.1.1 Applicability. Storage, use, and handling of hazardous materials in any quantity shall comply with 60.5.1 and the applicable material-specific requirements in Chapters 11 through 21 of NFPA 400. [**400**:6.1.1]

Table 60.4.2.1.5.3(b) Maximum Allowable Quantity (MAQ) per Indoor and Outdoor Control Area for Selected Hazard Categories in Mercantile and Storage Occupancies

Hazard Category	Maximum Allowable Quantity[a,b]			
	Solids		Liquids	
	lb	kg	gal	L
Physical Hazard Materials: Nonflammable and Noncombustible Solids and Liquids				
Unstable (reactive)				
Class 3	550	250	55	208
Class 2	1,150	522	115	435
Water-reactive				
Class 3	550	250	55	208
Class 2	1,150	522	115	435
Health Hazard Materials: Nonflammable and Noncombustible Solids and Liquids				
Corrosive	10,000	4,536	1,000	3,785
Highly toxic[c]	20	9	2	8
Toxic[c]	1,000	454	100	378

Note: Maximum quantities for hazard categories not shown are required to be in accordance with Table 60.4.2.1.1.3.
[a]Maximum quantities are permitted to be increased 100 percent in buildings that are sprinklered in accordance with NFPA 13. This increase shall not apply to highly toxic solids and liquids. Where footnote b also applies, the increase for both footnotes is permitted to be applied.
[b]Maximum quantities are permitted to be increased 100 percent where stored in approved storage cabinets in accordance with this *Code*. This increase shall not apply to highly toxic solids and liquids. Where footnote a also applies, the increase for both footnotes is permitted to be applied.
[c]Toxic or highly toxic solids or liquids displayed in original packaging in mercantile or storage occupancies and intended for maintenance, operation of equipment, or sanitation when contained in individual packaging not exceeding 100 lb (45.4 kg) shall be limited to an aggregate of 1200 lb (544.3 kg) or 120 gal (454.2 L). [**400:**5.2.1.5.3(b)]

Table 60.4.2.2.1 Design and Number of Control Areas

Floor Level	Maximum Allowable Quantity per Control Area (%)*	Number of Control Areas per Floor	Fire Resistance Rating for Fire Barriers† (hr)
Above grade			
>9	5.0	1	2
7–9	5.0	2	2
4–6	12.5	2	2
3	50.0	2	1
2	75.0	3	1
1	100.0	4	1
Below grade			
1	75.0	3	1
2	50.0	2	1
Lower than 2	NP	NP	N/A

NP: Not permitted. N/A: Not applicable.
*Percentages represent the applicable MAQ per control area shown in Table 60.4.2.1.1.3 or Table 60.4.2.1.2.1 with all the increases permitted in the footnotes of that table.
†Fire barriers are required to include floors and walls, as necessary, to provide a complete separation from other control areas. [**400:**Table 5.2.2.1]

HAZARDOUS MATERIALS

Δ **Table 60.4.3.7 Detached Buildings Required Where Quantity of Material Exceeds Amount Shown**

		Quantity of Material	
Material	Class	Solids and Liquids (tons)	Gases ft³ (m³)[a]
Individual bulk hydrogen compressed gas systems	N/A	N/A	15,000 (425)
Oxidizers	3	1,200	N/A
	2	2,000	N/A
Organic peroxides	I, IIA, IIB, III	1[b], 25[b], 40[b], 50[b]	N/A
Unstable (reactive) materials	3, nondetonable	1	2,000 (57)[c]
	2	25	10,000 (283)[c]
Water-reactive materials	3	1	N/A
	2, deflagrating	25	N/A
Pyrophoric gases	N/A	N/A	2,000 (57)

For SI units, 1 ton = 0.9 met ton.
N/A: Not applicable.
[a]See Table 21.2.5 of NFPA 400.
[b]Where two or more different classes of organic peroxide formulations are stored, see 14.3.2.5 of NFPA 400.
[c]Nondetonable.
[**400**:Table 5.3.7]

60.5.1.1.1* Storage of hazardous materials in quantities exceeding the MAQ set forth in Section 60.4 shall comply with Section 6.2 of NFPA 400 and the applicable material specific requirements in Chapters 11 through 21 of NFPA 400. [**400**:6.1.1.1]

60.5.1.1.2* The use, dispensing, and handling of hazardous materials in quantities exceeding the MAQ set forth in Section 60.4 shall comply with Section 6.3 of NFPA 400 and the applicable material specific requirements in Chapters 11 through 21 of NFPA 400. [**400**:6.1.1.2]

60.5.1.2* Safety Data Sheets (SDS). Safety data sheets (SDS) shall be available on the premises for hazardous materials regulated by this *Code*. When approved, SDSs shall be permitted to be retrievable by electronic access. [**400**:6.1.2]

60.5.1.3 Release of Hazardous Materials.

60.5.1.3.1 Prohibited Releases. Hazardous materials shall not be released into a sewer, storm drain, ditch, drainage canal, lake, river, or tidal waterway; upon the ground, a sidewalk, a street, or a highway; or into the atmosphere, unless such release is permitted by the following:

(1) Federal, state, or local governing regulations
(2) Permits of the jurisdictional air quality management board
(3) National Pollutant Discharge Elimination System permit
(4) Waste discharge requirements established by the jurisdictional water quality control board
(5) Sewer pretreatment requirements for publicly or privately owned treatment works

[**400**:6.1.3.1]

60.5.1.3.2 Control and Mitigation of Unauthorized Releases. Provisions shall be made for controlling and mitigating unauthorized releases. [**400**:6.1.3.2]

60.5.1.3.3 Records of Unauthorized Releases. Accurate records of the unauthorized release of hazardous materials shall be kept by the permittee. [**400**:6.1.3.3]

60.5.1.3.4* Notification of Unauthorized Releases. The fire department shall be notified immediately or in accordance with approved emergency procedures when an unauthorized release becomes reportable under state, federal, or local regulations. [**400**:6.1.3.4]

60.5.1.3.5 Container Failure. When an unauthorized release due to primary container failure is discovered, the involved primary container shall be repaired or removed from service. [**400**:6.1.3.5]

60.5.1.3.6 Overpack Containers. Overpack containers shall be permitted to be used as a means to provide protection for primary containers to be transported for repair or removal from service. [**400**:6.1.3.6]

60.5.1.3.7 Responsibility for Cleanup of Unauthorized Releases.

60.5.1.3.7.1 The person, firm, or corporation responsible for an unauthorized release shall institute and complete all actions necessary to remedy the effects of such unauthorized release, whether sudden or gradual, at no cost to the AHJ. [**400**:6.1.3.7.1]

60.5.1.3.7.2 When deemed necessary by the AHJ, cleanup of an unauthorized release shall be permitted to be initiated by the fire department or by an authorized individual or firm, and costs associated with such cleanup shall be borne by the owner, operator, or other person responsible for the unauthorized release. [**400**:6.1.3.7.2]

Δ **60.5.1.4* Personnel Training.** Persons in areas where hazardous materials are stored, dispensed, handled, or used shall be trained in the hazards of the materials employed and actions required by the emergency plan. The level of training to be conducted shall be consistent with the responsibilities of the persons to be trained in accordance with 60.5.1.4.1 through 60.5.1.4.5. [**400**:6.1.4]

60.5.1.4.1 Awareness. The training provided for persons designated in 60.5.1.4 shall include awareness training in accordance with 60.5.1.4.1.1 through 60.5.1.4.1.3. [**400**:6.1.4.1]

60.5.1.4.1.1 Completion. Initial training shall be completed prior to beginning work in the work area. [**400**:6.1.4.1.1]

60.5.1.4.1.2 Hazard Communications. Training shall be provided prior to beginning work in the work area to enable personnel to recognize and identify hazardous materials stored, dispensed, handled, or used on site and where to find safety information pertaining to the hazards of the materials employed. [**400**:6.1.4.1.2]

60.5.1.4.1.3 Emergency Plan. Training shall be provided prior to beginning work in the work area to enable personnel to implement the emergency plan. [**400**:6.1.4.1.3]

60.5.1.4.2 Operations Personnel. Persons engaged in storing, using, or handling hazardous materials shall be designated as operations personnel and shall be trained in accordance with 60.5.1.4.1 and 60.5.1.4.2.1 through 60.5.1.4.2.6. [**400**:6.1.4.2]

Δ **Table 60.4.4.1.2 Maximum Allowable Quantities of Hazardous Materials per Outdoor Control Area**

Material	Class	Storage Solid Pounds	Storage Liquid Gallons (lb)	Storage Gas (at NTP) ft^3 (lb)	Use — Closed Systems Solid Pounds	Use — Closed Systems Liquid Gallons (lb)	Use — Closed Systems Gas (at NTP) ft^3 (lb)	Use — Open Systems Solid Pounds	Use — Open Systems Liquid Gallons (lb)
Physical Hazard Materials									
Flammable gas									
Gaseous		N/A	N/A	3000	N/A	N/A	1500	N/A	N/A
Liquefied		N/A	N/A	(300)	N/A	N/A	(150)	N/A	N/A
Flammable solid		500	N/A	N/A	250	N/A	N/A	50	N/A
Organic peroxide	Detonable	1	(1)	N/A	¼	(¼)	N/A	¼	(¼)
Organic peroxide	I	20	(20)	N/A	10	(10)	N/A	2	(2)
	IIA	100	(200)	N/A	100	(100)	N/A	100	(100)
	IIB	400	(400)	N/A	400	(400)	N/A	400	(400)
	III	NL	NL	N/A	NL	NL	N/A	NL	NL
	IV	NL	NL	N/A	NL	NL	N/A	NL	NL
	V	NL	NL	N/A	NL	NL	N/A	NL	NL
Oxidizer	4	2	(2)	N/A	1	(¼)	N/A	¼	(¼)
	3	40	(40)	N/A	20	(2)	N/A	2	(2)
	2	1000	(1000)	N/A	500	(250)	N/A	50	(50)
	1	NL	NL	N/A	NL	NL	N/A	NL	NL
Oxidizing gas									
Gaseous		N/A	N/A	6000	N/A	N/A	6000	N/A	N/A
Liquefied		N/A	N/A	(600)	N/A	N/A	(300)	N/A	N/A
Pyrophoric		8	(8)	100	4	(4)	10	0	0
Unstable (reactive)	4	2	(2)	20	1	(1)	2	¼	(¼)
	3	20	(20)	200	10	(10)	10	1	(1)
	2	200	(200)	1000	100	(100)	250	10	(10)
	1	NL	NL	1500	NL	NL	NL	NL	NL
Water-reactive	3	20	(20)	N/A	10	(10)	N/A	1	(1)
	2	200	(200)	N/A	100	(100)	N/A	10	(10)
	1	NL	NL	N/A	NL	NL	N/A	NL	NL
Health Hazard Materials									
Corrosive		20,000	2000	N/A	10,000	1000	N/A	1000	100
Corrosive gas									
Gaseous		N/A	N/A	1620	N/A	N/A	810	N/A	N/A
Liquefied		N/A	N/A	(300)	N/A	N/A	(150)	N/A	N/A
Highly toxic		20	(20)	N/A	10	(10)	N/A	3	(3)
Highly toxic gas									
Gaseous		N/A	N/A	40*	N/A	N/A	20*	N/A	N/A
Liquefied		N/A	N/A	(8)*	N/A	N/A	(4)*	N/A	N/A
Toxic		1000	(1000)	N/A	500	50	N/A	125	(125)
Toxic gas									
Gaseous		N/A	N/A	1620	N/A	N/A	810	N/A	N/A
Liquefied		N/A	N/A	(300)	N/A	N/A	(150)	N/A	N/A

For SI units, 1 lb = 0.454 kg; 1 gal = 3.785 L; 1 ft^3 = 0.0283 m^3.
N/A: Not applicable. NL: Not limited.
NTP: Measured at normal temperature and pressure [70°F (21°C) and 14.7 psi (101 kPa)].
Notes:
(1) Table values in parentheses correspond to the unit name in parentheses at the top of the column.
(2) For gallons of liquids, divide the amount in pounds by 10.
(3) The aggregate quantities in storage and use cannot exceed the quantity listed for storage.
(4) The aggregate quantity of nonflammable solid and nonflammable or noncombustible liquid hazardous materials allowed in outdoor storage per single property under the same ownership or control used for retail or wholesale sales is permitted to exceed the MAQ where such storage is in accordance with 60.4.2.1.5.3.
*Permitted only where stored or used in approved exhausted gas cabinets, exhausted enclosures, or fume hoods. [400:Table 5.4.1.2]

60.5.1.4.2.1 Physical and Health Hazard Properties. Operations personnel shall be trained in the chemical nature of the materials, including their physical hazards and the symptoms of acute or chronic exposure as provided by the safety data sheet (SDS) furnished by the manufacturer or other authoritative sources. [**400**:6.1.4.2.1]

60.5.1.4.2.2 Dispensing, Using, and Processing. Operations personnel shall be trained in the use of specific safeguards applicable to the dispensing, processing, or use of the materials and equipment employed. [**400**:6.1.4.2.2]

60.5.1.4.2.3 Storage. Operations personnel shall be trained in the application of storage arrangements and site-specific limitations on storage for the materials employed. [**400**:6.1.4.2.3]

60.5.1.4.2.4 Transport (Handling). Operations personnel involved in materials handling shall be trained in the requirements for on-site transport of the materials employed. [**400**:6.1.4.2.4]

60.5.1.4.2.5 Actions in an Emergency. Operations personnel shall be trained in the necessary actions to take in the event of an emergency, including the operation and activation of emergency controls prior to evacuation. [**400**:6.1.4.2.5]

60.5.1.4.2.6 Changes. Training shall be provided whenever a new hazardous material is introduced into the work area that presents a new physical or health hazard, or when new information is obtained pertaining to physical or health hazards of an existing hazardous material that has not been included in previous training, and when there are changes in any of the following:

(1) Equipment
(2) Operations
(3) Hazardous materials
[**400**:6.1.4.2.6]

60.5.1.4.3 Emergency Response Liaison.

60.5.1.4.3.1 Responsible persons shall be designated and trained to be emergency response (ER) liaison personnel. [**400**:6.1.4.3.1]

60.5.1.4.3.2 Emergency response liaison personnel shall do the following:

(1) Aid emergency responders in pre-planning responses to emergencies
(2) Identify locations where hazardous materials are located
(3) Have access to safety data sheets
(4) Be knowledgeable in the site emergency response procedures

[**400**:6.1.4.3.2]

60.5.1.4.4 Emergency Responders. On-site emergency response teams shall be trained in accordance with NFPA 400.

60.5.1.4.5 Documentation. Training shall be documented and the documentation made available to the AHJ upon written request. [**400**:6.1.4.6]

60.5.1.5 Ignition Source Controls.

60.5.1.5.1 Smoking. Smoking shall be prohibited in the following locations:

(1) Within 25 ft (7.6 m) of outdoor storage areas, dispensing areas, or open use areas
(2) In rooms or areas where hazardous materials are stored or dispensed or used in open systems in amounts requiring a permit in accordance with Section 1.8 of NFPA 400 [**400**:6.1.5.1]

60.5.1.5.2 Open Flames and High-Temperature Devices. Open flames and high-temperature devices shall not be used in a manner that creates a hazardous condition. [**400**:6.1.5.2]

60.5.1.5.3 Energy-Consuming Equipment. Energy-consuming equipment with the potential to serve as a source of ignition shall be listed or approved for use with the hazardous materials stored or used. [**400**:6.1.5.3]

60.5.1.5.3.1* Powered Industrial Trucks. Powered industrial trucks shall be operated and maintained in accordance with NFPA 505 and Section 10.18.

60.5.1.6 Systems, Equipment, and Processes. Processes, methods, specifications, equipment testing and maintenance, design standards, performance, installation, equipment design and construction, and other pertinent criteria shall be in accordance with this section. [**400**:6.1.6]

60.5.1.6.1 Design and Construction of Containers and Tanks. Containers, cylinders, and tanks shall be designed and constructed in accordance with approved standards. Containers, cylinders, tanks, and other means used for containment of hazardous materials shall be of an approved type. [**400**:6.1.6.1]

60.5.1.6.2 Piping, Tubing, Valves, and Fittings. Piping, tubing, valves, fittings, and related components used for hazardous materials shall be in accordance with the following:

(1) Piping, tubing, valves, fittings, and related components shall be designed and fabricated from materials compatible with the material to be contained and shall be of a strength and durability to withstand the pressure, structural and seismic stress, and exposure to which they are subject.
(2) Piping and tubing shall be identified in accordance with ASME A13.1, *Scheme for the Identification of Piping Systems*, to indicate the material conveyed.
(3) Accessible manual valves, or fail-safe emergency shutoff valves operated by a remotely located manually or automatically activated shutdown control, shall be installed on supply piping and tubing at the following locations:
    (a) Point of use
    (b) Tank or bulk source
(4) Manual emergency shutoff valves and remotely located manually activated shutdown controls for emergency shutoff valves shall be identified, and the location shall be clearly visible, accessible, and indicated by means of a sign.
(5) Backflow prevention or check valves shall be provided when the backflow of hazardous materials could create a hazardous condition or cause the unauthorized discharge of hazardous materials.
(6) Liquids classified in accordance with NFPA 704 shall be carried in pressurized piping above a gauge pressure of 15 psi (103 kPa) having a hazard ranking as follows:
    (a) Health hazard Class 3 or Class 4
    (b) Flammability Class 4
    (c) Instability Class 3 or Class 4
(7) The pressurized piping specified in 60.5.1.6.2(6) shall be provided with an approved means of leak detection and

emergency shutoff or excess flow control in accordance with the following:

(a) Where the piping originates from within a hazardous material storage room or area, the excess flow control shall be located within the storage room or area.
(b) Where the piping originates from a bulk source, the excess flow control shall be located at the bulk source.
(c) Piping for inlet connections designed to prevent backflow shall not be required to be equipped with excess flow control.

[**400:**6.1.6.2]

60.5.1.6.3 Additional Regulations for Supply Piping for Health Hazard Materials. Supply piping and tubing for liquids or solids having a health hazard ranking of Class 3 or Class 4 in accordance with NFPA 704 shall be in accordance with ASME B31.3, *Process Piping*, and the following:

(1) Piping and tubing utilized for the transmission of highly toxic, toxic, or highly volatile corrosive liquids shall have welded, threaded, or flanged connections throughout, except for connections located within a ventilated enclosure, or an approved method of drainage or containment.
(2) Piping and tubing shall not be located within corridors, within any portion of a means of egress required to be enclosed in fire resistance–rated construction, or in concealed spaces in areas not classified as Protection Level 1 through Protection Level 4 occupancies.

[**400:**6.1.6.3]

60.5.1.6.4 Equipment, Machinery, and Alarms. Equipment, machinery, and required detection and alarm systems associated with the use, storage, or handling of hazardous materials shall be listed or approved. [**400:**6.1.6.4]

60.5.1.7 Empty Containers and Tanks. Empty containers and tanks previously used for the storage of hazardous materials shall be free from residual material and vapor as defined by DOT, the *Resource Conservation and Recovery Act (RCRA)*, or other regulating authority or shall be maintained as specified for the storage of hazardous material. [**400:**6.1.7]

60.5.1.8 Signs.

60.5.1.8.1 General.

60.5.1.8.1.1 Design and Construction. Signs shall be durable, and the size, color, and lettering of signs shall be in accordance with nationally recognized standards. [**400:**6.1.8.1.1]

60.5.1.8.1.2 Language. Signs shall be in English as the primary language or in symbols permitted by this *Code*. [**400:**6.1.8.1.2]

60.5.1.8.1.3 Maintenance. Signs shall meet the following criteria:

(1) They shall not be obscured.
(2) They shall be maintained in a legible condition.
(3) They shall not be removed, unless for replacement.

[**400:**6.1.8.1.3]

60.5.1.8.2 Hazard Materials Identification.

60.5.1.8.2.1 NFPA 704 Placard. Visible hazard identification signs in accordance with NFPA 704 shall be placed at the following locations, except where the AHJ has received a hazardous materials management plan and a hazardous materials inventory statement in accordance with 60.1.6 and 60.1.7 and has determined that omission of such signs is consistent with safety:

(1) On stationary aboveground tanks
(2) On stationary aboveground containers
(3) At entrances to locations where hazardous materials are stored, dispensed, used, or handled in quantities requiring a permit
(4) At other entrances and locations designated by the AHJ

[**400:**6.1.8.2.1]

60.5.1.8.2.2 Identification of Containers, Cartons, and Packages. Individual containers, cartons, or packages shall be conspicuously marked or labeled in accordance with nationally recognized standards. [**400:**6.1.8.2.2]

60.5.1.8.3 No Smoking Signs. Where "no smoking" is not applicable to an entire site or building, signs shall be provided as follows:

(1) In rooms or areas where hazardous materials are stored or dispensed or used in open systems in amounts requiring a permit in accordance with Section 1.8 of NFPA 400
(2) Within 25 ft (7.6 m) of outdoor storage, dispensing, or open-use areas

[**400:**6.1.8.3]

60.5.1.9 Protection from Vehicles.

60.5.1.9.1 Guard posts or other approved means shall be provided to protect the following where subject to vehicular damage:

(1) Storage tanks and connected piping, valves, and fittings
(2) Storage areas containing tanks or portable containers except where the exposing vehicles are powered industrial trucks used for transporting the hazardous materials
(3) Use areas

[**400:**6.1.9.1]

60.5.1.9.2 Where guard posts are installed, the posts shall meet the following criteria:

(1) They shall be constructed of steel not less than 4 in. (102 mm) in diameter and concrete filled.
(2) They shall be spaced not more than 4 ft (1.2 m) between posts on center.
(3) They shall be set not less than 3 ft (0.9 m) deep in a concrete footing of not less than a 15 in. (381 mm) diameter.
(4) They shall be set with the top of the posts not less than 3 ft (0.9 m) above ground.
(5) They shall be located not less than 3 ft (0.9 m) from the tank.

[**400:**6.1.9.2]

60.5.1.10 Electrical Wiring and Equipment.

Δ **60.5.1.10.1 General.**

Electrical wiring and equipment shall be installed in accordance with *NFPA 70*. [**400:**6.1.10.1]

60.5.1.10.2 Static Accumulation. When processes or use conditions exist where flammable gases, dusts, or vapors can be ignited by static electricity, means shall be provided to prevent the accumulation of a static charge and to dissipate the static charge to ground. [**400:**6.1.10.2]

60.5.1.11 Protection from Light. Materials that are sensitive to light shall be stored in containers designed to protect them from such exposure. [**400**:6.1.11]

60.5.1.12 Separation of Incompatible Materials.

60.5.1.12.1 Incompatible materials in storage and storage of materials incompatible with materials in use shall be separated when the stored materials are in containers having a capacity of more than 5 lb (2.268 kg) or ½ gal (1.89 L). [**400**:6.1.12.1]

60.5.1.12.2 Separation shall be accomplished by one of the following methods:

(1) Segregating incompatible materials storage by a distance of not less than 20 ft (6.1 m)
(2) Isolating incompatible materials storage by a noncombustible partition extending not less than 18 in. (457 mm) above and to the sides of the stored material or by a noncombustible partition that interrupts the line of sight between the incompatible materials
(3) Storing liquid and solid materials in hazardous materials storage cabinets complying with 60.5.1.18
(4) Storing compressed gases in gas cabinets or exhausted enclosures complying with Chapter 21 of NFPA 400

[**400**:6.1.12.2]

60.5.1.12.3 Materials that are incompatible shall not be stored within the same cabinet or enclosure. [**400**:6.1.12.3]

60.5.1.13 General Storage.

60.5.1.13.1 Storage. The storage arrangement of materials shall be in accordance with this section and the material specific requirements of Chapters 11 through 21 of NFPA 400 as applicable. [**400**:6.1.13.1]

60.5.1.13.2 Shelf Storage. Shelving shall be constructed to carry the design loads and shall be braced and anchored in accordance with the seismic design requirements of the applicable building code. [**400**:6.1.13.2]

60.5.1.13.2.1 Shelf Construction.

60.5.1.13.2.1.1 Shelving shall be treated, coated, or constructed of materials that are compatible with the hazardous materials stored. [**400**:6.1.13.2.1.1]

60.5.1.13.2.1.2 Shelves shall be provided with a lip or guard where used for the storage of individual containers, except under either of the following conditions:

(1) Where storage is located in hazardous materials storage cabinets or laboratory furniture specifically designed for such use
(2) Where amounts of hazardous materials in storage do not exceed the quantity threshold for requiring a permit in accordance with Section 1.8 of NFPA 400

[**400**:6.1.13.2.1.2]

60.5.1.13.2.2 Shelf storage of hazardous materials shall be maintained in an orderly manner. [**400**:6.1.13.2.2]

60.5.1.14 Seismic Protection. If seismic protection is provided it shall be maintained.

60.5.1.15 Outdoor Storage and Use Areas. Outdoor storage and use areas for hazardous materials shall comply with the following:

(1) Outdoor storage and use areas shall be kept free of weeds, debris, and common combustible materials not necessary to the storage or use of hazardous materials.
(2) The area surrounding an outdoor storage and use area shall be kept clear of weeds, debris, and common combustible materials not necessary to the storage or use of hazardous materials for a minimum distance of 15 ft (4.5 m).
(3) Outdoor storage and use areas for hazardous materials shall be located not closer than 20 ft (6.1 m) from a property line that can be built upon, a street, an alley, or a public way, except that a 2-hour fire barrier wall, without openings and extending not less than 30 in. (762 mm) above and to the sides of the storage area, shall be permitted in lieu of such distance.

[**400**:6.1.15]

60.5.1.16 Maintenance Required.

60.5.1.16.1 Equipment, machinery, and required detection and alarm systems associated with hazardous materials shall be maintained in an operable condition. [**400**:6.1.16.1]

60.5.1.16.2 Stationary tanks not used for a period of 90 days shall be safeguarded or removed in an approved manner. [**400**:6.1.16.2]

60.5.1.16.2.1 The tanks specified in 60.5.1.16.2 shall have the fill line, gauge opening, and pump connection secured against tampering. [**400**:6.1.16.2.1]

60.5.1.16.2.2 Vent lines shall be maintained. [**400**:6.1.16.2.2]

60.5.1.16.2.3* Tanks that are to be placed back in service shall be tested in an approved manner. [**400**:6.1.16.2.3]

60.5.1.16.3 The following shall apply to defective containers, cylinders, and tanks:

(1) They shall be removed from service, repaired, or disposed of in an approved manner.
(2) Overpack containers shall be permitted to be used as a means to provide protection for primary containers that are transported for repair or removal from service.

[**400**:6.1.16.3]

60.5.1.16.4 Defective equipment or machinery shall be removed from service and repaired or replaced. [**400**:6.1.16.4]

60.5.1.16.5 Required detection and alarm systems that are defective shall be replaced or repaired. [**400**:6.1.16.5]

60.5.1.17 Testing.

60.5.1.17.1 The equipment, devices, and systems listed in 60.5.1.17.2.1 shall be tested at one of the intervals listed in 60.5.1.17.2.2. Written records of the tests conducted or maintenance performed shall be maintained. [**400**:6.1.17.1]

60.5.1.17.2 Testing shall not be required under the following conditions:

(1) Where approved written documentation is provided that testing will damage the equipment, device, or system and the equipment, device, or system is maintained as specified by the manufacturer
(2) Where equipment, devices, and systems fail in a fail-safe manner
(3) Where equipment, devices, and systems self-diagnose and report trouble, with records of the self-diagnosis and trouble reporting made available to the AHJ

(4) Where system activation occurs during the required test cycle for the components activated during the test cycle
(5) Where approved maintenance in accordance with 60.5.1.16.1 is performed not less than annually or in accordance with an approved schedule, in which case the testing requirements set forth in 60.5.1.17.2.1 and 60.5.1.17.2.2 are permitted to apply.

[**400**:6.1.17.2]

60.5.1.17.2.1 Equipment, Devices, and Systems Requiring Testing. The following equipment, devices, and systems shall be tested in accordance with 60.5.1.17 and 60.5.1.17.2.2:

(1) Limit control systems for liquid level, temperature, and pressure required by 6.2.1.7 and 6.3.1.2 of NFPA 400
(2) Monitoring and supervisory systems required by 6.2.1.1 and 6.3.2.1.1 of NFPA 400

[**400**:6.1.17.2.1]

60.5.1.17.2.2 Testing Frequency. The equipment, systems, and devices listed in 60.5.1.17.2.1 shall be tested at one of the following frequencies:

(1) Not less than annually
(2) In accordance with the approved manufacturer's requirements
(3) In accordance with approved recognized industry standards
(4) In accordance with an approved schedule

[**400**:6.1.17.2.2]

60.5.1.18 Hazardous Materials Storage Cabinets. When storage cabinets are used to increase MAQ per control area or to otherwise comply with a specific provision in Section 60.5, such cabinets shall be in accordance with the following:

(1) Cabinets shall be constructed of metal.
(2) The interior of cabinets shall be treated, coated, or constructed of materials that are nonreactive with the hazardous material stored, and such treatment, coating, or construction shall include the entire interior of the cabinet.
(3) Cabinets shall be either listed as suitable for the intended storage or constructed in accordance with the following:
   (a) Cabinets shall be of steel having a thickness of not less than 0.044 in. (1.12 mm) (18 gauge).
   (b) The cabinet, including the door, shall be double-walled with 1½ in. (38.1 mm) airspace between the walls.
   (c) Joints shall be riveted or welded and shall be tight-fitting.
   (d) Doors shall be well fitted, self-closing, and equipped with a self-latching device.
   (e) The bottoms of cabinets utilized for the storage of liquids shall be liquidtight to a minimum height of 2 in. (51 mm).
   (f) For requirements regarding electrical equipment and devices within cabinets used for the storage of hazardous liquids, compressed gases, or cryogenic fluids, see *NFPA 70*.
(4) Cabinets shall be marked in conspicuous lettering that reads as follows: HAZARDOUS — KEEP FIRE AWAY

[**400**:6.1.18]

60.5.1.19 Installation of Tanks. Installation of tanks shall be in accordance with 60.5.1.19.1 through 60.5.1.19.2. [**400**:6.1.19]

60.5.1.19.1 Underground Tanks.

60.5.1.19.1.1 Underground tanks used for the storage of liquid hazardous materials shall be provided with secondary containment. [**400**:6.1.19.1.1]

60.5.1.19.1.2 In lieu of providing secondary containment for an underground tank, an aboveground tank in an underground vault complying with NFPA 30 shall be permitted. [**400**:6.1.19.1.2]

60.5.1.19.2 Aboveground Tanks. Aboveground stationary tanks installed outdoors and used for the storage of hazardous materials shall be located and protected in accordance with the requirements for outdoor storage of the particular material involved and in accordance with the requirements of Chapters 11 through 21 of NFPA 400. [**400**:6.1.19.2]

60.5.1.19.2.1 Aboveground tanks that are installed in vaults complying with NFPA 30 shall not be required to comply with location and protection requirements for outdoor storage. [**400**:6.1.19.2.1]

60.5.1.19.2.2 Aboveground tanks that are installed inside buildings and used for the storage of hazardous materials shall be located and protected in accordance with the requirements for indoor storage of the particular material involved. [**400**:6.1.19.2.2]

60.5.1.19.2.3 Marking. Aboveground stationary tanks shall be marked as required by 60.5.1.8.2.1. [**400**:6.1.19.2.3]

60.5.1.20 When required, fire alarm systems and smoke detection systems shall be installed in accordance with *NFPA 72*. [**400**:6.1.20]

60.6 Emergency Action Planning, Fire Risk Control, and Chemical Hazard Requirements for Industrial Processes. Emergency planning, fire risk control, and chemical hazard requirements associated with industrial processes where the quantities of materials in use require compliance with Protection Level 1, Protection Level 2, Protection Level 3, or Protection Level 4 based on materials exceeding the maximum allowable quantities (MAQ) in the following categories shall comply with the requirements of Chapter 7 of NFPA 400:

(1) Unpackaged organic peroxide formulations that are capable of explosive decomposition in their unpackaged state
(2) Oxidizer Class 3 and Class 4: solids and liquids
(3) Pyrophoric solids, liquids, and gases
(4) Unstable reactive Class 3 and Class 4: solids, liquids, and gases
(5) Highly toxic solids, liquids, and gases
(6) Water-reactive liquids, Class 3

60.7 Performance Alternative. In lieu of complying with Chapter 60 in its entirety, occupancies containing high hazard Level 1 to high hazard Level 5 contents shall be permitted to comply with Chapter 10 of NFPA 400.

Chapter 61 Aerosol Products

61.1 General Provisions.

61.1.1 Application.

61.1.1.1* The manufacture, storage, use, handling, and display of aerosol products shall comply with the requirements of Chapter 61, NFPA 30B, and Sections 60.1 through 60.4 of this *Code*.

61.1.1.2 Where the provisions of Chapter 61 or NFPA 30B conflict with the provisions of Chapter 60, the provisions of Chapter 61 and NFPA 30B shall apply.

Δ **61.1.1.3*** Chapter 61 shall apply to the storage and display of products whose contents are comprised entirely of compressed or liquefied gas, provided that the containers meet the requirements of 3.3.5 through 3.3.8. [**30B:**1.1.2]

61.1.1.4 Chapter 61 shall not apply to post-consumer processing of aerosol containers. [**30B:**1.1.3]

61.1.1.5* Chapter 61 shall not apply to containers that do not meet the definition of *Aerosol Container* (*see 3.3.1 of NFPA 30B*). [**30B:**1.1.4]

61.1.1.5.1 Containers that contain a product that meets the definitions in 3.3.2 and 3.3.3 of NFPA 30B, but are larger than the limits specified in 3.3.1 of NFPA 30B, shall not be classified as aerosol products, and Chapter 61 shall not apply to the manufacture, storage, and display of such products. [**30B:**1.1.4.1]

Δ **61.1.2 Permits.**

N **61.1.2.1** Permits shall be required in accordance with this chapter and Table 1.13.8(a) through Table 1.13.8(d).

N **61.1.2.2** Permits, where required, shall comply with Section 1.13.

61.1.3* Classification of Aerosol Products in Metal Containers of Not More Than 33.8 fl oz (1000 ml) and in Plastic or Glass Containers of Not More Than 4 fl oz (118 ml). See Annex E of NFPA 30B. [**30B:**4.2]

61.1.3.1 Aerosol products shall be classified by means of the calculation of their chemical or theoretical heats of combustion and shall be designated Level 1, Level 2, or Level 3 in accordance with 61.1.3.2 through 61.1.3.5.1.2 and Table 61.1.3.1. [**30B:**4.2.1]

Δ **61.1.3.1.1** In lieu of classification by means of the chemical heats of combustion, aerosol products shall be permitted to be classified by means of data obtained from properly conducted full-scale fire tests that utilize a 12-pallet test array. [**30B:**4.2.1.1]

61.1.3.1.2 The fire tests shall be conducted at an approved testing laboratory. (*See Annex C of NFPA 30B for information on the 12-pallet test array.*) [**30B:**4.2.1.2]

N **61.1.3.1.3** The requirement in 61.1.3.1.1 shall not apply to Aerosol Cooking Spray Products. (*See 61.1.3.5.*) [**30B:**4.2.1.3]

61.1.3.2 Level 1 Aerosol Products. Level 1 Aerosol Products shall be defined as those products with a total chemical heat of combustion that is less than or equal to 20 kJ/g (8600 Btu/lb). [**30B:**4.2.2]

61.1.3.3 Level 2 Aerosol Products. Level 2 Aerosol Products shall be defined as those products with a total chemical heat of combustion that is greater than 20 kJ/g (8600 Btu/lb), but less than or equal to 30 kJ/g (13,000 Btu/lb). [**30B:**4.2.3]

61.1.3.4 Level 3 Aerosol Products. Level 3 Aerosol Products shall be defined as those products with a total chemical heat of combustion that is greater than 30 kJ/g (13,000 Btu/lb). [**30B:**4.2.4]

Δ **61.1.3.5 Aerosol Cooking Spray Products.** Aerosol Cooking Spray Products shall be defined as those aerosol products designed to deliver a vegetable oil or a solid or nonflammable liquid to reduce sticking on cooking and baking surfaces, or to be applied to food, or both. [**30B:**4.2.5]

N **61.1.3.5.1** These products shall have a chemical heat of combustion that is greater than 20 kJ/g (8600 Btu/lb) and shall contain not more than 18 percent by weight of flammable propellant. [**30B:**4.2.5.1]

61.1.3.5.1.1 If the Aerosol Cooking Spray Product has a chemical heat of combustion that does not exceed 20 kJ/g (8600 Btu/lb), it shall be considered a Level 1 Aerosol Product. [**30B:**4.2.5.1.1]

61.1.3.5.1.2 If the Aerosol Cooking Spray Product contains more than 18 percent by weight of flammable propellant, it shall be classified in accordance with its chemical heat of combustion, as set forth in Table 61.1.3.1. [**30B:**4.2.5.1.2]

61.1.4 Classification of Aerosol Products in Plastic Containers Larger Than 4 fl oz (118 ml) and Smaller Than 33.8 oz (1000 ml).

Δ **61.1.4.1 Plastic Aerosol 1 Products.** Plastic Aerosol 1 products shall be defined as those that meet one of the following criteria:

(1) The base product has no fire point when tested in accordance with ASTM D92, *Standard Test Method for Flash and Fire Points by Cleveland Open Cup Tester*, and the propellant is nonflammable.

(2) The base product does not exhibit sustained combustion when tested in accordance with 49 CFR 173, Appendix H, "Method of Testing for Sustained Combustibility," or the *UN Recommendations on the Transport of Dangerous Goods*, and the propellant is nonflammable.

(3)* The base product contains not more than 20 percent by volume (15.8 percent by weight) of ethanol or propanol, or mixtures thereof in an aqueous mix, and the propellant is nonflammable.

(4)* The base product contains not more than 4 percent by weight of an emulsified liquefied flammable gas propel-

Δ **Table 61.1.3.1 Aerosol Classification**

If the chemical heat of combustion is		Aerosol Classification Level
>	≤	
0	20 kJ/g (8,600 Btu/lb)	1
20 kJ/g (8,600 Btu/lb)	30 kJ/g (13,000 Btu/lb)	2
30 kJ/g (13,000 Btu/lb)	—	3

[**30B:**Table 4.2.1]

lant within an aqueous base, and the propellant remains emulsified for the life of the product. [**30B:**4.3.1]

N **61.1.4.1.1** Where the propellant in 61.1.4.1(4) is not permanently emulsified, the propellant shall be nonflammable. [**30B:**4.3.1.1]

N **61.1.4.2 Plastic Aerosol 2 Products.** Plastic Aerosol 2 Products shall be defined as those products that meet one of the following criteria:

(1) The base product contains greater than 20 percent by volume (15.8 percent by weight) up to 50 percent by volume (39.5 percent by weight) of ethanol, propanol, other water miscible alcohols, or mixtures thereof in an aqueous mix, and the propellant is nonflammable compressed gas.
(2) The base product contains greater than 20 percent by volume (15.8 percent by weight) up to 50 percent by volume (39.5 percent by weight) of ethanol, propanol, other water miscible alcohols, or mixtures thereof in an aqueous mix; is packaged in a compartmented container that separates the product from the propellant as typified by a bag-on-valve (BOV) package, bag-in-container package, or piston-in-container package; and the propellant is nonflammable compressed gas, nonflammable liquefied gas, or mixtures thereof.

[**30B:**4.3.2]

61.1.4.3* Plastic Aerosol 3 Products. Plastic Aerosol 3 Products shall be defined as those that meet one of the following criteria:

(1) The base product has no fire point when tested in accordance with ASTM D92, *Standard Test Method for Flash and Fire Points by Cleveland Open Cup Tester*, and there is not more than 10 percent by weight flammable propellant.
(2) The base product does not exhibit sustained combustion when tested in accordance with 49 CFR 173, Appendix H, "Method of Testing for Sustained Combustibility," on the *UN Recommendations on the Transport of Dangerous Goods*, and there is not more than 10 percent weight flammable propellant.
(3) The base product contains not more than 50 percent by volume of flammable or combustible, water-miscible alcohols in an aqueous mix, and there is not more than 10 percent by weight flammable propellant.
(4) The base product contains greater than 50 percent by volume (39.5 percent by weight) up to 100 percent of ethanol, propanol, other water miscible alcohols, or mixtures thereof in an aqueous mix; is packaged in a compartmented container that separates the product from the propellant as typified by a bag-on-valve (BOV) package, bag-in-container package, or piston-in-container package; and the propellant is nonflammable compressed gas, nonflammable liquefied gas, or mixtures thereof.
(5) The base product contains not greater than 10 percent by weight of an emulsified, liquefied flammable gas propellant within an aqueous base.

[**30B:**4.3.3]

61.1.4.4 Plastic Aerosol X Products. Plastic Aerosol X Products shall be defined as those products that do not meet any of the criteria provided in 61.1.4.1, 61.1.4.2, or 61.1.4.3 [**30B:**4.3.4]

N **61.1.4.5 Plastic Aerosol Cooking Spray Products.** Plastic Aerosol Cooking Spray Products shall be defined as those that meet one of the following criteria:

(1) The base product is Aerosol Cooking Spray with a closed cup flash point of greater than 212°C (414°F), and the propellant is nonflammable compressed gas.
(2) The base product is Aerosol Cooking Spray with a closed cup flash point of greater than 212°C (414°F); is packaged in a compartmented container that separates the product from the propellant as typified by a bag-on-valve (BOV) package, bag-in-container package, or piston-in-container package; and the propellant is nonflammable compressed gas, nonflammable liquefied gas, or mixtures thereof.

[**30B:**4.3.5]

61.1.5 Marking of Packages of Aerosol Products.

61.1.5.1 Manufacturers of aerosol products shall ensure that all cartons or packages of aerosol products are identified on at least one exterior side with the classification of the aerosol products contained therein, in accordance with 61.1.3 and 61.1.4. [**30B:**4.4.1]

61.1.5.2 Cartons or packages containing aerosol products in metal containers or glass and plastic containers 4 fl oz (118 ml) or less shall be clearly marked as follows:

Level _____ Aerosols

[**30B:**4.4.2]

61.1.5.3 Cartons or packages containing Aerosol Cooking Spray Products in metal containers shall be clearly marked as follows:

Aerosol Cooking Spray

[**30B:**4.4.3]

61.1.5.4 Cartons or packages containing aerosol products in plastic containers greater than 4 fl oz (118 ml) shall be clearly marked on the exterior of the carton as follows:

Plastic Aerosol 1, 2, 3 (or X)

[**30B:**4.4.4]

61.2 Basic Requirements.

61.2.1 Building Construction.

61.2.1.1 Openings in fire walls or fire barriers shall be kept to a minimum. [**30B:**5.2.1]

61.2.1.1.1 All openings (i.e., personnel doorways, ductwork, conveyor line, etc.) shall be protected with automatic-closing or self-closing fire doors or dampers. [**30B:**5.2.1.1]

61.2.1.1.2 Fire doors shall be installed in accordance with NFPA 80. [**30B:**5.2.1.2]

61.2.1.1.3 Fire dampers shall be installed in accordance with manufacturer's instructions and NFPA 90A. [**30B:**5.2.1.3]

61.2.1.2 Means of Egress.

61.2.1.2.1 Means of egress shall comply with applicable provisions of NFPA *101*. [**30B:**5.2.2.1]

61.2.1.2.2 The design and construction of conveyor lines and other physical obstacles, such as in the flammable propellant charging and pump rooms, shall not allow entrapment of personnel and shall provide for direct access to exits. [**30B:**5.2.2.2]

61.2.2 Electrical Installations.

61.2.2.1 All electrical equipment and wiring, including heating equipment, shall be installed in accordance with *NFPA 70*. [**30B:**5.3.1]

61.2.2.1.1 Electrical equipment and wiring in areas where flammable liquids or flammable gases are handled shall meet the additional requirements of Articles 500 and 501 of *NFPA 70*. [**30B:**5.3.1.1]

61.2.2.2 Aerosol product storage and display areas shall be considered unclassified for purposes of electrical installation. [**30B:**5.3.2]

Δ **61.2.3 Heating Equipment.**

Heating equipment shall be installed in accordance with the applicable requirements of NFPA 31, NFPA 54, NFPA 58, and NFPA 85. [**30B:**5.4]

Δ **61.2.4 Flammable Liquids and Gases.** Areas in which flammable liquids and flammable gases are handled or stored shall meet the applicable requirements of NFPA 30 and NFPA 58. [**30B:**5.5]

61.2.5 Fire Protection.

61.2.5.1 Automatic Sprinkler Protection. Installations of automatic sprinklers, where required by this *Code* and NFPA 30B, shall be installed in accordance with Section 13.3 and NFPA 13 and the provisions of NFPA 30B. [**30B:**5.6.1]

61.2.5.1.1 Where the provisions of Chapter 61 and NFPA 13 differ, the provisions of Chapter 61 shall prevail. [**30B:**5.6.1.1]

61.2.5.1.2 Where Chapter 61 does not address specific automatic sprinkler protection criteria, the provisions of NFPA 13 shall prevail. [**30B:**5.6.1.2]

61.2.5.1.3 Production areas that contain base product fillers, button tippers, valve crimpers, test baths, and aerosol product packaging equipment shall be protected by a wet-pipe automatic sprinkler system installed in accordance with NFPA 13. The sprinkler system shall be designed to protect the highest level of storage or production hazard that is present. [**30B:**6.8.2]

61.2.5.1.3.1 Level 2 and Level 3 Aerosol Products shall be permitted to be stored in production areas, such as staging areas (e.g., awaiting transfer to a warehouse), provided all of the following are met:

(1) They are stacked no more than 5 ft (1.5 m) high.
(2) There is no warehouse storage of aerosol products within 25 ft (7.6 m) of the production line.

[**30B:**6.8.2.1]

Δ **61.2.5.1.3.2** Aerosol Cooking Spray Product containers shall be permitted to be stored in production areas, such as staging areas (e.g., awaiting transfer to a warehouse), up to a maximum quantity of 1000 lb (454 kg), provided all of the following are met:

(1) They are stacked no more than 5 ft (1.5 m) high.
(2) There is no warehouse storage of aerosol products within 25 ft (7.6 m) of the production line.

[**30B:**6.8.2.2]

N **61.2.5.1.3.3** Plastic Aerosol 3 Product containers of capacity larger than 118 ml (4 fl oz) shall be permitted to be stored in production areas, such as staging areas (e.g., awaiting transfer to a warehouse), up to a maximum quantity of 454 kg (1000 lb), provided all of the following are met:

(1) (1) They are stacked no more than 1.5 m (5 ft) high.
(2) (2) There is no warehouse storage of aerosol products within 7.6 m (25 ft) of the production line.

[**30B:**6.8.2.3]

N **61.2.5.1.3.4** Plastic Aerosol X Product containers of capacity larger than 118 ml (4 fl oz) shall be permitted to be stored in production areas, such as staging areas (e.g., awaiting transfer to a warehouse), up to a maximum quantity of 45 kg (100 lb), provided all of the following are met:

(1) They are stacked no more than 1.5 m (5 ft) high.
(2) There is no warehouse storage of aerosol products within 7.6 m (25 ft) of the production line.

[**30B:**6.8.2.4]

N **61.2.5.1.3.5** The maximum quantity in 61.2.5.1.3.1 and 61.2.5.1.3.3 do not apply to Level 1 Aerosol Products and Plastic Aerosol 1 Products, which are both treated as Class III commodities. [**30B:**6.8.2.6]

61.2.5.1.3.6 All other storage shall be protected in accordance with Table 7.4.2.7(a) through Table 7.4.2.7(m) of NFPA 30B, as applicable. [**30B:**6.8.2.6]

N **61.2.5.1.3.7** Storage exceeding quantities in 61.2.5.1.3.1 and 61.2.5.1.3.3 shall be protected in accordance with Table 7.4.2.7(a) through Table 7.4.2.7(m) in NFPA 30B, as applicable. [**30B:**6.8.2.7]

N **61.2.5.1.3.8** Storage exceeding quantities in 61.2.5.1.3.2 shall be protected in accordance with Table 7.3.2.3(a) and Table 7.3.2.3(b) in NFPA 30B, as applicable. [**30B:**6.8.2.8]

61.2.5.2 Standpipe and Hose System. Installations of standpipe and hose systems, where required by this *Code* and NFPA 30B, shall be designed and installed in accordance with Section 13.2 and NFPA 14 and with the provisions of NFPA 30B. Only combination or spray hose nozzles shall be used. [**30B:**5.6.2]

61.2.5.3 Portable Fire Extinguishers. Fire extinguishers shall be provided in accordance with Section 13.6 and NFPA 10. [**30B:**5.6.3]

61.2.6 Fire Alarms. Fire alarm systems shall be installed, tested, and maintained in accordance with applicable requirements of Section 13.7 and *NFPA 72*. [**30B:**5.7]

61.2.7 Sources of Ignition.

61.2.7.1 In areas where flammable gases or flammable vapors might be present, precautions shall be taken to prevent ignition by eliminating or controlling sources of ignition. [**30B:**5.8.1]

61.2.7.2 Sources of ignition shall include, but are not limited to, the following:

(1) Open flames

(2) Lightning
(3) Hot surfaces
(4) Radiant heat
(5) Smoking
(6) Cutting and welding
(7) Spontaneous ignition
(8) Frictional heat or sparks
(9) Static electricity
(10) Electrical arcs and sparks
(11) Stray currents
(12) Ovens, furnaces, and other heating equipment
(13) Automotive vehicles
(14) Material-handling equipment [**30B:**5.8.2]

61.3 Storage in Warehouses and Storage Areas.

61.3.1 Basic Requirements.

61.3.1.1 The protection criteria in Section 61.3 shall apply to the following:

(1) Level 1 Aerosol Products in metal containers up to and including 33.8 fl oz (1000 ml) capacity, in accordance with 61.3.2
(2) Aerosol Cooking Spray Products in metal containers up to and including 33.8 fl oz (1000 ml) capacity, in accordance with 61.3.3
(3) Level 2 and Level 3 Aerosol Products in metal containers up to and including 33.8 fl oz (1000 ml) capacity, in accordance with Section 7.4 of NFPA 30B
(4) Aerosol products in glass and plastic containers not more than 4 fl oz (118 ml) capacity, in accordance with Section 7.4 of NFPA 30B
(5) Plastic Aerosol 1 Products in plastic containers greater than 4 fl oz (118 ml) capacity and up to and including 33.8 fl oz (1000 ml) capacity, in accordance with 61.3.4
(6) Plastic Aerosol 2 Products in plastic containers greater than 4 fl oz (118 ml) capacity and not more than 33.8 fl oz (1000 ml) capacity, in accordance with Section 7.4 of NFPA 30B
(7) Plastic Aerosol 3 Products in plastic containers greater than 4 fl oz (118 ml) capacity and up to and including 33.8 fl oz (1000 ml) capacity, in accordance with Section 7.4 of NFPA 30B
(8) Plastic Aerosol Cooking Spray Products in plastic containers greater than 118 ml (4 fl oz) capacity and not more than 1000 ml (33.8 fl oz) in accordance with 7.3.2.3 of NFPA 30B

[**30B:**7.1.1]

61.3.1.2 All outer packaging of aerosol products, including cartons, trays, shrouds, or other packaging, shall be identified on at least one side with the classification of the aerosol products in accordance with 61.1.5 and with one of the following, whichever is appropriate:

(1) Level _____ Aerosols
(2) Aerosol Cooking Spray
(3) Plastic Aerosol 1
(4) Plastic Aerosol 2
(5) Plastic Aerosol 3
(6) Plastic Aerosol X
(7) Plastic Aerosol Cooking Spray

[**30B:**7.1.2]

61.3.1.3* Fire-retardant cartons shall not be considered an acceptable alternative to the protection requirements of Section 61.3. [**30B:**7.1.3]

61.3.2 Storage of Level 1 Aerosol Products.

61.3.2.1 Level 1 Aerosol Products shall be considered equivalent to Class III commodities, as defined in NFPA 13. [**30B:**7.2.1]

61.3.2.2 In cases where the storage of Level 1 Aerosol Products is required to be protected, such storage shall be protected in accordance with the requirements for Class III commodities set forth in NFPA 13. [**30B:**7.2.2]

61.3.2.3 Solid shelving that is installed in racks that contain Level 1 Aerosol Products shall be protected in accordance with the provisions of NFPA 13. [**30B:**7.2.3]

61.3.3 Storage of Aerosol Cooking Spray Products.

61.3.3.1 General.

61.3.3.1.1 Aerosol Cooking Spray Products in metal containers or Plastic Aerosol Cooking Spray Products shall be permitted to be stored in a general-purpose warehouse. [**30B:**7.3.1.1]

61.3.3.1.2 Aerosol Cooking Spray Products in metal containers or Plastic Aerosol Cooking Spray Products shall be permitted to be stored mixed with other higher hazard aerosols as long as the provided isolation, storage height restrictions, and protection are based on the highest hazard aerosol product present. [**30B:**7.3.1.2]

61.3.4 Aerosol Products in Plastic Containers Greater Than 4 fl oz (118 ml) and Not More Than 33.8 fl oz (1000 ml).

61.3.4.1 Fire Protection — Plastic Aerosol 1 Products.

61.3.4.1.1 Plastic Aerosol 1 Products shall be permitted to be stored in a general-purpose warehouse without isolation. [**30B:**7.5.1.1]

61.3.4.1.2* Plastic Aerosol 1 Products shall be considered equivalent to Class III commodities, as defined in NFPA 13. [**30B:**7.5.1.2]

61.3.4.1.3 In cases where the storage of Plastic Aerosol 1 Products is required to be protected, they shall be protected in accordance with the requirements of NFPA 13. [**30B:**7.5.1.3]

61.3.4.1.4 Solid shelving that is installed in racks that contain Plastic Aerosol 1 Products shall be protected in accordance with the provisions of NFPA 13. [**30B:**7.5.1.4]

61.3.4.2 Fire Protection — Plastic Aerosol X Products.

61.3.4.2.1 Storage of Plastic Aerosol X Products in occupancies other than warehouses or mercantile occupancies, such as in assembly, business, educational, industrial, and institutional occupancies, shall be permitted up to a maximum of 100 lb (45 kg) net weight. [**30B:**7.5.2.1]

61.3.4.2.2 Solid pile, palletized, or rack storage of Plastic Aerosol X Products shall be permitted in a general-purpose warehouse or an aerosol warehouse regardless of protection level up to a maximum of 250 lb (115 kg). [**30B:**7.5.2.2]

61.4 Mercantile Occupancies.

61.4.1 Plastic Aerosol X Products. Plastic Aerosol X Products shall be permitted to be stored in mercantile occupancies up to a maximum quantity of 100 lb (45 kg) net weight. [**30B**:8.1]

61.4.2 Sales Display Areas — Aerosol Storage Not Exceeding 8 ft (2.4 m) High.

61.4.2.1 Level 1 Aerosol Products and Plastic Aerosol 1 Products in sales display areas shall not be limited in quantity. [**30B**:8.2.1]

61.4.2.2 When located in sales display areas, Aerosol Cooking Spray Products in metal containers and, Plastic Aerosol Cooking Spray, Plastic Aerosol 2, Plastic Aerosol 3, and Level 2 and Level 3 Aerosol Products shall be removed from combustible cartons or the combustible cartons shall be display-cut, except as provided for in 61.4.2.2.1, 61.4.2.2.2, 61.4.2.2.3, respectively. [**30B**:8.2.2]

61.4.2.2.1 Cartoned Aerosol Cooking Spray Products in metal containers and Plastic Aerosol Cooking Spray Products shall be permitted in the sales display area, provided that the area is protected in accordance with one of the following:

(1) Table 7.3.2.3(a) or Table 7.3.2.3(b) of NFPA 30B
(2) Paragraph 61.4.2.3.1

[**30B**:8.2.2.1]

61.4.2.2.1.1 Protection in accordance with Table 6.4.2.7(a) through Table 6.4.2.7(l) of NFPA 30B shall also be permitted for Aerosol Cooking Spray Products in metal containers and Plastic Aerosol Cooking Spray Products. [**30B**:8.2.2.1.1]

61.4.2.2.2 Cartoned Level 2 and Level 3 Aerosol Products and Cartoned Plastic Aerosol 2 Products shall be permitted in the sales display area, provided that the area is protected in accordance with one of the following:

(1) Table 7.4.2.7(a) through Table 7.4.2.7(m) of NFPA 30B
(2) Paragraph 61.4.2.3.1

[**30B**:8.2.2.2]

61.4.2.2.3 Cartoned Plastic Aerosol 3 Products shall be permitted in the sales display area, provided that the area is protected in accordance with one of the following:

(1) Table 7.4.2.7(m) of NFPA 30B
(2) Paragraph 61.4.2.3.1
[**30B**:8.2.2.3]

61.4.2.3 Aerosol Cooking Spray Products, in metal containers and Plastic Aerosol Cooking Spray, Plastic Aerosol 2, Plastic Aerosol 3, and Level 2 and Level 3 Aerosol Products in sales display areas shall not exceed the maximum quantities given in 61.4.2.3.1 and 61.4.2.3.2 according to the protection provided. [**30B**:8.2.3]

61.4.2.3.1 In sales display areas that are nonsprinklered or whose sprinkler system does not meet the requirements of 61.4.2.3.2, the total aggregate quantity of Aerosol Cooking Spray Products in metal containers and Plastic Aerosol Cooking Spray, Plastic Aerosol 2, Plastic Aerosol 3, and Level 2 and Level 3 Aerosol Products shall not exceed 2 lb/ft^2 (9.8 kg/m^2) of total sales display area, up to the quantities specified in Table 61.4.2.3.1. [**30B**:8.2.3.1]

61.4.2.3.1.1 No single 10 ft × 10 ft (3 m × 3 m) section of sales display area shall contain an aggregate quantity of more than

Δ **Table 61.4.2.3.1 Maximum Quantity per Floor of Aerosol Cooking Spray Products, in Metal Containers and Plastic Aerosol Cooking Spray, Plastic Aerosol 2, Plastic Aerosol 3, and Level 2 and Level 3 Aerosol Products**

Floor	Maximum Net Weight per Floor	
	lb	kg
Basement	Not Permitted	
Ground	2500	1135
Upper	500	227

[**30B**:Table 8.2.3.1]

1000 lb (454 kg) net weight of Aerosol Cooking Spray Products in metal containers and Plastic Aerosol Cooking Spray, Plastic Aerosol 2, Plastic Aerosol 3, and Level 2 and Level 3 Aerosol Products. [**30B**:8.2.3.1.1]

61.4.2.3.2 In sales display areas that are sprinklered in accordance with NFPA 13 for at least ordinary hazard (Group 2) occupancies, the total aggregate quantity of Aerosol Cooking Spray Products in metal containers and Plastic Aerosol Cooking Spray, Plastic Aerosol 2, Plastic Aerosol 3, and Level 2 and Level 3 Aerosol Products shall not exceed 2 lb/ft^2 (9.8 kg/m^2) of total sales display area. [**30B**:8.2.3.2]

61.4.2.3.2.1 No single 10 ft × 10 ft (3 m × 3 m) section of sales display area shall contain an aggregate quantity of more than 1000 lb (454 kg) net weight of Aerosol Cooking Spray Products in metal containers and Plastic Aerosol Cooking Spray, Plastic Aerosol 2, Plastic Aerosol 3, and Level 2 and Level 3 Aerosol Products. [**30B**:8.2.3.2.1]

61.4.2.4 Aerosol Cooking Spray Products, in metal containers and Plastic Aerosol Cooking Spray, Plastic Aerosol 2, Plastic Aerosol 3, and Level 2 and Level 3 Aerosol Products shall be securely stacked to not more than 6 ft (1.8 m) high from base to top of the storage array unless on fixed shelving. [**30B**:8.2.4]

61.4.2.4.1 Shelving shall be of stable construction, and storage shall not exceed 8 ft (2.4 m) in height. [**30B**:8.2.4.1]

61.4.3 Sales Display Areas — Aerosol Storage Exceeding 8 ft (2.4 m) High.

61.4.3.1 Storage and display of Level 1 Aerosol Products and Plastic Aerosol 1 Products in sales display areas shall not be limited. [**30B**:8.3.1]

61.4.3.2 Uncartoned or display-cut (case-cut) Aerosol Cooking Spray Products in metal containers and Plastic Aerosol Cooking Spray, Plastic Aerosol 2, Plastic Aerosol 3, and Level 2 and Level 3 Aerosol Products that are stored for display no more than 6 ft (1.8 m) above the floor shall be permitted where protection is installed in accordance with 8.3.3 of NFPA 30B, based on the highest level of aerosol product in the array and the packaging method of the storage above 6 ft (1.8 m). [**30B**:8.3.2]

61.4.4 Back Stock Storage Areas.

61.4.4.1 Where back stock areas are separated from sales display areas by construction having a minimum 1-hour fire resistance rating, storage of Aerosol Cooking Spray Products in metal containers and Plastic Aerosol Cooking Spray, Plastic Aerosol 2, Plastic Aerosol 3, and Level 2 and Level 3 Aerosol

Products shall meet the requirements of Chapter 7 of NFPA 30B. [**30B**:8.4.1]

61.4.4.2 Where back stock areas are not separated from sales display areas by construction having a minimum 1-hour fire resistance rating, the quantity of Aerosol Cooking Spray Products in metal containers and Plastic Aerosol Cooking Spray, Plastic Aerosol 2, Plastic Aerosol 3, and Level 2 and Level 3 Aerosol Products in back stock areas shall be included in the total allowable quantities specified in 61.4.2.3 or 8.3.4 of NFPA 30B. [**30B**:8.4.2]

61.4.4.2.1 Protection shall be provided in accordance with 61.4.3.3. [**30B**:8.4.2.1]

61.4.4.3 An additional quantity of Aerosol Cooking Spray Products in metal containers and Plastic Aerosol Cooking Spray, Plastic Aerosol 2, Plastic Aerosol 3, and Level 2 and Level 3 Aerosol Products, up to a maximum of 500 lb (227 kg) net weight, shall be permitted in back stock areas where the additional quantities are stored in flammable liquid storage cabinets that meet the requirements of Section 9.5 of NFPA 30. [**30B**:8.4.3]

61.4.4.4 Storage of Aerosol Cooking Spray Products in metal containers and Plastic Aerosol Cooking Spray, Plastic Aerosol 2, Plastic Aerosol 3, and Level 2 and Level 3 Aerosol Products in separate, inside flammable liquids storage rooms shall meet the requirements of 7.4.7 of NFPA 30B. [**30B**:8.4.4]

61.5 Operations and Maintenance.

61.5.1 Means of Egress. Means of egress and exits shall be maintained in accordance with NFPA *101*. [**30B**:9.1]

61.5.2 Powered Industrial Trucks.

61.5.2.1 The use and selection of powered industrial trucks shall comply with Section 10.18. [**30B**:9.2.1]

61.5.2.2 Only trained and authorized operators shall be allowed to operate powered industrial trucks. [**30B**:9.2.2]

61.5.2.3 Operator training shall be equivalent to that specified by ANSI/ASME B56.1, *Safety Standard for Low-Lift and High-Lift Trucks*. [**30B**:9.2.3]

61.5.2.4 Loads.

61.5.2.4.1 If the type of load handled presents a hazard of backward falls, the powered industrial truck shall be equipped with a vertical load backrest extension. [**30B**:9.2.4.1]

61.5.2.4.2 For loads that are elevated above the mast of the truck, the backrest extension shall reach at least halfway into the uppermost pallet load. [**30B**:9.2.4.2]

61.5.3 Control of Ignition Sources.

61.5.3.1 Sources of Ignition.

61.5.3.1.1 In areas where flammable gases or flammable vapors might be present, precautions shall be taken to prevent ignition by eliminating or controlling sources of ignition. Sources of ignition include, but are not limited to, the following:

(1) Open flames
(2) Lightning
(3) Hot surfaces
(4) Radiant heat
(5) Smoking
(6) Cutting and welding
(7) Spontaneous ignition
(8) Frictional heat or sparks
(9) Static electricity
(10) Electrical arcs and sparks
(11) Stray currents
(12) Ovens, furnaces, and other heating equipment
(13) Automotive vehicles
(14) Material-handling equipment [**30B**:9.3.1.1]

61.5.3.2 Smoking shall be strictly prohibited, except in designated smoking areas. [**30B**:9.3.2]

61.5.3.3* Welding, cutting, and similar spark-producing operations shall not be permitted in areas that contain aerosol products, until a written permit authorizing the work has been issued. [**30B**:9.3.3]

61.5.3.3.1 The permit shall be issued by a person in authority following an inspection of the area to assure that proper precautions have been taken and will be followed until completion of the work. [**30B**:9.3.3.1]

61.5.4 Aisles. Storage in aisles shall be prohibited so as to permit access for fire fighting, salvage, and removal of stored commodities. [**30B**:9.4]

61.5.5 Waste Disposal and Recycling.

N **61.5.5.1** This section shall apply to aerosol product manufacturing sites and provides requirements for the disposal and reclamation of aerosol products from the production process that contain ignitible (flammable or combustible) base products or Class I liquid propellants. [**30B**:9.5.1]

N **61.5.5.1.1** Damaged, leaking, or out-of-spec aerosol products shall be disposed of in a safe manner, in accordance with applicable laws and regulations. [**30B**:9.5.1.1]

61.5.5.2 This section shall apply to storage sites engaged in the disposal and reclamation of aerosol products. [**30B**:9.5.2]

61.5.5.2.1 Damaged or leaking aerosol products shall be separated from other materials and trash. [**30B**:9.5.2.1]

61.5.6 Inspection and Maintenance.

61.5.6.1 A written and documented preventive maintenance program shall be developed for equipment, machinery, and processes that are critical to fire-safe operation of the facility. [**30B**:9.6.1]

61.5.6.2 Critical detection systems and their components, emergency trips and interlocks, alarms, and safety shutdown systems shall be inspected on a regularly scheduled basis, and any deficiencies shall be immediately corrected. [**30B**:9.6.2]

61.5.6.2.1 Items in this inspection schedule shall include, but are not limited to, the following:

(1) Gas detection systems
(2) Deflagration suppression systems
(3) Deflagration vent systems
(4) Ventilation and local exhaust systems
(5) Propellant charging room door interlocks
(6) Process safety devices
(7) Fire alarm systems

[**30B**:9.6.2.1]

61.5.6.3 Maintenance.

Δ **61.5.6.3.1** Vent closure maintenance shall be performed after every act of nature or process upset condition to ensure that the closure has not been physically damaged and there are no obstructions, including but not limited to snow, ice, water, mud, or process material, that could lessen or impair the efficiency of the vent closure. [**30B**:9.6.3.1]

Δ **61.5.6.3.2** An inspection shall be performed in accordance with 11.4.4 of NFPA 68 after every process maintenance turnaround. [**30B**:9.6.3.2]

Δ **61.5.6.3.3** If process material has a tendency to adhere to the vent closure, the vent closure shall be cleaned periodically to maintain vent efficiency. [**30B**:9.6.3.3]

Δ **61.5.6.3.4** Process interlocks, if provided, shall be verified. [**30B**:9.6.3.4]

Δ **61.5.6.3.5** Known potential ignition sources shall be inspected and maintained. [**30B**:9.6.3.5]

Δ **61.5.6.3.6** Records shall be kept of any maintenance and repairs performed. [**30B**:9.6.3.6]

61.5.7* **Static Electricity.** All process equipment and piping involved in the transfer of flammable liquids or gases shall be connected to a static-dissipating earth ground system to prevent accumulations of static charge. [**30B**:9.7]

Chapter 62 Reserved

Chapter 63 Compressed Gases and Cryogenic Fluids

63.1 General Provisions.

63.1.1 Application.

63.1.1.1* The installation, storage, use, and handling of compressed gases and cryogenic fluids in portable and stationary containers, cylinders, equipment, and tanks in all occupancies shall comply with the requirements of Chapter 63; NFPA 55, and Sections 60.1 through 60.4 of this *Code*.

63.1.1.2 Where the provisions of Chapter 63 or NFPA 55 conflict with the provisions of Chapter 60, the provisions of Chapter 63 and NFPA 55 shall apply.

63.1.1.3 The requirements in this chapter shall apply to the installation, storage, use, and handling of compressed gases and cryogenic fluids in portable and stationary cylinders, containers, equipment, and tanks in all occupancies. [**55**:1.3.1]

63.1.1.4 Specific Applications. Chapter 63 shall not apply to the following:

(1)* Off-site transportation of materials covered by Chapter 63
(2) Storage, use, and handling of radioactive gases in accordance with NFPA 801
(3)* Use and handling of medical compressed gases at health care facilities in accordance with NFPA 99, except as specified in Chapter 17 of NFPA 55
(4) Systems consisting of cylinders of oxygen and cylinders of fuel gas used for welding and cutting in accordance with NFPA 51
(5)* Flammable gases used as a vehicle fuel when stored on a vehicle
(6)* Storage, use, and handling of liquefied and nonliquefied compressed gases in laboratory work areas in accordance with NFPA 45
(7) Storage, use, and handling of liquefied petroleum gases in accordance with NFPA 58
(8) Storage, use, and handling of compressed gases within closed-cycle refrigeration systems complying with the mechanical code
(9) Liquefied natural gas (LNG) storage at utility plants under NFPA 59A
(10) Compressed natural gas (CNG) and LNG utilized as a vehicle fuel in accordance with NFPA 52
(11)* Compressed hydrogen gas (GH$_2$), or liquefied hydrogen gas (LH$_2$) generated, installed, stored, piped, used, or handled in accordance with NFPA 2 when there are no specific or applicable requirements in NFPA 55
(12) Nonflammable mixtures of ethylene oxide with other chemicals
(13) Ethylene oxide in chambers 10 scf (0.283 Nm^3) or less in volume or for containers holding 7.05 oz (200 g) of ethylene oxide or less

[**55**:1.3.2]

Δ **63.1.2 Permits.**

N **63.1.2.1** Permits shall be required in accordance with this chapter and Table 1.13.8(a) through Table 1.13.8(d).

N **63.1.2.2** Permits, where required, shall comply with Section 1.13.

63.1.2.3 The permit applicant shall apply for approval to close storage, use, or handling facilities at least 30 days prior to the termination of the storage, use, or handling of compressed or liquefied gases.

63.1.2.4 Such application shall include any change or alteration of the facility closure plan filed pursuant to 60.1.4.7.

63.1.2.5 This 30-day period shall be permitted to be waived by the AHJ if special circumstances require such waiver.

63.1.2.5.1 Permits shall not be required for routine maintenance.

63.1.2.5.2 For repair work performed on an emergency basis, application for permit shall be made within 2 working days of commencement of work.

63.1.3 General Definitions.

63.1.3.1 Absolute Pressure. See 3.3.1.

63.1.3.2 ASTM. See 3.3.20.

63.1.3.3 Automatic Emergency Shutoff Valve. See 3.3.21.

63.1.3.4 Bulk Hydrogen Compressed Gas System. See 3.3.283.1.

63.1.3.5 Bulk Inert Gas System. See 3.3.283.2.

63.1.3.6 Bulk Liquefied Hydrogen System. See 3.3.283.3.

63.1.3.7 Bulk Oxygen System. See 3.3.283.4.

63.1.3.8 Cathodic Protection. See 3.3.43.

63.1.3.9 Cathodic Protection Tester. See 3.3.44.

63.1.3.10 CGA. See 3.3.47.

63.1.3.11 Compressed Gas Container. See 3.3.73.2.

63.1.3.12 Compressed Gas System. See 3.3.283.6.

63.1.3.13 Continuous Gas Detection System. See 3.3.283.7.

63.1.3.14 Cryogenic Fluid. See 3.3.80.

63.1.3.14.1 Flammable Cryogenic Fluid. See 3.3.80.1.

63.1.3.14.2 Inert Cryogenic Fluid. See 3.3.80.2.

63.1.3.14.3 Oxidizing Cryogenic Fluid. See 3.3.80.3.

63.1.3.15 Cylinder. See 3.3.82.

63.1.3.16 Cylinder Containment Vessel. See 3.3.83.

63.1.3.17 Cylinder Pack. See 3.3.84.

63.1.3.18 Distributor. See 3.3.94.

63.1.3.19 Emergency Shutoff Valve. See 3.3.102.

63.1.3.20 Ethylene Oxide Drum. See 3.3.104.

63.1.3.21 Excess Flow Control. See 3.3.105.

63.1.3.22 Exhausted Enclosure. See 3.3.107.

63.1.3.23 Explosion Control. See 3.3.114.

63.1.3.24 Gallon. See 3.3.144.

63.1.3.25 Gas. See 3.3.146.

63.1.3.25.1 Compressed Gas. See 3.3.146.1.

63.1.3.25.2 Corrosive Gas. See 3.3.146.2.

63.1.3.25.3 Flammable Gas. See 3.3.146.3.

63.1.3.25.4 Flammable Liquefied Gas. See 3.3.146.4.

63.1.3.25.5 Highly Toxic Gas. See 3.3.146.5.

63.1.3.25.6 Inert Gas. See 3.3.146.6.

63.1.3.25.7 Nonflammable Gas. See 3.3.146.10.

63.1.3.25.8 Other Gas. See 3.3.146.11.

63.1.3.25.9 Oxidizing Gas. See 3.3.146.12.

63.1.3.25.10 Pyrophoric Gas. See 3.3.146.13.

63.1.3.25.11 Toxic Gas. See 3.3.146.16.

63.1.3.25.12 Unstable Reactive Gas. See 3.3.146.17.

63.1.3.26 Gas Cabinet. See 3.3.147.

63.1.3.27 Gas Manufacturer/Producer. See 3.3.148.

63.1.3.28 Gas Room. See 3.3.149.

63.1.3.29 Gaseous Hydrogen System. See 3.3.150.

63.1.3.30 Hazard Rating. See 3.3.155.

63.1.3.31 Immediately Dangerous to Life and Health (IDLH). See 3.3.165.

63.1.3.32 Indoor Area. See 3.3.17.5.

63.1.3.33 ISO Module. See 3.3.176.

63.1.3.34 Liquid Oxygen Ambulatory Container. A container used for liquid oxygen not exceeding 0.396 gal (1.5 L) specifically designed for use as a medical device as defined by 21 USC Chapter 9, the United States Food, Drug and Cosmetic Act that is intended for portable therapeutic use and to be filled from its companion base unit which is liquid oxygen home care container.

63.1.3.35 Liquid Oxygen Home Care Container. A container used for liquid oxygen not exceeding 15.8 gal (60 L) specifically designed for use as a medical device as defined by 21 USC Chapter 9, the United States Food, Drug and Cosmetic Act that is intended to deliver gaseous oxygen for therapeutic use in a home environment.

63.1.3.36 Manual Emergency Shutoff Valve. See 3.3.184.

63.1.3.37 Mechanical Code. See 3.3.57.3.

Δ **63.1.3.38 Mobile Supply Unit.** See 3.3.196.

63.1.3.39 Nesting. See 3.3.199.

63.1.3.40 Normal Temperature and Pressure (NTP). See 3.3.200.

63.1.3.41 OSHA. See 3.3.210.

63.1.3.42 Outdoor Area. See 3.3.17.7.

63.1.3.43 Permissible Exposure Limit (PEL). See 3.3.178.2.

63.1.3.44 Portable Tank. See 3.3.284.4.

63.1.3.45 Pressure Vessel. See 3.3.226.

63.1.3.46 Short-Term Exposure Limit (STEL). See 3.3.178.3.

63.1.3.47 Stationary Tank. See 3.3.284.6.

63.1.3.48 TC. See 3.3.285,

63.1.3.49 Treatment System. See 3.3.283.14.

63.1.3.50 Tube Trailer. See 3.3.292.

63.1.3.51 Valve Outlet Cap or Plug. See 3.3.300.3

63.1.3.52 Valve Protection Cap. See 3.3.300.4.

63.1.3.53 Valve Protection Device. See 3.3.300.5.

63.1.4 Hazardous Materials Classification.

63.1.4.1* Pure Gases. Hazardous materials shall be classified according to hazard categories as follows:

(1) Physical hazards, which shall include the following:
 (a) Flammable gas
 (b) Flammable cryogenic fluid
 (c) Oxidizing gas
 (d) Oxidizing cryogenic fluid
 (e) Pyrophoric gas
 (f) Unstable reactive (detonable) gas, Class 3 or Class 4
 (g) Unstable reactive (nondetonable) gas, Class 3
 (h) Unstable reactive gas, Class 1 or Class 2
(2) Health hazards, which shall include the following:
 (a) Corrosive gas
 (b) Cryogenic fluids
 (c) Highly toxic gas
 (d) Toxic gas

[55:5.1.1]

63.1.4.2 Other Hazards. Although it is possible that there are other known hazards, the classification of such gases is not within the scope of Chapter 63 and they shall be handled, stored, or used as an *other gas*. [**55:**5.1.2]

63.1.4.3 Mixtures. Mixtures shall be classified in accordance with the hazards of the mixture as a whole. [**55:**5.1.3]

63.1.4.4 Responsibility for Classification. Classification shall be performed by an approved organization, individual, or testing laboratory. [**55:**5.1.4]

Δ **63.1.4.4.1 Toxicity of Gas Mixtures.** The toxicity of gas mixtures shall be classified in accordance with NFPA 400 or the requirements of 29 CFR 1910.1200, 49 CFR 173.115, or ISO 10298, *Gas cylinders — Gases and gas mixtures — Determination of toxicity for the selection of cylinder valve outlets*. [**55:**5.1.4.1]

Δ **63.1.4.4.2 Flammability of Gas Mixtures.** For gas mixtures other than those containing ammonia and nonflammable gases, flammability of gas mixtures shall be classified in accordance with CGA P-23, *Standard for Categorizing Gas Mixtures Containing Flammable and Nonflammable Components*; or by physical testing in accordance with the requirements of ASTM E681, *Standard Test Method for Concentration Limits of Flammability of Chemicals (Vapors and Gases)*, or ISO 10156, *Gas Cylinders — Gases and gas mixtures — Determination of fire potential and oxidizing ability for the selection of cylinder valve outlets*. [**55:**5.1.4.2]

63.2 Building-Related Controls.

63.2.1 General.

63.2.1.1 Occupancy.

63.2.1.1.1 Occupancy Requirements. Occupancies that contain compressed gases or cryogenic fluids shall comply with Section 63.2 in addition to other applicable requirements of NFPA 55. [**55:**6.1.1.1]

63.2.1.1.2 Occupancy Classification. The occupancy of a building or structure, or portion of a building or structure, shall be classified in accordance with the building code. [**55:**6.1.1.2]

63.2.2 Control Areas.

63.2.2.1 Construction Requirements. Control areas shall be separated from each other by fire barriers in accordance with Table 60.4.2.2.1. [**55:**6.2.1]

63.2.2.2 Number of Control Areas. The maximum number of control areas within a building shall be in accordance with Table 60.4.2.2.1. [**400:**5.2.2.1]

63.2.2.3 Where only one control area is present in a building, no special construction provisions shall be required. [**400:**5.2.2.2]

63.2.2.4 Quantities Less Than or Equal to the MAQ. Indoor control areas with compressed gases or cryogenic fluids stored or used in quantities less than or equal to those shown in Table 63.2.3.1.1 shall be in accordance with 63.2.3.1.6 and 63.2.3.1.7, and subsections 63.2.1, 63.2.7, 63.2.8, 63.2.12, 63.2.15, 63.2.16, and the applicable provisions of Chapters 1 through 5 and Chapters 7 through 16 of NFPA 55. [**55:**6.2.4]

63.2.3 Occupancy Protection Levels.

63.2.3.1 Quantity Thresholds for Compressed Gases and Cryogenic Fluids Requiring Special Provisions.

Δ **63.2.3.1.1* Threshold Exceedances.** Where the quantities of compressed gases or cryogenic fluids stored or used within an indoor control area exceed those shown in Table 63.2.3.1.1, the area shall meet the requirements for Protection Levels 1 through 5 in accordance with the building code based on the requirements of 63.2.3.2. [**55:**6.3.1.1]

63.2.3.1.2 Quantities Greater Than the MAQ. Building-related controls in areas with compressed gases or cryogenic fluids stored or used within an indoor area in quantities greater than those shown in Table 63.2.3.1.1 shall be in accordance with the requirements of Section 63.2. [**55:**6.3.1.2]

63.2.3.1.3 Aggregate Allowable Quantities. The aggregate quantity in use and storage shall not exceed the quantity listed for storage. [**55:**6.3.1.3]

63.2.3.1.4 Incompatible Materials. When the classification of materials in individual containers requires the area to be placed in more than one protection level, the separation of protection levels shall not be required, provided the area is constructed to meet the requirements of the most restrictive protection level and that the incompatible materials are separated as required by 63.3.1.12.2. [**55:**6.3.1.4]

63.2.3.1.5 Multiple Hazards. When a compressed gas or cryogenic fluid has multiple hazards, all hazards shall be addressed and controlled in accordance with the provisions for the protection level for which the threshold quantity is exceeded. [**55:**6.3.1.5]

63.2.3.1.6 Flammable and Oxidizing Gases.

63.2.3.1.6.1 Flammable and oxidizing gases shall not be stored or used in other than industrial or storage occupancies. [**55:**6.3.1.6.1]

63.2.3.1.6.2 Cylinders, containers, or tanks not exceeding 250 scf (7.1 Nm^3) content at normal temperature and pressure (NTP) and used for maintenance purposes, patient care, or operation of equipment shall be permitted. [**55:**6.3.1.6.2]

63.2.3.1.6.3 Hydrogen gas systems located in a hydrogen gas room that meet the requirements of Section 6.5 of NFPA 55 shall be permissible in quantities up to those allowed by Table 63.2.3.1.1 in assembly, educational, institutional, residential, or business occupancies. [**55:**6.3.1.6.3]

63.2.3.1.7 Toxic and Highly Toxic Compressed Gases. Except for containers or cylinders not exceeding 20 scf (0.6 Nm^3) content at NTP stored or used within gas cabinets or exhausted enclosures of educational occupancies, toxic or highly toxic compressed gases shall not be stored or used in other than industrial and storage occupancies. [**55:**6.3.1.7]

63.2.3.2 Classification of Protection Levels. The protection level required shall be based on the hazard class of the material involved as indicated in 63.2.3.2.1 through 63.2.3.2.5. [**55:**6.3.2]

Δ **Table 63.2.3.1.1 Maximum Allowable Quantity (MAQ) of Hazardous Materials per Control Area**

Material	Class	High Hazard Protection Level	Storage Solid Pounds	Storage Liquid Gallons	Storage Gas[a] scf (lb)	Use — Closed Systems Solid Pounds	Use — Closed Systems Liquid Gallons	Use — Closed Systems Gas[a] scf (lb)	Use — Open Systems Solid Pounds	Use — Open Systems Liquid Gallons
Cryogenic fluid	Flammable	2	NA	45[b,c]	NA	NA	45[b,c]	NA	NA	45[b,c]
	Oxidizing	3	NA	45[d,e]	NA	NA	45[d,e]	NA	NA	45[d,e]
	Inert	NA	NA	NL	NA	NA	NL	NA	NA	NL
Flammable, gas[f]	Gaseous Category 1A and 1B (High BV)[l]	2	NA	NA	1000[d,e]	NA	NA	1000[d,e]	NA	NA
	Gaseous Category 1B (Low BV)[l]	2	NA	NA	162,500[d,e]	NA	NA	162,500[d,e]	NA	NA
	Liquefied Category 1A and 1B (High BV)[l]	2	NA	NA	(150)[d,e]	NA	NA	(150)[d,e]	NA	NA
		2	NA	NA	(10,000)[d,e,i]	NA	NA	(10,000)[d,e,i]	NA	NA
	Liquefied Category 1B (Low BV)[l] LP	2	NA	NA	(300)[g,h,i]	NA	NA	(300)[g]	NA	NA
Inert gas	Gaseous	NA	NA	NA	NL	NA	NA	NL	NA	NA
	Liquefied	NA	NA	NA	NL	NA	NA	NL	NA	NA
Oxidizing gas	Gaseous	3	NA	NA	1500[d,e]	NA	NA	1500[d,e]	NA	NA
	Liquefied	3	NA	NA	(150)[d,e]	NA	NA	(150)[d,e]	NA	NA
Pyrophoric gas	Gaseous	2	NA	NA	50[d,j]	NA	NA	50[d,j]	NA	NA
	Liquefied	2	NA	NA	(4)[d,j]	NA	NA	(4)[d,j]	NA	NA
Unstable (reactive) gas	Gaseous									
	4 or 3 detonable	1	NA	NA	10[d,j]	NA	NA	10[d,j]	NA	NA
	3 nondetonable	2	NA	NA	50[d,e]	NA	NA	50[d,e]	NA	NA
	2	3	NA	NA	750[d,e]	NA	NA	750[d,e]	NA	NA
	1	NA	NA	NA	NL	NA	NA	NL	NA	NA
Unstable (reactive) gas	Liquefied									
	4 or 3 detonable	1	NA	NA	(1)[d,j]	NA	NA	(1)[d,j]	NA	NA
	3 nondetonable	2	NA	NA	(2)[d,e]	NA	NA	(2)[d,e]	NA	NA
	2	3	NA	NA	(150)[d,e]	NA	NA	(150)[d,e]	NA	NA
	1	NA	NA	NA	NL	NA	NA	NL	NA	NA
Corrosive gas	Gaseous	4	NA	NA	810[d,e]	NA	NA	810[d,e]	NA	NA
	Liquefied		NA	NA	(150)[d,e]	NA	NA	(150)[d,e]	NA	NA
Highly toxic gas	Gaseous	4	NA	NA	20[e,k]	NA	NA	20[e,k]	NA	NA
	Liquefied		NA	NA	(4)[e,k]	NA	NA	(4)[e,k]	NA	NA
Toxic gas	Gaseous	4	NA	NA	810[d,e]	NA	NA	810[d,e]	NA	NA
	Liquefied		NA	NA	(150)[d,e]	NA	NA	(150)[d,e]	NA	NA

NA: Not applicable within the context of NFPA 55 (refer to the applicable building or fire code for additional information on these materials).
NL: Not limited in quantity.
Notes:
(1) For use of control areas (see Section 6.2 of NFPA 55).
(2) Table values in parentheses or brackets correspond to the unit name in parentheses or brackets at the top of the column.
(3) The aggregate quantity in use and storage is not permitted to exceed the quantity listed for storage. In addition, quantities in specific occupancies are not permitted to exceed the limits in the building code.
[a]Measured at NTP [70°F (20°C) and 14.7 psi (101.3 kPa)].
[b]None allowed in unsprinklered buildings unless stored or used in gas rooms or in approved gas cabinets or exhausted enclosures as specified in this code.
[c]With pressure-relief devices for stationary or portable containers vented directly outdoors or to an exhaust hood.
[d]Quantities are permitted to be increased 100 percent where stored or used in approved cabinets, gas cabinets, exhausted enclosures, or gas rooms as appropriate for the material stored. Where Footnote e also applies, the increase for the quantities in both footnotes is permitted to be applied accumulatively.
[e]Maximum quantities are permitted to be increased 100 percent in buildings equipped throughout with automatic sprinkler systems in accordance with NFPA 13. Where Footnote d also applies, the increase for the quantities in both footnotes is permitted to be applied accumulatively.
[f]Flammable gases in the fuel tanks of mobile equipment or vehicles are permitted to exceed the MAQ where the equipment is stored and operated in accordance with the applicable fire code.
[g]See NFPA 58 and Chapter 69 for requirements for liquefied petroleum gas (LP-Gas). LP-Gas is not within the scope of NFPA 55 or Chapter 63.
[h]Additional storage locations are required to be separated by a minimum of 300 ft (92 m).
[i]In mercantile occupancies, storage of LP-Gas is limited to a maximum of 200 lb (91 kg) in nominal 1 lb (0.45 kg) LP-Gas containers.
[j]Permitted only in buildings equipped throughout with automatic sprinkler systems in accordance with NFPA 13.
[k]Allowed only where stored or used in gas rooms or in approved gas cabinets or exhausted enclosures as specified in this code.
[l]High BV Category 1B flammable gas has a burning velocity greater than 3.9 in./s (10 cm/s). Low BV Category 1B flammable gas has a burning velocity 3.9 in./s (10 cm/s) or less.
[**55**:Table 6.3.1.1]

63.2.3.2.1 Protection Level 1. Occupancies used for the storage or use of unstable reactive Class 4 and unstable reactive Class 3 detonable compressed gases in quantities that exceed the quantity thresholds for gases requiring special provisions shall be classified Protection Level 1. [55:6.3.2.1]

63.2.3.2.2 Protection Level 2. Occupancies used for the storage or use of flammable, pyrophoric, and nondetonable, unstable reactive Class 3 compressed gases or cryogenic fluids in quantities that exceed the quantity thresholds for gases requiring special provisions shall be classified as Protection Level 2. [55:6.3.2.2]

63.2.3.2.3 Protection Level 3. Occupancies used for the storage or use of oxidizing and unstable reactive Class 2 compressed gases or cryogenic fluids in quantities that exceed the quantity thresholds for gases requiring special provisions shall be classified as Protection Level 3. [55:6.3.2.3]

63.2.3.2.4 Protection Level 4. Occupancies used for the storage or use of toxic, highly toxic, and corrosive compressed gases in quantities that exceed the quantity thresholds for gases requiring special provisions shall be classified as Protection Level 4. [55:6.3.2.4]

63.2.3.2.5 Protection Level 5. Buildings and portions thereof used for fabrication of semiconductors or semiconductor research and development and containing quantities of hazardous materials exceeding the maximum allowable quantities of high hazard level 5 contents permitted in control areas shall be classified as Protection Level 5. [55:6.3.2.5]

Δ **63.2.4 Gas Rooms.** Where a gas room is used to increase the threshold quantity for a gas requiring special provisions or where otherwise required by the material or application specific requirements of Chapters 7 through 16 of NFPA 55, the room shall meet the requirements of 63.2.4.1 through 63.2.4.5. [55:6.4]

63.2.4.1 Pressure Control. Gas rooms shall operate at a negative pressure in relationship to the surrounding area. [55:6.4.1]

63.2.4.2 Exhaust Ventilation. Gas rooms shall be provided with an exhaust ventilation system. [55:6.4.2]

63.2.4.3 Construction. Gas rooms shall be constructed in accordance with the building code. [55:6.4.3]

63.2.4.4 Separation. Gas rooms shall be separated from other occupancies by a minimum of 1-hour fire resistance. [55:6.4.4]

63.2.4.5 Limitation on Contents. The function of compressed gas rooms shall be limited to storage and use of compressed gases and associated equipment and supplies. [55:6.4.5]

63.2.5* Detached Buildings. Occupancies used for the storage or use of compressed gases, including individual bulk hydrogen compressed gas systems in quantities exceeding those specified in Table 63.2.5, shall be in detached buildings constructed in accordance with the provisions of the building code. [55:6.6]

63.2.6 Weather Protection.

63.2.6.1 For other than explosive materials and hazardous materials presenting a detonation hazard, a weather protection structure shall be permitted to be used for sheltering outdoor storage or use areas, without requiring such areas to be classified as indoor storage or use. [55:6.7.1]

Δ **Table 63.2.5 Detached Buildings Required Where Quantity of Material Exceeds Amount Shown**

Gas Hazard	Class	scf	Nm³
Individual bulk hydrogen compressed gas systems	N/A	15,000	425
Unstable reactive (detonable)	4 or 3	Quantity thresholds for gases requiring special provisions*	
Unstable reactive (nondetonable)	3	2,000	57
Unstable reactive (nondetonable)	2	10,000	283
Pyrophoric gas[†]	NA	2,000	57

NA: Not applicable.
*See Table 63.2.3.1.1.
[†]Detached buildings are not required for gases in high-hazard gas rooms that support Protection Level 5 fabrication facilities separated from other areas by a fire barrier with a fire resistance rating of not less than 2 hours, where the gas is located in internally sprinklered gas cabinets equipped with continuous leak detection and automatic shutdown, where the supply is from cylinders that do not exceed 125 lb (57 kg) water capacity per 49 CFR 173.192 for Hazard Zone A toxic gases, and where the gas cabinets are not manifolded upstream of pressure control devices.
[55: Table 6.6]

63.2.6.2 Weather protected areas constructed in accordance with 63.2.6.4 shall be regulated as outdoor storage or use. [55:6.7.2]

63.2.6.3 Weather protected areas that are not constructed in accordance with 63.2.6.4 shall be regulated as indoor storage or use. [55:6.7.2.1]

63.2.6.4 Buildings or structures used for weather protection shall be in accordance with the following:

(1) The building or structure shall be constructed of noncombustible materials.
(2) Walls shall not obstruct more than one side of the structure.
(3) Walls shall be permitted to obstruct portions of multiple sides of the structure, provided that the obstructed area does not exceed 25 percent of the structure's perimeter area.
(4) The building or structure shall be limited to a maximum area of 1500 ft² (140 m²), with increases in area allowed by the building code based on occupancy and type of construction.
(5) The distance from the structure constructed as weather protection to buildings, lot lines, public ways, or means of egress to a public way shall not be less than the distance required for an outside hazardous material storage or use area without weather protection based on the hazard classification of the materials contained.
(6) Reductions in separation distance shall be permitted based on the use of fire barrier walls where permitted for specific materials in accordance with the requirements of Chapters 7 through 11 of NFPA 55.

[55:6.7.3]

63.2.7* Electrical Equipment. Electrical wiring and equipment shall be in accordance with subsection 63.2.7, *NFPA 70*, and NFPA 79, as applicable. [**55:**6.8]

63.2.7.1 Standby Power.

63.2.7.1.1 Where the following systems are required by NFPA 55 for the storage or use of compressed gases or cryogenic fluids that exceed the quantity thresholds for gases requiring special provisions, such systems shall be connected to a standby power system in accordance with *NFPA 70*:

(1) Mechanical ventilation
(2) Treatment systems
(3) Temperature controls
(4) Alarms
(5) Detection systems
(6) Other electrically operated systems

[**55:**6.8.1.1]

63.2.7.1.2 The requirements of 63.2.7.1.1 shall not apply where emergency power is provided in accordance with 63.2.7.2 and *NFPA 70*. [**55:**6.8.1.2]

63.2.7.1.3 When standby power is required, the system shall meet the requirements for a Level 2 system in accordance with NFPA 111. [**55:**6.8.1.3]

63.2.7.2 Emergency Power. When emergency power is required, the system shall meet the requirements for a Level 2 system in accordance with NFPA 110 or NFPA 111. [**55:**6.8.2]

63.2.8* Employee Alarm System. Where required by government regulations, an employee alarm system shall be provided to allow warning for necessary emergency action as called for in the emergency action plan required by 4.2.1.1 of NFPA 55, or for reaction time for safe egress of employees from the workplace or the immediate work area, or both. [**55:**6.9]

63.2.9 Explosion Control. Explosion control shall be provided as required by Table 63.2.9 in accordance with NFPA 68 or NFPA 69 where amounts of compressed gases in storage or use exceed the quantity thresholds requiring special provisions. [**55:**6.10]

63.2.10* Fire Protection Systems. Except as provided in 63.2.10.1, buildings or portions thereof required to comply with Protection Levels 1 through 5 shall be protected by an approved automatic fire sprinkler system complying with Section 13.3 and NFPA 13. [**55:**6.11]

63.2.10.1 Rooms or areas that are of noncombustible construction with wholly noncombustible contents shall not be required to be protected by an automatic fire sprinkler system. [**55:**6.11.1]

63.2.10.2 Sprinkler System Design.

63.2.10.2.1 Where sprinkler protection is required, the area in which compressed gases or cryogenic fluids are stored or used shall be protected with a sprinkler system designed to be not less than that required by 11.2.3.1.1 of NFPA 13 for the Ordinary Hazard Group 2 density/area curve. [**55:**6.11.2.1]

63.2.10.2.2 Where sprinkler protection is required, the area in which the flammable or pyrophoric compressed gases or cryogenic fluids are stored or used shall be protected with a sprinkler system designed to be not less than that required by 11.2.3.1.1 of NFPA 13 for the Extra Hazard Group 1 density/area curve. [**55:**6.11.2.2]

Table 63.2.9 Explosion Control Requirements

		Explosion Control Methods	
Material	Class	Barricade Construction	Explosion Venting or Prevention Systems
Flammable cryogenic fluid	—	Not required	Required
Flammable gas	Nonliquefied	Not required	Required
	Liquefied	Not required	Required
Pyrophoric gas	—	Not required	Required
Unstable reactive gas	4	Required	Not required
	3 (detonable)	Required	Not required
	3 (nondetonable)	Not required	Required

[55: Table 6.10]

63.2.11 Lighting. Approved lighting by natural or artificial means shall be provided for areas of storage or use. [**55:**6.12]

63.2.12 Hazard Identification Signs.

63.2.12.1 Location. Hazard identification signs shall be placed at all entrances to locations where compressed gases are produced, stored, used, or handled in accordance with NFPA 704. [**55:**6.13.1]

63.2.12.1.1 Ratings shall be assigned in accordance with NFPA 704. [**55:**6.13.1.1]

63.2.12.1.2 The AHJ shall be permitted to waive 63.2.12.1 where consistent with safety. [**55:**6.13.1.2]

63.2.12.2 Application. Signage shall be provided as specified in 63.2.12.2.1 and 63.2.12.2.2. [**55:**6.13.2]

63.2.12.2.1 Signs. Signs shall not be obscured or removed. [**55:**6.13.2.1]

63.2.12.2.2 No Smoking. Signs prohibiting smoking or open flames within 25 ft (7.6 m) of area perimeters shall be provided in areas where toxic, highly toxic, corrosive, unstable reactive, flammable, oxidizing, or pyrophoric gases are produced, stored, or used. [**55:**6.13.2.2]

63.2.13 Spill Control, Drainage, and Secondary Containment. Spill control, drainage, and secondary containment shall not be required for compressed gases. [**55:**6.14]

63.2.14 Shelving.

63.2.14.1 Shelves used for the storage of cylinders, containers, and tanks shall be of noncombustible construction and designed to support the weight of the materials stored. [**55:**6.15.1]

63.2.14.2 Shelves and containers shall be secured from overturning. [**55:**6.15.2]

63.2.15 Vent Pipe Termination. The termination point for piped vent systems serving cylinders, containers, tanks, and gas systems used for the purpose of operational or emergency venting shall be located to prevent impingement exposure on the system served and to minimize the effects of high temperature thermal radiation or the effects of contact with the gas from the escaping plume to the supply system, personnel, adjacent structures, and ignition sources. [55:6.16]

63.2.16 Ventilation. Indoor storage and use areas and storage buildings for compressed gases and cryogenic fluids shall be provided with mechanical exhaust ventilation or fixed natural ventilation, where natural ventilation is shown to be acceptable for the material as stored. [55:6.17]

63.2.16.1 Compressed Air. The requirements of 63.2.16 shall not apply to cylinders, containers, and tanks containing compressed air. [55:6.17.1]

63.2.16.2 Ventilation Systems. In addition to the requirements of 63.2.16, ventilation systems shall be designed and installed in accordance with the requirements of the mechanical code. [55:6.17.2]

63.2.16.3 Mechanical Exhaust Ventilation. Where mechanical exhaust ventilation is provided, the system shall be operational during the time the building or space is occupied. [55:6.17.3]

63.2.16.4 Continuous Operation. When operation of ventilation systems is required, systems shall operate continuously unless an alternative design is approved by the AHJ. [55:6.17.3.1]

63.2.16.5 Ventilation Rate Mechanical exhaust or fixed natural ventilation shall be provided at a rate of not less than 1 scf/min/ft^2 (0.0051 m^3/sec/m^2) of floor area over the area of storage or use. [55:6.17.3.2]

63.2.16.6 Shutoff Controls. Where powered ventilation is provided, a manual shutoff switch shall be provided outside the room in a position adjacent to the principal access door to the room or in an approved location. [55:6.17.3.3]

63.2.16.7 Manual Shutoff Switch. The switch shall be the breakglass or equivalent type and shall be labeled as follows:

WARNING:
VENTILATION SYSTEM EMERGENCY SHUTOFF

[55:6.17.3.3.1]

63.2.16.8 Inlets to the Exhaust System.

63.2.16.8.1 The exhaust ventilation system design shall take into account the density of the potential gases released. [55:6.17.4.1]

63.2.16.8.2* For gases that are heavier than air, exhaust shall be taken from a point within 12 in. (305 mm) of the floor. The use of supplemental inlets shall be allowed to be installed at points above the 12 in. (305 mm) threshold level. [55:6.17.4.2]

63.2.16.8.3* For gases that are lighter than air, exhaust shall be taken from a point within 12 in. (305 mm) of the ceiling. The use of supplemental inlets shall be allowed to be installed at points below the 12 in. (305 mm) threshold level. [55:6.17.4.3]

63.2.16.8.4 The location of both the exhaust and inlet air openings shall be designed to provide air movement across all portions of the floor or ceiling of the room or area to prevent the accumulation of vapors within the ventilated space. [55:6.17.4.4]

63.2.16.9 Recirculation of Exhaust. Exhaust ventilation shall not be recirculated. [55:6.17.5]

63.2.16.10 Ventilation Discharge. Ventilation discharge systems shall terminate at a point not less than 50 ft (15 m) from intakes of air-handling systems, air-conditioning equipment, and air compressors. [55:6.17.6]

63.2.16.11 Air Intakes. Storage and use of compressed gases shall be located not less than 20 ft (6 m) from air intakes. *(See 63.3.5 through 63.3.11 for material-specific requirements.)* [55:6.17.7]

63.2.17 Gas Cabinets. Where a gas cabinet is required, is used to provide separation of gas hazards, or is used to increase the threshold quantity for a gas requiring special provisions, the gas cabinet shall be in accordance with the requirements of 63.2.17.1 through 63.2.17.5. [55:6.18]

63.2.17.1 Construction.

63.2.17.1.1 Materials of Construction. The gas cabinet shall be constructed of not less than 0.097 in. (2.46 mm) (12 gauge) steel. [55:6.18.1.1]

63.2.17.1.2 Access to Controls. The gas cabinet shall be provided with self-closing limited access ports or noncombustible windows to give access to equipment controls. [55:6.18.1.2]

63.2.17.1.3 Self-Closing Doors. The gas cabinet shall be provided with self-closing doors. [55:6.18.1.3]

63.2.17.2 Ventilation Requirements.

63.2.17.2.1 The gas cabinet shall be provided with an exhaust ventilation system designed to operate at a negative pressure relative to the surrounding area. [55:6.18.2.1]

63.2.17.2.2 Where toxic, highly toxic, pyrophoric, unstable reactive Class 3 or Class 4, or corrosive gases are contained, the velocity at the face of access ports or windows, with the access port or window open, shall not be less than 200 ft/min (61 m/min) average, with not less than 150 ft/min (46 m/min) at any single point. [55:6.18.2.2]

63.2.17.3 Fire Protection. Gas cabinets used to contain toxic, highly toxic, or pyrophoric gases shall be internally sprinklered. [55:6.18.3]

Δ **63.2.17.4 Quantity Limits.**

N **63.2.17.4.1** Gas cabinets shall contain not more than three cylinders, containers, or tanks, where each contains greater than or equal to 10 scf (0.28 m^3). [55:6.18.4.1]

N **63.2.17.4.2** Gas cabinets shall contain not more than 30 cylinders, containers, or tanks, where the capacity of each is less than 10 scf (0.28 m^3) in place of a cylinder, container, or tank containing greater than or equal to 10 scf (0.28 m^3). [55:6.18.4.2]

63.2.17.5 Separation of Incompatibles. Incompatible gases, as defined by Table 63.3.1.12.2, shall be stored or used within separate gas cabinets. [55:6.18.5]

N **63.2.17.6*** All cylinders in gas cabinets shall be individually secured to prevent falling or rolling and designed to allow exhaust airflow around the cylinders. [55:6.18.6]

N **63.2.17.7*** The interior of gas cabinets handling flammable gases or flammable liquefied gases shall be electrically classified as determined by a qualified individual in accordance with the requirements of *NFPA 70*. [55:6.18.7]

63.2.18 Exhausted Enclosures.

63.2.18.1 Ventilation Requirements. Where an exhausted enclosure is required or used to increase the threshold quantity for a gas requiring special provisions, the exhausted enclosure shall be provided with an exhaust ventilation system designed to operate at a negative pressure in relationship to the surrounding area. [55:6.19.1]

63.2.18.1.1 Control Velocity at Access Openings. Where toxic, highly toxic, pyrophoric, unstable reactive Class 3 or Class 4, or corrosive gases are contained, the velocity at the face openings providing access shall be not less than 200 ft/min (61 m/min) average, with not less than 150 ft/min (46 m/min) at any single point. [55:6.19.1.1]

63.2.18.1.2 Separation of Incompatible Gases Within Enclosures. Cylinders, containers, and tanks within enclosures shall be separated in accordance with Table 63.3.1.12.2. [55:6.19.1.2]

63.2.18.1.3 Fire Protection. Exhausted enclosures shall be internally sprinklered. [55:6.19.1.3]

63.2.18.2 Separation. Incompatible gases, as defined by Table 63.3.1.12.2, shall be stored or used within separate exhausted enclosures. [55:6.19.2]

63.2.19* Source Valve. Bulk gas systems shall be provided with a source valve. [55:6.20]

63.2.19.1 The source valve shall be marked. [55:6.20.1]

63.2.19.2 The source valve shall be designated on the design drawings for the installation. [55:6.20.2]

63.3 Compressed Gases.

63.3.1 General. The storage, use, and handling of compressed gases in cylinders, containers, and tanks shall be in accordance with the provisions of Chapters 1 through 7 of NFPA 55. [55:7.1]

N **63.3.1.1** Where the primary supply of compressed gas is stored in a bulk liquid form, the provisions of Chapter 8 of NFPA 55 shall apply to piping and other gaseous system components downstream of the liquid vaporizer and upstream of the source valve. [55:7.1.1]

63.3.1.2 Compressed Gas Systems.

63.3.1.2.1 Design. Compressed gas systems shall be designed for the intended use and shall be designed by persons competent in such design. [55:7.1.2.1]

63.3.1.2.2 Installation. Installation of bulk compressed gas systems shall be supervised by personnel knowledgeable in the application of the standards for their construction and use. [55:7.1.2.2]

N **63.3.1.2.3** Tube trailers used as gas supply systems shall comply with the mandatory requirements of CGA P-74, *Standard for Tube Trailer Supply Systems at Customer Sites*. [55:7.1.2.3]

63.3.1.3 Insulated Liquid Carbon Dioxide Systems. Insulated liquid carbon dioxide systems shall be in accordance with Chapter 13 of NFPA 55. [55:7.1.3]

63.3.1.4 Insulated Liquid Nitrous Oxide Systems. Insulated liquid nitrous oxide systems shall be in accordance with Chapter 16 of NFPA 55. [55:7.1.4]

63.3.1.5* Listed or Approved Hydrogen Equipment.

63.3.1.5.1 Listed or approved hydrogen–generating and hydrogen–consuming equipment shall be in accordance with the listing requirements and manufacturers' instructions. [55:10.2.8.1]

63.3.1.5.2 Such equipment shall not be required to meet the requirements of Chapter 7 of NFPA 55. [55:10.2.8.2]

63.3.1.6* Metal Hydride Storage Systems.

63.3.1.6.1 General Requirements.

63.3.1.6.1.1 Metal Hydride Storage System Requirements. The storage and use of metal hydride storage systems shall be in accordance with 63.3.1.6. [55:10.2.9.1.1]

63.3.1.6.1.2 Metal Hydride Systems Storing or Supplying Hydrogen. Those portions of the system that are used as a means to store or supply hydrogen shall also comply with Chapter 7 and Chapter 10 of NFPA 55 as applicable. [55:10.2.9.1.2]

63.3.1.6.1.3 Classification. The hazard classification of the metal hydride storage system, as required by 63.1.4.1 and 63.1.4.3, shall be based on the hydrogen stored without regard to the metal hydride content. [55:10.2.9.1.3]

63.3.1.6.1.4 Listed or Approved Systems. Metal hydride storage systems shall be listed or approved for the application and designed in a manner that prevents the addition or removal of the metal hydride by other than the original equipment manufacturer. [55:10.2.9.1.4]

63.3.1.6.1.5 Containers, Design, and Construction. Compressed gas cylinders, containers, and tanks used for metal hydride storage systems shall be designed and constructed in accordance with 63.3.1.7.1. [55:10.2.9.1.5]

63.3.1.6.1.6 Service Life and Inspection of Containers. Metal hydride storage system cylinders, containers, and tanks shall be inspected at intervals not to exceed 5 years. [55:10.2.9.1.6]

63.3.1.6.1.7 Marking and Labeling. Marking and labeling of cylinders, containers, tanks, and systems shall be in accordance with 63.3.1.7 and the requirements in 63.3.1.6.1.7.1 through 63.3.1.6.1.7.4. [55:10.2.9.1.7]

63.3.1.6.1.7.1 System Marking. Metal hydride storage systems shall be marked with the following:

(1) Manufacturer's name
(2) Service life indicating the last date the system can be used
(3) A unique code or serial number specific to the unit
(4) System name or product code that identifies the system by the type of chemistry used in the system
(5) Emergency contact name, telephone number, or other contact information
(6) Limitations on refilling of containers to include rated charging pressure and capacity

[55:10.2.9.1.7.1]

63.3.1.6.1.7.2 Valve Marking. Metal hydride storage system valves shall be marked with the following:

(1) Manufacturer's name
(2) Service life indicating the last date the valve can be used

(3) Metal hydride service in which the valve can be used or a product code that is traceable to this information
[**55:**10.2.9.1.7.2]

63.3.1.6.1.7.3 Pressure Relief Device Marking. Metal hydride storage system pressure relief devices shall be marked with the following:

(1) Manufacturer's name
(2) Metal hydride service in which the device can be used or a product code that is traceable to this information
(3) Activation parameters to include temperature, pressure, or both

[**55:**10.2.9.1.7.3]

(A) Pressure Relief Devices Integral to Container Valves. The required markings for pressure relief devices that are integral components of valves used on cylinders, containers, and tanks shall be allowed to be placed on the valve. [**55:**10.2.9.1.7.3(A)]

63.3.1.6.1.7.4 Pressure Vessel Markings. Cylinders, containers, and tanks used in metal hydride storage systems shall be marked with the following:

(1) Manufacturer's name
(2) Design specification to which the vessel was manufactured
(3) Authorized body approving the design and initial inspection and test of the vessel
(4) Manufacturer's original test date
(5) Unique serial number for the vessel
(6) Service life identifying the last date the vessel can be used
(7) System name or product code that identifies the system by the type of chemistry used in the system

[**55:**10.2.9.1.7.4]

63.3.1.6.1.8 Temperature Extremes. Metal hydride storage systems, whether full or partially full, shall not be exposed to temperatures exceeding the range stipulated by the manufacturer. [**55:**10.2.9.1.8]

63.3.1.6.1.9 Falling Objects. Metal hydride storage systems shall not be placed in areas where they are capable of being damaged by falling objects. [**55:**10.2.9.1.9]

63.3.1.6.1.10 Piping Systems. Piping, including tubing, valves, fittings, and pressure regulators, serving metal hydride storage systems shall be maintained gastight to prevent leakage. [**55:**10.2.9.1.10]

63.3.1.6.1.10.1 Leaking Systems. Leaking systems shall be removed from service. [**55:**10.2.9.1.10.1]

63.3.1.6.1.11 Refilling of Containers. The refilling of listed or approved metal hydride storage systems shall be in accordance with the listing requirements and manufacturers' instructions. [**55:**10.2.9.1.11]

63.3.1.6.1.11.1 Industrial Trucks. The refilling of metal hydride storage systems serving powered industrial trucks shall be in accordance with NFPA 2. [**55:**10.2.9.1.11.1]

63.3.1.6.1.11.2 Hydrogen Purity. The purity of hydrogen used for the purpose of refilling containers shall be in accordance with the listing and the manufacturers' instructions. [**55:**10.2.9.1.11.2]

63.3.1.6.1.12 Electrical. Electrical components for metal hydride storage systems shall be designed, constructed, and installed in accordance with *NFPA 70.* [**55:**10.2.9.1.12]

63.3.1.6.2 Portable Containers or Systems.

63.3.1.6.2.1 Securing Containers. Cylinders, containers, and tanks shall be secured in accordance with 63.3.1.10.5. [**55:**10.2.9.2.1]

63.3.1.6.2.1.1 Use on Mobile Equipment. Where a metal hydride storage system is used on mobile equipment, the equipment shall be designed to restrain cylinders, containers, or tanks from dislodgement, slipping, or rotating when the equipment is in motion. [**55:**10.2.9.2.1.1]

63.3.1.6.2.1.2 Motorized Equipment. Metal hydride storage systems used on motorized equipment shall be installed in a manner that protects valves, pressure regulators, fittings, and controls against accidental impact. [**55:**10.2.9.2.1.2]

(A) Protection from Damage. Metal hydride storage systems, including cylinders, containers, tanks, and fittings, shall not extend beyond the platform of the mobile equipment. [**55:**10.2.9.2.1.2(A)]

63.3.1.6.2.2 Valves. Valves on cylinders, containers, and tanks shall remain closed except when containers are connected to closed systems and ready for use. [**55:**10.2.9.2.2]

63.3.1.7 Cylinders, Containers, and Tanks.

63.3.1.7.1 Design and Construction. Cylinders, containers, and tanks shall be designed, fabricated, tested, and marked (i.e., stamped) in accordance with Department of Transportation (DOT) regulations, Transport Canada's (TC) *Transportation of Dangerous Goods Regulations,* or the ASME *Boiler and Pressure Vessel Code.* [**55:**7.1.5.1]

63.3.1.7.2 Defective Cylinders, Containers, and Tanks.

63.3.1.7.2.1 Defective cylinders, containers, and tanks shall be returned to the supplier. [**55:**7.1.5.2.1]

63.3.1.7.2.2 Suppliers shall repair the cylinders, containers, and tanks, remove them from service, or dispose of them in an approved manner. [**55:**7.1.5.2.2]

63.3.1.7.2.3 Suppliers shall ensure that defective cylinders, containers, and tanks that have been repaired are evaluated by qualified individuals to verify that the needed repairs and any required testing has been performed and that those repaired or tested are in a serviceable condition before returning them to service. [**55:**7.1.5.2.3]

63.3.1.7.3 Supports. Stationary cylinders, containers, and tanks shall be provided with engineered supports of noncombustible material on noncombustible foundations. [**55:**7.1.5.3]

63.3.1.7.4 Cylinders, Containers, and Tanks Containing Residual Gas. Compressed gas cylinders, containers, and tanks containing residual product shall be treated as full except when being examined, serviced, or refilled by a gas manufacturer, authorized cylinder requalifier, or distributor. [**55:**7.1.5.4]

63.3.1.7.5 Pressure Relief Devices.

63.3.1.7.5.1 When required by 63.3.1.7.5.2, pressure relief devices shall be provided to protect containers and systems containing compressed gases from rupture in the event of overpressure from thermal exposure. [**55:**7.1.5.5.1]

63.3.1.7.5.2 Pressure relief devices to protect containers shall be designed and provided in accordance with CGA S-1.1, *Pressure Relief Device Standards — Part 1 — Cylinders for Compressed*

Gases, for cylinders; CGA S-1.2, *Pressure Relief Device Standards — Part 2 — Portable Containers for Compressed Gases,* for portable tanks; and CGA S-1.3, *Pressure Relief Device Standards — Part 3 — Stationary Storage Containers for Compressed Gases,* for stationary tanks or in accordance with applicable equivalent requirements in the country of use. [55:7.1.5.5.2]

63.3.1.7.5.3 Pressure relief devices shall be sized in accordance with the specifications to which the container was fabricated. [55:7.1.5.5.3]

63.3.1.7.5.4 The pressure relief device shall have the capacity to prevent the maximum design pressure of the container or system from being exceeded. [55:7.1.5.5.4]

63.3.1.7.5.5 Pressure relief devices shall be arranged to discharge unobstructed to the open air in such a manner as to prevent any impingement of escaping gas upon the container, adjacent structures, or personnel. This requirement shall not apply to DOT specification containers having an internal volume of 2.0 scf (0.057 Nm^3) or less. [55:7.1.5.5.5]

63.3.1.7.5.6 Pressure relief devices or vent piping shall be designed or located so that moisture cannot collect and freeze in a manner that would interfere with operation of the device. [55:7.1.5.5.6]

N **63.3.1.7.5.7 Shutoffs Between Pressure Relief Devices and Containers.**

N **63.3.1.7.5.7.1 General.** Shutoff valves installed between pressure relief devices and containers shall be in accordance with 63.3.1.7.5.7.2 through 63.3.1.7.5.7.4. [55:7.1.5.5.7.1]

N **63.3.1.7.5.7.2 Location.** Shutoff valves shall not be installed between pressure relief devices and containers unless the valves or their use meet the requirements of 63.3.1.7.5.7.3 or 63.3.1.7.5.7.4. [55:7.1.5.5.7.2]

N **63.3.1.7.5.7.3* Security.** Shutoff valves, where used, shall be locked in the open position, and their use shall be limited to service-related work performed by the supplier under the requirements of the ASME *Boiler and Pressure Vessel Code.* [55:7.1.5.5.7.3]

N **63.3.1.7.5.7.4 Multiple Pressure Relief Devices.** Shutoff valves controlling multiple pressure relief devices on a container shall be installed so that either the type of valve installed or the arrangement provides the full required flow through the relief devices at all times. [55:7.1.5.5.7.4]

63.3.1.8 Cathodic Protection. Where required, cathodic protection shall be in accordance with 63.3.1.8. [55:7.1.6]

63.3.1.8.1 Operation. Where installed, cathodic protection systems shall be operated and maintained to continuously provide corrosion protection. [55:7.1.6.1]

63.3.1.8.2 Inspection. Container systems equipped with cathodic protection shall be inspected for the intended operation by a cathodic protection tester. The frequency of inspection shall be determined by the designer of the cathodic protection system. [55:7.1.6.2]

63.3.1.8.2.1 The cathodic protection tester shall be certified as being qualified by the National Association of Corrosion Engineers, International (NACE). [55:7.1.6.2.1]

63.3.1.8.3 Impressed Current Systems. Systems equipped with impressed current cathodic protection systems shall be inspected in accordance with the requirements of the design and 63.3.1.8.2. [55:7.1.6.3]

63.3.1.8.3.1 The design limits of the cathodic protection system shall be available to the AHJ upon request. [55:7.1.6.3.1]

63.3.1.8.3.2 The system owner shall maintain the following records to demonstrate that the cathodic protection is in conformance with the requirements of the design:

(1) The results of inspections of the system
(2) The results of testing that has been completed
[55:7.1.6.3.2]

63.3.1.8.4 Repairs, maintenance, or replacement of a cathodic protection system shall be under the supervision of a corrosion expert certified by NACE. [55:7.1.6.4]

63.3.1.8.4.1 The corrosion expert shall be certified by NACE as a senior corrosion technologist, a cathodic protection specialist, or a corrosion specialist or shall be a registered engineer with registration in a field that includes education and experience in corrosion control. [55:7.1.6.4.1]

63.3.1.9 Labeling Requirements.

63.3.1.9.1 Containers. Individual compressed gas cylinders, containers, and tanks shall be marked or labeled in accordance with DOT requirements or those of the applicable regulatory agency. [55:7.1.7.1]

63.3.1.9.2 Label Maintenance. The labels applied by the gas manufacturer to identify the liquefied or nonliquefied compressed gas cylinder contents shall not be altered or removed by the user. [55:7.1.7.2]

63.3.1.9.3 Stationary Compressed Gas Cylinders, Containers, and Tanks.

63.3.1.9.3.1 Stationary compressed gas cylinders, containers, and tanks shall be marked in accordance with NFPA 704. [55:7.1.7.3.1]

63.3.1.9.3.2 Markings shall be visible from any direction of approach. [55:7.1.7.3.2]

63.3.1.9.4 Piping Systems.

63.3.1.9.4.1 Except as provided in 63.3.1.9.4.2, piping systems shall be marked in accordance with ASME A13.1, *Scheme for the Identification of Piping Systems,* or other applicable approved standards as follows:

(1) Marking shall include the name of the gas and a direction-of-flow arrow.
(2) Piping that is used to convey more than one gas at various times shall be marked to provide clear identification and warning of the hazard.
(3) Markings for piping systems shall be provided at the following locations:

    (a) At each critical process control valve
    (b) At wall, floor, or ceiling penetrations
    (c) At each change of direction
    (d) At a minimum of every 20 ft (6.1 m) or fraction thereof throughout the piping run

[55:7.1.7.4.1]

63.3.1.9.4.2 Piping within gas manufacturing plants, gas processing plants, refineries, and similar occupancies shall be marked in an approved manner. [55:7.1.7.4.2]

63.3.1.10 Security.

63.3.1.10.1 General. Compressed gas cylinders, containers, tanks, and systems shall be secured against accidental dislodgement and against access by unauthorized personnel. [55:7.1.8.1]

63.3.1.10.2* Security of Areas. Storage, use, and handling areas shall be secured against unauthorized entry. [55:7.1.8.2]

63.3.1.10.3 Administrative controls shall be allowed to be used to control access to individual storage, use, and handling areas located in secure facilities not accessible by the general public. [55:7.1.8.2.1]

63.3.1.10.4 Physical Protection.

63.3.1.10.4.1 Compressed gas cylinders, containers, tanks, and systems that could be exposed to physical damage shall be protected. [55:7.1.8.3.1]

63.3.1.10.4.2 Guard posts or other means shall be provided to protect compressed gas cylinders, containers, tanks, and systems indoors and outdoors from vehicular damage in accordance with Section 4.11 of NFPA 55. [55:7.1.8.3.2]

63.3.1.10.5 Securing Compressed Gas Cylinders, Containers, and Tanks. Compressed gas cylinders, containers, and tanks in use or in storage shall be secured to prevent them from falling or being knocked over by corralling them and securing them to a cart, framework, or fixed object by use of a restraint, unless otherwise permitted by 63.3.1.10.5.1 and 63.3.1.10.5.2. [55:7.1.8.4]

63.3.1.10.5.1 Compressed gas cylinders, containers and tanks in the process of examination, servicing, and refilling shall not be required to be secured. [55:7.1.8.4.1]

63.3.1.10.5.2 At cylinder-filling plants, authorized cylinder requalifier's facilities, and distributors' warehouses, the nesting of cylinders shall be permitted as a means to secure cylinders. [55:7.1.8.4.2]

63.3.1.11 Valve Protection.

63.3.1.11.1 General. Compressed gas cylinder, container, and tank valves shall be protected from physical damage by means of protective caps, collars, or similar devices. [55:7.1.9.1]

63.3.1.11.1.1 Valve protection of individual valves shall not be required to be installed on individual cylinders, containers, or tanks installed on tube trailers or similar transportable bulk gas systems equipped with manifolds that are provided with a means of physical protection that will protect the valves from physical damage when the equipment is in use. Protective systems required by DOT for over the road transport shall provide an acceptable means of protection. [55:7.1.9.1.1]

63.3.1.11.1.1.1 Valve protection of individual valves shall not be required on cylinders, containers, or tanks that comprise bulk or non-bulk gas systems where the containers are stationary, or portable equipped with manifolds, that are provided with physical protection in accordance with Section 4.11 of NFPA 55 and 63.3.1.10.4 or other approved means. Protective systems required by DOT for over the road transport shall provide an acceptable means of protection. [55:7.1.9.1.1.1]

63.3.1.11.2 Valve-Protective Caps. Where compressed gas cylinders, containers, and tanks are designed to accept valve-protective caps, the user shall keep such caps on the compressed gas cylinders, containers, and tanks at all times, except when empty, being processed, or connected for use. [55:7.1.9.2]

63.3.1.11.3 Valve Outlet Caps or Plugs.

63.3.1.11.3.1 Gastight valve outlet caps or plugs shall be provided and in place for all full or partially full cylinders, containers, and tanks containing toxic, highly toxic, pyrophoric, or unstable reactive Class 3 or Class 4 gases that are in storage. [55:7.1.9.3.1]

63.3.1.11.3.2 Valve outlet caps and plugs shall be designed and rated for the container service pressure. [55:7.1.9.3.2]

63.3.1.12 Separation from Hazardous Conditions.

63.3.1.12.1 General. Compressed gas cylinders, containers, tanks, and systems in storage or use shall be separated from materials and conditions that present exposure hazards to or from each other. [55:7.1.10.1]

63.3.1.12.2* Incompatible Materials. Gas cylinders, containers, and tanks shall be separated in accordance with Table 63.3.1.12.2. [55:7.1.10.2]

Table 63.3.1.12.2 Separation of Gas Cylinders, Containers, and Tanks by Hazard Class

Gas Category	Other Gas	Unstable Reactive Class 2, Class 3, or Class 4 ft	m	Corrosive ft	m	Oxidizing ft	m	Flammable ft	m	Pyrophoric ft	m	Toxic or Highly Toxic ft	m
Toxic or highly toxic	NR	20	6.1	20	6.1	20	6.1	20	6.1	20	6.1	—	—
Pyrophoric	NR	20	6.1	20	6.1	20	6.1	20	6.1	—	—	20	6.1
Flammable	NR	20	6.1	20	6.1	20	6.1	—	—	20	6.1	20	6.1
Oxidizing	NR	20	6.1	20	6.1	—	—	20	6.1	20	6.1	20	6.1
Corrosive	NR	20	6.1	—	—	20	6.1	20	6.1	20	6.1	20	6.1
Unstable reactive Class 2, Class 3, or Class 4	NR	—	—	20	6.1	20	6.1	20	6.1	20	6.1	20	6.1
Other gas	—	NR		NR		NR		NR		NR		NR	

NR: No separation required.
[55: Table 7.1.10.2]

63.3.1.12.2.1 Subparagraph 63.3.1.12.2 shall not apply to gases contained within closed piping systems. [**55:**7.1.10.2.1]

63.3.1.12.2.2 The distances shown in Table 63.3.1.12.2 shall be permitted to be reduced without limit where compressed gas cylinders, containers, and tanks are separated by a barrier of noncombustible construction that has a fire resistance rating of at least 0.5 hour and interrupts the line of sight between the containers. [**55:**7.1.10.2.2]

N **63.3.1.12.2.3*** The distances shown in Table 63.3.1.12.2 shall be permitted to be reduced without limit where it has been determined that compressed gas cylinders, containers, and tanks are not incompatible. [**55:**7.1.10.2.3]

63.3.1.12.2.4 The 20 ft (6.1 m) distance shall be permitted to be reduced to 5 ft (1.5 m) where one of the gases is enclosed in a gas cabinet or without limit where both gases are enclosed in gas cabinets. [**55:**7.1.10.2.4]

63.3.1.12.2.5 Cylinders without pressure relief devices shall not be stored without separation from flammable and pyrophoric gases with pressure relief devices. [**55:**7.1.10.2.5]

63.3.1.12.2.6* Spatial separation shall not be required between cylinders deemed to be incompatible in gas production facilities where cylinders are connected to manifolds for the purposes of filling, analysis of compressed gases, or manufacturing procedures, assuming the prescribed controls for the manufacture of gas mixtures are in place. [**55:**7.1.10.2.6]

63.3.1.12.3* Clearance from Combustibles and Vegetation. Combustible waste, vegetation, and similar materials shall be kept a minimum of 10 ft (3.1 m) from compressed gas cylinders, containers, tanks, and systems. [**55:**7.1.10.3]

63.3.1.12.3.1 A noncombustible partition without openings or penetrations and extending not less than 18 in. (457 mm) above and to the sides of the storage area shall be permitted in lieu of the minimum distance. [**55:**7.1.10.3.1]

63.3.1.12.3.2 The noncombustible partition shall be either an independent structure or the exterior wall of the building adjacent to the storage area. [**55:**7.1.10.3.2]

63.3.1.12.4 Ledges, Platforms, and Elevators. Compressed gas cylinders, containers, and tanks shall not be placed near elevators, unprotected platform ledges, or other areas where compressed gas cylinders, containers, or tanks could fall distances exceeding one-half the height of the container, cylinder, or tank. [**55:**7.1.10.4]

63.3.1.12.5 Temperature Extremes. Compressed gas cylinders, containers, and tanks, whether full or partially full, shall not be exposed to temperatures exceeding 125°F (52°C) or subambient (low) temperatures unless one of the following apply:

(1) The compressed gas cylinders, containers, or tanks are designed for use under such exposure
(2) The compressed gas cylinders, containers, or tanks are located at compressed gas manufacturing facilities where all of the following apply:
 (a) Temperatures above 125°F (52°C) and below subambient (low) temperatures are permitted for the purposes of filling, analysis, and other related procedures
 (b) Engineering controls are employed to prevent any hazards
 (c) The temperature extremes will not degrade the original mechanical properties of the containers, cylinders, or tanks
[**55:**7.1.10.5]

Δ **63.3.1.12.5.1** Compressed gas cylinders, containers, and tanks that have not been designed for use under elevated temperature conditions shall not be exposed to direct sunlight outdoors where ambient temperatures exceed 125°F (52°C). [**55:**7.1.10.5.1]

N **63.3.1.12.5.2** The use of a weather protection structure or shaded environment for storage or use shall be permitted as a means to protect against direct exposure to sunlight. [**55:**7.1.10.5.2]

63.3.1.12.6 Falling Objects. Compressed gas cylinders, containers, and tanks shall not be placed in areas where they are capable of being damaged by falling objects. [**55:**7.1.10.6]

63.3.1.12.7 Heating. Compressed gas cylinders, containers, and tanks, whether full or partially full, shall not be heated by devices that could raise the surface temperature of the container, cylinder, or tank to above 125°F (52°C). [**55:**7.1.10.7]

63.3.1.12.7.1 Electrically Powered Heating Devices. Electrical heating devices shall be in accordance with *NFPA 70*. [**55:**7.1.10.7.1]

63.3.1.12.7.2 Fail-Safe Design. Devices designed to maintain individual compressed gas cylinders, containers, and tanks at constant temperature shall be designed to be fail-safe. [**55:**7.1.10.7.2]

63.3.1.12.8 Sources of Ignition. Open flames and high-temperature devices shall not be used in a manner that creates a hazardous condition. [**55:**7.1.10.8]

63.3.1.12.9 Exposure to Chemicals. Compressed gas cylinders, containers, and tanks shall not be exposed to corrosive chemicals or fumes that could damage cylinders, containers, tanks, or valve-protective caps. [**55:**7.1.10.9]

N **63.3.1.12.9.1** Compressed gas cylinders shall not be located where they could be exposed to spills of flammable and combustible liquids. [**55:**7.1.10.9.1]

63.3.1.12.10 Exposure to Electrical Circuits. Compressed gas cylinders, containers, and tanks shall not be placed where they could become a part of an electrical circuit. [**55:**7.1.10.10]

63.3.1.12.10.1* Electrical devices mounted on compressed gas piping, cylinders, containers, or tanks shall be installed, grounded, and bonded in accordance with the methods specified in *NFPA 70(NEC)*. [**55:**7.1.10.10.1]

63.3.1.13 Service and Repair. Service, repair, modification, or removal of valves, pressure relief devices, or other compressed gas cylinder, container, and tank appurtenances shall be performed by trained personnel and with the permission of the container owner. [**55:**7.1.11]

63.3.1.14 Unauthorized Use. Compressed gas cylinders, containers, and tanks shall not be used for any purpose other than to serve as a vessel for containing the product for which it was designed. [**55:**7.1.12]

63.3.1.15 Cylinders, Containers, and Tanks Exposed to Fire. Compressed gas cylinders, containers, and tanks exposed to fire shall not be used or shipped while full or partially full until they are requalified in accordance with the pressure vessel code under which they were manufactured. [55:7.1.13]

63.3.1.16 Leaks, Damage, or Corrosion.

63.3.1.16.1 Removal from Service. Leaking, damaged, or corroded compressed gas cylinders, containers, and tanks shall be removed from service. [55:7.1.14.1]

63.3.1.16.2 Replacement and Repair. Leaking, damaged, or corroded compressed gas systems shall be replaced or repaired. [55:7.1.14.2]

63.3.1.16.3* Handling of Cylinders, Containers, and Tanks Removed from Service. Compressed gas cylinders, containers, and tanks that have been removed from service shall be handled in an approved manner. [55:7.1.14.3]

63.3.1.16.4 Leaking Systems. Compressed gas systems that are determined to be leaking, damaged, or corroded shall be repaired to a serviceable condition or shall be removed from service. [55:7.1.14.4]

63.3.1.17 Surfaces.

63.3.1.17.1 To prevent bottom corrosion, cylinders, containers, and tanks shall be protected from direct contact with soil or surfaces where water might accumulate. [55:7.1.15.1]

63.3.1.17.2 Surfaces shall be graded to prevent accumulation of water. [55:7.1.15.2]

63.3.1.18 Storage Area Temperature.

63.3.1.18.1 Compressed Gas Containers. Storage area temperatures shall not exceed 125°F (52°C). [55:7.1.16.1]

63.3.1.19 Installation of Underground Piping.

63.3.1.19.1 Underground piping shall be of welded construction without valves, unwelded mechanical joints, or connections installed underground. [55:7.1.17.1]

63.3.1.19.1.1 Valves or connections located in boxes or enclosures shall be permitted to be installed underground where such boxes or enclosures are accessible from above ground and where the valves or connections contained are isolated from direct contact with earth or fill. [55:7.1.17.1.1]

63.3.1.19.1.1.1 Valve boxes or enclosures installed in areas subject to vehicular traffic shall be constructed to resist uniformly distributed and concentrated live loads in accordance with the building code for areas designated as vehicular driveways and yards, subject to trucking. [55:7.1.17.1.1.1]

63.3.1.19.1.2* Piping installed in trench systems located below grade where the trench is open to above shall not be considered to be underground. [55:7.1.17.1.2]

63.3.1.19.2 Gas piping in contact with earth or other material that could corrode the piping shall be protected against corrosion in an approved manner. [55:7.1.17.2]

63.3.1.19.2.1 When cathodic protection is provided, it shall be in accordance with 63.3.1.8. [55:7.1.17.2.1]

Δ **63.3.1.19.3** Underground piping shall be installed on at least 6 in. (150 mm) of well-compacted bedding material. [55:7.1.17.3]

Δ **63.3.1.19.4** In areas subject to vehicle traffic, the pipe trench shall be deep enough to permit a cover of at least 18 in. (450 mm) of well-compacted backfill material and pavement. [55:7.1.17.4]

Δ **63.3.1.19.5** In paved areas where a minimum 2 in. (50 mm) of asphalt is used, backfill between the pipe and the asphalt shall be permitted to be reduced to 8 in. (200 mm) minimum. [55:7.1.17.5]

Δ **63.3.1.19.6** In paved areas where a minimum 4 in. (100 mm) of reinforced concrete is used, backfill between the pipe and the asphalt shall be permitted to be reduced to 4 in. (100 mm) minimum. [55:7.1.17.6]

63.3.1.19.7 In areas not subject to vehicle traffic, the pipe trench shall be deep enough to permit a cover of at least 12 in. (300 mm) of well-compacted backfill material. [55:7.1.17.7]

Δ **63.3.1.19.8** A greater burial depth shall be provided when required by the manufacturer's instructions or where frost conditions are present. [55:7.1.17.8]

Δ **63.3.1.19.9** Piping within the same trench shall be separated horizontally by at least two pipe diameters. Separation shall need not exceed 9 in. (230 mm). [55:7.1.17.9]

Δ **63.3.1.19.10** Two or more levels of piping within the same trench shall be separated vertically by a minimum 6 in. (150 mm) of well-compacted bedding material. [55:7.1.17.10]

63.3.1.20 Cleaning and Purging of Gas Piping Systems.

63.3.1.20.1 General.

63.3.1.20.1.1 Piping systems shall be cleaned and purged in accordance with the requirements of 63.3.1.20 when one or more of the following conditions exist:

(1) The system is installed and prior to being placed into service
(2) There is a change in service
(3)* There are alterations or repair of the system involving the replacement of parts or addition to the piping system and prior to returning the system to service
(4)* The design standards or written procedures specify cleaning and purging

[55:7.1.18.1.1]

63.3.1.20.1.2 Cleaning and purging of the internal surfaces of piping systems shall be conducted by qualified individuals trained in cleaning and purging operations and procedures, including the recognition of potential hazards associated with cleaning and purging. [55:7.1.18.1.2]

63.3.1.20.1.3* A written cleaning or purging procedure shall be provided to establish the requirements for the cleaning and purging operations to be conducted. [55:7.1.18.1.3]

63.3.1.20.1.3.1* An independent or third-party review of the written procedure shall be conducted after the procedure has been written and shall accomplish the following:

(1) Evaluate hazards, errors, and malfunctions related to each step in the procedure
(2) Review the measures prescribed in the procedure for applicability
(3) Make recommendations for additional hazard mitigation measures if deemed necessary

[55:7.1.18.1.3.1]

63.3.1.20.1.3.2 The completed written procedure shall be as follows:

(1) Maintained on site by the facility owner/operator
(2) Provided to operating personnel engaged in cleaning or purging operations
(3) Made available to the AHJ upon request
[**55:**7.1.18.1.3.2]

63.3.1.20.1.3.3 Where generic cleaning or purging procedures have been established, a job-specific operating procedure shall not be required. [**55:**7.1.18.1.3.3]

63.3.1.20.1.3.4 Generic procedures shall be reviewed when originally published or when the procedure or operation is changed. [**55:**7.1.18.1.3.4]

63.3.1.20.1.4 Written procedures to manage a change in process materials, technology, equipment, procedures, and facilities shall be established by the facility owner/operator. [**55:**7.1.18.1.4]

63.3.1.20.1.4.1 The management-of-change procedures shall ensure that the following topics are addressed prior to any change in the configuration or design of the piping system:

(1) The technical basis for the proposed change
(2) The safety and health implications
(3) Whether the change is permanent or temporary
(4) Whether modifications to the cleaning and purging procedures are required as a result of the identified changes
[**55:**7.1.18.1.4.1]

63.3.1.20.1.4.2 When modifications to the cleaning and purging procedures are required, the written procedure shall be updated to incorporate any elements identified by the management-of-change procedures. [**55:**7.1.18.1.4.2]

63.3.1.20.1.5 Prior to cleaning or purging, piping systems shall be inspected and tested to determine that the installation, including the materials of construction, and method of fabrication, comply with the requirements of the design standard used and the intended application for which the system was designed. [**55:**7.1.18.1.5]

63.3.1.20.1.5.1 Inspection and testing of piping systems shall not be required to remove a system from service. [**55:**7.1.18.1.5.1]

63.3.1.20.1.5.2 Purging of piping systems shall not be required for systems that are utilized for operations designated by written operating procedures in accordance with the requirements of the cleaning or purging procedure specified in 63.3.1.20.1.1. [**55:**7.1.18.1.5.2]

63.3.1.20.1.5.3* Personnel in the affected area(s), as determined by the cleaning or purging procedure, shall be informed of the hazards associated with the operational activity and notified prior to the initiation of any such activity. [**55:**7.1.18.1.5.3]

63.3.1.20.2* Cleaning. Piping system designs shall be documented to specify the requirements for the internal cleaning of the piping system prior to installation and initial use. [**55:**7.1.18.2]

63.3.1.20.2.1 The internal surfaces of gas piping systems shall be cleaned to ensure that the required standard of cleanliness specified by the design is met prior to placing the gas piping system into service. [**55:**7.1.18.2.1]

63.3.1.20.2.2* When piping systems are cleaned in stages during installation or assembly, the interior of the cleaned piping shall be protected against the infiltration of unwanted contaminants. [**55:**7.1.18.2.2]

63.3.1.20.3* Purging. Piping systems used to contain gases with a physical or health hazard in any of the categories specified by 63.1.4 shall be purged prior to being placed into service for initial use. [**55:**7.1.18.3]

63.3.1.20.3.1 Piping systems shall be purged to remove the internal contents preceding the following activities or operations:

(1) Activating or placing a piping system into service
(2) Deactivating or removing a piping system from service
(3) Changing the service of a piping system from one gas to another, except when such gas is supplied to a manifold or piping system designed for the purpose of filling or otherwise processing cylinders, containers, or tanks in a process with established procedures
(4) Performing service, maintenance, or modifications on a system where personnel or designated areas will potentially be exposed to the internal contents of the piping system
(5) Performing hot work, including but not limited to welding, cutting or brazing on the piping system
[**55:**7.1.18.3.1]

63.3.1.20.3.2 The termination point for the release of purged gases shall be in accordance with 63.2.15. [**55:**7.1.18.3.2]

63.3.1.20.3.2.1 The release of purged gases or mixtures containing any quantity of corrosive, toxic, or highly toxic gases shall be through a treatment system in accordance with the applicable requirements of 63.3.6.3.4 or 63.3.10.3. [**55:**7.1.18.3.2.1]

63.3.1.20.3.2.2 The termination point for the release of purged gases resultant from the purging of piping systems out of service, other than those in accordance with 63.3.1.20.3.2.1, shall not be required to be in accordance with 63.2.15 where the contained volume of the piping system (when released to indoor areas) does not result in a concentration in the room or area that will reduce the oxygen concentration in the room or area below a level of 19.5 percent or that exceeds any of the following limits:

(1) Ceiling limit
(2) Permissible exposure limit
(3) Short-term exposure limit
(4) Twenty-five percent of the lower flammable limit
[**55:**7.1.18.3.2.2]

***N* 63.3.2 Subatmospheric Gas Sources (SAGS).**

***N* 63.3.2.1** The storage and use of subatmospheric gas sources (type 1 or 2) with compatible gases shall meet all the requirements of this *Code* based on the assigned hazard categories listed in Section 5.1 of NFPA 55. [**55:**7.2.1]

***N* 63.3.2.2** SAGS cylinders with incompatible gases shall meet the requirements of 17.14.2.1 through 17.14.2.6 in NFPA 318. [**55:**7.2.2]

63.3.3 Storage.

63.3.3.1 General.

63.3.3.1.1 Applicability. The storage of compressed gas cylinders, containers, and tanks shall be in accordance with 63.3.3. [**55:**7.3.1.1]

63.3.3.1.2 Upright Storage Flammable Gas in Solution and Liquefied Flammable Gas. Cylinders, containers, and tanks containing liquefied flammable gases and flammable gases in solution shall be positioned in the upright position. [**55:**7.3.1.2]

63.3.3.1.2.1 Cylinders and Containers of 1.3 Gal (5 L) or Less. Containers with a capacity of 1.3 gal (5 L) or less shall be permitted to be stored in a horizontal position. [**55:**7.3.1.2.1]

63.3.3.1.2.2 Cylinders, Containers, and Tanks Designed for Horizontal Use. Cylinders, containers, and tanks designed for use in a horizontal position shall be permitted to be stored in a horizontal position. [**55:**7.3.1.2.2]

63.3.3.1.2.3 Palletized Cylinders, Containers, and Tanks. Cylinders, containers, and tanks, with the exception of those containing flammable liquefied compressed gases, that are palletized for transportation purposes shall be permitted to be stored in a horizontal position. [**55:**7.3.1.2.3]

63.3.3.1.3 Classification of Weather Protection as an Indoor Versus an Outdoor Area. For other than explosive materials and hazardous materials presenting a detonation hazard, a weather protection structure shall be permitted to be used for sheltering outdoor storage or use areas without requiring such areas to be classified as indoor storage. [**55:**7.3.1.3]

63.3.3.2 Material-Specific Regulations.

63.3.3.2.1 Indoor Storage. Indoor storage of compressed gases shall be in accordance with the material-specific provisions of 63.3.5 through 63.3.11. [**55:**7.3.2.1]

63.3.3.2.2 Exterior Storage.

63.3.3.2.2.1 General. Exterior storage of compressed gases shall be in accordance with the material-specific provisions of 63.3.5 through 63.3.11. [**55:**7.3.2.2.1]

63.3.3.2.2.2 Separation. Distances from property lines, buildings, and exposures shall be in accordance with the material-specific provisions of 63.3.5 through 63.3.11. [**55:**7.3.2.2.2]

63.3.4 Use and Handling.

63.3.4.1 General.

63.3.4.1.1 Applicability. The use and handling of compressed gas cylinders, containers, tanks, and systems shall be in accordance with 63.3.4.1. [**55:**7.4.1.1]

63.3.4.1.2 Controls.

63.3.4.1.2.1 Compressed gas system controls shall be designed to prevent materials from entering or leaving the process at an unintended time, rate, or path. [**55:**7.4.1.2.1]

63.3.4.1.2.2 Automatic controls shall be designed to be fail-safe. [**55:**7.4.1.2.2]

63.3.4.1.3 Piping Systems. Piping, tubing, fittings, and related components shall be designed, fabricated, and tested in accordance with the requirements of the applicable parts in ASME B31.3, *Process Piping*. [**55:**7.4.1.3]

63.3.4.1.3.1 Integrity. Piping, tubing, pressure regulators, valves, and other apparatus shall be kept gastight to prevent leakage. [**55:**7.4.1.3.1]

63.3.4.1.3.2 Backflow Prevention. Backflow prevention or check valves shall be provided where the backflow of hazardous materials could create a hazardous condition or cause the unauthorized discharge of hazardous materials. [**55:**7.4.1.3.2]

63.3.4.1.4 Valves.

63.3.4.1.4.1 Valves utilized on compressed gas systems shall be designed for the gas or gases and pressure intended and shall be accessible. [**55:**7.4.1.4.1]

63.3.4.1.4.2 Valve handles or actuators for required shutoff valves shall not be removed or otherwise altered to prevent access. [**55:**7.4.1.4.2]

63.3.4.1.5 Vent Pipe Termination.

63.3.4.1.5.1 Venting of gases shall be directed to an approved location. [**55:**7.4.1.5.1]

63.3.4.1.5.2 The termination point for piped vent systems serving cylinders, containers, tanks, and gas systems used for the purpose of operational or emergency venting shall be in accordance with 63.2.15. [**55:**7.4.1.5.2]

63.3.4.1.6 Upright Use.

63.3.4.1.6.1 Compressed gas cylinders, containers, and tanks containing flammable liquefied gas, except those designed for use in a horizontal position and those compressed gas cylinders, containers, and tanks containing nonliquefied gases, shall be used in a "valve end up" upright position. [**55:**7.4.1.6.1]

63.3.4.1.6.2 An upright position shall include a position in which the cylinder, container, or tank axis is inclined as much as 45 degrees from the vertical and in which the relief device is always in direct communication with the gas phase. [**55:**7.4.1.6.2]

63.3.4.1.7 Inverted Use. Cylinders, containers, and tanks containing nonflammable liquefied gases shall be permitted to be used in the inverted position when the liquid phase is used. [**55:**7.4.1.7]

63.3.4.1.7.1 Flammable liquefied gases at processing plants shall be permitted to use this inverted position method while transfilling. [**55:**7.4.1.7.1]

63.3.4.1.7.2 The cylinder, container, or tank shall be secured, and the dispensing apparatus shall be designed for use with liquefied gas. [**55:**7.4.1.7.2]

63.3.4.1.8 Cylinders and Containers of 1.3 Gal (5 L) or Less. Cylinders or containers with a water volume of 1.3 gal (5 L) or less shall be permitted to be used in a horizontal position. [**55:**7.4.1.8]

63.3.4.1.9 Transfer. Transfer of gases between cylinders, containers, and tanks shall be performed by qualified individuals using equipment and operating procedures in accordance with CGA P-1, *Safe Handling of Compressed Gases in Containers*. [**55:**7.4.1.9]

63.3.4.1.10 Use of Compressed Gases for Inflation. Inflatable equipment, devices, or balloons shall only be pressurized or filled with compressed air or inert gases. [55:7.4.1.10]

63.3.4.1.11 Emergency Shutoff Valves.

63.3.4.1.11.1 Accessible manual or automatic emergency shutoff valves shall be provided to shut off the flow of gas in case of emergency. [55:7.4.1.11.1]

63.3.4.1.11.1.1* Manual emergency shutoff valves or the device that activates an automatic emergency shutoff valve on a bulk source or piping system serving the bulk supply shall be identified by means of a sign. [55:7.4.1.11.1.1]

63.3.4.1.11.2 Emergency shutoffs shall be located at the point of use and at the tank, cylinder, or bulk source, and at the point where the system piping enters the building. [55:7.4.1.11.2]

63.3.4.1.12 Emergency Isolation.

63.3.4.1.12.1 Where compressed gases from sources in excess of the quantity thresholds in Table 63.2.3.1.1 having a hazard ranking in one or more of the following hazard classes in accordance with NFPA 704 are carried in pressurized piping above a gauge pressure of 15 psi (103 kPa), an approved method of emergency isolation shall be provided:

(1) Health hazard Class 3 or Class 4
(2) Flammability Class 4
(3) Instability Class 3 or Class 4

[55:7.4.1.12.1]

63.3.4.1.12.2 Approved means of meeting the requirements for emergency isolation shall include any of the following:

(1) Automatic shutoff valves, located as close to the bulk source as practical, tied to leak detection systems
(2) Attended control stations where trained personnel can monitor alarms or supervisory signals and can trigger emergency responses
(3) A constantly monitored control station with an alarm and remote shutoff of the gas supply system
(4) Excess flow valves at the bulk source

[55:7.4.1.12.2]

63.3.4.1.12.3 The requirements of 63.3.4.1.12 shall not be required for the following:

(1) Piping for inlet connections designed to prevent backflow at the source
(2) Piping for pressure relief devices

[55:7.4.1.12.3]

63.3.4.1.12.4 Location Exemptions. The requirements of 63.3.4.1.12 shall not apply to the following:

(1) Piping for inlet connections designed to prevent backflow
(2) Piping for pressure relief devices
(3) Systems containing 430 scf (12.7 Nm^3) or less of flammable gas

[55:7.4.1.12.4]

63.3.4.2 Material-Specific Regulations.

63.3.4.2.1 Indoor Use. Indoor use of compressed gases shall be in accordance with the requirements of 63.3.5 through 63.3.11. [55:7.4.2.1]

63.3.4.2.2 Exterior Use.

63.3.4.2.2.1 General. Exterior use of compressed gases shall be in accordance with the requirements of 63.3.5 through 63.3.11. [55:7.4.2.2.1]

63.3.4.2.2.2 Separation. Distances from property lines, buildings, and exposure hazards shall be in accordance with the material-specific provisions of 63.3.5 through 63.3.11. [55:7.4.2.2.2]

63.3.4.3 Handling.

63.3.4.3.1 Applicability. The handling of compressed gas cylinders, containers, and tanks shall be in accordance with 63.3.4.3. [55:7.4.3.1]

63.3.4.3.2 Carts and Trucks.

63.3.4.3.2.1 Cylinders, containers, and tanks shall be moved using an approved method. [55:7.4.3.2.1]

63.3.4.3.2.2 Where cylinders, containers, and tanks are moved by hand cart, hand truck, or other mobile device, such carts, trucks, or devices shall be designed for the secure movement of cylinders, containers, and tanks. [55:7.4.3.2.2]

63.3.4.3.3 Lifting Devices. Ropes, chains, or slings shall not be used to suspend compressed gas cylinders, containers, and tanks unless provisions at time of manufacture have been made on the cylinder, container, or tank for appropriate lifting attachments, such as lugs. [55:7.4.3.3]

63.3.5 Medical Gas Systems. Medical gas systems for health care shall be in accordance with NFPA 99. [55:7.5]

63.3.6 Corrosive Gases.

63.3.6.1 General. The storage or use of corrosive compressed gases exceeding the quantity thresholds for gases requiring special provisions as specified in Table 63.2.3.1.1 shall be in accordance with Chapters 1 through 6 of NFPA 55 and subsections 63.3.1 through 63.3.4 and 63.3.6. [55:7.6.1]

63.3.6.2 Distance to Exposures. The outdoor storage or use of corrosive compressed gas shall not be within 20 ft (6.1 m) of buildings not associated with the manufacture or distribution of corrosive gases, lot lines, streets, alleys, public ways, or means of egress. [55:7.6.2]

63.3.6.2.1 A 2-hour fire barrier wall without openings or penetrations and that extends not less than 30 in. (762 mm) above and to the sides of the storage or use area shall be permitted in lieu of the 20 ft (6.1 m) distance. [55:7.6.2.1]

63.3.6.2.1.1* Where a fire barrier is used to protect compressed gas systems, the system shall terminate downstream of the source valve. [55:7.6.2.1.1]

63.3.6.2.1.2 The fire barrier wall shall be either an independent structure or the exterior wall of the building adjacent to the storage or use area. [55:7.6.2.1.2]

63.3.6.2.1.3 The 2-hour fire barrier shall be located at least 5 ft (1.5 m) from any exposure. [55:7.6.2.1.3]

63.3.6.2.1.4 The 2-hour fire barrier wall shall not have more than two sides at approximately 90 degree (1.57 rad) directions or not more than three sides with connecting angles of approximately 135 degrees (2.36 rad). [55:7.6.2.1.4]

63.3.6.3 Indoor Use. The indoor use of corrosive gases shall be provided with a gas cabinet, exhausted enclosure, or gas room. [**55:7.6.3**]

63.3.6.3.1 Gas Cabinets. Gas cabinets shall be in accordance with 63.2.17. [**55:7.6.3.1**]

63.3.6.3.2 Exhausted Enclosures. Exhausted enclosures shall be in accordance with 63.2.18. [**55:7.6.3.2**]

63.3.6.3.3 Gas Rooms. Gas rooms shall be in accordance with 63.2.4. [**55:7.6.3.3**]

63.3.6.3.4 Treatment Systems. Treatment systems, except as provided for in 63.3.6.3.4.1, gas cabinets, exhausted enclosures, and gas rooms containing corrosive gases in use shall be provided with exhaust ventilation, with all exhaust directed to a treatment system designed to process the accidental release of gas. [**55:7.6.3.4**]

63.3.6.3.4.1 Treatment systems shall not be required for corrosive gases in use where provided with the following:

(1) Gas detection in accordance with 63.3.10.3.2.1.1
(2) Fail-safe automatic closing valves in accordance with 63.3.10.3.2.2

[**55:7.6.3.4.1**]

63.3.6.3.4.2 Treatment systems shall be capable of diluting, adsorbing, absorbing, containing, neutralizing, burning, or otherwise processing the release of corrosive gas in accordance with 63.3.10.3.4.1. [**55:7.6.3.4.2**]

63.3.6.3.4.3 Treatment system sizing shall be in accordance with 63.3.10.3.4. [**55:7.6.3.4.3**]

63.3.7 Flammable Gases.

63.3.7.1 Storage, Use, and Handling.

63.3.7.1.1* The storage or use of flammable gases exceeding the quantity thresholds for gases requiring special provisions as specified in Table 63.2.3.1.1 shall be in accordance with Chapters 1 through 6 of NFPA 55 and subsections 63.3.1 through 63.3.4 and 63.3.7. [**55:7.7.1.1**]

63.3.7.1.2 Storage, use, and handling of gaseous hydrogen shall be in accordance with 63.3.7.1 and Chapter 10 of NFPA 55. [**55:7.7.1.2**]

63.3.7.1.3 Storage, use, and handling of compressed natural gas shall be in accordance with 63.3.7.1. [**55:7.7.1.3**]

63.3.7.2 Distance to Exposures. The outdoor storage or use of non-bulk flammable compressed gas shall be located from lot lines, public streets, public alleys, public ways, or buildings not associated with the manufacture or distribution of such gases in accordance with Table 63.3.7.2. [**55:7.7.2**]

63.3.7.2.1 Bulk hydrogen gas installations shall be in accordance with Chapter 10 of NFPA 55. [**55:7.7.2.1**]

63.3.7.2.1.1* Where a protective structure is used to protect compressed gas systems, the system shall terminate downstream of the source valve. [**55:7.7.2.1.1**]

63.3.7.2.1.2 The fire barrier wall shall be either an independent structure or the exterior wall of the building adjacent to the storage or use area. [**55:7.7.2.1.2**]

Δ **63.3.7.2.2*** Bulk gas systems for flammable gases shall be in accordance with Table 10.4.2.2.1(a), Table 10.4.2.2.1(b), or Table 10.4.2.2.1(c) of NFPA 55 where the quantity of flammable compressed gas exceeds 5000 scf (141.6 Nm^3). [**55:7.7.2.2**]

63.3.7.2.2.1 Where fire barriers are used as a means of distance reduction, fire barriers shall be in accordance with 10.4.2.2.4 of NFPA 55. [**55:7.7.2.2.1**]

63.3.7.2.2.2 Mobile acetylene trailer systems (MATS) shall be located in accordance with 15.2.3 of NFPA 55. [**55:7.7.2.2.2**]

63.3.7.2.3 The configuration of the protective structure shall be designed to allow natural ventilation to prevent the accumulation of hazardous gas concentrations. [**55:7.7.2.3**]

63.3.7.2.4 Storage and use of flammable compressed gases shall not be located within 50 ft (15.2 m) of air intakes or the minimum distance from a hydrogen bulk storage system as specified in Table 10.4.2.2.1(a), Table 10.4.2.2.1(b), or Table 10.4.2.2.1(c) of NFPA 55, whichever is less. [**55:7.7.2.4**]

63.3.7.2.5 Storage and use of flammable gases outside of buildings shall also be separated from building openings by 25 ft (7.6 m) or the minimum distance from a hydrogen bulk storage system as specified in Table 10.4.2.2.1(a), Table 10.4.2.2.1(b), or Table 10.4.2.2.1(c) of NFPA 55, whichever is less. [**55:7.7.2.5**]

Δ **Table 63.3.7.2 Distance to Exposures for Non-Bulk Flammable Gases**

Maximum Amount per Storage Area (scf)	Minimum Distance Between Storage Areas (ft)	Minimum Distance to Lot Lines of Property That Can Be Built Upon (ft)	Minimum Distance to Public Streets, Public Alleys or Public Ways (ft)	Minimum Distance to Buildings on the Same Property — Less Than 2-Hour Construction	2-Hour Construction	4-Hour Construction
0–4225	5	5	5	5	0	0
4226–21,125	10	10	10	10	5	0
21,126–50,700	10	15	15	20	5	0
50,701–84,500	10	20	20	20	5	0
84,501–200,000	20	25	25	20	5	0

For SI units, 1 ft = 304.8 mm; 1 scf = 0.02832 Nm^3.
Note: The minimum required distances does not apply where fire barriers without openings or penetrations having a minimum fire-resistive rating of 2 hours interrupt the line of sight between the storage and the exposure. The configuration of the fire barriers shall be designed to allow natural ventilation to prevent the accumulation of hazardous gas concentrations. [**55:Table 7.7.2**]

N **63.3.7.2.5.1** Fire barriers shall be permitted to be used as a means to separate storage areas from openings or a means of egress used to access the public way. [**55:**7.7.2.5.1]

N **63.3.7.2.6** Vents from tube trailers and fixed storage systems under weather protection shall discharge outside the weather protection. [**55:**7.7.2.6]

63.3.7.3 Indoor Non-Bulk Hydrogen Compressed Gas System Location.

Δ **63.3.7.3.1** Hydrogen systems of less than 5000 scf (141.6 Nm^3) and greater than the MAQ, where located inside buildings, shall be in accordance with the following:

(1) In a ventilated area in accordance with the provisions of 63.2.16
(2) Separated from incompatible materials in accordance with the provisions of 63.3.1.12.2
(3) A distance of 25 ft (7.6 m) from open flames and other sources of ignition
(4) A distance of 50 ft (15 m) from intakes of ventilation, air-conditioning equipment, and air compressors located in the same room or area as the hydrogen system
  (a) The distance shall be permitted to be reduced to 10 ft (3.1 m) where the room or area in which the hydrogen system is installed is protected by a listed detection system per Article 500.7(K) of *NFPA 70* and the detection system shuts down the fuel supply in the event of a leak that results in a concentration that exceeds 25 percent of the LFL
  (b) Emergency shutoff valves shall be provided in accordance with 63.3.4.1.11.
(5) A distance of 50 ft (15 m) from other flammable gas storage
(6) Protected against damage in accordance with the provisions of 63.3.1.10.4.

[**55:**10.3.5.1]

63.3.7.3.2 Systems Installed in One Room.

63.3.7.3.2.1 More than one system of 5000 scf (141.6 Nm^3) or less shall be permitted to be installed in the same room or area, provided the systems are separated by at least 50 ft (15 m) or a full-height fire-resistive partition having a minimum fire resistance rating of 2 hours is located between the systems. [**55:**10.3.5.2.1]

63.3.7.3.2.2 The separation distance between multiple systems of 5000 scf (141.6 Nm^3) or less shall be permitted to be reduced to 25 ft (7.6 m) in buildings where the space between storage areas is free of combustible materials and protected with a sprinkler system designed for Extra Hazard, Group 1 occupancies in accordance with the requirements of 63.2.10. [**55:**10.3.5.2.2]

63.3.7.3.2.3 The required separation distance between individual portable systems in the process of being filled or serviced in facilities associated with the manufacture or distribution of hydrogen and its mixtures shall not be limited by 63.3.7.3.2.1 or 63.3.7.3.2.2 when such facilities are provided with Protection Level 2 controls and the applicable requirements of Chapters 1 through 7 of NFPA 55. [**55:**10.3.5.2.3]

N **63.3.7.4 Outdoor Non-Bulk Hydrogen Compressed Gas Location.**

N **63.3.7.4.1** The outdoor storage or use of non-bulk gaseous hydrogen shall be in accordance with 63.3.7.2. [**55:**10.3.6.1]

Δ **63.3.7.5 Maintenance.**

63.3.7.5.1 Maintenance shall be performed annually by a qualified representative of the equipment owner. [**55:**10.3.7.1]

63.3.7.5.2 The maintenance shall include inspection for physical damage, leak tightness, ground system integrity, vent system operation, equipment identification, warning signs, operator information and training records, scheduled maintenance and retest records, alarm operation, and other safety-related features. [**55:**10.3.7.2]

63.3.7.5.3 Scheduled maintenance and retest activities shall be formally documented, and records shall be maintained a minimum of 3 years. [**55:**10.3.7.3]

63.3.7.6 Ignition Source Control. Ignition sources in areas containing flammable gases shall be in accordance with 63.3.7.6. [**55:**7.7.3]

63.3.7.6.1 Static Producing Equipment. Static producing equipment located in flammable gas areas shall be grounded. [**55:**7.7.3.1]

63.3.7.6.2 No Smoking or Open Flame. Signs shall be posted in areas containing flammable gases stating that smoking or the use of open flame, or both, is prohibited within 25 ft (7.6 m) of the storage or use area perimeter. [**55:**7.7.3.2]

63.3.7.6.3 Heating. Heating, where provided, shall be by indirect means. Equipment used for heating applications in rooms or areas where flammable gases are stored or used shall be listed and labeled for use in hazardous environments established by the gases present and shall be installed in accordance with the conditions of the listing and the manufacturer's installation instructions. [**55:**7.7.3.3]

63.3.7.7 Electrical. Areas in which the storage or use of compressed gases exceeds the quantity thresholds for gases requiring special provisions shall be in accordance with *NFPA 70*. [**55:**7.7.4]

63.3.7.8 Maintenance of Piping Systems.

63.3.7.8.1 Maintenance of flammable gas system piping and components shall be performed annually by a qualified representative of the equipment owner. [**55:**7.7.5.1]

63.3.7.8.2 This maintenance shall include inspection for physical damage, leak tightness, ground system integrity, vent system operation, equipment identification, warning signs, operator information and training records, scheduled maintenance and retest records, alarm operation, and other safety-related features. [**55:**7.7.5.2]

63.3.7.8.3 Scheduled maintenance and retest activities shall be formally documented, and records shall be maintained a minimum of 3 years. [**55:**7.7.5.3]

63.3.8 Oxidizing Gases.

63.3.8.1 General. The storage or use of oxidizing compressed gases exceeding the quantity thresholds for gases requiring special provisions as specified in Table 63.2.3.1.1 shall be in accordance with Chapters 1 through 6 of NFPA 55 and 63.3.1 through 63.3.4 and 63.3.8. [55:7.8.1]

63.3.8.2 Distance to Exposures. The outdoor storage or use of oxidizing compressed gas shall be in accordance with Table 63.3.8.2. [55:7.8.2]

63.3.8.2.1 The distances shall not apply where fire barriers having a minimum fire resistance of 2 hours interrupt the line of sight between the container and the exposure. [55:7.8.2.1]

63.3.8.2.1.1* Where a fire barrier is used to protect compressed gas systems, the system shall terminate downstream of the source valve. [55:7.8.2.1.1]

63.3.8.2.1.2 The fire barrier wall shall be either an independent structure or the exterior wall of the building adjacent to the storage or use area. [55:7.8.2.1.2]

63.3.8.2.2 The fire barrier shall be at least 5 ft (1.5 m) from the storage or use area perimeter. [55:7.8.2.2]

63.3.8.2.3 The configuration of the fire barrier shall allow natural ventilation to prevent the accumulation of hazardous gas concentrations. [55:7.8.2.3]

63.3.9 Pyrophoric Gases.

63.3.9.1 General. Pyrophoric compressed gases exceeding the quantity thresholds for gases requiring special provisions as specified in Table 63.2.3.1.1 shall be stored and used in accordance with Chapters 1 through 6 of NFPA 55 and 63.3.1 through 63.3.4 and 63.3.9. [55:7.9.1]

63.3.9.2 Silane and Silane Mixtures. Silane and silane mixtures shall be stored, used, and handled in accordance with the provisions of ANSI/CGA G-13, *Storage and Handling of Silane and Silane Mixtures*. [55:7.9.2]

63.3.9.3 Distance to Exposures. The outdoor storage or use of pyrophoric compressed gas shall be in accordance with Table 63.3.9.3. [55:7.9.3]

63.3.9.3.1 The distances shall be allowed to be reduced to 5 ft (1.5 m) where fire barriers having a minimum fire resistance of 2 hours interrupt the line of sight between the container and the exposure. [55:7.9.3.1]

63.3.9.3.1.1* Where a fire barrier is used to protect compressed gas systems, the system shall terminate downstream of the source valve. [55:7.9.3.1.1]

63.3.9.3.1.2 The fire barrier shall be either an independent structure or the exterior wall of the building adjacent to the storage or use area. [55:7.9.3.1.2]

63.3.9.3.1.3 The fire barrier shall be at least 5 ft (1.5 m) from the storage or use area perimeter. [55:7.9.3.1.3]

63.3.9.3.1.4 The configuration of the fire barrier shall allow natural ventilation to prevent the accumulation of hazardous gas concentrations. [55:7.9.3.1.4]

63.3.9.3.2 Storage and use of pyrophoric gases outside buildings shall be separated from building openings by 25 ft (7.6 m). [55:7.9.3.2]

63.3.9.3.2.1 Fire barriers shall be permitted to be used as a means to separate storage areas from building openings that are used to access the public way. [55:7.9.3.2.1]

63.3.10 Toxic and Highly Toxic Gases.

63.3.10.1 General. The storage or use of toxic or highly toxic gases exceeding the quantity thresholds for gases that require special provisions as specified in Table 63.2.3.1.1 shall be in accordance with Chapters 1 through 6 of NFPA 55 and 63.3.1 through 63.3.4 and 63.3.10. [55:7.10.1]

Δ **Table 63.3.8.2 Distance to Exposures for Oxidizing Gases**

Quantity of Gas Stored (at NTP)		Distance to a Building Not Associated with the Manufacture or Distribution of Oxidizing Gases or to a Public Way or Property Line		Minimum Distance Between Storage Areas	
scf	Nm³	ft	m	ft	m
0–50,000	0–1416	5	1.5	5	1.5
50,001–100,000	1417–2832	10	3.0	10	3.0
≥100,001	≥2833	15	4.6	15	4.6

[55: Table 7.8.2]

Δ **Table 63.3.9.3 Distance to Exposures for Pyrophoric Gases**

Maximum Amount per Storage Area		Minimum Distance Between Storage Areas		Minimum Distance to Property Lines		Minimum Distance to Public Ways		Minimum Distance to Buildings on the Same Property					
									Less Than 2-Hour Construction		2-Hour Construction		4-Hour Construction	
scf	Nm³	ft	m	ft	m	ft	m	ft	m	ft	m	ft	m
250	7.1	5	1.5	25	7.6	5	1.5	5	1.5	0	0	0	0
>250 to 2500	>7.1 to 71.0	10	3.0	50	15.2	10	3.0	10	3.0	5	1.5	0	0
>2500 to 7500	>71.0 to 212.4	20	6.0	100	30.5	20	6.0	20	6.0	10	3.0	0	0

[55:Table 7.9.3]

63.3.10.2 Ventilation and Arrangement.

63.3.10.2.1 Indoors. The indoor storage or use of highly toxic gases or toxic gases shall be provided with a gas cabinet, exhausted enclosure, or gas room. [55:7.10.2.1]

63.3.10.2.1.1 Gas cabinets shall be in accordance with 63.2.17. [55:7.10.2.1.1]

63.3.10.2.1.2 Exhausted enclosures shall be in accordance with 63.2.18. [55:7.10.2.1.2]

63.3.10.2.1.3 Gas rooms shall be in accordance with 63.2.4. [55:7.10.2.1.3]

63.3.10.2.2 Distance to Exposures. The outdoor storage or use of toxic or highly toxic compressed gases shall not be within 75 ft (23 m) of lot lines, streets, alleys, public ways or means of egress, or buildings not associated with such storage or use. [55:7.10.2.2]

63.3.10.2.2.1 A 2-hour fire barrier wall without openings or penetrations that extends not less than 30 in. (762 mm) above and to the sides of the storage or use area and that interrupts the line of sight between the storage or use area and the exposure shall be permitted in lieu of the 75 ft (23 m) distance. [55:7.10.2.2.1]

63.3.10.2.2.1.1* Where a fire barrier is used to protect compressed gas systems, the system shall terminate downstream of the source valve. [55:7.10.2.2.1.1]

63.3.10.2.2.1.2 The fire barrier wall shall be either an independent structure or the exterior wall of the building adjacent to the storage or use area. [55:7.10.2.2.1.2]

63.3.10.2.2.1.3 The 2-hour fire barrier wall shall be located at least 5 ft (1.5 m) from any exposure. [55:7.10.2.2.1.3]

63.3.10.2.2.1.4 The 2-hour fire barrier wall shall not have more than two sides at approximately 90 degree (1.5 rad) directions or more than three sides with connecting angles of approximately 135 degrees (2.36 rad). [55:7.10.2.2.1.4]

N 63.3.10.2.2.1.5 The minimum distance requirement for exposures shall be reduced to 5 ft (1.5 m) from buildings and 25 ft (7.6 m) from exit discharges where gases are stored in gas cabinets as specified in this *Code*. [55:7.10.2.2.1.5]

63.3.10.2.2.2 Where the storage or use area is located closer than 75 ft (23 m) to a building not associated with the manufacture or distribution of toxic or highly toxic compressed gases, openings in the building other than for piping shall not be permitted above the height of the top of the 2-hour fire barrier wall or within 50 ft (15 m) horizontally from the storage area, regardless of whether the openings are shielded by a fire barrier. [55:7.10.2.2.2]

63.3.10.2.3 Air Intakes. Storage and use of toxic or highly toxic compressed gases shall not be located within 75 ft (23 m) of air intakes. [55:7.10.2.3]

63.3.10.3 Treatment Systems. Except as provided in 63.3.10.3.1 and 63.3.10.3.2, gas cabinets, exhausted enclosures, and gas rooms containing toxic or highly toxic gases shall be provided with exhaust ventilation, with all exhaust directed to a treatment system designed to process accidental release of gas. [55:7.10.3]

63.3.10.3.1 Storage of Toxic or Highly Toxic Gases. Treatment systems shall not be required for toxic or highly toxic gases in storage where cylinders, containers, and tanks are provided with the controls specified in 63.3.10.3.1.1 through 63.3.10.3.1.3. [55:7.10.3.1]

63.3.10.3.1.1 Valve Outlets Protected. Valve outlets shall be equipped with outlet plugs or caps, or both, rated for the container service pressure. [55:7.10.3.1.1]

63.3.10.3.1.2 Handwheels Secured. Where provided, handwheel-operated valves shall be secured to prevent movement. [55:7.10.3.1.2]

63.3.10.3.1.3 Containment Devices Provided. Approved cylinder containment vessels or cylinder containment systems shall be provided at an approved location. [55:7.10.3.1.3]

63.3.10.3.2 Use of Toxic Gases. Treatment systems shall not be required for toxic gases in use where cylinders, containers, and tanks are provided with the controls specified in 63.3.10.3.2.1 and 63.3.10.3.2.2. [55:7.10.3.2]

63.3.10.3.2.1 Gas Detection.

63.3.10.3.2.1.1 A gas detection system with a sensing interval not exceeding 5 minutes shall be provided. [55:7.10.3.2.1.1]

63.3.10.3.2.1.2 The gas detection system shall monitor the exhaust system at the point of discharge from the gas cabinet, exhausted enclosure, or gas room. [55:7.10.3.2.1.2]

63.3.10.3.2.2 Fail-Safe Automatic Closing Valve. An approved automatic-closing fail-safe valve shall be located on or immediately adjacent to and downstream of active cylinder, container, or tank valves. [55:7.10.3.2.2]

63.3.10.3.2.2.1 The fail-safe valve shall close when gas is detected at the permissible exposure limit, short-term exposure limit (STEL), or ceiling limit by the gas detection system. [55:7.10.3.2.2.1]

63.3.10.3.2.2.2 For attended operations, a manual closing valve shall be permitted when in accordance with 63.3.10.3.4.3. [55:7.10.3.2.2.2]

63.3.10.3.2.2.3 For gases used at unattended operations for the protection of public health, such as chlorine at water or wastewater treatment sites, the automatic valve shall close if the concentration of gas detected by a gas detection system reaches one-half of the IDLH. [55:7.10.3.2.2.3]

63.3.10.3.2.2.4 The gas detection system shall also alert persons on-site and a responsible person off-site when the gas concentration in the storage/use area reaches the OSHA PEL, OSHA ceiling limit, or OSHA STEL for the gas employed. [55:7.10.3.2.2.4]

63.3.10.3.3 Treatment System Design and Performance. Treatment systems shall be capable of diluting, adsorbing, absorbing, containing, neutralizing, burning, or otherwise processing stored or used toxic or highly toxic gas, or both. [55:7.10.3.3]

63.3.10.3.3.1 Where a total containment system is used, the system shall be designed to handle the maximum anticipated pressure of release to the system when it reaches equilibrium. [55:7.10.3.3.1]

63.3.10.3.3.2 Treatment systems shall be capable of reducing the allowable discharge concentrations to one-half the IDLH threshold at the point of discharge. [55:7.10.3.3.2]

63.3.10.3.4 Treatment System Sizing.

63.3.10.3.4.1 Worst-Case Release of Gas. Treatment systems shall be sized to process the maximum worst-case release of gas based on the maximum flow rate of release from the largest vessel utilized in accordance with 63.3.10.3.4.2. [55:7.10.3.4.1]

63.3.10.3.4.2 Largest Compressed Gas Vessel. The entire contents of the single largest compressed gas vessel shall be considered. [55:7.10.3.4.2]

63.3.10.3.4.3 Attended Operations — Alternative Method of System Sizing.

63.3.10.3.4.3.1 Where source cylinders, containers, and tanks are used in attended process operations, with an operator present at the enclosure where the activity occurs, the volume of the release shall be limited to the estimated amount released from the process piping system within a period not to exceed 5 minutes. [55:7.10.3.4.3.1]

63.3.10.3.4.3.2 Such process piping systems shall comply with the requirements of 63.3.10.3.4.3.2(A) through 63.3.10.3.4.3.2(E). [55:7.10.3.4.3.2]

(A) Local Exhaust. All gas transfer operations shall be conducted within a zone of local exhaust that is connected to a treatment system. [55:7.10.3.4.3.2(A)]

(B) Gas Detection. Gas detection shall be used to provide a warning to alert the operators to emission of gas into the zone of local exhaust, and the following requirements also shall apply:

(1) The system shall be capable of detecting gas at the PEL or the ceiling limit for the gas being processed.
(2) Activation of the gas detection system shall provide a local alarm.

[55:7.10.3.4.3.2(B)]

(C) Process Shutdown. Operations involving the gas detected shall be shut down and leaks repaired. [55:7.10.3.4.3.2(C)]

(D) Piping System Construction. Piping systems used to convey gases shall be of all-welded construction throughout, with the exception of fittings used to connect cylinders, containers, or tanks, or any combination thereof, to the process system. [55:7.10.3.4.3.2(D)]

(E) Piping System Accessibility. Piping systems shall be designed to provide for readily accessible manual shutdown controls. [55:7.10.3.4.3.2(E)]

63.3.10.3.5 Rate of Release. The time release shall be in accordance with Table 63.3.10.3.5 for the type of container indicated. [55:7.10.3.5]

63.3.10.3.6* Maximum Flow Rate of Release.

63.3.10.3.6.1 For portable cylinders, containers, and tanks, the maximum flow rate of release shall be calculated based on assuming the total release from the cylinder or tank within the time specified. [55:7.10.3.6.1]

Δ **63.3.10.3.6.2*** When portable cylinders, containers, or tanks are equipped with reduced flow orifices, the worst-case rate of

Δ **Table 63.3.10.3.5 Rate of Release**

	Time Release	
Container Type	Nonliquefied Gases	Liquefied Gases
Cylinders without restrictive flow orifices	5 minutes	30 minutes
Portable tanks without restrictive flow orifices	40 minutes	240 minutes
All others	Based on peak flow from maximum valve orifice	Based on peak flow from maximum valve orifice

[55: Table 7.10.3.5]

release shall be determined by the maximum achievable flow from the valve based on the following formula:

[63.3.10.3.6.2]

$$CFM = (767 \times A \times P)\frac{(28.96/MW)^{1/2}}{60}$$

where:
CFM = standard cubic feet per minute of gas of concern under flow conditions
A = area of orifice in square inches *(See Table A.63.3.10.3.6 for areas of typical restricted flow orifices.)*
P = supply pressure of gas at NTP in pounds per square inch absolute
MW = molecular weight

[55:7.10.3.6.2]

63.3.10.3.6.3 For mixtures, the average of the molecular weights shall be used. [55:7.10.3.6.3]

63.3.10.4 Leaking Cylinders, Containers, and Tanks. When cylinders, containers, or tanks are used outdoors in excess of the quantities specified in Table 63.2.3.1.1 in the column for unsprinklered areas (unprotected by gas cabinets or exhausted enclosures), a gas cabinet, exhausted enclosure, or containment vessel or system shall be provided to control leaks from leaking cylinders, containers, and tanks in accordance with 63.3.10.4.1 through 63.3.10.4.2.3. [55:7.10.4]

63.3.10.4.1 Gas Cabinets or Exhausted Enclosures. Where gas cabinets or exhausted enclosures are provided to handle leaks from cylinders, containers, or tanks, exhaust ventilation shall be provided that is directed to a treatment system in accordance with the provisions of 63.3.10.3. [55:7.10.4.1]

63.3.10.4.2 Containment Vessels or Systems. Where containment vessels or containment systems are provided, they shall comply with the requirements of 63.3.10.4.2.1 through 63.3.10.4.2.3. [55:7.10.4.2]

63.3.10.4.2.1 Performance. Containment vessels or containment systems shall be capable of fully containing or terminating a release. [55:7.10.4.2.1]

63.3.10.4.2.2 Personnel. Trained personnel capable of operating the containment vessel or containment system shall be available at an approved location. [55:7.10.4.2.2]

63.3.10.4.2.3 Location. Containment vessels or systems shall be capable of being transported to the leaking cylinder, container, or tank. [55:7.10.4.2.3]

63.3.10.5 Emergency Power.

63.3.10.5.1 General. Emergency power shall comply with the requirements of 63.3.10.5 in accordance with *NFPA 70*. [55:7.10.5.1]

63.3.10.5.2 Alternative to Emergency Power. Emergency power shall not be required where fail-safe engineering is provided for mechanical exhaust ventilation, treatment systems, and temperature control, and standby power is provided to alternative systems that utilize electrical energy. [55:7.10.5.2]

63.3.10.5.3 Where Required. Emergency power shall be provided for the following systems:

(1) Exhaust ventilation
(2) Treatment system
(3) Gas detection system
(4) Temperature control system
(5) Required alarm systems

[55:7.10.5.3]

63.3.10.5.4 Level. Emergency power systems shall comply with the requirements for a Level 2 system in accordance with NFPA 110. [55:7.10.5.4]

63.3.10.6 Gas Detection. Except as provided in 63.3.10.6.1, a continuous gas detection system in accordance with the requirements of 63.3.10.6.2 through 63.3.10.6.6 shall be provided for the indoor storage or use of toxic or highly toxic compressed gases. [55:7.10.6]

63.3.10.6.1 Where Gas Detection Is Not Required. A gas detection system shall not be required for toxic gases where the physiological warning properties for the gas are at a level below the accepted PEL or the ceiling limit for the gas. [55:7.10.6.1]

63.3.10.6.2 Local Alarm. The gas detection system shall initiate a local alarm that is both audible and visible. [55:7.10.6.2]

63.3.10.6.3 Alarm Monitored. The gas detection system shall transmit a signal to a constantly attended control station for quantities exceeding one toxic or highly toxic compressed gas cylinder. [55:7.10.6.3]

63.3.10.6.4 Automatic Shutdown.

63.3.10.6.4.1 Activation of the gas detection system shall automatically shut off the flow of gas related to the system being monitored. [55:7.10.6.4.1]

63.3.10.6.4.2 An automatic shutdown shall not be required for reactors utilized for the production of toxic or highly toxic gases when such reactors are operated at gauge pressures less than 15 psi (103.4 kPa), constantly attended, and provided with readily accessible emergency shutoff valves. [55:7.10.6.4.2]

63.3.10.6.5 Detection Points. Detection shall be provided at the locations specified in 63.3.10.6.5.1 through 63.3.10.6.5.4. [55:7.10.6.5]

63.3.10.6.5.1 Treatment System Discharge. Detection shall be provided at the discharge from the treatment system. [55:7.10.6.5.1]

63.3.10.6.5.2 Point of Use. Detection shall be provided in the room or area in which the gas is used. [55:7.10.6.5.2]

63.3.10.6.5.3 Source. Detection shall be provided at the source cylinder, container, or tank used for delivery of the gas to the point of use. [55:7.10.6.5.3]

63.3.10.6.5.4 Storage. Detection shall be provided in the room or area in which the gas is stored. [55:7.10.6.5.4]

63.3.10.6.6 Level of Detection. The gas detection system shall detect the presence of gas at or below the PEL or the ceiling limit of the gas for those points identified in 63.3.10.6.5.2 and 63.3.10.6.5.3 and at not less than one-half the IDLH level for points identified in 63.3.10.6.5.1. [55:7.10.6.6]

63.3.10.7 Automatic Smoke Detection System. An automatic smoke detection system shall be provided for the indoor storage or use of highly toxic compressed gases in accordance with *NFPA 72*. [55:7.10.7]

63.3.11 Unstable Reactive Gases (Nondetonable). The storage or use of unstable reactive (nondetonable) gases exceeding the quantity thresholds for gases requiring special provisions as specified in Table 63.2.3.1.1 shall be in accordance with Chapters 1 through 6 of NFPA 55 and 63.3.1 through 63.3.4 and 63.3.11. [55:7.11]

63.3.11.1 Distances to Exposures for Class 2.

63.3.11.1.1 The outdoor storage or use of unstable reactive Class 2 compressed gas shall not be within 20 ft (6 m) of buildings, lot lines, streets, alleys, or public ways or means of egress. [55:7.11.1.1]

63.3.11.1.2 A 2-hour fire barrier wall without openings or penetrations shall be permitted in lieu of the 20 ft (6 m) distance required by 63.3.11.1.1. [55:7.11.1.2]

63.3.11.1.2.1* Where a fire barrier wall is used to protect compressed gas systems, the system shall terminate downstream of the source valve. [55:7.11.1.2.1]

63.3.11.1.2.2 The fire barrier wall shall be either an independent structure or the exterior wall of the building. [55:7.11.1.2.2]

63.3.11.1.2.3 The 2-hour fire barrier wall shall be located at least 5 ft (1.5 m) from any exposure. [55:7.11.1.2.3]

63.3.11.1.2.4 The 2-hour fire barrier wall shall not have more than two sides at approximately 90 degree (1.57 rad) directions or not more than three sides with connecting angles of approximately 135 degrees (2.36 rad). [55:7.11.1.2.4]

63.3.11.2 Distances to Exposures for Class 3.

63.3.11.2.1 The outdoor storage or use of unstable reactive Class 3 (nondetonable) compressed gas shall not be within 75 ft (23 m) of buildings, lot lines, streets, alleys, or public ways or means of egress. [55:7.11.2.1]

63.3.11.2.2 A 2-hour fire barrier wall without openings or penetrations, extending not less than 30 in. (762 mm) above and to the sides of the storage or use area, that interrupts the line of sight between the storage or use and the exposure shall be permitted in lieu of the 75 ft (23 m) distance specified in 63.3.11.2.1. [55:7.11.2.2]

63.3.11.2.2.1* Where a fire barrier wall is used to protect compressed gas systems, the system shall terminate downstream of the source valve. [55:7.11.2.2.1]

63.3.11.2.2.2 The fire barrier wall shall be either an independent structure or the exterior wall of the building adjacent to the storage or use area. [55:7.11.2.2.2]

63.3.11.2.2.3 The 2-hour fire barrier wall shall be located at least 5 ft (1.5 m) from any exposure. [55:7.11.2.2.3]

63.3.11.2.2.4 The 2-hour fire barrier wall shall not have more than two sides at approximately 90 degree (1.57 rad) directions or more than three sides with connecting angles of approximately 135 degrees (2.36 rad). [55:7.11.2.2.4]

63.3.11.3 Storage Configuration.

63.3.11.3.1 Unstable reactive Class 3 compressed gases stored in cylinders, containers, or tanks shall be arranged to limit individual groups of cylinders, containers, or tanks to areas not exceeding 100 ft^2 (9.3 m^2). [55:7.11.3.1]

63.3.11.3.2 Multiple areas shall be separated by aisles. [55:7.11.3.2]

63.3.11.3.3 Aisle widths shall not be less than the height of the cylinders, containers, or tanks or 4 ft (1.2 m), whichever is greater. [55:7.11.3.3]

63.3.11.4 Basements. Unstable reactive compressed gases shall not be stored in basements. [55:7.11.4]

63.3.11.5 Unstable Reactive Gases (Detonable).

63.3.11.5.1 Storage or Use. The storage or use of unstable reactive (detonable) gases exceeding the quantity thresholds for gases requiring special provisions as specified in Table 63.2.3.1.1 shall be in accordance with Chapters 1 through 6 of NFPA 55, 63.3.1 through 63.3.4, and 63.3.11.5. [55:7.11.5.1]

63.3.11.5.2 Location. The location of storage areas shall be determined based on the requirements of the building code for explosive materials. [55:7.11.5.2]

N **63.3.12 Subatmospheric Gas (Type 1 and Type 2) Sources.**

N **63.3.12.1 General.** The storage and use of subatmospheric gas (type 1 and type 2) sources shall meet the requirements of 7.14.2.1 through 7.14.2.6 in NFPA 318. [55:7.12.1]

N **63.3.12.1.1** Where the storage and use of subatmospheric gas (type 1 and type 2) sources do not meet the requirement in 63.3.11.1.1, the storage and use of subatmospheric gas (type 1 and type 2) shall meet all the requirements of this standard based on the assigned hazard categories listed in Section 5.1 of NFPA 55. [55:7.12.1.1]

63.4 Cryogenic Fluids.

Δ **63.4.1 General.** This section shall apply to all cryogenic fluids, including those fluids regulated elsewhere in this *Code*, except that where specific requirements are provided in other sections, those specific requirements shall apply in accordance with the applicable chapter. [55:8.1]

63.4.1.1 Storage, use, and handling of cryogenic fluids shall be in accordance with Chapters 1 through 6 of NFPA 55 and Section 63.4 as applicable. [55:8.1.1]

N **63.4.1.2** Storage, use, and handling of inert cryogenic fluids shall be in accordance with CGA P-18, *Standard for Bulk Inert Gas Systems*. [55:8.1.2]

N **63.4.1.3** Storage, use, and handling of inert cryogenic fluids in medical gas applications shall be in accordance with Chapter 17 and ANSI/CGA M-1, *Standard for Medical Gas Supply Systems at Health Care Facilities*, in addition to the provisions stated herein. [55:8.1.3]

Δ **63.4.2* Containers — Design, Construction, and Maintenance.** Containers employed for the storage or use of cryogenic fluids shall be designed, fabricated, tested, marked (i.e., stamped), and maintained in accordance with Department of Transportation (DOT) regulations, Transport Canada's (TC) *Transportation of Dangerous Goods Regulations*, the ASME *Boiler and Pressure Vessel Code*, or regulations of other administering agencies. [55:8.2]

63.4.2.1 Aboveground Tanks. Aboveground tanks for the storage of cryogenic fluids shall be in accordance with 63.4.2.1. [55:8.2.1]

63.4.2.1.1 Construction of the Inner Vessel. The inner vessel of storage tanks in cryogenic fluid service shall be designed and constructed in accordance with the ASME *Boiler and Pressure Vessel Code* and shall be vacuum jacketed in accordance with 63.4.2.1.2. [55:8.2.1.1]

63.4.2.1.2 Construction of the Vacuum Jacket (Outer Vessel).

63.4.2.1.2.1 The vacuum jacket used as an outer vessel for storage tanks in cryogenic fluid service shall be designed to withstand the maximum internal and external pressure to which it will be subjected under operating conditions, including emergency pressure relief of the annular space between the inner vessel and the outer vessel. [55:8.2.1.2.1]

63.4.2.1.2.2 The jacket shall be designed to withstand a minimum collapsing pressure differential of 30 psi (207 kPa). [55:8.2.1.2.2]

63.4.2.1.2.3 Vacuum Level Monitoring.

63.4.2.1.2.3.1 A connection shall be provided on the exterior of the vacuum jacket to allow measurement of the pressure within the annular space between the inner vessel and the outer vessel. [55:8.2.1.2.3.1]

63.4.2.1.2.3.2 The connection shall be fitted with a bellows-sealed or diaphragm-type valve equipped with a vacuum gauge tube that is shielded to protect against damage from impact. [55:8.2.1.2.3.2]

63.4.2.2 Nonstandard Containers.

63.4.2.2.1 Containers, equipment, and devices that are not in compliance with recognized standards for design and construction shall be permitted if approved by the AHJ upon presentation of evidence that they are designed and constructed for safe operation. [55:8.2.2.1]

63.4.2.2.2 The following data shall be submitted to the AHJ with reference to the deviation from the standard with the application for approval:

(1) Type and use of container, equipment, or device
(2) Material to be stored, used, or transported
(3) Description showing dimensions and materials used in construction
(4) Design pressure, maximum operating pressure, and test pressure
(5) Type, size, and setting of pressure relief devices

[**55:8.2.2.2**]

63.4.2.3 Foundations and Supports. Stationary tanks shall be provided with concrete or masonry foundations or structural steel supports on firm concrete or masonry foundations, and the requirements of 63.4.2.3.1 through 63.4.2.3.5 also shall apply. [**55:8.2.3**]

63.4.2.3.1 Excessive Loads. Stationary tanks shall be supported to prevent the concentration of excessive loads on the supporting portion of the shell. [**55:8.2.3.1**]

63.4.2.3.2 Expansion and Contraction. Foundations for horizontal containers shall be constructed to accommodate expansion and contraction of the container. [**55:8.2.3.2**]

63.4.2.3.3* Support of Ancillary Equipment.

63.4.2.3.3.1 Foundations shall be provided to support the weight of vaporizers or heat exchangers. [**55:8.2.3.3.1**]

63.4.2.3.3.2 Foundations shall be designed to withstand soil and frost conditions as well as the anticipated seismic, snow, wind, and hydrostatic loading under operating conditions. [**55:8.2.3.3.2**]

63.4.2.3.4 Temperature Effects. Where drainage systems, terrain, or surfaces beneath stationary tanks are arranged in a manner that can subject stationary tank foundations or supports to temperatures below −130°F (−90°C), the foundations or supports shall be constructed of materials that are capable of withstanding the low-temperature effects of cryogenic fluid spillage. [**55:8.2.3.4**]

63.4.2.3.5 Corrosion Protection. Portions of stationary tanks in contact with foundations or saddles shall be painted to protect against corrosion. [**55:8.2.3.5**]

63.4.2.4 Pressure Relief Devices.

63.4.2.4.1 General.

N **63.4.2.4.1.1** Where a bulk gas source system is connected to an indoor cryogenic fluid piping system protected by a pressure relief device that is designed to protect against exceeding the maximum allowable working pressure or maximum process operating pressure, releases shall be directed to a safe location outdoors to the open air. [**55:8.2.4.1.1**]

63.4.2.4.1.2 Pressure relief devices shall be provided to protect containers and piping systems containing cryogenic fluids from damage due to overpressure. [**55:8.2.4.1.2**]

63.4.2.4.1.3 Pressure relief devices shall be designed in accordance with CGA S-1.1, *Pressure Relief Device Standards — Part 1 — Cylinders for Compressed Gases*, and CGA S-1.2, *Pressure Relief Device Standards — Part 2 — Portable Containers for Compressed Gases*, for portable tanks; and CGA S-1.3, *Pressure Relief Device Standards — Part 3 — Stationary Storage Containers for Compressed Gases*, for stationary tanks. [**55:8.2.4.1.3**]

63.4.2.4.2 Containers Open to the Atmosphere. Portable containers that are open to the atmosphere and are designed to contain cryogenic fluids at atmospheric pressure shall not be required to be equipped with pressure relief devices. [**55:8.2.4.2**]

63.4.2.4.3 Equipment Other Than Containers. Heat exchangers, vaporizers, insulation casings surrounding containers, vessels, and coaxial piping systems in which liquefied cryogenic fluids could be trapped due to leakage from the primary container shall be provided with a pressure relief device. [**55:8.2.4.3**]

63.4.2.4.4 Sizing.

63.4.2.4.4.1 Pressure relief devices shall be sized in accordance with the specifications to which the container was fabricated. [**55:8.2.4.4.1**]

63.4.2.4.4.2 The pressure relief device shall have the capacity to prevent the maximum design pressure of the container or system from being exceeded. [**55:8.2.4.4.2**]

63.4.2.4.5 Accessibility. Pressure relief devices shall be located such that they are accessible for inspection and repair. [**55:8.2.4.5**]

63.4.2.4.5.1* ASME pressure relief valves shall be made to be tamper resistant in order to prevent adjusting of the set pressure by other than authorized personnel. [**55:8.2.4.5.1**]

63.4.2.4.5.2 Non-ASME pressure relief valves shall not be field adjusted. [**55:8.2.4.5.2**]

63.4.2.4.6 Arrangement.

63.4.2.4.6.1 Pressure Relief Devices. Pressure relief devices shall be arranged to discharge unobstructed to the open air in such a manner as to prevent impingement of escaping gas on personnel, containers, equipment, and adjacent structures or its entrance into enclosed spaces. [**55:8.2.4.6.1**]

63.4.2.4.6.2 Portable Containers with Volume Less Than 2.0 scf (0.057 Nm³).

63.4.2.4.6.2.1 The arrangement of the discharge from pressure relief devices from DOT-specified containers with an internal water volume of 2.0 scf (0.057 Nm³) or less shall be incorporated in the design of the container. [**55:8.2.4.6.2.1**]

63.4.2.4.6.2.2 Additional safeguards regarding placement or arrangement shall not be required. [**55:8.2.4.6.2.2**]

63.4.2.4.7 Shutoffs Between Pressure Relief Devices and Containers.

63.4.2.4.7.1 General. Shutoff valves installed between pressure relief devices and containers shall be in accordance with 63.4.2.4.7. [**55:8.2.4.7.1**]

63.4.2.4.7.2 Location. Shutoff valves shall not be installed between pressure relief devices and containers unless the valves or their use meet the requirements of 63.4.2.4.7.2.1 or 63.4.2.4.7.2.2. [**55:8.2.4.7.2**]

63.4.2.4.7.2.1* Security. Shutoff valves shall be locked in the open position, and their use shall be limited to service-related work performed by the supplier under the requirements of the ASME *Boiler and Pressure Vessel Code*. [55:8.2.4.7.2.1]

63.4.2.4.7.2.2 Multiple Pressure Relief Devices. Shutoff valves controlling multiple pressure relief devices on a container shall be installed so that either the type of valve installed or the arrangement provides the full required flow through the relief devices at all times. [55:8.2.4.7.2.2]

63.4.2.4.8 Temperature Limits. Pressure relief devices shall not be subjected to cryogenic fluid temperatures except when operating. [55:8.2.4.8]

63.4.3 Pressure Relief Vent Piping.

63.4.3.1 General. Pressure relief vent piping systems shall be constructed and arranged to direct the flow of gas to a safe location and in accordance with 63.4.3. [55:8.3.1]

63.4.3.2 Sizing. Pressure relief device vent piping shall have a cross-sectional area not less than that of the pressure relief device vent opening and shall be arranged so as not to restrict the flow of escaping gas. [55:8.3.2]

63.4.3.3 Arrangement. Pressure relief device vent piping and drains in vent lines shall be arranged so that escaping gas discharges unobstructed to the open air and does not impinge on personnel, containers, equipment, and adjacent structures or enter enclosed spaces. [55:8.3.3]

63.4.3.4 Installation. Pressure relief device vent lines shall be installed in a manner that excludes or removes moisture and condensation to prevent malfunction of the pressure relief device due to freezing or ice accumulation. [55:8.3.4]

63.4.3.5 Overfilling. Controls shall be provided to prevent overfilling of stationary containers. [55:8.3.5]

63.4.4 Marking.

63.4.4.1 General. Cryogenic containers and systems shall be marked in accordance with nationally recognized standards and in accordance with 63.4.4. [55:8.4.1]

63.4.4.1.1 Portable Containers.

63.4.4.1.1.1 Portable cryogenic containers shall be marked in accordance with CGA C-7, *Guide to Classification and Labeling of Compressed Gases*. [55:8.4.1.1.1]

63.4.4.1.1.2* All DOT-4L/TC-4LM liquid cylinders shall have product identification visible from all directions with minimum 2 in. (51 mm) high letters. [55:8.4.1.1.2]

63.4.4.1.2 Stationary Tanks. Stationary tanks shall be marked in accordance with NFPA 704. [55:8.4.1.2]

63.4.4.1.3 Identification Signs. Visible hazard identification signs shall be provided in accordance with NFPA 704 at entrances to buildings or areas in which cryogenic fluids are stored, handled, or used. [55:8.4.1.3]

63.4.4.2 Identification of Contents. Stationary containers shall be placarded with the identity of their contents to indicate the name of the material contained. [55:8.4.2]

63.4.4.3 Container Specification. Stationary containers shall be marked with the manufacturing specification and maximum allowable working pressure on a permanent nameplate. [55:8.4.3]

63.4.4.3.1 The nameplate shall be installed on the container in an accessible location. [55:8.4.3.1]

63.4.4.3.2 The nameplate shall be marked in accordance with nationally recognized standards. [55:8.4.3.2]

63.4.4.4 Identification of Container Connections.

63.4.4.4.1 Container inlet and outlet connections, liquid-level limit controls, valves, and pressure gauges shall be identified using one of the methods prescribed by 63.4.4.4.1.1 through 63.4.4.4.1.2. [55:8.4.4.1]

63.4.4.4.1.1 They shall be marked with a permanent tag or label identifying their function. [55:8.4.4.1.1]

63.4.4.4.1.2 They shall be identified by a schematic drawing that indicates their function and designates whether they are connected to the vapor or liquid space of the container. [55:8.4.4.1.2]

63.4.4.4.1.2.1 When a schematic drawing is provided, it shall be attached to the container and maintained in a legible condition. [55:8.4.4.1.2.1]

63.4.4.5 Identification of Piping Systems. Piping systems shall be identified in accordance with ASME A13.1, *Scheme for the Identification of Piping Systems*. [55:8.4.5]

63.4.4.6 Identification of Emergency Shutoff Valves. Emergency shutoff valves on stationary containers shall be identified, visible, and indicated by means of a sign. [55:8.4.6]

63.4.5 Security.

63.4.5.1 General. Cryogenic containers and systems shall be secured against accidental dislodgement and against access by unauthorized personnel in accordance with 63.4.5. [55:8.5.1]

63.4.5.2* Security of Areas. Areas used for the storage of containers and systems shall be secured against unauthorized entry. [55:8.5.2]

63.4.5.2.1 Administrative controls shall be allowed to be used to control access to individual storage areas located in secure facilities not accessible by the general public. [55:8.5.2.1]

63.4.5.3 Securing of Containers. Stationary containers shall be secured to foundations in accordance with the building code. [55:8.5.3]

63.4.5.3.1 Portable containers subject to shifting or upset shall be secured. [55:8.5.3.1]

63.4.5.3.2 Nesting shall be permitted as a means of securing portable containers. [55:8.5.3.2]

63.4.5.4 Securing of Vaporizers. Vaporizers, heat exchangers, and similar equipment shall be secured to foundations, and their connecting piping shall be designed and constructed to provide for the effects of expansion and contraction due to temperature changes. [55:8.5.4]

63.4.5.5 Physical Protection. Containers, piping, valves, pressure relief devices, regulating equipment, and other appurtenances shall be protected against physical damage and tampering. [55:8.5.5]

63.4.6 Separation from Hazardous Conditions.

63.4.6.1 General. Cryogenic containers and systems in storage or use shall be separated from materials and conditions that present exposure hazards to or from each other in accordance with 63.4.6. [55:8.6.1]

63.4.6.2* Stationary Cryogenic Containers. Stationary containers located outdoors shall be separated from exposure hazards in accordance with the minimum separation distances indicated in Table 63.4.6.2. [55:8.6.2]

63.4.6.2.1 Fire Barriers. A 2-hour fire barrier wall shall be permitted in lieu of the distances specified in Table 63.4.6.2 for items 1, 4, 7, 8 and 9, where in accordance with the provisions of 63.4.6.2.1.1 through 63.4.6.2.1.4. [55:8.6.2.1]

63.4.6.2.1.1 The fire barrier wall shall be without openings or penetrations. [55:8.6.2.1.1]

63.4.6.2.1.1.1 Penetrations of the fire barrier wall by conduit or piping shall be permitted provided that the penetration is protected with a firestop system in accordance with the building code. [55:8.6.2.1.1.1]

63.4.6.2.1.2 The fire barrier wall shall be either an independent structure or the exterior wall of the building adjacent to the storage system. [55:8.6.2.1.2]

63.4.6.2.1.3 The fire barrier wall shall be located not less than 5 ft (1.5 m) from any exposure. [55:8.6.2.1.3]

63.4.6.2.1.4 The fire barrier wall shall not have more than two sides at 90 degree (1.57 rad) directions or not more than three sides with connecting angles of 135 degrees (2.36 rad). [55:8.6.2.1.4]

63.4.6.2.1.4.1* The connecting angles between fire barrier walls shall be permitted to be reduced to less than 135 degrees (2.36 rad) for installations consisting of three walls when in accordance with 63.4.12.2.7.2. [55:8.6.2.1.4.1]

63.4.6.2.1.5 Where the requirement of 63.4.6.2.1.4 is met, the bulk system shall be a minimum distance of 1 ft (0.3 m) from the fire barrier wall. [55:8.6.2.1.5]

63.4.6.2.2 Point-of-Fill Connections. Point-of-fill connections serving stationary containers filled by mobile transport equipment shall not be positioned closer to exposures than the minimum distances in Table 63.4.6.2. [55:8.6.2.2]

63.4.6.2.3 Surfaces Beneath Containers. The surface of the area on which stationary containers are placed, including the surface of the area located below the point at which connections are made for the purpose of filling such containers, shall be compatible with the fluid in the container. [55:8.6.2.3]

63.4.6.3 Portable Cryogenic Containers. Portable containers used for cryogenic fluids located outdoors shall be separated from exposure hazards in accordance with Table 63.4.6.3. [55:8.6.3]

63.4.6.3.1 Non-bulk portable containers of liquefied hydrogen shall be separated from exposure hazards in accordance with Table 63.4.6.3.1. [55:8.6.3.1]

63.4.6.3.2 Fire Barriers. A 2-hour fire barrier wall shall be permitted in lieu of the distances specified by Table 63.4.6.3 or Table 63.4.6.3.1 when in accordance with the provisions of 63.4.6.3.2.1 through 63.4.6.3.2.4. [55:8.6.3.2]

63.4.6.3.2.1 The fire barrier wall shall be without openings or penetrations. [55:8.6.3.2.1]

63.4.6.3.2.1.1 Penetrations of the fire barrier wall by conduit or piping shall be permitted provided that the penetration is protected with a firestop system in accordance with the building code. [55:8.6.3.2.1.1]

63.4.6.3.2.2 The fire barrier wall shall be either an independent structure or the exterior wall of the building adjacent to the storage system. [55:8.6.3.2.2]

63.4.6.3.2.3 The fire barrier wall shall be located not less than 5 ft (1.5 m) from any exposure. [55:8.6.3.2.3]

63.4.6.3.2.4 The fire barrier wall shall not have more than two sides at approximately 90 degree (1.57 rad) directions or not more than three sides with connecting angles of approximately 135 degrees (2.36 rad). [55:8.6.3.2.4]

63.4.7 Electrical Wiring and Equipment.

63.4.7.1 General. Electrical wiring and equipment shall be in accordance with *NFPA 70* and NFPA 79, as applicable, and 63.4.7. [55:8.7.1]

Table 63.4.6.2 Minimum Separation Distance Between Stationary Cryogenic Containers and Exposures

Exposure	Minimum Distance ft	Minimum Distance m
(1) Buildings, regardless of construction type	1	0.3
(2) Wall openings	1	0.3
(3) Air intakes	10	3.1
(4) Property lines	5	1.5
(5) Places of public assembly (assembly occupancies)	50	15
(6) Nonambulatory patient areas	50	15
(7) Combustible materials, (e.g., paper, leaves, weeds, dry grass, debris)	15	4.5
(8) Incompatible hazardous materials	20	6.1
(9) Building exits	10	3.1

[55: Table 8.6.2]

Δ **Table 63.4.6.3 Minimum Separation Distance Between Portable Cryogenic Containers and Exposures**

Exposure	Minimum Distance ft	Minimum Distance m
(1) Building exits	10	3.1
(2) Wall openings	1	0.3
(3) Air intakes	10	3.1
(4) Property lines	5	1.5
(5) Room or area exits	3	0.9
(6) Combustible materials, (e.g., paper, leaves, weeds, dry grass, debris)	15	4.5
(7) Incompatible hazardous materials	20	6.1

[55: Table 8.6.3]

Δ Table 63.4.6.3.1 Distance to Exposures for Non-Bulk Liquefied Hydrogen (LH$_2$)

Maximum Amount per Storage Area (gal)	Minimum Distance Between Storage Areas (ft)	Minimum Distance to Lot Lines of Property That Can Be Built Upon (ft)	Minimum Distance to Public Streets, Public Alleys, or Public Ways (ft)	Minimum Distance to Buildings on the Same Property Less than 2-Hour Construction	2-Hour Construction	4-Hour Construction
0–39.7	5	5	5	5	0	0
39.8–186.9	10	10	10	10	5	0
187–448.7	10	15	15	20	5	0
448.8–747.8	10	20	20	20	5	0
>747.8	20	25	25	20	5	0

For SI units: 1 ft = 305 mm.

Notes:
(1) For requirements on minimum distance to air intakes, see 63.3.7.2.4.
(2) For requirements on minimum distance to building openings including exits, see 63.3.7.2.5.
(3) When 63.4.6.3.2 is used as a means of distance reduction, the configuration of the fire barriers should be designed to allow natural ventilation to prevent the accumulation of hazardous gas concentrations.

[**55**:Table 8.6.3.1]

63.4.7.2 Location. Containers and systems shall not be located where they could become part of an electrical circuit. [**55**:8.7.2]

63.4.7.3 Electrical Grounding and Bonding. Containers and systems shall not be used for electrical grounding. [**55**:8.7.3]

63.4.7.3.1 When electrical grounding and bonding are required, the system shall be in accordance with *NFPA 70*. [**55**:8.7.3.1]

63.4.7.3.2 The grounding system shall be protected against corrosion, including corrosion caused by stray electrical currents. [**55**:8.7.3.2]

63.4.8 Service and Repair. Service, repair, modification, or removal of valves, pressure relief devices, or other container appurtenances shall be in accordance with nationally recognized codes and standards. [**55**:8.8]

63.4.8.1 Containers. Containers that have been removed from service shall be handled in an approved manner. [**55**:8.8.1]

63.4.8.1.1 Testing. Containers out of service in excess of 1 year shall be inspected and tested as required in 63.4.8.1.2. [**55**:8.8.1.1]

63.4.8.1.2 Pressure Relief Device Testing. The pressure relief devices shall be tested for operability and to determine if they are set at the relief pressure required by the tank design. [**55**:8.8.1.2]

63.4.8.1.3 Containers that have previously been used for flammable cryogenic fluids and have been removed from service shall be purged with an inert gas to remove residual flammable gas and stored with all valves closed and the valve outlets plugged. [**55**:8.8.1.3]

63.4.8.2 Systems. Service and repair of containers or systems shall be performed by trained personnel in accordance with nationally recognized standards and with the permission of the container owner. [**55**:8.8.2]

63.4.9 Unauthorized Use. Containers shall not be used for any purpose other than to serve as a vessel for containing the product for which it is designated. [**55**:8.9]

63.4.10 Leaks, Damage, and Corrosion.

63.4.10.1 Leaking, damaged, or corroded containers shall be removed from service. [**55**:8.10.1]

63.4.10.2 Leaking, damaged, or corroded systems shall be replaced, repaired, or removed from service. [**55**:8.10.2]

63.4.11 Lighting. Where required by the AHJ, lighting, including emergency lighting, shall be provided for fire appliances and operating facilities such as walkways, control valves, and gates ancillary to stationary containers. [**55**:8.11]

63.4.12 Storage.

63.4.12.1 Indoor Storage.

Δ **63.4.12.1.1 Installation.** Stationary containers indoors shall be installed in accordance with Chapters 9 and 11 of NFPA 55 or with CGA P-18, *Standard for Bulk Inert Gas Systems*. [**55**:8.12.1.1]

63.4.12.1.2 Stationary Containers. Stationary containers shall be in accordance with 63.4.2. [**55**:8.12.1.2]

63.4.12.1.3 Cryogenic Fluids. Cryogenic fluids in stationary or portable containers stored indoors shall be stored in buildings, rooms, or areas constructed in accordance with the building code. [**55**:8.12.1.3]

63.4.12.1.4 Ventilation. Ventilation shall be in accordance with 63.2.16. [**55**:8.12.1.4]

63.4.12.2 Outdoor Storage.

63.4.12.2.1 General. Cryogenic fluids in stationary or portable containers stored outdoors shall be in accordance with 63.4.12.2. [**55**:8.12.2.1]

63.4.12.2.2 Access. Stationary containers shall be located to provide access by mobile supply equipment and authorized personnel. [**55:**8.12.2.2]

63.4.12.2.2.1 Where exit access is provided to serve areas in which equipment is installed, the minimum width shall be not less than 28 in. (710 mm). [**55:**8.12.2.2.1]

63.4.12.2.3 Physical Protection. Cryogenic fluid containers, cylinders, tanks, and systems that could be exposed to physical damage shall be protected. [**55:**8.12.2.3]

63.4.12.2.3.1 Guard posts or other means shall be provided to protect cryogenic fluid containers, cylinders, tanks, and systems indoors and outdoors from vehicular damage. *(See Section 4.11 of NFPA 55.)* [**55:**8.12.2.3.1]

63.4.12.2.4 Diked Areas Containing Other Hazardous Materials. Containers of cryogenic fluids shall not be located within diked areas with other hazardous materials. [**55:**8.12.2.4]

63.4.12.2.5* Areas Subject to Flooding. Stationary containers located in flood hazard areas shall be anchored to prevent flotation during conditions of the design flood as designated by the building code. [**55:**8.12.2.5]

63.4.12.2.5.1 Elevated Tanks. Structures supporting elevated tanks and tanks that are supported at a level above that designated in the design flood shall be anchored to resist lateral shifting due to flood and other hydrostatic effects. [**55:**8.12.2.5.1]

63.4.12.2.5.2 Underground Tanks. Underground tanks in flood hazard areas shall be anchored to prevent flotation, collapse, or lateral movement resulting from hydrostatic loads, including the effects of buoyancy, during conditions of the design flood. [**55:**8.12.2.5.2]

63.4.12.2.6 Drainage.

63.4.12.2.6.1 The area surrounding stationary and portable containers shall be provided with a means to prevent accidental discharge of fluids from endangering personnel, containers, equipment, and adjacent structures and from entering enclosed spaces in accordance with this *Code*. [**55:**8.12.2.6.1]

63.4.12.2.6.2 The stationary container shall not be placed where spilled or discharged fluids will be retained around the container. [**55:**8.12.2.6.2]

63.4.12.2.6.3 The provisions of 63.4.12.2.6.2 shall be permitted to be altered or waived where the AHJ determines that the container does not constitute a hazard after consideration of special features such as the following:

(1) Crushed rock utilized as a heat sink
(2) Topographical conditions
(3) Nature of occupancy
(4) Proximity to structures on the same or adjacent property
(5) Capacity and construction of containers and character of fluids to be stored

[**55:**8.12.2.6.3]

63.4.12.2.6.4 The grade for a distance of not less than 50 ft (15.2 m) from where cryogenic fluid storage or delivery systems are installed shall be higher than the grade on which flammable or combustible liquids are stored or used. [**55:**8.12.2.6.4]

63.4.12.2.6.4.1* Drainage Control.

(A) Where the grade differential between the storage or delivery system and the flammable or combustible liquids storage or use area is not in accordance with 63.4.12.2.6.4, diversion curbs or other means of drainage control shall be used to divert the flow of flammable or combustible liquids away from the cryogenic system. [**55:**8.12.2.6.4.1(A)]

(B) The means of drainage control shall prevent the flow of flammable or combustible liquid to a distance not less than 50 ft (15.2 m) from all parts of the delivery system. [**55:**8.12.2.6.4.1(B)]

63.4.12.2.7 Outdoor Installations.

63.4.12.2.7.1* Enclosed Courts. Stationary containers shall not be installed within enclosed courts. [**55:**8.12.2.7.1]

63.4.12.2.7.2* Courts. Stationary containers shall be sited so that they are open to the surrounding environment except that encroachment by building walls of unlimited height shall be permitted when in accordance with the distances specified by Table 63.4.6.2 or the material-specific tables in Chapters 9, 11, 13, and 16 of NFPA 55. [**55:**8.12.2.7.2]

63.4.12.2.7.2.1* Where exterior building walls encroach on the system to form a court, the system shall be located at a distance not less than the height of the wall from at least two court walls. [**55:**8.12.2.7.2.1]

63.4.12.2.7.2.2 The required distance between the exterior walls of the building forming the court and the container shall be determined independently without regard to fire barrier walls used to allow encroachment by fire exposure hazards. [**55:**8.12.2.7.2.2]

Δ **63.4.12.2.7.3 Fire Department Access.** Fire department access roadways or other approved means shall be in accordance with this *Code*. [**55:**8.12.2.7.3]

63.4.13 Use and Handling.

63.4.13.1 General. Use and handling of containers and systems shall be in accordance with 63.4.13. [**55:**8.13.1]

63.4.13.1.1 Operating Instructions. Operating instructions shall be provided for installations that require the operation of equipment. [**55:**8.13.1.1]

63.4.13.1.2 Attended Delivery. A qualified individual shall be in attendance at all times cryogenic fluid is transferred from mobile supply units to a storage system. [**55:**8.13.1.2]

63.4.13.1.3 Cleaning and Purging of Gas Piping Systems. Cleaning and purging of piping systems shall be in accordance with 63.3.1.20. [**55:**8.13.1.3]

63.4.13.1.4 Inspection.

63.4.13.1.4.1 Cryogenic fluid storage systems shall be inspected and maintained by a qualified representative of the equipment owner as required by the material-specific requirements of Chapters 9, 11, 13, and 16 of NFPA 55. [**55:**8.13.1.4.1]

63.4.13.1.4.2* The interval between inspections other than those specified by material-specific requirements shall be based on nationally recognized good practices or standards. [**55:**8.13.1.4.1.1]

63.4.13.1.4.3 A record of the inspection shall be prepared and provided to the user or the AHJ upon request. [**55:**8.13.1.4.2]

63.4.13.1.5 Design.

63.4.13.1.5.1 Nationally Recognized Good Practices. Where nationally recognized good practices or standards have been established for the process employed, such practices and standards shall be followed. [**55:**8.13.1.5.1]

63.4.13.1.5.2 Piping Systems. Piping, tubing, fittings, and related components shall be designed, fabricated, and tested in accordance with the requirements of ASME B31.3, *Process Piping*, or other approved standards and shall be in accordance with 63.4.13.2. [**55:**8.13.1.5.2]

63.4.13.2 Piping and Appurtenances.

63.4.13.2.1 Piping systems shall be designed for the use intended through the full range of pressure and temperature to which they will be subjected. [**55:**8.13.2.1]

63.4.13.2.2 Piping systems shall be designed and constructed to allow for expansion, contraction, vibration, settlement, and fire exposure. [**55:**8.13.2.2]

63.4.13.3 Joints. Joints in piping and tubing shall be in accordance with the requirements of ASME B31.3, *Process Piping*, or other approved standards. [**55:**8.13.3]

63.4.13.4 Valves and Accessory Equipment. Valves and accessory equipment shall be acceptable for the intended use at the temperatures of the application and shall be designed and constructed to withstand the maximum pressure at the minimum temperature to which they will be subjected. [**55:**8.13.4]

63.4.13.5 Shutoff Valves on Containers. Shutoff valves shall be provided on all container connections, except for pressure relief devices. [**55:**8.13.5]

63.4.13.5.1 Shutoff valves for containers with multiple pressure relief devices shall be permitted in accordance with 63.4.2.4.7. [**55:**8.13.5.1]

63.4.13.5.2 Shutoff valves shall be accessible and located as close as practical to the container. [**55:**8.13.5.2]

63.4.13.6 Shutoff Valves on Piping.

63.4.13.6.1 Shutoff valves shall be installed in piping containing cryogenic fluids where needed to limit the volume of liquid discharged in the event of piping or equipment failure. [**55:**8.13.6.1]

63.4.13.6.2 Pressure relief valves shall be installed where liquid or cold gas can be trapped between shutoff valves in the piping system. *(See 63.4.2.4.)* [**55:**8.13.6.2]

63.4.13.7 Physical Protection and Support.

63.4.13.7.1 Aboveground piping systems shall be supported and protected from physical damage. [**55:**8.13.7.1]

63.4.13.7.2 Piping passing through walls shall be protected from mechanical damage. [**55:**8.13.7.2]

63.4.13.8 Corrosion Protection.

63.4.13.8.1 Aboveground piping that is subject to corrosion shall be protected against corrosion. [**55:**8.13.8.1]

63.4.13.8.2 Belowground piping shall be protected against corrosion. [**55:**8.13.8.2]

63.4.13.9 Cathodic Protection. Where required, cathodic protection shall be in accordance with 63.4.13.9. [**55:**8.13.9]

63.4.13.9.1 Operation. Where installed, cathodic protection systems shall be operated and maintained to continuously provide corrosion protection. [**55:**8.13.9.1]

63.4.13.9.2 Inspection.

63.4.13.9.2.1 Container systems equipped with cathodic protection shall be inspected for the intended operation by a cathodic protection tester. [**55:**8.13.9.2.1]

N **63.4.13.9.2.1.1** The examinations shall be documented. [**55:**8.13.9.2.1.1]

N **63.4.13.9.2.1.2** A record of the examination history shall be maintained by the owner and shall be available to the AHJ upon request. [**55:**8.13.9.2.1.2]

63.4.13.9.2.2 The cathodic protection tester shall be certified as being qualified by the National Association of Corrosion Engineers, International (NACE). [**55:**8.13.9.2.2]

63.4.13.9.3 Impressed Current Systems.

63.4.13.9.3.1 Systems equipped with impressed current cathodic protection systems shall be inspected in accordance with the requirements of the design and 63.4.13.9.2. [**55:**8.13.9.3.1]

63.4.13.9.3.2 The design limits shall be available to the AHJ upon request. [**55:**8.13.9.3.2]

63.4.13.9.3.3 The system owner shall maintain the following records to demonstrate that the cathodic protection is in conformance with the requirements of the design:

(1) The results of inspections of the system
(2) The results of testing that has been completed
[**55:**8.13.9.3.3]

63.4.13.9.4 Repairs, maintenance, or replacement of a cathodic protection system shall be under the supervision of a corrosion expert certified by NACE. [**55:**8.13.9.4]

63.4.13.9.4.1 The corrosion expert shall be certified by NACE as a senior corrosion technologist, a cathodic protection specialist, or a corrosion specialist or shall be a registered engineer with registration in a field that includes education and experience in corrosion control. [**55:**8.13.9.4.1]

63.4.13.10 Testing.

63.4.13.10.1 Piping systems shall be tested and proved free of leaks after installation as required by the codes and standards to which they are designed and constructed. [**55:**8.13.10.1]

63.4.13.10.2 Test pressures shall not be less than 150 percent of the maximum allowable working pressure when hydraulic testing is conducted or 110 percent when testing is conducted pneumatically. [**55:**8.13.10.2]

63.4.13.11 Material-Specific Requirements.

Δ **63.4.13.11.1 Indoor Use.** Indoor use of cryogenic fluids shall be in accordance with the material-specific provisions of Chapters 9, 11, 13, and 16 of NFPA 55 or with CGA P-18, *Standard for Bulk Inert Gas Systems*, and 63.4.13.2. [**55:**8.13.11.1]

63.4.13.11.2 Outdoor Use.

Δ **63.4.13.11.2.1 General.** Outdoor use of cryogenic fluids shall be in accordance with the material-specific provisions of Chapters 9, 11, 13, and 16 of NFPA 55 or with CGA P-18, *Standard for Bulk Inert Gas Systems*, and 63.4.13.2. [**55**:8.13.11.2.1]

Δ **63.4.13.11.2.2 Separation.** Distances from property lines, buildings, and exposure hazards shall be in accordance with Table 63.4.6.2 and Table 63.4.6.3 and the material-specific provisions of Chapters 9, 11, 13, and 16 of NFPA 55 or with CGA P-18, *Standard for Bulk Inert Gas Systems*. [**55**:8.13.11.2.2]

63.4.13.11.2.3 Emergency Shutoff Valves.

63.4.13.11.2.3.1* Accessible manual or automatic emergency shutoff valves shall be provided to shut off the cryogenic fluid supply in case of emergency. [**55**:8.13.11.2.3.1]

(A) Manual emergency shutoff valves or the device that activates an automatic emergency shutoff valve on a bulk source or piping systems serving the bulk supply shall be identified by means of a sign. [**55**:8.13.11.2.3.1(A)]

63.4.13.11.2.3.2 Emergency shutoff valves shall be located at the point of use, at the source of supply, and at the point where the system piping enters the building. [**55**:8.13.11.2.3.2]

63.4.13.11.3 Filling and Dispensing.

63.4.13.11.3.1 General. Filling and dispensing of cryogenic fluids shall be in accordance with 63.4.13.1.2. [**55**:8.13.11.3.1]

63.4.13.11.3.2 Dispensing Areas. Dispensing of cryogenic fluids associated with physical or health hazards shall be conducted in approved locations. [**55**:8.13.11.3.2]

63.4.13.11.3.2.1 Indoor Dispensing Areas. Dispensing indoors shall be conducted in areas constructed in accordance with the building code. [**55**:8.13.11.3.2.1]

63.4.13.11.3.2.2 Ventilation. Indoor areas in which cryogenic fluids are dispensed shall be ventilated in accordance with the requirements of 63.2.16 and the mechanical code. [**55**:8.13.11.3.2.2]

63.4.13.11.3.2.3 Piping Systems. Piping systems utilized for filling or dispensing of cryogenic fluids shall be designed and constructed in accordance with 63.4.13.2. [**55**:8.13.11.3.2.3]

Δ **63.4.13.11.3.3 Vehicle Loading and Unloading Areas.** Loading and unloading areas shall be constructed in accordance with the requirements of Chapter 9 of NFPA 55 for liquid oxygen, Chapter 11 of NFPA 55 for liquid hydrogen, Chapter 13 of NFPA 55 for liquid carbon dioxide, and Chapter 16 of NFPA 55 for liquid nitrous oxide or CGA P-18, *Standard for Bulk Inert Gas Systems*, for inert cryogenic fluids, as applicable. [**55**:8.13.11.3.3]

Δ **63.4.13.11.3.4*** A noncombustible, delivery vehicle spill pad shall be provided when required by the material-specific requirements of Chapter 9 of NFPA 55 for liquid oxygen, Chapter 11 of NFPA 55 for liquid hydrogen, and Chapter 16 of NFPA 55 for liquid nitrous oxide. [**55**:8.13.11.3.4]

63.4.13.11.3.4.1* A noncombustible spill pad shall be provided for delivery areas where bulk liquid helium is transferred from delivery vehicles. [**55**:8.13.11.3.4.1]

63.4.13.11.3.5 Filling Controls. A pressure gauge and full trycock valve shall be provided and shall be visible from the delivery point to allow the delivery operator to monitor the internal pressure and liquid level of stationary containers during filling. [**55**:8.13.11.3.5]

63.4.13.11.3.5.1 When the containers being filled are remote from the delivery point and pressure gauges or full trycock valves are not visible, redundant gauges and valves shall be installed at the filling connection. [**55**:8.13.11.3.5.1]

63.4.13.11.4 Handling.

63.4.13.11.4.1 Applicability. Handling of cryogenic containers shall be in accordance with 63.4.13.11.4. [**55**:8.13.11.4.1]

63.4.13.11.4.2 Carts and Trucks.

63.4.13.11.4.2.1 Cryogenic containers shall be moved using an approved method. [**55**:8.13.11.4.2.1]

63.4.13.11.4.2.2 Where cryogenic containers are moved by hand cart, hand truck, or other mobile device, that device shall be designed for the secure movement of the container. [**55**:8.13.11.4.2.2]

63.4.13.11.4.3 Design. Carts and trucks used to transport cryogenic containers shall be designed to provide a stable base for the commodities to be transported and shall have a means of restraining containers to prevent accidental dislodgement. [**55**:8.13.11.4.3]

63.4.13.11.4.4 Closed Containers.

63.4.13.11.4.4.1 Pressurized containers shall be closed while being transported. [**55**:8.13.11.4.4.1]

63.4.13.11.4.4.2 Containers designed for use at atmospheric conditions shall be transported with appropriate loose-fitting covers in place to prevent spillage. [**55**:8.13.11.4.4.2]

63.5 Bulk Oxygen Systems.

63.5.1 Bulk oxygen systems shall comply with Chapter 9 of NFPA 55.

63.5.2 Cleaning and Purging of Gas Piping Systems. Cleaning and purging of piping systems shall be in accordance with 63.3.1.20. [**55**:9.4.1.9]

63.5.3 Cleaning of oxygen systems used in medical gas service shall be in accordance with NFPA 99. *(See also 9.4.3.1 of NFPA 55.)* [**55**:9.4.1.9.1]

63.6 Gas Hydrogen Systems.

63.6.1 Bulk hydrogen compressed gas systems shall comply with NFPA 2 and Chapter 10 of NFPA 55.

63.6.2 Cleaning and purging of piping systems shall be in accordance with 63.3.1.20. [**55**:10.2.3.2]

63.7 Bulk Liquefied Hydrogen Systems.

63.7.1 Bulk liquefied hydrogen systems shall comply with NFPA 2 and Chapter 11 of NFPA 55.

63.7.2 Cleaning and purging of piping systems shall be in accordance with 63.3.1.20. [**55**:11.2.3.9]

63.8 Gas Generation Systems.

63.8.1 General. Gas generation systems shall comply with NFPA 2 and Chapter 12 of NFPA 55.

63.9 Insulated Liquid Carbon Dioxide Systems. Insulated liquid carbon dioxide systems shall comply with Chapter 13 of NFPA 55.

63.9.1 General. The storage, use, and handling of liquid carbon dioxide in insulated systems shall be in accordance with the provisions of Chapter 13 and Chapters 1 through 7 of NFPA 55, as applicable.

63.9.2 Permits.

63.9.2.1 For other than vehicles equipped for and using compressed gas as a fuel for propelling the vehicle, an operational permit shall be required for liquid carbon dioxide systems in excess of 100 lb (45.4 kg) of carbon dioxide.

63.9.2.2 A construction permit shall be required for the installation of, or modification to, a liquid carbon dioxide (CO_2) system where the quantity exceeds the amount listed in 63.9.2.

63.9.2.3 The following information shall be provided to the authority having jurisdiction with the application for permit:

(1) Total aggregate quantity of liquid CO_2 in pounds or cubic feet at normal temperature and pressure
(2) Location and total volume of the room where the liquid CO_2 will be located and whether the room is at or below grade
(3) Location of containers relative to equipment, building openings, and means of egress
(4) Manufacturer's specifications and pressure rating, including cut sheets, of all piping and/or tubing to be used
(5) A piping and instrumentation diagram that shows piping support and remote fill connections
(6) Details of container venting, including, but not limited to, vent line size, material, and termination location
(7) Alarm and detection system and equipment, if applicable
(8) Seismic support for containers

63.9.3 Pressure Relief Devices. Containers used for liquid carbon dioxide shall be equipped with pressure relief devices piped from the uppermost part of the containers and communicating with the vapor space. [55:13.4.1]

63.9.4 Physical Protection.

63.9.4.1 Pressure relief devices shall be located to minimize tampering, damage, and obstruction to flow. [55:13.4.1.1.1]

63.9.4.2 The inlet and outlet of the relief devices shall not be blocked by a valve or plug during normal operation. [55:13.4.1.1.2]

63.9.5 Vent Pipe Systems. Pressure relief devices shall be piped to the outdoors where the discharge will not impinge on the structure, personnel, or means of egress and will not create a hazardous concentration of carbon dioxide. [55:13.4.1.2]

63.9.5.1 Pressure relief devices from portable DOT 4L containers that are not a component of a stationary system shall not be required to meet the requirements of 63.9.5. [55:13.4.1.2.1]

63.9.5.2* Vent piping systems serving pressure relief devices shall be protected from water intrusion to prevent moisture or solid carbon dioxide from collecting and freezing and interfering with the operation of the pressure relief device. [55:13.4.1.2.2]

63.9.5.3* Vent piping systems serving pressure relief devices shall be designed to prevent backflow restrictions exceeding 10 percent backpressure on the pressure relief device under full flow conditions. [55:13.4.1.2.3]

63.9.6 Pressure and Level Indicators.

63.9.6.1 Cylinders, containers, and tanks shall be provided with a pressure gauge and a level gauge or device for indicating the quantity of liquid carbon dioxide. [55:13.4.2.1]

63.9.6.2 These devices shall be designed for the temperatures and pressures associated with liquid carbon dioxide service. [55:13.4.2.2]

63.9.6.3 Where cylinders, containers, and tanks are in locations remote from the filling connection, a means to determine when the containers have been filled to their design capacity shall be provided and shall be verifiable from the filling connection. [55:13.4.2.3]

63.9.7 Piping Systems.

63.9.7.1 Carbon dioxide piping shall be located and supported to protect against damage from strain on piping and fittings; the effects of expansion, contraction, and vibration; mechanical damage; and heat sources. [55:13.4.3.1]

63.9.7.2 Piping, tubing, and hoses and fittings shall be designed to a bursting pressure of at least four times the system design pressure. [55:13.4.3.2]

63.9.7.3* Materials of Construction. Materials of construction shall be employed for potential exposure to a temperature of −109.3°F (−78.5°C). [55:13.5]

63.9.7.4 Operating Instructions. Operating instructions shall account for potential exposure of personnel to extremely low temperatures in accordance with 13.7.3 of NFPA 55. [55:13.6]

N **63.9.7.5 Small Insulated Liquid Carbon Dioxide Indoor Systems.**

N **63.9.7.5.1*** Container foundations or floors in multistoried buildings shall be designed to support the weight of the system at its full capacity in accordance with the building code. [55:13.7.1]

N **63.9.7.5.2*** Rooms or areas where container systems are filled and used indoors or in enclosed outdoor locations shall be provided with a gas detection and alarm system that shall be capable of detecting and notifying the building occupants of a gas release of carbon dioxide at, or in excess of, the Time-Weighted Average–Permissible Exposure Limit (TWA-PEL) published by the Occupational Safety and Health Administration (OSHA) and the Threshold Limit Value–Short Term Exposure Limit (TLV-STEL) published by the American Conference of Governmental Industrial Hygienists (ACGIH). More conservative set points shall be permitted to be used. [55:13.7.2]

N **63.9.7.5.2.1*** Activation of the gas detection system shall initiate an audible alarm within the room or area in which the system is installed. [55:13.7.2.1]

N **63.9.7.5.2.2** Subsection 63.9.7.5.2 shall not apply to manufacturer locations where containers are filled indoors and distributed for use. [55:13.7.2.2]

N **63.9.7.5.2.3** Activation of the gas detection system shall sound a local alarm to notify persons responsible for system operation of a hazard condition in the area in which the system is installed. [55:13.7.2.3]

N 63.9.7.5.3 A warning sign shall be posted at the entrance to the building, room, enclosure, or confined area where the container is located. [**55:**13.7.3]

N 63.9.7.5.3.1 The warning sign shall be at least 8 in. (200 mm) wide and 6 in. (150 mm) high and state the following:

CAUTION — CARBON DIOXIDE GAS

Ventilate the area before entering.

A high carbon dioxide (CO_2) gas concentration in this area can cause suffocation.

[**55:**13.7.3.1]

63.9.8 Safety Measures.

63.9.8.1 Rooms or areas inside assembly, business, educational, institutional, and residential occupancies containing a liquid carbon dioxide (CO_2) system shall comply with the safety measures in 63.9.9.1.

63.9.8.2 The provisions of 63.9.9.1 shall not apply to liquid carbon dioxide (CO_2) systems located above grade in outdoor areas with enclosure walls obstructing on no more than 75 percent of the perimeter at ground level.

63.9.8.3 Gas Detection System.

63.9.8.3.1 A continuous gas detection system shall be provided in the room or area where container systems are filled and used, and in areas where the heavier-than-air gas can congregate.

63.9.8.3.2 Carbon dioxide (CO_2) sensors shall be provided within 12 in. (305 mm) of the floor in the area where the gas is most likely to accumulate or leaks are most likely to occur.

63.9.8.3.3 The system shall be designed to detect and notify at a low-level alarm and high-level alarm.

63.9.8.4 The threshold for activation of the low-level alarm shall not exceed a carbon dioxide concentration of 5,000 ppm TWA (9,000 mg/m^3). When carbon dioxide is detected at the low-level alarm, the system shall activate a signal at a normally attended location within the building.

63.9.8.5 The threshold for activation of the high-level alarm shall not exceed a carbon dioxide concentration of 30,000 ppm (54,000 mg/m^3). When carbon dioxide is detected at the high-level alarm, the system shall activate an audible and visual alarm in an approved location.

63.9.9 Signage.

63.9.9.1 Hazard identification signs shall be posted at the entrance to the room and confined to the area where liquid carbon dioxide containers are located. The sign shall be a minimum 8 in. (200 mm) wide and 6 in. (150 mm) high and indicate:

CAUTION – CARBON DIOXIDE GAS
Ventilate the area before entering.
A high carbon dioxide (CO_2) gas concentration
in this area can cause asphyxiation.

63.9.10 Performance Design Option.

63.9.10.1 Carbon dioxide (CO_2) systems shall not be required to be provided with a gas detection system where a complete discharge of the stored carbon dioxide cannot result in a concentration exceeding 5,000 ppm in the room where the container is located or the area where the carbon dioxide is likely to congregate. The maximum concentration (ppm) shall be determined as follows:

(1) Calculate the volume (scf) of CO_2 gas at standard temperature and pressure that is contained in the storage containers as follows:

   (a) To convert pounds of liquid to volume (scf) of CO_2 gas, multiply the pounds by 8.741.
   (b) To convert gallons of liquid to volume (scf) of CO_2 gas, multiply the gallons by 74.04.

(2) Calculate the volume of the room containing the CO_2 containers, or the area where the CO_2 is likely to congregate, in cubic feet as follows:

   (a) The volume of the room or area shall be based on a height limitation of 5 ft (1524 mm) or the ceiling, whichever is less.
   (b) The boundary of the area shall be to walls or partitions 5 ft (1524 mm) or more in height that obstruct gas dispersion at the floor level.
   (c) All doors in the boundary walls shall be considered closed.
   (d) CO_2 shall be assumed to congregate in basements, pits, or lower floors where openings are present between the containers and the lower floor.

(3) Divide the volume of CO_2 gas by the volume of the room. If the result does not exceed 0.005 (5,000 ppm), the design meets the performance option criteria.

63.9.11 Seismic and Structural Design.

63.9.11.1 Liquid carbon dioxide system containers and piping shall comply with the seismic design requirements in accordance with the building code and shall not exceed the floor loading limitation of the building.

63.9.11.2 Container foundations or floors in multistoried buildings shall be designed to support the weight of the system at its full capacity in accordance with the building code.

63.9.12 Small Insulated Liquid Carbon Dioxide Outdoor Systems.

63.9.12.1 Container systems located in enclosed spaces shall be in accordance with Section 13.7 of NFPA 55 for indoor systems. [**55:**13.8.1]

63.9.12.1.1* Aboveground outdoor locations shall not be required to be provided with a gas detection and alarm system in accordance with 13.7.2 of NFPA 55 where the system is unenclosed. [**55:**13.8.1.1]

63.9.12.1.1.1 To be considered unenclosed, enclosures constructed to limit access or otherwise provide a visual or architectural barrier for the installation shall be constructed in accordance with the requirements in 63.2.6 for weather protection or with the following:

(1) The enclosure shall be constructed without a roof or overhead cover.
(2) Supports and walls shall not obstruct more than three sides nor more than 75 percent of the perimeter of the storage or use area, with 25 percent of the perimeter being open to the atmosphere.

[**55:**13.8.1.1.1]

63.9.12.1.1.2 Enclosures that do not meet the requirements of 63.9.12.1.1.1 shall be permitted when constructed in accordance with the following:

(1) The enclosure shall be constructed without a roof or overhead cover.
(2) Continuous mechanical exhaust ventilation shall be provided.

[**55:**13.8.1.1.2]

63.9.12.1.1.2.1 Where mechanical exhaust ventilation is provided, it shall be in accordance with the following:

(1) The exhaust system shall be installed in accordance with the requirements of the mechanical code.
(2) The exhaust system shall be designed to consider the density of the potential vapors released with exhaust taken from a point within 12 in. (305 mm) of the floor.
(3) The location of both the exhaust and the inlet air openings shall be designed to provide air movement across all portions of the enclosure to prevent the accumulation of vapors.
(4) The rate of exhaust ventilation shall be not less than 1 scf/min/ft^2 (0.028 Nm^3/min/m^2) of floor area within the enclosure.

[**55:**13.8.1.1.2.1]

63.9.13 Large Indoor Insulated Liquid Carbon Dioxide Systems. (Reserved)

63.9.14 Large Outdoor Insulated Liquid Carbon Dioxide Systems.

63.9.14.1 Location. Outdoor stationary large insulated liquid carbon dioxide systems shall be located in accordance with Table 63.9.14.1. [**55:**13.10.1]

63.9.14.2 Point-of-Fill Connections. Point-of-fill connections serving stationary containers filled by mobile transport equipment shall not be positioned closer to exposures than the minimum distances in Table 63.9.14.1. [**55:**13.10.1.1]

Δ **Table 63.9.14.1 Minimum Separation Distance Between Outdoor Stationary Large Insulated Liquid Carbon Dioxide Containers and Exposures**

Exposure	Minimum Distance ft	Minimum Distance m
(1) Buildings, regardless of construction type	2	0.6
(2) Wall openings other than building exits	2	0.6
(3) Air intakes	10	3.1
(4) Property lines	5	1.5
(5) Places of public assembly (assembly occupancies)	50	15
(6) Nonambulatory patient areas	50	15
(7) Combustible materials (e.g., paper, leaves, weeds, dry grass, debris)	15	4.5
(8) Incompatible hazardous materials	20	6.1
(9) Building exits	10	3.1

[**55:**Table 13.10.1]

63.9.14.3 Fire Barriers. A 2-hour fire barrier wall shall be permitted in lieu of the distances specified by Table 63.9.14.1 when in accordance with the provisions of 63.9.14.3.1 through 63.9.14.3.4. [**55:**13.10.2]

63.9.14.3.1 The fire barrier wall shall be without openings or penetrations. [**55:**13.10.2.1]

63.9.14.3.1.1 Penetrations of the fire barrier wall by conduit or piping shall be permitted provided that the penetration is protected with a firestop system in accordance with the building code. [**55:**13.10.2.1.1]

63.9.14.3.2 The fire barrier wall shall be either an independent structure or the exterior wall of the building adjacent to the storage system. [**55:**13.10.2.2]

63.9.14.3.3 The fire barrier wall shall be located not less than 5 ft (1.5 m) from any exposure. [**55:**13.10.2.3]

63.9.14.3.4 The fire barrier wall shall not have more than two sides at approximately 90 degree (1.57 rad) directions or not more than three sides with connecting angles of approximately 135 degrees (2.36 rad). [**55:**13.10.2.4]

63.10 Storage, Handling, and Use of Ethylene Oxide for Sterilization and Fumigation.

63.10.1 General. Storage, handling, and use of ethylene oxide for sterilization and fumigation shall comply with Chapter 14 of NFPA 55.

63.10.2 Cleaning and Purging of Gas Piping Systems.

63.10.2.1 Cleaning and purging of piping systems shall be in accordance with 63.3.1.20. [**55:**14.4.1.3]

63.10.2.2 Piping and valves that have been used to transport ethylene oxide to or from a sterilizer to the emission control or release point shall be drained and purged in accordance with 63.3.1.20 prior to dismantling. [**55:**14.4.3.1]

Δ **63.11 Carbon Dioxide Beverage Systems.**

63.11.1 General. Systems with more than 100 lb (45 kg) of carbon dioxide used in beverage dispensing applications shall comply with 63.11.2 through 63.11.4. [**55:**13.11.1]

63.11.2 Equipment. The storage, use, and handling of carbon dioxide shall be in accordance with Chapters 1 through 7 of NFPA 55 and the requirements of this chapter, as applicable. [**55:**13.11.2]

63.11.3 Protection from Damage. Carbon dioxide system storage tanks, cylinders, piping, and fittings shall be installed so they are protected from damage by occupants or equipment during normal facility operations. [**55:**13.11.3]

63.11.4 Required Protection. Carbon dioxide storage tanks, cylinders, piping, and equipment located indoors, in rooms, and other areas where a leak of carbon dioxide can collect shall be provided with either ventilation in accordance with 63.11.4.1 or an emergency alarm system in accordance with 63.11.4.2. [**55:**13.11.4]

63.11.4.1 Ventilation. Mechanical ventilation shall be in accordance with the Uniform Mechanical Code and shall comply with all of the following:

(1) Mechanical ventilation in a room or area shall be at a rate of not less than 1 ft^3/min/ft^2 (0.00508 m^3/s/m^2).

(2) Exhaust shall be taken from a point within 12 in. (305 mm) of the floor.
(3) The ventilation system shall be designed to operate with a negative pressure in relation to the surrounding area.

[55:13.11.4.1]

63.11.4.2 Emergency Alarm System. Emergency alarm systems shall comply with all of the following:

(1) Areas where carbon dioxide can accumulate, continuous gas detection shall be provided.
(2) The system shall be capable of detecting and notifying the building occupants of a gas release of carbon dioxide at, or in excess of, the Time-Weighted Average–Permissible Exposure Limit (TWA–PEL) published by the Occupational Safety and Health Administration (OSHA) and the Threshold Limit Value–Short Term Exposure Limit (TLV®–STEL) published by the American Conference of Governmental Industrial Hygienists (ACGIH). More conservative set points shall be permitted to be used.
(3) The emergency alarm system activation shall initiate a local alarm within the room or area in which the system is installed.

[55:13.11.4.2]

63.12 Liquid Oxygen in Home Care.

63.12.1 General. The storage and use of liquid oxygen (LOX) in home care shall comply with Sections 63.4 and 63.12.

63.12.1.1 Gas equipment used in the home for health care shall conform to applicable requirements of NFPA 99.

63.12.2 Information and Instructions. The seller of liquid oxygen shall provide the user with information in written form that includes, but is not limited to, the following:

(1) Manufacturer's instructions and labeling for storage and use of the containers
(2) Locating containers away from ignition sources, exits, electrical hazards, and high temperature devices in accordance with 63.12.3.2
(3) Restraint of containers to prevent falling in accordance with 63.12.3.3
(4) Requirements for handling containers in accordance with 63.12.3.4
(5) Safeguards for refilling of containers in accordance with 63.12.3.5

63.12.3 Containers. Containers of liquid oxygen in home care shall be in accordance with 63.12.3.1 through 63.12.3.5.

63.12.3.1* Containers shall be stored, used, and operated in accordance with the manufacturer's instructions and labeling.

63.12.3.2 Containers shall not be located in areas as follows:

(1) Where they can be overturned due to operation of a door
(2) Where they are in the direct path of egress
(3) Where they are subject to damage from falling objects
(4) Where they can become part of an electrical circuit
(5) Where open flames and high temperature devices could cause a hazard

63.12.3.3* Liquid oxygen home care containers shall be restrained by one of the following methods while in storage or use to prevent falling caused by contact, vibration, or seismic activity:

(1) Restraining containers to a fixed object with one or more restraints
(2) Restraining containers within a framework, stand, or assembly designed to resist container movement
(3) Restraining containers by locating a container against two points of contact

63.12.3.4 Containers shall be transported by use of a cart or hand truck designed for such use.

63.12.3.4.1 Liquid oxygen home care containers equipped with a roller base shall not be required to be transported by use of a cart or truck.

63.12.3.4.2 Liquid oxygen ambulatory containers shall be permitted to be hand carried.

63.12.3.5 The filling of containers shall be in accordance with 63.12.3.5.1 through 63.12.3.5.2.

63.12.3.5.1 Liquid oxygen home care containers shall be filled outdoors.

63.12.3.5.1.1* A drip pan compatible with liquid oxygen shall be provided under home care container filling and vent connections used during the filling process.

63.12.3.5.2 Liquid oxygen ambulatory containers shall be allowed to be filled indoors when the supply container is designed for filling such containers and written instructions are provided by the container manufacturer.

63.12.3.5.3* The use of open flames and high temperature devices shall be in accordance with the adopted fire prevention code.

63.12.4 Maximum Quantity. The maximum aggregate quantity of liquid oxygen allowed in storage and in use in a single dwelling unit shall be 31.6 gal (120 L).

63.12.4.1 The maximum aggregate quantity of liquid oxygen allowed in day care occupancies shall be limited by the maximum allowable quantity set forth in the adopted fire prevention code or building code.

63.12.4.2 Where individual sleeping rooms are separated from the remainder of the dwelling unit by fire barriers and horizontal assemblies having a minimum fire-resistance rating of 1 hour in accordance with the adopted building code, the maximum aggregate quantity per dwelling unit shall be allowed to be increased to a maximum of 31.6 gal (120 L) of liquid oxygen per sleeping room.

63.12.5 Smoking. Smoking shall be prohibited in rooms or areas where liquid oxygen is in use.

63.12.5.1* A sign stating "OXYGEN — NO SMOKING" shall be posted in the room or area where the liquid oxygen containers are stored or used.

Chapter 64 Corrosive Solids and Liquids

64.1 General.

Δ **64.1.1** The storage, use, and handling of corrosive solids and liquids shall comply with the requirements of Chapter 60.

Δ **64.1.2** The storage, use, and handling of corrosive solids and liquids in amounts exceeding the maximum allowable quantities permitted in control areas set forth in Chapter 60 shall comply with the requirements of NFPA 400.

N **64.1.3** Permits shall be required in accordance with this chapter and Table 1.13.8(a) through Table 1.13.8(d).

N **64.1.4** Permits, where required, shall comply with Section 1.13.

Chapter 65 Explosives, Fireworks, and Model Rocketry

65.1 General.

65.1.1* The storage, use, and handling of explosives, fireworks, and model rocketry shall comply with the requirements of this chapter, NFPA standards referenced within this chapter, and Sections 60.1 through 60.4 of this *Code*.

65.1.2 Where the provisions of this chapter or NFPA standards referenced herein conflict with the provisions of Chapter 60, the provisions of this chapter and referenced NFPA standards shall apply.

N **65.1.3** Permits shall be required in accordance with this chapter and Table 1.13.8(a) through Table 1.13.8(d).

N **65.1.4** Permits, where required, shall comply with Section 1.13.

65.2 Display Fireworks.

65.2.1 The construction, handling, and use of fireworks intended solely for outdoor display as well as the general conduct and operation of the display shall comply with the requirements of NFPA 1123.

65.2.2 All storage of display fireworks shall comply with NFPA 1124.

65.2.3 Permits. Permits, where required, shall comply with Section 1.13.

65.3 Pyrotechnics Before a Proximate Audience.

65.3.1 The use of pyrotechnic special effects in the performing arts in conjunction with theatrical, musical, or any similar productions before a proximate audience, performers, or support personnel shall comply with NFPA 1126.

65.3.2 Where any of the following conditions exist, they shall comply with NFPA 1126:

(1) Any indoor display of pyrotechnic special effects
(2) Any outdoor use of pyrotechnic special effects at distances less than those required by NFPA 1123
(3) The use of pyrotechnic special effects during any videotaping, audiotaping, or filming of any television, radio, or movie production if such production is before a proximate audience
(4) The rehearsal of any production in which pyrotechnic special effects are used

65.3.3 Permits. Permits, where required, shall comply with Section 1.13.

65.4 Flame Effects Before an Audience.

65.4.1 The use of flame effects before an audience shall comply with NFPA 160.

65.4.2 Permits. Permits, where required, shall comply with Section 1.13.

65.5 Fireworks Manufacturing.

65.5.1 The manufacture, transportation, or storage of fireworks shall comply with NFPA 1124.

65.5.2 Permits. Permits, where required, shall comply with Section 1.13.

65.6 Model Rocketry.
The design, construction, limitations of propellant mass and power, and reliability of model rocket motors and model rocket motor reloading kits and their components produced commercially for sale to or use by the public for purposes of education, recreation, and sporting competition shall comply with NFPA 1122.

65.7 Rocketry Manufacturing.

65.7.1 The manufacture of model rocket motors designed, sold, and used for the purpose of propelling recoverable aero models shall comply with NFPA 1125.

65.7.2 Permits. Permits, where required, shall comply with Section 1.13.

65.8 High Power Rocketry.

65.8.1 The design, construction, limitations of propellant mass and power, and reliability of all high-power rocket motors and motor components produced commercially for sale to or use by the certified user for education, recreation, and sporting competition shall comply with NFPA 1127.

65.8.2 Permits. Permits, where required, shall comply with Section 1.13.

65.9 Explosives.

65.9.1 The manufacture, transportation, storage, sale, and use of explosive materials shall comply with NFPA 495 and NFPA 498.

65.9.2 Permits.

65.9.2.1 Permits, where required, shall comply with Section 1.13.

65.9.2.2 A separate permit shall be required to conduct blasting operations.

Chapter 66 Flammable and Combustible Liquids

66.1 General.

66.1.1* The storage, handling, and use of flammable and combustible liquids, including waste liquids, as herein defined and classified, shall comply with this chapter; NFPA 30, and Sections 60.1 through 60.4 of this *Code*.

66.1.2 Where the provisions of this chapter or NFPA 30 conflict with the provisions of Chapter 60, the provisions of this chapter and NFPA 30 shall apply.

△ **66.1.3** This chapter shall not apply to the following:

(1)* Any liquid that has a melting point of 100°F (37.8°C) or greater
(2)* Any liquid that does not meet the criteria for fluidity given in the definition of *liquid* in Chapter 3 of NFPA 30 and in the provisions of Chapter 4 of NFPA 30
(3) Any cryogenic fluid or liquefied gas, as defined in Chapter 3
(4)* Any liquid that does not have a flash point, but which is capable of burning under certain conditions
(5)* Any aerosol product
(6) Any mist, spray, or foam
(7)* Transportation of ignitible (flammable or combustible) liquids as governed by the US Department of Transportation
(8)* Use of alcohol-based hand rub (ABHR) dispensers that comply with the applicable provisions of NFPA *101* or the adopted fire code for ABHR dispensers
(9) Liquids in the fuel tanks of motor vehicles, aircraft, boats, or portable or stationary engines
(10) Liquids that have no fire point when tested in accordance with ASTM D92, *Standard Test Method for Flash and Fire Points by Cleveland Open Cup Tester*, up to the boiling point of the liquid or up to a temperature at which the liquid shows an obvious physical change
(11) Liquids with a flash point greater than 95°F (35°C) in a water-miscible solution or water-miscible dispersion with a water and noncombustible solids content of more than 80 percent by weight, and which does not sustain combustion when tested in accordance with "Method of Testing for Sustained Combustibility," in accordance with 49 CFR 173, Appendix H, or the UN publication, *Recommendations on the Transport of Dangerous Goods*
(12)* Unstable liquids
[**30**:1.1.2]

N **66.1.4** The storage of ABHR solution shall be in accordance with NFPA 30.

△ **66.1.5** Installations made in accordance with the applicable requirements of the following standards shall be deemed to be in compliance with this *Code*:

(1) NFPA 1
(2) NFPA 20
(3) NFPA 30A
(4) NFPA 31
(5) NFPA 32
(6) NFPA 33
(7) NFPA 34
(8) NFPA 35
(9) NFPA 36
(10) NFPA 37
(11) NFPA 45
(12) NFPA 99
(13) NFPA *101*
[**30**:1.5.3]

△ **66.1.6 Permits.**

N **66.1.6.1** Permits shall be required in accordance with this chapter and Table 1.13.8(a) through Table 1.13.8(d).

N **66.1.6.2** Permits, where required, shall comply with Section 1.13.

66.2 Reserved.

66.3 Definitions.

66.3.1 (Reserved)

66.3.2 (Reserved)

66.3.3 General Definitions.

66.3.3.1 Alcohol-Based Hand Rub. See 3.3.14.

66.3.3.2 Area.

66.3.3.2.1 Fire Area. See 3.3.17.3.

66.3.3.3 Barrel. See 3.3.24.

66.3.3.4 Basement. See 3.3.25.

66.3.3.5 Boiling Point. See 3.3.30.

66.3.3.6* Boil-Over. See 3.3.31.

66.3.3.7 Building.

66.3.3.7.1* Important Building. See 3.3.32.7.

66.3.3.7.2 Storage Tank Building. See 3.3.32.11.

66.3.3.8 Chemical Plant. See 3.3.50.

66.3.3.9 Closed-Top Diking. See 3.3.56.

66.3.3.10 Container. A vessel of 119 gal (450 L) or less capacity used for transporting or storing liquids, excluding intermediate bulk containers. [**30**,2021]

66.3.3.10.1 Closed Container. See 3.3.73.3.1.

66.3.3.10.2 Intermediate Bulk Container. See 3.3.73.5.

66.3.3.11 Control Area. For this chapter, a building or portion of a building within which liquids are allowed to be stored, dispensed, and used or handled in quantities that do not exceed the maximum allowable quantity (MAQ). [**30**,2021]

66.3.3.12 Crude Petroleum. See 3.3.79.

66.3.3.13 Cryogenic Fluid. See 3.3.80.

66.3.3.14 Damage-Limiting Construction. See 3.3.85.

66.3.3.15 Distillery. See 3.3.93.

66.3.3.16 Fire Point. See 3.3.133.

66.3.3.17 Flash Point. See 3.3.140.

66.3.3.18* Fugitive Emissions. See 3.3.143.

66.3.3.19* Hazardous Material or Hazardous Chemical. Material presenting dangers beyond the fire problems relating to flash point and boiling point. [**30**,2021]

66.3.3.20 Hazardous Materials Storage Locker. See 3.3.158.

66.3.3.21 Hazardous Reaction or Hazardous Chemical Reaction. See 3.3.159.

66.3.3.22 Heat Transfer Fluid (HTF). See 3.3.160.

66.3.3.23 High-Hazard Level 2 Contents. Contents that present a deflagration hazard or a hazard from accelerated burning, which, for this chapter, includes Class I, Class II, or Class IIIA liquids [FP < 200°F (93°C)] that are used or stored in normally open containers or systems, or in closed containers or systems at gauge pressures 15 psi (103 kPa) or greater. [**30**,2021]

66.3.3.24 High-Hazard Level 3 Contents. Contents that readily support combustion or that present a physical hazard, which, for this chapter, includes Class I, Class II, or Class IIIA liquids [FP < 200°F (93°C)] that are used or stored in normally closed containers or in closed systems at gauge pressures of less than 15 psi (103 kPa). [**30**,2021]

66.3.3.25 Incidental Liquid Use or Storage. See 3.3.170.

66.3.3.26 Liquid.

66.3.3.26.1 Combustible Liquid. See 3.3.180.1.

66.3.3.26.2 Flammable Liquid. See 3.3.180.2.

66.3.3.26.3 Stable Liquid. See 3.3.180.6.

66.3.3.27* Operating Unit (Vessel) or Process Unit (Vessel). See 3.3.207.

66.3.3.28 Operations. See 3.3.208.

66.3.3.29* Process or Processing. See 3.3.228.

66.3.3.30 Protection for Exposures. See 3.3.231.

66.3.3.31 Refinery. See 3.3.240.

66.3.3.32* Safety Can. See 3.3.249.

66.3.3.33 Storage Tank. See 3.3.284.7.

66.3.3.33.1 Aboveground Tank. See 3.3.284.2.

66.3.3.33.1.1 Protected Aboveground Tank. See 3.3.284.2.1.

66.3.3.33.2 Low-Pressure Tank. For the purposes of this chapter, a storage tank designed to withstand an internal pressure above a gauge pressure of 1.0 psi (6.9 kPa) but not more than a gauge pressure of 15 psi (103 kPa) measured at the top of the tank. [**30**,2021]

66.3.3.33.3 Portable Tank. See 3.3.284.4.

66.3.3.33.3.1* Nonmetallic Portable Tank. A portable tank, as herein defined, constructed of plastic, fiber, or a material other than metal. [**30**,2021]

66.3.3.33.4 Secondary Containment Tank. See 3.3.284.5.

66.3.3.34 Unit Operation or Unit Process. See 3.3.294.

66.3.3.35 Vapor Pressure. See 3.3.301.

66.3.3.36 Vapor Processing Equipment. Those components of a vapor processing system designed to process vapors or liquids captured during transfer or filling operations. [**30**,2021]

66.3.3.37* Vapor Processing System. See 3.3.283.15.

66.3.3.38 Vapor Recovery System. See 3.3.283.16.

66.3.3.39 Vent.

66.3.3.39.1 Emergency Relief Vent. See 3.3.101.

66.3.3.40* Warehouse.

66.3.3.40.1 General-Purpose Warehouse. See 3.3.305.1.

66.3.3.40.2 Liquid Warehouse. See 3.3.305.2.

66.4 Classification of Liquids.

66.4.1 Classification Scheme.

66.4.1.1 Class I Liquids.

66.4.1.1.1 A liquid with a closed-cup flash point below 100°F (37.8°C) shall be designated as a Class I liquid (i.e., flammable liquid), as determined by the test procedures and apparatus set forth in 66.4.3 and a Reid vapor pressure that does not exceed an absolute pressure of 40 psi (276 kPa) at 100°F (37.8°C), as determined by ASTM D323, *Standard Test Method for Vapor Pressure of Petroleum Products (Reid Method).* [**30**:4.2.1.1]

66.4.1.1.2 Class I liquids shall be further subclassified in accordance with the following:

(1) *Class IA Liquid.* A liquid that has a flash point below 73°F (22.8°C) and a boiling point below 100°F (37.8°C).
(2) *Class IB Liquid.* A liquid that has a flash point below 73°F (22.8°C) and a boiling point at or above 100°F (37.8°C).
(3) *Class IC Liquid.* A liquid that has a flash point at or above 73°F (22.8°C), but below 100°F (37.8°C).

[**30**:4.2.1.2]

66.4.1.2 Class II Liquids. A liquid with a closed-cup flash point at or above 100°F (37.8°C) but below 140°F (60°C) shall be designated as a Class II liquid (i.e., combustible liquid), as determined by the test procedures and apparatus set forth in 66.4.3. [**30**:4.2.2]

66.4.1.3 Class III Liquids.

66.4.1.3.1 A liquid with a closed-cup flash point at or above 140°F (60°C) shall be designated as a Class III liquid (i.e., combustible liquid), as determined by the test procedures and apparatus set forth in 66.4.3. [**30**:4.2.3.1]

66.4.1.3.2 Class III liquids shall be further subclassified in accordance with the following:

(1) *Class IIIA Liquid.* A liquid that has a flash point at or above 140°F (60°C), but below 200°F (93°C).
(2) *Class IIIB Liquid.* A liquid that has a flash point at or above 200°F (93°C).

[**30**:4.2.3.2]

66.4.2 Determination of Boiling Point (BP).

66.4.2.1 For defining the boiling point, atmospheric pressure shall be considered to be an absolute pressure of 14.7 psi (101.4 kPa). [**30**:4.3.1]

66.4.2.2 For mixtures that do not have a constant boiling point, the 20 percent evaporated point of a distillation performed in accordance with ASTM D86, *Standard Test Method for Distillation of Petroleum Products at Atmospheric Pressure,* shall be considered to be the boiling point. [**30**:4.3.2]

66.4.3 Determination of Flash Point (FP). The flash point of a liquid shall be determined according to the methods specified in 66.4.3.1 through 66.4.3.4. [**30**:4.4]

66.4.3.1 Except as specified in 66.4.3.1.1, the flash point of a liquid having a viscosity below 5.5 centiStokes at 104°F (40°C) or below 9.5 centiStokes at 77°F (25°C) shall be determined in accordance with ASTM D56, *Standard Test Method for Flash Point by Tag Closed Cup Tester*. [**30**:4.4.1]

66.4.3.1.1 Cut-back asphalts, liquids that tend to form a surface film, and liquids that contain suspended solids shall not be tested in accordance with ASTM D56, *Standard Test Method for Flash Point by Tag Closed Cup Tester*, even if they otherwise meet the viscosity criteria. [**30**:4.4.1.1]

66.4.3.1.2 Such liquids as stated in 66.4.3.1.1 shall be tested in accordance with 66.4.3.2. [**30**:4.4.1.2]

66.4.3.2 The flash point of a liquid having a viscosity of 5.5 centiStokes or more at 104°F (40°C) or 9.5 centiStokes or more at 77°F (25°C) or a flash point of 200°F (93.4°C) or higher shall be determined in accordance with ASTM D93, *Standard Test Methods for Flash Point by Pensky-Martens Closed Cup Tester*. [**30**:4.4.2]

66.4.3.3 As an alternative, ASTM D3278, *Standard Test Methods for Flash Point of Liquids by Small Scale Closed-Cup Apparatus*, shall be permitted to be used for paints, enamels, lacquers, varnishes, and related products and their components that have flash points between 32°F (0°C) and 230°F (110°C) and viscosities below 150 Stokes at 77°F (25°C). [**30**:4.4.3]

66.4.3.4 As an alternative, ASTM D3828, *Standard Test Methods for Flash Point by Small Scale Closed Cup Tester*, shall be permitted to be used for materials other than those for which ASTM D3278 is specifically required. [**30**:4.4.4]

66.5 Reserved.

66.6 Fire and Explosion Prevention and Risk Control.

66.6.1* **Scope.** This subsection shall apply to the hazards associated with storage, processing, handling, and use of ignitible (flammable or combustible) liquids. This subsection shall also apply when specifically referenced by another section. [**30**:6.1]

66.6.2 Reserved.

66.6.3* Management of Fire and Explosion Hazards. This subsection shall apply to the management methodology used to identify, evaluate, and control the hazards involved in the processing and handling of ignitible (flammable or combustible) liquids. These hazards include, but are not limited to, preparation, separation, purification, and change of state, energy content, or composition. [**30**:6.3]

66.6.4 Hazards Analysis.

66.6.4.1 General. Operations involving ignitible (flammable or combustible) liquids shall be reviewed to ensure that fire and explosion hazards are addressed by fire prevention, fire control, and emergency action plans, except as provided in 66.6.4.1.1. [**30**:6.4.1]

66.6.4.1.1 The requirement in 66.6.4.1 shall not apply to the following:

(1) Operations where liquids are used solely for on-site consumption as fuels.
(2) Operations where Class II or Class III liquids [FP ≥ 100°F (37.8°C)] are stored in atmospheric tanks or transferred at temperatures below their flash points.
(3) Mercantile occupancies, crude petroleum exploration, drillings, and well servicing operations, and normally unoccupied facilities in remote locations.

[**30**:6.4.1.1]

66.6.4.1.2 Engineering Evaluation.

66.6.4.1.2.1* The extent of fire prevention and control that is provided shall be determined in consultation with the AHJ or by means of an engineering evaluation of the operation and application of sound fire protection and process engineering principles. [**30**:6.4.1.2.1]

66.6.4.1.2.2 An engineering evaluation shall include, but not be limited to, the following:

(1) Analysis of the fire and explosion hazards of the operation
(2) Analysis of emergency relief from process vessels, taking into consideration the properties of the materials used and the fire protection and control measures taken
(3) Analysis of applicable facility design requirements in Chapters 17, 18, 19, 28, and 29 of NFPA 30
(4) Analysis of applicable requirements for liquid handling, transfer, and use, as covered in Chapters 17, 18, 19, 28, and 29 of NFPA 30
(5) Analysis of local conditions, such as exposure to and from adjacent properties and exposure to floods, earthquakes, and windstorms
(6) Analysis of the emergency response capabilities of the local emergency services

[**30**::6.4.1.2.2]

N **66.6.4.1.2.3** Explosion hazards shall be evaluated, at a minimum, if any of the following conditions exist:

(1) Class IA liquids [FP < 73°F (22.8°C) and BP < 100°F (37.8°C)] are stored in containers larger than 1 gal (4 L) or in quantities exceeding the MAQ
(2) Class I liquids [FP <100°F (37.8°C)] are handled, transferred, or used in quantities exceeding the MAQ
(3) Class II or Class III liquids [FP ≥100°F (37.8°C)] are handled, transferred, or used at quantities exceeding the MAQ at temperatures at or above their flash point or above atmospheric pressure
(4) Class II or Class III liquids [FP ≥100°F (37.8°C)] are handled, transferred, or used for operations at temperatures at or above their boiling point in any quantity
(5) Runaway reactions or creation of ignitible vapors can occur because of normal mixing operations
(6) Ignitible liquids can enter in contact with incompatible material under abnormal conditions

[**30**:6.4.1.2.3]

N **66.6.4.1.2.4** Where an explosion hazard is determined to exist by the evaluation in 66.6.4.1.2, explosion protection shall be provided in accordance with 66.6.8. [**30**:6.4.1.2.4]

66.6.4.1.3* Storage, processing, handling, and use of Class II and Class III liquids [FP ≥ 100°F (37.8°C)] heated at or above their flash point shall follow the requirements for Class I liquids [FP < 100°F (37.8°C)], unless an engineering evaluation conducted in accordance with Section 66.6 justifies following the requirements for some other liquid class. [**30**:6.4.1.3]

66.6.4.2 Management of Change. The hazards analysis shall be repeated whenever the hazards leading to a fire or explosion change significantly. Conditions that might require repeating a review shall include, but are not limited to, the following:

(1) When changes occur in the materials in process
(2) When changes occur in process equipment
(3) When changes occur in process control
(4) When changes occur in operating procedures or assignments

[**30:**6.4.2]

66.6.5 Control of Ignition Sources.

66.6.5.1 General. Precautions shall be taken to prevent the ignition of flammable vapors by sources such as the following:

(1) Open flames
(2) Lightning
(3) Hot surfaces
(4) Radiant heat
(5) Smoking
(6) Cutting and welding
(7) Spontaneous ignition
(8)* Frictional heat or sparks
(9) Static electricity
(10) Electrical sparks
(11) Stray currents
(12) Ovens, furnaces, and heating equipment

[**30:**6.5.1]

66.6.5.2 Smoking. Smoking shall be permitted only in designated and identified areas. [**30:**6.5.2]

66.6.5.3* Hot Work.

66.6.5.3.1 Welding, cutting, and similar spark-producing operations shall not be permitted in areas containing Class I liquids [FP < 100°F (37.8°C)] until a written permit authorizing such work has been issued. [**30:**6.5.3.1]

66.6.5.3.2 The permit shall be issued by a person in authority following inspection of the area to ensure that permit requirements have been implemented and will be followed until the job is completed. [**30:**6.5.3.2]

66.6.5.4 Static Electricity.

N **66.6.5.4.1*** The prevention of electrostatic ignition shall apply when either of the following are transferred, handled, or used:

(1) Class I liquids [FP < 100°F (37.8°C)]
(2) Class II or Class III liquids [FP ≥ 100°F (37.8°C)] at or above their flash points

[**30:**6.5.4.1]

66.6.5.4.2 All equipment such as tanks, machinery, and piping shall be designed and operated to limit the generation of static electricity. [**30:**6.5.4.2.1]

Δ **66.6.5.4.3** All metallic equipment such as tanks, machinery, and piping shall be bonded and grounded. [**30:**6.5.4.3]

Δ **66.6.5.4.4** The bond and ground shall be either physically applied or inherently present by the nature of the installation. [**30:**6.5.4.3.1]

Δ **66.6.5.4.5** Any electrically isolated section of metallic piping or equipment shall be bonded and grounded. [**30:**6.5.4.3.2]

66.6.5.4.6* All nonmetallic containers, equipment, and piping shall be designed and operated to prevent electrostatic ignition where the potential for an ignitible mixture exists. [**30:**6.5.4.4]

66.6.5.5 Electrical Systems. Design, selection, and installation of electrical wiring and electrical utilization equipment shall meet the requirements of Section 66.7. [**30:**6.5.5]

66.6.6 Detection and Alarm Systems and Procedures.

66.6.6.1* An approved means shall be provided for prompt notification of fire or other emergency to those identified in the emergency action plan in accordance with Section 66.6.9. [**30:**6.6.1]

66.6.6.2 Those areas, including buildings, where a potential exists for a Class I liquid [flash point < 100°F (37.8°C)] spill shall be monitored as appropriate. The following methods shall be permitted to be used:

(1) Personnel observation or patrol
(2) Process-monitoring equipment that would indicate a spill or leak could have occurred
(3) Provision of gas detectors to continuously monitor the area where facilities are unattended

[**30:**6.6.2]

66.6.7 Fire Protection and Fire Suppression Systems.

66.6.7.1* This section identifies recognized fire protection and fire suppression systems and methods used to prevent or minimize the loss from fire or explosion in ignitible (flammable or combustible) liquid-processing facilities. The application of one or a combination of these systems and methods as well as the use of fire-resistive materials shall be determined in accordance with Sections 66.6.3 and 66.6.4. [**30:**6.7.1]

66.6.7.2 A reliable water supply or other suitable fire control agent shall be available in pressure and quantity to meet the fire demands indicated by the specific hazards of liquids-processing operations, storage, or exposure. [**30:**6.7.2]

66.6.7.3* Permanent connections between the fire water system and any process system shall be prohibited, to prevent contamination of fire water with process fluids. [**30:**6.7.3]

Δ **66.6.7.4** Where required by this section, hydrants, with or without fixed monitor nozzles, shall be provided in accordance with NFPA 24. The number and placement shall depend on the hazards of the facility. [**30:**6.7.4]

66.6.7.5 Where the need is indicated by the hazards of ignitible (flammable or combustible) liquid processing, storage, or exposure as determined by 66.6.4, fixed protection shall be provided. [**30:**6.7.5]

N **66.6.7.6*** Where provided, fire control systems shall be designed, installed, and maintained in accordance with the following NFPA standards, as applicable:

(1) NFPA 11
(2) NFPA 12
(3) NFPA 12A
(4) NFPA 13
(5) NFPA 15
(6) NFPA 17
(7) NFPA 750

(8) NFPA 770
(9) NFPA 2001
[**30:**6.7.6]

Δ **66.6.7.7** Where required by this section, standpipe and hose systems shall be installed in accordance with NFPA 14 or hose connections from sprinkler systems using combination spray and straight stream nozzles shall be installed in accordance with NFPA 13. [**30:**6.7.7]

66.6.7.8* Where required by this section, listed portable fire extinguishers shall be provided in such quantities, sizes, and types as are needed for the specific hazards of operation and storage. [**30:**6.7.8]

66.6.7.9 Where provided, mobile foam apparatus and supplies of foam concentrate shall be appropriate to the specific hazards. [**30:**6.7.9]

N **66.6.8 Explosion Protection Systems.**

N **66.6.8.1** The application of one or a combination of recognized explosion protection and explosion suppression systems and methods used to prevent or minimize the loss from explosion in ignitible (flammable or combustible) liquid facilities, as well as the use of fire-resistive materials, shall be determined in accordance with Sections 66.6.3 and 66.6.4. [**30:**6.8.1]

N **66.6.8.2** Where required by the engineering evaluation specified in 66.6.4.1.2, or where otherwise provided, explosion protection systems shall incorporate one or more of the following methods of protection:

(1) Deflagration venting in accordance with NFPA 68
(2) Deflagration venting through listed flame-arresting devices in accordance with NFPA 68
(3) Oxidant concentration reduction in accordance with NFPA 69
(4) Deflagration pressure containment in accordance with NFPA 69
(5) Deflagration suppression system in accordance with NFPA 69
(6) Approved engineered damage-limiting construction designed in accordance with available standards

[**30:**6.8.2]

66.6.9 Emergency Planning and Training.

66.6.9.1 A written emergency action plan that is consistent with available equipment and personnel shall be established to respond to fires and related emergencies and include the following:

(1) Procedures to be followed in case of fire or release of liquids or vapors, such as sounding the alarm, notifying the fire department, evacuating personnel, and controlling and extinguishing the fire
(2) Procedures and schedules for conducting drills of these procedures
(3) Appointment and training of personnel to carry out assigned duties, including review at the time of initial assignment, as responsibilities or response actions change, and whenever anticipated duties change
(4) Procedures for maintenance and operation of (a) fire protection equipment and systems, (b) drainage and containment systems, and (c) dispersion and ventilation equipment and systems
(5) Procedures for shutting down or isolating equipment to reduce, mitigate, or stop the release of liquid or vapors, including assigning personnel responsible for maintaining critical plant functions or shutdown of plant processes and safe start-up following isolation or shutdown
(6) Alternate measures for the safety of occupants

[**30:**6.9.1]

66.6.9.2 Personnel responsible for the use and operation of fire protection equipment shall be trained in the use of that equipment. Refresher training shall be conducted at least annually. [**30:**6.9.2]

66.6.9.3 Planning of effective fire control measures shall be coordinated with local emergency response agencies. [**30:**6.9.3]

Δ **66.6.9.4** Procedures shall be established to provide for safe shutdown of operations under emergency conditions and for safe start-up following cessation of emergencies. [**30:**6.9.4]

N **66.6.9.5** Provisions shall be made for training of personnel in shutdown and start-up procedures, and in activation, use, and deactivation of associated alarms, interlocks, and controls. [**30:**6.9.5]

N **66.6.9.6** Procedures shall also be made for inspection and testing of associated alarms, interlocks, and controls. [**30:**6.9.6]

66.6.9.7 The emergency procedures shall be kept readily available in the operating areas and shall be updated when conditions change, as identified in 66.6.4.2. [**30:**6.9.7]

66.6.9.7.1 Where premises are likely to be unattended for considerable periods of time, a summary of the emergency plan shall be posted or located in a strategic and accessible location. [**30:**6.9.7.1]

66.6.10 Inspection and Maintenance.

Δ **66.6.10.1** All fire protection equipment shall be properly maintained, and periodic inspections and tests shall be done in accordance with both standard practice and the equipment manufacturers recommendations. Water-based fire protection systems shall be inspected, tested, and maintained in accordance with NFPA 25. [**30:**6.10.1]

66.6.10.2 Maintenance and operating practices shall be established and implemented to prevent and control leakage and spillage of ignitible (flammable or combustible) liquids. [**30:**6.10.2]

66.6.10.3 Combustible waste material and residues in operating areas shall comply with the requirements in 66.6.10.3.1 through 66.6.10.3.3. [**30:**6.10.3]

N **66.6.10.3.1** Combustible waste material shall be kept to a minimum and stored in metal waste receptacles or listed combustible waste receptacles. [**30:**6.10.3.1]

N **66.6.10.3.2*** Rags, wipes, and waste with ignitible (flammable or combustible) liquid residues shall be kept to a minimum and stored in listed oily waste receptacles. [**30:**6.10.3.2]

N **66.6.10.3.3** Waste receptacles in operating areas subject to 66.6.10.3.1 and 66.6.10.3.2 shall be emptied daily. [**30:**6.10.3.3]

66.6.10.4 Ground areas around facilities where liquids are stored, handled, or used shall be kept free of weeds, trash, or other unnecessary combustible materials. [**30:**6.10.4]

66.6.10.5 Aisles established for movement of personnel shall be kept clear of obstructions to permit orderly evacuation and ready access for manual fire-fighting activities. [**30:**6.10.5]

66.6.11 Management of Security.

66.6.11.1 Scope.

66.6.11.1.1 This section shall apply to the management methodology used to identify, evaluate, and control the security hazards involved in the processing, storage, and handling of ignitible (flammable or combustible) liquids. [**30:**6.11.1.1]

66.6.11.1.2 These hazards include, but are not limited to, vulnerability to terrorist or other malicious attacks. [**30:**6.11.1.2]

66.6.11.2 General. The methodology used shall incorporate a risk-based approach to site security and shall have the following objectives:

(1) Identification and evaluation of security risks
(2) Evaluation of the security performance of the facility
(3) Evaluation of protection for employees, the facility itself, the surrounding communities, and the environment. *(See Annex I of NFPA 30 for more detailed information.)*

[**30:**6.11.2]

66.6.11.3 Specific Requirements.

66.6.11.3.1 Operations involving ignitible (flammable or combustible) liquids shall be reviewed to ensure that security vulnerabilities identified during the security vulnerability assessment (SVA) are addressed in a facility security program, with corresponding fire prevention and emergency action plans and drills. [**30:**6.11.3.1]

66.6.11.3.2 The balance of physical, electronic, and personnel techniques used to respond to the SVA shall be determined by means of an engineering evaluation of the operation and application of sound security principles. This evaluation shall include, but not be limited to, the following:

(1) Assessing overall facility
(2) Evaluating vulnerabilities
(3) Assessing threats/consequences
(4) Assessing physical factors/attractiveness
(5) Identifying mitigation factors
(6) Conducting security assessment or gap analysis

[**30:**6.11.3.2]

66.6.11.3.3 A written emergency action plan that is consistent with available equipment and personnel shall be established to respond to fires, security, and related emergencies. This plan shall include the following:

(1) Procedures to be followed such as initiating alarms, notifying appropriate agencies, evacuating personnel, and controlling and extinguishing the fire
(2) Procedures and schedules for conducting drills of these procedures
(3) Appointment and training of personnel to carry out assigned duties
(4) Maintenance of fire protection and response equipment
(5) Procedures for shutting down or isolating equipment to reduce the release of liquid
(6) Alternate measures for the safety of occupants

[**30:**6.11.3.3]

66.6.11.3.4 Specific duties of personnel shall be reviewed at the time of initial assignment, as responsibilities or response actions change, and whenever anticipated duties change. [**30:**6.11.3.4]

66.6.11.3.5 The security management review conducted in accordance with this section shall be repeated under the following conditions:

(1) For an initial review of all new relevant facilities and assets
(2) When substantial changes to the threat or process occur
(3) After a significant security incident
(4) For periodic revalidation of the SVA

[**30:**6.11.3.5]

N **66.6.12* Containment, Drainage, and Spill Control.** Ignitible (flammable or combustible) liquids shall not be released into a sewer, storm drain, ditch, drainage canal, lake, river, or tidal waterway; upon the ground, a sidewalk, a street, or a highway; or into the atmosphere, unless such release is permitted by the relevant federal, state, and local governing regulations. [**30:**6.12]

N **66.6.12.1* Design Intent.** The facility shall be designed and operated to prevent the discharge of liquids to public waterways, public sewers, or adjoining property as determined by regulatory requirements and the requirements of 66.6.11. [**30:**6.12.1]

N **66.6.12.2 Spill Control.** Where required by other chapters, spill control shall be provided in accordance with 66.6.12. [**30:**6.12.2]

N **66.6.12.2.1** Buildings, or portions thereof, used for storage of ignitible (flammable or combustible) liquids in individual containers having a capacity of more than 55 gal (208.2 L) shall be provided with spill control to prevent the flow of liquids to adjoining areas. [**30:**6.12.2.1]

N **66.6.12.2.2** Where spill control is required, floors in indoor locations and similar surfaces in outdoor locations shall be constructed to contain a spill from the largest single vessel by one of the following methods:

(1) Liquidtight sloped or recessed floors in indoor locations or similar areas in outdoor locations
(2) Liquidtight floors in indoor locations or similar areas in outdoor locations provided with liquidtight raised or recessed sills or dikes
(3) Sumps and collection systems
(4) Other approved systems

[**30:**6.12.2.2]

N **66.6.12.2.3** Except for drains, both of the following shall apply:

(1) Solid floors shall be liquidtight.
(2) Walls shall be liquidtight where they join the floor and for at least 4 in. (100 mm) above the floor.

[**30:**6.12.2.3]

N **66.6.12.2.4** Means shall be provided to prevent ignitible (flammable or combustible) liquid spills from running into basements. [**30:**6.12.2.4]

N **66.6.12.3 Secondary Containment.** Where required, secondary containment shall be provided in accordance with this section. [**30:**6.12.3]

N **66.6.12.3.1** Buildings, or portions thereof, used to store liquids where the capacity of an individual vessel exceeds 55 gal (208.2 L) or the aggregate capacity of multiple vessels exceeds 1000 gal (3785 L) shall be provided with secondary containment. [**30:**6.12.3.1]

N 66.6.12.3.2* Where secondary containment is required, floors in indoor locations and similar surfaces in outdoor locations shall be constructed to contain a spill from the largest single vessel by one of the following methods:

(1) Liquidtight sloped or recessed floors in indoor locations or similar areas in outdoor locations
(2) Liquidtight floors in indoor locations or similar areas in outdoor locations provided with liquidtight raised or recessed sills or dikes
(3) Sumps and collection systems
(4) Other approved systems

[**30**:6.12.3.2]

N 66.6.12.3.3 Where secondary containment is provided, it shall have a capacity that is not less than the largest single container, intermediate bulk container, bulk container, vessel, or tank that can drain into it, plus the capacity to contain the fire protection water that can reasonably be expected to contain a fire occurring within the secondary containment area, plus the volume occupied by anything that is, or could be sitting in the containment were a spill to occur. [**30**:6.12.3.3]

N 66.6.12.4 Drainage. If drainage is used it shall meet the requirements of 66.6.12. [**30**:6.12.4]

N 66.6.12.4.1 Where a drainage system is used to remove liquids from the fire area, it shall direct liquid leakage and fire protection water to an approved safe location without creating any additional exposure hazards. [**30**:6.12.4.1]

N 66.6.12.4.2 If drainage systems are connected to public or private sewers, or discharged into waterways, the drainage system shall be equipped with traps and separators. [**30**:6.12.4.2]

N 66.6.12.4.3 Drainage systems shall be designed to handle the anticipated liquid flow, including fire protection water. [**30**:6.12.4.3]

N 66.6.12.4.4 Curbs, scuppers, or special drainage systems shall be permitted to be used. [**30**:6.12.4.4]

N 66.6.12.4.4.1 An open-grated trench across the width of the opening inside of the room that drains to a safe location shall be permitted to be used as an alternative to a sill or ramp. [**30**:6.12.4.4.1]

66.7 Electrical Systems.

66.7.1 Scope. This section shall apply to areas where Class I liquids [FP < 100°F (37.8°C)] are stored, handled, or used and to areas where Class II or Class III liquids [FP ≥ 100°F (37.8°C)] are stored, handled, or used at or above their flash points. [**30**:7.1]

66.7.2 Reserved.

66.7.3 General Requirements.

66.7.3.1 Electrical utilization equipment and wiring shall not constitute a source of ignition for any ignitible vapor that might be present under normal operation or because of a spill. Compliance with 66.7.3.2 through 66.7.3.7.1 shall be deemed as meeting the requirements of this section. [**30**:7.3.1]

66.7.3.2 All electrical utilization equipment and wiring shall be of a type specified by and installed in accordance with *NFPA 70*. [**30**:7.3.2]

66.7.3.3* Table 66.7.3.3 shall be used to delineate and classify areas for installation of electrical utilization equipment and wiring under normal operating conditions. [**30**:7.3.3]

66.7.3.4 A classified area shall not extend beyond a floor, wall, roof, or other solid partition that has no openings within the classified area. [**30**:7.3.4]

66.7.3.5 The designation of classes, divisions, and zones shall be as defined in Chapter 5 of *NFPA 70*. [**30**:7.3.5]

66.7.3.6 The area classifications listed in Table 66.7.3.3 are based on the premise that all applicable requirements of this *Code* have been met; if this is not the case, the AHJ shall have the authority to classify the extent of the area. [**30**:7.3.6]

66.7.3.7* Where the provisions of 66.7.3.1 through 66.7.3.6 require the installation of electrical equipment suitable for Class I, Division 1 or 2, or Zone 1 or 2 locations, ordinary electrical equipment, including switchgear, shall be permitted to be used if installed in a room or enclosure that is maintained under positive pressure with respect to the classified area. [**30**:7.3.7]

66.7.3.7.1 Ventilation make-up air shall be taken from an uncontaminated source. [**30**:7.3.7.1]

66.8 Application of Area Classification. Area classification shall be used to assure that fixed electrical utilization equipment, electrical fixtures, and wiring are installed within Class I, Division 1; Zone 1; Class I, Division 2; or Zone 2 designated areas, as defined by Article 500 of *NFPA 70*. [**30**:7.4]

66.9 Storage of Ignitible (Flammable or Combustible) Liquids in Containers — General Requirements.

66.9.1 Scope.

66.9.1.1 This section shall apply to the storage of ignitible (flammable or combustible) liquids in:

(1) Drums or other containers that do not exceed 119 gal (450 L) individual capacity
(2) Portable tanks that do not exceed 660 gal (2500 L) individual capacity
(3) Intermediate bulk containers that do not exceed 793 gal (3000 L)

[**30**:9.1.1]

66.9.1.2 This section shall also apply to limited transfer of ignitible (flammable or combustible) liquids incidental thereto. [**30**:9.1.2]

66.9.1.3 This section shall also apply to overpack drums when used for temporary containment of containers that do not exceed 60 gal (230 L) capacity. Such overpack containers shall be treated as containers as defined in 66.3.3.10. [**30**:9.1.3]

Δ Table 66.7.3.3 Electrical Area Classifications

Location	NEC Class I, Division	Zone	Extent of Classified Area
Indoor equipment installed in accordance with 66.7.3 where flammable vapor–air mixtures can exist under normal operation	1	0	The entire area associated with such equipment where flammable gases or vapors are present continuously or for long periods of time
	1	1	Area within 5 ft of any edge of such equipment, extending in all directions
	2	2	Area between 5 ft and 8 ft of any edge of such equipment, extending in all directions; also, space up to 3 ft above floor or grade level within 5 ft to 25 ft horizontally from any edge of such equipment*
Outdoor equipment of the type covered in 66.7.3 where flammable vapor–air mixtures can exist under normal operation	1	0	The entire area associated with such equipment where flammable gases or vapors are present continuously or for long periods of time
	1	1	Area within 3 ft of any edge of such equipment, extending in all directions
	2	2	Area between 3 ft and 8 ft of any edge of such equipment, extending in all directions; also, space up to 3 ft above floor or grade level within 3 ft to 10 ft horizontally from any edge of such equipment
Tank storage installations inside buildings	1	1	All equipment located below grade level
	2	2	Any equipment located at or above grade level
Tank — aboveground, fixed roof	1	0	Inside fixed-roof tank
	1	1	Area inside dike where dike height is greater than the distance from the tank to the dike for more than 50 percent of the tank circumference
	2	2	Within 10 ft from shell, ends, or roof of tank; also, area inside dike up to top of dike wall
	1	0	Area inside of vent piping or vent opening
	1	1	Within 5 ft of open end of vent, extending in all directions
	2	2	Area between 5 ft and 10 ft from open end of vent, extending in all directions
Tank — aboveground, floating roof With fixed outer roof	1	0	Area between the floating and fixed-roof sections and within the shell
With no fixed outer roof	1	1	Area above the floating roof and within the shell
Tank vault — interior	1	1	Entire interior volume, if Class I liquids [FP < 100°F (37.8°C)] are stored within
Underground tank fill opening	1	1	Any pit, box, or space below grade level, if any part is within a Division 1 or 2 or Zone 1 or 2 classified location
	2	2	Up to 18 in. above grade level within a horizontal radius of 10 ft from a loose fill connection and within a horizontal radius of 5 ft from a tight fill connection
Vent — discharging upward	1	0	Area inside of vent piping or opening
	1	1	Within 3 ft of open end of vent, extending in all directions
	2	2	Area between 3 ft and 5 ft of open end of vent, extending in all directions
Drum and container filling — outdoors or indoors	1	0	Area inside the drum or container
	1	1	Within 3 ft of vent and fill openings, extending in all directions

(continues)

Δ Table 66.7.3.3 Continued

Location	NEC Class I, Division	Zone	Extent of Classified Area
	2	2	Area between 3 ft and 5 ft from vent or fill opening, extending in all directions; also, up to 18 in. above floor or grade level within a horizontal radius of 10 ft from vent or fill opening
Pumps, bleeders, withdrawal fittings			
Indoor	2	2	Within 5 ft of any edge of such devices, extending in all directions; also, up to 3 ft above floor or grade level within 25 ft horizontally from any edge of such devices
Outdoor	2	2	Within 3 ft of any edge of such devices, extending in all directions; also, up to 18 in. above grade level within 10 ft horizontally from any edge of such devices
Pits and sumps			
Without mechanical ventilation	1	1	Entire area within a pit or sump if any part is within a Division 1 or 2 or Zone 1 or 2 classified location
With adequate mechanical ventilation	2	2	Entire area within a pit or sump if any part is within a Division 1 or 2 or Zone 1 or 2 classified location
Containing valves, fittings, or piping, and not within a Division 1 or 2 or Zone 1 or 2 classified location	2	2	Entire pit or sump
Drainage ditches, separators, impounding basins			
Outdoor	2	2	Area up to 18 in. above ditch, separator, or basin; also, area up to 18 in. above grade within 15 ft horizontally from any edge
Indoor			Same as pits and sumps
Tank vehicle and tank car[†]			
Loading through open dome	1	0	Area inside of the tank
	1	1	Within 3 ft of edge of dome, extending in all directions
	2	2	Area between 3 ft and 15 ft from edge of dome, extending in all directions
Loading through bottom connections with atmospheric venting	1	0	Area inside of the tank
	1	1	Within 3 ft of point of venting to atmosphere, extending in all directions
	2	2	Area between 3 ft and 15 ft from point of venting to atmosphere, extending in all directions; also, up to 18 in. above grade within a horizontal radius of 10 ft from point of loading connection
Loading through closed dome with atmospheric venting	1	1	Within 3 ft of open end of vent, extending in all directions
	2	2	Area between 3 ft and 15 ft from open end of vent, extending in all directions; also, within 3 ft of edge of dome, extending in all directions
Loading through closed dome with vapor control	2	2	Within 3 ft of point of connection of both fill and vapor lines, extending in all directions
Bottom loading with vapor control or any bottom unloading	2	2	Within 3 ft of point of connections, extending in all directions; also, up to 18 in. above grade within a horizontal radius of 10 ft from point of connections
Storage and repair garage for tank vehicles	1	1	All pits or spaces below floor level
	2	2	Area up to 18 in. above floor or grade level for entire storage or repair garage

(continues)

Δ Table 66.7.3.3 *Continued*

Location	NEC Class I, Division	Zone	Extent of Classified Area
Garages for other than tank vehicles	Ordinary		If there is any opening to these rooms within the extent of an outdoor classified location, the entire room shall be classified the same as the area classification at the point of the opening
Outdoor drum storage	Ordinary		
Liquid storage rooms or storage lockers used for the storage of Class I liquids [FP < 100°F (37.8°C)]	2	2	Entire room or locker
Indoor warehousing where there is no Class I liquid [FP < 100°F (37.8°C)] transfer	Ordinary		If there is any opening to these rooms within the extent of an indoor classified location, the classified location shall extend through the opening to the same extent as if the wall, curb, or partition did not exist
Office and rest rooms	Ordinary		If there is any opening to these rooms within the extent of an indoor classified location, the room shall be classified the same as if the wall, curb, or partition did not exist
Piers and wharves			See Figure 29.3.22 of NFPA 30.

For SI units, 1 in. = 25 mm; 1 ft = 0.3 m.
*The release of Class I liquids [FP < 100°F (37.8°C)] can generate vapors to the extent that the entire building, and possibly an area surrounding it, should be considered a Class I, Division 2, or Zone 2 location.
†When classifying extent of area, consideration should be given to the fact that tank cars or tank vehicles can be spotted at varying points. Therefore, the extremities of the loading or unloading positions should be used. [30:Table 7.3.3]

Δ **66.9.1.4** This section shall not apply to the following:

(1) Containers, intermediate bulk containers, and portable tanks that are used in operations areas, as covered by Section 66.17
(2) Liquids in the fuel tanks of motor vehicles, aircraft, boats, or portable or stationary engines
(3) Beverages, medicines, foodstuffs, cosmetics, and other products that do not contain more than 20 percent by volume of water-miscible ignitible (flammable or combustible) liquids, with the remainder of the product consisting of components that do not burn
(4) Liquids that have no fire point when tested in accordance with ASTM D92, *Standard Test Method for Flash and Fire Points by Cleveland Open Cup Tester*, up to the boiling point of the liquid or up to a temperature at which the liquid shows an obvious physical change
(5) Liquids with a flash point greater than 95°F (35°C) in a water-miscible solution or water-miscible dispersion with a water and noncombustible solids content of more than 80 percent by weight, and which does not sustain combustion when tested in accordance with "Method of Testing for Sustained Combustibility," in accordance with 49 CFR 173, Appendix H, or the UN publication, *Recommendations on the Transport of Dangerous Goods*
[30:9.1.4]

66.9.2 General Requirements.

Δ **66.9.2.1** The general requirements of this section shall be applicable to the storage of ignitible (flammable or combustible) liquids in control areas, liquid storage rooms, and liquid warehouses as covered in Chapters 10 through 14 of NFPA 30, regardless of the quantities being stored. [30:9.3.1]

N **66.9.2.1.1** Where more stringent requirements are set forth in Chapters 10 through 14 of NFPA 30, those requirements shall take precedence. [30:9.3.1.1]

66.9.2.2 Means of egress shall meet applicable requirements of NFPA *101*. [30:9.3.2]

66.9.2.3 Wood of at least 1 in. (25 mm) nominal thickness shall be permitted to be used for shelving, racks, dunnage, scuffboards, floor overlay, and similar installations. [30:9.3.4]

66.9.2.4 Class I liquids [FP < 100°F (37.8°C)] shall not be permitted to be stored in basements as defined in 3.3.25. [30:9.3.4]

66.9.2.5 Class II and Class IIIA liquids [100°F (37.8°C) ≤ FP < 200°F (93°C)] shall be permitted to be stored in basements as defined in 3.3.25, provided the basement is protected in accordance with Section 66.16. [30:9.3.5]

66.9.2.6 Class IIIB liquids [FP ≥ 200°F (93°C)] shall be permitted to be stored in basements as defined in 3.3.25. [30:9.3.6]

66.9.2.7 Where containers, intermediate bulk containers, or portable tanks are stacked, they shall be stacked so that stability is maintained and excessive stress on container walls is prevented. [30:9.3.7]

66.9.2.7.1 Portable tanks and intermediate bulk containers stored more than one high shall be designed to stack securely, without the use of dunnage. [30:9.3.7.1]

66.9.2.7.2 Materials-handling equipment shall be capable of handling containers, portable tanks, and intermediate bulk containers that are stored at all storage levels. [30:9.3.7.2]

66.9.2.7.3* Power-operated industrial trucks used to move Class I liquids [FP < 100°F (37.8°C)] shall be selected, operated, and maintained in accordance with NFPA 505. [**30:**9.3.7.3]

66.9.2.8 Containers, intermediate bulk containers, and portable tanks in unprotected control areas, liquid storage rooms, and liquid warehouses shall not be stored closer than 36 in. (915 mm) to the nearest beam, chord, girder, or other roof or ceiling member. [**30:**9.3.8]

Δ **66.9.2.9** Liquids used for building maintenance, painting, or other similar infrequent maintenance purposes shall be permitted to be stored in closed containers outside of storage cabinets or liquid storage rooms and liquid warehouses, if limited to an amount that does not exceed a 10-day supply at anticipated rates of use. [**30:**9.3.9]

66.9.2.10 Storage, handling, and use of Class II and Class III liquids [FP ≥ 100°F (37.8°C)] heated at or above their FP shall follow the requirements for Class I liquids [FP < 100°F (37.8°C)], unless an engineering evaluation conducted in accordance with Section 66.6 justifies following the requirements for some other liquid class. *(See 66.6.4.1.3 and A.66.6.4.1.3.)*[**30:**9.3.10]

66.9.3 Acceptable Containers.

Δ **66.9.3.1*** Only the following approved containers, intermediate bulk containers, and portable tanks shall be used for Class I, Class II, and Class IIIA liquids [FP < 200°F (93.3°C)]:

(1) Metal containers, metal intermediate bulk containers, and metal portable tanks meeting the requirements of, and containing products authorized by, the US Department of Transportation Hazardous Materials Regulations in 49 CFR 100–199, or by Part 6 of the UN *Recommendations on the Transport of Dangerous Goods*

(2) Plastic or metal consumer-use containers meeting the requirements of, and used within the scope of, ASTM F852, *Standard Specification for Portable Gasoline, Kerosene and Diesel Containers for Consumer Use*

(3) Nonmetallic or metallic commercial/industrial safety cans meeting the requirements of, and used within the scope of, one or more of the following specifications:

  (a) UL 30, *Metal Safety Cans*
  (b) UL 1313, *Nonmetallic Safety Cans for Petroleum Products*
  (c) UL/ULC 30, *Metallic and Nonmetallic Safety Cans for Flammable and Combustible Liquids*
  (d) FM Global *Approval Standard for Safety Containers and Filling, Supply, and Disposal Containers* — Class Number 6051 and 6052

(4) Plastic containers that meet requirements set by, and contain products authorized by, the following:

  (a) The US Department of Transportation Hazardous Materials Regulations in 49 CFR 100–199, or by Part 6 of the UN publication *Recommendations on the Transport of Dangerous Goods*
  (b) Items 256 or 258 of the *National Motor Freight Classification* (NMFC) for liquids that are not classified as hazardous by the US Department of Transportation Hazardous Materials Regulations in 49 CFR 100–199, or by Part 6 of the UN publication *Recommendations on the Transport of Dangerous Goods*

(5) Fiber drums that meet the following:

  (a) Requirements of Items 294 and 296 of the *National Motor Freight Classification* (NMFC) or of Rule 51 of the *Uniform Freight Classification* (UFC), for Types 2A, 3A, 3B-H, 3B-L, or 4A
  (b) Requirements of, and containing liquid products authorized by, either the US Department of Transportation Hazardous Materials Regulations in 49 CFR Chapter I, or by the US Department of Transportation exemption

(6)* Rigid nonmetallic intermediate bulk containers that meet requirements set by, and contain products authorized by, the following:

  (a) The US Department of Transportation Hazardous Materials Regulations in 49 CFR 100–199, or by Part 6 of the UN publication, *Recommendations on the Transport of Dangerous Goods,* for Classes 31H1, 31H2, and 31HZ1
  (b) The *National Motor Freight Classification* (NMFC), or the International Safe Transit Association for liquids that are not classified as hazardous by the US Department of Transportation Hazardous Materials Regulations in 49 CFR 100–199, or by Part 6 of the UN publication *Recommendations on the Transport of Dangerous Goods*

(7) Glass containers up to the capacity limits stated in Table 66.9.3.3 and in accordance with US Department of Transportation Hazardous Materials Regulations in 49 CFR 100–199

(8) Other nonmetallic intermediate bulk containers that comply with 66.9.3.1.1

[**30:**9.4.1]

66.9.3.1.1 For protected storage, nonmetallic intermediate bulk containers shall comply with Table 66.9.3.3 and shall be listed and labeled in accordance with UL 2368, *Fire Exposure Testing of Intermediate Bulk Containers for Flammable and Combustible Liquids;* FM 6020, *Approval Standard for Composite Intermediate Bulk Containers;* or an equivalent test procedure. [**30:**9.4.1.1]

66.9.3.1.2 Medicines, beverages, foodstuffs, cosmetics, and other common consumer products, where packaged according to commonly accepted practices for retail sales, shall be exempt from the requirements of 66.9.3.1 and 66.9.3.3. [**30:**9.4.1.2]

66.9.3.2 Each portable tank or intermediate bulk container shall be provided with one or more devices installed in the top with sufficient emergency venting capacity to limit internal pressure under fire exposure conditions to a gauge pressure of 10 psi (70 kPa) or 30 percent of the bursting pressure of the portable tank, whichever is greater. [**30:**9.4.2]

66.9.3.2.1 The total venting capacity shall be not less than that specified in 22.7.3.2 or 22.7.3.4 of NFPA 30. [**30:**9.4.2.1]

66.9.3.2.2 At least one pressure-actuated vent having a minimum capacity of 6000 ft^3 (170 m^3) of free air per hour at an absolute pressure of 14.7 psi (101 kPa) and 60°F (15.6°C) shall be used. The vent shall be set to open at not less than a gauge pressure of 5 psi (35 kPa). [**30:**9.4.2.2]

66.9.3.2.3 If fusible vents are used, they shall be actuated by elements that operate at a temperature not exceeding 300°F (150°C). Where plugging of a pressure-actuated vent can occur, such as when used for paints, drying oils, and similar materials, fusible plugs or venting devices that soften to failure at a maximum of 300°F (150°C) under fire exposure shall be permitted to be used for the entire emergency venting requirement. [**30**:9.4.2.3]

Δ **66.9.3.3** The maximum allowable size of a container, intermediate bulk container, or metal portable tank for Class I, Class II, and Class IIIA liquids [FP < 200°F (93°C)] shall not exceed that specified in Table 66.9.3.3. [**30**:9.4.3]

N **66.9.3.3.1** Table 66.9.3.3 shall not apply to containers that meet the requirements of 66.9.1, 66.9.3.3.2, 66.9.3.3.4, or 66.9.3.3.5. [**30**:9.4.3.1]

66.9.3.3.2 Class IB and Class IC [FP < 100°F (37.8°C) and BP ≥ 100°F (37.8°C)] water-miscible liquids shall be permitted to be stored in plastic containers up to 60 gal (230 L) in size, if stored and protected in accordance with Table 66.16.5.3.7. [**30**:9.4.3.2]

66.9.3.3.3 Nonmetallic intermediate bulk containers, as permitted by Table 66.9.3.3, shall be listed and labeled in accordance with UL 2368, *Fire Exposure Testing of Intermediate Bulk Containers for Flammable and Combustible Liquids*; FM 6020, *Approval Standard for Composite Intermediate Bulk Containers*; or an equivalent test procedure. [**30**:9.4.3.3]

66.9.3.3.4 Class IA and Class IB [FP < 73°F (22.8°C)] liquids shall be permitted to be stored in glass containers of not more than 1.3 gal (5 L) capacity if the required liquid purity (such as American Chemical Society analytical reagent grade or higher) would be affected by storage in metal containers or if the liquid can cause excessive corrosion of a metal container. [**30**:9.4.3.4]

66.9.3.3.5 Leaking or damaged containers up to 60 gal (230 L) capacity shall be permitted to be stored temporarily in accordance with this section and Chapters 10 through 12 of NFPA 30, provided they are enclosed in overpack containers. [**30**:9.4.3.5]

66.9.3.3.5.1 To be considered protected storage as defined in 9.2.1 of NFPA 30 and in accordance with Section 66.16, an overpack container shall be constructed of the same material as the leaking or damaged container. [**30**:9.4.3.5.1]

66.9.3.3.5.2 Metal overpack containers shall be considered non-relieving style containers. [**30**:9.4.3.5.2]

N **66.9.3.4*** Plastic pallets shall not be permitted. [**30**:9.4.4]

66.9.4* Liquid Storage Cabinets.

Δ **66.9.4.1** The volume of Class I, Class II, and Class IIIA liquids [FP < 200°F (93°C)] stored in an individual storage cabinet shall not exceed 120 gal (460 L). [**30**:9.5.1]

66.9.4.2 The total aggregate volume of Class I, Class II, and Class IIIA liquids [FP < 200°F (93°C)] in a group of storage cabinets shall not exceed the maximum allowable quantity of

Δ **Table 66.9.3.3 Maximum Allowable Size — Containers, Intermediate Bulk Containers (IBCs), and Portable Tanks**

Container Type	Class IA#	Class IB#	Class IC#	Class II#	Class IIIA#
Glass	1 pt (0.5 L)	1 qt (1 L)	1.3 gal (5 L)	1.3 gal (5 L)	5.3 gal (20 L)
Metal (other than drums) or approved plastic	1.3 gal (5 L)	6.5 gal (20 L)	6.5 gal (20 L)	6.5 gal (20 L)	6.5 gal (20 L)
Safety cans	2.6 gal (10 L)	5.3 gal (20 L)	5.3 gal (20 L)	5.3 gal (20 L)	5.3 gal (20 L)
Metal drum (e.g., UN 1A1/1A2)	119 gal (450 L)	119 gal (450 L)	119 gal (450 L)	119 gal (450 L)	119 gal (450 L)
Approved metal portable tanks and IBCs	793 gal (3000 L)	793 gal (3000 L)	793 gal (3000 L)	793 gal (3000 L)	793 gal (3000 L)
Rigid plastic IBCs (UN 31H1 or 31H2) and composite IBCs with rigid inner receptacle (UN31HZ1)†	NP	NP	NP	793 gal (3000 L)	793 gal (3000 L)
Composite IBCs with flexible inner receptacle (UN31HZ2), DOT/UN-approved flexible IBCs, and NMFC/ISTA-compliant IBCs†	NP	NP	NP	331 gal (1300 L)	331 gal (1300 L)
Non-bulk bag-in-box	NP	NP	NP	NP	NP
Polyethylene UN1H1 and UN1H2, or as authorized by DOT special permit or approval	1.3 gal (5 L)	5.3 gal (20 L)*	5.3 gal (20 L)*	119 gal (450 L)	119 gal (450 L)
Fiber drum NMFC or UFC Type 2A; Types 3A, 3B-H, or 3B-L; or Type 4A	NP	NP	NP	119 gal (450 L)	119 gal (450 L)

NP: Not permitted for the container categories so classified unless a fire protection system is provided that is developed in accordance with 66.16.3.5 and is approved for the specific container and protection against static electricity is provided.
*See 66.9.3.3.1.
†See 66.9.3.3.2.
#See 66.4.1 for details on the classification scheme.
[**30**:Table 9.4.3]

ignitible (flammable or combustible) liquids per control area based on the occupancy where the cabinets are located. [30:9.5.2]

66.9.4.3 Storage cabinets that meet at least one of the following sets of requirements shall be acceptable for storage of ignitible (flammable or combustible) liquids:

(1) Storage cabinets designed and constructed to limit the internal temperature at the center of the cabinet and 1 in. (25 mm) from the top of the cabinet to not more than 325°F (163°C), when subjected to a 10-minute fire test that simulates the fire exposure of the standard time–temperature curve specified in ASTM E119, *Standard Test Methods for Fire Tests of Building Construction and Materials,* shall be acceptable. All joints and seams shall remain tight and the door shall remain securely closed during the test.
(2) Metal storage cabinets constructed in the following manner shall be acceptable:
  (a) The bottom, top, door, and sides of the cabinet shall be at least No. 18 gauge sheet steel and shall be double-walled, with 1½ in. (38 mm) air space.
  (b) Joints shall be riveted, welded, or made tight by some equally effective means.
  (c) The door shall be provided with a three-point latch arrangement, and the door sill shall be raised at least 2 in. (50 mm) above the bottom of the cabinet to retain spilled liquid within the cabinet.
  (d) New cabinets shall have self-closing doors.
(3) Wooden cabinets constructed in the following manner shall be acceptable:
  (a) The bottom, sides, and top shall be constructed of exterior-grade plywood that is at least 1 in. (25 mm) thick and of a type that will not break down or delaminate under fire conditions.
  (b) All joints shall be rabbeted and shall be fastened in two directions with wood screws.
  (c) Where more than one door is used, there shall be a rabbetted overlap of not less than 1 in. (25 mm).
  (d) Doors shall be equipped with a means of latching, and hinges shall be constructed and mounted in such a manner as to not lose their holding capacity when subjected to fire exposure.
  (e) A raised sill or pan capable of containing a 2 in. (50 mm) depth of liquid shall be provided at the bottom of the cabinet to retain spilled liquid within the cabinet.
  (f) New cabinets shall have self-closing doors.
(4) Listed storage cabinets that have been constructed and tested in accordance with UL 1275, *Flammable Liquid Storage Cabinets*; FM 6050, *Approval Standard for Storage Cabinets for Ignitable (Flammable Liquids)*; or equivalent shall be acceptable.

[30:9.5.3]

66.9.4.4* Storage cabinets shall not be required by this *Code* to be ventilated for fire protection purposes. [30:9.5.4]

66.9.4.4.1 If a storage cabinet is not ventilated, the vent openings shall be sealed with the bungs supplied with the cabinet or with bungs specified by the cabinet manufacturer. [30:9.5.4.1]

66.9.4.4.2* If a storage cabinet is ventilated for any reason, the vent openings shall be ducted directly to a safe location outdoors or to a treatment device designed to control volatile organic compounds (VOCs) and ignitible vapors in such a manner that will not compromise the specified performance of the cabinet and in a manner that is acceptable to the AHJ. [30:9.5.4.2]

N **66.9.4.4.2.1*** Storage cabinet vent ducting shall be noncombustible. [30:9.5.4.2.1]

66.9.4.5* Storage cabinets shall include the following marking:

FLAMMABLE
KEEP FIRE AWAY

[30:9.5.5]

66.9.4.5.1 The minimum letter height for FLAMMABLE (signal word) shall be 2.0 in. (50 mm) and the minimum letter height for KEEP FIRE AWAY (message) shall be 1.0 in. (25 mm). [30:9.5.5.1]

66.9.4.5.2 All letters shall be uppercase and in contrasting color to the background. [30:9.5.5.2]

66.9.4.5.3 The marking shall be located on the upper portion of the cabinet's front door(s) or frame. [30:9.5.5.3]

66.9.4.5.4 Use of other languages, the international symbol for "flammable" (a flame in a triangle), the international symbol for "keep fire away" (a burning match in "no" circle) shall be permitted. [30:9.5.5.4]

N **66.9.4.6*** Storage cabinets shall be located on a stable and level surface. [30:9.5.6]

N **66.9.4.6.1*** Cabinets shall only be used for liquid storage in closed containers or original shipping packaging. [30:9.5.6.1]

N **66.9.4.6.2*** Material shall not be stored on top of cabinets. [30:9.5.6.2]

N **66.9.4.6.3*** Cabinets or vent ducting that have obvious defects or loss of integrity (e.g., spill retention, door closure, latches, etc.) shall be repaired or replaced. [30:9.5.6.3]

66.9.5 Maximum Allowable Quantities (MAQs) per Control Area.

Δ **66.9.5.1 General Occupancy Limits.** The maximum allowable quantities (MAQs) of ignitible (flammable or combustible) liquids allowed in each control area shall not exceed the amounts specified in Table 66.9.5.1, Table 66.9.5.2.1, and Chapters 10 through 14 of NFPA 30 as applicable. [30:9.6.1]

66.9.5.2 Special Occupancy Limits.

66.9.5.2.1 For the following occupancies, the MAQs per control area shall not exceed the amounts specified in Table 66.9.5.2.1:

(1) Assembly
(2) Ambulatory health care
(3) Business
(4) Day care
(5) Detention and correctional
(6) Educational
(7) Health care
(8) Residential

[30:9.6.2.1]

Δ **Table 66.9.5.1 MAQ of Ignitible (Flammable or Combustible) Liquids per Control Area**

Liquid Class(es)#	Quantity gal	L	Notes
IA	30	115	1, 2
IB and IC	120	460	1, 2, 3
IA, IB, IC combined	120	460	1, 2, 4
II	120	460	1, 2
IIIA	330	1,265	1, 2
IIIB	13,200	50,600	1, 2, 5

#See 66.4.1 for details on the classification scheme.
Notes:
(1) Quantities are permitted to be increased 100 percent where stored in approved liquid storage cabinets or in safety cans in accordance with this *Code*. Where Notes 2 and 3 also apply, the increase for Notes 1, 2, and 3 is permitted to be applied accumulatively.
(2) Quantities are permitted to be increased 100 percent in buildings equipped throughout with an automatic sprinkler system installed in accordance with NFPA 13. Where Note 1 also applies, the increase for Notes 1, 2, and 3 is permitted to be applied accumulatively.
(3) Quantities of Class IB or IC [FP < 100°F (37.8°C) / BP ≥ 100°F (37.8°C)] liquids are permitted to be increased 100 percent for beverages, medicine, foodstuff, cosmetics, and other consumer products with up to 50 percent by volume ethanol in water and in containers up to 1.3 gal (5 L). Where Notes 1 and 2 also apply, the increase for Notes 1, 2, and 3 is permitted to be applied accumulatively.
(4) Containing not more than the maximum allowable quantity per control area of Class IA, Class IB, or Class IC [FP < 100°F (37.8°C)] liquids, individually.
(5) Quantities are not limited in a building equipped throughout with an automatic sprinkler system installed in accordance with NFPA 13 and designed in accordance with the protection criteria contained in Section 66.16 of this *Code*. [**30**:Table 9.6.1]

Table 66.9.5.2.1 MAQs — Special Occupancy Limits

Liquid Class(es)#	Quantity gal	L
I and II	10	38
IIIA	60	227
IIIB	120	454

#See 66.4.1 for details on the classification scheme.
Note: The MAQs provided in Table 66.9.5.1 are permitted to be used for beverages that are Class IB or IC [FP < 100°F (37.8°C) / BP ≥ 100°F (37.8°C)] liquids with up to 50 percent by volume ethanol in water and in containers up to 0.99 gal (3.785 L) for assembly or business occupancies.
[**30**:Table 9.6.2.1]

66.9.5.2.2 For the occupancies specified in 66.9.5.2.1, storage in excess of 10 gal (38 L) of Class I and Class II liquids [FP < 140°F (60°C)] combined or in excess of 60 gal (227 L) of Class IIIA liquids [140°F (60°C) ≤ FP < 200°F (93°C)] shall be permitted where stored in ignitible (flammable or combustible) liquid storage cabinets and where the total aggregate quantity does not exceed 180 gal (680 L). [**30**:9.6.2.2]

66.9.5.2.3 Fuel in the tanks of operating mobile equipment shall be permitted to exceed the quantities specified in Table 66.9.5.1, where the equipment is operated in accordance with this *Code*. [**30**:9.6.2.3]

Δ **66.9.5.2.4** For the occupancies specified in 66.9.5.2.1, the MAQ for Class IIIB liquids [FP ≥ 200°F (93°C)] shall be permitted to be increased 100 percent if the building is protected throughout with an automatic sprinkler system installed in accordance with NFPA 13. [**30**:9.6.2.4]

66.9.6 Control Areas.

66.9.6.1 For the purpose of this *Code*, a control area shall be a space within a building where quantities of ignitible (flammable or combustible) liquids that do not exceed the maximum quantities allowed by Table 66.9.5.1 or Table 66.9.5.2.1 are stored. [**30**:9.7.1]

Δ **66.9.6.2** Where more than one control area is present in a building, control areas shall be separated from each other by fire barriers in accordance with Table 60.4.2.2.1. [**30**:9.7.2]

66.9.6.3 Control areas located below grade that are considered basements, as defined in 3.3.25, shall not be utilized for the storage of Class I liquids [FP < 100°F (37.8°C)]. [**30**:9.7.3]

66.9.7 Classification of Occupancies That Exceed the Maximum Allowable Quantities of Ignitible (Flammable or Combustible) Liquids per Control Area.

66.9.7.1* Occupancy Classifications. Buildings and portions of buildings where liquids are stored shall be classified as Protection Level 2 or Protection Level 3, as established in this section, when the MAQs per control area are exceeded. [**30**:9.8.1]

66.9.7.1.1 Protection Level 2. Buildings and portions thereof storing quantities of ignitible (flammable or combustible) liquids that are considered as High-Hazard Level 2 liquids and that exceed the maximum allowable quantities per control area shall be classified as Protection Level 2 occupancies. [**30**:9.8.1.1]

66.9.7.1.2 Protection Level 3. Buildings and portions thereof storing quantities of ignitible (flammable or combustible) liquids that are considered as High-Hazard Level 3 liquids and that exceed the maximum allowable quantities per control area shall be classified as Protection Level 3 occupancies. [**30**:9.8.1.2]

66.9.7.2* Requirements for Specific Occupancies. Ignitible (flammable or combustible) liquids stored in Protection Level 2 or Protection Level 3 occupancies shall meet the applicable requirements for storage in a Liquid Storage Room or Liquid Warehouse as defined in this *Code* and in *NFPA 5000*. [**30**:9.8.2]

66.9.8 Construction Requirements.

66.9.8.1 Fire resistance ratings for liquid storage rooms and liquid warehouses shall comply with Table 66.9.8.1. [**30**:9.9.1]

Δ **66.9.8.2** Acceptable methods for determining fire resistance shall be in accordance with the building code. [**30**:9.9.2]

66.9.8.3 Openings in interior walls to adjacent rooms or buildings and openings in exterior walls with fire resistance ratings shall be provided with normally closed, listed fire doors with fire protection ratings that correspond to the fire resistance rating of the wall as specified in Table 66.9.8.3. [**30**:9.9.3]

66.9.8.3.1 Such doors shall be permitted to be arranged to stay open during material-handling operations if the doors are

Δ **Table 66.9.8.1 Fire Resistance Ratings for Liquid Storage Rooms and Liquid Warehouses**

Type of Storage Area	Interior Walls, Ceilings, Intermediate Floors[a]	Roofs	Exterior Walls
Liquid storage room			
Floor area ≤ 150 ft^2	1	NR	NR
Floor area > 150 ft^2, but ≤ 500 ft^2	2	NR	NR
Liquid warehouse	4[b]	NR	4[c]

For SI units, 1 ft^2 = 0.09 m^2.
NR: No requirement.
[a]Between either a liquid storage room or a liquid warehouse and any adjacent areas not dedicated to liquid storage.
[b]A 4-hour fire wall, in accordance with NFPA 221, is required except as follows:
1) Where storage of liquids in a liquid warehouse is limited to Class IIIB liquids [FP ≥ 200°F (93°C)] that are not heated above their FP, 2-hour fire walls or fire barriers are permitted.
2) Where a liquid warehouse is protected in accordance with Section 66.16, 2-hour fire walls or fire barriers are permitted.
3) Where a liquid warehouse is protected in accordance with Section 66.16, accessory use areas, such as offices and restrooms, having a combined area of less than 10 percent of the area of the liquid warehouse do not require a fire resistance rating for the interior walls and ceilings.
[c]The fire resistance rating for walls that are located more than 10 ft (3 m) but less than 50 ft (15 m) from an important building or line of adjoining property that can be built upon is permitted to be 2 hours. Walls located 50 ft (15 m) or more from an important building or line of adjoining property that can be built upon do not require a fire resistance rating.
[**30**:Table 9.9.1]

Table 66.9.8.3 Protection Ratings for Fire Doors

Fire Resistance Rating of Wall as Required by Table 66.9.8.1 (hr)	Fire Protection Rating of Door (hr)
1	¾
2	1½
4	3*

*One fire door required on each side of interior openings for attached liquid warehouses. [**30**:Table 9.9.3]

designed to close automatically in a fire emergency by provision of listed closure devices. [**30**:9.9.3.1]

66.9.8.3.2 Fire doors shall be installed in accordance with NFPA 80. [**30**:9.9.3.2]

Δ **66.9.8.4** Exterior walls shall be constructed to provide ready access for firefighting operations by means of access openings, windows, or lightweight, noncombustible wall panels except if the liquid storage room is totally enclosed within a building.

N **66.9.8.5** A minimum of 25 percent of the perimeter of the liquid warehouse shall be an exterior wall. [**30**:9.9.5]

66.9.9 Fire Protection.

66.9.9.1 Protected Storage. Fire protection requirements for protected storage shall meet the requirements of 66.9.9.2 and Section 66.16. [**30**:9.10.1]

66.9.9.2 Manual Fire Protection.

Δ **66.9.9.2.1** Portable fire extinguishers shall be provided in accordance with NFPA 10 and NFPA 30. [**30**:9.10.2.1]

Δ **66.9.9.2.2** Portable fire extinguishers shall meet the following requirements:

(1) At least one portable fire extinguisher having a capability of not less than 40:B shall be located outside of, but not more than 10 ft (3 m) from, the door opening into a liquid storage room or liquid warehouse.
(2) At least one portable fire extinguisher having a capability of not less than 40:B shall be located within 30 ft (9 m) of any Class I or Class II liquids [FP < 140°F (60°C)] located outside of a liquid storage room or liquid warehouse or at least one portable fire extinguisher having a capacity of 80:B located within 50 ft (15 m) of such a storage area.

[**30**:9.10.2.2]

Δ **66.9.9.2.3** Where provided, hose connections supplied from sprinkler systems shall be installed in accordance with NFPA 13. [**30**:9.10.2.3]

Δ **66.9.9.2.4** Where provided, hose connections supplied by a standpipe system shall be installed in accordance with NFPA 14. [**30**:9.10.2.4]

66.9.9.2.5 Where hose connections are provided, the water supply shall be sufficient to meet the fixed fire protection demand plus a total of at least 500 gpm (1900 L/min) for inside and outside hose connections for at least 2 hours, unless otherwise specified in Section 66.16. [**30**:9.10.2.5]

Δ **66.9.10*** **Emergency Control Systems.**

66.9.11 Electrical Systems.

66.9.11.1 Electrical area classification shall not be required for control areas, liquid storage rooms, or liquid warehouses where all containers, intermediate bulk containers, and portable tanks are sealed and are not opened, except as provided for in 66.9.11.2. [**30**:9.12.1]

Δ **66.9.11.2** For liquid storage rooms that are totally enclosed within the building, electrical wiring and utilization equipment for Class I liquid [FP < 100°F (37.8°C)] storage shall be Class I, Division 2 (Zone 2). [**30**:9.12.2]

N **66.9.11.3** Electrical wiring and utilization equipment in liquid storage rooms used for the storage of Class II and Class III liquids [FP ≥ 100°F (37.8°C)] shall be suitable for ordinary purpose. [**30**:9.12.3]

N **66.9.11.4** Class I, Division 2 (Zone 2) requirements shall apply to Class II and Class III liquids [FP ≥ 100°F (37.8°C)] when stored at temperatures above their FP. [**30**:9.12.4]

66.9.12 Containment, Drainage, and Spill Control.

66.9.12.1 Where the maximum allowable quantity (MAQ) is exceeded, spill control shall be required in accordance with 66.6.11.2. [**30**:9.13.1]

△ **66.9.12.2** Where the MAQ is exceeded, secondary containment shall comply with 66.6.11.3 and any additional requirements of this section. [**30:**9.13.2]

66.9.12.3 Where used, drainage shall comply with 66.6.11.4. [**30:**9.13.3]

66.9.12.4 Where only Class IIIB liquids [FP ≥ 200°F (93°C)] are stored, spill control, secondary containment, and drainage shall not be required. [**30:**9.13.4]

66.9.12.5 Where only unsaturated polyester resins (UPRs) containing not more than 50 percent by weight of Class IC, Class II, or Class IIIA liquid [73°F (22.8°C) ≤ FP < 200°F (93°C)] constituents are stored and are protected in accordance with 66.16.5.3.11, spill control, secondary containment, and drainage shall not be required. [**30:**9.13.5]

66.9.13 Ventilation. Control areas, liquid storage rooms, or liquid warehouses where dispensing is conducted shall be provided with ventilation that meets the requirements of 66.18.6. [**30:**9.14]

66.9.14 Exhausted Enclosures. (Reserved)

66.9.15 Explosion Control. The extent of required explosion control shall be determined in accordance with 66.6.4.1.2.3. [**30:**9.16]

66.9.16 Separation from Incompatible Materials.

66.9.16.1 Except as provided for in 66.9.16.3, ignitible (flammable or combustible) liquids shall be separated from incompatible materials where the stored materials are in containers having a capacity of more than 5 lb (2.268 kg) or ½ gal (1.89 L). [**30:**9.17.1]

66.9.16.1.1 Separation shall be accomplished by one of the following methods:

(1) Segregating incompatible materials storage by a distance of not less than 20 ft (6.1 m)
(2) Isolating incompatible materials storage by a noncombustible partition extending not less than 18 in. (460 mm) above and to the sides of the stored materials
(3) Storing liquid materials in Class I liquids [FP < 100°F (37.8°C)] storage cabinets in accordance with 66.9.4

[**30:**9.17.1.1]

66.9.16.2 Ignitible (flammable or combustible) liquids shall be separated from Level 2 and Level 3 aerosols in accordance with Chapter 61 and NFPA 30B. [**30:**9.17.2]

66.9.16.3 Liquids shall be separated from oxidizers by at least 25 ft (7.6 m). [**30:**9.17.3]

66.9.16.4* Materials that are water-reactive, as described in NFPA 704, shall not be stored within 25 ft (7.6 m) of ignitible (flammable or combustible) liquids. [**30:**9.17.4]

N **66.9.16.5** The design of floor slope, drains, or containment systems shall prevent the mixing of incompatible materials while they remain reactive. [**30:**9.17.5]

66.9.17 Dispensing, Handling, and Use of Ignitible (Flammable or Combustible) Liquids in Storage Areas.

66.9.17.1 Dispensing, handling, and use of ignitible (flammable or combustible) liquids shall meet all applicable requirements of Section 66.18. [**30:**9.18.1]

66.9.17.2 Dispensing of Class I liquids [FP < 100°F (37.8°C)] or Class II and Class III liquids [FP ≥ 100°F (37.8°C)] at temperatures at or above their FP shall not be permitted in storage areas that exceed 1000 ft^2 (93 m^2) in floor area unless the dispensing area is separated from the storage areas in accordance with Table 66.9.8.1 and meets all other requirements of 66.9.8. [**30:**9.18.2]

66.9.18 Outdoor Storage of Ignitible (Flammable or Combustible) Liquids. Storage of ignitible (flammable or combustible) liquids outside of buildings shall meet the requirements of Section 66.14 or 66.15, whichever is applicable. [**30:**9.19]

66.10 Reserved.

66.11 Reserved.

66.12 Reserved.

66.13 Reserved.

66.14 Hazardous Materials Storage Lockers.

66.14.1* Scope. This section shall apply to the storage of ignitible (flammable or combustible) liquids in movable, modular, prefabricated storage lockers, also known as hazardous materials storage lockers (hereinafter referred to as lockers), specifically designed and manufactured for storage of hazardous materials, in the following:

(1) Containers that do not exceed 119 gal (450 L) individual capacity
(2) Portable tanks that do not exceed 660 gal (2500 L) individual capacity
(3) Intermediate bulk containers that do not exceed 793 gal (3000 L) individual capacity

[**30:**14.1]

66.14.2 Reserved.

66.14.3 General Requirements.

66.14.3.1 Lockers that are used as liquid storage rooms shall meet the requirements of Chapters 9 and 12 of NFPA 30, 66.14.4, and 66.14.6. [**30:**14.3.1]

△ **66.14.3.2** Lockers that are located outside shall meet the requirements of 66.14.4 and 66.14.4.6. [**30:**14.3.2]

66.14.4 Design and Construction of Hazardous Materials Storage Lockers.

66.14.4.1 The design and construction of a locker shall meet all applicable local, state, and federal regulations and requirements and shall be subject to the approval of the AHJ. [**30:**14.4.1]

66.14.4.2 Movable prefabricated structures that have been examined, listed, or labeled by an organization acceptable to the AHJ for use as a hazardous materials storage facility shall be acceptable. [**30:**14.4.2]

66.14.4.3 Lockers shall not exceed 1500 ft^2 (140 m^2) gross floor area. [**30:**14.4.3]

66.14.4.4 Vertical stacking of lockers shall not be permitted. [**30:**14.4.4]

66.14.4.5 Where electrical wiring and electrical utilization equipment are required, they shall comply with Section 66.7 and 66.9.11. [**30:**14.4.5]

66.14.4.6 Where dispensing or filling is permitted inside a locker, operations shall comply with the provisions of Section 66.18. [**30**:14.4.6]

66.14.4.7 Ventilation shall be provided in accordance with 66.18.6. [**30**:14.4.7]

66.14.4.8 Lockers shall include a spill containment system to prevent the flow of ignitible (flammable or combustible) liquids from the locker under emergency conditions. [**30**:14.4.8]

66.14.4.8.1 The containment system shall have sufficient capacity to contain 10 percent of the volume of containers allowed in the locker or the volume of the largest container, whichever is greater. [**30**:14.4.8.1]

66.14.5 Designated Sites for Hazardous Materials Storage Lockers.

66.14.5.1 Lockers shall be located on a designated approved site on the property. [**30**:14.5.1]

66.14.5.2 The designated site shall be arranged to provide the minimum separation distances specified in Table 66.14.5.2 between individual lockers, from locker to property line that is or can be built upon, and from locker to nearest side of public ways or to important buildings on the same property. [**30**:14.5.2]

66.14.5.3 Once the designated site is approved, it shall not be changed without the approval of the AHJ. [**30**:14.5.3]

66.14.5.4 More than one locker shall be permitted on a designated site, provided that the separation distance between individual lockers is maintained in accordance with Table 66.14.5.2. [**30**:14.5.4]

66.14.5.5 Where the approved designated storage site is accessible to the general public, it shall be protected from tampering or trespassing. [**30**:14.5.5]

66.14.6 Storage Requirements.

66.14.6.1 Containers of ignitible (flammable or combustible) liquid in their original shipping packages shall be permitted to be stored either palletized or solid piled within the locker. [**30**:14.6.1]

66.14.6.2 Unpackaged containers shall be permitted to be stored on shelves or directly on the floor of the locker. [**30**:14.6.2]

66.14.6.3 Containers over 30 gal (114 L) capacity storing Class I or Class II liquids [FP < 140°F (60°C)] shall not be stored more than two containers high. [**30**:14.6.3]

66.14.6.4 In all cases, the storage arrangement shall provide unrestricted access to and egress from the locker. [**30**:14.6.4]

66.14.6.5 Miscellaneous combustible materials, including but not limited to idle pallets, excessive vegetation, and packing materials, shall not be permitted within 5 ft (1.5 m) of the designated site approved for lockers. [**30**:14.6.5]

66.14.6.6 Warning signs for lockers shall be in accordance with applicable local, state, and federal regulations or with NFPA 704. [**30**:14.6.6]

Δ **Table 66.14.5.2 Designated Sites**

Area of Designated Site[a] (ft^2)	Between Individual Lockers	From Locker to Property Line That Is or Can Be Built Upon[b]	From Locker to Nearest Side of Public Ways or to Important Buildings on Same Property[b,c]
≤100	5	10	5
>100 and ≤500	5	20	10
>500 and ≤1500[d]	5	30	20

For SI units, 1 ft = 0.3 m; 1 ft^2 = 0.09 m^2.
[a]Site area limits are intended to differentiate the relative size and thus the number of lockers that are permitted in one designated site.
[b]Distances apply to properties that have protection for exposures, as defined. If there are exposures and such protection for exposures does not exist, the distances should be doubled.
[c]Separation distances in the table can be reduced by half, to a minimum of 5 ft (1.5 m), if the following are met:

(1) Either the building or the locker has a fire resistance rating of 2 hours.
(2) The building has no openings to above grade areas within 10 ft (3 m) horizontally.
(3) The building has no openings to below grade areas within 50 ft (15 m) horizontally of the designated area.

[d]Where a single locker has a gross single-story floor area that will require a site area limit of greater than 1500 ft^2 (140 m^2) or where multiple units exceed the area limit of 1500 ft^2 (140 m^2), the AHJ should be consulted for approval of distances. [**30**:Table 14.5.2]

66.15 Outdoor Storage.

66.15.1 Scope. This section shall apply to the storage of ignitible (flammable or combustible) liquids outdoors in the following:

(1) Drums or other containers that do not exceed 119 gal (450 L) individual capacity
(2) Portable tanks that do not exceed 660 gal (2500 L) individual capacity
(3) Intermediate bulk containers that do not exceed 793 gal (3000 L) individual capacity

[**30**:15.1]

66.15.2 Reserved.

66.15.3 General Requirements. Outdoor storage of ignitible (flammable or combustible) liquids in containers, intermediate bulk containers, and portable tanks shall comply with Table 66.15.3 and with all applicable requirements of this section. [**30**:15.3]

66.15.3.1 Where two or more classes of liquids are stored in a single pile, the maximum quantity permitted in that pile shall be that of the most hazardous class of liquid present. [**30**:15.3.1]

66.15.3.2 No container, intermediate bulk container, or portable tank in a pile shall be more than 200 ft (60 m) from a minimum 20 ft (6 m) wide access way to permit approach of fire control apparatus under all weather conditions. [**30**:15.3.2]

66.15.3.3 The distances specified in Table 66.15.3 shall apply to properties that have protection for exposures as defined. If

Table 66.15.3 Storage Limitations for Outside Storage

	Containers		Portable Tanks and Metal IBCs		Rigid Plastic and Composite IBCs		Minimum Separation Distance (ft)		
Liquid Class[#]	Maximum Quantity per Pile (gal)[a,b,c]	Maximum Storage Height (ft)	Maximum Quantity per Pile (gal)	Maximum Storage Height (ft)	Maximum Quantity per Pile (gal)[a,c]	Maximum Storage Height (ft)	Between Piles or Rack Sections	To Property Line That Is or Can Be Built Upon[b,d]	To Street, Alley, or Public Way[b]
IA	1,100	10	2,200	7	NP	NP	5	50	10
IB	2,200	12	4,400	14	NP	NP	5	50	10
IC	4,400	12	8,800	14	NP	NP	5	50	10
II	8,800	12	17,600	14	8,800	14	5	25	5
III	22,000	18	44,000	14	22,000	18	5	10	5

For SI units, 1 ft = 0.3 m; 1 gal = 3.8 L.
NP: Not permitted.
[#]See 66.4.1 for details on the classification scheme.
[a]See 66.15.3.1 regarding mixed-class storage.
[b]See 66.15.3.4 for smaller pile sizes.
[c]For storage in racks, the quantity limits per pile do not apply, but the rack arrangements should be limited to a maximum of 50 ft (15 m) in length and two rows or 9 ft (2.7 m) in depth.
[d]See 66.15.3.3 regarding protection for exposures. [30:Table 15.3]

there are exposures and protection for exposures does not exist, the distance to the property line that is or can be built upon shall be doubled. [30:15.3.3]

66.15.3.4 Where total quantity stored does not exceed 50 percent of the maximum quantity per pile, as specified in Table 66.15.3, the distances to a property line that is or can be built upon and to streets, alleys, or public ways shall be permitted to be reduced by 50 percent but in no case to less than 3 ft (0.9 m). [30:15.3.4]

66.15.3.5 The storage area shall be graded in a manner to divert possible spills away from buildings or other exposures or shall be surrounded by a curb at least 6 in. (150 mm) high. [30:15.3.5]

66.15.3.6 When accessible to the public, the storage area shall be protected against tampering and trespassing. [30:15.3.6]

66.15.3.7 The storage area shall be kept free of weeds, debris, and other combustible materials not necessary to the storage for a distance of at least 10 ft (3 m) around the perimeter of the stored materials. [30:15.3.7]

66.15.3.8 The storage area shall be permitted to be protected from the weather by a canopy or roof that does not limit the dissipation of heat or dispersion of flammable vapors and does not restrict firefighting access and control. [30:15.3.8]

N **66.15.3.9 Containment, Drainage, and Spill Control.** Where the maximum quantity per pile established in Table 66.15.3 is exceeded, spill control and secondary containment shall be provided in accordance with 66.6.11.2 or 66.6.11.3. [30:15.3.9]

N **66.15.3.9.1** The storage area shall be either graded in a manner to divert possible spills away from buildings or other exposures or surrounded by a curb at least 6 in. (150 mm) high. [30:15.3.9.1]

N **66.15.3.9.2** Where used, drainage shall comply with 66.6.12.4. [30:15.3.9.2]

N **66.15.3.10** Where curbs, dikes, or similar containment barriers are used, provisions shall be made to drain accumulations of groundwater, rainwater, or spills of ignitible (flammable or combustible) liquids. [30:15.3.10]

N **66.15.3.10.1** The design of the containment for outside storage shall include the additional volume required to account for the accumulation of rainfall for a minimum of 24 hours in a 25-year reoccurrence. [30:15.3.10.1]

N **66.15.3.10.2** Larger quantities used to account for local meteorological conditions shall be considered where appropriate. [30:15.3.10.2]

N **66.15.3.10.3** Where the design of the containment for outside storage includes the fire suppression water volume, a means for its drainage shall be provided. [30:15.3.10.3]

N **66.15.3.11** Drains shall both terminate at a safe location and flow freely under fire conditions. [30:15.3.11]

66.15.4 Outdoor Storage Adjacent to a Building.

66.15.4.1 A maximum of 1100 gal (4160 L) of ignitible (flammable or combustible) liquids in containers, intermediate bulk containers, or portable tanks shall be permitted to be stored adjacent to a building under the same management, provided the following conditions apply:

(1) The adjacent building wall has an exterior fire resistance rating of 2 hours.
(2) The adjacent building wall has no openings at grade or above grade that are within 10 ft (3 m) horizontally of the storage.
(3) The adjacent building wall has no openings directly above the storage.
(4) The adjacent building wall has no openings below grade within 50 ft (15 m) horizontally of the storage.

[30:15.4.1]

66.15.4.2 The provisions of 66.15.4.1(1) through 66.15.4.1(4) shall be permitted to be waived, subject to the approval of the AHJ, if the building in question is one story, is of fire-resistive or noncombustible construction, and is devoted principally to the storage of ignitible (flammable or combustible) liquids. [**30:**15.4.2]

66.15.4.3 The quantity of ignitible (flammable or combustible) liquid stored adjacent to a building that meets the conditions of 66.15.4.1(1) through 66.15.4.1(4) shall be permitted to exceed that permitted in 66.15.4.1, provided the maximum quantity per pile does not exceed 1100 gal (4160 L) and each pile is separated by a 10 ft (3 m) minimum clear space along the common wall. [**30:**15.4.3]

66.15.4.4 The quantity of ignitible (flammable or combustible) liquid stored shall be permitted to exceed the 1100 gal (4160 L) quantity specified by 66.15.4.1 where a minimum distance equal to that specified by Table 66.15.3 for distance to property line shall be maintained between buildings and the nearest container or portable tank. [**30:**15.4.4]

66.15.4.5 Where the provisions of 66.15.4.1 cannot be met, a minimum distance equal to that specified by Table 66.15.3 for distance to property line shall be maintained between buildings and the nearest container or portable tank. [**30:**15.4.5]

66.16 Automatic Fire Protection for Inside Liquid Storage Areas.

66.16.1 Scope.

66.16.1.1* This section shall apply to automatic fire protection systems for all inside storage of ignitible (flammable or combustible) liquids in containers, intermediate bulk containers, and portable tanks as specified in 66.9.3. [**30:**16.1.1]

Δ **66.16.1.2*** This section shall not apply to Class IA liquids [FP < 73°F (22.8°C) and BP < 100°F (37.8°C)]. [**30:**16.1.2]

66.16.1.3 Storage of ignitible (flammable or combustible) liquids that is protected in accordance with the applicable requirements of this section shall be considered protected, as defined in 66.16.2.1. All other storage shall be considered unprotected unless an alternate means of protection has been approved by the AHJ. [**30:**16.1.3]

66.16.2 Definitions Specific to Section 66.16. For the purpose of this section, the terms in this section shall have the definitions given. [**30:**16.2]

66.16.2.1* Protected. For the purposes of 66.16, this term shall apply to the storage of containers that meet the appropriate provisions of 66.16 or alternate provisions that have been approved by the AHJ *(see 66.16.3.5 and 66.16.9)*. [**30:**16.2.2]

66.16.2.2* Unprotected. For the purposes of this section, this term shall apply to the storage of containers that do not meet the criteria to be considered protected, as defined in 66.16.2.1. [**30:**16.2.3]

66.16.2.3* Relieving-Style Container. A metal container, a metal intermediate bulk container, or a metal portable tank that is equipped with at least one pressure-relieving mechanism at its top that is designed, sized, and arranged to relieve the internal pressure generated due to exposure to fire so that violent rupture is prevented. [**30:**16.2.4]

Δ **66.16.2.4* Unsaturated Polyester Resin (UPR).** A resin that contains up to 50 percent by weight of Class IC, Class II, or Class III liquid [FP > 73°F (22.8°C)], but no Class IA or Class IB liquid [FP < 73°F (22.8°C)]. [**30:**16.2.5]

66.16.2.5 Viscous Liquid. A liquid that gels, thickens, or solidifies when heated or whose viscosity at room temperature versus weight percent content of Class I, Class II, or Class III liquid (any FP or BP) is in the shaded portion of Figure 66.16.2.5. [**30:**16.2.6]

66.16.2.6 Water-Miscible Liquid. A liquid that mixes in all proportions with water without the use of chemical additives, such as emulsifying agents. [**30:**16.2.7]

66.16.3 General Requirements.

66.16.3.1 Where different classes of liquids, container types, and storage configurations are stored in the same protected area, protection shall meet either of the following:

(1) Requirements of this section for the most severe storage fire hazard present
(2) Where areas are not physically separated by a barrier or partition capable of delaying heat from a fire in one hazard area from fusing sprinklers in an adjacent hazard area, the required protection for the more demanding hazard shall:

(a) Extend 20 ft (6 m) beyond its perimeter, but not less than the required minimum sprinkler design area
(b) Be provided with means to prevent the flow of burning ignitible (flammable or combustible) liquid under emergency conditions into adjacent hazard areas
(c) Provide containment and drainage as required by 66.16.8

[**30:**16.3.1]

66.16.3.2 Unless otherwise specified in this section, single-row racks shall not be more than 4.5 ft (1.4 m) in depth and double-row racks shall not be more than 9 ft (2.8 m) in depth. [**30:**16.3.2]

66.16.3.3 When applying the fire protection criteria of this section, a minimum aisle space of 6 ft (1.8 m) shall be provided between adjacent piles or adjacent rack sections, unless otherwise specified in the tables in 66.16.5. [**30:**16.3.3]

Δ **FIGURE 66.16.2.5** Viscous Liquid: Viscosity Versus Weight Percent Ignitible (Flammable or Combustible) Component. [**30:**Figure 16.2.6]

Δ **66.16.3.4** Viscous liquids, as defined in 66.16.2.5, shall be permitted to be protected using one of the following:

(1) For metal containers, the criteria for Class IIIB liquids [FP ≥ 200°F (93°C)], as determined by Figure 66.16.4.1(a)
(2) For nonmetallic containers, the criteria for Class IIIB liquids [FP ≥ 200°F (93°C)], as determined by Figure 66.16.4.1(b)

[**30:**16.3.4]

66.16.3.5 Protection systems that are designed and developed based on full-scale fire tests performed at an approved test facility or on other engineered protection schemes shall be considered an acceptable alternative to the protection criteria set forth in this section. Such alternative protection systems shall be approved by the AHJ. [**30:**16.3.5]

66.16.3.6 For relieving-style containers of greater than 6.5 gal (25 L) and up to 119 gal (450 L) capacity, the following shall apply:

(1) The pressure-relieving mechanism shall be listed and labeled in accordance with FM Global *Approval Standard for Plastic Plugs for Steel Drums*, Class Number 6083, or equivalent.
(2) The pressure-relieving mechanism shall not be painted, and cap seals, if used, shall be made of thermoplastic material.
(3) For metal containers greater than 6.5 gal (25 L) capacity, the pressure-relieving mechanism shall be unobstructed or an additional pressure-relieving mechanism shall be provided.

[**30:**16.3.6]

66.16.3.7 To be considered protected by Table 66.16.5.3.9 and Table 66.16.5.3.10, rigid nonmetallic intermediate bulk containers shall be listed and labeled in accordance with UL 2368, *Fire Exposure Testing of Intermediate Bulk Containers for Flammable and Combustible Liquids*; FM 6020, *Approval Standard for Composite Intermediate Bulk Containers*; or an equivalent test procedure. [**30:**16.3.7]

66.16.4 Automatic Sprinkler and Foam-Water Sprinkler Fire Protection Systems.

66.16.4.1 Where automatic sprinkler systems or low-expansion foam-water sprinkler systems are used to protect storage of ignitible (flammable or combustible) liquids, Figure 66.16.4.1(a), Figure 66.16.4.1(b), or Figure 66.16.4.1(c), whichever is applicable, and the appropriate table in 66.16.5 shall be used to determine protection criteria. [**30:**16.4.1]

66.16.4.1.1* Figure 66.16.4.1(a) shall be used for miscible and nonmiscible ignitible (flammable or combustible) liquids in metal containers, metal portable tanks, and metal intermediate bulk containers. [**30:**16.4.1.1]

66.16.4.1.2 Figure 66.16.4.1(b) shall be used for miscible and nonmiscible ignitible (flammable or combustible) liquids in nonmetallic containers and in nonmetallic intermediate bulk containers. [**30:**16.4.1.2]

66.16.4.1.3 Figure 66.16.4.1(c) shall be used for water-miscible ignitible (flammable or combustible) liquids in nonmetallic containers and in nonmetallic intermediate bulk containers. [**30:**16.4.1.3]

66.16.4.2 Automatic sprinkler and foam-water fire protection systems shall be wet pipe, deluge, or preaction systems. [**30:**16.4.2]

66.16.4.2.1 If a preaction system is used, it shall be designed so that water or foam solution will immediately discharge from the sprinkler upon sprinkler actuation. [**30:**16.4.2.1]

66.16.4.2.2 A foam-water sprinkler system that meets any of the design criteria specified in the water sprinkler tables in this section shall be acceptable, provided that the system is installed in accordance with NFPA 11. [**30:**16.4.2.2]

N **66.16.4.2.3*** Sprinkler system design criteria for foam-water systems found in Section 66.16.5 shall be based upon the use of aqueous film forming foam concentrates containing PFAS that are listed in accordance with UL 162, *Standard for Foam Equipment and Liquid Concentrates*, or FM 5130, *Approval Standard for Foam Extinguishing Systems*. [**30:**16.4.2.3]

N **66.16.4.2.4** Foam concentrates other than aqueous film forming foam in accordance with 66.16.4.2.3 shall be used with the sprinkler system design criteria for foam-water systems found in Section 66.16.5 only where specifically listed for that application. [**30:**16.4.2.4]

66.16.4.3 Water-based fire protection systems shall be inspected, tested, and maintained in accordance with NFPA 25. [**30:**16.4.3]

66.16.5 Fire Protection System Design Criteria.

66.16.5.1 General. Subsections 66.16.5.3.1 through 66.16.5.3.18 and their related tables, Table 66.16.5.3.1 through Table 66.16.5.3.18, shall be used to determine the protection criteria and storage arrangement for the applicable liquid class, container type, and storage configuration, as described in 66.16.5.3.1 through 66.16.5.3.18 and subject to the provisions of 66.16.5.1. [**30:**16.5.1]

66.16.5.1.1 The protection criteria in Table 66.16.5.3.1 through Table 66.16.5.3.18 shall only be used with ceilings having a pitch of 2 in 12 or less. [**30:**16.5.1.1]

66.16.5.1.2 When foam or foam-water fire protection systems are provided, discharge densities shall be determined based on the listing criteria of the foam discharge devices selected, the foam concentrate, the specific ignitible (flammable or combustible) liquids to be protected, and the criteria in the appropriate table in this section. Where the discharge densities given in the tables differ from those in the listing criteria for the discharge devices, the greater of the two shall be used. [**30:**16.5.1.2]

△ **FIGURE 66.16.4.1(a)** Fire Protection Criteria Decision Tree for Miscible and Nonmiscible Ignitible (Flammable or Combustible) Liquids in Metal Containers. [30:Figure 16.4.1(a)]

△ **FIGURE 66.16.4.1(b)** Fire Protection Criteria Decision Tree for Miscible and Nonmiscible Ignitible (Flammable or Combustible) Liquids in Nonmetallic Containers. [30:Figure 16.4.1(b)]

△ **66.16.5.1.3** In-rack sprinklers shall be installed in accordance with the provisions of NFPA 13. In addition, the following modifications shall apply:

(1) In-rack sprinklers shall be laid out in accordance with 66.16.5.1.10 and 66.16.6, as applicable.
(2) Sprinklers in multiple-level in-rack sprinkler systems shall be provided with water shields unless they are separated by horizontal barriers or are specifically listed for installation without water shields.
(3) A vertical clear space of at least 6 in. (150 mm) shall be maintained between the sprinkler deflector and the top tier of storage.
(4) Sprinkler discharge shall not be obstructed by horizontal rack structural members.
(5) Where in-rack sprinklers are installed below horizontal barriers, the deflector shall be located a maximum of 7 in. (180 mm) below the barrier.
(6) Longitudinal and transverse flue spaces of at least 6 in. (150 mm) shall be maintained between each rack load.

[**30**:16.5.1.3]

△ **66.16.5.1.4** Ceiling sprinklers shall be installed in accordance with NFPA 13 and shall be permitted to have the following maximum head spacing:

(1) Class I, Class II, and Class IIIA liquids [FP < 200°F (93°C)]: 100 ft² (9.3 m²) per sprinkler
(2) Class IIIB liquids [FP ≥ 200°F (93°C)]: 120 ft² (11.1 m²) per sprinkler

[**30**:16.5.1.4]

66.16.5.1.4.1 Ordinary or intermediate temperature–rated K-25 extended-coverage sprinklers shall be permitted to be used as standard response high temperature sprinklers at greater than 144 ft² (13 m²) coverage, with 12 ft (3.7 m) minimum spacing and a maximum coverage area of 196 ft² (18 m²) coverage. [**30**:16.5.1.4.1]

Shaded text = Revisions.   △ = Text deletions and figure/table revisions.   • = Section deletions.   *N* = New material.   2024 Edition

Note: For SI units, 1 gal = 3.8 L.

Δ FIGURE 66.16.4.1(c) Fire Protection Criteria Decision Tree for Water-Miscible Ignitible (Flammable or Combustible) Liquids in Nonmetallic Containers. [30:Figure 16.4.1(c)]

Δ **66.16.5.1.5** The ceiling heights given in Table 66.16.5.3.1 through Table 66.16.5.3.12, excluding Table 66.16.5.3.8, shall be permitted to be increased by a maximum of 10 percent if an equivalent percent increase in ceiling sprinkler design density is provided. [30:16.5.1.5]

66.16.5.1.6 Foam-water sprinkler systems shall be installed in accordance with NFPA 11. [30:16.5.1.6]

66.16.5.1.6.1 Foam-water sprinkler systems shall have at least 15 minutes of foam concentrate, based on the required design flow rate. [30:16.5.1.6.1]

66.16.5.1.6.2* Foam-water sprinkler systems shall provide foam solution at the minimum required concentration with as few as four sprinklers flowing. [30:16.5.1.6.2]

66.16.5.1.7 When relieving style containers are used, both ¾ in. (20 mm) and 2 in. (50 mm) listed and labeled pressure-relieving mechanisms are required on containers greater than 6.5 gal (25 L) capacity. [30:16.5.1.7]

66.16.5.1.8 For the purposes of 66.16.5, a rigid nonmetallic intermediate bulk container is one that meets the maximum allowable capacity criteria of Table 66.9.3.3 and has been listed and labeled in accordance with UL 2368, *Fire Exposure Testing of Intermediate Bulk Containers for Flammable and Combustible Liquids*; FM 6020, *Approval Standard for Composite Intermediate Bulk Containers*; or an equivalent test procedure. [30:16.5.1.8]

66.16.5.1.9 For the purposes of 66.16.5, the following shall apply:

(1) 1 gal = 3.8 L; 1 ft = 0.3 m; 1 ft^2 = 0.09 m^2
(2) 1 gpm/ft^2 is equivalent to 40.7 L/min/m^2 or 40.7 mm/min
(3) A gauge pressure of 1 psi is equivalent to a gauge pressure of 6.9 kPa
(4) SR = standard response sprinkler; QR = quick response sprinkler; ESFR = early suppression fast-response sprinkler; OT = ordinary temperature; HT = high temperature
(5) Where an ordinary-temperature sprinkler is indicated, an intermediate-temperature sprinkler shall be used where ambient conditions require.

[30:16.5.1.9]

Δ **66.16.5.1.10** For 66.16.5, the following shall apply to the in-rack sprinkler design layouts specified in Table 66.16.5.3.1 through Table 66.16.5.3.12:

(1) Layout 1, as referenced in Table 66.16.5.3.1, shall mean one line of in-rack sprinklers at approximately 8 ft (2.4 m) above the floor in the longitudinal flue space, with sprinklers spaced not more than 10 ft (3 m) on center.
(2) Layout 2, as referenced in Table 66.16.5.3.1, shall mean one line of in-rack sprinklers at approximately 6 ft (1.8 m) above the floor and one line of in-rack sprinklers at approximately 12 ft (3.6 m) above the floor in the longitudinal flue space, with sprinklers spaced not more than 10 ft (3 m) on center, and sprinklers staggered vertically.
(3) Layout 3, as referenced in Table 66.16.5.3.1 and Table 66.16.5.3.3, shall mean one line of in-rack sprinklers in the longitudinal flue space every 4 ft to 6 ft (1.2 m to 1.8 m) above the floor and positioned to coincide with a storage level except above the top tier, with sprinklers spaced not more than 10 ft (3 m) on center and sprinklers staggered vertically, where more than one level of in-rack sprinklers is installed.
(4) Layout 4, as referenced in Table 66.16.5.3.1 and Table 66.16.5.3.3, shall mean one line of in-rack sprinklers in the longitudinal flue space at every 8 ft to 12 ft (2.4 m to 3.6 m) above the floor and positioned to coincide with a storage level except above the top tier, with the first level beginning at an elevation of approximately 4 ft to 6 ft (1.2 m to 1.8 m) above the floor and positioned to coincide with a storage level, with sprinklers spaced not more than 10 ft (3 m) on center and sprinklers staggered vertically, where more than one level of in-rack sprinklers is installed.
(5) Layout 5, as referenced in Table 66.16.5.3.1, shall mean one line of in-rack sprinklers in the longitudinal flue space at every 4 ft to 6 ft (1.2 m to 1.8 m) above the floor and positioned to coincide with a storage level except above the top tier and face sprinklers at the first in-rack sprinkler level at each rack upright, with in-rack sprinklers spaced not more than 9 ft (2.7 m) on center and staggered vertically, where more than one level of in-rack sprinklers is installed.
(6) Layout 6, as referenced in Table 66.16.5.3.1, shall mean one line of in-rack sprinklers in the longitudinal flue space at every 8 ft to 12 ft (2.4 m to 3.6 m) above the floor and positioned to coincide with storage level except the top tier and face sprinklers at the first in-rack sprinkler level at each rack upright, with in-rack sprinklers spaced not more than 10 ft (3 m) on center and staggered vertically, where more than one level of in-rack sprinklers is installed.

[30:16.5.1.10]

66.16.5.1.11 For each entry in Table 66.16.5.3.1 through Table 66.16.5.3.18 the "Fire Test Ref." number shall be used to identify the information in Section E.2 of NFPA 30 about the fire tests on which the protection criteria for that entry are based. [30:16.5.1.11]

66.16.5.1.12 The water supply shall be sufficient to meet the fixed fire protection demand plus a total of at least 500 gpm (1900 L/min) for inside and outside hose connections for at least 2 hours, unless otherwise specified in this section. [30:16.5.1.12]

N **66.16.5.2** Section 66.16.10 and its related tables, Table 66.16.10.1.4, Table 66.16.10.1.5.4, and Table 66.16.10.2.4, shall be used to determine protection criteria for the palletized and rack storage of distilled spirits, up to 75 percent by volume ethanol in wooden barrels. [30:16.5.2]

66.16.5.3 Specific Design Criteria.

Δ **66.16.5.3.1** Table 66.16.5.3.1 shall apply to the following:

(1) Automatic sprinkler protection
(2) Single- or double-row rack storage
(3) All liquid classes except Class IA liquids [FP < 73°F (22.8°C) and BP < 100°F (37.8°C)]
(4) Metal containers, metal portable tanks, metal intermediate bulk containers
(5) Relieving- or nonrelieving-style containers

[30:16.5.3.1]

Δ **Table 66.16.5.3.1** Design Criteria for Sprinkler Protection of Single- and Double-Row Rack Storage of Class IB, Class IC, Class II, Class IIIA, and Class IIIB Liquids [Any FP, BP ≥ 100°F (37.8°C)] in Metal Containers, Portable Tanks, and IBCs

Liquid Type/Flash Point	Container Capacity	Container Type	Maximum Ceiling Height ft (m)	Maximum Storage Height ft (m)	Ceiling: K-factor gpm/psi$^{1/2}$ (L/min/bar$^{1/2}$)	Ceiling: Response/Nominal Temperature Rating/Orientation	Design Density gpm/ft^2 (mm/min)	Area ft^2 (m^2)	In-Rack: K-factor gpm/psi$^{1/2}$ (L/min/bar$^{1/2}$)	In-Rack: Response/Nominal Temperature Rating/Orientation	Minimum Discharge Flow gpm (L/min)	Layout (See 16.5.1.10)	Notes	Fire Test Ref. [See Table E.2(a)]
Class IB, Class IC, Class II, and Class IIIA Liquids [FP < 200°F (93°C) and BP ≥ 100°F (37.8°C)]	≤1.3 gal (5 L)	Nonrelieving	30 (9.1)	16 (4.9)	K≥11.2 (160)	QR/High/Any	0.60 (24)	2000 (190)	K≥5.6 (80)	QR/Ordinary/Any	30 (110)	1	1, 2, 7	1
				20 (6.1)	K≥11.2 (160)	SR or QR/High/Any	0.60 (24)	2000 (190)	K≥5.6 (80)	QR/Ordinary/Any	30 (110)	2	1, 2, 7	2
	≤6.5 gal (25 L)	Nonrelieving	30 (9.1)	25 (7.6)	K≥8.0 (115)	SR or QR/High/Any	0.30 (12)	3000 (280)	K≥5.6 (80)	QR/Ordinary/Any	30 (110)	7	1, 7	14
		Relieving	18 (5.5)	14 (4.3)	K≥11.2 (160)	QR/High/Pendent	0.65 (26.5)	2000 (190)	No in-rack sprinklers required			4		
			30 (9.1)	25 (7.6)	K≥8.0 (115)	SR or QR/High/Any	0.30 (12)	3000 (280)	K≥5.6 (80)	QR/Ordinary/Any	30 (110)	7	1, 5, 7	14
	>6.5 and ≤60 gal (>25 and ≤230 L)	Nonrelieving	30 (9.1)	25 (7.6)	K≥11.2 (160)	SR/High/Any	0.40 (16)	3000 (280)	K≥5.6 (80)	SR or QR/Ordinary/Any	30 (110)	5	1, 7	5
	(>25 and ≤230 L)	Relieving	30 (9.1)	25 (7.6)	K≥11.2 (160)	SR/High/Any	0.60 (24)	3000 (280)	K≥5.6 (80)	QR/Ordinary/Any	30 (110)	6	1, 7	10
	Portable tanks and IBCs	Relieving	30 (9.1)	25 (7.6)	K≥11.2 (160)	SR/High/Any	0.60 (24)	3000 (280)	K≥5.6 (80)	SR or QR/Ordinary/Any	30 (110)	5	1, 7	12
Class IIIB Liquids [FP ≥ 200°F (93°C)]	≤6.5 gal (25 L)	Nonrelieving	50 (15)	40 (12)	K≥8.0 (115)	SR or QR/High/Any	0.30 (12)	2000 (190)	K≥5.6 (80)	QR/Ordinary/Any	30 (110)	4	1, 3, 7	4
		Relieving	50 (15)	40 (12)	K≥8.0 (115)	SR or QR/High/Any	0.30 (12)	2000 (190)	K≥5.6 (80)	QR/Ordinary/Any	30 (110)	4	1, 7	9
	>6.5 and ≤60 gal (>25 and ≤230 L)	Nonrelieving	50 (15)	40 (12)	K≥8.0 (115)	SR/High/Any	0.30 (12)	3000 (280)	K≥5.6 (80)	QR/Ordinary/Any	30 (110)	4	1, 3, 7	6
		Relieving	50 (15)	40 (12)	K≥8.0 (115)	SR/High/Any	0.30 (12)	3000 (280)	K≥5.6 (80)	QR/Ordinary/Any	30 (110)	4	1, 3, 7	11
	Portable tanks and IBCs	Relieving	50 (15)	40 (12)	K≥8.0 (115)	SR/High/Any	0.30 (12)	3000 (280)	K≥5.6 (80)	QR/Ordinary/Any	30 (110)	4	1, 6, 7	13

For definitions of abbreviations used in the Response column, see 66.16.5.1.9(4). See also 66.16.5.1.9(5).

Notes:
See 66.16.5.3.1.1 for additional design criteria.

(1) Protection for uncartoned or case-cut nonsolid shelf display up to 6.5 ft (2 m) and storage above on pallets in racking and stored on shelf materials, including open wire mesh, or 2 in. × 6 in. (50 mm × 150 mm) wooden slats, spaced a minimum of 2 in. (50 mm) apart.
(2) Increase ceiling density to 0.60 gpm/ft2 (24 mm/min) if more than one level of storage exists above the top level of in-rack sprinklers.
(3) Double-row racks limited to maximum 6 ft (1.8 m) depth.
(4) For K=8.0 (115) and larger ceiling sprinklers, increase ceiling density to 0.60 gpm/ft^2 (24 mm/min) over 2000 ft^2 (190 m^2) if more than one level of storage exists above the top level of in-rack sprinklers.
(5) Reduce in-rack sprinkler spacing to maximum 9 ft (2.7 m) centers.
(6) See 66.16.5.3.1.2 for additional design criteria.
(7) See 66.16.5.3.1.3 for additional design criteria.

[30:Table 16.5.3.1]

N **66.16.5.3.1.1** Where noted in Table 66.16.5.3.1, in-rack sprinkler design shall include the following based on the number of levels of in-rack sprinklers:

(1) Where one level of in-rack sprinklers is installed, the eight most hydraulically remote sprinklers.
(2) Where two levels of in-rack sprinklers are installed, the six most hydraulically remote sprinklers on each level.
(3) Where three or more levels of in-rack sprinklers are installed, the six most hydraulically remote sprinklers on the top three levels.

[**30**:16.5.3.1.1]

N **66.16.5.3.1.2** Where noted in Table 66.16.5.3.1, the minimum in-rack discharge pressure shall not be less than 10 psi (0.69 bar). [**30**:16.5.3.1.2]

N **66.16.5.3.1.3** Where noted in Table 66.16.5.3.1, the sprinkler layout for Layout 7 shall mean the following:

(1) One line of in-rack sprinklers in the longitudinal flue space at every storage level above the floor except above the top tier and face sprinklers above either the second or third storage level.
(2) In-rack sprinklers in the longitudinal flue spaced not more than 9 ft (2.7 m) on-center and staggered vertically, where more than one level of in-rack sprinklers is installed.
(3) In-rack sprinklers located at the rack face spaced not more than 5 ft (1.5 m) on-center.

[**30**:16.5.3.1.3]

66.16.5.3.2 Table 66.16.5.3.2 shall apply to the following:

(1) Automatic sprinkler protection
(2) Palletized or stacked storage
(3) All liquid classes except Class IA liquids [FP < 73°F (22.8°C) and BP < 100°F (37.8°C)]
(4) Metal containers, metal portable tanks, metal intermediate bulk containers
(5) Relieving- or nonrelieving-style containers

[**30**:16.5.3.2]

66.16.5.3.3 Table 66.16.5.3.3 shall apply to the following:

(1) Foam-water sprinkler protection
(2) Single- or double-row rack storage
(3) All liquid classes except Class IA liquids [FP < 73°F (22.8°C) and BP < 100°F (37.8°C)]
(4) Metal containers, metal portable tanks, metal intermediate bulk containers
(5) Relieving- or nonrelieving-style containers

[**30**:16.5.3.3]

N **66.16.5.3.3.1** Where noted in Table 66.16.5.3.3, the minimum in-rack pressure shall not be less than a gauge pressure of 10 psi (0.69 bar). [**30**:16.5.3.3.1]

66.16.5.3.4 Table 66.16.5.3.4 shall apply to the following:

(1) Foam-water sprinkler protection
(2) Palletized or stacked storage
(3) All liquid classes except Class IA liquids [FP < 73°F (22.8°C) and BP < 100°F (37.8°C)]
(4) Metal containers, metal portable tanks, metal intermediate bulk containers
(5) Relieving- or nonrelieving-style containers

[**30**:16.5.3.4]

66.16.5.3.5 Table 66.16.5.3.5 shall apply to the following:

(1) Automatic sprinkler protection
(2) Single-, double-, or multiple-row rack storage
(3) Class IIIB liquids [FP ≥ 200°F (93°C)]
(4) Nonmetallic containers or intermediate bulk containers
(5) Cartoned or uncartoned

[**30**:16.5.3.5]

66.16.5.3.6 Table 66.16.5.3.6 shall apply to the following:

(1) Automatic sprinkler protection
(2) Shelf storage
(3) All liquid classes except Class IA liquids [FP < 73°F (22.8°C) and BP < 100°F (37.8°C)]
(4) Metal containers
(5) Nonrelieving-style containers

[**30**:16.5.3.6]

Δ **66.16.5.3.7** Table 66.16.5.3.7 shall apply to the following:

(1) Automatic sprinkler protection
(2) Single- or double-row rack storage
(3) Water-miscible ignitible (flammable or combustible) liquids
(4) Glass or plastic containers
(5) Cartoned or uncartoned

[**30**:16.5.3.7]

66.16.5.3.8 Table 66.16.5.3.8 shall apply to the following:

(1) Automatic sprinkler protection
(2) Single- or double-row rack storage or palletized storage
(3) All liquid classes except Class IA liquids [FP < 73°F (22.8°C) and BP < 100°F (37.8°C)]
(4) Metal containers
(5) Relieving-style containers

[**30**:16.5.3.8]

N **66.16.5.3.8.1** The in-rack sprinkler water demand shall be based on the simultaneous operation of the most hydraulically remote sprinklers as follows:

(1) Seven sprinklers where only one level of in-rack sprinklers is installed
(2) Fourteen sprinklers (seven on each of the two top levels) where more than one level of in-rack sprinklers is installed

[**30**:16.5.3.8.1]

N **66.16.5.3.8.2** Where noted in Table 66.16.5.3.8, the minimum in-rack pressure shall not be less than a gauge pressure of 10 psi (0.69 bar). [**30**:16.5.3.8.2]

66.16.5.3.9 Table 66.16.5.3.9 shall apply to the following:

(1) Automatic sprinkler protection
(2) Palletized storage
(3) Class II and III nonmiscible and Class II and III miscible liquids [FP ≥ 100°F (37.8°C)]
(4) Listed and labeled rigid nonmetallic intermediate bulk containers

[**30**:16.5.3.9]

66.16.5.3.9.1 Foam-water sprinkler protection shall be permitted to be substituted for water sprinkler protection, provided the same design criteria are used. [**30**:16.5.3.9.1]

Δ Table 66.16.5.3.2 Design Criteria for Sprinkler Protection of Palletized and Stacked Storage of Class IB, Class IC, Class II, Class IIIA, and Class IIIB Liquids [Any FP, BP ≥ 100°F (37.8°C)] in Metal Containers, Portable Tanks, and IBCs

Liquid Type/Flash Point	Container Capacity	Container Type	Packaging	Maximum Ceiling Height ft (m)	Maximum Storage Height ft (m)	K-factor gpm/psi^(1/2) (L/min/bar^(1/2))	Response/ Nominal Temperature Rating/ Orientation	Density gpm/ft² (mm/min)	Area ft² (m²)	Number of Sprinklers @ Pressure psi (bar)	Notes	Fire Test Ref. [See Table E.2(b)]
Class IB, Class IC, Class II, and Class IIIA Liquids [FP < 200°F (93°C) and BP ≥ 100°F (37.8°C)]	1.3 gal (5 L)	Relieving	Cartoned Only	30 (9.1)	12 (3.7)	K≥11.2 (160)	SR/ Ordinary/ Any	0.6 (24)	3000 (280)	—	—	18
						K25.2EC (360EC)	QR/ Ordinary/ Any	0.6 (24)	3000 (280)	—	—	18
	≤6.5 gal (25 L)	Nonrelieving	Uncartoned and/or cartoned	18 (5.5)	4 (12)	K≥8.0 (115)	SR or QR/ High/Any	0.21 (8.6)	1500 (140)	—	1	1
					5 (1.5)	K≥8.0 (115)	SR or QR/ High/Any	0.30 (12)	3000 (280)	—	—	2
				30 (9.1)	5 (1.5)	K14 (200)	FR/ Ordinary/ Any	—	—	—	—	—
						K16.8 (240)	FR/ Ordinary/ Any	—	—	30 @ 18 (1.2)	—	18
						K≥22.4 (320)	FR/ Ordinary/ Any	—	—	30 @ 7 (0.5)	—	18
		Relieving	Uncartoned and/or cartoned	30 (9.1)	5 (1.5)	K14 (200)	FR/ Ordinary/ Any	—	—	30 @ 18 (1.2)	—	18
						K16.8 (240)	FR/ Ordinary/ Any	—	—	30 @ 13 (0.9)	—	18
						K≥22.4 (320)	FR/ Ordinary/ Any	—	—	30 @ 7 (0.5)	—	18
	>6.5 and ≤60 gal (>25 and ≤230 L)	Nonrelieving	Uncartoned and/or cartoned	18 (5.5)	5 (1.5)	K≥11.2 (160)	SR/High/Any	0.40 (16.3)	3000 (280)	—	—	4
		Relieving	Uncartoned and/or cartoned	30 (9.1)	5 (1.5)	K≥11.2 (160)	SR/High/Any	0.40 (16.3)	3000 (280)	—	—	9
				30 (9.1)	6.5 (2.0)	K≥11.2 (160)	SR/High/Any	0.60 (24.4)	3000 (280)	—	3	10
	Portable tanks and IBCs	Relieving	—	30 (9.1)	1–high	K≥8.0 (115)	SR/High/Any	0.30 (12.2)	3000 (280)	—	—	14
				30 (9.1)	2–high	K≥11.2 (160)	SR/High/Any	0.60 (24.4)	3000 (280)	—	—	15
Class IIIB Liquids [FP ≥ 200°F (93°C)]	≤6.5 gal (25 L)	Any	Uncartoned and/or cartoned	30 (9.1)	5 (1.5)	K14 (200)	FR/ Ordinary/ Any	—	—	30 @ 18 (1.2)	—	18
						K16.8 (240)	FR/ Ordinary/ Any	—	—	30 @ 13 (0.9)	—	18
						K≥22.4 (320)	FR/ Ordinary/ Any	—	—	30 @ 7 (0.5)	—	18
	>6.5 and ≤60 gal (>25 and ≤230 L)	Nonrelieving	Uncartoned and/or cartoned	20 (6.1)	10 (3.0)	K≥8.0 (115)	SR/High/Any	0.25 (10.2)	3000 (280)	—	—	6
				30 (9.1)	18 (5.5)	K≥8.0 (115)	SR/High/Any	0.35 (14.2)	3000 (280)	—	—	7
		Relieving	Uncartoned and/or cartoned	20 (6.1)	10 (3.0)	K≥8.0 (115)	SR/High/Any	0.25 (10.2)	3000 (280)	—	—	12
				30 (9.1)	18 (5.5)	K≥8.0 (115)	SR/High/Any	0.25 (10.2)	3000 (280)	—	—	12
	Portable tanks and IBCs	Relieving	—	30 (9.1)	1-high	K≥8.0 (115)	SR/High/Any	0.25 (10.2)	3000 (280)	—	—	16
	—	—	—	30 (9.1)	2-high	K≥11.2 (160)	SR/High/Any	0.50 (20.4)	3000 (280)	—	—	17

For definitions of abbreviations used in the Response column, see 66.16.5.1.9(4). See also 66.5.1.9(5).

Notes:
(1) Minimum hose stream demand can be reduced to 250 gpm (950 L/min) for 2 hours.
(2) Sprinklers must also be hydraulically calculated to provide a density of 0.80 gpm/ft² (33 mm/min) over 1000 ft² (93 m²).
(3) Drums must be placed on open slatted pallet, not nested, to allow pressure relief from drums on lower levels.

[30:Table 16.5.3.2]

Δ **Table 66.16.5.3.3 Design Criteria for Foam-Water Sprinkler Protection of Single- or Double-Row Rack Storage of Class IB, Class IC, Class II, Class IIIA, and Class IIIB Liquids [Any FP, BP ≥ 100°F (37.8°C)] Liquids in Metal Containers, Portable Tanks, and IBCs**

Liquid Type/Flash Point	Container Capacity	Container Type	Maximum Ceiling Height ft (m)	Maximum Storage Height ft (m)	Ceiling Sprinkler Protection — K-factor gpm/psi$^{1/2}$ (L/min/bar$^{1/2}$)	Ceiling Sprinkler Protection — Response/Nominal Temperature Rating/Orientation	Design Density gpm/ft² (mm/min)	Design Area ft² (m²)	In-Rack Sprinkler Protection — K-factor gpm/psi$^{1/2}$ (L/min/bar$^{1/2}$)	In-Rack Sprinkler Protection — Response/Nominal Temperature Rating/Orientation	Minimum Discharge Flow gpm (L/min)	Layout (See 66.16.5.1.10)	Notes	Fire Test Ref. [See Table E.2(c)]
Class IB, Class IC, Class II, and Class IIIA Liquids [FP < 200°F (93°C) and BP ≥ 100°F (37.8°C)]	≤6.5 gal (25 L)	Nonrelieving	30 (9.1)	25 (7.6)	K≥8.0 (115)	SR or QR/High/Any	0.30 (12)	2000 (190)	K≥5.6 (80)	SR or QR/Ordinary/Any	30 (110)	3	1, 2, 4, 5	1
		Relieving	30 (9.1)	25 (7.6)	K≥8.0 (115)	SR or QR/High/Any	0.30 (12)	2000 (190)	K≥5.6 (80)	SR or QR/Ordinary/Any	30 (110)	4	1, 2, 4, 5	4
	>6.5 and ≤60 gal (>25 and ≤230 L)	Nonrelieving	30 (9.1)	25 (7.6)	K≥8.0 (115)	SR/High/Any	0.30 (12)	3000 (280)	K≥5.6 (80)	SR or QR/Ordinary/Any	30 (110)	3	1, 3, 4, 5	2
		Relieving	30 (9.1)	25 (7.6)	K≥8.0 (115)	SR/High/Any	0.30 (12)	3000 (280)	K≥5.6 (80)	SR or QR/Ordinary/Any	30 (110)	4	1, 3, 4, 5	5
	Portable tanks and IBCs	Relieving	30 (9.1)	25 (7.6)	K≥8.0 (115)	SR/High/Any	0.30 (12)	3000 (280)	K≥5.6 (80)	SR or QR/Ordinary/Any	30 (110)	4	1, 3, 4, 5	5
Class IIIB Liquids [FP ≥ 200°F (93°C)]	≤60 gal (230 L)	Nonrelieving	50 (15)	40 (12)	K≥8.0 (115)	SR/High/Any	0.30 (12)	2000 (190)	K≥5.6 (80)	SR or QR/Ordinary/Any	30 (110)	4	1, 5	3
		Relieving	50 (15)	40 (12)	K≥8.0 (115)	SR/High/Any	0.30 (12)	2000 (190)	K≥5.6 (80)	SR or QR/Ordinary/Any	30 (110)	4	1, 5	6

For definitions of abbreviations used in the Response column, see 66.16.5.1.9(4). See also 66.16.5.1.9(5).

Notes:
(1) In-rack sprinkler design based on the six most hydraulically remote sprinklers in each of the upper three levels.
(2) Design area can be reduced to 1500 ft² when using a preprimed foam-water system installed in accordance with NFPA 11 and maintained according to NFPA 25.
(3) Design area can be reduced to 2000 ft² when using a preprimed foam-water system installed in accordance with NFPA 11 and maintained according to NFPA 25.
(4) In-rack sprinkler hydraulic design can be reduced to three sprinklers operating per level, with three levels operating simultaneously, when using a preprimed foam-water sprinkler system designed in accordance with NFPA 11 and maintained in accordance with NFPA 25.
(5) See 66.16.5.3.3.1 for additional design criteria.
[**30:**Table 16.5.3.3]

Δ **66.16.5.3.9.2** Rigid nonmetallic intermediate bulk containers shall be listed and labeled in accordance with UL 2368, *Fire Exposure Testing of Intermediate Bulk Containers for Flammable and Combustible Liquids*; FM 6020, *Approval Standard for Composite Intermediate Bulk Containers*; or an equivalent test procedure. [**30:**16.5.3.9.2]

66.16.5.3.9.3 The sprinkler operating gauge pressure shall be a minimum 30 psi (207 kPa). [**30:**16.5.3.9.3]

66.16.5.3.10 Table 66.16.5.3.10 shall apply to the following:

(1) Automatic sprinkler protection
(2) Single- or double-row rack storage
(3) Class II and III nonmiscible and Class II and III miscible liquids [FP ≥ 100°F (37.8°C)]
(4) Listed and labeled rigid nonmetallic intermediate bulk containers

[**30:**16.5.3.10]

N **66.16.5.3.10.1** Foam-water sprinkler protection shall be permitted to be substituted for water sprinkler protection, provided the same design criteria are used. [**30:**16.5.3.10.1]

N **66.16.5.3.10.2** Rigid nonmetallic intermediate bulk containers shall be listed and labeled in accordance with UL 2368, *Fire Exposure Testing of Intermediate Bulk Containers for Flammable and Combustible Liquids*; FM 6020, *Approval Standard for Composite Intermediate Bulk Containers*; or an equivalent test procedure. [**30:**16.5.3.10.2]

66.16.5.3.11 Table 66.16.5.3.11 shall apply to the following:

(1) Automatic sprinkler protection
(2) Palletized or stacked storage
(3) Unsaturated polyester resins (UPRs) with not more than 50 percent by weight of Class IC, Class II, or Class IIIA liquid [73°F (22.8°C) ≤ FP < 200°F (93°C)]
(4) Metal containers
(5) Relieving-style metal containers; nonrelieving-style allowed only up to 6 gal (23 L)

[**30:**16.5.3.11]

N **66.16.5.3.11.1** Containers that exceed 6.5 gal (25 L) capacity shall have both 3⁄4 in. (20 mm) and 2 in. (50 mm) listed and labeled pressure-relieving devices. [**30:**16.5.3.11.1]

Δ **Table 66.16.5.3.4 Design Criteria for Foam-Water Sprinkler Protection of Palletized and Stacked Storage of Class IB, Class IC, Class II, and Class IIIA Liquids [FP < 200°F (93°C) and BP ≥ 100°F (37.8°C)] in Metal Containers, Portable Tanks, and IBCs**

Liquid Type/ Flash Point	Container Capacity	Container Type	Packaging	Maximum Ceiling Height ft (m)	Maximum Storage Height ft (m)	K-factor gpm/psi$^{1/2}$ (L/min/bar$^{1/2}$)	Response/ Nominal Temperature Rating/ Orientation	Density gpm/ft^2 (mm/min)	Area ft^2 (m^2)	Notes	Fire Test Ref. [See Table E.2(d)]
Class IB, Class IC, Class II, and Class IIIA Liquids [FP < 200°F (93°C) and BP ≥ 100°F (37.8°C)]	≤6.5 gal (25 L)	Nonrelieving	Cartoned	30 (9.1)	11 (3.4)	K≥11.2 (160)	SR or QR/ High/Any	0.40 (16)	3000 (280)	1	1
			Uncartoned	30 (9.1)	12 (3.7)	K≥8.0 (115)	SR or QR/ High/Any	0.30 (12)	3000 (280)	1	2
	>6.5 and ≤60 gal (>25 and ≤230 L)	Nonrelieving	Cartoned or uncartoned	30 (9.1)	5 (1.5) [1-high]	K≥8.0 (115)	SR/High/Any	0.30 (12)	3000 (280)	1	3
		Relieving	Cartoned or uncartoned	30 (9.1)	6.5 (2.0) [2-high]	K≥8.0 (115)	SR/High/Any	0.30 (12)	3000 (280)	2, 3	4
				33 (10.1)	10 (3.0) [3-high]	K≥11.2 (160)	SR/High/Any	0.45 (18.3)	3000 (280)	2, 3	6
					13.75 (4.2) [4-high]	K≥11.2 (160)	SR/High/Any	0.60 (24)	3000 (280)	2, 3	7
	Portable tanks and IBCs	Relieving	—	30 (9.1)	1- or 2-high	K≥8.0 (115)	SR/High/Any	0.30 (12)	3000 (280)	—	5

For definitions of abbreviations used in the Response column, see 66.16.5.1.9(4). See also 66.16.5.1.9(5).

Notes:
(1) Design area can be reduced to 2000 ft^2 (190 m^2) when using a preprimed foam-water system installed in accordance with NFPA 11 and maintained according to NFPA 25.
(2) Both ¾ in. (20 mm) and 2 in. (50 mm) listed and labeled pressure-relieving mechanisms are required on containers greater than 6.5 gal (25 L) capacity. See 66.16.3.6.
(3) Drums placed on open slatted pallet, not nested, to allow pressure relief from drums on lower levels.

[**30**:Table 16.5.3.4]

Δ **Table 66.16.5.3.5 Design Criteria for Sprinkler Protection of Single-, Double-, and Multiple-Row Rack Storage of Class IIIB Liquids [FP ≥ 200°F (93°C)] in Nonmetallic Containers**

Liquid Type/Flash Point	Container Capacity	Packaging	Maximum Ceiling Height ft (m)	Maximum Storage Height ft (m)	Rack Depth ft (m)	Minimum Aisle Width ft (m)	K-factor gpm/psi$^{1/2}$ (L/min/bar$^{1/2}$)	Response/ Nominal Temperature Rating/ Orientation	Number of Sprinklers @ Pressure psi (bar)	K-factor gpm/psi$^{1/2}$ (L/min/bar$^{1/2}$)	Response/ Nominal Temperature Rating/ Orientation	Minimum Discharge Flow gpm (L/min)	Layouts	Notes	Fire Test Ref. [See Table E.2(e)]
Class IIIB [FP ≥ 200°F (93°C)]	≤5 gal (19 L)	Plastic containers, cartoned or uncartoned	Unlimited	Unlimited	Any	4 (1.2)			See 66.16.6.1						1
Class IIIB [FP ≥ 375°F (190°C)]	≤6 gal (23 L)	Flexible plastic liner within a composite corrugated paperboard box	Unlimited	Unlimited	Any	8 (2.4)			See 66.16.6.3					1	2
	≤275 gal (1045 L)	Flexible plastic liner within a composite continuously wound corrugated paperboard intermediate bulk container	30 (9.1)	28 (8.5)	Any	8 (2.4)			See 66.16.6.3					1, 2	2

Note:
(1) This is a subgroup of Class IIIB tied to the flashpoint of the liquids that were tested.
(2) Construction of intermediate bulk container to be a minimum of 8 layers of paperboard, with a minimum nominal thickness of 1.5 in. (38 mm) at the center of any side panel.

[**30**:Table 16.5.3.5]

△ **Table 66.16.5.3.6 Design Criteria for Sprinkler Protection of Shelf Storage of Class IB, Class IC, Class II, Class IIIA, and Class IIIB Liquids [Any FP, BP ≥ 100°F (37.8°C)] in Metal Containers**

Liquid Type/ Flash Point	Container Capacity	Container Type	Maximum Ceiling Height ft (m)	Maximum Storage Height ft (m)	Minimum Aisle Width ft (m)	K-factor gpm/psi$^{1/2}$ (L/min/bar$^{1/2}$)	Response/ Nominal Temperature Rating/ Orientation	Density gpm/ft^2 (mm/min)	Area ft^2 (m^2)	Notes	Fire Test Ref. [See Table E.2(f)]
Class IB, Class IC, Class II, Class IIIA, and Class IIIB Liquids [Any FP, BP ≥ 100°F (37.8°C)]	≤1.3 gal (5 L)	Nonrelieving	18 (5.5)	6 (1.8)	5 (1.5)	K≥5.6 (80)	SR or QR/ High/Any	0.19 (7.7)	1500 (140)	1, 2	1

For definitions of abbreviations used in the Response column, see 66.16.5.1.9(4). See also 66.16.5.1.9(5).

Notes:
(1) Protection limited to mercantile shelving that is 2 ft (600 mm) or less in depth per side, with backing between each side.
(2) Minimum hose stream demand can be reduced to 250 gpm for 2 hours.

[**30**:Table 16.5.3.6]

△ **Table 66.16.5.3.7 Design Criteria for Sprinkler Protection of Single- and Double-Row Rack Storage of Water-Miscible Class IB, Class IC, Class II, Class IIIA, and Class IIIB Liquids [Any FP, BP ≥ 100°F (37.8°C)] Liquids in Glass or Plastic Containers**

Liquid Type/ Flash Point	Container Capacity	Packaging	Maximum Ceiling Height ft (m)	Maximum Storage Height ft (m)	Maximum Rack Depth ft (m)	Minimum Aisle Width ft (m)	K-factor gpm/psi$^{1/2}$ (L/min/bar$^{1/2}$)	Response/ Nominal Temperature Rating/ Orientation	Number of Sprinklers @ Pressure psi (bar)	K-factor gpm/psi$^{1/2}$ (L/min/bar$^{1/2}$)	Response/ Nominal Temperature Rating/ Orientation	Minimum Discharge Flow gpm (L/min)	Layout	Fire Test Ref. [See Table E.2(g)]
Water-miscible Class IB, Class IC, Class II, Class IIIA, and Class IIIB Liquids [Any FP, BP ≥ 100°F (37.8°C)]	≤16 oz (450 mL)	Cartoned	Unlimited	Unlimited	9 (2.7)	8 (2.4)						See 66.16.6.1			3
	≤1 gal (3.8 L)	Cartoned	Unlimited	Unlimited	9 (2.7)	8 (2.4)						See 66.16.6.2			1
	≤60 gal (230 L)	Cartoned or uncartoned	30 (9.1)	25 (7.6)	9 (2.7)	8 (2.4)						See 66.16.6.2			2

[**30**:Table 16.5.3.7]

66.16.5.3.12 Table 66.16.5.3.12 shall apply to the following:

(1) Automatic sprinkler protection
(2) Palletized or stacked storage
(3) Miscible liquids with concentration of ignitible (flammable or combustible) no greater than 80 percent by volume
(4) Glass or plastic containers

[**30**:16.5.3.12]

N **66.16.5.3.13** Table 66.16.5.3.13 shall apply to the following:

(1) Automatic sprinkler protection or foam-water sprinkler protection
(2) Single- and double-row rack storage
(3) Class II and Class III liquids [FP ≥ 100°F (37.8°C)]
(4) Metal containers
(5) Relieving- and nonrelieving-style containers

[**30**:16.5.3.13]

N **66.16.5.3.14** Table 66.16.5.3.14 shall apply to the following:

(1) Automatic sprinkler protection
(2) Single-, double-, or multiple-row rack storage
(3) Class IB, Class IC, Class II, and Class IIIA liquids [FP < 200°F (93°C) and BP ≥ 100°F (37.8°C)]
(4) Glass and plastic containers
(5) Cartoned packaging

[**30**:16.5.3.14]

Δ Table 66.16.5.3.8 Design Criteria for Sprinkler Protection of Single-Row Rack, Double-Row Rack, and Palletized Storage of Class IB, Class IC, Class II, Class IIIA, and Class IIIB Liquids [Any FP, BP ≥ 100°F (37.8°C)] in Relieving-Style Metal Containers

Liquid Type/Flash Point	Storage Arrangement	Container Capacity	Packaging	Maximum Ceiling Height ft (m)	Maximum Storage Height ft (m)	Maximum Rack Depth ft (m)	Minimum Aisle Width ft (m)	K-factor gpm/psi$^{1/2}$ (L/min/bar$^{1/2}$)	Response/Nominal Temperature Rating/Orientation	Number of Sprinklers @ Pressure psi (bar kPa)	K-factor gpm/psi$^{1/2}$ (L/min/bar$^{1/2}$)	Response/Nominal Temperature Rating/Orientation	Minimum Discharge Flow gpm (L/min)	Layout (See 66.16.6.7)	Notes	Fire Test Ref.
Class IB, Class IC, Class II, Class IIIA, and Class IIIB Liquids [Any FP, BP ≥ 100°F (37.8°C)]	Rack	≤1.3 gal (5 L)	Cartoned	30 (9.1)	20 (6.1)	9 (2.7)	8 (2.4)	K≥14 (200)	ESFR/Ordinary/Pendent	12 @ 75 (5.2)	No in-rack sprinklers required			—		3
					25 (7.6)	9 (2.7)	8 (2.4)	K≥14 (200)	ESFR/Ordinary/Pendent	12 @ 50 (3.4)	K8.0 (115)	QR/Ordinary/Any	31 (117)	8	1, 2, 6	4
		≤6.5 gal (25 L)	Cartoned or uncartoned	24 (7.3)	14 (4.3)	6 (1.8)	7.5 (2.3)	K≥14 (200)	ESFR/Ordinary/Pendent	12 @ 50 (3.4)	K11.2 (160)	QR/Ordinary/Any	36 (136)	7	1, 2, 3, 4, 5, 6	1
								K≥25.2 (360)	ESFR/Ordinary/Pendent	12 @ 25 (1.7)	No in-rack sprinklers required				2, 3, 4, 5	2
				30 (9.1)	25 (7.6)	9 (2.7)	8 (2.4)	K≥14 (200)	ESFR/Ordinary/Pendent	12 @ 75 (5.2)	K8.0 (115)	QR/Ordinary/Any	44 (167)	9	1, 2, 6	5
	Palletized	≤1.3 gal (5 L)	Cartoned	30 (9.1)	8 (2.4)	—	7.5 (2.3)	K≥14 (200)	ESFR/Ordinary/Pendent	12 @ 50 (3.4)	—	—	—	—		6
		≤6.5 gal (25 L)	Cartoned or uncartoned	30 (9.1)	12 (3.7)	—	7.5 (2.3)	K≥14 (200)	ESFR/Ordinary/Pendent	12 @ 75 (5.2)	—	—	—	—		7

For definitions of abbreviations used in the Response column, see 66.16.5.1.9(4). See also 66.16.5.1.9(5).

Notes:
(1) See 66.16.5.3.8.1 for additional design criteria.
   (a) Seven sprinklers where only one level of in-rack sprinklers is installed.
   (b) Fourteen sprinklers (seven on each of the two top levels) where more than one level of in-rack sprinklers is installed.
(2) The in-rack sprinkler water demand should be balanced with the ceiling sprinkler water demand at their point of connection.
(3) Containers with a capacity of up to 1.3 gal (5 L) are not required to be relieving style.
(4) Provide minimum 3 in. (76 mm) transverse flue at rack uprights.
(5) Racks can have open-mesh wire intermediate shelving on lower levels.
(6) See 66.16.5.3.8.2 for additional design criteria.
[**30**:Table 16.5.3.8]

Δ Table 66.16.5.3.9 Design Criteria for Sprinkler Protection of Palletized Storage of Class II and III Liquids [FP ≥ 100°F (37.8°C)] in Listed and Labeled Rigid Nonmetallic IBCs

Liquid Type/Flash Point	Container Capacity	Maximum Ceiling Height ft (m)	Maximum Storage Height ft (m)	K-factor gpm/psi$^{1/2}$ (L/min/bar$^{1/2}$)	Response/Nominal Temperature Rating/Orientation	Density gpm/ft^2 (mm/min)	Area ft^2 (m^2)	Notes	Fire Test Ref. [See Table E.2(i).]
Class II and III Liquids [FP ≥ 100°F (37.8°C)]	≤793 gal (3000 L)	30 (9.1)	1-high	K≥11.2 (160)	SR/High/Any	0.45 (18.3)	3000 (280)	1	1
			2-high	K≥11.2 (160)	SR/High/Any	0.60 (24)	3000 (280)	1	2

For definitions of abbreviations used in the Response column, see 66.16.5.1.9(4). See also 66.16.5.1.9(5).

Note:
(1) See also 66.16.5.3.1 through 66.16.5.3.3.
[**30**:Table 16.5.3.9]

Δ **Table 66.16.5.3.10 Design Criteria for Sprinkler Protection of Single- and Double-Row Rack Storage of Class II and III Liquids [FP ≥ 100°F (37.8°C)] in Listed and Labeled Rigid Nonmetallic IBCs**

						Ceiling Sprinkler Protection			In-Rack Sprinkler Protection				
						Sprinkler Type		Design	Sprinkler Type		Design		
Liquid Type/Flash Point	Container Capacity	Maximum Ceiling Height ft (m)	Maximum Storage Height ft (m)	Maximum Rack Depth ft (m)	Minimum Aisle Width ft (m)	K-factor gpm/psi$^{1/2}$ (L/min/bar$^{1/2}$)	Response/ Nominal Temperature Rating/ Orientation	Number of Sprinklers @ Pressure psi (bar)	K-factor gpm/psi$^{1/2}$ (L/min/bar$^{1/2}$)	Response/ Nominal Temperature Rating/ Orientation	Minimum Discharge Flow gpm (L/min)	Layout	Fire Test Ref. [See Table E.2(j)]
Class II and III Liquids [FP ≥ 100°F (37.8°C)]	≤793 gal (3000 L)	30 (9.1)	25 (7.6)	9 (2.7)	8 (2.4)				See 66.16.6.2.				1

[**30**:Table 16.5.3.10]

Δ **Table 66.16.5.3.11 Design Criteria for Sprinkler Protection of Palletized or Stacked Storage of Unsaturated Polyester Resins in Metal Containers**

				Ceiling Sprinkler Protection					
				Sprinkler Type		Design			
Liquid Type/ Flash Point	Container Capacity	Maximum Ceiling Height ft (m)	Maximum Storage Height ft (m)	K-factor gpm/psi$^{1/2}$ (L/min/bar$^{1/2}$)	Response/ Nominal Temperature Rating/ Orientation	Density gpm/ft^2 (mm/min)	Area ft^2 (m^2)	Notes	Fire Test Ref. [See Table E.2(k).]
Unsaturated Polyester Resins	>6.5 and ≤60 gal (>25 and ≤230 L)	33 (10.1)	10 (3.0)	K≥11.2 (160)	SR/Any/Any	0.45 (18.3)	3000 (280)	1, 2, 3	1

For definitions of abbreviations used in the Response column, see 66.16.5.1.9(4). See also 66.16.5.1.9(5).
Notes:
(1) Drums placed on open, slatted pallet, not nested, to allow pressure relief from drums on lower levels.
(2) Storage areas containing unsaturated polyester resin (UPR) should not be located in the same spill containment area or drainage path of other Class I or Class II liquids [FP < 140°F (60°C)], unless protected as required for such other liquids.
(3) See 66.16.5.3.11.1 for additional design criteria.
[**30**:Table 16.5.3.11]

Δ **Table 66.16.5.3.12 Design Criteria for Sprinkler Protection of Palletized or Stacked Storage of Water-Miscible Class IB, Class IC, Class II, Class IIIA, and Class IIIB Liquids [Any FP, BP ≥ 100°F (37.8°C)] in Glass or Plastic Containers**

				Ceiling Sprinkler Protection				
				Sprinkler Type		Design		
Liquid Type/Flash Point	Container Capacity	Maximum Ceiling Height ft (m)	Maximum Storage Height ft (m)	K-factor gpm/psi$^{1/2}$ (L/min/bar$^{1/2}$)	Response/Nominal Temperature Rating/Orientation	Density gpm/ft^2 (mm/min)	Area ft^2 (m^2)	Fire Test Ref. [See Table E.2(l).]
Water-miscible Class IB, Class IC, Class II, Class IIIA, and Class IIIB Liquids [Any FP, BP ≥ 100°F (37.8°C)]	≤8 oz (240 ml)	38 (11.6)	5 (1.5)	K≥11.2 (160)	QR/Ordinary/Any	0.47 (19.2)	2000 (190)	P60 and P61

For definitions of abbreviations used in the Response column, see 66.16.5.1.9(4). See also 66.16.5.1.9(5).
[**30**:Table 16.5.3.12]

N 66.16.5.3.15 Table 66.16.5.3.15 shall apply to the following:

(1) Automatic sprinkler protection
(2) Single- or double-row rack storage
(3) Liquids with a FP greater than or equal to 450°F (230°C)
(4) Plastic containers
(5) Cartoned or uncartoned

[**30**:16.5.3.15]

N 66.16.5.3.16 Table 66.16.5.3.16 shall apply to the following:

(1) Automatic sprinkler protection
(2) Single- or double-row rack storage
(3) Storage of 100 percent or less of ethanol/propanol/methanol
(4) Plastic or glass containers
(5) Cartoned packaging

[**30**:16.5.3.16]

N 66.16.5.3.17 Table 66.16.5.3.17 shall apply to the following:

(1) Automatic sprinkler protection
(2) Single-, double-, or multiple-row rack storage
(3) 50 percent/50 percent mixture of ethanol/propanol/methanol/water
(4) Plastic or glass containers
(5) Cartoned packaging

[**30**:16.5.3.17]

N 66.16.5.3.18 Table 66.16.5.3.18 shall apply to the following:

(1) Automatic sprinkler protection
(2) Palletized storage
(3) 50 percent/50 percent mixture of ethanol/propanol/methanol/water
(4) Plastic or glass containers
(5) Cartoned packaging

[**30**:16.5.3.18]

N Table 66.16.5.3.13 Design Criteria for Sprinkler Protection or Foam-Water Sprinkler Protection of Single- and Double-Row Rack Storage of Class II and Class III Liquids [FP ≥ 100°F (37.8°C)] in Metal Containers

Liquid Type/Flash Point	Container Capacity	Maximum Ceiling Height ft (m)	Maximum Storage Height ft (m)	Maximum Rack Depth ft (m)	Minimum Aisle Width ft (m)	Ceiling Sprinkler Protection — K-factor gpm/psi$^{1/2}$ (L/min/bar$^{1/2}$)	Ceiling — Response/Nominal Temperature Rating/Orientation	Ceiling Design — Number of Sprinklers @ Pressure psi (bar)	In-Rack K-factor gpm/psi$^{1/2}$ (L/min/bar$^{1/2}$)	In-Rack Response/Nominal Temperature Rating/Orientation	In-Rack Minimum Discharge Flow gpm (L/min)	Layout	Fire Test Reference
Class II and III Liquids [FP ≥ 100°F (37.8°C)]	>6.5 and ≤60 gal (>25 and ≤230 L)	48 (14.6 m)	34 (10.4)	9 (2.7)	6 (1.8)				See 66.16.6.5.				See Section E.5

[**30**:Table 16.5.3.13]

N Table 66.16.5.3.14 Design Criteria for Sprinkler Protection for Rack Storage of Class IB, Class IC, Class II, and Class IIIA Liquids [FP < 200°F (93°C) and BP ≥ 100°F (37.8°C)]

Liquid Type/Flash Point	Container Capacity	Packaging	Maximum Ceiling Height ft (m)	Maximum Storage Height ft (m)	Maximum Rack Depth ft (m)	Minimum Aisle Width ft (m)	Ceiling K-factor gpm/psi$^{1/2}$ (L/min/bar$^{1/2}$)	Ceiling Response/Nominal Temperature Rating/Orientation	Ceiling Design — Number of Sprinklers @ Pressure psi (bar)	In-Rack K-factor gpm/psi$^{1/2}$ (L/min/bar$^{1/2}$)	In-Rack Response/Nominal Temperature Rating/Orientation	In-Rack Minimum Discharge Flow gpm (L/min)	Layout	Fire Test Reference [See Table E.2(m)]
Class IB, Class IC, Class II, and Class IIIA Liquids [FP < 200°F (93°C) and BP ≥ 100°F (37.8°C)]	<2 oz (60 ml)	Cartoned	Unlimited	Unlimited	Any	4 (1.2)				See 66.16.6.1.				1

[**30**:Table 16.5.3.14]

N **Table 66.16.5.3.15 Water Sprinkler Protection for Single- or Double-Row Rack Storage of Class IIIB Liquids [FP ≥ 450°F (230°C)] in Plastic Containers**

Liquid Type/Flash Point	Container Capacity	Packaging	Maximum Ceiling Height ft (m)	Maximum Storage Height ft (m)	Maximum Rack Depth ft (m)	Minimum Aisle Width ft (m)	Ceiling Sprinkler Protection — Sprinkler Type K-factor gpm/psi$^{1/2}$ (L/min/bar$^{1/2}$)	Ceiling Sprinkler Protection — Sprinkler Type Response/Nominal Temperature Rating/Orientation	Ceiling Sprinkler Protection — Design Number of Sprinklers @ Pressure psi (bar)	In-Rack Sprinkler Protection — Sprinkler Type K-factor gpm/psi$^{1/2}$ (L/min/bar$^{1/2}$)	In-Rack Sprinkler Protection — Sprinkler Type Response/Nominal Temperature Rating/Orientation	In-Rack Sprinkler Protection — Design Minimum Discharge Flow gpm (L/min)	Layout (See 66.16.6.7)	Fire Test Reference [See Table E.2(n)]
Class IIIB [FP ≥ 450°F (230°C)]	≤5 gal (19 L)	Cartoned	30 (9.1)	15 (4.6)	9 (2.7)	8 (2.4)	K14 (200)	ESFR/Ordinary/Pendent	12 @ 50 (3.4)	No in-rack sprinklers required				1
				25 (7.6)	9 (2.7)	8 (2.4)	K14 (200)	ESFR/Ordinary/Pendent	12 @ 75 (5.2)	No in-rack sprinklers required See 66.16.6.1. See 66.16.6.4.				
		Uncartoned or mixed cartoned and uncartoned	30 (9.1)	25 (7.6)	9 (2.7)	8 (2.4)				See 66.16.6.1. See 66.16.6.4.				
	≤48 oz (≤1.4 L)	Cartoned	40 (12)	35 (10.7)	9 (2.7)	4 (1.2)	K25.2 (360)	ESFR/Ordinary/Pendent	12 @ 40 (2.8)	See 66.16.6.4 [only 1 level of in-rack sprinklers at approximately 15 ft (4.6 m) level].				

[30:Table 16.5.3.15]

N **Table 66.16.5.3.16 Design Criteria for Sprinkler Protection of Rack Storage of 100 Percent or Less Ethanol/Propanol/Methanol in Plastic or Glass Containers**

Liquid Type/Flash Point	Container Capacity	Packaging	Maximum Ceiling Height ft (m)	Maximum Storage Height ft (m)	Minimum Aisle Width ft (m)	Ceiling — K-factor gpm/psi$^{1/2}$ (L/min/bar$^{1/2}$)	Ceiling — Response/Nominal Temperature Rating/Orientation	Design — Density gpm/ft² (mm/min)	Design — Area ft² (m²)	Design — Number of Sprinklers @ Pressure psi (bar)	In-Rack — K-factor gpm/psi$^{1/2}$ (L/min/bar$^{1/2}$)	In-Rack — Response/Nominal Temperature Rating/Orientation	Minimum Discharge Flow gpm (L/min)	Layout (See 66.16.6.7)	Notes	Fire Test Reference [See Table E.2(o)]
100 Percent or Less Ethanol/Propanol/Methanol	≤6 oz (180 ml)	Cartoned	30 (9.1)	25 (7.6)	8 (2.4)	K11.2 (160)	SR/Ordinary/Any	0.60 (24)	2000 (190)	—	K≥8.0 (115)	1	45 (170)	9	1	1
						K≥11.2 (160)	SR/Ordinary/Any	0.30 (12)	2000 (190)	—	K≥8.0 (115)	1	45 (170)	8	1	—
						K14 (200)	ESFR/Ordinary/Pendent	—	—	12 @ 50 (3.4)	No in-rack sprinklers required					
						K16.8 (240)		—	—	12 @ 35 (2.4)						
						K22.4 (320)		—	—	12 @ 25 (1.7)						
						K25.2 (360)		—	—	12 @ 20 (1.4)						
			40 (12)	35 (10.7)	8 (2.4)	K14 (200)	ESFR/Ordinary/Pendent	—	—	12 @ 75 (5.2)	No in-rack sprinklers required					
						K16.8 (240)		—	—	12 @ 52 (3.6)						
						K22.4 (320)		—	—	12 @ 45 (3.1)						
						K25.2 (360)		—	—	12 @ 40 (2.8)						

(1) Base the in-rack sprinkler water demand on the simultaneous operation of the most hydraulically remote sprinklers as follows:
    (a) Eight (8) sprinklers where only one level of in-rack sprinklers is installed
    (b) Fourteen (14) sprinklers (seven on each of the two top levels) where two levels of in-rack sprinklers are installed

[30:Table 16.5.3.16]

N Table 66.16.5.3.17 Design Criteria for Sprinkler Protection of Rack Storage of 50 Percent/50 Percent Mixture of Ethanol/Propanol/Methanol/Water in Plastic or Glass Containers

							Ceiling Sprinkler Protection					In-Rack Sprinkler Protection				
							Sprinkler Type		Design			Sprinkler Type		Design		
Liquid Type/Flash Point	Container Capacity	Packaging	Maximum Ceiling Height ft (m)	Maximum Storage Height ft (m)	Minimum Aisle Width ft (m)	Maximum Rack Depth ft (m)	K-factor gpm/psi$^{1/2}$ (L/min/bar$^{1/2}$)	Response/Nominal Temperature Rating/Orientation	Density gpm/ft² (mm/min)	Area ft² (m²)	Number of Sprinklers @ Pressure psi (bar)	K-factor gpm/psi$^{1/2}$ (L/min/bar$^{1/2}$)	Response/Nominal Temperature Rating/Orientation	Minimum Discharge Flow gpm (L/min)	Layout (See 66.16.6.7)	Fire Test Reference [See Table E.2(p)]
50 Percent/50 Percent Mixture of Ethanol/Propanol/Methanol/Water	≤1 gal (3.8 L)	Cartoned	30 (9.1)	25 (7.6)	8 (2.4)	9 (2.7)	K≥11.2 (160)	SR/Ordinary/Any	0.60 (24)	2000 (190)	—	K≥8.0 (115)	QR/Ordinary/Any	45 (170)	9	1
							K≥14 (200)	ESFR/Ordinary/Pendent	—	—	12 @ 75 (5.2)	No in-rack sprinklers required				
	≤59 oz (1.75 L)	Cartoned	Unlimited	Unlimited	4 (1.2)	Any	K≥11.2 (160)	SR/Ordinary/Any	0.30 (12)	2000 (190)	—	See 66.16.6.6. <5 ft (1.5 m) storage above top level of in-rack sprinklers				
									0.60 (24)	2000 (190)	—	See 66.16.6.6. <10 ft (3.0 m) storage above top level of in-rack sprinklers				

[30:Table 16.5.3.17]

N Table 66.16.5.3.18 Design Criteria for Sprinkler Protection of Palletized Storage of 50 Percent/50 Percent Mixture of Ethanol/Propanol/Methanol/Water in Plastic or Glass Containers

					Ceiling Sprinkler Protection			
					Sprinkler Type		Design	
Liquid Type/Flash Point	Container Capacity	Packaging	Maximum Ceiling Height ft (m)	Maximum Storage Height ft (m)	K-factor gpm/psi$^{1/2}$ (L/min/bar$^{1/2}$)	Response/Nominal Temperature Rating/Orientation	Number of Sprinklers @ Pressure psi (bar)	Fire Test Reference [See Table E.2(q)]
50 Percent/50 Percent Mixture of Ethanol/Propanol/Methanol/Water	≤59 oz (1.75 L)	Cartoned	30 (9.1)	5 (1.5)	K14 (200)	ESFR/Ordinary/Any	20 @ 18 (1.2)	1
				17 (5.2)	K14 (200)	ESFR/Ordinary/Any	12 @ 50 (3.4)	-
			40 (12)	5 (1.5)	K14 (200)	ESFR/Ordinary/Any	20 @ 18 (1.2)	-
				17 (5.2)	K14 (200)	ESFR/Ordinary/Any	12 @ 75 (5.2)	-

[30:Table 16.5.3.18]

66.16.6 Fire Protection System Design Schemes.

66.16.6.1 Fire Protection System Design Scheme "A."

△ **66.16.6.1.1** Horizontal barriers of plywood having a minimum thickness of ⅜ in. (10 mm) or of sheet metal of minimum 22 gauge thickness shall be installed in accordance with Figure 66.16.6.1.1(a), Figure 66.16.6.1.1(b), or Figure 66.16.6.1.1(c), whichever is applicable. All ignitible (flammable or combustible) liquid storage shall be located beneath a barrier. *[See also 66.16.6.1.9 for liquids with flash points equal to or greater than 450°F (230°C).]* [30:16.6.1.1]

66.16.6.1.2 In-rack sprinklers shall be installed in accordance with Figure 66.16.6.1.1(a), Figure 66.16.6.1.1(b), or Figure 66.16.6.1.1(c), whichever is applicable. [30:16.6.1.2]

66.16.6.1.3 Vertical barriers shall not be provided between in-rack sprinklers. [30:16.6.1.3]

△ **66.16.6.1.4** In-rack sprinklers shall meet the following requirements:

(1) In-rack sprinklers shall be ordinary temperature–rated quick-response sprinklers and shall have a nominal K-factor equal to or greater than 8.0. Intermediate-temperature sprinklers shall be used where ambient conditions require.

(2) In-rack sprinklers shall be installed below each barrier level.

(3) In-rack sprinklers shall provide a minimum operating flow of 57 gpm (220 L/min) out of each of the hydraulically most remote six sprinklers (six on one line or three on two lines) if one barrier level is provided, or out of each of the hydraulically most remote eight sprinklers (eight on one line or four on two lines on the same level) if two or more barrier levels are provided. The minimum in-rack sprinkler discharge pressure shall not be less than a gauge pressure of 10 psi (0.69 bar).

[30:16.6.1.4]

FIGURE 66.16.6.1.1(a) Single-Row Rack Sprinkler Layout for Design Scheme "A." [30:Figure 16.6.1.1(a)]

Notes: (1) For SI units, 1 in. = 25 mm; 1 ft = 0.3 m.
(2) X denotes K-8.0, ordinary, QR in-rack sprinkler.

FIGURE 66.16.6.1.1(b) Double-Row Rack Sprinkler Layout for Design Scheme "A." [30:Figure 16.6.1.1(b)]

Notes: (1) For SI units, 1 in. = 25 mm; 1 ft = 0.3 m.
(2) ● denotes K-8.0, ordinary, QR longitudinal flue sprinkler.
(3) X denotes K-8.0, ordinary, QR face sprinkler.

FIGURE 66.16.6.1.1(c) Multiple-Row Rack Sprinkler Layout for Design Scheme "A." [30:Figure 16.6.1.1(c)]

Notes: (1) For SI units, 1 in. = 25 mm; 1 ft = 0.3 m.
(2) X denotes K-8.0, ordinary, QR in-rack sprinkler.

66.16.6.1.5* Where adjacent rack bays are not dedicated to storage of ignitible (flammable or combustible) liquids, the barrier and in-rack sprinkler protection shall be extended at least 8 ft (2.4 m) beyond the area devoted to ignitible (flammable or combustible) liquid storage. In addition, barrier and in-rack sprinkler protection shall be provided for any rack across the aisle within 8 ft (2.4 m) of the perimeter of the ignitible (flammable or combustible) liquid storage in accordance with 66.16.6.1. [**30:**16.6.1.5]

66.16.6.1.6 Ceiling sprinkler demand shall not be included in the hydraulic calculations for in-rack sprinklers. [**30:**16.6.1.6]

66.16.6.1.7 Water demand at point of supply shall be calculated separately for in-rack and ceiling sprinklers and shall be based on the greater demand. [**30:**16.6.1.7]

Δ **66.16.6.1.8** Ceiling sprinklers shall meet the following requirements:

(1) Ceiling sprinkler protection shall be designed to protect the surrounding occupancy.
(2) Any sprinkler type shall be acceptable.
(3) If standard spray sprinklers are used, they shall be capable of providing not less than 0.20 gpm/ft^2 over 3000 ft^2 (8 mm/min over 270 m^2).
(4) If the ignitible (flammable or combustible) liquid storage does not extend to the full height of the rack, protection for commodities stored above the top horizontal barrier shall meet the requirements of NFPA 13 for the commodities stored, based on the full height of the rack.

[**30:**16.6.1.8]

66.16.6.1.9 Barriers shall not be required for liquids with closed-cup flash points of 450°F (230°C) or greater. If barriers are omitted, the following shall apply:

(1) Ceiling sprinkler protection shall provide a minimum density of 0.3 gpm/ft^2 over the most hydraulically remote 2000 ft^2 (12 mm/min over 180 m^2) using ordinary temperature, standard-response sprinklers. Sprinklers shall have a nominal K-factor equal to or greater than 8.0. Intermediate-temperature sprinklers shall be used where ambient conditions require.
(2) The ceiling sprinkler water demand and the in-rack water demand shall be balanced at their point of connection.
(3) The sprinklers located at the rack face shall be staggered vertically.

[**30**:16.6.1.9]

66.16.6.1.10 A 500 gpm (1900 L/min) hose stream allowance shall be provided. [**30**:16.6.1.10]

66.16.6.2 Fire Protection System Design Scheme "B."

66.16.6.2.1 Horizontal barriers of plywood having a minimum thickness of ⅜ in. (10 mm) or of sheet metal of minimum 22 gauge thickness shall be installed in accordance with Figure 66.16.6.2.1(a), Figure 66.16.6.2.1(b), or Figure 66.16.6.2.1(c), whichever is applicable. All ignitible (flammable or combustible) liquid storage shall be located beneath a barrier. [**30**:16.6.2.1]

66.16.6.2.2 In-rack sprinklers shall be installed in accordance with Figure 66.16.6.2.1(a), Figure 66.16.6.2.1(b), or Figure 66.16.6.2.1(c), whichever is applicable. [**30**:16.6.2.2]

FIGURE 66.16.6.2.1(b) Single-Row Rack Sprinkler Layout for Design Scheme "B" — Sprinklers on Face of Rack. [**30**:Figure 16.6.2.1(b)]

FIGURE 66.16.6.2.1(a) Single-Row Rack Sprinkler Layout for Design Scheme "B" — Sprinklers in Center of Rack. [**30**:Figure 16.6.2.1(a)]

FIGURE 66.16.6.2.1(c) Double-Row Rack Sprinkler Layout for Design Scheme "B." [**30**:Figure 16.6.2.1(c)]

66.16.6.2.3 Vertical barriers shall not be provided between in-rack sprinklers. [**30**:16.6.2.3]

Δ **66.16.6.2.4** In-rack sprinklers shall meet the following requirements:

(1) In-rack sprinklers shall be ordinary temperature–rated quick-response sprinklers and shall have a nominal K-factor equal to or greater than 8.0. Intermediate-temperature sprinklers shall be used where ambient conditions require.

(2) In-rack sprinklers shall be installed below each barrier level.

(3) For containers that do not exceed 60 gal (230 L) capacity, in-rack sprinklers shall provide a minimum discharge flow of 57 gpm (220 L/min) out of each of the hydraulically most remote six sprinklers (six on one line or three on two lines) if one barrier level is provided, or out of each of the hydraulically most remote eight sprinklers (eight on one line or four on two lines on the same level) if two or more barrier levels are provided. The minimum in-rack sprinkler discharge pressure shall not be less than a gauge pressure of 10 psi (0.69 bar).

(4) For containers that exceed 60 gal (230 L) capacity, but do not exceed 793 gal (3000 L), in-rack sprinklers shall provide a minimum discharge flow of 57 gpm (220 L/min) out of each of the hydraulically most remote 12 sprinklers (12 on one line or six on two lines on the same level). The minimum in-rack sprinkler discharge pressure shall not be less than a gauge pressure of 10 psi (0.69 bar).

[**30**:16.6.2.4]

Δ **66.16.6.2.5** If there are adjacent rack bays that are not dedicated to storage of ignitible (flammable or combustible) liquids, the barrier and in-rack sprinkler protection shall be extended beyond the area devoted to ignitible (flammable or combustible) liquid storage as follows:

(1) For containers that do not exceed 1 gal (3.8 L) capacity, protection shall be extended at least 8 ft (2.4 m) beyond the area devoted to ignitible (flammable or combustible) liquid storage. In addition, adjacent racks across the aisles on each side of the ignitible (flammable or combustible) liquid storage shall be protected in accordance with NFPA 13 for the commodity stored.

(2) For containers that exceed 1 gal (3.8 L) capacity, but do not exceed 793 gal (3000 L), protection shall be extended at least 8 ft (2.4 m) beyond the area devoted to ignitible (flammable or combustible) liquid storage. In addition, protection shall be provided for any rack across the aisle within 8 ft (2.4 m) of the perimeter of the ignitible (flammable or combustible) liquid storage in accordance with 66.16.6.2.

[**30**:16.6.2.5]

66.16.6.2.6 Ceiling sprinklers for containers that do not exceed 1 gal (3.8 L) capacity shall meet the following requirements:

(1) Ceiling sprinklers shall be designed to protect the surrounding occupancy.

(2) Ceiling sprinkler water demand shall not be included in the hydraulic calculations for the in-rack sprinkler protection.

(3) Water demand at the point of supply shall be calculated separately for in-rack and ceiling sprinklers and shall be based on the greater of the two.

(4) Any sprinkler type shall be acceptable for the ceiling sprinkler protection.

(5) If standard spray sprinklers are used, they shall be capable of providing not less than 0.20 gpm/ft^2 over 3000 ft^2 (8 L/min over 270 m^2).

(6) If the ignitible (flammable or combustible) liquid storage does not extend to the full height of the rack, protection for commodities stored above the top horizontal barrier shall meet the requirements of Section 13.3 and NFPA 13 for the commodities stored, based on the full height of the rack.

[**30**:16.6.2.6]

66.16.6.2.7 Ceiling sprinklers for containers that exceed 1 gal (3.8 L) capacity, but do not exceed 60 gal (230 L), shall meet the following requirements:

(1) Ceiling sprinkler protection shall provide a minimum density of 0.45 gpm/ft^2 (18.3 mm/min) over the most hydraulically remote 3000 ft^2 (270 m^2), using high-temperature, standard-response sprinklers of nominal K-factor of 11.2 or greater. Other types of sprinklers shall not be used.

(2) Ceiling sprinkler water demand and the in-rack sprinkler demand shall be balanced at the point of connection.

[**30**:16.6.2.7]

66.16.6.2.8 Ceiling sprinklers for containers that exceed 60 gal (230 L) capacity, but do not exceed 793 gal (3000 L), shall meet the following requirements:

(1) Ceiling sprinklers shall be designed to provide a minimum density of 0.60 gpm/ft^2 over 3000 ft^2 (24 mm/min over the most remote 270 m^2), using high-temperature–rated, standard-response sprinklers of nominal K-factor of 11.2 or greater. Other types of sprinklers shall not be used.

(2) Ceiling sprinkler water demand and the in-rack sprinkler demand shall be balanced at the point of connection.

[**30**:16.6.2.8]

66.16.6.2.9 A 500 gpm (1900 L/min) hose stream allowance shall be provided. [**30**:16.6.2.9]

66.16.6.3 Fire Protection System Design Scheme "C."

66.16.6.3.1 Horizontal barriers of plywood having a minimum thickness of 3/8 in. (10 mm) or of sheet metal of minimum 22 gauge thickness shall be installed in accordance with Figure 66.16.6.3.1(a), Figure 66.16.6.3.1(b), or Figure 66.16.6.3.1(c), whichever is applicable. All ignitible (flammable or combustible) liquid storage shall be located beneath a barrier. [**30**:16.6.3.1]

66.16.6.3.2 Vertical baffles shall not be installed between in-rack sprinklers. [**30**:16.6.3.2]

Δ **66.16.6.3.3** In-rack sprinklers shall meet the following requirements:

(1) In-rack sprinklers shall be ordinary temperature–rated, quick-response sprinklers. Sprinklers shall have a nominal K-factor equal to or greater than 8.0. An intermediate-temperature sprinkler shall be used where ambient conditions require.

(2) In-rack sprinklers shall be installed below each barrier level.

(3) In-rack sprinklers shall provide a minimum discharge flow of 30 gpm (110 L/min) out of each of the hydraulically most remote six sprinklers (six on one line or three on two lines), if one barrier level is provided, or out of each of the hydraulically most remote eight sprinklers (eight on one line or four on two lines on the same level) if two or more barrier levels are provided. The minimum in-rack sprinkler discharge pressure shall not be less than a gauge pressure of 10 psi (0.69 bar). [**30**:16.6.3.3]

66.16.6.3.4 If there are adjacent bays of in-rack arrays that are not dedicated to storage of ignitible (flammable or combustible) liquids, the barrier and in-rack sprinkler protection shall be extended at least 8 ft (2.4 m) beyond the area devoted to ignitible (flammable or combustible) liquid storage. [**30**:16.6.3.4]

66.16.6.3.5 Ceiling sprinkler demand shall not be included in the hydraulic calculations for in-rack sprinklers. [**30**:16.6.3.5]

66.16.6.3.6 Water demand at point of supply shall be calculated separately for in-rack and ceiling sprinklers and shall be based on the greater demand. [**30**:16.6.3.6]

66.16.6.3.7 Ceiling sprinklers shall meet the following requirements:

(1) Ceiling sprinkler protection shall be designed to protect the surrounding occupancy.
(2) Any sprinkler type shall be acceptable.
(3) If standard spray sprinklers are used, they shall be capable of providing not less than 0.20 gpm/ft² over 3000 ft² (8 mm/min over 270 m²).
(4) If the ignitible (flammable or combustible) liquid storage does not extend to the full height of the rack, protection

FIGURE 66.16.6.3.1(a) Single-Row Rack Sprinkler Layout for Design Scheme "C." [**30**:Figure 16.6.3.1(a)]

FIGURE 66.16.6.3.1(b) Double-Row Rack Sprinkler Layout for Design Scheme "C." [**30**:Figure 16.6.3.1(b)]

FIGURE 66.16.6.3.1(c) Multiple-Row Rack Sprinkler Layout for Design Scheme "C." [30:Figure 16.6.3.1(c)]

Notes: (1) For SI units, 1 in. = 25 mm; 1 ft = 0.3 m.
(2) X denotes K-8.0, ordinary, QR face sprinkler.
● denotes K-8.0, ordinary, QR flue sprinkler.

for commodities stored above the top horizontal barrier shall meet the requirements of Section 13.3 and NFPA 13 for the commodities stored, based on the full height of the rack. [**30**:16.6.3.7]

66.16.6.3.8 A 500 gpm (1900 L/min) hose stream allowance shall be provided. [**30**:16.6.3.8]

66.16.6.4 Fire Protection System Design Scheme "D."

66.16.6.4.1 In-rack sprinklers shall meet the following requirements:

(1) In-rack sprinklers shall be installed in accordance with Figure 66.16.6.4.1(a) or Figure 66.16.6.4.1(b), whichever is applicable.
(2) In-rack sprinklers shall be ordinary-temperature-rated, quick-response sprinklers.
(3) In-rack sprinklers shall have a K-factor of 8.0 (115).
(4) In-rack sprinklers shall provide a minimum discharge flow of 30 gpm (113 L/min) out of the hydraulically most remote:

   (a) Eight sprinklers on one level if one level of in-racks (8 total)
   (b) Seven sprinklers on two levels if two or more levels of in-racks (14 total)

[**30**:16.6.4.1]

66.16.6.4.2 If there are adjacent bays of in-rack arrays that are not dedicated to ignitible (flammable or combustible) storage of liquids, in-rack sprinkler protection shall be extended at least 8 ft (2.4 m) beyond the area devoted to ignitible (flammable or combustible) liquid storage. [**30**:16.6.4.2]

66.16.6.4.3 Ceiling sprinklers shall be designed to provide a minimum density of 0.3 gpm/ft^2 (12.2 mm/min) over the most remote 2000 ft^2 (185 m^2) using ordinary-temperature-rated, standard-response spray sprinklers, having a nominal K-factor of 8.0 or 11.2. [**30**:16.6.4.3]

66.16.6.4.4 The ceiling and in-rack sprinkler water demands shall be balanced at the point of connection to the water supply. [**30**:16.6.4.4]

66.16.6.4.5 A 500 gpm (1890L/min) hose stream allowance shall be provided. [**30**:16.6.4.5]

66.16.6.4.6 A 1-hour duration shall be provided for the fire protection water demand. [**30**:16.6.4.6]

66.16.6.5 Fire Protection System Design Scheme "E."

66.16.6.5.1 Horizontal barriers of plywood having a minimum thickness of ⅜ in. (10 mm) or of sheet metal of minimum 22 gauge thickness shall be installed in accordance with Figure 66.16.6.5.1(a) or Figure 66.16.6.5.1(b), whichever is applicable. [**30**:16.6.5.1]

66.16.6.5.2 All ignitible (flammable or combustible) liquid storage shall be located beneath a barrier. [**30**:16.6.5.2]

66.16.6.5.3 Vertical baffles shall not be installed between in-rack sprinklers. [**30**:16.6.5.3]

Notes: (1) For SI units, 1 in. = 25 mm; 1 ft = 0.3 m.
(2) • Denotes K-25.2 extended coverage pendent CMDA storage sprinkler

FIGURE 66.16.6.4.1(a) Single-Row Rack Sprinkler Layout for Fire Protection System Design Scheme "D." [30:Figure 16.6.4.1(a)]

FLAMMABLE AND COMBUSTIBLE LIQUIDS 1-443

Plan View labels:
- Solid barrier with max. 2 in. gaps at vertical penetrations
- 9 ft (max)
- Rack upright
- 8 ft – 10 ft

PLAN VIEW

Elevation View labels:
- Deflector a maximum of 7 in. below barrer
- Deflector a minimum of 6 in. above top of storage
- 15 ft (max.) vert. distance between barriers
- Barrier always required above top tier of liquids storage
- Height of array not limited
- 15 ft (max.) vert. distance between barriers

ELEVATION VIEW

Notes: (1) For SI units, 1 in. = 25 mm; 1 ft = 0.3 m.
 (2) • Denotes K-25.2 extended coverage pendent CMDA storage sprinkler

FIGURE 66.16.6.4.1(b) Double-Row Rack Sprinkler Layout for Fire Protection System Design Scheme "D." [30:Figure 16.6.4.1(b)]

Notes:
(1) For SI units, 1 in. = 25 mm; 1 ft = 0.3 m.
(2) • denotes K25.2 extended coverage pendent CMDA storage sprinkler.

N FIGURE 66.16.6.5.1(a) Single-Row Rack Sprinkler Layout for Design Scheme "E." [30:Figure 16.6.5.1(a)]

FLAMMABLE AND COMBUSTIBLE LIQUIDS   1-445

PLAN VIEW
- Solid barrier with max. 2 in. gaps at vertical penetrations
- Rack upright
- 10 ft (max)
- 9 ft (max)

ELEVATION VIEW
- Deflector a maximum of 7 in. below barrier
- Barrier always required above top tier of liquids storage
- Deflector a minimum of 6 in. above top of storage
- 15 ft (max.) vertical distance between barriers
- 15 ft (max.) vertical distance between barriers

Notes:
(1) For SI units, 1 in. = 25 mm; 1 ft = 0.3 m.
(2) • denotes K25.2 extended coverage pendent CMDA storage sprinkler.

N FIGURE 66.16.6.5.1(b)   Double-Row Rack Sprinkler Layout for Design Scheme "E." [30:Figure 16.6.5.1(b)]

Shaded text = Revisions.   Δ = Text deletions and figure/table revisions.   • = Section deletions.   N = New material.   2024 Edition

Δ **66.16.6.5.4** In-rack sprinklers shall meet the following requirements:

(1) In-rack sprinklers shall be intermediate temperature–rated, pendent sprinklers with a nominal K-factor of 25.2, RTI of 50 $(m/sec)^{1/2}$ or less, and be listed as extended coverage control mode density/area storage sprinklers.
(2) In-rack sprinklers shall be installed below each barrier level.
(3) The minimum in-rack sprinkler discharge pressure shall not be less than a gauge pressure of 30 psi.
(4) Where one level of in-rack sprinklers is installed, the design shall include the four most hydraulically remote sprinklers (i.e., four on one line).
(5) Where two levels of in-rack sprinklers are installed, the design shall include the three most hydraulically remote sprinklers on each level.
(6) Where three or more levels of in-rack sprinklers are installed, the design shall include the three most hydraulically remote sprinklers on the top three levels.
(7) Foam-water sprinkler protection shall be permitted to be substituted for water sprinkler protection, provided the same design criteria is used.

[30:16.6.5.4]

66.16.6.5.5 If there are adjacent bays of in-rack arrays that are not dedicated to storage of ignitible (flammable or combustible) liquids, the barrier and in-rack sprinkler protection shall be extended at least 8 ft (2.4 m) beyond the area devoted to ignitible (flammable or combustible) liquid storage. [30:16.6.5.5]

66.16.6.5.6 Ceiling sprinkler demand shall not be included in the hydraulic calculations for in-rack sprinklers where standard-response sprinklers are used for ceiling-level protection. [30:16.6.5.6]

66.16.6.5.7 Water Demand.

66.16.6.5.7.1 Water demand at the point of supply shall be calculated separately for in-rack and ceiling sprinklers. [30:16.6.5.7.1]

66.16.6.5.7.2 Water demand shall be based on the greater demand between in-rack and ceiling sprinklers. [30:16.6.5.7.2]

66.16.6.5.8 Ceiling sprinklers shall meet the following requirements:

(1) Ceiling sprinkler protection shall be designed to protect the surrounding occupancy.
(2) Any sprinkler type shall be acceptable.
(3)* If standard spray sprinklers are used, they shall be capable of providing not less than 0.30 gpm/ft² over 3000 ft² (8 mm/min over 270 m²) when supplied with water.
(4) If the ignitible (flammable or combustible) liquid storage does not extend to the full height of the rack, protection for commodities stored above the top horizontal barrier shall meet the requirements of NFPA 13 for the commodities stored, based on the full height of the rack.

[30:16.6.5.8]

66.16.6.5.9 A 500 gpm (1900 L/min) hose stream allowance shall be provided. [30:16.6.5.9]

66.16.6.6 Fire Protection System Design Scheme "F."

66.16.6.6.1 In-rack sprinklers shall meet the following requirements:

(1) In-rack sprinklers shall be ordinary temperature-rated, quick-response sprinklers.
(2) In-rack sprinklers shall have a K-factor of 8.0 (115) or 11.2 (160).
(3) In-rack sprinklers shall be installed on 20 ft (6 m) vertical increments in accordance with Figure 66.16.6.6.1(a) and Figure 66.16.6.6.1(b) with the in-rack pattern shown in Figure 66.16.6.6.1(b) repeated from rack face to rack face for multiple-row racks.
(4) In-rack sprinklers shall provide a minimum discharge flow of 30 gpm (110 L/min) out of the hydraulically most remote sprinkler as follows:
   (a) Six in-rack sprinklers on one level if one level of in-racks (6 total)
   (b) Six in-rack sprinklers on two levels if two levels of in-racks (12 total)
   (c) Six in-rack sprinklers on three levels if three or more levels of in-racks (18 total)

[30:16.6.6.1]

66.16.6.6.2 If there are adjacent bays of rack storage that are not dedicated to ignitible (flammable or combustible) liquid storage, the in-rack sprinkler protection shall be extended at least 8 ft (2.4 m) beyond the area devoted to ignitible (flammable or combustible) liquid storage. [30:16.6.6.2]

66.16.6.6.3 The ceiling and in-rack sprinkler demands shall be balanced at the point of connection to the water supply. [30:16.6.6.3]

66.16.6.6.4 A 500 gpm (1890L/min) hose stream allowance shall be provided. [30:16.6.6.4]

66.16.6.6.5 A 1-hour duration shall be provided for the fire protection water demand. [30:16.6.6.5]

Δ **66.16.6.7 In-Rack Sprinkler Layouts for Table 66.16.5.3.8.** Where indicated in Table 66.16.5.3.8 of this *Code* and Table 16.5.3.16 of NFPA 30, in-rack sprinklers shall be as follows:

(1) Where Layout 7 is required, in-rack sprinklers shall be installed in accordance with Figure 66.16.6.7(a).
(2) Where Layout 8 is required, in-rack sprinklers shall be installed in accordance with Figure 66.16.6.7(b) or Figure 66.16.6.7(c).
(3) Where Layout 9 is required, in-rack sprinklers shall be installed in accordance with Figure 66.16.6.7(d) or Figure 66.16.6.7(e), whichever is applicable.

[30:16.6.7]

66.16.7 Water Supply. Water supplies for automatic sprinklers, other water-based protection systems, hose streams, and hydrants shall be capable of supplying the anticipated water flow demand for a minimum of 2 hours. [30:16.7]

66.16.8 Containment, Drainage, and Spill Control.

66.16.8.1 Secondary containment or secondary containment and drainage shall be provided in accordance with Figure 66.16.8.1, where protection systems are installed in accordance with the provisions of this section. [30:16.8.1]

66.16.8.2* Where control of the spread of liquid is required, means to limit the spread of liquid to an area not greater than the design discharge area of the ceiling sprinkler system shall be provided. [30:16.8.2]

FIGURE 66.16.6.6.1(a) Single-Row Rack Sprinkler Layout for Design Scheme "F." [30:Figure 16.6.6.1(a)]

FIGURE 66.16.6.6.1(b) Double-Row Rack Sprinkler Layout for Design Scheme "F." (Multiple row racks shall extend the same sprinkler pattern through the rack.) [30:Figure 16.6.6.1(b)]

FLAMMABLE AND COMBUSTIBLE LIQUIDS 1-449

FIGURE 66.16.6.7(a) Double-Row Rack Sprinkler Layout 7. [30:Figure 16.6.7(a)]

Notes: (1) For SI units, 1 in. = 25 mm; 1 ft = 0.3 m.
(2) X denotes K-11.2, ordinary, QR in-rack sprinkler.

FIGURE 66.16.6.7(b) Double-Row Rack Sprinkler Layout 8 — Option #1. [30:Figure 16.6.7(b)]

Notes: (1) For SI units, 1 in. = 25 mm; 1 ft = 0.3 m.
(2) ● and X denote K-8.0, QR in-rack sprinklers.

FIGURE 66.16.6.7(c) Double-Row Rack Sprinkler Layout 8 — Option #2. [30:Figure 16.6.7(c)]

Notes: (1) For SI units, 1 in. = 25 mm; 1 ft = 0.3 m.
(2) X denotes K-8.0, QR in-rack sprinkler.

FIGURE 66.16.6.7(d) Double-Row Rack Sprinkler Layout 9 — Option #1. [30:Figure 16.6.7(d)]

Notes: (1) For SI units, 1 in. = 25 mm; 1 ft = 0.3 m.
(2) ● and X denote K-8.0, QR in-rack sprinklers.

Shaded text = Revisions. Δ = Text deletions and figure/table revisions. • = Section deletions. *N* = New material.   2024 Edition

FIGURE 66.16.6.7(e) Double-Row Rack Sprinkler Layout 9 — Option #2. [30:Figure 16.6.7(e)]

Notes: (1) For SI units, 1 in. = 25 mm; 1 ft = 0.3 m.
(2) X denotes K-8.0, QR in-rack sprinkler.

66.16.9 Other Automatic Fire Protection Systems. Alternate fire protection systems, such as automatic water spray systems, automatic water mist systems, high-expansion foam systems, dry chemical extinguishing systems, alternate sprinkler system configurations, or combinations of systems shall be permitted if approved by the AHJ. Such alternate systems shall be designed and installed in accordance with the appropriate NFPA standard and with manufacturer's recommendations for the system(s) selected. [30:16.9]

N **66.16.10 Distilled Spirits in Wooden Barrels.**

N **66.16.10.1 Palletize Storage Arrays.**

N **66.16.10.1.1** Palletized storage arrays of barrels stored on-end shall be limited to a maximum of 7 pallets high. [30:16.10.1.1]

N **66.16.10.1.2** Flue spaces with a minimum width of 6 in. (152 mm) shall be maintained between adjacent pallets. [30:16.10.1.2]

N **66.16.10.1.3** Palletized storage that is provided with a defined loading aisle between pallet storage areas shall be arranged using one of the following:

(1) Draft curtains shall be provided along the side of palletized storage facing the loading aisle to separate the fast-response sprinklers and standard-response sprinklers.
(2) A trench drain shall be provided on each side of the loading aisle, arranged to capture any spilled distilled spirits in the aisle space and remove them from the building to prevent spills from spreading into the barrel storage area.
(3) Barrels shall be banded on each pallet to prevent barrels from falling off pallets during transportation and loading into the storage racks.

[30:16.10.1.3]

N **66.16.10.1.3.1** Draft curtains shall meet the requirements provided in NFPA 204. [30:16.10.1.3.1]

N **66.16.10.1.4** Palletized storage of on-end wooden barrels storing distilled spirits shall be protected in accordance with Table 66.16.10.1.4 and 66.16.10.1.4.1 through 66.16.10.1.4.4. [30:16.10.1.4]

N **66.16.10.1.4.1** The storage and automatic sprinkler requirements in Table 66.16.10.1.5.4 shall apply to alcohol-water mixtures greater than 20 percent and up to 75 percent alcohol by volume in wooden barrel sizes not exceeding 130 gal (492 L). [30:16.10.1.4.1]

N **66.16.10.1.4.2** The water supply shall meet the fixed fire protection demand plus at least 500 gpm (1900 L/min) for inside and outside hose connections for at least 1 hour. [30:16.10.1.4.2]

N **66.16.10.1.4.3** Where a permanent loading aisle is provided with a separate automatic sprinkler system on the ceiling, the barrel storage automatic sprinkler design and the loading aisle automatic sprinkler design are not required to be balanced at the point of connection. [30:16.10.1.4.3]

N **66.16.10.1.4.4** Where dry-pipe sprinkler systems are installed, the sprinkler system shall be designed to deliver water to the most remote four sprinklers within 40 seconds. [30:16.10.1.4.4]

N **66.16.10.1.5** Palletized storage of distilled spirits in small, distilled spirits facilities is permitted to be in accordance with 66.16.10.1.5.1 through 66.16.10.1.5.4 and Table 66.16.10.1.5.4. [30:16.10.1.5]

N **66.16.10.1.5.1** A small, distilled spirits facility shall be a maximum of 7,500 ft^2 (697 m^2). [30:16.10.1.5.1]

N **66.16.10.1.5.2** The clearance from the top of storage to the deflector of the automatic sprinklers at the ceiling shall be a minimum of 18 in. (457 mm) and a maximum of 10 ft (3048 mm). [30:16.10.1.5.2]

N **66.16.10.1.5.3** The automatic sprinkler coverage area shall not exceed 80 ft^2 (7.4 m^2) per sprinkler. [30:16.10.1.5.3]

N **66.16.10.1.5.4** The storage arrangement and automatic sprinkler system design shall be in accordance with Table 66.16.10.1.5.4. [30:16.10.1.5.4]

N **66.16.10.2 Rack Storage Arrays.**

N **66.16.10.2.1** Rack storage arrangements with on-side wooden barrels shall be provided with a minimum width of 8 in. (203 mm) between adjacent rows of barrels. [30:16.10.2.1]

N **66.16.10.2.2** Rack storage arrangements with on-end wooden barrels shall be provided with transverse and longitudinal flue spaces with a minimum width of 6 in. (15 cm). [30:16.10.2.2]

N **66.16.10.2.3** Where provided, elevated walkways between barrels shall be constructed in accordance with one of the following:

(1) Noncombustible materials that are 50 percent open shall be used.
(2) Noncombustible materials that are open less than 50 percent provided the walkway has a maximum width of 1 ft (0.3 m) and a minimum gap of 3 in. (76 mm) is provided between the walkway and the barrel storage shall be used.

[30:16.10.2.3]

△ **FIGURE 66.16.8.1** Spill Containment and Liquid Spread Control for Protected Storage. [30:Figure 16.8.1]

N Table 66.16.10.1.4 Palletized Storage of Distilled Spirits with up to 75 Percent Alcohol by Volume in Wooden Barrels

				Ceiling Sprinkler Protection						
				Sprinkler Type		Design				
Protection Area	System Type	Ceiling Height ft (m)	Storage Height ft (m)/# drums	Response/ Nominal Temperature Rating/ Orientation	K-factor gpm/psi$^{1/2}$ (L/min/ bar$^{1/2}$)	Density gpm/ft^2 (mm/min)	Area ft^2 (m^2)	# of Sprinklers @ Pressure psi (bar)	Notes	Fire Test Reference (Table E.2(r))
Barrel Storage	Wet	30 ft (9 m)	24 ft (7.3 m)/ 7 drums	FR/Ordinary/ Pendent	14.0 (202)	—	—	12 @ 18 (1.25)	1	1
	Dry			SR/High/ Upright	16.8 (240)	0.6 (24)	2400 (220)	—	1	
Loading Aisle w/ Draft Curtain	Wet/Dry	-	NA	SR/High/Any	≥ 5.6 (80)	0.2 (8)	10,000 (930)	—	1	
Loading Aisle w/ Trench Drains Or Banded Barrels or No Permanent Loading Aisle			Provide the palletized storage design across the entire roof area (i.e., storage area and loading aisle)							

Notes:
(1) See 66.16.5.1.9 for abbreviations.
[30:Table16.10.1.4]

N Table 66.16.10.1.5.4 Palletized Storage of Distilled Spirits in Wooden Barrels in Small Distilled Spirits Facilities

				Ceiling Sprinkler Protection					
				Sprinkler Type		Design			
Protection Area	Sprinkler System Type	Maximum Ceiling Height ft (m)	Maximum Storage Height ft (m)/# drums	Response/ Nominal Temperature Rating/ Orientation	K-factor gpm/psi$^{1/2}$ (L/min/ bar$^{1/2}$)	Density gpm/psi$^{1/2}$ (L/min/ bar$^{1/2}$)	Area ft^2 (m^2)	Notes	Fire Test Reference (Table E.2(s))
Barrel Storage	Wet	24 (7.3)	12 (3.7)	SR/High/Any	≥ 11.2 (161)	0.35 (14.5)	4000 (370)	1	1
				SR/Ordinary/Any	≥ 11.2 (161)	0.35 (14.5)	7500 (700)	1	

Notes:
(1) See 66.16.5.1.9 for abbreviations.
[30:Table16.10.1.5.4]

N 66.16.10.2.4 Rack storage arrangements of alcohol-water mixtures up to 75 percent alcohol in wooden barrels with sizes not exceeding 130 gal (492 L) shall be protected in accordance with 66.16.10.2.4.1 through 66.16.10.2.4.3 and Table 66.16.10.2.4. [30:16.10.2.4]

N 66.16.10.2.4.1 The water supply shall meet the fixed fire protection demand plus at least 500 gpm (1900 L/min) for inside and outside hose connections for at least two hours. [30:16.10.1.4.1]

N 66.16.10.2.4.2 Where dry-pipe automatic sprinkler systems are installed, the automatic sprinkler system shall be designed to deliver water to the most remote four sprinklers within 40 seconds. [30:16.10.2.4.2]

N 66.16.10.2.4.3 The automatic sprinkler system installed at the ceiling and the in-rack sprinkler system shall be balanced at the point of connection. [30:16.10.2.4.3]

N 66.16.10.3 Fire Protection Layouts for Distilled Spirits in Wooden Barrels.

N 66.16.10.3.1 In-Rack Layouts for Rack Storage of On-Side Wooden Barrels. In-rack layouts for rack storage of on-side wooden barrels are shown in Figure 66.16.10.3.1(a) and Figure 66.16.10.3.1(b). [30:16.10.3.1]

N 66.16.10.3.2 In-Rack Layouts for Rack Storage of On-End Wooden Barrels. In-rack layouts for rack storage of on-end wooden barrels are shown in Figure 66.16.10.3.2(a) and Figure 66.16.10.3.2(b). [30:16.10.3.2]

66.17 Processing Facilities.

66.17.1 Scope.

66.17.1.1* This section shall apply where the processing of ignitible (flammable or combustible) liquids is the principal activity, except as covered elsewhere in this *Code* or in other NFPA standards. *(See 66.1.5.)* [30:17.1.1]

N Table 66.16.10.2.4 Rack Storage of Distilled Spirits in Wooden Barrels

Barrel Arrangement	Sprinkler System Type	Maximum Ceiling Height ft (m)	Maximum Storage Height ft (m)/# Barrels	Minimum Aisle Width ft (m)	Response/ Nominal Temperature Rating/ Orientation	K-factor gpm/ psi$^{1/2}$ (L/min/ bar$^{1/2}$)	Density gpm/ft^2 (mm/ min)	Area ft^2 (m^2)	# of Sprinklers @ Pressure psi (bar)	Response/ Nominal Temperature Rating	K-factor gpm/ psi$^{1/2}$ (L/min/ bar$^{1/2}$)	Flow gpm (L/min)	Layout	Notes	Fire Test Reference (Table E.2(t))
On-Side	Wet	40 (12)	33 (10)/9 barrels	NA	QR/Ordinary/Pendent	14.0 (200)	—	—	12 @ 37 (2.5)	None				1	1
					SR/High/Any	≥ 11.2 (160)	0.3 (12)	2000	—	QR/Ordinary/Any	8.0 (115)	45 (170)	Fig 66.16.10.3.1(1) 66.16.10.3.1(2)	1	
	Dry	40 (12)	33 (10)/9 barrels	NA	SR/High/Upright	16.8 (240)	0.85 (34.6)	2400	—	None				1	
					SR/High/Upright	≥ 11.2 (160)	0.3 (12)	2000	—	QR/Ordinary/Upright	8.0 (115)	45 (170)	Fig 66.16.10.3.1(1) 66.16.10.3.1(2)	1	
On-End	Wet	30 (9.1)	25 (7.6)/5 barrels	8 (2.4)	SR/High/Any	≥ 11.2 (160)	0.3 (12)	5000	—	QR/Ordinary/Any	≥ 8.0 (115)	6 @ 25 (95) [one level] 12 @ 25 (95) [greater than one level]	Fig 66.16.10.3.2(1) 66.16.10.3.2(2)	1	

Notes:
(1) See 66.16.5.1.9 for abbreviations.
[**30:**Table 16.10.2.4]

N FIGURE 66.16.10.3.1(a) In-Rack Sprinkler Layout for On-Side Wooden Barrels (Plan View).
[**30:**Figure 16.10.3.1(a)]

N **FIGURE 66.16.10.3.1(b)** In-Rack Sprinkler Layout for On-Side Wooden Barrels (Elevation View). [30:Figure 16.10.3.1(b)]

66.17.1.2 Provisions of this section shall not prohibit the use of movable tanks for the dispensing of ignitible (flammable or combustible) liquids into fuel tanks of motorized equipment outside on premises not accessible to the public, where such use has the approval of the AHJ. [30:17.1.2]

66.17.2 Reserved.

66.17.3 General Requirements.

66.17.3.1 Ignitible (flammable or combustible) liquid processing operations shall be located and operated so that they do not constitute a significant fire or explosion hazard to life, to property of others, or to important buildings or facilities within the same plant. [30:17.3.1]

66.17.3.2 Specific requirements shall depend on the inherent risk in the operations themselves, including the ignitible (flammable or combustible) liquids being processed, operating temperatures and pressures, and the capability to control any ignitible (flammable or combustible) liquid or vapor releases or fire incidents that could occur. [30:17.3.2]

66.17.3.3 The interrelationship of the many factors involved shall be based on good engineering and management practices to establish suitable physical and operating requirements. [30:17.3.3]

66.17.3.4 Process facilities shall comply with the applicable requirements for specific operations set forth in Sections 66.18, 66.19, 66.28, or 66.29. [30:17.3.4]

66.17.3.5 Process facilities shall comply with the applicable requirements for procedures and practices for fire and explosion prevention, protection, and control set forth in Section 66.6. [30:17.3.5]

66.17.3.6 Processing and handling of Class II and Class III liquids [FP ≥ 100°F (37.8°C)] heated at or above their flash points shall follow the requirements for Class I liquids [FP < 100°F (37.8°C)], unless an engineering evaluation conducted in accordance with Section 66.6 justifies following the requirements for some other liquid class. *(See 66.6.4.1.3 and A.66.6.4.1.3.)* [30:17.3.6]

66.17.3.7 When a process heats an ignitible (flammable or combustible) liquid to a temperature at or above its flash point, the following shall apply:

(1) The process vessel shall be closed to the room in which it is located and vented to the outside of the building.
(2) If the vessel needs to be opened to add ingredients, the room ventilation shall meet the requirements of 66.17.11 and the process heating controls will be interlocked with the ventilation such that the process heat will shut down if the ventilation fails or is turned off.
(3) The process vessel shall be equipped with an excess temperature control set to limit excessive heating of the ignitible (flammable or combustible) liquid and the subsequent release of vapors.
(4) If a heat transfer medium is used to heat the ignitible (flammable or combustible) liquid and the heat transfer fluid can heat the ignitible (flammable or combustible) liquid to its boiling point on failure of the process and excess temperature heat controls, a redundant excess temperature control shall be provided.

FIGURE 66.16.10.3.2(a) In-Rack Sprinkler Layout for Single-Row Rack of On-End Wooden Barrels (Plan View). [30:Figure 16.10.3.2(a)]

(5) The extent of required explosion control shall be determined in accordance with 66.6.4.1.2.
[**30**:17.3.7]

66.17.4 Location of Process Vessels and Equipment.

66.17.4.1 Ignitible (flammable or combustible) liquid-processing vessels and equipment shall be located in accordance with the requirements of this section. [**30**:17.4.1]

66.17.4.2 Processing vessels and buildings containing such processing vessels shall be located so that a fire involving the vessels does not constitute an exposure hazard to other occupancies. [**30**:17.4.2]

66.17.4.3* The minimum distance of a processing vessel to a property line that is or can be built upon, including the opposite side of a public way; to the nearest side of a public way; or to the nearest important building on the same property shall be determined by one of the following:

(1) In accordance with Table 66.17.4.3
(2) In accordance with an engineering evaluation of the process, followed by application of sound fire protection and process engineering principles

[**30**:17.4.3]

66.17.4.3.1 Processing vessels used solely to process stable Class IIIB liquids [FP ≥ 200°F (93°C)] shall be located in accordance with Table 66.22.4.1.5. [**30**:17.4.3.1]

66.17.4.4 Where process vessels are located in a building and the exterior wall facing the exposure (line of adjoining property that is or can be built upon or nearest important building on the same property) is greater than 25 ft (7.6 m) from the exposure and is a blank wall having a fire resistance rating of not less than 2 hours, any greater distances required by Table 66.17.4.3 shall be permitted to be waived. If the exterior wall is a blank wall having a fire resistance rating of not less than 4 hours, all distances required by Table 66.17.4.3 shall be permitted to be waived. [**30**:17.4.4]

66.17.4.5 All the distances given in Table 66.17.4.3 shall be doubled where protection for exposures is not provided. [**30**:17.4.5]

66.17.4.6* Ignitible (flammable or combustible) liquid-processing equipment, such as pumps, heaters, filters, and exchangers, shall not be located closer than 25 ft (7.6 m) to property lines where the adjoining property is or can be built upon or to the nearest important building on the same property that is not an integral part of the process. This spacing

FIGURE 66.16.10.3.2(b) In-Rack Sprinkler Layout for Double-Row Rack of On-End Wooden Barrels. [30:Figure 16.10.3.2(b)]

requirement shall be permitted to be waived where exposures are protected in accordance with 66.17.4.3. [30:17.4.6]

66.17.5 Accessibility. Each process unit or building containing ignitible (flammable or combustible) liquid-processing equipment shall be accessible from at least one side for firefighting and fire control. [30:17.5]

66.17.6 Construction Requirements.

66.17.6.1 Process buildings or structures used for ignitible (flammable or combustible) liquid operations shall be constructed as follows:

(1) Consistent with the operations being conducted and with the classes of liquids handled

(2) To minimum Type II (000) construction, as defined in *NFPA 5000*

(3) In accordance with Table 66.17.6.1

[30:17.6.1]

66.17.6.2 Construction types shall be as defined in *NFPA 5000*. [30:17.6.2]

66.17.6.3 Where protection for exposures is not provided, the applicable distances given in Table 66.17.6.1 shall be doubled. [30:17.6.3]

Δ Table 66.17.4.3 Location of Process Vessels with Respect to Property Lines, Public Ways, and the Nearest Important Building on the Same Property — Protection for Exposures Is Provided

	Minimum Distance (ft)			
	From Property Line that Is or Can Be Built upon, Including Opposite Side of Public Way		From Nearest Side of Any Public Way or from Nearest Important Building on Same Property that Is Not an Integral Part of the Process	
	Emergency Relief*		Emergency Relief*	
Vessel Maximum Operating Liquid Capacity (gal)	Not Over 2.5 psi	Over 2.5 psi	Not Over 2.5 psi	Over 2.5 psi
275 or less	5	25	5	25
276 to 750	10	25	5	25
751 to 12,000	15	25	5	25
12,001 to 30,000	20	30	5	25
30,001 to 50,000	30	45	10	25
50,001 to 100,000	50	75	15	25
Over 100,000	80	120	25	40

For SI units, 1 gal = 3.8 L; 1 ft = 0.3 m; 1 psi = a gauge pressure of 6.9 kPa.
Note: Double all of above distances where protection for exposures is not provided.
*Gauge pressure. [30:Table 17.4.3]

Δ Table 66.17.6.1 Minimum Separation Distances for Buildings or Structures Used for Ignitible (Flammable or Combustible) Liquid Handling and Operations

		Minimum Separation Distance (ft)	
Liquid Class	Minimum Type of Construction*	To Street, Alley, or Public Way	To Adjacent Property Line that Is or Can Be Built Upon
Class I liquids [FP < 100°F (37.8°C)]; liquids of any class heated above their flash points†	II (222) II (111) II (000)	5 5 10	10 25 50
Class II liquids [100°F (37.8°C) ≤ FP < 140°F (60°C)]	II (111) II (000)	5 5	10 25
Class III [FP ≥ 140°F (60°C)]	II (000)	5	10

For SI units, 1 ft = 0.3 m.
Note: Distances apply to properties that have protection for exposures, as defined in this code. If there are exposures for which protection does not exist, the distances should be doubled, in accordance with 66.17.6.3.
*Construction types are defined in NFPA 220.
†For stable liquids of any class heated above their flash points, see 66.6.4.1.3 and A.66.6.4.1.3.
[30:Table 17.6.1]

66.17.6.4 For buildings or structures that are not provided with approved automatic sprinkler protection, the separation distances otherwise required by Table 66.17.6.1 shall be determined by an engineering evaluation of the process, but shall not be less than the separation distances required by Table 66.17.4.3. [30:17.6.4]

66.17.6.5 Buildings or structures used solely for blending, mixing, or dispensing of Class IIIB liquids [FP ≥ 200°F (93°C)] at temperatures below their flash points shall be permitted to be constructed of combustible construction, subject to the approval of the AHJ. [30:17.6.5]

66.17.6.6 Buildings or structures used for processing or handling of ignitible (flammable or combustible) liquids where the quantities of ignitible (flammable or combustible) liquids do not exceed 360 gal (1360 L) of Class I and Class II liquids [FP < 140°F (60°C)] and 720 gal (2725 L) of Class IIIA liquids [140°F (60°C) ≤ FP < 200°F (93°C)] shall be permitted to be constructed of combustible construction, subject to the approval of the AHJ. [30:17.6.6]

66.17.6.7 Buildings or structures used for processing or handling of ignitible (flammable or combustible) liquids protected with automatic sprinklers or equivalent fire protection systems shall be permitted to be constructed of combustible construction, subject to the approval of the AHJ. [30:17.6.7]

66.17.6.8* Load-bearing building supports and load-bearing supports of vessels and equipment capable of releasing quantities of ignitible (flammable or combustible) liquids that could result in a fire capable of causing substantial property damage shall be protected by one or more of the following:

(1) Drainage to a safe location to prevent ignitible (flammable or combustible) liquids from accumulating under vessels or equipment or around load-bearing supports
(2) Fire-resistive construction
(3) Fire-resistant protective coatings or systems

(4) Water spray systems designed and installed in accordance with NFPA 15
(5) Other alternate means acceptable to the AHJ

[**30**:17.6.8]

66.17.6.9 Class I liquids [FP < 100°F (37.8°C)] shall not be handled or used in basements. [**30**:17.6.9]

66.17.6.9.1 Where Class I liquids [FP < 100°F (37.8°C)] are handled or used above grade within buildings with basements or closed pits into which flammable vapors can travel, such belowgrade areas shall be provided with mechanical ventilation designed to prevent the accumulation of flammable vapors. [**30**:17.6.9.1]

66.17.6.9.2 Means shall be provided to prevent ignitible (flammable or combustible) liquid spills from running into basements. [**30**:17.6.9.2]

66.17.6.10* Smoke and heat venting shall be permitted to be used where it assists access for firefighting. [**30**:17.6.10]

66.17.6.11* Areas shall have exit facilities arranged to prevent occupants from being trapped in the event of fire. [**30**:17.6.11]

66.17.6.11.1 Exits shall not be exposed by the drainage facilities described in 66.17.10. [**30**:17.6.11.1]

66.17.6.12 Aisles shall be maintained for unobstructed movement of personnel and fire protection equipment. [**30**:17.6.12]

Δ **66.17.6.13** Indoor areas where Class IA liquids [FP < 73°F (22.8°C) and BP < 100°F (37.8°C)] or other liquids intentionally heated to or above their BP are in use shall be designed to direct flame, combustion gases, and pressures resulting from a deflagration away from important buildings or occupied areas through the use of damage-limiting construction in accordance with NFPA 68. [**30**:17.6.13]

Δ **66.17.6.13.1** The damage-limiting construction design shall be both of the following:

(1) In accordance with recognized standards
(2) Acceptable to the AHJ

[**30**:17.6.13.1]

66.17.7* Fire Protection.

N **66.17.7.1 Interior.**

N **66.17.7.1.1** A hazard analysis shall be performed in accordance with 66.6.4 to determine the facility's fixed fire protection systems. [**30**:A.17.7.1.1]

N **66.17.7.1.1.1** Where required by the AHJ, or indicated by the hazard analysis, automatic sprinkler protection shall be provided in accordance with the requirements in 66.17.7.1.1.1.1 and 66.17.7.1.1.1.2. [**30**:A.17.7.1.1.1]

N **66.17.7.1.1.1.1** The demand area shall be based on the credible area of spill determined in the hazard analysis. [**30**:A.17.7.1.1.1.1]

N **66.17.7.1.1.1.2** Areas that have chemicals incompatible with water shall be provided with an alternative fire extinguishing system as determined in the hazard analysis. [**30**:A.17.7.1.1.1.2]

N **66.17.7.2 Exterior.** A hazard analysis shall be performed in accordance with 66.6.4 to determine the exterior fire protection system requirements. [**30**:A.17.7.2]

66.17.8* Emergency Control Systems.

66.17.9 Electrical Systems. Electrical wiring and electrical utilization equipment shall comply with Section 66.7. [**30**:17.9]

66.17.10 Containment, Drainage, and Spill Control.

66.17.10.1 A facility shall be designed and operated to prevent the discharge of ignitible (flammable or combustible) liquids to public waterways, public sewers, or adjoining property. [**30**:17.10.1]

66.17.10.2 Where spill control is used, it shall comply with the requirements of 66.6.11 and any additional requirements of this section. [**30**:17.10.2]

66.17.10.3* Where containment is used, it shall comply with the requirements of 66.6.11, and any additional requirements of this section. [**30**:17.10.3]

N **66.17.10.4** Where used, drainage shall comply with 66.6.11. [**30**:17.10.4]

N **66.17.10.5** Where only Class IIIB liquids [FP ≥ 200°F (93°C)] are handled, spill control, secondary containment, and drainage shall not be required. [**30**:17.10.5]

N **66.17.10.6** Where only unsaturated polyester resins (UPRs) containing not more than 50 percent by weight of Class IC, Class II, or Class IIIA liquid [73°F (22.8°C) ≤ FP < 200°F (93°C)] constituents are handled and are protected in accordance with 66.16.5.3.11, spill control, secondary containment, and drainage shall not be required. [**30**:17.10.6]

66.17.11 Ventilation.

66.17.11.1 Enclosed processing areas handling or using Class I liquids [FP < 100°F (37.8°C)], or Class II or Class III liquids [FP ≥ 100°F (37.8°C)] heated to temperatures at or above their FP, shall be ventilated at a rate sufficient to maintain the concentration of vapors within the area at or below 25 percent of the lower flammable limit (LFL). Compliance with 66.17.11.2 through 66.17.11.10 shall be deemed as meeting the requirements of this section. [**30**:17.11.1]

N **66.17.11.2*** Ventilation requirements shall be confirmed by one of the following:

(1) Calculations based on the anticipated fugitive emissions *(see Annex H in NFPA 30 for calculation method)*.
(2) Sampling of the actual vapor concentration under normal operating conditions. Sampling shall be conducted at a 5 ft (1.5 m) radius from each potential vapor source extending to or toward the bottom and the top of the enclosed processing area. The vapor concentration used to determine the required ventilation rate shall be the highest measured concentration during the sampling procedure.

[**30**:17.11.2]

N **66.17.11.3** A ventilation rate of not less than 1 ft^3/min/ft^2 (0.3 m^3/min/m^2) of solid floor area shall be considered as meeting the requirements of 66.17.11.1. [**30**:17.11.3]

66.17.11.4 Ventilation shall be accomplished by mechanical or natural means. [**30**:17.11.4]

66.17.11.5 Exhaust ventilation discharge shall be to a safe location outside the building. [**30**:17.11.5]

66.17.11.6 Recirculation of the exhaust air shall be permitted only when it is monitored continuously using a fail-safe system that is designed to automatically sound an alarm, stop recirculation, and provide full exhaust to the outside in the event that vapor–air mixtures in concentrations over one-fourth of the lower flammable limit are detected. [30:17.11.6]

66.17.11.7* Provision shall be made for introduction of make-up air in such a manner as to avoid short-circuiting the ventilation. [30:17.11.7]

66.17.11.8 Ventilation shall be arranged to include all floor areas or pits where flammable vapors can collect. [30:17.11.8]

66.17.11.9 Local or spot ventilation to control special fire or health hazards, if provided, shall be permitted to be utilized for up to 75 percent of the required ventilation. [30:17.11.9]

66.17.11.10 Where equipment such as dispensing stations, open centrifuges, plate and frame filters, and open vacuum filters is used in a building, the equipment and ventilation of the building shall be designed to limit flammable vapor–air mixtures under normal operating conditions to the interior of equipment and to not more than 5 ft (1.5 m) from equipment that exposes Class I liquids [FP < 100°F (37.8°C)] to the air. [30:17.11.10]

N **66.17.11.11** The mechanical ventilation system for processing areas shall be designed to provide an alarm notification upon loss of airflow. [30:17.11.11]

66.17.12 Explosion Control. The extent of required explosion control shall be determined in accordance with 66.6.4.1.2.3. [30:17.12]

66.17.13 Reserved.

66.17.14* Process Equipment and Vessels. Equipment shall be designed and arranged to prevent the unintentional escape of ignitible (flammable or combustible) liquids and vapors and to minimize the quantity escaping in the event of accidental release. [30:17.14]

66.17.15 Management of Operations Hazards.

Δ **66.17.15.1*** This section shall apply to the management methodology used to identify, evaluate, and control the hazards involved in processing and handling of ignitible (flammable or combustible) liquids. [30:17.15.1]

Δ **66.17.15.2** Operations involving ignitible (flammable or combustible) liquids shall be reviewed to ensure that fire and explosion hazards resulting from loss of containment of liquids are provided with corresponding fire prevention and emergency action plans in accordance with 66.6.4.1. [30:17.15.2]

Δ **66.17.15.3** The extent of fire and explosion prevention and risk control that is provided shall be determined in accordance with 66.6.4.1.2.3. [30:17.15.3]

Δ **66.17.15.4** A written emergency action plan that is consistent with available equipment and personnel shall be established to respond to fires and related emergencies, in accordance with 66.6.8. [30:17.15.4]

Δ **66.17.15.5** The fire hazards management review conducted in accordance with 66.17.15 shall be repeated in accordance with the requirements of 66.6.4.2. [30:17.15.5]

66.18 Dispensing, Handling, Transfer, and Use of Ignitible (Flammable or Combustible) Liquids.

66.18.1 Scope. This section applies where ignitible (flammable or combustible) liquids are handled, dispensed, transferred, or used, including in process areas. [30:18.1]

66.18.2 Reserved.

Δ **66.18.3 General Requirements.**

N **66.18.3.1** Rooms for ignitible liquid handling, dispensing, transfer, or use shall be designed in accordance with the applicable requirements of Sections 66.17 and 66.18, unless an engineering evaluation of fire and explosion hazards conducted in accordance with 66.6.4.1.2 justifies a different level of protection. [30:18.3.2]

N **66.18.3.2** Processing and handling of Class II and Class III liquids [FP ≥ 100°F (37.8°C)] heated at or above their FP shall follow the requirements for Class I liquids [FP < 100°F (37.8°C)], unless an engineering evaluation conducted in accordance with Section 66.6 justifies following the requirements for some other liquid class. *(See 66.6.4.1.3 and A.66.6.4.1.3.)* [30:18.3.2]

66.18.4 Dispensing, Handling, Transfer, and Use.

66.18.4.1 Class I liquids [FP < 100°F (37.8°C)] shall be kept in closed tanks or containers when not actually in use. Class II and Class III liquids [FP ≥ 100°F (37.8°C)] shall be kept in closed tanks or containers when not actually in use when the ambient or process temperature is at or above their FP. [30:18.4.1]

66.18.4.2 Where ignitible (flammable or combustible) liquids are used or handled, provisions shall be made to promptly and safely mitigate and dispose of leakage or spills. [30:18.4.2]

66.18.4.3 Class I liquids [FP < 100°F (37.8°C)] shall not be used outside closed systems where there are open flames or other ignition sources within the classified areas set forth in Section 66.7. [30:18.4.3]

66.18.4.4 Transfer of ignitible (flammable or combustible) liquids among vessels, containers, tanks, and piping systems by means of air or inert gas pressure shall be permitted only under all of the following conditions:

(1) The vessels, containers, tanks, and piping systems shall be designed for such pressurized transfer and shall be capable of withstanding the anticipated operating pressure.
(2) Safety and operating controls, including pressure-relief devices, shall be provided to prevent overpressure of any part of the system.
(3) Only inert gas shall be used to transfer Class I liquids [FP < 100°F (37.8°C)]. Only inert gas shall be used to transfer Class II and Class III liquids [FP ≥ 100°F (37.8°C)] that are heated above their FP.

[30:18.4.4]

66.18.4.4.1 Dispensing of Class I liquids [FP < 100°F (37.8°C)] from a container by means of air shall be permitted under the following conditions:

(1) The pressure shall be generated by means of a listed hand-operated device.
(2) Pressure shall not exceed a gauge pressure of 6 psi (41 kPa) and pressure relief shall be provided.

(3) The container shall not exceed 119 gal (450 L) and shall be capable of withstanding the maximum pressure generated by the device.
(4) The device shall be bonded and grounded or shall be demonstrated as not being capable of generating a static charge under any operating condition.
(5) The device shall be constructed of material compatible with the ignitible (flammable or combustible) liquid dispensed.
[30:18.4.4.1]

66.18.4.5 Positive displacement pumps shall be provided with pressure relief that discharges back to the tank, pump suction, or other suitable location or shall be provided with interlocks to prevent overpressure. [30:18.4.5]

66.18.4.6 Piping, valves, and fittings shall meet the requirements of Section 66.27. [30:18.4.6]

66.18.4.7 Approved hose shall be permitted to be used at transfer stations. [30:18.4.7]

66.18.4.8* The staging of ignitible (flammable or combustible) liquids in containers, intermediate bulk containers, and portable tanks shall be limited to the following:

(1) Containers, intermediate bulk containers, and portable tanks that are in use
(2) Containers, intermediate bulk containers, and portable tanks that were filled during a single shift
(3) Containers, intermediate bulk containers, and portable tanks needed to supply the process for one continuous 24-hour period
(4) Containers, intermediate bulk containers, and portable tanks that are stored in accordance with Section 66.9

[30:18.4.8]

66.18.4.9 Class I, Class II, or Class IIIA liquids [FP < 200°F (93°C)] used in a process and staged in the process area shall not be filled in the process area. [30:18.4.9]

66.18.4.9.1 Intermediate bulk containers and portable tanks that meet the requirements of Section 66.9 shall be permitted to be filled in the process area. [30:18.4.9.1]

66.18.4.9.2 Intermediate products that are manufactured in the process area shall be permitted to be filled in the process area. [30:18.4.9.2]

66.18.5 Incidental Operations.

66.18.5.1* This section shall apply to areas where the use, handling, and storage of ignitible (flammable or combustible) liquids is only a limited activity to the established occupancy classification. [30:18.5.1]

66.18.5.2 Class I liquids [FP < 100°F (37.8°C)] or Class II and Class III liquids [FP ≥ 100°F (37.8°C)] that are heated up to or above their FP shall be drawn from or transferred into vessels, containers, or portable tanks as follows:

(1) From original shipping containers with a capacity of 5.3 gal (20 L) or less
(2) From safety cans
(3) Through a closed piping system
(4) From portable tanks or containers by means of a device that has antisiphoning protection and that draws through an opening in the top of the tank or container
(5) By gravity through a listed self-closing valve or self-closing faucet

[30:18.5.2]

66.18.5.2.1 If hose is used in the transfer operation, it shall be equipped with a self-closing valve without a hold-open latch in addition to the outlet valve. Only listed or approved hose shall be used. [30:18.5.2.1]

Δ **66.18.5.2.2** Means that meet the requirements of 66.6.5.4 shall be provided to minimize generation of and safely dissipate static electricity. [30:18.5.2.2]

66.18.5.2.3 Where pumps are used for ignitible (flammable or combustible) liquid transfer, means shall be provided to deactivate liquid transfer in the event of an ignitible (flammable or combustible) liquid spill or fire. [30:18.5.2.3]

66.18.5.3 Storage of ignitible (flammable or combustible) liquids other than those governed by 66.18.5.4 and 66.18.5.5 shall comply with Section 66.9. [30:18.5.3]

66.18.5.4 The maximum allowable quantities (MAQs) of ignitible (flammable or combustible) liquids in containers in use in incidental operations in a control area shall not exceed the greater of the following:

(1)* The amount required to supply incidental operations for one continuous 24-hour period, provided the hazard analysis required in Section 66.6 accounts for these quantities
(2) The aggregate sum of the quantities provided in Table 66.18.5.4

[30:18.5.4]

66.18.5.4.1 Where the quantities of ignitible (flammable or combustible) liquids in incidental operations are governed by 66.18.5.4(2), the aggregate quantity of liquids in storage and in use shall not exceed the maximum allowable quantity per control area in Section 66.9. [30:18.5.4.1]

Table 66.18.5.4 MAQ of Liquids Per Control Area for Incidental Operations

Liquid Class(es)#	Open Use gal	Open Use L	Use — Closed Containers gal	Use — Closed Containers L
IA	10	38	30	115
IB and IC	30	115	120	460
II	30	115	120	460
IIIA	80	300	330	1,265
IIIB	3,300	12,650	13,200	50,600

#See 66.4.1 for details on the classification scheme.
Notes:
Quantities are permitted to be increased 100 percent where stored in approved Class I liquids [FP < 100°F (37.8°C)] storage cabinets or in safety cans. Where note (2) also applies, the increase for both notes is permitted to be applied accumulatively.
Quantities are permitted to be increased 100 percent in buildings equipped throughout with an approved automatic sprinkler system installed in accordance with NFPA 13. Where Note (1) also applies, the increase for both notes is permitted to be applied accumulatively.
[30:18.5.4]

66.18.5.4.2 Control areas shall be in accordance with Section 66.9. [**30**:18.5.4.2]

Δ **66.18.5.5** Where quantities of ignitible (flammable or combustible) liquids in excess of the limits in 66.18.5.4.1 are necessary, storage shall be in tanks that meet all applicable requirements of Section 66.17, Sections 66.21 through 66.25, and Section 66.27. [**30**:18.5.5]

66.18.5.6 Areas in which ignitible (flammable or combustible) liquids are transferred from one tank or container to another container shall be provided with the following:

(1) Separation from other operations where potential ignition sources are present by distance or by fire-resistant construction
(2) Drainage or other means to control spills, in accordance with 66.6.11
(3) Natural or mechanical ventilation that meets the requirements of 66.17.11

[**30**:18.5.6]

Δ **66.18.6 Ventilation for Dispensing Areas.**

66.18.6.1 Ventilation Type.

66.18.6.1.1 Areas where dispensing is conducted shall be provided with either a gravity system or a continuous mechanical exhaust ventilation system. [**30**:18.6.1.1]

66.18.6.1.2 Mechanical ventilation shall be used if Class I liquids [FP < 100°F (37.8°C)] are dispensed within the room. [**30**:18.6.1.2]

66.18.6.2 Exhaust air shall be taken from a point near a wall on one side of the room and within 12 in. (300 mm) of the floor, with one or more make-up inlets located on the opposite side of the room within 12 in. (300 mm) of the floor. [**30**:18.6.2]

66.18.6.3 The location of both the exhaust and inlet air openings shall be arranged to provide air movement across all portions of the floor to prevent accumulation of flammable vapors. [**30**:18.6.3]

66.18.6.4* Exhaust ventilation discharge shall be to a safe location outside the building. [**30**:18.6.4]

66.18.6.4.1 Recirculation of the exhaust air shall be permitted only when it is monitored continuously using a fail-safe system that is designed to automatically sound an alarm, stop recirculation, and provide full exhaust to the outside in the event that vapor-air mixtures in concentrations over one-fourth of the lower flammable limit are detected. [**30**:18.6.4.1]

66.18.6.5 If ducts are used, they shall not be used for any other purpose and shall comply with NFPA 91. [**30**:18.6.5]

66.18.6.5.1 If make-up air to a mechanical system is taken from within the building, the opening shall be equipped with a fire door or damper, as required in NFPA 91. [**30**:18.6.5.1]

66.18.6.5.2 For gravity systems, the make-up air shall be supplied from outside the building. [**30**:18.6.5.2]

66.18.6.6 Mechanical ventilation systems shall provide at least 1 cfm of exhaust air for each square foot of floor area (0.3 m^3/min/m^2), but not less than 150 cfm (4 m^3/min). [**30**:18.6.6]

66.18.6.6.1 The mechanical ventilation system for dispensing areas shall be designed to provide an alarm notification upon loss of airflow. [**30**:18.6.6.1]

66.18.6.6.2 Dispensing operations shall be stopped upon loss or failure of the ventilation. [**30**:18.6.6.2]

66.19 Specific Operations.

66.19.1 Scope. This section shall apply to the handling and use of liquids in specific operations as herein described. [**30**:19.1]

66.19.2 Definitions Specific to Section 66.19.

66.19.2.1* Cooking Oil. Where used in this section, cooking oil shall be classified as a Class IIIB liquid [FP ≥ 200°F (93°C)]. This definition shall apply to both fresh, or new, cooking oil and waste, or used, cooking oil. [**30**:19.2.1]

66.19.3 Reserved.

66.19.4 Recirculating Heat Transfer Systems.

66.19.4.1 Scope.

66.19.4.1.1 This section shall apply only to recirculating heat transfer systems that use a heat transfer fluid that is heated up to or above its flash point under normal operation. [**30**:19.4.1.1]

66.19.4.1.2 This section shall not apply to process streams used as a means of heat transfer or to any heat transfer system of 60 gal (230 L) capacity or less. [**30**:19.4.1.2]

66.19.4.2* General Requirements. A heater or vaporizer for heat transfer fluid that is located inside a building shall meet all applicable requirements of Section 66.17. [**30**:19.4.2]

66.19.4.3* System Design.

66.19.4.3.1* Drainage shall be provided at strategic low points in the heat transfer system. Drains shall be piped to a safe location that is capable of accommodating the total capacity of the system or the capacity of that part of the system that is isolated. [**30**:19.4.3.1]

66.19.4.3.2* Where the heat transfer system expansion tank is located above floor level and has a capacity of more than 250 gal (950 L), it shall be provided with a low-point drain line that can allow the expansion tank to drain to a drain tank on a lower level. The drain line valve shall be operable from a safe location. [**30**:19.4.3.2]

66.19.4.3.3 A heat transfer fluid system shall not be used to provide direct building heat. [**30**:19.4.3.3]

66.19.4.3.4 All pressure-relief device outlets shall be piped to a safe location. [**30**:19.4.3.4]

66.19.4.4* Fuel Burner Controls and Interlocks. Oil- or gas-fired heaters or vaporizers shall be designed and installed in accordance with the applicable requirements of NFPA 31 or NFPA 85, whichever is applicable. Wood dust suspension-fired heaters or vaporizers shall be designed and installed in accordance with the applicable requirements of NFPA 85. [**30**:19.4.4]

66.19.4.5 Piping.

66.19.4.5.1* Piping shall meet all applicable requirements of Section 66.27. [**30**:19.4.5.1]

66.19.4.5.2 All pipe connections shall be welded. [**30**:19.4.5.2]

66.19.4.5.2.1 Welded, threaded connections shall be permitted to be used for piping 2 in. (50 mm) and smaller. [**30**:19.4.5.2.1]

66.19.4.5.2.2 Mechanical joints shall be permitted to be used at pump, valve, and equipment connections. [**30**:19.4.5.2.2]

66.19.4.5.3 New piping that is to be insulated with permanent insulation and existing piping that has been disturbed and is to be reinsulated with permanent insulation shall be covered with a closed-cell, nonabsorbent insulation material. [**30**:19.4.5.3]

66.19.4.5.3.1 Where all pipe joints are welded and where there are no other points in the system subject to leakage, such as at valves or pumps, other types of insulation shall be permitted. [**30**:19.4.5.3.1]

66.19.4.5.3.2 Where dams are formed around possible leak-producing areas, using metal "donut" flanges that are welded to the pipe or using a "donut" segment of nonabsorbent insulation sealed to the pipe to prevent migration of leakage into adjacent insulation, the piping from dam to dam shall be considered to be a closed system and other types of insulation shall be permitted. The area subject to leakage where the dam has been constructed shall be insulated with nonabsorbent insulation or a nonabsorbent insulation system. [**30**:19.4.5.3.2]

66.19.4.5.3.3 Where removable, reusable insulated covers are required for access, the covers shall be fabricated of flexible or rigid insulation that is encapsulated in a manner to provide a nonabsorbent insulation system to prevent absorption of leakage into the insulation. [**30**:19.4.5.3.3]

66.19.4.6 Fire Protection.

66.19.4.6.1* Automatic sprinkler protection meeting the requirements of Section 13.3 and NFPA 13 for Extra Hazard (Group I) Occupancies shall be provided for building areas containing a heat transfer system heater or vaporizer. [**30**:19.4.6.1]

66.19.4.6.2 An alternate fire protection system shall be permitted to be used, if approved by the AHJ. Such alternate system shall be designed and installed in accordance with the appropriate NFPA standard and with manufacturer's recommendations for the system selected. [**30**:19.4.6.2]

66.19.4.7 Operation.

66.19.4.7.1* Operations involving heat transfer fluid systems and equipment shall be reviewed in accordance with 66.6.4.1.2.3 to ensure that the fire and explosion hazards resulting from loss of containment of the fluid or failure of the system are provided with corresponding fire prevention and emergency action plans. [**30**:19.4.7.1]

66.19.4.7.2 Operators of heat transfer systems shall be trained in the hazards of improper operation of the system and leakage and shall be trained to recognize upset conditions that can lead to dangerous situations. [**30**:19.4.7.2]

66.19.4.7.3 Safety interlocks shall be inspected, calibrated, and tested annually or at other intervals established in accordance with other applicable standards to determine that they are in proper operating condition. [**30**:19.4.7.3]

66.19.5 Vapor Recovery and Vapor Processing Systems.

66.19.5.1 Scope.

66.19.5.1.1 This section shall apply to vapor recovery and vapor processing systems where the vapor source operates at pressures from vacuum up to and including a gauge pressure of 1.0 psi (6.9 kPa), or where there is a potential for vapor mixtures in the flammable range. [**30**:19.5.1.1]

66.19.5.1.2 This section shall not apply to the following:

(1) Marine systems that comply with US Department of Transportation Regulations in Title 33, Code of Federal Regulations, Parts 154, 155, and 156, and US Coast Guard Regulations in Title 46, Code of Federal Regulations, Parts 30, 32, 35, and 39
(2) Marine and automotive service station systems that comply with Chapter 30 and NFPA 30A

[**30**:19.5.1.2]

66.19.5.2 Overpressure Protection and Vacuum Protection.

66.19.5.2.1 Tanks and equipment shall have independent venting for overpressure or vacuum conditions that could occur from malfunction of the vapor recovery or vapor processing system. [**30**:19.5.2.1]

66.19.5.2.2 Venting of tanks shall comply with 66.21.4.3. [**30**:19.5.2.2]

66.19.5.3 Vent Location.

66.19.5.3.1 Vents on vapor processing systems shall be not less than 12 ft (3.7 m) from adjacent ground level, with outlets located and directed so that ignitible vapors will disperse to a concentration below the lower flammable limit before reaching any location that contains an ignition source. [**30**:19.5.3.1]

66.19.5.3.2 Vent outlets shall be located so that vapors will not be trapped by eaves or other obstructions and shall be at least 5 ft (1.5 m) from building openings and at least 15 ft (4.5 m) from powered ventilation air intake devices. [**30**:19.5.3.2]

66.19.5.3.3 Vapor processing equipment and their vents shall be located in accordance with 66.17.3. [**30**:19.5.3.3]

66.19.5.4 Vapor Collection Systems.

66.19.5.4.1 Vapor collection piping shall be designed to prevent trapping ignitible (flammable or combustible) liquid. [**30**:19.5.4.1]

66.19.5.4.2 Vapor recovery and vapor processing systems that are not designed to handle ignitible (flammable or combustible) liquid shall be provided with a means to eliminate any ignitible (flammable or combustible) liquid that carries over to or condenses in the vapor collection system. [**30**:19.5.4.2]

66.19.5.5 Liquid Level Monitoring.

Δ **66.19.5.5.1*** A liquid knock-out vessel used in the vapor collection system shall have means to verify the ignitible (flammable or combustible) liquid level and a high liquid level sensor that activates an alarm. [**30**:19.5.5.1]

66.19.5.5.2 For unattended facilities, the high liquid level sensor shall initiate shutdown of ignitible (flammable or combustible) liquid transfer into the vessel and shutdown of vapor recovery or vapor processing systems. [**30**:19.5.5.2]

66.19.5.6 Overfill Protection.

Δ 66.19.5.6.1 Storage tanks served by vapor processing or vapor recovery systems shall be equipped with overfill protection in accordance with 66.21.7.1. [**30**:19.5.6.1]

66.19.5.6.2 Overfill protection of tank vehicles shall be in accordance with applicable provisions of 66.28.11.1. [**30**:19.5.6.2]

66.19.5.7 Sources of Ignition.

Δ 66.19.5.7.1 Vapor Release. Tank or equipment openings provided for purposes of vapor recovery shall be protected against possible vapor release in accordance with 23.13.7 of NFPA 30 and 66.28.11.1.8.1. [**30**:19.5.7.1]

66.19.5.7.2* Electrical Area Classification. Electrical area classification shall be in accordance with Section 66.7. [**30**:19.5.7.2]

66.19.5.7.3* Static Electricity. Vapor collection and vapor processing equipment shall be protected against static electricity in accordance with 66.6.5.4. [**30**:19.5.7.3]

66.19.5.7.4* Spontaneous Ignition. Equipment shall be designed or written procedures established and implemented to prevent ignition where the potential exists for spontaneous ignition. [**30**:19.5.7.4]

66.19.5.7.5* Friction Heat or Sparks from Mechanical Equipment. Mechanical equipment used to move vapors that are in the flammable range shall be designed to prevent sparks or other ignition sources under both normal and equipment malfunction conditions. [**30**:19.5.7.5]

66.19.5.7.6* Flame Propagation. Where there is reasonable potential for ignition of a vapor mixture in the flammable range, means shall be provided to stop the propagation of flame through the vapor collection system. The means chosen shall prevent flame propagation under the conditions with which they will be used. [**30**:19.5.7.6]

66.19.5.7.7 Explosion Protection. The extent of required explosion control shall be determined in accordance with 66.6.4.1.2.3. [**30**:19.5.7.7]

66.19.5.8 Emergency Shutdown Systems.
Emergency shutdown systems shall be designed to fail to a safe position in the event of loss of normal system power (i.e., air or electric) or equipment malfunction. [**30**:19.5.8]

66.19.6 Solvent Distillation Units.

66.19.6.1 Scope.

66.19.6.1.1 This section shall apply to solvent distillation units having distillation chambers or still pots that do not exceed 60 gal (227 L) nominal capacity and are used to recycle Class I, Class II, or Class IIIA liquids [FP < 200°F (93°C)]. [**30**:19.6.1.1]

66.19.6.1.2 This section shall not apply to research, testing, or experimental processes; to distillation processes carried out in petroleum refineries, chemical plants, or distilleries; or to distillation equipment used in dry cleaning operations. [**30**:19.6.1.2]

66.19.6.2 Equipment. Solvent distillation units shall be approved or shall be listed in accordance with UL 2208, *Solvent Distillation Units*. [**30**:19.6.2]

66.19.6.3 Solvents. Solvent distillation units shall only be used to distill liquids for which they have been investigated and that are listed on the unit's marking or contained within the manufacturers' literature. [**30**:19.6.3]

66.19.6.4 Location.

66.19.6.4.1 Solvent distillation units shall be located and operated in locations in accordance with their approval or listing. [**30**:19.6.4.1]

66.19.6.4.2 Solvent distillation units shall not be used in basements. [**30**:19.6.4.2]

66.19.6.4.3 Solvent distillation units shall be located away from potential sources of ignition, as indicated on the unit's marking. [**30**:19.6.4.3]

66.19.6.5 Liquid Storage. Distilled liquids and liquids awaiting distillation shall be stored in accordance with this *Code*. [**30**:19.6.5]

66.19.7 Cooking Oil Storage Tank Systems in Commercial Kitchens.

66.19.7.1 Scope.

66.19.7.1.1 This section shall apply to storage tank systems for cooking oil, as defined in 66.19.2.1, located in commercial kitchens where tank capacities are greater than 60 gal (227 L). [**30**:19.7.1.1]

66.19.7.1.2 This section shall apply to both fresh and waste cooking oil storage tank systems. [**30**:19.7.1.2]

66.19.7.1.3* Where there are conflicts between the requirements of this section and requirements of other sections of this *Code*, the requirements of this section shall take precedence. [**30**:19.7.1.3]

66.19.7.2 Design and Construction of Cooking Oil Storage Tanks.

66.19.7.2.1 Materials of Construction. Tanks shall be of metallic or nonmetallic construction. [**30**:19.7.2.1]

66.19.7.2.1.1 Tanks and their appurtenances shall be constructed of materials compatible with cooking oil. [**30**:19.7.2.1.1]

66.19.7.2.1.2* For tanks storing waste cooking oil, the tanks and their appurtenances shall be constructed of materials compatible with cooking oil at a minimum temperature of 140°F (60°C) continuous and 235°F (113°C) intermittent. [**30**:19.7.2.1.2]

66.19.7.2.2 Design Standards.

66.19.7.2.2.1* Metallic cooking oil storage tanks shall be listed in accordance with UL 142, *Steel Aboveground Tanks for Flammable and Combustible Liquids*, or UL 80, *Steel Tanks for Oil-Burner Fuels and Other Combustible Liquids*. [**30**:19.7.2.2.1]

66.19.7.2.2.2 Nonmetallic cooking oil storage tanks shall comply with both of the following:

(1) Be listed in accordance with CAN/UL/ULC 2152, *Special Purpose Nonmetallic Containers and Tanks for Specific Combustible or Noncombustible Liquids*
(2) Not exceed 200 gal (757 L) per tank

[**30**:19.7.2.2.2]

66.19.7.2.3 Normal Venting.

66.19.7.2.3.1 The normal vent(s) shall be located above the maximum normal liquid level. [**30**:19.7.2.3.1]

66.19.7.2.3.2 The normal vent shall be at least as large as the largest filling or withdrawal connection. [**30**:19.7.2.3.2]

66.19.7.2.3.3 Where used, normal vents, including vent piping, that are smaller than 1.25 in. (32 mm) nominal inside diameter shall be tested to verify that internal tank pressures will remain below a gauge pressure of 0.5 psi (3.5 kPa) under maximum expected flow rates for tank filling and withdrawal. These tests shall be permitted to be conducted by a qualified outside agency or by the manufacturer, if certified by a qualified observer. [**30**:19.7.2.3.3]

66.19.7.2.3.4* Normal vents shall be permitted to discharge inside the building. [**30**:19.7.2.3.4]

66.19.7.2.4 Emergency Venting.

66.19.7.2.4.1 Cooking oil storage tanks shall be provided with emergency relief venting in accordance with Section 66.22. [**30**:19.7.2.4.1]

66.19.7.2.4.2 For nonmetallic cooking oil storage tanks, emergency relief venting by form of construction shall be permitted. This shall include the low melting point of the material of construction of the tank. [**30**:19.7.2.4.2]

66.19.7.2.4.3 For metallic cooking oil storage tanks, emergency relief venting by form of construction shall be prohibited. [**30**:19.7.2.4.3]

66.19.7.2.4.4 Emergency vents shall be permitted to discharge inside the building. [**30**:19.7.2.4.4]

66.19.7.2.5* Prevention of Overfilling of Cooking Oil Storage Tanks. Every cooking oil storage tank shall be provided with means to prevent an accidental overfill. Such means shall be automatic and fail-safe in nature. [**30**:19.7.2.5]

66.19.7.2.6 Tank Heating.

66.19.7.2.6.1* Electrical equipment used for heating cooking oil shall be listed to UL 499, *Electrical Heating Appliances*, and shall comply with *NFPA 70*. [**30**:19.7.2.6.1]

66.19.7.2.6.2* Electrical equipment used for heating cooking oil shall comply with *NFPA 70* and shall be equipped with automatic means to limit the temperature of the oil to less than 140°F (60°C). [**30**:19.7.2.6.2]

66.19.7.2.6.3 Use of electrical immersion heaters in nonmetallic tanks shall be prohibited. [**30**:19.7.2.6.3]

66.19.7.3 Tank Installation and Testing.

66.19.7.3.1 Location of Cooking Oil Storage Tanks. Tanks shall be installed in locations appropriate for storage of foodstuffs or inventory and shall not be installed in areas designated as cooking areas. [**30**:19.7.3.1]

66.19.7.3.1.1* Tanks shall be spaced at least 3 ft (0.9 m) away from any cooking appliance or any surface heated to a temperature above 140°F (60°C) continuous and at least 6 ft (1.8 m) away from any open flame. [**30**:19.7.3.1.1]

66.19.7.3.1.2* Tanks shall not be installed under commercial kitchen ventilation hoods. [**30**:19.7.3.1.2]

66.19.7.3.1.3 Tanks shall not be required to be separated from one another. [**30**:19.7.3.1.3]

66.19.7.3.2 Foundations for and Anchoring of Cooking Oil Storage Tanks.

66.19.7.3.2.1* Tanks shall be secured to prevent the tank from tipping over. [**30**:19.7.3.2.1]

66.19.7.3.2.2 In areas subject to earthquakes, tank supports, the foundation, and anchoring shall meet the requirements of the applicable building code for the specific seismic zone. Engineering evaluation by a qualified, impartial outside agency shall be an acceptable method of meeting this requirement. [**30**:19.7.3.2.2]

66.19.7.3.2.3 Where a tank is located in areas subject to flooding, the method for anchoring the tank shall be capable of preventing the tank, either full or empty, from floating during a rise in water level up to the established maximum flood stage. Engineering evaluation by a qualified, impartial outside agency shall be an acceptable method of meeting this requirement. [**30**:19.7.3.2.3]

66.19.7.3.3 Tank Openings Other than Vents.

66.19.7.3.3.1 Each connection to the tank below the normal liquid level through which liquid can normally flow shall be provided with an internal or external valve located as close as possible to the shell of the tank, in accordance with Section 66.22. [**30**:19.7.3.3.1]

66.19.7.3.3.2* Connections to the tank above the normal liquid level through which liquid can normally flow shall not be required to have a valve, provided there exists a liquidtight closure at the opposite end of the line. The liquidtight closure shall be in the form of a valve, a plug, or a coupling or fitting with positive shutoff. [**30**:19.7.3.3.2]

66.19.7.3.4 Field Testing.

66.19.7.3.4.1* As an alternate method to the testing requirements in Section 66.21, cooking oil storage tanks shall be tested for leaks at the time of installation by filling the tank with cooking oil to a liquid level above the highest tank seam or connection within the normal liquid level. Before the tank is placed in service, all leaks shall be corrected in an approved manner or the tank shall be replaced. [**30**:19.7.3.4.1]

66.19.7.3.4.2 An approved listing mark on a cooking oil storage tank shall be considered to be evidence of compliance with tank testing requirements. [**30**:19.7.3.4.2]

66.19.7.4 Fire Protection for Cooking Oil Storage Tanks.

Δ **66.19.7.4.1 Identification for Emergency Responders.** A sign or marking that meets the requirements of NFPA 704 or another approved system shall be applied to each cooking oil storage tank in accordance with Section 66.21. Additional signage shall be applied to each tank identifying the contents of the tank as cooking oil, either fresh or waste. [**30**:19.7.4.1]

66.19.7.4.2* In areas where tanks are located, no additional ventilation shall be required beyond that necessary for comfort ventilation, provided that all cooking equipment is equipped with exhaust systems in accordance with NFPA 96. [**30**:19.7.4.2]

66.19.7.4.3 If ventilation is not provided as specified in 66.19.7.4.2, then the tank shall be vented to another room inside the building that meets these requirements, or the tank shall be vented to the outside of the building. [**30**:19.7.4.3]

66.19.7.5 Transfer Lines.

Δ **66.19.7.5.1* Design and Construction of Fresh Cooking Oil Transfer Lines.** Transfer lines for fresh cooking oil shall be permitted to be constructed of metallic or nonmetallic materials that are compatible with cooking oil and food products. Nonmetallic transfer lines shall also meet the following requirements:

(1) Transfer lines in pressure applications shall be rated for a working gauge pressure of 100 psi (689 kPa) at 70°F (21°C) or the maximum output pressure of the transfer pump, whichever is higher.
(2) Transfer lines in suction applications shall be rated for full vacuum at 70°F (21°C).
(3) Transfer lines shall be rated for temperatures up to 120°F (49°C) continuous.
(4) The maximum nominal inside diameter shall be no larger than 1.25 in. (32 mm).
(5) Leakage shall be controlled through the use of check valves or antisiphon valves at points where the lines connect to the fresh oil tank.

[**30**:19.7.5.1]

66.19.7.5.2* Design and Construction of Waste Cooking Oil Transfer Lines. Waste cooking oil transfer lines shall be permitted to be constructed of metallic or nonmetallic materials that are compatible with cooking oil. [**30**:19.7.5.2]

66.19.7.5.2.1 Transfer lines shall be rated for use with cooking oil at elevated temperatures of 275°F (135°C) continuous and 350°F (177°C) intermittent. [**30**:19.7.5.2.1]

66.19.7.5.2.2 Nonmetallic transfer lines shall be rated for working pressures up to 250 psi (1724 kPa) at 275°F (135°C). [**30**:19.7.5.2.2]

66.19.7.5.3 Flow Control. Cooking oil transfer lines shall be equipped with means to prevent unintended transfer or dispensing of cooking oil. These means shall be permitted to be in the form of momentary control switches, valves, check valves, antisiphon valves, plugs, couplings, fittings, or any combination thereof that are fail-safe in nature. [**30**:19.7.5.3]

66.19.7.5.4 Pressure Control. Pumping systems used to transfer cooking oil shall have means to prevent overpressurization of transfer lines. These means shall be in the form of relief valves, bypass valves, pressure sensor devices, or the pressure limitation of the pump itself. [**30**:19.7.5.4]

66.19.7.5.5 Installation of Cooking Oil Transfer Lines in Plenum-Rated Spaces. Cooking oil transfer lines installed in plenum-rated spaces shall be enclosed in noncombustible raceways or enclosures, or shall be covered with a material listed and labeled for installation within a plenum. [**30**:19.7.5.5]

66.19.7.5.6 Testing of Cooking Oil Transfer Lines. Cooking oil transfer lines shall be tested after installation and prior to use. Testing shall be with cooking oil at the normal operating pressures. Any leaks discovered in transfer lines as a result of testing shall be repaired or the transfer lines replaced prior to placing the transfer lines into service. [**30**:19.7.5.6]

66.20 Reserved.

66.21 Storage of Ignitible (Flammable or Combustible) Liquids in Tanks — Requirements for All Storage Tanks.

66.21.1 Scope. This section shall apply to the following:

(1) The storage of liquids, as defined in 3.3.33 of NFPA 30 and Section 66.4, in fixed tanks that exceed 60 gal (230 L) capacity
(2) The storage of liquids in portable tanks that exceed 660 gal (2500 L) capacity
(3) The storage of liquids in intermediate bulk containers that exceed 793 gal (3000 L) capacity
(4) The design, installation, testing, operation, and maintenance of such tanks, portable tanks, and bulk containers

[**30**:21.1]

66.21.2 Definitions Specific to Section 66.21. For the purpose of this section, the following definitions shall apply. [**30**:21.2]

66.21.2.1 Compartmented Tank. A tank that is divided into two or more compartments intended to contain the same or different liquids. [**30**:21.2.1]

66.21.3 General Requirements.

66.21.3.1 Storage of Class II and Class III liquids [FP ≥ 100°F (37.8°C)] heated at or above their FP shall follow the requirements for Class I liquids [FP < 100°F (37.8°C)], unless an engineering evaluation conducted in accordance with Section 66.6 and 66.21.6 justifies following the requirements for some other liquid class. [**30**:21.3.1]

Δ **66.21.3.2** Tanks shall be permitted to be of any shape, size, or type consistent with recognized engineering standards. Metal tanks shall be welded, riveted and caulked, or bolted or constructed using a combination of these methods. [**30**:21.3.2]

66.21.3.3 Tanks designed and intended for aboveground use shall not be used as underground tanks. [**30**:21.3.3]

66.21.3.4 Tanks designed and intended for underground use shall not be used as aboveground tanks. [**30**:21.3.4]

66.21.3.5 Tanks shall be designed and built in accordance with recognized engineering standards for the material of construction being used. [**30**:21.3.5]

66.21.4 Design and Construction of Storage Tanks.

66.21.4.1 Materials of Construction. Tanks shall be of steel or other approved noncombustible material in accordance with 66.21.4.1.1 through 66.21.4.1.4, or of combustible materials in accordance with 66.21.4.1.1 and 66.21.4.1.3 through 66.21.4.1.5. [**30**:21.4.1]

66.21.4.1.1 The materials of construction for tanks and their appurtenances shall be compatible with the liquid to be stored. In case of doubt about the properties of the liquid to be stored, the supplier, producer of the liquid, or other competent authority shall be consulted. [**30**:21.4.1.1]

66.21.4.1.2 Unlined concrete tanks shall be permitted to be used for storing liquids that have a gravity of 40°API or heavier. Concrete tanks with special linings shall be permitted to be used for other liquids, provided they are designed and constructed in accordance with recognized engineering standards. [**30**:21.4.1.2]

66.21.4.1.3 Tanks shall be permitted to have combustible or noncombustible linings. The selection, specification, and type of lining material and its required thickness shall be based on the properties of the liquid to be stored. When there is a change in the characteristics of the liquid to be stored, the compatibility of the lining and the liquid shall be verified. [30:21.4.1.3]

66.21.4.1.4 An engineering evaluation shall be made if the specific gravity of the liquid to be stored exceeds that of water or if the tank is designed to contain liquids at a liquid temperature below 0°F (–18°C). [30:21.4.1.4]

66.21.4.1.5 Combustible Materials.

66.21.4.1.5.1 Tanks shall be permitted to be constructed of combustible materials where approved. [30:21.4.1.5.1]

66.21.4.1.5.2 Tanks constructed of combustible materials shall be limited to any of the following:

(1) Underground installation
(2) Use where required by the properties of the ignitible (flammable or combustible) liquid stored
(3) Aboveground storage of Class IIIB liquids [FP ≥ 200°F (93°C)] in areas not exposed to a spill or leak of Class I or Class II liquids [FP < 140°F (60°C)]
(4) Storage of Class IIIB liquids [FP ≥ 200°F (93°C)] inside a building protected by an approved automatic fire-extinguishing system

[30:21.4.1.5.2]

66.21.4.1.5.3* Use of electrical immersion heaters in nonmetallic tanks shall be prohibited. [30:21.4.1.5.3]

66.21.4.1.5.4 Exposed combustible components of nonmetallic tanks shall be spaced at least 3 ft (0.9 m) away from any surface heated to a temperature above 140°F (60°C) and at least 6 ft (1.8 m) away from any open flame. [30:21.4.1.5.4]

66.21.4.2 Design Standards for Storage Tanks.

66.21.4.2.1 Design Standards for Atmospheric Tanks.

66.21.4.2.1.1* Atmospheric tanks designed and constructed in accordance with any of the following recognized engineering standards shall be deemed as meeting the requirements of 66.21.4.2.1:

(1) API Specification 12B, *Bolted Tanks for Storage of Production Liquids*
(2) API Specification 12D, *Field Welded Tanks for Storage of Production Liquids*
(3) API Specification 12F, *Shop Welded Tanks for Storage of Production Liquids*
(4) API Standard 650, *Welded Tanks for Oil Storage*
(5) UL 58, *Steel Underground Tanks for Flammable and Combustible Liquids*
(6) UL 80, *Steel Tanks for Oil-Burner Fuels and Other Combustible Liquids*
(7) UL 142, *Steel Aboveground Tanks for Flammable and Combustible Liquids*
(8) UL 142A, *Safety for Special Purpose Aboveground Tanks for Specific Flammable or Combustible Liquids*
(9) UL 1316, *Glass-Fiber Reinforced Plastic Underground Storage Tanks for Petroleum Products, Alcohols, and Alcohol-Gasoline Mixtures*
(10) UL 2080, *Fire Resistant Tanks for Flammable and Combustible Liquids*
(11) UL 2085, *Protected Aboveground Tanks for Flammable and Combustible Liquids*
(12) UL 2258, *Aboveground Nonmetallic Tanks for Fuel Oil and Other Combustible Liquids*, where used in accordance with the provisions in 66.21.4.1.5

[30:21.4.2.1.1]

66.21.4.2.1.2 Tanks shall be limited to operation from atmospheric to a gauge pressure of 0.5 psi (3.5 kPa) unless permitted in 66.21.4.2.1.3 through 66.21.4.2.1.5. [30:21.4.2.1.2]

66.21.4.2.1.3 Atmospheric tanks designed and constructed in accordance with Annex F of API Standard 650, *Welded Tanks for Oil Storage*, shall be permitted to operate at pressures from atmospheric to a gauge pressure of 2.5 psi (17.2 kPa). [30:21.4.2.1.3]

66.21.4.2.1.3.1 Tanks shall be anchored as required by Annex F of API Standard 650, *Welded Tanks for Oil Storage*. [30:21.4.2.1.3.1]

66.21.4.2.1.4 Atmospheric tanks that are not designed and constructed in accordance with Annex F of API Standard 650, *Welded Tanks for Oil Storage*, shall be permitted to operate at pressures from atmospheric to a gauge pressure of 1.0 psi (6.9 kPa) only if an engineering analysis is performed to determine that the tank can withstand the elevated pressure. [30:21.4.2.1.4]

66.21.4.2.1.5 Horizontal cylindrical and rectangular tanks built according to any of the standards specified in 66.21.4.2.1.1 shall be permitted to operate at pressures from atmospheric to a gauge pressure of 1.0 psi (6.9 kPa) and shall be limited to a gauge pressure of 2.5 psi (17 kPa) under emergency venting conditions. [30:21.4.2.1.5]

66.21.4.2.1.6 Low-pressure tanks and pressure vessels shall be permitted to be used as atmospheric tanks. [30:21.4.2.1.6]

66.21.4.2.1.7 Atmospheric tanks shall not be used to store an ignitible (flammable or combustible) liquid at a temperature at or above its boiling point. [30:21.4.2.1.7]

66.21.4.2.2 Design Standards for Low-Pressure Tanks.

66.21.4.2.2.1 Low-pressure tanks shall be designed and constructed in accordance with recognized engineering standards. Low-pressure tanks that meet either of the following standards shall be deemed as meeting the requirements of 66.21.4.2.2:

(1) API 620, *Design and Construction of Large, Welded, Low-Pressure Storage Tanks*
(2) ASME *Code for Unfired Pressure Vessels*, Section VIII, Division 1

[30:21.4.2.2.1]

66.21.4.2.2.2 Low-pressure tanks shall not be operated above their design pressures. [30:21.4.2.2.2]

66.21.4.2.2.3 Pressure vessels shall be permitted to be used as low-pressure tanks. [30:21.4.2.2.3]

66.21.4.2.3 Design Standards for Pressure Vessels.

66.21.4.2.3.1 Tanks with storage pressures above a gauge pressure of 15 psi (100 kPa) shall be designed and constructed in accordance with recognized engineering standards. Pressure vessels that meet any of the following standards shall be deemed as meeting the requirements of 66.21.4.2.3:

(1) Fired pressure vessels shall be designed and constructed in accordance with Section I (Power Boilers), or Section VIII, Division 1 or Division 2 (Pressure Vessels), as applicable, of the ASME *Boiler and Pressure Vessel Code*.

(2) Unfired pressure vessels shall be designed and constructed in accordance with Section VIII, Division 1 or Division 2, of the ASME *Boiler and Pressure Vessel Code*. [**30:**21.4.2.3.1]

66.21.4.2.3.2 Pressure vessels that do not meet the requirements of 66.21.4.2.3.1(1) or 66.21.4.2.3.1(2) shall be permitted to be used, provided they are approved by the AHJ. [**30:**21.4.2.3.2]

66.21.4.2.3.3 Pressure vessels shall not be operated above their design pressures. The normal operating pressure of the vessel shall not exceed the design pressure of the vessel. [**30:**21.4.2.3.3]

66.21.4.3 Normal Venting for Storage Tanks.

66.21.4.3.1 Storage Tank Venting.

66.21.4.3.1.1* Storage tanks shall be vented to prevent the development of vacuum or pressure that can distort the tank or exceed the rated design vacuum or rated design pressure of the tank when the tank is filled or emptied or because of atmospheric temperature changes. [**30:**21.4.3.1.1]

N **66.21.4.3.1.1.1*** Where used, pressure-vacuum vent devices shall be listed or approved. [**30:**21.4.3.1.1.1]

N **66.21.4.3.1.1.2** The requirement in 66.21.4.3.1.1.1 does not apply to tanks for upstream production liquids. [**30:**21.4.3.1.1.2]

66.21.4.3.1.2 Normal vents shall be located above the maximum normal liquid level. [**30:**21.4.3.1.2]

66.21.4.3.2* Atmospheric storage tanks shall be vented so as not to exceed the tank's design operating pressure or a gauge pressure of 1.0 psi (6.9 kPa), whichever is less, and shall be vented to prevent the development of vacuum. [**30:**21.4.3.2]

66.21.4.3.3 Low-pressure tanks and pressure vessels shall be vented to prevent the development of pressure or vacuum that exceeds the rated design pressure of the tank or vessel. Means shall also be provided to prevent overpressure from any pump discharging into the tank or vessel when the pump discharge pressure can exceed the design pressure of the tank or vessel. [**30:**21.4.3.3]

66.21.4.3.4 If any tank or pressure vessel has more than one fill or withdrawal connection and simultaneous filling or withdrawal can be made, the vent size shall be based on the maximum anticipated simultaneous flow. [**30:**21.4.3.4]

66.21.4.3.5 For tanks equipped with vents that permit pressures to exceed a gauge pressure of 2.5 psi (17 kPa) and for low-pressure tanks and pressure vessels, the outlet of all vents and vent drains shall be arranged to discharge in a manner that prevents localized overheating of or flame impingement on any part of the tank, if vapors from the vents are ignited. [**30:**21.4.3.5]

66.21.4.3.6 Tanks and pressure vessels that store Class IA liquids [FP < 73°F (22.8°C) and BP < 100°F (37.8°C)] shall be equipped with venting devices that are closed, except when venting under pressure or vacuum conditions. [**30:**21.4.3.6]

66.21.4.3.7 Tanks and pressure vessels that store Class IB and Class IC liquids [FP < 100°F (37.8°C) and BP ≥ 100°F (37.8°C)] shall be equipped with venting devices or with listed flame arresters. When used, vent devices shall be closed, except when venting under pressure or vacuum conditions. [**30:**21.4.3.7]

Δ **66.21.4.3.8** Tanks of 3000 barrels (bbl) [126,000 gal (475 m^3)] capacity or less that store crude petroleum in crude-producing areas and outside aboveground atmospheric tanks of less than 1000 gal (3785 L) capacity that contain other than Class IA liquids [FP < 73°F (22.8°C) and BP < 100°F (37.8°C)] shall be permitted to have open vents. [**30:**21.4.3.8]

66.21.4.3.9* Flame arresters or venting devices required in 66.21.4.3.6 and 66.21.4.3.7 shall be permitted to be omitted on tanks that store Class IB or Class IC liquids [FP < 100°F (37.8°C) and BP ≥ 100°F (37.8°C)] where conditions are such that their use can, in case of obstruction, result in damage to the tank. [**30:**21.4.3.9]

66.21.4.3.10 Piping for normal vents shall be designed in accordance with Section 66.27. [**30:**21.4.3.10]

Δ **66.21.4.4 Tank Fill Pipes.**

N **66.21.4.4.1** Fill pipes that enter the top of a tank shall terminate within 6 in. (150 mm) of the bottom of the tank. [**30:**21.4.4.1]

N **66.21.4.4.2** Fill pipes in tanks whose vapor space under the expected range of operating conditions is not in the flammable range or is inerted shall not need to meet 66.21.4.4.1. [**30:**21.4.4.2]

N **66.21.4.4.3*** Fill pipes in tanks handling ignitible (flammable or combustible) liquids with minimal potential for accumulation of static charge shall not need to meet 66.21.4.4.1, provided that the fill line is designed and the system is operated to avoid mist generation and to provide residence time downstream of filters or screens to allow dissipation of the generated static charge. [**30:**21.4.4.3]

N **66.21.4.4.4** Fill pipes shall be installed or arranged so that vibration is minimized. [**30:**21.4.4.4]

66.21.4.5* Corrosion Protection.

66.21.4.5.1 Corrosion protection shall meet the requirements of 66.21.4.5.2 or 66.21.4.5.3, whichever is applicable. [**30:**21.4.5.1]

66.21.4.5.2 Internal Corrosion Protection for Metal Storage Tanks. Where tanks are not designed in accordance with standards of the American Petroleum Institute, the American Society of Mechanical Engineers, or Underwriters Laboratories Inc., or if corrosion is anticipated beyond that provided for in the design formulas or standards used, additional metal thickness or approved protective coatings or linings shall be provided to compensate for the corrosion loss expected during the design life of the tank. [**30:**21.4.5.2]

66.21.4.5.3 Internal Corrosion Protection for Nonmetallic Tanks. Where tanks are not designed in accordance with standards of the American Petroleum Institute, the American Society of Mechanical Engineers, ASTM International, or Underwriters Laboratories Inc., or if degradation is anticipated beyond that provided for in the design formulas or standards used, degradation shall be compensated for by providing additional tank material thickness or by application of protective coatings or linings, as determined by an engineering analysis. [30:21.4.5.3]

66.21.5 Testing Requirements for Tanks.

66.21.5.1 General. All tanks, whether shop-built or field-erected, shall be tested before they are placed in service in accordance with the requirements of the code under which they were built. [30:21.5.1]

66.21.5.1.1 An approved listing mark on a tank shall be considered to be evidence of compliance with 66.21.5.1.1. Tanks not so marked shall be tested before they are placed in service in accordance with the applicable requirements for testing in the standards listed in 66.21.4.2.1.1, 66.21.4.2.2.1, or 66.21.4.2.3.1 or in accordance with recognized engineering standards. Upon satisfactory completion of testing, a permanent record of the test results shall be maintained by the owner. [30:21.5.1.1]

N **66.21.5.1.2** Where the vertical length of the fill and vent pipes is such that, when filled with liquid, the static head imposed on the bottom of the tank exceeds a gauge pressure of 10 psi (70 kPa), the tank and its related piping shall be tested hydrostatically to a pressure equal to the static head thus imposed by using recognized engineering standards. [30:21.5.1.2]

N **66.21.5.1.3** Before the tank is initially placed in service, all leaks or deformations shall be corrected in an approved manner. Mechanical caulking shall not be permitted for correcting leaks in welded tanks except for pinhole leaks in the roof. [30:21.5.1.3]

N **66.21.5.1.4** Tanks to be operated at pressures below their design pressure shall be tested by the applicable provisions of 66.21.5.1.1 or 66.21.5.1.2 based upon the pressure developed under full emergency venting of the tank. [30:21.5.1.4]

66.21.5.2* Tightness Testing. In addition to the tests called for in 66.21.5.1, all tanks and connections shall be tested for tightness after installation and before being placed in service in accordance with 66.21.5.2.3 through 66.21.5.2.11, as applicable. [30:21.5.2]

N **66.21.5.2.1** Except for underground tanks, the test required in 66.21.5.2 shall be made at operating pressure with air, inert gas, or water. [30:21.5.2.1]

N **66.21.5.2.2 Conditions Where Field Testing Is Not Required.**

N **66.21.5.2.2.1** Testing required by 66.21.5.2 shall not be required for a primary tank or an interstitial space that continues to maintain a factory-applied vacuum in accordance with the manufacturer's instructions. [30:21.5.2.2.1]

N **66.21.5.2.2.2** Such components as stated in 66.21.5.2.2.1 shall be considered to be tight until such time that the vacuum is broken. [30:21.5.2.2.2]

N **66.21.5.2.2.3** Final tightness testing of an interstitial space shall not be required if the factory-applied vacuum is maintained until one of the following conditions is met:

(1) For aboveground tanks, the tank is set on the site at the location where it is intended to be installed.
(2) For underground tanks, backfill has been completed to the top of the tank.

[30:21.5.2.2.3]

66.21.5.2.3 Air pressure shall not be used to test tanks that contain liquids or vapors. *(See Section 27.7 of NFPA 30 for testing pressure piping.)* [30:21.5.2.3]

66.21.5.2.4 For field-erected tanks, the tests required by 66.21.5.1.1 or 21.5.1.2 of NFPA 30 shall be permitted to be considered the test for tank tightness. [30:21.5.2.4]

66.21.5.2.5 Horizontal shop-fabricated aboveground tanks shall be tested for tightness either hydrostatically or with air pressure at not less than a gauge pressure of 3 psi (20 kPa) and not more than a gauge pressure of 5 psi (35 kPa). [30:21.5.2.5]

66.21.5.2.6 Vertical shop-fabricated aboveground tanks shall be tested for tightness either hydrostatically or with air pressure at not less than a gauge pressure of 1.5 psi (10 kPa) and not more than a gauge pressure of 2.5 psi (17 kPa). [30:21.5.2.6]

N **66.21.5.2.7** Rectangular shop-fabricated aboveground tanks shall be tested for tightness either hydrostatically or with air pressure at not less than a gauge pressure of 0.5 psi (3 kPa) and not more than a gauge pressure of 1.5 psig (10 kPa) or in accordance with the tank's listing or the manufacturer's instructions. [30:21.5.2.7]

66.21.5.2.8 Single-wall underground tanks and piping, before being covered, enclosed, or placed in use, shall be tested for tightness either hydrostatically or with air pressure at not less than a gauge pressure of 3 psi (20 kPa) and not more than a gauge pressure of 5 psi (35 kPa). [30:21.5.2.8]

66.21.5.2.9* Underground secondary containment tanks and horizontal aboveground secondary containment tanks shall have the primary (inner) tank tested for tightness either hydrostatically or with air pressure at not less than a gauge pressure of 3 psi (20 kPa) and not more than a gauge pressure of 5 psi (35 kPa). [30:21.5.2.9]

Δ **66.21.5.2.9.1*** The interstitial space of such tanks shall be tested either hydrostatically or with air pressure at a gauge pressure of 3 to 5 psi (20 to 35 kPa), by vacuum at 5.3 in. Hg (18 kPa), or in accordance with the tank's listing or the manufacturer's instructions. [30:21.5.2.9.1]

66.21.5.2.9.2 The pressure or vacuum shall be held for not less than 1 hour or for the duration specified in the listing procedures for the tank. [30:21.5.2.9.2]

N **66.21.5.2.10*** The interstitial space of such tanks shall be tested either hydrostatically or with air pressure at a gauge pressure of 0.5 to 1.5 psi (10 to 17 kPa), by vacuum at 5.3 in. Hg (18 kPa), or in accordance with the tank's listing or manufacturer's instructions. [30:21.5.2.10]

66.21.5.2.11 Vertical aboveground secondary containment–type tanks shall have their primary (inner) tank tested for tightness either hydrostatically or with air pressure at not less than a gauge pressure of 1.5 psi (10 kPa) and not more than a gauge pressure of 2.5 psi (17 kPa). [30:21.5.2.11]

Δ **66.21.5.2.11.1*** The interstitial space of such tanks shall be tested either hydrostatically or with air pressure at a gauge pressure of 1.5 to 2.5 psi (10 to 17 kPa), by vacuum at 5.3 in. Hg (18 kPa), or in accordance with the tank's listing or manufacturer's instructions. [**30**:21.5.2.11.1]

66.21.5.2.11.2 The pressure or vacuum shall be held for not less than 1 hour or for the duration specified in the listing procedures for the tank. [**30**:21.5.2.11.2]

66.21.5.3* Periodic Testing. Each tank shall be tested when required by the manufacturer's instructions and applicable standards to ensure the integrity of the tank. [**30**:21.5.3]

66.21.6 Fire Prevention and Control.

66.21.6.1 General Requirements. Management techniques and fire control methods shall be in accordance with NFPA 30.

N **66.21.6.1.1** This section shall apply to the commonly recognized management techniques and fire control methods used to prevent or minimize the loss from fire or explosion in tank storage facilities. The wide range in size, design, and location of tank storage facilities shall preclude the inclusion of detailed fire prevention and control methods applicable to all such facilities. [**30**:21.6.1.1]

N **66.21.6.1.2** Tank storage facilities shall establish and implement fire prevention and control methods for life safety, for minimizing property loss, and for reducing fire exposure to adjoining facilities resulting from fire and explosion. Compliance with 66.21.6.2 through 66.21.6.6 shall be deemed as meeting the requirements of 66.21.6.1. [**30**:21.6.1.2]

N **66.21.6.2 Control of Ignition Sources.** In order to prevent the ignition of flammable vapors in tank storage facilities, ignition sources shall be controlled in accordance with Section 66.6. [**30**:21.6.2]

N **66.21.6.3 Management of Fire and Explosion Hazards.** The extent of required fire and explosion control shall be determined in accordance with 66.6.4.1.2.3. [**30**:21.6.3]

N **66.21.6.4 Fire Control.** Tank storage facilities for liquids shall be reviewed to ensure that fire and explosion hazards resulting from loss of containment of liquids are provided with corresponding fire prevention and emergency action plans. *(See also 66.6.3.)* [**30**:21.6.4]

66.21.6.5 Emergency Planning and Training.

66.21.6.5.1 Emergency procedures shall be kept available in an operating area. The procedures shall be reviewed and updated in accordance with 66.6.4.2. [**30**:21.6.5.5]

66.21.6.5.2 Where tank storage facilities are unattended, a summary of the emergency plan shall be posted or located in a strategic location that is accessible to emergency responders. [**30**:21.6.5.6]

66.21.6.6 Inspection and Maintenance of Fire Protection and Emergency Response Equipment.

66.21.6.6.1* All fire protection and emergency response equipment shall be maintained, inspected, and tested in accordance with regulatory requirements, standard practices, and equipment manufacturers' recommendations. [**30**:21.6.6.1]

66.21.6.6.2 Maintenance and operating procedures and practices at tank storage facilities shall be established and implemented to control leakage and prevent spillage and release of ignitible (flammable or combustible) liquids. [**30**:21.6.6.2]

66.21.6.6.3 Ground areas around tank storage facilities shall be kept free of weeds, trash, and other unnecessary combustible materials. [**30**:21.6.6.3]

66.21.6.6.4 Accessways established for movement of personnel shall be maintained clear of obstructions to permit evacuation and access for manual fire fighting and emergency response in accordance with regulatory requirements and the emergency plan. [**30**:21.6.6.4]

66.21.6.6.5 Combustible waste material and residues in operating areas shall be kept to a minimum, stored in covered metal containers, and disposed of daily. [**30**:21.6.6.5]

66.21.6.6.6 Personnel responsible for the inspection and maintenance of fire protection and emergency response equipment shall be trained and shall be able to demonstrate knowledge of the inspection and maintenance of that equipment. Refresher training shall be conducted as needed to maintain proficiency. [**30**:21.6.6.6]

66.21.7 Operation of Storage Tanks.

66.21.7.1 Prevention of Overfilling of Storage Tanks. The procedures or equipment to prevent the overfilling of storage tanks shall comply with NFPA 30.

66.21.7.2 Identification and Security.

Δ **66.21.7.2.1 Identification for Emergency Responders.** A sign or marking that meets the requirements of NFPA 704 or another approved system shall be applied to storage tanks containing ignitible (flammable or combustible) liquids. The marking shall be located where it can be seen, such as on the side of the tank, the shoulder of an accessway or walkway to the tank or tanks, or on the piping outside of the diked area. If more than one tank is involved, the markings shall be so located that each tank can be identified. [**30**:21.7.2.1]

66.21.7.2.2* Security for Unsupervised Storage Tanks. Unsupervised, isolated aboveground storage tanks shall be secured and shall be marked to identify the fire hazards of the tank and the tank's contents to the general public. Where necessary to protect the tank from tampering or trespassing, the area where the tank is located shall be secured. [**30**:21.7.2.2]

66.21.7.3 Storage Tanks in Areas Subject to Flooding.

66.21.7.3.1 Tank Loading.

66.21.7.3.1.1 The filling of a tank to be protected by water or product loading shall be started as soon as floodwaters are predicted to reach a dangerous flood stage. [**30**:21.7.3.1.1]

66.21.7.3.1.2 Where independently fueled pumps are relied on, sufficient fuel shall be available at all times to permit continuing operations until all tanks are filled. [**30**:21.7.3.1.2]

66.21.7.3.1.3 Tank valves shall be locked in a closed position when loading has been completed. [**30**:21.7.3.1.3]

66.21.7.3.2 Operating Instructions. Operating instructions or procedures to be followed in a flood emergency shall be established and implemented by personnel identified in 66.21.7.3.3. [**30**:21.7.3.2]

66.21.7.3.3 Personnel Training. Personnel responsible for activating and performing flood emergency procedures shall be trained in their implementation and shall be informed of the location and operation of valves and other controls and equipment necessary to effect the intent of these procedures. Personnel shall also be trained in the procedures required to place the facility back into service following a flood emergency. [30:21.7.3.3]

N **66.21.7.4 Removal from Service of Storage Tanks.**

N **66.21.7.4.1* Closure of Aboveground Storage Tanks.** Aboveground tanks taken out of service or abandoned shall be emptied of ignitible (flammable or combustible) liquid, rendered vapor-free, and safeguarded against trespassing in accordance with NFPA 326 or in accordance with the requirements of the authority having jurisdiction. [30:21.7.4.1]

N **66.21.7.4.2 Reuse of Aboveground Storage Tanks.** Aboveground tanks shall be permitted to be reused for liquids service provided they comply with applicable sections of this *Code* and are approved. [30:21.7.4.2]

N **66.21.7.4.3 Removal from Service of Underground Storage Tanks.**

N **66.21.7.4.3.1* General.** Underground tanks taken out of service or abandoned shall be emptied of ignitible (flammable or combustible) liquid, rendered vapor-free, and safeguarded against trespassing in accordance with this section and in accordance with NFPA 326 or the requirements of the authority having jurisdiction. The procedures outlined in this section shall be followed when taking underground tanks temporarily out of service, closing them in place permanently, or removing them. [30:21.7.4.3.1]

N **66.21.7.4.3.2 Temporary Closure.** Underground tanks shall be rendered temporarily out of service only when it is planned that they will be returned to active service, closed in place permanently, or removed within an approved period not exceeding 1 year. The following requirements shall be met:

(1) Corrosion protection and release detection systems shall be maintained in operation.
(2) The vent line shall be left open and functioning.
(3) The tank shall be secured against tampering.
(4) All other lines shall be capped or plugged.
[30:21.7.4.3.2]

N **66.21.7.4.3.2.1** Tanks remaining temporarily out of service for more than 1 year shall be permanently closed in place or removed in accordance with 66.21.7.4.3.3 or 66.21.7.4.3.4, as applicable. [30:21.7.4.3.2.1]

N **66.21.7.4.3.3 Permanent Closure in Place.** Underground tanks shall be permitted to be permanently closed in place if approved by the authority having jurisdiction. All of the following requirements shall be met:

(1) All applicable authorities having jurisdiction shall be notified.
(2)* A safe workplace shall be maintained throughout the prescribed activities.
(3) All liquids and residues shall be removed from the tank, appurtenances, and piping and shall be disposed of in accordance with regulatory requirements and industry practices, using a written procedure.
(4) The tank, appurtenances, and piping shall be made safe by either purging them of flammable vapors or inerting the potential explosive atmosphere. Confirmation that the atmosphere in the tank is safe shall be by testing of the atmosphere using a combustible gas indicator if purging, or an oxygen meter if inerting, at intervals in accordance with written procedures.
(5) Access to the tank shall be made by careful excavation to the top of the tank.
(6) All exposed piping, gauging and tank fixtures, and other appurtenances, except the vent, shall be disconnected and removed.
(7) The tank shall be completely filled with an inert solid material.
(8) The tank vent and remaining underground piping shall be capped or removed.
(9) The tank excavation shall be backfilled.
[30:21.7.4.3.3]

N **66.21.7.4.3.4 Removal and Disposal.** Underground tanks and piping shall be removed in accordance with the following requirements:

(1) The steps described in 66.21.7.4.3.3(1) through 66.21.7.4.3.3(5) shall be followed.
(2) All exposed piping, gauging and tank fixtures, and other appurtenances, including the vent, shall be disconnected and removed.
(3) All openings shall be plugged, leaving a ¼ in. (6 mm) opening to avoid buildup of pressure in the tank.
(4) The tank shall be removed from the excavated site and shall be secured against movement.
(5) Any corrosion holes shall be plugged.
(6) The tank shall be labeled with its former contents, present vapor state, vapor-freeing method, and a warning against reuse.
(7) The tank shall be removed from the site as authorized by the authority having jurisdiction, preferably the same day.
[30:21.7.4.3.4]

N **66.21.7.4.3.5 Temporary Storage of Removed Tanks.** If it is necessary to temporarily store an underground tank that has been removed, it shall be placed in a secure area where public access is restricted. A ¼ in. (6 mm) opening shall be maintained to avoid buildup of pressure in the tank. [30:21.7.4.3.5]

N **66.21.7.4.3.6 Disposal of Tanks.** Disposal of underground tanks shall meet the following requirements:

(1) Before a tank is cut up for scrap or landfill, the atmosphere in the tank shall be tested in accordance with 66.21.7.4.3.3(4) to ensure that it is safe.
(2) The tank shall be made unfit for further use by cutting holes in the tank heads and shell.
[30:21.7.4.3.6]

N **66.21.7.4.3.7 Documentation.** All necessary documentation shall be prepared and maintained in accordance with all federal, state, and local rules and regulations. [30:21.7.4.3.7]

N **66.21.7.4.3.8 Reuse of Underground Storage Tanks.** Underground tanks shall be permitted to be reused for underground storage of liquids provided they comply with applicable sections of this code and are approved. [30:21.7.4.3.8]

66.21.7.5* Leak Detection and Inventory Records for Underground Storage Tanks. Accurate inventory records or a leak detection program shall be maintained on all Class I liquid [FP < 100°F (37.8°C)] storage tanks for indication of leakage from the tanks or associated piping. [30:21.7.5]

N **66.21.8 Inspection and Maintenance of Storage Tanks and Storage Tank Appurtenances.**

N **66.21.8.1*** Each storage tank constructed of steel shall be inspected and maintained in accordance with API Standard 653, *Tank Inspection, Repair, Alteration, and Reconstruction,* or STI SP001, *Standard for the Inspection of Aboveground Storage Tanks,* whichever is applicable. [**30:**21.8.1]

N **66.21.8.2** Each storage tank constructed of other materials shall be inspected and maintained in accordance with the manufacturer's instructions and applicable standards to ensure compliance with the requirements of this *Code*. [**30:**21.8.2]

N **66.21.8.3** Testing of storage tanks shall meet the requirements of 66.21.5. [**30:**21.8.3]

N **66.21.8.4** Each storage tank shall be maintained liquidtight. Each storage tank that is leaking shall be emptied of ignitible (flammable or combustible) liquid or repaired in a manner acceptable to the authority having jurisdiction. [**30:**21.8.4]

N **66.21.8.5** Each storage tank that has been structurally damaged, repaired, reconstructed, relocated, jacked, or damaged by impact, flood, or other trauma, or is suspected of leaking shall be inspected and tested in accordance with 66.21.5 or in a manner acceptable to the authority having jurisdiction. [**30:**21.8.5]

N **66.21.8.6*** Storage tanks and their appurtenances, including normal vents, emergency vents, overfill prevention devices, and related devices, shall be inspected and maintained to ensure that they function as intended in accordance with written procedures. [**30:**21.8.6]

N **66.21.8.7** Openings for gauging on storage tanks storing Class I liquids [FP < 100°F (37.8°C)] shall be provided with a vaportight cap or cover. Such covers shall be closed when not gauging. [**30:**21.8.7]

N **66.21.8.8*** Facilities with aboveground storage tanks shall establish and implement a procedure to check for and remove water from the bottom of storage tanks that contain nonmiscible ignitible (flammable or combustible) liquids. [**30:**21.8.8]

66.21.9 Change of Stored Liquid. Storage tanks that undergo any change of stored liquid shall be re-evaluated for compliance with Sections 66.21 through 66.25, as applicable. [**30:**21.9]

66.22 Storage of Ignitible (Flammable or Combustible) Liquids in Tanks — Aboveground Storage Tanks.

66.22.1 Scope. This section shall apply to the following:

(1) The storage of liquids, as defined in 3.3.33 of NFPA 30 and Section 66.4, in fixed tanks that exceed 60 gal (230 L) capacity
(2) The storage of liquids in portable tanks that exceed 660 gal (2500 L) capacity
(3) The storage of liquids in intermediate bulk containers that exceed 793 gal (3000 L)
(4) The design, installation, testing, operation, and maintenance of such tanks, portable tanks, and bulk containers

[**30:**22.1]

66.22.2 Definitions Specific to Section 66.22. For the purpose of this section, the terms in this section shall have the definitions given. [**30:**22.2]

66.22.2.1 Fire-Resistant Tank. An atmospheric aboveground storage tank with thermal insulation that has been evaluated for resistance to physical damage and for limiting the heat transferred to the primary tank when exposed to a hydrocarbon fuel fire and is listed in accordance with UL 2080, *Fire Resistant Tanks for Flammable and Combustible Liquids,* or an equivalent test procedure. [**30:**22.2.1]

66.22.2.2 Floating Roof Tank. An aboveground storage tank that incorporates one of the following designs:

(1) A closed-top pontoon or double-deck metal floating roof in an open-top tank constructed in accordance with API Standard 650, *Welded Steel Tanks for Oil Storage*
(2) A fixed metal roof with ventilation at the top and roof eaves constructed in accordance with API Standard 650 and containing a closed-top pontoon or double-deck metal floating roof meeting the requirements of API Standard 650
(3) A fixed metal roof with ventilation at the top and roof eaves constructed in accordance with API Standard 650 and containing a metal floating cover supported by liquidtight metal floating devices that provide buoyancy to prevent the liquid surface from being exposed when half of the flotation is lost

[**30:**22.2.2]

66.22.2.2.1 For the purposes of this section, an aboveground storage tank with an internal metal floating pan, roof, or cover that does not meet 66.22.2.2 or one that uses plastic foam (except for seals) for flotation, even if encapsulated in metal or fiberglass, shall meet the requirements for a fixed roof tank. [**30:**22.2.2.1]

66.22.2.3 Protected Aboveground Tank. An atmospheric aboveground storage tank with integral secondary containment and thermal insulation that has been evaluated for resistance to physical damage and for limiting the heat transferred to the primary tank when exposed to a hydrocarbon pool fire and is listed in accordance with UL 2085, *Protected Aboveground Tanks for Flammable and Combustible Liquids,* or an equivalent test procedure. [**30:**22.2.3]

66.22.3 General Requirements. Storage of Class II and Class III liquids [FP ≥ 100°F (37.8°C)] heated at or above their FP shall follow the requirements for Class I liquids [FP < 100°F (37.8°C)], unless an engineering evaluation conducted in accordance with Section 66.6 justifies following the requirements for some other liquid class. [**30:**22.3]

66.22.4* Location of Aboveground Storage Tanks.

66.22.4.1 Location with Respect to Property Lines, Public Ways, and Important Buildings.

66.22.4.1.1 Tanks storing Class I, Class II, or Class IIIA stable liquids [FP < 200°F (93°C)] whose internal pressure is not permitted to exceed a gauge pressure of 2.5 psi (17 kPa) shall be located in accordance with Table 66.22.4.1.1(a) and Table 66.22.4.1.1(b). Where tank spacing is based on a weak roof-to-shell seam design, the user shall present evidence certifying such construction to the AHJ upon request. [**30:**22.4.1.1]

Δ Table 66.22.4.1.1(a) Location of Aboveground Storage Tanks Storing Stable Liquids — Internal Pressure Not to Exceed a Gauge Pressure of 2.5 psi (17 kPa)

Type of Tank	Protection	Minimum Distance (ft) From Property Line That Is or Can Be Built Upon, Including the Opposite Side of a Public Way[a]	From Nearest Side of Any Public Way or from Nearest Important Building on the Same Property[a]
Floating roof	Protection for exposures[b]	½ × diameter of tank	⅙ × diameter of tank
	None	Diameter of tank but need not exceed 175 ft	⅙ × diameter of tank
Vertical with weak roof-to-shell seam	Approved foam or inerting system[c] on tanks not exceeding 150 ft in diameter[d]	½ × diameter of tank	⅙ × diameter of tank
	Protection for exposures[b]	Diameter of tank	⅓ × diameter of tank
	None	2 × diameter of tank but need not exceed 350 ft	⅓ × diameter of tank
Horizontal and vertical tanks with emergency relief venting to limit pressures to 2.5 psi (gauge pressure of 17 kPa)	Approved inerting system[c] on the tank or approved foam system on vertical tanks	½ × value in Table 66.22.4.1.1(b)	½ × value in Table 66.22.4.1.1(b)
	Protection for exposures[b]	Value in Table 66.22.4.1.1(b)	Value in Table 66.22.4.1.1(b)
	None	2 × value in Table 66.22.4.1.1(b)	Value in Table 66.22.4.1.1(b)
Protected aboveground tank	None	½ × value in Table 66.22.4.1.1(b)	½ × value in Table 66.22.4.1.1(b)

For SI units, 1 ft = 0.3 m.
[a]The minimum distance cannot be less than 5 ft (1.5 m).
[b]See definition 3.3.46 of NFPA 30, Protection for Exposures.
[c]See NFPA 69.
[d]For tanks over 150 ft (45 m) in diameter, use "Protection for Exposures" or "None," as applicable.
[30:Table 22.4.1.1(a)]

Table 66.22.4.1.1(b) Reference Table for Use with Tables 66.22.4.1.1(a), 66.22.4.1.3, and 66.22.4.1.5

Tank Capacity (gal)	Minimum Distance (ft) From Property Line that Is or Can Be Built Upon, Including the Opposite Side of a Public Way	From Nearest Side of Any Public Way or from Nearest Important Building on the Same Property
275 or less	5	5
276 to 750	10	5
751 to 12,000	15	5
12,001 to 30,000	20	5
30,001 to 50,000	30	10
50,001 to 100,000	50	15
100,001 to 500,000	80	25
500,001 to 1,000,000	100	35
1,000,001 to 2,000,000	135	45
2,000,001 to 3,000,000	165	55
3,000,001 or more	175	60

For SI units, 1 ft = 0.3 m; 1 gal = 3.8 L.
[30:Table 22.4.1.1(b)]

66.22.4.1.2 Vertical tanks with weak roof-to-shell seams *(see 22.7.2 of NFPA 30)* that store Class IIIA liquids [FP < 200°F (93°C)] shall be permitted to be located at one-half the distances specified in Table 66.22.4.1.1(a), provided the tanks are not within the same diked area as, or within the drainage path of, a tank storing a Class I or Class II liquid [FP < 140°F (60°C)]. [**30:**22.4.1.2]

66.22.4.1.3 Tanks storing Class I, Class II, or Class IIIA stable liquids [FP < 200°F (93°C)] and operating at pressures that exceed a gauge pressure of 2.5 psi (17 kPa), or are equipped with emergency venting that will permit pressures to exceed a gauge pressure of 2.5 psi (17 kPa), shall be located in accordance with Table 66.22.4.1.3 and Table 66.22.4.1.1(b). [**30:**22.4.1.3]

Δ **66.22.4.1.4 Tank Storage of Liquids with Boil-Over Characteristics.**

N **66.22.4.1.4.1** Tanks storing ignitible (flammable or combustible) liquids with boil-over characteristics shall be located in accordance with Table 66.22.4.1.4.1. [**30:**22.4.1.4.1]

N **66.22.4.1.4.2** Liquids with boil-over characteristics shall not be stored in fixed roof tanks larger than 150 ft (45 m) in diameter, unless an approved inerting system is provided on the tank. [**30:**22.4.1.4.2]

66.22.4.1.5 Tanks storing Class IIIB stable liquids [FP ≥ 200°F (93°C)] shall be located in accordance with Table 66.22.4.1.5, except if located within the same diked area as, or within the drainage path of, a tank storing a Class I or Class II liquid [FP < 140°F (60°C)]. [**30:**22.4.1.5]

N **66.22.4.1.5.1** Tanks storing Class IIIB liquid [FP ≥ 200°F (93°C)] that are located within the same diked area as, or within the drainage path of, a tank storing a Class I or Class II liquid [FP < 140°F (60°C)] shall be located in accordance with 66.22.4.1.1. [**30:**22.4.1.5.1]

66.22.4.1.6 Where two tank properties of diverse ownership have a common boundary, the AHJ shall be permitted, with the written consent of the owners of the two properties, to substitute the distances provided in 66.22.4.2 for the minimum distances set forth in 66.22.4.1.1. [**30:**22.4.1.6]

Table 66.22.4.1.3 Location of Aboveground Storage Tanks Storing Stable Liquids — Internal Pressure Permitted to Exceed a Gauge Pressure of 2.5 psi (17 kPa)

		Minimum Distance (ft)	
Type of Tank	Protection	From Property Line that Is or Can Be Built Upon, Including the Opposite Side of a Public Way	From Nearest Side of Any Public Way or from Nearest Important Building on the Same Property
Any type	Protection for exposures*	1½ × value in Table 66.22.4.1.1(b) but not less than 25 ft	1½ × value in Table 66.22.4.1.1(b) but not less than 25 ft
	None	3 × value in Table 66.22.4.1.1(b) but not less than 50 ft	1½ × value in Table 66.22.4.1.1(b) but not less than 25 ft

For SI units, 1 ft = 0.3 m.
*See definition 3.3.46 of NFPA 30, Protection for Exposures.
[**30:**Table 22.4.1.3]

Δ **Table 66.22.4.1.4.1 Location of Aboveground Storage Tanks Storing Boil-Over Ignitible (Flammable or Combustible) Liquids**

		Minimum Distance (ft)	
Type of Tank	Protection	From Property Line that Is or Can Be Built Upon, Including the Opposite Side of a Public Way[a]	From Nearest Side of Any Public Way or from Nearest Important Building on the Same Property[a]
Floating roof	Protection for exposures[b]	½ × diameter of tank	⅙ × diameter of tank
	None	Diameter of tank	⅙ × diameter of tank
Fixed roof	Approved foam or inerting system[c]	Diameter of tank	⅓ × diameter of tank
	Protection for exposures[b]	2 × diameter of tank	⅔ × diameter of tank
	None	4 × diameter of tank but need not exceed 350 ft	⅔ × diameter of tank

For SI units, 1 ft = 0.3 m.
[a]The minimum distance cannot be less than 5 ft.
[b]See definition 3.3.46 of NFPA 30, Protection for Exposures.
[c]See NFPA 69.
[**30:**Table 22.4.1.4.1]

Δ **Table 66.22.4.1.5 Location of Aboveground Storage Tanks Storing Class IIIB Liquids [FP ≥ 200°F (93°C)]**

Tank Capacity (gal)	Minimum Distance (ft) From Property Line that Is or Can Be Built Upon, Including the Opposite Side of a Public Way	From Nearest Side of Any Public Way or from Nearest Important Building on the Same Property
12,000 or less	5	5
12,001 to 30,000	10	5
30,001 to 50,000	10	10
50,001 to 100,000	15	10
100,001 or more	15	15

For SI units, 1 ft = 0.3 m; 1 gal = 3.8 L.
[**30**:Table 22.4.1.5]

66.22.4.1.7 Where end failure of a horizontal pressure tank or vessel can expose property, the tank or vessel shall be placed with its longitudinal axis parallel to the nearest important exposure. [**30**:22.4.1.7]

66.22.4.2 Shell-to-Shell Spacing of Adjacent Aboveground Storage Tanks.

66.22.4.2.1* Tanks storing Class I, Class II, or Class IIIA stable liquids [FP < 200°F (93°C) and any BP] shall be separated by the distances given in Table 66.22.4.2.1. [**30**:22.4.2.1]

66.22.4.2.1.1 Tanks that store crude petroleum, have individual capacities not exceeding 3000 bbl [126,000 gal (480 m³)], and are located at production facilities in isolated locations shall not be required to be separated by more than 3 ft (0.9 m). [**30**:22.4.2.1.1]

66.22.4.2.1.2 Tanks used only for storing Class IIIB liquids [FP ≥ 200°F (93°C)] shall not be required to be separated by more than 3 ft (0.9 m) provided they are not within the same diked area as, or within the drainage path of, a tank storing a Class I or Class II liquid [FP < 140°F (60°C)]. If located within the same diked area as, or within the drainage path of, a tank storing a Class I or Class II liquid [FP < 140°F (60°C)], the tank storing Class IIIB liquid [FP ≥ 200°F (93°C)] shall be spaced in accordance with the requirements for Class IIIA liquids [140°F (60°C) ≤ FP < 200°F (93°C)] in Table 66.22.4.2.1. [**30**:22.4.2.1.2]

66.22.4.2.2 Where tanks are in a diked area containing Class I or Class II liquids [FP < 140°F (60°C)] or in the drainage path of Class I or Class II liquids [FP < 140°F (60°C)] and are compacted in three or more rows or in an irregular pattern, greater spacing or other means shall be permitted to be required by the AHJ to make tanks in the interior of the pattern accessible for firefighting purposes. [**30**:22.4.2.2]

66.22.4.2.3* The minimum horizontal separation between an LP-Gas container and a Class I, Class II, or Class IIIA [FP< 200°F (93°C)] liquid storage tank shall be 20 ft (6 m). [**30**:22.4.2.3]

Δ **Table 66.22.4.2.1 Minimum Shell-to-Shell Spacing of Aboveground Storage Tanks**

Tank Diameter	Floating Roof Tanks	Fixed Roof or Horizontal Tanks Class I or Class II Liquids [FP < 140°F (60°C)]	Class IIIA Liquids [140°F (60°C) ≤ FP < 200°F (93°C)]
All tanks not over 150 ft (45 m) in diameter	⅙ × sum of adjacent tank diameters but not less than 3 ft (0.9 m)	⅙ × sum of adjacent tank diameters but not less than 3 ft (0.9 m)	⅙ × sum of adjacent tank diameters but not less than 3 ft (0.9 m)
Tanks larger than 150 ft (45 m) in diameter:			
If remote impounding is provided in accordance with 66.22.11.1	⅙ × sum of adjacent tank diameters	¼ × sum of adjacent tank diameters	⅙ × sum of adjacent tank diameters
If open diking is provided in accordance with 66.22.11.2	¼ × sum of adjacent tank diameters	⅓ × sum of adjacent tank diameters	¼ × sum of adjacent tank diameters

Notes:
(1) The "sum of adjacent tank diameters" means the sum of the diameters of each pair of tanks that are adjacent to each other. See also A.66.22.4.2.1.
(2) The separation distances in Table 66.22.4.2.1 are minimum requirements. Where thermal radiant heat flux modeling completed as part of an engineering evaluation shows potential escalation to adjacent tanks, distances could be increased, or mitigation measures could be implemented. (See Annex F of NFPA 30.)

[**30**:Table 22.4.2.1]

66.22.4.2.3.1 Means shall be provided to prevent Class I, Class II, or Class IIIA liquids [FP < 200°F (93°C)] from accumulating under adjacent LP-Gas containers by means of dikes, diversion curbs, or grading. [30:22.4.2.3.1]

66.22.4.2.3.2 Where liquid storage tanks are within a diked area, the LP-Gas containers shall be outside the diked area and at least 10 ft (3 m) away from the centerline of the wall of the diked area. [30:22.4.2.3.2]

Δ **66.22.4.2.4** If a tank storing a Class I, Class II, or Class IIIA liquid [FP < 200°F (93°C)] operates at pressures exceeding a gauge pressure of 2.5 psi (17 kPa) or is equipped with emergency relief venting that will permit pressures to exceed a gauge pressure of 2.5 psi (17 kPa), it shall be separated from an LP-Gas container by the appropriate distance given in Table 66.22.4.2.1. [30:22.4.2.4]

66.22.4.2.5 The requirements of 66.22.4.2.3 shall not apply where LP-Gas containers of 125 gal (475 L) or less capacity are installed adjacent to fuel oil supply tanks of 660 gal (2500 L) or less capacity. [30:22.4.2.5]

66.22.5 Installation of Aboveground Storage Tanks.

66.22.5.1 Tank Supports.

66.22.5.1.1 Tank supports shall be designed and constructed in accordance with recognized engineering standards. [30:22.5.1.1]

66.22.5.1.2 Tanks shall be supported in a manner that prevents excessive concentration of loads on the supported portion of the shell. [30:22.5.1.2]

66.22.5.1.3 In areas subject to earthquakes, tank supports and connections shall be designed to resist damage as a result of such shocks. [30:22.5.1.3]

66.22.5.2 Foundations for and Anchoring of Aboveground Storage Tanks.

66.22.5.2.1* Tanks shall rest on the ground or on foundations made of concrete, masonry, piling, or steel. [30:22.5.2.1]

66.22.5.2.2 Tank foundations shall be designed to minimize the possibility of uneven settling of the tank and to minimize corrosion in any part of the tank resting on the foundation. [30:22.5.2.2]

Δ **66.22.5.2.3** Where tanks storing Class I, Class II, or Class IIIA liquids [FP < 200°F (93°C)] are supported above their foundations, tank supports shall be of concrete, masonry, or protected steel.

N **66.22.5.2.4** Single wood timber supports (not cribbing), laid horizontally, shall be permitted to be used for outside aboveground tanks if not more than 12 in. (300 mm) high at their lowest point. [30:22.5.2.4]

Δ **66.22.5.2.5*** Steel support structures or exposed piling for tanks storing Class I, Class II, or Class IIIA liquids [FP < 200°F (93°C)] shall be protected by materials having a fire resistance rating of not less than 2 hours. [30:22.5.2.5]

N **66.22.5.2.5.1** Steel saddles less than 12 in. (300 mm) high at their lowest point shall not require fire protection per 66.22.5.2.5. [30:22.5.2.5.1]

N **66.22.5.2.5.2** At the discretion of the AHJ, water spray protection in accordance with NFPA 15 or NFPA 13 shall be permitted to be used. [30:22.5.2.5.2]

66.22.5.2.6 Where a tank is located in an area subject to flooding, provisions shall be taken to prevent tanks, either full or empty, from floating or sliding during a rise in water level up to the established maximum flood stage. *(See 66.21.7.3.)* [30:22.5.2.6]

N **66.22.5.3** Flat bottom, vertical cylindrical tanks constructed in accordance with API 650, *Welded Tanks for Oil Storage*, shall be anchored to a concrete ringwall or other suitable foundation under the following conditions:

(1) The tank internal pressure exceeds the equivalent pressure of the weight of the tank shell, roof, and roof framing.
(2) The tank must be anchored to comply with the weak roof-to-shell criteria.
(3) Under the design criteria for the tank, including all applicable load combinations, anchorage is required to prevent overturning due to wind or seismic loads.

[30:22.5.3]

66.22.6 Vent Piping for Aboveground Tanks. Piping for normal and emergency relief venting shall be constructed in accordance with Section 66.27. [30:22.6]

66.22.7 Emergency Relief Venting for Fire Exposure for Aboveground Storage Tanks.

66.22.7.1 General.

66.22.7.1.1* Every aboveground storage tank shall have emergency relief venting in the form of construction or a device or devices that will relieve excessive internal pressure caused by an exposure fire. [30:22.7.1.1]

66.22.7.1.1.1 The requirement in 66.22.7.1.1 shall apply to each compartment of a compartmented tank, the interstitial space (i.e., annulus) of a secondary containment–type tank, and the enclosed space of tanks of closed-top dike construction. [30:22.7.1.1.1]

Δ **66.22.7.1.1.2 Spaces or Enclosed Volumes.**

N **66.22.7.1.1.2.1** The requirement in 66.22.7.1.1 shall also apply to spaces or enclosed volumes, such as those intended for insulation, membranes, or weather shields, that are capable of containing liquid because of a leak from the primary vessel. [30:22.7.1.1.2.1]

N **66.22.7.1.1.2.2** The insulation, membrane, or weather shield shall not interfere with emergency venting. [30:22.7.1.1.2.2]

66.22.7.1.1.2.3 Tanks storing Class IIIB liquids [FP ≥ 200°F (93°C)] that are larger than 12,000 gal (45,400 L) capacity and are not within the diked area or the drainage path of tanks storing Class I or Class II liquids [FP < 140°F (60°C)] shall not be required to meet the requirements of 66.22.7.1.1. [30:22.7.1.1.2.3]

66.22.7.1.2 For vertical tanks, the emergency relief venting construction referred to in 66.22.7.1.1 shall be permitted to be a floating roof, a lifter roof, a weak roof-to-shell seam, or another approved pressure-relieving construction. [30:22.7.1.2]

N **66.22.7.1.3** If two-phase flow is anticipated during emergency venting, an engineering evaluation shall be conducted in order to size the pressure-relieving devices. [**30:**22.7.1.3]

N **66.22.7.2 Weak Roof-to-Shell Seam Construction.** If used, a weak roof-to-shell seam shall be constructed to fail preferential to any other seam and shall be designed in accordance with API Standard 650, *Welded Steel Tanks for Oil Storage*. [**30:**22.7.2]

66.22.7.3 Pressure-Relieving Devices.

66.22.7.3.1* Where entire dependence for emergency relief venting is placed upon pressure-relieving devices, the total venting capacity of both normal and emergency vents shall be sufficient to prevent rupture of the shell or bottom of a vertical tank or of the shell or heads of a horizontal tank. [**30:**22.7.3.1]

N **66.22.7.3.2** Except as provided for in 22.7.3.5, 22.7.3.6, and 22.7.3.7 in NFPA 30, the total emergency relief venting capacity of both normal and emergency venting devices shall be not less than that determined in Table 66.22.7.3.2. *(See Annex C in NFPA 30 for the square footage of typical tank sizes.)*

66.22.7.3.2.1 Emergency relief vent devices shall be vaportight and restricted to one of the following:

(1) Self-closing manway cover
(2) Manway cover provided with long bolts that permit the cover to lift under internal pressure
(3) Additional or larger relief valve or valves
[**30:**22.7.3.2.1]

66.22.7.3.3 The outlets of all vents and vent drains on tanks equipped with emergency relief venting that permits pressures to exceed a gauge pressure of 2.5 psi (17.2 kPa) shall be arranged to discharge so that localized overheating of or flame impingement on any part of the tank will not occur if vapors from the vents are ignited. [**30:**22.7.3.9]

66.22.7.3.4* Each commercial tank venting device shall have the following information either stamped or cast into the metal body of the device or included on a metal nameplate permanently affixed to it:

(1) Start-to-open pressure
(2) Pressure at which the valve reaches the full open position
(3) Flow capacity at the pressure indicated by 66.22.7.3.4(2)
[**30:**22.7.3.10]

N **66.22.7.3.4.1** Where used, emergency vent devices shall be listed or approved. [**30:**22.7.3.10.1]

N **66.22.7.3.4.1.1** The requirement in 66.22.7.3.4.1 does not apply to tanks for upstream production liquids. [**30:**22.7.3.10.1.1]

N **66.22.7.3.4.2** If the start-to-open pressure is less than a gauge pressure of 2.5 psi (17.2 kPa) and the pressure at the full open position is greater than a gauge pressure of 2.5 psi (17.2 kPa), the flow capacity at a gauge pressure of 2.5 psi (17.2 kPa) shall also be stamped on the venting device. [**30:**22.7.3.10.2]

N **66.22.7.3.4.3** The flow capacity shall be expressed in cubic feet per hour of air at 60°F (15.6°C) and an absolute pressure of 14.7 psi (101 kPa). [**30:**22.7.3.10.3]

N **66.22.7.3.4.4** The flow capacity of tank venting devices less than 8 in. (200 mm) in nominal pipe size shall be determined by actual test *(see 66.22.7.3.4.5)*. [**30:**22.7.3.10.4]

N **66.22.7.3.4.5** The tests referenced in 66.22.7.3.4.4 shall be permitted to be conducted by a qualified, impartial outside agency or by the manufacturer if certified by a qualified, impartial observer. [**30:**22.7.3.10.5]

N **66.22.7.3.4.6*** The flow capacity of tank venting devices equal to or greater than 8 in. (200 mm) nominal pipe size, including manway covers with long bolts, shall be determined by test or by calculation. [**30:**22.7.3.10.6]

N **66.22.7.3.4.7** If the flow capacity referenced in 66.22.7.3.4.6 is determined by calculation, all of the following shall apply:

(1) The opening pressure shall be measured by test.
(2) The calculation shall be based on a flow coefficient of 0.5 applied to the rated orifice.
(3) The rating pressure and corresponding free orifice area shall be stated.
(4) The word calculated shall appear on the nameplate.
[**30:**22.7.3.10.7]

66.22.7.4* Extension of Emergency Vent Piping. Piping to or from approved emergency vent devices for atmospheric and low-pressure tanks shall be sized to provide emergency vent flows that limit the back pressure to less than the maximum pressure permitted by the design of the tank. Piping to or from approved emergency vent devices for pressure vessels shall be sized in accordance with the ASME *Boiler and Pressure Vessel Code*. [**30:**22.7.4]

Δ **66.22.8* Fire Protection for Aboveground Storage Tanks.**

Δ **66.22.8.1** A fire-extinguishing system or exposure protection system in accordance with NFPA 11 or NFPA 15 shall be provided or made available for a storage tank where all of the following conditions apply:

(1) The tank is a vertical atmospheric storage tank that has a capacity of 50,000 gal (190 m³) or more.
(2) The tank contains a Class I liquid [FP < 100°F (37.8°C)].

N **Table 66.22.7.3.2 Required Emergency Relief Venting — Cubic Feet of Free Air per Hour (CFH) versus Wetted Area of Tank Shell (ft²)**

ft²	CFH	ft²	CFH	ft²	CFH
20	21,100	160	168,000	900	493,000
30	31,600	180	190,000	1000	524,000
40	42,100	200	211,000	1200	557,000
50	52,700	250	239,000	1400	587,000
60	63,200	300	265,000	1600	614,000
70	73,700	350	288,000	1800	639,000
80	84,200	400	312,000	2000	662,000
90	94,800	500	354,000	2400	704,000
100	105,000	600	392,000	2800	742,000
120	126,000	700	428,000	and over	
140	147,000	800	462,000		

For SI units, 10 ft² = 0.93 m²; 36 ft³ = 1.0 m³.

Notes:
(1) Interpolate for intermediate values not specified in the table.
(2) CFH is flow capacity at absolute pressure of 14.7 psi (101 kPa) and 60°F (15.6°C). See 22.7.3.10.2 of NFPA 30.

(3) The tank is located in a congested area where there is an unusual exposure hazard to the tank from adjacent property or to adjacent property from the tank.

(4) The tank has a fixed-roof or a combination fixed- and floating-roof that does not meet the requirements of 66.22.2.2(2) or 66.22.2.2(3) to be classified as a floating roof tank.

[30:22.8.1]

66.22.9 Additional Requirements for Fire-Resistant Aboveground Storage Tanks.

66.22.9.1 Fire-resistant tanks shall be tested and listed in accordance with UL 2080, *Fire Resistant Tanks for Flammable and Combustible Liquids.* [30:22.9.1]

N **66.22.9.2** Fire-resistant tanks shall also meet both of the following requirements:

(1) The construction that provides the required fire-resistive protection shall reduce the heat transferred to the primary tank in order to limit the temperature of the primary tank to an average maximum rise of 800°F (430°C) and a single point maximum rise of 1000°F (540°C) and to prevent release of liquid, failure of the primary tank, failure of the supporting structure, and impairment of venting for a period of not less than 2 hours when tested using the fire exposure specified in UL 2080.

(2) Reduction in sizing of the emergency vents in accordance with 22.7.3.5 of NFPA 30 shall not be permitted.

[30:22.9.2]

66.22.10 Additional Requirements for Protected Aboveground Storage Tanks.

66.22.10.1 Protected aboveground tanks shall be tested and listed in accordance with UL 2085, *Protected Aboveground Tanks for Flammable and Combustible Liquids.* [30:22.10.1]

N **66.22.10.2** Protected aboveground tanks shall also meet both of the following requirements:

(1) The construction that provides the required fire-resistive protection shall reduce the heat transferred to the primary tank in order to limit the temperature of the primary tank to an average maximum rise of 260°F (144°C) and a single point maximum rise of 400°F (204°C) and to prevent release of ignitible (flammable or combustible) liquid, failure of the primary tank, failure of the supporting structure, and impairment of venting for a period of not less than 2 hours when tested using the fire exposure specified in UL 2085, *Protected Aboveground Tanks for Flammable and Combustible Liquids.*

(2) Reduction in sizing of the emergency vents in accordance with 22.7.3.5 of NFPA 30 shall not be permitted.

[30:22.10.2]

66.22.11* Control of Spills from Aboveground Storage Tanks. Every tank that contains a Class I, Class II, or Class IIIA liquid [FP < 200°F (93°C)] shall be provided with means to prevent an accidental release of liquid from endangering important facilities and adjoining property or from reaching waterways. Such means shall meet the requirements of 66.22.11.1, 66.22.11.2, 66.22.11.3, or 66.22.11.4, whichever is applicable. [30:22.11]

66.22.11.1 Remote Impounding. Where control of spills is provided by drainage to a remote impounding area so that spilled ignitible (flammable or combustible) liquid does not collect around tanks, the requirements of 66.22.11.1.1 through 66.22.11.1.4 shall apply. [30:22.11.1]

66.22.11.1.1 The drainage route shall have a slope of not less than 1 percent away from the tank for at least 50 ft (15 m) toward the impounding area. [30:22.11.1.1]

Δ **66.22.11.1.2** The impounding area shall have a capacity not less than that of the largest tank that drains into it. [30:22.11.1.2]

N **66.22.11.1.2.1** "Partial" remote impounding for a percentage of the required capacity shall be permitted where compliance with 66.22.11.1.2 is not possible. [30:22.11.1.2.1]

N **66.22.11.1.2.2** Where "partial" remote impounding is used, open diking meeting the requirements of 66.22.11.1.2 shall be permitted for the remainder of the spill control volume. [30:22.11.1.2.2]

66.22.11.1.3 The drainage route shall be located so that, if the liquid in the drainage system is ignited, the fire will not seriously expose tanks or adjoining property. [30:22.11.1.3]

Δ **66.22.11.1.4** The impounding area shall be located so that, when filled to capacity, the liquid will not be closer than 50 ft (15 m) from any property line that is or can be built upon or from any tank. [30:22.11.1.4]

N **66.22.11.1.4.1** Where partial remote impounding as provided for in 66.22.11.1.2.1 and 66.22.11.1.2.2 is used, the liquid in the partial remote impounding area shall meet the requirements of 66.22.11.1.4. [30:22.11.1.4.1]

N **66.22.11.1.4.2** Tank spacing shall be determined based on the diked tank provisions of Table 66.22.4.2.1.

66.22.11.2 Impounding Around Tanks by Open Diking. Where control of spills is provided by means of impounding by open diking around the tanks, such systems shall meet the requirements of 22.11.2.1 through 22.11.2.8 of NFPA 30. [30:22.11.2]

N **66.22.11.2.1** A slope of not less than 1 percent away from the tank shall be provided for at least 50 ft (15 m) or to the dike base, whichever is less. [30:22.11.2.1]

N **66.22.11.2.2*** The volumetric capacity of the diked area shall not be less than the greatest amount of ignitible (flammable or combustible) liquid that can be released from the largest tank within the diked area, assuming a full tank. [30:22.11.2.2]

N **66.22.11.2.2.1** To allow for volume occupied by tanks, the capacity of the diked area enclosing more than one tank shall be calculated after deducting the volume of the tanks, other than the largest tank, below the height of the dike. [30:22.11.2.2.1]

N **66.22.11.2.3** To permit access, the outside base of the dike at ground level shall be no closer than 10 ft (3 m) to any property line that is or can be built upon. [30:22.11.2.3]

N **66.22.11.2.4** Walls of the diked area shall be of earth, steel, concrete, or solid masonry designed to be liquidtight and to withstand a full hydrostatic head. [30:22.11.2.4]

N **66.22.11.2.4.1*** Earthen walls 3 ft (0.9 m) or more in height shall have a flat section at the top not less than 2 ft (0.6 m) wide and shall have a slope that is consistent with the angle of repose of the material of which the wall is constructed. [**30:**22.11.2.4.1]

N **66.22.11.2.5** Where the average interior height of the walls of the diked area exceeds 6 ft (1.8 m), provisions shall be made for normal access; necessary emergency access to tanks, valves, and other equipment; and egress from the diked enclosure. The following requirements shall apply:

(1) Where the average height of a dike containing Class I liquids [FP < 100°F (37.8°C)] is over 12 ft (3.6 m) high, measured from interior grade, or where the distance between any tank and the top inside edge of the dike wall is less than the height of the dike wall, provisions shall be made for operation of valves and for access to tank roof(s) without entering below the top of the dike. These provisions shall be permitted to be met through the use of remote-operated valves, elevated walkways, or other arrangements.
(2) Piping passing through dike walls shall be designed to withstand imposed stresses as a result of settlement or fire exposure.
(3) The distance between the shell of any tank and the toe of the interior of the dike wall shall be not less than 5 ft (1.5 m).

[**30:**22.11.2.5]

N **66.22.11.2.6** Each diked area containing two or more tanks shall be subdivided, preferably by drainage channels or at least by intermediate dikes, in order to prevent minor spills from a tank from endangering adjacent tanks within the diked area. [**30:**22.11.2.6]

N **66.22.11.2.6.1** The drainage channels or intermediate dikes shall be located between tanks so as to take full advantage of the space with due regard for the individual tank capacities. [**30:**22.11.2.6.1]

N **66.22.11.2.6.2** Intermediate dikes shall be not less than 18 in. (450 mm) in height. [**30:**22.11.2.6.2]

N **66.22.11.2.6.3** Subdivision shall be provided according to the requirements of 66.22.11.2.6.3.1, 66.22.11.2.6.3.2, 66.22.11.2.6.3.3, or 66.22.11.2.6.3.4, whichever is applicable. [**30:**22.11.2.6.3]

N **66.22.11.2.6.3.1** Where stable liquids are stored in vertical cone roof tanks of weak roof-to-shell seam design or in floating roof tanks, one subdivision shall be provided for each tank greater than 10,000 bbl (420,000 gal or 1590 m^3) capacity. In addition, one subdivision shall be provided for each group of tanks [with no individual tank exceeding 10,000 bbl (420,000 gal or 1590 m^3) capacity] having an aggregate capacity not greater than 15,000 bbl (630,000 gal or 2385 m^3). [**30:**22.11.2.6.3.1]

N **66.22.11.2.6.3.2** Where crude petroleum is stored in producing areas in any type of tank, one subdivision shall be provided for each tank greater than 10,000 bbl (420,000 gal or 1590 m^3) capacity. In addition, one subdivision shall be provided for each group of tanks [with no individual tank exceeding 10,000 bbl (420,000 gal or 1590 m^3) capacity] having an aggregate capacity not greater than 15,000 bbl (630,000 gal or 2385 m^3). [**30:**22.11.2.6.3.2]

N **66.22.11.2.6.3.3** Where stable liquids are stored in tanks not covered in 66.22.11.2.6.3.1, one subdivision shall be provided for each tank greater than 2380 bbl (100,000 gal or 380 m^3) capacity. In addition, one subdivision shall be provided for each group of tanks [with no individual tank exceeding 2380 bbl (100,000 gal or 380 m^3) capacity] having an aggregate capacity not greater than 3750 bbl (150,000 gal or 570 m^3). [**30:**22.11.2.6.3.3]

N **66.22.11.2.6.3.4** Whenever two or more tanks storing Class I liquids [FP < 100°F (37.8°C)], any one of which is over 150 ft (45 m) in diameter, are located in a common diked area, intermediate dikes shall be provided between adjacent tanks to hold at least 10 percent of the capacity of the tank so enclosed, not including the volume displaced by the tank. [**30:**22.11.2.6.3.4]

66.22.11.2.7 Where provision is made for draining water from diked areas, such drains shall be controlled to prevent ignitible (flammable or combustible) liquids from entering natural water courses, public sewers, or public drains. [**30:**22.11.2.7]

66.22.11.2.7.1 Control of drainage shall be accessible under fire conditions from outside the dike. [**30:**22.11.2.7.1]

66.22.11.2.7.2 Storage of combustible materials, empty drums, full drums, or barrels shall not be permitted within the diked area. [**30:**22.11.2.8]

66.22.11.3 Impounding Around Tanks by Closed-Top Diking. Where control of spills is provided by means of impounding by closed-top diking around the tanks, such systems shall meet all of the requirements of 66.22.11.4 or shall meet the requirements of 66.22.11.3.1 through 66.22.11.3.4. [**30:**22.11.3]

N **66.22.11.3.1*** The volumetric capacity of the diked area shall not be less than the greatest amount of ignitible (flammable or combustible) liquid that can be released from the largest tank within the diked area, assuming a full tank. [**30:**22.11.3.1]

N **66.22.11.3.2** To allow for volume occupied by tanks, the capacity of the diked area enclosing more than one tank shall be calculated after deducting the volume of the tanks, other than the largest tank, below the height of the dike. [**30:**22.11.3.2]

N **66.22.11.3.3** To permit access, the outside base of the dike at ground level shall be no closer than 10 ft (3 m) to any property line that is or can be built upon. [**30:**22.11.3.3]

N **66.22.11.3.4*** Walls of the diked area shall be of steel, concrete, or solid masonry designed to be liquidtight and to withstand a full hydrostatic head. [**30:**22.11.3.4]

N **66.22.11.3.5** Where provision is made for draining water from diked areas, such drains shall be controlled to prevent ignitible (flammable or combustible) liquids from entering natural water courses, public sewers, or public drains. [**30:**22.11.3.5]

66.22.11.3.5.1 Control of drainage shall be accessible under fire conditions from outside the dike. [**30:**22.11.3.5.1]

66.22.11.3.6 Storage of combustible materials, empty drums, full drums, or barrels shall not be permitted within the diked area. [**30:**22.11.3.6]

N **66.22.11.3.7** The capacity of the primary tank shall not exceed that given in 66.22.11.4.1. [**30:**22.11.3.7]

N **66.22.11.3.8** All piping connections to the tank shall be made above the normal maximum liquid level. [**30:**22.11.3.8]

N **66.22.11.3.9** The tank shall be capable of resisting the damage from the impact of a motor vehicle, or collision barriers shall be provided. [**30:**22.11.3.9]

N **66.22.11.3.10** Where the means of secondary containment is enclosed, it shall be provided with emergency venting in accordance with 66.22.7. [**30:**22.11.3.10]

N **66.22.11.3.11** Means shall be provided to establish the integrity of the secondary containment, in accordance with Chapter 21 of NFPA 30. [**30:**22.11.3.11]

N **66.22.11.3.12** Where the normal vent or the emergency vent device or both discharge outside the enclosure created by the closed-top diking, the tank within the enclosure shall comply with 66.22.11.4.4 and 66.22.11.4.5. [**30:**22.11.3.12]

N **66.22.11.3.13** Where the fill connection for the tank within the enclosure created by the closed-top diking is not located within the enclosure, the tank shall meet the requirements of 66.22.11.4.4 and 66.22.11.4.5. [**30:**22.11.3.13]

66.22.11.4 Secondary Containment–Type Aboveground Storage Tanks. Where a secondary containment–type tank is used to provide spill control, the tank shall meet all of the requirements of 66.22.11.4.1 through 66.22.11.4.10. [**30:**22.11.4]

N **66.22.11.4.1** The capacity of the listed primary tank for Class I, Class II, and Class IIIA liquids [FP < 200°F (93°C)] shall not exceed 50,000 gal (189,000 L). [**30:**22.11.4.1]

N **66.22.11.4.2** All piping connections to the tank shall be made above the maximum liquid level. [**30:**22.11.4.2]

N **66.22.11.4.3** Means shall be provided to prevent the release of liquid from the tank by siphon flow. [**30:**22.11.4.3]

N **66.22.11.4.4** Means shall be provided for determining the level of liquid in the tank. This means shall be accessible to the delivery operator. [**30:**22.11.4.4]

N **66.22.11.4.5** Means shall be provided to prevent overfilling by sounding an alarm when the liquid level in the tank is no more than 90 percent of capacity or by automatically stopping delivery of liquid to the tank when the liquid level in the tank is no more than 95 percent of capacity. [**30:**22.11.4.5]

N **66.22.11.4.5.1** In no case shall these provisions restrict or interfere with the functioning of the normal vent or the emergency vent. [**30:**22.11.4.5.1]

N **66.22.11.4.5.2*** When used, overfill prevention devices shall be listed or approved (*see 66.22.11.4.5.2.1*). [**30:**22.11.4.5.2]

N **66.22.11.4.5.2.1** The requirement in 66.22.11.4.5.2 does not apply to tanks in API 620, *Design and Construction of Large, Welded, Low-pressure Storage Tanks*, and API 650, *Welded Tanks for Oil Storage*, or tanks for upstream production liquids. [**30:**22.11.4.5.2.1]

66.22.11.4.6 Spacing between adjacent tanks shall comply with Table 66.22.4.2.1. [**30:**22.11.4.6]

66.22.11.4.7 The tank shall be capable of resisting the damage from the impact of a motor vehicle, or collision barriers shall be provided. [**30:**22.11.4.7]

66.22.11.4.8 Where the means of secondary containment is enclosed, it shall be provided with emergency venting in accordance with 66.22.7. [**30:**22.11.4.8]

N **66.22.11.4.9** Means shall be provided to establish the integrity of the secondary containment, in accordance with Chapter 21 of NFPA 30. [**30:**22.11.4.9]

N **66.22.11.4.10** The secondary containment shall be designed to withstand the hydrostatic head resulting from a leak from the primary tank of the maximum amount of liquid that can be stored in the primary tank. [**30:**22.11.4.10]

66.22.12 Equipment, Piping, and Fire Protection Systems in Remote Impoundment Areas and Diked Areas.

Δ **66.22.12.1 Location of Piping.**

N **66.22.12.1.1** Only piping for product, utility, or fire protection purposes directly connected to a tank or tanks within a single diked area shall be routed through a diked area, a remote impoundment area, a spillway draining to a remote impoundment area, or above a storage tank drainage area where the piping can be exposed to a fire. [**30:**22.12.1.1]

N **66.22.12.1.2*** Piping for other product lines and from adjacent tanks is permitted to be routed through such areas if engineering designs are provided to incorporate features to prevent the piping from creating an exposure hazard. [**30:**22.12.1.2]

66.22.12.2 Drainage.

66.22.12.2.1 Drainage shall be provided to prevent accumulation of any ignitible (flammable or combustible) liquid under the piping by providing a slope of not less than 1 percent away from the piping for at least 50 ft (15 m). [**30:**22.12.2.1]

66.22.12.2.2 Corrosion-resistant piping and piping that is protected against corrosion shall be permitted to be buried where such drainage is not provided. [**30:**22.12.2.2]

66.22.12.3* Location of Equipment. If located in a remote impoundment area, a diked area, or a spillway draining to a remote impoundment area, process equipment, pumps, instrumentation, and electrical utilization equipment shall be located or protected so that a fire involving such equipment does not constitute an exposure hazard to the tank or tanks in the same area for a period of time consistent with emergency response capabilities. [**30:**22.12.3]

66.22.12.4 Fire Protection Systems. Hose connections, controls, and control valves for application of fire protection foam or water to tanks shall be located outside remote impoundment areas, diked areas, or spillways draining to a remote impoundment area. [**30:**22.12.4]

66.22.12.5 Combustible Materials. Structures such as stairways, walkways, instrumentation shelters, and supports for piping and equipment that are located in a remote impoundment area, diked area, or spillway draining to a remote impoundment area shall be constructed of noncombustible materials. [**30:**22.12.5]

66.22.13 Tank Openings Other Than Vents.

66.22.13.1 Each connection to an aboveground tank through which liquid can normally flow shall be provided with an internal or an external valve located as close as practical to the shell of the tank. [**30:**22.13.1]

66.22.13.2 Each connection below the liquid level through which liquid does not normally flow shall be provided with a liquidtight closure such as a valve, plug, or blind, or a combination of these. [**30:**22.13.2]

66.22.13.3 Openings for gauging on tanks storing Class I liquids [FP < 100°F (37.8°C)] shall be provided with a vapor-tight cap or cover. [**30**:22.13.3]

66.22.13.4 Filling and emptying connections for Class I, Class II, and Class IIIA liquids [FP < 200°F (93°C)] that are connected and disconnected shall be located outside of buildings at a location free from any source of ignition. [**30**:22.13.4]

66.22.13.4.1 Such connections shall be located not less than 5 ft (1.5 m) away from any building opening. [**30**:22.13.4.1]

66.22.13.4.2 Such connections for any ignitible (flammable or combustible) liquid shall be closed and liquidtight when not in use and shall be properly identified. [**30**:22.13.4.2]

66.22.14 Aboveground Storage Tanks Located in Areas Subject to Flooding.

66.22.14.1 Vertical tanks shall be located so that the tops of the tanks extend above the maximum flood stage by at least 30 percent of their allowable storage capacity. [**30**:22.14.1]

66.22.14.2 Horizontal tanks that are located where more than 70 percent of the tank's storage capacity will be submerged at the established flood stage shall be secured by one of the following methods:

(1) Anchored to resist movement
(2) Attached to a foundation of steel and concrete or of concrete having sufficient weight to provide load for the tank when filled with liquid and submerged by flood water to the established flood stage
(3) Secured from floating by other means

[**30**:22.14.2]

66.22.14.3 Tank vents or other openings that are not liquid-tight shall extend above the maximum flood stage water level. [**30**:22.14.3]

Δ **66.22.14.4** A dependable water supply shall be used for filling an empty or partially filled tank. [**30**:22.14.4]

N **66.22.14.5** Where filling the tank with water is impractical or hazardous because of the contents of the tank, the tank should be protected by other means against movement or collapse. [**30**:22.14.5]

66.22.14.6 Spherical or spheroid tanks shall be protected by any of the methods specified in 66.22.14. [**30**:22.14.6]

66.22.15 Collision Protection for Aboveground Storage Tanks. Where a tank is exposed to vehicular impact, protection shall be provided to prevent damage to the tank. [**30**:22.15]

66.22.16 Installation Instructions for Aboveground Storage Tanks. Factory-built aboveground tanks shall be provided with instructions for testing the tanks and for installation of the normal and emergency vents. [**30**:22.16]

66.22.17 Inspection and Maintenance of Aboveground Storage Tanks.

66.22.17.1 Inspection and maintenance of aboveground tanks shall meet the requirements of 66.21.8.

66.23 Storage of Ignitible (Flammable or Combustible) Liquids in Tanks — Underground Tanks.

66.23.1 Underground Storage Tanks Located in Areas Subject to Flooding.

66.23.1.1* Tanks shall be anchored or shall be secured by approved means to resist movement when subjected to hydrostatic forces associated with high groundwater or floodwater. [**30**:23.14.1]

66.23.1.1.1 The design of the anchoring or securing method shall be based on the buoyancy of an empty tank that is fully submerged. [**30**:23.14.1.1]

66.23.1.1.2 Tank vents and other openings that are not liquid-tight shall be extended above maximum flood stage water level. [**30**:23.14.1.2]

66.23.1.1.3 Each tank shall be so constructed and installed that it will safely resist external pressures if submerged. [**30**:23.14.1.3]

66.23.2 Reserved.

66.23.3 Installation Instructions for Underground Storage Tanks. Factory-built underground tanks shall be provided with instructions for testing and for installation of the normal vents. [**30**:23.16]

Δ **66.23.4 Inspection and Maintenance of Underground Storage Tanks.**

N **66.23.4.1** Inspection and maintenance for underground tanks shall meet the requirements of 66.21.8. [**30**:23.17.1]

N **66.23.4.2** Overfill protection devices or systems shall be inspected and tested annually to ensure proper operation. [**30**:23.17.2]

66.24 Storage Tank Buildings.

66.24.1 Storage tank buildings shall be in accordance with NFPA 30.

N **66.24.1.1** This chapter shall apply to installations of tanks storing Class I, Class II, and Class IIIA liquids [FP < 200°F (93°C)] in storage tank buildings. [**30**:24.1.1]

N **66.24.1.2** This chapter shall also apply to installations of aboveground storage tanks storing Class II, Class IIIA, or Class IIIB liquids [FP < 200°F (93°C)] in storage tank buildings where the liquids are heated at or above their flash points. In such cases, the liquids shall be regulated as Class I liquids [FP < 100°F (37.8°C)] unless an engineering evaluation conducted in accordance with Chapter 6 of NFPA 30 justifies following the requirements for some other liquid class. [**30**:24.1.2]

N **66.24.1.3** This chapter shall not apply to the following:

(1) Tanks covered by Chapters 17, 18, and 19 of NFPA 30.
(2) A tank that has a canopy or roof that does not limit the dissipation of heat or dispersion of flammable vapors and does not restrict firefighting access and control. Such tanks shall comply with the provisions of Chapter 22 of NFPA 30.

[**30**:24.1.3]

66.24.2 Definitions Specific to Section 66.24. (Reserved)

N **66.24.3 General Requirements. (Reserved)**

N **66.24.4 Location of Storage Tank Buildings.**

N **66.24.4.1** Tanks and associated equipment within the storage tank building shall be so located that a fire in the area shall not constitute an exposure hazard to adjoining buildings or tanks for a period of time consistent with the response and suppression capabilities of the firefighting operations available to the location. Compliance with 66.24.4.2 through 66.24.4.8 shall be deemed as meeting the requirements of 66.24.4.1. [**30**:24.4.1]

N **66.24.4.2** The minimum distance from exposed property lines and buildings for tank installations within structures having walls with a fire resistance rating of less than 2 hours shall be in accordance with Table 66.24.4.2. [**30**:24.4.2]

N **66.24.4.3** The capacity of any individual tank shall not exceed 100,000 gal (380 m^3) without the approval of the authority having jurisdiction. [**30**:24.4.3]

N **66.24.4.4** Where protection for exposures is not provided, the distances given in Table 66.24.4.2 shall be doubled. The distances shall not be required to exceed 300 ft (90 m). [**30**:24.4.4]

N **66.24.4.5** Where a storage tank building has an exterior wall facing an exposure, the distances in Table 66.24.4.2 shall be permitted to be modified as follows:

(1) Where the wall is a blank wall having a fire resistance rating of not less than 2 hours, separation distance between the storage tank building and its exposure shall not be required to be greater than 25 ft (7.6 m).
(2) Where a blank wall having a fire resistance rating of not less than 4 hours is provided, the distance requirements of Table 66.24.4.2 shall not apply.

[**30**:24.4.5]

N **66.24.4.6** If the explosion control methods provided in NFPA 68 are used, the wall facing an exposure shall be pressure resistant unless another approach in accordance with 66.6.8 is approved. [**30**:24.4.6]

N **66.24.4.7** Other equipment associated with tanks, such as pumps, heaters, filters, and exchangers, shall not be located closer than 25 ft (7.6 m) to property lines where the adjoining property is or can be built upon or to the nearest important building on the same property that is not an integral part of the storage tank building. This spacing requirement shall not apply where exposures are protected as outlined in 66.24.4.2. [**30**:24.4.7]

N **66.24.4.8** Each storage tank building and each tank within the building shall be accessible from at least two sides for firefighting and fire control. [**30**:24.4.8]

N **66.24.4.9** Class I liquids [FP < 100°F (37.8°C)] and Class II or Class IIIA liquids [100°F (37.8°C) ≤ FP < 200°F (93°C)] heated above their flash points shall not be stored in basements. [**30**:24.4.9]

N **66.24.5 Construction of Storage Tank Buildings.**

N **66.24.5.1** Storage tank buildings shall be constructed so as to maintain structural integrity for 2 hours under fire exposure conditions and to provide access and egress for unobstructed movement of all personnel and fire protection equipment. Compliance with 66.24.5.2 through 66.24.5.6 shall be deemed as meeting the requirements of 66.24.5.1. [**30**:24.5.1]

N **66.24.5.2*** Buildings or structures shall be of at least 2-hour fire resistance rating. [**30**:24.5.2]

N **66.24.5.2.1** Noncombustible or combustible construction shall be permitted when protected by automatic sprinklers or equivalent protection subject to the approval of the authority having jurisdiction. [**30**:24.5.2.1]

N **66.24.5.3** Where Class I liquids [FP < 100°F (37.8°C)] are stored above grade within buildings with basements or other belowgrade areas into which flammable vapors can travel, such belowgrade areas shall be provided with mechanical ventilation

N **Table 66.24.4.2 Location of Storage Tank Buildings with Respect to Property Lines, Public Ways, and the Nearest Important Building on the Same Property**

Largest Tank — Operating Liquid Capacity (gal)	Minimum Distance from Property Line that Is or Can Be Built Upon, Including Opposite Side of Public Way (ft) Stable Liquid Emergency Relief Not over 2.5 psi	Stable Liquid Emergency Relief Over 2.5 psi	Minimum Distance from Nearest Side of Any Public Way or from Nearest Important Building on Same Property (ft) Stable Liquid Emergency Relief Not over 2.5 psi	Stable Liquid Emergency Relief Over 2.5 psi
Up to 12,000	15	25	5	10
12,001 to 30,000	20	30	5	10
30,001 to 50,000	30	45	10	15
50,001 to 100,000	50	75	15	25

For SI units, 1 gal = 3.8 L; 1 ft = 0.3 m; 1 psi = 6.9 kPa.
[**30**:Table 24.4.2]

designed to prevent the accumulation of flammable vapors. Enclosed storage tank pits shall not be considered basements. [**30**:24.5.3]

N **66.24.5.4** The extent of required damage-limiting construction for storage tank buildings shall be determined in accordance with 66.6.4.1.2.3 and 66.6.8. [**30**:24.5.4]

N **66.24.5.5*** Access aisles not less than 3 ft (0.9 m) in width shall be provided and maintained from the exterior of the storage tank building into the building and around all storage tanks. [**30**:24.5.5]

N **66.24.5.6** A clear space of at least 3 ft (0.9 m) shall be maintained between the top of each tank and the building structure for buildings protected in accordance with 66.24.6.2.3. For buildings without fixed fire suppression systems, sufficient clear space shall be provided to allow for the application of hose streams to the top of the tank(s) for cooling purposes. [**30**:24.5.6]

66.24.6 Fire Protection for Storage Tank Buildings.

66.24.6.1 Manual Fire Control Equipment for Storage Tank Buildings.

66.24.6.1.1* Listed portable fire extinguishers shall be provided for facilities in such quantities, sizes, and types as could be needed for special storage hazards as determined in accordance with 21.6.1.2 of NFPA 30. [**30**:24.6.1.1]

66.24.6.1.2* Where the need is indicated in accordance with 21.6.3 of NFPA 30, water shall be utilized through standpipe and hose systems, or through hose connections from sprinkler systems using combination spray and straight stream nozzles to permit effective fire control. [**30**:24.6.1.2]

66.24.6.1.3 Where the need is indicated in accordance with 21.6.3 of NFPA 30, mobile foam apparatus shall be provided. [**30**:24.6.1.3]

66.24.6.2 Fixed Fire Control Equipment for Tank Buildings.

66.24.6.2.1 A reliable water supply or other suitable fire control agent shall be available in pressure and quantity to meet the fire demands indicated by special storage hazards or exposure as determined by 21.6.3 of NFPA 30. [**30**:24.6.2.1]

66.24.6.2.2* Hydrants, with or without fixed monitor nozzles, shall be provided in accordance with accepted practice. The number and placement shall depend on the hazard of the storage, or exposure, as determined by 21.6.3 of NFPA 30. [**30**:24.6.2.2]

66.24.6.2.3* Where the need is indicated by the hazards of storage or exposure as determined by 21.6.3 of NFPA 30, fixed protection shall be required utilizing approved foam, foam-water sprinkler systems, sprinkler systems, water spray systems, deluge systems, gaseous extinguishing systems, dry chemical extinguishing systems, fire-resistive materials, or a combination of these. [**30**:24.6.2.3]

66.24.6.2.3.1 When foam or foam-water fire protection systems are provided, discharge densities shall be determined based on the listing criteria for selected foam discharge devices, the foam concentrate, and the specific liquids to be protected. [**30**:24.6.2.3.1]

Δ **66.24.6.2.4** If provided, fire control systems shall be designed, installed, and maintained in accordance with the following NFPA standards:

(1) NFPA 11
(2) NFPA 12
(3) NFPA 12A
(4) NFPA 13
(5) NFPA 15
(6) NFPA 17
(7) NFPA 25
[**30**:24.6.2.4]

66.24.7 Electrical Systems for Storage Tank Buildings.

66.24.7.1 Installation of electrical utilization equipment and wiring shall meet the requirements of Section 66.7. [**30**:24.8.1]

66.24.7.2 Section 66.7 shall be used to determine the extent of classified locations for the purpose of installation of electrical equipment. [**30**:24.8.2]

66.24.7.2.1 In establishing the extent of a classified location, it shall not extend beyond a floor, wall, roof, or other solid partition that has no openings within the classified area. [**30**:24.8.2.1]

66.24.8 Containment, Drainage, and Spill Control from Storage Tank Buildings.

Δ **66.24.8.1** Where the maximum allowable quantity (MAQ) is exceeded, spill control shall be required in accordance with 66.6.11.2. [**30**:24.9.1]

66.24.8.2 Where the MAQ is exceeded, secondary containment shall comply with 66.6.11.3 and any additional requirements of 66.24.5. [**30**:24.9.2]

66.24.8.3 Where used, drainage shall comply with 66.6.11.4. [**30**:24.9.3]

66.24.8.4 Where only Class IIIB liquids [FP ≥ 200°F (93°C)] are stored, spill control, secondary containment, and drainage shall not be required. [**30**:24.9.4]

66.24.8.5 Where only unsaturated polyester resins (UPRs) containing not more than 50 percent by weight of Class IC, Class II, or Class IIIA liquid [73°F (22.8°C) ≤ FP < 200°F (93°C)] constituents are stored and are protected in accordance with 16.5.3.11 of NFPA 30, spill control, secondary containment, and drainage shall not be required. [**30**:24.9.5]

66.24.8.6* Emergency drainage systems shall be provided to direct ignitible (flammable or combustible) liquid leakage and fire protection water to a safe location. [**30**:24.9.6]

66.24.9 Ventilation for Storage Tank Buildings. Storage tank buildings storing Class I liquids [FP < 100°F (37.8°C)] or Class II or Class III liquids [FP ≥ 100°F (37.8°C)] at temperatures at or above their flash points shall be ventilated at a rate sufficient to maintain the concentration of vapors within the building at or below 25 percent of the lower flammable limit. Compliance with 24.10.2 through 24.10.7 of NFPA 30 shall be deemed as meeting the requirements of 66.24.9. [**30**:24.10.1]

66.24.10 Reserved.

66.24.11 Explosion Control. The extent of required explosion control shall be determined in accordance with 66.6.4.1.2.3. [**30**:24.12]

66.24.12 Vents for Tanks Inside Storage Tank Buildings.

66.24.12.1 Vents for tanks inside tank buildings shall be designed to ensure that vapors are not released inside the building. Compliance with 66.24.12.2 through 66.24.12.6 shall be deemed as meeting the requirements of 66.24.12.1. [**30:**24.13.1]

66.24.12.2 Vents for tanks inside tank buildings shall be as required in 66.21.4.3 and 66.22.7. [**30:**24.13.2]

66.24.12.3 Emergency venting by the use of a weak roof-to-shell seam shall not be permitted. [**30:**24.13.3]

66.24.12.4 Automatic sprinkler systems designed in accordance with the requirements of Section 13.3 and NFPA 13 shall be accepted by the AHJ as equivalent to water spray systems for purposes of calculating the required airflow rates for emergency vents in 22.7.3.5 of NFPA 30, provided the density and coverage requirements of NFPA 15 are met. [**30:**24.13.4]

66.24.12.5 Vents shall terminate outside the building in accordance with 66.27.8.1. [**30:**24.13.5]

66.24.12.5.1 Emergency relief vents on protected aboveground tanks complying with UL 2085 containing Class II and Class III liquids [FP ≥ 100°F (37.8°C)] shall be allowed to discharge inside the building. [**30:** 24.13.5.1]

66.24.12.6 Piping for normal and emergency relief venting shall meet the requirements of Section 66.27. [**30:**24.13.6]

Δ **66.24.13 Tank Openings Other than Vents for Tanks Inside Storage Tank Buildings.**

N **66.24.13.1** Tank openings other than vents for tanks inside tank buildings shall be designed to ensure that Class I liquids [FP < 100°F (37.8°C)] or vapors are not released inside the building. Compliance with 66.24.13.2 through 66.24.13.9 shall be deemed as meeting the requirements of 66.24.13.1. [**30:**24.14.1]

N **66.24.13.2** All tank openings that are located at or below the maximum liquid level shall be liquidtight. Those that are located above the maximum liquid level shall be normally closed and shall be mechanically secured to prevent release of vapors. [**30:**24.14.2]

N **66.24.13.3** Each liquid transfer connection on any tank storing Class I or Class II liquids [FP < 140°F (60°C)] inside buildings shall be provided with one of the following:

(1) A normally closed, remotely activated valve
(2) An automatic-closing, heat-activated valve
(3) Another approved device
[**30:**24.14.3]

N **66.24.13.4** Connections used for emergency disposal or to provide for quick cutoff of flow in the event of fire in the vicinity of the tank shall not be required to meet the requirement of 66.24.13.3. [**30:**24.14.4]

N **66.24.13.5** Each connection through which liquid can gravity flow from a tank inside a building shall be provided with an internal or an external valve located as close as practical to the shell of the tank. This valve shall be considered to be in compliance with 66.24.13.3. If a separate valve is used, both valves shall be located adjacent to each other. [**30:**24.14.5]

N **66.24.13.6*** Openings for manual gauging of Class I or Class II liquids [FP < 140°F (60°C)], if independent of the fill pipe, shall be provided with a vaportight cap or cover that shall be kept closed when not in use. [**30:**24.14.6]

N **66.24.13.6.1** Each such opening for any liquid shall be protected against liquid overflow and possible vapor release by means of a spring-loaded check valve or other approved device. [**30:**24.14.6.1]

N **66.24.13.7** The inlet of the fill pipe and the outlet of a vapor recovery line for which connections to tank vehicles and tank cars are made and broken shall be as follows:

(1) Located outside of buildings at a location free from any source of ignition
(2) Located not less than 5 ft (1.5 m) away from any building opening
(3) Closed tight and protected against tampering when not in use
(4) Identified
[**30:**24.14.7]

N **66.24.13.8*** Tanks storing Class I, Class II, or Class IIIA liquids [FP < 200°F (93°C)] inside buildings shall be equipped with a device, or other means shall be provided, to prevent overflow into the building. [**30:**24.14.8]

N **66.24.13.9** Tank openings provided for purposes of vapor recovery shall be protected against possible vapor release by means of a spring-loaded check valve or dry-break connection or other approved device, unless the opening is pipe-connected to a vapor processing system. [**30:**24.14.9]

N **66.24.13.9.1** Openings designed for combined fill and vapor recovery shall also be protected against vapor release unless connection of the liquid delivery line to the fill pipe simultaneously connects the vapor recovery line. [**30:**24.14.9.1]

N **66.24.13.9.2** All connections shall be vaportight. [**30:**24.14.9.2]

66.24.14 Detection and Alarm Systems for Storage Tank Buildings.

66.24.14.1 An approved means shall be provided to promptly notify those within the plant and the available public or mutual aid fire department of any fire or other emergency. [**30:**24.15.1]

66.24.14.2 Those areas, including buildings, where the potential exists for a Class I liquid [FP < 100°F (37.8°C)] spill shall be monitored as appropriate. Such methods shall include both of the following:

(1) Personnel observation or patrol
(2) Monitoring equipment that indicates a spill or leak has occurred in an unattended area
[**30:**24.15.2]

66.24.15 Inspection and Maintenance for Storage Tank Buildings.

66.24.15.1 Combustible waste material and residues in operating areas shall be kept to a minimum, stored in covered metal containers, and disposed of daily. [**30:**24.16.1]

66.24.15.2 Storage of combustible materials and empty or full drums or barrels shall not be permitted within the storage tank building. [**30:**24.16.2]

66.25 Storage Tank Vaults.

66.25.1 Scope. This section shall apply to the design, construction, and installation of vaults for aboveground tanks. [30:25.1]

66.25.2 Definitions Specific to Section 66.25. (Reserved)

66.25.3 General Requirements.

66.25.3.1* Storage Tank Selection and Arrangement.

66.25.3.1.1 Aboveground tanks shall be permitted to be installed in vaults that meet the requirements of this section. [30:25.3.1.1]

66.25.3.1.2 Vaults shall be constructed and listed in accordance with UL 2245, *Below-Grade Vaults for Flammable Liquid Storage Tanks*. [30:25.3.1.2]

66.25.3.1.3 Except as modified by the provisions of this section, vaults shall meet all other applicable provisions of this *Code*. [30:25.3.1.3]

66.25.3.1.4 Tanks installed in storage tank vaults shall be listed for aboveground use. [30:25.3.1.4]

66.25.3.1.5 Each tank shall be in its own vault and shall be completely enclosed by the vault. [30:25.3.1.5]

66.25.3.1.6 Sufficient clearance between the tank and the vault shall be provided to allow for visual inspection and maintenance of the tank and its appurtenances. [30:25.3.1.6]

66.25.3.1.7 Backfill shall not be permitted around the tank. [30:25.3.1.7]

66.25.3.1.8 Dispensing devices shall be permitted to be installed on the tops of vaults. Dispensing devices used for motor fuels shall be installed in accordance with NFPA 30A. [30:25.3.1.8]

66.25.3.1.9 At each entry point into the vault, a warning sign indicating the need for procedures for safe entry into confined spaces shall be posted. Each entry point shall be secured against unauthorized entry and vandalism. [30:25.3.1.9]

66.25.3.2 Storage Tank Appurtenances.

66.25.3.2.1 An approved means of overfill protection shall be provided for the tanks in the vaults. The use of ball float valves shall be prohibited. [30:25.3.2.1]

66.25.3.2.2 Fill connections for vaults installed inside buildings shall comply with 66.22.13.4. [30:25.3.2.2]

66.25.3.3 Vault Arrangement.

66.25.3.3.1 Vaults shall be permitted to be either above or below grade. [30:25.3.3.1]

66.25.4 Location of Storage Tank Vaults. In lieu of the separation distance requirements given in 66.22.4, separation distances between the vault and any of the following shall be permitted to be reduced to 0 ft (0 m), as measured from the outer perimeter of the vault wall:

(1) Any property line that is or can be built upon
(2) The near and far sides of a public way
(3) The nearest important building on the same property

[30:25.4]

Δ **66.25.5 Construction and Installation of Storage Tank Vaults.**

N **66.25.5.1 Construction Requirements.** Vaults shall be designed and constructed in accordance with 66.25.5.1.1 through 66.25.5.1.4. [30:25.5.1]

N **66.25.5.1.1** The top of an abovegrade vault that contains a tank storing Class I liquid [FP < 100°F (37.8°C)] or Class II liquid [100°F (37.8°C) ≤ FP < 140°F (60°C)] stored at a temperature above its flash point shall be constructed of noncombustible material and shall be designed to be weaker than the walls of the vault to ensure that the thrust of any explosion occurring inside the vault is directed upward before destructive internal pressure develops within the vault. [30:25.5.1.1]

N **66.25.5.1.2** The top of an at-grade or belowgrade vault that contains a tank storing Class I liquid [FP < 100°F (37.8°C)] or Class II liquid [100°F (37.8°C) ≤ FP < 140°F (60°C)] stored at a temperature above its flash point shall be designed to relieve or contain the force of any explosion occurring inside the vault. [30:25.5.1.2]

N **66.25.5.1.3** Adjacent vaults shall be permitted to share a common wall. [30:25.5.1.3]

N **66.25.5.1.4** Where required, the vault shall be wind and earthquake resistant, in accordance with recognized engineering standards. [30:25.5.1.4]

N **66.25.5.2 Installation Requirements.** Storage tank vaults shall be installed in accordance with the requirements of 66.25.5.2.1 and 66.25.5.2.2. [30:25.5.2]

N **66.25.5.2.1** Each vault and its tank shall be anchored to resist uplifting by groundwater or flooding, including when the tank is empty. [30:25.5.2.1]

N **66.25.5.2.2** Vaults that are not resistant to damage from the impact of a motor vehicle shall be protected by collision barriers. [30:25.5.2.2]

N **66.25.6 Fire Protection for Storage Tank Vaults.** Each vault shall be provided with means to admit a fire suppression agent. [30:25.6]

N **66.25.7 Emergency Controls for Storage Tank Vaults.** (Reserved)

N **66.25.8 Electrical Systems for Storage Tank Vaults.**

N **66.25.8.1** Installation of electrical utilization equipment and wiring shall meet the requirements of Chapter 7 of NFPA 30. [30:25.5.8.1]

N **66.25.8.2** Chapter 7 of NFPA 30 shall be used to determine the extent of classified locations for the purpose of installation of electrical equipment. [30:25.5.8.2]

N **66.25.9 Containment, Drainage, and Spill Control for Storage Tank Vaults.**

N **66.25.9.1** Means shall be provided to recover liquid from the vault. [30:25.5.9.1]

N **66.25.9.2** If a pump is used to meet this requirement, the pump shall not be permanently installed in the vault. [30:25.5.9.2]

N **66.25.9.3** Electric-powered portable pumps shall be approved for use in Class I, Division 1 locations, as defined in *NFPA 70*. [30:25.5.9.3]

N **66.25.10 Ventilation Systems for Storage Tank Vaults.**

N **66.25.10.1** Vaults that contain tanks storing Class I liquids [FP < 100°F (37.8°C)] shall be ventilated at a rate of not less than 1 cfm/ft² of floor area (0.3 m³/min/m²), but not less than 150 cfm (4 m³/min). [**30**:25.5.10.1]

N **66.25.10.2** Such ventilation shall operate continuously or shall be designed to operate upon activation of a vapor and liquid detection system. [**30**:25.5.10.2]

N **66.25.10.3** Failure of the exhaust airflow shall automatically shut down the dispensing system. [**30**:25.5.10.3]

N **66.25.10.4** The exhaust system shall be designed to provide air movement across all parts of the vault floor. [**30**:25.5.10.4]

N **66.25.10.5** Supply and exhaust ducts shall extend to within 3 in. (75 mm), but not more than 12 in. (300 mm) of the floor. [**30**:25.5.10.5]

N **66.25.10.6** The exhaust system shall be installed in accordance with the provisions of NFPA 91. [**30**:25.5.10.6]

N **66.25.11 Reserved.**

N **66.25.12 Explosion Control.** The extent of required explosion control shall be determined in accordance with 66.6.4.1.2.3. [**30**:25.5.12]

N **66.25.13 Vents for Tanks Inside Storage Tank Vaults.**

N **66.25.13.1** Vent pipes that are provided for normal tank venting shall terminate outside the vault and at least 12 ft (3.6 m) above ground level and shall meet the requirements of 27.8.1 of NFPA 30. [**30**:25.5.13.1]

N **66.25.13.2** Emergency vents shall be vaportight and shall be permitted to discharge inside the vault. Long-bolt manhole covers shall not be permitted for this purpose. [**30**:25.5.13.2]

66.25.14 Reserved.

66.25.15 Detection and Alarm Systems for Storage Tank Vaults.

66.25.15.1 Each vault shall be provided with an approved vapor and liquid detection system that is equipped with on-site audible and visual warning devices with battery backup. [**30**:25.15.1]

66.25.15.2 The vapor detection system shall sound an alarm when the system detects vapors that reach or exceed 25 percent of the lower flammable limit of the liquid stored. [**30**:25.15.2]

66.25.15.3 Vapor detectors shall be located no higher than 12 in. (300 mm) above the lowest point in the vault. [**30**:25.15.3]

66.25.15.4 The liquid detection system shall sound an alarm upon detection of any liquid, including water. [**30**:25.15.4]

66.25.15.5 Liquid detectors shall be located in accordance with the manufacturer's instructions. [**30**:25.15.5]

66.25.15.6 Activation of either the vapor detection system or the liquid detection system shall cause a signal to be sounded at an approved, constantly attended location within the facility serving the tanks or at an approved location. [**30**:25.15.6]

66.25.16 Inspection and Maintenance of Storage Tank Vaults and Equipment. Vaults and their required equipment shall be maintained in accordance with the requirements of this section. [**30**:25.16]

66.26 Reserved.

66.27 Piping Systems.

66.27.1 Scope.

66.27.1.1 This section shall apply to the design, installation, testing, operation, and maintenance of piping systems for liquids or flammable vapors. Such piping systems shall include, but not be limited to, pipe, tubing, flanges, bolting, gaskets, valves, fittings, flexible connectors; the pressure-containing parts of other components including, but not limited to, expansion joints and strainers; and devices that serve such purposes as mixing, separating, snubbing, distributing, metering, control of flow, or secondary containment piping. [**30**:27.1.1]

66.27.1.2 This section shall not apply to any of the following:

(1) Tubing or casing on any oil or gas wells and any piping connected directly thereto
(2) Motor vehicles, aircraft, boats, or piping that is integral to a stationary engine assembly
(3) Piping within the scope of any applicable boiler and pressure vessel code

[**30**:27.1.2]

66.27.2 Definitions Specific to Section 66.27. For the purpose of this section, terms in this section shall have the definitions given. [**30**:27.2]

66.27.2.1 Corrosion Protection. A means to lessen or prevent the deterioration of the piping system from exposure to its contents or its environment. [**30**:27.2.1]

66.27.2.2 Flexible Connector. A connection joint in a piping system that allows differential movement of the piping system and limits system stress and mechanical damage. [**30**:27.2.2]

66.27.2.3 Leak. An unintended release of ignitible (flammable or combustible) liquid or vapor from the piping system due to failure of the piping system. [**30**:27.2.3]

66.27.2.4 Low Melting Point Materials. Materials that melt at a low temperature, including but not limited to aluminum, copper, or brass; materials that soften on fire exposure, such as plastics; or nonductile materials, such as cast iron. [**30**:27.2.4]

66.27.2.5 Secondary Containment. Containment that is external to and separate from the primary piping system. [**30**:27.2.5]

66.27.3 General Requirements.

66.27.3.1 Performance Standards.

66.27.3.1.1 The design, fabrication, assembly, test, and inspection of piping systems shall be suitable for the working pressures and structural stresses to be encountered by the piping system. [**30**:27.3.1.1]

66.27.3.1.2 Compliance with ASME B31.1, *Power Piping*; ASME B31.3, *Process Piping*; or ASME B31.4, *Pipeline Transportation Systems for Liquids and Slurries*, and the provisions of this section shall be considered *prima facie* evidence of compliance with the foregoing provisions. [**30**:27.3.1.2]

66.27.3.2 Tightness of Piping. Piping systems shall be maintained liquidtight. A piping system that has leaks that constitute a hazard shall be repaired in a manner acceptable to the AHJ, or it shall be emptied of liquid, vapor freed, and no longer used. [30:27.3.2]

66.27.4 Materials of Construction for Piping Systems.

Δ **66.27.4.1 Materials Specifications.** Pipe, valves, faucets, couplings, flexible connectors, fittings, and other pressure-containing parts shall meet the material specifications and pressure and temperature limitations of ASME B31.1, *Power Piping*; ASME B31.3, *Process Piping*; or ASME B31.4, *Pipeline Transportation Systems for Liquids and Slurries*, except as provided for in 66.27.4.2, 66.27.4.3, 66.27.4.4, and 66.27.4.7. [30:27.4.1]

66.27.4.2 Ductile Iron. Ductile (nodular) iron shall meet the specifications of ASTM A395/A395M, *Standard Specification for Ferritic Ductile Iron Pressure-Retaining Castings for Use at Elevated Temperatures*. [30:27.4.2]

66.27.4.3 Materials of Construction for Valves. Valves at storage tanks, as required by 22.14 of NFPA 30 and 66.22.13, and their connections to the tank shall be of steel or ductile iron, except as provided for in 66.27.4.3.1, 66.27.4.3.2, or 66.27.4.4. [30:27.4.3]

66.27.4.3.1 Valves at storage tanks shall be permitted to be other than steel or ductile iron where the chemical characteristics of the liquid stored are not compatible with steel or where the valves are installed internally to the tank. [30:27.4.3.1]

66.27.4.3.2* Valves installed externally to the tank shall be permitted to be other than steel or ductile iron if the material of construction has a ductility and melting point comparable to steel or ductile iron and is capable of withstanding the stresses and temperatures involved in fire exposure or the valves are otherwise protected from fire exposures, such as by materials having a fire resistance rating of not less than 2 hours. [30:27.4.3.2]

66.27.4.3.3 Cast iron, brass, copper, aluminum, malleable iron, and similar materials shall be permitted to be used on tanks described in 66.22.4.2.1.1 or on tanks storing Class IIIB liquids [flash point ≥ 200°F (93°C)] where the tanks are located outdoors and not within a diked area or drainage path of a tank storing a Class I, Class II, or Class IIIA liquid [FP < 200°F (93°C)]. [30:27.4.3.3]

66.27.4.4 Low Melting Point Materials.

66.27.4.4.1 Low melting point materials, as defined in 66.27.2.4, shall be compatible with the ignitible (flammable or combustible) liquids being handled and shall be used within the pressure and temperature limitations of ASME B31.1, *Power Piping*; ASME B31.3, *Process Piping*; or ASME B31.4, *Pipeline Transportation Systems for Liquids and Slurries*. [30:27.4.4.1]

66.27.4.4.2 Low melting point materials shall not be used as part of a tank's normal or emergency vent piping. [30:27.4.4.2]

66.27.4.4.3 Low melting point materials shall be permitted to be used underground. [30:27.4.4.3]

66.27.4.4.4 Low melting point materials shall be permitted to be used outdoors aboveground, outside a dike, outside a remote impounding area, or inside buildings, provided they meet one of the following conditions:

(1) They are resistant to damage by fire.
(2) They are located so that any leakage resulting from failure will not expose persons, important buildings, tanks, or structures.
(3) They are located where leakage can be controlled by operation of one or more accessible, remotely located valves.
(4)* They are included in valves or piping components connected to an aboveground secondary containment tank and located above the tank and within ten feet of a thermally activated fire valve that is upstream of the low melting point materials.

[30:27.4.4.4]

66.27.4.4.5 Low melting point materials shall be permitted to be used within a dike or within a remote impounding area, provided they meet one of the following:

(1) They are connected above the normal operating liquid level of the tank.
(2) They are connected below the normal operating liquid level of the tank and one of the following conditions is met:
   (a) The stored liquid is a Class IIIB liquid [FP ≥ 200°F (93°C)], the tank is located outdoors, and the piping is not exposed to a potential spill or leak of a Class I, Class II or Class IIIA liquid [FP < 200°F (93°C)]
   (b) The low melting point material is protected from fire exposure, such as by using materials that have a fire resistance rating of not less than 2 hours.

[30:27.4.4.5]

66.27.4.4.6 Piping systems of these materials shall be designed and built in accordance with recognized standards of design for the particular materials chosen or with approved equivalent standards or shall be listed. [30:27.4.4.6]

66.27.4.5 Lining Materials. Piping, valves, and fittings shall be permitted to have combustible or noncombustible linings. [30:27.4.5]

66.27.4.6 Nonmetallic Piping.

66.27.4.6.1 Piping systems of nonmetallic materials, including piping systems incorporating secondary containment piping, shall be designed and built in accordance with recognized standards of design or approved equivalents and shall be installed in accordance with 66.27.4.4. [30:27.4.6.1]

66.27.4.6.2 Nonmetallic piping shall be built and used within the scope of their approvals or within the scope of UL 971, *Nonmetallic Underground Piping for Flammable Liquids*. [30:27.4.6.2]

66.27.4.6.3 Nonmetallic piping systems and components shall be installed in accordance with manufacturer's instructions. [30:27.4.6.3]

N **66.27.4.7 Metallic/Nonmetallic Composite Piping.**

N **66.27.4.7.1** Underground metallic/nonmetallic composite piping systems shall be either listed in accordance with UL 971A, *Metallic Underground Fuel Pipe for Flammable Liquids*, or be approved. [30:27.4.7.1]

N **66.27.4.7.2** Aboveground metallic/nonmetallic composite piping systems shall be either listed in accordance UL/ULC 1369, *Above Ground Piping for Flammable and Combustible Liquids*, or be approved. [30:27.4.7.2]

N 66.27.4.7.3 Metallic/nonmetallic composite piping systems and components shall be installed in accordance with the manufacturers' instructions. [30:27.4.7.3]

66.27.5 Pipe Joints.

66.27.5.1 Tightness of Pipe Joints.

66.27.5.1.1 Joints shall be made liquidtight and shall be welded, flanged, threaded, or mechanically attached. [30:27.5.1.1]

66.27.5.1.2* Joints shall be designed and installed so that the mechanical strength of the joint will not be impaired if exposed to a fire. [30:27.5.1.2]

66.27.5.1.3 Threaded joints shall be made with a suitable thread sealant or lubricant. [30:27.5.1.3]

66.27.5.1.4 Joints in piping systems handling Class I liquids [FP < 100°F (37.8°C)] shall be welded when located in concealed spaces within buildings. [30:27.5.1.4]

66.27.5.2 Flexible Connectors. Flexible connectors shall be listed and labeled in accordance with UL 2039, *Flexible Connector Pipe for Fuels*. [30:27.5.2]

Δ **66.27.5.3 Friction Joints.**

N 66.27.5.3.1 Pipe joints dependent upon the friction characteristics of combustible materials for mechanical continuity or liquidtightness of piping shall only be used outside of buildings above ground, except as provided for in 66.27.5.3.3, or below ground. [30:27.5.3.1]

N 66.27.5.3.2 Where such joints are used aboveground, either the piping shall be secured to prevent disengagement at the fitting or the piping system shall be so designed that any spill or leak resulting from disengagement will not expose persons, important buildings, or structures and can be controlled by remote valves. [30:27.5.3.2]

N 66.27.5.3.3 Pipe joints dependent on the friction characteristics of their components shall be permitted to be used inside buildings provided both of the following are met:

(1) They are located where leakage can be controlled by operation of an accessible, remotely located valve that is outside the fire risk area.
(2) The mechanical strength and liquidtightness of the joint is not dependent on the resiliency of a combustible material or component.

[30:27.5.3.3]

66.27.6 Installation of Piping Systems. Piping systems shall be in accordance with NFPA 30.

N 66.27.6.1 Piping systems shall be supported and protected against physical damage, including damage from stresses arising from settlement, vibration, expansion, or contraction. The installation of nonmetallic piping shall be in accordance with the manufacturer's instructions. [30:27.6.1]

N 66.27.6.2* Load-bearing piping supports that are located in areas with a high fire exposure risk shall be protected by one or more of the following:

(1) Drainage to a safe location to prevent ignitible (flammable or combustible) liquid from accumulating under pipeways (*see also, Section 6.12 of NFPA 30*)
(2) Fire-resistive construction
(3) Fire-resistant protective coatings or systems
(4) Water spray systems designed and installed in accordance with NFPA 15
(5) Other alternate means acceptable to the authority having jurisdiction

[30:27.6.2]

N 66.27.6.3 Piping that passes through or pierces a dike wall or the wall of a structure shall be designed to prevent damaging stresses and leakage due to settlement or fire exposure. [30:27.6.3]

N 66.27.6.4* Aboveground piping systems that are subject to external corrosion shall be suitably protected. Underground piping systems shall be protected against corrosion in accordance with 23.3.5 of NFPA 30. [30:27.6.4]

Δ **66.27.6.5 Installation of Underground Piping.**

N 66.27.6.5.1 Underground piping shall be installed on at least 6 in. (150 mm) of well-compacted bedding material. [30:27.6.5.1]

N 66.27.6.5.2 In areas subject to vehicle traffic, the pipe trench shall be deep enough to permit a cover of at least 18 in. (450 mm) of well-compacted backfill material and pavement. [30:27.6.5.2]

N 66.27.6.5.3 In paved areas where a minimum 2 in. (50 mm) of asphalt is used, backfill between the pipe and the asphalt shall be permitted to be reduced to 8 in. (200 mm) minimum. [30:27.6.5.3]

N 66.27.6.5.4 In paved areas where a minimum 4 in. (100 mm) of reinforced concrete is used, backfill between the pipe and the asphalt shall be permitted to be reduced to 4 in. (100 mm) minimum. [30:27.6.5.4]

N 66.27.6.5.5 In areas not subject to vehicle traffic, the pipe trench shall be deep enough to permit a cover of at least 6 in. (150 mm) of well-compacted backfill material. [30:27.6.5.5]

N 66.27.6.5.6 A greater burial depth shall be provided when required by the manufacturer's instructions or where frost conditions are present. [30:27.6.5.6]

N 66.27.6.5.7 Piping within the same trench shall be separated horizontally by at least two pipe diameters. Separation need not exceed 9 in. (230 mm). [30:27.6.5.7]

N 66.27.6.5.8 Two or more levels of piping within the same trench shall be separated vertically by a minimum 6 in. (150 mm) of well-compacted bedding material. [30:27.6.5.8]

N 66.27.6.6 Valves.

N 66.27.6.6.1 Piping systems shall contain valves to operate the system properly and to isolate the equipment in the event of an emergency. [30:27.6.6.1]

N 66.27.6.6.2 Piping systems in connection with pumps shall contain valves to properly control the flow of ignitible (flammable or combustible) liquid both in normal operation and in the event of an emergency. [30:27.6.6.2]

N 66.27.6.6.3 Each connection to a piping system by which equipment such as tank cars, tank vehicles, or marine vessels discharges ignitible (flammable or combustible) liquids into storage tanks shall be provided with a check valve for automatic protection against back flow if the piping arrangement is such that backflow from the system is possible. *(See also 66.22.13.1.)* [**30:**27.6.6.3]

N **66.27.6.7 Common Loading and Unloading Piping.** If loading and unloading is done through a common pipe system, a check valve shall not be required. However, an isolation valve shall be provided. This valve shall be located so that it is accessible or shall be remotely operable. [**30:**27.6.7]

N **66.27.7 Testing of Piping Systems.**

N **66.27.7.1 Initial Testing.** Unless tested in accordance with the applicable sections of ASME B31.1, *Power Piping*; B31.3, *Process Piping*; or B31.4, *Pipeline Transportation Systems for Liquids and Slurries*, all piping shall be tested before being covered, enclosed, or placed in use. [**30:**27.7.1]

N **66.27.7.1.1** Testing shall be done hydrostatically to 150 percent of the maximum anticipated pressure of the system or pneumatically to 110 percent of the maximum anticipated pressure of the system, and the test pressure shall be maintained while a complete visual inspection of all joints and connections is conducted. [**30:**27.7.1.1]

N **66.27.7.1.2** In no case shall the test pressure be less than a gauge pressure of 5 psi (35 kPa) measured at the highest point of the system, and in no case shall the test pressure be maintained for less than 10 minutes. [**30:**27.7.1.2]

N **66.27.7.2 Initial Testing of Secondary Containment Piping.** The interstitial space of secondary containment–type piping shall be tested hydrostatically or with air pressure at a gauge pressure of 5 psi (35 kPa) or shall be tested in accordance with its listing or with the manufacturer's instructions. [**30:**27.7.2]

N **66.27.7.2.1** The pressure source shall be disconnected from the interstitial space to ensure that the test is being conducted on a closed system. [**30:**27.7.2.1]

N **66.27.7.2.2** The pressure shall be maintained for a minimum of 1 hour. [**30:**27.7.2.2]

N **66.27.7.3 Testing During Maintenance.** Existing piping shall be tested in accordance with this subsection if the piping is leaking. [**30:**27.7.3]

N **66.27.7.3.1** Piping that could contain a Class I, Class II, or Class IIIA liquid [FP < 200°F (93°C)] or vapor shall not be tested using air. [**30:**27.7.3.1]

66.27.8 Vent Piping. Vent piping shall be designed, constructed, and installed in accordance with this section. [**30:**27.8]

66.27.8.1 Vent Piping for Aboveground Storage Tanks.

66.27.8.1.1 Where the outlets of vent pipes for tanks storing Class I liquids [FP < 100°F (37.8°C)] are adjacent to buildings or public ways, they shall be located so that vapors are released at a safe point outside of buildings and not less than 12 ft (3.6 m) above the adjacent ground level. [**30:**27.8.1.1]

66.27.8.1.2 Vapors shall be discharged upward or horizontally away from adjacent walls. [**30:**27.8.1.2]

66.27.8.1.3 Vent outlets shall be located so that vapors will not be trapped by eaves or other obstructions and shall be at least 5 ft (1.5 m) from building openings and at least 15 ft (4.5 m) from powered ventilation air intake devices. [**30:**27.8.1.3]

66.27.8.1.4 Manifolding of vent piping shall be prohibited except where required for special purposes such as vapor recovery, vapor conservation, or air pollution control. [**30:**27.8.1.4]

66.27.8.1.4.1 Where vent piping is manifolded, pipe sizes shall be capable of discharging, within the pressure limitations of the system, the vapors they are required to handle when all manifolded tanks are subject to the same fire exposure. [**30:**27.8.1.4.1]

66.27.8.1.5 Vent piping for tanks storing Class I liquids [FP < 100°F (37.8°C)] shall not be manifolded with vent piping for tanks storing Class II or Class III liquids [FP ≥ 100°F (37.8°C)] unless positive means are provided to prevent the following:

(1) Vapors of Class I liquids [FP < 100°F (37.8°C)] from entering tanks storing Class II or Class III liquids [FP ≥ 100°F (37.8°C)]
(2) Contamination
(3) Possible change in classification of the less volatile liquid
[**30:**27.8.1.5]

66.27.8.1.6* Extension of Emergency Vent Piping. Piping to or from approved emergency vents for atmospheric and low-pressure tanks shall be sized to provide emergency vent flows that limit the back pressure to less than the maximum pressure permitted by the design of the tank. Piping to or from approved emergency vents for pressure vessels shall be sized in accordance with the ASME *Boiler and Pressure Vessel Code*. Calculations demonstrating compliance with this paragraph shall include the start-to-open pressure of an approved emergency vent device, where provided. [**30:**27.8.1.6]

66.27.8.2 Vent Piping for Underground Tanks.

66.27.8.2.1* Vent pipes from underground tanks storing Class I liquids [FP < 100°F (37.8°C)] shall be located so that the discharge point is outside of buildings, higher than the fill pipe opening, and not less than 12 ft (3.6 m) above the adjacent ground level. [**30:**27.8.2.1]

66.27.8.2.2 Vent pipe outlets shall be located and directed so that vapors will not accumulate or travel to an unsafe location, enter building openings, or be trapped under eaves and shall be at least 5 ft (1.5 m) from building openings and at least 15 ft (4.5 m) from powered ventilation air intake devices. [**30:**27.8.2.2]

66.27.8.2.3 Vent pipes shall not be obstructed by devices provided for vapor recovery or other purposes unless the tank and associated piping and equipment are otherwise protected to limit back-pressure development to less than the maximum working pressure of the tank and equipment by the provision of pressure-vacuum vents, rupture discs, or other tank-venting devices installed in the tank vent lines. [**30:**27.8.2.3]

66.27.8.2.4 Vent outlets and devices shall be protected to minimize the possibility of blockage from weather, dirt, or insect nests. [**30:**27.8.2.4]

66.27.8.2.5 Vent piping shall be sized in accordance with Table 23.6.2 of NFPA 30. [**30:**27.8.2.5]

66.27.8.2.6 Vent pipes from tanks storing Class II or Class IIIA liquids [100°F (37.8°C) ≤ FP < 200°F (93°C)] shall terminate outside of the building and higher than the fill pipe opening. [**30:**27.8.2.6]

66.27.8.2.7 Vent outlets shall be above normal snow level. [**30:**27.8.2.7]

66.27.8.2.8 Vent pipes shall be permitted to be fitted with return bends, coarse screens, or other devices to minimize ingress of foreign material. [**30:**27.8.2.8]

66.27.8.2.9 Vent pipes and vapor return piping shall be installed without sags or traps in which liquid can collect. [**30:**27.8.2.9]

66.27.8.2.10 Condensate tanks, if utilized, shall be installed and maintained so that blocking of the vapor return piping by liquid is prevented. [**30:**27.8.2.10]

66.27.8.2.11 Vent pipes and condensate tanks shall be located so that they will not be subjected to physical damage. The tank end of the vent pipe shall enter the tank through the top. [**30:**27.8.2.11]

66.27.8.2.12 Where tank vent piping is manifolded, pipe sizes shall be such as to discharge, within the pressure limitations of the system, the vapors they could be required to handle when manifolded tanks are filled simultaneously. [**30:**27.8.2.12]

66.27.8.2.12.1 Float-type check valves installed in tank openings connected to manifolded vent piping to prevent product contamination shall be permitted to be used, provided that the tank pressure will not exceed that permitted by 23.5.3.2 of NFPA 30 when the valves close. [**30:**27.8.2.12.1]

66.27.8.2.13 Vent piping for tanks storing Class I liquids [FP < 100°F (37.8°C)] shall not be manifolded with vent piping for tanks storing Class II or Class III liquids [FP ≥ 100°F (37.8°C)] unless positive means are provided to prevent the following:

(1) Vapors of Class I liquids [FP < 100°F (37.8°C)] from entering tanks storing Class II or Class III liquids [FP ≥ 100°F (37.8°C)]
(2) Contamination
(3) Possible change in classification of the less volatile liquid

[**30:**27.8.2.13]

66.27.9 Bonding and Grounding. Piping systems shall be bonded and grounded in accordance with 66.6.5.4. [**30:**27.9]

66.27.10* Identification and Marking of Piping Systems. Each loading and unloading riser shall be marked to identify the product for which it is to be used. [**30:**27.10]

66.27.11 Special Requirements for Marine Piping Systems.

66.27.11.1 Where piping is from a floating structure or pier, an approved flexible connector shall be permitted between the fixed shore piping and the piping on the floating structure or pier and between separate sections of the floating structure to accommodate changes in water level. [**30:**27.11.1]

66.27.11.2 The interior of the flexible connectors shall be compatible with the ignitible (flammable or combustible) liquid handled. [**30:**27.11.2]

66.27.11.3* The exterior of the flexible connectors shall be resistant to or shielded from salt water and fresh water, ultraviolet radiation, physical damage, and damage by fire. [**30:**27.11.3]

66.27.11.4 The flexible connectors shall be suitable for the intended pressures and shall be tested in accordance with 27.7 of NFPA 30. [**30:**27.11.4]

N **66.27.12** Piping systems taken out of service or abandoned shall be temporarily or permanently closed in accordance with this section. [**30:**27.12]

66.28 Bulk Loading and Unloading Facilities for Tank Cars and Tank Vehicles.

66.28.1 Scope. This section shall apply to operations involving the loading or unloading of tank cars and tank vehicles. [**30:**28.1]

66.28.2 Definitions Specific to 66.28. (Reserved)

66.28.3 General Requirements.

66.28.3.1 Bonding and Grounding and Stray Currents.

Δ **66.28.3.1.1*** Bonding and grounding in accordance with 66.6.5.4 for the control of static electricity shall not be required where the tank cars and tank vehicles are only loaded or unloaded with Class II and Class III liquids [FP ≥ 100°F (37.8°C)] at temperatures below their flash points and Class I liquids [FP < 100°F (37.8°C)] are not handled at the loading facility. [**30:**28.3.1.1]

66.28.3.1.2* Loading and unloading facilities that are used to load liquids not excluded by 66.28.3.1.1 into tank vehicles through open domes shall be provided with a means for electrically bonding and grounding the fill pipe to protect against static electricity hazards. [**30:**28.3.1.2]

66.28.3.1.2.1 Such means shall consist of a metallic bonding wire that is permanently electrically connected to the fill pipe assembly or to some part of the rack structure that is in electrical contact with the fill pipe assembly. [**30:**28.3.1.2.1]

66.28.3.1.2.2 The other end of the bonding wire shall be provided with an opposed-point-type clamp, or an equivalent device, for convenient attachment to the tank compartment being loaded. [**30:**28.3.1.2.2]

66.28.3.1.2.3 All parts of the fill pipe assembly, including, but not limited to, the drop tube, rack structure and piping, shall form a continuous electrically conductive path that is directed to ground through the rack assembly or by conductive wiring. [**30:**28.3.1.2.3]

66.28.3.1.3 Stray current protection shall be provided by permanently bonding the fill pipe to at least one rail and to an available metal facility component at loading and unloading facilities where liquids are transferred into and from tank cars through open domes. [**30:**28.3.1.3]

66.28.3.1.3.1 Multiple pipelines that enter the area shall be permanently bonded together. [**30:**28.3.1.3.1]

Δ **66.28.3.1.3.2** In areas where excessive stray currents are known to exist, all pipelines entering the area shall be provided with insulating sections to electrically isolate them from the facility piping. [**30:**28.3.1.3.2]

66.28.4 Location of Loading and Unloading Facilities.

66.28.4.1 Tank vehicle and tank car loading and unloading facilities shall be separated from aboveground tanks, warehouses, other plant buildings, or the nearest line of adjoining property that can be built upon by a distance of at least 25 ft (7.6 m) for Class I liquids [FP < 100°F (37.8°C)] and for Class II and Class III liquids [FP ≥ 100°F (37.8°C)] handled at temperatures at or above their FP and at least 15 ft (4.6 m) for Class II and Class III liquids [FP ≥ 100°F (37.8°C)] handled at temperatures below their FP, measured from the nearest fill spout or transfer connection. [**30:**28.4.1]

66.28.4.2* These distances shall be permitted to be reduced if there is suitable protection for exposures. [**30:**28.4.2]

66.28.4.3 Buildings for pumps or shelters for personnel shall be permitted to be a part of the facility. [**30:**28.4.3]

66.28.5 Roofed Structures. A loading or unloading facility that has a canopy or roof that does not limit the dissipation of heat or dispersion of flammable vapors and does not restrict firefighting access and control shall be treated as an outdoor facility. [**30:**28.5]

66.28.6 Reserved.

66.28.7 Reserved.

66.28.8 Reserved.

66.28.9* Containment, Drainage, and Spill Control. Loading and unloading facilities shall be provided with drainage systems or other means to contain spills. [**30:**28.9]

66.28.10 Equipment.

66.28.10.1 Equipment such as piping, pumps, and meters used for the transfer of Class I liquids [FP < 100°F (37.8°C)] between storage tanks and the fill stem of the loading facility shall not be used for the transfer of Class II or Class III liquids [FP ≥ 100°F (37.8°C)] unless one of the following conditions exists:

(1) Only water-miscible ignitible (flammable or combustible) liquid mixtures are handled, and the class of the mixture is determined by the concentration of liquid in water.
(2) The equipment is cleaned between transfers.
[**30:**28.10.1]

66.28.10.2 Remote pumps located in underground tanks shall have a listed leak detection device installed on the pump discharge side that will indicate if the piping system is not essentially liquidtight. [**30:**28.10.2]

66.28.10.2.1 This device shall be checked and tested at least annually according to the manufacturer's specifications to ensure proper installation and operation. [**30:**28.10.2.1]

66.28.11 Operating Requirements.

66.28.11.1 Loading and Unloading of Tank Vehicles.

66.28.11.1.1 Ignitible (flammable or combustible) liquids shall be loaded only into cargo tanks whose material of construction is compatible with the chemical characteristics of the liquid. The liquid being loaded shall also be chemically compatible with the liquid hauled on the previous load unless the cargo tank has been cleaned. [**30:**28.11.1.1]

Δ **66.28.11.1.2** Before loading tank liquids not excluded by 66.28.3.1.1 into vehicles through open domes, a bonding connection shall be made to the vehicle or tank before dome covers are raised and remain in place until filling is completed and all dome covers have been closed and secured. [**30:**28.11.1.2]

66.28.11.1.3 When transferring Class I liquids [FP < 100°F (37.8°C)], or Class II or Class III liquids [FP ≥ 100°F (37.8°C)] at temperatures at or above their FP, engines of tank vehicles or motors of auxiliary or portable pumps shall be shut down during the making and breaking of hose connections. [**30:**28.11.1.3]

66.28.11.1.4 If loading or unloading is done without requiring the use of the motor of the tank vehicle, the motor shall be shut down throughout any transfer operations involving Class I liquids [FP < 100°F (37.8°C)]. [**30:**28.11.1.4]

66.28.11.1.5* Filling through open domes into tank vehicles that contain vapor–air mixtures within the flammable range or where the liquid being filled can form such a mixture shall be by means of a downspout that extends to within 6 in. (150 mm) of the bottom of the tank unless the liquid is conductive, or the operation is performed with the end of the downspout submerged in liquid. [**30:**28.11.1.5]

66.28.11.1.6 When top loading a tank vehicle with Class I or Class II liquids [FP < 140°F (60°C)] without a vapor control system, valves used for the final control of flow shall be of the self-closing type and shall be manually held open except where automatic means are provided for shutting off the flow when the vehicle is full. [**30:**28.11.1.6]

66.28.11.1.6.1 Automatic shutoff systems shall be provided with a manual shutoff valve located at a safe distance from the loading nozzle to stop the flow if the automatic system fails. [**30:**28.11.1.6.1]

66.28.11.1.6.2 When top loading a tank vehicle with vapor control, flow control shall be in accordance with 66.28.11.1.8 and 66.28.11.1.9. [**30:**28.11.1.6.2]

66.28.11.1.7 When bottom loading a tank vehicle, a positive means shall be provided for loading a predetermined quantity of ignitible (flammable or combustible) liquid, together with a secondary automatic shutoff control to prevent overfill. [**30:**28.11.1.7]

66.28.11.1.7.1 The connecting components between the loading rack and the tank vehicle that are required to operate the secondary control shall be functionally compatible. [**30:**28.11.1.7.1]

66.28.11.1.7.2 The connection between the liquid loading hose or pipe and the tank vehicle piping shall be by means of a dry disconnect coupling. [**30:**28.11.1.7.2]

66.28.11.1.8 When bottom loading a tank vehicle that is equipped for vapor control, but when vapor control is not used, the tank shall be vented to the atmosphere, at a height not lower than the top of the cargo tank of the vehicle, to prevent pressurization of the tank. [**30:**28.11.1.8]

66.28.11.1.8.1 Connections to the facility's vapor control system shall be designed to prevent the escape of vapor to the atmosphere when the system is not connected to a tank vehicle. [**30:**28.11.1.8.1]

66.28.11.1.9 When bottom loading is used, reduced flow rates (until the fill opening is submerged), splash deflectors, or other devices shall be used to prevent splashing and to minimize turbulence. [**30:**28.11.1.9]

Δ **66.28.11.1.10*** Metal or conductive objects, such as gauge tapes, sample containers, and thermometers, shall not be lowered into or suspended in a compartment while the compartment is being filled or immediately after to permit the relaxation of charge. [**30:**28.11.1.10]

66.28.11.1.11 Hose materials used for transfer shall be compatible with the ignitible (flammable or combustible) liquids being handled. [**30:**28.11.1.11]

66.28.11.2 Loading and Unloading of Tank Cars.

66.28.11.2.1 Ignitible (flammable or combustible) liquids shall be loaded only into tank cars whose material of construction is compatible with the chemical characteristics of the liquid. The liquid being loaded shall also be chemically compatible with the liquid hauled on the previous load unless the tank car has been cleaned. [30:28.11.2.1]

Δ **66.28.11.2.2*** Filling through open domes into tank cars that contain vapor–air mixtures within the flammable range, or where the liquid being filled can form such a mixture, shall be by means of a downspout that extends to within 6 in. (150 mm) of the bottom of the tank unless the liquid is conductive, or the operation is performed with the end of the downspout submerged in liquid. [30:28.11.2.2]

66.28.11.2.3 When bottom loading is used, reduced flow rates (until the fill opening is submerged), splash deflectors, or other devices shall be used to prevent splashing and to minimize turbulence. [30:28.11.2.3]

Δ **66.28.11.2.4*** Metal or conductive objects, such as gauge tapes, sample containers, and thermometers, shall not be lowered into or suspended in a compartment while the compartment is being filled or immediately after to permit the relaxation of charge. [30:28.11.2.4]

66.28.11.2.5 Hose materials used for transfer shall be compatible with the ignitible (flammable or combustible) liquids being handled. [30:28.11.2.5]

66.28.11.3* Switch Loading. To prevent hazards due to a change in flash point of liquids, any tank car or tank vehicle that has previously contained a Class I liquid [FP < 100°F (37.8°C)] shall treat the loading of Class II or Class III liquids [FP ≥ 100°F (37.8°C)] as Class I liquids. [30:28.11.3]

Δ **66.28.11.4** The person responsible for loading or unloading shall remain in attendance during the operation or be able to locally or remotely monitor and control the operation for the duration of the operation. [30:28.11.4]

N **66.28.11.4.1** A responsible person shall not be required where a hazards analysis conducted in accordance with 66.6.4 shows that the loading or unloading operation can be safely shut down in an emergency. [30:28.11.4.1]

66.28.11.4.2* The responsible person shall be trained to recognize unsafe conditions and take appropriate actions. [30:28.11.4.2]

66.29 Wharves.

66.29.1 Scope.

66.29.1.1 This section shall apply to all wharves, as defined in 3.3.307, whose primary purpose is the bulk transfer of ignitible (flammable or combustible) liquids. [30:29.1.1]

66.29.1.2 This section shall not apply to the following:

(1) Marine service stations, as covered in Chapter 30 and NFPA 30A
(2) Marinas and boatyards, as covered in Chapter 28 and NFPA 303
(3) Wharves that handle liquefied petroleum gas, as covered in Chapter 69 and NFPA 58, or liquefied natural gas, as covered in NFPA 59A

[30:29.1.2]

66.29.2 Definitions Specific to 66.29. (Reserved)

66.29.3 General Requirements.

66.29.3.1 General-purpose wharves that handle bulk transfer of ignitible (flammable or combustible) liquids and other commodities shall meet the requirements of Section 28.2 and NFPA 307. [30:29.3.1]

66.29.3.2 Incidental handling of packaged cargo of ignitible (flammable or combustible) liquids and loading or unloading of general cargo, such as ships' stores, during transfer of liquids shall be conducted only when approved by the wharf supervisor and the senior officer of the vessel. [30:29.3.2]

66.29.3.3 Wharves at which ignitible (flammable or combustible) liquid cargoes are to be transferred in bulk to or from tank vessels shall be at least 100 ft (30 m) from any bridge over a navigable waterway or from any entrance to or superstructure of a vehicular or railroad tunnel under a waterway. [30:29.3.3]

66.29.3.4 The termination of the loading or unloading fixed piping shall be at least 200 ft (60 m) from any bridge or from any entrance to or superstructure of a tunnel. [30:29.3.4]

66.29.3.5 The substructure and deck of the wharf shall be designed for the use intended. [30:29.3.5]

66.29.3.6 The deck of the wharf shall be permitted to be of any material that will afford the desired combination of flexibility, resistance to shock, durability, strength, and fire resistance. [30:29.3.6]

66.29.3.7 Heavy timber construction shall be permitted. [30:29.3.7]

66.29.3.8 Tanks used exclusively for ballast water or Class II or Class III liquids [FP ≥ 100°F (37.8°C)] stored at temperatures below their flash points shall be permitted to be installed on a wharf designed to support the weight of the tanks and their contents. [30:29.3.8]

66.29.3.9 Loading pumps capable of building up pressures that exceed the safe working pressure of cargo hose or loading arms shall be provided with bypasses, relief valves, or other arrangements to protect the loading facilities against excessive pressure. [30:29.3.9]

66.29.3.9.1 Relief devices shall be tested at least annually to determine that they function satisfactorily at their set pressure. [30:29.3.9.1]

66.29.3.10 All pressure hose and couplings shall be inspected at intervals recommended by the manufacturer for the service in which they are used. [30:29.3.10]

66.29.3.10.1 With the hose extended, the hose and couplings shall be tested using the in-service maximum operating pressure. [30:29.3.10.1]

66.29.3.10.2 Any hose showing material deterioration, signs of leakage, or weakness in its carcass or at the couplings shall be withdrawn from service and repaired or discarded. [30:29.3.10.2]

66.29.3.10.3 The hose materials used for transfer shall be compatible with the ignitible (flammable or combustible) liquids being handled. [30:29.3.10.3]

66.29.3.11 Piping, valves, and fittings shall meet applicable requirements of Section 66.27 and shall also meet the following requirements:

(1) Flexibility of piping shall be assured by layout and arrangement of piping supports so that motion of the wharf structure resulting from wave action, currents, tides, or the mooring of vessels will not subject the piping to excessive strain.
(2) Pipe joints that depend on the friction characteristics of combustible materials or on the grooving of pipe ends for mechanical continuity of piping shall not be permitted.
(3) Swivel joints shall be permitted to be used in piping to which hose are connected and for articulated swivel-joint transfer systems, provided the design is such that the mechanical strength of the joint will not be impaired if the packing materials should fail, for example, by exposure to fire.
(4) Each line conveying Class I or Class II liquids [FP < 140°F (60°C)] leading to a wharf shall be provided with a readily accessible block valve located on shore near the approach to the wharf and outside of any diked area. Where more than one line is involved, the valves shall be identified as to their specific lines and grouped in one location.
(5) Means shall be provided for easy access to any cargo line valves that are located below the wharf deck.

[30:29.3.11]

Δ **66.29.3.12** Pipelines on wharves that handle Class I or Class II liquids [FP < 140°F (60°C)] or Class III liquids [FP ≥ 140°F (60°C)] at temperatures at or above their FP, shall be bonded and grounded. [30:29.3.12]

66.29.3.12.1 Insulating flanges or joints shall be installed for protection against stray currents. [30:29.3.12.1]

66.29.3.12.2 Bonding and grounding connections on all pipelines shall be located on the wharf side of insulating flanges, if used, and shall be accessible for inspection. [30:29.3.12.2]

66.29.3.12.3 Bonding between the wharf and the vessel shall not be required. [30:29.3.12.3]

66.29.3.13 Hose or articulated swivel-joint pipe connections used for cargo transfer shall be capable of accommodating the combined effects of change in draft and change in tide. Hose shall be supported to avoid kinking and damage from chafing. [30:29.3.13]

66.29.3.14 Mooring lines shall be kept adjusted to prevent surge of the vessel from placing stress on the cargo transfer system. [30:29.3.14]

66.29.3.15 Material shall not be placed on wharves in such a manner as to obstruct access to firefighting equipment or important pipeline control valves. [30:29.3.15]

66.29.3.16 Where the wharf is accessible to vehicle traffic, an unobstructed roadway to the shore end of the wharf shall be maintained for access of firefighting apparatus. [30:29.3.16]

66.29.3.17 Loading or unloading shall not commence until the wharf supervisor and the person in charge of the tank vessel agree that the tank vessel is properly moored and all connections are properly made. [30:29.3.17]

66.29.3.18 Mechanical work shall not be performed on the wharf during cargo transfer, except under special authorization based on a review of the area involved, methods to be employed, and precautions necessary. [30:29.3.18]

66.29.3.19 Sources of ignition shall be controlled during transfer of liquids. [30:29.3.19]

66.29.3.20 Vehicular traffic and mechanical work including, but not limited to, welding, grinding, and other hot work, shall not be performed during cargo transfer except as authorized by the wharf supervisor and the senior officer on the vessel. [30:29.3.20]

66.29.3.21 Smoking shall be prohibited at all times on the wharf during cargo transfer operations. [30:29.3.21]

66.29.3.22 For marine terminals handling Class I liquids [FP < 100°F (37.8°C)] and Class II and Class III liquids [FP ≥ 100°F (37.8°C)] at temperatures at or above their FP, Figure 66.29.3.22 shall be used to determine the extent of classified areas for the purpose of installation of electrical equipment. [30:29.3.22]

66.29.3.23 Where a flammable atmosphere can exist in the vessel cargo compartment, cargo transfer systems shall be designed to limit the velocity of the incoming ignitible (flammable or combustible) liquid stream to 3 ft (0.9 m) per second until the compartment inlet opening is sufficiently submerged to prevent splashing. [30:29.3.23]

66.29.3.24 Filters, pumps, wire screens, and other devices that can produce static electric charges through turbulence shall be so located to allow a minimum of 30 seconds of relaxation time prior to discharging cargo into the compartment. [30:29.3.24]

66.29.3.25* Spill collection shall be provided around manifold areas to prevent spread of ignitible (flammable or combustible) liquids to other areas of the wharf or under the wharf. [30:29.3.25]

66.29.3.26 Vapor seals shall be provided on all drain lines leaving the wharf. [30:29.3.26]

66.29.3.27 Where required, wharves shall have a system to isolate and shut down the loading operation in the event of failure of a hose, loading arm, or manifold valve. This system shall meet all of the following requirements:

(1) If the protective system closes a valve on a gravity-fed or pipeline-fed loading system, it shall be designed to ensure the line is not subjected to damage from pressure surges.
(2) Emergency shutdown systems shall be permitted to be automatically or manually activated.

[30:29.3.27]

66.29.3.27.1 Manually activated device(s) shall be identified and accessible during an emergency. [30:29.3.27.1]

66.29.3.28* Fire protection and emergency response equipment for wharves shall be related to the products being handled, emergency response capability, size, location, frequency of use, and adjacent exposures. [30:29.3.28]

66.29.3.28.1 Where a fire water main is provided, the main shall be permitted to be wet or dry. In all cases, isolation valves and fire department connections shall be provided at the wharf-to-shore connection. [**30**:29.3.28.1]

66.29.3.28.2 Where a fire water main is provided, hydrants and monitors shall also be provided so that effective fire water streams can be applied to any berth or loading manifold from two directions. [**30**:29.3.28.2]

66.29.3.28.3 Fire water pumps, fire hose, fire water mains, foam systems, and other fire suppression equipment shall be maintained and tested in accordance with NFPA 25. [**30**:29.3.28.3]

66.29.3.28.4 Where no fire water main is provided, a minimum of two wheeled dry chemical extinguishers with minimum ratings of 240-B:C each shall be provided. The extinguishers shall be located within 50 ft (15 m) of pump or manifold areas and shall be easily reached along emergency access paths. Existing 150 lb (68 kg) dry chemical extinguishers that continue to be maintained in accordance with NFPA 10 shall be permitted to remain in service. [**30**:29.3.28.4]

△ **FIGURE 66.29.3.22** Area Classification for a Marine Terminal Handling Class I Liquids [FP < 100°F (37.8°C)]. [30:Figure 29.3.22]

Chapter 67 Flammable Solids

67.1 General.

67.1.1 The storage, use, and handling of flammable solids shall comply with the requirements of Chapter 60.

67.1.2 The storage, use, and handling of flammable solids in amounts exceeding the maximum allowable quantity permitted in control areas as set forth in Chapter 60 shall also comply with the requirements of NFPA 400.

N **67.1.3** Permits shall be required in accordance with this chapter and Table 1.13.8(a) through Table 1.13.8(d).

N **67.1.4** Permits, where required, shall comply with Section 1.13.

Chapter 68 Highly Toxic and Toxic Solids and Liquids

68.1 General.

68.1.1 The storage, use, and handling of highly toxic and toxic solids and liquids shall comply with Chapter 60.

68.1.2 The storage, use, and handling of highly toxic and toxic solids and liquids in amounts exceeding the maximum allowable quantity permitted in control areas as set forth in Chapter 60 shall also comply with the requirements of NFPA 400.

N **68.1.3** Permits shall be required in accordance with this chapter and Table 1.13.8(a) through Table 1.13.8(d).

N **68.1.4** Permits, where required, shall comply with Section 1.13.

Chapter 69 Liquefied Petroleum Gases and Liquefied Natural Gases

69.1 General Provisions.

69.1.1* Application.

69.1.1.1 The storage, use, and handling of liquefied petroleum gases (LP-Gas) shall comply with the requirements of this chapter; NFPA 58 and Sections 60.1 through 60.4 of this *Code*.

69.1.1.2 Where the provisions of Chapter 69 or NFPA 58 conflict with the provisions of Chapter 60, the provisions of this chapter and NFPA 58 shall apply.

69.1.1.3 Stationary Installations. Plans for stationary installations utilizing storage containers with aggregate water capacity exceeding 4000 gal (15.2 m³), and all rooftop installations of ASME containers shall be submitted to the AHJ before the installation is started by the person or company that either installs or contracts to have the containers installed. *[See also 6.22.11.1(F) of NFPA 58.]* [58:4.3.1]

Δ **69.1.2 Permits.**

N **69.1.2.1** Permits shall be required in accordance with this chapter and Table 1.13.8(a) through Table 1.13.8(d).

N **69.1.2.2** Permits, where required, shall comply with Section 1.13.

69.2 LP-Gas Equipment and Appliances.

69.2.1 Containers.

69.2.1.1 General.

Δ **69.2.1.1.1*** Containers shall be designed, fabricated, tested, and marked or stamped in accordance with the regulations of the US Department of Transportation (DOT 49 CFR); Federal Aviation Administration (FAA 14 CFR); Section VIII, "Rules for the Construction of Unfired Pressure Vessels," of ASME's *Boiler and Pressure Vessel Code*; or the *API-ASME Code for Unfired Pressure Vessels for Petroleum Liquids and Gases*, except for UG-125 through UG-136. [58:5.2.1.1]

69.2.1.1.1.1 Used containers constructed to specifications of the Association of American Railroads shall not be installed. [58:5.2.1.1(A)]

69.2.1.1.1.2 Adherence to the case interpretations and addenda of the applicable ASME Code that has been adopted and published within 180 calendar days prior to the effective date of NFPA 58 shall be considered compliance with the ASME Code. [58:5.2.1.1(B)]

Δ **69.2.1.1.1.3** The requirements of Section 1.4 of NFPA 58 shall apply where containers are fabricated to earlier editions of regulations, rules, or codes listed in 69.2.1.1.1, or to the Interstate Commerce Commission (ICC) *Rules for Construction of Unfired Pressure Vessels* prior to April 1, 1967. [58:5.2.1.1(I)]

69.2.1.1.2 Containers that have been involved in a fire and show no distortion shall be requalified for continued service before being used or reinstalled. [58:5.2.1.2]

69.2.1.1.2.1 Cylinders shall be requalified by a manufacturer of that type of cylinder or by a repair facility approved by DOT. [58:5.2.1.2(A)]

69.2.1.1.2.2 ASME or API-ASME containers shall be retested using the hydrostatic test procedure applicable at the time of the original fabrication. [58:5.2.1.2(B)]

69.2.1.1.2.3 All container appurtenances shall be replaced. [58:5.2.1.2(C)]

69.2.1.1.2.4 DOT 4E specification (aluminum) cylinders and composite cylinders involved in a fire shall be permanently removed from service. [58:5.2.1.2(D)]

69.2.1.1.3 ASME paragraph U-68 or U-69 containers shall be permitted to be continued in use, installed, reinstalled, or placed back into service. Installation of containers shall be in accordance with all provisions listed in NFPA 58. *(See Section 5.2, Table 5.2.4.3, Table 5.9.2.5(A), and Annex D of NFPA 58.)* [58:5.2.1.3]

69.2.1.1.4 Containers that show excessive denting, bulging, gouging, or corrosion shall be removed from service. [58:5.2.1.4]

69.2.1.1.5 Except for containers used in cargo tank vehicle service, ASME containers of 3000 gal (11.4 m³) water capacity or less used to store anhydrous ammonia shall not be converted to LP-Gas fuel service. [58:5.2.1.5]

69.2.1.1.6 Repairs or alteration of a container shall comply with the regulations, rules, or code under which the container was fabricated. Repairs or alteration to ASME containers shall be in accordance with the NBBI NB23, *National Board Inspection Code*. [58:5.2.1.6]

69.2.1.1.7 Field welding shall be permitted only on saddle plates, lugs, pads, or brackets that are attached to the container by the container manufacturer. [**58:**5.2.1.7]

69.2.1.1.8 Containers for general use shall not have individual water capacities greater than 120,000 gal (454 m³). [**58:**5.2.1.8]

Δ **69.2.1.1.9** Dispensing systems not located in LP-Gas bulk plants or industrial plants shall have an aggregate water capacity not greater than 30,000 gal (114 m³). [**58:**5.2.1.9]

69.2.1.1.10 Heating or cooling coils shall not be installed inside storage containers. [**58:**5.2.1.10]

69.2.1.1.11 ASME containers installed underground, partially underground, or as mounded installations shall incorporate provisions for cathodic protection and shall be coated with a material recommended for the service that is applied in accordance with the coating manufacturer's instructions. [**58:**5.2.1.11]

69.2.1.2 Portable Container Appurtenance Physical Damage Protection.

69.2.1.2.1 Cylinders shall incorporate protection against physical damage to cylinder appurtenances and immediate connections to such appurtenances when not in use by any of the following means:

(1) A ventilated cap
(2) A ventilated collar
(3) A cylinder valve providing inherent protection as defined by DOT in 49 CFR 173.301(h)(3) [**58:**5.2.6.1]

69.2.1.2.2 Protection of appurtenances of portable containers, skid tanks, and tanks for use as cargo tanks of more than 1000 lb (454 kg) water capacity [nominal 420 lb (191 kg) propane capacity] shall comply with 69.2.1.2.2.1 through 69.2.1.2.2.3. [**58:**5.2.6.2]

69.2.1.2.2.1 Appurtenance protection from physical damage shall be provided by recessing, by protective housings, or by location on the vehicle. [**58:**5.2.6.2(A)]

69.2.1.2.2.2 Appurtenance protection shall comply with the provisions under which the containers are fabricated. [**58:**5.2.6.2(B)]

69.2.1.2.2.3 Appurtenance protection shall be secured to the container in accordance with the ASME code under which the container was designed and built. [**58:**5.2.6.2(C)]

69.2.1.3 Portable Storage Containers.

69.2.1.3.1 The legs or supports, or the lugs for the attachment of legs or supports, shall be secured to the container in accordance with the ASME code under which the container was designed and built. [**58:**5.2.7.1]

69.2.1.3.2 The attachment of a container to either a trailer or semitrailer running gear, or the attachments to the container to make it a vehicle, so that the unit can be moved by a conventional over-the-road tractor, shall comply with the DOT requirements for cargo tank service. [**58:**5.2.7.2]

69.2.1.3.3 Portable tank design and construction of a full framework, skids, or lugs for the attachment of skids, and protection of fittings shall be in accordance with DOT portable tank specifications. The bottom of the skids shall be not less than 2 in. (51 mm) or more than 12 in. (300 mm) below the outside bottom of the tank shell. [**58:**5.2.7.3]

69.2.1.4 Container Marking.

69.2.1.4.1 Cylinders shall be marked as provided in the regulations, rules, or code under which they are fabricated. [**58:**5.2.8.1]

69.2.1.4.1.1 Where LP-Gas and one or more other compressed gases are to be stored or used in the same area, the cylinders shall be marked "Flammable" and either "LP-Gas," "Propane," or "Butane," or shall be marked in accordance with the requirements of 49 CFR, "Transportation." [**58:**5.2.8.1(A)]

69.2.1.4.1.2 When being transported, cylinders shall be marked and labeled in accordance with 49 CFR, "Transportation." [**58:**5.2.8.1(B)]

69.2.1.4.2* Cylinders shall be marked with the following information:

(1) Water capacity of the cylinder in pounds
(2) Tare weight of the cylinder in pounds, fitted for service [**58:**5.2.8.2]

69.2.1.4.3* The markings specified for ASME containers shall be on a stainless steel metal nameplate attached to the container, located to remain visible after the container is installed. [**58:**5.2.8.3]

69.2.1.4.3.1 The nameplate shall be attached in such a way as to minimize corrosion of the nameplate or its fastening means and not contribute to corrosion of the container. [**58:**5.2.8.3(A)]

69.2.1.4.3.2 Where the container is buried, mounded, insulated, or otherwise covered so the nameplate is obscured, the information contained on the nameplate shall be duplicated and installed on adjacent piping or on a structure in a clearly visible location. [**58:**5.2.8.3(B)]

Δ **69.2.1.4.3.3** ASME containers shall be marked with the following information:

(1) All ASME container nameplate requirements
(2) Service (i.e., aboveground, underground, or both)
(3) Water capacity of container in pounds or US gallons
(4) Wording that reads "This container shall not contain a product that has a vapor pressure in excess of ___ psig at 100°F" *(see Table 5.2.4.3 of NFPA 58)*
(5) Outside surface area in square feet
(6) Shell thickness and head thickness
(7) Overall length (OL), outside diameter (OD), and head design (HD)

[**58:**5.2.8.3(C)]

69.2.1.4.3.4 In addition to the markings required by this *Code*, nameplates on cargo tanks shall include the markings required by the ASME Code and the DOT. [**58:**5.2.8.3(D)]

69.2.1.4.4 Warning labels shall meet the following requirements:

(1) Warning labels shall be applied to all cylinders of 100 lb (45.4 kg) propane capacity or less that are not filled on-site.
(2) Warning labels shall include information on the potential hazards of LP-Gas. [**58:**5.2.8.4]

69.2.1.4.5 All containers that contain unodorized LP-Gas products shall be marked "NOT ODORIZED." [**58:**5.2.8.5]

69.2.1.4.5.1 The marking shall have a contrasting background surrounded by a rectangular red border and with red letters in the sizes shown in Table 69.2.1.4.5.1. [**58:**5.2.8.5(A)]

69.2.1.4.5.2 The markings shall be on both ends or on both sides of a container or on both sides and the rear of cargo tanks. [**58:**5.2.8.5(B)]

69.2.2 Reserved.

69.2.3 Reserved.

69.2.4 Reserved.

69.2.5 Reserved.

69.2.6 Containers with Attached Supports.

69.2.6.1 Vertical ASME Containers. Vertical ASME containers of over 125 gal (0.5 m³) water capacity for use in permanent installations in stationary service shall be designed with steel supports that allow the container to be installed on and fastened to concrete foundations or supports. [**58:**5.6.1]

69.2.6.1.1 Steel supports shall be designed to make the container self-supporting without guy wires and to withstand the wind and seismic (earthquake) forces anticipated at the site. [**58:**5.6.1.1]

69.2.6.1.2 Steel supports shall be protected against fire exposure with a material having a fire resistance rating of at least 2 hours. [**58:**5.6.1.2]

69.2.6.1.3 Continuous steel skirts having only one opening of 18 in. (460 mm) or less in diameter shall have 2-hour fire protection applied to the outside of the skirt. [**58:**5.6.1.3]

69.2.6.2 Skid Tanks. Skid tanks shall have a secure steel frame to allow transportation of the skid tank when not filled with LP-Gas. [**58:**5.6.2]

69.2.6.3 Porta-Pacs.

69.2.6.3.1 The legs or supports, or the lugs for the attachment of legs or supports, shall be secured to the container in accordance with the ASME code under which the container was designed and built. [**58:**5.6.3.1]

69.2.6.3.2 The ASME container shall be attached to either of the following:

(1) A trailer or semitrailer running gear, or the attachments to the container to make it a vehicle, so that the unit can be moved by a conventional over-the-road tractor.
(2) A metal frame such that the container can be moved as a trailer if wheels are added, which is approved for stationary use, or on a flat rail car.

[**58:**5.6.3.2]

69.2.6.3.3 Protection of appurtenances shall be in accordance with 69.2.1.2. [**58:**5.6.3.3]

69.2.6.3.4 Movable fuel storage tenders shall be secured to the trailer support structure for the service involved. [**58:**5.6.3.4]

69.2.7 Reserved.

69.2.8 Reserved.

69.2.9 Container Appurtenances.

69.2.9.1 Materials.

69.2.9.1.1 Container appurtenances and regulators shall be fabricated of materials that are compatible with LP-Gas and shall be resistant to the action of LP-Gas under service conditions. [**58:**5.9.1.1]

(A) The following materials shall not be used:

(1) Gray cast iron
(2) Nonmetallic materials for bonnets or bodies of valves or regulators

[**58:**5.9.1.1(A)]

69.2.9.1.2* Pressure-containing metal parts of appurtenances shall have a minimum melting point of 1500°F (816°C), except for the following:

(1) Fusible elements
(2) Approved or listed variable liquid level gauges used in containers of 3500 gal (13.2 m³) water capacity or less

[**58:**5.9.1.2]

69.2.9.1.3 Container appurtenances shall have a service pressure of at least 250 psig (1.7 MPag). [**58:**5.9.1.3]

69.2.9.1.4 Gaskets used to retain LP-Gas in containers shall be resistant to the action of LP-Gas. [**58:**5.9.1.4]

69.2.9.1.4.1 Gaskets shall be made of metal or other material confined in metal having a melting point over 1500°F (816°C) or shall be protected against fire exposure. [**58:**5.9.1.4(A)]

69.2.9.1.4.2 When a flange is opened, the gasket shall be replaced. [**58:**5.9.1.4(B)]

69.2.9.1.4.3 Aluminum O-rings and spiral-wound metal gaskets shall be permitted. [**58:**5.9.1.4(C)]

69.2.9.1.4.4 Gaskets for use with approved or listed liquid level gauges for installation on a container of 3500 gal (13.2 m³) water capacity or less shall be exempt from the minimum melting point requirement. [**58:**5.9.1.4(D)]

69.2.10 Piping (Including Hose), Fittings, and Valves. Piping (including hose), fittings, and valves shall comply with Section 5.11 of NFPA 58.

69.3 Installation of LP-Gas Systems.

69.3.1* Application. Section 69.3 applies to the following:

(1) Location and field installation of LP-Gas systems that use components, subassemblies, container assemblies, and container systems that are fabricated in accordance with Chapter 5 of NFPA 58
(2) Location of containers and liquid transfer systems
(3) Installation of container appurtenances and regulators
(4) Installation of piping (including flexible connectors and hose), hydrostatic relief valves, and piping service limitations

Δ Table 69.2.1.4.5.1 Size of "NOT ODORIZED" Marking

Water Capacity		Letter Height		Border Width	
gal	m³	in.	mm	in.	mm
≥499	≥1.89	4	100	½	13
49–498	0.19–1.88	1½	37	⁵⁄₁₆	8
2.6–48	0.01–0.1	¾	0.18	¼	6
1–2.5	0.004–0.009	⅜	10	¹⁄₁₆	2

[**58:**Table 5.2.8.5(A)]

(5) Installation of equipment
(6) Testing of piping systems
(7) Location of containers not connected for use
[**58:**6.1.1]

69.3.2 Nonapplication. This chapter does not apply to the following:

(1) Refrigerated containers
(2) Installation of systems used in the highway transportation of LP-Gas
[**58:**6.1.2]

69.3.3 Location of Containers.

69.3.3.1 LP-Gas containers shall be located outside of buildings unless they are specifically allowed to be located inside of buildings. [**58:**6.2.1]

69.3.3.2 LP-Gas containers shall be allowed in buildings only for the following applications:

(1) Cylinders as specifically provided for in Section 6.23 of NFPA 58
(2) Containers of less than 125 gal (0.5 m^3) water capacity for the purposes of being filled in buildings or structures complying with Chapter 10 of NFPA 58
(3) Containers on LP-Gas vehicles complying with, and parked or garaged in accordance with, Chapter 9 of NFPA 58
(4) Containers used with LP-Gas portable engine fuel systems complying with 11.13.1 of NFPA 58
(5) Containers used with LP-Gas stationary engine fuel systems complying with Section 6.29 of NFPA 58
(6) Containers used with LP-Gas–fueled industrial trucks complying with 11.11.4 of NFPA 58
(7) Containers on LP-Gas–fueled vehicles garaged in accordance with Section 11.14 of NFPA 58
(8) Cylinders awaiting use, resale, or exchange when stored in accordance with 69.5.2 and 69.5.3
[**58:**6.2.2]

69.3.4 Location of Containers Not Connected for Use.

69.3.4.1 Cylinders awaiting use, resale, or exchange shall be stored in accordance with Chapter 8 of NFPA 58. [**58:**6.3.1]

69.3.4.2 ASME containers of 4,000 gal (15.2 m^3) or less that have been removed from service but that contain LP-Gas shall be stored outside of buildings in accordance with either 69.3.4.2(1) or 69.3.4.2(2):

(1) Containers shall be located either at a bulk plant or in an approved area.
(2) Containers not complying with 69.3.4.2(1) shall comply with the following:

   (a) Containers shall be located in a manner that will minimize exposure to physical damage.
   (b) Containers shall be oriented so that the pressure relief valve remains in communication with the vapor space.
   (c) Containers shall not be located on roofs of buildings.
   (d) Valve outlets on ASME containers shall be plugged or capped.
   (e) Where screw-on-type caps or collars are utilized on ASME containers, they shall be in place whenever this type of container is stored regardless of the fill level of the container.
   (f) The location of ASME containers shall comply with the "Aboveground Containers" column and the "Between Containers" column of Table 69.3.5.1.1 with respect to important buildings and lines of adjoining property that can be built upon.
   (g) Where the provisions of 69.3.4.2(2)(f) are impractical, alternative storage locations for containers shall be approved by the AHJ.

[**58:**6.3.2]

69.3.5 Container Separation Distances.

69.3.5.1 Aboveground Containers.

69.3.5.1.1* Containers installed outside of buildings, whether of the portable type replaced on a cylinder exchange basis or permanently installed and refilled at the installation, shall be located with respect to the adjacent containers, important building, group of buildings, or line of adjoining property that can be built upon, in accordance with Table 69.3.5.1.1, Table 69.3.6.1.2, 69.3.5.1.2 through 69.3.5.1.3, 69.3.5.3, 69.3.5.4.1 through 69.3.5.4.4, and 69.3.6.3.6 through 69.3.6.3.11. [**58:**6.4.1.1]

69.3.5.1.2 When the provisions of 6.31.3 through 6.31.5 of NFPA 58 are met, the minimum distance from an ASME container to a building or adjoining property line that can be built upon shall be reduced by one-half for ASME containers of 2001 gal through 30,000 gal (7.6 m^3 through 114 m^3) water capacity. [**58:**6.4.1.2]

69.3.5.1.3 The 25 ft (7.6 m) minimum distance from aboveground ASME containers of 501 gal through 2000 gal (1.9 m^3 through 7.6 m^3) water capacity to buildings, a group of buildings, or the line of adjoining property that can be built upon shall be reduced to 10 ft (3 m) for a single ASME container of 1200 gal (4.5 m^3) or less water capacity where such container is at least 25 ft (7.6 m) from any other LP-Gas container of more than 125 gal (0.5 m^3) water capacity. [**58:**6.4.1.3]

69.3.5.2 Underground or Mounded ASME Containers.

Δ **69.3.5.2.1** Minimum distances from important buildings and the line of adjoining property that can be built upon for underground or mounded ASME containers larger than 2000 gal (7.6 m^3) water capacity incorporating all the provisions of Section 6.31 of NFPA 58, shall be reduced to 10 ft (3 m). [**58:**6.4.2.1]

69.3.5.2.2 Distances for all underground and mounded ASME containers shall be measured from the container surface. [**58:**6.4.2.2]

69.3.5.2.3 No part of an underground or mounded ASME container shall be less than 10 ft (3 m) from a building or line of adjoining property that can be built upon. [**58:**6.4.2.3]

69.3.5.3 Multiple Containers Less Than 125 gal (0.5 m^3) Individual Water Capacity. Multiple containers, each having a water capacity less than 125 gal (0.5 m^3) and installed in an aboveground group as a manifolded single service or as individual services, shall comply with the following:

(1) Where the aggregate water capacity of all containers in any group is 500 gal (1.9 m^3) or less, the minimum separation distances required by Table 69.3.5.1.1 for each container shall be 0 ft (0 m) for each container in the group from an important building or line of adjoining property that can be built upon.

Table 69.3.5.1.1 Separation Distances Between Containers, Important Buildings, and Line of Adjoining Property That Can Be Built Upon

Water Capacity per Container		Minimum Distances					
		Mounded or Underground Containers[a]		Aboveground Containers		Between Containers[b]	
gal	m³	ft	m	ft	m	ft	m
<125[c]	<0.5[c]	10	3	0[d]	0[d]	0	0
125–250	0.5–1.0	10	3	10	3	0	0
251–500	>1.0–1.9	10	3	10	3	3	1
501–2,000	>1.9–7.6	10	3	25[e]	7.6	3	1
2,001–30,000	>7.6–114	50	15	50	15	5	1.5
30,001–70,000	>114–265	50	15	75	23		
70,001–90,000	>265–341	50	15	100	30	¼ of sum of diameters of adjacent containers	
90,001–120,000	>341–454	50	15	125	38		
120,001–200,000	>454–757	50	15	200	61		
200,001–1,000,000	>757–3785	50	15	300	91		
>1,000,000	>3785	50	15	400	122		

[a]See 69.3.5.2.1.
[b]See 69.3.5.4.5.
[c]See 69.3.5.4.4.
[d]See 69.3.5.4.1, 69.3.5.4.2, 69.3.5.4.3, 69.3.5.4.4.
[e]See 69.3.5.1.3.
[58:Table 6.4.1.1]

(2) Where the aggregate water capacity of all containers in the group is greater than 500 gal (1.9 m³), the minimum separation distances in Table 69.3.5.1.1 for each container shall be based on the aggregate capacity.
(3) There shall be no separation required between individual containers within the group.
(4)* For the application of 69.3.5.3(1) and 69.3.5.3(2), the number of containers in a single group is determined by the number of containers that are less than 10 ft (3 m) from any other container in the group.
[58:6.4.3]

69.3.5.4 Separation Distance Between Container Pressure Relief Valve and Building Openings.

69.3.5.4.1 Cylinders shall not be located and installed underneath any building unless the space is open to the atmosphere for 50 percent of its perimeter or more. [58:6.4.4.1]

69.3.5.4.2 ASME containers of less than 125 gal (0.5 m³) water capacity shall be located and installed so that the discharge from pressure relief devices shall not terminate in or beneath any building. [58:6.4.4.2]

69.3.5.4.3* The distance measured horizontally from the point of discharge of a container pressure relief valve to any building opening below the level of such discharge shall be in accordance with Table 69.3.5.4.3. [58:6.4.4.3]

69.3.5.4.4 The distance measured in any direction from the point of discharge of a container pressure relief valve, vent of a fixed maximum liquid level gauge on a container, and the container filling connection to exterior sources of ignition, openings into direct-vent (sealed combustion system) appliances, and mechanical ventilation air intakes shall be in accordance with Table 69.3.5.4.3. [58:6.4.4.4]

69.3.5.4.5 Access at the ends or sides of individual underground containers having a water capacity of 125 gal (0.5 m³) or more shall be provided in multicontainer installations to facilitate working with cranes or hoists. [58:6.4.4.5]

69.3.6 Other Container Location Requirements.

69.3.6.1 ASME Multicontainer Requirements.

69.3.6.1.1 Where storage containers having an aggregate water capacity of more than 4000 gal (15.2 m³) are located in

Table 69.3.5.4.3 Separation Distance Between Container Pressure Relief Valve and Building Openings

Container Type	Exchange or Filled at Point of Use	Distance Horizontally from Relief Valve Discharge to Opening Below Discharge		Discharge from Relief Valve, Vent Discharge, and Filling Connection to Exterior Source of Ignition, Openings into Direct-Vent Appliances, and Mechanical Ventilation Air Intakes	
		ft	m	ft	m
Cylinder	Exchange	3	0.9	5	1.5
Cylinder	Filled at the point of use	3	0.9	10	3.0
ASME	Filled at the point of use	5	1.5	10	3.0

[58:Table 6.4.4.3]

heavily populated or congested areas, the siting provisions of 69.3.5.1.1 and Table 69.3.5.1.1 shall be permitted to be modified as indicated by the fire safety analysis described in 6.30.3 of NFPA 58. [58:6.5.1.1]

69.3.6.1.2 Aboveground multicontainer installations comprised of ASME containers having an individual water capacity of 12,000 gal (45 m³) or more and installed for use in a single location shall be limited to the number of containers in one group, with each group separated from the next group in accordance with the degree of fire protection provided in Table 69.3.6.1.2. [58:6.5.1.2]

69.3.6.1.3 Where the provisions of 6.31.3 and 6.31.4 of NFPA 58 are met, the minimum separation distance between groups of ASME containers protected by hose stream only shall be one-half the distances required in Table 69.3.6.1.2. [58:6.5.1.3]

69.3.6.2 Underground and Mounded ASME Containers.

69.3.6.2.1 Underground or mounded ASME containers shall be located in accordance with 69.3.6.2.2 and 69.3.6.2.3. [58:6.5.2.1]

69.3.6.2.2 Underground or mounded containers shall be located outside of any buildings. [58:6.5.2.2]

69.3.6.2.3 Buildings shall not be constructed over any underground or mounded containers. [58:6.5.2.3]

69.3.6.2.4 The sides of adjacent containers shall be separated in accordance with Table 69.3.5.1.1 but shall not be separated by less than 3 ft (1 m). [58:6.5.2.4]

69.3.6.2.5 Where containers are installed parallel with ends in line, the number of containers in one group shall not be limited. [58:6.5.2.5]

69.3.6.2.6 Where more than one row of containers is installed, the adjacent ends of the containers in each row shall be separated by not less than 10 ft (3 m). [58:6.5.2.6]

69.3.6.3 Additional Container Installation Requirements.

69.3.6.3.1 Additional container installation requirements shall comply with 69.3.6.3.2 through 69.3.6.3.13 and 69.3.6.4. [58:6.5.3.1]

Δ **Table 69.3.6.1.2 Maximum Number of Containers in a Group and Their Separation Distances**

Fire Protection Provided by	Maximum Number of Containers in One Group	Minimum Separation Between Groups ft	Minimum Separation Between Groups m
Hose streams only (see 6.5.1.2 and 6.30.3.1 of NFPA 58)	6	50	15
Fixed monitor nozzles per 6.30.6.3 of NFPA 58	6	25	7.6
Fixed water spray per 6.30.6.1 of NFPA 58	9	25	7.6
Insulation per 6.30.5.1 of NFPA 58	9	25	7.6

[58:Table 6.5.1.2]

69.3.6.3.2 Containers shall not be stacked one above the other. [58:6.5.3.2]

69.3.6.3.3* Combustible materials shall not accumulate or be stored within 10 ft (3 m) of a container. [58:6.5.3.3]

69.3.6.3.4* The area under containers shall be graded or shall have dikes or curbs installed so that the flow or accumulation of flammable liquids with flash points below 200°F (93.4°C) is prevented. [58:6.5.3.4]

69.3.6.3.5* LP-Gas containers shall be located at least 10 ft (3 m) from the centerline of the wall of diked areas containing Class I flammable or Class II combustible liquids. [58:6.5.3.5]

69.3.6.3.6 The minimum horizontal separation between aboveground LP-Gas containers and aboveground tanks containing liquids having flash points below 200°F (93.4°C) shall be 20 ft (6 m). [58:6.5.3.6]

69.3.6.3.7 The requirements of 69.3.6.3.6 shall not apply where LP-Gas containers of 125 gal (0.5 m³) or less water capacity are installed adjacent to fuel oil supply tanks of 660 gal (2.5 m³) or less capacity. [58:6.5.3.7]

69.3.6.3.8 No horizontal separation shall be required between aboveground LP-Gas containers and underground tanks containing flammable or combustible liquids installed in accordance with NFPA 30. [58:6.5.3.8]

69.3.6.3.9* The minimum separation between LP-Gas containers and oxygen or gaseous hydrogen containers shall be in accordance with NFPA 55. [58:6.5.3.9]

69.3.6.3.10 Where protective structures having a minimum fire resistance rating of 2 hours interrupt the line of sight between uninsulated portions of the oxygen or hydrogen containers and the LP-Gas containers, no minimum distance shall apply. [58:6.5.3.10]

69.3.6.3.11 The minimum separation between LP-Gas containers and liquefied hydrogen containers shall be in accordance with NFPA 55. [58:6.5.3.11]

69.3.6.3.12 Where LP-Gas cylinders are to be stored or used in the same area with other compressed gases, the cylinders shall be marked to identify their content in accordance with CGA C-7, *Guide to Classification and Labeling of Compressed Gases*. [58:6.5.3.12]

69.3.6.3.13 An aboveground LP-Gas container and any of its parts shall not be located within 6 ft (1.8 m) of a vertical plane beneath overhead electric power lines that are over 600 volts, nominal. [58:6.5.3.13]

69.3.6.3.14 The minimum separation distances specified in Table 69.3.5.1.1 between containers and buildings of noncombustible construction devoted exclusively to gas manufacturing and distribution operations shall be reduced to 10 ft (3 m). [58:6.5.3.14]

69.3.6.4* Structure Requirements.

69.3.6.4.1 Structures such as fire walls, fences, earth or concrete barriers, and other similar structures shall be permitted around installed nonrefrigerated containers in accordance with all of the following:

(1) Clearance shall be provided around the container for inspection and maintenance.

(2) The structure shall be open on at least one side that includes the longest dimension of the container.
(3) The top of the container shall be capable of being wetted by an emergency response hose stream.
[58:6.5.4.1]

69.3.6.4.2 Structures used to prevent flammable or combustible liquid accumulation or flow shall be permitted in accordance with 69.3.6.3.4. [58:6.5.4.2]

69.3.6.4.3 Structures between LP-Gas containers and gaseous hydrogen containers shall be permitted in accordance with 69.3.6.3.10. [58:6.5.4.3]

69.3.6.4.4 Structures such as fences shall be permitted in accordance with 6.22.4 of NFPA 58. [58:6.5.4.4]

69.3.7 Location of Transfer Operations.

69.3.7.1 Transfer of Liquids.

69.3.7.1.1* Liquid shall be transferred into containers, including containers mounted on vehicles, only outdoors, under weather canopies, or in structures in accordance with Chapter 10 of NFPA 58. [58:6.7.1.1]

Δ **69.3.7.1.2** The transfer of liquid into containers on the roofs of structures shall be permitted, provided that the installation conforms to the requirements specified in 6.8.9 and 6.23.11 in NFPA 58. [58:6.7.1.2]

69.3.7.1.3 The transfer hose shall not be routed in or through any buildings except those specified in 6.7.1.1 of NFPA 58. [58:6.7.1.3]

69.3.7.1.4 Filling of containers located outdoors in stationary installations in accordance with Section 6.4 of NFPA 58 shall be permitted to be filled at that location. [58:6.7.1.4]

69.3.7.1.5 The transfer hose shall not be routed in or through any building except those specified in 69.3.7.1.3. [58:6.7.1.3]

69.3.7.1.6 Filling of containers located outdoors in stationary installations in accordance with 69.3.5 shall be permitted to be filled at that location. [58:6.7.1.4]

69.3.7.2 Container Point of Transfer Location Requirements.

69.3.7.2.1* If the point of transfer of containers located outdoors in stationary installations is not located at the container, it shall be located in accordance with Table 69.3.7.2.1. [58:6.7.2.1]

69.3.7.2.2 Containers not located in stationary installations shall be filled at a location determined by the point of transfer in accordance with Table 69.3.7.2.1. [58:6.7.2.2]

69.3.7.3 Separation Distance from Point of Transfer.

69.3.7.3.1 If the point of transfer is a component of a system covered by Section 6.27 or Chapter 11 of NFPA 58, the requirements of parts A, B, and C of Table 69.3.7.2.1 shall not apply to the structure containing the point of transfer. [58:6.7.3.1]

Δ Table 69.3.7.2.1 Distance Between Point of Transfer and Exposures

Part	Exposure	Minimum Horizontal Distance ft	m
A	Buildings,[a] mobile homes, recreational vehicles, and modular homes with at least 1-hour fire-rated walls	10	3.1
B	Buildings[a] with other than at least 1-hour fire-rated walls	25[b]	7.6[b]
C	Building wall openings or pits at or below the level of the point of transfer	25[b]	7.6[b]
D	Line of adjoining property that can be built upon	25[b]	7.6[b]
E	Outdoor places of public assembly, including schoolyards, athletic fields, and playgrounds	50[b]	15[b]
F	Public ways, including public streets, highways, thoroughfares, and sidewalks		
	(1) From points of transfer for LP-Gas dispensing systems	10	3.1
	(2) From other points of transfer	25[b]	7.6[b]
G	Driveways[c]	5	1.5
H	Mainline railroad track centerlines	25	7.6
I	Containers[d] other than those being filled	10	3.1
J	Flammable and Class II combustible liquid[e] dispensers and the fill connections of containers	10[b]	3.1[b]
K	Flammable and Class II combustible liquid[e] aboveground containers and filling connections of underground containers	20	6.1
L	Stored or accumulated combustible materials	10	3.1

[a]For the purpose of this table, buildings also include structures such as tents and box trailers at construction sites.
[b]See 69.3.7.3.4.
[c]Not applicable to driveways and points of transfer at vehicle fuel dispensers.
[d]Not applicable to filling connections at the storage container or to dispensing vehicle fuel dispenser units of 4000 gal (15.2 m^3) water capacity or less when used for filling containers not mounted on vehicles.
[e]NFPA 30 defines Class I flammable liquids as including those having a flash point below 100°F (37.8°C) and having a vapor pressure not exceeding 40 psia (276 kPa) at 100°F (37.8°C). NFPA 30 defines Class II combustible liquids as including those having a flash point at or above 100°F (37.8°C) and below 140°F (60°C).
[58:Table 6.7.2.1]

69.3.7.3.2 If LP-Gas is vented to the atmosphere under the conditions stipulated in 7.3.1.1(4) of NFPA 58, the distances in Table 69.3.7.2.1 shall be doubled. [**58:**6.7.3.2]

69.3.7.3.3 If the point of transfer is housed in a structure complying with Chapter 10 of NFPA 58, and the common walls comply with 10.2.1 of NFPA 58, separation distances in Table 69.3.7.2.1 shall not be required where the common walls comply with 10.3.1.3 of NFPA 58. [**58:**6.7.3.3]

69.3.7.3.4 The distances in Table 69.3.7.2.1, parts B, C, D, E, F(2), and J, shall be reduced by one-half where the system incorporates the provisions of low-emission transfer as provided in 6.31.5 of NFPA 58. [**58:**6.7.3.4]

69.3.8 Installation of Containers.

69.3.8.1 General Requirements.

69.3.8.1.1 Containers shall be positioned so that the pressure relief valve is in direct communication with the vapor space of the container. [**58:**6.8.1.1]

69.3.8.1.2 LP-Gas containers or systems that are installed within 10 ft (3 m) of public vehicular thoroughfares shall be provided with a means of vehicular barrier protection. [**58:**6.8.1.2]

69.3.8.1.3 Field welding on containers shall be limited to nonpressure parts such as saddle plates, wear plates, or brackets installed by the container manufacturer. [**58:**6.8.1.3]

69.3.8.1.4* Aboveground containers shall be painted. [**58:**6.8.1.4]

69.3.8.1.5 Containers shall be installed so that all container operating appurtenances are accessible. [**58:**6.8.1.5]

69.3.8.1.6 Where necessary to prevent flotation due to possible high flood waters around aboveground or mounded containers, or high water table for those underground and partially underground, containers shall be securely anchored. [**58:**6.8.1.6]

69.3.8.1.7 ASME containers that have liquid interconnections shall be installed so that the maximum permitted filling level of each container is at the same elevation. [**58:**6.8.1.7]

69.3.8.2 Installation of Cylinders.

69.3.8.2.1 Cylinders shall be installed only above ground and shall be set upon a firm foundation or otherwise be firmly secured. *(See 69.3.8.2.2.)* [**58:**6.8.2.1]

69.3.8.2.2 The cylinder shall not be in contact with the soil. [**58:**6.8.2.2]

69.3.8.2.3 Flexibility shall be provided in the connecting piping. *(See 69.3.8.2.4.)* [**58:**6.8.2.3]

69.3.8.2.4 Where flexible connectors are used, they shall comply with 6.11.7 of NFPA 58. [**58:**6.8.2.4]

69.3.9 Internal Valves.

69.3.9.1 The requirements of 69.3.9.2 through 69.3.9.5 shall be required for internal valves in liquid service that are installed in containers of over 4000 gal (15.2 m^3) water capacity by July 1, 2003. [**58:**6.13.1]

69.3.9.2 Internal valves shall be installed in accordance with 5.9.4.2 and Table 5.9.4.2 of NFPA 58 on containers of over 4000 gal (15.2 m^3) water capacity. [**58:**6.13.2]

69.3.9.3 Thermal Activation.

69.3.9.3.1 Automatic shutdown of internal valves in liquid service shall be provided using thermal (fire) actuation. [**58:**6.13.3.1]

69.3.9.3.2 The thermal sensing element of the internal valve shall be within 5 ft (1.5 m) of the internal valve. [**58:**6.13.3.2]

69.3.9.4 Emergency Remote Shutdown of Internal Valves. Where emergency remote shutdown devices are required to operate valves or electrical equipment, they shall comply with the following requirements:

(1) The devices shall be readily accessible.
(2) The devices shall be located along a path of egress.
(3) The devices shall be installed not less than 20 ft (6 m) or more than 100 ft (30 m) from the point of transfer controlled by the valve or electrical equipment.
(4) The devices shall be identified by a sign incorporating the words "[name of the LP-Gas] Emergency Shutoff" in block letters at least 2 in. (51 mm) in height on a background of contrasting color to the letters.
(5) Where the facility provides a single product or a single emergency shutoff controlling multiple products, the "[name of the LP-Gas]" designation in accordance with 69.3.9.4(4) shall not be required.
(6) The sign required by 69.3.9.4(4) shall be located at the device.
(7) The devices shall be installed outside of buildings except as in 69.3.9.4(8).
(8) The devices shall be permitted to be installed within the structure where the point of transfer is located within a structure complying with Chapter 10 of NFPA 58.

[**58:**4.10]

Δ **69.3.9.4.1** At least one remote emergency shutdown device in accordance with 69.3.9.4 shall be installed for internal valves in liquid service. [**58:**6.13.4.1]

69.3.9.4.2 The requirements of 69.3.9.4.1 shall be retroactive to all internal valves required by NFPA 58 within 3 years of the first adoption of this edition. [**58:**6.13.4.2]

69.3.9.5 Remote shutdown equipment operating valves specified in 5.9.4.2 of NFPA 58 shall be tested for proper operation monthly, with the results documented, except as specified in 69.3.9.6. [**58:**6.13.4.3]

N **69.3.9.6** If the interval between transfers exceeds 30 days, the test shall be performed prior to the next transfer. [**58:**6.13.4.4]

N **69.3.9.7*** Internal valves and emergency shutoff valves installed in lieu of internal valves in liquid service shall be visually verified for closure during the monthly inspection, except as specified in 69.3.9.6. [**58:**6.13.4.5]

N **69.3.9.8** Remote shutdown of internal valves and emergency shutoff valves as specified in Section 6.14 of NFPA 58 shall be permitted to be incorporated into the same remote shutdown station. [**58:**6.13.4.6]

69.3.10 Emergency Shutoff Valves.

Δ **69.3.10.1** Stationary container storage systems with an aggregate water capacity of more than 4000 gal (15.2 m^3) utilizing a liquid transfer line that is 1½ in. (39 mm) or larger and a pressure equalizing vapor line that is 1¼ in. (32 mm) or larger shall be equipped with emergency shutoff valves. [58:6.15.1]

69.3.10.2 An emergency shutoff valve shall be installed in the transfer lines of the fixed piping transfer system within 20 ft (6 m) of lineal pipe from the nearest end of the hose or swivel-type piping connections. [58:6.15.2]

69.3.10.3 When the flow is only into the container, a backflow check valve shall be permitted to be used in lieu of an emergency shutoff valve if installed in the piping transfer system downstream of the hose or swivel-type piping connections. [58:6.15.3]

69.3.10.4 The backflow check valve shall have a metal-to-metal seat or a primary resilient seat with metal backup, not hinged with combustible material, and shall be designed for this specific application. [58:6.15.4]

69.3.10.5 Where there are two or more liquid or vapor lines with hoses or swivel-type piping connected of the sizes designated, an emergency shutoff valve or a backflow check valve, where allowed, shall be installed in each leg of the piping. [58:6.15.5]

Δ **69.3.10.6** Emergency shutoff valves shall be installed so that the temperature-sensitive element in the valve, or a supplemental temperature-sensitive element connected to actuate the valve, is not more than 5 ft (1.5 m) from the nearest end of the hose or swivel-type piping connected to the line in which the valve is installed. [58:6.15.6]

69.3.10.7 Temperature-sensitive elements of emergency shutoff valves shall not be painted or coated after manufacture. [58:6.15.7]

69.3.10.8* The emergency shutoff valves or backflow check valves shall be installed in the fixed piping so that any break resulting from a pull will occur on the hose or swivel-type piping side of the connection while retaining intact the valves and piping on the plant side of the connection. [58:6.15.8]

69.3.10.9 Where emergency shutoff valves are required to be installed in accordance with 69.3.10.2, a means shall be incorporated to actuate the emergency shutoff valves in the event of a break of the fixed piping resulting from a pull on the hose. [58:6.15.9]

69.3.10.10 Emergency shutoff valves required by NFPA 58 shall be tested monthly for the functions required by 5.15.2.3(2) and 5.15.2.3(3) of NFPA 58, with the results documented, except as specified in 6.15.10.1 of NFPA 58. [58:6.15.10]

69.3.10.11 Backflow check valves installed in lieu of emergency shutoff valves shall be checked annually for proper operation, and the results of the test shall be documented. [58:6.15.11]

69.3.10.12 All new and existing emergency shutoff valves shall comply with 69.3.10.12.1 through 69.3.10.12.2. [58:6.15.12]

69.3.10.12.1 At least one remote emergency shutdown device in accordance with 69.3.9.4 shall be installed for each emergency shutoff valve. [58:6.15.12.1]

Δ **69.3.10.12.2** Where an emergency shutoff valve is used in lieu of an internal valve in compliance with 5.9.4.2(D)(2) of NFPA 58, the remote shutoff device shall be installed in accordance with 69.3.9.4. [58:6.15.12.2]

69.3.10.13 Emergency shutoff valves for railroad tank car transfer systems shall be in accordance with 6.22.2.6, 6.31.4, 7.2.3.7, and 7.2.3.8 of NFPA 58. [58:6.15.13]

69.3.11 Installation in Areas of Heavy Snowfall.

69.3.11.1* In areas where the ground snow load is equal to or exceeds 100 psf (488 kg/m^2), piping, regulators, meters, and other equipment installed in the piping system shall be protected from the forces of accumulated snow. [58:6.19.1]

69.3.12 LP-Gas Systems in Buildings or on Building Roofs or Exterior Balconies.

69.3.12.1 Application.

69.3.12.1.1 Subsection 69.3.12 shall apply to the installation of the following LP-Gas systems in buildings or structures:

(1) Cylinders inside of buildings or on the roofs or exterior balconies of buildings
(2) Systems in which the liquid is piped from outside containers into buildings or onto the roof

[58:6.23.1.1]

69.3.12.1.2 The phrase *cylinders in use* shall mean connected for use. [58:6.23.1.2]

69.3.12.1.2.1 The use of cylinders indoors shall be only for the purposes specified in 6.23.4 through 6.23.10 of NFPA 58. [58:6.23.1.2(A)]

69.3.12.1.2.2 The use of cylinders indoors shall be limited to those conditions where operational requirements make the indoor use of cylinders necessary and location outside is impractical. [58:6.23.1.2(B)]

69.3.12.1.2.3 The use of cylinders on roofs shall be limited to those conditions where operational requirements make the use of cylinders necessary and location other than on roofs of buildings or structures is impractical. [58:6.23.1.2(C)]

69.3.12.1.2.4 Liquid LP-Gas shall be piped into buildings or structures only for the purposes specified in 6.11.1.1(E) of NFPA 58. [58:6.23.1.2(D)]

69.3.12.1.3 Storage of cylinders awaiting use shall be in accordance with Chapter 8 of NFPA 58. [58:6.23.1.3]

69.3.12.1.4 Transportation of cylinders within a building shall be in accordance with 6.23.3.6 of NFPA 58. [58:6.23.1.4]

69.3.12.1.5 The following provisions shall be required in addition to those specified in Sections 6.2 and 6.4 of NFPA 58:

(1) Liquid transfer systems shall be in accordance with Chapter 7 of NFPA 58.
(2) Engine fuel systems used inside buildings shall be in accordance with Chapter 11 of NFPA 58.
(3) LP-Gas transport or cargo tank vehicles stored, serviced, or repaired in buildings shall be in accordance with Chapter 9 of NFPA 58.

[58:6.23.1.5]

69.3.12.2 Additional Equipment Requirements for Cylinders, Equipment, Piping, and Appliances Used in Buildings, Building Roofs, and Exterior Balconies.

Δ **69.3.12.2.1** Cylinders shall be in accordance with the following:

(1) Cylinders shall not exceed 245 lb (111 kg) water capacity [nominal 100 lb (45 kg) propane capacity] each.
(2) Cylinders shall comply with applicable requirements of Section 5.2 of NFPA 58 and be equipped as provided in Section 5.9 of NFPA 58.
(3) Cylinders shall be marked in accordance with 5.2.8.1 and 5.2.8.2 of NFPA 58.
(4) Cylinders with propane capacities greater than 2 lb (0.9 kg) shall be equipped as provided in Table 5.9.4.1(B) of NFPA 58.
(5) Cylinders with propane capacities greater than 2 lb (0.9 kg) shall be equipped with an excess-flow valve installed at the cylinder discharge when used indoors for vapor service.
(6) Cylinder valves shall be protected in accordance with 5.2.6.1 of NFPA 58.
(7) Cylinders having water capacities greater than 2.7 lb (1.2 kg) and connected for use shall stand on a firm and substantially level surface.
(8) Cylinders shall be secured in an upright position if necessary.
(9) Cylinders and the valve-protecting devices used with them shall be oriented to minimize the possibility of impingement of the pressure relief device discharge on the cylinder and adjacent cylinders.

[58:6.23.2.1]

69.3.12.2.2 Manifolds and fittings connecting cylinders to pressure regulator inlets shall be designed for at least 250 psig (1.7 MPag) service pressure. [58:6.23.2.2]

69.3.12.2.3 Piping shall comply with Section 5.11 of NFPA 58 and shall have a pressure rating of 250 psig (1.7 MPag). [58:6.23.2.3]

69.3.12.2.4 Liquid piping and vapor piping at pressures above 125 psig (0.9 MPag) shall be installed in accordance with 6.11.3 of NFPA 58. [58:6.23.2.4]

69.3.12.2.5 Hose, hose connections, and flexible connectors shall comply with the following:

(1) Hose used at pressures above 5 psig (34 kPag) shall be designed for a pressure of at least 350 psig (2.4 MPag).
(2) Hose used at a pressure of 5 psig (34 kPag) or less and used in agricultural buildings not normally occupied by the public shall be designed for the operating pressure of the hose.
(3) Hose shall comply with 5.11.7 of NFPA 58.
(4) Hose shall be installed in accordance with 6.24.4 of NFPA 58.
(5) Hose shall be as short as practical, without kinking or straining the hose or causing it to be close enough to a burner to be damaged by heat.
(6) Hoses greater than 10 ft (3 m) in length shall be protected from damage.

[58:6.23.2.5]

69.3.12.2.6* Portable heaters, including salamanders, shall comply with the following:

(1) Portable heaters shall be equipped with an approved automatic device to shut off the flow of gas to the main burner and to the pilot, if used, in the event of flame extinguishment or combustion failure.
(2) Portable heaters shall be self-supporting unless designed for cylinder mounting.
(3) Portable heaters shall not be installed utilizing cylinder valves, connectors, regulators, manifolds, piping, or tubing as structural supports.
(4) Portable heaters having an input of more than 50,000 Btu/hr (53 MJ/hr) shall be equipped with either a pilot that must be lighted and proved before the main burner can be turned on or an approved electric ignition system.

[58:6.23.2.6]

69.3.12.2.7 The provisions of 69.3.12.2.6 shall not be applicable to the following:

(1) Tar kettle burners, hand torches, or melting pots
(2) Portable heaters with less than 7500 Btu/hr (8 MJ/hr) input if used with cylinders having a maximum water capacity of 2.7 lb (1.2 kg) and filled with not more than 16.8 oz (0.522 kg) of LP-Gas

[58:6.23.2.7]

69.3.12.3 Buildings Under Construction or Undergoing Major Renovation.

69.3.12.3.1 Where cylinders are used and transported in buildings or structures under construction or undergoing major renovation and such buildings are not occupied by the public, the requirements of 69.3.12.3.2 through 69.3.12.3.10 shall apply. [58:6.23.4.1]

69.3.12.3.2 The use and transportation of cylinders in the unoccupied portions of buildings or structures under construction or undergoing major renovation that are partially occupied by the public shall be approved by the AHJ. [58:6.23.4.2]

69.3.12.3.3 Cylinders, equipment, piping, and appliances shall comply with 69.3.12.2. [58:6.23.4.3]

69.3.12.3.4 Heaters used for temporary heating shall be located at least 6 ft (1.8 m) from any cylinder. (*See 69.3.12.3.5 for an exception to this requirement.*) [58:6.23.4.4]

69.3.12.3.5 Integral heater-cylinder units specifically designed for the attachment of the heater to the cylinder, or to a supporting standard attached to the cylinder, and designed and installed to prevent direct or radiant heat application to the cylinder shall be exempt from the spacing requirement of 69.3.12.3.4. [58:6.23.4.5]

69.3.12.3.6 Blower-type and radiant-type units shall not be directed toward any cylinder within 20 ft (6.1 m). [58:6.23.4.6]

69.3.12.3.7 If two or more heater-cylinder units of either the integral or nonintegral type are located in an unpartitioned area on the same floor, the cylinder(s) of each such unit shall be separated from the cylinder(s) of any other such unit by at least 20 ft (6.1 m). [58:6.23.4.7]

69.3.12.3.8 If heaters are connected to cylinders manifolded together for use in an unpartitioned area on the same floor, the total water capacity of cylinders manifolded together serving any one heater shall not be greater than 735 lb (333 kg) [nominal 300 lb (136 kg) propane capacity]. If there is more than one such manifold, it shall be separated from any other by at least 20 ft (6.1 m). [58:6.23.4.8]

69.3.12.3.9 Where cylinders are manifolded together for connection to a heater(s) on another floor, the following shall apply.

(1) Heaters shall not be installed on the same floors with manifolded cylinders.
(2) The total water capacity of the cylinders connected to any one manifold shall not be greater than 2450 lb (1111 kg) [nominal 1000 lb (454 kg) propane capacity].
(3) Manifolds of more than 735 lb (333 kg) water capacity [nominal 300 lb (136 kg) propane capacity], if located in the same unpartitioned area, shall be separated from each other by at least 50 ft (15 m).

[58:6.23.4.9]

69.3.12.3.10 Where compliance with the provisions of 69.3.12.3.6 through 69.3.12.3.9 is impractical, alternate installation provisions shall be allowed with the approval of the AHJ. [58:6.23.4.10]

69.3.12.4 Buildings Undergoing Minor Renovation When Frequented by the Public.

69.3.12.4.1 Cylinders used and transported for repair or minor renovation in buildings frequented by the public during the hours the public normally occupies the building shall comply with the following:

(1) The maximum water capacity of individual cylinders shall be 50 lb (23 kg) [nominal 20 lb (9.1 kg) propane capacity], and the number of cylinders in the building shall not exceed the number of workers assigned to the use of the propane.
(2) Cylinders having a water capacity greater than 2.7 lb (1.2 kg) shall not be left unattended.

[58:6.23.5.1]

69.3.12.4.2 During the hours the building is not open to the public, cylinders used and transported within the building for repair or minor renovation and with a water capacity greater than 2.7 lb (1.2 kg) shall not be left unattended. [58:6.23.5.2]

69.3.12.5 Buildings Housing Industrial Occupancies.

69.3.12.5.1 Cylinders used in buildings housing industrial occupancies for processing, research, or experimental purposes shall comply with 69.3.12.5.1.1 and 69.3.12.5.1.2. [58:6.23.6.1]

69.3.12.5.1.1 If cylinders are manifolded together, the total water capacity of the connected cylinders shall be not more than 735 lb (333 kg) [nominal 300 lb (136 kg) propane capacity]. If there is more than one such manifold in a room, it shall be separated from any other by at least 20 ft (6.1 m). [58:6.23.6.1(A)]

69.3.12.5.1.2 The amount of LP-Gas in cylinders for research and experimental use in the building shall be limited to the smallest practical quantity. [58:6.23.6.1(B)]

69.3.12.5.2 The use of cylinders to supply fuel for temporary heating in buildings housing industrial occupancies with essentially noncombustible contents shall comply with the requirements in 69.3.12.3 for cylinders in buildings under construction. [58:6.23.6.2]

69.3.12.5.3 The use of fuel cylinders for temporary heating shall be permitted only where a portable appliance for space heating is essential and a permanent heating installation is not practical. [58:6.23.6.3]

69.3.12.6 Buildings Housing Educational and Institutional Occupancies.

69.3.12.6.1 The use of cylinders in classrooms shall be prohibited unless they are used temporarily for classroom demonstrations in accordance with 69.3.12.8.1. [58:6.23.7.1]

69.3.12.6.2 Where cylinders are used in buildings housing educational and institutional laboratory occupancies for research and experimental purposes, the following shall apply:

(1) The maximum water capacity of individual cylinders used shall be 50 lb (23 kg) [nominal 20 lb (9.1 kg) propane capacity] if used in educational occupancies and 12 lb (5.4 kg) [nominal 5 lb (2 kg) propane capacity] if used in institutional occupancies.
(2) If more than one such cylinder is located in the same room, the cylinders shall be separated by at least 20 ft (6.1 m).
(3) Cylinders not connected for use shall be stored in accordance with Chapter 8 of NFPA 58.
(4) Cylinders shall not be stored in a laboratory room.

[58:6.23.7.2]

69.3.12.7 Temporary Heating and Food Service Appliances in Buildings in Emergencies.

69.3.12.7.1 Cylinders shall not be used in buildings for temporary emergency heating purposes except when all of the following conditions are met:

(1) The permanent heating system is temporarily out of service.
(2) Heat is necessary to prevent damage to the buildings or contents.
(3) The cylinders and heaters comply with, and are used and transported in accordance with, 69.3.12.2 and 69.3.12.3.
(4) The temporary heating appliance is not left unattended.
(5) Air for combustion and ventilation is provided in accordance with NFPA 54.

[58:6.23.8.1]

69.3.12.7.2 When a public emergency has been declared and gas, fuel, or electrical service has been interrupted, portable listed LP-Gas commercial food service appliances meeting the requirements of 69.3.12.8.4 shall be permitted to be temporarily used inside affected buildings. [58:6.23.8.2]

69.3.12.7.3 The portable appliances used shall be discontinued and removed from the building at the time the permanently installed appliances are placed back in operation. [58:6.23.8.3]

69.3.12.8 Use in Buildings for Demonstrations or Training, and Use of Small Cylinders for Self-Contained Torch Assemblies and Food Service Appliances.

69.3.12.8.1 Cylinders used temporarily inside buildings for public exhibitions or demonstrations, including use in classroom demonstrations, shall be in accordance with the following:

(1) The maximum water capacity of a cylinder shall be 12 lb (5.4 kg) [nominal 5 lb (2 kg) propane capacity].

(2) If more than one such cylinder is located in a room, the cylinders shall be separated by at least 20 ft (6.1 m).
[58:6.23.9.1]

69.3.12.8.2 Cylinders used temporarily in buildings for training purposes related to the installation and use of LP-Gas systems shall be in accordance with the following:

(1) The maximum water capacity of individual cylinders shall be 245 lb (111 kg) [nominal 100 lb (45 kg) propane capacity], but not more than 20 lb (9.1 kg) of propane shall be placed in a single cylinder.
(2) If more than one such cylinder is located in the same room, the cylinders shall be separated by at least 20 ft (6.1 m).
(3) The training location shall be acceptable to the AHJ.
(4) Cylinders shall be promptly removed from the building when the training class has terminated.

[58:6.23.9.2]

69.3.12.8.3* Cylinders used in buildings as part of approved self-contained torch assemblies or similar appliances shall be in accordance with the following:

(1) Cylinders used in buildings shall comply with UL 147A, *Nonrefillable (Disposable) Type Fuel Gas Cylinder Assemblies*.
(2) Cylinders shall have a maximum water capacity of 2.7 lb (1.2 kg).

[58:6.23.9.3]

69.3.12.8.4 Cylinders used with commercial food service appliances shall be used inside restaurants and in attended commercial food catering operations in accordance with the following:

(1) Cylinders and appliances shall be listed.
(2) Commercial food service appliances shall not have more than two 10 oz (296 ml) nonrefillable butane gas cylinders, each having a maximum capacity of 1.08 lb (0.490 kg).
(3) Cylinders shall comply with UL 147B, *Nonrefillable (Disposable) Type Metal Container Assemblies for Butane*.
(4) Cylinders shall be connected directly to the appliance and shall not be manifolded.
(5) Cylinders shall be an integral part of the listed, approved, commercial food service device and shall be connected without the use of a rubber hose.
(6) Storage of cylinders shall be in accordance with 8.3.1 of NFPA 58.

[58:6.23.9.4]

69.3.12.9 Cylinders on Roofs or Exterior Balconies.

69.3.12.9.1 Where cylinders are installed permanently on roofs of buildings, the buildings shall be of fire-resistant construction or noncombustible construction having essentially noncombustible contents, or of other construction or contents that are protected with automatic sprinklers. [58:6.23.11.1]

69.3.12.9.1.1 The total water capacity of cylinders connected to any one manifold shall be not greater than 980 lb (445 kg) [nominal 400 lb (181 kg) propane capacity]. If more than one manifold is located on the roof, it shall be separated from any other by at least 50 ft (15 m). [58:6.23.11.1(A)]

69.3.12.9.1.2 Cylinders shall be located in areas where there is free air circulation, at least 10 ft (3 m) from building openings (such as windows and doors), and at least 20 ft (6.1 m) from air intakes of air-conditioning and ventilating systems. [58:6.23.11.1(B)]

69.3.12.9.1.3 Cylinders shall not be located on roofs that are entirely enclosed by parapets more than 18 in. (460 mm) high unless the parapets are breached with low-level ventilation openings not more than 20 ft (6.1 m) apart, or unless all openings communicating with the interior of the building are at or above the top of the parapets. [58:6.23.11.1(C)]

69.3.12.9.1.4 Piping shall be in accordance with 69.3.12.2.3 through 69.3.12.2.5. [58:6.23.11.1(D)]

69.3.12.9.1.5 Hose shall not be used for connection to cylinders. [58:6.23.11.1(E)]

69.3.12.9.1.6 The fire department shall be advised of each installation. [58:6.23.11.1(F)]

69.3.12.9.2 Cylinders having water capacities greater than 2.7 lb (1 kg) [nominal 1 lb (0.5 kg) LP-Gas capacity] shall not be located on decks or balconies of dwellings of two or more living units above the first floor unless they are served by exterior stairways. [58:6.23.11.2]

Δ 69.3.13 Installation of Appliances Other Than on Vehicles.

Δ 69.3.13.1 Patio Heaters.

69.3.13.1.1 Patio heaters utilizing an integral LP-Gas container greater than 1.08 lb (0.49 kg) propane capacity shall comply with 69.3.13.1.2 and 69.3.13.1.3. [58:6.24.1.1]

69.3.13.1.2 Patio heaters shall be listed and used in accordance with their listing and the manufacturer's instructions. [58:6.24.1.2]

69.3.13.1.3 Patio heaters shall not be located within 5 ft (1.5 m) of exits from an assembly occupancy. [58:6.24.1.3]

69.3.13.2 Hose for Portable Appliances.

69.3.13.2.1 The requirements of 69.3.13 shall apply to hoses used on the low-pressure side of regulators to connect portable appliances. [58:6.24.4.1]

69.3.13.2.2 Where used inside buildings, the following shall apply:

(1) The hose shall be the minimum practical length and shall be in accordance with 69.3.12.2.5.
(2) The hose shall not extend from one room to another or pass through any partitions, walls, ceilings, or floors except as provided by 69.3.12.3.9.
(3) The hose shall not be concealed from view or used in concealed locations.

[58:6.24.4.2]

69.3.13.2.3 Where installed outside of buildings, the following shall apply:

(1) The hose length shall be permitted to exceed 10 ft (3.3 m).
(2) The hose shall be as short as practical.

[58:6.24.4.3]

69.3.13.2.4 Hose shall be securely connected to the appliance. [58:6.24.4.4]

69.3.13.2.5 The use of rubber slip ends shall not be permitted. [58:6.24.4.5]

69.3.13.2.6 A shutoff valve shall be provided in the piping immediately upstream of the inlet connection of the hose. [58:6.24.4.6]

Δ **69.3.13.2.7** Where more than one appliance shutoff valve in accordance with 6.24.4.6 of NFPA 58 is located near another, the valves shall be marked to indicate which appliance is connected to each valve. [**58:**6.24.4.7]

69.3.13.2.8 Hose shall be protected against physical damage. [**58:**6.24.4.8]

69.3.14 LP-Gas Systems on Vehicles (Other Than Engine Fuel Systems).

Δ **69.3.14.1* Application.** This section shall apply to nonengine fuel systems on all vehicles. [**58:**6.27.1]

Δ **69.3.14.2 Nonapplication.** Subsection 69.3.14 shall not apply to the following:

(1) Systems installed on mobile homes
(2) Systems installed on recreational vehicles
(3) Systems installed on mobile food facilities *(see Chapter 16 of NFPA 58)*
(4) Cargo tank vehicles, including trailers and semitrailers, and similar units used to transport LP-Gas as cargo *(see Chapter 9 of NFPA 58)*
(5) LP-Gas engine fuel systems on the vehicles *(see Chapter 11 of NFPA 58)*
[**58:**6.27.2]

69.3.14.3 Container Installation Requirements.

69.3.14.3.1 Containers shall comply with 69.3.14.3.1.1 through 69.3.14.3.1.5. [**58:**6.27.3.1]

69.3.14.3.1.1 ASME mobile containers shall be in accordance with one of the following:

(1) A MAWP of 312 psig (2.2 MPag) or higher where installed in enclosed spaces of vehicles
(2) A MAWP of 312 psig (2.2 MPag) or higher where installed on passenger vehicles
(3) A MAWP of 250 psig (1.7 MPag) or higher for containers where installed on the exterior of nonpassenger vehicles
[**58:**6.27.3.1(A)]

69.3.14.3.1.2 LP-Gas fuel containers used on passenger-carrying vehicles shall not exceed 200 gal (0.8 m³) aggregate water capacity. [**58:**6.27.3.1(B)]

69.3.14.3.1.3 The capacity of individual LP-Gas containers on highway nonpassenger vehicles shall be either less than or equal to 1000 gal (3.8 m³) water capacity or be in accordance with US Department of Transportation regulations. [**58:**6.27.3.1(C)]

69.3.14.3.1.4 The capacity of cargo tank motor vehicles shall not be limited by NFPA 58. [**58:**6.27.3.1(D)]

69.3.14.3.1.5 Containers designed for stationary service only and not in compliance with the container appurtenance protection requirements of 5.2.6 of NFPA 58 shall not be used. [**58:**6.27.3.1(E)]

69.3.14.3.2 Containers used for the purposes covered by 69.3.14 shall not be installed, transported, or temporarily or permanently stored inside any vehicle covered by 69.3.14, except for ASME containers installed in accordance with 69.3.14.3.4.8, Chapter 9 of NFPA 58, or DOT regulations. [**58:**6.27.3.2]

Δ **69.3.14.3.3** LP-Gas containers and pressure regulators shall be installed either on the outside of the vehicle or in a recess or cabinet vaportight to the inside of the vehicle but accessible from and vented to the outside, with the vents located near the top and bottom of the enclosure and 3 ft (1 m) horizontally away from any opening into the vehicle below the level of the vents. [**58:**6.27.3.3]

Δ **69.3.14.3.4**

69.3.14.3.4.1 Containers shall be installed with road clearance in accordance with 11.8.3 of NFPA 58. [**58:**6.27.3.3(A)]

Δ **69.3.14.3.4.2** Fuel containers shall be installed to prevent recess or cabinet or rotating, with the fastenings designed and constructed to withstand, without permanent visible deformation, static loading in any direction equal to four times the weight of the container filled with fuel. [**58:**6.27.3.3(B)]

69.3.14.3.4.3 Where containers are installed within a vehicle housing, the securing of the housing to the vehicle shall comply with this provision. Any removable portions of the housing or cabinet shall be secured while in transit. [**58:**6.27.3.3(C)]

Δ **69.3.14.3.4.4** Field welding on containers shall be limited to attachments to nonpressure parts applied by the container manufacturer. [**58:**6.27.3.3(D)]

69.3.14.3.4.5 All container valves, appurtenances, and connections shall be protected to prevent damage from accidental contact with stationary objects; from loose objects, stones, mud, or ice thrown up from the ground or floor; and from an overturn or similar vehicular accident. [**58:**6.27.3.3(E)]

69.3.14.3.4.6 Cylinders shall have permanent protection for cylinder valves and connections. [**58:**6.27.3.3(F)]

69.3.14.3.4.7 Where cylinders are located on the outside of a vehicle, weather protection shall be provided. [**58:**6.27.3.3(G)]

69.3.14.3.4.8 Containers installed on the interior of passenger-carrying vehicles shall be installed in compliance with Section 11.9 of NFPA 58, with pressure relief valve installations in compliance with 11.8.5 of NFPA 58. [**58:**6.27.3.3(H)]

69.3.14.3.5 Cylinders installed on portable tar kettles alongside the kettle, on the vehicle frame, or on road surface heating equipment shall be protected from radiant or convected heat from open flame or other burners by the use of a heat shield or by the location of the cylinder(s) on the vehicle. In addition, the following shall apply:

(1) Cylinder valves shall be closed when burners are not in use.
(2) Cylinders shall not be refilled while burners are in use as provided in 7.2.3.2(B) of NFPA 58.
[**58:**6.27.3.4]

69.3.14.4 Installation of Container Appurtenances.

69.3.14.4.1 Container appurtenances shall be installed in accordance with the following:

(1) Pressure relief valve installation on ASME containers installed in the interior of vehicles complying with Section 11.9 of NFPA 58 shall comply with 11.8.5 of NFPA 58.
(2) Pressure relief valve installations on ASME containers installed on the outside of vehicles shall comply with 11.8.5 of NFPA 58 and 69.3.14.3.3.
(3) Main shutoff valves on containers for liquid and vapor shall be readily accessible.

(4) Cylinders shall be designed to be filled in either the vertical or horizontal position, or if they are the universal type, they are permitted to be filled in either position.
(5) All ASME container inlets, outlets, or valves installed in container inlets or outlets, except pressure relief devices and gauging devices, shall be labeled to designate whether they communicate with the vapor or liquid space.
(6) Containers from which only vapor is to be withdrawn shall be installed and equipped with connections to minimize the possibility of the accidental withdrawal of liquid.

[58:6.27.4.1]

69.3.14.4.2 Regulators shall be installed in accordance with 6.10.2 of NFPA 58 and 69.3.14.4.2.1 through 69.3.14.4.2.5. [58:6.27.4.2]

69.3.14.4.2.1 Regulators shall be installed with the pressure relief vent opening pointing vertically downward to allow for drainage of moisture collected on the diaphragm of the regulator. [58:6.27.4.2(A)]

69.3.14.4.2.2 Regulators not installed in compartments shall be equipped with a durable cover designed to protect the regulator vent opening from sleet, snow, freezing rain, ice, mud, and wheel spray. [58:6.27.4.2(B)]

Δ **69.3.14.4.2.3** Regulators installed at or below the floor level shall be installed in a compartment that provides protection against the weather and wheel spray. [58:6.27.4.2(C)]

69.3.14.4.2.4 Regulator compartments shall comply with the following:

(1) The compartment shall be of sufficient size to allow tool operation for connection to and replacement of the regulator(s).
(2) The compartment shall be vaportight to the interior of the vehicle.
(3) The compartment shall have a 1 in.^{2} (650 mm^2) minimum vent opening to the exterior located within 1 in. (25 mm) of the bottom of the compartment.
(4) The compartment shall not contain flame or spark-producing equipment.

[58:6.27.4.2(D)]

69.3.14.4.2.5 A regulator vent outlet shall be at least 2 in. (51 mm) above the compartment vent opening. [58:6.27.4.2(E)]

69.3.14.5 Piping.

69.3.14.5.1 Piping shall be installed in accordance with 6.11.3 of NFPA 58 and 69.3.14.5.1.1 through 69.3.14.5.1.13. [58:6.27.5.1]

69.3.14.5.1.1 Steel tubing shall have a minimum wall thickness of 0.049 in. (1.2 mm). [58:6.27.5.1(A)]

69.3.14.5.1.2 A flexible connector shall be installed between the regulator outlet and the fixed piping system to protect against expansion, contraction, jarring, and vibration strains. [58:6.27.5.1(B)]

69.3.14.5.1.3 Flexibility shall be provided in the piping between a cylinder and the gas piping system or regulator. [58:6.27.5.1(C)]

69.3.14.5.1.4 Flexible connectors shall be installed in accordance with 6.11.7 of NFPA 58. [58:6.27.5.1(D)]

69.3.14.5.1.5 Flexible connectors longer than the length allowed in the *Code*, or fuel lines that incorporate hose, shall be used only where approved. [58:6.27.5.1(E)]

69.3.14.5.1.6 The fixed piping system shall be designed, installed, supported, and secured to minimize the possibility of damage due to vibration, strains, or wear and to preclude any loosening while in transit. [58:6.27.5.1(F)]

69.3.14.5.1.7 Piping shall be installed in a protected location. [58:6.27.5.1(G)]

69.3.14.5.1.8 Where piping is installed outside the vehicle, it shall be installed as follows:

(1) Piping shall be under the vehicle and below any insulation or false bottom.
(2) Fastening or other protection shall be installed to prevent damage due to vibration or abrasion.
(3) At each point where piping passes through sheet metal or a structural member, a rubber grommet or equivalent protection shall be installed to prevent chafing.

[58:6.27.5.1(H)]

69.3.14.5.1.9 Gas piping shall be installed to enter the vehicle through the floor directly beneath or adjacent to the appliance served. [58:6.27.5.1(I)]

69.3.14.5.1.10 If a branch line is installed, the tee connection shall be located in the main gas line under the floor and outside the vehicle. [58:6.27.5.1(J)]

69.3.14.5.1.11 Exposed parts of the fixed piping system either shall be of corrosion-resistant material or shall be coated or protected to minimize exterior corrosion. [58:6.27.5.1(K)]

69.3.14.5.1.12 Hydrostatic relief valves shall be installed in isolated sections of liquid piping as provided in Section 6.16 of NFPA 58. [58:6.27.5.1(L)]

69.3.14.5.1.13 Piping systems, including hose, shall be proven free of leaks in accordance with Section 6.17 of NFPA 58. [58:6.27.5.1(M)]

69.3.14.5.2 There shall be no fuel connection between a tractor and trailer or other vehicle units. [58:6.27.5.2]

69.3.14.6 Equipment Installation. Equipment shall be installed in accordance with Section 6.21 of NFPA 58 and 69.3.14.6.1 and 69.3.14.6.2. [58:6.27.6]

69.3.14.6.1 Installation shall be made in accordance with the manufacturer's recommendations and, in the case of approved equipment, as provided in the approval. [58:6.27.6.1]

69.3.14.6.2 Equipment installed on vehicles shall be protected against vehicular damage as provided for container appurtenances and connections in 69.3.14.3.4.5. [58:6.27.6.2]

69.3.14.7 Appliance Installation on Vehicles.

69.3.14.7.1 Paragraph 69.3.14.7 shall apply to the installation of all appliances on vehicles. It shall not apply to engines. [58:6.27.7.1]

69.3.14.7.2 All appliances covered by 69.3.14.7 installed on vehicles shall be approved. [58:6.27.7.2]

69.3.14.7.3 Where the device or appliance, such as a cargo heater or cooler, is designed to be in operation while the vehicle is in transit, means, such as an excess-flow valve to stop the flow of gas in the event of a line break, shall be installed. [**58:**6.27.7.3]

69.3.14.7.4 Gas-fired heating appliances shall be equipped with shutoffs in accordance with 5.24.8(A) of NFPA 58, except for portable heaters used with cylinders having a maximum water capacity of 2.7 lb (1.2 kg), portable torches, melting pots, and tar kettles. [**58:**6.27.7.4]

69.3.14.7.5 Gas-fired heating appliances, other than ranges and illuminating appliances installed on vehicles intended for human occupancy, shall be designed or installed to provide for a complete separation of the combustion system from the atmosphere inside the vehicle. [**58:**6.27.7.5]

69.3.14.7.6* Where unvented-type heaters that are designed to protect cargo are used on vehicles not intended for human occupancy, provisions shall be made to provide air from the outside for combustion and dispose of the products of combustion to the outside. [**58:**6.27.7.6]

69.3.14.7.7 Appliances installed in the cargo space of a vehicle shall be readily accessible whether the vehicle is loaded or empty. [**58:**6.27.7.7]

69.3.14.7.8 Appliances shall be constructed or otherwise protected to minimize possible damage or impaired operation due to cargo shifting or handling. [**58:**6.27.7.8]

69.3.14.7.9 Appliances shall be located so that a fire at any appliance will not block egress of persons from the vehicle. [**58:**6.27.7.9]

69.3.14.7.10 A permanent caution plate shall be affixed to either the appliance or the vehicle outside of any enclosure. [**58:**6.27.7.10]

69.3.14.7.10.1 The caution plate shall be adjacent to the container(s). [**58:**6.27.7.10.1]

69.3.14.7.10.2 The caution plate shall include the following text:

   CAUTION:
   (1) Be sure all appliance valves are closed before opening container valve.
   (2) Connections at the appliances, regulators, and containers shall be checked periodically for leaks with soapy water or its equivalent.
   (3) Never use a match or flame to check for leaks.
   (4) Container valves shall be closed when equipment is not in use.
   [**58:**6.27.7.10.2]

69.3.14.7.11 Gas-fired heating appliances and water heaters shall be equipped with automatic devices designed to shut off the flow of gas to the main burner and the pilot in the event the pilot flame is extinguished. [**58:**6.27.7.11]

69.3.14.8 Parking, Servicing, and Repair.

69.3.14.8.1 Where vehicles with LP-Gas fuel systems used for purposes other than propulsion are parked, serviced, or repaired inside buildings, the requirements of 69.3.14.8.2 through 69.3.14.8.4 shall apply. [**58:**6.27.8.1]

69.3.14.8.2 The fuel system shall be leak-free, and the container(s) shall not be filled beyond the limits specified in Chapter 7 of NFPA 58. [**58:**6.27.8.2]

69.3.14.8.3 The container shutoff valve shall be closed, except that the container shutoff valve shall not be required to be closed when fuel is required for test or repair. [**58:**6.27.8.3]

69.3.14.8.4 The vehicle shall not be parked near sources of heat, open flames, or similar sources of ignition, or near unventilated pits. [**58:**6.27.8.4]

69.3.14.8.5 Vehicles having containers with water capacities larger than 300 gal (1.1 m^3) shall comply with the requirements of Section 9.7 of NFPA 58. [**58:**6.27.8.5]

69.3.15 Vehicle Fuel Dispenser and Dispensing Systems.

69.3.15.1 Application.

69.3.15.1.1 Subsection 69.3.15 includes the location, installation, and operation of vehicle fuel dispensers and dispensing systems. [**58:**6.28.1.1]

69.3.15.1.2 The provisions of 69.3.3 and 69.3.5, as modified by 69.3.15, shall apply. [**58:**6.28.1.2]

69.3.15.2 Location.

69.3.15.2.1 Location of vehicle fuel dispensers and dispensing systems shall be in accordance with Table 69.3.7.2.1. [**58:**6.28.2.1]

69.3.15.2.2 Vehicle fuel dispensers and dispensing systems shall be located away from pits in accordance with Table 69.3.7.2.1, with no drains or blow-offs from the unit directed toward or within 15 ft (4.6 m) of a sewer system's opening. [**58:**6.28.2.2]

69.3.15.3 General Installation Provisions.

69.3.15.3.1 Vehicle fuel dispensers and dispensing systems shall be installed in accordance with the manufacturer's installation instructions. [**58:**6.28.3.1]

69.3.15.3.2 Vehicle fuel dispensers and dispensing systems shall not be located within a building or structure, unless they comply with Chapter 10 of NFPA 58. [**58:**6.28.3.2]

69.3.15.3.3 No more than 50 percent of the perimeter of an area where a dispenser or dispensing system is located shall be enclosed. [**58:**6.28.3.3]

69.3.15.3.4 A weather shelter or canopy shall be permitted to cover the working space for the filling operation. [**58:**6.28.3.4]

69.3.15.3.5 Control for the pump used to transfer LP-Gas through the unit into containers shall be provided at the device in order to minimize the possibility of leakage or accidental discharge. [**58:**6.28.3.5]

69.3.15.3.6 A device that shuts off the flow of gas when flow exceeds the predetermined flow rate shall be installed as close as practical to the point where the dispenser hose connects to the liquid piping and upstream of the hose. [**58:**6.28.3.6]

69.3.15.3.7 Piping and the dispensing hose shall be provided with hydrostatic relief valves in accordance with Section 6.16 of NFPA 58. [**58:**6.28.3.7]

69.3.15.3.8 Protection against trespassing and tampering shall be in accordance with 6.22.4 of NFPA 58. [**58:**6.28.3.8]

69.3.15.3.9 The container liquid withdrawal opening used with vehicle fuel dispensers and dispensing systems shall be equipped with one of the following:

(1) An internal valve fitted for remote closure and automatic shutoff using thermal (fire) actuation
(2) A positive shutoff valve that is located as close to the container as practical and an excess-flow valve installed in the container, plus an emergency shutoff valve that is fitted for remote closure and installed downstream in the line as close as practical to the positive shutoff valve

[**58**:6.28.3.9]

Δ **69.3.15.3.10** At least one remote shutdown device shall be installed for either the internal valve or the emergency shutoff valve required by 69.3.15.3.9(1) or 69.3.15.3.9(2). [**58**:6.28.3.10]

N **69.3.15.3.10.1** The shutdown device shall comply with the requirements of 69.3.9.4 except as permitted by 69.3.15.3.10.2. [**58**:6.28.3.10.1]

N **69.3.15.3.10.2** The minimum distance required by 69.3.9.4(3) shall be permitted to be reduced to 3 ft (0.9 m). [**58**:6.28.3.10.2]

69.3.15.3.11 Emergency shutoff valves and internal valves that are fitted for remote closure as required in this section shall be tested annually for proper operation. [**58**:6.28.3.11]

69.3.15.3.12 A manual shutoff valve and an excess-flow check valve shall be located in the liquid line between the pump and the dispenser inlet where the dispensing device is installed at a remote location and is not part of a complete storage and dispensing unit mounted on a common base. [**58**:6.28.3.12]

Δ **69.3.15.3.13** All dispensers shall be installed on a concrete foundation or shall be part of a complete storage and dispensing unit on a common base and installed in accordance with 6.8.3.5 of NFPA 58. [**58**:6.28.3.13]

69.3.15.3.14 Vehicle barrier protection (VBP) shall be provided for containers serving liquid dispensers where those containers are located within 10 ft (3 m) of a vehicle thoroughfare or parking location in accordance with 69.3.15.3.14.1 or 69.3.15.3.14.2. [**58**:6.28.3.14]

Δ **69.3.15.3.14.1** Concrete filled guard posts shall be constructed of steel not less than 4 in. (102 mm) in diameter with the following characteristics:

(1) Spaced not more than 4 ft (1200 mm) between posts on center
(2) Set not less than 3 ft (900 mm) deep in a concrete footing of not less than 15 in. (380 mm) diameter
(3) Set with the top of the posts not less than 3 ft (900 mm) above ground
(4) Located not less than 3 ft (900 mm) from the protected installation

[**58**:6.28.3.14(A)]

69.3.15.3.14.2* Equivalent protection in lieu of guard posts shall be approved. [**58**:6.28.3.14(B)]

Δ **69.3.15.3.15** Where the dispenser is not on a common base with its storage container and the dispensing unit is located within 10 ft (3 m) of a vehicle thoroughfare, parking location, or an engine fuel filling station, the dispenser shall be provided with VBP. [**58**:6.28.3.15]

69.3.15.3.16 Dispensers shall be protected from physical damage. [**58**:6.28.3.16]

69.3.15.3.17 A listed quick-acting shutoff valve shall be installed at the discharge end of the transfer hose. [**58**:6.28.3.17]

69.3.15.3.18 At least one remote shutdown device in accordance with 69.3.9.4 shall be installed for the electrical supply. [**58**:6.28.3.18]

69.3.15.3.19 The markings for the switches or breakers shall be visible at the point of liquid transfer. [**58**:6.28.3.19]

69.3.15.4 Installation of Vehicle Fuel Dispensers.

69.3.15.4.1 Hose shall comply with the following:

(1) Hose length shall not exceed 18 ft (5.5 m) unless approved by the AHJ.
(2) All hose shall be listed.
(3) When not in use, the hose shall be secured to protect the hose from damage.

[**58**:6.28.3.20]

69.3.15.4.2 A listed emergency breakaway device shall be installed and shall comply with UL 567, *Emergency Breakaway Fittings, Swivel Connectors, and Pipe-Connection Fittings for Petroleum Products and LP-Gas,* and be designed to retain liquid on both sides of the breakaway point, or other devices affording equivalent protection approved by the AHJ. [**58**:6.28.4.1]

69.3.15.4.3 Vehicle fuel dispensers shall be located as follows:

(1) Conventional systems shall be at least 10 ft (3.0 m) from any dispensing device for Class I or Class II liquids.
(2) Low-emission transfer systems in accordance with 6.31.5 of NFPA 58 shall be at least 5 ft (2 m) from any dispensing device for Class I or Class II liquids.

[**58**:6.28.4.2]

69.4 LP-Gas Liquid Transfer.

69.4.1* Scope.

69.4.1.1 Section 69.4 applies to the following types of transfers:

(1) Transfer of liquid LP-Gas from one container to another wherever such a transfer involves connections and disconnections in the transfer system or the venting of LP-Gas to the atmosphere
(2) Transfer of LP-Gas vapor between containers and from containers to the atmosphere

[**58**:7.1.1]

69.4.1.2 Section 69.4 also applies to operational safety and methods for determining the quantity of LP-Gas permitted in containers. [**58**:7.1.2]

69.4.2 Operational Safety.

69.4.2.1 Transfer Personnel.

69.4.2.1.1 Transfer operations shall be conducted by qualified personnel meeting the provisions of Section 4.4 of NFPA 58. [**58**:7.2.1.1]

69.4.2.1.2 At least one qualified person shall remain in attendance at the transfer operation from the time connections are made until the transfer is completed, shutoff valves are closed, and lines are disconnected. [**58**:7.2.1.2]

69.4.2.1.3 Transfer personnel shall exercise caution to ensure that the LP-Gases transferred are those for which the transfer system and the containers to be filled are designed. [58:7.2.1.3]

69.4.2.2 Filling and Evacuating of Containers.

69.4.2.2.1 Transfer of LP-Gas to and from a container shall be accomplished only by qualified individuals trained in proper handling and operating procedures meeting the requirements of Section 4.4 of NFPA 58 and in emergency response procedures. [58:7.2.2.1]

69.4.2.2.2 When noncompliance with Section 5.2 or Section 5.9 of NFPA 58 is found or it is determined in accordance with 69.4.2.2.7 that the container will not be filled, the container owner and user shall be notified in writing. [58:7.2.2.2]

69.4.2.2.3 Injection of compressed air, oxygen, or any oxidizing gas into containers to transfer LP-Gas liquid shall be prohibited. [58:7.2.2.3]

69.4.2.2.4 When evacuating a container owned by others, the qualified person(s) performing the transfer shall not inject any material other than LP-Gas into the container. [58:7.2.2.4]

69.4.2.2.5* Valve outlets on refillable cylinders of 108 lb (49 kg) water capacity [nominal 45 lb (20 kg) propane capacity] or less shall be equipped with a redundant pressure-tight seal or one of the following listed connections: CGA 790, CGA 791, or CGA 810, as described in CGA V-1, *Standard for Compressed Gas Cylinder Valve Outlet and Inlet Connections*. [58:7.2.2.5]

69.4.2.2.6 Where redundant pressure seals are used, they shall be in place whenever the cylinder is not connected for use. [58:7.2.2.6]

69.4.2.2.7* Damage.

69.4.2.2.7.1 Prior to filling cylinders with CGA 791 and CGA 793 connections, the face seal shall be visually inspected for visible damage. [58:7.2.2.7(A)]

69.4.2.2.7.2 If visible damage on the face seal is found, the cylinder shall not be filled. [58:7.2.2.7(B)]

69.4.2.2.8 Nonrefillable (disposable) and new unused cylinders shall not be required to be equipped with valve outlet seals. [58:7.2.2.8]

69.4.2.2.9 Containers shall be filled only after determination that they comply with the design, fabrication, inspection, marking, and requalification provisions of NFPA 58. [58:7.2.2.9]

69.4.2.2.10 Prior to refilling a cylinder that has a cylinder sleeve, the cylinder sleeve shall be removed to facilitate the visual inspection of the cylinder. [58:7.2.2.10]

69.4.2.2.11 Cylinders required to have an overfilling prevention device (OPD) shall not be filled unless they are equipped with this device and a fixed maximum liquid level gauge. [58:7.2.2.11]

69.4.2.2.12 The requirements of 69.4.2.2.10 shall not apply to containers that comply with 5.2.9 of NFPA 58 and are included in the flight log of a hot air balloon. [58:7.2.2.12]

69.4.2.2.13 Hot air balloon containers shall not be required to be removed from the aircraft for filling. [58:7.2.2.13]

69.4.2.2.14 "Single trip," "nonrefillable," or "disposable" cylinders shall not be refilled with LP-Gas. [58:7.2.2.14]

69.4.2.2.15 Containers shall comply with the following with regard to service or design pressure requirements:

(1) The service pressure marked on the cylinder shall be not less than 80 percent of the vapor pressure of the LP-Gas for which the cylinder is designed at 130°F (54°C).
(2) The maximum allowable working pressure (MAWP) for ASME containers shall be in accordance with Table 5.2.4.3 of NFPA 58.

[58:7.2.2.15]

69.4.2.2.16 Universal cylinders shall be permitted to be filled when in the vertical position or in the horizontal position when the positioning slot is in the correct orientation. [58:7.2.2.16]

69.4.2.2.17 Transfer of refrigerated LP-Gas shall be made only into systems that are designed to accept refrigerated LP-Gas. [58:7.2.2.17]

69.4.2.2.18 A container shall not be filled if the container assembly does not meet the requirements for continued service. [58:7.2.2.18]

69.4.2.2.19 Transfer hoses larger than ½ in. (12 mm) internal diameter shall not be used for making connections to individual cylinders being filled indoors. [58:7.2.2.19]

69.4.2.3 Arrangement and Operation of Transfer Systems.

69.4.2.3.1 Public access to areas where LP-Gas is stored and transferred shall be prohibited, except where necessary for the conduct of normal business activities. [58:7.2.3.1]

69.4.2.3.2 Sources of ignition shall be turned off during transfer operations, while connections or disconnections are made, or while LP-Gas is being vented to the atmosphere. [58:7.2.3.2]

69.4.2.3.2.1 Internal combustion engines within 15 ft (4.6 m) of a point of transfer shall be shut down while such transfer operations are in progress, with the exception of the following:

(1) Engines of LP-Gas cargo tank vehicles, constructed and operated in compliance with Chapter 9 of NFPA 58, while such engines are driving transfer pumps or compressors on these vehicles to load containers in accordance with 6.7.2.2 of NFPA 58
(2) Portable engines with shielded ignition systems and exhaust system spark-arresters located at least 10 ft (3 m) from a point of transfer while such engines are driving transfer pumps or compressors
(3) Engines for industrial (and forklift) trucks powered by LP-Gas used in buildings as provided in Section 11.11 of NFPA 58

[58:7.2.3.2(A)]

69.4.2.3.2.2 Smoking, open flame, portable electrical tools, and extension lights capable of igniting LP-Gas shall not be permitted within 25 ft (7.6 m) of a point of transfer while filling operations are in progress. [58:7.2.3.2(B)]

69.4.2.3.2.3 Metal cutting, grinding, oxygen–fuel gas cutting, brazing, soldering, or welding shall not be permitted within 35 ft (10.7 m) of a point of transfer while filling operations are in progress. [58:7.2.3.2(C)]

69.4.2.3.2.4 Materials that have been heated above the ignition temperature of LP-Gas shall be cooled before LP-Gas transfer is started. [58:7.2.3.2(D)]

69.4.2.3.2.5 Sources of ignition shall be turned off during the filling of any LP-Gas container on the vehicle. [**58:**7.2.3.2(E)]

69.4.2.3.3 Cargo tank vehicles unloading into storage containers shall be at least 10 ft (3.0 m) from the container and so positioned that the shutoff valves on both the truck and the container are readily accessible. [**58:**7.2.3.3]

Δ **69.4.2.3.4** The cargo tank vehicle shall not transfer LP-Gas into dispensing system storage while parked on a public way. [**58:**7.2.3.4]

69.4.2.3.5 Transfers to containers serving agricultural or industrial equipment requiring refueling in the field shall comply with 69.4.2.3.5.1 and 69.4.2.3.5.2. [**58:**7.2.3.5]

69.4.2.3.5.1* Where the intake of air-moving equipment is less than 50 ft (15 m) from a point of transfer, it shall be shut down while containers are being refilled. [**58:**7.2.3.5(A)]

69.4.2.3.5.2 Equipment employing open flames or equipment with integral containers shall be shut down while refueling. [**58:**7.2.3.5(B)]

69.4.2.3.6 From the time railroad tank cars are delivered to sidings and disconnected from the motive force for loading or unloading until they are again connected to the motive force for removal, the following shall apply:

(1) A caution sign, with wording such as "STOP. TANK CAR CONNECTED," shall be placed at the active end(s) of the siding while the car is connected for LP-Gas transfer, as required by DOT regulations.
(2) Wheel chocks shall be placed to prevent movement of the car in either direction.
(3) Access to the track shall be secured to prevent entry by other rail equipment while the car is connected for LP-Gas transfer.
(4) The requirements of 69.4.2.3.6(2) shall not apply to movement on the siding to facilitate loading or unloading.

[**58:**7.2.3.6]

69.4.2.3.7 Where a hose or swivel-type piping is used for loading or unloading railroad tank cars, it shall be protected as follows:

(1) An emergency shutoff valve shall be installed at the railroad tank car end of the hose or swivel-type piping where flow into or out of the railroad tank car is possible.
(2) An emergency shutoff valve or a backflow check valve shall be installed on the railroad tank car end of the hose or swivel piping where flow is only into the railroad tank car.

[**58:**7.2.3.7]

69.4.2.3.8 Where cargo tank vehicles are filled directly from railroad tank cars on a private track with nonstationary storage tanks involved, the following requirements shall be met:

(1) Transfer protection shall be provided in accordance with 69.3.10.
(2) Ignition source control shall be in accordance with Section 6.26 of NFPA 58.
(3) Control of ignition sources during transfer shall be provided in accordance with 69.4.2.3.2.
(4) Fire extinguishers shall be provided in accordance with 9.4.7 of NFPA 58.
(5) Transfer personnel shall meet the provisions of 69.4.2.1.
(6) Cargo tank vehicles shall meet the requirements of 69.4.2.3.
(7) The points of transfer shall be located in accordance with Table 69.3.7.2.1 with respect to exposures.
(8) Provision for anchorage and breakaway shall be provided on the cargo tank vehicle side for transfer from a railroad tank car directly into a cargo tank vehicle.
(9) The provisions of Chapter 15 of NFPA 58 shall apply to all LP-Gas transfers performed in accordance with 69.4.2.3.8.

[**58:**7.2.3.8]

69.4.2.3.9 Where cargo tank vehicles are filled from other cargo tank vehicles or cargo tanks, the following requirements shall apply:

(1) Transfer between cargo tanks or cargo tank vehicles where one is used as a bulk plant shall be temporary installations that comply with 4.3.2, 6.22.1, 6.22.2, 6.22.4 through 6.22.6 of NFPA 58, and 69.4.2.3.1.
(2) Arrangements and operations of the transfer system shall be in accordance with the following:
    (a) The point of transfer shall be in accordance with Table 69.3.7.2.1.
    (b) Sources of ignition within the transfer area shall be controlled during the transfer operation as specified in 69.4.2.3.2.
    (c) Fire extinguishers shall be provided in accordance with 9.4.7 of NFPA 58.
(3) Cargo tanks shall comply with the requirements of 69.4.2.2.9.
(4) Provisions designed either to prevent a pull-away during a transfer operation or to stop the flow of LP-Gas from both cargo tank vehicles or cargo tanks in the event of a pull-away shall be incorporated.
(5) Off-truck remote shutoff devices that meet 49 CFR 173.315(n) requirements and are installed on the cargo tank vehicle unloading the LP-Gas shall satisfy the requirements of 69.4.2.3.9(4).
(6) Cargo tank vehicle LP-Gas transfers that are for the sole purpose of testing, maintaining, or repairing the cargo tank vehicle shall be exempt from the requirements of 69.4.2.3.9(1).

[**58:**7.2.3.9]

69.4.2.4 Hose Inspection.

69.4.2.4.1 Transfer hose assemblies shall be observed for leakage or for damage that could impair their integrity before each use. [**58:**7.2.4.1]

69.4.2.4.2 Transfer hose assemblies shall be inspected at least annually. [**58:**7.2.4.2]

69.4.2.4.3 Inspection of pressurized hose assemblies shall include inspection for the following:

(1) Damage to outer cover that exposes reinforcement
(2) Kinked or flattened hose
(3) Soft spots or bulges in hose
(4) Couplings that have slipped on the hose, are damaged, have missing parts, or have loose bolts
(5) Leakage other than permeability leakage

[**58:**7.2.4.3]

69.4.2.4.4 Hose assemblies shall be replaced, repaired, or continued in service based on the results of the inspection. [**58:**7.2.4.4]

69.4.2.4.5 Leaking or damaged hose shall be immediately repaired or removed from service. [58:7.2.4.5]

69.4.3 Venting LP-Gas to the Atmosphere.

69.4.3.1 Outdoors.

Δ **69.4.3.1.1** LP-Gas in liquid or vapor form shall be vented to the atmosphere only under the following conditions:

(1) Where the maximum flow from fixed liquid level, rotary, or slip tube gauges does not exceed that from a No. 54 drill orifice
(2) Between shutoff valves before disconnecting the liquid transfer line from the container
(3) By the use of vent valves
(4) Where the rate of discharge does not exceed the discharge from a No. 31 drill size orifice, from listed liquid transfer pumps manufactured before January 1, 2000, using such vapor as a source of energy
(5) For purging in accordance with 7.3.3 of NFPA 58
(6) In emergencies
(7) Where used as the pressure source in remote shutdown systems for internal valves and emergency shutoff valves

[58:7.3.1.1]

69.4.3.1.2 Venting of compressor liquid traps shall be attended. [58:7.3.1.2]

69.5 Storage of Cylinders Awaiting Use, Resale, or Exchange.

69.5.1 Scope.

69.5.1.1 The provisions of Section 69.5 apply to the storage of cylinders of 1000 lb (454 kg) water capacity or less, whether filled, partially filled, or empty, as follows:

(1) At consumer sites or dispensing systems, where not connected for use
(2) In storage for resale or exchange by dealer or reseller

[58:8.1.1]

69.5.1.2 Section 69.5 does not apply to new or unused cylinders. [58:8.1.2]

69.5.1.3 Section 69.5 does not apply to cylinders stored at bulk plants. [58:8.1.3]

69.5.2 General Provisions.

69.5.2.1 General Location of Cylinders.

69.5.2.1.1 Cylinders in storage shall be located to minimize exposure to excessive temperature rises, physical damage, or tampering. [58:8.2.1.1]

69.5.2.1.2 Cylinders in storage having individual water capacity greater than 2.7 lb (1.1 kg) [nominal 1 lb (0.45 kg) LP-Gas capacity] shall be positioned so that the pressure relief valve is in direct communication with the vapor space of the cylinder. [58:8.2.1.2]

69.5.2.1.3 Cylinders stored in buildings in accordance with 69.5.3 shall not be located near exits, near stairways, or in areas normally used, or intended to be used, for the safe egress of occupants. [58:8.2.1.3]

69.5.2.1.4 If empty cylinders that have been in LP-Gas service are stored indoors, they shall be considered as full cylinders for the purposes of determining the maximum quantities of LP-Gas permitted by 69.5.3.1, 69.5.3.2.1, and 69.5.3.4.1. [58:8.2.1.4]

69.5.2.1.5 Cylinders shall not be stored on roofs. [58:8.2.1.5]

69.5.2.2 Protection of Valves on Cylinders in Storage.

69.5.2.2.1 Cylinder valves shall be protected as required by 69.2.1.2.1 and 69.4.2.2.5. [58:8.2.2.1]

69.5.2.2.2 Screw-on-type caps or collars shall be in place on all cylinders stored, regardless of whether they are full, partially full, or empty, and cylinder outlet valves shall be closed. [58:8.2.2.2]

69.5.2.2.3 Valve outlets on cylinders less than 108 lb (49 kg) water capacity [nominal 45 lb (20 kg) propane capacity] shall be plugged, capped, or sealed in accordance with 69.4.2.2.5. [58:8.2.2.3]

69.5.3 Storage Within Buildings.

69.5.3.1 General. Storage of cylinders in buildings shall be in accordance with Table 69.5.3.1(a) or Table 69.5.3.1(b) or the requirements of 69.5.3. [58:8.3.1]

69.5.3.2 Storage Within Buildings Frequented by the Public.

Δ **69.5.3.2.1** The quantity of LP-Gas in cylinders stored or displayed shall not exceed 200 lb (91 kg) in one location, with additional storage separated by 50 ft (15 m). [58:8.3.2.1]

N **69.5.3.2.1.1** The maximum quantity to be stored in one building shall not exceed 1000 lb (454 kg). [58:8.3.2.1(A)]

69.5.3.2.1.2 Where the total quantity stored in a mercantile occupancy exceeds 200 lb (91 kg), an approved sprinkler system that, at a minimum, meets the ordinary hazard (Group 2) requirement of NFPA 13 shall be installed. [58:8.3.2.1(B)]

Δ **Table 69.5.3.1(a) Maximum Allowable Quantity (MAQ) of LP-Gas Storage for Maximum 1 lb Cylinders Without Protection, in Cabinets, or in Areas Protected by Suppression in Other Than Industrial, Storage, and Mercantile Occupancies**

Assembly	Educational	Day Care	Health Care	Ambulatory Health Care	Detention and Correctional	One- and Two-Family Dwellings	Lodging or Rooming House	Hotel and Dormitory	Apartment	Residential Board and Care	Business
2 lb (1 kg)[a]	2 lb (1 kg)[b]	2 lb (1 kg)	2 lb (1 kg)[c]	2 lb (1 kg)	2 lb (1 kg)	2 lb (1 kg)	2 lb (1 kg)	2 lb (1 kg)	2 lb (1 kg)	2 lb (1 kg)	2 lb (1 kg)

Note: Additional 15 lb (7 kg) in restaurants and food service in accordance with 69.5.3.2.3 in 10 oz (0.4 kg) maximum cylinders; one additional 15 lb (7 kg) unit where protected by 2-hour fire wall protection.
[a]Additional 20 lb (9 kg) in assembly occupancies used for flame effects per NFPA 160; additional 20 lb units with 20 ft (6 m) separation.
[b]Additional 20 lb (9 kg) in educational occupancies (in labs, not in classrooms); additional 20 lb (9 kg) units with 20 ft (6 m) separation.
[c]Additional 5 lb (2 kg) in health care occupancies in labs only; additional 5 lb (2 kg) units with 20 ft (6 m) separation.
[58:Table 8.3.1(a)]

Δ **Table 69.5.3.1(b) Maximum Allowable Quantity (MAQ) of LP-Gas Storage in Containers with No Protection, in Cabinets, and Where Protected by Suppression in Mercantile, Industrial, and Storage Occupancies**

Mercantile	Industrial	Storage
200 lb (91 kg) [1 lb (0.5 kg) maximum/cylinder][a]	300 lb (136 kg)[b]	300 lb (136 kg)[c]

[a] A total of 1000 lb (454 kg) in 200 lb (91 kg) units with additional units with a 200 ft (60 m) separation and with suppression in accordance with 69.5.3.2.1.
[b] Additional 300 lb (136 kg) with 300 ft (91 m) separation.
[c] A total of 10,000 lb (454 kb) in special rooms in accordance with Chapter 10 of NFPA 58.
[58:Table 8.3.1(b)]

69.5.3.2.1.3 The sprinkler density shall be 0.300 gpm/ft^2 (12.2 mm/min) over the most remote 2000 ft^2 (18.6 m^2) area, and the hose stream allowance shall be 250 gpm (946 L/min). [58:8.3.2.1(C)]

69.5.3.2.2 The cylinders shall not exceed a water capacity of 2.7 lb (1.1 kg) [nominal 1 lb (0.45 kg) LP-Gas]. [58:8.3.2.2]

Δ **69.5.3.3 Storage in Restaurants and Food Service Locations.** In restaurants and at food service locations, storage of 10 oz (283 g) butane nonrefillable containers shall be limited to not more than 24 containers and 24 additional 10 oz (283 g) butane nonrefillable containers stored in another location within the building constructed with at least 2-hour fire wall protection. [58:8.3.3]

69.5.3.4 Storage Within Buildings Not Frequented by the Public.

69.5.3.4.1 The maximum quantity of LP-Gas allowed in one storage location shall not exceed 735 lb (334 kg) water capacity [nominal 300 lb (136 kg) propane capacity]. [58:8.3.4.1]

69.5.3.4.2 Where additional storage locations are required on the same floor within the same building, they shall be separated by a minimum of 300 ft (91.4 m). [58:8.3.4.2]

69.5.3.4.3 Storage beyond the limitations described in 69.5.3.4.2 shall comply with 69.5.3.5. [58:8.3.4.3]

69.5.3.4.4 Cylinders carried as part of the service equipment on highway mobile vehicles shall not be part of the total storage capacity requirements of 69.5.3.4.1, where such vehicles are stored in private garages and carry no more than three cylinders with a total aggregate capacity per vehicle not exceeding 100 lb (45.4 kg) of propane. [58:8.3.4.4]

69.5.3.4.5 Cylinder valves shall be closed when not in use. [58:8.3.4.5]

69.5.3.5 Storage Within Special Buildings or Rooms.

69.5.3.5.1 The maximum quantity of LP-Gas stored in special buildings or rooms shall be 10,000 lb (4540 kg). [58:8.3.5.1]

69.5.3.5.2 Special buildings or rooms for storing LP-Gas cylinders shall not be located where the buildings or rooms adjoin the line of property occupied by schools, churches, hospitals, athletic fields, or other points of public gathering. [58:8.3.5.2]

69.5.3.5.3 The construction of all special buildings and rooms specified in 69.5.3.5.2 shall comply with Chapter 10 of NFPA 58 and the following:

(1) Vents to the outside only shall be provided at both the top and bottom of the building and shall be located at least 5 ft (1.5 m) from any building opening.
(2) The entire area shall be classified for purposes of ignition source control in accordance with Section 6.26 of NFPA 58.

[58:8.3.5.3]

69.5.3.6 Storage Within Residential Buildings. Storage of cylinders within a residential building, including the basement or any storage area in a common basement of a multiple-family building and attached or detached garages, shall be limited to cylinders each with a maximum water capacity of 2.7 lb (1.2 kg) and shall not exceed 5.4 lb (2.4 kg) aggregate water capacity per each living space unit. [58:8.3.6]

69.5.4 Storage Outside of Buildings.

69.5.4.1* Location of Storage Outside of Buildings.

69.5.4.1.1 Storage outside of buildings for cylinders awaiting use or resale or that are part of a cylinder exchange point shall be located as follows:

(1) At least 5 ft (1.5 m) from any doorway or opening in a building frequented by the public where occupants have at least two means of egress as defined by NFPA *101*
(2) At least 10 ft (3 m) from any doorway or opening in a building or sections of a building that has only one means of egress
(3) At least 20 ft (6.1 m) from any automotive service station fuel dispenser

[58:8.4.1.1]

69.5.4.1.2 Distances from cylinders in storage outside of buildings shall be in accordance with Table 69.5.4.1.2 with respect to the following:

(1) Nearest important building or group of buildings
(2) Line of adjoining property that can be built upon
(3) Busy thoroughfares or sidewalks on other than private property
(4) Line of adjoining property occupied by schools, churches, hospitals, athletic fields, or other points of public gathering
(5) Dispenser

[58:8.4.1.2]

69.5.4.1.3 Fire-Resistive Protective Structure.

69.5.4.1.3.1 The distances in Table 69.5.4.1.2 shall be reduced to 0 where a 2-hour fire-resistive protective structure made of noncombustible materials is provided that breaks the line of sight of the storage and the building. [58:8.4.1.3(A)]

Table 69.5.4.1.2 Distances from Cylinders in Storage and Exposures

Quantity of LP-Gas Stored		Horizontal Distance to …					
		(1) and (2)		(3) and (4)		(5)*	
lb	kg	ft	m	ft	m	ft	m
≤720	≤227	0	0	0	0	5	1.5
721–2,500	>227–1,134	0	0	10	3	10	3
2,501–6,000	>1,134–2,721	10	3	10	3	10	3
6,001–10,000	>2,721–4,540	20	6.1	20	6.1	20	6.1
>10,000	>4,540	25	7.6	25	7.6	25	7.6

*The minimum distance from a point of transfer associated with a dispensing system must comply with Table 69.3.7.2.1. [58:Table 8.4.1.2]

69.5.4.1.3.2 For buildings with exterior walls rated 2-hour fire resistance and constructed of noncombustible materials not provided with eaves over the storage, the exterior wall shall be allowed in lieu of a protective structure to reduce the distance to 0. [58:8.4.1.3(B)]

69.5.4.1.4 Cylinders in the filling process shall not be considered to be in storage. [58:8.4.1.4]

69.5.4.2 Protection of Cylinders.

69.5.4.2.1* Cylinders at a location open to the public shall be placed on shelves constructed of materials with a flame spread index of less than 25, in accordance with ASTM E84, *Standard Test Method for Surface Burning Characteristics of Building Materials*, or UL 723, *Test for Surface Burning Characteristics of Building Materials*, and shall be of sufficient strength to support the cylinders. [58:8.4.2.1]

69.5.4.2.2 Cylinders at a location open to the public shall be protected by either of the following:

(1) An enclosure in accordance with 6.22.4.2 of NFPA 58
(2) A lockable ventilated enclosure of metal exterior construction

[58:8.4.2.2]

69.5.4.2.3* Vehicular barrier protection (VBP) shall be provided where vehicle traffic is expected at the location, except where cylinders are protected in accordance with 69.5.4.2.2(2). [58:8.4.2.3]

69.5.4.3 Alternative Location and Protection of Storage. Where the provisions of 69.5.4.1 and 69.5.4.2.2 are impractical at construction sites or at buildings or structures undergoing major renovation or repairs, alternative storage of cylinders shall be acceptable to the AHJ. [58:8.4.3]

69.5.5 Fire Protection and Electrical Area Classification.

69.5.5.1* Retail cylinder exchange locations having aggregate quantities of 720 lb (327 kg) or more of propane shall be provided with at least one portable fire extinguisher having a minimum dry chemical agent capacity of 10 lb (4.5 kg) dry chemical per Section 4.7 of NFPA 58. [58:8.5.1]

69.5.5.2 Other than those complying with 69.5.5.1, propane storage locations having aggregate quantities of propane exceeding 720 lb (327 kg), shall be provided with at least one approved portable fire extinguisher having a minimum dry chemical agent capacity of 18 lb (8.2 kg) per Section 4.7 of NFPA 58. [58:8.5.2]

69.5.5.3 The required fire extinguisher shall be located within 50 ft (15 m) travel distance of the propane storage location. [58:8.5.3]

69.5.5.4 The storage of cylinders awaiting resale shall be exempt from the electrical classification requirements of NFPA 58. [58:8.5.4]

69.5.6 Automated Cylinder Exchange Stations.

69.5.6.1 Cylinder exchange cabinets that include an automated vending system for exchanging cylinders shall comply with the requirements in 69.5.6.2 through 69.5.6.6. [58:8.6.1]

69.5.6.2 Electrical equipment installed in cylinder storage compartments shall comply with the requirements for Class I, Division 2 equipment in accordance with *NFPA 70*. [58:8.6.2]

69.5.6.3 Cabinets shall be designed such that cylinders can be placed inside only in the upright position. [58:8.6.3]

69.5.6.4 Door releases for access to stored cylinders shall be permitted to be pneumatic, mechanical, or electrically powered. [58:8.6.4]

69.5.6.5 A manual override control shall be permitted for use by authorized personnel. [58:8.6.5]

69.5.6.6 The vending system shall not be capable of returning to automatic operation after a manual override until the system has been inspected and reset by authorized personnel. [58:8.6.6]

69.6 Vehicular Transportation of LP-Gas.

69.6.1 Transportation in Portable Containers.

69.6.1.1 Transportation of Cylinders.

69.6.1.1.1 Cylinders having an individual water capacity not exceeding 1000 lb (454 kg) [nominal 420 lb (191 kg) propane capacity], when filled with LP-Gas, shall be transported in accordance with the requirements of 69.6.1. [58:9.3.2.1]

69.6.1.1.2 Cylinders shall be constructed as provided in 69.2.1 and equipped in accordance with Section 5.9 of NFPA 58 for transportation as cylinders. [58:9.3.2.2]

69.6.1.1.3 The quantity of LP-Gas in cylinders shall be in accordance with Chapter 7 of NFPA 58. [58:9.3.2.3]

69.6.1.1.4 Cylinder valves shall comply with the following:

(1) Valves of cylinders shall be protected in accordance with 69.2.1.2.1.
(2) Screw-on-type protecting caps or collars shall be secured in place.
(3) The provisions of 69.4.2.2.5 shall apply.

[58:9.3.2.4]

69.6.1.1.5 The cargo space of the vehicle shall be isolated from the driver's compartment, the engine, and the engine's exhaust system. [58:9.3.2.5]

69.6.1.1.5.1 Open-bodied vehicles shall be considered to be in compliance with 69.6.1.1.5. [58:9.3.2.5(A)]

69.6.1.1.5.2 Closed-bodied vehicles having separate cargo, driver, and engine compartments shall be considered to be in compliance with 69.6.1.1.5. [58:9.3.2.5(B)]

69.6.1.1.5.3 Closed-bodied vehicles, such as passenger cars, vans, and station wagons, shall not be used for transporting more than 215 lb (98 kg) water capacity [nominal 90 lb (41 kg) propane capacity], but not more than 108 lb (49 kg) water capacity [nominal 45 lb (20 kg) propane capacity] per cylinder, unless the driver and engine compartments are separated from the cargo space by a vaportight partition that contains no means of access to the cargo space. [**58:**9.3.2.5(C)]

69.6.1.1.6 Cylinders and their appurtenances shall be determined to be leak-free before being loaded into vehicles. [**58:**9.3.2.6]

69.6.1.1.7 Cylinders shall be loaded into vehicles with flat floors or equipped with racks for holding cylinders. [**58:**9.3.2.7]

69.6.1.1.8 Cylinders shall be fastened in position to minimize the possibility of movement, tipping, and physical damage. [**58:**9.3.2.8]

69.6.1.1.9 Cylinders being transported by vehicles shall be positioned in accordance with Table 69.6.1.1.9. [**58:**9.3.2.9]

69.6.1.1.10 Vehicles transporting cylinders where the total weight is more than 1000 lb (454 kg), including the weight of the LP-Gas and the cylinders, shall be placarded as required by DOT regulations or state law. [**58:**9.3.2.10]

69.6.1.2 Fire Extinguishers.

69.6.1.2.1 Each truck or trailer transporting portable containers in accordance with 69.6.1.1 or 69.6.1.2 shall be equipped with at least one portable fire extinguisher in accordance with Section 4.7 of NFPA 58 having a minimum capacity of 18 lb (8.2 kg) dry chemical. [**58:**9.3.5.1]

69.6.2 Parking and Garaging Vehicles Used to Carry LP-Gas Cargo.

69.6.2.1 Application. Subsection 69.6.2 applies to the parking and garaging of vehicles used for the transportation of LP-Gas. [**58:**9.7.1]

69.6.2.2 Parking Outdoors.

69.6.2.2.1 Vehicles shall not be left unattended on any street, highway, avenue, or alley, except for necessary absences from the vehicle associated with drivers' normal duties, including stops for meals and rest stops during the day or night, except as follows:

(1) This requirement shall not apply in an emergency.

(2) This requirement shall not apply to vehicles parked in accordance with 69.6.2.2.3 and 69.6.2.2.4. [**58:**9.7.2.1]

69.6.2.2.2* Vehicles shall not be parked in congested areas. [**58:**9.7.2.2]

69.6.2.2.3 Where vehicles are parked off the street in uncongested areas, they shall be at least 50 ft (15 m) from any building used for assembly, institutional, or multiple residential occupancy. [**58:**9.7.2.3]

69.6.2.2.4 Where vehicles carrying portable containers or cargo tank vehicles of 3500 gal (13 m^3) water capacity or less are parked on streets adjacent to the driver's residence in uncongested residential areas, the parking locations shall be at least 50 ft (15 m) from a building used for assembly, institutional, or multiple residential occupancy. [**58:**9.7.2.4]

69.6.2.3 Parking Indoors.

69.6.2.3.1 Cargo tank vehicles parked in any public garage or building shall have LP-Gas liquid removed from the following:

(1) Cargo tank
(2) Piping
(3) Pump
(4) Meter
(5) Hose
(6) Related equipment

[**58:**9.7.3.1]

69.6.2.3.2 Vehicles used to carry portable containers shall not be moved into any public garage or building for parking until all portable containers have been removed from the vehicle. [**58:**9.7.3.2]

69.6.2.3.3 The pressure in the delivery hose and related equipment shall be reduced to approximately atmospheric. [**58:**9.7.3.3]

69.6.2.3.4 All valves shall be closed before the vehicle is moved indoors. [**58:**9.7.3.4]

69.6.2.3.5 Delivery hose or valve outlets shall be plugged or capped before the vehicle is moved indoors. [**58:**9.7.3.5]

69.6.2.3.6 Vehicles carrying or containing LP-Gas shall only be parked in buildings complying with Chapter 10 of NFPA 58 and located on premises owned or under the control of the operator of such vehicles where the following provisions are met:

(1) The public shall be excluded from such buildings.
(2) Floor level ventilation shall be provided in all parts of the building where such vehicles are parked.
(3) Leaks in the vehicle LP-Gas systems shall be repaired before the vehicle is moved indoors.
(4) Primary shutoff valves on cargo tanks and other LP-Gas containers on the vehicle (except propulsion engine fuel containers) shall be closed and delivery hose outlets plugged or capped to contain system pressure before the vehicle is moved indoors.
(5) Primary shutoff valves on LP-Gas propulsion engine fuel containers shall be closed while the vehicle is parked.
(6) No LP-Gas container shall be located near a source of heat or within the direct path of hot air being blown from a blower-type heater.

Table 69.6.1.1.9 Orientation of Cylinders on Vehicles

| Propane Capacity of Cylinder | | Open Vehicles | Enclosed Spaces of Vehicles |
lb	kg		
≤45	≤20	Any position	
>45	>20	Relief valve in communication with the vapor space	
≤4.2	≤1.9		Any position
>4.2	>1.9		Relief valve in communication with the vapor space

[**58:**Table 9.3.2.9]

(7)* LP-Gas containers shall be gauged or weighed to determine that they are not filled beyond the maximum filling limit according to Section 7.4 of NFPA 58.
[58:9.7.3.6]

69.6.2.3.7 Where vehicles are serviced or repaired indoors, the following shall apply:

(1) When it is necessary to move a vehicle into any building located on premises owned or operated by the operator of such vehicle for service on engine or chassis, the provisions of 69.6.2.3.6 shall apply.

(2) When it is necessary to move a vehicle carrying or containing LP-Gas into any public garage or repair facility for service on the engine or chassis, the provisions of 69.6.2.3.1 shall apply, or the driver or a qualified representative of an LP-Gas operator shall be in attendance at all times while the vehicle is indoors, and the following shall apply:

   (a) Leaks in the vehicle LP-Gas systems shall be repaired before the vehicle is moved indoors.
   (b) Primary shutoff valves on cargo tanks, portable containers, and other LP-Gas containers installed on the vehicle (other than propulsion engine fuel containers) shall be closed.
   (c) LP-Gas liquid shall be removed from the piping, pump, meter, delivery hose, and related equipment and the pressure therein reduced to approximately atmospheric before the vehicle is moved inside.
   (d) Delivery hose or valve outlets shall be plugged or capped before the vehicle is moved indoors.
   (e) No container shall be located near a source of heat or within the direct path of hot air blown from a blower or from a blower-type heater.
   (f) LP-Gas containers shall be gauged or weighed to determine that they are not filled beyond the maximum filling capacity in accordance with Section 7.4 of NFPA 58.
   [58:9.7.3.7]

69.6.2.3.8 If repair work or servicing is to be performed on a cargo tank vehicle system, all LP-Gas shall be removed from the cargo tank and piping, and the system shall be thoroughly purged before the vehicle is moved indoors. [58:9.7.3.8]

69.7 LP-Gases at Utility Plants. The design, construction, location, installation, and operation of refrigerated and nonrefrigerated liquefied petroleum gas systems at utility gas plants shall be in accordance with NFPA 59.

69.8 Liquefied Natural Gas (LNG) Facilities. The design, location, construction, and operation of liquefied natural gas facilities shall be in accordance with NFPA 59A.

Chapter 70 Oxidizer Solids and Liquids

70.1 General.

70.1.1 The storage, use, and handling of oxidizer solids and liquids shall comply with the requirements of Chapter 60.

70.1.2 The storage, use, and handling of oxidizer solids and liquids in amounts exceeding the maximum allowable quantity permitted in control areas as set forth in Chapter 60 shall also comply with the requirements of NFPA 400.

70.1.3 The display and storage of Class 1 through Class 3 oxidizer solids and liquids in mercantile, storage, or industrial occupancies where the general public has access to the material for sale, and to the storage of oxidizing solid and liquid materials in such occupancies in areas that are not accessible to the public, shall comply with the requirements of NFPA 400.

N **70.1.4** Permits shall be required in accordance with this chapter and Table 1.13.8(a) through Table 1.13.8(d).

N **70.1.5** Permits, where required, shall comply with Section 1.13.

Chapter 71 Pyrophoric Solids and Liquids

71.1 General.

71.1.1 The storage, use, and handling of pyrophoric solids and liquids shall comply with the requirements of Chapter 60.

71.1.2 The storage, use, and handling of pyrophoric solids and liquids in amounts exceeding the maximum allowable quantity permitted in control areas as set forth in Chapter 60 shall also comply with the requirements of NFPA 400.

N **71.1.3** Permits shall be required in accordance with this chapter and Table 1.13.8(a) through Table 1.13.8(d).

N **71.1.4** Permits, where required, shall comply with Section 1.13.

Chapter 72 Unstable (Reactive) Solids and Liquids

72.1 General.

72.1.1 The storage, use, and handling of unstable (reactive) solids and liquids shall comply with the requirements of Chapter 60.

72.1.2 The storage, use, and handling of unstable (reactive) solids and liquids in amounts exceeding the maximum allowable quantity permitted in control areas as set forth in Chapter 60 shall also comply with the requirements of NFPA 400.

N **72.1.3** Permits shall be required in accordance with this chapter and Table 1.13.8(a) through Table 1.13.8(d).

N **72.1.4** Permits, where required, shall comply with Section 1.13.

Chapter 73 Water-Reactive Solids and Liquids

73.1 General.

73.1.1 The storage, use, and handling of water-reactive solids and liquids shall comply with the requirements of Chapter 60.

73.1.2 The storage, use, and handling of water-reactive solids and liquids in amounts exceeding the maximum allowable quantity permitted in control areas as set forth in Chapter 60 shall also comply with the requirements of NFPA 400.

N **73.1.3** Permits shall be required in accordance with this chapter and Table 1.13.8(a) through Table 1.13.8(d).

N **73.1.4** Permits, where required, shall comply with Section 1.13.

Chapter 74 Ammonium Nitrate

74.1 General.

74.1.1 The storage, use, and handling of ammonium nitrate (solid oxidizer) shall comply with Chapter 60.

74.1.2 The storage of ammonium nitrate in the form of crystals, flakes, grains, or prills including fertilizer grade, dynamite grade, nitrous oxide grade, technical grade, and other mixtures containing 60 percent or more by weight of ammonium nitrate shall comply with NFPA 400.

N **74.1.3** Permits shall be required in accordance with this chapter and Table 1.13.8(a) through Table 1.13.8(d).

N **74.1.4** Permits, where required, shall comply with Section 1.13.

Chapter 75 Organic Peroxide Solids and Liquids

75.1 General.

75.1.1 The storage, use, and handling of organic peroxide solids and liquids shall comply with the requirements of Chapter 60.

75.1.2 The storage, use, and handling of organic peroxide solids and liquids in amounts exceeding the maximum allowable quantity permitted in control areas as set forth in Chapter 60 shall also comply with the requirements of NFPA 400.

N **75.1.3** Permits shall be required in accordance with this chapter and Table 1.13.8(a) through Table 1.13.8(d).

N **75.1.4** Permits, where required, shall comply with Section 1.13.

Annex A Explanatory Material

Annex A is not a part of the requirements of this NFPA document but is included for informational purposes only. This annex contains explanatory material, numbered to correspond with the applicable text paragraphs.

A.1.1.1 The scope of this document is not intended to include primary consideration for conditions related to hazard assessment, planning, resource or incident management, construction features, protection features, features of occupancy, or practices that are primarily intended to reduce security vulnerabilities to life and property.

Security threat mitigation actions are primarily addressed through NFPA 730. Development of an Active Shooter/Hostile Event Response program is primarily addressed through NFPA 3000.

Security should be considered an ancillary component of the requirements in this *Code* to mitigate hazards from fire, explosions, and dangerous conditions.

A.1.2 Consideration for life safety could include occupants, fire department personnel, fire brigade members, employees, responsible parties, and the general public.

A.1.3.2 This *Code* is partially composed of limited text references extracted from other NFPA codes and standards in an effort to bring together information useful during field inspections.

With respect to hazardous materials, provisions in Chapters 60, 61, 63, 65, 66, and 69, are partial extracts of materials from NFPA standards referenced in each of these chapters. These extracts are included in NFPA 1 to assist users of the document by providing ready access to provisions that could be routinely referenced by fire code enforcers. However, through their adoption by reference in NFPA 1, the NFPA standards identified in these chapters apply in their entirety.

A.1.3.2.2 This section provides a basis for regulating an occupancy or hazard not specifically regulated by NFPA 1 or its referenced standards (e.g., retail sales and associated storage of consumer fireworks; wind turbines; amusement structures not defined as special amusement buildings, such as outdoor roller coasters and water slides). The AHJ has the authority to use any available resource and its own discretion to develop an appropriate protection scheme, including use of the provisions of Chapter 1, Administration; Chapter 4, Goals and Objectives; Chapter 5, Performance-Based Option; or other nationally recognized standards as indicated in 1.3.2.2 to regulate such occupancies or hazards.

A.1.3.6.2 A limited but reasonable time should be allowed for compliance with any part of this *Code* for existing buildings, commensurate with the magnitude of expenditure, disruption of services, and degree of hazard. Occupied existing buildings should comply with 10.3.3.

A.1.4.1.1 New editions of referenced publications incorporate advances in knowledge, best practices, and technology. Therefore, if an owner or contractor provides compliance with a new edition of a referenced publication that is specified by this *Code*, the AHJ should accept the new edition as evidence of full compliance with the *Code*.

A.1.4.1.1.1 The intent of 1.4.1.1 and 1.4.1.1.1 is that an AHJ should approve the use of subsequent editions of referenced publications only when the entire new edition of the referenced standard is used. This paragraph is not intended to permit the use of "cherry-picking" specific sections of one edition of a referenced standard but to use the entire subsequent edition of the referenced standard.

A.1.4.1.1.2 In circumstances where the AHJ is requested to use a specific section in a subsequent edition of a referenced publication and not the entire subsequent edition, the AHJ should require technical documentation submitted in compliance with 1.4.1 or 1.4.2. Before approving the use of specific sections of subsequent editions of referenced documents and not the entire edition of the subsequent edition, the AHJ should ensure that other changes did not occur to the subsequent edition that might affect the overall level of fire and life safety protection.

A.1.4.3 The term *practical difficulties* is meant to convey that there is a significant physical impediment to complying with the *Code* due to existing construction features, topography, or other existing constraints that would make compliance technically infeasible. Physical limitations can cause the need for disproportionate effort or expense with little increase in safety. A claimed financial hardship, without a corresponding technical compliance difficulty, would not be justification for requesting a modification to the *Code* or for an AHJ to grant such a modification under 1.4.3.

A.1.7.2 For additional information on qualifications of code enforcement personnel, see NFPA 1030, NFPA 1033, and NFPA 1035.

A.1.7.6.1 The AHJ enforcing NFPA 1 may not have the technical expertise, required certifications, licensure, or legal authority to enforce all of the provisions and subject matter contained therein. As an example, Chapter 11 contains references to codes and standards that regulate specific building subsystems. These subsystems could be regulated by electrical, mechanical, plumbing, or other specialty enforcement officials with technical expertise or legal authority in the specific area of the subsystem. This paragraph authorizes the AHJ enforcing NFPA 1 to rely on the opinion and authority of these specialty enforcement officials in order to determine compliance.

A.1.7.7.1 New construction and existing occupancy inspection services should comply with NFPA 1730.

N A.1.7.7.6 AHJs should have the authority to respond to declared disaster environments by modifying inspection requirements, including schedule and scope, due to a disaster impacting the jurisdiction enforcing this *Code*. The types of inspections that can be modified or delayed by the AHJ include those performed by or on behalf of the AHJ, and inspection, testing, and maintenance (ITM) activities by owners, tenants, or contractors. During a declared disaster, the AHJ should clearly convey the scope and expectations of the modification or delay to affected parties.

It is important to note that 1.7.7.6 is intended to apply to only jurisdictions included in the formal disaster declaration issued by the emergency management authority of the respective jurisdiction, whether at the local, state, or federal level. Once the disaster declaration expires, the authority granted to the AHJ under 1.7.7.6 of this *Code* expires, and normal inspection schedules should resume without further action required by the AHJ.

A.1.7.8.3 Utility types could include, but are not limited to, electric, gas, water, sanitary sewer, or other types of utility services provided by private or public utilities.

A.1.7.17.3 Before each performance or the start of such activity, such individuals should inspect the required fire appliances provided to see that they are properly located and in good working order, and should keep diligent watch for fires during the time such place is open to the public or such activity is being conducted and take prompt measures for extinguishment of fires that can occur.

A.1.11.4.3 No additional information should be submitted to review by the Board of Appeals without the information submitted to the AHJ for their review prior to the hearing date. Additional information submitted after the filing of the appeal to the Board and AHJ should be made available to the Board and AHJ in a time frame that permits adequate review before the hearing date.

A.1.13.6.13 Figure A.1.13.6.13 shows a sample permit.

A.1.14.5.2 The following is provided for information purposes only and has been provided by outside sources. Information concerning the noted services has not been independently verified, nor have the services been endorsed by the NFPA or any of its technical committees.

Examples of certification programs for fireworks displays include those conducted through the American Pyrotechnics Association (APA) and the Pyrotechnics Guild International (PGI). Both programs are recognized by several state fire marshals' offices throughout the United States. Authorities having jurisdiction should contact the applicable trade organizations or groups that cover each of the activities listed in 1.14.1 for information on recognized certification program(s).

A.1.14.5.4 An example of suggested requirements for licensing operators who perform fireworks displays can be found in Annex C, Suggested Requirements for Operator Licensing, of NFPA 1123, 2010 edition.

A.1.15.6 The AHJ should consider the risk, complexity of the design, qualifications of the AHJ's review staff, and state registration laws/rules to determine if requiring plans/design documents to be prepared by a registered design professional is appropriate.

A.1.18 The schedule of fees should be established to cover the cost of services required to enforce this *Code* by conducting plans review and inspection services. The level of service provided is discussed in detail within NFPA 1730. If fees do not cover the cost of services, then the jurisdiction can choose to subsidize such fees by funding the inspection and plans review services from the general fund or other revenue funding mechanism.

A.2.1(1) For example, Chapter 2 references NFPA 10. Such reference does not mean that all buildings must be provided with portable fire extinguishers. Rather, portable fire extin-

---

Side 1

PERMIT FOR CUTTING AND WELDING WITH PORTABLE GAS OR ARC EQUIPMENT

Date _____
Building _____
Dept. _____ Floor _____
Work to be done _____
_____
Special precautions _____
_____
Is fire watch required? _____
The location where this work is to be done has been examined and necessary precautions taken, and permission is granted for this work. (See other side.)
Permit expires _____
         Signed _____
             (Individual responsible for
             authorizing welding and cutting)
Time Started _____ Completed _____

FINAL CHECK

Work area and all adjacent areas to which sparks and heat might have spread [including floors above and below and on opposite side of wall(s)] were inspected 30 minutes after the work was completed and were found firesafe.

         Signed _____
             (Supervisor or Fire Watcher)

Side 2

ATTENTION

Before approving any cutting and welding permit, the fire safety supervisor or appointee shall inspect the work area and confirm that precautions have been taken to prevent fire in accordance with NFPA 51B.

PRECAUTIONS
❑ Sprinklers in service
❑ Cutting and welding equipment in good repair

WITHIN 35 FT (10.7 M) OF WORK
❑ Floors swept clean of combustibles
❑ Combustible floors wet down and covered with damp sand, metal, or other shields
❑ All wall and floor openings covered
❑ Covers suspended beneath work to collect sparks

WORK ON WALLS OR CEILINGS
❑ Construction noncombustible and without combustible covering
❑ Combustibles moved away from opposite side of wall

WORK ON ENCLOSED EQUIPMENT
(Tanks, containers, ducts, dust collectors, etc.)
❑ Equipment cleaned of all combustibles
❑ Containers purged of flammable vapors

FIRE WATCH
❑ To be provided during and 30 minutes after operation
❑ Supplied with extinguisher and small hose
❑ Trained in use of equipment and in sounding fire alarm

FINAL CHECK
❑ To be made 30 minutes after completion of any operation unless fire watch is provided

         Signed _____
                  (Supervisor)

△ **FIGURE A.1.13.6.13 Sample Permit.**

guishers are mandatory only to the extent called for elsewhere in the *Code*.

A.2.1.1 New editions of referenced publications incorporate advances in knowledge, best practices, and technology. Therefore, if an owner or contractor provides compliance with a new edition of a referenced publication that is specified by this *Code*, the AHJ should accept the new edition as evidence of full compliance with the *Code*.

A.2.1.1.1 The intent of 2.1.1 and 2.1.1.1 is that an AHJ should approve the use of subsequent editions of referenced publications only when the entire new edition of the referenced standard is used. This paragraph is not intended to permit the use of "cherry-picking" specific sections of one edition of a referenced standard but to use the entire subsequent edition of the referenced standard.

A.2.1.1.2 In circumstances where the AHJ is requested to use a specific section in a subsequent edition of a referenced publication and not the entire subsequent edition, the AHJ should require technical documentation submitted in compliance with 1.4.1 or 1.4.2. Before approving the use of specific sections of subsequent editions of referenced documents and not the entire edition of the subsequent edition, the AHJ should ensure that other changes did not occur to the subsequent edition that might affect the overall level of fire and life safety protection.

N **A.2.1.2** To determine the applicable edition of a publication referenced within an extracted section, the user should go to the relevant extract document to determine the applicable edition of the reference publication.

A.3.2.1 Approved. The National Fire Protection Association does not approve, inspect, or certify any installations, procedures, equipment, or materials; nor does it approve or evaluate testing laboratories. In determining the acceptability of installations, procedures, equipment, or materials, the authority having jurisdiction may base acceptance on compliance with NFPA or other appropriate standards. In the absence of such standards, said authority may require evidence of proper installation, procedure, or use. The authority having jurisdiction may also refer to the listings or labeling practices of an organization that is concerned with product evaluations and is thus in a position to determine compliance with appropriate standards for the current production of listed items.

A.3.2.2 Authority Having Jurisdiction (AHJ). The phrase "authority having jurisdiction," or its acronym AHJ, is used in NFPA documents in a broad manner, since jurisdictions and approval agencies vary, as do their responsibilities. Where public safety is primary, the authority having jurisdiction may be a federal, state, local, or other regional department or individual such as a fire chief; fire marshal; chief of a fire prevention bureau, labor department, or health department; building official; electrical inspector; or others having statutory authority. For insurance purposes, an insurance inspection department, rating bureau, or other insurance company representative may be the authority having jurisdiction. In many circumstances, the property owner or his or her designated agent assumes the role of the authority having jurisdiction; at government installations, the commanding officer or departmental official may be the authority having jurisdiction.

A.3.2.3 Code. The decision to designate a standard as a "code" is based on such factors as the size and scope of the document, its intended use and form of adoption, and whether it contains substantial enforcement and administrative provisions.

A.3.2.6 Listed. The means for identifying listed equipment may vary for each organization concerned with product evaluation; some organizations do not recognize equipment as listed unless it is also labeled. The authority having jurisdiction should utilize the system employed by the listing organization to identify a listed product.

A.3.3.1 Absolute Pressure. Measured from this reference point, the standard atmospheric pressure at sea level is an absolute pressure of 14.7 psi (101.3 kPa). [55, 2023]

N **A.3.3.5 Aerosol Container.** Maximum sizes, minimum strengths, and other critical limitations for aerosol containers are set by the US Department of Transportation (49 CFR). These regulations ensure that aerosol products can be safely transported in interstate commerce. Aerosol products are generally classified as Other Regulated Materials — Class D (ORM-D). A cutaway drawing of a typical aerosol container is shown in Figure A.3.3.5. Labeling of aerosol products, including precautionary language for flammability and other hazards, is regulated by a number of federal authorities, including the Consumer Product Safety Commission, the Food and Drug Administration, the Environmental Protection Agency, the Occupational Safety and Health Administration, and the Federal Trade Commission. [30B, 2023] (FCC-HAZ)

Additional information on the labeling of aerosol products is given in Annex F (of NFPA 30B), Flammability Labeling of Aerosol Products. [30B, 2023] (FCC-HAZ)

A.3.3.6 Aerosol Products. The base product can be dispensed from the container in such form as a mist, spray, foam, gel, or aerated powder. [30B, 2023]

N **FIGURE A.3.3.5** One Type of Aerosol Container (Cutaway View). When the plunger (1) is pressed, a hole in the valve (2) allows a pressurized mixture of product and propellant (3) to flow through the plunger's exit orifice. [Source: Fire Protection Handbook, 20th edition] [30B:Figure A.3.3.1] (FCC-HAZ)

N A.3.3.8 Aerosol Valve. The product can be dispensed continuously or as a metered dose. Examples include liquid, gas, foam, paste, powder, or gel. [*30B*, 2023] (FCC-HAZ)

A.3.3.11 Aisle Width. See Figure A.3.3.11. [*13*, 2022]

A.3.3.17.11 Spray Area. This definition identifies the areas in which vapors, residue, and combustible powders might exist, either in suspension or on surfaces, as a result of the normal operation of the equipment. The presence of these materials requires various protection measures as identified later in this *Code*, such as the installation of fire suppression systems. [*33*, 2021]

For the purpose of this *Code*, the AHJ can define the limits of the spray area in any specific case. The spray area in the vicinity of spray application operations will necessarily vary with the design and arrangement of the equipment and with the method of operation. Where spray application operations are strictly confined to predetermined spaces that are provided with adequate and reliable ventilation, such as a properly designed and constructed spray booth, the spray area ordinarily will not extend beyond this space. When spray application operations are *not* confined to an adequately ventilated space, then the spray area might extend throughout the room or building area where the spraying is conducted. [*33*, 2021]

The following areas are typically not considered part of the spray area:

(1) Fresh air make-up units
(2) Air supply ducts and air supply plenums
(3) Recirculation air supply ducts downstream of recirculation particulate filters
(4) Exhaust ducts from solvent concentrator (i.e., pollution abatement) units

[*33*, 2021]

Spray booth recirculation systems contain a recirculation particulate filter, or series of filters, that have a minimum removal efficiency intended to minimize the potential for particulate accumulation in downstream areas. The reduction of particulates downstream of these filters reduces the hazards that are found in spray areas. [*33*, 2021]

A.3.3.23 Baled Cotton. See Table A.3.3.23.

The Joint Cotton Industry Bale Packaging Committee (JCIBPC) specifications for baling of cotton now requires that all cotton bales be secured with wire bands, polyester plastic strapping, or cold-rolled high tensile steel strapping, and then covered in fully coated or strip-coated woven polypropylene, polyethylene film, or burlap.

A.3.3.23.2 Densely Packed Baled Cotton. Experimental work by the US Department of Agriculture, and others (Wakelyn and Hughs, 2002), investigated the flammability of cotton bales with a packing density of at least 22 lb/ft^3 (360 kg/m^2). The research showed that such cotton bales (densely packed cotton bales) did not undergo self-heating or spontaneous combustion, and that the likelihood of sustained smoldering combustion internal to the cotton bale, creating a delayed fire hazard, was extremely low. The same research also showed that, when the cotton bales were exposed to smoldering cigarettes, matches, and open flames (including the gas burner ignition source used for the mattress tests, ASTM E1590, *Standard Test Method for Fire Testing of Mattresses*, and California Technical Bulletin 129), the probability of initiating flaming combustion was at such a low level as not to qualify the densely packed cotton bales as flammable solids. These investigations resulted in harmonization between the US Department of Transportation (49 CFR 172.102, note 137), the United Nations *Recommendations on the Transport of Dangerous Goods,* the International Maritime Organization (the *International Maritime Dangerous Goods Code*), and the International Civil Aviation Organization's *Technical Instructions,* with the removal of the flammable solid designation from densely packed cotton bales, complying with ISO 8115, *Cotton Bales — Dimensions and Density,* and the exemption of such cotton bales from the corresponding transportation hazardous materials regulations.

A.3.3.27.4 Valve-Regulated (VRLA). In VRLA batteries, the liquid electrolyte in the cells is immobilized in an absorptive glass mat (AGM cells or batteries) or by the addition of a gelling agent (gel cells or gelled batteries).

A.3.3.30 Boiling Point. (BP) At the boiling point, the surrounding atmospheric pressure can no longer hold the liquid in the liquid state and the liquid boils. A low boiling point is indicative of a high vapor pressure and a high rate of evaporation. [*30*:A.4.3]

A.3.3.31 Boil-Over. Boil-over occurs when the residues from surface burning become more dense than the unburned oil and sink below the surface to form a hot layer, which progresses downward much faster than the regression of the liquid surface. When this hot layer, called a "heat wave," reaches water or water-in-oil emulsion in the bottom of the tank, the water is first superheated and then boils almost explosively, overflowing the tank. Oils subject to boil-over consist of components having a wide range of boiling points, including both light ends and viscous residues. These characteristics are present in most crude oils and can be produced in synthetic mixtures. [*30*, 2024]

A boil-over is an entirely different phenomenon from a slop-over or froth-over. Slop-over involves a minor frothing that occurs when water is sprayed onto the hot surface of a burning oil. Froth-over is not associated with a fire but results when water is present or enters a tank containing hot viscous oil. Upon mixing, the sudden conversion of water to steam causes a portion of the tank contents to overflow. [*30*, 2024]

A.3.3.32 Building. The term *building* is to be understood as if followed by the words *or portions thereof. (See also A.3.3.280, Structure.)* [*101*, 2024]

A.3.3.32.1 Airport Terminal Building. The term *terminal* is sometimes applied to airport facilities other than those serving passengers, such as cargo- and freight-handling facilities and

FIGURE A.3.3.11 Illustration of Aisle Width. [*13*:Figure A.3.3.4]

fuel-handling facilities. These facilities are covered by other NFPA standards, such as NFPA 30. [**415,** 2022]

A.3.3.32.5 Existing Building. With respect to judging whether a building should be considered existing, the deciding factor is not when the building was designed or when construction started but, rather, the date plans were approved for construction by the appropriate AHJ. [***101,*** 2024]

A.3.3.32.6 High-Rise Building. It is the intent of this definition that, in determining the level from which the highest occupiable floor is to be measured, the enforcing agency should exercise reasonable judgment, including consideration of overall accessibility to the building by fire department personnel and vehicular equipment. Where a building is situated on a sloping terrain and there is building access on more than one level, the enforcing agency might select the level that provides the most logical and adequate fire department access. [***5000,*** 2024]

A.3.3.32.7 Important Building. Examples of important buildings include occupied buildings where egress within 2 minutes cannot be reasonably expected and control buildings that require presence of personnel for orderly shutdown of important or hazardous processes. Important buildings can also include unprotected storage where products from fire can harm the community or the environment or buildings that contain high-value contents or critical equipment or supplies. [***30,*** 2024]

A.3.3.32.10 Special Amusement Building. Special amusement buildings include amusements typically found in theme parks such as a roller coaster–type ride within a building, a multilevel play structure within a building, a submarine ride, and similar amusements where the occupants are not in the open air and might or might not be confined to a ride vehicle and/or unable to self-evacuate. Examples of temporary special amusement buildings include mobile fun houses typically found in carnivals or a gymnasium converted to a haunted house for Halloween. [***101,*** 2024]

Three conditions are essential to the definition of a special amusement building:

First, the area might be either an entire building or a portion of a building. A rollercoaster within a theme park would not be a special amusement building if it is open to the air along its entire length. On the other hand, if portions of the rollercoaster were partially enclosed within buildings that house the show elements, it would then be a special amusement building. [***101,*** 2024]

Second, a special amusement building contains either an amusement ride or device, or a walkway over a course intended to provide amusement or entertainment. A theater with fixed seats and a performance platform or stage would typically not be a special amusement building because there is no amusement ride or device, and there is no walkway that is used to provide amusement or entertainment. [***101,*** 2024]

Third, a special amusement building is intended to either divert the patron's attention away from the egress path, either through audio or visual distractions or by intentionally confounding the patron, or it contains or restrains the patron such that the patron is unable to self-evacuate when the amusement ride has ceased motion. A carousel or small train inside a shopping mall might not be considered to be a special amusement building if, once ride motion has ceased, the patron can step out of the vehicle without assistance and is aware of the egress path. [***101,*** 2024]

Other occupancies might also fall into the classification of special amusement building if the conditions described in the definition apply. Escape rooms are an example of where such conditions might exist. It is incumbent on the AHJ to inquire if the conditions in the escape room meet the definition of a special amusement building. Where such conditions exist, escape rooms should be classified as special amusement buildings. Where such conditions do not exist, escape rooms might be classified as another occupancy type, such as business. [***101,*** 2024]

It is important for the AHJ to recognize that the *Code* requires an occupancy to be classified as a special amusement building if the conditions in the space meet the definition of *special amusement building*, regardless of the occupant load of the space. No minimum occupant load threshold must be met for a space to be classified as a special amusement building. A space could be classified as a special amusement building even where the occupant load is significantly fewer than the 50 occupants required for classification of other assembly occupancies. [***101,*** 2024]

The requirements for special amusement buildings are not intended to apply to the design of the actual amusement ride or device, but rather that of the facility that houses the ride or device. The design of an amusement ride or device, including all platforms and stairs that are attached to the ride structure, is governed by other standards, such as ASTM F2291, *Standard Practice for Design of Amusement Rides and Devices*. The design of facilities elements around the ride, including stairs and platforms that are not part of the ride structure, should be in accordance with the applicable requirements of this *Code*. [***101,*** 2024]

Table A.3.3.23 Typical Cotton Bale Types and Approximate Sizes

Bale Type	Dimensions in.	Dimensions mm	Average Weight lb	Average Weight kg	Volume ft^3	Volume m^3	Density lb/ft^3	Density kg/m^3
Compressed, standard	57 × 29 × 23	1448 × 736 × 584	500	226.8	22.0	0.62	22.7	366
Gin, standard	55 × 31 × 21	1397 × 787 × 533	500	226.8	20.7	0.58	24.2	391
Compressed, universal	58 × 25 × 21	1475 × 635 × 533	500	226.8	17.6	0.50	28.4	454
Gin, universal	55 × 26 × 21	1397 × 660 × 533	500	226.8	17.4	0.49	28.7	463
Compressed, high density	58 × 22 × 21	1473 × 559 × 533	500	226.8	15.5	0.44	32.2	515
Densely packed baled cotton	55 × 21 × 27.6 to 35.4	1400 × 530 × 700 to 900	500	226.8	21.1	0.60	22.0	360

A.3.3.43 Cathodic Protection. This protection renders a metallic container or piping system or component negatively charged with respect to its surrounding environment. [55, 2023]

A.3.3.51 Chip. Chips are usually ¼ in. to 1¼ in. (6.4 mm to 31.8 mm) in size, with nothing finer than that which is retainable on a ¼ in. (6.4 mm) screen; however, blower and conveyor systems can create some fine dust particles after screening.

A.3.3.52 Cleaning Media. Cleaning methods that incorporate chemical washing techniques can include the use of chemical substances, usually liquid, capable of dissolving or dispersing a foreign substance or contaminants and techniques such as rinsing, heating, steaming, or vacuuming applied either individually or in combination with other techniques. Air, inert gas, steam, and water are acceptable cleaning media. [55, 2023]

A.3.3.61 Combustible Dust. The term *combustible dust* when used in this standard includes powders, fines, fibers, etc. [652, 2019]

Dusts traditionally were defined as material 420 μm or smaller (i.e., capable of passing through a US No. 40 standard sieve). For consistency with other standards, 500μm (i.e., capable of passing through a US No. 35 standard sieve) is now considered an appropriate size criterion. Particle surface area-to-volume ratio is a key factor in determining the rate of combustion. Combustible particulate solids with a minimum dimension more than 500 μm generally have a surface-to-volume ratio that is too small to pose a deflagration hazard. Flat platelet-shaped particles, flakes, or fibers with lengths that are large compared to their diameter usually do not pass through a 500 μm sieve, yet could still pose a deflagration hazard. Many particulates accumulate electrostatic charge in handling, causing them to attract each other, forming agglomerates. Often, agglomerates behave as if they were larger particles, yet when they are dispersed they present a significant hazard. Therefore, it can be inferred that any particulate that has a minimum dimension less than or equal to 500 μm could behave as a combustible dust if suspended in air or the process-specific oxidizer. If the minimum dimension of the particulate is greater than 500 μm, it is unlikely that the material would be a combustible dust, as determined by test. The determination of whether a sample of combustible material presents a flash-fire or explosion hazard could be based on a screening test methodology such as provided in ASTM E1226, *Standard Test Method for Explosibility of Dust Clouds*. Alternatively, a standardized test method such as ASTM E1515, *Standard Test Method for Minimum Explosible Concentration of Combustible Dusts*, could be used to determine dust explosibility. Chapter 5 of NFPA 652 has additional information on testing requirements. [652, 2019]

There is some possibility that a sample will result in a false positive in the 20 L sphere when tested by the ASTM E1226 screening test or the ASTM E1515 test. This is due to the high energy ignition source overdriving the test. When the lowest ignition energy allowed by either method still results in a positive result, the owner/operator can elect to determine whether the sample is a combustible dust with screening tests performed in a larger scale (≥1 m³) enclosure, which is less susceptible to overdriving and thus will provide more realistic results. [652, 2019]

This possibility for false positives has been known for quite some time and is attributed to "overdriven" conditions that exist in the 20 L chamber due to the use of strong pyrotechnic igniters. For that reason, the reference method for explosibility testing is based on a 1 m³ chamber, and the 20 L chamber test method is calibrated to produce results comparable to those from the 1 m³ chamber for most dusts. In fact, the US standard for 20 L testing (ASTM E1226) states, "The objective of this test method is to develop data that can be correlated to those from the 1 m³ chamber (described in ISO 6184-1 and VDI 3673)…" ASTM E1226 further states, "Because a number of factors (concentration, uniformity of dispersion, turbulence of ignition, sample age, etc.) can affect the test results, the test vessel to be used for routine work must be standardized using dust samples whose K_{St} and P_{max} parameters are known in the 1 m³ chamber." [652, 2019]

NFPA 68 also recognizes this problem and addresses it stating that "the 20 L test apparatus is designed to simulate results of the 1 m³ chamber; however, the igniter discharge makes it problematic to determine K_{St} values less than 50 bar-m/sec. Where the material is expected to yield K_{St} values less than 50 bar-m/sec, testing in a 1 m³ chamber might yield lower values." [652, 2019]

Any time a combustible dust is processed or handled, a potential for deflagration exists. The degree of deflagration hazard varies, depending on the type of combustible dust and the processing methods used. [652, 2019]

A dust deflagration has the following four requirements:

(1) Combustible dust
(2) Dust dispersion in air or other oxidant
(3) Sufficient concentration at or exceeding the minimum explosible concentration (MEC)
(4) Sufficiently powerful ignition source such as an electrostatic discharge, an electric current arc, a glowing ember, a hot surface, welding slag, frictional heat, or a flame

[652, 2019]

If the deflagration is confined and produces a pressure sufficient to rupture the confining enclosure, the event is, by definition, an "explosion." [652, 2019]

Evaluation of the hazard of a combustible dust should be determined by the means of actual test data. Each situation should be evaluated and applicable tests selected. The following list represents the factors that are sometimes used in determining the deflagration hazard of a dust:

(1) MEC
(2) MIE
(3) Particle size distribution
(4) Moisture content as received and as tested
(5) Maximum explosion pressure at optimum concentration
(6) Maximum rate of pressure rise at optimum concentration
(7) K_{St} (normalized rate of pressure rise) as defined in ASTM E1226, *Standard Test Method for Explosibility of Dust Clouds*
(8) Layer ignition temperature
(9) Dust cloud ignition temperature
(10) Limiting oxidant concentration (LOC) to prevent ignition
(11) Electrical volume resistivity
(12) Charge relaxation time
(13) Chargeability

[652, 2019]

It is important to keep in mind that as a particulate is processed, handled, or transported, the particle size generally decreases due to particle attrition. Therefore, it is often necessary to evaluate the explosibility of the particulate at multiple points along the process. Where process conditions dictate the use of oxidizing media other than air, which is nominally taken as 21 percent oxygen and 79 percent nitrogen, the applicable tests should be conducted in the appropriate process-specific medium. [*652*, 2019]

A.3.3.62 Combustible Fiber. Combustible fibers can include cotton, sisal, henequen, ixtle, jute, hemp, tow, cocoa fiber, oakum, baled waste, baled wastepaper, kapok, hay, straw, excelsior, Spanish moss, or other like materials.

A.3.3.66 Combustible Waste. These materials include but are not limited to all combustible fibers, hay, straw, hair, feathers, down, wood shavings, turnings, all types of paper products, soiled cloth trimmings and cuttings, rubber trimmings and buffings, metal fines, and any mixture of the previously listed items, or any other salvageable combustible waste materials.

A.3.3.69 Common Path of Travel. Common path of travel is measured in the same manner as travel distance but terminates at that point where two separate and distinct routes become available. Paths that merge are common paths of travel. [*101*, 2024]

A.3.3.70.1 Fire Compartment. Additional fire compartment information is contained in 8.2.2 of NFPA *101*. [*101*, 2024]

In the provisions for fire compartments utilizing the outside walls of a building, it is not intended that the outside wall be specifically fire resistance rated, unless required by other standards. Likewise, it is not intended that outside windows or doors be protected, unless specifically required for exposure protection by another section of this *Code*, by NFPA *101*, or by other standards. [*101*, 2024]

A.3.3.70.2 Smoke Compartment. Where smoke compartments using the outside walls or the roof of a building are provided, it is not intended that outside walls or roofs, or any openings therein, be capable of resisting the passage of smoke. Application of smoke compartment criteria where required elsewhere in NFPA *101*, should be in accordance with Section 8.5 of NFPA *101*. [*101*, 2024]

A.3.3.73.3 Container (Flammable or Combustible Liquid). The US DOT defines *non-bulk packaging* as having up to 119 gal (450 L) capacity in 49 CFR 171.8. [*30*, 2024]

A.3.3.75 Conventional Pallet. See Figure A.3.3.75. [*13*, 2022]

A.3.3.81 Cultural Resource Properties. Such properties include, but are not limited to, museums, libraries, historic structures, and places of worship. [*914*, 2023]

A.3.3.84 Cylinder Pack. *Six-packs* and *twelve-packs* are terms used to further define cylinder packs with a specific number of cylinders. The characteristic internal water volume of individual cylinders in a cylinder pack ranges from 1.52 scf to 1.76 scf (43 L to 50 L) or a water capacity of 95 lb to 110 lb (43 kg to 50 kg). [*55*, 2023]

N **A.3.3.86 Deficiency.** See NFPA 25 for additional guidance and examples of deficiencies.

A.3.3.90.4 Combination Detector. These detectors do not utilize a mathematical evaluation principle of signal processing

Conventional pallet

Solid flat bottom wood pallet (slave pallet)

△ **FIGURE A.3.3.75 Typical Pallets.** [13:Figure A.3.3.154.1]

more than a simple "or" function. Normally, these detectors provide a single response resulting from either sensing method, each of which operates independent of the other. These detectors can provide a separate and distinct response resulting from either sensing method, each of which is processed independent of the other. [*72*, 2019]

A.3.3.90.7 Fixed-Temperature Detector. The difference between the operating temperature of a fixed-temperature device and the surrounding air temperature is proportional to the rate at which the temperature is rising. The rate is commonly referred to as *thermal lag*. The air temperature is always higher than the operating temperature of the device. [*72*, 2019]

Typical examples of fixed-temperature sensing elements are as follows:

(1) *Bimetallic.* A sensing element comprised of two metals that have different coefficients of thermal expansion arranged so that the effect is deflection in one direction when heated and in the opposite direction when cooled.
(2) *Electrical Conductivity.* A line-type or spot-type sensing element in which resistance varies as a function of temperature.
(3) *Fusible Alloy.* A sensing element of a special composition metal (eutectic) that melts rapidly at the rated temperature.
(4) *Heat-Sensitive Cable.* A line-type device in which the sensing element comprises, in one type, two current-carrying wires separated by heat-sensitive insulation that softens at the rated temperature, thus allowing the wires to make electrical contact. In another type, a single wire is centered in a metallic tube, and the intervening space is filled with a substance that becomes conductive at a critical temperature, thus establishing electrical contact between the tube and the wire.
(5) *Liquid Expansion.* A sensing element comprising a liquid that is capable of marked expansion in volume in response to an increase in temperature.

[*72*, 2019]

A.3.3.90.8 Flame Detector. Flame detectors are categorized as ultraviolet, single wavelength infrared, ultraviolet infrared, or multiple wavelength infrared. [*72*, 2019]

A.3.3.90.12 Multi-Criteria Detector. A multi-criteria detector is a detector that contains multiple sensing methods that respond to fire signature phenomena and utilizes mathematical evaluation principles to determine the collective status of the device and generates a single output. Typical examples of multi-criteria detectors are a combination of a heat detector with a smoke detector, or a combination rate-of-rise and fixed-temperature heat detector that evaluates both signals using an algorithm to generate an output such as pre-alarm or alarm. The evaluation can be performed either at the detector or at the control unit. Other examples are detectors that include sensor combinations that respond in a predictable manner to any combination of heat, smoke, carbon monoxide, or carbon dioxide. [*72*, 2019]

A.3.3.90.13 Multi-Sensor Detector. Typical examples of multi-sensor detectors are a combination of a heat detector with a smoke detector, or a combination rate-of-rise and fixed-temperature heat detector that evaluates both signals using an algorithm to generate an output such as pre-alarm or alarm. The evaluation can be performed either at the detector or at the control unit. Other examples are detectors that include sensor combinations that respond in a predictable manner to any combination of heat, smoke, carbon monoxide, or carbon dioxide. [*72*, 2019]

A.3.3.90.18 Rate Compensation Detector. A typical example of a rate compensation detector is a spot-type detector with a tubular casing of a metal that tends to expand lengthwise as it is heated and an associated contact mechanism that closes at a certain point in the elongation. A second metallic element inside the tube exerts an opposing force on the contacts, tending to hold them open. The forces are balanced in such a way that, on a slow rate-of-temperature rise, there is more time for heat to penetrate to the inner element, which inhibits contact closure until the total device has been heated to its rated temperature level. However, on a fast rate-of-temperature rise, there is not as much time for heat to penetrate to the inner element, which exerts less of an inhibiting effect so that contact closure is achieved when the total device has been heated to a lower temperature. This, in effect, compensates for thermal lag. [*72*, 2019]

A.3.3.90.19 Rate-of-Rise Detector. Typical examples of rate-of-rise detectors are as follows:

(1) *Pneumatic Rate-of-Rise Tubing.* A line-type detector comprising small-diameter tubing, usually copper, that is installed on the ceiling or high on the walls throughout the protected area. The tubing is terminated in a detector unit that contains diaphragms and associated contacts set to actuate at a predetermined pressure. The system is sealed except for calibrated vents that compensate for normal changes in temperature.
(2) *Spot-Type Pneumatic Rate-of-Rise Detector.* A device consisting of an air chamber, a diaphragm, contacts, and a compensating vent in a single enclosure. The principle of operation is the same as that described for pneumatic rate-of-rise tubing.
(3) *Electrical Conductivity–Type Rate-of-Rise Detector.* A line-type or spot-type sensing element in which resistance changes due to a change in temperature. The rate of change of resistance is monitored by associated control equipment, and an alarm is initiated when the rate of temperature increase exceeds a preset value.

[*72*, 2019]

A.3.3.99 Dwelling Unit. It is not the intent of the *Code* that the list of spaces in the definition of the term *dwelling unit* to be all inclusive. It is the intent of the *Code* that the list of spaces is a minimal set of criteria that must be provided to be considered a dwelling unit and, therefore, the dwelling unit can contain other spaces that are typical to a single-family dwelling. [*5000*, 2024]

A.3.3.103 Energy Storage Systems (ESS). ESS include, but are not limited to, the following categories:

(1) Chemical: hydrogen storage
(2) Thermal: thermal energy storage
(3) Electrochemical:

   (a) Batteries
   (b) Flow batteries

(4) Mechanical:

   (a) Flywheel
   (b) Pumped hydro
   (c) Compressed air energy storage (CAES)

(5) Electrical:

   (a) Capacitors
   (b) Superconducting magnetic energy storage (SMES)

These systems can have ac or dc output for utilization and can include inverters and converters to change stored energy into electrical energy. It is not the intention for ESS to include energy generation systems. [*855*, 2020]

Energy storage systems can include, but are not limited to, batteries, capacitors, and kinetic energy devices (e.g., flywheels). Energy storage systems can include inverters or converters to change voltage levels or to make a change between an ac or a dc system. These systems differ from other storage systems such as a UPS system, which is a power supply used to provide alternating-current power to a load for some period of time in the event of a power failure.

[*855*, 2023]

A.3.3.107 Exhausted Enclosure. Such enclosures include laboratory hoods, exhaust fume hoods, and similar appliances and equipment used to retain and exhaust locally the gases, fumes, vapors, and mists that could be released. Rooms or areas provided with general ventilation, including rooms, such as control areas, with dedicated hazardous vapor/gas exhaust systems, in and of themselves, are not exhausted enclosures. [*55*, 2023]

A.3.3.108 Existing. See A.3.3.32.5, Existing Building. [*101*, 2024]

A.3.3.110 Exit. Exits include exterior exit doors, exit passageways, horizontal exits, exit stairs, and exit ramps. In the case of a stairway, the exit includes the stair enclosure, the door to the stair enclosure, the stairs and landings inside the enclosure, the door from the stair enclosure to the outside or to the level of exit discharge, and any exit passageway and its associated doors, if such are provided, so as to discharge the stair directly to the outside. In the case of a door leading directly from the street floor to the street or open air, the exit comprises only the door. *(See also 7.2.2.6.3.1 and A.7.2.2.6.3.1 of NFPA 101.)* [*101*, 2024]

Doors of small individual rooms, as in hotels, while constituting exit access from the room, are not referred to as exits, except where they lead directly to the outside of the building from the street floor. [*101*, 2024]

A.3.3.110.1 Horizontal Exit. Horizontal exits should not be confused with egress through doors in smoke barriers. Doors in smoke barriers are designed only for temporary protection against smoke, whereas horizontal exits provide protection against serious fire for a relatively long period of time in addition to providing immediate protection from smoke. *(See 7.2.4 of NFPA 101.)* [*101*, 2024]

A.3.3.114 Explosion Control. NFPA 68 provides guidance on the use of deflagration venting systems in buildings and other enclosures. The primary purpose of a venting system is to relieve the overpressure produced in an explosion to limit the potential damage to the building where the explosion occurs. Although some structural damage can be anticipated, the use of relief venting is expected to prevent massive building failure and collapse. In cases where detonation is probable, venting is often used in conjunction with barricade construction where the pressure-resistant portions of the building have been constructed to resist the pressures anticipated should an explosive event occur. Design of barricade systems is highly specialized and the subject of military standards applicable to the subject. NFPA 69 provides guidance on the use of suppression, ventilation systems, and the limiting of oxidants as a means to prevent the occurrence of an explosion. When relief vents are to be used as a means to provide explosion relief, the fundamental requirements of the building code for structural elements, including snow, wind, and seismic events, should be considered. In some instances, the requirements for wind resistance can impose more rigorous requirements on the relief vents than required by the engineering analysis used to determine the relief pressure. In such cases, users must demonstrate that the relief vents will not become airborne or release in such a manner as to create secondary hazards within or external to the building in which they are installed. Specific designs might require approval by the AHJ. [*55*, 2023]

A.3.3.115 Explosive Material. The term *explosive material* includes, but is not limited to, dynamite, black powder, pellet powder, initiating explosives, detonators, safety fuses, squibs, detonating cord, igniter cord, igniters, and Display Fireworks 1.3G (Class B, Special). The term *explosive* includes any material determined to be within the scope of Title 18, United States Code, Chapter 40, and also includes any material classified as an explosive by the Hazardous Materials Regulations of the US Department of Transportation (DOT) in 49 CFR. [*5000*, 2024]

The former classification system used by DOT included the terms *high explosive* and *low explosive*, as further defined in A.3.3.414.3.2 of *NFPA 5000®*. These terms remain in use by the US Bureau of Alcohol, Tobacco, Firearms, and Explosives. Explosive materials classified as hazard Class 1 are further defined under the current system applied by DOT. Compatibility group letters are used in concert with division numbers to specify further limitations on each division noted. For example, the letter G (as in 1.4G) identifies substances or articles that contain a pyrotechnic substance and similar materials. UN/DOT Class 1 Explosives are defined as follows:

(1) Division 1.1 explosives are explosives that are a mass explosion hazard, which is a hazard that instantaneously affects almost the entire load.
(2) Division 1.2 explosives are explosives that are a projection hazard but not a mass explosion hazard.
(3) Division 1.3 explosives are explosives that are a fire hazard and either a minor blast hazard or a minor projection hazard, or both, but not a mass explosion hazard.
(4) Division 1.4 explosives are explosives that pose a minor explosion hazard and meet both of the following criteria:
   (a) The explosive effects are largely confined to the package, and no projection of fragments of appreciable size or range is to be expected.
   (b) An external fire cannot cause virtually instantaneous explosion of almost the entire contents of the package.
(5) Division 1.5 explosives are very insensitive explosives that are comprised of substances that are a mass explosion hazard, but are so insensitive that there is very little probability of initiation or of transition from burning to detonation under normal conditions of transport.
(6) Division 1.6 explosives are extremely insensitive articles that are not a mass explosion hazard, that are comprised of articles that contain only extremely insensitive detonating substances, and that demonstrate a negligible probability of accidental initiation or propagation.

[*5000*, 2024]

A.3.3.119 Festival Seating. Festival seating describes situations in assembly occupancies where live entertainment events are held that are expected to result in overcrowding and high audience density that can compromise public safety. It is not the intent to apply the term *festival seating* to exhibitions; sports events; conventions; and bona fide political, religious, and educational events. Assembly occupancies with 15 ft² (1.4 m²) or more per person should not be considered festival seating. [*101*, 2024]

A.3.3.121.2 Interior Finish. Interior finish is not intended to apply to surfaces within spaces such as those that are concealed or inaccessible. Furnishings that, in some cases, might be secured in place for functional reasons should not be considered as interior finish. [*101*, 2024]

A.3.3.121.3 Interior Floor Finish. Interior floor finish includes coverings applied over a normal finished floor or stair treads and risers. [*101*, 2024]

A.3.3.121.4 Interior Wall Finish. Such partitions are intended to include washroom water closet partitions. [*101*, 2024]

A.3.3.130 Fire Hydrant. See Figure A.3.3.130(a) and Figure A.3.3.130(b). [*25*, 2023]

△ FIGURE A.3.3.130(a) Typical Fire Hydrant Connection. [25:Figure A.3.3.14(a)]

A.3.3.131 Fire Lane. The traditional term *fire lane* is no longer utilized in this *Code*. However, a fire apparatus access road that is marked and prohibits obstructions in accordance with 18.2.3.6 would meet the traditional intent of a fire lane.

A.3.3.136 Fireworks. Toy caps for use in toy pistols, toy canes, toy guns, and novelties and trick noisemakers are not considered to be fireworks *(see Annex C of NFPA 1124)*. The regulations referred to limit the explosive content of each toy cap to not more than an average of 0.25 gr (16.2 mg). Also, each package containing such caps has to be labeled to indicate the maximum explosive content per cap. For information on the use of model rockets and model rocket motors, see NFPA 1122. For information on the use of high-power rockets and high-power rocket motors, see NFPA 1127. Model rockets, model rocket motors, high-power rockets, and high-power rocket motors designed, sold, and used for the purpose of propelling recoverable aero models are not considered to be fireworks. [1124, 2022]

A.3.3.136.1 Display Fireworks. Display fireworks are described as Fireworks, UN0335 and are classified as Explosives, 1.3G by the US Department of Transportation (US DOT) *(see Annex C of NFPA 1124)*.

Display fireworks include, but are not limited to, the following:

(1) Salutes or firecrackers containing more than 2 gr (130 mg) of explosive composition (salute powder)
(2) Aerial shells containing more than 2.1 oz (60 g) of total pyrotechnic and explosive composition
(3) Other display pieces that exceed the limits for classification as consumer fireworks

Such fireworks are also described as fireworks, 49 CFR 172 by the US DOT.

[1124, 2022]

A.3.3.137 Flame Spread. See Section 10.2 of NFPA *101*. [*101*, 2024]

A.3.3.141.1 Gross Floor Area. Where the term *floor area* is used, it should be understood to be gross floor area, unless otherwise specified. [5000, 2024]

A.3.3.143 Fugitive Emissions. These include leaks from pump seals, valve packing, flange gaskets, compressor seals, process drains, and so forth. [30, 2024]

A.3.3.146.1 Compressed Gas. The states of a compressed gas are categorized as follows:

(1) Nonliquefied compressed gases are gases, other than those in solution, that are in a packaging under the charged pressure and are entirely gaseous at a temperature of 68°F (20°C).
(2) Liquefied compressed gases are gases that, in a packaging under the charged pressure, are partially liquid at a temperature of 68°F (20°C). Cryogenic fluids represent a transient state of a gas that is created through the use of refrigeration. Cryogenic fluids cannot exist in the liquid form or partial liquid form at temperatures of 68°F (20°C); hence, they are not "compressed gases" as defined.
(3) Compressed gases in solution are nonliquefied gases that are dissolved in a solvent.
(4) Compressed gas mixtures consist of a mixture of two or more compressed gases contained in a packaging, the hazard properties of which are represented by the properties of the mixture as a whole.

[55, 2023]

N **A.3.3.146.3 Flammable Gas.** The term *flammable gas* includes both Category 1A flammable gas and Category 1B flammable gas where not otherwise specified in this *Code*. [55, 2023]

A.3.3.146.6 Inert Gas. Inert gases do not react readily with other materials under normal temperatures and pressures. For example, nitrogen combines with some of the more active metals such as lithium and magnesium to form nitrides, and at high temperatures it will also combine with hydrogen, oxygen, and other elements. The gases neon, krypton, and xenon are considered rare due to their scarcity. Although these gases are commonly referred to as inert gases, the formation of compounds is possible. For example, xenon combines with fluorine to form various fluorides and with oxygen to form oxides; the compounds formed are crystalline solids. Radon is inert under the definition provided, but because it is radioactive, it is not considered inert for the purposes of NFPA 55. [55, 2023]

A.3.3.146.9 Liquefied Petroleum Gas (LP-Gas). In the pure state propylene (Chemical Abstract Service 105-07-01) has a vapor pressure of 132.8 psig (915.72 kPa) at 70°F (21.1°C). The vapor pressure of commercial propane (Chemical Abstract Service 74-98-6) at 70°F 21.1°C) is 124 psig (855 kPa). Although commercial propane can contain some propylene, as

Δ **FIGURE A.3.3.130(b)** Flush-Type Hydrant. [25:Figure A.3.3.14(b)]

in impurity, propylene in the pure state does not meet the definition of LP-Gas. Propylene in the pure state is commonly found in use as an industrial fuel gas. *(See NFPA 51.)* [**58,** 2024]

A.3.3.146.11 Other Gas. A gas classified as an "other gas" might be a nonflammable gas or an inert gas. [**55,** 2023]

A.3.3.146.17 Unstable Reactive Gas. Unstable reactive materials are subdivided into five classifications. Class 4 materials are materials that in themselves are readily capable of detonation or explosive decomposition or explosive reaction at normal temperatures and pressures. They include the following:

(1) Materials that are sensitive to localized thermal or mechanical shock at normal temperatures and pressures
(2) Materials that have an instantaneous power density (product of heat of reaction and reaction rate) at 482°F (250°C) of 1000 W/mL or greater

[**55,** 2023]

Class 3 materials are materials that in themselves are capable of detonation or explosive decomposition or explosive reaction but require a strong initiating source or heat under confinement before initiation. Class 3 materials include the following:

(1) Materials that have an instantaneous power density (product of heat of reaction and reaction rate) at 482°F (250°C) at or above 100 W/mL and below 1000 W/mL
(2) Materials that are sensitive to thermal or mechanical shock at elevated temperatures and pressures
(3) Materials that react explosively with water without requiring heat or confinement

[**55,** 2023]

Class 2 materials are materials that readily undergo violent chemical change at elevated temperatures and pressures, including the following:

(1) Materials that have an instantaneous power density (product of heat of reaction and reaction rate) at 482°F (250°C) at or above 10 W/mL and below 100 W/mL
(2) Materials that react violently with water or form potentially explosive mixtures with water

[**55,** 2023]

Class 1 materials are materials that in themselves are normally stable but that can become unstable at elevated temperatures and pressures, including the following:

(1) Materials that have an instantaneous power density (product of heat of reaction and reaction rate) at 482°F (250°C) at or above 0.01 W/mL and below 10 W/mL
(2) Materials that react vigorously with water, but not violently
(3) Materials that change or decompose on exposure to air, light, or moisture

[**55,** 2023]

Class 0 materials are materials that in themselves are normally stable, even under fire conditions, including the following:

(1) Materials that have an instantaneous power density (product of heat of reaction and reaction rate) at 482°F (250°C) below 0.01 W/mL
(2) Materials that do not react with water
(3) Materials that do not exhibit an exotherm at temperatures less than or equal to 932°F (500°C) when tested by differential scanning calorimetry

[**55,** 2023]

A.3.3.147 Gas Cabinet. Doors and access ports for exchanging cylinders and accessing pressure-regulating controls are permitted to be included as part of a gas cabinet. [**55,** 2023]

A.3.3.150 Gaseous Hydrogen (GH$_2$) System. The system includes stationary or portable containers, pressure regulators, pressure-relief devices, manifolds, interconnecting piping, and controls as required. [**55,** 2023]

A.3.3.151 Grade Plane. See 7.1.4 of *NFPA 5000* for provisions for establishing the grade plane. Vertical measurements might be used in determining the number of stories or building height. [**5000,** 2024]

A.3.3.154 Hazard of Contents. Hazardous materials are materials that present physical or health hazards and are regulated by the *Code*. The categories of materials classified as physical hazards, health hazards, or both have been established in concert with those categories identified by OSHA in 29 CFR that are used by preparers of material safety data sheets (MSDS). In some cases, the hazard categories are further subdivided into classes that have long been established by NFPA standards. For example, while OSHA recognizes flammable liquids as a broad class, including those that are combustible, such liquids are further categorized by building and fire codes with respect to degree of hazard under the system of classification used by NFPA to include Class I, Class II, and Class III liquids. They are further subdivided within these classes to Class IA, Class IB and so forth. A similar approach is used for materials in other categories where there are subcategories of hazard established by existing NFPA standards, including oxidizers, unstable reactives, organic peroxides, water reactives, and others. [**5000:**A.6.3.2]

Under the classification system used by OSHA, a hazardous material can have one or more physical or health hazards in categories not currently regulated by the *Code*; for example, irritants, sensitizers, radioactive materials, etiological agents, and others. This is not to say that these materials are not hazardous materials, but rather that the *Code* does not provide specific regulation for the hazard category represented. [**5000:**A.6.3.2]

The *Code* defines contents as either high hazard, low hazard, or ordinary hazard. The category of high hazard, which includes hazardous materials, is subdivided into groups in which the hazards of the groups are comparable, for example, high hazard Level 1 through Level 5. *(See also A.34.1.1 of NFPA 5000®.)* [**5000:**A.6.3.2]

A.3.3.154.2 Low Hazard Contents. Chapter 30 of *NFPA 5000* recognizes storage of noncombustible materials as low hazard. In other occupancies, it is assumed that, even where the actual contents hazard is normally low, there is sufficient likelihood that some combustible materials or hazardous operations will be introduced in connection with building repair or maintenance, or some psychological factor might create conditions conducive to panic, so that the egress facilities cannot safely be reduced below those specified for ordinary hazard contents. [**5000:**A.6.3.2.2]

A.3.3.154.3 Ordinary Hazard Contents. Ordinary hazard classification represents the conditions found in most buildings and is the basis for the general requirements of NFPA *101*. [***101:***A.6.2.2.3]

The fear of poisonous fumes or explosions is necessarily a relative matter to be determined on a judgment basis. All smoke contains some toxic fire gases but, under conditions of ordinary hazard, there should be no unduly dangerous exposure during the period necessary to escape from the fire area, assuming there are proper exits. [*101*:A.6.2.2.3]

A.3.3.155 Hazard Rating. The criteria for hazard rating are as defined in NFPA 704. [55, 2023]

A.3.3.159 Hazardous Reaction or Hazardous Chemical Reaction. These dangers might include, but are not limited to, toxic effects, reaction speed (including detonation), exothermic reaction, or production of unstable or reactive materials. [30, 2024]

A.3.3.161 Heliport. The term *heliport* applies to all sites used or intended to be used for the landing and takeoff of helicopters. [418, 2016]

A.3.3.165 Immediately Dangerous to Life and Health (IDLH). This level is established by the National Institute for Occupational Safety and Health (NIOSH). If adequate data do not exist for precise establishment of IDLH, an independent certified industrial hygienist, industrial toxicologist, or appropriate regulatory agency should make such determination. [55, 2023]

A.3.3.166 Imminent Danger. A use of a building or portion of a building that is inconsistent with the approved use under the Certificate of Occupancy could qualify as an imminent danger.

Δ **A.3.3.169 Incident Commander (IC).** This position is equivalent to the on-scene Incident Commander as defined in OSHA 1910.120(8), Hazardous Waste Operations and Emergency Response. The Incident Commander (IC) has overall authority and responsibility for conducting incident operations and is responsible for the management of all incident operations at the incident site. [470, 2022]

A.3.3.176 ISO Module. The characteristic internal water volume of individual tubular cylinders is 43 scf (1218 L) or a water capacity of 2686 lb (1218 kg). The frame of an ISO container module and its corner castings are specially designed and dimensioned to be used in multimodal transportation service on container ships, special highway chassis, and container-on-flatcar railroad equipment. [55, 2023]

A.3.3.178.1 Ceiling Limit. The ceiling limits utilized are to be those published in 29 CFR 1910.1000. [5000, 2024]

A.3.3.178.2 Permissible Exposure Limit (PEL). The maximum permitted time-weighted average exposures to be utilized are those published in 29 CFR 1910.1000. [55, 2023]

A.3.3.178.3 Short-Term Exposure Limit (STEL). STEL limits are published in 29 CFR 1910.1000. [55, 2023]

A.3.3.180.4 Ignitible Liquid. Unless otherwise specified, the term *liquid* means an ignitible liquid. [30, 2024]

The term *ignitible liquid* refers to any liquid that has a measurable closed-cup flash point. Class I liquids [FP < 100°F (37.8°C)], Class II and Class III liquids [FP ≥ 100°F (37.8°C)], and inflammable liquids are all ignitible liquids. *(See Annex B of NFPA 30 for more information.)* [30, 2024]

Δ **A.3.3.189.3 Corrosive Material.** A chemical is considered to be corrosive if it destroys or irreversibly changes the structure of the tissue at the site of contact within a specified period of time using one of the *in vivo* or *in vitro* OECD test methods authorized in 49 CFR Part 173.137. For purposes of this *Code*, this term does not refer to action on inanimate surfaces (e.g., steel or aluminum). Available testing data produced prior to September 30, 1995 from the test method in Appendix A to 49 CFR 173 in effect on October 1, 1994 can also be used to determine the corrosivity of a material. [400, 2022]

A.3.3.189.4 Hazardous Material. Hazardous wastes might or might not be classified as hazardous materials. Management and disposal of hazardous waste is regulated by the EPA under the Resource Conservation and Recovery Act (RCRA). EPA requires wastes identified as hazardous to be handled, stored, treated, and disposed of according to the stipulations of the RCRA hazardous waste program in 40 CFR 260–299, "Solid Wastes." [400, 2022]

A.3.3.189.7 Highly Toxic Material. While categorization is basically simple in application, the degree of hazard depends on many variables that should be carefully considered individually and in combination. Some examples include the following:

(1) Materials wherein the highly toxic component or mixtures thereof are inextricably bound and cannot be released so there is little or no potential for exposure
(2) Nonfriable solid hazardous materials existing in product forms and in the demonstrated absence of inhalable particles that might not present the same inhalation hazard as the chemical components existing in a friable state
(3) Mixtures of highly toxic materials with ordinary materials, such as water, that might not warrant classification as highly toxic

[400, 2022]

Any hazard evaluation that is required for the precise categorization of highly toxic material is required to be performed by experienced, technically competent persons. [400, 2022]

A.3.3.189.9 Incompatible Material. Information on incompatible materials can be found in safety data sheets (SDS) or manufacturers' product bulletins. [400, 2022]

A.3.3.189.14 Toxic Material. While categorization is basically simple in application, the degree of hazard depends on many variables that should be carefully considered individually and in combination. Some examples include the following:

(1) Materials wherein the toxic component or mixtures thereof are inextricably bound and cannot be released so there is little or no potential for exposure
(2) Nonfriable solid hazardous materials existing in product forms and in the demonstrated absence of inhalable particles that might not present the same inhalation hazard as the chemical components existing in a friable state
(3) Mixtures of toxic materials with ordinary materials, such as water, that might not warrant classification as toxic

[400, 2022]

Any hazard evaluation that is required for the precise categorization of toxic material is required to be performed by experienced, technically competent persons. [400, 2022]

A.3.3.189.15 Unstable (Reactive) Material. Unstable (reactive) material is classified as follows:

(1) Class 4 unstable (reactive) materials are those that, in themselves, are readily capable of detonation, explosive decomposition, or explosive reaction at normal temperatures and pressures and include, among others, materials

that are sensitive to localized thermal or mechanical shock at normal temperatures and pressures.
(2) Class 3 unstable (reactive) materials are those that, in themselves, are capable of detonation, explosive decomposition, or explosive reaction, but that require a strong initiating source or that must be heated under confinement before initiation, and include, among others, materials that are sensitive to thermal or mechanical shock at elevated temperatures and pressures.
(3) Class 2 unstable (reactive) materials are those that readily undergo violent chemical change at elevated temperatures and pressures and include, among others, materials that exhibit an exotherm at temperatures less than or equal to 30°F (−1°C) when tested by differential scanning calorimetry.
(4) Class 1 unstable (reactive) materials are those that, in themselves, are normally stable, but that can become unstable at elevated temperatures and pressures and include among others, materials that change or decompose on exposure to air, light, or moisture and that exhibit an exotherm at temperatures greater than 30°F (−1°C), but less than or equal to 57°F (14°C), when tested by differential scanning calorimetry.

[400, 2022]

A.3.3.189.16 Water-Reactive Material. Class 1 water-reactive materials are materials whose heat of mixing is at or above 30 cal/g and less than 100 cal/g. Class 2 water-reactive materials are materials whose heat of mixing is at or above 100 cal/g and less than 600 cal/g. Class 3 water-reactive materials are materials whose heat of mixing is greater or equal to 600 cal/g. [400, 2022]

A.3.3.190 Maximum Allowable Quantity (MAQ). Quantities are permitted to exceed the MAQ when they are located in an area complying with Protection Levels 1–5 in accordance with the building code.

A.3.3.191 Means of Egress. A means of egress comprises the vertical and horizontal travel and includes intervening room spaces, doorways, hallways, corridors, passageways, balconies, ramps, stairs, elevators, enclosures, lobbies, escalators, horizontal exits, courts, and yards. [101, 2024]

N **A.3.3.194 Micromobility Device, Powered.** Micromobility devices are not intended to include motor vehicles that are required to be registered with a governmental agency. Nor is it intended to include motorized wheelchairs, medical scooters, shopping carts, golf carts, or electrical convenience vehicles.

A.3.3.196 Mobile Supply Unit. Examples include ISO modules, tube trailers, and cylinder packs. [55, 2023]

A.3.3.197 Mobile or Temporary Cooking. Mobile or temporary cooking can include self-propelled trucks and vehicles; trailered units; push carts; equipment located under cover of awnings, canopies, or pop-up tents; or other structures for which a building permit has not been issued.

A.3.3.200 Normal Temperature and Pressure (NTP). There are different definitions of normal conditions. The normal conditions defined here are the ones most commonly used in the compressed gas and cryogenic fluid industry. [55, 2023]

N **A.3.3.201 Nuisance Alarm.** Nuisance alarms are unwanted alarms. Sometimes nuisance alarms might be called false alarms. In this *Code*, any unwanted alarm is considered false because they are not indicative of real hazards. Because the term false has been used by many people to mean many different things, this *Code* is instead using the terms unwanted, nuisance, and malicious to categorize the different types of alarms. They occur when some condition simulates a fire or other hazardous condition. For example, cigarette smoke can activate smoke detectors and smoke alarms. In that case, there might not be anything wrong with the smoke detector or smoke alarm — it is doing its job responding to the condition or stimulus that it was designed to detect. Another example would be a heat detector or heat alarm that activates when someone inadvertently points a hair dryer towards it. A malicious alarm occurs when someone intentionally activates the detector or alarm when there is no fire hazard. See the definitions of malicious, unintentional, unknown, and unwanted alarms. [72, 2022]

A.3.3.203.1 Ambulatory Health Care Occupancy. It is not the intent that occupants be considered to be incapable of self-preservation just because they are in a wheelchair or use assistive walking devices, such as a cane, a walker, or crutches. Rather it is the intent to address treatment centers that receive patients who have been rendered incapable of self-preservation, such as being rendered unconscious as a result of an accident or being unable to move due to sudden illness. [101, 2024]

It is not the intent that the term *anesthesia* be limited to general anesthesia. [101, 2024]

A.3.3.203.2 Apartment Building. The *Code* specifies that, wherever there are three or more living units in a building, the building is considered an apartment building and is required to comply with either Chapter 30 or Chapter 31 of NFPA *101*, as appropriate. Townhouse units are considered to be apartment buildings if there are three or more units in the building. The type of wall required between units in order to consider them to be separate buildings is normally established by the AHJ. If the units are separated by a wall of sufficient fire resistance and structural integrity to be considered as separate buildings, then the provisions of Chapter 24 of NFPA *101*, apply to each townhouse. Condominium status is a form of ownership, not occupancy; for example, there are condominium warehouses, condominium apartments, and condominium offices. [101, 2024]

Δ **A.3.3.203.3 Assembly Occupancy.** Assembly occupancies might include the following:
(1) Armories
(2) Assembly halls
(3) Auditoriums
(4) Bowling lanes
(5) Club rooms
(6) College and university classrooms, 50 persons and over
(7) Conference rooms
(8) Courtrooms
(9) Dance halls
(10) Drinking establishments
(11) Exhibition halls
(12) Gymnasiums
(13) Libraries
(14) Mortuary chapels
(15) Museums
(16) Nightclubs

(17) Passenger stations and terminals of air, surface, underground, and marine public transportation facilities
(18) Places of religious worship
(19) Pool rooms
(20) Recreation piers
(21) Restaurants
(22) Skating rinks
(23) Special amusement buildings, regardless of occupant load
(24) Theaters

[*101,* 2024]

Assembly occupancies are characterized by the presence or potential presence of crowds with attendant panic hazard in case of fire or other emergency. They are generally open or occasionally open to the public, and the occupants, who are present voluntarily, are not ordinarily subject to discipline or control. Such buildings are ordinarily not used for sleeping purposes. Special conference rooms, snack areas, and other areas incidental to, and under the control of, the management of other occupancies, such as offices, fall under the 50-person limitation. [*101,* 2024]

Restaurants and drinking establishments with an occupant load of fewer than 50 persons should be classified as mercantile occupancies. [*101,* 2024]

Occupancy of any room or space for assembly purposes by fewer than 50 persons in another occupancy, and incidental to such other occupancy, should be classified as part of the other occupancy and should be subject to the provisions applicable thereto. [*101,* 2024]

For special amusement buildings, see 12.4.9 and 13.4.9 of NFPA *101*. [*101,* 2024]

A.3.3.203.5 Business Occupancy. Business occupancies include the following:

(1) Airport traffic control towers (ATCTs)
(2) City halls
(3) College and university instructional buildings, classrooms under 50 persons, and instructional laboratories
(4) Courthouses
(5) Dentists' offices
(6) Doctors' offices
(7) General offices
(8) Outpatient clinics (ambulatory)
(9) Town halls

[*101,* 2024]

Doctors' and dentists' offices are included, unless of such character as to be classified as ambulatory health care occupancies. *(See 3.3.203.1.)* [*101,* 2024]

Birth centers should be classified as business occupancies if they are occupied by fewer than four patients, not including infants, at any one time; do not provide sleeping facilities for four or more occupants; and do not provide treatment procedures that render four or more patients, not including infants, incapable of self-preservation at any one time. For birth centers occupied by patients not meeting these parameters, see Chapter 18 or Chapter 19 of NFPA *101*, as appropriate. [*101,* 2024]

Service facilities common to city office buildings such as newsstands, lunch counters serving fewer than 50 persons, barber shops, and beauty parlors are included in the business occupancy group. [*101,* 2024]

City halls, town halls, and courthouses are included in this occupancy group, insofar as their principal function is the transaction of public business and the keeping of books and records. Insofar as they are used for assembly purposes, they are classified as assembly occupancies. [*101,* 2024]

A.3.3.203.6 Day-Care Home. A day-care home is generally located within a dwelling unit. [*101,* 2024]

A.3.3.203.7 Day-Care Occupancy. Day-care occupancies include the following:

(1) Adult day-care occupancies, except where part of a health care occupancy
(2) Child day-care occupancies
(3) Day-care homes
(4) Kindergarten classes that are incidental to a child day-care occupancy
(5) Nursery schools

[*101,* 2024]

In areas where public schools offer only half-day kindergarten programs, many child day-care occupancies offer state-approved kindergarten classes for children who need full-day care. Because these classes are normally incidental to the day-care occupancy, the requirements of the day-care occupancy should be followed. [*101,* 2024]

A.3.3.203.8 Detention and Correctional Occupancy. Detention and correctional occupancies include the following:

(1) Adult and juvenile substance abuse centers
(2) Adult and juvenile work camps
(3) Adult community residential centers
(4) Adult correctional institutions
(5) Adult local detention facilities
(6) Juvenile community residential centers
(7) Juvenile detention facilities
(8) Juvenile training schools

[*101,* 2024]

Detention and correctional occupancies do not include psychiatric and dementia units in hospitals, emergency rooms in hospitals, ambulatory health care occupancies, nursing homes, and residential board and care occupancies where persons can be lawfully detained. [*101,* 2024]

See A.22.1.1.1.6 and A.23.1.1.1.6 of NFPA *101*. [*101,* 2024]

A.3.3.203.9 Dormitory. Rooms within dormitories intended for the use of individuals for combined living and sleeping purposes are guest rooms or guest suites. Examples of dormitories are college dormitories, fraternity and sorority houses, and military barracks. [*101,* 2024]

A.3.3.203.10 Educational Occupancy. Educational occupancies include the following:

(1) Academies
(2) Kindergartens
(3) Schools

[*101,* 2024]

An educational occupancy is distinguished from an assembly occupancy in that the same occupants are regularly present. [*101,* 2024]

A.3.3.203.11 Health Care Occupancy. Health care occupancies include the following:

(1) Hospitals
(2) Limited care facilities
(3) Nursing homes

[*101,* 2024]

Occupants of health care occupancies typically have physical or mental illness, disease, or infirmity. They also include infants, convalescents, or infirm aged persons. It is not the intent to consider occupants incapable of self-preservation because they are in a wheelchair or use assistive walking devices, such as a cane, a walker, or crutches. [*101,* 2024]

A.3.3.203.12 High-Risk Occupancy. Examples of high-risk occupancies could include multiple-family dwellings, high-rise buildings, hotels, dormitories, lodging and rooming, assembly, child care, detention, educational, health care, and industrial. [*1730,* 2019]

A.3.3.203.14 Hotel. So-called apartment hotels should be classified as hotels, because they are potentially subject to the same transient occupancy as hotels. Transients are those who occupy accommodations for less than 30 days. [*101,* 2024]

A.3.3.203.15 Industrial Occupancy. Industrial occupancies include the following:

(1) Drycleaning plants
(2) Factories of all kinds
(3) Food processing plants
(4) Gas plants
(5) Hangars (for servicing/maintenance)
(6) Laundries
(7) Power plants
(8) Pumping stations
(9) Refineries
(10) Sawmills
(11) Telephone exchanges

[*101,* 2024]

In evaluating the appropriate classification of laboratories, the AHJ should treat each case individually, based on the extent and nature of the associated hazards. Some laboratories are classified as occupancies other than industrial; for example, a physical therapy laboratory or a computer laboratory. [*101,* 2024]

A.3.3.203.16 Limited Care Facility. Limited care facilities and residential board and care occupancies both provide care to people with physical and mental limitations. However, the goals and programs of the two types of occupancies differ greatly. The requirements in NFPA *101* for limited care facilities are based on the assumption that these are medical facilities, that they provide medical care and treatment, and that the patients are not trained to respond to the fire alarm; that is, the patients do not participate in fire drills but, rather, await rescue. *(See Section 18.7 of NFPA 101.)* [*101,* 2024]

The requirements for residential board and care occupancies are based on the assumption that the residents are provided with personal care and activities that foster continued independence, that the residents are encouraged and taught to overcome their limitations, and that most residents, including all residents in prompt and slow homes, are trained to respond to fire drills to the extent they are able. Residents are required to participate in fire drills. *(See Section 32.7 of NFPA 101.)* [*101,* 2024]

Persons with Alzheimer's and related illnesses might be located in a nursing home, limited care facility, or board and care facility. For such persons, it is the level of care provided, not the medical diagnosis, that matters for the purposes of determining whether the facility should meet the requirements for limited care. Where personal care is provided but medical or custodial care is not, the limited care definition does not typically apply. It is the intent of this definition that it not apply to persons not receiving medical or custodial care, provided they are able to assist in their own evacuation, regardless of their medical diagnosis. [*101,* 2024]

A.3.3.203.18 Low-Risk Occupancy. Examples of low-risk occupancies could include storage, mercantile, and business. [*1730,* 2019]

A.3.3.203.19 Mercantile Occupancy. Mercantile occupancies include the following:

(1) Auction rooms
(2) Department stores
(3) Drugstores
(4) Restaurants with fewer than 50 persons
(5) Shopping centers
(6) Supermarkets

[*101,* 2024]

Office, storage, and service facilities incidental to the sale of merchandise and located in the same building should be considered part of the mercantile occupancy classification.

[*101,* 2024]

A.3.3.203.21 Moderate-Risk Occupancy. Examples of moderate-risk occupancies could include ambulatory health care and industrial occupancies that do not maintain, store, use, or handle hazardous materials in excess of exempt amounts. [*1730,* 2019]

A.3.3.203.22.3 Motor Fuel Dispensing Facility Located Inside a Building. The motor fuel dispensing facility can be either enclosed or partially enclosed by the building walls, floors, ceilings, or partitions or can be open to the outside. The motor fuel dispensing area is that area required for dispensing of fuels to motor vehicles. Dispensing of fuel at manufacturing, assembly, and testing operations is not included within this definition. [*30A,* 2024]

A.3.3.203.26 Parking Structure. A parking structure is permitted to be enclosed or open, use ramps, and use mechanical control push-button-type elevators to transfer vehicles from one floor to another, or mechanical or stacker systems. Motor vehicles are permitted to be parked by the driver or by an attendant where a mechanical or stacker parking system is used. Motor fuel is permitted to be dispensed, and motor vehicles are permitted to be serviced in a parking structure in accordance with NFPA 30A. [*88A,* 2023]

A.3.3.203.28 Residential Board and Care Occupancy. The following are examples of facilities that are classified as residential board and care occupancies:

(1) Group housing arrangement for persons with physical or intellectual disabilities who normally attend school in the community, attend worship in the community, or otherwise use community facilities
(2) Group housing arrangement for persons with physical or intellectual disabilities who are undergoing training in

preparation for independent living, for paid employment, or for other normal community activities
(3) Group housing arrangement for the elderly that provides personal care services but that does not provide nursing care
(4) Facility for social rehabilitation of individuals with alcohol or substance use disorders or mental health conditions that contains a group housing arrangement and that provides personal care services but does not provide acute care
(5) Assisted living facilities
(6) Other group housing arrangements that provide personal care services but not nursing care

[*101*, 2024]

A.3.3.203.29 Residential Occupancy. Residential occupancies are treated as separate occupancies in this *Code* as follows:

(1) One- and two-family dwellings (Chapter 24 of NFPA *101*)
(2) Lodging or rooming houses (Chapter 26 of NFPA *101*)
(3) Hotels, motels, and dormitories (Chapters 28 and 29 of NFPA *101*)
(4) Apartment buildings (Chapters 30 and 31 of NFPA *101*)

[*101*, 2024]

A.3.3.203.31 Storage Occupancy. Storage occupancies include the following:

(1) Barns
(2) Bulk oil storage
(3) Cold storage
(4) Freight terminals
(5) Grain elevators
(6) Hangars (for storage only)
(7) Parking structures
(8) Truck and marine terminals
(9) Warehouses

[*101*, 2024]

Storage occupancies are characterized by the presence of relatively small numbers of persons in proportion to the area.

[*101*, 2024]

A.3.3.203.31.1 Mini-Storage Building. Mini-storage buildings are typically designed to accommodate relatively small transient tenants who are often private individuals or persons who own small businesses and need additional storage space that is generally very small in area to accommodate their short-term storage needs. This definition is not intended to apply to large warehouse buildings designed to be rented or leased to relatively large multiple tenants who are generally storing their wares in conjunction with their businesses. Garage units that are primarily intended for vehicular storage as part of a multi-family development are not intended to be classified as mini-storage buildings. [**5000**, 2024]

A.3.3.207 Operating Unit (Vessel) or Process Unit (Vessel). Unit operations include, but are not limited to, distillation, oxidation, cracking, and polymerization. [**30**, 2024]

A.3.3.212 Oxidizer. Examples of other oxidizing gases include bromine, chlorine, and fluorine. [**400**, 2022]

The classification of oxidizers is based on the technical committee's evaluation of available scientific and technical data, actual experience, and its considered opinion. Classification refers to the pure oxidizer. Gross contamination can cause oxidizers of all classes to undergo exothermic or explosive reaction, particularly if they also are subjected to confinement and heating. *(See G.2.2 through G.2.5 of NFPA 400 for oxidizer classifications.)* [**400**, 2022]

The classification of oxidizers is based on the degree to which an oxidizing chemical increases, if at all, the burning rate of available combustible fuels. Factors that can influence the burning rate of oxidizers are concentration, particle size, product form, product packaging, and packaging configuration. Examples of Class 1, 2, 3, and 4 chemical oxidizers are listed in Section G.2 of NFPA 400. The definition of the current classes and the oxidizers listed as typical of each Class in Section G.2 of NFPA 400 are based on the technical committee's evaluation of available data, experience, and results of tests done by the Bureau of Mines and GE Research in the 1970s. [**400**, 2022]

The definition of Class 1, 2, 3, and 4 oxidizers is subjective. Currently, there is no bench scale test method that adequately measures the burning rate of oxidizers for large-scale storage. The UN's *Recommendations on the Transport of Dangerous Goods, Model Regulations,* includes a bench scale test method (Test O.1) to assign packing groups to solid oxidizers. Thirty grams (1.06 oz) of a mixture of the test substance and cellulose powder is ignited with a Nichrome wire. The time from ignition to the end of visible burning of the mixture is compared with the burning time of several different mixtures of potassium bromate (Class 3) and cellulose powder. The test does not characterize chemical reactivity or thermal stability. The test is not representative of packaged oxidizers. The determination of burning time is strongly dependent on test conditions, particle size, and the test operator's perception of the end of active burning. [**400**, 2022]

The Fire Protection Research Foundation (FPRF) published *National Oxidizing Pool Chemicals Storage Fire Test Project* in August 1998. The technical report includes literature abstracts, large-scale calorimetry test data, and intermediate scale rack storage tests. The peak rate of heat release of packaging and packaged oxidizers trichloroisocyanuric acid (Trichlor, Class 1) and calcium hypochlorite (available chlorine >68%, Class 3) are summarized in Table A.3.3.212. [**400**, 2022]

The Class 1 Trichlor did not increase the burning rate of the combustible packaging. Class 3 calcium hypochlorite (available chlorine >68%) caused a severe increase in the burning rate of the combustible packaging. In 2006, the FPRF published a report on the *Development of an Enhanced Hazard Classification System for Oxidizers.* The report includes a review of fire losses, historical test data, and current test methods for oxidizing materials used by transportation and environmental regulatory agencies. Two classification schemes with multiple test methods and performance-based criteria were proposed to distinguish between Class 1, 2, 3, and 4 oxidizers in a storage situation. [**400**, 2022]

Future FPRF effort is proposed to define an appropriate bench scale test, validated by medium scale free burn testing, for oxidizers. The goal of the enhanced classification system would be to prescribe tests and use performance-based criteria to define the different classes of oxidizers based on the degree of burning rate enhancement, chemical reactivity, and thermal stability. [**400**, 2022]

The FPRF completed a project that resulted in the development of a bench-scale test, validated by intermediate scale testing, for solid oxidizers. An enhanced classification system with prescribed tests and performance-based criteria to define the different classes of oxidizers based on the degree of burning rate enhancement was developed. [Buc, Elizabeth C., *Oxidizer Classification Research Project: Tests and Criteria*, Fire Protection Research Foundation, November 2009] [**400,** 2022]

A.3.3.219 Personal Care. Personal care involves responsibility for the safety of the resident while inside the building. Personal care might include daily awareness by management of the resident's functioning and whereabouts, making and reminding a resident of appointments, the ability and readiness for intervention in the event of a resident experiencing a crisis, supervision in the areas of nutrition and medication, and actual provision of transient medical care, including limited periodic skilled nursing care. [*101,* 2024]

A.3.3.222 Pier. The terms *pier* and *wharf* are used interchangeably. [307, 2021]

A.3.3.226 Pressure Vessel. Pressure vessels of any type can be subject to additional regulations imposed by various states or other legal jurisdictions. Users should be aware that compliance with DOT or ASME requirements might not satisfy all of the required regulations for the location in which the vessel is to be installed or used. [55:A.8.2]

A.3.3.228 Process or Processing. The sequence can include both physical and chemical operations, unless the term is modified to restrict it to one or the other. The sequence can involve, but is not limited to, preparation, separation, purification, or change in state, energy content, or composition. [30, 2024]

A.3.3.237 Rack. Some rack structures use solid shelves. Racks are permitted to be fixed, portable, or movable. Loading is permitted to be either manual, using lift trucks, stacker cranes, or hand placement, or automatic, using machine-controlled storage and retrieval systems. *[See Figure A.34.8.3.1(a) through Figure A.34.8.3.1(k).]*

Table A.3.3.212 Results of Large-Scale Calorimetry Tests with Packaging and Packaged Oxidizers on Wood Pallets

Oxidizer and Packaging	Total Weight with Pallets (lb)	Peak Convective HRR (kW)
40 cartons of empty HDPE 2 lb capacity containers	300	1736
40 cartons of pea gravel filled HDPE 2 lb capacity containers	1631	464
40 cartons of granular Trichlor in HDPE 2 lb capacity containers	1891	649
40 cartons of tablet form Trichlor in HDPE 2 lb capacity containers	1882	877
48 cartons of granular calcium hypochlorite in 1 lb capacity Surlin (plastic) bags	1468	6696
36 cartons of granular calcium hypochlorite in HDPE 1 lb capacity containers	1452	16,184

For SI units, 1 lb = 0.45 kg.
Source: FPRF, *National Oxidizing Pool Chemicals Storage Fire Test Project,* Aug. 1998.
[**400,** Table A.3.3.73]

A.3.3.237.2 Movable Racks. Movable racks can be moved back and forth only in a horizontal, two-dimensional plane. A moving aisle is created as abutting racks are either loaded or unloaded, then moved across the aisle to abut other racks.

N **A.3.3.237.4 Portable Racks.** Portable racks can be arranged in any number of configurations.

A.3.3.238 Ramp. See 7.2.5 of NFPA *101.* [*101,* 2024]

A.3.3.249 Safety Can. Safety cans listed to UL 30, *Metal Safety Cans,* or *FM Approval Class Number 6051-6052, Standard Safety Containers and Filling, Supply and Disposal Containers for Ignitable (Flammable) Liquids,* are limited to 5 US gal (19 L). UL 1313, *Nonmetallic Safety Cans for Petroleum Products,* allows for capacities up to 5 Imperial gal (23 L). UL/ULC 30, *Metallic and Nonmetallic Safety Cans for Flammable and Combustible Liquids,* limits a maximum of 5 US gal (19 L) and incorporates requirements from the previous versions of UL 30 and UL 1313. The new flame mitigation device (FMD) term is inclusive of different devices that prevent an external ignition source from igniting the container contents, which is evaluated for effectiveness in UL/ULC 30. FMDs include traditional flame arresters (e.g., screen or strainer) and newer designs, such as mesh screen or sintered metal and materials, such as expanded metal mesh. [30, 2024]

A.3.3.250 Safety Data Sheet (SDS). SDSs in the United States are prepared in accordance with the Occupational Safety and Health Administration (OSHA) hazard communication standard (29 CFR 1910.1200, "Hazard Communication"). Chemicals transported internationally might include additional requirements. *(See Annex B of NFPA 400 for additional information regarding SDSs.)* [**400,** 2022]

A.3.3.256 Signal.

A.3.3.256.1 Alarm Signal. Examples of alarm signals include outputs of activated alarm initiating devices, the light and sound from actuated alarm notification appliances, alarm data transmission to a supervising station, and so forth. [72, 2016]

A.3.3.256.2 Fire Alarm Signal. Examples include outputs from activated fire alarm initiating devices (manual fire alarm box, automatic fire detector, waterflow switch, etc.), the light and sound from actuated fire alarm notification appliances, fire alarm data transmission to a supervising station, and so forth. [72, 2016]

A.3.3.256.3 Supervisory Signal. Examples include activated supervisory signal-initiating device outputs, supervisory data transmissions to supervising stations, the light and sound from actuated supervisory notification appliances, a delinquency signal indicating a guard's tour supervisory condition, and so forth. [72, 2016]

The term *guard's tour supervisory signal*, associated with systems supporting guard's tour supervisory service, is a message indicating that a guard has activated a guard's tour reporting station (not in itself an indication of a supervisory condition). Guard's tour supervisory signals are not a subset of the general category of supervisory signals as used in this *Code.* [72, 2016]

A.3.3.256.4 Trouble Signal. Examples include off-normal outputs from integrity monitoring circuits, the light and sound from actuated trouble notification appliances, trouble data transmission to a supervising station, and so forth. [72, 2016]

A.3.3.259 Smoke Barrier. A smoke barrier, such as a wall, floor, or ceiling assembly, might be aligned vertically or horizontally. A smoke barrier might or might not have a fire resistance rating. Application of smoke barrier criteria where required elsewhere in the *Code* should be in accordance with Section 12.9. [*5000*, 2024]

A.3.3.261 Smoke Partition. A smoke partition is not required to have a fire resistance rating. [*101*, 2024]

A.3.3.264.1 Combustible Particulate Solid. Combustible particulate solids include dusts, fibers, fines, chips, chunks, flakes, and mixtures of these. A definition of this breadth is necessary because it is crucial to address the fact that there is attrition of the material as it is conveyed. Pieces and particles rub against each other and collide with the walls of the duct as they travel through the system. The rubbing and collision break down the material and produce a mixture of pieces and much finer particles, called dusts. Consequently, it is expected that every conveying system produces dusts, regardless of the starting size of the material, as an inherent by-product of the conveying process. [*69*, 2019]

A.3.3.264.2 Flammable Solid. Flammable solids include finely divided solid materials that, when dispersed in air as a cloud, could be ignited and cause an explosion. [*400*, 2022]

A.3.3.266 Solid Shelving. The placement of loads affects the calculated area of the shelf. It is the intent to apply this definition to loads on the rack where 6 in. (150 mm) nominal flues are not provided on all four sides, regardless of whether shelving materials are present. See 20.5.3.1.2 of NFPA 13 for additional allowances for double-row racks up 25 ft (7.6 m) and for multiple-row racks of any height without a longitudinal flue space. [*13*, 2022]

A.3.3.269 Spray Booth. Spray booths are manufactured in a variety of forms, including automotive refinishing, downdraft, open-face, traveling, tunnel, and updraft booths. This definition is not intended to limit the term *spray booth* to any particular design. The entire spray booth is part of the spray area. A spray booth is not a spray room. [*33*, 2021]

A.3.3.270 Spray Room. The entire spray room is considered part of the spray area. A spray booth is not a spray room. [*33*, 2021]

A.3.3.275.7 Miscellaneous Tire Storage. The limitations on the type and size of storage are intended to identify those situations where tire storage is present in limited quantities and incidental to the main use of the building. Occupancies such as aircraft hangars, automobile dealers, repair garages, retail storage facilities, automotive and truck assembly plants, and mobile home assembly plants are types of facilities where miscellaneous storage could be present. [*13*, 2022]

A.3.3.278 Street Floor. Where, due to differences in street levels, two or more stories are accessible from the street, each is a street floor. Where there is no floor level within the specified limits for a street floor above or below ground level, the building has no street floor. [*101*, 2024]

A.3.3.280 Structure. The term *structure* is to be understood as if followed by the words *or portion thereof. (See also 3.3.32, Building.)* [*101*, 2024]

A.3.3.280.1 Open Structure. Open structures are often found in oil refining, chemical processing, or power plants. Roofs or canopies without enclosing walls are not considered an enclosure. [*101*, 2024]

A.3.3.281 Suburb or Suburban. Suburban areas can include populous towns or large villages or be located outside the official limits of a densely settled city of 2500 to 50,000 people per census block, or those areas that interface with the outer rim of an urban cluster (UC). Suburban communities usually exist within commuting distance of urban areas but exhibit their own jurisdictional autonomy. [*1142*, 2017]

A.3.3.283.1 Bulk Hydrogen Compressed Gas System. The bulk system terminates at the source valve, which is the point where the gas supply, at service pressure, first enters the supply line, or at a piece of equipment that utilizes the hydrogen gas, such as a hydrogen dispenser. The containers are either stationary or movable, and the source gas for the system is stored as a compressed gas. [*55*, 2023]

Bulk hydrogen compressed gas systems can include a bulk storage source, transfer piping and manifold system, compression system, and other components. The gaseous source can include a tube trailer, tube bank, or other high pressure storage vessels used to serve the piping system that transports hydrogen to the end user. Compressors can be installed downstream of the storage supply to boost the pressure of the source gas, and intermediate high pressure storage might be present. This is done where the end use requires hydrogen at a pressure higher than that of the bulk supply. In these instances, there may be intermediate storage vessels used to store the gas at elevated pressures. It is not uncommon for the bulk supply as delivered to be furnished at nominal gauge pressure of 3000 psi (20,684 kPa), and the intermediate high pressure storage to be stored at gauge pressures up to 15,000 psi (103,421 kPa). See Figure A.3.3.283.1(a) through Figure A.3.3.283.1(f). [*55*, 2023]

N **A.3.3.283.2 Bulk Inert Gas System.** The bulk system terminates at the source valve, which is commonly the point where the gas supply, at service pressure, first enters the supply line or a piece of equipment that utilizes the gas or the liquid. The containers are either stationary or movable, and the source gas is stored as a compressed gas or cryogenic fluid. [*55*, 2023]

Bulk inert gas systems can be used to supply gas in either its compressed gaseous or liquefied form. Systems that may be used to supply both gaseous and liquid forms are referred to as hybrid systems. The following bulk inert gas systems are typical of those in use:

When the primary supply of the gas as stored is from a compressed gaseous source that is used in the compressed and gaseous form, the bulk inert gas system is said to be a bulk inert compressed gas system.

When the primary supply of the gas as stored is in a liquid form and the system is designed to transfer only liquid, the system is said to be a bulk liquefied inert gas system.

When the primary supply of the gas as stored is in a liquid form and the system is designed to transfer or store the gas in a compressed gaseous form, with or without a feature that may also allow the subsequent transfer and use of liquid, the bulk inert gas system is said to be a hybrid bulk inert gas system.

For the purposes of the application of the code, a hybrid system is viewed as a bulk liquefied inert gas system.

[*55*, 2023]

- (PI) Pressure indicator
- (PSH) Pressure switch high
- (TI) Temperature indicator
- Excess flow valve (EFV)
- Reducer
- Filter
- Heat exchanger
- Strainer
- Flow orifice
- Rupture disk [pressure safety element (PSE)]
- Source valve (SV)
- Hand control valve (HCV)
- Check valve (CV)
- Needle valve (NV)
- Angle valve
- Ball valve (BV)
- Pressure safety valve (PSV)
- Automatic valve
- Pressure control valve
- Low pressure vent
- Instrument air
- Threaded end cap
- Flex hose (FH)
- Area break/piping specification

FIGURE A.3.3.283.1(a) Symbol Legend for Figure A.3.3.274.1(b) through Figure A.3.3.274.1(f). [55:Figure A.3.3.95.9.1(a)]

Notes:
1. System designed, as-built, and installed per NFPA 55.
2. ●— To vent stack, vent system designed per CGA G-5.5, *Hydrogen Vent Systems*.
3. Fitting count for the tube trailer is 125 joints.
4. Pipe sizes used for this system with respect to gauge pressure:

250 psi (1724 kPa) — 2.07 in. (52.50 mm)
3,000 psi (20,684 kPa) — 0.75 in. (18.97 mm)
7,500 psi (51,711 kPa) — 0.31 in. (7.92 mm)
12,000 psi (82,737.1 kPa) — 0.28 in. (7.16 mm)

FIGURE A.3.3.283.1(b) Typical Tube Trailer. [55:Figure A.3.3.95.9.1(b)]

FIGURE A.3.3.283.1(c) Typical Bulk Compressed Gaseous Storage System. [55:Figure A.3.3.95.9.1(c)]

N **A.3.3.283.3 Bulk Liquefied Hydrogen System.** The bulk system terminates at the source valve, which is commonly the point where the gas supply, at service pressure, first enters the supply line or a piece of equipment that utilizes the gas or the liquid, such as a hydrogen dispenser. The containers are either stationary or movable, and the source gas for the system is stored as a cryogenic fluid. [55, 2023]

A bulk liquefied hydrogen system can include a liquid source where the liquid is vaporized and subsequently compressed and transferred to storage in the compressed gaseous form. It is common for liquid hydrogen systems to be equipped with vaporizers that are used to gasify the cryogen for ultimate use in the compressed state; however, there are also systems that can be used to transfer liquid in the cryogenic state. For systems that are composed of combined gaseous and liquefied hydrogen storage systems and have separate source valves for both systems, the system can be viewed as having two source valves for determining minimum separation distances for bulk storage systems in accordance with 10.4.2.2 and 11.3.2.2 of NFPA 55. Identifying two source valves means that each portion of the system is subject to its respective minimum separation distances in accordance with 10.4.2.2 or 11.3.2.2 of NFPA 55. [55, 2023]

A.3.3.283.4 Bulk Oxygen System. The bulk oxygen system terminates at the source valve, which is commonly the point where oxygen at service pressure first enters the supply line or a piece of equipment that utilizes the oxygen gas or liquid. The oxygen containers are either stationary or movable, and the oxygen is stored as a compressed gas or cryogenic fluid. [55, 2023]

Bulk oxygen systems can be used to supply gas in either its compressed gaseous or liquefied form. Systems that may be used to supply both gaseous and liquid forms are referred to as hybrid systems. The following bulk oxygen systems are typical of those in use:

(1) When the primary supply of the gas as stored is from a compressed gaseous source that is used in the compressed and gaseous form, the bulk oxygen system is said to be a bulk compressed oxygen gas system.
(2) When the primary supply of the gas as stored is in a liquid form and the system is designed to transfer only liquid, the system is said to be a bulk liquefied oxygen system.
(3) When the primary supply of the gas as stored is in a liquid form and the system is designed to transfer or store the gas in a compressed gaseous form, with or without a feature that may also allow the subsequent transfer and use of liquid, the bulk oxygen system is said to be a hybrid

Notes:
1. System designed, as-built, and installed per NFPA 55.
2. ⟶ To vent stack, vent system designed per CGA G-5.5, *Hydrogen Vent Systems.*
3. Fitting count for the pressure control manifold is 111 joints.
4. Fitting count for the stanchion is 29 joints.
5. Pipe sizes used for analysis for this system with respect to gauge pressure:
   250 psi (1724 kPa) — 2.07 in. (52.50 mm)
   3,000 psi (20,684 kPa) — 0.75 in. (18.97 mm)
   7,500 psi (51,711 kPa) — 0.31 in. (7.92 mm)
   12,000 psi (82,737.1 kPa) — 0.28 in. (7.16 mm)

FIGURE A.3.3.283.1(d) Typical Tube Trailer Discharge Stanchion and Pressure Control Manifold. [55:Figure A.3.3.95.9.1(d)]

bulk oxygen system. For the purposes of the application of the *Code*, a hybrid system is viewed as a bulk liquefied oxygen system. [55, 2023]

A.3.3.283.13 Standpipe System. This arrangement is accomplished by means of connections to water supply systems or by means of pumps, tanks, and other equipment necessary to provide an adequate supply of water to the hose connections. A building can have multiple horizontal standpipes, vertical standpipes system zones, and/or multiple types of standpipe systems. [14, 2023]

A.3.3.283.15 Vapor Processing System. Examples are systems using blower-assist for capturing vapors and refrigeration, absorption, and combustion systems for processing vapors. [30, 2024]

A.3.3.283.16 Vapor Recovery System. Examples are balanced-pressure vapor displacement systems and vacuum-assist systems without vapor processing. [30, 2024]

A.3.3.284.4 Portable Tank. A portable tank does not include any cylinder having less than 1000 lb (453.5 kg) water capacity, cargo tank, tank car tank, or trailers carrying cylinders of over 1000 lb (453.5 kg) water capacity. [55, 2023]

A.3.3.284.6 Stationary Tank. A stationary tank does not include a cylinder having less than 1000 lb (453.5 kg) water capacity. [55, 2023]

A.3.3.290 Traffic Calming Device. Traffic calming devices typically consist of, but are not limited to, speed bumps, speed humps, and traffic circles.

A.3.3.291 Transfilling. Transfilling usually occurs from a bulk container to a smaller container, such as filling a small compressed gas cylinder.

A.3.3.292 Tube Trailer. The characteristic internal water volume of individual tubular cylinders ranges from 43 scf to 93 scf (1218 L to 2632 L) or a water capacity of 2686 lb to 5803 lb (1218 kg to 2632 kg). [55, 2023]

A.3.3.298 Use [Hazardous Materials]. Examples of use include, but are not limited to, blending, mixing, reacting, distillation, heating or cooling, pumping, compressing, drying, screening, filling, loading and unloading, repackaging, scrubbing, absorbing, neutralizing, and incineration. [400, 2022]

A.3.3.298.1 Closed System Use. Examples of closed systems for solids and liquids include reaction process operations and product conveyed through a piping system into a closed vessel, system, or piece of equipment. [400, 2022]

A.3.3.298.2 Open System Use. Examples of open systems for solids and liquids include dispensing from or into open beakers or containers, and dip tank and plating tank operations. [400, 2022]

FIGURE A.3.3.283.1(e) Typical Chemical Energy Storage Module (CESM). [55:Figure A.3.3.95.9.1(e)]

N **A.3.3.305.2 Liquid Warehouse.** A liquid warehouse is generally a large space where the quantity of stored ignitible liquids exceeds the MAQ. The legacy term *attached building* most closely resembles the current definition of liquid warehouse. A space designed for ignitible (flammable and combustible) liquid storage will be considered a control area, a liquid storage room, or a liquid warehouse. [30, 2024]

A.3.3.307 Wharf. The terms *wharf* and *pier* are used interchangeably. [307, 2021]

Δ **A.3.3.308 Wildland/Urban Interface.** The term *wildland/urban interface* can distort the perception of the primary issue. It can direct attention to "where" structures are located (e.g., at the edge of communities near the wildland) rather than if the structures are highly ignitable. This can cause emergency planners to focus on things that will not make a significant impact on reducing structure loss (e.g., how firefighters and equipment get there, what type of fire equipment is needed, and the location of fire hydrants and water sources) if there are more structures at risk than equipment to protect them, or if it becomes too dangerous for firefighting forces to be present. [1140, 2022]

The essence of this issue is not where structures and domestic landscapes adjoin wildland, but the location, density, and availability of ignitable structures. Which structures are at the greatest risk: ignition-resistant homes bordering the wildland or a dense subdivision with wood shingle roofs several miles away from wildland fuels? The wildland/urban interface is not a geographic location, but rather a set of conditions that can exist in many communities. [1140, 2022]

Δ **A.3.4.5 Design Specification.** Design specifications include both hardware and human factors, such as the conditions produced by maintenance and training. For purposes of performance-based design, the design specifications of interest are those that affect the ability of the building to meet the stated goals and objectives. [*101*, 2024]

A.3.4.7 Exposure Fire. An exposure fire usually refers to a fire that starts outside a building, such as a wildlands fire or vehicle fire, and that, consequently, exposes the building to a fire. [*101*, 2024]

A.3.4.8 Fire Model. Due to the complex nature of the principles involved, models are often packaged as computer software. Any relevant input data, assumptions, and limitations needed to properly implement the model will be attached to the fire models. [*101*, 2024]

A.3.4.9 Fire Scenario. A fire scenario defines the conditions under which a proposed design is expected to meet the fire safety goals. Factors typically include fuel characteristics, ignition sources, ventilation, building characteristics, and occupant locations and characteristics. The term *fire scenario* includes more than the characteristics of the fire itself but excludes design specifications and any characteristics that do not vary from one fire to another; the latter are called assumptions. The term *fire scenario* is used here to mean only those specifications required to calculate the fire's development and effects, but, in other contexts, the term might be used to mean both the initial

FIGURE A.3.3.283.1(f) Typical Compressor Module. [55:Figure A.3.3.95.9.1(f)]

Notes:
1. System designed, as-built, and installed per NFPA 55.
2. →●To vent stack, vent system designed per CGA G-5.5, *Hydrogen Vent Systems*.
3. Fitting count for the compression system is 225 joints.
4. Pipe sizes used for analysis for this system with respect to gauge pressure:

250 psi (1724 kPa) — 2.07 in. (52.50 mm)
3,000 psi (20,684 kPa) — 0.75 in. (18.97 mm)
7,500 psi (51,711 kPa) — 0.31 in. (7.92 mm)
12,000 psi (82,737.1 kPa) — 0.28 in. (7.16 mm)

specifications and the subsequent development and effects (i.e., a complete description of fire from conditions prior to ignition to conditions following extinguishment). [*101*, 2024]

Δ **A.3.4.10 Fuel Load.** Fuel load includes interior finish and trim. [*101*, 2024]

A.3.4.14 Performance Criteria. Performance criteria are stated in engineering terms. Engineering terms include temperatures, radiant heat flux, and levels of exposure to fire products. Performance criteria provide threshold values used to evaluate a proposed design. [*101*, 2024]

A.3.4.15 Proposed Design. The design team might develop a number of trial designs that will be evaluated to determine whether they meet the performance criteria. One of the trial designs will be selected from those that meet the performance criteria for submission to the AHJ as the proposed design. [*101*, 2024]

The proposed design is not necessarily limited to fire protection systems and building features. It also includes any component of the proposed design that is installed, established, or maintained for the purpose of life safety, without which the proposed design could fail to achieve specified performance criteria. Therefore, the proposed design often includes emergency procedures and organizational structures that are needed to meet the performance criteria specified for the proposed design. [*101*, 2024]

A.4.1 The overall goals of this *Code* are presented in 4.1.1. These overall goals are treated in greater depth in 4.1.3 through 4.1.5. In each of these subsections, an overall goal for the subsection is defined, specific goals relating to the overall goal are presented next, and the objectives that relate to the specific goal follow. This format is intended to enhance the usability of the *Code*.

The subjects addressed in Chapter 4 are general in nature and supplement the provisions of Chapter 1, Administration. NFPA publication style dictates that Chapter 1 of all codes and standards is to include only title, scope, purpose, application, equivalency, units and formulas, and enforcement sections. All other general provisions are to be contained in Chapter 4, General Requirements, which follows Chapter 2, Referenced Publications, and Chapter 3, Definitions.

Chapter 4 provides general information about the *Code's* goals and objectives, inherent assumptions, options that can be applied for compliance with life safety and property protection requirements, and information regarding how the *Code* is applied *(see Sections 4.1 through 4.5)*. These goals and objectives establish the broad areas that this *Code* governs. They can be achieved via prescriptive-based options or performance-based options. Additionally, the goals and objectives can be reviewed to determine whether satisfactory conditions are being provided when equivalency options are being considered.

General administrative and application requirements that apply to all facilities and buildings are also included in this chapter *(see Section 4.5)*.

A.4.1.1 These highest level goals are intentionally general in nature. Each includes a broad spectrum of topics as shown in 4.1.3. The property protection goal is not just a goal unto itself, as it is also achieved in part as a result of designing to achieve the other stated goals. A reasonable level of safety is further defined by subsequent language in the *Code*. The facility/property owner or an insurance representative might also have other goals, which might necessitate more stringent objectives as well as more demanding criteria.

A.4.1.2 The objectives apply regardless of which option a user of the *Code* selects for a design — the performance-based option or the prescriptive-based option. The objectives are stated in more specific terms than the goals and tend to be more quantitative. The goals and objectives, taken together, form the broad, general targets at which a performance-based design can take aim. Specific criteria for design follow in Chapter 5.

A.4.1.3 The concept of providing for safety applies not only to safety during a fire, explosion, or hazardous materials incident, but also during the normal use of a building or facility. A reasonable level of safety should be provided for occupants in and individuals near the facility or building in question. The resultant design in addition to providing for occupant's safety also promotes the public welfare. Public welfare is also provided as a result of the mission continuity provisions of this *Code*.

A.4.1.3.1.1 The phrase *reasonably safe* from fire is defined by subsequent language in this *Code*, primarily in the objectives.

A.4.1.3.1.2.2 In many cases, the provisions of the *Code* to provide safety for occupants satisfies this goal for protection of emergency responders.

A.4.1.3.1.2.5 This provision addresses the fire safety objectives of operations addressed elsewhere in the *Code*, such as hot work, tar kettle operation, and so forth, that are not directly related to building construction and use.

A.4.1.3.2.1 The phrase *reasonably safe during normal use* is defined by subsequent language in this *Code*, primarily in the objectives. Certain requirements, such as heights of guards and stair dimensions, are provided to ensure that the occupants are safe during nonemergency use of the buildings. Failure to address these features could result in falls or other injuries to occupants in their normal day-to-day activities in the building.

A.4.1.3.3.2.2 For item 3, the phrase *external force* refers to the application of factors such as heat, water, shock, or other phenomenon onto hazardous materials that are sensitive to such factors and could react vigorously to produce unsafe conditions.

A.4.1.4.2.1 Ignition occurs when combustible materials come into contact with a source of heat of sufficient temperature and power for a requisite time in an atmosphere where oxygen is present. Combustible material does not necessarily ignite immediately upon contact with a source of heat.

A.4.1.4.2.2 Examples of specific conditions to avoid include, but are not limited to, flashover, fire spread beyond the item or room of fire origin, overheating of equipment, and overpressure of exterior walls.

A.4.1.5.1 This goal is applicable to certain buildings and facilities that have been deemed to be necessary to the continued welfare of a community. Depending on the nature of the critical mission provided by the building, various stakeholders, including community leaders, AHJs, and owners will identify the mission critical buildings. Mission critical areas should be identified and appropriately protected. The objectives for property protection and mission continuity are sometimes difficult to differentiate. Achieving the objectives for property protection could, to a certain extent, accomplish the objectives for mission continuity.

A.4.1.5.2 Examples of buildings and facilities that provide a public welfare role for a community could include hospitals, police and fire stations, evacuation centers, schools, water and sewerage facilities, and electrical generating plants. Also included are buildings and facilities with significant impact on the economic viability of the community. This objective is intended to ensure that such buildings and facilities are capable of providing essential services following a disaster since the community's well-being depends on such service being available.

A.4.1.6 Additional information on building security is provided in NFPA 730, NFPA 731, and NFPA 3000.

A.4.2.1 Additional assumptions that need to be identified for a performance-based design are addressed in Chapter 5.

A.4.2.2 It is not assumed that a design scenario will be considered that simulates the hazards produced when unauthorized releases of hazardous materials occur simultaneously at different locations within a facility, unless it is reasonable to expect that a single incident, such as a fork lift accident or pipe failure, could be expected to create such a condition. However, when hazardous materials are in close proximity to one another, such as on a shelf or in adjacent storage cabinets, it could be reasonable to apply a design scenario where multiple releases of the hazardous materials occur simultaneously from these close proximity areas. In this case, it is not unreasonable to expect the shelf to collapse or a forklift to damage adjacent hazardous materials containers.

A.4.2.3 It is not assumed that a design scenario will be considered that simulates the hazards produced when a fire, explosion, or external force that creates a dangerous condition occurs at the same time that hazardous materials have been subject to an unauthorized release. This does not preclude considering a scenario where a fire or explosion occurs and impinges on hazardous materials that are in their normal storage, use, or handling conditions.

The phrase *external force that creates a dangerous condition* refers to the application of factors such as heat, water, shock, or other phenomenon onto hazardous materials that are sensitive to such factors and could react vigorously to produce unsafe conditions.

A.4.4.4 Fire alarms alert occupants to initiate emergency procedures, facilitate orderly conduct of fire drills, and initiate response by emergency services.

A.4.5.7 Examples of changes from one occupancy subclassification to another subclassification of the same occupancy could include a change from a Class B to a Class A mercantile occupancy. Hospitals and nursing homes are both health care occupancies and are defined separately, but they are not established as separate suboccupancies; thus, a change from one to the other does not constitute a change of occupancy subclassification.

For example, a building was used as a hospital but has been closed for 4 years. It is again to be used as a hospital. As long as the building was not used as another occupancy during the time it was closed, it would be considered an existing hospital.

Hotels and apartments, although both residential occupancies, are treated separately, and a change from one to the other constitutes a change of occupancy.

A.4.5.8.3 Examples of such features include automatic sprinklers, fire alarm systems, standpipes, and portable fire extinguishers. The presence of a life safety feature, such as sprinklers or fire alarm devices, creates a reasonable expectation by the public that these safety features are functional. When systems are inoperable or taken out of service but the devices remain, they present a false sense of safety. Also, before taking any life safety features out of service, extreme care needs to be exercised to ensure that the feature is not required, was not originally provided as an alternative or equivalent, or is no longer required due to other new requirements in the current *Code*. It is not intended that the entire system or protection feature be removed. Instead, components such as sprinklers, initiating devices, notification appliances, standpipe hose, and exit systems should be removed to reduce the likelihood of relying on inoperable systems or features. Conversely, equipment, such as fire or smoke dampers, that is not obvious to the public should be able to be taken out of service if no longer required by this *Code*. Where a door that is not required to be fire protection rated is equipped with a fire protection listing label, it is not the intent of 4.5.8.3 to require such door to be self- or automatic-closing due merely to the presence of the label. [*101*:A.4.6.12.3]

A.4.5.8.4 In some cases, the requirements for new construction are less restrictive, and it might be justifiable to permit an existing building to use the less restrictive requirements. However, extreme care needs to be exercised when granting such permission, because the less restrictive provision might be the result of a new requirement elsewhere in the *Code*. For example, in editions of the *Code* prior to 1991, corridors in new health care occupancies were required to have a 1-hour fire resistance rating. Since 1991, such corridors have been required only to resist the passage of smoke. However, this provision is based on the new requirement that all new health care facilities be protected throughout by automatic sprinklers. (*See A.4.5.8.5.*) [*101*:A.4.6.7.4]

A.4.5.8.5 An example of what is intended by 4.5.8.4 and 4.5.8.5 follows. In a hospital that has 6 ft (1830 mm) wide corridors, such corridors cannot be reduced in width, even though the provisions for existing hospitals do not require 6 ft (1830 mm) wide corridors. However, if a hospital has 10 ft (3050 mm) wide corridors, they are permitted to be reduced to 8 ft (2440 mm) in width, which is the requirement for new construction. If the hospital corridor is 36 in. (915 mm) wide, it would have to be increased to 48 in. (1220 mm), which is the requirement for existing hospitals. [*101*:A.4.6.7.5]

A.4.5.9.1(1) Examples of such materials include steel, concrete, masonry, and glass. [*5000*:A.7.1.4.1.1(1)]

N **A.4.5.10** Material subject to increase in combustibility or flame spread index beyond the limits herein established through the effects of age, moisture, or other atmospheric condition is considered combustible. (*See NFPA 259 and NFPA 220.*) [*5000*:A.7.1.4.2]

A.5.1 The performance option of this *Code* establishes acceptable levels of risk for facilities (i.e., buildings and other structures and the operations therewith associated) as addressed in Section 1.3. (Note that "facility" and "building" can be used interchangeably with facility being the more general term.) While the performance option of this *Code* does contain goals, objectives, and performance criteria necessary to provide for an acceptable level of risk, it does not describe how to meet these goals, objectives, and performance criteria. Design and engineering are needed to meet the provisions of Chapter 5. For fire protection designs, the *SFPE Engineering Guide to Performance-Based Fire Protection* provides a framework for these assessments.

Pre-construction design requirements address those issues, which have to be considered before the certificate of occupancy is issued for a facility.

A.5.1.3 Qualifications should include experience, education, and credentials that demonstrate knowledgeable and responsible use of applicable models and methods.

A.5.1.4 The *SFPE Engineering Guide to Performance-Based Fire Protection* outlines a process for using a performance-based approach in the design and assessment of building fire safety design and identifies parameters that should be considered in the analysis of a performance-based design. As can be seen this process requires the involvement of all stakeholders who have a share or interest in the successful completion of the project. The steps that are recommended by the *SFPE Engineering Guide to Performance-Based Fire Protection* for this process are shown in Figure A.5.1.4.

The guide specifically addresses building fire safety performance-based design. It might not be directly applicable to performance-based designs involving other systems and operations covered within this *Code*, such as hot work operations or hazardous materials storage. However, the various steps for defining, developing, evaluating, and documenting the performance-based design should still provide a useful framework for the overall design process.

The steps in the performance-based design process are as follows:

(1) *Step 1: Defining Project Scope*. The first step in a performance-based design is to define the scope of the project. Defining the scope consists of identifying and documenting the following:

    (a) Constraints on the design and project schedule
    (b) The stakeholders associated with project
    (c) The proposed building construction and features desired by the owner or tenant
    (d) Occupant and building characteristics
    (e) The intended use and occupancy of the building
    (f) Applicable codes and regulations
    An understanding of these items is needed to ensure that a performance-based design meets the stakeholders' needs.

(2) *Step 2: Identifying Goals*. Once the scope of the project is defined, the next step in the performance-based design

process is to identify and document the fire safety goals of various stakeholders. Fire safety goals could include levels of protection for people and property, or they could provide for continuity of operations, historical preservation, and environmental protection. Goals could be unique for different projects, based on the stakeholders needs and desires. The stakeholders should discuss which goals are the most important for the project. In order to avoid problems later in the design process, all stakeholders should be aware of and agree to the goals prior to proceeding with the performance-based design process *(see Step 7)*.

(3) *Step 3: Defining Stakeholder and Design Objectives.* The third step in the design process is to develop objectives. The objectives are essentially the design goals that are further refined into tangible values that can be quantified in engineering terms. Objectives could include mitigating the consequences of a fire expressed in terms of dollar values, loss of life, or other impact on property operations, or maximum allowable conditions, such as extent of fire spread, temperature, spread of combustion products, and so forth.

(4) *Step 4: Developing Performance Criteria.* The fourth step in the design process is the development of performance criteria to be met by the design. These criteria are a further refinement of the design objectives and are numerical values to which the expected performance of the trial designs can be compared. Performance criteria could include threshold values for temperatures of materials, gas temperatures, carboxyhemoglobin (COHb) levels, smoke obscuration, and thermal exposure levels.

(5) *Step 5: Developing Design Scenarios.* Once the performance criteria have been established, the engineer will develop and analyze design alternatives to meet performance criteria. The first part of this process is the identification of possible scenarios and design scenarios. Fire scenarios are descriptions of possible fire events, and consist of fire characteristics, building characteristics (including facility operations), and occupant characteristics. The fire scenarios identified will subsequently be filtered (i.e., combined or eliminated) into a subset of design fire scenarios against which trial designs will be evaluated. Hazardous materials scenarios can be treated similarly.

(6) *Step 6: Developing Trial Design(s).* Once the project scope, performance criteria, and design scenarios are established, the engineer develops preliminary designs, referred to as trial designs, intended to meet the project requirements. The trial design(s) include proposed fire protection systems, construction features, and operation that are provided in order for a design to meet the performance criteria when evaluated using the design fire scenarios. The evaluation method should also be determined at this point. The evaluation methods used should be appropriate for the situation and agreeable to the stakeholders.

(7) *Step 7: Developing a Fire Protection Engineering Design Brief.* At this point in the process a fire protection engineering design brief should be prepared and provided to all stakeholders for their review and concurrence. This brief should document the project scope, goals, objectives, trial designs, performance criteria, design fire scenarios, and analysis methods. Documenting and agreeing upon these factors at this point in the design process will help avoid possible misunderstandings later.

(8) *Step 8: Evaluating Trial Designs.* Each trial design is then evaluated using each design scenario. The evaluation results will indicate whether the trial design will meet the performance criteria. Only trial design(s) that meet the performance criteria can be considered as final design proposals. Yet, the performance criteria can be revised with the stakeholders' approval. The criteria cannot be arbitrarily changed to ensure that a trial design meets a criterion, but can be changed based on additional analysis and the consideration of additional data.

(9) *Step 9: Modifying Designs or Objectives.* If none of the trial designs evaluated comply with the previously agreed upon performance criteria, it could be necessary to either develop and evaluate new trial designs, or revisit the objectives and performance criteria previously agreed upon by the stakeholders to determine if stakeholder objectives and performance criteria should be modified.

(10) *Step 10: Selecting the Final Design.* Once an acceptable trial design is identified using the evaluation, it can be considered for the final project design. If multiple trial designs are evaluated, further analysis will be needed to select a final design. The selection of an acceptable trial design for the final design could be based on a variety of factors, such as financial considerations, timeliness of installation, system and material availability, ease of installation, maintenance and use, and other factors.

(11) *Step 11: Preparing Performance-Based Design Report.* Once the final design is identified, design documents need to be prepared. Proper documentation will ensure that all stakeholders understand what is necessary for the design implementation, maintenance, and continuity of the fire protection design. The documentation should include the fire protection engineering design brief, a performance design report, detailed specifications and drawings, and a facility operations and maintenance manual.

(12) *Step 12: Preparing Specifications, Drawings, and Operations and Maintenance Manual.* The specifications and drawings portion of the performance-based design report convey to building and system designers and installing contractors how to implement the performance design. Specifications and drawings could include required sprinkler densities, hydraulic characteristics and spacing requirements, the fire detection and alarm system components and programming, special construction requirements including means of egress and location of fire-resistive walls, compartmentation, and the coordination of interactive systems. The detailed specifications are the implementation document of the performance-based design report. The detailed drawings will graphically represent the results of the performance design. The Operations and Maintenance (O&M) Manual clearly states the requirement of the facility operator to ensure that the components of the performance design are in place and operating properly. The O&M Manual describes the commissioning requirements and the interaction of the different systems' interfaces. All subsystems are identified, and inspection and testing regimes and schedules are created.

The O&M Manual also gives instruction to the facility operator on restrictions placed on facility operations. These limitations are based on the engineering assumptions made during the design and analysis. These limiting factors could include critical fire load, sprinkler design requirements, building use and occupancy, and reliability and maintenance of systems. The O&M Manual can be used to communicate to tenants and occupants these limits and their responsibilities as a tenant. It could also be used as a guide for renovations and changes. It also can be used to document agreements between stakeholders.

A.5.1.5 A third-party reviewer is a person or group of persons chosen by the AHJ to review proposed performance-based designs. Qualifications of the third-party reviewer should include experience, education, and credentials that demonstrate knowledgeable and responsible use of applicable models and methods. The *SFPE Guide for Peer Review in the Fire Protection Design Process* provides a method for the initiation, scope, conduct, and report of a peer review for a fire protection engineering design.

A.5.1.8 See Step 12 of A.5.1.4 for a description of these documents.

A.5.1.9 Information that could be needed by the fire service arriving at the scene of a fire in a performance-based designed facility includes, but is not limited to, the following:

(1) Safe shutdown procedures of equipment and processes
(2) Facility personnel responsible for assisting the fire service
(3) Operating procedures required to maintain the effectiveness of the performance-based designed fire protection system: when it is and is not appropriate to alter, shut down, or turn off a design feature; assumptions that have to be maintained if a fire occurs; suggested fire-fighting tactics that relate to the specific nature of the performance-based design

The design specifications and O&M Manual documentation described in 5.1.8 should provide a guide for the facility owner and tenants to follow in order to maintain the required level of safety anticipated by the original design. It should also provide a guide for the AHJ to use in conducting ongoing inspections of the facility.

A.5.1.10 Continued compliance with the goals and objectives of the *Code* involves many factors. The building construction, including openings, interior finish, and fire- and smoke-resistive construction, and the building and fire protection systems need to retain at least the same level of performance as is provided for by the original design parameters. The use and occupancy should not change to the degree that assumptions made about the occupant characteristics, combustibility of furnishings, and existence of trained personnel are no longer valid. In addition, actions provided by other personnel, such as emergency responders, should not be diminished below the documented assumed levels. Also, actions needed to maintain reliability of systems at the anticipated level need to meet the initial design criteria.

Subsection 5.1.10 deals with issues that arise after the facility has been constructed and a certificate of occupancy has been issued. Therefore, any changes to the facility or the operations conducted therein, up to and including the demolition of the facility, that affect the assumptions of the original design are considered as part of the management of change.

The following is a process for evaluating performance-based facilities:

(1) Review of original design analysis and documentation as follows:

    (a) Assumptions
    (b) Input parameter values
    (c) Predictions and/or results of other calculations

(2) Review of design analysis and documentation for any subsequent renovations, additions, modifications, and so forth, as in Step 1 of A.5.1.4
(3) Review of the facility's operations and maintenance manual, including any and all revisions to it
(4) On-site inspection, involving the following:

    (a) Consideration of "prescriptive" issues (e.g., blocked egress paths, poor maintenance of systems)
    (b) Comparison of assumptions to specific, pertinent on-site conditions
    (c) Comparison of input parameter values to pertinent on-site conditions
    (d) Review of maintenance and testing documentation to ensure adherence to the schedules detailed in the facility's O&M Manual

(5) Reconciliation of discrepancies as follows:

    (a) Develop a list of discrepancies
    (b) Consultation with the facility owner and/or their representative
    (c) Preparation of a schedule that reconciles the discrepancies

A.5.1.11 Private fire inspection services can be used to meet this provision provided that they are qualified to assess the impact of changes on the performance-based design and assumptions.

A.5.2.2 The performance criteria in 5.2.2 define an acceptable level of performance that should be agreed upon by the stakeholders, including the owner and the AHJ. The acceptable level of performance can vary widely between different facilities based on a number of factors, including the existence of potential ignition sources, potential fuel loads present, reactivity and quantity of hazardous materials present, the nature of the operations conducted at the facility, and the characteristics and number of personnel likely to be present at the facility.

A.5.2.2.1 Many of the performance criteria related to safety from fire can also be found in the annex of NFPA *101*.

A.5.2.2.2 It is anticipated that the design provides protection for occupants who are not intimate with the initial unintentional detonation or deflagration of explosive materials, and individuals immediately adjacent to the property. It is recognized that employees should be trained and knowledgeable in the hazards of the materials present in the workplace. It is recognized that some of these individuals could experience psychological and physical injuries, such as hearing problems, on either a short- or long-term basis. However, the intent is that they do not experience thermal burns or loss of life or limb as a direct result of the explosion.

It is not the intent of the *Code* to provide protection against explosions caused by acts of terrorism. This would involve the introduction of an unknown quantity of explosives in an unknown location within or adjacent to a building. Where protection is needed against such acts of terrorism, the appropriate military and law enforcement agencies should be consulted.

FIGURE A.5.1.4 Steps in the Performance-Based Analysis and the Conceptual Design Procedure for Fire Protection Design.

A.5.2.2.3 Given the nature and variety of hazardous materials, more than one performance criterion for a specific facility could need to be developed. Criteria have to be developed for each hazardous material and possibly for different personnel; for example, higher levels of exposure can be tolerated by personnel that are in some way protected than those personnel having no protection. Development of performance criteria for hazardous materials should be developed by the facility owner and the facility's safety personnel in conjunction with the AHJ and the emergency response personnel expected to respond to an incident.

It is anticipated that the design provides protection for occupants inside or immediately adjacent to the facility who are not intimate with the initial unauthorized release of hazardous materials, or the initial unintentional reaction of hazardous materials. However, it is assumed that these individuals depart from the area of the incident in a time frame reasonable for their circumstances, based on their observation of the event, or some other form of notification.

It is also anticipated that employees and emergency response personnel are trained and aware of the hazardous materials present in the facility, and the potential consequences of their involvement in the incident, and take appropriate measures to ensure their own safety during search and rescue operations.

It is not the intent of the *Code* to provide protection against acts of terrorism involving the introduction of hazardous materials into a facility. This involves the introduction of an unknown quantity of materials in an unknown location within or adjacent to a building. Where protection is needed against such acts of terrorism, the appropriate military and law enforcement agencies should be consulted.

A.5.2.2.4 Each facility designed using a performance-based approach most likely has different levels of acceptable and unacceptable property damage. This reflects the unique aspects of the performance-based designed facility and the reasons for pursuing a performance-based design. Therefore, the definition of an acceptable and an unacceptable level of property damage results from discussions between the facility's owner, manager and engineer, the designer, (possibly) the insurance underwriter and field engineer, and the AHJ. There could be cases where a property damage criterion is not needed.

Note that the structural integrity performance criteria for property damage most likely differs from the structural integrity performance criteria for life safety. This reflects the difference in the associated objectives: a life safety criterion probably is more restrictive than one for property damage.

A.5.2.2.5 Each facility designed using a performance-based approach most likely has a different level of acceptable and unacceptable interruption of the facility's mission. This reflects the unique aspects of the performance-based designed facility and the reasons for pursuing a performance-based design. Therefore, the definition of an acceptable and an unacceptable interruption of the facility's mission results from discussions between the facility's owner, manager and engineer, the designer, (possibly) the insurance underwriter and field engineer, and the AHJ. There could be cases where a mission continuity criterion is not needed.

A.5.2.2.8 Performance-based design of structural fire resistance requires three major steps:

(1) Determination of the thermal exposure to a structure resulting from a fire
(2) Determination of the temperature history within the structure, or portion thereof
(3) Determination of the structural response

SFPE Standard S.01, *Calculating Fire Exposures to Structures*, provides methodologies to predict thermal boundary conditions for fully developed fires to a structure (Step 1). SFPE Standard S.02, *Calculation Methods to Predict the Thermal Performance of Structural and Fire Resistive Assemblies*, provides methodologies to predict the thermal response of structures (Step 2). Appendix E, *Performance-Based Design Procedures for Fire Effects on Structures*, of ASCE/SEI 7, *Minimum Design Loads and Associated Criteria for Buildings and Other Structures*, provides methodologies to predict the structural response (Step 3).

A.5.4 Many events can occur during the life of a facility; some have a higher probability of occurrence than others. Some events, though not typical, could have a devastating effect on the facility. A reasonable design should be able to achieve the goals, objectives, and performance criteria of this *Code* for any typical or common design scenario and for some of the nontypical, potentially devastating scenarios, up to some level commensurate with society's expectations as reflected in this *Code*.

The challenge in selecting design scenarios is finding a manageable number that are sufficiently diverse and representative so that, if the design is reasonably safe for those scenarios, it should then be reasonably safe for all scenarios, except for those specifically excluded as being unrealistically severe or sufficiently infrequent to be fair tests of the design.

A.5.4.1.2 The *SFPE Engineering Guide to Performance-Based Fire Protection* identifies methods for evaluating fire scenarios.

A.5.4.1.3 It is desirable to consider a wide variety of different design scenarios to evaluate the complete capabilities of the building or structure. Design scenarios should not be limited to a single or a couple of worst-case events.

A.5.4.2.1 An example of such a scenario for a health care occupancy involves a patient room with two occupied beds with a fire initially involving one bed and the room door open. This is a cursory example in that much of the explicitly required information indicated in 5.4.2.1 can be determined from the information provided in the example. Note that it is usually necessary to consider more than one scenario to capture the features and conditions typical of an occupancy.

A.5.4.2.2 Examples of such scenarios are a fire involving ignition of gasoline as an accelerant in a means of egress, clothing racks in corridors, renovation materials, or other fuel configurations that can cause an ultrafast fire. The means of egress chosen is the doorway with the largest egress capacity among doorways normally used in the ordinary operation of the building. The baseline occupant characteristics for the property are assumed. At ignition, doors are assumed to be open throughout the building.

A.5.4.2.3 An example of such a scenario is a fire in a storage room adjacent to the largest occupiable room in the building. The contents of the room of fire origin are specified to provide the largest fuel load and the most rapid growth in fire severity consistent with the normal use of the room. The adjacent occupiable room is assumed to be filled to capacity with occupants. Occupants are assumed to be somewhat impaired in whatever form is most consistent with the intended use of the building. At ignition, doors from both rooms are assumed to be open. Depending on the design, doorways connect the two rooms or they connect via a common hallway or corridor.

For purposes of this scenario, an occupiable room is a room that could contain people (i.e., a location within a building where people are typically found).

A.5.4.2.4 An example of such a scenario is a fire originating in a concealed wall- or ceiling-space adjacent to a large, occupied function room. Ignition involves concealed combustibles, including wire or cable insulation and thermal or acoustical insulation. The adjacent function room is assumed to be occupied to capacity. The baseline occupant characteristics for the property are assumed. At ignition, doors are assumed to be open throughout the building.

A.5.4.2.5 An example of such a scenario is a cigarette fire in a trash can. The trash can is close enough to room contents to ignite more substantial fuel sources but is not close enough to any occupant to create an intimate-with-ignition situation. If the intended use of the property involves the potential for some occupants to be incapable of movement at any time, then the room of origin is chosen as the type of room likely to have such occupants, filled to capacity with occupants in that condition. If the intended use of the property does not involve the potential for some occupants to be incapable of movement, then the room of origin is chosen to be an assembly or function area characteristic of the use of the property, and the trash can is placed so that it is shielded by furniture from suppression systems. At ignition, doors are assumed to be open throughout the building.

A.5.4.2.6 An example of such a scenario is a fire originating in the largest fuel load of combustibles possible in normal operation in a function or assembly room or in a process/manufacturing area, characteristic of the normal operation of the property. The configuration, type, and geometry of the combustibles are chosen so as to produce the most rapid and severe fire growth or smoke generation consistent with the normal operation of the property. The baseline occupant characteristics for the property are assumed. At ignition, doors are assumed to be closed throughout the building.

This scenario includes everything from a big couch fire in a small dwelling to a rack storage fire in combustible liquids stock in a big box retail store.

A.5.4.2.7 An example of such a scenario is an exposure fire. The initiating fire is the closest and most severe fire possible consistent with the placement and type of adjacent properties and the placement of plants and combustible adornments on the property. The baseline occupant characteristics of the property are assumed.

This category includes wildland/urban interface fires and exterior wood shingle problems, where applicable.

A.5.4.2.8 This scenario addresses a set of conditions with a typical fire originating in the building with any one passive or active fire protection system or feature being ineffective. Examples include unprotected openings between floors or between fire walls or fire barrier walls, rated fire doors that fail to close automatically or are blocked open, sprinkler system water supply that is shut off, fire alarm system that's nonoperative, smoke management system that is not operational, or automatic smoke dampers that are blocked open. This scenario should represent a reasonable challenge to the other building features provided by the design and presumed to be available.

The exemption from Fire Design Scenario 8 is applied to each active or passive fire protection system individually and requires two different types of information to be developed by analysis and approved by the AHJ. System reliability is to be analyzed and accepted. Design performance in the absence of the system is also to be analyzed and accepted, but acceptable performance does not require fully meeting the stated goals and objectives. It might not be possible to meet fully the goals and objectives if a key system is unavailable, and yet no system is totally reliable. The AHJ determines which level of performance, possibly short of the stated goals and objectives, is acceptable, given the very low probability (that is, the system's unreliability probability) that the system will not be available.

A.5.4.3.1 This scenario is intended to address facilities where explosives, and products containing explosives, are manufactured, stored, sold, or handled. From an overall safety standpoint, the operations being performed at these facilities should include stringent safety procedures that significantly reduce the likelihood of an explosion from occurring. However, if an explosion does occur, protection methods such as storage magazines, property set backs, deflagration, and explosion venting and containment need to be in place, as appropriate, to minimize potential injury and loss of life and property.

Where products containing explosives, such as pyrotechnic displays or fireworks, are stored, handled, or used in buildings, such as arenas, an explosion scenario should not result in significant injuries to occupants not intimate with the materials.

A.5.4.4 Design hazardous materials scenarios should explicitly account for the following:

(1) Occupant activities, training, and knowledge
(2) Number and location of occupants
(3) Discharge location and surroundings
(4) Hazardous materials' properties
(5) Ventilation, inerting, and dilution systems and conditions
(6) Normal and emergency operating procedures
(7) Safe shutdown and other hazard mitigating systems and procedures
(8) Weather conditions affecting the hazard
(9) Potential exposure to off-site personnel

Design hazardous materials scenarios should be evaluated as many times as necessary by varying the factors previously indicated. Design hazardous materials scenarios could need to be established for each different type of hazardous material stored or used at the facility.

A.5.4.4.4.2 This provision should be applied to each protection system individually and requires two different types of information to be developed by analysis and approved by the AHJ. System reliability is to be analyzed and accepted. Design performance in the absence of the system is also to be analyzed and accepted, but acceptable performance does not require fully meeting the stated goals and objectives. It might not be possible to meet fully the goals and objectives if a key system is unavailable, and yet no system is totally reliable. The AHJ determines which level of performance, possibly short of stated goals and objectives, is acceptable, given the very low probability (that is, the systems' unreliability probability) that the system will be unavailable.

A.5.4.5.1 An example of such a scenario would involve a fire or earthquake effectively blocking the principal entrance/exit but not immediately endangering the occupants. The full occupant load of the assembly space has to exit using secondary means.

A.5.5.3.1 The *SFPE Handbook of Fire Protection Engineering* provides a listing of typical input data that can be used in a performance-based fire protection design.

A.5.5.5 The *SFPE Guidelines for Substantiating a Fire Model for a Given Application* provides a framework for ensuring a selected fire model is valid and verified for a specific application.

A.5.6 The assessment of precision required in 5.7.2 requires a sensitivity and uncertainty analysis, which can be translated into safety factors.

Sensitivity Analysis. The first run a model user makes should be labeled as the base case, using the nominal values of the various input parameters. However, the model user should not rely on a single run as the basis for any performance-based fire safety system design. Ideally, each variable or parameter that the model user made to develop the nominal input data should have multiple runs associated with it, as should combinations of key variables and parameters. Thus, a sensitivity analysis should be conducted that provides the model user with data that indicates how the effects of a real fire could vary and how the response of the proposed fire safety design could also vary.

The interpretation of a model's predictions can be a difficult exercise if the model user does not have knowledge of fire dynamics or human behavior.

Reasonableness Check. The model user should first try to determine whether the predictions actually make sense, that is, they don't upset intuition or preconceived expectations. Most likely, if the results don't pass this test, an input error has been committed.

Sometimes the predictions appear to be reasonable but are, in fact, incorrect. For example, a model can predict higher temperatures farther from the fire than close to it. The values themselves could be reasonable, for example, they are not hotter than the fire, but they don't "flow" down the energy as expected.

A margin of safety can be developed using the results of the sensitivity analysis in conjunction with the performance criteria to provide the possible range of time during which a condition is estimated to occur.

Safety factors and margin of safety are two concepts used to quantify the amount of uncertainty in engineering analyses. Safety factors are used to provide a margin of safety and represent, or address, the gap in knowledge between the theoretically perfect model, that is, reality and the engineering models that can only partially represent reality.

Safety factors can be applied to either the predicted level of a physical condition or to the time at which the condition is predicted to occur. Thus, a physical or a temporal safety factor, or both, can be applied to any predicted condition. A predicted condition (that is, a parameter's value) and the time at which it occurs are best represented as distributions. Ideally, a computer fire model predicts the expected or nominal value of the distribution. Safety factors are intended to represent the spread of these distributions.

Given the uncertainty associated with data acquisition and reduction, and the limitations of computer modeling, any condition predicted by a computer model can be thought of as an expected or nominal value within a broader range. For example, an upper layer temperature of 1110°F (600°C) is predicted at a given time. If the modeled scenario is then tested (that is, full-scale experiment based on the computer model's input data), the actual temperature at that given time could be 1185°F or 1085°F (640°C or 585°C). Therefore, the temperature should be reported as 1110°F + 75°F, −25°F (600°C + 40°C, −15°C) or as a range of 1085°F to 1184°F (585°C to 640°C).

Ideally, predictions are reported as a nominal value, a percentage, or an absolute value. As an example, an upper layer temperature prediction could be reported as 1112°F (600°C), 86°F (30°C) or 1112°F (600°C), 5 percent. In this case, the physical safety factor is 0.05 (that is, the amount by which the nominal value should be degraded and enhanced). Given the state-of-the-art of computer fire modeling, this is a very low safety factor. Physical safety factors tend to be on the order of tens of percent. A safety factor of 50 percent is not unheard of.

Part of the problem in establishing safety factors is that it is difficult to state the percentage or range that is appropriate. These values can be obtained when the computer model predictions are compared to test data. However, using computer fire models in a design mode does not facilitate this since (1) the room being analyzed has not been built yet and (2) test scenarios do not necessarily depict the intended design.

A sensitivity analysis should be performed based on the assumptions that affect the condition of interest. A base case that uses all nominal values for input parameters should be developed. The input parameters should be varied over reasonable ranges, and the variation in predicted output should be noted. This output variation can then become the basis for physical safety factors.

The temporal safety factor addresses the issue of when a condition is predicted and is a function of the rate at which processes are expected to occur. If a condition is predicted to occur 2 minutes after the start of the fire, then this can be used as a nominal value. A process similar to that described for physical safety factors can also be employed to develop temporal safety factors. In this case, however, the rates (for example, of heat release and toxic product generation) will be varied instead of absolute values (for example, material properties).

The margin of safety can be thought of as a reflection of societal values and can be imposed by the AHJ for that purpose. Since the time for which a condition is predicted is most likely the focus of the AHJ (for example, the model predicts occupants have 5 minutes to safely evacuate), the margin of safety is characterized by temporal aspects and tacitly applied to the physical margin of safety.

Escaping the harmful effects of fire (or mitigating them) is, effectively, a race against time. When assessing fire safety system designs based on computer model predictions, the choice of an acceptable time is important. When an AHJ is faced with the predicted time of untenability, a decision needs to be made regarding whether sufficient time is available to ensure the safety of facility occupants. The AHJ is assessing the margin of safety. Is there sufficient time to get everyone out safely? If the

AHJ feels that the predicted egress time is too close to the time of untenability, then the AHJ can impose an additional time that the designer has to incorporate into the system design. In other words, the AHJ can impose a greater margin of safety than that originally proposed by the designer.

The *SFPE Handbook of Fire Protection Engineering* has a discussion on the use of safety factors and the evaluation of uncertainty in a performance-based design.

A.5.7.1 The *SFPE Engineering Guide to Performance-Based Fire Protection* describes the documentation that should be provided for a performance-based design.

Proper documentation of a performance design is critical to the design acceptance and construction. Proper documentation also ensures that all parties involved understand what is necessary for the design implementation, maintenance, and continuity of the fire protection design. If attention to details is maintained in the documentation, then there should be little dispute during approval, construction, start-up, and use.

Poor documentation could result in rejection of an otherwise good design, poor implementation of the design, inadequate system maintenance and reliability, and an incomplete record for future changes or for testing the design forensically.

A.5.7.2 The sources, methodologies, and data used in performance-based designs should be based on technical references that are widely accepted and used by the appropriate professions and professional groups. This acceptance is often based on documents that are developed, reviewed, and validated under one of the following processes:

(1) Standards developed under an open consensus process conducted by recognized professional societies, codes or standards organizations, or governmental bodies
(2) Technical references that are subject to a peer review process and published in widely recognized peer-reviewed journals, conference reports, or other publications
(3) Resource publications such as the *SFPE Handbook of Fire Protection Engineering*, which are widely recognized technical sources of information

The following factors are helpful in determining the acceptability of the individual method or source:

(1) Extent of general acceptance in the relevant professional community. Indications of this acceptance include peer-reviewed publication, widespread citation in the technical literature, and adoption by or within a consensus document.
(2) Extent of documentation of the method, including the analytical method itself, assumptions, scope, limitations, data sources, and data reduction methods.
(3) Extent of validation and analysis of uncertainties. This includes comparison of the overall method with experimental data to estimate error rates as well as analysis of the uncertainties of input data, uncertainties and limitations in the analytical method, and uncertainties in the associated performance criteria.
(4) Extent to which the method is based on sound scientific principles.
(5) Extent to which the proposed application is within the stated scope and limitations of the supporting information, including the range of applicability for which there is documented validation. Factors such as spatial dimensions, occupant characteristics, and ambient conditions can limit valid applications.

In many cases, a method is built from and includes numerous component analyses. These component analyses should be evaluated using the same factors that are applied to the overall method as outlined in items (1) through (5).

A method to address a specific fire safety issue, within documented limitations or validation regimes, might not exist. In such a case, sources and calculation methods can be used outside of their limitations, provided that the design team recognizes the limitations and addresses the resulting implications.

The technical references and methodologies to be used in a performance-based design should be closely evaluated by the design team and the AHJ, and possibly by a third-party reviewer. The strength of the technical justification should be judged using criteria in items (1) through (5). This justification can be strengthened by the presence of data obtained from fire testing.

A.5.7.11 Documentation for modeling should conform to ASTM E1472, *Standard Guide for Documenting Computer Software for Fire Models*, and the *SFPE Guide for Substantiating a Fire Model for a Given Application*.

Δ A.6.1.2.1 Assembly Occupancy. Assembly occupancies might include the following:

(1) Armories
(2) Assembly halls
(3) Auditoriums
(4) Bowling lanes
(5) Club rooms
(6) College and university classrooms, 50 persons and over
(7) Conference rooms
(8) Courtrooms
(9) Dance halls
(10) Drinking establishments
(11) Exhibition halls
(12) Gymnasiums
(13) Libraries
(14) Mortuary chapels
(15) Museums
(16) Nightclubs
(17) Passenger stations and terminals of air, surface, underground, and marine public transportation facilities
(18) Places of religious worship
(19) Pool rooms
(20) Recreation piers
(21) Restaurants
(22) Skating rinks
(23) Special amusement buildings, regardless of occupant load
(24) Theaters

[*101*:A.6.1.2.1]

Assembly occupancies are characterized by the presence or potential presence of crowds with attendant panic hazard in case of fire or other emergency. They are generally or occasionally open to the public, and the occupants, who are present voluntarily, are not ordinarily subject to discipline or control. Such buildings are ordinarily not used for sleeping purposes. Special conference rooms, snack areas, and other areas incidental to, and under the control of, the management of other occupancies, such as offices, fall under the 50-person limitation. [*101*:A.6.1.2.1]

Restaurants and drinking establishments with an occupant load of fewer than 50 persons should be classified as mercantile occupancies. [*101*:A.6.1.2.1]

Occupancy of any room or space for assembly purposes by fewer than 50 persons in another occupancy, and incidental to such other occupancy, should be classified as part of the other occupancy and should be subject to the provisions applicable thereto. [*101*:A.6.1.2.1]

For special amusement buildings, see 12.4.9 and 13.4.9 of NFPA *101*. [*101*:A.6.1.2.1]

Δ **A.6.1.3.1 Educational Occupancy.** Educational occupancies include the following:

(1) Academies
(2) Kindergartens
(3) Schools
[*101*:A.6.1.3.1]

An educational occupancy is distinguished from an assembly occupancy in that the same occupants are regularly present. [*101*:A.6.1.3.1]

Δ **A.6.1.4.1 Day-Care Occupancy.** Day-care occupancies include the following:

(1) Adult day-care occupancies, except where part of a health care occupancy
(2) Child day-care occupancies
(3) Day-care homes
(4) Kindergarten classes that are incidental to a child day-care occupancy
(5) Nursery schools
[*101*:A.6.1.4.1]

In areas where public schools offer only half-day kindergarten programs, many child day-care occupancies offer state-approved kindergarten classes for children who need full-day care. Because these classes are normally incidental to the day-care occupancy, the requirements of the day-care occupancy should be followed. [*101*:A.6.1.4.1]

Δ **A.6.1.5.1 Health Care Occupancy.** Health care occupancies include the following:

(1) Hospitals
(2) Limited care facilities
(3) Nursing homes
[*101*:A.6.1.5.1]

Occupants of health care occupancies typically have physical or mental illness, disease, or infirmity. They also include infants, convalescents, or infirm aged persons. [*101*:A.6.1.5.1]

A.6.1.6.1 Ambulatory Health Care Occupancy. It is not the intent that occupants be considered to be incapable of self-preservation just because they are in a wheelchair or use assistive walking devices, such as a cane, a walker, or crutches. Rather, it is the intent to address emergency care centers that receive patients who have been rendered incapable of self-preservation due to the emergency, such as being rendered unconscious as a result of an accident or being unable to move due to sudden illness. [*101*:A.6.1.6.1]

Δ **A.6.1.7.1 Detention and Correctional Occupancy.** Detention and correctional occupancies include the following:

(1) Adult and juvenile substance abuse centers
(2) Adult and juvenile work camps
(3) Adult community residential centers
(4) Adult correctional institutions
(5) Adult local detention facilities
(6) Juvenile community residential centers
(7) Juvenile detention facilities
(8) Juvenile training schools
[*101*:A.6.1.7.1]

Detention and correctional occupancies do not include psychiatric and dementia units in hospitals, emergency rooms in hospitals, ambulatory health care occupancies, nursing homes, and residential board and care occupancies where persons can be lawfully detained. [*101*:A.6.1.7.1]

See A.22.1.1.1.6 and A.23.1.1.1.6 of NFPA *101*. [*101*:A.6.1.7.1]

A.6.1.7.2 Chapters 22 and 23 of NFPA *101* address the residential housing areas of the detention and correctional occupancy as defined in 3.3.178.5 of NFPA *101*. Examples of uses, other than residential housing, include gymnasiums or industries. [*101*:A.6.1.7.2]

A.6.1.8.1.1 One- and Two-Family Dwelling Unit. The application statement of 24.1.1.1 of NFPA *101* limits each dwelling unit to being "occupied by members of a single family with not more than three outsiders." This *Code* and NFPA *101* do not define the term *family*. The definition of family is subject to federal, state, and local regulations and might not be restricted to a person or a couple (two people) and their children. The following examples aid in differentiating between a single-family dwelling and a lodging or rooming house:

(1) An individual or a couple (two people) who rent a house from a landlord and then sublease space for up to three individuals should be considered a family renting to a maximum of three outsiders, and the house should be regulated as a single-family dwelling in accordance with Chapter 24 of NFPA *101*.
(2) A house rented from a landlord by an individual or a couple (two people) in which space is subleased to four or more individuals, but not more than 16, should be considered and regulated as a lodging or rooming house in accordance with Chapter 26 of NFPA *101*.
(3) A residential building that is occupied by four or more individuals, but not more than 16, each renting from a landlord, without separate cooking facilities, should be considered and regulated as a lodging or rooming house in accordance with Chapter 26 of NFPA *101*.

[*101*:A.6.1.8.1.1]

A.6.1.8.1.3 Hotel. So-called apartment hotels should be classified as hotels, because they are potentially subject to the same transient occupancy as hotels. Transients are those who occupy accommodations for less than 30 days. [*101*:A.6.1.8.1.3]

A.6.1.8.1.4 Dormitory. Rooms within dormitories intended for the use of individuals for combined living and sleeping purposes are guest rooms or guest suites. Examples of dormitories include college dormitories, fraternity and sorority houses, and military barracks. [*101*:A.6.1.8.1.4]

A.6.1.9.1 Residential Board and Care Occupancy. The following are examples of facilities classified as residential board and care occupancies:

(1) Group housing arrangement for physically or mentally handicapped persons who normally attend school in the community, attend worship in the community, or otherwise use community facilities
(2) Group housing arrangement for physically or mentally handicapped persons who are undergoing training in preparation for independent living, for paid employment, or for other normal community activities
(3) Group housing arrangement for the elderly that provides personal care services but that does not provide nursing care
(4) Facility for social rehabilitation of individuals with alcohol or substance use disorders or mental health conditions that contains a group housing arrangement and that provides personal care services but does not provide acute care
(5) Assisted living facilities
(6) Other group housing arrangements that provide personal care services but not nursing care

[*101*:A.6.1.9.1]

Δ **A.6.1.10.1 Mercantile Occupancy.** Mercantile occupancies include the following:

(1) Auction rooms
(2) Department stores
(3) Drugstores
(4) Restaurants with fewer than 50 persons
(5) Shopping centers
(6) Supermarkets

[*101*:A.6.1.10.1]

Office, storage, and service facilities incidental to the sale of merchandise and located in the same building should be considered part of the mercantile occupancy classification. [*101*:A.6.1.10.1]

Δ **A.6.1.11.1 Business Occupancy.** Business occupancies include the following:

(1) Airport traffic control towers (ATCTs)
(2) City halls
(3) College and university instructional buildings, classrooms under 50 persons, and instructional laboratories
(4) Courthouses
(5) Dentists' offices
(6) Doctors' offices
(7) General offices
(8) Outpatient clinics (ambulatory)
(9) Town halls

[*101*:A.6.1.11.1]

Doctors' and dentists' offices are included, unless of such character as to be classified as ambulatory health care occupancies. (*See 3.3.198.1 of NFPA 101.*) [*101*:A.6.1.11.1]

Birth centers should be classified as business occupancies if they are occupied by fewer than four patients, not including infants, at any one time; do not provide sleeping facilities for four or more occupants; and do not provide treatment procedures that render four or more patients, not including infants, incapable of self-preservation at any one time. For birth centers occupied by patients not meeting these parameters, see Chapter 18 or Chapter 19 of NFPA *101*, as appropriate. [*101*:A.6.1.11.1]

Service facilities common to city office buildings, such as newsstands, lunch counters serving fewer than 50 persons, barber shops, and beauty parlors are included in the business occupancy group. [*101*:A.6.1.11.1]

City halls, town halls, and courthouses are included in this occupancy group, insofar as their principal function is the transaction of public business and the keeping of books and records. Insofar as they are used for assembly purposes, they are classified as assembly occupancies. [*101*:A.6.1.11.1]

Δ **A.6.1.12.1 Industrial Occupancy.** Industrial occupancies include the following:

(1) Drycleaning plants
(2) Factories of all kinds
(3) Food processing plants
(4) Gas plants
(5) Hangars (for servicing/maintenance)
(6) Laundries
(7) Power plants
(8) Pumping stations
(9) Refineries
(10) Sawmills
(11) Telephone exchanges

[*101*:A.6.1.12.1]

In evaluating the appropriate classification of laboratories, the AHJ should treat each case individually, based on the extent and nature of the associated hazards. Some laboratories are classified as occupancies other than industrial; for example, a physical therapy laboratory or a computer laboratory. [*101*:A.6.1.12.1]

Δ **A.6.1.13.1 Storage Occupancy.** Storage occupancies include the following:

(1) Barns
(2) Bulk oil storage
(3) Cold storage
(4) Freight terminals
(5) Grain elevators
(6) Hangars (for storage only)
(7) Parking structures
(8) Truck and marine terminals
(9) Warehouses

[*101*:A.6.1.13.1]

Storage occupancies are characterized by the presence of relatively small numbers of persons in proportion to the area. [*101*:A.6.1.13.1]

A.6.1.14.1.1 Where a building is subdivided for occupancy by multiple tenants, the presence of rated fire barriers between occupancies and independent exit access for each occupancy does not mandate the use of the separated occupancy provisions of 6.1.14.4. [*101*:A.6.1.14.1.1]

A.6.1.14.1.3 Examples of uses that might be incidental to another occupancy include the following:

(1) Newsstand (mercantile) in an office building
(2) Giftshop (mercantile) in a hotel
(3) Small storage area (storage) in any occupancy
(4) Minor office space (business) in any occupancy
(5) Maintenance area (industrial) in any occupancy

[*101*:A.6.1.14.1.3]

A.6.1.14.1.3(2) Examples of uses that have occupant loads below the occupancy classification threshold levels include the following:

(1) Assembly use with fewer than 50 persons within a business occupancy
(2) Educational use with fewer than 6 persons within an apartment building.

[*101*:A.6.1.14.1.3(2)]

A.6.1.14.3.2 For example, a common path of travel that occurs wholly in a business tenant space, in a multiple occupancy building containing assembly and business occupancies, should not have to meet the assembly occupancy common path of travel limitation. [*101*:A.6.1.14.3.2]

A.6.1.14.4.5 Where the *Code* text states that the provision has applicability to the building, rather than just to the occupancy, the provision applies to the entire building, regardless of whether the separated occupancies form of protection is used. For example, the provision of 18.3.5.1 of NFPA *101* requires that the entire building housing a health care occupancy be sprinklered. Contrast that with the requirement of 20.3.4.1 of NFPA *101*, which requires an ambulatory health care facility, and not the entire building, to be provided with a fire alarm system. [*101*:A.6.1.14.4.5]

A.10.1.2 It is the intent of this *Code* that all existing buildings comply with the referenced edition of NFPA *101*.

A.10.3.3 The AHJ should take into account the maintenance of required means of egress and fire protection systems during the construction, repair, alteration, or addition to the building. If necessary, alternative protection features can be required to ensure that no imminent hazards exist as the result of modifications.

A.10.4.2.1 Items to be considered in preparing an emergency plan should include the following:

(1) Purpose of plan
(2) Building description, including certificate of occupancy
(3) Appointment, organization, and contact details of designated building staff to carry out the emergency duties
(4) Identification of events (man-made and natural) considered life safety hazards impacting the building
(5) Responsibilities matrix (role-driven assignments)
(6) Policies and procedures for those left behind to operate critical equipment
(7) Specific procedures to be used for each type of emergency
(8) Requirements and responsibilities for assisting people with disabilities
(9) Procedures for accounting for employees
(10) Training of building staff, building emergency response teams, and other occupants in their responsibilities
(11) Documents, including diagrams, showing the type, location, and operation of the building emergency features, components, and systems
(12) Practices for controlling life safety hazards in the building
(13) Inspection and maintenance of building facilities that provide for the safety of occupants
(14) Conducting fire and evacuation drills
(15) Interface between key building management and emergency responders
(16) Names or job titles of persons who can be contacted for further information or explanation of duties
(17) Post-event (including drill) critique/evaluation, as addressed in Chapter 9 of *NFPA 1600*
(18) Means to update the plan, as necessary

[*101*:A.4.8.2.1]

A.10.4.2.1(3) It is assumed that a majority of buildings will use a total evacuation strategy during a fire. It should be noted that evacuation from a building could occur for reasons other than a fire, but such other reasons are not the primary focus of the *Code*. As used herein, total evacuation is defined as the process in which all, or substantially all, occupants leave a building or facility in either an unmanaged or managed sequence or order. An alternative to total evacuation, is partial evacuation, which can be defined as the process in which a select portion of a building or facility is cleared or emptied of its occupants while occupants in other portions mostly carry on normal activity. In either case, the evacuation process can be ordered or managed in accordance with an established priority in which some or all occupants of a building or facility clear their area and utilize means of egress routes. This is typically done so that the more-endangered occupants are removed before occupants in less-endangered areas. Alternative terms describing this sequencing or ordering of evacuation are *staged evacuation* and *phased evacuation*. [*101*:A.4.8.2.1(3)]

Table A.10.4.2.1(3) illustrates options for extent of management and extent of evacuation. Some of the options shown might not be appropriate. As noted in Table A.10.4.2.1(3), either total or partial evacuation can include staged (zoned) evacuation or phased evacuation, which is referred to as managed or controlled evacuation. It should also be noted that the evacuation process might not include relocation to the outside of the building but might instead include relocation to an area of refuge or might defend the occupants in place to minimize the need for evacuation. [*101*:A.4.8.2.1(3)]

The different methods of evacuation are also used in several contexts throughout NFPA *101*. Though most of the methods of evacuation are not specifically defined or do not have established criteria, various sections of NFPA *101* promulgate them as alternatives to total evacuation. The following sections of NFPA *101* discuss these alternatives in more detail:

(1) Section 4.7 — Provides requirements for fire and relocation drills
(2) 7.2.12 — Provides requirements for area of refuge
(3) 7.2.4 — Provides requirements for horizontal exits
(4) 9.6.3.7— Provides the alarm signal requirements for different methods of evacuation
(5) 9.6.3.10 — Permits automatically transmitted or live voice evacuation or relocation instructions to occupants and requires them in accordance with *NFPA 72*
(6) 14.3.4.2.3 (also Chapter 15) — Describes alternative protection systems in educational occupancies
(7) 18.1.1.2/18.1.1.3/Section 18.7 (also Chapter 19) — Provide methods of evacuation for health care occupancies
(8) Chapters 22 and 23 — Provide methods of evacuation for detention and correctional occupancies, including the five groups of resident user categories
(9) Chapters 32 and 33 — Provide methods of evacuation for residential board and care occupancies
(10) 32.1.5/33.1.5 — For residential board and care occupancies, state that "no means of escape or means of egress shall be considered as complying with the minimum

criteria for acceptance, unless emergency evacuation drills are regularly conducted"

(11) 40.2.5.2.2 — For industrial occupancies, states that "ancillary facilities in special-purpose industrial occupancies where delayed evacuation is anticipated shall have not less than a 2-hour fire-resistance-rated separation from the predominant industrial occupancy and shall have one means of egress that is separated from the predominant industrial occupancy by 2-hour fire-resistance-rated construction"

[*101*:A.4.8.2.1(3)]

The method of evacuation should be accomplished in the context of the physical facilities, the type of activities undertaken, and the provisions for the capabilities of occupants (and staff, if available). Therefore, in addition to meeting the requirements of the *Code*, or when establishing an equivalency or a performance-based design, the following recommendations and general guidance information should be taken into account when designing, selecting, executing, and maintaining a method of evacuation:

(1) When choosing a method of evacuation, the available safe egress time (ASET) must always be greater than the required safe egress time (RSET).
(2) The occupants' characteristics will drive the method of evacuation. For example, occupants might be incapable of evacuating themselves because of age, physical or mental disabilities, physical restraint, or a combination thereof. However, some buildings might be staffed with people who could assist in evacuating. Therefore, the method of evacuation is dependent on the ability of occupants to move as a group, with or without assistance. For more information, see the definitions under the term *Evacuation Capability* in Chapter 3 of NFPA *101*.
(3) An alternative method of evacuation might or might not have a faster evacuation time than a total evacuation. However, the priority of evacuation should be such that the occupants in the most danger are given a higher priority. This prioritization will ensure that occupants more intimate with the fire will have a faster evacuation time.
(4) Design, construction, and compartmentation are also variables in choosing a method of evacuation. The design, construction, and compartmentation should limit the development and spread of a fire and smoke and reduce the need for occupant evacuation. The fire should be limited to the room or compartment of fire origin. Therefore, the following factors need to be considered:
    (a) Overall fire resistance rating of the building
    (b) Fire-rated compartmentation provided with the building
    (c) Number and arrangement of the means of egress
(5) Fire safety systems should be installed that complement the method of evacuation and should include consideration of the following:
    (a) Detection of fire
    (b) Control of fire development
    (c) Confinement of the effects of fire
    (d) Extinguishment of fire
    (e) Provision of refuge or evacuation facilities, or both
(6) One of the most important fire safety systems is the fire alarm and communications system, particularly the notification system. The fire alarm system should be in accordance with *NFPA 72* and should take into account the following:
    (a) Initial notification of only the occupants in the affected zone(s) (e.g., zone of fire origin and adjacent zones)
    (b) Provisions to notify occupants in other unaffected zones to allow orderly evacuation of the entire building
    (c) Need for live voice communication
    (d) Reliability of the fire alarm and communications system
(7) The capabilities of the staff assisting in the evacuation process should be considered in determining the method of evacuation.
(8) The ability of the fire department to interact with the evacuation should be analyzed. It is important to determine if the fire department can assist in the evacuation or if fire department operations hinder the evacuation efforts.
(9) Evacuation scenarios for hazards that are normally outside of the scope of the *Code* should be considered to the extent practicable. (*See 4.3.1 of NFPA 101.*)
(10) Consideration should be given to the desire of the occupants to self-evacuate, especially if the nature of the building or the fire warrants evacuation in the minds of the occupants. Self-evacuation might also be initiated by communication between the occupants themselves through face-to-face contact, mobile phones, and so forth.
(11) An investigation period, a delay in the notification of occupants after the first activation of the fire alarm, could help to reduce the number of false alarms and unnecessary evacuations. However, a limit to such a delay should be established before a general alarm is sounded, such as positive alarm sequence, as defined in *NFPA 72*.
(12) Consideration should be given to the need for an evacuation that might be necessary for a scenario other than a fire (e.g., bomb threat, earthquake).
(13) Contingency plans should be established in the event the fire alarm and communication system fail, which might facilitate the need for total evacuation.
(14) The means of egress systems should be properly maintained to ensure the dependability of the method of evacuation.
(15) Fire prevention policies or procedures, or both, should be implemented that reduce the chance of a fire (e.g., limiting smoking or providing fire-safe trash cans).
(16) The method of evacuation should be properly documented, and written forms of communication should be provided to all of the occupants, which might include sign postings throughout the building. Consideration should be given to the development of documentation for an operation and maintenance manual or a fire emergency plan, or both.
(17) Emergency egress drills should be performed on a regular basis. For more information, see Section 4.7 of NFPA *101*.
(18) The AHJ should also be consulted when developing the method of evacuation.

[*101*:A.4.8.2.1(3)]

Measures should be in place and be employed to sequence or control the order of a total evacuation, so that such evacuations proceed in a reasonably safe, efficient manner. Such measures include special attention to the evacuation capabilities and needs of occupants with disabilities, either permanent or temporary. For comprehensive guidance on facilitating life safety for such populations, go to www.nfpa.org. For specific guidance on emergency stair travel devices, see ANSI/RESNA ED-1, *Emergency Stair Travel Devices Used by Individuals with Disabilities*. [*101*:A.4.8.2.1(3)]

In larger buildings, especially high-rise buildings, it is recommended that all evacuations — whether partial or total — be managed to sequence or control the order in which certain occupants are evacuated from their origin areas and to make use of available means of egress. In high-rise buildings, the exit stairs, at any level, are designed to accommodate the egress flow of only a very small portion of the occupants — from only one or a few stories, and within a relatively short time period — on the order of a few minutes. In case of a fire, only the immediately affected floor(s) should be given priority use of the means of egress serving that floor(s). Other floors should then be given priority use of the means of egress, depending on the anticipated spread of the fire and its combustion products, and for the purpose of clearing certain floors to facilitate eventual fire service operations. Typically, this means that the one or two floors above and below a fire floor will have secondary priority immediately after the fire floor. Depending on where combustion products move — for example, upward through a building with cool-weather stack effect — the next priority floors will be the uppermost occupied floors in the building. [*101*:A.4.8.2.1(3)]

Generally, in order to minimize evacuation time for most or all of a relatively tall building to be evacuated, occupants from upper floors should have priority use of exit stairs. For people descending many stories of stairs, this priority will maximize their opportunity to take rest stops without unduly extending their overall time to evacuate a building. Thus, the precedence behavior of evacuees should be that people already in an exit stair should normally not defer to people attempting to enter the exit stair from lower floors, except for those lower floors most directly impacted by a fire or other imminent danger. Notably, this is contrary to the often observed behavior of evacuees in high-rise building evacuations where lower floor precedence behavior occurs. (Similarly, in the most commonly observed behavior of people normally disembarking a passenger airliner, people within the aisle defer to people entering the aisle, so that the areas closest to the exit typically clear first.) Changing, and generally managing, the sequence or order within which egress occurs will require effectively informing building occupants and evaluating resulting performance in a program of education, training, and drills. [*101*:A.4.8.2.1(3)]

When designing the method of evacuation for a complex building, all forms of egress should be considered. For example, consideration could be given to an elevator evacuation system. An elevator evacuation system involves an elevator design that provides protection from fire effects so that elevators can be used safely for egress. See 7.2.13 and A.7.2.12.2.4 of NFPA *101* for more information. [*101*:A.4.8.2.1(3)]

For further guidance, see the following publications:

(1) *SFPE Engineering Guide to Human Behavior in Fire*, which provides information on occupant characteristics, response to fire cues, decision making in fire situations, and methods for predicting evacuation times

(2) NFPA *Fire Protection Handbook*, 20th edition, Section 1, Chapter 9, which provides good methodology for managing exposures and determining the method of evacuation

(3) NFPA *Fire Protection Handbook*, 20th edition, Section 20, which provides further commentary on methods of evacuation for different occupancies

(4) *SFPE Handbook of Fire Protection Engineering*, Volume II, Chapters 58–61, which provide an overview of some of the research on methods of evacuation and methods for predicting evacuation times

[*101*:A.4.8.2.1(3)]

A.10.4.2.3 Emergency action plans are a critical component of ensuring life safety in buildings. Life safety is the result of an interaction of technical and social systems within the building and in the community. Gathering information to evaluate the performance and effectiveness of emergency action plans is important for verifying system performance and as a basis for improvement. Such reports should be retained by building management and used to inform the process for revision of the building emergency action plan. [*101*:A.4.8.2.3]

Following any drill or actual emergency or reported emergency occurring in the building, an after action report should be prepared by the building owner or designated representative to document the function of the building's life safety hardware, procedures, and occupant emergency organization. [*101*:A.4.8.2.3]

For ordinary drills and reported emergencies, areas of success and areas for improvement should be identified. [*101*:A.4.8.2.3]

For actual emergencies in the building, where there is major occupant movement, damage, or casualties, additional information should be collected. This includes questions concerning the event, as well as performance of life safety systems. It also

Δ **Table A.10.4.2.1(3) Occupant Evacuation Strategies**

	Managed Sequence	**Unmanaged Sequence**
Shelter in place	No movement — Shelter in place upon direction	No movement — Shelter in place per prior instruction
Relocation or partial evacuation	Managed or controlled partial evacuation •In-building relocation on same floor •In-building relocation to different floors •Occupants of some floors leave building	Unmanaged movement
Total evacuation	Managed or controlled total evacuation	Unmanaged or uncontrolled total evacuation

[*101*:Table A.4.8.2.1(3)]

identifies improvements in areas such as training, maintenance, interaction with local emergency response organizations, or occupant management. The reports from these significant events should be shared with the local emergency response organization. [*101*:A.4.8.2.3]

A.10.5.2 Premises are deemed to be overcrowded when the occupant load exceeds the exit capacity or the posted occupant load.

A.10.5.3 The requirement in 10.5.3 is not intended to apply to facilities utilizing a "defend in place" strategy or other occupancies where total evacuation is not intended or desired (e.g., detention, health care, high rise). A written emergency response plan can clarify how a facility can conform to this requirement.

Occupancies required to have an emergency action plan are listed in 10.4.1 and the requirements for the contents of an emergency action plan are listed in 10.4.2.

A.10.6 The purpose of emergency egress and relocation drills is to educate the participants in the fire safety features of the building, the egress facilities available, and the procedures to be followed. Speed in emptying buildings or relocating occupants, while desirable, is not the only objective. Prior to an evaluation of the performance of an emergency egress and relocation drill, an opportunity for instruction and practice should be provided. This educational opportunity should be presented in a nonthreatening manner, with consideration given to the prior knowledge, age, and ability of audience. [*101*:A.4.7]

The usefulness of an emergency egress and relocation drill, and the extent to which it can be performed, depends on the character of the occupancy. [*101*:A.4.7]

In buildings where the occupant load is of a changing character, such as hotels or department stores, no regularly organized emergency egress and relocation drill is possible. In such cases, the emergency egress and relocation drills are to be limited to the regular employees, who can be thoroughly schooled in the proper procedure and can be trained to properly direct other occupants of the building in case of emergency evacuation or relocation. In occupancies such as hospitals, regular employees can be rehearsed in the proper procedure in case of fire; such training is always advisable in all occupancies, regardless of whether regular emergency egress and relocation drills can be held. [*101*:A.4.7]

A.10.6.2 If an emergency egress and relocation drill is considered merely as a routine exercise from which some persons are allowed to be excused, there is a grave danger that, in an actual emergency, the evacuation and relocation will not be successful. However, there might be circumstances under which all occupants do not participate in an emergency egress and relocation drill; for example, infirm or bedridden patients in a health care occupancy. [*101*:A.4.7.2]

A.10.6.4 Fire is always unexpected. If the drill is always held in the same way at the same time, it loses much of its value. When, for some reason during an actual fire, it is not possible to follow the usual routine of the emergency egress and relocation drill to which occupants have become accustomed, confusion and panic might ensue. Drills should be carefully planned to simulate actual fire conditions. Not only should drills be held at varying times, but different means of exit or relocation areas should be used, based on an assumption that fire or smoke might prevent the use of normal egress and relocation avenues. [*101*:A.4.7.4]

A.10.6.6 The written record required by this paragraph should include such details as the date, time, participants, location, and results of that drill. [*101*:A.4.7.6]

A.10.7.1.3 This requirement should not be construed to forbid the owner, manager, or other person in control of the aforementioned building or premises from using all diligence necessary to extinguish such fire prior to the arrival of the fire department.

A.10.10.2 Hazardous conditions could include extreme drought or red-flag-type conditions that can result in rapidly developing wildfires.

A.10.10.3.1 Areas for such use can include inhabited premises or designated campsites where such fires are built in a permanent barbecue, portable barbecue, outdoor fireplace, incinerator, or grill.

Δ **A.10.10.6.3** It is not the intent of 10.10.6.3 to allow the permanent installation of portable equipment unless it is permitted by its listing.

A.10.10.9.1 Areas for such use can include inhabited premises or designated campsites that maintain a defensible space in accordance with NFPA 1140.

A.10.10.10 A hazardous condition is intended to include any fire that generates smoke or products of combustion that could obstruct visibility in traffic, create health issues, damage property, or contribute to conditions that create property, safety, or health hazards. As numerous variables can go into this determination, the AHJ will need to evaluate each situation on a case-by-case basis.

Smoke can potentially create its own hazardous conditions such as blocking visibility on roadways.

A.10.11.1 An additional means to identify the locations of new and existing buildings is to co-geolocate each building with US National Grid 108 ft^2 (10 m^2) coordinates to the primary entrance.

A.10.11.1.1 Where a building is not routinely identified by a street address, other means of building identification such as building name or number should be permitted.

A.10.11.1.5 E911, or Enhanced 911, attempts to automatically associate a location with a call's origin. The location could be a physical address or a geographic reference point. When E911 is in place, the address or geographic reference point is transmitted to the public safety answering point (PSAP). Paragraph 10.11.1.xx ensures that telecommunications equipment that is part of the transmission path is programmed to communicate correct address information to the E911 PSAP. It is not the intent of this provision to require E911 capability of the telecommunications equipment where the PSAP is not capable of receiving such data.

A.10.11.3 Figure A.10.11.3 shows an example of a stairway marking sign. [*101*:A.7.2.2.5.4]

A.10.11.3.1.13 It is not the intent to require a sign that reads ROOF ACCESS, as such message might be misinterpreted by building occupants as an alternative egress route. However, signs that read ROOF ACCESS are not prohibited, as many such signs have been installed in existing buildings so as to

NORTH STAIR

FLOOR

5

SUB-BASEMENT TO 24TH FLOOR
NO ROOF ACCESS
↓ DOWN TO FIRST FLOOR
FOR EXIT DISCHARGE

FIGURE A.10.11.3 Example of a Stairway Marking Sign. [*101*:Figure A.7.2.2.5.4]

make a requirement for removal impractical. Historically, the ROOF ACCESS sign has provided information for the fire department. Where there is no roof access, such information will be posted via a NO ROOF ACCESS sign. The absence of the NO ROOF ACCESS sign should be understood by the fire department to mean that roof access is possible. [*101*:A.7.2.2.5.4.1(M)]

A.10.12.2.1 Issues to be considered by the AHJ should include, but not be limited to, the availability of utilities to the building.

△ **A.10.14.3.1** Life safety evaluations are examples of performance-based approaches to life safety. In this respect, significant guidance in the form and process of life safety evaluations is provided by Chapter 5 of NFPA *101*, keeping in mind the fire safety emphasis in Chapter 5 of NFPA *101*. Performance criteria, scenarios, evaluation, safety factors, documentation, maintenance, and periodic assessment (including a warrant of fitness) all apply to the broader considerations in a life safety evaluation. A life safety evaluation deals not only with fire but also with storms, collapse, crowd behavior, and other related safety considerations for which a checklist is provided in A.10.14.3.3. Chapter 5 of NFPA *101* provides guidance, based on fire safety requirements, for establishing a documented case showing that products of combustion in all conceivable fire scenarios will not significantly endanger occupants using means of egress in the facility (for example, due to fire detection, automatic suppression, smoke control, large-volume space, or management procedures). Moreover, means of egress facilities plus facility management capabilities should be adequate to cope with scenarios where certain egress routes are blocked for some reason. [*101*:A.12.4.2.1]

In addition to making realistic assumptions about the capabilities of persons in the facility (e.g., an assembled crowd including many disabled persons or persons unfamiliar with the facility), the life safety evaluation should include a factor of safety of not less than 2.0 in all calculations relating to hazard development time and required egress time (the combination of flow time and other time needed to detect and assess an emergency condition, initiate egress, and move along the egress routes). The factor of safety takes into account the possibility that half of the egress routes might not be used (or be usable) in certain situations. [*101*:A.12.4.2.1]

Regarding crowd behavior, the potential hazards created by larger masses of people and greater crowd densities (which can be problematic during ingress, occupancy, and egress) demand that technology be used by designers, managers, and authorities responsible for buildings to compensate for the relaxed egress capacity provisions of Table 12.4.3.3 of NFPA *101*. In very large buildings for assembly use, the hazard of crowd crushes can exceed that of fire or structural failure. Therefore, the building designers, managers, event planners, security personnel, police authorities, and fire authorities, as well as the building construction authorities, should understand the potential problems and solutions, including coordination of their activities. For crowd behavior, this understanding includes factors of design, information, management, and expectations during ingress, circulation, and egress. Published guidance on these factors and techniques is found in ANSI ES1.9, *Crowd Management;* the *SFPE Handbook of Fire Protection Engineering*, in Chapter 56, Egress Concepts and Design Approaches; Chapter 58, Human Behavior in Fire; and Chapter 59, Employing the Hydraulic Model in Assessing Emergency Movement; and the SFPE *Guide to Human Behavior in Fire* and the publications referenced therein. [*101*:A.12.4.2.1]

Table 12.2.3.2 and Table 12.4.3.3 of NFPA *101* are based on a linear relationship between number of seats and nominal flow time, with not less than 200 seconds (3.3 minutes) for 2000 seats plus 1 second for every additional 50 seats up to 25,000. Beyond 25,000 total seats, the nominal flow time is limited to 660 seconds (11 minutes). Nominal flow time refers to the flow time for the most able group of patrons; some groups less familiar with the premises or less able groups might take longer to pass a point in the egress system. Although three or more digits are noted in the tables, the resulting calculations should be assumed to provide only two significant figures of precision. [*101*:A.12.4.2.1]

A.10.14.3.3 Factors to be considered in a life safety evaluation include the following:

(1) Nature of the events being accommodated, including the following:

    (a) Ingress, intra-event movement, and egress patterns
    (b) Ticketing and seating policies/practices
    (c) Event purpose (e.g., sports contest, religious meeting)
    (d) Emotional qualities (e.g., competitiveness) of event
    (e) Time of day when event is held
    (f) Time duration of single event
    (g) Time duration of attendees' occupancy of the building

(2) Occupant characteristics and behavior, including the following:

    (a) Homogeneity
    (b) Cohesiveness
    (c) Familiarity with building
    (d) Familiarity with similar events
    (e) Capability (as influenced by factors such as age, physical abilities)
    (f) Socioeconomic factors
    (g) Small minority involved with recreational violence
    (h) Emotional involvement with the event and other occupants

(i) Use of alcohol or drugs
(j) Food consumption
(k) Washroom utilization

(3) Management, including the following:

(a) Clear, contractual arrangements for facility operation/use as follows:
  i. Between facility owner and operator
  ii. Between facility operator and event promoter
  iii. Between event promoter and performer
  iv. Between event promoter and attendee
  v. With police forces
  vi. With private security services
  vii. With ushering services
(b) Experience with the building
(c) Experience with similar events and attendees
(d) Thorough, up-to-date operations manual
(e) Training of personnel
(f) Supervision of personnel
(g) Communications systems and utilization
(h) Ratios of management and other personnel to attendees
(i) Location/distribution of personnel
(j) Central command location
(k) Rapport between personnel and attendees
(l) Personnel support of attendee goals
(m) Respect of attendees for personnel due to the following:
  i. Dress (uniform) standards
  ii. Age and perceived experience
  iii. Personnel behavior, including interaction
  iv. Distinction between crowd management and control
  v. Management concern for facility quality (e.g., cleanliness)
  vi. Management concern for entire event experience of attendees (i.e., not just during the occupancy of the building)

(4) Emergency management preparedness, including the following:

(a) Complete range of emergencies addressed in operations manual
(b) Power loss
(c) Fire
(d) Severe weather
(e) Earthquake
(f) Crowd incident
(g) Terrorism
(h) Hazardous materials
(i) Transportation accident (e.g., road, rail, air)
(j) Communications systems available
(k) Personnel and emergency forces ready to respond
(l) Attendees clearly informed of situation and proper behavior

(5) Building systems, including the following:

(a) Structural soundness
(b) Normal static loads
(c) Abnormal static loads (e.g., crowds, precipitation)
(d) Dynamic loads (e.g., crowd sway, impact, explosion, wind, earthquake)
(e) Stability of nonstructural components (e.g., lighting)
(f) Stability of movable (e.g., telescoping) structures
(g) Fire protection
(h) Fire prevention (e.g., maintenance, contents, housekeeping)
(i) Compartmentation
(j) Automatic detection and suppression of fire
(k) Smoke control
(l) Alarm and communications systems
(m) Fire department access routes and response capability
(n) Structural integrity
(o) Weather protection
(p) Wind
(q) Precipitation (attendees rush for shelter or hold up egress of others)
(r) Lightning protection
(s) Circulation systems
(t) Flowline or network analysis
(u) Waywinding and orientation
(v) Merging of paths (e.g., precedence behavior)
(w) Decision/branching points
(x) Route redundancies
(y) Counterflow, crossflow, and queuing situations
(z) Control possibilities, including metering
(aa) Flow capacity adequacy
(bb) System balance
(cc) Movement time performance
(dd) Flow times
(ee) Travel times
(ff) Queuing times
(gg) Route quality
(hh) Walking surfaces (e.g., traction, discontinuities)
(ii) Appropriate widths and boundary conditions
(jj) Handrails, guardrails, and other rails
(kk) Ramp slopes
(ll) Step geometries
(mm) Perceptual aspects (e.g., orientation, signage, marking, lighting, glare, distractions)
(nn) Route choices, especially for vertical travel
(oo) Resting/waiting areas
(pp) Levels of service (overall crowd movement quality)
(qq) Services
(rr) Washroom provision and distribution
(ss) Concessions
(tt) First aid and EMS facilities
(uu) General attendee services

[*101*:A.12.4.2.3]

A scenario-based approach to performance-based fire safety is addressed in Chapter 5 of NFPA *101*. In addition to using such scenarios and, more generally, the attention to performance criteria, evaluation, safety factors, documentation, maintenance, and periodic assessment required when the Chapter 5 of NFPA *101* option is used, life safety evaluations should consider scenarios based on characteristics important in assembly occupancies. These characteristics include the following:

(1) Whether there is a local or mass awareness of an incident, event, or condition that might provoke egress
(2) Whether the incident, event, or condition stays localized or spreads
(3) Whether or not egress is desired by facility occupants

(4) Whether there is a localized start to any egress or mass start to egress
(5) Whether exits are available or not available

[*101*:A.12.4.2.3]

Examples of scenarios and sets of characteristics that might occur in a facility follow. [*101*:A.12.4.2.3]

Scenario 1. Characteristics: mass start, egress desired (by management and attendees), exits not available, local awareness. [*101*:A.12.4.2.3]

Normal egress at the end of an event occurs just as a severe weather condition induces evacuees at the exterior doors to retard or stop their egress. The backup that occurs in the egress system is not known to most evacuees, who continue to press forward, potentially resulting in a crowd crush. [*101*:A.12.4.2.3]

Scenario 2. Characteristics: mass start, egress not desired (by management), exits possibly not available, mass awareness. [*101*:A.12.4.2.3]

An earthquake occurs during an event. The attendees are relatively safe in the seating area. The means of egress outside the seating areas are relatively unsafe and vulnerable to aftershock damage. Facility management discourages mass egress until the means of egress can be checked and cleared for use. [*101*:A.12.4.2.3]

Scenario 3. Characteristics: local start, incident stays local, egress desired (by attendees and management), exits available, mass awareness. [*101*:A.12.4.2.3]

A localized civil disturbance (e.g., firearms violence) provokes localized egress, which is seen by attendees, generally, who then decide to leave also. [*101*:A.12.4.2.3]

Scenario 4. Characteristics: mass start, egress desired (by attendees), incident spreads, exits not available, mass awareness. [*101*:A.12.4.2.3]

In an open-air facility unprotected from wind, precipitation, and lightning, sudden severe weather prompts egress to shelter, but not from the facility. The means of egress congest and block quickly as people in front stop once they are under shelter while people behind them continue to press forward, potentially resulting in a crowd crush. [*101*:A.12.4.2.3]

These scenarios illustrate some of the broader factors to be taken into account when assessing the capability of both building systems and management features on which reliance is placed in a range of situations, not just fire emergencies. Some scenarios also illustrate the conflicting motivations of management and attendees, based on differing perceptions of danger and differing knowledge of hazards, countermeasures, and capabilities. Mass egress might not be the most appropriate life safety strategy in some scenarios, such as Scenario 2. [*101*:A.12.4.2.3]

Table A.10.14.3.3 summarizes the characteristics in the scenarios and provides a framework for developing other characteristics and scenarios that might be important for a particular facility, hazard, occupant type, event, or management. [*101*:A.12.4.2.3]

A.10.14.12.3.1 Visitors to the crop maze should only use flashlights, chemical lights, or similar devices to illuminate their travel through the maze. Candles, gas-fired lanterns, cigarette lighters, or similar open flame or flame-producing devices are prohibited for use inside a crop maze at all times.

A.10.15.5.1 The measurement should be taken from the building opening to the exhaust outlet of the generator. The 20 ft (6.1 m) separation is intended to minimize the carbon monoxide hazard associated with portable and vehicle-mounted generators. Consideration should also be given to the orientation of the generator exhaust.

A.10.15.5.2 It is not the intent of this section to prohibit the installation or use of portable and vehicle-mounted generators within outside structures such as lean-tos or sheds intended solely to provide weather protection for the generator.

A.10.15.8 Section 702.5 of *NFPA 70* requires transfer equipment (switches) for all standby systems, including portable and vehicle-mounted generators. Transfer switches are designed to prevent the inadvertent interconnection of normal and alternate (temporary) sources of supply in any operation of the transfer equipment. The inadvertent interconnection of the utility source and the portable generator can result in energizing the utility system from the generator when the utility power is off, or overloading the generator when the utility power is restored. This condition creates an electrical shock and fire hazard for utility workers and the public. Additionally, 406.7(B) of *NFPA 70* prohibits the practice of backfeeding a receptacle directly from a portable generator. While backfeeding is sometimes done as a common practice, it is an unsafe way to connect a portable generator to a building's electrical system, and this section is intended to prohibit this unsafe practice.

A.10.15.10(1) Power should not be provided in a manner that backfeeds receptacles or the premise wiring system.

A.10.16 For additional guidance, see Chapter 34 for provisions for indoor and outdoor storage of material. Chapter 33 contains provisions for outside storage of tires.

A.10.19 See A.10.16.

Table A.10.14.3.3 Life Safety Evaluation Scenario Characteristics Matrix

					Management		Occupants						
Scenario	Local Awareness	Mass Awareness	Incident Localized	Incident Spreads	Egress Desired	Egress Not Desired	Egress Desired	Egress Not Desired	Local Start	Mass Start	Exits Available	Exits Not Available	Other
1	X	—	—	—	X	—	X	—	—	X	—	X	—
2	—	X	—	—	—	X	—	—	—	X	—	X	—
3	—	X	X	—	X	—	X	—	X	—	X	—	—
4	—	X	—	X	—	—	X	—	—	X	—	X	—

[*101*:Table A.12.4.2.3]

A.10.20.1.2 The flame-retardant requirements for light-transmitting plastics can also be found in Chapter 48 of *NFPA 5000*.

A.10.20.1.5 A fire hazards analysis is an assessment of the potential for a fire at any location to ensure that the possibility of injury to people or damage to buildings, equipment, or the environment is within acceptable limits.

N **A.10.22** The total quantities of ignitible (flammable or combustible) liquids in any area should comply with the provisions of other recognized codes, including NFPA 1 and NFPA 30. In addition, special consideration should be given to the following:

(1) Obstructions created by the installation of hand-rub solution dispensers
(2) Location of dispensers with regard to adjacent combustible materials and potential sources of ignition, especially where dispensers are mounted on walls of combustible construction
(3) Requirements for other fire protection features, including complete automatic sprinkler protection, to be installed throughout the compartment
(4) Amount and location of the flammable solutions, both in use and in storage, particularly with respect to potential for leakage or failure of the dispenser

[*101*:A.8.7.3.3]

A.11.1.2.2.1 In most cases, the AHJ for enforcement of NFPA 1 might not have the technical expertise on existing electrical wiring, appliances, or equipment to effectively evaluate whether existing conditions are unsafe and mitigation actions need to be taken by an owner or tenant. This section authorizes the AHJ to require an individual with sufficient expertise to evaluate existing conditions. It is important to note that the AHJ must first have some evidence that the existing electrical wiring, fixtures, appliances, or equipment is potentially unsafe in order to require the evaluation. This section is not intended to provide the AHJ with blanket authority to require an evaluation when such evidence is lacking.

A.11.1.5 A portable appliance as used in this section is synonymous with the term *portable equipment* as used in *NFPA 70*. Portable equipment in Article 513 of *NFPA 70* is equipment with electrical components suitable to be moved by a single person without mechanical aids. The service conditions and portable appliances for which extension cords can be used temporarily or permanently are established in 11.1.5.1 through 11.1.5.6.

A.11.1.5.6 The spacing of receptacles varies according to the occupancy type and date of construction. Where fixed receptacles do not exist, 11.1.5.6 does not permit the permanent use of extension cords.

A.11.1.7.1 Section 230.70 of *NFPA 70 (NEC)*, includes requirements for the location and marking of service disconnect means. *NFPA 70* applies to most public and private buildings, structures, yards, parking lots, and similar installations. It does not apply to certain electrical installations under the exclusive control of communications utilities or electric utilities, and other specific installations. *(See NFPA 70, 90.2.)* Multiple service disconnect means could be provided as allowed by *NFPA 70*.

A.11.3.3 Continued operation of solid-state elevator equipment is contingent on maintaining the ambient temperature in the range specified by the elevator manufacturer. If the machine room ventilation/air-conditioning is connected to the general building system, and that system is shut down during a fire, the fire department might lose the use of elevators due to excessive heat in the elevator machine room. [*101*:A.9.4.5]

A.11.5.1.5 Examples of portable devices not covered by NFPA 31 are blowtorches, melting pots, and weed burners. [**31**:A.1.1.5]

A.11.5.1.10.1 See Chapter 11 of NFPA 31 for additional requirements for oil-burning stoves, kerosene-burning room heaters, and kerosene-burning portable heaters. See Chapter 12 of NFPA 31 for additional requirements for used oil–burning appliances. See Chapter 13 of NFPA 31 for additional requirements for combination oil-and-gas–burning appliances. [**31**:A.4.5.1]

Acceptable liquid fuels for use in oil-burning equipment are the liquid fuels for which the appliance is listed by an approved listing agency such as UL, based on testing to an accepted standard, or as approved and stipulated by the oil burner manufacturer. The fuels that are commonly used are No. 2 distillate fuel oil, ultra-low sulfur No. 2 distillate fuel oil, kerosene in residential oil burners, and other fuels listed in 11.5.1.10.1 for a range of burner applications. Not all fuels are approved for all applications. For example, 11.5.1.10.1 recently added ASTM D7666, *Standard Specification for Triglyceride Burner Fuel*, but this burner fuel might not be approved for, and cannot be burned in, residential oil-heating equipment. In addition, the biodiesel content for residential oil burners typically is limited by the burner manufacturer to 5 percent by volume in fuel oil, which is accepted by UL as equivalent to a heating oil without biodiesel content. Research is ongoing for use of B20 and higher biodiesel fuel blends in residential heating equipment, which require approval by the burner manufacturer. Equipment installers should refer to the installation instructions of the burner manufacturer regarding acceptable fuels to be used that are part of the burner's listing. [**31**:A.4.5.1]

A.11.5.1.10.3 Where heavy oils are used, provisions should be made to maintain the oil within the recommended temperature range indicated in Table A.11.5.1.10.3 so that proper atomization is maintained. [**31**:A.4.5.3]

A.11.5.1.10.3(4) UL 296A, *Waste Oil-Burning Air Heating Appliances*, specifies that a burner provided with preheating means for the fuel oil can be provided with an oil temperature interlock device to prevent delivery of the fuel oil to the firing portion of the burner until the fuel oil has reached a predetermined minimum temperature. On a burner that is not equipped with oil-preheating equipment, an oil temperature interlock device should not be provided on the burner and should be bypassed during any firing tests of the burner. [**31**:A.4.5.3(4)]

N **A.11.7.2** For additional information, see UL 2200, *Standard for Stationary Engine Generator Assemblies*.

A.11.8 NFPA 92 provides guidance in implementing systems using pressure differentials to accomplish one or more of the following:

(1) Maintain a tenable environment in the means of egress during the time required for evacuation
(2) Control and reduce the migration of smoke from the fire area

Table A.11.5.1.10.3 Recommended Temperature Range for Proper Atomization of Heavy Oils

Fuel No.	Viscosity in SSU at 100°F	Low Temperature Limit (°F)	High Temperature Limit (°F)
4	45	35*	50
	50	35*	65
	60	45*	85
	75	62	105
	100	80	125
5	150	100	145
	200	112	160
	300	130	180
	400	140	190
	500	150	200
6	1,000	170	225
	2,000	190	245
	3,000	205	260
	4,000	212	270
	5,000	218	275
	10,000	240	290

*At these temperatures, proper operation of the appliance might not be attained because of unsatisfactory atomization of the fuel. For this reason, the fuel oil should be kept at the high end of the recommended temperature range.
[31:Table A.4.5.3]

(3) Provide conditions outside the fire zone that assist emergency response personnel to conduct search and rescue operations and to locate and control the fire
(4) Contribute to the protection of life and reduction of property loss

A.11.10 Two-way radio communication enhancement systems provide for greater flexibility and safety for emergency responders during in-building operations.

N A.11.10.2 AHJs are cautioned against requiring two-way radio communications enhancement systems in locations such as telecommunications facility equipment rooms where the operation of two-way radio devices could impair telecommunication services due to interference. Telecommunications facilities are essential elements of the public safety network, providing communities with connectivity to 911 and E911, as well as processing of alarms and other signals. The telephone network has a large, embedded base of legacy electronic equipment that has not been designed or tested for immunity at the power levels and frequencies commonly used in responder radios. As a result, the use of radios in telecommunications equipment rooms can result in a phone service outage. A 2010 joint study of the effects of responder radios on telecommunications equipment was sponsored by several telecommunications carriers and performed by UL. This study confirmed that telecommunications equipment can be functionally impaired and damaged by close proximity radio operation at common frequencies. To help assure reliability of the phone network, it is recommended that responder radios not be utilized in telecommunications equipment areas. Telecommunications equipment rooms are not publicly accessible areas and the number of incidents requiring responder access are low compared to other commercial occupancies. As these facilities are unique occupancies with such an important role, close cooperation between the telecommunications carrier and the AHJ should be encouraged to assure responder activities are not unduly impaired.

A.11.12.2.1 Marking is needed to provide emergency responders with appropriate warning and guidance with respect to working around and isolating the solar electric system. This can facilitate identifying energized electrical lines that connect the solar modules to the inverter, which should not be cut when venting for smoke removal during fire-fighting operations.

A.11.12.2.1.1 To clarify what the labels described in the text of 11.12.2.1.1 should look like, this annex information provides a pictorial depiction of the sign to be similarly replicated for compliance with 11.12.2.1.1. Figure A.11.12.2.1.1(a) depicts the sign required by 11.12.2.1.1.1. Figure A.11.12.2.1.1(b) depicts the sign required by 11.12.2.1.1.2.

A.11.12.3.2.3 Figure A.11.12.3.2.3(a) through Figure A.11.12.3.2.3(c) are intended to provide visuals for the requirements of 11.12.3.2.3. In these figures, the PV array is greater than 33 percent of the roof area and therefore also has a 36 in. (914 mm) setback on either side of the horizontal ridge as required by 11.12.3.2.3.2.

A.11.12.3.3.4.2(1) Figure A.11.12.3.3.4.2(1) shows an array on a commercial building with an axis less than 250 ft (76.2 m). Per 11.12.3.3.4.1, 48 in. (1219 mm) pathways are provided around the perimeter, and per 11.12.3.3.4.2(1), 96 in. (2438 mm) pathways are provided for ventilation.

A.11.12.3.3.4.2(2) Figure A.11.12.3.3.4.2(2) shows an array on a commercial building with an axis greater than 250 ft (76.2 m). Per 11.12.3.3.4.2, 6 ft. (1829 mm) pathways are provided around the perimeter, and per 11.12.3.3.4.2(1), 96 in. (2438 mm) pathways are provided for ventilation. And per 11.12.3.3.4.2(2), 48 in. (1219 mm) pathways are provided at existing roof skylights at intervals not greater than 150 ft (46 m).

A.11.12.3.3.4.2(3) Figure A.11.12.3.3.4.2(3)(a) shows an array on a commercial building with an axis less than 250 ft (76.2 m). Per 11.12.3.3.2.1, 48 in. (1219 mm) pathways are provided around the perimeter, and per 11.12.3.3.4.2(3), 48 in. (1219 mm) pathways with ventilation opportunities provided every 20 ft (6096 mm).

Figure A.11.12.3.3.4.2(3)(b) shows an array on a commercial building with an axis greater than 250 ft (76.2 m). Per 11.12.3.3.4.2, 6 ft. (1829 mm) pathways are provided around the perimeter, and per 11.12.3.3.4.2(3), 48 in. (1219 mm) pathways with ventilation opportunities provided every 20 ft (6096 mm).

A.11.12.4.1 The zoning regulations of the jurisdiction setback requirements between buildings or property lines, and accessory structures might apply.

A.11.12.4.2 Though dirt with minor growth is not considered noncombustible, the AHJ might approve dirt bases as long as any growth is maintained under and around the installation to reduce the risk of ignition from the electrical system. This could be a serious consideration for large ground-mounted photovoltaic systems. Not only should the base be considered under the systems, but also around the systems to the point that the risk of fire from growth or other ignition sources will be reduced.

ANNEX A 1-561

Δ FIGURE A.11.12.2.1.1(a)   Sign Required by 11.12.2.1.1.1.

Δ FIGURE A.11.12.2.1.1(b)   Sign Required by 11.12.2.1.1.2.

FIGURE A.11.12.3.2.3(a) Pathways on a Cross-Gable Roof with a Valley. *(Source: Cal Fire.)*

FIGURE A.11.12.3.2.3(b) Pathways on a Full Gable Roof. *(Source: Cal Fire.)*

FIGURE A.11.12.3.2.3(c) Pathways on a Full Hip Roof. *(Source: Cal Fire.)*

FIGURE A.11.12.3.3.4.2(1) Commercial Array with an Axis Less Than 250 ft (76.2 m) and with 8 ft (2.4 m) Walkways. *(Source: Cal Fire.)*

FIGURE A.11.12.3.3.4.2(2) Commercial Array with an Axis Greater Than 250 ft (76.2 m), with 8 ft (2.4 m) Walkways, and 4 ft (1.2 m) Pathways to Existing Roof Hatches. *(Source: Cal Fire.)*

Δ **FIGURE A.11.12.3.3.4.2(3)(a)** Commercial Array with an Axis Less Than 250 ft (76.2 m) and with 4 ft (1.2 m) Pathways with Ventilation Opportunities every 20 ft (6096 mm). *(Source: Cal Fire.)*

FIGURE A.11.12.3.3.4.2(3)(b) Commercial Array with an Axis Greater Than 250 ft (76.2 m) and with 4 ft (1.2 m) Pathways with Ventilation Opportunities Every 20 ft (6096 mm). *(Source: Cal Fire.)*

A.12.2 Table A.12.2 provides a cross reference from the NFPA construction types to the model building codes. [**220**:A.4.1.1]

A.12.2.1 Building construction types are defined in NFPA 220. The following material is extracted verbatim from NFPA 220 and is included here as a convenience for users of this *Code*. Any requests for Formal Interpretations (FIs) or Tentative Interim Amendments (TIAs) on the following material should be directed to the Technical Committee on Building Construction. See Table A.12.2.1 for fire resistance ratings for each building construction type.

Type I and Type II Construction. Type I (442 or 332) and Type II (222, 111, or 000) construction shall be those types in which the fire walls, structural elements, walls, arches, floors, and roofs are of approved noncombustible or limited-combustible materials. [**220**:4.3.1]

Type III Construction. Type III (211 or 200) construction shall be that type in which exterior walls and structural elements that are portions of exterior walls are of approved noncombustible or limited-combustible materials, and in which fire walls, interior structural elements, walls, arches, floors, and roofs, are entirely or partially of wood of smaller dimensions than required for Type IV construction or are of approved noncombustible, limited-combustible, or other approved combustible materials. [**220**:4.4.1]

Type IV Construction. Type IV (2HH) construction shall be that type in which fire walls, exterior walls, and interior bearing

Δ **Table A.12.2 Cross Reference of Building Construction Types**

Code Source NFPA 220	I(442)	I(332)	II(222)	II(111)	II(000)	III(211)	III(200)	IV(2HH)	V(111)	V(000)
UBC	—	I FR	II FR	II 1 hr	II N	III 1 hr	III N	IV HT	V 1 hr	V N
B/NBC	1A	1B	2A	2B	2C	3A	3B	4	5A	5B
SBC	I	II	—	IV 1 hr	IV UNP	V 1 hr	V UNP	III	VI 1 hr	VI UNP
IBC	—	IA	IB	IIA	IIB	IIIA	IIIB	IV	VA	VB

UBC: Uniform Building Code.
FR: Fire rated.
N: Nonsprinklered.
HT: Heavy timber.
B/NBC: BOCA/National Building Code.
SBC: Standard Building Code.
IBC: International Building Code.
UNP: Unprotected.
[**220**:Table A.4.1.1]

walls and structural elements that are portions of such walls are of approved noncombustible or limited-combustible materials, except as allowed for exterior walls in 4.5.6.7 of NFPA 220. Other interior structural elements, arches, floors, and roofs shall be of solid or laminated wood or cross-laminated timber without concealed spaces or with concealed spaces conforming to 4.5.6.7 of NFPA 220 and shall comply with the allowable dimensions of 4.5.6.7 of NFPA 220. [**220**:4.5.1]

Type V (111 or 000) Construction. Type V (111 or 000) construction shall be that type in which structural elements, walls, arches, floors, and roofs are entirely or partially of wood or other approved material. [**220**:4.6]

A.12.3.3 Fire-resistive construction also includes fire-resistive coatings and sprayed fire-resistive materials, as well as membrane and through-penetration firestops and fire-resistive joint systems. It is important to conduct periodic inspections of fire-resistive construction, especially these elements and components that are directly visible or readily accessible for inspection.

Inspections of sprayed fire-resistive materials and coatings are especially important since they can be subject to delamination, removal, physical abuse, deterioration, and degradation over time. Periodic inspections should be able to identify apparent deficiencies, especially where they crumble or fall off when touched. When such conditions are identified, they should be further inspected or tested by qualified third parties to verify their integrity and effectiveness. Where they are found to be deficient, appropriate corrective action should be taken to restore them to their original condition.

Tested and listed firestop systems should be installed to the listing in order to perform as expected. Systems installed in accordance with an engineering judgment (EJ) should be installed in accordance with the EJ. The firestop systems should be inspected periodically to assure continued performance. To inspect firestops, the listed system design or EJ should be acces-

Δ Table A.12.2.1 Fire Resistance Ratings for Type I Through Type V Construction (hr)

Construction Element	Type I		Type II			Type III		Type IV	Type V	
	442	332	222	111	000	211	200	2HH	111	000
Exterior Bearing Walls[a]										
Supporting more than one floor, columns, or other bearing walls	4	3	2	1	0[b]	2	2	2	1	0[b]
Supporting one floor only	4	3	2	1	0[b]	2	2	2	1	0[b]
Supporting a roof only	4	3	1	1	0[b]	2	2	2	1	0[b]
Interior Bearing Walls										
Supporting more than one floor, columns, or other bearing walls	4	3	2	1	0	1	0	2	1	0
Supporting one floor only	3	2	2	1	0	1	0	1	1	0
Supporting roofs only	3	2	1	1	0	1	0	1	1	0
Columns										
Supporting more than one floor, columns, or other bearing walls	4	3	2	1	0	1	0	H	1	0
Supporting one floor only	3	2	2	1	0	1	0	H	1	0
Supporting roofs only	3	2	1	1	0	1	0	H	1	0
Beams, Girders, Trusses, and Arches										
Supporting more than one floor, columns, or other bearing walls	4	3	2	1	0	1	0	H	1	0
Supporting one floor only	2	2	2	1	0	1	0	H	1	0
Supporting roofs only	2	2	1	1	0	1	0	H	1	0
Floor/Ceiling Assemblies	2	2	2	1	0	1	0	H	1	0
Roof/Ceiling Assemblies	2	1½	1	1	0	1	0	H	1	0
Interior Nonbearing Walls	0	0	0	0	0	0	0	0	0	0
Exterior Nonbearing Walls[c]	0[b]	0[b]	0[b]	0[b]	0[b]	0[b]	0[b]	0[b]	0[b]	0[b]

H = Heavy timber members *(see NFPA 220 text for requirements)*.
[a]See 7.3.2.1 of *NFPA 5000*.
[b]See Section 7.3 of *NFPA 5000*.
[c]See 4.3.2.12, 4.4.2.3, and 4.5.6.8 of NFPA 220.
[**220**:Table 4.1.1]

sible. Firestop installations are only able to be identified by the listing design, the listing references, the materials to be used, and installation parameters. Without the listing, neither the inspector, building owner, nor building management company has any idea how to inspect or repair the firestop systems.

Firestop systems can be marked at the location of the installation using a variety of methods from paper labels to complex plastic tear-away labels, ceramic fiber, or metal tags. These can be attached to the assembly or to the penetrating item(s). A variety of marking methods can be used and they should provide important information, such as the listing number, date, manufacturer, and installing contractor.

A.12.4.1 See Annex K of NFPA 80 for general information about fire doors. [**80:**A.1.1]

A.12.4.1.1 No fire test standard requirement currently exists to which fabric fire safety curtain assemblies can be tested. Only the curtain fabric is tested in accordance with ASTM E119, *Standard Test Methods for Fire Tests of Building Construction and Materials,* or UL 263, *Fire Tests of Building Construction and Materials.* The perimeter and internal framework and all supporting, guide, and operating components used in specific applications are not tested. Variations in size of proscenium openings and the amount of side and head clearances available for individual stages dictate the number of variations in design of the assemblies. [**80:**A.1.1.1]

A.12.4.1.2 For requirements on their installation, see NFPA 82 and NFPA 232. [**80:**A.1.1.2]

Δ **A.12.4.1.3** For requirements on the installation of hoistway doors for elevators and dumbwaiters, see the applicable sections of ASME A17.1/CSA B44, *Safety Code for Elevators and Escalators,* or ASME A17.3, *Safety Code for Existing Elevators and Escalators.* [**80:**A.1.1.3]

Δ **A.12.4.1.4** The fire performance evaluation of these assemblies is tested in accordance with ASTM E119, *Standard Test Methods for Fire Tests of Building Construction and Materials,* or UL 263, *Fire Tests of Building Construction and Materials,* for horizontal access doors; NFPA 252, UL 10B, *Fire Tests of Door Assemblies,* or UL 10C, *Positive Pressure Fire Tests of Door Assemblies,* for fire doors and shutters; NFPA 257 or UL 9, *Fire Tests of Window Assemblies,* for fire windows and glass block; and NFPA 288 for doors in horizontal fire-rated assemblies. It is not the intent of this section to establish the degree of protection required or to constitute the approval of any product. These are determined by the AHJ. [**80:**A.1.1.4]

Δ **A.12.4.2.1** See Chapter 19 of NFPA 80 for fire dampers, and Chapter 20 of NFPA 80 for fabric fire safety curtains. [**80:**A.5.1.1.1]

A.12.4.2.3.1 Operability issues may include proper operation and function of latching hardware and closing devices. Latching hardware should not be modified to prevent positive latching. [**80:**A.5.1.2.1]

A.12.4.2.6 Field modifications beyond the scope of the prescriptive allowances permitted by 5.1.5.2.2 through 5.1.5.2.2.5 of NFPA 80 typically result in voiding the fire rating of the assembly. Paragraph 12.4.2.6 provides an alternative method whereby proposed modifications can be documented and presented to the labeling agency prior to work commencing. Where the proposed modification(s) are within the parameters of the manufacturer's procedures and will not degrade the fire resistance of the assembly, the labeling agency is permitted to authorize such modifications without a requirement for a subsequent field inspection. [**80:**A.5.1.5.1]

Generally, the replacement of hardware components on swinging doors (hinges, pivots, door closers, etc.) is not considered to be a field modification, provided the replacement hardware does not require additional cutting, mortising, or boring into the doors and frames and the hardware meets the criteria specified elsewhere in NFPA 80. Likewise, the installation of surface-mounted items like protection plates is not considered to be field modifications. Cutting doors for vision panels, enlarging existing cutouts for vision panels, and trimming doors in height or width are examples of field modifications. Similarly, installing hardware components that require additional cutting and mortising of the doors or frames are examples of field modifications. [**80:**A.5.1.5.1]

A.12.4.2.8 Doors, shutters, and windows are of no value unless they are properly maintained and closed or are able to close at the time of fire. A periodic inspection and maintenance program is generally the responsibility of the building owner. [**80:**A.5.2]

A.12.4.2.8.1 Hinges, catches, closers, latches, and stay rollers are especially subject to wear. [**80:**A.5.2.1]

A.12.4.2.8.2 Newer technology includes use of barcodes and other electronic devices. This section recognizes that completed and filed barcode reports should be considered signed by the inspector. [**80:**A.5.2.2]

Some inspection organizations will utilize inspection markers or tags to identify completion of the inspections. These markers are intended to be different from any approved or listed field labeling service. The marker or tag is not to take the place of the inspection records as required by 12.4.2.8.2. [**80:**A.5.2.2]

A.12.4.2.8.2.2 In many cases, AHJs are not able to inspect each building in their jurisdiction each year. Inspection and testing records need to be retained during the intervening periods between the AHJ's formal visits to provide evidence that the inspections and testing were performed as required by this *Code.* Additionally, maintenance records documenting that the necessary corrective actions have been made in accordance with this *Code* should be stored with the inspection and testing records for the same period of time. Retaining the records for 7 years allows the AHJ the ability to look back over an extended period of time to verify that the fire door assemblies are being properly maintained. [**80:**A.5.2.2.2]

A.12.4.2.8.2.3 Installation of new fire door assemblies should be documented in the same manner and level of detail as the periodic inspections and testing of fire door assemblies required by 12.4.2.8.3 and 12.4.2.8.4. Records of new fire door assemblies should be retained with the periodic inspections and testing records for the facility. [**80:**A.5.2.2.3]

A.12.4.2.8.2.4(8) Each fire door assembly inspected and tested should be assigned a unique identifier code (e.g., door number as assigned by the facility) that can be used to track the assembly's compliance and maintenance records throughout the lifetime of its installation. Identifier codes could be a door assembly number, barcode, or other code that is unique to each fire door assembly. [**80:**A.5.2.2.4(8)]

A.12.4.2.8.2.4(9) To aid the AHJ during the review of the inspections and testing reports, the records should include a description of the type of fire door assembly as follows:

Type 6: Swinging door with builders hardware

Type 7: Swinging fire door with fire door hardware

Type 8: Horizontally sliding fire door

Type 9: Special purpose horizontally accordion or folding door

Type 10: Vertically sliding fire door

Type 11: Rolling steel door

Type 12: Fire shutter

Type 13: Service counter fire door

Type 14: Hoistway doors for elevators and dumbwaiter

Type 15: Chute door

Type 16: Access door

Type 17: Fire window

[80:A.5.2.2.4(9)]

A.12.4.2.8.2.4(10) Functional operation of fire door assemblies should include testing of the closing device, complete closure of the fire door, and full engagement of latch(es) where required by door type. Functional testing of automatic-closing or power-operated fire door assemblies and electrically controlled latching hardware or release devices might need to be coordinated with the facility during other electrically controlled system tests. [80:A.5.2.2.4(10)]

A.12.4.2.8.3.1 Visual inspection and functional testing of fire door and fire window assemblies require the persons performing the inspections and testing to be thoroughly knowledgeable of the various components and systems that are used to create fire-rated assemblies. In the case of swinging doors with builders hardware, these assemblies are comprised of labeled and listed components from several manufacturers. Often, the listing of the door leaf determines which products are permitted to be installed on an assembly. Inspectors of swinging doors with builders hardware need be able to recognize which components can or cannot be used on specific assemblies, which requires training and experience on behalf of the persons performing the inspections. Additionally, AHJs need to be able to rely on the competency, expertise, experience, and knowledge of the fire door inspectors in their jurisdiction. [80:A.5.2.3.1]

A.12.4.2.8.3.2 Any fire door or fire window assembly or component that has a history of reoccurring failures should be evaluated for possible replacement or other corrective measures. [80:A.5.2.3.2]

A.12.4.2.8.3.5.2 Where a previously applied inspection mark exists, it should be updated or replaced to record the most recent inspection. [80:A.5.2.3.5.3]

A.12.4.2.8.3.9 Moveable parts of the door assembly can include, but are not limited to, stay rollers, gears, and closing mechanisms. [80:A.5.2.3.9]

N **A.12.4.2.8.4** While the requirement to inspect fire doors applies to new and existing doors, one must consider both the retroactivity clause in Chapter 1 and the applicable code requirements at the time the door was installed when conducting the inspection. There was a time when this *Code* did not require wired glass to be labeled. It would be inappropriate, for example, to cite a door with wired glass that is not labeled as being deficient if it was installed at a time when labeling was not required. In addition, NFPA *101* permits protective plates up to 48 in. (1220 mm) above the bottom of the door for some existing doors. Where NFPA *101* takes precedent over the referenced standard, it would be inappropriate to cite a door as being deficient in applications where a 48 in. (1220 mm) protective plate is permitted. [80:A.5.2.4]

A.12.4.2.8.4.1 Doors subject to high-volume use and abuse might warrant an increased frequency of inspection. Components including, but not limited to, hinges, catches, closers, latches, and stay rollers are especially subject to wear. [80:A.5.2.4.1]

N **A.12.4.2.8.4.2** Rolling steel fire doors are unique with respect to other fire door types because of the complexity of tension release and automatic closing systems of these doors as opposed to other types of doors that typically open and close as entire units. Special training for periodic inspection and testing is necessary because of the multitude of components involved that must work together for the door to be tested and reset correctly. It is essential that the rolling steel fire door industry maintain oversight of any person involved in periodic inspection and testing of such products. When requested, such a person should be able to produce documented evidence of training. Recognized industry organizations and manufacturers of listed rolling steel fire doors with appropriate training materials and programs are viable options for training individuals about the proper performance of rolling steel fire doors and their applicable codes and standards. Periodic inspection and testing should be documented on a form that complies with industry standards. The door should be provided with an inspection mark that complies with industry standards indicating when it was last inspected and tested and refers to the inspection and test form for additional information. [80:A.5.2.4.2]

A.12.4.2.8.4.7 The determination of the time required for corrective action should be based on a risk analysis and availability of replacement materials. [80:A.5.2.4.5]

A.12.4.2.10 See Annex J of NFPA 80 for information regarding performance-based inspection, testing, and maintenance options for fire door assemblies. [80:A.5.4]

A.12.4.2.11.1 The determination of the time required for corrective action should be based on a risk analysis and availability of replacement materials. [80:A.5.5.1]

A.12.4.2.11.4 The determination of the time required for corrective action should be based on a risk analysis and availability of replacement materials. [80:A.5.5.4]

△ **A.12.4.2.11.10** Existing fire door assemblies that have been repaired should be inspected and tested immediately upon completion of the repair work to ensure that they are in compliance with this *Code*. Records of maintenance work should be maintained with the periodic inspections and testing records for the facility. [80:A.5.5.10]

A.12.4.2.11.10.2(8) See A.12.4.2.8.2.4(8). [**80:**A.5.5.10.2(8)]

A.12.4.2.11.10.2(9) See A.12.4.2.8.2.4(9). [**80:**A.5.5.10.2(9)]

A.12.4.2.11.10.2(10) When maintenance work on an existing fire door assembly is required as the result of a periodic inspections and testing report to correct deficiencies, the maintenance report should reference the inspections and testing report where the deficiencies were cited to show that the follow up work was performed. Descriptions of the work performed on fire door assemblies should document the nature of the work (i.e., replaced surface mounted door closer, installed new gasketing). Where the work performed included field modifications permitted by the laboratory, in accordance with 12.4.2.6.2 and approved by the AHJ, documentation of the permission and approval should be attached to the maintenance report. [**80:**A.5.5.10.2(10)]

A.12.5 The requirements pertaining to interior finish are intended to restrict the spread of fire over the continuous surface forming the interior portions of a building. [*101:*A.10.2]

The requirements are based on fire testing to NFPA 286 (with the criteria of 12.5.4.2), which apply to all interior finish materials. Many interior finish materials are permitted to be tested based on other fire tests, such as ASTM E84, *Standard Test Method for Surface Burning Characteristics of Building Materials,* UL 723, *Test for Surface Burning Characteristics of Building Materials,* or NFPA 265 as provided in the relevant subsection of Section 12.5. [*101:*A.10.2]

A.12.5.2 The requirements pertaining to interior finish are intended to restrict the spread of fire over the continuous surface forming the interior portions of a building. The presence of multiple paint layers has the potential for paint delamination and bubbling or blistering of paint. Testing (NFPA *Fire Technology,* August 1974, "Fire Tests of Building Interior Covering Systems," David Waksman and John Ferguson, Institute for Applied Technology, National Bureau of Standards) has shown that adding up to two layers of paint with a dry film thickness of about 0.007 in. (0.18 mm) will not change the fire properties of surface-covering systems. Testing has shown that the fire properties of the surface-covering systems are highly substrate dependent and that thin coatings generally take on the characteristics of the substrate. When exposed to fire, the delamination, bubbling, and blistering of paint can result in an accelerated rate of flame spread. [*101:*A.10.2.1]

A.12.5.3 Table A.12.5.3 provides a compilation of the interior finish requirements of 7.1.4 of NFPA *101* and the occupancy chapters (Chapters 12 through 42) of NFPA *101*. [*101:*A.10.2.2]

A.12.5.3.2 This paragraph recognizes that traditional finish floors and floor coverings, such as wood flooring and resilient floor coverings, have not proved to present an unusual hazard. [*101:*A.10.2.2.2]

A.12.5.4 ASTM E84, *Standard Test Method of Surface Burning Characteristics of Building Materials,* and UL 723, *Test for Surface Burning Characteristics of Building Materials,* are considered nationally recognized consensus standard test methods for determining the flame spread index and smoke developed index of building materials and are likely to yield equivalent test results. *(See also A.12.5.5.4.1.)* [*101:*A.10.2.3]

Δ **Table A.12.5.3 Interior Finish Classification Limitations**

Occupancy	Exits	Exit Access Corridors	Other Spaces
Assembly — new			
>300 occupant load	A	A or B	A or B
	I or II	I or II	NA
≤300 occupant load	A	A or B	A, B, or C
	I or II	I or II	NA
Assembly — existing			
>300 occupant load	A	A or B	A or B
≤300 occupant load	A	A or B	A, B, or C
Educational — new	A	A or B	A or B; C on low partitions*
	I or II	I or II	NA
Educational — existing	A	A or B	A, B, or C
Day-care centers — new	A	A	A or B
	I or II	I or II	NA
Day-care centers — existing	A or B	A or B	A or B
Day-care homes — new	A or B	A or B	A, B, or C
	I or II		NA
Day-care homes — existing	A or B	A, B, or C	A, B, or C
Health care — new	A	A	A
	NA	B on lower portion of corridor wall*	B in small individual rooms*
	I or II	I or II	NA
Health care — existing	A or B	A or B	A or B
Detention and correctional — new (sprinklers mandatory)	A or B	A or B	A, B, or C
	I or II	I or II	NA
Detention and correctional — existing	A or B	A or B	A, B, or C
	I or II	I or II	NA
One- and two-family dwellings and lodging or rooming houses	A, B, or C	A, B, or C	A, B, or C
Hotels and dormitories — new	A	A or B	A, B, or C
	I or II	I or II	NA
Hotels and dormitories — existing	A or B	A or B	A, B, or C
	I or II*	I or II*	NA
Apartment buildings — new	A	A or B	A, B, or C
	I or II	I or II	NA
Apartment buildings — existing	A or B	A or B	A, B, or C
	I or II*	I or II*	NA
Residential board and care — *(See 20.5.3.3.)*			
Mercantile — new	A or B	A or B	A or B
	I or II		NA
Mercantile — existing			
Class A or class B stores	A or B	A or B	Ceilings — A or B; walls — A, B, or C
Class C stores	A, B, or C	A, B, or C	A, B, or C
Business and ambulatory health care — new	A or B	A or B	A, B, or C
	I or II		NA

(continues)

Δ Table A.12.5.3 Continued

Occupancy	Exits	Exit Access Corridors	Other Spaces
Business and ambulatory health care — existing	A or B	A or B	A, B, or C
Industrial	A or B I or II	A, B, or C I or II	A, B, or C NA
Storage	A or B I or II	A, B, or C	A, B, or C NA

*See corresponding chapters for details.
NA: Not applicable.
Notes:
(1) Class A interior wall and ceiling finish — flame spread index, 0–25 (new applications); smoke developed index, 0–450.
(2) Class B interior wall and ceiling finish — flame spread index, 26–75 (new applications); smoke developed index, 0–450.
(3) Class C interior wall and ceiling finish — flame spread index, 76–200 (new applications); smoke developed index, 0–450.
(4) Class I interior floor finish — critical radiant flux, not less than 0.45 W/cm^2.
(5) Class II interior floor finish — critical radiant flux, not less than 0.22 W/cm^2, but less than 0.45 W/cm^2.
(6) Automatic sprinklers — where a complete standard system of automatic sprinklers is installed, interior wall and ceiling finish with a flame spread rating not exceeding Class C is permitted to be used in any location where Class B is required, and Class B interior wall and ceiling finish is permitted to be used in any location where Class A is required; similarly, Class II interior floor finish is permitted to be used in any location where Class I is required, and no interior floor finish classification is required where Class II is required. These provisions do not apply to new detention and correctional occupancies.
(7) Exposed portions of structural members complying with the requirements for heavy timber construction are permitted.
[*101*:Table A.10.2.2]

A.12.5.4.1.2 Materials tested per NFPA 286 and meeting the criteria of 12.5.4.2 are considered Class A materials. However, not all materials that meet the requirements for Class A based on testing per ASTM E84 or UL 723 will meet the requirements of this *Code* for testing in accordance with NFPA 286. [*101*:A.10.2.3.1.2]

A.12.5.4.3 It has been shown that the method of mounting interior finish materials usually affects actual performance. The use of standard mounting methods will be helpful in determining appropriate fire test results. Where materials are tested in intimate contact with a substrate to determine a classification, such materials should be installed in intimate contact with a similar substrate. Such details are especially important for "thermally thin" materials. For further information, see ASTM E84, *Standard Test Method for Surface Burning Characteristics of Building Materials*. [*101*:A.10.2.3.3]

Some interior wall and ceiling finish materials, such as fabrics not applied to a solid backing, do not lend themselves to a test made in accordance with ASTM E84. In such cases, the large-scale test outlined in NFPA 701 is permitted to be used. In 1989 the NFPA Technical Committee on Fire Tests eliminated the so-called "small-scale test" from NFPA 701 because the results had been shown not to represent a fire performance that corresponded to what happened in real scale. Since then, NFPA 701 no longer contains a "small-scale test" but it now contains two tests (Test 1 and Test 2), which apply to materials as a function of their areal density. Thus NFPA 701 Test 1 applies to fabrics (other than vinyl-coated fabric blackout linings) having an areal density less than or equal to 21 oz/yd^2 (700 g/m^2), while NFPA 701 Test 2 applies to fabrics with an areal density greater than 21 oz/yd^2 (700 g/m^2), vinyl-coated fabric blackout linings, decorative objects, and films. Representations that materials or products have been tested to the small-scale test in NFPA 701 normally refer to the pre-1989 small-scale test, which no longer exists and which does not represent acceptable fire performance. [*101*:A.10.2.3.3]

Prior to 1978, the test report described by ASTM E84 included an evaluation of the fuel contribution as well as the flame spread index and the smoke developed index. However, it is now recognized that the measurement on which the fuel contribution is based does not provide a valid measure. Therefore, although the data are recorded during the test, the information is no longer normally reported. Classification of interior wall and ceiling finish thus relies only on the flame spread index and smoke developed index. [*101*:A.10.2.3.3]

The 450 smoke developed index limit is based solely on obscuration. (*See A.10.2.4.4 of NFPA 101.*) [*101*:A.10.2.3.3]

A.12.5.5 Surface nonmetallic raceway products, as permitted by *NFPA 70*, are not interior finishes and are not subject to the provisions of Chapter 10 of NFPA *101*. [*101*:A.10.2.4]

A.12.5.5.2 Paragraph 12.5.5.2 does not require Type IV (2HH), heavy timber, other than that used in interior exit stairs, interior exit ramps, and exit passageways be tested by either ASTM E84 or UL 723 to determine a flame spread rating. Taller wood buildings and new technology, primarily new "mass timber," make taller buildings of Type IV possible. To that end, the requirements for Type IV have been changed to require the testing for components in the egress system such that they too need to be tested and meet the appropriate classification required in this section. This means that Type IV is "presumed" to comply with the finish requirements in this section for the purpose of meeting the requirements of this section for any wall or ceiling finish of elements other than interior exit stairways, interior exit ramps, and exit passageways. [*101*:A.10.2.4.2]

A.12.5.5.3.3 See A.12.5.5.3.3.2. [*101*:A.10.2.4.3.3]

A.12.5.5.3.3.2 Both NFPA 286 and UL 1715, *Fire Test of Interior Finish Material*, contain smoke obscuration criteria. UL 1040, *Fire Test of Insulated Wall Construction*, and ANSI/FM Approvals 4880, *American National Standard for Evaluating the Fire Performance of Insulated Building Panel Assemblies and Interior Finish Materials*, do not. Smoke obscuration is an important component of the fire performance of cellular or foamed plastic materials. [*101*:A.10.2.4.3.3.2]

A.12.5.5.4 Previous editions of the *Code* have regulated textile materials on walls and ceilings using ASTM E84, *Standard Test Method for Surface Burning Characteristics of Building Materials*, or UL 723, *Test for Surface Burning Characteristics of Building Materials*. Full-scale room/corner fire test research has shown that flame spread indices produced by ASTM E84 or UL 723 might not reliably predict all aspects of the fire behavior of textile wall and ceiling coverings. [*101*:A.10.2.4.4]

NFPA 265 and NFPA 286, both known as room/corner tests, were developed for assessing the fire and smoke obscuration performance of textile wall coverings and interior wall and ceiling finish materials, respectively. As long as an interior wall or ceiling finish material is tested by NFPA 265 or NFPA 286, as appropriate, using a mounting system, substrate, and adhesive (if appropriate) that are representative of actual use, the room/corner test provides an adequate evaluation of a product's flammability and smoke obscuration behavior. Manufacturers, installers, and specifiers should be encouraged to use NFPA 265 or NFPA 286, as appropriate (but not both), because each of these standard fire tests has the ability to characterize actual product behavior, as opposed to data generated by tests using ASTM E84 or UL 723, which only allow comparisons of one product's performance with another. If a manufacturer or installer chooses to test a wall finish in accordance with NFPA 286, additional testing in accordance with ASTM E84 or UL 723 is not necessary. [*101*:A.10.2.4.4]

The test results from ASTM E84 or UL 723 are suitable for classification purposes but should not be used as input into fire models, because they are not generated in units suitable for engineering calculations. Actual test results for heat, smoke, and combustion product release from NFPA 265, and from NFPA 286, are suitable for use as input into fire models for performance-based design. [*101*:A.10.2.4.4]

A.12.5.5.4.1 The methodology specified in NFPA 265 includes provisions for measuring smoke obscuration. [*101*:A.10.2.4.4.1]

A.12.5.5.4.2 See A.12.5.5.4.1 and A.12.5.5.4. [*101*:A.10.2.4.4.2]

A.12.5.5.5 Expanded vinyl wall covering consists of a woven textile backing, an expanded vinyl base coat layer, and a nonexpanded vinyl skin coat. The expanded base coat layer is a homogeneous vinyl layer that contains a blowing agent. During processing, the blowing agent decomposes, which causes this layer to expand by forming closed cells. The total thickness of the wall covering is approximately 0.055 in. to 0.070 in. (1.4 mm to 1.8 mm). [*101*:A.10.2.4.5]

A.12.5.5.15 Light-transmitting plastics are used for a variety of purposes, including light diffusers, exterior wall panels, skylights, canopies, glazing, and the like. Previous editions of the *Code* have not addressed the use of light-transmitting plastics. Light-transmitting plastics will not normally be used in applications representative of interior finishes. Accordingly, ASTM E84, *Standard Test Method for Surface Burning Characteristics of Building Materials*, or UL 723, *Test for Surface Burning Characteristics of Building Materials*, can produce test results that might or might not apply. [*101*:A.10.2.4.15]

Light-transmitting plastics are regulated by model building codes such as *NFPA 5000*. Model building codes provide adequate regulation for most applications of light-transmitting plastics. Where an AHJ determines that a use is contemplated that differs from uses regulated by model building codes, light-transmitting plastics in such applications can be substantiated by fire tests that demonstrate the combustibility characteristics of the light-transmitting plastics for the use intended under actual fire conditions. [*101*:A.10.2.4.15]

For additional information on light transmitting plastics, see Section 48.7 of *NFPA 5000*. [*101*:A.10.2.4.15]

A.12.5.7 Fire-retardant coatings need to be applied to surfaces properly prepared for the material, and application needs to be consistent with the product listing. Deterioration of coatings applied to interior finishes can occur due to repeated cleaning of the surface or painting over applied coatings. [*101*:A.10.2.6]

A.12.5.7.1 It is the intent of NFPA *101* to mandate interior wall and ceiling finish materials that obtain their fire performance and smoke developed characteristics in their original form. However, in renovations, particularly those involving historic buildings, and in changes of occupancy, the required fire performance or smoke developed characteristics of existing surfaces of walls, partitions, columns, and ceilings might have to be secured by applying approved fire-retardant coatings to surfaces having higher flame spread ratings than permitted. Such treatments should comply with the requirements of NFPA 703. When fire-retardant coatings are used, they need to be applied to surfaces properly prepared for the material, and application needs to be consistent with the product listing. Deterioration of coatings applied to interior finishes can occur due to repeated cleaning of the surface or painting over applied coatings, but permanency must be assured in some appropriate fashion. Fire-retardant coatings must possess the desired degree of permanency and be maintained so as to retain the effectiveness of the treatment under the service conditions encountered in actual use. [*101*:A.10.2.6.1]

A.12.5.7.2 The intent of this section is that factory-applied fire-retardant-coated products, such as panels or tiles applied to walls or ceilings, replace the existing finish and are not applied on top of the existing finish. [*101*:A.10.2.6.2]

A.12.5.8 The flooring radiant panel provides a measure of a floor covering's tendency to spread flames when located in a corridor and exposed to the flame and hot gases from a room fire. The flooring radiant panel test method is to be used as a basis for estimating the fire performance of a floor covering installed in the building corridor. Floor coverings in open building spaces and in rooms within buildings merit no further regulation, provided that it can be shown that the floor covering is at least as resistant to spread of flame as a material that meets the US federal flammability standard 16 CFR 1630, "Standard for the Surface Flammability of Carpets and Rugs" (FF 1-70). All carpeting sold in the United States since 1971 is required to meet this standard and, therefore, is not likely to become involved in a fire until a room reaches or approaches flashover. Therefore, no further regulations are necessary for carpet, other than carpet in exitways and corridors. [*101*:A.10.2.7]

It has not been found necessary or practical to regulate interior floor finishes on the basis of smoke development. [*101*:A.10.2.7]

Full-scale fire tests and fire experience have shown that floor coverings in open building spaces merit no regulation beyond the US federally mandated DOC FF 1-70 "pill test." This is because floor coverings meeting the pill test will not spread flame significantly until a room fire approaches flashover. At flashover, the spread of flame across a floor covering will have minimal impact on the already existing hazard. The minimum critical radiant flux of a floor covering that will pass the FF 1-70 test has been determined to be approximately 0.04 W/cm^2 (Tu, King-Mon and Davis, Sanford, "Flame Spread of Carpet Systems Involved in Room Fires," NFSIR 76-1013, Center for Fire Research, National Bureau of Standards, June 1976). The flooring radiant panel is only able to determine critical radiant flux values to 0.1 W/cm^2. This provision will prevent use of a noncomplying material, which can create a problem, especially when the *Code* is used outside the United States where US federal regulation FF 1-70 (16 CFR 1630) is not mandated. [*101*:A.10.2.7]

A.12.5.8.1 Compliance with 16 CFR 1630, "Standard for the Surface Flammability of Carpets and Rugs" (FFI-70), is considered equivalent to compliance with ASTM D2859, *Standard Test Method for Ignition Characteristics of Finished Textile Floor Covering Materials.* [*101*:A.10.2.7.1]

A.12.5.8.3 ASTM E648, *Standard Test Method for Critical Radiant Flux of Floor-Covering Systems Using a Radiant Heat Energy Source,* and NFPA 253 are considered nationally recognized consensus standard test methods for determining the critical radiant flux from floor covering systems and are likely to yield equivalent test results. [*101*:A.10.2.7.3]

A.12.6.1 Testing per NFPA 701 applies to textiles and films used in a hanging configuration. If the textiles are to be applied to surfaces of buildings or backing materials as interior finishes for use in buildings, they should be treated as interior wall and ceiling finishes in accordance with 12.5.2 of this *Code*, and they should then be tested for flame spread index and smoke developed index values in accordance with ASTM E84, *Standard Test Method for Surface Burning Characteristics of Building Materials,* or UL 723, *Test for Surface Burning Characteristics of Building Materials,* or for flame spread and flashover in accordance with NFPA 265. Films and other materials used as interior finish applied to surfaces of buildings should be tested for flame spread index and smoke developed index values in accordance with ASTM E84 or UL 723 or for heat and smoke release and flashover in accordance with NFPA 286. [*101*:A.10.3.1]

The test results from NFPA 701 are suitable for classification purposes but should not be used as input into fire models, because they are not generated in units suitable for engineering calculations. [*101*:A.10.3.1]

A.12.6.2.1 The Class I requirement associated with testing in accordance with NFPA 260 and the char length of not more than 1½ in. (38 mm) required with testing in accordance with NFPA 261 are indicators that the furniture item or mattress is resistant to a cigarette ignition. A fire that smolders for an excessive period of time without flaming can reduce the tenability within the room or area of fire origin without developing the temperatures necessary to operate automatic sprinklers. [*101*:A.10.3.2.1]

The test results from NFPA 260 and from NFPA 261 are suitable for classification purposes but should not be used as input into fire models because they are not generated in units suitable for engineering calculations. [*101*:A.10.3.2.1]

Traditionally, NFPA 260 was equivalent to ASTM E1353, *Standard Test Methods for Cigarette Ignition Resistance of Components of Upholstered Furniture,* and NFPA 261 was equivalent to ASTM E1352, *Standard Test Method for Cigarette Ignition Resistance of Mock-Up Upholstered Furniture Assemblies.* However, that changed temporarily when NFPA 260 and NFPA 261 adopted the new NIST standard reference material (SRM 1196) as the igniting cigarette and ASTM E1352 and ASTM E1353 did not, meaning that ASTM E1352 and ASTM E1353 were using commercial cigarettes that are low-ignition propensity and have a low likelihood of properly assessing smoldering potential. The 2016 editions of ASTM E1352 and ASTM E1353 adopted the NIST SRM 1196 cigarette as the igniting cigarette, making them, once more, equivalent to NFPA 261 and NFPA 260, respectively. [*101*:A.10.3.2.1]

A.12.6.2.2 The intent of the provisions of 12.6.2.2 is as follows:

(1) The peak heat release rate of not more than 80 kW by a single upholstered furniture item was chosen based on maintaining a tenable environment within the room of fire origin, and the sprinkler exception was developed because the sprinkler system helps to maintain tenable conditions, even if the single upholstered furniture item were to have a peak rate of heat release in excess of 80 kW.

(2) The total heat release of not more than 25 MJ by the single upholstered furniture item during the first 10 minutes of the test was established as an additional safeguard to protect against the adverse conditions that would be created by an upholstered furniture item that released its heat in other than the usual measured scenario, and the following should also be noted:

   (a) During the test for measurement of rate of heat release, the instantaneous heat release value usually peaks quickly and then quickly falls off, so as to create a triangle-shaped curve.

   (b) In the atypical case, if the heat release were to peak and remain steady at that elevated level, as opposed to quickly falling off, the 80 kW limit would not ensure safety.

   (c) Only a sprinkler exception is permitted in lieu of the test because of the ability of the sprinkler system to control the fire.

Actual test results for heat, smoke, and combustion product release from ASTM E1537, *Standard Test Method for Fire Testing of Upholstered Furniture,* might be suitable for use as input into fire models for performance-based design. Furthermore, California Technical Bulletin 133, "Flammability Test Procedure for Seating Furniture for Use in Public Occupancies," includes pass/fail criteria for a single upholstered furniture item of 80 kW peak heat release rate and 25 MJ total heat release over the first 10 minutes of the test.

[*101*:A.10.3.2.2]

A.12.6.3.1 The char length of not more than 2 in. (51 mm) required in 16 CFR 1632, "Standard for the Flammability of Mattresses and Mattress Pads" (FF 4-72, Amended), is an indicator that the mattress is resistant to a cigarette ignition. United States federal regulations require mattresses in this country to comply with 16 CFR 1632. [*101*:A.10.3.3.1]

A.12.6.3.2 The intent of the provisions of 12.6.3.2 is as follows:

(1) The peak heat release rate of not more than 100 kW by a single mattress was chosen based on maintaining a tenable environment within the room of fire origin, and the sprinkler exception was developed because the sprinkler system helps to maintain tenable conditions, even if the single mattress were to have a peak rate of heat release in excess of 100 kW.

(2) The total heat release of not more than 25 MJ by the single mattress during the first 10 minutes of the test was established as an additional safeguard to protect against the adverse conditions that would be created by a mattress that released its heat in other than the usual measured scenario, and the following should also be noted:

   (a) During the test for measurement of rate of heat release, the instantaneous heat release value usually peaks quickly and then quickly falls off, so as to create a triangle-shaped curve.

(b) In the atypical case, if the heat release were to peak and remain steady at that elevated level, as opposed to quickly falling off, the 100 kW limit would not ensure safety.

(c) Only a sprinkler exception is permitted in lieu of the test because of the ability of the sprinkler system to control the fire.

Actual test results for heat, smoke, and combustion product release from ASTM E1590, *Standard Test Method for Fire Testing of Mattresses,* might be suitable for use as input into fire models for performance-based design. Furthermore, California Technical Bulletin 129, "Flammability Test Procedure for Mattresses for Use in Public Buildings," includes pass/fail criteria for a single mattress of 100 kW peak heat release rate and 25 MJ total heat release over the first 10 minutes of test.

[*101*:A.10.3.3.2]

A.12.6.4 Natural cut Christmas trees that are not effectively treated to improve fire performance, ordinary crepe paper decorations, and pyroxylin plastic decorations might be classified as highly flammable. See 12.6.9 for requirements for combustible artificial decorative vegetation. See 12.6.9 for provisions for natural cut Christmas trees. [*101*:A.10.3.4]

A.12.6.6 Neither UL 1975, *Fire Tests for Foamed Plastics Used for Decorative Purposes,* nor NFPA 289 is intended for evaluating interior wall and ceiling finish materials. Actual test results for heat, smoke, and combustion product release from UL 1975 or from NFPA 289 might be suitable for use as input into fire models intended for performance-based design. [*101*:A.10.3.6]

A.12.6.9.6.4 A method to check for dryness is to grasp a tree branch with a reasonably firm pressure and pull your hand to you, allowing the branch to slip through your grasp. If the needles fall off readily, the tree does not have adequate moisture content and should be removed.

A.12.7.2 To ensure that a fire barrier is continuous, it is necessary to seal completely all openings where the fire barrier abuts other fire barriers, the exterior walls, the floor below, and the floor or ceiling above. In 12.7.2(2), the fire resistance rating of the bottom of the interstitial space is provided by that membrane alone. Ceilings of rated floor/ceiling and roof/ceiling assemblies do not necessarily provide the required fire resistance. [*101*:A.8.3.1.2]

A.12.7.5.1.1 Fire-resistance-rated glazing complying with 12.7.5, where not installed in a door, is considered a wall, not an opening protective. [*101*:A.8.3.2.1.1]

A.12.7.6.2.2 Longer ratings might be required where opening protectives are provided for property protection as well as life safety. NFPA 80 should be consulted for standard practice in the selection and installation of fire door assemblies and fire window assemblies. [*101*:A.8.3.3.2.2]

A vision panel in a fire door is not a fire window, and, thus, it is not the intent of the "NP" notations in the "Fire Window Assemblies" column of Table 12.7.6.2.2 to prohibit vision panels in fire doors. [*101*:A.8.3.3.2.2]

Table 12.7.6.2.2 with regard to glazing is intended for new construction and could have limited application to existing glazing installations. For example, existing vision panels of 100 in.^{2} (0.065 m^2) of wired glass in 60-minute and 90-minute doors and existing vision panels of 1296 in.^{2} (0.84 m^2) wired glass in doors 45 minutes or less have been accepted. [*101*:A.8.3.3.2.2]

Historically, installations of wired glass did not require marking. There could be existing installations of other glazing products used as opening protectives (e.g., vision panels, side lights, or transom panels) that also might not have markings. It is the building owner's responsibility to provide documentation acceptable to the AHJ regarding the product used and its compliance with the applicable provisions of this *Code.* [*101*:A.8.3.3.2.2]

Existing fire windows, where permitted, were traditionally allowed to have up to 1296 in.^{2} (0.84 m^2) of wired glass per panel. [*101*:A.8.3.3.2.2]

A.12.7.6.3 Some door assemblies have been tested to meet the conditions of acceptance of ASTM E119, *Standard Test Methods for Fire Tests of Building Construction and Materials,* or UL 263, *Fire Tests of Building Construction and Materials.* Where such assemblies are used, the provisions of 12.7.5 should be applied instead of those of 12.7.6.3. [*101*:A.8.3.3.3]

In existing installations, steel door frames that are well set in the wall might be judged as acceptable even if the frame label is not legible. [*101*:A.8.3.3.3]

A.12.7.6.3.1 Where a door or door frame is not required to be fire protection rated and is equipped with a fire protection listing label, the door and the door frame are not required to comply with NFPA 80. [*101*:8.3.3.3.1]

A.12.7.6.5.3 Some doors and glazing assemblies have been tested to meet the conditions of acceptance of ASTM E119, *Standard Test Methods for Fire Tests of Building Construction and Materials,* or UL 263, *Fire Tests of Building Construction and Materials.* Where such assemblies are used, the provisions of 12.7.5 should be applied instead of those of 12.7.6.6.6. [*101*:A.8.3.3.5.3]

Δ **A.12.7.6.6.6** Some window assemblies have been tested to meet the conditions of acceptance of ASTM E119, *Standard Test Methods for Fire Tests of Building Construction and Materials,* or UL 263, *Fire Tests of Building Construction and Materials.* Where such assemblies are used, the provisions of 12.7.5 should be applied instead of those of 12.7.6.6.6. [*101*:A.8.3.3.6.6]

A.12.7.8.7.3(1)(c) Criteria associated with fireblocking can be found in 8.14.2 of *NFPA 5000.* [*101*:A.8.3.4.7.3(1)(c)]

A.12.7.9.4 The provisions of 12.7.9.4 are intended to restrict the interior vertical passage of flame and hot gases from one floor to another at the location where the floor intersects the exterior wall assembly. The requirements of 12.7.9.4 mandate sealing the opening between a floor and an exterior wall assembly to provide the same fire performance as that required for the floor. ASTM E2307, *Standard Test Method for Determining Fire Resistance of Perimeter Fire Barrier Systems Using Intermediate-Scale, Multi-story Test Apparatus,* is a test method for evaluating the performance of perimeter fire barrier systems. Some laboratories have tested and listed perimeter fire barrier systems essentially in accordance with the ASTM method. The ASTM test method evaluates the performance of perimeter fire barrier systems in terms of heat transfer and fire spread inside a building through the floor/exterior wall intersection. The current test method does not assess the ability of perimeter fire barrier systems to prevent the spread of fire from story to story via the exterior. However, some laboratories have included additional temperature measurement criteria in their evaluation of the exterior wall and evaluation of vision glass breakage as additional pass/fail criteria in an attempt to at least partially address this "leapfrog" effect. [*101*:A.8.3.5.4]

A.12.8.1 Although a smoke partition is intended to limit the free movement of smoke, it is not intended to provide an area that would be free of smoke. [*101*:A.8.4.1]

A.12.8.2(2) The provision for terminating the smoke partition at the ceiling is not intended to prevent the wall from extending above the ceiling. [*101*:8.4.2(2)]

An architectural, exposed, suspended-grid acoustical tile ceiling with penetrations for sprinklers, ducted HVAC supply and return-air diffusers, speakers, and recessed light fixtures is capable of limiting the transfer of smoke. [*101*:A.8.4.2(2)]

A.12.8.3.4 Gasketing of doors should not be necessary, as the clearances in NFPA 80 effectively achieve resistance to the passage of smoke if the door is relatively tight-fitting. [*101*:A.8.4.3.4]

A.12.8.6.2 An air-transfer opening, as defined in NFPA 90A, is an opening designed to allow the movement of environmental air between two contiguous spaces. [*101*:A.8.4.6.2]

A.12.9.1 Wherever smoke barriers and doors therein require a degree of fire resistance, as specified by requirements in the various occupancy chapters (Chapter 12 through Chapter 42 of NFPA *101*), the construction should be a fire barrier that has been specified to limit the spread of fire and restrict the movement of smoke. [*101*:A.8.5.1]

Although a smoke barrier is intended to restrict the movement of smoke, it might not result in tenability throughout the adjacent smoke compartment. The adjacent smoke compartment should be safer than the area on the fire side, thus allowing building occupants to move to that area. Eventually, evacuation from the adjacent smoke compartment might be required. [*101*:A.8.5.1]

A.12.9.2 To ensure that a smoke barrier is continuous, it is necessary to seal completely all openings where the smoke barrier abuts other smoke barriers, fire barriers, exterior walls, the floor below, and the floor or ceiling above. It is not the intent to prohibit a smoke barrier from stopping at a fire barrier if the fire barrier meets the requirements of a smoke barrier (i.e., the fire barrier is a combination smoke barrier/fire barrier). [*101*:A.8.5.2]

A.12.9.4.1 For additional information on the installation of smoke-control door assemblies, see NFPA 105. [*101*:A.8.5.4.1]

A.12.9.4.4 Where, because of operational necessity, it is desired to have smoke barrier doors that are usually open, such doors should be provided with hold-open devices that are activated to close the doors by means of the operation of smoke detectors and other alarm functions. [*101*:A.8.5.4.4]

A.13.1.3.2 It is intended that the requirements in 13.1.3.1.2 be applied to retesting of any integrated systems following repair or replacement of equipment in lieu of applying retesting provisions in NFPA 4. [*101*:A.9.11.4.2]

N **A.13.1.9** A generally accepted practice is for critical deficiencies to be corrected or repaired within 30 days, noncritical deficiencies should be corrected or repaired within 90 days, and impairments should be corrected as soon as practical.

A.13.1.12 Such safeguards or fire safety equipment can include, but should not be limited to, automatic fire alarm systems, automatic sprinkler or water spray systems, standpipe and hose, fixed or portable fire extinguishers, breathing apparatus, manual or automatic covers, smoke and heat vents, and carbon dioxide, foam, halogenated, dry chemical, or other special fire-extinguishing systems.

A.13.2.2.2(3) Building height should be measured in accordance with the building code adopted in the jurisdiction.

A.13.2.2.5 It is not the intent of 13.2.2.5 to permit the removal of portions of the existing standpipe system other than hose lines, and that such remaining system components be maintained and available for use by the fire department or other appropriate fire suppression personnel.

N **A.13.2.3.4.3** After the tragic February 23, 1991, One Meridian Plaza fire, the maximum standpipe pressure requirements were adjusted to better reflect national fire service operating pressures based on the recommendations found in USFA-TR-049, "Highrise Office Building Fire One Meridian Plaza." The intent of 13.2.3.4.3 is to afford the AHJ the option of utilizing those higher pressures adopted in NFPA 14 only where they do not exceed the current 175 psi (12.1 bar) maximum for hose valve outlet pressure.

A.13.3.1.1 This *Code* contains requirements for automatic sprinkler protection that might not be required by other NFPA codes. These requirements are included in this *Code* from a property protection standpoint in an effort to reduce property damage due to fires as well as to reduce the costs of manual fire suppression in years to come.

A.13.3.1.6 Properly designed automatic sprinkler systems provide the dual function of both automatic alarms and automatic extinguishment. Dual function is not provided in those cases where early detection of incipient fire and early notification of occupants are needed to initiate actions in behalf of life safety earlier than can be expected from heat-sensitive fire detectors. [*101*:A.9.7.1.4]

N **A.13.3.1.8.1.1** Valve supervisory switches, pressure switches, and waterflow switches, are examples of supervisory attachments, or more appropriately defined by *NFPA 72* as supervisory signal initiating devices. System components and parameters that are required to be supervised should also include, but not be limited to, levels and temperatures of water in tanks, tank pressure, and air pressure on dry-pipe and preaction valves.

A.13.3.2.5.3(1) It is the intent to permit a single multipurpose room of less than 12,000 ft^2 (1115 m^2) to have certain small rooms as part of the single room. These rooms could be a kitchen, an office, an equipment room, and the like. It is also the intent that an addition could be made to an existing building, without requiring that the existing building be sprinklered, where both the new and existing buildings have independent means of egress and a fire-rated separation is provided to isolate one building from the other. [*101*:A.12.3.5.3(1)]

A school gymnasium with egress independent of, and separated from, the school would be included in this exception, as would a function hall attached to a church with a similar egress arrangement. [*101*:A.12.3.5.3(1)]

A.13.3.2.5.3(3) Examples of low fire hazard uses include spectator sporting events, concerts, and performances on platforms. [*101*:A.12.3.5.3(3)]

The following uses are not low fire hazard uses: concerts and performances on stages; tradeshows; exhibition and display of combustible items; displays of vehicles, boats, or similar items; or events using open flames or pyrotechnic effects. [*101*:A.12.3.5.3(3)]

A.13.3.2.9.1 In areas where the replenishment of water supplies is not immediately available from on-site sources, alternate provisions for the water-fill rate requirements of NFPA 13 and NFPA 22 that are acceptable to the AHJ should be provided. Appropriate means for the replenishment of these supplies from other sources, such as fire department tankers, public safety organizations, or other independent contractors should be incorporated into the overall fire safety plan of the facility. [*101*:A.18.3.5.1]

With automatic sprinkler protection required throughout new health care facilities and quick-response sprinklers required in smoke compartments containing patient sleeping rooms, a fire and its life-threatening by-products can be reduced, thereby allowing the defend-in-place concept to continue. The difficulty in maintaining the proper integrity of life safety elements has been considered, and it has been judged that the probability of a sprinkler system operating as designed is equal to or greater than other life safety features. [*101*:A.18.3.5.1]

A.13.3.2.9.4 The requirements for use of quick-response sprinklers intend that quick-response sprinklers be the predominant type of sprinkler installed in the smoke compartment. It is recognized, however, that quick-response sprinklers might not be approved for installation in all areas such as those where NFPA 13 requires sprinklers of the intermediate- or high-temperature classification. It is not the intent of the 13.3.2.9.4 requirements to prohibit the use of standard sprinklers in limited areas of a smoke compartment where intermediate- or high-temperature sprinklers are required. [*101*:A.18.3.5.6]

Residential sprinklers are considered acceptable in patient sleeping rooms of all health care facilities, even though not specifically listed for this purpose in all cases. [*101*:A.18.3.5.6]

Where the installation of quick-response sprinklers is impracticable in patient sleeping room areas, appropriate equivalent protection features acceptable to the AHJ should be provided. It is recognized that the use of quick-response sprinklers might be limited in facilities housing certain types of patients or by the installation limitations of quick-response sprinklers. [*101*:A.18.3.5.6]

A.13.3.2.9.5 This exception is limited to hospitals, as nursing homes and many limited care facilities might have more combustibles within the closets. The limited amount of clothing found in the small clothes closets in hospital patient rooms is typically far less than the amount of combustibles in casework cabinets that do not require sprinkler protection, such as nurse servers. In many hospitals, especially new hospitals, it is difficult to make a distinction between clothes closets and cabinet work. The exception is far more restrictive than similar exceptions for hotels and apartment buildings. NFPA 13 already permits the omission of sprinklers in wardrobes. It is not the intent of 13.3.2.9.5 to affect the wardrobe provisions of NFPA 13. It is the intent that the sprinkler protection in the room covers the closet as if there were no door on the closet. [*101*:A.18.3.5.10]

A.13.3.2.9.6 For the proper operation of sprinkler systems, cubicle curtains and sprinkler locations need to be coordinated. Improperly designed systems might obstruct the sprinkler spray from reaching the fire or might shield the heat from the sprinkler. Many options are available to the designer including, but not limited to, hanging the cubicle curtains 18 in. (455 mm) below the sprinkler deflector; using a ½ in. (13 mm) diagonal mesh or a 70 percent open weave top panel that extends 18 in. (455 mm) below the sprinkler deflector; or designing the system to have a horizontal and minimum vertical distance that meets the requirements of NFPA 13. The test data that form the basis of the NFPA 13 requirements are from fire tests with sprinkler discharge that penetrated a single privacy curtain. [*101*:A.18.3.5.11]

A.13.3.2.10.7 It is not the intent to require existing standard sprinklers in existing sprinkler systems to be replaced with listed quick-response or listed residential sprinklers. It is the intent that new sprinkler systems installed in existing buildings comply with the requirements of Chapter 18 of NFPA *101*, including 18.3.5.6. [*101*:A.19.3.5.4]

A.13.3.2.10.9 It is intended that any valve that controls automatic sprinklers in the building or portions of the building, including sectional and floor control valves, be electrically supervised. Valves that control isolated sprinkler heads, such as in laundry and trash chutes, are not required to be electrically supervised. Appropriate means should be provided to ensure that valves that are not electrically supervised remain open. [*101*:A.19.3.5.7]

A.13.3.2.10.10 The provisions of 13.3.2.10.10(6) and 13.3.2.10.10(7) are not intended to supplant NFPA 13, which requires that residential sprinklers with more than a 10°F (5.6°C) difference in temperature rating not be mixed within a room. Currently there are no additional prohibitions in NFPA 13 on the mixing of sprinklers having different thermal response characteristics. Conversely, there are no design parameters to make practical the mixing of residential and other types of sprinklers. [*101*:A.19.3.5.8]

Residential sprinklers are considered acceptable in patient sleeping rooms of all health care facilities, even though not specifically listed for this purpose in all cases. [*101*:A.19.3.5.8]

A.13.3.2.10.10(6) It is not the intent of the *Code* to permit standard-response sprinklers to meet the criteria of 13.3.2.10.10 just because the sprinklers were installed before quick-response sprinklers were invented or listed. The intent of 13.3.2.10.10(6) is to permit older quick-response systems to be credited, even though there might be some standard-response sprinklers in existence due to the fact that quick-response sprinklers were unavailable for those specific locations at the time. For example, in the early days of quick-response sprinklers, there were no high-temperature quick-response sprinklers available. [*101*:A.19.3.5.8(6)]

A.13.3.2.10.12 This exception is limited to hospitals, as nursing homes and many limited care facilities might have more combustibles within the closets. The limited amount of clothing found in the small clothes closets in hospital patient rooms is typically far less than the amount of combustibles in casework cabinets that do not require sprinkler protection, such as nurse servers. In many hospitals, especially new hospitals, it is difficult to make a distinction between clothes closets and cabinet work. The exception is far more restrictive than similar exceptions for hotels and apartment buildings. NFPA 13 already permits the omission of sprinklers in wardrobes. It is not the intent of 13.3.2.10.12 to affect the wardrobe provisions of NFPA 13. It is the intent that the sprinkler protection in the room covers the closet as if there were no door on the closet. [*101*:A.19.3.5.10]

A.13.3.2.10.13 For the proper operation of sprinkler systems, cubicle curtains and sprinkler locations need to be coordinated. Improperly designed systems might obstruct the sprinkler spray from reaching the fire or might shield the heat from the sprinkler. Many options are available to the designer including, but not limited to, hanging the cubicle curtains 18 in. (455 mm) below the sprinkler deflector; using ½ in. (13 mm) diagonal mesh or a 70 percent open weave top panel that extends 18 in. (455 mm) below the sprinkler deflector; or designing the system to have a horizontal and minimum vertical distance that meets the requirements of NFPA 13. The test data that forms the basis of the NFPA 13 requirements is from fire tests with sprinkler discharge that penetrated a single privacy curtain. [*101*:A.19.3.5.11]

A.13.3.2.12.1 Where the openings in ceilings or partitions are ¼ in. (6.3 mm) or larger in the smallest dimension, where the thickness or depth of the material does not exceed the smallest dimension of the openings, and where such openings constitute not less than 70 percent of the area of the ceiling or partition material, the disruption of sprinkler spray patterns is permitted to be disregarded. [*101*:A.23.3.5.2]

A.13.3.2.14.2 Although not required by NFPA *101*, the use of residential sprinklers or quick-response sprinklers is encouraged for new installations of sprinkler systems within dwelling units, apartments, and guest rooms. Caution should be exercised, as the system needs to be designed for the sprinkler being used. [*101*:A.29.3.5.3]

A.13.3.2.15.3 The 12 ft² (1.1 m²) closet sprinkler exemption differs from requirements in NFPA 13 because fire loss data supports the long-standing position of NFPA *101*, since the 1976 edition of NFPA *101*, to omit sprinklers from such closets. The provision is further supported by the lack of losses in buildings protected in accordance with NFPA 13D and NFPA 13R which permit the omission of sprinklers from closets not exceeding 24 ft² (2.2 m²). [*101*:A.30.3.5.3]

A.13.3.2.16.1 Although not required by NFPA *101*, the use of residential sprinklers or quick-response sprinklers is encouraged for new installations of sprinkler systems within dwelling units, apartments, and guest rooms. Caution should be exercised, because the system needs to be designed for the sprinkler being used. [*101*:A.31.3.5.2]

A.13.3.2.16.3 NFPA *101* and NFPA 13 both allow sprinklers to be omitted in small bathrooms in dwelling units. Historically, NFPA 13 sometimes differed in this requirement. Maintaining this provision in NFPA *101* allows all previously approved sprinkler installations to remain compliant. [*101*:A.31.3.5.4]

A.13.3.2.16.7 For example, if an Option 3 sprinkler system were being used to justify use of Class C wall finish in an exit enclosure, the sprinkler system would need to be extended into the exit enclosure, even if the rest of the requirements for Option 3 did not require the sprinklers in the exit enclosure. [*101*:A.31.3.5.8]

A.13.3.2.17.2.3 The decision to permit the use of the criteria from NFPA 13D in these occupancies is based on the following:

(1) The desire to obtain a level of fire suppression and control that is approximately equivalent to that delivered by residential facilities protected by such systems (*see A.1.1 in NFPA 13D*)
(2) The fact that potential fire exposure and challenge to the suppression system in a small lodging and rooming occupancy is of the same nature and no more severe than that found in residences

[*101*:A.26.3.6.2.3]

A.13.3.2.19.2.1 Where any provision requires the use of an automatic sprinkler system in accordance with 13.3.2.19.2, the provision of 13.3.2.19.2.2 is not permitted to be used. [*101*:A.32.2.3.5.1]

A.13.3.2.19.2.2 Where a facility utilizing the provision of 13.3.2.19.2.2 contains residents who can no longer comply with the 3-minute evacuation response, 33.1.8 of NFPA *101* requires the facility to comply with the requirements for new construction, including automatic sprinkler protection. (See also A.33.1.8 of NFPA *101*.) [*101*:A.32.2.3.5.2]

Δ **A.13.3.2.19.2.3.2** The decision to permit the use of the criteria from NFPA 13D in these occupancies is based on the following:

(1) The desire to obtain a level of fire suppression and control approximately equivalent to that delivered by residential facilities protected by such systems (*see A.1.1 in NFPA 13D*)
(2) The fact that potential fire exposure and challenge to the suppression system in a small board and care facility are of the same nature and are no more severe than those found in residences

[*101*:A.32.2.3.5.3.2]

Chapter 13 permits the use of NFPA 13D and NFPA 13R outside of their scopes. This permission is based on a review of the occupancy and a recognition that the fires in board and care facilities are similar to those of other residential occupancies and that the level of protection is appropriate. The requirements of NFPA 13D and NFPA 13R have been supplemented with requirements for additional water supplies to compensate for the special needs of the board and care occupancy. [*101*:A.32.2.3.5.3.2]

NFPA 13D contains additional requirements for a piping system serving both sprinkler and domestic needs. [*101*:A.32.2.3.5.3.2]

A.13.3.2.20.1.1 It is intended that this requirement apply to existing small facilities that are converted to large facilities. [*101*:A.33.3.3.5.1]

Chapter 13 permits the use of NFPA 13D and NFPA 13R outside of their scopes. This permission is based on a review of the occupancy and a recognition that the fires in board and care facilities are similar to those of other residential occupancies and that the level of protection is appropriate. In some circumstances, such as those for impractical evacuation capabilities, the requirements of NFPA 13D and NFPA 13R have been supplemented with requirements for additional water supplies to compensate for the special needs of the board and care occupancy. [*101*:A.33.3.3.5.1]

Δ **A.13.3.2.20.2.1.1** The decision to permit the use of the criteria from NFPA 13D in these occupancies is based on the following:

(1) The desire to obtain a level of fire suppression and control approximately equivalent to that delivered by residential facilities protected by such systems (see A.1.1 in NFPA 13D)
(2) The fact that potential fire exposure and challenge to the suppression system in a small board and care facility are of the same nature and are no more severe than those found in residences
[*101*:A.33.2.3.5.3.1]

Chapter 13 permits the use of NFPA 13D and NFPA 13R outside of their scopes. This permission is based on a review of the occupancy and a recognition that the fires in board and care facilities are similar to those of other residential occupancies and that the level of protection is appropriate. In some circumstances, such as those for impractical evacuation capabilities, the requirements of NFPA 13D and NFPA 13R have been supplemented with requirements for additional water supplies to compensate for the special needs of the board and care occupancy. [*101*:A.33.2.3.5.3.1]

A.13.3.2.24.2 The enabling legislation adopting this *Code* should specify a specific date for compliance with 13.3.2.24.2. Building owners and managers should be notified of this requirement within 180 days of code adoption. The following items should be considered by the AHJ as guidance in evaluating compliance plans:

(1) Shortage of qualified contractors to install sprinkler systems
(2) Impact on owners and tenants as a result of existing conditions contained in lease agreements
(3) Environmental constraints resulting from contaminated material being removed from limited areas of the building during installation of sprinklers and attendant activity
(4) Available time to install sprinklers in the occupied spaces
(5) Financial constraints of owners being able to fund the cost of installing automatic sprinklers with associated costs
(6) Ability of the owner to coordinate general building remodeling with the actual sprinkler retrofit process

A.13.3.2.24.2.3 Examples of retrofit schedules can include the following:

(1) Plan submitted and approved within 1 year; 33 percent of square footage completed within 4 years; 66 percent of square footage completed within 8 years; 100 percent of square footage completed within 12 years.
(2) Plans submitted and approved with 1 year; all common areas completed within 4 years; 50 percent of remaining area completed within 8 years; 100 percent of remaining area completed within 12 years.
(3) An alternative schedule can be approved by the AHJ that does not have any intermediary stages but has to be 100 percent complete within 8 years.

N **A.13.3.2.25** For the purpose of the requirements in 13.3.2.25.1 through 13.3.2.25.3, combustibles include all combustible materials in storage as well as noncombustible materials that are enclosed, encapsulated, or packaged in combustible materials.

A.13.3.2.25.2 Portions of structures that are subdivided by fire walls can be considered to be separate buildings for the purpose of applying this *Code*. Fire walls by their definition have sufficient structural stability to maintain the integrity of the wall in the event of the collapse of the building construction on either side of the wall.

Δ **A.13.3.3.4.1.1** Any portion of or all inspection, testing, and maintenance is permitted to be contracted out to an inspection, testing, and maintenance service company. [**25**:A.4.1.1]

Δ **A.13.3.3.4.1.1.3.1** Water-based systems rely on the adequacy and ongoing maintenance of drainage systems — such as roof drains, storm drains, and floor drains — during water flow as part of system tests. These systems are often used for purposes other than fire system testing and are not part of the fire protection system. They are often designed and maintained as part of a building's plumbing systems. [**25**:A.4.1.1.4]

A.13.3.3.4.1.1.4 Examples of designated representatives can include the occupant, management firm, or managing individual through specific provisions in the lease, written use agreement, or management contract. [**25**:A.4.1.1.5]

A.13.3.3.4.1.2 In areas that have the potential for freezing temperatures below the level that can be adequately protected by an allowable antifreeze solution, supplemental heat can be provided when temperatures fall below the level of the antifreeze solution. Other means of freeze protection for water-filled piping, including heated valve enclosures, heat tracing, insulation, or other methods are allowed by the applicable installation standard. Installation standards require heat tracing protecting fire protection piping against freezing to be supervised. [**25**:A.4.1.2]

A.13.3.3.4.1.2.1 In order to ensure compliance, the owner should verify that windows, skylights, doors, ventilators, other openings and closures, concealed spaces, unused attics, stair towers, roof houses, and low spaces under buildings do not expose water-filled piping to freezing. This should occur prior to the onset of cold weather and periodically thereafter. [**25**:A.4.1.2.1]

A.13.3.3.4.1.2.2 There are locations where water-filled piping was approved for installation and temperatures cannot be maintained at 40°F (4°C). For example, NFPA 13 permits water-filled piping in areas where temperatures are less than 40°F (4°C) and heat loss calculations verify that the system will not freeze. [**25**:A.4.1.2.2]

A.13.3.3.4.1.3 The components are not required to be open or exposed. Doors, removable panels, or valve pits can be permitted to satisfy the need for accessibility. Such equipment should not be obstructed by features such as walls, ducts, columns, direct burial, or stock storage. [**25**:A.4.1.3]

N **A.13.3.3.4.1.4.3** NFPA 13 permits systems designed with nitrogen to benefit from a higher *C* value. [**25**:A.4.1.4.3]

A.13.3.3.4.1.5 Needed corrections and repairs should be classified as an impairment, critical deficiency, or noncritical deficiency according to the effect on the fire protection system and the nature of the hazard protected. [**25**:A.4.1.5]

Impairments are the highest priority problem found during inspection, testing, and maintenance and should be corrected as soon as possible. The fire protection system cannot provide an adequate response to a fire, and implementation of impairment procedures outlined in 13.3.3.6 is required until the impairment is corrected. [**25**:A.4.1.5]

Critical deficiencies need to be corrected in a timely fashion. The fire protection system is still capable of performing, but its performance can be impacted and the implementation of impairment procedures might not be needed. However, special consideration must be given to the hazard in the determination of the classification. A deficiency that is critical for one hazard might be an impairment in another. [25:A.4.1.5]

Noncritical deficiencies do not affect the performance of the fire protection system but should be corrected in a reasonable time period so that the system can be properly inspected, tested, and maintained. [25:A.4.1.5]

Assembly occupancies, health care facilities, prisons, high-rise buildings, other occupancies where the life safety exposure is significant, or facilities that cannot be evacuated in a timely manner require special consideration. As an example, a nonfunctioning waterflow alarm might be considered a critical deficiency in a storage warehouse but an impairment in a hospital. [25:A.4.1.5]

High-hazard occupancies where early response to a fire is critical also require special consideration. A small number of painted sprinklers could be considered an impairment for a system protecting a high-hazard occupancy but might be considered a critical deficiency in a metal working shop. [25:A.4.1.5]

Classifications of needed corrections and repairs are shown in Table A.3.3.8 of NFPA 25. [25:A.4.1.5]

Δ **A.13.3.3.4.1.5.1** System deficiencies not explained by normal wear and tear, such as hydraulic shock or internal pipe corrosion, can often be indicators of system problems and should be investigated and evaluated by qualified personnel or engineer. Failure to address these issues could lead to catastrophic failure. Examples of deficiencies that can be caused by issues beyond normal wear and tear are as follows:

(1) Pressure gauge deficiencies, as follows:
   (a) Gauge not returning to zero
   (b) Gauge off scale
   (c) Gauge with bent needle
(2) Support devices deficiencies, as follows:
   (a) Bent hangers and/or rods
   (b) Hangers pulled out/off structure
   (c) Indication of pipe or hanger movement, such as the following:
      i. Hanger scrape marks on pipe, exposed pipe surface where pipe and hangers are painted
      ii. Firestop material damaged at pipe penetration of fire-rated assembly
(3) Unexplained system damage, as follows:
   (a) Unexplained system damage beyond normal wear and tear, such as holes or pinholes
   (b) Bent or broken shafts on valves
   (c) Bent or broken valve clappers
   (d) Unexplained leakage at branch lines, cross main, or feed main piping
   (e) Unexplained leakage at close nipples, pipe connections to fittings, and sprinklers
   (f) Loose bolts on flanges and couplings
(4) Fire pump deficiencies, as follows:
   (a) Fire pump driver out of alignment
   (b) Vibration of fire pump and/or driver
   (c) Unusual sprinkler system piping noises (i.e., sharp report, loud bang)

[25:A.4.1.5.1]

A.13.3.3.4.1.5.1.1 For examples of a reference sources containing lists of links to manufacturers' information regarding components that are recalled or part of a replacement program, see the manufacturers' websites or other applicable websites. [25:A.4.1.5.1.1]

A.13.3.3.4.1.5.1.2 Remedies for equipment under recall include entrance into a program for scheduled replacement. Such replacement or remedial product should be installed in accordance with the manufacturer's instructions and the appropriate NFPA installation standards. A recalled product is a product subject to a statute or administrative regulation specifically requiring the manufacturer, importer, distributor, wholesaler, or retailer of a product, or any combination of such entities, to recall the product, or a product voluntarily recalled by a combination of such entities. [25:A.4.1.5.1.2]

A.13.3.3.4.1.6 The inspections and tests specified in this *Code* do not address the adequacy of design criteria or the capability of the fire protection system to protect the building or its contents. It is assumed that the original system design and installation were appropriate for the occupancy and use of the building and were approved by all applicable AHJs. If no changes to the water supply or to the building or its use have transpired since it was originally occupied, no evaluation is required. If changes are contemplated, it is the owner's responsibility to arrange for the evaluation of the fire protection system(s). In such a case, Figure A.13.3.3.4.1.6 provides an example of a questionnaire that the owner could use. Where the inspections and tests specified in the *Code* have been contracted to a qualified inspection provider or contractor, it is not the role of the inspector or contractor to determine if any changes have been made or the subsequent evaluation of the fire protection system. The evaluation of any building changes should be conducted before any proposed change is incorporated and should utilize the appropriate installation standard and input from applicable AHJs. [25:A.4.1.6]

Fire protection systems should not be removed from service when the building is not in use; however, where a system that has been out of service for a prolonged period (such as in the case of idle or vacant properties) is returned to service, it is recommended that a responsible and experienced contractor be retained to perform all inspections and tests. [25:A.4.1.6]

A.13.3.3.4.1.6.2 Fire protection systems are designed and installed based on a specific set of circumstances and building uses. For example, the volume of water needed for a sprinkler system to control a fire in the built environment is based upon the intended use of the facility known at the time the sprinkler system was designed and installed. Revisions to properties used for storage represent one of the most common scenarios that impact the ability of systems to provide adequate protection. Some of the most common changes include raising the storage height, changing the storage method arrangement such as adding racks, installing solid shelves in rack structures, or decreasing the aisle widths between racks. Changes in product packaging with the use of foam inserts, bubble wrap, or other plastics or encapsulated storage can significantly increase the fire hazard. Changing from wood pallets to plastic pallets, converting to the use of plastic bin boxes, or revising or adding material handling systems such as conveyors could severely

Owner's Questionnaire

A. Is the building occupied? ☐ Yes ☐ No

B. Has the occupancy and hazard of contents remained the same since the last inspection? ☐ Yes ☐ No

C. Are all fire protection systems in service? ☐ Yes ☐ No

D. Has the system remained in service without modification since the last inspection? ☐ Yes ☐ No

E. Was the system free of actuation of devices or alarms since the last inspection? ☐ Yes ☐ No

Explain any "no" answers:

_____
_____
_____
_____
_____

Owner or Designated Representative (print)   Signature and Date

© 2019 National Fire Protection Association   NFPA 25

Δ FIGURE A.13.3.3.4.1.6 Owner's Questionnaire. [25:Figure A.4.1.6]

impact the effectiveness of the fire protection systems. [25:A.4.1.6.2]

A.13.3.3.4.1.7 See Annex E of NFPA 25 for an example of a hazard evaluation form. A hazard evaluation is not part of a system inspection. [25:A.4.1.7]

A.13.3.3.4.1.9 Systems installed in accordance with the 2007 and subsequent editions of NFPA 13 should have a general information sign. It is not the intent of the committee for a system to have both the information sign required by NFPA 25 and the general information sign required by NFPA 13. The information sign required by NFPA 25 is intended to be provided for systems installed prior to the 2007 edition of NFPA 13. Systems installed under the 2007 and subsequent editions of NFPA 13 should have a general information sign. [25:4.1.9]

A.13.3.3.4.1.10 The hydraulic design information sign should be secured to the riser with durable wire, chain, or equivalent. *(See Figure A.13.3.3.4.1.10.)* [25:A.5.2.5]

A.13.3.3.4.3.1 Typical records include, but are not limited to, valve inspections; flow, drain, and pump tests; and trip tests of dry pipe, deluge, and preaction valves. [25:A.4.3.1]

Acceptance test records should be retained for the life of the system or its special components. Subsequent test records should be retained for a period of 1 year after the next test. The comparison determines deterioration of system performance or condition and the need for further testing or maintenance. [25:A.4.3.1]

A.13.3.3.4.3.1.1 Records required to be maintained should be transferred to the new property owner when a property changes ownership. [25:A.4.3.1.1]

This system as shown on _____ company

print no. _____ dated _____

for _____

at _____ contract no. _____

is designed to discharge at a rate of _____

gpm per ft^2 (L/min per m^2) of floor area over a maximum

area of _____ ft^2 (m^2) when supplied

with water at a rate of _____ gpm (L/min)

at _____ psi (bar) at the base of the riser.

Hose stream allowance of _____

gpm (L/min) is included in the above.

FIGURE A.13.3.3.4.1.10 Sample Hydraulic Design Information Sign. [25:Figure A.5.2.5]

A.13.3.3.4.3.1.2 Computer programs that file inspection and test results should provide a means of comparing current and past results and should indicate the need for corrective maintenance or further testing. [25:A.4.3.1.2]

N **A.13.3.3.4.3.3** See Section B.3 of NFPA 25 for information regarding sample forms. [25:A.4.3.3]

N **A.13.3.3.5.1.1(4)** In the event of a fire, all sprinklers within the fire area should be inspected after the incident. In situations where the fire was quickly controlled or extinguished by one or two sprinklers, it might be necessary only to replace the activated sprinklers. Replacement sprinklers should be of the same make and model or have compatible performance characteristics (*see 13.3.3.5.1.2*). Soot-covered sprinklers should be replaced because deposits can result in the corrosion of operating parts. In the event of a substantial fire, special consideration should be given to also replacing the first ring of sprinklers surrounding the activated sprinklers due to the potential for excessive thermal exposure, which could weaken the response mechanisms. [25:A.5.4.1.1(4)]

N **A.13.3.3.5.1.2** Flexible hose connections are considered a fitting. [25:A.5.4.1.2]

A.13.3.3.5.1.3 To help in the replacement of like sprinklers, unique sprinkler identification numbers (SINs) are provided on all sprinklers manufactured after January 1, 2001. The SIN accounts for differences in K-factor, deflector characteristics, pressure rating, and thermal sensitivity. [25:A.5.4.1.3]

A.13.3.3.5.1.3.1 Old-style sprinklers are permitted to replace existing old-style sprinklers. Old-style sprinklers should not be used to replace standard sprinklers without a complete engineering review of the system. The old-style sprinkler is the type manufactured before 1953. It discharges approximately 40 percent of the water upward to the ceiling, and it can be installed in either the upright or pendent position. [25:A.5.4.1.3.1]

A.13.3.3.5.1.3.2 It is recognized that the flow and pressure available to the replacement sprinkler might be less than its current flow and pressure requirement. [25:A.5.4.1.3.2]

A.13.3.3.5.1.5 It is imperative that any replacement sprinkler have the same characteristics as the sprinkler being replaced. If the same temperature range, response characteristics, spacing requirements, flow rates, and K-factors cannot be obtained, a sprinkler with similar characteristics should be used, and the system should be evaluated to verify the sprinkler is appropriate for the intended use. With regard to response characteristics, matching identical response time index (RTI) and conductivity factors is not necessary unless special design considerations are given for those specific values. [25:A.5.4.1.5]

A.13.3.3.5.1.6 A minimum of two sprinklers of each type and temperature rating installed should be provided. [25:A.5.4.1.6]

A.13.3.3.5.1.6.5 One sprinkler wrench design can be appropriate for many types of sprinklers, and multiple wrenches of the same design should not be required. [25:A.5.4.1.6.5]

A.13.3.3.5.1.6.6.1 The minimum information in the list contained in the spare sprinkler cabinet should be marked with the following:

(1) General description of the sprinkler, including upright, pendent, residential, ESFR, and so forth

(2) Quantity of sprinklers that is to be maintained in the spare sprinkler cabinet.
[25:A.5.4.1.5.6.1]

An example of the list is shown in Figure A.13.3.3.5.1.6.6.1. [25:A.5.4.1.6.6.1]

A.13.3.3.5.1.7 Corrosion-resistant or specially coated sprinklers should be installed in locations where chemicals, moisture, or other corrosive vapors exist. [25:A.5.4.1.7]

A.13.3.3.5.1.10.1 Typical sandwich bags purchased in a grocery store are generally plastic, not cellophane. Plastic bags have a tendency to shrink and adhere to the sprinkler prior to sprinkler activation, creating the potential for disruption of sprinkler spray patterns. Bags placed over sprinklers need to be true cellophane or paper. [25:A.5.4.1.10.1]

A.13.3.3.5.2 Conversion of dry pipe systems to wet pipe systems on a seasonal basis causes corrosion and accumulation of foreign matter in the pipe system and loss of alarm service. [25:A.5.4.2]

A.13.3.3.6.3.1 A clearly visible tag alerts building occupants and the fire department that all or part of the water-based fire protection system is out of service. The tag should be weather resistant, plainly visible, and of sufficient size [typically 4 in. × 6 in. (100 mm × 150 mm)]. The tag should identify which system is impaired, the date and time impairment began, and the person responsible. Figure A.13.3.3.6.3.1 illustrates a typical impairment tag. [25:A.15.3.1]

A.13.3.3.6.3.2 An impairment tag should be placed on the fire department connection to alert responding firefighters of an abnormal condition. An impairment tag that is located on the system riser only could go unnoticed for an extended period if firefighters encounter difficulty in gaining access to the building or sprinkler control room. [25:A.15.3.2]

A.13.3.3.6.5 The need for temporary fire protection, termination of all hazardous operations, and frequency of inspections in the areas involved should be determined. All work possible should be done in advance to minimize the length of the impairment. Where possible, temporary feedlines should be used to maintain portions of systems while work is completed. [25:A.15.5]

Water-based fire protection systems should not be removed from service when the building is not in use. Where a system that has been out of service for a prolonged period, such as in

Sprinklers Contained in this Cabinet			
Sprinkler Identification, SIN	General Description	Temperature Rating, °F	Sprinkler Quantity Maintained
TY9128	Extended Coverage, K-25, upright	165	6
VK494	Residential concealed pendent	155	6
Issued: 8/31/19	Revised:		

△ **FIGURE A.13.3.3.5.1.6.6.1** Sample List. [25:Figure A.5.4.1.6.6.1]

ATTACH TO VALVE
• READ INSTRUCTIONS ON OTHER SIDE •

SPRINKLER VALVE
SHUT

THIS VALVE CONTROLS SPRINKLERS IN BUILDING(S):

SHUT BY (SIGNATURE) | DATE

→ After valve is opened, make 2 in. (50 mm) drain test. Drop in pressure should be normal. If pressure drop is extreme and does not build up, the system is impaired and immediate investigation is necessary.

DRAIN TEST RESULTS

STATIC PRESSURE psi (bar) | FLOWING PRESSURE psi (bar)

DRAIN TEST MADE BY (SIGNATURE) | DATE

FIGURE A.13.3.3.6.3.1 Sample Impairment Tag. [25:Figure A.15.3.1]

the case of idle or vacant properties, is returned to service, qualified personnel should be retained to inspect and test the systems. [**25:**A.15.5]

A.13.3.3.6.5.2(4)(b) A fire watch should consist of trained personnel who continuously patrol the affected area. Ready access to fire extinguishers and the ability to promptly notify the fire department are important items to consider. During the patrol of the area, the person should not only be looking for fire, but making sure that the other fire protection features of the building such as egress routes and alarm systems are available and functioning properly. [**25:**A.15.5.2(4)(b)]

A.13.3.3.6.5.2(4)(c) Temporary water supplies are possible from a number of sources, including use of a large-diameter hose from a fire hydrant to a fire department connection, use of a portable tank and a portable pump, or use of a standby fire department pumper and/or tanker. [**25:**A.15.5.2(4)(c)]

A.13.3.3.6.5.2(4)(d) Depending on the use and occupancy of the building, it could be enough in some circumstances to stop certain processes in the building or to cut off the flow of fuel to some machines. It is also helpful to implement "No Smoking" and "No Hot Work" (cutting, grinding, or welding) policies while the system is out of service because these activities are responsible for many fire ignitions. [**25:**A.15.5.2(4)(d)]

A.13.3.3.6.6 Emergency impairments include, but are not limited to, system leakage, interruption of water supply, frozen or ruptured piping, equipment failure, or other impairments found during inspection, testing, or maintenance activities. [**25:**A.15.6]

A.13.3.3.6.6.2 When one or more impairments are discovered during inspection, testing, and maintenance activities, the owner or owner's authorized representative should be notified in writing. See Figure A.13.3.3.6.6.2 for an example of written notification. [**25:**A.15.6.2]

Δ **A.13.3.3.6.7** Occasionally, fire protection systems in idle or vacant buildings are shut off and drained. When the equipment is eventually restored to service after a long period of not being maintained, it is recommended that qualified personnel or a qualified contractor perform the work. The following is an example of a procedure:

(1) All piping should be traced from the extremities of the system to the main connections with a careful check for blank gaskets in flanges, closed valves, corroded or damaged sprinklers, nozzles or piping, insecure or missing hangers, and insufficient support. Proper repairs or adjustments should be made, and needed extensions or alterations for the equipment should be completed.

(2) An air test at low pressure (40 psi) should be conducted prior to allowing water to fill the system. When the piping has been proven tight by passing the air test, water can be introduced slowly into the system, with proper precautions against damage by escape of water from previously undiscovered defects. When the system has been filled under normal service pressure, drain valve tests should be

IMPAIRMENT NOTICE

DURING A RECENT INSPECTION OF YOUR FIRE PROTECTION SYSTEM(S), AN *EMERGENCY IMPAIRMENT* WAS DISCOVERED AND INDICATED ON THE INSPECTION REPORT. AS DEFINED BY NFPA 25, AN *EMERGENCY IMPAIRMENT* IS "A CONDITION WHERE A WATER-BASED FIRE PROTECTION SYSTEM OR PORTION THEREOF IS OUT OF ORDER DUE TO AN UNEXPECTED OCCURRENCE, SUCH AS A RUPTURED PIPE, OPERATED SPRINKLER, OR AN INTERRUPTION OF WATER SUPPLY TO THE SYSTEM." NFPA 25 FURTHER STATES, "EMERGENCY IMPAIRMENTS INCLUDE BUT ARE NOT LIMITED TO SYSTEM LEAKAGE, INTERRUPTION OF WATER SUPPLY, FROZEN OR RUPTURED PIPING, AND EQUIPMENT FAILURE."

WE RECOMMEND THAT IMMEDIATE STEPS BE TAKEN, AS DESCRIBED IN THE ATTACHED COPY OF CHAPTER 15 OF NFPA 25, TO CORRECT THE FOLLOWING IMPAIRMENT(S) TO YOUR FIRE PROTECTION SYSTEM(S):

[ ] CONTROL VALVE SHUT. SYSTEM OUT OF SERVICE.
[ ] LOW WATER PRESSURE DURING FLOW TEST. POSSIBLE OBSTRUCTION IN WATER SUPPLY OR PARTIALLY SHUT VALVE.
[ ] PIPE(S) FROZEN.
[ ] PIPE(S) LEAKING.
[ ] PIPE(S) ARE OBSTRUCTED.
[ ] SYSTEM PIPING OR PORTIONS OF SYSTEM PIPING ARE DISCONNECTED.
[ ] FIRE DEPT. CONNECTION MISSING OR DAMAGED OR OBSTRUCTED.
[ ] DRY PIPE VALVE CANNOT BE RESET.
[ ] DRY PIPE SYSTEM QUICK OPENING DEVICE IS OUT OF SERVICE.
[ ] SPRINKLERS ARE PAINTED, CORRODED, DAMAGED, OR LOADED.
[ ] FIRE PUMP IS OUT OF SERVICE.
[ ] DETECTION/ACTUATION SYSTEM IS OUT OF SERVICE.
[ ] OTHER: _____

FIGURE A.13.3.3.6.6.2 Sample Impairment Notice. [25:Figure A.15.6.2]

made to detect any closed valve that possibly could have been overlooked. All available pipes should be flushed, and an obstruction investigation completed to make sure that the system is clear of debris.

(3) Where the system was known to have been damaged by freezing or where other extensive damage might have occurred, a full hydrostatic test can be performed in accordance with NFPA 13 to determine whether the system integrity has been maintained.

(4) Dry pipe valves, quick-opening devices, alarm valves, and all alarm connections should be examined, put in proper condition, and tested.

(5) Fire pumps, pressure and gravity tanks, reservoirs, and other water supply equipment should receive proper attention before being placed in service. Each supply should be tested separately and then together if they are designed to work together.

(6) All control valves should be operated from the closed to fully open position and should be left sealed, locked, or equipped with a tamper switch.

[25:A.15.7]

A.13.4.2 Isolation valves and control valves are considered to be identical when used in conjunction with a backflow prevention assembly. [20:A.4.18]

A.13.4.3.2 If a complete fire pump submittal package is available, it should provide for comparison of the equipment specified. Such a package should include an approved copy of the fire pump room general arrangement drawings, including the electrical layout, the layout of the pump and water source, the layout of the pump room drainage details, the pump foundation layout, and the mechanical layout for heat and ventilation. [20:A.14.2.4]

A.13.5.3 The installation of backflow prevention devices on services supplying water to existing fire protection systems can result in excessive pressure losses. Therefore, installation of backflow prevention devices to protect public health has to be accomplished with due regard for the implications on fire protection. The provisions of AWWA M14, *Backflow Prevention and Cross-Connection Control: Recommended Practices*, should be used as a guide for determining the appropriate protection for public health. Hydraulic calculations and water supply analysis should be conducted prior to installation to determine the impact on fire protection.

A.13.6.1.2 Employees expected or anticipated to use fire extinguishers should be instructed on the hazards of fighting fire, how to properly operate the fire extinguishers available, and what procedures to follow in alerting others to the fire emergency.

The intended application of footnote e in Table 13.6.1.2 is for warehouse areas that are generally unoccupied except by operators on forklifts or similar vehicles or occasional workers or maintenance personnel. The footnote is not intended to apply to office or process areas. Office and process areas have to be provided with fixed extinguishers in accordance with NFPA 10 and applicable provisions in this *Code*.

A.13.6.1.3.1 Listed and labeled halon portable fire extinguishers currently comply with Section 13.6 and have demonstrated compliance with the requirements of UL-1093, *Standard for Halogenated Agent Fire Extinguishers*, which also includes fire testing and rating criteria. As a result of the "Montreal Protocol on Substances that Deplete the Ozone Layer", UL has withdrawn UL-1093. This does not imply that extinguishers that are listed and labeled to the requirements of UL-1093 are unsafe for use as fire extinguishers, nor does it mean that UL or the EPA is requiring that halon extinguishers be removed from service. It does mean that UL will not accept new designs of halon extinguishers for testing or UL listing. It also means that no changes or updates are allowed to models that are currently listed and that had previously demonstrated compliance with UL 1093. [10:A.4.1.1]

Extinguisher manufacturers are allowed to manufacture their current design of UL-listed halon extinguishers with the UL listing mark until October 2025. Halon extinguishers currently in use will continue to be listed beyond the 2025 date and should be permitted to be used to comply with the requirements of NFPA 10 and this *Code* when installed, inspected, and maintained in accordance with NFPA 10 and this *Code*. [10:A.4.1.1]

A.13.6.1.3.2 AHJs should determine the acceptability and credibility of the organization listing or labeling fire extinguishers. Authorities should determine if the organization tests to all the requirements of NFPA 10. Factors such as the structure of the organization, its principal fields of endeavor, its reputation and established expertise, its involvement in the standards-writing process, and the extent of its follow-up service programs should all be assessed before recognition is given. [10:A.4.1.2]

The listing and labeling organization identification marking might be in the form of a symbol of the organization. The product category marking should identify the extinguisher, for example, "Carbon Dioxide Fire Extinguisher," "Dry Chemical Fire Extinguisher," or "Clean Agent Fire Extinguisher." Extinguisher ratings should indicate the classification of fire type, such as A, B, or C, and the associated fire size. An example of an extinguisher rating is 1-A: 5-B:C, which designates a Class A fire (wood) rating with an associated fire size of 1, as described in UL711, CAN/ULC-S508, *Standard for the Rating and Fire Testing of Fire Extinguishers*; a Class B fire (flammable liquid) rating with an associated fire size of 5, as described in UL711, CAN/ULC-S508; and a Class C compatible rating as described in UL711, CAN/ULC-S508. [10:A.4.1.2]

A.13.6.1.4 Federal OSHA regulations require that manufacturers communicate information as to the type of chemicals in a product that can be hazardous and the level of hazard. This information is contained in the MSDS created for each chemical or mixture of chemicals and is summarized on labels or tags attached to the product. Additionally, state and local authorities have enacted similar acts and regulations requiring identification of chemicals and hazardous ingredients in products. MSDSs for fire extinguisher agents are available on request from fire equipment dealers or distributors or the fire equipment manufacturer. [10:A.4.2]

The identification of contents information enables determination of the type of chemicals contained in the fire extinguisher and helps to resolve complications arising from an unusual use of the agent. The *Hazardous Materials Identification System (HMIS)*, developed by the American Coatings Association, uses a three-place format with numerical indexes from 0 to 4. The first place is for "toxic properties," the second place is for "flammability," and the third place is for "reactivity" with other chemicals. Most fire extinguishers have a 0 numerical index in the second and third places because they are nonflammable and relatively inert. [10:A.4.2]

Information on the HMIS can be obtained from Label Master, Inc., in Chicago, IL, or from the American Coatings Association in Washington, DC. Extinguisher contents information can be integrated into the standard fire extinguisher label in some form, or it can be on a separate label or tag. The following example is a typical chemical contents identification marking:

CONTENTS: ABC DRY CHEMICAL/HMIS 1-0-0
MUSCOVITE MICA, MONOAMMONIUM PHOSPHATE
AMMONIUM SULFATE/NUISANCE DUST
IRRITANT/CONTENTS UNDER PRESSURE
[Manufacturer's Name, Mailing Address, Phone Number]

[10:A.4.2]

Δ **A.13.6.1.5.2** Fire extinguishers manufactured by companies that are no longer in business can remain in use if they meet the requirements of NFPA 10 and this *Code* and are maintained in accordance with the manufacturer's service manual. When these extinguishers require recharging or maintenance and the required extinguishing agent or necessary repair parts are not available, the extinguishers should be removed from service. [10:A.4.4.2]

A.13.6.2.3.2.1 Examples of extinguishers for protecting Class A hazards are as follows:

(1) Water type
(2) Halogenated agent type *(For halogenated agent–type fire extinguishers, see 13.6.2.3.2.6.)*
(3) Multipurpose dry chemical type
(4) Wet chemical type

[10:A.5.3.2.1]

A.13.6.2.3.2.2 Examples of extinguishers for protecting Class B hazards are as follows:

(1) Aqueous film-forming foam (AFFF)
(2) Film-forming fluoroprotein foam (FFFP)
(3) Carbon dioxide
(4) Dry chemical type
(5) Halogenated agent type *(For halogenated agent–type fire extinguishers, see 13.6.2.3.2.6.)*

[10:A.5.3.2.2]

A.13.6.2.3.2.3 The use of dry chemical fire extinguishers on wet energized electrical equipment (such as rain-soaked utility poles, high-voltage switch gear, and transformers) could aggravate electrical leakage problems. The dry chemical in combination with moisture provides an electrical path that can reduce the effectiveness of insulation protection. The removal of all traces of dry chemical from such equipment after extinguishment is recommended. [10:A.5.3.2.3]

A.13.6.2.3.2.4 The following information pertains to Class D hazards:

(1) Chemical reaction between burning metals and many extinguishing agents (including water) can range from explosive to inconsequential, depending in part on the type, form, and quantity of metal involved. In general, the hazards from a metal fire are significantly increased when such extinguishing agents are applied. The advantages and limitations of a wide variety of commercially available metal fire extinguishing agents are discussed in NFPA 484 and in Section 6, Chapter 9, of the NFPA *Fire Protection Handbook*. The MSDS of the Class D hazard being protected or the extinguisher manufacturer should be consulted.
(2) The agents and fire extinguishers discussed in this section are of specialized types, and their use often involves special techniques peculiar to a particular combustible metal. A given agent will not necessarily control or extinguish all metal fires. Some agents are valuable in working with several metals; others are useful in combating only one type of metal fire. The AHJs should be consulted in each case to determine the desired protection for the particular hazard involved.
(3) Certain combustible metals require special extinguishing agents or techniques. See NFPA 484 for additional information. If there is doubt, NFPA 484 or the NFPA *Fire Protection Guide to Hazardous Materials* should be consulted. (NFPA 49 and NFPA 325 have been officially withdrawn from the *National Fire Codes*, but the information is contained in the NFPA *Fire Protection Guide to Hazardous Materials*.)
(4) Reference should be made to the manufacturer's recommendations for use and special techniques for extinguishing fires in various combustible metals.
(5) Fire of high intensity can occur in certain metals. Ignition is generally the result of frictional heating, exposure to moisture, or exposure from a fire in other combustible materials. The greatest hazard exists when these metals are in the molten state or in finely divided forms of dust, turnings, or shavings.

[10:A.5.3.2.4]

The properties of a wide variety of combustible metals and the agents available for extinguishing fires in these metals are discussed in NFPA 484, the NFPA *Fire Protection Handbook*, and the SFPE *Handbook of Fire Protection Engineering*. [10:A.5.3.2.4]

A.13.6.2.3.2.6 Halon agent is highly effective for extinguishing fire and evaporates after use, leaving no residue. Halon agent is, however, included in the Montreal Protocol list of controlled substances developed under the United Nations Environment Program. Where agents other than halon can satisfactorily protect the hazard, they should be used instead of halon. Halon use should be limited to extinguishment of unwanted fire; it should not be used for routine training of personnel. [10:A.5.3.2.6]

A.13.6.2.3.2.6.1 UL 2129, ULC/CAN-S566, *Standard for Halocarbon Clean Agent Fire Extinguishers*, and ULC/CAN-S512, *Standard for Halogenated Agent Hand and Wheeled Fire Extinguishers*, require halocarbon and halogenated agent nameplates to provide safety guidelines for avoiding overexposure to agent vapors when the agents are discharged into confined spaces. The UL minimum volume requirement for confined spaces is based on exposure to the agent in the absence of a fire and does not include considerations of fire or agent decomposition products. ULC/CAN-S512 has been withdrawn from the standards directory and although new listings to this standard are not anticipated, extinguishers listed prior to the Montreal Protocol are still listed. [10:A.5.3.2.6.1]

A.13.6.2.3.2.7 Wheeled fire extinguishers are available in capacities of 33 gal (125 L) for foam units and range from 30 lb to 350 lb (13.6 kg to 158.8 kg) for other types of extinguishers. These fire extinguishers are capable of delivering higher agent flow rates and greater agent stream range than normal portable-type fire extinguishers. Wheeled fire extinguishers are capable of furnishing increased fire-extinguishing effectiveness for high hazard areas and have added importance where a limited number of people are available. [**10**:A.5.3.2.7]

A.13.6.2.4.1.1 Light hazard occupancies can include some buildings or rooms occupied as offices, classrooms, churches, assembly halls, guest room areas of hotels or motels, and so forth. This classification anticipates that the majority of content items are either noncombustible or so arranged that a fire is not likely to spread rapidly. Small amounts of Class B flammables used for duplicating machines, art departments, and so forth, are included, provided that they are kept in closed containers and safely stored. [**10**:A.5.4.1.1]

A.13.6.2.4.1.2 Ordinary hazard occupancies could consist of dining areas, mercantile shops and allied storage, light manufacturing, research operations, auto showrooms, parking garages, workshop or support service areas of light hazard occupancies, and warehouses containing Class I or Class II commodities as defined by NFPA 13. [**10**:A.5.4.1.2]

A Class I commodity is defined by NFPA 13 as a noncombustible product that meets one of the following criteria:

(1) It is placed directly on wooden pallets.
(2) It is placed in single-layer corrugated cartons, with or without single-thickness cardboard dividers, with or without pallets.
(3) It is shrink-wrapped or paper-wrapped as a unit load, with or without pallets.

[**10**:A.5.4.1.2]

A Class II commodity is defined by NFPA 13 as a noncombustible product that is in slatted wooden crates, solid wood boxes, multiple-layered corrugated cartons, or equivalent combustible packaging material, with or without pallets. [**10**:A.5.4.1.2]

A.13.6.2.4.1.3 Extra hazard occupancies could consist of woodworking; vehicle repair; aircraft and boat servicing; cooking areas; individual product display showrooms; product convention center displays; and storage and manufacturing processes such as painting, dipping, and coating, including flammable liquid handling. Also included is warehousing or in-process storage of other than Class I and Class II commodities. [**10**:A.5.4.1.3]

N **A.13.6.2.4.2** All buildings have Class A fire hazards. In any occupancy, there could be a predominant hazard as well as special hazard areas requiring extinguishers with ratings to match those hazards. For example, a hospital will have need for Class A fire extinguishers covering patient rooms, corridors, offices, and so forth, but will need Class B fire extinguishers in laboratories and where flammable anesthetics are stored or handled, Class C fire extinguishers in electrical switch gear or generator rooms, and Class K extinguishers in kitchens. [**10**:A.5.5]

A.13.6.2.5.1.1 Pressurized flammable liquids and pressurized gas fires are considered to be a special hazard. Class B fire extinguishers containing agents other than dry chemical are relatively ineffective on this type of hazard due to stream and agent characteristics. The system used to rate the effectiveness of fire extinguishers on Class B fires (flammable liquids in depth) is not applicable to these types of hazards. It has been determined that special nozzle design and rates of agent application are required to cope with such hazards. [**10**:A.5.5.4.1]

A.13.6.2.5.1.1.1 A three-dimensional Class B fire involves Class B materials in motion, such as pouring, running, or dripping flammable liquids, and generally includes vertical as well as one or more, horizontal surfaces. Fires of this nature are considered to be a special hazard. The system used to rate fire extinguishers on Class B fires (flammable liquids in depth) is not directly applicable to this type of hazard. The installation of fixed systems should be considered where applicable. [**10**:A.5.5.4.2]

A.13.6.2.5.2(2) Where multiple extinguishers are utilized, simultaneous discharge from multiple locations to eliminate any blind spots created by an obstacle should be employed. [**10**:A.5.5.4.3(2)]

N **A.13.6.2.5.3** Examples of water-soluble flammable liquids include alcohols, acetone, esters, and ketones. [**10**:A.5.5.4.4]

A.13.6.2.5.4 Fire extinguishers for cooking media (vegetable or animal oils and fats) traditionally followed Table 6.3.1.1 of NFPA 10 for extra hazard, requiring a minimum 40-B -rated sodium bicarbonate or potassium bicarbonate dry chemical extinguisher. The evolution of high-efficiency cooking appliances and the change to hotter-burning vegetable shortening has created a more severe fire hazard. Testing has shown that wet chemical extinguishers have several times the cooking fire-extinguishing capability of a minimum 40-B rated sodium bicarbonate or potassium bicarbonate dry chemical extinguisher, which has prompted the creation of a new classification and a new listing test protocol. The test protocol is found in UL 711, CAN/ULC-S508. [**10**:A.5.5.4.5]

See NFPA 96 for further information. Persons in cooking areas need specific training on the use of extinguishers as an essential step for personal safety. Class K fire extinguishers equipped with extended wand–type discharge devices should not be used in a manner that results in subsurface injection of wet chemical extinguishing agents into hot cooking media. Subsurface injection causes a thermodynamic reaction comparable to an explosion. Class K fire extinguishers are no longer manufactured with extended wand–type discharge devices. [**10**:A.5.5.4.5]

A.13.6.2.5.4.3 Figure A.13.6.2.5.4.3(a) and Figure A.13.6.2.5.4.3(b) show the recommended wording for the Class K placard. Recommended size is 7⅝ in. × 11 in. (194 mm × 279 mm). [**10**:A.5.5.5.3]

A.13.6.2.5.5 Occupancies are required to have extinguishers installed, this section is applicable to areas where the electronic equipment is located. Delicate electronic equipment includes, but is not limited to, telecommunications, computers, servers, robotics, and reproduction equipment. [**10**:A.5.5.4.6]

Extinguishers provided for the protection of delicate electronic equipment are typically halogenated agent and water mist extinguishers with Class A ratings [**10**:A.5.5.4.6]

A.13.6.2.5.5.2 Dry chemical residue will probably not be able to be completely and immediately removed, and, in addition, multipurpose dry chemical exposed to temperatures in excess of 250°F (121°C) or relative humidity in excess of 50 percent can cause corrosion. The use of other clean agent types of extinguishing agents can help to minimize or eliminate collateral equipment damage and associated clean-up concerns. [**10**:A.5.5.4.6.2]

△ FIGURE A.13.6.2.5.4.3(a)   Typical Class K Placard in English and Spanish. [10:Figure A.5.5.4.5.3(a)]

△ FIGURE A.13.6.2.5.4.3(b)   Typical Class K Placard in English and French. [10:Figure A.5.5.4.5.3(b)]

A.13.6.2.5.7.2 Other nonlisted agents can be used if acceptable to the AHJ. Other nonlisted agents include specially dried sand, dolomite, soda ash, lithium chloride, talc, foundry flux, and zirconium silicate or other agents shown to be effective. Consult NFPA 484 for use and limitations of these agents and other nonlisted alternatives. [**10:**A.5.5.4.8.2]

Δ **A.13.6.2.6.1** Where portable fire extinguishers are required to be installed, the following documents should be reviewed for the occupancies outlined in their respective scopes:

(1) NFPA 77
(2) NFPA 402
(3) NFPA 610
(4) NFPA 850
(5) NFPA 921
(6) NFPA 1452

[**10:**A.5.5.5.1]

A.13.6.3.1.1 The following items affect distribution of portable fire extinguishers:

(1) Area and arrangement of the building occupancy conditions
(2) Severity of the hazard
(3) Anticipated classes of fire
(4) Other protective systems or devices
(5) Distances to be traveled to reach fire extinguishers

[**10:**A.6.1.1]

In addition, the following factors should be considered:

(1) Anticipated rate of fire spread
(2) Intensity and rate of heat development
(3) Smoke contributed by the burning materials

[**10:**A.6.1.1]

Wheeled fire extinguishers have additional agent and range and should be considered for areas where the additional protection is needed. Portable fire extinguishers offer the occupant a means to assist in evacuation of a building or occupancy. They are useful to knock down the fire if it occurs along the evacuation route. If possible, the individual property should be surveyed for actual protection requirements. [**10:**A.6.1.1]

A.13.6.3.1.3.3.2 The primary means for identifying locations of fire extinguishers should be by the installation of the fire extinguisher signs that are specifically designed for that purpose. Examples of other means of identifying the fire extinguisher locations include arrows, lights, or coding of the wall or column. [**10:**A.6.1.3.3.2]

Δ **A.13.6.3.1.3.4** In situations where it is necessary that fire extinguishers be provided temporarily, a good practice is to provide portable stands on which the fire extinguishers can be installed. Portable stands should be designed to comply with the mounting heights for extinguishers. *(See 13.6.3.1.3.9.)* [**10:**A.6.1.3.4]

N **A.13.6.3.1.3.4(1)** Hangers not intended for extinguishers should not be installed [e.g., a 5 lb (2.3 kg) extinguisher hanger should not be used with a 10 lb (4.5 kg) extinguisher]. [**10:**A.6.1.3.4(1)]

N **A.13.6.3.1.3.10.3** An example of an inventory control label could be a label or sticker with a number, symbol, or barcode that correlates with a specific extinguisher's details and location. [**10:**A.6.1.3.10.3]

A.13.6.3.1.3.11.4 Vented fire extinguisher cabinets should utilize tinted glass and should be constructed to prevent the entrance of insects and the accumulation of water. Vented fire extinguisher cabinets constructed in this manner lower the maximum internal temperature by 10°F to 15°F (5.6°C to 8.3°C). [**10:**A.6.1.3.11.4]

A.13.6.3.1.3.11.6 Certain fire resistance–rated cabinets are intended for installation into fire resistance–rated walls. Cabinets that are not fire resistance–rated make the entire fire resistance–rated wall noncompliant, so only surface-mounted cabinets or fire resistance–rated cabinets are appropriate for installation in fire resistance–rated walls. [**10:**A.6.1.3.11.6]

A.13.6.3.1.3.12 The following precautions should be noted where fire extinguishers are located in areas that have temperatures outside the range of 40°F to 120°F (4°C to 49°C):

(1) AFFF and FFFP fire extinguishers cannot be protected against temperatures below 40°F (4°C) by adding an antifreeze charge, because it tends to destroy the effectiveness of the extinguishing agent.
(2) Plain water fire extinguishers should not be protected against temperatures below 40°F (4°C) with ethylene glycol antifreeze. Calcium chloride solutions should not be used in stainless steel fire extinguishers.
(3) Fire extinguishers installed in machinery compartments, diesel locomotives, automotive equipment, marine engine compartments, and hot processing facilities can easily be subjected to temperatures above 120°F (49°C). Selection of fire extinguishers for hazard areas with temperatures above the listed limits should be made on the basis of recommendations by manufacturers of this equipment.

[**10:**A.6.1.3.12]

A.13.6.3.4 Electrical equipment should be de-energized as soon as possible to prevent reignition. [**10:**A.6.4]

A.13.6.3.5.3 See NFPA 484 for additional information. [**10:**A.6.5.3]

A.13.6.3.5.4 See NFPA 484 for additional information. [**10:**A.6.5.4]

A.13.6.4.1 Subsection 13.6.4 is concerned with the rules governing inspection, maintenance, and recharging of fire extinguishers. These factors are of prime importance in ensuring operation at the time of a fire. The procedure for inspection and maintenance of fire extinguishers varies considerably. Minimal knowledge is necessary to perform a monthly "quick check" or inspection in order to follow the inspection procedure as outlined in 13.6.4.2. [**10:**A.7.1]

A.13.6.4.1.2.1 Persons performing maintenance and recharging of extinguishers should meet one of the following criteria:

(1) Factory training and certification for the specific type and brand of portable fire extinguisher being serviced
(2) Certification by an organization acceptable to the AHJ
(3) Registration, licensure, or certification by a state or a local AHJ

[**10:**A.7.1.2.1]

Certification confirms that a person has fulfilled specific requirements as a fire extinguisher service technician and has earned the certification. For the purpose of Section 13.6, certification is the process of an organization issuing a document confirming that an applicant has passed a test based on the chapters and annexes of NFPA 10. The organization administering the test issues an official document that is relied upon as proof of passing the test. Ultimately, the document issued by the organization administering the test must be acceptable to the AHJ. Some AHJs do not rely on outside organizations and establish their own local licensing programs that include a test. [**10**:A.7.1.2.1]

A.13.6.4.1.2.3 This requirement is not intended to prevent service technicians from performing the inspections. [**10**:A.7.1.2.3]

A.13.6.4.2.1.1 Frequency of fire extinguisher inspections should be based on the need of the area in which fire extinguishers are located. The required monthly inspection is a minimum. [**10**:A.7.2.1.1]

A.13.6.4.2.1.2 Inspections should be performed on extinguishers 12 times per year, at regular intervals not exceeding 31 days. [**10**:A.7.2.1.2]

A.13.6.4.2.1.3 Inspections should be more frequent if any of the following conditions exist:

(1) High frequency of fires in the past
(2) Severe hazards
(3) Susceptibility to tampering, vandalism, or malicious mischief
(4) Possibility of, or history of, theft of fire extinguishers
(5) Locations that make fire extinguishers susceptible to mechanical injury
(6) Possibility of visible or physical obstructions
(7) Exposure to abnormal temperatures or corrosive atmospheres
(8) Characteristics of fire extinguishers, such as susceptibility to leakage

[**10**:A.7.2.1.3]

More frequent inspections could be enhanced through electronic monitoring of the fire extinguisher. [**10**:A.7.2.1.3]

A.13.6.4.2.2.3 Fire extinguishers in vehicles should be inspected at the beginning of a shift or whenever the vehicle is used. The inspection should ensure that the extinguisher is charged and ready for use. Extinguishers in compartments or trunks can become damaged or otherwise compromised because of weather exposure, other items in the compartment that are not secured, or other factors. [**10**:A.7.2.2.3]

N A.13.6.4.2.4.2 All buildings have Class A fire hazards. In any occupancy, there could be a predominant hazard as well as special hazard areas requiring extinguishers with ratings to match those hazards. For example, a hospital will have need for Class A fire extinguishers covering patient rooms, corridors, offices, and so forth, but will need Class B fire extinguishers in laboratories and where flammable anesthetics are stored or handled, Class C fire extinguishers in electrical switch gear or generator rooms, and Class K extinguishers in kitchens. [**10**:A.5.5]

A.13.6.4.3.2 In addition to the required tag or label, a permanent file record should be kept for each fire extinguisher. This file record should include the following information, as applicable:

(1) Maintenance date and the name of the person and the agency performing the maintenance
(2) Date of the last recharge and the name of the person and the agency performing the recharge
(3) Hydrostatic retest date and the name of the person and the agency performing the hydrostatic test
(4) Description of dents remaining after passing of the hydrostatic test
(5) Date of the 6-year maintenance for stored-pressure dry chemical and halogenated agent types (*See 13.6.4.3.6.*)

[**10**:A.7.3.4]

It is recognized that an electronic bar coding system is often acceptable to the AHJ in lieu of a tag or label for maintenance record keeping. [**10**:A.7.3.4]

Under special circumstances, or when local requirements are in effect, additional information can be desirable or required. [**10**:A.7.3.4]

Δ **A.13.7.1.2** The following functions are included in Annex A to provide guidelines for utilizing building systems and equipment in addition to proprietary fire alarm equipment in order to provide life safety and property protection. Building functions that should be monitored, initiated, or controlled during a fire alarm condition include, but should not be limited to, the following:

(1) Elevator operation consistent with ANSI/ASME A17.1/CSA B44, *Safety Code for Elevators and Escalators*
(2) Unlocking of stairwell and exit doors (*see NFPA 80 and NFPA 101*)
(3) Release of fire and smoke dampers (*see NFPA 90A and NFPA 90B*)
(4) Monitoring and initiating of automatic fire extinguishing system(s) or suppression system(s) and equipment in accordance with the applicable NFPA standard(s)

[**72**:A.23.3.3.1]

A.13.7.1.4.2 Records of conducted maintenance and testing and a copy of the certificate of compliance should be maintained. [**101**:A.9.6.1.5]

A.13.7.1.5 Requirements to address impaired fire alarm systems, and fire alarm systems prone to chronic nuisance alarms are provided in 13.7.1.5. In many situations, the problems can be corrected by ensuring the systems are maintained, serviced, and tested by an approved fire alarm service company. However, in some cases, the system problems may be attributed to aging for which suitable replacement parts are no longer available.

N A.13.7.1.5.5 Prior to a fire alarm system being classified as a chronic-nuisance-alarm-prone system, the owner should assess the environment, ITM, and system condition to determine if the nuisance alarms can be mitigated prior to the fifth nuisance alarm. As part of the fire alarm service company ITM assessment after the fifth alarm, the fire alarm service company should make a determination as to if the cause for the nuisance alarm is environmental or a fault with the fire alarm system. An environmental issue might require the owner or tenant to modify their policies or practices in an attempt to mitigate future nuisance alarms. There might be times in which a qualified individual or firm other than the fire alarm service company, acceptable to the AHJ, can be retained to assist with the mitigation of the nuisance alarms.

N A.13.7.1.5.6 It is not the intention of the code to prohibit building owners from operating chronic nuisance alarm systems that are not immediately resolved by the actions denoted in 13.7.1.5.5.

A.13.7.1.5.7 This paragraph allows the AHJ to require chronic nuisance alarm prone systems to comply with the *NFPA 72*, Section 26.3 requirements for central station service. Central station service, as compared to other supervising service, requires the system to be covered by a systematic follow-up program under the control of the organization that has listed the prime contractor. This will ensure that not only is the system being maintained, serviced, and periodically tested by an approved alarm service company, but it is also under an ongoing audit program by the company that listed the central station. Many jurisdictions that require central station service on fire alarm systems also communicate directly with the listing organization concerning the systems monitored in their jurisdiction.

A.13.7.1.5.8 It is not always practical for the AHJ to continually verify that required monitoring, testing, service, and maintenance are provided. It is also difficult for the AHJ to determine if older systems are no longer able to be serviced or repaired to keep them operational and resistant to nuisance alarms, particularly if spare parts are no longer available. Paragraph 13.7.1.5.8 requires the fire alarm companies to notify the AHJ when required services have been discontinued, or when systems can no longer be serviced and maintained in an operational condition, free from chronic nuisance alarms. It is not the intent of this paragraph to prevent system owners from getting a second opinion on the system status from another approved fire alarm service provider.

A.13.7.1.6 The requirement of 13.7.1.6 recognizes there will be instances where, for example, a facility owner would want to apply detection to meet certain performance goals and to address a particular hazard or need, but that detection is not required. Once installed, of course, acceptance testing, annual testing, and ongoing maintenance in accordance with this *Code* is expected. The intent of this section is to allow the use of a single detector, or multiple detectors provided for specific protection, with spacing to meet specific fire safety objectives as determined in accordance with 17.6.1.1 and 17.7.1.1 of *NFPA 72*. [**72**:A.17.5.3.3]

A.13.7.1.7.5 It is not the intent of 13.7.1.7.5 to require manual fire alarm boxes to be attached to movable partitions or to equipment, nor is it the intent to require the installation of permanent structures for mounting purposes only. [*101*:A.9.6.2.5]

A.13.7.1.7.6 The manual fire alarm box required by 13.7.1.7.6 is intended to provide a means to manually activate the fire alarm system when the automatic fire detection system or waterflow devices are out of service due to maintenance or testing, or where human discovery of the fire precedes automatic sprinkler system or automatic detection system activation. Where the fire alarm system is connected to a monitoring facility, the manual fire alarm box required by 13.7.1.7.6 should be connected to a separate circuit that is not placed "on test" when the detection or sprinkler system is placed "on test." The manual means is only intended for use by the system technician or the building owner and should be located by the sprinkler riser or fire alarm control unit. [*101*:A.9.6.2.6]

A.13.7.1.7.7 Manual fire alarm boxes can include those with key-operated locks for detention areas or psychiatric hospitals, manual fire alarm boxes in areas where explosive vapors or dusts might be a hazard, or manual fire alarm boxes in areas with corrosive atmospheres. The appearance of manual fire alarm boxes for special uses often differs from those used in areas of normal occupancy. Manual fire alarm boxes, such as those with locks, that are located in areas where the general public has limited access might need to have signage advising persons to seek assistance from staff in the event a fire is noted. [*101*:A.9.6.2.7]

Δ **A.13.7.1.8.4** Per 13.7.1.8.1, the residential occupancy requirements determine whether smoke alarms are needed within sleeping rooms. Paragraph 13.7.1.8.4 limits the requirement for interconnection of smoke alarms to those in new construction. This *Code* does not intend to require compliant, existing smoke alarm installations to be interconnected. This *Code* is periodically revised to add retrospective requirements only where the need is clearly substantiated. [*101*:A.9.6.2.10.7.1]

A.13.7.1.8.5.3 Smoke detectors and smoke alarms should be installed in those locations recommended by the manufacturer's published instructions, except in those cases where the space above the ceiling is open to the outside and little or no insulation is present over the ceiling. Such cases result in the ceiling being excessively cold in the winter or excessively hot in the summer. Where the ceiling is significantly different in temperature from the air space below, smoke and heat have difficulty reaching the ceiling and a detector that is located on that ceiling. [**72**:A.29.11.3.4(3)]

Δ **A.13.7.1.8.5.4** As per annex material located in A.29.8.1 of NFPA 72, it is not normally recommended that smoke alarms or smoke detectors be placed in kitchen spaces. This section of the code provides guidelines for safe installation if a need exists to install a smoke alarm or smoke detector in a residential kitchen space or cooking area. [**72**:A.29.11.3.4(4)]

Within this *Code* section, a fixed cooking appliance is any appliance that is intended to be permanently connected electrically to the wiring system or the fuel source. A stationary cooking appliance is any appliance that is intended to be fastened in place or located in a dedicated space, and is connected to the supply circuit or fuel source. [**72**:A.29.11.3.4(4)]

Smoke alarms and smoke detectors that are currently available to consumers are susceptible to particles released into the air during normal cooking procedures. If smoke alarms and smoke detectors are placed too close to the area where the cooking source originates, a high level of nuisance alarms can occur. Frequent nuisance alarms can result in an occupant disabling the smoke alarm or smoke detector. [**72**:A.29.11.3.4(4)]

Nuisance alarm studies show that commercially available residential smoke alarms and smoke detectors are susceptible to nuisance alarms when installed too close to cooking appliances. As the horizontal distance between the smoke alarm or smoke detectors and the cooking appliance increases, the frequency of nuisance alarms decreases. Smoke alarms or smoke detectors that use ionization smoke detection have been shown to be more susceptible to cooking nuisance alarms than those that use photoelectric smoke detection when the alarms or detectors are installed within 10 ft (3.0 m) along a horizontal smoke travel path from a cooking appliance. Smoke alarms or smoke detectors that use photoelectric smoke detection produce nuisance alarms when installed less than 10 ft (3.0 m) from a cooking appliance, though to a lesser degree. [**72**:A.29.11.3.4(4)]

The occurrence of the higher frequency of nuisance alarms observed in smoke alarms or smoke detectors that use ionization detection have been documented in the fire research data. Due to the differences in technology between ionization detection and photoelectric detection, the sensitivity typically used for ionization detection is much higher than that used for photoelectric detection. This sensitivity difference is a result of each type of the detection being required to satisfy UL 217 performance tests. Removing detection technology from consideration, the frequency of nuisance alarms is solely due to the sensitivity of the detection method used. Thus, both ionization and photoelectric detector technologies will produce nuisance alarms due to cooking, but currently available smoke alarms and smoke detectors that use ionization detection typically produce more cooking-related nuisance alarms. [72:A.29.11.3.4(4)]

The higher sensitivities of currently available smoke alarms and smoke detectors that use ionization detection do provide a benefit at the expense of a potentially higher rate of cooking-related nuisance alarms. Research has demonstrated that ionization detection will typically respond faster than photoelectric detection to flaming fires, providing earlier warning to occupants that might allow for quicker intervention or faster egress. In general, the installation of smoke alarms or smoke detectors that use ionization detection will result in increased fire safety at the risk of a higher frequency of nuisance alarms. The installation of smoke alarms or smoke detectors that use photoelectric detection will result in reduced fire safety for flaming fires and a reduced risk of nuisance alarms. Based on the trade-off between faster response to fires and the frequency of nuisance alarms, detectors that utilize both technologies (i.e., ionization, photoelectric, and a combination) are allowed to be installed between 10 ft (3.0 m) and 20 ft (6.1 m) along a horizontal flow path from a standard or fixed cooking appliance if the specific detector is equipped with an alarm silencing means or is of the photoelectric-type. [72:A.29.11.3.4(4)]

Nuisance alarm studies provide data on cooking nuisances that emanate from both fixed cooking appliances and stationary cooking appliances (e.g., stove, oven) as well as portable cooking appliances (e.g., toaster). Based on these studies, which demonstrate the potential of all cooking appliances to generate nuisance sources, a zone of exclusion has been specified surrounding each stationary or fixed cooking appliance. The purpose of this zone is to limit the installation of smoke alarms and detectors in areas where stationary, fixed, or portable cooking appliances will be located within the residential kitchen space such that potential nuisance alarms are minimized. The size of the zone of exclusion is specified to attempt to take into account the unknown and transitory locations of portable cooking appliances. This zone of exclusion is determined by measuring a 10 ft (3.0 m) radial distance from the closest edge of a stationary or fixed cooking appliance. The zone of exclusion is not intended to pass through walls or doorways. Figure A.13.7.1.8.5.4(a) provides an example of the zone of exclusion in a generalized residential kitchen. [72:29.11.3.4(4)]

If other areas of this code require that a smoke alarm or smoke detector be placed within a horizontal flow path distance between 10 ft (3.0 m) and 20 ft (6.1 m) from a stationary or fixed cooking appliance, the following method should be used to determine the distance, and only photoelectric detection or smoke alarms/detectors with alarm silencing means can be installed in this area. [72:A.29.11.3.4(4)]

To install a smoke alarm or detector between 10 ft (3.0 m) and 20 ft (6.1 m) from the cooking appliance, an installer must first determine the 10 ft (3.0 m) area of exclusion. Once the area of exclusion is determined, an installer must then determine the horizontal flow distance. This is the horizontal distance along the ceiling from the closest edge of the cooking appliance to the smoke alarm or detector. The horizontal distance can consist of line segments due to impediments, such as interior partitions. Once an impediment is met, the measurement of the distance will then continue along the new horizontal path segment until the distance requirement is met or another impediment is encountered. Figure A.13.7.1.8.5.4(b) provides an example for placement outside a kitchen in a nearby hallway. Figure A.13.7.1.8.5.4(c) provides another example of appropriate placement outside of a kitchen in an adjacent room. [72:A.29.11.3.4(4)]

At a horizontal flow path distance of greater than 20 ft (6.1 m), any type of smoke alarm or smoke detector can be installed. [72:A.29.11.3.4(4)]

In rare cases, a residential dwelling can be of such size and configuration that an area of exclusion of 10 ft (3.0 m) from a stationary or fixed cooking appliance excludes the placement of a smoke alarm or smoke detector required by other areas of this *Code*. In these cases, a smoke alarm or smoke detector using photoelectric detection can be installed at least 72 in. (1.83 m) from the fixed or stationary cooking appliance. Figure A.13.7.1.8.5.4(d) provides an example of this situation in practice where a smoke alarm or smoke detector is required outside of the sleeping area, but the space is in close proximity to the kitchen space. [72:A.29.11.3.4(4)]

In response to the above noted nuisance alarm studies, the 8th edition of UL 217, *Smoke Alarms*, and the 7th edition of UL 268, *Smoke Detectors for Fire Alarm Systems*, have added a new performance test to help reduce nuisance alarms from normal cooking. This end-product performance and listing requirement aligns with 13.7.1.8.5.6 of this *Code*. Smoke alarms complying with these UL standards will be listed "for resistance to common nuisance sources from cooking" and are suitable for installation at distances from cooking appliances outlined in this *Code*. [72:A.29.11.3.4(4)]

N **A.13.7.1.8.5.6** Studies indicate that smoke alarms and smoke detectors that use ionization detection, photoelectric detection, or a combination of ionization and photoelectric detection, are susceptible to nuisance alarms caused by steam. Some research has been done on the comparative response of these types of detection to steam. Steam particles, in general, are visible, reflect light easily, and are typically produced in a size range that has been shown to be more likely to actuate a photoelectric sensor (Dinaburg and Gottuk, 2015). Thus, it is required that smoke alarms and smoke detectors be installed greater than 36 in. (910 mm) from the bathroom door where possible. Increasing the distance between the smoke alarm or smoke detector and the bathroom door can reduce the frequency of nuisance alarms from bathroom steam. Frequent nuisance alarms can result in the occupant disabling the smoke alarm. Each incremental increase in separation, up to 10 ft (3.0 m), between the bathroom door and the smoke alarm or smoke detector is expected to reduce the frequency of nuisance alarms. [72:A.29.11.3.4(6)]

N **A.13.7.1.8.5.7** There are circumstances in which the placement of smoke alarms and detectors cannot physically meet the requirement to be 36 in. (910 mm) or further away from the

FIGURE A.13.7.1.8.5.4(a) Example of Zone of Exclusion (gray area) Within Typical Residential Kitchen. [72:Figure A.29.11.3.4(4)(a)]

tip of the fan blade. Consequently, there is an irreconcilable conflict in enforcing all siting requirements of this standard, so the requirement of 13.7.1.8.5.9 only applies where possible to allow compliance with this standard. A limited study (Gottuk and Gottuk 2015) has indicated that placing alarms closer than 36 in. (910 mm) is not expected to produce an unacceptable risk, and in some cases, could improve performance. [72:A.29.11.3.4(8)]

N **A.13.7.1.8.5.11** Figure A.13.7.1.8.5.11 illustrates acceptable smoke alarm or smoke detector mounting locations for tray-shaped ceilings. [72:A.29.11.3.4(11)]

A.13.7.1.8.8 A dwelling unit is that structure, area, room, or combination of rooms, including hotel rooms/suites, in which a family or individual lives. A dwelling unit includes living areas only and not common usage areas in multifamily buildings, such as corridors, lobbies, and basements. [101:A.9.6.2.10.7.2]

A.13.7.1.9.2.1 Elevator lobbies have been considered areas subject to unwanted alarms due to factors such as low ceilings and smoking. In the past several years, new features have become available to reduce this problem. These features are, however, not necessarily included in any specific installation. [101:A.9.6.3.2.1]

A.13.7.1.9.2.2 The concept addressed is that detectors used for releasing service, such as door or damper closing and fan shutdown, are not required to sound the building alarm. [101:A.9.6.3.2.2]

A.13.7.1.9.2.3 The concept addressed is that detectors used for releasing service, such as door or damper closing and fan shutdown, are not required to sound the building alarm. [101:A.9.6.3.2.3]

A.13.7.1.9.6.7 Visual notification appliances installed in large-volume spaces, such as arenas, stadiums, mall concourses and atriums, can be alternative devices which are not listed as visible notification appliances for fire alarm systems provided that the notification objective of the visual signal is reasonably achieved. Examples of alternative devices include, but are not limited to, scoreboards, message boards, and other electronic devices that meet the performance objectives of visible fire alarm appliances in large-volume spaces. [101:A.9.6.3.6.7]

It is the intent to permit the omission of visible notification appliances as identified in 13.7.1.9.6.7, provided that the adjacent areas that have not been specifically designated as exempt are provided with visible notification as required by 13.7.1.9.6. [101:A.9.6.3.6.7]

A.13.7.1.9.6.8 Documentation should be maintained with the as-built drawings so that inspection and testing personnel understand that the visible appliances have been exempted from certain areas and, therefore, can note the deviation on the acceptance test documentation and ongoing inspection reports. This will provide inspection and testing personnel with necessary details regarding the omission of visible notification appliances. [101:A.9.6.3.6.8]

A.13.7.1.9.7.2 To approve an evacuation plan to selectively notify building occupants, the AHJ should consider several building parameters, including building compartmentation,

FIGURE A.13.7.1.8.5.4(b) Example of Smoke Alarm or Smoke Detector Placement Between 10 ft (3.0 m) and 20 ft (6.1 m) Away in Hallway from Center of Stationary or Fixed Cooking Appliance. [72:Figure A.29.11.3.4(4)(b)]

FIGURE A.13.7.1.8.5.4(c) Example of Smoke Alarm or Smoke Detector Placement Between 10 ft (3.0 m) and 20 ft (6.1 m) Away in Hallway from Center of Stationary or Fixed Cooking Appliance. [72:Figure A.29.11.3.4(4)(c)]

FIGURE A.13.7.1.8.5.4(d) Example of Exception Placement of Photoelectric Smoke Alarm or Smoke Detector at 72 in. (1.83 m) from Stationary or Fixed Cooking Appliance. [72:Figure A.29.11.3.4(4)(d)]

detection and suppression system zones, occupant loads, and the number and arrangement of the means of egress. [*101*:A.9.6.3.7.2]

In high-rise buildings, it is typical to evacuate the fire floor, the floor(s) above, and the floor immediately below. Other areas are then evacuated as the fire develops. [*101*:A.9.6.3.7.2]

A.13.7.1.10.5 The concern is the possible use of systems that include monitor-it-yourself (MIY) network-type systems that transmit directly to the emergency forces call center. These systems do not comply with the various transmission methods that are identified within *NFPA 72*. The use of these systems should first receive the approval of the local fire authority prior to being programed with the dispatch call center number.

A.13.7.1.13.4 The primary purpose of annunciation is to enable responding personnel to quickly and accurately determine the status of equipment or emergency control functions that might affect the safety of occupants. [72:A.10.18.3]

A.13.7.1.13.6 Fire alarm system annunciation should, as a minimum, be sufficiently specific to identify a fire alarm signal in accordance with the following:

(1) If a floor exceeds 22,500 ft² (2090 m²) in area, the floor should be subdivided into detection zones of 22,500 ft² (2090 m²) or less, consistent with the existing smoke and fire barriers on the floor.
(2) If a floor exceeds 22,500 ft² (2090 m²) in area and is undivided by smoke or fire barriers, detection zoning should be determined on a case-by-case basis in consultation with the AHJ.
(3) Waterflow switches on sprinkler systems that serve multiple floors, areas exceeding 22,500 ft² (2090 m²), or areas

N **FIGURE A.13.7.1.8.5.11 Locations Permitted for Smoke Alarms and Smoke Detectors on Tray-Shaped Ceilings.** [72:Figure A.29.11.3.4(11)]

inconsistent with the established detection system zoning should be annunciated individually.

(4) In-duct smoke detectors on air-handling systems that serve multiple floors, areas exceeding 22,500 ft² (2090 m²), or areas inconsistent with the established detection system zoning should be annunciated individually.

(5) If a floor area exceeds 22,500 ft² (2090 m²), additional zoning should be provided. The length of any zone should not exceed 300 ft (91 m) in any direction. If the building is provided with automatic sprinklers throughout, the area of the alarm zone should be permitted to coincide with the allowable area of the sprinkler zone.

[72:A.10.18.5]

A.13.7.1.15 This section does not require mass notification systems, it only provides direction for the risk analysis. Where the risk analysis and resulting action plan identifies a need for a mass notification system, NFPA 72 should be used for design and installation requirements. [*101*:A.9.14]

A.13.7.1.15.1 A risk analysis will determine whether a mass notification system is required in addition to the life safety emergency communication systems required by this *Code*. The risk analysis might show that no additional notification is required. [*101*:A.9.14.1]

A.13.7.2.1.2.3 The intent is to require detectors only in nonsprinklered hazardous areas that are unoccupied. When the building is occupied, the detectors in the unoccupied, unsprinklered hazardous areas will initiate occupant notification. If the building is unoccupied, the fire in the nonsprinklered hazardous area is not a life safety issue, and the detectors, upon activation, are not required to notify anyone. The signal from a detector is permitted to be sent to a control panel in an area that is occupied when the building is occupied, but that is unoccupied when the building is unoccupied, without the need for central station monitoring or the equivalent. [*101*:A.12.3.4.2.3]

A.13.7.2.1.3.5 Examples of devices that might be used to provide alternative visible means include scoreboards, message boards, and other electronic devices. [*101*:A.12.3.4.3.5]

A.13.7.2.1.4.1(3) The intent is to require CO detectors in occupiable spaces immediately adjacent, vertically or horizontally, to attached garages, regardless of the presence of openings between the garage and the adjacent occupiable spaces. Other occupiable spaces that are not adjacent to the attached garage do not require CO detectors. [*101*:A.12.3.4.4.1(3)]

A.13.7.2.2.3 The intent is to require detectors only in nonsprinklered hazardous areas that are unoccupied. Where the building is occupied, the detectors in the unoccupied, unsprinklered hazardous areas will initiate occupant notification. If the building is unoccupied, the fire in the nonsprinklered hazardous area is not a life safety issue, and the detectors, upon activation, are not required to notify anyone. The signal from a detector is permitted to be sent to a control panel in an area that is occupied when the building is occupied, but that is unoccupied when the building is unoccupied, without the need for central station monitoring or the equivalent. [*101*:A.13.3.4.2.3]

A.13.7.2.3.2.3.1 Occupied portions of the building should have access to a central point for manual activation of the evacuation signal. [*101*:A.14.3.4.2.3.1]

A.13.7.2.3.2.3.2 Occupied portions of the building should have access to a central point for manual activation of the evacuation signal. [*101*:A.14.3.4.2.3.2]

A.13.7.2.4.2.3.1 Occupied portions of the building should have access to a central point for manual activation of the evacuation signal. [*101*:A.15.3.4.2.3.1]

A.13.7.2.4.2.3.2 Occupied portions of the building should have access to a central point for manual activation of the evacuation signal. [*101*:A.15.3.4.2.3.2]

A.13.7.2.4.3.1.1 The audible occupant notification signal for evacuation of an educational occupancy building should be the distinctive three-pulse temporal pattern fire alarm evacuation signal that is required of new systems by *NFPA 72*. The temporal pattern will help educate students to recognize the need to evacuate when they are in other occupancies. Existing fire alarm systems should be modified, as feasible, to sound the three-pulse temporal pattern. [*101*:A.15.3.4.3.1.1]

A.13.7.2.7.2 It is not the intent of this *Code* to require single-station smoke alarms that might be required by local codes to be connected to or to initiate the building fire alarm system. [*101*:A.18.3.4.2]

A.13.7.2.7.3.1(2) In health care occupancies, fire alarm system notification is often designed primarily to notify staff who are responsible for the occupants in their care. The staff can be used as an alternate means for notifying others who might need to relocate or evacuate. [*101*:A.18.3.4.3.1(2)]

A.13.7.2.7.5.3 The requirement for smoke detectors in spaces open to the corridors eliminates the requirements of 18.3.6.1(1)(c), 18.3.6.1(2)(b), and 18.3.6.1(5)(b) of NFPA *101* for direct supervision by the facility staff of nursing homes. [*101*:A.18.3.4.5.3]

A.13.7.2.8.2 It is not the intent of this *Code* to require single-station smoke alarms, which might be required by local codes, to be connected to or to initiate the building fire alarm system. [*101*:A.19.3.4.2]

A.13.7.2.8.3.1(1) It is the intent of this provision to permit a visible fire alarm signal instead of an audible signal to reduce interference between the fire alarm and medical equipment monitoring alarms. [*101*:A.19.3.4.3.1(1)]

A.13.7.2.8.3.1(4) In health care occupancies, fire alarm system notification is often designed primarily to notify staff who are responsible for the occupants in their care. The staff can be used as an alternate means for notifying others who might need to relocate or evacuate. [*101*:A.19.3.4.3.1(4)]

A.13.7.2.9.3.1.2 In ambulatory health care occupancies, fire alarm system notification is often designed primarily to notify staff who are responsible for the occupants in their care. The staff can be used as an alternate means for notifying others who might need to relocate or evacuate. [*101*:A.20.3.4.3.1.2]

A.13.7.2.10.3.1.2 In ambulatory health care occupancies, fire alarm system notification is often designed primarily to notify staff who are responsible for the occupants in their care. The staff can be used as an alternate means for notifying others who might need to relocate or evacuate. [*101*:21.3.4.3.1.2]

A.13.7.2.11.3.1(2) The staff at the constantly attended location should have the capability to promptly initiate the general alarm function and contact the fire department or have direct communication with a control room or other location that can initiate the general alarm function and contact the fire department. [*101*:A.22.3.4.3.1(2)]

A.13.7.2.11.4 Examples of contiguous common spaces are galleries and corridors. [*101*:A.22.3.4.4]

A.13.7.2.11.4.3 An open dormitory is a dormitory that is arranged to allow staff to observe the entire dormitory area at one time. [*101*:A.22.3.4.4.3]

A.13.7.2.12.3.1(2) The staff at the constantly attended location should have the capability to promptly initiate the general alarm function and contact the fire department or have direct communication with a control room or other location that can initiate the general alarm function and contact the fire department. [*101*:A.23.3.4.3.1(2)]

A.13.7.2.12.4.3 An open dormitory is a dormitory that is arranged to allow staff to observe the entire dormitory area at one time. [*101*:A.23.3.4.4.3]

A.13.7.2.13.1.1 Paragraph 11.5.1.3 of *NFPA 72* contains related requirements. They specify that, where the interior floor area for a given level of a dwelling unit, excluding garage areas, is greater than 1000 ft^2 (93 m^2), smoke alarms are to be installed as follows:

(1) All points on the ceiling are to have a smoke alarm within a distance of 30 ft (9.1 m), measured along a path of travel, or to have one smoke alarm per 500 ft^2 (46.5 m^2) of floor area, which is calculated by dividing the total interior floor area per level by 500 ft^2 (46.5 m^2).
(2) Where dwelling units include great rooms or vaulted/cathedral ceilings extending over multiple floors, smoke alarms located on the upper floor that are intended to protect the aforementioned area are permitted to be considered as part of the lower floor(s) protection scheme used to meet the requirements of A.13.7.2.13.1.1(1).

[*101*:A.24.3.4.1.1]

A.13.7.2.13.1.1(2) Paragraphs 11.5.1.1(2) and 11.5.1.2 of *NFPA 72* contain related requirements. The requirement of 11.5.1.1(2) of *NFPA 72* specifies that an alarm is to be installed outside of each separate dwelling unit sleeping area, within 21 ft (6.4 m) of any door to a sleeping room, with the distance measured along a path of travel. The requirement in 11.5.1.2 of *NFPA 72* specifies that, where the area addressed in 11.5.1.1(2) of *NFPA 72* is separated from the adjacent living areas by a door, a smoke alarm is to be installed in the area between the door and the sleeping rooms, and additional alarms are to be installed on the living area side of the door. [*101*:A.24.3.4.1.1(2)]

A.13.7.2.13.2.2 The placement requirements of *NFPA 72* are modified specifically for one- and two-family dwellings as required by this *Code* and do not affect other regulations within a jurisdiction. [*101*:A.24.3.4.2.2]

A.13.7.2.14.3.1 The proprietor is the owner or owner's agent with responsible charge. [*101*:A.26.3.4.3.1]

A.13.7.2.14.6.2 The placement requirements of *NFPA 72* are modified to accommodate lodging or rooming house occupancies that are part of multiple occupancy buildings (e.g., an on-call physicians' sleeping room in a hospital). The placement requirements of *NFPA 72* are modified specifically for lodging or rooming houses as required by this *Code* and do not affect other regulations within a jurisdiction. [*101*:A.26.3.4.6.2]

A.13.7.2.15.3.1 Visible signaling appliances might be governed by provisions of federal regulations in 28 CFR 36, Appendix A, "Americans with Disabilities Act Accessibility Guidelines for Buildings and Facilities," Section 4.28, Alarms. [*101*:A.28.3.4.3.1]

A.13.7.2.15.3.4 A quantity of such rooms and suites might be required to be equipped with accessible communication features based on the total number of rooms in a transient lodging facility. *(See 28 CFR Parts 35 and 36, "2010 ADA Standards for Accessible Design.")* [*101*:A.28.3.4.3.4]

A.13.7.2.15.5 Caution needs to be exercised in locating smoke alarms with regard to their proximity to bathrooms, cooking facilities, and HVAC outlets in order to prevent nuisance alarms. [*101*:A.28.3.4.6]

A.13.7.2.16.3.6 The provision for immediate notification of the public fire department is intended to include, but is not limited to, all of the arrangements in 13.7.1.10.2. Other arrangements that depend on a clerk or other member of the staff to notify the fire department might also be permitted. In such cases, however, it is essential that a trained staff member and an immediately available means of calling the fire department are continuously available. If a telephone is to be used, it should not be of any type or arrangement that requires a coin or the unlocking of a device to contact the fire department. [*101*:A.29.3.4.3.6]

A.13.7.2.16.5 Caution needs to be exercised in locating smoke alarms with regard to their proximity to bathrooms, cooking facilities, and HVAC outlets in order to prevent nuisance alarms. [*101*:A.29.3.4.5]

A.13.7.2.17.3.2 The standard audible alarm signal used in all fire alarm horns and integral sounders of smoke detectors for the past 30 years utilized a typical frequency of approximately 3 KHz. Peer-reviewed research has concluded the waking effectiveness of a 520 Hz low-frequency signal is superior to the standard 3 KHz audible alarm signal for waking high-risk segments of the population such as people over 65, people who are hard of hearing, school-age children, and people who are alcohol impaired. Therefore, the 520 Hz low-frequency audible alarm signal is now required in areas intended for sleeping within apartment buildings that are required to have a fire alarm system. The following product solutions are currently available in the market to produce the 520 Hz low-frequency audible alarm signal in sleeping rooms:

(1) Smoke detectors with integral sounder bases
(2) Fire alarm system horns and horn/strobes
(3) Speakers connected to an in-building fire alarm emergency voice alarm communication (EVAC) system

[*101*:A.30.3.4.3.2]

The peer-reviewed research project — *Optimizing Fire Alarm Notification for High Risk Groups: Waking Effectiveness of Alarms (Auditory, Visual and Tactile) for Adults Who Are Hard of Hearing* and *Waking Effectiveness of Alarms (Auditory, Visual and Tactile) for the Alcohol Impaired* — was conducted under the auspices of the Fire Protection Research Foundation. [*101*:A.30.3.4.3.2]

A.13.7.2.17.5 Previous editions of NFPA *101* permitted the single-station smoke alarm required by 13.7.2.17.5 to be omitted from each apartment where a complete automatic smoke detection system was installed throughout the building. With such a system, when one detector is activated, an alarm is sounded throughout the building. Experience with complete smoke detection systems in apartment buildings has shown that numerous nuisance alarms are likely to occur. Where there is a problem with frequent nuisance alarms, occupants ignore the alarm, or the system is either disconnected or otherwise rendered inoperative. [*101*:A.30.3.4.5]

A.13.7.2.17.5.1 The standard audible alarm signal used in all smoke alarms for the past 30 years utilized a typical frequency of approximately 3 KHz. Peer-reviewed research has concluded the waking effectiveness of the 520 Hz low-frequency signal is superior to the standard 3 KHz audible alarm signal for waking high-risk segments of the population such as people over 65, people who are hard of hearing, school-age children, and people who are alcohol impaired. Therefore, the 520 Hz low-frequency audible alarm signal is now required for smoke alarms in areas intended for sleeping within apartment buildings that are required to have a fire alarm system. If smoke alarms that are capable of producing the low-frequency audible alarm signal are not available, smoke detectors arranged to function in the same manner as smoke alarms in accordance with 13.7.1.8.6 would be required. The following product solutions are currently available in the market if the smoke alarm is unable to produce the 520 Hz low-frequency audible alarm signal in sleeping rooms:

(1) Smoke detectors with integral sounder bases
(2) Fire alarm system horns and horn/strobes
(3) Speakers connected to an in-building fire alarm emergency voice alarm communication (EVAC) system

[*101*:A.30.3.4.5.1]

The peer-reviewed research project — *Optimizing Fire Alarm Notification for High Risk Groups: Waking Effectiveness of Alarms (Auditory, Visual and Tactile) for Adults Who Are Hard of Hearing* and *Waking Effectiveness of Alarms (Auditory, Visual and Tactile) for the Alcohol Impaired* — was conducted under the auspices of the Fire Protection Research Foundation. [*101*:A.30.3.4.5.1]

A.13.7.2.17.6.4 Where fuel-burning appliances or fuel-burning fireplaces are located outside but attached to the dwelling unit, the area or room containing the fuel-burning appliance or fuel-burning fireplace could be considered part of the attached dwelling unit(s). In this application, either carbon monoxide alarms or carbon monoxide detectors are permitted to be installed in the attached dwelling unit(s) in accordance with 13.7.2.17.6. [*101*:A.30.3.4.6.4]

A.13.7.2.18.4.1 It is intended that a building compliant with Option 2, as defined in Chapter 31 of NFPA *101*, function as described in the paragraph that follows. [*101*:A.31.3.4.4.1]

Occupants within a living unit become aware of a fire emergency, either through personal awareness or through being alerted by the smoke alarm(s) installed within the living unit. Other building occupants are alerted to the fire emergency by the building fire alarm system that is initiated by manual fire alarm boxes adjacent to the exits, heat detection within the living unit where the fire emergency exists, smoke detection in the common areas outside the living unit, or a combination thereof. The installation of system heat detectors versus smoke detectors within the living unit is intended to eliminate nuisance-type alarms and reduce occupant complacency from frequent false alarms. The installation of smoke detection within the living unit should only be contemplated after a careful analysis of the goals and with the approval of the AHJ. [*101*:A.31.3.4.4.1]

A.13.7.2.18.5.1 NFPA *101* provides adequate, balanced fire protection and takes into consideration the passive and active systems required in a given occupancy. The level of protection prescribed by *NFPA* 72 which includes smoke alarms in all sleeping rooms, without exception, does not necessarily take into consideration the complete protection package mandated by NFPA *101*. [*101*:A.31.3.4.5.1]

A.13.7.2.20.6 Positive alarm sequence applies only to emergency forces notification. Occupant notification is required to occur immediately upon activation of the detection device or system. [*101*:A.32.3.3.4.6]

A.13.7.2.21.4 Most often, smoke alarms sounding an alarm at 85 dBA or greater, installed outside the bedroom area, will meet the intent of this requirement. Smoke alarms remotely located from the bedroom might not be loud enough to awaken the average person. In such cases, it is recommended that smoke alarms be interconnected so that the activation of any smoke alarm will cause all smoke alarms to activate. [*101*:A.33.2.3.4.4]

NFPA *101* provides adequate, balanced fire protection and takes into consideration the passive and active systems required in a given occupancy. The level of protection prescribed by *NFPA* 72 which includes smoke alarms in all sleeping rooms, without exception, does not necessarily take into consideration the complete protection package prescribed by NFPA *101*. [*101*:A.33.2.3.4.4]

A.13.7.2.22.6.1 See A.13.7.2.16.3.6. [*101*:A.33.3.3.4.6.1]

A.13.7.2.25.5 It is not the intent of this paragraph to require a new risk analysis where an existing risk analysis addresses the issues or arrangements associated with a new building. [*101*:A.38.3.4.5]

A.13.7.2.29.3.1 The need for voice communication can be based on a decision regarding staged or partial evacuation versus total evacuation of all floors. The determination of need is a function of occupancy classification and building height. [*101*:A.11.8.4.1]

N A.13.7.2.30.1 Additional documents such as NEMA SB-7, *Applications Guide for Carbon Monoxide Alarms and Detectors*, and the NFPA Fire Protection Research Foundation (FPRF) technical report, *Development of a Technical Basis for Carbon Monoxide Detector Siting*, can also be used as supplemental resources to help with risk assessment, siting, and application considerations. [**72**:A.17.12.1]

A.13.7.2.30.1(1) Both permanent and temporary carbon-monoxide-producing devices need to be considered when locating carbon monoxide detectors. This includes accounting for all carbon-monoxide-producing appliances and equipment and temporary/mobile equipment, including vehicles, generators, machinery, engines, internal combustion engines, propane equipment, space heaters, engine-driven tools, grills, fire pits, systems used to generate hydrogen, fuel-burning equipment, and any other permanent and/or transient-type equipment and appliances that can be sources of carbon monoxide. [**72**:A.17.12.1(1)]

By placing carbon monoxide detectors close to all permanent as well as all temporary carbon-monoxide-producing sources, early detection of carbon monoxide is more likely to occur. Detectors should therefore be located as close as practicable to the carbon-monoxide-producing source, taking into account such factors as detector accessibility for inspection, testing, and maintenance; potential sources of detector damage or contamination; potential nuisance alarm sources; transient backdrafting spillage of flue gases during startup and operation; and ventilation supply and exhaust vents. For early detection, carbon monoxide detectors should be located on the ceiling over carbon-monoxide-producing sources. There is often some buoyancy of the heated combustion gases that can help carry the carbon monoxide to the detector. [**72**:A.17.12.1(1)]

Carbon monoxide detectors should also be considered throughout the room/space that contains the carbon-monoxide-producing source to help address either limited or no buoyancy of the carbon monoxide, adverse impacts by HVAC systems, as well as ambient airflows in the space that can carry carbon monoxide away from the source rather than up to the ceiling directly over the source.

[**72**:A.17.12.1(1)]

A.13.7.2.30.1(2) Carbon monoxide can follow flow paths from its original source to adjacent areas in the building, including moving horizontally and vertically throughout the space, building, and structure, and where carbon monoxide detectors should be located in these adjacent areas needs to be considered. Detector location and spacing should be based on an engineering evaluation that considers potential sources and migration of carbon monoxide, including through exhaust ductwork, HVAC equipment, openings in walls and floors, unprotected penetrations, and elevator shafts. [**72**:A.17.12.1(2)]

As some of the higher carbon monoxide concentrations are often at the source and within the exhaust ductwork and venting equipment, carbon monoxide detectors should be located along the exhaust path of any carbon-monoxide-producing equipment, appliances, and so forth, extending from the source of the carbon monoxide through the building to the termination of the exhaust at an exterior wall or roof. This should include detectors along any duct branch lines and interconnections to any ductwork and piping used in the exhaust system so carbon monoxide that might exist outside the exhaust path (due to leaks, damage, obstructions, rust, corrosion, etc.) can be detected. [**72**:A.17.12.1(2)]

The impact of HVAC systems should be taken into account when locating carbon monoxide detectors. HVAC systems can transport as well as mix and dilute carbon monoxide. Consideration should be given to the layout and operation of the HVAC system and whether the HVAC is constantly running or only runs for a portion of the time and, therefore, is not constantly distributing or mixing air in the building. When locating carbon monoxide detectors, other considerations include the presence and impact of closed doors and walls. These can compartmentalize areas within an individual HVAC zone or floor and prevent spread. Their presence can also allow carbon monoxide to accumulate more rapidly in given areas if doors are closed to contain it and not allow it to spread and dilute the concentration. [**72**:A.17.12.1(2)]

Carbon monoxide can potentially enter the building from an exterior source, such as through make-up air systems. Some of the external sources that should be considered when locating carbon monoxide detectors include adjacent structures, exterior systems, equipment such as vehicles and generators, and interconnections to underground spaces or parking garages. [**72**:A.17.12.1(2)]

N A.13.7.2.30.1(3) Carbon monoxide detectors should also be located and installed as recommended by the manufacturer's published instructions, including those specific requirements for the spacing between detectors, minimum/maximum spacings to walls and obstructions, minimum/maximum height of a detector in a space, minimum/maximum distances to HVAC vents, reductions in spacing required for high ceilings, and other pertinent information required to help properly design, assess, and install detectors to achieve their intent of detecting carbon monoxide early on to warn occupants of a hazard. [**72**:A.17.12.1(3)]

N A.13.7.2.30.1(4) Carbon monoxide detectors should also be located and installed as recommended by the manufacturer's published instructions, including those specific requirements for the spacing between detectors, minimum/maximum spacings to walls and obstructions, minimum/maximum height of a detector in a space, minimum/maximum distances to HVAC vents, reductions in spacing required for high ceilings, and other pertinent information required to help properly design, assess, and install detectors to achieve their intent of detecting carbon monoxide early on to warn occupants of a hazard. [**72**:A.17.12.1(4)]

N A.13.7.2.30.7 At present there is no product performance listing for duct-mounted carbon monoxide detectors because there is no peer-reviewed research to determine what the alarm thresholds for duct-mounted carbon monoxide detectors should be. There are considerable differences between the operation of a spot-type carbon monoxide detector and a duct-mounted carbon monoxide detector. The environment in ducts can be very harsh and could impact the carbon monoxide detector's sensing element. Furthermore, in most buildings, there are periods when the HVAC system is not moving significant quantities of air from the compartments it serves. As a result, the carbon monoxide detection system cannot be designed to rely on the HVAC system operation for the transport of carbon monoxide to the carbon monoxide detectors. [**72**:A.17.12.3]

A.13.7.3.1.1.3 This requirement does not apply to notification appliance circuits. [72:A.10.3.3]

N **A.13.7.3.2.2.1(1)** The purpose for a written narrative is to provide a description of the work to be performed and could be as simple as "Install additional three smoke detectors to provide coverage for newly installed meeting room." However, it could be desirable to include why or by whose direction the work is being done, such as "at owner's request," "per specifications dated …," or "at the direction of … ." See also Section 23.3 of *NFPA 72* for additional system feature documentation requirements. [72:7.2.1(1)]

N **A.13.7.3.2.2.1(12)** Paragraph 26.6.2.5 of *NFPA 72* allows for the following three communications pathway options when a supervising station fire alarm system is provided:

(1) Performance-based technologies
(2) Digital alarm communicator systems
(3) Radio systems, which includes one-way private and two-way RF systems

[72:7.2.1(12)]

Chapter 26 of *NFPA 72* includes several requirements specific to each of these communications pathway alternatives. In order to verify the provided communication path(s), and any shared equipment, comply with Code requirements, the following are examples of information that should be submitted as the minimum documentation for a supervising station fire alarm system:

(1) Performance-based technologies
   (a) The type of performance-based transmitter(s) to be used such as IP communicators, cellular radios, and so forth
   (b) Whether communications with the supervising station will be via a single pathway or a multiple pathway
   (c) An indication of the use, where applicable, of shared equipment such as routers, modems, and LANs within the protected premises
   (d) Battery calculations for the shared equipment, which should meet the requirements of 26.6.3.13 of *NFPA 72*
(2) Digital alarm communicator system
   (a) The primary communications pathway, which should be a telephone line
   (b) The secondary communications pathway, which should comply with 26.6.4.2.4 of *NFPA 72*
(3) Radio system
   (a) The type of radio system that will be used (private one-way or two-way RF)
   (b) The secondary power provided for the radio transmitter

[72:7.2.1(12)]

Where the transmitter equipment is located separately from the main fire alarm control unit, an indication of its protection in accordance with 10.4.4 of *NFPA 72* should also be provided within the minimum documentation. [72:7.2.1(12)]

N **A.13.7.3.2.3.6.6.3** It is the intent that if an original or current record of completion is not available for the overall system, the installer would provide a new record of completion that addresses items discovered about the system. The installer will complete the respective sections related to the overall system that have been discovered under the current scope of work. It is not the intent of this section to require an in-depth evaluation of an existing system solely for the purpose of completing a system-wide record of completion. [72:A.7.5.6.6.3]

A.13.7.3.2.3.8 This section is intended to provide a basis for the authority having jurisdiction to require third-party verification and certification that the authority having jurisdiction and the system owner can rely on to reasonably assure that the fire alarm system installation complies with the applicable requirements. Where the installation is an extension, modification, or reconfiguration of an existing system, the intent is that the verification be applicable only to the new work and that reacceptance testing be acceptable. [72:A.7.5.8]

A.13.7.3.2.5.1.2 It is intended that archived records be allowed to be stored in electronic format as long as hard copies can be made from them when required. [72:A.7.7.1.2]

A.13.7.3.2.5.2.3 The intent is that paper and/or electronic documents should not be stored inside the control unit because control units are not typically approved for the storage of combustible material. [72:A.7.7.2.3]

Examples of system documents include the following:

(1) Record drawings (as-builts)
(2) Equipment technical data sheets
(3) Alternative means and methods, variances, appeals, approvals, and so forth
(4) Performance-based design documentation in accordance with 7.3.7 of *NFPA 72*
(5) Risk analysis documentation in accordance with 7.3.6 of *NFPA 72*
(6) Emergency response plan in accordance with 7.3.8 of *NFPA 72*
(7) Evaluation documentation in accordance with 7.3.9 of *NFPA 72*
(8) Software and firmware control documentation in accordance with 23.2.2 of *NFPA 72*

[72:A.7.7.2.3]

A.13.7.3.2.5.2.6 Documentation stored in electronic media can become obsolete, for example, 5.25 in. and 3.5 in. disks and tape drives are not supported by current technology. Updating the stored media to current technology concerns the programs used to operate them, and the computer or hardware used to interface to the system installed. Thus, it is necessary to ensure that all components are still compatible with the installed system. [72:A.7.7.2.6]

A.13.7.3.2.5.3.2 It is recognized that there are circumstances in which the security and protection of some system documents will require measures other than that prescribed in *NFPA 72*. Since a common expectation of a mass notification system is to function during security and/or terrorist events, it could be crucial that system design be protected. [72:A.7.7.3.2]

Where such conditions have been identified, the stakeholders should clearly identify what and how system documents should be maintained to satisfy the integrity of this section regarding reviews, future service, modifications, and system support. [72:A.7.7.3.2]

Due to freedom of information laws allowing for public access to documents submitted to and retained by code officials, it could be necessary for secure documents to be reviewed by code officials at alternate locations. Such conditions should be identified by the stakeholders and discussed with the authorities having jurisdiction(s) in advance. [72:A.7.7.3.2]

A.13.7.3.3.8 Protective covers, also called pull station protectors can be installed over manually actuated alarm initiating devices to provide mechanical protection, environmental protection, and to reduce the likelihood of accidental or malicious activation. The protective covers must be listed to ensure that they do not hinder the operation of the pull stations and to ensure that they meet accessibility requirements for activation by persons with physical disabilities. The *Code* explicitly permits installing them over single- or double-action devices. When installed over a double-action device, the assembly effectively becomes a triple-action device. Some units include battery-operated audible warning signals that have been shown to deter malicious activations. To be effective, it is important that the regular staff or occupants be aware of the sound and investigate immediately in order to catch someone who might otherwise actuate the device without cause or to ensure that the device is actuated if there is a legitimate reason. [72:A.17.15.8]

A.13.7.3.3.9.3 In environments where red paint or red plastic is not suitable, an alternative material, such as stainless steel, could be used as long as the box meets the requirements of 13.7.3.3.9.2. [72:A.17.15.9.3]

A.13.7.3.3.9.5 It is not the intent of 13.7.3.3.9.5 to require manual fire alarm boxes to be attached to movable partitions or to equipment, nor to require the installation of permanent structures for mounting purposes only. [72:A.17.15.9.5]

A.13.7.3.4 The terms *certificated* and *placarded*, which appeared in previous editions of *NFPA 72*, were considered by some to be too specific to two listing organizations and were replaced with more generic wording. The concept of providing documentation to indicate ongoing compliance of an installed system continues to be reflected by the current language. [72:A.26.3.4]

There are two distinct services offered by organizations that list fire alarm service provided by prime contractors and central stations. The first is the listing of these alarm services, which requires the companies to demonstrate they have the knowledge and ability to install, test, service, and maintain central station alarm systems and/or monitor and appropriately retransmit on receipt of various signals from protected premises alarm systems. [72:A.26.3.4]

The second part of the service provided by listing organizations is the certification of individual protected premises fire alarm systems to bring the alarm systems under their ongoing audit inspection program or systematic follow-up program. Under this program, systems are certified by the listing organization, and documentation of this is to be provided, posted, and handled as described in 13.7.3.4 through 13.7.3.4.8. The method used to document compliance with this portion of the program varies among listing organizations and includes the issuance of certificates, placards, or other documentation. [72:A.26.3.4]

There is nothing in this Code that requires all protected premises alarm systems monitored by a listed central station to be tested, maintained, serviced, monitored, and responded to in accordance with Section 26.3 of *NFPA 72*. This is often misunderstood by code users, owners, and AHJs, who think that merely specifying that these systems be monitored by a central station with a fire alarm listing gets them full central station service. Full compliance with central station alarm system requirements involves using alarm companies with fire alarm listings and having the listing organization certify the protected premises alarm system. [72:A.26.3.4]

A.13.7.3.4.2(2) The record of completion *(see Chapter 10 of NFPA 72)* can be used to fulfill this requirement. [72:A.26.3.4.2(2)]

A.13.7.3.4.5 It is the prime contractor's responsibility to remove all compliance markings (certification markings or placards) when a service contract goes into effect that conflicts in any way with the requirements of 13.7.3.4. [72:A.26.3.4.5]

A.13.7.3.4.6 The prime contractor should be aware of statutes, public agency regulations, or certifications regarding alarm systems that might be binding on the subscriber. The prime contractor should identify for the subscriber which agencies could be an AHJ and, if possible, advise the subscriber of any requirements or approvals being mandated by these agencies. [72:A.26.3.4.6]

The subscriber has the responsibility for notifying the prime contractor of those private organizations that are being designated as an AHJ. The subscriber also has the responsibility to notify the prime contractor of changes in the AHJ, such as where there is a change in insurance companies. Although the responsibility is primarily the subscriber's, the prime contractor should also take responsibility for seeking out these private AHJs through the subscriber. The prime contractor is responsible for maintaining current records on the AHJ for each protected premises. [72:A.26.3.4.6]

The most prevalent public agency involved as an AHJ with regard to alarm systems is the local fire department or fire prevention bureau. These are normally city or county agencies with statutory authority, and their approval of alarm system installations might be required. At the state level, the fire marshal's office is most likely to serve as the public regulatory agency. [72:A.26.3.4.6]

The most prevalent private organizations involved as AHJs are insurance companies. Others include insurance rating bureaus, insurance brokers and agents, and private consultants. It is important to note that these organizations have no statutory authority and become AHJs only when designated by the subscriber. [72:A.26.3.4.6]

With both public and private concerns to satisfy, it is not uncommon to find multiple AHJs involved with a particular protected premises. It is necessary to identify all AHJs in order to obtain all the necessary approvals for a central station alarm system installation. [72:A.26.3.4.6]

The phrase "in writing" can include any form of correspondence that can be verified upon request, such as a letter, fax, email, or other means of documented transfer of information from one entity to another. [72:A.26.3.4.6]

A.13.7.4.1.2.3 Situations exist where supplemental enclosures are necessary to protect the physical integrity of an initiating device. Protective enclosures should not interfere with the performance characteristics of the device. If the enclosure degrades the performance, methods should be detailed in the manufacturer's published instructions of the protection device that clearly identify the degradation. In some cases, adjustments to initiating device sensitivity or range of operation are necessary to ensure the objective and performance of the system. [**72:**A.17.4.2.3]

A.13.7.4.2.2 This requirement is based on the generally accepted principle that the ceiling jet is approximately 10 percent of the distance from the base of the fire to the ceiling. To this figure, an additional safety factor of 50 percent has been added. Performance-based methods are available to predict the impact of partitions on the flow of smoke to detectors and can be used to substantiate a less restrictive design criterion. [**72:**A.17.5.2]

A.13.7.4.3.1 Figure A.13.7.4.3.1 illustrates the proper mounting placement for detectors. [**72:**A.17.6.3.1.3.1]

A.13.7.4.3.3 In high-ceiling areas, such as atriums, where spot-type smoke detectors are not accessible for periodic maintenance and testing, projected beam–type or air sampling–type detectors should be considered where access can be provided. [**72:**A.17.7.4.2]

A.13.7.4.3.3.1 Refer to Figure A.13.7.4.3.3.1 for an example of proper mounting for detectors. Sidewall detectors mounted closer to the ceiling will respond faster. [**72:**A.17.7.4.2.1]

A.13.7.4.3.3.2 Figure A.13.7.4.3.3.2 illustrates under-floor mounting installations. [**72:**A.17.7.4.2.2]

A.13.7.4.3.3.3.1 The 30 ft (9.1 m) spacing is a guide for prescriptive designs. The use of such a spacing is based upon customary practice in the fire alarm community. [**72:**A.17.7.4.2.3.1]

△ FIGURE A.13.7.4.3.3.1 Example of Proper Mounting of Smoke Detectors. [72: Figure A.17.7.4.2.1]

Where there are explicit performance objectives for the response of the smoke detection system, the performance-based design methods outlined in Annex B of *NFPA 72* should be used. [**72:**A.17.7.4.2.3.1]

For the purposes of this section, "nominal 30 ft (9.1 m)" should be determined to be 30 ft (9.1 m) ±5 percent [±18 in. (460 mm)]. [**72:**A.17.7.4.2.3.1]

A.13.7.4.3.3.3.1(2) This is useful in calculating locations in corridors or irregular areas *[see 17.6.3.1.1 of NFPA 72 and Figure A.17.6.3.1.1(h) of NFPA 72]*. For irregularly shaped areas, the spacing between detectors can be greater than the selected spacing, provided the maximum spacing from a detector to the farthest point of a sidewall or corner within its zone of protection is not greater than 0.7 times the selected spacing (0.7S). [**72:**A.17.7.4.2.3.1(2)]

A.13.7.4.3.3.4 Detectors are placed at reduced spacings at right angles to joists or beams in an attempt to ensure that detection time is equivalent to that which would be experienced on a flat ceiling. It takes longer for the combustion products (smoke or heat) to travel at right angles to beams or joists because of the phenomenon wherein a plume from a relatively hot fire with significant thermal lift tends to fill the pocket between each beam or joist before moving to the next beam or joist. [**72:**A.17.7.4.2.4]

Though it is true that this phenomenon might not be significant in a small smoldering fire where there is only enough thermal lift to cause stratification at the bottom of the joists, reduced spacing is still recommended to ensure that detection time is equivalent to that which would exist on a flat ceiling, even in the case of a hotter type of fire. [**72:**A.17.7.4.2.4]

A.13.7.4.3.3.4.2(3) The geometry and reservoir effect is a significant factor that contributes to the development of velocity, temperature, and smoke obscuration conditions at smoke detectors located on the ceiling in beam pocket areas or at the bottom of beams as smoke collected in the reservoir volume spills into adjacent pockets. The waffle- or pan-type ceiling created by beams or solid joists, although retarding the initial flow of smoke, results in increased optical density, temperature

FIGURE A.13.7.4.3.1 Example of Proper Mounting for Heat Detectors. [72: Figure A.17.6.3.1.3.1]

rise, and gas velocities comparable to unconfined smooth ceilings. [**72:**A.17.7.4.2.4.2(3)]

For waffle- or pan-type ceilings with beams or solid joists, an alternative smoke detector grid arrangement (such as a shifted grid), with detectors located to take advantage of the channeling effect due to the reservoirs created by the beam pockets, will improve detector response and might allow greater spacing. See Figure A.13.7.4.3.3.4.2(3)(a) and Figure A.13.7.4.3.3.4.2(3)(b) for an example of shifted grids. The alternative smoke detector grid arrangement and spacing should be justified by an engineering analysis comparing the alternative smoke detector grid arrangement with the performance of smoke detectors on a level ceiling of equal height using 30 ft (9.1 m) smoke detector spacing. [**72:**A.17.7.4.2.4.2(3)]

Figure A.13.7.4.3.3.4.2(3)(a) illustrates the reservoir and channeling effect that results from the deep beam configuration. The strongest gas flows occur in a direction perpendicular to the beam opposite the fire location. The weaker flow occurs in a directional 45 degrees off the beam grid; however, the reservoir effect accounts for higher concentrations of smoke eventually flowing from the strong area reservoirs into the weak area reservoirs. [**72:**A.17.7.4.2.4.2(3)]

Figure A.13.7.4.3.3.4.2(3)(b) is a generic example illustrating how a smoke detection grid using 30 ft (9.1 m) spacing can be shifted to take advantage of the channeling and reservoir effect to optimize detection response. In the circle, the fire is split into four beam bays that must fill with smoke before appreciable flows occur into the next adjoining eight beam bays. This represents the worst case scenario for smoke to reach the detectors on the circle. The three other fire locations shown require the fire to initially fill only one or two bays before spilling to adjacent bays. [**72:**A.17.7.4.2.4.2(3)]

A.13.7.4.3.3.4.2(4) Corridor geometry is a significant factor that contributes to the development of velocity, temperature, and smoke obscuration conditions at smoke detectors located along a corridor. This is based on the fact that the ceiling jet is confined or constrained by the nearby walls without opportunity for entrainment of air. For corridors of approximately 15 ft (4.6 m) in width and for fires of approximately 100 kW or greater, modeling has demonstrated that the performance of smoke detectors in corridors with beams has been shown to be comparable to spot smoke detector spacing on an unconfined smooth ceiling surface. [**72:**A.17.7.4.2.4.2(4)]

A.13.7.4.3.3.4.3 A smoke detector should be placed within each beam channel. Computer modeling has shown that parallel beams (upslope) are very effective at channeling smoke, and smoke spillover is rarely detectable in adjacent parallel pockets. [**72:**A.17.7.4.2.4.3]

A.13.7.4.3.3.4.4 Irregular area spacing guidance for level beam ceilings can be used. Computer modeling has shown that spot-type detectors should be located on the bottom of perpendicular beams. [**72:**A.17.7.4.2.4.4]

A.13.7.4.3.3.4.5 Computer modeling has shown that spot-type detectors should be located on the bottom of perpendicular beams and should be aligned with the center of pocket, as shown, in Figure A.13.7.4.3.3.4.5. [**72:**A.17.7.4.2.4.5]

A.13.7.4.3.3.4.2.6 Identification can include means such as marking or use of a configuration management program that identifies locations. [**72:**A.17.7.4.6.2.6]

Δ **FIGURE A.13.7.4.3.3.2** Mounting Installations Permitted (*top*) and Not Permitted (*bottom*). [72: Figure A.17.7.4.2.2]

△ FIGURE A.13.7.4.3.3.4.2(3)(a)   Reservoir and Channeling Effect of Deep Beams. [72: Figure A.17.7.4.2.4.2(3)(a)]

△ FIGURE A.13.7.4.3.3.4.2(3)(b)   Shifted Smoke Detection Grid to Optimize Detection for Deep Beam Effects. [72: Figure A.17.7.4.2.4.2(3)(b)]

△ FIGURE A.13.7.4.3.3.4.5   Spot-Type Detector Spacing for Sloping Ceilings with Beam Pockets. [72: Figure A.17.7.4.2.4.5]

A.13.7.4.3.4.2.7 A benchmark test point should be provided at the furthest end of each pipe run, opposite the end of the air sampling–type smoke detector apparatus. This remote test point is intended to benchmark system performance at the time of initial commissioning and during routine test and inspection. The test point should be labeled to document benchmark system performance at the time of commissioning, using manufacturer-supplied labels intended for this purpose. Benchmark labels should be placed just above test points and be positioned so that they are visible without obstruction. [**72:**A.17.7.4.6.2.7]

A.13.7.4.3.4.2.9 Where installed in areas having environmental conditions such as high temperature or humidity, radiation or corrosive atmospheres, all pipe network materials should be suitable for the specific environmental conditions anticipated. [**72:**A.17.7.4.6.2.9]

A.13.7.4.3.5 On smooth ceilings, a spacing of not more than 60 ft (18.3 m) between projected beams and not more than one-half that spacing between a projected beam and a sidewall (i.e., wall parallel to the beam travel) should be used as a guide. Other spacing should be determined based on ceiling height, airflow characteristics, and response requirements. [**72:**A.17.7.4.7]

In some cases, the light beam projector is mounted on one end wall, with the light beam receiver or reflector mounted on the opposite wall. However, it is also permitted to suspend the projector and receiver/reflector from the ceiling at a distance from the end walls not exceeding one-quarter the selected spacing (S). *(See Figure A.13.7.4.3.5.)* [**72:**A.17.7.4.7]

A.13.7.4.3.5.8 Where the light path of a projected beam–type detector is abruptly interrupted or obscured, the unit should not initiate an alarm. It should give a trouble signal after verification of blockage. [**72:**A.17.7.4.7.8]

A.13.7.4.3.6 Construction debris, dust (especially gypsum dust and the fines resulting from the sanding of drywall joint compounds), and aerosols can affect the sensitivity of smoke detectors and, in some instances, cause deleterious effects to

FIGURE A.13.7.4.3.5 Maximum Distance at Which Ceiling-Suspended Light Projector and Receiver Can Be Positioned from End Wall Is One-Quarter Selected Spacing (S). [72:Figure A.17.7.4.7]

S = Selected detector spacing

the detector, thereby significantly reducing the expected life of the detector. [*72*:A.17.7.2]

A.13.7.4.3.8.2 Smoke detector spacing depends on the movement of air within the room. [*72*:A.17.7.7.3.3]

A.14.3.1(1) In existing buildings, existing walls in good repair and consisting of lath and plaster, gypsum panel products, or masonry units can usually provide satisfactory protection for the purposes of this requirement where a 1-hour fire resistance rating is required. Further evaluation might be needed where a 2-hour fire resistance rating is required. Additional guidelines can be found in Annex O of NFPA 914 and in the *SFPE Handbook of Fire Protection Engineering*. [*101*:A.7.1.3.2.1(1)]

A.14.3.1(3) In existing buildings, existing walls in good repair and consisting of lath and plaster, gypsum panel products, or masonry units can usually provide satisfactory protection for the purposes of this requirement where a 1-hour fire resistance rating is required. Further evaluation might be needed where a 2-hour fire resistance rating is required. Additional guidelines can be found in Annex O of NFPA 914 and in the *SFPE Handbook of Fire Protection Engineering*. [*101*:A.7.1.3.2.1(3)]

A.14.3.1(5) It is not the intent to require the structural elements supporting outside stairs, or structural elements that penetrate within exterior walls or any other wall not required to have a fire resistance rating, to be protected by fire-resistance-rated construction. [*101*:A.7.1.3.2.1(5)]

A.14.3.1(8) Means of egress from the level of exit discharge is permitted to pass through an exit stair enclosure or exit passageway serving other floors. Doors for convenience purposes and unrelated to egress also are permitted to provide access to and from exit stair enclosures and exit passageways, provided that such doors are from corridors or normally occupied spaces. It is also the intent of this provision to prohibit exit enclosure windows, other than approved vision panels in doors, that are not mounted in an exterior wall. [*101*:A.7.1.3.2.1(8)]

A.14.3.1(9)(b) The intent of this provision is to prevent the exit enclosure from being used as a vertical chase for building services. Penetrations for electrical wiring are permitted where the wiring serves equipment permitted by the AHJ to be located within the exit enclosure. [*101*:A.7.1.3.2.1(9)(b)]

A.14.3.1(9)(d) This provision will allow security cameras, public address systems, emergency communication systems, telephone repeaters and similar life safety devices in the exit enclosure, and wiring and similar pathways for such devices, to penetrate the fire barrier serving the exit enclosure. It is the intent of this provision to prevent the exit enclosure from being used as a vertical chase for building services. [*101*:A.7.1.3.2.1(9)(d)]

A.14.3.3 This provision prohibits the use of exit enclosures for storage or for installation of equipment not necessary for safety. Occupancy is prohibited other than for egress, refuge, and access. The intent is that the exit enclosure essentially be "sterile" with respect to fire safety hazards. [*101*:A.7.1.3.2.3]

A.14.4.1 A proper means of egress allows unobstructed travel at all times. Any type of barrier including, but not limited to, the accumulations of snow and ice in those climates subject to such accumulations is an impediment to free movement in the means of egress. Another example of an obstruction or impediment to full instant use of means of egress is any security device or system that emits any medium that could obscure a means of egress. It is, however, recognized that obstructions occur on a short-duration basis. In these instances, awareness training should be provided to ensure that blockages are kept to a minimum and procedures are established for the control and monitoring of the area affected. [*101*:A.7.1.10.1]

A.14.5.1.1 Where doors are subject to two-way traffic, or where their opening can interfere with pedestrian traffic, an appropriately located vision panel can reduce the chance of accidents. [*101*:A.7.2.1.4.1]

Swinging doors in horizontal- or vertical-rolling partitions should be permitted in a means of egress where the following criteria are met:

(1) The door or doors comply with 14.5.1.
(2) The partition in which the doors are mounted complies with the applicable fire protection rating and closes upon smoke detection or power failure at a speed not exceeding 9 in./s (230 mm/s) and not less than 6 in./s (150 mm/s).
(3) The doors mounted in the partition are self-closing or automatic-closing in accordance with 14.5.4.1.

[*101*:A.7.2.1.4.1]

Pivoted-swinging-type doors include balanced doors. [*101*:A.7.2.1.4.1]

A.14.5.1.2 See 7.4.2.1.2 and 7.4.2.2.2 of NFPA *101* for door swing direction requirements for working space about electrical equipment. [*101*:A.7.2.1.4.2]

A.14.5.1.3 The requirements of 14.5.1.3 are not intended to apply to the swing of cross-corridor doors, such as smoke barrier doors and horizontal exits. Neither are the requirements intended to apply to doors from rooms that are typically unoccupied, such as janitor's closets, electrical closets, or telecommunications closets. [*101*:A.7.2.1.4.3]

A.14.5.2.3 Examples of devices that might be arranged to release locks and latches include knobs, levers, and bars. This requirement is permitted to be satisfied by the use of conventional types of hardware, whereby the door is released by turning a lever, knob, or handle or by pushing against a bar, but not by unfamiliar methods of operation such as a blow to break glass. It is also within the intent of this requirement that switches integral to traditional doorknobs, lever handles, or bars, and that interrupt the power supply to an electrical lock, be permitted, provided that they are affixed to the door leaf. [*101*:A.7.2.1.5.3]

A.14.5.2.3.2 An example of a releasing motion in a single linear direction, as described in ANSI/BHMA A156.41, *Standard for Door Hardware Single Motion to Egress*, is pushing on a panic bar to release the locking/latching hardware to allow a door to be opened. An example of a releasing motion in a single rotational direction is turning a lever-operated handle of a door lockset in either a clockwise direction or a counterclockwise direction, but not both directions, to unlock/unlatch the door. [*101*:A.7.2.1.5.3.2]

Δ **A.14.5.2.3.4** Examples of devices that, when used with a latch, can be arranged to require not more than one additional releasing operation include dead bolts, security chains, swing door locks, and privacy door guards. [*101*:A.7.2.1.5.3.4]

A.14.5.2.5 Some fire door assemblies are listed for use with fire pins or fusible links that render the door leaf release inoperative upon exposure to elevated temperature during a fire. The door leaf release mechanism is made inoperative where conditions in the vicinity of the door opening become untenable for human occupancy, and such door opening no longer provides a viable egress path. [*101*:A.7.2.1.5.5]

A.14.5.2.6.2 Where the entrance consists of an exterior vestibule, the locking arrangement should be permitted on the egress side of either the interior or exterior door of the vestibule. [*101*:A.7.2.1.5.6.2]

A.14.5.2.7 It is intended that the re-entry provisions apply only to enclosed exit stairs, not to outside stairs. This arrangement makes it possible to leave the stairway at such floor if the fire renders the lower part of the stair unusable during egress or if the occupants seek refuge on another floor. [*101*:A.7.2.1.5.7]

A.14.5.2.10 Examples of devices prohibited by this requirement include locks, padlocks, hasps, bars, chains, or combinations thereof. [*101*:A.7.2.1.5.10]

A.14.5.3 None of the special locking arrangements addressed in 14.5.3 are intended to allow *credentialed egress* or similar provisions, where an occupant cannot leave the building without swiping a card through a reader. Where such an arrangement is desired to keep track of occupants, the swiping of cards needs to be procedural but not necessary for releasing the door lock or latch. Egress needs to be available at all times as required by this *Code*. [*101*:A.7.2.1.6]

A.14.5.3.1 Delayed-egress electrical locking systems function as the name suggests: these electrical locking systems delay egress through the door. However, 14.5.3.1.1(1) and 14.5.3.1.1(2) identify situations where the delay of these locking systems must be deactivated, facilitating immediate and unobstructed egress. Delayed-egress electrical locking systems are most commonly installed where there are concerns for internal security, such as theft from a store through required perimeter exits. Delayed-egress electrical locking systems might also be installed where occupants might benefit by being protected from their actions. [*101*:A.7.2.1.6.1]

A.14.5.3.1.1(3) It is not the intent to require a direct physical or electrical connection between the door release device and the lock. It is the intent to allow door movement initiated by operating the door release device required in 14.5.2.3 as the primary option to initiate the irreversible process. [*101*:A.7.2.1.6.1.1(3)]

Delayed-egress electrical locking systems commonly employ a mechanical latch and/or lock in addition to an electrical lock. The use of a mechanical latch/lock in addition to an electrical lock such as a magnetic lock allows a door to be mechanically locked preventing uncontrolled ingress should the electrical lock be de-energized as in a power failure. [*101*:A.7.2.1.6.1.1(3)]

Several factors need to be considered in approving an increase in delay time from 15 seconds to 30 seconds. Some of those factors include occupancy, occupant density, ceiling height, fire hazards present, fire protection features provided, and the location of the delayed-egress locks. An example of a location where the increase on delay time might not be approved is at an exit stair discharge door. [*101*:A.7.2.1.6.1.1(3)]

A.14.5.3.1.1(4) In the event that the AHJ has permitted increased operation time, the sign should reflect the appropriate time. [*101*:A.7.2.1.6.1.1(4)]

N **A.14.5.3.1.1(6)** The electrical locking hardware might be a component of an electrical locking system, or it might be a device with an individual listing. Depending on the electrical locking system or component, either UL 294 or UL 1034 is the pertinent standard for the required listing. [*101*:A.7.2.1.6.1.1(6)]

A.14.5.3.2 Doors with a sensor-release electrical locking system are equipped with an electrical locking system that is released by a sensor activated by the normal motions of an occupant egressing through that door. The activation of the sensor to cause the electrical lock to release is usually by passive action by the occupant, such as walking to the door. A manual release device, such as a push-button switch that directly interrupts the power to the electrical lock, is required by item (3) as a backup. With most sensor-release electrical locking systems, the occupant might not notice the door is electrically locked in the direction of egress. Doors equipped with these locking systems provide unobstructed, immediate egress. [*101*:A.7.2.1.6.2]

These provisions were previously titled "Access-Controlled Egress Door Assemblies" as these doors typically have some type of access control system, such as a key pad, card scanner, or fob scanner controlling access (ingress) into the building or space. Because access control systems can be installed on essentially any door, the previous title resulted in differing interpretations, applications, and enforcement of permitted locking systems, and they were retitled in the 2018 edition of the *Code*. [*101*:A.7.2.1.6.2]

N **A.14.5.3.2.1(8)** The electrical locking hardware might be a component of an electrical locking system, or it might be a device with an individual listing. Depending on the electrical locking system or component, either UL 294 or UL 1034 is the pertinent standard for the required listing. [*101*:A.7.2.1.6.2.1(8)]

A.14.5.3.3.1(5) It is critical that the electrical lock be arranged to release upon loss of power to the releasing hardware to ensure occupants can egress in the event of a power failure. [*101*:A.7.2.1.6.3.1(5)]

A.14.5.3.4 The electrical locking provisions of 14.5.3.4 for elevator lobby exit access door assemblies are similar to, but different from, the electrical locking systems of 14.5.3.1, 14.5.3.2, and 14.5.3.3. [*101*:A.7.2.1.6.4]

On doors to tenant spaces from the elevator lobby, it is not the intent to prohibit these doors from being equipped with access control systems, such as card readers controlling access to the tenant spaces, provided that the door leading from the elevator lobby is not in the path to the exit access required by 14.9.1.6.1. [*101*:A.7.2.1.6.4]

It is acceptable to use a sensor-release electrical locking system from a tenant space into the elevator lobby with the sensor on the tenant (egress)side of the door to allow free access to the elevator lobby. [*101*:A.7.2.1.6.4]

A.14.5.3.5 See 14.9.2.1.2 and 14.9.2.2.2 for door unlatching requirements for working space about electrical equipment. [*101*:A.7.2.1.7]

A.14.5.3.5.3 The presence of fire exit hardware on a door does not imply the door is required to be a fire protection-rated door. [*101*:A.7.2.1.7.3]

A.14.5.4.1 Examples of doors designed to normally be kept closed include those to a stair enclosure or horizontal exit. [*101*:A.7.2.1.8.1]

A.14.5.5 Special-purpose horizontally sliding accordion or folding door assemblies installed in accordance with 14.5.9 should not be considered powered doors subject to the provisions of 14.5.5. [*101*:A.7.2.1.9]

Powered doors are divided into two categories — power-assisted or low-energy power-operated doors and power-operated doors. Doors that conform to ANSI/BHMA A156.19, *Power Assist and Low Energy Power Operated Doors*, or ANSI/BHMA A156.38, *Low Energy Power Operated Sliding and Folding Doors*, use limited power to operate the door. These door operators are for swinging, sliding, or folding doors. Power-assisted and low-energy power-operated doors require fewer safeguards as compared to power-operated doors. Doors that conform to ANSI/BHMA A156.10, *Power Operated Pedestrian Doors*, require more power to operate the door and require additional safeguards to provide protection against personal injury. Power-operated doors can be swinging, sliding, or folding doors. [*101*:A.7.2.1.9]

A.14.5.5.1 An example of the type of door addressed by 14.5.5.1 is one actuated by a motion-sensing device upon the approach of a person. [*101*:A.7.2.1.9.1]

A.14.5.5.1.8 Although a single power-operated door leaf located within a two-leaf opening might alone not provide more than 30 in. (760 mm) of clear width in the emergency breakout mode, where both leaves are broken out to become side hinged, the required egress width is permitted to be provided by the width of the entire opening. [*101*:A.7.2.1.9.1.8]

A.14.5.7.1.3 Security access turnstiles are designed to control security access into and out of buildings. Security access turnstiles might utilize physical barriers consisting of arms, wings, gates, or panels. The subject physical barriers come in various heights and function by retracting or opening in the direction of travel. [*101*:A.7.2.1.11.1.3]

Δ **A.14.5.10.1** Door assemblies within the required means of egress (e.g., door assemblies that discharge from exit enclosures) require a higher level of care and maintenance throughout the life of their installations to ensure they perform as intended by the *Code*. Annual inspection and functional testing of these door assemblies is necessary to verify that they are maintained in proper working condition. Panic hardware and fire exit hardware devices are specifically required to be used in assembly and educational occupancies. However, door leaves that are equipped with panic hardware or fire exit hardware, in areas not specifically required by the *Code* (e.g., stairwell entry doors and double-egress cross-corridor door assemblies not serving an assembly occupancy), should be subject to annual inspection and functional testing to ensure that the operating hardware functions correctly in accordance with 14.5.3.4, since the presence of panic hardware and fire exit hardware implies it is required by the *Code*. [*101*:A.7.2.1.14.1]

Additionally, door assemblies that are door hardware-release of electrically locked egress door assemblies in accordance with 14.5.3.3 and door assemblies that are equipped with special locking arrangements in accordance with 14.5.3.3 are outfitted with electrified hardware and devices that are susceptible to wear and abuse. Consequently, these door assemblies need to be inspected and tested on an annual basis, regardless of the occupant load being served. [*101*:A.7.2.1.14.1]

In cases where the AHJ determines there is a distinct hazard to building occupant safety, the inspection requirements of 7.2.1.14 in NFPA *101* should be applied to other exit access, exit, and exit discharge door assemblies. [*101*:A.7.2.1.14.1]

A.14.5.10.2 See NFPA 80, Annex J, for information pertaining to performance-based inspection, testing, and maintenance of door assemblies. See NFPA 105, Annex B, for information pertaining to performance-based inspection, testing, and maintenance of smoke door assemblies. [*101*:A.7.2.1.14.2]

A.14.5.10.7 Performing corrective action work on door assemblies frequently requires ordering replacement components that might take time to produce, ship, and install. Consideration of the time it takes to procure and install components should be included in the timeline for restoring the door assemblies to normal working condition. [*101*:A.7.2.1.14.7]

A.14.6.2 The purpose of this provision is to protect the exterior wall of a stairway from fires in other portions of the building. If the exterior wall of the stair is flush with the building exterior wall, the fire would need to travel around 180 degrees in order to impact the stair. This has not been a problem in existing buildings, so no protection is required. However, if the angle of exposure is less than 180 degrees, protection of either the stair wall or building wall is required. [*101*:A.7.2.2.5.2]

Figure A.14.6.2(a), Figure A.14.6.2(b), and Figure A.14.6.2(c) illustrate the requirement, assuming nonrated glass on the exterior wall of the stair is used. [*101*:A.7.2.2.5.2]

A.14.6.3 An example of a use with the potential to interfere with egress is storage. [*101*:A.7.2.2.5.3]

A.14.7 An exit passageway serves as a horizontal means of exit travel that is protected from fire in a manner similar to an enclosed interior exit stair. Where it is desired to offset exit stairs in a multistory building, an exit passageway can be used to preserve the continuity of the protected exit by connecting the bottom of one stair to the top of the stair that continues to the street floor. Probably the most important use of an exit passageway is to satisfy the requirement that at least 50 percent of the exit stairs discharge directly outside from multistory

FIGURE A.14.6.2(a) Stairway with Nonrated Exterior Wall in Same Plane as Building Exterior Wall. [*101*:Figure A.7.2.2.5.2(a)]

FIGURE A.14.6.2(b) Stairway with Unprotected Exterior Perimeter Protruding Past Building Exterior Wall. [*101*:Figure A.7.2.2.5.2(b)]

FIGURE A.14.6.2(c) Stairway with Nonrated Exterior Wall Exposed by Adjacent Exterior Wall of Building. [*101*:Figure A.7.2.2.5.2(c)]

buildings (*see 7.7.2 of NFPA 101*). Thus, if it is impractical to locate the stair on an exterior wall, an exit passageway can be connected to the bottom of the stair to convey the occupants safely to an outside exit door. In buildings of extremely large area, such as shopping mall concourses and some factories, the exit passageway can be used to advantage where the travel distance to reach an exit would otherwise be excessive. [*101*:A.7.2.6]

A.14.7.1 Examples of building elements that might be arranged as exit passageways include hallways, corridors, passages, tunnels, underfloor passageways, or overhead passageways. [*101*:A.7.2.6.1]

A.14.7.4.1(1) Where an exit passageway serves occupants on the level of exit discharge as well as other floors, it should not be required that the occupant loads be added, thus increasing the width of the exit passageway. The situation is the same as that in which occupants from the level of exit discharge join occupants from upper floors for a few feet of horizontal travel through a stair enclosure. [*101*:A.7.2.6.4.1(1)]

Δ **A.14.8.1.2** When using Table 14.8.1.2, the actual use of the space and not the occupancy classification should be considered. [*101*:A.7.3.1.2]

The normal occupant load is not necessarily a suitable criterion, because the greatest hazard can occur when an unusually large crowd is present, which is a condition often difficult for AHJs to control by regulatory measures. The principle of this *Code* is to provide means of egress for the maximum probable number of occupants, rather than to attempt to limit occupants to a number commensurate with available means of egress. However, limits of occupancy are specified in certain special cases for other reasons. [*101*:A.7.3.1.2]

Suggested occupant load factors for components of large airport terminal buildings are given in Table A.14.8.1.2. However, the AHJ might elect to use different occupant load factors, provided that egress requirements are satisfied. [*101*:A.7.3.1.2]

The figure used in determining the occupancy load for mall shopping centers of varying sizes was arrived at empirically by surveying over 270 mall shopping centers, by studying mercantile occupancy parking requirements, and by observing the number of occupants per vehicle during peak seasons. [*101*:A.7.3.1.2]

These studies show that, with an increase in shopping center size, there is a decrease in the number of occupants per square foot of gross leasable area. [*101*:A.7.3.1.2]

This phenomenon is explained when one considers that, above a certain shopping center gross leasable area [approximately 600,000 ft^2 (56,000 m^2)], there exists a multiplicity of the same types of stores. The purpose of duplicate types of stores is to increase the choices available to a customer for any given type of merchandise. Therefore, when shopping center size increases, the occupant load increases as well, but at a declining rate. In using Figure 14.8.1.2(a) or Figure 14.8.1.2(b), the occupant load factor is applied only to the gross leasable area that uses the mall concourse as a means of egress. [*101*:Table A.7.3.1.2]

The value for concentrated business use is intended to address business use spaces with a higher density of occupants than would normally be expected in a general business occupancy. Where furnishings and floor layouts are arranged to maximize the number of occupants in the space, the value for concentrated business use should be applied. Examples of concentrated business use areas are call centers, trading floors, and data processing centers. [*101*:A.7.3.1.2]

Collaboration rooms/spaces are common to office buildings. Their principal function is to permit collaboration among occupants in the privacy of a small room/space. These rooms/

spaces are primarily used by occupants of the business occupancy to transition temporarily from their regular workstation area in order to obtain privacy and to avoid disturbing other employees located in the open office environment. Collaboration rooms/spaces have been commonly referred to as quiet rooms, focus rooms, huddle rooms, and team rooms. [*101*:A.7.3.1.2]

Collaboration rooms/spaces are not considered conference rooms, since a conference room's principal function is to be used for assembly purposes. [*101*:A.7.3.1.2]

A.14.8.3 In egress capacity calculations, standard rounding should be used. [*101*:7.3.3]

Δ **A.14.8.3.2** The effective capacity of stairways has been shown by research to be proportional to the effective width of the stairway, which is the nominal width minus 12 in. (305 mm). This phenomenon, and the supporting research, were described in Chapter 59, "Employing the Hydraulic Model in Assessing Emergency Movement," in the fifth edition of the *SFPE Handbook of Fire Protection Engineering* and was also addressed in Appendix D of the 1985 edition of NFPA *101*, among several other publications. In 1988, this appendix was moved to form Chapter 2 of the 1988 edition of NFPA 101M. (This document was later designated as NFPA 101A, and this chapter remained in the document through the 1998 edition.) In essence, the effective width phenomenon recognizes that there is an edge or boundary effect at the sides of a circulation path. It has been best examined in relation to stairway width, where the edge effect was estimated to be 6 in. (150 mm) on each side, but a similar phenomenon occurs with other paths, such as corridors and doors, although quantitative estimates of their edge effect are not as well established as they have been for stairways, at least those stairways studied in Canada during the late 1960s through the 1970s in office building evacuation drills and in crowd movement in a variety of buildings with assembly occupancy. [*101*:A.7.3.3.2]

More recent studies have not been performed to determine how the edge effect might be changing (or has changed) with demographic changes to larger, heavier occupants moving more slowly, and thus swaying laterally, to maintain balance when walking. The impact of such demographic changes, which are significant and influential for evacuation flow and speed of movement on stairs, for example, has the effect of increasing the time of evacuation in a way that affects all stair widths, but will be most pronounced for nominal widths less than 56 in. (1422 mm). [*101*:A.7.3.3.2]

Without taking into account occupant demographic changes in the last few decades that affect evacuation performance, especially on stairs, the formula for enhanced capacity of stairways wider than 44 in. (1120 mm) assumes that any portion of the nominal width greater than 44 in. (1120 mm) is as effective proportionally as the effective width of a nominal 44 in. (1120 mm) stair, that is, 32 in. (810 mm). Thus, the denominator (0.218) in the equation is simply the effective width of 32 in. (810 mm) divided by the capacity of 147 persons that is credited, by the 0.3 in. (7.6 mm) capacity factor in Table 14.8.3.1, to the corresponding nominal width, 44 in. (1120 mm). [*101*:A.7.3.3.2]

The resulting permitted stairway capacities, based on occupant load of single stories (in accordance with 7.3.1.4 of NFPA *101*), for several stairway widths are shown in Table A.14.8.3.2. [*101*:A.7.3.3.2]

A.14.8.3.4.1.1 The criteria of 14.8.3.4.1.1, as initially written, were intended to provide for minimum widths for small spaces such as individual offices. The intent is that these reductions in required width apply to spaces formed by furniture and movable walls, so that accommodations can easily be made for individuals using wheelchairs or other mobility devices. One side of a path could be a fixed wall, provided that the other side is movable. This does not exempt the door widths or widths of fixed-wall corridors, regardless of the number of people or length. The allowance for reduction in width has been expanded to include all exit accesses serving not more than six people where the travel length along the reduced-width path does not exceed 50 ft (15 m), regardless of occupancy or use of the space. [*101*:A.7.3.4.1.1]

Table A.14.8.3.2 Stairway Capacities

Permitted Capacity (no. of persons)	Nominal Width in.	Nominal Width mm	Clear Width Between Handrails[a] in.	Clear Width Between Handrails[a] mm	Effective Width in.	Effective Width mm
120[b]	36	915	28	710	24	610
147	44	1120	36	915	32	810
202	56	1420	48	1220	44	1120
257	68	1725	60[c]	1525[c]	56	1420

[a] A reasonable handrail incursion of only 4 in. (100 mm), into the nominal width is assumed on each side of the stair, although 7.3.2.2 of NFPA *101* permits a maximum incursion of 4½ in. (114 mm) on each side.
[b] Other *Code* sections limit the occupant load for such stairs more severely (e.g., 50 persons in 7.2.2.2.1.2 of NFPA *101*). Such lower limits are partly justified by the relatively small effective width of such stairs, which, if taken into account by Table 14.8.3.1, would result in a correspondingly low effective capacity of only 110 persons (24 divided by 0.218), or a more realistic capacity factor of 0.327, applicable to nominal width.
[c] A clear width of 60 in. (1525 mm) is the maximum permitted by the handrail reachability criteria of 7.2.2.4.1.2 of NFPA *101*. Although some prior editions of the *Code* permitted wider portions of stairs [up to 88 in. (2240 mm), between handrails], such wider portions are less effective for reasonably safe crowd flow and generally should not be used for major crowd movement. To achieve the maximum possible, reasonably safe egress capacity for such stairs, retrofit of an intermediate — not necessarily central — handrail is recommended; for example, with an intermediate handrail located 36 in. (915 mm) from the closest side handrail. In this case, the effective capacity would be 358 persons for the formerly permitted, now retrofitted, stair. This is based on a retrofitted, effective width of about 78 in. (1980 mm) [subtracting 2 in. (51 mm) from each usable side of a handrail and assuming a 2 in. (51 mm) wide, retrofitted intermediate handrail].
[*101*:Table A.7.3.3.2]

Table A.14.8.1.2 Airport Terminal Occupant Load Factors

Airport Terminal Area	ft² (gross)	m² (gross)
Concourse	100	9.3
Waiting areas	15	1.4
Baggage claim	20	1.9
Baggage handling	300	27.9

[*101*:Table A.7.3.1.2]

Figure A.14.8.3.4.1.1(a) and Figure A.14.8.3.4.1.1(b) present selected anthropometric data for adults. The male and female figures depicted in the figures are average, 50th percentile, in size. Some dimensions apply to very large, 97.5 percentile, adults (noted as 97.5 P). [*101*:A.7.3.4.1.1]

A.14.10.1.1.1 See A.14.10.1.2.1. [*101*:A.7.5.1.1.1]

A.14.10.1.2.1 The terms *dead end* and *common path of travel* are commonly used interchangeably. Although the concepts of each are similar in practice, they are two different concepts. [*101*:A.7.5.1.2.1]

A common path of travel exists where a space is arranged so that occupants within that space are able to travel in only one direction to reach any of the exits or to reach the point at which the occupants have the choice of two paths of travel to remote exits. Part (a) of Figure A.14.10.1.2.1 is an example of a common path of travel. [*101*:A.7.5.1.2.1]

While a dead end is similar to a common path of travel, a dead end can exist where there is no path of travel from an occupied space but can also exist where an occupant enters a corridor thinking there is an exit at the end and, finding none, is forced to retrace his or her path to reach a choice of exits.

FIGURE A.14.8.3.4.1.1(a) Anthropometric Data (in in.) for Adults; Males and Females of Average, 50th Percentile, Size; Some Dimensions Apply to Very Large, 97.5 Percentile (97.5 P), Adults. [*101*:Figure A.7.3.4.1.1(a)]

FIGURE A.14.8.3.4.1.1(b) Anthropometric Data (in mm) for Adults; Males and Females of Average, 50th Percentile, Size; Some Dimensions Apply to Very Large, 97.5 Percentile (97.5 P), Adults. [*101*:Figure A.7.3.4.1.1(b)]

Part (b) of Figure A.14.10.1.2.1 is an example of such a dead-end arrangement. [*101*:A.7.5.1.2.1]

Combining the two concepts, part (c) of Figure A.14.10.1.2.1 is an example of a combined dead-end/common path of travel problem. [*101*:A.7.5.1.2.1]

Common paths of travel and dead-end travel are measured using the same principles used to measure travel distance as described in Section 7.6 of NFPA *101*. Starting in the room shown in part (d) of Figure A.14.10.1.2.1, measurement is made from the most remote point in the room, A, along the natural path of travel, and through the doorway along the centerline of the corridor to point C, located at the centerline of the corridor, which then provides the choice of two different paths to remote exits; this is common path of travel. The space between point B and point C is a dead end. *(See 3.3.69 for the definition of common path of travel.)* [*101*:A.7.5.1.2.1]

A.14.10.1.3.2 Figure A.14.10.1.3.2(a) through Figure A.14.10.1.3.2(e) illustrate the method of measurement intended by 14.10.1.3.2. [*101*:A.7.5.1.3.2]

A.14.10.1.3.4 Figure A.14.10.1.3.4 illustrates the method of measuring exit separation distance along the line of travel within a minimum 1-hour fire-resistance-rated corridor. [*101*:A.7.5.1.3.4]

FIGURE A.14.10.1.2.1 Common Paths of Travel and Dead-End Corridors. [*101*:Figure A.7.5.1.2.1]

FIGURE A.14.10.1.3.2(a) Diagonal Rule for Exit Remoteness. [*101*:Figure A.7.5.1.3.2(a)]

FIGURE A.14.10.1.3.2(b) Diagonal Rule for Exit and Exit Access Door Remoteness. [*101*:Figure A.7.5.1.3.2(b)]

△ **A.14.10.1.4.2** It is difficult in actual practice to construct scissor stairs so that products of combustion that have entered one stairway do not penetrate into the other. Their use as separate required exits is discouraged. The term *limited-combustible* is intentionally not included in 14.10.1.4.2. The user's attention is directed to the provisions for limited-combustible and noncombustible in 4.5.9 and 4.5.10 in NFPA *101*, respectively. [*101*:A.7.5.1.4.2]

A.14.10.2.1 It is not the intent that an area with equipment such as a beverage brew pot, microwave oven, and a toaster be considered a kitchen. [*101*:A.7.5.2.1]

A.14.10.2.2 Doors that lead through wall paneling, and that harmonize in appearance with the rest of the wall to avoid detracting from some desired aesthetic or decorative effect, are not acceptable, because casual occupants might not be aware of such means of egress even though it is visible. [*101*:A.7.5.2.2]

A.14.10.4.1 An accessible means of egress should comply with the accessible route requirements of ICC A117.1, *Accessible and Usable Buildings and Facilities*. [*101*:A.7.5.4.1]

FIGURE A.14.10.1.3.2(c) Diagonal Rule for Exit and Access Remoteness. [*101*:Figure A.7.5.1.3.2(c)]

FIGURE A.14.10.1.3.2(d) Exit Separation and Diagonal Measurement of Area Served. [*101*:Figure A.7.5.1.3.2(d)]

FIGURE A.14.10.1.3.2(e) Diagonal Measurement for Unusually Shaped Areas. [*101*:Figure A.7.5.1.3.2(e)]

FIGURE A.14.10.1.3.4 Exit Separation Measured Along Corridor Path. [*101*:A.7.5.1.3.4]

A.14.11.1 An exit from the upper stories in which the direction of egress travel is generally downward should not be arranged so that it is necessary to change to travel in an upward direction at any point before discharging to the outside. A similar prohibition of reversal of the vertical component of travel should be applied to exits from stories below the floor of exit discharge. However, an exception is permitted in the case of stairs used in connection with overhead or underfloor exit passageways that serve the street floor only. [*101*:A.7.7.1]

It is important that ample roadways be available from buildings in which there are large numbers of occupants so that exits will not be blocked by persons already outside. Two or more avenues of departure should be available for all but very small places. Location of a larger theater — for example, on a narrow dead-end street — might be prohibited by the AHJ under this rule, unless some alternate way of travel to another street is available. [*101*:A.7.7.1]

Exterior walking surfaces within the exit discharge are not required to be paved and often are provided by grass or similar surfaces. Where discharging exits into yards, across lawns, or onto similar surfaces, in addition to providing the required width to allow all occupants safe access to a public way, such access also is required to meet the following:

(1) Provisions of 7.1.7 of NFPA *101* with respect to changes in elevation
(2) Provisions of 7.2.2 of NFPA *101* for stairs, as applicable
(3) Provisions of 7.2.5 of NFPA *101* for ramps, as applicable
(4) Provisions of 7.1.10 of NFPA *101* with respect to maintaining the means of egress free of obstructions that would prevent its use, such as snow and the need for its removal in some climates

[*101*:A.7.7.1]

A.14.11.3.3 Examples include partitions and gates. The design should not obstruct the normal movement of occupants to the exit discharge. Signs, graphics, or pictograms, including tactile types, might be permitted for existing exit enclosures where partitions or gates would obstruct the normal movement of occupants to the exit discharge. [*101*:A.7.7.3.3]

A.14.12.1.1 Illumination provided outside the building should be to either a public way or a distance away from the building that is considered safe, whichever is closest to the building being evacuated. [*101*:A.7.8.1.1]

A.14.12.1.2.2 Photoluminescent materials and battery-powered luminaires require some period of time to restore themselves to full operational capacity after being de-energized. [*101*:A.7.8.1.2.2]

Photoluminescent products rely on nearby luminaires to maintain their full capacity. When those luminaires are de-energized, the photoluminescent product will gradually deplete its capacity. Listed photoluminescent exit signs and path markers are restored to full rated capacity within one hour, and there is no known limit to the number of times they can be discharged and recharged, nor any known degradation of overall capacity or lifetime as a result of discharge/charge cycles. [*101*:A.7.8.1.2.2]

De-energizing the normal (utility) power source will automatically begin the battery discharge cycle of emergency luminaires, unit equipment, and exit signs provided with battery backup. Once drained, these batteries will typically require between 24 and 72 hours, depending on the battery technology and charging circuitry design, to regain full capacity. Frequent discharge/charge cycles can reduce overall battery lifetime and, depending on battery technology, might also prematurely reduce overall battery capacity. [*101*:A.7.8.1.2.2]

A.14.12.1.2.3 A consideration for the approval of automatic, motion sensor–type lighting switches, controls, timers, or controllers is whether the equipment is listed as a fail-safe device for use in the means of egress. [*101*:A.7.8.1.2.3]

A.14.12.1.3(4) Some processes, such as manufacturing or handling of photosensitive materials, cannot be performed in areas provided with the minimum specified lighting levels. The use of spaces with lighting levels below 1 foot-candle (10.8 lux) might necessitate additional safety measures, such as written emergency action plans, training of new employees in emergency evacuation procedures, and periodic fire drills. [*101*:A.7.8.1.3(4)]

A.14.12.1.4 Failure of a lighting unit is deemed to have occurred when the light output drops below 70 percent of its original level. [*101*:A.7.8.1.4]

A.14.13.1.1 Emergency lighting outside the building should provide illumination to either a public way or a distance away from the building that is considered safe, whichever is closest to the building being evacuated. [*101*:A.7.9.1.1]

A.14.14.1.2.1 Where a main entrance also serves as an exit, it will usually be sufficiently obvious to occupants so that no exit sign is needed. [*101*:A.7.10.1.2.1]

The character of the occupancy has a practical effect on the need for signs. In any assembly occupancy, hotel, department store, or other building subject to transient occupancy, the need for signs will be greater than in a building subject to permanent or semipermanent occupancy by the same people, such as an apartment house where the residents are presumed to be familiar with exit facilities by reason of regular use thereof. Even in a permanent residence–type building, however, there is need for signs to identify exit facilities such as outside stairs that are not subject to regular use during the normal occupancy of the building. [*101*:A.7.10.1.2.1]

The requirement for the locations of exit signs visible from any direction of exit access is illustrated in Figure A.14.14.1.2.1. [*101*:A.7.10.1.2.1]

A.14.14.1.2.2 The direction of travel to the exit discharge within a stair enclosure with horizontal components in excess of the typical landings might need additional signage to be readily visible or obvious. Exit signs should be installed above doors through which the egress path leads. Directional exit signs should be installed where the horizontal egress path changes directions. The stairway marking signs required by 10.11.3, provided within the stair enclosure at each floor landing, indicate the vertical direction to exit discharge. [*101*:A.7.10.1.2.2]

A.14.14.1.5.2 For externally illuminated signs in accordance with 14.14.6 and internally illuminated signs listed without a marked viewing distance, the rated viewing distance should be considered to be 100 ft (30 m). Where placing signs at their rated viewing distance requires them to be placed above the line of sight, consideration should be given to proportionally increasing the size of the exit legend to compensate for the additional straight-line distance between the viewer and the sign. [*101*:A.7.10.1.5.2]

A.14.14.1.6 See 14.14.3. [*101*:A.7.10.1.6]

A.14.14.1.7 See 3.3.158.2 of NFPA *101* for the definition of *internally illuminated*. [*101*:A.7.10.1.7]

A.14.14.1.8 In stores, for example, an otherwise adequate exit sign could be rendered inconspicuous by a high-intensity illuminated advertising sign located in the immediate vicinity. [*101*:A.7.10.1.8]

Red is the traditional color for exit signs and is required by law in many places. However, at an early stage in the development of NFPA *101*, a provision made green the color for exit signs, following the concept of traffic lights in which green indicates safety and red is the signal to stop. During the period when green signs were specified by NFPA *101*, many such signs were installed, but the traditional red signs also remained. In 1949, the Fire Marshals Association of North America voted to request that red be restored as the required exit sign color, because it was found that the provision for green involved difficulties in law enactment that were out of proportion to the importance of safety. Accordingly, the 10th edition of NFPA *101* specified red where not otherwise required by law. The present text avoids any specific requirement for color, based on the assumption that either red or green will be used in most cases and that there are some situations in which a color other than red or green could actually provide better visibility. [*101*:A.7.10.1.8]

A.14.14.3 Where graphics are used, the symbols provided in NFPA 170 should be used. Such signs need to provide equal visibility and illumination and are to comply with the other requirements of Section 14.14. [*101*:A.7.10.3]

A.14.14.3.2 Pictograms are permitted to be used in lieu of, or in addition to, signs with text. [*101*:A.7.10.3.2]

A.14.14.4 It is not the intent of this paragraph to require emergency lighting but only to have the sign illuminated by emergency lighting if emergency lighting is required and provided. [*101*:A.7.10.4]

It is not the intent to require that the entire stroke width and entire stroke height of all letters comprising the word EXIT be visible per the requirements of 14.14.6.3 under normal or emergency lighting operation, provided that the sign is visible and legible at a 100 ft (30 m) distance under all room illumination conditions. [*101*:A.7.10.4]

A.14.14.5.1 See A.14.12.1.3(4). [*101*:A.7.10.5.1]

FIGURE A.14.14.1.2.1   Location of Exit Signs. [*101*:Figure A.7.10.1.2.1]

A.14.14.5.2 It is the intent to prohibit a freely accessible light switch to control the illumination of either an internally or externally illuminated exit sign. [*101*:A.7.10.5.2]

A.14.14.5.2.2 The flashing repetition rate should be approximately one cycle per second, and the duration of the off-time should not exceed ¼ second per cycle. During on-time, the illumination levels need to be provided in accordance with 14.14.6.3. Flashing signs, when activated with the fire alarm system, might be of assistance. [*101*:A.7.10.5.2.2]

A.14.14.6.1 Experience has shown that the word EXIT, or other appropriate wording, is plainly legible at 100 ft (30 m) if the letters are as large as specified in 14.14.6.1. [*101*:A.7.10.6.1]

A.14.14.6.2 Figure A.14.14.6.2 shows examples of acceptable locations of directional indicators with regard to left and right orientation. Directional indicators are permitted to be placed under the horizontal stroke of the letter T, provided that spacing of not less than ⅜ in. (10 mm) is maintained from the horizontal and vertical strokes of the letter T. [*101*:A.7.10.6.2]

A.14.14.6.3 Colors providing a good contrast are red or green letters on matte white background. Glossy background and glossy letter colors should be avoided. [*101*:A.7.10.6.3]

The average luminance of the letters and background is measured in footlamberts or candela per square meter. The contrast ratio is computed from these measurements by the following formula:

$$\text{Contrast} = \frac{L_g - L_e}{L_g} \quad [\text{A.14.14.6.3}]$$

Where L_g is the greater luminance and L_e is the lesser luminance, either the variable L_g or L_e is permitted to represent the letters, and the remaining variable will represent the background. The average luminance of the letters and background can be computed by measuring the luminance at the positions indicated in Figure A.14.14.6.3 by numbered circles. [*101*:A.7.10.6.3]

A.14.14.7.2 Photoluminescent signs need a specific minimum level of light on the face of the sign to ensure that the sign is charged for emergency operation and legibility in both the normal and emergency modes. Additionally, the type of light source (e.g., incandescent, fluorescent, halogen, metal halide) is important. Each light source produces different types of visible and invisible light (e.g., UV) that might affect the ability of some photoluminescent signs to charge and might also affect the amount of light output available during emergency mode. This type of sign would not be suitable where the illumination levels are permitted to decline. The charging light source should not be connected to automatic timers, because the continuous illumination of the sign is needed; otherwise, the sign illumination would not be available, because it would be discharged. [*101*:A.7.10.7.2]

A.14.14.8.1.1 Special signs require sufficient illumination in order for them to be readable at close proximity. They are not expected to be of a size or illumination level necessary to be readable from a distance, as is the case for an exit sign. [*101*:A.7.10.8.1.1]

A.14.14.8.3 The likelihood of occupants mistaking passageways or stairways that lead to dead-end spaces for exit doors and becoming trapped governs the need for exit signs. Thus, such areas should be marked with a sign that reads as follows:

NO EXIT

Supplementary identification indicating the character of the area, such as TO BASEMENT, STOREROOM, LINEN CLOSET, or the like, is permitted to be provided. [*101*:A.7.10.8.3]

A.15.1.1.3 Examples of such operational challenges might include, but not be limited to, special amusement occupancies, high-rise buildings, high-angle rescue environments, and high-hazard occupancies. The intent of this section is to capture uses for which either additional fire department training or resources are necessary to protect the proposed development with effective fire department operational deployment.

A.16.1.3 See also NFPA 241. [*101*:A.4.6.10.3]

A.16.5.2.4.2 Appropriate means should be provided to prevent portable fire extinguishers from damage and secured from falling when roofing operations are being conducted.

N A.16.5.3.2.2 Any use of torches or burners will require a separate permit.

Δ A.17.1.2 Figure A.17.1.2 and Table A.17.1.2 are examples of two different approaches to hazard assessment. [*1140*:A.24.2.2]

Figure A.17.1.2 is an example of an assessment guide with assessment information based on observation of the areas around the structure. This form, intended to be given to the resident, can be very useful by indicating the most serious hazards and the mitigation recommendation(s) that can be taken to reduce the ignition hazard. In this example, samples of the kind of information noted in an assessment are given as observations and suggestions for mitigation. [*1140*:A.24.2.2]

EXIT▷
◁EXIT
◁EXIT▷

FIGURE A.14.14.6.2 Directional Indicators. [*101*:Figure A.7.10.6.2]

FIGURE A.14.14.6.3 Measurement of Exit Sign Luminance. [*101*:Figure A.7.10.6.3]

This example of an assessment guide is designed to help determine how vulnerable the structure will be during a wildland fire and to convey to the resident those items that should be corrected (mitigated) so that their home will have a better chance to survive a wildland fire. This form is offered as an example of the kind of tool that might be useful during a site visit as a guide for assessing the structure ignition zone. Remember, the following assessment items are for *prevention/ mitigation* measures to be done *well in advance* of wildland fire season. [1140:A.24.2.2]

Figure A.17.1.2 is a form used to document observations, collect data, provide a hazard assessment, and give mitigation recommendations for the resident. From the mitigation recommendations, a mitigation plan and schedule is developed in accordance with 17.1.10. [1140:A.24.2.2]

Table A.17.1.2 is a modified rating form based on the previous edition of NFPA 1144. Infrastructure elements of water supply, signage, and other fire suppression resources have been deleted, since the presence or absence of such resources does not modify the existing hazards of the structure. The table is presented only as an example of a rating system and should be modified to meet the environmental conditions of the area under consideration. [1140:A.24.2.2]

A numeric rating form that will yield a hazard rating number can have a variety of uses, for example, determining relative hazards among several properties and mapping overall hazard ratings on a map. However, residents and homeowners often accept the rating number as finite and undertake mitigation measures that will merely reduce the rating rather than actually reduce the ignition potential of the structure. [1140:A.24.2.2]

A.17.1.4 It is critical to keep in mind that the ignition of the structure might occur from one or more of the following sources:

(1) Big flames (crown fire or intense surface fire). One objective of observation of the conditions and elements and subsequent mitigation recommendations is to keep crown fire and high intensity surface fire at a distance of 100–200 ft (30–60 m) or more from home and other potential hazards (combustibles, buildings, etc.).
(2) Small flames (surface fire). Another objective is to keep small flames at a distance of 30 ft (9 m) or more from home(s) and combustible attachments (decks).
(3) Firebrands (embers). A final and essential objective is to eliminate beds of fine fuel and entry points for firebrands on and near home(s).

[1140:A.24.3]

A.17.1.5.1 Wildland fire dangers exist in flat land areas, as well as in mountainous terrain. In addition, property line limitations often preclude effective vegetation mitigation, and alternatives for mitigation are needed. [1140:A.24.3.1.1]

A.17.1.5.2 Local weather conditions or prevailing winds play a role in fire behavior (e.g., from which direction a fire is most likely to come, to the intensity and speed of fire travel, depending on the degree of slope), and the direction from which a wildland fire is most likely to approach the structure is an important exposure consideration. Sources of local weather records and fire weather history from the National Weather Service, National Oceanic and Atmospheric Administration (NOAA), local weather bureaus, or wildland fire agencies can be a valuable resource in assessing existing structures or in planning for new construction. [1140:A.24.3.1.2]

A.17.1.5.3 Adjacent ignitible structures (garages, carports, sheds, gazebos, utility cabinets) can contribute to heat intensity, flame contact, and fire spread from firebrands. [1140:A.24.3.1.3]

A.17.1.5.4 Overlapping zones could have a positive result in that the outermost extent of a structure ignition zone might be a neighboring parking lot or already treated vegetation area, such as a fuel modification. On the other hand, the overlap might include other private or public lands, which could make mitigation more difficult because it could involve state or federal agencies or absentee landowners who do little or no vegetation management or hazard mitigation. [1140:A.24.3.1.4]

A.17.1.5.5 Structure location on a slope increases the structure's exposure to heat (e.g., structure setback from the slope is sufficient to reduce its radiant heat exposure). Setback distances of the structure can be measured in accordance with A.25.1.3.2 of NFPA 1140. [1140:A.24.3.1.5]

A.17.1.6.1 All common coverings (composition shingles, tile, and, in many cases, metal) typically have a fire-resistive roofing classification adequate for interface fire protection if the covering material is tightly assembled to resist firebrand intrusion. [1140:A.24.3.2.1]

Untreated wood roofing is easily ignited and a major hazard. The only wood roof coverings that can be considered acceptable are wood shakes or shingles that have been treated at the factory by a pressure-impregnation fire-retardant process, tested for fire resistance, and certified with a fire-resistant roofing classification of Class A, Class B, or Class C. Pressure-treated wood roofing looks very similar to the hazardous untreated wood roofing, and currently there is no permanent identification method. If in doubt, assume wood roofing is untreated unless documentation is provided. [1140:A.24.3.2.1]

A.17.1.6.2 Look for gaps in the roof covering that might allow small wind-blown firebrands to penetrate under the covering and ignite material below. [1140:A.24.3.2.2]

Some fire-resistive roof coverings are designed or installed with gaps that allow firebrand intrusion under the covering and have resulted in firebrand intrusion and ignition of the building under the roof covering. The worst example is roof coverings that allow combustible debris to blow under the covering or that allow rodents and birds to bring nesting material in under the roof covering. Clay (Spanish or straight barrel mission) tile roof covering can have this problem unless eave closures or "bird stops" are used to close the convex opening created by the shape of the tile at the eave. Metal tile roofing installed on top of old wood roofing left in place has been a problem. If you can see wood through gaps in metal tile roof covering, firebrands can penetrate and ignite the building. [1140:A.24.3.2.2]

A.17.1.6.3 Plastic skylights can melt from radiant heat or flaming embers or both. Deformation can result in large openings that can allow the entry of embers and other flaming materials. Skylights constructed of multilayered glazed panels or tempered glass provide increased protection from heat and embers. [1140:A.24.3.2.3]

Δ **Table A.17.1.2 Example of Structure Assessment Rating Form**

Rating Values by Areas Assessed	Overview of Surrounding Environment (24.3.1)	From Chimney to Eaves (24.3.2)	From Top of the Exterior Wall to Foundation (24.3.3)	From Foundation to Immediate Landscaped Area (24.3.4)	From Immediate Landscaped Area to Extent of Structure Ignition Zone (24.3.5)
Topographical Features					
(1) Topographical features that adversely affect wildland fire behavior (24.3.1)	0–5				
(2) Areas with history of high fire occurrence (24.4.4)	0–5				
(3) Areas exposed to unusually severe fire weather and strong, dry winds (24.3.1.3)	0–5				
(4) Local weather conditions and prevailing winds (24.3.1.2)	0–5				
(5) Separation of structure on adjacent property that can contribute to fire spread/behavior (24.3.1.3)	0–5			0–5	0–5
Vegetation — Characteristics of predominant vegetation					
(1) Light (e.g., grasses, forbs, sawgrasses, and tundra) NFDRS Fuel Models A, C, L, N, S, and T	5			15	5
(2) Medium (e.g., light brush and small trees) NFDRS Fuel Models D, E, F, H, P, Q, and U	10			20	5
(3) Heavy (e.g., dense brush, timber, and hardwoods) NFDRS Fuel Models B, G, and O	15			25	15
(4) Slash (e.g., timber harvesting residue) NFDRS Fuel Models J, K, and L	15			30	20
Topography (24.3.1.1, 24.3.4, 24.3.5)					
(1) Slope 5–9%				1	1
(2) Slope 10–20%				4	2
(3) Slope 21–30%				7	3
(4) Slope 31–40%				10	6
(5) Slope >41%				15	10
Building Setback, relative to slopes of 30% or more (24.3.1.5, 25.1.3.2)					
(1) 30 ft (9.14 m) to slope	1				
(2) 30 ft (9.14 m) to slope	5				
Roofing Materials and Assembly, nonrated (424.3.2.1, 24.3.2.3)			50*		
Ventilation Soffits, without metal mesh or screening (24.3.3.4)			20		

(continues)

Table A.17.1.2 Continued

Rating Values by Areas Assessed	Overview of Surrounding Environment (24.3.1)	From Chimney to Eaves (24.3.2)	From Top of the Exterior Wall to Foundation (24.3.3)	From Foundation to Immediate Landscaped Area (24.3.4)	From Immediate Landscaped Area to Extent of Structure Ignition Zone (24.3.5)
Gutters, combustible (24.3.2.4, 24.3.2.5)		5			
Building Construction (predominant)† (24.3.4)					
(1) Noncombustible/fire-resistive/ignition-resistant siding and deck			Low		
(2) Noncombustible/fire-resistive/ignition-resistant siding and combustible deck			Medium		
(3) Combustible siding and deck			High		
Fences and Attachments, combustible (24.3.4.3)				15	
Placement of Gas and Electric Utilities					
(1) One underground, one aboveground	3				
(2) Both aboveground	5				
Fuel Modification within the structure ignition zone (24.3.4, 24.3.5)					
(1) 71–100 ft (21–30 m) of vegetation treatment from the structure(s)					5
(2) 30–70 ft (9–21 m) of vegetation treatment from the structure(s)				7	
(3) <30 ft (9 m) of vegetation treatment from the structure(s)				15	
No Fixed Fire Protection (NFPA 13, 13R, 13D sprinkler system)			5		
TOTALS (if numerical ranking is desired)					
Hazard Rating Scale (Compare with above totals)					
Slight Structure Ignition Hazards from Wildland Fire	0–14	0–14	0–14	0–14	0–14
Moderate Structure Ignition Hazards from Wildland Fire	15–29	15–29	15–29	15–29	15–29
Significant Structure Ignition Hazards from Wildland Fire	30–49	30–49	30–49	30–49	30–49
Severe Structure Ignition Hazards from Wildland Fire	50+	50+	50+	50+	50+

*Nonrated and combustible roof assemblies are predominantly structural exposures and severely increase the ignition hazard from wildland fire.
†The table provides both numerical and value rankings (low, medium, high). The user is urged to assign the value ranking of low, medium, or high based on the other ignition factors prevalent at the assessment site. For example, a deck made of combustible materials might rank low if it is small in size and the rest of the site is in a low fuel loading area that will not promote a large amount of firebrands. That same deck might rate high if it is in an area of high fuel loading that will promote numerous firebrands. Numeric values can be substituted as a local option. [**1140:**Table A.24.2.2]

STRUCTURE ASSESSMENT GUIDE

Date of assessment: _22 Nov_ Property address: _70 Norris Rd._
Resident: _John and Jane Doe_ Property owner: _Same_

PRIMARY INFORMATION

Assessment Items	Mitigation Recommendations
1. OVERVIEW OF SURROUNDINGS	
How is the structure positioned in relationship to severe fire behavior? *The house is located near peak of a ridge at local map reference Q-4-12. The setbacks from the lot lines are approximately 15–20 ft. There is a slight sloping of the lot away from the house within 50 ft of the lot line on the north.*	*Since prevailing winds during fire season are most likely from the west-southwest, keep pine needles and leaf litter cleaned up on roadside berm.*
Type of construction: *Wood frame construction with brick façade on the front. Vinyl siding on back and two sides.*	
2. CHIMNEY TO EAVES	
Inspect the roof — noncombustible? shingles missing? shingles flat with no gaps? *Noncombustible roofing in good shape.*	*Inspect roof each spring for damage, especially after a hard winter or wind storm.*
Gutters — present? Noncombustible? *Aluminum gutters at all eaves. No overhanging limbs nearby. Pine needles and leaf litter not likely to collect in deep quantities.*	*Keep gutters free of pine needles and leaves. Check early spring and fall.*
Litter on roof, in gutters, and crevices? *Fairly clean. Not much of a concern. Easy to maintain.*	
3. TOP OF THE EXTERIOR WALL TO FOUNDATION	
Attic, eave, soffit vents, and crawl spaces: *Not much of a concern.*	
Inspect windows and screens — metal screens? Multi-paned windows? Picture windows facing vegetation? *Metal screens on all windows. Some windows on west side are double-paned. Some high vegetation near front windows. Low vegetation in rear.*	*Keep front bushes pruned and watered during fire season. Replace any missing or torn screens immediately, especially the front.*
Walls and attachments — noncombustible? Will they collect litter? *Not much of a concern.*	
Decks — combustible materials? *Wooden deck and privacy fence on south side. No skirting or screening beneath deck. Deck in good condition. Small vegetation around deck but overhanging tree limbs. Some collection of leaves and needles near deck and wooden stairs.*	*Prune trees closest to deck and privacy fence. Remove the pine needles and leaves. Store combustibles elsewhere — perhaps the shed in the backyard — especially during high fire danger periods. Put skirting or 1/4" wire mesh around deck openings.*

© 2017 National Fire Protection Association NFPA 1144 (p. 1 of 2)

Δ **FIGURE A.17.1.2** Structure Assessment Guide — Example with Notations. [1140:Figure A.24.2.2]

STRUCTURE ASSESSMENT GUIDE (continued)

Assessment Items	Mitigation Recommendations
3. TOP OF THE EXTERIOR WALL TO FOUNDATION *(continued)*	
Fences. *Wooden stockade fence joins house on north side. Wooden fencing also on south side. Chain link in rear along lot line. Neighbor's wooden fence is less than 2–3 ft from their wooden fence — will allow leaves and embers to accumulate.*	*Keep wooden fence perimeter clear of dry leaves and other combustible materials like chairs, wood, etc. If the chance presents itself to use noncombustible materials to separate fence from house, you should consider it.*
Flammable material next to or under the structure. *None observed.*	
Combustible materials near or on the structure where walls meet roof or decking surfaces. *Plastic outdoor furniture pads on deck might pose problem from ember shower.*	*Keep combustible chair pads put away except when in use.*
Crawl space, attic vents, soffits. *All appear to be in excellent condition and protected.*	
Nooks and crannies and other small spaces. *All appear to be in excellent condition and protected.*	
4. FOUNDATION TO IMMEDIATE LANDSCAPED AREA	
Landscaped (managed) vegetation — separation distances, maintenance, plant selection? Firewise Landscaping Zones? *Lawn well cared for. Leaf and needle accumulation along east side (rear of property) with small stand of trees. Front and south side have mix of pine and other vegetation.*	*Be sure to keep these areas well tended, pine needles cleared and limbs pruned. Lawn needs to be kept green and mowed. Plants irrigated, pruned and raked — especially during high fire danger periods.*
Propane tanks. *No large ones. Outdoor grill small tank.*	*Make sure this area is kept clear of any combustibles — especially when using the grill.*
Vehicle and RV use and parking, including lawn mowers, etc. *Parking in front. Mower storage in shed which is 40–50 ft from NE corner of house. Plastic children's play house etc. near wooden fence along north side but over 30 ft from house.*	
5. IMMEDIATE LANDSCAPED AREA TO EXTENT OF THE HOME IGNITION ZONE	
Inspect vegetation clearance and crown separation. *Lot is rather small and the neighboring properties' vegetation is more dense than this one. Trees in back should pose little concern as prevailing winds will not communicate fire towards house.*	*Work with neighbors to improve all three lots to reduce the hazards on this corner. The neighbors behind this address and those on either side might benefit from some clearance that might take place but the separation of those properties appears to be sufficient.*

© 2017 National Fire Protection Association

NFPA 1144 (p. 2 of 2)

Δ **FIGURE A.17.1.2** Continued

A.17.1.6.4 The roof is the most vulnerable part of the structure and is subject to the collection of combustible vegetative litter (e.g., leaves, pine needles) or other debris and buildup that can be ignited by firebrands. Can litter build up and accumulate on surfaces next to combustible, perpendicular walls? Will combustible decking or roofing provide ember beds next to combustible, perpendicular walls? [1140:A.24.3.2.4]

Heat trapping under eaves does not occur until the wall supports flaming combustion as indicated by the portions of the wall that were protected (shaded) and did not char during experiments conducted by the USDA Forest Service Fire Sciences Lab in Missoula, MT. [1140:A.24.3.2.4]

A.17.1.6.5 Gutters and downspouts collect leaves and pine needles. Gutters and eave troughs made from combustible materials (e.g., wood, vinyl) are as vulnerable to firebrand collection as the roof and other parts of the structure. If leaf litter is allowed to gather in gutters, firebrands or embers can ignite the leaf litter, which in turn could ignite combustible eave materials or overhangs. If gutters are attached to combustible fascia boards, the fascia board should be considered as a possible fuel that can be ignited by fine fuels burning in the gutters. [1140:A.24.3.2.5]

Gutters that pose a fire threat from an approaching wildland fire are often pulled down by attending firefighters. For the resident, an alternative might be to remove the gutters along the side(s) of the house most prone to the collection of leaves and needles and install a noncombustible drip line shown in Figure A.17.1.6.5. Removing gutters eliminates the collection of dry leaves and needles along the roof line and fascia board. Also reduced is the possibility of ice damage to the roof in the winter. The use of a gravel bed for drip lines along the leeward side(s) of the house provides reduced ignition potential and reduced wind hazard, since the gravel would be less likely to be blown by high winds on the leeward elevations. The windward sides of the house can be landscaped with mulch (less impact damage in case of wind events) if protected with low volume sprinklers to raise the fine fuel moisture levels in times of high fire danger. [1140:A.24.3.2.5]

A.17.1.6.6 Eaves should be boxed to prevent flying embers from entering small spaces. [1140:A.24.3.2.6]

FIGURE A.17.1.6.5 Mitigating Risk of Leaf- and Needle-Filled Gutters. [1140: Figure A.24.3.2.5]

A.17.1.7.1 Identify the wall covering or siding (e.g., wood, vinyl, brick, stucco) and determine the possibility of litter buildup and accumulation on surfaces next to walls. Under low radiant heat levels, vinyl siding is damaged and falls off a wall, which can leave openings for firebrands exposing the interior of the home to ignition through eave vents and other possible openings. Vinyl is difficult to ignite by firebrands or radiant heat, but will sustain combustion when directly contacted by flames. [1140:A.24.3.3.1]

Hanging ½ in. (12.5 mm) or thicker drywall on the exterior wall studs prior to adding stucco, siding, and so forth can increase the fire rating. [1140:A.24.3.3.1]

A.17.1.7.3 Windows should be constructed of multi-paned or tempered glass that will resist fracture from intense heat in accordance with 25.7.1 of NFPA 1140, and window screens made from a material that will not allow hot firebrands to enter the home's interior in accordance with 25.7.2 of NFPA 1140. [1140:A.24.3.3.3]

A.17.1.7.4 Check attic, crawl space, eave, and soffit vents for appropriate protection (e.g., metal screening, noncombustible skirting) to prevent entry of firebrands. Roof turbine vents should be screened to prevent the entry of firebrands into attic spaces. [1140:A.24.3.3.4]

A.17.1.7.5 Examples of attached structures include decks, lean-to overhangs, patio covers, carports, balconies, fences, and similar structures that could be ignited by convection or firebrands. [1140:A.24.3.3.5]

A.17.1.7.6 Areas on, next to, or under a structure should be kept free of combustible fuel such as debris, vegetation, wooden furniture, brooms, welcome mats, furniture cushions, gasoline cans, firewood stacks, or piled construction materials. Look for combustible walkways, fencing, or decking attached to the structure, highly combustible fuels adjacent to the structure (e.g., junipers near decks and walkways), combustible materials (e.g., building materials, firewood) stored under decks or adjacent to the structure, animal nests among combustible structural fuels, and landscaping materials (e.g., bark mulch, ground cover plants) near the structure and surrounding plants that might support flaming combustion or that could easily be ignited by firebrands. [1140:A.24.3.3.6]

A.17.1.8 The structure ignition zone includes the spatially arranged traditional landscaping zones, but can exceed the extent of the property line. Figure A.17.1.8 illustrates the relationship of the structure and immediate landscaped area to the larger structure ignition zone. Within the immediate landscaped area [from the structure to approximately 30 ft (9 m)], often referred to as the defensible space, special consideration should be given that any combustible materials (e.g., plants, lawn furniture, litter, construction materials) should be removed in the 0 ft to 5 ft (0 m to 1.5 m) zone immediately adjacent to the structure and reduced in the zone from 5 ft to 30 ft (1.5 m to 9 m) to minimize the chance for ignition of the structure. The total structure ignition zone includes any spatially arranged landscaping area and can exceed the extent of the property line. The level of risk of ignition within the total area of the ignition zone depends on the type of construction and is further influenced by slope, soils, and other site-specific conditions. [1140:A.24.3.4]

The AHJ should require the development of a landscape plan for the property. Such plans should address four zones around the property as follows:

(1) The most immediate landscaped area is the closest to the house and includes the area encircling the structure for at least 30 ft (9 m) on all sides. The landscaped vegetation within 30 ft (9 m) of structures should be irrigated as needed, cleared of dead vegetation, and/or planted with succulents and other plants (where appropriate) that are low in combustibility potential. Plantings should be limited to carefully spaced, low-growing, low-combustibility species, grasses, and lawns. Shrubs planted next to the structure should be of low combustibility, no more than 18 in. (45 cm) in height, and not planted against the home. The planting bed should be noncombustible (e.g., stone, gravel, bare ground) or irrigated if combustible materials (e.g., bark mulch) are used.

All highly combustible plants, such as junipers and ornamental conifers, should be removed or trimmed and maintained to be ignition-resistant. Vegetation deposits (dry leaf and pine litter) that can support surface fire and flames should be removed regularly. Areas of vegetation (natural areas, undeveloped areas, landscaped areas, fields, etc.) that exist near the structure should be evaluated for the possibility of causing ignition of the structure.

(2) Progressing outward from the structure, the types and densities of vegetation should change to reduce the continuity of vegetation fuels. For example, plantings can be done in islands. Trees can be introduced into this zone with careful consideration of their combustibility and continued maintenance to separate crowns and avoid ladder fuels. Tree placement should be planned so that the edge of the canopy of the tree when fully mature is no closer than 10 ft (3 m) to the edge of the structure.

(3) Progressing even farther from the structure, more medium-sized plants and well-spaced trees can be planted in well-spaced groupings to reduce exposure to wildland fire and help maintain privacy. The volume of vegetation (i.e., fuel) should be kept as low as possible or practical.

(4) The most distant area [100 ft to 200 ft (30 m to 60 m)] from the structure determines the extent of the structure ignition zone. Plants in this furthermost area should be carefully pruned and thinned, and highly combustible vegetation removed. Particular attention should be paid to the types and densities of the vegetation in this area. For example, some vegetation and trees generate more firebrands than others and require additional thinning, removal, or replacement.

[**1140**:A.24.3.4]

A.17.1.8.1 Vegetative fuels include live vegetation, mulch and landscaping materials, slash piles, composting piles, and firewood storage. [**1140**:A.24.3.4.1]

Combustible vegetation close enough to windows to provide intense radiant heat or flame contact should be pruned, moved, or substituted with smaller, lower combustibility plants. Figure A.17.1.8.1(a) illustrates the use of low combustibility plants separated by a gravel area next to the foundation. [**1140**:A.24.3.4.1]

Mulch is an alternative to noncombustible landscaping materials such as gravel and rock. The size and texture of mulching materials affects its ignition and fire spread potential. Larger organic materials are preferable to smaller materials. [**1140**:A.24.3.4.1]

Landscaping with mulch can be acceptable if the mulch is protected with low volume sprinklers to raise the fine fuel moisture levels and offset its combustibility in times of high fire danger. The installation of sprinklers for areas using mulch for landscaping is shown in Figure A.17.1.8.1(b). [**1140**:A.24.3.4.1]

Figure A.17.1.8.1(c) describes the physical similarities of the NFDRS fuel models with fire behavior fuel models. See Annex I of NFPA 1140 for fuel model classifications. [**1140**:A.24.3.4.1]

Δ **FIGURE A.17.1.8** The Structure Ignition Zone. (*Source: Firewise Communities Program.*) [**1140**:Figure A.24.3.4]

FIGURE A.17.1.8.1(a) Foundation Planting and Landscaping. (*Courtesy of Firewise Communities Program. Photo by K. Clineff.*) [1140:Figure A.24.3.4.1(a)]

FIGURE A.17.1.8.1(b) Use of Low Volume Sprinklers in Organic Material. (*Courtesy of Firewise Communities Program. Photo by G. Johnston.*) [1140:Figure A.A.24.3.4.1(b)]

A.17.1.8.2 Typical heat and flame sources include, but are not limited to, propane heaters, barbecue cookers, and grills. [1140:A.24.3.4.2]

A.17.1.8.3 Attachments include, but are not limited to, permanent and temporary construction such as decks, fences, awnings, lean-to buildings; and combustible walkways, fencing, or decking attached to the home. [1140:A.24.3.4.3]

Figure A.17.1.8.3(a) shows a typical deck where combustible decking materials could result in the gathering of embers next to combustible walls and where the construction and design of decks, balconies, and porches with open spaces underneath could allow leaf and needle debris and embers to collect. [1140:A.24.3.4.3]

Figure A.17.1.8.3(b) illustrates one method of separating a combustible fence from the structure by the installation of a transitional section of noncombustible (iron) fencing. Similar use of masonry or stone can provide the same fire-resistant separation. [1140:A.24.3.4.3]

A.17.1.8.4 Examples of such structures include, but are not limited to, hot tubs, utility sheds, outbuildings, detached garages and carports, gazebos, trellises, auxiliary structures, stables, barns and other structures within 30 ft (9 m) of the primary structure, outdoor furniture, and recreational structures (e.g., children's playhouses, swing sets). In some cases, separation distances from lot lines might require the inclusion of neighboring residential structures in the assessment. [1140:A.24.3.4.4]

A.17.1.8.5 Parking vehicles on areas of dry grasses and fine fuels could result in ignition by hot exhaust systems or firebrands. Also, a fire that originates from a parked vehicle could present an exposure hazard to the primary structure or nearby vegetation. Any dry vegetation beneath the vehicle could cause ignition of the vehicle, which in turn could cause structure ignition; conversely, the ignition of the structure could cause ignition of the vehicle, which could present additional dangers to responding firefighters. [1140:A.24.3.4.5]

A.17.1.9.1 Evaluation of the vegetative fuels should include the following:

(1) Can vegetative fuels lead surface fire and flames to the structure?
(2) Have ladder fuels been eliminated within the structure ignition zone?
(3) Are tree crowns separated enough to prevent big flames from coming within 30 ft (9 m) of the structure?

[1140:A.24.3.5.1]

A.17.1.9.2 The location (placement) of trees and the separation between them is important to prevent ignition of the structure from radiant heat and to reduce the concentration of leaf fall and needle drop near the structure. Adequate separation and control of ignition potential are factors that affect fire intensity and are dependent on the size, density, and species of trees and vegetation. [1140:A.24.3.5.2]

Consider using islands of trees that offer separation of trees from the structure and other combustibles. Figure A.17.1.9.2(a) illustrates the use of such planting islands that preserve key trees for aesthetics while providing shade and exposure separation from structures. Figure A.17.1.9.2(b) shows that small planting islands within an expanse of main-

Physical Description Similarity Chart of NFDRS and FBO Fuel Models
NFDRS Models Realigned to Fuels Controlling Spread Under Severe Burning Conditions

NFDRS Fuel Models	1	2	3	4	5	6	7	8	9	10	11	12	13	
A Western Annuals	X													Grass
L Western Perennial	X													
S Tundra	X					3rd			2nd					
C Open Pine with Grass		X							2nd					
T Sagebrush with Grass		X				3rd	2nd							
N Sawgrass			X											
B Mature Brush over 6 ft (1.8 m)				X										Shrub
O High Pocosin				X										
F Intermediate Brush						2nd	X							
Q Alaskan Black Spruce							X	2nd						
D Southern Rough							2nd	X						
H Short-Needle Closed (Normal Dead)									X					Timber
R Hardwood Litter (Summer)									X					
U Western Long-Needle Pine										X				
P Southern Long-Needle Pine										X				
E Hardwood Litter (Fall)										X				
G Short-Needle Closed (Heavy Dead)										X				
K Light Slash											X			Slash
J Medium Slash												X		
I Heavy Slash													X	

Grass — Shrub — Timber — Slash

△ FIGURE A.17.1.8.1(c) Sample of a Physical Description Similarity Chart of NFDRS and FBO Fuel Models. [1140:Figure A.24.3.4.1(c)]

tained lawn provides both separation and low combustibility protection from ignition close the structure. [1140:A.24.3.5.2]

A.17.1.9.3 Typical heat and flame sources include, but are not limited to, propane- and charcoal-fired barbecue cookers, heaters, and grills. [1140:A.24.3.5.3]

A.17.1.9.4 Examples of such structures include, but are not limited to, hot tubs, utility sheds, outbuildings, detached garages and carports, gazebos, trellises, auxiliary structures, stables, barns and other structures between the immediate landscaped area and the extent of structure ignition zone, outdoor furniture, recreational structures (children's playhouses, swing sets). In some cases, separation distances from lot lines might require the inclusion of neighboring residential structures in the assessment. [1140:A.24.3.5.4]

N **A.17.1.9.5** See A.17.1.8.5. [1140:A.24.3.5.5]

A.17.1.9.6 Attachments include, but are not limited to, permanent and temporary construction such as decks, fences, awnings, and lean-to buildings. [1140:A.24.3.5.6]

△ **A.17.1.10.3** Access and evacuation concerns along with fire suppression capabilities (such as fire station location, water supply, road widths, and grades) are important to overall fire protection and safety. Likewise, vegetation clearance and maintenance along private roadways, driveways, and water supplies are important elements in fire suppression and emergency evacuation. Since these elements do not relate specifically to reducing the ignition potential of the structure, these are covered in NFPA 1140 and 17.3.5.3. [1140:A.24.4.3]

A.17.1.10.4 The frequency of wildland fire occurrence will affect the priorities of the mitigation measures and the periodic maintenance schedule of the property being assessed. [1140:A.24.4.4]

△ FIGURE A.17.1.8.3(a) Leaf Litter and Needles Collect in Small Spaces. *(Courtesy of Firewise Communities Program.)* [1140:Figure A.24.3.4.3(a)]

△ FIGURE A.17.1.9.2(a) Planting Islands Offer Exposure Protection, Preserve Aesthetics. *(Courtesy of Firewise Communities Program. Photo by G. Johnston.)* [1140:Figure A.24.3.5.2(a)]

△ FIGURE A.17.1.8.3(b) Transition Fence Separates Combustible Fence from Structure. *(Courtesy of Firewise Communities Program. Photo by G. Johnston.)* [1140:Figure A.24.3.4.3(b)]

△ FIGURE A.17.1.9.2(b) Small Planting Islands Within an Expanse of Maintained Lawn. *(Courtesy of Firewise Communities Program. Photo by D. Frazier.)* [1140:Figure A.24.3.5.2(b)]

A.17.1.10.5 Chapters 10 through 18 in NFPA 1140 provide guidance on planning and installing fire protection infrastructure. [1140:A.24.4.5]

A.17.3.1 The unrestricted use of grass-, grain-, brush-, or forest-covered lands under the jurisdiction of the AHJ presents a potential hazard to life and property from fire and resulting erosion.

A.17.3.2 Possible uses include recreation (e.g., camping, hunting, hiking), construction, and seasonal habitation.

A.17.3.5.1.5 An emergency can include situations such as trees falling into power lines or trees' location in violation of Table 17.3.5.1.3.1.

A.17.3.5.2.1.1 Acceptable methods of fuel treatment include, but are not limited to, prescribed burning by qualified personnel, mowing, pruning, removing, substitution, mulching, converting to compost, and grazing. [1140:A.26.2.1]

Vegetation. Fire resistance in plants depends on many variables, including location, growing conditions, and maintenance. Plants should be chosen that are suitable for the geographic region and the location in the landscape, and plants with similar needs should be grouped to minimize care. Plant characteristics that reduce maintenance needs include the following:

(1) Drought-resistant
(2) Pest-resistant
(3) Native
(4) Noninvasive
(5) Slow-growing
(6) Wind-resistant
(7) Thriving without supplemental fertilizing

[1140:A.26.2.1]

High Combustibility (fire-prone, fire-tolerant) Plants. Some plants burn readily because they are adapted to survive in fire-dependent ecosystems and can contain volatile compounds that support fire. Fire-prone plants have traits (i.e., adaptations) that help them to survive fire, such as thick bark or extensive roots. They often contain resins, oils, or waxes that ignite easily and burn intensely. Fire-prone plants will flame, not smolder, when preheated and ignited with a match. They should be removed from Zone 1 of the landscape, as illustrated in Figure A.17.1.8, Figure A.17.1.9.2(a), and Figure A.17.1.9.2(b). Where it is not practical or desirable to remove a fire-prone plant, surrounding it with open space or fire-resistant plants can reduce the hazard. Typical characteristics of fire-prone plants include the following:

(1) Volatile resins, oils, or waxes, indicated by leaves that are aromatic when crushed
(2) Narrow leaves or needles (often evergreen)
(3) Waxy or fuzzy leaves
(4) Accumulation of fine, twiggy, dry, or dead material on the plant or on the ground under the plant
(5) Loose, papery, or thick bark

[1140:A.26.2.1]

Low Combustibility Plants. In place of fire-prone plants, landscapers and homeowners should use low combustibility plants, often referred to as fire-resistant plants. Although all plants will burn at some point, wildland fire researchers have shown that some types of plants, including many native plants, resist burning more than others. Additionally, some ornamental plants, when properly irrigated and maintained, are more resistant to fire than others. Low combustibility plants are typically low fuel volume, non-oily, nonresinous plants that are also drought-resistant, have small thick leathery leaves, and produce very little dead plant material. Typical characteristics of fire-resistant plants include the following:

(1) High moisture content in leaves
(2) Low oil or resin content (not aromatic)
(3) Drought tolerance or drought resistance
(4) Minimal seasonal accumulation of dead vegetation, or accumulation of dead leaves that are somewhat resistant to fire because they hold moisture in the soil (large, flat leaves)
(5) Limited foliage and few dead branches
(6) Open or loose branching habit
(7) Easy maintenance and pruning

[1140:A.26.2.1]

A.17.3.5.2.1.5 Studies of structural ignition from radiant heat indicate that ignitions are unlikely to occur from burning vegetation beyond 120 ft (36.6 m) from a structure. Therefore, clearing of vegetation and thinning of trees to a distance of 120 ft (36.6 m) from a dwelling — as in a zoned Firewise landscape — will prevent ignition of a structure from the radiant heat from a flame front in a high-risk ecosystem (Cohen and Butler, 1996). [1140:A.26.2.5]

A tree crown spacing of 18 ft (5.5 m) for trees within the Zone 1 defensible space [within 30 ft (9 m) of a structure] will reduce radiant heat to at or below the level where ignition of wood occurs, with closer spacing of trees allowed in the zones further from the structure, as described in Table A.17.3.5.2.1.5. These tree-spacing recommendations apply equally to thinning of mature trees or planting of new trees in high- or extreme-risk areas. Tree spacing is measured between the outer edges of the crowns of mature trees, so new trees must be planted with spacing equivalent to the estimated diameter of the mature crown. [1140:A.26.2.5]

Table A.17.3.5.2.1.5 illustrates general clearance distances for tree crowns. However, these distances can be adjusted by the AHJ in consideration of species of trees and understory vegetation, slope of the property, the proximity to other neighboring structures, overlapping ignition zones, and other site-specific factors. [1140:A.26.2.5]

A.17.3.5.2.1.8 Accessory structures include, but are not limited to, outbuildings, patio covers, gazebos, palapas, and similar outdoor structures. [1140:A.25.9]

A.17.3.5.2.1.11.1 Unprotected heat and flame sources include, but are not limited to, open burning without spark protection, barbecue pits, clay or stone fireplaces, and fire pits. Supervision of burning includes the presence of a source of water or other extinguishing equipment. [1140:A.25.12.1]

Δ Table A.17.3.5.2.1.5 Recommended Tree Crown Spacing to Prevent Structural Ignition from Wildland Fire Radiant Heat

Zone	Distance from Structure	Recommended Tree Crown Spacing
1	0–30 ft (0–9 m)	18 ft (5.5 m)
2	30–60 ft (9–18 m)	12 ft (3.7 m)
3	60–100 ft (18–30 m)	6 ft (1.8 m)
4	Beyond 100 ft (30 m)	No restrictions

[1140:Table A.26.2.5]

A.18.2.2 Access control devices take many forms such as remote opening devices, card keys, key codes, keys, and so forth.

A.18.2.3.1.3 The intent of 18.2.3.1.3 is to not require fire apparatus access roads to detached gazebos and ramadas, independent buildings associated with golf courses, parks, and similar uses such as restrooms or snack shops that are 400 ft² (37 m²) or less in area, and detached equipment or storage buildings for commercial use that are 400 ft² (37 m²) or less in area.

A.18.2.3.3 Access roads that are below the 100-year base flood elevation and roadways that could be blocked by frequent rail traffic are two conditions that could limit access in an emergency and warrant an additional access roadway. Requiring additional access roads because of possible congestion should be based on a traffic impact analysis of the proposed development. This type of analysis is typically conducted by a transportation or traffic engineer and occurs at the cost of the developer. This *Code* avoids establishing a specific threshold for mandating multiple-access roads; potential congestion conditions are so variable that prescriptive language is not justified. The AHJ has the authority to require a study of the traffic conditions resulting from a development and the subsequent need for additional access via Section 1.16.

A.18.2.3.5.1.1 Where parking is permitted along the access road, the unobstructed width is not intended to include the width of the parking.

A.18.2.3.5.1.1.1 One condition to consider in reducing access road width would be intended travel in one direction only.

A.18.2.3.5.2 It is not the intent of 18.2.3.5.2 to restrict the design of fire apparatus access roads to traditional, non-permeable materials such as asphalt or concrete. Permeable materials, pavers, or other designs can be used if approved by the AHJ and meet the loading requirements in all weather conditions. In considering whether to approve non-traditional materials, the AHJ should consider maintenance issues due to weather and traffic.

The designer and AHJ should consider the point loads created by fire department aerial apparatus stabilizers in the design of fire apparatus access roads. NFPA 1900 limits the pressure exerted over the ground contact under the apparatus stabilizer to 75 psi (517 kPa). The 75 psi (517 kPa) design specification, along with a safety margin, should be included in the design of fire apparatus access roads that would be used as a base to operate fire department aerial apparatus.

A.18.2.3.5.6.2 The design limits of fire department apparatus should take into account mutual aid companies and other response agencies that might respond to emergencies.

A.18.2.4 Fire apparatus access roads should be kept clear of obstructions such as parked vehicles, fences and other barriers, dumpsters, and excess vegetation. However, it should be understood that a severe snowstorm can make these roads temporarily inaccessible. In many parts of the country, the annual snowfall is of such magnitude that alternative arrangements such as temporary roads over the snow accumulation could be necessary.

A.18.2.4.1.3 These obstructions include those obscuring or interfering with fire department connections to sprinkler systems or standpipe systems or both.

A.18.3.1 See Section 18.4 for determining required fire flow.

A.18.3.1.1 NFPA 1140 and NFPA 1142 can serve as references for additional water supply and fire flow information.

A.18.4.1 Section 18.4 and the associated tables are only applicable for determining minimum water supplies for manual fire suppression efforts. Water supplies for fire protection systems are not addressed by this section. It is not the intent to add the minimum fire protection water supplies, such as for a fire sprinkler system, to the minimum fire flow for manual fire suppression purposes required by this section.

A.18.4.1.1 For the purpose of this section, a building subdivided by fire walls constructed in accordance with the building code is considered to be a separate building.

A.18.4.2.1.1 The intent of 18.4.2.1.1 is to provide some limited flexibility in those circumstances where there is no water supply available and the fire department's capabilities to deliver water via a tanker shuttle or drafting operation are also limited. The AHJ should consider establishing additional conditions, such as those contained in 18.4.2.1.2, prior to permitting decreased fire flow capability.

A.18.4.4.1.2 Approved automatic sprinkler systems for one- and two-family dwellings include those meeting the requirements of NFPA 13, NFPA 13D, and NFPA 13R.

A.18.4.4.1.3 Approved automatic sprinkler systems for one- and two-family dwellings include those meeting the requirements of NFPA 13, NFPA 13D, and NFPA 13R.

A.18.4.4.1.5 The fire flow reductions specified in 18.4.4.1.2, 18.4.4.1.3, and 18.4.4.1.4 are permitted to be combined. However, where the reductions are combined, the resulting required fire flow is not permitted to be reduced to less than 500 gpm (1900 L/min) for 1 hour.

A.18.4.4.2.5 The fire flow reductions specified in 18.4.4.2.2 and 18.4.4.2.3 are permitted to be combined. However, where the reductions are combined, the resulting required fire flow is not permitted to be reduced to less than 500 gpm (1900 L/min) for 1 hour.

A.18.4.4.3.1 Table A.18.4.4.3.1 provides a comparison of the types of construction for various model building codes. [5000:A.7.2.1.1]

A.18.4.4.3.4 The provision of 18.4.4.3.4 is intended to limit the required fire flow duration to not more than 2 hours where the building is sprinklered. The 2000 gpm (7571 L/min) limit is based on a 75 percent reduction of 8000 gpm (30,283 L/min), which is the maximum fire flow required by Table 18.4.4.2.1. The required 2-hour duration is consistent with the maximum hose stream duration requirements of NFPA 13.

A.18.4.4.4 The fire sprinkler system demand is generally significantly less than the demands in Table 18.4.4.2.1, even after hose stream demands are applied. The sprinkler system demand can be a part of the overall flow available to a building site. There is no need to add these flow demands together, which would penalize the building owner that has decided to put fire sprinkler systems in place.

A.18.5.1.2 The conditions where a local jurisdiction might determine that a modification or extension of the water distribution system is deemed to be impractical are varied and should be evaluated on a case-by-case basis. Conditions that

Table A.18.4.4.3.1 Cross-Reference of Building Construction Types

NFPA 5000	I (442)	I (332)	II (222)	II (111)	II (000)	III (211)	III (200)	IV (2HH)	V (111)	V (000)
UBC	—	I FR	II FR	II 1 hr	II N	III 1 hr	III N	IV HT	V 1 hr	V N
B/NBC	1A	1B	2A	2B	2C	3A	3B	4	5A	5B
SBC	I	II	—	IV 1 hr	IV UNP	V 1 hr	V UNP	III	VI 1 hr	VI UNP
IBC	—	IA	IB	IIA	IIB	IIIA	IIIB	IV	VA	VB

UBC: *Uniform Building Code.*
FR: Fire rated.
N: Nonsprinklered.
HT: Heavy timber.
B/NBC: *National Building Code.*
SBC: *Standard Building Code.*
UNP: Unprotected.
IBC: *International Building Code.*
[**5000**:Table A.7.2.1.1]

should be considered in determining if an extension is impractical should include, but not be limited to, the following:

(1) Distance required to extend the water distribution system
(2) Capability of the existing water distribution system to meet the fire flow demand
(3) Density and occupancy of the proposed development
(4) Potential additional future development in the area of the extension
(5) Other codes and standards, which might warrant extension of the water distribution system
(6) Future anticipated improvements to the water distribution system
(7) Buildings within a previously approved development

A.18.5.1.4 Fire apparatus access roads are intended to include public streets provided they meet the requirements of 18.2.3.

A.18.5.4.3 It is not the intent of Table 18.5.4.3 to limit the actual fire flow capacity of a fire hydrant, only the fire flow capacity for which a fire hydrant is credited based on its distance from the building.

A.18.5.10.3 Color coding or stenciling a fire hydrant with the actual flow capacity are two methods to accomplish the capacity marking of fire hydrants when it is required by the AHJ. NFPA 291 specifies the following approach to hydrant marking for flow indication:

Classification of Hydrants. Hydrants should be classified in accordance with their rated capacities [at 20 psi (1.4 bar) residual pressure or other designated value] as follows:

(1) Class AA — Rated capacity of 1500 gpm (5680 L/min) or greater
(2) Class A — Rated capacity of 1000–1499 gpm (3785–5675 L/min)
(3) Class B — Rated capacity of 500–999 gpm (1900–3780 L/min)
(4) Class C — Rated capacity of less than 500 gpm (1900 L/min)

The tops and nozzle caps should be painted with the following capacity-indicating color scheme:

(1) Class AA — Light blue
(2) Class A — Green
(3) Class B — Orange
(4) Class C — Red paint

The capacity colors should be of a reflective-type paint.

A.19.2.1.2.1 Nonmetallic or plastic rubbish containers should be limited in their combustibility and should be tested for heat release with the cone calorimeter, to the recognized standard of ASTM E1354 referred to as the cone or oxygen consumption calorimeter. The cone calorimeter test standard does not indicate the exact conditions (heat flux and orientation) needed for testing. This test is intended to give detailed information as to how the fire performance of materials perform under actual fire conditions. The value of 300 kW/m^2 for peak rate of heat release of the rubbish container material corresponds to the value that Douglas fir wood emits under the same conditions. Rubbish containers are often manufactured of polyethylene [effective heat of combustion ca. 19,000 Btu/lb (45 MJ/kg)], which releases much more heat in a fire than the typical contents of the container, much of which is paper (effective heat of combustion ca. 6400 Btu/lb (15 MJ/kg)]. For comparison purposes, Table A.19.2.1.2.1 shows peak heat release rates of a series of materials (34 plastics and Douglas fir wood) at an incident heat flux of 40 kW/m^2, in the horizontal orientation and at a thickness of 0.25 in. (6 mm) [Hirschler 1992]. For further comparison, a fire test conducted with a small ignition source on a 22.4 lb polyethylene rubbish container resulted in the release of 1.34 MW within 13.35 minutes of ignition (before it had to be manually extinguished) and caused flashover in the test room. The maximum a container can release is 300 kW/m^2 or maximum heat release rate. Douglas fir has a constant of 300 kW/m^2 where polyethylene has a peak heat release rate of 1268 kW/m^2. Nonmetallic containers such as polyethylene can represent more fuel than their contents (high density polyethylene 19,994 Btu/lb versus newsprint at 8000). A detailed review of listings or approvals is advised prior to acceptance.

A.20.1.4 Where a special amusement building is installed inside another building on a temporary basis, such as within an exhibit hall, the special amusement building requirements apply only to the portions of the building used as a special amusement. For example, the smoke detectors required by 20.1.4.4.3 are not required to be connected to the building's fire alarm system. Where installed in an exhibit hall, such smoke detectors are also required to comply with the provisions applicable to an exhibit. [***101***:A.12.4.9; ***101***:A.13.4.9]

A.20.1.4.1.1 The aggregate horizontal projections of a multilevel play structure are indicative of the number of children who

Table A.19.2.1.2.1 Peak Rate of Heat Release of Materials in the Cone Calorimeter at an Incident Heat Flux of 40 kW/m^2, in the Horizontal Orientation, at a Thickness of 6 mm

	Material Description	Abbreviation	Peak Rate of Heat Release (kW/m^2)
1	Polytetrafluorethylene	PTFE	14
2	Poly(vinyl chloride) flexible 1	PVC Plenum 1	43
3	Poly(vinyl chloride) flexible 2	PVC Plenum 2	64
4	Poly(vinyl chloride) flexible 3	PVC Plenum 3	87
5	Polycarbonate 1	PolyCarb 1	429
6	Poly(vinyl chloride) flexible 4	PVC Plenum 4	77
7	Chlorinated PVC	CPVC	84
8	Poly(vinyl chloride) rigid computer housing	PVC computer	175
9	Poly(vinyl chloride) flexible wire FR	PVC flex FR	92
10	Poly(vinyl chloride) rigid low smoke	PVC low smoke	111
11	Cross linked polyethylene FR	XLPE FR	192
12	Poly(vinyl chloride) flexible wire semi FR	PVC Flex semi FR	142
13	Poly(vinyl chloride) rigid window	PVC window	183
14	Poly(vinyl chloride) flexible wire non FR	PVC Flex non FR	167
15	Poly(methyl methacrylate) FR Blend	PMMA FR	176
16	Polycarbonate 2	Polycarb 2	420
17	Polyphenylene Oxide FR Blend 1	PPO/PS 1	276
18	Polyphenylene Oxide FR Blend 2	PPO/PS 2	265
19	Acrylonitrile butadiene styrene FR 1	ABS FR 1	291
20	Acrylonitrile butadiene styrene FR 2	ABS FR 2	402
21	Poly(vinyl chloride) flexible bath curtain	PVC Flex Poor	237
22	Douglas fir	D Fir	221
23	Polystyrene FR	PS FR	334
24	Polyacetal	P Acetal	360
25	Polyurethane Flexible Foam non FR	PU	710
26	Poly(methyl methacrylate)	PMMA	665
27	Polyurethane Thermoplastic	TPU	221
28	Nylon	Nylon	1313
29	Acrylonitrile butadiene styrene	ABS	944
30	Polystyrene	PS	1101
31	Styrene acrylonitrile EPDM blend	EPDM SAN	956
32	Poly(butylene terephthalate)	PBT	1314
33	Poly(ethylene terephthalate)	PET	534
34	Polyethylene	PE	1408
35	Polypropylene	PP	1509

Source: Hirschler 1992. "Heat release from plastic materials", M.M. Hirschler, Chapter 12 a, in "Heat Release in Fire," Elsevier, London, UK, Eds. V. Babrauskas and S.J. Grayson, 1992. pp. 375–422.

might be within the structure and at risk from a fire or similar emergency. The word "aggregate" is used in recognition of the fact that the platforms and tubes that make up the multilevel play structure run above each other at various levels. In calculating the area of the projections, it is important to account for all areas that might be expected to be occupied within, on top of, or beneath the components of the structure when the structure is used for its intended function. [*101*:A.12.4.9.1.1; *101*:A.13.4.9.1.1]

A.20.1.4.1.2 An example of a Class A special amusement building would be a theme park attraction or dark ride where patrons are restrained inside a ride vehicle and guided through a building on a track. [*101*:A.12.4.9.1.2; *101*:A.13.4.9.1.2]

An example of a Class B special amusement building would be an escape room or theme park attraction where a patron can exit the building once the amusement or effects are stopped. Temporary rides such as a merry-go-round or train located in a mall would not meet the definition of a Class B special amusement building unless there was an element to the ride where a patron would become confused or is otherwise confined to the ride vehicle and unable to self-evacuate. See A.3.3.32.10. [*101*:A.12.4.9.1.2; *101*:A.13.4.9.1.2]

An example of a Class C special amusement building would be a temporary haunted house, maze, or carnival attraction. [*101*:A.12.4.9.1.2; *101*:A.13.4.9.1.2]

A.20.1.4.2.1.3 Consideration should be given to the provision of directional exit marking on or adjacent to the floor. [*101*:A.12.4.9.2.1.3; *101*:A.13.4.9.2.1.3]

A.20.1.4.2.2.1 Lighting levels within special amusement buildings might be reduced to levels that are lower than those required by Section 7.8 of NFPA *101* for show purposes. In addition, projections, special effects, haze, and other theatrical elements might be combined, which can disorient occupants who are unfamiliar with the egress route. The activation of the automatic sprinkler system or smoke detection system should immediately increase illumination to the required levels and stop all show elements that would continue to disorient or confuse occupants. [*101*:A.12.4.9.2.2.1; *101*:A.13.4.9.2.2.1]

Because of the delay in verification or cross-zoning of smoke detectors, positive alarm sequence should not be utilized when alarm-verification or cross-zoned smoke detectors is selected. [*101*:A.12.4.9.2.2.1; *101*:A.13.4.9.2.2.1]

In the context of a special amusement building, a conflicting or confusing sound or visual is any audio or visual device that is intended to quickly distract the attention the patron of a special amusement building for the purpose of frightening, confounding, disorienting, or otherwise capturing the attention of the patron. Examples of this include strobing and flashing lights, loud sound effects, scare or jump effects, loud music, animated figures, projected animation, and interactive games. These can all interfere with the fire alarm notification devices and live announcements from the attraction operator for the patron's attention. In addition, effects that simulate the sound, sight, and smell of flames or smoke will confuse the patron if they continue to operate when the fire alarm system has been activated. [*101*:A.12.4.9.2.2.1; *101*:A.13.4.9.2.2.1]

Some examples of audio and visuals that might occur in a special amusement building, but that might not constitute a conflicting sound or visual, include static or very slow-moving video or projected images, background music, steady state lighting, and ride vehicle triggered effects. [*101*:A.12.4.9.2.2.1; *101*:A.13.4.9.2.2.1]

A.20.1.4.2.2.2 Amusement rides and devices that contain or restrain their patrons such that they are unable to evacuate without the assistance of a ride operator present a unique challenge during an emergency. While ASTM F2291, *Standard Practice for Design of Amusement Rides and Devices*, provides for the design of evacuation paths in case the ride stops before completing its full cycle. The safest and fastest way to exit patrons during an emergency might be to "cycle out" by continuing ride operation until all patrons have exited the ride at the normal exit point (at the unload platform). If a patron were to attempt to exit the ride vehicle while the ride continues operation during an emergency, the patron may potentially be struck by the ride vehicle, or the ride's safety systems might stop all ride motion, potentially extending the evacuation period. Because increasing the illumination of the means of egress along the ride and terminating any conflicting or confusing sounds or visuals while the ride is cycling out might entice the patrons to attempt to self-evacuate while the ride is in motion, the AHJ and the owner are encouraged to work closely to develop a plan that implements the safest and most efficient method to exit the patrons from the ride, which might include continuing normal show operation during cycle out. In addition, the plan should assure that all ride operators and emergency responders understand their roles during cycle out, or during an evacuation if the ride cycle out is interrupted. [*101*:12.4.9.2.2.2; *101*:A.13.4.9.2.2.2]

The ride owner should work with the AHJ from an early stage to develop a pre-incident plan in accordance with NFPA 1620 and any required or applicable provisions of 12.4.2.5.2 and 13.4.2.5.2 of NFPA *101*. [*101*:12.4.9.2.2.2; *101*:A.13.4.9.2.2.2]

A.20.1.4.4.2 Special amusement attractions might contain an operator console or "tower," which might also serve as a constantly attended location when the ride is operating. [*101*:A.12.4.9.4.2; *101*:A.13.4.9.4.2]

A.20.1.4.4.4 Notification in special amusement buildings should be considered carefully depending on the operation of the special amusement. Voice announcements are the required method. However, automatically transmitted evacuation instructions might not be appropriate in some rides when occupants are confined to a ride vehicle and unable to self-evacuate. In order to avoid confusion, manual voice announcements from the ride operator might be preferable to pre-recorded evacuation instructions for some rides. [*101*:A.12.4.9.4.4, *101*:A.13.4.9.4.4]

A.20.1.4.4.4.3 Special amusement buildings that contain rides tend be occupied after operating hours by maintenance staff. After-hours maintenance work might take place along the ride track or in an attached maintenance bay where ride vehicles are moved on and off spur tracks. When no ride operator is located at the constantly attended location to receive alarm signals, a means of automatically sounding the general evacuation signal should be provided for after-hours occupants. [*101*:A.12.4.9.4.4.3, *101*: A.13.4.9.4.4.3]

A.20.1.4.5.1 See A.20.1.4.1.1. [*101*:A.12.4.9.5.1; *101*:A.13.4.9.5.1]

A.20.1.4.6.1 Special amusement buildings might simulate different structures, such as an outdoor scene where false walls and ceilings, commonly known as sets, are recreated indoors with various fabrics and materials used to simulate trees, leaves, or other items. Sets in special amusement buildings are often designed by entertainment companies familiar with Broadway-style stage productions. However, unlike stages and theaters, there are no requirements for smoke control or proscenium protection. The AHJ should consider and evaluate the total quantity of material introduced into the space. [*101*:A.12.4.9.6.1, *101*:A.13.4.9.6.1]

A.20.1.4.6.2 The evacuation plan for special amusement buildings should consider the safest and fastest way to remove occupants from the structure. When a ride stops within the special amusement building, removing occupants from the ride system might present an extended evacuation. Additionally, hazards associated with the ride and show system might present electrical and entanglement challenges to occupants unfamiliar with the building. Evacuation of special amusement buildings can also pose challenges to the local fire department if they are not familiar with the nature of the building or ride system. Specialized equipment for rescue, ride vehicle-specific tools for releasing doors, and high-energy ride vehicle hazard awareness might all be required when evacuating from a location other than a load/unload station. [*101*:A.12.4.9.6.2, *101*:A.13.4.9.6.2]

The ride owner should work with the AHJ from an early stage to develop a pre-incident plan in accordance with NFPA 1620 and any required or applicable provisions of 10.14.3.5.2. [*101*:A.12.4.9.6.2, *101*:A.13.4.9.6.2]

A.20.1.5.3(3)(a) Securely supported altar candles in churches that are well separated from any combustible material are permitted. On the other hand, lighted candles carried by children wearing cotton robes present a hazard too great to be permitted. There are many other situations of intermediate hazard where the AHJ will have to exercise judgment. [*101*:A.12.7.3(3)(a); *101*:A.13.7.3(3)(a)]

A.20.1.5.4.1 Fabric applied over unused seating sections should meet the requirements of 20.1.5.4. [*101*:A.12.7.4.1; *101*:A.13.7.4.1]

A.20.1.5.4.3 The phrase "unprotected materials containing foamed plastic" is meant to include foamed plastic items covered by "thermally thin" combustible fabrics or paint. *(See A.12.5.4.3.)* [*101*:A.12.7.4.3; *101*:A.13.7.4.3]

A.20.1.5.5.4.7.1(3) See A.10.14.3.1. [*101*:A.12.7.5.3.7.1(3); *101*:A.13.7.5.3.7.1(3)]

A.20.1.5.6.2 Crowd managers and crowd manager supervisors need to clearly understand the required duties and responsibilities specific to the venue's emergency plan. The crowd management training program should include a clear appreciation of crowd dynamics factors including space, energy, time, and information, as well as specific crowd management techniques, such as metering. Training should involve specific actions necessary during normal and emergency operations, and include an assessment of people-handling capabilities of a space prior to its use, the identification of hazards, an evaluation of projected levels of occupancy, the adequacy of means of ingress and egress and identification of ingress and egress barriers, the processing procedures such as ticket collection, and the expected types of human behavior. Training should also involve the different types of emergency evacuations and, where required by the emergency plan, relocation and shelter-in-place operations, and the challenges associated with each. [*101*:A.12.7.6.2; *101*:A.13.7.6.2]

A.20.1.5.6.4 In large facilities, crowd managers typically have a specific area of responsibility. In such facilities, the requirements of 20.1.5.6.4 might apply only to the crowd managers' area of responsibility. [*101*:A.12.7.6.4; *101*:A.13.7.6.4]

A.20.1.5.7 Because of the variety of types of places of assembly covered in this *Code*, no general requirement for patrols or fire watchers has been included. The NFPA 102 Committee fully recognizes the importance of this feature of fire protection, however, and believes that a system of well-trained patrols or fire watchers should be maintained in every place of assembly where fire hazards might develop. Such locations would include, among others, the spaces underneath grandstands and the areas inside and outside tents and air-supported structures. The fire watchers serve to detect incipient fires and to prevent an accumulation of materials that will carry fire. The number of such watchers required will, of course, vary for the different types of assembly occupancies, depending upon the combustibility of the construction and the number of persons accommodated. Provided with an adequate supply of portable fire extinguishing equipment located at readily accessible points, such a fire watch or detail should be able to prevent small fires from reaching serious proportions.

A.20.1.5.8 It is important that an adequate number of competent attendants is on duty at all times when the assembly occupancy is occupied. [*101*:A.12.7.7; *101*:A.13.7.7]

A.20.1.5.8.3 It is not the intent of this provision to require an announcement in bowling alleys, cocktail lounges, restaurants, or places of worship. [*101*:A.12.7.7.3; *101*:A.13.7.7.3]

Δ **A.20.2.4.2.1** The requirements are, of necessity, general in scope, because it is recognized that they apply to all types of educational occupancies as well as conditions of occupancies, such as truant schools; schools for students with intellectual, vision, hearing, and speech disabilities; and public schools. It is fully recognized that no one code can meet all the conditions of the various buildings involved, and it will be necessary for site administrators to issue supplements to these requirements; however, all supplements should be consistent with these requirements. [*101*:A.14.7.2.1; *101*:A.15.7.2.1]

A.20.2.4.2.4 Many jurisdictions are now conducting other drills in addition to emergency egress drills. Targeted violence events can include everything from active shooters to use of other weapons intended to cause harm. Natural hazard drills generally consist of tornado or earthquake drills. [*101*:A.14.7.2.4; *101*:A.15.7.2.4]

A.20.2.4.3.1 Particular attention should be given to keeping all doors unlocked; keeping doors that serve to protect the safety of paths of egress closed and under no conditions blocked open, such as doors on stairway enclosures; keeping outside stairs and fire escape stairs free from all obstructions and clear of snow and ice; and allowing no accumulation of snow or ice or materials of any kind outside exit doors that might prevent the opening of the door or interfere with rapid escape from the building. [*101*:A.14.7.3.1; *101*:A.15.7.3.1]

Any condition likely to interfere with safe egress should be corrected immediately, if possible, or otherwise should be reported at once to the appropriate authorities. [*101*:A.14.7.3.1; *101*:A.15.7.3.1]

A.20.3.1.3 The definition of day-care occupancy is intended to exclude day-care uses that are part of some other occupancy. In such cases, the requirements of the predominant occupancy apply. Examples of excluded facilities include the following:

(1) Rooms located within places of worship used as nurseries or for supervision of children or religious education while services are being held in the building.
(2) Rooms used for temporary child care during short-term recreational activities of the child's relative or guardian, such as within a health club or park district.
(3) Rooms used for temporary child care during short-term activities such as court hearings, medical appointments, libraries, or other similar circumstances.

[*101*:A.16.1.1.7; *101*:A.17.1.1.7]

A.20.3.2.2 The purpose of this requirement is to prevent arrangements whereby a client can be trapped in a space or area. It is intended that this provision be broadly interpreted by the AHJ to include equipment such as refrigerators and freezers. [*101*:A.16.2.2.2.4; *101*:A.17.2.2.2.4]

A.20.3.4.1.2 Day-care homes do not provide for the full-time maintenance of a client. Day-care occupancies that provide a primary place of residence are addressed in other occupancy chapters. *(See Chapters 24 through 33 of NFPA 101.)* [*101*:A.17.6.1.1.2]

Δ **A.20.3.4.2.1.1** The requirements are, of necessity, general in scope, because it is recognized that they apply to all types of day-care occupancies as well as conditions of occupancies, such as truant day-care occupancies; occupancies for persons with intellectual, vision, hearing, and speech disabilities; adult day-care; care of infants; and day-care occupancies. It is fully recognized that no one code can meet all the conditions of the various buildings involved, and it will be necessary for site administrators, through the written fire emergency response plan, to issue supplements to these requirements; however, all supplements should be consistent with these requirements. Additionally, it is recommended that fire safety be a part of the educational programs of the occupancy for clients. [*101*:A.16.7.1; *101*:A.17.7.1]

Fire emergency response plans need to be written and made available to all employees, including temporary or substitute staff, so that all employees know what is expected of them during a fire emergency. The elements needed in the written plan should be identified in coordination with the AHJ. [*101*:A.16.7.1; *101*:A.17.7.1]

The facility fire emergency response plan might be a module of a facility disaster plan that covers other emergencies. [*101*:A.16.7.1; *101*:A.17.7.1]

The proper safeguarding of clients during a fire emergency requires prompt and effective response by the facility employees in accordance with the fire emergency response plan. Duties covered under the plan should be assigned by position rather than by employee name. Such assignment ensures that, in the absence of an employee, the duties of the position will be performed by a substitute or temporary employee assigned to the position. Temporary or substitute employees should be instructed in advance regarding their duties under the plan for the position to which they are assigned. [*101*:A.16.7.1; *101*:A.17.7.1]

Written fire emergency response plans should include, but should not be limited to, information for employees regarding methods and devices available for alerting occupants of a fire emergency. Employees should know how the fire department is to be alerted. Even where automatic systems are expected to alert the fire department, the written plan should provide for backup alerting procedures by staff. Other responses of employees to a fire emergency should include the following:

(1) Removal of clients in immediate danger to areas of safety, as set forth in the plan
(2) Methods of using building features to confine the fire and its by-products to the room or area of origin
(3) Control of actions and behaviors of clients during removal or evacuation activities and at predetermined safe assembly areas

[*101*:A.16.7.1; *101*:A.17.7.1]

The written plan should state clearly the facility policy regarding the actions staff are to take or not take to extinguish a fire. It should also incorporate the emergency egress and relocation drill procedures set forth in 20.3.4.2.2. [*101*:A.16.7.1; *101*:A.17.7.1]

For additional guidance on emergency action plans, see *NFPA 1600*. This standard establishes a common set of criteria for disaster management, emergency management, and business continuity programs. [*101*:A.16.7.1; *101*:A.17.7.1]

Δ **A.20.3.4.2.2.1** The requirements are, of necessity, general in scope, because it is recognized that they apply to all types of day-care occupancies as well as conditions of occupancies, such as truant day-care occupancies; and day-care occupancies for persons with intellectual, vision, hearing, and speech disabilities. It is fully recognized that no one code can meet all the conditions of the various buildings involved, and it will be necessary for site administrators to issue supplements to these requirements, but all supplements should be consistent with these requirements. [*101*:A.16.7.2.1; *101*:A.17.7.2.1]

A.20.3.4.2.3.2 Particular attention should be given to keeping all doors unlocked; keeping doors that serve to protect the safety of paths of egress closed and under no conditions blocked open, such as doors on stairway enclosures; keeping outside stairs and fire escape stairs free from all obstructions and clear of snow and ice; and allowing no accumulation of snow or ice or materials of any kind outside exit doors that might prevent the opening of the door or interfere with rapid escape from the building. [*101*:A.16.7.3.2; *101*:A.17.7.3.2]

A.20.3.4.2.3.6 It is the intent that the requirement for adequate adult staff to be awake at all times when clients are present be applied to family day-care and group day-care homes that are operated at night, as well as day-care occupancies. [*101*:A.16.7.5; *101*:A.17.7.5]

A.20.4.2 Health care occupants have, in large part, varied degrees of physical disability, and their removal to the outside, or even their disturbance caused by moving, is inexpedient or impractical in many cases, except as a last resort. Similarly, recognizing that there might be an operating necessity for the restraint of the mentally ill, often by use of barred windows and locked doors, fire exit drills are usually extremely disturbing, detrimental, and frequently impracticable. [*101*:A.18.7; *101*:A.19.7]

In most cases, fire exit drills, as ordinarily practiced in other occupancies, cannot be conducted in health care occupancies. Fundamentally, superior construction, early discovery and extinguishment of incipient fires, and prompt notification need to be relied on to reduce the occasion for evacuation of buildings of this class to a minimum. [*101*:A.18.7; *101*:A.19.7]

A.20.4.2.1.5 Many health care occupancies conduct fire drills without disturbing patients by choosing the location of the simulated emergency in advance and by closing the doors to patients' rooms or wards in the vicinity prior to initiation of the drill. The purpose of a fire drill is to test and evaluate the efficiency, knowledge, and response of institutional personnel in implementing the facility fire emergency action plan. Its purpose is not to disturb or excite patients. Fire drills should be scheduled on a random basis to ensure that personnel in health care facilities are drilled not less than once in each 3-month period. [*101*:A.18.7.1.4; *101*:A.19.7.1.4]

Drills should consider the ability to move patients to an adjacent smoke compartment. Relocation can be practiced using simulated patients or empty wheelchairs. [*101*:A.18.7.1.4; *101*:A.19.7.1.4]

A.20.4.2.2.1 Each facility has specific characteristics that vary sufficiently from other facilities to prevent the specification of a universal emergency procedure. The recommendations that follow, however, contain many of the elements that should be considered and adapted, as appropriate, to the individual facility. [*101*:A.18.7.2.1; *101*:A.19.7.2.1]

Upon discovery of fire, personnel should immediately take the following action:

(1) If any person is involved in the fire, the discoverer should go to the aid of that person, calling aloud an established code phrase, which provides for both the immediate aid of any endangered person and the transmission of an alarm.
(2) Any person in the area, upon hearing the code called aloud, should activate the building fire alarm using the nearest manual fire alarm box.

(3) If a person is not involved in the fire, the discoverer should activate the building fire alarm using the nearest manual fire alarm box.
(4) Personnel, upon hearing the alarm signal, should immediately execute their duties as outlined in the facility fire safety plan.
(5) The telephone operator should determine the location of the fire as indicated by the audible signal.
(6) In a building equipped with an uncoded alarm system, a person on the floor of fire origin should be responsible for promptly notifying the facility telephone operator of the fire location.
(7) If the telephone operator receives a telephone alarm reporting a fire from a floor, the operator should regard that alarm in the same fashion as an alarm received over the fire alarm system and should immediately notify the fire department and alert all facility personnel of the place of fire and its origin.
(8) If the building fire alarm system is out of order, any person discovering a fire should immediately notify the telephone operator by telephone, and the operator should then transmit this information to the fire department and alert the building occupants.

[*101*:A.18.7.2.1; *101*:A.19.7.2.1]

A.20.4.2.3.3 The purpose of this requirement is to provide a means for building designers, occupants, and operators to clearly designate approved egress corridors that can be identified even though physical or other obvious barriers might not be present to indicate their location. Floor plans used to satisfy this requirement might incorporate more than one function and more than one smoke compartment of the building, provided egress corridors are clearly identified where no fixed barriers are present. Such plans should be accessible to the AHJ but should not be required to be posted. [*101*:A.18.7.3.3; *101*:A.19.7.3.3]

A.20.4.2.4 The most rigid discipline with regard to prohibition of smoking might not be nearly as effective in reducing incipient fires from surreptitious smoking as the open recognition of smoking, with provision of suitable facilities for smoking. Proper education and training of the staff and attendants in the ordinary fire hazards and their abatement is unquestionably essential. The problem is a broad one, varying with different types and arrangements of buildings; the effectiveness of rules of procedure, which need to be flexible, depends in large part on the management. [*101*:A.18.7.4; *101*:A.19.7.4]

A.20.4.2.5.1 In addition to the provisions of 12.6.1, which deal with ignition resistance, additional requirements with respect to the location of cubicle curtains relative to sprinkler placement are included in NFPA 13. [*101*:A.18.7.5.1; *101*:A.19.7.5.1]

A.20.4.2.5.6(2) The user should verify that the products meet the referenced test methods of NFPA 701, and not the small-scale test procedure that was previously eliminated from NFPA 701. [*101*:A.18.7.5.6(2); *101*:A.19.7.5.6(2)]

A.20.4.2.5.6(4) The percentage of decorations should be measured against the area of any wall or ceiling, not the aggregate total of walls, ceilings, and doors. The door is considered part of the wall. The decorations must be located such that they do not interfere with the operation of any door, sprinkler, smoke detector, or any other life safety equipment. Other art might include hanging objects or three-dimensional items. [*101*:A.18.7.5.6(4); *101*:A.19.7.5.6(4)]

N **A.20.4.2.5.6(5)** When determining if the hazard for fire development or spread is present, consideration should be given to whether the building or area being evaluated is sprinklered. [*101*:A.19.7.5.6(5)]

A.20.4.2.5.7.1 It is not the intent to permit collection receptacles with a capacity greater than 64 gal (242 L) to be positioned at or near a nurses' station based on the argument that such nurses' station is constantly attended. The large collection receptacle itself needs to be actively attended by staff. Staff might leave the large receptacle in the corridor outside a patient room while entering the room to collect soiled linen or trash, but staff is expected to return to the receptacle, move on to the next room, and repeat the collection function. Where staff is not actively collecting material for placement in the receptacle, the receptacle is to be moved to a room protected as a hazardous area. [*101*:A.18.7.5.7.1; *101*:A.19.7.5.7.1]

A.20.4.2.5.7.2 It is the intent that this provision permits recycling of bottles, cans, paper and similar clean items that do not contain grease, oil, flammable liquids, or significant plastic materials using larger containers or several adjacent containers and not require locating such containers in a room protected as a hazardous area. Containers for medical records awaiting shredding are often larger than 64 gal (242 L). These containers are not to be included in the calculations and limitations of 20.4.2.5.7.1. There is no limit on the number of these containers, as FM Approvals 6920/6921, *Oily Waste Cans and Containers for Combustible Waste*, ensures that the fire will not spread out of the container. FM approval standards are written for use with FM Approvals. The tests can be conducted by any approved laboratory. The portions of the standard referring to FM Approvals are not included in this reference. [*101*:A.18.7.5.7.2; *101*:A.19.7.5.7.2]

A.20.4.2.6 Portable space heaters complying with 20.4.2.6 should be permitted to be located in office areas, nurses stations, and other similar nonpatient spaces within the same smoke compartment as patient sleeping rooms. [*101*:A.18.7.8; *101*:A.19.7.8]

A.20.5.2.1.1 Where residents require evacuation or relocation assistance, the plan should address the specific needs for each resident, and adequate staffing should be provided as necessary to implement the plan. [*101*:A.32.7.1.1; *101*:A.33.7.1.1]

A.20.5.2.3.3 An assembly point can be located outside the building, in a separate building, or in an adjacent smoke compartment in the same building. [*101*:A.32.7.3.3]

A.20.5.2.4.1 Smoking regulations should include the following:

(1) Smoking should be prohibited in any room, compartment, or area where flammable or combustible liquids, combustible gases, or oxygen is used or stored and in any other hazardous location, and the following also should apply:

  (a) Such areas should be posted with signs that read NO SMOKING or the international symbol for no smoking.
  (b) In residential board and care facilities where smoking is totally prohibited and signs so indicating are placed at all major entrances, secondary signs with language that prohibits smoking are not required.

(2) Smoking by residents classified as not responsible with regard to their ability to safely use and dispose of smoking materials should be prohibited.
(3) Where a resident, as specified in A.20.5.2.4.1(2), is under direct supervision by staff or by a person approved by the administration, smoking might be permitted.
(4) Smoking materials should not be provided to residents or maintained by residents without the approval of the administration.
(5) Areas where smoking is permitted should be clearly identified.
(6) Ashtrays of noncombustible material and safe design should be provided and required to be used in all areas where smoking is permitted.
(7) Self-closing cover devices into which ashtrays can be emptied should be made available to all areas where smoking is permitted and should be required to be used.

[*101*:A.32.7.4.1; *101*:A.33.7.4.1]

A.20.5.2.5 The requirements applicable to draperies/curtains, upholstered furniture, and mattresses apply only to new draperies/curtains, new upholstered furniture, and new mattresses. The word *new* means unused, normally via procurement from the marketplace, either by purchase or donation, of items not previously used. Many board and care facilities allow residents to bring into the board and care home upholstered furniture items from the resident's previous residence. Such items are not new and, thus, are not regulated. On the other hand, some of the larger board and care homes purchase contract furniture, as is done in hotels. Such new, unused furniture, whether purchased or received as a donation, is regulated by the requirements of 20.5.2.5.2. By federal law, mattresses manufactured and sold within the United States must pass testing per 16 CFR 1632, "Standard for the Flammability of Mattresses and Mattress Pads" (FF4-72). [*101*:A.32.7.5; *101*:A.33.7.5]

Δ **A.20.5.2.5.2** New upholstered furniture within board and care homes should be tested for rates of heat release in accordance with 12.6.3.2.1. [*101*:A.32.7.5.2; *101*:A.33.7.5.2]

A.20.5.2.5.2.3 New mattresses within board and care homes should be tested for rates of heat release in accordance with 12.6.3.2.2. [*101*:A.32.7.5.3; *101*:A.33.7.5.3]

A.20.6.2 Ambulatory health care occupants have, in large part, varied degrees of physical disability, and their removal to the outside, or even their disturbance caused by moving, is inexpedient or impractical in many cases, except as a last resort. Similarly, recognizing that there might be an operating necessity for the restraint of the mentally ill, often by use of barred windows and locked doors, fire exit drills are usually extremely disturbing, detrimental, and frequently impracticable. [*101*:A.20.7; *101*:A.21.7]

In most cases, fire exit drills, as ordinarily practiced in other occupancies, cannot be conducted in ambulatory health care occupancies. Fundamentally, superior construction, early discovery and extinguishment of incipient fires, and prompt notification need to be relied on to reduce the occasion for evacuation of buildings of this class to a minimum. [*101*:A.20.7; *101*:A.21.7]

A.20.6.2.1.5 Many ambulatory health care occupancies conduct fire drills without disturbing patients by choosing the location of the simulated emergency in advance and by closing the doors in the vicinity prior to the initiation of the drill. The purpose of a fire drill is to test and evaluate the efficiency, knowledge, and response of personnel in implementing the facility fire emergency plan. Its purpose is not to disturb or excite patients. Fire drills should be scheduled on a random basis to ensure that personnel in ambulatory health care facilities are drilled not less than once in each 3-month period. [*101*:A.20.7.1.4; *101*:A.21.7.1.4]

Drills should consider the ability to move patients to an adjacent smoke compartment. Relocation can be practiced using simulated patients or empty wheelchairs. [*101*:A.20.7.1.4; *101*:A.21.7.1.4]

A.20.6.2.2.1 Each facility has specific characteristics that vary sufficiently from other facilities to prevent the specification of a universal emergency procedure. The recommendations that follow, however, contain many of the elements that should be considered and adapted, as appropriate, to the individual facility. [*101*:A.20.7.2.1; *101*:A.21.7.2.1]

Upon discovery of fire, personnel should immediately take the following action:

(1) If any person is involved in the fire, the discoverer should go to the aid of that person, calling aloud an established code phrase, which provides for both the immediate aid of any endangered person and the transmission of an alarm.
(2) Any person in the area, upon hearing the code called aloud, should activate the building fire alarm using the nearest manual fire alarm box.
(3) If a person is not involved in the fire, the discoverer should activate the building fire alarm using the nearest manual fire alarm box.
(4) Personnel, upon hearing the alarm signal, should immediately execute their duties as outlined in the facility fire safety plan.
(5) The telephone operator should determine the location of the fire as indicated by the audible signal.
(6) In a building equipped with an uncoded alarm system, a person on the floor of fire origin should be responsible for promptly notifying the facility telephone operator of the fire location.
(7) If the telephone operator receives a telephone alarm reporting a fire from a floor, the operator should regard that alarm in the same fashion as an alarm received over the fire alarm system and should immediately notify the fire department and alert all facility personnel of the place of fire and its origin.
(8) If the building fire alarm system is out of order, any person discovering a fire should immediately notify the telephone operator by telephone, and the operator should then transmit this information to the fire department and alert the building occupants.

[*101*:A.20.7.2.1; *101*:A.21.7.2.1]

A.20.6.2.4 The most rigid discipline with regard to prohibition of smoking might not be nearly as effective in reducing incipient fires from surreptitious smoking as the open recognition of smoking, with provision of suitable facilities for smoking. Proper education and training of the staff and attendants in the ordinary fire hazards and their abatement is unquestionably essential. The problem is a broad one, varying with different types and arrangements of buildings; the effectiveness of rules of procedure, which need to be flexible, depends in large part on the management. [*101*:A.20.7.4; *101*:A.21.7.4]

A.20.6.2.5.1 In addition to the provisions of 12.6.1, which deal with ignition resistance, additional requirements with respect to the location of cubicle curtains relative to sprinkler placement are included in NFPA 13. [*101*:A.20.7.5.1; *101*:A.21.7.5.1]

A.20.6.2.5.4(4) The percentage of decorations should be measured against the area of any wall or ceiling, not the aggregate total of walls, ceilings, and doors. The door is considered part of the wall. The decorations must be located such that they do not interfere with the operation of any door, sprinkler, smoke detector, or any other life safety equipment. Other art might include hanging objects or three-dimensional items. [*101*:A.20.7.5.4(4); *101*:A.21.7.5.4(4)]

A.20.6.2.5.5.2 It is the intent that this provision permits recycling of bottles, cans, paper, and similar clean items that do not contain grease, oil, flammable liquids, or significant plastic materials using larger containers or several adjacent containers and not require locating such containers in a room protected as a hazardous area. Containers for medical records awaiting shredding are often larger than 64 gal (242 L). These containers are not to be included in the calculations and limitations of 20.6.2.5.5.1. There is no limit on the number of these containers, as FM Approvals 6920/6921, *Oily Waste Cans and Containers for Combustible Waste*, ensures that the fire will not spread outside of the container. FM approval standards are written for use with FM Approvals. The tests can be conducted by any approved laboratory. The portions of the standard referring to FM Approvals are not included in this reference. [*101*:A.20.7.5.5.2; *101*:A.21.7.5.5.2]

A.20.7.2.1.2 This requirement is permitted to be met by electronic or oral monitoring systems, visual monitoring, call signals, or other means. [*101*:A.22.7.1.2; *101*:A.23.7.1.2]

A.20.7.2.1.3 Periodic, coordinated training should be conducted and should involve detention and correctional facility personnel and personnel of the fire department legally committed to serving the facility. [*101*:A.22.7.1.3; *101*:A.23.7.1.3]

A.20.7.2.2 Personal property provides combustible contents for fire development. Therefore, adequate controls are needed to limit the quantity and combustibility of the fuels available to burn to reduce the probability of room flashover. The provisions of 20.7.2.4 will not, by themselves, prevent room flashover if personal property controls are not provided. [*101*:A.22.7.2; *101*:A.23.7.2]

Δ **A.20.7.2.4** The type, quantity, and arrangement of furniture and other combustibles are important factors in determining how fast the fire will develop. Furnishings, including upholstered items and wood items, such as wardrobes, desks, and bookshelves, might provide sufficient fuel to result in room flashover, which is the full fire involvement of all combustibles within a room once sufficient heat has been built up within the room. [*101*:A.22.7.4]

A.20.8.2.1.1 Employers are obligated to determine the degree to which employees are to participate in emergency activities. Regulations of the US Department of Labor (OSHA) govern these activities and provide options for employers, from total evacuation to aggressive structural fire fighting by employee brigades. *(For additional information, see 29 CFR 1910, Subparts E and L, "OSHA Regulations for Emergency Procedures and Fire Brigades.")* [*101*:A.28.7.1.1; *101*:A.29.7.1.1]

A.20.8.2.1.2 Emergencies should be assumed to have arisen at various locations in the occupancy in order to train employees in logical procedures. [*101*:A.28.7.1.2; *101*:A.29.7.1.2]

A.20.8.2.4.1 Floor diagrams should reflect the actual floor arrangement and should be oriented with the actual direction to the exits. [*101*:A.28.7.4.1; *101*:A.29.7.4.1]

A.20.8.2.4.2 Factors for developing the fire safety information include such items as construction type, suppression systems, alarm and detection systems, building layout, and building HVAC systems. [*101*:A.28.7.4.2; *101*:A.29.7.4.2]

A.20.11.4.4 Materials such as wood I-Joist, wood or steel trusses, or cold formed steel would not typically be considered equivalent.

A.20.15.5.1 Examples of facilities covered by NFPA 61 include, but are not limited to, bakeries, grain elevators, feed mills, flour mills, milling, corn milling (dry and wet), rice milling, dry milk products, mix plants, soybean and other oilseed preparation operations, cereal processing, snack food processing, tortilla plants, chocolate processing, pet food processing, cake mix processing, sugar refining and processing, and seed plants. [**61**:A.1.3.1]

A.20.15.6.2 See NFPA 232 where large archives or records storage buildings are involved.

A.20.17.3(2) See also NFPA 914.

A.21.1.4 For further information on aircraft hangars, see NFPA 409. [*101*:A.40.6]

A.21.1.5 For further information on aircraft hangars, see NFPA 409. [*101*:A.42.6]

A.21.2.4.2 Furniture, floor and wall coverings, and other furnishings in airport terminal occupancies, including passenger holding lounges, waiting areas, restaurant dining rooms, bars, and retail stores, should not be made of materials that have high combustibility, smoke-development characteristics, or both, for example, some plastic foams, latex-rubber foam, some plastics, and some synthetic fibers. Such materials have a tendency to release combustible gases at relatively low temperatures, making them easily ignitible. When burning, these materials also release high amounts of heat energy at rapid rates, thereby contributing greatly to fire propagation. [**415**:A.4.1.2]

Interior finish Class A and Class B are described in NFPA *101*. [**415**:A.4.1.2]

A.21.2.5.2 Examples of points of flammable vapor release are fuel tank vent openings and fuel hydrant pits. Air supply intake and exhaust openings for air-conditioning or ventilating equipment serving the terminal building should not be located on the ramp side of an airport terminal building. Fixed air-conditioning and ventilating equipment serving only aircraft should be in a room that has no openings communicating with the remainder of the terminal building. [**415**:A.4.2.2]

A.21.2.5.3 Rooms that contain coal-, gas-, or oil-fired equipment or any other open-flame device should not have openings on the ramp side of the building. Combustion and ventilation air should be supplied from the street side or the roof of the building or through a gravity louver from a nonhazardous area in the building. [**415**:A.4.2.3]

A.21.2.6.2 The hazards to persons from jet intakes and blast, noise, propellers, and so forth, on the ramp should be taken into consideration in locating emergency exit points leading to ramps from the airport terminal building. A means of notification of unauthorized usage (such as an alarm system) of these emergency exits may be desirable. [415:A.4.3.2]

A.21.2.7 The assembly portion of the terminal building can include areas such as the concourse waiting areas, baggage claim areas, and restaurants. The assembly portion should exclude kitchens, toilets, small office areas, and other areas not normally accessible to the public. [415:A.4.5.1]

A.21.2.7.5 The exposure to the airport terminal building from the airport ramp is significant. The number of building sprinklers operating from the exposure fire could be greater than the number of building sprinklers operating from an internal ignition source. [415:A.4.5.1.5]

A.21.2.8.2 If the public fire department is responding to the "street" side of the airport terminal building, timely access to the normal alarm receiving point might be limited by emergency conditions or distance. Planned radio communication with a constantly attended alarm-receiving point can assist in a more efficient response by the public fire department. The remote annunciator on the street side of the terminal building can provide building condition information not otherwise available. [415:A.4.5.2.2]

A.21.3.3.1 FAA AC 150/5390-2C, *Heliport Design Advisory Circular*, contains design and construction information on heliports. This advisory circular provides for adequate clearance between operating aircraft and buildings or structures located at the heliport. The FAA advisory circular should be consulted to ensure that adequate safe practice and facilities are maintained. [418:A.4.2]

A.21.3.3.7 The two means of egress can also be used for access to the landing pad for firefighting and/or rescue operations. Where doors accessing the interior of the building are locked, an approved means should be provided for entry of emergency responders. [418:A.4.8]

A.21.3.3.7.1 Figure A.21.3.3.7.1(a) and Figure A.21.3.3.7.1(b) are examples of acceptable configurations of egress points on landing pads. The geometry of the landing pad in Figure A.21.3.3.7.1(b) is such that it has no sides and does not comply with 21.3.3.7.3; however, it does comply with the 90-degree rule in 21.3.3.7.1. Figure A.21.3.3.7.1(c) is an example of an unacceptable configuration, due to both egress points being on the same side of the landing pad. [418:A.4.8.1]

FIGURE A.21.3.3.7.1(a) Example of an Acceptable Configuration of Egress Points on a Landing Pad. [418:Figure A.4.8.1(a)]

FIGURE A.21.3.3.7.1(b) Example of an Acceptable Configuration of Egress Points on a Landing Pad with No Sides. [418:Figure A.4.8.1(b)]

FIGURE A.21.3.3.7.1(c) Example of an Unacceptable Configuration of Egress Points on a Landing Pad. [418:Figure A.4.8.1(c)]

A.21.3.4.1 Where the landing pad is nonporous, fuel-tight, and provided with a proper drainage system, and where fuel cannot flow to support members, the main structural support members would not need to be fire rated. [418:A.5.2]

A.21.3.4.4 Design of the means of egress from a rooftop landing pad might involve a compromise among several different code requirements. Rooftop landing pads bring with them an inherent risk. The means of egress must be provided for safety to human life. Strict compliance with a code's requirement for rated stairways off the landing pad is not the intent of this standard. The intent of this standard is to provide a minimum safeguard to provide a reasonable degree of safety to all persons on the roof. The building's egress system is dictated by the adopted building code. Once those persons enter the building's egress system, they are away from the FATO area. [418:A.5.5]

A.21.3.4.4.1 See Figure A.21.3.3.7.1(a) through Figure A.21.3.3.7.1(c) for examples of acceptable configurations of egress points on landing pads. The geometry of the landing pad in Figure A.21.3.3.7.1(b) is such that it has no sides and cannot comply with 21.3.4.4.3; however, it does comply with the 90-degree rule in 21.3.4.4.1. Figure A.21.3.3.7.1(c) is not an acceptable configuration due to both egress points being on the same side of the landing pad. [418:A.5.5.1]

A.21.3.4.4.4 When considering the means of egress from the landing pad and for the rooftop, obstructions to the FATO need to be avoided since they can create unsafe flight conditions that have been shown to cause aircraft accidents. Exterior, open stairways leading to the building's egress system should not encroach into the FATO. [**418**:A.5.5.4]

A.21.3.4.6.1.2 The design density is for synthetic foam concentrates, not fluoroprotein or protein foam products. [**418**:A.5.7.1.3]

A.21.3.4.6.2.2 Consideration should be given to the environmental conditions of the rooftop landing pad in the design of the system, including wind, exhaust fans, and other factors that affect the distribution of the foam on the rooftop landing pad. [**418**:A.5.7.2.2]

A.21.3.4.6.2.6.1 Training on the operation of the fire protection system should be in accordance with Annex B of NFPA 418. [**418**:A.5.7.2.6.1]

A.21.3.4.6.2.6.2 It is acceptable for the rooftop landing pad to be viewed using video or other acceptable means. [**418**:A.5.7.2.6.2]

A.21.3.4.6.3.1 The area of application and the duration where using a hose line system is reduced because foam is applied efficiently and directly on the fire by trained personnel. [**418**:A.5.7.3.1]

A.25.1.4.2 NFPA 58 permits the use of portable butane-fueled appliances in restaurants and in attended commercial food catering operations where fueled by a maximum of two 10 oz (0.28 kg) LP-Gas capacity, nonrefillable butane containers with a water capacity not in excess of 1.08 lb (0.4 kg) per container. Containers are required to be directly connected to the appliance, and manifolding of containers is not permitted. Storage of cylinders is also limited to 24 containers, with an additional 24 permitted where protected by a 2-hour fire-resistance-rated barrier. *(See 4.1.3 of NFPA 101 and Annex C of NFPA 101 for referenced documents on hazardous materials.)* [*101*:A.8.7.3.2]

A.25.1.8 Because of the variety of types of places of assembly covered by this *Code*, no general requirement for patrols or fire watchers has been included. The committee fully recognizes the importance of this feature of fire protection, however, and believes that a system of well-trained patrols or fire watchers should be maintained in every place of assembly where fire hazards might develop. Such locations would include, among others, the spaces underneath grandstands and the areas inside and outside tents and air-supported structures. The fire watchers serve to detect incipient fires and to prevent an accumulation of materials that will carry fire. The number of such watchers required will, of course, vary for the different types of assembly occupancies, depending upon the combustibility of the construction and the number of persons accommodated. Provided with an adequate supply of portable fire-extinguishing equipment located at readily accessible points, such a fire watch or detail should be able to prevent small fires from reaching serious proportions.

A.25.1.12.2 The 20 ft (6.1 m) separation is intended to minimize the carbon monoxide hazard and fire hazard associated with portable generators.

A.25.5.3.3.1 The requirements of 25.5.3.3.1 can be considered as a Class 4, Type 60, system per NFPA 110. [*101*:A.11.9.3.3.1]

A.26.1.4(1) Either condition of 26.1.4(1) meeting the minimum quantity will bring the lab within the scope of Chapter 26. A school lab with a low pressure natural gas system supplying Bunsen burners (with less than the minimum quantities of combustible or flammable liquids and less than the minimum quantities of other flammable gases) is an example of a lab outside the scope of Chapter 26. [**45**:A.1.1.3(1)]

A.26.1.4(2) The hazards of pilot plants are primarily based on the process, the chemistry, and the equipment, not the laboratory environment. Laboratories that have pilot plants within the laboratory unit should apply NFPA 45 to the laboratory portion. NFPA 45 should not be used to justify applying laboratory requirements, such as a general-purpose-area electrical classification, to the pilot plant itself. [**45**:A.1.1.3(2)]

A.26.1.4(7) NFPA 801 provides direction for controlling hazards associated with radioactive materials. NFPA 801 should be used only for issues related to radioactive materials in a laboratory. All other nonradioactive, laboratory issues are covered by NFPA 45. [**45**:A.1.1.3(7)]

A.26.1.6.1 Laboratory buildings, laboratory units, and laboratory work areas need to have clearly developed plans for fire prevention, maintenance, and emergency procedures. Guidance of the development of these plans and procedures can be found in NFPA 45.

A.28.1.2.2 Where fixed fire-extinguishing system components are installed in areas subjecting these components to corrosion or other atmospheric damage, special considerations might be necessary. Corrosion-resistant types of pipe, fittings, and hangers or protective corrosion-resistant coatings should be used where corrosive conditions exist. [**303**:A.6.2]

A.28.1.2.2.1.3 Where clearly impractical for economic or physical reasons, the AHJ could permit the omission of an automatic fire-extinguishing system when considering water supply availability and adequacy and size of facility. [**303**:A.6.2.1.3]

A.28.1.2.2.2 It is not the intent of this paragraph to limit the types of fire protection systems to automatic sprinklers in order to comply with the requirements of 28.1.2.2.2. Other types of automatic fire-extinguishing systems, such as foam/water, expanded foam, or clean agents, can be used for compliance provided that the system is applicable to the hazard present; automatically provides for the detection, control, and extinguishment of fires involving the hazards that might be present in the building; and is acceptable to the AHJ. The combustibility of the boats in storage should be considered in determining the hazard classification for appropriate sprinkler system design. [**303**:A.6.2.2]

A.28.1.2.2.2.2 See A.28.1.2.2.1.3. [**303**:A.6.2.2.2]

A.28.1.2.2.3.4 See A.28.1.2.2.1.3. [**303**:A.6.2.3.4]

A.28.1.2.2.4.1 Compliance with the requirements of Chapter 17 of NFPA 13 for the protection of Group A plastics stored on solid shelves should be considered for the design and installation of automatic sprinkler systems provided for the protection of buildings housing boats stored on multilevel racks. The combustibility of the boats in storage should be considered in determining hazard classifications. Plan view configuration of the boats in storage should be reviewed to determine whether in-rack sprinklers are needed and to aid in the proper design of the in-rack portion of the sprinkler system. Sound engineering judgment is necessary in selecting sprinkler spacing, placement, and design criteria. [**303**:A.6.2.4.1]

A.28.1.2.2.4.3 See A.28.1.2.2.1.3. [**303**:A.6.2.4.3]

A.28.1.2.2.5 To comply with this requirement, water supplies can consist of a hydrant that is part of an approved water supply system, drafting hydrant, or drafting site. [303:A.6.2.5]

A.28.1.2.3 The 2019 edition of NFPA 14 has incorporated a chapter specific to standpipes and hose systems installed at marinas, boatyards, and marine terminals or on piers, docks, and wharves. This chapter addresses the unique concerns of these systems, including corrosion resistance, flexibility, and other issues specific to the maritime environment. [303:A.6.3]

A.28.1.2.4.1.2 A portable fire extinguisher can be either hand carried or on wheels. [303:A.6.4.1.2]

A.28.1.2.6 See NFPA 80A. [303:A.6.7]

A.28.1.2.7.2(3) EMS and police numbers should be displayed in addition to fire department numbers unless 9-1-1 (E-9-1-1) is in use.

A.28.1.3.1.3 It is recommended that an auxiliary power supply be provided to ensure lighting in the event of a power failure. [303:A.7.1.3]

A.28.1.3.2.1.5(4) Where fuel tanks and fuel systems are susceptible to damage by certain fuel additives or fuel blends, special considerations might be required to prevent damage to tanks and fuel systems that could lead to fuel leaks. Such considerations might include, but are not limited to, completely emptying and purging the fuel tank and/or more frequent inspections to detect damage and leakage from the fuel tank and fuel system that are stored at least 95 percent full in accordance with NFPA 303. [303:A.7.2.1.5(4)]

A.28.1.3.2.4 Batteries should be removed for storage and charging wherever practical. [303:A.7.2.4]

A.28.1.4.1 Marinas and boatyard owners and operators are encouraged to be familiar with the requirements of NFPA 302. It is recommended that marina and boatyard owners and operators encourage vessel owners and occupants to practice proper fire prevention aboard moored and stored vessels. [303:A.8.1]

A.28.1.4.2.6(6) See 42.9.10.8 for the list of the fuel dispensing requirements that are to be provided to boat operators using the marina or boatyard. [303:A.8.2.6]

A.28.1.4.2.6(7) For the purpose of this requirement, the emergency contact information should only include the means to contact the fire department or emergency services and the marina or boatyard address. [303:A.8.2.6(7)]

A.28.2.2 See NFPA 303. [307:A.1.3.2]

A.28.2.3(1) See NFPA 30. [307:A.1.3.3(1)]

A.28.2.3(2) See NFPA 59A or NFPA 58. [307:A.1.3.3(2)]

A.28.3.1 Many vessels undergoing construction, conversion, or repairs, and vessels laid up in a shipyard or elsewhere are readily vulnerable to fire, due to the quantity and character of combustible materials used in building. Long passageways, unenclosed stairways, hatches, and hoistways facilitate the rapid spread of fire throughout the vessel. Often the location of the vessel is isolated so that private protection is the main source of fire-fighting services. Even where major municipal protection is available, material damage or complete destruction before effective means of extinguishment are brought into action often results from the following:

(1) Possible delayed response, due either to late discovery of the fire or to the absence of means for quick notification
(2) Lack of special equipment in many municipal fire departments for combating shipboard fires
(3) An unfamiliarity with ship construction due to the transitory nature of the risk

[312:A.1.2]

A.30.1.5.1 Additional fire protection considerations can include items such as fixed suppression systems, automatic fire detection, manual fire alarm stations, transmission of alarms to off-site locations, and limiting volume delivered per transaction. [30A:A.7.3.5.1]

A.30.1.6.7 Natural ventilation can normally be expected to dissipate any fuel vapors before they reach ignitible concentrations if at least two sides of the dispensing area are open to the building exterior. [30A:A.7.3.6.7]

A.30.1.6.9 Oil/water separators might not be designed to remove or separate flammable or combustible liquids other than oil. [30A:A.7.3.6.9]

A.30.2.7 The ventilation requirements contained in this subsection do not consider exhaust emissions from motor vehicle engines. An appropriate professional should be consulted to determine precautions necessary to protect against this health hazard. [30A:A.7.5]

A.30.2.7.1 Manual control switches for supply and exhaust ventilating systems should be located close to the entrance to the area served. In buildings protected by automatic sprinklers or fire alarm systems, it is recommended that the necessary interlocks be provided to shut down supply and exhaust fans when the sprinklers or fire alarms operate. For service facilities for CNG-fueled vehicles and LNG-fueled vehicles, see NFPA 52. [30A:A.7.5.1]

A.30.2.7.4 Lighter-than-air fuels include fuels such as hydrogen and natural gas, but not LP-Gas. [30A:A.7.5.4]

A.30.2.8.6 Enclosed rooms or spaces storing CNG- or LNG-fueled vehicles should prohibit the transmission of gases to other areas of the building. Other areas outside of the enclosure, if not used for repairing or storing CNG- or LNG-fueled vehicles, can use other heating methods. Note that, according to A.1.1 of NFPA 52, CNG weighs about two-thirds as much as air and, therefore, as a gas, will rise in a room. LNG at a temperature of less than or equal to −170°F (−112°C) is heavier than ambient air [at 60°F (15°C)], but as the LNG's temperature rises, the gas becomes lighter than air. Determination of the potential for gas accumulation should be based on an engineering analysis. (Guidance for classification of hazardous locations is available in NFPA 497.) [30A:A.7.6.6]

A.30.3.3.7.2 Roof and ceiling designs should minimize the potential impact of pockets and recesses in roofs and ceilings, such as those created by skylights, ceiling geometry, or other features, and should be ventilated, if necessary, to prevent gas buildup. Gas holdup areas such as those created by mezzanines, subfloors, gaps or spaces between beams and ceilings, holes along the beams' neutral axes, and other features should include provisions for ventilation and gas detection, if required, to prevent gas buildup. [30A:A.7.8.7.2]

A.30.3.3.8.1 Other garage spaces, such as parts rooms and mechanical rooms that are not continuously occupied, should support repair operations. [30A:A.7.8.8.1]

A.30.3.3.11.2 Automatic actions can be implemented by installing power isolation systems, such as normally closed solenoids or other devices, that do not require power to activate. [30A:A.7.8.11.2]

Δ **A.30.3.3.12.4.2** For vehicle repair garages, the International Mechanical Code requires a ventilation rate of 0.75 cfm/ft² (0.23 m³/min per m²) minimum. At a ceiling height of 23 ft (7 m), this translates to an air change rate of two ACH. [30A:A.7.8.12.4.2]

A.31.1 Each individual property has its own special conditions of stock handling, exposure, and topography. For this reason, only basic fire protection principles are discussed herein and are intended to be applied with due consideration of all local factors involved. The AHJ should be consulted.

A.31.3.2.1.1 Good housekeeping should be maintained at all times, including regular and frequent cleaning of materials-handling equipment.

A.31.3.2.1.6.1 See NFPA 505.

A.31.3.2.1.10.1 See NFPA 82 for small rubbish burners.

A.31.3.2.2.1 Saw mills, planing mills, treating plants, adzing mills, and similar buildings without blank walls should be separated from yard storage by a clear space in accordance with the recommendations of NFPA 80A.

Unsprinklered manufacturing buildings and other large structures with combustible contents represent a severe exposure to yard storage, unless the exterior walls have the necessary fire resistance to act as a fire separation and are essentially absent of unprotected openings.

A.31.3.2.2.2 Weeds, grass, and similar vegetation should be prevented throughout the entire yard, and any vegetation growth should be sprayed as often as needed with an herbicide or ground sterilizer, or should be grubbed out. Dead weeds should be removed after destruction. Weed burners should not be used.

A.31.3.2.3 Where practical, some form of fixed system of alarm notification or communication equipment should be provided within the storage yard (e.g., telephones, radios).

Portable fire extinguishers suitable for the fire hazard involved should be provided at convenient, conspicuously accessible locations in the yard. Approved portable fire-extinguishing equipment should be located so that the travel distance to the nearest unit is not more than 75 ft (23 m). See Section 13.6. Approved fire extinguishers suitable for the fire hazard involved should be provided on all power vehicles and units, including haulage or private locomotives in the yard.

A.31.3.3.1.2 The type of operations at properties where the provisions of 31.3.4 apply vary widely. Retail lumber and building material operations are often characterized by large area buildings with minor outside storage areas. On the other hand, wholesale and distribution yards can involve large outside storage areas that present fire protection problems similar to mill yards.

A.31.3.3.2.1 Fire loss experience in lumberyards indicates that the following are the principal factors that allow lumberyard fires to reach serious proportions:

(1) Large, undivided stacks
(2) Congested storage conditions
(3) Delayed fire detection
(4) Inadequate fire protection
(5) Ineffective fire-fighting tactics

A.31.3.3.2.2 It is recognized that retail and wholesale lumber storage yards are normally located within municipal system boundaries, where the system should be capable of supplying not less than four 2½ in. (65 mm) hose streams simultaneously [1000 gpm (4000 L/min)]. Where large-scale fire-fighting operations can be expected, larger water supplies are needed. Where protection from municipal water supplies and hydrant systems is not provided or is not considered adequate by the AHJ, a yard fire hydrant system should be provided and installed in accordance with NFPA 24.

A.31.3.3.3.1 Where the danger of underground fire is present, refuse-filled or sawdust-filled land should not be used.

A.31.3.3.3.3 Air-dried stickered stacks are subject to rapid-fire spread through the air spaces and should therefore be kept as low as practicable.

A.31.3.3.4.2 Because of the large quantities of material generally involved in lumberyard fires, some form of exposure protection for adjoining properties is recommended. Clear spaces or walls capable of providing fire barriers between yard storage and the exposed properties should be used. The responsibility for the protection of properties adjoining a lumberyard is often a joint responsibility to be worked out between the lumberyard and adjoining property owners. The AHJ should be consulted.

A.31.3.4.1 Each individual property has its own special conditions of yard use, material-handling methods, and topography. For this reason, only basic fire protection principles are discussed herein and are intended to be applied with due consideration of all local factors involved. The AHJ should be consulted.

A.31.3.4.2 Fire loss experience in lumber storage yards indicates that the following are the principal factors that allow lumberyard fires to reach serious proportions:

(1) Large, undivided stacks
(2) Congested storage conditions
(3) Delayed fire detection
(4) Inadequate fire protection
(5) Ineffective fire-fighting tactics

A.31.3.4.3 Refuse-filled or sawdust-filled land, swampy ground, or areas where the hazard of underground fire is present should not be used as a storage site.

A.31.3.4.3.1 For basic fire protection, the hydrant system should be capable of supplying not less than four 2½ in. (65 mm) hose streams simultaneously [1000 gpm (4000 L/min)] while maintaining a positive residual pressure in the fire protection hydrant system of not less than 20 psi (1.38 bar).

Where large-scale fire-fighting operations can be expected, larger water supplies with adequate mains are needed.

For early extinguishment with basic fire protection, hydrants should be spaced with sufficient 2½ in. (65 mm) hose attached to allow rapid hose laying to all parts of the stacking areas. For this reason, the hydrants should be spaced at about 250 ft (76 m) intervals so that any part of the yard can be reached with 250 ft (60 m) of hose. Hydrants preferably should be located at fire apparatus access road intersections. A hydrant hose house with not less than 250 ft (60 m) of fire hose and auxiliary equipment should be provided at each hydrant. *(See NFPA 24.)*

A.31.3.5.1.1 Each individual property has its own special conditions of yard use, stock-handling methods, and topography. For this reason, only basic fire protection principles are discussed herein, and are intended to be applied with due consideration of all local factors involved. Ties, as used herein, include ties, poles, piles, posts, and other similar forest products. Treated ties are ties that are pressure impregnated with preservatives.

A.31.3.5.2 Fire loss experience in tie storage yards indicates that the following are the principal factors that allow fires to reach serious proportions:

(1) Large, undivided stacks
(2) Congested storage conditions
(3) Delayed fire detection
(4) Inadequate fire protection
(5) Ineffective fire-fighting tactics

A.31.3.5.3 Refuse-filled or sawdust-filled land, swampy ground, or areas where the hazard of underground fire is present should not be used as storage site.

A.31.3.5.3.1 With relatively open stacking (that is, stacking that allows for penetration of fire-extinguishing streams), sufficient alleyway width can usually be accomplished by providing a not-less-than 4 ft (1.2 m) alleyway width between alternate rows of tie stacks. *[See Figure A.31.3.5.3.1(a).]* Flat crib-style stacking without space between the stacks that forms solid packed rows should require a not-less-than 4 ft (1.2 m) alleyway width between each row. *[See Figure A.31.3.5.3.1(b).]*

FIGURE A.31.3.5.3.1(a) Relatively Open Stacking Methods.

FIGURE A.31.3.5.3.1(b) Crib-Style Stacking into Solid Rows.

A.31.3.5.3.2 For basic fire protection, the hydrant system should be capable of supplying not less than four 2½ in. (65 mm) hose streams simultaneously [not less than 1000 gpm (4000 L/min)] while maintaining a positive residual pressure in the fire protection hydrant system of not less than 20 psi (1.38 bar).

Where large-scale fire-fighting operations can be expected, larger water supplies with adequate mains are needed.

For early extinguishment with basic fire protection, hydrants should be spaced with sufficient 2½ in. (65 mm) hose attached to allow rapid hose laying to all parts of the stacking areas. For this reason, hydrants should be spaced at about 250 ft (76 m) intervals so that any part of the yard can be reached with 200 ft (60 m) of hose. Hydrants preferably should be located at fire apparatus access road intersections. A hydrant hose house with not less than 200 ft (60 m) of fire hose and auxiliary equipment should be provided at each hydrant. *(See NFPA 24.)*

A.31.3.5.3.5 Heights in excess of 20 ft (6 m) seriously restrict effective extinguishing operations.

A.31.3.6.1 Each individual property has its own special conditions of yard use, stock-handling methods, and topography. It is recognized that climate conditions, wood species, and the age of piles are all factors affecting fire safety. For these reasons, only basic fire protection principles are discussed herein, and are intended to be applied with due consideration of all local factors involved. Except for the surface layer, the moisture content of a pile of wood chips or hogged material is quite high, so surface fires do not generally penetrate more than a few inches into the pile. Fire tests indicate that, for areas of average humidity conditions, the flame propagation over the surface is relatively slow. These conditions allow ready extinguishment, provided that there is early detection and good access. It is expected that, in areas where long periods of low humidity prevail, faster surface flame spread can be anticipated, increasing the importance of early detection and good access.

A.31.3.6.2.1 Fire experience and fire tests indicate that two completely different types of fires can occur in storage piles — surface fires and internal fires. Fire prevention activities and fire protection facilities should, therefore, include preparations for coping with both situations.

Internal heating is a hazard inherent to long-term bulk storage of chips and hogged material that progresses to spontaneous combustion under certain pile conditions. Internal fires are difficult to detect and extinguish. Unless provisions are made for measuring internal temperatures, such fires can burn for long periods before emission of smoke at the surface indicates an internal fire.

Extinguishment then becomes a lengthy and expensive loss-control and operating problem requiring equipment and manpower to move large portions of the pile, either by digging out the burning portions or removing the unburned portions of the pile. Experience has shown that these conditions create very large losses, and special attention should be given to the prevention of spontaneous combustion and to pre-fire planning where evaluating how best to handle an imminent or actual fire in a particular pile.

A.31.3.6.2.2 Prevention of internal fires requires an understanding of the factors that cause exothermic oxidation so that steps can be taken to minimize this hazard and to provide means of monitoring temperature conditions inside the pile. Refuse and old chips should not be permitted in the chip pile base. The storage site should be thoroughly cleaned before starting a new pile.

The quality of chip supplies should be controlled in terms of percentage of fines. The concentration of fines should not be allowed during pile buildup.

Pneumatic systems produce an air classification of stored materials that should be recognized, and appropriate steps should be taken to minimize concentration of fines.

It is preferable to spread new stored materials in a relatively even layer over the pile.

Vehicles used on all piles should be of a type that minimizes compaction.

Veneer chip piles should be limited to 50 ft (15 m) in height.

A.31.3.6.2.2(4) For example, whole-tree chip piles containing bark, leaves, and other extraneous or hogged material can be subject to greater degrees of spontaneous heating and thermal degradation and should be reclaimed more frequently.

A.31.3.6.2.2(5) Fundamentally, several small piles are better than one large pile.

A.31.3.6.2.2(8) Minimizing the diffusion of water from wet, stored material into dry fires is important to reduce exothermic heating caused by adsorption effects. Maintaining surface moisture content is also important so as to reduce the hazard of surface fires during periods of hot, dry weather.

A.31.3.6.3 A high standard of housekeeping should be maintained around all potential heat sources.

Care should be exercised to prevent tramp metal from entering the piles, or sections of blower pipes from being buried in the piles.

A.31.3.6.3.1 For very large piles, two or more access roadways should be provided on opposite sides of the pile.

A.31.3.6.3.2 Narrow, low piles facilitate fire extinguishment.

A.31.3.6.3.4 Due to the size and configuration of piles, providing portable fire extinguishers within 75 ft (23 m) of travel distance to any point is not practical.

A.31.3.6.3.5 Fire hydrants connected to yard mains should be provided so that any part of the pile(s) can be reached by hose equipment provided in each hydrant hose house. Each hydrant hose house should be equipped with a complement of 2½ in. (65 mm) and 1½ in. (38 mm) hose, a 2½ in. (65 mm) and 1½ in. (38 mm) gated wye, and 1½ in. (38 mm) combination nozzles.

Hydrants should be spaced at about 250 ft (76 m) intervals so that any part of the yard can be reached with 200 ft (60 m) of hose.

Where pile configurations are such that all parts of the pile cannot be reached by the hose, a fire hose cart(s) equipped with an ample supply of hose and nozzles should be strategically placed in the storage area.

The amount of water needed to control a pile fire varies substantially depending on the size of the pile. Weather conditions, operating methods, geographic location, type of material stored, and the degree to which wetting can be employed affect the potential for a large area surface fire. Experience indicates that exposure to long periods of hot, dry weather with no regular surface wetting creates conditions under which fast-spreading surface fires, which require many hose streams for control depending on the size of the pile, can occur.

Likewise, the frequency of pile turnover and operating methods affect the potential for serious internal fires. Piles built using methods that allow a concentration of fines and piles stored for long periods of time with no turnover are subject to internal heating that, if undetected, can create intense internal fires.

A flow of not less than 500 gpm (2000 L/min) should be provided at any fire hydrant in the pile area. Additional flows should be provided as needed where conditions are likely to produce serious surface fires or large internal fires. Fire mains should be engineered to deliver the recommended gallonage plus allowance for operational uses and special extinguishing equipment at a residual pressure of 60 psi to 100 psi (4.1 bar to 6.9 bar) at the hydrants.

A.31.3.6.3.7 With the use of the equipment specified in 31.3.6.3.7, surface types of pile fires can usually be removed from the affected areas and extinguished.

Where deep-seated fires occur within the pile or under the pile in tunnels or other enclosures, this equipment is invaluable in breaking down the entire pile and spreading it out in a safe yard area, which allows firefighters using hand hose lines or deluge units to extinguish both the pile and ground-spread stored material.

A.31.3.6.4.1 Experience indicates that radiated heat from exposing fires in storage piles does not ordinarily pose a serious ignition threat to other piles, provided that recommended clear spaces are maintained. Flying brands from exposing fires, especially during high winds, do present a hazardous ignition source. Upwind forest or brush fires can also present a problem in relation to flying sparks and brands.

A.31.3.6.4.2 Buildings or other structures near storage piles can pose a serious exposure hazard to the pile.

A.31.3.6.4.3 Greater clearance is desirable when piles are high and side slopes are greater than 60 degrees.

A.31.3.7 This type of chip has a much higher aliphatic hydrocarbon (sugar) content and spontaneously ignites readily. Lumber chips are debarked and thus lose the cambium layer associated with stored sugars. It is these sugars that start the bacterial decomposition that proceeds to spontaneous ignition.

A.31.3.8.1.1 Each individual property has its own special conditions for yard use, stock-handling methods, and topography. For this reason, only basic fire protection principles are discussed herein, and are intended to be applied with due consideration of all local factors involved.

A.31.3.8.2 Fire loss experience in outside storage of logs indicates that the following are the principal factors that allow log pile fires to reach serious proportions:

(1) Large, undivided piles
(2) Congested storage conditions
(3) Delayed fire detection
(4) Inadequate fire protection
(5) Ineffective fire-fighting tactics

A.31.3.8.3 Refuse-filled or sawdust-filled land, swampy ground, or areas where the hazard of underground fire is present should not be used as a storage site.

A.31.3.8.3.3 Where practical, greater widths should be provided to minimize the effects of radiated heat, particularly in high-piled yards.

A.31.3.8.3.3.2 Heights in excess of 20 ft (6 m) seriously restrict effective extinguishing operations, since successful extinguishment of log pile fires requires penetration of the pile from the side by hose streams.

A.31.3.8.3.3.3 See Figure A.31.3.8.3.3.3.

A.31.3.8.3.3.4 For basic fire protection, the hydrant system should be capable of supplying not less than four 2½ in. (65 mm) hose streams simultaneously [not less than 1000 gpm (4000 L/min)] while maintaining a positive residual pressure in the fire protection hydrant system of not less than 20 psi (1.38 bar).

Where large-scale fire-fighting operations can be expected, larger water supplies with adequate mains are needed.

For early extinguishment with basic fire protection, hydrants should be spaced with sufficient 2½ in. (65 mm) hose attached to allow rapid hose laying to all parts of the piling areas. For this reason, hydrants should be spaced at about 250 ft (76 m) intervals so that any part of the yard can be reached with 200 ft (60 m) of hose. Hydrants should be located at fire apparatus access road intersections. A hydrant hose house with not less than 200 ft (60 m) of fire hose and auxiliary equipment should be provided at each hydrant. *(See NFPA 24.)*

A.31.3.8.3.6 The installation of a portable piping system equipped with irrigation or lawn-type sprinklers on the top of each log pile is recommended.

A.32.7 The AHJ, when granting a permit to a production company to film on location, should consider the placement of the support equipment. Typically, the production support vehicles are numerous, and unregulated placement of these vehicles could impede emergency access or egress. Additionally, the types of support vehicles need to be arranged so that a hazardous operation (e.g., fueling or special effects) is distant from sources of ignition and crew gathering areas (e.g., catering locations). The location permit should include a plot plan so the AHJ can adequately assess potential problems. [140:A.5.9]

A.32.9.2.2 This requirement does not prohibit the use of mobile generators for auxiliary power. [140:A.4.8.2]

FIGURE A.31.3.8.3.3.3 Layout of Log Storage Yard.

A.32.9.4.1.3.1 Paragraphs 32.9.4.1.3.1 and 32.9.4.1.3.2 recognize motion picture and television industry practices that require sets to change constantly and that sets are "temporary" construction not subject to building codes or standards. Solid ceilings that obstruct the stage sprinklers are "flown" (moved) in or out to permit special shooting angles or lighting requirements, often on a scene-by-scene basis. With temporary walls and ceilings, it would be impractical to install a sprinkler system in a constantly changing structure. Therefore, one or more of the following mitigation techniques should be used to compensate for the areas shielded from sprinkler spray by solid or hard ceilings or platforms:

(1) Approved and listed heat detectors or smoke detectors can be installed beneath such solid or hard ceilings in excess of 600 ft^2 (55.7 m^2) in area and platforms in excess of 600 ft^2 (55.7 m^2) in area and 3 ft (0.9 m) in height. Detectors should be connected to an approved and listed central, proprietary, or remote station service or to a local alarm that will provide an audible signal (i.e., a bell or horn) at a constantly attended location. The detector system, including the alarm panel, is defined as a portable system because it is intended to be reinstalled when platforms or sets are changed. The detectors that are secured to standard outlet boxes and the listed fire alarm panels can be temporarily supported by sets, platforms, or pedestals. Spacing of detectors should be per manufacturers' requirements.
(2) The ceiling can be positioned to allow for the operation of the building's automatic fire sprinkler system after videotaping, filming, or broadcasting of programs has been completed for the day.
(3) A fire watch should be provided when the set is not in use.
(4) No combustible materials should be stored under any platforms. Consideration should be given to secure such covered areas with screen wire or other materials that will permit visual inspection and emergency access.
(5) Approved/listed fire retardants can be applied beneath combustible platforms.
(6) Approved/listed fire retardants can be applied to scenery, props, framework and deck of combustible platforms, and the hard ceilings of combustible sets.

[140:A.4.11.1.3.1]

A.32.9.4.1.3.2 See A.32.9.4.1.3.1. [140:A.4.11.1.3.2]

A.32.10.1.3 The AHJ might approve the routing of power cables through fire-rated windows or doors if standby fire personnel or other approved safeguards are provided during such periods. [140:A.5.8.3]

A.32.10.2 Where a production company films *on location*, such activity might interfere with, or prevent, the normal use of the facility or area. As such, the facility being occupied as a production location is often used for a purpose different from that of its normal use. Where the production company filming causes the facility or area to curtail normal operations, the facility should not be required to meet the life safety provisions applicable to the normal occupancy. Rather, life safety features should be maintained consistent with provisions required for the temporary use. For example, consider a single story assembly occupancy building with occupant load of 600 persons that has three exits for compliance with the provision of NFPA *101* that requires a minimum of three exits where the occupant load of a floor exceeds 500 persons. The assembly occupancy building is used as a production location for a total of 200 persons. The production crew presents, for approval of the AHJ, a plan to block off one of the three exits while maintaining compliance with the requirements for egress width, travel distance, common path of travel, and dead-end corridors. The AHJ approves the proposed means of egress as appropriate for the intended use as required by 32.10.2. [140:A.5.10]

A.32.10.3.1 The phrase "intimate with the initial fire development" refers to the person(s) at the ignition source or first materials burning, not to all persons within the same room or area. [140:A.5.11.1]

The occupant protection requirement of 32.10.3.1 is the same as that required for all occupancies by NFPA *101*. The activities associated with filming at a production location without an audience are characteristic of the occupancy classification of industrial occupancy. Industrial occupancies are not required by NFPA *101* to be sprinklered. The objective of protecting occupants not intimate with the initial fire development for the time needed to evacuate, relocate, or defend in place is accomplished for industrial occupancies by prescriptive provisions not dependent on sprinkler protection. [140:A.5.11.1]

Where production location filming occurs in a building area not provided with the life safety systems required for industrial occupancies (e.g., in a tower with a single means of egress provided by an unenclosed stair), sprinklers, a fire alarm system, or other mitigation techniques acceptable to the AHJ will need to be employed for compliance with 32.10.3.1. Where sprinklers are provided, see 32.10.3.2 and 32.10.3.6. [140:A.5.11.1]

A.32.10.3.4 See A.32.9.4.1.3.1. [140:A.5.11.4]

A.32.10.3.5 See A.32.9.4.1.3.1. [140:A.5.11.5]

A.32.10.4.4 Special attention should be focused on any possible obstructions to the means of egress. The means of egress and the marking of it might be confusing to the audience due to the numerous bright lights, scenery, video and film cameras, and other equipment in and around the soundstage. [140:A.6.4]

A.33.1 Fire service professionals who have managed major scrap tire piles believe that the best approach is to allow the tire pile to burn while protecting exposures like buildings, heavy equipment, and surrounding tire piles. Once the tire pile is in a smoldering stage, heavy equipment can be used to pull the pile apart and the tire material can be extinguished incrementally. For additional information, see *Rings of Fire: Tire Fire Prevention and Suppression.*

A.33.4.3 This can include but is not limited to the availability of earth-moving equipment or other approved means of controlling a fire.

A.33.7.5 Altered tire material piles have been known to spontaneously combust after a heavy precipitation. Investigators have considered anaerobic action and potential heat from oxidation of steel belts as the source of exothermic reaction.

A.34.1.1.2(6) The limitations on the type and size of storage are intended to identify those situations where tire storage is present in limited quantity and incidental to the main use of the building. Occupancies such as aircraft hangars, automobile dealers, repair garages, retail storage facilities, automotive and truck assembly plants, and mobile home assembly plants are types of facilities where miscellaneous tire storage could be present. The fire protection sprinkler design densities specified by NFPA 13 are adequate to provide protection for the storage heights indicated. Storage beyond these heights or areas presents hazards that are addressed by this *Code* and are outside the scope of NFPA 13.

A.34.1.3 The plan should be of sufficient size to be legible. Typical content to be included on the floor plan might include, but not be limited to, the following:

(1) Locations, dimensions, and height limits of piled, palletized, and rack storage
(2) Commodity classification permitted to be stored in each area
(3) Required clearances between top of storage and sprinkler deflectors
(4) Required clearances between top of storage and ceiling
(5) Aisle dimensions between storage arrays
(6) Location of any required fire department access doors
(7) Location of valves controlling ceiling and in-rack sprinkler water supplies

A.34.2.1 Unit loads and pallet loads are examples of individual storage units. [13:A.20.3.1]

Δ **A.34.3** Specification of the type, amount, and arrangement of combustibles for any commodity classification is essentially an attempt to define the potential fire severity, based on its burning characteristics, so the fire can be successfully controlled by the prescribed sprinkler protection for the commodity class. In actual storage situations, however, many storage arrays do not fit precisely into one of the fundamental classifications; therefore, the user needs to make judgments after comparing each classification to the existing storage conditions. Storage arrays consist of thousands of products, which makes it impossible to specify all the acceptable variations for any class. As an alternative, a variety of common products are classified in this annex based on judgment, loss experience, and fire test results. [13:20.4]

Table A.34.3(a) provides examples of commodities not addressed by the classifications in Section 34.3. The commodities listed in Table A.34.3(a) are outside the scope of NFPA 13 protection. [13:20.4]

Table A.34.3(a) includes lithium ion batteries. Lithium ion batteries have been a research project within the NFPA Research Foundation. As a result, the following reports have been published:

(1) *Lithium Ion Batteries Hazard and Use Assessment*, published July 2011 and available at the NFPA Research Foundation web site.
(2) *Flammability Characterization of Lithium-ion Batteries in Bulk Storage,* published March 2013; and available at www.fmglobal.com/researchreports.
(3) *Lithium Ion Batteries Hazard and Use Assessment Phase IIB, Flammability Characterization of Li-ion Batteries for Storage Protection,* published April 2013 and available at the NFPA Research Foundation web site.
(4) *Lithium Ion Batteries Hazard and Use Assessment — Phase III,* published November 2016 and available at the NFPA Research Foundation web site.

[13:20.4]

Table A.34.3(b) is an alphabetized list of commodities with corresponding classifications. [13:20.4]

Table A.20.4.1, Table A.20.4.2, Table A.20.4.3, Table A.20.4.4, and Table A.20.4.5.1 of NFPA 13 provide examples of commodities within a specific class. [13:20.4]

A.34.3.1 See NFPA 13, Table A.20.4.1. [13:A.20.4.1]

A.34.3.2 See NFPA 13, Table A.20.4.2. [13:20.4.2]

A.34.3.3 See NFPA 13, Table A.20.4.3. [13:20.4.3]

A.34.3.4 See NFPA 13, Table A.20.4.4.

A.34.3.5 The categories listed in 34.3.5.1, 34.3.6, and 34.3.7 are based on unmodified plastic materials. The use of fire- or flame-retarding modifiers or the physical form of the material could change the classification. [13:A.20.4.5]

The addition of fire retardants to plastic should not be relied upon as the sole basis for a reduction in classification given the unknown performance of the fire retardant under a storage scenario. It is expected that full-scale or commodity classification type testing would be necessary to justify any such reduction in classification. No reduction in classification should be given for plastics simply because they contain a fire retardant. [13:A.20.4.5]

Plastic materials not specifically classified in 34.3.5 should be protected as Group A plastics unless full-scale or commodity classification type testing demonstrates otherwise. It is not possible to classify full-scale fire performance of plastics by looking solely at heat of combustion. Plastic materials should not be categorized into a Group (A, B, or C) based upon comparing heat of combustion with values for plastics already classified in NFPA 13. [13:A.20.4.5]

A.34.3.5.2 See Section 20.3 of NFPA 13 for commodity classification guidance.

A.34.3.8 All arrangements of exposed plastics cannot be protected with all types of sprinklers. Only certain combinations of ceiling sprinklers and in-rack sprinklers have been found to provide acceptable protection. No full-scale fire testing has been performed that has determined acceptable criteria for exposed expanded plastics. Factory Mutual has published criteria in its data sheets to protect exposed expanded plastics based on a risk analysis and small/intermediate-scale test data. Some authorities having jurisdiction accept that criteria as an alternative to the intent of NFPA 13. [13:A.20.4.8]

Table A.34.3(a) Examples of Commodities Not Addressed by Classifications in Section 34.3

Ammunition Components
 - Bulk primers and powder
Batteries
 - Lithium and other similar exotic metals
 - Lithium-ion and other rechargeable batteries that contain combustible electrolyte
Boat Storage
 - Stored on racks
Boxes, Crates
 - Empty, wood slatted*
Carpet Rolls
Combustible Metals — unless specifically identified otherwise
Compressed or Liquefied Flammable Gases (i.e., filled propane cylinders) — unless specifically identified otherwise
Explosives
 - Blasting primers and similar items
Fertilizers (nitrates)
Fireworks
 - Consumer and display
Flammable and Combustible Liquids — unless specifically identified otherwise
 - Liquids that contain greater than 20 percent alcohol
Hanging Garments, Bulk Storage
Lighters (butane)
 - Loose in large containers (Level 3 aerosol)
Storage Container
 - Large container storage of household goods

*Should be treated as idle pallets.
[13:Table A.20.4(a)]

Table A.34.3(b) Alphabetical Listing of Commodity Classes

Product Heading	Product	NFPA 13
Batteries	Dry cells (excludes lithium, lithium-ion, and other similar exotic metals or combustible electrolyte); without blister packing (if blister packed refer to commodity classification definitions)	Class I
	Vehicle; any size (e.g., automobile or truck); empty plastic casing	Group A Nonexpanded
	Vehicle; large (e.g., truck or larger); dry or wet (excludes lithium-ion and other cells containing combustible electrolyte) cells	Group A Nonexpanded
	Vehicle; small (e.g., automobile); wet (excludes lithium-ion and other cells containing combustible electrolyte) cells	Class I
Empty Containers	Noncombustible	Class I
	PET, bottles or jars	Class IV
	Rigid plastic (not including PET), up to 32 oz. (1 L)	Group A Nonexpanded
	Rigid plastic (not including PET), greater than 32 oz. (1 L)	Group A Expanded
	Wood; solid sided (e.g., crates, boxes)	Class II
Film Rolls, Including Photographic	Film (polypropylene, polyester, polyethylene); rolled on any reel type	Group A Nonexpanded
	Film; 35 mm metal film cartridges in polyethylene cans; cartoned	Class III
	Film; motion picture or bulk rolls in polycarbonate, polyethylene or in metal cans; polyethylene bagged; cartoned	Class II
	Film; rolls in polycarbonate plastic cassettes; cartoned	Class IV
	Photographic paper; sheets; bagged in polyethylene; cartoned	Class III
Flammable/ Combustible Liquids	Aerosol; Level 1	Class III
	Lighters; butane; blister-packed; cartoned	Group A Nonexpanded
	Liquids; up to 20 percent alcohol (e.g., alcoholic beverages, flavoring extracts); greater than 5 gal (20 L) plastic containers with wall thickness greater than ¼ in. (6 mm)	Group A Nonexpanded
	Liquids; up to 20 percent alcohol (e.g., alcoholic beverages, flavoring extracts); metal, glass or ceramic containers	Class I
	Liquids; up to 20 percent alcohol (e.g., alcoholic beverages, flavoring extracts); plastic containers greater than 5 gal (20 L) and wall thickness up to ¼ in. (6 mm)	Class II
	Liquids; up to 20 percent alcohol (e.g., alcoholic beverages, flavoring extracts); up to 5 gal (20 L) plastic bottles or jars	Class I
	Liquids; up to 20 percent alcohol (e.g., alcoholic beverages, flavoring extracts); wood containers	Class II
Food Products — Frozen	Frozen foods; nonwaxed or nonplastic packaging	Class I
	Frozen foods; plastic trays	Class III
	Frozen foods; waxed or plastic-coated paper packaging	Class II
Food Products — Non-Frozen	Butter (stick or whipped spread) or margarine (up to 50 percent oil)	Class III
	Dry foods (such as baked goods, candy, cereals, cheese, chocolate, cocoa, coffee, grains, granular sugar, nuts, etc.); bagged or cartoned	Class III
	Foods (e.g., coffee, fish products, fruit, meat products, nuts, poultry, etc.); metal cans	Class I
	Fruits and vegetables (noncombustible semi-liquids); crushed; plastic containers up to 5 gal (20 L)	Class I
	Fruits and vegetables; fresh; wood spacers, non-plastic trays or containers	Class I
	Margarine; over 50 and up to 80 percent oil	Group A Nonexpanded
	Meat; fresh; no plastic packaging; exposed	Class I
	Meat; fresh; no plastic packaging; cartoned	Class II
	Meat; fresh; plastic trays	Class III
	Milk; any container; stored in solid plastic crates	Group A Nonexpanded
	Milk; paper containers, or plastic bottles or jars up to 5 gal (20 L) plastic bottles or jars	Class I

(continues)

Table A.34.3(b) Continued

Product Heading	Product	NFPA 13
	Salt; bagged	Class I
	Salt; cartoned	Class II
	Snack foods (e.g., potato chips); plasticized aluminum bags; cartoned	Group A Nonexpanded
	Syrup; wooden container	Class II
Furniture and Bedding	Furniture and bedding; with foam cushioning	Group A Expanded
	Furniture; metal (e.g., file cabinets or desks with plastic trim); cartoned	Class I
	Furniture; wood (e.g., doors, windows, cabinets, etc.); no plastic coverings or foam cushioning	Class III
	Furniture; wood; plastic coverings nonexpanded plastic trim	Class IV
	Box spring; standard (minimal plastic materials)	Class III
	Box spring; wrapped in plastic cover	Class IV
	Mattress; foam (in finished form)	Group A Expanded
Housing Materials/ Appliances	Appliances; major (e.g., stoves, refrigerators); no appreciable plastic interior or exterior trim; cartoned	Class II
	Appliances; major (e.g., stoves, refrigerators); no appreciable plastic interior or exterior trim; exposed	Class I
	Appliances; no appreciable plastic exterior trim (interior of unit can have appreciable plastic)	Class III
	Carpet tiles; cartoned	Group A Nonexpanded
	Fiberglass insulation; paper-backed rolls; bagged or unbagged	Class IV
	Floor coverings; vinyl, stacked tiles	Class IV
	Floor coverings; vinyl; rolled	Group A Nonexpanded
	Gypsum board	Class I
	Housing materials (such as sinks, countertops, etc.); noncombustible, cartoned or crated	Class II
	Paint; oil-based; friction-top metal containers; cartoned	Class IV
	Paint; water-based (latex); friction-top metal containers; cartoned	Class I
	Roofing shingles; asphalt-coated fiberglass	Class III
	Roofing shingles; asphalt-impregnated felt	Class IV
Miscellaneous	Ammunition; small arms and shotgun; cartoned	Class IV
	Charcoal; mineral spirit impregnated; bagged	Group A Expanded
	Charcoal; standard (non-mineral spirit impregnated); bagged	Class III
	Leather hides; baled	Class II
	Leather; finished products (e.g., shoes, jackets, gloves, bags, luggage, belts)	Class III
	Motors; electric	Class I
	Shock absorbers; metal dust cover	Class II
	Shock absorbers; plastic dust cover	Class III
	Skis; composite materials (plastic, fiberglass, foam, etc.)	Class IV
	Tobacco products; cartoned	Class III
	Toys; stuffed; foam or synthetic	Group A Expanded
	Transformer; dry or empty (i.e., void of oil)-filled	Class I
Noncombustible Liquids	Liquids or semi-liquids; PET containers greater than 5 gal (20 L) having a nominal wall thickness greater than 0.25 in. (6 mm)	Class IV
	Liquids or semi-liquids; PET containers up to 5 gal (20 L) or greater than 5 gal (20 L) having a nominal wall thickness up to 0.25 in. (6 mm)	Class I
	Liquids or semi-liquids (e.g., crushed fruits and vegetables); plastic containers up to 5 gal (18.9 L) capacity	Class I
	Liquids or semi-liquids; plastic (except PET) containers greater than 5 gal (20 L) capacity having a nominal wall thickness greater than 0.25 in. (6 mm)	Group A Nonexpanded
	Liquids or semi-liquids; plastic (except PET) containers greater than 5 gal (20 L) capacity having a nominal wall thickness up to 0.25 in. (6 mm)	Class II

(continues)

Shaded text = Revisions.   Δ = Text deletions and figure/table revisions.   • = Section deletions.   *N* = New material.

Table A.34.3(b) Continued

Product Heading	Product	NFPA 13
	Liquids; cardboard drink boxes, plastic-coated, wax-coated, and/or aluminum-lined; exposed or on corrugated carton trays with plastic sheeting	Class I
	Liquids; cardboard drink boxes, plastic-coated, wax-coated, and/or aluminum-lined; stored in plastic containers	Group A Nonexpanded
	Liquids; glass bottles or jars; cartoned	Class I
	Liquids; pharmaceuticals (nonflammable); glass bottles or jars; cartoned	Class II
	Liquids; plastic bottles or jars; stored in open or solid plastic crates	Group A Nonexpanded
Paper Products	Book signatures (paper part of book without hard cover)	Class II
	Cartons (i.e., cardboard flats); corrugated; partially assembled	Class IV
	Cartons (i.e., cardboard flats); corrugated; unassembled in neat piles	Class III
	Cartons; wax-coated, single-walled corrugated	Group A Nonexpanded
	Cellulosic paper products; nonwax-coated (e.g., books, cardboard games, cartoned tissue products, magazines, newspapers, paper cups, paper plates, paper towels, plastic-coated paper food containers, stationery)	Class III
	Cellulosic paper products; wax-coated (e.g., paper plates, cups); loosely packed; cartoned	Group A Nonexpanded
	Cellulosic paper products; wax-coated (e.g., paper plates, cups); nested; cartoned	Class IV
	Matches; paper-type; cartoned	Class IV
	Matches; wooden; cartoned	Group A Nonexpanded
	Rolled; lightweight; in storage racks	Class IV
	Rolled; medium or heavyweight; in storage racks or on-side	Class III
	Tissue products; plastic-wrapped; cartoned	Class III
	Tissue products; plastic-wrapped; exposed	Group A Nonexpanded
Plastic/Rubber	ABS (Acrylonitrile-butadiene-styrene copolymer)	Group A Nonexpanded
	Acetal (polyformaldehyde)	Group A Nonexpanded
	Acrylic (polymethyl methacrylate)	Group A Nonexpanded
	Automobile bumpers and dashboards	Group A Expanded
	Butyl rubber	Group A Nonexpanded
	Cellulose Acetate	Class IV
	Cellulose Acetate Butyrate	Group A Nonexpanded
	Chloroprene rubber	Class IV
	Containers; nonexpanded plastic gridded or solid; collapsed or nested with no air spaces	Group A Nonexpanded
	ECTFE (ethylene-chlorotrifluoro-ethylene copolymer)	Class IV
	EPDM (ethylene-propylene rubber)	Group A Nonexpanded
	ETFE (ethylene-tetrafluoroethylene copolymer)	Class IV
	Ethyl Cellulose	Group A Nonexpanded
	FEP (fluorinated ethylene-propylene copolymer)	Class IV
	FRP (fiberglass-reinforced polyester)	Group A Nonexpanded
	Melamine (melamine formaldehyde)	Class III
	Nitrile Rubber (acrylonitrile-butadiene rubber)	Group A Nonexpanded
	Nylon (nylon 6, nylon 6/6)	Group A Nonexpanded
	PCTFE (polychlorotrifluoroethylene)	Class III
	PET (Polyethylene Terephthalate — thermoplastic polyester)	Group A Nonexpanded
	Phenolic	Class III
	Plastics; stored in fully closed and solid (no openings), metal containers	Class I
	Polybutadiene	Group A Nonexpanded
	Polycarbonate	Group A Nonexpanded
	Polyester elastomer	Group A Nonexpanded
	Polyethylene	Group A Nonexpanded
	Polypropylene	Group A Nonexpanded

(continues)

Table A.34.3(b)   Continued

Product Heading	Product	NFPA 13
	Polystyrene; foam products (plates, cups, etc.)	Group A Expanded
	Polystyrene; rigid products	Group A Nonexpanded
	Polyurethane	Group A Expanded
	PTFE (polytetrafluoroethylene)	Class III
	PVC (polyvinyl chloride) products, up to 20 percent plasticizer	Class III
	PVC (polyvinyl chloride) products, greater than 20 percent plasticizer	Group A Nonexpanded
	PVC resins; bagged	Class III
	PVDC (polyvinylidene chloride)	Class III
	PVDF (polyvinylidene fluoride)	Class III
	PVF (polyvinyl fluoride)	Group A Nonexpanded
	Rubber; natural in blocks; cartoned	Group A Nonexpanded
	Rubber; natural; expanded	Group A Expanded
	Rubber; natural; nonexpanded	Group A Nonexpanded
	Rubber; synthetic (santoprene)	Group A Nonexpanded
	SAN (styrene acrylonitrile)	Group A Nonexpanded
	SBR (styrene-butadiene rubber)	Group A Nonexpanded
	Silicone rubber	Class IV
	Urea (urea formaldehyde)	Class III
Plastic Containers	Bottles or jars (except PET) greater than 1 gal (4 L) containing noncombustible solids	Group A Nonexpanded
	Bottles or jars (except PET) up to 1 gal (4 L) containing noncombustible solids	Group A, cartoned (treat as cartoned even if exposed) Nonexpanded
Powders/Pills	Pharmaceutical pills; glass bottles or jars; cartoned	Class II
	Pharmaceuticals pills; plastic bottles or jars; cartoned	Class IV
	Polyvinyl Alcohol (PVA) resins; bagged	Class IV
	Powders; combustible (ordinary such as sugar or flour); free-flowing; bagged	Class II
	Powders; noncombustible free-flowing powdered or granular materials (cement, calcium chloride, clay, iron oxide, sodium chloride, sodium silicate, etc.)	Class I
	Powders; noncombustible; glass bottles or jars; cartoned	Class I
	Powders; noncombustible; PET bottles or jars	Class II
	Powders; noncombustible; plastic (other than PET) bottles or jars; exposed	Group A Nonexpanded
	Powders; noncombustible; plastic bottles or jars greater than 1 gal (4 L) capacity	Group A Nonexpanded
	Powders; noncombustible; plastic bottles or jars up to 1 gal (4 L) capacity; cartoned	Class IV
Textile Materials/Products	Cloth; natural fibers; baled	Class III
	Cloth; synthetic cloth	Group A Nonexpanded
	Clothing; natural fibers (e.g., wool, cotton) and viscose	Class III
	Cotton; cartoned	Class III
	Diapers; cotton or linen	Class III
	Diapers; plastic or nonwoven fabric; cartoned	Class IV
	Diapers; plastic or nonwoven fabric; plastic-wrapped; exposed	Group A Nonexpanded
	Fabric; rayon and nylon	Group A Nonexpanded
	Fabric; synthetic (except rayon and nylon); greater than 50/50 blend	Group A Nonexpanded
	Fabric; synthetic (except rayon and nylon); up to 50/50 blend	Group A Nonexpanded
	Fabric; vinyl-coated (e.g., tablecloth); cartoned	Group A Nonexpanded
	Fibers; rayon and nylon; baled	Class IV
	Fibers; synthetic (except rayon and nylon); baled	Group A Nonexpanded
	Thread or yarn; rayon and nylon; wood or paper spools	Class IV
	Thread or yarn; rayon or nylon; plastic spools	Group A Nonexpanded

(continues)

Shaded text = Revisions.   Δ = Text deletions and figure/table revisions.   • = Section deletions.   *N* = New material.

Table A.34.3(b) Continued

Product Heading	Product	NFPA 13
	Thread or yarn; synthetic (except rayon and nylon); greater than 50/50 blend; paper or wood spools	Group A Nonexpanded Plastic
	Thread or yarn; synthetic (except rayon and nylon); greater than 50/50 blend; plastic spools	Group A Nonexpanded
	Thread or yarn; synthetic (except rayon and nylon); up to 50/50 blend; plastic spools	Group A Nonexpanded
	Thread or yarn; synthetic (except rayon and nylon); up to 50/50 blend; wood or paper spools	Group A Nonexpanded Plastic
Wax Products	Candles	Group A Expanded
	Paraffin or petroleum wax; blocks	Group A Expanded
Wire/Cable/Spools	Spools; plastic; empty	Group A Nonexpanded
	Spools; wood; empty	Class III
	Wire or cable; PVC insulated; metal or wood spools	Class II
	Wire or cable; PVC insulated; plastic spools	Class IV
	Wire; bare; metal spools, exposed	Class I
	Wire; bare; metal spools; cartoned	Class II
	Wire; bare; plastic spools; cartoned	Class IV
	Wire; bare; plastic spools; exposed	Group A Nonexpanded
	Wire; bare; wood or cardboard spools	Class II
Wood Products	Wood patterns	Class IV
	Wood products (e.g., fiberboard, lumber, particle board, plywood, pressboard with smooth ends and edges); bundled solid blocks	Class II
	Wood products (e.g., fiberboard, lumber, particle board, plywood, pressboard with smooth ends and edges); unbundled or non-solid blocks	Class III
	Wood products (e.g., toothpicks, clothespins and hangers)	Class III

[13:Table A.20.4(b)]

Δ **A.34.3.10** *Paper Classification.* These classifications were derived from a series of large-scale and laboratory-type small-scale fire tests. It is recognized that not all paper in a class burns with exactly the same characteristics. [13:A.20.4.10]

Paper can be soft or hard, thick or thin, or heavy or light and can also be coated with various materials. The broad range of papers can be classified according to various properties. One important property is basis weight, which is defined as the weight of a sheet of paper of a specified area. Two broad categories are recognized by industry — paper and paperboard. Paperboard normally has a basis weight of 20 lb (9.1 kg) or greater measured on a 1000 ft^2 (93 m^2) sheet. Stock with a basis weight less than 20 lb/1000 ft^2 (0.1 kg/m^2) is normally categorized as paper. The basis weight of paper is usually measured on a 3000 ft^2 (280 m^2) sheet. The basis weight of paper can also be measured on the total area of a ream of paper, which is normally the case for the following types of printing and writing papers:

(1) *Bond paper* — 500 sheets, 17 in. × 22 in. (425 mm × 550 mm) = 1300 ft^2 (120 m^2) per ream
(2) *Book paper* — 500 sheets, 25 in. × 38 in. (625 mm × 950 mm) = 3300 ft^2 (305 m^2) per ream
(3) *Index paper* — 500 sheets, 25½ in. × 30½ in. (640 mm × 765 mm) = 2700 ft^2 (250 m^2) per ream
(4) *Bristol paper* — 500 sheets, 22½ in. × 35 in. (565 mm × 890 mm) = 2734 ft^2 (255 m^2) per ream
(5) *Tag paper* — 500 sheets, 24 in. × 36 in. (600 mm × 900 mm) = 3000 ft^2 (280 m^2) per ream

[13:A.20.4.10]

For the purposes of this *Code*, all basis weights are expressed in lb/1000 ft^2 (kg/93 m^2) of paper. To determine the basis weight per 1000 ft^2 (93 m^2) for papers measured on a sheet of different area, the following formula should be applied:

[A.34.3.10a]

$$\frac{\text{Base weight}}{1000 \text{ ft}^2} = \text{basis weight} \times 1000 \text{ measured area}$$

Example: To determine the basis weight per 1000 ft^2 (93 m^2) of 16 lb (7.3 kg) bond paper:

[A.34.3.10b]

$$\left(\frac{16 \text{ lb}}{1300 \text{ ft}^2}\right) 1000 = \frac{12.3 \text{ lb}}{1000 \text{ ft}^2}$$

[13:A.20.4.10]

Large- and small-scale fire tests indicate that the burning rate of paper varies with the basis weight. Heavyweight paper burns more slowly than lightweight paper. Full-scale roll paper fire tests were conducted with the following types of paper:

(1) *Linerboard* — 42 lb/1000 ft^2 (0.2 kg/m^2) nominal basis weight
(2) *Newsprint* — 10 lb/1000 ft^2 (50 g/m^2) nominal basis weight
(3) *Tissue* — 5 lb/1000 ft^2 (20 g/m^2) nominal basis weight

[**13:**A.20.4.10]

The rate of firespread over the surface of the tissue rolls was extremely rapid in the full-scale fire tests. The rate of firespread over the surface of the linerboard rolls was slower. Based on the overall results of these full-scale tests, along with additional data from small-scale testing of various paper grades, the broad range of papers has been classified into three major categories as follows:

(1) *Heavyweight* — Basis weight of 20 lb/1000 ft^2 (100 g/m^2) or greater
(2) *Mediumweight* — Basis weight of 10 lb to 20 lb/1000 ft^2 (100 g/m^2 to 0.098 kg/m^2)
(3) *Lightweight* — Basis weight of less than 10 lb/1000 ft^2 (50 gm^2) and tissues regardless of basis weight

[**13:**A.20.4.10]

The following SI units were used for conversion of US customary units:

1 lb = 0.45 kg

1 in. = 25 mm

1 ft = 0.3 m

1 ft^2 = 0.09 m^2

[**13:**A.20.4.10]

The various types of papers normally found in each of the four major categories are provided in Table A.34.3.10. [**13:**A.20.4.10]

A.34.3.11 Exposed, expanded Group A plastic dunnage, instrument panels, and plastic bumper facia were the automotive components with their related packaging that were utilized in the fire tests. This test commodity used in the large-scale sprinklered fire test proved to be the worst challenge per the large-scale calorimeter tests of available components. See *Technical Report of Fire Testing of Automotive Parts in Portable Storage Racking*, prepared by Underwriters Laboratories, Project 99NK29106, NC4004, January 5, 2001, and *Commodity Hazard Comparison of Expanded Plastic in Portable Bins and Racking*, Project 99NK29106, NC4004, September 8, 2000. [**13:**A.20.7]

A.34.4.1 With protection installed in accordance with this *Code*, fire protection of overhead steel and steel columns might not be necessary. Consideration should be given to subdividing large area warehouses in order to reduce the amount of merchandise that could be affected by a single fire.

Walls or partitions are recommended to be provided to separate the storage area from mercantile, manufacturing, or other occupancies to prevent the possibility of transmission of fire or smoke between the two occupancies. Door openings should be equipped with automatic-closing fire doors appropriate for the fire resistance rating of the wall or partition.

A.34.4.3 Since most of the fire tests were conducted without heat and smoke venting and draft curtains, protection specified in NFPA 13 was developed without their use.

For guidance on smoke and heat venting, see NFPA 204.

Smoke removal is important to manual fire fighting and overhaul. Vents through eave-line windows, doors, monitors, or gravity or mechanical exhaust systems facilitate smoke removal after control of the fire is achieved.

Results of tests organized by the Fire Protection Research Foundation and the Retail Committee on Group A Plastics to study the interaction of sprinklers, vents, and draft curtains indicate that the impact of automatic vents on sprinkler performance is neutral when automatic sprinkler discharge is adequate for the hazard and that draft curtains are potentially negative. Test results show that the placement of sprinklers and the thermal sensitivity of sprinklers and vents should be considered. Care should be exercised in the placement of draft curtains. Where required to be installed, draft curtains should be aligned where possible with aisles or other clear spaces in storage areas. Draft curtains where positioned over storage could adversely affect sprinkler operations. The number of operating sprinklers increased and led to a fire that consumed more commodity compared to other tests with fires ignited away from the draft curtains.

A.34.5.1 Commodities that are particularly susceptible to water damage should be stored on skids, dunnage, pallets, or

Table A.34.3.10 Paper Classification

Heavyweight	Mediumweight	Lightweight	Tissue
Linerboards	Bond and reproduction	Carbonizing tissue	Toilet tissue
Medium	Vellum	Cigarette	Towel tissue
Kraft roll wrappers	Offset	Fruit wrap	
Milk carton board	Tablet	Onion skin	
Folding carton board	Computer		
Bristol board	Envelope		
Tag	Book		
Vellum bristol board	Label		
Index	Magazine		
Cupstock	Butcher		
Pulp board	Bag		
	Newsprint (unwrapped)		

[**13:**Table A.20.4.10]

elevated platforms in order to maintain at least 4 in. (100 mm) clearance from the floor.

A.34.5.2.2 Protection for exposed steel structural roof members could be needed and should be provided as indicated by the AHJ.

A.34.5.2.5 Incandescent light fixtures should have shades or guards to prevent the ignition of commodity from hot bulbs where possibility of contact with storage exists.

A.34.6.1 Wet systems are recommended for storage occupancies. Dry systems are permitted only where it is impractical to provide heat. Preaction systems should be considered for storage occupancies that are unheated, particularly where in-rack sprinklers are installed or for those occupancies that are highly susceptible to water damage.

A.34.6.4.2 See Annex B of NFPA 13E.

A.34.7.3.2 The use of welding, cutting, soldering, or brazing torches in the storage areas introduces a severe fire hazard and, when possible, should be relocated to a designated area. The use of mechanical fastenings and mechanical saws or cutting wheels is recommended.

A.34.7.6 Periodic inspections of all fire protection equipment should be made in conjunction with regular inspections of the premises. Unsatisfactory conditions should be reported immediately and necessary corrective measures taken promptly.

A.34.7.6.2 All fire-fighting and safety personnel should realize the great danger in shutting off sprinklers once opened by heat from fire. Shutting off sprinklers to locate fire could cause a disaster. Ventilation, use of smoke masks, smoke removal equipment, and removal of material are more safe. *(See NFPA 1660.)*

Sprinkler water should be shut off only after the fire is extinguished or completely under the control of hose streams. Even then, rekindling is a possibility. To be ready for prompt valve reopening if fire rekindles, a person stationed at the valve, a fire watch, and dependable communications between them are needed until automatic sprinkler protection is restored.

Prefire emergency planning is important and should be done by management and fire protection personnel, and the action to be taken discussed and correlated with the local fire department personnel. The critical time during any fire is in the incipient stage, and the action taken by fire protection personnel upon notification of fire can allow the fire to be contained in its early stages.

Pre-emergency planning should incorporate the following:

(1) Availability of hand fire-fighting equipment for the height and type of commodity involved
(2) Availability of fire-fighting equipment and personnel trained for the type of storage arrangement involved
(3) Assurance that all automatic fire protection equipment, such as sprinkler systems, water supplies, fire pumps, and hand hose, is in service at all times

Sprinkler protection installed as required in this *Code* is expected to protect the building occupancy without supplemental fire department activity. Fires that occur in rack storage occupancies protected in accordance with this *Code* are likely to be controlled. Fire department activity can, however, minimize the extent of loss. The first fire department pumper arriving at a rack storage–type fire should connect immediately to the sprinkler system's fire department connection and start pumping operations.

In the test series for storage up to 25 ft (7.6 m), the average time from ignition to smoke obscuration in the test building was about 13 minutes. The first sprinkler operating time in these same fires averaged about 3 minutes. Considering response time for the waterflow device to transmit a waterflow signal, approximately 9 minutes remains between the time of receipt of a waterflow alarm signal at fire department headquarters and the time of smoke obscuration within the building as an overall average.

In the test series for storage over 25 ft (7.6 m), the visibility time was extended. If the fire department facility emergency personnel arrive at the building in time to have sufficient visibility to locate the fire, suppression activities with small hose lines should be started. (Self-contained breathing apparatus is recommended.) If, on the other hand, the fire is not readily visible, hose should be laid to exterior doors or exterior openings in the building and charged lines provided to these points, ready for ultimate mop-up operations. Manual fire-fighting operations in such a warehouse should not be considered a substitute for sprinkler protection.

Important: The sprinkler system should be kept in operation during manual fire-fighting and mop-up operations.

During the testing program, the installed automatic extinguishing system was capable of controlling the fire and reducing all temperatures to ambient within 30 minutes of ignition. Ventilation operations and mop-up were not started until this point. The use of smoke removal equipment is important.

Smoke removal capability should be provided. Examples of smoke removal equipment include the following:

(1) Mechanical air-handling systems
(2) Powered exhaust fans
(3) Roof-mounted gravity vents
(4) Perimeter gravity vents

Whichever system is selected, it should be designed for manual actuation by the fire department, thus allowing personnel to coordinate the smoke removal (ventilation) with mop-up operations.

See also NFPA 600 and Annex B of NFPA 13E and NFPA 1030.

N **A.34.7.6.3.2** The building owner or a designated representative initiates this annual evaluation, either through an in-house process or through an outside entity. Upon completion, the evaluation should be documented and provided to the AHJ when requested. Changes or differences from the posted plan should be reviewed with the AHJ. The purpose of the annual evaluation of the storage plan is to ensure that the approved protection levels for the current commodities and occupant classifications are still being adhered to and that no deviations from that approved storage plan have taken place. This evaluation is not intended to replace the hazard evaluation required by NFPA 25 when hazards or processes change. In that event, NFPA 25 requires the owner to take the necessary steps outlined in that standard and to notify the AHJ.

A.34.8.3.1 Rack storage as referred to in this *Code* contains commodities in a rack structure, usually steel. Many variations of dimensions are found. Racks can be single-row, double-row, or multiple-row, with or without solid shelves. The standard commodity used in most of the tests was 42 in. (1.07 m) on a side. The types of racks covered in this *Code* are as follows:

(1) Double-row racks, in which pallets rest on two beams parallel to the aisle. Any number of pallets can be supported by one pair of beams. *[See Figure A.34.8.3.1(a) through Figure A.34.8.3.1(d).]*
(2) Automatic storage-type rack, in which the pallet is supported by two rails running perpendicular to the aisle. *[See Figure A.34.8.3.1(e).]*
(3) Multiple-row racks more than two pallets deep, measured aisle to aisle, which include drive-in racks, drive-through racks, flow-through racks, and portable racks arranged in the same manner, and conventional or automatic racks with aisles less than 42 in. (1.07 m) wide. *[See Figure A.34.8.3.1(f) through Figure A.34.8.3.1(j).]*
(4) Movable racks, which are racks on fixed rails or guides. They can be moved back and forth only in a horizontal two-dimensional plane. A moving aisle is created as abutting racks are either loaded or unloaded, then moved across the aisle to abut other racks. *[See Figure A.34.8.3.1(k).]*
(5) Solid shelving, which are conventional pallet racks with plywood shelves on the shelf beams *[see Figure A.34.8.3.1(c) and Figure A.34.8.3.1(d)]*. These are used in special cases.
(6) Cantilever rack, in which the load is supported on arms that extend horizontally from columns. The load can rest on the arms or on the shelves supported by the arms. *[See Figure A.34.8.3.1(l).]*

Load depth in conventional or automatic racks should be considered a nominal 4 ft (1.22 m). *[See Figure A.34.8.3.1(b).]*

A.34.8.3.2 Fixed rack structures should be designed to facilitate removal or repair of damaged sections without resorting to flame cutting or welding in the storage area. Where sprinklers are to be installed in racks, rack design should anticipate the additional clearances necessary to facilitate installation of sprinklers. The rack structure should be anchored to prevent damage to sprinkler lines and supply piping in racks.

Rack structures should be designed for seismic conditions in areas where seismic resistance of building structure is required.

FIGURE A.34.8.3.1(a) Conventional Pallet Rack.

FIGURE A.34.8.3.1(b) Double-Row Racks Without Solid or Slatted Shelves.

Legend
A — Load depth
B — Load width
E — Storage height
F — Commodity
G — Pallet
H — Rack depth
L — Longitudinal flue space
T — Transverse flue space

FIGURE A.34.8.3.1(c) Double-Row Racks with Solid Shelves.

Legend
A — Shelf depth
B — Shelf height
E — Storage height
F — Commodity
H — Rack depth
L — Longitudinal flue space
T — Transverse flue space

FIGURE A.34.8.3.1(d) Double-Row Racks with Slatted Shelves.

Legend
A — Shelf depth
B — Shelf height
E — Storage height
F — Commodity
H — Rack depth
L — Longitudinal flue space
T — Transverse flue space

A.34.8.3.3 Storage in aisles can render protection ineffective and should be discouraged.

A.34.8.3.3.3 See Chapter 12 of NFPA 13.

A.34.8.3.4.1.1 Detection systems, concentrate pumps, generators, and other system components essential to the operation of the system should have an approved standby power source.

A.34.8.3.4.2.1(1) Where high-expansion foam is contemplated as the protection media, consideration should be given to possible damage to the commodity from soaking and corrosion. Consideration also should be given to the problems associated with removal of foam after discharge.

A.34.9.1 Illustrations of some, but not necessarily all, tire storage arrangements are shown in Figure A.34.9.1(a) through Figure A.34.9.1(g).

A.34.9.2.3 NFPA *101* accurately reflects the travel distance requirements as follows:

(1) Tire storage is classified as ordinary hazard.
(2) Tire fires begin burning slowly. In combination with an acceptable automatic sprinkler system, this slower burning allows time for egress.
(3) Tire storage warehouses have a low occupant load.
(4) Large aisle widths [8 ft (2.4 m) minimum] required in 34.9.3.1.4 of this *Code* facilitate egress.

A.34.9.3.1.1 Limiting the pile length is not intended. (*See Figure A.34.9.3.1.1.*)

FIGURE A.34.8.3.1(e) Automatic Storage-Type Rack.

End View / Aisle View

Legend
A — Load depth
B — Load width
E — Storage height
F — Commodity
G — Pallet
L — Longitudinal flue space
T — Transverse flue space

FIGURE A.34.8.3.1(f) Multiple-Row Rack to be Served by a Reach Truck.

End View
L — Longitudinal flue space

FIGURE A.34.8.3.1(g) Flow-Through Pallet Rack.

FIGURE A.34.8.3.1(h) Drive-In Rack — Two or More Pallets Deep (Fork Truck Drives into the Rack to Deposit and Withdraw Loads in the Depth of the Rack).

FIGURE A.34.8.3.1(i) Flow-Through Rack.

FIGURE A.34.8.3.1(j) Portable Racks.

A.34.10.2 With protection installed in accordance with this *Code*, fire protection of overhead steel and steel columns is not necessary. However, some lightweight beams and joists can distort and necessitate replacement, particularly following fires involving plastic-wrapped rolls stored 20 ft (6.1 m) and higher.

A.34.11.1 Idle pallet storage introduces a severe fire condition. Stacking idle pallets in piles is the best arrangement of combustibles to promote rapid spread of fire, heat release, and complete combustion. After pallets are used for a short time in warehouses, they dry out and edges become frayed and splintered. In this condition they are subject to easy ignition from a small ignition source. Again, high piling increases considerably both the challenge to sprinklers and the probability of involving a large number of pallets when fire occurs. Therefore storing idle pallets outdoors where possible is preferable. A fire in idle plastic or wooden pallets is one of the greatest challenges to sprinklers. The undersides of the pallets create a dry area on which a fire can grow and expand to other dry or partially wet areas. This process of jumping to other dry, closely located, parallel, combustible surfaces continues until the fire bursts through the top of the stack. Once this happens, very little water is able to reach the base of the fire. The only practical method of stopping a fire in a large concentration of pallets with ceiling sprinklers is by means of prewetting. In high stacks, prewetting cannot be done without abnormally high water supplies. The storage of idle pallets should not be permitted in an unsprinklered warehouse containing other storage.

FIGURE A.34.8.3.1(k) Movable Rack.

Legend
T — Transverse flue space
L — Longitudinal flue space

FIGURE A.34.9.1(a) Typical Open Portable Rack Unit.

FIGURE A.34.9.1(b) Typical Palletized Portable Rack Units.

FIGURE A.34.8.3.1(l) Cantilever Rack.

FIGURE A.34.9.1(c) Open Portable Tire Rack.

Legend
A — Load depth   G — Pallet
B — Load width   H — Rack depth
E — Storage height   L — Longitudinal flue space
F — Commodity   T — Transverse flue space

FIGURE A.34.9.1(d) Double-Row Fixed Rack Tire Storage.

FIGURE A.34.9.1(e) Palletized Portable Rack On-Side Tire Storage Arrangement (Banded or Unbanded).

FIGURE A.34.9.1(f) On-Tread, On-Floor Tire Storage Arrangement (Normally Banded).

FIGURE A.34.9.1(g) Typical Laced Tire Storage.

Legend
L — Length
W — Width

FIGURE A.34.9.3.1.1 Typical Tire Piling Arrangement.

A.34.11.3 The practice that some materials are stored on pallets in an open yard is recognized. Since stacks of idle pallets present a severe fire problem, attention needs to be paid to the storage arrangements of the pallets. Manual outside open sprinklers generally are not a reliable means of protection unless property is attended to at all times by plant emergency personnel. Open sprinklers with a deluge valve are preferred.

A.34.11.4.1 Pallets staged outdoors at pallet manufacturing and recycling facilities should not be defined as idle (i.e., not active or not in use) considering that these facilities stage work-in-process pallets in an active management environment according to the following:

(1) Pallets are the primary business activity at these manufacturing and recycling facilities.
(2) Pallet inventories are organized in a specific manner based on size and quality.
(3) Pallet inventories are rotated on a routine basis.
(4) Personnel are a frequent presence in the staging area during hours of operation.

Combustible pallets listed and labeled to ANSI/FM 4996, *Classification of Pallets and Other Material Handling Products as Equivalent to Wood Pallets,* or to UL 2335, *Fire Tests of Storage Pallets,* should be treated as wood pallets.

A.34.11.4.9 The access to the individual pallet stacks within a pallet array is based upon water stream reach. The 30 ft (9 m) depth in 34.11.4.9(1) using an 8 ft (2.4 m) wide aisle is based upon hand hose line stream reach. The 50 ft (15 m) depth in 34.11.4.9(2) is based upon master stream reach whether from a deck gun mounted upon an engine or from an aerial device.

The arrangement can be in any configuration as long the measurement to the individual pallet stack within the pallet array meets 34.11.4.9(1) or 34.11.4.9(2). The configuration can be with 8 ft or 50 ft (2.4 m or 15 m) aisle on one side, an 8 ft or 50 ft (2.4 m or 15 m) aisles on both sides, or a combination of aisle widths.

A.34.11.4.10 The required fire flow should be based on available water supplies, fire department response capabilities, and exposure hazards.

N **A.34.11.4.12** Other protection measures can include the following:

(1) The storage yard areas and materials-handling equipment selection, design, and arrangement are based upon an approved risk assessment.
(2) Automatic fire detection transmits an alarm signal to a supervising station in accordance with *NFPA 72.*
(3) Fire apparatus access roads are provided around all storage areas.

A.38.1 Processing of other agricultural products not addressed by this chapter should comply with other applicable sections of this *Code.*

A.38.1.1 For the purposes of this *Code,* the term *cannabis* includes all forms of cannabis, including hemp.

A.38.1.5 Occupancy classification should take into consideration the hazards associated with the process occurring in the facility and the quantities of high-hazard contents.

A.38.4 Due to security of growing and processing operations, access control, electromagnetic locks, and other locking arrangements are used. Chapter 14 addresses the installation of specialized locking devices.

A.38.5.5.1 Fumigation for cannabis growing, processing, or extraction facility includes the production or use of sulfur dioxide.

A.38.5.5.2 Fires, open flames, and similar sources of ignition should be eliminated from the space under fumigation or insecticidal fogging. Electricity in any part of the building, structure, or space where operation of switches or electrical devices, equipment, or systems could serve as a source of ignition should be shut off. In addition, electronic devices, including portable equipment and cellular phones, should be shut off and telephone lines should be disconnected from telephones.

A.38.6 Flammable or combustible liquids, flammable gases, liquefied petroleum gases, or nonflammable gases used in extraction processing of oils and fats are hereinafter referred to as "solvents."

The extraction process includes extracting the oils and fats by use of a solvent, desolventizing the raw material and producing the miscella, distilling the solvent from the miscella, and recovering the solvent.

A.38.6.1.1.2 The dedicated room should not be used for any other purpose, including storage. Materials that might interfere with the operation of exhaust systems should be prohibited, such as acoustical ceiling tiles.

A.38.6.1.1.4 Examples of rooms using hazardous materials for extraction are those using flammable and combustible liquids and CO_2.

A.38.6.1.2.1 Nonhazardous processes might not warrant constant attendance by trained personnel.

A.38.6.1.2.2 Staff monitoring the extraction process do not need to meet the training requirements of 38.6.1.4.

A.38.6.1.2.2(2) The transfer of solvent includes LPG liquid transfilling.

A.38.6.1.4.2 Examples of these programs include, but are not limited to, the following:

(1) Training programs developed by extraction equipment manufacturers
(2) Compressed Gas Association CGA P-1, *Safe Handling of Compressed Gases in Containers,* for operators of CO_2 equipment
(3) Programs by governmental organizations

A.38.6.1.6.2.3 The provisions for container (i.e., tank) construction are applicable to the working tank or the supply tank that is connected to the extraction equipment.

A.38.6.1.6.4 The technical report documenting the design or peer review should be submitted for review and approval to the AHJ prior to the equipment being located or installed at the facility.

Where a technical report is required to be submitted for review and approval by the AHJ, the following should occur:

(1) Prior to submittal of the technical report, the engineer should submit to the AHJ any educational background and professional experience specific to the review and approval of system, equipment, and processes with like hazards of those associated with the cannabis extraction system.
(2) Once the proof of qualifications are found acceptable by the AHJ, the engineer of record should produce the technical report and the report should be signed and sealed in accordance with respective state requirements.

All of, but not limited to, the following items should be included in the technical report:

(1) Manufacturer information.
(2) Engineer of record information.
(3) Date of review and report revision history
(4) Signature page, which should include the following:

　(a) Author of the report
　(b) Date of report
　(c) Seal, date, and signature of engineer of record performing the design or peer review
　(d) Date and signature of the engineer performing the engineering check of the report (which cannot be performed by the authoring engineer though it can be from the same firm as the authoring engineer)

(5) Model number of the item evaluated. If the equipment is provided with a serial number, the serial number should be included for verification at time of site inspection.
(6) Methodology of the design or peer review process used to determine minimum safety requirements. Methodology should consider the basis of design, and should include a code analysis and code path to demonstrate the reason as to why specific code or standards are applicable or not.
(7) Equipment description. A list of all components and subassemblies of the system or equipment, indicating the materials, solvent compatibility, maximum temperature, and pressure limits.
(8) A general flow schematic or general process flow diagram (PFD) of the process. All primary components of the process equipment should be identified and match the aforementioned list. Operating temperatures, pressures, and solvent state of matter should be identified in each primary step or component. A piping and instrumentation diagram (PID or PI&D) might be provided but is not required.
(9) Analysis of the vessel(s) if pressurized beyond standard atmospheric pressure. Analysis should include purchased and fabricated components.
(10) Structural analysis for the frame system supporting the equipment.
(11) Process safety analysis of the extraction equipment, from the introduction of raw product to the end of the extraction process.
(12) Comprehensive process hazard analysis considering failure modes and points of failure throughout the process. This portion of the review should include review of emergency procedure information provided by the manufacturer of the equipment or process and not that of the facility, building, or room.
(13) Review of the assembly instructions, and operational and maintenance manuals provided by the manufacturer.
(14) Findings and observations of the analysis.
(15) List of references used in the analysis.

If the technical report or manufacturer's literature indicate specific requirements for the location, room, space, or building where the extraction process is to occur, the engineer of record, as approved, should review the construction documents of such location, room, space, or building and provide a report of their findings and observations to the AHJ.

The findings and observations should include the following:

(1) Process safety analysis of the entire process from raw material to finished product.
(2) Comprehensive process hazard analysis considering failure modes and points throughout the process and a review of emergency procedures as related to the equipment or process and the facility.

A.38.6.2.4.2 The purpose of alerting the extraction operator is to provide notification that the operator is in a flammable environment because the LP gas used is not odorized. This could be in the form of a visual warning, local alarm, or other approved means. However, it is not intended for evacuation or to dispatch the fire department.

A.38.6.3.2.1 The intent of this section is to require an exhaust system utilization to capture velocities across the work area. Standard laboratory capture velocity is between 80 and 100 ft/min (24 and 30 m/min).

Most flammable liquid extractions and post oil processing are bench-top process that can be conducted in a chemical fume hood. Larger operations might need larger hoods or special full-room exhaust systems in compliance with NFPA 91 or the mechanical code. The exception is intended for small unheated processes where plant material might be soaked in flammable liquid and directly transferred to a food product.

A.38.6.4.4 Exhaust piping can be of the flexible type as long as the piping or hose is capable of handling the force of the exhaust. Relief devices include spring-loaded pressure relief valves or rupture disks.

A.38.7 The intent of this section is for filling the working container (i.e., tank) connected to the extraction equipment.

A.40.4 See ANSI/AIHA Z10-2012, *Occupational Health and Safety Management Systems.* [652:A.8.2]

A.40.5.1 This section provides the minimum requirements for performing a hazard assessment to identify and analyze the hazards presented by the presence of combustible particulate solids for the purpose of identifying relevant management strategies necessary to provide a reasonable degree of protection to life and property. [652:A.7.1]

The intent of this section is to establish a requirement to analyze the potential hazards of an operation regardless of size. The dust hazards analysis methodology is not necessarily the same as that in the OSHA process safety management (PSM) regulation and is not intended to trigger such a requirement. Annex B provides an example of how one might perform a DHA. [652:A.7.1]

A.40.5.1.1.1 A DHA is a careful review of the fire and explosion hazards to determine the consequences of what could go wrong and to determine what safeguards could be implemented to prevent or mitigate those consequences. DHA should be completed as soon as possible. For existing facilities, those processes with the greatest perceived risk should be evaluated first. [652:A.7.1.1.1]

A.40.5.1.1.2 The deadline for completing initial DHAs is 5 years after the effective date of the first edition of this standard. [652:A.7.1.1.2]

This edition extends the first edition's period of 3 years for completion of all DHAs to 5 years. It is not the intent of this requirement to permit a delay in the completion of all DHA until the fifth year. [652:A.7.1.1.2]

A.40.5.2.1 NFPA standards rely on the determination of "where an explosion hazard or deflagration hazard exists." There are other physical and health hazards to consider such as toxicity, reactivity with water, and so forth that can be considered when conducting a DHA. The DHA should consider the four conditions that are required for a deflagration:

(1) A combustible particulate solid of sufficiently small particle size to deflagrate
(2) A combustible particulate solid suspended in air to deflagrate (or other oxidizing medium)
(3) A combustion particulate solid suspension of sufficiently high concentration to deflagrate

(4) A competent igniter applied to the suspension of combustible particulate solids where the concentration is sufficient for flame propagation.
[**652:**A.7.2.1]

A deflagration leading to an explosion will occur whenever all four criteria occur within a compartment or container at the same time. Since gravity is a concentrating effect and we always assume an ignition source is present unless we can prove one cannot exist, even under conditions of equipment failure, this list reduces to:

(1) A combustible particulate solid of sufficiently small particle size to deflagrate
(2) A means for suspending the combustible particulate solid in air (or other oxidizing medium)
(3) A sufficient concentration can be achieved
[**652:**A.7.2.1]

Most dust explosions occur as a series of deflagrations leading to a series of explosions in stages. While a single explosion is possible, it is the exception rather than the rule. Most injuries are the result of the "secondary" deflagrations rather than the initial event. Most "explosion" events are a series of deflagrations each causing a portion of the process or facility to explode. Primary deflagrations lead to secondary deflagrations, usually fueled by accumulated fugitive dust that has been suspended by the following:

(1) Acoustic impulse waves of the initial, primary, deflagration
(2) Entrainment by deflagration pressure front
[**652:**A.7.2.1]

The majority of the property damage and personnel injury is due to the fugitive dust accumulations within the building or process compartment. The elimination of accumulated fugitive dust is CRITICAL and the single most important criterion for a safe workplace. [**652:**A.7.2.1]

A.40.5.2.2 The qualified person who is leading or performing the DHA should be familiar with conducting a DHA. The qualified person should also be familiar with the hazards of combustible dusts. Typically, a team performs a DHA. For some processes this team might be a little as two persons, or for larger and more complex processes, the team might require many more than two persons. This team is made of a variety of persons whose background and expertise can include the following:

(1) Familiarity with the process
(2) Operations and maintenance
(3) Process equipment
(4) Safety systems
(5) History of operation
(6) The properties of the material
(7) Emergency procedures
[**652:**A.7.2.2]

The individuals involved in the DHA could include facility operators, engineers, owners, equipment manufacturers, or consultants. [**652:**A.7.2.2]

A.40.5.3.1(2)(b) The hazard management document for all the areas of the process or facility compartment determined to be combustible dust hazards should include, but not be limited to, the following:

(1) Test reports
(2) Drawings
(3) Sizing calculations
[**652:**A.7.3.1(2)(b)]

Methods to prevent or mitigate the consequences of combustible dust hazards can be developed by using the methods permitted in this standard or other industry- or commodity-specific NFPA standards. Subsection 40.5.3.1 outlines the minimum steps of a dust hazards analysis. [**652:**A.7.3.1(2)(b)]

A.40.5.3.3.1 This includes the process systems and ancillary equipment such as dust collection systems. Where multiple compartments present essentially the same hazard, a single evaluation might be appropriate. [**652:**A.7.3.3.1]

A.40.5.3.3.3 Each and every process component should be evaluated, including ducts, conveyors, silos, bunkers, vessels, fans, and other pieces of process equipment. Each point along the process should be described, and hazards at each point should be identified. Remedial measures for each hazard should be identified and documented. The means by which the hazard should be managed is then determined. Usually the relevant industry or commodity-specific NFPA standard will provide options. The process and process equipment will often determine which option is most appropriate. (Refer to Annex B of NFPA 652 for an example of a process hazard analysis.) [**652:**7.3.3.3]

A.40.5.3.4.2 Each and every facility compartment containing combustible particulate solids should be evaluated. The complete contents of the compartment should be considered, including hidden areas. Each area in the compartment should be described, and hazards at each point should be identified. Remedial measures for each hazard should be identified and documented. The means by which the hazard should be managed is then determined. Usually the relevant industry or commodity-specific NFPA standard will provide options. *(See Annex C of NFPA 652.)* [**652:**A.7.3.4.2]

A.40.5.3.4.2.1 Refer to 6.1.1.3 and 6.1.1.8 of NFPA 654 and 6.4.2.2 of NFPA 664 for examples of methods to determine acceptable threshold accumulation level. [**652:**A.7.3.4.2.1]

A.40.6.1 The operating procedures should address both the normal operating conditions and the safe operating limits. Where possible, the basis for establishing the limits and the consequences of exceeding the limits should also be described. The operating procedures should address all aspects of the operation, including the following (as applicable):

(1) Normal startup
(2) Continuous operation
(3) Normal shutdown
(4) Emergency shutdown
(5) Restart after normal or emergency shutdown
(6) Anticipated process upset conditions
(7) System idling
[**652:**A.8.3.1]

For manual operations, the procedures and practices should describe techniques, procedural steps, and equipment that are intended to minimize or eliminate combustible dust hazards. [**652:**A.8.3.1]

Operating procedures and practices should be reviewed on a periodic basis, typically annually, to ensure they are current and accurate. [**652:**A.8.3.1]

A.40.6.2 Safe work practices include, but are not limited to, hot work, confined space entry, and lockout/tagout, and the use of personal protective equipment. *(See NFPA 51B.)* Consideration for extending the duration of the fire watch could be warranted based on characteristics of the material, equipment configuration, and conditions. For example, the PRB Coal Users' Group practice for hot work suggests fire watches could be warranted for 2 to 12 hours following the completion of hot work due to the exothermic chemical reaction of subbituminous coals. In addition to the hazards of combustible dust, safe work practices should address the hazards of mitigation systems such as inerting and suppression. [652:A.8.3.2]

A.40.7.2 Model Programs Annex. (Reserved)

A.40.7.2.1.1 Items that should be included in the housekeeping procedure include the following:

(1) A risk assessment that considers the specific characteristics of the dust being cleaned (particle size, moisture content, MEC, MIE) and other safety risks introduced by the cleaning methods used
(2) Personal safety procedures, including fall protection when working at heights
(3) Personal protective equipment (PPE), including flame-resistant garments in accordance with the hazard analysis required by NFPA 2113
(4) Cleaning sequence
(5) Cleaning methods to be used
(6) Equipment, including lifts, vacuum systems, attachments, and so forth
(7) Cleaning frequency

[652:A.8.4.2.1.1]

A.40.7.2.1.2 For information on selection of housekeeping methods, refer to 2.2.4 of FM Data Sheet 7-76, "Prevention and Mitigation of Combustible Dust Explosions and Fires." Other factors can be considered in the selection of a housekeeping method, such as the effectiveness or compatibility of certain methods with the material. Cleaning should be comprehensive and should remove dust from the facility versus relocating it to other surfaces in the area. For the purposes of this standard, the concern is about dust that either propagates flame or that can be dispersed by credible disturbances. For accumulations that are not easy to disperse, the fire hazard should be considered *(see Section 40.13)*. [652:A.8.4.2.1.2]

The accumulation of a dust layer on a surface that is subject to heating (e.g., the surface of a bearing, an electrical motor, or a heater) could insulate the surface, increasing the surface temperature above the equipment "T" rating, to the point where the dust could self-ignite and smolder. [652:A.8.4.2.1.2]

Housekeeping of a dust layer that has self-ignited and started smoldering could result in full-ignition as the dust disperses during the housekeeping process. The burning dust could damage the housekeeping equipment, ignite a larger dust cloud or a flammable gas release in the area, or initiate smoldering in other dust layers. Before performing housekeeping of a dust layer on a potentially hot surface, the dust should be tested to confirm whether self-ignition and smoldering has initiated. Note that housekeeping of dust layers settling after a dust flash-fire should also consider the dust to be smoldering. [652:A.8.4.2.1.2]

A.40.7.2.2.1 Portable vacuum cleaners are self-contained units that typically utilize either an electrically or compressed air powered (with venturi) vacuum source (AMD) and an air-material separator (AMS) that is either wet (i.e., liquid) or dry (i.e., filter media). A single hose connection is normally provided, but larger semiportable units (either on trucks or moved by forklifts) can allow use of more than one simultaneous operator. Typically, when dry filter media is used there is no automatic filter cleaning method; however, with the larger semiportable units automatic filter cleaning is usually provided due to the higher air flows and material/dust loading. [652:A.8.4.2.2.1]

A.40.7.2.2.1.2 Using a portable vacuum cleaner with metal dusts and particles can have risks that are not adequately covered in NFPA 652. However, NFPA 484 has specific sections for use of wet and dry portable vacuum cleaning equipment and on their use with the more exotic metals and alloys such as titanium, aluminum, and so forth. [652:A.8.4.2.2.1.2]

A.40.7.2.2.1.3 Use of portable vacuum cleaning equipment for housekeeping of combustible dusts is subject to the same dust hazards analysis (DHA) as would be a centralized vacuum cleaning system. The combustible dust characteristics, hazards, and risks should be analyzed to determine the best type of portable unit to use and the restrictions on their use. This should also consider the classification of the area of use, personnel protective equipment, and so forth. [652:A.8.4.2.2.1.3]

A.40.7.2.2.1.6 Verification of the path to ground can be visual. [652:A.8.4.2.2.1.6]

A.40.7.2.2.1.7 If a large quantity of material is spilled in an unclassified area, the bulk material should be collected by sweeping or shoveling or with a portable vacuum cleaner listed as suitable for Class II locations. Vacuum cleaners meeting the requirements in 40.7.2.2.1 can be used to clean up residual material after the bulk of the spill has been collected. [652:A.8.4.2.2.1.7]

A.40.7.2.2.1.7(6) Liquids or wet material can weaken paper filter elements causing them to fail, which can allow combustible dust to reach the fan and motor. [652:A.8.4.2.2.1.7(6)]

A.40.7.2.2.2 The Committee is not aware of vendors providing equipment listed for Class III electrically classified (hazardous) locations. A common practice is to use equipment listed for Class II in areas classified as Class III. [652:A.8.4.2.2.2]

A.40.7.2.3 With manual cleaning, such as using a scoop and brush, generating a dust cloud should be avoided. Where appropriate for the specific commodity, the use of natural bristle brushes should be considered to reduce the risk of static sparking. [652:A.8.4.2.3]

A.40.7.2.4 Use of high-pressure water can generate dust clouds, and care should be taken when using this method. Use of water wash-down for some metal dusts can result in hydrogen generation. Refer to NFPA 484 for restrictions on the use of water wash-down. [652:A.8.4.2.4]

A.40.7.2.4.3 Examples of additional precautions to be taken can include, but are not limited to, the following:

(1) Operating management has full knowledge of and has granted approval for the use of water.
(2) Ventilation, either natural or forced, is sufficient to maintain concentrations of flammable or toxic gasses at safe levels.

(3) Complete drainage of all water effluent to a safe, contained area is available.

[**652**:A.8.4.2.4.3]

A.40.7.2.6.1 Compressed air blowdown used for cleaning purposes has been demonstrated to present significant hazards and should be employed when other cleaning methods present higher risk. Compressed air blowdown does not remove accumulated dust, it simply moves the dust to another area, which will then have to be cleaned. It is preferable to use engineering design controls to eliminate areas that can be inaccessible or difficult to clean by other methods. [**652**:A.8.4.2.6.1]

A.40.7.2.6.2 All of the listed precautions might not be required for limited use of compressed air for cleaning minor accumulations of dust from machines or other surfaces between shifts. A risk assessment should be conducted to determine which precautions are required for the specific conditions under which compressed air is being used. [**652**:A.8.4.2.6.2]

A.40.7.6.1 Surfaces on which dust can accumulate can include walls, floors, and horizontal surfaces, such as equipment, ducts, pipes, hoods, ledges, beams, and above suspended ceilings and other concealed surfaces such as the interior of electrical enclosures. [**652**:A.8.4.6.1]

Factory Mutual recommends that surfaces should be cleaned frequently enough to prevent hazardous accumulations (FM Data Sheet 7-76, *Prevention and Mitigation of Combustible Dust Explosives and Fire*, 2.3.5). Housekeeping for fugitive dusts is most important where the operational intent is that the dust accumulations are not normally present in the occupancy and the building has no deflagration protection features, such as damage limiting/explosion venting construction or classified electrical equipment, and additional personal protection from dust deflagration hazards is also not provided. Factors that should be considered in establishing the housekeeping frequency include the following:

(1) Variability of fugitive dust emissions
(2) Impact of process changes and non-routine activities
(3) Variability of accumulations on different surfaces within the room (i.e., walls, floors, overheads)

[**652**:A.8.4.6.1]

A.40.7.6.3 One example of a transient release of dust is a temporary loss of containment due to a failure of a seal in process equipment or conveying systems. Table A.40.7.6.3 provides an example of an unscheduled housekeeping procedure to limit the time that a local spill or transient releases of dust are allowed to remain before cleaning the local area to less than the threshold housekeeping dust accumulation. The "level accumulation" of combustible dust should be established in the housekeeping program based on the risk of flash fires and secondary explosions from the dust hazards analysis. [**652**:A.8.4.6.3]

A.40.7.7.1 Typically, the housekeeping effectiveness is verified on an annual basis or after a significant change in the operation. If transient releases are becoming more frequent, the housekeeping effectiveness and equipment integrity should be verified. [**652**:A.8.4.7.1]

A.40.8.1 Hot work activities include the following:

(1) Cutting and welding

Table A.40.7.6.3 Unscheduled Housekeeping

Level Accumulation	Longest Time to Complete Unscheduled Local Cleaning of Floor-Accessible Surfaces (hours)	Longest Time to Complete Unscheduled Local Cleaning of Remote Surfaces (hours)
1	8	24
2	4	12
3	1	3

[**652**:Table A.8.4.6.3]

(2) Other maintenance, modification, or repair activities involving the application of an open flame or the generation of hot sparks

[**652**:A.8.5.1]

A.40.8.2 The hot work area specified in NFPA 51B is 11 m (35 ft). [**652**:A.8.5.2]

A.40.9.1.1 A specific evaluation of the work environment to determine the requirement for the wearing of flame-resistant garments should be based on the potential hazards that workers are exposed to as part of their work duties. [**652**:A.8.6.1.1]

A.40.9.1.3 It is important to distinguish between the different PPE requirements in NFPA 2112 and *NFPA 70E* for different exposure hazards. The PPE requirements in NFPA 2112 are not the same requirements in *NFPA 70E* and might not be sufficient protection for electric arc. [**652**:A.8.6.1.3]

A.40.9.1.4 Portions of this list are taken from Section 4.3 of NFPA 2113. [**652**:A.8.6.1.4]

A.40.9.1.6 At a minimum, the policy should address who is responsible for laundering, inspecting, repairing, and retiring garments. See also Section 6.1 from NFPA 2113. If flame-resistant clothing becomes contaminated with combustible particulate solids, the protective performance of the garments could be compromised. Wearers should maintain an awareness of and take precautions against the accumulation of combustible particulate solids on their protective clothing. [**652**:A.8.6.1.6]

A.40.9.2.1 This section does not include an incidental amount of elastic used in nonmelting fabric, underwear, or socks. [**652**:A.8.6.2.1]

A.40.9.2.2 See also Section 5.1 from NFPA 2113. [**652**:A.8.6.2.2]

A.40.10.1 Process interlocks and protection systems should be inspected, calibrated, and tested in the manner in which they are intended to operate, with written records maintained for review. In this context, "test" implies a nondestructive means of verifying that the system will operate as intended. For active explosion protection systems, this can involve the disconnection of final elements (i.e., suppression discharge devices or fast-acting valve actuators) and the use of a simulated signal to verify the correct operation of the detection and control system. Testing can also include slow-stroke activation of fast acting valves to verify unrestricted travel. Some devices, such as explosion vent panels, suppression discharge devices, and some fast-acting valve actuators, cannot be functionally "tested" in a nondestructive manner, and so only periodic, preventive, and predictive inspection, maintenance, and replacement (if necessary) are applied. [652:A.8.7.1]

Inspection and maintenance requirements for explosion vents and other explosion protection systems are found in NFPA 68, and NFPA 69, respectively. [652:A.8.7.1]

A.40.10.2(5) Process interlocks should be calibrated and tested in the manner in which they are intended to operate, with written test records maintained for review by management. Testing frequency should be determined in accordance with the AIChE Center for Chemical Process Safety, *Guidelines for Safe Automation of Chemical Processes*. [654:A.8.7.1.2(5)]

A.40.10.4 Corrective actions should be expedited on high-risk hazards (those that could result in a fatality or serious injury). Where in-kind repairs cannot be promptly implemented, consideration should be given to providing alternate means of protection. [652:A.8.7.4]

A.40.10.5 See Section 40.16 for information regarding document retention. [652:A.8.7.5]

A.40.11.1 Safety of a process depends on the employees who operate it and the knowledge and understanding they have of the process. It is important to maintain an effective and ongoing training program for all employees involved. Operator response and action to correct adverse conditions, as indicated by instrumentation or other means, are only as good as the frequency and thoroughness of training provided. [652:A.8.8.1]

A.40.11.2 All plant personnel, including management; supervisors; and operating, housekeeping, and maintenance personnel should receive general awareness training for combustible dust hazards, commensurate with their job responsibilities, including training on locations where hazards can exist on site, appropriate measures to minimize hazards, and response to emergencies. [652:A.8.8.2]

A.40.11.2.1 Safe work habits are developed and do not occur naturally. The training program should provide enough background information regarding the hazards of the materials and the process so that the employees can understand why it is important to follow the prescribed procedures. Training should address the following:

(1) The hazards of their working environment and procedures in case of emergencies, including fires, explosions, and hazardous materials releases
(2) Operating, inspection, testing, and maintenance procedures applicable to their assigned work
(3) Normal process procedures as well as emergency procedures and changes to procedures
(4) Emergency response plans, including safe and proper evacuation of their work area and the permissible methods for fighting incipient fires in their work area
(5) The necessity for proper functioning of related fire and explosion protection systems
(6) Safe handling, use, storage, and disposal of hazardous materials used in the employees' work areas
(7) The location and operation of fire protection equipment, manual pull stations and alarms, emergency phones, first-aid supplies, and safety equipment
(8) Equipment operation, safe startup and shutdown, and response to upset conditions

[652:A.8.8.2.1]

A.40.11.2.3 The extent of this training should be based on the level of interaction the person is expected to have with the system. For example, operators need to be aware of the hazards presented by explosion suppression systems but might not need to know how to operate the suppression system (e.g., interfacing with the system control panel or locking out devices). Maintenance personnel, on the other hand, might need to know how and when to lock out the devices and how to return the system to its operational state. [652:A.8.8.2.3]

A.40.12.2 Qualified contractors should have proper credentials, which include applicable American Society of Mechanical Engineers (ASME) stamps, professional licenses, and so forth. [652:A.8.9.2]

A.40.12.3 It is suggested that annual meetings be conducted with regular contractors to review the facility's safe work practices and policies. Some points to cover include to whom the contractors would report at the facility, who at the facility can authorize hot work or fire protection impairments, and smoking and nonsmoking areas. The owner/operator does not necessarily need to provide the training to the contractor. [652:A.8.9.3]

A.40.12.3.3 In addition to the combustible dust fire and explosion hazards, contractors should also be made aware of other potential process and occupational hazards. There can be combustible materials other than combustible dusts in the equipment or immediate vicinity where contractors might be working. Combustion of dusts can generate toxic products, and some combustible dusts are acutely toxic. [652:A.8.9.3.3]

A.40.13.1 All plant personnel, including management, supervisors, and maintenance and operating personnel, should be trained to participate in plans for controlling plant emergencies. [652:A.8.10.1]

The emergency plan should contain the following elements:

(1) A signal or alarm system
(2) Identification of means of egress
(3) Minimization of effects on operating personnel and the community
(4) Minimization of property and equipment losses
(5) Interdepartmental and interplant cooperation
(6) Cooperation of outside agencies
(7) The release of accurate information to the public

[652:A.8.10.1]

Emergency drills should be performed annually by plant personnel. Malfunctions of the process should be simulated and emergency actions undertaken. Disaster drills that simulate a major catastrophic situation should be undertaken periodically with the cooperation and participation of public fire, police, and other local community emergency units and nearby cooperating plants. [652:A.8.10.1]

Specialized training for the public fire department(s) and industrial fire brigades can be warranted due to facility specific hazards where the methods to control and extinguish a fire can be outside of their normal arena of traditional fire fighting. *(See OSHA's publication, Firefighting Precautions at Facilities with Combustible Dust, for additional information.)* [652:A.8.10.1]

A.40.14 To thoroughly assess the risks, analyze the incident, and take any corrective steps necessary, investigations should be conducted promptly based on the nature of the incident and in coordination with the AHJ (as applicable). [652:A.8.11]

The investigation should include root cause analysis and should include a review of existing control measures and underlying systemic factors. Appropriate corrective action should be taken to prevent recurrence and to assess and monitor the effectiveness of actions taken. [652:A.8.11]

Such investigations should be carried out by trained persons (internal or external) and include participation of workers. All investigations should conclude with a report on the action taken to prevent recurrence. [652:A.8.11]

Investigation reports should be reviewed with all affected personnel and their representatives (including contract employees where applicable) whose job tasks are relevant to the incident findings, and with the health and safety committee, to make any appropriate recommendations. Any recommendations from the safety and health committee should be communicated to the appropriate persons for corrective action, included in the management review, and considered for continual improvement activities. [652:A.8.11]

A system should be established to promptly address and resolve the incident report findings and recommendations. [652:A.8.11]

Corrective actions resulting from investigations should be implemented in all areas where there is a risk of similar incidents and subsequently checked to avoid repetition of injuries and incidents that gave rise to the investigation. [652:A.8.11]

Reports produced by external investigation agencies should be acted upon in the same manner as internal investigations. [652:A.8.11]

Incident investigation reports should be made available to affected employees and their representatives at no cost. [652:A.8.11]

A.40.14.1 Events where there are injuries, equipment damage, or significant business interruption are subject to investigation. [652:A.8.11.1]

In addition to investigation of fires and explosions, it is also a good practice to investigate near misses (events that could have resulted in fires or explosions under different circumstances) and all activations of active fire and explosion mitigation systems. It is important to educate facility personnel on the concept of what a near miss is and to clearly communicate their responsibility for reporting both incidents and near misses. [652:A.8.11.1]

Near-miss events often indicate an underlying problem that should be corrected. See NFPA 654 for additional information. Barriers to reporting should be removed, as described in ANSI/AIHA Z10, *Occupational Health and Safety Management Systems*. Investigations should include workers and their representatives, as appropriate. [652:A.8.11.1]

A.40.14.4 The term *affected personnel* is intended to include members of employee organizations such as safety committees and employee representatives of various types. [652:A.8.11.4]

A.40.15.1 It is essential to have thorough written documentation, as the slightest changes to procedures, processes, resources, staffing, and equipment, including equipment from suppliers, can have a dramatic impact on the overall hazard analysis. Change includes something as benign as process materials sourcing from a different manufacturer, the same raw material manufacturer using new methods to produce the product, or changes in formulation. These changes from a supplier's end can impact the characteristics of the processes and materials. Individuals involved should include those involved in the process such as maintenance, engineering, and purchasing personnel, and all others as deemed necessary. Staffing and job tasks are not intended for shift changes, but for overall staff and their representative tasks. For reference, see the documentation form in ANSI/AIHA Z10, *Occupational Health and Safety Management Systems*. [652:A.8.12.1]

The following changes in material or process should warrant a management of change review per Section 40.15, and new samples should be collected and analyzed:

(1) New process equipment is installed that presents new hazards.
(2) New operating conditions for existing equipment create a new hazard.
(3) A new material is used in the process.

[652:A.8.12.1]

A.40.15.2(1) The proposed change and why it is needed should be described. It should include sufficient technical information to facilitate review by the approvers, address adverse effects that could occur, and describe how such effects would be mitigated by the proposed change. [652:A.8.12.2(1)]

A.40.15.2(2) Some fire and explosion protection systems introduce additional hazards into the process environment. These hazards can include, but are not limited to, energy in suppression canisters, asphyxiation hazards from inert gases, and mechanical laceration/amputation hazards from explosion isolation systems. While these are not fire or explosion hazards, they should be addressed as part of the management of change review per this document so that appropriate controls can be applied. [652:A.8.12.2(2)]

A.40.15.3 While implementation of the management of change procedure is not required for replacement in kind, it is critical that only qualified personnel are the ones who determine if the replacement is "in kind." These qualified personnel should be intimately familiar with the items listed in 40.15.2, as well as the broad scope of hazards associated with the particular process. [652:A.8.12.3]

Replacement "in kind" for raw materials. Care must be taken when substituting raw materials. There have been cases where a seemingly equivalent material substitution resulted in a large change in the process hazard. Not all safety properties of a material are characterized in, for example, an MSDS. Chemical composition might be identical, but quite different static ignition hazards due to bulk resistivity and charge relaxation rate can appreciably increase the hazard. Flowability differences can affect the hazard probability too. Differences in natural raw materials are generally less of a concern than manufactured materials in this regard. [652:A.8.12.3]

A.40.16 The creation and retention of documentation is necessary in order to implement and periodically evaluate the effectiveness of the management systems presented in this *Code*. Documentation in any form (e.g., electronic) should remain legible and be readily identifiable and accessible. The documentation should be protected against damage, deterioration, or loss, and retained for the applicable period specified in this *Code*. [652:A.8.13]

A.40.16.1(3) Incident investigation reports should be maintained for review during cyclical hazards evaluation reviews at least until the changes are incorporated in the dust hazards analysis and for compliance with other regulatory requirements. [652:A.8.13.1(3)]

A.40.16.1(5) Process and technology information includes process performance parameters, properties of the materials being handled, and documents such as design drawings, design codes and standards used as the basis for both the process and the equipment, equipment manufacturers' operating and maintenance manuals, standard operating procedures, and safety systems operation. [652:A.8.13.1(5)]

A.40.16.1(6) Management of change documents should be retained until the changes are incorporated into the next dust hazards analysis. [652:A.8.13.1(6)]

A.40.16.1(8) Contractor records typically include information such as the contract documentation with scope of work and necessary insurance coverage, the contractor's safety programs, records demonstrating the contractor's safety performance, qualifications and certifications necessary for the work to be done, periodic evaluations of the contractor's work performance, and records demonstrating that the employees of the contractor have been trained to safely perform the assigned work. [652:A.8.13.1(8)]

A.40.18 Effective employee participation is an essential element of the Occupational Health and Safety Management System (OHSMS) to achieve continuous improvement in risk reduction, as described in ANSI/AIHA Z10-2012, *Occupational Health and Safety Management Systems*. The OHSMS ensures that employees and their authorized representatives are involved, informed, and trained on all aspects of health associated with their work, including emergency arrangements. Employee participation includes items such as, but not limited to, the following:

(1) Involving employees and their authorized representatives, where they exist, in establishing, maintaining, and evaluating the OSHMS
(2) An occupational health and safety committee
(3) Access to safety and health information
(4) Risk assessment, implementation, and review of risk control measures
(5) Incident and near-miss investigations
(6) Inspections and audits
(7) Reporting unsafe conditions, tools, equipment, and practices
(8) Mentoring of new employees, apprentices, and for onsite orientation
(9) Identifying hazards with strong emphasis on high-risk jobs and the application of the hierarchy of controls
(10) In accordance with established and maintained procedures, appropriate arrangements to ensure that concerns, ideas, and input that employees and their representatives share are received, considered, and responded to
(11) Employees removing themselves from work situations that they have reasonable justification to believe present an imminent and serious danger to their safety or health

[652:A.8.15]

Employees who justifiably take those actions by notifying their supervisor should be protected from discrimination by removing those barriers as outlined in the OHSMS. [652:A.8.15]

Where this *Code* and annex refer to employees and their representatives (where representatives exist), the intention is that they should be consulted as the primary means to achieve appropriate participation in the development and implementation of all aspects of the OHSMS. In some instances, it might be appropriate to involve all employees and all representatives. [652:A.8.15]

Employee participation is a key component of an OHSMS. When employees and their representatives are engaged and their contributions are taken seriously, they tend to be more satisfied and committed to the OHSMS, and the system is more effective. Engaging employees and their representatives in dialogue with management and each other about safety and health can lead to improved relationships, better overall communication, improved compliance, and reduced rates of injury, illness, and death. The improved morale translates to greater safety and health results. [652:A.8.15]

Employees and their representatives need to be trained about how the OHSMS works and to evaluate it periodically to determine whether improvements need to be made. The information needs to be presented in a form and language that employees and their representatives easily understand. *(See also A.40.14.4.)*

[652:A.8.15]

A.41.1.2(7) There are more detailed, and in some cases more stringent, requirements for torch-applied roofing found in Section 16.4 and NFPA 241. [51B:A.1.3.1(7)]

A.41.2.1 The Technical Committee on Hot Work Operations (NFPA 51B) recognizes that management might not always have expertise in hot work and, therefore, would need a knowledgeable designated agent or contractor to act on its behalf. Examples of those who might not have the expertise can include owners of small retail shops, a small apartment complex manager, or a grocery store owner who has no knowledge of hot work safe practices. [51B:A.4.1]

Management should ensure that the contractor has evidence of financial responsibility, which can take the form of an insurance certificate or other document attesting to coverage or responsibility. [51B:A.4.1]

A.41.2.2.1 Other special hazards can include, but are not limited to, lead, noise, and radiation. Sometimes these special hazards require disposable outer garments that can catch fire. [51B:A.4.2.1]

A.41.2.2.3(1) Alternatives to hot work can include the following:

(1) Mechanical removal and relocation of frozen piping to a heated area
(2) Manual hydraulic shears
(3) Mechanical bolting
(4) Screwed, flanged, or clamped pipe
(5) Reciprocating saw
(6) Mechanical pipe cutter
(7) Approved self-drilling or compressed air-actuated fasteners

[51B:A.4.2.3(1)]

A.41.2.2.7 The inspection is usually made ½ hour after the completion of hot work to detect and extinguish possible smoldering fires. The inspector should be alert for circumstances that can require an extension of the final inspection interval. [51B:A.4.2.7]

A.41.2.4.1 The fire watch duties can be assigned to anyone who understands the hazard of the hot work being performed and the limitations placed on that hot work operation by the person issuing the hot work permit (PAI). The fire watch has the responsibility to make certain the hot work area is maintained in a fire-safe condition throughout performance of the hot work and has the authority to stop the hot work if unsafe conditions are observed. The fire watch must understand the basic hazards of any combustible construction involved with the hot work area, the fire exposure hazard that hot work creates to occupancies adjacent to or below the hot work operation, the hazards associated with the occupancy, and the need to maintain proper isolation of all hot work operations from combustible or flammable materials. The fire watch should also be properly trained in use of manual, portable fire extinguishers and emergency notification procedures within the facility. The fire watch is not a replacement for proper planning to prevent conditions that allow a fire to develop, regardless of the fire-fighting equipment available and the capabilities of the individuals involved. [51B:A.4.4.1]

A.41.2.4.4 The fire watch should have experience with test fires. [51B:A.4.4.4]

A.41.2.4.7 These tasks might include moving partitions relating to the hot work, sweeping in the immediate area, and minimal assistance to the operator. [51B:A.4.4.7]

Δ **A.41.2.5** The trend toward outsourcing facility maintenance and renovations can influence the risks associated with hot work. A contractor might have the technical expertise to perform hot work but is not likely to have a full understanding of fire prevention or of the specific combustible hazards within a client property. Additional safeguards to be considered include, but are not limited to, how the hot work should be isolated to prevent fire hazards; who will be assigned as the fire watch for the hot work operations; the facility emergency notification procedures; available manual fire-fighting tools (like portable fire extinguishers and small hose stations); identification of all areas where hot work is not allowed; connecting hot work equipment to existing utility systems (gas or electricity); and review of any requirements for completion of hot work by a certain time each day. [51B:A.4.5]

Hot work loss incidents involving contractors occur with regular frequency. For many of these incidents, facility management has not implemented a process for managing the fire hazards associated with the proposed contract work activity, views the contractor's personnel as the recognized subject matter experts, and is either ignorant of potential fire hazards with the planned contract activity or presumes the contractor is expert in all associated safety regulations and requirements and will address hazards accordingly. [51B:A.4.5]

A.41.3.1 At a work site, hazards other than hot work, such as radiation, lead, or noise, are often present. Any additional personal protective equipment (PPE) donned for protection against these other hazards should also be appropriate for hot work. Heavier materials, such as woolen clothing or heavy cotton, are preferable to lighter materials because they are more difficult to ignite. Cotton clothing, if used for protection, should be chemically treated to reduce its combustibility. Clothing treated with flame-resistant materials can lose some of its protective characteristics after repeated washing or cleaning. Materials that can melt and cause severe burns should not be used as clothing when the wearer will be welding or cutting. [51B:A.5.1]

Sparks can lodge in rolled-up sleeves, pockets of clothing, or cuffs of overalls or trousers. Therefore, it is recommended that sleeves and collars be kept buttoned and pockets be eliminated from the front of clothing. Where pockets are present, they should be emptied of flammable or readily combustible materials. Trousers or overalls should not have cuffs and should not be turned up on the outside. Trousers should overlap shoe tops to prevent spatter from getting inside shoes. [51B:A.5.1]

Frayed clothing is particularly susceptible to ignition and burning and should not be worn when welding or cutting. [51B:A.5.1]

A.41.3.3.2.2 An example of a hot work permit is shown in Figure A.41.3.3.2.2. This permit can be modified to suit local conditions. [51B:A.5.3.2.2]

Δ **A.41.3.4** For additional information on cutting and welding of containers that have held flammable materials, see NFPA 326 and AWS F4.1, *Safe Practices for the Preparation of Containers and Piping for Welding and Cutting and Allied Processes.* [51B:A.5.4]

Additional consideration should be given when hot work is performed in areas near the storage of large quantities of exposed, readily ignitable materials such as bulk sulfur, baled paper, or cotton. For additional information on welding and cutting in storage areas, refer to Chapter 34 and NFPA 655. [51B:A.5.4]

A.41.3.4(2) Precautions in addition to those in 41.3.5 for hot work performed during fire protection system impairments can include the following:

(1) Charged hose lines
(2) Additional fire extinguishers
(3) Fire department/brigade presence
(4) Discontinuation of hazardous operations
(5) Additional fire watch personnel
(6) Isolation of combustibles with a 30-minute fire-rated barrier
(7) More frequent inspections by the PAI
(8) Temporary fire detection
(9) Personnel stationed at manual fire protection release stations

[51B:A.5.4(2)]

A.41.3.4(3) Examples of explosive atmospheres include mixtures of flammable gases, vapors, liquids, or combustible dusts with air. [51B:A.5.4(3)]

A.41.3.5 The decision tree in Figure A.41.3.5 can be used to determine if a hot work permit is necessary. [51B:A.5.5]

N **A.41.3.5.1.2.1** One such listing includes ANSI/FM 4950, *American National Standard for Evaluating Welding Pads, Welding Blankets and Welding Curtains for Hot Work Operations.* [51B:5.5.1.2.1]

A.41.3.5.1.3 When hot work is performed at an elevated level, it should be noted that sparks or slag can fall at a trajectory and land farther than 35 ft (11 m) horizontally from a point directly under the hot work operator. [51B:A.5.5.1.3]

HOT WORK PERMIT

Seek an alternative/safer method if possible!

Before initiating hot work, ensure precautions are in place as required by NFPA 51B and ANSI Z49.1.
Make sure an appropriate fire extinguisher is readily available.

This Hot Work Permit is required for any operation involving open flame or producing heat and/or sparks. This work includes, but is not limited to, welding, brazing, cutting, grinding, soldering, thawing pipe, torch-applied roofing, or chemical welding.

Date _____	Hot work by ❏ employee ❏ contractor
Location/Building and floor _____	Name (print) and signature of person doing hot work _____
Work to be done _____	I verify that the above location has been examined, the precautions marked on the checklist below have been taken, and permission is granted for this work.
Time started _____ Time completed _____	Name (print) and signature of permit-authorizing individual (PAI)
THIS PERMIT IS GOOD FOR ONE DAY ONLY	_____

- ❏ Available sprinklers, hose streams, and extinguishers are in service and operable.
- ❏ Hot work equipment is in good working condition in accordance with manufacturer's specifications.
- ❏ Special permission obtained to conduct hot work on metal vessels or piping lined with rubber or plastic.

Requirements within 35 ft (11 m) of hot work
- ❏ Flammable liquid, dust, lint, and oily deposits removed.
- ❏ Explosive atmosphere in area eliminated.
- ❏ Floors swept clean and trash removed.
- ❏ Combustible floors wet down or covered with damp sand or fire-resistive/noncombustible materials or equivalent.
- ❏ Personnel protected from electrical shock when floors are wet.
- ❏ Other combustible storage material removed or covered with listed or approved materials (welding pads, blankets, or curtains; fire-resistive tarpaulins), metal shields, or noncombustible materials.
- ❏ All wall and floor openings covered.
- ❏ Ducts and conveyors that might carry sparks to distant combustible material covered, protected, or shut down.

Requirements for hot work on walls, ceilings, or roofs
- ❏ Construction is noncombustible and without combustible coverings or insulation.
- ❏ Combustible material on other side of walls, ceilings, or roofs is moved away.

Requirements for hot work on enclosed equipment
- ❏ Enclosed equipment is cleaned of all combustibles.
- ❏ Containers are purged of flammable liquid/vapor.
- ❏ Pressurized vessels, piping, and equipment removed from service, isolated, and vented.

Requirements for hot work fire watch and fire monitoring
- ❏ Fire watch is provided during and for a minimum of 30 min. after hot work, including any break activity.
- ❏ Fire watch is provided with suitable extinguishers and, where practical, a charged small hose.
- ❏ Fire watch is trained in use of equipment and in sounding alarm.
- ❏ Fire watch can be required in adjoining areas, above and below.
- ❏ Yes ❏ No   Per the PAI/fire watch, monitoring of hot work area has been extended beyond the 30 min.

© 2023 National Fire Protection Association   NFPA 51B

Δ **FIGURE A.41.3.3.2.2**   Sample of a Hot Work Permit. [51B:Figure A.5.3.2.2]

FIGURE A.41.3.5 Hot Work Permit Decision Tree. [51B: Figure A.5.5]

Decision tree steps:
1. Is there an acceptable alternative to hot work? — Yes → Complete job with cold work. No hot work permit is needed. No →
2. Can hot work be performed in a designated area (e.g., maintenance shop)? — Yes → Examine designated area, then complete hot work there. No hot work permit is needed. No →
3. Is the proposed work to be performed in a permit-required area (e.g., NOT in a maintenance shop)? — Yes → Obtain a written hot work permit. No →
4. Is the proposed work to be performed in a nonpermissible area? — Yes → Hot work and permit are not authorized. No →
5. Obtain a written hot work permit.

N **A.41.3.5.1.3.1** One such listing includes ANSI/FM 4950, *American National Standard for Evaluating Welding Pads, Welding Blankets and Welding Curtains for Hot Work Operations.* [51B:A.5.5.1.3.1]

N **A.41.3.5.1.6** One such listing includes ANSI/FM 4950, *American National Standard for Evaluating Welding Pads, Welding Blankets and Welding Curtains for Hot Work Operations.* [51B:A.5.5.1.6]

N **A.41.3.5.1.7** Where a wall or similar structure is noncombustible and is so large that the PAI determines that combustibles on the opposite side from where the hot work is being performed pose no risk of ignition, then the combustible materials need not be moved and a fire watch is not required. [51B:A.5.5.1.7]

A.41.3.5.1.12 Implementing precautions against accidental activation of automatic fire detection and suppression systems should occur near the hot work operation. For example, a wet rag could be laid over a sprinkler head or a detector could be individually disabled, covered, or removed. Any such precautions taken during hot work operations need to be removed when the hot work operation is complete. [51B:A.5.5.1.12]

Automatic sprinkler systems should not have the water supply shutoff during hot work operation. [51B:A.5.5.1.12]

A.41.3.5.1.14 Hot work operations that might fall into the category where the 35 Foot Rule could be enlarged include, but are not limited to, elevated hot work and windy areas. [51B:A.5.5.1.14]

A.41.3.5.1.15 Hot work operations that might fall into the category where the 35 Foot Rule could be reduced include, but are not limited to, torch soldering, gas tungsten arc welding, heat gun operations, and handheld pen-type soldering. [51B:A.5.5.1.15]

A.41.3.5.5 The time period between PAI inspections of the hot work area should not exceed 8 hours. [51B:A.5.5.5]

A.41.3.6.1 The decision tree in Figure A.41.3.6.1 can be used to determine if a fire watch is necessary. [51B:A.5.6.1]

A.41.3.6.1(1) Figure A.41.3.6.1(1)(a) and Figure A.41.3.6.1(1)(b) demonstrate the hot work 35 Foot Rule. [51B:A.5.6.1(1)]

A.41.3.6.2 An additional fire watch(es) might be necessary in certain situations, such as where hot work is performed near open shafts or at elevated heights or where sparks can travel through spaces such as openings. [51B:A.5.6.2]

A.41.3.6.3 The provision of additional hot work area monitoring should be determined based on conditions that will support hidden, smoldering fire conditions such as combustible construction, storage of bulk materials such as baled wastepaper or piled trash, or concealed spaces within building construction. [51B:A.5.6.3]

Hot work area monitoring can be provided by any of the following:

(1) Personnel working in the area
(2) Automatic smoke detection
(3) Security or maintenance rounds through the hot work area every 30 minutes
(4) Security cameras with smoke or fire detection capability

[51B:A.5.6.3]

A.41.3.7 For hot tapping on a gas pipeline, see ASME B31.8, *Gas Transmission and Distribution Piping Systems.* [51B:A.5.7]

For hot tapping on a liquid pipeline, see API RP 2201, *Safe Hot Tapping Practices in the Petroleum and Petrochemical Industries.* [51B:A.5.7]

A.41.4.1 A common example of a situation where Section 41.4 would apply is work performed in a single-dwelling home by a plumber sweating a pipe. Another example is the repair of a wrought iron railing used for steps in a single-dwelling home. A third example is welding performed on construction or agricultural equipment on site. The NFPA 51B committee recognizes that it is not always practical to have more than one individual present, and completing a job with one person is a common practice. The NFPA 51B committee stresses that it is always better to have more than one individual present to ensure fire safety but realizes that it is not always practical to do so. [51B:A.6.1]

A.41.5.5.2.3 The preferred location for cylinder storage is in an approved storage area outdoors. [51B:A.7.5.2.3]

A.42.2.1.3 See NFPA 2, NFPA 52, and NFPA 58 for requirements for facilities where only these fuels are dispensed. [30A:A.1.1.3]

Δ **A.42.3.3.1** PEI RP200, *Recommended Practices for Installation of Aboveground Storage Systems for Motor Vehicle Fueling*, provides information on proper installation, inspection, and maintenance of aboveground storage systems for motor vehicle fueling, including associated devices and components. The US

FIGURE A.41.3.6.1 Fire Watch Decision Tree. [51B:Figure A.5.6.1]

Environmental Protection Agency's regulation for Spill Prevention Control and Countermeasure (SPCC) Plans found in 40 CFR 112 provides additional requirements. [30A:A.4.3.2]

A.42.3.3.6.2 The top of the posts should be set not less than 3 ft (0.9 m) above ground and should be located not less than 5 ft (1.5 m) from the tank. Other approved means to protect tanks subject to vehicular damage include vehicle impact resistance testing such as that prescribed in UL 2085, *Protected Aboveground Tanks for Flammable and Combustible Liquids*, for protected aboveground tanks. [30A:A.4.3.7.2]

N **A.42.4.4.2** When testing with air, the pressure should be maintained at the initial pressure setting or within a range that can be accounted for by temperature changes held for a minimum of 1 hour. [30A:A.5.4.2]

A.42.5.3.6.1 Useful forms for documentation can be found in PEI RP500, *Recommended Practices for Inspection and Maintenance of Motor Fuel Dispensing Equipment*, and are available at www.pei.org/rp500. [30A:A.6.3.6.1]

A.42.5.3.6.2 See A.42.5.3.6.1. [30A:A.6.3.6.2]

A.42.5.6.2 The flow of fuel can be stopped by dispensers used in self-serve motor fuel dispensing facilities. The nozzle can be returned to the dispenser in the latched-open position. Subsequent activation of the dispenser would then immediately release fuel from the latched-open nozzle, creating a hazardous situation. [30A:A.6.6.2]

A.42.7.2.1 API RP 1621, *Bulk Liquid Stock Control at Retail Outlets*, provides information on this subject. [30A:A.9.2.1]

FIGURE A.41.3.6.1(1)(a) The 35 Foot Rule Illustrated. [51B:Figure A.5.6.1(1)(a)]

Callouts:
1. Close doors, seal floor openings, post copy of permit, shut down conveyers, and prevent general access.
2. If possible, position operator to redirect spatter during work, or add an additional fire curtain or equivalent.
3. Relocate combustible storage or separate with approved barriers (seal area below dividers) or cover with approved welding pads, blankets, curtains, or fire-resistive tarpaulins.
4. Position fire watch with suitable fire extinguishers to protect potential hazard area and equip fire watch with means for emergency communications.

35 ft (11 m)

FIGURE A.41.3.6.1(1)(b) Example of Where Multiple Fire Watches Are Needed. [51B:Figure A.5.6.1(1)(b)]

Callouts:
1. Application of 35 Foot Rule involving elevated work — additional safeguards will apply. Close doors, seal floor openings, post copy of permit, shut down conveyers, and prevent general access. Consider whether areas can be tented to contain spatter. PAI will determine how many additional fire watchers will be required.
2. If possible, position operator to redirect (limit) spatter during work.
3. Relocate combustible storage or separate with approved barriers (seal area below dividers) or cover with approved welding pads, blankets, curtains, or fire-resistive tarpaulins.
4. Equipment below might need to be protected.
5. Position fire watchers with suitable fire extinguishers to protect potential hazard areas and equip them with means for emergency communications.
6. The PAI can extend the 35 Foot Rule as necessary (e.g., because of wind or elevation).

35 ft (11 m)

2024 Edition   Shaded text = Revisions.   Δ = Text deletions and figure/table revisions.   • = Section deletions.   *N* = New material.

A.42.7.2.2.3.2 If the tank is situated in a dike, the dike wall meets this requirement. For secondary containment-type tanks, drainage, curbing, or other approved means can be used. [30A:A.9.2.2.3.2]

A.42.7.2.3.1 See Chapter 9 of NFPA 30 for further information. [30A:A.9.2.3.1]

A.42.7.2.5 Many fuel stations display items such as wood, bagged ground cover, cartons of consumable products, and other combustibles that create vision obstructions, excessive fire load, and other hazards in and around dispensing islands and pumps. [30A:A.9.2.5.6]

N **A.42.7.2.6.2** Examples include, but are not limited to, emergency generators, pumps, emergency vehicles, and refrigeration equipment. [30A:A.9.2.5.2]

A.42.7.2.6.3 This provision is not intended to prohibit a facility from having extra numbers or types of fire extinguishers provided that the code minimum rated portable fire extinguishers are provided at the specified travel distances. [30A:A.9.2.5.3]

A.42.7.2.6.5 The following language includes both the mandatory requirements and some optional text that could be used to comply with the requirements in 42.7.2.6.5:

WARNING

It is unlawful and dangerous to dispense gasoline into unapproved containers.
No smoking.
Stop motor.
No filling of portable containers in or on a motor vehicle.
Place container on ground before filling.
Discharge your static electricity before fueling by touching a metal surface away from the nozzle.
Before using pump, touch any metal on the car away from your vehicle's fuel filler with bare hand. This will discharge static electricity on your body. Failure to fully discharge may ignite gasoline vapors.
Do not re-enter your vehicle while gasoline is pumping. This can re-charge your body with static electricity. If you must re-enter your vehicle, discharge static electricity again before touching the pump nozzle.
If a fire starts, **do not** remove nozzle — back away immediately and tell attendant. If no attendant is on site, use the emergency shut-off button to stop pump.
Do not allow individuals under licensed age to use the pump.
Only persons of licensed age should use pump.
Keep children away from the pump area.
Do not allow children to use pump.

[30A:A.9.2.5.5]

A.42.7.5.6 Additional fire protection considerations can include fixed suppression systems, automatic fire detection, manual fire alarm stations, transmission of alarms to off-site locations, and limitation of the quantity of motor fuel delivered per transaction. [30A:A.9.5.6]

N **A.42.7.8.1.1** See A.7.1 of NFPA 30A.

N **A.42.7.8.2.3** The ground wire should never be attached to the chassis if welding a fender, as the electrical resistance between the two could be sufficient to cause a fire or personal injury. The monorail and hoist should not be used as the ground side for the same reason.

A.42.7.9.1 This requirement would apply whether or not the LNG tank was required to be drained. Management of the LNG tank could include the use of a "captive vent" that safely conducts the boil-off gas to the atmosphere at a safe location outside the building.

A.42.8.2.3 Not all fuels have equipment that is currently listed. As technology develops, this provision will allow the AHJs the latitude to approve systems and equipment that cannot be currently listed. [30A:A.12.2.3]

A.42.8.2.4 See A.42.8.2.3. [30A:A.12.2.4]

A.42.8.3.4 The selection of the 20 ft (6 m) separation distance between storage containers of different gaseous fuels is based on long-standing requirements in NFPA 2, NFPA 52, and NFPA 58. The separation distance between containers storing gaseous fuels and liquid motor fuel dispensers is based on the maximum 18 ft length of dispenser hose attached to the liquid fuel dispenser and the potential for a liquid pool fire to affect the gaseous fuel storage containers. [30A:A.12.3.4]

A.42.8.6.2 The designation of classes and divisions of classified locations is defined in Article 500 of *NFPA 70*. [30A:A.12.6.2]

A.42.9.2.2 Cases where the length of the supply line to dispensing devices would result in insufficient pressure for operational purposes or would increase the potential for leakage due to the increased number of fittings or exposure of the line can warrant location of the supply on the pier. [30A:A.11.2.2]

A.42.9.5.4 Due to the unique nature of both the wiring and marine fuel piping at a marina, the systems should be protected in the event either is damaged. Protection could consist of separation, physical barriers, or other means. The intent is to prevent damaged electrical wiring from becoming an ignition source in the event of a release of flammable liquid. [30A:A.11.5.4]

N **A.42.9.5.6** Examples include, but are not limited to, emergency generators, pumps, emergency vessels, and refrigeration equipment. [30A:A.11.5.6]

A.42.9.6.2 NFPA 77 contains information on this subject. [30A:A.8.5.2]

A.42.9.6.4 Where excessive stray currents are encountered, piping handling Class I and Class II liquids should be electrically isolated from the shore piping. This requirement prevents stray currents originating in the vessel's electrical system from causing an electrical arc or spark. [30A:A.11.6]

A.42.9.6.4.1 NFPA 77 contains information on this subject. [30A:A.11.6.1]

A.42.9.8.2 See Section 9.4 of NFPA 30 for further information. [30A:A.11.8.2]

A.42.10.2.1.3 The section on aircraft refueling hose has been altered extensively by referencing EI 1529. NFPA 407 formerly contained many requirements for hose, but these were intended to address only those features that could be related to a fire or the results of a fire. It was not until 1982 that a comprehensive aircraft refueling hose specification was published by the American Petroleum Institute (API). Prior to that time, NFPA 407 was the only document in existence that addressed this subject. In 2010, the API transferred responsibility for aviation fuel-handling standards to the Energy Institute (EI). [407:A.4.1.4]

EI 1529 deals with all aspects of hose safety, including the couplings that are acceptable. [407:A.4.1.4]

NFPA 407 recognizes the need for an extensive document such as EI 1529 and requires hoses that meet that standard. However, it is important to recognize that EI does not perform testing and that it does not regulate those manufacturers who claim to sell hose that meets EI 1529. The hose user and the cognizant authority having jurisdiction could find it prudent to require hose manufacturers to produce copies of test reports or documents that certify that hoses of identical construction and compounds have been tested and have passed all requirements of EI 1529 satisfactorily. [407:A.4.1.4]

N **A.42.10.2.1.3.3.6** Splicing of a hose with couplings alters the design bend radius of the hose, creating two kinks when the hose is wound on a drum. [407:A.4.1.4.3.6]

A.42.10.2.1.4.9 The charge on the fuel can be reduced by the use of a static dissipater additive that increases the electrical conductivity of the fuel and thereby allows the charge to relax or dissipate more quickly, or by the use of a relaxation chamber that increases the residence time of the fuel downstream of the filter to at least 30 seconds, thereby allowing most of the charge to dissipate before the fuel arrives at the receiving tank. [407:A.4.1.5.9]

API RP 2003 recommends a 30-second relaxation time for loading tank trucks and refuelers. However, it has not been a common practice to require a similar relaxation time for aircraft refueling, primarily because of the relatively few electrostatic incidents that have occurred during aircraft fueling. (For additional information on this topic, see CRC Report No. 583.) [407:A.4.1.5.9]

In filling tank trucks or storage tanks, API RP 2003 recommends that at least 30 seconds of residence time be provided downstream of a filter in order to allow static charges generated in flowing fuel to relax before fuel enters the tank. [407:A.4.1.5.9]

The reason it is possible to fuel aircraft safely with low conductivity fuel without providing 30 seconds of relaxation time is due primarily to the difference in the geometry of aircraft tanks as compared with tank truck compartments. Flow into the aircraft normally is subdivided into several tanks simultaneously and also distributed into adjoining compartments of each tank by a multihole inlet. Bachman and Dukek (1972) conducted full-scale research using a simulated large aircraft tank and concluded that none of the tanks or compartments hold sufficient fuel to allow enough charges to accumulate and create large surface voltages. Slower fill rates per compartment also allow more charge to relax. [407:A.4.1.5.9]

Additionally, the inlet system of most aircraft tanks directs fuel toward the bottom of the tank to avoid splashing that generates more charge. Finally, while the hoses that connect the fueler to the aircraft provide only a few seconds of residence time for charge relaxation at high rates of flow, the actual relaxation volume in the system is significantly greater where a coated screen is used as a second stage water barrier. In this case, the vessel's volume after the first stage filter coalescer could represent an additional 15 seconds of residence time for charge relaxation. (The coated screen, unlike other water barriers, does not generate charge.) [407:A.4.1.5.9]

A flammable vapor space in the tank due to the presence of JET B or JP-4 fuels still constitutes a potential hazard. Therefore, to minimize the chance for static ignition, FAA regulations require that fueling be conducted at half of the rated flow where civil aircraft have used such fuels. [407:A.4.1.5.9]

A.42.10.2.1.6.1 Carbon dioxide extinguishers should not be selected due to their limited range and effectiveness in windy conditions. [407:A.4.1.10.1]

A.42.10.2.1.6.3 Multipurpose dry chemical (ammonium phosphate) fire-extinguishing agent is known to cause corrosion to aircraft components. Although the agent is capable of extinguishing fires on or near aircraft, it is likely that the agent will spread to other, uninvolved aircraft, causing damage from corrosion. [407:A.4.1.10.3]

A.42.10.2.1.8.2 The beam of radar equipment has been known to cause ignition of flammable vapor–air mixtures from inductive electric heating of solid materials or from electrical arcs or sparks from chance resonant conditions. The ability of an arc to ignite flammable vapor–air mixtures depends on the total energy of the arc and the time lapse involved in the arc's duration, which is related to the dissipation characteristics of the energy involved. The intensity or peak power output of the radar unit, therefore, is a key factor in establishing safe distances between the radar antenna and fueling operations, fuel storage or fuel loading rack areas, fuel tank truck operations, or any operations where flammable liquids and vapors could be present or created. [407:A.4.1.12.2]

Most commercially available weather-mapping airborne radar equipment operates at peak power outputs, varying from 25 kW to 90 kW. Normally this equipment should not be operated on the ground. Tests have shown that the beam of this equipment can induce energy capable of firing flash bulbs at considerable distances. If the equipment is operated on the ground for service checking or for any other reason, the beam should not be directed toward any of the hazards described in the previous paragraph that are located within 30 m (100 ft). Higher power radar equipment can require greater distances. [407:A.4.1.12.2]

Airport surface detection radar operates under a peak power output of 50 kW. It is fixed rather than airborne equipment. [407:A.4.1.12.2]

Airborne surveillance radar of the type currently carried on military aircraft has a high peak power output. Aircraft carrying this type of radar can be readily distinguished by radomes atop or below the fuselage, or both. [407:A.4.1.12.2]

Aircraft warning radar installations are the most powerful. Most of these installations are, however, remotely located from the hazards specified in the first paragraph and therefore are not covered herein. Ground radar for approach control or traffic pattern surveillance is considered the most fire hazardous type of radar normally operating at an airport. The latter type of equipment has a peak power output of 5 MW. Where possible, new installations of this type of equipment should be located at least 150 m (500 ft) from any of the hazards described in the first paragraph. [407:A.4.1.12.2]

A.42.10.2.2.1.1 Records should be kept of personnel training. These records should be made available to the authority having jurisdiction upon request. [407:A.4.2.2.1]

A.42.10.2.2.1.2 Fuel servicing personnel should be given adequate training with extinguishers so that such equipment is used effectively in an emergency. Such training should be given on fires of the type that could be encountered on the job. To ensure prompt action in the event of a spill or other hazardous condition developing during fueling operations, aircraft servicing personnel also should be trained in the operation of emergency fuel shutoff controls. Each new fuel servicing employee should be given indoctrination training covering these and similar safety essentials that are related to the job. Follow-up and advanced training should be given as soon as the employee is sufficiently acquainted with the work to benefit from such training. Supervisors should be given training in the more technical aspects of fire safety so that they understand the reason for these and similar requirements and have an appreciation for the responsibility of a supervisor and the safety of an operation. [407:A.4.2.2.2]

A.42.10.2.2.2 The following actions are appropriate in the event of a fuel spill, although each spill should be treated as an individual case due to such variables as the size of the spill, type of flammable or combustible liquid involved, wind and weather conditions, equipment arrangement, aircraft occupancy, emergency equipment, and personnel available:

(1) The flow of fuel should be stopped, if possible. If the fuel is discovered leaking or spilling from fuel servicing equipment or hoses, the emergency fuel shutoff should be operated at once. If the fuel is discovered leaking or spilling from the aircraft at the filler opening, vent line, or tank seams during fueling operations, fueling should be stopped immediately. Evacuation of the aircraft should be ordered when necessary. The aircraft then should be thoroughly checked for damage or entrance of flammable liquid or vapors into any concealed wing or fuselage area, and corrective action should be taken as necessary before it is returned to normal operational service.

(2) The airport fire crew should be notified if the spill presents a fire hazard. The only routine exceptions are for small spills. Supervisory personnel should be notified to ensure that operations in progress can be continued safely or halted until the emergency is past and that corrective measures can be taken to prevent recurrence of a similar accident.

(3) It could be necessary to evacuate the aircraft if the spill poses a serious fire exposure to the aircraft or its occupants. Walking through the liquid area of the fuel spill should not be permitted. Persons who have been sprayed with fuel or had their clothing soaked with fuel should go to a place of refuge, remove their clothing, and wash. Individuals whose clothing has been ignited should be wrapped in blankets, coats, or other items or should be told to or forced to roll on the ground.

(4) Mobile fueling equipment and all other mobile equipment should be withdrawn from the area or left as is until the spilled fuel is removed or made safe. No fixed rule can be made as fire safety varies with circumstances. Shutting down equipment or moving vehicles can provide a source of ignition if no fire immediately results from the spillage.

(5) Aircraft, automotive, or spark-producing equipment in the area should not be started before the spilled fuel is removed or made safe. If a vehicle or cart engine is running at the time of the spill, it normally is good practice to drive the vehicle away from the hazard area unless the hazard to personnel is judged too severe. Fuel servicing vehicles or carts in operation at the time of the spill should not be moved until a check is made to verify that any fuel hose that could have been in use or connected between the vehicle and the aircraft is safely stowed.

(6) If any aircraft engine is operating at the time of the spill, it normally is good practice to move the aircraft away from the hazard area unless air currents set up by operating power plants would aggravate the extent or the nature of the existing vapor hazard.

(7) If circumstances dictate that operating internal combustion engine equipment within a spill area that has not ignited should be shut down, engine speeds should be reduced to idle prior to cutting ignition in order to prevent backfire.

(8) The volatility of the fuel can be a major factor in the initial severity of the hazard created by a spill. Gasoline and other low flash point fuels at normal temperatures and pressures produce vapors that are capable of forming ignitable mixtures with the air near the surface of the liquid, whereas this condition does not normally exist with kerosene fuels (JET A or JET A-1) except where ambient temperatures are 38°C (100°F) or above or where the liquid has been heated to a similar temperature.

(9) Spills of gasoline and low flash point turbine fuels (JET B) greater than 3 m (10 ft) in any dimension and covering an area of over 5 m^2 (50 ft^2) or that are of an ongoing nature should be blanketed or covered with foam. The nature of the ground surface and the existing exposure conditions dictate the exact method to be followed. Such fuels should not be washed down sewers or drains. The decision to use a sewer or drain should be made only by the chief of the airport fire brigade or the fire department. If fuels do enter sewers, either intentionally or unintentionally, large volumes of water should be introduced to flush such sewers or drains as quickly as possible to dilute the flammable liquid content of the sewer or drain to the maximum possible extent. Normal operations involving ignition sources (including aircraft and vehicle operations) should be prohibited on surface areas adjacent to open drains or manholes from which flammable vapors could issue due to the introduction of liquids into the sewer system until it can be established that no flammable vapor–air mixture is present in the proximity. (NOTE: NFPA 415 provides further information on aircraft fueling ramp drainage designs to control the flow of fuel that could be spilled on a ramp and to minimize the resulting possible danger.)

(10) Spills of kerosene grades of aviation fuels (JET A or JET A-1) greater than 3 m (10 ft) in any dimension and covering an area of over 5 m^2 (50 ft^2) or that are of an ongoing nature and that have not ignited should be blanketed or covered with foam if there is danger of ignition. If there is no danger of ignition, an absorbent compound or an emulsion-type cleaner can be used to clean the area. Kerosene does not evaporate readily at normal temperatures and should be cleaned up. Smaller spills can be cleaned up using an approved, mineral type, oil absorbent.

(11) Aircraft on which fuel has been spilled should be inspected thoroughly to ensure that no fuel or fuel vapors have accumulated in flap well areas or internal wing sections not designed for fuel tankage. Any cargo, baggage, express, mail sacks, or similar items that have been

wetted by fuel should be decontaminated before being placed aboard any aircraft. [**407**:A.4.2.3]

N **A.42.10.2.2.4** Hydrocarbon fuels, such as aviation gasoline and JET A, generate electrostatic charge when passing through the pumps, filters, and piping of a fuel transfer system. (The primary electrostatic generator is the filter/separator that increases the level of charge on a fuel by a factor of 100 or more as compared with pipe flow.) Splashing, spraying, or free-falling of the fuel further enhances the charge. When charged fuel arrives at the receiving tank (cargo tank or aircraft fuel tank), one of two possible events will occur:

(1) The charge will relax harmlessly to ground.
(2) If the charge or the fuel is sufficiently high, a spark discharge can occur. Whether or not an ignition follows depends on the energy (and duration) of the discharge and the composition of the fuel-air mixture in the vapor space (i.e., whether or not it is in the flammable range).

[**407**:A.4.2.5]

The amount of charge on a fuel when it arrives at the receiving tank, and hence its tendency to cause a spark discharge, depends on the nature and amount of impurities in the fuel, its electrical conductivity, the nature of the filter media (if present), and the relaxation time of the system [i.e., the residence time of the fuel in the system between the filter (separator) and the receiving tank]. The time needed for this charge to dissipate is dependent upon the conductivity of the fuels; it could be a fraction of a second or several minutes. [**407**:A.4.2.5]

No amount of bonding or grounding prevents discharges from occurring inside a fuel tank. Bonding ensures that the fueling equipment and the receiving tank (aircraft or fueler) are at the same potential and provides a path for the charges separated in the fuel transfer system (primarily the filter/separator) to combine with and neutralize the charges in the fuel. Also, in overwing fueling and in top loading of cargo tanks, bonding ensures that the fuel nozzle or the fill pipe is at the same potential as the receiving tank, so that a spark does not occur when the nozzle or fill pipe is inserted into the tank opening. For this reason, the bonding wire has to be connected before the tank is opened. [**407**:A.4.2.5]

Grounding during aircraft fueling or fuel servicing vehicle loading is no longer required because of the following:

(1) Grounding does not prevent sparking at the fuel surface (*see NFPA 77*).
(2) Grounding is not required by NFPA 77.
(3) The static wire might not be able to conduct the current in the event of an electrical fault in the ground support equipment connected to the aircraft and could constitute an ignition source if the wire fuses. If ground support equipment is connected to the aircraft or if other operations are being conducted that necessitate electrical earthing, separate connections should be made for this purpose. Static electrical grounding points can have high resistance and, therefore, are unsuitable for grounding. For a more complete discussion of static electricity in fuels, see NFPA 77.

[**407**:A.4.2.5]

A.42.10.2.2.4.3.1 Ordinary plastic funnels or other nonconducting materials can increase static generation. The use of chamois as a filter is extremely hazardous. [**407**:A.4.2.5.3.1]

A.42.10.2.2.6.1 Portable fire extinguishers for ramps where fueling operations are conducted are intended to provide an immediate means of fire protection in an area likely to contain a high concentration of personnel and valuable equipment. The prominent and strategic positioning of portable fire extinguishers is essential for them to be of maximum value in the event of an emergency. Extinguishers should not be located in probable spill areas. For normal single parking configurations, extinguishers specified for protection of fuel servicing operations should be located along the fence, at terminal building egress points, or at emergency remote control stations of airport fixed-fuel systems. To provide accessibility from adjoining gates, particularly where more than one unit is specified, extinguishers can be permitted to be located approximately midway between gate positions. Where this is done, the maximum distance between extinguishers should not be over 60 m (200 ft). Where the specified extinguishers are not located along the fence but are brought into the servicing area prior to the fueling operation, they should be located upwind not over 30 m (100 ft) from the aircraft being serviced. For protection of fuel servicing of aircraft that are double parked or triple parked, extinguishers should be located upwind not over 30 m (100 ft) from the aircraft being serviced. [**407**:A.4.2.7.1]

A.42.10.2.2.6.2 During inclement weather, extinguishers not in enclosed compartments can be permitted to be protected by canvas or plastic covers. [**407**:A.4.2.7.2]

A.42.10.2.2.8 Failure of an aircraft fueling hose in service is a potential source of fuel spillage and a potential fire hazard. The principal reasons for failure of aircraft fueling hoses include the following:

(1) Using damaged hoses
(2) Using aged hoses
(3) Exceeding hose pressure limits
(4) Installing hoses improperly

[**407**:A.4.2.9]

A.42.10.2.2.8.5.1 Particular attention should be paid to the 305 mm (12 in.) adjacent to the couplings. These areas are prone to premature failure. [**407**:A.4.2.9.5.1]

A.42.10.2.2.9 Establishing precise rules for fueling is impossible when the electrical storms are in the vicinity of the airport. The distance of the storm from the airport, the direction in which it is traveling, and its intensity are all factors to be weighed in making the decision to suspend fueling operations temporarily. Experience and good judgment are the best guides. Sound travels approximately 322 m/sec ($\frac{1}{5}$ mi/sec). The approximate number of miles to the storm can be determined by counting the seconds between a flash of lightning and the sound of thunder and dividing by 5. [**407**:A.4.2.10]

Δ **A.42.10.2.2.10.1.3** The precautions in 42.10.2.2.11.1.3 and 42.10.2.2.11.1.4 are intended to minimize the danger of the ignition of any flammable vapors discharged during fueling and of fuel spills by sources of ignition likely to be present in airport terminal buildings. [**407**:A.4.2.11.1.3]

A.42.10.2.2.11.1 Electric hand lamps used in the immediate proximity of the fueling operation should be of the type approved for use in *NFPA 70*, Class I, Division 1, Group D hazardous locations. No supportable basis exists for requiring, in the petroleum industry, the use of approved, listed, or permitted two- or three-cell flashlights to avoid igniting Class I, Group D vapors. [**407**:A.4.2.12.1]

A.42.10.2.2.11.1.2 Aircraft ground-power generators should be located as far as practical from aircraft fueling points and tank vents to reduce the danger of igniting flammable vapors that could be discharged during fueling operations at sparking contacts or on hot surfaces of the generators. [**407**:A.4.2.12.1.2]

A.42.10.2.2.11.1.5 For further information on intrinsically safe apparatus, see UL 913, FM Approval 3610, or UL 60079-11. [**407**:A.4.2.12.1.5]

A.42.10.3.1.2.1 Where pressure tanks are used, details on construction, spacing, and location should be in accordance with industry good practice and approved by the authority having jurisdiction. When AVGAS, MOGAS, or JET B turbine fuels are stored in bulk quantities in aboveground tanks, they should be stored in floating roof-type tanks. Covered floating roof tanks minimize the hazardous flammable vapor–air space above the liquid level. The vapor spaces of underground tanks storing fuels should not be interconnected. [**407**:A.5.1.2.1]

Δ **A.42.10.3.1.3.14** Flanged connections should be provided for ease of dismantling and to avoid cutting and welding after the system has been placed in service. The location of these isolation devices depends upon the size and character of each system, but the following locations generally apply (*see Figure A.42.10.3.1.3.14*):

(1) At each storage tank
(2) At each pump
(3) At each filter separator
(4) At each hydrant or on each hydrant lateral
(5) At each flow regulator or pressure control valve

[**407**:A.5.1.3.14]

A.42.10.3.1.3.17 Cathodic protection is recommended for metal components of airport fueling systems and fuel storage facilities that are in contact with the ground. The two types of cathodic protection are as follows:

(1) Galvanic anode method, which generates its own current
(2) Impressed current method, which has an external current source

[**407**:A.5.1.3.17]

A.42.10.3.1.6.1 Deadman controls should be designed so that the operator can use them comfortably while wearing gloves and hold them for the time needed to complete the operation. A pistol grip deadman device that is squeezed to operate is preferable to a small button that needs to be held by a thumb or finger. [**407**:A.5.1.7.1]

Note: No dimensional relationship exists between elements in this figure. Refer to this standard; NFPA 30, *Flammable and Combustible Liquids Code*; NFPA 70, *National Electrical Code*; and FAA Regulations for separations and clearances.

Key:
1. Check valve at tank inlet
2. Isolation valve at tank inlet/outlet
3. Pumping system
4. Pump discharge control valve or hydrant system shutoff valve (alternate location)
5. Hydrant system shutoff valve (alternate location)
6. Hydrant shutoff valve
7. Hydrant pit valve
8. Hydrant fueling servicing vehicle
9. Emergency fuel shutoff station
10. Valve box
11. Hydrant pit

N **FIGURE A.42.10.3.1.3.14** Typical Fixed Airport Fueling System Isolation Valving Operating and Emergency Controls.[**407**:Figure A.5.1.3.14]

A.42.10.3.1.6.2.2 The overshoot of pressure control release, V_{max}, should be calculated by the following equation:

$$V_{max} = Q \times 1 \text{ min} \times 0.05 \qquad [A.42.10.3.1.6.2.2]$$

where:
Q = actual fuel flow rate, L/min (gal/min)

Example

If the actual fuel flow rate at the time of deadman control release is 1500 L/min (400 gpm), total overshoot must not exceed 75 L/min (20 gal/min). [**407**:A.5.1.7.2.2]

A.42.10.3.1.6.3 Hydrant valves and couplers should be in accordance with EI 1584. [**407**:A.5.1.7.3]

A.42.10.3.1.6.5 Where surge suppressors are necessary, they should be located so that exposure to vehicular traffic, weather conditions, and the result of accidental rupture is minimized. [**407**:A.5.1.7.5]

N **A.42.10.3.1.8.2** The following times should be considered reasonable fuel shutoff times for certain diameter valves. This information is based on testing double block and bleed valves.

(1) 10 in. and smaller-diameter valves = 29 seconds
(2) 12 in.-diameter valves = 41 seconds
(3) 14 in. and larger-diameter valves = 45 seconds

[**407**:A.5.1.9.2]

A.42.10.3.1.8.4 Fuel transfer by pumping is the more common procedure and normally is preferred from a fire protection standpoint, since it allows rapid shutdown of fuel flow through pump shutdown. Gravity transfer is the simplest method but normally is limited to relatively low flow rates. Because the static head does exert some pressure in the system, a safety shutdown should include a valve or valves located as close to the tank as practicable. [**407**:A.5.1.9.4]

A.42.10.3.1.8.6 The operation of the emergency shutoff control should sound an alarm at the airport fire crew station and at the fuel storage facility. [**407**:A.5.1.9.6]

N **A.42.10.3.1.9** Fire extinguishers with a rated discharge of at least 0.4536 kg/sec (1 lb/sec) in accordance with the requirements of NFPA 10 should be considered. [**407**:A.5.1.10]

N **A.42.10.3.1.9.1** The locations of fire extinguishers at fixed sites can be combined. For example, two loading racks on opposite sides of a fueling island can share one fire extinguisher mounted on the island. [**407**:A.5.1.10.1]

A.42.10.3.2.1 The airport perimeter fence can be sufficient to meet this requirement. [**407**:A.5.2.1]

A.42.10.4.1.3.12.2.3 An optional precaution against misfueling of aircraft fuel servicing tank vehicles is to equip the coupler and truck fitting with coded lugs or a mechanical device to ensure product selection and to prevent mixing of products. This might not be feasible on over-the-road-type tank vehicles. [**407**:A.6.1.3.12.2.3]

A.42.10.4.1.5.4 Electrical equipment contained in aircraft fuel servicing vehicles or cart engine compartments and located 460 mm (18 in.) or more above ground can be permitted to be of the general-purpose type. [**407**:A.6.1.6.4]

A.42.10.4.1.6.1 See A.42.10.3.1.7.1. [**407**:A.6.1.7.1]

A.42.10.4.1.6.4.2 See A.42.10.3.1.7.2.2. [**407**:A.6.1.7.4.2]

N **A.42.10.4.1.9** Fire extinguishers with a rated discharge of at least 0.4536 kg/sec (1 lb/sec) in accordance with the requirements of NFPA 10 should be considered. [**407**:A.6.1.10]

A.42.10.4.1.9.8.1 It is not the intent of 42.10.4.1.9.8.1 to prohibit 12 V power outlets. The intent is to prohibit glowing elements. [**407**:A.6.1.10.8.1]

A.42.10.4.1.12.1 Wherever possible, flexible engine exhaust pipe should be avoided due to the potential of breaking. Where used, stainless steel is preferable, and the length should be limited to approximately 460 mm (18 in.). [**407**:A.6.1.13.1]

A.42.10.4.1.12.7 The requirement for spark-arresting exhaust systems is not intended to extend to diesel engines equipped with turbochargers. The USDA Forest Service, the governmental body that regulates the spark arrester standard, clearly identifies that all diesel engines with a turbocharger and no waste gate (also clearly identified therein) are exempt from the requirements to have an additional spark-arresting device. [**407**:A.6.1.13.7]

A.42.10.4.2.1.3 The use of tunnels or enclosed roadways is discouraged. Where there is no alternate route, and the fuel servicing vehicle requires the use of a tunnel or enclosed roadway, the authority having jurisdiction should examine the following considerations:

(1) Length
(2) Clearances
(3) Fixed fire suppression or extinguishing systems
(4) Frequency of use
(5) Ventilation
(6) Overlying structures and operations
(7) Other traffic
(8) Fire department access
(9) Emergency egress
(10) Drainage
(11) Other conditions

[**407**:A.6.2.1.3]

A.42.10.4.2.4.4 The size of the DPF regeneration area depends on the equipment being used (fleet size). The authority having jurisdiction should designate the size and number of DPF regeneration pads and determine whether a centralized facility is advantageous. [**407**:A.6.2.10.4]

N **A.42.10.6.1.5** Fire extinguishers with a rated discharge of at least 0.4536 kg/sec (1 lb/sec) in accordance with the requirements of NFPA 10 should be considered. [**407**:A.8.1.10]

A.42.11.1.1 Natural gas is a flammable gas. It is colorless, tasteless, and nontoxic. It is a light gas, weighing about two-thirds as much as air. As used in the systems covered by NFPA 52, it tends to rise and diffuses rapidly in air when it escapes from the system. [**52**:A.1.1]

Natural gas burns in air with a luminous flame. At atmospheric pressure, the ignition temperature of natural gas–air mixtures has been reported to be as low as 900°F (482°C). The flammable limits of natural gas–air mixtures at atmospheric pressure are about 5 percent to 15 percent by volume natural gas. [**52**:A.1.1]

Natural gas is nontoxic but can cause anoxia (asphyxiation) when it displaces the normal 21 percent oxygen in air in a confined area without adequate ventilation. [**52:**A.1.1]

The concentrations at which flammable or explosive mixtures form are much lower than the concentration at which asphyxiation risk is significant. [**52:**A.1.1]

NFPA 704 rating is as follows:

(1) Health — 0
(2) Flammability — 4
(3) Reactivity — 0
(4) Special — None
[**52:**A.1.1]

Cryogenic fluids are gases that have been liquefied by having their temperature brought below –130°F (–90°C). They are typically stored at low pressures in vacuum jacketed containers. Some of the potential hazards of cryogenic fluids are the following:

(1) Extreme cold that freezes or damages human skin on contact and can embrittle metals
(2) Extreme pressure resulting from rapid vaporization of the fluid during a leak or release of the cryogenic fluid
(3) Asphyxiation resulting from a release of the cryogenic fluid that vaporizes and displaces air
[**52:**A.1.1]

Personnel handling cryogenic fluids should use the protective clothing prescribed on the material safety data sheet (MSDS). This clothing typically includes heavy leather gloves, aprons, and eye protection. [**52:**A.1.1]

A.42.11.1.1.3 Current DOT specifications do not address the use of cylinders that are approved for the transportation of natural gas to be used in CNG service. [**52:**A.15.4.3.1.5]

The following Compressed Gas Association publications are relevant cylinder inspection standards:

(1) CGA C-6, *Standard for Visual Inspection of Steel Compressed Gas Cylinders*
(2) CGA C-6.1, *Standard for Visual Inspection of High Pressure Aluminum Compressed Gas Cylinders*
(3) CGA C-6.2, *Standard for Visual Inspection and Requalification of Fiber Reinforced High Pressure Cylinders*
(4) CGA C-10, *Guideline to Prepare Cylinders and Tubes for Gas Service and Changes in Gas*
[**52:**A.15.4.3.1.5]

The Compressed Gas Association publication CGA C-6.4, *Methods for External Visual Inspection of Natural Gas Vehicle (NGV) and Hydrogen Gas Vehicle (HGV) Fuel Containers and Their Installations*, is specified in CSA/ANSI NGV 2, *Compressed natural gas vehicle fuel containers*, as appropriate for CNG container inspection.

[**52:**A.15.4.3.1.5]

A.42.11.3 For information on on-site storage of LNG in ASME tanks larger than 70,000 gal (265 m³) and in tanks built to API or other standards, see NFPA 59A.

Prior to the time NFPA 52 was developed, the use of LNG as an aviation fuel, fueling site liquefaction facilities, and the use of residential LNG fueling facilities were not being considered actively. The NFPA 52 committee intends to provide coverage for these applications at the appropriate time.

A.42.12.1 This section addresses mobile fueling activities governed by NFPA 30A. Other local, state, and federal requirements are applicable. [**30A:**A.14.1]

A.42.12.2.3 The safety and emergency response plan is intended to be completed, maintained, and updated by the mobile fueling operator to help ensure that fueling operations are conducted in a safe manner that is acceptable to the AHJ. Such a plan might include some or all of the following elements:

(1) Written safety and emergency response plan that establishes policies and procedures for fire safety, spill prevention and control, personnel training, and compliance with other applicable requirements of this *Code*.
(2) Where required by the AHJ, a site plan for each location at which mobile fueling occurs. The site plan should be in sufficient detail to indicate all buildings, structures, lot lines, property lines, and appurtenances on site and their use or function; all uses adjacent to the lot lines of the site; fueling locations, the locations of all storm drain openings, and adjacent waterways or wetlands; information regarding slope, natural drainage, curbing, impounding, and how a spill will be retained upon the site property; and the scale of the site plan.
(3) If the AHJ does not require site plans of approved fueling locations, the safety and emergency response plan should include guidelines for locations within the jurisdiction where mobile fueling can and cannot be provided, such as on residential streets, on school grounds, and so on.
[**30A:**A.14.2.3]

A.42.12.2.4.1 In addition to any other training, education, and certifications that might be required by federal regulations and HAZCOM, the operator should also be trained on the requirements of this *Code*. [**30A:**A.14.2.4.1]

N **A.42.12.2.7.1** Because legacy and current building codes restrict motor fuel dispensing in certain parking structures, the original design of a building and the codes in effect at the time of construction, in addition to the existing conditions, should be considered prior to approving new operational activity. [**30A:**A.14.2.7.1]

N **A.42.12.2.7.2** Subsection 42.12.2.7.2 provides minimum requirements to conduct on-demand mobile fueling in aboveground open parking structures in accordance with 42.12.2.7.2.1. The authority having jurisdiction can require a mobile fueling operational permit to set forth further requirements and constraints due to local geography, culture, weather, and other considerations. In addition to the requirements in 42.12.2.7.2, mobile fueling operations should comply with all applicable local, state, and federal traffic safety requirements. [**30A:**A.14.2.7.2]

N **A.42.12.2.7.2.1** Where a jurisdiction does not have an adopted building code, the definition of *Open Parking Structure* in NFPA 88A can be used. [**30A:**A.14.2.7.2.1]

N **A.42.12.2.7.2.9** A ramp over a hose is sufficient to comply with 42.12.2.7.2.9. [**30A:**A.14.2.7.2.9]

N **A.42.12.2.7.2.12** Considerations for accessibility include, but are not limited to, an approved driving surface capable of supporting the fire apparatus, required turning radius, and reach of the aerial ladder. [**30A:**A.14.2.7.2.12]

A.42.12.2.9 Paragraph 42.12.2.9 provides minimum requirements to conduct on-demand mobile fueling on public roads and public ways. The AHJ can require a mobile fueling operational permit to set forth further requirements and constraints due to local geography, culture, weather, and other considerations. In addition to the requirements in 42.12.2.9, mobile fueling operations should comply with all applicable local, state, and federal traffic safety requirements. [**30A**:A.14.2.9]

A.42.12.2.9(2) A ramp over a hose is sufficient to comply with this requirement. [**30A**:A.14.2.9(2)]

Δ **A.42.12.3.1** In addition to the requirements in 42.12.3.1, mobile fueling vehicles should comply with all applicable local, state, and federal requirements, including DOT requirements for vehicles used to transport gasoline and diesel fuel. [**30A**:A.14.3.1]

A.42.12.4.5 The listed hose and nozzle assembly provides for bonding. However, where there is a plastic insert that prohibits an electrical/metallic connection with the customer vehicle while filling, then a separate means of bonding is required. [**30A**:A.14.4.5]

A.43.1.1 The risk to life and property because of the fire and explosion hazards of spray application of flammable and combustible materials varies depending on the arrangement and operation of the particular process and on the nature of the material being sprayed. The principal hazards addressed in this *Code* are those of the materials being sprayed: flammable and combustible liquids and combustible powders, as well as their vapors, mists, and dusts, and the highly combustible deposits and residues that result from their use. Properly designed, constructed, and ventilated spray areas are able to confine and control combustible residues, dusts, or deposits and to remove vapors and mists from the spray area and discharge them to a safe location, thus reducing the likelihood of fire or explosion. Likewise, accumulations of overspray residues, some of which are not only highly combustible but also subject to spontaneous ignition, can be controlled. [**33**:A.1.1]

The control of sources of ignition in spray areas and in areas where flammable and combustible liquids or powders are handled, together with constant supervision and maintenance, is essential to safe spray application operations. The human element requires careful consideration of the location of spray application operations and the installation of fire extinguishing systems so that the potential for spread of fire to other property and damage to property by extinguishing agent discharge is reduced. [**33**:A.1.1]

A.43.1.1.1 Refer to Figure A.43.1.1.1 for assistance in determining whether Chapter 43 applies to a particular spray application process. [**33**:A.1.1.1]

A.43.1.1.6(1) There are many industrial applications that involve routine use of small quantities of flammable or combustible liquids (e.g., coatings, lubricants, adhesives) on a regular or periodic basis. An example would be touch-up of manufactured articles using aerosol containers or small, portable spray application equipment. The intent of this provision is to allow such use without having to comply with the requirements of Chapter 43. [**33**:A.1.1.4]

A.43.1.1.6(2) Chapter 43 does not cover spray application operations that are conducted outdoors on buildings, bridges, tanks, or similar structures. These situations occur only occasionally for any given structure and overspray deposits are not likely to present a hazardous condition. Also, the space where there might be an ignitible vapor air or dust air mixture is very limited due to atmospheric dilution. [**33**:A.1.1.6]

A.43.1.1.6(3) The occasional use of portable spray equipment or aerosol spray containers is not likely to result in hazardous accumulations of overspray. Therefore, such operations are not within the scope of this *Code*. The following safeguards, however, should be observed:

(1) Adequate ventilation should be provided at all times, particularly where spray application is conducted in relatively small rooms or enclosures.
(2) Spray application should not be conducted in the vicinity of open flames or other sources of ignition. Either the spray operation should be relocated or the source of ignition should be removed or turned off.
(3) Containers of coating materials, thinners, or other hazardous materials should be kept tightly closed when not actually being used.
(4) Oily or coating-laden rags or waste should be disposed of promptly and in a safe manner at the end of each day's operations, due to the potential for spontaneous ignition.
(5) The same fundamental rules for area cleanliness and housekeeping that are required for industrial spray application operations should be observed.

[**33**:A.1.1.7]

Δ **FIGURE A.43.1.1.1 Decision Tree — Does Chapter 43 Apply?** [**33**:Figure A.1.1.1]

A.43.1.2.1 Fires involving spray application operations and processes can be expected to develop rapidly and to generate copious quantities of heat and smoke. In sprinklered buildings, such fires can also result in the operation of a greater-than-normal number of sprinklers. Operations and equipment should be arranged and located so that there is adequate egress for personnel and adequate access for fire-fighting operations.

Where spray application operations are extensive, they should be located in a separate building or in an area that is separated by fire-rated construction from all other operations or storage. [33:A.4.1]

N **A.43.1.2.2** The use of proper cutoff between hazards and exposures depends on many factors. Where the exposure hazard is high or severe, the authority having jurisdiction might require protection beyond the indicated 2-hour fire resistance rating.

A.43.1.2.3 Spray application operations that incorporate assembly lines or conveyor systems present special problems. If conveyor systems extend between separate buildings, a sprinklered, noncombustible, connecting passageway is advisable. If conveyor systems pass through floors, the openings should be surrounded by deep [greater than 18 in. (460 mm)] draft curtains on the underside of the floor deck and should be provided with automatic high-velocity spray nozzles arranged to create a counterdraft. If conveyor systems pass through fire walls or fire barrier walls, it is most desirable to provide a short gap in the conveyor to allow automatic fire doors to close. Interlocks might be necessary to stop conveyors moving toward the fire walls and clear the conveyors moving away from the fire walls in order to prevent fire doors from dropping on conveyed materials and thereby preventing complete closure. Another option is to provide a noncombustible or limited-combustible, sprinkler-protected tunnel on both sides of the opening. [33:A.4.2]

Rooms that house spray application operations should be separated from other occupancies or operations by construction that meets the requirements of 43.1.3. [33:A.4.2]

In sprinklered buildings where spray application operations occupy one portion of an open area, the spray application operations should be surrounded by noncombustible or limited-combustible draft curtains extending downward at least 18 in. (460 mm) from the ceiling, but deeper if practical. The draft curtains aid in preventing the activation of sprinklers outside the area enclosed by the curtains and tend to confine the discharge of water to the immediate area of the fire. Additional consideration might be given to the use of heat and smoke vents to aid in fire control. [33:A.4.2]

Sprinkler discharge should be drained to the outside of the building, to an internal drain system, or to some other suitable location. Properly designed and installed floor drains and scuppers of sufficient number and size to handle expected sprinkler discharge should be provided. Where spray application operations are located on an upper floor, they should not be located directly above goods or equipment that are subject to water damage. In addition, the floor should be made watertight and means should be provided to drain sprinkler discharge directly from the area. [33:A.4.2]

A.43.1.3.1 Spray booths can be of a wide variety of shapes and sizes to accommodate the various industrial applications of spray application. Without the use of a spray booth, the spray area, as defined in 3.3.17.11, can constitute a considerable area, with all the requirements for a spray area then becoming applicable. It is important that only equipment suitable for specific purposes be utilized in connection with the handling and application of flammable or combustible liquids or powders. [33:A.5.1]

A.43.1.4.1 Because of the requirements for special safeguards, electrostatic apparatus; drying, curing, and fusing apparatus; and vehicle undercoating and body lining operations are covered in other chapters of NFPA 33. [33:A.6.2]

A.43.1.4.1.2 In the Division system, areas are classified as either Division 1 or Division 2, depending on whether ignitible gases or vapors are always present or likely to be present (Division 1) or whether ignitible gases or vapors are not normally present (Division 2). The Zone system identifies hazardous locations as Zone 0, Zone 1, or Zone 2, depending on whether the ignitible atmosphere will always be present (Zone 0), is likely to be present (Zone 1), or is not normally present (Zone 2). The Zone system is based on International Electrotechnical Commission (IEC) standards and was incorporated into *NFPA 70* in 1996. [33:A.6.2.2]

A.43.1.4.1.5 There should be no open flames, hot surfaces, or spark-producing equipment in the spray area or in any area where they might be exposed to combustible residues. Open flames or spark-producing equipment should not be located where they can be exposed to deposits of combustible residues. Some residues can be ignited at low temperatures, such as those produced by steam pipes, incandescent luminaires, and power tools. In powder coating applications, the temperature of the object or material being coated should be maintained at least 50°F (28°C) below the autoignition temperature of the powder. [33:A.6.2.5]

A.43.1.4.1.6 Areas that are above or adjacent to spray areas and where materials are located, stored, mixed, or processed should be ventilated. Equipment that is known to produce flame, sparks, or particles of hot metal, including luminaires, that are adjacent to areas that are safe under normal operating conditions but which can become dangerous due to accident or careless operation should not be installed in such areas unless the equipment is totally enclosed or is separated from the area by partitions that will prevent the sparks or particles from entering the area. [33:A.6.2.6]

A.43.1.4.2.1 See *NFPA 70*. [33:A.6.3.1]

A.43.1.4.2.1.1 This classification usually includes the following locations:

(1) Where volatile flammable liquids or liquefied flammable gases are transferred from one container to another
(2) Interiors of spray booths and areas in the vicinity of spraying and painting operations where volatile flammable solvents are used
(3) Locations containing open tanks or vats of volatile flammable liquids
(4) Drying rooms or compartments for the evaporation of flammable solvents
(5) All other locations where ignitible concentrations of flammable vapors or gases are likely to occur in the course of normal operations

[33:A.6.3.1.1]

In some Division 1 locations, ignitible concentrations of flammable gases or vapors might be present continuously or for long periods of time. Examples include the following:

(1) The inside of inadequately vented enclosures containing instruments normally venting flammable gases or vapors to the interior of the enclosure
(2) Inadequately ventilated areas within spraying or coating operations using volatile flammable fluids

(3) The interior of an exhaust duct that is used to vent ignitible concentrations of vapors
[**33:**A.6.3.1.1]

A.43.1.4.2.1.2 This classification usually includes locations where volatile flammable liquids or flammable gases or vapors are used but that, in the judgment of the AHJ, would become hazardous only in case of an accident or of some unusual operating condition. The quantity of flammable material that might escape in case of accident, the adequacy of ventilating equipment, the total area involved, and the record of the industry or business with respect to explosions or fires are all factors that merit consideration in determining the classification and extent of each location. [**33:**A.6.3.1.2]

Piping without valves, checks, meters, and similar devices would not ordinarily introduce a hazardous condition even though used for flammable liquids or gases. Depending on factors such as the quantity and size of the containers and ventilation, locations used for the storage of flammable liquids or liquefied or compressed gases in sealed containers may be considered either hazardous (classified) or unclassified locations. See NFPA 30-2018, *Flammable and Combustible Liquids Code,* and NFPA 58-2017, *Liquefied Petroleum Gas Code.* [**33:**A.6.3.1.2]

A.43.1.4.2.1.3 This classification includes locations inside vented tanks or vessels that contain volatile flammable liquids; inside inadequately vented spraying or coating enclosures, where volatile flammable solvents are used; inside open vessels, tanks and pits containing volatile flammable liquids; and the interior of an exhaust duct that is used to vent ignitible concentrations of vapors. [**33:**A.6.3.1.3]

It is not good practice to install electrical equipment in Zone 0 locations except when the equipment is essential to the process or when other locations are not feasible. [*See NFPA 70, 505.5(A) Informational Note No. 2.*] If it is necessary to install electrical systems in a Zone 0 location, it is good practice to install intrinsically safe systems as described by NFPA 70, Article 504. [**33:**A.6.3.1.3]

A.43.1.4.2.1.4 Normal operation is considered the situation when plant equipment is operating within its design parameters. Minor releases of flammable material may be part of normal operations. Minor releases include the releases from mechanical packings on pumps. Failures that involve repair or shutdown (such as the breakdown of pump seals and flange gaskets, and spillage caused by accidents) are not considered normal operation. [**33:**A.6.3.1.4]

This classification usually includes locations where volatile flammable liquids are transferred from one container to another; areas in the vicinity of spraying and painting operations where flammable solvents are used; adequately ventilated drying rooms or compartments for evaporation of flammable solvents; inadequately ventilated pump rooms for volatile flammable liquids; and other locations where ignitible concentrations of flammable vapors or gases are likely to occur in the course of normal operation but not classified Zone 0. [**33:**A.6.3.1.4]

A.43.1.4.2.2.1 Dusts containing magnesium or aluminum are particularly hazardous, and the use of extreme precaution is necessary to avoid ignition and explosion. [**33:**A.6.3.2.1]

A.43.1.4.2.2.2 The quantity of combustible dust that may be present and the adequacy of dust removal systems are factors that merit consideration in determining the classification and may result in an unclassified area. [**33:**A.6.3.2.2]

Where products such as seed are handled in a manner that produces low quantities of dust, the amount of dust deposited may not warrant classification. [**33:**A.6.3.2.2]

A.43.1.4.2.2.3 As a guide to classification of Zone 20 locations, refer to ANSI/ISA 60079-10-2 (12.10.05)-2013, *Explosive Atmospheres — Part 10-2: Classification of areas — Combustible dust atmospheres.* [**33:**A.6.3.2.3]

Zone 20 classification includes locations inside dust containment systems; hoppers, silos, etc., cyclones and filters, dust transport systems, except some parts of belt and chain conveyors, etc.; blenders, mills, dryers, bagging equipment, etc. [**33:**A.6.3.2.3]

A.43.1.4.2.2.4 This classification usually includes locations outside dust containment and in the immediate vicinity of access doors subject to frequent removal or opening for operation purposes when internal combustible mixtures are present; locations outside dust containment in the proximity of filling and emptying points, feed belts, sampling points, truck dump stations, belt dump over points, etc. where no measures are employed to prevent the formation of combustible mixtures; locations outside dust containment where dust accumulates and where due to process operations the dust layer is likely to be disturbed and form combustible mixtures; locations inside dust containment where explosive dust clouds are likely to occur (but neither continuously, nor for long periods, nor frequently) as, for example, silos (if filled and/or emptied only occasionally) and the dirty side of filters if large self-cleaning intervals are occurring. [**33:**A.6.3.2.4]

See also A.43.1.4.2.2.3. [**33:**A.6.3.2.4]

A.43.1.4.2.2.5 Zone 22 locations usually include outlets from bag filter vents, because in the event of a malfunction there can be emission of combustible mixtures; locations near equipment that has to be opened at infrequent intervals or equipment that from experience can easily form leaks where, due to pressure above atmospheric, dust will blow out; pneumatic equipment, flexible connections that can become damaged, etc.; storage locations for bags containing dusty product, since failure of bags can occur during handling, causing dust leakage; and locations where controllable dust layers are formed that are likely to be raised into explosive dust–air mixtures. Only if the layer is removed by cleaning before hazardous dust–air mixtures can be formed is the area designated unclassified. [**33:**A.6.3.2.5]

Locations that normally are classified as Zone 21 can fall into Zone 22 when measures are employed to prevent the formation of explosive dust–air mixtures. Such measures include exhaust ventilation. The measures should be used in the vicinity of (bag) filling and emptying points, feed belts, sampling points, truck dump stations, belt dump over points, etc. [**33:**A.6.3.2.5]

See also A.43.1.4.2.2.3. [**33:**A.6.3.2.5]

Δ **A.43.1.4.3.3** Equipment that is both listed for accumulation of deposits of combustible residues and listed for Class I, Division 1; Zone 1; Class II, Division 1; or Zone 21 locations can be installed in the spray area. *(See NFPA 70.)* [**33:**A.6.4.3]

A.43.1.4.4.4(2) Access doors into a spray area that must be closed to allow normal automated spray application operations to occur should not be considered an opening. The door should be considered a maintenance access and never open while a hazardous condition exists in the booth. Therefore, the area outside the door/maintenance access should be considered unclassified. [33:A.6.5.4(2)]

A.43.1.4.4.5 Supply containers include paint pressure pots, paint pressure tanks, and any container with attached pumping equipment. [33:A.6.5.5]

A.43.1.4.6 During operation of any electrostatic equipment, electrically conductive isolated objects within the process area are influenced by the process and can become charged to voltages that result in spark discharges capable of igniting flammable or combustible substances. Objects commonly involved in such incidents include workpieces on conveyor racks that have fouled contact points; solvent containers or tools placed on nonconducting paint residues, cardboard, or wooden rests; spray booth components such as loose floor grates; and human beings insulated from ground by rubber footwear, paint residue accumulations on floors, and gloves. [33:A.6.7]

Even in spray painting environments where there is no electrostatic equipment in operation but where sticky, electrically nonconductive paint residues have accumulated on the floor, a significant hazard is associated with static electrification of human bodies that results from walking across such a floor. As few as two or three steps can produce sufficient voltage on the body of a worker to create an incendive spark when he or she approaches a grounded object. If this spark occurs in a flammable vapor such as is found surrounding a solvent container or a freshly painted object, a fire results. See NFPA 77 for additional information. [33:A.6.7]

N **A.43.1.4.7** See Article 400 of *NFPA 70*, which covers general requirements, applications, and construction specifications for flexible cords and flexible cables. [33:A.6.8]

N **A.43.1.4.7(5)** See Article 500 of *NFPA 70*, which covers the requirements for electrical and electronic equipment and wiring for all voltages in Class I, Divisions 1 and 2; Class II, Divisions 1 and 2; and Class III, Divisions 1 and 2 locations where fire or explosion hazards might exist due to flammable gases, flammable liquid-produced vapors, combustible liquid-produced vapors, combustible dust, or ignitible fibers/flyings. [33:A.6.8(5)]

A.43.1.5.2.1 Acceptable means to comply with 43.1.5.2.1 include, but are not limited to, visible gauges, audible alarms, approved interlocks, or an effective inspection program. [33:A.7.2.1]

A.43.1.5.3 All spray areas require make-up air, and since the air exhausted from spray application operations is normally contaminated and can be recirculated only under rigidly controlled conditions, the source of the make-up air should be given careful consideration. When the capacity of the ventilating fan is low and the area where the exhaust system is located is large, sufficient make-up air often can be provided by natural infiltration of air through building walls, windows, doors, and so forth. In general, if the volume of the room or building where the exhaust system is located is not equal to at least 20 times the volumetric capacity of the fans (three air changes per hour), then additional make-up air should be provided. Outside air should be tempered and might have to be dehumidified or chilled for proper operation of the spray application apparatus. Automatic controls, including a high-temperature-limit switch, fan interlocks, and safety shutoff valves, should be provided for safe operation. [33:A.7.3]

The method of distributing the make-up air requires careful consideration. If the velocities and distribution of air through baffles, filters, and registers have not been carefully designed, the spray application operation can be inefficient. The velocity of the air through filters, and so forth, should not exceed 200 ft/min (60 m/min). Higher velocities can disrupt spray application operations due to turbulent airflow in the vicinity of the spray apparatus. This turbulence can also cause a properly designed exhaust system to fail to confine and remove vapors or to fail to confine and control residues, dusts, and deposits. [33:A.7.3]

In some heating arrangements, forced make-up or replacement air directly compensating for the contaminated air exhausted from spray application operations is used in place of or to augment general area heating and ventilation. [33:A.7.3]

With the many variables that can be encountered in heating and ventilating systems, it generally is advisable to engage the services of a qualified ventilating engineer to obtain a safe and efficient installation. [33:A.7.3]

The features that should be considered include the following:

(1) Location of sources of heat to comply with 43.1.4
(2) Locating air intakes to prevent recalculation of contaminated air, and equipping air intakes with appropriate screens or filters
(3) Automatic temperature and proportioning controls, including an independent excess temperature limit control
(4) A safety system interlocked with the heater to automatically provide for its safe ignition and to minimize the hazards that might result from failure of its proper operating cycle, proper pressure of fuel supply, ventilation, and electrical power
(5) An interlock between the spray booth exhaust system and the make-up air system to ensure that both systems are operable and provide a proper balance of supply and replacement air
(6) In the case of direct-fired units, operating controls that ensure that concentrations of unburned fuel or products of combustion, if inhaled, are kept to levels that are safe for operating personnel

[33:A.7.3]

A.43.1.5.5 If air exhausted from the spray area is permitted to be recirculated, as provided for in 43.1.5.5, it is critical for effective monitoring that sensors be protected from obstruction and contamination. See *NFPA 72* for recommended maintenance and calibration procedures. [33:A.7.5]

A.43.1.5.5(6) If recirculated air is used for make-up air for occupied spaces, including spray areas, spray booths, spray rooms, and other process areas, the requirements for decontamination and maximum allowable concentrations of solvents are far more stringent than those required by this *Code* for fire and explosion prevention. Refer to appropriate occupational safety and health and industrial hygiene standards for permissible exposure limits. One such standard is ASSP Z9.7, *Recirculation of Air from Industrial Process Exhaust Systems*. [33:A.7.5(6)]

N **A.43.1.5.6** If air exhausted from the spray area is permitted to be recirculated, as provided for in Section 7.5 of NFPA 33, indirect heaters are allowed to be located within the recirculated air path as long as the surface temperature of the indirect heater does not exceed 105°C (221°F). This temperature limit addresses the hazards associated with the possible accumulation of combustible residue on the heater surface in the event of a failure of the filter system during spray application operations. [**33**:A.7.6(3)]

A.43.1.5.7 Exhaust systems should be individually ducted to the outside of the building. Where treatment of the exhaust airstream is necessary to satisfy environmental regulations or where energy conservation measures are used, this might not be practical, and manifolding of the exhaust ducts might be necessary. It should be understood that manifolding of exhaust ducts increases the fire hazard. A fire starting in one booth can spread through the exhaust system and involve other spray areas. Heat exchangers, which are sometimes used to preheat exhaust air before it enters an incinerator, are subject to fires from the spontaneous ignition of residue that collects on heat exchanger surfaces. [**33**:A.7.7]

A.43.1.5.8 For ducts for powder coating systems, the strength of the materials of construction should be considered, since the duct might have to contain the pressure of a deflagration. *(See NFPA 68.)* [**33**:A.7.8]

A.43.1.5.9 The designer of the exhaust ducts and fasteners should refer to appropriate design guides, such as the ANSI/SMACNA 005, *Round Industrial Duct Construction Standards* and the ANSI/SMACNA 002, *Rectangular Industrial Duct Construction Standards*, published by the Sheet Metal and Air Conditioning Contractors National Association. [**33**:A.7.9]

A.43.1.5.12 If there are other operations that give off ignitible vapors in the vicinity of a spray application operation, they should be provided with independent mechanical ventilation. [**33**:A.7.12]

A.43.1.6.1 For large spray operations, coatings, thinners, and solvents can be stored in one of the following locations:

(1) Underground storage tanks
(2) Aboveground storage tanks
(3) Separate buildings
(4) Separate dedicated rooms within the facility
[**33**:A.8.1]

In some cases, liquids are pumped to a mixing room or paint kitchen, where they are mixed and then pumped to the spray area. For smaller operations, separate storage and mixing areas might not be justified. However, it is desirable to minimize the fire loading in or near the spray area by one or a combination of the following methods:

(1) Flammable liquid storage cabinets
(2) A protected enclosed metal structure
(3) Use of metal containers with limitations on the quantity of liquid located near the spray area
[**33**:A.8.1]

A.43.1.6.4.1 Examples of comparable properties and materials resistant to heat include those listed in FM 6036, *Flexible Hose Assemblies for Flammable Gases and/or Ignitable Liquids*, and SAE J343, *Test and Test Procedures for SAE 100R Series Hydraulic Hose and Hose Assemblies*. [**33**:A.8.4.1]

N **A.43.1.6.4.1.1** NFPA 77 provides information on bonding and grounding. [**33**:A.8.4.1.1]

A.43.1.6.4.2 Valves should be kept shut when spray application operations are not being conducted, to minimize the release of coating material in the event of fire. [**33**:A.8.4.2]

A.43.1.6.4.3 If plastic tubing leaks within shielded areas, such as within color changers, the resulting spray fire will destroy all tubing, releasing large quantities of coating material in an area that cannot be reached by the booth protection system. Automatic protection systems should be provided for these areas. [**33**:A.8.4.3]

A major cause of fire in automatic electrostatic spray booths has been the replacement of original equipment plastic tubing with other types of tubing. Such replacement tubing, particularly if conductive coatings are used, is susceptible to the development of pinhole leaks. [**33**:A.8.4.3]

N **A.43.1.6.4.4** The use of a spring-loaded pressure relief valve might create a situation in which the piping system experiences pressure hammer due to the cycling of the pressure relief valve. In cases where this is possible, added effort might be necessary to ensure the system is shut down before the components fail. [**33**:A.8.4.4]

A.43.1.6.5.2 NFPA 77 provides information on static protection. [**33**:A.8.5.2]

△ **A.43.1.7.1** As indicated in 43.1.6, it is not advisable to keep large quantities of flammable or combustible liquids in areas that expose personnel or important property to injury or loss. The primary reason is that fires in flammable liquids are difficult to extinguish by the usual methods, and if large quantities are involved, they can spread the fire by flowing over large areas. For fires in small amounts of flammable or combustible liquids, hand extinguishers or large extinguishers on wheels especially designed for such fires are effective. If large quantities of liquids are to be protected, suitable automatic equipment should be provided and special attention should be given to proper dikes, curbs, and drains to prevent the flow to other property. [**33**:A.9.1]

For the extinguishment of fire in spray residues, handheld fire extinguishers suitable for fire in ordinary combustibles or hose streams are effective. [**33**:A.9.1]

Depending on the level of filtration, residues could accumulate in the exhaust ductwork. Because the ductwork is part of the spray area, it must be protected in accordance with 43.1.7. This includes the ductwork from a water-wash booth. [**33**:A.9.1]

Because the particulate filters will accumulate paint residue, they must be protected. The solvent concentrator units, by their design, contain high concentrations of solvent, so they also must be protected. Additionally, the most commonly used solvent concentrators use activated carbon as the adsorption medium. This medium is highly combustible, especially with high levels of solvents absorbed. Ketone solvents pose an even greater risk. [**33**:A.9.1]

Because suppression media other than water might damage the carbon bed, water-based suppression systems (wet pipe sprinklers, preaction sprinklers, dry pipe sprinklers, and open-head deluge systems) are recommended for this application. [**33**:A.9.1]

The recirculated air supply unit must be protected because of the filter media it contains. Also, many large air supply units have gas-fired heaters to heat outside make-up air. [**33**:A.9.1]

Air supply ducts from the particulate filter to the air supply unit and from the air supply unit to the spray booth are not normally protected, since all particulates have been filtered. [**33:**A.9.1]

The choice of the automatic fire protection system should always be based on good engineering practice. Generally, for most spray areas, automatic sprinklers are considered most appropriate *(see A.43.1.7.7)*. However, consideration must be given to how much water is likely to flow and how much water is to be contained. [**33:**A.9.1]

Dry chemical extinguishing systems are most appropriate for small spray application operations (e.g., automotive refinishing, furniture refinishing, and similar processes) that utilize dry filters to capture overspray. These systems provide economical adequate protection. They are a viable alternative for any facility without sufficient water supply to support an automatic sprinkler system. [**33:**A.9.1]

Carbon dioxide or clean agent extinguishing systems should be used for open area protection only after careful consideration. Holding the required concentration of agent for the period of time needed for extinguishment in a spray booth environment can be difficult. In addition, total flooding with carbon dioxide in normally or potentially occupied areas presents serious health concerns. The time delay required prior to discharge can allow a fire time to grow and spread. Carbon dioxide and clean agent systems, however, are an appropriate choice for protecting electrostatic equipment enclosures inside or immediately outside the spray area. [**33:**A.9.1]

N **A.43.1.7.2.1** During a fire condition, an interlock should shut down the recirculation air so as not to return smoke to the spray booth or spray room. The air make-up system and exhaust system should remain in operation. [**33:** A.9.2.1]

A.43.1.7.3 The severity and extent of fires in spray application operations have substantially increased when rubber or plastic supply hose were burned off, resulting in the addition of the entire contents of the supply system to the fire. By limiting the amount of fuel available, the magnitude of the fire can be held to more manageable limits. The shutoff should be accomplished by means of an interlock with a fire detection system or the automatic fire extinguishing system for the spray area. This shutoff is normally accomplished by shutting the distribution pumps. In some cases, it is also advisable to limit the flow from the solvent piping system. This can be accomplished with properly specified check valves in the pipe "drops." [**33:**A.9.3]

A.43.1.7.7 Spray application operations should be located only in buildings that are completely protected by an approved system of automatic sprinklers. If the operations are located in unsprinklered buildings, sprinklers should be installed to protect spray application processes where practical. Because of the rapidity and intensity of fires that involve spray operations, the available water should be ample to simultaneously supply all sprinklers likely to open in one fire without depleting the available water for use by hose streams. Noncombustible draft curtains can be used to limit the number of sprinklers that will open. [**33:**A.9.5.1]

Even when areas adjacent to coating operations are considered under reasonably positive fire control by adequate automatic sprinkler protection, damage is possible if operations are conducted on floors above those containing contents that are highly susceptible to water damage. Waterproofing and drainage of spray room floors can assist in reducing water damage on floors below. Proper drainage of the large volume of water frequently necessary to extinguish spray finishing room fires often presents considerable difficulty. [**33:**A.9.5.1]

Automatic sprinklers in spray areas, including the interior of spray booths and exhaust ducts, should be wet pipe, preaction, or deluge system so that water can be placed on the fire in the shortest possible time. Automatic sprinklers in spray booths and exhaust ducts should be of the lowest practical temperature rating. The delay in application of water with ordinary dry pipe sprinklers can permit a fire to spread so rapidly that final extinguishment is difficult without extensive resulting damage. [**33:**A.9.5.1]

The location of the sprinklers inside spray booths should be selected with care to avoid heads being placed in the direct path of spray and yet afford protection for the entire booth interior. When sprinklers are in the direct path of spray, even one day's operation can result in deposits on the sprinklers that insulate the fusible link or choke open head orifices to the extent that sprinklers cannot operate efficiently. [**33:**A.9.5.1]

Automatic sprinklers should also be located so that areas subject to substantial accumulations of overspray residue are protected. Generally, sprinklers are located no more than 4 ft (1220 mm) from side walls of booths and rooms and from dry overspray collectors (where applicable). Sprinklers in booths or rooms should be on Extra Hazard occupancy spacing of 100 ft^2 (9.3 m^2). [**33:**A.9.5.1]

All sprinkler systems in spray areas should be controlled by an accessible indicating control valve. [**33:**A.9.5.1]

Use of water as the extinguishing agent for solvent and coating material fires might, in some cases, cause problems with splashing and "floating" of flaming liquids and residues. This possibility should be included with the other factors that are normally considered in the selection of an extinguishing agent. In addition, water from sprinkler or deluge systems, after coming into contact with coating materials, residues, or solvents, might have to be collected and treated as hazardous waste. [**33:**A.9.5.1]

A.43.1.7.7.1 Paragraph 43.1.7.7.1 lists four types of automatic sprinkler systems and requires that the one "most appropriate for the portion of the spray area being protected" be used. Generally, an open-head deluge system provides the highest level of protection, given that all sprinklers in the protected area flow simultaneously. This type of system is most appropriate for large, downdraft, water-wash spray booths when protecting automatic electrostatic spray application zones. [**33:**A.9.5.1.1]

Wet pipe automatic sprinkler systems are appropriate for protecting spray booths that utilize nonelectrostatic application processes or operations using listed electrostatic application processes. Wet pipe systems are also generally used to protect exhaust plenums (eliminator or scrubber sections), exhaust ducts, and air recirculation filter houses. [**33:**A.9.5.1.1]

Dry pipe systems have been included because some exhaust duct designs include sections that are subject to freezing. [**33:**A.9.5.1.1]

Preaction systems have been included because some spray application processes and equipment can be damaged by unwanted water discharge. This damage can be disruptive and costly. Powder spray booths and solvent concentrator (air pollution abatement) systems are examples of systems where it is appropriate to use a preaction system. [**33:**A.9.5.1.1]

A.43.1.7.7.3 Determining the water supply requirements for a paint spray application system requires identification of the credible fire scenario that results in the greatest water demand. In small booths, this is typically a combination of the sprinklers within the booth and those in the exhaust plenum and stack. [**33:**A.9.5.1.3]

Large or complex paint spray systems can include some of the following features that require careful evaluation in determining the total system water demand in the event of a fire:

(1) *Multiple (primary and secondary) fire protection systems.* A common example is a wet pipe system combined with a deluge or water mist system. These systems can operate simultaneously, and this possibility should be evaluated to ensure that the water supply is adequate.
(2) *Large booths with multiple protection zones.* The fire scenario determining the required water supply needs to take into account the likelihood of involving more than one water-based fire protection system. This is especially true where optical flame detection is used to activate deluge systems. Consider the following:
   (a) If optical flame detection can "view" a fire in adjacent zone
   (b) Proximity of two zones
   (c) Airflow between zones transporting hot gases to adjacent zone
(3) *Recirculating or interconnected exhaust systems.* In simple exhaust systems, a developing fire tends to follow the airflow from the source to the exhaust point. However, in recirculating or interconnected systems, the possibility exists that airflow will also draw the fire into adjacent systems.
(4) *Multiple exhaust plenum areas.* Supply plenums are usually devoid of paint or coating residue and cannot be expected to be part of a single fire scenario involving a spray booth or area. Exhaust plenums, including water wash/eliminator sections in downdraft booths, can contain a build-up of combustible residue and the airflow naturally draws a fire from the booth into the plenum and then on to the exhaust system. As in the multiple spray zone example, it is possible that more than one exhaust plenum could become involved.
(5) *Concealed spaces.* In some booths, external or internal enclosures are provided for the purposes of paint and solvent supply, mixing, and recirculation. These enclosures are often protected by wet pipe sprinkler systems independent of the primary booth protection systems. Their operation might or might not be likely during a booth fire depending on the fire separation of these systems from the spray area.

[**33:**A.9.5.1.3]

Building areas outside of the spray area or paint booth are not included in the demand calculation, as the fire suppression systems and booth/spray area construction are intended to contain a fire until manual fire-fighting efforts can achieve final fire extinguishment. [**33:**A.9.5.1.3]

Figure A.43.1.7.7.3(a) and Figure A.43.1.7.7.3(b) show two examples of demand calculation worksheets to demonstrate how both simple and complex systems can be evaluated. Note that the accuracy of the decisions made in determining the water supply demand depends on the expertise of the evaluator. [**33:**A.9.5.1.3]

A.43.1.7.7.6 Water supply requirements for most industrial paint spray operations should be adequate to supply all automatic sprinklers in the spray area. Loss experience has shown that fires starting in the exhaust duct can spread to the spray booth and that fires starting in the booth can spread to the exhaust duct. [**33:**A.9.5.1.6]

Sprinklers or sprinkler systems protecting stacks or ducts should be of a type not subject to freezing. Automatic systems are preferred, but manual systems are also acceptable. Nonfreeze or dry-type sprinkler systems can be used in ducts subject to freezing. For some industries, such as the automotive industry, manually operated open-head systems have proved to be effective protection for ducts and stacks. [**33:**A.9.5.1.6]

Ductwork in powder coating applications does not require fire protection. Based on design duct velocity, there is no accumulation of residual powder. [**33:**A.9.5.1.6]

N **A.43.1.7.7.6(6)** Consideration should be given to duct areas resulting in the highest sprinkler discharge demand. This might actually include multiple paths of ducts, provided the total length of the ducts considered does not exceed 30.5 m (100 linear ft) and all subsections of ducts are interconnected. [**33:**A.9.5.1.6(6)]

While a developing fire might follow the direction of airflow and vertical rise in the ducts, it should not be assumed that a fire will only occur while the system is operating. Operations such as cutting and welding can result in ignition of residues inside the duct while equipment is idle. [**33:**A.9.5.1.6(6)]

It is not anticipated that both the building ceiling and spray area systems will operate simultaneously if installed in accord-

Spray Area/Spray Booth Water Demand Calculation Worksheet		
		Flow
Total Demand:		695 gpm
1. Spray area demand*		
a.	1st Zone:	
b.	2nd Zone:	
c.	Sprinkler system:	130 gpm
2. Exhaust system demand		65 gpm
3. Eliminator/scrubber		
4. Hose stream		500 gpm

Assumptions:
(1) Small booth with straight airflow path into the booth through filter to plenum and then through stack (direct to atmosphere).
(2) Demands for booth and exhaust (stack) sprinklers are totaled (assumes all sprinklers operate).

△ **FIGURE A.43.1.7.7.3(a)** Spray Area/Spray Booth Water Demand Calculation Worksheet for a Simple Booth. [**33:**Figure A.9.5.1.3(a)] ance with both this standard and NFPA 13, so a total demand including both building ceiling and spray area systems is not required by this section. [**33**:A.9.5.1.6(6)]

N **A.43.1.7.7.6(7)** Minimal hose streams might be needed to effect final extinguishment if the fire is limited to inside the stack alone. To determine water supply requirements, see 43.1.7.7.3 and A.43.1.7.7.3 for guidance. [**33**:A.9.5.1.6(7)]

N **A.43.1.7.7.7.1** Plastic bags should not be used for this purpose, as shrinkage prior to reaching the temperatures necessary to ensure sprinkler activation can interfere with proper sprinkler operation and the development of spray patterns. The ban on plastic bags should include polypropylene or other petroleum-based plastic bags commonly marketed as comparable to cellulose-based bags. Thin, clear, cellulose-based material degrades rather than melting and, like paper, does not experience shrinkage. [**33**:A.9.5.1.7.1]

A.43.1.7.8 This discharge is typically accomplished by means of a piping network from the fire protection system into all parts of the spray area. To avoid potential flashback of an unextinguished fire, modular fire protection units should not be used to protect areas with ducts or plenums, or areas that exceed the listing of the system. They might, however, be suited for smaller open spray areas that fall within the limits of the listing. [**33**:A.9.5.2]

A.43.1.7.9 Unlike powder application systems, the make-up air and exhaust systems for a liquid application system have to continue to function, unless there is a compelling reason to shut them down. [**33**:A.9.6.2]

Spray Area/Spray Booth Water Demand Calculation Worksheet		Flow	PSI
Total Demand:		1,974 gpm	103 psi
1.	Spray area demand		
a.	1st Zone:	488 gpm	96 psi
b.	2nd Zone:	605 gpm	103 psi
c.	Sprinkler system:		
2.	Exhaust system demand		
a.	Path 1	360 gpm	75 psi
b.	Path 2		
c.	Path 3		
3.	Eliminator/scrubber	521 gpm	88 psi

Assumptions:
(1) Deluge systems in two zones operate because optical flame detectors are not sufficiently isolated from adjacent zones.
(2) Ceiling closed-head (wet) system does not operate because deluge systems are effective in controlling the fire and cooling the spray area.
(3) Exhaust demand is based upon all heads operating along the airflow path from the fire origin to the termination of the exhaust stack.

Δ **FIGURE A.43.1.7.7.3(b)** Spray Area/Spray Booth Water Demand Calculation Worksheet for a Complex System. [**33**:Figure A.9.5.1.3(b)]

N **A.43.1.7.10.4** Exposed areas downstream of a work piece and upstream of a dry filtration system are susceptible to build-up of paint overspray. These areas include, but are not limited to sheet metal shrouding around filter elements, guide plates that direct air flow into the dry filtration system, and maintenance walkways. Commonly, removable coatings such as plastic sheeting, foils, or greases are applied over these exposed areas to facilitate cleaning of the overspray build-up. As these coatings are intended to be removed at discrete intervals, a finite amount of overspray build-up will be present in these exposed areas during normal booth operation, requiring the need for fire protection over these areas. Depending upon the design of the dry filtration system, some or all portions of these exposed areas can be adequately protected by the main spray booth fire suppression system. In some cases, permanent design features of the dry filtration system, such as sheet metal air guide plates, baffles, or filter shrouds, obstruct the main spray booth fire suppression system from adequately protecting all exposed areas. In these cases, additional fire protection is needed to ensure all exposed areas are adequately protected. [**33**:A.9.6.3.4]

N **A.43.1.7.10.6(2)** When recirculation is stopped, ventilation might need to be diverted to atmosphere to maintain ventilation in accordance with 43.1.7.2. [**33**:A.9.6.3.6(2)]

N **A.43.1.7.11.2.1** A fire detection system might be but does not have to be of the smoke, air aspirating, heat, or flame detection type or a combination of them. Special consideration should be given for the location of the detection units as residue built up can block the sensing elements or reduce their sensitivity. Periodic cleaning should be performed. [**33**:A.9.7.2.1]

N **A.43.1.7.11.3** See A.43.1.7.10.4. [**33**:A.9.7.3]

N **A.43.1.7.11.5(3)** When recirculation is stopped, ventilation might need to be diverted to atmosphere to maintain ventilation in accordance with Section 9.2 of NFPA 33. [**33**:A.9.7.5(3)]

N **A.43.1.7.12.3** See A.43.1.7.10.4. [**33**:A.9.8.3]

N **A.43.1.7.12.4** When recirculation is stopped, ventilation might need to be diverted to atmosphere to maintain ventilation in accordance with 43.1.7.2. [**33**:A.9.8.4]

A.43.1.8.1 The materials used in spray application processes can create serious fire hazards. For example, the vapors and mists created by the atomization of flammable and combustible liquids can form explosive mixtures in air. In addition, deposits of residues can ignite spontaneously or be easily ignited. Finally, fires involving flammable and combustible liquids or combustible residues can spread rapidly and can produce intense heat and smoke. Properly designed equipment can do much to lessen these hazards but cannot eliminate them. These inherent characteristics should make it obvious that supervision of operations, maintenance of equipment, and daily cleaning are essential to a safe operation. [**33**:A.10.1]

It is important that some type of periodic inspection be conducted and recorded as part of the maintenance procedures. It is also important that any inspections of spray application equipment be conducted by competent and reliable personnel who have knowledge of the equipment and the inherent characteristics of the materials used. [**33**:A.10.1]

The frequency of the inspections depends on the individual components of the spray application process. For example, it might be acceptable to check sprinkler control valves or other control mechanisms for approved fire protection systems on a weekly or even monthly basis. However, this frequency would not be acceptable for ensuring adequate airflow through collector filters of a spray booth. At a minimum, that should be done at the beginning of each operating shift. Similarly, the buildup of residues would also need to be checked on a per-shift basis. Individual plant operations might dictate that either of these items (airflow and residue buildup) be checked every few hours. [33:A.10.1]

A.43.1.8.1.1 The use of the term *predetermined* is intended to convey the idea that one cannot arbitrarily locate or conduct spray application operations without thought to the hazards and special requirements that such operations demand. Requirements regarding electrical equipment and ventilation are of primary concern. This *Code* also specifies requirements that can vary based on the type of equipment used, the type of material being spray applied, and even the type of operation. Any spray application operation should also consider the storage, handling, and distribution of the coating materials used in the process. Certainly there are other factors, but these examples should adequately explain the need for predetermining the spray area and why operations should be confined to those areas. [33:A.10.1.1]

Δ **A.43.1.8.2** In the spray finishing of any workpiece, there is frequently a portion of the spray that does not deposit directly on the object or material being coated but does deposit on adjacent surfaces as residue material. This is referred to as *overspray*. Many of these residues are highly combustible, igniting at very low temperatures or spontaneously, resulting in fast-spreading fires. To limit the duration and intensity of fires, the accumulation of deposits has to be minimized and controlled as much as practical. The accumulation of residues represents one of the most significant challenges to fire control. [33:A.10.3]

Cleaning. The interior of spray booths, exhaust fan blades, and exhaust ducts should be cleaned regularly to avoid the accumulation of residues. Either spray operators should be allowed ample time for this cleaning, or a special maintenance crew should be provided for cleaning at the close of each day's operation. If equipment is so designed that during cleanup hose streams or fixed water nozzles can be used in ducts and spray booths without water damage to building and contents, cleaning operations are greatly facilitated. Many plants have found that by coating the interior of spray booths with a suitable soap-like or water-soluble material immediately after cleaning, adhesive spray deposits can be removed the following day with the use of water streams. Other materials, such as plastics that can be readily peeled off the interior of the spray booth, can also be used to facilitate cleaning of the overspray residue. [33:A.10.3]

Properly maintained water-wash booths offer lower fire loading than dry booths. To maintain this advantage, it is necessary to perform regular and scheduled maintenance. This maintenance schedule should be recorded and the records filed. When the nozzles, jets or orifices, eliminator packs, and strainer screens become fouled with accumulated sludge or overspray, combustible residues will be deposited on the interior of the exhaust duct and fan blades. The nozzles, jets, orifices, and eliminator packs should be inspected each work shift. Strainer screens should be removed and cleaned each work shift. [33:A.10.3]

The booth interior, exhaust stack, and fan blades should be checked periodically, and accumulations of overspray and dirt should be removed as required. Exhaust ducts or stacks should not be entered for cleaning or repairs unless they are free from flammable vapors and have been thoroughly wet down. [33:A.10.3]

A.43.1.8.5 Many fires have originated from the spontaneous ignition of fabric and waste impregnated with coating materials. When sprayed articles are rubbed with rags or waste, all unclean rags and waste should be immediately placed in approved waste cans and removed from the premises at least daily at the close of each shift. When employees change clothes on plant premises, soiled clothing should be kept in metal lockers provided in a segregated dressing room. [33:A.10.6]

A.43.1.8.5.3 See NFPA 77 for information on bonding and grounding. [33:A.10.6.3]

A.43.1.8.7.4 See NFPA 77 for information on bonding and grounding. [33:A.10.8.4]

A.43.1.8.9 Bleaching compounds, such as hydrogen peroxide, hypochlorites, perchlorates, or other oxidizing compounds, can cause fires when in contact with organic finishing materials. Hence, if bleaching compounds are to be used in spray booths, the booths should be thoroughly cleaned and used only for that purpose. The alternate use of spray booths for bleaching compounds and other finishing materials or the alternate use of finishing materials containing nitrocellulose and other types of finishing materials containing drying oils, such as varnishes, oil-based stains, air-drying enamels, primers, and so forth, without first thoroughly removing all traces of deposits can result in a spontaneous ignition fire. [33:A.10.10]

A.43.1.8.10 Stricter environmental regulation has given rise to the increased use of chlorinated solvents, such as 1,1,1-trichloroethane and methylene chloride. These solvents are not photochemically reactive and, therefore, can be useful in helping to meet standards regarding volatile organic compound emissions. However, these solvents have a well-documented characteristic of being chemically reactive with aluminum. The reaction that occurs is unpredictable both in terms of when it will occur and to what degree it will proceed. In most situations there is no apparent reaction. Other situations have noted effects ranging from simple corrosion to catastrophic explosion-like failure accompanied by considerable shrapnel and a fireball. Understanding and controlling the subsequent hazard is hindered by this unpredictability. Although there is some understanding of the actual reaction, the following factors acting as independent variables have been found to have an effect on the initiation and rate of reaction:

(1) Heat
(2) Pressure
(3) Ratio of aluminum surface area to volume of solvent, presence of moisture (condensation), aluminum alloy content, metal content of the coating, and the introduction of other solvents or materials

[33:A.10.11]

Therefore, the only assuredly safe condition is to keep these materials separate. [33:A.10.11]

It is important to realize that aluminum has been used as a primary material for spray equipment construction over many years. Incorporating these solvents into existing spray systems cannot be done safely without first determining the construction material of the equipment and then replacing those components where contact with aluminum and chlorinated solvent will occur within a pressurizable device (e.g., pumps, heaters, piping, fluid valves, and spray gun cups). [33:A.10.11]

A.43.1.8.12 If repairs or changes are to be made to equipment, care should be taken to see that all residue deposits are removed and the area wet down with water beforehand in order to avoid a fire. During such repairs, no spraying should be conducted, all flammable and combustible liquids and portable combustible material should be removed from the vicinity, and suitable fire extinguishers should be kept readily available. [33:A.10.13]

The use of welding or cutting torches should be prohibited except under the supervision of a competent person familiar with the fire hazards involved. *(See NFPA 51B.)* [33:A.10.13]

A.43.5.3.2(4) For dry chemical fire protection systems, it might be prudent to double the quantity of agent and its flowrate, compared to a similar size fully enclosed spray booth to achieve the desired degree of protection. This is due to the relatively unenclosed nature of a limited finishing workstation compared to a traditional spray booth. [33:A.14.3.2(4)]

This recommendation is based on a white paper provided by the Fire Equipment Manufacturers' Association titled "Recommendations for Protection of Curtained Limited Finishing Workstations." [33:A.14.3.2(4)]

A.43.5.3.8.2 A means of showing that the limited finishing workstation is in the drying or curing mode of operation can be, but is not limited to, having the lighting of the workstation go out, use of a flashing light or strobe, or use of an audible device. [33:A.14.3.8.2]

A.43.7.1 Organic peroxides are a group of chemicals that are used as catalysts (chain reaction initiators) in the polymerization of plastics monomers and resins. Commercially, they are available as numerous formulations that differ not only in chemical species but also in concentration, type, and amount of diluent. [33:A.16.1]

The rapidly expanding reinforced styrene–polyester composites industry is one of the larger users of organic peroxide formulations. The formulations are used to catalyze (harden) the styrene–polyester resin. Frequently, the resin mixture and the catalyst are spray-applied to the reinforcing matrix using an automatic proportioning spray applicator. The most widely used catalyst systems are formulations of methyl ethyl ketone peroxide (MEKP), in varying concentrations with different diluents, usually dibutyl phthalate. For transportation purposes, the US Department of Transportation classifies these formulations as "organic peroxides" or "flammable liquids." [33:A.16.1]

For purposes of storage and warehousing, NFPA 400 classifies these materials using a five-tiered system, depending on their relative hazard as packaged for shipment. Thus, NFPA 400 recognizes that the different formulations available differ widely in fire hazard. In many cases, the "active oxygen," a measure of the material's catalytic activity and one measure of its reactivity hazard, has been reduced, thus reducing any explosion hazard. [33:A.16.1]

The following precautions are recommended:

(1) Organic peroxide formulations should be stored in a cool, dry location that is separated from the work area. The formulations should not be stored with materials with which they might not be compatible. Storage quantity limitations and fire protection requirements are contained in NFPA 400.
(2) The amount of organic peroxide formulation kept in the work area should be limited to that needed for a single day's use. Any formulation remaining at the end of a workday should be returned to the storage area.
(3) All necessary precautions, as recommended by the supplier, should be taken when organic peroxide formulations are used. Good housekeeping should be strictly observed, and spills should be immediately cleaned. Spilled material or material (such as resin) that has been contaminated with organic peroxide formulations has to be properly disposed of immediately. Trained personnel and safe operating procedures are essential for safe operation. The user should refer to the material safety data sheet (MSDS) or its equivalent for safety and handling information for the specific formulation being used. [33:A.16.1]

A.43.7.3.2 Such mixing can result in a spontaneous fire or explosion. [33:A.16.3.2]

A.43.7.6 The chemical and thermal stability of organic peroxide formulations is markedly reduced by contact or contamination with strong acids or bases, sulfur compounds, amines, and reducing agents of any type. Decomposition gases or vapors produced by some organic peroxide formulations can present a fire or explosion hazard. For example, the decomposition of benzoyl peroxide produces highly flammable vapors. [33:A.16.6]

Heat, including heat from fire exposure, is an important factor in the decomposition of organic peroxide formulations. Some formulations decompose quietly when exposed to a slow, gradual increase in temperature. However, these same formulations can decompose violently or even explode when subjected to a rapid, excessive increase in temperature, such as from fire exposure. [33:A.16.6]

In general, an organic peroxide that is formulated with a diluent into a dilute solution or paste burns more slowly than the concentrated or pure material and is less sensitive to shock or impact. [33:A.16.6]

A.43.9.1 The reinforced styrene–polyester composites industry uses a variety of fabrication techniques to manufacture a wide range of useful products. Most of these products are fabricated with polyester- or vinyl ester–based resins and a fiber reinforcement, most commonly glass fiber. The resins contain a monomer, usually styrene, and are mixed with a catalyst to initiate curing. Other volatile organic chemicals used include the organic peroxide formulations, such as MEKP, used to cure the resin, and various dyes and admixtures. [33:A.17.1]

Open molding is the predominant molding method, with mold sizes ranging from less than 1 ft² (0.1 m²) to very large structures, such as boat hulls over 100 ft (30 m) in length. The two most widely used application methods are hand lay-up and spray-up. In the hand lay-up fabrication method, a glass fiber mat is saturated with the resin by direct spray application or by manual application of the liquid resin. The spray-up fabrication method employs a "chopper gun" that simultaneously applies catalyzed resin and chopped glass fiber to a mold. In addition, many operations use a spray-applied polyester resin gelcoat, as for in-mold coating. Products produced by this industry include boats, bathtubs and shower enclosures, sinks and lavatories, underground storage tanks, auto and truck bodies, recreational vehicles, pollution control equipment, piping, and other specialized parts. [33:A.17.1]

A.43.9.3 The determination by the Technical Committee on Finishing Processes that Ordinary Hazard (Group 2) sprinkler design density is sufficient for protecting spray application of styrene cross-linked thermoset resins (commonly known as glass fiber–reinforced plastics) is based on the following factors:

(1) Although the styrene monomer that is a component in unsaturated polyester resin is a Class I flammable liquid by definition, actual burn tests reveal that the resin does not readily ignite and burns slowly when it does ignite.
(2) Tests of resin application areas have shown that the processes do not produce vapors that exceed 25 percent of the lower flammable limit (LFL). Resin application tests have also indicated that the maximum levels of vapor concentrations are about 690 parts per million (ppm) for spray application. The tests were conducted in an enclosed area with no ventilation. The LFL concentration for styrene is 11,000 ppm. Twenty-five percent of the LFL is 2,750 ppm.

[33:A.17.3]

A.43.9.5.3 NFPA 77 contains information on static electricity. [33:A.17.5.3]

N **A.43.10.1** Where a requirement applies to a particular process, the name of that process will be stated. [34:A.1.1.1]

A.43.10.1.6 See NFPA 86.

A.43.10.2 Section 43.10 anticipates conditions of average use.

A.43.11.1 The safety of a spray application process depends on the employees who operate it and the knowledge and understanding they have of the process and equipment involved. Therefore, it is important to maintain an effective and ongoing training program for all employees involved in such work. New employees should be effectively trained before being assigned to a job. After the initial training, employees should receive periodic retraining to ensure their knowledge and understanding of normal process procedures as well as with emergency procedures or changes in procedures. Safe work habits are developed; they do not occur naturally. [33:A.19.1]

All training should be provided by qualified personnel knowledgeable in the processes and operations involved. Appropriate training should be provided for all employees involved in or affected by spray application processes. This includes, but is not limited to, operating, supervisory, housekeeping, and maintenance personnel. [33:A.19.1]

A.43.11.1.2 Any work requiring entry of employees into confined spaces should be conducted in accordance with a written procedure that is rigidly followed. This procedure should include, but not be limited to, the following:

(1) Analysis of confined space atmosphere for flammable, combustible, toxic, or oxygen-deficient conditions
(2) Rescue, fire, and emergency procedures
(3) Locking and tagging procedures for all power and process hazard sources
(4) Ventilation
(5) Personal protective equipment
(6) Proper tools and electrical equipment

(7) Written entry authorization by a qualified responsible individual

[33:A.19.1.2]

N **A.44.2.1(1)** Extraction processes that use flammable liquids but are not within the scope of NFPA 36 might be within the scope of NFPA 30, and the user is referred to that document for guidance. *(See Chapter 3 of NFPA 36 for definitions of terms, including "extraction process" and "solvent.")* [36:A.1.1.1]

A.45.1.2 The use of automatic sprinkler protection in accordance with NFPA 13 is recommended for all storage of combustible fibers.

A.46.3.8 Where required by the AHJ, a report evaluating the acceptability of technologies, processes, products, facilities, materials, and uses associated with the operation should be provided in accordance with Section 1.4 and approved. The evaluation could be conducted in accordance with the UL 3400, *Additive Manufacturing Facility Safety Management*, requirements by an approved agency.

A.50.1.1 These requirements include, but are not limited to, all manner of cooking equipment, exhaust hoods, grease removal devices, exhaust ductwork, exhaust fans, dampers, fire-extinguishing equipment, and all other auxiliary or ancillary components or systems that are involved in the capture, containment, and control of grease-laden cooking effluent. [96:A.1.1.1]

A.50.1.5 The AHJ can exempt temporary facilities, such as a tent, upon evaluation for compliance to the applicable portions of NFPA 96 or this *Code*. [96:A.1.1.3]

Although it might not be practical to enforce all requirements of NFPA 96 in temporary facilities, the AHJ should determine that all necessary provisions that affect the personal safety of the occupants are considered. [96:A.1.1.3]

Δ **A.50.1.7** This judgment should take into account the type of cooking being performed, the items being cooked, and the frequency of cooking operations. Examples of operations that might not require compliance with Chapter 50 include the following:

(1) Day care centers warming bottles and lunches
(2) Therapy cooking facilities in health care occupancies
(3) Churches and meeting operations that are not cooking meals that produce grease-laden vapors
(4) Employee break rooms where food is warmed

[96:A.1.1.5]

In non-assembly occupancies where residential equipment is utilized, the AHJ may consider requiring protection of the cooking surface with a listed residential range top extinguishing unit as an alternative to no protection or requiring full protection in accordance with this *Code*.

[96:A.1.1.5]

A.50.2.1.1.1 As referenced in UL 197, some products evaluated using the emission test procedure EPA 202, as described in UL 710B, are listed in the UL directory under the category KNLZ, Commercial, with Integral Systems for Limiting the Emission of Grease-laden Air. [96:A.4.1.1.1]

N **A.50.2.1.5.1** Inspection of exhaust systems for compliance with the design, fabrication, and installation requirements of this standard, including the hood, duct, fan, auxiliary equipment, and clearance to combustible construction, should be performed by properly trained and qualified persons familiar with the commercial kitchen exhaust system design and installation requirements of this standard and acceptable to the authority having jurisdiction (AHJ). Inspection of existing installations should occur when changes in ownership, tenants, or cookline arrangements occur. [96:A.4.1.5.1]

N **A.50.2.1.5.2** A service contractor with only periodic access to the equipment, such as the exhaust system cleaner and fire extinguishing system contractor, does not assume this responsibility.

N **A.50.2.2.1** The measurement of clearance to combustible or limited-combustible material is intended to be measured from the closest point of the exhaust system component to that material. Example: The clearance where ceramic tile is installed over gypsum board that extends behind the hood should be measured from the hood to the gypsum board. Placing a noncombustible material over a combustible or limited-combustible material does not permit a zero clearance installation. [96:A.4.2.1]

A.50.4.3.2 Examples of cooking equipment that produce grease-laden vapors include, but are not limited to, deep fat fryers, ranges, griddles, broilers, woks, tilting skillets, and braising pans. [96:A.10.1.2]

A.50.4.4.2 NFPA 10, Annex A, provides recommendations for placards. [96:A.10.2.2]

Δ **A.50.4.4.3** ANSI/CAN/UL/ULC 300 primarily addresses the method of fire testing for self-contained chemical extinguishing systems commonly referred to as pre-engineered systems. ANSI/CAN/UL/ULC 300 has been identified as a baseline for testing fire-extinguishing systems intended for the protection of commercial cooking–related hazards. Additional equivalent testing standards for other types of fire-extinguishing systems not considered pre-engineered that demonstrate equivalent fire testing severity to the ANSI/CAN/UL/ULC 300 test standard include ANSI/CAN/UL/ULC 199, UL 199B, 199E, and UL 710B. [96:A.10.2.3]

A.50.4.4.3.1 A change from rendered animal fat to cooking oil likely will increase autoignition temperatures, and a change to insulated energy-efficient cooking equipment that does not allow ease of cooling likely will result in difficulties sustaining extinguishment with systems not complying with ANSI/CAN/UL/ULC 300, ANSI/CAN/UL/ULC 199, UL 199B, UL 199E, or UL 710B. [96:A.10.2.3.1]

A.50.4.4.10(4) An approved weekly recorded inspection could consist of a log of entries that would display the date and time of each inspection and the initials of the person(s) conducting the visual inspection. Attaching the log to a clipboard and mounting it near the valve in question serves as a convenient reminder of the need to conduct the inspection. [96:A.10.2.10(4)]

N **A.50.4.7.1.1** Mounting location is recommended to be a minimum of 10 ft (3 m) and a maximum of 20 ft (6 m) from the protected hood. [96:A.10.5.1.1]

A.50.4.7.1.3 Installing a guard should reduce the likelihood of an unwanted discharge of the fire-extinguishing system. [96:A.10.5.1.3]

A.50.4.10.2 Although training and qualification might be available elsewhere, the manufacturer of the equipment being installed should be considered an appropriate source of training and qualification. [96:A.10.8.2]

A.50.4.11.1 The system used to rate extinguishers for Class B fires (flammable liquids in depth) does not take into consideration the special nature of heated grease fires. Cooking-grease fires are a special hazard requiring agents that saponify (make a soap foam layer to seal the top surface of the grease) for this application. [96:A.10.9.1]

A.50.5.1.2 Examples of cooking equipment that produce grease-laden vapors include, but are not limited to, deep fat fryers, ranges, griddles, broilers, woks, tilting skillets, and braising pans. [96:A.11.1.2]

A.50.5.2.1 NFPA 10, Annex A, provides recommendations for placards. [96:A.11.2.1]

A.50.5.2.2 ANSI/CAN/UL/ULC 300 primarily addresses the method of fire testing for self-contained chemical extinguishing systems commonly referred to as pre-engineered systems. ANSI/CAN/UL/ULC 300 has been identified as a baseline for testing fire-extinguishing systems intended for the protection of commercial cooking–related hazards. Additional equivalent testing standards for other types of fire-extinguishing systems not considered pre-engineered that demonstrate equivalent fire testing severity to the ANSI/CAN/UL/ULC 300 test standard include ANSI/CAN/UL/ULC 199, UL 199B, UL 199E, and UL 710B. [96:A.11.2.2]

A.50.5.4.1.1 Mounting location is recommended to be a minimum of 10 ft (3 m) and a maximum of 20 ft (6 m) from the protected hood. [96:A.11.4.1.1]

A.50.5.4.1.3 Installing a guard should reduce the likelihood of an unwanted discharge of the fire-extinguishing system. [96:A.11.4.1.3]

A.50.5.6.2 Although training and qualification might be available elsewhere, the manufacturer of the equipment being installed should be considered an appropriate source of training and qualification. [96:11.6.2]

A.50.5.7.1 The system used to rate extinguishers for Class B fires (flammable liquids in depth) does not take into consideration the special nature of heated grease fires. Cooking-grease fires are a special hazard requiring agents that saponify (i.e., make a soap foam layer to seal the top surface of the grease) for this application. [96:A.11.7.1]

A.50.6.1.4 It is important that all kitchen employees be instructed that the fire-extinguishing system is the primary protection and how to respond appropriately to a fire. If the fire cannot be extinguished by shutting off the fuel source to a pan of burning grease and covering the pan, then employees should perform the following:

(1) Operate the manual actuation device for the fire-extinguishing system to suppress the fire and automatically shut off fuel to the appliances.
(2) Call the fire department and report the fire.
(3) Evacuate personnel and guests, as needed.
(4) Stand by with a Class K fire extinguisher to be used if the fire is not fully extinguished by the fire-extinguishing system.

[96:A.12.1.4]

A.50.6.2.1 It is recommended that such training and qualification be performed by the manufacturer of the equipment being inspected and serviced. The various electrical, mechanical, and filtration components of the systems should be inspected and tested as required to ensure that they continue to function according to original design. [96:A.12.2.1]

A.50.6.2.2 It is not intended that actual discharge of agent occur to test all components, but where pressure from the discharging agent or from compressed gas actuators is needed to actuate control components, an alternate means for testing those components should be provided and used. [96:A.12.2.2]

A.50.6.2.4 The date of manufacture marked on fusible metal alloy sensing elements does not limit when they can be used. These devices have unlimited shelf life. The intent of 50.6.2.4 is to require semiannual replacement of fusible metal alloy sensing elements that have been installed in environments that subject them to contaminant loading, such as grease in restaurant hoods and ducts, that could adversely affect their proper operation. [96:A.12.2.4]

A.50.6.3.4 See A.50.6.2.4. [96:A.12.3.4]

A.50.6.4 The primary focus of an inspection for cleanliness is to establish whether the volume of grease buildup within the exhaust system warrants cleaning and to determine whether adequate access is available throughout the exhaust system to remove the grease buildup. [96:A.12.4]

ANSI/IKECA I10 provides guidance for inspection of the exhaust system. [96:A.12.4]

N **A.50.6.6.1** ANSI/IKECA C10 provides guidance for cleaning the exhaust system.

A good operating practice is for cleaning personnel of commercial kitchen exhaust systems to have personal protective equipment (PPE) and height access equipment. The following items should be considered as a minimum:

(1) Eye protection
(2) Hand protection
(3) Head protection
(4) Foot protection
(5) Respiratory protection
(6) Fall protection
(7) Ladders
(8) Lock-out/tag-out kit

Preparation. The fan should be turned off, locked out, and tagged out. Open flames should be extinguished, and switches/breakers serving the appliance and cooking area outlets should be locked out. If the switches/breakers are not capable of being locked out and tagged out, any solid-fuel cooking appliances should be extinguished and the solid fuel removed.

Removal or Covering of Equipment. Food products, cookware, and cooking support equipment that can be removed should be removed from the cleaning area. Equipment that cannot be removed should be covered.

Cleaning Methods. The following methods for cleaning surfaces covered with grease and contaminants have been proved to be effective:

(1) Manual cleaning by scraping, grinding, or scrubbing
(2) Chemical cleaning with agents and water
(3) Pressure washing with pressurized water or pressurized water and agents
(4) Steam cleaning with pressurized steam

Waste Water and Solid Waste. Water and agents used in the cleaning process and solid waste should be collected for disposal. [96:A.12.6.1]

N **A.50.6.6.13.1(1)** Such as is done via hand punch.

N **A.50.6.7.2** Once the agent has fully discharged and if the fire has not been extinguished, the fire can continue to burn and spread. This can occur if the fire starts in or before system discharge and spreads to an area outside the protected area. Examples of areas outside the zone of protection include the flue of a gas-fired fryer, the area below the cooking surface of a griddle, inside the grease drip collectors, and any area behind or below an appliance. To minimize the probability of a fire spreading out of control, it is important that these areas outside the zone of protection be kept clean of grease and other combustible cooking residues. [96:A.12.7.2]

Δ **A.50.7.1.1** Cooking appliances that are designed for permanent installation, including, but not limited to, ranges, ovens, stoves, broilers, grills, fryers, griddles, and barbecues, should be installed in accordance with the manufacturer's installation instructions.

(1) Commercial electric cooking appliances should be listed and labeled in accordance with UL 197.
(2) Microwave cooking appliances should be listed and labeled in accordance with UL 923.
(3) Oil-burning stoves should be listed and labeled in accordance with UL 896.
(4) Wood-fired cooking appliances should be listed and labeled in accordance with UL 737 or UL 2162, depending on exact appliance type.
(5) Gas-fired cooking appliances should be listed and labeled in accordance with ANSI Z83.11.
(6) Gas-wood-fired cooking appliances should be listed and labeled in accordance with ANSI Z83.11, UL 737, and/or UL 2162, depending on exact appliance type.

[96:A.13.1.1]

A.50.7.1.2.1 Gas-fueled appliances should be installed to the requirements of NFPA 54 or NFPA 58. [96:A.13.1.2.1]

A.50.7.1.2.2 The effectiveness of an automatic extinguishing system is affected by the placement of the nozzles. For this reason, it is essential that cooking appliances be situated in the area in which they were when the extinguishing equipment was designed and installed. If an appliance is moved from under the equipment for cleaning or any other reason, it should be returned to its original position prior to initiation of a cooking operation. [96:A.13.1.2.2]

When appliances are on wheels or casters for ease of cleaning, it is important that the appliance be placed in its design position to ensure that the fire-extinguishing system will be effective. An approved method should ensure that the appliance is returned to its appropriate position before cooking takes place. Channels, markings, or other approved methods assist in ensuring proper placement. [96:A.13.1.2.2]

A.50.7.1.2.3.1 Wheel chocks that can be fastened to the floor should be installed to ensure that an appliance with casters is returned to its approved design location. [96:A.13.1.2.3.1]

A.50.8.2.1 Although 10 ft (3 m) clearance is considered reasonable to accommodate most fire departments, the AHJ should be allowed to determine if local fire service operations can accommodate vehicles parked closer than 10 ft (3 m). [96:A.17.2.1]

N **A.50.8.8.2.3** The phrase "each use" is intended to mean that a visual inspection is needed each day, prior to the cooking appliances being used. Visually inspecting for a leak can be done using a soapy solution and looking for bubbles. [96:A.17.8.2.3]

N **A.50.8.11.6** The address required to be posted in 50.8.11.6 is so that anyone helping with the operation of the mobile or temporary cooking operation can quickly and correctly share their location with the 911 operator or emergency responders if assistance is needed. A suggested method for a vehicle with a regular route would be to create a flip chart with the regularly visited locations on durable pages that can be fastened in a prominent location. [96:A.17.11.6]

A.52.1.1 This Chapter 52 regulates the design, commissioning, construction, installation, maintenance, testing, and decommissioning of stationary and mobile energy storage systems.

It is not the intent of Chapter 52 to regulate equipment with integral standby power systems below the amounts in Table 1.3 of NFPA 855, such as emergency lighting units, fire alarm control units, and other appliances and equipment.

A.52.1.8 This includes installations in the following locations:

(1) Indoor installations in dedicated-use buildings (see Table 4.4.2 of NFPA 855)
(2) Indoor installations in nondedicated-use buildings (see Table 4.4.2 of NFPA 855)
(3) Outdoor installations near exposures (see Table 4.4.3 of NFPA 855)
(4) Outdoor installations in remote locations (see Table 4.4.3 of NFPA 855)
(5) Rooftop installations (see Table 4.4.4 of NFPA 855)
(6) Installations in open parking garages (see Table 4.4.4 of NFPA 855)
(7) One- and two-family dwellings and townhouse unit installations (see Chapter 15 of NFPA 855)

Δ **A.52.1.12.2.3** This is in line with the scope of 90.2(D)(5) of *NFPA 70* and applies to lead-acid or nickel-cadmium batteries. [855:A.4.7.7.3(2)]

N **A.52.1.14** Installations of communications equipment, including batteries, under the exclusive control of communications utilities located outdoors or in building spaces used exclusively for such installations are not covered by *NFPA 70* and need not comply with the requirements of *NFPA 70*. [855:A.4.7.1]

Adequate working space is vital for electrical safety-related work practices. Articles 110 and 706 of *NFPA 70* provide working space requirements for electrical equipment. NECA 416 is another installation standard that provides guidelines for working space requirements. [855:A.4.7.1]

A.52.1.19.2 This sign can be broken into multiple segments. An example of this would be if the manufacturer provides their own separate signage about the fire suppression system. [855:A.4.7.4.2]

N **A.52.1.23** This section addresses hazards associated with the release of flammable gases from ESS during normal charging, discharging, and use conditions. Similar requirements have been in fire codes for many years primarily to address off-gassing of hydrogen from stationary vented lead-acid battery systems but not limited to that technology. [855:A.9.6.5.1]

This section is not intended to provide protection against the release of flammable gases during abnormal charging or thermal runaway conditions. Those conditions are addressed in 9.6.5.6 of NFPA 855. In addition, this section does not regulate ventilation of toxic and highly toxic gases, which are regulated by 4.6.11 of NFPA 855. [855:A.9.6.5.1]

N **A.52.2.2** Based on the system design and features, remote monitoring and controls that provide additional safety benefits can be used by the AHJ to determine the level of onsite monitoring required. [855:A.9.6.6.2.4]

N **A.52.2.3** Hazard support personnel should be able to provide support to the AHJ in reoccupying the space, implementing the decommissioning plan, and deenergizing the battery modules for a safe means of transportation. [855:A.9.6.6.2.5]

Hazard support personnel are not expected to perform any fire suppression duties but can do so if properly trained and equipped. [855:A.9.6.6.2.5]

A.53.1 See the mechanical code for refrigerant group descriptions.

A.53.1.1.1 Refrigerant safety groups are established by ANSI/ASHRAE 34, *Designation and Safety Classification of Refrigerants*. Safety groups are based on the relative safety with respect to toxicity and flammability. The classification groups include a letter designation that indicates the toxicity (A is "lower toxicity" and B is "higher toxicity") and a number that indicates flammability (1 indicates no flame propagation in air when tested by prescribed methods at specified conditions, 2 is "lower flammability," and 3 is "higher flammability").

A.53.2.3.1.4 See A.53.1.1.1.

A.53.2.3.2 See A.53.1.1.1.

A.54.2.2.2 NEMA 250, *Enclosures for Electrical Equipment*, is intended for use as a guide in the design, fabrication, testing, and use of equipment regulated by Chapter 54.

A.60.1.6.1 See NFPA 400 for a model hazardous materials management plan (HMMP). [400:A.1.11.1]

A.60.1.7 See NFPA 400 for a model hazardous materials inventory statement (HMIS). [400:A.1.12]

A.60.3.3 Where a conflict exists between applicable requirements, an analysis should be made and the proper applicable requirement should be implemented or conformed to subject to the approval of the AHJ. [400:A.4.4]

N **A.60.3.4** The safe handling, collection, and disposal of hazardous waste can be accomplished only if the physical, chemical, and hazardous properties of its components are known and that information is properly applied. The categorization of a material as waste is normally under the purview of the user. In some cases the waste might be contaminated or "off spec" material, or material where the concentration of the hazardous components has been diluted. In other cases the waste might consist of cleaning materials that have become contaminated with a hazardous material. [400:A.4.5]

The classifiers of waste are cautioned that the classification of hazardous waste under the requirements of the Environmental Protection Agency (EPA) or Department of Transportation

(DOT) for labeling required for shipping purposes might not correspond to the system of classification incorporated into Section 4.1 of NFPA 400. In addition, some judgment is needed to apply the code in circumstances where the waste material is not in a form that is normally encountered when the hazardous material employed is in its virgin state. For example, a material that might not have been hazardous in its pure form might become hazardous when it becomes contaminated as use occurs. A tank of water used for rinsing parts on a plating line will eventually become contaminated by the materials that are being rinsed from parts as they travel through the line. If the concentration of the material being rinsed from parts becomes high enough, the content of hazardous materials in the rinse tank might be present in a concentration sufficient enough to cause the waste rinse water to be classified as hazardous. See Section B of NFPA 400 for examples on the classification of dilute solutions of common corrosive materials. [400:A.4.5]

In many cases the waste material could be a mixture of materials that must be classified in accordance with the requirements of Section 4.3 of NFPA 400. [400:A.4.5]

A.60.4.4 Where a detached building is required for indoor storage in accordance with Table 60.4.3.7, detached outdoor storage can be used in lieu of indoor storage. Where detached outdoor storage is implemented, the outdoor storage requirements in Chapters 5 and 6 of NFPA 400, and any material-specific chapters of NFPA 400 apply. [400:A.5.4]

A.60.5.1.1.1 Outdoor control areas are not classified with protection levels. [400:A.6.1.1.1]

A.60.5.1.1.2 Outdoor control areas are not classified with protection levels. [400:A.6.1.1.2]

A.60.5.1.2 *Readily available* can mean access to the product manufacturer's or user's paper or electronic copies of SDSs. [400:A.6.1.2]

A.60.5.1.3.4 There might be additional regulations that must be complied with to notify other agencies. [400:A.6.1.3.4]

A.60.5.1.4 The hazard potential of a facility is not dependent on any single factor. Physical size, number of employees, and the quantity and the nature of the hazardous materials are important considerations. The level of training can vary with the complexity of the facility under consideration. [400:A.6.1.4]

A.60.5.1.5.3.1 The approved powered industrial trucks addressed in NFPA 505 are trucks that are listed by a testing laboratory for the use intended and should be tested and labeled in accordance with UL 558, *Safety Industrial Trucks, Internal Combustion Engine-Powered*, or UL 583, *Safety Electric-Battery-Powered Industrial Trucks*. [400:6.1.5.3.1]

A.60.5.1.16.2.3 Testing can include visual inspection, x-ray, spark testing, pressure testing, leak testing, or other nondestructive methods. [400:A.6.1.16.2.3]

A.61.1.1.1 Chapter 61 provides minimum acceptable requirements for fire prevention and protection in facilities that manufacture and store aerosol products and in mercantile occupancies where aerosol products are displayed and sold. As explained in A.6.1 of NFPA 30B, the hazards presented by each stage of the manufacturing process will vary, depending on the flammability of the base product and on the flammability of the propellant. Considerable judgment will be required of the designer and of the AHJ to provide an adequate level of fire protection. *(See also Annex B of NFPA 30B.)* [30B:A.1.2]

Aerosol products in storage or mercantile occupancies complying with this chapter, and covered by 60.1.2(9), are not required to comply with Sections 60.1 through 60.4.

A.61.1.1.3 For products that do not meet this requirement, see NFPA 55 and NFPA 58. [30B:A.1.1.2]

A.61.1.1.5 Chapter 61 does not apply to products that can be dispensed as aerosolized sprays that are not packaged in aerosol containers as defined in 3.3.1 of NFPA 30B. Chapter 61 is not applicable to other applications such as industrial spray adhesives that are dispensed from large [5–125 gal (18.9 L–475 L)] pressurized gas cylinders. There is no assurance that the protection specified in Chapter 61 will be adequate. [30B:A.1.1.4]

N A.61.1.3 Tests have shown that aerosol products in plastic containers with a heat of combustion of 10.5 kJ/g have been adequately protected as determined by fire tests. See Annex C for a description of the testing of aerosol products in plastic containers. *(See also Annex E of NFPA 30B for information on determining the classification level of aerosol products in metal containers.)* [30B:A.4.2]

N A.61.1.4.1(3) Fire testing with alcohol and water at this percentage in plastic bottles has been successful. Small-scale burn tests of aerosol products in plastic containers have shown the aerosol with a nonflammable propellant to behave the same as the aerosol with no propellant. [30B:A4.3.1(3)]

N A.61.1.4.1(4) A fire test with a formula of this type using liquefied petroleum gas was successful. An emulsion in an aerosol product is a mixture of two or more liquids, one of which is present as droplets of microscopic or ultramicroscopic size distributed throughout the other. Emulsions are formed from the component liquids either spontaneously or, more often, by mechanical means such as agitation, provided that the liquids that are mixed have no (or a very limited) mutual solubility. Emulsions are stabilized by agents that form films at the surface of the droplets (e.g., soap molecules) or that impart to them a mechanical stability (e.g., colloidal carbon or bentonite). Colloidal distributions or suspension of one or more liquid(s) with another liquid will have a shelf life that varies with the efficiency of the recipe used. [30B:A.4.3.1(4)]

N A.61.1.4.3 The aerosol industry might work on a plastic aerosol product with a formula requiring greater protection than Plastic Aerosol 1, but less protection than that required for Plastic Aerosol 3. By designating the product in 61.1.4.3 as Plastic Aerosol 3, it will not lead to a conflict for a later formula in regard to carton marking and sprinkler protection requirements. [30B:A.4.3.3]

A.61.3.1.3 At the present time there have been no fire-retardant packaging systems tested that have demonstrated substantial mitigation of the fire hazards presented by aerosol products. [30B:A.7.1.3]

A.61.3.4.1.2 The maximum quantity of storage of Plastic Aerosol X Products is limited to what is provided in 61.3.4.1.2 because no demonstrated protection criteria are available. [30B:A.7.5.1.2]

A.61.5.3.3 See NFPA 51B for further information. [30B:A.9.3.3]

A.61.5.7 See NFPA 77 for further information. [30B:A.9.7]

A.63.1.1.1 See A.1.3.2.

A.63.1.1.4(1) For regulations on the transportation of gases, see 49 CFR 100–185, "Transportation," and *Transportation of Dangerous Goods Regulations*. [55:A.1.3.2(1)]

A.63.1.1.4(3) Cryogenic fluid central supply system installations are intended to be covered by the requirements of this *Code*. Instrumentation and alarms that are attendant to the system and designed to interface with the application in a health care facility are to be retained within the purview of NFPA 99. See Section 17.1.2 of NFPA 55. [55:A.1.3.2(3)]

Refer to Section 63.12 for requirements for liquid oxygen (LOX) in home health care.

A.63.1.1.4(5) For information, see NFPA 52, or NFPA 58. [55:A.1.3.2(5)]

A.63.1.1.4(6) The storage and use of compressed gases and cryogenic fluids outside the boundaries of laboratory work areas are covered by NFPA 55. [55:A.1.3.2(6)]

A.63.1.1.4(11) NFPA 55 is used as the source document for the fundamental requirements for compressed hydrogen gas (GH_2), or liquefied hydrogen gas (LH_2) system installations. Correlation between NFPA 55 and NFPA 2 is the responsibility of the two technical committees involved. The installation requirements for bulk GH_2 or LH_2 are viewed as fundamental provisions. On the other hand, use-specific requirements for designated applications such as vehicular fueling are not resident in NFPA 55 and are under the purview of the NFPA 2 Technical Committee. Where there are specific provisions or controls included in NFPA 55, the specific controls of NFPA 55 will govern except that modifications made to provisions that have been extracted can be followed when the modifications have been made within NFPA's extract procedure as indicated in the *Manual of Style for NFPA Technical Committee Documents*. [55:A.1.3.2(11)]

A.63.1.4.1 Not all hazardous materials are placed into the high hazard category, and some of these materials have been recognized as being of low ordinary hazard, depending on their nature in a fire. Inert compressed gases and cryogenic fluids are one example; there are others. Compressed gases and cryogenic fluids represent the gas phase of an array of hazardous materials. As the genre of hazardous materials is expanded, there are other materials in hazard categories or hazard classes that may in fact be high hazard materials by definition, but which in some cases do not have a MAQ and, therefore, are not required to comply with the requirements for high hazard occupancies. Examples of such materials are Class IIIB combustible liquids, Class 1 unstable reactive materials (including gases), Class 1 water-reactive solids and liquids, Class 1-3 water-reactive gases, Class 1 oxidizing solids and liquids, and Class IV and V organic peroxides. [55:A.5.1.1]

N A.63.2.3.1.1 Maximum Allowable Quantity. Table 63.2.3.1.1 allows for a 100 percent increase in the MAQ for quantities stored in approved cabinets or other specified control. A combination of storage both inside and outside approved cabinets within the control area is permitted. Storage amounts up to the MAQ are allowed outside of cabinets where the 100 percent increase is applied. Footnotes (^{d}) and (^{e}) allow quantities to be increased by an additional 100 percent where sprinklers are installed throughout the building. [55:A.6.3.1.1]

As an example, Table A.63.2.3.1.1 shows the MAQ for oxidizing gas with various control scenarios. [55:A.6.3.1.1]

Δ A.63.2.5 Bulk hydrogen compressed gas systems terminate at the source valve. In cylinder filling or packaging operations, cylinders located on filling manifolds located downstream of the source valve are not considered to be part of the bulk gas system. For definitions of *source valve* and *bulk hydrogen compressed gas system*, see 3.3.94 and 3.3.100.9.1 of NFPA 55. Additional requirements for source valves can be found in 63.2.19. The 15,000 scf (425 Nm^3) threshold only applies to the supply and not to cylinders being filled from the system. An example of an individual bulk hydrogen system would be supply containers manifolded together into an individual system, such as a bundle or a tube trailer that exceeds 15,000 scf and which is intended to feed a process. [55:A.6.6]

A.63.2.7 Electrical and electronic equipment and wiring for use in hazardous locations as defined in Article 500 of *NFPA 70* should meet the requirements of Articles 500 and 501 of *NFPA 70*. Note that Article 505 also details requirements for this equipment and wiring in hazardous locations and uses a zone classification method rather than the division method of Article 500. [55:A.6.8]

A.63.2.8 Under the requirements of 29 CFR 1910.38 established by OSHA regulations, employers must establish an employee alarm system that complies with 29 CFR 1910.165. The requirements of 29 CFR 1910.165 for the employee alarm system include, but are not limited to, systems that are capable of being perceived above ambient noise or light levels by all employees in the affected portions of the workplace. Tactile devices should be used to alert those employees who would not otherwise be able to recognize the audible or visual alarm. The alarm system can be electrically powered or powered by pneumatic or other means. State, local, or other governmental regu-

N Table A.63.2.3.1.1 Oxidizing Gas with Various Control Scenarios

Controls	Maximum Allowed Outside Cabinets scf	Maximum Allowed Outside Cabinets Nm^3	Maximum Total Allowed scf	Maximum Total Allowed Nm^3
No cabinets, no sprinklers	1500	42.48	1500	42.48
No cabinets, fully sprinklered	3000	84.96	3000	84.96
Cabinets, no sprinklers	1500	42.48	3000	84.96
Cabinets, fully sprinklered	3000	84.96	6000	169.92

[55:Table A.6.3.1.1]

lations might also establish requirements for employee alarm systems. [55:A.6.9]

A.63.2.10 The intent of this section is to require a water-based fire extinguishing system to keep vessels containing compressed gases cool in the event of an exposure fire, thereby minimizing the likelihood of a release and associated consequences. Accordingly, alternative fire extinguishing systems, such as dry-chemical or gaseous agent systems, should not be substituted. [55:A.6.11]

A.63.2.16.8.2 Examples of gases that are heavier than air include, but are not limited to, carbon dioxide, argon, and nitrous oxide. [55:A.6.17.4.2]

A.63.2.16.8.3 Examples of gases that are lighter than air include, but are not limited to, hydrogen, helium, and methane. [55:A.6.17.4.3]

N **A.63.2.17.6** Cylinders should be secured with straps, chains, or racks installed in gas cabinets to prevent falling or rolling. Racks should be of open design that allows air to move through the cabinet. [55:A.6.18.6]

N **A.63.2.17.7** It is prudent that all electrical equipment inside a gas cabinet meets at least a Class I, Division 2 classification unless a hazard analysis and risk assessment indicate another classification is more prudent. The area outside the gas cabinet should be classified based on the situation and activities occurring in that area independent of the gas cabinet itself. NFPA 497 can also be a valuable source for proper classifications. [55:A.6.18.7]

A.63.2.19 Figure A.63.2.19 shows three possible locations of the source valve. [55:A.6.20]

A.63.3.1.5 The compressed gas system equipment referenced is intended to include fuel cell applications, generation of hydrogen from portable or transportable hydrogen generation equipment, batteries, and similar devices and equipment that utilize hydrogen for the purpose of power generation. It does not include hydrogen production facilities intended to produce hydrogen used for distribution or repackaging operations operated by gas producers, distributors, and repackagers. [55:A.10.2.8]

A.63.3.1.6 Numerous metal hydrides are currently being tested for gaseous hydrogen storage applications. While certain Class D extinguishing agents have been effective on some metal hydride materials, they have not been tested on the wide range of hydrides. It is crucial to understand any adverse chemical reactions between the hydride and the agent prior to using the fire suppressant. Additionally, it is important to understand that the application should be limited to small incipient stage fires. Larger fires would require the use of personal protective equipment in the application of the extinguishing agent. [55:A.10.2.9]

N **A.63.3.1.7.5.7.3** Where multiple valves or pressure relief devices are connected to a vent stack or common header, the potential exists for one valve to discharge into the header or stack while personnel are performing maintenance on another valve or pressure relief device. One solution is to install valves on the inlet and outlet of pressure relief devices for maintenance. Closing a full-area stop valve on the outlet of a pressure relief device that is being replaced prevents the backflow of gas from another device connected to the same stack or header. The ASME *Boiler and Pressure Vessel Code* requires that full-area stop valves be locked open and provided with manual vent valves for maintaining pressure during maintenance operations. Further, the ASME Code requires that if the full-area stop valve is closed, an operator must be present at all times to maintain the vessel pressure within acceptable limits and must lock the full-area stop valve in the open position before leaving the station. See the *ASME Boiler and Pressure Vessel Code* for complete details and requirements. [55:A.7.1.5.5.7.3]

A.63.3.1.10.2 The goal of this requirement is to prevent unauthorized personnel or those unfamiliar with gas storage systems from tampering with the equipment as well as to prevent the inadvertent or unauthorized removal or use of compressed gases from storage areas. Where the compressed gases are located in an area open to the general public, a common practice is to fence and lock the storage or use area, with access restricted to supplier and user personnel. When the storage or use area is located within the user's secure area and is not accessible by the general public, it is not always necessary to fence or otherwise secure the individual gas storage or use areas. Personnel access patterns may still mandate that the system be fenced, as determined by the supplier and the user. [55:A.7.1.8.2]

A.63.3.1.12.2 Figure A.63.3.1.12.2 is a schematic showing the separation distances required by 63.3.1.12.2. [55:A.7.1.10.2]

N **A.63.3.1.12.2.3** The NFPA *Fire Protection Guide to Hazardous Materials* can be used for guidance on compatibility. Additionally, safety data sheets and other sources such as the Hazardous Materials Expert Assistant (HMEX) provide information about the compatibility of chemicals. [55:A.7.1.10.2.3]

A.63.3.1.12.2.6 Analysis of gas mixtures often includes the analysis of individual cylinders that have been disconnected from the filling manifolds. The analysis procedure is a production step where cylinders of many different types and contents are processed. It is not unusual for an individual gas mixture to contain gases otherwise deemed to be incompatible in the pure state. For example, a mixture of hydrogen and air is routinely manufactured for use as a calibrating gas mixture used to validate the operation of flammable gas detection systems. Analytical operations involving incompatible gases, which may be located within an individual laboratory, typically require that the gases being analyzed be connected to individual work stations or analytical instruments as the process is conducted. The typical analytical process is an attended process where technicians have "hands on" control of the cylinder under examination, which serves to mitigate events that may otherwise occur in unattended operations, including storage or the use of an unattended source of supply. [55:A.7.1.10.2.6]

A.63.3.1.12.3 Clearance is required from combustible materials to minimize the effects of exposure fires to the materials stored or used. The requirement to separate the materials from vegetation should not be interpreted to mean that the area is maintained free of all vegetation. In some settings, gas systems are located on grounds that are maintained with formal landscaping. Some judgment must be exercised to determine whether the vegetation poses what might be viewed as an exposure hazard to the materials stored. Cut lawns, formal landscaping, and similar vegetation do not ordinarily present a hazard and should be allowed. On the other hand, tall, dry grass or weeds and vegetation that fringes on the border of an urban–wildland interface might be viewed as a hazard. [55:A.7.1.10.3]

(a) JTG Liquid Supply System(s)

(b) JTG Tube Trailer Offloading Station

(c) JTG Tube Trailer Supply System

⟶ Piping within the scope of NFPA 55
---⟶ Piping within the scope of NFPA 52
⟶ Optional piping within the scope of NFPA 55

FIGURE A.63.2.19 Three Examples of Source Valve Locations. [55: Figure A.6.20]

FIGURE A.63.3.1.12.2 Separation of Gas Cylinders by Hazard. [55:Figure A.7.1.10.2]

A.63.3.1.12.10.1 Electrical devices can include pressure transducers, signal transmitters, shutoff controls, and similar devices. Some of these devices may be nonincendive and suitable for use in hazardous areas. Flammability of gases is not the only concern with respect to electrical circuits, because piping serving systems in use can act as conductors of electrical energy, exposing unrelated portions of the system to electrical hazards if improperly installed. [55:A.7.1.10.10.1]

A.63.3.1.16.3 The gas supplier should be consulted for advice under these circumstances. [55:A.7.1.14.3]

A.63.3.1.19.1.2 Underground piping systems are those systems that are buried and in contact with earth fill or similar materials. Piping located in open-top or grated-top trenches is not considered to be underground although it may be below grade. [55:A.7.1.17.1.2]

A.63.3.1.20.1.1(3) The replacement of parts in a system to repair leaks, the addition of gaskets, and similar routine maintenance is not intended to establish the need for cleaning of the entire piping system. The requirement is to not introduce new containments during the repair (e.g., cutting oils, grinding debris, contaminated hardware). Conversely, when a piping system is extended, or when the system needs to be rendered safe for maintenance purposes, purging the system before disassembly likely will be required as will internal cleaning if new piping or materials of construction are introduced. [55:A.7.1.18.1.1(3)]

A.63.3.1.20.1.1(4) Cleaning and purging of piping systems can be conducted as individual functions, that is, just cleaning, just purging, or in combination as required to satisfy the requirements of the procedures. [55:A.7.1.18.1.1(4)]

A.63.3.1.20.1.3 It is not intended that a new written procedure be required each time the activity occurs within a facility. [55:A.7.1.18.1.3]

A.63.3.1.20.1.3.1 The review of the written procedures should not be performed solely by the same person(s) responsible for developing the procedures. It can be performed by an independent person or group within the company or department or by a third-party consultant. [55:A.7.1.18.1.3.1]

Δ **A.63.3.1.20.1.5.3** The notification is given to warn personnel that such procedures are about to occur so they will be out of zones potentially affected by the cleaning or purging procedure. The intended notification is to be commensurate with the operation to be conducted, and the timing of the notification should be relevant to the activity conducted so that personnel in the area can respond in a timely manner. Notification could be an audible and/or visible alarm or an announcement over a public address system, private network, radio, or similar and reliable means of electronic transmission. [55:A.7.1.18.1.5.3]

Verbal notification can be used in operations where the piping system is limited to the area occupied by those that will be conducting the cleaning or purging procedures and related operating personnel. These areas frequently are found in occupancies where the gas used to charge the piping system is supplied from portable containers, as well as those areas where the piping system is located primarily in the occupied work area. [55:A.7.1.18.1.5.3]

A.63.3.1.20.2 For additional information on cleaning techniques used for stainless steel parts and equipment, see ASTM A380/A380 M, *Standard Practice for Cleaning, Descaling, and Passivation of Stainless Steel Parts, Equipment, and Systems.* [55:A.7.1.18.2]

Δ **A.63.3.1.20.2.2** During construction, visual inspection should be performed on sections of pipe as the piping system is being assembled to ensure that no gross contamination is left in the pipe. Where the standard of cleanliness is high, fabrication techniques should be utilized that do not introduce contamination into the pipe. Examples of these techniques can include, but are not limited to, constant inert gas purging or assembly in a particulate-controlled environment. The use of piping and components with a high-quality interior surface finish and high-quality materials of construction all have an effect on the ability to maintain a high degree of cleanliness. [55:A.7.1.18.2.2]

Cleaning after construction can typically be accomplished by one or more of the following methods:

(1) Pigging
(2) Mechanical scraping
(3) High-velocity gas flow
(4) Liquid washing
(5) Use of cleaning media
(6) Application of high vacuum
(7) Solvent cleaning
(8) Water washing
(9) Steam cleaning

[55:A.7.1.18.2.2]

A.63.3.1.20.3 Purging can be accomplished by continuous media or gas flow, evacuation or vacuum, or repeated pressurizing and venting cycles commonly referred to as pulse purging or cycle purging. In some cases, purge procedures can involve more than one type of purging technique. Purging can be accomplished by manual or automatic means. Automated purge panels or manifold systems operated by a programmable logic controller are commonly used as a means to enhance the results of a purging process where high purity gas delivery systems are employed. [55:A.7.1.18.3]

A.63.3.4.1.11.1.1 In operations where an automatic emergency shutoff valve is activated by a control system that is operated from a remote station or by remote station software, the software system should be designed to provide a visual indication of the emergency shutdown control system. The visual emergency shutdown function should be able to be identified by trained operators and recognizable to emergency response personnel. [55:A.7.4.1.11.1.1]

A.63.3.6.2.1.1 Portions of the system upstream of the source valve include the containers or bulk supply as well as control equipment designed to control the flow of gas into a piping system. The piping system downstream of the source valve is protected by excess flow control should failure occur in the piping system and is not required to be protected by the fire barrier. The fire barrier serves to protect those portions of the system that are the most vulnerable along with the necessary controls used to operate the system. [55:A.7.6.2.1.1]

A.63.3.7.1.1 All liquefied and nonliquefied flammable compressed gases are regulated by 63.3.7 unless they are specifically indicated as not applicable in accordance with 63.1.1.4. [55:A.7.7.1.1]

A.63.3.7.2.1.1 See A.63.3.6.2.1.1. [55:A.7.7.2.1.1]

N **A.63.3.7.2.2** Even though Chapter 10 of NFPA 55 is specific to hydrogen gas systems, the tables referenced in 63.3.7.2.2 [e.g., Table 10.4.2.2.1(a) through Table 10.4.2.2.1(c) of NFPA 55] can be used for all flammable gases, including hydrogen. [55:A.7.7.2.2]

A.63.3.8.2.1.1 See A.63.3.6.2.1.1. [55:A.7.8.2.1.1]

A.63.3.9.3.1.1 See A.63.3.6.2.1.1. [55:A.7.9.3.1.1]

A.63.3.10.2.2.1.1 See A.63.3.6.2.1.1. [55:A.7.10.2.2.1.1]

A.63.3.10.3.6 The areas for typical restricted flow orifices are shown in Table A.63.3.10.3.6. [55:A.7.10.3.6]

A.63.3.10.3.6.2 The formula has been taken from industry publications including the Scott Specialty Gases *Design and Safety Handbook*. It is based on estimated flow rates for air at 70°F (21°C) discharging to normal atmospheric pressure through an average shape and quality orifice. It can be assumed to be ±15 percent accurate. Correction factors have been built into the formula as presented in 63.3.10.3.6.2 to accommodate the use of gases other than air (e.g., use of specific gravity data). [55:A.7.10.3.6.2]

Δ **Table A.63.3.10.3.6 Typical Orifice Areas**

Orifice Diameter		Area	
in.	cm	in.^{2}	cm^2
0.006	0.015	2.83×10^{-5}	1.83×10^{-4}
0.010	0.025	7.85×10^{-5}	5.06×10^{-4}
0.014	0.036	1.54×10^{-4}	9.93×10^{-4}

[55:Table A.7.10.3.6]

A.63.3.11.1.2.1 See A.63.3.6.2.1.1. [55:A.7.11.1.2.1]

A.63.3.11.2.2.1 See A.63.3.6.2.1.1. [55:A.7.11.2.2.1]

A.63.4.2 Pressure vessels of any type can be subject to additional regulations imposed by various states or other legal jurisdictions. Users should be aware that compliance with DOT or ASME requirements might not satisfy all the required regulations for the location in which the vessel is to be installed or used. [55:A.8.2]

A.63.4.2.3.3 Vaporizers or heat exchangers used to vaporize cryogenic fluids can accumulate a large load of ice during operation. Additional requirements to be considered in the design include snow load for the area where the installation is located as well as the requirements for seismic conditions. The operating conditions of systems vary, and the designer has a responsibility to consider all the loads that might be imposed. Foundations that could be used to support delivery vehicles as well might require special consideration relevant to live loads as well as for the dead loads imposed by the equipment itself. [55:A.8.2.3.3]

A.63.4.2.4.5.1 Pressure relief valves typically are spring-loaded valves where the relief pressure is set by adjustment of a spring. Valves should be made to be tamper resistant in order to prevent adjustment by other than authorized personnel typically found at a retest facility. An ASME pressure relief valve is designed to comply with the requirements of the ASME *Boiler and Pressure Vessel Code* and typically is equipped with a wire and lead seal to resist tampering. [55:A.8.2.4.5.1]

A.63.4.2.4.7.2.1 The ASME *Boiler and Pressure Vessel Code* requires that full-area stop valves be locked open and provided with manual vent valves for maintaining pressure during maintenance operations. Further, the ASME Code requires that if the full-area stop valve is closed, an operator must be present at all times to maintain the vessel pressure within acceptable limits and must lock the full-area stop valve in the open position before leaving the station. See the ASME *Boiler and Pressure Vessel Code* for complete details and requirements. [55:A.8.2.4.7.2.1]

A.63.4.4.1.1.2 An example of this identification is 360 degree wraparound tape. [55:A.8.4.1.1.2]

A.63.4.5.2 The purpose of this requirement is to prevent unauthorized personnel or those unfamiliar with cryogenic storage systems from tampering with the equipment. Where the bulk storage system is located in an area open to the general public, a common practice is to fence the system and lock it, with access restricted to supplier personnel and sometimes user personnel. When the bulk storage system is located within the user's secure area and is not open to the general public, it is not always necessary to fence the bulk storage system. Personnel access patterns may still mandate that the system be fenced, as determined by the supplier and the user. [55:A.8.5.2]

A.63.4.6.2 It is not uncommon to have inert cryogenic fluids used to provide stage effects for theatrical performances that are conducted within assembly occupancies. The fluids are sometimes placed within these occupancies with special controls, including ventilation systems, fire detection systems, monitors for oxygen deficiency, warning signs, and remote fill indicating devices that indicate tank volume when a remote filling point is provided and stationary tanks are involved. Such installations are normally permitted on a case-by-case basis under the requirements of Section 1.6 of NFPA 55. [55:A.8.6.2]

Clearance is required from combustible materials to minimize the effects of exposure fires to the materials stored or used. The requirement to separate the materials from vegetation should not be interpreted to mean that the area is maintained free of all vegetation. In some settings, gas systems are located on grounds that are maintained with formal landscaping. Some judgment must be exercised to determine whether the vegetation poses what might be viewed as an exposure hazard to the materials stored. Cut lawns, formal landscaping, and similar vegetation do not ordinarily present a hazard, and should be allowed. On the other hand, tall, dry grass or weeds and vegetation that fringes on the border of an urban–wildland interface might be viewed as a hazard. [55:A.8.6.2]

A.63.4.6.2.1.4.1 See Figure A.63.4.12.2.7.2.1, which addresses bulk cryogenic systems located in a courtyard. This figure also applies to the case where any or all of the three walls are constructed as fire barrier walls. [55:A.8.6.2.1.4.1]

A.63.4.12.2.5 Flood hazard areas typically are identified on either (1) the special flood hazard area shown on the flood insurance rate map or (2) the area subject to flooding during the design flood and shown on a jurisdiction's flood hazard map or otherwise legally designated. [55:A.8.12.2.5]

A.63.4.12.2.6.4.1 The intent of these provisions is to make certain that the cryogenic installation is not exposed to the potential of a pool fire from the release of flammable or combustible liquids. Cryogenic fluids are not diked in order that they are allowed to dissipate should leakage occur. Studies conducted by NASA (NSS 1740.16, *Safety Standard for Hydrogen and Hydrogen Systems,* 1997) show that the use of dikes around liquid hydrogen storage facilities serves to prolong ground-level flammable cloud travel and that the dispersion mechanism is enhanced by vaporization-induced turbulence. The travel of spilled or leaked cryogenic fluid to distances greater than a few feet (meters) from the source given the nature of the typical leak is considered to be implausible due to the character of cryogenic fluids and their ability to quickly absorb heat from the surrounding environment. [55:A.8.12.2.6.4.1]

A.63.4.12.2.7.1 CGA P-41, *Locating Bulk Storage Systems in Courts,* provides guidance to determine the suitability of a court or enclosed court. [55:A.8.12.2.7.1]

A.63.4.12.2.7.2 The placement of stationary containers is limited with respect to exposure hazards. Table 63.4.6.2 establishes the minimum separation distance between a building and any stationary tank at 1 ft (0.3 m). Additional limitations are placed on wall openings, air intakes, and other exposures. The material-specific tables for liquid oxygen and flammable cryogenic liquids specify increased distances according to the type of construction adjacent to the tank. A problem arises when courtyards are configured so as to interrupt the free movement of air around a tank where an asphyxiation hazard, a flammable hazard, or an oxygen-enriched environment can be created. [55:A.8.12.2.7.2]

Placement of stationary containers proximate to the wall of the building served is allowable, provided the minimum separation distances for exposure hazards are met. When additional walls encroach on the installation to form a court, the focus of concern shifts away from the exposure hazards associated with the building itself to the hazards associated with personnel due to hazardous atmospheres that can be created due to the lack of free air movement and ventilation. [55:A.8.12.2.7.2]

By specifying the minimum distance between the tank and the encroaching walls that form the court, the circulation of adequate air is ensured. Placing the tank at not less than the height of two of the three encroaching walls results in creating an opening such that the angular dimension between the top of two of the three encroaching walls and the point over which the tank is placed is not greater than 45 degrees, thereby allowing the circulation of air through the space in which the tank is installed. [55:A.8.12.2.7.2]

A.63.4.12.2.7.2.1 The separation distances shown in Figure A.63.4.12.2.7.2.1 are required to provide for ventilation in the space in order to avoid creating a confined space. Chapter 8 of NFPA 55 is a generic chapter used to establish minimum requirements for all cryogens. Material-specific requirements for oxygen, hydrogen, or other gases might require greater separation distances based on the type of construction or the related exposure. For example, wall number 3 shown in Figure A.63.4.12.2.7.2.1 could be an exterior building wall, and the gas could be hydrogen. Refer to Table 63.4.6.2 of this *Code*, and Table 9.3.2, Table 11.3.2.2, Table 13.10.1, and Table 16.2 of NFPA 55 for specific details regarding building walls, wall openings, air intakes, and similar conditions. [55:A.8.12.2.7.2.1]

Δ **A.63.4.13.1.4.2** CGA P-18, *Standard for Bulk Inert Gas Systems,* recommends periodic inspection intervals for inert gas systems. [55:A.8.13.1.4.1.1]

A.63.4.13.11.2.3.1 In operations where an automatic emergency shutoff valve is activated by a control system that is operated from a remote station or by remote station software, the software system should be designed to provide a visual indication of the emergency shutdown control system. The visual emergency shutdown function should be able to be identified by trained operators and recognizable to emergency response personnel. [55:A.8.13.11.2.3.1]

A.63.4.13.11.3.4 The inert cryogens, nitrogen and argon, do not require the installation of a noncombustible spill pad,

FIGURE A.63.4.12.2.7.2.1 Bulk Cryogenic System Located in a Courtyard. [55:Figure A.8.12.2.7.2.1]

because they do not typically condense oxygen from the air in sufficient quantities to pose a hazard during transfer. [55:A.8.13.11.3.4]

A.63.4.13.11.3.4.1 The noncombustible spill pad is provided for liquid helium transfer operations, because the cryogen is at a temperature that is sufficiently low enough to liquefy oxygen, presenting a hazard when in contact with combustible surfaces. [55:A.8.13.11.3.4.1]

N **A.63.9.5.2** Vent pipes must be protected to prevent the intrusion of water that can freeze and interfere with the operation of the pressure relief device. Covers can be employed to protect the vent pipe against the elements. Carbon dioxide released through vent pipes can be transformed to the solid state through the production of what is dry ice in the form of "snow." It is possible for dry ice to form a plug in the vent line system. For this reason, designers might choose to locate the pressure relief device at the end of a vent line rather than on the unit itself. There are alternative designs that accomplish this intent. It is important that the system designer provide a system that is not susceptible to the formation of ice plugs due to moisture or solid carbon dioxide so that vent lines function as intended. [55:A.13.4.1.2.2]

N **A.63.9.5.3** Where cylinders, containers, and tanks are in locations remote from the filling connection, a means to determine when the containers have been filled to their design capacity should be provided and be verifiable from the filling connection. A functional pressure gauge equipped on the filling equipment connected to the fill box on the outside of the building is one method used to determine when the container being filled and the delivery vehicle pressures quickly equalize and the transfer of product is complete. [55:A.13.4.1.2.3]

N **A.63.9.7.3** Materials used in the system can become brittle and fail if subjected to low temperatures. Maintain the system at or above the minimum design temperature by appropriate design materials or operating instructions to prevent system failure. [55:A.13.5]

In North America, the majority of the containers in refrigerated carbon dioxide service are fabricated using low-alloy carbon steels such as SA-212, SA-515, SA-516, and SA-612. Containers manufactured before 1990 typically had a minimum design metal temperature (MDMT), the lowest temperature at which a container is designed to operate at a given pressure at −20°F (−28.9°C). When the container wall is at an operating temperature colder than the MDMT, it is out of its intended operating condition. [55:A.13.5]

N **A.63.9.7.5.1** The building code establishes requirements for the structure based on loads imposed by the elements of construction as well as for the loads that could be imposed by machinery or equipment. Building owners are responsible for understanding the limitations of loads on the building in which these installations are to be located. A professional engineer representing the building owner might have to make a determination as to the adequacy of the structure regarding the loads that are to be imposed for systems of this nature. [55:A.13.7.1]

N **A.63.9.7.5.2** Enclosed areas can include indoor as well as outdoor locations such as one with four solid walls and no roof or ceiling. The PEL is established by OSHA in 29 CFR 1910.1000, Table Z-1. [55:A.13.7.1]

N **A.63.9.7.5.2.1** The American Conference of Governmental Industrial Hygienists (ACGIH), in *TLVs® and BEIs®, Threshold Limit Values for Chemical Substances and Physical Agents and Biological Exposure Indices*, has established threshold limit values (TLVs®). The threshold limit value–time weighted average basis (TLV-TWA®) for CO_2 has been established at 5000 ppm, with a short-term exposure limit (STEL-TLV®) value of 30,000 ppm. [55:A.13.7.2.1]

As stated by ACGIH, the TLV-TWA represents a time-weighted average concentration for a conventional 8-hour workday and a 40-hour workweek to which it is believed that nearly all workers can be repeatedly exposed, day after day, without adverse effect. The STEL-TLV is the concentration to which it is believed that workers can be exposed continuously for a short period of time without suffering from irritation, chronic or irreversible tissue damage, or narcosis of sufficient degree to increase the likelihood of accidental injury, to impair self-rescue, or to materially reduce work efficiency, provided that the daily TLV-TWA is not exceeded. The STEL-TLV is not a separate, independent exposure guideline; rather, it supplements the TLV-TWA where there are recognized acute effects from a substance whose toxic effects are primarily of a chronic nature. TLV-STELs are recommended only where toxic effects have been reported from high short-term exposures in either humans or animals. [55:A.13.7.2.1]

A.63.9.12.1.1 Aboveground locations include locations that are above grade. Although some installations may be above ground, the actual grade of the terrain on which the installation is located could result in entrapment of vapors. Designers should avoid locating enclosures in areas where natural terrain features or other impediments serve to act as impediments to the dissipation of vapors should a release occur. [55:A.13.8.1.1]

A.63.12.3.1 The seller has a responsibility to provide written instructions to the user in accordance with 63.12.2. In fulfilling this responsibility the seller should explain to the user the use of the equipment being delivered and precautions that are to be taken. The seller's written instructions are intended to make the user aware of the hazards of the material and to provide recommendations that will address the location, restraint, movement, and refill of ambulatory containers when these containers are to be refilled by the user. However, the user has the responsibility to receive, read, and understand the written material regarding storage and use of liquid oxygen and the containers and equipment that is furnished by the seller. In addition to specific information or instructions provided by the seller or equipment manufacturer regarding the storage or use of the equipment and of the liquid oxygen or the containers used, the user remains responsible to see that the containers are used or maintained in accordance with the seller's instructions to ensure that they are as follows:

(1) Located and maintained in accordance with the requirements of 63.12.3.2
(2) Restrained in accordance with the requirements of 63.12.3.3
(3) Handled or transported in accordance with the requirements of 63.12.3.4
(4) When liquid oxygen ambulatory containers are to be refilled by the user, that the containers are refilled in accordance with the requirements of 63.12.3.5 and the manufacturer's instructions

A.63.12.3.3 Two points of contact can be provided by using elements of a room or furnishings in the room such as the walls of a corner of a room or a wall and a furnishing or object such as a table or a desk.

A.63.12.3.5.1.1 Drip pans or similar containment devices are used in order to protect against liquid oxygen spillage from coming into contact with combustible surfaces, including asphalt thereby elevating the potential for ignition.

A.63.12.3.5.3 Oxygen is not a flammable gas, and ignition of the gas itself is not the primary hazard. When oxygen is present in concentrations that exceed normal ambient concentrations of approximately 21 percent (by volume), ordinary combustible materials can be ignited more easily, and when combustion occurs, the combustion is more vigorous. As a general rule, the higher the concentration of oxygen present, the more likely ignition of ordinary combustibles will occur if ignition sources are present, and the more rapid the combustion process. Fire prevention codes frequently contain general statements cautioning against the use of open flames, and warnings are designed to prevent a hazardous condition caused by ignition sources. On the other hand, these codes assume that the normal ambient atmosphere is present, and they do not typically warn of the hazards of an oxygen-enriched atmosphere, which represents a condition out of the ordinary.

A.63.12.5.1 A sign prohibiting smoking in areas where oxygen is used may be provided by the seller. However, the posting of the sign within the user's premises and observing the prohibitions and precautionary information printed on the sign remains the responsibility of the user.

A.65.1.1 Chapter 65 does not contain any prescriptive technical provisions to address the retail sale and associated storage of consumer fireworks. The AHJ can utilize 1.3.2.2 to develop a protection approach for new and existing consumer fireworks retail sale and storage facilities.

A.66.1.1 See A.1.3.2.

A.66.1.3(1) Liquids that are solid at 100°F (37.8°C) or above, but are handled, used, or stored at temperatures above their FP, should be reviewed against pertinent sections of this *Code*. [**30**:A.1.1.2(1)]

A.66.1.3(2) The information in A.66.1.3(1) also applies here. [**30**:A.1.1.2(2)]

A.66.1.3(4) Certain mixtures of flammable or combustible (ignitible) liquids and halogenated hydrocarbons either do not exhibit a FP using the standard closed-cup test methods or will exhibit elevated FP. However, if the halogenated hydrocarbon is the more volatile component, preferential evaporation of this component can result in a liquid that does have a FP or has a FP that is lower than the original mixture. In order to evaluate the fire hazard of such mixtures, FP tests should be conducted after fractional evaporation of 10, 20, 40, 60, or even 90 percent of the original sample or other fractions representative of the conditions of use. For systems such as open process tanks or spills in open air, an open-cup test method might be more appropriate for estimating the fire hazard. [**30**:A.1.1.2(4)]

A.66.1.3(5) See NFPA 30B. [**30**:A.1.1.2(5)]

A.66.1.3(7) Requirements for transportation of flammable and combustible (ignitible) liquids can be found in NFPA 385 and in the US Department of Transportation's Hazardous Materials Regulations, Title 49, Code of Federal Regulations, Parts 100–199. [**30**:A.1.1.2(7)]

A.66.1.3(8) This scope exclusion only applies to the use of alcohol-based hand rub (ABHR) dispensers, as covered in other codes such as NFPA *101*. The storage of ABHR not in use is subject to the requirements of NFPA 30, including maximum allowable quantities, storage arrangement and required protection features. See Figure A.66.1.3(8) for high-level guidance on the code regulation of ABHR. [**30**:A.1.1.2(8)]

N **A.66.1.3(12)** Requirements for unstable liquids are found in NFPA 400.

A.66.3.3.6 See A.3.3.31.

A.66.3.3.7.1 See A.3.3.32.7.

A.66.3.3.18 See A.3.3.143.

A.66.3.3.19 Hazardous Material or Hazardous Chemical. These dangers can arise from, but are not limited to, toxicity, reactivity, instability, or corrosivity. [**30**,2021]

A.66.3.3.27 See A.3.3.207.

A.66.3.3.29 See A.3.3.228.

A.66.3.3.32 See A.3.3.249.

A.66.3.3.33.3.1 Nonmetallic Portable Tank. Permissible nonmetallic portable tanks for shipping Class I, Class II, and Class IIIA liquids [FP < 200°F (93°C) and any BP] are governed by hazardous materials transportation regulations promulgated by the United Nations (UN) and the US Department of Transportation (DOT). Small tanks for Class IIIB liquids [FP ≥ 200°F (93°C)] are not governed by either UN or DOT hazardous materials regulations. Fiber portable tanks for Class IIIB liquids [FP ≥ 200°F (93°C)] include composite designs consisting of a multi-ply corrugated box with a rigid or flexible inner plastic bladder. [**30**,2021]

A.66.3.3.37 See A.3.3.283.15.

A.66.3.3.40 Warehouse. Warehousing operations referred to in these definitions are those operations not accessible to the public and include general-purpose, merchandise, distribution, and industrial warehouse–type operations. [**30**,2021]

A.66.6.1 These provisions might not provide adequate protection for all operations involving hazardous materials or chemical reactions, nor do they consider health hazards resulting from exposure to such materials. [**30**:A.6.1]

A.66.6.3 The evaluation for management of fire hazards should consider probability of an ignitible mixture, the presence of a credible ignition source, and consequences of an ignition. Where the risk is unacceptable to the AHJ, explosion protection in accordance with NFPA 69, or deflagration venting in accordance with NFPA 68, or a combination of the two should be provided. See also *Guidelines for Chemical Process Quantitative Risk Analysis*, 2nd edition, from the Center for Chemical Process Safety/American Institute of Chemical Engineers. [**30**:A.6.3]

A.66.6.4.1.2.1 The wide range in size, design, and location of liquid-processing facilities precludes the inclusion of detailed fire and hazard prevention and control systems and methods applicable to all such facilities. The user should seek further guidance from documents such as NFPA 551 and the SFPE's *Engineering Guide to Fire Risk Assessment*. [**30**:A.6.4.1.2.1]

FIGURE A.66.1.3(8) High-Level Guidance Flowchart on the Code Regulation of ABHR. [30:Figure A.1.1.2(8)]

A.66.6.4.1.3 Storage, processing, handling, and use of Class II and Class III liquids [FP ≥ 100°F (37.8°C)] at temperatures above the FP can produce ignitible vapors if the liquid is released or vessels are vented. Class I liquid [FP < 100°F (37.8°C)] requirements address such events to minimize the likelihood of ignition and the consequences if ignition occurs, thus becoming a benchmark for design features when Class II and Class III liquids [FP ≥ 100°F (37.8°C)] are handled above the FP. However, their characteristics differ from those of Class I liquids [FP < 100°F (37.8°C)]. For example, the extent of travel of the Class II and III vapors is limited by the quick condensation of released vapors as they cool to lower temperatures. This might justify a more limited electrical area classification, different ventilation, elimination of explosion venting, and so forth. In addition, the process handling these Class II and Class III heated liquids could incorporate safety design features that accomplish the intent of NFPA 30, that is to address the hazards of released vapors. Further, the more restrictive building construction requirements in Table 17.6.1 of NFPA 30 might not be necessary for a particular process involving Class II and Class III liquids [FP ≥ 100°F (37.8°C)] heated above the FP. The option of conducting an engineering evaluation in accordance with Section 66.6 was included to allow the use of alternative designs to address the level of hazards identified. The SFPE's *Engineering Guide to Performance-Based Fire Protection* provides a methodology on how to perform an alternative design. [30:A.6.4.1.3]

Users of the code should be aware that there might be other applicable requirements. For example, in the US OSHA Flammable Liquids Standard (1910.106), processing Category 3 and Category 4 liquids (which approximate Class IC through Class IIIA liquids in NFPA 30) is prescriptively managed, and requires actions when the liquid is heated for use to within 30°F (16.7°C) of its flash point. [30:A.6.4.1.3]

Δ **A.66.6.5.1(8)** With respect to frictional heat or sparks, it is recognized that there is a need to control sources of ignition, including mechanical sparks from hand tools, that have sufficient energy to ignite flammable vapors. Studies, anecdotes, codes, referenced standards, and other historical documents (e.g., API 2214, *Spark Ignition Properties of Hand Tools*) show that there is a potential for hand tool sparks to ignite flammable vapors from a limited number of chemicals and under certain unique conditions. These include Class I liquids [FP < 100°F (37.8°C)] with low minimum ignition energies, operations in which liquids are heated, and atypical spark generation that can occur between specific types of hand tools and struck surfaces (i.e., thermite reactions or impact of steel tools on quartzitic materials). Even spark-resistant tools might not provide suitable protection against ignition. For example, hard metal particles can become imbedded in the relatively soft metal of spark-resistant tools, and these particles can cause sparks when the tools are used. [30:A.6.5.1(8)]

NFPA 30 requires analyses, such as job safety analyses or activity hazard analyses, of the hazards and risks of a given task and the application of appropriate protective measures to prevent or mitigate the hazards and risks. This includes identification and mitigation of ignition risk from multiple sources, including hand tools. Due to the complexity of the numerous operations involving Class I liquids [FP < 100°F (37.8°C)], NFPA 30 cannot address all conditions in which spark-resistant tools should be made mandatory, might be advisable, or are unnecessary to help control the ignition risk of any given operation. [30:A.6.5.1(8)]

It is recognized that the adoption of the new Globally Harmonized System for labeling by the US Occupational Safety and Health Administration (29 CFR 1910.1200, Appendix C) creates a generalized mandate for the use of spark-resistant tools. However, based on available technical information, this mandate goes beyond what is considered necessary for fire safety, given the fact that it applies to liquids that present little risk of ignition unless heated to or above their flash points. *(See A.66.6.4.1.3.)* [**30**:A.6.5.1(8)]

A.66.6.5.3 See NFPA 51B. [**30**:A.6.5.3]

A.66.6.5.4.1 The prevention of electrostatic ignition in equipment is a complex subject. Refer to NFPA 77 for guidance. [**30**:A.6.5.4.1]

N **A.66.6.5.4.6** Table 66.7.3.3 lists typical areas where ignitible mixtures would be expected to exist under normal operating conditions. [**30**:A.6.5.4.4]

In these areas, configurations of nonmetallic containers, equipment, and piping should be designed and operated to prevent static accumulation that can lead to electrostatic ignition of vapors. This is typically accomplished by using nonmetallic components constructed of materials that have surface resistivity less than 10^9 ohms per square (conductive or static dissipative) and are connected to ground. Additional techniques are detailed in NFPA 77. [**30**:A.6.5.4.4]

A.66.6.6.1 One method of complying with this requirement could be through the installation of an automatic and/or manual fire alarm system as covered in *NFPA 72*. [**30**:A.6.6.1]

A.66.6.7.1 Other recognized fire prevention and control factors, involving construction, location, and separation, are addressed elsewhere in Section 66.6. [**30**:A.6.7.1]

A.66.6.7.3 Permanent connections to process water lines from the fire water system present an opportunity for contamination of the fire water with process fluids. Incidents have occurred where fire water was contaminated with flammable process liquids, with subsequent increased fire damage and, in some cases, injury. Temporary connections are permitted to meet extraordinary needs, as in turnaround and inspection periods, tank cleaning, and so forth. However, care should be taken to address the potential for contamination. Where such use occurs frequently enough to justify a more robust arrangement, double block-and-bleed valves, removable spool pieces, or other means should be used to assure that no contamination can occur. Check valves alone are not sufficient. [**30**:A.6.7.3]

Use of utility water sources, such as boiler feedwater, that are not contaminated, is acceptable for use as a supplemental fire water supply. [**30**:A.6.7.3]

N **A.66.6.7.6** The facility owner should perform hazard recognition of the type of foam used on site, as some legacy foams contain per- or polyfluoroalkylated substances (PFAS), which are being evaluated for environmental and human health hazards. *(See Annex E of NFPA 11 for more information.)* [**30**:A.6.7.6]

A.66.6.7.8 NFPA 10 provides information on the suitability of various types of extinguishers. [**30**:A.6.7.8]

N **A.66.6.10.3.2** The self-closing lid and metal construction of an oily waste receptacle prevents spontaneous combustion. The ongoing exothermic reaction can generate a large amount of smoke, which can fill a facility. [**30**:A.6.10.3.2]

One of the main safety features of an oily waste can is the self-close lid. Cans allowed to be overfilled will prevent the lid from closing. It is recommended if the rags and wipes cannot be removed safely from the site, they should be stored in a noncombustible container with a tight-fitting lid outdoors away from other combustible materials. [**30**:A.6.10.3.2]

N **A.66.6.12** Examples of relevant regulations include the following:

(1) Permits of the jurisdictional air quality management board
(2) National Pollutant Discharge Elimination System permit
(3) Waste discharge requirements established by the jurisdictional water quality control board
(4) Sewer pretreatment requirements for publicly or privately owned treatment works

[**30**:A.6.12]

N **A.66.6.12.1** Containment of spills, leaks, or other container failures can be accomplished by any of the following:

(1) Listed liquid drainage floor assemblies — FM Approval Standard 6090, *Approval Standard for Ignitable Liquid Drainage Floor Assemblies,* is one example of a listing standard
(2) Noncombustible, liquidtight raised sills, curbs, or ramps of suitable height at exterior openings
(3) Noncombustible, liquidtight raised sills, curbs, or ramps of suitable height, or other flow-diverting structures at interior openings
(4) Sloped floors
(5) Open-grate trenches or floor drains that are connected to a properly designed drainage system
(6) Wall scuppers that discharge to a safe location or to a properly designed drainage system
(7) Other means that are acceptable to the authority having jurisdiction

[**30**:A.6.12.1]

Where sills, curbs, or ramps are used, the appropriate height will depend on a number of factors, including the maximum expected spill volume, the floor area, and the existence of any drainage systems. Historically, curbs and sills have been 4 in. (100 mm) high. [**30**:A.6.12.1]

A variety of curb, sill, and ramp heights can be used to obtain the desired secondary containment volume. As a guide, 1 ft^2 of water at a depth of 1 in. equals 0.6 gal (1 m^2 of water @ 25 mm = 25 L). Once the total quantity of liquid containment has been established, the necessary curb, sill, or ramp height can then be calculated. [**30**:A.6.12.1]

Liquid drainage flooring assemblies are designed based on a volumetric flow rate rather than a static volume. Thus, liquid drainage floor assemblies should have a volumetric flow capacity of at least 150 percent of the required fire protection at maximum anticipated flow rates. [**30**:A.6.12.1]

Where open-grate trenches are used, the volume of the trench should be able to contain the maximum expected spill volume or otherwise be connected to a properly designed drainage system. [**30**:A.6.12.1]

It should be noted that these containment and drainage provisions address only fire protection concerns. Consult the appropriate environmental regulations for other restrictions that could apply. [**30**:A.6.12.1]

N **A.66.6.12.3.2** The requirement in 66.6.12.3.2 is based on NFPA 400 and *NFPA 5000*. [**30:**A.6.12.3.2]

A.66.7.3.3 For additional information, see NFPA 497. [**30:**A.7.3.3]

A.66.7.3.7 NFPA 496 provides details for these types of installations. [**30:**A.7.3.7]

A.66.9.2.7.3 Section 5.1 of NFPA 505 states, "In locations used for the storage of Class I liquids [FP < 100°F (37.8°C)] in sealed containers or liquefied or compressed flammable gases in containers, approved power-operated industrial trucks designated as Types CNS, DS, ES, GS, LPS, GS/CNS, or GS/LPS shall be permitted to be used where approved by the AHJ." Compared to the above types, industrial trucks that are designated DY and EE have significantly less potential for igniting flammable vapors (such as might result from a spill of Class I liquid [FP < 100°F (37.8°C)]) and should be used in control areas, liquid storage rooms, and liquid warehouses where conditions warrant. [**30:**A.9.3.7.3]

A.66.9.3.1 It is not the intent of 66.9.3 to regulate containers and packaging systems for Class IIIB liquids [FP ≥ 200°F (93°C)], except as required for protected storage in accordance with Section 66.16. [**30:**A.9.4.1]

A.66.9.3.1(6) The term *rigid nonmetallic intermediate bulk container* is used to describe intermediate bulk containers that have a plastic vessel that serves as the primary liquid-holding component. This vessel can be enclosed in or encased by an outer structure consisting of a steel cage, a single-wall metal or plastic enclosure, a double wall of foamed or solid plastic, or a paperboard enclosure. These are often called *composite IBCs*, which is the term used by the US Department of Transportation (DOT) to describe them. The term *rigid nonmetallic intermediate bulk container* also denotes an all-plastic single-wall IBC that might or might not have a separate plastic base and for which the containment vessel also serves as the support structure. IBCs and portable tanks with a nonmetallic inner liner that have an outer metal enclosure that is sufficient, in and of itself, to be compliant with the appropriate DOT/UN designation for a metal IBC or metal portable tank are considered metal IBCs or metal portable tanks as designated under 66.9.3.1(1). [**30:**A.9.4.1(6)]

N **A.66.9.3.4** FM Approvals Class 4996 pallets are evaluated from a fire severity standpoint as compared to wood pallets; however, the pallets ability to maintain its structural integrity when exposed to a liquid pool fire is not evaluated. [**30:**A.9.4.4]

A.66.9.4 The requirements in 66.9.4 are based on hazards associated with fixed Class I liquids [FP < 100°F (37.8°C)] storage cabinets. They do not address potential hazards associated with mobile storage cabinets (i.e., cabinets with integral wheels) such as the following:

(1) Increased risk of spills
(2) Potential for tipover or blockage of egress
(3) Maintenance of vent and grounding integrity
(4) Variable condition of exposed floor surfaces under the cabinet

[**30:**A.9.5]

A.66.9.4.4 Venting of storage cabinets has not been demonstrated to be necessary for fire protection purposes. Additionally, venting a cabinet could compromise the ability of the cabinet to adequately protect its contents from involvement in a fire, because cabinets are not generally tested with any venting. Therefore, venting of storage cabinets is not recommended. [**30:**A.9.5.4]

However, it is recognized that some jurisdictions might require storage cabinets to be vented and that venting can also be desirable for other reasons, such as health and safety. In such cases, the venting system should be installed so as to not affect substantially the desired performance of the cabinet during a fire. Means of accomplishing this can include thermally actuated dampers on the vent openings or sufficiently insulating the vent piping system to prevent the internal temperature of the cabinet from rising above that specified. Any make-up air to the cabinet should also be arranged in a similar manner. [**30:**A.9.5.4]

If vented, the cabinet should be vented from the bottom with make-up air supplied to the top. Also, mechanical exhaust ventilation is preferred and should comply with NFPA 91. Manifolding the vents of multiple storage cabinets should be avoided. [**30:**A.9.5.4]

A.66.9.4.4.2 A "safe location" should be selected as the location of a vent discharge to minimize the potential for ignitible vapors to travel to a source of ignition after discharge from the vent. Electrical equipment that does not meet the requirements for hazardous locations can serve as an ignition source. The Technical Committee advises that vent discharge locations should consider such factors as the following:

(1) Characteristics of the exhausted material (vapor density, toxicity, velocity of discharge, etc.)
(2) Proximity to potential ignition sources
(3) Building openings such as doors, windows, air intakes, and so forth
(4) Dispersion characteristics (distance to discharge within the flammable range, direction of discharge, atmospheric conditions, and the influence of building and neighboring buildings on discharged vapors)
(5) Likelihood of vapor accumulation following discharge, such as accumulation under building eaves
(6) Likelihood of sufficient discharge volume to allow an ignitible concentration to reach an ignition source

[**30:**A.9.5.4.2]

Historically, NFPA 30 has provided prescriptive guidance, often based on area classification requirements, and results have been acceptable. Closer distances should be accepted only if an analysis by a qualified person justifies closer distances. Similarly, the specified distances might not be acceptable for all installations, thus the guidance provided above. [**30:**A.9.5.4.2]

N **A.66.9.4.4.2.1** Duct material should be rigid metallic or similar construction to provide similar fire survivability to that of the cabinet. [**30:**A.9.5.4.2.1]

A.66.9.4.5 ANSI Z535.2.2007, Environmental and Facility Safety Signs, Section 9.2, was used to determine the letter height, based on a safe viewing distance of 25 ft (7.5 m). Markings can be reflective to improve visibility. See ASTM D4956, *Standard Specification for Retroreflective Sheeting for Traffic Control*, for more information on providing reflective surfaces. If international symbols are used, they should be a minimum of 2.0 in. (50 mm) in size. [**30:**A.9.5.5]

N **A.66.9.4.6** Only countertop-style cabinets should be placed on top of other items. Floor model cabinets should not be placed on top of pallets, spill pallets, workbenches, tool boxes, or similar. A clear working area should be maintained in front of the cabinet doors to avoid spills while moving individual containers in and out. [**30:**A.9.5.6]

N **A.66.9.4.6.1** Cabinets are not intended for the storage of paper, cardboard, or other ordinary combustibles. If shipping packaging becomes saturated due to leaks or spills, it should be removed from the cabinet. [**30:**A.9.5.6.1]

N **A.66.9.4.6.2** Cabinets should not be stacked unless approved/listed for stacked service. [**30:**A.9.5.6.2]

N **A.66.9.4.6.3** Cabinets or vent ducting that have obvious defects or loss of integrity (e.g., spill retention, door closure, latches, etc.) shall be repaired or replaced. [**30:**9.5.6.3]

A.66.9.7.1 The Protection Level classifications are taken from *NFPA 5000*. Protection Levels 1, 4, and 5 do not apply to the storage of flammable and combustible (ignitible) liquids and are, therefore, not extracted here. [**30:**A.9.8.1]

A.66.9.7.2 See *NFPA 5000* for additional requirements. [**30:**A.9.8.2]

N **A.66.9.10** See A.17.8 of NFPA 30 for additional information. [**30:**9.11]

N **A.66.9.16.4** In the unique situation of water reactive ignitible (flammable or combustible) liquids, a specific risk assessment should be performed. [**30:**A.9.17.4]

A.66.14.1 Environmental concerns have dictated special handling of hazardous materials, chemicals, and wastes. Some of these have flammable and combustible (ignitible) liquid characteristics, in addition to their environmental and health problems, thus causing some questions as to how they should be stored and handled. [**30:**A.14.1]

Several manufacturers have met this problem by designing and manufacturing movable, modular prefabricated storage lockers, working diligently with various building officials and AHJs. This results in a product that is intended to meet government standards and regulations for hazardous materials storage. Several municipalities have passed model ordinances covering the design, construction, and location of hazardous materials storage lockers. Design features can include, but are not limited to, the following:

(1) Secondary spill containment sumps
(2) Deflagration venting
(3) Ventilation requirements, including mechanical ventilation where dispensing operations are expected
(4) Electrical equipment for hazardous locations in accordance with *NFPA 70*
(5) Static electricity control
(6) Fire suppression systems (dry chemical or sprinklers)
(7) Heavy structural design for the following:
   (a) Security provisions
   (b) Doors that lock and permit pallet loading
   (c) Wind load, snow load, and storage load conditions
   (d) Anchorage provisions
   (e) Skid design, permitting relocation using lift trucks
(8) Fire-related exterior walls, if required
(9) Interior partitions to segregate incompatible materials
(10) Size limits to limit quantities that can be stored within preassembled or ready-to-assemble designs
(11) Nonsparking floors
(12) Shelving, if required
(13) Heating or cooling units, if needed
(14) Corrosion protection as required
(15) Employee safety provisions (eye/face wash)
(16) NFPA 704 hazard symbols
[**30:**A.14.1]

Features provided are determined by specific storage requirements and needs of the owner, keeping in mind applicable regulations and ordinances that apply and the approval requirements of the AHJ. [**30:**A.14.1]

Several testing laboratories have developed internal procedures for the examination, testing, and listing or labeling of hazardous materials storage lockers submitted by manufacturers. [**30:**A.14.1]

Δ **A.66.16.1.1** See Annex E of NFPA 30 for limitations of the protection criteria of Table 16.5.3.1 through Table 16.5.3.12 of NFPA 30, particularly for intermediate bulk containers and portable tanks having capacities greater than 60 gal (230 L). [**30:**A.16.1.1]

Protected storage allowed under previous editions of NFPA 30 can be continued if the class of liquids stored, the quantity of liquids stored, fire protection, and building configuration remain unchanged. Table A.66.16.1.1(a) and Table A.66.16.1.1(b), reprinted here from the 1993 edition of NFPA 30, can be used as a reference for storage arrangements in previously approved, protected, liquid storage rooms or liquid warehouses. [**30:**A.16.1.1]

For certain liquids such as ketones, esters, and alcohols, the minimum required densities established in the listing criteria for foam discharge devices are often higher than the general densities specified for protection of flammable and combustible (i.e., ignitible) liquids. When determining the design criteria for extinguishing systems using foam, it is important to ensure that the listing criteria, which are typically based on empirical data from fire tests, are not overlooked. Otherwise, the fire protection system design can be inadequate for proper protection. [**30:**A.16.1.1]

Early suppression fast-response (ESFR) sprinklers have been tested for protection of liquids only to the extent reflected in the tables in Section 66.16.5. Any other use of ESFR sprinklers for protection of liquids should be based on an engineering analysis that evaluates the potential failure of the sprinkler system based on a rapid-growth fire or a large pool fire that would operate more sprinklers than are accommodated by the design area. The use of ESFR protection, particularly without provisions for the control of spread of liquid, presents the possibility of a liquid pool fire that could exceed the limited design operating area of an ESFR system. [**30:**A.16.1.1]

The information in Table 66.16.5.3.1 through Table 66.16.5.3.12 was developed from full-scale fire tests. Where only one K-factor sprinkler is allowed, this was the only size proven to provide fire control. Where a choice of K-factors is allowed by the tables, each was able to provide fire control; however, the larger K-factor sprinklers sometimes demonstrated better fire control and further limited fire damage. Where only one type of response sprinkler is allowed, this is the only type of sprinkler proven to provide fire control. Where a choice of response characteristics (SR or QR) is allowed by the tables, each was able to provide fire control; however, the QR sprinklers sometimes demonstrated better fire control and further limited fire damage. [**30:**A.16.1.1]

In the testing involving metal containers, only steel containers were tested. Other metal containers, such as aluminum, have not been tested. [30:A.16.1.1]

Where test and protection criteria are provided for glass or plastic containers, it is acceptable to use these criteria for protection of steel containers of the same size for storage configurations that meet the test configuration. [30:A.16.1.1]

Δ **A.66.16.1.2** To date, there has been no full-scale testing to determine appropriate fire protection design criteria for Class IA liquids [FP < 73°F (22.8°C) and BP < 100°F (37.8°C)]. [30:A.16.1.2]

A.66.16.2.1 The term *protected* indicates that the fire risk is managed so as to control the fire and prevent it from spreading beyond the design area of the automatic fire protection system. [30:A.16.2.2]

A.66.16.2.2 The term *unprotected* indicates that the growth of a fire might exceed the capabilities of the automatic fire protection system and extend beyond the design area of the system. In such cases, the total contents of the fire area might become involved in a fire, regardless of the protection features provided. [30:A.16.2.3]

A.66.16.2.3 Table A.66.16.2.3 provides examples of commonly used metal containers that are considered either relieving style or nonrelieving style for use in developing protected storage arrangements in accordance with Table 16.5.3.1 through Table 16.5.3.12 of NFPA 30. [30:A.16.2.4]

Table A.66.16.1.1(b) Storage Arrangements for Protected Rack Storage of Liquids in Containers and Portable Tanks

Liquid Class	Type Rack	Storage Level	Maximum Storage Height of Containers (ft)	Maximum Quantity of Containers (gal)*†
IA	Double row	Ground floor	25	7,500
	or	Upper floors	15	4,500
	single row	Basement	NP	—
IB	Double row	Ground floor	25	15,000
IC	or	Upper floors	15	9,000
	single row	Basement	NP	—
II	Double row	Ground floor	25	24,000
	or	Upper floors	25	24,000
	single row	Basement	15	9,000
III	Multirow,	Ground floor	40	55,000
	double row,	Upper floors	20	55,000
	or single row	Basement	20	25,000

For SI units, 1 ft = 0.3 m; 1 gal = 3.8 L.
NP: Not permitted.
*Maximum quantity allowed on racks in cut-off rooms and attached buildings.
†Maximum quantity allowed per rack section in liquid warehouses.
[30:Table A.16.1.1(b)]

Table A.66.16.1.1(a) Storage Arrangements for Protected Palletized or Solid Pile Storage of Liquids in Containers and Portable Tanks

Liquid Class	Storage Level	Maximum Storage Height (ft) Containers	Maximum Storage Height (ft) Portable Tanks	Maximum Quantity per Pile (gal) Containers	Maximum Quantity per Pile (gal) Portable Tanks	Maximum Quantity* (gal) Containers	Maximum Quantity* (gal) Portable Tanks
IA	Ground floor	5	—	3,000	—	12,000	—
	Upper floors	5	—	2,000	—	8,000	—
	Basement	NP	NP	—	—	—	—
IB	Ground floor	6½	7	5,000	20,000	15,000	40,000
	Upper floors	6½	7	3,000	10,000	12,000	20,000
	Basement	NP	NP	—	—	—	—
IC	Ground floor	6½†	7	5,000	20,000	15,000	40,000
	Upper floors	6½†	7	3,000	10,000	12,000	20,000
	Basement	NP	NP	—	—	—	—
II	Ground floor	10	14	10,000	40,000	25,000	80,000
	Upper floors	10	14	10,000	40,000	25,000	80,000
	Basement	5	7	7,500	20,000	7,500	20,000
III	Ground floor	20	14	15,000	60,000	55,000	100,000
	Upper floors	20	14	15,000	60,000	55,000	100,000
	Basement	10	7	10,000	20,000	25,000	40,000

For SI units, 1 ft = 0.3 m; 1 gal = 3.8 L.
NP: Not permitted.
*Applies only to cut-off rooms and attached buildings.
†These height limitations can be increased to 10 ft for containers of 5 gal capacity or less. [30:Table A.16.1.1(a)]

Δ **Table A.66.16.2.3 Common Relieving- and Nonrelieving-Style Metal Containers**

Container Type	Relieving Style	Nonrelieving Style
≤1 qt[a]	All	N/A
>1 qt and ≤6 gal[a]	Metal containers with plastic cap, or flexible or rigid plastic spout with plastic cap	Metal containers with steel spout and steel screw cap
≤1 gal, friction lid	Metal containers with metal friction-fit covers (e.g., paint can lid)	N/A
1 gal and ≤6 gal (lug cover)	Metal containers with metal covers held in place with a mechanical friction-fit (e.g., lug-type) closure mechanism	N/A
>6 gal and ≤60 gal[b,c] (drums)	Metal containers, tight or open-head (drums) having at least one 2 in. plastic plug (Note: Cap seals, if used, need to be plastic and nonmetallic.)	Open head metal containers with steel covers having no steel flange openings; or open head and tight head metal containers with steel flange openings where only steel plugs and/or cap seals are used
>60 gal and ≤793 gal	Metal portable tanks or metal intermediate bulk containers with at least one relief device conforming to the design, construction, and capacity of the container's section	N/A

For SI units, 1 gal = 3.8 L, 1 qt = 1 L.
N/A: Not applicable.
[a]All containers ≤1 qt are considered relieving style because their failure is inconsequential.
[b]In full-scale fire tests, where containers were provided with both ¾ in. (19 mm) and 2 in. (50 mm) relieving vent openings and, in some cases, both vents were obstructed by pallet slats, rupture of containers did not occur. Because it is not possible to determine if all conceivable obstruction scenarios were represented, where drums are stacked more than one high, provide an additional ¾ in. (19 mm) or 2 in. (50 mm) pressure-relieving mechanism.
[c]The use of plastic plugs instead of steel plugs (bungs) in a steel drum in order to achieve a relieving-style container should contemplate the following issues in order to assure the safe storage of liquids:
  (1) The compatibility of the plastic plug materials and gaskets with the liquids being stored.
  (2) The stability and shelf life of the liquids being stored as the plastic plugs can admit water vapor, oxygen, and light.
  (3) The difference in expansion coefficients for plastic plugs and steel drums for those drums subject to temperature variations and hot or cold conditions.
  (4) The tooling issues involved with the use of plastic plugs as the torque levels are different from those levels used for steel plugs.
  (5) The training of fill line operators in order to avoid cross-threading and/or the stripping of threads.
  (6) The voiding of the United Nations (UN) rating on the steel drum by installing plastic plugs. If the user needs to install a plug other than the one originally provided by the container manufacturer, then the user should contact the manufacturer to ensure that the UN rating will still be valid.
[30:Table A.16.2.4]

A.66.16.2.4 Unsaturated polyester resins (UPRs) are high molecular weight unsaturated polymers dissolved in a reactive monomer, usually styrene, in concentrations of 50 percent or less by weight. UPRs are combined with reinforcements such as fiberglass and/or fillers to produce a wide range of products. Examples of such products include automobile parts, bathroom tubs and shower stalls, cultured marble, and many products for architectural, recreational, construction, and corrosion-resistant applications. UPRs are normally packaged in 55 gal (208 L) drums. The US Department of Transportation classification for UPRs is "UN 1866, Resin Solution"; however, it should be noted that this classification includes many materials that are not unsaturated polyester resins. [30:A.16.2.5]

N **A.66.16.4.1.1** For liquid concentration equal to or less than 20 percent as shown in Figure 66.16.4.1(c), see Table A.20.4(b) of NFPA 13. [30:A.16.4.1.1]

N **A.66.16.4.2.3** Existing PFAS foam-based concentrates can be based on C6 or C8 molecules. Within the US, C8 foams are no longer produced, but might be present in legacy systems. The C6-based foams continue to be listed by UL and FM Approvals. Both foam types are considered valid for the fire protection systems in Chapter 16. [30:A.16.4.2.3]

A.66.16.5.1.6.2 Most fire tests using foam-water protection schemes have been conducted with immediate foam solution discharge from the operating sprinklers. If an appreciable delay is encountered before properly proportioned foam is discharged, control of the fire might not be established. One method of accomplishing immediate foam solution discharge is by using an in-line balanced pressure (ILBP) proportioning system. [30:A.16.5.1.6.2]

A.66.16.6.1.5 The 8 ft (2.4 m) separation distance required in 66.16.6.1.5 is measured from the face of liquid storage in one rack to the face of liquid storage and/or other storage across the aisle in an adjacent rack. Rack designers, code officials, and plan reviewers are cautioned to the fact that many rack storage arrangements involve the storage of pallets that overhang the face of the rack. Therefore, although the structural rack members might be arranged to have an 8 ft (2.4 m) aisle between the racks, the distance between the face of the stored materials in the racks could be less than 8 ft (2.4 m) when the racks are filled with pallets. This will not be in compliance with the requirements of 66.16.6.1.5, unless the barrier and in-rack sprinkler protection is extended. [30:A.16.6.1.5]

A.66.16.6.5.8(3) Design area can be reduced to 2000 ft² when using a preprimed foam-water system installed in accordance with NFPA 11 and maintained in accordance with NFPA 25. [30:A.16.6.5.8(3)]

Δ **A.66.16.8.2** Subsection 66.16.8 requires that control of liquid spread be provided to prevent a pool fire on the floor from spreading and opening more sprinkler heads than the design of the sprinkler system anticipates. For example, if the sprinkler system is designed to provide 0.45 gpm/ft² over 3000 ft² (18 mm/min over 280 m²), 66.16.8.2 requires that the spread of liquid also be limited to 3000 ft² (280 m²). Various means are available to achieve this control. [30:A.16.8.2]

Typical methods use trench or spot drains that divide the floor of the storage area into rectangles having areas equal to or less than the design area of the sprinkler system. Drains are centered under racks, and the floor is sloped toward the drain trenches with a minimum slope of 1 percent. The floor is made highest at the walls. See Figure A.66.16.8.2(a) and Figure A.66.16.8.2(b). Trenches are arranged as described in NFPA 15 and as shown in Figure A.66.16.8.2(c). Note particularly the dimensions of the trenches, and note that the solid covering spans one-third of the width on either side of the open grate and the open grate spans the middle third. Spot drains can be similarly arranged. Another method, shown in Figure A.66.16.8.2(d), uses spot drains located at building columns, where the area between any four columns does not exceed the design area of the sprinkler system. The floor is sloped to direct water flow to the drains. [30:A.16.8.2]

Connections to the drains are provided at trapped sumps, arranged as described in NFPA 15. See Figure A.66.16.8.2(e). To provide a safety factor, the drain pipes are sometimes sized to carry 150 percent of anticipated sprinkler discharge. The following equation can be used to calculate the flow of the drain pipe:

[A.66.16.8.2]
$$F = 1.5DA$$

where:
F = flow (gpm or L/min)
D = sprinkler design density (gpm/ft² or L/min/m²)
A = sprinkler design area (ft² or m²)

Additional information can be found in *Guidelines for Safe Warehousing of Chemicals*, Center for Chemical Process Safety, American Institute of Chemical Engineers. [30:A.16.8.2]

A.66.17.1.1 Facilities designed in accordance with Chapter 17 of NFPA 30 do not use the maximum allowable quantity and control area concepts found in the building code. [30:A.17.1.1]

N **A.66.17.4.3** Minimum distances provided in Table 66.17.4.3 are extracts from similar tables in Chapter 22 in NFPA 30. Process vessels are at greater risk of upset and experience a wider range of process parameters (e.g., flow, temperature, pressure, level, reactivity, vapor density, and potential for vapors to reach ignition sources if released) when compared to storage tanks. Evaluations for minimum distance should take these factors into account and establish the "stability" of the material and the maximum pressure in the vessel(s), taking into consideration credible process deviations and the design and reliability of safeguards that prevent or control process upsets. Minimum distances to property lines, important buildings, and public ways should consider the risk (i.e., likelihood and consequence) to persons, property, and adjacent processes and storage from vapor cloud ignition, blast overpressure, and thermal flux (i.e., burn injury and adjacent structure fire). See also 66.17.4.3. [30:A.66.17.4.3]

Additional guidance can be found in the following documents:

(1) NFPA 497
(2) NFPA 551
(3) AIChE *Guidelines for Evaluating Process Plant Buildings for External Explosions and Fires*
(4) AIChE *Guidelines for Siting and Layout of Facilities*
(5) AIChE *Guidelines for Vapor Cloud Explosion, Pressure Vessel Burst, BLEVE and Flash Fire Hazards*

FIGURE A.66.16.8.2(a) General Scheme for Warehouse Spill Control of Liquids. [30: Figure A.16.8.2(a)]

FIGURE A.66.16.8.2(b) Plan View of Warehouse Spill Control of Liquids. [30: Figure A.16.8.2(b)]

FIGURE A.66.16.8.2(c) Details of Drainage Trench Design. [30: Figure A.16.8.2(c)]

FIGURE A.66.16.8.2(d) Typical Arrangement of Floor Drains. [30: Figure A.16.8.2(d)]

FIGURE A.66.16.8.2(e) Details of Liquid-Seal Trap. [30: Figure A.16.8.2(e)]

(6) SFPE *Handbook of Fire Protection Engineering*
(7) SFPE *Engineering Standard on Calculating Fire Exposures to Structures*
(8) SFPE *Engineering Standard on Calculation Methods to Predict the Thermal Performance of Structural and Fire Resistive Assemblies*
(9) SFPE *Engineering Guide to Predicting 1st and 2nd Degree Skin Burns from Thermal Radiation*
(10) SFPE *Engineering Guide to Fire Exposures to Structural Elements*
(11) SFPE *Engineering Guide to Assessing Flame Radiation to External Targets from Pool Fires*
(12) SFPE *Engineering Guide to Fire Risk Assessment*
(13) API RP 500, *Recommended Practice for Classification of Locations for Electrical Installations at Petroleum Facilities Classified as Class I, Division 1 and Division 2*
(14) ANSI/API RP 505, *Recommended Practice for Classification of Locations for Electrical Installations at Petroleum Facilities Classified as Class I, Zone 0, Zone 1 and Zone 2*
(15) API RP 752, *Management of Hazards Associated with Location of Process Plant Buildings*
(16) API RP 753, *Management of Hazards Associated with Location of Process Plant Portable Buildings*

[**30:**A.66.17.4.3]

A.66.17.4.6 Equipment operated at gauge pressures that exceed 1000 psi (6900 kPa) might require greater spacing. [**30:**A.17.4.6]

A.66.17.6.8 API 2218, *Fireproofing Practices in Petroleum and Petrochemical Processing Plants*, contains guidance on selecting and installing fire-resistant coatings to protect exposed steel supports from a high-challenge fire exposure. It also contains a general discussion on determining need for such protection and estimating the extent of the area exposed. [**30:**A.17.6.8]

A.66.17.6.10 NFPA 204 provides information on this subject. [**30:**A.17.6.10]

A.66.17.6.11 NFPA *101* provides information on this subject. [**30:**A.17.6.11]

N **A.66.17.7** At a minimum, a hazard analysis in accordance with 66.6 *(see also, 66.17.15.3)* should be conducted to determine the proper fire suppression system. [**30:**A.17.7]

Historically, extra hazard (Group 2) (EH2) has been used as a design basis for process areas with ignitible (flammable and combustible) liquids. However, NFPA 13 data for EH2 sprinkler protection should be used with caution. These data were first introduced in the 1978 edition of NFPA 13, and no substantiation or fire test data was provided for its basis. An occupancy definition for EH2 is provided in NFPA 13, which states, "Occupancies or portions of other occupancies with moderate to substantial amounts of flammable or combustible liquids or occupancies where shielding of combustibles is extensive." Recognizing there is no definition quantifying "moderate to substantial amounts of flammable or combustible liquids," this lack of clarity presents a dilemma for users of this provision. [**30:**A.17.7]

The following Items can impact the size of a fire event and the effectiveness of the sprinkler system, and should be included in the hazard analysis:

(1) Protection goals and objectives
(2) Maximum liquid pool size as influenced by potential spill volume, drainage systems, interlocks, and other liquid containment methods
(3) Water miscibility
(4) Operating temperature of the liquid
(5) Amount of storage in area *(see 66.16 for design criteria)*
(6) Ceiling/roof height
(7) Sprinkler characteristics
(8) Anticipated fire size (i.e., area and intensity) and duration
(9) Important buildings or exterior processes, and liquid storage areas adjacent to buildings or exterior processes
(10) Exposure limits to adjacent buildings, process areas, or storage
(11) Response time and capabilities of onsite fire brigade or local fire department
    (a) Hard-piped liquid transfer systems
    (b) Air-operated fail closed valves interlocked in the event of a spill or fire
    (c) Liquid level control interlocks on production vessels
    (d) Overpressure protection of processing equipment and piping
    (e) Process control systems
    (f) Process safety systems

[**30:**A.17.7]

The following references can be consulted when conducting the hazard analysis:

(1) NFPA 13
(2) NFPA 15
(3) FM Global Property Loss Prevention Data Sheet 7-14, *Fire Protection for Chemical Plants*
(4) FM Global Property Loss Prevention Data Sheet 7-32, *Ignitable Liquid Operations*
(5) API RP 2001, *Fire Protection in Refineries*
(6) API RP 2030, *Application of Fixed Water Spray Systems for Fire Protection in the Petroleum and Petrochemical Industries*
(7) National Fire Protection Research Foundation, *International Foam-Water Sprinkler Research Project, Task 1 Technical Report: Literature Search & Technical Analysis*
(8) Also see A.66.17.4.3 for further references

[**30:**A.17.7]

A couple examples of how to design sprinkler protection criteria for process area protection are FM Global Property Loss Prevention Data Sheets 7-32 and 7-14. Data sheet 7-32 looks at roof height, sprinkler characteristics, automatic isolation of liquid holdup, drainage, and other factors to limit potential pool size. The protection criteria use the operation of automatic sprinklers over large sprinkler operating areas, but not assuming that all sprinklers will operate. Data sheet 7-14, on the other hand, assumes the ability to control or shut down ignitible (flammable and combustible) liquid flow is limited, requiring the use of deluge sprinkler designs. Both documents have used various types of fire tests to frame out the protection approaches that are recommended. [**30:**A.17.7]

Sprinklered fire test data relevant to operations areas, and released into the public domain, are very limited. Several sprinklered pool fire tests data for aircraft hangars generated in the 1970s have been released into the public domain. These tests used automatic sprinkler systems. A selection of fire tests conducted on small volume spills and pool fires illustrated they are the easiest type of liquid fires to control or extinguish. Had these fires involved much larger volumes typically found in production facilities the area of operating sprinklers could have been much larger. Additionally, if the fire type would have also involved flowing spills, pressurized releases, or obstructed fires those factors would have magnified the associated fire risk. [**30:**A.17.7]

The discharge of plain water onto an ignitible (flammable or combustible) liquid fire can expect to spread the fire involving low viscosity liquids having a specific gravity less than water. Therefore, the merits of spill containment and drainage features vertically aligned with ceiling mounted draft curtains should not be overlooked. [**30:**A.17.7]

N **A.66.17.8** Most industrial processes have control systems intended to maintain the normal and proper operation of the process. An emergency control system should ideally be a system that is reliable and separate from the normal process control system with set points that represent a situation that is no longer something that can be brought back to the target operation level. This system is designed to act to shut down the process, or elements thereof, to attempt to make the situation "safe." The emergency control system should be fail-safe. Examples of fail-safe include: (1) loss of critical utilities would result in a shutdown of the process, (2) reactor emergency shutdown system, or (3) emergency shut down valves will fail in a safe condition (fail-closed or fail-open depending on what was deemed safe). [**30:**A.17.8]

A.66.17.10.3 This might require curbs, scuppers, or special drainage systems to control the spread of fire. Annex A of NFPA 15 provides information on this subject. [**30:**A.17.10.3]

N **A.66.17.11.2** Equipment in enclosed processing areas can deteriorate over time, and periodic evaluation should be conducted to ensure that leakage rates have not increased or that the ventilation rate is adequate for any increase in leakage rates. [**30:**A.17.11.2]

A.66.17.11.7 NFPA 91 and NFPA 90A provide information on this subject. [**30:**A.17.11.7]

A.66.17.14 Where the vapor space of equipment is usually within the flammable range, the probability of explosion damage to the equipment can be limited by inerting, by providing an explosion suppression system, or by designing the equipment to contain the peak explosion pressure that can be modified by explosion relief. Where the special hazards of operation, sources of ignition, or exposures indicate a need, consideration should be given to providing protection by one or more of the above means. [**30:**A.17.14]

See NFPA 68 and NFPA 69 for additional information on various methods of mitigating losses from explosions. [**30:**A.17.14]

N **A.66.17.15.1** Hazards can be present in operations such as preparation; separation; purification; and change of state, energy content, or composition. Hazards also can be present in other operations not listed in this annex. [**30:**A.17.15.1]

A.66.18.4.8 The process area is not intended to be a storage area for liquid containers. However, it is recognized that containers will be brought into the process area either for transfer of liquids to the process or for dispensing liquids from the process to the containers. [**30:**A.18.4.8]

The amount of liquid in containers in the process area should be limited as much as possible. Full containers should not be stored in the process area but can be staged there. Only the amount of liquid needed for one continuous 24-hour period should be brought into the process area in full containers. Partial containers can remain in the process area as long as they do not increase the hazard present. Containers that were filled in the process area can remain there during the shift that they were filled but should be relocated to the appropriate storage area before the end of the workday or shift in the case of 24-hour-a-day operations. [**30:**A.18.4.8]

Δ **A.66.18.5.1** Incidental operations are operations that utilize liquids only as a limited activity to that which establishes the occupancy classification. Examples include automobile assembly, assembly of electronic equipment, furniture manufacturing, and areas within refineries, distilleries, and chemical plants where the use of liquids is incidental, such as in maintenance shops, offices, or vehicle repair shops. Some more detailed descriptions follow:

(1) *Vehicle Assembly.* Vehicle assembly operations usually involve both process and incidental use of liquids. An example of a process operation would be paint storage and mixing utilized for application of the vehicle primer, color coats, and clear coats. For these operations, the requirements of Section 66.17 apply. Examples of incidental use would be sealer deck wipedown operations, windshield washer solvent dispensing, brake fluid filling, and final line paint repair operations. These operations might be continuous. However, the quantities of liquids used and the vapor exposures are significantly reduced from larger volume usage found within vehicle body component paint mixing and storage operations.
(2) *Assembly of Electrical Equipment.* Examples of incidental use of liquids in these types of occupancies might include "photoresist" coating operations, "softbaking" operations, wave solder operations, and wipedown operations.
(3) *Chemical Plant Maintenance Shop.* Incidental use of liquids is commonplace in maintenance shops located within a chemical plant. Examples are cutting oils used in a machine shop, Class II solvents for degreasing, and Class I and Class II paint solvents and fuels associated with automotive and industrial truck repair.
(4) *Cleaning and Sanitation.* Under provisions established by the US Food and Drug Administration (FDA) in 21 CFR, "GMP for Medical Devices," Class I and Class II liquids [FP < 140°F (60°C)] can be used for cleaning and sanitation purposes. Limited quantities are used to remove manufacturing materials, mold release compounds, and other contaminants not intended to be on the final product. An example would be the use of isopropyl alcohol (IPA), transferred to a cleaning wipe via a plunger-type liquid-dispensing container. The cleaning wipe is then used to remove manufacturing materials not intended to be on the final product. The key point here is not that the liquid is not part of the final product, but that limited quantities of liquid are used and the use is incidental to the manufacturing operation that produces the product. [**30:**A.18.5.1]

A.66.18.5.4(1) The intent of this requirement is to allow the quantities of flammable and combustible (ignitible) liquids needed to safely and efficiently operate for the actual operating hours in any 24-hour period. As an example, if the facility operates only 8 hours out of 24 (i.e., a single shift) and uses 50 gal (190 L) of liquid during that time, then 50 gal (190 L) is the allowable quantity for the continuous 24-hour period. If the facility increases operations to two shifts, then the allowable quantity doubles to 100 gal (380 L). [**30:**A.18.5.4(1)]

Δ **A.66.18.6.4** A "safe location" should be selected as the location of a vent discharge to minimize the potential for ignitible vapors to travel to a source of ignition after discharge from the vent. Electrical equipment that does not meet the requirements for hazardous locations can serve as an ignition source. The Technical Committee advises that vent discharge locations should consider factors such as the following:

(1) Characteristics of the exhausted material (vapor density, toxicity, velocity of discharge, etc.)
(2) Proximity to potential ignition sources
(3) Building openings such as doors, windows, air intakes, and so forth
(4) Dispersion characteristics (distance to discharge within the flammable range, direction of discharge, atmospheric conditions, and the influence of building and neighboring buildings on discharged vapors)
(5) Likelihood of vapor accumulation following discharge, such as accumulation under building eaves
(6) Likelihood of sufficient discharge volume to allow an ignitible concentration to reach an ignition source

[**30:**A.18.6.4]

Historically, NFPA 30 has provided prescriptive guidance, often based on area classification requirements, and results have been acceptable. Closer distances should be accepted only if an engineering study by a qualified engineer justifies closer distances. Similarly, the specified distances might not be acceptable for all installations, thus the guidance provided above. [**30:**A.18.6.4]

A.66.19.2.1 Cooking oil is a Class IIIB liquid [FP ≥ 200°F (93°C)] with a high FP typically above 500°F (260°C). Because of its high FP, cooking oil presents a lower fire hazard than Class IIIB liquids [FP ≥ 200°F (93°C)] having FP lower than 500°F (260°C). Fresh, or new, cooking oil is supplied to the user for cooking operations. As the oil becomes degraded through repeated use, it must be replaced with fresh oil. This waste, or used, cooking oil is recovered from the cooking appliance and temporarily stored for offsite removal. To maintain fluidity in the transfer process, the waste oil is heated to approximately 100°F (38°C), well below the FP temperature. [**30:**A.19.2.1]

A.66.19.4.2 Mist explosions have occurred when heat transfer fluid that is above its boiling point has been released in an enclosed area. Consideration should be given to locating heaters or vaporizers either in a detached building or in a room with damage-limiting construction. [**30:**A.19.4.2]

A.66.19.4.3 The system should be interlocked to stop circulation of the heat transfer fluid through the system and to shut off the system heater or vaporizer in the event of a fire, abnormally low pressure in the system, or operation of an approved heat detection system. Where the refractory inside the heater or vaporizer can retain enough heat to cause either breakdown of the heat transfer fluid or tube fouling if fluid circulation through the unit is stopped, circulation could have to be continued. In the event of a confirmed fire, it is desirable to subdivide the piping system by means of interlocked safety shutoff valves. A practical way of accomplishing this is to isolate all secondary circulating loops from the primary loop that runs into and out of the vaporizer or heater. [30:A.19.4.3]

A well-marked remote emergency shutoff switch or electrical disconnect should be provided to shut down the entire system in the event of an emergency. This should be located either in a constantly attended location or at a location that would be accessible in the event of a leak or a fire. [30:A.19.4.3]

If there are any process or utility lines running in or through rooms or areas containing parts of the heat transfer system, consideration should be given to providing emergency shutoff valves. They should be located so they are readily accessible in the event of a fire. [30:A.19.4.3]

Where the liquid level in the system expansion tank is maintained by an automatically actuated supply pump taking suction from the heat transfer fluid storage tank, an interlock should be provided to shut down the supply pump when a high level indicator is actuated, regardless of whether the pump is in automatic or manual mode. [30:A.19.4.3]

A.66.19.4.3.1 Heat transfer fluid systems have the potential for releasing large quantities of heated flammable or combustible (ignitible) liquids. Low-point drains piped to a safe location provide the ability to remove heat transfer fluid from a breached piping system in order to minimize the total quantity of fluid released. An engineering analysis should be used to determine the location and design of low-point drains. The engineering analysis should consider system inventory, the amount of heat transfer fluid that can be released in a specific fire area, the exposure created by a release, and the fire protection provided. [30:A.19.4.3.1]

A.66.19.4.3.2 Where possible, the drain tank(s) should be located below the lowest system drain opening to permit gravity flow. Breather vents should be provided based on the maximum emptying or filling rates. [30:A.19.4.3.2]

A.66.19.4.4 If stack gas from a heater or vaporizer is recovered to provide auxiliary heat for other equipment (e.g., rotary dryers), suitable dampers, isolation gates, burner control logic, or other means should be provided to ensure that all equipment is properly purged and will operate in a safe manner. The control logic should anticipate all possible operating modes of the individual pieces of equipment, whether operating singly or together, to ensure safe startup and shutdown under normal or upset conditions. [30:A.19.4.4]

Instrumentation and interlocks should be provided to sound an alarm and to automatically shut down the fuel source to the heater or vaporizer when any of the following conditions are detected:

(1) Low flow of heat transfer fluid through the heat exchange tubes of the heater, as measured at the discharge.
(2) High temperature or pressure of the fluid at the heater or vaporizer outlet. The high-temperature interlock should be set at or below the manufacturer's maximum recommended bulk fluid temperature.
(3) Low pressure at the heater or vaporizer outlet or elsewhere in the system. This interlock could require a bypass to allow for startup.
(4) Low fluid level in the expansion tank.
(5) Low liquid level in the vaporizer.
(6) Sprinkler system flow in any area containing the heat transfer equipment or piping.

[30:A.19.4.4]

Alarm set points should be provided at levels below or above the automatic shutoff setpoints to monitor the abovementioned variables and provide an opportunity for operators to correct the problem before conditions reach an unsafe level. [30:A.19.4.4]

A.66.19.4.5.1 Where possible, piping should be run underground, outside, or in floor trenches. Overhead routing of heat transfer fluid piping should be minimized. [30:A.19.4.5.1]

A.66.19.4.6.1 Historical records show that fires involving heat transfer fluids can be very severe and long lasting. It is recommended that automatic sprinkler or deluge protection be provided throughout all building areas potentially exposed to a heat transfer fluid spill fire. [30:A.19.4.6.1]

A.66.19.4.7.1 Some factors that should be considered as part of such a review include the following:

(1) Infiltration of material being heated into the heat transfer system. In this case, the system should be shut down and the internal leak point found and repaired as soon as possible.
(2) Leaks in the system. Any leak should be corrected promptly regardless of how small. Corrections should be permanent, such as repacking valve stems and replacing leaky gaskets. Any heat transfer fluid released as a result of a leak or operation of a safety valve should be cleaned up immediately if it is or can come in contact with a hot surface. Other spills can be cleaned up at the first available opportunity.
(3) Pipe or equipment insulation that is soaked with heat transfer fluid. In this case, the cause of the leak should be corrected promptly and the insulation replaced with clean, dry insulation.
(4) High temperature anywhere in the system. In this case, operating procedures should specify shutdown of the heater or vaporizer fuel supply as soon as the temperature of the heat transfer fluid exceeds the manufacturer's recommended maximum bulk fluid temperature. Any corrective actions taken to correct a high temperature condition should only be done with the heat source shut off.

[30:A.19.4.7.1]

A.66.19.5.5.1 If the liquid knock-out vessel utilizes a pump for automatic liquid removal, consideration should be given to a low-level alarm and shutdown to avoid running the pump dry, resulting in a potential source of ignition. [30:A.19.5.5.1]

A.66.19.5.7.2 Electrical enclosures that need to be opened frequently for maintenance (i.e., enclosures housing vapor processing system controls) have a higher potential for mechanical damage that could render the enclosures unable to contain an explosion. Additional inspection could be needed to ensure the integrity of the enclosure. [30:A.19.5.7.2]

A.66.19.5.7.3 NFPA 77 and API 2003, *Protection Against Ignition Arising Out of Static, Lightning, and Stray Currents*, can be used as a reference for protections against static ignition. [**30:**A.19.5.7.3]

A.66.19.5.7.4 Spontaneous ignition can be a problem in the following:

(1) Facilities where pyrophoric deposits can accumulate from the handling of oxygen-deficient vapors containing sulfur compounds or asphaltic materials. When air is introduced into the system, the pyrophoric materials can react, resulting in potential ignition and fire.
(2) Facilities that handle fluids in such a way that mixing of hypergolic or otherwise incompatible materials can occur. Such mixing could occur with fluids remaining in the vapor recovery system from prior loading activities.
(3) Facilities handling oxygenated hydrocarbons in carbon absorption units. Higher heats of absorption for these types of vapors can potentially lead to overheated carbon beds and increase the chance that an oxidation reaction can be initiated. (For further information, refer to API Report, "An Engineering Analysis of the Effects of Oxygenated Fuels on Marketing Vapor Recovery Equipment.")

[**30:**A.19.5.7.4]

A.66.19.5.7.5 US Coast Guard Regulations in Title 33, Code of Federal Regulations, Part 154, Section 154.826(b), (c), and (d), can be used as a reference for vapor mover designs that minimize the potential for ignition. [**30:**A.19.5.7.5]

A.66.19.5.7.6 The potential for ignition in the vapor collection system needs to be evaluated on a case-by-case basis. If ignition occurs, flame propagation in piping systems containing vapor mixtures in the flammable range normally starts with low-speed burning (deflagration). As the flame moves through the piping, it accelerates and, within a short distance, can reach supersonic speeds (detonation). Initial low-speed flame propagation can be stopped by flame arresters, liquid seals, or automatic fast-acting valve systems where designed, operated, and tested within the requirements of NFPA 69. Flame propagation can also be stopped for both deflagrations and detonations by use of detonation arresters tested in accordance with US Department of Transportation Coast Guard Regulations of the 33 CFR 154, Appendix A, or other procedures acceptable to the AHJ, or automatic fast-acting valve systems tested under the appropriate conditions. [**30:**A.19.5.7.6]

A.66.19.7.1.3 The goal of 66.19.7 is to consolidate in one location all requirements for commercial kitchen cooking oil storage and operations. There are a number of chapters in NFPA 30 that apply to these systems, including chapters on storage tanks and piping systems, transferring and dispensing of liquids, and so forth. Many of these requirements are more applicable to industrial or process situations and commercial kitchen cooking oil storage and use was not anticipated. All applicable chapters have been assessed in detail. Those specific requirements in this section that are in potential conflict with other sections of this *Code* have been identified and alternate methods or exceptions have been developed where appropriate. This approach eliminates the need to add exceptions throughout the existing *Code*, improving ease of use particularly for fire officials. [**30:**A.19.7.1.3]

A.66.19.7.2.1.2 Waste oil is drained from commercial cooking equipment via a transfer pump and transfer lines to a waste oil storage tank. The oil might be as hot as 375°F (190°C), still well below the oil's FP. Experience shows that the oil loses significant heat in the transfer process. The maximum temperature of waste cooking oil entering the storage tank is typically below 235°F (113°C). The storage tank should be constructed of materials compatible with cooking oil in that temperature range. [**30:**A.19.7.2.1.2]

A.66.19.7.2.2.1 Existing steel tanks listed for flammable and combustible (ignitible) liquids are considered acceptable for waste oil use. These tank standards contain design and construction requirements that would not meet food code requirements, making the tanks unacceptable for storage of liquid food products (i.e., fresh cooking oil). [**30:**A.19.7.2.2.1]

A.66.19.7.2.3.4 High flash point cooking oils do not create ignitable vapors when stored under the conditions specified in 66.19.7. [**30:**A.19.7.2.3.4]

A.66.19.7.2.5 Although generally not required for tanks storing Class IIIB liquids [FP ≥ 200°F (93°C)], overfill protection is considered necessary for cooking oil storage tanks to prevent inadvertent spillage. [**30:**A.19.7.2.5]

A.66.19.7.2.6.1 The prohibition of electrical immersion heaters in nonmetallic tanks eliminates a primary ignition source for the oil stored in the tank. [**30:**A.19.7.2.6.1]

A.66.19.7.2.6.2 The temperature limitation of 140°F (60°C) corresponds to ASTM C1055 (ISO 13732-1) restrictions for maximum allowable temperatures of nonmetallic industrial surfaces for human contact. [**30:**A.19.7.2.6.2]

A.66.19.7.3.1.1 The kitchen cooking area has historically been an area where fires occur. Tanks should, therefore, be located away from the kitchen cooking area. [**30:**A.19.7.3.1.1]

A.66.19.7.3.1.2 The area beneath the ventilation hood is another area of potential accidental ignition. [**30:**A.19.7.3.1.2]

A.66.19.7.3.2.1 Guidance on securing tanks from tipping over is provided by the manufacturer's instructions in accordance with the tank listing. [**30:**A.19.7.3.2.1]

A.66.19.7.3.3.2 An example of a fitting with a positive shutoff is a spring-loaded check valve or a hydraulic quick-coupling with a spring-loaded poppet. [**30:**A.19.7.3.3.2]

A.66.19.7.3.4.1 Cooking oil storage tanks are atmospheric tanks with open vents. The requirement in Section 66.21 to pressurize the tank for leak testing would be difficult to achieve in the field, due to tank construction and configuration. It is also desirable to prevent water contamination of the cooking oil. A more appropriate test would be to fill the tank with cooking oil to cover all connections and seams below the normal liquid level. [**30:**A.19.7.3.4.1]

A.66.19.7.4.2 Supplemental ventilation, as is required for cooking operations, is not needed for cooking oil storage tanks. [**30:**A.19.7.4.2]

A.66.19.7.5.1 Waste oil lines are generally pumped until there is little residual oil remaining in the lines. Fresh cooking oil lines are likely to contain residual oil after fill and removal operations. Restricting the fresh oil line size to 1.25 in. (32 mm) maximum inside diameter limits the amount of oil in the line. Additionally, the requirement for check valves or anti-siphon valves on the lines at points where the lines connect to the tank eliminates the possibility of a compromised line siphoning the contents of the tank. To the extent possible, transfer lines should avoid being routed over seating areas. These requirements are designed to minimize fire risk by limiting cooking oil quantities in transfer lines that could become involved in a fire. In buildings protected by automatic sprinklers, the need to add sprinklers in previously unprotected spaces (assuming the transfer lines are located in these spaces) should be considered in accordance with the requirements of NFPA 13. [**30:**A.19.7.5.1]

A.66.19.7.5.2 The temperature and pressure ratings for the waste oil lines are consistent with the maximum expected conditions. [**30:**A.19.7.5.2]

A.66.21.4.1.5.3 Electrical immersion heaters pose a potential hazard to melt through plastic tanks and/or cause ignition. If these heaters are proposed for use in plastic tanks because of operational needs, a hazard analysis required by 66.6.4.1 should consider engineering controls such as, but not limited to, the following:

(1) Low-liquid-level alarm
(2) High-temperature alarm
(3) Over-temperature and low-liquid-level automatic shutoff of the immersion heater

[**30:**A.21.4.1.5.3]

A.66.21.4.2.1.1 Atmospheric tanks include tanks of compartmented design and tanks that incorporate secondary containment. [**30:**A.21.4.2.1.1]

UL 142A, *Special Purpose Aboveground Tanks for Specific Flammable or Combustible Liquids*, covers shop-fabricated steel special-purpose generator base, work bench, lube oil, used oil, process, and day tank types. [**30:**A.21.4.2.1.1]

A.66.21.4.3.1.1 Normal venting is not required for the interstitial space of a secondary containment tank. [**30:**A.21.4.3.1.1]

N **A.66.21.4.3.1.1.1** UL/ULC 2583, *Fuel Tank Accessories for Flammable and Combustible Liquids*, contains functional testing requirements for pressure/vacuum vent devices to ensure they meet the pressure- and vacuum-relieving pressures in 66.21.4.3.2 at the time of installation. [**30:**A.21.4.3.1.1.1]

A.66.21.4.3.2 Tanks intended for normal operation at pressures greater than a gauge pressure of 1.0 psi (6.9 kPa) are designed in accordance with 66.21.4.2.3. It is recognized that a slight vacuum is necessary to operate a vacuum vent. [**30:**A.21.4.3.2]

A.66.21.4.3.9 Liquid properties that justify omitting such devices include, but are not limited to, condensation, corrosiveness, crystallization, polymerization, freezing, or plugging. When any of these conditions exist, consideration should be given to heating, use of devices that employ special materials of construction, use of liquid seals, or inerting. See NFPA 69. [**30:**A.21.4.3.9]

A.66.21.4.4.3 Examples of liquids with minimal potential for accumulation of static charge include crude oil, asphalt, and water-miscible liquids. For additional information, see NFPA 77. [**30:**A.21.4.4.3]

A.66.21.4.5 Other means of internal corrosion protection include protective coatings and linings and cathodic protection. [**30:**A.21.4.5]

N **A.66.21.5.2** See PEI RP200, *Recommended Practices for Installation of Aboveground Storage Systems for Motor Vehicle Fueling*, and STI R912, *Installation Instructions for Shop-Fabricated Stationary Aboveground Storage Tanks for Flammable, Combustible Liquids*, for additional requirements to test secondary containment tanks. [**30:**A.21.5.2]

A.66.21.5.2.9 Underground double-wall tanks can be considered to be a type of secondary containment. The terms "double-wall tank" and "jacketed tank" are sometimes used to describe underground secondary containment tanks. [**30:**A.21.5.2.9]

N **A.66.21.5.2.9.1** The limits stated in 66.21.5.2.9.1 should not exceed the values of the selected test method. [**30:**A.21.5.2.9.1]

N **A.66.21.5.2.10** The limits stated in 66.21.5.2.10 should not exceed the values of the selected test method. [**30:**A.21.5.2.10]

To assure structural integrity of the primary rectangular storage tank, the interstitial space should be tested only while the primary tank is still under test pressure. See rectangular tank manufacturer instructions for procedure to verify containment tightness, and see STI R912, *Installation Instructions for Shop-Fabricated Stationary Aboveground Storage Tanks for Flammable, Combustible Liquids*, for additional guidance with testing secondary contained rectangular tanks. [**30:**A.21.5.2.10]

N **A.66.21.5.2.11.1** The limits stated in 66.21.5.2.11.1 should not exceed the values of the selected test method. [**30:**A.21.5.2.11.1]

A.66.21.5.3 For information on testing of underground tanks, see NFPA 329. For information on testing aboveground tanks, see API 653, *Tank Inspection, Repair, Alteration, and Reconstruction*. [**30:**A.21.5.3]

A.66.21.6.6.1 See NFPA 25 or other specific fire protection system standards. [**30:**A.21.6.6.1]

A.66.21.7.2.2 Protection from tampering or trespassing might include one or more of the following: appropriate fencing around isolated tanks in remote areas; "No Trespassing" signs; warning signs indicating the fire hazard of the tank or its contents; locked or secured access to stairways and ladders; locked or secured hatches, valves, and so forth. [**30:**A.21.7.2.2]

N **A.66.21.7.4.1** For further information, see API 2015, *Cleaning Petroleum Storage Tanks*; and API 2016, *Guidelines and Procedures for Entering and Cleaning Petroleum Storage Tanks*. [**30:**A.21.7.4.1]

N **A.66.21.7.4.3.1** See API 1604, *Closure of Underground Petroleum Storage Tanks*, and Annex D of NFPA 30 for additional information. [**30:**A.21.7.4.3.1]

N **A.66.21.7.4.3.3(2)** Special training might be required.

A.66.21.7.5 See NFPA 329 for information on testing methods. [**30:**A.21.7.5]

N **A.66.21.8.1** Regular inspections of aboveground storage tanks, including shop fabricated aboveground storage tanks, performed in accordance with national standards, provide a means to ensure system maintenance. Acceptable standards include, but are not limited to, the following:

(1) API 653, *Tank Inspection, Repair, Alteration, and Reconstruction*
(2) STI SP001, *Standard for Inspection of Aboveground Storage Tanks*
(3) API RP 12R1, *Setting, Maintenance, Inspection, Operation, and Repair of Tanks in Production Service*

(4) API RP 2350, *Overfill Protection for Storage Tanks in Petroleum Facilities*
[**30:**A.21.8.1]

N A.66.21.8.6 For additional information, see API 653, *Tank Inspection, Repair, Alteration, and Reconstruction*, API RP 2350, *Overfill Protection for Storage Tanks in Petroleum Facilities*, and PEI RP600, *Recommended Practices for Overfill Prevention for Shop-Fabricated Aboveground Tanks*. [**30:**A.21.8.6]

N A.66.21.8.8 The accumulation of water in the bottom of a tank encourages microbial activity that hampers operations and increases the risk of product release. It is imperative that tank owners and operators routinely monitor the tank bottom for accumulation of water and establish a procedure for when and how the water is to be removed. Additional information can be found in API 1501, *Filtration and Dehydration of Aviation Fuels*; API RP 1621, *Bulk Liquid Stock Control at Retail Outlets*; and API Standard 2610, *Design, Construction, Operation, Maintenance, and Inspection of Terminal and Tank Facilities*. Other sources of information are ASTM D6469, *Standard Guide for Microbial Contamination in Fuels and Fuel Systems*; the National Oilheat Research Alliance, *Oilheat Technician's Manual*; and the STI publication, *Keeping Water Out of Your Storage System*. [**30:**A.21.8.8]

A.66.22.4 See PEI RP200, *Recommended Practices for Installation of Aboveground Storage Systems for Motor Vehicle Fueling*, for additional information. [**30:**A.22.4]

A.66.22.4.2.1 Where more than two tanks are involved, the sum of the diameters of each possible pair of tanks is calculated. For example, assume four tanks in a common diked area, numbered 1 through 4 clockwise from tank #1. The diameter of each pair of tanks is summed, as follows: 1 and 2, 1 and 3, 1 and 4, 2 and 3, 2 and 4, and 3 and 4. [**30:**A.22.4.2.1]

Regarding note (2) in Table 66.22.4.2.1, see 66.6.4 for engineering evaluations. Tank shell and roof exposure protection (such as cooling rings) can be used on existing tanks to control exposure protection and prevent escalation. [**30:**A.22.4.2.1]

N A.66.22.4.2.3 Thermal radiation modeling completed as an engineering evaluation in 66.6.4 could demonstrate that a higher separation distance is necessary to prevent escalation. Tank shell exposure protection, such as fixed water sprays, can be used on existing tanks to control exposure and prevent escalation. Refer to NFPA 15 for additional information. [**30:**A.22.4.2.3]

A.66.22.5.2.1 Appendix E of API Standard 650, *Welded Steel Tanks for Oil Storage*, and Appendix B of API 620, *Design and Construction of Large, Welded, Low-Pressure Storage Tanks*, provide information on tank foundations. [**30:**A.22.5.2.1]

A.66.22.5.2.5 For further information, see ASTM E119, *Standard Test Methods for Fire Tests of Building Construction and Materials*, and UL 1709, *Rapid Rise Fire Tests of Protection Materials for Structural Steel*. [**30:**A.22.5.2.5]

N A.66.22.7.1.1 Typically, during an exposure fire, the tank contents will be boiled and the pressure in the tank will be limited by a relief device sized per 66.22.7.1.1. The temperature of the tank shell in contact with the contents will be limited to the boiling point of the contents at the relief pressure. [**30:**A.22.7.1.1]

Under certain circumstances, conventional emergency relief venting will not provide adequate protection for aboveground storage tanks impacted by an exposure fire. Tanks have both a maximum allowable working pressure (MAWP) and a corresponding temperature at which that pressure was calculated, the maximum allowable working temperature (MAWT). At temperatures above the MAWT, the effective pressure rating will decrease, and ultimately could drop below the MAWP or perhaps even below the operating pressure of the tank.

If 66.22.7.1.1 cannot be applied, a hazard analysis completed per Section 6.4 can reveal cases where such relief venting is not an adequate safeguard for an exposure fire. [**30:**A.22.7.1.1]

Examples of such cases include, but are not limited to, the following:

(1) Fire exposure of tanks containing fluids with a boiling point at relief conditions which is higher than the MAWT (sometimes referred to as high boiling materials) can result in the shell of the tank being heated to the point of failure before the pressure in the tank reaches the relief device set pressure. Alternative means of protecting a tank should be considered if:

[A.66.22.7.1.1a]

$$T_{boil} > MAWT$$

(2) Nonferrous tanks (e.g., aluminum or copper) can have MAWTs which are significantly lower than ferrous tanks. Therefore, many chemicals will likely have boiling points higher than the MAWT of these tanks. During an exposure fire, excessive temperature can result in weakening and possible failure of the tank shell, potentially at a pressure below the relief device set pressure. The guidance in A.66.22.7.1.1(1) is applicable, but the MAWT could be significantly lower.

(3) Liquids that are heated to a temperature and pressure higher than their critical temperature and critical pressure become supercritical fluids. Supercritical materials exhibit no heat of vaporization. An exposure fire that heats a material to supercritical conditions can cause the tank shell to weaken and possibly fail due to excessive temperature before reaching the relief set pressure. This situation occurs when:

[A.66.22.7.1.1b]

$$P_{tank} > P_{critical}$$

and

$$T_{tank} > T_{critical}$$

(4) Excessive shell temperature due to an exposure fire on areas of unwetted shell can lead to weakening of the shell and the potential for a boiling liquid expanding vapor explosion (BLEVE). Identification of this scenario typically requires detailed simulation of the temperature of the vessel shell during an exposure fire.
[**30:**A.22.7.1.1]

In cases such as those identified in A.66.22.7.1.1(1) through A.66.22.7.1.1(4), depending on the tank temperature and pressure ratings and the qualities of the liquids being handled, the tank shell might see elevated temperatures, which could result in failure at a pressure above, equal to, or below the rated pressure of the tank. In extreme cases, the tank shell might experience temperatures that could result in failure at a pressure not only below the relief set pressure, but also below the normal operating pressure. [**30:**A.22.7.1.1]

In cases such as these, when the conventional approach of 66.22.7.1.1 will not provide adequate protection for the tank, alternative approaches to emergency venting should be considered. One approach to addressing such cases of exposure fires is via extinguishment of the fire by the application of an automatic, fixed foam fire protection system designed, installed, operated, and maintained per NFPA 11. Such a solution might meet the requirements of equivalency *(see Section 1.5 of NFPA 30)*. [**30**:A.22.7.1.1]

Δ **A.66.22.7.3.1** An engineering evaluation should be performed whenever two-phase flow is anticipated. The objective of the engineering evaluation determining emergency vent requirements and design of the relief system is to protect against catastrophic failure resulting in unacceptable risk to persons or to the facility. Factors that should be included in the evaluation are as follows:

(1) Properties of the materials including evaluated influence of two-phase flow and thermally induced instability. See the following references from the Design Institute for Emergency Relief Systems of the Center for Chemical Process Safety/American Institute of Chemical Engineers:

  (a) Fisher, H. G. and Forrest, H. S., "Protection of Storage Tanks from Two-Phase Flow Due to Fire Exposure"
  (b) Houser, J., et al, "Vent Sizing for Fire Considerations: External Fire Duration, Jacketed Vessels, and Heat Flux Variations Owing to Fuel Consumption"
  (c) *Guidelines for Pressure Relief and Effluent Handling Systems*

(2) Rate of heat input to the tank and contents. Computer models such as PLGS (supported by the UK Health and Safety Executive) can be useful in making the analysis.

(3) Fire duration. For pool fires this analysis can be based on burning rate and pool depth. Computer programs can be useful in making this analysis.

[**30**:A.22.7.3.1]

N **A.66.22.7.3.4** UL/ULC 2583, *Fuel Tank Accessories for Flammable and Combustible Liquids*, contains functional testing requirements for emergency vent devices to ensure they meet the relieving pressure in 66.22.7.3.4.2 and the minimum flow rate in 66.22.7.3.4.3 at the time of installation based on testing and calculations in 66.22.7.3.4.4 and 66.22.7.3.4.6. [**30**:A.22.7.3.10]

N **A.66.22.7.3.4.6** The following is a suitable formula for this calculation:

[A.66.22.7.3.4.6]

$$CFH = 1667 C_f A \sqrt{P_t - P_a}$$

where:
CFH = venting requirement (ft³ of free air per hour)
C_f = flow coefficient of 0.5
A = orifice area (in.²)
P_t = absolute pressure inside the tank (in. of water)
P_a = absolute atmospheric pressure outside the tank (in. of water)
[**30**:A.22.7.3.10.6]

A.66.22.7.4 Vent sizing formulae and prescriptive vent sizes, such as those established by UL 142, *Steel Aboveground Tanks for Flammable and Combustible Liquids*, are typically based on the direct installation of a venting device on to a tank with a nipple not exceeding 12 in. (300 mm). When the outlet of a vent must be extended to a remote location, such as for tanks located in buildings, which require vent discharges to be located outside, a significant reduction in vent flow can occur unless the size of the vent and connecting piping is increased. In such cases, the size of vents and vent pipe extensions should be calculated to ensure that a tank will not be over-pressurized during a fire exposure. [**30**:A.22.7.4]

Δ **A.66.22.8** Requirements in this section might also apply to Class II and Class III liquids [FP ≥ 100°F (37.8°C)] that are heated at or above their flashpoint. This was previously stated in 66.22.8.2 in the 2018 edition and in prior editions, but was later deleted because 66.22.3 had been added to apply that requirement to the entirety of Chapter 22 of NFPA 30. [**30**:A.22.8]

Protection against fire or explosion required for large liquid storage tanks should consider the use of a fixed, semi-fixed, or portable protection system designed in conformance with good engineering practice such as those described in NFPA 11, NFPA 15, and NFPA 69. Ordinary combustibles (such as wood) would be subject to radiant heat unpiloted ignition from a burning tank, when such exposures are located a distance of less than about 150 percent of the tank diameter (assuming no wind effects). Exposure from adjacent property to the tanks would depend on the specific products and storage arrangement and could require some engineering analysis based on the occupancy and its exposure potential. [**30**:A.22.8]

A.66.22.11 "Accidental release" includes, but is not limited to, the following:

(1) Leakage from the tank shell
(2) Overfill
(3) Leakage from piping connected to the tank

[**30**:A.22.11]

N **A.66.22.11.2.2** An aboveground storage tank dike is normally sized to contain the entire contents of the largest single tank within it. Some designs incorporate sufficient freeboard (additional capacity) to accommodate precipitation or firefighting water. The amount of this freeboard is usually governed by local conditions. [**30**:A.22.11.2.2]

N **A.66.22.11.2.4.1** Diked areas for tanks containing Class I liquids [FP < 100°F (37.8°C)] located in extremely porous soils might require special treatment to prevent seepage of hazardous quantities of liquids to low-lying areas or waterways in case of spills. [**30**:A.22.11.2.4.1]

N **A.66.22.11.3.1** See A.66.22.11.2.2. [**30**:A.22.11.3.1]

N **A.66.22.11.3.4** Where elastomeric seals are used in concrete diking joints, consideration should be given to using a high-temperature-rated elastomer, providing protection by insulation or steel covers, or providing backup strips to prevent leakage in the event of a fire exposure. During the Buncefield 2005 incident, the secondary containment failed because the elastomeric joints melted from radiant heat from the flames burning in the secondary containment. An appropriate solution should meet two criteria: the joints of the secondary containment wall should be water tight and the joint should not melt. Both can be accomplished by shielding elastomeric joints with stainless steel sheet metal that is bolted to the concrete but which covers the elastomeric joint to shield it from radiant energy. For new construction, a solution is to install a water stop made of stainless steel sheet metal. [**30:**A.22.11.3.4]

N **A.66.22.11.4.5.2** UL/ULC 2583, *Fuel Tank Accessories for Flammable and Combustible Liquids*, contains functional testing requirements for overfill prevention devices to ensure they meet the alarm or shutoff functions at the tank capacity levels in 66.22.11.4.5 at the time of installation. [**30:**A.22.11.4.5.2]

A.66.22.12.1.2 Engineering designs that can reduce exposure hazards include use of sealed sleeve piping and secondary containment piping to prevent leakage and the use of remotely controlled isolation valves on product lines to stop the flow of liquids when the piping is subjected to fire exposure. [**30:**A.22.12.1.2]

A.66.22.12.3 Methods of preventing an exposure hazard include intermediate diking, drainage, or fire protection features such as water spray systems, monitors, or fire-resistive coatings. High integrity pumps or equipment also constitute a method of limiting exposure hazards. [**30:**A.22.12.3]

A.66.23.1.1 Anchoring can be accomplished using nonmetallic straps or metallic straps that are separated from the tank shell by inert insulating dielectric material. The straps should be connected to a bottom hold-down pad or deadman anchors. For additional information, see reference to API RP 1615, *Installation of Underground Petroleum Storage Systems*; PEI RP100, *Recommended Practices for Installation of Underground Liquid Storage Systems*; and STI RP R011, *Recommended Practice for Anchoring of Steel Underground Storage Tanks*. [**30:**A.23.14.1]

Previous editions of NFPA 30 included provisions for the use of water ballast as a means to weight a tank to prevent movement during a flood. In anticipation of a flood event, water could be used to fill the tank to reduce buoyancy. While this approach remains technically viable for existing tanks that are not properly secured to prevent movement, the use of water as a means of providing ballast is no longer considered an acceptable basis of design for new tank installations. [**30:**A.23.14.1]

It is not the intent of this section to prohibit the use of water as ballast in underground tanks during system installation and prior to the initial introduction of the stored liquid. [**30:**A.23.14.1]

N **A.66.24.5.2** See NFPA 220. [**30:**A.24.5.2]

N **A.66.24.5.5** The purpose of the access aisles is to provide for ease of maintenance and emergency operations. [**30:**A.24.5.5]

A.66.24.6.1.1 NFPA 10 provides information on the suitability of various types of extinguishers. [**30:**A.24.6.1.1]

A.66.24.6.1.2 See NFPA 13 and NFPA 14. [**30:**A.24.6.1.2]

A.66.24.6.2.2 See NFPA 24 for information on this subject. [**30:**A.24.6.2.2]

A.66.24.6.2.3 See NFPA 11, NFPA 13, and NFPA 15 for information on these subjects. [**30:**A.24.6.2.3]

For certain fuel types, such as ketones, esters, and alcohols, the minimum required densities established in the listing criteria for foam discharge devices are often higher than the general densities specified for protection of flammable and combustible (ignitable) liquids. When determining the design criteria for extinguishing systems using foam, it is important to ensure that the listing criteria, which are typically based on empirical data from fire tests, are not overlooked. Otherwise, the fire protection system design can be inadequate for proper protection. [**30:**A.24.6.2.3]

N **A.66.24.8.6** This might require curbs, scuppers, or special drainage systems to control the spread of fire. Annex A of NFPA 15 provides information on this subject. [**30:**A.24.9.6]

N **A.66.24.13.6** Substitutes for manual gauging include, but are not limited to, heavy-duty flat gauge glasses; magnetic, hydraulic, or hydrostatic remote reading devices; and sealed float gauges. [**30:**A.24.14.6]

N **A.66.24.13.8** Suitable devices include, but are not limited to, a float valve; a preset meter on the fill line; a low head pump incapable of producing overflow; or a liquidtight overflow pipe, sized at least one pipe size larger than the fill pipe, that discharges by gravity back to the outside source of liquid or to an approved location. [**30:**A.24.14.8]

A.66.25.3.1 Inspections are recommended for shop fabricated aboveground tanks. One guide is SP001, *Standard for Inspection of Aboveground Storage Tanks*, which is published by the Steel Tank Institute. In addition, the tank owner may desire to conduct additional inspections to ensure the ongoing integrity of tanks and equipment. Because the interior of a vault will ordinarily remain dry and temperature-moderated, environmental effects on tanks and equipment inside vaults will be reduced as compared to aboveground tanks that are not protected from weather exposure. Accordingly, inspection and maintenance frequencies for exterior surfaces of tanks and piping in vaults are typically less critical than for aboveground tanks installed outdoors. Nevertheless, inspection and maintenance of emergency vents and overfill prevention devices are still necessary. [**30:**A.25.3.1]

Clearance between the shell of a tank or equipment in a vault and the interior vault wall should be sufficient to accommodate visual inspections and maintenance that may be needed. In addition, consideration should be given to the need for inspection and maintenance of tank interior surfaces that may be impacted by internal corrosion. [**30:**A.25.3.1]

Clearance should be adequate to permit the following:

(1) Entry into the vault interior by an inspector or maintenance worker
(2) Access to manipulate, repair, or replace any equipment or fittings in the vault
(3) Access within the vault to visually inspect, either by direct sight or with the aid of an optical vision extension tools, interior vault surfaces and exterior surfaces of tanks and equipment, to determine the source of any leakage that may occur, and to conduct any needed repairs

[**30:**A.25.3.1]

Because vaults are designed to provide for entry by inspectors or maintenance workers, consideration should also be given to providing access for rescue by emergency responders who may be called upon to rescue an individual from a vault. Such consideration may include providing a minimum access hatch dimension of 36 in. (915 mm) and a minimum dimension for walkways in vault interior spaces of 30 in. (760 mm) to permit an emergency responder with an SCBA to maneuver and providing, in some cases, a second means of access to the vault interior. [**30:**A.25.3.1]

A.66.27.4.3.2 For further information, see ASTM E119, *Standard Test Methods for Fire Tests of Building Construction and Materi-*

als, UL 263, *Fire Tests of Building Construction and Materials*, and UL 1709, *Rapid Rise Fire Tests of Protection Materials for Structural Steel*. [**30:**A.27.4.3.2]

A.66.27.4.4.4(4) A thermally activated fire valve is a valve that meets UL 842, *Valves for Flammable Fluids*; FM 7400, *Liquid and Gas Safety Shutoff Valves*; or API 607, *Fire Tests for Quarter-turn Valves and Valves Equipped with Nonmetallic Seats*. [**30:**A.27.4.4.4(4)]

A.66.27.5.1.2 It is expected that some joints may leak under fire conditions but will not come apart. [**30:**A.27.5.1.2]

N **A.66.27.6.2** API 2218, *Fireproofing Practices in Petroleum and Petrochemical Processing Plants*, contains guidance on selecting and installing fire-resistant coatings to protect exposed steel supports from a high-challenge fire exposure. It also contains a general discussion on determining need for such protection and estimating the extent of the area exposed. [**30:**A.27.6.2]

N **A.66.27.6.4** Buried steel piping should be coated with a suitable material and should be cathodically protected. Galvanized steel pipe, by itself and without other corrosion protection methods, is not acceptable for underground piping. Steel swing joints and stainless steel flexible connectors should also be made corrosion resistant when in contact with the soil. Thus, such fittings should also be coated and cathodically protected when installed between nonmetallic, compatible tanks and piping, such as fiberglass-reinforced plastic. [**30:**A.27.6.4]

A.66.27.8.1.6 Vent sizing formulas and prescriptive vent sizes, such as those established by UL 142, *Steel Aboveground Tanks for Flammable and Combustible Liquids*, are typically based on the direct installation of a venting device onto a tank. When the outlet of a vent must be extended to a remote location, such as for tanks located in buildings, which require vent discharges to be located outside, a significant reduction in vent flow can occur unless the size of the vent and connecting piping is increased. In such cases, the size of vents and vent pipe extensions should be calculated to ensure that a tank will not be over-pressurized during a fire exposure. [**30:**A.27.8.1.6]

A.66.27.8.2.1 API RP 500, *Recommended Practice for Classification of Locations for Electrical Installations at Petroleum Facilities Classified as Class I, Division 1 and Division 2*, and API RP 505, *Recommended Practice for Classification of Locations for Electrical Installations at Petroleum Facilities Classified as Class I, Zone 0, Zone 1, and Zone 2*, establish a 10 ft (3 m) classified zone around most tank vents that are potential sources of ignitible vapors. However, neither document provides specific distances for a belowgrade tank. Applying these strategies to 66.27.8.2.1 resulted in a minimum height for these tank vents of 10 ft (3 m) above grade. Since the majority of these vents exist at retail service station tanks, and since vehicles and other publicly introduced ignition sources could be located close to the vent, an additional 2 ft (0.6 m) was added to the minimum height as a safety factor to ensure the vehicle does not introduce a potential ignition source into the vapor space surrounding the vent. This results in a total height for the vent stack from a belowgrade tank of 12 ft (3.6 m). [**30:**A.27.8.2.1]

A.66.27.10 Where loading and unloading risers for Class II or Class IIIA liquids [100°F (37.8°C) ≤ FP < 200°F (93°C)] are located in the same immediate area as loading and unloading risers for Class I liquids [FP < 100°F (37.8°C)], consideration should be given to providing positive means, such as different pipe sizes, connection devices, special locks, or other methods designed to prevent the erroneous transfer of Class I liquids [FP < 100°F (37.8°C)] into or from any container or tank used for Class II or Class IIIA liquids [100°F (37.8°C) ≤ FP < 200°F (93°C)]. Note that such consideration might not be necessary for water-miscible liquids, where the class is determined by the concentration of liquid in water, or where the equipment is cleaned between transfers. [**30:**A.27.10]

A.66.27.11.3 A special marina use rating for aboveground piping systems is addressed in UL 1369, *Above Ground Piping for Flammable and Combustible Liquids*. [**30:**A.27.11.3]

N **A.66.28.3.1.1** If local ambient weather conditions bring the liquid temperature above the flash point of the liquid, the user should handle the liquid as a Class I liquid [FP < 100°F (37.8°C)]. [**30:**A.28.3.1.1]

A.66.28.3.1.2 The use of nonconductive materials in the fill pipe assembly should be avoided to prevent any electrical discontinuity in the piping of the system. Serious accidents have occurred when nonconductive materials, such as plastic or rubber hose, have been used in the fill pipe assembly. [**30:**A.28.3.1.2]

A.66.28.4.2 Use of fixed fire protection systems, dikes, fire-rated barriers, or a combination of any of these can provide suitable protection from exposures. [**30:**A.28.4.2]

A.66.28.9 The intent of this requirement is to prevent the spread of uncontrolled, spilled liquid from traveling beyond the loading or unloading area and exposing surrounding equipment and buildings. [**30:**A.28.9]

A.66.28.11.1.5 NFPA 77 provides additional information on static electricity protection and defines conductive liquids as liquids possessing a conductivity greater than 10^4 picosiemens per meter (pS/m). [**30:**A.28.11.1.5]

N **A.66.28.11.1.10** Relaxation time is dependent on the conductivity of the liquid. See NFPA 77 for guidance on determining appropriate relaxation times. [**30:**A.28.11.1.10]

A.66.28.11.2.2 NFPA 77 provides additional information on static electricity protection and defines conductive liquids as liquids possessing a conductivity greater than 10^4 picosiemens per meter (pS/m). [**30:**A.28.11.2.2]

N **A.66.28.11.2.4** Relaxation time is dependent on the conductivity of the liquid. See NFPA 77 for guidance on determining appropriate relaxation times. [**30:**A.28.11.2.4]

A.66.28.11.3 The term *switch loading* describes a situation that warrants special consideration. [**30:**A.28.11.3]

When a tank is emptied of a cargo of Class I liquid [FP < 100°F (37.8°C)], a mixture of vapor and air is left, which can be, and often is, within the flammable range. When such a tank is refilled with a Class I liquid [FP < 100°F (37.8°C)], any charge that reaches the tank shell will be bled off by the required bond wire. Also, there will be no flammable mixture at the surface of the rising oil level because the Class I liquid [FP < 100°F (37.8°C)] produces at its surface a mixture too rich to be ignitible. This is the situation commonly existing in tank vehicles in gasoline service. If, as occasionally happens, a static charge does accumulate on the surface sufficient to produce a spark, it occurs in a too-rich, nonignitible atmosphere and thus causes no harm. [**30:**A.28.11.3]

A very different situation arises if the liquid is "switch loaded," that is, when a Class II or Class III liquid [FP ≥ 100°F (37.8°C)] is loaded into a tank vehicle that previously contained a Class I liquid [FP < 100°F (37.8°C)]. [**30:**A.28.11.3]

Class II or Class III liquids [FP ≥ 100°F (37.8°C)] are not necessarily more potent static generators than the Class I liquid [FP < 100°F (37.8°C)] previously loaded, but the atmosphere in contact with the rising oil surface is not enriched to bring it out of the flammable range. If circumstances are such that a spark should occur either across the oil surface or from the oil surface to some other object, the spark occurs in a mixture that can be within the flammable range, and an explosion can result. [**30:**A.28.11.3]

It is emphasized that bonding the tank to the fill stem is not sufficient; a majority of the recorded explosions have occurred when it was believed the tank had been adequately bonded. The electrostatic potential that is responsible for the spark exists inside the tank on the surface of the liquid and cannot be removed by bonding. Measures to reduce the change of such internal static ignition can be one or more of the following:

(1) Avoid spark promoters. Conductive objects floating on the oil surface increase the charge of sparking to the tank wall. Metal gauge rods or other objects projecting into the vapor space can create a spark gap as the rising liquid level approaches the projection. A common precaution is to require that fill pipes (downspouts) reach as close to the bottom of the tank as practicable. Any operation such as sampling, taking oil temperature, or gauging that involves lowering a conductive object through an opening into the vapor space on the oil should be deferred until at least 1 minute after flow has ceased. This will permit any surface charge to relax.
(2) Reduce the static generation by one or more of the following:
    (a) Avoid splash filling and upward spraying of oil where bottom filling is used.
    (b) Employ reduced fill rates at the start of filling through downspouts, until the end of the spout is submerged. Some consider 3 ft/sec (0.9 m/sec) to be a suitable precaution.
    (c) Where filters are employed, provide relaxation time in the piping downstream from the filters. A relation time of 30 seconds is considered by some to be a suitable precaution.
(3) Eliminate the flammable mixture before switch loadings by gas freeing or inerting. [**30:**A.28.11.3]

See NFPA 77 and NFPA 385 for further information. [**30:**A.28.11.3]

A.66.28.11.4.2 Emergency and safety procedures include, but are not limited to, the following:

(1) Procedures for bonding and grounding the tank vehicle
(2) Proper use of portable extinguishers
(3) Procedures for recognizing and eliminating sources of ignition
(4) Procedures for recognizing and understanding contingency plans for handling a spill or leak
(5) Procedures for notifying the appropriate agencies in an emergency

[**30:**A.28.11.4.2]

N **A.66.29.3.25** Where practical, the collection basin should be drained to a remote location. [**30:**A.29.3.25]

A.66.29.3.25 Where practical, the collection basin should be drained to a remote location. [**30:**A.29.3.25]

A.66.29.3.28 Because of the many variables involved, exact requirements cannot be provided. However, Table A.66.29.3.28 provides guidance on the level of fire protection typically provided at wharves and marine terminals handling Class I liquids [FP < 100°F (37.8°C)]. [**30:**A.29.3.28]

A.69.1.1 See A.1.3.2.

A.69.2.1.1.1 Prior to April 1, 1967, regulations of the US Department of Transportation were promulgated by the Interstate Commerce Commission. In Canada, the regulations of the Canadian Transport Commission apply and are available from the Canadian Transport Commission, Union Station, Ottawa, Canada. [**58:**A.5.2.1.1]

Table A.66.29.3.28 Typical Fire Protection for Wharves and Marine Terminals

Locations	Water Demand (gpm)	Hydrant Monitors[a] (gpm)	Hose Reels	Fire Extinguisher Dry Chemical 120-B:C	240-B:C Wheeled	International Shore Connection	Emergency Equipment Lockers	Monitors and Hose Foam Concentrate Required (gal)	Fire Boat Connection
Barge terminals	500–1000	Two 500	Two 1¼	2	NR	NR	1	100[b]	NR
Tankers 20,000 DWT and under	1000–2000	Two 500	Two 1¼	2	1	1	1	300[b]	2
20,001–70,000 DWT	2000	Two 1000	Four 1¼[c]	2	2[d]	2	1	2000	2
70,001 DWT and over	2000[e]	Two 1000	Four 1¼[c]	3	2[d]	2	1	2000[f]	2
Sea islands	2000–4000[e]	Three 1000	Four 1¼[c]	4	2	3	2	3000	2

For SI units, 1 gpm = 3.8 L/min; 1 gal = 3.8 L; 1 lb = 0.45 kg.
NR: Not required.
[a]A minimum of two 1½ in. (38 mm) hydrant outlets should be provided at each monitor riser.
[b]This can be provided by onshore mobile equipment.
[c]One hose reel at each berth should have foam capability.
[d]The proximity of adjacent berths can reduce the total required.
[e]Under-dock systems are optional. Add water for under-dock system (0.16 × area).
[f]Under-dock systems are optional. Add foam for under-dock system (0.16 × 0.3 × 30 × area). [**30:**Table A.29.3.28]

Construction of containers to the *API-ASME Code for Unfired Pressure Vessels for Petroleum Liquids and Gases* has not been authorized after July 1, 1961. [**58**:A.5.2.1.1]

A.69.2.1.4.2 The tare weight is the cylinder weight plus the weight of all permanently attached valves and other fittings but does not include the weight of protecting devices that are removed in order to load the cylinder. [**58**:A.5.2.8.2]

A.69.2.1.4.3 Head design refers to the shape of the head. Shapes include hemispherical, semi-ellipsoidal, and others. *(Refer to the API-ASME Code for Unfired Pressure Vessels for Petroleum Liquids and Gases for more information.)* [**58**:A.5.2.8.3]

A.69.2.9.1.2 Materials with melting points exceeding 1500°F (816°C) include steel, ductile (nodular) iron, malleable iron, or brass, as follows:

(1) Ductile iron should meet the requirements of ASTM A395/A395M, *Standard Specification for Ferritic Ductile Iron Pressure-Retaining Castings for Use at Elevated Temperatures,* or equivalent, and malleable iron should meet the requirements of ASTM A47/A47M, *Standard Specification for Ferritic Malleable Iron Castings,* or equivalent.
(2) Approved or listed variable liquid level gauges used in containers of 3500 gal (13.2 m^3) water capacity or less are exempt from the minimum melting point requirement.
(3) Cast-iron should not be used.
(4) Nonmetallic materials should not be used for bonnets or bodies of valves or regulators.

[**58**:A.5.9.1.2]

A.69.3.1 Section 6.5 of NFPA 58 includes general provisions that are applicable to most stationary systems. Sections 6.7 through 6.16 of NFPA 58 extend and modify Section 6.5 of NFPA 58 for systems installed for specific purposes. [**58**:A.6.1.1]

Δ **A.69.3.5.1.1** When applying Table 69.3.5.1.1 to cylinders, which have their capacities expressed in pounds, the first table entry, <125 gal (<0.5 m^3), includes all cylinders. Cylinders have a maximum capacity of 1000 lb or 119 gal (454 kg or 3.8 m^3) (water capacity). [**58**:A.6.4.1.1]

The "Line of Adjoining Property That Can Be Built Upon" refers to the property boundaries of the property adjacent to the one where the container is located. This is illustrated in Figure A.69.3.5.1.1 and in Figure I.1(a), Figure I.1(b), and Figure I.1(c) of NFPA 58, taking into consideration a condition that involves property on the other side of a street, highway, navigable waterway, or other right of way. The minimum distance limitation is from the container to the property line where that property line is common to plots of ground of different ownership and would also apply between the container and the property line of the far side of a street or other public right of way. [**58**:A.6.4.1.1]

Regarding "Important Building," a building can be important for any number of reasons, including the following:

(1) Human occupancy
(2) Replacement value
(3) Value of the contents
(4) Vital role of its production equipment or business records to a business
(5) The effect of building location on product release and fire control activities by firefighters and other emergency responders

[**58**:A.6.4.1.1]

Human occupancy in a building does not automatically make it important. Occupancy for brief periods, such as one might find in a garage while a vehicle is being loaded, should not be a factor in classifying a building as important. [**58**:A.6.4.1.1]

Clearly, buildings that house assembly occupancies, such as theaters and churches, are "important" because the general public will be there, as well as at mercantile occupancies (stores). Homes, apartments, hotels, dormitories, and prisons should also be considered "important." Storage occupancies might not be considered "important" if workers only occasionally enter the building. [**58**:A.6.4.1.1]

Buildings with characteristics that (1) hinder emergency responders from being able to gain access to a position where they can safely apply water to a tank or (2) act as an impediment to applying water should also be considered a part of this category. There is such a wide assortment of physical configurations of industrial and bulk plant sites that each location must be considered on its own. Items such as railroad tracks, containers for storage of other fuels, fences obstructing access from preferred directions, topography, and even rows of trees can present unique challenges for access and, with the location of buildings on congested sites, can by themselves, or in combination, make applying water on the tanks extremely difficult. [**58**:A.6.4.1.1]

A.69.3.5.3(4) Figure A.69.3.5.3(4)(a) and Figure A.69.3.5.3(4)(b) depict the requirements of 69.3.5.3(4). [**58**:A.6.4.3(4)]

A.69.3.5.4.3 Building openings in the context of 69.3.5.4.3 are any opening that communicates air from the exterior to the interior of the building, including windows, doors, or dryer vent terminations below the level of the relief valve discharge. [**58**:A.6.4.4.3]

A.69.3.6.3.3 Clearance is required between combustible materials and propane containers in order to minimize the effects of fires on the container. The requirement to maintain separation between the container and stored combustible materials is needed so that an accumulation of materials that might represent a hazard to the container does not occur. The term *stored* is intended to denote materials that are purposely placed. The term *accumulate* is intended to denote materials that are there by other than being purposely placed. Vegetation of any type located near or under the container is not considered to be a hazard. [**58**:A.6.5.3.3]

A.69.3.6.3.4 For information on determination of flash points, see NFPA 30. [**58**:A.6.5.3.4]

A.69.3.6.3.5 Examples of Class I flammable liquids are gasoline and methanol. Examples of Class II combustible liquids are diesel, kerosene, or fuel oils. [**58**:A.6.5.3.5]

A.69.3.6.3.9 Also see NFPA 51. [**58**:A.6.5.3.9]

A.69.3.6.4 The presence of such structures can create significant hazards, such as the following:

(1) Pocketing of escaping gas
(2) Interference with application of cooling water by fire departments
(3) Redirection of flames against containers
(4) Impeding the egress of personnel in an emergency

[**58**:A.6.5.4]

Δ **FIGURE A.69.3.5.1.1** Illustration of Separation Distances from Containers to the Line of Adjoining Property That Can Be Built Upon. [58:Figure A.6.4.1.1]

FIGURE A.69.3.5.3(4)(a) Separation Between Containers 10 ft (3 m) or Greater.

[Diagram showing Case 2: Two groups of 120 gal (0.45 m³) water capacity containers 10 ft (3 m) or more from each other, making the aggregate capacity of each group (8 × 120) = 960 gal (3.6 m³). Table 6.4.1.1 requires minimum 25 ft (7.6 m) from the building for an aggregate capacity between 501 and 2000 gal (1.9 and 7.6 m³). Shows Building with 25 ft (7.6 m) separation to containers. Less than 10 ft (3 m) separation between two groups. Each container is 120 gal (0.45 m³) water capacity [420 lb (190.51 kg)]. (Not to scale)]

FIGURE A.69.3.5.3(4)(b) Separation Between Containers Less Than 10 ft (3 m).

A.69.3.7.1.1 It is the intent to allow transfer of liquid into containers in open areas under canopies or roofs where 50 percent or more of the perimeter is not enclosed. [58:A.6.7.1.1]

A.69.3.7.2.1 Examples of Class I flammable liquids, as referenced in Table 69.3.7.2.1 Part J, are gasoline and methanol; examples of Class II combustible liquids, as referenced in Table 69.3.7.2.1 Part K, are diesel, kerosene, and fuel oils. [58:A.6.7.2.1]

A.69.3.8.1.4 Generally, a light-reflecting color paint is preferred unless the system is installed in an extremely cold climate. [58:A.6.8.1.4]

N **A.69.3.9.7** An option for visual verification could consist of an inspection of the actuator to verify it moved into the fully closed position. [58:A.6.13.4.5]

A.69.3.10.8 Anchorage can be accomplished by the use of concrete bulkheads or equivalent anchorage or by the use of a weakness or shear fitting. [58:A.6.15.8]

A.69.3.11.1 The variables that affect the potential for damage to outdoor gas system components present in areas where heavy snowfalls occur are numerous. Therefore, the selection of an appropriate method to mitigate potential damage from snow and ice should be based upon the characteristics of the installation site and the forces that are anticipated. Some alternatives include the following:

(1) Locating aboveground piping, regulators, and meters above snow levels
(2) Locating aboveground piping, regulators, and meters on the gable end of buildings
(3) Adding support to aboveground piping, regulators, and meters or securing them to the structure to withstand snow and ice load
(4) Installing dedicated covers for regulators and meters that are designed to withstand a vertical static load equal to two times the ground snow load (psf) for the area but not less than 350 psf
(5) Locating aboveground piping, regulators, and meters in an elevated and protected location under extended roof overhangs and eaves. The equipment should be located near the elevation of the bottom of the eave or overhang. If the equipment is located too far below the eave or overhang, snow shedding from the roof can curl back under the eave and impact equipment. See Figure A.6.19.1 of NFPA 58.

[58:A.6.19.1]

A.69.3.12.2.6 The requirement for a pilot or an electronic ignition system became effective for heaters with inputs over 50,000 Btu/hr (53 MJ/hr) manufactured on or after May 17, 1967. [58:A.6.23.2.6]

A.69.3.12.8.3 The weight of the cylinders will be affected by the specific gravity of the LP-Gas. Weights varying from 16.0 oz to 16.8 oz (454 g to 476 g) are recognized as being within the range of what is nominal. [58:A.6.23.9.3]

A.69.3.14.1 Typical nonengine fuel systems include those on commercial, industrial, construction, and public service vehicles such as trucks, semitrailers, trailers, portable tar kettles, road surface heating equipment, mobile laboratories, clinics, and mobile cooking units (such as catering and canteen vehicles). [58:A.6.27.1]

A.69.3.14.7.6 Requirements for the design of containers are located in Section 5.2 of NFPA 58. Requirements for container appurtenances are located in Section 5.9 of NFPA 58. [58:A.6.27.7.6]

N **A.69.3.15.3.14.2** Other barriers are designed to be equal in proportion to the anticipated damages. For example, the height of a commonly used concrete "Jersey barrier" or heavy concrete blocks is typically less than 3 ft (0.9 m) tall and both have been effectively used as alternative means of equivalent protection in lieu of guard posts. Other examples of equivalent vehicle barrier protection include the guardrails and guard cables that are commonly seen along highways that help keep vehicles from leaving the roadway. [58:A.6.28.3.14(B)]

A.69.4.1 Ignition source control at transfer locations is covered in Section 6.26 of NFPA 58. Fire protection is covered in Section 6.30 of NFPA 58. [58:A.7.1]

A.69.4.2.2.5 Examples of an effective seal are a POL plug or cap. Listed quick-closing couplings with CGA V-1 connection numbers 790 (forklift ACME connection), 791 (portable cylinder ACME/POL connection), and 810 (socket/plug quick connection) have secondary seals. Therefore, plugs or caps for these connections are not required or recommended. [58:A.7.2.2.5]

Δ **A.69.4.2.2.7** CGA 791 and 793 connections are primarily used on consumer LP-Gas equipment. Both connection designs employ the use of a face seal to seal the male and female sides of the connection before gas flow occurs. Damage to the face seal (e.g., cracking, gouging, tearing, roping) affects the sealing surfaces and could result in a leak. Examples of cracking, gouging/tearing, roping, filling double seal, and missing face seal are shown in Figure A.69.4.2.2.7. [58:A.7.2.2.7]

This inspection is intended to identify visible damage to the face seal, not to confirm whether the CGA 791 or CGA 793 connections are within dimensional tolerance. [58:A.7.2.2.7]

The photographs below depict examples of visible damage to a face seal that resulted in leakage when connected to an appliance. [58:A.7.2.2.7]

Training materials regarding the pre-fill inspection of cylinders, including the face seals, can be found in the Propane Education and Research Council (PERC) training program "Dispensing Propane Safely." [58:A.7.2.2.7]

The CGA 791 and 793 connections as manufactured do not permit the replacement of the face seal, and the face seal design is not the same for all manufacturers. Therefore, if the face seal has been compromised, the cylinder should not be filled. [58:A.7.2.2.7]

A.69.4.2.3.5.1 Air-moving equipment includes large blowers on crop dryers, space heaters, and some central heating equipment. Equipment employing open flames includes flame cultivators, weed burners, and tar kettles. [58:A.7.2.3.5(A)]

A.69.5.4.1 The filling process in 69.5.4.1.4 refers to the time period beginning when a cylinder or cylinders are brought to a dispensing station to be filled and ending when the last cylinder is filled and all the cylinders are removed from the filling area. This is meant to define a continuous process, with the cylinders being unattended for only brief periods, such as operator breaks or lunch. [58:A.8.4.1]

A.69.5.4.2.1 It has been shown that when tested in accordance with ASTM E84, *Standard Test Method for Surface Burning Characteristics of Building Materials*, or UL 723, *Test for Surface Burning Characteristics of Building Materials*, materials such as steel, concrete, gypsum board, and aluminum will meet the requirements of a flame spread index of 25 or less. In contrast, the flame spread indices of some combustible materials can be much higher. Typically, untreated wood products will exhibit a flame spread index ranging between 50 and 200. [58:A.8.4.2.1]

Cracking

Gouging/tearing

Roping

Filling double seal

Missing face seal

Δ **FIGURE A.69.4.2.2.7** Examples of Defects. [Figure 58:A.7.2.2.7]

A.69.5.4.2.3 Research conducted demonstrated that lockable, ventilated enclosures of aluminum or steel construction protect cylinders stored within those cabinets from potentially catastrophic damage due to impact from a motor vehicle. The report, "Evaluation of Collision Protection Provided by Vehicle Impact Bollards and Propane Cylinder Exchange Cabinets," was prepared for the National Propane Gas Association and is available from NFPA. [58:A.8.4.2.3]

Where cylinders are not stored in lockable, ventilated metal enclosures, 69.5.4.2.2(1) requires them to be stored in a fenced enclosure *(see 6.22.4.2 of NFPA 58)*, which could provide sufficient protection for the cylinders. Where fenced enclosures warrant additional vehicular barrier protection (VBP), the following provide such protection:

(1) Guardrails
(2) Steel bollards
(3) Raised sidewalks [minimum of 6 in. (150 mm) in height]
(4) Fencing
(5) Ditches
(6) Berms (not to exceed 50 percent of the container perimeter)
(7) Jersey barriers
(8) Parking bumpers [minimum of 6 in. (150 mm) in height]
(9) Fencing/gates

[58:A.8.4.2.3]

A.69.5.5.1 Although fire extinguishers are required in locations where cylinders are stored and awaiting use or resale, the specific site characteristics should be considered. For example, where the installation is a retail exchange cabinet, cylinders will be locked inside and will typically contain either a CGA 791, CGA 793, or CGA 810 valve connection, all of which have redundancy built into them that prevents the flow of gas unless connected to an appliance. As such, any cylinder fire in a retail facility cabinet should never be extinguished by anyone other than fire service personnel because the source of the gas cannot be turned off. The sole function for fire extinguishers in these locations is to extinguish incipient fires in the vicinity of the cabinet. [58:A.8.5.1]

Δ **A.69.6.2.2.2** The term *congested area* is intended to describe situations where access to the vehicle during an emergency or where moving the vehicle away from an emergency could be impeded. [58:A.9.7.2.2]

N **A.69.6.2.3.6(7)** The proper fill level of propane containers that are permanently installed on vehicles, can be determined by using the fixed maximum liquid level gauge or any other approved method. Fill levels of portable containers can be determined by using the fixed maximum liquid level gauge, by weighing the cylinder, or any other approved method. [58:A.9.7.3.6(7)]

Annex B Sample Ordinance Adopting the NFPA 1, *Fire Code*

This annex is not a part of the requirements of this NFPA document but is included for informational purposes only.

Δ **B.1** The following sample ordinance is provided to assist a jurisdiction in the adoption of this *Code* and is not part of this *Code*.

ORDINANCE NO. _____

An ordinance of the *[jurisdiction]* adopting the *[year]* edition of NFPA 1, *Fire Code*, and documents listed in Chapter 2 of that *Code*, prescribing regulations governing conditions hazardous to life and property from fire or explosion; providing for the issuance of permits and collection of fees; repealing Ordinance No. _____ of the [jurisdiction] and all other ordinances and parts of ordinances in conflict therewith; providing a penalty; providing a severability clause; and providing for publication; and providing an effective date.

BE IT ORDAINED BY THE *[governing body]* **OF THE** *[jurisdiction]*:

SECTION 1 That the _____ *[year]* edition of NFPA 1, *Fire Code*, and documents adopted by Chapter 2, three (3) copies of which are on file and are open to inspection by the public in the office of the *[jurisdiction's keeper of records]* of the *[jurisdiction]*, are hereby adopted and incorporated into this ordinance as fully as if set out at length herein, and from the date on which this ordinance shall take effect, the provisions thereof shall be controlling within the limits of the *[jurisdiction]*. The same are hereby adopted as the code of the *[jurisdiction]* for the purpose of prescribing regulations governing conditions hazardous to life and property from fire or explosion and providing for issuance of permits and collection of fees.

SECTION 2 Any person who shall violate any provision of this *Code* or standard hereby adopted or fail to comply therewith; or who shall violate or fail to comply with any order made thereunder; or who shall build in violation of any detailed statement of specifications or plans submitted and approved thereunder; or fail to operate in accordance with any certificate or permit issued thereunder; and from which no appeal has been taken; or who shall fail to comply with such an order as affirmed or modified by a court of competent jurisdiction, within the time fixed herein, shall severally for each and every such violation and noncompliance, respectively, be guilty of a misdemeanor, punishable by a fine of not less than $ _____ nor more than $ _____ or by imprisonment for not less than _____ days nor more than _____ days or by both such fine and imprisonment. The imposition of one penalty for any violation shall not excuse the violation or permit it to continue; and all such persons shall be required to correct or remedy such violations or defects within a reasonable time; and when not otherwise specified the application of the above penalty shall not be held to prevent the enforced removal of prohibited conditions. Each day that prohibited conditions are maintained shall constitute a separate offense.

SECTION 3 Additions, insertions, and changes — that the _____ *[year]* edition of NFPA 1, *Fire Code*, is amended and changed in the following respects:

[List Amendments]

SECTION 4 That ordinance No. _____ of *[jurisdiction]* entitled *[fill in the title of the ordinance or ordinances in effect at the present time]* and all other ordinances or parts of ordinances in conflict herewith are hereby repealed.

SECTION 5 That if any section, subsection, sentence, clause, or phrase of this ordinance is, for any reason, held to be invalid or unconstitutional, such decision shall not affect the validity or constitutionality of the remaining portions of this ordinance. The *[governing body]* hereby declares that it would have passed this ordinance, and each section, subsection, clause, or phrase hereof, irrespective of the fact that any one or more sections, subsections, sentences, clauses, and phrases be declared unconstitutional.

SECTION 6 That the *[jurisdiction's keeper of records]* is hereby ordered and directed to cause this ordinance to be published.

[NOTE: An additional provision may be required to direct the number of times the ordinance is to be published and to specify that it is to be in a newspaper in general circulation. Posting may also be required.]

SECTION 7 That this ordinance and the rules, regulations, provisions, requirements, orders, and matters established and adopted hereby shall take effect and be in full force and effect *[time period]* from and after the date of its final passage and adoption.

Annex C Fire Fighter Safety Building Marking System

This annex is not a part of the requirements of this NFPA document unless specifically adopted by the jurisdiction.

C.1 Firefighter Safety Building Marking System (FFSBMS).

C.1.1 General.

C.1.1.1 The firefighter safety building marking system provides basic building information for firefighters responding to the building or structure.

C.1.1.2 Where required by the AHJ, buildings and structures shall have the firefighter safety building marking system sign installed.

C.1.2 Sign.

C.1.2.1 The approved firefighter safety building marking system sign shall be placed in a position to be plainly legible and visible from the street or road fronting the property or as approved by the fire department.

C.1.2.2 The firefighter safety building marking system sign shall consist of the following:

(1) White reflective background with black letters
(2) Durable material
(3) Arabic numerals or alphabet letters
(4) Permanently affixed to the building or structure in an approved manner

C.1.2.3 The firefighter safety building marking system shall be a Maltese cross as shown in Figure C.1.2.3.

C.1.2.4 The minimum size of the firefighter safety building marking system sign and lettering shown in Figure C.1.2.4 shall be in accordance with the following or as approved by the fire department:

(1) A shall be 5 in. × 5 in.
(2) B shall be 1¼ in.
(3) C shall be 2½ in.
(4) Letters shall be 1 in. height with a stroke of ¼ in.

C.1.3 Ratings.

C.1.3.1 Ratings shall be determined by the construction type, hazards of contents, automatic fire sprinkler systems and standpipe systems, occupancy/life safety, and special hazards in accordance with this section.

C.1.3.1.1 Where multiple ratings occur within a classification category, a determination shall be made by the AHJ of the rating that shall be based on the greatest potential risk for the specific category. *(See Note 1 in C.2.1.)*

FIGURE C.1.2.3 Sample Sign for Firefighter Safety Building Marking System.

△ FIGURE C.1.2.4 Dimensions for Firefighter Safety Building Marking System Signs.

C.1.3.2 Construction Type. The construction type shall be designated by assigning the appropriate lettering to the top of the Maltese cross as follows:

(1) FR — Fire-resistive construction
(2) NC — Noncombustible construction
(3) ORD — Ordinary construction
(4) HT — Heavy timber construction
(5) C — Combustible construction

C.1.3.3 Hazards of Contents. The hazards of contents shall be rated by determining its hazard and assigning the appropriate rating to the left of the Maltese cross as follows *(see Note 2 in C.2.2)*:

L — Low hazard. Low hazard contents shall be classified as those of such low combustibility that no self-propagating fire therein can occur.

M — Moderate hazard. Moderate hazard contents shall be classified as those that are likely to burn with moderate rapidity or to give off a considerable volume of smoke.

H — High hazard. High hazard contents *(see Note 3 in C.2.3)* shall be classified as those that are likely to burn with extreme rapidity or from which explosions are likely.

C.1.3.4 Automatic Fire Sprinkler and Standpipe System. The automatic fire sprinkler system and standpipe system shall be rated by determining its level of protection and assigning the appropriate rating to the right of the Maltese cross. If multiple systems are provided, all systems shall be included in the Maltese cross as follows:

(1) A — Automatic fire sprinkler system installed throughout
(2) P — Partial automatic fire sprinkler system or other suppression system installed
(3) S — Standpipe system installed
(4) N — None

C.1.3.5 Occupancy/Life Safety Issues. The occupancy/life safety type shall be rated by determining the level of difficulty in evacuating occupants from the building and the occupancy type by assigning the appropriate rating to the bottom of the Maltese cross as follows:

(1) L — Business, industrial, mercantile, residential, and storage occupancies

(2) M — Ambulatory health care, assembly, educational, and day care occupancies
(3) H — Detention and correction facilities, health care, and board and care occupancies

C.1.3.6 Special Designations. The special hazards can be assigned to the center of the Maltese cross *(see Note 4 in C.2.4)*.

C.1.4 Installation and Maintenance.

C.1.4.1 Fire departments that implement the firefighter safety building marking system (FFSBMS) shall provide written instructions to the owner/operator of a facility equipped with a firefighter safety building marking system sign regarding the information to be included on the sign, and the fire department shall perform annual inspections to verify continued compliance with the information shown on the sign *(see Note 5 in C.2.5)*.

C.1.4.2 Installation and maintenance of the sign shall be the responsibility of the owner/operator.

C.1.4.3 The fire department shall enact procedures to identify changes of occupancy that could establish a need to update information on the sign and shall notify the owner/operator when changes are necessary.

C.1.5 Training.

C.1.5.1 Training shall be provided to all fire department personnel responding to buildings using the FFSBMS sign.

C.2 Notes. The following notes are explanatory and are not part of the mandatory text for Annex C.

C.2.1 Note 1. An example of the greatest potential risk for construction type where an FR and an NC are present, the ranking on the FFSBMS sign would be NC.

C.2.2 Note 2. Hazard of contents are described as follows:

Low hazard recognizes storage of noncombustible materials as low hazard. In other occupancies it is assumed that, even where the actual contents hazard is normally low, there is sufficient likelihood that some combustible materials or hazardous operations will be introduced in connection with building repair or maintenance, or some psychological factor might create conditions conducive to panic, so that the egress facilities cannot safely be reduced below those specified for ordinary hazard contents.

Moderate hazard classification represents the conditions found in most buildings and is the basis for the general requirements of this *Code*.

The fear of poisonous fumes or explosions is necessarily a relative matter to be determined on a judgment basis. All smoke contains some toxic fire gases but, under conditions of moderate hazard, there should be no unduly dangerous exposure during the period necessary to escape from the fire area, assuming there are proper exits.

C.2.3 Note 3. High hazard contents include occupancies where flammable liquids are handled or used or are stored under conditions involving possible release of flammable vapors; where grain dust, wood flour or plastic dust, aluminum or magnesium dust, or other explosive dusts are produced; where hazardous chemicals or explosives are manufactured, stored, or handled; where cotton or other combustible fibers are processed or handled under conditions producing flammable flyings; and other situations of similar hazard.

C.2.4 Note 4. The center of the firefighter safety building marking system sign has been left empty to permit the local jurisdiction space to provide for additional information that they may wish to add. The NFPA 704 marking system can be incorporated into the center of the firefighter safety building marking system sign if all the applicable provisions of NFPA 704 are met including lettering size and so forth.

C.2.5 Note 5. The intent of this provision is to verify that the information on the FFSBMS sign is correct on a regular basis. Fire departments responding to facilities equipped with a FFSBMS sign should verify signage and preplans annually. Other means of verifying the information on the FFSBMS sign could include mailings, outside consultants, and community service programs.

Δ **Annex D Firefighter Breathing-Air Replenishment Systems**

This annex is not a part of the requirements of this NFPA document unless specifically adopted by the jurisdiction.

D.1 General. Where required by the AHJ, firefighter breathing-air replenishment systems shall comply with Appendix F of the *Uniform Plumbing Code*.

N **D.2 Permit.**

N **D.2.1** A permit shall be required for the installation of a firefighter breathing-air replenishment system.

N **D.2.2** The permit shall comply with Section 1.13.

Annex E Fire Sprinkler Disclosure Statement for One- and Two-Family Dwellings

This annex is not a part of the requirements of this NFPA document unless specifically adopted by the jurisdiction.

E.1 Where automatic sprinkler systems are not required in new one- and two-family dwellings, a disclosure statement shall be provided to the buyer in accordance with Sections E.2 and E.3.

E.2 Prior to agreeing on final pricing for the construction of a new one- or two-family dwelling with a buyer, the builder shall provide the buyer with a copy of written materials approved by the AHJ, which details the benefits of an automatic sprinkler system.

E.3 Concurrent with providing the information approved by the AHJ, as required in E.2, a builder shall provide a quote for the cost associated with the installation of an automatic sprinkler system. Upon request of the buyer, the builder shall, at the buyer's expense, install an automatic sprinkler system.

E.4 The provisions of Section E.3 shall only apply to the execution of contracts for new one- and two-family dwellings that have not yet been constructed. Homes that are already constructed by a builder, typically called *spec homes,* shall not fall under the provisions of Section E.3 because they received permits prior to buyers executing contracts.

Annex F Informational References

F.1 Referenced Publications. The documents or portions thereof listed in this annex are referenced within the informational sections of this *Code* and are not part of the requirements of this document unless also listed in Chapter 2 for other reasons.

Δ **F.1.1 NFPA Publications.** National Fire Protection Association, 1 Batterymarch Park, Quincy, MA 02169-7471.

NFPA 2, *Hydrogen Technologies Code*, 2023 edition.

NFPA 3, *Standard for Commissioning of Fire Protection and Life Safety Systems*, 2024 edition.

NFPA 4, *Standard for Integrated Fire Protection and Life Safety System Testing*, 2024 edition.

NFPA 10, *Standard for Portable Fire Extinguishers*, 2022 edition.

NFPA 11, *Standard for Low-, Medium-, and High-Expansion Foam*, 2021 edition.

NFPA 13, *Standard for the Installation of Sprinkler Systems*, 2022 edition.

NFPA 13D, *Standard for the Installation of Sprinkler Systems in One- and Two-Family Dwellings and Manufactured Homes*, 2022 edition.

NFPA 13E, *Recommended Practice for Fire Department Operations in Properties Protected by Sprinkler and Standpipe Systems*, 2020 edition.

NFPA 13R, *Standard for the Installation of Sprinkler Systems in Low-Rise Residential Occupancies*, 2022 edition.

NFPA 14, *Standard for the Installation of Standpipe and Hose Systems*, 2024 edition.

NFPA 15, *Standard for Water Spray Fixed Systems for Fire Protection*, 2022 edition.

NFPA 17, *Standard for Dry Chemical Extinguishing Systems*, 2024 edition.

NFPA 17A, *Standard for Wet Chemical Extinguishing Systems*, 2024 edition.

NFPA 20, *Standard for the Installation of Stationary Pumps for Fire Protection*, 2022 edition.

NFPA 22, *Standard for Water Tanks for Private Fire Protection*, 2023 edition.

NFPA 24, *Standard for the Installation of Private Fire Service Mains and Their Appurtenances*, 2022 edition.

NFPA 25, *Standard for the Inspection, Testing, and Maintenance of Water-Based Fire Protection Systems*, 2023 edition.

NFPA 30, *Flammable and Combustible Liquids Code*, 2024 edition.

NFPA 30A, *Code for Motor Fuel Dispensing Facilities and Repair Garages*, 2024 edition.

NFPA 30B, *Code for the Manufacture and Storage of Aerosol Products*, 2023 edition.

NFPA 31, *Standard for the Installation of Oil-Burning Equipment*, 2020 edition.

NFPA 33, *Standard for Spray Application Using Flammable or Combustible Materials*, 2021 edition.

NFPA 45, *Standard on Fire Protection for Laboratories Using Chemicals*, 2024 edition.

NFPA 51, *Standard for the Design and Installation of Oxygen–Fuel Gas Systems for Welding, Cutting, and Allied Processes*, 2023 edition.

NFPA 51B, *Standard for Fire Prevention During Welding, Cutting, and Other Hot Work*, 2024 edition.

NFPA 52, *Vehicular Natural Gas Fuel Systems Code*, 2023 edition.

NFPA 54, *National Fuel Gas Code*, 2024 edition.

NFPA 55, *Compressed Gases and Cryogenic Fluids Code*, 2023 edition.

NFPA 58, *Liquefied Petroleum Gas Code*, 2024 edition.

NFPA 59A, *Standard for the Production, Storage, and Handling of Liquefied Natural Gas (LNG)*, 2023 edition.

NFPA 61, *Standard for the Prevention of Fires and Dust Explosions in Agricultural and Food Processing Facilities*, 2020 edition.

NFPA 68, *Standard on Explosion Protection by Deflagration Venting*, 2023 edition.

NFPA 69, *Standard on Explosion Prevention Systems*, 2019 edition.

NFPA 70®, *National Electrical Code*®, 2023 edition.

NFPA 70E®, *Standard for Electrical Safety in the Workplace*®, 2024 edition.

NFPA 72®, *National Fire Alarm and Signaling Code*®, 2022 edition.

NFPA 77, *Recommended Practice on Static Electricity*, 2024 edition.

NFPA 80, *Standard for Fire Doors and Other Opening Protectives*, 2022 edition.

NFPA 80A, *Recommended Practice for Protection of Buildings from Exterior Fire Exposures*, 2022 edition.

NFPA 82, *Standard on Incinerators and Waste and Linen Handling Systems and Equipment*, 2019 edition.

NFPA 86, *Standard for Ovens and Furnaces*, 2023 edition.

NFPA 90A, *Standard for the Installation of Air-Conditioning and Ventilating Systems*, 2024 edition.

NFPA 90B, *Standard for the Installation of Warm Air Heating and Air-Conditioning Systems*, 2024 edition.

NFPA 91, *Standard for Exhaust Systems for Air Conveying of Vapors, Gases, Mists, and Particulate Solids*, 2020 edition.

NFPA 92, *Standard for Smoke Control Systems*, 2021 edition.

NFPA 96, *Standard for Ventilation Control and Fire Protection of Commercial Cooking Operations*, 2024 edition.

NFPA 99, *Health Care Facilities Code*, 2024 edition.

NFPA 101®, *Life Safety Code*®, 2024 edition.

NFPA 101A, *Guide on Alternative Approaches to Life Safety*, 2022 edition.

NFPA 102, *Standard for Grandstands, Folding and Telescopic Seating, Tents, and Membrane Structures*, 2021 edition.

NFPA 105, *Standard for Smoke Door Assemblies and Other Opening Protectives*, 2022 edition.

NFPA 110, *Standard for Emergency and Standby Power Systems*, 2022 edition.

NFPA 170, *Standard for Fire Safety and Emergency Symbols*, 2021 edition.

NFPA 204, *Standard for Smoke and Heat Venting*, 2021 edition.

NFPA 220, *Standard on Types of Building Construction*, 2024 edition.

NFPA 232, *Standard for the Protection of Records*, 2022 edition.

NFPA 241, *Standard for Safeguarding Construction, Alteration, and Demolition Operations*, 2022 edition.

NFPA 252, *Standard Methods of Fire Tests of Door Assemblies*, 2022 edition.

NFPA 257, *Standard on Fire Test for Window and Glass Block Assemblies*, 2022 edition.

NFPA 259, *Standard Test Method for Potential Heat of Building Materials*, 2023 edition.

NFPA 260, *Standard Methods of Tests and Classification System for Cigarette Ignition Resistance of Components of Upholstered Furniture*, 2024 edition.

NFPA 261, *Standard Method of Test for Determining Resistance of Mock-Up Upholstered Furniture Material Assemblies to Ignition by Smoldering Cigarettes*, 2023 edition.

NFPA 265, *Standard Methods of Fire Tests for Evaluating Room Fire Growth Contribution of Textile or Expanded Vinyl Wall Coverings on Full Height Panels and Walls*, 2023 edition.

NFPA 286, *Standard Methods of Fire Tests for Evaluating Contribution of Wall and Ceiling Interior Finish to Room Fire Growth*, 2024 edition.

NFPA 288, *Standard Methods of Fire Tests of Horizontal Fire Door Assemblies Installed in Horizontal Fire Resistance–Rated Assemblies*, 2022 edition.

NFPA 289, *Standard Method of Fire Test for Individual Fuel Packages*, 2023 edition.

NFPA 291, *Recommended Practice for Water Flow Testing and Marking of Hydrants*, 2022 edition.

NFPA 302, *Fire Protection Standard for Pleasure and Commercial Motor Craft*, 2020 edition.

NFPA 303, *Fire Protection Standard for Marinas and Boatyards*, 2021 edition.

NFPA 326, *Standard for the Safeguarding of Tanks and Containers for Entry, Cleaning, or Repair*, 2020 edition.

NFPA 329, *Recommended Practice for Handling Releases of Flammable and Combustible Liquids and Gases*, 2020 edition.

NFPA 385, *Standard for Tank Vehicles for Flammable and Combustible Liquids*, 2022 edition.

NFPA 400, *Hazardous Materials Code*, 2022 edition.

NFPA 402, *Guide for Aircraft Rescue and Fire-Fighting Operations*, 2019 edition.

NFPA 409, *Standard on Aircraft Hangars*, 2022 edition.

NFPA 415, *Standard on Airport Terminal Buildings, Fueling Ramp Drainage, and Loading Walkways*, 2022 edition.

NFPA 418, *Standard for Heliports*, 2021 edition.

NFPA 484, *Standard for Combustible Metals*, 2022 edition.

NFPA 495, *Explosive Materials Code*, 2023 edition.

NFPA 496, *Standard for Purged and Pressurized Enclosures for Electrical Equipment*, 2024 edition.

NFPA 497, *Recommended Practice for the Classification of Flammable Liquids, Gases, or Vapors and of Hazardous (Classified) Locations for Electrical Installations in Chemical Process Areas*, 2024 edition.

NFPA 499, *Recommended Practice for the Classification of Combustible Dusts and of Hazardous (Classified) Locations for Electrical Installations in Chemical Process Areas*, 2024 edition.

NFPA 505, *Fire Safety Standard for Powered Industrial Trucks Including Type Designations, Areas of Use, Conversions, Maintenance, and Operations*, 2024 edition.

NFPA 600, *Standard on Facility Fire Brigades*, 2020 edition.

NFPA 601, *Standard for Security Services in Fire Loss Prevention*, 2020 edition.

NFPA 610, *Guide for Emergency and Safety Operations at Motorsports Venues*, 2024 edition.

NFPA 654, *Standard for the Prevention of Fire and Dust Explosions from the Manufacturing, Processing, and Handling of Combustible Particulate Solids*, 2020 edition.

NFPA 655, *Standard for Prevention of Sulfur Fires and Explosions*, 2017 edition.

NFPA 701, *Standard Methods of Fire Tests for Flame Propagation of Textiles and Films*, 2023 edition.

NFPA 703, *Standard for Fire-Retardant-Treated Wood and Fire-Retardant Coatings for Building Materials*, 2024 edition.

NFPA 704, *Standard System for the Identification of the Hazards of Materials for Emergency Response*, 2022 edition.

NFPA 730, *Guide for Premises Security*, 2023 edition.

NFPA 731, *Standard for the Installation of Premises Security Systems*, 2023 edition.

NFPA 801, *Standard for Fire Protection for Facilities Handling Radioactive Materials*, 2020 edition.

NFPA 850, *Recommended Practice for Fire Protection for Electric Generating Plants and High Voltage Direct Current Converter Stations*, 2020 edition.

NFPA 855, *Standard for the Installation of Stationary Energy Storage Systems*, 2023 edition.

NFPA 914, *Code for the Protection of Historic Structures*, 2023 edition.

NFPA 921, *Guide for Fire and Explosion Investigations*, 2021 edition.

NFPA 1030, *Standard for Professional Qualifications for Fire Prevention Program Positions*, 2024 edition.

NFPA 1033, *Standard for Professional Qualifications for Fire Investigator*, 2022 edition.

NFPA 1122, *Code for Model Rocketry*, 2018 edition.

NFPA 1123, *Code for Fireworks Display*, 2022 edition.

NFPA 1124, *Code for the Manufacture, Transportation, and Storage of Fireworks and Pyrotechnic Articles*, 2022 edition.

NFPA 1127, *Code for High Power Rocketry*, 2018 edition.

NFPA 1140, *Standard for Wildland Fire Protection*, 2022 edition.

NFPA 1142, *Standard on Water Supplies for Suburban and Rural Fire fighting*, 2022 edition.

NFPA 1225, *Standard for Emergency Services Communications*, 2022 edition.

NFPA 1660, *Standard on Community Risk Assessment, Pre-Incident Planning, Mass Evacuation, Sheltering, and Re-entry Programs*, 2024 edition.

NFPA 1730, *Standard on Organization and Deployment of Fire Prevention Inspection and Code Enforcement, Plan Review, Investigation, and Public Education Operations*, 2019 edition.

NFPA 2112, *Standard on Flame-Resistant Clothing for Protection of Industrial Personnel Against Short-Duration Thermal Exposures from Fire*, 2023 edition.

NFPA 2113, *Standard on Selection, Care, Use, and Maintenance of Flame-Resistant Garments for Protection of Industrial Personnel Against Short-Duration Thermal Exposures from Fire*, 2020 edition.

NFPA 3000®, *Standard for an Active Shooter/Hostile Event Response (ASHER) Program*, 2021 edition.

NFPA 5000®, *Building Construction and Safety Code®*, 2024 edition.

NFPA *Fire Protection Guide to Hazardous Materials*, 2010 edition.

NFPA *Fire Protection Handbook*, 20th edition, 2008.

NFPA *Fire Technology*, August 1974, "Fire Tests of Building Interior Covering Systems."

F.1.2 Other Publications.

△ **F.1.2.1 AIChE Publications.** American Institute of Chemical Engineers, 120 Wall Street, FL 23, New York, NY 10005-4020.

Guidelines for Safe Warehousing of Chemicals, 1998.

F.1.2.2 AIHA Publications. American Industrial Hygiene Association, 3141 Fairview Park Drive, Suite 777, Falls Church, VA 22042.

ANSI/AIHA Z10.0, *Occupational Health and Safety Management Systems*, 2019.

△ **F.1.2.3 ANSI Publications.** American National Standards Institute, Inc., 25 West 43rd Street, 4th Floor, New York, NY 10036.

ANSI/BHMA A156.41, *Standard for Door Hardware Single Motion to Egress*, 2020.

ANSI/ISA12.10.05, *Explosive Atmospheres — Part 10-2: Classification of Areas — Combustible Dust Atmospheres*, 2013.

ANSI/AIHA Z9.7, *Recirculation of Air from Industrial Process Exhaust Systems*, 2007.

ANSI Z83.11/CSA 1.8, *Gas Food Service Equipment*, 2016.

ANSI Z400.1/Z129.1, *Hazardous Workplace Chemicals — Hazard Evaluation and Safety Data Sheet and Precautionary Labeling Preparation*, 2010.

ANSI/ISA 60079-10-2 (12.10.05), *Explosive Atmospheres — Part 10-2: Classification of areas — Combustible dust atmospheres*, 2015.

△ **F.1.2.4 API Publications.** American Petroleum Institute, 1220 L Street, NW, Washington, DC 20005-4070.

API RP 500, *Recommended Practice for Classification of Locations for Electrical Installations at Petroleum Facilities Classified as Class I, Division I and Division 2*, 3rd edition, addendum 1 (2021), 2020.

ANSI/API RP 505, *Recommended Practice for Classification of Locations for Electrical Installations at Petroleum Facilities Classified as Class I, Zone 0, Zone 1, and Zone 2*, 2018.

API 620, *Design and Construction of Large, Welded, Low-Pressure Storage Tanks*, 12th edition, addendum 2 (2018), 2013.

API 650, *Welded Tanks for Oil Storage*, 12th edition, errata 1 (2021), 2020.

API 653, *Tank Inspection, Repair, Alteration, and Reconstruction*, 5th edition, addendum 1 (2014), addendum 2 (2018), addendum 3 (2021), 2014.

API RP 1615, *Installation of Underground Petroleum Storage Systems*, 6th edition, 2011, reaffirmed 2022.

API RP 1621, *Bulk Liquid Stock Control at Retail Outlets*, 5th edition, 1993, reaffirmed 2020.

API 2003, *Protection Against Ignition Arising Out of Static, Lightning, and Stray Currents*, 8th edition, 2015, reaffirmed 2020.

API 2218, *Fireproofing Practices in Petroleum and Petrochemical Processing Plants*, 3rd edition, 2013, reaffirmed 2020.

API 2214, *Spark Ignition Properties of Hand Tools*, 4th edition, 2004, reaffirmed 2010.

"An Engineering Analysis of the Effects of Oxygenated Fuels on Marketing Vapor Recovery Equipment," September 1990.

API-ASME *Code for Unfired Pressure Vessels for Petroleum Liquids and Gases*, Pre-July 1, 1961.

F.1.2.5 ASCE Publications. American Society of Civil Engineers, 1801 Alexander Bell Drive, Reston, VA 20191-4400.

ASCE/SEI 7, *Minimum Design Loads and Associated Criteria for Buildings and Other Structures*, 2016 edition.

F.1.2.6 ASHRAE Publications. ASHRAE, 1791 Tullie Circle, NE, Atlanta, GA 30329-2305.

ANSI/ASHRAE 34, *Designation and Safety Classification of Refrigerants*, 2019.

△ **F.1.2.7 ASME Publications.** American Society of Mechanical Engineers, Two Park Avenue, New York, NY 10016-5990.

ASME A17.1/CSA B44, *Safety Code for Elevators and Escalators*, 2019.

ASME A17.3, *Safety Code for Existing Elevators and Escalators*, 2020.

ANSI/ASME B31.8, *Gas Transmission and Distribution Piping Systems*, 2020.

ASME *Boiler and Pressure Vessel Code*, 2021.

Δ **F.1.2.8 ASTM Publications.** ASTM International, 100 Barr Harbor Drive, P.O. Box C700, West Conshohocken, PA 19428-2959.

ASTM A380/A380M, *Standard Practice for Cleaning, Descaling, and Passivation of Stainless Steel Parts, Equipment, and Systems*, 2017.

ASTM C1055, *Standard Guide for Heated System Surface Conditions that Produce Contact Burn Injuries*, 2020.

ASTM D2859, *Standard Test Method for Ignition Characteristics of Finished Textile Floor Covering Materials*, 2021.

ASTM D4956, *Standard Specification for Retroreflective Sheeting for Traffic Control*, 2019.

ASTM D6469, *Standard Guide for Microbial Contamination in Fuels and Fuel Systems*, 2020.

ASTM D7666, *Standard Specification for Triglyceride Burner Fuel*, 2019.

ASTM E84, *Standard Test Method of Surface Burning Characteristics of Building Materials*, 2021a.

ASTM E119, *Standard Test Methods for Fire Tests of Building Construction and Materials*, 2020.

ASTM E648, *Standard Test Method for Critical Radiant Flux of Floor Covering Systems Using a Radiant Heat Energy Source*, 2019ae1.

ASTM E814, *Standard Test Method for Fire Tests of Through Penetration Firestop Systems*, 2013a (2017).

ASTM E1226, *Standard Test Method for Explosibility of Dust Clouds*, 2019.

ASTM E1352, *Standard Test Method for Cigarette Ignition Resistance of Mock-Up Upholstered Furniture Assemblies*, 2016.

ASTM E1353, *Standard Test Methods for Cigarette Ignition Resistance of Components of Upholstered Furniture*, 2021.

ASTM E1354, *Standard Test Method for Heat and Visible Smoke Release Rates for Materials and Products Using an Oxygen Consumption Calorimeter*, 2017.

ASTM E1472, *Standard Guide for Documenting Computer Software for Fire Models*, 2007 (withdrawn 2011).

ASTM E1491, *Test Method for Minimum Autoignition Temperature of Dust Clouds*, 2006 (2019).

ASTM E1515, *Standard Test Method for Minimum Explosible Concentration of Combustible Dusts*, 2014.

ASTM E1537, *Standard Test Method for Fire Testing of Upholstered Furniture*, 2016.

ASTM E1590, *Standard Test Method for Fire Testing of Mattresses*, 2022.

ASTM E2019, *Standard Test Method for Minimum Ignition Energy of a Dust Cloud in Air*, 2003 (2019).

ASTM E2021, *Standard Test Method for Hot-Surface Ignition of Dust Layers*, 2015.

ASTM E2030, *Guide for Recommended Uses of Photoluminescent (Phosphorescent) Safety Markings*, 2009a (withdrawn 2018).

ASTM E2174, *Standard Practice for On-Site Inspection of Installed Firestops*, 2020a.

ASTM E2393, *Standard Practice for On-Site Inspection of Installed Fire Resistive Joint Systems and Perimeter Fire Barriers*, 2020a.

ASTM F1870, *Standard Guide for Selection of Fire Test Methods for the Assessment of Upholstered Furnishings in Detention and Correctional Facilities*, 2016.

ASTM F2291, *Standard Practice for Design of Amusement Rides or Devices*, 2021.

F.1.2.9 AWS Publications. American Welding Society, 8669 NW 36 Street, #130, Miami, FL 33166-6672.

AWS F4.1, *Recommended Safe Practices for the Preparation for Welding and Cutting Containers and Piping*, 2017.

F.1.2.10 AWWA Publications. American Water Works Association, 6666 West Quincy Avenue, Denver, CO 80235.

AWWA M14, *Backflow Prevention and Cross-Connection Control: Recommended Practices*, 4th edition, 2015.

F.1.2.11 California Department of Consumer Affairs Publications. Bureau of Home Furnishings and Thermal Insulation, 3485 Orange Grove Avenue, North Highlands, CA 95660-5595.

Technical Bulletin CA TB 129, "Flammability Test Procedure for Mattresses for Use in Public Buildings," 1992.

F.1.2.12 CGA Publications. Compressed Gas Association, 14501 George Carter Way, Suite 103, Chantilly, VA 20151.

CGA C-6, *Standards for Visual Inspection of Steel Compressed Gas Cylinders*, 2019.

CGA C-6.1, *Standards for Visual Inspection of High Pressure Aluminum Compressed Gas Cylinders*, 2019.

CGA C-6.2, *Guidelines for Visual Inspection and Requalification of Fiber Reinforced High Pressure Cylinders*, 2019.

CGA C-10, *Recommended Procedures for Changes of Gas Service for Compressed Gas Cylinders*, 2013.

F.1.2.13 CSFM Publications. California State Fire Marshal Publications, Office of the State Fire Marshal, 2251 Harvard Street, Sacramento, CA 95811.

Rings of Fire: Tire Fire Prevention and Suppression, 2005.

F.1.2.14 FAA Publications. Federal Aviation Administration, US Department of Transportation, 800 Independence Avenue, SW, Washington, DC 20591.

FAA AC 150/5390-2C, *Heliport Design Advisory Circular*, April 24, 2012.

Δ **F.1.2.15 FM Publications.** FM Global, 270 Central Avenue, P.O. Box 7500, Johnston, RI 02919-4949.

ANSI/FM 4880, *American National Standard for Evaluating the Fire Performance of Insulated Building Panel Assemblies and Interior Finish Materials*, 2018.

ANSI/FM 4996, *Classification of Pallets and Other Material Handling Products as Equivalent to Wood Pallets*, 2015.

Flammability Characterization of Lithium-ion Batteries in Bulk Storage, FM Global Research Report, March 2013.

FM 6921, *Approval Standard for Containers for Combustible Waste*, 2004.

FM Data Sheet 7-76, "Prevention and Mitigation of Combustible Dust Explosions and Fire," 2020.

FM 6090, *Approval Standard for Ignitable Liquid Drainage Floor Assemblies*, 2017.

F.1.2.16 FPRF Publications. Fire Protection Research Foundation, 1 Batterymarch Park, Quincy, MA 02169-7471.

Buc, Elizabeth, *Oxidizer Classification Research Project: Tests and Criteria, Final Report*, Fire and Materials Research Laboratory, November 2, 2009.

Development of an Enhanced Hazard Classification System for Oxidizers, 2006.

Fire Protection Research Foundation, *Optimizing Fire Alarm Notification for High Risk Groups: Waking Effectiveness of Alarms (Auditory, Visual and Tactile) for Adults Who Are Hard of Hearing*, 2007.

Fire Protection Research Foundation, *Optimizing Fire Alarm Notification for High Risk Groups: Waking Effectiveness of Alarms (Auditory, Visual and Tactile) for the Alcohol Impaired*, 2007.

Fire Protection Research Foundation (FPRF) Report, *Development of Technical Basis for Carbon Monoxide Detector Siting*, prepared by C. Beyler and D. Gottuk, 2007.

National Oxidizing Pool Chemicals Storage Fire Test Project, August 1998.

F.1.2.17 IAPMO Publications. International Association of Plumbing and Mechanical Officials, 4755 E. Philadelphia Street, Ontario, CA 91761.

UPC, *Uniform Plumbing Code*, 2021.

F.1.2.18 ICAO Publications. International Civil Aviation Organization, Document Sales Unit, 999 University Street, Montréal, Quebec, Canada, H3C 5H7, icaohq@icao.int

Technical Publications.

N **F.1.2.19 ICC Publications.** International Code Council, 500 New Jersey Avenue, NW, 6th Floor, Washington, DC 20001-2070.

ICC A117.1, *Standard for Accessible and Usable Buildings and Facilities*, 2017.

International Building Code, 2024.

F.1.2.20 IEC Publications. International Electrotechnical Commission, 3, rue de Varembé, P.O. Box 131, CH-1211 Geneva 20, Switzerland.

IEC 61340-4-4, *Electrostatics—Part 4-4: Standard Test Methods for Specific Applications — Electrostatic Classification of Flexible Intermediate Bulk Containers (FIBC)*, 2018.

F.1.2.21 IEEE Publications. IEEE, 3 Park Avenue, 17th Floor, New York, NY 10016-5997.

IEEE 1635/ASHRAE 21, *Guide to Battery Room Ventilation and Thermal Management*, 2012.

F.1.2.22 IMO Publications. International Maritime Organization, 4 Albert Embankment, London SE1 7SR, United Kingdom, publications-sales@imo.org.

International Maritime Dangerous Goods Code, 2020.

F.1.2.23 ISO Publications. International Organization for Standardization, ISO Central Secretariat, BIBC II, Chemin de Blandonnet 8, CP 401, 1214 Vernier, Geneva, Switzerland.

ISO 8115, *Cotton Bales — Dimensions and Density*, 1986.

ISO 13732-1, *Ergonomics of the Thermal Environment — Methods for the Assessment of Human Responses to Contact with Surfaces, Part 1: Hot Surfaces*, 2006.

Δ **F.1.2.24 NACE Publications.** NACE International, 15835 Park Ten Place, Houston, TX 77084-4906.

NACE SP0169, *Control of External Corrosion of Underground or Submerged Metallic Piping Systems*, 2013.

F.1.2.25 PEI Publications. Petroleum Equipment Institute, 6931 S. 66th E. Ave., Suite 200, Tulsa, OK 74101-2380.

PEI/RP100, *Recommended Practices for Installation of Underground Liquid Storage Systems*, 2020.

PEI/RP200, *Recommended Practices for Installation of Aboveground Storage Systems for Motor Vehicle Fueling*, 2019.

PEI/RP500, *Recommended Practices for Inspection and Maintenance of Motor Fuel Dispensing Equipment*, 2019.

PEI/RP600, *Recommended Practices for Overfill Prevention for Shop-Fabricated Aboveground Tanks*, 2018.

F.1.2.26 Scott Specialty Gases Publications. Scott Specialty Gases, 6141 Easton Road, Box 310, Plumsteadville, PA 18949.

Design and Safety Handbook, 2006.

F.1.2.27 SFPE Publications. Society of Fire Protection Engineers, 9711 Washingtonian Blvd, Suite 380, Gaithersburg, MD 20878.

SFPE Standard S.01, *Calculating Fire Exposures to Structures*, 2011.

SFPE Standard S.02, *Calculation Methods to Predict the Thermal Performance of Structural and Fire Resistive Assemblies*, 2015.

SFPE Engineering Guide to Fire Risk Assessment, 2021.

SFPE Engineering Guide to Performance-Based Fire Protection, 2007.

SFPE Guidelines for Peer Review in the Fire Protection Design Process, 2020.

SFPE Guide for Substantiating a Fire Model for a Given Application, 2011.

SFPE Guide to Human Behavior in Fire, 2018.

SFPE Handbook of Fire Protection Engineering, 5th edition, 2016.

F.1.2.28 STI/SPFA Publications. Steel Tank Institute/Steel Plate Fabricators Association, 944 Donata Court, Lake Zurich, IL 60047.

STI R 931, *Double Wall AST Installation and Testing Instructions*, 2011.

STI RP R011, *Recommended Practice for Anchoring of Steel Underground Storage Tanks*, 2010.

Keeping Water Out of Your Storage System, 2006.

F.1.2.29 TC Publications. Transport Canada, 330 Sparks Street, Ottawa, ON K1A 0N5, Canada. webfeedback@tc.gc.ca

Transportation of Dangerous Goods Regulations.

Δ **F.1.2.30 UL Publications.** Underwriters Laboratories Inc., 333 Pfingsten Road, Northbrook, IL 60062-2096.

Commodity Hazard Comparison of Expanded Plastic in Portable Bins and Racking, Underwriters Laboratories, Project 99NK29106, NC4004, September 8, 2000.

Technical Report of Fire Testing of Automotive Parts in Portable Storage Racking, Underwriters Laboratories, Project 99NK29106, NC4004, January 5, 2001.

UL 9, *Fire Tests of Window Assemblies*, 2009, revised 2020.

UL 10B, *Fire Tests of Door Assemblies*, 2008, revised 2020.

UL 10C, *Positive Pressure Fire Tests of Door Assemblies*, 2016, revised 2021.

UL 30, *Metal Safety Cans*, 1995, revised 2019.

UL 142, *Steel Aboveground Tanks for Flammable and Combustible Liquids*, 2019, revised 2021.

UL 197, *Commercial Electric Cooking Appliances*, 2010, revised 2020.

UL 199, *Automatic Sprinklers for Fire-Protection Service*, 2022.

UL 199B, *Control Cabinets for Automatic Sprinkler Systems Used for Protection of Commercial Cooking Equipment*, 2015.

UL 199E, *Outline of Investigation for Fire Testing of Sprinklers and Water Spray Nozzles for Protection of Deep Fat Fryers*, 2004.

UL 263, *Fire Tests of Building Construction and Materials*, 2011, revised 2021.

UL 296A, *Waste Oil-Burning Air-Heating Appliances*, 2018.

UL 300, *Fire Testing of Fire Extinguishing Systems for Protection of Commercial Cooking Equipment*, 2019.

UL 558, *Industrial Trucks, Internal Combustion Engine-Powered*, 2012, revised 2021.

UL 647, *Unvented Kerosene-Fired Room Heaters and Portable Heaters*, 1993, revised 2010.

UL 710B, *Recirculating Systems*, 2011, revised 2021.

UL 711, *Rating and Fire Testing of Fire Extinguishers*, 2018.

UL 723, *Test for Surface Burning Characteristics of Building Materials*, 2018.

UL 737, *Fireplace Stoves*, 2011, revised 2020.

UL 896, *Oil-Burning Stoves*, 1993, revised 2016.

UL 913, *Intrinsically Safe Apparatus and Associated Apparatus for Use in Class I, II, and III Division 1, Hazardous (Classified) Locations*, 2013, revised 2019.

UL 923, *Microwave Cooking Appliances*, 2013, revised 2020.

UL 969, *Marking and Labeling Systems*, 2017, revised 2018.

UL 1040, *Fire Test of Insulated Wall Construction*, 1996, revised 2022.

UL 1278, *Movable and Wall- or Ceiling-Hung Electric Room Heaters*, 2014, revised 2022.

UL 1313, *Nonmetallic Safety Cans for Petroleum Products*, 2015.

UL 1479, *Fire Tests of-Penetration Firestops*, 2015, revised 2021.

UL 1709, *Rapid Rise Fire Tests of Protection Materials for Structural Steel*, 2017.

UL 1715, *Fire Test of Interior Finish Material*, 1997, revised 2022.

UL 1975, *Fire Tests for Foamed Plastics Used for Decorative Purposes*, 2006.

UL 2085, *Protected Aboveground Tanks for Flammable and Combustible Liquids*, 1997, revised 2010.

UL 2129, *Halocarbon Clean Agent Fire Extinguishers*, 2017, revised 2021.

UL 2162, *Commercial Wood-Fired Baking Ovens — Refractory Type*, 2014, revised 2019.

UL 2200, *Standard for Stationary Engine Generator Assemblies*, 2020.

UL 2335, *Fire Tests of Storage Pallets*, 2010, revised 2017.

UL 2436, *Outline of Investigation for Spill Containment for Stationary Acid and Alkaline Electrolyte Battery Systems*, 2020.

UL 60079-11, *Explosive Atmospheres — Part 11: Equipment Protection by Intrinsic Safety 'i'*, 2013, revised 2018.

F.1.2.31 United Nations Publications. United Nations Publications, United Nations Plaza, Room DC2–853, New York, NY 10017.

ST/SG/AC.10/40/Add.2, *Report of the Committee of Experts on the Transport of Dangerous Goods and on the Globally Harmonized System of Classification and Labelling of Chemicals on its Sixth Session*, December 14, 2012, Geneva, Switzerland. Addendum, Annex II, Amendments to the Fifth Revised Edition of the Recommendations on the Transport of Dangerous Goods, Manual of Tests and Criteria (ST/SG/AC.10/11/Rev.5).

UN Recommendations on the Transport of Dangerous Goods, 2011.

F.1.2.32 US Government Publications. US Government Publishing Office, 732 North Capitol St., NW, Washington, DC 20401-0001.

OSHA *Firefighting Precautions at Facilities with Combustible Dust*, 2013.

Title 16, Code of Federal Regulations, Part 1500, Commercial Practices, Chapter 11.

Title 16, Code of Federal Regulations, Part 1630, "Standard for the Surface Flammability of Carpets and Rugs."

Title 16, Code of Federal Regulations, Part 1632, "Standard for the Flammability of Mattresses and Mattress Pads."

Title 18, Code of Federal Regulations, "Importation, Manufacture, Distribution and Storage of Explosive Materials."

Title 21, Code of Federal Regulations, "GMP for Medical Devices."

Title 28, Code of Federal Regulations, Part 36, Appendix A, "Americans with Disabilities Act Accessibility Guidelines for Buildings and Facilities."

Title 29, Code of Federal Regulations, Part 1910, "OSHA Regulations for Emergency Procedures and Fire Brigades."

Title 29, Code of Federal Regulations, Part 1910.38.

Title 29, Code of Federal Regulations, Part 1910.100.

Title 29, Code of Federal Regulations, Part 1910.106.

Title 29, Code of Federal Regulations, Part 1910.165.

Title 29, Code of Federal Regulations, Part 1910.1000.

Title 29, Code of Federal Regulations, Part 1910.1200.

Title 30, Code of Federal Regulations, Part 36, "Approved Requirements for Permissible Mobile Diesel-Powered Transportation Equipment."

Title 33, Code of Federal Regulations, Part 154, Appendix A.

Title 40, Code of Federal Regulations, Parts 260–299, "Solid Wastes."

Title 40, Code of Federal Regulations, Part 355.

Title 40, Code of Federal Regulations, Part 370.3.

Title 49, Code of Federal Regulations, Parts 105–110.

Title 49, Code of Federal Regulations, Parts 100–185, Transportation.

Title 49, Code of Federal Regulations, Parts 100–199.

Title 49, Code of Federal Regulations, Part 171.8.

Title 49, Code of Federal Regulations, Part 172.

Title 49, Code of Federal Regulations, Part 172.102.

Title 49, Code of Federal Regulations, Part 173.120.

Title 49, Code of Federal Regulations, Part 173.137.

Title 49, Code of Federal Regulations, Part 173.150.

Title 49, Code of Federal Regulations, Part 173.225.

Title 49, Code of Federal Regulations, Part 173, Appendix A.

Δ **F.1.2.33 Other Publications.**

Bachman, K. C., and W. G. Dudek, *Static Electricity in Fueling Superjets*, 1972. Exxon Research and Engineering Co., Linden, NJ.

BOCA/National Building Code.

CRC Report No. 583.

CSA B44, *Safety Code for Elevators and Escalators.*

Fire Equipment Manufacturers' Association, "Recommendations for Protection of Curtained Limited Finishing Workstations."

Fisher, H. G. and Forrest, H. S., "Protection of Storage Tanks from Two-Phase Flow Due to Fire Exposure."

Hirschler, 1992: "Heat release from plastic materials."

Houser, J. et al, "Vent Sizing for Fire Considerations: External Fire Duration, Jacketed Vessels, and Heat Flux Variations Owing to Fuel Consumption."

NASA, NSS 1740.16, *Safety Standard for Hydrogen and Hydrogen Systems*, 2004.

Oilheat Research Alliance, *Oilheat Technician's Manual.*

ANSI/SMACNA 002, *Rectangular Industrial Duct Construction Standards*, 2011.

SMACNA Round Industrial Duct Construction Standards.

Standard Building Code.

ULC-S603, *Galvanic Corrosion Protection Systems for Steel Underground Tanks for Flammable and Combustible Liquids.*

Uniform Building Code.

Wakelyn, P. J., and S. E. Hughs, "Evaluation of the Flammability of Cotton Bales," *Fire and Materials*, Vol. 26, pp. 183–189, 2002.

F.2 Informational References. (Reserved)

Δ **F.3 References for Extracts in Informational Sections.**

NFPA 10, *Standard for Portable Fire Extinguishers*, 2022 edition.

NFPA 13, *Standard for the Installation of Sprinkler Systems*, 2022 edition.

NFPA 14, *Standard for the Installation of Standpipe and Hose Systems*, 2024 edition.

NFPA 20, *Standard for the Installation of Stationary Pumps for Fire Protection*, 2022 edition.

NFPA 25, *Standard for the Inspection, Testing, and Maintenance of Water-Based Fire Protection Systems*, 2023 edition.

NFPA 30, *Flammable and Combustible Liquids Code*, 2024 edition.

NFPA 30A, *Code for Motor Fuel Dispensing Facilities and Repair Garages*, 2024 edition.

NFPA 30B, *Code for the Manufacture and Storage of Aerosol Products*, 2023 edition.

NFPA 31, *Standard for the Installation of Oil-Burning Equipment*, 2020 edition.

NFPA 33, *Standard for Spray Application Using Flammable or Combustible Materials*, 2021 edition.

NFPA 45, *Standard on Fire Protection for Laboratories Using Chemicals*, 2024 edition.

NFPA 51B, *Standard for Fire Prevention During Welding, Cutting, and Other Hot Work*, 2024 edition.

NFPA 52, *Vehicular Natural Gas Fuel Systems Code*, 2023 edition.

NFPA 55, *Compressed Gases and Cryogenic Fluids Code*, 2023 edition.

NFPA 58, *Liquefied Petroleum Gas Code*, 2024 edition.

NFPA 61, *Standard for the Prevention of Fires and Dust Explosions in Agricultural and Food Processing Facilities*, 2020 edition.

NFPA 69, *Standard on Explosion Prevention Systems*, 2019 edition.

NFPA 70®, *National Electrical Code®*, 2023 edition.

NFPA 72®, *National Fire Alarm and Signaling Code*, 2022 edition.

NFPA 80, *Standard for Fire Doors and Other Opening Protectives*, 2022 edition.

NFPA 88A, *Standard for Parking Structures*, 2023 edition.

NFPA 96, *Standard for Ventilation Control and Fire Protection of Commercial Cooking Operations*, 2024 edition.

NFPA 101®, *Life Safety Code®*, 2024 edition.

NFPA 140, *Standard on Motion Picture and Television Production Studio Soundstages, Approved Production Facilities, and Production Locations*, 2024 edition.

NFPA 220, *Standard on Types of Building Construction*, 2024 edition.

NFPA 241, *Standard for Safeguarding Construction, Alteration, and Demolition Operations*, 2022 edition.

NFPA 303, *Fire Protection Standard for Marinas and Boatyards*, 2021 edition.

NFPA 307, *Standard for the Construction and Fire Protection of Marine Terminals, Piers, and Wharves*, 2021 edition.

NFPA 312, *Standard for Fire Protection of Vessels During Construction, Conversion, Repair, and Lay-Up*, 2021 edition.

NFPA 400, *Hazardous Materials Code*, 2022 edition.

NFPA 407, *Standard for Aircraft Fuel Servicing*, 2017 edition.

NFPA 415, *Standard on Airport Terminal Buildings, Fueling Ramp Drainage, and Loading Walkways*, 2022 edition.

NFPA 418, *Standard for Heliports*, 2021 edition.

NFPA 470, *Hazardous Materials/Weapons of Mass Destruction (WMD) Standard for Responders*, 2022 edition.

NFPA 652, *Standard on the Fundamentals of Combustible Dust*, 2019 edition.

NFPA 654, *Standard for the Prevention of Fire and Dust Explosions from the Manufacturing, Processing, and Handling of Combustible Particulate Solids*, 2020 edition.

NFPA 855, *Standard for the Installation of Stationary Energy Storage Systems*, 2023 edition.

NFPA 914, *Code for the Protection of Historic Structures*, 2023 edition.

NFPA 1124, *Code for the Manufacture, Transportation, and Storage of Fireworks and Pyrotechnic Articles*, 2022 edition.

NFPA 1140, *Standard for Wildland Fire Protection*, 2022 edition.

NFPA 1142, *Standard on Water Supplies for Suburban and Rural Fire Fighting*, 2022 edition.

NFPA 1730, *Standard on Organization and Deployment of Fire Prevention Inspection and Code Enforcement, Plan Review, Investigation, and Public Education Operations*, 2019 edition.

NFPA 5000®, *Building Construction and Safety Code®*, 2024 edition.

Index

Copyright © 2023 National Fire Protection Association. All Rights Reserved.

The copyright in this index is separate and distinct from the copyright in the document that it indexes. The licensing provisions set forth for the document are not applicable to this index. This index may not be reproduced in whole or in part by any means without the express written permission of NFPA.

-3-

3D Printer
- Definition, 3.3.287

-A-

Absolute Pressure
- Definition, 3.3.1, A.3.3.1

Access Box
- Definition, 3.3.2

Addition
- Definition, 3.3.3

Additive Manufacturing
- Definition, 3.3.4
- Industrial Additive Manufacturing
  - Definition, 3.3.4.1
- Nonindustrial Additive Manufacturing
  - Definition, 3.3.4.2

Additive Manufacturing (3D Printing), Chap. 46
- Application, 46.1
  - Installation, Operation, and Maintenance, 46.1.3
  - Permits, 46.1.2
- Industrial Additive Manufacturing, 46.3
- Nonindustrial Additive Manufacturing, 46.2

Administration, Chap. 1
- Application, 1.3
  - Buildings, 1.3.6
  - Conflicts, 1.3.3
  - Multiple Occupancies, 1.3.4
  - Referenced Standards, 1.3.2, A.1.3.2
    - Retroactivity of Referenced Standards to Existing Conditions, 1.3.2.4
  - Severability, 1.3.7
  - Vehicles and Vessels, 1.3.5
- Authority, 1.7
  - Administration, 1.7.1
  - Authority to Order Corrections and Abate, 1.7.8
  - Certificate of Occupancy, 1.7.14
  - Delegation of Authority, 1.7.5
  - Enforcement Assistance, 1.7.4
  - Imminent Dangers and Evacuation, 1.7.16
  - Impersonation, 1.7.10
  - Inspection, 1.7.7
  - Inspection of Construction and Installation, 1.7.13
  - Interference with Enforcement, 1.7.9
  - Interpretations, Rules, and Regulations, 1.7.3
  - Investigation, 1.7.11
    - Authority, 1.7.11.1
    - Evidence, 1.7.11.2
    - Limiting Access, 1.7.11.3
  - Minimum Qualifications to Enforce This Code, 1.7.2, A.1.7.2
  - Plans and Specifications, 1.7.12
  - Public Fire Education, 1.7.18
  - Reliance on Other Enforcement Officials, 1.7.6
  - Standby and Fire Watch Personnel, 1.7.17
  - Stop Work Order, 1.7.15
- Certificates of Fitness, 1.14
  - Authorization, 1.14.1
  - Certification of Applicant, 1.14.5
  - Mandatory, 1.14.2
  - Revocation or Suspension of Certificates of Fitness, 1.14.12
- Duties and Powers of the Incident Commander, 1.8
  - Authority, 1.8.1
  - Controlling Scene, 1.8.2
  - Obstruction of Operations, 1.8.3
  - Scene Barrier, 1.8.4
- Enforcement, 1.6
- Equivalencies, Alternatives, and Modifications, 1.4
  - Alternatives, 1.4.2
  - Approval, 1.4.6
  - Equivalencies, 1.4.1
    - Compliance with Subsequent Editions of Referenced Publications, 1.4.1.1, A.1.4.1.1
  - Modifications, 1.4.3, A.1.4.3
  - Tests, 1.4.7
- Fees, 1.18, A.1.18
- Fire Code Board of Appeals, 1.11
  - Authority of the Board of Appeals, 1.11.3
  - Decisions, 1.11.6
  - Establishment of Fire Code Board of Appeals, 1.11.1
    - Membership, 1.11.1.1
  - Means of Appeals, 1.11.4
  - Meetings and Records, 1.11.5
  - Rules and Procedures of the Board of Appeals, 1.11.2
- Liability, 1.9
- Notice of Violations and Penalties, 1.17
  - Abatement, 1.17.5
  - Destruction or Removal of Notice, 1.17.3
  - Penalties, 1.17.4
  - Serving Notice of Violation, 1.17.2
  - Where Required, 1.17.1
- Permits and Approvals, 1.13
  - Approvals by Other AHJs, 1.13.4
  - Conditions of Approval, 1.13.3
  - Misrepresentation, 1.13.5
  - Permits, 1.13.6
  - Revocation or Suspension of Permits, 1.13.7
- Plan Review, 1.15
- Pre-incident Planning, 1.10
- Purpose, 1.2, A.1.2
- Records and Reports, 1.12

INDEX

Emergency Response Records, 1.12.4
Scope, 1.1
    Title, 1.1.2
Technical Assistance, 1.16
Units, 1.5
    International System of Units, 1.5.1
    Primary and Equivalent Values, 1.5.2

Aerosol Container
    Definition, 3.3.5, A.3.3.5

Aerosol Products
    Definition, 3.3.6, A.3.3.6

Aerosol Products, Chap. 61
    Basic Requirements, 61.2
        Building Construction, 61.2.1
            Means of Egress, 61.2.1.2
        Electrical Installations, 61.2.2
        Fire Alarms, 61.2.6
        Fire Protection, 61.2.5
            Automatic Sprinkler Protection, 61.2.5.1
            Portable Fire Extinguishers, 61.2.5.3
            Standpipe and Hose System, 61.2.5.2
        Flammable Liquids and Gases, 61.2.4
        Heating Equipment, 61.2.3
        Sources of Ignition, 61.2.7
    General Provisions, 61.1
        Application, 61.1.1
        Classification of Aerosol Products in Metal Containers of Not More Than 33.8 fl oz (1000 ml) and in Plastic or Glass Containers of Not More Than 4 fl oz (118 ml), 61.1.3, A.61.1.3
            Aerosol Cooking Spray Products, 61.1.3.5
            Level 1 Aerosol Products, 61.1.3.2
            Level 2 Aerosol Products, 61.1.3.3
            Level 3 Aerosol Products, 61.1.3.4
        Classification of Aerosol Products in Plastic Containers Larger Than 4 fl oz (118 ml) and Smaller Than 33.8 oz (1000 ml), 61.1.4
            Plastic Aerosol 1 Products, 61.1.4.1
            Plastic Aerosol 2 Products, 61.1.4.2
            Plastic Aerosol 3 Products, 61.1.4.3, A.61.1.4.3
            Plastic Aerosol Cooking Spray Products, 61.1.4.5
            Plastic Aerosol X Products, 61.1.4.4
        Marking of Packages of Aerosol Products, 61.1.5
        Permits, 61.1.2
    Mercantile Occupancies, 61.4
        Back Stock Storage Areas, 61.4.4
        Plastic Aerosol X Products, 61.4.1
        Sales Display Areas — Aerosol Storage Exceeding 8 ft (2.4 m) High, 61.4.3
        Sales Display Areas — Aerosol Storage Not Exceeding 8 ft (2.4 m) High, 61.4.2
    Operations and Maintenance, 61.5
        Aisles, 61.5.4
        Control of Ignition Sources, 61.5.3
            Sources of Ignition, 61.5.3.1
        Inspection and Maintenance, 61.5.6
            Maintenance, 61.5.6.3
        Means of Egress, 61.5.1

        Powered Industrial Trucks, 61.5.2
            Loads, 61.5.2.4
        Static Electricity, 61.5.7, A.61.5.7
        Waste Disposal and Recycling, 61.5.5
    Storage in Warehouses and Storage Areas, 61.3
        Aerosol Products in Plastic Containers Greater Than 4 fl oz (118 ml) and Not More Than 33.8 fl oz (1000 ml), 61.3.4
            Fire Protection — Plastic Aerosol 1 Products, 61.3.4.1
            Fire Protection — Plastic Aerosol X Products, 61.3.4.2
        Basic Requirements, 61.3.1
        Storage of Aerosol Cooking Spray Products, 61.3.3
            General, 61.3.3.1
        Storage of Level 1 Aerosol Products, 61.3.2

Aerosol Propellant
    Definition, 3.3.7

Aerosol Valve
    Definition, 3.3.8, A.3.3.8

Airport (Aerodrome)
    Definition, 3.3.9

Airport Ramp
    Definition, 3.3.10

Airports and Heliports, Chap. 21
    Hangars, 21.1
        Fire Department Access, 21.1.2
        Means of Egress Provisions for Aircraft Servicing Hangars, 21.1.4, A.21.1.4
        Means of Egress Provisions for Aircraft Storage Hangars, 21.1.5, A.21.1.5
        Permits, 21.1.1
        Smoking, 21.1.3
    Rooftop Heliport Construction and Protection, 21.3
        Application, 21.3.1
        General, 21.3.2
            Fire Department Access, 21.3.2.2
            Permits, 21.3.2.1
            Smoking, 21.3.2.3
        General Requirements — Land-Based Facilities, 21.3.3
            Firefighting Access, 21.3.3.3
            Fuel Spill Control, 21.3.3.4
            Fueling System, 21.3.3.6
            Means of Egress, 21.3.3.7, A.21.3.3.7
            No Smoking, 21.3.3.5
            Plans, 21.3.3.1, A.21.3.3.1
            Tank and Equipment Locations, 21.3.3.2
        Portable Fire Extinguishers, 21.3.5
            Extinguishers Subject to Damage, Theft, or Tampering, 21.3.5.2
            Minimum Requirement, 21.3.5.1
        Rooftop Landing Facilities, 21.3.4
            Fire Protection, 21.3.4.6
                Acceptance Testing, 21.3.4.6.9
                Fixed Foam Fire-Extinguishing Systems, 21.3.4.6.9.1
                Manual Firefighting Equipment, 21.3.4.6.9.2
                Fire Alarm, 21.3.4.6.8
                Fixed Foam Fire-Extinguishing Systems, 21.3.4.6.2
                Activation of Systems, 21.3.4.6.2.6

2024 Edition

Foam Concentrate Supply, 21.3.4.6.6
General, 21.3.4.6.1
Inspection, Testing, and Maintenance, 21.3.4.6.10
Manual Fire-Fighting Equipment, 21.3.4.6.3
Supplementary Protection, 21.3.4.6.3.2
Water Supply, 21.3.4.6.5
Fire-Fighting Access, 21.3.4.5
Landing Pad Construction Materials, 21.3.4.3
Landing Pad Pitch, 21.3.4.2
Means of Egress, 21.3.4.4, A.21.3.4.4
Structural Support, 21.3.4.1, A.21.3.4.1
Terminals, 21.2
Application, 21.2.1
Exits, 21.2.6
Fire Alarm and Communications Systems, 21.2.8
Fire Hydrants, 21.2.9
Fire Protection — Sprinkler Systems, 21.2.7, A.21.2.7
Covered Plane-Loading Positions, 21.2.7.6
General, 21.2.4
Glazing Material–Covered Openings Facing the Ramp, 21.2.4.5
General, 21.2.2
Fire Department Access, 21.2.2.2
Permits, 21.2.2.1
Heating, Ventilating, and Air Conditioning, 21.2.5
Portable Fire Extinguishers, 21.2.11
Smoking, 21.2.3
Standpipe and Hose Systems, 21.2.10

Aisle Width
Definition, 3.3.11, A.3.3.11
Alarm
Definition, 3.3.12
Alarm Signal
Definition, 3.3.13
Alcohol-Based Hand Rub
Definition, 3.3.14
Alleyway
Definition, 3.3.15
Alternative Calculation Procedure
Definition, 3.4.1
Ammonium Nitrate, Chap. 74
General, 74.1
Analysis
Definition, 3.4.2
Sensitivity Analysis
Definition, 3.4.2.1
Uncertainty Analysis
Definition, 3.4.2.2
Animal Housing Facilities, Chap. 35
General, 35.1
Permits, 35.2
ANSI/ASME
Definition, 3.3.16
Approved
Definition, 3.2.1, A.3.2.1

Area
Back Stock Area
Definition, 3.3.17.1
Control Area
Definition, 3.3.17.2
Definition, 3.3.17
Fire Area
Definition, 3.3.17.3
Fire Flow Area
Definition, 3.3.17.4
Indoor Area
Definition, 3.3.17.5
Organic Peroxide Storage Area
Definition, 3.3.17.6
Outdoor Area
Definition, 3.3.17.7
Permissible Areas
Definition, 3.3.17.8
Sales Display Area
Definition, 3.3.17.9
Smoking Area
Definition, 3.3.17.10
Spray Area
Definition, 3.3.17.11, A.3.3.17.11
ASME
Definition, 3.3.18
ASME Container (or Tank)
Definition, 3.3.19
ASTM
Definition, 3.3.20
Authority Having Jurisdiction (AHJ)
Definition, 3.2.2, A.3.2.2
Automatic Emergency Shutoff Valve
Definition, 3.3.21
Automatic Sprinkler
Definition, 3.3.22
Automobile Wrecking Yards, Chap. 22
Burning Operations, 22.8
Fire Apparatus Access Roads, 22.3
Fire Extinguishers, 22.6
General, 22.1
Housekeeping, 22.5
Motor Vehicle Fluids and Hazardous Materials, 22.9
Air Bag Systems, 22.9.4
General, 22.9.1
Lead-Acid Batteries, 22.9.5
Mitigation for Vehicle Fluid Leaks, 22.9.3
Motor Vehicle Fluids, 22.9.2
Other Battery Technologies, 22.9.6
Permits, 22.2
Tire Storage, 22.7
Welding and Cutting, 22.4

-B-

Baled Cotton
Block
Definition, 3.3.23.1

Definition, 3.3.23, A.3.3.23
Densely Packed Baled Cotton
  Definition, 3.3.23.2, A.3.3.23.2
Fire-Packed Baled Cotton
  Definition, 3.3.23.3
Naked Cotton Bale
  Definition, 3.3.23.4
Barrel
  Definition, 3.3.24
Basement
  Definition, 3.3.25
Battery System
  Definition, 3.3.26
Battery Types, Stationary
  Definition, 3.3.27
  Lithium Metal Polymer Battery
    Definition, 3.3.27.2
  Lithium-Ion Battery
    Definition, 3.3.27.1
  Nickel Cadmium (NiCad) Battery
    Definition, 3.3.27.3
  Valve-Regulated (VRLA)
    Definition, 3.3.27.4, A.3.3.27.4
Block
  Definition, 3.3.28
Board of Appeals
  Definition, 3.3.29
Boil-Over
  Definition, 3.3.31, A.3.3.31
Boiling Point (BP)
  Definition, 3.3.30, A.3.3.30
Building
  Airport Terminal Building
    Definition, 3.3.32.1, A.3.3.32.1
  Apartment Building
    Definition, 3.3.32.2
  Attached Building
    Definition, 3.3.32.3
  Bulk Merchandising Retail Building
    Definition, 3.3.32.4
  Definition, 3.3.32, A.3.3.32
  Existing Building
    Definition, 3.3.32.5, A.3.3.32.5
  High-Rise Building
    Definition, 3.3.32.6, A.3.3.32.6
  Important Building
    Definition, 3.3.32.7, A.3.3.32.7
  Mini-Storage Building
    Definition, 3.3.32.8
  Satellite
    Definition, 3.3.32.9
  Special Amusement Building
    Definition, 3.3.32.10, A.3.3.32.10
  Storage Tank Building
    Definition, 3.3.32.11
Building Services, Chap. 11
  Electrical Fire Safety, 11.1

Building Disconnect, 11.1.7
  Identification of Disconnecting Means, 11.1.7.3
Covers, 11.1.8
Extension Cords, 11.1.5, A.11.1.5
General, 11.1.1
Multiplug Adapters, 11.1.3
Permanent Wiring, Fixtures, and Equipment, 11.1.2
Relocatable Power Taps, 11.1.4
Temporary Installations, 11.1.6
  All Wiring Installations, 11.1.6.2
    Approval, 11.1.6.2.2
    Other Articles, 11.1.6.2.1
  Scope, 11.1.6.1
  Time Constraints, 11.1.6.3
    90 Days, 11.1.6.3.2
    During the Period of Construction, 11.1.6.3.1
    Emergencies and Tests, 11.1.6.3.3
    Removal, 11.1.6.3.4
Elevators, Escalators, and Conveyors, 11.3
  Elevator Machine Rooms, 11.3.3, A.11.3.3
  Elevator Testing, 11.3.4
  Elevators for Occupant-Controlled Evacuation Prior to Phase I Emergency Recall Operations and Fire Service Access Elevators, 11.3.7
  Fire Fighters' Emergency Operations, 11.3.1
  Number of Cars, 11.3.2
  Openings to Exit Enclosures, 11.3.5
  Standardized Fire Service Elevator Keys, 11.3.6
    Existing Buildings, 11.3.6.3
Emergency Command Center, 11.9
  Emergency Command Center Acceptance Testing, 11.9.6
Heating Appliances, 11.5
  General, 11.5.1
    Acceptable Liquid Fuels, 11.5.1.10
    Clothes Dryers, 11.5.1.11
    Permits, 11.5.1.8
  Kerosene Burners and Oil Stoves, 11.5.2
  Portable Electric Heater, 11.5.3
  Vents, 11.5.4
Heating, Ventilation, and Air-Conditioning, 11.2
  Air-Conditioning, Heating, Ventilating Ductwork, and Related Equipment, 11.2.1
  Ventilating or Heat-Producing Equipment, 11.2.2
In-Building Emergency Responder Communication Enhancement Systems, 11.10, A.11.10
  Listed and Labeled, 11.10.4
  Permits, 11.10.1
Medical Gas and Vacuum Systems, 11.11
Photovoltaic Systems, 11.12
  Building-Mounted Photovoltaic (PV) and Building Integrated Photovoltaic (BIPV) Installations, 11.12.2
    Marking, 11.12.2.1, A.11.12.2.1
      Identification of Power Sources, 11.12.2.1.4
      Installer Information, 11.12.2.1.5
      Marking, 11.12.2.1.2
      Marking and Labeling Required, 11.12.2.1.3
        Marking and Labeling Required, 11.12.2.1.3.1

Markings for Building Integrated PV (BIPV) Systems, 11.12.2.1.6
Rapid Shutdown Marking, 11.12.2.1.1, A.11.12.2.1.1
Buildings with More Than One Rapid Shutdown Type, 11.12.2.1.1.7
Rapid Shutdown Switch, 11.12.2.1.1.8
Rapid Shutdown Type, 11.12.2.1.1.1

Buildings with Rapid Shutdown 11.12.2.1.1.1.1
- General, 11.12.1
- Ground-Mounted Photovoltaic System Installations, 11.12.4
  - Clearances, 11.12.4.1, A.11.12.4.1
  - Vegetation Management Plan, 11.12.4.2, A.11.12.4.2
- Rooftop Access and Ventilation, 11.12.3
  - Buildings Other Than One- and Two-Family Dwellings and Townhouses, 11.12.3.3
    - Minimizing Obstructions in Pathways, 11.12.3.3.5
    - Other Pathways, 11.12.3.3.3
    - Perimeter Pathways, 11.12.3.3.2
    - Roof Access, 11.12.3.3.1
    - Smoke Ventilation, 11.12.3.3.4
  - Emergency Escape and Rescue Openings, 11.12.3.4
  - General, 11.12.3.1
  - One- and Two-Family Dwellings and Townhouses, 11.12.3.2
    - Access Pathways, 11.12.3.2.3, A.11.12.3.2.3
    - Alternative Setbacks at Ridge, 11.12.3.2.5
    - Setbacks at Ridge, 11.12.3.2.4
- Smoke Control, 11.8, A.11.8
- Stationary Generators and Standby Power Systems, 11.7
  - Emergency and Legally Required Standby Power Systems, 11.7.3
    - Acceptance, 11.7.3.2
    - General, 11.7.3.1
  - Maintenance and Testing, 11.7.5
  - Scope, 11.7.1
  - Stationary Combustion Engines and Gas Turbines Installation, 11.7.2, A.11.7.2
  - Stored Electrical Energy Emergency and Legally Required Standby Power System Installation, 11.7.4
- Utilities, 11.4
- Waste Chutes, Incinerators, and Laundry Chutes, 11.6
  - Enclosure, 11.6.1
  - Installation and Maintenance, 11.6.2

Bulk Hydrogen Compressed Gas System
Definition, 3.3.33

Bulk Inert Gas System
Definition, 3.3.34

Bulk Liquefied Hydrogen Gas System
Definition, 3.3.35

Bulk Oxygen System
Definition, 3.3.36

Bulk Plant or Terminal
Definition, 3.3.37

Burn-It
Definition, 3.3.38

Bury-It
Definition, 3.3.39

-C-

Cannabis Extraction Equipment
Definition, 3.3.40

Cannabis Extraction Facility
Definition, 3.3.41

Cannabis Growing, Processing, or Extraction Facilities, Chap. 38
- Application, 38.1, A.38.1
- Fire Protection Systems, 38.3
- Growing or Production of Cannabis, 38.5
  - Carbon Dioxide Enrichment Equipment, 38.5.3
    - Container Refilling, 38.5.3.5
    - Equipment, 38.5.3.1
    - Gas Detection System, 38.5.3.2
      - System Activation, 38.5.3.2.2
      - System Design, 38.5.3.2.1
    - Pressurization and Ventilation, 38.5.3.3
    - Signage, 38.5.3.4
  - Fumigation, 38.5.5
    - General, 38.5.5.1, A.38.5.5.1
    - Maintenance of Openings, 38.5.5.8
    - Notification, 38.5.5.3
    - Occupancy During Fumigation, 38.5.5.6
    - Sealing of Building Structure, or Space, 38.5.5.7
    - Signage, 38.5.5.4
    - Sources of Ignition, 38.5.5.2, A.38.5.5.2
    - Venting and Cleanup, 38.5.5.9
    - Watch Personnel, 38.5.5.5
  - Interior Finish, Contents, and Furnishings, 38.5.4
  - Odor Control, 38.5.2
  - Pesticide Application, 38.5.6
  - Ventilation for Light Fixtures, 38.5.1
- Means of Egress, 38.4, A.38.4
- Permits, 38.2
- Processing or Extraction, 38.6, A.38.6
  - Carbon Dioxide Extraction, 38.6.4
    - CO2 Discharges, 38.6.4.4, A.38.6.4.4
    - CO2 Gas Detection, 38.6.4.3
    - General, 38.6.4.1
    - Storage and Handling, 38.6.4.2
  - Flammable and Combustible Liquid Extraction, 38.6.3
    - Exhaust, 38.6.3.2
    - General, 38.6.3.1
    - Storage and Handling, 38.6.3.3
  - General, 38.6.1
    - Extraction Room, 38.6.1.1
      - Means of Egress, 38.6.1.1.4, A.38.6.1.1.4
    - Indoor Horticultural Grow Structures, 38.6.1.3
      - Area Limits, 38.6.1.3.8
      - Clearance from Ignition Sources, 38.6.1.3.7
      - Electrical Wiring and Equipment, 38.6.1.3.3
      - Fire Protection Systems, 38.6.1.3.6
      - Heating Appliances, 38.6.1.3.5
      - Horticultural Lighting, 38.6.1.3.4
      - Materials, 38.6.1.3.2
    - Operator Training, 38.6.1.4
    - Signage, 38.6.1.5
    - Staffing, 38.6.1.2

Systems, Equipment, and Processes, 38.6.1.6
    Approval for Systems and Equipment with No Listing, 38.6.1.6.3
    Change of Extraction Medium, 38.6.1.6.5
    Documentation for Equipment with No Listing, 38.6.1.6.4, A.38.6.1.6.4
    Equipment, 38.6.1.6.2
    Equipment Field Verification, 38.6.1.6.6
    General, 38.6.1.6.1
Liquefied Petroleum Gas (LPG) Extraction, 38.6.2
    Electrical, 38.6.2.3
    Exhaust, 38.6.2.2
    Extraction Room Gas Detection System, 38.6.2.4
    Facility Piping Systems, 38.6.2.7
    General, 38.6.2.1
    Protection, 38.6.2.5
    Storage, 38.6.2.6
Transfilling, 38.7, A.38.7

Carbon Dioxide Enrichment Process
Definition, 3.3.42

Cathodic Protection
Definition, 3.3.43, A.3.3.43

Cathodic Protection Tester
Definition, 3.3.44

Certificate of Fitness
Definition, 3.3.45

CFR
Definition, 3.3.46

CGA
Definition, 3.3.47

Chemical Fume Hood
Definition, 3.3.48

Chemical Name
Definition, 3.3.49

Chemical Plant
Definition, 3.3.50

Chip
Definition, 3.3.51, A.3.3.51

Classification of Occupancy, Chap. 6
Classification of Occupancy, 6.1
  Ambulatory Health Care, 6.1.6
    Definition — Ambulatory Health Care Occupancy, 6.1.6.1, A.6.1.6.1
  Assembly, 6.1.2
    Definition — Assembly Occupancy, 6.1.2.1, A.6.1.2.1
  Business, 6.1.11
    Definition — Business Occupancy, 6.1.11.1, A.6.1.11.1
  Day Care, 6.1.4
    Definition — Day-Care Occupancy, 6.1.4.1, A.6.1.4.1
  Detention and Correctional, 6.1.7
    Definition — Detention and Correctional Occupancy, 6.1.7.1, A.6.1.7.1
    Nonresidential Uses, 6.1.7.2, A.6.1.7.2
  Educational, 6.1.3
    Definition — Educational Occupancy, 6.1.3.1, A.6.1.3.1
    Incidental Instruction, 6.1.3.3
    Other Occupancies, 6.1.3.2
  General, 6.1.1
    Occupancy Classification, 6.1.1.1
    Special Structures, 6.1.1.2
  Health Care, 6.1.5
    Definition — Health Care Occupancy, 6.1.5.1, A.6.1.5.1
  Industrial, 6.1.12
    Definition — Industrial Occupancy, 6.1.12.1, A.6.1.12.1
  Mercantile, 6.1.10
    Definition — Mercantile Occupancy, 6.1.10.1, A.6.1.10.1
  Multiple Occupancies, 6.1.14
    Definitions, 6.1.14.2
      Mixed Occupancy, 6.1.14.2.2
      Multiple Occupancy, 6.1.14.2.1
      Separated Occupancy, 6.1.14.2.3
    General, 6.1.14.1
    Mixed Occupancies, 6.1.14.3
    Separated Occupancies, 6.1.14.4
  Residential, 6.1.8
    Definition — Residential Occupancy, 6.1.8.1
      Definition — Apartment Building, 6.1.8.1.5
      Definition — Dormitory, 6.1.8.1.4, A.6.1.8.1.4
      Definition — Hotel, 6.1.8.1.3, A.6.1.8.1.3
      Definition — Lodging or Rooming House, 6.1.8.1.2
      Definition — One- and Two-Family Dwelling Unit, 6.1.8.1.1, A.6.1.8.1.1
  Residential Board and Care, 6.1.9
    Definition — Residential Board and Care Occupancy, 6.1.9.1, A.6.1.9.1
  Storage, 6.1.13
    Definition — Storage Occupancy, 6.1.13.1, A.6.1.13.1

Cleaning and Purging of Flammable Gas Piping Systems, Chap. 55
Application, 55.1
Permits, 55.2

Cleaning Media
Definition, 3.3.52, A.3.3.52

Cleanroom
Definition, 3.3.53

Cleanrooms, Chap. 23
Applicability, 23.2
General, 23.1
Permits, 23.3

Clear Space
Definition, 3.3.54

Closed System Use
Definition, 3.3.55

Closed-Top Diking
Definition, 3.3.56

Code
Definition, 3.2.3, A.3.2.3

Code
Building Code
  Definition, 3.3.57.1
Definition, 3.3.57
Electrical Code
  Definition, 3.3.57.2
Mechanical Code
  Definition, 3.3.57.3

Plumbing Code
  Definition, 3.3.57.4
Cold Deck
  Definition, 3.3.58
Column (Paper)
  Definition, 3.3.59
Combustible (Material)
  Definition, 3.3.60
Combustible Dust
  Definition, 3.3.61, A.3.3.61
Combustible Fiber
  Definition, 3.3.62, A.3.3.62
Combustible Fibers, Chap. 45
  Baled Storage, 45.6
    Blocks or Piles, 45.6.1
    Sisal and Other Fibers, 45.6.2
  Electrical Wiring, 45.2
  General, 45.1
    Permits, 45.1.4
  Hazardous Materials, 45.8
  Loose Storage of Combustible Fibers, 45.5
    Loose House, 45.5.6
    Rooms or Compartments for Quantities of Loose Combustible Fibers Ranging Between 100 ft3 (2.8 m3) and 500 ft3 (14.2 m3), 45.5.3
    Storage Vaults for Quantities of Loose Combustible Fibers Exceeding 1000 ft3 (28.3 m3), 45.5.5
    Storage Vaults for Quantities of Loose Combustible Fibers Ranging Between 500 ft3 (14.2 m3) and 1000 ft3 (28.3 m3), 45.5.4
  No Smoking, 45.3
  Storage of Hay, Straw, and Other Similar Agricultural Products, 45.7
  Vehicles and Material Handling Equipment, 45.4
Combustible Liquid
  Definition, 3.3.63
Combustible Particulate Solid
  Definition, 3.3.64
Combustible Refuse
  Definition, 3.3.65
Combustible Waste
  Definition, 3.3.66, A.3.3.66
Combustible Waste and Refuse, Chap. 19
  Combustible Waste and Refuse, 19.2
    Rubbish Containers, 19.2.1
      Commercial Rubbish-Handling Operations, 19.2.1.5
      General, 19.2.1.1
      Nonmetallic Containers, 19.2.1.2
      Removal, 19.2.1.3
      Rubbish Within Dumpsters, 19.2.1.4
    General, 19.1
      Permits, 19.1.1
    Vehicles or Conveyances Used to Transport Combustible Waste or Refuse, 19.1.6
Combustion
  Definition, 3.3.67
Commercial Cooking, Chap. 50
  Application, 50.1
  Fire-Extinguishing Equipment for Cooking Operations in Buildings, 50.4
    Fuel and Electric Power Shutoff, 50.4.6
    General Requirements, 50.4.3
    Manual Actuation, 50.4.7
    Permits, 50.4.2
    Portable Fire Extinguishers, 50.4.11
    Review and Certification, 50.4.10
      Installation Requirements, 50.4.10.2, A.50.4.10.2
    Simultaneous Operation, 50.4.5
    Special Design and Application, 50.4.9
    System Annunciation, 50.4.8
    Types of Equipment, 50.4.4
      Hoods with Water Wash, 50.4.4.8
      Modifications to Existing Hood Systems, 50.4.4.7
      Water Valve Supervision, 50.4.4.10
      Water-Based Fire-Extinguishing System, 50.4.4.9
  Fire-Extinguishing Equipment for Mobile and Temporary Cooking Operations, 50.5
    Fuel and Electric Power Shutoff, 50.5.3
    General Requirements, 50.5.1
    Manual Actuation, 50.5.4
    Portable Fire Extinguishers, 50.5.7
    Review and Certification, 50.5.6
      Installation Requirements, 50.5.6.2, A.50.5.6.2
    System Annunciation, 50.5.5
    Types of Equipment, 50.5.2
      Modifications to Existing Hood Systems, 50.5.2.3
  General Requirements for Cooking Operations in Buildings and Mobile and Temporary Cooking Operations, 50.2
    AHJ Notification, 50.2.4
    Clearance, 50.2.2
    Drawings, 50.2.3
    General, 50.2.1
      Responsibility, 50.2.1.5
  Minimum Safety Requirements for Cooking Equipment, 50.7
    Commercial Kitchen Cooking Oil Storage Tank Systems, 50.7.2
    Cooking Equipment, 50.7.1
      Installation, 50.7.1.2
  Mobile and Temporary Cooking Operations, 50.8
    Appliance Installation on Vehicles, 50.8.4
    Carbon Monoxide Detectors, 50.8.10
    Electrical Wiring, 50.8.9
    General, 50.8.1
      Communications, 50.8.1.5
      Fire Department Access, 50.8.1.4
      Storage of Flammable and Combustible Liquids, 50.8.1.6
    General Precautions, 50.8.13
    Internal Combustion Engine Power Sources, 50.8.6
    Location of Mobile and Temporary Cooking Operations, 50.8.2
      Relative to Buildings, 50.8.2.1, A.50.8.2.1
      Relative to Other Mobile or Temporary Cooking, 50.8.2.2
    LP-Gas Cooking Appliances, 50.8.5
    LP-Gas Systems, 50.8.8
      LP-Gas System Leak Detection, 50.8.8.2

INDEX

LP-Gas Systems on Vehicles (Other than Engine Fuel Systems), 50.8.8.3
    LP-Gas Container Installation Requirements, 50.8.8.3.1
Parking, Servicing, and Repair, 50.8.12
Tents, 50.8.3
Training, 50.8.11
Vehicle-Mounted Generators, 50.8.7
Procedures for the Use, Inspection, Testing, and Maintenance of Equipment, 50.6
    Cleaning of Exhaust Systems, 50.6.6
    Cooking Equipment Maintenance, 50.6.7
    Inspection for Grease Buildup, 50.6.4, A.50.6.4
    Inspection of Fire Dampers, 50.6.3
        Documentation Tag, 50.6.3.4, A.50.6.3.4
        Replacement of Fusible Links, 50.6.3.3
    Inspection, Testing, and Maintenance of Fire-Extinguishing Systems, 50.6.2
    Inspection, Testing, and Maintenance of Listed Hoods Containing Mechanical, Water Spray, or Ultraviolet Devices, 50.6.5
    Operating Procedures, 50.6.1
Protection of Coverings and Enclosure Materials, 50.3

Commodity
Definition, 3.3.68

Common Path of Travel
Definition, 3.3.69, A.3.3.69

Compartment
Definition, 3.3.70
Fire Compartment
    Definition, 3.3.70.1, A.3.3.70.1
Smoke Compartment
    Definition, 3.3.70.2, A.3.3.70.2

Compressed Gases and Cryogenic Fluids, Chap. 63
Building-Related Controls, 63.2
    Control Areas, 63.2.2
        Construction Requirements, 63.2.2.1
        Number of Control Areas, 63.2.2.2
        Quantities Less Than or Equal to the MAQ, 63.2.2.4
    Detached Buildings, 63.2.5, A.63.2.5
    Electrical Equipment, 63.2.7, A.63.2.7
        Emergency Power, 63.2.7.2
        Standby Power, 63.2.7.1
    Employee Alarm System, 63.2.8, A.63.2.8
    Exhausted Enclosures, 63.2.18
        Separation, 63.2.18.2
        Ventilation Requirements, 63.2.18.1
            Control Velocity at Access Openings, 63.2.18.1.1
            Fire Protection, 63.2.18.1.3
            Separation of Incompatible Gases Within Enclosures, 63.2.18.1.2
    Explosion Control, 63.2.9
    Fire Protection Systems, 63.2.10, A.63.2.10
        Sprinkler System Design, 63.2.10.2
    Gas Cabinets, 63.2.17
        Construction, 63.2.17.1
            Access to Controls, 63.2.17.1.2
            Materials of Construction, 63.2.17.1.1
            Self-Closing Doors, 63.2.17.1.3
        Fire Protection, 63.2.17.3
        Quantity Limits, 63.2.17.4
        Separation of Incompatibles, 63.2.17.5
        Ventilation Requirements, 63.2.17.2
    Gas Rooms, 63.2.4
        Construction, 63.2.4.3
        Exhaust Ventilation, 63.2.4.2
        Limitation on Contents, 63.2.4.5
        Pressure Control, 63.2.4.1
        Separation, 63.2.4.4
    General, 63.2.1
        Occupancy, 63.2.1.1
            Occupancy Classification, 63.2.1.1.2
            Occupancy Requirements, 63.2.1.1.1
    Hazard Identification Signs, 63.2.12
        Application, 63.2.12.2
            No Smoking, 63.2.12.2.2
            Signs, 63.2.12.2.1
        Location, 63.2.12.1
    Lighting, 63.2.11
    Occupancy Protection Levels, 63.2.3
        Classification of Protection Levels, 63.2.3.2
            Protection Level 1, 63.2.3.2.1
            Protection Level 2, 63.2.3.2.2
            Protection Level 3, 63.2.3.2.3
            Protection Level 4, 63.2.3.2.4
            Protection Level 5, 63.2.3.2.5
        Quantity Thresholds for Compressed Gases and Cryogenic Fluids Requiring Special Provisions, 63.2.3.1
            Aggregate Allowable Quantities, 63.2.3.1.3
            Flammable and Oxidizing Gases, 63.2.3.1.6
            Incompatible Materials, 63.2.3.1.4
            Multiple Hazards, 63.2.3.1.5
            Quantities Greater Than the MAQ, 63.2.3.1.2
            Threshold Exceedances, 63.2.3.1.1, A.63.2.3.1.1
            Toxic and Highly Toxic Compressed Gases, 63.2.3.1.7
    Shelving, 63.2.14
    Source Valve, 63.2.19, A.63.2.19
    Spill Control, Drainage, and Secondary Containment, 63.2.13
    Vent Pipe Termination, 63.2.15
    Ventilation, 63.2.16
        Air Intakes, 63.2.16.11
        Compressed Air, 63.2.16.1
        Continuous Operation, 63.2.16.4
        Inlets to the Exhaust System, 63.2.16.8
        Manual Shutoff Switch, 63.2.16.7
        Mechanical Exhaust Ventilation, 63.2.16.3
        Recirculation of Exhaust, 63.2.16.9
        Shutoff Controls, 63.2.16.6
        Ventilation Discharge, 63.2.16.10
        Ventilation Rate, 63.2.16.5
        Ventilation Systems, 63.2.16.2
    Weather Protection, 63.2.6
Bulk Liquefied Hydrogen Systems, 63.7
Bulk Oxygen Systems, 63.5

Cleaning and Purging of Gas Piping Systems, 63.5.2
Carbon Dioxide Beverage Systems, 63.11
   Equipment, 63.11.2
   General, 63.11.1
   Protection from Damage, 63.11.3
   Required Protection, 63.11.4
      Emergency Alarm System, 63.11.4.2
      Ventilation, 63.11.4.1
Compressed Gases, 63.3
   Corrosive Gases, 63.3.6
      Distance to Exposures, 63.3.6.2
      General, 63.3.6.1
      Indoor Use, 63.3.6.3
         Exhausted Enclosures, 63.3.6.3.2
         Gas Cabinets, 63.3.6.3.1
         Gas Rooms, 63.3.6.3.3
         Treatment Systems, 63.3.6.3.4
   Flammable Gases, 63.3.7
      Distance to Exposures, 63.3.7.2
      Electrical, 63.3.7.7
      Ignition Source Control, 63.3.7.6
         Heating, 63.3.7.6.3
         No Smoking or Open Flame, 63.3.7.6.2
         Static Producing Equipment, 63.3.7.6.1
      Indoor Non-Bulk Hydrogen Compressed Gas System Location, 63.3.7.3
         Systems Installed in One Room, 63.3.7.3.2
      Maintenance, 63.3.7.5
      Maintenance of Piping Systems, 63.3.7.8
      Outdoor Non-Bulk Hydrogen Compressed Gas Location, 63.3.7.4
      Storage, Use, and Handling, 63.3.7.1
   General, 63.3.1
      Cathodic Protection, 63.3.1.8
         Impressed Current Systems, 63.3.1.8.3
         Inspection, 63.3.1.8.2
         Operation, 63.3.1.8.1
      Cleaning and Purging of Gas Piping Systems, 63.3.1.20
         Cleaning, 63.3.1.20.2, A.63.3.1.20.2
         General, 63.3.1.20.1
         Purging, 63.3.1.20.3, A.63.3.1.20.3
      Compressed Gas Systems, 63.3.1.2
         Design, 63.3.1.2.1
         Installation, 63.3.1.2.2
      Cylinders, Containers, and Tanks, 63.3.1.7
         Cylinders, Containers, and Tanks Containing Residual Gas, 63.3.1.7.4
         Defective Cylinders, Containers, and Tanks, 63.3.1.7.2
         Design and Construction, 63.3.1.7.1
         Pressure Relief Devices, 63.3.1.7.5
            Shutoffs Between Pressure Relief Devices and Containers, 63.3.1.7.5.7

General 63.3.1.7.5.7.1 Location 63.3.1.7.5.7.2 Multiple Pressure Relief Devices 63.3.1.7.5.7.4 Security 63.3.1.7.5.7.3, A.63.3.1.7.5.7.3

         Supports, 63.3.1.7.3
      Cylinders, Containers, and Tanks Exposed to Fire, 63.3.1.15
      Installation of Underground Piping, 63.3.1.19
      Insulated Liquid Carbon Dioxide Systems, 63.3.1.3
      Insulated Liquid Nitrous Oxide Systems, 63.3.1.4
      Labeling Requirements, 63.3.1.9
         Containers, 63.3.1.9.1
         Label Maintenance, 63.3.1.9.2
         Piping Systems, 63.3.1.9.4
         Stationary Compressed Gas Cylinders, Containers, and Tanks, 63.3.1.9.3
      Leaks, Damage, or Corrosion, 63.3.1.16
         Handling of Cylinders, Containers, and Tanks Removed from Service, 63.3.1.16.3, A.63.3.1.16.3
         Leaking Systems, 63.3.1.16.4
         Removal from Service, 63.3.1.16.1
         Replacement and Repair, 63.3.1.16.2
      Listed or Approved Hydrogen Equipment, 63.3.1.5, A.63.3.1.5
      Metal Hydride Storage Systems, 63.3.1.6, A.63.3.1.6
         General Requirements, 63.3.1.6.1
            Classification, 63.3.1.6.1.3
            Containers, Design, and Construction, 63.3.1.6.1.5
            Electrical, 63.3.1.6.1.12
            Falling Objects, 63.3.1.6.1.9
            Listed or Approved Systems, 63.3.1.6.1.4
            Marking and Labeling, 63.3.1.6.1.7

Pressure Relief Device Marking 63.3.1.6.1.7.3 Pressure Vessel Markings 63.3.1.6.1.7.4 System Marking 63.3.1.6.1.7.1 Valve Marking 63.3.1.6.1.7.2

            Metal Hydride Storage System Requirements, 63.3.1.6.1.1
            Metal Hydride Systems Storing or Supplying Hydrogen, 63.3.1.6.1.2
            Piping Systems, 63.3.1.6.1.10

Leaking Systems 63.3.1.6.1.10.1

            Refilling of Containers, 63.3.1.6.1.11

Hydrogen Purity 63.3.1.6.1.11.2 Industrial Trucks 63.3.1.6.1.11.1

            Service Life and Inspection of Containers, 63.3.1.6.1.6
            Temperature Extremes, 63.3.1.6.1.8
         Portable Containers or Systems, 63.3.1.6.2
            Securing Containers, 63.3.1.6.2.1

Motorized Equipment 63.3.1.6.2.1.2 Use on Mobile Equipment 63.3.1.6.2.1.1

            Valves, 63.3.1.6.2.2
      Security, 63.3.1.10
         General, 63.3.1.10.1
         Physical Protection, 63.3.1.10.4
         Securing Compressed Gas Cylinders, Containers, and Tanks, 63.3.1.10.5
         Security of Areas, 63.3.1.10.2, A.63.3.1.10.2
      Separation from Hazardous Conditions, 63.3.1.12
         Clearance from Combustibles and Vegetation, 63.3.1.12.3, A.63.3.1.12.3
         Exposure to Chemicals, 63.3.1.12.9

INDEX

Exposure to Electrical Circuits, 63.3.1.12.10
Falling Objects, 63.3.1.12.6
General, 63.3.1.12.1
Heating, 63.3.1.12.7
    Electrically Powered Heating Devices, 63.3.1.12.7.1
    Fail-Safe Design, 63.3.1.12.7.2
Incompatible Materials, 63.3.1.12.2, A.63.3.1.12.2
Ledges, Platforms, and Elevators, 63.3.1.12.4
Sources of Ignition, 63.3.1.12.8
Temperature Extremes, 63.3.1.12.5
Service and Repair, 63.3.1.13
Storage Area Temperature, 63.3.1.18
    Compressed Gas Containers, 63.3.1.18.1
Surfaces, 63.3.1.17
Unauthorized Use, 63.3.1.14
Valve Protection, 63.3.1.11
    General, 63.3.1.11.1
    Valve Outlet Caps or Plugs, 63.3.1.11.3
    Valve-Protective Caps, 63.3.1.11.2
Medical Gas Systems, 63.3.5
Oxidizing Gases, 63.3.8
    Distance to Exposures, 63.3.8.2
    General, 63.3.8.1
Pyrophoric Gases, 63.3.9
    Distance to Exposures, 63.3.9.3
    General, 63.3.9.1
    Silane and Silane Mixtures, 63.3.9.2
Storage, 63.3.3
    General, 63.3.3.1
        Applicability, 63.3.3.1.1
        Classification of Weather Protection as an Indoor Versus an Outdoor Area, 63.3.3.1.3
        Upright Storage Flammable Gas in Solution and Liquefied Flammable Gas, 63.3.3.1.2
            Cylinders and Containers of 1.3 Gal (5 L) or Less, 63.3.3.1.2.1
            Cylinders, Containers, and Tanks Designed for Horizontal Use, 63.3.3.1.2.2
            Palletized Cylinders, Containers, and Tanks, 63.3.3.1.2.3
    Material-Specific Regulations, 63.3.3.2
        Exterior Storage, 63.3.3.2.2
            General, 63.3.3.2.2.1
            Separation, 63.3.3.2.2.2
        Indoor Storage, 63.3.3.2.1
Subatmospheric Gas (Type 1 and Type 2) Sources, 63.3.12
    General, 63.3.12.1
Subatmospheric Gas Sources (SAGS), 63.3.2
Toxic and Highly Toxic Gases, 63.3.10
    Automatic Smoke Detection System, 63.3.10.7
    Emergency Power, 63.3.10.5
        Alternative to Emergency Power, 63.3.10.5.2
        General, 63.3.10.5.1
        Level, 63.3.10.5.4
        Where Required, 63.3.10.5.3
    Gas Detection, 63.3.10.6
        Alarm Monitored, 63.3.10.6.3
        Automatic Shutdown, 63.3.10.6.4
        Detection Points, 63.3.10.6.5
            Point of Use, 63.3.10.6.5.2
            Source, 63.3.10.6.5.3
            Storage, 63.3.10.6.5.4
            Treatment System Discharge, 63.3.10.6.5.1
        Level of Detection, 63.3.10.6.6
        Local Alarm, 63.3.10.6.2
        Where Gas Detection Is Not Required, 63.3.10.6.1
    General, 63.3.10.1
    Leaking Cylinders, Containers, and Tanks, 63.3.10.4
        Containment Vessels or Systems, 63.3.10.4.2
            Location, 63.3.10.4.2.3
            Performance, 63.3.10.4.2.1
            Personnel, 63.3.10.4.2.2
        Gas Cabinets or Exhausted Enclosures, 63.3.10.4.1
    Treatment Systems, 63.3.10.3
        Maximum Flow Rate of Release, 63.3.10.3.6, A.63.3.10.3.6
        Rate of Release, 63.3.10.3.5
        Storage of Toxic or Highly Toxic Gases, 63.3.10.3.1
            Containment Devices Provided, 63.3.10.3.1.3
            Handwheels Secured, 63.3.10.3.1.2
            Valve Outlets Protected, 63.3.10.3.1.1
        Treatment System Design and Performance, 63.3.10.3.3
        Treatment System Sizing, 63.3.10.3.4
            Attended Operations — Alternative Method of System Sizing, 63.3.10.3.4.3
            Largest Compressed Gas Vessel, 63.3.10.3.4.2
            Worst-Case Release of Gas, 63.3.10.3.4.1
        Use of Toxic Gases, 63.3.10.3.2
            Fail-Safe Automatic Closing Valve, 63.3.10.3.2.2
            Gas Detection, 63.3.10.3.2.1
    Ventilation and Arrangement, 63.3.10.2
        Air Intakes, 63.3.10.2.3
        Distance to Exposures, 63.3.10.2.2
        Indoors, 63.3.10.2.1
Unstable Reactive Gases (Nondetonable), 63.3.11
    Basements, 63.3.11.4
    Distances to Exposures for Class 2, 63.3.11.1
    Distances to Exposures for Class 3, 63.3.11.2
    Storage Configuration, 63.3.11.3
    Unstable Reactive Gases (Detonable), 63.3.11.5
        Location, 63.3.11.5.2
        Storage or Use, 63.3.11.5.1
Use and Handling, 63.3.4
    General, 63.3.4.1
        Applicability, 63.3.4.1.1
        Controls, 63.3.4.1.2
        Cylinders and Containers of 1.3 Gal (5 L) or Less, 63.3.4.1.8
        Emergency Isolation, 63.3.4.1.12
            Location Exemptions, 63.3.4.1.12.4
        Emergency Shutoff Valves, 63.3.4.1.11
        Inverted Use, 63.3.4.1.7
        Piping Systems, 63.3.4.1.3
            Backflow Prevention, 63.3.4.1.3.2
            Integrity, 63.3.4.1.3.1

Transfer, 63.3.4.1.9
Upright Use, 63.3.4.1.6
Use of Compressed Gases for Inflation, 63.3.4.1.10
Valves, 63.3.4.1.4
Vent Pipe Termination, 63.3.4.1.5
Handling, 63.3.4.3
　Applicability, 63.3.4.3.1
　Carts and Trucks, 63.3.4.3.2
　Lifting Devices, 63.3.4.3.3
Material-Specific Regulations, 63.3.4.2
　Exterior Use, 63.3.4.2.2
　　General, 63.3.4.2.2.1
　　Separation, 63.3.4.2.2.2
　Indoor Use, 63.3.4.2.1
Cryogenic Fluids, 63.4
　Containers — Design, Construction, and Maintenance, 63.4.2, A.63.4.2
　　Aboveground Tanks, 63.4.2.1
　　　Construction of the Inner Vessel, 63.4.2.1.1
　　　Construction of the Vacuum Jacket (Outer Vessel), 63.4.2.1.2
　　　　Vacuum Level Monitoring, 63.4.2.1.2.3
　　Foundations and Supports, 63.4.2.3
　　　Corrosion Protection, 63.4.2.3.5
　　　Excessive Loads, 63.4.2.3.1
　　　Expansion and Contraction, 63.4.2.3.2
　　　Support of Ancillary Equipment, 63.4.2.3.3, A.63.4.2.3.3
　　　Temperature Effects, 63.4.2.3.4
　　Nonstandard Containers, 63.4.2.2
　　Pressure Relief Devices, 63.4.2.4
　　　Accessibility, 63.4.2.4.5
　　　Arrangement, 63.4.2.4.6
　　　　Portable Containers with Volume Less Than 2.0 scf (0.057 Nm3), 63.4.2.4.6.2
　　　　Pressure Relief Devices, 63.4.2.4.6.1
　　　Containers Open to the Atmosphere, 63.4.2.4.2
　　　Equipment Other Than Containers, 63.4.2.4.3
　　　General, 63.4.2.4.1
　　　Shutoffs Between Pressure Relief Devices and Containers, 63.4.2.4.7
　　　　General, 63.4.2.4.7.1
　　　　Location, 63.4.2.4.7.2

Multiple Pressure Relief Devices63.4.2.4.7.2.2Security63.4.2.4.7.2.1, A.63.4.2.4.7.2.1

　　　Sizing, 63.4.2.4.4
　　　Temperature Limits, 63.4.2.4.8
　Electrical Wiring and Equipment, 63.4.7
　　Electrical Grounding and Bonding, 63.4.7.3
　　General, 63.4.7.1
　　Location, 63.4.7.2
　General, 63.4.1
　Leaks, Damage, and Corrosion, 63.4.10
　Lighting, 63.4.11
　Marking, 63.4.4
　　Container Specification, 63.4.4.3
　　General, 63.4.4.1

Identification Signs, 63.4.4.1.3
Portable Containers, 63.4.4.1.1
Stationary Tanks, 63.4.4.1.2
Identification of Container Connections, 63.4.4.4
Identification of Contents, 63.4.4.2
Identification of Emergency Shutoff Valves, 63.4.4.6
Identification of Piping Systems, 63.4.4.5
Pressure Relief Vent Piping, 63.4.3
　Arrangement, 63.4.3.3
　General, 63.4.3.1
　Installation, 63.4.3.4
　Overfilling, 63.4.3.5
　Sizing, 63.4.3.2
Security, 63.4.5
　General, 63.4.5.1
　Physical Protection, 63.4.5.5
　Securing of Containers, 63.4.5.3
　Securing of Vaporizers, 63.4.5.4
　Security of Areas, 63.4.5.2, A.63.4.5.2
Separation from Hazardous Conditions, 63.4.6
　General, 63.4.6.1
　Portable Cryogenic Containers, 63.4.6.3
　　Fire Barriers, 63.4.6.3.2
　Stationary Cryogenic Containers, 63.4.6.2, A.63.4.6.2
　　Fire Barriers, 63.4.6.2.1
　　Point-of-Fill Connections, 63.4.6.2.2
　　Surfaces Beneath Containers, 63.4.6.2.3
Service and Repair, 63.4.8
　Containers, 63.4.8.1
　　Pressure Relief Device Testing, 63.4.8.1.2
　　Testing, 63.4.8.1.1
　Systems, 63.4.8.2
Storage, 63.4.12
　Indoor Storage, 63.4.12.1
　　Cryogenic Fluids, 63.4.12.1.3
　　Installation, 63.4.12.1.1
　　Stationary Containers, 63.4.12.1.2
　　Ventilation, 63.4.12.1.4
　Outdoor Storage, 63.4.12.2
　　Access, 63.4.12.2.2
　　Areas Subject to Flooding, 63.4.12.2.5, A.63.4.12.2.5
　　　Elevated Tanks, 63.4.12.2.5.1
　　　Underground Tanks, 63.4.12.2.5.2
　　Diked Areas Containing Other Hazardous Materials, 63.4.12.2.4
　　Drainage, 63.4.12.2.6
　　General, 63.4.12.2.1
　　Outdoor Installations, 63.4.12.2.7
　　　Courts, 63.4.12.2.7.2, A.63.4.12.2.7.2
　　　Enclosed Courts, 63.4.12.2.7.1, A.63.4.12.2.7.1
　　　Fire Department Access, 63.4.12.2.7.3
　　Physical Protection, 63.4.12.2.3
Unauthorized Use, 63.4.9
Use and Handling, 63.4.13
　Cathodic Protection, 63.4.13.9
　　Impressed Current Systems, 63.4.13.9.3
　　Inspection, 63.4.13.9.2

INDEX

Operation, 63.4.13.9.1
Corrosion Protection, 63.4.13.8
General, 63.4.13.1
    Attended Delivery, 63.4.13.1.2
    Cleaning and Purging of Gas Piping Systems, 63.4.13.1.3
    Design, 63.4.13.1.5
        Nationally Recognized Good Practices, 63.4.13.1.5.1
        Piping Systems, 63.4.13.1.5.2
    Inspection, 63.4.13.1.4
    Operating Instructions, 63.4.13.1.1
Joints, 63.4.13.3
Material-Specific Requirements, 63.4.13.11
    Filling and Dispensing, 63.4.13.11.3
        Dispensing Areas, 63.4.13.11.3.2

Indoor Dispensing Areas 63.4.13.11.3.2.1 Piping Systems 63.4.13.11.3.2.3 Ventilation 63.4.13.11.3.2.2

        Filling Controls, 63.4.13.11.3.5
        General, 63.4.13.11.3.1
        Vehicle Loading and Unloading Areas, 63.4.13.11.3.3
    Handling, 63.4.13.11.4
        Applicability, 63.4.13.11.4.1
        Carts and Trucks, 63.4.13.11.4.2
        Closed Containers, 63.4.13.11.4.4
        Design, 63.4.13.11.4.3
    Indoor Use, 63.4.13.11.1
    Outdoor Use, 63.4.13.11.2
        Emergency Shutoff Valves, 63.4.13.11.2.3
        General, 63.4.13.11.2.1
        Separation, 63.4.13.11.2.2
Physical Protection and Support, 63.4.13.7
Piping and Appurtenances, 63.4.13.2
Shutoff Valves on Containers, 63.4.13.5
Shutoff Valves on Piping, 63.4.13.6
Testing, 63.4.13.10
Valves and Accessory Equipment, 63.4.13.4
Gas Generation Systems, 63.8
    General, 63.8.1
Gas Hydrogen Systems, 63.6
General Provisions, 63.1
    Application, 63.1.1
        Specific Applications, 63.1.1.4
    General Definitions, 63.1.3
        Absolute Pressure, 63.1.3.1
        ASTM, 63.1.3.2
        Automatic Emergency Shutoff Valve, 63.1.3.3
        Bulk Hydrogen Compressed Gas System, 63.1.3.4
        Bulk Inert Gas System, 63.1.3.5
        Bulk Liquefied Hydrogen System, 63.1.3.6
        Bulk Oxygen System, 63.1.3.7
        Cathodic Protection, 63.1.3.8
        Cathodic Protection Tester, 63.1.3.9
        CGA, 63.1.3.10
        Compressed Gas Container, 63.1.3.11
        Compressed Gas System, 63.1.3.12
        Continuous Gas Detection System, 63.1.3.13
        Cryogenic Fluid, 63.1.3.14
            Flammable Cryogenic Fluid, 63.1.3.14.1
            Inert Cryogenic Fluid, 63.1.3.14.2
            Oxidizing Cryogenic Fluid, 63.1.3.14.3
        Cylinder, 63.1.3.15
        Cylinder Containment Vessel, 63.1.3.16
        Cylinder Pack, 63.1.3.17
        Distributor, 63.1.3.18
        Emergency Shutoff Valve, 63.1.3.19
        Ethylene Oxide Drum, 63.1.3.20
        Excess Flow Control, 63.1.3.21
        Exhausted Enclosure, 63.1.3.22
        Explosion Control, 63.1.3.23
        Gallon, 63.1.3.24
        Gas, 63.1.3.25
            Compressed Gas, 63.1.3.25.1
            Corrosive Gas, 63.1.3.25.2
            Flammable Gas, 63.1.3.25.3
            Flammable Liquefied Gas, 63.1.3.25.4
            Highly Toxic Gas, 63.1.3.25.5
            Inert Gas, 63.1.3.25.6
            Nonflammable Gas, 63.1.3.25.7
            Other Gas, 63.1.3.25.8
            Oxidizing Gas, 63.1.3.25.9
            Pyrophoric Gas, 63.1.3.25.10
            Toxic Gas, 63.1.3.25.11
            Unstable Reactive Gas, 63.1.3.25.12
        Gas Cabinet, 63.1.3.26
        Gas Manufacturer/Producer, 63.1.3.27
        Gas Room, 63.1.3.28
        Gaseous Hydrogen System, 63.1.3.29
        Hazard Rating, 63.1.3.30
        Immediately Dangerous to Life and Health (IDLH), 63.1.3.31
        Indoor Area, 63.1.3.32
        ISO Module, 63.1.3.33
        Liquid Oxygen Ambulatory Container, 63.1.3.34
        Liquid Oxygen Home Care Container, 63.1.3.35
        Manual Emergency Shutoff Valve, 63.1.3.36
        Mechanical Code, 63.1.3.37
        Mobile Supply Unit, 63.1.3.38
        Nesting, 63.1.3.39
        Normal Temperature and Pressure (NTP), 63.1.3.40
        OSHA, 63.1.3.41
        Outdoor Area, 63.1.3.42
        Permissible Exposure Limit (PEL), 63.1.3.43
        Portable Tank, 63.1.3.44
        Pressure Vessel, 63.1.3.45
        Short-Term Exposure Limit (STEL), 63.1.3.46
        Stationary Tank, 63.1.3.47
        TC, 63.1.3.48
        Treatment System, 63.1.3.49
        Tube Trailer, 63.1.3.50
        Valve Outlet Cap or Plug, 63.1.3.51
        Valve Protection Cap, 63.1.3.52
        Valve Protection Device, 63.1.3.53

2024 Edition

Hazardous Materials Classification, 63.1.4
      Mixtures, 63.1.4.3
      Other Hazards, 63.1.4.2
      Pure Gases, 63.1.4.1, A.63.1.4.1
      Responsibility for Classification, 63.1.4.4
         Flammability of Gas Mixtures, 63.1.4.4.2
         Toxicity of Gas Mixtures, 63.1.4.4.1
   Permits, 63.1.2
Insulated Liquid Carbon Dioxide Systems, 63.9
   General, 63.9.1
   Large Outdoor Insulated Liquid Carbon Dioxide Systems, 63.9.14
      Fire Barriers, 63.9.14.3
      Location, 63.9.14.1
      Point-of-Fill Connections, 63.9.14.2
   Performance Design Option, 63.9.10
   Permits, 63.9.2
   Physical Protection, 63.9.4
   Piping Systems, 63.9.7
      Materials of Construction, 63.9.7.3, A.63.9.7.3
      Operating Instructions, 63.9.7.4
      Small Insulated Liquid Carbon Dioxide Indoor Systems, 63.9.7.5
   Pressure and Level Indicators, 63.9.6
   Pressure Relief Devices, 63.9.3
   Safety Measures, 63.9.8
      Gas Detection System, 63.9.8.3
   Seismic and Structural Design, 63.9.11
   Signage, 63.9.9
   Small Insulated Liquid Carbon Dioxide Outdoor Systems, 63.9.12
   Vent Pipe Systems, 63.9.5
Liquid Oxygen in Home Care, 63.12
   Containers, 63.12.3
   General, 63.12.1
   Information and Instructions, 63.12.2
   Maximum Quantity, 63.12.4
   Smoking, 63.12.5
Storage, Handling, and Use of Ethylene Oxide for Sterilization and Fumigation, 63.10
   Cleaning and Purging of Gas Piping Systems, 63.10.2
   General, 63.10.1
Condition, Existing
   Definition, 3.3.71
Construction Documents
   Definition, 3.3.72
Container
   [LP-Gas] Container
      Definition, 3.3.73.6
   ASME Container
      Definition, 3.3.73.1
   Compressed Gas Container
      Definition, 3.3.73.2
   Container (Flammable or Combustible Liquid)
      Definition, 3.3.73.3, A.3.3.73.3
   Cryogenic Fluids Container
      Definition, 3.3.73.4
   Definition, 3.3.73

   Intermediate Bulk Container
      Definition, 3.3.73.5
Control Area
   Definition, 3.3.74
Conventional Pallet
   Definition, 3.3.75, A.3.3.75
Cooking Fire
   Definition, 3.3.76
Cordwood
   Definition, 3.3.77
Corrosive Material
   Definition, 3.3.78
Corrosive Solids and Liquids, Chap. 64
   General, 64.1
Crude Petroleum
   Definition, 3.3.79
Cryogenic Fluid
   Definition, 3.3.80
   Flammable Cryogenic Fluid
      Definition, 3.3.80.1
   Inert Cryogenic Fluid
      Definition, 3.3.80.2
   Oxidizing Cryogenic Fluid
      Definition, 3.3.80.3
Cultural Resource Properties
   Definition, 3.3.81, A.3.3.81
Cylinder
   Definition, 3.3.82
Cylinder Containment Vessel
   Definition, 3.3.83
Cylinder Pack
   Definition, 3.3.84, A.3.3.84

-D-

Damage-Limiting Construction
   Definition, 3.3.85
Data Conversion
   Definition, 3.4.3
Deficiency
   Critical Deficiency
      Definition, 3.3.86.1
   Definition, 3.3.86, A.3.3.86
   Noncritical Deficiency
      Definition, 3.3.86.2
Definitions, Chap. 3
Deflagration
   Definition, 3.3.87
Delivered Audio Quality (DAQ)
   Definition, 3.3.88
Design Fire Scenario
   Definition, 3.4.4
Design Specification
   Definition, 3.4.5, A.3.4.5
Design Team
   Definition, 3.4.6
Desolventizing
   Definition, 3.3.89

INDEX

Detector
    Air Sampling–Type Detector
        Definition, 3.3.90.1
    Automatic Fire Detector
        Definition, 3.3.90.2
    Automatic Fire Extinguishing or Suppression System Operation Detector
        Definition, 3.3.90.3
    Combination Detector
        Definition, 3.3.90.4, A.3.3.90.4
    Definition, 3.3.90
    Electrical Conductivity Heat Detector
        Definition, 3.3.90.5
    Fire–Gas Detector
        Definition, 3.3.90.6
    Fixed-Temperature Detector
        Definition, 3.3.90.7, A.3.3.90.7
    Flame Detector
        Definition, 3.3.90.8, A.3.3.90.8
    Gas Detector
        Definition, 3.3.90.9
    Heat Detector
        Definition, 3.3.90.10
    Line-Type Detector
        Definition, 3.3.90.11
    Multi-Criteria Detector
        Definition, 3.3.90.12, A.3.3.90.12
    Multi-Sensor Detector
        Definition, 3.3.90.13, A.3.3.90.13
    Other Fire Detectors
        Definition, 3.3.90.14
    Pneumatic Rate-of-Rise Tubing Heat Detector
        Definition, 3.3.90.15
    Projected Beam–Type Detector
        Definition, 3.3.90.16
    Radiant Energy–Sensing Fire Detector
        Definition, 3.3.90.17
    Rate Compensation Detector
        Definition, 3.3.90.18, A.3.3.90.18
    Rate-of-Rise Detector
        Definition, 3.3.90.19, A.3.3.90.19
    Smoke Detector
        Definition, 3.3.90.20
    Spark/Ember Detector
        Definition, 3.3.90.21
    Spot-Type Detector
        Definition, 3.3.90.22

Detonation
    Definition, 3.3.91

Dispensing
    Definition, 3.3.92

Distillery
    Definition, 3.3.93

Distributor
    Definition, 3.3.94

Donor Antenna
    Definition, 3.3.95

Dormitory
    Definition, 3.3.96

DOT
    Definition, 3.3.97

Driveway
    Definition, 3.3.98

Drycleaning, Chap. 24
    General, 24.1
    Permits, 24.2

Dust Explosion and Fire Prevention, Chap. 40
    Application, 40.1
    Contractors, 40.12
        Contractor Training, 40.12.3, A.40.12.3
    Documentation Retention, 40.16, A.40.16
    Dust Hazards Analysis (DHA), 40.5
        Criteria, 40.5.2
            Documentation, 40.5.2.3
            Overview, 40.5.2.1, A.40.5.2.1
            Qualifications, 40.5.2.2, A.40.5.2.2
        General Requirements, 40.5.1, A.40.5.1
            Retroactivity, 40.5.1.1
        Methodology, 40.5.3
            Building or Building Compartments, 40.5.3.4
            General, 40.5.3.1
            Material Evaluation, 40.5.3.2
            Process Systems, 40.5.3.3
    Emergency Planning and Response, 40.13
    Employee Participation, 40.18, A.40.18
    General, 40.4, A.40.4
    Hot Work, 40.8
    Housekeeping, 40.7
        Auditing and Documentation, 40.7.7
        Frequency and Goal, 40.7.6
        General, 40.7.1
        Methodology, 40.7.2, A.40.7.2
            Compressed Air Blowdown Method, 40.7.2.6
            Procedure, 40.7.2.1
            Sweeping, Shoveling, Scoop, and Brush Cleaning Method, 40.7.2.3, A.40.7.2.3
            Vacuum Cleaning Method, 40.7.2.2
                Portable Vacuum Cleaners, 40.7.2.2.1, A.40.7.2.2.1
            Water Washdown Cleaning Method, 40.7.2.4, A.40.7.2.4
        Training, 40.7.3
        Vacuum Trucks, 40.7.5
    Incident Investigation, 40.14, A.40.14
    Inspection, Testing, and Maintenance, 40.10
    Management of Change, 40.15
    Management Systems Review, 40.17
    Operating Procedures and Practices, 40.6
    Permits, 40.2
    Personal Protective Equipment, 40.9
        Limitations of PPE Application. (Flame-Resistant Garments), 40.9.2
        Workplace Hazard Assessment, 40.9.1
    Retroactivity, 40.3
    Training and Hazard Awareness, 40.11

2024 Edition

Dwelling Unit
   Definition, 3.3.99, A.3.3.99
   One- and Two-Family Dwelling Unit
      Definition, 3.3.99.1

-E-

Emergency
   Definition, 3.3.100
Emergency Relief Vent
   Definition, 3.3.101
Emergency Shutoff Valve
   Definition, 3.3.102
Energy Storage Systems, Chap. 52
   Capacitor Energy Storage Systems, 52.6
   Electrochemical Energy Storage Systems, 52.5
   Fuel Cell Energy Storage Systems, 52.7
   General, 52.1
      Combustible Storage, 52.1.11
      Documentation Location, 52.1.4
      Electrical Installation, 52.1.14, A.52.1.14
      Emergency Operations Plan, 52.1.5
      Environment, 52.1.15
      Equipment, 52.1.12
         Repairs, 52.1.12.1
         Replacements, 52.1.12.3
         Retrofits, 52.1.12.2
      Exhaust Ventilation During Normal Operation, 52.1.23, A.52.1.23
      Fire Command Centers, 52.1.17
      Fire Suppression and Control, 52.1.24
      Impact Protection, 52.1.20
      Increase in Power Rating or Maximum Stored Energy, 52.1.13
      Installations and Locations, 52.1.8, A.52.1.8
      Means of Egress, 52.1.21
      Mobile ESS Equipment and Operations, 52.1.9
      One- and Two-Family Dwelling and Townhouse Units, 52.1.2
      Operation, Maintenance, and Testing, 52.1.7
      Permits, 52.1.3
      Reused Equipment, 52.1.18
      Security of Installations, 52.1.16
      Signage, 52.1.19
      Smoke and Fire Detection, 52.1.26
      Spill Control, 52.1.22
      System Commissioning and Decommissioning, 52.1.6
         Commissioning Plan, 52.1.6.1
      System Interconnections, 52.1.10
      Ventilation, 52.1.25
      Water Supply, 52.1.27
   Operation and Maintenance, 52.4
   Remediation Measures, 52.2
      Hazard Support Personnel, 52.2.1
   Storage of Used or Off-Specification Batteries, 52.8
   System Interconnection, 52.3
Energy Storage Systems (ESS)
   Definition, 3.3.103, A.3.3.103

Ethylene Oxide Drum
   Definition, 3.3.104
Excess Flow Control
   Definition, 3.3.105
Excess Flow Valve
   Definition, 3.3.106
Exhausted Enclosure
   Definition, 3.3.107, A.3.3.107
Existing
   Definition, 3.3.108, A.3.3.108
Existing Condition
   Definition, 3.3.109
Exit
   Definition, 3.3.110, A.3.3.110
   Horizontal Exit
      Definition, 3.3.110.1, A.3.3.110.1
Exit Access
   Definition, 3.3.111
Exit Discharge
   Definition, 3.3.112
Explanatory Material, Annex A
Explosion
   Definition, 3.3.113
Explosion Control
   Definition, 3.3.114, A.3.3.114
Explosive Material
   Definition, 3.3.115, A.3.3.115
Explosives, Fireworks, and Model Rocketry, Chap. 65
   Display Fireworks, 65.2
      Permits, 65.2.3
   Explosives, 65.9
      Permits, 65.9.2
   Fireworks Manufacturing, 65.5
      Permits, 65.5.2
   Flame Effects Before an Audience, 65.4
      Permits, 65.4.2
   General, 65.1
   High Power Rocketry, 65.8
      Permits, 65.8.2
   Model Rocketry, 65.6
   Pyrotechnics Before a Proximate Audience, 65.3
      Permits, 65.3.3
   Rocketry Manufacturing, 65.7
      Permits, 65.7.2
Exposure Fire
   Definition, 3.4.7, A.3.4.7
Extraction Room (Cannabis)
   Definition, 3.3.116

-F-

Facility
   Animal Housing Facility
      Definition, 3.3.117.1
   Definition, 3.3.117
   Hazardous Material Storage Facility
      Definition, 3.3.117.2

Limited Care Facility
    Definition, 3.3.117.3
Motor Fuel Dispensing Facility
    Definition, 3.3.117.4
Fail-Safe
    Definition, 3.3.118
Features of Fire Protection, Chap. 12
    Construction, 12.2, A.12.2
    Contents and Furnishings, 12.6
        Combustible Vegetation, 12.6.9
            Electrical Equipment, 12.6.9.7
            Flammability of Combustible Artificial Decorative Vegetation, 12.6.9.5
            Open Flames, 12.6.9.8
            Provisions for Natural Cut Trees, 12.6.9.6
                Fire-Retardant Treatments for Natural Cut Christmas Trees, 12.6.9.6.5
        Containers for Waste or Linen, 12.6.8
        Draperies, Curtains, and Other Hanging or Suspended Furnishings and Decorations, 12.6.1, A.12.6.1
        Explosive or Highly Flammable Furnishings or Decorations, 12.6.4, A.12.6.4
        Fire-Retardant Coatings, 12.6.5
        Foamed Plastics, 12.6.6, A.12.6.6
        Lockers, 12.6.7
        Mattresses, 12.6.3
            Rate of Heat Release and Mass Loss Testing of Mattresses, 12.6.3.2, A.12.6.3.2
            Smoldering Ignition of Mattresses, 12.6.3.1, A.12.6.3.1
        Upholstered Furniture, 12.6.2
            Rate of Heat Release Testing of Upholstered Furniture, 12.6.2.2, A.12.6.2.2
            Smoldering Ignition of Upholstered Furniture, 12.6.2.1, A.12.6.2.1
    Fire Barriers, 12.7
        General, 12.7.1
        Joints, 12.7.9
            Exterior Curtain Walls and Perimeter Joints, 12.7.9.4, A.12.7.9.4
            General, 12.7.9.1
            Joint System Requirements, 12.7.9.2
        Opening Protectives, 12.7.6
            Fire Doors, 12.7.6.3, A.12.7.6.3
            Fire Windows, 12.7.6.5
            Floor Fire Door Assemblies, 12.7.6.4
            General, 12.7.6.1
            Glazing, 12.7.6.6
            Minimum Fire Protection Rating, 12.7.6.2
            Sidelights and Transoms, 12.7.6.7
        Opening Protectives, 12.7.7
        Penetrations, 12.7.8
            Ducts and Air-Transfer Openings, 12.7.8.8
            Firestop Systems and Devices Required, 12.7.8.2
                Alternative Firestop Requirements, 12.7.8.2.5
                F Ratings, 12.7.8.2.3
                T Ratings, 12.7.8.2.4
                Testing, 12.7.8.2.2
            General, 12.7.8.1
            Insulation and Coverings, 12.7.8.4
            Membrane Penetrations, 12.7.8.7
            Sleeves, 12.7.8.3
            Transitions, 12.7.8.6
            Vibration Isolation Equipment or Systems, 12.7.8.5
        Smoke Barrier Used as a Fire Barrier, 12.7.4
        Walls, 12.7.5
    Fire Doors and Other Opening Protectives, 12.4
        Care and Maintenance of Fire Doors and Other Opening Protectives, 12.4.2
            Field Labeling, 12.4.2.5
            Field Modifications, 12.4.2.6, A.12.4.2.6
            Inspection and Testing, 12.4.2.8, A.12.4.2.8
                Acceptance Testing, 12.4.2.8.3
                    Closing Devices, 12.4.2.8.3.8
                    Rolling Steel Fire Doors12.4.2.8.3.8.3
                    Horizontally Sliding, Vertically Sliding, and Rolling Doors, 12.4.2.8.3.7
                    Swinging Doors with Builders Hardware or Fire Door Hardware, 12.4.2.8.3.5
                        Inspection Mark12.4.2.8.3.5.2, A.12.4.2.8.3.5.2
                    Swinging Doors with Fire Door Hardware. [80:5.2.3.6], 12.4.2.8.3.6
                Inspection Records, 12.4.2.8.2, A.12.4.2.8.2
                Installation Inspection, 12.4.2.8.1, A.12.4.2.8.1
                Periodic Inspection and Testing, 12.4.2.8.4, A.12.4.2.8.4
            Maintenance, 12.4.2.11
            Operability, 12.4.2.3
                Prevention of Door Blockage, 12.4.2.3.3
            Performance-Based Option, 12.4.2.10, A.12.4.2.10
            Removal of Door or Window, 12.4.2.7
            Replacement, 12.4.2.4
            Retrofit Operators, 12.4.2.9
    Fire-Resistive Materials and Construction, 12.3
        Maintenance of Fire-Resistive Construction, Draft-Stop Partitions, and Roof Coverings, 12.3.3, A.12.3.3
        Quality Assurance for Penetrations and Joints, 12.3.2
    General, 12.1
    Interior Finish, 12.5, A.12.5
        Automatic Sprinklers, 12.5.9
        Fire-Retardant Coatings, 12.5.7, A.12.5.7
        General, 12.5.2, A.12.5.2
        Interior Floor Finish Testing and Classification, 12.5.8, A.12.5.8
        Interior Wall and Ceiling Finish Materials with Special Requirements, 12.5.5, A.12.5.5
            Cellular or Foamed Plastic, 12.5.5.3
            Decorations and Furnishings, 12.5.5.16
            Expanded Vinyl Ceiling Coverings, 12.5.5.7
            Expanded Vinyl Wall Coverings, 12.5.5.5, A.12.5.5.5
            Exposed Portions of Structural Members, 12.5.5.2, A.12.5.5.2
            Facings or Wood Veneers Intended to be Applied on Site over a Wood Substrate, 12.5.5.14
            Laminated Products Factory Produced with a Wood Substrate, 12.5.5.13
            Light-Transmitting Plastics, 12.5.5.15, A.12.5.5.15
            Lockers, 12.5.5.8

Combustible Lockers, 12.5.5.8.1
Wood Lockers, 12.5.5.8.2
Metal Ceiling and Wall Panels, 12.5.5.12
Reflective Insulation Materials, 12.5.5.11
Site-Fabricated Stretch Systems, 12.5.5.10
Solid Thermoplastics, 12.5.5.9
Textile Ceiling Coverings, 12.5.5.6
Textile Wall Coverings, 12.5.5.4, A.12.5.5.4
Thickness Exemption, 12.5.5.1
Interior Wall or Ceiling Finish Testing and Classification, 12.5.4, A.12.5.4
Acceptance Criteria for NFPA 286, 12.5.4.2
Interior Wall and Ceiling Finish Materials Tested in Accordance with ASTM E84 or UL 723, 12.5.4.3, A.12.5.4.3
Interior Wall and Ceiling Finish Materials Tested in Accordance with NFPA 286, 12.5.4.1
Trim and Incidental Finish, 12.5.6
Bulletin Boards, Posters, and Paper, 12.5.6.3
General, 12.5.6.1
Wall Base, 12.5.6.2
Use of Interior Finishes, 12.5.3, A.12.5.3
Smoke Barriers, 12.9
Continuity, 12.9.2, A.12.9.2
Ducts and Air-Transfer Openings, 12.9.5
Access and Identification, 12.9.5.5
Identification. , 12.9.5.5.3
General, 12.9.5.1
Installation, Testing, and Maintenance, 12.9.5.4
Smoke Damper Exemptions, 12.9.5.3
Smoke Damper Ratings, 12.9.5.6
Smoke Dampers, 12.9.5.2
Smoke Detectors, 12.9.5.7
Fire Barrier Used as Smoke Barrier, 12.9.3
General, 12.9.1, A.12.9.1
Joints, 12.9.7
Opening Protectives, 12.9.4
Penetrations, 12.9.6
Vibration Isolation Equipment or Systems, 12.9.6.6
Smoke Partitions, 12.8
Air-Transfer Openings, 12.8.6
General, 12.8.6.1
Smoke Damper Ratings, 12.8.6.3
Smoke Dampers, 12.8.6.2, A.12.8.6.2
Smoke Detectors, 12.8.6.4
Continuity, 12.8.2
General, 12.8.1, A.12.8.1
Joints, 12.8.5
Opening Protectives, 12.8.3
Penetrations, 12.8.4
Vibration Isolation Equipment or Systems, 12.8.4.2
Festival Seating
Definition, 3.3.119, A.3.3.119
Fines (Wood)
Definition, 3.3.120
Finish
Definition, 3.3.121

Interior Ceiling Finish
Definition, 3.3.121.1
Interior Finish
Definition, 3.3.121.2, A.3.3.121.2
Interior Floor Finish
Definition, 3.3.121.3, A.3.3.121.3
Interior Wall Finish
Definition, 3.3.121.4, A.3.3.121.4
Fire Alarm System
Definition, 3.3.124
Fire Apparatus Access Road
Definition, 3.3.125
Fire Compartment
Definition, 3.3.126
Fire Department Access and Water Supply, Chap. 18
Fire Department Access, 18.2
Access to Structures or Areas, 18.2.2, A.18.2.2
Access Box(es), 18.2.2.1
Access Maintenance, 18.2.2.3
Access to Gated Subdivisions or Developments, 18.2.2.2
Fire Apparatus Access Roads, 18.2.3
Access to Building, 18.2.3.2
Marking of Fire Apparatus Access Road, 18.2.3.6
Multiple Access Roads, 18.2.3.3, A.18.2.3.3
Required Access, 18.2.3.1
Specifications, 18.2.3.5
Bridges, 18.2.3.5.5
Dead Ends, 18.2.3.5.4
Dimensions, 18.2.3.5.1
Grade, 18.2.3.5.6
Surface, 18.2.3.5.2, A.18.2.3.5.2
Traffic Calming Devices, 18.2.3.5.7
Turning Radius, 18.2.3.5.3
Traffic Signal Pre-emption, 18.2.3.4
Obstruction and Control of Fire Apparatus Access Road, 18.2.4, A.18.2.4
Closure of Accessways, 18.2.4.2
General, 18.2.4.1
Fire Flow Requirements for Buildings, 18.4
Fire Flow Area, 18.4.3
General, 18.4.3.1
Type I (443), Type I (332), and Type II (222) Construction, 18.4.3.2
Fire Flow Requirements for Buildings, 18.4.4
Buildings Other Than One- and Two-Family Dwellings, 18.4.4.3
One- and Two-Family Dwellings Exceeding 5000 ft2 (464.5 m2), 18.4.4.2
One- and Two-Family Dwellings Not Exceeding 5000 ft2 (464.5 m2), 18.4.4.1
Required Fire Flow and Automatic Sprinkler System Demand, 18.4.4.4, A.18.4.4.4
Modifications, 18.4.2
Decreases in Fire Flow Requirements, 18.4.2.1
Increases in Fire Flow Requirements, 18.4.2.2
Scope, 18.4.1, A.18.4.1
Fire Hydrants, 18.5
Accessibility, 18.5.6

INDEX

Buildings Other than Detached One- and Two-Family Dwellings, 18.5.3
Clear Space Around Hydrants, 18.5.7
Detached One- and Two-Family Dwellings, 18.5.2
Fire Hydrant Locations and Distribution, 18.5.1
Hydrants Out of Service, 18.5.9
Inspection, Testing, and Maintenance, 18.5.5
Marking of Hydrants, 18.5.10
Minimum Number of Fire Hydrants for Fire Flow, 18.5.4
Protection, 18.5.8
General, 18.1
Application, 18.1.1
Permits, 18.1.2
Plans, 18.1.3
Fire Apparatus Access, 18.1.3.1
Fire Hydrant Systems, 18.1.3.2
Water Supplies, 18.3

Fire Department Service Delivery Concurrency Evaluation, Chap. 15
Application, 15.1
Approval, 15.6
Evaluator Qualifications, 15.3
Fire Department Service Delivery Concurrency Evaluation Documentation, 15.4
Independent Review, 15.5
Level of Service Objectives, 15.2

Fire Door Assembly
Definition, 3.3.127

Fire Fighter Breathing-Air Replenishment Systems, Annex D
General, D.1
Permit, D.2

Fire Fighter Safety Building Marking System, Annex C
Fire Fighter Safety Building Marking System (FFSBMS), C.1
General, C.1.1
Installation and Maintenance, C.1.4
Ratings, C.1.3
Automatic Fire Sprinkler and Standpipe System, C.1.3.4
Construction Type, C.1.3.2
Hazards of Contents, C.1.3.3
Occupancy/Life Safety Issues, C.1.3.5
Special Designations, C.1.3.6
Sign, C.1.2
Training, C.1.5
Notes, C.2
Note 1, C.2.1
Note 2, C.2.2
Note 3, C.2.3
Note 4, C.2.4
Note 5, C.2.5

Fire Flow
Definition, 3.3.128

Fire Hazard
Definition, 3.3.129

Fire Hydrant
Definition, 3.3.130, A.3.3.130

Fire Lane
Definition, 3.3.131, A.3.3.131

Fire Model
Definition, 3.4.8, A.3.4.8

Fire Monitoring
Definition, 3.3.132

Fire Point
Definition, 3.3.133

Fire Protection Systems, Chap. 13
Detection, Alarm, and Communications Systems, 13.7
Automatic Fire Detectors, 13.7.4
General Requirements. , 13.7.4.1
Duct Detector Installation, 13.7.4.1.5
Mechanical Protection, 13.7.4.1.2
Inspection, Testing, and Maintenance, 13.7.4.4
Location, 13.7.4.3
Air Sampling–Type Smoke Detector, 13.7.4.3.4
General, 13.7.4.3.4.1
Pipe Network, 13.7.4.3.4.2
Ceiling Tiles and Ceiling Assemblies, 13.7.4.3.7
High Air Movement Areas, 13.7.4.3.8
Location, 13.7.4.3.8.1
Spacing, 13.7.4.3.8.2, A.13.7.4.3.8.2
Projected Beam–Type Smoke Detectors, 13.7.4.3.5, A.13.7.4.3.5
Protection During Construction, 13.7.4.3.6, A.13.7.4.3.6
Spot-Type Smoke Detectors, 13.7.4.3.3, A.13.7.4.3.3
Requirements for Smoke and Heat Detectors, 13.7.4.2
Partitions, 13.7.4.2.2, A.13.7.4.2.2
Recessed Mounting, 13.7.4.2.1
Fire Alarm Systems, 13.7.3
Automatic Fire Detection and Alarm Service, 13.7.3.5
Documentation and Notification, 13.7.3.2
Approval and Acceptance, 13.7.3.2.1
Completion Documentation, 13.7.3.2.3
Record Drawings (As-Builts), 13.7.3.2.3.5
Record of Completion, 13.7.3.2.3.6
Electronic Record of Completion 13.7.3.2.3.6.7 Revisions 13.7.3.2.3.6.6
Site-Specific Software, 13.7.3.2.3.7
Verification of Compliant Installation, 13.7.3.2.3.8, A.13.7.3.2.3.8
Forms, 13.7.3.2.6
Forms for Documentation, 13.7.3.2.6.2
General, 13.7.3.2.6.1
Inspection, Testing, and Maintenance Documentation, 13.7.3.2.4
Record of Inspection and Testing, 13.7.3.2.4.6
Minimum Required Documentation, 13.7.3.2.2
Records, Record Retention, and Record Maintenance, 13.7.3.2.5
Document Accessibility, 13.7.3.2.5.2
Document Security, 13.7.3.2.5.3
Records, 13.7.3.2.5.1
General, 13.7.3.1
Equipment, 13.7.3.1.1
Indication of Central Station Service, 13.7.3.4, A.13.7.3.4
Manually Actuated Alarm-Initiating Devices, 13.7.3.3
General, 13.7.1

2024 Edition

Annunciation, 13.7.1.13
    Alarm Annunciation, 13.7.1.13.2
    Alarm Annunciation Display, 13.7.1.13.5
    Annunciation Zoning, 13.7.1.13.6, A.13.7.1.13.6
    Annunciator Access and Location, 13.7.1.13.4, A.13.7.1.13.4
    Supervisory and Trouble Annunciation, 13.7.1.13.3
Building Alarm and Signaling Systems, 13.7.1.2, A.13.7.1.2
Carbon Monoxide (CO) Detection and Warning Equipment, 13.7.1.14
Emergency Control Functions, 13.7.1.11
Emergency Forces Notification, 13.7.1.10
Impaired and Nuisance Alarm Prone Systems, 13.7.1.5, A.13.7.1.5
Location of Controls, 13.7.1.12
Nonrequired Coverage, 13.7.1.6, A.13.7.1.6
Occupant Notification, 13.7.1.9
Risk Analysis for Mass Notification Systems, 13.7.1.15, A.13.7.1.15
Signal Initiation, 13.7.1.7
Smoke Alarms, 13.7.1.8
    Smoke Alarms in Sleeping Rooms, 13.7.1.8.3
    Specific Location Requirements. , 13.7.1.8.5
Where Required and Occupancy Requirements, 13.7.2
    Carbon Monoxide Detectors, 13.7.2.30
        Carbon Monoxide Detectors for Control of Carbon Monoxide Spread, 13.7.2.30.9
        Protection During Construction, 13.7.2.30.8
    Existing Ambulatory Health Care Occupancies, 13.7.2.10
        Emergency Control Functions, 13.7.2.10.4
        General, 13.7.2.10.1
        Initiation, 13.7.2.10.2
        Notification, 13.7.2.10.3
            Emergency Forces Notification, 13.7.2.10.3.2
            Occupant Notification, 13.7.2.10.3.1
    Existing Apartment Buildings, 13.7.2.18
        Detection, 13.7.2.18.4
        General, 13.7.2.18.1
        Initiation, 13.7.2.18.2
        Notification, 13.7.2.18.3
        Smoke Alarms, 13.7.2.18.5
    Existing Assembly Occupancies, 13.7.2.2
        General, 13.7.2.2.1
        Initiation, 13.7.2.2.2
        Notification, 13.7.2.2.3
    Existing Business Occupancies, 13.7.2.26
        Emergency Forces Notification, 13.7.2.26.4
        General, 13.7.2.26.1
        Initiation, 13.7.2.26.2
        Occupant Notification, 13.7.2.26.3
    Existing Day-Care Occupancies, 13.7.2.6
        Detection, 13.7.2.6.5
        Emergency Forces Notification, 13.7.2.6.4
        Existing Day-Care Homes, 13.7.2.6.6
        General, 13.7.2.6.1
        Initiation, 13.7.2.6.2
        Occupant Notification, 13.7.2.6.3
    Existing Detention and Correctional Occupancies, 13.7.2.12
        Detection, 13.7.2.12.4
        General, 13.7.2.12.1
        Initiation, 13.7.2.12.2
        Notification, 13.7.2.12.3
            Emergency Forces Notification, 13.7.2.12.3.2
            Occupant Notification, 13.7.2.12.3.1
    Existing Educational Occupancies, 13.7.2.4
        General, 13.7.2.4.1
        Initiation, 13.7.2.4.2
            Alternative Protection System, 13.7.2.4.2.3
            Automatic Initiation, 13.7.2.4.2.2
            General, 13.7.2.4.2.1
        Notification, 13.7.2.4.3
            Emergency Forces Notification, 13.7.2.4.3.2
            Occupant Notification, 13.7.2.4.3.1
    Existing Health Care Occupancies, 13.7.2.8
        Detection, 13.7.2.8.5
            Corridors, 13.7.2.8.5.1
            Detection in Spaces Open to Corridors, 13.7.2.8.5.2
        Emergency Control Functions, 13.7.2.8.4
        General, 13.7.2.8.1
        Initiation, 13.7.2.8.2, A.13.7.2.8.2
        Notification, 13.7.2.8.3
            Emergency Forces Notification, 13.7.2.8.3.2
            Occupant Notification, 13.7.2.8.3.1
    Existing Hotels and Dormitories, 13.7.2.16
        Carbon Monoxide Alarms and Carbon Monoxide Detection Systems, 13.7.2.16.6
        General, 13.7.2.16.1
        Initiation, 13.7.2.16.2
        Notification, 13.7.2.16.3
        Smoke Alarms, 13.7.2.16.5, A.13.7.2.16.5
    Existing Mercantile Occupancies, 13.7.2.24
        General, 13.7.2.24.1
        Initiation, 13.7.2.24.2
        Notification, 13.7.2.24.3
            Emergency Forces Notification, 13.7.2.24.3.2
            Occupant Notification, 13.7.2.24.3.1
    Existing, Large (More Than 16 Residents) Residential Board and Care Occupancies, 13.7.2.22
        Emergency Forces Notification, 13.7.2.22.6
        General, 13.7.2.22.1
        Initiation, 13.7.2.22.2
        Occupant Notification, 13.7.2.22.4
        Smoke Alarms, 13.7.2.22.7
        Smoke Detection Systems, 13.7.2.22.8
    Existing, Small (Not More Than 16 Residents) Residential Board and Care Occupancies, 13.7.2.21
        Fire Alarm Systems, 13.7.2.21.1
        Initiation, 13.7.2.21.2
        Occupant Notification, 13.7.2.21.3
        Smoke Alarms, 13.7.2.21.4, A.13.7.2.21.4
    New Ambulatory Health Care Occupancies, 13.7.2.9
        Carbon Monoxide Detection, 13.7.2.9.4

Emergency Control Functions, 13.7.2.9.5
General, 13.7.2.9.1
Initiation, 13.7.2.9.2
Notification, 13.7.2.9.3
  Emergency Forces Notification, 13.7.2.9.3.2
  Occupant Notification, 13.7.2.9.3.1
New and Existing Industrial Occupancies, 13.7.2.27
General, 13.7.2.27.1
Initiation, 13.7.2.27.2
Notification, 13.7.2.27.3
New and Existing Lodging or Rooming Houses, 13.7.2.14
  Carbon Monoxide Alarms and Carbon Monoxide Detection Systems, 13.7.2.14.6
General, 13.7.2.14.1
Initiation, 13.7.2.14.2
Notification, 13.7.2.14.3
Smoke Alarms, 13.7.2.14.5
New and Existing One- and Two-Family Dwellings, 13.7.2.13
  Carbon Monoxide and Carbon Monoxide Detection Systems, 13.7.2.13.2
New and Existing Storage Occupancies, 13.7.2.28
General, 13.7.2.28.1
Initiation, 13.7.2.28.2
Notification, 13.7.2.28.3
New Apartment Buildings, 13.7.2.17
  Carbon Monoxide Alarms and Carbon Monoxide Detection Systems, 13.7.2.17.6
General, 13.7.2.17.1
Initiation, 13.7.2.17.2
Notification, 13.7.2.17.3
Smoke Alarms, 13.7.2.17.5, A.13.7.2.17.5
New Assembly Occupancies, 13.7.2.1
  Carbon Monoxide Detection, 13.7.2.1.4
General, 13.7.2.1.1
Initiation, 13.7.2.1.2
Notification, 13.7.2.1.3
Risk Analysis for Mass Notification Systems, 13.7.2.1.5
New Business Occupancies, 13.7.2.25
  Emergency Forces Notification, 13.7.2.25.4
General, 13.7.2.25.1
Initiation, 13.7.2.25.2
Occupant Notification, 13.7.2.25.3
Risk Analysis for Mass Notification, 13.7.2.25.5, A.13.7.2.25.5
New Day-Care Occupancies, 13.7.2.5
Detection, 13.7.2.5.5
Emergency Forces Notification, 13.7.2.5.4
General, 13.7.2.5.1
Initiation, 13.7.2.5.2
New Day-Care Homes, 13.7.2.5.6
Occupant Notification, 13.7.2.5.3
New Detention and Correctional Occupancies, 13.7.2.11
Detection, 13.7.2.11.4, A.13.7.2.11.4
General, 13.7.2.11.1
Initiation, 13.7.2.11.2
Notification, 13.7.2.11.3
  Emergency Forces Notification, 13.7.2.11.3.2

Occupant Notification, 13.7.2.11.3.1
New Educational Occupancies, 13.7.2.3
  Carbon Monoxide Alarms and Carbon Monoxide Detection Systems, 13.7.2.3.4
General, 13.7.2.3.1
Initiation, 13.7.2.3.2
  Alternative Protection System, 13.7.2.3.2.3
  Automatic Initiation, 13.7.2.3.2.2
  General, 13.7.2.3.2.1
Notification, 13.7.2.3.3
  Emergency Forces Notification, 13.7.2.3.3.2
  Occupant Notification, 13.7.2.3.3.1
Risk Analysis for Mass Notification Systems, 13.7.2.3.5
New Health Care Occupancies, 13.7.2.7
Detection, 13.7.2.7.5
  Carbon Monoxide Detection, 13.7.2.7.5.4
  Detection in Spaces Open to Corridors, 13.7.2.7.5.2
  General, 13.7.2.7.5.1
  Nursing Homes, 13.7.2.7.5.3, A.13.7.2.7.5.3
Emergency Control Functions, 13.7.2.7.4
General, 13.7.2.7.1
Initiation, 13.7.2.7.2, A.13.7.2.7.2
Notification, 13.7.2.7.3
  Annunciation and Annunciation Zoning, 13.7.2.7.3.3
  Emergency Forces Notification, 13.7.2.7.3.2
  Occupant Notification, 13.7.2.7.3.1
New Hotels and Dormitories, 13.7.2.15
  Carbon Monoxide Alarms and Carbon Monoxide Detection Systems, 13.7.2.15.6
Detection, 13.7.2.15.4
General, 13.7.2.15.1
Initiation, 13.7.2.15.2
Notification, 13.7.2.15.3
Risk Analysis for Mass Notification, 13.7.2.15.7
Smoke Alarms, 13.7.2.15.5, A.13.7.2.15.5
New Mercantile Occupancies, 13.7.2.23
General, 13.7.2.23.1
Initiation, 13.7.2.23.2
Notification, 13.7.2.23.3
  Emergency Forces Notification, 13.7.2.23.3.2
  Occupant Notification, 13.7.2.23.3.1
New, Large (More than 16 Residents) Residential Board and Care Occupancies, 13.7.2.20
Annunciator Panel, 13.7.2.20.3
Carbon Monoxide Alarms and Carbon Monoxide Detection Systems, 13.7.2.20.9
Emergency Forces Notification, 13.7.2.20.6, A.13.7.2.20.6
General, 13.7.2.20.1
High-Rise Buildings, 13.7.2.20.5
Initiation, 13.7.2.20.2
Occupant Notification, 13.7.2.20.4
Smoke Alarms, 13.7.2.20.7
Smoke Detection Systems, 13.7.2.20.8
New, Small (Not More Than 16 Residents) Residential Board and Care Occupancies, 13.7.2.19

Carbon Monoxide Alarms and Carbon Monoxide Detection Systems, 13.7.2.19.4
  General, 13.7.2.19.1
  Initiation, 13.7.2.19.2
  Occupant Notification, 13.7.2.19.3
  Smoke Alarms, 13.7.2.19.5
 Special Structures and High-Rise Buildings, 13.7.2.29
  New High-Rise Buildings, 13.7.2.29.3
  Open Structures, 13.7.2.29.1
  Towers, 13.7.2.29.2
Fire Pumps, 13.4
 Component Replacement, 13.4.5
 Diesel Engine Driver System Operation, 13.4.3
  Certified Pump Curve, 13.4.3.2, A.13.4.3.2
  Emergency Starting and Stopping, 13.4.3.1
 General, 13.4.1
  Permits, 13.4.1.2
  Pump Operation, 13.4.1.3
   Service Personnel Qualifications and Experience, 13.4.1.3.1
 Periodic Inspection, Testing, and Maintenance, 13.4.4
 Valve Supervision, 13.4.2, A.13.4.2
  Supervised Closed, 13.4.2.2
  Supervised Open, 13.4.2.1
General, 13.1
 Integrated Fire Protection and Life Safety System Test, 13.1.3
  Basic Testing, 13.1.3.1
  NFPA 4 Testing, 13.1.3.2, A.13.1.3.2
 Records, 13.1.6
Non-Listed Fire Protection or Suppression Devices and Equipment, 13.9
Other Fire Protection Systems, 13.8
Portable Fire Extinguishers, 13.6
 General Requirements, 13.6.1
  Identification of Contents, 13.6.1.4, A.13.6.1.4
  Listing and Labeling, 13.6.1.3
   Electrical Conductivity, 13.6.1.3.3
  Obsolete Fire Extinguishers, 13.6.1.5
  Scope, 13.6.1.1
  Where Required, 13.6.1.2, A.13.6.1.2
 Inspection, Maintenance, and Recharging, 13.6.4
  Extinguisher Maintenance, 13.6.4.3
   Annual Maintenance Record Keeping, 13.6.4.3.2, A.13.6.4.3.2
   Maintenance Procedures, 13.6.4.3.1
  General, 13.6.4.1, A.13.6.4.1
   Personnel, 13.6.4.1.2
   Replacement Fire Extinguishers, 13.6.4.1.3
   Responsibility, 13.6.4.1.1
   Tags or Labels, 13.6.4.1.4
  Inspection, 13.6.4.2
   Corrective Action, 13.6.4.2.3
    Nonrechargeable Dry Chemical Fire Extinguisher, 13.6.4.2.3.2
    Nonrechargeable Halon Agent Fire Extinguisher, 13.6.4.2.3.3
    Rechargeable Fire Extinguishers, 13.6.4.2.3.1
   Inspection Frequency, 13.6.4.2.1

Inspection Procedures, 13.6.4.2.2
   Inspection Procedure for Containers of Class D Extinguishing Agent, 13.6.4.2.2.5
  Inspection Record Keeping, 13.6.4.2.4
   Electronic Inspection Records, 13.6.4.2.4.2, A.13.6.4.2.4.2
   Manual Inspection Records, 13.6.4.2.4.1
 Installation of Portable Fire Extinguishers, 13.6.3
  General, 13.6.3.1
   Antifreeze, 13.6.3.1.4
   Electronic Monitoring and Alarm System, 13.6.3.1.5
   Extinguisher Readiness, 13.6.3.1.2
   Number of Extinguishers, 13.6.3.1.1, A.13.6.3.1.1
   Placement, 13.6.3.1.3
    Cabinets, 13.6.3.1.3.11

Location 13.6.3.1.3.11.2 Locked Cabinets 13.6.3.1.3.11.1

    Installation Height, 13.6.3.1.3.9
    Label Visibility, 13.6.3.1.3.10
    Visibility, 13.6.3.1.3.3
  Installations for Class A Hazards, 13.6.3.2
   Fire Extinguisher Size and Placement for Class A Hazards, 13.6.3.2.1
  Installations for Class B Hazards, 13.6.3.3
   Flammable Liquids of Appreciable Depth, 13.6.3.3.2
   Obstacle, Gravity/Three-Dimensional, and Pressure Fire Hazards, 13.6.3.3.3
   Spill Fires, 13.6.3.3.1
  Installations for Class C Hazards, 13.6.3.4, A.13.6.3.4
  Installations for Class D Hazards, 13.6.3.5
  Installations for Class K Hazards, 13.6.3.6
  Solid-Fuel Cooking Appliances, 13.6.3.7
 Selection of Portable Fire Extinguishers, 13.6.2
  Classification of Fires, 13.6.2.2
  Classification of Hazards, 13.6.2.4
   Classifying Occupancy Hazard, 13.6.2.4.1
    Extra Hazard, 13.6.2.4.1.3, A.13.6.2.4.1.3
    Light Hazard, 13.6.2.4.1.1, A.13.6.2.4.1.1
    Ordinary Hazard, 13.6.2.4.1.2, A.13.6.2.4.1.2
   Selection of Fire Extinguishers, 13.6.2.4.2, A.13.6.2.4.2
    General, 13.6.2.4.2.1
    Selection for Building Protection, 13.6.2.4.2.2
    Selection for Occupancy Hazards, 13.6.2.4.2.3
  Extinguisher Classification System, 13.6.2.3
  General Requirements, 13.6.2.1
  Selection for Specific Hazards, 13.6.2.5
   Areas Containing Oxidizers, 13.6.2.5.6
   Class B Fires, 13.6.2.5.1
    Extinguishers for Pressurized Liquid and Pressurized Gas Fires, 13.6.2.5.1.1, A.13.6.2.5.1.1

Thee-Dimensional Fires 13.6.2.5.1.1.1, A.13.6.2.5.1.1.1

   Class D Combustible Metal Fires, 13.6.2.5.7
   Class K Cooking Media Fires, 13.6.2.5.4, A.13.6.2.5.4
   Electronic Equipment Fires, 13.6.2.5.5, A.13.6.2.5.5
   Obstacle Fires, 13.6.2.5.2
   Water-Soluble Liquid Fires (Polar Solvents), 13.6.2.5.3, A.13.6.2.5.3
  Selection for Specific Locations, 13.6.2.6

Sprinkler Systems, 13.3
  General, 13.3.1
    Supervision, 13.3.1.8
      Alarm Signal Transmission, 13.3.1.8.2
      Supervisory Signals, 13.3.1.8.1
  Inspection, Testing, and Maintenance, 13.3.3
    Ceiling Tiles and Ceiling Assemblies, 13.3.3.3
    General Requirements, 13.3.3.4
      Manufacturer's Corrective Action, 13.3.3.4.2
      Records, 13.3.3.4.3
      Responsibility of the Property Owner or Designated Representative, 13.3.3.4.1
        Addressing Changes in Hazard, 13.3.3.4.1.7, A.13.3.3.4.1.7
        Antifreeze Information Sign, 13.3.3.4.1.11
        Changes in Occupancy, Use, Process, or Materials, 13.3.3.4.1.6, A.13.3.3.4.1.6
        Control Valve Location, 13.3.3.4.1.8
        Corrections and Repairs, 13.3.3.4.1.5, A.13.3.3.4.1.5
        Freeze Protection, 13.3.3.4.1.2, A.13.3.3.4.1.2
        Hydraulic Design Information Sign, 13.3.3.4.1.10, A.13.3.3.4.1.10
        Impairments, 13.3.3.4.1.12
        Information Sign, 13.3.3.4.1.9, A.13.3.3.4.1.9
        Notification of System Shutdown or Testing, 13.3.3.4.1.4
        Responsibility for Inspection, Testing, Maintenance, and Impairment, 13.3.3.4.1.1, A.13.3.3.4.1.1
          Accessibility. , 13.3.3.4.1.3, A.13.3.3.4.1.3
  Impairments, 13.3.3.6
    Emergency Impairments, 13.3.3.6.6, A.13.3.3.6.6
    General, 13.3.3.6.1
      Minimum Requirements, 13.3.3.6.1.1
    Impaired Equipment, 13.3.3.6.4
    Impairment Coordinator, 13.3.3.6.2
    Preplanned Impairment Programs, 13.3.3.6.5, A.13.3.3.6.5
    Restoring Systems to Service, 13.3.3.6.7, A.13.3.3.6.7
    Tag Impairment System, 13.3.3.6.3
  Sprinkler Systems, 13.3.3.5
    Maintenance — Dry Pipe Systems, 13.3.3.5.2, A.13.3.3.5.2
    Maintenance — Sprinklers, 13.3.3.5.1
      Protective Coverings, 13.3.3.5.1.10
      Replacement Sprinklers, 13.3.3.5.1.1
      Stock of Spare Sprinklers, 13.3.3.5.1.6, A.13.3.3.5.1.6
  Where Required, 13.3.2
    Existing Apartment Buildings, 13.3.2.16
    Existing Assembly Occupancies, 13.3.2.6
      Fire Protection, 13.3.2.6.5
    Existing Detention and Correctional Facilities, 13.3.2.12
    Existing Educational Occupancies, 13.3.2.8
    Existing Health Care Occupancies, 13.3.2.10
    Existing Hotels and Dormitories, 13.3.2.14
    Existing Mercantile Occupancies, 13.3.2.22
    Existing Residential Board and Care Facilities, 13.3.2.20
      Large Facilities, 13.3.2.20.1
        Domestic Water Supply Option, 13.3.2.20.1.6
        General, 13.3.2.20.1.1, A.13.3.2.20.1.1
        High-Rise Buildings, 13.3.2.20.1.3
        Impractical Evacuation Capability, 13.3.2.20.1.2
        Supervision, 13.3.2.20.1.5
      Small Facilities, 13.3.2.20.2
    High-Rise Buildings, 13.3.2.24
    Lodging or Rooming Houses, 13.3.2.17
    New and Existing Day Care, 13.3.2.27
      Existing Day Care, 13.3.2.27.2
      New Day Care, 13.3.2.27.1
    New Apartment Buildings, 13.3.2.15
      Attics, 13.3.2.15.2
      Convenience Openings, 13.3.2.15.4
    New Assembly Occupancies, 13.3.2.5
      Fire Protection, 13.3.2.5.5
    New Detention and Correctional Facilities, 13.3.2.11
    New Educational Occupancies, 13.3.2.7
    New Health Care Occupancies, 13.3.2.9
    New Hotels and Dormitories, 13.3.2.13
    New Industrial Occupancies, 13.3.2.28
    New Mercantile Occupancies, 13.3.2.21
      Extinguishing Requirements, 13.3.2.21.2
      Mall Buildings, 13.3.2.21.3
        Automatic Extinguishing Systems, 13.3.2.21.3.1
        Hose Connections, 13.3.2.21.3.2
    New Residential Board and Care Occupancies, 13.3.2.19
      Large Facilities, 13.3.2.19.1
        General, 13.3.2.19.1.1
        Supervision, 13.3.2.19.1.2
      Small Facilities, 13.3.2.19.2
    New Storage Occupancies, 13.3.2.25, A.13.3.2.25
      Bulk Storage of Tires, 13.3.2.25.4
      General Storage, 13.3.2.25.2, A.13.3.2.25.2
      High-Piled Storage, 13.3.2.25.1
      Mini-Storage Building, 13.3.2.25.5
    One- and Two-Family Dwellings, 13.3.2.18
    Underground and Limited Access Structures, 13.3.2.23
    Woodworking Operations, 13.3.2.26
Standpipe Systems, 13.2
  General, 13.2.1
  Inspection, Testing, and Maintenance, 13.2.3
    Existing Systems, 13.2.3.4
  Where Required, 13.2.2
    New and Existing Detention and Correctional Facilities, 13.2.2.4
Water Supply, 13.5
  Inspection, Testing, and Maintenance, 13.5.4
Fire Retardant
Definition, 3.3.134
Fire Scenario
Definition, 3.4.9, A.3.4.9
Design Fire Scenario
  Definition, 3.4.9.1

Fire Sprinkler Disclosure Statement for One- and Two-Family Dwellings, Annex E
Fire Watch
    Definition, 3.3.135
Fire, Recreational
    Definition, 3.3.123
Fires, Classification of
    Class A Fires
        Definition, 3.3.122.1
    Class B Fires
        Definition, 3.3.122.2
    Class C Fires
        Definition, 3.3.122.3
    Class D Fires
        Definition, 3.3.122.4
    Class K Fires
        Definition, 3.3.122.5
    Definition, 3.3.122
Fireworks
    Definition, 3.3.136, A.3.3.136
    Display Fireworks
        Definition, 3.3.136.1, A.3.3.136.1
Fixed Guideway Transit and Passenger Rail Systems, Chap. 37
    General, 37.1
Flame Spread
    Definition, 3.3.137, A.3.3.137
Flame Spread Index
    Definition, 3.3.138
Flammable and Combustible Liquids, Chap. 66
    Application of Area Classification, 66.8
    Automatic Fire Protection for Inside Liquid Storage Areas, 66.16
        Automatic Sprinkler and Foam-Water Sprinkler Fire Protection Systems, 66.16.4
        Containment, Drainage, and Spill Control, 66.16.8
        Definitions Specific to Section 66.16, 66.16.2
            Protected, 66.16.2.1, A.66.16.2.1
            Relieving-Style Container, 66.16.2.3, A.66.16.2.3
            Unprotected, 66.16.2.2, A.66.16.2.2
            Unsaturated Polyester Resin (UPR), 66.16.2.4, A.66.16.2.4
            Viscous Liquid, 66.16.2.5
            Water-Miscible Liquid, 66.16.2.6
        Distilled Spirits in Wooden Barrels, 66.16.10
            Fire Protection Layouts for Distilled Spirits in Wooden Barrels, 66.16.10.3
                In-Rack Layouts for Rack Storage of On-End Wooden Barrels, 66.16.10.3.2
                In-Rack Layouts for Rack Storage of On-Side Wooden Barrels, 66.16.10.3.1
            Palletize Storage Arrays, 66.16.10.1
            Rack Storage Arrays, 66.16.10.2
        Fire Protection System Design Criteria, 66.16.5
            General, 66.16.5.1
            Specific Design Criteria, 66.16.5.3
        Fire Protection System Design Schemes, 66.16.6
            Fire Protection System Design Scheme "A.", 66.16.6.1
            Fire Protection System Design Scheme "B.", 66.16.6.2
            Fire Protection System Design Scheme "C.", 66.16.6.3
            Fire Protection System Design Scheme "D.", 66.16.6.4
            Fire Protection System Design Scheme "E.", 66.16.6.5
                Water Demand, 66.16.6.5.7
            Fire Protection System Design Scheme "F.", 66.16.6.6
            In-Rack Sprinkler Layouts for Table 66.16.5.3.8, 66.16.6.7
        General Requirements, 66.16.3
        Other Automatic Fire Protection Systems, 66.16.9
        Scope, 66.16.1
        Water Supply, 66.16.7
    Bulk Loading and Unloading Facilities for Tank Cars and Tank Vehicles, 66.28
        Containment, Drainage, and Spill Control, 66.28.9, A.66.28.9
        Equipment, 66.28.10
        General Requirements, 66.28.3
            Bonding and Grounding and Stray Currents, 66.28.3.1
        Location of Loading and Unloading Facilities, 66.28.4
        Operating Requirements, 66.28.11
            Loading and Unloading of Tank Cars, 66.28.11.2
            Loading and Unloading of Tank Vehicles, 66.28.11.1
            Switch Loading, 66.28.11.3, A.66.28.11.3
        Roofed Structures, 66.28.5
        Scope, 66.28.1
    Classification of Liquids, 66.4
        Classification Scheme, 66.4.1
            Class I Liquids, 66.4.1.1
            Class II Liquids, 66.4.1.2
            Class III Liquids, 66.4.1.3
        Determination of Boiling Point (BP), 66.4.2
        Determination of Flash Point (FP), 66.4.3
    Definitions, 66.3
        General Definitions, 66.3.3
            Alcohol-Based Hand Rub, 66.3.3.1
            Area, 66.3.3.2
                Fire Area, 66.3.3.2.1
            Barrel, 66.3.3.3
            Basement, 66.3.3.4
            Boil-Over, 66.3.3.6, A.66.3.3.6
            Boiling Point, 66.3.3.5
            Building, 66.3.3.7
                Important Building, 66.3.3.7.1, A.66.3.3.7.1
                Storage Tank Building, 66.3.3.7.2
            Chemical Plant, 66.3.3.8
            Closed-Top Diking, 66.3.3.9
            Container, 66.3.3.10
                Closed Container, 66.3.3.10.1
                Intermediate Bulk Container, 66.3.3.10.2
            Control Area, 66.3.3.11
            Crude Petroleum, 66.3.3.12
            Cryogenic Fluid, 66.3.3.13
            Damage-Limiting Construction, 66.3.3.14
            Distillery, 66.3.3.15
            Fire Point, 66.3.3.16
            Flash Point, 66.3.3.17
            Fugitive Emissions, 66.3.3.18, A.66.3.3.18
            Hazardous Material or Hazardous Chemical, 66.3.3.19, A.66.3.3.19
            Hazardous Materials Storage Locker, 66.3.3.20

Hazardous Reaction or Hazardous Chemical Reaction, 66.3.3.21
Heat Transfer Fluid (HTF), 66.3.3.22
High-Hazard Level 2 Contents, 66.3.3.23
High-Hazard Level 3 Contents, 66.3.3.24
Incidental Liquid Use or Storage, 66.3.3.25
Liquid, 66.3.3.26
    Combustible Liquid, 66.3.3.26.1
    Flammable Liquid, 66.3.3.26.2
    Stable Liquid, 66.3.3.26.3
Operating Unit (Vessel) or Process Unit (Vessel), 66.3.3.27, A.66.3.3.27
Operations, 66.3.3.28
Process or Processing, 66.3.3.29, A.66.3.3.29
Protection for Exposures, 66.3.3.30
Refinery, 66.3.3.31
Safety Can, 66.3.3.32, A.66.3.3.32
Storage Tank, 66.3.3.33
    Aboveground Tank, 66.3.3.33.1
        Protected Aboveground Tank, 66.3.3.33.1.1
    Low-Pressure Tank, 66.3.3.33.2
    Portable Tank, 66.3.3.33.3
        Nonmetallic Portable Tank, 66.3.3.33.3.1, A.66.3.3.33.3.1
    Secondary Containment Tank, 66.3.3.33.4
Unit Operation or Unit Process, 66.3.3.34
Vapor Pressure, 66.3.3.35
Vapor Processing Equipment, 66.3.3.36
Vapor Processing System, 66.3.3.37, A.66.3.3.37
Vapor Recovery System, 66.3.3.38
Vent, 66.3.3.39
    Emergency Relief Vent, 66.3.3.39.1
Warehouse, 66.3.3.40, A.66.3.3.40
    General-Purpose Warehouse, 66.3.3.40.1
    Liquid Warehouse, 66.3.3.40.2
Dispensing, Handling, Transfer, and Use of Ignitible (Flammable or Combustible) Liquids, 66.18
Dispensing, Handling, Transfer, and Use, 66.18.4
General Requirements, 66.18.3
Incidental Operations, 66.18.5
Scope, 66.18.1
Ventilation for Dispensing Areas, 66.18.6
    Ventilation Type, 66.18.6.1
Electrical Systems, 66.7
General Requirements, 66.7.3
Scope, 66.7.1
Fire and Explosion Prevention and Risk Control, 66.6
Containment, Drainage, and Spill Control, 66.6.12, A.66.6.12
    Design Intent, 66.6.12.1, A.66.6.12.1
    Drainage, 66.6.12.4
    Secondary Containment, 66.6.12.3
    Spill Control, 66.6.12.2
Control of Ignition Sources, 66.6.5
    Electrical Systems, 66.6.5.5
    General, 66.6.5.1
    Hot Work, 66.6.5.3, A.66.6.5.3
    Smoking, 66.6.5.2
    Static Electricity, 66.6.5.4
Detection and Alarm Systems and Procedures, 66.6.6
Emergency Planning and Training, 66.6.9
Explosion Protection Systems, 66.6.8
Fire Protection and Fire Suppression Systems, 66.6.7
Hazards Analysis, 66.6.4
    General, 66.6.4.1
        Engineering Evaluation, 66.6.4.1.2
    Management of Change, 66.6.4.2
Inspection and Maintenance, 66.6.10
Management of Fire and Explosion Hazards, 66.6.3, A.66.6.3
Management of Security, 66.6.11
    General, 66.6.11.2
    Scope, 66.6.11.1
    Specific Requirements, 66.6.11.3
Scope, 66.6.1, A.66.6.1
General, 66.1
Permits, 66.1.6
Hazardous Materials Storage Lockers, 66.14
Design and Construction of Hazardous Materials Storage Lockers, 66.14.4
Designated Sites for Hazardous Materials Storage Lockers, 66.14.5
General Requirements, 66.14.3
Scope, 66.14.1, A.66.14.1
Storage Requirements, 66.14.6
Outdoor Storage, 66.15
General Requirements, 66.15.3
    Containment, Drainage, and Spill Control, 66.15.3.9
Outdoor Storage Adjacent to a Building, 66.15.4
Scope, 66.15.1
Piping Systems, 66.27
Bonding and Grounding, 66.27.9
Definitions Specific to Section 66.27, 66.27.2
    Corrosion Protection, 66.27.2.1
    Flexible Connector, 66.27.2.2
    Leak, 66.27.2.3
    Low Melting Point Materials, 66.27.2.4
    Secondary Containment, 66.27.2.5
General Requirements, 66.27.3
    Performance Standards, 66.27.3.1
    Tightness of Piping, 66.27.3.2
Identification and Marking of Piping Systems, 66.27.10, A.66.27.10
Installation of Piping Systems, 66.27.6
    Common Loading and Unloading Piping, 66.27.6.7
    Installation of Underground Piping, 66.27.6.5
    Valves, 66.27.6.6
Materials of Construction for Piping Systems, 66.27.4
    Ductile Iron, 66.27.4.2
    Lining Materials, 66.27.4.5
    Low Melting Point Materials, 66.27.4.4
    Materials of Construction for Valves, 66.27.4.3
    Materials Specifications, 66.27.4.1
    Metallic/Nonmetallic Composite Piping, 66.27.4.7
    Nonmetallic Piping, 66.27.4.6
Pipe Joints, 66.27.5
    Flexible Connectors, 66.27.5.2
    Friction Joints, 66.27.5.3

2024 Edition

Tightness of Pipe Joints, 66.27.5.1
Scope, 66.27.1
Special Requirements for Marine Piping Systems, 66.27.11
Testing of Piping Systems, 66.27.7
    Initial Testing, 66.27.7.1
    Initial Testing of Secondary Containment Piping, 66.27.7.2
    Testing During Maintenance, 66.27.7.3
Vent Piping, 66.27.8
    Vent Piping for Aboveground Storage Tanks, 66.27.8.1
        Extension of Emergency Vent Piping, 66.27.8.1.6, A.66.27.8.1.6
    Vent Piping for Underground Tanks, 66.27.8.2
Processing Facilities, 66.17
    Accessibility, 66.17.5
    Construction Requirements, 66.17.6
    Containment, Drainage, and Spill Control, 66.17.10
    Electrical Systems, 66.17.9
    Emergency Control Systems, 66.17.8, A.66.17.8
    Explosion Control, 66.17.12
    Fire Protection, 66.17.7, A.66.17.7
        Exterior, 66.17.7.2
        Interior, 66.17.7.1
    General Requirements, 66.17.3
    Location of Process Vessels and Equipment, 66.17.4
    Management of Operations Hazards, 66.17.15
    Process Equipment and Vessels, 66.17.14, A.66.17.14
    Scope, 66.17.1
    Ventilation, 66.17.11
Specific Operations, 66.19
    Cooking Oil Storage Tank Systems in Commercial Kitchens, 66.19.7
        Design and Construction of Cooking Oil Storage Tanks, 66.19.7.2
            Design Standards, 66.19.7.2.2
            Emergency Venting, 66.19.7.2.4
            Materials of Construction, 66.19.7.2.1
            Normal Venting, 66.19.7.2.3
            Prevention of Overfilling of Cooking Oil Storage Tanks, 66.19.7.2.5, A.66.19.7.2.5
            Tank Heating, 66.19.7.2.6
        Fire Protection for Cooking Oil Storage Tanks, 66.19.7.4
            Identification for Emergency Responders, 66.19.7.4.1
        Scope, 66.19.7.1
        Tank Installation and Testing, 66.19.7.3
            Field Testing, 66.19.7.3.4
            Foundations for and Anchoring of Cooking Oil Storage Tanks, 66.19.7.3.2
            Location of Cooking Oil Storage Tanks, 66.19.7.3.1
            Tank Openings Other than Vents, 66.19.7.3.3
        Transfer Lines, 66.19.7.5
            Design and Construction of Fresh Cooking Oil Transfer Lines, 66.19.7.5.1, A.66.19.7.5.1
            Design and Construction of Waste Cooking Oil Transfer Lines, 66.19.7.5.2, A.66.19.7.5.2
            Flow Control, 66.19.7.5.3
            Installation of Cooking Oil Transfer Lines in Plenum-Rated Spaces, 66.19.7.5.5
            Pressure Control, 66.19.7.5.4

            Testing of Cooking Oil Transfer Lines, 66.19.7.5.6
    Definitions Specific to Section 66.19, 66.19.2
        Cooking Oil, 66.19.2.1, A.66.19.2.1
    Recirculating Heat Transfer Systems, 66.19.4
        Fire Protection, 66.19.4.6
        Fuel Burner Controls and Interlocks, 66.19.4.4, A.66.19.4.4
        General Requirements, 66.19.4.2, A.66.19.4.2
        Operation, 66.19.4.7
        Piping, 66.19.4.5
        Scope, 66.19.4.1
        System Design, 66.19.4.3, A.66.19.4.3
    Scope, 66.19.1
    Solvent Distillation Units, 66.19.6
        Equipment, 66.19.6.2
        Liquid Storage, 66.19.6.5
        Location, 66.19.6.4
        Scope, 66.19.6.1
        Solvents, 66.19.6.3
    Vapor Recovery and Vapor Processing Systems, 66.19.5
        Emergency Shutdown Systems, 66.19.5.8
        Liquid Level Monitoring, 66.19.5.5
        Overfill Protection, 66.19.5.6
        Overpressure Protection and Vacuum Protection, 66.19.5.2
        Scope, 66.19.5.1
        Sources of Ignition, 66.19.5.7
            Electrical Area Classification, 66.19.5.7.2, A.66.19.5.7.2
            Explosion Protection, 66.19.5.7.7
            Flame Propagation, 66.19.5.7.6, A.66.19.5.7.6
            Friction Heat or Sparks from Mechanical Equipment, 66.19.5.7.5, A.66.19.5.7.5
            Spontaneous Ignition, 66.19.5.7.4, A.66.19.5.7.4
            Static Electricity, 66.19.5.7.3, A.66.19.5.7.3
            Vapor Release, 66.19.5.7.1
        Vapor Collection Systems, 66.19.5.4
        Vent Location, 66.19.5.3
Storage of Ignitible (Flammable or Combustible) Liquids in Containers — General Requirements, 66.9
    Acceptable Containers, 66.9.3
    Classification of Occupancies That Exceed the Maximum Allowable Quantities of Ignitible (Flammable or Combustible) Liquids per Control Area, 66.9.7
        Occupancy Classifications, 66.9.7.1, A.66.9.7.1
            Protection Level 2, 66.9.7.1.1
            Protection Level 3, 66.9.7.1.2
        Requirements for Specific Occupancies, 66.9.7.2, A.66.9.7.2
    Construction Requirements, 66.9.8
    Containment, Drainage, and Spill Control, 66.9.12
    Control Areas, 66.9.6
    Dispensing, Handling, and Use of Ignitible (Flammable or Combustible) Liquids in Storage Areas, 66.9.17
    Electrical Systems, 66.9.11
    Emergency Control Systems, 66.9.10, A.66.9.10
    Explosion Control, 66.9.15
    Fire Protection, 66.9.9
        Manual Fire Protection, 66.9.9.2

INDEX

Protected Storage, 66.9.9.1
General Requirements, 66.9.2
Liquid Storage Cabinets, 66.9.4, A.66.9.4
Maximum Allowable Quantities (MAQs) per Control Area, 66.9.5
    General Occupancy Limits, 66.9.5.1
    Special Occupancy Limits, 66.9.5.2
Outdoor Storage of Ignitible (Flammable or Combustible) Liquids, 66.9.18
Scope, 66.9.1
Separation from Incompatible Materials, 66.9.16
Ventilation, 66.9.13
Storage of Ignitible (Flammable or Combustible) Liquids in Tanks — Aboveground Storage Tanks, 66.22
    Aboveground Storage Tanks Located in Areas Subject to Flooding, 66.22.14
    Additional Requirements for Fire-Resistant Aboveground Storage Tanks, 66.22.9
    Additional Requirements for Protected Aboveground Storage Tanks, 66.22.10
    Collision Protection for Aboveground Storage Tanks, 66.22.15
    Control of Spills from Aboveground Storage Tanks, 66.22.11, A.66.22.11
        Impounding Around Tanks by Closed-Top Diking, 66.22.11.3
        Impounding Around Tanks by Open Diking, 66.22.11.2
        Remote Impounding, 66.22.11.1
        Secondary Containment–Type Aboveground Storage Tanks, 66.22.11.4
    Definitions Specific to Section 66.22, 66.22.2
        Fire-Resistant Tank, 66.22.2.1
        Floating Roof Tank, 66.22.2.2
        Protected Aboveground Tank, 66.22.2.3
    Emergency Relief Venting for Fire Exposure for Aboveground Storage Tanks, 66.22.7
        Extension of Emergency Vent Piping, 66.22.7.4, A.66.22.7.4
        General, 66.22.7.1
        Pressure-Relieving Devices, 66.22.7.3
        Weak Roof-to-Shell Seam Construction, 66.22.7.2
    Equipment, Piping, and Fire Protection Systems in Remote Impoundment Areas and Diked Areas, 66.22.12
        Combustible Materials, 66.22.12.5
        Drainage, 66.22.12.2
        Fire Protection Systems, 66.22.12.4
        Location of Equipment, 66.22.12.3, A.66.22.12.3
        Location of Piping, 66.22.12.1
    Fire Protection for Aboveground Storage Tanks, 66.22.8, A.66.22.8
    General Requirements, 66.22.3
    Inspection and Maintenance of Aboveground Storage Tanks, 66.22.17
    Installation Instructions for Aboveground Storage Tanks, 66.22.16
    Installation of Aboveground Storage Tanks, 66.22.5
        Foundations for and Anchoring of Aboveground Storage Tanks, 66.22.5.2
        Tank Supports, 66.22.5.1
    Location of Aboveground Storage Tanks, 66.22.4, A.66.22.4

        Location with Respect to Property Lines, Public Ways, and Important Buildings, 66.22.4.1
        Tank Storage of Liquids with Boil-Over Characteristics, 66.22.4.1.4
        Shell-to-Shell Spacing of Adjacent Aboveground Storage Tanks, 66.22.4.2
    Scope, 66.22.1
    Tank Openings Other Than Vents, 66.22.13
    Vent Piping for Aboveground Tanks, 66.22.6
Storage of Ignitible (Flammable or Combustible) Liquids in Tanks — Requirements for All Storage Tanks, 66.21
    Change of Stored Liquid, 66.21.9
    Definitions Specific to Section 66.21, 66.21.2
        Compartmented Tank, 66.21.2.1
    Design and Construction of Storage Tanks, 66.21.4
        Corrosion Protection, 66.21.4.5, A.66.21.4.5
            Internal Corrosion Protection for Metal Storage Tanks, 66.21.4.5.2
            Internal Corrosion Protection for Nonmetallic Tanks, 66.21.4.5.3
        Design Standards for Storage Tanks, 66.21.4.2
            Design Standards for Atmospheric Tanks, 66.21.4.2.1
            Design Standards for Low-Pressure Tanks, 66.21.4.2.2
            Design Standards for Pressure Vessels, 66.21.4.2.3
        Materials of Construction, 66.21.4.1
            Combustible Materials, 66.21.4.1.5
        Normal Venting for Storage Tanks, 66.21.4.3
            Storage Tank Venting, 66.21.4.3.1
        Tank Fill Pipes, 66.21.4.4
    Fire Prevention and Control, 66.21.6
        Control of Ignition Sources, 66.21.6.2
        Emergency Planning and Training, 66.21.6.5
        Fire Control, 66.21.6.4
        General Requirements, 66.21.6.1
        Inspection and Maintenance of Fire Protection and Emergency Response Equipment, 66.21.6.6
        Management of Fire and Explosion Hazards, 66.21.6.3
    General Requirements, 66.21.3
    Inspection and Maintenance of Storage Tanks and Storage Tank Appurtenances, 66.21.8
    Operation of Storage Tanks, 66.21.7
        Identification and Security, 66.21.7.2
            Identification for Emergency Responders, 66.21.7.2.1
            Security for Unsupervised Storage Tanks, 66.21.7.2.2, A.66.21.7.2.2
        Leak Detection and Inventory Records for Underground Storage Tanks, 66.21.7.5, A.66.21.7.5
        Prevention of Overfilling of Storage Tanks, 66.21.7.1
        Removal from Service of Storage Tanks, 66.21.7.4
            Closure of Aboveground Storage Tanks, 66.21.7.4.1, A.66.21.7.4.1
            Removal from Service of Underground Storage Tanks, 66.21.7.4.3
                Disposal of Tanks, 66.21.7.4.3.6
                Documentation, 66.21.7.4.3.7
                General, 66.21.7.4.3.1, A.66.21.7.4.3.1
                Permanent Closure in Place, 66.21.7.4.3.3
                Removal and Disposal, 66.21.7.4.3.4

Reuse of Underground Storage Tanks, 66.21.7.4.3.8
Temporary Closure, 66.21.7.4.3.2
Temporary Storage of Removed Tanks, 66.21.7.4.3.5
Reuse of Aboveground Storage Tanks, 66.21.7.4.2
Storage Tanks in Areas Subject to Flooding, 66.21.7.3
Operating Instructions, 66.21.7.3.2
Personnel Training, 66.21.7.3.3
Tank Loading, 66.21.7.3.1
Scope, 66.21.1
Testing Requirements for Tanks, 66.21.5
General, 66.21.5.1
Periodic Testing, 66.21.5.3, A.66.21.5.3
Tightness Testing, 66.21.5.2, A.66.21.5.2
Conditions Where Field Testing Is Not Required, 66.21.5.2.2
Storage of Ignitible (Flammable or Combustible) Liquids in Tanks — Underground Tanks, 66.23
Inspection and Maintenance of Underground Storage Tanks, 66.23.4
Installation Instructions for Underground Storage Tanks, 66.23.3
Underground Storage Tanks Located in Areas Subject to Flooding, 66.23.1
Storage Tank Buildings, 66.24
Construction of Storage Tank Buildings, 66.24.5
Containment, Drainage, and Spill Control from Storage Tank Buildings, 66.24.8
Detection and Alarm Systems for Storage Tank Buildings, 66.24.14
Electrical Systems for Storage Tank Buildings, 66.24.7
Explosion Control, 66.24.11
Fire Protection for Storage Tank Buildings, 66.24.6
Fixed Fire Control Equipment for Tank Buildings, 66.24.6.2
Manual Fire Control Equipment for Storage Tank Buildings, 66.24.6.1
Inspection and Maintenance for Storage Tank Buildings, 66.24.15
Location of Storage Tank Buildings, 66.24.4
Tank Openings Other than Vents for Tanks Inside Storage Tank Buildings, 66.24.13
Ventilation for Storage Tank Buildings, 66.24.9
Vents for Tanks Inside Storage Tank Buildings, 66.24.12
Storage Tank Vaults, 66.25
Construction and Installation of Storage Tank Vaults, 66.25.5
Construction Requirements, 66.25.5.1
Installation Requirements, 66.25.5.2
Containment, Drainage, and Spill Control for Storage Tank Vaults, 66.25.9
Detection and Alarm Systems for Storage Tank Vaults, 66.25.15
Electrical Systems for Storage Tank Vaults, 66.25.8
Explosion Control, 66.25.12
Fire Protection for Storage Tank Vaults, 66.25.6
General Requirements, 66.25.3
Storage Tank Appurtenances, 66.25.3.2
Storage Tank Selection and Arrangement, 66.25.3.1, A.66.25.3.1

Vault Arrangement, 66.25.3.3
Inspection and Maintenance of Storage Tank Vaults and Equipment, 66.25.16
Location of Storage Tank Vaults, 66.25.4
Scope, 66.25.1
Ventilation Systems for Storage Tank Vaults, 66.25.10
Vents for Tanks Inside Storage Tank Vaults, 66.25.13
Wharves, 66.29
General Requirements, 66.29.3
Scope, 66.29.1
Flammable Solids, Chap. 67
General, 67.1
Flammable Vapors
Definition, 3.3.139
Flash Point (FP)
Definition, 3.3.140
Floor Area
Definition, 3.3.141
Gross Floor Area
Definition, 3.3.141.1, A.3.3.141.1
Net Floor Area
Definition, 3.3.141.2
Forecasting
Definition, 3.3.142
Forest Products and Biomass Feedstocks, Chap. 31
General, 31.1, A.31.1
Permits, 31.2
Protection of Storage of Forest Products, 31.3
Application, 31.3.1
General Fire Protection, 31.3.2
Exposure Protection, 31.3.2.2
Fire Detection and Extinguishment, 31.3.2.3, A.31.3.2.3
Operational Fire Prevention, 31.3.2.1
Outside Storage of Biomass Feedstock, 31.3.10
Outside Storage of Logs, 31.3.8
Application, 31.3.8.1
General, 31.3.8.2, A.31.3.8.2
Log Yard Protection, 31.3.8.3, A.31.3.8.3
Outside Storage of Lumber and Wood Panel Products at Other Than Retail and Wholesale Storage Yards, 31.3.4
Application, 31.3.4.1, A.31.3.4.1
General, 31.3.4.2, A.31.3.4.2
Open Yard Storage, 31.3.4.3, A.31.3.4.3
Outside Storage of Lumber and Wood Panel Products at Retail and Wholesale Storage Yards, 31.3.3
Application, 31.3.3.1
Exposure Protection, 31.3.3.4
Exposure from the Yard, 31.3.3.4.2, A.31.3.3.4.2
Exposure to the Yard, 31.3.3.4.1
General, 31.3.3.2
Open Yard Storage, 31.3.3.3
Outside Storage of Ties, Poles, Piles, Posts, and Other Similar Forest Products at Pressure-Treating Plant Yards, 31.3.5
Application, 31.3.5.1
General, 31.3.5.2, A.31.3.5.2
Tie Yard Protection, 31.3.5.3, A.31.3.5.3

INDEX

Outside Storage of Wood Chips and Hogged Material, 31.3.6
    Application, 31.3.6.1, A.31.3.6.1
    Emergency Action Plan, 31.3.6.5
    Exposure Protection, 31.3.6.4
    General, 31.3.6.2
    Pile Protection, 31.3.6.3, A.31.3.6.3
Storage and Processing of Wood Chips, Hogged Material, Fines, Compost, and Raw Products at Yard Waste Recycling Facilities, 31.3.7, A.31.3.7
    Fire Protection, 31.3.7.4
    Static Pile Protection, 31.3.7.3
Wood Processing and Woodworking Facilities, 31.3.9

Fuel Load
    Definition, 3.4.10, A.3.4.10

Fugitive Emissions
    Definition, 3.3.143, A.3.3.143

-G-

Gallon, US Standard
    Definition, 3.3.144

Garage
    Definition, 3.3.145

Gas
    Compressed Gas
        Definition, 3.3.146.1, A.3.3.146.1
    Corrosive Gas
        Definition, 3.3.146.2
    Definition, 3.3.146
    Flammable Gas
        Definition, 3.3.146.3, A.3.3.146.3
    Flammable Liquefied Gas
        Definition, 3.3.146.4
    Highly Toxic Gas
        Definition, 3.3.146.5
    Inert Gas
        Definition, 3.3.146.6, A.3.3.146.6
    Liquefied Gas
        Definition, 3.3.146.7
    Liquefied Natural Gas (LNG)
        Definition, 3.3.146.8
    Liquefied Petroleum Gas (LP-Gas)
        Definition, 3.3.146.9, A.3.3.146.9
    Nonflammable Gas
        Definition, 3.3.146.10
    Other Gas
        Definition, 3.3.146.11, A.3.3.146.11
    Oxidizing Gas
        Definition, 3.3.146.12
    Pyrophoric Gas
        Definition, 3.3.146.13
    Scavenged Gas
        Definition, 3.3.146.14
    Simple Asphyxiant Gas
        Definition, 3.3.146.15
    Toxic Gas
        Definition, 3.3.146.16

Unstable Reactive Gas
    Definition, 3.3.146.17, A.3.3.146.17

Gas Cabinet
    Definition, 3.3.147, A.3.3.147

Gas Manufacturer/Producer
    Definition, 3.3.148

Gas Room
    Definition, 3.3.149

Gaseous Hydrogen (GH2) System
    Definition, 3.3.150, A.3.3.150

General Requirements, Chap. 4
    Assumptions, 4.2
        Incidents Impinging on Hazardous Materials, 4.2.3, A.4.2.3
        Single Fire Source, 4.2.1, A.4.2.1
        Single Hazardous Material Release, 4.2.2, A.4.2.2
    Compliance Options, 4.3
        Performance-Based Option, 4.3.2
        Prescriptive-Based Option, 4.3.1
    Fundamental Requirements, 4.4
        Appropriateness of Safeguards, 4.4.2
        Means of Egress, 4.4.3
            Awareness of Egress System, 4.4.3.2
                Lighting, 4.4.3.2.3
            Unobstructed Egress, 4.4.3.1
        Multiple Safeguards, 4.4.1
        Occupant Notification, 4.4.4, A.4.4.4
        System Design/Installation, 4.4.6
        Vertical Openings, 4.4.5
    General Requirements, 4.5
        Authority Having Jurisdiction (AHJ), 4.5.1
        Changes of Occupancy, 4.5.7, A.4.5.7
        Conditions for Occupancy, 4.5.4
        Construction, Repair, and Improvement Operations, 4.5.6
            Escape Facilities, 4.5.6.2
        Historic Structures and Cultural Resource Buildings, 4.5.2
        Limited-Combustible Material, 4.5.10, A.4.5.10
        Maintenance, Inspection, and Testing, 4.5.8
        Noncombustible Material, 4.5.9
        Provisions in Excess of Code Requirements, 4.5.3
        Warrant of Fitness, 4.5.5
    Goals and Objectives, 4.1, A.4.1
        Goals, 4.1.1, A.4.1.1
        Objectives, 4.1.2, A.4.1.2
        Property Protection, 4.1.4
            Property Protection Goal, 4.1.4.1
            Property Protection Objectives, 4.1.4.2
                Fire Spread and Explosions, 4.1.4.2.2, A.4.1.4.2.2
                Hazardous Materials, 4.1.4.2.4
                Prevention of Ignition, 4.1.4.2.1, A.4.1.4.2.1
                Structural Integrity, 4.1.4.2.3
        Public Welfare, 4.1.5
        Public Welfare Goal, 4.1.5.1, A.4.1.5.1
        Public Welfare Objective, 4.1.5.2, A.4.1.5.2
        Safety, 4.1.3, A.4.1.3
            Safety During Building Use, 4.1.3.2
                Safety-During-Building-Use Goal, 4.1.3.2.1, A.4.1.3.2.1
                Safety-During-Building-Use Objectives, 4.1.3.2.2

2024 Edition

Safety from Fire, 4.1.3.1
  Safety-from-Fire Goals, 4.1.3.1.1, A.4.1.3.1.1
  Safety-from-Fire Objectives, 4.1.3.1.2
Safety from Hazardous Materials, 4.1.3.3
  Safety-from-Hazardous-Materials Goal, 4.1.3.3.1
  Safety-from-Hazardous-Materials Objectives, 4.1.3.3.2
Security Features, 4.1.6, A.4.1.6

General Safety Requirements, Chap. 10
Alcohol-Based Hand-Rub (ABHR) Dispensers, 10.22, A.10.22
  ABHR Dispenser Capacity, 10.22.2
  ABHR Dispenser Location, 10.22.3
  ABHR Dispenser Operation and Testing, 10.22.4
  Personal Use Containers, 10.22.1
  Spill Containment and Maintenance, 10.22.5
Building Evacuation, 10.5
Combustible Vegetation, 10.13
  Exterior Vegetation, 10.13.2
  Interior Vegetation, 10.13.1
Emergency Action Plans, 10.4
  Plan Requirements, 10.4.2
  Where Required, 10.4.1
Fire Drills, 10.6, A.10.6
  Drill Frequency, 10.6.2, A.10.6.2
  Orderly Evacuation, 10.6.3
  Relocation Area, 10.6.5
  Simulated Conditions, 10.6.4, A.10.6.4
  Where Required, 10.6.1
Fire Protection Markings, 10.11
  Premises Identification, 10.11.1, A.10.11.1
  Shaftways to Be Marked for Fire Fighter Safety, 10.11.2
  Stairway Identification, 10.11.3, A.10.11.3
Fundamental Requirements, 10.1
  Building Code, 10.1.3
  Life Safety Code, 10.1.2, A.10.1.2
  Listed and Labeled, 10.1.7
  Structural Hazards, 10.1.4
Indoor Play Structures, 10.20
Occupancy, 10.3
  Change of Use or Occupancy Classification, 10.3.4
Open Flames, Candles, Open Fires, and Incinerators, 10.10
  Cooking Equipment, 10.10.6
  Discontinuance, 10.10.10, A.10.10.10
  Fire Attendant, 10.10.5
  Incinerators and Fireplaces, 10.10.8
  Installation of Patio Heaters, 10.10.7
  Open Fires, 10.10.4
  Open-Flame Devices, 10.10.9
  Outdoor Fires, 10.10.3
  Permits, 10.10.1
Outside Storage, 10.16, A.10.16
Owner/Operator/Tenant Responsibilities, 10.2
  Minimum Fire Prevention Inspection Frequencies for Existing Occupancies, 10.2.7
Parade Floats, 10.17
  Fire Protection, 10.17.2
  Permits, 10.17.1
Portable and Vehicle-Mounted Generators, 10.15
  Operation of Portable and Vehicle-Mounted Generators, 10.15.5
  Scope, 10.15.1
Powered Industrial Trucks, 10.18
Powered Micromobility Devices, 10.21
  Battery Charging, 10.21.4
  Charging Equipment, 10.21.2
  General, 10.21.1
  Listing, 10.21.3
Reporting of Fires and Other Emergencies, 10.7
  Fire Reporting, 10.7.1
Seasonal and Vacant Buildings and Premises, 10.12
Smoking, 10.9
Special Outdoor Events, Carnivals, and Fairs, 10.14
  Carbon Monoxide Alarm, 10.14.7
  Communications, 10.14.10
  Cooking, 10.14.9
  Crop Maze, 10.14.12
    Fireworks, 10.14.12.4
    General, 10.14.12.2
      Employee Monitor, 10.14.12.2.3
      Public Address System, 10.14.12.2.7
    Permits, 10.14.12.1
    Prohibited, 10.14.12.3
  Electrical Equipment, 10.14.8
  Internal Combustion Power Sources, 10.14.11
    Fire Extinguishers, 10.14.11.4
    Fueling, 10.14.11.1
    Protection, 10.14.11.3
    Refueling, 10.14.11.2
  Life Safety Evaluation, 10.14.3
    Building Systems and Facility Management Assessments, 10.14.3.3, A.10.14.3.3
      Building Systems. , 10.14.3.3.1
      Facility Management, 10.14.3.3.2
      Life Safety Evaluation, 10.14.3.3.3
    Conditions to Be Assessed, 10.14.3.2
    General, 10.14.3.1, A.10.14.3.1
    Life Safety Building Systems Document, 10.14.3.4
      Document Distribution, 10.14.3.4.1
      Engineering Analysis and Calculations, 10.14.3.4.4
      Life Safety Floor Plans, 10.14.3.4.3
      Life Safety Narrative, 10.14.3.4.2
    Life Safety Management Document. , 10.14.3.5
      Building Systems Reference Guide, 10.14.3.5.4
      Document Distribution, 10.14.3.5.1
      Facility Management and Operational Plans, 10.14.3.5.2
      Records, 10.14.3.5.3
  Permits, 10.14.1
  Portable Fire Extinguishers, 10.14.5
  Smoke Alarms, 10.14.6
  Standby Fire Personnel, 10.14.4
Storage of Combustible Materials, 10.19, A.10.19
  Attic, Under-Floor, and Concealed Spaces, 10.19.6
  Ceiling Clearance, 10.19.3
  Equipment Rooms, 10.19.5
  Fueled Equipment, 10.19.7

General, 10.19.1
Means of Egress, 10.19.4
Permits, 10.19.2
Tampering with Fire Safety Equipment, 10.8
General Storage, Chap. 34
    Building Construction, 34.4
        Construction Type, 34.4.1, A.34.4.1
        Emergency Smoke and Heat Venting, 34.4.3, A.34.4.3
        Fire-Fighting Access, 34.4.2
    Building Equipment, Maintenance, and Operations, 34.7
        Building Service Equipment, 34.7.2
        Cutting and Welding Operations, 34.7.3
        Industrial Trucks, 34.7.1
        Lighting, 34.7.8
        Maintenance and Inspection, 34.7.6, A.34.7.6
            Storage Plan Maintenance, 34.7.6.3
        Refrigeration Systems, 34.7.7
        Smoking, 34.7.5
        Waste Disposal, 34.7.4
    Classification of Commodities, 34.2
        Pallet Types, 34.2.2
            General, 34.2.2.1
            Plastic Pallet, 34.2.2.2
    Commodity Classes, 34.3, A.34.3
        Carton Records Storage, 34.3.13
        Classification of Plastics, Elastomers, and Rubber, 34.3.5, A.34.3.5
            Group A, 34.3.5.1
        Classification of Rolled Paper Storage, 34.3.10, A.34.3.10
            Heavyweight Class, 34.3.10.1
            Lightweight Class, 34.3.10.3
            Mediumweight Class, 34.3.10.2
            Tissue.[13:20.4.10.4], 34.3.10.4
        Class I, 34.3.1, A.34.3.1
        Class II, 34.3.2, A.34.3.2
        Class III, 34.3.3, A.34.3.3
        Class IV. [13:20.4.4], 34.3.4, A.34.3.4
        Display/Storage of Up to Group A Plastics, 34.3.12
            Baled Cotton, 34.3.12.1
        Group B, 34.3.6
        Group C, 34.3.7
        Mixed Commodities. [13:20.4.13], 34.3.14
            Mixed Commodity Segregation, 34.3.14.4
        Plastic Motor Vehicle Components, 34.3.11, A.34.3.11
        Rubber Tires, 34.3.9
    General, 34.1
        Application, 34.1.1
        Approved Storage Floor Plan, 34.1.3, A.34.1.3
        Permits, 34.1.2
    General Fire Protection, 34.6
        Alarm Service, 34.6.5
        Fire Organization, 34.6.4
        High-Expansion Foam, 34.6.2
        Manual Protection, 34.6.3
            Hydrants, 34.6.3.2
            Portable Fire Extinguishers, 34.6.3.1
        Security Service, 34.6.6
        Sprinkler Systems, 34.6.1, A.34.6.1
    Protection of Rack Storage, 34.8
        Application, 34.8.1
        Building Construction, 34.8.2
        Storage Arrangement, 34.8.3
            Aisle Widths, 34.8.3.3, A.34.8.3.3
            General Fire Protection, 34.8.3.4
                High-Expansion Foam, 34.8.3.4.1
                High-Expansion Foam Submergence, 34.8.3.4.2
            Rack Loading, 34.8.3.2, A.34.8.3.2
            Rack Structure, 34.8.3.1, A.34.8.3.1
    Protection of Roll Paper, 34.10
        Application, 34.10.1
        Building Construction, 34.10.2, A.34.10.2
        Storage Arrangement, 34.10.3
    Protection of Rubber Tires, 34.9
        Application, 34.9.1, A.34.9.1
        Building Arrangement, 34.9.2
            Fire Walls, 34.9.2.2
            Steel Columns, 34.9.2.1
            Travel Distance to Exits, 34.9.2.3, A.34.9.2.3
        Storage Arrangement, 34.9.3
            Clearances, 34.9.3.2
            Piling Procedures, 34.9.3.1
    Storage Arrangement, 34.5
        Aisles, 34.5.3
        Commodity Clearance, 34.5.2
        Flammable and Combustible Liquids, 34.5.4
        Piling Procedures and Precautions, 34.5.1, A.34.5.1
    Storage of Idle Pallets, 34.11
        General, 34.11.1, A.34.11.1
        Indoor Storage, 34.11.2
        Outdoor Storage, 34.11.3, A.34.11.3
        Outside Storage at Pallet Manufacturing and Pallet Recycling Facilities, 34.11.4
Grade Plane
    Definition, 3.3.151, A.3.3.151
Grandstands and Bleachers, Folding and Telescopic Seating, Tents, and Membrane Structures, Chap. 25
    Folding and Telescopic Seating, 25.4
        Guards and Railings, 25.4.2
        Maintenance and Operation of Folding and Telescopic Seating, 25.4.3
        Seating, 25.4.1
    General, 25.1
        Cooking, 25.1.11
        Detection, Alarm, and Communications Systems, 25.1.7
        Electrical Installations, 25.1.9
            Electrical Systems, 25.1.9.1
        Extinguishment Requirements, 25.1.6
            Portable Fire Extinguishers, 25.1.6.3
        Fire Detail, 25.1.8, A.25.1.8
        Fire Hazards, 25.1.5
            Open Flame Devices and Pyrotechnics, 25.1.5.4
        Flammable Liquids and Gases, 25.1.4
        Generators, 25.1.12
            Fire Extinguishers, 25.1.12.4

Fueling, 25.1.12.3
Heating Devices, 25.1.10
　Electric Heaters, 25.1.10.2
　Fired Heaters, 25.1.10.1
　　Air-Conditioning, Heating, Ventilating Ductwork, and Related Equipment, 25.1.10.1.4
　　Ventilating or Heat-Producing Equipment, 25.1.10.1.5
Means of Egress, 25.1.3
Permits, 25.1.2
Grandstands, 25.3
　Guards and Railings, 25.3.5
　Maintenance of Outdoor Grandstands, 25.3.6
　Seating, 25.3.1
　Spaces Underneath Grandstands, 25.3.4
　Special Requirements — Portable Grandstands, 25.3.3
　Special Requirements — Wood Grandstands, 25.3.2
Permanent Membrane Structures, 25.5
　Air-Supported and Air-Inflated Structures, 25.5.3
　　General, 25.5.3.1
　　Pressurization (Inflation) System, 25.5.3.2
　　Standby Power System, 25.5.3.3
　Application, 25.5.1
　　Flame Propagation Performance, 25.5.1.5
　　Flame Spread Index, 25.5.1.3
　　Roof Covering Classification, 25.5.1.4
　　Testing, 25.5.1.2
　　Use of Membrane Roofs, 25.5.1.1
　Maintenance and Operation, 25.5.4
　Tensioned-Membrane Structures, 25.5.2
Temporary Membrane Structures, 25.6
　Air-Supported and Air-Inflated Structures, 25.6.5
　　General, 25.6.5.1
　　Pressurization (Inflation) System, 25.6.5.2
　　Standby Power System, 25.6.5.3
　Application, 25.6.1
　　Alternative Requirements, 25.6.1.2
　　Flame Propagation Performance, 25.6.1.4
　　Required Approval, 25.6.1.1
　　Roof Covering Classification, 25.6.1.3
　Fire Hazards, 25.6.2
　Fire-Extinguishing Equipment, 25.6.3
　Maintenance and Operation, 25.6.6
　Tensioned-Membrane Structures, 25.6.4
Tents, 25.2
　Fire Hazards, 25.2.4
　　Smoking, 25.2.4.2
　Fire-Extinguishing Equipment, 25.2.5
　Flame Propagation Performance, 25.2.2
　General, 25.2.1
　Location and Spacing, 25.2.3

Ground Kettle
Definition, 3.3.152
Guide
Definition, 3.2.4

-H-

Handling
Definition, 3.3.153
Hazard of Contents
Definition, 3.3.154, A.3.3.154
High Hazard
　Definition, 3.3.154.1
Low Hazard Contents
　Definition, 3.3.154.2, A.3.3.154.2
Ordinary Hazard Contents
　Definition, 3.3.154.3, A.3.3.154.3
Hazard Rating
Definition, 3.3.155, A.3.3.155
Hazardous Material
Definition, 3.3.156
Hazardous Material Storage Facility
Definition, 3.3.157
Hazardous Materials, Chap. 60
　Classification of Materials, Wastes, and Hazard of Contents, 60.3
　　Classification of High-Hazard Contents, 60.3.1
　　　General, 60.3.1.1
　　Classification of Waste, 60.3.4, A.60.3.4
　　Mixtures, 60.3.2
　　Multiple Hazards, 60.3.3, A.60.3.3
　Emergency Action Planning, Fire Risk Control, and Chemical Hazard Requirements for Industrial Processes, 60.6
　Fundamental Requirements, 60.5
　　General Requirements, 60.5.1
　　　Applicability, 60.5.1.1
　　　Electrical Wiring and Equipment, 60.5.1.10
　　　　General, 60.5.1.10.1
　　　　Static Accumulation, 60.5.1.10.2
　　　Empty Containers and Tanks, 60.5.1.7
　　　General Storage, 60.5.1.13
　　　　Shelf Storage, 60.5.1.13.2
　　　　　Shelf Construction, 60.5.1.13.2.1
　　　　Storage, 60.5.1.13.1
　　　Hazardous Materials Storage Cabinets, 60.5.1.18
　　　Ignition Source Controls, 60.5.1.5
　　　　Energy-Consuming Equipment, 60.5.1.5.3
　　　　　Powered Industrial Trucks, 60.5.1.5.3.1, A.60.5.1.5.3.1
　　　　Open Flames and High-Temperature Devices, 60.5.1.5.2
　　　　Smoking, 60.5.1.5.1
　　　Installation of Tanks, 60.5.1.19
　　　　Aboveground Tanks, 60.5.1.19.2
　　　　　Marking, 60.5.1.19.2.3
　　　　Underground Tanks, 60.5.1.19.1
　　　Maintenance Required, 60.5.1.16
　　　Outdoor Storage and Use Areas, 60.5.1.15
　　　Personnel Training, 60.5.1.4, A.60.5.1.4
　　　　Awareness, 60.5.1.4.1
　　　　　Completion, 60.5.1.4.1.1
　　　　　Emergency Plan, 60.5.1.4.1.3
　　　　　Hazard Communications, 60.5.1.4.1.2
　　　　Documentation, 60.5.1.4.5

Emergency Responders, 60.5.1.4.4
Emergency Response Liaison, 60.5.1.4.3
Operations Personnel, 60.5.1.4.2
 Actions in an Emergency, 60.5.1.4.2.5
 Changes, 60.5.1.4.2.6
 Dispensing, Using, and Processing, 60.5.1.4.2.2
 Physical and Health Hazard Properties, 60.5.1.4.2.1
 Storage, 60.5.1.4.2.3
 Transport (Handling), 60.5.1.4.2.4
Protection from Light, 60.5.1.11
Protection from Vehicles, 60.5.1.9
Release of Hazardous Materials, 60.5.1.3
 Container Failure, 60.5.1.3.5
 Control and Mitigation of Unauthorized Releases, 60.5.1.3.2
 Notification of Unauthorized Releases, 60.5.1.3.4, A.60.5.1.3.4
 Overpack Containers, 60.5.1.3.6
 Prohibited Releases, 60.5.1.3.1
 Records of Unauthorized Releases, 60.5.1.3.3
 Responsibility for Cleanup of Unauthorized Releases, 60.5.1.3.7
Safety Data Sheets (SDS), 60.5.1.2, A.60.5.1.2
Seismic Protection, 60.5.1.14
Separation of Incompatible Materials, 60.5.1.12
Signs, 60.5.1.8
 General, 60.5.1.8.1
  Design and Construction, 60.5.1.8.1.1
  Language, 60.5.1.8.1.2
  Maintenance, 60.5.1.8.1.3
 Hazard Materials Identification, 60.5.1.8.2
  Identification of Containers, Cartons, and Packages, 60.5.1.8.2.2
  NFPA 704 Placard, 60.5.1.8.2.1
 No Smoking Signs, 60.5.1.8.3
Systems, Equipment, and Processes, 60.5.1.6
 Additional Regulations for Supply Piping for Health Hazard Materials, 60.5.1.6.3
 Design and Construction of Containers and Tanks, 60.5.1.6.1
 Equipment, Machinery, and Alarms, 60.5.1.6.4
 Piping, Tubing, Valves, and Fittings, 60.5.1.6.2
Testing, 60.5.1.17
General Requirements, 60.1
 Applicability, 60.1.1
 Applicability of Sections, 60.1.4
  Limited Applicability of this Chapter for Specific Material Classes, 60.1.4.3
  Quantities Exceeding the Maximum Allowable Quantities per Control Area, 60.1.4.2
  Quantities Not Exceeding the Maximum Allowable Quantities per Control Area, 60.1.4.1
 Facility Closure, 60.1.5
 Hazardous Materials Inventory Statement (HMIS), 60.1.7, A.60.1.7
 Hazardous Materials Management Plan (HMMP), 60.1.6
 Permits, 60.1.3
 Subjects Not Regulated, 60.1.2

Performance Alternative, 60.7
Permissible Storage and Use Locations, 60.4
 Control Areas, 60.4.2
  Construction Requirements for Control Areas, 60.4.2.2
  Number of Control Areas, 60.4.2.2.1
 General, 60.4.1
  Control Areas or Special Protection Required, 60.4.1.1
  High-Hazard Contents, 60.4.1.3
  Weather Protection Structures, 60.4.1.2
 Outdoor Areas, 60.4.4, A.60.4.4
  Outdoor Control Areas, 60.4.4.1
   General, 60.4.4.1.1
   Maximum Allowable Quantity per Outdoor Control Area, 60.4.4.1.2
   Number of Outdoor Control Areas, 60.4.4.1.3
  Outdoor Storage and Use Areas, 60.4.4.2
 Protection Levels, 60.4.3
  Detached Building Required for High-Hazard Level 2 and High-Hazard Level 3 Materials, 60.4.3.7
  Protection Level 1, 60.4.3.3
  Protection Level 2, 60.4.3.4
  Protection Level 3, 60.4.3.5
  Protection Level 4, 60.4.3.6
Special Definitions, 60.2
 Chemical Name, 60.2.1
 Closed System Use, 60.2.2
 Control Area, 60.2.3
 Dispensing, 60.2.4
 Flammable Solid, 60.2.5
 Hazardous Material, 60.2.6
 Health Hazard Material, 60.2.7
 Highly Toxic Material, 60.2.8
 Incompatible Material, 60.2.9
 Liquid, 60.2.10
 Open System Use, 60.2.11
 Organic Peroxide, 60.2.12
  Organic Peroxide Formulation, 60.2.12.1
   Class I, 60.2.12.1.1
   Class II, 60.2.12.1.2
   Class III, 60.2.12.1.3
   Class IV, 60.2.12.1.4
   Class V, 60.2.12.1.5
 Oxidizer, 60.2.13
  Class 1, 60.2.13.1
  Class 2, 60.2.13.2
  Class 3, 60.2.13.3
  Class 4, 60.2.13.4
 Physical Hazard Material, 60.2.14
 Pyrophoric Material, 60.2.15
 Solid Material, 60.2.16
 Toxic Material, 60.2.17
 Unstable (Reactive) Material, 60.2.18
 Use, 60.2.19
 Water-Reactive Material, 60.2.20
Hazardous Materials Storage Locker
 Definition, 3.3.158

2024 Edition

Hazardous Reaction or Hazardous Chemical Reaction
  Definition, 3.3.159, A.3.3.159
Heat Transfer Fluid (HTF)
  Definition, 3.3.160
Heliport
  Definition, 3.3.161, A.3.3.161
Highly Toxic and Toxic Solids and Liquids, Chap. 68
  General, 68.1
Hogged Material
  Definition, 3.3.162
Home
  Day-Care Home
    Definition, 3.3.163.1
  Definition, 3.3.163
  Nursing Home
    Definition, 3.3.163.2
Horizontal Exit
  Definition, 3.3.164

-I-

Immediately Dangerous to Life and Health (IDLH)
  Definition, 3.3.165, A.3.3.165
Imminent Danger
  Definition, 3.3.166, A.3.3.166
Impairment
  Definition, 3.3.167
In-Building Emergency Responder Communications Enhancement System
  Definition, 3.3.168
Incapacitation
  Definition, 3.4.11
Incident Commander (IC)
  Definition, 3.3.169, A.3.3.169
Incidental Liquid Use or Storage
  Definition, 3.3.170
Indicating Valve
  Definition, 3.3.171
Indoor Horticultural Grow Structure
  Definition, 3.3.172
Industrial Ovens and Furnaces, Chap. 51
  General, 51.1
    Application, 51.1.1
    Permits, 51.1.2
  Location, 51.2
  Safety Controls, 51.3
Informational References, Annex F
Initiating Device
  Definition, 3.3.173
Initiating Device Circuit
  Definition, 3.3.174
Input Data Specification
  Definition, 3.4.12
Inside Liquid Storage Area
  Definition, 3.3.175
ISO Module
  Definition, 3.3.176, A.3.3.176

-J-

Jurisdiction
  Definition, 3.3.177

-L-

Labeled
  Definition, 3.2.5
Laboratories Using Chemicals, Chap. 26
  General, 26.1
    Plans and Procedures, 26.1.6
  Permits, 26.2
Limit
  Ceiling Limit
    Definition, 3.3.178.1, A.3.3.178.1
  Definition, 3.3.178
  Permissible Exposure Limit (PEL)
    Definition, 3.3.178.2, A.3.3.178.2
  Short-Term Exposure Limit (STEL)
    Definition, 3.3.178.3, A.3.3.178.3
Limited-Combustible (Material)
  Definition, 3.3.179
Liquefied Petroleum Gases and Liquefied Natural Gases, Chap. 69
  General Provisions, 69.1
    Application, 69.1.1, A.69.1.1
      Stationary Installations, 69.1.1.3
    Permits, 69.1.2
  Installation of LP-Gas Systems, 69.3
    Application, 69.3.1, A.69.3.1
    Container Separation Distances, 69.3.5
      Aboveground Containers, 69.3.5.1
      Multiple Containers Less Than 125 gal (0.5 m3) Individual Water Capacity, 69.3.5.3
      Separation Distance Between Container Pressure Relief Valve and Building Openings, 69.3.5.4
      Underground or Mounded ASME Containers, 69.3.5.2
    Emergency Shutoff Valves, 69.3.10
    Installation in Areas of Heavy Snowfall, 69.3.11
    Installation of Appliances Other Than on Vehicles, 69.3.13
      Hose for Portable Appliances, 69.3.13.2
      Patio Heaters, 69.3.13.1
    Installation of Containers, 69.3.8
      General Requirements, 69.3.8.1
      Installation of Cylinders, 69.3.8.2
    Internal Valves, 69.3.9
      Emergency Remote Shutdown of Internal Valves, 69.3.9.4
      Thermal Activation, 69.3.9.3
    Location of Containers, 69.3.3
    Location of Containers Not Connected for Use, 69.3.4
    Location of Transfer Operations, 69.3.7
      Container Point of Transfer Location Requirements, 69.3.7.2
      Separation Distance from Point of Transfer, 69.3.7.3
      Transfer of Liquids, 69.3.7.1
    LP-Gas Systems in Buildings or on Building Roofs or Exterior Balconies, 69.3.12
      Additional Equipment Requirements for Cylinders, Equipment, Piping, and Appliances Used in

INDEX

Buildings, Building Roofs, and Exterior Balconies, 69.3.12.2
Application, 69.3.12.1
Buildings Housing Educational and Institutional Occupancies, 69.3.12.6
Buildings Housing Industrial Occupancies, 69.3.12.5
Buildings Under Construction or Undergoing Major Renovation, 69.3.12.3
Buildings Undergoing Minor Renovation When Frequented by the Public, 69.3.12.4
Cylinders on Roofs or Exterior Balconies, 69.3.12.9
Temporary Heating and Food Service Appliances in Buildings in Emergencies, 69.3.12.7
Use in Buildings for Demonstrations or Training, and Use of Small Cylinders for Self-Contained Torch Assemblies and Food Service Appliances, 69.3.12.8
LP-Gas Systems on Vehicles (Other Than Engine Fuel Systems), 69.3.14
Appliance Installation on Vehicles, 69.3.14.7
Application, 69.3.14.1, A.69.3.14.1
Container Installation Requirements, 69.3.14.3
Equipment Installation, 69.3.14.6
Installation of Container Appurtenances, 69.3.14.4
Nonapplication, 69.3.14.2
Parking, Servicing, and Repair, 69.3.14.8
Piping, 69.3.14.5
Nonapplication, 69.3.2
Other Container Location Requirements, 69.3.6
Additional Container Installation Requirements, 69.3.6.3
ASME Multicontainer Requirements, 69.3.6.1
Structure Requirements, 69.3.6.4, A.69.3.6.4
Underground and Mounded ASME Containers, 69.3.6.2
Vehicle Fuel Dispenser and Dispensing Systems, 69.3.15
Application, 69.3.15.1
General Installation Provisions, 69.3.15.3
Installation of Vehicle Fuel Dispensers, 69.3.15.4
Location, 69.3.15.2
Liquefied Natural Gas (LNG) Facilities, 69.8
LP-Gas Equipment and Appliances, 69.2
Container Appurtenances, 69.2.9
Materials, 69.2.9.1
Containers, 69.2.1
Container Marking, 69.2.1.4
General, 69.2.1.1
Portable Container Appurtenance Physical Damage Protection, 69.2.1.2
Portable Storage Containers, 69.2.1.3
Containers with Attached Supports, 69.2.6
Porta-Pacs, 69.2.6.3
Skid Tanks, 69.2.6.2
Vertical ASME Containers, 69.2.6.1
Piping (Including Hose), Fittings, and Valves, 69.2.10
LP-Gas Liquid Transfer, 69.4
Operational Safety, 69.4.2
Arrangement and Operation of Transfer Systems, 69.4.2.3
Filling and Evacuating of Containers, 69.4.2.2
Damage, 69.4.2.2.7, A.69.4.2.2.7
Hose Inspection, 69.4.2.4

Transfer Personnel, 69.4.2.1
Scope, 69.4.1, A.69.4.1
Venting LP-Gas to the Atmosphere, 69.4.3
Outdoors, 69.4.3.1
LP-Gases at Utility Plants, 69.7
Storage of Cylinders Awaiting Use, Resale, or Exchange, 69.5
Automated Cylinder Exchange Stations, 69.5.6
Fire Protection and Electrical Area Classification, 69.5.5
General Provisions, 69.5.2
General Location of Cylinders, 69.5.2.1
Protection of Valves on Cylinders in Storage, 69.5.2.2
Scope, 69.5.1
Storage Outside of Buildings, 69.5.4
Alternative Location and Protection of Storage, 69.5.4.3
Location of Storage Outside of Buildings, 69.5.4.1, A.69.5.4.1
Fire-Resistive Protective Structure, 69.5.4.1.3
Protection of Cylinders, 69.5.4.2
Storage Within Buildings, 69.5.3
General, 69.5.3.1
Storage in Restaurants and Food Service Locations, 69.5.3.3
Storage Within Buildings Frequented by the Public, 69.5.3.2
Storage Within Buildings Not Frequented by the Public, 69.5.3.4
Storage Within Residential Buildings, 69.5.3.6
Storage Within Special Buildings or Rooms, 69.5.3.5
Vehicular Transportation of LP-Gas, 69.6
Parking and Garaging Vehicles Used to Carry LP-Gas Cargo, 69.6.2
Application, 69.6.2.1
Parking Indoors, 69.6.2.3
Parking Outdoors, 69.6.2.2
Transportation in Portable Containers, 69.6.1
Fire Extinguishers, 69.6.1.2
Transportation of Cylinders, 69.6.1.1

Liquid
Combustible Liquid
Definition, 3.3.180.1
Definition, 3.3.180
Flammable Liquid
Definition, 3.3.180.2
Highly Volatile Liquid
Definition, 3.3.180.3
Ignitible Liquid
Definition, 3.3.180.4, A.3.3.180.4
Liquid Class
Definition, 3.3.180.5
Stable Liquid
Definition, 3.3.180.6
Listed
Definition, 3.2.6, A.3.2.6
Log
Definition, 3.3.181
Loose House
Definition, 3.3.182

Lumber
    Definition, 3.3.183

-M-

Manual Emergency Shutoff Valve
    Definition, 3.3.184
Manual Fire Alarm Box
    Definition, 3.3.185
Manual Pull Station
    Definition, 3.3.186
Manufactured Home and Recreational Vehicle Sites, Chap. 27
    General, 27.1
    Manufactured Home Sites, 27.2
    Recreational Vehicle Parks and Campgrounds, 27.3
Marinas, Boatyards, Marine Terminals, Piers, and Wharves, Chap. 28
    Construction, Conversion, Repair, and Lay-Up of Vessels, 28.3
    Marinas, Boatyards, and Other Recreational Marine Facilities, 28.1
        Berthing and Storage, 28.1.3
            Dry Storage, 28.1.3.2
                Battery Storage, 28.1.3.2.4, A.28.1.3.2.4
                General, 28.1.3.2.1
                    Fire Department Access, 28.1.3.2.1.8
                    Heaters, 28.1.3.2.1.1
                In-Out Dry Storage and Rack Storage, 28.1.3.2.3
                Indoors, 28.1.3.2.2
            Wet Storage and Berthing, 28.1.3.1
        Fire Protection, 28.1.2
            Automatic Fire Detectors, 28.1.2.8
            Exposure Protection, 28.1.2.6, A.28.1.2.6
            Fire Standpipe Systems, 28.1.2.3, A.28.1.2.3
            Fixed Fire-Extinguishing Systems, 28.1.2.2, A.28.1.2.2
                Buildings Exceeding 5000 ft2 (465 m2), 28.1.2.2.2, A.28.1.2.2.2
                Buildings on Piers and Covered Piers, 28.1.2.2.1
                Combustible Piers and Substructures, 28.1.2.2.3
                Indoor Rack Storage, 28.1.2.2.4
            Hydrants and Water Supplies, 28.1.2.5
            In-Out Dry Storage and Rack Storage, 28.1.2.4
            Portable Fire Extinguishers, 28.1.2.1
                Placement, 28.1.2.1.1
                Visibility and Identification, 28.1.2.1.2
            Transmittal of Fire Emergency, 28.1.2.7
        Operational Hazards, 28.1.4
            Conditions on Individual Boats, 28.1.4.1, A.28.1.4.1
            General Precautions, 28.1.4.2
        Scope, 28.1.1
    Marine Terminals, Piers, and Wharves, 28.2
Marine Terminal
    Definition, 3.3.187
Marine Vessel
    Definition, 3.3.188
Material
    Combustible (Material)
        Definition, 3.3.189.1
    Compatible Material
        Definition, 3.3.189.2
    Corrosive Material
        Definition, 3.3.189.3, A.3.3.189.3
    Definition, 3.3.189
    Hazardous Material
        Definition, 3.3.189.4, A.3.3.189.4
    Hazardous Production Material (HPM)
        Definition, 3.3.189.5
    Health Hazard Material
        Definition, 3.3.189.6
    Highly Toxic Material
        Definition, 3.3.189.7, A.3.3.189.7
    Hogged Material
        Definition, 3.3.189.8
    Incompatible Material
        Definition, 3.3.189.9, A.3.3.189.9
    Limited-Combustible (Material)
        Definition, 3.3.189.10
    Noncombustible Material
        Definition, 3.3.189.11
    Physical Hazard Material
        Definition, 3.3.189.12
    Pyrophoric Material
        Definition, 3.3.189.13
    Toxic Material
        Definition, 3.3.189.14, A.3.3.189.14
    Unstable (Reactive) Material
        Definition, 3.3.189.15, A.3.3.189.15
    Water-Reactive Material
        Definition, 3.3.189.16, A.3.3.189.16
Maximum Allowable Quantity (MAQ)
    Definition, 3.3.190, A.3.3.190
Means of Egress
    Definition, 3.3.191, A.3.3.191
Means of Egress, Chap. 14
    Application, 14.1
    Arrangement of Means of Egress, 14.10
        Accessible Means of Egress, 14.10.4
        Exterior Ways of Exit Access, 14.10.3
        General, 14.10.1
        Impediments to Egress, 14.10.2
    Capacity of Means of Egress, 14.8
        Egress Capacity, 14.8.3, A.14.8.3
            Minimum Width, 14.8.3.4
        Measurement of Means of Egress, 14.8.2
        Occupant Load, 14.8.1
            Capacity from a Point of Convergence, 14.8.1.5
            Egress Capacity from Balconies and Mezzanines, 14.8.1.6
            Exits Serving More than One Story, 14.8.1.4
            Occupant Load Factor, 14.8.1.2, A.14.8.1.2
            Occupant Load Increases, 14.8.1.3
            Sufficient Capacity, 14.8.1.1
    Discharge from Exits, 14.11
        Arrangement and Marking of Exit Discharge, 14.11.3
        Components of Exit Discharge, 14.11.4
        Discharge to Roofs, 14.11.6
        Exit Discharge Through Interior Building Areas, 14.11.2
        Exit Termination, 14.11.1, A.14.11.1

Signs, 14.11.5
Door Openings, 14.5
    Door Openings in Folding Partitions, 14.5.8
    Inspection of Door Openings, 14.5.10
    Locks and Latches, 14.5.2
        Key-Operated Locks, 14.5.2.6
        Latch-Release Devices, 14.5.2.3, A.14.5.2.3
        Stair Enclosure Re-entry, 14.5.2.7, A.14.5.2.7
    Powered Door Leaf Operation, 14.5.5, A.14.5.5
        General, 14.5.5.1, A.14.5.5.1
        Self-Closing or Self-Latching Door Leaf Operation, 14.5.5.2
    Revolving Door Assemblies, 14.5.6
    Self-Closing Devices, 14.5.4
        Delayed Action Closers, 14.5.4.4
    Special Locking Arrangements, 14.5.3, A.14.5.3
        Delayed-Egress Electrical Locking Systems, 14.5.3.1, A.14.5.3.1
        Door Hardware Release of Electrically Locked Egress Door Assemblies, 14.5.3.3
        Elevator Lobby Exit Access Door Assemblies Locking, 14.5.3.4, A.14.5.3.4
        Panic Hardware and Fire Exit Hardware, 14.5.3.5, A.14.5.3.5
        Sensor-Release of Electrical Locking Systems, 14.5.3.2, A.14.5.3.2
    Special-Purpose Horizontally Sliding Accordion or Folding Door Assemblies, 14.5.9
    Swing and Force to Open, 14.5.1
        Door Leaf Encroachment, 14.5.1.3, A.14.5.1.3
        Door Leaf Swing Direction, 14.5.1.2, A.14.5.1.2
        Door Unlatching and Leaf Operating Forces, 14.5.1.5
        Screen Door Assemblies and Storm Door Assemblies, 14.5.1.4
        Swinging-Type Door Assembly Requirement, 14.5.1.1, A.14.5.1.1
    Turnstiles and Similar Devices, 14.5.7
Emergency Lighting, 14.13
    General, 14.13.1
    Periodic Testing of Emergency Lighting Equipment, 14.13.2
Enclosure and Protection of Stairs, 14.6
    Enclosures, 14.6.1
    Exposures, 14.6.2, A.14.6.2
    Usable Space, 14.6.3, A.14.6.3
Exit Access Corridors, 14.2
Exit Passageways, 14.7, A.14.7
    Enclosure, 14.7.2
    General, 14.7.1, A.14.7.1
    Stair Discharge, 14.7.3
    Width, 14.7.4
Exits, 14.3
Illumination of Means of Egress, 14.12
    General, 14.12.1
    Sources of Illumination, 14.12.2
Marking of Means of Egress, 14.14
    Directional Signs, 14.14.2
    Externally Illuminated Signs, 14.14.6
        Level of Illumination, 14.14.6.3, A.14.14.6.3
        Size and Location of Directional Indicator, 14.14.6.2, A.14.14.6.2
        Size of Signs, 14.14.6.1, A.14.14.6.1
    General, 14.14.1
        Existing Exemption, 14.14.1.4
        Exit Access, 14.14.1.5
        Exit Stair Door Tactile Signage, 14.14.1.3
        Exits, 14.14.1.2
        Floor Proximity Egress Path Marking, 14.14.1.7, A.14.14.1.7
        Floor Proximity Exit Signs, 14.14.1.6, A.14.14.1.6
        Mounting Location, 14.14.1.9
        Visibility, 14.14.1.8, A.14.14.1.8
        Where Required, 14.14.1.1
    Illumination of Signs, 14.14.5
        Continuous Illumination, 14.14.5.2, A.14.14.5.2
        General, 14.14.5.1, A.14.14.5.1
    Internally Illuminated Signs, 14.14.7
        Listing, 14.14.7.1
        Photoluminescent Signs, 14.14.7.2, A.14.14.7.2
    Power Source, 14.14.4, A.14.14.4
    Sign Legend, 14.14.3, A.14.14.3
    Special Signs, 14.14.8
        Characters, 14.14.8.2
        No Exit, 14.14.8.3, A.14.14.8.3
        Sign Illumination, 14.14.8.1
Means of Egress Reliability, 14.4
    Furnishings and Decorations in Means of Egress, 14.4.2
    Impediments to Egress, 14.4.3
    Maintenance, 14.4.1, A.14.4.1
Number of Means of Egress, 14.9
    General, 14.9.1
        Elevator Landing and Lobby Exit Access, 14.9.1.6
    Spaces About Electrical Equipment, 14.9.2
        600 Volts, Nominal, or Less, 14.9.2.1
            Door Unlatching and Direction of Door Swing, 14.9.2.1.2
            Number of Means of Egress, 14.9.2.1.1
        Over 600 Volts, Nominal, 14.9.2.2
            Door Unlatching and Direction of Door Swing, 14.9.2.2.2
            Number of Means of Egress, 14.9.2.2.1
Secondary Means of Escape, 14.15

Means of Escape
    Definition, 3.3.192

Mechanical Refrigeration, Chap. 53
    General, 53.1, A.53.1
        Applicability, 53.1.1
            Ammonia Refrigeration, 53.1.1.3
        Permits and Plans, 53.1.2
        Reference Codes and Standards. , 53.1.3
    Operations, Maintenance, Testing, and Decommissioning, 53.3
        Operations and Maintenance, 53.3.1
            Access to System, 53.3.1.2
            Changing of Refrigerant Type, 53.3.1.4
            General, 53.3.1.1
            Notification of Fugitive Releases, 53.3.1.7
            Permissible Refrigerant Discharges, 53.3.1.6

Records of Refrigerant Quantities, 53.3.1.5
Storage in Machinery Rooms, 53.3.1.3
Testing of Equipment, 53.3.2
Acceptance Testing, 53.3.2.1
Periodic Testing, 53.3.2.2
Records of Required Testing, 53.3.2.3
Testing Personnel Qualifications, 53.3.2.4
Safety Features, 53.2
Emergency Pressure Control System, 53.2.1
High- and Intermediate-Pressure Zones, 53.2.1.1
Automatic Emergency Stop, 53.2.1.1.4
Manual Operation, 53.2.1.1.2
Overpressure Limit Set Point for Crossover Valves, 53.2.1.1.1
System Design Pressure, 53.2.1.1.3
Low-Pressure Zone, 53.2.1.2
Automatic Emergency Stop, 53.2.1.2.2
Overpressure Limit Set Point for Emergency Stop, 53.2.1.2.1
Refrigeration Machinery Rooms, 53.2.3
Electrical, 53.2.3.4
Prohibited Sources of Ignition, 53.2.3.2, A.53.2.3.2
Refrigerant Vapor Detection, Monitoring, Alarm, and Electrical Systems, 53.2.3.1
Alarm Threshold, 53.2.3.1.1
Audibility, 53.2.3.1.3
Emergency Shutoff Interface, 53.2.3.1.4, A.53.2.3.1.4
Installation and Maintenance, 53.2.3.1.7
Location of Signaling Devices, 53.2.3.1.2
Monitoring and Annunciation, 53.2.3.1.6
Power and Supervision, 53.2.3.1.5
Ventilation Systems, 53.2.3.3
Signs and Labels, 53.2.4
General, 53.2.4.1
Systems with More Than 110 lb (50 kg) of Refrigerant, 53.2.4.2
Treatment, Flaring, and Diffusion Systems for Refrigerant Discharge, 53.2.2
Design of Flaring Systems, 53.2.2.2
Required Systems, 53.2.2.1
Flammable Refrigerants, 53.2.2.1.2
Toxic and Highly Toxic Refrigerants, 53.2.2.1.1

Mezzanine
Definition, 3.3.193

Micromobility Device, Powered
Definition, 3.3.194, A.3.3.194

Miscella
Definition, 3.3.195

Mobile or Temporary Cooking
Definition, 3.3.197, A.3.3.197

Mobile Supply Unit
Definition, 3.3.196, A.3.3.196

Motion Picture and Television Production Studio Soundstages and Approved Production Facilities, Chap. 32
Decorative Materials, 32.4
Fire Department Access, 32.7, A.32.7
Fire Watch, 32.3
Other Hazards, 32.3.3
General, 32.1
Housekeeping, 32.8
Permits, 32.2
Production Locations, 32.10
Electrical Requirements, 32.10.1
Fire Protection, 32.10.3
Fire Hydrants and Fire Appliances, 32.10.3.8
Means of Egress, 32.10.2, A.32.10.2
Operating Features, 32.10.4
Audience Life Safety, 32.10.4.4, A.32.10.4.4
Emergency Services Notification, 32.10.4.5
Ignitible (Flammable or Combustible) Liquids, 32.10.4.2
Waste or Refuse, 32.10.4.1
Welding, 32.10.4.3
Pyrotechnic Special Effects and Open Flames, 32.6
Smoking, 32.5
Soundstages and Approved Production Facilities, 32.9
Air Conditioning, Heating, and Ventilating, 32.9.5
Electrical Requirements, 32.9.2
Fire Protection, 32.9.4
Extinguishment Requirements, 32.9.4.1
Fire Alarm System, 32.9.4.2
General, 32.9.1
Means of Egress, 32.9.3
Emergency Instruction to Audience, 32.9.3.7

Motor Fuel Dispensing Facilities and Repair Garages, Chap. 30
Motor Fuel Dispensing Facilities, 30.1
Application, 30.1.1
Permits, 30.1.1.3
Drainage, 30.1.4
Fixed Fire Protection, 30.1.5
Fuel Dispensing Areas Inside Buildings, 30.1.6
Mechanical Exhaust System, 30.1.6.7, A.30.1.6.7
Number of Vehicles Simultaneously Served, 30.1.6.6
Means of Egress, 30.1.3
Occupancy Classification, 30.1.2
Operational Requirements, 30.4
Repair Garages for Vehicles Powered by Alternate Fuels, 30.3
Battery-Powered Electric Vehicles, 30.3.4
Construction, 30.3.4.3
Fixed Fire Protection, 30.3.4.4
Means of Egress, 30.3.4.2
Occupancy Classification, 30.3.4.1
CNG Fueled Vehicles and LNG Fueled Vehicles, 30.3.3
Applicability, 30.3.3.1
CNG and LNG Defueling Equipment, 30.3.3.14
Bonding and Grounding, 30.3.3.14.6
Captive Vent Systems, 30.3.3.14.7
General, 30.3.3.14.1
Construction Requirements of CNG and LNG Repair Areas, 30.3.3.6
Definition and Classification of Repair Areas Serving CNG and LNG Vehicle Repair, 30.3.3.4
Applicability, 30.3.3.4.1
CNG Repair Area Classification, 30.3.3.4.2
LNG Repair Area Classification, 30.3.3.4.3
Drainage, 30.3.3.5

Fixed Fire Protection, 30.3.3.10
Gas Detection System, 30.3.3.11
Failure of the Gas Detection System, 30.3.3.11.3
Operation, 30.3.3.11.2, A.30.3.3.11.2
System Design, 30.3.3.11.1
System Integrity, 30.3.3.11.4
Heat-Producing Appliances and Other Sources of Ignition, 30.3.3.13
Fired Heating Equipment, 30.3.3.13.4
Heating, Ventilating, and Air Conditioning, 30.3.3.12
Means of Egress, 30.3.3.3
Occupancy Classification, 30.3.3.2
Pits, Belowgrade Work Areas, and Subfloor Work Areas, 30.3.3.9
Roofs and Ceilings — Major and Minor Repair Areas, 30.3.3.7
Walls and Partitions — Major and Minor Repair Areas, 30.3.3.8
Hydrogen, 30.3.1
Means of Egress, 30.3.1.2
LP-Gas-Fueled Vehicles, 30.3.2
Drainage, 30.3.2.3
Fixed Fire Protection, 30.3.2.5
Gas Detection System, 30.3.2.6
Failure of the Gas Detection System, 30.3.2.6.3
Operation, 30.3.2.6.2
System Design, 30.3.2.6.1
System Integrity, 30.3.2.6.4
General Construction Requirements, 30.3.2.1
Heat-Producing Appliances, 30.3.2.8
Listing and Restricted Locations, 30.3.2.8.2
Heating, Ventilating, and Air-Conditioning, 30.3.2.7
Means of Egress, 30.3.2.2
Pits, Belowgrade Work Areas, and Subfloor Work Areas for LP-Gas Powered Vehicles, 30.3.2.4
Repair Garages for Vehicles Powered by Flammable and Combustible Liquids, 30.2
Application, 30.2.1
Permits, 30.2.1.1
Drainage, 30.2.4
Fixed Fire Protection, 30.2.5
Gas Detection System, 30.2.6
Failure of the Gas Detection System, 30.2.6.3
Operation, 30.2.6.2
System Design, 30.2.6.1
System Integrity, 30.2.6.4
Heat-Producing Appliances, 30.2.8
Listing and Restricted Locations, 30.2.8.2
Heating, Ventilating, and Air-Conditioning, 30.2.7, A.30.2.7
Means of Egress, 30.2.3
Occupancy Classification, 30.2.2
Motor Vehicle Fluid
Definition, 3.3.198

-N-

Nesting
Definition, 3.3.199

Normal Temperature and Pressure (NTP)
Definition, 3.3.200, A.3.3.200
Nuisance Alarm
Definition, 3.3.201, A.3.3.201

-O-

Observation
Definition, 3.3.202
Occupancy
Ambulatory Health Care Occupancy
Definition, 3.3.203.1, A.3.3.203.1
Apartment Building
Definition, 3.3.203.2, A.3.3.203.2
Assembly Occupancy
Definition, 3.3.203.3, A.3.3.203.3
Bulk Merchandising Retail Building
Definition, 3.3.203.4
Business Occupancy
Definition, 3.3.203.5, A.3.3.203.5
Day-Care Home
Definition, 3.3.203.6, A.3.3.203.6
Day-Care Occupancy
Definition, 3.3.203.7, A.3.3.203.7
Definition, 3.3.203
Detention and Correctional Occupancy
Definition, 3.3.203.8, A.3.3.203.8
Dormitory
Definition, 3.3.203.9, A.3.3.203.9
Educational Occupancy
Definition, 3.3.203.10, A.3.3.203.10
Health Care Occupancy
Definition, 3.3.203.11, A.3.3.203.11
High-Risk Occupancy
Definition, 3.3.203.12, A.3.3.203.12
Hospital
Definition, 3.3.203.13
Hotel
Definition, 3.3.203.14, A.3.3.203.14
Industrial Occupancy
Definition, 3.3.203.15, A.3.3.203.15
Limited Care Facility
Definition, 3.3.203.16, A.3.3.203.16
Lodging or Rooming House
Definition, 3.3.203.17
Low-Risk Occupancy
Definition, 3.3.203.18, A.3.3.203.18
Mercantile Occupancy
Definition, 3.3.203.19, A.3.3.203.19
Mixed Occupancy
Definition, 3.3.203.20
Moderate-Risk Occupancy
Definition, 3.3.203.21, A.3.3.203.21
Motor Fuel Dispensing Facility
Definition, 3.3.203.22
Multiple Occupancy
Definition, 3.3.203.23

2024 Edition

Nursing Home
  Definition, 3.3.203.24
One- and Two-Family Dwelling
  Definition, 3.3.203.25
Parking Structure
  Definition, 3.3.203.26, A.3.3.203.26
Repair Garages
  Definition, 3.3.203.27
Residential Board and Care Occupancy
  Definition, 3.3.203.28, A.3.3.203.28
Residential Occupancy
  Definition, 3.3.203.29, A.3.3.203.29
Separated Occupancy
  Definition, 3.3.203.30
Storage Occupancy
  Definition, 3.3.203.31, A.3.3.203.31

Occupancy Fire Safety, Chap. 20
  Ambulatory Health Care Centers, 20.6
    Application, 20.6.1
    Interior Finish, 20.6.3
      General, 20.6.3.1
      Interior Wall and Ceiling Finish, 20.6.3.2
      New Interior Floor Finish, 20.6.3.3
    Operating Features, 20.6.2, A.20.6.2
      Evacuation and Relocation Plan and Fire Drills, 20.6.2.1
      Furnishings, Mattresses, and Decorations, 20.6.2.5
        Soiled Linen and Trash Receptacles, 20.6.2.5.5
      Integrated Fire Protection and Life Safety Systems, 20.6.2.7
      Maintenance of Exits, 20.6.2.3
      Portable Space-Heating Devices, 20.6.2.6
      Procedure in Case of Fire, 20.6.2.2
        Fire Safety Plan, 20.6.2.2.2
        Protection of Patients, 20.6.2.2.1, A.20.6.2.2.1
        Staff Response, 20.6.2.2.3
      Smoking, 20.6.2.4, A.20.6.2.4
  Apartment Buildings, 20.9
    Application, 20.9.1
    Contents and Furnishings, 20.9.4
    Interior Finish, 20.9.3
      Existing Interior Floor Finish, 20.9.3.5
      Existing Interior Wall and Ceiling Finish, 20.9.3.3
      General, 20.9.3.1
      New Interior Floor Finish, 20.9.3.4
      New Interior Wall and Ceiling Finish, 20.9.3.2
    Operating Features, 20.9.2
      Emergency Instructions for Residents of Apartment Buildings, 20.9.2.1
      Fuel-Fired Heaters, 20.9.2.2
      Inspection of Door Openings, 20.9.2.3
      Integrated Fire Protection and Life Safety Systems, 20.9.2.4
  Assembly Occupancies, 20.1
    Application, 20.1.1
      Permits, 20.1.1.1
    Flame-Retardant Requirements, 20.1.2
    Interior Finish, 20.1.3
      Assembly Areas, 20.1.3.3
      Corridors, Lobbies, and Enclosed Stairways, 20.1.3.2
      General, 20.1.3.1
      Interior Floor Finish, 20.1.3.5
        Existing Interior Floor Finish, 20.1.3.5.4
      Screens, 20.1.3.4
    Operating Features, 20.1.5
      Clothing, 20.1.5.11
      Crowd Managers, 20.1.5.6
      Drills, 20.1.5.8, A.20.1.5.8
      Fire Detail, 20.1.5.7, A.20.1.5.7
      Furnishings, Decorations, and Scenery, 20.1.5.4
      Integrated Fire Protection and Life Safety Systems, 20.1.5.13
      Means of Egress Inspection, 20.1.5.1
        Inspection of Door Openings, 20.1.5.1.3
      Open Flame Devices and Pyrotechnics, 20.1.5.3
        Permits, 20.1.5.3.1
      Projection Rooms, 20.1.5.12
      Seating, 20.1.5.10
        Festival Seating, 20.1.5.10.3
        Occupant Load Posting, 20.1.5.10.4
        Secured Seating, 20.1.5.10.1
        Unsecured Seating, 20.1.5.10.2
      Smoking, 20.1.5.9
      Special Provisions for Exposition Facilities, 20.1.5.5
        Exhibits, 20.1.5.5.4
          Prohibited Materials, 20.1.5.5.4.13
          Vehicles, 20.1.5.5.4.12
        General, 20.1.5.5.2
        Materials Not on Display, 20.1.5.5.3
        Permits, 20.1.5.5.1
      Special Provisions for Food Service Operations, 20.1.5.2
    Special Amusement Buildings, 20.1.4, A.20.1.4
      Detection, Alarm, and Communications Systems, 20.1.4.4
        General, 20.1.4.4.1
        Initiation, 20.1.4.4.2, A.20.1.4.4.2
        Notification, 20.1.4.4.4, A.20.1.4.4.4
        Smoke Detection, 20.1.4.4.3
      Extinguishment Requirements, 20.1.4.5
        Automatic Sprinklers, 20.1.4.5.1, A.20.1.4.5.1
      General, 20.1.4.1
      Interior Finish, 20.1.4.3
      Means of Egress, 20.1.4.2
        Exit Marking, 20.1.4.2.1
        Illumination, 20.1.4.2.2
      Operating Features, 20.1.4.6
        Emergency Action Plan, 20.1.4.6.2, A.20.1.4.6.2
        Furnishings, Decorations, and Scenery, 20.1.4.6.1, A.20.1.4.6.1
  Business Occupancies, 20.13
    Application, 20.13.1
    Interior Finish, 20.13.3
      General, 20.13.3.1
      Interior Floor Finish, 20.13.3.3
        Existing Interior Floor Finish, 20.13.3.3.4
      Interior Wall and Ceiling Finish, 20.13.3.2

Operating Features, 20.13.2
    Drills, 20.13.2.2
    Emergency Action Plans, 20.13.2.1
    Food Service Operations, 20.13.2.4
    Inspection of Door Openings, 20.13.2.5
    Portable Fire Extinguisher Training, 20.13.2.3
Day-Care Occupancies, 20.3
    Application, 20.3.1
        Adult Day-Care Occupancies, 20.3.1.5
        General, 20.3.1.4
    Day-Care Homes, 20.3.4
        Classification, 20.3.4.1
        Operating Features, 20.3.4.2
            Emergency Action Plans, 20.3.4.2.1
            Emergency Egress and Relocation Drills, 20.3.4.2.2
            Inspections, 20.3.4.2.3
                Day-Care Staff, 20.3.4.2.3.6, A.20.3.4.2.3.6
                Furnishings and Decorations, 20.3.4.2.3.5
                Inspection of Door Openings, 20.3.4.2.3.4
                Integrated Fire Protection and Life Safety Systems, 20.3.4.2.3.7
    General Requirements, 20.3.2
        Bathroom Doors, 20.3.2.3
        Door Latches, 20.3.2.2, A.20.3.2.2
        Flexible Plan and Open Plan Buildings, 20.3.2.4
    Interior Finish, 20.3.3
        Existing Interior Wall and Ceiling Finish, 20.3.3.3
        General, 20.3.3.1
        Interior Floor Finish, 20.3.3.4
            Existing Interior Floor Finish, 20.3.3.4.4
        New Interior Wall and Ceiling Finish, 20.3.3.2
Detention and Correctional Occupancies, 20.7
    Application, 20.7.1
    Interior Finish, 20.7.3
        Existing Interior Floor Finish, 20.7.3.5
        Existing Interior Wall and Ceiling Finish, 20.7.3.3
        General, 20.7.3.1
        Interior Finish (Nonsprinklered Existing Building Renovations), 20.7.3.6
            Interior Floor Finish, 20.7.3.6.2
            Interior Wall and Ceiling Finish, 20.7.3.6.1
        New Interior Floor Finish, 20.7.3.4
        New Interior Wall and Ceiling Finish, 20.7.3.2
    Operating Features, 20.7.2
        Attendants, Evacuation Plan, and Fire Drills, 20.7.2.1
        Combustible Personal Property, 20.7.2.2, A.20.7.2.2
        Door Inspection, 20.7.2.7
        Furnishings, Mattresses, and Decorations, 20.7.2.4, A.20.7.2.4
        Heat-Producing Appliances, 20.7.2.3
        Integrated Fire Protection and Life Safety Systems, 20.7.2.8
        Keys, 20.7.2.5
        Portable Space-Heating Devices, 20.7.2.6
Educational Occupancies, 20.2
    Application, 20.2.1
    Flexible Plan and Open Plan Buildings, 20.2.2
    Interior Finish, 20.2.3
        General, 20.2.3.1
        Interior Floor Finish, 20.2.3.3
            Existing Interior Floor Finish, 20.2.3.3.4
        Interior Wall and Ceiling Finish, 20.2.3.2
    Operating Features, 20.2.4
        Emergency Action Plan, 20.2.4.1
        Emergency Egress Drills, 20.2.4.2
        Furnishings and Decorations, 20.2.4.4
        Inspection, 20.2.4.3
            Inspection of Door Openings, 20.2.4.3.3
        Integrated Fire Protection and Life Safety Systems, 20.2.4.6
        Unvented Fuel-Fired Heating Equipment, 20.2.4.5
Health Care Occupancies, 20.4
    Application, 20.4.1
    Interior Finish, 20.4.3
        General, 20.4.3.1
        Interior Finish (Nonsprinklered Smoke Compartment Rehabilitation), 20.4.3.4
            General, 20.4.3.4.1
            Interior Wall and Ceiling Finish, 20.4.3.4.2
        Interior Floor Finish, 20.4.3.5
            Existing Interior Floor Finish, 20.4.3.5.3
        Interior Floor Finish, 20.4.3.3
        New Interior Wall and Ceiling Finish, 20.4.3.2
            Existing Interior Wall and Ceiling Finish, 20.4.3.2.3
    Operating Features, 20.4.2, A.20.4.2
        Evacuation and Relocation Plan and Fire Drills, 20.4.2.1
        Furnishings, Mattresses, and Decorations, 20.4.2.5
            Soiled Linen and Trash Receptacles, 20.4.2.5.7
        Integrated Fire Protection and Life Safety Systems, 20.4.2.7
        Maintenance of Means of Egress, 20.4.2.3
        Portable Space-Heating Devices, 20.4.2.6, A.20.4.2.6
        Procedure in Case of Fire, 20.4.2.2
            Fire Safety Plan, 20.4.2.2.2
            Protection of Patients, 20.4.2.2.1, A.20.4.2.2.1
            Staff Response, 20.4.2.2.3
        Smoking, 20.4.2.4, A.20.4.2.4
Historic Buildings and Cultural Resources, 20.17
Hotels and Dormitories, 20.8
    Application, 20.8.1
    Interior Finish, 20.8.3
        Existing Interior Wall and Ceiling Finish, 20.8.3.3
        General, 20.8.3.1
        Interior Floor Finish (Existing Nonsprinklered Buildings), 20.8.3.5
        New Interior Floor Finish, 20.8.3.4
        New Interior Wall and Ceiling Finish, 20.8.3.2
    Operating Features, 20.8.2
        Contents and Furnishings, 20.8.2.5
            Upholstered Furniture and Mattresses, 20.8.2.5.2
        Drills in Dormitories, 20.8.2.3
        Emergency Duties, 20.8.2.2
        Emergency Instructions for Residents or Guests, 20.8.2.4
            Emergency Action Plans, 20.8.2.4.3
        Fuel-Fired Heaters, 20.8.2.6
        Hotel Emergency Organization, 20.8.2.1

Integrated Fire and Life Safety Protection
    Systems, 20.8.2.7
Industrial Occupancies, 20.14
  Application, 20.14.1
  Interior Finish, 20.14.4
    General, 20.14.4.1
    Interior Floor Finish, 20.14.4.3
    Interior Wall and Ceiling Finish, 20.14.4.2
  Operating Features, 20.14.3
    Inspection of Door Openings, 20.14.3.1
    Integrated Fire Protection and Life Safety
      Systems, 20.14.3.2
  Permits, 20.14.2
Lodging or Rooming Houses, 20.10
  Application, 20.10.1
  Fuel-Fired Heaters, 20.10.2
  Interior Finish, 20.10.3
    General, 20.10.3.1
    Interior Floor Finish, 20.10.3.3
    Interior Wall and Ceiling Finish, 20.10.3.2
Mercantile Occupancies, 20.12
  Application, 20.12.1
  Interior Finish, 20.12.3
    General, 20.12.3.1
    Interior Floor Finish, 20.12.3.3
      Existing Interior Floor Finish, 20.12.3.3.4
    Interior Wall and Ceiling Finish, 20.12.3.2
  Operating Features, 20.12.2
    Drills, 20.12.2.2
    Emergency Plans, 20.12.2.1
    Extinguisher Training, 20.12.2.3
    Food Service Operations, 20.12.2.4
    Inspection of Door Openings, 20.12.2.5
    Integrated Fire Protection and Life Safety
      Systems, 20.12.2.6
One- and Two-Family Dwellings and Manufactured
    Housing, 20.11
  Application, 20.11.1
  Fire Protection of Floors, 20.11.4
  Fuel-Fired Heaters, 20.11.2
  Interior Finish, 20.11.3
    General, 20.11.3.1
    Interior Wall and Ceiling Finish, 20.11.3.2
  Manufactured Housing, 20.11.5
Residential Board and Care Occupancies, 20.5
  Application, 20.5.1
  Interior Finish, 20.5.3
    Apartment Buildings Housing Board and Care
      Occupancies, 20.5.3.3
      Existing Interior Finish, 20.5.3.3.2
      New Interior Finish, 20.5.3.3.1
    Large Facilities, 20.5.3.2
      Existing Interior Wall and Ceiling Finish, 20.5.3.2.3
      General, 20.5.3.2.1
      Interior Floor Finish, 20.5.3.2.4
        Existing Interior Floor Finish, 20.5.3.2.4.4
      New Interior Wall and Ceiling Finish, 20.5.3.2.2
    Small Facilities, 20.5.3.1

Existing Interior Wall and Ceiling Finish, 20.5.3.1.3
General, 20.5.3.1.1
Interior Floor Finish, 20.5.3.1.4
  Existing Interior Floor Finish, 20.5.3.1.4.3
New Interior Wall and Ceiling Finish, 20.5.3.1.2
  Operating Features, 20.5.2
    Emergency Action Plan, 20.5.2.1
    Emergency Egress and Relocation Drills, 20.5.2.3
    Furnishings, Bedding, and Decorations, 20.5.2.5,
      A.20.5.2.5
    Resident Training, 20.5.2.2
    Smoking, 20.5.2.4
Special Structures and High-Rise Buildings, 20.16
  Application, 20.16.1
Storage Occupancies, 20.15
  Application, 20.15.1
  Bulk Storage Elevators, 20.15.5
    Applicability, 20.15.5.3
    Application, 20.15.5.1, A.20.15.5.1
  Cellulose Nitrate Motion Picture Film Storage, 20.15.7
    Application, 20.15.7.1
    Permits, 20.15.7.2
  High-Piled Storage, 20.15.8
    Application, 20.15.8.1
    Permits, 20.15.8.2
  Interior Finish, 20.15.4
    General, 20.15.4.1
    Interior Floor Finish, 20.15.4.3
    Interior Wall and Ceiling Finish, 20.15.4.2
  Operating Features, 20.15.3
    Inspection of Door Openings, 20.15.3.1
    Integrated Fire Protection and Life Safety
      Systems, 20.15.3.2
  Permits, 20.15.2
  Record Storage, 20.15.6
Occupant Characteristics
  Definition, 3.4.13
Occupant Load
  Definition, 3.3.204
Open System Use
  Definition, 3.3.205
Operating Pressure
  Definition, 3.3.206
Operating Unit (Vessel) or Process Unit (Vessel)
  Definition, 3.3.207, A.3.3.207
Operations
  Definition, 3.3.208
Organic Peroxide
  Definition, 3.3.209
  Organic Peroxide Formulation
    Definition, 3.3.209.1
  Organic Peroxide Storage Area
    Definition, 3.3.209.2
Organic Peroxide Solids and Liquids, Chap. 75
  General, 75.1
OSHA
  Definition, 3.3.210

Outside Storage of Tires, Chap. 33
    Emergency Response Plan, 33.3
    Fire Control Measures, 33.4
        Manual Fire-Fighting Equipment, 33.4.1
    General, 33.1, A.33.1
        Ignition Sources, 33.1.6
        Permits, 33.1.2
    Individual Piles, 33.2
        Existing Individual Piles, 33.2.2
        New Outside Tire Storage Sites and Piles, 33.2.1
    Outdoor Storage of Altered Tire Material, 33.7
    Signs and Security, 33.6
        Access, 33.6.3
    Site Access, 33.5

Overcrowded
    Definition, 3.3.211

Oxidizer
    Class 1
        Definition, 3.3.212.1
    Class 2
        Definition, 3.3.212.2
    Class 3
        Definition, 3.3.212.3
    Class 4
        Definition, 3.3.212.4
    Definition, 3.3.212, A.3.3.212

Oxidizer Solids and Liquids, Chap. 70
    General, 70.1

Ozone Gas–Generating Equipment, Chap. 54
    Automatic Shutdown, 54.4
    Location, 54.2
        Cabinets, 54.2.2
        General, 54.2.1
        Ozone Generator Rooms, 54.2.3
    Manual Shutdown, 54.5
    Piping, Valves, and Fittings, 54.3
        General, 54.3.1
        Identification, 54.3.4
        Materials, 54.3.3
        Secondary Containment, 54.3.2
    Scope, 54.1

Ozone Generator
    Definition, 3.3.213

-P-

Paper
    Definition, 3.3.214

Parking Garages, Chap. 29
    General, 29.1

Patch Kettle
    Definition, 3.3.215

Performance Criteria
    Definition, 3.4.14, A.3.4.14

Performance-Based Option, Chap. 5
    Design Scenarios, 5.4, A.5.4
        General, 5.4.1
        Required Design Scenarios — Explosion, 5.4.3
            Explosion Design Scenario 1, 5.4.3.1, A.5.4.3.1
        Required Design Scenarios — Fire, 5.4.2
            Fire Design Scenario 1, 5.4.2.1, A.5.4.2.1
            Fire Design Scenario 2, 5.4.2.2, A.5.4.2.2
            Fire Design Scenario 3, 5.4.2.3, A.5.4.2.3
            Fire Design Scenario 4, 5.4.2.4, A.5.4.2.4
            Fire Design Scenario 5, 5.4.2.5, A.5.4.2.5
            Fire Design Scenario 6, 5.4.2.6, A.5.4.2.6
            Fire Design Scenario 7, 5.4.2.7, A.5.4.2.7
            Fire Design Scenario 8, 5.4.2.8, A.5.4.2.8
        Required Design Scenarios — Hazardous Materials, 5.4.4, A.5.4.4
            Hazardous Materials Design Scenario 1, 5.4.4.1
            Hazardous Materials Design Scenario 2, 5.4.4.2
            Hazardous Materials Design Scenario 3, 5.4.4.3
            Hazardous Materials Design Scenario 4, 5.4.4.4
        Required Design Scenarios — Safety During Building Use, 5.4.5
            Building Use Design Scenario 1, 5.4.5.1, A.5.4.5.1
            Building Use Design Scenario 2, 5.4.5.2
    Documentation Requirements, 5.7
        Design Scenarios, 5.7.6
        Evidence of Modeler Capability, 5.7.12
        Facility Design Specifications, 5.7.3
        General, 5.7.1, A.5.7.1
        Input Data, 5.7.7
        Modeling Features, 5.7.11, A.5.7.11
        Occupant Characteristics, 5.7.5
        Output Data, 5.7.8
        Performance Criteria, 5.7.4
        Performance Evaluation, 5.7.13
        Prescriptive Requirements, 5.7.10
        Safety Factors, 5.7.9
        Technical References and Resources, 5.7.2, A.5.7.2
        Use of Performance-Based Design Option, 5.7.14
    Evaluation of Proposed Designs, 5.5
        General, 5.5.1
        Input Data, 5.5.3
            Data, 5.5.3.1, A.5.5.3.1
            Data Requirements, 5.5.3.2
            Uncertainty and Conservatism of Data, 5.5.3.3
        Output Data, 5.5.4
        Use, 5.5.2
        Validity, 5.5.5, A.5.5.5
    General, 5.1, A.5.1
        Annual Certification, 5.1.11, A.5.1.11
        Application, 5.1.1
        Approved Qualifications, 5.1.3, A.5.1.3
        Design Feature Maintenance, 5.1.10, A.5.1.10
        Final Determination, 5.1.7
        Goals and Objectives, 5.1.2
        Hazardous Materials, 5.1.12
        Independent Review, 5.1.5, A.5.1.5
        Information Transfer to the Fire Service, 5.1.9, A.5.1.9
        Operations and Maintenance Manual, 5.1.8, A.5.1.8
        Plan Submittal Documentation, 5.1.4, A.5.1.4
        Sources of Data, 5.1.6

Special Definitions, 5.1.13
Performance Criteria, 5.2
   General, 5.2.1
   Specific Performance Criteria, 5.2.2, A.5.2.2
      Emergency Responder Protection, 5.2.2.7
      Explosion Conditions, 5.2.2.2, A.5.2.2.2
      Fire Conditions, 5.2.2.1, A.5.2.2.1
      Hazardous Materials Exposure, 5.2.2.3, A.5.2.2.3
      Occupant Protection from Structural Failure, 5.2.2.8, A.5.2.2.8
      Occupant Protection from Untenable Conditions, 5.2.2.6
      Property Protection, 5.2.2.4, A.5.2.2.4
      Public Welfare, 5.2.2.5, A.5.2.2.5
Retained Prescriptive Requirements, 5.3
   Electrical Systems, 5.3.2
   Equivalency, 5.3.5
   General, 5.3.3
   Means of Egress, 5.3.4
   Systems and Features, 5.3.1
Safety Factors, 5.6, A.5.6

Permissible Exposure Limit (PEL)
   Definition, 3.3.216

Permit
   Definition, 3.3.217

Peroxide-Forming Chemical
   Definition, 3.3.218

Personal Care
   Definition, 3.3.219, A.3.3.219

Pesticide
   Definition, 3.3.220

Physical Hazard
   Definition, 3.3.221

Pier
   Definition, 3.3.222, A.3.3.222

Portable Generator
   Definition, 3.3.223

Pre-Incident Plan
   Definition, 3.3.224

Pressure Vessel
   Definition, 3.3.226, A.3.3.226

Pressure-Regulating Device
   Definition, 3.3.225
   Pressure-Reducing Valve
      Definition, 3.3.225.1
   Pressure-Restricting Device
      Definition, 3.3.225.2

Primary Containment
   Definition, 3.3.227

Process or Processing
   Definition, 3.3.228, A.3.3.228

Process Unit (Vessel)
   Definition, 3.3.229

Proposed Design
   Definition, 3.4.15, A.3.4.15

Proprietary Information
   Definition, 3.3.230

Protection for Exposures
   Definition, 3.3.231

Public Way
   Definition, 3.3.232

Purging
   Definition, 3.3.233

Pyrophoric
   Definition, 3.3.234

Pyrophoric Solids and Liquids, Chap. 71
   General, 71.1

-Q-

Quality Assurance
   Definition, 3.3.235

Quality Assurance Program
   Definition, 3.3.236

-R-

Rack
   Definition, 3.3.237, A.3.3.237
   Double-Row Racks
      Definition, 3.3.237.1
   Movable Racks
      Definition, 3.3.237.2, A.3.3.237.2
   Multiple-Row Racks
      Definition, 3.3.237.3
   Portable Racks
      Definition, 3.3.237.4, A.3.3.237.4
   Single-Row Racks
      Definition, 3.3.237.5

Ramp
   Definition, 3.3.238, A.3.3.238

Recommended Practice
   Definition, 3.2.7

Recreational Fire
   Definition, 3.3.239

Referenced Publications, Chap. 2

Refinery
   Definition, 3.3.240

Refrigerant Concentration Limit (RCL)
   Definition, 3.3.241

Refueling, Chap. 42
   Additional Requirements for CNG, LNG, Hydrogen, and LP-Gas, 42.8
      Dispenser Installations Beneath Canopies, 42.8.4
      Electrical Equipment, 42.8.6
      Fuel Storage, 42.8.3
      General Requirements, 42.8.2
      Scope, 42.8.1
      Specific Requirements for LP-Gas Dispensing Devices, 42.8.5
   Aircraft Fuel Servicing, 42.10
      Airport Fueling Vehicles, 42.10.4
         Design and Construction, 42.10.4.1
            Bonding, 42.10.4.1.4
            Control of Fuel Flow, 42.10.4.1.6
                Air Elimination, 42.10.4.1.6.6

Pressure Fuel Servicing System Controls, 42.10.4.1.6.4
Drive Train, 42.10.4.1.11
Electrical System, 42.10.4.1.5
  Battery Compartments, 42.10.4.1.5.1
  Tractor Trailer Wiring, 42.10.4.1.5.9
  Wiring, 42.10.4.1.5.2
Emergency Fuel Shutoff Systems, 42.10.4.1.8
Exhaust System, 42.10.4.1.12
Filters and Ancillary Equipment, 42.10.4.1.7
  Cabinets, 42.10.4.1.7.1
  Product Recovery Tanks, 42.10.4.1.7.2
Fire Protection, 42.10.4.1.9, A.42.10.4.1.9
  Smoking Equipment, 42.10.4.1.9.8
General Requirements, 42.10.4.1.1
Marking and Labeling, 42.10.4.1.10
  Emergency Fuel Shutoff Signs, 42.10.4.1.10.4
  Signage, 42.10.4.1.10.3
Pumps and Piping System, 42.10.4.1.3
  Loading System, 42.10.4.1.3.12

Bottom Loading 42.10.4.1.3.12.2 Top Loading 42.10.4.1.3.12.1

Tanks, 42.10.4.1.2
  Baffles, 42.10.4.1.2.6
  Fill Openings and Top Flashings, 42.10.4.1.2.9
  Tanks for Flammable Liquids Other than Fuel, 42.10.4.1.2.10
  Tests, 42.10.4.1.2.11
Operations, 42.10.4.2
  Control of Fuel Flow, 42.10.4.2.2
  Exhaust System, 42.10.4.2.4
    Vehicle Regeneration Area, 42.10.4.2.4.4, A.42.10.4.2.4.4
  Loading and Unloading, 42.10.4.2.5
    Bottom Loading, 42.10.4.2.5.11
    Top Loading, 42.10.4.2.5.10
  Maintenance, 42.10.4.2.3
  Positioning of Aircraft Fuel Servicing Vehicles and Carts During Fueling, 42.10.4.2.6
  Security, 42.10.4.2.1
    Parking of Aircraft Fuel Servicing Hydrant Vehicles and Carts, 42.10.4.2.1.2
    Parking of Aircraft Fuel Servicing Tank Vehicles, 42.10.4.2.1.1
Application, 42.10.1
Aviation Fueling Facilities, 42.10.3
  Design and Construction, 42.10.3.1
    Aircraft Fuel Servicing Vehicle Loading and Unloading Racks, 42.10.3.1.11
    Control of Fuel Flow, 42.10.3.1.6
      Deadman Controls, 42.10.3.1.6.1, A.42.10.3.1.6.1
      Flow Control Valves, 42.10.3.1.6.4
      Fuel Pressure, 42.10.3.1.6.5, A.42.10.3.1.6.5
      Hydrant Valves, 42.10.3.1.6.3, A.42.10.3.1.6.3
      Pressure Fuel Servicing System Controls, 42.10.3.1.6.2
    Electrical Systems, 42.10.3.1.5
      Electrical Equipment, 42.10.3.1.5.1
    Electrostatic Hazards and Bonding, 42.10.3.1.4
    Emergency Fuel Shutoff Systems, 42.10.3.1.8
    Filters and Ancillary Equipment, 42.10.3.1.7
    Fire Protection, 42.10.3.1.9, A.42.10.3.1.9
    Fuel Servicing Hydrants, Pits, and Cabinets, 42.10.3.1.12
    Fuel Storage Tanks, 42.10.3.1.2
    General Requirements, 42.10.3.1.1
      System Design and Approval, 42.10.3.1.1.6

Design Approval 42.10.3.1.1.6.1 Hydrostatic Test 42.10.3.1.1.6.3 System Approval 42.10.3.1.1.6.2

    Marking and Labeling, 42.10.3.1.10
    Pumps and Piping Systems, 42.10.3.1.3
  Operations, 42.10.3.2
    Control of Fuel Flow, 42.10.3.2.2
    Fire Protection, 42.10.3.2.3
    Security, 42.10.3.2.1, A.42.10.3.2.1
  General Requirements, 42.10.2
    Design and Construction, 42.10.2.1
      Aircraft Fueling Ramps, 42.10.2.1.8
        Aircraft Radar Equipment, 42.10.2.1.8.1
        Emergency Fire Equipment Accessibility, 42.10.2.1.8.3
        Ground Radar Equipment, 42.10.2.1.8.2, A.42.10.2.1.8.2
        Ramp and Apron Drainage, 42.10.2.1.8.4
      Electrostatic Hazards and Bonding, 42.10.2.1.4
      Filters and Ancillary Equipment, 42.10.2.1.5
      Fire Extinguishers, 42.10.2.1.6
      Fuel Dispensing Systems, 42.10.2.1.2
      Fueling Hose, 42.10.2.1.3, A.42.10.2.1.3
        Additional Requirements, 42.10.2.1.3.3

Hydrostatic Testing 42.10.2.1.3.3.7

        Fueling Hose Apparatus, 42.10.2.1.3.2
        Performance Requirements, 42.10.2.1.3.1
      General Requirements, 42.10.2.1.1
      Marking and Labeling, 42.10.2.1.7
    Operations, 42.10.2.2
      Aircraft Fuel Servicing, 42.10.2.2.10
        Aircraft Occupancy During Fuel Servicing, 42.10.2.2.10.2
        Location of Aircraft During Fuel Servicing, 42.10.2.2.10.1
      Aircraft Fueling Hose, 42.10.2.2.8, A.42.10.2.2.8
        Daily Inspection, 42.10.2.2.8.4
        Monthly Inspection, 42.10.2.2.8.5
        Quarterly Inspection, 42.10.2.2.8.6
      Bonding, 42.10.2.2.4, A.42.10.2.2.4
        Bonding for Overwing Fueling, 42.10.2.2.4.2
      Control of Fuel Flow, 42.10.2.2.5
      Defueling of Aircraft, 42.10.2.2.12
      Emergency Fuel Shutoff, 42.10.2.2.3
      Fire Hazards on Aircraft Fuel Servicing Ramps, 42.10.2.2.11
        Electrical Equipment Operated on Aircraft Fuel Servicing Ramps or Aprons, 42.10.2.2.11.1, A.42.10.2.2.11.1

Open Flames on Aircraft Fuel Servicing Ramps, 42.10.2.2.11.2
Operation of Aircraft Engines and Heaters, 42.10.2.2.11.3
Fire Protection, 42.10.2.2.6
Lightning, 42.10.2.2.9, A.42.10.2.2.9
Maintenance, 42.10.2.2.7
Prevention and Control of Spills, 42.10.2.2.2, A.42.10.2.2.2
Fuel Spill Procedures, 42.10.2.2.2.5
Rapid Refueling, 42.10.2.2.13
Training, 42.10.2.2.1
Rooftop Heliports, 42.10.5
Design and Construction, 42.10.5.1
Emergency Fuel Shutoff Systems, 42.10.5.1.4
Fire Protection, 42.10.5.1.5
Fuel Storage Tanks, 42.10.5.1.2
General Requirements, 42.10.5.1.1
System Design and Approval, 42.10.5.1.1.1
Pumps and Piping Systems, 42.10.5.1.3
Operations, 42.10.5.2
Emergency Fuel Shutoff, 42.10.5.2.2
Personnel, 42.10.5.2.1
Self-Service Aircraft Fueling, 42.10.6
Design and Construction, 42.10.6.1
Emergency Fuel Shutoff Systems, 42.10.6.1.4
Fire Protection, 42.10.6.1.5, A.42.10.6.1.5
Fuel Storage Tanks, 42.10.6.1.2
General Requirements, 42.10.6.1.1
System Design and Approval, 42.10.6.1.1.1
Marking and Labeling, 42.10.6.1.6
Operating Instructions, 42.10.6.1.6.3
Pumps and Piping Systems, 42.10.6.1.3
Operations, 42.10.6.2
Occupancy, 42.10.6.2.2
Security, 42.10.6.2.1
Alternate Fuels, 42.11
Compressed Natural Gas (CNG) Vehicular Fuel Systems, 42.11.1
Scope, 42.11.1.1, A.42.11.1.1
Liquefied Natural Gas (LNG), 42.11.3, A.42.11.3
Liquefied Petroleum Gas (LP-Gas), 42.11.2
Automotive Fuel Servicing, 42.2
Applicability, 42.2.1
General Requirements, 42.2.2
Plans and Specifications, 42.2.2.1
Building Construction Requirements, 42.6
Fuel Dispensing Systems, 42.5
Emergency Electrical Disconnects, 42.5.7
Unattended Motor Fuel Dispensing Facilities, 42.5.7.11
General Requirements, 42.5.2
Requirements for Dispensing Devices, 42.5.3
Inspections, 42.5.3.6
Exterior Inspection, 42.5.3.6.1, A.42.5.3.6.1
Internal Dispenser Cabinet Inspection, 42.5.3.6.2, A.42.5.3.6.2
Maintenance, 42.5.3.6.3
Requirements for Dispensing Hose, 42.5.5

Requirements for Fuel Delivery Nozzles, 42.5.6
Automatic Closing Valve, 42.5.6.3
Requirements for Remote/Submersible Pumps, 42.5.4
Leak Detection, 42.5.4.2
Scope, 42.5.1
Vapor Recovery Systems, 42.5.8
General, 42.1
Permits, 42.1.2
Scope, 42.1.1
Marine Fueling, 42.9
Cargo Tank Fueling Facilities, 42.9.9
Containers and Movable Tanks, 42.9.8
Electrical Installations, 42.9.6
Bonding and Grounding, 42.9.6.4, A.42.9.6.4
Fuel Dispensing System, 42.9.4
Operating Requirements, 42.9.10
Piping Systems, 42.9.3
Portable Fire Extinguishers, 42.9.7
Scope, 42.9.1
Sources of Ignition, 42.9.5
Continuing Operation, 42.9.5.6, A.42.9.5.6
Storage, 42.9.2
Tanks at Elevation, 42.9.2.5
On-Demand Mobile Fueling, 42.12
Approvals and Mobile Fueling Locations, 42.12.2
Buildings and Parking Structures, 42.12.2.7
Safety and Emergency Response Plan, 42.12.2.3, A.42.12.2.3
Training, 42.12.2.4
Mobile Fueling Vehicles and Equipment, 42.12.3
Operations, 42.12.4
Inspection Program, 42.12.4.10
Operations Using Metal Safety Cans, 42.12.4.11
Scope, 42.12.1, A.42.12.1
Dispensing Class I and Class II Liquids for On-Demand Mobile Fueling, 42.12.1.2
Operational Requirements, 42.7
Basic Requirements, 42.7.2
Basic Fire Control, 42.7.2.6
Continuing Operation, 42.7.2.6.2, A.42.7.2.6.2
Fire Extinguishers, 42.7.2.6.3, A.42.7.2.6.3
Gaseous Fuel Dispensing Areas, 42.7.2.6.3.8
Indoor Liquid Motor Fuel Dispensing Areas, 42.7.2.6.3.6
New Fire Extinguishers, 42.7.2.6.3.4
Outdoor Liquid Motor Fuel Dispensing Areas, 42.7.2.6.3.7
Repair Garages, 42.7.2.6.3.5
Fire Suppression Systems, 42.7.2.6.4
Signs, 42.7.2.6.5, A.42.7.2.6.5
Sources of Ignition, 42.7.2.6.1
Dispensing from a Tank That Does Not Exceed 120 Gal (454 L) and from Containers Inside Buildings, 42.7.2.4
Dispensing into Containers, 42.7.2.3
Display of Materials, 42.7.2.5, A.42.7.2.5
Fire Doors, 42.7.2.9
Housekeeping, 42.7.2.8

Inventory Control, 42.7.2.1, A.42.7.2.1
Maintenance of Aboveground Storage Tank Appurtenances, 42.7.2.10
Tank Filling and Bulk Delivery, 42.7.2.2
Delivery Vehicle Location, 42.7.2.2.4
Waste Handling, 42.7.2.7
LNG Vehicle Fueling System Monitoring and Management, 42.7.9
Operating Requirements for Attended Self-Service Motor Fuel Dispensing Facilities, 42.7.4
Operating Requirements for Fleet Vehicle Motor Fuel Dispensing Facilities, 42.7.6
Operating Requirements for Full-Service Motor Fuel Dispensing Facilities, 42.7.3
Operating Requirements for Unattended Self-Service Motor Fuel Dispensing Facilities, 42.7.5
Refueling from Tank Vehicles, 42.7.7
Portable Fire Extinguishers, 42.7.7.10
Repair Areas, 42.7.8
Chassis Cleaning, 42.7.8.7
Drying Apparatus, 42.7.8.4
General, 42.7.8.1
Housekeeping, 42.7.8.9
Parts Cleaning, 42.7.8.6
Repair of Fuel Tanks Containing Flammable or Combustible Liquids, 42.7.8.5
Spray Painting and Undercoating, 42.7.8.3
Storage and Handling of Flammable and Combustible Liquids, Liquefied Petroleum Gases, and Compressed Natural Gases, 42.7.8.8
Welding and Open Flame Operations, 42.7.8.2
Scope, 42.7.1
Piping for Liquids, 42.4
Detector Maintenance, 42.4.5
General Requirements for All Piping Systems, 42.4.2
Installation of Piping Systems, 42.4.3
Bends, 42.4.3.1
Flexible Connections, 42.4.3.2
Scope, 42.4.1
Testing, 42.4.4
General, 42.4.4.1
Leak Detection, 42.4.4.4
Maintenance Testing, 42.4.4.3
Secondary Containment Piping, 42.4.4.2, A.42.4.4.2
Vapor Recovery Piping, 42.4.7
Vent Piping, 42.4.6
Storage of Liquids, 42.3
General Requirements, 42.3.2
Scope, 42.3.1
Storage of Liquids, 42.3.3
Aboveground Storage Tanks, 42.3.3.1, A.42.3.3.1
Spill Control, 42.3.3.1.7
Additional Requirements for All Aboveground Tanks, 42.3.3.5
Additional Requirements for Protected Aboveground Storage Tanks, 42.3.3.4
Corrosion Protection, 42.3.3.7
Physical Protection for All Outside Aboveground Tanks, 42.3.3.6

Security, 42.3.3.6.1
Storage of Liquids Inside Buildings, 42.3.3.8
Class I, II, and IIIA Liquids in Tanks Exceeding 120 Gal (454 L) Capacity, 42.3.3.8.2
Class I, II, and IIIA Liquids in Tanks Not Exceeding 120 Gal (454 L) Capacity and in Containers, 42.3.3.8.1
Class IIIB Liquids, 42.3.3.8.3
Temporary Storage of Liquid Fuels, 42.3.3.9
Vaults for Aboveground Tanks, 42.3.3.2
Construction and Installation of Storage Tank Vaults, 42.3.3.2.3
Construction Requirements, 42.3.3.2.3.1
Installation Requirements, 42.3.3.2.3.2
Detection and Alarm Systems for Storage Tank Vaults, 42.3.3.2.7
General, 42.3.3.2.2
Inspection and Maintenance of Storage Tank Vaults and Equipment, 42.3.3.2.9
Location of Storage Tank Vaults, 42.3.3.2.8
Scope, 42.3.3.2.1
Storage Tank Selection and Arrangement, 42.3.3.2.4
Tank Appurtenances, 42.3.3.2.5
Ventilation Systems for Storage Tank Vaults, 42.3.3.2.6
Additional Requirements for Fire-Resistant Aboveground Storage Tanks, 42.3.3.3
Registered Design Professional (RDP)
Definition, 3.3.242
Relocatable Power Tap
Definition, 3.3.243
RF Emitting Device
Active RF Emitting Device
Definition, 3.3.244.1
Definition, 3.3.244
Passive RF Emitting Device
Definition, 3.3.244.2
RF Radio Frequency (RF)
Definition, 3.3.245
Row
Definition, 3.3.246
Rubberized Asphalt Melter (Melter)
Definition, 3.3.247
Rural
Definition, 3.3.248

-S-

Safe Location
Definition, 3.4.16
Safeguarding Construction, Alteration, and Demolition Operations, Chap. 16
Alteration of Buildings, 16.2
Asbestos Removal, 16.6
Notification, 16.6.1
Permits, 16.6.2
Signs, 16.6.3
Fire Safety During Demolition, 16.3
General Requirements, 16.1
Lead Removal, 16.7

                    Notification, 16.7.1
                    Permits, 16.7.2
                    Signs, 16.7.3
            Tar Kettles and Rubberized Asphalt Melters, 16.5
                    General, 16.5.1
                            Permits, 16.5.1.2
                    Rubberized Asphalt Melters for Roof Deck Systems, 16.5.3
                            Exits, 16.5.3.4
                            Fire Extinguishers, 16.5.3.5
                            Fuel System, 16.5.3.8
                            General, 16.5.3.1
                            Maintenance, 16.5.3.9
                            Melter Operation, 16.5.3.6
                            Melter Supervision, 16.5.3.7
                            Minimum Requirements, 16.5.3.10
                            Permits, 16.5.3.2
                            Rubberized Asphalt Melter Location, 16.5.3.3
                    Tar Kettles, 16.5.2
                            Construction, 16.5.2.13
                                    Minimum Requirements, 16.5.2.13.2
                            Exits, 16.5.2.5
                            Fire Extinguishers, 16.5.2.4
                            Fuel System, 16.5.2.6
                            Kettle Supervision, 16.5.2.3
                            Maintenance, 16.5.2.10
                            Roofing Kettle Doors, 16.5.2.11
                            Tar Kettle Location, 16.5.2.2
            Torch-Applied Roofing Systems, 16.4
                    Permits, 16.4.1
Safety Can
            Definition, 3.3.249, A.3.3.249
Safety Data Sheet (SDS)
            Definition, 3.3.250, A.3.3.250
Safety Factor
            Definition, 3.4.17
Safety Margin
            Definition, 3.4.18
Sales Display Area
            Definition, 3.3.251
Salvage Vehicle
            Definition, 3.3.252
Sample Ordinance Adopting the NFPA 1, Fire Code, Annex B
Self-Closing
            Definition, 3.3.253
Sensitivity Analysis
            Definition, 3.4.19
Separation of Hazards
            Definition, 3.3.254
Shall
            Definition, 3.2.8
Shop Drawings
            Definition, 3.3.255
Should
            Definition, 3.2.9
Signal
            Alarm Signal
                    Definition, 3.3.256.1, A.3.3.256.1

            Definition, 3.3.256, A.3.3.256
            Fire Alarm Signal
                    Definition, 3.3.256.2, A.3.3.256.2
            Supervisory Signal
                    Definition, 3.3.256.3, A.3.3.256.3
            Trouble Signal
                    Definition, 3.3.256.4, A.3.3.256.4
Simple Asphyxiant Gas
            Definition, 3.3.257
Smoke Alarm
            Definition, 3.3.258
Smoke Barrier
            Definition, 3.3.259, A.3.3.259
Smoke Compartment
            Definition, 3.3.260
Smoke Partition
            Definition, 3.3.261, A.3.3.261
Smoking
            Definition, 3.3.262
Smoking Area
            Definition, 3.3.263
Solid
            Combustible Particulate Solid
                    Definition, 3.3.264.1, A.3.3.264.1
            Definition, 3.3.264
            Flammable Solid
                    Definition, 3.3.264.2, A.3.3.264.2
Solid Material
            Definition, 3.3.265
Solid Shelving
            Definition, 3.3.266, A.3.3.266
Solvent Extraction, Chap. 44
            Application, 44.2
            General, 44.1
            Permits, 44.3
            Special Requirements, 44.4
Special Use
            Definition, 3.3.267
Spray Area
            Definition, 3.3.268
Spray Booth
            Definition, 3.3.269, A.3.3.269
Spray Room
            Definition, 3.3.270, A.3.3.270
Spraying, Dipping, and Coating Using Flammable or Combustible Materials, Chap. 43
            Application, 43.1
                    Construction and Design of Spray Areas, Spray Rooms, and Spray Booths, 43.1.3
                            Conveyor Openings, 43.1.3.4
                            Illumination and Observation Panels, 43.1.3.6
                            Separation from Other Occupancies, 43.1.3.5
                            Spray Areas, 43.1.3.1, A.43.1.3.1
                            Spray Booths, 43.1.3.3
                            Spray Rooms, 43.1.3.2
                            Ventilation, 43.1.3.7
                    Electrical and Other Sources of Ignition, 43.1.4

Electrical Area Classification, 43.1.4.2
  Class I Locations, 43.1.4.2.1, A.43.1.4.2.1
    Class I, Division 1 Locations, 43.1.4.2.1.1, A.43.1.4.2.1.1
    Class I, Division 2 Locations, 43.1.4.2.1.2, A.43.1.4.2.1.2
    Zone 0 Locations, 43.1.4.2.1.3, A.43.1.4.2.1.3
    Zone 1 Locations, 43.1.4.2.1.4, A.43.1.4.2.1.4
    Zone 2 Locations, 43.1.4.2.1.5
  Class II Locations, 43.1.4.2.2
    Class II, Division 1 Locations, 43.1.4.2.2.1, A.43.1.4.2.2.1
    Class II, Division 2 Locations, 43.1.4.2.2.2, A.43.1.4.2.2.2
    Zone 20, 43.1.4.2.2.3, A.43.1.4.2.2.3
    Zone 21, 43.1.4.2.2.4, A.43.1.4.2.2.4
    Zone 22, 43.1.4.2.2.5, A.43.1.4.2.2.5
  Electrical Devices in Areas Adjacent to or Connected to Spray Areas, 43.1.4.4
  Electrical Devices in Spray Areas, 43.1.4.3
  Flexible Power Cords, 43.1.4.7, A.43.1.4.7
  General, 43.1.4.1, A.43.1.4.1
  Illumination, 43.1.4.5
  Movement of Powered Vehicles, 43.1.4.9
  Portable Electric Luminaires, 43.1.4.8
  Static Electricity, 43.1.4.6, A.43.1.4.6
General Requirements, 43.1.2
  Location of Spray Application Operations, 43.1.2.1, A.43.1.2.1
  Locations in Other Occupancies, 43.1.2.2, A.43.1.2.2
  Separation, 43.1.2.3, A.43.1.2.3
Operations and Maintenance, 43.1.8
  Chlorinated Solvents, 43.1.8.10, A.43.1.8.10
  Cleaning Operations, 43.1.8.7
    Equipment, 43.1.8.7.4, A.43.1.8.7.4
    Liquid Storage, 43.1.8.7.6
    Liquids, 43.1.8.7.2
    Location, 43.1.8.7.3
    Manual Cleaning, 43.1.8.7.5
    Scope, 43.1.8.7.1
  Clothing, 43.1.8.6
  Combustible Deposits, 43.1.8.2, A.43.1.8.2
  General, 43.1.8.1, A.43.1.8.1
    Inspection, Testing, and Maintenance. [33:10.2], 43.1.8.1.3
  High-Pressure Hose Lines, 43.1.8.3
  Hot Work, 43.1.8.12, A.43.1.8.12
  Maintenance Procedures, 43.1.8.4
  Smoking, 43.1.8.11
  Solvent Distillation Units (Solvent Recyclers), 43.1.8.8
    Equipment, 43.1.8.8.2
    Liquid Storage, 43.1.8.8.5
    Location, 43.1.8.8.4
    Scope, 43.1.8.8.1
    Solvents, 43.1.8.8.3
  Spontaneous Ignition Hazards, 43.1.8.9, A.43.1.8.9
  Waste Containers, 43.1.8.5, A.43.1.8.5
Protection, 43.1.7
  Automated Spray Application Operations, 43.1.7.6
    Emergency Shutdown, 43.1.7.6.2
    Interlock, 43.1.7.6.1
  Automatic Carbon Dioxide, Dry Chemical, and Clean Agent Systems, 43.1.7.8, A.43.1.7.8
  Automatic Sprinkler Systems, 43.1.7.7, A.43.1.7.7
    Dust Protection, 43.1.7.7.6, A.43.1.7.7.6
  Coating Material Delivery Systems, 43.1.7.3, A.43.1.7.3
  Conveyors, 43.1.7.4
  General, 43.1.7.1, A.43.1.7.1
    Mix Rooms. [33:9.1.2], 43.1.7.1.3
    Portable Fire Extinguishers, 43.1.7.1.6
  Protection for Automated Liquid Electrostatic Spray Application Equipment, 43.1.7.9, A.43.1.7.9
  Protection for Dry Particulate Scrubber, 43.1.7.10
  Protection for Electrostatic Precipitator Scrubber, 43.1.7.11
  Protection for High-Capacity Dry Paint Arrestor, 43.1.7.12
  Protection Systems, 43.1.7.5
  Ventilation Systems, 43.1.7.2
Storage, Handling, and Distribution of Flammable and Combustible Liquids, 43.1.6
  Distribution Systems — General, 43.1.6.5
  Distribution Systems — Piping, 43.1.6.4
  General, 43.1.6.1, A.43.1.6.1
  General Occupancy Limits, 43.1.6.2
  Mixing, 43.1.6.3
Ventilation, 43.1.5
  Drying Areas, 43.1.5.12, A.43.1.5.12
  Exhaust Duct Access Openings, 43.1.5.10
  Exhaust Fans and Drives, 43.1.5.11
  General, 43.1.5.1
  Make-Up Air, 43.1.5.3, A.43.1.5.3
  Manifolding of Exhaust Ducts, 43.1.5.7, A.43.1.5.7
  Materials of Construction, 43.1.5.8, A.43.1.5.8
  Performance Requirements, 43.1.5.2
    Powder Coating Systems, 43.1.5.2.2
  Recirculation of Exhaust, 43.1.5.5, A.43.1.5.5
  Routing of Exhaust Ducts, 43.1.5.4
  Support of Exhaust Ducts, 43.1.5.9, A.43.1.5.9
Automated Electrostatic Spray Equipment, 43.2
Containers. [33:17.7.2], 43.8
Dipping, Coating, and Printing Processes, 43.10
Drying, Curing, and Fusion Processes, 43.4
Handheld Electrostatic Spray Equipment, 43.3
Miscellaneous Spray Operations, 43.5
  Limited Finishing Workstations, 43.5.3
  Preparation Workstations, 43.5.2
  Vehicle Undercoating and Body Lining, 43.5.1
    Noncomplying Undercoating Operations, 43.5.1.2
Organic Peroxides and Plural Component Coatings, 43.7
  General, 43.7.2
  Handling of Organic Peroxides, 43.7.5
  Material Safety Data Sheets, 43.7.9
  Mixing of Organic Peroxides with Promoters, 43.7.6, A.43.7.6
  Prevention of Contamination, 43.7.3
  Scope, 43.7.1, A.43.7.1

Smoking, 43.7.7
Storage of Organic Peroxides, 43.7.4
Trained Personnel, 43.7.8
Powder Coating, 43.6
Styrene Cross-Linked Composites Manufacturing (Glass Fiber–Reinforced Plastics), 43.9
Electrical and Other Hazards, 43.9.5
Fire Protection, 43.9.3, A.43.9.3
Resin Application Equipment, 43.9.2
Resin Storage, 43.9.4
Scope, 43.9.1, A.43.9.1
Use and Handling, 43.9.7
Ventilation, 43.9.6
Training, 43.11
General, 43.11.1, A.43.11.1

Sprinkler System
Definition, 3.3.271
Sprinkler System (NFPA 13/13R)
Definition, 3.3.271.1
Sprinkler System (NFPA 13D)
Definition, 3.3.271.2

Stakeholder
Definition, 3.4.20

Standard
Definition, 3.2.10

Standard Cubic Foot (scf) of Gas
Definition, 3.3.272

Standard Temperature and Pressure (STP)
Definition, 3.3.273

Standpipe System
Definition, 3.3.274

Storage
Banded Tire Storage
Definition, 3.3.275.1
Cartoned Storage
Definition, 3.3.275.2
Definition, 3.3.275
Detached Storage
Definition, 3.3.275.3
High-Piled Storage
Definition, 3.3.275.4
Isolated Storage
Definition, 3.3.275.5
Laced Tire Storage
Definition, 3.3.275.6
Miscellaneous Tire Storage
Definition, 3.3.275.7, A.3.3.275.7
On-Side Tire Storage
Definition, 3.3.275.8
On-Tread Tire Storage
Definition, 3.3.275.9
Palletized Tire Storage
Definition, 3.3.275.10
Segregated Storage
Definition, 3.3.275.11
Yard Storage
Definition, 3.3.275.12

Story
Definition, 3.3.276
Occupiable Story
Definition, 3.3.276.1

Street
Definition, 3.3.277

Street Floor
Definition, 3.3.278, A.3.3.278

Structural Element
Definition, 3.3.279

Structure
Definition, 3.3.280, A.3.3.280
Open Structure
Definition, 3.3.280.1, A.3.3.280.1

Suburb or Suburban
Definition, 3.3.281, A.3.3.281

Summarily Abate
Definition, 3.3.282

System
Bulk Hydrogen Compressed Gas System
Definition, 3.3.283.1, A.3.3.283.1
Bulk Inert Gas System
Definition, 3.3.283.2, A.3.3.283.2
Bulk Liquefied Hydrogen System
Definition, 3.3.283.3, A.3.3.283.3
Bulk Oxygen System
Definition, 3.3.283.4, A.3.3.283.4
Central Station Service Alarm System
Definition, 3.3.283.5
Compressed Gas System
Definition, 3.3.283.6
Continuous Gas Detection System
Definition, 3.3.283.7
Cylinder Containment System
Definition, 3.3.283.8
Dedicated Smoke-Control System
Definition, 3.3.283.9
Definition, 3.3.283
Fire Alarm System
Definition, 3.3.283.10
Fire Protection System
Definition, 3.3.283.11
Nondedicated Smoke-Control System
Definition, 3.3.283.12
Standpipe System
Definition, 3.3.283.13, A.3.3.283.13
Treatment System
Definition, 3.3.283.14
Vapor Processing System
Definition, 3.3.283.15, A.3.3.283.15
Vapor Recovery System
Definition, 3.3.283.16, A.3.3.283.16

-T-

Tank
Aboveground Storage Tank
Definition, 3.3.284.1

Aboveground Tank
    Definition, 3.3.284.2
ASME Tank
    Definition, 3.3.284.3
Definition, 3.3.284
Portable Tank
    Definition, 3.3.284.4, A.3.3.284.4
Secondary Containment Tank
    Definition, 3.3.284.5
Stationary Tank
    Definition, 3.3.284.6, A.3.3.284.6
Storage Tank
    Definition, 3.3.284.7
TC
    Definition, 3.3.285
Telecommunication Facilities and Information Technology Equipment, Chap. 36
    General, 36.1
Temporary Wiring
    Definition, 3.3.286
Tire
    Definition, 3.3.288
    Rubber Tires
        Definition, 3.3.288.1
    Scrap Tire
        Definition, 3.3.288.2
Toxic Material
    Definition, 3.3.289
Traffic Calming Device
    Definition, 3.3.290, A.3.3.290
Transfilling
    Definition, 3.3.291, A.3.3.291
Tube Trailer
    Definition, 3.3.292, A.3.3.292

-U-

Unauthorized Discharge
    Definition, 3.3.293
Uncertainty Analysis
    Definition, 3.4.21
Unit (Vessel), Operating or Process
    Definition, 3.3.296
Unit Operation or Unit Process
    Definition, 3.3.294
Unit Process
    Definition, 3.3.295
Unstable (Reactive) Material
    Definition, 3.3.297
Unstable (Reactive) Solids and Liquids, Chap. 72
    General, 72.1
Use [Hazardous Materials]
    Closed System Use
        Definition, 3.3.298.1, A.3.3.298.1
    Definition, 3.3.298, A.3.3.298
    Open System Use
        Definition, 3.3.298.2, A.3.3.298.2

Special Use
    Definition, 3.3.298.3

-V-

Valet Trash Collection
    Definition, 3.3.299
Valve
    Definition, 3.3.300
    Indicating Valve
        Definition, 3.3.300.1
    Reduced Flow Valve
        Definition, 3.3.300.2
    Valve Outlet Cap or Plug
        Definition, 3.3.300.3
    Valve Protection Cap
        Definition, 3.3.300.4
    Valve Protection Device
        Definition, 3.3.300.5
Vapor Pressure
    Definition, 3.3.301
Vapor Processing System
    Definition, 3.3.302
Vapor Recovery System
    Definition, 3.3.303
Vehicle-Mounted Generator
    Definition, 3.3.304
Verification Method
    Definition, 3.4.22

-W-

Warehouse
    Definition, 3.3.305
    General-Purpose Warehouse
        Definition, 3.3.305.1
    Liquid Warehouse
        Definition, 3.3.305.2, A.3.3.305.2
Wastewater Treatment and Collection Facilities, Chap. 39
    General, 39.1
Water Capacity
    Definition, 3.3.306
Water-Reactive Solids and Liquids, Chap. 73
    General, 73.1
Welding, Cutting, and Other Hot Work, Chap. 41
    Arc Welding Equipment, 41.6
        Installation, 41.6.1
    Fire Prevention Precautions, 41.3
        Cylinders, 41.3.8
        Fire Extinguishers, 41.3.2
        Fire Watch and Fire Monitoring, 41.3.6
        Hot Tapping, 41.3.7, A.41.3.7
        Hot Work Permit, 41.3.5, A.41.3.5
        Nonpermissible Areas, 41.3.4, A.41.3.4
        Permissible Areas, 41.3.3
            Designated or Permit-Required Areas, 41.3.3.2
                Designated Areas, 41.3.3.2.1
                Permit-Required Areas, 41.3.3.2.2, A.41.3.3.2.2
            General, 41.3.3.1

Personal Protective Clothing, 41.3.1, A.41.3.1
General, 41.1
   Permits, 41.1.5
Public Exhibitions and Demonstrations, 41.5
   Application, 41.5.1
   Cylinders, 41.5.5
      Cylinder Protection, 41.5.5.7
      Cylinder Valves, 41.5.5.5
      Gas Capacity Limitation, 41.5.5.1
      Process Hose, 41.5.5.4
      Storage, 41.5.5.2
      Transporting Cylinders, 41.5.5.3
      Valve Caps, 41.5.5.6
   Fire Protection, 41.5.4
      Fire Department Notification, 41.5.4.3
      Fire Extinguishers, 41.5.4.1
      Shielding, 41.5.4.2
   Site, 41.5.3
      Design, 41.5.3.2
      Location, 41.5.3.1
   Supervision, 41.5.2
Responsibility for Hot Work, 41.2
   Contractors, 41.2.5, A.41.2.5
   Fire Watch, 41.2.4
   Hot Work Operator, 41.2.3
   Management, 41.2.1, A.41.2.1
   Mutual Responsibility, 41.2.6
   Permit Authorizing Individual (PAI), 41.2.2
Sole Proprietors and Individual Operators, 41.4
   Assignment of PAI and Fire Watch, 41.4.1, A.41.4.1
   Documented Hot Work Permit, 41.4.2

Wharf
   Definition, 3.3.307, A.3.3.307
Wildland Urban Interface, Chap. 17
   General, 17.1
      Development of Wildland Fire Hazard Mitigation Plan, 17.1.10
      From Chimney to Eaves, 17.1.6
      From Foundation to the Immediate Landscaped Area, 17.1.8, A.17.1.8
      From the Immediate Landscaped Area to the Extent of the Structure Ignition Zone, 17.1.9
      From Top of Exterior Wall to Foundation, 17.1.7
      Mitigation Implementation and Enforcement, 17.1.11
      Overview of the Surrounding Environment, 17.1.5
      Structure Assessment Elements and Conditions, 17.1.4, A.17.1.4
   Plans, 17.2
   Wildland Fire–Prone Areas, 17.3
      Clearance of Brush and Vegetative Growth, 17.3.5
         Electrical Transmission Lines, 17.3.5.1
            Electrical Power Line Emergencies, 17.3.5.1.5, A.17.3.5.1.5
            Trimming Clearance, 17.3.5.1.3
         Roadways, 17.3.5.3
         Structures, 17.3.5.2
      Fire Roads, Firebreaks, and Emergency Access, 17.3.7
      Maintenance, 17.3.9
      Permits and Approvals, 17.3.2, A.17.3.2
      Restricted Entry, 17.3.3
         Signs, 17.3.3.3
      Safeguards, 17.3.1, A.17.3.1
      Tampering with Fire Safety Equipment, 17.3.8
      Unusual Circumstances, 17.3.6
      Use of Flammable Materials and Procedures, 17.3.4
         Apiaries, 17.3.4.5
         Explosives and Blasting, 17.3.4.3
         Fireworks, 17.3.4.4
         Smoking, 17.3.4.1
         Tracer Bullets, Tracer Charges, Rockets, and Model Aircraft, 17.3.4.2
Wildland/Urban Interface
   Definition, 3.3.308, A.3.3.308
Wood Panel
   Definition, 3.3.309
Written Notice
   Definition, 3.3.310

Submitting Public Input / Public Comment Through the Online Submission System

Following publication of the current edition of an NFPA standard, the development of the next edition begins and the standard is open for Public Input.

Submit a Public Input

NFPA accepts Public Input on documents through our online submission system at www.nfpa.org. To use the online submission system:

- Choose a document from the List of NFPA codes & standards or filter by Development Stage for "codes accepting public input."
- Once you are on the document page, select the "Next Edition" tab.
- Choose the link "The next edition of this standard is now open for Public Input." You will be asked to sign in or create a free online account with NFPA before using this system.
- Follow the online instructions to submit your Public Input (see www.nfpa.org/publicinput for detailed instructions).
- Once a Public Input is saved or submitted in the system, it can be located on the "My Profile" page by selecting the "My Public Inputs/Comments/NITMAMs" section.

Submit a Public Comment

Once the First Draft Report becomes available there is a Public Comment period. Any objections or further related changes to the content of the First Draft must be submitted at the Comment Stage. To submit a Public Comment follow the same steps as previously explained for the submission of Public Input.

Other Resources Available on the Document Information Pages

Header: View document title and scope, access to our codes and standards or NFCSS subscription, and sign up to receive email alerts.

Current & Prior Editions	Research current and previous edition information.
Next Edition	Follow the committee's progress in the processing of a standard in its next revision cycle.
Technical Committee	View current committee rosters or apply to a committee.
Ask a Technical Question	For members, officials, and AHJs to submit standards questions to NFPA staff. Our Technical Questions Service provides a convenient way to receive timely and consistent technical assistance when you need to know more about NFPA standards relevant to your work.
News	Provides links to available articles and research and statistical reports related to our standards.
Purchase Products & Training	Discover and purchase the latest products and training.
Related Products	View related publications, training, and other resources available for purchase.